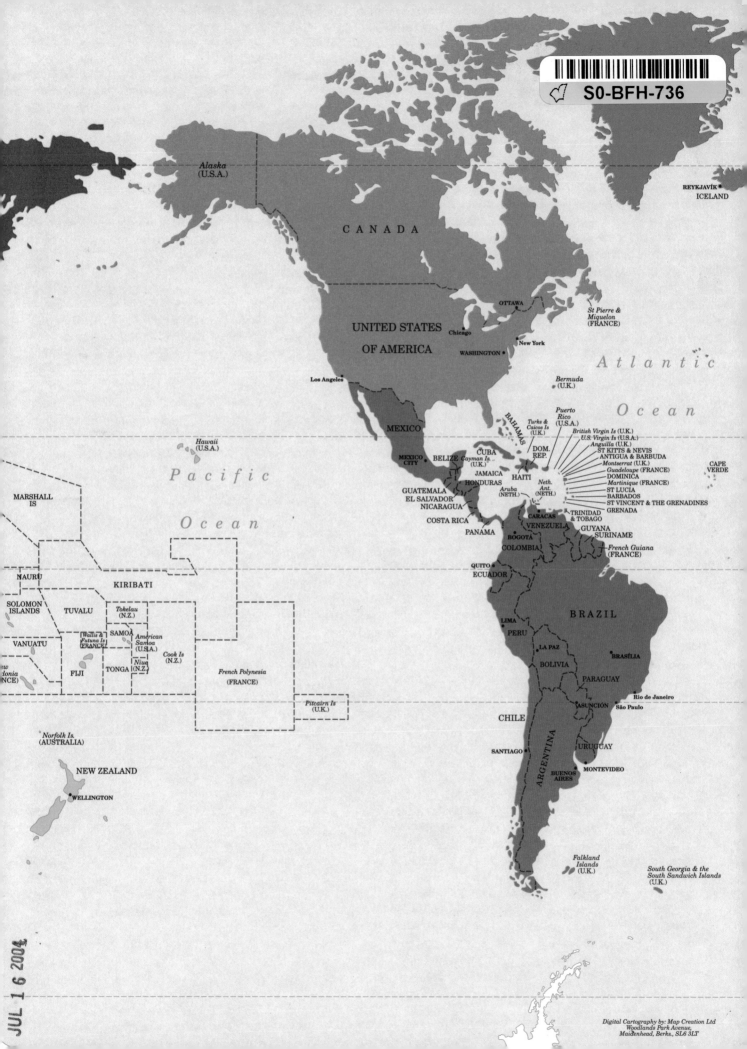

Eastern Europe, Russia and
Central Asia
2004

# Eastern Europe, Russia and Central Asia 2004

4th Edition

Europa Publications
Taylor & Francis Group

LONDON AND NEW YORK

**Fourth edition 2003**

ISBN 1-85743-187-1
ISSN 1470-5702

Typeset and printed by Unwin Brothers Limited
The Gresham Press
Old Woking, Surrey

# FOREWORD

In 1990 Europa Publications began to prepare the first edition of what became EASTERN EUROPE AND THE COMMONWEALTH OF INDEPENDENT STATES, which had been intended to encompass just eight countries; the second edition covered 27. In recent years the contrast between developments in most of the countries of the former USSR and those located in Central and South-Eastern Europe has increased. Thus, the former Soviet republics of Estonia, Latvia and Lithuania are included in the sister volume to this book, CENTRAL AND SOUTH-EASTERN EUROPE. This, the fourth edition of EASTERN EUROPE, RUSSIA AND CENTRAL ASIA, covers the 12 member states of the Commonwealth of Independent States, providing a comprehensive description and analysis of each, and placing them within their international, regional and historical context. Russia continues to dominate the region, whether the countries that come under its influence wish it to or not. Moreover, although parliamentary and presidential elections took place in several countries in 2003 (and were to take place in Russia in 2003–04), for the most part the old Soviet demagogues continued to govern the region. Indeed, some observers claimed that Azerbaijan was moving towards 'monarchy', with the election to the presidency of the ailing incumbent's son in mid-October 2003. Earlier, referendums held in Kyrgyzstan and Tajikistan approved constitutional amendments, widely interpreted as increasing their Presidents' hold on power. Meanwhile, despite the constitutional referendum held in Chechnya in March, and the republican presidential election in October, prospects for stability in the republic remained remote.

Part One comprises nine articles by specialist writers, which discuss various topics of relevance to the region, ranging from international relations and militant Islam to the politics of energy and economic development. Part Two comprises chapters on each of the 12 states, including information on the country, its people, its history, its politics and its economy: a geography and map is followed by a chronology and then two essays, one a political narrative, the other an examination of the economy, each of which is, again, written by an acknowledged expert. The detailed statistical and directory sections give data on major companies, other financial and business organizations, state institutions, religion, culture, the media and environmental organizations, to list but a few. The information on government provides data on local administration, including detailed surveys of each of the 89 constituent units of the Russian Federation, for example, and coverage of a number of polities with varying degrees of official recognition. Each chapter concludes with a bibliography. Part Three is an up-to-date Political Profiles section, including biographical outlines of individuals prominent in the region. Regional Information (Part Four), provides details of the principal organizations and research institutes that are active in the region, and select bibliographies of books and periodicals.

The Editor is grateful to all the contributors for their articles and help and to the numerous governments and organizations that provided statistical and other information.

October 2003

# ACKNOWLEDGEMENTS

The editors gratefully acknowledge the co-operation, interest and advice of all the authors who contributed to this volume. We are also indebted to many organizations connected with the region, particularly the national statistical offices, whose help is greatly appreciated. We owe special thanks to a number of embassies and ministries. In addition, we are grateful to Edward Oliver, who prepared the maps that are included in this volume.

We are most grateful for permission to make extensive use of material from the following sources: the United Nations' *Demographic Yearbook, Statistical Yearbook, Monthly Bulletin of Statistics, International Trade Statistics Yearbook* and *Industrial Commodity Statistics Yearbook*; the United Nations Educational, Scientific and Cultural Organization's *Statistical Yearbook*; the Food and Agriculture Organization of the United Nations' Statistical Database and *Yearbook of Fishery Statistics*; the International Labour Office's Statistical Database and *Yearbook of Labour Statistics*; the World Bank's *World Bank Atlas, Global Development Finance, World Development Report* and *World Development Indicators*; the International Monetary Fund's Statistical Database and *International Financial Statistics* and *Government Finance Statistics Yearbook*; the World Tourism Organization's *Yearbook of Tourism Statistics*; and *The Military Balance 2002–2003*, a publication of the International Institute for Strategic Studies, Arundel House, 13–15 Arundel Street, London WC2R 3DX.

# HEALTH AND WELFARE STATISTICS: SOURCES AND DEFINITIONS

**Fertility** Source: WHO, *The World Health Report* (2002). The number of children that would be born per woman, assuming no female mortality at child-bearing ages and the age-specific fertility rates of a specified country and reference period.

**Under-5 mortality rate** Source: UNDP, *Human Development Report* (2003). The ratio of registered deaths of children under 5 years to the total number of registered live births over the same period.

**HIV/AIDS** Source: UNDP, *Human Development Report* (2002). Estimated percentage of adults aged 15 to 49 years living with HIV/AIDS. < indicates 'fewer than'.

**Health expenditure** Source: WHO, *The World Health Report* (2002).
*US $ per head (PPP)*
International dollar estimates, derived by dividing local currency units by an estimate of their purchasing-power parity (PPP) compared with the US dollar. PPPs are the rates of currency conversion that equalize the purchasing power of different currencies by eliminating the differences in price levels between countries.
*% of GDP*
GDP levels for OECD countries follow the most recent UN System of National Accounts. For non-OECD countries a value was estimated by utilizing existing UN, IMF and World Bank data.
*Public expenditure*
Government health-related outlays plus expenditure by social schemes compulsorily affiliated with a sizeable share of the population, and extrabudgetary funds allocated to health services. Figures include grants or loans provided by international agencies, other national authorities, and sometimes commercial banks.

**Access to water and sanitation** Source: WHO, *Global Water Supply and Sanitation Assessment* (2000 Report). Defined in terms of the type of technology and levels of service afforded. For water, this includes house connections, public standpipes, boreholes with handpumps, protected dug wells, protected spring and rainwater collection; allowance is also made for other locally defined technologies. 'Access' is broadly defined as the availability of at least 20 litres per person per day from a source within 1 km of the user's dwelling. Sanitation is defined to include connection to a sewer or septic tank system, pour-flush latrine, simple pit or ventilated improved pit latrine, again with allowance for acceptable local technologies. Access to water and sanitation does not imply that the level of service or quality of water is 'adequate' or 'safe'.

**Human Development Index (HDI)** Source: UNDP, *Human Development Report* (2002). A summary of human development measured by three basic dimensions: prospects for a long and healthy life, measured by life expectancy at birth; knowledge, measured by adult literacy rate (two-thirds' weight) and the combined gross enrolment ratio in primary, secondary and tertiary education (one-third weight); and standard of living, measured by GDP per head (PPP US $). The index value obtained lies between zero and one. A value above 0.8 indicates high human development, between 0.5 and 0.8 medium human development, and below 0.5 low human development. Countries with insufficient data were excluded from the HDI. In total, 173 countries were ranked for 2000.

# CONTENTS

# CONTENTS

# THE CONTRIBUTORS

**Shirin Akiner.** School of Oriental and African Studies, University of London.

**John Anderson.** University of St Andrews.

**Annette Bohr.** Royal Institute of International Affairs, London, and University of Manchester.

**Helen Boss.** Vienna Institute of Comparative Economic Studies.

**Michael Bourdeaux.** Keston Institute, Oxford.

**Aleg Cherp.** Central European University, Budapest.

**Jane Falkingham.** Professor at University of Southampton.

**Philip Hanson.** Professor at University of Birmingham.

**Edmund Herzig.** Royal Institute of International Affairs, London, and University of Manchester.

**Taras Kuzio.** University of Toronto.

**Margot Light.** Professor at London School of Economics and Political Science, University of London.

**Tamara Makarenko.** University of St Andrews.

**Neil Melvin.** University of Leeds, and Senior Adviser to the Organization for Security and Co-operation in Europe High Commissioner on National Minorities.

**Ruben Mnatsakanian.** Central European University, Budapest.

**Steven D. Roper.** Eastern Illinois University.

**Angus Roxburgh.** Journalist, broadcaster and author.

**Andrew Ryder.** University of Portsmouth.

**Veronica Schneider.** Journalist.

**George Tarkhan-Mouravi.** Director, Institute for Policy Studies, Tbilisi.

**Phil Williams.** Professor at Matthew B. Ridgway Center for International Security Studies, University of Pittsburgh, Pennsylvania.

**Andrew Yorke.** Political and economic analyst.

# ABBREVIATIONS

| | |
|---|---|
| Acad. | Academician; Academy |
| AD | anno domini |
| ADB | Asian Development Bank |
| Adm. | Admiral |
| admin. | administration |
| AH | Anno Hegirae |
| a.i. | ad interim |
| AID | (US) Agency for International Development |
| AIDS | Acquired Immunodeficiency Syndrome |
| Alt. | Alternate |
| AM | Amplitude Modulation |
| amalg. | amalgamated |
| AO | Avtonomnyi Oblast (Autonomous Oblast) |
| AOK | Avtonomnyi Okrug (Autonomous Okrug) |
| approx. | approximately |
| ASEAN | Association of South East Asian Nations |
| asscn | association |
| assoc. | associate |
| ASSR | Autonomous Soviet Socialist Republic |
| asst | assistant |
| Aug. | August |
| auth. | authorized |
| Ave | Avenue |
| | |
| b. | born |
| BC | before Christ |
| Bd | Board |
| Bd, Blvd | Bulevardi, Boulevard |
| b/d | barrels per day |
| Bldg | Building |
| br.(s) | branch(es) |
| Brig. | Brigadier |
| BSE | bovine spongiform encephalopathy |
| BSEC | (Organization of the) Black Sea Economic Co-operation |
| bul. | bulvar (boulevard) |
| | |
| C | Centigrade |
| c. | circa; child, children |
| cap. | capital |
| Capt. | Captain |
| Cdre | Commodore |
| Cen. | Central |
| CEO | Chief Executive Officer |
| CFE | Conventional Forces in Europe |
| Chair. | Chairman/woman |
| c.i.f. | cost, insurance and freight |
| CIS | Commonwealth of Independent States |
| C-in-C | Commander-in-Chief |
| circ. | circulation |
| cm | centimetre(s) |
| CMEA | Council for Mutual Economic Assistance |
| c/o | care of |
| Co | Company; County |
| Col | Colonel |
| Commdr | Commander |
| Commdt | Commandant |
| Commr | Commissioner |
| Corpn | Corporation |
| CP | Communist Party |
| CPSU | Communist Party of the Soviet Union |
| CSCE | Conference on Security and Co-operation in Europe |
| Cttee | Committee |
| cu | cubic |
| cwt | hundredweight |
| | |
| d. | daughter(s) |
| DDR | Deutsche Democratische Republik (German Democratic Republic) |
| Dec. | December |
| Dep. | Deputy |
| dep. | deposits |
| Dept | Department |
| devt | development |
| Dir | Director |
| DM | Deutsche Mark (German mark) |
| Dr | Doctor |

| | |
|---|---|
| dwt | dead weight tons |
| | |
| E | East; Eastern |
| EBRD | European Bank for Reconstruction and Development |
| EC | European Community |
| ECE | (United Nations) Economic Commission for Europe |
| ECO | Economic Co-operation Organization |
| Econ. | Economist; Economics |
| ECOSOC | (United Nations) Economic and Social Council |
| ECU | European Currency Unit |
| edn | edition |
| EEC | European Economic Community |
| EFTA | European Free Trade Association |
| e.g. | exempli gratia (for example) |
| eKv | electron kilovolt |
| e-mail | electronic mail |
| eMv | electron megavolt |
| Eng. | Engineer; Engineering |
| ESCAP | Economic and Social Commission for Asia and the Pacific |
| est. | established; estimate; estimated |
| et al. | et alii (and others) |
| etc. | et cetera |
| EU | European Union |
| excl. | excluding |
| exec. | executive |
| | |
| F | Fahrenheit |
| f. | founded |
| FAO | Food and Agriculture Organization |
| Feb. | February |
| FDI | foreign direct investment |
| FM | frequency modulation |
| fmrly | formerly |
| f.o.b. | free on board |
| Fr | Father |
| FRG | Federal Republic of Germany |
| Fri. | Friday |
| FRY | Federal Republic of Yugoslavia |
| ft | foot (feet) |
| | |
| g | gram(s) |
| GATT | General Agreement on Tariffs and Trade |
| GDP | gross domestic product |
| GDR | German Democratic Republic |
| Gen. | General |
| GNI | gross national income |
| GNP | gross national product |
| Gov. | Governor |
| Govt | Government |
| grt | gross registered tons |
| GWh | gigawatt hours |
| | |
| ha | hectares |
| HE | His (or Her) Eminence; His (or Her) Excellency |
| HIV | human immunodeficiency virus |
| hl | hectolitre(s) |
| HM | His (or Her) Majesty |
| Hon. | Honorary (or Honourable) |
| hp | horsepower |
| HQ | Headquarters |
| HRH | His (or Her) Royal Highness |
| | |
| IAEA | International Atomic Energy Agency |
| ibid | ibidem (from the same source) |
| IBRD | International Bank for Reconstruction and Development (World Bank) |
| ICC | International Chamber of Commerce |
| ICFTU | International Confederation of Free Trade Unions |
| ICRC | International Committee of the Red Cross |
| IDA | International Development Association |
| i.e. | id est (that is to say) |
| ILO | International Labour Organization/Office |
| IMF | International Monetary Fund |
| in (ins) | inch (inches) |

# ABBREVIATIONS

| | |
|---|---|
| Inc, Incorp., Incd | Incorporated |
| incl. | including |
| Ind. | Independent |
| INF | Intermediate-range Nuclear Forces |
| Ing. | Engineer |
| Insp. | Inspector |
| Int. | International |
| IRF | International Road Federation |
| irreg. | irregular |
| Is | Islands |
| IUCN | International Union for the Conservation of Nature and Natural Reserves |
| Jan. | January |
| Jr | Junior |
| Jt | Joint |
| kg | kilogram(s) |
| KGB | Komitet Gosudarstvennoi Bezopasnosti (Committee for State Security) |
| kHz | kilohertz |
| km | kilometre(s) |
| kom. | komnata (room) |
| kv. | kvartira (apartment); kvartal (apartment block) |
| kW | kilowatt(s) |
| kWh | kilowatt hours |
| lb | pound(s) |
| Lt, Lieut | Lieutenant |
| Ltd | Limited |
| m | metre(s) |
| m. | married; million |
| Maj. | Major |
| Man. | Manager; managing |
| mem. | member |
| MEV | mega electron volts |
| mfrs | manufacturers |
| Mgr | Monseigneur; Monsignor |
| MHz | megahertz |
| Mil. | Military |
| mm | millimetre(s) |
| Mon. | Monday |
| MP | Member of Parliament |
| MSS | Manuscripts |
| MW | megawatt(s); medium wave |
| MWh | megawatt hour(s) |
| N | North; Northern |
| n.a. | not available |
| nab. | naberezhnaya (embankment, quai) |
| Nat. | National |
| NATO | North Atlantic Treaty Organization |
| NCO | Non-Commissioned Officer |
| NGO | non-governmental organization |
| NMP | net material product |
| no. | number |
| Nov. | November |
| nr | near |
| nrt | net registered tons |
| Obl. | Oblast (region) |
| Oct. | October |
| OECD | Organisation for Economic Co-operation and Development |
| OIC | Organization of the Islamic Conference |
| Ok | okrug (district) |
| OPEC | Organization of the Petroleum Exporting Countries |
| opp. | opposite |
| Org. | Organization |
| OSCE | Organization for Security and Co-operation in Europe |
| p. | page |
| p.a. | per annum |
| Parl. | Parliament(ary) |
| per. | pereulok (lane, alley) |
| Perm. Rep. | Permanent Representative |
| pl. | ploshchad (square) |
| PLC | Public Limited Company |
| PLO | Palestine Liberation Organization |
| POB | Post Office Box |

| | |
|---|---|
| pr. | prospekt (avenue) |
| Pres. | President |
| Prin. | Principal |
| Prof. | Professor |
| prov. | provulok (lane) |
| Pte | Private |
| p.u. | paid up |
| publ. | publication; published |
| Publr | Publisher |
| q.v. | quod vide (to which refer) |
| Rd | Road |
| reg., regd | register; registered |
| reorg. | reorganized |
| Rep. | Republic; Representative |
| res | reserve(s) |
| retd | retired |
| Rev. | Reverend |
| Rm. | Room |
| RSFSR | Russian Soviet Federative Socialist Republic |
| s. | son(s) |
| S | South; Southern; San |
| SARS | Severe Acute Respiratory Syndrome |
| SDR(s) | Special Drawing Right(s) |
| Sec. | Secretary |
| Secr. | Secretariat |
| Sen. | Senior |
| Sept. | September |
| Soc. | Society |
| Sq. | Square |
| sq | square (in measurements) |
| SS | Saints |
| SSR | Soviet Socialist Republic |
| St | Saint; Street |
| START | Strategic Arms' Reduction Treaty |
| Str. | Strada (street) |
| Sun. | Sunday |
| Supt | Superintendent |
| tech., techn. | technical |
| tel. | telephone |
| Thurs. | Thursday |
| Treas. | Treasurer |
| Tues. | Tuesday |
| TV | television |
| u/a | unit of account |
| UK | United Kingdom |
| ul. | ulica, ulice (street) |
| UN | United Nations |
| UNAIDS | United Nations Joint Programme on HIV/AIDS |
| UNCTAD | United Nations Conference on Trade and Development |
| UNDP | United Nations Development Programme |
| UNEP | United Nations Environment Programme |
| UNESCO | United Nations Educational, Scientific and Cultural Organization |
| UNHCR | United Nations High Commissioner for Refugees |
| UNICEF | United Nations Children's Fund |
| Univ. | University |
| UNPA | United Nations Protected Area |
| USA | United States of America |
| USAID | United States Agency for International Development |
| USSR | Union of Soviet Socialist Republics |
| VAT | value added tax |
| Ven. | Venerable |
| VHF | Very High Frequency |
| viz. | videlicet (namely) |
| vol.(s) | volume(s) |
| vul. | vulitsa (street) |
| W | West; Western |
| WCL | World Confederation of Labour |
| Wed. | Wednesday |
| WFTU | World Federation of Trade Unions |
| WHO | World Health Organization |
| WTO | World Trade Organization |
| yr | year |

# INTERNATIONAL TELEPHONE CODES

To make international calls to telephone and fax numbers listed in *Eastern Europe, Russia and Central Asia*, dial the international code of the country from which you are calling, followed by the appropriate country code for the organization you wish to call (listed below), followed by the area code (if applicable) and telephone or fax number listed in the entry.

| | Country code | + GMT* |
|---|---|---|
| Armenia | 374 | +4 |
| Azerbaijan | 994 | +5 |
| Belarus | 375 | +2 |
| Georgia | 995 | +4 |
| Kazakhstan | 7 | +6 |
| Kyrgyzstan | 996 | +5 |
| Moldova | 373 | +2 |
| Russia | 7 | +2 to +12 |
| Tajikistan | 992 | +5 |
| Turkmenistan | 993 | +5 |
| Ukraine | 380 | +2 |
| Uzbekistan | 998 | +5 |

\* Time difference in hours + Greenwich Mean Time (GMT). The times listed compare the standard (winter) times. Some countries adopt Summer (Daylight Saving) Times—i.e. + 1 hour—for part of the year.

# EXPLANATORY NOTE ON THE DIRECTORY SECTION

The Directory section of each chapter is arranged under the following headings, where they apply:

THE CONSTITUTION

THE GOVERNMENT
HEAD OF STATE
CABINET/COUNCIL OF MINISTERS
MINISTRIES

PRESIDENT AND LEGISLATURE

LOCAL GOVERNMENT

POLITICAL ORGANIZATIONS

DIPLOMATIC REPRESENTATION

JUDICIAL SYSTEM

RELIGION

THE PRESS

PUBLISHERS

BROADCASTING AND COMMUNICATIONS
TELECOMMUNICATIONS
RADIO
TELEVISION

FINANCE
CENTRAL BANK
STATE BANKS
DEVELOPMENT BANKS
COMMERCIAL BANKS
STOCK EXCHANGE
INSURANCE

TRADE AND INDUSTRY
GOVERNMENT AGENCIES
DEVELOPMENT ORGANIZATIONS

CHAMBERS OF COMMERCE
INDUSTRIAL AND TRADE ASSOCIATIONS
EMPLOYERS' ASSOCIATIONS
UTILITIES
STATE HYDROCARBONS COMPANIES
MAJOR COMPANIES
TRADE UNIONS

TRANSPORT
RAILWAYS
ROADS
INLAND WATERWAYS
SHIPPING
CIVIL AVIATION

TOURISM

CULTURE
NATIONAL ORGANIZATIONS
CULTURAL HERITAGE
SPORTING ORGANIZATIONS
PERFORMING ARTS
ASSOCIATIONS

EDUCATION
UNIVERSITIES

SOCIAL WELFARE
NATIONAL AGENCIES
HEALTH AND WELFARE ORGANIZATIONS

ENVIRONMENT
GOVERNMENT ORGANIZATIONS
ACADEMIC INSTITUTIONS
NON-GOVERNMENTAL ORGANIZATIONS

DEFENCE

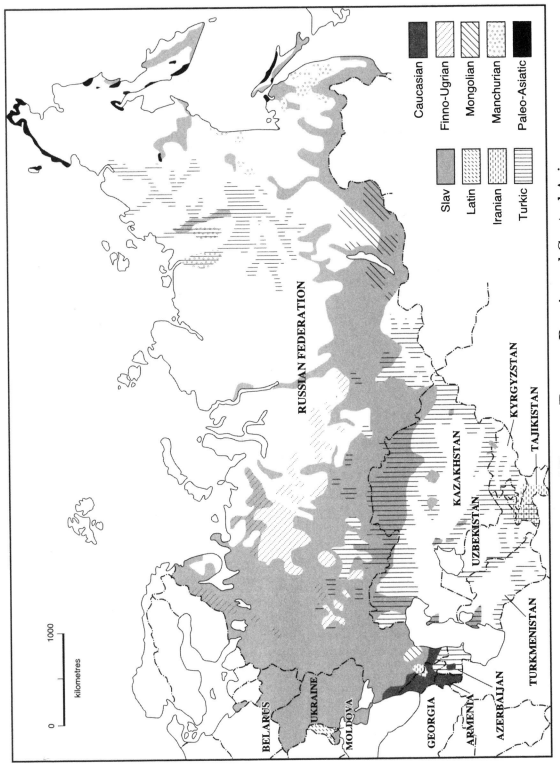

Ethnic Groups of Eastern Europe, Russia and Central Asia

# PART ONE

# General Survey

# INTERNATIONAL RELATIONS OF RUSSIA AND THE COMMONWEALTH OF INDEPENDENT STATES

## Prof. MARGOT LIGHT

### INTRODUCTION

Of the 15 independent countries that emerged from the disintegration of the USSR in late 1991, 11 immediately formed the Commonwealth of Independent States (CIS). A 12th, Georgia, joined at the end of 1993. However, the governments of all the successor states were initially too preoccupied with establishing independent statehood and disentangling themselves from the institutions of the former USSR to attend much to foreign policy. In some cases they also had to deal with severe domestic conflicts. Once they turned their attention to the outside world, however, it became clear that Russia, by far the most powerful of the post-Soviet states in terms of size, military strength and economic potential, would dominate the international relations of the area. To a large extent, therefore, their policies towards one another and towards the wider world were a function of their relationship with Russia. In subsequent years, a number of regional groupings were formed. Even when it is not a member, the Russian Federation has a strong influence on the policies of these organizations. Similarly, Russia plays an important role in their bilateral relations with one another and with the outside world.

The President and Government of Russia, the prime movers in the events that led to the final disintegration of the USSR, similarly soon discovered that some of Russia's most acute foreign-policy problems emanated from the other successor states. Russia's identity as a state was, historically and culturally, bound up with the existence of a Russian empire. The majority of the Russian population, including the political leaders instrumental in dissolving the USSR, found it difficult to accept the loss of that empire. The adoption of two distinct terms, 'near' and 'far' abroad, to refer to the former Soviet republics and to the outside world, respectively, symbolizes the perceptual and practical problems Russians had in converting the relationships between the old Union Republics into foreign policy and accepting that the other successor states were fully independent. Moreover, conflicts between and within those states, some of which had erupted before the USSR disintegrated, were exacerbated by its dissolution. It soon became apparent that the 'new world order' (as the President of the USA in 1989–93, George Bush, optimistically dubbed the international system after the Cold War) in the former USSR was characterized by confusion, disorder and conflict.

With regard to the far abroad, the new Russian leaders had, rather naively, expected that independence, democratization and the introduction of market reforms would ensure that Russia's interests would coincide with those of the powerful industrialized Western countries. However, differences soon appeared, the most serious of which concerned the eastward expansion of the North Atlantic Treaty Organization (NATO). In Russia there was a strong perception that the West was wilfully neglecting the genuine threats to Russian security caused by conflicts on its periphery and by the expansion of NATO. Outside Russia, by contrast, there was increasing apprehension that Russian foreign policy was becoming more assertive.

By the end of the 1990s NATO had expanded to include the Czech Republic, Hungary and Poland. It had also adopted a new military strategy, and in March 1999 it had launched a prolonged air attack on Serbia, the Federal Republic of Yugoslavia, in an attempt to prevent the continuing repression of the predominantly ethnic Albanian population of the province of Kosovo and Metohija. Relations between Russia and the West were at their lowest point since the end of the Cold War. Furthermore, Russia was engaged in a second ferocious war against separatists in the Republic of Chechnya. A new East–West division threatened to separate Russia from Western, Central and South-Eastern Europe, and the independent states on Russia's western border (Belarus, Moldova, Ukraine and the three Baltic states of Estonia, Latvia and Lithuania) were left in a precarious 'no-man's land' between East and West. Following the suicide attacks on the US cities of New York and Washington, DC, on 11 September 2001, however, Russian President Vladimir Putin supported the rapidly assembled US-led coalition against global terrorism, and relations between Russia and the USA, and between Russia and NATO improved, despite the announcement in November 2002 that the Baltic states would be admitted to NATO in a second round of expansion by May 2004, and despite the US-led military intervention to remove the regime of Iraqi President Saddam Hussain that commenced in March 2003 (and which was opposed by Russia). Nevertheless, a number of contentious issues remain unresolved, which are capable of undermining the new spirit of East-West co-operation.

In the first section of the following account of the international relations of the post-Soviet states, their initial difficulties in consolidating their independence and establishing independent foreign policies are examined in more detail. The problems obstructing the development of the CIS into an effective multilateral organization, the bilateral relations of the newly independent states, and the other regional groupings they have formed, are considered in the second section. A major obstacle to the effective integration of the CIS is the large number of internal and inter-state disputes, which hinder economic recovery and the establishment of peaceful international relations. The most intractable of these conflicts are surveyed in the third section of the chapter. The fourth turns to the relations of the successor states with the wider world. The chapter concludes with a brief assessment of future prospects for the international relations of Russia and the CIS.

### FOREIGN POLICY AND THE ESTABLISHMENT OF INDEPENDENT STATEHOOD

Apart from Estonia, Latvia and Lithuania, which essentially reverted to the independence that they had lost when they were incorporated into the USSR in 1940 (and which will not be considered in this chapter), the non-Russian successor states had never before enjoyed independent statehood in the modern international system. The symbols of external sovereignty—international recognition and individual membership of international organizations such as the UN—were granted immediately. Internal sovereignty, however, was more difficult to assert, either because a sense of statehood barely existed (this was the case, for example, in Belarus) or because there were violent conflicts between different groups within the state (for example, in Georgia). The establishment of an active and independent foreign policy proved to be no simple matter. All the Union Republics that formed the USSR had, in theory, possessed ministries of foreign affairs. Only Belarus and Ukraine, however, had any experience of foreign representation, having held separate seats at the UN since its inception and having contributed staff to its international civil service and to its specialized agencies. In many of the newly independent states there was a small educated élite and, since pay and conditions of work in the public sector were inferior to the opportunities available in the new business world, it was sometimes difficult for ministries of foreign affairs to recruit suitably qualified personnel. Lack of diplomatic expertise and the shortage of experienced staff were compounded by the great material difficulties presented by establishing representation abroad. Moreover, at first, foreign representatives accredited to the governments of the newly independent states continued to operate from Moscow, the Soviet as well as the Russian capital, thus inadvertently contributing to the sense that Russian interests took precedence over their own. Russia began from a far more advantageous position. Foreign embassies, international agencies, prominent non-governmental organizations and media representatives were already located in Moscow. The Russian Ministry of Foreign Affairs took over the buildings and most of the personnel of the Soviet Ministry of Foreign Affairs. Soviet embassies and trade missions abroad, with some personnel changes, immediately began to represent the Russian Federation. Russia also inherited valuable intangible assets, such as highly professional diplomats with experience of the international system and well-established channels of communication. Moreover, as the recognized legal heir to the USSR, a permanent member of the UN Security Council and the only successor state with recognized nuclear status, Russia immediately occupied a more prominent role in the international system than did any other successor state.

This does not mean that the consolidation of independent statehood in Russia was free from problems. Many Russians found it difficult to accept that some areas that had previously always been part of Russia (particularly those where there were large Russian populations) were now legally within foreign countries. Russia had never before been a nation-state and there was uncertainty and disagreement about the country's new identity, and about the role it should play both within the former USSR and in the world as a whole. Moreover, the foreign-policy expertise that Russia inherited from the USSR was of little help in dealing with the CIS: few diplomats knew anything about the other former Soviet republics and Russia was rather slow to develop formal diplomatic relations with the near abroad. With regard to the West, the Russian President, Boris Yeltsin, and his Government not only wanted to continue the friendly relations established by Mikhail Gorbachev, the last Soviet leader (1985–91), but they also hoped to have access to Western aid. This entailed the rapid establishment of a market economy. The pace and nature of the economic reforms adopted to meet this requirement inevitably had serious repercussions on Russia's relations with the other former Soviet republics.

The economic conditions under which the newly independent states attempted to establish their statehood and formulate independent foreign policies were inauspicious. The Soviet economy had been in steep decline for a number of years and by 1991 economic conditions were catastrophic. In many of the new states economic chaos was exacerbated by domestic political turmoil. None of the conflicts that had characterized the last years of the existence of the USSR had

been resolved by its disintegration and new disputes appeared almost immediately. The CIS proved woefully inadequate for either facilitating the disintegration of the USSR or providing a framework for reintegration, and incapable of dealing with the new problems that arose almost as soon as it was established.

## MULTILATERAL AND BILATERAL RELATIONS IN THE CIS

The CIS provides an intergovernmental framework for the multilateral co-operation of its 12 members. It consists of a Council of Heads of State, assisted by Councils of Heads of Government, of Foreign Ministers, of Defence Ministers and of Ministers of Internal Affairs. There is also an Inter-parliamentary Assembly. None of the Councils has supranational powers: decisions are taken by consensus and any member may refrain from participating in a decision to which it objects. The CIS established numerous bodies to provide co-ordination in various sectors of the economy, as well as in other fields. Despite these elaborate institutional arrangements, CIS members do not wish to sacrifice their individual sovereignty in order to achieve supranational efficiency. As a result, only about one-half of the agreements the organization has reached have been signed by all CIS members; an even smaller proportion have been ratified by all the signatories and only a few have been implemented.

One reason why the CIS developed so slowly is that its founding members did not share the same goals for its future. The intention of some of its original signatories (for example, Ukraine) was to use the organization to effect an orderly disintegration of the centralized, interdependent economy of the USSR. Other members (for example, Kazakhstan) hoped that it would provide a framework for close economic, political and military integration. However, even those states that are the most enthusiastic participants in the CIS fear Russian hegemony. It is not just a question of Russia's size compared with that of the other CIS members, and its relative military and economic power. There is also the problem of the 25m. ethnic Russians and Russian-speakers who live in the other countries of the CIS. Russian policy-makers regularly assert that protection of diaspora Russians is the most vital of Russia's national interests. Although these statements have remained in the realm of rhetoric rather than being translated into active policy, they suggest that Russia claims the right to intervene in the domestic affairs of its neighbours. Paradoxically, however, it is Russia itself that demonstrates most ambivalence about the CIS. Although the Russian Government frequently announces ambitious programmes for the establishment of a single economic space and an effective military alliance, there is considerable apprehension in Russia that the CIS will become a financial burden and a vehicle for Russian subsidies to the other members.

The result of this equivocation and mixture of motives is that the CIS has divided into an inner core of states that desire closer ties (Armenia, Belarus, Kazakhstan, Kyrgyzstan, Russia and Tajikistan), two states that resist integration (Turkmenistan and Ukraine) and, between them, a group of increasingly reluctant members (Azerbaijan, Georgia, Moldova and Uzbekistan). This division is reflected in the number of states that adhere to various agreements within the CIS. Only six states acceded to the CIS Collective Security Treaty, for example, which was signed in Tashkent, Uzbekistan, in May 1992. Three further states joined in 1993, but Moldova, Ukraine and Turkmenistan refused to co-operate. When the Treaty became due for renewal in 1999, Azerbaijan, Georgia and Uzbekistan effectively seceded from the agreement. In May 2002 the six remaining members decided to upgrade the Treaty to a regional defence organization, the Collective Security Treaty Organization. They did not, however, agree to implement a parallel proposal to create a joint military force under the command of the Russian army's General Staff. In May 2001 the six original signatories had created a joint 3,000-strong rapid reaction force primarily to deal with incursions into Central Asia by Islamist militants, which held a series of command-and-staff exercises in 2001 and 2002. Azerbaijan, Moldova, Turkmenistan, Ukraine and Uzbekistan did not sign a treaty providing for the defence of the Commonwealth's external borders in May 1995, or for the common air defence system agreed in February 1996 (although by early 1998 all CIS members, except Azerbaijan and Moldova, were participants). In June 2000 the entire membership of the CIS, with the exception of Turkmenistan, agreed to establish an Anti-Terrorist Centre, which opened in Bishkek, Kyrgyzstan, in September 2001. Although five signatories of the Collective Security Treaty agreed to establish joint peace-keeping forces, few are in a position to contribute troops. Consequently, Russia has become the principal CIS peace-keeper, and this has raised suspicions, both within and outside the CIS, that Russia has neo-imperialist designs in the former USSR.

Russia proved to be the main obstacle to the establishment of effective economic integration within the CIS. In January 1995 a CIS Customs Union was founded by Belarus, Kazakhstan and Russia; it was renamed the Free Trade Zone in 1996 and the Eurasian Economic Community (EURASEC) in October 2000 (despite the name, however, by that time only Belarus, Kazakhstan, Kyrgyzstan, Russia and Tajikistan were full members). Moldova, Ukraine and Armenia were granted observer status in 2002–03. Changing the name did not make economic integration more effective, primarily because the Russian Government regularly attached conditions and reservations that deprived the Free Trade Zone/EURASEC of any real meaning.

Confusingly, some CIS members have also concluded parallel multilateral and bilateral agreements that appear to have nothing to do with the CIS framework. Thus, in February 1995 the Presidents of Kazakhstan, Kyrgyzstan and Uzbekistan established a Central Asian Economic Union (later the Central Asian Union), with the avowed objective of achieving economic integration by 2000. By mid-1998 Tajikistan had joined the Union, although its economic ambitions had been reduced in scale. In June 1999 the four Presidents granted Georgia and Turkey observer status in the Union, but they were no closer to their goal of forming a common Central Asian economic space that would include a common market for goods, services, and capital. Having renamed it the Central Asian Economic Community, established the Central Asian Reconstruction Bank and adopted a Strategy of Integrated Development for 2000–05, in 2001 the Presidents of its member states admitted that it had accomplished none of its aims, and agreed to turn it into a far looser Economic Forum, a debating body with diluted functions, broader non-governmental participation and a more flexible agenda. However, under the threat of cross-border incursions from Afghanistan by Islamist forces, in April 2000 the four Central Asian Presidents agreed on joint action to combat terrorism; political, religious and other forms of extremism; and transborder organized crime. In February 2002 the organization once again adopted a new name, the Central Asian Co-operation Organization, with a wider remit—in addition to accelerating regional economic integration, it was charged with focusing on security issues.

The Central Asian states (with the exception of Turkmenistan), together with the People's Republic of China and Russia, are also members of the Shanghai Co-operation Organization (initially established in 1996 as the Shanghai Forum), which became a fully fledged international organization in June 2002, when it adopted a formal Charter and signed an agreement on the establishment of a Regional Anti-Terrorist Centre. In May 2003 its leaders agreed to turn it into a formal international organization by May 2004, with a permanent secretariat located in Beijing, China.

In 1996 the Presidents of Russia and Belarus founded a Community of Sovereign Republics. One year later it became a Union of Sovereign Republics, and the two Presidents adopted a Union Treaty and a Union Charter. In December 1999 they signed a further treaty that created—in theory, at least—a confederal Russian-Belarusian state. The unification treaty provided for a Higher State Council, made up of the presidents, prime ministers and chairmen of both chambers of each country's parliament; a Council of Ministers, the chairman of which would be appointed by the Higher State Council; a bicameral union parliament, consisting of a House of Representatives of elected members and a House of the Union, the members of which would be appointed by the executive branch; a Supreme Court; and an Accounting Chamber to oversee the implementation of the Union's budget. It was envisaged that the two states would adopt the Russian rouble as their common currency in 2005. Implementation of the Union would require the harmonization of the two countries' legal and economic systems, but Belarus has been slow to reform. As a result, by late 2003 little real progress had been made towards the implementation of the Union. Moreover, President Putin appeared to envisage a Union on the basis of a unified federal state, according to which Belarus would, in effect, be incorporated into the Russian Federation. The Belarusian President is unlikely to find this an acceptable condition.

At the end of 1997 the Governments of Azerbaijan, Georgia, Moldova and Ukraine established an informal and consultative grouping within the CIS. Known by the acronym of GUAM, it united the four countries that have been most resistant to closer CIS integration and that share, therefore, common security and economic concerns (among them, the transportation of petroleum from the Caspian Sea oilfields via a route that avoids Russia). In April 1999, when Uzbekistan joined the group, the acronym expanded to GUUAM. After three years as an informal grouping, in June 2001 its members signed a Charter creating three levels of institution: a conference of heads of state, to meet annually; a twice-yearly conference of ministers of foreign affairs, to act as an executive; and a Committee of National Co-ordinators, to act as GUUAM's permanent staff. Like the other regional groupings in the former USSR, GUUAM has done little to implement its stated aims, and its institutionalization did not serve to make it more effective.

The proliferation of treaties and arrangements within the CIS and outside its framework, coupled with multiple bilateral agreements between individual members, compounds the organization's decision-making incoherence and legal disorder and is a symptom of its ineffectiveness. There are three main obstacles to effective integration within the CIS: first, the variable pace at which member states have set about reforming their economies; second, the dependence of most of the other members on Russian energy supplies; and third, the preference all CIS members have for redirecting their economic and political relations to countries outside the former USSR.

In 1992 the Russian Government embarked on economic reform immediately, freeing prices without waiting until the other successor states were ready to follow suit. The result was an extremely high rate of inflation in Russia and severe economic consequences for those former Soviet republics that still used the Soviet and Russian currency unit, the rouble. When it became clear that Russia could not implement macroeconomic reform while the rouble remained the official currency of other countries, the Russian Government effectively dissolved the 'rouble zone'. However, the other former republics were still dependent on Russia for their energy supplies and, as prices rose, they became increasingly indebted to it. In many cases the Russian Government began to offer 'debt-for-equity' deals, thereby acquiring valuable economic interests in the other successor states. In order to reduce their dependence on Russia, all CIS members have attempted to diversify their economic and political relations, hoping to attract external investment and assistance. As a result, intra-CIS trade has declined year-on-year since the disintegration of the USSR.

Despite its sponsorship of various multilateral proposals, the Russian Government has preferred to rely on bilateral arrangements with CIS members, particularly to agree on combined control of the external borders of the CIS and to negotiate basing agreements for Russian troops. At a conference of the Organization for Security and Co-operation in Europe (OSCE) held in İstanbul, Turkey, in November 1999, the Russian Government agreed to withdraw troops from two of its four remaining military bases in Georgia by July 2001, and from the Transnistria (Transdnestria) region of Moldova by December 2002. Russian troops vacated the Vaziani base, near the Georgian capital, Tbilisi, according to schedule, and in June 2002 the OSCE confirmed that, after some delays, Russia had completed its withdrawal of arms and personnel from the Gudauta military base in Abkhazia, Georgia. Nevertheless, in 2003 the Georgian Government continued to complain that Russia was delaying compliance with its obligations to close its bases in Georgia. Similarly, Russia did not fulfil its undertaking to withdraw from Transnistria by the end of 2002. Buying into the near abroad by forgiving debts in return for shares (in, for example, a number of Armenian companies), maintaining military bases and negotiating separate, bilateral agreements appeared to be a less expensive way of achieving leadership within the CIS than through the implementation of economic integration.

Within the CIS the most important (and the most contentious) bilateral relations are between Russia and Ukraine. Ukraine, the second largest of the former Soviet republics, is a reluctant member of the CIS and participates fully in few of its agreements. Without Ukrainian participation, however, effective military or economic integration of the CIS is impossible. The Russian leadership is also aware that Ukraine is becoming an increasingly important partner to Western countries. From the Ukrainian point of view, there is fear of Russian hegemony and apprehension that Russia might attempt to coerce Ukraine into a military alliance when NATO expanded further. Even if Ukraine resisted, it would be isolated in a vulnerable, exposed position as a neutral buffer between Russia and the West. When Leonid Kuchma, known to be sympathetic to Russia, was elected Ukrainian President in July 1994, both sides expected relations to improve. The most controversial territorial issue that divided the two countries, the status of Crimea, became less acute. Other difficulties remained, however, and it took until May 1997 to negotiate a mutually acceptable division of the Black Sea fleet and to agree on the location and status of naval bases for Russia's share of the fleet in Sevastopol. Even after the agreements were ratified by both parliaments, however, difficulties continued with regard to the naval bases and because Ukraine was heavily indebted to Russia for its energy supplies. Moreover, on his re-election in November 1999 Kuchma reaffirmed Ukraine's 'European choice' (the name he gave to Ukraine's strategy of attempting to achieve membership of the European Union—EU—and closer co-operation with NATO), a policy that increases Russian fears of being isolated on the periphery of an expanding Europe. A domestic political crisis in Ukraine in early 2001 seemed to portend a move away from the West and towards Russia. However, President Kuchma continued to act as the prime mover in GUUAM and

to resist closer integration within the CIS. As long as Ukraine remains a reluctant member of the CIS, there is little prospect that the organization will develop into the counterpart of the EU that its most ardent supporters would like. At the same time, no matter how ineffective it is in bringing about integration, it is unlikely to be disbanded, even if only because it provides a useful multilateral forum for the exchange of views. The CIS is, however, severely tested by the intractable, violent conflicts that afflict its members, and it is these that will now be addressed.

## INTERNAL AND INTER-STATE CONFLICT IN THE CIS

Few empires have disintegrated with as little violence as the USSR did in 1991. At the time of its dissolution, however, a number of conflicts had already broken out or were on the point of doing so. There was, for example, a bitter dispute between Armenia and Azerbaijan over Nagornyi Karabakh (known as Artsakh by the Armenians), and there was strife within Georgia both between rival factions, and between the South Ossetian Autonomous Oblast and the central Government of Georgia. Several more conflicts occurred thereafter: between rival factions in Tajikistan; between the Autonomous Republic of Abkhazia and the central Georgian Government; between Transnistrian separatists and the Moldovan Government; and between Chechen secessionists and the Russian state. Although uneasy cease-fire agreements brought the fighting to a halt in most cases (the war in Chechnya ended in 1996, but a second war began in 1999), it has not been possible to reach a permanent or effective political settlement to any of the conflicts. Russia is involved in peace-keeping (either on its own behalf or as part of CIS forces) and/or mediation efforts in all of the conflicts in the former USSR apart from in Chechnya, where it is a direct participant.

This ubiquitous activity, together with claims that Russia is responsible for security in the post-Soviet area (and demands that the UN and other international organizations recognize and support that responsibility), has caused alarm within and outside the CIS. There are accusations that Russia uses (or has instigated) the conflicts to fulfil neo-imperialist aims. It is true that some of the conflicts have proved politically useful to the Russian Government (it was only because Russian help was required to bring the Georgian–Abkhazian conflict to an end, for example, that Georgia was persuaded to join the CIS). It is also the case that the Russian style of peace-keeping and peace-making often bears little relation to what the UN understands by those activities. However, the UN has sent observers, but has been unable to commit troops to the territory of the former USSR, and the OSCE, while active in mediation efforts in all the conflicts, has no troops at its disposal to monitor cease-fire agreements. It is, therefore, difficult to see any credible alternative peace-keeper to Russia in the area. Nor can Russian claims that protracted conflict prevents economic regeneration and threatens to spread into other states be discounted.

The conflicts in Georgia and Tajikistan were essentially between rival clans, over who held political power in those countries. In the case of Georgia, the conflict began before the USSR disintegrated. It came to an uncertain end when Eduard Shevardnadze, who had been First Secretary of the Georgian Communist Party before becoming Soviet Minister of Foreign Affairs, returned and took control of the country in March 1992. He was helped by the death of Zviad Gamsakhurdia, a nationalist leader and the first popularly elected President of Georgia, in January 1994. In Tajikistan the situation was more complicated, because refugees and forces supporting the Government ousted in November 1992 fled across the border into Afghanistan. From there they organized armed resistance, raising the spectre of another Afghan war. Russian border troops were rushed in to seal the border with Afghanistan and, together with small contingents from Kazakhstan, Kyrgyzstan and Uzbekistan, the Russian army has monitored the numerous cease-fire agreements that have been implemented. The Russian Government was also instrumental in arranging negotiations between the Government of Tajikistan and its opposition, which finally produced a peace agreement in May 1997, and multi-party elections in March 2000. None the less, violence has not completely disappeared from the area and, following an Islamist insurgency in 1999 that initially targeted Kyrgyzstan, with Uzbekistan as the real goal, there is little pressure on Russia from Tajikistan (or Kazakhstan, Kyrgyzstan and Uzbekistan) to withdraw the 25,000 Russian troops stationed in Tajikistan. However, Russia no longer exercises sole influence in Central Asia; after the suicide attacks on the USA in September 2001, Kyrgyzstan, Tajikistan and Uzbekistan granted the USA and its allies access to their bases, in order to facilitate the US-led 'war on terrorism', initially focused on Afghanistan. (Kazakhstan also made an offer of assistance, although, in the event, the US-led coalition required access only to its airspace.)

The conflict between Azerbaijan and Nagornyi Karabakh, like the conflicts between Georgia and South Ossetia and Abkhazia, is an ethnic dispute that began when the central Government reduced the degree of autonomy the disputed area had enjoyed in the old Soviet system. In the case of Nagornyi Karabakh, a predominantly Armenian enclave within Azerbaijan, local people requested the transfer of the area from Azerbaijani to Armenian jurisdiction in 1988. The Azeris responded by attacking ethnic Armenians living in Azerbaijan and the conflict subsequently escalated into a war between Armenia and Azerbaijan. By the end of 1993 Armenia had captured a large swathe of Azerbaijani territory that had previously separated Nagornyi Karabakh from Armenia itself. There has been a military impasse ever since. A cease-fire agreement implemented in 1994 has been respected, and in mid-1995 political negotiations began, under the combined auspices of the 'Minsk Group' of the OSCE and Russia. A draft settlement, formally proposed at the beginning of 1996, provided for the autonomy of Nagornyi Karabakh, the return and demilitarization of occupied territory, and assured access from Karabakh to Armenia, all monitored by OSCE peace-keeping forces. However, the three parties to the dispute, Armenia, Azerbaijan and Nagornyi Karabakh, could not make the necessary compromises to finalize a settlement. Bilateral, private negotiations between Presidents Heydar Aliyev of Azerbaijan and Robert Kocharian of Armenia intermittently produced optimistic hopes of a settlement, but it will remain difficult to reach agreement on the future status of Nagornyi Karabakh.

Hostilities between the Georgian central Government and the South Ossetian Autonomous Oblast, caused by the abolition of South Ossetia's autonomy by the Georgian authorities in 1990, also pre-date the disintegration of the USSR. After two years of sporadic conflict, a cease-fire, policed by Georgian, Russian and South Ossetian troops, was agreed. The peace-keepers are monitored, in turn, by the OSCE, which took the lead in convening political negotiations. Here too, however, a mutually acceptable compromise to the problem that caused the conflict—South Ossetia's future status— remains elusive. Russian involvement was far more direct in the war between Georgia and the Autonomous Republic of Abkhazia, and President Shevardnadze, probably with good reason, frequently accuses the Russians of assisting the Abkhazians. By September 1993 Georgian troops (and ethnic Georgian inhabitants of Abkhazia) had been evicted from Abkhazia, the Georgian state seemed on the brink of collapse and President Shevardnadze had suffered a humiliating defeat. Russia intervened and, under CIS auspices and with

some UN co-operation, contributed peace-keeping forces and took the leading mediating role. The presence of Russian peace-keepers has been the subject of continual dispute between Georgia and Russia, and the difficulty of returning Georgian refugees to Abkhazia has complicated the negotiations and has continued to be a controversial issue. A considerable distance remains between Georgia's offer of an 'asymmetric federation' and Abkhazia's demand for a loose confederation. In early 2002 the USA sent military advisers to Georgia to help train its forces for anti-terrorism operations and to help address the increasing lawlessness in the country's notorious Pankisi Gorge region, close to the border with Chechnya. In the southern Caucasus, as in Central Asia, therefore, Russia no longer exercises uncontested influence.

The Russian army also played a more direct role in the conflict that erupted in the Moldovan region of Transnistria. In 1992 the majority ethnic-Russian population feared that the central Government of Moldova intended to unite with Romania, and asserted its independence as the 'Dnestr Republic'. Soldiers stationed in the area, from the Russian 14th Army, were accused of fighting with the Transnistrian separatists. When a cease-fire agreement was negotiated in June 1992, Russian troops were entrusted with keeping the peace. Protracted negotiations, in which Russia accepted Ukraine as a co-mediator in 1996, failed to resolve the issue of Transnistria's future status. With the former Prime Minister, Yevgenii Primakov, as the Chairman of Russia's state commission on Transnistria, the Russian Government proposed that Moldova and Transnistria accept the formula of a 'common state'. However, this formula proved unacceptable. In July 2002 the OSCE proposed a federative solution, according to which areas of Moldovan territory would have the right to their own legislation and Constitution, but the Moldovan Constitution and laws would prevail. Under the proposal, the agreement would be guaranteed by Russia, Ukraine and the OSCE, and the OSCE would provide peace-keeping troops during the transition period. The Moldovan Government appeared to be prepared to accept the proposal, but Transnistria continued to insist on a confederation, although it did not reject the OSCE proposal outright.

The refusal of the President of the unrecognized Chechen Republic of Ichkeriya, Gen. Dzhokhar Dudayev, to accept that Chechnya was a member of the Russian Federation, was reluctantly tolerated by the federal authorities until an attack by his opponents (supported by the Russians) failed to oust him in October 1994. In December federal forces intervened in Chechnya. Despite terrible destruction and heavy losses on both sides, including the death of Dudayev in April 1996, the federal troops were unable to beat the Chechens into submission. Finally, after the loss of 60,000–100,000 lives, a cease-fire, negotiated by a former general, Aleksandr Lebed (briefly President Yeltsin's security adviser in 1996, and the Governor of Krasnoyarsk Krai until his death in 2002), came into operation on 23 August 1996; a peace accord was signed on 31 August. The accord provided for the withdrawal of Russian troops, but postponed a decision about Chechnya's status for a period of five years. In mid-1999 Chechen rebels attacked the neighbouring Republic of Dagestan (Daghestan), announcing that they wanted to establish an Islamist state, before being defeated and driven back by federal troops. Following bomb attacks, blamed on Chechen dissidents, in Moscow and elsewhere in Russia in September, the Russian air force attacked Chechnya, and a second ferocious war was launched against the Republic, ostensibly targeting terrorists, but, inevitably, killing large numbers of civilians and causing immense damage to buildings and the local infrastructure. Although the Russian army claimed to have defeated the rebels by early 2000, guerrilla attacks against Russian forces continued and, since Russia continued to accuse Georgia of harbouring Chechen terrorists (particularly in the Pankisi Gorge), the conflict intermittently adversely affected Russian-Georgian relations. There were few signs that the Russian Government was prepared to negotiate with the separatists to bring about an end to the conflict. Nevertheless, the Russian Government held a referendum in March 2003, in which a purported 96.0% of participating Chechen voters approved a new draft constitution, stipulating that Chechnya is a constituent part of the Russian Federation. The first presidential elections under the new Constitution were held in October.

The reason why durable political settlements have proved elusive in Abkhazia, Chechnya, Nagornyi Karabakh, South Ossetia and Transnistria is that the secessionist forces all demand self-determination and independence, while the governments of the countries from which they wish to secede will grant autonomy, but insist on preserving the territorial integrity of the country. There is no easy solution to the problem of reconciling these mutually exclusive demands. As a result, although those cease-fires that have been reached may prevent further violence, the underlying political conflicts are unlikely to be completely resolved in the foreseeable future.

The wars in Chechnya were considered, by the Russian Government at least, to be domestic matters that did not concern foreign policy. However, the first war had profound consequences for post-Cold War international relations. As far as the near abroad was concerned, it made the Russian Government more wary of supporting separatist movements in neighbouring countries. It also increased the anxiety of other governments that Russia might use violence to reinstate the USSR. Moreover, it enhanced a perception, already extensively held in the wider world, that Russian policy had become more aggressive. The governments of the former Soviet bloc of Eastern Europe renewed their petitions for early membership of NATO, and Western countries became more sympathetic to their pleas. The ferocity of the second war, and Russia's disregard of international demands that the Government should negotiate with the separatists and that it should investigate accusations of human rights abuses perpetrated by Russian forces in Chechnya, exacerbated the perception that Russia had become aggressive and intransigent. As a result, Russia's relations with both its neighbours and with the wider world were profoundly affected by the wars in Chechnya. In the interests of ensuring Russian co-operation in the war on terrorism, international criticism of Russian policy in Chechnya subsided for a while, but it resumed from mid-2002.

## THE FAR ABROAD

At first, the Russian Government assumed that its relations with the far abroad would be orientated towards the West. Moreover, it naively expected that, since it had democratized and was introducing market reforms, its foreign-policy interests would coincide with those of the West. It gradually became clear that these hopes were misguided, and when Russia began to assert its own interests strains started to appear in Russian-Western relations. Russia turned its attention to other states, reviving relations with some of the USSR's former allies. At the same time, the West, which had initially concentrated on Russia, began to develop relations with the other successor states to the USSR.

President Yeltsin, like President Gorbachev before him, relied on arms control to provide dramatic symbols of Russia's good relations with the USA. Russian-US military relations began with a flourish, when the second Strategic Arms' Reduction Treaty (START 2—which was to reduce each side's nuclear arsenal to 3,000–3,500 warheads, eliminate multiple warheads and Russian heavy land-based intercontinental missiles, and reduce US submarine-launched nuclear warheads by 50%) was signed in January 1993. However, it could

not come into effect before the reductions agreed by the USSR in START 1 had been completed by the successor states, and there was a delay while both Russia and the USA persuaded Ukraine to ratify START 1. By then, however, ratification of START 2 by the Russian State Duma (the lower house of parliament) had turned into a lengthy and controversial process, which was affected both by proposals to expand NATO and by domestic politics. When Putin was elected as Russian President in March 2000, he persuaded the Duma to ratify the Treaty: in April both START 2 and the multilateral Comprehensive Test Ban Treaty (concluded in 1996) were ratified. However, Putin warned the USA that if it abrogated the 1972 Anti-Ballistic Missile (ABM) Treaty and proceeded to develop its planned national missile defence, Russia would cease to consider itself bound by Russian-US arms-control agreements. The declared determination of US President George W. Bush to develop and deploy a missile defence system, with or without the approval of the European allies of Russia and the USA, and his intention to ignore the limitations imposed by the ABM Treaty should the Russian Government refuse to negotiate modifications to it, created considerable tension in bilateral US-Russian relations following Bush's inauguration in January 2001. However, by December, when Bush finally announced his intention unilaterally to withdraw the USA from the ABM Treaty, Russian-US relations had improved to the extent that a new strategic arms-limitation treaty was signed in May 2002, in which each side undertook to reduce its nuclear arsenal to between 1,700 and 2,200 warheads; the two Presidents also signed a declaration on the new strategic relations between Russia and the USA. Nevertheless, the Russian Government believed the USA's abrogation of the ABM Treaty to be an error, and in June, in a largely symbolic gesture, it announced Russia's withdrawal from START 2.

Fulfilment of the terms of the 1990 Conventional Forces in Europe (CFE) agreement also became a protracted issue. When the USSR disintegrated, the forces permitted it under the terms of the CFE agreement had to be divided between the European successor states. By then, there were a number of conflicts on Russia's southern perimeter. As a result, the Russian Government believed that the forces it was permitted on its southern flank were inadequate to deal with the evident threats to Russian security. Since CFE had taken many years to conclude, there was a marked reluctance in the West to renegotiate it (although various suggestions were made about how Russia might circumvent the limits). The Russian Government interpreted the Western response as a lack of sympathy for the genuine threats facing Russia. The issue had not yet been resolved by the deadline for full compliance with the treaty in November 1995. Moreover, like START 2, CFE became hostage to NATO expansion: Russia argued that, in the event of enlargement, the deployment of arms on the territory of new NATO members would contravene the CFE treaty. To the disquiet of countries bordering Russia, NATO members became more flexible about changing the flank levels set in the 1990 treaty. In May 1996 the 30 signatories of the CFE agreement increased the number of soldiers and arms Russia was permitted to station in its Leningrad and North Caucasus military districts, and negotiations to revise the treaty began in Vienna, Austria, in January 1997. The new CFE agreement was adopted at the OSCE conference of heads of state and of government in November 1999.

The other significant arms agreement of the post-Cold War world is known as the Wassenaar Arrangement (also as the New Forum), after the suburb of The Hague, Netherlands, where it was agreed in December 1995. A multilateral arrangement on export controls for conventional weapons and sensitive dual-use goods and technologies, it received final approval by 33 co-founding countries in July 1996. One of the problems in negotiating the arrangement was the suspicion held by Russian officials (and shared by the French) that US proposals to include certain clauses had more to do with reducing commercial competition in a lucrative arms market dominated by the USA, than with international security. Despite the procedures established by the agreement, Russian arms and nuclear-technology (purportedly for civilian use) sales are an issue of frequent contention in relations between Russia and the USA.

Arms-control problems were symptomatic of a division within Russia about what its foreign-policy interests were and of a general disillusionment with the outcome of reform. Although President Yeltsin was far more successful than Gorbachev had been in securing multilateral and bilateral aid, the conditions for receiving aid were perceived to be stringent and unnecessarily invasive. Moreover, there was resentment at the unexpected barriers to Russian exports and fear that Russia's reliance on petroleum and natural gas exports meant that the country was becoming a commodity-producing economy of a type usually associated with the developing world. This is one reason why attempts to prevent Russia selling arms (arms production is the only branch of manufacturing in which Russian goods are competitive on the world market) caused great irritation within the Russian Federation. Other differences had also begun to appear between Russian and Western policy (towards Serbia and Iraq, for example). The Russian leadership took active measures to improve the country's relations with the People's Republic of China, with Japan and with traditional Soviet partners such as Cuba, the Democratic People's Republic of Korea (North Korea), India and Iraq. The high point of Russia's *rapprochement* with China was a Friendship and Co-operation Treaty, signed by President Putin and the Chinese leader, Jiang Zemin, in Moscow in July 2001. Increasingly, however, security issues became more prominent in Russia's relations with the outside world.

After the collapse of the communist system, NATO undertook a series of measures to reassure the former socialist states, without explicitly offering them security guarantees. The North Atlantic Co-operation Council (NACC, succeeded in 1997 by the Euro-Atlantic Partnership Council—EAPC), for example, offered consultation and co-operation with the Alliance. Extended first to the countries of Eastern Europe, upon the disintegration of the USSR all the former Soviet republics were invited to join. The invitation was accepted happily in Russia. When the 'Partnership for Peace', a more active programme of co-operation with NATO, was proposed in January 1994, however, Russia demanded special terms that would demonstrate that it was a great power. The Russian Government eventually signed a Partnership agreement, but Russia's membership meant that such agreements were no longer sufficient to allay the anxieties of the Eastern European former socialist states with regard to the perceived increasing assertiveness of Russian foreign policy. Eastern European demands for full NATO membership became more urgent, particularly when Russian federal forces attacked Chechnya. NATO politicians responded positively. Russia's objections were vehement and they were voiced by the entire political spectrum: the eastward expansion of NATO was interpreted as a new version of containment, designed to exclude and isolate Russia. The issue soon dominated both Russia's relations with the outside world and the international relations of Eastern Europe.

In July 1997 NATO invited the Czech Republic, Hungary and Poland to join the Alliance. In the preceding months intensive negotiations had taken place on a charter to formalize the relationship between Russia and NATO. The Founding Act on Mutual Relations, Co-operation and Security was agreed by NATO's 16 members and signed by President Yeltsin and the Secretary-General of NATO at a meeting in Paris, France, in May 1997. It established a NATO-Russian Permanent Joint Council that would give Russia a voice, but not a veto, in the Alliance's affairs. The Founding Act was intended to ameliorate Russian anxiety about NATO expansion. Russian criticism of expansion did not abate, however, particularly when NATO announced that it would remain open to membership by other countries and adopted a new strategic doctrine in April 1999, which envisaged 'out of area' military action (in other words, military operations in non-NATO member countries). Since NATO had already launched an attack against Serbia (without the approval of the UN Security Council, which would have made the attack legitimate in international law), Russians of all political persuasions interpreted the doctrine as a direct threat to Russian security. The conflict with Serbia came to an end in June, in large part owing to Russian mediation, and Russia agreed to co-operate with NATO in supplying forces to police the peace in Kosovo and to enable Kosovar refugees to return to their homes. However, co-operation with NATO in the NATO-Russian Permanent Joint Council was temporarily suspended and vociferous criticism of NATO continued to characterize Russia's official public statements on foreign policy, until Russia's support for the war on international terrorism brought that country closer to NATO member states.

As a result of the improvement in relations after 11 September 2001, in late May 2002 Russia and the 19 NATO member countries signed the Rome Declaration, in Italy, establishing a new mechanism for co-operation, the NATO-Russia Council, which replaced the Permanent Joint Council. In the new NATO-Russia Council, Russia would have an equal voice on issues such as combating international terrorism, peace-keeping, civil emergency planning, defence modernization and preventing the proliferation of weapons of mass destruction. Although the Russian Government continued to express its opposition to further NATO expansion, when the announcement was made in November 2002 that the Baltic states would be admitted to NATO in a second round of expansion by May 2004, the decision was accepted in Russia with regret rather than anger.

Russia was not the only successor state to feel concerned about NATO expansion. While the Baltic states petitioned for early inclusion in the Alliance, the Governments of Belarus and Ukraine were faced with the prospect of becoming vulnerable 'buffer' states between an expanded Western Alliance and a more belligerent Russia. Belarus aligned itself ever closer with Russia, but Ukraine was a declared neutral state, anxious to preserve its independence and resistant to a military alliance with Russia. The Ukrainian Government had long believed that the West's policy of relegating Ukraine to a subsidiary position and neglecting it in favour of relations with the Russian Federation was short-sighted, since it ignored the new geopolitical threats of post-Cold War Europe. The West gradually began to respond to Ukraine's predicament. By the beginning of 1996 Ukraine had become a major recipient of US (and, more reluctantly, IMF) aid and it had become regularly included on the itinerary of Western politicians visiting Russia. Parallel to the Founding Act with Russia, NATO concluded a special charter with Ukraine in 1997 and, after Kuchma was re-elected President in November 1999, the Alliance embarked on an active programme of co-operation with that country. In May 2002 President Kuchma declared that Ukraine's long-term strategy was to achieve full membership of NATO.

The Central Asian states were less directly concerned by the prospect of NATO expansion and, with the exception of Turkmenistan, not averse to a closer military relationship with Russia. All six states of the former USSR where Muslims form the majority of the population (the five Central Asian states and Azerbaijan) fear the influence of fundamentalism from abroad, although the 'Islamist threat' is also often used by these regimes as a pretext to justify domestic policies that might otherwise be subjected to criticism. The Islamist threat is a fear that is shared by the Russian Government (since Russia has a sizeable Muslim population), as well as the USA. As mentioned above, in the weeks following the terrorist attacks of 11 September 2001 on New York and Washington, DC, four of the five Central Asian Governments offered the USA and its allies the use of their military facilities. In 2002 the US aid budget for the region increased by US \$200m., to \$442m., and the Central Asian Governments were delighted to receive US protection against both internal and external Islamist fundamentalism, together with the opportunity to counterbalance Russian influence in the region.

Like the European states of the former USSR, the states of Central Asia and the south Caucasus have developed relations with the wider world. Turkey has been active in seeking links with Central Asia and the states of the south Caucasus, concentrating on the Turkic-speaking countries. Black Sea Economic Co-operation (now the Organization of the Black Sea Economic Co-operation—BSEC) was launched by the 11 littoral states in 1992, and in May 1998 they signed a charter, permitting the group's elevation to the status of an official international organization. In 1992 the Economic Co-operation Organization (ECO), originally comprising Iran, Pakistan and Turkey, was expanded to include Afghanistan, Azerbaijan, Kazakhstan, Kyrgyzstan, Tajikistan, Turkmenistan and Uzbekistan. Moreover, as part of its programme of Technical Assistance to the CIS, in May 1993 the EU launched Transport Corridor Europe–Caucasus–Central Asia (TRACECA), a project that aimed to develop a transport corridor on an east–west axis from the five Central Asian republics, across the Caspian Sea, through the three Caucasian republics and across the Black Sea to Europe.

Azerbaijan, Kazakhstan and Turkmenistan have rich reserves of petroleum and natural gas that are of interest to multinational energy companies and to the countries in which their headquarters are based. The Caspian Sea, in particular, is the focus of international attention—from multinationals, from the developed industrial countries, from the People's Republic of China and from surrounding countries that wish to provide lucrative transit facilities for the export of the Caspian resources. Indeed, the Caspian Sea is the focus of so much attention that it is likely to engender the most contentious international problems of the former Soviet states. Already there are disagreements about whether its status is that of an inland lake or a sea (which has implications for the ownership of the resources and how they are exploited) and there are contending views about the best route for transporting its resources to the world market.

Russia is one of the Caspian littoral states and the Russian Government is determined that the Russian Federation should have a major share of the Sea's resources and the power to decide how those resources reach the market. The USA is determined both that alternative routes should also be used, and that no routes should transverse Iran. To US delight and Russian displeasure, in November 1999 the Presidents of Azerbaijan, Georgia, and Turkey agreed on a legal framework for the construction and operation of a petroleum pipeline from Baku, in Azerbaijan, via Tbilisi, in Georgia, to the Turkish terminal at Ceyhan, on the Mediterranean Sea. However, work towards the construction of the pipeline only began in September 2002. Meanwhile, the President of Turkmenistan and his Azerbaijani, Georgian, and Turkish counterparts had signed a letter of intent on building an underwater trans-Caspian pipeline to export natural gas from Turkmenistan, via Azerbaijan and Georgia, to Turkey. Numerous other potential pipelines are also under discussion.

## FUTURE PROSPECTS

By 2003, despite all predictions to the contrary, the CIS had survived and there was little reason to expect it to disintegrate. Indeed, if Russia's relations with NATO deteriorate, Russia may become less ambivalent about the costs of further CIS integration and willing and able to invest more than simple rhetoric to strengthen it. Without full Ukrainian participation, however, the CIS will have difficulty becoming a credible counterpart to the EU and/or NATO.

Whether or not the CIS endures, Russia will continue to identify the other successor states as areas of vital interest; President Putin was more assertive in this regard than his predecessor, but no Russian leadership can afford to be indifferent to the fate of diaspora Russians. The perception that Russia can only be defended by protecting the external borders of the former USSR will prevail, and the conviction that conflict in neighbouring states threatens the integrity of the Russian Federation will remain. Moreover, Russia's economic and strategic interests in the Caspian Sea will continue as long as there are valuable resources to be extracted.

In Russia's relations with the Western world, it seems unlikely that the optimism of the immediate post-Cold War period will be recaptured. Despite the vast improvement in relations after 2001, Russia vehemently opposed the intervention in Iraq in 2003, although Putin, a realist, recognized that Russia's status in the international system benefits from co-operation with the West. However, co-operation does not necessarily denote approval of Western or, more particularly, US policies, and there are a number of contentious issues that can put the relationship under strain. The international relations of Russia and the CIS require careful management by all concerned.

## BIBLIOGRAPHY

Bowker, M., and Ross, C. (Eds). *Russia after the Cold War*. London, Longman, 2000.

Kanet, R. E., and Kozhemiakin, A. V. (Eds). *The Foreign Policy of the Russian Federation*. Basingstoke, Macmillan, 1997.

Malcolm, N., Pravda, A., Allison, R., and Light, M. *Internal Factors in Russian Foreign Policy: Domestic Influences in the Post-Soviet Setting*. Oxford, Oxford University Press, 1996.

Trenin, D. *The End of Eurasia: Russia and the Border Between Geopolitics and Globalization*. Washington, DC, Carnegie Endowment for International Peace, 2001.

Webber, M. *The International Politics of Russia and the Successor States*. Manchester, Manchester University Press, 1996.

# POLITICS OF ENERGY IN THE CASPIAN SEA REGION

## Dr SHIRIN AKINER

### GEOGRAPHY

The Caspian Sea is the largest inland sea in the world. With a surface area of approximately 371,000 sq km (143,244 sq miles), it is some five times bigger than Lake Superior, in Canada, which is the world's second largest land-locked stretch of water. It is larger, too, than open seas such as the Baltic Sea and the Persian (Arabian) Gulf. From north to south the Caspian Sea measures some 1,171 km (728 miles); its maximum width from east to west is about 435 km (measurements are subject to cyclical variation). The Sea, which contains six hydrocarbons basins, is supplied by several rivers. These include, in the north, the Volga, Ural and Emba, which together account for some 80% of the river-water supplies to the Sea. In the west, the Kura and other rivers supply about 7% of river water, while in the south the Iranian rivers account for a further 5%. The Caspian Sea has no outlets or tides and salinity is low. In winter the northern coastal waters can be frozen for several months. The Sea has a complex hydrogeology and divides naturally into three sections:

the shallow northern section, bordered by Kazakhstan and Russia, has a depth of 25 m (82 ft), and reaches just 5 m in depth near the coast; this is being rapidly eroded by deposits from the Volga and other large rivers that flow into this section;

the central section, stretching between Azerbaijan and northern Turkmenistan, has a depth that varies in places from 170 m to 790 m;

the southern, deepest section, bordered by Iran and southern Turkmenistan, has a depth of between 334 m and 980 m; it is separated from the central stretch by the Apsheron Peninsula and a massive submarine ridge.

The water level in the Caspian Sea rises and falls in an irregular cycle that lasts between 50 and 170 years. During 1960–75 the level dropped very considerably, but throughout the 1980s it rose at an alarming rate (rising by more than 1.5 m over a period of 12 years), causing severe flooding along the southern coastline. This flooding gradually spread to the central section, inundating parts of the coast of Azerbaijan, Russia (especially the republic of Kalmykiya) and Turkmenistan. By the mid-1990s the level had begun to fall, and between 1996 and 2001 a decrease of some 0.5 m was recorded. However, by 2002 there were indications that this trend might once again be reversed.

The Caspian Sea has great economic and strategic significance. Apart from possessing significant hydrocarbons reserves, it has several other assets. These include a great diversity of fish species, some 30 of which have commercial value. The most highly prized fish is the sturgeon, which produces the world-famous Beluga caviar. The Caspian Sea also provides an important maritime alternative to overland cargo routes between Russia and the Middle East. During the Soviet era transborder traffic across the Sea was severely restricted, but in the 1990s the littoral states evinced new interest in developing transport links using barges and steamers. Concurrently, there was an upsurge in maritime piracy and smuggling and stringent measures were required to police the Sea.

However, the Caspian basin is best known for its resources of petroleum and natural gas (a substantial proportion of which are located offshore). In 1991, at the time of the collapse of the USSR, many areas had not yet been fully explored. Estimates of the size of these reserves varied hugely. At the end of 2001 there were proven petroleum reserves in Azerbaijan of 7,000m. barrels; proven reserves of natural gas were assessed at 850,000m. cu m (some 30,000,000m. cu ft). Kazakhstan's proven petroleum reserves were assessed at 8,000m. barrels, and its gas reserves at 1,840,000m. cu m. Turkmenistan's proven petroleum reserves were assessed at 500m. barrels, and its gas reserves at 2,860,000m. cu m. Caspian petroleum and gas reserves in the south (the Iranian sector) and the north-west (the Russian sector) were thought to be limited; thus, these estimates, taken together, placed petroleum reserves in the range of importance of the North Sea area, rather than Iran or Saudi Arabia, while gas reserves were regarded as being comparable to those of North America.

### FOREIGN INVESTMENT

Following the disintegration of the USSR, Kazakhstan was the first, and the most significant, recipient of foreign investment in the hydrocarbons sector, among the member countries of the Commonwealth of Independent States (CIS). The first major agreement was reached in May 1992, with the US petroleum company, Chevron Corporation, and provided for the development of the huge Tengiz field on the Caspian's north-eastern littoral. A joint venture, Tengizchevroil, was established between Chevron and Kazakhstan, to manage the project. Other petroleum companies later bought into the venture; in 1999 the Government of Kazakhstan began to consider selling part of its shareholding in the consortium (then valued at between US $500m. and $1,000m.). With regard to the gas sector, in 1992 British Gas and its partner, Azienda Generale Italiana Petroli SA (Agip SA of Italy), began to invest in the huge Karachaganak gas field in north-west Kazakhstan. In 1993 the Caspian Shelf Consortium (a seven-member group, consisting of Agip, British Gas, British Petroleum—BP, Mobil of France, Anglo-Dutch Royal Dutch/Shell, Statoil of Norway and Total of France) was created to explore an offshore area of 100,000 sq km in the north-eastern (Kazakh) sector of the Caspian Sea. In 1997, after having completed a four-year seismic survey, the consortium was dissolved, to be reformed as the North Caspian Project Consortium. Also in 1997 several new companies became involved in Kazakhstan. The Government of Kazakhstan awarded the China National Petroleum Company exclusive negotiating rights for a contract to develop the Uzen field (the country's second largest, after Tengiz). Another newcomer to the petroleum industry in Kazakhstan that year was the Spanish company, Repsol, which, in partnership with British Enterprise Oil, signed an agreement with Kazakhstan for the right to explore the Baiganinsk field in the north-west of the country. India's Oil and Natural Gas Corporation was, likewise, awarded a licence to explore a 10,000 sq km area in the Pavlodar basin. These and other deals, together with the discovery of large petroleum reserves in Kazakhstan's offshore Kashagan field in July 2000, gave the Government grounds to believe that it could become the sixth largest petroleum producer in the world by 2010.

In 1994, after many delays, a Western petroleum consortium, led by BP, finally signed a US $8,000m. contract with the Government of Azerbaijan to develop offshore fields (Azeri, Chirag and deepwater Guneshli) in the western (Azerbaijani) sector of the Caspian. In October 1995 the Azerbaijan International Operating Company (AIOC), a consortium of companies from Azerbaijan, Japan, Norway, Russia, Saudi Arabia, Turkey, the United Kingdom and the USA, was established to develop the offshore fields; it finally started producing small volumes of petroleum for export in November 1997. Several other consortiums signed further contracts with Azerbaijan (more than 20 had been signed by 1999) and by the end of the century most major international petroleum companies were involved in the Azerbaijani sector of the Caspian Sea. In July 1999 BP Amoco (created through the merger of BP and Amoco of the USA) announced that gas resources of some 400,000m. cu m had been discovered in the offshore prospect of Shah Deniz, representing the first confirmed discovery of new energy resources in the region since the dissolution of the USSR.

Turkmenistan took longer than Kazakhstan and Azerbaijan to attract foreign investment to its petroleum and gas fields. However, in the second half of the 1990s interest began to increase. In 1996 an agreement covering the development of three large offshore petroleum and gas deposits (Barinov, Livonov and Shafag) was concluded with Petronas, the Malaysian state energy company; an exploration and production-sharing agreement for oilfields in the Nebitdag region (western Turkmenistan) was also reached with Monument Oil and Gas Plc of the United Kingdom. Other deals included a concession to the Argentine company, Bridas, to develop the Keimir and Ak-Patlauk oilfields and, likewise, to prospect in south-eastern Turkmenistan (where it discovered new gas deposits in the Yashlar area). In 1998 an agreement was signed with the National Iranian Drilling Company to drill four petroleum wells in the coastal region of Turkmenistan.

Both the Russian and the Iranian sectors remained largely underdeveloped in the late 1990s. However, foreign investment in Caspian petroleum and gas in the aftermath of the collapse of the USSR was, as indicated above, considerable. Nevertheless, exploitation of the region's hydrocarbons resources proceeded more slowly than had initially been anticipated. This was partly because of unforeseen technical obstacles, and there were also problems associated with the weak local infrastructure. Legal systems were in flux and laws and regulations were frequently ambiguous and contradictory. There was, too, a general lack of familiarity with Western business practices; moreover, corruption was rife. Such factors created an environment that was far from conducive to the smooth functioning of agreements. These difficulties were compounded by the unusually low price of petroleum in the late 1990s. However, there were three particular issues that delayed the region's development: disputes over the legal status of the Caspian Sea; lack of adequate export facilities; and fears over regional stability.

## LEGAL STATUS

In the early 19th century, after having annexed most of Transcaucasia and much of western Kazakhstan, Russia became the major power on the Caspian Sea. The Gulistan Pact (1813) and the Treaty of Turkmanchai (1828) allowed Persia (as Iran was known until 1935) some rights of access to the Sea, but gave Russia the exclusive right to maintain a fleet of warships. After the Bolshevik revolution these unequal arrangements (always much resented by Persia) were abrogated, to be replaced in 1921 by the Iranian-Soviet Friendship Treaty. In theory, this gave equal rights of access to the Sea to both countries (at this period, the only littoral states). In practice, however, the USSR continued to play the dominant role; this was scarcely surprising, given the relative strengths of the two countries and the fact that the USSR controlled all but the southern rim of the Caspian littoral. Subsequent agreements with Iran regarding the Sea were confined to such matters as the development of fish stocks and the protection of the environment. Soviet exploitation of the offshore petroleum and gas fields, located in the central and northern sections of the Sea, was not discussed: this was treated by both sides as a matter of Soviet domestic policy. There was, therefore, implicit recognition of a 'Soviet sector' in the Caspian Sea. Yet, neither the question of national sovereignty nor the delimitation of the Sea was raised in official exchanges between Iran and the USSR. Thus, there was no formal definition of the legal status of the Caspian Sea.

In December 1991, following the dissolution of the USSR, three new littoral states came into existence: Azerbaijan, Kazakhstan and Turkmenistan. Independence was followed by massive economic disruption in all three countries. The exploitation of the rich, offshore hydrocarbons reserves of the Caspian Sea came to be seen as the only solution to the deepening economic crisis. However, several obstacles prevented this, in particular the lack of clarity, at national and international level, regarding the status of the Caspian Sea. There was no unanimity between the five littoral states as to what type of legal regime should apply (whether it should be subject to the law of the sea, of frontier lakes, of a condominium or of some other regime). Past practice (between Persia and the Russian Empire and, subsequently, between Iran/Persia and the USSR) had followed a condominium-type model of joint use and joint sovereignty. Russia and Iran favoured a continuation of this approach, arguing that the Sea should be treated as an 'indivisible reservoir', the object of common use by all the littoral states, to be utilized with the agreement of all.

However, any common zone would, effectively, be under Russian control, since the Russian Federation maintained the only substantial military forces in the area. Moreover, such a regime would have excluded Western petroleum companies from any exploitation of resources and left the remaining littoral states as junior partners in Russian- and Iranian-led projects. This approach would have retained Russian domination of the region, since Russia could use its right of veto on the development of offshore petroleum resources to exert pressure on other governments. The proposed arrangement was, therefore, unacceptable to the newly emergent states of Azerbaijan, Kazakhstan and Turkmenistan. They put forward various proposals for the delimitation of the Sea into exclusive national sectors. This was to entail the demarcation of seven international boundaries: Iran–Azerbaijan, Azerbaijan–Russia, Russia–Kazakhstan, Kazakhstan–Turkmenistan, Turkmenistan–Iran, Azerbaijan–Turkmenistan and Azerbaijan–Kazakhstan. Kazakhstan took the most extreme position, proposing not only that the Sea be divided into national sectors, but also that the Volga river, its delta, and the Volga–Don and Volga–Baltic canals be internationalized, on the grounds that all the former Soviet republics had contributed to the construction of these waterways and, consequently, should have joint ownership. If this argument were deemed valid, it would provide the Caspian Sea with outlets to the open seas and, hence, it could not be defined as a land-locked, internal 'lake'. The same criteria could then be used for delimitation as had been used for maritime areas such as the Persian Gulf.

In November 1996, after lengthy negotiation, preliminary agreement was reached between all the states, except Azerbaijan, on the partial division of the Sea into national sectors. Each sector was to extend 45 nautical miles (75 km) from the coast, with the middle of the Sea to be preserved as a common economic zone, shared equally between the littoral states. Unilateral hydrocarbons-extraction projects in the central waters that were at, or about to reach, the development stage, would be allowed to continue, but in future such enterprises were to be owned by joint-stock companies of the five states. However, Azerbaijan declined to accept this compromise, although it did agree to the creation of a Special Working Group (SWG) to develop a related convention.

At the end of January 1997 a new issue arose that greatly complicated the situation. Turkmenistan laid claim to off-shore oilfields that were already being developed on Azerbaijan's behalf by an international consortium. Both states insisted that the fields lay within their sovereign waters (although the whole question of 'sovereign waters' was still open to dispute, since no legal regime had yet been agreed for the Caspian). Turkmenistan's position was supported by neither Russia nor Iran; however, Russia did try to act as a mediator. Its role was somewhat compromised when, in July, two Russian petroleum companies, Rosneft and LUKoil, concluded an agreement with the State Oil Company of the Azerbaijan Republic (SOCAR), to develop one of the disputed fields (known as Kyapaz by Azerbaijan and Serdar by Turkmenistan). The Russian companies later withdrew from the contract and Azerbaijan appeared to be gaining the advantage, especially after that country's President, Heydar Aliyev, visited Washington, DC, USA, for talks. Subsequently, however, a number of large investors began to give support to Turkmenistan, owing to their eagerness to exploit that country's rich on and offshore resources. Tensions between the two countries remained unresolved. In mid-2001 Turkmenistan closed its embassy in the Azerbaijani capital, Baku, ostensibly owing to 'temporary financial difficulties'. However, many commentators associated this measure with the continuing dispute between the two countries over the ownership of petroleum deposits in the central Caspian Sea.

In September 1998 the Minister of Foreign Affairs of Kazakhstan addressed the UN General Assembly and called for a decision to be reached on the legal status of the Caspian Sea. However, by 2001 little progress had been made. A summit meeting of the leaders of the Caspian littoral states (Azerbaijan, Iran, Kazakhstan, Russia and Turkmenistan) was scheduled for March of that year, but was repeatedly postponed. The meeting finally took place in Ashghabat, the capital of Turkmenistan, on 23–24 April 2002. The stated aim of the summit was to decide on a legal regime for the Sea. Azerbaijan, Kazakhstan and Russia had, by this time, reached a common standpoint (largely owing to energetic lobbying by President Vladimir Putin of Russia's special envoy on Caspian issues, Viktor Kaluzhnii), based on the principle that the surface be used in common, but the seabed be divided into national sectors, corresponding to each country's coastline, along a median line. This division would award Kazakhstan approximately 29% of the Sea, Azerbaijan 20%, Russia 16%, Turkmenistan 21% and Iran 14%. Iran rejected the idea of such a division, advocating, instead, an equal division of the seabed and the surface of the Sea into national sectors, with each littoral state to hold 20%. The Turkmen stance was less clear, but for the most part appeared to be close to that of Iran. There were indications from 2001 that the Iranian position might be modified, as officials began to speak of the need for a more flexible approach to Caspian issues. Nevertheless, despite much preparatory work, the April summit did not yield conclusive results. The assembled heads of state failed to sign any agreement; not even a joint declaration was produced.

The lack of progress in multilateral negotiations contrasted with heightened bilateral activity between the Caspian states. Kazakhstan and Russia had for some time been working towards a full resolution of demarcation issues. On 13 May 2002 the leaders of the two countries signed a protocol setting out the geographical co-ordinates of the modified median line; this supplemented an historic agreement, reached in July 1998, on the bilateral demarcation of the seabed. In September 2002 Presidents Aliyev and Putin likewise signed a bilateral demarcation agreement (initially drafted in November 2001). On the basis of these separate bilateral agreements, a trilateral document was signed on 14 May 2003. This, in effect, completed the division of the seabed in the North Caspian into national sectors.

In the South Caspian, no formal demarcation agreements had been concluded. However, in March 2003 Iran and Turkmenistan began discussions on the delimitation of their respective sectors. In July Kazakhstani and Turkmenistani officials held similar negotiations, following which it was announced that a bilateral agreement on national sectors was expected to be signed by Presidents Nursultan Nazarbayev and Saparmyrat Niyazov, respectively, later in the year. Relations between Iran and Azerbaijan and, likewise, between Azerbaijan and Turkmenistan, remained tense (see below), but constructive diplomatic efforts were being made to resolve their differences.

At the multilateral level, the SWG on the legal regime of the Caspian Sea, comprising senior government officials and academics from all the littoral states, convened on a fairly regular basis. Its joint efforts resulted in the preparation of a draft convention on the legal status of the Caspian Sea, presented at the eighth session of the SWG in Baku on 26–27 February 2003. The document identified issues on which there was already common agreement, such as the need for the demilitarization of the Sea, free commercial shipping for the littoral states, and protection of the environment. Wide divergences of opinion on several vital questions remained, however, and these continued to be discussed at subsequent sessions of the SWG.

Meanwhile, there were concerns over the growing environmental problems associated with the Sea. In September 1998 it was announced that the five littoral states had approved a comprehensive plan to reduce pollution levels and to draw up a balanced and sustainable plan for the use of the biological resources of the Sea, and in July 2003 a draft convention on environmental protection of the Caspian Sea was agreed, although it had still to be signed by the Heads of State of the littoral states.

In 2000 the Sea was affected by a mysterious epidemic that caused the deaths of some 30,000 seals. Kazakh environmentalists blamed the petroleum industry for the deaths, but scientists believed cumulative poisoning by toxic elements, such as mercury, to be a more likely cause. Further seal deaths were reported in 2001; some 5,000 dead seals were washed ashore in Azerbaijan alone. Stocks of Caspian sturgeon had long been under threat from pollution and the mismanagement of bio-resources. The total legal catch of Caspian sturgeon declined from 22,000 metric tons per year in 1970 to an estimated 12,000 tons in the late 1990s (some sources claimed the decline to have been even more dramatic). In June 2001 Azerbaijan, Kazakhstan and Russia agreed to a moratorium on sturgeon fishing until the end of the year, and agreed to allow officials affiliated to the UN, under the Convention on International Trade in Endangered Species of Wild Flora and Fauna, to inspect their sturgeon-management work. Exports of caviar for the remainder of the year were confined to existing stocks. However, poachers' catches were known to be up to 12 times greater than the legally approved limits. In 2001 the official retail price for caviar was US $2,000 per kg; the 'black' (unofficial) market price in Baku or the Russian capital, Moscow, was between $20 and $70. The moratorium was lifted in March 2002, since international inspectors were satisfied that the littoral states had made significant improvements in their fisheries policies. However, environmentalists feared that the situation was far from stable and that allowing exports of caviar to resume would have a devastating impact on the sturgeon population.

A worrying development at the end of the 1990s was the incipient militarization of the Sea. In October 1999 President Niyazov of Turkmenistan decreed the establishment of a 'national service' for the development of the Turkmen sector of the Caspian Sea—a sector which, the decree proclaimed, was 'an inalienable part of Turkmenistan'. What precise form the proposed national service was to take was not clear. National commentators suggested that it would be empowered to issue permits and licences for fishing and navigation in the relevant sector of the Sea. There was speculation that, to be effective, some kind of fisheries' protection vessels (probably armed) would be required. The publication of the decree evoked an angry response from the Russian Ministry of Foreign Affairs, which declared that it would not recognize attempts by 'certain Caspian states' to extend their sovereignty to the waters of the Caspian, until the legal status of that Sea had been determined. Russia warned that if any other littoral state tried to limit these freedoms, it would take 'adequate measures' to ensure compliance. In 2001, however, both Azerbaijan and Turkmenistan purchased speedboats from the USA in order to patrol the Caspian. Turkmenistan purchased 20 additional boats from Ukraine, including 40-metric ton vessels capable of carrying large calibre guns. Russia was also reported to be reinforcing its Caspian flotilla. In late July Iran, which had previously expressed concern over these measures, initiated a confrontation with two Azerbaijani boats. The vessels, on lease to BP (the company had reverted to its original name in mid-2000), were in a part of the Sea that was disputed by Azerbaijan and Iran; they were evicted from the area by an armed Iranian patrol boat, supported by military aircraft, prompting BP to suspend its petroleum-exploration activities in the southern Caspian. Azerbaijan angrily denounced Iran's action. Coincidentally, in August 2001 the Turkish air force staged a display over Baku; the event had allegedly been planned a year in advance, but the timing implied Turkish readiness to defend Azerbaijani interests. At the beginning of August 2002 Russia staged large-scale exercises in the Caspian, designed to demonstrate Russia's ability to combat such threats as terrorism and large-scale poaching. Azerbaijan and Kazakhstan also took part in the operations; Iran sent observers, but Turkmenistan declined to participate on account of its declared stance of neutrality. The Russian Minister of Defence, Sergei Ivanov, indicated that Russia might establish a permanent military force in the region to guarantee stability.

## PIPELINE POLITICS

Another issue that hindered the exploitation of the hydrocarbons resources of the Caspian basin was the lack of an adequate export infrastructure. In the past, petroleum and gas pipelines from the region were linked to the internal Soviet network. After the collapse of the USSR, Russia used the situation to exert political and economic leverage over the newly independent states. This was highly unsatisfactory not only for these states, but also for foreign investors, who wanted to export hydrocarbons from the Caspian without the potential threat of Russian interference. However, there were several concerns regarding the construction of new pipelines. Key factors were the distance from world markets and the consequent high cost of such projects; environmental problems related to the export of petroleum through the Bosphorus; US sanctions against Iran; and regional instability that could threaten the transboundary transportation of hydrocarbons. Multiple routes were proposed, but few had

progressed beyond the stages of memoranda of intent and preliminary feasibility studies.

### Azerbaijan

There were three possible destinations for pipelines from Baku's offshore oilfields: the Black Sea, the Mediterranean Sea and the Persian Gulf. The distance to the Black Sea was shorter than that to the Mediterranean, but pipelines terminating on this coast would attract the major disadvantage of increasing oil-tanker traffic through the Bosphorus and the Dardanelles. The Turkish authorities were bound by the 1936 Montreux Convention to allow free passage for all merchant ships through the Straits of Marmara, but the traffic had reached such a volume that it could no longer be managed safely. Moreover, the constant movement of large tankers was causing severe environmental damage. The use of the Straits for the transportation of Caspian petroleum would further augment these problems.

There was fierce competition between Iran, Russia and Turkey (supported by the West, in particular the USA) to secure pipeline routes that would cross their respective territories and, thus, yield lucrative transit fees. In October 1995, after months of campaigning by the concerned parties, and the personal intervention of the US President, Bill Clinton, in an urgent telephone call to President Aliyev of Azerbaijan, it was finally announced that two routes to the Black Sea had been chosen for the initial 'early oil' stage. The northern route, from Baku to Novorossiisk, would run into Russia, the southern route, from Baku to Supsa, into Georgia. The latter route was the AIOC's preferred choice for the main export pipeline, although there were some who believed that, from an economic point of view, the route to the Persian Gulf would have been a more rational choice. However, that was not a feasible option while US sanctions against Iran remained in force.

### *Existing Routes and Routes Under Construction from Azerbaijan*

**Baku–Groznyi (Russia)–Novorossiisk (on Russia's Black Sea coast):** Selected as the northern 'early oil' route, in the early 1990s this was the only pipeline that was almost ready for use, with only a small section (of under 30 km) remaining to be added. The pipeline became operational in November 1997. At 1,400 km, it was the longest of the Black Sea routes but, geographically, the terrain was the easiest. However, the political risk associated with the pipeline remained very high, as a section of it ran through the Chechen capital, Groznyi, at the heart of the armed hostilities with Russian federal forces in 1994–96, and again from 1999. In mid-1999 the Chechen section of the pipeline was closed, owing to violence and the threat of sabotage in the region. A new section of the pipeline, avoiding the republic of Chechnya, was completed in April 2000.

**Baku–Supsa (Georgia):** Selected as the southern 'early oil' route, this represented the shortest distance to the Black Sea, at some 830 km. Originally, it had been planned to incorporate some of the existing pipelines, but these proved to be beyond repair. Consequently, the pipeline project had exceeded its original budget by some US $200m. by the time it became operational in April 1999. It was later upgraded, expanding its capacity from 115,000 barrels per day (b/d) to 145,000 b/d.

**Baku–Tbilisi (Georgia)–Ceyhan (Turkey):** Despite concerns over its economic viability, this was selected as the route for the main export pipeline. It was to cover a distance of 1,730 km, running from the Caspian Sea to the Mediterranean; the cost of construction was estimated at US $2,900m. In October 1998 the Governments of Azerbaijan, Georgia, Kazakhstan, Turkey and Turkmenistan signed the Ankara Declaration, in support of this route, which was also favoured by the US Government. In November 1999 a further intergovernmental agreement on the construction of the pipeline was signed in İstanbul, Turkey; a financial agreement was signed in Washington, in April 2000, and a detailed engineering study was initiated in 2001. There was strong pressure from the US Government to realize this project, but initially petroleum companies were seriously concerned as to whether or not the pipeline was commercially viable. It did not seem likely that Azerbaijan alone would be able to produce sufficient petroleum, and representatives of the Kazakh petroleum industry were reluctant to commit to the project. In early 2002, however, as the significant size of the recently discovered Kashagan deposit became clear, they showed greater enthusiasm. In May the European Bank for Reconstruction and Development (EBRD) agreed to provide $300m. in funding (about 10% of the estimated cost of construction); the World Bank also indicated its willingness to support the project. The Baku–Tbilisi–Ceyhan Company, a BP-led multinational consortium, was formed to construct the pipeline, and an historic ceremony was held at the Baku terminal in September. The project was due for completion in 2005. However, from late 2002 a coalition of local and international non-governmental organizations, including Amnesty International, Campagna per la Riforma della Banca Mondiale, Friends of the Earth, and WWF (formerly known as the World Wildlife Fund) launched a vigorous campaign to draw attention to the potential environmental dangers and human rights abuses that they believed were associated with the construction of the pipeline. As a result, the international financial organizations that had originally been prepared to support the project decided to await the outcome of further environmental and social-impact assessments before making a final committment to the release of funds.

### Proposed Routes from Azerbaijan

**Baku–Armenia (along the Araks river valley)–Ceyhan:** Geographically, this would have been the easiest route, but it involved political risks in crossing Armenia and eastern Turkey (although one group of supporters believed that it could encourage regional co-operation, dubbing it the 'Peace Line').

**Baku–Iran–Ceyhan:** This was technically and economically feasible, but unacceptable to Western investors while sanctions against Iran remained in place.

**Baku–Groznyi–Novorossiisk–Trabzon or Samsun or Zonguldak (Turkey)–Mediterranean Sea:** This proposed pipeline could transport petroleum overland to the Russian Black Sea coast, then by tanker (or, eventually, pipeline) to a Turkish Black Sea port (such as Trabzon, Samsun or Zonguldak, or possibly a port to the west of İstanbul), then overland to a terminal on the Mediterranean coast. It would have the advantage of avoiding the Straits; moreover, both Turkey and Russia would profit from the transit fees. The main disadvantage was the cost of constructing the pipelines and the two new terminals required. There were also serious security concerns associated with crossing Chechen territory.

**Baku–Groznyi–Novorossiisk–Burgas (Bulgaria, Black Sea coast)–Aleksandroupolis (Greece, Aegean coast):** This route found favour with member states of the European Union.

Other options for avoiding the Bosphorus included routes via Constanţa (Romania) to Trieste (Italy), and to Ukraine, via the Odessa–Brody pipeline, which opened in 2002 (see below).

### Kazakhstan

**Tengiz–Novorossiisk:** The Caspian Pipeline Consortium (CPC) was created in 1992 as a joint venture between the Governments of Kazakhstan and Oman, acting through the Oman Oil Company. Subsequently, Azerbaijan and Russia joined the group, along with Western companies. The CPC initially proposed the construction of a pipeline from the Tengiz oilfield on the northern littoral to the Russian Black Sea port of Novorossiisk. The original plan was to route the pipeline through Groznyi to the Black Sea. In July 1993, however, a more northerly course, via the Republic of Dagestan (Daghestan), was agreed, in order to avoid Chechnya. The 1,580 km-pipeline (about one-half of which was to use existing pipes) was scheduled for completion in 1996 and was to have an initial capacity of 28m. metric tons per year, rising to 67m. tons by 2010. However, its construction was subject to many delays, which included major disagreements over the ownership structure. In particular, the conditions offered to the US company, Chevron, were considered to be highly unsatisfactory.

In October 1995 the Government of Kazakhstan decided to terminate the original agreement and to relaunch the project in a new form. A revised share structure was finally accepted in mid-May 1997, with Russia acquiring 24% of shares, Kazakhstan 19%, Oman 7%, and with the remaining 50% to be shared between a number of foreign companies, headed by Chevron (with 15%). Later that year the CPC suddenly suspended construction work, owing to unresolved financial and legal disputes with the Russian local authorities. In November 1998 the first major contract for the implementation of the pipeline was signed in Moscow and the project began to make progress in 1999, following a successful feasibility study. The pipeline was inaugurated in late March 2001, and by August it had been filled with some 900,000 metric tons of petroleum. However, political differences between Russia and Kazakhstan caused delays; the first consignment of Kazakh petroleum was to have left Novorossiisk on 6 August, but shortly before this could take place it was announced that loading had been deferred indefinitely. A further delay was caused by the theft of two loading hoses. Eventually the pipeline became fully operational on 3 September. It was formally opened on 27 November, at a ceremony held near Novorossiisk, and attended by the Russian Minister of Energy, the Kazakh Minister of Energy and Natural Resources, and the US Secretary of Energy. By that time the pipeline had been thoroughly tested and six tanker loads of Kazakh petroleum had already been delivered to world markets.

### Other Export Routes from Kazakhstan

The difficulties with pipeline routes did not prevent the export of petroleum from Kazakhstan in the 1990s. The first regular shipments (using Azerbaijani tankers) of crude petroleum from the Tengiz field began at the end of July 1997, delivering 100,000–150,000 b/d to the Black Sea terminals at Novorossiisk and Batumi (Georgia). It was then shipped through the Bosphorus Straits to world markets. In 1996 test shipments had been sent to Azerbaijan, where crude petroleum was processed for local use; an equivalent swap of Azerbaijani petroleum was sent by rail to Batumi for onward shipment. In 1998 Kazakhstan concluded an agreement with three Western companies (Royal Dutch/Shell, Mobil and Chevron) for a feasibility study on parallel petroleum and gas pipelines under the Caspian Sea to Azerbaijan.

Other export facilities included a swap deal with Iran, concluded in 1996. The agreement allowed Kazakhstan to ship across the Caspian an initial 2m. metric tons of petroleum per year (increasing, eventually, to 6m. tons per year) for refining and distribution in northern Iran; in exchange, Iran was to assign an equivalent amount of crude petroleum to Kazakhstan at a terminal in the Gulf, or at one of its European storage facilities. The deal was suspended the following year because Iran's refineries refused to accept Kazakh petroleum, owing to the high sulphur content. In 2002, after the Iranian refineries had been upgraded, swaps were reinstated. By early 2003 Iran was importing about 50,000 b/d from Kazakhstan. An upgraded pipeline running from the Iranian port of Neka on the Caspian Sea to the Rey refinery near the Iranian capital, Tehran, was completed in September 2003. This had an initial capacity of 120,000 b/d, later to rise to 370,000 b/d. Construction of a pipeline from western Kazakhstan via Turkmenistan to Tehran, and then to Kharg Island in the Persian Gulf was also under consideration; the French company TotalFinaElf (as Total was known until mid-2003, following its merger, in 1999–2000, with PetrolFina and Elf Aquitaine) carried out the feasibility study.

In 1997 Kazakhstan also began transporting crude petroleum by rail to the People's Republic of China. The first shipment, of 1,400 metric tons, arrived in Xinjiang in October. It was anticipated that export volumes would increase significantly in the future. Later the same year, Canada's Hurricane Hydrocarbons registered a joint venture with a Kazakh company to complete the construction of a rail transhipment terminal on the China–Kazakhstan border.

Existing pipelines, meanwhile, continued to be used. The main western pipeline, which after upgrading was capable of transporting 310,000 b/d, ran 3,000 km from Atyrau to Samara (in the Volga region); the Kenkiyak–Omsk pipeline (of some 400 km) carried petroleum from the Aktyubinsk fields to a Siberian refinery. The Odessa–Brody pipeline, part of Ukraine's Eurasian Oil Transport Corridor, was completed in mid-2002; the first consignment of Caspian oil (from the Tengiz field) was unloaded at the southern terminal in early August.

## Turkmenistan

In the 1990s the main customers for Turkmen gas were other members of the CIS, such as Armenia, Azerbaijan, Georgia and Ukraine. However, these countries were unable to meet payments and fell deeply into arrears. By the end of 1995 Turkmenistan was owed little short of US $2,000m., and the establishment of export outlets to Europe, the Middle East and South Asia became a priority. Several projects were under consideration by the end of the decade, but most proposals were long term, with limited hope of implementation in the near future.

**Turkmenistan–Iran–Turkey–Western Europe:** This was the Turkmen Government's favoured option for an export route. In 1994 financing for the first segment of a 1,400-km gas pipeline was secured and construction commenced. The Turkmenistan–Iran section, which had a capacity of 8,000m. cu m per year, became operational in December 1997. The US Government was initially opposed to an extension of this pipeline to Turkey and Europe, because of Iran's involvement, but it abandoned its objections in mid-1997. The project aroused international interest, with companies such as Royal Dutch/Shell and the French company, Sofregaz, bidding for the construction contract. However, it was not clear how soon work would begin.

**Turkmenistan–People's Republic of China(–Japan):** In 1992 the Japanese Mitsubishi Corporation and the China National Petroleum Corporation began to undertake feasibility studies regarding the construction of a trans-Asia gas pipeline. In August 1995 they were joined by Esso China, a unit of Exxon Corporation of the USA. The intention was that the gas pipeline would terminate at a port on the Yellow Sea, with the possibility of onshipment to Japan and, perhaps, the Republic of Korea. In early 1997 it was announced that the Mitsubishi Group had formed a consortium, with Exxon and the China National Petroleum Company, to develop a pilot project for the trans-Asia gas pipeline, to connect gas fields in Uzbekistan and Turkmenistan with China's Pacific coast, via

Kazakhstan and mainland China (with an estimated length of 6,130 km, and at an estimated cost of US $9,500m.). Three possible routes were under consideration by Japanese experts. The political risk was difficult to calculate, since much would depend on internal developments in the People's Republic of China. The benefits of opening up Central Asian hydrocarbons to Pacific markets might, however, eventually outweigh the disadvantages of this route. The project was technically viable, but the distance and difficult geographic conditions made it extremely costly.

**Turkmenistan–Afghanistan–Pakistan:** In May 1997 the US petroleum company, Unocal, and its strategic partner, the Saudi Arabian company, Delta Nimir, signed a memorandum of agreement with the Turkmen Government, regarding projects for the construction of petroleum and gas pipelines from Turkmenistan's eastern gas fields to Pakistan, via Afghanistan (the estimated length of the pipeline was 1,043 km, and its estimated cost was US $1,900m.), with a possible extension to India. Bridas, which had previously put forward a similar proposal, continued to make preliminary preparations for construction, in the hope of participating in the project. However, distance, terrain, climatic conditions and, above all, the chronic instability in the region, made this route seem impractical. In 2002, however, following the US-led intervention in Afghanistan from October 2001, and the collapse of that country's Taliban regime, hopes for a more peaceful and prosperous future began to revive. Consequently, there was renewed interest in the proposed pipeline. At a meeting held in Islamabad, Pakistan, in May 2002, the Presidents of Afghanistan, Pakistan and Turkmenistan agreed to pursue the project, and in July the Asian Development Bank provided funding for a feasibility study.

**Turkmenistan–Azerbaijan–Georgia–Turkey:** In August 1999 Royal Dutch/Shell took on a major new role in the development of Turkmen gas resources, when it joined a consortium to build a Trans-Caspian Gas Pipeline under the Sea, from Turkmenistan to Turkey, via Azerbaijan. Royal Dutch/Shell became a 'strategic partner' of Turkmenistan in developing the various gas deposits that were to be the main source of supply for the pipeline. On the eve of the signing ceremony, which took place in November, the President of SOCAR indicated that, although Azerbaijan was prepared to act as a transit country for Turkmen gas in the initial stages, in the longer term provision must also be made for the export of Azerbaijani gas via this route. This view was prompted by the fact that Azerbaijan had recently discovered substantial gas reserves in the offshore Caspian waters of Shah Deniz and expected to become a major exporter in its own right within a few years. In early 2000 negotiations over how the pipeline's anticipated 30m. cu m of annual throughput should be divided resulted in serious disagreements between Azerbaijan and Turkmenistan. The President of Georgia, Eduard Shevardnadze, warned that if Azerbaijan and Turkmenistan failed to reach an agreement, an alternative project for the export of Azerbaijani gas to Turkey (entailing the construction of a new pipeline across Georgia) would be implemented, without the participation of Turkmenistan. In February 2003 it was announced that work was to begin in 2004 on the construction of the 690-km pipeline from Baku via Tbilisi to Erzurum (Turkey), and the Trans-Caspian Gas Pipeline project was postponed indefinitely in March 2003, when Royal Dutch/Shell decided to reduce its activities in Turkmenistan.

Meanwhile, a rival project had been developed. In December 1997 the Turkish Prime Minister, Mesut Yılmaz, signed an agreement with his Russian counterpart, Viktor Chernomyrdin, to build the so-called Blue Stream natural gas pipeline. This was to be the world's deepest underwater gas pipeline, running from Russia to Turkey, via the Black Sea. In early 2000 Boras Hatları ile Petrol Taşıma AŞ (BOTAŞ) of

Turkey and Russia's Gazprom began work on the project, which was completed in late 2002. The transportation of gas via the pipeline commenced in December.

## REGIONAL POLITICS

In the early 2000s the most obvious cause for concern in the Caspian basin was the war in Chechnya. Despite the gutting of the capital, Groznyi, and the great loss of human life, neither the Chechens, intent on full independence, nor the Russian Government, determined to preserve the integrity of the Russian Federation, were prepared to contemplate compromise solutions. The desire to secure control over the export pipeline, with the economic and political power that that would give, was undoubtedly a major factor in the struggle. Conditions in Dagestan and Kalmykiya, the other autonomous republics of the Russian Federation that bordered the Caspian Sea, were more stable.

In Azerbaijan, President Aliyev, the survivor of several attempted *coups d'état*, was re-elected in 1998 for a new term of office, with a substantial majority. However, the war with Armenia, a possible transit country, over Nagornyi Karabakh, had still not been resolved, and relations remained tense. Moreover, Aliyev's health was increasingly unreliable in the months preceding the presidential election due to take place in October 2003 and, in the event, his son was elected in his place (see the chapter on Azerbaijan). In Georgia, another transit country, the situation was also fragile. President Shevardnadze was the subject of a number of assassination attempts in the late 1990s, and the conflict with the separatist Autonomous Republic of Abkhazia remained an ongoing matter of concern. In Kazakhstan, President Nazarbayev stood for re-election in 1999, and was returned to office with a large proportion of the votes cast. In Turkmenistan, the incumbent leader, Saparmyrat Niyazov, was confirmed as President for life in December 1999. Nevertheless, the deteriorating economic situation in these states was beginning to cause real hardship among the population and there were fears that this could lead to serious social and political unrest. The situation was especially fragile in Azerbaijan, giving rise to considerable speculation about possible successors and their policies.

Russia's relationship with Azerbaijan, Kazakhstan and Turkmenistan was ambiguous and fluid. Following the election of Putin in March 2000, some feared that Russia would attempt to regain hegemony over the Caspian basin by force; the war in Chechnya seemed to lend credence to this view. Others believed that it was unlikely that Russia would be able to bear the expense, let alone muster the necessary forces, to carry out such a plan. However, on a bilateral basis, a gradual *rapprochement* was already taking place between Russia and these states. This was most obvious in the case of Kazakhstan, which by the mid-1990s had moved closer to the Russian Federation in economic and defence matters than had seemed conceivable in the immediate aftermath of independence. Azerbaijan and particularly Turkmenistan espoused a more overtly nationalist agenda. Yet beneath the official rhetoric, there was an awareness that a friendly relationship with Russia could be mutually beneficial.

Iran's relationship with the other Caspian states was cordial, but not especially close. Some Western analysts had feared that Iran would attempt to spread Islamist extremism throughout the Caspian basin. However, there was little evidence of this, and Iranian activities from the 1990s were directed primarily towards establishing good-neighbourly relations, particularly in the spheres of economic co-operation and the establishment of cultural contacts. Issues relating to the Caspian Sea were a priority. The Caspian Sea Co-operation Zone (CSCZ), which included all five littoral states, was created, on Iran's initiative, in February 1992. Its aim was to provide a forum for the discussion of matters of common interest. However, the CSCZ did not succeed in playing a leading role regarding the delimitation of the Sea, nor was it actively involved in negotiations concerning the exploitation of the Sea's hydrocarbons resources. The CSCZ gradually ceded its role to the Economic Co-operation Organization (ECO), a larger grouping of regional states (members comprised the former Soviet Central Asian states, Afghanistan, Azerbaijan, Iran, Pakistan and Turkey).

## OUTLOOK

By the beginning of the 21st century the excitement that had surrounded the initial stages of Western involvement in the development of the hydrocarbons resources of the Caspian basin had evaporated somewhat, and there was potential for disillusionment among the population in the newly independent states, owing to endemic corruption and the lack of democracy. The international rivalry over pipeline routes and the dispute over the legal status of the Caspian Sea increased the risks for foreign investors and raised tensions throughout the region. All the countries in the Caspian region were affected by corruption, and there were serious concerns about the rise in the smuggling of contraband, large-scale poaching and other illegal activities. Moreover, there was unease regarding the increasing pollution of the environment. However, there appeared to be some impetus towards the resolution of such issues. Important steps had been taken to create a serviceable infrastructure and officials from the host countries and foreign investors in the petroleum industry were beginning to gain a better understanding of each other's working practices. The political situation was calmer than had been anticipated (with the obvious exception of Chechnya) and there was a manifest desire for multilateral co-operation. Interest in the region increased dramatically in July 2000, when a nine-member consortium, the Offshore Kazakhstan International Operating Company (OKIOC, known as the Agip Kazakhstan North Caspian Operating Company—Agipko—from mid-2001), announced the discovery of large reserves of petroleum. Kazakhstan's Kashagan field, located in the north-east sector of the Caspian Sea, was estimated to have recoverable reserves of up to 20,000m. barrels. However, in 2001 two companies, BP and Statoil, left the consortium. The remaining members redistributed the stakes among themselves, giving TotalFinaElf, Royal Dutch/Shell, ENI (of Italy, which incorported Agip in 1998—the field operator), ExxonMobil (formed in 1999 by the merger of Exxon and Mobil) and the BG Group (formerly British Gas) 16.7% each, while the Phillips Petroleum Company (USA) and Inpex (Japan) each held 8.3%. Petroleum was expected to begin flowing from Kashagan in 2005. In March 2003 Sinopec (China Petroleum and Chemical Corporation—the People's Republic of China's second largest petroleum and gas producer) and China National Offshore Oil Corporation (CNOOC—China's third largest petroleum company) each attempted to acquire one-half of BG's stake in the Kashagan field, but they were thwarted by the other consortium partners, which exercised pre-emptive rights to buy the shares. Shortly afterwards, in June Sinopec signed an agreement with SOCAR and became the operator of a consortium to develop the Pirsaat field (with recoverable reserves estimated at 1.5m. metric tons), some 70 km south of Baku.

# MILITANT ISLAM IN CENTRAL ASIA AND THE CAUCASUS

## Dr TAMARA MAKARENKO

### INTRODUCTION

Targeted as strategic allies by the Administration of US President George W. Bush in the aftermath of the suicide attacks perpetrated by the Islamist fundamentalist al-Qa'ida (Base) organization on the US cities of New York and Washington, DC, on 11 September 2001, the countries of Central Asia and the Caucasus provided essential staging grounds for military operations in Afghanistan (the Taliban regime of which was harbouring al-Qa'ida). By 2003 many countries in the region continued to support and participate in the US-led 'war on terrorism' by sharing intelligence and seeking to reform domestic counter-terrorism legislation in response to UN Security Council Resolution 1373, a wide-ranging anti-terrorism resolution, adopted on 28 September 2001. Despite this demonstration of international co-operation, it had become increasingly clear that regional government élites in Central Asia and the Caucasus had prospered from their participation. First, regional regimes, recipients of Western military aid, received widespread support for their attempts to counter domestic terrorist threats, including imported radical and militant Islamist groups. Second, the leaders of several republics successfully manipulated the objectives of the 'war on terrorism' to intensify their own attempts to suppress political opposition. Indirectly using the USA's doctrine of pre-emptive strikes to gain legitimacy, states such as Russia and Uzbekistan have increased the use of repressive tactics against groups and individuals deemed to pose a threat to national security. Thus, instead of alleviating terrorism in Central Asia and the Caucasus, the prevailing post-11 September environment in the regions has served to promote the rise of militancy.

Although it would be difficult to dispute the existence of radical and militant Islam in the Caucasus and Central Asia, and equally difficult to argue that Islamist movements do not pose a genuine threat, the rise of militant Islam in the region continues to warrant little understanding. One of the greatest misperceptions about militant Islam among the countries of the Commonwealth of Independent States (CIS) is that it is comparable to the experience of the Middle East. Despite sharing some historical commonalities, the practice and understanding of Islam in the CIS has been significantly affected by a history marked by successive conquests, the Soviet experience and legacy, and the subsequent uncertainty of independence, together with unrelenting political unrest. It is, therefore, imperative that radical and militant Islam in this unique geographical space be predominantly regarded as a phenomenon combining ideology, nationalism, political aspirations and varying degrees of criminality. As a consequence, any analysis of the emergence and subsequent growth of Islamist groups in the region necessitates making a distinction between legitimate Islamic revival and political or criminal groups, which seek to take advantage of an unstable environment by adopting the veneer of Islam.

### THE ORIGINS OF ISLAM IN THE CIS

The long histories of the Caucasus and Central Asia are intimately interwoven with the gradual penetration of Islam. Dating back over 1,000 years, nomadic Muslim tribes travelled across the Eurasian landmass to spread the word of the Prophet Muhammad. Although these nomadic tribes mostly comprised peaceful emissaries, who also traded consumer goods along the ancient 'Silk Road', others, such as the Arab armies of the 7th century, forced adherence by conquest. Unlike the situation in the Middle East, however, Islam did not have a timeless legacy. For example, the geographical realities of Central Asia, combined with the developments of modernity, inevitably led to its isolation. As new maritime trade routes emerged, land-locked Central Asia was increasingly bypassed and, thus, had little contact with the remainder of the Muslim world. As a result, by the 16th century much of the Caucasus and Central Asia appeared to be Muslim only in name.

Muslim traditions in the CIS are arguably weak compared with those in the Middle East, despite the fact that local populations have continued to abide by Islamic laws, and have sought to retain forms of a Muslim education. The practice of Islam throughout the region, however, was distorted over the centuries, as it was combined with traditional pagan religious beliefs and practices. Furthermore, efforts to preserve Islam encountered numerous obstacles by the 18th century, with the expansion of the (Christian) Russian Empire. External attempts to suppress a strong Muslim following in Central Asia and parts of the Caucasus directly created the roots of both radical and militant Islam. Although the majority of the Muslim communities in these regions were compliant to Russian Europeanization efforts, small elements of rebellion did emerge; these movements were unorganized, and failed to co-ordinate any serious form of opposition. It was not until the advent of Soviet power that organized and violent radical Muslim resistance movements emerged. For example, Muslim *basmachi* insurgents organized armed attacks against the Soviet presence in the Fergana valley (a region that comprises parts of Kyrgyzstan, Tajikistan and Uzbekistan) and southern Tajikistan until the 1930s, when they were eventually quashed.

The Soviet authorities asserted their dominance throughout the Caucasus and Central Asia by eliminating all social vestiges of religion. Thus, Muslim leaders were forced into exile, theological schools (*madrassahs*) were closed and religious literature was confiscated. However, there were sporadic shifts in communist religious policy. For example, in an attempt to gain support from Soviet Muslims and mobilize Muslim communities during the Second World War (1939–45), the authorities established a more conciliatory religious attitude. This policy was strengthened by the creation of 'official' Islam, which included the formation of four Islamic spiritual directorates, each responsible for state-supported *madrassahs* and state-registered mosques throughout the regions.

One of the most important consequences of this policy was the creation of a dichotomy between 'official' and 'parallel', or 'underground', Islam. As with most religions suppressed in the USSR, clandestine movements focused on preserving the true faith. In Uzbekistan, for example, it is estimated that 600 unregistered mosques existed in 1945, and by 1960 there were an estimated 6,000 unregistered mosques operating in Tajikistan. Considering the historical difficulties of maintaining the theological doctrines of Islam, however, underground movements concentrated almost exclusively on ritual and symbol—and, thus, Islam increasingly became associated with ethnic identity, and became an expression of political and social discontent. Clandestine groups emerged predominantly in Central Asia, in the search for moral regeneration and the revival of Islam beyond its cultural foundations.

Added to this environment, and exacerbating the plight of Islamic radicals, was the Soviet invasion of Afghanistan. Throughout the 1980s Soviet Muslims were drafted by the Red Army to fight the Afghan *mujahidin* resisting Soviet penetration. As a result, although fighting on the side of the USSR, Soviet Muslims were reintroduced to the wider Muslim world. Furthermore, many Soviet Muslim soldiers were deeply affected by the dedication of the *mujahidin*. Thus, as the war progressed growing numbers of Muslims—particularly from Central Asia—travelled clandestinely to Pakistan and Saudi Arabia to study in *madrassahs* and/or to train as guerrilla fighters, as a show of support for the Afghan cause. Consequently, the Islamist sects of 'Deobandism' and 'Wahhabism' were imported into the Caucasus and Central Asia, further radicalizing the existing clandestine movements. In many respects, the Soviet–Afghan conflict revealed to the Muslims of the USSR that Islamic solidarity could be mobilized as a political and, if necessary, militant force for change.

## INDEPENDENCE AND THE RISE OF MILITANT ISLAM

Most practising Muslims in the Caucasus and Central Asia follow liberal forms of Islam, such as Hanafism. In general, Muslims in the CIS consider their religion as one of many defining aspects of their identity. Depending on particular events and situations, identity is also based on association with a specific linguistic or cultural group, membership of a blood-based clan, being part of an urban or rural population, or residence in a particular village or region. Being Muslim in the CIS is, therefore, comparable in meaning and action to being Christian in Western Europe or North America.

Although this is a widely accepted truism, several other, ideological interpretations of Islam penetrated the Caucasus and Central Asia from the late 1980s, and increasingly after 1991. Many of these radical forms of Islam, such as Wahhabism, have been linked with fundamentalism. Unable to exist in a vacuum, the rise of radical Islam has been facilitated by several contemporary factors since the collapse of the USSR. Most important have been the prevailing post-independence order throughout the CIS; the end of geographic isolation; and the civil wars in Afghanistan, the Russian republic of Chechnya, the southern Caucasus and Tajikistan.

Following the demise of the USSR, former Soviet republics were faced with an environment historically associated with the rise of radical ideological movements. Deteriorating living standards, rising unemployment and generally inexperienced and corrupt governments became the norm and, subsequently, the cause of growing frustration and dissatisfaction among the population. In areas that suffered the worst rates of unemployment and social conditions, such as Chechnya and Tajikistan, people were driven to criminal activities as a means to attain some degree of financial security. This prevailing environment was also the cause of rising dissatisfaction with democratization efforts. In many regions democracy and attempts to adopt a market economy have been blamed for increasing economic, political and social problems. Equally troubling, however, is the fact that the worst-affected segments of the population have become susceptible to radical movements, which promise to restructure society, to develop one based on equality and morality.

Despite the deteriorating living conditions in the post-independence CIS, one of the primary factors that allowed external interpretations of Islam to penetrate the region was the opening of borders. Non-existent borders, and the power vacuum created by the fall of communism, combined with the geopolitical importance of the region (as a natural land 'corridor' between East and West, and with an abundance of lucrative natural resources), attracted numerous actors interested in replacing the dominant regional ideology with their own. The USA and Western Europe sought to promote democracy, whereas states such as Iran, Pakistan, Saudi Arabia and Turkey sought to export their own political and social orders, all of which combine varying degrees of Islamic penetration. Taking advantage of post-independence vulnerabilities, foreign Muslim actors found that one of the most effective ways to influence the future development of the Caucasus and the Central Asian republics was through the construction of local mosques. Local *madrassahs*, established with foreign support, subsequently attracted large numbers of students, owing to their offer of free education, and the opportunity to receive a scholarship for continued study abroad (usually in Pakistan, Saudi Arabia or Turkey). Thus, as occurred during earlier centuries, the Muslim states of the CIS experienced a new succession of 'ideological' conquests.

The immediate post-Soviet era was, therefore, crucial for radical Islamist movements, if only because it created an environment characterized by weak states, growing public discontent and competition for influence by external states. One particular factor, however, which acted as a catalyst to the establishment of radical—and subsequently militant—Islam, was the outbreak of the civil conflict that raged throughout parts of the region from the 1990s. Thus, in Chechnya (1994–96 and 1999–) and the Central Asian republic of Tajikistan (1992–97), for example, radical movements increased their ties with Afghanistan, and acted as a source of inspiration for the emergence of militant Islamist groups seeking to initiate change.

As is characteristic of civil conflict, the war in Tajikistan displaced an estimated 500,000, most of whom fled over the border to Afghanistan. Regional analysts estimated that among the refugees were approximately 60,000 members of the Islamic Renaissance Party (IRP), which formed part of the opposition forces (the United Tajik Opposition—UTO) embroiled in the conflict. It was further believed that as many as 6,000 of these displaced individuals received training in *mujahidin* camps run by Jamiat-i Islami, a guerrilla group, and Hizb-i Islami (Islamic Party) Afghanistan. Guerrilla training helped the UTO to engineer an impasse in the civil war and, thus, helped usher in the peace agreement that was signed in June 1997. The Tajik peace process, however, was regarded as a severe compromise by the more radical elements of the IRP. As such, these elements, characterized by Wahhabist and pan-Islamist beliefs, sought to maintain close contacts with Afghanistan, and subsequently joined other emerging radical parties, such as Tauba and Islom Lashkarlary, which were directly connected to the most militant grouping to emerge in Central Asia: the Islamist Movement of Uzbekistan (IMU).

In contrast, in the Caucasus militant Islam was predominantly influenced by the ongoing conflict in Chechnya. Although the unresolved dispute between the separatist republic and the federal Government largely concerned the issue of independence, Islamist rhetoric was mobilized from the mid-1990s for a number of reasons. First, unable to secure support from Western states—despite widespread acknowledgement of the human rights abuses perpetrated by federal military forces—Chechen rebels sought assistance from the Islamic world (Afghanistan, Pakistan, Saudi Arabia and Turkey) by focusing on Muslim affinity and brotherhood. Second, Islam represented an effective mobilizing ideology; for example, Chechen fighters drew inspiration from the successes of their Afghan counterparts. Attempts to secure support from the international militant Islamist community for the Chechen war effort and rising interest in seeking ties with Afghanistan thus created a façade of Islamic revivalism masking ethno-nationalist, and at times criminal, motivations.

## CONTEMPORARY DYNAMICS

By the mid-1990s the prospect of Islamist militancy gaining strength throughout the Caucasus and Central Asia, specifically in Chechnya, Georgia's Pankisi Gorge (close to the Chechen border), Tajikistan and the Fergana valley, was increasing. With little hope of economic, political or social conditions improving, the persistence of political unrest—characterized by repression and human rights abuses—merely serves to provide an accessible recruitment and support base. Considering the evolution of militant Islamist groups in the CIS over past decades, it remains evident that political dynamics continue to have a profound effect on the activities and organization of such movements.

Despite international determination to fight the scourge of terrorism at its roots—a rhetorical motivation used to drive the US-led invasion of Afghanistan and the subsequent military campaign to remove the Iraqi regime of President Saddam Hussein in 2003—the very roots of terrorism in Central Asia and the Caucasus remain intact. As socioeconomic conditions continue to deteriorate throughout these areas, despite increased international involvement, parts of the indigenous population have increasingly related their worsening position to the relationship that is being fostered between the USA and their own governments. This perception, combined with indications that commitments to help restructure Afghanistan and Iraq are faltering, fuels strengthened radical militant Islamist movements. Thus, the failure to learn from past experience, to understand the driving forces of militant Islam, or to confront overarching fears of legitimate political opposition ensures that the security policy of regional governments advance the creation of their worst security fears. Although this situation has not fully materialized in Central Asia, recent dynamics in Chechnya provide a distinct warning of what the future may hold.

### The Origins of Militant Islam in Central Asia

As indicated in the previous section, the most militant Islamist group operating in Central Asia is the IMU. Although the IMU could be considered a descendant of extremist factions of the IRP, the unofficial origins of the group have been traced back to demonstrations that took place in Namangan, Uzbekistan, in 1991. These protests were led by Tahirjon Yuldashev and other local Islamists, including Jumaboy (Juma) A. Khojiyev (Namanganiy), who sought to establish Muslim self-government in the city. Although this early movement quickly collapsed, the Muslim activists did establish an Islamist political party, known as Adolat (Justice).

Encountering rising government repression of political opposition in Uzbekistan, Yuldashev and Namanganiy—the future leadership of the IMU—moved to Tajikistan, where they joined the IRP and enlisted in the civil war. Namanganiy, a former Soviet paratrooper, with extensive combat experience in Afghanistan, was recruited as a military commander, and Yuldashev acted as an IRP emissary on trips to centres of radical Islam, including Afghanistan, Pakistan, Saudi Arabia, Turkey and the Caucasus. As a result of his extensive travels, between 1992 and 1995 Yuldashev learned about the organizational and operational dynamics of radical and militant Islamist groups, and secured a network of contacts.

After the establishment of peace in Tajikistan in 1997, Yuldashev and Namanganiy, who opposed the settlement, severed their ties with the IRP. Yuldashev subsequently pursued his personal objective of establishing an Islamist movement, and Namanganiy remained in Tajikistan, where he became involved in the trafficking of illicit narcotics from Afghanistan. Although Namanganiy appeared to have withdrawn from active combat for the promotion of Islamism in the region, his renown as a militant Islamist meant that he attracted a considerable following, including Uzbek dissidents, disillusioned Tajik Islamists and Arab *mujahidin* searching for a new cause.

Namanganiy's charisma, and his ability to attract a wide following, as well as his previous relationship with Yuldashev in both Adolat and the IRP, were factors that probably led Yuldashev to seek Namanganiy's co-operation in establishing a militant Islamist movement. Having returned to Tajikistan in 1997, Yuldashev successfully convinced Namanganiy to help launch a new movement that would focus on removing the corrupt leadership of their native land, Uzbekistan, and replacing it with an Islamist state. Although Yuldashev capitalized on his contacts in Afghanistan and settled in the Afghan capital, Kabul, Namanganiy utilized his relations with IRP leaders in the newly formed Tajik Government to centre his operations in the Tavildera valley. Having secured operational 'havens' and an initial following of militants, estimated at no more than 400, in mid-1998 Yuldashev and Namanganiy announced the creation of the IMU. Thus, the priority for the next two years was to build a solid membership and secure ideological and financial support.

The spiritual roots of the IMU lie in the Wahhabi movements that emerged in the USSR in the 1980s. Wahhabists (superficially similar to members of the Saudi Arabian movement of the same name) follow a strict religious doctrine that takes literally the words of the Prophet Muhammad. As such, they renounce the main schools of Sunni Islam and condemn Sufism. Wahhabism places great importance on the concept of holy war (*jihad*) against non-believers and Muslims who deviate from the principles of Islam. Although, historically, Wahhabism was focused on the religious imperative, modern movements influenced by Wahhabism focus almost exclusively on a political ideology, which normally seeks to base society on religion. This understanding of Islam played a determining role in the aims and motivations espoused by the IMU.

Placed on the US Department of State's list of terrorist organizations in September 2000, there existed no conclusive evidence implicating the IMU in acts of terrorism (the use or threat of violence to intimidate). The group was, however, held responsible for planning and conducting terrorist campaigns, which included an attack on police-officers in Namangan in 1997, and a series of bomb attacks in Tashkent, the Uzbek capital, in early 1999. The Uzbek Government attributed these attacks to 'Islamist extremists', thereby helping to discredit any form of political opposition that threatened to emerge in that country. By 2000, however, the Government had focused on the IMU, in response to the group's official declaration, which was anti-Uzbek and which sought to remove Uzbek President Islam Karimov from power, thus justifying the subsequent widespread repression of, and perpetration of human rights abuses against, suspected Islamist radicals, who were often members of opposition groups.

By late 2000 the IMU was guilty of undertaking guerrilla operations and trafficking illicit narcotics, not necessarily guilty of conducting significant acts of terrorism. Careful analysis of the activities of the IMU revealed that the driving motivation for its militant incursions into Kyrgyzstan and Uzbekistan in August 1999 and August–September 2000 was not the establishment of an Islamic state, but the destabilization of border areas, in order to maintain and secure routes for the transportation of narcotics. In other words, the IMU successfully manipulated the political situation to further criminal activity. This does not mean that many members of the IMU did not have legitimate political grievances; however, it does reveal that the group has operated as two separate entities, operating from two different countries, which share little more than a common name and contacts.

Based in Afghanistan while Namanganiy and his followers were conducting their incursions and intensifying their involvement in the illegal drugs trade, Yuldashev and his supporters focused on developing links with the international Islamist militant network as a means to neutralize the criminal allegations pitted against the IMU in Central Asia and to ensure that the ideological component of the IMU was not compromised. However, suggestions that the profits accrued by Namanganiy were not directed towards the overall funding of the IMU merely serve to emphasize that the two men ran separate operations. This allegation became further apparent in 2001, following announcements that the IMU had changed its name to the Islamist Movement of Turkestan, and subsequently sought to establish an Islamist state that would stretch from the Caspian Sea to the Xinjiang Uygur (Uigur) Autonomous Region of the People's Republic of China. This name change was understood to have been instigated by Yuldashev as a means to distance himself further from Namanganiy's predominantly criminal faction. Furthermore, it revealed that Yuldashev was beginning to espouse a pan-Islamist ideology as a result of the contacts he had developed throughout his travels and during his stays in Afghanistan and Pakistan.

This ideological element within the IMU, however, was most evident during the US-led counter-terrorist campaign that was launched in Afghanistan in late 2001. Media accounts of the Afghan campaign frequently suggested that IMU forces were fighting alongside supporters of Afghanistan's Taliban regime in the Mazar-i-Sharif region. Although this comment was largely accurate, the IMU did not remain in Afghanistan as a united group. In fact, the only militants to remain in Afghanistan to engage in military activities were Namanganiy and his followers. Yuldashev was believed to have left Afghanistan for Pakistan at the beginning of the military campaign. Fully committed to the goals of the IMU, he could only secure the future of the movement by leading the core group of ideological militants within the IMU to safety. Furthermore, depending on the outcome in Afghanistan, the only way for Yuldashev to ensure that reprisals would be taken against Central Asian Governments for their co-operation with the US-led coalition was by regrouping in a new 'safe haven', from which future terrorist acts could be co-ordinated.

The counter-terrorist campaign conducted by the Western coalition forces in Afghanistan had several important implications for the IMU. At an operational level, the Movement's most significant reverse was the loss of its training camps in Afghanistan; organizationally, the reported death of Namanganiy in late 2001 also gave rise to concerns that the IMU would collapse for lack of a charismatic leader to attract and maintain a large following. At the same time, however, the series of events that followed the suicide attacks on the USA in September 2001 created conditions conducive to the emergence of a group strictly (and, thus, more dangerously) motivated by radical Islamist ideals; moreover, it created groups of Afghan Arab militants seeking a new cause for which to fight—just as had been the case at the end of the Soviet–Afghan war.

Most accounts of the IMU after September 2001 and the US-led bombing campaign in Afghanistan concluded that the loss of Afghanistan represented the single greatest threat to the group's survival. Not only were IMU training camps allegedly destroyed, but the IMU—as was the case with other

militant Islamist groups seeking refuge in Afghanistan—had also lost a support base and a centre that ensured access to international contacts. Although Afghanistan was, without a doubt, irreplaceable as a terrorist haven, remnants of the group took advantage of several areas of operation that had not been targeted seriously by counter-terrorist operations. A resurgent IMU, therefore, is believed to have made use of its fortified camps in the Tavildera and Karategin valleys in Tajikistan, the mountains of the Surkhandarin Oblast in Uzbekistan, and the North-West Frontier Province of Pakistan.

### The IMU after the US-led Intervention in Afghanistan

Although the IMU suffered serious operational losses, including the death of its military commander, Namanganiy, it was these very losses that appeared to be leading to the creation of a potentially stronger group, which could lead to more regional instability than initially predicted. First, the death of Namanganiy did not eliminate the role his followers played in drugs-trafficking operations. Namanganiy's absence simply created criminal competition for control over several strategic trafficking routes between Afghanistan, Kyrgyzstan, Tajikistan and Uzbekistan. Second, the elimination of Namanganiy from the structure of the IMU gave Yuldashev an unhindered opportunity to regain control over the Movement, and thus finally to distance himself from the criminal component fostered by Namanganiy. With a reduced membership base, and limited training facilities, in 2003 there were already indications that Yuldashev might refocus a resurgent IMU on small-scale acts of insurgency that would be capable of striking at the heart of the Central Asian republics, thus spreading greater fear than did the armed incursions of 1999 and 2000.

It can be argued that after September 2001 Yuldashev had, intentionally or otherwise, risen in status within regional ideological circles. His apparently unequivocal dedication to the ideals of the IMU, as it was originally perceived, ensured the group's survival. Thus, over the following two years, most probably under his guidance, analysis suggested that the IMU consolidated its membership base, to form one highly committed to radical Islamist ideals. At the core of the group are believed to be an increasing number of Afghan-Arab militants displaced from Afghanistan. This shift in membership was further enhanced by regional allegations that Gulbuddin Hekmatyar, a radical Afghan-Pashtun leader of the Hizb-i Islami, expressed an interest in joining forces with the IMU. In February 2003 Hekmatyar was added to the US Department of State's list of terrorists, owing to his links with al-Qa'ida. In response to this announcement, Hekmatyar released a *fatwa* (a decree pertaining to a point of Islamic law) stating that *jihad* against US troops far outweighed the *jihad* Afghans waged against the USSR, thereby indicating his continued support for the use of violence. Thus, the combined force of Hekmatyar and IMU militants could prove to be a significant threat to the region. Contributing to this allegation were equivalent unconfirmed reports that Uygur militants and the Islamist extremist Hizb-i Tahrir had officially joined the IMU, thus creating a resurgent Islamic Movement of Turkestan (see above). Regardless of how accurate these assessments are, what is clear is that the IMU has not disappeared. Although by late 2003 there had been no confirmed attacks attributed directly to the IMU, the Kyrgyz security services blamed a series of bomb attacks on the group, including an explosion at Bishkek's Dordoy market in late December 2002, which killed seven people and injured more than 40; and the bombing of a currency-exchange office in Osh in May 2003, which killed one person. (Responsibility for the latter incident, however, was also attributed to criminal rivalries in southern Kyrgyzstan between groups seeking to control the currency-exchange business.) Although not large-scale acts of terrorism, if the perpetrators of these acts were proven to be members of the IMU, it would be an indication that the group was beginning to reassert itself. Contrary to the proven operational capabilities of other active terrorist groups world-wide, a resurgent IMU would be unlikely to be capable of conducting devastating acts of terrorism, leading to mass casualties. Based on the IMU's aims and motivations, it appears likely that the group will focus its future activities on attacking Western, and particularly US targets in Central Asia. This concern was supported by warnings released by the US Department of State, which advised those travelling to Kyrgyzstan and Uzbekistan to exercise caution. For example, in April 2003, following the discovery of bomb-like material in the basement of a hotel in Tashkent, the USA warned that the IMU was planning to target Uzbek hotels frequented by Western citizens; and one month later the USA warned of an imminent IMU threat to Kyrgyzstan, based on intelligence that the group was planning acts of terrorism against US citizens and interests.

## Militant Islam in the Caucasus

Unlike the experience in Central Asia, militant Islam in the Caucasus cannot be isolated to one operational group. On the contrary, the post-1991 environment laid the foundations for the penetration of several forms of Islamist militancy—most of which were referred to in terms of 'Wahhabism', because of their loose ideological affiliation. Although traces of militant Islam exist in Azerbaijan, and Georgia's Pankisi Gorge was believed to have been infiltrated by both organized criminals and Islamist militants, it may be argued that the centre of Caucasian Islamist militancy is located in the northern regions, specifically in the Russian republics of Chechnya and Dagestan (Daghestan). In fact, it is as a result of the Chechen conflict that Islamist militancy was viewed as a security threat to the region. However, it would be inaccurate to suggest that instability in the Caucasus was caused solely by the presence of militant Islamist groups. Comparable to the Central Asian experience, a thorough understanding of militant Islam in the Caucasus must acknowledge that the issue of Chechnya never attracted a strong Islamist following and, simultaneously, take into account the role of ethno-nationalism, ideas of political secession and the dominating lure of criminality in the ongoing instability.

Although militant Islamist groups commonly operate under a specific name, such as the IMU, militant groups in the Caucasus have tended to operate under the name of their leader, for example Shamil Basayev in Chechnya. An ethnic Chechen, Basayev rose to prominence as a field commander during the civil conflict of 1994–96, and gained notoriety in 1995 after leading a group of militants into Budennovsk, in Stavropol Krai, Russia, where some 1,500 Russian civilians were taken hostage at the local hospital. Despite adopting a Muslim identity during the Chechen–Russian war, Basayev was not primarily attracted to Islam—as such, any rhetoric on establishing an Islamist state came second to his desire to fight Russia (particularly given the fact that his home village of Vedeno had been destroyed following its aerial bombardment by Russian federal forces). In addition to Basayev, there were a significant number of other militant groups operating in the region under the leadership of individuals such as Salman Raduyev (who died in December 2002), Movladi Udugov and Ruslan Gelayev.

Frequently classified as radical Islamists interested in establishing a new political and social order according to *Shari'a* (Islamic law), it could be concluded that these groups were primarily motivated by ethno-nationalist sentiments and driven by the desire to secure independence from the federal Government. By espousing the radical Islamic language of *jihad* and describing themselves as *mujahidin*, Islam has been manipulated as an effective tool, in order to raise additional sources of revenue from Muslim sympathizers worldwide. Indeed, the operational use of Islam became evident at the end of the first Chechen conflict in 1996, when attempts to introduce *Shari'a* failed. Although religion was used to mobilize Chechen militants, in the absence of a threat the Chechens reverted to traditional methods of social control, with disputes settled by respected elders or by the use of firearms.

One militant leader operating in the unstable Chechen environment who was dedicated solely to Islam, until his assassination by federal security services (confirmed in April 2002), was the guerrilla leader ibn al-Khattab, thought to have been born in Saudi Arabia. A dedicated Wahhabist, Khattab moved to Chechnya in 1995 with a small militant following, after having previously fought in Afghanistan and Tajikistan. Attracted by the war of resistance against Russia, his declared intention in Chechnya was to dispel Russian forces from the northern Caucasus and install an Islamist Republic that would include Dagestan, Karachayevo-Cherkessiya, Kabardino-Balkariya (the Kabardino-Balkar Republic), North Osetiya—Alaniya and Ingushetiya, with Chechnya playing the leading role. With his relative pan-Islamist aims, Khattab added a legitimate militant Islamist component to the Chechen cause. Furthermore, owing to his connections with the international network of militant Islamist groups, Khattab was believed to have been responsible for securing financial support from al-Qa'ida, and from radical sources in the Middle East (for example, Jordan, Saudi Arabia, Turkey and the United Arab Emirates). These strategic resources ensured that Khattab and his militants won important successes against the federal forces in Chechnya immediately upon their arrival, thus earning him renown throughout the region, and inevitably drawing him closer to Basayev.

It was when Basayev and Khattab joined forces in the late 1990s that widespread criminality and the sporadic guerrilla activities conducted by various Chechen groups became overshadowed by the spectre of 'Islamist' terrorism. In August 1999 Basayev and Khattab are believed to have led an incursion into Dagestan, as a result of which several villages were seized, and an Islamic territory declared. Although the militants were dispelled by federal troops one month later, the incursion was followed by a series of terrorist attacks throughout Russia, which were attributed by the Government to Chechen militants. The attacks included the bombings in August–September 1999 of a federal military-housing complex in Buinaksk, Dagestan; a shopping centre and two apartment buildings in Moscow; and an apartment building in Volgodonsk, in southern Russia; in addition to further bomb attacks in 2000, which targeted the central market in Vladikavkaz in July and Moscow's Pushkinskaya metro station in August. From 1999 Chechen militants also adopted the strategic use of suicide bombings to eliminate federal troop leaders and military unit commanders in Chechnya, to attack military and administrative facilities, and to eliminate so-called 'traitors of the nation'. Most attacks were believed to have been conducted by one of two suicide battalions, known as 'Shakhid', and formed by Basayev in September 1999. Over a two-day period in July 2001, Russian sources reported five suicide attacks, which killed 33 people and wounded a further 84.

Evidently, radical militant Islam has played an important role in the recent Chechen instability. However, it is also important to understand the rise of Chechen militancy in the context of widespread criminality. The decline of state-sponsored terrorism following the end of the Cold War forced many militant groups to resort to criminal activities as a primary source of funding. Chechen militants organizing themselves and their operations in Russia from the early 1990s were no different. In fact, groups in the northern

Caucasus benefited substantially from the unprecedented growth of criminality in Chechnya under the leadership of Gen. Dzhokhar Dudayev (who died in a missile attack in 1996).

Commonly referred to as a haven for organized crime, Chechnya has provided insurgents with the opportunity to profit from the illegal sale of petroleum, trafficking in illicit narcotics and weapons, and kidnapping. Although the responsibility for most kidnappings was attributed to criminal groups, it was recognized that the forces of Basayev and Khattab regularly engaged in criminal activities. In a video-recording confiscated by Russian troops in Chechnya in May 2001, Basayev acknowledged his role in organizing many of the kidnappings that had taken place in Chechnya.

Although it was rarely contested that Chechen militants engaged in crime to finance their activities, it was rather difficult to distinguish confidently the primary motivation of rebel commanders. For example, prior to joining forces with Khattab, Basayev was not regarded as a radical Islamist. The question, therefore, remained as to whether Basayev was driven by ethno-nationalism, radical Islam or the creation of an environment conducive to his criminal activities in Chechnya and the region, through the manipulation of the hostilities.

With the death of Khattab, it remained largely unknown how militant Islam in the Caucasus would be affected. Despite leaving a legacy as a successful guerrilla leader, and attracting a small number of Arab fighters to the Chechen cause, it had yet to be proven whether Khattab's presence had sparked the emergence of a dedicated group of radical Islamist soldiers engaged in *jihad*. Considering the growing number of civilian casualties in Chechnya from 1999 (with an estimated 5,000 civilian deaths, and over 200,000 internally displaced persons), it appeared radical Islam had become attractive to a younger generation, seeking retribution and stability. However, this fear may have been overstated. Apart from the Islamist militants that have gathered in the region from around the world—including Afghanistan—preliminary evidence suggested that conflict in the Caucasus was reorganizing along ethno-nationalist lines. For example, following the suicide attacks on the USA in September 2001, the subsequent death of Khattab and the growing US involvement in the southern Caucasus, it was reported that Basayev had rejoined the Chechen nationalist leader and President of the unrecognized 'Chechen Republic of Ichkeriya', Khalid 'Aslan' Maskhadov.

## Chechnya after the US-led Intervention in Afghanistan

Militant Islam in Chechnya, and similarly the Chechen experience of insurgency, has undergone a transition, to match the environmental conditions in which it seeks to operate. This evolution accelerated in the aftermath of the US-led campaign in Afghanistan as a result of several fundamental factors, such as intensified human rights violations by federal forces (for example, through reports of 'cleansing' operations and the disappearance of key Chechen figures); rising civilian casualties in federal counter-terrorism operations; the assassination of Khattab; and the anticipated repercussions of government-initiated political solutions unrepresentative of all the warring factions, such as the referendum on a draft constitution for Chechnya, held in March 2003. Responding to this operational environment, the emerging form of Chechen insurgency was characterized by the desire to conduct maximum-casualty attacks against federal military and civilian targets. Supporting this perception was the increased tendency of Chechen militants, notably war widows (often referred to as the 'Black Widows'), to conduct suicide missions, as exemplified by the crisis of 23–26 October 2002, when over 40 militants, armed with explosive devices, took hostage more than 800 people in Moscow's Nord-Ost theatre, and demanded the immediate withdrawal of all federal forces from Chechnya (the militants and some 129 hostages were killed during a rescue operation). Subsequently, on 27 December the headquarters of the pro-Moscow republican Government was targeted by suicide bombers, resulting in at least 83 deaths. As a result of this general trend, the increased lethality of Chechen terrorism since 1999 can be accounted for. According to figures from the Russian Ministry of Internal Affairs, recorded acts of terrorism increased three-fold between 1999 and 2002, from 100 to 272. These figures are likely to continue to rise as a new generation of insurgents, raised in an environment of violence, joins the rank and file of Chechen militancy.

Clarity can be gained by dividing rebel groups into those primarily motivated by nationalism, and those driven by radical Islamist beliefs. Although this distinction lacks detail about the nature of individual groups, there are inherent difficulties associated with attempts to identify specific groups. In part, this is the result of the operational dynamics of the Chechen situation; violent campaigns in both the first and second wars have resulted in the rapid turnover of unit commanders at every level. None the less, the US Department of State's designation, in February 2003, of three separate groups as terrorist organizations can be used as a guide to examine the intricacies of the existing state of Chechen militancy. The key to assessing these groups, as illustrated below, is the sliding scale of motivation espoused by the militants, which is, therefore, exemplified by a loose confederation of groups that operate both in unison and independently from one another.

*The Islamic International Brigade (IIB)*. Led by Khattab until his assassination in 2002, the IIB was considered to be the most violent group in Chechnya. With a following of an estimated 200 to 300 foreign *mujahidin*, and believed to include a greater number of indigenous fighters, IIB militants are well versed in sabotage and subversive activity; its most notable campaign was the 1999 rebel incursion into Dagestan (see above). Shamil Basayev played a formative role in the group; in joining forces with Khattab, Basayev provided the IIB with a political dimension and a direct link to Chechnya. Basayev remained commander of the Chechen units after Khattab's death, and Abu al-Walid (Abd al-Aziz al-Ghamidi) took overall control of the IIB. Born and raised in Saudi Arabia, and allegedly of Chechen ancestry, Walid was believed to have met Khattab in 1995, and to have become his deputy in 1999, before the Dagestani incursion that acted as a catalyst to the second Chechen war. Following a period of relative inactivity after the death of Khattab, Walid was believed successfully to have attracted fresh external Wahhabi support to secure future IIB operations. His potential success as commander was proven with the shooting down of a military helicopter in August 2002, which killed 118 soldiers. Despite conducting equally devastating acts of insurgency under Walid as had occurred under Khattab, the IIB had been reorganized to meet the demands of the evolving operational environment. Perhaps the most significant change within the IIB was the fact that Walid had begun to co-operate with Maskhadov, an enemy of Khattab. Indeed, in mid-2002 it was reported that individual IIB units had joined the Eastern Front of the regular forces of the Chechen rebel army. The implications of this could risk the future of IIB operations, particularly the IIB's ability to attract foreign support and foreign fighters. Although Maskhadov was fighting for an independent Chechnya, his predominantly nationalist aims did not comply with the pan-Islamic, Wahhabi ideology of IIB supporters fighting for an Islamic caliphate, initially to encompass the Caucasus, before spreading further afield.

*Riyadus-Salikhin Reconnaissance and Sabotage Battalion of Chechen Martyrs*. Also known as Riyadus-as-Saliheen (RAS), this group officially emerged in October 2002, when its existence was announced by Basayev, at the commencement of the theatre hostage situation. Initially believed to be led by Movsar Barayev, the commander of the theatre operation, it was subsequently recognized that the RAS was under the leadership of Basayev. At the time of the theatre incident, Basayev led Maskhadov's Military Committee and was in charge of the Chechen fighters of the IIB—two positions that overlapped, given the relationship established between Walid and Maskhadov. Prior to joining forces with Khattab, thus immediately turning into an enemy of many Chechen nationalists, Basayev had been one of Maskhadov's trusted subordinates. His agreement to attempt to co-operate with Maskhadov between July and October 2002 was thus not wholly out of character; however, the co-operative façade was rapidly destroyed after Maskhadov publicly denounced the hostage-taking incident. Basayev responded by affirming that he was abandoning his other commitments to operate independently as the head of the newly formed RAS. Confirming the role that Basayev held in the RAS, Barayev and other theatre hostage-takers had stated that they were acting on the orders of Basayev. This is important to note, because it emphasizes the fact that Basayev commanded a group of dedicated militants, with the resolve to engage in mass-casualty acts. Estimates indicated that the RAS had approximately 200 militants, including a female division. However, since Basayev previously commanded one-third of all Chechen militants, it remained to be seen whether any more would join the ranks of the RAS. Given that the RAS had been operational for less than one year, the group appeared to be very loosely organized. That said, there was evidence that the RAS was slowly evolving into a structure with affiliated *mujahidin* units. In many respects, the RAS may be considered as an emerging military-guerrilla unit and the only 'real' armed structure developing among Chechen militants. Based on the commitment Basayev had shown to Wahhabism in the past, and the focus placed on suicide missions, it was apparent that the group was officially motivated by radical Islamist ideals, including the establishment of a Chechen state based on *Shari'a* law. Confirming this view, Basayev stated in an interview that 'anything that does not agree with the *Shari'a* does not belong to our policies'. If the RAS continues to co-ordinate acts such as the Moscow theatre crisis and the suicide bombing of the republican government building, it is increasingly likely that Basayev will have the potential to attract external support. According to analysts and journalists in the region, Basayev was perhaps the only commander capable of inspiring respect from young and emerging Chechen fighters. Thus, in addition to impressing the international radical Islamist militant community, he was *en route* to accessing a large number of indigenous recruits, increasingly fuelled by a sense of hopeless revenge in a militarized society that offered few options for a stable future life.

*Special Purpose Islamic Regiment (SPIR)*. The third Chechen group to be designated as terrorist by the US Department of State was the SPIR. According to US sources, the SPIR was also led by Basayev; however some US analysts allocated the leadership of the SPIR to Khamzat Gelayev. Furthermore, the same sources suggested that members of the SPIR were Wahhabi radicals, seeking to establish a Caucasian caliphate. Although these conclusions were partly indisputable, the roots of the SPIR and its recent manifestation consisted of a network of motivations, players and alliances. Several accounts indicated that the

SPIR was formed in 1996 by Arbi Barayev, as a criminal organization engaged in kidnapping and the smuggling of petroleum, although it also operated as part of the Chechen resistance organized by Maskhadov. Following a dispute with Maskhadov, there were reports that Basayev expanded his criminal group by enlisting the support of Islamist militants, including the Chechen separatist leader Zelimkhan Yandarbiyev (Dzhokar Dudayev's successor until 1997), and Khattab. Tracing the operations of Arbi Barayev and Khattab until 2002, it is unlikely that the two worked closely together; Khattab's dedication to Islam conflicted with Arbi Barayev's strictly criminal motivations. Based on several accounts, it thus appears that the SPIR has been misunderstood, and in fact encompasses a vastly different group of militants, controlled by the Military Committee of the Majlis al-Shura of the Chechen Republic of Ichkeriya, led by Aslan Maskhadov. Although Maskhadov was specifically seeking national independence from Russia, after Dudayev sought the support of radical Islam following the first military intervention by federal forces in 1994, Maskhadov continued to embrace Islamism for two primary reasons. First, it attracted potential Chechen recruits who wanted more than a separate state, thus providing a justifiable ideology for opposition; and second, it has secured a previously inaccessible source of international funding. Despite considering co-operation with Islamist militants, Maskhadov consistently distanced himself from extreme radicals from abroad. For example, he maintained a distance from Khattab, as well as from RAS suicide attacks. Maskhadov was extremely reluctant to lose any of his fighters to suicide missions. It was thus evident that Maskhadov had, in part, succesfully commandeered Islam—albeit a moderate form—to secure his group and mission.

The way in which the Chechen resistance has organized itself post-11 September 2001 is significant for numerous reasons. First, a clearer delineation of interests and leadership appears to be emerging. Consolidated aims and motivations, especially those focused around radical forms of Islam, have been proven to pose unprecedented threats, as illustrated by the elimination of barriers to the perpetration of mass-casualty suicide attacks. The examples given above are illustrative of the increasing intensity of insurgency emerging from Chechnya, and there are numerous other examples: in September 2002 a passenger bus was the target of a bomb attack, which killed approximately 20 people; in October an attack was perpetrated outside a police station in Groznyi, killing around 25; in April 2003 a bus carrying construction workers from Groznyi was targeted by a remote-controlled bomb, leaving six people dead; in May suicide bombers drove a truck bomb into the district headquarters of the Federal Security Committee at Znamenskoye, killing at least 59 people; in the same month there was a suicide attack at an Islamic festival in Ilishkan Yurt, which killed 16 (the attack had been intended to assassinate Akhmed haji Kadyrov, the Governor and Head of Administration of Chechnya); in June a female suicide bomber killed at least 17 bus passengers (mainly airmen and airbase personnel) near Mozdok, close to the Chechen border; and in July two female suicide bombers detonated explosives outside an annual music festival at the Tushino airfield, Moscow, and approximately 16 people were killed. Thus, the future of Chechnya continued to occupy a precarious position, wavering between peace and the emergence of an unprecedented campaign of terrorism.

## FUTURE PROSPECTS

Unquestionably, the future development of radical and militant Islam in Central Asia and the Caucasus will continue to be influenced by the activities of the Western-led counter-terrorism coalition throughout the region, the subsequent counter-terrorism policy followed by the regional governments, and the associated reaction of the local population. The most disquieting conclusion to result from the response to the suicide attacks of September 2001 was that counter-terrorist operations had done little to target the endless regional grievances that were attracting increasing numbers of followers to radical forms of political Islam. These grievances included the dire (and deteriorating) economic and social conditions, incessant corruption among government and law-enforcement officials, and the perpetration of unchecked human rights abuses as the foremost method of controlling society and displacing political opposition. By late 2003 the Western-led coalition remained unresponsive to these conditions, contributing to the emergence of an environment favouring the growth of radical and, most threateningly, militant Islam. Western rhetoric, promoting peace, and economic and political reform in the region, has come to be regarded by many as paradoxical, and might eventually compel growing numbers of disaffected people to perceive membership of Islamist opposition groups as their only opportunity to initiate change.

## BIBLIOGRAPHY

Akiner, Shirin. 'Islamic Fundamentalism in Central Asia: Historical Background and Contemporary Context'. Geneva, *UNHCR Centre for Documentation and Research Writenet Paper*, No. 13/2000, May 2001.

Arutiunov, Sergei. 'Ethnicity and Conflict in the Caucasus', in Fred Wehling (Ed.), *Ethnic Conflict and Russian Intervention in the Caucasus*. San Diego, CA, University of California Institute for the Study of Global Conflict and Co-operation, 1995.

Baev, Pavel. *Will Russia go for a Military Victory in Chechnya?* Sandhurst, Conflict Studies Research Centre, Jan. 2000.

Blandy, Charles. *Daghestan: The Gathering Storm*. Sandhurst, Conflict Studies Research Centre, June 1998.

Bremer, Ian, and Ray, Taras (Eds). *New States New Politics*. Cambridge, Cambridge University Press, 1997.

Cornell, Svante, and Regine, Spectre. 'Central Asia: More Than Islamic Radicals', in *The Washington Quarterly*. Vol. 25, No. 1 (Winter), 2002.

de Waal, Thomas. 'Fighting for Chechnya: Is Islam a Factor?' (*PBS Wide Angle Briefing*). New York, NY, Thirteen/WNET New York, 28 Aug. 2002.

Fredholm, Michael. *Uzbekistan and the Threat from Islamic Extremism*. Sandhurst, Conflict Studies Research Centre. March 2003.

Haghayeghi, Mehrdad. *Islam and Politics in Central Asia*. London, Macmillan, 1995.

Howard, Shawn. 'The Afghan Connection', in *National Security Studies*. Vol. 6, No. 3 (Summer), 2000.

Ignatenko, Alexander. 'Ordinary Wahhabism', in *Russian Journal*. 1 Dec. 2001.

Kulikov, Anatoliy. 'Trouble in the North Caucasus', in *Military Review*. July–Aug. 1999.

Jersild, Austin Lee. 'Who Was Shamil? Russian Colonial Rule and Sufi Islam in the North Caucasus, 1859-1917', in *Central Asia Survey*. Vol. 14, No. 2, 1995.

Lieven, Anatol. 'Nightmare in the Caucasus', in *The Washington Quarterly*. Vol. 23, No. 1, 2000.

'Chechnya After September 11th', statement before the Commission for Security and Co-operation in Europe. 9 May 2002.

Makarenko, Tamara. 'Crime and Terrorism in Central Asia', in *Jane's Intelligence Review*. Vol. 12, No. 7, July 2000.

'Drugs in Central Asia: Security Implications and Political Manipulations', in *Cahiers d'Etudes sur la Méditerrannée orientale et le monde turco-iranien (CEMOTI)*. No. 32, 2002.

'Foreign Bases Complicate Terror Assessments in Central Asia', in *Jane's Intelligence Review*. Vol. 15, No. 6, July 2003.

'Chechen Militants Threaten Increased Terrorism', in *Jane's Intelligence Review*. Vol. 15, No. 5, May 2003.

Mann, Poonam. 'Islamic Movement of Uzbekistan: Will it Strike Back?', in *Strategic Analysis: A Monthly Journal of the Institute for Defence Studies and Analyses*. Vol. 26, No. 2, April–June 2002.

Pain, Emil. 'The Second Chechen War: The Information Component', in *Military Review*. July–Aug. 2000.

Rashid, Ahmed. *Jihad: The Rise of Militant Islam in Central Asia*. New Haven, CT, and London, Yale University Press, 2002.

Weir, Fred. 'A New Terror-War Front: The Caucasus', in *The Christian Science Monitor*. 26 Feb. 2002.

# THE ECONOMIES OF THE COMMONWEALTH OF INDEPENDENT STATES: AN OVERVIEW

## Prof. PHILIP HANSON

Revised for this edition by the Editor

### OVERVIEW

After 1991 there were 15 sovereign states in the territory once occupied by the Union of Soviet Socialist Republics (USSR). Relations between them were neither uniform across the vast former Soviet empire nor stable over time. The most important distinction was between, on the one hand, the three Baltic states, Estonia, Latvia and Lithuania, which firmly rejected all organizational connections with the Russian Federation and, on the other, the remaining 12 states. By late 1993 all of those 12 had become members of the Commonwealth of Independent States (CIS). At the end of 2001 these countries' total population numbered some 282m., of which Russia accounted for just over one-half.

The CIS was not a confederation, not a military alliance and not a common market—it was chiefly a forum for policy discussions. Membership in it implied an acceptance of a common past and a recognition that there might be some gains to be had from joint action. The stance of the Baltic states, the population of which constituted only about 3% of the total population of the former USSR, reflected their history in the 20th century. Independent in 1918–40, they were forcibly annexed by the USSR. Their economic development after 1991 (discussed here for comparative reasons only), as well as their policy towards Russia, differed markedly from that of any of the CIS countries. By the early 2000s the three Baltic economies had become much closer, in organizational and production structure, to Western European economies, and were poised to become full members of the European Union (EU) in May 2004. The CIS nations, in contrast, remained, at best, half-reformed—and in several cases a good deal less than that. The widespread use of barter, money surrogates and the US dollar left internal price structures in the CIS countries still somewhat different to those in the West. State control of foreign trade was much reduced, but still significant. All the CIS states had begun to use Western-style national income accounting, but in none of them was the statistical system fully adapted to internationally acceptable levels of reporting. In short, the old problems of comparison of economic data were still present.

At the same time, the beginnings of economic transformation brought new difficulties for statisticians. The decline in economic activity in the CIS states, between 1989 and 2001, appeared to be enormous, at about 38%. In fact, this post-communist decline in economic activity was exaggerated in the available data. Indeed, even that part of the measured decline that was real had less impact on people's welfare than the figures might suggest—although for large numbers of people there was still real hardship. The new private sector was inadequately covered by statistical reporting. Part of officially reported output in the past had been a statistical mirage, which disappeared along with producers' needs to exaggerate their output in order to qualify for plan-fulfilment bonuses. One part of the officially reported decline in output was real enough, but consisted merely of a loss of wasteful economic activity that had been generated by the old system. Another part of the officially recorded 'slump' was a loss of arms production, of no value to consumers. Meanwhile, some economic activity that was of the greatest value to households in the CIS states, such as subsistence food production, was substantial, but had never been properly covered in the statistics. This activity almost certainly increased. None the less, the official figures are the only guidance available, and they show, for the CIS countries as a group, no clear recovery at all until 1999. In 1997, for the first time since the dissolution of the USSR, total officially recorded output grew, albeit by only 1%. This evidence of economic progress, however, was swiftly followed by a renewed decline in output from the second quarter of 1998, a deterioration that was made worse by the Russian financial crisis of August. That crisis dragged the output of the entire CIS down by 3.5% in 1998. The devaluation of the Russian currency, the rouble, and petroleum-price increases lifted the Russian economy once more by 1999, and with it the CIS as a whole. Although the recovery continued, by 2002 GDP in the CIS economies, taken together, was equivalent to 75.1% of its 1991 level, in real terms.

The economic development of the remaining CIS countries was closely tied to that of Russia. The total output of the group turned upwards when output increased in Russia—briefly in 1997, and then continuously from 1999; in other years the decline in output was similar. This was true for the CIS as a whole, but not for each individual country. For several, including Ukraine and Kazakhstan, the next largest CIS economies after the Russian Federation, trade with Russia represented a significant part of their overall economic activity—hence the close alignment of changes in output—but this was not so in every case. Apart from the difference in degree of interdependence with Russia, two other factors produced divergences within the group of states in post-communist development. Some CIS countries experienced damaging wars (Tajikistan, Armenia, Azerbaijan and Georgia); and some, most strikingly Belarus and Uzbekistan, attempted to avoid economic reform altogether.

The living standards of households in the former USSR were exceptionally difficult to measure to begin with; and the decline in general economic conditions after 1989 was, at the same time, exaggerated by the available figures. In the case of Russia, officially measured gross domestic product (GDP) per head of population in 2001, if converted to US dollars at a rate reflecting the rouble's domestic purchasing power, was about US $7,100, according to UN Development Programme (UNDP) figures. That put Russia in the same category as Colombia or Brazil, at about one-fifth the US level. The figure for Belarus was slightly higher ($7,620), and the figures for the remaining CIS member states were between $6,500 (Kazakhstan) and a very low $1,170 (Tajikistan).

It might appear that a decline of almost 50% in production, accompanied, as it was, by a decrease in foreign trade, would entail the most severe of economic reverses for most, if not all, of the population, and particularly for low-income families with large numbers of children, and pensioners not supported by other members of an extended family. However, the decline experienced by most households, for the reasons given above, was considerably less than the official percentage decreases in GDP until 1999 would suggest. In addition, investment fell dramatically in the CIS countries; although this was damaging for the future of those countries, it was not so for the welfare of their inhabitants in the short term.

The extreme economic turbulence that followed the formal dissolution of the USSR, in December 1991, continued an earlier unravelling that had begun in about 1988. That, in turn, could be seen as an outcome of destabilizing efforts to reverse the long-term deterioration in Soviet economic performance. Between the 1920s and the early 1970s the Soviet economy had, on the whole, grown relatively quickly. One result was that, according to most assessments, the difference between GDP per head in the USSR and in the USA showed a tendency to decline. Thus, the famous objective of Soviet leader Stalin (Iosif V. Dzhugashvili), of 'catching up and over-taking' the developed capitalist countries, was, for a long time, something that Soviet socialism was, indeed, achieving.

From the late 1950s, however, the growth of Soviet output and productivity slowed remorselessly. By the early 1970s, according to official Soviet measurements, the difference between the USSR and the USA was no longer being eroded. For the long-term survival of a regime with ideological claims to economic superiority, this was an ominous development. For a military 'superpower', the prospect of gradually comparing increasingly unfavourably with other national economies was even more ominous. However, no serious attempt was made to tackle the problem until the mid-1980s. Early in Leonid Brezhnev's term as Communist Party leader (1964–82), there was an attempt at economic reform. Thereafter, the main impulse in policy-making was not to disturb the status quo.

In 1983, under Yurii Andropov, and from March 1985 until the USSR's collapse in December 1991, under Mikhail Gorbachev, there were serious and increasingly radical attempts by the country's leadership to improve Soviet economic performance. At first there was little agreement on the causes of the slowing of growth, so that remedial efforts were constantly being redirected. Among the causes suggested, with some degree of plausibility, were: major economic policy errors (such as in the choice of investment priorities); an excessive military burden; semi-isolation from Western trade and technology; and an erosion of discipline in an economic and political system that relied heavily on authority to function.

In 1987, however, when Gorbachev's early efforts at change began to seem ineffectual, a consensus developed among policy-makers that it was, above all, the centrally administered economic system that was responsible for the relative economic decline. It followed that a shift from 'planning' to the 'market' was needed. What that meant, however, was not clear to most of the politicians and economists who were accustomed to the traditional system. For some time they aimed to establish a 'half-way house' economy, in which there would be markets for products, but state ownership of nearly all farms and factories would continue. Experience in countries such as Poland and Hungary, however, supported the view of some Western economists that a 'Third Way' of this sort, where there was a market for products, but not for land or capital, was not viable.

In the Soviet capital, Moscow, from about 1989 the idea of a transformation to a Western type of private-enterprise economy began increasingly to be accepted. This remarkable shift in thinking was reflected in a large volume of legislation designed to create the legal framework of a full market economy with, among other features, various forms of private enterprise, commercial banks, stock markets, anti-monopoly rules, contract law and a convertible currency. Such a deliberate transformation of an entire economic system in peacetime was unprecedented, and it was not surprising that it proved to be a turbulent process. In the decade that followed only the Baltic states seemed to have begun to make clear economic gains out of the general upheaval. In principle, a successful transformation of the economic system was a change from which, in the long term, all were likely to benefit. In practice, and in the short term, there were many people whose position would deteriorate, and there was greater uncertainty for everyone concerning jobs and prices. Moreover, the political liberalization that accompanied the economic changes released hitherto suppressed separatist tendencies and ethnic animosities among the peoples of the USSR.

In 1990–91, amid increasing economic disarray, inter-ethnic and national separatist tensions increased. The failed *putsch* attempt by traditionalists in the Soviet leadership, in August 1991, precipitated the Union's final dissolution. Most of the 15 republics increased their pressure for greater powers at the expense of the centre. Within weeks of the suppression of the coup attempt, the three Baltic states regained the independent status that they had enjoyed in the period between the two World Wars. In December the Russian leadership, under its President, Boris Yeltsin, effectively signalled that an end to the USSR had been decided.

Even before the formal dissolution of the USSR, most of the republics had agreed to join the CIS. By the end of 1993 all of the former Union Republics had joined, or rejoined, the CIS, except for the three Baltic countries. The motives of the non-Russian CIS states for preserving at least a loose association with the Russian Federation varied considerably. All but Azerbaijan, Kazakhstan and Turkmenistan had begun their independent existence with a very strong reliance on supplies of fuel (chiefly petroleum and natural gas) from Russia. These supplies came at well below world market prices and used an infrastructure of pipelines, pumping stations and refineries that was orientated to supplies from Russia. The poorest of the CIS states, Kyrgyzstan, Tajikistan, Turkmenistan and Uzbekistan, had also been the beneficiaries of large budget transfers within the USSR. In some cases the motives were, primarily, to do with security. Armenia, for example, was dangerously isolated as a result of the war in neighbouring Azerbaijan over the ethnically Armenian enclave of Nagornyi Karabakh (Artsakh to the Armenians). Similarly, Georgia found its territorial integrity threatened by secessionist movements that received covert Russian support, and eventually capitulated to this pressure by accepting membership of the CIS.

Russia accounted for just over one-half of the population and about three-fifths of the output of the CIS grouping. Ukraine, with about 17% of combined CIS gross national product (GNP) in 1993, was the second largest economy. By that time the 12 states no longer shared the rouble currency, and difficulties in intra-CIS payments were prominent. All had currencies that were inconvertible or of only limited convertibility. In none of the CIS economies was the necessary liberalization of prices, stabilization of price levels, privatization of ownership, opening to the world economy and restructuring of economic activity pursued in a systematic and determined way. In some, they were simply deferred, so that the economy drifted in a 'systemic vacuum': no longer a centrally planned economy, but not a market economy either.

Nowhere was resistance to market reform the result of an explicit adoption of the old, communist, ideological stance by the leadership. The situation, broadly, was that policy-making was dominated by traditionalists from the old élite, who spoke of the need to proceed cautiously with reform, but did not openly repudiate reform in general. Market reform had become the new orthodoxy. The real division among policy-makers was between those who were serious about it and those who were unenthusiastic and nervous about their chances of keeping power if they embarked on substantial change.

In these circumstances, financial discipline was weak. For all the CIS states a rapid rate of increase in consumer prices was, for most of 1991–96, a common experience. This inflation rate was typically around 2,000%–2,500% in 1992, but it decreased thereafter. By 1995 the average inflation rate for consumer prices in the 12 CIS countries (weighted by the size of their economies) was about 170%. By 1999 inflation had become more modest. In the CIS as a whole, the rate of increase in consumer prices in 2000 was some 27%. There remained a great deal of individual variation, however. In Belarus, for example, the rate of inflation was about 169%.

Despite the apparent collapse in output, officially recorded unemployment figures remained comparatively low in the CIS countries. In Russia, at the end of 2001 a labour-force survey measured unemployment at 9.0%—a figure that was low when the scale of the decline in recorded output was taken into account. In most of the other CIS countries the officially reported rates of unemployment were substantially lower, at around 3.7% in Ukraine, 2.3% in Belarus, and 1.3% in Azerbaijan. Typically, this was partly the result of reporting procedures and partly the result of the genuine retention of labour by enterprises that had not yet been obliged to restructure. In other words, the low unemployment rates could, in most cases, be seen as symptomatic of a lack of economic adjustment, and as a signal that reductions in the labour force were yet to come.

However, the low official unemployment figures did not entirely misrepresent the situation across most of the former USSR. Few state or newly privatized enterprises were being closed down. Nor were they being forced to make mass redundancies. For a long time, outside the Baltic states, monetary policies had remained lenient, and many producers continued to be supported by a combination of budget subsidies, easy credits, and being left to accumulate tax- and electricity-payment arrears with impunity. Estonia and Latvia pioneered tougher policies from 1992, and Lithuania and Armenia, Azerbaijan, Georgia, Kazakhstan, Kyrgyzstan and Moldova followed later. Russia began in 1992, but pursued an intermittent approach to financial stabilization. From 1995 its fiscal and monetary policies were tightened, bringing inflation down to below 10% by early 1998. This apparent progress, however, proved to be largely illusory (see below).

Throughout the CIS, therefore, the application of financial discipline was, for several years, delayed or wavering. That produced results that were far from benign. Producers were not under much pressure to reduce employment, but output and, therefore, real incomes, decreased anyway. The restructuring of the economy that was necessary for a sustained recovery was largely deferred. Lenient ('soft') financial policies kept people nominally employed, but the resulting high inflation deterred the investment that would have helped to build a new economy. From 1995, however, tougher stabilization policies were pursued in most of the CIS—Belarus, Tajikistan, Turkmenistan and Uzbekistan being the exceptions.

## GROSS DOMESTIC PRODUCT

The structure of economic activity in the former USSR as a whole could not be depicted with any precision after its fragmentation. Data from some successor states were lacking; in others, divergences in statistical concepts and measures were reducing comparability between the different countries. Even if these problems had not existed, variations among the states in the extent and pattern of price liberalization made any compilation of figures unreliable.

In 1990 the composition of Soviet GDP by sector of origin, at current prices, was: industry 32%, agriculture 18%, construction 10%, transport and communications 6%, retail and wholesale trade 12%, and other services 22%. At that time the farming sector's contribution was probably understated. For the reasons given above, it is not possible to reconstruct the pattern of output for the former Soviet states combined at a recent date. The change in Russia, however, gives some indication of the likely overall change in structure for the CIS group. Between 1989 and 1998 the proportion of GDP held by industry, measured in current prices, declined, the proportion held by distribution and of other services rose, and the proportion held by the farming sector declined sharply. As these proportions were in current prices, the changes in them reflected the movement of relative prices, as well as output. Data on employment and on the volume of output suggested that, in real terms, industry contracted more than did most other sectors. The farming sector's 'share' in current-price output declined largely because agricultural prices did not keep pace with most other prices. Employment and real output in the farming sector performed comparatively well, although the sector's financial condition was very poor. The most significant advance was made in the business-services sector, especially financial services. Together with distribution, this was probably the only sector in which employment increased over the period discussed. Within the industrial sector, the decline in output in the Russian petroleum, gas and raw-materials industries was substantially less than in the engineering or textiles and clothing industries. That pattern of change, above all, provoked alarm about the 'deindustrialization' of Russia: a concern that might have been misplaced if (as many suspected) most of Russian manufacturing was uncompetitive to begin with. After the devaluation of the rouble in August 1998, Russian official figures showed industrial output to be growing rapidly (by some 6.0%, for example, in 2001). This rebound increased industry's share of GDP, after a long decline.

As a guide to changes in the overall composition of output in the CIS countries, these tendencies can give only a rather approximate idea of what was happening on the territory of the former USSR as a whole. Broadly speaking, however, states with a strong natural-resource base (such as Kazakhstan, Russia, Turkmenistan and Uzbekistan) fared better than those that were specialized in manufacturing, and the human capital of which was not markedly above the Soviet average.

The composition of Soviet total final domestic expenditure, by end-use, in 1990, according to official sources, was: household consumption 50.2%; public-sector consumption 19.7%; gross fixed investment 23.0%; and changes in inventories 7.1%. The one thing that is certain about subsequent changes in the relative importance of these final spending categories across the successor states is that real fixed investment decreased sharply until 1999. Indeed, it is clear that in many sectors gross investment was less than retirement of capital assets, so that the capital stock was shrinking. One effect was to reduce capacity in some branches of production. Another was to reduce technological change, since much new technology would have had to be embodied in new machinery.

The share of household consumption in total final expenditure appeared to have increased. This does not automatically follow from the relative decline in investment, since other final end-use categories exist, but it was implied by the evidence both of a relatively modest decline in agricultural output and a lesser decline in the output of manufactured consumer goods than of manufacturing in total. A more complete and accurate picture than that provided by the official data could be expected to strengthen this conclusion. Underrecorded activities, in other words, tended to be related to consumption.

## DIFFERENT TENDENCIES AMONG THE CIS STATES

The economies of individual CIS states are discussed in the

relevant chapters in Part Two. The broad picture shows rather little uniformity among them, beyond their common heritage and the continuing close economic links that most of them retain with Russia. The dissolution of the USSR was widely expected to cause very great damage for all the republics except the Russian Federation. As has already been mentioned, the poorer countries, especially those in Central Asia, had benefited from budget transfers from the all-Union Government under the old order. They had to endure severe budgetary problems when those transfers ceased, weakening their chances of maintaining a politically viable minimum of social services or of avoiding highly inflationary budgetary deficits—or both.

All the former Soviet countries had generally had, according to official figures, a deficit in the deliveries of merchandise between Russia and themselves, if the goods in question were valued at world prices. This was not, obviously, the case when these flows were measured in Soviet rouble prices; the main source of this discrepancy was the underpricing in roubles of petroleum and gas, of which Russia was the dominant supplier. This assessment, however, was always problematic.

First, all Soviet prices were distorted in a variety of ways, and not easily placed in the context of the world-price valuations that the Russian statisticians were using. The flows of services, as distinct from goods, were neglected. In several cases, such as Ukrainian provision of transit and port services, these could be the source of substantial net earnings for the states in question under a liberalized regime. Second, and more fundamentally, there was no reason to suppose that the previous pattern of flows of goods, set by the Soviet planners, would have much justification in a market economy. Some of the desirable adjustment involved, however, could only occur as the structure of production capacities changed. That, in turn, would require investment and would not, therefore, occur immediately. A third expected source of difficulty for most of the former Soviet republics was their transactions with the outside world. With a few exceptions, notably Russia, they had generated only small export flows to the outside world under the Soviet order, compared with the imports allocated to them by Soviet planners. Moreover, it was widely believed that no republic, apart from Russia, could be expected to inherit useful reserves of gold and 'hard' (convertible) currency net of foreign debt, since the USSR as a whole was widely understood, from the available data, to have bequeathed net liabilities to its successor states (Russia subsequently negotiated a so-called 'zero option' with many of the successor states, whereby it assumed responsibility for their share of the Soviet debt in exchange for their renunciation of any claim to Soviet assets—see below).

In the event, the varying economic fortunes of the successor countries in 1991–92 could not be explained by the disintegration of the USSR. All showed a severe decline in economic activity, of course, and the dissolution of the USSR played its part in that. However, the variations among them in the depth of that decline did not coincide with projections of their degree of 'dependency' on Russia or on the rest of the former USSR. Small states with large budget transfers from the central Soviet government in the past, and very large shares of output, dependent on transactions with the rest of the USSR, did not necessarily fare worse than the others. One reason for this was that failures in supplies of materials and components occurred between production units within each successor state, and by no means only in cross-border flows. At the same time other internal factors, specific to each state, rather than the links between them, had powerful effects on the course of economic events.

Particularly important were: war and civil war; and the presence of reformist or traditionalist leaderships. Countries engulfed in conflict suffered both from the direct effects of war

on economic activity and from an inability to put efforts into economic reorganization. The most systematic reformers succeeded in reducing inflation, but at the cost of substantial declines in economic activity. States that embarked on reform, but failed in stabilization, had high rates of inflation, but slightly less of a decline in output. The most unreconstructed of the successor states at first exhibited somewhat lower rates of inflation than the would-be reformers and substantially less of a decline in output than any of the other states. This 'advantage', if such it was, endured. If the overall level of GDP in 2001, as a percentage of the 1989 level, was 62% for both Russia and the CIS as a whole, the minimal reformers had much higher ratios: 103% in the case of Uzbekistan, 88% for Belarus and 84% for Turkmenistan. Finally, there were some special instances, where factors unique to a particular state played a role.

The main economic casualties of war were mentioned earlier: Armenia, Azerbaijan, Georgia and Tajikistan. In Armenia and Georgia, officially recorded output in 1992 was one-half or less than the 1989 level. By 1995 Georgia had experienced the most spectacular economic collapse of all: GDP had declined, officially at least, to below one-fifth of its 1989 level. Azerbaijan and Armenia by that date were, according to official data, operating at between one-third and two-fifths of their 1989 levels. Moldova, where fighting had been localized and brought to a halt, showed a less severe decline.

Both Armenia and Georgia, with traditionally entrepreneurial cultures and, in the case of the former, a large and wealthy diaspora, had more potential for economic modernization than the rest of the CIS. In both cases, land and housing privatization, requiring less elaborate policy-making than industrial privatization, developed relatively well, despite the disruption of war. However, both suffered, not only from the direct effects of war, but from having supply routes from the outside world blocked for reasons associated with the fighting. Nevertheless, by 1995 both had demonstrated their capacity for adaptation by bringing inflation under control. The two countries, both pursuing financial stringency and accelerated structural reform, began to experience real economic growth from the second half of the 1990s; this recovery was maintained, despite the impact of the Russian financial crisis.

Tajikistan, like Belarus, Turkmenistan and Uzbekistan was, quite apart from the conflict on its soil, reluctant to reform. These countries remained, by 2003, the least reconstructed of all the former Soviet economies. Their low private-sector shares of GDP (of between 20% and 45%) revealed their comparative underdevelopment in reform. In addition, inflation in these states tended to remain comparatively high until 2000, while levels of output, as mentioned above, were maintained more successfully. This was one benefit of resisting reform. It was associated, however, with autocratic rule; and this avoidance of reform offered no basis for later recovery and sustained growth. Nevertheless, even in these countries there were changes. In 2001 the Belarusian Government finally liberalized the foreign-exchange market, moderated the high rate of growth of the money supply and announced plans to end remaining price controls; however, many other controls remained. The Uzbek Government and Central Bank undertook to liberalize the exchange-rate regime in 2002. Again, however, the remaining controls were extensive; Uzbek farms, for example, had to sell one-half of their grain and cotton harvest to the state, at fixed prices.

In Kazakhstan and Kyrgyzstan, price liberalization was more cautious than in Russia, but reform policy, in the sense of privatization, was quite active. Policy-makers in Kazakhstan, where there was a well-endowed natural-resource base, were able to convince some major Western energy companies that the country was politically more stable and better-administered than Russia. They were also less wary of foreign ownership and control. Accordingly, Kazakhstan began to attract some significant foreign direct investment (FDI).

Russia naturally had a large influence on all the other former Soviet states. Its leadership approached reform more seriously from the start than that of any other CIS nation. Russia's reformers, however, encountered powerful domestic resistance to liberalization and stabilization. The privatization of large and medium-sized enterprises was enacted very rapidly in Russia, as significant groups within the old élite came to believe they could gain from it. It was carried out in a way that gave large initial advantages to insiders, particularly the incumbent state-enterprise managers. Financial discipline—the reduction of subsidies, of the budgetary deficit and of money-supply growth—was much more strongly resisted by powerful lobbies. It, therefore, moved in distinct phases, with gains coming particularly in early 1992, in late 1993 after President Yeltsin's dissolution of a hostile parliament, and again from 1995 onwards. The reduction of inflation in 1995–98, however, was achieved by monetary policy, with fiscal policy remaining loose. The general government deficits that resulted were financed by an unsustainable emission of short-term government paper—treasury bills (known by their Russian acronym, GKOs)—at yields that eventually made it impossible for the authorities to keep 'rolling over' (postponing their obligations on) the debt. This was at the root of the financial crisis of August 1998. After the four-fold devaluation of the rouble in 1998, accompanied by partial defaults on government debt, continued debt financing of the state budgetary deficit became impossible. At the same time, the Government was saved from the highly inflationary alternative—printing money—by the boost to Russian exporters and producers of import-substitutes given by the devaluation, as well as by a recovery in world petroleum prices. These stimulated economic activity, reduced imports (helping the Government to finance its servicing of foreign debt) and increased budget revenues and, as a result, GDP registered positive growth in 1999–2002.

Ukraine adhered to moderately traditionalist policies, and exhibited smaller initial declines in output than Russia. Early Ukrainian experiments with a separate national currency were particularly ill-conceived and damaging to stability. There was some progress in 1996, but reforms were subsequently restrained by the determined opposition of the Rada (parliament), which was dominated by conservatives and had more power than its Russian counterpart. For several years Ukraine's 'oligarchs' (politically influential business magnates), many of whom had made their fortunes trading in Russian gas, blocked more thorough reform. They had prospered from a system based on price and other market controls and did not want to see an end to these convenient arrangements. In 1999–2000, however, the Government of Prime Minister Viktor Yushchenko managed to push through reforms that helped to liberalize the economy. Partly for this reason, and partly because of Russia's growth, output increased in 2000, when Ukrainian GDP registered growth for the first time since the collapse of the USSR, and strong growth was maintained in 2001.

By 2001–02 most CIS states were experiencing respectable and, in some cases, even dramatic economic growth. In 2002, according to CIS figures, GDP registered a year-on-year increase of 12.9% in Armenia, of 10.6% in Azerbaijan, of 9.5% in Kazakhstan, of 9.1% in Tajikistan, of 7.2% in Moldova, and of between 4.1% and 5.4% in Ukraine, Russia, Belarus and Georgia.

One common feature of economic life in all of these countries was corruption. However, it did not necessarily always take the same form. In mid-1999 the World Bank and the European Bank for Reconstruction and Development under-

took a joint survey of firms in 22 former communist countries, which showed some interesting differences. The results of the survey were used to construct a 'state-capture' index, reflecting the proportion of respondents who had stated that their businesses were directly affected by private payments made to officials to influence decisions taken in parliament, government, the central bank, the courts and/or political parties. Whereas Azerbaijan, Kyrgyzstan, Moldova, Russia and Ukraine had high state-capture indexes, Belarus and Uzbekistan had low indexes: where the private sector had remained small-scale it appeared to have been unable to buy influence.

## ECONOMIC RELATIONS BETWEEN THE SUCCESSOR STATES

In late 1991, as the USSR was in the last stages of disintegration, strenuous efforts were made to establish an economic union. Grigorii Yavlinskii, the economist who led the negotiations on behalf of the Soviet Government, said at the time that some sort of economic community was the most that could, by then, be negotiated; in his view, mistrust and mutual animosities precluded the salvaging of even a loose political confederation. What he and his allies—including, at that stage, the IMF—hoped for, was the maintenance of a 'single economic space': essentially, a single currency and an area in which goods, labour and capital could move freely. The project failed.

To keep a single currency and also stabilize it (that is, reduce inflation to a low level) required close co-ordination of monetary and budgetary policies. It also required that those policies be kept restrictive. If co-ordination were lacking, growing budgetary deficits and credit creation in some of the states would have inflationary effects on all of them. Indeed, the temptation for each state to pursue inflationary fiscal policies was strong, since the inflationary consequences of its deficits would be spread across the whole currency area. Only Russia was so large a part of the ex-Soviet economy that its policy-makers could reasonably identify their national inflationary tendencies with those of the whole region. Yavlinskii and others drafted plans for an inter-state bank, under which monetary policy would be controlled for the whole 'rouble zone'. Using the analogy of the US Federal Reserve system, this would have been a central bank, jointly controlled by the Soviet republics.

There were three fundamental difficulties with this project. First, there were suspicions and animosities between many of the states and a widespread reclaiming of national identity, which made co-operation politically difficult to achieve. Second, the differences in development level and location relative to other, non-Soviet states were very great. Output per head in Tajikistan was well under one-half that of Russia. The gravitational pull of trade with 'outside' partners would, in the long term, be very different for different successor states: for Kazakhstan, with the People's Republic of China and the countries of southern Asia; for Ukraine, with Central Europe; and so on. Finally, the huge size and traditional dominance of Russia were such as to create particular difficulties. For nationalist leaders in many of the successor states, Russia represented the imperial power against which they were asserting their identity; and it was, in addition, such a large part of the total that it was bound to dominate any 'Commonwealth' or 'economic union'.

When the former Soviet states embarked on their separate national existences, the rouble remained their common currency. Links between producers and customers in different successor states were close and well-established. There was, moreover, a high degree of monopoly in some of the sectors in various states. This resulted in part from the traditional Leninist obsession with economies of scale, and in part from the central planners' need to deal with as small a number of production units as possible. Monopoly power was not an economic problem when the central authorities set all prices and output levels. In the absence of such controls, many felt it became a serious issue; there was, for example, only one producer of tractor-feed computer-printer paper in the USSR.

The scope for rapid adjustment of the pattern of production and supply was, therefore, limited. It was not as limited as it might at first appear to have been, however, for two reasons. First, many Soviet enterprises produced for their own use a great many items that were outside their official 'profile'. These included components, specialized machinery and even food for their own work-force—all characteristically supplied to their Western counterparts by separate, specialist businesses. Second, much of what was produced was wasted, or not wanted at all, and the transportation of many supplies was also unnecessarily circuitous and costly. Therefore, some adjustment of the pattern of output and delivery was already occurring in 1991 and continued to develop thereafter, without additional investment being needed to support a restructuring of capacity.

In the long term, with market economies established, production capacities reshaped and a reorientation of trade relationships permitted, it was likely that trade among the former Soviet countries would decline and trade with the outside world expand. Two independent projections of the effects of such changes, made in 1992, suggested a broadly similar picture: eventually, with market economies and a general opening to world trade, trade between the former Soviet republics would be likely to reach some 20%–40% of its 1987 level and the proportion of trade that was conducted with the outside world would become correspondingly larger.

Even so, inter-republic trade could usefully continue at relatively high levels for a time. The adjustments to a new environment would take several years. The changes in trade patterns that could be made in the short term were limited by the inherited structure and location of capacity. Given those limitations, the maintenance of open trading among the successor states and, above all, an effective system of payments were desirable. Moreover, fragmentation into different currencies would put a great strain on the skills and institutions available to operate so many different monetary systems. Such expertise as there was, was mainly to be found in Moscow. The IMF's initial support for a single rouble currency zone was understandable. However, the necessary coordination of monetary policies was, for political reasons, not feasible.

Although the Russian central banking authorities retained the sole right to issue rouble notes and coins, credit expansion was the responsibility of the new central banks in the remaining states. Budgetary policy, likewise, was the responsibility of their governments and parliaments. Goods deliveries were largely at the discretion of individual enterprises, but state and, often, local authorities took control of some of the output of enterprises on their territory and traded it themselves, or tried to impose control on enterprise transactions through licensing. Meanwhile, border controls at the new inter-state boundaries were rare and, where they did exist, of an improvised character.

All the states tried to impose some sort of control on cross-border flows, mainly on exports of food, consumer goods and principal raw materials. In conditions of shortage and sellers' markets, the governments concerned were trying to raise apparent domestic availability of these items, regardless of the damage done to each country's gains from trade. Thus, Russia first introduced export licences for deliveries outside the former USSR, and then extended the licensing system to exports to other former Soviet republics. For some products, this may have worked. For many others, the customs controls

were inadequate. Trade agreements were signed between the various states, but the implementation of them was low. In general, governments had insufficient control over production and distribution on their own territories to be able to deliver what they had promised.

Prices in inter-republic trade were, for the most part, in 1992–93, not world market prices; settlement was initially in roubles. By mid-1992, however, the Russian administration had come to view the 'rouble zone' as a threat to its own efforts to control inflation. Poorly controlled credit expansion in other states allowed their enterprises to buy supplies from Russia with rouble settlement through the banking system. On the Russian side, at least in early 1992, a serious attempt was being made to control credit. Thus, most of the other former Soviet states were operating trade deficits with Russia, and rouble bank accounts were being established in Russia from the credit expansion in Russia's partners. The Russian authorities moved to curb this by requiring all cross-border rouble bank payments to go through correspondent accounts at the Central Bank of the Russian Federation and by imposing upper limits on the imbalance that could be accumulated in these correspondent accounts.

The idea of the limits was to restrict the growth of Russia's money supply that was arising because of excess money creation in the other states. Accordingly, the limits were made adjustable, supposedly to reflect each partner's monetary behaviour—although this was not the way it worked in reality. If one of the other states was willing to allow its money supply to be controlled, in effect, by Russia, the limit could be raised; if not, it would be lowered. The third possibility was that the other country might introduce its own currency; if it did so, settlement with Russia might still be carried out through the correspondent account, but the other state would be under pressure to introduce its own currency in such a way as to keep the inflationary effect on Russia to a minimum—for example, by withdrawing its cash roubles from circulation and handing them over to the Russian Central Bank, rather than letting them flood into Russia as they ceased to be legal tender in the other state. This approach was applied rather more seriously from mid-1993, by which time other currencies were beginning to be introduced.

The rouble thus ceased to be a common currency, freely exchangeable across the whole of what had been a single rouble zone. In 1992 there were two types of new currency: those that had been introduced as the sole legal tender and those that had been introduced as a parallel currency to circulate alongside the rouble. The Ukrainian karbovanets (from September 1996 the hryvnya) and several others were, initially, less successful than the Estonian and Latvian currencies, for example. Gradually, however, the new currencies became established, although they were often neither stable nor convertible. The last to be introduced was the Tajik rouble, in May 1995 (replaced by the somoni—equivalent to 1,000 Tajik roubles—in October 2000).

From mid-1992 even those states outside Russia still using currency known as 'roubles' were, in reality, outside a single rouble currency area. This became more firmly the case from mid-1993. It remained open to all former Soviet states, however, with or without new currencies, to continue to trade with Russia on the basis of rouble settlement. Their correspondent accounts with the Russian Central Bank would then be their reserves, supporting trade with Russia and with each other. This option was akin to the sterling area of 1931–68, although the United Kingdom's pound sterling in the last years of the sterling area was a convertible currency, while the rouble had by 1995 attained only resident, current-account convertibility.

The other main options were the use of US dollars for inter-state settlement, the revival of the rouble zone in some new guise, or the establishment of a payments union, under which net balances outstanding would be periodically settled in a mixture of hard currency and credit. The restoration of the rouble zone would require the establishment of a joint, inter-state bank, upon which it proved impossible to agree. Even very limited schemes, such as a monetary union between Russia and Belarus, although discussed, were not implemented. Dollar settlement would require quantities of dollars that would be impossible for some of the states to provide. The clearing-union scheme would need less hard currency, but would require a degree of co-operation and appropriate expertise to operate it. These were not forthcoming.

In the course of 1992–93 payments arrangements were a shifting mixture of rouble zone, rouble area and dollar settlement. Arrangements varied over time, among different groups of states and across different types of transaction. In addition, many transactions across the new state borders were carried out on a barter basis or with the use of cash roubles. In a formal, contractual sense, prices tended to move towards world-market levels, but only in stages. Moreover, arrears of payment in a highly inflationary environment (unless payment was to be made in dollars or other convertible currencies) meant that the effective price received was often far less in real terms than the contract price.

A combination of real economic contraction, some reorientation of trade towards the outside world, the abandonment of wasteful and unwanted transactions and the disintegration of the rouble zone led to a decline in the volume of trade among the former Soviet republics until the mid-1990s. Thereafter, intra-CIS trade fluctuated, declining in 1997–99, and then rising, as the CIS region began its economic recovery. By 1997 such trade had, as predicted, become the lesser part of CIS countries' foreign trade. In the first 11 months of 2002 Russia delivered only 14.8% of its exports to other CIS countries, and received only 22.2% of its imports from them. The other CIS countries, taken together, were rather more CIS-orientated in terms of trade, but they still performed more than one-half of their external trade outside the CIS. In 1998, in the CIS countries as a whole, 26.6% of exports were reciprocal, as were 36.7% of imports—the higher import figure reflecting, in particular, the continued dependence of several CIS countries on Russian petroleum and gas. Those countries, however, were, largely, not paying Russia for their fuel supplies, and this was a constant source of friction, and of reductions in Russian supplies.

Early on, Russia sought to make its trade terms less attractive for non-CIS members than for its CIS partners. The main lever, in so far as these terms were concerned, was the threat to shift to world prices and hard-currency settlement. At the end of 1998 overdue payments from other CIS countries to Russian entities (mostly for petroleum and gas) totalled US $118m. This was not a large sum in relation to total Russian trade and payments, but that was the result, in part, of the debts being denominated in roubles. A few months earlier, before the devaluation of the rouble, the total in dollar terms was much larger.

In general, a pattern rather reminiscent of the old Council of Mutual Economic Assistance (CMEA) was emerging. The Soviet authorities in the 1970s, on a steeply rising energy market, had complained about the costs of supplying Eastern Europe (that is, the communist bloc of Central Europe and the Balkans) on preferential terms, but, nevertheless, continued to do so, raising the energy price for their CMEA partners, but still keeping it well below world levels and not insisting on hard-currency payment. It was only when real energy prices on world markets declined, in the 1980s, that this gap began to be closed. The other former Soviet states, or at least those that entered and remained in the CIS, similarly received better terms for Russian energy than those available on the world market. Even those, like Ukraine, with which Russia

had poor relations, were not simply required to pay world prices and settle debts in convertible currency. The common elements in the CMEA and CIS relationships were the relative weakness of Russia's partners, and Russia's security interests in maintaining links with them.

In 2001 the average price per barrel for Russian crude petroleum exported outside the CIS was US $21.28, while for export to CIS partners it was $17.19. However, only about 13% of Russia's exports of crude petroleum were purchased by other CIS countries; for the most part, crude petroleum was delivered to Belarus and Ukraine, natural gas to Ukraine, and petroleum products to Belarus, Ukraine and Kazakhstan.

Payment problems within the CIS remained a contentious issue. For most of the post-Soviet period Russia ran a merchandise trade surplus with the other CIS countries, and continued to be the main energy supplier to most of them. In 1995, however, as Russian deliveries of petroleum and gas to other CIS states continued to be reduced, the merchandise trade surplus decreased. This indicated a degree of success for Russia in persuading its CIS partners to repay their debts with increased export deliveries. That, however, did not last long, and the Russian surplus increased in 1996 and 1997.

In the mid-1990s a free-trade area was negotiated between Belarus, Kazakhstan and Russia (known as the Eurasian Economic Community—EURASEC from October 2000, by which time Kyrgyzstan and Tajikistan were also members). The first two were, for rather different reasons, the CIS countries most disposed towards close co-operation with Russia. The absence of Ukraine from EURASEC limited its importance; in 2000 only three-fifths of Russia's intra-CIS trade turnover was with its EURASEC partners. However, the lack of systematic policing of border crossing points between CIS states made for rather more free trade in practice—among all CIS countries—than was officially sanctioned. This circumstance also meant that reported trade volumes between CIS countries should be treated with caution.

Russia's ambition to join the World Trade Organization (WTO) had implications for these somewhat ill-defined arrangements. Between December 1998 and February 2003 Kyrgyzstan, Georgia, Moldova and Armenia secured membership of the WTO, but these countries were not asked very searching questions before being invited to join, because they appeared neither threatening nor particularly useful to existing members. Russia was being taken more seriously. One of many pre-conditions for Russia's membership required it to ensure that any existing free-trade area of which it was a member was 'clean'—that is, internal discrimination. The loose, *ad hoc* arrangement of organizations such as EURASEC would not easily pass this test.

An even more unorthodox arrangement existed, at least in theory, between Russia and Belarus. In December 1999 there was formal agreement on the eventual creation of a Russia-Belarus economic and political union. In June 2002 the two countries' Prime Ministers, the Chairman of the Russian Central Bank and the First Deputy Chairman of the Belarusian National Bank confirmed proposals to introduce a common currency in 2008. The plans provided for the prior unification of the countries' banking systems and the convergence of inflation rates; to help reduce inflation, Belarus undertook to stop printing money to cover budgetary deficits in 2004. However, the terms of the agreement, and the timescale envisaged for its implementation, indicated that the arrangement was symbolic rather than practical. In September 2003 Belarus, Kazakhstan, Russia and Ukraine launched an new initiative, to be known as the United Economic Space, which was to involve the co-ordination of economic policy and a free-trade area, but no common currency.

## FOREIGN TRADE AND PAYMENTS

Before the dissolution of the USSR, Russia was the predominant source of hard-currency earnings for the whole country. There are considerable difficulties in identifying a meaningful Russian share in Soviet merchandise exports, but one not unreasonable Russian estimate put it at about 81% of the Soviet total in 1990, along with about a two-thirds share in Soviet gold sales, which were counted separately from exports of merchandise. Russia was not, however, so predominant in the receipt of imports. According to the same source, the Russian share of merchandise imports in 1990 was 67%. This situation, when taken in conjunction with Russia's supply of energy, on generous terms, to the rest of the former USSR, provided grounds for assertions that Russia was 'exploited' by the other Soviet republics, and that the latter would find themselves in severe external financial difficulties after the USSR disintegrated. In the event, all the CIS states experienced balance-of-payments difficulties in 1992–93.

The USSR had bequeathed to its successor states low foreign-exchange reserves, modest gold reserves (in comparison with the position in 1980), debts to Western banks and governments that were moderately large by international standards, arrears of payments to many companies and outstanding credits to a number of developing countries—credits that were reckoned to be mostly irrecoverable. When the USSR ceased to exist, in December 1991, the most optimistic estimate of its outstanding debt to Western banks and governments was US $65,300m. There were also Soviet payments due to Eastern Europe, the valuation of which was in dispute. Offsetting this was $8,800m. in foreign currency, 240 metric tons of gold and the possibly worthless 'asset' of debt owed to the USSR by developing countries, plus some assets overseas, such as embassy premises.

In October 1991 a formula was calculated for the distribution of the debt burden among the former Soviet states. According to this formula, Russia was allocated 61% of the debt, Ukraine 16% and Belarus and Kazakhstan about 4% each. Of the three treaties relating to the joint servicing of this debt, only nine of the 15 states signed at least one. Russia and Ukraine, although they both signed all three treaties, were unable to reach agreement on how to manage the debt servicing. Meanwhile, arrears of commercial payments to Western suppliers, which had begun to accumulate in 1990–91, continued to build up.

Increasingly, in practice, the debt to the West came to be seen as Russia's debt. In June 1992 Russia formally proposed that it take over all the old Soviet debt, on condition that the other former Soviet republics renounced all claim to Soviet foreign assets. Superficially, this so-called zero option was a generous offer. However, the information on foreign assets was weak and mutual suspicions were strong. Most countries declined the offer, although some subsequently agreed to it. Thus, in 1992–93 that debt was virtually unserviced, and increased steadily. By mid-1993 the gross debt to the West may have been in the order of US $80,000m. By the end of 2001 Russia's gross external debt, composed of the inherited Soviet debt (with accrued interest) and newly contracted debt (including short-term debt), was some $152,649m. Western creditors that had inherited the Soviet-era debt were organized in two groups, representing commercial banks and governments, for purposes of debt negotiations. In 1996–97 Russia negotiated restructuring agreements with both these groups of creditors, postponing the main burden of debt-service on the 'inherited' debt until 2003. However, even these deals proved insufficient. In 1999 the Russian Government adopted the policy of discriminating between inherited, Soviet-era debt and its own, post-Soviet debt: it defaulted on the former and continued to service the latter, while calling for a restructuring of its debts to the so-called 'London Club'

and 'Paris Club' of commercial and official creditors, respectively. In February 2000 a preliminary agreement was reached in the London Club, under which some of the London Club debt would be cancelled and the balance rescheduled over 30 years. The Russian Government initially aimed to negotiate a similar deal with the Paris Club, but faced considerable difficulties in doing so. Russia began 2001 in selective default, but, thereafter, its robust external finances made further efforts towards debt restructuring or partial default extremely unconvincing. These attempts were duly abandoned, and Russia subsequently succeeded in meeting its debt commitments without assistance.

Exports from the CIS countries to the rest of the world declined in the early 1990s, but began to recover in the mid-1990s. By 2001 they totalled US $108,771m. (excluding figures for Turkmenistan and Uzbekistan), with the dominant goods being petroleum, natural gas, timber, diamonds and metals. Part of the recovery came from a diversion of exportables away from intra-CIS deliveries, towards the rest of the world. At the same time, the decline in production reduced export-supply capacity, while also reducing CIS demand for materials and intermediate goods. In particular, this was the case for the staple export of crude petroleum, on which Soviet hard-currency earnings had depended so heavily in the past. The earlier dismantling of the CMEA, and the unresolved payments problems between the former USSR and the old communist bloc countries, curtailed transactions with previously socialist (communist) trading partners. Concern over debt-servicing and over making payments for current imports induced successor-state governments to maintain control over imports and to tax export revenues.

The CIS states, for the most part, had serious external financing problems, for the reasons already mentioned. Western financial assistance was made available, but both its scale and its composition were called into question by critics. The Group of Seven (G7) leading Western economies announced a series of measures, worth US $24,000m. in aid to Russia, in April 1992. This was followed by a further $43,000m., announced in 1993. These seemed to be substantial amounts, capable of delivering real assistance to the former USSR. (Assistance to Russia was considered likely, to some extent, to 'trickle down' to other former Soviet states.) Moreover, disbursement was close to, or more than, the amount pledged. The best 1993 estimates, from various sources, of assistance disbursed in 1992, ranged from about $17,000m. to over $30,000m. Economists in the IMF, in many ways the leading organization in the whole Western assistance effort, put the total disbursed at slightly above the amount pledged.

The reality, however, was much less helpful than the appearance. A large part of the sums disbursed consisted of debt relief. In other words, it was a recognition of the fact that the debt was not going to be serviced anyway. Another large part consisted of Western governments' export credits, designed primarily to promote each country's capital-goods exports, and with conditions close to market terms. Very little of the aid pledged or disbursed consisted of grants; nearly all of it was loans, generating a later balance-of-payments burden. In this respect, the arrangements bore no resemblance to the USA's 'Marshall Plan' (European Reconstruction Program) aid to Western Europe after the Second World War, which was predominantly in the form of grants. A relatively small proportion of the Russian aid was technical assistance, ranging from guidance on macroeconomic policy to assistance with schemes of food packaging and distribution. Some of this was useful, but much of it came in for strong criticism for being delayed, misdirected and chiefly benefiting the consultants who were paid to provide it.

Some of the potentially most helpful forms of assistance—stand-by loans, currency stabilization funds and Extended Fund Facilities (EFF) to be provided by the IMF—were not disbursed to the main Soviet successor states until 1995. In the most important case, that of Russia, this was because conditions of prior policy achievements, set by the Russian Government in agreement with the IMF, were not met. In particular, the Russian Government was unable to reduce its budgetary deficit and inflation rate in 1992, in the manner it had promised to do. Eventually, however, an IMF stand-by loan was given to Russia in early 1995 and a large EFF almost one year later. The disbursement of the EFF was in tranches, subject on each occasion to IMF monitoring of Russian policy performance. The delaying of tranches became the norm, and there were accusations of misuse of those funds that were received—most spectacularly from Russia's state auditor in September 1998, following the aid given after the collapse of the rouble.

In 1996–98 Russia began to exploit the potential of private and commercial financing through the international financial markets, issuing Eurobonds and obtaining bank-consortium loans for the national and local governments. Some of the biggest and best-known Russian companies also followed these routes. The Asian financial crisis of 1997, however, raised the cost of such borrowing and left Russia and the other former Soviet states once more looking mainly to Western governments and to international lending institutions for external finance. With the Russian financial crisis of 1998 the situation deteriorated still further, and an IMF loan was cancelled. Thereafter, the unintended but benign effects of rouble devaluation, reinforced by a subsequent rise in petroleum prices, largely solved Russia's external financing problems, and dependence on the IMF came to an end.

For the other CIS states, assistance from the international financial organizations, such as the IMF, or from creditor nations remained an objective. However, in 2001–03 the disbursement of loans to Armenia, Azerbaijan, Moldova and Tajikistan was suspended, when government policy failed to meet the conditions imposed by the international lending institutions. The smaller CIS states—even Kazakhstan and Ukraine—were often treated more strictly in this respect than Russia. This was because they were, in general, regarded as less dangerous if neglected. In contrast, Russia tended, at least until 1998, to be given the benefit of the doubt in loan disbursements, for foreign-policy reasons.

Official aid was by no means the only, or the most important, channel through which Western countries could contribute to the economic transformation and recovery of the former Soviet states. Access for those countries' exports to Western markets was of much greater consequence and, in the long term, private FDI, it was hoped, would play a major role in transforming the old Soviet economies. In both these areas, however, experience in 1992–93 was sobering. It is true that, even in 1992, the much-reduced merchandise exports of the former USSR amounted to a sum (US $54,900m.) that was large relative to their output: large, that is, if the latter was measured at current market exchange rates. Export earnings, moreover, were at the disposal of the firms and governments of the countries that had earned them, and carried no future debt-service burden with them.

The inflow of FDI to the CIS states remained comparatively modest. In 2001 the annual flow was estimated at US $5,831m., less than one-third the level of FDI into Central and South-Eastern Europe (including the Baltic states). Joint ventures with foreign partners, registered on the territory of the former USSR, together with the wholly owned subsidiaries of foreign firms, were certainly numerous. However, most were small and far more were registered, but not functioning, than were actually operational. Reliable information about such firms was lacking. Official data indicated a cumulative total of $34,318m. in FDI in the CIS by the end of 2001. Portfolio investment from abroad began, effectively, in 1994, but remained modest for a time. However, it increased rapidly in 1997, greatly exceeding FDI. This reflected the liberalization of capital markets, principally in Russia. It also left these economies more vulnerable to the volatility of world financial markets than they had been previously. This was demonstrated in 1998–99, when portfolio investment into the CIS collapsed.

A perception of political stability was considered important in attracting Western interest. The broad indications were that Kazakhstan had been more successful than Russia in attracting at least some large-scale Western investment in the energy sector, and interest in the country increased following the discovery of substantial petroleum reserves in the Kazakh sector of the Caspian Sea in July 2000. Likewise, Azerbaijan attracted interest in its petroleum sector, particularly with the end of fighting over Nagornyi Karabakh in 1994 (if not the conclusion of a final settlement of the conflict). Frequent and unpredictable changes in tax regimes, informally preferential treatment of domestic competitors and a lack of transparency and reliability in the dealings of local business partners, however, all tended to deter or limit foreign investment in most of the CIS countries.

Russia is not the main attraction for FDI within the CIS. At the end of 2001 total cumulative FDI was estimated at US $11,001m. in Kazakhstan, $9,702m. in Russia and $4,062m. in Azerbaijan. Considered on a per-head basis, or as a proportion of total investment or of GDP, FDI is much more substantial in Kazakhstan than it is in Russia. This appears mainly to be the result of the greater readiness of those initially in charge of petroleum and natural gas assets in Kazakhstan to share control with foreigners, perhaps owing to the more acute need for foreign expertise in that country. Latterly, however, Kazakhstan's businesspeople have become more confident and more acquisitive, and foreign investors have been encountering an increased number of difficulties.

## PROBLEMS AND PROSPECTS

As was noted at the beginning of this article, by 1995 it had already become difficult to generalize across the 12 CIS states. They had always differed substantially in development levels, resource endowments and cultural inheritance. By 2003, with separate currencies and substantial differences in economic policies, the scope for further divergence had greatly increased.

In all of them, the institutions and regulations of the economic system were moving in the general direction of private enterprise and the market. However, the 12 states were moving not only at different speeds, but along somewhat different routes. In some countries, movement towards the market was extremely slow—most notably in Belarus and Uzbekistan. In both of these countries, enterprises operated mainly through informal negotiation with the state, and were not driven by concerns about customers, competitors and suppliers.

Approaches to privatization varied a great deal: from the minimalist (Belarus, Tajikistan and Turkmenistan), to mass privatization favouring insiders (Russia), to a greater reliance on selling assets to foreign investors (Kazakhstan). Furthermore, clarity of property-rights legislation, the effectiveness of its enforcement and the openness and liquidity of financial markets varied enormously. Except in Armenia, privatization was particularly weak and problem-ridden with respect to land and agriculture.

In the opinion of lawyers, nevertheless, several of the successor states had, as early as 1993, approved an 'adequate first generation' of commercial and property law. The property-rights problems in such cases were more to do with interpretation and an underdeveloped judicial system than the official legislation. This unevenly developed nature of the judicial system was an example of a general and fundamental problem: completely new institutions and skills could not come into being quickly. Many commercial banks were former branches of the state bank or 'pocket banks' set up by a small group of producers. Most enterprises, even after they were officially privatized, had the same internal organization as before, the same management, and often the same propensity to look for state subsidies when financial troubles were imminent. If the subsidies were no longer directly from the state budget, but took the opaque form of officially tolerated arrears, tax offsets and settlement in barter with over-valued goods, the effect in reducing pressures to restructure and become efficient was much the same.

The tendency of managers in privatized firms to expect state help was apparent in several of the ex-Soviet states, notably Russia. From 1995 continued macroeconomic discipline and the gradual development of market institutions and patterns of behaviour were expected to reduce the scale of this problem. Russian policy-makers had designed the privatization process so that it favoured initial ownership by the managers and workers of each firm. However, a strong regime of financial stringency would force even state enterprises to behave in a more cost-effective way and should, in principle, have the same effect on worker-owned firms. It would also make them more amenable to acquisition by outside investors, able to bring in new capital and expertise. By 1995 the main problem in the states in which reform was relatively advanced was that uncertainties continued to deter investment and recovery, and that effective capital markets were slow in developing. Thereafter, improvements in capital markets continued in Russia and some other CIS countries, but they remained narrow, illiquid and lacked transparency, impeding the development of an effective market for corporate control and, therefore, impeding the restructuring of enterprises. The 1998 Russian crisis produced further reverses, although from 1999 Russia's recovery sent more encouraging signals. On the whole, the remaining CIS economies were less advanced in reforms than Russia.

Three broad conclusions can be drawn. First, the process of economic change in the former USSR, outside the Baltic states, was bedevilled by the strong political constituencies opposed to it and by the lack of political coherence of reform movements. Taken in conjunction with the actual and potential ethnic conflicts in the former USSR, they made economic transformation considerably more difficult than in Central and South-Eastern Europe. Second, if the political process of reform from above was handicapped, change from below could still continue. Throughout the former USSR, household behaviour was adapting to new conditions and a new business class was emerging. Third, the recovery of the Russian economy after 1998, encouraged by rouble devaluation and higher petroleum prices, but subsequently sustained by rising domestic confidence and accelerated reform, influenced the economic environment in the rest of the CIS relatively quickly, despite the large differences between national business environments within the region.

# RUSSIA'S NEW FEDERALISM

## Dr NEIL MELVIN

### INTRODUCTION

Historically, the territories currently constituted as the Russian Federation were dominated by a highly centralized state system, with little autonomy exercised by the regions. The collapse of the USSR and the emergence of Russia as an independent state marked an important change in the long tradition of centralized control. Although formed as a federative state following the creation of the USSR, Russia only acquired the characteristics of a genuine federation with the political developments of the late 1980s and early 1990s. In the 1990s Russia's regions came to exercise an unparalleled degree of autonomy. In recent years, however, the central authorities in Moscow have made considerable efforts to reclaim the powers lost to the regions and to establish a more stable and institutionalized form of federal relations.

The federal Government's initial response to the increased power of the regions was defensive and incoherent. Several attempts were made to codify the nature of centre-regional relations (notably, the Federation Treaty of March 1992, the Constitution of December 1993 and a series of bilateral treaties concluded between the central Government and leading territories from 1994). The new arrangements between the centre and the regions did not, however, prove to be durable, because they failed to resolve the principal disputes between the federal Government and the provinces. In the first decade of independence relations were, therefore, characterized by instability and the lack of a clear legal basis on which to determine the division of powers between the different subjects of the Federation.

The election of Vladimir Putin as federal President, on 26 March 2000, led to renewed efforts to tackle the Federation's problems. The federal Government sought to impose a greater degree of centralized control on the regions. Significant reforms were introduced, notably a programme to develop a more coherent legal and institutional basis for centre-regional relations. Although during the early years of the Putin presidency considerable progress was achieved in restricting the influence of the regional élite at the political centre of the Russian system and placing federal relations on a firmer basis, challenging the regional leaders' control over their own regions initially proved more problematic. Subsequently, additional reforms were introduced to tighten central control. A particular focus of attention was the relationship between the municipal and regional levels of government. Despite several stages of attempted reform of centre-regional relations the considerable dissolution of power that accompanied the fragmentation of the USSR, and the subsequent policies of reform, ensured that the federal authorities were unable to engineer a return to the historic pattern of central dominance. At the same time, the complex institutional legacy of the Soviet-era federation and the entrenched power of the regional élite ensured that forging a new and stable federal system remained a critical issue.

### HISTORICAL BACKGROUND

In the medieval period, the European lands of contemporary Russia were divided into a series of feudal principalities. The dissolution of the early Slavic state of Kievan Rus, following its conquest by the Mongol Tatars in 1237–40, produced a loose confederation of large Russian principalities, independent of each other, but subordinate to Tatar control. By 1400 the relatively small principality of Muscovy (based in the town of Moscow—Moskva) had emerged as the most powerful region among the Russian provinces, after it began to conquer its neighbours, including, in 1364, the powerful principality of Vladimir. Muscovy eventually defeated the armies of the Golden Horde (as the regional Mongol leader, the Khan, and his entourage were known) at the Battle of Kulikovo in 1380.

In the 15th and 16th centuries Muscovy expanded its borders further, conquering all the remaining major Russian principalities. The rise of Muscovy, under rulers such as Ivan III and Vasilii III, saw the emergence of a powerful system of monarchical centralism, as part of which other groups, such as the aristocracy (boyars), were subordinated to the monarchy. Particularly important in the growth of Muscovy was the reign of Ivan IV ('the Terrible', 1533–84), who consolidated autocratic rule by means of policies that undermined both the boyars and the Russian Orthodox Church. Under Ivan IV, Muscovy conquered the first Muslim lands, taking the Khanate of Kazan in 1552, and that of Astrakhan in 1556.

The elimination of regionalism was a primary condition for the consolidation of the powerful Russian empire-state. Regional reform under Ivan IV witnessed the development of centralized control over the territories under Muscovy's control. Peter (Petr) I ('the Great', 1682–1725) undertook further reform of regional government, designed to enhance the state's ability to raise taxes and military strength from the regions. Governors-general were placed in charge of the newly organized regional units of Russia (gubernia). Under Catherine (Yekaterina) II ('the Great', 1762–96), the Pugachev riot (1773–75), a peasant rebellion that directly threatened the state, led to the gentry playing an increased role in local government.

The transformation of Muscovy into the Russian Empire occurred with the extensive territorial expansion of the 18th and 19th centuries. The borders of the Russian Empire were extended into Ukraine, Finland, Bessarabia, Central Asia, the Far East and Transcaucasia. As new territories were added to the core European lands of the Empire, centralized and bureaucratic practices were projected into the conquered regions. In the late 19th century a movement for greater regional autonomy (oblastnichestvo) emerged, particularly in Siberia. In the years preceding the collapse of the tsarist system, regional discontent increased throughout the Russian Empire, but the regions remained bound firmly to its political centre.

The dislocation and collapse that accompanied the revolutions of 1917 and the subsequent civil war (1918–21) led to a considerable de facto decentralization of power. Following the consolidation of Bolshevik rule (under Lenin—Vladimir Ilych Ulyanov), a process of recentralization was launched. Political autonomy was undermined, including the structure of the soviets. The core territories of the former Russian Empire were organized formally as a federation (the USSR), although, in practice, the republics exercised very little autonomy. Within the USSR, the territories of Russia were also constituted as a federal system (the Russian Soviet Federative Socialist Republic—RSFSR or Russian Federation). The Federation was based on an asymmetrical administrative structure, with the ethno-territorially defined republics enjoying greater formal powers than the predominately ethnically Russian regions (oblasts) and provinces (krais).

Despite its formally federal structure, the RSFSR operated as the core of the unitary system that underpinned the USSR. The power of the Communist Party and state economic control ensured that the regions of the RSFSR enjoyed little autonomy. At the heart of the Soviet subordination of the regions was the system of appointment (*nomenklatura*), whereby the federal authorities determined all key positions in the regions. The high degree of centralization was further exacerbated by the policies of repression employed under Stalin (Iosif V. Dzhugashvili).

Even after Stalin, there was little significant change in the nature of territorial politics in the RSFSR. Nikita Khrushchev (1953–64) experimented with a reorganization of the territorial management of the Soviet economy, and Leonid Brezhnev (1964–82) pursued a policy of ensuring stability in the regions through a system that guaranteed long-term tenure for regional leaders.

## THE COLLAPSE OF THE USSR

The radical regionalism that developed in Russia in the early 1990s evolved from relations between the Soviet centre and the Soviet republics after 1986. In the late 1980s the concept of economic self-sufficiency for the republics became popular and the Soviet leader, Mikhail Gorbachev, began to grant responsibility for regional development to provincial leaders, based on the idea of full cost-accounting. At the same time, the programme of democratization of local government that was initiated in 1987 transferred power to regional parliaments, at the expense of the bureaucrats. Together, these changes promoted a contest between Gorbachev and regional party leaders, who were usually more conservative. In the late 1980s many regional leaders were replaced by means of an ongoing purge of Brezhnev-era appointments.

In 1990 a new factor began to influence the already unstable relationship between the centre and the regions: the struggle for power between Soviet President Gorbachev and Boris Yeltsin, who was committed to democratic reform and who, in May 1990, was elected Chairman of the Supreme Soviet (legislature) of the Russian Federation. Yeltsin combined his democratic programme with the idea of increased sovereignty for the national republics, including Russia, and for both ethnically populated republics and Russian regions in the Russian Federation. As the republics of the USSR began to move towards increased autonomy and even independence, in Russia some of the ethnic regions also began to debate issues of sovereignty. A declaration of Russian sovereignty within the USSR was issued on 12 June 1990, which included the aim to broaden substantially the rights of the subjects of the Federation.

Yeltsin did not object to the declarations of state sovereignty made by a number of autonomous republics in the Russian Federation, such as Bashkortostan (Bashkiriya), Kalmykiya, Marii-El and Chuvashiya, in October 1990. Indeed, travelling through Russia in mid-1991, Yeltsin sought to strengthen his political position with respect to the Soviet centre by gaining the support of the emerging regional movements. Most famously, in Tatarstan, in a phrase that he was not to be permitted to forget, Yeltsin encouraged the republican leadership to 'take as much sovereignty as you can'. Consequently, 24 subjects of the Russian Federation declared their sovereignty. Gorbachev also put forward his own ideas for increased autonomy in various territories. As a result of this attention, in mid-1991 the national republics of the Russian Federation became directly involved in the broader debate about the future of the USSR.

Shortly after the failure of the August 1991 coup and the subsequent demise of the USSR, regionalization swept across Russia. Weakened by the political struggles against Soviet institutions, Russian President Yeltsin's new regime had little leverage over the regions. Moreover, many in Yeltsin's Government viewed the transfer of power from the federal Government to the regions as a means to undermine further the tradition of autocracy in the country, and so did not oppose it.

The leading exponents of the transfer of power to the regions were the leaders of Russia's ethno-national territories. In the early 1990s all the ethno-territorial regions, with the exception of the Jewish Autonomous Oblast, proclaimed themselves to be full republics. The regions leading this movement were Tatarstan, Bashkortostan, and Chechnya; the latter, under Dzhokhar Dudayev, a former Soviet air-force general, went so far as to declare complete independence from Russia. The lack of a clear constitutional basis for the new Russian state also led many of the republics to introduce their own laws.

Initially, the federal Government rejected the use of coercion in response to the actions of the regions. Instead, in 1992–93 the struggle for political dominance between the President and parliament led Yeltsin to make concessions to the ethnic republics, in the hope of obtaining increased support. On 31 March 1992 Yeltsin endorsed the Federation Treaty, which enshrined a strong form of sovereignty for the ethnic republics. Chechnya and Tatarstan, however, refused to sign the Treaty. With the republics demonstrating growing assertiveness, other Russian regions began to demand increased rights vis-à-vis the centre. As a result, fears emerged that increased regional autonomy would lead to separatism.

In September–October 1993 regionalist sentiment seemed to reach its highest level, as Sverdlovsk Oblast sought to raise its administrative status by declaring itself the 'Ural Republic', in order to obtain the same rights as the ethnic republics; however, the declaration was revoked by presidential decree. The violent confrontation between President Yeltsin and the national legislature, which began in September, appeared to undermine the regionalist movement, and a more balanced federal system was introduced in the new Constitution adopted on 12 December. The apparent uniformity of status imposed by the Constitution was, however, short-lived. Within months of its passage Yeltsin began a process of concluding treaties (*dogovory*) and agreements (*soglasheniya*) with the republics and, subsequently, with many of the other regions of the Federation. In February 1994 the first bilateral treaty was concluded with Tatarstan. There followed a series of agreements with Bashkortostan, Buryatiya, Kabardino-Balkariya, Sakha (Yakutiya), and other ethno-republics.

The renewed asymmetry within the federal system introduced by the agreements of 1994–96 caused support for regionalism to increase once again. Renewed regionalism was also stimulated by pressure for the election of regional leaders, which began in earnest in 1995. As the federal Government lost its ability to appoint the heads of local administrations, a new, autonomous élite developed, focused on the regional executive. In December 1994 the federal authorities became engaged in the first Chechen war. The federal army's humiliating withdrawal from the republic under the terms of the peace agreement reached on 31 August 1996 further weakened the central Government's influence over the regions.

During much of Yeltsin's tenure as President, the federal authorities lacked a clear vision of the future of the Federation. The Government lost much of its political and cultural significance in the provinces, and also lost its leading role in the economic sphere as a result of privatization. In this environment, centre-peripheral relations came to be based primarily on agreements about the redistribution of resources (fiscal federalism) and *ad hoc* agreements between President Yeltsin and regional leaders. As a result of the presidential election of July 1996, the President grew particularly dependent on the regional élite, on whose support he had been compelled to rely. In the final years of the Yeltsin presidency the power of the regions, notably Tatarstan and Bashkortostan, effective defeat in the war with Chechnya, and the inability of the centre to impose its policies on the regions suggested that it was this regional élite that determined policy in most parts of Russia. Some even speculated that the country would eventually disintegrate along the lines of the USSR before it.

In the late 1990s a consensus began to develop that changes were required in the nature of the Federation to establish greater co-ordination and stability. During his brief tenure as Prime Minister, in 1998–99, Yevgenii Primakov raised the issue of reforming centre-peripheral relations by, in particular, consolidating existing regions and reverting to appointed regional leaders. With the appointment, in August 1999, of Vladimir Putin as Prime Minister and, following Yeltsin's unexpected resignation on 31 December, as acting President, the debate about the future of the Federation intensified. From late September Putin launched a second war with Chechnya, which initially appeared to be more successful than the previous campaign.

During the presidential election campaign of early 2000 the regional élite sought to shape the future direction of regional policy by promoting their own vision of centre-regional relations. In an open letter to Vladimir Putin a number of governors argued that Russia should become a presidential republic with a strong executive branch. The governors' suggestions had a common theme: they were politically conservative, and marked by a statism resembling the strict state administration in the political and social spheres that was characteristic of the Soviet-era. The governors were concerned that it was no longer possible to manage Russia and that the state had been deprived of levers for controlling society.

## PUTIN'S NEW FEDERALISM

Following the election of Vladimir Putin as President, in March 2000, regional reform became one of the central elements of his policy programme. The immediate objectives of the reform were two-fold:

To create a 'single economic and legal field' and to put an end to 'legal chaos'.

To strengthen the executive 'power vertical'.

There was also a third, unstated objective:

To reduce the power of the country's regional leaders.

The broad aim of the reforms was to reverse the processes that had led to an apparent unravelling of the Federation. Although the core elements were specified in Putin's address to the nation, the new measures did not constitute a single programme of reform, but rather a loose collection of initiatives designed to curtail the influence of the regional élite.

The reform of centre-regional relations in Russia involved a number of different dimensions:

The creation of seven 'federal districts'.

The appointment of 'federal inspectors'.

Reform of the Federation Council, the upper chamber of the two-tier Federal Assembly (parliament).

Harmonization of legislation.

Control of federal appointments.

Strengthening control over regional transfers.

Weakening the 'political influence' of governors.

In May 2000 the President announced the creation of seven large federal districts, which encompassed all 89 subjects of the Federation. This measure was designed to counter some of the problems that stemmed from the asymmetrical nature of the Federation. The position of 'presidential representative' was established for each district. A central task of the presidential representatives was to ensure that regional constitutions and legislation conformed to federal laws. While many oblasts and krais rapidly implemented measures to harmonize their legislation, the republics of Tatarstan, Bashkortostan and Ingushetiya sought to resist changes to their laws. In June 2001 the federal Government announced that existing legal arrangements would continue, but in a hierarchy, with the Constitution serving as the fundamental basis of federal relations, and bilateral treaties as the least important element.

In May 2000 legislation was also introduced to reform the involvement of the regional élite in the Federal Assembly. Under the Yeltsin-era interpretation of the Constitution, the Federation Council was composed of regional executives and chairmen of the regional legislatures. Putin ensured that the regional élite was removed from this national institution, and a new session of the Federation Council, composed, instead, of their full-time appointees, opened in January 2002. Meanwhile, a largely symbolic State Council was established in September 2000, as a forum for regional leaders to advise the President on issues concerning the relationship between the central administration and Russia's regions.

During the Yeltsin years, regional leaders gained control over the appointment of key federal officers in each district, including regional police-officers, media officials and tax police. Manipulation of the system of appointments was an important component of the regional élite's ability to resist federal government initiatives to control them. During his first 18 months in office, President Putin gradually reclaimed the power to control the appointment of federal officers in the regions.

The single most important element of Putin's new policy towards the regions was tighter control over fiscal federalism. The federal Government became far more active in monitoring the raising of taxes in the regions, through the federal Treasury, and also exercised greater control over the redistribution of tax revenues. From the 2002 budget the federal authorities retained 55% of the budget and the regions only 45%; prior to the implementation of reform the regions had retained well over 50%. Together with the drive to establish a unified legal space and enhance the authority of the federal authorities in the regions, these measures placed significant constraints on the autonomy of the regional élite.

Reflecting the need to make concessions to gain the support of regional leaders for other elements of Putin's reform agenda, in early 2001 the President signed a law to allow such leaders to stand for three or more terms of office, thereby permitting many of the most powerful to prolong their hold over their regions. This measure suggested a willingness to compromise on the earlier, more radical ambitions behind regional reform. However, in July 2002 the Constitutional Court upheld a law passed by the national parliament in 1999, limiting regional leaders to two terms of office, but ruled that the two terms should be calculated from October 1999, the month in which the original law came into effect. Thus, many regional leaders were still to be permitted to serve for three, or even four terms of office. Meanwhile, in October 2001 the Ministry for Federal Affairs and National and Migration Policy was abolished, and its responsibilities redistributed between the Ministries of Internal Affairs, Economic Development and Trade, and Foreign Affairs.

In 2002, halfway through his first term of office and two years after the introduction of radical regional reform, in his annual 'state of the nation' address Putin undertook a preliminary evaluation of the restructuring of regional power structures, and outlined the way forward. The President signalled clearly the end of the practice of concluding bilateral treaties between the federal Government and the regions, which had been at the core of Yeltsin-era regional policy. He indicated that although the existence of such agreements had been constitutional, they had led to 'inequality between subjects of the Federation' and, therefore, inequality between citizens. The repudiation of the power-sharing agreements and the abolition of the Ministry of Federal Affairs and National and Migration Policy marked further progress in Putin's effort to redefine regional-federal relations and signaled Putin's intention to integrate regional and national policy. Reflecting on these and earlier regional reforms, Putin indicated that he was satisfied that the 'organizational work' associated with the establishment of the seven federal districts had been accomplished. However, despite the President's optimism about the results of regional reform, the initiative to increase central control over the regions had produced mixed results.

In their first two years in office, the presidential representatives failed to curtail dramatically the autonomy that regional leaders had acquired during the Yeltsin presidency. Although the reform of the Federation Council deprived governors of direct access to the process of federal policy-making, regional leaders maintained the right to appoint the senators representing the executive branch of each constituent member of the Russian Federation and, therefore, retained a channel for lobbying in the capital. At the same time, the regional élite increased its power at local level, to an extent unanticipated by the federal centre, through the consolidation of powerful ruling coalitions, comprising political leaders, representatives of large-scale industrial enterprises and members of law-enforcement agencies.

The process of legislative harmonization also experienced difficulties. For example, 18 months after the initiation of a campaign to bring Bashkortostan's legislation into conformity with federal law, it was estimated that 72% of the republic's legislation continued to violate federal norms—a higher percentage than at the beginning of the initiative. The republican authorities continued to consider Bashkortostan to be a sovereign republic and refused to recognize a ruling of the federal Constitutional Court that stated the opposite.

Although President Putin's reform programme did much to institute a more stable Federation and to limit the power of the regional élite, the initial reform programme was unable to re-establish full control over the regions. Federal structures failed to exercise clear authority over the regional leaders, and initial attempts to secure support for state-sponsored candidates in gubernatorial elections were rarely successful. Most significantly, in February 2001, following a severe energy shortage in Primorskii Krai, in the Far East, the Governor, Yevgenii Nazdratenko, resigned from office, under pressure from Putin. Subsequently, however, the federal Government was unable to ensure the election of its preferred candidate to the governorship (while Nazdratenko was awarded appointment as Chairman of the State Fisheries Committee).

In other regional elections, incumbency, rather than the endorsement of the federal authorities, emerged as the single most important factor in determining electoral outcome. Although in April 2002 the Constitutional Court confirmed the recently established right of the President to dismiss errant governors (and that of the President and the State Duma to dissolve regional legislatures), governors tended to be removed from office through the offer of an important position in Moscow or the threat of a criminal investigation, rather than the complex procedure foreseen by the law.

Centralization of the tax system proved a more effective instrument for the central Government. Value-added tax revenue of 15% was withdrawn from the regional budget, resulting in a reduction in regional resources and the diversion of 11% of tax revenue from the regions to the centre. Owing to the economic growth registered in 2000–02, however, political

opposition to the change was muted, as many regions did not immediately feel its full effects.

Presidential representatives blamed their limited success in imposing control over the regions on the lack of comprehensive legislation to make explicit the competencies of the regional and federal authorities. As a result, the federal authorities' attempts to impose a coherent discipline across the Federation were weakened, as threats made to law-violating regions were rarely followed by measures to implement them. In 2001 concern about the failure to bring regions under closer control led Putin to ask his deputy chief of staff, Dmitrii Kozak, to head a commission that was to recommend additional structural changes to federal-regional relations, with the aim of establishing a 'single legal space for Russia'. The Kozak Commission experienced considerable difficulties in developing its proposals, but by early 2003 a comprehensive law, designed to delineate clearly authority between the federal authorities, the regional powers and local government across Russia, had been drafted. A central aim of the law was to establish a more stable financial framework for local government. Meanwhile, a number of observers suggested that stability would be bought at the cost of further centralizing authority—the 'vertical' structure of power—and diminishing local democracy. After the limited success of candidates supported by the federal Government in regional elections held during the first years of Putin's presidency, in 2002–03 the central Government began to intervene more actively in the conduct of regional elections. The precedent was established in November 2000, when, the day before the gubernatorial election in Kursk Oblast, federal officials urged the removal of the incumbent candidate, Aleksandr Rutskoi, owing to a legal technicality. In April 2002 a similar scenario was repeated in the republic of Ingushetiya, and in October the federal Government intervened to resolve a dispute over the result of the gubernatorial elections held in Krasnoyarsk Krai. By 2003 there were signs that the Government's agenda for regional reform was beginning to produce results. A number of regions had been forced to alter their basic constitutional order to conform to federal legislation; most notable in this respect was the progress made in Dagestan towards the introduction of a directly elected president, replacing the previous collective presidency, based upon a parliamentary-style system. The federal Government also expressed strong support for the candidacy of the presidential envoy for the North-Western Federal District, Valentina Matviyenko, in the gubernatorial elections held in St Petersburg in September–October.

However, the federal Government's image continued to be tarnished by the failure to secure a durable peace in Chechnya, despite devoting massive financial and military resources to this end. By mid-2003, four years after launching a renewed conflict in Chechnya (the first had taken place in 1994–96), a means to resolve the future of the separatist republic and to reintegrate it within the broader Federation continued to elude the federal authorities. The federal Government sought to promote the belief that stability had been restored in the republic and that the war was over, supported by a widely criticized referendum on a new constitution in March 2003, in which, according to the official results, more than 96% of those whose voted endorsed the draft constitution and two further questions (on the method of electing a president and parliament for the republic), as well as the drafting of a Chechen-Russian power-sharing treaty, and the announcement that presidential elections were to be held in the republic in October (the candidate favoured by the federal Government was duly elected). The federal Government's position was challenged, however, by the actions of Chechen suicide bombers outside the republic, including a large-scale hostage-taking incident at a Moscow theatre in October 2002, and the continuing high death toll in Chechnya.

The difficulties that the federal Government continued to encounter in ensuring its control over Russia's regions three years after the initiation of reform led to the suggestion in 2003 that Putin planned to introduce a more comprehensive reorganization of the Federation. Such a reorganization, which had been mooted at various points throughout the 1990s, would focus on the amalgamation of the existing 89 federal subjects, possibly reducing this number by as much as one-half.

## CONCLUSION

The end of Soviet power represented a radical departure for relations between the federal Government and the regions of the Russian Federation. Following the collapse of the USSR, Russia's regions were able to fashion a high degree of autonomy from central interference. By the end of the first decade of independence, the regional élite had emerged as a powerful, autonomous political force. Control over regional economic resources, local taxes, federal appointments and the local media ensured that regional executives dominated events in most regions. At the end of the 1990s the regional leadership appeared to be in position to determine the direction of Russia's national politics.

The President elected in 2000, Vladimir Putin, made challenging the power of the regional élite and bringing greater stability to centre-peripheral relations a priority of his Government. Early in his term of office a series of measures was announced that did much to restrict the influence of regional leaders at the federal level and to establish a common legal system throughout the country. Resentment among the regional élite about these actions led to growing disenchantment with the President. However, despite important successes, the federal Government seemed unable to tackle the power of the regional regimes. Republican executives continued to exercise enormous discretion over their internal affairs, reflecting the critical role played by their resources. With this power base largely untouched, the federal Government was not easily able to unseat regional leaders. It also proved difficult for the federal authorities to influence significantly the results of gubernatorial elections, without resort to manipulation through the courts. Furthermore, the weak state of political parties in Russia meant that to help secure a pro-presidential majority in the parliamentary elections that were due to take place in December 2003, the federal Government would have to rely on support from the regional leaders.

Many of the reforms introduced by President Putin could, however, have a significant impact only in the medium and long term. In particular, control over regional budgets through taxation and the redistribution of resources began to serve as an important restraint on regional leaders only from 2002. In the first years of his initiative to reshape federal relations Putin achieved many of his objectives by pursuing a gradual process of reform, rather than through radical restructuring. Although such measures were successful in instilling greater stability in the Federation, any further reform appeared likely to demand a more fundamental change to Russia's constitutional order.

# POVERTY AND SOCIAL WELFARE IN THE COMMONWEALTH OF INDEPENDENT STATES

## Prof. JANE FALKINGHAM

### INTRODUCTION

At independence in 1991, the 15 new countries that had been part of the former USSR enjoyed relatively high levels of human development. Extensive social investment during the Soviet period meant that literacy was almost universal, and well above the rate in other countries with comparable levels of income per head, while life expectancy averaged 68 years. Unemployment was unheard of and—at least officially— poverty did not exist. Few could have foreseen that the process of transition towards market economies and democratic governments would have such high human cost. The virtual collapse of economic output in many countries following independence, along with 'hyperinflation', which eroded individual savings, resulted in a dramatic decline in living standards for many people. By 1996 about two-thirds of the population of Georgia had incomes below the official poverty line, while in Ukraine the rate was about one-half (UN Development Programme—UNDP, 1999). The severity of the situation was emphasized by the reversal in life expectancy, primarily owing to increasing mortality among young and middle-aged men, reported in several major countries in the region. In 1995 male life expectancy in Russia was just 58 years, 10 years lower than male life expectancy in the People's Republic of China.

After 1998, however, there was some cause for optimism. The region as a whole enjoyed unprecedented economic stability after the Russian financial crisis of 1998. A return to positive economic growth was observed in almost every country of the region, and in some countries democratic elections had taken place, giving new impetus for reform, while ethnic tensions had also abated in many places.

However, significant progress in improving the material and social welfare of ordinary people remains illusive. An estimated 50m. people continue to live in severe poverty. Moreover, in some countries of the region, the proportion of the population living below the poverty line has increased, despite economic growth, and inequality in income has continued to rise. The public sector continues to experience privation. Real spending on health and education remains low by international standards, and in some cases has actually declined, despite economic growth. The proportion of births taking place without skilled attendants, a key indicator of quality of health-care services, has increased. In many countries educational standards have fallen, as schools continue to lack basic supplies and infrastructure deteriorates.

There are also worrying signs of new hazards, with a rise in organized crime, increasing drug use and an escalation of the HIV epidemic in many parts of the region. Thus, in many cases, the real objective of transition—improving the lives of ordinary people—appears to have taken second place to the imperative of economic growth.

This essay focuses on trends in the indicators of well-being in the countries of the former USSR (excluding the Baltic states of Estonia, Latvia and Lithuania) since independence. The essay is divided into four sections, each dealing with a different aspect of welfare. The first section examines changes in national income and in expenditure on key social sectors, including education and health. The second section discusses changes in material living conditions and the extent and depth of poverty in the region. It is increasingly recognized that material resources, or the lack thereof, reflect just one, albeit very important, dimension of poverty. Being poor goes well beyond a narrow lack of material consumption to encompass poor health outcomes, low achievement in education and increased vulnerability to external shocks. The third section, therefore, looks at changes in life expectancy and infant mortality, along with other indicators of health and access to health-care services. Trends in education enrolment and attendance rates are discussed in the fourth and final section.

### ECONOMIC GROWTH AND PUBLIC SPENDING

Following independence, the withdrawal of subsidies from Russia, combined with the interruption of inter-republican trade within the former USSR and the impact of tight government stabilization policies, resulted in a dramatic reduction in output across the region. In some areas, the severe economic impact accompanying the collapse of the USSR was further exacerbated by natural disasters and by armed conflicts and border disputes (for example, between Armenia and Azerbaijan, particularly in 1988–94; in South Ossetia and Abkhazia, Georgia, especially in 1989–94; in the Transnistria region of Moldova in 1991–92; in Tajikistan in 1992–97; and in the Fergana valley region of Kyrgyzstan, Tajikistan and Uzbekistan in 1989–91). All parts of the region experienced a marked contraction in output per head during the early 1990s, followed by recovery. From 1999, output increased in almost all the 12 countries of the Commonwealth of Independent States (CIS). However, despite this growth, the real value of gross domestic product (GDP) per head remained significantly lower than its pre-transition level (even in the Baltic states). In the Caucasus (Armenia, Azerbaijan and Georgia), where the decline in output was more extreme, and where recovery took place later, in the early 2000s GDP per head remained around 40% lower than its pre-transition level.

However, there were significant differences in experience between sub-regions. Strong economic growth, coupled with a reduction in overall population size, resulted in GDP per head that was 6% higher than the 1989 level being recorded in Kazakhstan in 2002. In the rest of the region, GDP per head remained lower than the 1989 figure, with output per head in Georgia, Moldova and Tajikistan at less than one-half the 1989 level, despite negative population growth in both Georgia and Moldova. According to estimates by the UNDP, in 2001 the Central Asian republic of Tajikistan recorded the lowest level of GDP per head among the countries of the region. Tajikistan recorded an estimated annual GDP per head of just US $169 (or $1,170 in terms of purchasing-power parity—with figures adjusted to take into account differences in the cost of living). Indeed, after taking price differences into account, the Tajikistani population were estimated to be living on just over $3 per person per day.

It is important to note that the above estimates reflect measured output only, and may overestimate the decline in output and underestimate subsequent economic growth, as they may exclude some, or all, informal-sector activity. However, even after accepting that there may be measurement problems, it remains clear that the region has suffered a severe decline in economic output.

Furthermore, the ability of governments to respond to depressed economic activity by increasing public expenditure has been severely constrained, with a dwindling tax base and poor tax-collection rates. The level of general government spending as a percentage of GDP declined between 1991 and 2002 in many countries of the region. Since one of the aims of transition is to reduce the once all-encompassing role of the state, a decrease in government spending is to be expected. However, in a number of CIS countries the proportion of government spending has become so low that the functioning of vital state services may be impaired. Furthermore, it is important to remember that social spending comprises a diminishing share of a significantly reduced real GDP.

Once again, there are marked differences between sub-regions, with social spending being generally higher in the western CIS (Belarus, Moldova, Russia and Ukraine) than in the Caucasus and Central Asia (Kazakhstan, Kyrgyzstan, Tajikistan, Turkmenistan and Uzbekistan). Public expenditure on health and education was at critically low levels in Armenia (where spending in 2001 accounted for 1.2% and 2.3% of GDP, respectively), Georgia (0.9% and 2.1%) and Tajikistan (1.1% and 2.4%). In comparison, most member governments of the Organisation for Economic Co-operation and Development (OECD) spend between 5% and 7% of GDP on health care. With the decline in government expenditure in the CIS region, private spending has necessarily increased. However, the introduction of charges for health care, textbooks and school lunches, together with the increasing cost of public transport, all mean that access to basic social services has been severely eroded, particularly in the poorest countries, and it is likely that this will be reflected in a deterioration of the indicators of human development over time.

## INEQUALITY AND POVERTY

High levels of social expenditure and low wage differentials meant that the distribution of income within the USSR was significantly more egalitarian than in most market economies (Atkinson and Micklewright, 1992—see Bibliography). Unfortunately, the decline in measured output during the 1990s discussed above was accompanied by large increases in inequality in household incomes across the region. Inequality in household incomes can be measured in terms of the Gini coefficient, where 0 indicates absolute equality of the population and 1 indicates absolute inequality. In the mid-1990s the average value for the OECD countries was 0.31. In 1989 all the republics of the USSR, with the exception of Azerbaijan, experienced a lower rate of inequality than in the OECD. However, by 2001 most of the former Soviet countries, with the exception of Belarus, displayed values that exceeded even the top of the OECD range (in the 1980s the OECD country that displayed the greatest disparity in household incomes was the USA, with a Gini coefficient of 0.37). The increase in inequality was particularly marked in Armenia, where in 1998/99 the income Gini coefficient reached 0.57, a level akin to the level found among Latin American countries such as Chile (0.57) and Brazil (0.61).

Some increase in income inequality during transition was to be expected, as the market system allows rewards to be more closely associated with risk-taking, training, individual talent and effort. The emergence of open unemployment and the increasing inequality of income from sources other than employment further added to this trend. However, it is clear that the growth in inequality was far more rapid than anticipated, fuelled by a widespread failure to respect employment contracts, leading to the pervasive practice of wages being paid in arrears, especially for the less well-paid; and by the flawed privatization of public assets, leading to the concentration of wealth among very few people. The widening of the gap between those at the top and bottom of the scale has resulted in an acute sense of relative deprivation for those left behind.

Trends in income inequality and poverty are closely linked, and it is not surprising that both absolute and relative poverty levels have increased. As well as exacerbating the hardship of those groups traditionally thought of as being disadvantaged—pensioners, families with large numbers of children and single-parent families—the economic dislocation of transition has also given rise to new groups of poor, including the families of workers 'on leave without pay' or with low pay (especially agricultural and public-sector employees), the long-term unemployed, young people in search of their first job and a growing number of refugees, both economic refugees and persons displaced as a result of civil conflict.

A commonly used international definition of absolute poverty is survival on less than US $1 per person per day. This standard was developed by the World Bank in the 1980s, and was based on the average of the national poverty lines of 10 low-income countries, all of which were located wholly, or in part, within the tropics. In a 2000 report on poverty in Central and Eastern Europe and the CIS (see Bibliography), the World Bank argued that a higher poverty line was required for the region, given that its cooler climate necessitates additional expenditure on heat, winter clothing and food. A level of $2.15 a day was, therefore, interpreted as a low threshold. A higher threshold of $4.30 was also used, recognizing that what may be considered as a 'subsistence need' inevitably varies with the level of a country's development. Even the poorest households in the region will incur expenses on basic services such as the post, child care and health care, and need to cover the running costs of at least some basic consumer durables, such as a television and/or a refrigerator.

At the end of a decade of transition, an estimated 164m. people living in the countries of the former USSR were living in poverty, of whom over 50m. were living in extreme poverty. The problem of low living standards is endemic (and even in the relatively 'successful' Baltic states between one-fifth and one-third of the population are living on less than US $4.30 per person per day). Absolute poverty is greatest, however, in Tajikistan, Moldova, Armenia and Kyrgyzstan. According to World Bank figures, in Tajikistan 68.3% of the population lived in extreme poverty (less than $2.15 per person per day) in 1999, while 95.8% of the population survived on less than $4.30 per person per day. The corresponding figures were: 55.4% and 84.6% in Moldova; 49.1% and 84.1% in Kyrgyzstan; 43.5% and 86.2% in Armenia; 18.8% and 50.3% in Russia; 5.7% and 30.9% in Kazakhstan; 3.0% and 29.4% in Ukraine; and 1.0% and 10.4% in Belarus.

The situation is, however, improving. For those countries for which time series data are available, the proportions of the population living in poverty, according to nationally defined standards, appeared to peak in 1999, following the adverse impact of the Russian financial crisis, and in the following three years improvements were recorded in all the countries of the region, with the exception of Georgia, where the incidence of poverty appeared to have stabilized, but not yet begun to recover. In particular, Kyrgyzstan and Moldova both experienced strong economic growth from 2000, and both have recorded significant reductions in poverty (although figures indicating absolute change should be treated with caution, as data from different surveys are not strictly comparable over time).

## HEALTH AND POVERTY

Health is both a determinant and a dimension of poverty. Ill health and malnutrition are often reasons why households end up in poverty or descend further into it if they are already poor. Illness in the primary or sole wage-earner, and the consequent loss of income, can undermine a poor household's ability to cope financially. In a consultation exercise conducted by the World Bank in 1999, ill health emerged as one of the main reasons cited by households as a cause of poverty. Payments for health services, in particular hospital care, can make the difference between whether a household is able to cope or not. However, poverty is also a cause of ill health. Poor people suffer from a multiplicity of deprivations, which translates into ill health. Most obviously such people lack the financial resources to pay for food, clean water, adequate sanitation and health services, which constitute the key inputs to producing good health. It is not only lack of income that causes the high level of ill health among poor people. The health facilities serving them are often dilapidated, inaccessible, inadequately stocked with basic medicines and run by poorly trained staff.

Under the socialist system, access to health-care services was not a problem, with universal entitlement to comprehensive and free, but inefficient, health care, with excess human and physical infrastructure. Health-care utilization rates were high, and differences across groups, in terms of access to health services, were negligible. Indicators of population health were high by international standards. Tragically, in the last decade there have been remarkable reversals in both health and health care.

## Mortality

The most fundamental measure of the well-being of a population is how long its members can expect to live. Life expectancy at birth is a hypothetical measure, calculating the number of years a man or woman could expect to live, on average, if they were exposed to the risk of dying at the prevailing age-specific mortality rates throughout their entire life. The measure is hypothetical as no one individual lives their entire life in one calendar year, and it is sensitive to short-term changes in mortality rates. During 1989–95 the health of the population deteriorated across much of the CIS, with declines in life expectancy in the majority of the countries of the region. Proportionately, the declines were most marked among men, particularly in the countries of the western CIS. For example, between 1989 and 1995 life expectancy for Russian males declined by almost six years, from 64.2 years in 1989 to 58.3 years in 1995. From the mid-1990s, however, mortality rates appeared to begin to improve, although in many countries life expectancy remains lower than was the case in 1989. The 'mortality crisis' among Russian men has attracted considerable attention (Chen et al, 1996; Cornia and Paniccia, 1995), with much being written about its causes, and its relationship with poverty, unemployment, depression and, especially, alcohol (McKee, 1999; Shkolnikov et al, 2001; Walberg et al, 1998). However, the fact that male mortality also increased elsewhere in the region received less comment.

## Nutritional Status

There is a very real possibility that the level and depth of income poverty faced by households within the region is affecting children's nutritional status, with subsequent long-term developmental consequences. The three standard indices of physical growth are: height-for-age (arrested growth reflects chronic undernutrition), weight-for-height (reflecting acute or recent malnutrition), and weight-for-age (the percentage underweight is a good overall indicator of the child population's nutritional health). In a healthy, well-nourished child population, it is expected that 2.3% of children will fall below two standard deviations of the reference population and will be classified as stunted, wasted or underweight.

The figures for seven CIS countries, including Russia, demonstrate that the nutritional status of children in the region is a major cause for concern (Falkingham, 2003). The percentage

of children classified as stunted is significantly greater than the World Health Organization (WHO) standard of 2.3% in all instances. The rate of stunting in 2000 was 10.6% in Russia, 13.0% in Armenia and 19.6% in Azerbaijan. In Georgia the rate was 11.7% in 1999, and in children aged between 0 and 35 months the rate was 24.8% in Kyrgyzstan in 1999 and 31.3% in Uzbekistan in 1996. In Tajikistan the 2002 figure, of 30.9% (for children aged between six and 59 months), was a particular cause for concern, although it was an improvement on the rates recorded by previous nutritional surveys. The countries' rankings generally followed the rankings for material poverty discussed earlier. Countries with high levels of material poverty, such as Tajikistan and Kyrgyzstan, also have more malnourished children, emphasizing the link between low income and poor health. Unless something is done to improve material living standards, it is likely that rates of malnutrition will increase, with a concomitant increase in morbidity as these children enter young adulthood.

### Access to Health Care

An important determinant of good health is access to good-quality health care. Since independence health services in many countries have deteriorated rapidly, owing to the imposition of severe financial constraints, exacerbated in some areas by extensive damage to infrastructure during armed conflict. It is clear that the widening gap between the health-care budget and the actual costs of care has resulted in both a decline in the quality of services and an increased burden on the household, both in terms of official charges and, more commonly, informal payments. There is a small, but growing, body of evidence that cost represents an important barrier to health care within the region. Indicators of financial barriers to health care in six countries demonstrate that between 13% (in Russia) and 94% of respondents (in Georgia) were either unable to afford care, or compelled to borrow money or sell assets to obtain care, during the 1990s (Lewis, 2002).

## EDUCATION

As with health, the countries of the CIS began the transition with an enviable record on education, with near-universal literacy. Attendance at school was compulsory between the ages of seven and 15, and there was also an extensive system of kindergartens for pre-school-age children, and technical and vocational schools for post-compulsory education. However, over the subsequent decade there were serious reversals in several countries and it is unlikely that the high literacy rates of the past will be sustained in future generations.

The impact of economic decline on education outcomes may be thought of as being three-fold (Falkingham, 2000). First, decreased access (and increased costs) may reduce enrolment rates. Parents who are unable to afford the cost of textbooks, uniforms, or even shoes, may simply withdraw their children from education altogether. Second, even if enrolled, children may not attend school regularly, either for the reasons given above, or because they are needed as family labour (working in the home looking after younger children, or working on family land or in the hired labour market to supplement household income). Finally, children may attend school, but may not benefit from the education. The teacher may be absent, owing to a second job, or—reflecting decreasing public finance for education—there may be no textbooks, it may be too cold to concentrate as a result of a lack of adequate heating, or the child may be anaemic and/or malnourished, and too lethargic to learn. There is very little evidence concerning learning outcomes, so discussion here focuses on trends in kindergarten, primary- and secondary-school enrolment and attendance.

One of the most worrying trends is the decline in the proportion of children aged between three and six years enrolled in pre-primary school education. Prior to independence, attendance at kindergartens was widespread. In the western CIS in 1989, over 60% of children in the relevant age-group were enrolled at kindergartens, rising to nearly 75% in Russia. Enrolment rates were lower in the Caucasus and Central Asia, but even there, with the exception of Azerbaijan and Tajikistan, over 30% of children were enrolled in pre-schools. After independence, rates declined dramatically in almost all of the CIS countries; declines were especially steep in the poorest countries. This was partly a result of the closure of enterprise-based (employer-provided) kindergartens. However, enrolment fell by more than the reduction in capacity, suggesting a decline in demand for kindergarten places, as well as their supply. Such trends are of concern, given the role that kindergartens can play in increasing household welfare, both in terms of freeing the parent to participate in other activities, specifically paid employment, and the developmental role of pre-school education and nutritional and health interventions (Klugman et al, 1997).

Primary education continues to be compulsory, and enrolment rates in basic education have generally remained high. However, there were worrying declines in enrolment in basic education in Armenia and Turkmenistan; data from the UN Children's Fund (UNICEF) MONEE project (a regional 'monitoring' project for the countries of 'Eastern' Europe and the CIS) indicated that only four out of five children aged between seven and 15 years were enrolled in school in Armenia. Furthermore, enrolment rates reveal only part of the situation, and there is a growing problem of declining attendance.

Outside Russia and Ukraine, post-compulsory education enrolment also decreased dramatically. Once again, the decline was most marked in the countries with higher levels of poverty. Worryingly for future levels of human capital and associated prospects for economic growth, between 1989 and 2001 the proportion of 15–18-year-olds attending general secondary schools declined by more than 40% in Tajikistan, Turkmenistan and Uzbekistan, and by over 30% in Azerbaijan and Kyrgyzstan.

In contrast, there was significant growth in higher education in all but three countries. The expansion of higher education was particularly rapid in Kyrgyzstan, where the proportion of 19–24-year-olds in tertiary education increased more than two-fold (from 13.2% to 37.4%) between 1989 and 2000. Almost all of the growth in tertiary education was in the private sector, with a proliferation of private colleges in fields that were under-represented in the past—most notably business studies, economics and law. The quality of education provided varies enormously, and again cost presents a barrier to access for children from the poorest families.

In Kyrgyzstan, at the age of 15 years there was little difference in enrolment rates by sex or by income in 1998 (Falkingham et al, 2002). However, enrolment subsequently declined dramatically. There was a tendency for boys from poor households, in particular, to leave school at 15, whereas for girls, and for boys from wealthier households, the trend did not begin until one year later. By the age of 21, the greatest distinction in enrolment data was influenced by income, rather than sex, with the poor being much less likely to continue in education than the non-poor.

With rising costs at both school and college it is difficult to resist the conclusion put forward by the UNDP, that the education systems in the CIS are coming to reflect the increasing socio-economic stratification of these societies. Access to quality education has become confined substantially to those who can afford private fees and tuition. It is imperative that action is taken to ensure that the growing poverty and stratification outlined above does not result in the re-emergence of illiteracy within the region and the cycle of deprivation and social exclusion that accompany it.

## CONCLUSION

The preceding sections have provided a bleak picture of falling real incomes, growing poverty, declining life expectancy, rising child malnutrition and deteriorating educational status. Although from the beginning of the 2000s economic growth throughout the region demonstrated a positive trend, this alone is not sufficient. In countries where disparities in incomes are large, it will be difficult substantially to increase the incomes of poor families in the short and medium term without some reduction in those income differences. This will necessitate tackling the vested interests that are holding back restructuring, stifling small-scale private enterprise and frustrating efforts to improve public-expenditure management. Action is also required to protect and build capabilities, so that the poor are able to take advantage of new income-generating opportunities. Moreover, there remains an urgent need to invest in schools and primary health-care facilities and to strengthen public-expenditure management systems to ensure equality of access for all.

## BIBLIOGRAPHY

Atkinson, A. B., and Micklewright, J. *Economic Transformation in Eastern Europe and the Distribution of Income*. Cambridge, Cambridge University Press, 1992.

Chen, L., Wittgenstein, F., and McKeon, E. 'The Upsurge of Mortality in Russia: Causes and Policy Implications', in *Population and Development Review*. Vol. 22, No. 3, 1996.

Cornia, G., and Paniccia, R. 'The Demographic Impact of Sudden Impoverishment: Eastern Europe during the 1989–94 Transition'. *Innocenti Occasional Papers*, EPS 49. Florence, UNICEF Innocenti Research Centre, 1995.

Falkingham, J. 'From Security to Uncertainty: The Impact of Economic Change on Child Welfare in Central Asia'. *Innocenti Working Paper*, ESP 76. Florence, UNICEF Innocenti Research Centre, 2000.

'Inequality and Poverty in the CIS-7'. Paper prepared for the Lucerne Conference of the CIS-7 Initiative, 20–22 January 2003.

Falkingham, J., Namazie, C., and Siyam, A. 'Poverty and Vulnerability in the Kyrgyz Republic 1996–1998'. Mimeo paper. Washington, DC, World Bank, 2002.

Klugman, J., et al. 'The Impact of Kindergarten Divestiture on Household Welfare', in J. Falkingham, S. Marnie, and J. Micklewright (Eds). *Household Welfare in Central Asia*. Basingstoke, Macmillan, 1997.

Lewis, M. 'Informal Health Payments in Eastern Europe and Central Asia: Issues, Trends and Policy Implications', in E. Mossialos, A. Dixon, J. Figueras, and J. Kutzin (Eds). *Funding Health Care: Options for Europe*. Buckingham, Open University Press, 2002.

McKee, M. 'Unravelling the Enigma of the Russian Mortality Crisis: A Review Essay on Charles M. Becker and David Bloom (Eds). *The Demographic Crisis in the Former Soviet Union*', in *Population Development Review*. Vol. 25, No. 2, 1999.

Bureau of Economic Analysis (BEA). *Russian Economic Trends*. Moscow, BEA, June 2003.

Shkolnikov, V., McKee, M., Leon, D. A. 'Changes in Life Expectancy in Russia in the 1990s', in *The Lancet*. Vol. 357, 2001.

UNDP. *Transition 1999: Human Development Report for Central and Eastern Europe and the CIS*. New York, NY, UNDP, 1999.

*Human Development Report*. New York, NY, UNDP, 2003.

UNICEF. *Social Monitor 2003*. Florence, UNICEF Innocenti Research Centre, 2003.

Walberg, P., McKee, M., Shkolnikov, V., Chenet, L., and Leon, D. A. 'Economic Change, Crime, and Mortality Crisis in Russia: A Regional Analysis', in *British Medical Journal*. August 1998.

World Bank. *Making Transition Work for Everyone*. Oxford, Oxford University Press, 2000.

*Armenia Poverty Update*. Washington, DC, World Bank, 2002.

# TRENDS IN RELIGIOUS POLICY

### Rev. Canon MICHAEL BOURDEAUX

### FROM COMMUNISM TO RELIGION

The experiment forcibly to impose *gosateizm* (state atheism) in the USSR lasted just 70 years. Until Lenin—Vladimir Ilych Ulyanov's first Decree on the Separation of Church and State of January 1918, no government in history had sought to enforce a system that rejected all forms of religion. Soviet state atheism experienced variable degrees of success, but continued as the dominant policy, in one form or other, until 1988.

Every Soviet leader put his personal stamp on atheist policy (for example, Lenin's seizure of the property of the Russian Orthodox Church; Stalin—Iosif V. Dzhugashvili's purge of the whole Church leadership, moderated during the Second World War (1939–45); Nikita Khrushchev's renewed physical onslaught as leader of the USSR, 1953–64; and Leonid Brezhnev's hunting down of 'dissidents' as Soviet leader in 1964–82), but the long-term aim of eliminating religion from society continued to stand. Much of this policy was successful, at least outwardly. Every church institution at local, diocesan or national level was systematically destroyed. When churches of any denomination continued to exist up to the beginning of the Second World War, they were entirely isolated units and, therefore, all the more vulnerable to persecution. No literature, no teaching, no charitable work and no communal activities existed outside the walls of a registered church, although the numbers of the latter did, indeed, grow, as the result of Stalin's concessions during the last decade of his life (1943–53). Some institutions re-emerged after the War, such as eight theological seminaries, two academies, one heavily censored journal and a politically controlled central administration (the Patriarchate of the Orthodox Church in the Soviet and Russian capital, Moscow). The Baptists—the only legal Protestant group—were accorded some of these privileges, but without the theological education; the Roman Catholics had two churches on Russian soil and nothing else. Under Khrushchev all of these gains came under renewed threat, but his premature removal from office halted the Church's decline, without allowing any restitution of its recent losses.

Beneath the surface, however, the elimination of religion had not proceeded as smoothly as the propagandists consistently reported in the Soviet press. Despite the constant assertion that religion was dying out, there was evidence that the survival of religion had persisted long after the destruction of its institutions. In the process it was also revealed that the influence of the Orthodox Church, proclaimed throughout Siberia and the Russian south with the expansion of empire, was thin indeed, and recent observations provide evidence of the most remarkable revival of pre-Christian religion.

What of the survival of Orthodoxy itself in the Russian heartland during the communist period? The evidence is manifold and widespread, and is illustrated particularly well by Alexander Solzhenitsyn. His work published in Soviet times was suffused with an underlying allegiance to the Christian faith and later, during the long period when his works were banned, he revealed himself as an adherent, overtly. His first publication, the novella *One Day in the Life of Ivan Denisovich* (1962), an account of life in a labour camp, which Khrushchev permitted to be published in order to provide support for his anti-Stalin campaign, described the use of prayer by one of the inmates. An essay contained in his second and last-published work in the Soviet period, a collec-

tion of prose poems, expressed horror at the desecration of Russia's Christian architectural heritage, and its publication inspired a new generation to make efforts to preserve the remaining tatters. An extract gives the flavour:

'When you travel the by-roads of central Russia you begin to understand the secret of the pacifying Russian countryside. It's in the churches. . . they nod to each other from afar, from villages that are cut off and invisible to each other. . . But when you get into the village you find that not the living but the dead greeted you from afar. The crosses were knocked off the roof or twisted out of place long ago. The dome has been stripped and there are gaping holes between its rusty ribs. . . Our forefathers put all their understanding of life into these stones, into these bell-towers. . .'

The advent of Mikhail Gorbachev as General Secretary of the Communist Party put an end to official Soviet atheism three years into his rule. On 29 April 1988 Gorbachev received a group of leading Russian Orthodox bishops. His words marked the beginning of a new era:

'Not everything has been easy and simple in the sphere of church-state relations. Religious organizations have been affected by the tragic developments that occurred in the period of the cult of personality. Mistakes made in relation to the church and believers in the 1930s and subsequently are being rectified. . . Believers are Soviet people, workers, patriots, and they have the full right to express their convictions with dignity. *Perestroika* [restructuring], democratization and *glasnost* [openness] concern them as well—in full measure and without any restrictions. This is especially true of ethics and morals, a domain where universal norms and customs are so helpful for our common cause.'

'Our common cause'—never before had a communist leader in power spoken thus of religion. Gorbachev followed words with deeds, although his own experiment in democracy collapsed three years later (see Russian chapter in Part Two). Gorbachev made two promises: the right to celebrate officially the millennium of the baptism of Prince Volodymyr (Vladimir), which led to the conversion of the medieval Kievan state in 988, and the introduction of a new and just law on religion to replace that imposed by Stalin in 1929.

The first was soon implemented, as plans were already in existence for the celebration on 4 June 1988 of the conversion of the Eastern Slavs (the ancient land of 'Rus', based in what is now Ukraine). However, by that time what might have been a local celebration had expanded to become one of international significance. Guests from all over the world were expected, but they were surprised to find that the celebrations were the subject of extensive media coverage. Moscow and Russia received the acclaim that should rightly have belonged to Kiev and Ukraine, but, nevertheless, it felt as though the USSR had become a Christian country overnight. Russia would never be the same again.

Gorbachev's promise of a new law took longer to implement, but when it was promulgated in September 1990 it exceeded all expectations, proclaiming total freedom of religion (even permitting the teaching of religion in state schools in the Russian republic's version, although the text for the whole USSR did not go quite this far).

## RELIGIOUS REVIVAL AND THE NEW LAW OF 1997

Had Gorbachev's law remained in force for a reasonable period of time, it would have represented a major step in the painful evolution of Russia towards democracy. As it was, the religious revival, which had begun as early as the 1960s among the intelligentsia of Moscow and Leningrad (now St Petersburg), and which predated the advent of Gorbachev (to whom it is sometimes mistakenly ascribed) by some 20 years, continued steadily throughout the former USSR. What Gorbachev did was to facilitate the rebirth of religious institutions nation-wide and to give voice to the repressed spiritual aspirations of the Russian people (encouraged by the maxim of the time, *glasnost*).

One major effect of this, as well as promoting the expression of the hitherto covert religious beliefs of the populace (one-third of the population still considered itself to have a religious belief), was an influx of foreign missionaries of many denominations and religions. They were encouraged by the events of 1988, by the legislation of 1990 and, especially, by the collapse of the USSR at the end of 1991. At this time, too, Russia, Ukraine and other former constituent republics began urgently to turn to the West for advice and economic support, which soon led to a much more ready access and a partial relaxation of visa restrictions. This, however, was not to last. Internally, in the seven-year period between the enactment of Gorbachev's law and its repeal (under Russian President Boris Yeltsin), both Russia and the now independent countries of the Commonwealth of Independent States (CIS) had experienced a revival of indigenous religion.

The repeal of the 1990 law on religion was only one aspect of the gathering spirit of resentment against the West in Russia. In September 1997 Gorbachev's law was replaced by controversial legislation returning the regulation of religious organizations to the state, albeit in a different form from that formerly exercised by the Communist Party. Under the old system, every region of the USSR had local officials, who were responsible for controlling religious activities and reporting back to the Council for Religious Affairs in Moscow. This system had been abolished in 1990, but not, as it proved, swept away. Many officials continued to support the old regime and they joined the hierarchy of the Russian Orthodox Church in agitating for the introduction of the new law. Time might well have dictated that the threats introduced by external missionaries and the internal revival of sectarianism were perceived, rather than actual, and that the reaction was disproportionate, but the old atheist guard believed that their services were needed again. The complex text of the resulting new law was achieved by means of a secretive process and the machinations of bureaucracy, which excluded public debate.

There is not space here to discuss the new law in detail, although the debate concerning possible revisions has continued. However, it is worth pausing over the preamble—not, its defenders claim, part of the law itself, but merely the context in which the law is set:

> 'Confirming the right of each to freedom of conscience and freedom of creed, and also to equality before the law regardless of his attitudes to religion and his convictions; basing itself on the fact that the Russian Federation is a secular state; recognizing the special contribution of Orthodoxy to the history of Russia and to the establishment and development of Russia's spirituality and culture; respecting Christianity, Islam, Buddhism, Judaism and other religions and creeds which constitute an inseparable part of the historical heritage of Russia's peoples; considering it important to promote the achievement of mutual understanding, tolerance and respect in questions of freedom of conscience and freedom of creed; the Russian Federation hereby adopts this federal law.'

The other Christian dominations, separate from the Russian Orthodox Church, are undefined. One can only assume that the text refers to Roman Catholicism and Protestantism, the first of which had some influence in Russia before 1917, the second rather more. Representatives of Islam, Buddhism and Judaism were, naturally, appeased to find themselves named and protected under the new law. The identities of the other 'religions and creeds' remained unspecified.

The main text went on to demonstrate that there were to be three tiers of privilege. The Russian Orthodox Church, *de facto* if not *de jure*, claimed the right to decide which other religions or denominations were to be granted the right of registration, and local Orthodox clergy were frequently consulted by state officials, adding a decisive voice on which should or should not be registered. The new law appeared to grant the Russian Orthodox Church the first claim on the loyalty of some 160m. people. However, the text of the law made it clear that any religion might be considered 'traditional' if it was in existence in 1982, 15 years before the decree came into effect. This takes one back to the end of the Brezhnev era. As a result, the discrimination of that time, dictated by Soviet policy, can be seen to be perpetuated. Any group that was not in existence at that time was compelled to re-register, conditionally, each year for 15 years, in order to prove its credentials and, in the mean time, had virtually no rights: it was not to be permitted to print and distribute literature, own property, hire halls, invite foreign preachers into Russia, and much more. The selected year, 1982, was within the period of *zastoi* (stagnation), as Gorbachev called it. This was a time of widespread discrimination, with a ban on such groups as Methodists (except in Estonia); Lutherans (except in Estonia and Latvia); some groups of Baptists, which had separated from the Russian-dominated All-Union Council; Catholics of the Byzantine Rite (the 'Uniates', or 'Greek' Catholics of Ukraine); Jehovah's Witnesses, and many others. Some of these groups had, notably, been present before the Revolution: Lutherans existed in Siberia in the 18th century, and in St Petersburg from its foundation (as shown by the church, which has been fully restored, on Nevskii Prospekt).

The 1997 law also insisted that all registered congregations should re-register by 1 January 2000. This imposed inconvenience and bureaucratic restraint nation-wide. The Anglican Church had owned property in St Petersburg and Moscow, with flourishing congregations, before the Revolution. However, its application for re-registration in Moscow, where worship had taken place in its former church from 1991, was twice rejected at the end of 1999, before being accepted following considerable diplomatic dispute. Many Orthodox congregations failed to re-register by the due date and such was the confusion that in January 2000 the State Duma (lower house of parliament) voted to extend the deadline by one full year. The 1997 law provided grounds for protracted legal disputes. The best known was the prolonged scandal over the removal of the Salvation Army's registration in Moscow. This was eventually restored in March 2002, but the legal process nation-wide cost the denominations substantial sums in legal fees and considerable time in bureaucratic wrangling. President Vladimir Putin, while proclaiming himself to be an active member of the Orthodox Church, stood aside from these controversies.

The law did not seem to have inhibited the unrestrained revival of religious institutions of all kinds, Christian, Muslim, Buddhist, Jewish and pagan, throughout Russia, although it had certainly led to the increased surveillance of foreign missionaries in most places. There were some expulsions of Protestant missionaries, but the Roman Catholic Church was able to introduce some 300 foreign priests. In early 2002—and continuing in 2003—bitter controversy erupted between the Roman Catholic Church and the Moscow Patriarchate. Plans by the Catholic Church to upgrade its four apostolic administrations to the status of full canonical dioceses were strongly opposed by the Orthodox leadership, which claimed that Russian territory should be subject to one jurisdiction only—its own. This controversy prevented a visit to Russia by Pope John Paul II, thus thwarting the main ambition of the latter years of his papacy.

### AROUND THE CIS

The Orthodox Church was dominant in the Russian heartland, the territory stretching some 500 km (300 miles) to 600 km in all directions from Moscow. It was less dominant elsewhere, however. North of St Petersburg, east of the Volga river, right across Siberia and the whole of the south and south-east, the picture was very different. Both Protestantism and Roman Catholicism made significant progress in Siberia. Baptists were present in Soviet times in all major population centres and by the early 2000s they were building new churches and training a strong local leadership. The Pentecostal Church, banned in the Soviet period, rivalled them in many places and the Roman Catholic Church was well organized, opening new parishes in many places and establishing a Bishops' Conference in 1999.

Anti-Semitism (strongly present and often encouraged under the communist regime) has never entirely disappeared from Russia and Ukraine. It was present not least in church circles, although its most public proponent, Metropolitan Ioann of St Petersburg, died in 1995.

Buddhism was experiencing a major revival, not only in the traditional area of the Republic of Buryatiya, on the Mongolian border, south of Irkutsk Oblast in Siberia, but also in Europe. Kalmykiya was Europe's only Buddhist civilization in tsarist times. Eventually Buddhism was tolerated, although in the communist period not only was it eliminated, but the Kalmyks were deported to Siberia. By the early 2000s Buddhism had, once again, become an active force in this European stronghold.

Perhaps most surprising was the rise of traditional pre-Christian paganism in many areas where, in tsarist times, the missionary activity of the Russian Orthodox Church did little more than introduce a Christian overlay and administration in places where people, especially in rural areas, quietly preserved their ancient customs. This might not seem so surprising in the tribal areas of Siberia, where reindeer-herding and trapping in the forests remained the traditional way of life. That paganism was experiencing a major revival elsewhere was unexpected. It had become particularly popular in the Lower Volga, where the Republics of Chuvashiya, Marii-El and Udmurtiya are situated. In particular in Marii-El, pagan religion was making significant progress, not only in terms of cultural domination, but was also being promoted by politicians as a means to re-establish the identity of the peoples living in those areas.

The vast territories covered by the newly independent countries of the CIS presented a picture of even greater diversity, one not susceptible to generalization. The former imposition of state atheism had, of course, left its mark everywhere, but the speed with which the religious picture had changed in every new country was astonishing. Religion was acknowledged by the respective governments to be a major factor in these emerging societies, each one of which introduced legislation to control religion, and where the compulsion to register with the state, in order to achieve legitimacy, was universal.

Wherever one looked, however, religion was a defining feature and it was often allied with newly asserted nationalism. Religious intolerance in one form or another was present throughout the region. For example, Armenia strongly opposed the propagation of any religion other than the tradi-

tional Armenian Apostolic Church. It was the first state in history officially to adopt Christianity as its religion and its polices were partly a reaction, once it had achieved independence, to its treatment at the hands of first the Turks, and then the Soviet atheists, throughout the 20th century. The late head of the Church, Catholicos Karekin I, who died in 1999, after only a short period in office, was educated in the West, possessed great ecumenical experience and held moderate views, but even he was in favour of legislation to control sectarian activity and the work of foreign missionaries. In 2001 the Armenian Apostolic Church celebrated the 1,700th anniversary of its establishment as the official state religion.

The Georgian Orthodox Church emerged as a barely unifying factor in a country experiencing political turmoil, and the Georgian President and former Soviet foreign minister, Eduard Shevardnadze, was a convert. The Church became strongly nationalistic, even to the extent of severing most of its foreign ties, and reduced its ecumenical contact by leaving the World Council of Churches. However, bilateral relations with, for example, the Anglican Church survived. Minorities, such as the long-established Baptist Church under Bishop Malkhaz Songulashvili, were feeling the effects of intolerance, however much they wished to assert that they, too, were traditional Georgian churches. Throughout 2001–03 the situation worsened, with physical attacks on property (including that belonging to the Bible Society) and on individuals; the police made little effort to restrain the perpetrators.

In Moldova, the Orthodox Church predominated, but its religious, as well as its political, allegiance was torn between Romania, with which it shares a language, and Russia, where the Moscow Patriarchate was attempting to retain the adherence of the people; the law officially banned proselytism.

In Ukraine there were sharper divisions than elsewhere in the CIS. Stalin abolished the Ukrainian (so-called 'Greek') Catholic Church in 1946, but succeeded only in compelling it to operate clandestinely. When it emerged in the period of *glasnost*, it began to reclaim from the Moscow Patriarchate its lost churches (predominantly in the western region around Lviv). By the early 2000s in the centre (the Kiev region) and in the east of the country the Orthodox Church predominated, but the territory was still subject to disputes between different jurisdictions. The Moscow Patriarchate had fought a bitter, and largely successful, battle to retain the majority of its churches after being confronted by the emergence of an independent 'Kiev Patriarchate', led by the renegade Patriarch Filaret, whose conduct prompted a number of senior clergy to leave the Ukrainian Orthodox Church upon his election as Patriarch. In addition, there were probably more Protestants, mainly Baptists, in Ukraine, than in the rest of the countries of the CIS combined (including Russia) and the Protestant organizations were very active and well organized, in terms of building churches and re-establishing seminary education.

Belarus was notable for the strength of its churches, being influenced, respectively, by its Roman Catholic neighbours, Poland and Lithuania, to the west, and by Orthodox Russia to the east. State policy under its President, Alyaksandr Lukashenka, declared that Orthodoxy must predominate and, as a consequence, there was only limited tolerance of the strong Roman Catholic minority. The Orthodox Metropolitan, Filaret of Minsk, a resolute survivor of the Soviet period, was also a strong pro-Russian activist. Pro-Orthodox religious legislation, enacted in 2002, was the most discriminatory in the CIS. None the less, Metropolitan Filaret was cited as a possible successor to the patriarchal throne in Moscow.

After the revival of the Russian Orthodox Church, the rise of Islam in many parts of the region was the most important new factor, in religious terms, following the collapse of communism. This development originated some considerable time earlier, but the removal of the constraints imposed by communism accelerated the process. By 2001 the religious status quo of the communist period in the five states of Central Asia (Kazakhstan, Kyrgyzstan, Tajikistan, Turkmenistan and Uzbekistan) had already changed beyond recognition. Islam was universally present, and in some places dominant, a factor that was turning the focus of politics away from Russia and towards the Islamic states to the south.

During the Soviet period, Muslims in Central Asia, perhaps numbering up to 40m. adherents, were overtly quiescent. They were isolated from contact with mainstream Islam in Arab countries, Iran and Pakistan, and could not develop their own institutions, because of the dominance of Soviet atheism. The old regime constantly claimed success in its modernization programme for the region, particularly in terms of the liberation of women. However, a covert Islamic culture endured, with extensive devotion to domestic ritual. Travelling mullahs and the survival of secret Sufi ' brotherhoods' ensured that Islam was not dormant.

After independence in 1991, wealthy Arab states provided considerable resources for the building of mosques and theological schools (*madrassahs*). Throughout the region the governing élites, largely unchanged since the Soviet era, sought to control the revival of Islam for political purposes through semi-official Islamic religious administrations established in Soviet times. Increasingly, they also identified any form of opposition as Muslim extremism, under the all-embracing term, 'Wahhabism', and employed forceful methods to combat it. All the new states introduced religious controls of varying severity, favouring official Islam and Russian Orthodoxy. A law of 1998 in Uzbekistan banned all religious activity by unregistered congregations. There was relative tolerance between the Slav and indigenous peoples who had learned to live together during the Soviet period, but this has not prevented the widespread persecution of individual Baptist and Pentecostal congregations, especially in Turkmenistan and Uzbekistan.

Over the vast and sparsely populated territory of Kazakhstan there was greater religious tolerance, with Orthodox Russians and Muslim Kazakhs enjoying reasonable relations with each other. The Roman Catholic Church had established a regular jurisdiction and a theological seminary opened in 1999. The armed conflict between Armenia and Azerbaijan (the latter the only other predominantly Muslim territory outside Central Asia), over the primarily ethnic Armenian enclave of Nagornyi Karabakh (known as Artsakh by the Armenians) inside Azerbaijan, saw the expulsion of many Armenians from Muslim territory, but primarily on ethnic, rather than religious, grounds. Moreover, this area was much quieter from the mid-1990s.

The suicide attacks on the USA on 11 September 2001, and the subsequent invasion of Afghanistan by US and allied forces, had a huge and visibly destabilizing effect on the whole region, and not only the three Central Asian states that share a border with Afghanistan (Tajikistan, Turkmenistan and Uzbekistan). For example, in the Fergana valley, a heavily populated region divided between three states (Kyrgyzstan, Tajikistan and Uzbekistan), there was evidence of considerable opposition to US policy among leading members of the Muslim clergy, in contrast to the accommodation made by those countries' respective governments. In many places there were signs that there had been a new stimulus to Islamic revival. There was already an element of religious conflict in the war for independence from Russia fought in Chechnya, and Shi'ite Muslims from outside the republic had strongly

influenced the actions of local people. Every Orthodox Church in Chechnya was destroyed and its priests either murdered or expelled. It remained uncertain whether the devastated city of Groznyi was to be rebuilt, but, if so, Orthodox churches were certain to reappear. The issue of Islam was likely to remain symbolic for the Chechens beaten back into the mountains and they were retaining their sympathizers in the neighbouring republics of Dagestan (Daghestan) and Ingushetiya. In 2002–03 acts of aggression by secessionist Chechens became increasingly widespread. (See also the essay on Militant Islam in Central Asia and the Caucasus.)

Some other parts of Russia were also experiencing an Islamic revival. It was a strong feature in the Republic of Adygeya (Adygheya), the Black Sea region in the south. This was even more true in the Republic of Tatarstan, centred on Kazan, the ancient heartland of the Muslim faith in Russia. The Orthodox Church was strongly present here, too, and the two each commanded the loyalty of almost 50% of the population. These developments took place with some degree of co-operation between the two faiths.

With the exception of the Baltic states (Estonia, Latvia and Lithuania), the whole area of the former USSR had failed to implement the degree of religious liberty for which there was such a high hope in 1991, when communism and its atheist policies finally collapsed. However, the Christian Church in a variety of traditions, as well as the dominant Orthodox Church, was destined to be visibly and actively present in Russia in the 21st century. The failed experiment of state atheism destroyed so much, yet what it left behind proved that human agency, however systematic its efforts over a long period of time, was unable to eliminate faith. There was a certain degree of truth in the preamble to the 1997 law that the future of Russia and the future of Orthodoxy were inseparable. However, the Slav lands seemed destined to be pluralistic societies, in which the most disparate elements would have to learn to live together, not least Muslims alongside Christians. Laws favouring one group over another threatened to lead not only to heightened tensions, but to disaster caused by the exacerbation of ethnic conflict.

The countries of Central Asia, as a bloc, were more problematic. Even before September 2001 the full consequences of political realignment, as a result of the revival of Islam in all five countries, had been expected to be considerable, and the situation was likely to be influenced further by the Arab–Israeli conflict, which intensified in 2002, and the US-led military campaign in Iraq in 2003. Moreover, the harshness of the Central Asian regimes also threatened to provoke local conflicts, which could escalate.

## BIBLIOGRAPHY

Bourdeaux, M. (Ed.). *The Politics of Religion in Russia and the New States of Eurasia*. New York, NY, M. E. Sharpe, 1995.

Bourdeaux, M., and Witte, J. (Eds). *Proselytism and Orthodoxy in Russia: The New War for Souls*. Maryknoll, NY, Orbis Books, 1999.

Ellis, J. *The Russian Orthodox Church: A Contemporary History*. Beckenham, Croom Helm, 1986.

*The Russian Orthodox Church: Triumphalism and Defensiveness*. London, Macmillan, 1996.

Keston Institute. *Religion, State and Society*. Oxford, Keston Institute, quarterly.

Sawatsky, W. *Soviet Evangelicals since World War II*. Kitchener, ON, Herald Press, 1981.

# APPENDIX: THE RELIGIONS OF THE REGION

There is a vast range of religions, denominations and sects in the region, from the many Christian churches, through Islam, to the religions of Asia, such as Buddhism. A brief survey of the main groups follows.

## CHRISTIANITY

The Christian religion is a monotheistic faith, which evolved from Judaism in the first century AD. Christianity is based on a belief in the divinity and teachings of Jesus Christ, the Messiah or Son of God, through whom salvation (life after death) can be obtained. His followers established the institution of a single Church, originally based on the four leading cities of the Roman Empire: Antioch, Alexandria, Rome itself and Constantinople (from AD 330, the capital). Four distinct traditions emerged: the Syrian or Jacobite Church was based on Antioch; the Coptic Church was based on Alexandria; the Western, or Latin, Church was based on Rome and became known as the Roman Catholic Church (the Protestants sprang from this tradition too); and the Eastern, or Greek, Orthodox Church became centred on Constantinople (this is the tradition of most of the region's Orthodox Churches). Later divisions resulted in the emergence of the Armenian (Gregorian) Church and the Nestorian Church.

The Church also established the Christian era (a calendar of years denoted by *Anno Domini*), a reckoning that is now the most widely used international system and is in official use throughout the former USSR. Likewise, it was the Church that preserved the use of the ancient Roman, Julian calendar, which was used in the Russian Empire until the revolution. In 1582 a reformed Gregorian calendar (in normal use now) was first introduced, but by Pope Gregory XIII, so its adoption was initially resisted by non-Roman Catholic countries. For religious purposes, the Eastern Orthodox Church still uses a version of the old Julian calendar (and the Georgian Orthodox calendar is different again). The Muslims and Buddhists use a lunar calendar, which is about 10 days shorter than the solar calendar of the Gregorian reckoning. Islam dates its years from the date of the *Hijra*—the flight of the Prophet Muhammad from Mecca to Medina, so the year 1424 AH (*Anno Hegirae*) begins on AD 22 February 2004. The Buddhist era is usually dated from the death of Gautama Buddha, nominally reckoned to be 544 BC, with AD 2004 approximately conterminous with 2548. The Jewish calendar is luni-solar and reckons years in the Era of Creation (*Anno Mundi*)—the year AM 5765 begins on AD 16 September 2004.

### The Eastern Orthodox Church

In 1054 the split (schism) in the Church that had become established in the old Roman Empire became formal. The bishops of what had been the Latin-speaking West supported the authority of the Pope, the Roman patriarch, and the insertion of the *filioque* clause into the standard confession of faith, the Nicene Creed. (This claimed that the Holy Spirit, a constituent part of the triune deity, was a product of both the Father and the Son—*Logos*—not merely of the Father.) The bishops of the Greek-speaking Eastern Roman Empire, dominated by the Byzantine Patriarch of Constantinople (today still regarded as the Ecumenical Patriarch), rejected this, and so formalized a division of Europe into East and West. The Eastern, or Greek, Orthodox Church continued to use the Greek alphabet, but had also added to the success of its missionary work among the 'barbarian' peoples, on the Byzantine borders, by the introduction of the Cyrillic alphabet and a Slavonic liturgy. This powerful formative influence of the Church, particularly on culture, education and national identity, is still most relevant today. In Soviet Moldavia—now Moldova—the authorities forced the adoption of a Cyrillic alphabet to replace the traditional Latin one, although this was reversed after independence. The other Orthodox churches use the Cyrillic alphabet, the invention of which is attributed to the Byzantine missionaries, St Cyril (Constantine) and St Methodius, in the ninth century.

The Eastern Orthodox churches have a membership of some 200m., most of them in Eastern Europe and Russia. They are not formally linked save in acknowledging the pre-eminence of the Ecumenical Patriarch (Bartholomeos I of Constantinople and New Rome, since 1991), who convened a meeting of 12 of the highest Eastern Orthodox patriarchs in the Turkish city of İstanbul (formerly Constantinople) during 1992. They met regularly thereafter. The Russian Orthodox Church is the largest denomination and also assumed jurisdiction over the Orthodox of Soviet Moldavia, Trans-Carpathian Ukraine and Galicia. After the collapse of the USSR, however, it increasingly devolved power from the Moscow Patriarchate, in an attempt to retain the local Church's position in the more nationalist-charged atmosphere. All the countries of the region have at least some Orthodox Christians.

Within the former USSR, there are missions of the Eastern Orthodox Patriarchs of Antioch and Alexandria, but the other main Orthodox Church is the Georgian. The Primate of the Georgian Orthodox Church, the Catholicos-Patriarch, also enjoys jurisdiction over several Russian and Greek communities, but, under the communists, the Church was restricted by the lack of its own seminary and by the limited instruction in Georgian devotional literature and liturgical traditions. After independence, this position was reversed.

With the liberalization of religion, religious groups increasingly demanded greater autonomy and a reversal of russification, as with the Ukrainian Autocephalous Orthodox Church or the Gagauz Turkish-speaking Orthodox. There was also the return of those Orthodox who went into exile after the communists came to power (often forming rival hierarchies abroad) and the secession of the Uniates who had been forcibly amalgamated with the Orthodox. Even within the established Church, the end of a communist-imposed monopoly created strains. Moreover, the dissolution of the USSR threatened the Patriarch of Moscow's jurisdiction beyond the more limited borders of the Russian Federation.

### The Roman Catholic Church

The Western, or Roman Catholic Church, was distinguished by its use of a liturgy in Latin, which is still referred to as the Latin Rite, although most services are now conducted in the vernacular. The Latin Rite is not used by the adherents of the 'Greek Catholic' or 'Uniate' Church. This denomination is part of the Roman Catholic Church, but uses the Eastern or 'Byzantine' Rite; their Orthodox predecessors had acknowledged the primacy of the Roman pontiff, the Pope (also the existence of Purgatory, the doctrine of the *filioque* and the use of unleavened bread for communion), but retained their traditional liturgies and ecclesiastical organization. Not all Uniates use the Byzantine Rite; there are some from non-Orthodox traditions. In the region there are the Armenian Catholics and some Chaldean (Nestorian) Catholics, who also retain their Oriental customs and rites (the remaining Uniates are the Maronites, the Syrian Catholics and the Coptic Catholics).

## Protestant Churches

In the Reformation period of the 16th and 17th centuries some of the Western, or Catholic, Christians protested against the authority of the Roman pontiff, the Pope, and formed separate ('Protestant') sects. Most of these groups relied more on the authority of the Bible and rejected the episcopal organization of the Church. The main denominations are: Lutheran Evangelical (who define their faith by the Augsburg Confession of 1530); the more fundamentalist Calvinists and Presbyterians; Baptists; Pentecostalists; and Unitarians. There are also communities of Seventh-day Adventists (distinguished among Christians by their observance of the Sabbath on Saturday), Methodists, Mennonites (mainly of German descent, they combine characteristics of the Baptists and the Society of Friends—Quakers), Molokans (pacifist fundamentalists in the Caucasus) and many others.

## Other Christian Churches

The Armenian Apostolic, or Gregorian, Church is one of the Monophysite churches, like the Coptic and Syrian Jacobite Churches. It separated from the rest of the Church when it rejected the authority of the Council of Chalcedon in 451. (The Monophysites maintain that there is a single, divine nature in the person of the incarnate Christ, whereas Chalcedon decreed that Christ had two natures, both human and divine.) There are significant Armenian communities in the region and abroad, quite apart from in Armenia itself. In the 1950s there was an acrimonious schism in the Church, between the Supreme Patriarchate and the Catholicosate of Cilicia (based in Beirut, Lebanon). In 1995, however, the Catholicos of Cilicia was chosen as the new Supreme Patriarch, with the support of the Armenian Government, in an effort to end the schism; he died in 1999.

Another ancient Christian sect that differed from the orthodox on the nature of Christ, were the Nestorians (followers of a fifth-century Patriarch of Constantinople), some communities of whom live in the countries that once formed the USSR. The Nestorians once dominated Central Asia and much of the Middle East. The major split in the western Church was the Protestant defection from Rome. Both the Roman Catholic and the Orthodox Churches lost some members when they underwent reformation. There are Old Catholic communities in many of the countries of Eastern Europe (formed in the 19th century). The Old Believers (Raskolniki) of the Russian Orthodox tradition, who rejected reforms of the 18th century, have long had an eminent role in Russian cultural and spiritual life. The main Old Believer group, those of the Belokrinitskii Concord, elected their own patriarch, the Metropolitan of Moscow and All-Russia, in 1991.

## ISLAM

Islam means 'submission' or surrender to God. It is the preferred name for the monotheistic religion founded by Muhammad, the Prophet (AD 570–632), in Arabia. The unparalleled spread of the religion in its first centuries can be attributed to the concept of holy war (*jihad*).

The Five Pillars of the practice of Islam are: the Witness that 'there is no god but God' (*Allah*) and that 'Muhammad is His Prophet'; prayer, which takes place five times daily and includes prostration in the direction of the holy city of Mecca and recitation of set verses, and is also performed in congregational worship at a mosque on Fridays, the Muslim holy day; almsgiving; fasting, which must take place during the hours of daylight for the whole of the ninth month, Ramadan (some exceptions are allowed); finally, the Pilgrimage (*hajj*) to Mecca (Makkah), Saudi Arabia, which is incumbent at least once in the lifetime of a Muslim. The heart of Islam is contained in the Koran, which is considered above criticism as the very Word of God as uttered to his Prophet. This authority is supplemented by various traditions (*hadith*). To interpret the application of Islamic law (*Shari'a*) into normal activity, four main schools of thought emerged, the main one in the region being the Hanafi. An ideal of the Islamic community (*umma*) is that the brotherhood of Muslims is its basis and that the religion is international and beyond tribal division. However, there has not been an unchallenged Muslim leader since the Prophet, and the last of the caliphs (*khalifas* or 'successors' of Muhammad), who resided in Constantinople, had his office abolished by the Turkish Government in 1924.

Uzbekistan has the largest Muslim population in the region, although the other states in Central Asia and Azerbaijan are also predominantly Muslim. The North Caucasus is also an important Muslim region. In central Russia and Siberia there are large numbers of Volga Tatars, Chuvash and Bashkirs. There are a large number of Muslim Roma (Gypsies), mainly in Central Asia, some Chinese Muslims (Dungans) and a small number of Muslim Semites (most unusually in Uzbekistan, with the Arabs of Samarkand and the Chalas, Bukharan Jews who converted to Islam, but remained Jewish secretly).

## Sunni Muslims

Some 80% of the world's Muslims are Sunni, followers of 'the path' or customary way. They acknowledge the first four Caliphs as successors of Muhammad—Abu Bakr, 'Umar (Omar), 'Uthman (Othman) and 'Ali—and follow one of the four main schools of law. Other Muslims differ only in the interpretation of the true tradition (*sunna*). Except in the Iranian (Persian) influenced area of Azerbaijan, most of the region's Muslims are Sunni and of the Hanafi sect.

The so-called Wahhabi sect (not linked to, but superficially similar to, the Saudi Arabian movement of the same name) is often described as unitarian and 'fundamentalist'. The theologians of the Wahhabi *ikhwan* ('brotherhood') advocate the strictest observance of the principle of monotheism, rejecting the veneration of holy men and holy places, and the cleansing of Islam of late accretions and innovations. The movement was originally based mainly in Uzbekistan, but was considered increasingly influential in Tajikistan at the start of the civil wars. There are also what are described as Wahhabi groups in the Russian North Caucasus, in Chechnya and Dagestan (Daghestan). Such people might more accurately be described as Salafis, a general name for those who have urged a return to an early form of Islam. The definition of a Wahhabi is further complicated in the former USSR by its use as a generic description for those opposed to the official clergy or the establishment.

## Shi'a Muslims

The Shi'a, or 'followers' of 'Ali (cousin of Muhammad and husband of Fatima, the Prophet's daughter), reject the first three Caliphs of Sunni Islam and assert that the fourth Caliph was the rightful successor of Muhammad. 'Ali's son, Husain, is the great Shi'ite martyr. 'Ali's name is added after Muhammad's in the confession of faith, otherwise their beliefs are similar to the Sunnis. They instituted an *imam*, rather than a caliph, as their spiritual 'leader'. Most Shi'ites are 'Twelvers' and recognize a succession of 12 Imams, the last disappearing in AD 878; this occluded or hidden Imam, it is believed, will return as the *Mahdi* ('guided one').

Some Shi'ites, however, the Isma'ilis, are known as 'Seveners', because they believe that Isma'il, or one of his sons, was the seventh and last Imam, and disappeared in AD 765. There were political reasons for the schism, but the Isma'ilis also have a more mystical faith. There are several sects. The main group in the region is in Gornyi Badakhshon (Tajikistan), and they are Pamirs, followers of the Aga Khan (some Pamirs are Sunni).

## Sufis

The Sufis are mystics, found in all branches of Islam since very early in the religion's history. Named for their woollen (*suf*) monastic robes, the Sufis tempered orthodox formalism and deism with a quest for complete identification with the Supreme Being and annihilation of the self (the existence of the latter is known as polytheism—*shirk*), although this sometimes approached pantheism. The Sufis verged on the edge of acceptability for some time, but became an important influence. They are organized into what are loosely known as 'brotherhoods' (*turuq* or, singular, *tariqa*). In Soviet Central Asia clandestine Sufi groups were responsible for bolstering the officially tolerated Islamic institutions; they were fiercely anti-communist. After the dissolution of the USSR their influence became more apparent, not only in Central Asia, but also in the eastern Caucasus. Thus, Sufis (mainly of the *tariqa qadariya*) were predominant in the religious establishment of secessionist Chechnya.

### BUDDHISM

The number of Buddhists in Russia is uncertain, but there have been reports of up to 1m., mostly among the Buryats and Tyvans of Siberia. There are only small groups of Buddhist converts in Eastern Europe.

The founder of the faith, sometimes referred to as 'the Buddha', was a north Indian of the warrior caste, Siddhartha Gautama (usually ascribed the dates 563–483 BC). He renounced his privileges in the search for enlightenment, which he found under the Bo or Bodhi-tree; he understood the cycle of existence, the cycle of suffering and the way to Nirvana. He had become a Buddha or 'enlightened one' and, with the support of a monastic following, taught his *Dharma* (law, virtue, right, religion or truth), which must be followed on a Middle Way between the extremes of sensuality and asceticism. Gautama taught a scheme of moral and spiritual improvement by which the endless round of existence could be escaped and Nirvana or oblivion obtained. Sometimes described as agnostic, or even atheistic, this ignores the adoration of the Buddha himself. Furthermore, northern Buddhism, as practised in Siberia, has particularly retained and developed the hosts of celestial beings who can help. There are not only many Buddhas, but countless Bodhisattvas ('beings of enlightenment'), who have deferred their own salvation. The northern Buddhists describe themselves as of the Mahayana school, followers of the 'great vehicle' to salvation.

### OTHER RELIGIONS

Judaism is the oldest of the major monotheistic religions, and also advocates a code of morality and civil and religious duties. Its holy book (the Old Testament of the Christian Bible) is supported by traditions, which are expounded by the rabbis, who are doctors of the law and leaders of the Jewish congregations, which meet in synagogues. There are two main Jewish communities, which observe distinct rituals but have no doctrinal differences. The predominant European group is the Ashkenazim; there are some Sephardim in the Caucasian and Central Asian countries. Although both Christianity and Islam claim descent from, or to be the fulfilment of, Judaism, the Jews, as a race as well as a religion, have long been the victims of prejudice. Anti-Semitism has a long history in the Christian Church and, in Islam, the more recent Arab–Israeli conflict has bolstered the prejudice. The Jews are widespread throughout Eastern Europe and the Russian Federation. Their numbers, however, were seriously reduced during the Second World War, particularly in areas dominated by the Nazis. This holocaust of the Jewish people was the most extreme manifestation of the anti-Semitism that was endemic in Central and Eastern Europe and in the Russian Empire. These traditional prejudices were not completely rejected by the communist regimes, but, after the fall of these governments, anti-Semitism re-emerged strongly in some areas, despite the often small number of Jews. Emigration, usually to Israel, also reduced numbers. Some Turkic peoples of the region, notably a small minority of ethnic Azerbaijanis, practice Judaism, surviving since the times of the Khazar (Hazar) kaganate, an empire to the north of the Caucasus which disappeared in the 11th century.

There are few Hindus in the region, but missionary work was conducted by one such sect, the Hare Krishna (named for their chant) or Krishna Consciousness. They worship the Hindu pantheon and advocate a harmonious life-style, are vegetarian, and distinguished by the orange robes of their devotees. The communist authorities displayed an ambivalent attitude to them and they continued to experience difficulties in Russia after the collapse of the USSR. In October 2003 the Russian Orthodox hierarchy strongly objected to the proposed construction of a large Hare Krishna centre in Moscow.

Some traditional beliefs persist in Russia and other parts of the former USSR, including some shamanistic practices and ancestor worship. There are also some small Zoroastrian communities, to the north of Iran. This ancient religion is sometimes described as dualistic, but believes in the ultimate triumph of the principle of good. It is thought to have influenced both Judaism and Christianity and was once the state religion of Persia (Iran). Some of the Kurdish people are Yazidis, most of whom live in Armenia and Georgia. They are sometimes known as 'Devil-worshippers', owing to a mistaken understanding of their belief in the redemption of Lucifer, the fallen angel or evil principle of Christian and Zoroastrian cosmology. The Yazidi beliefs are a synthesis of Zoroastrian, Nestorian Christian, Jewish and Muslim traditions.

# ORGANIZED CRIME IN RUSSIA AND THE COMMONWEALTH OF INDEPENDENT STATES

## Prof. PHIL WILLIAMS

### INTRODUCTION

The election of Vladimir Putin as the President of the Russian Federation in March 2000 was greeted, by many Russians, with a considerable sense of hope. In his election campaign, Putin had emphasized not only the need to build Russia's wealth and strength, but also the urgency of reducing crime and corruption and containing the power of the 'oligarchs'. In effect, Putin offered strong, dynamic leadership and seemed willing to confront those forces in Russian society that inhibited the growth of the country's prosperity and influence. By 2003 Putin had clearly had some success. In 2002 amendments to Russia's criminal code came into effect, which paid more attention to the rights of the accused and to due process than had previously been the case. However, this did not obstruct vigorous efforts to deal with the power of the oligarchs. In 2002–03 efforts to reduce the power of the oligarchs continued, albeit somewhat selectively. Nor did the new criminal code prevent efforts to combat organized crime. As Stephen Handelman noted, 'A recharged police force has scored successes in breaking the power of several potent gangs, and the domestic business climate has become measurably safer for domestic and foreign investment, though it is still unpredictable' (Handelman, 2002—see Bibliography). Another area where some success was achieved was in efforts to combat trafficking in women for the commercial sex trade. This was an area where, nominally at least, Russia made considerable improvement. In its assessment of national efforts to combat trafficking in women in 2000 and 2001, the US Department of State ranked Russia as a tier 3 state (the lowest ranking). Knowing that this could have an adverse impact on economic assistance from the USA, Russia developed very strong anti-trafficking legislation. Although this had not been passed by the time the USA issued its 2003 report, the legal framework was regarded as positive progress, and Russia was upgraded. Implementation, however, remained uncertain. Indeed, it was significant that although in 2001–02 a Western European law-enforcement operation, led by Italy and co-ordinated by the European Union's European Police Force (Europol), broke up a major human-trafficking network organized largely by Russian organized crime groups, arrests of Russian criminals were very limited. Despite positive progress, therefore, efforts to combat the trafficking of women had a long way to go. Indeed, combating organized crime more generally remains a formidable task—more than one decade after the collapse of the USSR, criminal organizations remain a significant factor in political and economic life throughout the Commonwealth of Independent States (CIS). In November 2002 Putin reportedly criticized the Ministry of Internal Affairs (MVD) for its failure to reduce crime. The continued inability to contain crime, including organized crime, was also reflected in an opinion poll in mid-2003, which focused on control over Russia. Although 37% of respondents believed that Russia was ruled by 'large capital and oligarchs', 19% believed that 'organized criminal groups' ruled the country—4% more than believed that it was ruled by President Putin. This is not entirely surprising. During the 1990s criminal organizations became involved in a wide variety of economic and commercial activities and established an important, if ill-defined, presence in the political systems of former Soviet republics. In

Ukraine, for example, by the end of the 1990s corruption had become pervasive, threatening the integrity of government and making it difficult for the country to attract external investment. Moreover, Ukraine also played an important role in the trafficking of women to the West for prostitution (Ukraine was reported to be the most significant trafficker of women world-wide by 2002) and in the manufacturing of counterfeit compact discs (in late 2001 Ukraine submitted to pressure from the USA and other Western governments to introduce measures to combat compact-disc piracy). In Belarus, organized crime had fewer opportunities to embed itself as deeply as in Russia, partly because the transition process had been slower and firmly controlled by the authoritarian regime of President Alyaksandr Lukashenka. Even so, extortion, financial fraud and drugs-trafficking had become commonplace. Throughout these countries the law-enforcement agencies had been seriously impeded by a lack of resources, especially when compared with their opponents, the criminals, who had considerable financial power.

A similar situation prevailed in Central Asia, where drugs-trafficking, organized crime, corruption and violence were endemic—and were exacerbated by the region's proximity to Afghanistan. Although a Taliban ban on opium production led to a marked decline in the crop in 2001, with the overthrow of the country's Taliban regime, production once again increased. Indeed, according to the US Department of State's annual narcotics report, in 2002 Afghanistan was the largest producer of opium world-wide, and a significant cannabis producer (see Bibliography). The USA estimated that Afghanistan produced approximately 1,300 metric tons of opium per year; estimates by the UN Office for Drug Control and Crime Prevention, however, suggested that the figure was closer to 3,000 tons. What was not in doubt was the fact that Afghanistan's central role in the drugs business had a significant influence on stability in Central Asia. This was particularly important in the case of Tajikistan, which was still in the process of rebuilding, after a complex civil war fought, at least in part, for control of lucrative drugs-smuggling routes. Indeed, Tajikistan still suffered from the influence of dissident leaders—and organized crime, terrorism, insurgency, drugs-trafficking and political tensions were bound up together, as was the case in a number of African states. Moreover, Tajikistan was becoming increasingly involved in the Afghan drugs-trafficking business, as reflected by arrest statistics for drugs-trafficking in the Russian capital, Moscow, and elsewhere in the country. According to one report, 35% of Tajikistan's gross domestic product (GDP) came from drugs-trafficking (Paoli, 2000). It is not surprising, therefore, that influential figures from the civil conflict, including government officials, played an important role in the higher levels of the drugs trade (US Department of State, 2002). This might help to explain why, despite the increase in drugs production in Afghanistan, the volume of drugs seized in Tajikistan during 2002 actually declined for the first time in three years (US Department of State, 2003). Meanwhile, in Kyrgyzstan poverty remained widespread and, in some parts of the country, opium had become not only the drug of choice, but also the currency of choice. In Uzbekistan, too, criminal organizations maintained links with high-ranking politicians, providing financial support in return for political protection. Much of the opium and heroin produced in Afghanistan is trafficked to markets in Western Europe, although the Russian market has also grown enormously; in October 2001 the MVD reported that there were approximately 3m. drug addicts in Russia, a figure that was subsequently reiterated, but which could be an underestimation.

Organized crime was also extensive throughout the Caucasus, combining with separatism and political instability to create considerable volatility. In this regard, the Russian wars of 1994–96 and from 1999 in Chechnya were primarily attempts to combat secessionism, but they were also directed, at least in part, against Chechen organized crime, which had become a major problem in many parts of Russia, including Moscow. In Georgia, too, organized crime remained a major force. Many of the leading criminal authorities maintained close links with members of the political élite, who provided protection and support. Moreover, large segments of the economy continued to be exploited by criminal organizations, which controlled vehicle-manufacturing plants, and, reportedly, manganese-mining and ferrous-alloy-producing enterprises in western Georgia, and smuggled precious metals out of the country, despite government efforts to exert more control over the industry. In addition, Georgian organized crime was involved in extortion, money 'laundering' (the processing of illegally obtained funds into legitimate holdings), prostitution and car theft. Criminal groups not only controlled casinos, but also exerted considerable influence over the banking system. In July 2001 a crisis erupted in the Pankisi Gorge, an area in north-east Georgia that had become a 'safe haven' for organized crime, and was virtually free from government control. The situation subsequently became a source of tension between Georgia and Russia, as the Russian authorities claimed that Chechen rebels and terrorists were also operating from the Gorge. In January 2002 the Georgian Government began to undertake special operations intended to eradicate criminal activities in the Gorge and to prevent it from being a haven for Chechen and Arab fighters. These operations, however, had only partial success, and Russia continued to apply pressure for intervention. In August a more vigorous and concerted effort was undertaken to deal with the problems in the Gorge, and by November the Georgian Government claimed to have the situation under control. Russia, however, remained unconvinced; moreover, there was considerable speculation that stocks of the toxic chemical ricin, found in the possession of a number of people arrested in the United Kingdom in January 2003, had links with the Pankisi Gorge. During the Pankisi crisis, critics of the Georgian Government claimed that government officials were complicit in some of the criminal activities in the Gorge. Whatever the validity of these allegations, it was clear that organized crime continued to buttress the extensive corruption that had become one of the most salient characteristics of Georgian political, economic and social life—and which had become a major source of disillusionment with the increasingly fragile Government of President Eduard Shevardnadze.

In short, no understanding of political and economic developments in the former USSR would be complete without taking into account the scale, role and impact of organized crime. The focus here, however, is primarily on organized crime in Russia. Although there were national and regional variations in organized crime, developments in Russia were the most critical, not only because Russia remained the single most important country in the CIS, but also as a test of the capacity and will of a vigorous political leader to do something about the problem. The difficulty, however, was in providing an accurate appraisal of the challenge posed to Russia's future by organized crime.

There were several reasons for this. The first was the tendency of many Western, and some Russian, commentators to engage in hyperbole about Russian organized crime. In Russia, the term 'mafia' (mafiya) was used indiscriminately: almost any successful, wealthy businessman was regarded with immediate suspicion and assumed to be 'mafia'. Similarly, in the West there was a tendency to describe all criminal groups from the former USSR (be they from Armenia, Azerbaijan, Chechnya, Georgia, Tajikistan, Ukraine or Uzbekistan) as Russian organized crime, something that Russian officials bitterly resented. Moreover, the contrast between the orderly USSR and the lawlessness that characterized post-Soviet Russia lent itself to exaggeration, while the fact that Russian criminal organizations had become active and highly visible in other countries, such as Germany, Israel and the USA, greatly increased foreign sensitivities to the problem in Russia itself. Reports in 1999 that the Bank of New York had been used for money laundering and the 'flight' of capital (the export of funds for legitimate investment reasons, as well as tax avoidance) from Russia (see below), generated new concerns about the vulnerability of Western financial institutions to Russian organized crime. The scandal involving the Bank of New York also intensified the tendency in the USA to portray Russian organized crime as the new 'evil empire', the natural heir to the threat to freedom posed by the USSR. Such assessments almost invariably emphasized the central involvement of former agents of the secret service, the Committee for State Security (Komitet Gosudarstvennoi Bezopasnoti—KGB), in criminal activities, claimed that Russia had become a 'kleptocracy' or 'mafiocracy', and relied on facile labels rather than serious research and analysis.

The second obstacle to an accurate appraisal came from those who took an optimistic approach both about the future of Russia itself and about the capacity of the free market to curb organized crime. Indeed, some observers dismissed Russian organized crime as a temporary feature of the transition, rather than a long-term threat. The strengthening of state structures, the continued deregulation of the economy, and the natural evolution towards the Western model of political and economic governance, it was assumed, would lead inexorably to the decline of organized crime. Here, the tendency to exaggerate the capacity to deal with the problem was combined with a failure to understand the dynamics of the phenomenon, especially the capacity of organized crime to become entrenched in both political and economic life, and the subsequent difficulties of dislodging it.

Against this background of competing assessments, the purpose of this chapter is to separate the mythology and the reality of Russian organized crime and to offer a sober appraisal that avoids both exaggeration and underestimation. Consequently, the chapter explores the origins of Russian organized crime in the Soviet regime. It then identifies the particular characteristics of the transition process that provided both opportunities and incentives for the development of criminal organizations and criminal activities. The analysis subsequently focuses on some of the key dimensions of Russian organized crime, emphasizing both the organizations and the activities involved. In the final section, consideration is given to the future of crime and corruption in Russia and to the obstacles that the Government has to overcome, in order successfully to prevent the Russian state from being neutralized or controlled by organized crime.

## ORIGINS OF RUSSIAN ORGANIZED CRIME

Russian organized crime has a long tradition and did not simply rise out of nowhere in the aftermath of the collapse of the communist system and the disintegration of the USSR. As one observer noted, 'this is a society whose centuries-old tradition has never been characterized by the rule of law' (Galeotti, 1998). From the time of Tsar Nicholas (Nikolai) I (1825–55), who bemoaned the fact that he and his son were the only men in Russia who did not steal, to that of the Bolsheviks, who used bank robberies and other criminal activities to obtain the financing for their political campaigns, crime has played a large role in Russian society. Often part of the opposition to an absolutist or authoritarian state, Russian criminal organizations developed their own traditions and norms, as well as a regulatory apparatus that revolved around the *vory v zakone* (thieves professing the code), those with considerable status in criminal circles, who provided governance and helped to resolve disputes. The *vory* earned their status through a strict code of conduct, by time in gaol, an unwillingness to co-operate with the authorities and a rejection of traditional social norms, such as work and family. During the Soviet era, the *vory* were kept in check by a strong state.

If the Soviet state contained the traditional form of organized crime in Russia, however, it also incubated new forms of criminality. Indeed, the Soviet era saw the establishment of a profoundly significant political–criminal nexus (a term coined by Godson, 1997), albeit one that was dominated by the political élite. The Communist Party of the Soviet Union (CPSU), like many other authoritarian regimes, had the classic conditions that encourage corruption. As encapsulated by Robert Klitgaard (see Bibliography), these were: monopoly power, plus discretion about how to use this power, minus accountability. The result, as Konstantin Simis argued in 1982, was that the ruling élite in the USSR became infected by corruption and inequality, having access to goods and services that were simply not available to the ordinary citizen. A system that was supposedly designed to benefit the people became a means of benefiting party officials, particularly in the 1970s and 1980s, when the inadequacies of the economic system led to the growth of a 'black' market, a parallel economy, that not only functioned as a safety valve, but also a means of enriching the *nomenklatura*. In effect, the Soviet regime did not simply tolerate the black market, but actively encouraged the development of a symbiotic relationship between members of the party apparatus and various kinds of traffickers and illicit entrepreneurs. This included, but was certainly not confined to, the *vory*.

At the same time, it was clear where the power lay. As long as the CPSU remained the dominant force in Soviet society, criminals operated within a carefully circumscribed framework. With Mikhail Gorbachev's reforms (as Soviet leader, 1985–91) and the subsequent collapse of the USSR, organized crime changed from being a covert feature of Soviet life to a highly visible feature of Russian life. Transparency was perhaps the least important change, however. Much more significantly, the transition provided ideal conditions for the rapid growth of Russian criminal organizations as independent entities, no longer subject to the communist-imposed constraints and restrictions. The transition also encouraged criminality by members of the 'old guard', anxious to retain their wealth and privilege, even if they could no longer hold on to their power.

The Gorbachev era provided ample warning that the old system was coming to an end, thereby enabling senior communist officials to secrete thousands of millions of dollars abroad. Such funds were never properly traced. Furthermore, even after the collapse of the Soviet state, the old party members were among those best placed to exploit the new opportunities. Members of the *nomenklatura* who had obtained wealth through corruption or black market activities in the USSR, as well as many of their suppliers and other illicit entrepreneurs, were able to put this capital to use in the new capitalist system. Moreover, with the opening of the Russian economy, natural resources were exported on a large scale, with bureaucrats providing export licenses and other permits, in return for either part of the proceeds or substantial bribes. During the early stages of the move to capitalism, old alliances between bureaucrats and criminals were strengthened and new ones formed, leading to the rise of the 'comrade criminal' (Handelman, 1995), as 'a post-Soviet mafiya emerged, incorporating the most entrepreneurial elements of the former *nomenklatura* and the gangster capitalism of the new'.

If these developments suggested a perpetuation of much of the old system in a new guise, there were subtle but fundamental changes in the power relationship between the bureaucrats and the criminals. If Russian politics can be understood in terms of competing political–criminal oligarchies, the criminals had become much more dominant. From being subservient to the politicians and bureaucrats (who in the old regime had a powerful, coercive apparatus at their disposal) they had become arbiters of economic and political life, using force against those who opposed their activities. Individuals who opposed corruption and tried to initiate reform were either killed or intimidated, making it extremely difficult for reform efforts to develop any sustained momentum. An example of this was the murder, in August 1997, of Mikhail Manevich, Deputy Governor of St Petersburg, widely considered to be innovative and committed to combating corruption. Moreover, the perpetrators of such crimes were rarely brought to justice—a point that underlines the increase in power of the criminals and their ability to act with a high degree of impunity. However, this increase in power was not surprising, given the characteristics of the economic transition.

## THE TRANSITION AND THE RISE OF ORGANIZED CRIME

'The state of organized crime in any country depends in large part on the state of the state' (Rawlinson, 1996). Provided that the state is strong, organized crime will remain a minor nuisance. If the state is weak, organized crime ceases to operate at the margins of society and becomes a much more pervasive force. In this connection, the collapse of the Soviet state and the loss of a capacity to impose order on the population provided unprecedented opportunities for the flourishing of criminal organizations and drugs-trafficking groups. As Emile Durkheim, the French sociologist, observed, when a society is in a state of crisis or transition, then regulatory mechanisms to restrain criminal behaviour, through both formal sanctions and social norms, become far less effective, at least temporarily (Lotspeich, 1995).

One element of this weakness throughout most of the 1990s was an inadequate legal framework. The article against banditry in the old Soviet and, subsequently, Russian law was used primarily to deal with political nonconformity and was inadequate for dealing with criminal organizations in a nascent market economy. Although criminal organizations were not wholly immune from punishment in the new Russia, the legal instruments for their arrest, trial and detention were developed very slowly. This tardiness reflected the reluctance of some members of the lower chamber of parliament, the State Duma, to support the introduction of severe new measures (perhaps under criminal influence). The adoption of a new criminal code (see above) went some way to easing this problem, but its implementation remained uneven and its ultimate success uncertain.

Closely related to this legal weakness was the lack of an appropriate regulatory framework for business affairs in a capitalist system. The absence of effective mechanisms for debt collection and the failure to provide for arbitration of disputes created a regulatory vacuum in Russia that resembled that in Sicily over one century earlier (Gambetta, 1993). Consequently, organized crime became a surrogate for government, offering protection through the provision of a *krysha* ('roof') as well as contract enforcement. As a result, criminal organizations were provided with an entry into the business world, making it even more difficult to differentiate between the licit and the illicit, while even ostensibly legitimate businesses frequently resorted to violence against their competitors.

Nowhere, however, was the lack of an adequate legal and supervisory framework more marked than in the privatization process. The selling of state assets was implemented without sufficient safeguards and with a lack of oversight. There were three results of this. First, state assets were sold at unreasonably low prices, something that was particularly harmful to a Russian state lacking an adequate resource base. According to one report (from an article by the former Russian Minister of Internal Affairs, Col-Gen. Anatolii Kulikov, in January 1998), Kovrovskii Mechanical Plant, which supplied small arms to the military and to the MVD, was sold for around US $3m., while Uralmash, the Chelyabinsk Tractor Plant and the Chelyabinsk Metallurgical Combine were each sold for less than $4m. The six largest aluminium enterprises in the country were sold for a total of $62.2m. and most of Russia's 500 largest enterprises were sold at prices of less than $8m. A second consequence, stemming in part from the vagueness of the Law on Privatization, was that it became possible for the real owners to conceal themselves behind nominees, 'front men', and subsidiary firms, thereby allowing many of the officials responsible for managing the privatization process to become the beneficiaries. The MVD subsequently reported that one out of every 10 official crimes discovered between 1994 and mid-1997 was committed in the sphere of privatization (Satarov et al, 1998). A third consequence was that criminals, exploiting their links with officials, were able to benefit significantly. As one knowledgeable observer noted, 'Russian organized crime groups secured a massive transfer of state property because the privatization occurred rapidly, on a huge scale, without legal safeguards and without transparency. These groups used force, if necessary, but relied mainly on their large financial assets and their close ties to the former Communist Party élite, the military and the banking sector' (Louise Shelley, quoted in a Reuters report).

Another entry route for the criminals was provided by a taxation system that was simultaneously burdensome and ineffective. Taxation laws provided perverse incentives for tax evasion and criminal behaviour. Businesses typically evaded taxes; criminal organizations discovered this and then extorted the businesses, which found it cheaper to pay 'taxes' imposed by criminal organizations than those imposed by the Russian state. Consequently, Russia failed to develop a tax base adequate to fund government services in a variety of sectors, including law enforcement.

Lack of resources made it enormously difficult for the Russian police force to combat organized crime and drugs-trafficking. Perhaps nowhere was this more evident than the efforts to counter the drugs problem. Russia actually developed a sophisticated framework strategy to combat trafficking and the abuse of illegal drugs. Known as the Comprehensive Concept, the plan identified the need to reduce both supply and demand. Implementation, however, was sporadic and uneven and the counter-narcotics unit at the Ministry of Internal Affairs was hindered by the lack of resources available to fight drugs-trafficking and consumption.

As well as the lack of resources, law-enforcement agencies suffered from a lack of legitimacy. Initially distrusted because they were associated with authoritarianism and repression, law-enforcement agencies came to be regarded as incompetent and corrupt. Although some businesses (especially those owned by overseas companies) did turn to law enforcement for protection, the growth in private security companies was testimony to the continued inadequacy of the state's social-control agencies. Some private security companies were legitimate, but many others were fronts for criminal organizations, offering their services to firms that had been threatened by members of these very same organizations. In effect, private security companies became the public face of extortion. In what was perhaps an even more important development, police forces also became major players in the protection business, forcibly replacing some of the organized crime groups and obtaining lucrative recompense as a result. This trend became so pronounced that it prompted major efforts to reform parts of the Ministry of Internal Affairs. Increasing efforts were made to identify groups of police-officers who were, in effect, acting as organized criminals (described as 'werewolves' by the Minister of Internal Affairs, Boris Gryzlov). Following a series of arrests, more took place in August 2003, involving six police-officers, some of whom were connected to the so-called Orekhovskii criminal gang. According to Gryzlov, the group had used its position to attempt to gain control of representatives of small and medium-sized businesses, and fabricated evidence of crimes; members of the group were also suspected of carrying out contract killings.

Another form of weakness consisted of the state's inability to make provision for its citizenry, something that created pressure and incentives for citizens to engage in criminal activities. Unemployment and 'hyperinflation' encouraged extra-legal means of meeting basic needs. Illicit forms of behaviour offered rewards that were not easily available in the legitimate economy. This was particularly so for personnel in some of the central institutions of the state, such as the military and the scientific establishment, which suffered a precipitous decline in status and conditions. Consequently, members of the armed services at all ranks engaged in their own entrepreneurial activities. These ranged from a private who might sell light arms to local criminals, to the former Chief of Staff of the Russian Navy, Adm. Igor Khmelnov, who was convicted of charges of abuse of office in 1997. Although allegations that Khmelnov had illegally sold 64 ships from Russia's Pacific Fleet to India and the Republic of Korea (South Korea) were retracted, the case symbolized the extensive corruption in the Russian military. In this connection, it is worth noting that in October 1994 Dmitrii Kholodov, a journalist investigating corruption in the military, was killed when he was handed a suitcase that he had been told contained evidence of corruption, and that actually contained a hidden explosive device. In early 1998 two suspects, one formerly a colonel and the other formerly a major in military intelligence, were arrested for his murder. The tenacity with which the case was pursued was impressive. Nevertheless, the murder emphasized the willingness of the 'mafia in uniform' to use violence to protect their illicit entrepreneurial activities (Turbiville, 1995).

An inability to make provision for the citizenry during the economic upheaval became a significant characteristic of the transition in Russia and other states of the CIS. Thus, the Russian economy was characterized by a decline in production, hyperinflation, the growth of unemployment, new economic uncertainties, a lack of legitimate economic alternatives and a precipitous decline in living standards. Inflation in Russia was less rampant than in some of the other former Soviet republics, but still reached 1,529% in 1992, 800% in 1993 and 200% in 1994. By 1995 it had declined to 197%, and the rate stood at just 22% by 2001. Unemployment accounted for 4.5% of the labour force in 1992 and had reached 8.5% by 1996 (Layard and Parker, 1996). The rate was 9.8% in 2000, according to UN figures. These economic upheavals were accompanied by large-scale social and economic dislocation that inevitably encouraged a substantial, if undocumented, migration from the licit to the illicit economy. The migration from the legal economy to the illegal was given a further boost by the Russian economic crisis of 1998. Any gains that had been made in the previous few years were offset by the dislocation and disruption caused by the collapse of the economy, although, ironically, social unrest was kept to a minimum, in part because of the capacity of many people to use the illicit 'shadow', economy as a source of subsistence.

Another feature of states in transition is that they generally display a greater degree of openness to the outside world, designed, in part, to encourage foreign trade and investment. Such openness, however, attracts criminal enterprises as well as legitimate businesses. Among the foreign criminal organizations to have penetrated Russia were drugs-traffickers from the Democratic People's Republic of Korea (North Korea), Nigerians engaged in drugs-trafficking and financial crimes, and Italian criminal groups anxious to exploit new opportunities for counterfeiting and money laundering. Colombian drugs-trafficking organizations had also begun to see Russia as a developing market for their product and as a transhipment state for illicit drugs destined for Western Europe.

In addition, Russia had the problem of being host to a large number of citizens from the 'near abroad', individuals and groups from Central Asia and the Caucasus, which were responsible for a significant proportion of the drugs-trafficking and organized crime activity in Russia. According to the MVD, during 1997 foreign citizens and persons without citizenship committed approximately 28,000 crimes; of these over 86.6% were committed by residents of CIS countries. Such criminals were difficult to bring to justice, because the fragmentation of the USSR led to the replacement of a 'common judicial space' by a system characterized by a 'lack of border controls, no consistent legal norms and limited co-ordination among the justice systems of the successor states' (Shelley, 1995). Despite efforts to develop law-enforcement and intelligence co-ordination mechanisms among the intelligence agencies of the CIS states, the pace of co-operation was still behind that set by the criminals.

## THE DIMENSIONS OF ORGANIZED CRIME IN RUSSIA

### The Organizations

Figures on organized crime provided by the MVD suggested there had been a constant growth in the number of criminal organizations operating in the country. Some 3,000 groups in 1992 had increased to 5,700 in 1994, 8,000 in early 1996 and 9,000 by 1998. If these figures seemed to reveal a highly disturbing trend, however, there were several explanations for this apparent growth, not all of which were equally alarming. It is possible, of course, that the increase in numbers reflected an expanding and highly dynamic criminal world that was posing an increasingly obvious threat to the transition process. At the same time, the increase might have reflected fissiparous tendencies in many criminal organizations, indicating a process of fragmentation, rather than expansion. Another possibility was that the criteria for categorizing groups as criminal organizations had become more inclusive, incorporating groups with as few as two or three people. Including smaller groups in the assessment could also be a form of 'threat inflation', perhaps designed to obtain Western aid. Finally, the increase in numbers could also be a reflection of improved intelligence and analysis.

The difficulty is that there was not a standard baseline to determine whether the problem had increased, or the appraisal of the problem had become more accurate. The assessment was even more complex because the explanations were not mutually exclusive. Moreover, the situation was further confused by competing estimates. The MVD estimated that the 9,000 criminal organizations in Russia in 1998 employed around 100,000 people; yet on one occasion the Minister of Internal Affairs also stated that Russia had 12,500 organized crime groups and formations, with 60,000 active members.

One trend that many officials and observers often claimed to discern in the organized crime world, and one that ran counter to the fragmentation hypothesis referred to above, is that towards consolidation: organized crime groups, it was claimed, were being consolidated into a smaller number of larger criminal groupings, some of which had extensive international and transnational links. There were continuing reports that some organizations had formed large, loose associations. Common and co-operative arrangements included contributing to a common pool of resources (*obshak*), which was used to support the families of those in prison, for bribery and corruption, and to initiate new enterprises.

Even if a consolidation process was resulting in mergers among criminal groups, as figures suggested, organized crime in Russia remained highly diverse and fractured, with ethnic divisions, divisions based on territorial and sectoral control, and generational splits. Slavic groups and those from the Caucasus had waged an intense war against one another, especially in Moscow. Although this seemed to reach its peak during the first half of the 1990s, violent clashes continued, albeit more sporadically. As part of this struggle, one of the youngest organized crime leaders, Zelenyi (Vyacheslav Chuvarzin), was killed in 1997. Occasionally, the conflict went beyond Russian borders, as when a leading Slavic criminal, Andrei Isayev, was shot in Poland—a killing that reportedly led to retribution against the perpetrators by his followers. Some contract murders of criminal figures, however, had less to do with ethnic divisions than with a desire to take control of criminal activities. This may well have been the motive for the murder in January 1997 of Khudo Gasoyan (Khudo), who reputedly controlled many of the drugs shipments to Moscow from Kazakhstan and Kyrgyzstan.

Another division that occasionally resulted in open conflict was that between the *vory* and the new generation of criminals, who did not respect the traditions, were more entrepreneurial in their approach and, in some cases, had become 'authorities' because of wealth, rather than status accrued through time in prison and conformity with the criminal code. There is also an important distinction between those who had well-established symbiotic links with officials, and exploited these links for fraudulent financial schemes, and predatory groups that operated more like street gangs than sophisticated entrepreneurial businesses. In addition, there were several different categories of groups in terms of their scope or range: some were purely local or domestic, while others had transnational links. Another division that seemed to be emerging and that could become more important over time was that between those criminal organizations and criminal entrepreneurs trying to obtain legitimacy and those content to remain firmly within the criminal fraternity. These structural sources of conflict in the criminal world were often exacerbated by territorial rivalries and personal animosity among criminal leaders.

Indeed, in the early 2000s enmities in the criminal world often seemed as bitter as ever. In August 2001 it was reported that prominent 'thieves-in-law' had been killed in Moscow, Astrakhan and Sochi. Similarly, in March 2003 several Chechen *vory* were killed, and it was feared that Slavic criminal organizations, especially the Izmaylov group, had declared war on 'colleagues' from Chechnya and Azerbaijan. Killings of this kind contributed to a continued state of flux in the criminal world, with some groups becoming more prominent and others losing their dominant position. In St Petersburg, for example, the Tambov gang, which had long been the dominant criminal organization, was undermined as a result of concerted action by its rivals, reportedly including Azerbaijani, Chechen, Dagestani (Daghestani) and Tajikistani gangs. With government and law-enforcement authorities also targeting the Tambov group, it was significantly weakened.

If its power base was reduced, however, the Tambov organization remained a force to be reckoned with, and may have been responsible for the deaths of three people in Moscow in May 2003, including Konstantin Yakovlev (also known as Kostya Mogila—Kostya the Grave), a St Petersburg crime boss; one theory suggested that the Tambov gang, which had reportedly tried to eliminate Yakovlev in 2000 and 2001, had finally been successful (*Russian Reform Monitor* of the American Foreign Policy Council—see Bibliography).

Providing a definitive typology of Russian criminal organizations would require much more comprehensive information and analysis than can be presented here, and would need to take into account the various distinctions and differences identified above. Nevertheless, it is possible to identify at least seven different kinds of criminal group in Russia:

businesses that were ostensibly (and, in some instances, perhaps even predominantly) licit, but with their origin in criminal activities and with a residual tendency to resort to violence and corruption to protect and promote their activities and to deal with competitors. The 21st Century Association was perhaps the most well-known enterprise that at least some observers believed fitted into this category;

criminal organizations that had close links with officials and that were a key part of the competing administrative–financial–criminal oligarchies that were one of the dominant forces in Russia. These operated at local and regional levels, as well as nationally;

ethnic criminal organizations, which included Azeri, Chechen, Georgian and Slavic groups, and often specialized in one or more criminal activities;

what might be termed overarching criminal associations, which encompassed a wide range of smaller groups and engaged in a wide variety of criminal activities. Perhaps the exemplar of this kind of association was the Solntsevo group. One of Moscow's and, indeed, Russia's, foremost criminal organizations, Solntsevo was well entrenched, with several layers of strong leadership, a well-established structure and a high level of professionalism. It acted as a kind of 'co-operative' organization, co-ordinating some 300 individual crime groups, and had a wide diversity of criminal activities. Initially believed to be led by Sergei Mikhailov (Mikhas) and Viktor Averin (Avera, Sr), who were intent on moving in more entrepreneurial directions than the traditional *vory*, the Solntsevo organizations gradually dominated the south-western part of Moscow, taking control of Vietnamese drugs-trafficking groups and (through an affiliate crime leader) the Azerbaijani drugs-trafficking networks. The proceeds of criminal activities were invested in property, land and large commercial enterprises. Although Mikhailov was arrested and tried in Switzerland for criminal activities, he was acquitted and returned to Moscow, where he was reported to continue to play a role in the Solntsevo organization. Another figure, believed by some observers to be the key figure in the organization, was Semyon Mogilevich, who was based in Budapest, Hungary. Allegedly, Mogilevich, an educated Ukrainian, had developed an extensive 'and seemingly invincible business empire' that covered not only Moscow, Samara Oblast and the Autonomous Republic of Crimea (Ukraine), but also Hungary, Israel and the United Kingdom (Robinson, 1999). In 2003 there were reports that one of Mogilevich's companies was involved in a large-scale capital-flight scheme through the Russian gas monopoly, Gazprom. The Solntsevo organization reportedly controlled two hotels and several casinos; a car exchange; the non-food markets in the south-west district of Moscow; and commercial transportation to and from Vnukovo airport. In addition, it was believed to control freight passing through Moscow's Sheremetyevo International Airport (Robinson). The Solntsevo organization had also run very lucrative 'pyramid' investment schemes. It protected itself through bribing local investigators and prosecutors, but by the late 1990s it had been hurt by the indictment of at least some of the recipients of its largesse;

predatory criminal organizations that essentially engaged in small-scale criminal activities, such as localized extortion, car theft, etc., and that did not have links with corrupt officials. These organizations were more like street gangs than fully fledged organized crime groups, although the more successful among them tended to increase in sophistication and gradually developed links with the business, political and administrative élites;

specialized groups, including groups of contract killers (one of which was known as the Kurgatskaya), which were the equivalent of the old 'murder incorporated' in the US mafia. Several attempts by criminologists were made to develop a typology of such assassins or 'hit men'. One distinction, based largely on weapons, was between 'demolition men', who used explosives (there were 886 explosions in Russia in 1996, up from 18 in 1994) and 'snipers', who used firearms. The snipers were divided into 'professionals', whose fees could be in many thousands of US dollars, and 'infantry', who participated in the routine settling of grievances and were far less expensive to hire. Other analysts used as the basis for classification not the weapons, but the degree of professionalism and the fees charged. This yielded a four-fold typology: vagrants who would kill 'for a bottle of vodka'; members of crime groups who shot their victims on the orders of their leaders for a modest fee; 'professionals' who were usually former MVD and KGB operatives and were paid many thousands of dollars; and 'super-professionals', former members of special units of enforcement agencies, who were usually used by high-ranking officials in state organizations and who received fees in the hundreds of thousands of dollars. According to one estimate, there were only 100 professional 'hit men' on the entire territory of the CIS, and more than one-half of them were formerly officers in the 'S' unit of the KGB, where they developed their expertise;

groups of police-officers who have tacitly joined the ranks of the criminals and engaged in their own extortion and protection businesses. The extent of this phenomenon is difficult to assess, but according a report citing Vladimir Zhurkhov, head of Russia's Association of Small Businesses, abuses by law-enforcement officers had become 'quasi-systematic'. Although a purge of the police force took place in 2001, in an attempt to unearth corruption among law-enforcement representatives, it also meant a loss of expertise in crime-fighting. It was also clear that at least some former police-officers had either established criminal organizations of their own or joined existing organizations. In both cases they brought with them expertise concerning law-enforcement methods, and how best they could be countered. The result was that combating organized crime was likely to become an even more formidable task.

It is clear from this brief discussion that criminal groups in Russia varied enormously. Yet, this diversity was a source of strength and helped to explain the extensive penetration of the economy. Indeed, Russia and the other members of the CIS were perhaps unique in the extensive range of activities of organized crime. In Western countries, organized crime had generally involved the provision of illicit goods and services (including protection). In Russia it had gone far beyond this. The infiltration of licit business had become the norm rather than the exception. Although it was difficult to measure the scale of organized crime activity in Russia with great precision, in January 1998 Viktor Ilyukhin, Chairman of the Federal Security Committee (FSB—the successor to the KGB), claimed that approximately 40% of private enterprises, 60% of state-owned enterprises and between 55% and 85% of Russian banks were controlled by organized crime. Similar assessments continue to be made. Even though the basis for these judgments is rarely made explicit it is clear that the Russian economy has become heavily criminalized.

## Criminal Activities

### Extortion

Perhaps the most pervasive and significant activity of Russian organized crime was extortion of business. Both domestic and foreign firms were targets of extortion, with the criminals demanding about 10% of turnover. Although some groups actually provided protection and developed a vested interest in the success of the firm they 'protected' or extorted, others were simply parasitic, taking as much as they could and providing no service in return. In these cases, the payment was simply to make them desist from violence against the firm and its employees. Although the extent of extortion activities was impossible to gauge with accuracy, the MVD's 1997 report noted that, 'organized criminal formations continue to retain control over a significant part of the economic subjects in all forms of ownership, receiving significant financial support from them'. At the same time, there was a gradual change in the methodologies of the extortion business. Some criminal organizations became increasingly sophisticated and transformed themselves, at least ostensibly, into private security companies. Often in league with extortionists, the security firms, nevertheless, offered some possibility of a long-term transition towards more legitimate forms of business. As suggested above, police-officers also began to play a major role in the extortion business, prompting reports that, in some cases at least, they had replaced more traditional organized crime. Indeed, there was increasing evidence that this was the case, with police-officers not only using their official positions, but also resorting to violence to deal with competitors or recalcitrant businessmen. According to the INDEM Foundation, which focuses on corruption in Russia, it had become common for the police to become *krysha*, not only for legitimate businesses, but also for criminal activities. In this connection, INDEM analysts suggested that only about 40% of the earnings from the sale of contraband items went to the vendors; the remainder was used to pay the law-enforcement agencies (*Eurasia Security Trends*, published by the Jamestown Foundation).

### Economic Crime and Financial Fraud

One of the difficulties in assessing economic crime was that it was not clear that the definition had remained static over time. Similarly, it was difficult to know exactly what kinds of crime were being included at any one time. Nevertheless, it was clear that various kinds of fraud, embezzlement, money laundering, tax evasion and capital flight were included under this rubric. During 1997 2,900 cases of what the MVD described as unlawful and false entrepreneurship were identified, along with over 240 attempts at legalization of monetary gains obtained by unlawful means, over 60 criminal acts associated with unlawful receipt of credit and 470 cases of commercial bribery. In the credit-finance sphere, 29,200 crimes were uncovered, which was approximately five times

more than in 1993. Not surprisingly, given the economic crisis that began in August 1998, the situation subsequently deteriorated. According to the Minister of Internal Affairs, the number of registered economic crimes increased by an average of 18% during the first few months of 1999, with the spheres of finance and credit, and foreign trade, being particularly susceptible to problems, accounting for 20% and 30% of crimes, respectively. Although economic stabilization had some impact, economic crimes continued to pose a serious problem. In 2001 the Office of the Prosecutor-General investigated 361,000 economic crimes, representing an increase of 2.5% compared with 2000. There were 52,000 cases involving the illegal appropriation and expenditure of funds, a 3.7% increase compared with 2000, while the incidence of bribery increased by 13.7% compared with the previous year.

### Infiltration of the Property Market

Almost from the collapse of the USSR, citizens had been coerced or duped out of property they owned. In 1997, according to the MVD, 'around 1,000 crimes committed in the housing sphere were uncovered', including 400 cases of deception and over 60 murders. Before it was disbanded, one Moscow-based group, which specialized in the unlawful purchase of apartments, had acquired the ownership of over 100. In an expansive property market this kind of activity was enormously lucrative, and it was probably undertaken by both organized crime and by opportunist criminals who took advantage of gullible property-owners.

### Illicit Production and Sale of Vodka

About one-half of all the vodka in Russia was produced illegally, either domestically or smuggled through a variety of routes, including via the Arctic ports in the north-west and Krasnovodsk on the Caspian Sea, and through the borders with the People's Republic of China, Kazakhstan and Ukraine. The Republic of North Osetiya—Alaniya was the major domestic production centre, bottling about one-third of the illegal vodka that was supplied to some 60 Russian regions. Regarded as one of the major sources of revenue for criminal organizations in Russia, in 1997 the Ministry of Internal Affairs suppressed over 2,000 illegal producers of counterfeit alcoholic beverages, and seized 1.3m. decalitres. Despite these successes, however, in the early 2000s such activities continued to increase the funds of criminal organizations throughout significant parts of Russia.

### Automobile Theft

Another area in which organized crime had been very active was the theft and trafficking of automobiles. This had an international dimension, with luxury cars, in particular, being stolen from Western Europe and driven to Russia or other CIS countries. It was also a domestic problem that went beyond the theft of cars on the street. In one case, for example, a criminal group was accused of misappropriating 317 automobiles from the Volga Automotive Plant (as well as diesel engines from the Yaroslav Motor Plant and chemical products from the Sterlitamak Avangard Plant). Overlapping with this was robbery from car owners. One group was particularly active in this type of crime, and carried out 37 armed assaults and robberies of automobile owners in various Russian cities during 1995–96. Nor had the problem abated to any significant extent by the end of the 1990s. The number of car hijacks in Moscow, for example, was 1,217 in 1998 and 1,193 in 1999.

### Infiltration of the Banking System

During the 1990s considerable progress was made in Russia towards the development of a banking sector appropriate to a functioning and effective market economy. Russian banking, however, continued to suffer from several major problems, not the least of which was the infiltration of organized crime.

Indeed, banking was a high-risk profession, with bankers as one of the major targets for murder by organized crime groups. One analysis of the Russian banking system delineated four kinds of bank, depending on the degree of criminal penetration and the degree of criminality in their operations (Burlingame, 1998). Banks ranking high on both dimensions were characterized as predatory, while those ranking low could be regarded as 'clean' banks, albeit with the recognition that they could easily become targets for criminal influence. Banks that were not controlled by outside criminal groups, but in which the directors had criminal intent, were characterized as corrupt, while those where the management was basically honest, but had come under the control of outside criminal organizations fell into the fourth category, of corrupted banks. One of the reasons that there was so much violence in the banking sector was that some managers had resisted the process of external corruption—and paid the penalty for so doing.

The control of banks was an important asset for criminal organizations for various purposes, ranging from preferential credit arrangements to financial fraud. Infiltration of the banking sector also facilitated extortion, by providing details of businesses that were lucrative and that were vulnerable targets, because they had engaged in tax evasion. Finally, but no less importantly, it facilitated money laundering through the banking system, both by Russian criminal organizations and by those from elsewhere. This would become even more essential as Russian money-laundering legislation became increasingly stringent. Closely linked to this was capital flight, which remained a major problem for Russia. Indeed, it was sometimes difficult to distinguish between the laundering of the proceeds of crime and capital flight designed to evade taxes. This was certainly the case in the scandal concerning the Bank of New York, which became public in August 1999. Early reports suggested that about US $15,000m. had been laundered through the bank. Six months later, however, the estimated figure had been reduced by around one-half, and reports increasingly claimed that the majority of the funds was accounted for by capital flight, rather than the proceeds of crime. None the less, the scandal revealed the problems that could arise when Western banks developed correspondent banking relationships with Russian banks and failed to observe due diligence towards their partners. It also revealed that insiders could help to circumvent the normal processes of regulation and oversight. Perhaps most significantly of all, however, it illustrated the serious problems that remained in the Russian banking system.

### Infiltration of Industry and Commerce

It was not only the banking industry that had suffered from infiltration by criminal organizations. Criminal groups used violence and the threat of violence to dominate regional economies, particular industries or specific enterprises, such as the Volga Automobile Plant. In the latter case, local criminal groups consisting of about 1,000 persons effectively took control of distribution, and their permission was required for automobiles to go to customers (according to a 1997 interview with Vladimir Vasilev, a deputy minister heading the MVD's anti-mafia effort). Similarly, in the fuel and energy sectors, criminal enterprises attempted to establish control over the markets in Moscow, Ryazan, Samara, Tomsk, Tyumen, Ufa and elsewhere. In June 2003 the murders of two executives suggested that organized crime was becoming active in the defence sector. Police believed that the deaths of Igor Klimov, the acting director of Almaz-Antei, a major producer and exporter of air defence weapons, and Sergei Shchitko, the commercial director of Ratep, an affiliated business, were connected.

Criminal involvement in industry and commerce also brought with it a great deal of fraud. From 1995 to 1997, for example, members of one group, using forged documents, made a series of fraudulent deals and misappropriated petroleum products worth over 50,000m. roubles. Even more seriously, infiltration by organized crime was accompanied by considerable violence. During 1995, for example, several high-ranking officials in the aluminium industry were killed as part of what was clearly an effort by organized crime groups to establish control over a lucrative export industry. Subsequently, the hotel industry was a target, with four Moscow hotel executives being killed in an 18-month period. These included Paul Tatum, a US businessman who was in dispute with his Russian partners, and Yevgenii Tsimbalitov, Director of the Rossiya Hotel near Red Square. This is not surprising, as both Moscow and St Petersburg have lucrative hotel markets, but government or city authorities were still heavily involved in the hotel business. In this sector, as in others, Western investors found that local partners could be both unreliable and dangerous.

The economy in St Petersburg appeared to be particularly susceptible to this kind of infiltration: in the late 1990s the Tambov organized crime group, which was reputed to have between 300 and 400 'soldiers', was believed to control hotels, petroleum and petroleum products, and the production and sale of alcoholic beverages and confectionery. The group also illustrated the nexus between organized crime, business and politics. Vladimir Kumarin, regarded by many to be the group's leader, was also Vice-President of the St Petersburg Fuel Company, which controlled over two-thirds of the retail gasoline (petrol) market in the city, and had received numerous municipal contracts, largely because of its political links. In addition, the group was believed to have protectors in the St Petersburg Legislative Assembly. Elections and arrests depleted the ranks of the group's political supporters (in April 2000, for example, Sergei Shevchenko, a deputy of the municipal legislature, and one of the Tambov gang's protectors, was arrested), and by the early 2000s the influence of the Tambov gang had declined significantly. However, rather than representing a victory for the forces of law and order, this served to reflect the dynamism of the criminal world. Organized crime in St Petersburg had not been beaten; the patterns of dominance had simply changed.

Another area where organized crime seemed to have a particularly strong hold over both economic and political life was Smolensk Oblast. An investigation by representatives from the Main Administration for Combating Economic Crimes concluded that Smolensk was witnessing a transformation in the scale of the activity of criminal gangs, which had moved from individual cases of embezzlement to a tactic of establishing control over entire industrial enterprises and sectors. Embezzlement of budgetary funds was rife, and involved various sectors of the economy, including road construction and the provision of electricity. It was also believed that criminal organizations were working closely with officials. Indeed, there were allegations that the Oblast's Governor, Aleksandr Prokhorov, had offered protection to leading criminals, engaged in drugs-trafficking, extortion and cargo hijackings. In May 2002, however, Prokhorov was defeated in his bid for re-election, after an election campaign that was marred by violence and attempted killings, which continued in the months that followed; in August the Deputy Governor of Smolensk was murdered, in what was interpreted as an attempt to intimidate the new regime.

If events in Smolensk emphasized the symbiosis between politics, business and crime, events in Sakhalin Oblast revealed the willingness of criminals to resort to violence to protect their activities. In this case, the industry that was deeply penetrated by organized crime was fishing. Poaching, and the illegal export of caviar, in violation of the UN-administered Convention on International Trade in Endangered Species, has become a serious problem in and around the Caspian Sea region. In the Russian Far East, the evasion of export taxes on catches of fish provided enormously lucrative opportunities for trade between Sakhalin and Hokkaido, Japan. The Russian coastguard estimated that approximately US $1,000m. in revenues were lost each year, as a result of the illegal trade. Moreover, the 'fish mafia' has been willing to use violence to protect its illegal activities. In May 2002 Gen. Vitalii Gamov, who had been leading the attempts in Sakhalin to combat the illegal trade, was killed by a petrol bomb thrown into his home.

### Contract Killings

A major feature of criminal activity in Russia was the increased prevalence of contract killings. Although they accounted for only a very small proportion of the murders in Russia, contract killings had an import that transcended their number. In part, they reflected continued rivalry and conflict in the criminal world, but also the infiltration of both government and business. Although, initially, relatively few of these cases were solved, the record of law enforcement in this area had improved. In 1993 27 out of 228 contract murders were solved. In 1995 the figure was 60 out of 560. The largest increase came in 1997, when 132 contract killings were solved, almost twice as many as in 1996. In the short term, however, this did nothing to limit the phenomenon. Indeed, this was another area where the economic crisis of August 1998 greatly exacerbated the situation—largely because it led to an increase in the numbers of businessmen failing to meet their debt repayments. However, although in the first few months of 1999 567 people were murdered in contract killings in Russia, compared with 232 during the same period in 1998, the official total for 1999 as a whole was 591 (it is difficult not to regard this figure as a serious underestimate, given the extent of activity in the first half of the year). Official statistics suggested a further improvement in the situation in 2000, with only 386 contract killings (60 of which reportedly occurred in the petroleum industry). In 2001 327 contract killings were recorded, and 142 cases went to trial.

According to a 1999 report, citing an MVD official, such crimes were thoroughly planned, and customer and killer were separated by at least 10 intermediaries—the killer would, thus, be paid only a small fraction of the total fee. Moreover, the killers themselves were often recruited from former MVD, special services and special police personnel. According to the Office of the Prosecutor-General, about 70% of assassins are indicted, but only between 20% and 30% of those who order the assassinations are identified. Among the successes was the arrest in July 2001 of five members of a criminal group in Tolyatti, which numbered more than 10 professional killers, including former paratroopers and members of the 'special purpose' forces (*spetsnaz*). Several categories of victim were readily identifiable:

leaders of the criminal world who were killed as part of the struggle for power among criminal organizations, and whose death might result from business rivalries, ethnic clashes between Slavic groups and those from the Caucasus, personal animosities, or even such motives as revenge or professional jealousy. The victims included a significant number of the *vory-v-zakone*, as well as many new criminal authorities;

businessmen who resisted hostile take-overs by criminal organizations, who owed money and refused to pay, or who were killed as part of a struggle for power and control in a particular industrial sector, such as aluminium or the hotel sector;

journalists who were serious about exposing and eliminating corruption and who had been killed in an effort to prevent them investigating further;

bankers who either resisted the blandishments of criminal organizations or who become too deeply involved in criminal activities;

politicians and officials who resisted corruption, who investigated links between organized crime and corruption and who supported efforts to advance the process of reform, despite the economic and political obstacles. Perhaps the most notable of these was the killing in November 1998 of Galina Starovoitova, as she was entering her home in St Petersburg. A prominent reformist member of the Duma, and apparently resistant to corruption, Starovoitova was engaged in some significant corruption investigations that could have led to her murder.

In effect, the use of contract killing had been extended from an instrument of intergroup warfare to an instrument used to punish or eliminate those who were willing, in one way or another, to stand up to criminal organizations. Contract killings were used not only as a struggle for power and motivated by such factors as revenge, but also as an extension of business practices, contract enforcement and debt collection. Moreover, contract killings by Russians have spread to other countries, with cases in Germany, the Netherlands, Spain, the United Kingdom and the USA. It was in Russia, however, that they were most significant, not least because the range of victims reflected both the pervasiveness of organized crime in the Russian economy and the capacity of Russian criminal organizations to eliminate anyone who opposed them. Nor should too much comfort be taken from the decline in the number of contract killings in 2000–01. Although it is possible that these figures represented more effective law enforcement, a more plausible interpretation is that the influence of organized crime over particular industries had become sufficiently well-established that it was no longer necessary to remove obstacles to its control. The killings almost certainly had a salutary effect, creating sufficient fear that organized crime in Russia was able to operate with minimum opposition from those in legitimate industries. Similarly, the reduction in the number of contract killings suggested that in the criminal world many of the major spheres of influence—whether geographical or functional—had become well-established, and accepted by most criminal organizations. Criminal rivalries remained, but the brutality of the early 1990s had given way to a less violent phase.

None the less, contract killings continued to be widely reported by the media. Among the more prominent victims in 2001–02 were: Anatolii Tikhenko, President of the Federal Notary Public Chamber (FNP), who was shot and killed—probably owing to his efforts to combat corruption in the notary system; Tatyana Safronova, the head of Vladivostok's transportation department, who was killed after resisting efforts by organized criminals to control the city's commercial transport sector; and Yurii Belyakov, Deputy Mayor of Novosibirsk, who was probably killed as a result of his efforts to transfer Novosibirsk's largest open-air market to city government control. In Moscow, the victims included: Konstantin Georgiev, the head of a prominent hotel, in January 2002; Vladimir Kanevskii, the General Director of ATOR, Moscow's leading advertising company, who was murdered in February; and Andrei Petukhov, the head of the SOGAZ insurance company, a subsidiary of Gazprom, who was killed in May. In August Vladimir Golovlev, an associate of the controversial oligarch Boris Berezovskii and a Co-Chairman of the Liberal Russia party, was killed close to his home. The Governor of Magadan Oblast, Valentin Tsvetkov, who had attempted to combat organized crime, was murdered in October, and in December Duma aide Mikhail Grishankov was killed in St Petersburg. There were further high-profile murders in 2003. Among the victims were Duma member Sergei Yushenkov, who was killed in April outside his Moscow apartment, and

Igor Novik, the director of the Kristan furniture factory in St Petersburg, who was killed in August. Thus, although the number of contract killings had declined, they continued to be used to eliminate those regarded as threats or obstacles to criminal ambitions. The intersection of business, politics and crime remained a potentially deadly area.

### Drugs-trafficking

Drugs-trafficking in Russia had become a major activity, involving not only well-publicized links with Colombian cocaine traffickers, but also the supply of opium, heroin and marijuana from Central Asia, Afghanistan and Pakistan. In addition, there were several major cases involving large-scale trafficking in synthetic drugs. Control over the import and distribution of these drugs within Russia, however, was a matter of some debate

According to a report commissioned by the UN, the growth of drug use is not attributable to Russian organized crime. The local drugs markets of Russian cities are largely supplied by myriad dealers who tend to operate alone or in small groups and often consume illegal drugs themselves. In many cases, the dealers do not possess previous criminal expertise, and deal illegal drugs either to make a living or to supplement the meagre income they obtain from licit activities (Paoli). The US Department of State, however, contends that domestic distribution of illicit drugs is undertaken by the traditional Russian criminal organizations, and that trafficking into the country is frequently undertaken by members of various ethnic groups, which tend to specialize geographically in particular categories of drugs. For example, Afghans and Central Asians predominantly import heroin across the southern border with Kazakhstan into European Russia and western Siberia, while eastern Siberia is supplied with heroin, opium and ephedrine by Vietnamese and Chinese traffickers. The country's larger organized crime groups often allow small-scale traffickers to operate freely, in exchange for a share of their profits (US Department of State, 2003).

Whatever its precise structure, the drugs-trafficking industry in Russia continued to flourish. Russia was an increasingly attractive market for groups from the Caucasus, Central Asia and Ukraine, partly because of the strength of the rouble compared with currencies in other parts of the CIS, partly because courts often passed relatively lenient sentences on drugs dealers, and partly because of the ineffectiveness of interdiction. The establishment of a new State Committee for Combating Drugs-Trafficking, attached to the Ministry of Internal Affairs, gave some grounds for optimism, but the situation in Afghanistan ensured that combating drugs-trafficking remained a formidable undertaking.

### Counterfeiting and Intellectual Property Theft

Illegally copied, 'pirated', videotapes were not only for sale or shown in cinemas, they were also shown on television. The President of the USA's Motion Picture Association claimed that the US film industry lost US $300m. in profits in Russia each year, while another $250m. was believed to be lost to the Russian state in uncollected tax revenue. Illegal copying of computer software was also a major problem, with pirated copies accounting for a very high percentage of software in Russia. By the end of the 1990s new copyright laws and a public-education campaign had been initiated, but they had no more than a minor impact on the problem, at least in the short term.

### Corruption

Russia provided a very hospitable environment for the growth of organized crime. Criminal organizations, intent on ensuring that the congenial environment remained, resorted to corruption on a massive scale, with some reports suggesting that they spent 40%–50% and, in some cases, as much as 60% of their profits on bribing functionaries (cited in a 1997 interview with the Minister of Internal Affairs). Although such estimates may seem high, the bribery of officials could be used to minimize enforcement efforts, to obtain counter-intelligence that could neutralize genuine enforcement efforts, or to ensure that enforcement did not result in prosecution or conviction. In a sense, corruption was a way of keeping the state weak and acquiescent, and it was undertaken in a systematic manner. Thus, the Minister noted that when one criminal gang was arrested, the authorities found 'a computer programme on the methodological infiltration of the structures of power by criminal groups. Everything was minutely categorized: what must be done to gain control at a precisely defined time of this or that functionary'. This emphasized an important shift from the Soviet era: increasingly, the criminal organizations determined the rules. In post-Soviet Russia, corruption was designed not to overcome the inefficiencies of state control of economic life, but to protect criminal organizations from law enforcement. As the political élite was forced to accommodate those who had both the power to hurt and the wealth to purchase support, a new type of symbiotic relationship emerged, in which organized crime had become the dominant force. This is not to suggest that all corruption was organized crime-related. Clearly much of it was not. Indeed, one report emphasized 'the establishment of corruption networks—organized groups created for the collective derivation of income from corrupt activities. Any corruption network, according to the experts, must include three elements: a commercial or financial structure to implement privileges and advantages and turn them into money; a group of public officials making decisions securing the concealment of these activities; a group of law-enforcement officials protecting the corruption network' (INDEM Foundation, 2001).

### Trafficking in Nuclear Materials

An additional area of enormous potential significance was the trade in nuclear materials. While this was not a core activity of Russian criminal organizations, and seemed primarily to have been the preserve of amateur smugglers, there were some cases of organized crime involvement. In one case, in which members of a criminal organization were arrested, reports suggested that there was a clear division of roles and responsibilities. The implication was that this might not have been out of the ordinary. Even if it was a rare event, nuclear-material trafficking is a potential growth area for Russian organized crime, especially if criminal groups forged links with 'pariah' states, countries otherwise isolated internationally, and intent on developing weapons of mass destruction. Well-established smuggling routes from Russia through the Caucasus and Central Asia were difficult to police—it was likely that nuclear contraband was going in this direction, rather than through Central Europe and Germany. Indeed, open-source indicators suggested that from 1995 there was a shift towards the south, rather than the west, with an increase in the percentage of seizures taking place in the Balkans, the Caucasus, Central Asia and Turkey. What made this all the more significant was that it did not reflect an increase in law-enforcement capacity in these regions. With the exception of Turkey, law enforcement along these southern routes remained underfunded and inadequate.

### Trafficking in Arms

Following the collapse of the USSR, Russia also developed a significant problem with arms-trafficking. In large part, this stemmed from corruption in the military and the illegal sale of military equipment at all levels, from the illegal sale of single rifles to major weapons and equipment stocks. Moreover, the problem appeared to be showing little sign of diminishing. According to statistics from the Russian Supreme Court, 1.5 times more arrests were made for illegal arms-trading in 2001 than in 2000; in total, 26,113 people were arrested and 65,000 crimes were committed using illegal arms. In 2000 more than 300,000 unregistered firearms were seized, which represented a 37% increase compared with 1999. As with any criminal market, a significant portion of this trade was unorganized; however, it was also an activity in which organized crime played a significant role. Particularly prominent was Viktor Bout, a major arms trafficker who had been involved in trafficking arms to African conflicts and Afghanistan; although Bout had been indicted in Belgium, in late 2003 he remained at liberty in Russia.

### Computer Crime

The other area in which organized crime in Russia increasingly appeared to be involved was that of computer crime. Perhaps the earliest public example of this came in 1994, when the Citibank computer system in Boston, MA, USA, was infiltrated from St Petersburg, leading to the theft of US $10m. Although all but $400,000 was eventually recovered, there was considerable speculation that organized crime had been responsible for the incident. Subsequently, the growing number of unauthorized transactions suggested that Russian criminals were either recruiting or coercing 'hackers' to break into Western systems. Whether this was purely for criminal gain, for industrial espionage, or for state espionage was not always entirely clear. Given the seamless connections between crime, business and politics in Russia, however, it was likely that all three elements were involved. The USA appeared to be the major target. According to some reports, the USA's Federal Bureau of Investigation (FBI) believed that 40 companies in 20 states had been identified as targets for Russian organized crime groups. Activities included extortion, fraud and theft. In some cases, an incident of computer crime would be followed by an offer to remedy, for a large fee, the security weaknesses that had made intervention possible—a thinly disguised form of extortion. In other cases, credit card numbers were used for a series of frauds. Some of the perpetrators were simply individuals or small groups of hackers. At least some, however, were evidently working—either voluntarily or under duress—for criminal groups that had diversified their activities into yet another lucrative area. The other advantage of 'cybercrime' was that it was very low risk. The widespread availability of commercial establishments offering internet usage provided the opportunity to maintain anonymity and, although Russia had penalties for computer crime, effective and vigorous enforcement was rare. Furthermore, as in other areas, the possibility of official complicity could not be dismissed, thereby providing an extra layer of protection. Moreover, the internet provided the opportunity to commit crimes in other jurisdictions, while operating from what was, in effect, a 'safe haven' in Russia. There were also numerous intrusions into computer systems in the USA that were traced by US law-enforcement agencies to Russia and elsewhere in the former USSR. In March 2001 the FBI issued a warning that hackers in Russia and Eastern Europe had obtained illegal access to over 1m. credit card numbers, as well as other proprietary information, in over 40 electronic-commerce firms in the USA. Nor were these hackers inactive domestically. In August, for example, it was reported that the incidence of computer crime in Russia had increased two-fold over the previous two years.

This list of criminal activities is far from exhaustive. Nevertheless, it gives a flavour of the scope and scale of organized crime in Russia and, indeed, in other CIS countries. The problem also had a transnational dimension, beyond the 'near abroad'. Criminal organizations from Russia and elsewhere in the CIS had become active in Germany, Israel (which was attractive because of its lack of anti-money-laundering laws and its law of return) and the USA, as well as in Belgium and the Netherlands. In the USA, Russian criminals had become involved in lucrative fuel-tax evasion schemes, as well as in health care and insurance fraud. They had also become involved in the trafficking of women to the West for prostitution. In the first few years after the collapse of the USSR the trafficking of Slavic women to the West seemed to focus predominantly on the countries of Western Europe. Such trafficking subsequently became evident in Israel and the USA, as well as in Japan, South Korea, Poland, Turkey and South America. Although some of the traffickers resembled entrepreneurs rather than criminals, organized crime groups, at the very least, provided the manpower and control for such activities, and not only facilitated the passage of the women, but also exerted control over them once they arrived at their destination.

The other very obvious transnational dimension of Russian organized crime was money laundering. Although it was difficult to differentiate between flight capital and the profits of illegal transactions, there was evidence that Russian criminals laundered the proceeds of crime through a variety of foreign destinations. Money was sent to Israel both directly, and via Antwerp, the Netherlands; it went through international business companies in Gibraltar and into Spain; and it was detected in California, USA, in Germany, in the property market of London, United Kingdom, and in Viet Nam. In the mid-1990s Cyprus was a popular destination, but by the late 1990s the banking system there appeared to have tightened its regulations somewhat and, at the very least, the process had become rather less blatant. Some of the activity had shifted towards offshore financial centres in the Caribbean and, more recently, the South Pacific. The Cook Islands, Nauru, Niue and Vanuatu had all been used for Russian money laundering and capital flight, and some banks in these jurisdictions had even developed bilingual internet sites to attract Russian funds. There was also concern that Russian criminal organizations had helped Italians and, perhaps, even Colombians to launder their proceeds of crime through Russia. Whether or not such speculation was well-founded, it was clear that Russian criminals had established extensive links with their Italian and Colombian counterparts, a development that would make overcoming Russian organized crime even more of a challenge in the future. In mid-2002 law-enforcement agencies revealed the details of 'Operation Spider Web', which had uncovered a major Russian money-laundering scheme in Rimini, Italy, using import-export companies to legitimize criminal proceeds returning to Russia.

International concerns over Russian money laundering—and the Government's inability or unwillingness to fight it—became particularly clear in June 2000, when Russia was named by the Financial Action Task Force (FATF), a body established by the Group of Seven industrialized nations, as one of 15 non-co-operative financial centres. The concerns were well-founded, with Russian officials reporting 965 registered cases of money laundering in 2000—representing twice the figure registered in 1999—and a further 744 cases were registered in early 2001. In August 2001, however, partly as a result of the FATF's campaign and partly as a result of perceived discrimination against Russian banks, President Putin finally signed into law measures to combat money laundering. The new legislation required banks to report suspicious transactions, as well as all cash transactions exceeding approximately US $20,000, created a monitoring agency and brought Russia into greater conformity with international norms and standards. Although concerns remained about the effective implementation of the new law, as well as the continued influence of organized crime in the financial sector, the successful culmination of what had been a complex drafting and approval process represented significant progress, and Russia was removed from the FATF's list of non-co-operative states in October 2002.

## THE FUTURE OF ORGANIZED CRIME

What kind of future would organized crime have in Russia? The answer to this question would do much to determine the ultimate outcome of the economic transition, as well as act as an indicator for developments elsewhere in the CIS. It was possible to elaborate both positive and negative scenarios. The positive scenario envisaged a decline in Russian organized crime to what one analyst termed 'normal Western levels'—although precisely what this meant was uncertain (Leitzel, 1995). The underlying logic for predicting a positive outcome of this kind had several dimensions. In part, it suggested that the peculiarities of the early stages of a protracted transition process gave organized crime the opportunity to flourish, but that as the move to the free market and liberal democracy continued, temporary aberrations would be corrected and distortions would diminish or disappear. As the Russian state reasserted itself and established not only greater legitimacy and authority but, more specifically, effective legal and regulatory frameworks for business, the opportunities for organized crime to play a role in contract enforcement and dispute settlement would be constricted. Similarly, as the free market became truly free, opportunities for criminal activity would diminish. Unregulated capitalism, in which illicit business predominated, would give way to a more regulated form of capitalism, dominated by licit business. In short, there would be a gradual cleansing process.

This cleansing process, it could be argued, would be accompanied by a process of legitimization. Encouragement for this was often found in parallels between contemporary Russian businessmen and the 'robber barons' of the USA in the late 19th century. Thus, the first generation of capitalists were preoccupied solely with capital accumulation and had few, if any, scruples about the means of achieving it, but they would want differently for their sons and daughters. This theory supposed that the leaders of the mafia would not only wish to pass on their wealth, but would also wish to ensure that their heirs, untarnished by criminality, enjoyed high status within society. This would encourage a gradual transition from illicit to licit business.

Some comfort could also be derived from law-enforcement successes. Laws were becoming stronger, omissions of legislation were slowly being rectified and the criminal justice system was gradually beginning to function with greater integrity and effectiveness. One observer also contended that 'criminal justice in Russia, when it chooses to be, is still swift and summary, and defendants' rights are weak', so that organized crime could not use the law to defend itself as it could in the USA (Gustafson, 1999). The tax base was also being enhanced through a specific focus on tax evasion, while law-enforcement agencies were learning to co-operate more efficiently. During 1997, according to the MVD, over 16,000 participants in criminal formations were brought to justice in Russia, while 5,600 cases of bribery (an increase of 3%) were identified and over 480 corrupt officials were indicted. In short, progress was being made in showing that organized crime was not invincible, that criminals could not act with impunity and that the state was not helpless against the onslaught of crime and corruption. Moreover, the election of Putin to the presidency increased morale among law-enforcement personnel, who believed that he would not only provide strong, decisive leadership in the fight against organized crime, but would also ensure that a co-ordinated policy was vigorously implemented. Their argument was that if the requisite will was present, then the challenge posed by organized crime would not only be contained, but also significantly reduced.

None of the components of the optimistic scenario could be dismissed. Nevertheless, the scenario was not compelling, partly because it suffered from a fixation with both the virtues and the power of the market. It assumed that the market would tame organized crime; yet it was equally plausible that organized crime would continue to distort and dominate much of the market. The optimistic scenario also overlooked or minimized the capacity of organized crime to perpetuate itself, even when some of the market conditions that contributed so much to its emergence had disappeared. In addition, the theory ignored the capacity of organized crime to obstruct or even halt the movement towards reform. Organized crime groups might be entrepreneurial capitalists, but they inhibited legitimate entrepreneurial activity and the accumulation of investment capital by licit means. It was difficult for legitimate entrepreneurs to compete with those who had ready access to large financial resources obtained through illicit means. It was uncomfortable, to say the least, for them to compete with those who were willing to use violence as an extension of commerce. Furthermore, violence against businessmen and bankers inhibited the flow of foreign investment that was crucial to Russia's economic future.

The more pessimistic scenario of the future focused not on the market and the economy, but on the organized crime and corruption networks that had become a dominant and pervasive feature of Russian economic and political life. This was even more relevant in some other countries of the CIS. Symbiotic relationships between criminal organizations and the political and economic élites were generally regarded in the West as the most developed and mature stage of organized crime. Yet, largely because of its peculiar origins and its development in the transition, much organized crime in Russia had already reached this point. As a result, efforts to combat organized crime and corruption would continue to be hindered by the inadequacy of the legal framework, as well as by the desire of the 'comrade criminals', whether in political life or in the various bureaucracies, to perpetuate a corrupt system that provided considerable benefits.

Another obstacle was the lack of clarity about where legal transactions ended and criminal activities began. The connection between the legal and the illegal was reinforced by that between public and private: little was done to prevent conflicts of interests for those in political power, who typically used public office for private gain. Perhaps most important of all, however, was the 'iron triangle' that developed among the oligarchs and businessmen, organized criminals and political and bureaucratic élites, all of whom were working together in a symbiotic relationship that had become one of the most dominant characteristics of Russia in the first years of the 21st century. The consolidation of power by organized crime groups would make them virtually impossible to eradicate, yet was something that optimistic proponents of the market almost completely ignored. Indeed, the trend seemed to be going in the opposite direction, with the very distinct possibility that Russia would become—if it had not already—a neutralized or even captured state. It was arguable that the Russian state had been neutralized from the early 1990s: the criminal justice and law-enforcement systems were among the early casualties of the transition and had not yet fully recovered by the early 2000s. Perhaps even more seriously, there was some evidence that the state, in effect, had been captured by organized crime. The notion of 'state capture' had the following components: criminals had access to the resources of the state and were able to exploit these resources for their own purposes; the state could only act effectively, at least domestically, when its actions did not seriously impinge on the power and well-being of organized crime; state institutions could be used to mask organized crime activities; it was not clear where the state ended and organized crime began—or vice versa; organized crime usurped some of the functions of the state; and, finally, organized crime continued to be a major contributor to the Russian economy. Regarding this last characteristic, the central role played by organized crime in the Russian economy was emphasized by comments made in 2001 by Aleksandr Kulikov, the Chairman of the State Duma's security committee. Citing statistics provided by the MVD, Kulikov asserted that 40% of Russia's economy was engaged in the unofficial sector through parallel commercial structures (involving, for example, 'filial companies') in the entertainment and leisure sectors. In addition, he contended that between 50% and 85% of banks operating in Russia were under the control of organized crime, and that revenue from the shadow economy accounted for up to 40% of Russia's GDP, with nearly 9m. citizens involved in such activities. Kulikov also claimed that the number of organized crime groups had increased 17-fold during the preceding five years, while the number of groups with corrupt links had increased 170 times.

Another problem with the more hopeful vision of the future concerned the unwarranted parallels with US 'robber barons'. Ruthless as they were, such men built industry and infrastructure; for the most part, Russian criminals were more intent on robbing the Russian economy than building it. Moreover, even if some criminals did actually crave and achieve respectability, it was not clear that they would leave behind their old habits of violence against competitors. Even if there was an an ethos of betterment and escape at work, this could simply provide opportunities for more rapid promotion in the criminal world. The symbols of wealth and power displayed by organized crime figures in Russia were very attractive and almost invariably led to emulation. Recruitment for criminal organizations was easy, as illicit routes for advancement promised far greater and more immediate rewards than legitimate avenues. In short, even if some of the leading organized crime figures succeeded in becoming respectable, they would have more than enough successors to ensure that the problem would not go away. To conclude, organized crime could become the dominant force in Russian society. Instead of the legitimization of criminal capitalism and criminal organizations by the licit economy, the process could continue to move in the opposite direction, leading to a wholly collusive relationship in which the Russian state was subordinated to organized crime. Instead of the Russian state disciplining and containing such crime, as suggested above, organized crime might have already succeeded in capturing the Russian state and dominating the domestic economy.

In the final analysis, this pessimistic scenario may appear more compelling than more positive assessments. If this were so, the real transition would not be from authoritarianism to democracy or from a controlled economy to a free market, but simply from one form of criminal state to another. Although there were expectations that President Putin could somehow reverse this trend, by 2003 such expectations had certainly not been met. Putin reduced the power of the first generation of Russian oligarchs and encouraged initiatives against organized crime, which included a search of the home of Sergei Mikhailov, associated with the Solntsevo organization. In July 2002 Putin noted that 'special attention should be paid to the protection of the rights of owners. Entrepreneurs should be protected from pressure on the part of criminal groups'. Nevertheless, there was little evidence of a sustained and successful effort to provide the resources necessary to reduce the power of organized crime, and thereby provide such protection. Although Putin might yet be able to initiate such a campaign, by 2003 his anti-organized crime rhetoric had been little more than a triumph of hope over experience.

## BIBLIOGRAPHY

American Foreign Policy Council. *Russian Reform Monitor*. No. 1043, 27 May 2003.

Burlingame, Timothy M. 'Criminal Activity in the Russian Banking System', in *Transnational Organized Crime*. Vol. 3, No. 3, 1998.

Center for Strategic and International Studies. *Russian Organized Crime*, CSIS Task Force Report. Washington, DC, CSIS, 1997.

Galeotti, Mark. 'The Mafiya and the New Russia', in *Australian Journal of Politics and History*. Vol. 3, No. 3 (Sept.), Mimeo, 1998.

Gambetta, Diego. *The Sicilian Mafia: The Business of Private Protection*. Cambridge, MA, Harvard University Press, 1993.

Godson, Roy et al. 'Political–Criminal Nexus', in *Trends in Organized Crime*. Vol. 3, No. 1 (Autumn), 1997.

Gustafson, Thane. *Capitalism Russian-Style*. Cambridge, Cambridge University Press, 1999.

Handelman, Stephen. *Comrade Criminal: Russia's New Mafiya*. New Haven, CT, Yale University Press, 1995.

    'Russia's Terrorism—Organized Crime', in *Russia Watch*. No. 7, March 2002.

INDEM Foundation. *Diagnoses of Russian Corruption: Sociological Analysis on Moscow* (in Russian). Moscow, INDEM, 31 December 2001.

Jamestown Foundation. *Monitor*. Washington, DC, Jamestown Foundation, 13 July 2001.

    'Corruption Expert Takes Stock', in *Eurasia Security Trends*. Vol. 1, No. 1, March 2003.

Klitgaard, Robert. 'International Co-operation against Corruption', in *Finance and Development*. Vol. 35, No. 1 (March), 1998.

Layard, Richard, and Parker, John. *The Coming Russian Boom*. New York, NY, Free Press, 1996.

Leitzel, Jim. *Russian Economic Reform*. London, Routledge, 1995.

Lotspeich, Richard. 'Crime in the Transition Economies', in *Europe-Asia Studies*. Vol. 47, No. 4 (June), 1995.

Ministry of Internal Affairs (MVD) of the Russian Federation. 'Strategy is Aggressive: Results of Official Operations Activity of Internal Affairs Agencies and Military Service Activity of Internal Troops in 1997', MVD Report. Published in abbreviated form in *Moskovskaya Pravda* (in Russian). Moscow, 18 March 1998.

Norsk Utenrikspolitisk Institutt (NUPI). 'Chronology of Events', 2 November 2002 (online).

Paoli, Leticia. 'Illegal Drug Trade in Russia: Final Report'. Freiburg, Max Planck Institute, October 2000.

Rawlinson, Patricia. 'Russian Organized Crime: A Brief History', in *Transnational Organized Crime*. Vol. 2, Nos 2 and 3, 1996.

Robinson, Jeffrey. *The Merger*. London, Simon and Schuster, 1999.

Shelley, Louise. 'Transnational Organized Crime: An Imminent Threat to the Nation-State?' in *Journal of International Affairs*. Vol. 48, No. 1 (Jan.), 1995.

Simis, Konstantin. *USSR: The Corrupt Society*. New York, NY, Simon and Schuster, 1982.

Turbiville, Graham. 'Organized Crime and the Russian Armed Forces', in *Transnational Organized Crime*. Vol. 1, No. 4 (Winter), 1995.

US Department of State. *International Narcotics Control Strategy Report (INCSR)*. Washington, DC, US Department of State, 2002 and 2003.

# ENVIRONMENTAL DEGRADATION: PAST ROOTS, PRESENT TRANSITION AND FUTURE HOPES

## Dr ALEG CHERP and Dr RUBEN MNATSAKANIAN

### INTRODUCTION

The reforms of the Soviet political and economic systems initiated in the late 1980s and early 1990s were closely associated with environmental concerns. Support for these reforms was prompted by popular dissatisfaction with the environmental performance of the socialist economy. Politicians widely used environmental issues to challenge the existing political order and demand independence for the newly emerging nations. The old system, which was felt to be ineffective and disregardful of public opinion, was considered to be the main cause of the widespread environmental degradation. Naturally, there were abundant hopes that the reforms would deliver environmental improvements almost immediately.

As with many other expectations, this one was not fulfilled. After more than a decade of reform, reports of environmental disasters abound and positive news is rare. In order to explain why it has proved increasingly difficult to tackle environmental problems in post-Soviet countries, this essay first examines some of the root causes of these problems, before evaluating the extent to which recent developments have been able to reverse them.

This article argues that interaction between people and the environment in northern Eurasia has always been of a specific character, distorted, but not radically altered by socialism. The post-socialist transition provided many opportunities for environmental improvement, but also posed grave threats to the environment. Although the existing situation may not be as bleak as is often portrayed by the media, tremendous efforts will be required to ensure that environmental policies and management conform with international standards and protect the unique ecosystems of this part of the world.

The essay is divided into two principal parts: the first part deals with the historic roots of the existing environmental situation, in particular, the environmental legacy of the Soviet era. This legacy is especially important, since post-Soviet countries largely continue to operate institutions inherited from the USSR. The second section considers how the ongoing transition provides new opportunities and generates threats pertaining to the environment. Both sections have a similar structure of discussion. First, the context in which environmental problems unfolded is examined. Second, the ideas framing social attitudes towards the environment are discussed. Third, is an examination of the institutions that shaped the practices affecting the environment. Finally, there is an attempt to illustrate the environmental issues and problems that are the outcome of these conditions, ideas and institutions. The third and final section of the essay provides a summary and a conclusion, by pointing to key trends in the environmental situation and institutions of the newly independent states.

### ENVIRONMENTAL LEGACY

The countries of the former USSR are located in northern Eurasia, which, with its harsh climate and natural conditions, has historically determined specific patterns of human settle-ment and activity. Vast swathes of land were unable to sustain a considerable human population and remained untouched well into the 20th century, and even beyond. Many of these tracts are home to fragile, unique ecosystems, for example, permafrost taiga (boreal forest—marshy, predominantly pine forest) and tundra (plains), Lake Baikal in the Russian Far East, and the steppe (dry grasslands). In large areas, such as the steppe of Central Asia, or tundra, only nomadic pastoral agriculture was possible, which did not encourage the creation of stable human settlements. In other territories, such as European Russia, Belarus and Ukraine, agriculture was high risk, owing to the harsh winter climate and the short and unstable summer. Many of the abundant mineral resources of the region could not be used until modern times, because they required industrial means to extract and transport them to population and production centres. The virtual absence of natural barriers, such as seas or mountains, facilitated interaction between nomadic and settled cultures, but, at the same time, increased insecurity, by adding to the constant risk of invasion or war.

Until the early 20th century much productive land was found either in large estates or in communal village property, the latter ensuring the survival of families in areas where there was a high risk of crop failure. The institution of private land ownership did not extend beyond a very narrow circle of noble landowners in European Russia, and was even less developed in the more traditional societies of Siberia and Central Asia. At the same time, most mineral resources were controlled and exploited by the state. Thus, for the majority of the population, the idea of owning private property on agricultural or forested land was neither familiar nor particularly attractive. This attitude was reinforced by a strong dependence on foraging (for mushrooms, berries, fish, game, firewood, construction timber, and even iron—which until the end of the 18th century was predominantly extracted from peat bogs abundant in boreal forests) and on the freely accessible forests and rivers for day-to-day food requirements.

Surrounded by vast territories of uncultivated land, people often perceived these as being of marginal value, representing 'wild nature', which had to be 'conquered' or 'tamed'. The state further encouraged this 'frontier mentality' by promoting expansion into new areas, through the settlement of Siberia from the 16th century; the conquest of Central Asia and Caucasus in the 19th century; Prime Minister Pyotr Stolypin's (1862–1911) agrarian reforms in the 1900s, which encouraged the rural population to migrate from Central European Russia to Siberia and Central Asia; the ploughing of Kazakhstan's 'Virgin Lands' in the 1950s; the drainage of wetlands in the Polesie region of Belarus in 1966–90; and vast irrigation projects to facilitate cotton production in Central Asia in the 1960s and 1970s.

The social structure that emerged under these geographical and cultural conditions was a multinational, centralized empire, largely isolated from the rest of the world, undertaking continuous outward expansion in the perpetual quest for border security, suspicious of social innovation, and frequently attempting to implement forced modernization in order to maintain military and economic competitiveness with more developed countries. The Romanov Empire has been identified as 'the first developing country' (Shanin, 1985), in which changes that occurred gradually and organically in the West were aggressively introduced to the less-developed society by its ruling élite.

Shortly after the 1917 Revolution, Lenin's (Vladimir I. Ulyanov) Bolshevik Government became preoccupied with modernization and industrialization, with the aim of ending the economic underdevelopment of Russia. The notorious way in which the environment was treated during this period can be partially explained by the Bolsheviks' interpretation of Marxism, emphasizing the so-called labour theory of value. According to this theory, undeveloped land was valueless, and this approach almost entirely excluded environmental services, and even natural resources, from the Soviet Government's economic analyses and planning. As a result, natural resources were exploited and ecosystems destroyed, with little or no consideration of their economic worth, let alone their aesthetic and other values.

The industrialization of the USSR was led by the highly centralized state bureaucracy and primarily reflected the interests of this bureaucracy, with little regard for local concerns. For example, in the 1960s, during the assessment of the ambitious plans to develop enormous irrigation schemes in Central Asia in order to facilitate cotton production, it was noted that the Aral Sea (covering Kazakh and Uzbek territory) was likely to become dessicated. Although this enormous inland water body provided fish and other means of subsistence to large coastal communities, on a national scale cotton was deemed to be more important than fish (which could be obtained elsewhere). Therefore, it was decided to proceed with the irrigation plans, compensating local communities by shipping fish from the Arctic and the Far East for processing. The end result was one of the largest man-made environmental disasters of the 20th century, which inflicted tremendous suffering on former coastal inhabitants. Furthermore, the overall objectives of modernization were ideologically justified and, thus, often not subject to pragmatic analysis.

The inability of the state to halt environmental deterioration was further determined by its traditional suspicion of foreign, capitalist ideas. In particular, the communist ideology held that planned economies were inherently more environmentally friendly than capitalist ones, because they were not driven by the profit motive and were, therefore, able to ensure development that served economic, social and environmental objectives. Environmental pollution was often considered to be purely a 'capitalist' problem, which was simply not possible in a well-functioning socialist society. This resulted in an unwillingness to learn from the experience of Western countries, and justified only marginal participation by the USSR in international environmental agreements.

At the same time, certain unique streams of thought directed some environmental efforts in Soviet Russia. The Bolsheviks, with their 'scientific' approach to social development, sought to recruit scientists to various government bodies. One of these scientists, Vladimir Vernadskii, led a government committee, the task of which was to identify natural and other resources that could facilitate economic development. In the 1920s and 1930s Vernadskii developed the theory of the 'noosphere', based on the idea that humankind was becoming a 'geological force', transforming the Earth into a system in which natural and man-made factors would become equally important. A number of other scientists argued for the protection of certain ecosystems and landscapes for recreational, economic and scientific purposes. As a result, the USSR pioneered a unique network of nature protection reserves or *zapovedniks*. These were strictly protected

territories, with largely undisturbed natural ecosystems, useful in assessing long-term changes to the environment.

However, the overall record of the USSR in creating viable environmental-protection institutions was very poor. At the heart of the problem was the sector-based organization of the centrally planned economy, and the lack of checks and balances in the central government. The Soviet economy was managed by about 50 specialized ministries, each of which held an absolute monopoly within a particular branch of industry or agriculture. Any enterprise directly reporting to one of these ministries in the Russian and Soviet capital, Moscow, had little or no incentive to co-operate with local government or to consider local needs, including those relating to the environment. Co-operation between ministries, especially at the local level, was virtually non-existent, with all conflicts being referred to the central authorities in Moscow.

Another important factor was the very high degree of militarization of the Soviet economy (Smith and Moomaw—see Bibliography). In the military-industrial sector, production objectives had to be achieved without regard for the environmental, health or even economic consequences. Disregard for the environment and human health was reinforced by a system in which a significant proportion of the economy was operated by forced labour, through the infamous Gulag system of the 1930s, 1940s and 1950s.

The Government tended to consider the environment as yet another industrial sector, and manage it through specialized authorities (for example, the Committee for Water Works, the Main Hunting Authority, the Ministry of Fisheries, the Committee for Meteorology—also responsible for air and water quality—etc.). The widely accepted myth that socialism was incompatible with environmental problems explains the absence of an over-arching Ministry of the Environment, which would at least have united these diverse functions. However, although such agencies were able to achieve certain results within their own 'sectors' (for example, by ensuring the protection of game or fish from poaching), they had no mandate to influence other ministries and sectors, from which the most significant environmental impact originated.

The problem was exacerbated by the lack of accountability in the central government, where the Central Committee of the Communist Party was simultaneously responsible for all functions of society: industrial production, housing, health care, defence, education, the environment, etc. Whenever any conflict of interest arose between the environment and development, the non-transparent, informal policy process would almost always result in economic interests prevailing, except in such plainly catastrophic situations as the accident at the Chornobyl (Chernobyl) nuclear reactor in Ukraine in April 1986. The lack of democratic and participatory decision-making procedures, the disregard for public opinion and the reliance on Moscow-based experts to evaluate problems added to the anti-environmental bias of most economic decisions.

Another environmentally important institutional factor was the fact that innovation and the modernization of production facilities became progressively difficult to implement under the centrally planned economy. It was easier for the state to operate large, stable enterprises, with constant levels of inputs and outputs. For example, in the Urals, until the mid-1990s several factories were still working with equipment received in reparations from Germany after the Second World War (1939–45). Thus, the introduction of any progressive, environmentally clean technologies or management practices was extremely rare in the USSR.

At the same time, it would be inaccurate to state that the environment was entirely disregarded in industrial and agricultural activities. The Soviet system attempted to deal with it by imposing planning and design rules, and co-ordination procedures, by means of which new developments were required to satisfy minimum environmental and public-health criteria. A well-known element of these requirements was the adoption of so-called emission limit values (ELVs), determined for each enterprise, and based on the maximum permissible concentrations (MPCs) calculated for hundreds of individual chemical substances, with the aim of preventing harm to natural systems or human health. In practice, many MPCs and ELVs were exceeded, because there was no technical, economic or political means to enforce them. This system of regulating industrial pollution continues in post-Soviet countries, often utilizing the same MPCs.

Thus, the Soviet economy created a well-publicized pattern of environmental degradation, caused by a large number of negative factors, including the economic bias of central planners, the rapid and intense industrialization of designated areas, the highly inefficient use of energy and natural resources, and an almost complete disregard for public environmental concerns. 'The USSR generated waste on the scale of a highly industrialized country, but dealt with it in a fashion appropriate for a Third World nation' (Peterson, 1993). However, both positive and negative features of the Soviet environmental legacy can be identified.

The first feature, noted by many researchers, is the unique spatial pattern of environmental conditions. In some 'hot spots', or ecological disaster zones, usually found around large industrial centres or sites of environmental accidents and emergencies, environmental degradation was quite unprecedented. High levels of water and air pollution were combined with the destruction of the landscape and ecosystems, and a deterioration in the local economy and in health. Notorious examples of environmental disaster zones include the Aral Sea area; the areas surrounding the former Semipalatinsk nuclear test site in northern Kazakhstan; the areas around Norilsk in northern Siberia (Russia); industrial zones in the Kola Peninsula and the South Urals (Russia); the Donbass region of south-eastern Ukraine; the Sarasiya valley in Uzbekistan, adjacent to the Tajik Aluminium Plant; etc. (Mnatsakanian, 1992).

At the same time, post-Soviet countries feature large areas where ecosystems are relatively intact. In some regions, biodiversity was better protected than in the West, owing to lower population densities and restrictions in some areas on personal movement. The approach to biodiversity protection in the USSR benefited from the fact that the country retained sufficiently vast, and relatively untouched, ecosystems. Large areas of natural ecosystems were set aside as nature reserves, and this concept later engendered the international biosphere reserve programme, administered by the United Nations Educational, Scientific and Cultural Organization (UNESCO). The biodiversity protection areas of post-Soviet countries include the unique wetlands of Belarus; beech and pine forests and alpine meadows in the northern Caucasus; vast areas of primary forest in northern and central Russia; untouched steppe at Askania-Nova in Ukraine; the Volga river delta in the Caspian Sea; the Lena river delta in northern Siberia; and Lake Baikal, the world's largest freshwater body (Pryde, 1995). There are also significant areas of relatively unspoiled countryside and traditional land-use patterns.

The most notorious feature of the Soviet environmental legacy was the oversized heavy, especially military, industry, which resulted in tremendous environmental pressures, associated both with the nature of the production processes and their traditional secrecy. Another widely publicized environmental issue was the wastefulness of the socialist production processes, which resulted in one of the highest levels of energy intensity in the world. The centrally planned economy provided little or no incentive to conserve energy or raw materials or to minimize waste.

Although the USSR had established relatively strong public-health agencies (the so-called Sanitary-Epidemiological Service), which had largely managed to cope with the environmental and public-health issues typical of low-income societies, post-Soviet countries continue to encounter a distinctive mixture of issues, combining characteristics of both developed and developing countries. For example, some regions in Europe and the Urals are struggling with methods for the disposal of radioactive waste, chemical weapons and extremely toxic missile fuel, whereas in many areas of Central Asia the predominant problem is that of providing a basic rural water supply and sanitation. Such a combination resulted from the country's rapid and uneven modernization in the 20th century.

A number of urban environmental issues were caused by the specific pattern of urbanization in this part of the world. Unlike the situation in Western Europe, cities in Russia were almost never self-governed centres of trade, crafts and entrepreneurship, but, instead, performed the role of military outposts and factory towns. The rapid industrialization of the first half of the 20th century only strengthened this pattern. Soviet towns were typically provided with reasonable infrastructure and were free from slums. At the same time, the rapidly constructed cities provided bleak urban landscapes, dominated by concrete high-rise buildings and the almost universal pollution-emitting smokestacks of industrial facilities.

On the positive side, levels of consumer waste and motor-vehicle congestion were lower in the USSR than in most developed countries. Priority was given to the development of public means of transportation, and private car-ownership was regarded as a luxury, rather than the norm. Public-transportation networks, as well as systems for collecting, recycling and reusing consumer waste, were relatively well developed.

In summary, socialism left a mixed environmental legacy, unequally distributed between the regions and successor states of the USSR. The roots of the most prominent environmental issues can be traced far back to the history of the Soviet state and beyond, and linked to specific interaction between the environment and society in the 'first developing country', stretching across the tundra, forests, steppe and deserts of northern Eurasia.

## ENVIRONMENT IN TRANSITION

At the beginning of the reform process, popular opinion was sensitized to environmental problems, and closely associated these with the economic and political failures of socialism. Such high-profile events as the Chornobyl disaster catalyzed popular belief in the inability of the socialist system to ensure environmental safety. Observing the relatively cleaner environment in the West led the majority to assume that free-market and democratic reforms would deliver environmental improvements almost automatically.

In the early reform period, popular and political support for environmental causes was at an unprecedentedly high level. Many environmental activists or individuals with 'green' programmes were elected to the region's first democratic parliaments. Ministries of the Environment were created in all of the Soviet successor states. Environmental clauses were included in newly written constitutions, and framework laws on the environment were enacted. A large number of environmental non-governmental organizations (NGOs) commenced operations, especially in metropolitan areas. These included both rejuvenated nature protection groups (for example, the Socio-Ecological Union, the most powerful over-arching organization among the post-Soviet environmental NGOs), newly created domestic organizations and branches of international associations, such as Greenpeace and the World Wildlife Fund (WWF).

Many of the newly independent states participated in the Earth Summit, held in Rio de Janeiro, Brazil, in 1992, and enthusiastically participated in the international environmental agreements developed during the 1990s. In particular, the newly independent states took part in the UN Economic Commission for Europe's (ECE) Environment for Europe programme. As part of the framework for this process, the state of the environment in the region was properly assessed, and National Environmental Action Plans (NEAPs) drawn up. Although NEAPs rarely received adequate financial support or political commitment, they were important measures in the identification, evaluation and prioritization of key environmental tasks.

However, it soon became clear that legitimization of the environmental discourse and popular enthusiasm for environmental protection were, in themselves, insufficient to create viable institutions able to tackle the old systemic causes of environmental degradation, as well as newly emerging threats. Many of the newly independent states were either politically unstable or found it very difficult to establish viable national institutions when confronted with political and economic challenges. The environment had soon almost disappeared from political agendas, and the number of environmental NGOs declined.

Environmental-protection agencies and laws created in the 1990s secured some degree of environmental monitoring of economic activities, the basics of the 'polluter pays principle', as well as certain elements of public participation and access to environmental information. However, on the whole, they proved to be only marginally effective. In particular, the environmental agencies were underfunded, and often lacked both expertise and human capacity. Most laws attempted to achieve Western results by Soviet means, and were declaratory, non-specific or unenforceable. In many of the USSR's successor states environmental regulations was based on Soviet concepts, approaches, rules and standards (as outlined in the previous section) throughout the 1990s. In other words, they failed to challenge the systemic causes of environmental degradation associated with the lack of integration of environmental concerns into economic decision-making. Environmental-protection institutions were further weakened by the corruption characteristic of the post-Soviet states. As a result, by 2002 the Environmental Sustainability Index (ESI), designed by the World Economic Forum, ranked the Commonwealth of Independent States (CIS) countries much lower than the countries of Central and South-Eastern Europe, in terms of their institutional capacity to ensure environmental sustainability (World Economic Forum et al., 2002). A significant reverse for environmental institution-building was the disbandment of the Russian Ministry of the Environment in 2000, when all environmental responsibilities were transferred to the Ministry for Natural Resources. This measure was interpreted by many as undermining the fundamental principle of separation of control and management of environmental resources.

Nevertheless, some of the negative trends of environmental degradation were reversed from the early 1990s. The most remarkable development was the rapid reduction in levels of air and water pollution in many areas, associated with the abrupt decline in industrial output. In most cases this was a result of economic contraction, rather than the increasing effectiveness of environmental-protection measures. Thus, this positive trend may be reversed if production levels recover.

In the early 1990s it was widely believed that economic reform in the region would promote more efficient use of energy and resources, thereby reducing environmental problems. Indeed, in those sectors that were economically profitable and managed to attract foreign investment such resource gains did occur, and the environmental impact per unit of production decreased. Unfortunately, this trend was counterbalanced by the shift to more resource- and pollution-intensive branches of industry (such as electricity production and ferrous and non-ferrous metallurgy). As a result of free-market reforms, combined with globalization, many of the manufacturing industries subsidized by the Government in the past proved to be less competitive than typically more-polluting branches, associated with the extraction of raw materials.

Threats to other aspects of the environment in the CIS also emerged. Many of them concerned biodiversity, which, during Soviet times, was protected through the well-developed network of nature reserves. For example, historically, the unique biodiversity of the Kamchatka Peninsula, in the easternmost part of Russia, was preserved by an extensive system of protected areas, and by its remoteness, its rugged landscape and restrictions associated with the strategic military importance of the area. According to the UN Development Programme (UNDP) and the Global Environment Facility (GEF), from independence significant threats to biodiversity emerged as the accessibility of the area increased and the budgets of the protected areas were dramatically reduced (UNDP and GEF, 2000). A further threat to biodiversity has been the poaching of rare and endangered species on an unprecedented scale. In the early 2000s poaching in the Caspian Sea region led to curbs on the caviar trade, under the Convention on International Trade in Endangered Species of Wild Flora and Fauna. Post-independence, many nature reserves also suffered from military conflict in the proximity of biodiversity-rich areas (for example in the northern Caucasus, or Tigrovaya balka in Tajikistan). At the same time, there was a gradual return to wilderness in some areas, associated with the decline in agriculture and the abandonment of rural areas, and the withdrawal from military bases and other remote outposts that the state was no longer able to maintain.

The effect of the transition on urban environmental problems has been uneven. Most cities benefited from the decline in pollution associated with falling industrial production, and some metropolitan centres experienced rapid expansion of the property market and the rejuvenation of historic centres and infrastructure. At the same time, the growth in private motor-vehicle ownership threatens to reverse gains in air quality, and in many places crumbling infrastructure poses serious challenges to the health and well-being of urban dwellers.

The population of the ecological disaster zones has probably fared worst as a result of reform. The CIS countries have generally been unable to fund large-scale environmental remediation or local development in areas affected by the Chornobyl disaster, the nuclear testing at Semipalatinsk, the dessication of the Aral Sea and other examples of the Soviet environmental legacy. The population of such areas has entered a downward spiral of poverty, collapsing social structures, poor health and environmental degradation, from which it can only be rescued by means of concerted national and international efforts (UN, 2002).

## CONCLUSIONS: ENVIRONMENTAL OPPORTUNITIES AND THREATS OF TRANSITION

This essay has attempted to provide an overview of environmental degradation in the CIS that is somewhat broader than the conventional picture presented by media reports. The first conclusion is that although socialism was responsible for many of the existing environmental problems in the region, its environmental legacy has not been entirely negative, and it was not the sole cause of the widespread 'frontier mentality', suspicion of private ownership of land and low value placed on untouched areas of environment by society.

The recent political and economic changes in the CIS have not, thus far, significantly altered these systemic causes of environmental problems, although some progress has been made in increasing public participation, international co-operation, and the integration of environmental concerns into development decision-making. The process of transition presents significant opportunities for reversing environmental degradation, including administrative reforms and decentralization, social mobilization and democracy, and reduced subsidies to military and other heavy industries. Perhaps most significantly, the CIS countries are more prepared to accept international assistance, to learn from the experience of developed and developing countries and to adhere to international environmental agreements. Many of these states, particularly Moldova, Russia and Ukraine, are seeking to align their environmental legislation with that of the European Union (EU).

However, environmental threats associated with transition include the reduced time-scales of decision-makers, who are shifting their focus to the resolution of immediate economic and social problems, rather than longer-term environmental issues; globalization, which is threatening traditional lifestyles and encouraging the growth of resource- and pollution-intensive industries, a dependence on external markets, and a drive to overexploit natural resources; as well as political and social instability, and the marginalization of certain regions and groups.

As mentioned above, the changes to the overall environmental situation since independence have been mixed. While air and water pollution have tended to decline, pressures on undeveloped, biodiversity-rich regions have, in many instances, increased. Collapsing urban infrastructure and the rapid growth in private motor-vehicle ownership may undo the positive changes in urban air quality in the near future. Moreover, there is generally insufficient human and financial capacity to clean up environmental disaster zones and support the sustainable development of communities living there.

The ESI uses 20 main indicators to evaluate the progress made towards achieving environmental sustainability in 142 countries, and thus provide an international overview of environmental sustainability (World Economic Forum et al). Although the overall ESI was below median for all but four countries in the CIS in 2002, the CIS countries did fare relatively well in terms of 'environmental systems' and 'reducing environmental stresses', with the worst performances relating to the categories of 'social and institutional capacity' and 'global stewardship'. This indicates that, despite the widely reported problems, the environment remains a very significant and unique resource in the CIS. Untouched areas and unspoiled countryside have recreational, cultural, scientific and economic values, which can potentially be used to increase quality of life in the future.

Environmental institutions in the CIS also show signs of strengthening. If in the mid-1990s many environmental agencies were unwieldy, inefficient and excessively bureaucratic, by the early 2000s they were gradually reforming to conform to international standards and serve sustainable development. Although popular interest has focused on environmental issues of immediate concern, such as environmental health, the interest in wider and global causes has also increased. Traditional connections with the environment, in the form of dependence on forests and rivers for food and other basic needs, are being revived and can be used within the newly established institutions of public participation to ensure wider support and responsibility for environmental protection in the countryside and small towns.

In summary, in many countries and regions there are signs that the opportunities offered by the transition and by the positive legacies of the past can be wisely employed, and new threats can be avoided, in order to reverse the pattern of environmental degradation that developed throughout much of the 20th century.

## BIBLIOGRAPHY

Cherp, A., Mnatsakanian, R., and Kopteva, I. 'Economic Transition and Environmental Sustainability: Effects of Economic Restructuring on Air Pollution in the Russian Federation', in *Journal of Environmental Management*. Vol. 68, 2003.

Mnatsakanian, R. *Environmental Legacy of the Former Soviet Republics*. Edinburgh, Centre for Human Ecology, 1992.

Peterson, D. J. *Troubled Lands: The Legacy of Soviet Environmental Destruction*. Boulder, CO, Westview Press, 1993.

Pryde, P. (Ed.). *Environmental Resources and Problems in the Former Soviet Union*. Boulder, CO, Westview Press, 1995.

Shanin, T. *Russia as a 'Developing Society'*. Basingstoke, Macmillan, 1985.

Smith, W. D., and Moomaw, W. R. 'Making Peace with the Environment: Addressing the Military-Industrial Legacy in the Post-Soviet Era', in *Eastern Europe, Russia and Central Asia*. London, Europa Publications, 2000.

United Nations. *The Human Consequences of the Chernobyl Nuclear Accident. A Strategy for Recovery*. Minsk/Kiev/Moscow/New York, NY, UN, 2002.

United Nations Development Programme and Global Environmental Facility. *Demonstrating Sustainable Conservation of Biological Diversity in Four Protected Areas in Russia's Kamchatka Oblast* (Project Report). Moscow, UNDP, 2000.

World Economic Forum, Global Leaders of Tomorrow Environment Task Force and Yale Center for Environmental Law and Policy. *Environmental Sustainability Index* (Main Report). New Haven, CT, Yale Center for Environmental Law and Policy, 2002.

# PART TWO

# Country Surveys

# ARMENIA

## Geography

### PHYSICAL FEATURES

The Republic of Armenia (formerly the Armenian Soviet Socialist Republic, part of the USSR) is situated in south-west Transcaucasia, on the north-eastern border of Turkey. Its other borders are with Iran to the south, Azerbaijan to the east and Georgia to the north. The Nakhichevan Autonomous Republic, an Azerbaijani territory, is an enclave bordering Armenia, Iran and Turkey. The Republic of Armenia, which covers 29,800 sq km (11,508 sq miles), is the remnant of a much larger area of Armenian settlement that existed before the First World War and included many areas of eastern Turkey and other regions of the Caucasus. Nagornyi Karabakh (known to Armenians as Artsakh), is an autonomous oblast within Azerbaijan, mainly populated by Armenians. In 1989 conflict over the status of the enclave began, and from mid-1993 ethnic Armenian militia controlled not only Nagornyi Karabakh itself, but also areas of Azerbaijani territory around the disputed enclave.

The central physical feature of Armenia is Lake Sevan, a mountainous lake at an altitude of 1,924 m (6,313 ft), which is surrounded by high mountain ranges, reaching 4,090 m (13,419 ft) at Mt Aragats. The mountains are drained by numerous streams and rivers flowing into the River Araks (Aras), which empties into the Caspian Sea. The Araks marks the south-western border of the country and its basin forms a fertile lowland to the south of Yerevan called the Ararat plain.

### CLIMATE

The climate is typically continental: dry, with large variations in temperature. Winters are cold, the average January temperature in Yerevan being -3°C (26°F), but summers can be very warm, with August temperatures averaging 25°C (77°F), although high altitude moderates the heat in much of the country. Precipitation is low in the Yerevan area (annual average, 322 mm), but much higher in the mountains.

### POPULATION

At the 1989 census, 93.3% of the total *de facto* population of 3,287,677 were ethnic Armenians, 1.7% Kurds and 1.5% Russians. Other ethnic groups included Ukrainians (8,341), Assyrians (5,963), Greeks (4,650) and Georgians (1,364). As a result of inter-ethnic tension, almost the entire Azeri population (in 1989, 2.6% of the total) was reported to have left Armenia after the census was conducted, and Armenian refugees entered Armenia from Azerbaijan. There are many Armenians in neighbouring states, notably in Georgia and in Azerbaijan, although numbers in the latter decreased considerably after the inter-ethnic conflict of the late 1980s and early 1990s. There are also important Armenian communities abroad, particularly in the USA and France.

The official language is Armenian, the sole member of a distinct Indo-European language group. It is written in the Armenian script. Much of the population speak Russian as a second language, and Kurdish is used in some broadcasting and publishing. Most of the population are adherents of Christianity, the largest denomination being the Armenian Apostolic Church. There are also Russian Orthodox, Protestant, Islamic and Yazidi communities.

The total population at the census of 10 October 2001 was 3,210,606, according to provisional results. (However, this figure failed to take account of the migration of many Armenians in search of work abroad.) The capital is Yerevan, which had an estimated population of 1,246,100 at 1 January 2001. Other important towns include Gyumri (formerly Leninakan), with 210,100 inhabitants, and Vanadzor (formerly Kirovakan), with 170,800 inhabitants. In 1999 70% of the country's population lived in urban areas. Population density was 116.3 inhabitants per sq km at 10 October 2001, according to the provisional census results.

# Chronology

**c. 850 BC:** Indo-European tribes, Chaldeans, occupied territory to the south of the Caucasus, destroying the ancient kingdom of Urartu (Ararat); these two peoples were the ancestors of the Armenians.

**64:** The Roman Empire secured its pre-eminence in the region with the final defeat of the Kingdom of Pontus, to which the Armenians had been allied; parts of Armenia eventually became a Roman province.

**AD 117:** The Emperor Hadrian retracted the borders of the Roman Empire back to the River Euphrates (that is, still including what was known as Lesser Armenia), despite his predecessor Trajan's conquest of much territory to the east (Greater Armenia).

**c. 300:** St Gregory the Illuminator began the conversion of Armenia, which became the first Christian state at a time of renewed struggle for dominance in the region, between the Empires of Rome and Persia (Iran).

**451:** The Fourth Council of Chalcedon condemned Monophysitism, isolating the Armenians from the rest of the Christian Church.

**639:** The first Arab raids on Armenia marked the beginning of Muslim influence in the area.

**1071:** The Seljuq Turk victory at the Battle of Manzikert (now Malazgirt, Turkey) confirmed the Eastern Roman ('Byzantine') expulsion from Armenia and its environs and the dominance of the Sultanate of Iconium (Konya) or Rum.

**1375:** Mamelukes of Egypt conquered the Armenian capital of Sis and ended the country's nominal independence.

**1639:** After many years of dispute, Armenia was partitioned between the Turkish Ottoman Empire (which secured the larger, western part) and the Persian Empire, by the Treaty of Zuhab.

**1828:** Persia ceded Eastern Armenia to the Russian Empire by the Treaty of Turkmanchai.

**1878:** Russia gained the province of Kars from the Ottomans by the Congress of Berlin.

**1915:** The Ottoman massacres and persecution of Armenians, increasing since the 1890s, were at their most severe, rapidly depopulating Anatolian Armenia.

**22 April 1918:** Proclamation of a Transcaucasian federation (Armenia, Azerbaijan and Georgia), following the collapse of tsarist rule and the Soviet signing of the Treaty of Brest-Litovsk.

**28 May 1918:** Turkish menaces caused the collapse of Transcaucasia and the proclamation of an independent Armenia, which was governed by the Armenian Revolutionary Federation (ARF—Dashnaktsutiun, also known as Dashnaks); Armenia was forced to cede territory around Kars to the Turks.

**10 August 1920:** The Treaty of Sèvres, between the Allied Powers and the Ottoman authorities, recognized an independent Armenia, but the Treaty was rejected by the new Turkish leader, Mustafa Kemal (Atatürk).

**September 1920:** Turkish troops invaded Armenia after the ARF Government intervened in Anatolia, concerned at the savage persecution of ethnic Armenians there.

**29 November 1920:** Proclamation of the Soviet Republic of Armenia, following the invasion of Bolshevik troops.

**1921:** A series of treaties led to the establishment of Nagornyi Karabakh (Artsakh) as a mainly ethnic Armenian enclave within, and part of, Azerbaijan; Turkey recognized its borders with Soviet Transcaucasia.

**December 1922:** Armenia became a member of the Transcaucasian Soviet Federative Socialist Republic (TSFSR), which itself joined the Union of Soviet Socialist Republics (USSR).

**December 1936:** The new Soviet Constitution dissolved the TSFSR and Armenia became a full Union Republic in its own name.

**September 1987:** As a result of the policies of *glasnost* (openness) of the new leader of the USSR, Mikhail Gorbachev, Soviet Armenia experienced its first public demonstrations against ecological degradation and corruption in the local Communist Party of Armenia (CPA).

**February 1988:** The Nagornyi Karabakh Soviet passed a resolution demanding a transfer to Armenian jurisdiction. Armenians, led by a group of Yerevan intellectuals known as the Karabakh Committee, demonstrated in support. The demands led to anti-Armenian violence in Sumgait, Azerbaijan.

**December 1988:** Northern Armenia, particularly the city of Leninakan (now Gyumri), was devastated by an earthquake.

**1 December 1989:** The Armenian Supreme Soviet (republican legislature) declared Nagornyi Karabakh to be part of a unified Armenian Republic, following the end of direct rule in the enclave by the all-Union Government (since January) and the restoration of Azerbaijani authority.

**January 1990:** The all-Union Supreme Soviet declared that Armenia's December declaration was unconstitutional, whereupon the Armenian Supreme Soviet resolved that it had the power to veto central legislation.

**May 1990:** In the elections to the Armenian Supreme Soviet, the Armenian Pan-National Movement (APNM), the successor to the opposition Karabakh Committee, became the largest single party, obtaining some 35% of the votes cast; the APNM leader, Levon Ter-Petrossian, was elected Chairman of the Supreme Soviet (republican Head of State).

**23 August 1990:** The Armenian SSR declared its sovereignty and changed its name to the Republic of Armenia.

**March 1991:** Armenia refused to participate in the referendum on the Union, having declined to join negotiations since late 1990.

**August 1991:** Vazgen Manukian resigned as premier, being replaced by Khosrov Haroutunian.

**21 September 1991:** Armenia held a referendum on secession from the USSR; the new Soviet law on secession, involving a five-year transitional period, was expected to govern the process.

**23 September 1991:** The results of the referendum (94.4% of the electorate participated and, of them, 99.3% voted in favour of secession) prompted the republican Supreme Soviet (Supreme Council) immediately to declare Armenia an independent state.

**16 October 1991:** Ter-Petrossian remained Head of State after national elections for the post of President of the Republic.

**21 December 1991:** Armenia signed the Almaty Declaration, by which it became a member of the Commonwealth of Independent States (CIS), the formation of which effectively dissolved the USSR.

**February 1992:** Armenia was admitted to the Conference on Security and Co-operation in Europe (CSCE or, from December 1994, the Organization for Security and Co-operation in Europe—OSCE).

**March 1992:** Armenia became a member of the UN.

**May 1992:** Following months of full-scale conflict, Armenia and Azerbaijan negotiated a short-lived cease-fire, although Armenia claimed to have no control over the Nagornyi Karabakh militia, which had secured the whole enclave and a 'corridor' to Armenia.

**December 1992:** President Ter-Petrossian declared a national emergency in Armenia.

**February 1993:** Following the resignation of Khosrov Haroutunian, Hrant Bagratian was appointed as Prime Minister.

**30 April 1993:** The UN Security Council, under Resolution 822, demanded that all Armenian forces immediately withdraw from Azerbaijani territory and that a cease-fire be observed. Further motions were adopted on 29 July (Resolution 853) and 14 October (Resolution 874).

**24 May 1993:** The Armenian Government agreed to a CSCE-negotiated peace plan for Nagornyi Karabakh. Azerbaijan also signed the plan, but it was not accepted by the Nagornyi Karabakh leadership until June.

**August 1993:** Armenia, Russia and four other member states of the CIS signed a resolution on military co-operation, reinforcing the Collective Security Treaty signed in Tashkent, Uzbekistan, in May 1992.

**22 November 1993:** An Armenian currency, the dram, was introduced, despite previous agreements to participate in a rouble zone.

**9–11 May 1994:** Following protracted mediation by the CSCE and Russia, a new cease-fire agreement was signed by the Ministers of Defence of Armenia and Azerbaijan, and representatives of Nagornyi Karabakh. The agreement was formalized on 27 July.

**October 1994:** Armenia joined the North Atlantic Treaty Organization's (NATO) 'Partnership for Peace' programme.

**19 June 1995:** The Medzamor nuclear power station, closed since 1989, following the earthquake, was reopened, owing to severe energy shortages.

**5 July 1995:** In legislative elections the Republican (Hanrapetutiun) bloc, a coalition led by the APNM, won 119 of the 190 seats in the legislature. At the same time, a referendum on the Constitution was held: some 68% of those voting approved amendments that gave wider executive power to the President and reduced the number of seats in the National Assembly to 131, effective from the next general election.

**24 July 1995:** Hrant Bagratian was confirmed as premier by the new parliament.

**22 September 1996:** Presidential elections were held, with Ter-Petrossian obtaining 51.8% of the votes cast. In November the Constitutional Court rejected opposition appeals that the election results be declared invalid.

**4 November 1996:** Bagratian resigned as Prime Minister, allegedly because of opposition to his programme of economic reforms; Armen Sarkissian was appointed in his place on the same day.

**6 March 1997:** Sarkissian resigned as Prime Minister, and was replaced by Robert Kocharian (hitherto the President of Nagornyi Karabakh) on 20 March.

**April 1997:** The National Assembly ratified a treaty allowing Russia to maintain military bases in Armenia for a period of 25 years. In August Armenia and Russia signed a Treaty of 'Friendship, Co-operation and Mutual Understanding', signifying continuing close relations.

**3 February 1998:** Ter-Petrossian resigned as President, following disputes within the Government over his support for an OSCE peace settlement for Nagornyi Karabakh, which entailed some withdrawal of Armenian forces. The Chairman of the National Assembly, Babken Ararktsian, resigned the following day.

**30 March 1998:** Robert Kocharian, who, as Prime Minister, had been acting President since Ter-Petrossian's resignation, was confirmed as President following a second round of voting in the presidential election, with 59.5% of the votes cast. Of the registered electorate, 68.1% voted; despite some electoral irregularities, the results were considered valid.

**10 April 1998:** Armen Darbinian was appointed Prime Minister. In the same month President Kocharian met President Aliyev in Moscow, Russia, and agreed to recommence negotiations over the issue of Nagornyi Karabakh.

**8 September 1998:** Darbinian attended a summit meeting in Baku, Azerbaijan, at which Armenia, together with 11 other nations of Central Asia, the Caucasus and the Black Sea region, signed an agreement to recreate the 'Silk Road' trade route to Europe. This was the first high-level, governmental meeting between Armenia and Azerbaijan for four years.

**5 February 1999:** A controversial new law on electoral procedure, which provided for a 131-member legislature composed of 80 deputies elected by majority vote through single-mandate constituencies, with the remainder chosen under a system of proportional representation, on the basis of party lists, was fully adopted.

**May 1999:** Vano Siradeghian, the Chairman of the APNM and a former Minister of the Interior, was arrested for his alleged participation in a number of political murders in the mid-1990s; although his trial commenced in January 2000, he subsequently fled the country in April.

**30 May 1999:** Legislative elections were held. The Unity bloc (Miasnutiun), an alliance of the Republican Party of Armenia (RPA) and the People's Party of Armenia (PPA), proved successful, winning a total of 55 seats in the National Assembly.

**11 June 1999:** Armen Darbinian was replaced as Prime Minister by Vazgen Sarkissian, the unofficial leader of the RPA and hitherto the Minister of Defence.

**27 October 1999:** Five gunmen besieged the National Assembly. Eight people were killed during the attack, including Prime Minister Sarkissian and Karen Demirchian, Chairman of the National Assembly since June. Some 50 hostages were held for several hours until their release was negotiated by Kocharian; the President then assumed control of the Government until a new Prime Minister could be assigned. The assailants were subsequently charged with terrorist offences and murder.

**2 November 1999:** The National Assembly held an extraordinary sitting at which Armen Khachatrian, a member of the PPA, was elected Chairman. On the following day, President Kocharian appointed Aram Sarkissian, the younger brother of the murdered premier, as the new Prime Minister.

**12 May 2000:** Andranik Markarian was appointed Prime Minister, replacing Sarkissian, who had been removed from his post on 2 May. A cabinet reshuffle subsequently took place.

**25 January 2001:** Both Armenia and Azerbaijan were formally admitted to the Council of Europe.

**15 February 2001:** The trial commenced of 13 men accused of involvement in the parliamentary assassinations of October 1999.

**9 July 2001:** Senior government officials reached an agreement with their Turkish counterparts providing for the establishment of a Turkish-Armenian Reconciliation Commission (TARC). The first meeting of the 10-member Commission was held in İstanbul, Turkey, in late September; disagreements led to the dissolution of the TARC in December, although it reconvened in July 2002.

**7 September 2001:** The PPA left the Unity bloc, and subsequently joined two opposition parties in demanding the resignation of President Kocharian.

**14–15 September 2001:** The Russian President, Vladimir Putin, visited Armenia, and signed a 10-year economic agreement, which included proposals to transfer a number of state-owned enterprises to Russian ownership, in partial repayment of debts to Russia amounting to over US $90m.

**5 April 2002:** Some 10,000 people attended an opposition-sponsored protest against the closure of the country's only independent television station, A1+, which opposition parties claimed to be politically motivated. Demands were made for President Kocharian's resignation at a further large-scale protest held one week later, and demonstrations continued throughout April.

**3 July 2002:** Amendments to the electoral law, adopted in advance of the legislative election scheduled to take place in May 2003, provided for the election of 56 deputies by majority vote through single-mandate constituencies, with the remaining 75 to be elected under a system of proportional representation, on the basis of party lists.

**26 September 2002:** The Parliamentary Assembly of the Council of Europe adopted a resolution demanding that Armenia unconditionally abolish capital punishment by June 2003, or risk expulsion from that organization.

**20 October 2002:** Local elections took place, as a result of which the RPA consolidated its political strength.

**28 December 2002:** The Chairman of the board of Armenian Public Television and Radio, Tighran Naghdalian, was assassinated. In March 2003 Armen Sarkissian, the brother of former Prime Minister Aram Sarkissian, was one of a number of people to be arrested in connection with the murder.

**5 February 2003:** Armenia became a full member of the World Trade Organization.

**19 February and 5 March 2003:** In the presidential election Robert Kocharian received 49.5% of the votes cast in the first round of voting, fewer than the 50% necessary to secure an outright victory. Therefore, Kocharian and the second-placed candidate, Stepan Demirchian (the son of the murdered parliamentary Chairman, Karen Demirchian, with 28.2%), progressed to a second round of voting. At the 'run-off' election, Kocharian was re-elected as President, with 67.5% of the votes cast. However, there was strong international criticism of electoral procedure, and widespread protest demonstrations took place throughout the country.

**28 April 2003:** Representatives from Armenia, Belarus, Kazakhstan, Kyrgyzstan, Russia and Tajikistan formally inaugurated the successor to the Collective Security Treaty, a new regional defence organization known as the Collective Security Treaty Organization (CSTO). The membership agreement was ratified by the National Assembly in September.

**25 May 2003:** Legislative elections were held, in which the RPA obtained the largest number of seats in the National Assembly, followed by the Law-Governed Country Party of Armenia. The OSCE and opposition parties subsequently reported a number of electoral violations. A referendum on proposed constitutional amendments was also held on 25 May; however, fewer than the requisite one-third of registered voters approved the proposals.

**11 June 2003:** The RPA, the Law-Governed Country Party of Armenia and the RPA signed an agreement on the formation of a new, coalition Government; RPA leader Andranik Markarian retained the premiership, and Artur Baghdasarian, the Chairman of the Law-Governed Country Party of Armenia, assumed the post of Chairman of the National Assembly. The new National Assembly was the first in 85 years not to include any communist representation. Members of the opposition Justice (Artarutiun) bloc and the National Unity Party boycotted the opening session of the National Assembly when it convened on 12 June, and maintained their protest until September.

**9 September 2003:** The National Assembly approved a ban on capital punishment, formally ratifying Protocol 6 of the Convention for the Protection of Human Rights and Fundamental Freedoms of the Council of Europe, and abolishing the clause in the country's Criminal Code that had allowed for the enforcement of capital punishment in exceptional circumstances.

# History

## Dr EDMUND HERZIG

### EARLY HISTORY

Armenia and the Armenians first emerge clearly in historical records of the first millennium BC. In *circa* AD 314 Armenia became the first state to adopt Christianity. About one century later it developed a distinct alphabet and literary language, and religion and language have remained central to Armenian national identity ever since. Apart from brief periods of independence, for most of its history Armenia formed a borderland and battleground between more powerful, neighbouring states based on the Iranian plateau, in Mesopotamia, in Anatolia or Constantinople (now İstanbul, Turkey) and, more recently, in Russia.

The Treaties of Amasya (1555) and Zuhab (1639) led to the partition of Armenia, with the larger, western part being allotted to the Turkish Ottoman Empire and the eastern region becoming part of the Persian (Iranian) Safavid Empire. This division resulted in the development of distinct eastern and western Armenian languages. In 1828 the Russian Empire gained Eastern (Persian) Armenia by the Treaty of Turkmanchai, and in 1878 the Congress of Berlin transferred much of Western (Ottoman) Armenia (Kars province) to Russian control.

Over the centuries successive invasions and deportations, as well as the dynamics of international trade, in which Armenian merchants played an active role, resulted in the growth of an Armenian diaspora throughout Eastern Europe, the Middle East, the major commercial centres of Europe and the Indian Ocean, and, ultimately, North America.

In the late 19th century competing claims engendered by emerging Turkish and Armenian nationalism, coupled with the decline and dismemberment of the Ottoman Empire, led to increased tension, antagonism and conflict. This culminated in the 'genocide' of 1915, when the Ottoman authorities, fearing possible Armenian support for a Russian invasion, systematically deported or killed almost the entire Armenian population of Anatolia. More than 1m. people were estimated to have been massacred. As a consequence, the diaspora communities of France, Lebanon, Syria and the USA expanded, and the memory of the genocide became a defining element in the Armenian identity.

Following the collapse of Russian imperial power in 1917, Eastern Armenia became part of the short-lived anti-Bolshevik Transcaucasian federation, which also included Azerbaijan and Georgia. Subsequently, on 28 May 1918, after the dissolution of the federation, Armenia became an independent republic. The Government, dominated by the Armenian Revolutionary Federation (ARF—Dashnaktsutiun), had to contend with the problems of famine, a continuing Ottoman war and ethno-territorial disputes with Georgia and, more seriously, with Azerbaijan. Hopes that the future of an independent Armenia would be guaranteed by the Treaty of Sèvres, signed by the Allied Powers and the Ottomans on 10 August 1920, were quickly destroyed by the Bolsheviks' friendship treaty with the new Turkish leader, Mustafa Kemal (Atatürk), who rejected the Treaty. This was rapidly followed by a Turkish invasion of Armenia in September. In November the ARF Government resigned, preferring incorporation into the Union of Soviet Socialist Republics (USSR) to annihilation by the Turks. Bolshevik forces having secured the country, the Soviet Republic of Armenia was officially proclaimed on 29 November.

The ARF was excluded from Armenian politics throughout the period of Soviet rule, but remained a major political force in the diaspora, where it continued to espouse the cause of an independent, non-communist Armenia. Following the dissolution of the USSR in 1991, the ARF returned to Armenia, once more to become an important force in the country.

## SOVIET ARMENIA

The borders of Soviet Armenia were defined by a friendship treaty agreed in Moscow, Russia, in March 1921 and by the Treaty of Kars of October, under the terms of which the Bolsheviks ceded to Turkey the bulk of the Western Armenian territories that had been conquered by Imperial Russia. In addition, the Nakhichevan Autonomous Republic was established and placed under Azerbaijan's jurisdiction. Nagornyi Karabakh (Gharabagh or Artsakh, to Armenians) was also incorporated into Azerbaijan, although it was given the status of an autonomous oblast (region), in recognition of its mainly Armenian population. In December 1922 Armenia joined Azerbaijan and Georgia in the Transcaucasian Soviet Federative Socialist Republic. This was dissolved in December 1936 and Armenia became a full Union Republic of the USSR.

Armenia experienced rapid social and economic development during the Soviet period. Considerable advances were made in agriculture, industry, transport, education, health care, urban development and standards of living. This achievement was the more impressive given the extremely poor socio-economic conditions in Armenia at the beginning of the 1920s, but, as in other republics, the human and material costs of forced collectivization and industrialization were severe. Soviet rule brought security and stability to the truncated Armenia it had created and, to some extent, allowed the consolidation of Armenian national culture and identity through the promotion of the Armenian language and by the establishment of a number of cultural institutions. However, any nationalist expression that crossed the shifting and invisible line between the permissible and the forbidden was suppressed. The purges of 1936–38 and 1947–53 greatly reduced the ranks of the Communist Party of Armenia (CPA) and the republic's intelligentsia. The Armenian Apostolic Church was also persecuted severely.

## THE NATIONALIST MOVEMENT

From the mid-1980s the policies of the new Soviet leader, Mikhail Gorbachev, *perestroika* (restructuring) and *glasnost* (openness), permitted Armenian nationalists to give open expression to their views. There was considerable popular support for their demands, and what began as a loyal movement protesting a few specific issues was rapidly transformed into a campaign for national liberation and independence. Among the concerns voiced were the perceived threat to the future of the Armenian language and the problem of environmental damage caused by Soviet mismanagement and neglect. However, the primary issue that galvanized the Armenian national movement was that of Nagornyi Karabakh, the majority Armenian population of which was expressing deep dissatisfaction with Azerbaijani rule. In late 1987 there was increasing pressure in both Nagornyi Karabakh and Armenia for the reopening of the issue of the status of the enclave. There were also outbreaks of violence between ethnic Armenian and Azeri (ethnic Azerbaijani) villages in the region itself. In February 1988 the Nagornyi Karabakh Regional Soviet passed an unprecedented resolution demanding a transfer to Armenian jurisdiction. In Armenia, and in the Soviet capital, Moscow, Armenians demonstrated in support of the resolution. The number of participants in daily demonstrations in the Armenian capital, Yerevan, increased to hundreds of thousands within one week.

Initially, the Armenian people demonstrated against crimes committed against them before and during the period of Stalin—Iosif V. Dzhugashvili's rule, corruption in the higher echelons of the communist parties of Armenia and Azerbaijan, and the maladministration of Nagornyi Karabakh. The protests were generally spontaneous and optimistic, hopeful that Gorbachev would correct past injustices, and not antagonistic towards Azeri people in general. However, within a few days the mood in Armenia was transformed by anti-Armenian violence, in late February 1988, in the Azerbaijani town of Sumgait, in which, according to official reports, 26 Armenians died. This was followed by the exodus, often forced, of hundreds of thousands of Armenians from Azerbaijan and of Azeris from Armenia. The failure of local authorities to control the unrest led to the dismissal, in May, of the First Secretary of the CPA.

The demonstrations were organized by a number of Yerevan intellectuals, who formed a group known as the Karabakh Committee. The Committee included Levon Ter-Petrossian, Vazgen Sarkissian and Vazgen Manukian. Through strikes and demonstrations it forced the republican Government, in June 1988, to endorse Nagornyi Karabakh's demand for unification with Armenia, thus creating a major inter-republican crisis with Azerbaijan. In July the Presidium of the Supreme Soviet of the USSR rejected Nagornyi Karabakh's demands, bringing the Armenian national movement into direct confrontation with the Soviet authorities.

In December 1988 a strong earthquake occurred in northern Armenia, destroying the town of Spitak and badly damaging the country's second largest city, Leninakan (now Gyumri). More than 25,000 people died and some 500,000 were left homeless. Earthquake relief work and reconstruction, far from generating national unity, became a political issue. The CPA Government and the nationalist opposition each accused the other of incompetence and corruption.

Also in December 1988, the Soviet authorities ordered the arrest of the Karabakh Committee and the following month effectively placed Nagornyi Karabakh under direct rule. The crisis, however, continued. There was a general strike in Stepanakert, the enclave's capital, from May to August 1989, and continuing mass demonstrations in Yerevan and Baku, Azerbaijan, where, in January 1990, there were further anti-Armenian pogroms. In May 1989 the Karabakh Committee was released and renewed its campaign for the unification of Nagornyi Karabakh and Armenia. Although still fragmented, the opposition became better co-ordinated, forming the Armenian Pan-National Movement (APNM), which later became the party of government during the years of Levon Ter-Petrossian's presidency. By the end of 1989, with the decline of the communist system in Eastern Europe, demands for Armenian independence became stronger. In September Azerbaijan began a road, rail and pipeline blockade of Armenia, which remained in force in 2003, and caused immense damage to the Armenian economy, reducing energy supplies to a minimum and severely impeding the process of reconstruction following the earthquake.

In the period between the suppression of the Popular Front of Azerbaijan (PFA), and the restoration of communist rule, in January 1990, and the attempted *coup d'état* against Gorbachev in August 1991, there was an increasing alignment of all-Union authorities with Azerbaijan against Armenia. Soviet security forces supported Azerbaijan's efforts to reimpose control over Nagornyi Karabakh and Armenian villages outside the enclave. Stepanakert was effectively under siege and a number of other Armenian settlements were subjected to sustained bombardment and forced depopulation. The conflict escalated markedly, with an increasing use of rockets, artillery, armoured vehicles and even aircraft. In early and mid-1990 there were also outbreaks of fighting along Armenia's borders with Azerbaijan and Nakhichevan.

In Armenia the nationalist opposition retained the political initiative, with the APNM emerging as the strongest party in elections to the Armenian Supreme Soviet in May–July 1990, obtaining some 35% of the seats in the legislature. Levon Ter-Petrossian, leader of the APNM, defeated Vladimir Movsissian, First Secretary of the CPA, to become Chairman of the Supreme Soviet. Vazgen Manukian, also a leader of the APNM, was appointed Chairman of the Council of Ministers (Head of Government). On 23 August the Supreme Soviet adopted a resolution on sovereignty, including the right to maintain armed forces. The Armenian Soviet Socialist Republic was renamed the Republic of Armenia.

The existence of illegal Armenian armed formations, and Armenia's refusal to enter into the negotiations between the Soviet republics on a new treaty of union, or to participate in the referendum on the renewal of the USSR, which took place in March 1991, were the main issues of contention between the all-Union authorities and the Armenian Government in that year. In May Ter-Petrossian accused the USSR of having 'declared war on Armenia'. However, the failed coup attempt against Gorbachev in Moscow in August was followed by an improvement in relations between the central authorities and Armenia, with a consequent deterioration in all-Union relations with Azerbaijan.

## INDEPENDENT ARMENIA

Armenia's scheduled referendum on secession from the USSR took place on 21 September 1991. According to official figures, 94.4% of the electorate participated, with 99.3% of votes cast in favour of Armenian independence. Two days later the Supreme Soviet declared Armenia to be an independent state. This was followed, on 16 October, by a presidential election. Six candidates participated in the election, which was decisively won by Ter-Petrossian, with 87% of the total votes cast.

Armenia thus achieved independence relatively smoothly. Unlike in neighbouring Azerbaijan and Georgia, the transition to democracy was not characterized by coups, secessionist rebellions and the collapse of central authority. However, in late 1991 Ter-Petrossian's Government had some significant problems to resolve: first, the human and material costs of supporting the war effort of the Karabakh Armenians; second, the decline of the economy, owing to the dissolution of

the USSR in December and the economic blockade imposed by Azerbaijan (and supported by Turkey); and, finally, the task of reconstruction following the earthquake.

Living standards in Armenia deteriorated considerably in the early 1990s, reducing much of the population to poverty and reliance on international aid and remittances from relatives working abroad. The severe energy shortage was only partially alleviated by the controversial reopening of the Medzamor nuclear power station in 1995 (it had been closed after the earthquake of 1988). Far from fulfilling people's hopes of a better life, the experience of independence left many Armenians disillusioned, impoverished and disaffected. In the first 10 years of independence nearly 1m. Armenians (some 25% of the total population), mostly men of working age, often with good qualifications, emigrated in search of work in Russia.

In order to overcome these difficulties, Ter-Petrossian's Government pursued a programme of radical economic reform and developed generally moderate and pragmatic policies in other areas. The Government suffered internal upheaval, including the resignation as premier of Vazgen Manukian in August 1991 and of Khosrov Haroutunian in February 1993. The Government was also strongly opposed in the Supreme Council (formerly known as the Supreme Soviet) and on the streets of Yerevan. Opponents described the regime as corrupt, incompetent and authoritarian. However, by the mid-1990s the Government appeared to have succeeded in gaining support, if not from the masses, at least from the new elite, comprising bureaucrats, local administrators and the entrepreneurs of the new market economy.

## NAGORNYI KARABAKH

On the issue of Nagornyi Karabakh, President Ter-Petrossian was much more moderate in government than in opposition. Eventually, this cost him his office. Armenia provided substantial moral and material support for the separatists, but denied (although with little credibility) direct military involvement. By the mid-1990s the Armenian Government no longer demanded unification with the enclave, stating that it would accept any settlement that satisfied the Karabakh Armenians. It also resisted pressure to recognize the independent 'Republic of Nagornyi Karabakh' (declared in December 1991).

The nationalist opposition frequently attacked the Armenian Government for its lack of support of the Karabakh cause. Criticism was particularly strong following the launch of an intensive counter-offensive by Azerbaijani forces in June 1992, which resulted in several thousand people being expelled, exacerbating the already serious refugee crisis in Armenia. In mid-August the opposition held mass rallies in Yerevan in protest at the situation in Nagornyi Karabakh and the worsening economic crisis. Armenia's international reputation also suffered following the massacre of Azerbaijani civilians at Khojali on 25 February 1992, and declined further in April 1993, when the UN Security Council, under Resolution 822, demanded an Armenian withdrawal from occupied Azerbaijani territory outside the enclave and the implementation of a cease-fire. In July the UN Security Council's Resolution 853 demanded that Nagornyi Karabakh forces withdraw from Agdam, an Azerbaijani town east of the enclave.

Internal critics and its own disclaimers notwithstanding, the Armenian Government's support for the Karabakh Armenians proved vital. In early May 1994 a cease-fire agreement was signed by the Ministers of Defence of Armenia and Azerbaijan, and representatives of Nagornyi Karabakh. By this time, the Armenians had not only gained full control of the enclave, but also occupied extensive Azerbaijani territories outside its borders. There were some violations of the cease-fire, but not enough to prevent the agreement being formalized on 27 July. In September of the same year President Ter-Petrossian and the Azerbaijani President, Heydar Aliyev, reached agreement on some important provisions of a future peace treaty. Negotiations for a settlement had been in progress before the cease-fire, principally under the auspices of the Minsk Group of the Organization for Security and Co-operation in Europe (OSCE, until 1994 called the Conference on Security and Co-operation in Europe—CSCE), with the support of the UN. Simultaneous bilateral negotiations between presidential advisers also took place in 1994–96. In December 1994 Russia became a permanent co-chair of the 'Minsk Group', which helped bring its own mediation efforts more firmly into line with those of the OSCE, while in 1997 the USA and France joined Russia as co-chairs, adding to the Group's international significance.

However, a period of intense negotiation and increased international pressure on the parties to the conflict in 1996–97 resulted not in the resolution of the dispute, but in the emergence of a growing rift between the leaders of Armenia and Nagornyi Karabakh. President Ter-Petrossian conceded Azerbaijan's preference for a staged settlement, which would allow for the lifting of blockades, the deployment of a peace-keeping force, the return of most Azerbaijani territory outside the enclave, and the resettlement of the majority of refugees, in advance of a final resolution of Nagornyi Karabakh's future constitutional status. The Karabakh leadership preferred a 'package' settlement, which would not require it to surrender its perceived military advantage and security guarantees in advance of resolving the issue of status. The same division was reflected within the Armenian Government and, ultimately, precipitated President Ter-Petrossian's forced resignation in February 1998.

Ter-Petrossian's successor, Robert Kocharian, was a native of Nagornyi Karabakh and, indeed, had been its President before he became Prime Minister of Armenia in 1997. Kocharian's Government, which included another Karabakh Armenian, the influential Minister of Internal Affairs and National Security, Serge Sarkissian, was more sympathetic to the interests of the Karabakh Armenians and maintained a close alliance with the President of the unrecognized republic, Arkadii Ghukassian (who was re-elected for a second term in 2002). Certainly, President Kocharian was keen to avoid Ter-Petrossian's mistake of appearing to put pressure on the enclave's authorities to accept an unfavourable settlement. He strongly supported Nagornyi Karabakh's demands for direct negotiations with the Azerbaijani Government and insisted on a package settlement to the conflict, while continuing the previous Government's policy of non-recognition of independence for Nagornyi Karabakh and of stating that Armenia would accept any solution that was acceptable to the Karabakhs. Nevertheless, both in Armenia and in Nagornyi Karabakh itself, critics of the leadership (from within the ruling coalitions, as well as from the opposition) continued to focus on the Karabakh issue and the danger of submitting to Azerbaijan and to international pressure. In February 2001 the leading critic of Ghukassian in Nagornyi Karabakh was silenced when Samuel Babaian, the enclave's former Minister of Defence and army Commander-in-Chief, was gaoled for 14 years, for instigating an attempt to assassinate the republic's President in March 2000.

From mid-1998 President Kocharian, like his predecessor Ter-Petrossian, began to develop a dialogue with President Aliyev of Azerbaijan. Hopes for a resolution of the conflict remained centred on this presidential dialogue and on the continuing efforts of the Minsk Group. Negotiations succeeded in significantly reducing the gap between the positions of the Governments of Armenia and Azerbaijan, but, despite sustained diplomatic activity and several high-profile meetings, a final peace agreement remained elusive. After a nine-month interlude the two Presidents met again in August 2002, but failed to make any real further progress. In addition to the central issue of the eventual constitutional status of Nagornyi Karabakh, among the most difficult questions to be resolved were: the arrangements for the 'Lachin corridor', captured territory, which provided an overland link between the enclave and Armenia; reciprocal arrangements to guarantee Azerbaijani communication with Nakhichevan, via Armenian territory; guarantees for the security of the Armenians in Nagornyi Karabakh; and the return of Azeri refugees to the enclave. Meanwhile, the cease-fire remained subject to continuous minor violations, with frequent casualties resulting from sniper fire and occasional more serious hostilities. Opinion polls showed that the public continued to support a peaceful resolution, but were even less willing than the political leaders to make the necessary compromises. By the early 2000s there was increasing demand for a military solution among sections of the Azerbaijani opposition, as well as support for the revival of a phased approach, on the part of some Azerbaijani and international negotiators.

## POLITICAL DEVELOPMENTS

In July 1995 President Ter-Petrossian's party succeeded in winning another term in office, following the country's first post-Soviet general election. The Republican (Hanrapetutiun) bloc, an alliance of six groups led by Ter-Petrossian's party, the APNM, secured 119 of the 190 seats in parliament, by this time known as the National Assembly. In a simultaneous referendum, 68% of voters (56% of the electorate) supported a new Constitution, which had been strongly opposed at draft stage in the legislature and attracted international criticism for the wide-ranging powers it granted the presidency. Constitutional reform remained on the agenda thereafter, and in May 2003 a referendum was held on comprehensive proposals for reform. Some 600,000 people voted in favour of the proposed amendments, fewer than the 700,000 required, so the Constitution remained unchanged. Neither the Government nor the opposition had campaigned hard for the referendum, so there were no major immediate political consequences, although the failure to implement the changes had implications not only for domestic affairs, but also for Armenia's participation in the Council of Europe (to which it had acceded in January 2001), which required the introduction of some of the proposed reforms as a condition of membership.

In September 1996 Levon Ter-Petrossian was re-elected President, defeating Vazgen Manukian in the first round of voting, although he obtained only slightly more than the 50% of the votes required to avoid a second round. Both the elections and the constitutional referendum of 1996 were marred by electoral malpractice. The refusal of the Central Electoral Commission to register a large number of opposition parliamentary candidates, the Government's monopoly of television and radio broadcasts, and the falsification of results were among the most serious irregularities. Voters' choice was, in any case, significantly reduced by the suspension in December 1994 of the ARF. Although the election of 1996 was better conducted than that of 1995, the narrow margin of victory left the result open to question. Shortly after the election, opposition demonstrators attacked the parliament building and the Government imposed martial law for a short period to restore order. Several unpopular ministers were replaced, although this was not sufficient to rebuild the popularity and legitimacy of President Ter-Petrossian and his Government. The trials and imprisonment of ARF members continued until 1997, contributing to the political malaise of the last years of Ter-Petrossian's presidency. The ARF remained suspended until February 1998.

In 1995–97 President Ter-Petrossian's Government attracted increasing criticism from both the domestic opposition and the international community for its authoritarianism and weak commitment to democracy. These criticisms and concerns continued into the early 2000s, with all elections marred, to a greater or lesser extent, by malpractice, although Armenia's admission to the Council of Europe gave recognition to a degree of progress in the areas of democratization and human rights, as did its election to the UN's Commission on Human Rights in May 2001.

Levon Ter-Petrossian's political demise was precipitated in the latter part of 1997, when his disagreement with the leadership in Nagornyi Karabakh became clear, engendering divisions among his most senior ministers. The loss of the support of Robert Kocharian, the Prime Minister since March, the Minister of Defence, Vazgen Sarkissian, and the Minister of Internal Affairs and National Security, Serge Sarkissian, as well as the defection of a large number of his parliamentary supporters to the recently formed Yerkrapah parliamentary faction (which was loyal to the Minister of Defence) were decisive in persuading Ter-Petrossian that he had no choice but to resign in February 1998.

In the ensuing presidential election, the Prime Minister and acting President, Robert Kocharian, defeated Karen Demirchian, the First Secretary of the CPA for much of the 1970s and 1980s, with a large majority. The first post-Soviet change of president was achieved smoothly and within the framework of the Constitution (although Ter-Petrossian did not lose office through the electoral process).

Kocharian was committed to continuing many of the policies of his predecessor, but with a less compromising position on the issue of Nagornyi Karabakh, a more strongly professed commitment to open and democratic government, and certain differences of emphasis in foreign and economic policy (see below). The parliamentary election of May 1999 was won by a new force in Armenian politics, the Unity bloc, the principal components of which were the Republican Party of Armenia (RPA), unofficially led by Vazgen Sarkissian, and the People's Party of Armenia (PPA) of Karen Demirchian. Following the election, in which the Unity bloc won 55 seats in the 131-seat legislature, Sarkissian became Prime Minister and Demirchian was elected the Chairman of the National Assembly. Increased differences, having more to do with the control of political and economic resources than with policy issues, between the two men and President Kocharian soon emerged, and the President appeared increasingly weak and isolated. However, on 27 October Sarkissian and Demirchian, as well as six other deputies and officials, were assassinated, when gunmen stormed the National Assembly. The loss of the two leaders left both the Unity bloc and the Government in temporary disarray.

The murdered premier's younger brother, Aram, was appointed Prime Minister in early November 1999, but the tensions between the President and the National Assembly soon re-emerged, with the President coming under attack over his handling of the investigation into the assassinations, allegations of corruption, the continuing failure of the economic and social spheres, and reports that he was planning to compromise over Nagornyi Karabakh. In the last months of 1999 and in early 2000 President Kocharian was threatened with impeachment, but he was able to recover the political initiative, appointing Andranik Markarian, the leader of the RPA, as Prime Minister, and Serge Sarkissian as Minister of Defence, in May 2000. Parliamentary politics remained fluid in the early 2000s, with new parties and groupings emerging and old ones declining or disappearing, together with numerous defections. Among the most significant developments was the fading away of the Yerkrapah Union of Volunteers, members of which formed the Republic (Hanrapetutiun) party in early 2001, and simmering differences between the RPA and the PPA, with the former generally supportive of

Kocharian, and the latter becoming increasingly critical of both the Government and its Unity bloc partner. Eventually, in September 2001 the PPA split from the Unity bloc, although some of its deputies left the party in order to continue their support for Unity. By late 2001 it was clear that Kocharian had re-established control over the political situation, and that the opposition was too fragmented to offer a serious challenge, threats of impeachment notwithstanding. Kocharian won a second term in the second round of the presidential election held in March 2003, securing 67.5% of the votes cast. In the parliamentary elections held in May, the RPA emerged with the largest number of seats (with 23 of the 75 seats elected by proportional representation, and 32 overall), followed by the Law-Governed Country Party of Armenia (with 12 seats voted for by proportional representation and 18 overall), the Justice (Artarutiun) bloc (a coalition of the Armenian Democratic Party, the National Democratic Party, the People's Party of Armenia and the Union of National Democrats, with 14 of the seats elected by proportional representation, and 15 overall), and the ARF with a total of 11 seats. The coalition of pro-Government parties comprising the RPA, the Law-Governed Country Party of Armenia and the ARF emerged as the clear winners, and subsequently formed a new Government under Markarian, although there were the usual, and well-founded, accusations that the elections had not been fairly conducted.

## FOREIGN AFFAIRS

Armenia declared its independence in September 1991, but won international recognition only after the dissolution of the USSR in December of that year. Armenia was one of the original signatories of the Almaty Declaration that established the Commonwealth of Independent States (CIS). In February 1992 Armenia was admitted to the CSCE, and in March to the UN. On 15 May Armenia signed the CIS Collective Security Treaty in Tashkent, Uzbekistan, and in 1999 was one of only six CIS states to continue as a signatory of the agreement. In April 2003 the Treaty was formally superseded by the Collective Security Treaty Organization. Armenia also signed many other CIS agreements aimed at achieving closer co-operation among member states, although few of these had achieved significant results by 2003.

Armenia's foreign policy aimed to normalize relations with all neighbouring countries. Armenian-Russian relations were especially strong, both countries having a particular interest in security and military co-operation, and viewing each other as strategic partners. Armenia needed a safeguard against a perceived Turkish threat and to gain equipment, training and expertise for its own nascent armed forces, while Russia was interested in retaining control of the former Soviet external borders and in maintaining a forward air-defence zone. In 1994 and 1995 a series of agreements was signed, giving Russia 25-year basing rights in Armenia. Close military co-operation continued into the 2000s, with the implementation of a new, joint air-defence system in May 2001. There were limits, however, on how far Armenia would persist in its relations with Russia; neither Levon Ter-Petrossian nor Robert Kocharian favoured joining the Russia-Belarus Union, although this was advocated by some left-wing Armenian opposition politicians, and in mid-2001 Kocharian also rejected a proposal to make Russian Armenia's official second language. None the less, Armenia and Russia signed a 10-year economic co-operation programme in September, during a visit to the country by President Vladimir Putin of Russia.

Armenia also sought to diversify its foreign and security links, and in October 1994 joined the North Atlantic Treaty Organization's (NATO) 'Partnership for Peace' programme of military co-operation, although its membership remained, for the most part, passive until 2000, when Armenia began to take a more active interest. In June 2003 Armenia hosted NATO exercises for the first time, and the participation of the Turkish military in military exercises on Armenian territory was also unprecedented. In April 1996 Armenia, together with Azerbaijan and Georgia, signed an agreement on partnership and co-operation with the European Union, and in June 2000 the Parliamentary Assembly of the Council of Europe accepted Armenia's application for membership. Kocharian emphasized the importance of the European orientation of the country's foreign policy. In late September 2002, however, the Council of Europe warned that Armenia's membership could be suspended if the Government failed fully to abolish capital punishment by June 2003, after amendments to the Criminal Code, adopted in June 2002, permitted the death penalty to be enforced in exceptional circumstances. Armenia finally banned capital punishment in September 2003. Meanwhile, Armenia became a full member of the World Trade Organization in February 2003.

Relations with the USA, a substantial donor to Armenia, became closer during the 1990s, notwithstanding Armenian doubts about the overall direction of US policy in the Caucasus and the Caspian Sea basin, which was viewed as inclining dangerously towards the interests of Azerbaijan and Turkey, and US displeasure at Armenia's friendly relations with Iran, which, in the aftermath of the large-scale suicide attacks on the USA of 11 September 2001, US President George W. Bush had identified as one of three states forming an 'axis of evil'.

As indicated above, independent Armenia's relations with Iran had generally remained cordial, despite tension during the conflict in Nagornyi Karabakh, when Armenian successes threatened to send many thousands of Azeri refugees into Iran. The two countries signed numerous commercial and cultural agreements and there was increasing cross-border traffic. (There had been no crossing point on the Armenian–Iranian border during the Soviet period.) In December 1995 a permanent bridge across the River Araks (Araxes, Aras) was completed, replacing a temporary structure that had hitherto linked the two countries. The two countries' electricity grids were also linked in 1997 and there were plans for the construction of a gas pipeline, perhaps with European and Russian funding and support. In 2002 proposals were also under discussion for the joint construction of a hydroelectric plant on the Araks.

In contrast, relations with Azerbaijan and Turkey, Armenia's most important neighbours from an economic perspective, remained suspended owing to the Nagornyi Karabakh conflict. President Ter-Petrossian was criticized by the nationalist opposition for his pragmatic policy towards Turkey during the mid-1990s. He was accused of ignoring the historic issue of the 1915 'genocide' for the sake of contemporary economic and political benefits. This pragmatic policy was only partly successful. Although the approach was appreciated by Turkish officials and an informal dialogue was maintained, the Turkish Government insisted that the establishment of diplomatic relations and the opening of the border were conditional upon the resolution of the Nagornyi Karabakh issue. As Prime Minister, Robert Kocharian disagreed with Ter-Petrossian over relations between Azerbaijan and Turkey, arguing that Armenia could survive even if the blockades continued, but as President he came to appreciate the importance of the blockades in stifling Armenia's economic development. His Government gave a higher priority to seeking international and, ultimately, Turkish recognition of the 1915 'genocide', but it also supported new initiatives to improve Armenian-Turkish relations. Prominent among these was the Turkish-Armenian Reconciliation Commission, a non-governmental grouping of academics and retired diplomats, which gave impetus to the discussion of issues affecting bilateral relations. The Commission held its first meeting in September 2001, but its work was suspended between December and July 2002, following disagreement between its Armenian and Turkish members.

The Armenian Government's relations with the Armenian diaspora, which contributed significantly to aid programmes and to the finances of the Karabakh separatists, suffered in the mid-1990s. This was mainly owing to opposition in the diaspora to the 1994 suspension of the ARF, to the Ter-Petrossian Government's refusal to allow dual citizenship, and to what many viewed as the attempt to cultivate Armenian-Turkish relations at the expense of giving greater prominence to the massacres of 1915. President Kocharian's Government developed policies to help foster and consolidate relations with the Armenian diaspora in all of these areas, and improved its standing with overseas Armenian communities through major Armenian diaspora conferences in 1999 and 2002.

# The Economy

## Dr EDMUND HERZIG

### INTRODUCTION

Following the dissolution of the USSR in 1991, Armenia, like other former Soviet countries, was affected by a range of economic problems associated with the transition from a centralized, command economy to a market-orientated system. Armenia was particularly vulnerable following the collapse of the Soviet economic system as, in the Soviet period, it developed a primarily industrial economy, which was heavily dependent on inter-republican trade. In addition to the problems caused by the transition to a free-market system in the early 1990s, the Armenian economy was adversely affected by various other factors, not least the continuing costs of reconstruction after a severe earthquake in northern Armenia in December 1988. Equally serious was the cost of supporting the Karabakh Armenians' war effort in the disputed enclave (within Azerbaijan) of Nagornyi Karabakh, unofficially estimated at 30%–50% of the government budget

before the May 1994 cease-fire. By 2000 Armenia was still contributing at least one-half of the funds for the unrecognized republic of Nagornyi Karabakh's budget of US \$25m. An additional burden was the influx of refugees from both Nagornyi Karabakh and Azerbaijan. The imposition of a road, rail and pipeline blockade by Azerbaijan from September 1989, which was subsequently reinforced by Turkey, caused immense economic damage. Before this date, almost 90% of Armenia's imports from other Soviet republics came via Azerbaijan. Furthermore, in the early 1990s political instability in neighbouring Georgia resulted in a prolonged energy crisis in Armenia; main trade routes, both to traditional markets and suppliers in the former USSR and to potential new markets in the West, were closed, impeding deliveries of urgent supplies. Unlike some countries of the former USSR, Armenia was not richly endowed with petroleum, gas or other readily marketable natural resources. Moreover, in the Soviet period it imported many of its food requirements. The fact that it was land-locked made integration into the world economy difficult.

The combination of all these factors caused a severe economic decline in the early 1990s. Gross domestic product (GDP) in Armenia decreased, in real terms, by 52.4% in 1992 alone. At the beginning of 1994 it was calculated that the average Armenian was spending 80% of his or her income on food, an indication of very low living standards. A 1996 official survey of living conditions found that 55% of the population qualified as poor and 28% as very poor. Official figures put the rate of unemployment at between 9% and 11% of the workforce in 1994–2001, but the actual rate was probably two to three times higher. At the end of the 1990s only some 35% of the population was in employment and it was estimated that in 2001 50% of the population was still living below the poverty line. Basic social services, notably education and medicine, which were available to all in the Soviet period, were out of reach for a significant and growing proportion of the population, a particularly worrying development when the country's principal economic asset was its highly skilled and industrious work-force.

Social and economic pressures led to extensive emigration in the 1990s, and many Armenians, especially the young and the well-qualified, went abroad (mainly to Russia) in search of work. Independent Armenia conducted its first census in October 2001, the results of which indicated that the de facto population stood at a little over 3.0m.—substantially lower than the total of 3.3m. recorded at the last Soviet census, held in January 1989. Remittances from relatives working abroad, contributions from the Armenian diaspora, as well as Western humanitarian aid, went some way towards alleviating the severe social problems caused by the economic decline. The Government's social-welfare policy also underwent radical change, with successive legislation laying the foundations for a policy based on targeted, means-tested benefits for those deemed to be in greatest need. The large unofficial economy also made a significant contribution to many people's livelihood.

Recovery was slow. In 1994–2000 annual GDP growth averaged 5.4% (fluctuating between 3.3% and 7.3%), but by 2000 real GDP had recovered to only 63% of its 1989 level. The recovery in the rate of GDP per head improved more rapidly (estimated at some 8% per year over the same period). In 2002 GDP per head, in terms of international purchasing-power parity, was estimated at US $3,800, although this figure was still scarcely sufficient to meet basic needs.

## ECONOMIC POLICY

In the early 1990s the Government, unable to counteract the causes of the economic decline, took advantage of the situation in order to implement a radical economic-reform programme aimed at creating the legal, institutional and economic basis for a market economy. The reforms included the liberalization of prices, stabilization of the national currency, reduction of the budgetary deficit, promotion of privatization and rationalization of the taxation system. These measures, assisted by the May 1994 cease-fire in the Nagornyi Karabakh conflict and a slight improvement in energy supplies, allowed Armenia to become the first country among the Commonwealth of Independent States (CIS) to achieve growth in GDP.

After Armenia gained independence in 1991, President Levon Ter-Petrossian's Government (1991–98) pursued a privatization programme that was among the most radical in the former USSR. Privatization began with land and small-scale enterprises from 1991 and embraced housing in 1993. These early stages of the privatization process achieved a high level of success (by mid-1999 85% of small enterprises had been transferred to private ownership). However, the privatization of medium-sized and large enterprises, initiated in 1995,

proved to be more difficult and controversial, and the Government attracted criticism for its alleged failure to secure good prices or to safeguard the national interest through the sale of assets such as the telecommunications industry. Nevertheless, by mid-1999 75% of medium-sized and large enterprises had been privatized. In June 2001 President Robert Kocharian's Government (1998–) won parliamentary support for its plans to privatize remaining state-owned enterprises over a three-year period. Controversy has continued to surround the privatization of major state industries, with some foreign investors and managers being accused of failing to meet their commitments under the terms of privatization agreements. Privatization resulted in a dramatic shift in employment patterns: in 2001 74% of the work-force was employed in the private sector, whereas in 1995 the figure remained below 50%.

Armenia experienced very high rates of inflation in the early post-Soviet years. Salary increases, price liberalization from early 1992, shortages resulting from the economic blockade and the almost complete suspension of trade with other former Soviet territories all contributed to an increase in consumer prices. Until November 1993, when the Government introduced a national currency, the dram (see below), Armenia was adversely affected by Russia's financial and monetary policy. The average annual rate of increase in consumer prices was more than 5,000% in 1994, although this rate declined rapidly following the imposition of strict monetary policy, and had stabilized at a very low rate by the late 1990s. The annual rate of consumer-price inflation was less than 1% in 2000, increased to 3.1% in 2001, and was 1.1% in 2002. Progress was also made in reducing the budgetary deficit, which was equivalent to 56% of GDP in 1993, but which had declined to less than 4% of GDP by 2001. It was estimated that in 2003 government revenues would total some US $400m., while expenditure would amount to around $480m.

In November 1993 Armenia, like several other post-Soviet states, was forced to introduce a new national currency, when Russia refused to extend new rouble credits. (Armenia later also suffered the adverse effects of the Russian financial crisis of 1998.) The dram was introduced at a rate of 77 per US dollar, but declined to over 400 to the dollar within one year, stabilizing at about that level in 1994–95, before decreasing further, to around 500 to the dollar at the end of 1997. In 2002 the average rate of exchange was 573 drams to the dollar. Apart from the early rapid decline in value, the new currency could be considered one of the successes of government economic policy, which aimed to achieve economic competitiveness through a combination of a strong currency and low inflation.

Armenia's economic reforms achieved a relatively high degree of macroeconomic stability, and impressed the IMF, the World Bank and the European Bank for Reconstruction and Development (EBRD), all of which Armenia joined in 1992, and which, together with Russia and Western countries, extended major credits and technical assistance. Armenia's dependence on foreign creditors and donors meant that it had little choice but to adopt the economic policies that these organizations recommended. By the end of the first quarter of 2001, Armenia had accumulated some US $830m. in external debt, of which over 76% was owed to multilateral creditors (principally the World Bank and the IMF), nearly 14% to Russia, and over 7% to the USA. In November 2002 an agreement was signed with Russia, cancelling some US $98m. of Armenia's foreign debt, in exchange for which Russia was to obtain a controlling stake in a number of state-owned enterprises.

Foreign investment was slow in coming to Armenia. The absence of commercially attractive natural resources, the economic blockade, corruption, bureaucracy, and opaque and changing laws and regulations outweighed the advanced state of economic reform and the availability of cheap skilled labour in the calculations of most potential investors. Direct investment totalled just US $25m. in 1995, increasing to $221m. in 1998, before declining again, to $104m., in 2000. However, such short-term fluctuations were not overly significant, while the privatization of major enterprises was continuing, and while the overall level of direct investment remained so low. The importance of foreign investment, and of foreign economic relations more generally, was one of the more intensely debated issues in Armenian economic policy. President Levon Ter-Petrossian, like most Western analysts, considered that Armenia's only hope for sustained economic growth lay in dynamic trade relations with its neighbours in the region, since the domestic market was too small to stimulate growth and investment. From this perspective, resolution of the Karabakh conflict and the lifting of the Turkish and Azerbaijani blockades were essential prerequisites for economic recovery. Others argued that it was corruption and failure in the implementation of reforms that discouraged investment, and that if these problems were addressed, investment and growth would follow, irrespective of the blockades. Such commentators regarded any link between the Karabakh issue and economic recovery to be little more than a weak excuse.

## AGRICULTURE

Armenia's agricultural potential is constrained by the relatively small extent of its agricultural land (1.4m. hectares). Both during the Soviet period, and thereafter, Armenia has been heavily dependent on food imports (which accounted for 41% of the domestic market in 2000). The country's main agricultural products are fruits and vegetables grown in the fertile Ararat plain, and potatoes, grain, fodder and livestock from the uplands. Agriculture also provided the inputs for the food industry, which included important wine and cognac factories. The privatization of agricultural land in Armenia proceeded rapidly from 1991; by late 1992 approximately 90% of arable land was under private ownership. This had an immediate effect on production levels, which increased by a total of 15% in 1991. In the 1990s, however, the sector's progress was hampered by problems in land distribution, and in agricultural and market infrastructure. In 2000 these problems were exacerbated by severe drought. Nevertheless, with the industrial contraction of the early 1990s, agriculture and forestry came to occupy a very significant place in the national economy, accounting for 49% of GDP in 1993. With the beginnings of a recovery in the services and industrial sectors, agriculture's contribution to GDP moderated, to some 22.5% by 2000. In the course of the first decade of independence there was a shift within agriculture away from planted products, and towards meat and dairy production; this trend appeared to have peaked in 2000, when meat and dairy production accounted for around 50% of the value of agricultural output.

## MINING AND ENERGY

Armenia possesses significant mineral resources, notably copper, gold and molybdenum, and a variety of building stones, including tuff. There are also deposits of mineral salt, calcium oxide and carbon. Some of these were extracted and processed in the Soviet period, but the mining industry was largely inactive throughout the 1990s, although it began to show signs of recovery at the end of the decade.

The energy crisis was a major factor in Armenia's economic difficulties in the early 1990s. In the Soviet period, most of Armenia's energy requirements were imported in the form of natural gas from neighbouring Azerbaijan. However, this source was unavailable after Azerbaijan imposed its blockade in 1989. Following this, Armenia relied heavily on Turkmenistan and Russia for supplies of natural gas and petroleum, respectively. Unfortunately, the only gas pipeline bypassing Azerbaijan traversed a region of Georgia that was largely populated by Azeris (ethnic Azerbaijanis), and was subject to frequent sabotage. Georgia's internal unrest and alleged deliberate diversion of natural gas intended for Armenia also interrupted supplies, as did Armenia's occasional failure to meet payment conditions. In February 2001 Armenia and Russia reached an agreement, under the terms of which Russia was to cancel Armenia's gas arrears of US $7m., in return for obtaining a share of the infrastructure of the Armenian gas distribution company for the Russian companies, Gazprom and Itera. Armenia had also reached agreement with Iran on the construction of a 140-km gas pipeline, with an anticipated annual capacity of 35,300m. cu ft (1,000m. cu m), to allow imports of Iranian or Turkmen natural gas, although the project remained unrealized in 2003.

In the early 1990s domestic energy production was limited to a number of hydroelectric plants, which provided 68% of Armenia's electricity in 1993. By 1999 that proportion had declined to 21%, although there were plans significantly to extend Armenia's hydroelectric capacity. The country's only nuclear power plant, which was closed following the 1988 earthquake, was restarted in June 1995 and began generating later in the same year amid widespread international anxiety and protest. The Medzamor station was a VVER-440 pressurized-water reactor, of a different design to the Chornobyl (Chernobyl) reactor in Ukraine, which had failed, to notorious effect, in April 1986. Nevertheless, it was considered unsafe by many external specialists, owing to the absence of a containment dome and its location in an earthquake zone, as well as the possibility of other, unknown risks. By 2001 Medzamor was generating some 45% of Armenia's electricity. The Government came under pressure from the European Union (EU) to close the power station by 2004 but, despite initial agreement, it resisted, claiming that the station could be operated safely for a considerably longer period of time, following extensive renovation, and demanding international funds to allow it to develop alternative sources of power generation. This impasse remained unresolved in 2003. In September financial control of the plant was transferred to the Russian company Unified Energy Systems, for a period of five years, after that company took responsibility for the plant's arrears.

In 2000 Armenia's hydroelectric, thermal and nuclear power stations generated 5,958m. kWh of electricity, and 500m. kWh was exported in 1999. Iran and Armenia linked their electricity grids in 1997, allowing trade in electricity to follow patterns of seasonal demand, and Armenia also exported electricity to Georgia. In 2002 agreement was reached on the expansion of the exchange arrangement with Iran, and also on the construction of a hydroelectric plant on the River Araks (Araxes, Aras). In March Armenia's four regional electricity-distribution networks were merged to form a single entity, in preparation for their sale, following the failure of two international tenders in 2001. In August 2002 a Canadian-owned offshore company, the only bidder, acquired 81.1% of the network.

## INDUSTRY

Industry was the dominant sector in Soviet Armenia's economy, accounting for 57% of net material product (NMP) in 1980 and employing nearly 40% of the work-force. Both heavy and light industry were largely dependent on inputs from other Soviet republics, notably energy from Azerbaijan and Russia, as well as catalysts and iron ore for metallurgy, and fabrics and leather for the garment and footwear industries.

Armenia was also a major centre for the Soviet electronics industry, which relied on components from outside the republic, and which was integrated into the Soviet military-industrial complex. The main markets for all of these industries' products were other Soviet republics.

The collapse of the interdependent Soviet economy, therefore, affected Armenia's industrial sector especially acutely. However, it was the energy blockade that was the prime cause of the collapse in industrial output in the early 1990s. The sector contracted by almost 50% in 1992 alone, with many of Armenia's 450 factories inoperative, owing to lack of power. Industry recovered gradually, registering modest growth each year from 1994, with the exception of 1998, when Russia's financial crisis caused demand to contract (the average annual rate of growth was 2.4% in 1994–2000). Armenia's industrial growth was slower than that of most other CIS countries, and the continuing relative decline of the sector was indicated by the fact that in 2000 the sector (excluding construction) contributed 22.0% of GDP, whereas industry had contributed over 40% in 1990; industrial output in 2000 was just over one-half the level recorded one decade before. However, in the early 2000s the pace of industrial growth accelerated, and the annual rate of growth was estimated at 15% in 2002. The industrial sub-sectors that showed the greatest dynamism were those of food-processing and alcoholic beverages, precious stones, minerals and metallurgy, and chemicals.

## SERVICES AND TRADE

The services sector, comprising trade, transport and communications, social and financial services, as well as construction, grew more rapidly than did either agriculture or industry during most of the 1990s. Between 1994 and 2000 trade's share of overall value added rose from 4.5% to 10.0%; that of transport and communications increased from 4.2% to 7.8%; and that of construction increased from 6.7% to 11.1%. The contribution to GDP of the services sector as a whole was 55.6% in 2000.

Under Soviet rule Armenia's economy was heavily dependent on trade, with imports and exports each equivalent to more than 50% of GDP in the 1980s. The vast majority of trade was with other Soviet republics (98% of exports and 79% of imports in 1980–90). In the Soviet period Armenia's exports were dominated by light industrial goods, the production of which, like that of other industries, collapsed after independence. By the late 1980s Armenia already had a trade deficit, a problem that became increasingly serious in the 1990s. The deficit reached US $682m. in 1998, when the value of imports was more than three times the value of exports. In subsequent years the trade balance improved, with the deficit declining to $380m. in 2002.

Russia remained Armenia's most important trading partner throughout the 1990s, but its position was steadily eroded; in 1995 Russia absorbed 33.1% of Armenian exports, but it accounted for only 17.7% of export trade by 2001. In 1998, for the first time, the member countries of the EU accounted for a higher percentage of Armenia's imports (28.7%) than did the CIS countries (which accounted for 25.5%). This trend appeared to be stabilizing by the end of the

decade, and by 2000 the CIS countries accounted for 20% of external trade, and the EU countries for 35%. A considerable proportion of the EU countries' share was attributable to trade with Belgium in precious stones, which Armenia imported uncut for subsequent re-export. Largely because of the blockades by Azerbaijan and Turkey, Iran (and to a lesser extent Georgia) became increasingly important trading partners in the 1990s. The construction (completed in December 1995) of a permanent road bridge linking Armenia and Iran facilitated the further development of trade. There was also some limited indirect trade between both Turkey and Azerbaijan and Armenia via Georgia (as well as significant direct contraband trade in defiance of the blockades). The tariffs charged for transport through Georgia were high, however, while the new route to Iran was longer and more expensive than the old road and rail routes through Nakhichevan that had been closed by the blockade. In 2001 Iran accounted for 9.3% of Armenia's exports and 8.9% of its imports, less than the USA, which accounted for 15.3% of exports and 9.6% of imports.

An important objective for Armenia during the 1990s and early 2000s was membership of the World Trade Organization, to which it acceded on 5 February 2003.

## PROSPECTS

After independence Armenia made impressive progress in its transition towards a market economy, although it incurred significant social costs in the process. After more than 10 years of independence, macroeconomic stability had been achieved, and most sectors of the economy were registering steady growth. The continuing blockade by both Azerbaijan and Turkey, however, seemed likely to preclude any immediate dramatic improvement in the economy. Azerbaijan offered Armenia the best channel for trade and economic integration with other CIS countries, and Turkey provided the best route for developing economic links outside the former USSR. For a country with such a weak domestic market as Armenia, most analysts judge that integration into the larger regional economy is essential to attract and retain investment and talent, both foreign and domestic. If the Karabakh conflict could be resolved, Armenia's economic prospects would improve significantly. The country would regain access to many of the inputs and markets that were inaccessible while the conflict continued, and would have the possibility of participating in the regional network being developed to link the Caspian basin with Europe. Armenia would also be able to reclaim its historic economic function as a bridge between Anatolia, the Caucasus and Iran. In the absence of a resolution of the Karabakh conflict, Armenia could still enhance its economic prospects by further developing internal political stability, efficient institutions, and clear and consistently-applied laws and regulations, while taking steps to combat corruption, bureaucracy and favouritism. In the first years of the 2000s the country's economic development gained momentum and appeared less fragile, but it remained questionable whether the Government had the will or capacity to tackle the more difficult external and internal challenges, and whether the modest rate of recovery was sufficient to reverse a decade of social decline and emigration.

# Statistical Survey

Principal source: National Statistical Service of the Republic of Armenia, 375010 Yerevan, Republic Sq., Government House 3; tel. (1) 52-42-13; fax (1) 52-19-21; e-mail armstat@sci.am; internet www.armstat.am.

## Area and Population

### AREA, POPULATION AND DENSITY

| | |
|---|---:|
| Area (sq km) . . . . . . . . . . | 29,743* |
| Population (census results)† | |
| 12 January 1989 | |
| Males. . . . . . . . . . . . . | 1,619,308 |
| Females . . . . . . . . . . . | 1,685,468 |
| Total . . . . . . . . . . . . | 3,304,776 |
| 10 October 2001 (provisional) . . . . . . . | 3,210,606 |
| Population (official estimates at 1 January)‡ | |
| 2000 . . . . . . . . . . . . . | 3,803,400 |
| 2001 . . . . . . . . . . . . . | 3,802,400 |
| 2002 . . . . . . . . . . . . . | 3,800,000 |
| Density (per sq km) at 1 January 2002 . . . . . . | 127.8 |

\* 11,484 sq miles.

† Figures refer to *de jure* population. The *de facto* total was 3,287,677 in 1989 and 3,000,807 in 2001.

‡ The figures, which include persons temporarily absent (475,200 at 1 January 1999), have not been adjusted to take account of the October 2001 census results.

### POPULATION BY NATIONALITY

(permanent inhabitants, 1989 census)

| | % |
|---|---:|
| Armenian . . . . . . . . . . . . . . | 93.3 |
| Azerbaijani . . . . . . . . . . . . | 2.6 |
| Kurdish . . . . . . . . . . . . . | 1.7 |
| Russian . . . . . . . . . . . . . | 1.5 |
| Others . . . . . . . . . . . . . | 0.9 |
| **Total**. . . . . . . . . . . . . . | 100.0 |

### MARZER (PROVINCES)

(1 January 2001)

| Marz (Province) | Area (sq km)* | Estimated Population† | Density (per sq km) | Capital |
|---|---:|---:|---:|---|
| Yerevan . . . | 227 | 1,246,100 | 5,489.4 | Yerevan |
| Aragatsotn . . | 2,753 | 168,100 | 61.1 | Ashtarak |
| Ararat . . . | 2,096 | 311,400 | 148.6 | Artashat |
| Armavir . . | 1,242 | 323,300 | 260.3 | Armavir |
| Gegharkunik . | 5,348 | 278,600 | 67.8 | Gavar |
| Kotaik . . . | 2,089 | 328,900 | 157.4 | Hrazdan |
| Lori . . . . | 3,789 | 392,300 | 103.5 | Vanadzor |
| Shirak . . . | 2,681 | 3621,400 | 134.8 | Gyumri |
| Syunik . . . | 4,506 | 164,000 | 36.4 | Kapan |
| Tavush . . . | 2,704 | 156,500 | 57.9 | Ijevan |
| Vayots Dzor. . | 2,308 | 69,400 | 30.1 | Yeghegnadzor |
| **Total** . . . | 29,743 | 3,800,000 | 127.8 | |

\* Including inland water, totalling 1,278 sq km.

† Provisional figures, including persons temporarily absent from the country.

### PRINCIPAL TOWNS

(estimated population at 1 January 2001)

| | | | |
|---|---:|---|---:|
| Yerevan (capital). . | 1,246,100 | Vagarshapat (Echmiadzin) . . | 65,700 |
| Gyumri* . . . . | 210,100 | Hrazdan (Razdan) . | 63,400 |
| Vanadzor† . . . | 170,800 | Abovian . . . . | 60,600 |

\* Known as Leninakan between 1924 and 1991.

† Known as Kirovakan between 1935 and 1992.

### BIRTHS, MARRIAGES AND DEATHS*

| | Registered live births | | Registered marriages | | Registered deaths | |
|---|---:|---:|---:|---:|---:|---:|
| | Number | Rate (per 1,000) | Number | Rate (per 1,000) | Number | Rate (per 1,000) |
| 1994 . . | 51,143 | 13.7 | 17,118 | 4.6 | 24,652 | 6.6 |
| 1995 . . | 48,960 | 13.0 | 15,911 | 4.2 | 24,842 | 6.6 |
| 1996 . . | 48,134 | 12.8 | 14,234 | 3.8 | 24,936 | 6.6 |
| 1997 . . | 43,929 | 11.6 | 12,521 | 3.3 | 23,985 | 6.3 |
| 1998 . . | 39,366 | 10.4 | 11,365 | 3.0 | 23,210 | 6.1 |
| 1999 . . | 36,502 | 9.6 | 12,459 | 3.3 | 24,087 | 6.3 |
| 2000 . . | 34,276 | 9.0 | 10,986 | 2.9 | 24,025 | 6.3 |
| 2001† . . | 32,065 | 8.4 | 12,302 | 3.2 | 24,003 | 6.3 |

\* Rates are calculated from unrevised population estimates.

† Figures are provisional.

**Expectation of life** (WHO estimates, years at birth): 69.7 (males 66.2; females 73.0) in 2001 (Source: WHO, *World Health Report*).

### ECONOMICALLY ACTIVE POPULATION

(annual averages, '000 persons)

| | 1998 | 1999 | 2000† |
|---|---:|---:|---:|
| Material sphere . . . . . . | 987 | 956 | 946 |
| Agriculture . . . . . . | 566 | 560 | 554 |
| Forestry. . . . . . . | 2 | 2 | 2 |
| Industry* . . . . . . | 209 | 195 | 193 |
| Construction . . . . . | 57 | 54 | 53 |
| Transport and communications . | 28 | 26 | 26 |
| Trade and catering . . . . | 113 | 109 | 108 |
| Other activities . . . . | 12 | 10 | 10 |
| Non-material sphere. . . . . | 349 | 340 | 335 |
| Education, culture and art . . | 155 | 153 | 152 |
| Science . . . . . . | 17 | 16 | 16 |
| Health, physical culture and social welfare . . . . | 78 | 77 | 76 |
| Housing and personal services . | 43 | 38 | 38 |
| General administration . . . | 29 | 28 | 28 |
| Other activities . . . . | 27 | 28 | 25 |
| **Total employed**. . . . . | 1,337 | 1,298 | 1,283 |
| Registered unemployed . . . . | 139 | 164 | 170 |
| **Total labour force** . . . . | 1,476 | 1,462 | 1,453 |

\* Principally mining, manufacturing, electricity, gas and water.

† Preliminary figures.

Source: IMF, *Republic of Armenia: Recent Economic Developments and Selected Issues* (May 2001).

**2000** ('000 persons, annual averages): Agriculture 564.6; Forestry 2.1; Industry (including construction) 226.2; Transport and communications 46.6; Trade and catering 106.9; Education, culture and art 153.9; Other services 167.3; Activities not adequately defined 10.1; Registered unemployed 169.5; Total labour force 1,447.2.

**2001** ('000 persons, annual averages): Agriculture 567.9; Forestry 2.1; Industry (including construction) 210.8; Transport and communications 44.2; Trade and catering 110.5; Education, culture and art 155.2; Other services 162.8; Activities not adequately defined 11.4; Registered unemployed 146.8; Total labour force 1,411.7.

# Health and Welfare

## KEY INDICATORS

| | |
|---|---:|
| Total fertility rate (children per woman, 2001) . . . . . | 1.2 |
| Under-five mortality rate (per 1,000 live births, 2001) . . | 35 |
| HIV (% of persons aged 15–49, 2001) . . . . . . . | 0.15 |
| Physicians (per 1,000 head, 1998) . . . . . . . | 3.16 |
| Hospital beds (per 1,000 head, 1996) . . . . . . | 7.2 |
| Health expenditure (2000): US $ per head (PPP) . . . . | 192 |
| Health expenditure (2000): % of GDP . . . . . . | 7.5 |
| Health expenditure (2000): public (% of total) . . . . | 42.3 |
| Human Development Index (2001): ranking . . . . . | 100 |
| Human Development Index (2001): value . . . . . . | 0.729 |

For sources and definitions, see explanatory note on p. vi.

# Agriculture

## PRINCIPAL CROPS
('000 metric tons)

| | 1999 | 2000 | 2001 |
|---|---:|---:|---:|
| Wheat . . . . . . . . . | 214.4 | 177.8 | 241.7 |
| Barley . . . . . . . . | 65.1 | 32.9 | 107.4 |
| Maize . . . . . . . | 11.4 | 5.9 | 9.9 |
| Other cereals . . . . . . | 6.5 | 4.5* | 2.1* |
| Potatoes . . . . . . | 414.1 | 290.3 | 363.8 |
| Pulses . . . . . . . | 3.7 | 3.9 | 3.1 |
| Cabbages . . . . . | 94.0 | 51.5 | 80.4 |
| Tomatoes . . . . | 151.4 | 143.7 | 158.3 |
| Cauliflowers . . . . . | 2.4 | 2.2 | 3.8 |
| Cucumbers and gherkins . . | 55.3* | 30.0 | 49.6* |
| Dry Onions . . . . . | 40.5 | 31.3 | 33.0 |
| Garlic . . . . . . . | 7.0 | 6.1 | 6.7 |
| Peas (green) . . . . . | 0.1 | 1.2 | 0.7 |
| Carrots . . . . . . | 18.3 | 6.6 | 14.1 |
| Other vegetables* . . . . | 80.0 | 103.0 | 120.0 |
| Apples . . . . . . | 23.5 | 23.2 | 35.4 |
| Pears . . . . . . . | 16.5 | 16.3 | 9.8 |
| Apricots . . . . . | 15.4 | 36.7 | 10.8 |
| Peaches and nectarines . . . . | 11.5 | 26.8 | 16.0 |
| Plums . . . . . . . | 7.7 | 11.8 | 10.5 |
| Grapes . . . . . . | 114.8 | 115.8 | 116.5 |
| Watermelons† . . . . . | 88.5 | 52.8 | 54.8 |

* Unofficial figure(s).
† Including melons, pumpkins and squash.

Source: FAO.

## LIVESTOCK
('000 head, year ending September)

| | 1999 | 2000 | 2001 |
|---|---:|---:|---:|
| Horses . . . . . . . | 12 | 12 | 11 |
| Asses* . . . . . . . | 3 | 2 | 3 |
| Cattle . . . . . . | 469 | 479 | 485 |
| Pigs . . . . . . | 86 | 71 | 69 |
| Sheep . . . . . . | 508 | 497 | 540 |
| Goats . . . . . . | 12 | 11 | 10 |
| Rabbits* . . . . . | 5 | 5 | 5 |
| Chickens . . . . . | 3,190 | 4,255 | 4,300 |
| Turkeys* . . . . . . | 175 | 170 | 170 |

* FAO estimates.

Source: FAO.

## LIVESTOCK PRODUCTS
('000 metric tons)

| | 1999 | 2000 | 2001 |
|---|---:|---:|---:|
| Beef and veal . . . . . . | 32 | 33 | 32 |
| Mutton and lamb . . . . . | 5 | 6 | 7 |
| Pig meat . . . . . | 8 | 6 | 6 |
| Poultry meat . . . . . | 3 | 3 | 3 |
| Cows' milk . . . . . | 452 | 462 | 450 |
| Sheep's milk . . . . | 11 | 10 | 10 |
| Cheese* . . . . . | 3 | 3 | 3 |
| Hen eggs . . . . . | 18† | 22† | 19 |
| Wool: greasy . . . . | 1 | 1 | 1 |
| Wool: scoured* . . . . . | 1 | 1 | 1 |

* FAO estimates.
† Unofficial figure.

Source: FAO.

# Forestry

## ROUNDWOOD REMOVALS
('000 cubic metres, excluding bark)

| | 2000 | 2001 |
|---|---:|---:|
| **Total** (all fuel wood) . . . . . . . . | 57 | 42 |

Source: FAO.

# Fishing

(metric tons, live weight)

| | 1998 | 1999 | 2000 |
|---|---:|---:|---:|
| Capture . . . . . . . | 698 | 1,111 | 1,105 |
| Crucian carp . . . . . | 42 | 26 | 38 |
| Whitefishes . . . . . | 605 | 922 | 881 |
| Aquaculture . . . . . | 437 | 901 | 902 |
| Common carp . . . . | 101 | 352 | 381 |
| Silver carp . . . . . | 19 | 59 | 51 |
| Rainbow trout . . . . | 308 | 445 | 439 |
| **Total catch** . . . . . | 1,135 | 2,012 | 2,007 |

Source: FAO, *Yearbook of Fishery Statistics*.

# Mining

| | 1998 | 1999 | 2000 |
|---|---:|---:|---:|
| Copper concentrates (metric tons)*† . . . . . . . . . | 9,200 | 9,600 | 14,000 |
| Molybdenum concentrates (metric tons)* . . . . . | 2,500† | 5,403 | 6,044 |
| Silver ores (kg)* . . . . . | 1,000 | 1,200† | 1,300 |
| Gold ores (kg)* . . . . . | 350† | 400 | 400 |
| Salt ('000 metric tons) . . . . | 25 | 27 | 30 |

* Figures refer to the metal content of ores and concentrates.
† Estimated production.

Source: US Geological Survey.

# Industry

**SELECTED PRODUCTS**
('000 metric tons, unless otherwise indicated)

| | 1999 | 2000 | 2001 |
|---|---|---|---|
| Wheat flour | 148 | 152 | 112 |
| Wine ('000 hectolitres) | 48 | 26 | 60 |
| Beer ('000 hectolitres) | 84 | 79 | 100 |
| Mineral water ('000 hectolitres) | 106 | 180 | 197 |
| Soft drinks ('000 hectolitres) | 222 | 216 | 284 |
| Cigarettes (million) | 3,132 | 2,109 | 1,623 |
| Wool yarn—pure and mixed (metric tons) | 24 | 46 | 34 |
| Cotton yarn—pure and mixed (metric tons) | 55 | 80 | 60 |
| Woven cotton fabrics ('000 sq metres) | 157 | 219 | 147 |
| Silk fabrics ('000 sq metres) | 21 | 16 | n.a. |
| Woven woollen fabrics ('000 sq metres) | 9 | 48 | 28 |
| Carpets ('000 sq metres) | 18 | 19 | 18 |
| Leather footwear ('000 pairs) | 24 | n.a. | n.a. |
| Rubber tyres ('000)* | 5 | n.a. | n.a. |
| Rubber footwear ('000 pairs) | 12 | n.a. | n.a. |
| Cement | 287 | 219 | 276 |
| Electric energy (million kWh)‡ | 5,717 | 5,958 | 5,744 |

* For road motor vehicles.

‡ Source: IMF, *Republic of Armenia: Statistical Annex* (October 2002).

# Finance

**CURRENCY AND EXCHANGE RATES**

**Monetary Units**
100 louma = 1 dram.

**Sterling, Dollar and Euro Equivalents** (30 May 2003)
£1 sterling = 963.9 drams;
US $1 = 585.0 drams;
€1 = 691.6 drams;
1,000 drams = £1.037 = $1.709 = €1.446.

**Average Exchange Rate** (drams per US $)
2000    539.53
2001    555.08
2002    573.35

Note: The dram was introduced on 22 November 1993, replacing the Russian (formerly Soviet) rouble at a conversion rate of 1 dram = 200 roubles. The initial exchange rate was set at US $1 = 14.3 drams, but by the end of the year the rate was $1 = 75 drams. After the introduction of the dram, Russian currency continued to circulate in Armenia. The rouble had been withdrawn from circulation by March 1994.

**STATE BUDGET**
(million drams)*

| Revenue | 1999 | 2000 | 2001† |
|---|---|---|---|
| Tax revenue | 190,469 | 182,526 | 200,700 |
| Value-added tax | 68,270 | 67,491 | 79,500 |
| Excises | 21,677 | 25,403 | 31,000 |
| Enterprise profits tax | 21,499 | 20,320 | 16,300 |
| Personal income tax | 18,835 | 14,777 | 11,200 |
| Land tax | 1,471 | 1,473 | 1,700 |
| Customs duties | 8,051 | 8,672 | 9,800 |
| Payroll taxes | 25,085 | 23,480 | 26,600 |
| Other taxes | 25,582 | 20,909 | 24,400 |
| Other revenue | 18,813 | 12,897 | 17,000 |
| Grants | 15,100 | 6,582 | 18,500 |
| **Total** | 224,383 | 202,005 | 236,100 |

| Expenditure | 1999 | 2000 | 2001† |
|---|---|---|---|
| Current expenditure | 224,149 | 211,491 | 218,400 |
| Wages | 34,394 | 36,603 | 37,100 |
| Subsidies | 14,183 | 8,306 | 6,600 |
| Interest | 19,845 | 17,320 | 14,200 |
| Transfers | 72,978 | 66,273 | 73,000 |
| Pensions | 32,434 | 32,035 | 38,500 |
| Family allowances | 21,391 | 19,717 | 16,600 |
| Other transfers | 19,153 | 14,520 | 17,900 |
| Goods and services | 82,749 | 82,988 | 87,200 |
| Health | 14,257 | 14,576 | n.a. |
| Education | 7,654 | 8,717 | n.a. |
| Other | 60,838 | 59,695 | n.a. |
| Capital expenditure | 46,285 | 40,313 | 46,700 |
| Net lending | 26,686 | 15,607 | 16,000 |
| **Total** | 297,120 | 267,411 | 281,200 |

* Figures refer to the consolidated accounts of republican and local authorities, including the operations of the Pension and Employment Fund.
† Figures rounded to the nearest 100 million drams.

Sources: IMF, *Republic of Armenia: Recent Economic Developments and Selected Issues* (May 2001) and *Republic of Armenia: Statistical Appendix* (October 2002).

**INTERNATIONAL RESERVES**
(US $ million at 31 December)

| | 2000 | 2001 | 2002 |
|---|---|---|---|
| Gold* | 11.79 | 12.41 | 15.68 |
| IMF special drawing rights | 21.55 | 10.24 | 30.10 |
| Foreign exchange | 296.77 | 310.58 | 394.92 |
| **Total** | 330.11 | 333.23 | 440.70 |

* National valuation.

Source: IMF, *International Financial Statistics*.

**MONEY SUPPLY**
(million drams at 31 December)

| | 2000 | 2001 | 2002 |
|---|---|---|---|
| Currency outside banks | 59,486 | 65,037 | 88,553 |
| Demand deposits at commercial banks | 11,743 | 12,073 | 26,400 |
| **Total money** (incl. others) | 71,395 | 77,297 | 115,307 |

Source: IMF, *International Financial Statistics*.

**COST OF LIVING**
(Consumer Price Index; base: 1994 = 100)

| | 1999 | 2000 | 2001 |
|---|---|---|---|
| Food (incl. non-alcoholic beverages) | 362.4 | 340.9 | 357.0 |
| Electricity, gas and other fuels | 643.5 | 650.2 | 649.0 |
| Clothing (incl. footwear) | 231.5 | 222.8 | 220.3 |
| Rent | 12,391.6 | 12,447.3 | 12,464.5 |
| **All items** (incl. others) | 408.2 | 405.1 | 417.7 |

Source: ILO.

## NATIONAL ACCOUNTS
(million drams at current prices)

### Expenditure on the Gross Domestic Product

|  | 2000 | 2001 | 2002 |
|---|---|---|---|
| Government final consumption expenditure . . . . . | 121,791 | 132,708 | 137,575 |
| Private final consumption expenditure . . . . . | 1,001,704 | 1,100,035 | 1,215,835 |
| Increase in stocks . . . . | 2,149 | 24,304 | 21,123 |
| Gross fixed capital formation . . | 190,130 | 208,025 | 263,285 |
| **Total domestic expenditure** . | 1,315,774 | 1,465,072 | 1,637,818 |
| Exports of goods and services . . | 241,078 | 299,477 | 401,259 |
| *Less* Imports of goods and services | 521,272 | 542,653 | 640,380 |
| **Sub-total** . . . . . . | 1,035,580 | 1,221,896 | 1,398,697 |
| Statistical discrepancy* . . . | −4,241 | −46,020 | −41,714 |
| **GDP in purchasers' values** . . | 1,031,338 | 1,175,877 | 1,356,983 |

* Referring to the difference between the sum of the expenditure components and official estimates of GDP, compiled from the production approach.

Source: IMF, *International Financial Statistics*.

### Gross Domestic Product by Economic Activity

|  | 1998 | 1999 | 2000 |
|---|---|---|---|
| Agriculture and forestry . . . | 295,628 | 251,147 | 231,908 |
| Industry* . . . . . . . | 207,452 | 212,883 | 226,898 |
| Construction . . . . . | 80,936 | 93,360 | 112,743 |
| Transport and communications . | 48,528 | 73,978 | 71,698 |
| Trade and catering . . . . | 82,401 | 87,809 | 94,878 |
| Other services . . . . . | 243,847 | 268,897 | 294,331 |
| **Total** . . . . . . . | 958,791 | 988,074 | 1,032,455 |

* Principally mining, manufacturing, electricity, gas and water.

Source: IMF, *Republic of Armenia: Recent Economic Developments and Selected Issues* (May 2001).

## BALANCE OF PAYMENTS
(US $ million)

|  | 2000 | 2001 | 2002 |
|---|---|---|---|
| Exports of goods f.o.b. . . . . | 309.9 | 353.1 | 515.8 |
| Imports of goods f.o.b. . . . . | −773.4 | −773.3 | −895.8 |
| **Trade balance** . . . . . | −463.5 | −420.2 | −379.9 |
| Exports of services . . . . | 136.9 | 186.5 | 184.0 |
| Imports of services . . . . | −192.7 | −204.3 | −221.2 |
| **Balance on goods and services** | −519.3 | −438.0 | −417.1 |
| Other income received . . . | 103.7 | 103.1 | 128.0 |
| Other income paid . . . . | −50.8 | −39.6 | −40.3 |
| **Balance on goods, services and income** . . . . . . . | −466.4 | −374.5 | −329.4 |
| Current transfers received . . | 208.5 | 200.8 | 195.4 |
| Current transfers paid . . . . | −20.5 | −26.8 | −26.3 |
| **Current balance** . . . . | −278.4 | −200.5 | −160.3 |
| Capital account (net) . . . . | 28.3 | 30.1 | 68.1 |
| Direct investment from abroad. . | 104.2 | 69.9 | 109.7 |
| Portfolio investment assets . . | −19.1 | −5.8 | 3.5 |
| Portfolio investment liabilities . . | 0.3 | −0.1 | −0.2 |
| Other investment assets . . . | −9.5 | −18.2 | −91.0 |
| Other investment liabilities . . | 174.0 | 131.1 | 156.6 |
| Net errors and omissions . . | 17.0 | 12.1 | −12.5 |
| **Overall balance** . . . . | 16.9 | 18.6 | 73.9 |

Source: IMF, *International Financial Statistics*.

# External Trade

## PRINCIPAL COMMODITIES
(US $ '000)

| Imports c.i.f. | 1999 | 2000 | 2001 |
|---|---|---|---|
| **Live animals and animal products** . . . . . . | 41,485 | 33,612 | 30,816 |
| Meat and edible meat offal . . . | 25,937 | 20,477 | 20,940 |
| **Vegetable products** . . . . | 75,684 | 99,124 | 85,151 |
| Cereals. . . . . . . . | 47,297 | 64,425 | 48,170 |
| **Prepared foodstuffs; beverages, spirits and vinegar; tobacco and manufactured substitutes** . . . . . . | 76,991 | 69,802 | 76,889 |
| Tobacco and manufactured tobacco substitutes . . . . . . | 30,435 | 29,580 | 29,923 |
| **Mineral products** . . . . . | 176,039 | 179,251 | 188,191 |
| Mineral fuels, mineral oils and products of their distillation; bituminous substances; mineral waxes . . . . . . . . | 175,037 | 178,516 | 187,201 |
| **Products of chemical or allied industries** . . . . . . | 71,353 | 82,386 | 65,135 |
| Pharmaceutical products . . . | 32,441 | 42,290 | 28,945 |
| **Textiles and textile articles** | 30,040 | 32,058 | 35,963 |
| **Natural or cultured pearls, precious or semi-precious stones, precious metals and articles thereof; imitation jewellery; coins** . . . . . | 86,712 | 113,247 | 106,771 |
| **Base metals and articles thereof** . . . . . . . . | 23,835 | 24,363 | 36,056 |
| **Machinery and mechanical appliances; electrical equipment; sound and television apparatus** . . . | 81,403 | 117,234 | 88,366 |
| Nuclear reactors, boilers, machinery and mechanical appliances; parts thereof . . . | 49,215 | 50,130 | 48,529 |
| Electrical machinery, equipment and parts; sound and television apparatus, and parts and accessories . . . . . . | 32,188 | 67,104 | 39,836 |
| **Vehicles, aircraft, vessels and associated transport equipment** . . . . . . . | 33,146 | 23,202 | 25,897 |
| Vehicles other than railway or tramway rolling-stock, and parts and accessories thereof . . . | 30,945 | 21,859 | 24,619 |
| **Optical, photographic, measuring and medical instruments and apparatus; clocks and watches; musical instruments** . . . . . . | 12,959 | 12,342 | 26,953 |
| **Total** (incl. others) . . . . . | 811,268 | 884,674 | 877,434 |

| Exports f.o.b. | 1999 | 2000 | 2001 |
|---|---|---|---|
| **Prepared foodstuffs; beverages, spirits and vinegar; tobacco and manufactured substitutes** . . . . . | 15,917 | 27,334 | 47,978 |
| Beverages, spirits and vinegar . . | 9,792 | 22,473 | 39,119 |
| **Mineral products** . . . . | 30,996 | 37,194 | 37,885 |
| Ores, slag and ash . . . . | 7,752 | 15,241 | 20,493 |
| Mineral fuels, mineral oils and products of their distillation; bituminous substances; mineral waxes . . . . . . | 19,154 | 20,658 | 17,158 |
| **Plastics, rubber and articles thereof** . . . . . . | 9,110 | 9,049 | 13,068 |
| Rubber and articles thereof . . . | 8,898 | 8,802 | 12,405 |
| **Textiles and textile articles** . . | 13,585 | 13,184 | 24,288 |
| Non-knitted clothing and accessories . . . . . . | 10,980 | 9,029 | 15,543 |
| **Natural or cultured pearls, precious or semi-precious stones, precious metals and articles thereof; imitation jewellery; coins** . . . . | 99,879 | 121,452 | 122,848 |
| **Base metals and articles thereof** . . . . . . | 24,952 | 44,203 | 43,445 |
| Iron and steel . . . . . | 8,454 | 10,790 | 9,582 |
| Copper and articles thereof . . . | 5,448 | 15,999 | 12,882 |
| Aluminium and articles thereof | 9,155 | 14,366 | 17,865 |
| **Machinery and mechanical appliances; electrical equipment; sound and television apparatus** . . . | 17,488 | 31,020 | 28,474 |
| Nuclear reactors, boilers, machinery and mechanical appliances; parts thereof . . . | 8,644 | 9,657 | 15,081 |
| Electrical machinery, equipment and parts; sound and television apparatus, and parts and accessories . . . . . . | 8,843 | 21,363 | 13,394 |
| **Total** (incl. others) . . . . | 231,669 | 300,487 | 341,836 |

**PRINCIPAL TRADING PARTNERS**
(US $ '000)

| Imports c.i.f. | 1999 | 2000 | 2001 |
|---|---|---|---|
| Belgium . . . . . . . | 85,192 | 84,372 | 41,783 |
| Bulgaria . . . . . . | 12,082 | 7,216 | 6,424 |
| Canada . . . . . . . | 10,024 | 5,396 | 6,929 |
| France . . . . . . . | 12,340 | 17,559 | 12,048 |
| Georgia . . . . . . | 26,856 | 19,801 | 18,503 |
| Germany . . . . . . | 34,244 | 36,487 | 33,962 |
| Greece . . . . . . . | 13,029 | 54,003 | 13,579 |
| Iran . . . . . . . | 78,450 | 82,328 | 78,121 |
| Israel . . . . . . . | 2,425 | 19,378 | 27,593 |
| Italy . . . . . . . | 23,725 | 25,711 | 29,635 |
| Lebanon . . . . . . | 9,355 | 4,572 | 5,984 |
| Netherlands . . . . . | 5,123 | 12,427 | 6,958 |
| Panama . . . . . . | 23,581 | 20,957 | 19,331 |
| Russia . . . . . . . | 149,878 | 137,158 | 173,648 |
| Switzerland . . . . . | 16,415 | 22,920 | 26,516 |
| Turkey . . . . . . . | 40,152 | 40,462 | 33,756 |
| Ukraine . . . . . . | 7,926 | 12,342 | 22,102 |
| United Arab Emirates . . . | 40,196 | 41,728 | 47,422 |
| United Kingdom . . . . | 67,031 | 59,481 | 91,225 |
| USA . . . . . . . | 85,669 | 102,675 | 84,153 |
| **Total** (incl. others) . . . . | 811,268 | 884,733 | 877,434 |

| Exports f.o.b. | 1999 | 2000 | 2001 |
|---|---|---|---|
| Belgium . . . . . | 84,227 | 75,051 | 46,489 |
| Georgia . . . . . | 11,100 | 15,989 | 12,413 |
| Germany . . . . . | 10,201 | 12,918 | 11,122 |
| Iran . . . . . | 34,161 | 30,089 | 31,870 |
| Israel . . . . . | 2,225 | 17,300 | 33,391 |
| Italy . . . . . | 1,443 | 2,683 | 6,065 |
| Russia . . . . . | 33,856 | 44,560 | 60,501 |
| Switzerland . . . . | 3,749 | 8,830 | 8,937 |
| Turkmenistan . . . . | 6,069 | 5,544 | 813 |
| Ukraine . . . . . | 2,096 | 3,271 | 10,983 |
| United Arab Emirates . . . | 2,612 | 5,479 | 7,277 |
| United Kingdom . . . . | 9,444 | 10,099 | 20,116 |
| USA . . . . . | 16,008 | 37,861 | 52,268 |
| **Total** (incl. others) . . . . | 231,669 | 300,487 | 341,836 |

# Transport

**RAILWAYS**
(traffic)

| | 1999 | 2000 | 2001 |
|---|---|---|---|
| Passenger journeys ('000) . . . | 1,323.5 | 1,086.6 | 1,165.7 |
| Passenger-km (million) . . . . | 46.4 | 46.8 | 47.3 |
| Freight carried ('000 metric tons) | 1,389.3 | 1,423.5 | 1,394.3 |
| Freight ton-km (million) . . . | 323.9 | 353.6 | 344.2 |

**CIVIL AVIATION**
(traffic)

| | 1999 | 2000 | 2001 |
|---|---|---|---|
| Passengers carried ('000) . . . | 630 | 611 | 769 |
| Passengers-km (million) . . . | 646.8 | 579.2 | 714.4 |
| Cargo ton-kilometres ('000) . . | 12.8 | 9.6 | 9.2 |

# Tourism

**ARRIVALS BY NATIONALITY**

| | 1998 | 1999 | 2000 |
|---|---|---|---|
| CIS countries* . . . . . | 13,525 | 16,326 | 15,000 |
| France . . . . . . | 2,280 | 3,046 | 3,724 |
| Germany . . . . . . | 1,025 | 1,195 | 1,209 |
| Greece . . . . . . | 768 | 847 | 954 |
| Iran . . . . . . | 1,104 | 4,653 | 8,573 |
| Lebanon . . . . . . | 894 | 1,406 | 1,574 |
| Turkey . . . . . . | 714 | 823 | 427 |
| United Kingdom . . . . | 1,636 | 919 | 1,021 |
| USA . . . . . . | 3,804 | 5,151 | 6,804 |
| **Total** (incl. others) . . . . | 31,837 | 40,745 | 45,222 |

* Comprising Azerbaijan, Belarus, Georgia, Kazakhstan, Kyrgyzstan, Moldova, Russia, Tajikistan, Turkmenistan, Ukraine and Uzbekistan.

**Tourism receipts** (US $ million): 10 in 1998; 27 in 1999; 45 in 2000.

Sources: World Tourism Organization, *Yearbook of Tourism Statistics*, and World Bank, *World Development Indicators*.

**Tourist arrivals:** 123,263 in 2001; 162,089 in 2002.

Source: National Statistical Service of the Republic of Armenia.

## Communications Media

|  | 1998 | 1999 | 2000 |
|---|---|---|---|
| Television receivers ('000 in use) | 840 | 850 | 860 |
| Telephones ('000 main lines in use) | 557 | 547.3 | 533.4 |
| Facsimile machines (number in use) . | n.a. | 1,000* | n.a. |
| Mobile cellular telephones ('000 subscribers). . . . . . . | 7.0 | 8.1 | 17.4 |
| Personal computers ('000 in use) | 15 | 20 | n.a. |
| Internet users ('000) . . . . . | 30 | 30 | 50 |
| Book production†: |  |  |  |
| Titles . . . . . . . . | 535 | 571 | 657 |
| Copies ('000) . . . . . | 392 | 754 | 460 |
| Newspapers: |  |  |  |
| Titles . . . . . . . | 126 | 102 | 91 |
| Total circulation ('000 copies) . | 207 | 150 | 302 |
| Periodicals: |  |  |  |
| Titles . . . . . . . | 75 | 64 | 44 |
| Total circulation ('000 copies) . | 220 | 230 | 115 |

* Estimate.
† Including brochures.

**2001:** Telephones ('000 main lines in use) 531.5; Mobile cellular telephones ('000 subscribers) 25.0; Personal computers ('000 in use) 35.

**2002:** Mobile cellular telephones ('000 subscribers) 44.3.

Source: partly International Telecommunication Union.

## Education

(2000/01, unless otherwise indicated)

|  | Institutions | Teachers | Students |
|---|---|---|---|
| Pre-primary . . . . . | 769* | 7,585† | 46,600* |
| General . . . . . . . | 1,433 | 56,300 | 572,200 |
| Gymnasia and lyceums . | 48 | n.a. | 8,800 |
| Vocational . . . . | 56 | n.a. | 5,100 |
| Other specialized schools . | 75 | n.a. | 26,900 |
| State higher schools (incl. universities) . . . . . | 19 | 4,420* | 60,700 |

* Dec. 2000.
† 1998/99.

Source: partly UN, *Statistical Yearbook for Asia and the Pacific*.

**Adult literacy rate** (UNESCO estimates): 98.5% (males 99.3%; females 97.8%) in 2001 (Source: UN Development Programme, *Human Development Report*).

# Directory

## The Constitution

The Constitution was approved by some 68% of the electorate in a national referendum, held on 5 July 1995. It replaced the amended Soviet Constitution of 1978. The following is a summary of the new Constitution's main provisions:

### GENERAL PROVISIONS OF CONSTITUTIONAL ORDER

The Republic of Armenia is an independent democratic state; its sovereignty is vested in the people, who execute their authority through free elections, referendums and local self-government institutions and officials, as defined by the Constitution. Referendums, as well as elections of the President of the Republic, the National Assembly and local self-government bodies, are carried out on the basis of universal, equal, direct suffrage by secret ballot. Through the Constitution and legislation, the State ensures the protection of human rights and freedoms, in accordance with the principles and norms of international law. A multi-party political system is guaranteed. The establishment of political parties is a free process, but the activities of political parties must not contravene the Constitution and the law. The right to property is recognized and protected. Armenia conducts its foreign policy based on the norms of international law, seeking to establish neighbourly and mutually beneficial relations with all countries. The State ensures the protection of the environment, and historical and cultural monuments, as well as cultural values. The official language is Armenian.

### FUNDAMENTAL HUMAN AND CIVIL RIGHTS AND FREEDOMS

The acquisition and loss of citizenship are prescribed by law. A citizen of the Republic of Armenia may not be simultaneously a citizen of another country. The rights, liberties and duties of citizens of Armenia, regardless of nationality, race, sex, language, creed, political or other convictions, social origin, property and other status, are guaranteed. No one shall be subject to torture or cruel treatment. Every citizen has the right to freedom of movement and residence within the republic, as well as the right to leave the republic. Every citizen has the right to freedom of thought, speech, conscience and religion. The right to establish or join associations, trade unions, political organizations, etc., is guaranteed, as is the right to strike for protection of economic, social and labour interests. Citizens of the republic who have attained 18 years of age are entitled to participate in state government through their directly elected representatives or by expression of free will.

Every citizen has the right to social insurance in the event of old age, disability, sickness, widowhood, unemployment, etc. Every citizen has the right to education. Education is provided free at elementary and secondary state educational institutions. Citizens belonging to national minorities have the right to preserve their traditions and to develop their language and culture. Everyone charged with a penal offence has the right to be presumed innocent until proved guilty. The advocacy of national, racial and religious hatred, and the propagation of violence and war, are prohibited.

### THE PRESIDENT OF THE REPUBLIC

The President of the Republic of Armenia ensures the observance of the Constitution and the effective operation of the legislative, executive and juridical authorities. The President is the guarantor of the independence, territorial integrity and security of the republic. He/she is elected by citizens of the republic for a period of five years. Any person who has the right to participate in elections, has attained the age of 35 years, and has been a resident citizen of Armenia for the preceding 10 years is eligible for election to the office of President. No person may be elected to the office for more than two successive terms.

The President signs and promulgates laws adopted by the National Assembly, or returns draft legislation to the National Assembly for reconsideration; may dismiss the National Assembly and declare special elections to it, after consultation with the Prime Minister and the Chairman of the National Assembly; appoints and dismisses the Prime Minister; appoints and dismisses the members of the Government, upon the recommendation of the Prime Minister; appoints civil service officials; establishes deliberation bodies; represents Armenia in international relations, co-ordinates foreign policy, concludes international treaties, signs international treaties ratified by the National Assembly, and ratifies agreements between governments; appoints and recalls diplomatic representatives of Armenia to foreign countries and international organizations, and receives the credentials of diplomatic representatives of foreign countries; appoints the Procurator-General, as nominated by the Prime Minister; appoints members and the Chairman of the Constitutional Court; is the Supreme Commander-in-Chief of the Armed Forces; takes decisions on the use of the Armed Forces; grants titles of honour; and grants amnesties to convicts.

### THE NATIONAL ASSEMBLY

Legislative power in the Republic of Armenia is executed by the National Assembly. The Assembly comprises 131 deputies, elected for a four-year term. Any person who has attained the age of 25 years and has been a permanent resident and citizen of Armenia for the preceding five years is eligible to be elected a deputy.

The National Assembly deliberates and enacts laws; has the power to express a vote of 'no confidence' in the Government; confirms the state budget, as proposed by the Government; supervises the implementation of the state budget; elects its Chairman (Speaker) and two Deputy Chairmen; appoints the Chairman and

Deputy Chairman of the Central Bank, upon the nomination of the President; and appoints members of the Constitutional Court.

At the suggestion of the President of the Republic, the National Assembly declares amnesties; ratifies or declares invalid international treaties; and declares war. Upon the recommendation of the Government, the National Assembly confirms the territorial and administrative divisions of the republic.

### THE GOVERNMENT

Executive power is realized by the Government of the Republic of Armenia, which is composed of the Prime Minister and the Ministers. The Prime Minister is appointed by the President; upon the recommendation of the Prime Minister, the President appoints the remaining Ministers. The Prime Minister directs the current activities of the Government and co-ordinates the activities of the Ministers.

The Government presents the programme of its activities to the National Assembly for approval; presents the draft state budget to the National Assembly for confirmation, ensures implementation of the budget and presents a report on its implementation to the National Assembly; manages state property; ensures the implementation of state fiscal, loan and tax policies; ensures the implementation of state policy in the spheres of science, education, culture, health care, social security and environmental protection; ensures the implementation of defence, national security and foreign policies; and takes measures to strengthen adherence to the laws, to ensure the rights and freedoms of citizens, and to protect public order and the property of citizens.

### JUDICIAL POWER*

In the Republic of Armenia the courts of general competence are the tribunal courts of first instance, the review courts and the courts of appeal. There are also economic, military and other courts. The guarantor of the independence of judicial bodies is the President of the Republic. He/she is the Head of the Council of Justice. The Minister of Justice and the Procurator-General are the Deputy Heads of the Council of Justice. Fourteen members appointed by the President of the Republic for a period of five years are included in the Council. The Constitutional Court is composed of nine members, of whom the National Assembly appoints five and the President of the Republic appoints four. The Constitutional Court, *inter alia* , determines whether decisions of the National Assembly, decrees and orders of the President, and resolutions of the Government correspond to the Constitution; decides, prior to ratification of an international treaty, whether the obligations created in it correspond to the Constitution; resolves disputes relating to referendums and results of presidential and legislative elections; and decides on the suspension or prohibition of the activity of a political party.

### TERRITORIAL ADMINISTRATION AND LOCAL SELF-GOVERNMENT

The administrative territorial units of the Republic of Armenia are regions and communities. Regions are comprised of rural and urban communities. Local self-government takes place in the communities. Bodies of local self-government, community elders and the community head (city mayor or head of village) are elected for a three-year period to administer community property and solve issues of community significance. State government is exercised in the regions. The Government appoints and dismisses regional governors, who carry out the Government's regional policy and co-ordinate the performance of regional services by state executive bodies. The city of Yerevan has the status of a region.

* The new judicial system came into force in January 1999. The Supreme Court was replaced by the Court of Cassation, and Appellate Courts were to operate in the place of People's Courts. Members of the Court of Cassation were to be appointed by the President, for life.

# The Government

### HEAD OF STATE

**President:** ROBERT KOCHARIAN (acting from 3 February 1998, elected 30 March 1998, inaugurated 9 April 1998; re-elected 5 March 2003, inaugurated 9 April 2003).

### GOVERNMENT
(October 2003)

A coalition of the Republican Party of Armenia (RPA), the Armenian Revolutionary Federation (ARF) and the Law-Governed Country Party of Armenia (OY).

**Prime Minister:** ANDRANIK MARKARIAN (RPA).

**Minister of Foreign Affairs\*:** VARDAN OSKANIAN.

**Minister of Defence\*:** SERGE SARKISSIAN.

**Minister of Finance and the Economy:** VARDAN KHACHATRIAN (RPA).

**Minister of Justice\*:** DAVID HAROUTUNIAN.

**Minister of Energy:** ARMEN MOVSISSIAN (RPA).

**Minister of Regional Government and the Co-ordination of Infrastructure:** HOVIK ABRAHAMIAN (RPA).

**Minister of Urban Planning:** ARA ARAMIAN (OY).

**Minister of Social Security:** AGHVAN VARDANIAN (ARF).

**Minister of Health:** NORAIR DAVIDIAN (ARF).

**Minister of Agriculture:** DAVID LOKIAN (ARF).

**Minister of the Environment:** VARDAN AYVAZIAN (RPA).

**Minister of Trade and Economic Development:** KAREN CHSHMARITIAN (RPA).

**Minister of Education and Science:** SERGO YERITSIAN (OY).

**Minister of Culture and Youth Affairs:** TAMARA POGHOSSIAN (OY).

**Minister of Transport and Communications:** ANDRANIK MANUKIAN (RPA).

**Chairman of Committee on State Property Management:** DAVID VARDANIAN.

**Chairman of Committee on State Revenue:** FELIKS TSOLAKIAN.

**Cabinet Chief of Staff:** MANUK TOPUZIAN (RPA).

**Head of the Police of the Republic of Armenia\*:** Lt-Gen. HAIK HAROUTUNIAN.

**Head of the National Security Service:** Lt-Gen. KARLOS PETROSSIAN.

**Mayor of Yerevan\*:** YERVAND ZAKHARIAN.

* Presidentially appointed positions.

### MINISTRIES

**Office of the President:** 375077 Yerevan, Marshal Baghramian St 26; tel. (1) 52-02-04; fax (1) 52-15-51; internet www.president.am.

**Office of the Prime Minister:** 375010 Yerevan, Republic Sq. 1, Govt House; tel. (1) 52-03-60; fax (1) 15-10-35; internet www.gov.am/am/gov/premier.

**Ministry of Agriculture:** 375010 Yerevan, Nalbandian St 48; tel. (1) 52-46-41; fax (1) 15-10-86.

**Ministry of Culture and Youth Affairs:** 375010 Yerevan, Tumanian St 5; tel. (1) 52-93-49; fax (1) 52-39-22.

**Ministry of Defence:** Yerevan, Proshian Settlement, G. Shaush St 60; tel. (1) 28-94-52; fax (1) 28-16-74.

**Ministry of Education and Science:** 375010 Yerevan, Movses Khorenatsi St 13; tel. (1) 52-66-02; fax (1) 58-04-03; internet www.edu.am/mes.

**Ministry of Energy:** 375010 Yerevan, Republic Sq., Govt House 2; tel. (1) 52-19-64; fax (1) 15-16-87.

**Ministry of the Environment:** 375002 Yerevan, Moskovian St 35; tel. (1) 52-10-99; fax (1) 53-18-61; e-mail iac@mnpiac.am; internet www.mnpiac.am.

**Ministry of Finance and the Economy:** 375010 Yerevan, Melik-Adamian St 1; tel. (1) 52-70-82; fax (1) 52-37-45; e-mail staff@mf.gov.am; internet mfe.gov.am.

**Ministry of Foreign Affairs:** 375010 Yerevan, Republic Sq., Govt House 2; tel. (1) 54-40-41; fax (1) 54-39-25; e-mail info@armeniaforeignministry.com; internet www.armeniaforeignministry.am.

**Ministry of Health:** 375001 Yerevan, Tumanian St 8; tel. (1) 58-24-13; fax (1) 15-10-97; internet www.armhealth.am.

**Ministry of Justice:** 375010 Yerevan, Khorhrdaranayin St 8; tel. (1) 58-21-57; fax (1) 58-24-49.

**Ministry of Regional Government and the Co-ordination of Infrastructure:** 375010 Yerevan, Republic Sq., Govt House 3; tel. (1) 52-15-07.

**Ministry of Social Security:** 375025 Yerevan, Terian St 69; tel. (1) 52-68-31; fax (1) 15-19-20; internet www.mss.am.

**Ministry of Trade and Economic Development:** 375008 Yerevan, Hanrapetoutioun St 5; tel. (1) 52-61-34; fax (1) 15-16-75; internet www.minted.am.

**Ministry of Transport and Communications:** 375010 Yerevan, Nalbandian St 28; tel. (1) 52-38-62; fax (1) 54-59-79; e-mail traceca@arminco.am.

**Ministry of Urban Planning:** 375010 Yerevan, Republic Sq., Govt House; tel. (1) 58-90-80; fax (1) 52-32-00.

**Committee on State Property Management:** 375010 Yerevan, Republic Sq. 2, Govt House; tel. (1) 52-42-13; fax (1) 52-65-57; e-mail tender@privatization.am; internet www.privatization.am.

**Committee on State Revenue:** 375015 Yerevan, Movses Khorenatsi St 3; tel. (1) 53-91-95; fax (1) 53-82-26; internet www .taxservice.am.

**National Security Service:** Yerevan.

**Office of the Cabinet Chief of Staff:** 375010 Yerevan, Republic Sq., Govt House; tel. (1) 53-16-12; fax (1) 15-10-36.

**Office of the Mayor of Yerevan:** 375015 Yerevan, Grigor Lusavorichi St 13; tel. (1) 52-58-47; fax (1) 58-39-64.

**Police of the Republic of Armenia:** 375025 Yerevan, Nalbandian St 104; tel. (1) 56-09-08; fax (1) 57-84-40.

# President and Legislature

## PRESIDENT

### Presidential Election, First Ballot, 19 February 2003

| Candidates | % of votes |
| --- | --- |
| Robert Kocharian | 49.48 |
| Stepan Demirchian | 28.22 |
| Artashes Geghamian | 17.66 |
| Aram Karapetian | 2.95 |
| Others | 1.68 |
| Total | 100.00 |

### Second Ballot, 5 March 2003

| Candidates | % of votes |
| --- | --- |
| Robert Kocharian | 67.48 |
| Stepan Demirchian | 32.52 |
| Total | 100.00 |

## NATIONAL ASSEMBLY
### (Azgayin Zhoghov)

375095 Yerevan, Marshal Baghramian St 19; tel. (1) 58-82-25; fax (1) 52-98-26; internet www.parliament.am.

**Chairman:** ARTUR BAGHDASARIAN.

**Deputy Chairmen:** TIGRAN TOROSSIAN, VAHAN OVANESSIAN.

### General Election, 25 May 2003

| Parties and blocs | % of votes for seats by proportional representation | Number of seats by proportional representation | Total seats |
| --- | --- | --- | --- |
| Republican Party of Armenia | 23.6 | 23 | 32 |
| Law-Governed Country Party of Armenia | 13.0 | 12 | 18 |
| Justice bloc* | 13.6 | 14 | 15 |
| Armenian Revolutionary Federation | 11.5 | 11 | 11 |
| National Unity Party | 8.9 | 9 | 9 |
| United Labour Party | 5.7 | 6 | 6 |
| Independents and others | 24.0 | 0 | 37 |
| **Total** (incl. others) | 100.0 | 75 | 131† |

* A coalition of the Armenian Democratic Party, the National Democratic Party, the People's Party of Armenia and the Union of National Democrats.
† Results were annulled in three constituencies; the subsequent by-elections, which were held in June, were won by a member of the Law-Governed Country Party of Armenia, a member of the Republican Party of Armenia and an independent candidate.

# Local Government

Armenia is divided into 11 provinces (marzer), including the capital, Yerevan. Each provincial governor (marzpet) is appointed by the Government to carry out regional administration. The provinces are subdivided into 871 rural and 59 urban communities (hamaynkner). Local elections were held on 20 October 2002.

## MARZER

**Yerevan:** see section on The Government.

**Aragotsotn:** 387410 Ashtarak, Hanrapetoutioun St 4; tel. (32) 28-74-60; fax (32) 31-032; Gov. GABRIYEL GEZALIAN.

**Ararat:** Artashat; tel. (35) 25-216; Gov. ALIK SARGSIAN.

**Armavir:** Armavir; tel. (37) 63-716; Gov. ALBERT HEROIAN.

**Gegharkunik:** Gavar; tel. (64) 21-045; Gov. STEPAN BARSEGHIAN.

**Kotaik:** Hrazdan; tel. (23) 23-663; Gov. SAMUEL STEPANIAN.

**Lori:** 377200 Vanadzor, Hayk Sq. 1; tel. (51) 46-192; fax (51) 22-877; internet www.lori.am/eng/govern/marzpetaran.html; Gov. HENRIK KOCHINIAN.

**Shirak:** 377500 Gyumri, Garegin Nzhdeh 16; tel. (41) 22-310; fax (41) 37-390; internet www.shirakinfo.am; Gov. ROMIK MANOUKIAN.

**Syunik:** 377810 Kapan, G. Nzhdeh St 1; tel. (85) 62-010; fax (85) 62-443; Gov. EDIK BARSEGHIAN.

**Tavush:** 377260 Ijevan, Sahmanadrutian St 1; tel. (63) 32-356; fax (63) 32-203; internet www.tavush.am; Gov. ARMEN GULARIAN.

**Vayots Dzor:** 378140 Yeghegnadzor, Shahumian St 5; tel. (81) 22-522; fax (81) 25-595; Gov. SAMVEL SARKISSIAN.

# Political Organizations

At 1 January 2002 there were 107 political parties registered with the Ministry of Justice.

**Armenian Christian Democratic Union (HDQM):** Yerevan; tel. (1) 52-62-49; e-mail pride@freenet.am; f. 1990; Chair. KHOSROV HAROUTUNIAN.

**Armenian Democratic Party:** Yerevan, Koriun St 14; tel. (1) 52-52-73; f. 1992 by elements of Communist Party of Armenia; contested the parliamentary election of 2003 as part of the Justice (Artarutiun) bloc; Chair. ARAM SARKISSIAN.

**Armenian Liberal Democratic Party** (Ramgavar Azadagan—HRAK): 375009 Yerevan, Koriun St 19A; tel. and fax (1) 52-64-03; f. 1991; joined the Union of Social Democratic Forces in 2000; centre-right; Co-Chair. HARUTIUN ARAKELIAN, ARMEN STEPANIAN, MEKHAK GEVORGIAN; 1,100 mems.

**Armenian Pan-National Movement (APNM)** (Haiots Hamazgaien Sharjoum–HHSh): 375019 Yerevan, Khanjian St 27; tel. (1) 57-04-70; f. 1989; absorbed the 21st Century Party in March 2002; Pres. LEVON TER-PETROSSIAN; Chair. ALEKSANDR ARZUMANIAN.

**Armenian Revolutionary Federation (ARF)** (Hai Heghapokhakan Dashnaktsutiun): 375025 Yerevan, Miasniak Ave 2; internet www.arf.am; f. 1890; formed the ruling party in independent Armenia, 1918–20; prohibited under Soviet rule, but continued its activities in other countries; permitted to operate legally in Armenia from 1991; suspended in December 1994; legally reinstated 1998; 40,000 mems; Chair. RUBEN HAGOBIAN, VAHAN HOVHANISSIAN.

**Armenian Social Democratic Party** (Hunchakian): Yerevan, Aghbiur Serob St 7; tel. (1) 27-33-15; internet www.hunchak.org.au; Chair. ERNEST SOGOMONIAN.

**Communist Party of Armenia (CPA)** (HHK): Yerevan, Marshal Baghramian St 10; tel. (1) 56-79-33; fax (1) 53-38-55; f. 1920; dissolved 1991, relegalized 1992; c. 50,000 mems; Chair. RUBEN TOVMASSIAN.

**Law-Governed Country Party of Armenia** (Orinats Yerkir—OY): Yerevan; f. 1998; centrist; also known as the Rule of Law Party and the Legal State Party; Head ARTUR BAGHDASARIAN; 41,000 mems.

**Liberal Democratic Union of Armenia:** Yerevan; f. 2001 following the division of the National Democratic Union; also known as the People's Liberal Union; Leader SEYRAN AVAKIAN; 7,000 mems.

**Mighty Homeland Party** (Hzor Hayrenik): f. 1997; also known as Powerful Motherland Party; Chair. VARDAN VARAPETIAN; 11,500 mems.

**National Democratic Party:** Yerevan, Abovian St 12; tel. and fax (1) 56-31-88; e-mail adjm@arminco.com; f. 2001 following the division of the National Democratic Union; contested the 2003 parliamentary election as part of the Justice (Artarutiun) bloc; Leader SHAVARSH KOCHARIAN.

**National Unity Party** (Azgayin Miabanutiun): c/o National Assembly, 375095 Yerevan, Marshal Baghramian St 19; f. 1998; Leaders GARNIK ISAGULIAN, IGOR MURADIAN, GRANT KHACHATRIAN.

**People's Democratic Party:** Yerevan; f. 2001 following the split in the PPA; centrist; Leader GAGIK ASLANIAN; 1,250 mems.

**People's Party of Armenia (PPA)** (HzhK): Yerevan; f. 1998; contested the general election of May 2003 as part of the Justice (Artarutiun) bloc; Leader STEPAN DEMIRCHIAN.

**Republic** (Hanrapetutiun): Yerevan; f. 2001 by members of the Yerkrapah Union of Volunteers and former members of the Republican Party of Armenia; Leader ALBERT BAZEIAN.

**Republican Party of Armenia (RPA)** (HHK): Yerevan; tel. (1) 58-00-31; fax (1) 56-60-34; f. 1990 following a split in the UNS (see below); contested the general election of May 1999 as part of the Unity bloc, together with the People's Party of Armenia (PPA); the PPA left the coalition in Sept. 2001; 13 territorial orgs; 5,500 mems; Chair. ANDRANIK MARKARIAN.

**Union of National Democrats:** Yerevan; f. 2001 following a split in the National Democratic Union; contested the general election of May 2003 as part of the Justice (Artarutiun) bloc; Leader ARSHAK SADOIAN.

**Union for National Self-Determination (UNS):** 375013 Yerevan, Grigor Lusavorichi St 15; tel. (1) 52-55-38; Chair. PARUIR HAIRIKIAN.

**Union of Right Forces:** Yerevan; f. 2000 as an alliance of the Hazatutiun (Freedom) Party, the 21st Century Party (Democratic National Party), the Liberal Democratic Party and the Armat (Root) Party.

**Union of Socialist Forces:** Yerevan; f. 1997; left-wing; Leader ASHOT MANUCHARIAN.

**United Communist Party of Armenia:** Yerevan; f. 2003 by the merger of seven pro-communist parties, including the Renewed Communist Party of Armenia, the Party of Intellectuals, the Communist Party of the Working People and the United Progressive Communist; First Sec. YURI MANUKIAN.

**United Labour Party (MAK):** f. 2002; also known as United Workers' Party; Chair. GURGEN ARSENIAN.

# Diplomatic Representation

## EMBASSIES IN ARMENIA

**Belarus:** 375009 Yerevan, Abovian St 23–6; tel. (1) 59–73–09; fax (1) 56-70-18; e-mail armenia@arminco.com; Ambassador MARINA DOLGO-POLOVA.

**Bulgaria:** Yerevan, Nor Aresh 11 St, h. 85; tel. (1) 45–82–33; fax (1) 45-46-02; e-mail bularm@arminco.com; Chargé d'affaires STEFAN DIMITROV.

**China, People's Republic:** Yerevan, Marshal Baghramian St 12; tel. (1) 56-00-67; fax (1) 54-57-61; e-mail chiemb@mbox.amilink.net; Ambassador ZUO XUELIANG.

**France:** 375015 Yerevan, Grigor Lusavorichi St 8; tel. (1) 56-11-03; fax (1) 56-98-31; e-mail secretar@ambafran.am; internet www.ambafran.am; Ambassador HENRI CUNY.

**Georgia:** Yerevan, Arami St 42; tel. (1) 56-43-57; fax (1) 56-41-83; e-mail georgia@arminco.com; Ambassador NIKOLOZ NIKOLOZISHVILI.

**Germany:** 375025 Yerevan, Charents St 29; tel. (1) 52-32-79; fax (1) 52-47-81; e-mail germemb@arminco.com; internet www.deutschebotschaft-eriwan.am; Ambassador HANS-WULF BARTELS.

**Greece:** Yerevan, Proshian St 12; tel. (1) 53-00-51; fax (1) 53-00-49; e-mail grembarm@arminco.com; Ambassador ANTONIOS VLAVIANOS.

**India:** 375019 Yerevan 19, Pionerakan St 50/2; tel. (1) 53-82-88; fax (1) 53-39-84; e-mail inemyr@arminco.com; Ambassador DEEPAK VOHRA.

**Iran:** Yerevan, Budaghian St 1; tel. (1) 28-04-57; fax (1) 23-00-52; e-mail info@iranembassy.am; internet www.iranembassy.am; Ambassador MUHAMMAD FARHAD KOLEINI.

**Iraq:** Yerevan, Sevastopolian St 24; tel. (1) 27-51-45; fax (1) 26-13-22; Chargé d'affaires ABBAS MUZHAR AL-BADRY (pending new appointment).

**Italy:** 375010 Yerevan, Italia St 5; tel. (1) 54-23-35; fax (1) 54-23-41; e-mail ambitaly@arminco.com; Ambassador PAOLO ANDREA TRABALZA.

**Lebanon:** Yerevan, Vardanants St 7; tel. (1) 52-65-40; fax (1) 52-69-90; e-mail libarm@arminco.com; Ambassador JEBRAIL JAARAY.

**Poland:** Yerevan, Hanrapetutiun St 44A; tel. (1) 54-24-93; fax (1) 54-24-98; e-mail polemb@arminco.com; Ambassador VIKTOR ROSS.

**Romania:** Yerevan, Sepuhi St 3; tel. (1) 27-47-01; fax (1) 54-41-44; e-mail ambrom@netsys.am; Chargé d'affaires a.i. DORIN CIMPOEŞU.

**Russia:** 375015 Yerevan, Grigor Lusavorichi St 13A; tel. (1) 56-74-27; fax (1) 56-71-97; e-mail rossia@arminco.com; internet www.armenia.mid.ru; Ambassador ANATOLII DRYUKOV.

**Syria:** Yerevan, Marshal Baghramian St 14; tel. (1) 52-40-28; fax (1) 52-40-58; e-mail syria.em.arm@netsys.am; Chargé d'affaires a.i. HAMED HASAN.

**Turkmenistan:** Yerevan, Dzorapi St 72, Hotel Hrazdan; tel. (1) 53-05-12; fax (1) 52-52-35; e-mail serdar@arminco.com; Ambassador (vacant).

**Ukraine:** 375033 Yerevan, Yerznkian St 58; tel. (1) 58-68-56; fax (1) 22-82-96; e-mail ukremb@arminco.com; internet www.erevan.am/ukrembassy; Ambassador VOLODYMYR TYAGLO.

**United Kingdom:** Yerevan, Charents St 28; tel. (1) 55-30-81; fax (1) 54-38-20; e-mail britemb@arminco.com; Ambassador THORHILDA (THORDA) ABBOTT-WATT.

**USA:** Yerevan, Marshal Baghramian St 18; tel. (1) 52-46-61; fax (1) 52-08-00; e-mail usinfo@arminco.com; internet www.usa.am/index.html; Ambassador JOHN M. ORDWAY.

# Judicial System

A new judicial and legal system came into force in January 1999. The Supreme Court was replaced by the Court of Cassation, and Appellate Courts were to operate in the place of People's Courts. Members of the Court of Cassation were to be appointed by the President, for life.

### Constitutional Court

375019 Yerevan, Marshal Baghramian St 10; tel. (1) 58-81-40; fax (1) 52-99-91; e-mail armlaw@concourt.am; internet www.concourt.am.

f. 1996; Chair. GAGIK HAROUTUNIAN.

**Chairman of the Court of Cassation:** HANRIK DANIELIAN.

**Prosecutor-General:** ARAM TAMAZIAN.

# Religion

The major religion is Christianity. The Armenian Apostolic Church is the leading denomination and was widely identified with the movement for national independence. There are also Russian Orthodox and Islamic communities, although the latter lost adherents as a result of the departure of large numbers of Muslim Azeris from the republic. Most Kurds are also adherents of Islam, although some are Yazidis. In 2002 51 religious organizations were registered in Armenia, after legislative amendments were adopted, which increased the number of adherents required for registration from 50 to 200. (The Jehovah's Witness community was estimated to number 12,000, but failed to qualify for registration as its statutes were deemed to be in contravention of the Constitution.)

### GOVERNMENT AGENCY

**Council for the Affairs of the Armenian Church:** 375001 Yerevan, Abovian St 3; tel. (1) 56-46-34; fax (1) 56-41-81.

**Religious Council:** Yerevan; f. 2002 as a consultative council, to advise the Government on religious affairs; was to comprise representatives of the Government, the Office of the Prosecutor-General, the Armenian Apostolic Church, and the Catholic and Protestant Churches.

### CHRISTIANITY

**Armenian Apostolic Church:** Vagharshapat, Monastery of St Etchmiadzin; tel. (1) 28-57-37; fax (1) 15-10-77; e-mail holysee@etchmiadzin.am; internet www.holyetchmiadzin.com; nine dioceses in Armenia, four in other ex-Soviet republics and 25 dioceses and bishoprics in the rest of the world; 7m. members world-wide; 15 monasteries and three theological seminaries in Armenia; Supreme PATRIARCH KAREKIN II (Catholicos of All Armenians).

#### The Roman Catholic Church

##### Armenian Rite

Armenian Catholics in Eastern Europe are under the jurisdiction of an Ordinary (equivalent to a bishop with direct authority). At 31 December 2001 there were an estimated 220,000 adherents within this jurisdiction.

**Ordinary:** Most Rev. NERSES DER-NERSESSIAN (Titular Archbishop of Sebaste), Gyumri, Atarbekian St 82; tel. (41) 22-115; fax (41) 34-959; e-mail armorda@shirak.am.

##### Latin Rite

The Apostolic Administrator of the Caucasus is the Apostolic Nuncio (Ambassador of the Holy See) to Georgia, Armenia and Azerbaijan, who is resident in Tbilisi, Georgia.

# The Press

## PRINCIPAL NEWSPAPERS

In 2000 91 newspaper titles were published in Armenia, 74 of which were in Armenian. Those listed below are in Armenian except where otherwise stated.

**Ankakhutiun** (Independence): 375013 Yerevan, Grigor Lusavorichi St 15; tel. (1) 58-18-64; daily; organ of the Union for National Self-Determination; Editor PARUIR HAIRIKIAN.

**Aravot:** 375023 Yerevan, Arshakuniats Ave 2, 15th Floor; tel. (1) 56-89-68; fax (1) 52-87-52; e-mail news@aravot.am; internet www.aravot.am; daily; Editor A. ABRAMIAN.

**Avangard:** 375023 Yerevan, Arshakuniats Ave 2; f. 1923; 3 a week; organ of the Youth League of Armenia; Editor M. K. ZOHRABIAN.

**Azg** (The Nation): 375010 Yerevan, Hanrapetoutioun St 47; tel. (1) 52-16-35; fax (1) 56-29-41; e-mail azg2@arminco.com; internet www.azg.am; f. 1990; Editor HAGOP AVETIKIAN.

**Bravo:** Yerevan, Abovian St 12, Hotel Yerevan; tel. (1) 55-44-05; weekly; Editor K. KAZARIAN.

**Delovoi Express:** Yerevan, Zarian St 22, 2nd Floor; tel. (1) 25-26-83; fax (1) 25-90-23; e-mail eis@arminco.com; f. 1992; weekly; Editor E. NAGDALIAN.

**Epokha** (Epoch): 375023 Yerevan, Arshakuniats Ave 2; f. 1938; fmrly *Komsomolets*; weekly; Russian; organ of the Youth League of Armenia; Editor V. S. GRIGORIAN.

**Golos Armenii** (The Voice of Armenia): 375023 Yerevan, Arshakuniats Ave 2, 7th Floor; tel. (1) 52-77-23; fax (1) 52-89-08; e-mail root@goloss.arminco.com; f. 1934 as *Kommunist*; 3 a week; in Russian; Editor F. NASHKARIAN.

**Grakan Tert** (Literary Paper): 375019 Yerevan, Marshal Baghramian St 3; tel. (1) 52-05-94; f. 1932; weekly; organ of the Union of Writers; Editor ZAVEN HOVHANISSIAN.

**Haiastan** (Armenia): 375023 Yerevan, Arshakuniats Ave 2, 5th Floor; tel. (1) 52-84-50; f. 1920; 6 a week; in Russian; Editor TIGRAN NIKHOGOSSIAN.

**Haik** (Armenia): Yerevan; tel. (1) 52-77-01; e-mail root@hayk.arminco.com; weekly; organ of the Armenian Pan-National Movement; Editor V. DAVTIAN; circ. 30,000.

**Haiots Ashkhar:** Yerevan, Tumanian St 38; tel. (1) 53-32-11; fax (1) 53-88-65; e-mail hayashkh@armnico.com; f. 1997; Editor G. MKRTCHIAN; circ. 3,500.

**Hanrapetakan:** Yerevan; tel. (1) 58-00-31; fax (1) 56-60-34; organ of the Republican Party of Armenia.

**Hazatamart** (The Battle for Freedom): 375070 Yerevan, Atarbekian 181; organ of the Armenian Revolutionary Federation (ARF); Editor M. MIKAYELIAN.

**Hnchak Haiastani** (The Bell of Armenia): Yerevan; weekly.

**Marzakan Haiastan:** 375023 Yerevan, Arshakuniats Ave 5; tel. (1) 52-62-41; weekly; Editor S. MOURADIAN.

**Molorak:** 375023 Yerevan, Arshakuniats Ave 5; tel. (1) 52-62-12; daily; Editor H. GHAGHRINIAN.

**Respublika Armenia:** 375023 Yerevan, Arshakuniats Ave 2, 9th Floor; tel. (1) 52-69-69; e-mail root@ra.arminco.com; government publication; Editor A. KHANBABIAN.

**Ria Taze** (New Way): Yerevan; 2 a week; Kurdish.

**Vozny** (Hedgehog): 375023 Yerevan, Arshakuniats Ave 2, 12th Floor; tel. (1) 52-63-83; f. 1954; Editor A. SAHAKIAN.

**Yerevanian Orer** (Yerevan Days): Yerevan; Editor M. AIRAPETIAN.

**Yerkir** (Country): 375070 Yerevan, Zavarian St 181; tel. (1) 57-10-95; e-mail erkir@arminco.com; f. 1991; daily; organ of the ARF; publication temporarily suspended in January 2000.

**Yerokoian Yerevan** (Evening Yerevan): 375023 Yerevan, Arshakuniats Ave 2, 10th Floor; tel. (1) 52-97-52; weekly; organ of Yerevan City Council; Editor N. YENGIBARIAN.

**Yeter:** Yerevan, Manukian St 5; tel. (1) 55-34-13; weekly; Editor G. KAZARIAN.

**Zroutsakits:** 375023 Yerevan, Arshakuniats Ave 2, 2nd Floor; tel. (1) 52-84-30; weekly; Editor M. MIRIDJANIAN.

## PRINCIPAL PERIODICALS

In 2000 44 periodicals were published, of which 32 were in Armenian.

**Aghbiur** (Source): Yerevan; f. 1923, fmrly *Pioner*; monthly; for teenagers; Editor T. V. TONOIAN.

**Armenian Kommersant:** Yerevan, Koriuni St 19A; tel. (1) 52-79-77; monthly; Editor M. VARTANIAN.

**Aroghchapautiun** (Health): 376001 Yerevan, Tumanian St 8; tel. (1) 52-35-73; e-mail mharut@dmc.am; f. 1956; quarterly; journal of the Ministry of Health; Editor M. A. MURADIAN; circ. 2,000–5,000.

**Arvest** (Art): 375001 Yerevan, Tumanian St 5; f. 1932, fmrly *Sovetakan Arvest* (Soviet Art); monthly; publ. by the Ministry of Culture and Youth Affairs; Editor G. A. AZAKELIAN.

**Chetvertaya Vlast:** Yerevan, Abovian St 12, Rm 105, Hotel Yerevan 105; tel. (1) 59-73-81; monthly; Editor A. GEVORKIAN.

**Ekonomika** (Economics): Yerevan, Vardanants St 2; tel. (1) 52-27-95; f. 1957; monthly; government organ; Editor R. H. SHAKHKULIAN; circ. 1,500–2,000.

**Garoun** (Spring): 375015 Yerevan, Grigor Lusavorichi St 15; tel. (1) 56-29-56; e-mail garoun@garoun.am; f. 1967; monthly; independent; fiction, poetry and socio-political issues; Editor V. S. AYOUZIAN; circ. 1,500.

**Gitutyun ev Tekhnika** (Science and Technology): 375048 Yerevan, Komitasa Ave 49/3; tel. (1) 23-37-27; f. 1963; quarterly; journal of the Research Institute of Scientific-Technical Information and of Technological and Economic Research; Dir M.B. YEDILIAN; Editor M. A. CHUGURIAN; circ. 1,000.

**Hayastani Ashkhatavoruhi** (Working Women of Armenia): Yerevan; f. 1924; monthly; Editor A. G. CHILINGARIAN.

**Hayreniky Dzayn** (Voice of the Motherland): Yerevan; f. 1965; weekly; organ of the Armenian Committee for Cultural Relations with Compatriots Abroad; Editor L. H. ZAKARIAN.

**Iravunk:** 375002 Yerevan, Yeznik Koghbatsu St 50A; tel. (1) 53-27-30; fax (1) 53-41-92; e-mail info@iravunk.com; internet www.iravunk.com; f. 1989; weekly; Editor HAIK BABUKHANIAN; circ. 45,000.

**Literaturnaya Armeniya** (Literature of Armenia): 375019 Yerevan, Marshal Baghramian St 3; tel. (1) 56-36-57; f. 1958; monthly; journal of the Union of Writers; fiction; Russian; Editor A. M. NALBANDIAN.

**Nork:** Yerevan; f. 1934; fmrly *Sovetakan Grakanutyun* (Soviet Literature); monthly; journal of the Union of Writers; fiction; Russian; Editor R. G. OVSEPIAN.

**Novoye Vremya:** 375023 Yerevan, Arshakuniats Ave 2, 3rd Floor; tel. (1) 52-69-46; fax (1) 52-73-62; e-mail nvremya@arminco.com; f. 1992; 3 a week; Editor R. A. SATIAN; circ. 5,000.

**Veratsnvats Haiastan** (Reborn Armenia): Yerevan; f. 1945 as *Sovetakan Hayastan* (Soviet Armenia); monthly; journal of the Armenian Committee for Cultural Relations with Compatriots Abroad; fiction; Editor V. A. DAVITIAN.

**Yerevan Times:** 375009 Yerevan, Isaahakian St 28, 3rd Floor; tel. (1) 52-82-70; fax (1) 15-17-38; e-mail yertime@armpress.arminco.com; weekly; English; Editor T. HAKOBIAN.

### NEWS AGENCIES

**Arka News Agency:** 375010 Yerevan, Pavstos Byuzand St 1/3; tel. (1) 52-21-52; fax (1) 52-40-80; e-mail arka@arminco.com; internet www.arka.am; f. 1996; economic, financial and political news; Russian and English.

**Armenpress** (Armenian News Agency): 375009 Yerevan, Isaahakian St 28, 4th Floor; tel. (1) 52-67-02; fax (1) 52-57-98; e-mail contact@armenpress.am; internet www.armenpress.am; f. 1922 as state information agency, transformed into state joint-stock company in 1997; Armenian, English and Russian; Dir H. ZORIAN.

**Arminfo:** 375009 Yerevan, Isaahakian St 28, 2nd Floor; tel. (1) 52-20-34; fax (1) 54-31-72; e-mail news@arminfo.am; internet www.arminfo.am; f. 1991 as Snark; name changed as above in 2001; Dir EMMANUIL MKRTCHIAN; Editor ALEKSANDR AVANISOV.

**Mediamax** (Armenian Press Agency): Yerevan, Marshal Baghramian St 31A; tel. (1) 22-87-86; fax (1) 27-11-56; e-mail media@arminco.com; internet www.mediamax.am; Dir ARA TADEVOSIAN; Editor-in-Chief DAVID ALAVERDIAN.

**Noyan Tapan** (Noah's Ark): 375009 Yerevan, Isaahakian St 28, 3rd Floor; tel. (1) 56-59-65; fax (1) 52-42-79; e-mail contact@noyan-tapan.am; internet www.nt.am; also broadcaster, advertising agency, publisher and printing agency; Dir TIGRAN HAROUTUNIAN.

### PRESS ASSOCIATIONS

**Union of Journalists of Armenia:** Yerevan, Abovian St 64; tel. (1) 56-12-76; fax (1) 56-14-47; f. 1959; Dir ASTGHIK GEVORGIAN.

# Publishers

**Academy of Sciences Publishing House:** 375019 Yerevan, Marshal Baghramian St 24G; Dir KH.H. BARSEGHIAN.

**Arevik Publishing House:** 375009 Yerevan, Terian St 91; tel. (1) 52-45-61; fax (1) 52-05-36; e-mail arevikp@freenet.am; f. 1986; closed joint-stock co; political, scientific, fiction for children, textbooks; Pres. DAVID HOVHANNES; Exec. Dir ASTGHIK STEPANIAN.

**Hayastan** (Armenia Publishing House): 375009 Yerevan, Isaahakian St 28; tel. (1) 52-85-20; e-mail nunjan@hragir.aua.am; f. 1921; political and fiction; Dir VAHAGN SARKISSIAN.

**Haikakan Hanragitaran Hratarakchutioun** (Armenian Encyclopaedia Publishing House): 375001 Yerevan, Tumanian St 17; tel. (1) 52-43-41; fax (1) 52-06-67; e-mail encyclop@sci.am; internet www .encyclopedia.am; f. 1967; encyclopedias and other reference books; Editor H. M. AIVAZIAN.

**Hanragitaran—Armenica** (Encyclopaedia—Armenica LLC): 375001 Yerevan, Tumanian St 17; tel. (1) 52-43-41; fax (1) 52-06-67; e-mail e-armenica@yahoo.com; internet www.e_armenica.am; f. 1995; encyclopedias, other reference books; Dir S. A. KEROBIAN.

**Louys Publishing House:** 375009 Yerevan, Isaahakian St 28; tel. (1) 52-53-13; fax (1) 56-55-07; e-mail louys@arminco.com; internet www.spyur.am/luys.htm; f. 1955; textbooks; Dir H. Z. HAROUTUNIAN.

**Miva-Pres Publishing House:** 375009 Yerevan, Isahaakian St 28/21; tel. (1) 52-65-00; e-mail miva@noyan-tapan.am; translations of Armenian and world literature; Dir MICHAEL STEPANIAN.

**Nairi Ltd:** 375009 Yerevan, Terian St 91; tel. and fax (1) 56-58-54; e-mail nairi_hrat@rambler.ru; f. 1991; fiction, science, translations and reference; Pres. HRACHIA TAMRAZIAN.

**Noyan Tapan Publishing House:** 375009 Yerevan, Isahaakian St 28; tel. (1) 56-59-65; e-mail info@noyan-tapan.am; legal and medical literature; publishes magazines, booklets and a newspaper; Dir LILA KHALAPIAN.

**Tigran Mets Publishing House:** 375023 Yerevan, Arshakuniats St 2; tel. (1) 52-70-56; e-mail tigranmets2002@yahoo.com; fiction, poetry, science and children's books; Dir VREZH MARKOSSIAN.

**Yerevan State University Publishing House:** 375028 Yerevan, Aleks Manukian St 1; tel. (1) 55-28-84; e-mail pr-int@ysu.am; textbooks and reference books, history, literary criticism, science and fiction; Dir PERCH STEPANIAN.

## PUBLISHERS' ASSOCIATION

**National Book Chamber of Armenia:** 375009 Yerevan, G. Kochar St 21; tel. (1) 52-75-95; e-mail grapalat@arminco.com; f. 1922; centre of national bibliography, bibliographical information and statistics, and central depositary of publications; also incorporates the National Agency of ISBN; 2.5m. units.

**National Union of Armenian Publishers:** 375009 Yerevan, Isahaakian St 28; tel. (1) 56-31-57; fax (1) 56-55-07; e-mail gam@ arminco.com; internet www.magic.am/nuap; f. 1999; Pres. SOS MOVSISSIAN.

# Broadcasting and Communications

## TELECOMMUNICATIONS

**Armenia Telephone Co JV (ArmenTel):** Yerevan, Azatutiun Ave 24; tel. (1) 54-91-00; fax (1) 28-98-88; internet www.armentel.com; f. 1995 by the Government and TransWorld Telecom (USA); transferred to private ownership in 1998; 10% state-owned, 90% owned by OTE Hellenic Telecommunications Organization (Greece); restructuring of monopoly pending; Chief Exec. GEORGIOS VASILAKIS (acting); Chair. VASSILIS MAGLARAS; 7,159 employees (Dec. 2001).

**Arminco Global Telecommunications:** 375009 Yerevan, Isaahakian St 28, POB 10; tel. (1) 52-43-51; fax (1) 28-50-82; internet www .arminco.com; internet service provider; Gen. Dir ANDRANIK ALEKSANDRIAN.

**Netsys LLC:** Yerevan, Abovian St 38; tel. (1) 54-00-91; fax (1) 54-00-21; e-mail info@netsys.am; internet www.netsys.am; US-Armenian jt venture; internet service provider.

## BROADCASTING

### Radio

**Armenian Public Radio:** 375025 Yerevan, Alex Manogian St 5; tel. (1) 55-33-43; fax (1) 55-46-00; e-mail president@mediaconcern .am; internet www.mediaconcern.am; three programmes; broadcasts inside the republic in Armenian, Russian and Kurdish;

external broadcasts in Armenian, Russian, Kurdish, Azeri, Arabic, English, French, German, Spanish and Farsi; transformed into state joint-stock co in 1997; Dir-Gen. ARMEN AMIRIAN.

### Television

**Armenian Public Television:** 375047 Yerevan, Hovsepian St 26; tel. (1) 56-95-74; fax (1) 56-24-60; internet www.armtv.com; broadcasts in Armenian, and occasionally in Russian and English; transformed into state joint-stock co in 1997; Chair. of Council ALEKSAN HAROUTUNIAN; Exec. Dir ARMEN ARZUMANIAN.

# Finance

(cap. = capital; res = reserves; dep. = deposits; m. = million; brs = branches; amounts in drams, unless otherwise stated)

## BANKING

### Central Bank

**Central Bank of the Republic of Armenia:** 375010 Yerevan, V. Sarkissian St 6; tel. (1) 58-38-41; fax (1) 52-38-52; e-mail mcba@cba .am; internet www.cba.am; f. 1993 as successor to the Armenian Republic Bank; state-owned; cap. 100.0m., res 16,748.9m., dep. 26,588.5m. (Dec. 2001); Chair. Dr TIGRAN SARKISSIAN.

### Commercial Banks

In October 2002 there were 28 commercial banks in operation in Armenia. Some of the most influential of these are listed below:

**Agricultural Co-operative Bank of Armenia:** 375009 Yerevan, Byron St 1; tel. (1) 56-85-58; fax (1) 15-17-55; e-mail acba@arminco .com; internet www.acba.am; f. 1996; cap. 825m., res 2,300m., dep. 5,437m. (Dec. 2001); Gen. Man. STEPAN GISHIAN.

**Ardshininvestbank CJSC (ASHIB):** 375010 Yerevan, Deghatan St 3; tel. (1) 52-85-13; fax (1) 56-74-86; e-mail international@ashib .am; internet www.ashib.am; f. 1922, reorganized as joint-stock commercial bank, Bank for Industry and Construction, in 1992; restructured 1997; merged with Adana bank in Feb. 2002; second largest bank in Armenia; cap. 1,305.0m., res 412.8m., dep. 21,279.6m. (Dec. 2001); Chair. of Bd ARAM ANDREASSIAN; 25 brs.

**Armagrobank OJSC:** 375015 Yerevan, M. Khorenatsi St 7A; tel. (1) 53-43-42; fax (1) 53-09-97; e-mail agrobank@agrobank.am; internet www.agrobank.am; f. 1991, incorporated as joint-stock co in 1992; cap. 1,394.6m. (June 2001); Chair. GRIGOR GHONJEIAN; 36 brs.

**Armenian Development Bank:** 375015 Yerevan, Paronian St 21/1; tel. (1) 53-88-41; fax (1) 53-32-33; e-mail info@armdb.com; internet www.armdb.com; f. 1990; cap. US $3.0m., res $0.6m., dep. $12.2m. (2002); Chair. ALEKSANDR GRIGORIAN.

**Armenian Economy Development Bank (Armeconombank):** 375002 Yerevan, Amirian St 23/1; tel. (1) 56-27-05; fax (1) 53-89-04; e-mail bank@aeb.am; internet www.aeb.am; incorporated as joint-stock co in 1992; corporate banking; cap. 1,200m., res 29.8m., dep. 9,136.8m. (Dec. 2001); Chair. of Bd SARIBEK SUKIASSIAN; Chief Exec. ASHOT OSSIPIAN; 23 brs.

**Armenian Import-Export Bank CJSC (Armimpexbank):** 375010 Yerevan, Vazgen Sarkissian St 2; tel. (1) 58-99-06; fax (1) 56-48-87; e-mail office@impexbank.am; internet www.impexbank.am; f. 1992 by reorganization of Armenian br. of the Vneshekonombank of the former USSR; joint-stock co with foreign shareholding; cap. US $3.1m., dep. $14m. (Sept. 1999); Chair. of Bd B. ASATRIAN; 5 brs.

**Arminvestbank CJSC:** 375010 Yerevan, Vardanants St 13; tel. (1) 52-39-29; fax (1) 54-58-35; e-mail ibank@dolphin.am; f. 1992; cap. US $1.9m., res $0.3m., dep. $3.3m.; Chair. of Bd VAROUZHAN AMIRAGHIAN.

**Bank Mellat CJSC:** 375010 Yerevan, Amirian St 6, POB 24; tel. (1) 58-13-54; fax (1) 54-08-85; e-mail mellat@netsys.am; wholly owned by Bank Mellat (Iran); cap. and res 1,001.0m., dep. 6,418.4m. (Dec. 1999); Chair. ESSA GHAREMANI CHABOCK.

**Converse Bank Corpn:** 375010 Yerevan, Vazgen Sarkissian St 26; tel. (1) 56-92-48; fax (1) 54-09-20; e-mail post@cb.aic.net; internet www.cb.aic.net; f. 1994; reorganized in 1997; cap. 1,296.4m., res 195.2m., dep. 15,282.7m. (Dec. 2002); Pres. KHORI MODALAL; Chair. SMBAT NASIBIAN.

**Credit-Yerevan Joint-Stock Commercial Bank:** 375010 Yerevan, Amirian St 2/8; tel. (1) 58-90-65; fax (1) 15-18-20; e-mail garik@ mail.creyer.am; f. 1993; cap. US $2.1m. (Nov. 1998); Pres. MARTIN HOVHANNISIAN.

**HSBC Bank of Armenia cjsc:** 375010 Yerevan, Vazgen Sarkissian St 9; tel. (1) 56-32-29; fax (1) 52-69-49; e-mail hsbc@arminco.com; internet www.hsbc.com; f. 1996; cap. 2,438m., res 1,922m., dep. 33,156m. (July 2002); Chief Exec. CHARLES B. GREGORY; 2 brs.

**Prometey Bank LLC:** 375010 Yerevan, Hanrapetoutioun St 44/2; tel. (1) 56-20-36; fax (1) 54-57-19; e-mail office@prometeybank.am; internet www.prometeybank.am; f. 1990 as Prometheus Commercial Bank; name changed as above 2001; cap. 2,482.9m., res 52.1m., dep. 8,530.9m. (Dec. 2001); Chair. of Bd EMIL SOGHOMONIAN.

**Unibank CJSC:** 375001 Yerevan, Amiryan St 12; tel. (1) 53-98-70; fax (1) 53-30-52; e-mail unibank@unibank.am; internet www.unibank.am; f. 2001; Russian-owned; cap. US $5m., dep. $8m. (2002); Exec. Dir VARDAN G. ATAIAN; Chair. GAGIK ZAKARIAN; 5 brs.

**United Bank OJSC:** 375004 Yerevan, Spendiarov St 4; tel. (1) 53–90–41; fax (1) 53-69-055; e-mail ubank@netsys.am; internet www.ubank.am; f. 1996, as Haysnund, by merger; cap. 1,510m., res 221.2m., dep. 17,052.9m. (Dec. 1999); Chair. BENIK HAROUTUNIAN; Exec. Dir HOVSEP GALSTIAN.

### Savings Bank

**Armsavingsbank** (Armsberbank): 375010 Yerevan, Nalbandian St 46; tel. (1) 58-04-51; fax (1) 56-55-78; e-mail headoffice@asb.am; internet www.asb.am; reorganized 1996; privatized in 2001; cap. 444.4m., res 138.6m., dep. 3,320.1m. (Nov. 1998); Chair. of Bd MIKHAIL BAGDASAROV; Exec. Dir SEDA PETROSSIAN; 97 regional brs.

### Banking Union

**Union of Banks of Armenia:** 375009 Yerevan, Koriun St 19A; tel. (1) 52-77-31; fax (1) 56-75-86; e-mail root@tsark.arminco.com; internet www.bank.am; Pres. ARMEN YEGIAZARIAN.

## COMMODITY AND STOCK EXCHANGES

**Armenian Stock Exchange (Armex):** Yerevan, Mher Mkrtchyan St 5B , 6th Floor; tel. (1) 54-33-21; fax (1) 55-33-24; e-mail info@armex.am; internet www.armex.am; Man. Dir A. G. MELIKYAN.

**Gyumri Stock Exchange:** 375504 Gyumri, Abovian St 244; tel. (41) 2-31-09; fax (41) 2-10-23; f. 1995; Dir SISAK MCHITARIAN.

**Yerevan Commodity and Raw Materials Exchange 'Adamand':** Yerevan, Mkrtchian St 5; tel. (1) 56-31-15; fax (1) 56-30-51; e-mail ycre@cornet.am; internet www.yercomex.am; Dir GRIGOR VARDIKIAN.

**Yerevan Stock Exchange:** 375010 Yerevan, Hanrapetoutioun St 5; tel. (1) 52-32-01; fax (1) 15-15-48; internet www.yse.am; f. 1993; Pres. Dr SEDRAK SEDRAKIAN.

## INSURANCE

**Armenian Financial Insurance Co (AFIC):** 375010 Yerevan, Hanrapetoutioun St 5; tel. (1) 52-77-93; fax (1) 15-15-48; e-mail imamik@yse.armenia.su; f. 1996; Exec. Man. LEVON MAMIKONIAN.

**Asco-Pro Insurance Co Ltd:** Yerevan, Ghazar Parpetsu St 15, apt 3; tel. (1) 53-93-70; fax (1) 53-93-72; e-mail asco_pro@netsys.am; Dir G. AGHAJANIAN.

**Prime Insurance Co Ltd:** Yerevan, Charents St 1, 4th Floor; tel. (1) 57-51-18; fax (1) 55-94-73; e-mail prime@netsys.am; f. 1995; cargo, vehicle, aviation, construction, medical, property, and business-interruption insurance; Gen. Dir H. I. KARAPETIAN.

**Resolution Consultants Ltd:** Yerevan, Sayat Nova Ave 37, apt 60; tel. and fax (1) 55-79-37; e-mail recon@arminco.com; internet www.recon.am; f. 2000; Pres. JONATHAN STARK.

**State Insurance Armenia CJSC:** Yerevan, Zeytun, Karapet Ulnetsu St 31; tel. and fax (1) 24-94-83; e-mail petap@netsys.am; Russian-Armenian joint venture; Man. Dir V. H AVETISSIAN.

# Trade and Industry

## GOVERNMENT AGENCY

**Armenian Development Agency:** 375025 Yerevan, Charents St 17; tel. and fax (1) 54-22-72; e-mail ada@ada.am; internet www.ossada.am; Exec. Dir VAHAGN MOVSISSIAN.

## CHAMBER OF COMMERCE

**Chamber of Commerce and Industry of the Republic of Armenia:** 375010 Yerevan, Khanjian St 11; tel. (1) 56-01-84; fax (1) 58-78-71; e-mail chamber@arminco.com; f. 1959; Chair. MARTIN SARKISSIAN.

## EMPLOYERS' ORGANIZATIONS

**Armenian Business Forum:** Yerevan; tel. (1) 52-75-43; fax (1) 52-43-32; f. 1991; promotes joint ventures, foreign capital investments; Pres. VAHE JAZMADARIAN.

**Armenian Union of Manufacturers and Businessmen (Employers):** 375010 Yerevan, Khorenatsi St 26; tel. and fax (1) 56-29-21; e-mail umba@arminco.com; f. 1996; Chair. ARSEN KHAZARIAN.

## UTILITIES

**Armenian Energy Commission:** Yerevan, Isahaakian St 18; tel. (1) 59-25-44; fax (1) 52-55-63; e-mail eca@arminco.com; Chair. VARDAN MOVSISIAN.

### Electricity

In March 2002 Armenia's four state-owned regional electricity-distribution networks were merged to create a single entity, an 81.1% stake in which was divested to Midland Resources Holding (based in the United Kingdom) in August of that year.

**Armenergo CJSC:** 375009 Yerevan, Abovian St 27; tel. (1) 52-17-81; fax (1) 15-17-21; e-mail armenerg@arminco.com; transmission of electricity; Dir KAREN KARAPETIAN.

**Armenian Nuclear Power Plant (ANPP) Co:** 377766 Medzamor, Armavir; tel. (1) 28-18-80; fax (1) 28-06-69; e-mail anpp@lx2.yerphi.am; WWER-440 (V–270) pressurized water-reactor, with a 407.5 MW operating capacity; management transferred to Unified Energy Systems (Russia) in Sept. 2003; Gen. Dir GAGIK MARKOSIAN.

### Gas

**ArmGazProm CJSC:** Yerevan, Tbilisskoe St 43; tel. (1) 28-60-70; fax (1) 28-65-31; gas transmission and distribution company; state-owned until July 2001; subsequently 45% owned by Gazprom (Russia), 45% retained by the Government and 10% owned by Itera (Russia); Dir ROLAND ADONTS.

**ArmRusGazProm CJSC:** Yerevan, Tbilisian Kh. 43; tel. (1) 28-65-31; fax (1) 28-64-62; f. 1997; Armenian-Russian joint-stock co; Exec. Dir ROLAND ADONTS.

### Water

**Yerevan Water and Sewer CJSC:** Yerevan.

## MAJOR COMPANIES

Legislation to privatize state enterprises was enacted in July 1992. By September 2003 7,178 small firms and 1,789 medium-sized and large firms had been privatized, and the private sector was reported to generate more than 80% of national gross domestic product. The privatization process was expected to be completed by the end of 2004. The following is a selection of the principal industrial companies operating in Armenia.

### Chemicals

**Nairit-1:** 375029 Yerevan, Bagratounyats Ave 70; tel. (1) 48-31-21; fax (1) 44-25-99; f. as Nairit-1, after Nairit (f. 1933) divided into three separate cos in 2001; acquired by Ransat Plc (based in the United Kingdom) in mid-2002, but shares transferred to creditor Armsvyazbank in April 2003, pending new ownership; producer of chloroprene rubber.

**Prometey-Chimprom CJSC:** Vanadzhor; privatized in 1999; comprises complex of Vanadzhor chemical factories; produces carbide, corundum, ammonite, acetate thread and melamine.

### Electrical Goods

**Joint-Stock Company Armelektromash** (Armenian Scientific-Production Electronic Machinery Association): 375083 Yerevan, Manandian St 41; tel. (1) 42-45-83; fax (1) 42-16-79; e-mail info@armelectromash.ru; internet www.armelectromash.ru; f. 1940; manufactures synchronous generators, transformers and industrial goods; Exec. Dir G. M. GUKASSIAN.

**Armenmotor CJSC:** 375018 Yerevan, M. Khorenatsi St 28; tel. (1) 52-78-60; fax (1) 56-39-91; e-mail armmotor@netsys.am; internet www.armenmotor.am; f. 1920; manufacture and sale of motors, generators, pumps, electric meat mincers and ceiling fans; Pres. K. PETROSSIAN; 2,000 employees.

### Food and Beverages

**Yerevan Brandy Company (CJSC):** 375082 Yerevan, Isakov Ave 2; tel. (1) 54-00-00; fax (1) 58-77-13; e-mail info@ararat-intl.am; internet www.ybc.am; f. 1887; subsidiary of the Pernod Ricard Group (France); Pres. and Gen. Dir PIERRE LARRETCHE; Gen. Man. JEAN-FRANÇOIS ROUCOU; 500 employees.

### Metals

**Armenal:** 375051 Yerevan, Gribodoev St 25; tel. (1) 23-15-81; fax (1) 23-12-83; e-mail melkumyan_a@armenal.am; internet www.armenal.am; f. 1950 as Kanaker Aluminium Factory–KanAZ; name changed as above in 2000; Armenian-Russian foil-rolling enterprise;

74% owned by Russian Aluminium; Chair. Robert Yengoian; Gen. Dir Movses Dzavarian.

**Armzoloto:** 375051 Yerevan, Komitas Ave 49; tel. (1) 23-68-10; special state enterprise; gold-deposit prospecting, gold mine and open-deposit development.

**Mars State CJSC:** 375064 Yerevan, Raffu St 111; tel. (1) 73-83-23; fax (1) 74-37-50; e-mail robot@freenet.am; transferred to Russian ownership in 2003 as part of debt-reparation scheme; electrical engineering plant; Gen. Dir S. Demirchian.

**Pure Iron OJSC:** 375053 Yerevan, Artsakh Ave 75; tel. (1) 47-42-60; 48% owned by Khronomet (Germany); ferro-alloys, including ferromolybdenum and metal powders; Dir Henrikh Karapetian.

### Motor Vehicles

**Yeraz** (Yerevan Automobile Factory): 375014 Yerevan, Azatutioun St 27; tel. (1) 28-73-00; fax (1) 28-65-55; supplies Armenia (45%), the remainder of the Commonwealth of Independent States (54%) and Bulgaria (1%); Dir Eduard Babadzhian; 2,000 employees.

### Textiles and Clothing

**Armen-Carpet OJSC:** 375006 Yerevan, Chimiagortsneri St 9; tel. (1) 44-28-79; fax (1) 44-29-94; f. 1925; produces carpets; Gen. Man M. Stepanian; 1,500 employees.

**Garun:** 375023 Yerevan, Brusov St 26; tel. (1) 56-17-23; fax (1) 52-99-81; e-mail yenok@freenet.am; produces outdoor clothing; Gen. Dir G. Enokian.

**Tosp Open Stock Company:** 375065 Yerevan, Tichina St 2; tel. (1) 74-24-72; fax (1) 74-21-43; e-mail tosp@arminco.com; f. 1947; manufactures knitted textiles, underwear; Pres. S. Bekirski; 840 employees.

**Van:** 375020 Yerevan, Arshakuniats Ave 21; tel. (1) 56-23-45; manufactures a variety of textile products and footwear; Chair. Karen Grigorian.

### Miscellaneous

**Armenintorg—Armenian Foreign Trade Company Ltd:** 375012 Yerevan, Hr. Kochar St 25; tel. (1) 22-43-10; fax (1) 22-00-34; f. 1987; import and export, marketing, consultancy, auditing and other services; Gen. Dir G. B. Makarian; 20 employees.

**Impulse OJSC:** 377250 Dilijan, Shaumian St 17; tel. (720) 11-19; fax (720) 29-83; f. 1962; joint-stock co; owned by Armentrans; produces high-frequency communications systems; Gen. Dir Eduard Gurgeni Khanamirian; 2,500 employees.

**Jupiter Research and Development Company:** 375014 Yerevan Shirvanadze St 7 Kv.2; tel. (1) 58-54-34; fax (1) 52-89-74; e-mail jupiplus@freenet.am; f. 1994; state-owned; medical and pharmaceutical preparations; Gen. Dir Rafael Melkonian.

**Shoghakn Diamond Processing CJSC:** 378519 Kotaik Nor Hajen; tel. (24) 28-25-92; fax (24) 28-17-69; e-mail diamonds@shoghakn.am; internet www.shoghakn.am; f. 1971; owned by Lev Levaev Diamonds Ltd (Israel); diamond-cutting and -polishing; Dir Sergey Kasparian; 550 employees.

**Yerevan Jewellery Plant:** 375023 Yerevan, Arshakuniats Ave 12; tel. (1) 52-53-21; fax (1) 52-57-13; e-mail jewelsales@cornet.am; produces silver, gold and plastic jewellery; Dir E. Grigorian.

**Yerevan Paper and Container Mill:** 375085 Yerevan, Aeratsia St; tel. (1) 42-02-22; fax (1) 52-86-79; e-mail tuxtart@inbox.ru; f. 1995; Pres. Hripsineh Pogossian.

**Yerfrez OJSC:** 375014 Yerevan, Komitas St 60; tel. (1) 23-14-21; fax (1) 28-90-72; e-mail yerfrez@arminco.com; f. 1956; produces milling machines; Pres. E. Grigorian; 171 employees.

**Yerevan Cable Plant:** 375061 Yerevan, Tamantsineri St 55; tel. (1) 44-12-50; production of cables and wires; company restarted in 2001, fully modernized.

### TRADE UNIONS

At 1 January 2002 159 trade-union organizations were registered with the Ministry of Justice.

**Confederation of Trade Unions of Armenia:** 375010 Yerevan, Nalbandian St 26; tel. (1) 52-36-82; fax (1) 54-33-82; e-mail boris@xar.am; Chair. Martin Haroutunian.

**National Union of Farmers:** Yerevan, Sebastia St 3a; tel. and fax (1) 74-40-05; e-mail fam2002@infocom.am; f. 1998; Pres. Vanik Soghomonian.

**Union of Merchants of Armenia:** 375037 Yerevan, Azatutiun Ave 1/1; tel. (1) 25-28-54; fax (1) 25-91-76; e-mail merchants@netsys.am; f. 1993; Pres. Tsolvard Gevorgian.

# Transport

## RAILWAYS

In 2001 there were 711 km of railway track, 43.1 km of tram routes and 176.4 km of trolley bus routes. There are international lines to Iran and Georgia; lines to Azerbaijan and Turkey remained closed in 2003, as a result of those countries' continuing economic blockade of Armenia.

**Armenia Railways:** 375005 Yerevan, Tigran Mets St 50; tel. (1) 52-04-28; e-mail arway@mbox.amilink.net; f. 1992 following the dissolution of the former Soviet Railways; Pres. A. V. Khrimian.

### Metropolitan Railway

An initial 10-km route, with nine stations, opened in Yerevan in 1981, and a 10-km extension, with two stations, was under construction. A second line was planned, and proposals envisaged the installation of a 47-km network.

**Yermetro:** 375033 Yerevan, Marshal Baghramian St 76; tel. (1) 27-45-43; fax (1) 27-24-60; e-mail papiev@netsys.am; f. 1981; Gen. Man. P. Yayloian.

## ROADS

In 2000 there were an estimated 15,918 km of roads in Armenia (including 7,527 km of motorways, 3,360 km of highways and 4,167 km of secondary roads); 96.3% of roads were paved. In 1996 plans were made to upgrade existing roads, and to construct some 1,400 km of new roads over the next four years, with financial assistance from various international organizations. As a result of the economic blockade imposed in 1989 by Azerbaijan (and subsequently reinforced by Turkey), the Kajaran highway linking Armenia with Iran emerged as Armenia's most important international road connection; in December 1995 a permanent road bridge over the Araks (Aras) river was opened, strengthening this link. In mid-1997 a bus route to Syria was opened—the first overland route between the two countries.

## CIVIL AVIATION

Zvartnots International Airport, 15 km west of Yerevan, is the main national airport; there are also international airports in Shirak and Yerebuni.

**Civil Aviation Department:** 375042 Yerevan, Zvartnots International Airport; tel. (1) 28-57-68; fax (1) 15-11-23; government agency; Dir Hovhannes Yeritsian.

**National Aviation Union of Armenia:** Yerevan; Chair. Dmitri Atbashian.

**Armavia:** 375042 Yerevan, Zvartnots International Airport; tel. (1) 59-39-21; fax (1) 28-63-10; e-mail siberia@web.am; f. 2001; privately owned; operates flights to Russia and Turkey.

**Armenian Airlines:** 375042 Yerevan, Zvarnots Airport; tel. (1) 23-90-01; fax (1) 28-16-62; e-mail gendir@armenianairlines.am; f. 1993; operates scheduled and charter passenger services to countries of the CIS, Europe and the Middle East; privatization project approved by the Govt in 1997; Gen. Dir Arsen Avetissian.

**Armenian International Airways (AIA):** 375042 Yerevan, Zvartnots International Airport; tel. and fax (1) 28-76-37; e-mail aa@armenianairways.com; internet www.armenianairways.com; f. 2002; privately owned; flies to Europe and the Middle East; Man. Dir Versand Hakobian.

**Yer-Avia:** 375010 Yerevan, Busand St 1–3; tel. (1) 58-01-21; fax (1) 56-75-11; e-mail eravia@netsys.am; internet www.yer-avia.am; f. 1992; international cargo services; Chief Exec. Dr Arsen Aslanian.

# Tourism

Prior to secession from the USSR in 1991, Armenia attracted a number of tourists from the other Soviet republics. Following its independence, however, tourism severely declined, although by the late 1990s some European firms were beginning to introduce tours to the country. According to the World Tourism Organization, tourism receipts increased from about US $5m. in 1995 to $7m. in 1997. Receipts, according to the World Bank, increased rapidly thereafter, reaching $27m. in 1999 and $45m. in 2000. Armenia received an estimated 162,089 tourist arrivals in 2002. The major tourist attractions were the capital, Yerevan; Artashat, an early trading centre on the 'Silk Road'; and medieval monasteries. There was, however, little accommodation available outside the capital.

**Directorate of Trade, Tourism and Services:** Ministry of Industry and Trade, 375008 Yerevan, Hanrapetoutioun St 5; tel. (1) 58-94-94; fax (1) 56-61-23; e-mail garnikn@yahoo.com; Dir Artak Davtian.

**Armenian Tourism Association (ATA):** 375010 Yerevan, Amirian St 27; tel. (1) 53-45-01; fax (1) 52-25-83; e-mail ata@ tourismarmenia.com; f. 1997; non-governmental business association; Chair. ARTUR VOSKANIAN.

**Armenian Tourism Development Agency:** 375010 Yerevan, Nalbandian St 3; tel. (1) 57-80-01; fax (1) 54-23-03; e-mail help@ armeniainfo.com; internet www.armeniainfo.am; Dir NINA HOVNANIAN.

# Culture

## NATIONAL ORGANIZATIONS

**Ministry of Culture and Youth Affairs:** see section on The Government (Ministries).

**International Cultural Centre:** Yerevan; tel. (1) 52-39-30; fax (1) 90-72-23; Dir SAMUEL MAIRAPETIAN.

## CULTURAL HERITAGE

In 2000 there were 93 museums (which were attended by a total of 874,100 visitors in that year), 21 theatres (attended by 360,000 people), and 1,139 libraries.

**Egishe Charents State Museum of Literature and Art:** Yerevan, Aram St 1; tel. (1) 58-16-51; f. 1921; history of Armenian literature (18th–20th century), theatre, cinema and music; Dir H. BAKCHINIAN.

**Matenadaran Institute of Ancient Armenian Manuscripts:** 375009 Yerevan, Mashtots Ave 53; tel. (1) 58-32-92; internet www .matenadaran.am; f. 1920; 17,000 manuscripts and 300,000 archival documents on Armenian history, medieval science, culture and art; Dir SEN AREVSHATIAN.

**National Films Archive of Armenia (Filmodaran):** Yerevan; tel. (1) 8-54-06; Dir GAREGIN ZAKOIAN.

**National Gallery of Armenia:** 375010 Yerevan, Aram St 1; tel. (1) 58-08-12; fax (1) 56-36-61; e-mail nga@nga.sci.am; f. 1921; Western European, Armenian, Russian and Oriental art; Dir SHAKAR KHACHATURIAN.

**National Library of Armenia:** 375009 Yerevan, Terian St 72; tel. (1) 58-42-59; fax (1) 52-97-11; e-mail nla@arm.r.am; internet www .nla.am; f. 1919; over 6.2m. vols; Dir DAVIT SARGISSIAN.

**State History Museum of Armenia:** 375010 Yerevan, Republic Sq.; tel. (1) 58-27-61; fax (1) 50-60-98; f. 1919; 400,000 exhibits tracing the history of the Armenian people; Dir ANELKA GRIGORIAN; Vice-Dirs IVETA MKRTCHIAN, KAREN KHACHATRIAN.

**Yerevan Contemporary Art Museum:** Yerevan, Mashtots Ave 7; tel. (1) 53-53-59; fax (1) 56-48-51; e-mail harutmus@freenet.am; Dir H. S. IGITIAN.

## SPORTING ORGANIZATION

**National Olympic Committee of Armenia:** 375001 Yerevan, Abovian St 9; tel. (1) 52-07-70; fax (1) 15-15-80; e-mail armnoc@ arminco.com; Pres. ALEXAN AVETISSIAN; Gen. Sec. HAROUTHIOUN YAVRIAN.

## PERFORMING ARTS

**Alexander Spendiarov Opera and Ballet Theatre:** Yerevan, Mashtots Ave 35; tel. (1) 58-63-11; Dir TIGRAN LEVONIAN.

**Armenian National Academic Opera and Ballet Theatre:** Yerevan, Tumanian St 54; tel. (1) 52-79-92.

**Armenian Philharmonic Orchestra:** 375002 Yerevan, Mashtots Ave 46, Aram Khachaturian Concert Hall; tel. (1) 56-49-14; fax (1) 56-49-65; e-mail apo@arminco.com; internet www.apo.am; Artistic Dir EDUARD TOPJIAN.

**Armenian State Academic Choir:** Yerevan, Pushkin St 60; tel. (1) 58-63-03.

**H. Ghaplanian Drama Theatre:** 375009 Yerevan, Isaahakian St 28; tel. (1) 52-47-23.

**K. S. Stanislavsky State Drama Theatre:** Yerevan, Abovian St 7; tel. (1) 56-91-99; fax (1) 52-62-67; e-mail grigoryan@netsys.am; Dir A. S. GRIGORYAN.

**H. Tumanian State Puppet Theatre:** Yerevan, Sayat Nova Ave 4; tel. (1) 52-02-54; Dir RUBEN BABAIAN.

**Yerevan Chamber Theatre:** Yerevan, Mashtots Ave 58; tel. (1) 56-60-70; fax (1) 56-63-78; e-mail erkat@arminco.com; internet www .chambertheatre.am; Dir A. H. YERNJAKIAN.

**Yerevan Institute of Fine Arts and Theatre:** 375009 Yerevan, Isaahakian St 36; tel. (1) 56-07-26; f. 1944; training in all aspects of theatre and fine arts; Rector VAHAN MKRTOHIAN.

## ASSOCIATIONS

**Armenian Committee for Cultural Relations with Compatriots in Other Countries:** Yerevan; develops links with the Armenian diaspora.

**Benevolent Fund for Culture Development:** 375001 Yerevan, Tumanian St 5; tel. and fax (1) 56-21-31; e-mail mzbh@arminco.com; f. 1999; carries out cultural, educational and other charitable activities; Chair. SAMVEL MESROPIAN; Co-ordinator GOHAR SARKISSIAN.

**Union of Architects of Armenia:** Yerevan, Marshal Baghramian 17; tel. (1) 56-15-06.

**Union of Artists of Armenia:** Yerevan, Abovian St 16; tel. (1) 56-48-51; fax (1) 56-48-53.

**Union of Cinematographers of Armenia:** Yerevan, Vardanants St 18; tel. (1) 54-05-28; fax (1) 56-79-87.

**Union of Composers and Musicologists of Armenia:** Yerevan, Demirchian St 25; tel. (1) 52-47-02; fax (1) 52-42-92.

**Union of Writers of Armenia:** 375019 Yerevan, Marshal Baghramian Ave 3; tel. (1) 56-38-11; fax (1) 56-18-31.

# Education

Education is free and compulsory at primary and secondary levels. Until the early 1990s the general education system conformed to that of the centralized Soviet system. Extensive changes were subsequently made, with greater emphasis placed on Armenian history and culture. Armenia adopted an 11-year system of schooling in 2001/02. In 2000 total enrolment at pre-school establishments was equivalent to 17.2% of the relevant age-group. Primary enrolment in 1999 was equivalent to 86% of the age-group, while the comparable ratio for secondary enrolment was 88%. Most instruction is in Armenian, although Russian is widely learnt as a second language. In 2000/01 98.4% of students in general education schools were taught in Armenian, while for 1.3% Russian was the main language of instruction. In that year there were seven universities, with a total enrolment of 22,400 students. In addition, higher education was provided at 12 further institutes of higher education. In 2000/01 total enrolment in higher schools (including universities) was 43,600 students. Current expenditure on education at all levels of government, according to preliminary figures, was 8,717m. drams in 2000.

## UNIVERSITIES

**American University of Armenia:** 375019 Yerevan, Marshal Baghramian Ave 40; tel. (1) 51-25-26; fax (1) 51-28-40; internet www .aua.am; f. 1991; owned by American University of Armenia Corpn (USA); Pres. HAROUTUNE ARMENIAN.

**State Engineering University of Armenia:** 375009 Yerevan, Terian St 105; tel. (1) 52-05-20; fax (1) 15-10-68; e-mail politsch .yerevan@rex.iasnet.com; internet www.seua.am; f. 1991; fmrly Yerevan Polytechnic Institute (f. 1930); 8 faculties; 1,100 teachers; 11,000 students; brs in Goris, Gyumri and Vanadzor; Rector YURI L. SARKISSIAN.

**State Pedagogical University:** Yerevan, Khandjian St 13; tel. (1) 52-64-01; fax (1) 52-25-63; e-mail armped@netsys.am; Rector ARTYUSHA GUKASSIAN.

**Yerevan M. Heratsi State Medical University:** 375025 Yerevan, Korjun St 2; tel. (1) 52-17-11; fax (1) 15-18-12; e-mail meduni@moon .yerphi.am; internet www.medlib.am/ysmu; f. 1922; 568 teachers; 3,648 students; Rector V. P. HAKOPIAN.

**Yerevan State Academy of Fine Arts:** 375009 Yerevan, Isahakian St 36; tel. (1) 56-07-26; e-mail ysifa@edu.am; internet www.iatp .am/yafa; Rector Prof. ARAM ISSABEKIAN.

**Yerevan State Institute of National Economy:** 375025 Yerevan, Nalbandian St 128; tel. (1) 58-55-66; fax (1) 52-88-64; e-mail ysine@ edu.am.

**Yerevan State University:** 375025 Yerevan, Alex Manoogian St 1; tel. (1) 55-46-29; fax (1) 55-46-41; e-mail rector@ysu.am; internet www.ysu.am; f. 1919; language of instruction: Armenian; 21 faculties; 1,400 teachers; 9,000 students; Rector RADIK M. MARTIROSIAN.

# Social Welfare

In the 1990s much of Armenia's expenditure on health and welfare services was directed towards the survivors of the earthquake in northern Armenia in December 1998, which caused an estimated

25,000 deaths and 8,500m. roubles' worth of damage. A US $150m., three-year reconstruction programme commenced in 1999, and the Government planned to have completed the rebuilding of housing and infrastructure in the region by the end of 2002. Also in the 1990s, the escalation in the conflict with Azerbaijan and the collapse of the USSR encouraged a large number of refugees to flee to Armenia, creating new demands on the social-welfare system at a time of restricted government revenue, a situation that was exacerbated by the adaptation to a market economy and the economic blockade imposed on the country by neighbouring Azerbaijan and Turkey. In August 2003 the Government approved a Poverty Reduction Strategy, dependent on US $1,200m. pledged in external loans and grants, providing for social benefits to be increased by 400% over a period of 12 years.

The Pension Fund, established in 1991, merged with the Employment Fund, to create the Pension and Employment Fund in March 1992. In 1996 the retirement age was 65 years for men, and 63 years for women. At September 1997 607,111 people were in receipt of state pensions, 72% of which were provided on account of old age. In September 2003 the Government approved an increase in the state pension; the average old-age pension was to rise to some 7,900 drams per month.

In 1995 the Armenian Government adopted a programme for the development and reform of the health care system between 1996 and 2000, and the system was subsequently fully decentralized. In March 1996 the Medical Care Act was adopted, which authorized the provision of funding from a number of sources (from state and municipal budgets, medical insurance or private payments by patients). Two years later all state-owned health-care establishments were transformed into joint-stock companies. In 1999 there were 305 physicians and 620 hospital beds per 100,000 inhabitants, and a total of 174 hospitals in Armenia. In 2001 average life expectancy at birth was 66.2 years for males and 73.0 years for females in 2000. Of total current expenditure in 2000, 14,576m. (5.5% of expenditure) was allocated to health.

## GOVERNMENT AGENCIES

**Ministry of Social Security:** see section on The Government (Ministries).

**State Healthcare Agency:** Yerevan.

**Institute of Volunteers:** Yerevan; f. 1991 to train social workers and help the Government research social-issue priorities.

**Pension and Employment Fund:** 375025 Yerevan, Moskovian St 35; originally a branch of the USSR Pension Fund, a separate Armenian Pension Fund was established in 1991, and united with the Employment Fund in March 1992; largely funded by payroll contributions; Chair. Z. NUNUSHIAN.

## HEALTH AND WELFARE ORGANIZATIONS

**Armenian General Benevolent Union (AGBU):** 375019 Yerevan, Bagramian St 40; tel. (1) 27-11-65; fax (1) 27-08-10; e-mail agbua@aua.am; f. 1989; educational, cultural and humanitarian projects; Dir ASHOT GHASARIAN.

**Armenian Red Cross Society (ARCS):** 375015 Yerevan, Paronian St 21; tel. (1) 53-83-67; fax (1) 58-36-30; e-mail redcross@redcross .am; internet www.redcross.am; f. 1920; 12 regional and 6 community branches; Pres. Dr MKHTIAR MNATSAKANIAN.

**Armenian Relief Society:** Yerevan; tel. (1) 57-40-24; f. 1991; assists those needing medical and mental-health treatment.

**National Institute of Health (NIH):** 375051 Yerevan, Komitas Ave 49/4; tel. (2) 23-71-34; fax (2) 15-16-44; e-mail doumanian@nih .sci.am; internet www.medlib.am/nih; f. 1963; independent org. financed by the Ministry of Health; Dir D. H. DOUMANIAN.

**Project Hope:** Yerevan, Hin Echmiadzni Khjughi 109, Republic Rehabilitation Centre; tel. and fax (1) 15-10-61; f. 1988; supports reliable health-care programmes, including vaccinations.

**Unison:** 375033 Yerevan, H. Hakobian St 10/56; tel. (1) 22-64-70; fax (1) 40-35-18; e-mail unison@unison.am; internet www.unison .am; f. 2002; non-governmental org. for the support of people with special needs, including the disabled, the elderly, the homeless and minority groups; Pres. RASMILA ALAVERDIAN.

# The Environment

In the 1990s Yerevan experienced particularly severe pollution as a result of its high concentration of industrial enterprises and the surrounding mountains, which confined emissions. The influx of refugees and the shortage of fuel resulting from the conflict with Azerbaijan increased environmental degradation. In addition, the reopening of the Medzamor nuclear power station in mid-1995 raised fears of environmental damage. According to the terms of an

agreement signed with the European Union (EU) in April 1996, the power station was to be closed by 2004. The agreement was, however, dependent on the construction of adequate alternative energy facilities. The declining water level of Lake Sevan was also a cause for concern. A 10-year water-management programme was drafted in 2001, to be funded by contributions from the World Bank and the German Government.

## NATIONAL AGENCIES

**Ministry of the Environment:** see section on The Government (Ministries); includes Bio-resources Management Agency, Geology Agency, Hydrometeorological and Environment Monitoring Agency, Mineral Resources Agency, Water Resources Management Agency.
.

## ACADEMIC INSTITUTES

**Armenian Research Institute for Scientific Technical Information** (INFOTERRA National Focal Point): Yerevan; tel. (1) 23-67-74; e-mail nfp@globinfo; f. 1982; Dir MARAT B. EDILIAN.

**National Academy of Sciences of Armenia:** 375019 Yerevan, Marshal Baghramian Ave 24; tel. (1) 52-70-31; fax (1) 56-92-81; e-mail fsark@sci.am; internet www.sci.am; f. 1943; Pres. F. T. SARKISSIAN.

> **Centre for Ecological-Noosphere Studies:** 375025 Yerevan, Abovian St 68; tel. (1) 56-93-31; fax (1) 58-02-54; e-mail ecocentr@sci.am; internet www.sci.am/about/research/18-econoosf.html; f. 1989; carries out scientific and research activities; Dir Dr ARMEN K. SAGATELIAN; Dep. Dir Dr ROBERT H. REVAZIAN.

> **Institute of Botany and Botanical Garden:** 375063 Yerevan, Avan 63; tel. (1) 62-17-81; f. 1939; Dir ASHOT A. CHARCHOGLIAN.

> **Institute of Geological Sciences:** 375019 Yerevan, Marshal Baghramian Ave 24A; tel. (1) 52-44-26; fax (1) 56-80-72; e-mail hrshah@sci.am; internet www.sci.am/academy/7-geolo1.html; f. 1935; geological, geographical and ecological research; Dir R. T. DJRBASHIAN.

> **Institute of Zoology:** 375044 Yerevan, Sevak St 7; tel. (1) 28-14-70; Dir SERGEI H. MOVSESIAN.

> **Institute of Hydroecology and Ichthyology:** 375019 Yerevan, Rm 1112, Marshal Baghramian Ave 24D; tel. (1) 56-85-54; fax (1) 56-94-11; e-mail rhovan@sci.am; researches hydrobiology and fishery management; Dir RAFIK H. HOVHANISSIAN.

**Scientific Research Institute of Environmental Hygiene and Occupational Toxicology:** 375001 Yerevan, Tumanian St 8; tel. (1) 58-24-13; fax (1) 15-10-97; researches environmental pollution and toxic wastes; Dir VLADIMIR L. KOGAN.

**Scientific Centre for Agriculture and Plant Protection:** Echmiadzin, Isi-li-Mulino St 1; tel. (50) 53-454; Dir HRACHIK V. HOVSEPIAN; Dep. Dir SUREN A. SEMERDJAN.

**Scientific Centre of Hydrometeorology and Ecology:** State Dept of Hydrometeorology, Arshakunyats Ave 46/1; tel. (1) 44-66-11; Dir K. H. HAIRAPETIAN.

## NON-GOVERNMENTAL ORGANIZATIONS

**Armenian Ecological Benevolent Foundation:** tel. (1) 61-48-51; e-mail dovlatian@yahoo.com; Pres. ARMEN DOVLATIAN.

**Armenian Nature Protection Union:** Yerevan, Charents St 8; tel. (1) 55-67-78; e-mail anpuorg@freenet.am; Contact EDUARD YAVRUYAN.

**Association for Sustainable Human Development:** 375010 Yerevan, Khandjian St 33, Apt 18; tel. and fax (1) 52-23-27; e-mail ashd@freenet.am; internet users.freenet.am/~ashd; f. 1996; Chair. KARINE DANIELIAN.

**Ecology Fund of Armenia:** Yerevan, Komitas Ave 49, Rms 302–304; tel. (1) 23-69-00; fax (1) 22-30-58; Pres. BORIS MEHRABIAN.

**Ecoteam:** 375001 Yerevan, Abovian St 22A, Apt 53; tel. (1) 52-92-77; e-mail ecoteam@freenet.am; internet www.users.freenet.am/~ecoteam; f. 1996; energy and environmental NGO and information centre; Pres. ARTASHES SARKISSIAN.

**Ecotourism Association:** Yerevan, Shinararneri 22, Apt 32; tel. (1) 39-75-52; e-mail zhanna@freenet.am; Pres. ZHANNA GALIAN.

**EDEM Plant Protection Union:** Yerevan, Komitas St 58, Apt 53; tel. (1) 23-41-83; Pres. ARAMIS KHACHIKIAN.

**Environmental Survival Ecological Union:** 375019 Yerevan, Marshal Baghramian Ave 24D, Apt 908; tel. and fax (1) 52-38-30; e-mail esu@sci.am; internet caucasus.vitualave.net; f. 1997; Pres. Dr EVILINA GHUKASSIAN.

**Environmental Public Advocacy Center (EPAC):** Yerevan, Ghazar Par. 11, Apt 2; tel. (1) 58-25-31; e-mail epac@arminco.com; internet www.epac.am; f. 1997; Pres. AIDA ISKOIAN.

**Green Union of Armenia:** 375093 Yerevan, Mamikoniants St 47/13; tel. (1) 28-14-11; fax (1) 25-76-34; e-mail armgreen@ipia.sci .am; internet sci.am/armgreen; f. 1985; approx. 6,000 mems; Pres. HAKOB SANASARYAN.

**Union of Armenian Ecologists:** 375019 Yerevan, Marshal Bagh-ramian St 24D, Rm 1108; tel. (1) 56-85-54; e-mail grignan@sci.am; Pres. RAFAEL HOVHANISSIAN.

# Defence

Following the dissolution of the USSR in December 1991, Armenia became a member of the Commonwealth of Independent States and its collective security system, which was formally transformed into a regional defence organization, the Collective Security Treaty Organization (CSTO), in April 2003. The country also began to establish its own armed forces (estimated to number some 44,610 in August 2002). There was also a paramilitary force of about 1,000, attached to the Ministry of National Security. Military service is compulsory and lasts for two years (a law was passed in 2000, however, allowing for the exemption from military service of university graduates and those engaged in certain professions). There were approximately 2,900 Russian troops on Armenian territory in August 2002. The budget for 2002 allocated an estimated US $62m. of budgetary expenditure to defence. In 1994 Armenia joined the North Atlantic Treaty Organization's 'Partnership for Peace' pro-gramme of military co-operation.

**Commander-in-Chief of the Armed Forces:** President of the Republic.

**Chief of General Staff of the Armed Forces:** Maj.-Gen. MICHAEL HAROUTUNIAN.

# Bibliography

Adalian, R. P. (Ed.). *Armenia and Karabakh Factbook.* Washington, DC, Armenia Assembly of America, 1996.

Bournoutian, G. *A History of the Armenian People.* 2 vols. Costa Mesa, CA, Mazda Publishers, 1993.

Chorbajian, L., Dionabedian, P., and Mutafian, C. *The Caucasian Knot: The History and Geopolitics of Nagorno-Karabagh.* London, Zed Books, 1994.

Herzig, Edmund M., and Kurkchiyan, Marina. *The Armenians: A Handbook.* Richmond, Curzon Press, 2001.

Hewson, Robert H. *Armenia.* Chicago, IL, University of Chicago Press, 2000.

Hovannisian, R. G. (Ed.). *The Armenian People: From Ancient to Modern Times.* 2 vols. New York, NY, St Martin's Press, 1997.

Lang, D. M. *The Armenians: A People in Exile.* London, Unwin Paperbacks, 1988.

Libaridian, Gerard L. *The Challenge of Statehood.* Watertown, MA, Blue Crane Books, 1999.

Masih, Joseph R., and Krikorian, Robert O. *Armenia at the Cross-roads.* Amsterdam, Harwood Academic Publishers, 1999.

Matossian, M. K. *The Impact of Soviet Policies in Armenia.* Leiden, E. J. Brill, 1962.

Mouradian, C.-S. *De Staline...Gorbachev: histoire d'une république Sovietique: l'Armenie.* Paris, Editions Ramsay, 1990.

Suny, Ronald Grigor. *Armenia in the Twentieth Century.* Chicago, IL, Scholar's Press, 1983.

   *Looking Towards Ararat: Armenia in Modern History.* Bloo-mington and Indianapolis, IN, Indiana University Press, 1993.

Walker, C. *Armenia: The Survival of a Nation.* 2nd edn. London, Routledge, 1990.

Walker, C. J. (Ed.). *Armenia and Karabagh: The Struggle for Unity.* London, Minority Rights Publications, 1991.

de Waal, Thomas. *Black Garden: Armenia and Azerbaijan Through Peace and War.* New York, NY, and London, New York University Press, 2003.

Also see the Select Bibliography in Part Four.

# AZERBAIJAN

## Geography

### PHYSICAL FEATURES

The Azerbaijan Republic (formerly the Republic of Azerbaijan and, prior to that, the Azerbaijan Soviet Socialist Republic, a constituent unit of the USSR) is situated in eastern Transcaucasia, on the western coast of the Caspian Sea. There are international borders with Iran to the south, with Armenia to the west, with Georgia to the north-west and, to the north across the Caucasus, with the Russian Republic of Dagestan (Daghestan). The Nakhichevan Autonomous Republic is part of Azerbaijan, although it is separated from the rest of the country by Armenian territory. The enclave lies to the west of metropolitan Azerbaijan, with Iran to the south and west and Armenia to the north and east. There is a short border with Turkey at the north-western tip of Nakhichevan. Azerbaijan also includes the Nagorno-Karabakh Autonomous Oblast (Nagornyi Karabakh), which lies in the south-west of the country. It is largely populated by ethnic Armenians. Armed conflict over the status of Nagornyi Karabakh began in 1989 and by October 1993 Azerbaijan had lost control of about one-fifth of its own territory, including the entire Nagornyi Karabakh enclave, to Armenian militia. Nagornyi Karabakh, Upper or Mountainous Karabakh (Daglygh Karabakh in Azerbaijan), is known as Artsakh by the Armenians. The historical region of Azerbaijan also includes northern regions of Iran, where there is a significant ethnic Azerbaijani (Azeri) population. The country covers an area of 86,600 sq km (33,400 sq miles), 10% of which is forested. Nagornyi Karabakh covers 4,400 sq km of the total area and Nakhichevan 5,500 sq km.

The greater part of Azerbaijan is dominated by the lowlands around two rivers; the River Kura flows from the north-west into the Caspian Sea, and its tributary, the Araks (Araxes, Aras), runs along the border with Iran. North of the Kura lies the main axis of the Greater Caucasus mountain range (Bolshoi Kavkaz), the traditional boundary between Asia and Europe. This mountain range extends along the northern border of the country into north-east Azerbaijan and ends in the Apsheron Peninsula, a promontory in the Caspian Sea, which has significant petroleum reserves. Numerous mountain rivers flow into the Kura basin from the mountains of the Lesser Caucasus in the south-west. South of the mouth of the Kura, the Caspian littoral around the town of Lenkoran forms the Lenkoran plain.

### CLIMATE

The Kura plain has a hot, dry, temperate climate with an average July temperature of 27°C (80°F) and an average January temperature of 1°C (34°F). Average annual rainfall on the lowlands is 200 mm–300 mm, but the Lenkoran plain, noted for its subtropical climate, normally receives between 1,000 mm and 1,750 mm.

### POPULATION

According to the 1999 census, at which the total population was 7,953,438, Azeris formed the largest ethnic group (90.6% of the total population), followed by Lazs (Lezghis—2.4%), Russians (1.8%) and Armenians (1.5%). There were also small numbers of Talish, Avars, Turks, Tatars, Ukrainians, Sakhurs, Georgians, Kurds, Tats, Jews, Udins and others. Armenians predominate in Nagornyi Karabakh and Azeris in

Nakhichevan. After the outbreak of the conflict in Nagornyi Karabakh, many Armenians fled the country. Large numbers of Azeri refugees from the enclave entered Azerbaijan proper. The official language is Azerbaijani, one of the South Turkic group of languages. In 1989 27% of Azeris claimed to have a good knowledge of Russian, but fewer than 2% of Russians and 1% of Armenians in the republic claimed fluency in Azerbaijani. According to government sources, by the end of the 1990s Azerbaijani was spoken by 95% of the population. In 1992 parliament chose to abandon the Cyrillic alphabet (in use since 1939) and restore the Latin script. A presidential decree abolishing the use of Cyrillic for official and business purposes came into force on 1 August 2001. Religious adherence corresponds largely to ethnic origins: almost all ethnic Azerbaijanis are Muslims, some 70% being Shi'ite and 30% Sunni. There are also Christian communities, mainly representatives of the Russian Orthodox and Armenian Apostolic denominations.

At 1 January 2003 the total estimated population was 8,202,500. The capital is Baku (Baki), which had an estimated population of 1,817,900 in mid-2002. It is located on the coast of the Caspian Sea, near the southern shore of the Apsheron Peninsula. Other major cities include Gyanja (Ganca—formerly Kirovabad), an industrial town in the north-west of the country, in the foothills of the Lesser Caucasus (with an estimated population of 301,400 inhabitants in 2002), and Sumgait, a port on the Caspian Sea to the north of Baku (with an estimated 281,600 inhabitants in 1999). Nakhichevan town is the capital of the eponymous Autonomous Republic, and had an estimated 364,500 inhabitants in 2002. The chief town in Nagornyi Karabakh is Stepanakert (formerly Khankendi), with a population of 54,600 in 2002. In 1999 57% of the population lived in urban areas. Population density was 94.7 inhabitants per sq km at the beginning of 2003.

# Chronology

**625 BC–585 BC:** The Medes, under their ruler Cyaxares, with his capital at Ecbatana (now Hamadan, Iran), became a major power in the territories west of the River Tigris.

**550:** Cyrus II ('the Great') of Persia (Iran) conquered the kingdom of Media (Mada) and united the Medes and the Persians.

**323:** After the death of Alexander III ('the Great') of Macedon, who had conquered the Persian Empire, the satrap Atropates established an independent state in northern Media.

**AD 637:** The Persian Empire of the Sassanians, which had ruled Atropatene Media (from which is derived the name of Azerbaijan) since the third century AD, was conquered by the Arabs, under the Caliph 'Umar (Omar); the islamicization of the area began.

**11th century:** The assimilation of Turkic settlers by the previous population was to produce the Azeri people, distinct from the Persic people of modern Iran.

**1502:** The Safavids, an Azeri dynasty, assumed control of the Persian Empire.

**1828:** By the Treaty of Turkmanchai, following years of increasing Russian influence, Persia conceded the partition of Azerbaijan; territory to the north of the River Araks (Araxes, Aras) became part of the Russian Empire.

***c.* 1900:** The province of Azerbaijan was a major producer of petroleum, attracting increasing Slav immigration.

**1911:** The Musavat (Equality) party was founded, superseding the Himmat (Endeavour) party, formed by intellectuals in 1903–04. Musavat was a left-wing, nationalist movement, similar to the 'Young Turks' of the Ottoman Empire.

**1917:** The Russian Revolution impelled Musavat and the Bolsheviks to assume control in Baku, although Musavat withdrew from this administration shortly afterwards and established the Transcaucasian legislature.

**22 April 1918:** A Bolshevik and left-Menshevik soviet (council) was established in Baku; a Transcaucasian federation (Azerbaijan with Armenia and Georgia) was proclaimed, following the Soviet signing of the Treaty of Brest-Litovsk.

**28 May 1918:** The collapse of Transcaucasia forced Azerbaijan to establish its own government. Subsequently, Musavat began negotiations with the Turks; the Red Army was prevented from attempting to occupy Baku by a British military presence.

**September 1918:** The British left Baku, leaving anti-Bolshevik forces in charge, but were implicated in the execution of the Bolshevik leaders involved in the previous governments; this was accompanied by a massacre of Armenians.

**November 1918:** The British reoccupied Baku, but did not favour an independent Musavat regime's close links with Turkey (an ally of the Central Powers in the First World War); the United Kingdom did recognize a coalition Government in the following month.

**August 1919:** British forces left Baku, withdrawing to Persia.

**28 April 1920:** Following the occupation of Baku by the Red Army, a Soviet Republic of Azerbaijan was proclaimed.

**March 1921:** In a friendship treaty, the Turks and Soviet Russia agreed to guarantee that the enclave of Nakhichevan should fall under the jurisdiction of Azerbaijan.

**June 1921:** The arbitrating Soviet Bureau of Transcaucasian Affairs (Kavburo) voted to recommend the union of Nagornyi Karabakh (a predominantly ethnic Armenian enclave within Azerbaijan) with the Soviet Republic of Armenia, but the Soviet leader Stalin (Iosif V. Dzhugashvili) enforced the reversal of this decision; in 1923 Nagornyi Karabakh was granted special status within Azerbaijan, as an autonomous oblast (region).

**October 1921:** The Treaty of Kars agreed the borders of the Soviet Republics of Azerbaijan, Armenia and Georgia with Turkey, and the status of Nagornyi Karabakh and Nakhichevan as territories of Azerbaijan.

**December 1922:** The Soviet Socialist Republic (SSR) of Azerbaijan became a member of the Transcaucasian Soviet Federative Socialist Republic (TSFSR), which itself became a constituent member of the Union of Soviet Socialist Republics (USSR).

**December 1936:** The TSFSR was dissolved and the Azerbaijan SSR became a full Union Republic.

**1937–38:** Purges of the local communists included Azerbaijan's leader, Sultan Mejit Efendiyev.

**1946:** Following a protest to the UN by Iran, Allied pressure forced the USSR to end its attempts to integrate Iranian Azerbaijan with Soviet Azerbaijan.

**1969:** Heydar Aliyev became First Secretary of the Communist Party of Azerbaijan (CPA) and the republic's leader.

**October 1987:** Aliyev was dismissed, owing to corruption in government and in the Party.

**February 1988:** Nagornyi Karabakh's attempts to be transferred to Armenian jurisdiction caused increased inter-ethnic tension, culminating in anti-Armenian riots in Sumgait, in which 32 people were killed.

**12 January 1989:** The local authorities in Nagornyi Karabakh were suspended and the oblast was placed under the administration of a Special Administrative Committee (SAC), responsible to the all-Union Council of Ministers.

**September 1989:** A general strike secured the official recognition of the nationalist opposition movement, the Popular Front of Azerbaijan (PFA), established earlier in the year.

**23 September 1989:** Under increasing popular pressure, the Supreme Soviet, the legislature, of Azerbaijan effectively declared the republic's sovereignty and imposed an economic blockade on Armenia (Soviet troops maintained the Baku–Yerevan rail link).

**November 1989:** The SAC for Nagornyi Karabakh was replaced by a republican Organizing Committee, dominated by ethnic Azerbaijanis.

**1 December 1989:** The Armenian Supreme Soviet declared Nagornyi Karabakh to be part of a 'unified Armenian republic', a claim that was termed unconstitutional by the all-Union Supreme Soviet the following month.

**January 1990:** The PFA were prominent in attacks on government and party buildings, on Armenians and on the border posts with Iranian Azerbaijan; PFA demonstrators also attempted to declare the secession of Nakhichevan from the USSR. Soviet troops evacuated non-Azeris from Baku and enforced a state of emergency, amid some violence. On 20 January Abdul Vezirov was replaced by Ayaz Niyaz oglu Mutalibov as First Secretary of the CPA.

**18 May 1990:** Mutalibov was appointed Chairman of the Supreme Soviet (republican Head of State).

**September 1990:** In the elections to the Azerbaijan Supreme Soviet (postponed from February), the CPA, by this time resolved on the Nagornyi Karabakh issue, won some 80% of the seats; the opposition PFA, which had campaigned with other groups as the Democratic Alliance, alleged irregularities in the conduct of the elections and criticized the state of emergency.

**5 February 1991:** The Supreme Soviet convened, with the opposition deputies grouped as the Democratic Bloc of Azerbaijan.

**17 March 1991:** Azerbaijan participated in the Soviet referendum on the renewal of the Union; official results were that 93.3% of those who had voted (75.1% of the electorate) favoured remaining in the USSR, although in Nakhichevan only 20% supported this; the opposition claimed that only some 20% of the electorate had voted.

**30 August 1991:** Following the failure of a coup attempt in the Soviet and Russian capital, Moscow, and large anti-Government demonstrations, the Supreme Soviet of Azerbaijan voted in favour of claiming independence.

**2 September 1991:** Nagornyi Karabakh declared itself a republic.

**8 September 1991:** Mutalibov won 84% of the votes cast at elections to an executive presidency, which were boycotted by the opposition.

**18 October 1991:** The Supreme Soviet enacted legislation effecting the declaration of independence of 30 August. Later that month the PFA persuaded the Government and the Supreme Soviet to delegate some legislative powers to a smaller body, the Milli Majlis (National Assembly).

**10 December 1991:** In a referendum, residents of Nagornyi Karabakh voted overwhelmingly for independence; the Azerbaijani authorities considered the poll irregular, and the Karabakh Armenians secured no international recognition.

**21 December 1991:** President Mutalibov signed the Almaty Declaration, by which Azerbaijan became a founding member of the Commonwealth of Independent States (CIS).

**6 January 1992:** The new 'parliament' of Nagornyi Karabakh, elected on 28 December 1991, proclaimed the region's independence. In the same month President Mutalibov declared Nagornyi Karabakh to be under direct presidential rule.

**February 1992:** Azerbaijan was admitted to the Conference on Security and Co-operation in Europe (CSCE, from December 1994 the Organization for Security and Co-operation in Europe—OSCE) and signed, with eight other countries, the Black Sea Co-operation Accord.

**March 1992:** President Mutalibov resigned, owing to military reversals in Nagornyi Karabakh. (He was replaced on an interim basis by Yagub Mamedov.) In the same month CIS troops were withdrawn from the area as Armenian forces began to achieve some success against Azerbaijan. Azerbaijan became a member of the UN.

**May 1992:** By the time Armenia and Azerbaijan negotiated a short-lived cease-fire, the Nagornyi Karabakh militia had secured control over the whole enclave and a 'corridor' along the Lachin valley to Armenia. The Supreme Soviet voted to reinstate Mutalibov as President, but he was deposed after one day in office; this effective coup by the PFA was reinforced by the suspension of the Supreme Soviet and the transfer of its powers to the Milli Majlis.

**7 June 1992:** Abulfaz Elchibey (*né* Aliyev), leader of the PFA, was elected President of Azerbaijan by direct vote. Azerbaijan launched a counter-offensive in Nagornyi Karabakh.

**August 1992:** The Nagornyi Karabakh legislature declared a state of martial law; a State Defence Committee replaced the enclave's Government.

**October 1992:** Azerbaijan and Russia signed a Treaty of Friendship, Co-operation and Mutual Security. In the same

month the Milli Majlis voted overwhelmingly to withdraw Azerbaijan from the CIS.

**February 1993:** Col Surat Husseinov, who had successfully commanded Azerbaijani forces in the conflict over Nagornyi Karabakh, withdrew to Gyanja (Ganca), prompting allegations by President Elchibey that he was planning a military coup against the Government. Husseinov was subsequently dismissed from his posts and expelled from the PFA.

**April 1993:** President Elchibey declared a three-month state of emergency. Azerbaijan withdrew from CSCE-sponsored negotiations, in protest at a large-scale Armenian offensive.

**May 1993:** Azerbaijan approved a peace plan formulated by Russia, Turkey and the USA, and negotiated by the CSCE; it was not accepted by the Nagornyi Karabakh leadership until June.

**4 June 1993:** President Elchibey ordered a punitive attack in Gyanja by the Azerbaijani army on the 709th Brigade, a unit still loyal to their rebel leader, Col Surat Husseinov. Over 60 people were killed. Husseinov assumed control of the town.

**15 June 1993:** Heydar Aliyev, the former Communist Party leader, was elected Chairman of the Milli Majlis.

**17–18 June 1993:** President Elchibey fled to Nakhichevan.

**25 June 1993:** The Milli Majlis voted to transfer, on an acting basis, the majority of President Elchibey's powers to Aliyev and to impeach Elchibey. Three days later Husseinov's troops, having marched to Baku, pledged allegiance to acting President Aliyev.

**1 July 1993:** Aliyev nominated Husseinov as Prime Minister and Supreme Commander.

**23 August 1993:** Alikram Gumbatov, leader of the so-called 'Talysh-Mugan Autonomous Republic' (proclaimed during the Husseinov revolt of June), based in Lenkoran, fled the city after his headquarters were attacked by PFA supporters. He was sentenced to death in 1996; the sentence was later commuted to life imprisonment.

**1 September 1993:** The Milli Majlis endorsed the results of a referendum, in which 97.5% of participants voted in favour of President Elchibey's impeachment.

**20 September 1993:** A resolution for Azerbaijan to rejoin the CIS was adopted by the Milli Majlis; the country was officially admitted on 24 September and parliament ratified the Almaty Declaration, the Commonwealth Charter and the Tashkent Agreement on Collective Security on 29 September, despite PFA protests.

**3 October 1993:** Heydar Aliyev was elected President of Azerbaijan, with 98.8% of the votes cast.

**14 October 1993:** Resolution 874, adopted by the UN Security Council, endorsed the CSCE's schedule for implementing Resolutions 822 and 853, adopted earlier in the year and demanding, *inter alia*, an immediate cease-fire and the withdrawal of Armenian units from Azerbaijani territory.

**27 October 1993:** In reaction to CSCE cease-fire proposals, Armenia and Nagornyi Karabakh agreed to the schedule for the withdrawal of ethnic Armenian militia from Azerbaijani territory, but Azerbaijan rejected it as the CSCE plan did not envisage Armenian withdrawal from the Lachin corridor.

**November 1993:** The 'Minsk Group', established by the CSCE, organized a peace conference in Minsk, Belarus, on the issues concerning Nagornyi Karabakh.

**May 1994:** Azerbaijan joined the North Atlantic Treaty Organization's (NATO) 'Partnership for Peace' programme of military co-operation.

**9–11 May 1994:** Following protracted mediation by the CSCE and Russia, a new cease-fire agreement was finally signed by the Ministers of Defence of Azerbaijan and Armenia and representatives of Nagornyi Karabakh. The agreement was formalized on 27 July.

**20 September 1994:** Azerbaijan's state petroleum company and an international consortium signed an agreement establishing the Azerbaijan International Operating Company (AIOC), which was to develop Azerbaijani petroleum reserves.

**29 September 1994:** The Deputy Chairman of the Milli Majlis and the presidential security chief were assassinated, allegedly by members of special militia forces attached to the Ministry of Internal Affairs (known as OPON).

**2 October 1994:** In protest at the arrests of his men, the OPON military chief, Rovshan Javadov, attacked the offices of the Procurator-General, prompting President Aliyev to declare a state of emergency in Baku and Gyanja.

**5 October 1994:** Husseinov was dismissed as Prime Minister following allegations of a coup attempt, in Gyanja, reportedly led by a relative; he was replaced as premier by the First Deputy Prime Minister, Fuad Kuliyev.

**13–14 March 1995:** A decree disbanding the special militia forces prompted violent OPON protests; in the ensuing clashes with government troops on 17 March, at least 70 people, including Javadov, were killed. The PFA was accused of involvement in the insurrection and its activities temporarily suspended.

**12 November 1995:** Elections to the new 125-member Milli Majlis were held. Only eight of the country's official parties were permitted to participate and, of these, only two, the PFA and the National Independence Party (NIP), were opposition parties. At the same time a reported 91.9% of the electorate approved a new state Constitution in a nation-wide referendum; the country became the Azerbaijan Republic. Further rounds of voting for seats to the Milli Majlis were held on 26 November, 4 February 1996 and 18 February—the overwhelming majority of deputies elected were supporters of President Aliyev and his New Azerbaijan Party (NAP).

**14 April 1996:** The former defence minister, Rahim Gaziyev, and former President Mutalibov were arrested in Moscow, accused of plotting to overthrow the Azerbaijani Government (Mutalibov escaped extradition owing to ill health).

**19 July 1996:** Following accusations of economic mismanagement by President Aliyev, Fuad Kuliyev resigned as premier. Three other ministers were dismissed on charges of corruption. The First Deputy Prime Minister, Artur Rasizade, was appointed to head the Government; his appointment was confirmed in November.

**September 1996:** The Chairman of the Milli Majlis, Rasul Kuliyev, resigned. He was replaced by Murtuz Aleskerov. In April 1998 Kuliyev was charged with alleged abuses of power while in office.

**24 November 1996:** A presidential election in Nagornyi Karabakh was won by Robert Kocharian, already the *de facto* republican Head of State, with some 86% of the votes cast; the election was condemned by Azerbaijan and the OSCE as a hindrance to the peace process.

**January 1997:** Many opponents of Aliyev's regime were arrested, following allegations of foiled coup attempts, usually involving the former President, Mutalibov, and the former premier, Husseinov (the latter was extradited from Russia, where he had fled following his dismissal as premier, in March).

**20 March 1997:** Kocharian resigned the presidency of Nagornyi Karabakh upon his appointment as Prime Minister of Armenia; he was succeeded, on an acting basis, by Artur Tovmassian, the speaker of the legislature.

**1 September 1997:** Arkadii Ghukassian obtained some 90% of the votes cast in the Nagornyi Karabakh presidential election (he was inaugurated on 8 September).

**16 October 1997:** President Aliyev and President Ter-Petrossian of Armenia agreed to an OSCE proposal for a staged resolution of the conflict in Nagornyi Karabakh. Ter-Petrossian resigned in February 1998 following criticism of his moderate approach to the crisis.

**12 November 1997:** Despite security concerns, the AIOC officially began the first export of petroleum from the Caspian Sea, along the pipeline running from Baku to Novorossiisk, Russia, via the separatist Russian republic of Chechnya. (As a result of conflict in Chechnya from late 1999, a new section of the pipeline, avoiding the republic, was completed in March 2000).

**29 April 1998:** President Aliyev met the new Armenian President, Kocharian, at the CIS summit in Moscow, where it was agreed to resume negotiations on Nagornyi Karabakh.

**8 September 1998:** At a meeting held in Baku, Azerbaijan signed an agreement with 11 Asian and European countries, including Armenia, to recreate the 'Silk Road' trade route to Europe. This was the first high-level, governmental meeting between Azerbaijan and Armenia for four years.

**11 October 1998:** Aliyev was re-elected as Head of State with 77.6% of the total votes cast; the opposition protested the legitimacy of the elections and international observers noted a number of irregularities. Seven days later Aliyev was inaugurated for a second term. Rasizade was confirmed as premier on 23 October.

**December 1998:** The Milli Majlis approved a revised Constitution for Nakhichevan, endorsed by the Nakhichevan legislature, which defined the enclave as 'an autonomous state' within Azerbaijan.

**16 February 1999:** The Supreme Court sentenced Husseinov, the former Prime Minister, to life imprisonment, for his involvement in the October 1994 coup attempt. Also in February, it was reported that Azerbaijan was not to renew its membership of the CIS Collective Security Treaty for a second five-year period (subsequently signed in April by six countries), owing to the continued occupation of Nagornyi Karabakh by Armenian troops, and in protest at Russia's continuing supply of armaments to Armenia.

**17 April 1999:** A new pipeline, transporting crude petroleum from Baku to Supsa, Georgia, was inaugurated.

**July 1999:** After having been awarded observer status at NATO the previous month, Azerbaijan sent 30 troops to the Serbian province of Kosovo and Metohija, the Federal Republic of Yugoslavia, as part of a NATO peace-keeping force.

**18 November 1999:** At a summit meeting of the OSCE, held in İstanbul, Turkey, an agreement was signed by the Presidents of Azerbaijan, Georgia, Kazakhstan, Turkey and Turkmenistan, on the construction of a pipeline to transport petroleum from Baku, via Tbilisi, Georgia, to the Turkish port of Ceyhan.

**22 March 2000:** Arkadii Ghukassian, the President of Nagornyi Karabakh, was seriously wounded by gunmen in the territory's capital, Stepanakert. Over 20 people were arrested in connection with the incident, including Nagornyi Karabakh's former Minister of Defence, Samuel Babaian.

**5 November 2000:** Parliamentary elections were held. The NAP retained its majority, obtaining 79 seats in the Milli Majlis; the two main opposition parties, Musavat and the NIP, failed to secure any seats. Following allegations of electoral irregularities, in mid-November up to 10,000 people attended rallies to protest against the results. Further rounds of voting took place on 7 January 2001 in 11 districts where the results of the election had been annulled, owing to discrepancies.

**25 January 2001:** Azerbaijan was formally admitted to the Council of Europe.

**26 February 2001:** Babaian was found guilty of complicity in the attempt to assassinate Ghukassian in March 2000, and sentenced to 14 years' imprisonment.

**4 June 2001:** The Turkmenistani Ministry of Foreign Affairs closed its embassy in Baku, ostensibly owing to financial difficulties; the two countries were in dispute over ownership of Caspian oilfields.

**23 July 2001:** An armed Iranian patrol ship and military aircraft expelled a research vessel that was exploring potential oilfields in a disputed area of the southern Caspian Sea. The Iranian Government claimed that, since the maritime borders had not yet been agreed by all the nations surrounding the Caspian Sea, no country had the right to conduct petroleum-exploration operations.

**1 August 2001:** A presidential decree came into immediate force, according to which the Azerbaijani language was to use the Latin, rather than the Cyrillic, script.

**24–26 January 2002:** President Aliyev paid a state visit to Russia, at which seven bilateral agreements were signed, the most significant of which granted the Russian armed forces the right to use the Soviet-constructed Qabala radar station for a period of 10 years, while recognizing it as the property of Azerbaijan. Meanwhile, on 25 January, in recognition of Azerbaijan's support for the US-led campaign to combat international terrorism (initiated following large-scale terrorist attacks on the USA on 11 September 2001), US President George W. Bush signed a waiver to Section 907 of the Freedom Support Act, which barred direct US state aid to Azerbaijan while that country maintained its economic blockade of Armenia. The waiver was renewed in January 2003.

**11 August 2002:** Arkadii Ghukassian was re-elected as President of Nagornyi Karabakh. Ghukassian secured 88.4% of the votes cast, and the rate of participation by the electorate was some 75%.

**24 August 2002:** A referendum was held on proposed amendments to the Constitution, which would, *inter alia*, eliminate election by proportional representation, and allow for the transfer of power from the president to the prime minister (a presidential appointee), rather than the chairman of the Milli Majlis, in the event of the former's inability to govern. According to official results, 96% of the votes cast by 84% of the electorate were in favour of the amendments. Several large-scale opposition protests followed, amid allegations of fraud and procedural violations.

**23 September 2002:** The Presidents of Azerbaijan and Russia signed a bilateral agreement on the delimitation of the Caspian Sea, based on the principle that the surface be used in common, but the seabed be divided into national sectors, corresponding to each country's coastline, along a median line; a similar agreement had already been signed between Russia and Kazakhstan. A trilateral agreement was signed on 14 May 2003.

**21 April 2003:** President Aliyev collapsed during a televised speech. In July he was admitted to a Turkish hospital, owing to heart problems, prompting speculation as to whether he would be well enough to stand as a candidate in the presidential election, due to take place in October.

**28 April 2003:** Representatives from Armenia, Belarus, Kazakhstan, Kyrgyzstan, Russia and Tajikistan formally inaugurated the successor to the Collective Security Treaty, a new regional defence organization known as the Collective Security Treaty Organization (CSTO).

**27 May 2003:** The Milli Majlis passed a new electoral code, in conformity with the amendments approved in the referendum held in August, despite an opposition boycott.

**4 August 2003:** The Milli Majlis, meeting in emergency session, approved the appointment of the ailing President's son, Ilham Aliyev, as Prime Minister, following his nomination by his father. Two days later Ilham Aliyev undertook a leave of absence, in order to campaign for the presidential election; former premier Artur Rasizade became acting Prime Minister. Opposition demonstrations subsequently took place in protest against these developments.

**20 September 2003:** During opposition rallies held in advance of the presidential election, there were violent clashes with the security forces, resulting in hundreds of injuries.

**2 October 2003:** It was announced that Heydar Aliyev was to withdraw his candidacy for the presidential election, in favour of his son.

**15 October 2003:** At the presidential election, Ilham Aliyev was elected as the country's new President, obtaining some 80% of the votes cast. Members of the opposition alleged that widespread electoral violations had taken place, including intimidatory practices, and international observers declared the elections to have been neither free nor fair.

# History

## ANDREW YORKE

### INTRODUCTION

Present-day Azerbaijan occupies an area that has been inhabited for at least 3,000 years, and probably for far longer. However, in the modern era Azerbaijan has existed as an independent state for just two short periods: in 1918–20 and since October 1991. The country formed part of Persia for much of its history, although Turkic tribes from Central Asia had become a significant presence by the 11th century. Consequently, the Azeri language came to be dominated by Turkic rather than Persian influences. In the 19th century Azerbaijan experienced Russian domination, and was subsequently absorbed into the USSR. However, an area south of the river Araks (Araxes, Aras), which was also Azeri-populated, remained under Persian influence and now forms part of northern Iran. As a result, Azeri nationalists regard Azerbaijan as a nation divided by the great powers of Russia and Persia.

Islam replaced Orthodox Christianity in the territory that now constitutes Azerbaijan, following Arab domination in the seventh–ninth centuries. However, traditions of mysticism in the region made its people particularly receptive to Shi'a, the Islamic doctrine that remains dominant in the country. This was an important factor in setting Azerbaijan apart from Ottoman Turkey, where adherence was to the Sunni doctrine.

As the Persian Empire crumbled in the early 19th century, Russia came to dominate Azerbaijan as far south as the Araks river. However, the first major Russian incursion came under Tsar Peter (Petr) I ('the Great') in 1722, when Russian forces occupied Baku and other towns, until the reassertion of control by Persia in 1735. From the 1780s, the peoples of the south Caucasus (Armenia, Azerbaijan and Georgia) began to seek protection from Russia against an increasingly aggressive Persia. Owing to its history of Persian dominance and adherence to Islam, Azerbaijan was least inclined to regard Russia as a protector, but its nobles were unable to form a united front against the great power to the north. In the early 1800s Georgia was annexed by Russia under Alexander (Aleksandr) I, prompting the Azeris to turn to Persia for help. Following Russian victories in wars against Persia in 1804–13 and 1826–28, however, the territory came under Russian control.

Initially, Russia treated Azerbaijan merely as a military outpost, rather than a region with economic potential, and Azeris were effectively divested of their rights and property. In the 1840s, partly to counter a growing level of Ottoman sympathy in the region, Azeris were granted the same rights as Russian subjects, and some property was restored to Azeri nobles. Russian interest in the region accelerated rapidly, following the discovery of large reserves of petroleum and the denationalization of the industry in 1872. This led to an influx of Russians and Western entrepreneurs, who provided the expertise necessary to develop the oil industry. By the early 20th century Baku was a leading source of the world's petroleum. However, ethnic Azeris benefited little from the resultant wealth, and by the end of the 1870s only 13% of the country's oil industry was Azeri-owned. The majority of the petroleum profits were divided between two European companies: the Swedish Nobel brothers and the Royal Dutch company, which bought the local operations of the French Rothschilds and of the British company Shell shortly after the turn of the century. Despite the infrastructural improvements by the leading oil companies, Azerbaijan remained a low priority for Russia, and only became connected to Russia's vastly expanded rail network in 1890.

Baku developed rapidly as an urban centre, and attracted an influx of ethnic Armenians, who chiefly worked as merchants, industrial managers and Russian government administrators. Azeris became a minority in Baku (accounting for just 10% of the working-class population in 1907), largely holding menial jobs (for which they had to compete with immigrants from Iran, Russia and Turkey) and consigned to poverty, while the majority of Azeris were confined to the impoverished countryside. Resentment at their position in society and at the growing numbers of foreigners (especially Armenians) in the country led to riots and violent ethnic clashes in 1905.

The oppressive political environment in Baku meant that Azeri nationalism first flourished in European cities, such as Paris, France. However, the rapid urbanization that took place in Baku in the early 20th century encouraged the growth of an Azeri intelligentsia with a growing sense of national awareness. This new class was represented first by the Himmat (Endeavour) party, formed by intellectuals in 1903–04. Himmat was superseded in 1911 by the nationalist Musavat (Equality) party, which openly advocated independent statehood for Azerbaijan. In 1915 the party's armed wing, the Difay, proclaimed a 'republic of Azerbaijan' in Gyanja (Ganca), which was repressed by Russian troops a few weeks later.

The final collapse of imperial Russia following the October 1917 revolution provided Azerbaijan with its first experience of real independence. Although the 'Baku Bolsheviks', who were predominantly ethnic Russian or Armenian, declared a Soviet Government in November 1917, on 28 May 1918 Muslim nationalists declared an Azerbaijan People's Democratic Republic, effectively ending the authority in Azerbaijan of the fragile Transcaucasian federation, proclaimed in the previous month, and incorporating Armenia, Azerbaijan and Georgia. Once again, the north-western city of Gyanja became the parallel centre of power in the country. In Baku, mean-

while, a council (soviet), comprising a number of commissars, had been created under the leadership of the Armenian Bolshevik Anastas Mikoian. The commissars formed an executive committee, with *de facto* authority, but allowed the former district council to establish a provisional government under Stepan Shaumian, a moderate Armenian.

With Ottoman Turkish assistance, an International Islamic Army was formed in Gyanja, made up of some 7,000 élite troops and 14,000 volunteers. It entered Baku in September 1918, leading to clashes with Baku's Armenian population. A new Government was formed, dominated by Musavat, which ruled, in coalition with minor parties, in five successive Governments. The British military presence in Baku withdrew in September, after the collapse of the Baku soviet, although the British were implicated in the execution of 26 commissars, in an incident that would form part of Soviet martyrology and help to define the identity of Soviet Azerbaijan. The Turkish army subsequently occupied the country, until it was forced to withdraw following its defeat in the First World War. In November the British declared Azerbaijan under provisional British rule, and in December 1918 the first multi-party elections in Azerbaijan's history were held to a Musavat-dominated parliament. Meanwhile, the Bolsheviks began to win the support of left-wing factions in parliament and to smuggle arms from Russia.

## SOVIET RULE

The British forces withdrew in August 1919, apparently believing that the Bolsheviks would be driven out of Azerbaijan by an ascendant Turkey. Independent Azerbaijan was thus left increasingly vulnerable to attack by Soviet forces, which were consolidating their hold over a Russia that had been torn apart by civil war. On 1 April 1920 the last Musavat-dominated Government stood down, and the party's leadership took refuge in Tbilisi, Georgia. Armed Bolshevik forces took to the streets and proclaimed a Provisional Azerbaijani Military Revolutionary Committee. On 28 April the Soviet Red Army finally marched into Azerbaijan. It met little resistance, as much of the 30,000-strong Azerbaijani army was engaged in efforts to quell an uprising by ethnic Armenians in the enclave of Nagornyi Karabakh. By September the state of Azerbaijan had effectively been absorbed into the country that in 1922 became known as the Union of Soviet Socialist Republics (USSR).

In 1921 Azerbaijan was incorporated into a Transcaucasian Federated Republic (from 1922 the Transcaucasian Soviet Federative Socialist Republic—TSFSR), together with Georgia and Armenia. However, the republic was riven with tensions, and was abolished with the introduction of the so-called Stalin Constitution (after the Soviet leader, Iosif V. Dzhugashvili) in 1936. Thereafter, the Azerbaijan Soviet Socialist Republic (SSR) became a full Union Republic.

Throughout the 1920s and 1930s the Soviet leadership attempted to nurture a Soviet Azerbaijani identity, while persecuting nationalists and intellectuals who were opposed to communist rule. Religious leaders were persecuted and mosques were closed. The Azerbaijani people suffered as much as other Soviet peoples as a result of Stalin's policies of consignment to the prison and labour camps of the Gulag, the forced collectivization of agriculture between 1929 and 1935, and the 'Great Purges' of the late 1930s. (The islands of Nargen and Kum-Zirya became notorious prison colonies.) By 1940 approximately 120,000 Azerbaijanis had died as a result of repression. The purges and other repressive measures were co-ordinated by the First Secretary of the Communist Party of Azerbaijan (CPA), Mir Jafar Baghirov, although it was reputedly an appeal to Stalin by Baghirov that prevented Azeris sharing the fate of other Caucasian peoples deported towards the end of the Second World War (1939–45) in punishment for supposed collaboration with Nazi Germany.

However, Soviet rule did lead to a marked improvement in literacy rates and industrial development. At least until the Second World War, Baku literally helped to generate Stalin's rapid industrialization programme. Subsequently, the penetration of German forces deep into the north Caucasus prompted Stalin to seek alternative sources of energy, particularly in Russian Siberia, at a safer distance from foreign invasion.

Stalin's death in 1953 and his replacement by a collective leadership, which included Nikita Khrushchev, marked the end for Baghirov, who was executed in 1956. The same political 'thaw' that took place in the Russian and Soviet capital, Moscow, was felt in Azerbaijan, with the introduction of greater political freedoms and the rehabilitation of the victims of Stalin's rule. The economy also demonstrated an improvement in the 1960s, particularly in the sectors of agriculture and construction. Nevertheless, even in the 1970s purchasing power in the republic was just one-half of the Union average, indicating that the population was failing to benefit from much of its oil wealth.

In 1969 Heydar Aliyev took over from Imam D. Mustafayev, who had been accused of corruption, as First Secretary of the CPA. Aliyev had previously been head of the KGB (Committee for State Security) in the exclave of Nakhichevan, and had played an important role in the Soviet security services during the Second World War. In 1982 Aliyev was appointed to the Political Bureau (Politburo) of the Communist Party of the Soviet Union (CPSU) by the party's General Secretary, Yurii Andropov. None the less, in 1987 he fell victim to a corruption investigation launched by the Soviet President, Mikhail Gorbachev (1985–91). Aliyev, however, insisted that he had resigned for health reasons, and subsequently resigned from the CPSU, rather than waiting to be expelled. In 1988 he returned to his homeland of Nakhichevan, where he founded Yeni Azerbaijan (New Azerbaijan Party—NAP), which was to become the vehicle for his future political resurgence.

## NAGORNYI KARABAKH

The disputed enclave of Nagornyi Karabakh (or Artsakh in Armenian), located within Azerbaijani territory close to the border with Armenia, fuelled independence movements in both Armenia and Azerbaijan, and the failure of the Soviet authorities to control the situation contributed to the demise of the Union. The status of the enclave has proved an issue of contention for both newly independent states, hampering trade, deterring foreign investors and, by the early 2000s, continuing to pose the threat of renewed conflict.

Contrary to the assertions of some nationalists, the dispute over Nagornyi Karabakh is relatively recent. Although conflicts took place in the territory in previous centuries, as was the case elsewhere in the south Caucasus, the first real inter-ethnic conflict in the enclave did not occur until the early 20th century. The majority of ethnic Armenians had as their homeland Anatolia (now in Turkey) and Syria, with a relatively small community in present-day Armenia. This situation was to change when imperial Russia identified the Armenians as a potential source of support against the Ottoman Turks. Russia encouraged ethnic Armenians to settle in the south Caucasus, and over 500,000 did so in the first half of the 18th century. Russia also appears to have encouraged the activities of the extreme nationalist Armenian Revolutionary Federation (Dashnaktsutiun, also known simply as Dashnaks), which began to stage attacks against the Ottomans in eastern Anatolia in the early 1890s.

The first inter-ethnic clashes erupted in 1905, a time of political turmoil in St Petersburg (the Russian capital between 1712 and 1918). In February the murder by Dash-naktsutiun of a Muslim businessman in Baku led to violent clashes between Azeris and Armenians, which left over 300 dead. Similar confrontations quickly erupted in Yerevan, Armenia, where ethnic Azeris were murdered by armed Armenians. In August 1905 Dashnaktsutiun launched an attack in the Karabakh city of Shusha, leaving some 200 Azeris and 100 Armenians dead. In Baku Himmat responded with a general strike aimed at forcing the Russian overlords to act to restore order. Despite attempts by the Russian Governor-General to put an end to the disorder, in November further sporadic violence was reported in Gyanja and elsewhere. In mid-1906 a further Russian initiative to quell the unrest only led to an intensification of the two communities' conflict, in anticipation of the arrival of the Russians. Following three weeks of serious violence, in July Russia succeeded in regaining control, although the violence had claimed up to 10,000 lives.

During the interregnum between the collapse of imperial Russia and the imposition of Soviet control in the Caucasus, attempts were made to grant Nagornyi Karabakh independence under a joint presidency. However, the inter-ethnic violence continued in an increasingly extreme form. In 1918 the enclave became a battleground, in which Armenian forces seeking to incorporate it into their territory repelled Turkish-backed Azeri forces. The arrival of British forces in Azerbaijan prevented the complete takeover of Karabakh by Armenia. In January 1919 the British Governor-General appointed an Azeri landowner, Khosrovebek Sultanov, as Governor of Nagornyi Karabakh. However, Sultanov's offer of a cease-fire went unheeded, and Armenia retook much of the enclave. Finally, in May 1920 the area came under Red Army control.

The enclave was awarded to Azerbaijan in 1921, and acquired autonomous status in 1923. During the ensuing years of Soviet rule, Armenians campaigned hard, but unsuccessfully, to have the Nagorno-Karabakh Autonomous Oblast transferred from Azerbaijani control. During the 'thaw' of the 1960s thousands of Karabakh Armenians sent a petition to the Kremlin, claiming that Azerbaijan was neglecting the region, and there were at least two incidents of related violence. However, the Karabakh issue was not to pose a genuine challenge to Soviet authority until 1988.

As in other Soviet republics, the political and economic freedoms introduced by Gorbachev as part of his campaign for *glasnost* (openness) and *perestroika* (restructuring) led Azerbaijanis to revisit the question of national identity, and this growing sense of nationalism was accelerated by the Karabakh issue. Inspired by the resurgent nationalism and liberalism across the entire USSR, in February 1988 the Armenian-dominated Nagornyi Karabakh Soviet demanded that the territory be transferred to the jurisdiction of the Armenian SSR. These demands prompted violent attacks against Azeri settlements in Karabakh, as well as organized attacks against ethnic Armenians in the industrial city of Sumgait. Further clashes led to the exodus of Azeris from Nagornyi Karabakh and Armenia, and of ethnic Armenians from the rest of Azerbaijan. In mid-1988 both the Armenian Supreme Soviet and the Nagornyi Karabakh Soviet declared that the enclave had seceded from Azerbaijan and had been reintegrated with Armenia. A new party, called the Popular Front of Azerbaijan (PFA), which had been legalized as a result of *glasnost*, subsequently became an organ of Azeri nationalist sentiment, insisting that Azerbaijan's territorial integrity be preserved. Mass protests began in Baku and other cities, leading to hundreds of arrests by Soviet troops. After much prevarication in Moscow, Soviet troops finally intervened in Nagornyi Karabakh in early 1989, when the Soviet leadership imposed direct rule in the region. Nevertheless, tensions remained high, and Azerbaijan introduced an economic blockade of Armenia in September. In January 1990 Soviet troops finally entered Baku, which had become the scene of violent protests and pogroms, and over 120 protesters were killed. This incident was a major factor contributing to the alienation of Azeris from the USSR. Meanwhile, in the south of the country there were further PFA-inspired uprisings, demanding greater access to relatives living in northern Iran. A semblance of order was finally restored at the end of January, after leading PFA members had been arrested and a new leader of Azerbaijan, Ayaz Niyaz oglu Mutalibov, had been imposed by the Soviet authorities.

In August 1990 the Azerbaijani legislature voted to abolish the autonomous status of Nagornyi Karabakh; in September 1991 Nagornyi Karabakh responded by declaring the region a 'provisional republic'. By 1992 the situation had escalated into a state of full-scale conflict. During an ill-prepared military campaign hundreds of Azerbaijani troops were killed by the better-organized Armenian militia, and civilian casualties numbered in the thousands. Arguably the most notorious massacre of the war took place at Khojali, north-east of Stepanakert, in February 1992, when an Armenian assault was launched on the town, in which hundreds of Azeris had been resettled; approximately 485 Azeris were killed in the attack. By the end of February the Nagornyi Karabakh military controlled the entire enclave.

Mutalibov's successor Abulfaz Elchibey (*né* Aliyev), who was elected President of Azerbaijan in June 1992, made a number of ultimately unsuccessful attempts to retake the territory by force, and following intensive international mediation a cease-fire was finally announced by the Russian Minister of Defence, Pavel Grachev, in May 1994, and was formalized in July. It has held subsequently, albeit with frequent border violations and some exchanges of fire. As a result of the Nagornyi Karabakh conflict between 1m. and 1.5m. refugees and internally displaced persons were created, and at least 30,000 people died. Negotiations for a final settlement to the conflict continue under the auspices of the Organization for Security and Co-operation in Europe (OSCE), led by a 'troika' comprising representatives of France, Russia and the USA.

## EARLY INDEPENDENCE

In August 1991 an abortive coup against Gorbachev by 'hardliners' in Moscow led to large pro-independence demonstrations in Azerbaijan, which also called for Mutalibov's resignation. By the end of the month the Supreme Soviet had voted in favour of independence from the USSR. Presidential elections held in the following month led to Mutalibov being re-elected unchallenged, owing to an opposition boycott. Independence was formalized by the Supreme Soviet in October, and became a reality following the dissolution of the USSR in December 1991.

The outcry that followed the events at Khojali forced Mutalibov's resignation in March 1992. After a failed interim presidency by Yagub Mamedov, and an unsuccessful attempt by Mutalibov to recover his position, the nationalist PFA seized power in a coup in May. In June the leader of the PFA, Abulfaz Elchibey, a philologist with nationalist views, was elected President. However, he too failed to bring about a military resolution to the war in Nagornyi Karabakh, and his Government was given a sinister edge, owing to the appointment of Iskander Hamidov—leader of the Azeri branch of a Turkish paramilitary group—as Minister of Internal Affairs. Elchibey was ousted in June 1993 by a maverick military garrison, under Col Surat Husseinov (who had commanded Azerbaijani forces in the conflict over Nagornyi Karabakh), which Elchibey had attempted to disband. Elchibey subsequently fled to Nakhichevan, and the Milli Majlis (as the legislature was now known) awarded the acting presidency to the former Soviet-era leader, Heydar Aliyev, who had, by this

time, been recalled from Nakhichevan and appointed parliamentary Chairman (speaker). In order to avoid confrontation with Husseinov, Aliyev duly appointed him Prime Minister.

## THE ALIYEV ERA

Aliyev's first months in power were characterized by an assertion of control over the PFA and other opposition parties. Probably at the instigation of Husseinov, the Ministers of Defence, of Foreign Affairs and of Internal Affairs in the previous Government were imprisoned. Elchibey's removal from power was confirmed by a nation-wide referendum in August 1993, in which 98% of participants expressed 'no confidence' in the ousted President. This was followed by a victory for Aliyev in the presidential election held in October, in which he secured 99% of the votes cast. (The two candidates who stood against him were largely political unknowns.) In a further measure against the opposition, the Milli Majlis, under parliamentary Chairman Rasul Kuliyev, adopted a law on military censorship, which forbade the publication of any information deemed to damage the reputation of either the state or the President.

However, Aliyev faced a revolt in September–October 1994, after gunmen assassinated both the deputy speaker of parliament and Aliyev's head of security. The Procurator-General, Ali Omarov, a close ally of Husseinov, accused the Deputy Minister of Internal Affairs, Rovshan Javadov, of being responsible for the attack, and arrested members of the special police attached to the Ministry of Internal Affairs (known as OPON). Javadov responded by dispatching members of OPON to the Procuracy, where they kidnapped Omarov and released their colleagues. In response, Aliyev declared a state of emergency. There were suspicions that Husseinov and former President Mutalibov had co-ordinated the entire affair, possibly with Russian support. Both Omarov and Husseinov were subsequently dismissed from their positions, and the latter fled to Russia to avoid charges of treason.

In March 1995 Aliyev experienced further discord, when a presidential decree disbanding OPON prompted violent confrontation between the army and members of the OPON militia, as a result of which more than 50 people, including Javadov, were killed. Hundreds of people were arrested in the aftermath of the insurrection, among them the Minister of Internal Affairs. The PFA, which was accused of involvement in the incident, was temporarily banned.

In November 1995 the country held its first multi-party elections to the 125-member Milli Majlis. The majority of seats (60%) were won by Aliyev's NAP, and only two opposition parties, the PFA and the National Independence Party (NIP), led by Etibar Mamedov, were able to secure representation in the Milli Majlis. The voters also overwhelmingly approved a new Constitution, which granted wide-ranging powers to the President, including the right to appoint the prime minister and members of the Cabinet of Ministers, the prosecutor-general, and the Supreme Court and Constitutional Court judges. The international community criticized the voting as neither free nor fair.

In August 1996 Kuliyev published an accusatorial critique of Aliyev in a Russian journal. The following month Kuliyev resigned as speaker, and fled to the USA. His parliamentary immunity from prosecution was removed in March 1998, and the Prosecutor-General subsequently launched criminal proceedings against Kuliyev, who was charged with large-scale embezzlement during his tenure as head of a petroleum refinery. His replacement as parliamentary Chairman was an Aliyev loyalist, Murtuz Aleskerov.

In October 1998 Aliyev won a second term in office, securing 76% of the votes cast in the presidential election. Once again, the international community condemned the election, specifically owing to allegations of 'ballot-stuffing' and media bias in favour of the incumbent. Five major opposition parties, including the PFA and the Democrats, united to form the Movement for Democratic Elections and Electoral Reform (MDEER) prior to the election. As it approached, the MDEER announced a boycott, in protest at the Aliyev Government's perceived attempts to manipulate issues such as the composition of the Central Electoral Commission (CEC) and media coverage, and staged mass rallies in the capital, some of which led to clashes with the police. However, Etibar Mamedov fared well in the election, and claimed to have evidence that would compel Aliyev to progress to a second round of voting. None the less, the CEC subsequently announced Aliyev as the first-round winner, although it failed to provide a district-by-district analysis of the results.

Shortly afterwards, Aliyev was affected by his first major health problems since the heart attack that he claimed had prompted his resignation as First Secretary of the CPA in 1987. In subsequent years he received regular treatment at hospitals in both Turkey and the USA. Eventually, in April 2003 Aliyev collapsed while giving a televised speech, and spent much of the following months in hospital. For some time Aliyev's deteriorating health had prompted speculation about his likely successor, and in August 2002 constitutional amendments had been passed by referendum, providing for the prime minister to assume the role of acting president, pending new elections, in the event of the incumbent President's death or incapacitation. However, Aliyev's collapse led to uncertainties about the anticipated outcome of the presidential elections scheduled to take place on 15 October 2003. Heydar Aliyev's son, Ilham, was clearly his chosen successor, and was appointed Prime Minister at the beginning of August 2003, with the overwhelming approval of the Milli Majlis. Apparently with the intention of insuring against the possibility that the incumbent President might not be well enough to stand as a candidate in the presidential election, Ilham Aliyev also put forward his candidacy, and indeed in early October Heydar Aliyev released a statement announcing his withdrawal from the election.

Owing to widespread doubts that the forthcoming elections would be held under free and fair conditions, few observers had believed that any candidate from the opposition had a real chance of winning the election. These doubts were compounded by the fact that the opposition delayed uniting behind a single presidential candidate. Of the main challengers from the opposition, former parliamentary speaker Rasul Kuliyev, leader of the Democratic Party of Azerbaijan, and former President Ayaz Mutalibov (in exile in Russia) had been disqualified, as they did not satisfy residency criteria. Thus the main opposition candidates appeared to be Isa Gambar, the Chairman of Musavat, and Mamedov.

There were some doubts about the level of political authority wielded by Ilham Aliyev, and it had been considered conceivable (although unlikely) that the ruling élite might choose to consolidate behind a rival candidate. In the event, however, he was declared the victor in a single round of voting on 15 October 2003, with some 80% of the votes cast, although there were widespread allegations of electoral malpractice. Gambar was the second-placed candidate, with 12.8% of the votes cast, according to preliminary reports. In the immediate aftermath of the election, it remained to be seen whether the inauguration of Heydar Aliyev's heir would affect the political stability of the republic.

## FOREIGN RELATIONS

Azerbaijan's foreign policy has historically been defined by its relations with the three regional powers on or close to its borders: Iran, Russia and Turkey. Following the collapse of the USSR, relations with the USA also came to play an important role. Azerbaijan's first post-communist President,

Ayaz Mutalibov, was widely regarded as being controlled by the Soviet, and later Russian, authorities, and his successors have thus worked to strengthen the country's independence from its former rulers.

Mutalibov's immediate successor, Abulfaz Elchibey, regarded Turkey as Azerbaijan's chief ally. Elchibey was influenced by pan-Turkic ideology and favoured the cultivation of relations with Turkey, at the expense of relations with Iran and Russia. However, Elchibey's somewhat erratic leadership style meant that although Turkey may initially have offered its support, it was likely to have welcomed his succession by the more pragmatic Aliyev.

Foreign-policy priorities under Aliyev were generally orientated away from Russia, and even Turkey, in favour of the USA. The extremely lucrative contract signed in 1994 with an international consortium, established to develop the country's reserves, included the participation of the Russian petroleum company LUKoil (headed by an ethnic Azeri), but by 2003 LUKoil was indicating its intention to withdraw from all but one of its projects in Azerbaijan.

A more conciliatory line by the Russian side, particularly under the presidency of Vladimir Putin (2000–), had helped to stabilize bilateral relations. In particular, two recent events removed significant obstacles to the development of friendly Russian-Azerbaijani relations. First, in September 2002 the two sides signed a bilateral agreement on the division of their Caspian oil reserves. Second, in October an agreement came into effect, whereby Russia would pay for its continued use of the Qabala radar installation located on Azerbaijani territory. Nevertheless, Russia's perceived pro-Armenian orientation and its continued supply of military assistance to Armenia hindered the cultivation of more friendly ties. For example, Azerbaijan reacted angrily to the withdrawal of Russian equipment from military bases in Georgia, because that equipment was to be transferred to the Russian base situated in Gyumri, Armenia. Despite improved relations between Russia and the USA, and the involvement of both countries' interests in Azerbaijan's petroleum industry, Azerbaijan continued to struggle to balance the demands of both countries.

Relations with Turkey remained strong under Aliyev, and the commencement of construction work on the planned Baku–Tbilisi–Ceyhan (Turkey) petroleum pipeline and the planned Baku–Tbilisi–Erzurum (Turkey) gas pipeline was expected to help to cement the relationship between the two countries. However, signs that the new Turkish Government might be willing to remove its economic blockade of Armenia provoked an angry reaction in Azerbaijan, which believed that this would seriously weaken its bargaining position over the Karabakh issue.

Aliyev attempted to improve relations with Iran, which had been seriously undermined during Elchibey's pro-Turkish presidency. Given that the dominant Islamic doctrine in both countries is Shi'a, in addition to their common history and the fact that up to 20m. ethnic Azeris live in Iran, there is a potential for improved relations. However, in reality, these factors have served to contribute to tensions. Iran is wary of the ethnic Azeri population to the north, while Azerbaijan has accused Iran of fomenting unrest among its Shi'ite Muslim community. In particular, the Azerbaijani Government accused Iran of offering support to radical Islamist elements in the village of Nardaran, which became a focus for protests against the Aliyev regime in 2002–03. However, it was over the issue of the delimitation of the Caspian Sea that relations reached their nadir in July 2001, when Iran sent military patrol boats to threaten Azerbaijani survey vessels operating in the disputed sector of the sea. Iran claims a 20% territorial share of the Caspian, whereas Azerbaijan, Kazakhstan and Russia, which signed a trilateral agreement on the delimitation of their respective sectors in May 2003, believe that the seabed should be divided into national sectors, corresponding to each country's coastline, according to the so-called median line principle; according to this principle, Iran would be left with less than 14% of the seabed. Relations improved after 2001, with mutual visits by government delegations and the planned construction of a gas pipeline linking the two countries. However, a bilateral agreement on the division of the Caspian Sea remained a remote prospect.

The failure to reach agreement over the legal status of the Caspian Sea also posed an obstacle to relations with Turkmenistan, which sought an overarching agreement based on the median line principle, but with modifications that would allow it to lay claim to some of Azerbaijan's oilfields in the middle of the Caspian.

Relations with the USA were complicated by the ambiguity of US policy in the south Caucasus. On the one hand, the US Department of State has tended to follow a pro-Azerbaijan line, in support of US petroleum interests in the Azerbaijani sector of the Caspian Sea, although a strong pro-Armenian lobby exists within the US Congress. Given the strong lobbying power of US petroleum companies over the Administration of US President George W. Bush, as well as the increasingly pro-Russian orientation of Armenia, in the early 2000s relations between the USA and Azerbaijan were good. The economic sanctions imposed by the USA against Azerbaijan in 1992, under Section 907 of the Freedom Support Act (preventing direct US state aid to Azerbaijan while that country maintained an economic blockade of Armenia) were suspended in early 2002 to facilitate US-Azerbaijani co-operation in US-led efforts to combat international terrorism, following the suicide attacks on the USA of 11 September 2001. Azerbaijan received praise from the USA for its anti-terrorism efforts, and there was even speculation that US North Atlantic Treaty Organization (NATO) forces might eventually be relocated from Germany to Azerbaijan (and other Eastern European countries), although this would inevitably anger Russia.

In addition to its membership of the Commonwealth of Independent States (CIS), Azerbaijan is a member of the GUUAM grouping, a loose alliance of former Soviet states (Georgia, Ukraine, Uzbekistan, Azerbaijan, Moldova), drawn together by a pro-USA and anti-Russian orientation. From its inception in 1997, the grouping struggled to find common ground or achieve any meaningful co-operation. After the election of Putin as Russian President, several factors diminished the significance and viability of GUUAM: first, the new, pro-Russian orientation of Moldova and Ukraine; second, the improved relations between the USA and Russia; third, the vacillation of Uzbekistan, which joined in 1999, over whether to maintain its membership; and fourth, the fact that Russia has arguably adopted a more pragmatic approach to relations with the former Soviet republics. None the less, GUUAM showed signs of renewed activity in 2003, amid reports of US support for the grouping.

# The Economy

## ANDREW YORKE

### ECONOMIC INHERITANCE AND POLICY

Azerbaijan's geographical position and endowment with natural resources mean that it has significant economic potential. However, under imperial Russian, and later Soviet rule its economy was developed primarily in those sectors that were of use to the Empire or Union as a whole: notably petroleum, natural gas and chemical production. With the collapse of the command economy and the breakdown of official inter-republican trade, Azerbaijan experienced the 'transitional recession' that was shared by all the post-Soviet states. Indeed, gross domestic product (GDP) contracted by an average of almost 20% per year in the first four years of independence. A proportion of this decline can be attributed to the fact that Soviet GDP tended to be exaggerated, and to the large amount of economic activity that moved from the formal to the informal sphere.

Geography hindered the process of recovery from the recession, as independent Azerbaijan found itself surrounded by hostile states: Armenia, Iran and Russia. Moreover, the demise of the USSR meant that the Caspian Sea off Azerbaijan's eastern shore was surrounded by not two states (the USSR and Iran) but five (Azerbaijan, Iran, Kazakhstan, Russia and Turkmenistan), each of which laid claim to the Sea's oil and gas reserves. The ensuing unresolved dispute over the division of the Caspian Sea has hindered the exploitation of these deposits.

The war in Nagornyi Karabakh (see History) damaged the economy in several ways. In addition to the economic disruption that inevitably follows a war on a country's own territory, the additional pressure caused by more than 1m. Azeri refugees and internally displaced persons placed a considerable burden on the economy. The economic blockade imposed on Armenia also represented a significant barrier to trade.

The signing in 1994 of the petroleum deal often referred to as the 'contract of the century' marked a change in the country's economic fortunes. The agreement led to the formation of the Azerbaijan International Oil Consortium (AIOC), led by the British and US companies BP and Amoco (which subsequently merged), and separate deals were signed with other major foreign petroleum companies (see below). Petroleum production activities did not commence until 1997, but foreign investment began to flow into the country from 1994 in the form of 'bonus payments' to the Government, which helped to reverse the economic decline.

From 1996 GDP registered growth each year. Real GDP growth averaged 10% per year in the early 2000s, and it was expected to decelerate only slightly, to 9%, in 2003–04. However, this strong performance was not sufficient to offset the earlier decline. GDP continued to represent just 70% of its 1989 peak, and the average monthly wage was equivalent to approximately $70.

In 2002 the budgetary deficit was just US $44m., or approximately 0.5% of GDP. However, revenues remain highly dependent on the price of petroleum. This vulnerability was exposed in 1998 and 1999, when low global petroleum prices resulted in a substantial budget deficit, equivalent to of 4% and 5% of GDP, respectively.

As in many post-communist countries, the inflation rate soared out of control in the early years following the relaxation of price controls. It reached its peak in 1994 at 1,778%, but tight monetary policy had reduced it to single figures by 1996. In 2001 the annual rate of increase in consumer-price inflation was 1.5%, and the rate was 2.8% in 2002.

Azerbaijan reported a positive trade balance, of US $481.6m., in 2002. The country's primary exports are crude oil, petroleum products and natural gas (accounting for around 90% of all exports). Small amounts of machinery, cotton, foodstuffs and chemicals are also exported. The main imports are machinery and electrical equipment, mineral products, base metals, vehicles and transportation equipment, vegetable products and foodstuffs. The country's main trading partners in 2002 were Italy (accounting for 29% of total turnover), Russia (10%), France (8%) and Turkey (6%).

Owing to its petroleum and natural gas reserves, Azerbaijan is the leading former Soviet country in terms of foreign direct investment (FDI) per head, with a cumulative total of over US $600 per head by the end of 2002, compared with $180 in Russia. From 1994 the main foreign investors were the United Kingdom and the USA (each accounting for around 25% of cumulative FDI), Turkey (15%), Russia (7%), Norway (7%) and Japan (5%).

The most daunting challenge for Azerbaijan is the phenomenon known as 'Dutch Disease', which is common in countries where the economy is dominated by the energy sector, particularly in terms of exports. The influx of foreign currency from energy exports tends to drive up the value of the local currency, which, in turn, makes the country's goods less competitive both domestically and abroad. As a consequence, the Government becomes increasingly dependent on the energy sector for its revenues. Given that energy production is not a major employer, its dominance of the economy can lead to high rates of unemployment. Periods of low global energy prices can temporarily ease the upward pressure on the local currency and improve the competitiveness of non-energy exports, but are also likely to cause major declines in GDP and large budget deficits. (Two of the most notorious examples of economies damaged by 'Dutch Disease' are Nigeria and Venezuela.)

Finally, Azerbaijan's petroleum wealth is finite, and production is expected to peak as early as 2010, at four times existing levels, only to revert to similar levels as early as 2024. Consequently, there is only a limited period available in which to use petroleum exports as efficiently as possible, in order to bolster the long-term sustainability of the economy as a whole.

## TRANSPORT AND COMMUNICATIONS

The country's transport infrastructure includes extensive road and rail networks, which have suffered from years of underinvestment and poor maintenance. This situation was exacerbated by the closure of road and rail links with Russia (during the Chechen conflict of 1994–96) and Armenia (since 1994). Continuing security problems in Georgia also hinder transport links with the Black Sea. Moreover, since 1999 the renewed conflict in the separatist Russian republic of Chechnya has caused further disruption to road and rail links with Russia. Travel and freight traffic between Azerbaijan and the exclave of Nakhichevan remains possible only by air, or via Iran.

In 1999 the European Bank for Reconstruction and Development (EBRD) granted two loans, worth a total of US $36.4m., for transport projects: $20.2m. was allocated to the Azerbaijani sector of the trans-Caucasian railway, and $16.2m. for the modernization of the ferry terminal at Baku port. Both projects were intended to help realize the EU-sponsored project to develop a transport corridor, linking Europe, the Caucasus and Central Asia (TRACECA). That project has led to new investment in other areas of transport infrastructure, such as bridges.

The operation of the telecommunications sector has been marred by the continued tight control and monopolistic practices of the Ministry of Communications. Fixed-line telecommunications are run by Aztelecom, the planned privatization of which has been subject to repeated delays. Telephone usage remained low by 2000, with 49.1 telephone lines per 100 households, and 10.4 lines per 100 inhabitants; in Baku there were around 99.8 telephones per 100 families in the early 2000s. The mobile telecommunications sector is divided between two service providers: Azercell, a joint venture of Turkcell and the Ministry of Communications, with over 600,000 subscribers; and Bakcell, part-owned by Motorola of the USA, with over 200,000 subscribers. Internet usage in Azerbaijan was increasing, but remained low, although by 2002 there were approximately 300,000 internet users.

## AGRICULTURE

Agriculture is the second most important economic sector, after petroleum and gas. It remains the country's largest employer, providing approximately 39.6% of employment in 2002. However, agriculture's contribution to GDP had declined from 32.2% in 1994 to 15.2% in 2002. Land privatization was almost complete, with farmland apportioned as private property. However, progress was hindered by a lack of credit facilities for farmers, and production also suffered as a result of the Armenian occupation of much of Azerbaijan's most fertile land.

Under Soviet rule the crop mix in Azerbaijan was changed to provide species that were of benefit to the Union as a whole. Rice production, for example, was de-emphasized in favour of viniculture. After regaining independence Azerbaijan worked to alter its crop mix to enable it to regain a measure of self-sufficiency. However, it continues to import approximately 70% of food consumed.

The country's main agricultural products are cotton, grain, rice, grapes, fruit, vegetables, tea, tobacco, livestock and wine. Most agricultural production is from small, private producers rather than large-scale Soviet-style collective farms or Western-style agribusiness. The strong domestic currency (the manat) has led to substantial imports from Turkey, Russia and Iran.

Another principal reason for the high level of import trade was the fact that food-processing facilities were scarce, while those that do exist usually possess outdated technology. In 2002 the agriculture sector received just 0.8% of total investment, compared with 68.5% of investment in the petroleum and gas sector.

In recent years harvests have been reduced by natural disasters, most recently by severe flooding and locust infestation in early 2003. In previous years the World Bank, USAID and the International Fund for Agricultural Development (IFAD) had all provided loans to help reform the sector. The World Bank planned to lend an additional US $15m. to assist agricultural projects in 2004.

## INDUSTRY

In 2002 the contribution of industry to GDP was 49.5% (this figure includes industry related to the petroleum and gas sectors, discussed in the following section). Manufacturing accounted for just 6.7% of GDP in 2002, compared with 17.7% in 1991, as the booming petroleum and gas sector increasingly came to dominate the economy. In 2002 industrial production increased by 3.6%, compared with overall GDP growth of 10.6%. The main industrial products are oilfield equipment, steel, iron ore, cement, chemicals and petrochemicals, and textiles.

Chemicals and petrochemicals production is concentrated in the industrial city of Sumgait, located 30 km to the north of Baku. Founded in the late 1940s, most of its factories closed following the collapse of the USSR and the resulting economic decline. By 2003 only six factories remained in operation, but the city continued to suffer from serious environmental pollution. The oilfield equipment industry suffered from a lack of investment in new technologies. Furthermore, the foreign companies that operate many of the country's oilfields usually prefer to use Western suppliers of equipment.

The textiles industry, which was developed to take advantage of the country's cotton crops, has struggled to compete with inexpensive imports from Turkey and Iran. The country's textile plants are concentrated in the north-western city of Gyanja (Ganca).

In recent years the Government has attempted to privatize ageing factories, but it has received little interest from foreign buyers. Meanwhile, the IMF asked the Government to use a proportion of the funds accumulating in the State Oil Fund of Azerbaijan (SOFAZ—see below) to introduce tax reductions, in the hope of stimulating a revival in manufacturing and other non-petroleum sectors.

## PETROLEUM AND NATURAL GAS

As already noted, petroleum production has become the mainstay of Azerbaijan's economy, as well as an important instrument of foreign policy. The enthusiasm expressed in the 1990s that the Caspian region would become a new Persian Gulf has receded somewhat, but the true extent of Azerbaijan's Caspian reserves remains unknown. The country's onshore and offshore petroleum reserves are estimated at between 7,000m. and 13,000m. barrels. Domestically and abroad, attitudes to the industry and its effect on the economy have been divided between two extremes: those who regard petroleum as the key to the country's state-building project, its integration into the world economy and an improvement in living standards for its people; and those who regard it as a 'resource curse', which dooms the country to corrupt and authoritarian rule, as well as the predominance of an industry that pollutes the environment and concentrates wealth among a select few.

Petroleum production first began in earnest under Russian rule in the late 19th century. By the early 1900s Azerbaijan was a major global petroleum producer, with a high degree of involvement from foreign businesses, such as the Royal Dutch company and the Swedish Nobel brothers. Crude production in 1901 amounted to 11.7m. metric tons, compared with just 9.5m. tons in the USA. During the Soviet era, until the Second World War (1939–45), Azerbaijan's petroleum reserves fuelled the ambitious industrialization programme of the Soviet leader, Stalin (Iosif V. Dzhugashvili). However, the War convinced Stalin that Azerbaijan's oil reserves were vulnerable to foreign invasion. Thereafter, the focus of Soviet petroleum production was moved to the fields of Siberia, Russia, at a safer distance from hostile foreign powers.

In 1991, the final year of Soviet rule in Azerbaijan, petroleum production stood at 280,000 barrels per day (b/d). The catastrophic decline in GDP that followed the collapse of the USSR also affected petroleum production, with output reaching a low of 180,000 b/d in 1997. In the mean time, Azerbaijan's post-independence governments made various deals with foreign companies, in order to help revive production, as well as to help win strategic international allies. In September 1992 the State Oil Company of the Azerbaijan Republic (SOCAR) was founded, with responsibility for petroleum and gas production, refinery and pipelines; SOCAR is the sole operator of several ageing on- and offshore fields, but is also involved in the operation of all the international consortiums that have been established to undertake new projects since independence. There is a high degree of mutual involvement between SOCAR, the presidential administration and the Government. Indeed, until 2003 SOCAR's Vice-President was Ilham Aliyev, son of President Heydar Aliyev, and elected his successor in October of that year.

Deals reached in 1992–93 between SOCAR and Western companies under President Abulfaz Elchibey were annulled by Heydar Aliyev when he became President in late 1993. Instead, in 1994 a lucrative agreement was signed between SOCAR and a consortium of 11 companies, the Azerbaijan International Operating Company (AIOC), led by BP and Amoco. The consortium originally allocated a 10% stake to the Russian company LUKoil, in the hope that this would mute any Russian opposition to the deal. (LUKoil ultimately withdrew from the consortium in December 2002, selling its stake to the Japanese company Inpex). The deals signed in 1994 resulted in new production in 1997, and volumes subsequently increased each year, reaching 318,000 b/d in 2002. The bulk of the increase came from the Azeri-Chirag-Guneshli complex of oilfields, operated by BP on behalf of the AIOC, which had proven reserves of 5,400m. barrels.

Azerbaijani petroleum is exported via one pipeline running between Baku and Novorossiisk, Russia, and a second between Baku and Supsa, Georgia. However, the capacity of the two pipelines is insufficient to satisfy the anticipated boom in crude production. In 2002 construction work began on the so-called BTC pipeline, operated by a BP-led consortium, which was to transport petroleum from Baku to Ceyhan (Turkey), via Tbilisi (Georgia), to Western markets. A major advantage of this route was that it avoided the need for the subsequent transportation of petroleum by tanker through the narrow straits of the Bosphorus and the Dardanelles, and it received substantial political support from the USA, as it would avoid both Iran and Russia. The route of the pipeline has additional strategic significance for Azerbaijan as it also excludes Armenia, reinforcing that country's economic isolation. However, the high cost of construction and recent, more conservative estimates of Azerbaijan's Caspian reserves have cast into doubt the overall financial viability of the project. By mid-2003 the International Finance Corporation (the private-sector branch of the World Bank), the EBRD and other potential sponsors were continuing to prevaricate over the provision of financing. (The development of a proposed trans-Caspian petroleum pipeline from Aktau, Kazakhstan, to Baku would provide a considerable boost to the BTC pipeline's viability.) Moreover, improved relations between the USA and Russia, and the collapse, in 2003, of Saddam Hussain's regime in Iraq, also reduced the strategic significance of the pipeline to the USA. Nevertheless, the USA and Azerbaijan remained committed to the project, which appeared likely to be completed, despite protests from a wide range of international human rights and environmental non-governmental organizations. The BTC pipeline was expected to cost US $2,900m. to build. Construction work began in June 2003 and was expected to be completed by early 2005, with the first petroleum flowing in 2005 or 2006.

Very little of Azerbaijan's crude oil production is refined within the country. The state oil company SOCAR has two refineries in Baku: Azerneftyag, with a capacity of 240,000 b/d, and Azerneftyanayag, with a capacity of 203,000 b/d. However, in 2002 just 8,000 b/d of refined petroleum were produced, compared with 310,000 b/d of crude. A lack of investment at the plants left them outdated, and caused them to lose business to newly modernized refineries in Russia and Turkmenistan. However, the lack of domestic demand for petroleum products is the main factor responsible for the under-utilization of the refineries.

Azerbaijan is a net importer of natural gas, mostly from Russia. However, it also possesses unexploited reserves of gas in its sector of the Caspian sea. The country plans to become a major exporter of gas, and at the centre of this ambition is the Baku–Tbilisi (Georgia)–Erzurum (Turkey) pipeline consortium, also led by BP. The pipeline's route is to run parallel to the BTC petroleum pipeline for most of its length, and is expected to carry 6,600m. cu m of natural gas from the Shah Deniz field (containing an estimated 625,000m. of natural gas) to Turkey. However, since economic problems in Turkey had prompted that country to delay gas imports from Azerbaijan until 2006, construction was not scheduled to commence until 2004. A rival gas pipeline running from Russia to Turkey, known as 'Blue Stream', had been completed, but was unused in April–July 2003, while the Russian gas monopoly, Gazprom, attempted to resolve a price dispute with Turkey. Following a settlement of that dispute and the resumption of gas supplies from August, the likelihood that Turkey would also require large volumes of gas from Shah Deniz seemed increasingly remote. Consequently, Russia's Caspian envoy advised Azerbaijan to abandon its plans to build the Baku–Tbilisi–Erzurum pipeline and instead construct a pipeline linking to the Blue Stream channel. The Azerbaijani Government was unlikely to heed this advice, owing to the control it would grant to Russia over its gas exports.

## ELECTRICITY

Azerbaijan's electricity sector has a generating capacity of five gigawatts (GW), produced by eight thermal plants and six hydroelectric plants. Total generation in 2002 was 18,600m. kilowatt hours (kWh), compared with 18,800m. kWh in 2001. Economic growth stimulated consumption significantly, to 20,029m. kWh in 2002. Consequently, the country lost its self-sufficient status, particularly given that much of the electricity generated was lost in transmission, owing to the inefficient distribution network. As a result, electricity is imported from Russia, Iran, Turkey and Georgia. The exclave of Nakhichevan is supplied by imports from Turkey and Iran.

Generating technology is rapidly becoming obsolete, although there are long-term plans to privatize the entire sector. Initially, production will remain the responsibility of the domestic monopoly, Azerenerji, but the partial privatization of the distribution system had already taken place, with a Turkish company, Barmek Holding, taking over the management of two regional grids, covering Baku and Sumgait. Azerenerji has made little effort to compel customers to pay for electricity; despite low tariffs, only 35% of the electricity that it supplies is paid for by consumers.

The World Bank, the EBRD and the Islamic Development Bank provided grants to help improve the country's generating capacity. Foreign funding helped to finance the completion in 2000 of the 112 MW Yenikand hydroelectric station (a stalled Soviet-era project), a 100 MW thermal station in Baku, and the reconstruction of the Mingechaur hydroplant, which increased its capacity from 380 MW to 420 MW. In addition, the Japanese companies Mitsui and Mitsubishi participated in the construction of a 400 MW gas-fired block at the Severnaya regional electric power station, which was completed in December 2002.

## PROSPECTS

In an attempt to protect the economy from 'Dutch Disease' and the possible misuse of energy-export proceeds by future leaders, in December 1999 President Aliyev established SOFAZ. The aim of the Fund (which has been employed successfully in a similar form in oil-rich Norway), is to stabilize the domestic currency, by keeping foreign-currency proceeds out of the monetary system. Such funds also serve as a form of savings account, from which governments can draw during periods of low global petroleum prices, or as a source of investment in non-petroleum sectors of the economy. The IMF and World Bank were heavily involved in designing SOFAZ. Of the US $17,000m. which Azerbaijan is expected to earn in petroleum revenues between 2003 and 2010 (assuming a price of $25 per barrel), as much as $14,000m. was to go to SOFAZ, which had accumulated over $800m. by mid-2003.

Considerable controversy has already arisen over how the funds would be managed and spent. The Fund is directly subordinate to the President, raising questions about transparency, and as to whether the supervisory council established to oversee it will wield any real power. Moreover, the decision to spend some of the money already accumulated on financing for construction of the BTC petroleum pipeline led to criticism from the IMF, which argued that funds should be used exclusively to stimulate non-petroleum sectors of the economy, through tax reductions.

Like many resource-dependent countries, Azerbaijan is in a difficult situation. The lack of developed democratic institutions increases the likelihood that much of its hydrocarbons wealth will be diverted by corrupt politicians, bureaucrats or businessmen. At the same time, real democratic change is unlikely while the country's main economic resource is concentrated in the hands of the ruling élite.

Considerable progress has been made in recent years in reversing the country's decline and in building an economic basis for Azerbaijan's independent statehood. However, the majority of the population has barely benefited from the strong economic growth recorded from the latter part of the 1990s. A substantial amount of foreign petroleum investment is expected in the coming decades. Whether this influx will translate into a genuine improvement in living conditions for the general populace will depend on the management of SOFAZ. Unfortunately, this, in turn, will ultimately depend on the personal integrity of Aliyev and his successors, unless the political system undergoes a substantial shift towards democracy.

# Statistical Survey

Source (unless otherwise stated): State Statistical Committee of Azerbaijan Republic, 370136 Baku, Inshatchilar St; tel. (12) 38-64-98; fax (12) 38-24-42; e-mail ssc@azstat.org; internet www.azstat.org.

## Area and Population

### AREA, POPULATION AND DENSITY

| | |
|---|---:|
| Area (sq km) . . . . . . . . | 86,600* |
| Population (census results)† | |
| 12 January 1989 . . . . . . . . . | 7,021,178 |
| 27 January 1999 (provisional) | |
| Males . . . . . . . . . | 3,883,155 |
| Females . . . . . . . . . . | 4,070,283 |
| Total . . . . . . . . . | 7,953,438 |
| Population (official estimates at 1 January) | |
| 2001 . . . . . . . . . . | 8,081,000 |
| 2002 . . . . . . . . . | 8,141,400 |
| 2003 . . . . . . . . . | 8,202,500 |
| Density (per sq km) at 1 January 2003 . . . . . . . | 94.7 |

* 33,400 sq miles.
† Figures refer to *de jure* population. The *de facto* total at the 1989 census was 7,037,867.

Source: partly UN, *Population and Vital Statistics Report*.

### ETHNIC GROUPS
(permanent inhabitants, 1999 census)

| | Number ('000) | % |
|---|---:|---:|
| Azeri . . . . . . . . . . | 7,205.5 | 90.6 |
| Lazs (Lezghi) . . . . . . . | 178.0 | 2.2 |
| Russian . . . . . . . . . | 141.7 | 1.8 |
| Armenian . . . . . . . . . | 120.7 | 1.5 |
| Talish . . . . . . . . . . | 76.8 | 1.0 |
| Avar . . . . . . . . . . | 50.9 | 0.6 |
| Turkish . . . . . . . . . | 43.4 | 0.5 |
| Tatar . . . . . . . . . . | 30.0 | 0.4 |
| Ukrainian . . . . . . . . . | 29.0 | 0.4 |
| Sakhur . . . . . . . . . | 15.9 | 0.2 |
| Georgian . . . . . . . . . | 14.9 | 0.2 |
| Kurd . . . . . . . . . . | 13.1 | 0.2 |
| Tat . . . . . . . . . . | 10.9 | 0.1 |
| Jewish . . . . . . . . . | 8.9 | 0.1 |
| Udin . . . . . . . . . . | 4.2 | 0.1 |
| Others . . . . . . . . . | 9.5 | 0.1 |
| **Total** . . . . . . . . . | 7,953.4 | 100.0 |

### PRINCIPAL TOWNS
(estimated population at 1 January 2002)

| | | | | |
|---|---:|---|---|---:|
| Baki (Baku, the capital) . . . . | 1,817,900 | | Mingachevir (Mingechaur) . . | 94,600 |
| Nakhichevan . . . | 364,500 | | Ali Bayramli . . . | 70,900 |
| Gyanja (Ganca)* . . | 301,400 | | Stepanakert (Khankendi) . . | 54,600 |

* Known as Kirovabad between 1935 and 1989.

## BIRTHS, MARRIAGES AND DEATHS

| | Registered live births | | Registered marriages | | Registered deaths | |
|---|---:|---:|---:|---:|---:|---:|
| | Number | Rate (per 1,000) | Number | Rate (per 1,000) | Number | Rate (per 1,000) |
| 1995 . . | 143,315 | 18.9 | 43,130 | 5.7 | 50,828 | 6.7 |
| 1996 . . | 129,247 | 16.9 | 38,572 | 5.1 | 48,242 | 6.3 |
| 1997 . . | 132,052 | 17.1 | 46,999 | 6.1 | 46,962 | 6.1 |
| 1998 . . | 123,996 | 15.9 | 40,851 | 5.2 | 46,299 | 5.9 |
| 1999 . . | 117,539 | 14.9 | 37,382 | 4.8 | 46,295 | 5.9 |
| 2000 . . | 116,994 | 14.8 | 39,611 | 5.0 | 46,701 | 5.9 |
| 2001 . . | 110,356 | 13.8 | 41,861 | 5.2 | 45,284 | 5.7 |
| 2002* . . | 110,700 | 13.8 | 41,700 | 5.2 | 46,500 | 5.8 |

* Figures are rounded.

**Expectation of life** (WHO estimates, years at birth): 63.6 (males 60.7; females 66.6) in 2001 (Source: WHO, *World Health Report*).

### ECONOMICALLY ACTIVE POPULATION
(ISIC major divisions, annual average, '000 persons)

| | 2000 | 2001 | 2002 |
|---|---:|---:|---:|
| Agriculture, hunting and forestry | 1,517.2 | 1,482.0 | 1,495.0 |
| Fishing . . . . . . . . | 2.0 | 2.3 | 2.5 |
| Mining and quarrying . . . . | 39.6 | 42.1 | 42.2 |
| Manufacturing . . . . . | 169.3 | 163.9 | 169.5 |
| Electricity, gas and water supply | 40.5 | 41.0 | 39.9 |
| Construction . . . . . . | 153.6 | 155.0 | 178.0 |
| Wholesale and retail trade; repair of motor vehicles, motorcycles and household goods . . . . | 626.1 | 659.5 | 621.9 |
| Hotels and restaurants . . . . | 9.8 | 11.0 | 11.3 |
| Transport, storage and communications . . . . . | 167.0 | 167.5 | 169.8 |
| Financial intermediation . . . | 13.5 | 13.0 | 13.2 |
| Real estate, renting and business activities . . . . . . . | 98.0 | 97.0 | 97.2 |
| Public administration and defence; compulsory social security . . | 257.7 | 267.3 | 265.3 |
| Education . . . . . . . | 317.9 | 318.0 | 319.9 |
| Health and social work . . . | 168.9 | 170.0 | 173.6 |
| Other community, social and personal service activities . . | 123.2 | 125.0 | 126.7 |
| Extra-territorial organizations and bodies . . . . . . . | 0.2 | 0.4 | 0.5 |
| **Total employed** . . . . . | 3,704.5 | 3,715.0 | 3,726.5 |
| Unemployed . . . . . . | 43.7 | 48.4 | 51.0 |
| **Total labour force** . . . . . | 3,748.2 | 3,763.4 | 3,777.5 |

## Health and Welfare

### KEY INDICATORS

| | |
|---|---:|
| Total fertility rate (children per woman, 2001) . . . . . | 1.6 |
| Under-five mortality rate (per 1,000 live births, 2001) . . | 105 |
| HIV (% of persons aged 15–49, 2001) . . . . . . . | <0.10 |
| Physicians (per 1,000 head, 1998) . . . . . . . | 3.60 |
| Hospital beds (per 1,000 head, 1996) . . . . . . . | 9.69 |
| Health expenditure (2000): US $ per head (PPP) . . . . | 57 |
| Health expenditure (2000): % of GDP . . . . . . | 2.1 |
| Health expenditure (2000): public (% of total) . . . . . | 44.2 |
| Human Development Index (2001): ranking . . . . . . | 89 |
| Human Development Index (2001): value . . . . . . | 0.744 |

For sources and definitions, see explanatory note on p. vi.

# Agriculture

**PRINCIPAL CROPS**
('000 metric tons)

|  | 1999 | 2000 | 2001 |
|---|---|---|---|
| Wheat . . . . . . . . . | 865.7 | 1,150.3 | 1,500.0 |
| Rice (paddy) . . . . . . | 15.9 | 22.2 | 19.0 |
| Barley . . . . . . . | 102.3 | 219.5 | 360.0 |
| Maize . . . . . . . | 100.3 | 103.5 | 116.4 |
| Potatoes . . . . . . | 394.1 | 469.0 | 605.3 |
| Sugar beet . . . . . . | 42.2 | 46.7 | 40.8 |
| Pulses . . . . . . . | 12.4 | 15.6 | 21.1* |
| Hazelnuts . . . . . . | 12.6 | 13.3 | 15.0† |
| Other nuts† . . . . . . | 10.4 | 13.0 | 12.0 |
| Cottonseed . . . . . . | 59.1 | 54.9 | 52.2† |
| Cabbages . . . . . . | 58.1 | 72.4 | 78.6* |
| Tomatoes . . . . . . | 329.3 | 337.4 | 445.3* |
| Cucumbers and gherkins . . . | 70.7 | 80.5 | 95.6* |
| Dry onions . . . . . | 75.0 | 88.8 | 101.4* |
| Garlic . . . . . . . | 14.5 | 17.1 | 19.6* |
| Other vegetables* . . . . | 123.3 | 152.1 | 166.7 |
| Oranges* . . . . . . | 30.0 | 40.0 | 41.7 |
| Apples* . . . . . . . | 268.0 | 286.3 | 298.6 |
| Pears . . . . . . . | 28.5* | 33.4 | 34.8* |
| Apricots . . . . . . | 14.0* | 13.0 | 14.0* |
| Peaches and nectarines* . . . | 32.0 | 40.0 | 41.7 |
| Plums . . . . . . . | 17.4 | 18.1 | 18.8* |
| Grapes . . . . . . . | 112.5 | 76.8 | 63.1 |
| Watermelons‡ . . . . . | 206.3 | 261.0 | 290.5 |
| Other fruits* . . . . . | 35.2 | 46.3 | 47.9 |
| Tobacco (leaves) . . . . | 8.6 | 17.3 | 12.8 |
| Cotton (lint) . . . . . | 33.9 | 32.0 | 32.0* |

* Unofficial figure(s).
† FAO estimate(s).
‡ Including melons, pumpkins and squash.

Source: FAO.

**LIVESTOCK**
('000 head, year ending September)

|  | 1999 | 2000 | 2001 |
|---|---|---|---|
| Horses . . . . . . . . | 56 | 61 | 64 |
| Asses . . . . . . . . | 33 | 36 | 38 |
| Cattle . . . . . . . . | 1,913 | 1,961 | 2,022 |
| Buffaloes . . . . . . . | 297 | 299 | 306 |
| Pigs . . . . . . . . | 26 | 20 | 19 |
| Sheep . . . . . . . . | 5,131 | 5,280 | 5,553 |
| Goats . . . . . . . . | 381 | 494 | 533 |
| Chickens* . . . . . . . | 13,443 | 14,269 | 14,298 |
| Turkeys* . . . . . . . | 431 | 442 | 442 |

* Unofficial figures.

Source: FAO.

**LIVESTOCK PRODUCTS**
('000 metric tons)

|  | 1999 | 2000 | 2001 |
|---|---|---|---|
| Beef and veal . . . . . . | 52.0 | 574.0 | 56.6 |
| Mutton and lamb . . . . . | 34.8 | 36.1 | 37.9 |
| Pig meat . . . . . . . | 1.5 | 1.6 | 1.6 |
| Poultry meat . . . . . . | 16.3 | 16.9 | 17.7 |
| Cows' milk . . . . . . | 993.4 | 1,031.1 | 1,073.4 |
| Cheese . . . . . . . . | 10.5 | 10.3* | 10.8* |
| Butter . . . . . . . . | 4.9 | 4.9 | 5.0 |
| Hen eggs† . . . . . . . | 29.4 | 30.2 | 30.9 |
| Wool: greasy . . . . . . | 10.5 | 10.9 | 11.4 |
| Wool: scoured . . . . . . | 6.3 | 6.6 | 6.9 |
| Cattle hides (fresh)* . . . . | 8.9 | 9.3 | 9.7 |
| Sheepskins (fresh)* . . . . | 3.9 | 4.1 | 4.3 |

* FAO estimate(s).
† Unofficial figures.

Source: FAO.

# Forestry

**ROUNDWOOD REMOVALS**
('000 cubic metres, excl. bark)

|  | 1998 | 1999 | 2000 |
|---|---|---|---|
| Sawlogs, veneer logs and logs for sleepers* . . . . . . | 3,200 | 3,200 | 3,500 |
| Pulpwood* . . . . . . . | 3,200 | 3,200 | 3,500 |
| Other industrial wood . . . . | — | — | 100* |
| Fuel wood* . . . . . . | 6,200 | 6,200 | 6,400 |
| **Total** . . . . . . . | 12,600 | 12,600 | 13,500 |

* Unofficial figure(s).

Source: FAO.

# Fishing

(metric tons, live weight)

|  | 1998 | 1999 | 2000 |
|---|---|---|---|
| Capture . . . . . | 4,678 | 20,861 | 18,797 |
| Freshwater bream . . . . | 314 | 52 | 55 |
| Azov sea sprat . . . . | 4,043 | 20,460 | 18,520 |
| Aquaculture . . . . . | 211 | 235 | 120 |
| **Total catch** . . . . . . | 4,889 | 4,935 | 18,917 |

Source: FAO, *Yearbook of Fishery Statistics*.

# Mining

|  | 1999 | 2000 | 2001 |
|---|---|---|---|
| Crude petroleum ('000 metric tons) | 13,652 | 13,869 | 14,775 |
| Natural gas (million cu metres) . | 5,997 | 5,642 | 5,534 |

Source: Asian Development Bank, *Key Indicators of Developing Asian and Pacific Countries*.

# Industry

## SELECTED PRODUCTS
('000 metric tons, unless otherwise indicated)

| | 1998 | 1999 | 2000 |
|---|---|---|---|
| Margarine . . . . . . | 0.0 | 0.9 | 0.0 |
| Wheat flour . . . . . | 79 | 52 | 234 |
| Ethyl alcohol ('000 hectolitres) . . | 1 | 0 | 2 |
| Wine ('000 hectolitres) . . . . | 26 | 47 | 77 |
| Beer ('000 hectolitres) . . . . | 12 | 69 | 71 |
| Mineral water ('000 hectolitres) | 18 | 16 | 21 |
| Soft drinks ('000 hectolitres) . . | 569 | 326 | 466 |
| Cigarettes . . . . . . . | 241 | 416 | 2,362 |
| Wool yarn—pure and mixed (metric tons) . . . . . . . | 200 | 100 | 0 |
| Cotton yarn—pure and mixed (metric tons) . . . . . | 2,600 | 900 | 700 |
| Woven cotton fabrics ('000 metres) | 7,400 | 800 | 1,000 |
| Woollen woven fabrics ('000 sq metres) . . . . . . | 100 | 100 | 0 |
| Leather footwear ('000 pairs) . . | 315 | 54 | 122 |
| Aluminium plates, sheets, strip and foil . . . . . . . | 0.3 | 0 | 0.3 |
| Steel . . . . . . . . | 8 | 0 | 0 |
| Cement . . . . . . | 201 | 171 | 251 |
| Sulphuric acid . . . . . | 24 | 26 | 52 |
| Caustic soda (Sodium hydroxide) | 21 | 21 | 30 |
| Bricks (million) . . . . . | 14 | 10 | 7 |
| Television receivers ('000) . . . | 3 | 0 | 0 |
| Electric energy (million kWh) . . | 17,998 | 18,177 | n.a. |
| Jet fuels . . . . . . | 526 | 631 | n.a. |
| Motor spirit (petrol) . . . . | 630 | 354 | n.a. |
| Kerosene . . . . . . | 178 | 58 | n.a. |
| Gas-diesel (distillate fuel) oil . . | 2,057 | 2,121 | n.a. |
| Lubricants. . . . . . . | 82 | 45 | n.a. |
| Residual fuel oil (Mazout) . . . | 4,028 | 3,887 | n.a. |

Source: partly UN, *Industrial Commodity Statistics Yearbook*.

**2001** ('000 metric tons): Cement 523; Wheat flour 394; Sulphuric acid 9; Caustic soda (Sodium hydroxide) 22; Bricks (million) 12; Electric energy (million kWh) 18,970 (Source: partly Asian Development Bank, *Key Indicators of Developing Asian and Pacific Countries*).

# Finance

## CURRENCY AND EXCHANGE RATES

**Monetary Units**
100 gopik = 1 Azerbaijani manat.

**Sterling, Dollar and Euro Equivalents** (30 May 2003)
£1 sterling = 8,099.6 manats;
US $1 = 4,916.0 manats;
€1 = 5,811.6 manats;
10,000 manats = £1.235 = $2.034 = €1.721.

**Average Exchange Rate** (Azerbaijani manats per US $)
2000    4,474.2
2001    4,656.6
2002    4,860.8

Note: The Azerbaijani manat was introduced in August 1992, initially to circulate alongside the Russian (formerly Soviet) rouble, with an exchange rate of 1 manat = 10 roubles. In December 1993 Azerbaijan left the rouble zone, and the manat became the country's sole currency.

## STATE BUDGET
('000 million manats)

| Revenue | 1999 | 2000 | 2001 |
|---|---|---|---|
| Tax revenue . . . . . . | 2,338.9 | 2,872.2 | 3,570.4 |
| Other current revenue . . . | 397.4 | 589.6 | 321.8 |
| Capital revenue . . . . . | 61.3 | 114.4 | 27.7 |
| **Total** . . . . . . . | 2,797.6 | 3,576.2 | 3,919.9 |

| Expenditure | 2000 | 2001 | 2002 |
|---|---|---|---|
| General public services . . . . | 260.8 | 303.1 | 358.4 |
| Education . . . . . . . | 909.2 | 931.1 | 952.5 |
| Health . . . . . . . | 204.7 | 210.1 | 224.1 |
| Social security and welfare . . . | 696.7 | 730.7 | 951.2 |
| Economic services . . . . | 447.2 | 512.2 | 684.4 |
| Agriculture . . . . . | 157.4 | 158.8 | 211.7 |
| Other purposes . . . . . | 1,301.2 | 1,350.3 | 1,488.0 |
| **Total** . . . . . . | 3,819.8 | 4,037.5 | 4,658.6 |

Source: Asian Development Bank, *Key Indicators of Developing Asian and Pacific Countries*.

## INTERNATIONAL RESERVES
(US $ million at 31 December)

| | 2000 | 2001 | 2002 |
|---|---|---|---|
| IMF special drawing rights . . . | 6.60 | 2.49 | 0.70 |
| Reserve position in IMF . . . . | 0.01 | 0.01 | 0.01 |
| Foreign exchange . . . . . | 672.99 | 894.20 | 720.80 |
| **Total** . . . . . . | 679.61 | 896.70 | 721.51 |

Source: IMF, *International Financial Statistics*.

## MONEY SUPPLY
('000 million manats at 31 December)

| | 2000 | 2001 | 2002 |
|---|---|---|---|
| Currency outside banks . . . . | 1,349.81 | 1,468.99 | 1,668.73 |
| Demand deposits at commercial banks . . . . . . | 218.21 | 218.73 | 292.74 |
| **Total money** (incl. others) . . . | 1,569.81 | 1,693.10 | 1,967.27 |

Source: IMF, *International Financial Statistics*.

## COST OF LIVING
(Consumer Price Index; base: 1993 = 100)

| | 2000 | 2001 | 2002 |
|---|---|---|---|
| Food . . . . . . . | 9,853.0 | 10,117.3 | 10,489.5 |
| **All items** (incl. others) . . . . | 10,365.9 | 10,526.3 | 10,817.9 |

Source: UN, *Monthly Bulletin of Statistics*.

## NATIONAL ACCOUNTS
('000 million manats at current prices)

**Expenditure on the Gross Domestic Product**

| | 2000 | 2001 | 2002 |
|---|---|---|---|
| Government final consumption expenditure . . . . . | 1,401.8 | 1,458.3 | 1,523.2 |
| Private final consumption expenditure . . . . . | 17,367.0 | 18,512.5 | 20,216.5 |
| Increase in stocks . . . . | −581.0 | −586.2 | −592.0 |
| Gross fixed capital formation . . | 5,458.1 | 6,081.3 | 10,292.8 |
| **Total domestic expenditure** . . | 23,645.9 | 25,465.9 | 31,440.5 |
| Exports of goods and services . . | 9,476.8 | 11,029.9 | 12,963.9 |
| *Less* Imports of goods and services | 9,053.6 | 9,917.8 | 15,170.9 |
| Statistical discrepancy . . . . | −478.6 | — | 368.5 |
| **GDP in purchasers' values** . . | 23,590.5 | 26,578.0 | 29,602.0 |

Source: Asian Development Bank, *Key Indicators of Developing Asian and Pacific Countries*.

**Gross Domestic Product by Economic Activity**

| | 2000 | 2001 | 2002 |
|---|---|---|---|
| Agriculture and fishing . . . . | 3,755.1 | 3,901.19 | 4,150.2 |
| Mining . . . . . . . . | 6,522.5 | 7,880.3 | 8,120.7 |
| Manufacturing . . . . . . | 1,248.2 | 1,730.8 | 1,816.8 |
| Electricity, gas and water . . . | 724.0 | 387.4 | 382.8 |
| Construction . . . . . . | 1,539.6 | 1,553.6 | 3,185.0 |
| Trade . . . . . . . . | 1,574.9 | 2,072.7 | 2,354.3 |
| Transport and communications | 2,835.8 | 2,694.7 | 2,903.1 |
| Finance . . . . . . . | 219.1 | 325.4 | 332.6 |
| Public administration . . . . | 480.3 | 712.0 | 732.1 |
| Other . . . . . . . . | 3,235.0 | 3,228.0 | 3,320.4 |
| **GDP at factor cost** . . . . . | 22,134.5 | 24,486.0 | 27,298.0 |
| Indirect taxes *less* subsidies . . | 1,456.0 | 2,091.9 | 2,304.0 |
| **GDP in purchasers' values** . . | 23,590.5 | 26,578.0 | 29,602.0 |

Source: Asian Development Bank, *Key Indicators of Developing Asian and Pacific Countries.*

## BALANCE OF PAYMENTS
(US $ million)

| | 2000 | 2001 | 2002 |
|---|---|---|---|
| Exports of goods f.o.b. . . . . | 1,858.3 | 2,078.9 | 2,304.9 |
| Imports of goods f.o.b. . . . . | −1,539.0 | −1,465.1 | −1,823.3 |
| **Trade balance** . . . . . | 319.3 | 613.9 | 481.6 |
| Exports of services . . . . | 259.8 | 289.8 | 362.1 |
| Imports of services . . . . | −484.5 | −664.9 | −1,297.7 |
| **Balance on goods and services** | 94.6 | 238.8 | −454.0 |
| Other income received . . . . | 55.9 | 41.5 | 37.1 |
| Other income paid . . . . | −391.4 | −408.7 | −421.8 |
| **Balance on goods, services and income** . . . . . . . | −240.9 | −128.4 | −838.7 |
| Current transfers received . . . | 135.0 | 176.5 | 228.2 |
| Current transfers paid . . . | −62.0 | −99.9 | −157.9 |
| **Current balance** . . . . . | −167.8 | −51.8 | −768.4 |
| Capital account (net) . . . . | — | — | −28.7 |
| Direct investment abroad . . . | −0.8 | — | −325.6 |
| Direct investment from abroad . . | 129.9 | 226.5 | 1,392.4 |
| Portfolio investment assets . . | — | — | 0.4 |
| Other investment assets . . . | −114.2 | −394.0 | −302.9 |
| Other investment liabilities . . | 478.4 | 293.5 | 154.4 |
| Net errors and omissions . . . | — | −0.9 | −87.4 |
| **Overall balance** . . . . . | 325.6 | 73.4 | 34.2 |

Source: IMF, *International Financial Statistics.*

# External Trade

## PRINCIPAL COMMODITIES
(US $ million)

| Imports c.i.f. | 2000 | 2001 | 2002 |
|---|---|---|---|
| Vegetable products . . . . . | 119.5 | 116.8 | 106.1 |
| Prepared foodstuffs, beverages, spirits and vinegar; tobacco and manufactured substitutes . . | 59.5 | 69.7 | 84.0 |
| Mineral products . . . . . | 115.2 | 248.0 | 324.7 |
| Products of chemical or allied industries . . . . . . | 84.1 | 68.7 | 83.0 |
| Base metals and articles thereof | 123.4 | 132.1 | 281.1 |
| Machinery and mechanical appliances; electrical equipment; sound and television apparatus . | 362.8 | 353.8 | 395.9 |
| Vehicles, aircraft, vessels and associated transportation equipment . . . . . . | 100.0 | 198.6 | 123.5 |
| Optical, photographic, measuring and medical instruments and apparatus; clocks and watches; musical instruments . . . . | 35.8 | 35.9 | 28.8 |
| **Total** (incl. others) . . . . | 1,172.1 | 1,430.9 | 1,665.6 |

| Exports f.o.b. | 2000 | 2001 | 2002 |
|---|---|---|---|
| Vegetable products . . . . . | 22.5 | 20.7 | 35.6 |
| Prepared foodstuffs; beverages, spirits and vinegar; tobacco and manufactured substitutes . . | 24.2 | 31.6 | 27.7 |
| Mineral products . . . . . | 1,485.3 | 2,117.9 | 1,927.7 |
| Machinery and mechanical appliances; electrical equipment; sound and television apparatus . | 31.1 | 38.1 | 29.4 |
| **Total** (incl. others) . . . . . | 1,745.3 | 2,314.3 | 2,167.5 |

Source: Asian Development Bank, *Key Indicators of Developing Asian and Pacific Countries.*

## PRINCIPAL TRADING PARTNERS
(US $ million)

| Imports c.i.f. | 2000 | 2001 | 2002 |
|---|---|---|---|
| Bulgaria . . . . . . . | 11.8 | n.a. | n.a. |
| China, People's Repub. . . . . | 23.1 | n.a. | 51.0 |
| France . . . . . . . . | 19.0 | n.a. | 118.1 |
| Germany . . . . . . . | 67.6 | 95.9 | 83.5 |
| Iran . . . . . . . . | 56.8 | 66.2 | 57.9 |
| Italy . . . . . . . . | 28.1 | n.a. | 26.4 |
| Japan . . . . . . . . | 16.4 | n.a. | 48.4 |
| Kazakhstan . . . . . . | 57.6 | 90.3 | 149.8 |
| Netherlands . . . . . . | 18.9 | n.a. | 25.4 |
| Norway . . . . . . . | 6.0 | n.a. | 21.3 |
| Poland . . . . . . . | 20.7 | n.a. | n.a. |
| Russia . . . . . . . . | 249.3 | 143.1 | 280.9 |
| Singapore . . . . . . . | 13.2 | n.a. | 34.6 |
| Switzerland . . . . . . | 56.2 | 108.9 | 21.0 |
| Turkey . . . . . . . | 128.5 | 128.5 | 156.2 |
| Turkmenistan . . . . . . | 9.6 | n.a. | 119.8 |
| Ukraine . . . . . . . | 35.8 | 35.8 | 79.9 |
| United Arab Emirates . . . . | 19.9 | 27.5 | 19.2 |
| United Kingdom . . . . . | 58.9 | 62.9 | 85.2 |
| USA . . . . . . . . | 117.7 | 71.0 | 98.6 |
| **Total** (incl. others) . . . . . | 1,172.1 | 1,237.3 | 1,665.3 |

| Exports f.o.b. | 2000 | 2001 | 2002 |
|---|---|---|---|
| France . . . . . . . | 205.2 | 112.2 | 166.3 |
| Georgia . . . . . . | 74.7 | n.a. | 80.8 |
| Germany . . . . . . | 8.3 | 143.5 | 28.8 |
| Greece . . . . . . | 22.7 | n.a. | 54.1 |
| Iceland . . . . . . | 31.5 | n.a. | n.a. |
| Iran . . . . . . . | 7.7 | 7.7 | 29.9 |
| Israel . . . . . . | 135.2 | 270.3 | 154.1 |
| Italy . . . . . . | 762.5 | 547.6 | 1,082.7 |
| Malta . . . . . . | 25.4 | n.a. | 30.2 |
| Netherlands . . . . . | 26.2 | n.a. | 9.6 |
| Russia . . . . . . | 98.3 | 66.0 | 95.7 |
| Switzerland . . . . . | 45.8 | 54.9 | 20.4 |
| Tajikistan . . . . . | 19.6 | n.a. | 28.0 |
| Turkey . . . . . . | 105.0 | 140.9 | 83.4 |
| Ukraine . . . . . . | 23.6 | 23.6 | 13.0 |
| United Kingdom . . . . | 18.8 | 16.3 | 9.1 |
| USA . . . . . . . | 8.0 | n.a. | 52.0 |
| **Total** (incl. others) . . . . . | 1,745.3 | 1,757.1 | 2,167.5 |

Source: partly Asian Development Bank, *Key Indicators of Developing Asian and Pacific Countries.*

# Transport

## RAILWAYS

| | 2000 | 2001 | 2002 |
|---|---|---|---|
| Passengers carried ('000) . . | 4,250 | 4,646 | n.a. |
| Passenger-km (million) . . . | 493 | 537 | 583 |
| Freight carried (million metric tons) . . . . . . . . | 15.9 | 15.4 | 17.4 |
| Freight ton-km (million) . . . | 5,770 | 6,141 | 6,918 |

**ROAD TRAFFIC**
(vehicles in use at 31 December)

|  | 1998 | 1999 | 2000 |
|---|---|---|---|
| Passenger cars . . . . . | 281,320 | 306,993 | 332,026 |
| Buses | 13,666 | 14,941 | 16,756 |
| Lorries and vans . . . . . | 79,934 | 69,685 | 78,566 |
| Motorcycles and mopeds . . . | 9,271 | 9,269 | 8,016 |

Source: International Road Federation, *World Road Statistics*.

**2001:** Passenger cars 342,958; lorries ('000) 77,142; motorcycles 6,719.

**2002:** Passenger cars 350,600 (rounded figure); lorries 76,900 (rounded figure); motorcycles 8,278.

**SHIPPING**

**Merchant Fleet**
(registered at 31 December)

|  | 2000 | 2001 | 2002 |
|---|---|---|---|
| Number of vessels . . . . . | 284 | 283 | 285 |
| Total displacement ('000 grt) . . | 647.0 | 641.2 | 633.2 |

Source: Lloyd's Register-Fairplay, *World Fleet Statistics*.

**International Sea-borne Freight Traffic**
('000 metric tons)

|  | 1997 | 1998 | 1999 |
|---|---|---|---|
| Goods loaded . . . . . . | 7,128 | 7,812 | 7,176 |

Source: UN, *Monthly Bulletin of Statistics*.

**Sea-borne imports** ('000 metric tons): 5,118 in 2000; 7,029 in 2001; 7,853.4 in 2002.

**Sea-borne exports** ('000 metric tons): 703 in 2000; 996.3 in 2001; 1,057.3 in 2002.

**CIVIL AVIATION**
(traffic on scheduled services)

|  | 1999 | 2000 | 2001 |
|---|---|---|---|
| Kilometres flown (million) . . . | 21 | 17 | 9 |
| Passengers carried ('000) . . . | 697 | 701 | 701 |
| Passenger-km (million) . . . . | 835 | 798 | 827 |
| Total ton-km (million) . . . . | 112 | 102 | 76 |

**2002:** Passengers carried ('000) 735.

# Tourism

**FOREIGN TOURIST ARRIVALS**

| Country of residence | 2000 | 2001 | 2002 |
|---|---|---|---|
| CIS countries* . . . . . . | 346,483 | 320,229 | 288,428 |
| Iran . . . . . . . | 242,354 | 321,882 | 284,570 |
| Turkey . . . . . . . | 12,693 | 8,493 | 11,082 |
| **Total** (incl. others) . . . . | 680,909 | 766,992 | 793,345 |

* Comprising Armenia, Belarus, Georgia, Kazakhstan, Kyrgyzstan, Moldova, Russia, Tajikistan, Turkmenistan, Ukraine and Uzbekistan.

**Tourism receipts** (US $ million): 125 in 1998; 81 in 1999; 81 in 2000 (Sources: World Tourism Organization, *Yearbook of Tourism Statistics*, and World Bank, *World Development Indicators*).

# Communications Media

|  | 2000 | 2001 | 2002 |
|---|---|---|---|
| Television receivers ('000 in use) | 2,000 | n.a. | n.a. |
| Telephones ('000 main lines in use) | 801 | 865.5 | 989.2 |
| Mobile cellular telephones ('000 subscribers). . . . . . | 430.0 | 620.0 | 870.0 |
| Internet users ('000). . . . . | 12 | 25 | 300 |
| Book production (including pamphlets): titles . . . . | 400 | n.a. | n.a. |

**1994:** Facsimile machines (number in use) 2,500.

**1996:** Daily newspapers (number) 6; Non-daily newspapers (number) 251.

Sources: UN, *Statistical Yearbook*, UNESCO, *Statistical Yearbook*, and International Telecommunication Union.

# Education

(2001/02, unless otherwise indicated)

|  | Institutions | Teachers | Students* |
|---|---|---|---|
| Pre-primary . . . . . . . | 1,794 | 11,500† | 111,400 |
| Primary . . . . . . . | 446 | 39,780 | 13,000 |
| Secondary . . . . . . . | 3,149 | 109,600† | 1,516,000 |
| General . . . . . . . | 923 | 88,822 | 125,000 |
| Special needs schools . . . . | 20 | n.a. | 4,789 |
| Vocational . . . . . . . | 69 | n.a. | 49,200† |
| Higher . . . . . . . . | 40 | 11,216‡ | 120,500 |

* Figures are rounded to the nearest 100.
† 1999/2000.
‡ Excluding non-state institutions.

Source: partly UN, *Statistical Yearbook for Asia and the Pacific*.

**Adult literacy rate** (UNESCO estimates): 99.6% (males 99.7%; females 99.5%) in 1995 (Source: UNESCO, *Statistical Yearbook*).

# Directory

## The Constitution

The new Constitution was endorsed by 91.9% of the registered electorate in a national referendum, held on 12 November 1995. It replaced the amended Soviet Constitution of 1978. The following is a summary of the 1995 Constitution's main provisions:

### GENERAL PROVISIONS

The Azerbaijan Republic is a democratic, secular and unitary state. State power is vested in the people, who implement their sovereign right through referendums and their directly elected representatives. No individual or organization has the right to usurp the power of the people. State power is exercised on the principle of the division of powers between the legislature, the executive and the judiciary. The supreme aim of the state is to ensure human and civil rights and freedoms. The territory of the Azerbaijan Republic is inviolable and indivisible. Azerbaijan conducts its foreign policy on the basis of universally accepted international law. The state is committed to a market economic system and to freedom of entrepreneurial activity. Three types of ownership—state, private and municipal—are recognized; natural resources belong to the Azerbaijan Republic. The state promotes the development of art, culture, education, medical care and science, and defends historical, material and spiritual values. All religions are equal by law; the spread of religions that contradict the principles of humanity is prohibited. The state language is Azerbaijani, although the republic guarantees the free use of other languages. The capital is Baku (Baki).

### MAJOR RIGHTS, FREEDOMS AND RESPONSIBILITIES

Every citizen has inviolable, undeniable and inalienable rights and freedoms. Every person is equal before the law and the courts, regardless of sex, race, nationality, religion, origin, property and other status, and political or other convictions. Every person has the right to life. Any person charged with a penal offence is considered innocent until proven guilty. Capital punishment as an extreme measure of punishment, while still in force, can be applied for grave crimes. Every person has the right to freedom of thought, speech, conscience and religion. Everyone has the right to protect their national and ethnic affiliation. No one is to be subject to torture or the degradation of human dignity. The mass media are free, and censorship is prohibited. Every person has the right to freedom of movement and residence within the republic, and the right to leave the republic. The right to assemble publicly is guaranteed, and every person has the right to establish a political party, trade union or other organization; the activity of unions that seek to overthrow state power is prohibited. Citizens of the Azerbaijan Republic have the right to participate in the political life of society and the state, and the right to elect and to be elected to government bodies, and to participate in referendums. Every person has the right to health protection and medical aid, and the right to social security in old age, sickness, disability, unemployment, etc. The state guarantees the right to free secondary education.

### THE LEGISLATIVE

The supreme legislative body is the 125-member Milli Majlis (National Assembly). Deputies are elected by universal, equal, free, direct suffrage, and by secret ballot, for a five-year term. Any citizen who has reached the age of 25 years is eligible for election, with the exception of those possessing dual citizenship, those performing state service, and those otherwise engaged in paid work, unless employed in the creative, scientific and education sectors. The instigation of criminal proceedings against a deputy, and his or her detention or arrest, are only permitted on the decision of the Milli Majlis, on the basis of a recommendation by the Prosecutor-General. The Milli Majlis passes legislation, constitutional laws and resolutions; ratifies or denunciates treaties, agreements and conventions; ratifies the state budget; gives consent to declare war, on the recommendation of the President of the Republic; confirms administrative and territorial divisions; and declares amnesties. Upon the nomination of the President, the Milli Majlis is authorized to approve the appointment of the Prime Minister and the Prosecutor-General; appoint and dismiss members of the Constitutional Court and Supreme Court; and appoint and dismiss the Chairperson of the National Bank. It also has the power to express a vote of 'no confidence' in the Government; to call a referendum; to initiate impeachment proceedings against the President, on the recommendation of the Constitutional Court; and to introduce draft legislation and other issues for parliamentary discussion.

### EXECUTIVE POWER

The President, who is directly elected for a term of five years, is Head of State and Commander-in-Chief of the Armed Forces. Executive power is held by the President, who acts as guarantor of the independence and territorial integrity of the republic. Any university graduate aged 35 years or over, who has the right to vote, has been a resident of the republic for the preceding 10 years, has never been tried for a major crime, and who is exclusively a citizen of the Azerbaijan Republic, is eligible for election to the office of President. The President appoints and dismisses the Cabinet of Ministers, headed by the Prime Minister, which is the highest executive body.

The President calls legislative elections; concludes international treaties and agreements, and submits them to the Milli Majlis for ratification; signs laws or returns draft legislation to the Milli Majlis for reconsideration; proposes candidates for the Constitutional Court, the Supreme Court and the Economic Court, and nominates the Prosecutor-General and the Chairman of the National Bank; appoints and recalls diplomatic representatives of Azerbaijan to foreign countries and international organizations, and receives the credentials of diplomatic representatives; may declare a state of emergency or martial law; and grants titles of honour.

The President enjoys immunity from prosecution during his or her period in office. In the event that the President commits a grave crime, he may be removed from office on the recommendation of the Supreme Court and the Constitutional Court, and with the approval of the Milli Majlis.

### THE JUDICIARY

Judicial power is implemented only by the courts. Judges are independent and are subordinate only to the Constitution and the law; they are immune from prosecution. Trials are held in public, except in specialized circumstances.

The Constitutional Court is composed of nine members, appointed by the Milli Majlis on the recommendation of the President. It determines, among other things, whether presidential decrees, resolutions of the Milli Majlis and of the Cabinet of Ministers, laws of the Nakhichevan Autonomous Republic, and international treaties correspond to the Constitution; and decides on the prohibition of the activities of political parties. The Supreme Court is the highest judicial body in administrative, civil and criminal cases; the Economic Court is the highest legal body in considering economic disputes.

### AUTONOMOUS REPUBLIC OF NAKHICHEVAN

The Nakhichevan Autonomous Republic is an autonomous republic forming an inalienable part of the Azerbaijan Republic. It has its own Constitution, which must not contravene the Constitution and laws of Azerbaijan. Legislative power in Nakhichevan is vested in the 45-member Ali Majlis (Supreme Assembly), which serves a five-year term, and executive power is vested in the Cabinet of Ministers. The Ali Majlis elects a Chairman from among its members, as the highest official in the Republic of Nakhichevan. The Ali Majlis is responsible for the budget, the approval of economic and social programmes; and the approval of the Cabinet of Ministers. The Ali Majlis may dismiss its Chairman and express 'no confidence' in the Cabinet of Ministers, which is appointed by the Ali Majlis on the recommendation of the Prime Minister (the Chairman of the Cabinet of Ministers). The Prime Minister of Nakhichevan is, likewise, appointed by the Ali Majlis on the nomination of the President of Azerbaijan. Heads of local executive power in Nakhichevan are appointed by the President of Azerbaijan, after consultation with the Chairman of the Ali Majlis and the Prime Minister of Nakhichevan. Justice is administered by the courts of the Republic of Nakhichevan.

In December 1998 the Milli Majlis approved a revised Constitution for Nakhichevan, which defined the enclave as an 'autonomous state' within Azerbaijan.

### LOCAL SELF-GOVERNMENT

Local government in rural areas and towns, villages and settlements is exercised by elected municipalities.

### RIGHTS AND LAW

The Constitution has supreme legal force. Amendments and additions may only be introduced following a referendum.

# The Government

### HEAD OF STATE

**President:** ILHAM HEYDAR OGLU ALIYEV (elected by direct popular vote, 15 October 2003; inaugurated 31 October 2003).

### CABINET OF MINISTERS
(October 2003)

**Prime Minister:** ARTUR TAHIR OGLU RASIZADE (acting).

**First Deputy Prime Ministers:** ABBAS A. ABBASSOV, YAQUB ABDULLA OGLU AYYUBOV.

**Deputy Prime Ministers:** ELCHIN ILYAS OGLU EFENDIYEV, ABID QOCA OGLU SHARIFOV, ALI SAMIL OGLU HASANOV, HACIBALA IBRAHIM OGLU ABUTALIBOV.

**Minister of Public Health:** ALI BINNET OGLU INSANOV.

**Minister of Foreign Affairs:** VILAYAT MUKHTAR OGLU KULIYEV.

**Minister of Agriculture and Produce:** IRSHAD NADIR OGLU ALIYEV.

**Minister of Internal Affairs:** Col RAMIL IDRIS OGLU USUBOV.

**Minister of Culture:** POLAD OGLU BYUL-BYUL.

**Minister of Education:** MISIR CUMAYIL OGLU MARDANOV.

**Minister of Communications:** NADIR ALI OGLU AKHMEDOV.

**Minister of Finance:** AVAZ AKBAR OGLU ALEKPEROV.

**Minister of Justice:** FIKRET FARRUKH OGLU MAMMADOV.

**Minister of Labour and Social Protection:** ALI TEYMUR OGLU NAGIYEV.

**Minister of National Security:** Lt-Gen. NAMIK RASID OGLU ABBASOV.

**Minister of Defence:** Col-Gen. SAFAR AKHUNDBALA OGLU ABIYEV.

**Minister of Fuel and Energy:** MAJID KARIMOV.

**Minister of Taxes:** FAZIL MAMEDOV.

**Minister of Youth, Sport and Tourism:** ABULFAZ MURSAL OGLU KARAYEV.

**Minister of Economic Development:** FARKHAD SOKHRAT OGLU ALIYEV.

**Minister of Ecology and Natural Resources:** HUSSEIN BAGHIROV.

**Minister of Transport:** ZIYA MAMMEDOV.

#### Chairmen of State Committees

**Chairman of the State Committee for Securities:** HEYDAR BABAYEV.

**Chairman of the State Committee for Construction and Architectural Affairs:** ABID G. SHARIFOV.

**Chairman of the State Committee for Anti-monopoly Policy and Enterprise Support:** RAHIB GULIYEV.

**Chairman of the State Committee for Statistics:** ARIF A. VELIYEV.

**Chairman of the State Committee for Religious Affairs:** Dr RAFIK ALIYEV.

**Chairman of the State Committee for Geology and Mineral Resources:** ISLAM TAGIYEV.

**Chairman of the State Committee for Supervision of Safety at Work in Industry and Mining:** YAGUB EYYUBOV.

**Chairman of the State Committee for Material Resources:** HULMAMMAD JAVADOV.

**Chairman of the State Committee for Specialized Machinery:** SABIR ALEKPEROV.

**Chairman of the State Committee for Science and Technology:** AZAD MIRZAJANZADE.

**Chairman of the State Land and Mapping Committee:** HARIB MAMMADOV.

**Chairman of the State Customs Committee:** KAMALEDDIN HEYDAROV.

**Chairman of the State Committee for Veterinary Affairs:** MIRSALEH HUSSEINOV.

**Chairman of the State Committee for Hydrometeorology:** ZULFUGAR MUSAYEV.

**Chairman of the State Committee for the Protection and Refurbishment of Historical and Cultural Monuments:** FAKHREDDIN MIRALIYEV.

**Chairman of the State Committee for Refugees and Involuntary Migrants:** ALI HASANOV.

**Chairman of the State Committee for Improvements of Soil and Water Economy:** AHMED AHMEDZADE.

**Chairman of the State Committee for Women's Issues:** ZAHRA GULIYEVA.

## MINISTRIES

**Office of the President:** 370066 Baku, Istiklal St 19; tel. (12) 92-17-26; fax (12) 92-35-43; e-mail office@apparat.gov.az; internet www.president.az.

**Office of the Prime Minister:** 370066 Baku, Lermontov St 63; tel. (12) 92-66-23; fax (12) 92-91-79.

**Ministry of Agriculture and Produce:** 370016 Baku, Azadliq Sq. 1, Govt House; tel. (12) 93-53-55.

**Ministry of Communications:** 370139 Baku, Azerbaijan Ave 33; tel. (12) 93-00-04; fax (12) 98-79-12; e-mail mincom@azerin.com; internet www.azmincom.com.

**Ministry of Culture:** 370016 Baku, Azadliq Sq. 1, Govt House; tel. (12) 93-43-98; fax (12) 93-56-05; internet www.culture.az:8101.

**Ministry of Defence:** 370139 Baku, Azerbaijan Ave; tel. (12) 39-41-89; fax (12) 92-92-50.

**Ministry of Ecology and Natural Resources:** 370073 Baku, Bahram Agayev St 100A; tel. (12) 92-59-07; fax (12) 39–84–32.

**Ministry of Economic Development:** 370016 Baku, Azadliq Sq. 1, Govt House; tel. (12) 93-61-62; fax (12) 93-20-25; e-mail office@economy.gov.az; internet economy.gov.az.

**Ministry of Education:** 370016 Baku, Azadliq Sq. 1, Govt House; tel. (12) 93-72-66; fax (12) 98-75-69; e-mail edu_min@azeri.com; internet www.min.edu.az.

**Ministry of Finance:** 370022 Baku, Samed Vurghun St 83; tel. (12) 93-30-12; fax (12) 98-79-69; e-mail office@maliyye.gov.az; internet www.minfin-az.com.

**Ministry of Foreign Affairs:** 370004 Baku, Ghanjlar meydani 3; tel. (12) 92-68-56; fax (12) 92-56-06.

**Ministry of Fuel and Energy:** Baku, Gasanbek Zardabi St 88; tel. (12) 47-05-84; fax (12) 31–90–05; e-mail mfe@mfe.az; internet www.mfe.az.

**Ministry of Internal Affairs:** 370005 Baku, Gusi Hajiyev St 7; tel. (12) 92-57-54; fax (12) 98-22-85; internet www.mia.gov.az.

**Ministry of Justice:** 370601 Baku, Bul-Bul Ave 13; tel. (12) 93-97-85; fax (12) 98-49-41.

**Ministry of Labour and Social Protection:** 370016 Baku, Azadliq Sq. 1, Govt House; tel. (12) 93-05-42; fax (12) 93-94-72; e-mail mlspp@azerin.com; internet www.mlspp.az.

**Ministry of National Security:** 370602 Baku, Parliament Ave 2; tel. (12) 95-01-63; fax (12) 95-04-91.

**Ministry of Public Health:** 370014 Baku, Malaya Morskaya St 4; tel. (12) 93-29-77; fax (12) 93-76-47; e-mail mednet@mednet.az; internet www.mednet.az.

**Ministry of Taxes:** 370073 Baku, Landau St 16; tel. (12) 97-06-11; fax (12) 98-54-07; e-mail info@taxes.gov.az; internet www.taxes.gov.az.

**Ministry of Transport:** Baku.

**Ministry of Youth, Sport and Tourism:** 370072 Baku, Olympiya St 4; tel. (12) 65-64-42; fax (12) 65-64-38; e-mail myst@myst.gov.az; internet www.myst.gov.az.

# President and Legislature

## PRESIDENT

**Presidential Election, 15 October 2003**

| Candidates | Votes | % of votes |
|---|---|---|
| Ilham Aliyev (New Azerbaijan Party) . . | 2,438,787 | 79.53 |
| Isa Gambar (Musavat) . . . . . . . | 372,385 | 12.14 |
| Lala Shovkat Hajiyeva (Independent) . . | 100,558 | 3.28 |
| Etibar Mamedov (National Independence Party). . . . . . . . . . . | 82,401 | 2.69 |
| Ilyas Ismailov (Adalat Party) . . . . | 24,926 | 0.81 |
| Sabir Rustamkhanly (Civic Solidarity Party). . . . . . . . . . . | 23,730 | 0.77 |
| Gudrat Hasanguliyev (Popular Front of Azerbaijan) . . . . . . . . . | 13,624 | 0.44 |
| Hafiz Hadjiyev (Modern Musavat Party) . | 9,990 | 0.33 |
| Total . . . . . . . . . . . . | 3,066,401 | 100.00 |

## MILLI MAJLIS

### Milli Majlis
### (National Assembly)

370152 Baku, Mehti Hussein St 2; tel. (12) 92-79-45; fax (12) 98-02-42.

**Chairman (Speaker):** MURTUZ ALESKEROV.

**First Deputy Chairman:** ARIF RAHIMZADE.

Elections to Azerbaijan's new 125-member Milli Majlis were held on 5 November 2000. The electoral law of August 1995 provided for a mixed system of voting: 25 seats to be filled by proportional representation, according to party lists, the remaining 100 deputies to be elected in single-member constituencies. The latter included the constituencies of Armenian-held Nagornyi Karabakh and other occupied territories: refugees from those regions cast their votes in other parts of Azerbaijan (in anticipation of the eventual return of occupied areas to Azerbaijani jurisdiction). All 25 party seats were filled: the New Azerbaijan Party (NAP) obtained 17 seats, the Popular Front of Azerbaijan (PFA) four, and the Civic Solidarity Party (CSP) and independent candidates each secured two. Of the 88 constituency seats filled, 62 were reported to have been taken by the NAP and 26 by independent candidates. A further round of voting was held on 7 January 2000, in order to elect members for 11 vacant seats. The NAP obtained five seats, and five other parties and an independent candidate each obtained one seat. Thus, following all the rounds of voting, only one seat in the Majlis remained vacant (representing the Khankendi-Khojali-Khojavend constituency in Nagornyi Karabakh).

# Local Government

For the purposes of local government, Azerbaijan has 64 administrative districts. The country also includes one autonomous oblast, Nagornyi Karabakh, and one autonomous republic, the exclave of Nakhichevan (for details, see p. 130 below). There was some disruption to local government following the attempted secession of Nagornyi Karabakh and its occupation of some surrounding districts.

# Political Organizations

**Adalat Party** (Justice Party): f. 2001; Leader ILYAS ISMAILOV; 21,000 mems.

**Alliance for Azerbaijan Party:** Baku; f. 1994; Leader ABUTALYB SAMADOV.

**Azerbaijan Democratic Independence Party:** Baku; tel. (12) 98-78-23; in 1997 merged with Vahdat Party and one-half of the People's Freedom Party; Chair. LEYLA YUNUSOVA; Leader VAGIF KERIMOV.

**Azerbaijan National Democratic Party:** Baku; tel. (12) 94-89-37; fmrly the Grey Wolves Party (Boz Gurd); Leader ISKANDAR HAMIDOV.

**Azerbaijan National Equality Party:** Baku; tel. (12) 60-05-21; Leader FAHRADDIN AYDAYEV.

**Azerbaijani Democratic Left Party:** Baku; f. 1999; Chair. MEHMAN AMIRALIYEV.

**Azerbaijani Salvation Party** (Milly Qutulush): Baku; tel. (12) 98-73-96; f. 1999; nationalist; supports a united Azerbaijan; Chair. ELDAR GARADAGLY.

**Azerbaijan Social Democratic Party (ASDP):** 370014 Baku, 28 May St 3–11; tel. (12) 98-04-21; fax (12) 98-79-03; e-mail asdp@bakililar.az; internet www.soc-dem.org; f. 1989; formed a union with the Islamic Party of Azerbaijan and the Vahdat (Unity) Party in April 2000, as the Union of Pro-Azerbaijanist Forces; agreed merger with the Civic Unity Party in August 2003; Co-Chair. ARAZ ALIZADEH, AYAZ MUTALIBOV; Dep. Chair. SEYRAN MIRZOYEV, KHANHUSEIN ALIYEV, RENA GAVADOVA; 5,672 mems (2002).

**Civic Solidarity Party (CSP)** (Vatandash Hamrailiyi): Baku; tel. (12) 92-67-47; f. 1992; Chair. SABIR RUSTAMKHANLY.

**Civic Unity Party of Azerbaijan (CUPA):** Baku; merger with the Azerbaijan Social Democratic Party approved by the Chair. in August 2003, although this was disputed by the Secretary-General; Sec.-Gen. SABIR HAJIYEV; Chair. AYAZ MUTALLIBOV.

**Communist Party of Azerbaijan (CPA):** Baku; tel. (12) 94-89-37; disbanded Sept. 1991, re-established Nov. 1993; Chair. RAMIZ AHMADOV.

**Communist Workers' Party of Azerbaijan:** Baku; fmrly the United Communist Party of Azerbaijan; Leader SAYYAD SAYYADOV.

**Democratic Development Party:** Baku; f. 1999; Leader SABUHI ABDINOV.

**Democratic Party of Azerbaijan:** Baku, M. Huseinov St 5; tel. (12) 66-79-71; f. 1994; unregistered; merged with the Democratic Way Party in 2000; Chair. RASUL KULIYEV; Gen. Sec. SARDAR JALALOGLU.

**Heyrat Party:** Baku; Sec.-Gen. ASHRAF MEHDIYEV.

**Independent Azerbaijan Party:** Baku, A. Abbaszale 17; tel. (12) 39-30-96; fax (12) 39-53-55; Chair. NIZAMI SULEYMANOV.

**Islamic Party of Azerbaijan:** Baku; tel. (12) 93-72-61; f. 1992; forms part of the Union of Pro-Azerbaijanist Forces; Chair. ROVSAN AGAYEV; Leader ALI AKRAM ALIYEV (imprisoned 1997 on charges of treason, but pardoned in 1999; subsequently imprisoned in June 2002 for inciting public disorder); 50,000 mems (1997).

**Labour Party of Azerbaijan:** Baku; Leader SABUTAY MARNEDOV.

**Liberal Democratic Party:** Baku; divisions emerged in Nov. 2000.

**Liberal Party of Azerbaijan:** Baku, Azerbaijan Ave; tel. (12) 98-00-95; f. 1995; pro-Russian; Chair. (vacant).

**Modern Turan Party** (Chagdash-Turan): Baku; tel. (12) 73-16-79; Chair. ARIF ISLAM TAGIEV.

**Motherland Party** (Ana Vatan): Baku; tel. (12) 93-82-97; Leader FAZAIL AGAMALIYEV.

**Musavat** (Equality): Baku, Azerbaijan Ave 37; tel. (12) 47-46-56; fax (12) 47-43-75; e-mail ilkin@turgut.baku.az; f. 1911; in exile from 1920; re-established 1992; joined the United Opposition Movement (comprising 25 political parties) in Jan. 2002; Chair. ISA GAMBAR; Gen. Sec. VURGUN EYYUB.

**Namus Party** (Dignity): Baku; f. 1999; Chair. TOGRUL IBRAHIMOV.

**National Congress Party:** Baku; f. 1997 by disaffected members of Musavat; Chair. IHTIYAR SHIRINOV.

**National Independence Party (NIP)** (Milli Istiklal): Baku, Azadliq Ave 179; internet www.amip.info; f. 1992; Chair. ETIBAR MAMEDOV.

**National Statehood Party:** Baku; tel. (12) 67-71-74; f. 1994; unregistered from 1997; Chair. SABIR TARIVERDIYEV.

**New Azerbaijan Party (NAP)** (Yeni Azerbaijan): 370000 Baku, Bul-Bul Ave 13; tel. (12) 93-84-25; fax (12) 98-59-71; e-mail yap@bakinter.net; internet www.yap.org.az; f. 1992; internal divisions were reported to have emerged in 2001; Co-Chair. HEYDAR ALIYEV; First Dep. Chair. ILHAM ALIYEV; Dep. Chair. ALI NAGIYEV (Minister of Labour and Social Protection), MURTUZ ALESKEROV (Chairman of Milli Majlis), SIRUS TABRIZLI.

**Party for National Reconciliation:** Baku; f. 2000 by breakaway faction of the Liberal Democratic Party.

**People's Freedom Party** (Halg Azadliq): Baku; tel. (12) 98-31-45; Leader PANAH SHAHSEVENLI.

**People's Party of Azerbaijan:** Baku; f. 1998; Chair. PANAH HUSSEINOV.

**Popular Front of Azerbaijan (PFA)** (Azerbaijan Xalq Cabhasi): c/o Milli Majlis, 370152 Baku, Mehti Hussein St 2; tel. (12) 98-07-94; f. 1989; divided into reformist and conservative factions; the reformist faction was registered for the legislative election held in Nov. 2000, while the conservative faction entered into co-operation with Musavat; in Jan. 2002 the conservative faction of the PFA joined the United Opposition Movement, comprising a total of 25 parties; Chair. (reformist) ALI KERIMLI; Chair. (traditionalist) MURMAHMUD FATTAYEV.

**Progress Party** (Taraqqi): Baku; Chair. CHINGIZ SADIKHOV.

**Reformist Communist Party of Azerbaijan (CPA-2):** Baku; tel. (12) 94-89-37; f. 1998 as Communist Party of Azerbaijan 2; name changed 2001; Chair. FIRUDIN HASANOV.

**Republican Party:** Baku, Azadliq St 161; tel. (12) 61-98-19; f. 1999; Chair. RUFIZ GONAGOV.

**Social Justice Party:** Baku; Leader MATLAB MUTALLIMOV.

**Social Welfare Party:** Baku; Chair. KHANHUSEIN KAZYMLY.

**Socialist Party of Azerbaijan:** Baku; f. 1997; Co-Chair. SHAPUR GASIMI, MUBARIZ IBADOV; 2,000 mems.

**Turkic Nationalist Party:** Baku; Leader VUGAR BEYTURAN.

**Umid Party** (Hope Party): Baku; tel. (12) 38-57-35; f. 1993; socialist; Chair. IQBAL AGAZADA; Leader ABULFAR AHMADOV; 5,000 mems (1998).

**Vahdat Party** (Unity Party): Baku, Azerbaijan Ave, Dom 23, Rm 52/54; tel. (12) 98-00-44; e-mail vahdat@box.az; f. 1995; a splinter faction, the Unity Party II, emerged in April 2000 and subsequently merged with the PFA in December; member of the Union of Pro-Azerbaijanist Forces; Chair. TAHIR KARIMLI; 17,500 mems (2000).

**Workers' Party of Azerbaijan:** Sumgait; f. 1999; socialist; Chair. AKIF HASANOGLU.

**Yurdash Party** (Compatriot Party): Baku; tel. (12) 32-10-47; f. 1991; Chair. MAIS SAFARLI.

Other political groups include the Democratic Enlightenment Party, the Modern Musavat Party, the People's Democratic Party and the National Movement Party. The Azerbaijan Patriots' Party was founded in July 2000 and Alim Babayev was elected as its Chair.

# Diplomatic Representation

## EMBASSIES IN AZERBAIJAN

**China, People's Republic:** 370010 Baku, Khagani St 67; tel. (12) 98-62-57; fax (12) 98-00-10; e-mail chinaemb@azeurotel.com; Ambassador ZHANG XIYUN.

**Egypt:** Baku, Moscow Ave 50, 3rd Floor; tel. (12) 98-79-06; fax (12) 98-79-54; e-mail emb.egypt@azeuro.net; Ambassador JIHAN AMIN MEHMET ALI.

**France:** 370000 Baku, Rassoul Rza St 7, POB 36; tel. (12) 92-89-77; fax (12) 98-92-53; e-mail ambafranbakou@azerin.com; internet www.ambafranbakou.com; Ambassador CHANTAL POIRET.

**Georgia:** Baku, Asaf Zeynalli St 24; tel. (12) 97-45-58; fax (12) 97-45-61; e-mail emb@georgian.baku.az; Ambassador ZURAB GUMBERIDZE.

**Germany:** 370000 Baku, Mamedaliyev St 15; tel. (12) 98-78-19; fax (12) 98-54-19; e-mail post@bakudiplo.org; internet www.bakudiplo.org; Ambassador Prof. Dr KLAUS W. GREWLICH.

**Greece:** 370004 Baku, Icheri Sheher, Kichik Gala St 86/88; tel. (12) 92-46-80; fax (12) 92-48-35; e-mail greekemb@azeri.com; Ambassador Dr MERCOURIOS B. KARAFOTIAS.

**India:** 370069 Baku, Narimanov District, Oktay Karimov St 31/39; tel. (12) 47-41-86; fax (12) 47-25-72; e-mail eibaku@adanet.az; Ambassador JYOTI SWARUP PANDE.

**Iran:** Baku, B. Sadarov St 4; tel. (12) 92-64-53; fax (12) 98-07-33; e-mail iranemb@azerin.com; Ambassador AHAD QAZAIE.

**Israel:** 370073 Baku, Izmir St 1033, Hyatt Complex, 7th Floor; tel. (12) 90-78-81; fax (12) 90-78-92; e-mail israelembassy@azdata.net; Ambassador EITAN NA'EH.

**Italy:** 370004 Baku, Kichik Gala St 44; tel. (12) 97-51-33; fax (12) 97-52-02; e-mail ambbaku@azeuro.net; internet www.ambitalbaku.com; Ambassador MARGHERITA COSTA.

**Japan:** Baku, 1033 Izmir St, Hyatt Tower 3, 5th Floor; tel. (12) 90-78-18; fax (12) 90-78-20; e-mail japan@emb.baku.az; Ambassador TOSHIYUKI FUJIVARA.

**Kazakhstan:** Baku, Inglab St 889/82; tel. (12) 90-62-48; fax (12) 90-62-49; e-mail embassy@adanet.az; Ambassador ANDAR SHUKPUTOV.

**Korea, Democratic People's Republic:** Baku; Ambassador RI CHOL-GWANG.

**Libya:** Baku, Husein Javid Ave 520/20; tel. (12) 93-23-65; fax (12) 98-12-47; e-mail libiya@streamteach.net.az; Ambassador MUSTAFA SHAHTUR.

**Norway:** 370004 Baku, Vagif Mustafazade St 6–10; tel. (12) 97-43-25; fax (12) 97-37-98; e-mail emb.baku@mfa.no; Ambassador STEINAR GIL.

**Pakistan:** Baku, Atatürk Ave 30; tel. (12) 90-68-39; fax (12) 90-68-41; e-mail parepbaku@artel.net.az; Ambassador FAIZ MOHAMMED KHOSO.

**Poland:** 370069 Baku, Teymur Aliyev St 65; tel. (12) 61-22-42; fax (12) 41-09-57; e-mail embpol@azeurotel.com; internet www.embpol.azeurotel.com; Ambassador MARCIN NAWROT.

**Romania:** 370069 Baku, Tariverdiyev St 9A; tel. (12) 62-04-29; fax (12) 40-77-00; e-mail rom_amb_baku@azdata.net; Ambassador TASIN GEMIL.

**Russia:** 370022 Baku, Bakikhanov St 17; tel. (12) 98-60-16; fax (12) 97-36-08; e-mail embrus@embrus.baku.az; internet intrans.baku.az/embrus; Ambassador NIKOLAI RYABOV.

**Saudi Arabia:** Baku, S. Dadashov St 44/2; tel. (12) 97-23-05; fax (12) 97-23-02; e-mail najdiahbaku@azereurotel.com; Ambassador ALI HASAN JAFAR.

**Turkey:** 370000 Baku, Khagani St 27; tel. (12) 98-81-33; fax (12) 98-83-49; e-mail bakube@artel.net.az; Ambassador AHMET UNAL CEVIKOZ.

**Ukraine:** 37069 Baku, U. Vazirov St 49; tel. (12) 93-10-28; fax (12) 98-27-42; e-mail ukremb@azeurotel.com; internet www.ukremb.azeriland.com; Ambassador BORIS G. ALEKSENKO.

**United Kingdom:** 370065 Baku, Khagani St 45; tel. (12) 97-51-88; fax (12) 97-24-74; e-mail office@britemb.baku.az; internet www.britishembassy.az; Ambassador ANDREW TUCKER.

**USA:** 370007 Baku, Azadliq Ave 83; tel. (12) 98-03-36; fax (12) 98-37-55; internet www.usembassybaku.org; Ambassador RENO HARNISH.

**Uzbekistan:** Baku, Atatürk Ave 46; tel. (12) 97-25-49; fax (12) 97-25-48; e-mail embuzb@azeri.com; Ambassador ABDULGARUF ADUDRAKHMANOV.

# Judicial System

### Constitutional Court

Baku; internet www.constitutional-court-az.org.

Comprises a Chairman and eight judges, who are nominated by the President and confirmed in office by the Milli Majlis for a term of office of 10 years. Only the President, the Milli Majlis, the Cabinet of Ministers, the Procurator-General, the Supreme Court and the legislature of the Autonomous Republic of Nakhichevan are permitted to submit cases to the Constitutional Court.

**Chairman of the Constitutional Court and of the Supreme Court:** KHANLAR HAJIYEV.

**Prosecutor-General:** ZAKIR BEKIR OGLU GARALOV.

# Religion

### ISLAM

The majority (some 70%) of Azerbaijanis are Shi'ite Muslims; most of the remainder are Sunni (Hanafi school). The Spiritual Board of Muslims of the Caucasus is based in Baku. It has spiritual jurisdiction over the Muslims of Armenia, Georgia and Azerbaijan. The Chairman of the Directorate is normally a Shi'ite, while the Deputy Chairman is usually a Sunni.

**Spiritual Board of Muslims of the Caucasus:** Baku; Chair. Sheikh ALLASHUKUR PASHEZADE.

### CHRISTIANITY

### The Roman Catholic Church

The Church is represented in Azerbaijan by a Mission, established in October 2000. There were an estimated 200 adherents at 31 December 2001.

**Superior:** Rev. JOZEF DANIEL PRAVDA, 370069 Baku, Teimur Aliyev St 69b/1; tel. (12) 62-36-15; fax (12) 62-22-55; e-mail parish@catol.baku.az.

# The Press

In 1996 there were 257 newspaper titles, and in 1995 49 periodicals were officially registered in Azerbaijan. Owing to financial, political and technical difficulties, many publications reportedly suffered a sharp decrease in circulation. In August 1998 President Heydar Aliyev signed a decree abolishing censorship and ordering government bodies to provide support to the independent media.

### PRINCIPAL NEWSPAPERS

In Azerbaijani, except where otherwise stated.

**Ayna-Zerkalo:** 370138 Baku, Sharifzadeh St 1; tel. and fax (12) 97-71-23; e-mail gazeta@zerkalo.az; internet www.ayna.az; f. 1990; daily; independent; *Ayna* in Azerbaijani, *Zerkalo* in Russian; Editor-in-Chief ELCIN SIXLINSKI; circ. 4,500 (daily).

**Azadliq** (Liberty): 370000 Baku, Khagani St 33; tel. (12) 98-90-81; fax (12) 98-78-18; e-mail mail@azadliq.com; internet www.azadliq.az; f. 1989; weekly; independent; organ of the Popular Front of Azerbaijan; in Azerbaijani and Russian; Editor-in-Chief BAHADDIN HAZIYEV; circ. 9,034.

**Azerbaijan:** Baku, Metbuat Ave, Block 529; tel. (12) 39-44-91; fax (12) 39-43-23; e-mail azerbaijan_newspaper@azdata.net; internet www.azerbaijan.news.az; f. 1991; 5 a week; publ. by the Milli Majlis; in Azerbaijani and Russian; Editor-in-Chief BAKHTIYAR SADIGOV; circ. 10,242 (Azerbaijani), 3,040 (Russian).

**Azernews:** 370002 Baku, S. Askerova St 85, 3 et.; tel. (12) 94-93-73; fax (12) 95-85-37; e-mail azernews@azeurotel.com; internet www.azernews.net; f. 1997; weekly; Azeri, English and Russian; in association with AssA-Irada news agency; Editor-in-Chief FAZIL ABBASOV; circ. 5,000–6,000.

**Bakinskii Rabochii** (Baku Worker): 370146 Baku, Metbuat Ave, Block 529; tel. (12) 38-00-29; e-mail bakrab@azerin.com; internet www.br.az; f. 1906; 5 a week; govt newspaper; in Russian; Editor I. VEKILOVA; circ. 4,776.

**Baku Today:** 370000 Baku, A. Guliyev St 133, apt 23; tel. and fax (12) 98-68-69; e-mail editor@bakutoday.net; internet www.bakutoday.net; first online newspaper in English to cover the Caucasus and Caspian region; Azeri version on www.xeber.net; Editor-in-Chief MAHIR ISKENDER; circ. 1,500–3,000 daily.

**Baku Sun:** 370073 Baku, Inshaatchilar Ave 2, Office 42; tel. and fax (12) 97-55-31; e-mail editor@bakusun.baku.az; internet www.bakusun.az; f. 1998; weekly; free; in English; Editor VALENTINA HUBER.

**Bizim Asr:** 370141 Baku, A. Alekperov St 83/23; tel. (12) 97-88-99; fax (12) 97-88-98; e-mail bizim_asr@media-az.com; internet bizmasr.media-az.com; f. 1999; owned by Media Holding.

**Echo:** 370001 Baku, Sharifzadeh St 1; tel. (12) 97-51-74; fax (12) 47-41-50; e-mail gazeta@echo-az.com; internet www.echo-az.com; Editor-in-Chief RAUF TALISHINSKY.

**Express:** Baku, Khagani St 20B/43; tel. (12) 98–08–63; e-mail express@azeronline.com; internet www.express.com.az; Editor KH. BAYRAMOV.

**Ezhednevniye Novosti** (Daily News): Baku, Bratia Alibekovy St 43; tel. and fax (12) 92-12-24; e-mail alpha@azeri.com; internet www.alpha.azeri.com; in Russian; Editor EMIL ASADOV.

**525–ci Gazet:** 370033 Baku, S. Mustafayev St 27/121; tel. (12) 66-67-89; fax (12) 66-25-20; e-mail 525@azdata.net; internet www.525ci.com; f. 1992; 5 days a week; Azerbaijani, English and Russian; Editor-in-Chief RASHAD MAJID.

**Hayat** (Life): 370146 Baku, Metbuat Ave, Block 529; f. 1991; 5 a week; publ. by the Milli Majlis; Editor-in-Chief A. H. ASKEROV.

**Hurriyet** (Liberty): Baku; tel. (12) 67-53-22; fax (2) 98-82-27; organ of the Democratic Party of Azerbaijan; Editor-in-Chief AYDYN GULIEV.

**Intibakh** (Revival): Baku; independent; 3 a week; Editor-in-Chief MUSTAFA HAJIBEILI; circ. 10,000.

**Istiklal** (Independence): 370014 Baku, 28 May St 3–11; tel. (12) 93-33-78; fax (12) 98-75-55; e-mail istiklal@ngonet.baku.az; 4 a month; organ of the Azerbaijan Social Democratic Party; Editor ZARDUSHT ALIZADEH; circ. 5,000.

**Khalg Gazeti:** Baku, Bul-Bul Ave 18; tel. (12) 93-02-80; fax (12) 98-85-29; e-mail xalg-gazeti@azdata.net; f. 1919; fmrly *Kommunist*; 6 a week; organ of the office of the President; Editor HASAN HASANOV.

**Millat:** Baku; organ of the National Independence Party.

**Molodezh Azerbaijana** (Youth of Azerbaijan): 370146 Baku, Metbuat Ave, Block 529, 8th Floor; tel. (12) 39-00-51; f. 1919; weekly; in Russian; Editor V. EFENDIYEV; circ. 7,000.

**Respublika** (Republic): 370146 Baku, Metbuat Ave, Block 529; tel. (12) 38-01-14; fax (12) 38-01-31; f. 1996; daily; govt newspaper; Editor-in-Chief T. AHMADOV; circ. 5,500.

**Sharg:** Baku, Metbuat Ave, Block 529; tel. (12) 47-37-80; fax (12) 39-00-79; e-mail info@sherq.com; internet www.sherq.com.

**Veten Sesi** (Voice of the Motherland): 370146 Baku, Metbuat Ave, Block 529; f. 1990; weekly; publ. by the Society of Refugees of Azerbaijan; in Azerbaijani and Russian; Editor-in-Chief T. A. AHMEDOV.

**Yeni Azerbaijan:** Baku; tel. (12) 39-82-27; fax (12) 97-53-04; internet www.yeniazerbaycan.com; f. 1993; weekly; organ of the New Azerbaijan Party; Editor ALGYSH MUSAYEV; circ. 2,493.

**Yeni Müsavat:** Baku, Azerbaijan Ave 37, R. Beibutov St 3; tel. (12) 98-00-61; fax (12) 98-20-88; e-mail ymusavat@azeronline.com; internet www.yenimusavat.com; independent; opposition; Editor-in-Chief RAUF ARIFOGLU.

**Yeni Yuzil** (New Century): Baku; f. 2001 by the founder of Azadliq (q.v.); Editor-in-Chief GUNDUZ TAHIRLI.

### PRINCIPAL PERIODICALS

**Adabiyat** (Literature): 370146 Baku, Metbuat Ave, Block 529; tel. (12) 39-50-37; organ of the Union of Writers of Azerbaijan.

**Azerbaijan:** Baku; tel. (12) 92-59-63; f. 1923; monthly; publ. by the Union of Writers of Azerbaijan; recent works by Azerbaijani authors; Editor-in-Chief YUSIF SAMEDOGLU.

**Azerbaijan Gadyny** (Woman of Azerbaijan): Baku; f. 1923; monthly; illustrated; Editor H. M. HASILOVA.

**Dialog** (Dialogue): Baku; f. 1989; fortnightly; in Azerbaijani and Russian; Editor R. A. ALEKPEROV.

**Iki Sahil:** Baku, Nobel Ave 64; f. 1965; weekly; organ of the New Baku Oil-Refining Plant; Editor-in-Chief V. RAHIMZADEH; circ. 2,815.

**Kend Khayaty** (Country Life): Baku; f. 1952; monthly; journal of the Ministry of Agriculture and Produce; advanced methods of work in agriculture; in Azerbaijani and Russian; Editor D. A. DAMIRLI.

**Kirpi** (Hedgehog): Baku; f. 1952; fortnightly; satirical; Editor A. M. AIVAZOV.

**Literaturnyi Azerbaijan** (Literature of Azerbaijan): 370001 Baku, Khagani St 25; tel. (12) 93-51-00; e-mail sima@azeri.com; f. 1931; monthly; journal of the Union of Writers of Azerbaijan; fiction; in Russian; Editor-in-Chief M. F. VEKILOV.

**Monitor:** Baku, Islam Seferli St 54; tel. (12) 94-88-37; fax (12) 93-93-96; e-mail monitor-week@mail.ru; f. 2002; independent; Editor-in-Chief ELMAR HUSEINOV.

**Ulus:** Baku; tel. (12) 92-27-43; internet www.ulus-az.com; 2 a week; Editor TOFIK DADASHEV.

**Vyshka** (Oil derrick): Baku, Metbuat Ave, Block 529; tel. and fax (12) 39-96-97; e-mail medina@vyshka.com; internet vyshka.com; f. 1928; weekly; independent social-political newspaper; in Russian; Editor M. E. GASANOVA.

### NEWS AGENCIES

**ANIK 'Bilik Dunyasi':** Baku, D. Alievoli St 241, apt. 22; tel. (12) 93-55-61; fax (12) 98-18-41.

**AssA-Irada:** 370002 Baku, S. Askerova St 85, 3 et.; tel. (12) 94-93-73; fax (12) 95-85-37; e-mail azernews@azeurotel.com; internet www.azernews.net; f. 1991; Azeri, English and Russian.

**Azadinform Information Agency:** 370000 Baku, F. Amirov St 1; tel. (12) 98-48-59; fax (12) 98-47-60; e-mail azadinform@azerin.com; internet www.azadinform.baku-az.com; f. 1998; independent information agency; Chief Editor ASEF HAJIYEV.

**AzerTag** (Azerbaijan State News Agency): 370000 Baku, Bul-Bul Ave 18; tel. (12) 93-59-29; fax (12) 93-62-65; e-mail azertac@azdata.net; internet www.azertag.net; f. 1920; Gen. Dir SHAMIL MAMMAD OGLU SHAHMAMMADOV.

**Baku Telegraph:** see section on Telecommunications.

**Media-Press:** 370141 Baku, A. Alekperov 83/23; tel. (12) 97-07-05; fax (12) 97-88-98; e-mail news@mediapress.media-az.com; internet mediapress.media-az.com; f. 1999; owned by Media Holding; independent; Gen. Dir VUGAR GARADAGLY.

**Midiya Press Agency (MPA):** 370000 Baku, Bashir Safaroglu St 191/28; tel. (12) 97-42-45; fax (12) 97-33-59; e-mail agency@mpa.baku.az; internet www.az/mpa/; Azerbaijani, English and Russian.

**Sharg News Agency:** 370001 Baku, Mirza Shafi St 6; tel. (12) 92-69-80; fax (12) 92-46-23; e-mail sharg@azeri.com; internet www.azsharg.com; f. 1994; Correspondent K. MUSTAFAYEVA.

**Trend Information-Analytical Agency:** 370601 Baku, Fizuli St 69; tel. (12) 97-30-89; fax (12) 97-30-89; e-mail infotrend@azdata.net; internet www.trend-az.com; f. 1995; Russian and Turkish; Correspondent E. HUSSEINOV.

**Turan News Agency:** 370000 Baku, Khagani St 33; tel. (12) 98-42-26; fax (12) 98-38-17; e-mail root@turan.baku.az; internet www.turaninfo.com; f. 1990; independent news agency; Azerbaijani, English and Russian; Dir MEHMAN ALIYEV.

#### Foreign Bureaux

**Agence France-Presse (AFP):** Baku, Zargar Palan 128; tel. and fax (12) 47-07-18.

**Interfax-Azerbaijan:** Baku; tel. (12) 97-35-07; fax (12) 97-42-94; e-mail office1@interfax.baku.az; f. 2002; founded by the Interfax Group (Russia) and AzPetrol Azerbaijani Petroleum Co.

### PRESS ASSOCIATION

**Central Asian and Southern Caucasus Freedom of Expression Network:** Baku; tel. and fax (12) 38-32-56; e-mail azeri@ajip.baku.az; based in the office of the Trade Union of Journalists; members include the Azerbaijan National Committee of the International Press Institute, the Independent Association of Georgian Journalists, the Public Association of Journalists from Kyrgyzstan, the National Association of Independent Mass Media of Tajikistan and Union of Independent Journalists of Uzbekistan; Co-ordinator AZER H. HASRET.

## Publishers

**Azerbaijan Ensiklopediyasy** (Azerbaijan Encyclopedia): 370004 Baku, Boyuk Gala St 41; tel. (12) 92-87-11; fax (12) 92-77-83; e-mail azenciklop@ctc.net.az; f. 1965; encyclopedias and dictionaries; Gen. Dir I. O. VELIYEV.

**Azerneshr** (State Publishing House): 370005 Baku, Gusi Hajiyev St 4; tel. (12) 92-50-15; f. 1924; various; Dir A. MUSTAFAZADE; Editor-in-Chief A. KUSEINZADE.

**Elm** (Azerbaijani Academy of Sciences Publishing House): Baku; scientific books and journals.

**Gyanjlik** (Youth): 370005 Baku, Gusi Hajiyev St 4; books for children and young people; Dir E. T. ALIYEV.

**Ishyg** (Light): 370601 Baku, Gogol St 6; posters, illustrated publs; Dir G. N. ISMAILOV.

**Maarif** (State Publishing House of Educational Literature): 370111 Baku, A. Mageramov St 4; tel. and fax (12) 31-58-27; f. 1959; educational literature and materials; Dir ABAS ALI GIZI ALIYEVA SEVDA.

**Madani-maarif Ishi** (Education and Culture): 370146 Baku, Metbuat Ave, Block 529; tel. (12) 32-79-17; Editor-in-Chief ALOVSAT ATAMALY OGLU BASHIROV.

**Medeniyyat** (Publishing House of the 'Culture' Newspaper): 370146 Baku, Metbuat Ave 146; tel. (12) 32-98-38; Dir SHAKMAR AKPER OGLU AKPERZADE.

**Sada, Literaturno-Izdatelskyi Centr:** 370004 Baku, Bolshaya Krepostnaya St 28; tel. (12) 92-75-64; fax (12) 92-98-43; reference.

**Shur:** Baku; tel. (12) 92-93-72; f. 1992; Dir GASHAM ISA OGLU ISABEYLI.

**Yazychy** (Writer): 370005 Baku, Natavan St 1; fiction; Dir F. M. MELIKOV.

## Broadcasting and Communications

### TELECOMMUNICATIONS

**Azercell Telecom JV:** 370139 Baku, Tbilisi Ave 61A; tel. (12) 96-70-07; fax (12) 30-05-68; internet www.azercell.com; f. 1996; provides communication services with integrated voice and data transfer and internet services (Azeronline); joint-venture co between the Ministry of Communications and Fintur Holdings B.V. (Netherlands); 83.6% market share of mobile cellular telephone subscribers; Gen. Dir ESRA TAN; 295 employees.

**AzEuroTel JV:** 370001 Baku, B. Sardarov St 1; tel. (12) 97-07-07; fax (12) 97-01-01; e-mail aet@azeurotel.com; internet rus.azeurotel.com; f. 1995; established by the Ministry of Communications and LUKoil Europe Ltd (Russia) as a joint venture with the United Kingdom; digital, wireless, trunking and satellite communications and internet provider; Gen. Dir NURI AGAMIRZA AKHMEDOV.

**AzTelecom Production Management:** Baku, Tbilisi pr. 3166; tel. (12) 30-26-02; fax (12) 93-17-87; e-mail aztelecom@azerin.com; internet www.aztelecom.bakinter.net; national monopoly fixed-line telecommunications operator; f. 1992; owned by the Ministry of Communications; privatization pending; Dir NAZIM CAFAROV.

**Bakcell JV:** Baku, U. Hajibeyov St 24; tel. (12) 98-18-18; fax (12) 93-33-96; f. 1994; 25% owned by the Ministry of Communications and

25% owned by Motorola (USA); mobile telecommunications service provider; provides countrywide Global Mobile System (GSM) network coverage; Gen. Man. SHAI AVIGAL; 190 employees.

**Baku Telegraph Joint-Stock Co:** 370000 Baku, Azerbaijan Ave 41; tel. (12) 93-61-42; fax (12) 98-55-25; f. 1932; operates international telegraph, fax and telex services, and provides independent news services; Dir SABIRA AGARZAEVA.

### RADIO AND TELEVISION

**National Television and Radio Council:** Baku; f. 2003; regulatory body, comprising nine members, six of whom are presidential appointees; Chair. NUSHIRAVAN MAGERRAMOV.

**Radio and Television Company of Azerbaijan:** 370011 Baku, Mehti Hussein St 1; tel. (12) 92-72-53; fax (12) 39-54-52; f. 1956; state-owned; Dir NIZAMI MANAF OGLU KHUDIYEV; 2,490 employees.

**Azerbaijan National Television:** tel. (12) 39-77-72; fax (12) 97-20-20; internet www.aztv.az; f. 1956; programmes in Azerbaijani, English and Russian (14 hours a day); one regional channel and one national channel.

**Azerbaijan State Radio:** tel. (12) 92-87-68; fax (12) 39-72-48; f. 1926; broadcasts in Azerbaijani, Arabic, English and Turkish; two channels and one international broadcasting studio; Head MOVLUD SULEIMAN.

**ANS Independent Broadcasting and Media Co** (Azerbaijan News Service): 370073 Baku, Metbuat Ave 28/11; tel. (12) 97-72-68; fax (12) 98-94–98; internet www.ans-dx.com; f. 1999; joint-stock co, independent; Pres. VAHID MUSTAFAYEV.

**ANS TV:** tel. (12) 97-72-67; f. 1990.

**ANS-CHM Radio:** f. 1994; broadcasts in Azerbaijani, English, Russian and Turkish.

**Lider TV:** 370141 Baku, A. Alekperov 83/23; tel. (12) 97-88-99; fax (12) 97-87-77; e-mail mail@media-az.com; internet www.lidertv.com; f. 2000; owned by Media Holding.

**Lider 107 FM:** 370141 Baku, A. Alekperov 83/23; tel. (12) 97-07-05; fax (12) 97-88-98; e-mail lider@lider.fm; internet www.lider.fm; owned by Media Holding.

**Sara-TV:** Baku; entertainment programmes.

**Space TV and Radio:** 370073 Baku, H. Javid Ave 8; tel. (12) 33-00-66; fax (12) 92-76-65; e-mail info@space-az.com; internet www.space-az.com; f. 1997 (radio broadcasts commenced in 2001); Chair. ETIBAR ADIL BABAYEV.

# Finance

(cap. = capital; res = reserves; dep. = deposits; m. = million; brs = branches; amounts in manats, unless otherwise stated)

### BANKING

#### Central Bank

**National Bank of Azerbaijan:** 370014 Baku, R. Behbutov St 32; tel. (12) 93-11-22; fax (12) 93-55-41; e-mail mail@nba.az; internet www.nba.az; f. 1992 as central bank and supervisory authority; cap. 27,493m., res 401,096m., dep. 1,537,472m. (Dec. 2001); Chair. ELMAN RUSTAMOV.

#### State-owned Banks

**International Bank of Azerbaijan:** 370005 Baku, Nizami St 67; tel. (12) 93-00-91; fax (12) 93-40-91; e-mail ibar@ibar.az; internet www.ibar.az; f. 1992 to succeed br. of USSR Vneshekonombank; 50.2% owned by the Ministry of Finance, 9.24% owned by employees; carries out all banking services; cap. 50,000m., res 260,000m., dep. 382,000m. (Dec. 2002); Chair. of Bd JAHANGIR HAJIYEV; First Dep. Chair. RAUF RZAYEV; 32 brs.

**United Joint-Stock Bank:** Baku; f. 2000 by merger of Agroprombank (Agricultural bank), Prominvest (Industrial Investment Bank) and the Savings Bank; commenced operations 1 April; Pres. ZAKIR ZEYNALOV.

**United Universal JS Bank** (BUSBank): 370014 Baku, Fizuli St 71; tel. (12) 41-41-07; fax (12) 41-41-19; e-mail aibbank@artel.net.az; internet www.busb-az.com; f. 1992 to replace br. of USSR Sberbank; changed name from Amanatbank in 2000; largest state-owned bank; Chair. ZAKIR H. ZEYNALOV; 87 brs.

#### Other Banks

In January 2000 there were 70, mainly small, registered commercial banks operating in Azerbaijan, some of the most prominent of which are listed below:

**Azerbaijan Central Republican Bank:** 370088 Baku, Fizuli St 71; tel. (12) 93-05-61; fax (12) 93-94-89; Chair. HUSEYN SAFROV.

**Azerbaijan Industrial Bank:** 370010 Baku, Fizuli St 71; tel. (12) 93-17-01; fax (12) 93-12-66; f. 1992; joint-stock commercial bank; Chair. ORUJ H. HEYDAROV; 40 brs.

**Azerbaijan-Turkish Commercial Bank (Azer-Turk):** 1001 Baku, Islam Seferli St 5; tel. (12) 97-43-16; fax (12) 98-37-02; e-mail atb@azerturkbank.biz; internet www.azerturkbank.in-baku.com; f. 1995; cap. 12,848.0m., res 129.0m., dep. 22,104.0m. (Sept. 2003); Chair. MEHMET MUSAYEV QURBANOĞLU; Gen. Man. MEHMET SANI ACAROZMEN.

**Azerdemiryolbank:** 370008 Baku, Garabag St 31; tel. (12) 40-24-29; fax (12) 96-09-77; e-mail damir@azerdemiryolbank.am; internet www.azerdemiryolbank.am; f. 1989; largest private commercial bank; operates mainly in transport sector; cap. 12,717.2m., dep. 82,216.5m. (Dec. 2001); Chair. of Bd ROMAN AMIRDJANOV; 10 brs.

**Azerigazbank:** 370073 Baku, Landau St 16; tel. (12) 97-50-17; fax (12) 98-96-15; e-mail agbbank@azeri.com; internet www.azerigazbank.com; f. 1992; joint-stock investment bank; cap. 18,701.6m., dep. 21,607.1m. (Dec. 2001); Chair. AZER MOVSUMOV; 10 brs.

**Bakcoopbank (Baku Co-operative Bank):** Baku; tel. (12) 67-45-46; Gen. Dir ALIM I. AZIMOV.

**Baybank:** Baku; tel. (12) 93-50-07; fax (12) 98-57-76; e-mail baybank@artel.net.az; f. 1995; joint-stock bank, carries out all banking services; cap. US $1.5m., dep. $2.3m. (Dec. 1998); Pres., Gen. Man. and Chief Exec. T. SERDAR ERZURUMLU; Chair. HUSEYN BAYRAKTAR.

**Günay Bank:** 370095 Baku, Rasul Rza St 4/6; tel. (12) 98-04-55; fax (12) 98-14-39; e-mail gunaybank@azerin.com; internet www.gunaybank.com; f. 1992; first privately owned bank in Azerbaijan; cap. 11,071.4m., res 518.1m., dep. 17,460m. (Dec. 2001); Pres. AHAD SHIRINOV; 2 brs.

**Kauthar Bank:** 1009 Baku, B. Mejidov St 44/46; tel. (12) 97-30-34; fax (12) 97-30-29; e-mail bank@baku.usal.az; f. 1989; formerly Universal Commercial Bank; cap. 13,000m., res 1,019m., dep. 1,430m. (Sept. 2003); Pres. HEYDAR R. IBRAHIMOV.

**Rabitabank:** 370001 Baku, B. Sardarov St 1; tel. (12) 92-57-61; fax (12) 92-61-57; e-mail rbtbank@azevt.com; f. 1993; joint-stock commercial bank; operates mainly in telecommunications sector; Chair. ZAKIR NURIYEV; 4 brs.

**Ruzubank:** 370055 Baku, Istiglaliyat St 27; tel. (12) 92-42-58; fax (12) 92-78-12; f. 1992; joint-stock bank; cap. 216m., res 30.4m., dep. 1,834m.; Pres. S. A. ALIYEV; Chair. of Bd V. N. MUSAYEV.

**Trustbank JS Bank:** 370143 Baku, Firuddin Agayev St 9; tel. (12) 93-14-01; fax (12) 93-12-16; e-mail root@trustbank.baku.az; f. 1994; commercial bank; cap. 9,531m., res 175m., dep. 991m. (Sept. 2003); Pres. AZER AKHMEDOVICH ALIYEV; Chair. BAKHRAM ASLAN OGLU SULTANOV.

**Vostochniy Bank:** 370070 Baku, Kirova Ave 19; tel. (12) 93-22-47; fax (12) 93-11-81; Gen. Dir RAGIMOV A. ABBAL.

#### Association

**Azerbaijan Association of Banks:** Baku, B. Sardarov St 1; tel. (12) 97-58-29; fax (12) 97-15-15; e-mail bank_assoc@azeurotel.com; f. 1990; co-ordinates banking activity; Pres. ZAKIR NURIYEV; 49 mems.

### STOCK EXCHANGE

**Baku Stock Exchange** (Baki Fond Birjasi): 370070 Baku, Bul-Bul Ave 19; tel. (12) 98–85–22; fax (12) 93–77–93; e-mail info@bse.az; internet www.bse.az; closed joint-stock company; Pres. SALIM KRIMAN.

### INSURANCE

In January 2002 there were 38 insurance companies operating in Azerbaijan.

**Azergarant Joint-Stock Insurance Company:** Baku; tel. (12) 92-72-49; fax (12) 92-54-71; e-mail info@azerinvest.baku.az; f. 1993; Pres. Dr ALEKPER MAMEDOV; Gen. Dir FAIG HUSSEINOV.

**Azersigorta:** Baku.

**Günay Anadolu Sigorta JV:** 370005 Baku, Terlan Aliyarbekov St 3; tel. (12) 98-13-56; fax (12) 98-13-60; e-mail gunaysigorta@azdata.net; internet insurancegunayanadolu.com; f. 1992; serves major international cos operating in Azerbaijan; Gen. Man. ALOVSET GOJAYEV.

**Shafag:** Baku; f. 1998; medical insurance.

# Trade and Industry

## CHAMBER OF COMMERCE

**Chamber of Commerce and Industry:** 370601 Baku, Istiglaliyat St 31/33; tel. (12) 92-89-12; fax (12) 98-93-24; e-mail expo@chamber .baku.az; internet www.exhibition.azeri.com; Pres. Suleyman Bayram oglu Tatliyev.

## INDUSTRIAL AND TRADE ASSOCIATIONS

**National Confederation of Entrepreneurs (Employers') Organizations of Azerbaijan:** 370002 Baku, S. Askerova St 85, 9th Floor; tel. (12) 94-90-16; fax (12) 94-99-76; e-mail azerenterprise@artel.net.az; internet www.ask.org.az; f. 1999; Pres. Alekper Mamedov.

## UTILITIES

### Electricity

**Azerenerji JSC:** 370005 Baku, A. Alizade St 10; tel. (12) 98-29-11; fax (12) 98-55-23; e-mail azener@azener.in-baku.com; state-owned; power generation and transmission company; Pres. Etibar Pirverdiyev.

**AliBayramlielektrikshebeke JSC:** Ali Bayramli; f. 2001; comprising the Azerbaijani electricity network's southern zone; 25-year private management contract pending.

**Bakielektrikshebeke JSC** (Baku Electrical Grid): Baku; f. 2001 following the restructuring of the distribution assets of Azerenerji into five regional orgs; managed by Barmek Holding AS (Turkey) .

**Ganjaelektrikshebeke JSC:** Gyanja; f. 2001; comprising the Azerbaijani electricity distribution network's western zone; private management contract pending.

**Nakhichevan Electrikshebeke JSC:** f. 2001; state-owned open joint-stock co; one of the five transmission and distribution area networks into which the national grid was divided; approximately 60% of electricity imported from Iran.

**Sumgaitelektrikshebeke JSC:** Sumgait; f. 2001; covering the northern zone of the Azerbaijani electricity distribution network; 25-year private management contract pending.

### Gas

**AzeriGaz CJSC:** 370025 Baku, Yusif Safarov St 23; tel. (12) 90-42-52; fax (12) 90-42-55; e-mail azer_bayramov@azerigaz.org; f. 1992; transport, distribution, sale, compression and storage of natural gas; Chair. Alikhan Melikhov; 13,000 employees.

## PETROLEUM

Azerbaijan's petroleum reserves were estimated to total some 1,000m. metric tons at the end of 2001. Some 95% of petroleum extraction was in offshore fields in the Caspian Sea. In September 1994 Azerbaijan signed an agreement with 11 foreign petroleum companies which, together with the State Oil Company of the Azerbaijan Republic (SOCAR), made up the Azerbaijan International Operating Company (AIOC—see below). The agreement allowed for the exploration and development of three offshore fields containing an estimated 511m. tons of petroleum and 55,000m. cu m of natural gas. Production began in December 1997. Further production-sharing agreements were signed from 1995.

## STATE HYDROCARBONS COMPANIES

**Azerbaijan International Operating Company (AIOC):** 370003 Baku, Villa Petrolea, Neftchilar Ave 2; tel. (12) 91-21-02; fax (12) 75-96-02; e-mail bayatltf@bp.com; f. 1994 as a consortium of: SOCAR (q.v.), British Petroleum of the United Kingdom, Devon Energy, ExxonMobil and Unocal of the USA, Itochu and Inpex of Japan, Statoil of Norway, Türkiye Petrolleri (TPAO) of Turkey and the Delta Hess alliance of Saudi Arabia and the USA; exploration and development of Azerbaijani offshore petroleum reserves; Pres. David Woodward.

**State Committee for Geology and Mineral Resources of Azerbaijan:** 370073 Baku, Bakhram Agayev St 100A; tel. (12) 38-04-31; fax (12) 39-84-32; f. 1932; prospecting, research and surveys; Chair. Islam Tagiev.

**State Oil Company of the Azerbaijan Republic (SOCAR)** (GNKAR): 370004 Baku, Neftchilar Ave 73; tel. (12) 92-07-45; fax (12) 97-11-67; e-mail akhmedo@aiocaz.com; internet www.socar-cc .com; f. 1992, following a merger of the two state petroleum companies, Azerineft and Azneftkhimiya; conducts production and exploration activities, oversees refining and capital construction activities; includes the Azerneftyag and Azerneftyanayag refineries;

undergoing restructuring; Pres. Natik Aliyev; Exec. Dir Samir Rauf oglu Sharifov; 67,000 employees.

## Other Major Producers and Distributors

**Agip Azerbaijan:** 370000 Baku, 340 Nizami St, ISR Plaza, 11th Floor; tel. (12) 97-22-12; fax (12) 97-22-07; e-mail eros.agostinelli@ agipazerbaijan.com; internet www.eni.it; operate the offshore Kurdashi fields; member of the ENI Group of Italy.

**Azpetrol Group:** 370122 Baku, Zardaby 593; tel. (12) 97-69-74; fax (12) 97-68-64; e-mail azpetrol@1azpetrol.baku.az; f. 1997; includes the Azpetrol Oil Co and Azertrans hydrocarbons shipping and storage company; owns largest network of retail petrol stations in Azerbaijan; 3,000 employees.

**BP Caspian Sea Petroleum Ltd:** 370003 Baku, Neftchilar Ave 2, Villa Petrolea; tel. (12) 97-90-00; fax (12) 97-96-02; e-mail hallg@bp .com; f. Dec. 1998 by merger of British Petroleum and Amoco of the USA; Chief Exec. Andrew Hopwood; Country Man. Douglas Hill; 1,234 employees.

**ChevronTexaco Overseas Petroleum Azerbaijan Ltd:** 370000 Baku, 340 Nizami St, ISR Plaza, 10th Floor; tel. (12) 97-13-49; fax (12) 97-13-53; e-mail ismm@chevron.com; f. 1998; subsidiary of Chevron Overseas Petroleum Inc. of the USA; Man. J. Connor.

**Delta Hess:** Baku, Izmir St 1033, Hyatt Tower 2; tel. (12) 97-60-81; fax (12) 97-23-19; e-mail deltahess@azdata.net; f. 1998; owned by Amerada Hess Corpn (USA) and Delta Oil Central Asia Ltd (Saudi Arabia); 20% shareholder in the Garabakhli-Kursangli production-sharing agreement, 2.72% shareholder in the Azeri-Chirag-Guneshli project and equity holder in the Baku-Tbilisi (Georgia)-Ceyhan (Turkey) BTC petroleum pipeline; Country Man. Tom Springall.

**Devon Energy Caspian Corporation (DECC):** 370000 Baku, Nizami St 96, Landmark, 4th Floor; tel. (12) 97-10-79; fax (12) 98-48-83; subsidiary of US-based Devon Energy Corpn; merged with Pennzoil Company in 1999; 5.6% shareholder in the Azeri-Chirag-Guneshli project; Pres. Gregory Messner.

**ExxonMobil Ventures Azerbaijan Inc.:** 370004 Baku, Nizami St 96, Landmark Bldg, Suite 300; tel. (12) 98-24-60; fax (12) 98-24-72; subsidiary of ExxonMobil (USA); Gen. Man. Drew Goodbread.

**Inpex Southwest Caspian Sea, Ltd:** f. 1999; 51% owned by Inpex Corpn (Japan) and 49% owned by Japan National Oil Corpn; purchased 10% of the Azeri-Chirag-Guneshli petroleum project from LUKoil in 2003; Pres. Kunihiko Matsuo.

**Itochu Oil Exploration (Azerbaijan) Inc:** Baku, Izmir St 1033, Hyatt Tower 2, 5th Floor; tel. (12) 90-75-60; fax (12) 90-75-62; e-mail cieco@itochuoil.in-baku.com; f. 1996; 100% owned by Itochu Corpn (Japan); member of the AIOC (q.v.) and shareholder in the Azeri-Chirag-Guneshli project; Gen. Man. Kotaro Morishita.

**LUKoil Baku:** 370004 Baku, Taghiyev St 13; tel. (12) 92-32-35; fax (12) 93-48-30; e-mail office@lukoil.baku.az; subsidiary of LUKoil of Russia; Gen. Dir Fikrat Aliyev.

**Petroleum Geo-Services:** 370004 Baku, Boyuk Gala St 40, Norway House; tel. (12) 98-81-25; fax (12) 98-11-54; e-mail hassan .ahmadov@oslo.pgs.com; internet www.pgs.com; f. 1991; collates geophysical data for the petroleum and gas industries; Dir Hassan Akhmadov; 1,800 employees.

**Royal Dutch/Shell Azerbaijan Exploration and Production BV:** 370010 Baku, Izmir St 1033, Hyatt Tower 3; tel. (12) 97-06-61; fax (12) 97-06-65; e-mail saep@shell.az; Country Man. Rejep Aksulu.

**Statoil Caspian Region AS** (Den Norske Stats Oljeselskap as): 370010 Baku, Nizami St 96, Landmark Plaza, 5th Floor; tel. (12) 97-73-40; fax (12) 97-79-44; internet www.statoil.com; f. 1972; subsidiary of Statoil of Norway; Country Man. George Gundersen.

**Total Azerbaijan:** 370000 Baku, 340 Nizami St, ISR Plaza; tel. (12) 97-83-80; fax (12) 97-13-35; e-mail jean-claude.nawrot@total.com; internet www.total.com; subsidiary of Total (France); Gen. Man. Jean-Claude Nawrot.

**TPAO/TPOC** (Türkiye Petrolleri Anonim Ortaklığı): 37000 Baku, Nizami St 340, ISR Plaza, 4th Floor; tel. (12) 98-95-26; fax (12) 98-14-35; e-mail makaya@tpao-az.com; involved in four Exploration-, Development- and Production-sharing Agreements, including Azeri-Chirag-Guneshli (6.75%), Shah Deniz (9%), Kur Dashi (5%) and Alov (10%); shareholder in the Baku–Tbilisi (Georgia)–Ceyhan (Turkey) BTC Main Export Pipeline and the South Caucasus Natural Gas Pipeline Project.

**Unocal Khazar Ltd:** 370000 Baku, 340 Nizami St, ISR Plaza, 4th Floor; tel. (12) 97-50-22; fax (12) 97-50-23; e-mail mike.barnes@ unocal.com; internet www.unocal.com; Pres. Mike Barnes; Man. Bakhtiyar Akhdunov.

## Association

**Azneft Production Association:** 370004 Baku, Neftyanikov Ave 73; tel. (12) 92-06-85; fax (12) 92-32-04; represents petroleum and gas producers; a subsidiary of SOCAR (q.v.); Gen. Dir AKIF DZHAFAROV.

## MAJOR COMPANIES

By the early 2000s the majority of small enterprises were in the private sector. Most of the remaining larger state enterprises were to be privatized in the next phase of the privatization programme.

**Azerbaijan Aluminium Joint-Stock Co:** f. 2000 from Sumgaitalvanmetal (Sumgait Non-ferrous Metals), Gyandzha Clinozem Aluminium Production Association and Dashkesan alunite plant; owned by Fondel Metal Participations BW of the Netherlands.

**Azerbaijan Rolled Pipes Manufacture:** 373200 Sumgait, Mira Ave 1; tel. and fax (164) 557-65; f. 1952; manufactures rolled pipes, building materials and drilling equipment for the petroleum industry; Dir-Gen. E. A. DERVOYED; 10,000 employees.

**Azerbintorg:** Baku; tel. (12) 92-97-61; fax (12) 98-32-92; f. 1988; imports and exports a wide range of goods (90.4% of exports in 1995); Chair. KAMAL R. ABBASOV; Dir SADIKH KAMAL OGLU MAMEDOV.

**Azerbvneshservice:** 370001 Baku, Istigialiyat St 31–33; tel. (12) 92-15-92; fax (12) 98-93-24; e-mail expo@chamber.baku.az; involved in foreign trade, marketing, business consultancy for domestic and foreign cos, organizes exhibitions; Pres. M. M. AKHMEDOV.

**Azerelectromash JSC:** 370029 Baku, 4th Poperechnaya St 3, Keshla Settlement; tel. (12) 47-35-83; fax (12) 47-37-20; e-mail azema2002@rambler.ru; f. 1946; manufactures electric motors for the mechanical engineering, mining and petroleum industries; Gen. Dir JAVID GASHIMOV; 800 employees.

**Azerenergytikintigurashdirma JSC:** 370601 Baku, Azerbaijan Ave 20; tel. (12) 98-54-31; fax (12) 93-33-17; e-mail azetg@azdata.net; internet www.azetg.com; f. 1993; constructs and installs power-stations and electric facilities; seven subsidiary entities; Pres. RASUL HAMIDOV; 700 employees.

**Azerikhimia:** 373200 Sumgait, Samad Vurgun St 86; tel. (164) 594-01; fax (164) 598-17; e-mail root@qoch.sumgait.az; f. 1992; state-owned; chemical, pharmaceutical and plastic products; Pres. FIKRET MAMED OGLU SADYKHOV; 10,300 employees.

**Azerkontract:** 370141 Baku, A. Alekperov St 83/23; tel. (12) 594-01; fax (12) 598-17; Pres. MIRI AHAD OGLU GAMBAROV; 18,300 employees.

**Azertijaret:** 370000 Baku, Genjler Sq. 3; tel. (12) 92-66-67; fax (12) 98-07-56; e-mail aztij@azeri.com; Dir RAFIK SH. ALIYEV.

**Azertrans:** 370001 Baku, Istigialiyat St 31; tel. (12) 92-07-05; fax (12) 92-54-71; f. 1992; owner of the only tanker offload and rail facilities in Baku, and was to open similar facilities in Sangachal in 2003; freight forwarding and transport; 10 affiliated cos; Gen. Man. ELCHIN GULAMOV.

**Azinmash (Azerbaijan Petroleum Engineering Research and Design Institute):** 370029 Baku, Aras St 4; tel. and fax (12) 67-28-88; e-mail office@azinmash.azeri.com; f. 1930; designs and manufactures equipment for petroleum and natural-gas industries; organizes patents and licences; prospecting; state-owned; Dir RAUF DJAVADOVICH DJABAROV; 507 employees.

**Azneftkhimiamash Open Joint-Stock Co:** 370110 Baku, Academician Hasan Aliyev St 57; tel. (12) 41-17-16; fax (12) 41-17-23; e-mail azneftkimyamash@azdata.net; internet www.azneftkimyamash.com; f. 1936; designs and produces petroleum- and gas-related equipment; Chair. ALI YUSIF KARAKHANOV; 6,000 employees.

**Bakinsky Rabochy Engineering:** 370034 Baku, Proletarski St 10; tel. (12) 25-93-75; fax (12) 25-93-82; f. 1900; produces equipment for the petroleum industry, including pumping units and pipe transporters; state-owned; Dir MAMED AKPER OGLU VELIYEV; 1,200 employees.

**Bakkondisioner:** 370029 Baku, Asadov St 10; tel. (12) 66-60-57; fax (12) 66-83-25; manufactures air conditioners; Dir YASHAR BOYUK OGLU DEMIROV.

**Chinar:** 370029 Baku, N. Narimanov St 4; tel. and fax (12) 66-08-55; manufactures refrigerators; Dir ASHRAF MIAKHA OGLU KHADJIGERDIYEV.

**Compressor Manufacturing Plant:** 373200 Sumgait, Samad Vurgun St 1; tel. and fax (164) 30027; f. 1971; production and repair of industrial compressors, casting of various steel, cast-iron, plastic and copperware; Dir ELMAN HAJIBABA KAZIYEV.

**Improtex Group:** 370000 Baku, Azi Aslanov St 115; tel. (12) 98-02-27; fax (12) 93-29-97; e-mail haliev@azeurotel.com; internet www.improtex.net; f. 1991; holding group, which includes IMAIR (see Civil Aviation), Improtex Commerce (distributor), Improtex Motors

(importer), Improtex Trading (consumer-electronics retailer), Improtrans (transportation and logistics), and Improtex Travel (tour operator); Pres. FIZULI HASAN OGLU ALEKPEROV; Gen. Man. HIKMET ALIYEV; approx. 1,200 employees.

**Kaspmornefteflot:** 370025 Baku, Telnov St 13; tel. (12) 90-62-36; fax (12) 90-62-37; e-mail frd@kmnf.baku.az; internet www.kaspmornefteflot.baku-az.com; provides services for petroleum and natural gas production in the Caspian Sea, including construction, exploration, maintenance and transportation services; 318 vessels.

**Magistralkamarlari:** 370025 Baku, Najafgulu Rafiyev St 28; tel. (12) 66-56-96; fax (12) 66-35-88; constructs and services petroleum and gas pipelines; Gen. Dir TAFIQ AKHUNDOV; 1,100 employees.

**MIT International Trade Co:** 370148 Baku, Mehti Hussein St, Hotel Anba; tel. (12) 98-45-20; fax (12) 98-45-19; f. 1993; food products and consumer goods; Dir TAIR RAMAZAN OGLU ASADOV.

**Ulduz:** 370029 Baku, Khalglar Dostlugu Khiyabani St 1; tel. (12) 67-31-81; fax (12) 67-53-34; manufactures communications equipment; Dir ADIL MAMED OGLU MAGERRAMOV.

## TRADE UNIONS

**Association of Independent Workers of Azerbaijan:** Baku; Chair. NEYMAT PANAKHLI.

**Confederation of Azerbaijan Trade Unions:** Baku; tel. and fax (12) 92-72-68; Chair. SATTAR MEHBALIYEV.

**Free Trade Union of Teachers:** Baku; Chair. SEYRAN SEYRANOV.

**Trade Union of Journalists** (JuHI): 370000 Baku, Khagani St 33; tel. (50) 335-27-95; fax (12) 98-78-18; e-mail juhi@juhiaz.org; internet www.juhiaz.org; f. 1998; registered by Govt in March 2000; 654 mems; Chair. AZER HASRET.

**Trade Union of Oil and Gas Industry Workers:** 370033 Baku, Aga Neymatulla St 39; tel. (12) 67-69-53; fax (12) 47-15-85; e-mail oilunion@online.az; f. 1906; mems belong to 210 local organizations in the petroleum and gas sectors; 71,500 mems; Chair. JAHANGIR ALIYEV.

# Transport

## RAILWAYS

In 2002 there were 2,116 km of railway track, of which 1,269 km were electrified. The overwhelming majority of total freight traffic is carried by the railways. Railways connect Baku with Tbilisi (Georgia), Makhachkala (Dagestan, Russia) and Yerevan (Armenia). In 1997 passenger rail services between Moscow and Baku were resumed, and a service to Kiev (Ukraine) was inaugurated. The rail link with Armenia runs through the Autonomous Republic of Nakhichevan, but is currently disrupted, owing to Azerbaijan's economic blockade of Armenia. From Nakhichevan an international line links Azerbaijan with Tabriz (Iran). In 1991 plans were agreed with the Iranian Government for the construction of a rail line between Azerbaijan and Nakhichevan, which would pass through Iranian territory, thus bypassing Armenia. There is an underground railway in Baku (the Baku Metro); initially comprising two lines (total length 28 km), with 19 stations, a further 4.1 km, with three stations, was under construction.

**Azerbaijani Railways (AZ):** 370010 Baku, Dilara Aliyeva St 230; tel. (12) 98-44-67; fax (12) 98-85-47; e-mail info@addy.gov.az; internet addy.gov.az; f. 1992, following the dissolution of the former Soviet Railways; First Dep. Pres. and Chief Eng. M. M. MEHTIYEV.

**Baku Metropolitan:** 370602 Baku, H. Javid Ave 33A; tel. (12) 90-00-00; fax (12) 97-53-96; internet www.metro.gov.az:8101; f. 1967; Gen. Man. T. AKHMEDOV.

## ROADS

In 2000 the total length of roads in Azerbaijan was 24,981 km, of which 6,897 km were main roads; 92.3% of the road network was paved.

## SHIPPING

Shipping services on the Caspian Sea link Baku with Astrakhan (Russia), Turkmenbashi (Turkmenistan) and the Iranian ports of Bandar Anzali and Bandar Nowshar. At 31 December 2002 the Azerbaijani merchant fleet comprised 285 vessels, with a combined displacement of 633,189 grt. The total included 38 petroleum tankers (175,431 grt).

### Shipowning Company

**Baku Sea Port:** 370010 Baku, U. Hajibeyov St 72; tel. (12) 93-67-74; fax (12) 93-36-72; e-mail port@sea.baku.az; internet www.bakuport.com.

**Caspian Shipping Company (Caspar):** 370005 Baku, Mamma-demin Rasulzade St 5; tel. (12) 93-20-58; fax (12) 93-53-39; e-mail gkmp@caspar.baku.az; internet www.caspar.baku.az; f. 1858; nationalized by the Govt in 1991; transports crude petroleum and petroleum products; operates cargo and passenger ferries; fleet of 69 vessels; Pres. A. A. BASHIROV.

### CIVIL AVIATION

There are five airports in Azerbaijan, of which Baku (www.airport-baku.com) is the largest. A new air terminal was commissioned for the Bina-Baku airport in 1999. Nakhichevan also has its own airport.

**Civil Aviation Administration:** 370000 Baku, Azadliq Ave 11; tel. (12) 93-44-34; fax (12) 98-52-37; e-mail azal_coordpt@azerin.com; internet azaviation.com; Chief Inspector ILHAM G. AMIROV.

**Azerbaijan Airlines (AZAL)** (Azerbaijan Hava Yollari): 370000 Baku, Azadliq Ave 11; tel. (12) 93-44-34; fax (12) 98-52-37; e-mail azal@azal.baku.az; internet www.azal.az; f. 1992; formerly Aza-lavia; state airline operating scheduled and charter passenger ser-vices to Africa, the CIS, Europe, South-East Asia and the Middle East; Gen. Dir JAHANGIR ASKEROV.

    **Cargo Air Company (CAC):** 370109 Baku, Bina Airport; tel. and fax (12) 97-16-71; e-mail office@azavcar.baku.az; internet www.cacazal.com; state-owned; Dir YASHAR HASANOV.

**IMAIR Airlines:** 370000 Baku, Hazi Aslanov St 115; tel. (12) 93-41-71; fax (12) 93-27-77; e-mail root@imair.com; internet www.imair.com; f. 1995; independent airline operating international regular passenger and charter passenger and cargo services, mainly within the CIS region; Chair. and Pres. FIZOULI ALEKPEROV.

**Turan Air:** 370022 Baku, 102 Mardanov Bros St; tel. (12) 98-94-31; fax (12) 98-94-34; internet www.turan.com; f. 1994; operates sched-uled and charter passenger and cargo services, mainly within the former USSR.

# Tourism

Tourism is not widely developed. However, there are resorts on the Caspian Sea, including the Ganjlik international tourist centre, on the Apsheron Peninsula, near Baku, which has four hotels as well as camping facilities. There were 793,345 tourist arrivals in 2002.

**Council for Foreign Tourism:** 370004 Baku, Neftchilar Ave 65; tel. (12) 92-87-13; fax (12) 98-03-68; e-mail ff-com@azdata.net; under the Cabinet of Ministers.

# Culture

### NATIONAL ORGANIZATIONS

**Ministry of Culture:** see section on The Government (Ministries); organizes International Hari Bul-Bul Folk Festival, Kara Karayev International Festival of Modern Music, Musical September in Baku International Festival.

**Ministry of Youth, Sport and Tourism:** see section on the Gov-ernment (Ministries).

#### Nakhichevan Autonomous Republic

**Ministry of Culture:** 373630 Nakhichevan, Ave 1; tel. (136) 42252; Minister NIZAM IBRAHIM OGLU HAJIYEV.

### INTERNATIONAL ORGANIZATION

**Bakinets International Cultural Society:** 370000 Baku, Kha-gani St 16; tel. (12) 98-81-68; fax (12) 93-53-39; e-mail bakinez@azeurotel.com; internet bakinets.narod.ru/bakinets_society.htm; f. 1992; non-political non-commercial organization to promote Baku-nian culture; Pres. FIKRET SAIB OGLU ZARBALIYEV.

### CULTURAL HERITAGE

At the end of 2001 there were 156 museums and 4,152 public libraries in the country.

**Azerbaijan R. Mustafayev State Museum of Art:** 370001 Baku, Niyazi St 9–11; tel. (12) 92-57-89; f. 1924; Dir A. R. ASRAFILOV.

**Baku Museum of Education:** 370001 Baku, Niyazi St 11; tel. (12) 92-04-53; f. 1940; library of 52,000 vols; Dir T. Z. AHMEDZADE.

**Baku State University Central Library:** 370145 Baku, Z. Khalilova St 23; tel. (12) 39-08-58; fax (12) 38-05-82; f. 1919; 2.0m. vols; Librarian S. IBRAHIMOVA.

**Central Library of the Azerbaijan Academy of Sciences:** 370143 Baku, Narimanova pr. 31; tel. (12) 38-60-17; f. 1925; 2.5m. vols; Dir M. M. GASANOVA.

**Central State Archives of Literature and Art:** 370106 Baku, S. Bahlulzade Ave 3; tel. (12) 62-96-53; Dir LAYLA YUSIF KIZI GOFUROVA.

**J. Jabbarli State Theatre Museum:** 370004 Baku, Neftchilar Ave 123A; tel. (12) 93-40-98; Dir NURIDA GAMIDULLA KIZI NURULLAYEVA.

**M. F. Akhundov State Public Library:** 370601 Baku, Khagani St 29; tel. (12) 93-42-03; f. 1923; 4.4m. vols; Dir L. YU. GAFUROVA.

**Mähämmäd Füzuli Institute of Manuscripts of the Academy of Sciences:** 370001 Baku, Istiglaliyat St 8; tel. and fax (12) 92-31-97; f. 1950; manuscripts and historical documents relating to the history, philology and ethnology of Azerbaijani and other Muslim peoples; Vice-Dir M. M. ADILOV.

**Museum of the History of Azerbaijan of the Azerbaijan Academy of Sciences:** 370005 Baku, Malygin St 4; tel. (12) 93-36-48; f. 1920; 120,000 exhibits on the history of the Azerbaijani people from ancient times; Dir P. A. AZIZBEKOVA.

**Nizami Ganjavi State Museum of Azerbaijani Literature:** 370001 Baku, Istiglaliyat St 53; tel. (12) 92-18-64; f. 1939; 75,000 exhibits on the history of Azerbaijani literature; Dir I. R. ISRAFILOV.

**State Museum of Musical Culture:** 370004 Baku, R. Behbudov St 5; tel. (12) 98-69-72; internet www.citisight.com/baku/musculture.html; Dir ALLA GADJIAGA KIZI BAYRAMOVA.

**State Museum Palace of Shirvan-Shakh:** Baku, Zamkovaya Gora 76; tel. (12) 92-83-04; fax (12) 92-29-10; f. 1964; historical and architectural museum and national park; Dir DADASHEVA SEVDA.

#### Nakhichevan Autonomous Republic

**J. Mamedkuluzade State Museum of Literature:** 373630 Nakhichevan; tel. (136) 43942; Dir SUBHI FARRUKH OGLU KANKARLI.

**Nakhichevan State Museum:** 373630 Nakhichevan, Nizami St 31; tel. (136) 42369; Dir ISFANDIYAR MIR ISMAYIL OGLU ASADULLAYEV.

#### Stepanakert

**Stepanakert Museum of the History of Nagorno-Karabakh:** Stepanakert, Gorkogo St 4.

### SPORTING ORGANIZATION

**National Olympic Committee of Azerbaijan:** 370072 Baku, F. Khoyski St 98A; tel. (12) 90-64-42; fax (12) 90-64-38; Pres. Dr ILHAM ALIYEV; Gen. Sec. Prof. AGADJAN ABIYEV.

### PERFORMING ARTS

#### Drama, Opera, Dance

At the end of 2001 there were 27 professional theatres.

**Azerbaijan Marionette Theatre:** 370000 Baku, Khagani St 10; tel. (12) 98-65-94; Dir TARLAN BEYBALA OGLU GORCHIYEV.

**Baku Choreography School:** 370014 Baku, Bul-Bul Ave 54; tel. (12) 95-78-07; Dir N. I. KERIMOVA.

**F. Amirov State Song and Dance Ensemble:** 370001 Baku, Istiglaliyat St 2; tel. (12) 92-51-53; Dir GARKHMAZ AGABABA OGLU KURBANOV.

**Gek-Gel State Song and Dance Ensemble:** 374700 Gyanja, Atayevs St 135; tel. (522) 25289; Artistic Dir SHAHNAZ GASAN KIZI GASHIMOVA.

**Mirza Akhundov Opera and Ballet Theatre:** Baku, October St 8.

**Nizamy Poetry Theatre:** Gyanja, Baku St 38; tel. (522) 25188; Dir SURKHAY MOMIN OGLU SAFAROV.

**State Academic Drama Theatre:** 370000 Baku, Fizuli Sq.; tel. (12) 94-49-19; Dir GASAN SATTAR OGLU TURABOV.

**State Academic Opera and Ballet Theatre:** 370000 Baku, Nizami St 95; tel. (12) 93-16-51; f. 1959; Dir AKIF TARAN OGLU MELIKOV.

**State Dance Ensemble:** 370001 Baku, Istiglaliyat St 2; tel. (12) 92-51-53; Artistic Dir AFAK SULEYMAN KIZI MELIKOVA.

**State Musical Comedy Theatre:** 370056 Baku, Azerbaijan Ave 8; tel. (12) 93-24-11; Dir GADJYBABA AGARZA OGLU BAGIROV.

**State Musical Drama Theatre:**

    **Shusha State Musical Drama Theatre:** 370320 Sumgait, Aza-dliq Sq. 5; owing to the troubles in Nagornyi Karabakh, the Shusha co is based in Sumgait; Dir AGALAR IDRIS OGLU MEHTIYEV.

    **Sumgait State Musical Drama Theatre:** 373200 Sumgait, Aza-dliq Sq. 5; tel. (264) 59121; Dir and Artistic Man. AGALAR IDRIS OGLU MEHTIYEV.

**State Puppet Theatre:** 370004 Baku, Azerbaijan Ave 36; tel. (12) 92-64-35; Dir RAHMAN RAGIM OGLU HULIYEV.

**Gyanja State Puppet Theatre:** 374400 Gyanja, Djalil St 195; tel. (222) 35728; Dir BAYREM APREL OGLU FATALIYEV.

**State Russian Drama Theatre named after Samed Vurgun:** 370000 Baku, Khagani St 7; tel. (12) 93-40-48; e-mail rdt@azdata .net; internet www.rusdrama-az.com; f. 1920; Dir MARAT FARRUKH OGLU IBRAHIMOV.

**State Theatre for Young Spectators:** 370000 Baku, Nizami St 72; tel. (12) 93-88-52; Dir KAMAL GABIL OGLU AZIZOV.

**State Theatre of the Young:** 370001 Baku, M. Mukhtarov St 83; tel. (12) 94-48-47; Artistic Man. VAGIF IBRAHIM OGLU HASSANOV.

**State Youth Theatre:** 370000 Baku, Khagani St 10; tel. (12) 93-29-63; f. 1989; Dir HUSSEINAGA AGAHUSSEIN OGLU ATAKISHIYEV.

### Music

**Gaya State Variety Orchestra:** Baku; tel. (12) 92-48-30; Artistic Man. TEYMUR IBRAHIM OGLU MIRZOYEV.

**Gyanja Philharmonia Society State Chamber Orchestra:** 374400 Gyanja, Atayevs St 135; tel. (22) 25321; Artistic Man. RASIM ISA OGLU BAGIROV.

**K. Karayev State Chamber Orchestra:** 370001 Baku, Istiglaliyat St 2; tel. (12) 92-51-53; Artistic Dir YASHAR ABDULKHALIG OGLU IMANOV.

**Model Military Brass Band of the Ministry of Defence:** 370004 Baku, Samad Vurgun St 12; tel. (12) 93-64-20; Artistic Man. YUSIF YEVGENIYEVICH AKHUNDSADE.

**Muslim Magomayev Philharmonia:** 370001 Baku, Istiglaliyat St 2; tel. (12) 92-51-53; Dir RAFIG HUSSEIN OGLU SEIDZEDE.

**R. Beybutov State Theatre of Song:** 370000 Baku, R. Beybutov St 12; tel. (12) 93-94-15; Dir NIYAZI INGILAB OGLU ASLANOV.

**State Brass Band:** Baku; tel. (12) 94-90-40; Artistic Man. NAZIM MAGERRAM OGLU ALIYEV.

**State Conservatoire:** 370014 Baku, Sh. Badalbeyli St 98; tel. (12) 932248; Rector FARHAD SHAMSI OGLU BADALBEYLI.

**Uzeyir Hadjibekov State Symphony Orchestra:** 370001 Baku, Istiglaliyat St 2; tel. (12) 93-75-37; f. 1938; Artistic Man. RAUF ABDULLAYEV.

### Nakhichevan Autonomous Republic

**State Musical Drama Theatre:** 373630 Nakhichevan, A. Djavad St 2; tel. (236) 2589; Dir MAMED TAHIR OGLU GUMMATOV.

**State Philharmonia:** 373630 Nakhichevan; tel. (136) 56898; Dir MAMED TAHIR OGLU GUMBATOV.

**State Puppet Theatre:** 373630 Nakhichevan; tel. (136) 43217; Dir ALEKPER HAMED OGLU KASIMOV.

**State Song and Dance Ensemble:** Nakhichevan; tel. (236) 56898.

### ASSOCIATIONS

**Azconcert** (Concert Tours Union): 370010 Baku, Azerbaijan Ave 59; tel. (12) 93-81-00; Dir-Gen. ILDRIM ALINAZIR OGLU KASIMOV.

**Azerbaijan Musicians' Union:** 370000 Baku, A. Aliyev St 9; tel. (12) 92-67-04; fax (12) 98-13-30; Chair. FARHAD SHAMSI OGLU BADAL-BEYLI.

**Azerbaijan Society of Cultural Relations with Countrymen Abroad—Veten:** 370001 Baku, Istiglaliyat St 27; tel. (12) 92-60-66; fax (12) 92-55-82; f. 1987; cultural organization for developing contacts with Azerbaijanis in other countries; Chair. ELCHIN EFENDIYEV.

**Society for Contemporary Music** (Yeni Musiqi): 370141 Baku, Haqverdiyev St 3A –32; tel. (12) 39-06-70; fax (12) 38-76-01; Pres. Prof. FARAJ KARAYEV.

**Union of Actors of Azerbaijan:** 370000 Baku, Khagani St 10; tel. (12) 93-17-03; Pres. GASAN SATTAR OGLU TURABOV.

**Union of Artists of Azerbaijan:** 370000 Baku, Khagani St 19; tel. (12) 93-62-30; Chair. FARHAD KURBAN OGLU KHALILOV.

**Union of Composers of Azerbaijan:** 370001 Baku, M. Mukhtarov St 6; tel. (12) 92-65-75; e-mail info@musigi-dunya.az; internet composers.musigi-dunya.az; f. 1934; independent creative public organization of professional composers and musical experts; Chair. VASIF ADIGEZALOV.

**Union of Writers of Azerbaijan:** 370000 Baku, Khagani St 25; tel. (12) 93-66-40; Chair. ANAR RASUL OGLU RZAYEV.

# Education

Under Soviet rule a more extensive education system was introduced, and the level of literacy was greatly increased, from 8.1% in 1926 to 97.3% in 1989. Education is officially compulsory between the ages of six and 17 years. Primary education begins at the age of six years. Secondary education, comprising a first cycle of five years and a second cycle of two years, begins at the age of 10. In 2001 17% of children of the relevant age attended pre-primary schools. In 1999/2000 total net enrolment at primary schools was equivalent to 91% of the relevant age group; in 1998/99 the net rate of secondary enrolment was 78%. The main language of instruction is Azerbaijani, but there are also Russian-language schools and some teaching in Georgian and Armenian. From 1992 a Turkic version of the Latin alphabet was used in Azerbaijani-language schools (replacing the Cyrillic script). Almost all secondary schools use Azerbaijani as the language of instruction, and the percentage of pupils taught in Russian had declined from 13% in the mid-1990s to 6% by 2001. In higher education technical subjects were often taught in Russian, but there were demands for the greater use of Azerbaijani. There are 25 state-supported institutions of higher education, including the Azerbaijan State Petroleum Academy, which trains engineers for the petroleum industry, and 15 private universities. In 2001/02 there were 120,500 students in higher education. Government expenditure on education was estimated at 952,500m. manats in 2002 (representing 20.4% of total state spending).

### UNIVERSITIES

**Azerbaijan Medical University named after Nariman Narimanov:** 370022 Baku, Bakikhanov St 23; tel. (12) 95-43-24; fax (12) 40-27-70.

**Azerbaijan State Oil Academy (ASOA/ADNA):** 370010 Baku, Azadliq Ave 20; tel. (12) 93-45-57; fax (12) 98-29-41; e-mail ihm@ adna.baku.az; internet www.adna.baku.az; f. 1920; training and scientific research; 7 faculties; Rector Prof. SIYAVUSH F. QARAYEV.

**Azerbaijan State Pedagogical University:** 370000 Baku, Uzeir Hajibeyov St 34; tel. (12) 93-00-32.

**Azerbaijan Technical University (AzTU):** 370073 Baku, H. Javid Ave 25; tel. (12) 38-33-43; fax (12) 38-32-80; e-mail aztu@ aztu.org; internet www.aztu.org; f. 1950; 8 faculties; 835 teachers; 6,141 students; Rector Prof. H. A. MAMEDOV.

**Baku State University** (Baki Dovlat Universiteti): 370145 Baku, Z. Khalilov St 23; tel. (12) 38-64-58; fax (12) 98-33-76; e-mail bsu_international@lycos.com; internet bsu.in-baku.com; f. 1919; 16 faculties; 1,282 teachers; 11,101 students; Rector ABEL MAMMADALI MAHARRAMOV.

**Caucasus University:** 370010 Baku, Nariman Narimanov Ave 103; tel. (12) 38-72-46; fax (12) 98-14-87; e-mail admin@qafqaz.edu .az; internet www.qafqaz.edu.az; f. 1993; instruction in Turkish; five faculties; Rector Prof. EROL ORAL.

**Khazar University:** 370096 Baku, Mehseti St 11; tel. (12) 21-79-27; fax (12) 98-93-79; e-mail contact@khazar.org; internet www.khazar .org; f. 1991; private; five schools; 90 teachers; 970 students; Pres. Prof. HAMLET ISAXANLI.

**Western University:** 370010 Baku, Istiglaliyat St 27; tel. (12) 92-74-18; fax (12) 92-67-01; e-mail webmaster@wu.aznet.org; internet www.wu.aznet.org; f. 1991; private, non-profit institution; four schools; 180 faculties.

# Social Welfare

Azerbaijan has a comprehensive social-security system, which aims to ensure that every citizen receives at least a subsistence income and that health care and education are freely available. The system aims to cover all groups of the population. The social benefits are financed by three extrabudgetary funds, the Social Protection Fund, the Employment Fund and the Disabled Persons' Fund. The Social Protection Fund receives transfers from the republican budget as well as contributions from employers and employees, and the Employment Fund is financed by social-insurance contributions from employers. The first private hospital was opened in May 1998, in the Nakhichevan Autonomous Republic. In 1999 there were 890 hospital beds for every 100,000 inhabitants in Azerbaijan, and in 2002 there were 735 hospitals, and 29,090 physicians working in the country (one per 278 inhabitants). In 2002 government expenditure on health amounted to 224,100m. manats (representing 4.8% of total state spending), and expenditure on social security and welfare totalled 951,200m. manats (representing 20.4% of spending).

In 2001 life expectancy at birth was estimated to be 60.7 years for men and 66.6 years for women. The official retirement age is 62 for men and 57 for women. The extrabudgetary Social Protection Fund provides for old-age, disability and survivor pensions. Total expenditure by the Social Protection Fund totalled 1,330,000m. manats (5.6% of GDP) in 2000, including 783,000m. manats in pensions. Some 1.3m. people were receiving pensions at the end of 2002, according to official figures, of whom 743,000 were old-age pensioners. In 2002 the average monthly old-age pension totalled 92,000 manats.

## NATIONAL AGENCIES

**Ministry of Public Health:** see section on The Government (Ministries).

**Ministry of Labour and Social Protection** (see section on The Government (Ministries).):

**Employment Fund:** f. 1991; extrabudgetary govt fund intended to pay unemployment benefits, but insufficient transfers; pays for vocational training.

**Social Protection Fund:** f. 1992 by merger of Pension Fund and Social Insurance Fund; extrabudgetary govt fund.

**State Oil Fund of Azerbaijan (SOFAZ):** 370025 Baku, Sabit Orujov St 28; tel. (12) 90-57-30; fax (12) 90-57-31; e-mail office@oilfund.az; internet www.oilfund.az; f. 1999 to accumulate and manage energy-related revenue for the benefit of the country; Exec. Dir SAMIR SHARIFOV.

## HEALTH AND WELFARE ORGANIZATIONS

**People's Committee for Relief to Karabakh:** Baku; f. 1987; Chair. B. BAIRAMOV.

**Refugee Society:** Baku, pr. Karl Marx 48/54; tel. (12) 39-49-50; fax (12) 32-15-65; aids refugees and displaced people with housing, food and social services.

**Relief International (RI):** Baku; tel. (12) 98-42-76; e-mail root@relief.baku.az; delivers medical supplies and equipment and provides relief services.

**Relief Organization of the Azerbaijan Republic:** Baku, Gara Garayev St 114, kv. 37; tel. (12) 74-43-13; conducts social-welfare programmes and makes available emergency relief.

**Azerbaijani League for the Defence of the Rights of Children:** Baku, Mirzagi Aliyeva St 130, kv. 33; tel. (12) 98-81-42; individuals and organizations with an interest in the civil and human rights of children.

**CARE Azerbaijan:** Baku, U. Hajibeyov St 19, kv. 78/29; tel. (12) 98-20-81; e-mail root@care.baku.az; operates programmes in formal education, water sanitation, agroforestry and small-business management.

**Caritas—Azerbaijan:** Baku, Iskra St 6; tel. (12) 94-95-25; promotes awareness of, and efforts to, overcome poverty, hunger, oppression and injustice.

# The Environment

Considerable environmental damage has resulted from exploitation of the petroleum and gas resources of the Caspian Sea, and from the development of industrial areas in the east of the country. Baku and Sumgait (the Apsheron Peninsula) are particularly affected and are major sources of atmospheric, soil and marine pollution. In addition, excessive use of chemicals in agriculture has had a negative impact. Some regulation, including a Law on the Protection of the Environment, was introduced in 1992–93. The European Commission and the Global Environment Facility were implementing a Caspian Environment Programme in the five Caspian littoral states, to combat pollution and the rising water level; seven towns and 35 populated areas had already become submerged in Azerbaijan, owing to this problem. A World Bank project to build a sustainable sturgeon hatchery at Neftcala was planned for 2002. There were significant concerns over the environmental impact of major pipeline-construction projects under way in the Caucasus, particularly the planned Baku–Tbilisi (Georgia)–Ceyhan (Turkey) petroleum pipeline.

In 2001 there were 14 nature reserves (with a total area of 192.2 hectares) and one national park in Azerbaijan.

## GOVERNMENT ORGANIZATIONS

**Ministry of Ecology and Natural Resources:** see section on the Government (Ministries).

**State Committee for Ecology and Environment Protection:** 370001 Baku, Istiglaliyat St 31; tel. (12) 92-41-73; fax (12) 92-59-07.

**State Committee for Geology and Mineral Resources:** 370071 Baku, Bakhram Agayev St 100A; tel. (12) 38-54-54; fax (12) 39-84-32.

**State Committee for Improvement of Soil and Water Economy:** 370016 Baku, Azadliq Sq. 1, Govt House; tel. (12) 93-61-54; fax (12) 93-11-76; e-mail irriqation@azdata.net; f. 1923; Chair. AKHMED JUMA OGLU AKHMEDZADE.

## ACADEMIC INSTITUTES

**Academy of Sciences:** 370601 Baku, Istiglaliyat St 10; internet www.ab.az/asc/academy.htm; Pres. E. U. SALAYEV; institutes incl.:

**Botanical Garden:** Baku, Patamdartskoye Ave 40; Dir U. M. AGAMIROV.

**Commission on the Caspian Sea:** Baku, H. Javid St 31; tel. (12) 39-35-41; fax (12) 92-56-99; in the Dept of Earth Sciences; Chair. R. M. MAMEDOV.

**Commission on Nature Conservation:** 370001 Baku, Istiglaliyat St 10; in the Dept of Biological Sciences; Chair. G. A. ALIYEV.

**V. L. Komarov Institute of Botany:** 370073 Baku, Patamdartskoye Ave 40; tel. (12) 39-32-30; fax (12) 39-33-80; e-mail botanica@lan.ab.az; f. 1936; Dir V. D. O. GADJIYEV.

**Azerbaijan Energy Research Institute:** 370602 Baku, H. Zardabi Ave 94; tel. (12) 32-80-76; fax (12) 98-13-68; f. 1941; Dir KERIM NAZIR OGLU RAMAZANOV.

**Azerbaijan Research Institute of Water Economy:** 370012 Baku, Tbilisi Ave 69A; tel. (12) 31-69-90; f. 1961; Dir Dr ELCHIN SURKHOI OGLU GAMBAROV.

**National Centre on Climate Change:** 37000 Baku, R. Rza St 3; tel. (12) 93-29-05; fax (12) 98-51-76; e-mail mansimov@iglim.baku.az; internet www.az/climat; f. 1995; Head MIRZAKHAN MANSIMOV.

**Zashita Scientific Research Institute for Plant Protection:** Gyanja, Aziza St 57; tel. and fax (222) 57-47-94; f. 1959; Pres. Dr CIDIQE RZA GIZI MAMEDOVA.

### Non-Governmental Organizations

**Azerbaijan Green Movement (AGM) (DZA):** 370005 Baku, I. Zevin St 4; tel. (12) 94-99-97; fax (12) 67-33-81; e-mail guseynovafk@azdata.org; f. 1989; sustainable life association; Contact FARIDA GUSEINOVA.

**Caspian Environment Programme Thematic Centre:** 370016 Baku, Uzeir Hadjibeyov St 40, Rm 108; tel. (12) 97-17-85; fax (12) 97-17-86; e-mail caspian@caspian.in-baku.com; internet www.caspianenvironment.org; Scientific Liaison Officer VLADIMIR VLADYMYROV.

**Ecolex Environmental Law Centre (ELC):** e-mail ecolex@azdata.net; internet www.ecolex.aznet.org; f. 2000; non-commercial org.; Man. SAMIR ISAYEV.

**Ecosphere Social-Ecology Centre:** 370006 Baku, Lermontov St 3, Apt 61; tel. (12) 92-43-48; e-mail ecosfera@azeurotel.com; internet ecocaucasus.org; f. 1999; humanitarian org., focusing on education, health care and environmental protection; Chair. FIRUZA SULTAN-ZADEH.

# Defence

After gaining independence in 1991, Azerbaijan began forming a national army. This numbered 72,100 in August 2002 (an army of 62,000, a navy of 2,200 and air-defence forces of 7,900). The country has a share of the former Soviet Caspian Flotilla. Military service is for 17 months (but may be extended for ground forces). The Ministry of Internal Affairs controls a militia of an estimated 10,000. As a member of the Commonwealth of Independent States (CIS), Azerbaijan's naval forces operate under CIS (Russian) control. In May 1994 Azerbaijan joined the North Atlantic Treaty Organization's 'Partnership for Peace' programme. The 2002 budget allocated an estimated US $118m. to defence.

**Commander-in-Chief:** President of the Republic.

**Chief of the General Staff:** NEDZHMEDDIN HUSSEIN OGLU SADYKHOV.

# AUTONOMOUS TERRITORIES

Constitutionally, Azerbaijan is described as a unitary state, but two territories have had special status since the 1920s. The exclave of Nakhichevan has the status of an Autonomous Republic and Nagornyi Karabakh that of an Autonomous Oblast.

The regional assembly of the Nagorno-Karabakh Autonomous Oblast, which had a majority ethnic Armenian population, proclaimed a 'Republic of Nagornyi Karabakh' on 2 September 1991. Following a referendum and elections to a 'parliament', the independence of the Republic of Nagornyi Karabakh was declared on 6 January 1992. All such pronouncements were declared invalid by the Azerbaijani authorities. However, local forces gradually gained control of the region and secured a *de facto* independence. In addition to territory linking Nagornyi Karabakh with Armenia, other parts of Azerbaijan proper were occupied.

# AUTONOMOUS REPUBLIC OF NAKHICHEVAN

Nakhichevan lies to the west of 'metropolitan' Azerbaijan, separated from it by Armenian territory, which forms the northern and eastern borders of the exclave. Nakhichevan runs from the north-west to the south-east, following the course of the River Araks (Araxes, Aras), which forms its border with Turkey (at the north-west tip of the republic, on the Ararat plain) and with Iran. Its territory rises from the fertile lowlands of the Araks valley through the forested flanks of the Lesser Caucasus to the north. Nakhichevan covers an area of some 5,500 sq km (2,124 sq miles). Most of the population are ethnic Azerbaijani (Azeri), although at one time there was a sizeable Armenian community (comprising 45%–50% of the population in 1919), but this only provided some 5% of the total by the 1989 census. The chief town and capital is also called Nakhichevan, and is sited on the Araks. In the early 2000s the population of the exclave was estimated at some 300,000.

With the disintegration of the Ottoman and Russian Empires at the end of the First World War, conflicting historical claims to different areas exacerbated ethnic tensions and the process of forming nation states. Although Azerbaijan apparently surrendered its claims to Nakhichevan in 1920, it never became part of Soviet Armenia. Then, in 1921 it became recognized as part of Azerbaijan: the Soviet-Turkish Treaty of March granted Azerbaijani jurisdiction; and the October Treaty of Kars, which finally established the borders of Turkey and Soviet Transcaucasia, effectively made Russia and Turkey the international guarantors of Nakhichevan's status. This fact, and the decline in the numbers of the ethnic Armenian population under Soviet rule, rendered renewed Armenian claims to the republic in the late 1980s and early 1990s largely rhetorical (there was a short-lived threat from Armenian militia in mid-1992). Nakhichevan was affected by the economic blockade on Armenia, however, and had to rely on air links with Azerbaijan proper or on road routes through Iran.

Nakhichevan provided a source of strong support both for the nationalists who emerged in the late 1980s and for Heydar Aliyev, leader of Azerbaijan in 1969–87 and from 1993. In 1990 nationalist demonstrators seized buildings of the ruling Communist Party in Nakhichevan and attempted to declare the republic's secession from the USSR. This protest was suppressed, but the authorities continued to experience demonstrations and outright challenges along the border with Iran. In March 1991 Azerbaijan participated in the Soviet referendum on the renewal of the USSR; some 93.3% of those who voted favoured remaining in the Union, but in Nakhichevan support was only some 20%. The leader of the nationalist Popular Front of Azerbaijan, Abulfaz Elchibey (his original surname was Aliyev), was a native of Nakhichevan, as was Heydar Aliyev, who had retired to his home after his dismissal from office in 1987. Aliyev formed his New Azerbaijan Party in Nakhichevan, and in September 1991 was elected Chairman of the local Supreme Soviet. He again became involved in national politics in 1993, replacing Elchibey as President of Azerbaijan in that year. Elchibey, meanwhile, took refuge there, in his hometown of Keleki, and remained in effective internal exile until 1997, when he was permitted to return to Baku and active opposition politics until his death in 2000. The Azerbaijani Milli Majlis (National Assembly) approved a revised constitution for Nakhichevan in December 1998, which was endorsed by the republic's legislature, and which defined the enclave as an 'autonomous state' within Azerbaijan.

**Chairman of the Ali Majlis (Supreme Assembly):** VASIF TALIBOV.

**Prime Minister (Chairman of the Cabinet of Ministers):** ALI OSAT BAKHIYOV.

# NAGORNO-KARABAKH AUTONOMOUS OBLAST

Nagornyi Karabakh (Daglygh Karabakh) lies in south-west Azerbaijan (for further details, see below. The enclave was awarded to Azerbaijan in 1921 and acquired autonomous status in 1923. Although this autonomy was formally abolished by the legislature of Azerbaijan in August 1990, the Government remained willing to offer such a status to the enclave in any peace settlement. By 2003 no such agreement was forthcoming, however, and secessionist forces remained in control of the territory of the former autonomous oblast and of surrounding districts in Azerbaijan proper.

**Head of the Delegation of the Government of the Azerbaijan Republic to the Minsk Conference:** ARAZ AZIMOV.

# 'REPUBLIC OF NAGORNYI KARABAKH'

## Introduction

Nagornyi Karabakh, Upper or Mountainous Karabakh (Daglygh Karabakh in Azerbaijani, Artsakh in Armenian), is on the north-eastern slopes of the Lesser Caucasus. The region lies in the south-west of Azerbaijan; Nagornyi Karabakh's own south-western border, near the town of Lachin in Azerbaijan proper, is separated from the international frontier with Armenia only by a narrow strip of land along the Akera valley. The terrain consists of lowland steppe and heavily forested mountainsides, with much of the territory rising above the tree line, reaching 3,724 m (12,218 ft) at Mt Gyamysh. The old autonomous region covers an area of 4,400 sq km (1,698 sq miles), but the forces of the Republic of Nagornyi Karabakh actually occupy some 7,059 sq km or just over 8% of the territory of the Azerbaijan Republic. Historically, the Armenian population claims dominance in Shaumyan, on the north-western borders of the enclave, and in a wider 'Northern Nagornyi Karabakh', which stretches up as far as the town of Gyanja (Ganca, known as Gandzak by the Armenians—formerly Kirovabad). Following the troubles of the late 1980s and early 1990s, however, most ethnic Armenians had been expelled from areas still under the control of the Azerbaijani Government and Azeris had been expelled from the territories occupied by the Nagornyi Karabakh forces (Nagornyi Karabakh, the districts of Jebrail, Kelbadjar, Kubatli, Lachin and Zangelan and most of the districts of Agdam and Fizuli). In 1989, at the time of the last Soviet census, the population of the Autonomous Oblast was 189,085, 77% being ethnic Armenians and 22% Azeris. Even then, full account had not been taken of the disruption caused by refugees from ethnic disputes, and this situation was exacerbated by the open conflict of the early 1990s. By 2001 the total population was estimated to be 143,000, according to official sources, approximately one-half of whom resided in urban areas. The population consisted almost entirely of ethnic Armenians. There were also small numbers of Russians in the region, as well as Ukrainians, Belarusians, Greeks, Tatars and Georgians. The capital and chief town is Stepanakert (formerly Khankendi), with the other major towns being Mardakert, Martuni, Shushi, Askeran and Hadrut.

The Armenian principalities of Artsakh acknowledged Persian (Iranian) pre-eminence during the Middle Ages. Nagornyi Karabakh came under formal Russian control in the first decades of the 19th century, with the 1813 treaty between Russia and Persia being signed near the Karabakh village of Gulistan. The collapse of the Russian Empire with the revolutions of 1917 provoked Turkish intervention in Transcaucasia, to the detriment of the Armenian population, which suffered considerable loss of life in 1918–20. With the establishment of Bolshevik power, the Soviet Bureau of Transcaucasian Affairs (Kavburo) advised on the status of the autonomous protectorate. It recommended the union of Nagornyi Karabakh with the Soviet Republic of Armenia, but Stalin (Iosif V. Dzhugashvili) reversed the decision and the enclave formally came under the jurisdiction of Azerbaijan on 5 July 1921, with Shushi as its first capital. The borders of Soviet Transcaucasia and the status of Nagornyi Karabakh and Nakhichevan as territories of Azerbaijan were guaranteed by treaty with Turkey, at Kars, in October. Nagornyi Karabakh secured a distinct status within Azerbaijan when it was declared an autonomous oblast (region) in 1923.

The Soviet state did not tolerate open discontent, although there were appeals to the all-Union authorities to permit the union of Nagornyi Karabakh with Armenia in 1945, 1966 and 1977. There were also periods of ethnic tension, notably in 1967–68. From the mid-1980s, with a reformist Soviet leadership in power, the pressure to re-examine the status of Nagornyi Karabakh increased. However, the authorities persisted in their refusal to address the issue. This resulted in large-scale demonstrations by Armenians in Nagornyi Karabakh and violence between ethnic Armenian and Azerbaijani villages in the enclave. In February 1988 the Nagornyi Karabakh Soviet (council) passed a resolution demanding a transfer to Armenian jurisdiction, provoking anti-Armenian riots in Azerbaijan and much violence. Continued Armenian lobbying and unrest elicited a reaction from ethnic Azeris, with protests and rallies spreading to Kirovabad and other towns in November—in that month alone 14,000 ethnic Armenians fled Azerbaijan. Similar tensions and violence caused some 80,000 Azeris to leave Armenia in the same period. Many of these migrations were the result of forcible deportations.

On 12 January 1989 the Oblast's authorities were suspended and the region was placed under the jurisdiction of a Special Administrative Committee (SAC), responsible to the all-Union Council of Ministers. The imposition of direct rule, however, did little to alleviate tensions. Widespread public discontent forced the Azerbaijani authorities to recognize the nationalist opposition movement and to declare the sovereignty of the republic. In September they imposed an economic blockade of Armenia. In November the SAC was replaced by a republican Organizing Committee, mainly consisting of Azeris. This provoked the Armenian Supreme Soviet to declare on 1 December that the enclave was part of a 'unified Armenian republic'—the economic blockade was reimposed and there was violence in Nagornyi Karabakh and on the Armenian–Azerbaijani border. In January 1990 the all-Union Supreme Soviet deemed the Armenian declaration of December 1989 to be unconstitutional, but the Armenian legislature declared the primacy of its own legislation. In August 1990 the Azerbaijani legislature resolved to abolish the autonomous status of Nagornyi Karabakh.

In early 1991 a state of emergency was imposed in Nagornyi Karabakh, but Soviet troops failed to contain the increasing violence. There were also allegations of these troops aiding Azerbaijani attempts to expel ethnic Armenians from border areas. Meanwhile, in July the increasing activity of ethnic Armenian paramilitary units led the Soviet leader, Mikhail Gorbachev, to insist on their disarmament. However, by the end of the year, following the formation of the Commonwealth of Independent States (CIS) and Gorbachev's resignation, the USSR had ceased to exist. Despite Russian and Kazakhstani efforts to mediate an agreement (the initiative foundered after an aircraft carrying Azerbaijani and Russian negotiators crashed or was shot down), nationalist activism and violence continued to escalate. Moreover, with Azerbaijan moving towards claiming independence, a joint session of the Supreme Soviet of the Nagorno-Karabakh Autonomous Oblast and the district soviet of Shaumyan declared a 'Republic of Nagornyi Karabakh' on 2 September. In December a referendum indicated overwhelming support for independence and, following a general election on 28 December, a new 'parliament' formally proclaimed the independence of the Republic of Nagornyi Karabakh on 6 January 1992. The polity gained no international recognition, even from Armenia, which also renounced any territorial claims against Azerbaijan in March and denied that it had any control over the Nagornyi Karabakh Self-Defence Forces.

By 1992 sporadic clashes had developed into full-scale conflict. Stepanakert was, effectively, under siege by Azerbaijani forces and Shusha by Armenian paramilitaries. In January the President of Azerbaijan, Ayaz Mutalibov, placed the region under direct presidential rule and the Conference on Security and Co-operation in Europe (CSCE, later the Organization for Security and Co-operation in Europe—OSCE) began attempts to mediate a solution to the conflict. The following month the Nagornyi Karabakh Self-Defence Forces attacked the town of Khojali, defeating Azerbaijani troops and killing many civilians. The militia continued to gain territory, in May seizing control of the towns of Shusha (thus ending the bombardment of Stepanakert) and, in Azerbaijan proper, of Lachin. By the end of the month, when a short-lived cease-fire was negotiated, the Karabakh military was in control of the whole enclave and of a 'corridor' across the Lachin valley to Armenia.

There was a massive counter-offensive by Azerbaijani forces in June–October 1992, resulting in the exodus of several thousand people. In August the Nagornyi Karabakh legislature declared a state of martial law, with a State Defence Committee replacing the enclave's government. Its Chairman was Robert Kocharian, a member of the ruling faction, closely linked to the party of President Levon Ter-Petrossian of Armenia. Meanwhile, despite the latter's constant disclaimers of direct involvement, Armenian help was certainly important in resisting Azerbaijani attempts to close the Lachin corridor. However, in mid-1992 government forces did reoccupy almost one-half of the territory of the Republic of Nagornyi Karabakh, mainly in the north. This, in turn, led the Armenians to accuse Azerbaijan of receiving covert assistance from Turkey. Other sources attributed Azerbaijani success to improved morale after the *de facto* coup of the nationalists and the election of their leader, Abulfaz Elchibey, as President in June. Furthermore, the new commander and presidential plenipotentiary in Karabakh, Col Surat Husseinov, could bolster the regular army with forces equipped at his own expense.

In 1993 the Azerbaijani forces again lost ground, weakened by domestic political divisions. In early February Husseinov withdrew his forces from the occupied northern Karabakh town of Mardakert to Gyanja, for reasons that remain unclear. Certainly the move provided the Self-Defence Forces of Nagornyi Karabakh with the opportunity to embark on their own counter-offensive. By March they were occupying Azerbaijani territory outside the borders of the enclave, to the south (Fizuli) and to the west (Kelbajar). The Nagornyi Karabakh militias continued to make advances, seizing Agdam in July and Fizuli in August. Although they made no permanent claim on territory outside the existing borders, and withdrew from some villages in Kubatly, by October the ethnic Armenian forces had reached the Iranian border. By this time, the forces of Nagornyi Karabakh, in establishing their 'buffer zone', had occupied about one-fifth of Azerbaijani territory.

These advances caused widespread international concern. The UN passed Resolution 822 on 30 April 1993 (demanding an immediate cease-fire and the withdrawal of Armenian units from Azerbaijani territory), Resolution 853 on 29 July (condemning all hostilities and reiterating the demand for withdrawal, notably from Agdam), and Resolution 874 on 14 October (endorsing a CSCE schedule for the implementation of Resolutions 822 and 853). This last resolution also acknowledged the Karabakh Armenians as a separate party in the conflict, although the Azerbaijan and Nagornyi Karabakh leaderships had had their first direct negotiations in August. The weight of international opinion also encouraged Armenia to urge moderation on the Nagornyi Karabakh leadership. Continuing efforts by the CSCE, led by the 'Minsk Group' of interested parties, and a parallel initiative by Russia culminated in an agreement known as the Bishkek Declaration, signed in Kyrgyzstan on 5 May 1994. A cease-fire came into effect one week later and the agreement was formalized by the military authorities on 27 July. A political solution remained elusive, but the cease-fire, by and large, persisted. Prisoner-of-war exchanges took place in May 1995. By mid-1998 continuing OSCE efforts to mediate a settlement had caused the fall of President Ter-Petrossian and the accession of a less compromising Government in Armenia. This administration supported the Karabakh preference for a 'package' peace settlement, one which would not require Nagornyi Karabakh to relinquish its military advantages and security guarantees in advance of resolving the issue of its status. However, negotiations subsequently stalled, despite intensive international mediation.

Meanwhile, in April–June 1995 elections were held to the republican legislature, which was renamed the Azgayin Zhogov (National Assembly) in March 1996 and consisted of 33 members. This body renewed the state of martial law and instituted an executive presidency, to which post Kocharian was elected by parliament on 22 December 1995. On 24 November 1996 Kocharian secured an electoral mandate for remaining in the presidency, obtaining some 86% of the votes cast. On 20 March 1997, however, Kocharian was appointed Prime Minister of Armenia (he was elected President of Armenia on 30 March 1998). Arkadii Ghukassian was elected as the new President of Nagornyi Karabakh on 1 September 1997, with 89.3% of the votes cast. On 22 March 2000 Ghukassian was seriously wounded by gunmen in Stepanakert. The former republican Minister of Defence, Samuel Babaian, was subsequently charged with organizing the attack, in an attempt to carry out a *coup d'état*; he was sentenced to 14 years' imprisonment in February 2001. New parliamentary elections were held on 18 June 2000, at which the participation rate was 59.7%. On 11 August 2002 a presidential election took place; Ghukassian was re-elected to the presidency, with 88.4% of the votes cast. The rate of voter participation was some 75%.

The worst border skirmishes for several years were reported in mid-2003, prompting fears of a resumption of the conflict, particularly given uncertainties over the political continuity of Azerbaijan's leadership in the months preceding the presidential election scheduled for October; however, both sides sought to avoid renewed military activity, and it was anticipated that negotiations towards a peace settlement would resume following the presidential election.

# Directory

## The Government

**President:** Arkadii Ghukassian (elected by popular vote on 1 September 1997; re-elected 11 August 2002).

### Ministers
(October 2003)

**Prime Minister:** Anushavan Danielian.

**Deputy Prime Minister and Minister of Industrial Infrastructure and Urban Development:** Juri Gazarian.

**Deputy Prime Minister and Minister of Agriculture:** Benik Bakhshian.

**Minister of Health:** Zoya Lazarian.

**Minister of Foreign Affairs:** Ashot Ghulian.

**Minister of Internal Affairs:** Armen Isagulov.

**Minister of Defence:** Seyran Ohanian.

**Minister of Social Welfare:** Lenston Ghulian.

**Minister of Finance and Economy:** Spartak Tevosian.

**Minister of Education, Culture and Sport:** Armen Sarkisian.

**Minister of the Treasury:** Spartak Tevosian.

**Chief of Staff of the Government:** Souren Grigorian.

The Heads of the State Departments are: Robert Hayrapetian (Justice); Bako Sahakian (National Security); and Hakop Garamanian (Tax).

### Ministries

All Ministries and State Departments are located in Stepanakert.

**Office of the President:** Stepanakert, 20 February St 3; tel. and fax (1) 45-222; e-mail ps@president.nkr.am; internet www.president.nkr.am.

**Ministry of Foreign Affairs:** Stepanakert; tel. and fax (1) 71-551; e-mail info@mfa.nk.am; internet nkr.am.

## President and Legislature

### President of the Republic

**Presidential Election, 11 August 2002**

| Candidates | % of votes |
|---|---|
| Arkadii Ghukassian. | 88.4 |
| Artur Tovmassian | 8.2 |
| Albert Ghazarian | 2.1 |
| Grigorii Afanasian | 1.3 |
| Total | 100.0 |

### Azgayin Zhogov
(National Assembly)

**Chairman:** Oleg Yesayevich Yesaian.

**Deputy Chairman:** Moushegh Grigoryevich Ohanjanian.

There are 33 members of the Azgayin Zhogov, which was elected in June 2000.

## Local Government

The Nagorno-Karabakh Autonomous Oblast consisted of five districts (Askeran, Hadrut, Mardakert, Martuni and Shushi) and the city of Stepanakert. The Republic of Nagornyi Karabakh, as originally constituted, also included the district of Shaumyan. A new law on local government was enacted in January 1998.

**Mayor of Stepanakert:** Amik Avanesian.

## Political Organizations

Political organizations in Nagornyi Karabakh include: the Armenian Revolutionary Federation—Dashnaktsutyun, the Communist Party of Nagornyi Karabakh, Helsinki Initiative-92, the Popular Front of Artsakh, the Union of Greens of the Nagorno-Karabakh Republic and Veratsnoond—Revival Party.

# Bibliography

Chorbajian, Levon (Ed.). *The Making of Nagorno-Karabakh*. London, Palgrave, 2001.

Chorbajian, Levon, Donabedian, Patrick, and Mutafian, Claude. *The Caucasian Knot: The History and Geopolitics of Nagorno-Karabagh*. London, Zed Books, 1994.

Coppieters, Bruno (Ed.). *Contested Borders in the Caucasus*. Brussels, Vubpress, 1996.

Cox, C. *Ethnic Cleansing in Progress: War in Nagorno-Karabakh*. Zurich, Institute for Religious Minorities in the Islamic World, 1993.

Croissant, Michael P. *The Armenia-Azerbaijan Conflict*. Westport, CT, Praeger, 1998.

Fawcett, L. *Iran and the Cold War: The Azerbaijan Crisis of 1946*. Cambridge, Cambridge University Press, 1992.

Goldenburg, Susan. *The Caucasus and Post Soviet Disorder*. London, Zed Books, 1995.

Martin, Robert J. *The Economy and Foreign Relations of Azerbaijan*. London, Royal Institute of International Affairs, 1996.

Swietochowski, Tadeusz. *Russian Azerbaijan 1905–1920: The Shaping of National Identity in a Muslim Community*. Cambridge, Cambridge University Press, 1985.

Van Der Leeuw, Charles. *Azerbaijan: A Quest for Identity*. Richmond, Curzon, 1999.

de Waal, Thomas. *Black Garden: Armenia and Azerbaijan Through Peace and War*. New York, NY, and London, New York University Press, 2003.

Walker, C. (Ed.). *Armenia and Karabagh: The Struggle for Unity*. London, Minority Rights Publs, 1991.

Willerton, J. *Patronage and Politics in the USSR*. Cambridge, Cambridge University Press, 1992.

Also see the Select Bibliography in Part Four.

# BELARUS

## Geography

### PHYSICAL FEATURES

The Republic of Belarus (also known as Belorussia or Byelorussia and, formerly, the Byelorussian Soviet Socialist Republic, part of the USSR) is situated in north-eastern Europe. Historically, it was also known as White Russia or White Ruthenia. It is bounded by Latvia and Lithuania to the north-west, by Poland to the west, by Ukraine to the south and by Russia to the east. It covers an area of 207,595 sq km (80,153 sq miles).

The land is a plain with numerous lakes, swamps and marshes. There is an area of low hill country north of Minsk (Miensk), but the highest point, Mount Dzierżynski, is only 346 m (1,135 feet) above sea-level. The southern part of the country is a low, flat marshland. Forests covered some 34% of the territory in 1994, according to estimates by the UN's Food and Agriculture Organization (FAO). The main rivers are the Dnepr (Dnieper), which flows south to the Black Sea, and the Pripyat or Prypiać (Pripet), which flows eastwards, to the Dnepr, through a forested, swampy area, known as the Pripyat Marshes.

### CLIMATE

The climate is of a continental type, with an average January temperature, in Minsk, of –5°C (23°F) and an average for July of 19°C (67°F). Average annual precipitation is between 560 mm and 660 mm.

### POPULATION

Of a total population, at the 1999 census, of 10,045,237, 81% were ethnic Belarusians, 11% Russians, 4% Poles and 2% Ukrainians. There were also small numbers of Jews, Tatars, Roma (Gypsies), Lithuanians and other ethnic groups. From 1990 the official language of the republic was Belarusian, an Eastern Slavonic language written in the Cyrillic script (there is also a Belarusian version of the Latin alphabet). This, and the long domination of the area by Russia, complicates the naming and transliteration of places and people. Russified versions of names are often the most familiar, even in Belarus. Following a referendum in May 1995, Russian was reinstated as an official language. At the 1999 census, only 37% of Belarusians spoke Belarusian as their first language, and the remainder spoke Russian, although a far greater percentage regarded Belarusian to be their native language.

The major religion is Christianity, the Eastern Orthodox Church and the Roman Catholic Church being the largest denominations. There are also small Muslim and Jewish communities.

At 1 January 2002 the estimated total population was 9,899,000, giving a density of 47.7 people per sq km. In that year 71.1% of the population lived in urban areas. The capital is Minsk, which is situated in the centre of the country. Minsk was also declared to be the headquarters of the Commonwealth of Independent States (CIS). Official estimates indicated that it had a population of 1,699,100 on 1 January 2001. Other important towns are Gomel (Homiel—with an estimated population of 480,000 at January 2001), in the south-east of the country, Mogilev (Mahiloŭ, 360,600), near the eastern border with Russia, Vitebsk (Viciebsk, 341,500), in the north-east, and, near the border with Poland, Grodno (Horadnia, 307,100) and Brest (Bieraście—formerly Brest-Litovsk—291,400), in the south-west.

## Chronology

**c. 878:** Kievan Rus, the first unified state of the Eastern Slavs, was founded, with Kiev (Kyiv, now in Ukraine) as its capital.

**c. 988:** Vladimir, ruler of Kievan Rus, converted to Orthodox Christianity.

**10th century:** The principality of Polotsk (Polatsak or Połacak) became the main centre of power on Belarusian territory, rivalling Kiev and Novgorod for predominance within Rus.

**1054:** The death of Yaroslav I ('the Wise') signalled the dissolution of the Kievan state into rival principalities, the main ones in Belarus being those of Polotsk and Turov (Turau).

**1240–63:** Rule of Mindaugas (Mindouh), in Novogrudok (Navahradak), who formed the Grand Duchy of Lithuania (Litva) and Rus. His state covered the western territories of Rus, including Minsk (Miensk), Vitebsk (Viciebsk) and Polotsk, and eastern Lithuania. Orthodox Slavs predominated in the state and a precursor of Belarusian was the official language. The capital was later moved to Vilnius.

**1386:** Marriage of Jagiełło (Jahaila; baptized Władysław in 1386) of Lithuania and Jadwiga (Hedwig) of Poland established the union of the two states; subsequent treaties ensured Litva and Rus remained an autonomous Grand Duchy under Poland.

**1569:** The Grand Duchy of Litva, Rus and Samogitia (the latter—the 'lowlands', in western Lithuania—having been added in the 15th century) surrendered its separate status by the Union of Lublin, as part of an attempt to strengthen the Jagiellonian Polish-Lithuanian state, which was threatened by Sweden, the Ottoman Turks and the Russians.

**1596:** The Union of Brest ('Lithuanian' Brest or Brest-Litovsk) secured the allegiance of part of the Eastern Orthodox Church for the Pope, the head of the Roman Catholic Church; the creation of this 'Greek Catholic' or Uniate Church was part of a process of attempting to catholicize the confessionally mixed Polish state.

**1696:** Old Belarusian was replaced by Polish as the language of official documentation in the Grand Duchy.

**1772:** Parts of Belarus were incorporated into the Russian Empire (the ruler of which had been proclaimed 'Tsar of all the Russias' in 1721) at the First Partition of Poland.

**1793:** Second Partition of Poland; acquisition by Russia of the rest of Belarus.

**1839–40:** The tsarist authorities intensified russification in the North-Western Territories, as Belarusian lands were known: the Uniate Church was disbanded and the terms Belarus and Belarusian were banned.

**1861:** Emancipation of the serfs throughout the Russian Empire.

**1902:** The Belarusian Revolutionary (later Socialist) Hramada was founded; it became the leading Belarusian nationalist organization.

**1 August 1914:** Russia entered the First World War against Germany, Turkey and Austria-Hungary (the Central Powers); the tsarist military headquarters (Stavka) was based in Mogilev (Mahilioŭ); from 1915 western Belarus was occupied by the Germans.

**2 March (New Style 15 March) 1917:** Abdication of Tsar Nicholas II after demonstrations and strikes in Petrograd (St Petersburg), the imperial capital.

**5 August (18 August) 1917:** A Rada (Council) was proclaimed in Belarus, following the assembly of a 'national council' in the previous month; the Rada was predominantly Socialist Revolutionary in nature, aiming for an autonomous republic under the Petrograd Provisional Government.

**15 November (28 November) 1917:** Bolshevik troops arrived in Minsk from Petrograd, where Lenin (Vladimir Ilych Ulyanov) and his Bolshevik allies had assumed power; the Bolsheviks took control of the city against little resistance.

**28 December 1917 (10 January 1918):** An All-Belarusian Congress proclaimed Belarus a democratic republic and refused to recognize Bolshevik power on Belarusian territory; the Bolsheviks disbanded the Congress, but it elected a Rada, which continued to work in secret.

**14 February (Old Style 1 February) 1918:** First day upon which the Gregorian Calendar took effect in the Bolshevik territories.

**21 February 1918:** Bolshevik troops were forced to withdraw, as German forces occupied Minsk.

**3 March 1918:** By the Treaty of Brest-Litovsk, Soviet Russia ceded much territory to Germany, including Belarus, and recognized Ukrainian independence.

**25 March 1918:** The Belarusian Rada declared the independence of the state, as the Belarusian National Republic, but it only achieved limited autonomy under German military rule.

**23 December 1918:** Following the collapse of German power, the Russian communist leadership decided a Soviet Socialist Republic (SSR) should be established in the largely reoccupied Belarus.

**1 January 1919:** Proclamation of an independent Belarusian SSR, despite sentiments in Russia for the absorption of the territory.

**February 1919:** The Bolsheviks replaced the Belarusian SSR with a short-lived Lithuanian-Belarusian SSR ('Litbel'—in recognition of their common history).

**March 1919:** Polish armies invaded Belarus (declared part of Poland), Lithuania and Ukraine.

**11 July 1920:** Soviet troops recaptured Minsk, after more than one year of civil war and war with Poland; the following day, by the Treaty of Moscow, the Soviet regime recognized Lithuanian independence and subsequently ceded some Belarusian territory; the Belarusian SSR was re-established in the following month.

**16 January 1921:** Soviet Russia recognized the Belarusian SSR and signed an alliance with the nominally independent state.

**18 March 1921:** Poland retained about one-third of Belarus, in the west, by the Treaty of Rīga, which formally concluded the Soviet–Polish War.

**30 December 1922:** Four Soviet 'Union Republics' proclaimed the Union of Soviet Socialist Republics (USSR), of which the Belarusian SSR was a constituent and nominally independent member, despite a union with Russia being urged by Stalin (Iosif V. Dzhugashvili).

**1924:** The Belarusian SSR was virtually doubled in size when the territories of Vitebsk and Mogilev were formally transferred from Russian jurisdiction.

**October 1926:** Gomel (Homiel) was transferred from Russia to the Belarusian SSR.

**1933:** The Soviet Government claimed to discover a 'Belarusian National Centre', sponsored by Poland, which was the excuse for mass arrests of Belarusian officials and party members; furthermore, the peasantry were enduring much hardship during the forcible collectivization of agriculture.

**September 1939:** The Soviet army occupied western Belarus (Polish since 1921), in accordance with the Treaty of Non-Aggression with Germany (the Nazi-Soviet Pact), signed in August.

**3 November 1939:** The communists ensured that the new territories (which increased the Belarusian SSR by one-half in area) voted for incorporation into the USSR.

**22 June 1941:** The Germans violated the Nazi-Soviet Pact by invading the USSR in 'Operation Barbarossa'; according to the plans of the German leader, Adolf Hitler, Belarus was marked for ethnic German settlement (Ostland) and the expulsion of natives.

**28 June 1941:** Minsk was occupied by German forces; a 'puppet' regime under Ivan Yermachenko was subsequently established, although the Germans also encountered partisan resistance.

**December 1943:** At an Allied conference in Tehran, Iran, the USSR insisted that it should not only have all of Belarus and Ukraine, but its western border should be along the Oder (Odra) river.

**4 July 1944:** Soviet troops recaptured Minsk; during the war about one-quarter of the population of Belarus died (pre-1941 population levels were not regained until 1970) and massive damage was done throughout the republic.

**26 June 1945:** The USSR, the USA, the United Kingdom, China and 46 other countries, including the Belarusian and Ukrainian SSRs, in their own right, signed the Charter of the UN.

**1946–48:** A mass purge of the Communist Party of Belarus (CPB) resulted in the replacement of many ethnic Belarusian officials by Russians.

**October 1980:** Piotr Masherau, First Secretary of the CPB since 1965, was killed in suspicious circumstances, apparently after an argument with Leonid Brezhnev, General Secretary of the all-Union Communist Party.

**April 1986:** An explosion occurred at a nuclear reactor in Chornobyl (Chernobyl), Ukraine, 10 km south of the Belarusian border, which resulted in discharges of radioactive material; much of the 30-km exclusion zone around the disaster site was in Belarusian territory and over 20% of the republic was severely affected.

**30 October 1988:** A demonstration in Minsk to commemorate the victims of Stalinism (partly prompted by the discovery of mass graves at Kurapaty, near Minsk) was violently dispersed by security forces.

**June 1989:** The Belarusian Popular Front (BPF) held its inaugural congress in Vilnius, Lithuania. In February 1990 a BPF rally in Minsk was attended by some 150,000 protesters, demanding extra funds to deal with the consequences of the Chernobyl disaster.

**28 January 1990:** The Supreme Soviet (Supreme Council) enacted a law replacing Russian as the official language with Belarusian.

**4 March 1990:** For the elections to the republican Supreme Council, the BPF was obliged to join the Belarusian Democratic Bloc; although the Bloc won about one-quarter of the seats decided by popular ballot, the CPB still controlled some 84% of the total number of seats in the legislature.

**27 July 1990:** The Supreme Council, after increasing popular pressure, declared the state sovereignty of Belarus (claiming the right to form its own armed forces, issue its own currency and conduct its own foreign policy), but rejected the possibility of secession.

**17 March 1991:** In the all-Union referendum on the future of the USSR, 83% voted for a reformed Soviet federation, the highest proportion in any republic outside Central Asia.

**25 August 1991:** Following the collapse of the attempted coup in Moscow, Russia (the Soviet capital), the Supreme Council of Belarus adopted a declaration of independence; the communist leadership resigned and the CPB was suspended.

**19 September 1991:** Formal election of Stanislau Shushkevich, a physicist with a reputation as a reformist, as Chairman of the Supreme Council (Head of State), replacing Nikolai Dementei (Mikalai Dzemyantsei); the name of the state was changed to the Republic of Belarus.

**8 December 1991:** The leaders of Belarus, Russia and Ukraine met near Brest and agreed to form a Commonwealth of Independent States (CIS) to replace the USSR; the headquarters of the organization was to be in Minsk. On 21 December the leaders of 11 Soviet republics, including Belarus, signed a protocol, the Almaty (Alma-Ata) Declaration, on the formation of the CIS.

**20–22 July 1992:** A series of agreements between Belarus and Russia advocated increased co-operation and seemed to envisage some sort of confederation. The USA agreed to provide Belarus with US $59m., in order to assist with the removal of its nuclear weapons to Russia. The last remaining nuclear warhead was removed from Belarus on 26 November 1996.

**29 October 1992:** The Supreme Council rejected a petition, signed by 383,000 people, in support of the BPF's demand for new parliamentary elections.

**3 February 1993:** The Supreme Council approved adherence to the Treaty on the Non-Proliferation of Nuclear Weapons and ratified the first Strategic Arms Reduction Treaty (START 1). The following day the Supreme Council voted to end the suspension of the CPB, which had been in force since August 1991.

**26 January 1994:** Shushkevich, who had been in conflict with the conservative parliament for some time, also lost reformist support and was dismissed from office. Vyacheslau Kuznetsou, the First Deputy Chairman of the Supreme Council, became acting Head of State.

**28 January 1994:** Mechislau Gryb (Myacheslau Hryb), a pro-Russian conservative, was elected the new Chairman of the Supreme Council.

**15 March 1994:** The Supreme Council approved a new Constitution; it was formally adopted on 28 March and came into effect on 30 March.

**10 July 1994:** In the second round of voting in the presidential election (the first round was on 23 June) Alyaksandr Lukashenka, the head of the Supreme Council's anti-corruption committee and a conservative supporter of closer integration with Russia, received 85% of the votes cast. He was inaugurated as the first President of Belarus on 20 July.

**January 1995:** Belarus joined the 'Partnership for Peace' programme of military co-operation of the North Atlantic Treaty Organization (NATO).

**14 May 1995:** The results of a referendum enhanced presidential authority, restored Russian as an official language and approved a change to the state symbols and closer integration with Russia. The first round of parliamentary elections was held.

**28 May 1995:** After a second round of elections, only 119 deputies had been elected to the 260-member Supreme Council. Another two rounds of voting, on 29 November and 10 December, brought the total number of new deputies to a quorate 198; the CPB obtained the largest number of seats, followed by the Agrarian Party (AP), the United Civic Party of Belarus (UCP) and the Party of People's Accord.

**2 April 1996:** Despite nationalist protests, President Lukashenka and the Russian President, Boris Yeltsin, signed a Treaty on the Formation of a Community of Sovereign Republics, which expressed the intention of closer integration and eventual confederation; opposition rallies were dispersed by police, provoking accusations of brutality.

**9 August 1996:** President Lukashenka formally proposed a referendum on constitutional amendments to enhance his powers and increase his term of office (to 2001), after an increasing number of confrontations with parliament (the Constitutional Court ruled that the results of such a referendum were not legally binding, but the President revoked this decision by decree).

**18 November 1996:** Mikhail Chigir, who had been Lukashenka's first premier, was replaced by Syargey Ling, owing to his criticism of the President with regard to the referendum.

**24 November 1996:** Voting in the referendum on changes to the Constitution, despite drafts of the amendments being unavailable to the public and reports of widespread irregularities, indicated substantial support for the President; the impeachment proceedings against Lukashenka initiated by 75 parliamentary deputies were, therefore, halted.

**27 November 1996:** The amended Constitution was published and came into immediate effect; it provided for a bicameral National Assembly, the lower house of which, a 110-member House of Representatives, was established the previous day by the majority in the old Supreme Council. Fifty deputies denounced the referendum results and declared themselves the legitimate legislature; the Chairman of the Constitutional Court, Valery Tsikhinya, and several other judges subsequently resigned in protest at the imposition of the constitutional changes.

**13 December 1996:** The President approved legislation inaugurating the new upper house of parliament, the 64-

member Council of the Republic, consisting of regional representatives and presidential appointees.

**8 January 1997:** The deputies of a continuing 'Supreme Council' formed a 'shadow' cabinet, the Public Coalition Government—National Economic Council, chaired by Genadz Karpenka.

**2 April 1997:** Presidents Lukashenka and Yeltsin signed the Treaty of Union between Belarus and Russia and initialled the Charter of the Union; anti-Union demonstrations were suppressed by the security forces.

**29 July 1997:** Negotiations between representatives of the new and old legislatures, continued from June, collapsed, following disagreement over which Constitution (the 1994 version or the 1996 version) was to form the basis of the discussions.

**10 November 1997:** The BPF initiated a petition campaign, known as Charter-97 (Khartyya-97), with the aim of forcing new elections.

**2 April 1998:** On the anniversary of the Treaty of Union with Russia, anti-Government protestors disrupted celebrations with an unauthorized demonstration.

**22–29 June 1998:** Bulgaria, France, Germany, Greece, Italy, Japan, Poland, the United Kingdom and the USA withdrew their ambassadors from Belarus, in protest at the breach of international law involved in the effective eviction of the staff of 22 embassies housed in a residential compound outside Minsk. Subsequently, the European Union (EU) and the USA banned President Lukashenka and his ministers from entering their territory. In December Lukashenka gave assurances that, henceforth, he would comply with international agreements. (All ambassadors had returned to Minsk by September 1999.).

**2 November 1998:** The Parliamentary Assembly of the Russia-Belarus Union voted for the creation of a unified parliament, to consist of two chambers.

**15 December 1998:** A new law was approved by the House of Representatives, effectively banning candidates with a police record or fine from standing in local elections to be held in April 1999. Numerous opposition candidates who had incurred fines for participating in anti-Government demonstrations were, thus, excluded.

**10 January 1999:** The Central Electoral Commission of the former Supreme Council called a presidential election to be held in May, in accordance with the 1994 Constitution. Despite the arrest of its Chairman, Viktar Ganchar, the Commission registered two candidates, the exiled leader of the BPF, Zyanon Paznyak, and the former premier, Mikhail Chigir.

**27 January 1999:** President Lukashenka decreed that political parties, trade unions and other organizations must re-register by July; those failing to do so were to be disbanded. By September only 17 of the 28 existing official parties had been re-registered, owing to the imposition of stringent minimum levels of membership.

**6 April 1999:** The Chairman of the Public Coalition Government–National Economic Council, Genadz Karpenka, died. He was replaced on 21 April by Mechislau Gryb, who was officially elected to the post in November.

**6–16 May 1999:** The Central Electoral Commission of the former Supreme Council was unable to organize fixed polling stations for the presidential election, which neither the Government nor the international community recognized as valid.

**20 July 1999:** President Lukashenka did not stand down at the end of his five-year term, in contravention of the nullified 1994 Constitution. The following day over 2,000 people gathered in Minsk to protest at President Lukashenka's 'il-legitimate rule', leading to clashes with police and numerous arrests.

**22 July 1999:** Syamyon Sharetski, the leader of the AP and the former Chairman of the Supreme Council, fled to Lithuania to seek support, following his election as acting Head of State by the former Supreme Council.

**September 1999:** Nine independent newspapers were closed down by the Government, amid a climate of increased government control and the 'disappearances' of several opposition figures, including Viktar Ganchar, from May.

**26 September 1999:** Following an inconclusive leadership vote in July, members of the BPF formed a breakaway faction, known as the Conservative Christian Party of the BPF, with Paznyak as Chairman. Vintsuk Vyachorka was elected Chairman of the BPF in late October.

**17 October 1999:** Up to 20,000 demonstrators participated in an anti-Government Freedom March. Leading opposition officials were among the 90 protesters arrested.

**8 December 1999:** A Union Treaty was signed between Russia and Belarus which, ultimately, intended to merge the two countries.

**18 February 2000:** Syargey Ling resigned as Prime Minister. Parliament subsequently approved Uladzimir Yermoshin, hitherto the Governor of Minsk City, as his replacement.

**15 March 2000:** Up to 25,000 people took part in a second Freedom March in Minsk. Ten days later a demonstration in Minsk to mark the 82nd anniversary of the proclamation of the Belarusian National Republic was prevented from taking place, and up to 300 people were detained, attracting international criticism of what was deemed to be excessive police force. Despite the cancellation of the demonstration, up to 10,000 people gathered on the outskirts of the city.

**25 April 2000:** The joint Council of Ministers of Belarus and the Russian Federation met for the first time.

**19 May 2000:** The former premier, Mikhail Chigir, was convicted of abuse of office and received a three-year suspended prison sentence. The verdict, which was condemned as politically motivated by the international community, was overturned by the Supreme Court in December, pending a reinvestigation of the evidence, on the grounds that there had been legal irregularities during the trial.

**15 and 29 October 2000:** Despite a large anti-election rally and boycotts by a number of opposition parties, elections to the National Assembly were held. The Organization for Security and Co-operation in Europe (OSCE) declared the elections to be neither free, fair, nor open and the international community refused to recognize the results. After a second round of voting, 56 seats remained to be allocated, and further elections were scheduled for 18 March 2001.

**27 December 2000:** The Government and the central bank announced that the value of the Belarusian rouble would be linked to that of the Russian rouble, through a maximum permitted monthly devaluation of 3% (subsequently to be reduced to 2.5%), from January 2001, in order to facilitate the proposed full currency union between the two countries from 2008.

**1 January 2001:** A new, purportedly more liberal, criminal code was introduced.

**9 September 2001:** A presidential election was held; Lukashenka was re-elected, claiming 76% of the votes cast. However, international observers reported that the election was subject to serious irregularities, and the USA refused to recognize the results. Lukashenka was sworn in for a second term of office on 20 September; he appointed a new premier, Genadz Navitsky, on 1 October.

**22 December 2001:** Uladzimir Gancharyk, who had been the second-placed candidate in the presidential election, resigned as Chairman of the Federation of Trade Unions of Belarus, following government pressure.

**23 July 2002:** The former Prime Minister, Mikhail Chigir, was awarded a three-year, suspended prison sentence, following his trial on charges of tax evasion. (In March his son, Alyaksandr Chigir, had been sentenced to seven years in prison, after allegations of theft.) Chigir denounced both trials as politically motivated.

**14 August 2002:** At negotiations in Moscow, between Presidents Lukashenka and Putin, the latter proposed dramatic changes to the two countries' proposed Union, suggesting the creation of a unified, federal state, with common parliamentary and presidential elections to be held in 2003–04, and the adoption of the Russian rouble as a common currency in January 2004. Lukashenka, however, rejected the proposals, which he considered to represent a threat to Belarusian sovereignty.

**24 September 2002:** The Parliamentary Assembly of the Council of Europe established a 10-member commission to investigate the disappearances of high-profile political figures in Belarus.

**2 October 2002:** The Council of the Republic approved by a substantial majority a new bill that would introduce new restrictions on the practice of minority religions. The law came into effect on 16 November.

**20 February 2003:** The Parliamentary Assembly of the OSCE finally recognized the legitimacy of the Belarusian National Council. The OSCE representative office, closed since late October 2002, owing to the denial of accreditation to its officials, had reopened in January 2003, after agreement on its operation was reached with the Government. Meanwhile, travel bans on senior Belarusian officials, imposed by EU countries and the USA in November 2002, were withdrawn in April 2003.

**2 March and 11–16 March 2003:** Local elections took place in two rounds, amid international criticism of electoral irregularities; the vast majority of seats were won by the communist parties.

**17 April 2003:** The UN Commission for Human Rights passed a resolution, which urged the Government to investigate the disappearances of opposition figures and the alleged implication of senior government officials in politically motivated executions.

**28 April 2003:** Representatives from Armenia, Belarus, Kazakhstan, Kyrgyzstan, Russia and Tajikistan formally inaugurated the successor to the Collective Security Treaty, a new regional defence organization known as the Collective Security Treaty Organization (CSTO).

**10 July 2003:** President Lukashenka dismissed a number of government officials, including Prime Minister Navitsky, Deputy Prime Minister Alyaksandr Papkow and the Minister of Agriculture and Food, Mikhail Rusy. The First Deputy Prime Minister, Syarhey Sidorsky, was appointed acting Prime Minister, Raman Unuchka became a Deputy Prime Minister, and Zyanon Lomats was appointed Minister of Agriculture and Food. Navitsky was subsequently appointed Chairman of the Council of the Republic. Further appointments to the Government were made on 6 August.

# History
## Dr ANDREW RYDER

### EARLY HISTORY

The area of present-day Belarus was inhabited by Slavs from at least the ninth century, and probably earlier. At the end of the 13th century a Grand Duchy of Lithuania (Litva) and Rus was formed from Belarusian and Lithuanian lands, in which Belarus constituted the core. The Grand Duchy, in which Old Belarusian was the state language, united with Poland in the 16th century. Belarusian lands remained under Polish control until the partitions of Poland in 1772–95, when they became part of the Russian Empire. In the 19th century there was a growth of national consciousness among Belarusian intellectuals, but attempts to assert a Belarusian national identity were strongly opposed by the tsarist authorities, which considered the Belarusian language to be merely a dialect of Russian and refused to accept the concept of a Belarusian nation. Belarus had a distinct culture, mainly preserved by the peasantry, and a distinct language. However, the national movement did not gather significant popular support.

### SOVIET BELARUS

#### Establishment

With the collapse of tsarist authority, in July 1917 a Belarusian national council, or Rada, was formed in Minsk (Miensk); this appeared to have been inspired by the example of Ukraine to the south, which had established a similar body in April. However, the declaration of a Belarusian republic on 28 December, by an All-Belarusian Congress, had no lasting significance. Bolshevik forces loyal to the newly established regime of Lenin (Vladimir Ilych Ulyanov) in Petrograd (St Petersburg—then the Russian capital) had seized power in Minsk in November. They dissolved the Congress at the end of December. Bolshevik troops only withdrew from Minsk when German forces occupied the city in February 1918. German occupation was formalized by the Treaty of Brest-Litovsk, signed by Germany and the Soviet regime in March, in the city of Brest (Bieraście). The Treaty ceded Russian control of a large swathe of western territory, running from the Baltic to the Black Sea, including Belarus. On 25 March Belarus again declared its independence, as the Belarusian National Republic (BNR), but it achieved only a limited measure of autonomy under German military rule.

After Germany's defeat at the end of 1918, the Treaty of Brest-Litovsk was abrogated and German troops began to withdraw. Meanwhile, the Bolshevik Government of the newly created Russian Soviet Federative Socialist Republic (RSFSR) in Moscow, the new capital, had changed its policy towards Belarus. The communist leadership had been unwilling to recognize the existence of a Belarusian nation and its right to self-determination, but it now seemed that it wanted to create a semi-independent socialist Belarusian republic, as one in a series of 'buffer' states separating Soviet Russia from Germany and Central Europe. Accordingly, Bolshevik troops entered Belarus as the Germans withdrew, and a Belarusian Soviet Socialist Republic (SSR) was proclaimed on 1 January 1919.

However, in mid-January 1919 the Russian Communist Party (Bolsheviks)—RCP(B)—urged that the new SSR, as well as other newly established Soviet republics, be absorbed by the RSFSR. This scheme was soon replaced by a proposal for a military union of the two. In March, however, the Belarusian SSR was merged with Lithuania, which was also then under communist control, to form a new SSR, known as 'Litbel'. The new republic lasted less than one month, before Polish troops invaded in April 1919, occupied most of its territory and declared Belarus part of Poland. Until 1921 control of Belarus passed back and forth between Soviet and Polish forces. Minsk was retaken by Soviet forces in July 1920 and one month later the Belarusian SSR was re-established. Finally, in March 1921, the Treaty of Rīga was signed, which allocated the western one-third of Belarusian lands to Poland, while in the east the Belarusian SSR was firmly established.

## Belarus in the USSR

The formal attributes of independence did not give Belarus control over its own affairs. The Government of the Belarusian SSR was controlled by the Communist Party of Belarus (CPB), which, in turn, was an integral part of the RCP(B). Government and state bodies of the RSFSR increasingly took over responsibility for Belarusian affairs. However, the Belarusian SSR was permitted to enter into diplomatic relations with other countries and to formulate and conclude its own treaties with other states. This ambiguous situation was resolved on 30 December 1922, when the Union of Soviet Socialist Republics (USSR) was proclaimed, with the Belarusian SSR as one of six founding members. Belarusian affairs were now largely controlled by the all-Union authorities in Moscow. Nevertheless, as a Union Republic, Belarus retained some formal vestiges of autonomy.

Initially, the Belarusian SSR embraced the area around Minsk and territories extending south to the border of Ukraine. Under Soviet rule, the borders of Belarus were expanded three times. In 1924 Vitebsk (Viciebsk) and Mogilev (Mahiloŭ) provinces were transferred from Russia to Belarus. In 1926 Gomel (Homiel) province was also transferred from Russia. In 1939 the area of the republic was substantially increased when western Belarus, under Polish control since 1921, was annexed by the USSR under the terms of the Nazi-Soviet Pact and made part of the Belarusian SSR.

Under Soviet rule, Belarus suffered severely. In the early 1930s, during the programme of forced collectivization, many peasants were killed or deported. During the 1930s political repression engulfed the entire republic, although intellectual and political leaders suffered disproportionately, with most of the Belarusian cultural and political elite executed or imprisoned. During the Second World War the SSR was occupied by German forces from 1941 until 1944. Up to 2.2m. people were estimated to have died in Belarus during the War, representing some 25% of the population. The republic did not reach its pre-1941 population level until 1970. As much as 80% of the republic's housing was damaged and much of its industrial capacity and transport system was destroyed. The war caused significant ethnic changes in Belarus. The large Jewish population was almost eradicated by the Germans, and many Poles left the newly incorporated region of western Belarus to live in Poland. Thus, post-war Belarus had a high proportion of Belarusians in the population, although large-scale immigration by ethnic Russians after 1945 undermined Belarusian dominance.

Despite the destruction during the Second World War and relatively late industrialization, the Belarusian SSR was one of the most prosperous regions of the USSR. By the early 1980s it also had one of the most illiberal leaderships of any Union Republic. Perhaps as a result, the policies of Mikhail Gorbachev, the Soviet leader from 1985, of *glasnost* (openness) and *perestroika* (restructuring), initially had little impact in Belarus. However, towards the end of the 1980s there were growing demands for the preservation of the Belarusian language, prompted by the continuing russification of the republic. In 1989 29.9% of Belarusians spoke only

Russian and, of the remaining number, over 50% spoke Russian fluently. No other nationality of republican status in the USSR had such a high proportion of nationals unable to speak their own language, or such a high proportion of nationals speaking Russian. The main reason for this was the predominance of the Russian language in the education system. In 1980 only 35% of all pupils in the SSR were taught in Belarusian; the rest were taught in Russian. By 1989 the proportion of pupils taught in Belarusian had declined to just 20.8% and, in the republic's major cities, there were no Belarusian-language schools at all.

In addition to the language issue, in April 1986 the Chornobyl (Chernobyl) disaster, caused by an explosion in a Ukrainian nuclear reactor just south of the border with Belarus, resulted in severe radiation 'fall-out' and increased activity by environmental groups. However, overt political opposition or public criticism of the Government or of Communist Party policies was firmly stifled. An opposition political movement, the Belarusian Popular Front (BPF), was founded in June 1989, but its organizers were forced to hold the inaugural congress in Vilnius, Lithuania. The BPF's campaign on the use of Belarusian did have some success. The Supreme Soviet, or Supreme Council (the legislature), finally voted to adopt Belarusian as the state language (in place of Russian) on 28 January 1990, and mandated the use of Belarusian in education. The transitional period was, in some cases, to be as long as 10 years. The use of Russian and russified names remained prevalent, and government documents continued to be printed in Russian. In 1995 Russian was restored as an official language, alongside Belarusian and, thereafter, the use of Belarusian was steadily eroded. The 1999 census revealed that only 37% of Belarusians spoke Belarusian in everyday life, the remainder speaking Russian.

The first Belarusian grammar was written in the 1920s, but after the passage of a language law in 1933, Belarusian was marginalized in favour of Russian, and a new version of Belarusian was adopted. A complication in Belarusian is a popular form of speech, often called *trasyanka* (which translates as a mixture of hay and straw). Used mainly in rural areas, it is a mixture of Russian, Belarusian and Ukrainian, often used by politicians to promote a populist image. Opposition politicians have denounced *trasyanka* on the grounds that it is destroying pure Belarusian, and have adopted the pre-1933 version of the language. The Government, in turn, has denounced the pre-1933 version, those using it in public have been arrested, and publications that employ it have been prosecuted.

The BPF was not officially permitted to campaign in elections to the Belarusian Supreme Council and local councils on 4 March 1990. Instead, BPF candidates joined other opposition groups in the Belarusian Democratic Bloc. The democrats won approximately one-quarter of the 310 seats decided by popular vote (an additional 50 seats were filled by deputies delegated from the CPB). However, the Supreme Council was overwhelmingly dominated by deputies loyal to the CPB leadership (84% of deputies were members of the CPB), and the BPF faction in parliament had only about 30 members.

Despite limited numbers, the BPF deputies initially seemed to have considerable influence in the new legislature. They successfully campaigned for a declaration of state sovereignty, which the Belarusian Supreme Council adopted on 27 July 1990 (all deputies present voted for the document, but 115 did not take part in the debate). The declaration asserted the right of the republic to organize its own armed forces, create a national currency and manage its own domestic and foreign policies, but remained little more than a symbolic document.

Lack of popular support for secession from the USSR was evident at the referendum on the future of the Union in March 1991: 83% of voters supported a 'renewed union', the highest proportion in any Union Republic outside Central Asia. However, Belarus' reputation as one of the most stable of the Soviet republics was threatened by a series of strikes in April. The strikers held large demonstrations in Minsk, demanding wage rises and the cancellation of a new sales tax, but also announced political demands, including the resignation of the Government. The strikes ended when the Government made economic concessions, including high wage increases, but the political demands were rejected.

## INDEPENDENT BELARUS

During the attempted *coup d'état* in Moscow in August 1991, the leadership of the CPB supported the dissident State Committee for the State of Emergency (SCSE). Following the collapse of the coup, Nikolai Dementei (Mikalai Dzemyantsei), First Secretary of the CPB and Chairman of the Supreme Council, was forced to resign. On 25 August the Supreme Council declared the formal independence of Belarus, gave the 1990 Declaration of State Sovereignty constitutional force and temporarily suspended the activities of the CPB and the CPSU in Belarus. Dementei was replaced as Chairman of the Supreme Council (initially in an acting capacity) by Stanislau Shushkevich, a centrist politician well-known for his criticism of government negligence in the aftermath of the Chornobyl disaster. On 19 September he was formally elected to the post (equivalent to head of state) by the Supreme Council, which voted to change the name of the country to the Republic of Belarus. Belarusian independence was confirmed on 8 December 1991, when Belarus signed the Minsk Agreement (together with Russia and Ukraine), which established the Commonwealth of Independent States (CIS) and effectively dissolved the USSR. The headquarters of the new organization was to be in Minsk. The foundation of the CIS was confirmed by the Almaty (Alma-Ata) Declaration of 11 former Union Republics on 21 December, and the dissolution of the USSR was finalized by the resignation of Gorbachev as the last Soviet President four days later. Belarus then gained international recognition as an independent state.

Despite this, the Supreme Council remained dominated by conservatives, who retained the Soviet institutions of government. In January 1992 the BPF began a campaign for a referendum to support the scheduling of elections to the Supreme Council for late 1992 (more than two years earlier than required by the Constitution), and for the introduction of a new, more democratic electoral law. By May the campaigners had collected 383,000 signatures (after the Central Electoral Commission had disqualified some 58,000 signatures) on a petition demanding a referendum. However, when the Supreme Council convened in October, it rejected the petition, claiming that it suffered from irregularities. As a concession, deputies voted to permit new elections to the legislature in March 1994, one year earlier than scheduled, but failure to pass a parliamentary election law by late 1993 meant that the elections did not occur. Concern expressed by, among others, the US Government, at the refusal to hold a referendum, was dismissed by the Supreme Council as interference in the country's internal affairs.

Shushkevich appeared to have been chosen as Chairman of the Supreme Council because he was not part of the communist *apparat* (although he remained a member of the CPB until August 1991) and had no strong links with any major political movement. Although this might have initially been a favourable characteristic, it left Shushkevich disadvantaged in the Supreme Council. Confronted by the legislature's continued hostility towards reform, Shushkevich became more closely associated with the opposition BPF and its allies.

A new constitution was not adopted by the Supreme Council until 15 March 1994, after the rejection of two earlier versions

in late 1991 and late 1992. It was promulgated on 28 March 1994, and came into effect on 30 March. Based substantially on the old Soviet-era Constitution, the new Constitution provided for a directly elected executive President. By this time Shushkevich had been ousted from power and replaced, on 28 January 1994, by a conservative former police chief, Mechislau Gryb (Myacheslau Hryb), who supported closer integration with Russia. Gryb held power until the presidential election.

## THE LUKASHENKA PRESIDENCY

Presidential elections were held in June–July 1994. Alyaksandr Lukashenka, the former head of the Supreme Council's anti-corruption commission, obtained 47.1% of the votes cast in the first round of voting, whereas his closest contender, Vyacheslau Kebich, obtained only 18.2%. Lukashenka was elected the first President of Belarus on 10 July, with some 85% of the votes cast in the second round of voting. Lukashenka's victory consolidated power among the conservatives, who advocated closer relations with Russia, the supremacy of central over local authority and the primacy of the executive, as opposed to the legislature, in determining policy and action. The BPF was increasingly marginalized as President Lukashenka, with the support of the old *nomenklatura*, exploited the power that the unreconstructed state apparatus provided.

In May 1995 elections to a new 260-member Supreme Council were held. At the same time there was a referendum on increasing the powers of the presidency, on closer integration with Russia, on making Russian a state language and on restoring a version of the Soviet-era flag. The electorate overwhelmingly supported the referendum proposals but, although 61% participated in the first round of voting in the general election on 14 May, making it legally valid, only 18 candidates obtained the necessary simple majority of votes cast to secure election, and 242 seats in the legislature remained vacant. The state-owned media provided little coverage of the elections and the operating licence of the country's only private television station was suspended. In the second round of voting, on 28 May, 101 more seats were filled. However, the Supreme Council remained inquorate. Subsequent elections took place on 29 November and 10 December, after which 198 deputies had been elected, 24 more than the two-thirds' quorum required to allow parliament to function. The remaining 62 vacancies were ostensibly the result of low participation rates in certain electoral districts, areas in which the BPF had its strongest support, and were not finally filled until 1996. As a consequence, the BPF was not represented in the Supreme Council, having held 30 seats in the previous legislature.

In the intervening period, the paralysis of the legislature gave the executive considerable freedom in establishing policy, and enabled the President to arrogate more powers to himself. Lukashenka rapidly asserted control over the state-owned media. Responsibility for the security services was transferred from parliament to the President. They were largely unchanged from the Soviet era and continued to be known as the Committee for State Security (Komitet Gosudarstvennoi Bezopasnosti—KGB), and were split into two branches: one responsible for criminal affairs, the other for intelligence and state security. Lukashenka also created a new agency, the Control Service of the Office of the President, to deal with economic crime. At the same time actions were taken to outlaw, or render impotent, opposition or independent representative bodies.

After the four rounds of voting, the main parties represented in parliament were the CPB, with 42 seats (having won 21.2% of the votes cast in the first round of the elections); the Agrarian Party (AP), with 33 seats (16.7%); the United Civic

Party of Belarus (UCP) with nine seats; and the Party of People's Accord, with eight. The All-Belarusian Party of Popular Unity and Accord and the Belarusian Social Democratic Assembly each had two seats, and a further seven parties had one seat each; the remaining seats filled were occupied by 95 independents. Only two of the largest parties—the UCP and the Belarusian Social Democratic Assembly—were orientated towards democratic reform. The formation of parliamentary factions, which included the minor parties and most of the independents, led to the existence of five major groupings by early 1996: Accord (with 59 deputies); Agrarian (47); Communist (44); People's Unity (17); and the Belarus Social Democrats (15).

In mid-1996 confrontations between Lukashenka and parliament became increasingly frequent. In May the Supreme Council began an investigation into alleged human rights abuses, and in July Syamyon Sharetski, the parliamentary speaker, asked the Constitutional Court to examine the legality of several presidential decrees. In response, in early August the President proposed a referendum, to be held in November, on constitutional amendments, which would extend his term of office until 2001, give him extensive powers of appointment and allow him to rule by decree. The Supreme Council would be replaced with a bicameral National Assembly. Just before the referendum, the Constitutional Court ruled that the results would not be legally binding; President Lukashenka revoked the ruling by decree, provoking fierce criticism.

The referendum also contained three questions, proposed by the Supreme Council, designed to curtail the President's power. Voting began on 9 November 1996. Widespread violations of electoral law were reported by parliamentary observers. The Organization for Security and Co-operation in Europe (OSCE) refused to send monitors and the Council of Europe declared that the draft of the amended Constitution did not comply with European standards. The Chairman of the Central Electoral Commission, Viktar Ganchar, stated that he would not approve the referendum results and was dismissed shortly afterwards by Lukashenka. (Three years later, in mid-September 1999, Ganchar disappeared, following further opposition activity, and was never found.) Meanwhile, independent radio stations were closed down and some 200,000 copies of *Nasha Niva*, an independent weekly publication, were confiscated. The Chairman of the Council of Ministers (the Prime Minister), Mikhail Chigir, who had been appointed in July 1994, criticized the referendum, and was replaced by his deputy, Syargey Ling. A motion was submitted to the Constitutional Court by 75 Supreme Council deputies for the impeachment of the President. However, support for impeachment among the deputies rapidly dwindled and the Court abandoned further action after the referendum results appeared, despite overt procedural irregularities. According to official figures, some 84% of the electorate took part in the referendum, 70.5% of whom voted for the President's proposals, and only 7.9% of whom voted for those of the Supreme Council. The replacement of the elected parliament and the institution of a new constitution were unrecognized by many opposition leaders.

The amended Constitution was published on 27 November 1996 and came into immediate effect. Over 100 Supreme Council deputies declared their support for the President and passed legislation abolishing the Supreme Council and establishing the 110-member House of Representatives, the lower chamber of the new National Assembly. Existing deputies were invited to join the new legislature and their terms in office were confirmed for four years. Deputies who refused had their terms curtailed to only two months. The 64-member upper house, the Council of the Republic, convened for the first time in January 1997, with eight members appointed by

the President and 56 elected by regional councils. The Council of Europe suspended Belarus' 'guest' status, citing the lack of democracy in the new political structures. The only governments to recognize the legitimacy of the new government bodies were those of Iran, Iraq, Libya, Russia and Syria. Attempts to negotiate an end to the split between the new legislature and the deputies of the abolished 13th Supreme Soviet, mediated by the European Union (EU), were suspended in July, and later abandoned.

Repression of opponents of the Lukashenka regime continued, with frequent arrests and detentions. In 1997 legislation was introduced, which required all foreign journalists to renew their accreditation and, when the mid-September deadline had passed, it was reported that many had failed to observe correctly the new procedures. In November the BPF organized a petition campaign, called Charter-97 (Khartyya-97—deliberately recalling communist-era Czechoslovakia's Charter-77 movement), but, without access to the mass media or representation in public institutions, the opposition had become a marginalized, dissident movement, reminiscent of the situation prior to the collapse of the communist system.

The opposition refused to recognize either Lukashenka's dissolution of the parliament elected in 1995 or the new Constitution. Fifty deputies of the old Supreme Council denounced the referendum and, in early January 1997, established the Public Coalition Government—National Economic Council, a form of 'shadow' government, chaired by Genadz Karpenka. International organizations, including the EU and the OSCE, continued to deal exclusively with these elected deputies. In May 1999 the Central Electoral Commission of the former Supreme Council held a shadow presidential election in accordance with the 1994 Constitution, in which the former Prime Minister, Mikhail Chigir, was a leading candidate. However, by then he had been in pre-trial detention since the end of March 1999; his trial for abuse of office commenced in January 2000. He was eventually convicted of embezzlement, and, in May, given a three-year suspended prison sentence. The human rights group, Amnesty International, and the US embassy in Belarus criticized the trial, claiming it was politically motivated. Chigir appealed against the sentence, which was overturned by the Supreme Court in early December, although the Court returned the case to the prosecutor's office for further investigation; Chigir's wife received a two-year suspended sentence. Chigir's son was arrested in early 2001 for allegedly selling stolen cars, and in March 2002 was sentenced to seven years' imprisonment. In early 2002 Mikhail Chigir was charged with tax evasion, and he was given a three-year, suspended prison sentence in late July.

Zyanon Paznyak, a candidate in the 1994 presidential election, also stood as a candidate in the 1999 shadow presidential election, but withdrew in May, stating that the voting procedure violated the law; Paznyak later fled the country. The election resulted in the proclamation of Syamyon Sharetski, the leader of the AP, as acting President. However, he fled to Lithuania in mid-July, as he feared arrest, after demanding that Lukashenka leave office, according to the terms of the former Constitution, under which his term of office would have expired in July. In January 2000 the Council of Europe issued a statement condemning Belarus' position on human rights, democracy and the rule of law. However, in March 2001 Prime Minister Uladzimir Yermoshin insisted that the Government recognized 'constructive opposition', but would not tolerate opposition that constituted a threat to the 'Belarusian state'. Parliamentary elections were held on 15 and 29 October 2000, despite opposition demands for a boycott; of the 562 candidates contesting the 110 seats available, only 60 were not supporters of Lukashenka, and about half the prospective opposition candidates were denied permission to register. Official figures showed that over 60% of the electorate voted, but unofficial estimates suggested that the participation rate was as low as 40%, technically rendering the poll invalid. The OSCE, the Council of Europe and the European Parliament (the so-called 'parliamentary troika') criticized the elections, and the USA refused to recognize the results.

In advance of the presidential election scheduled to take place in September 2001, opposition parties participated in a Consultative and Co-ordinating Council of Democratic Forces, to ensure that votes cast against Lukashenka would not be divided between a number of candidates. In July the opposition parties finally selected Uladzimir Gancharyk (Hancharyk), the leader of the Federation of Trade Unions of Belarus, to oppose Lukashenka, although his campaign was hampered by the Government's successful efforts to silence his supporters among the media and civic groups.

In mid-March 2001 Lukashenka signed a decree banning the use of foreign financial assistance for activities relating to political campaigns and other forms of mass propaganda, including the provision of funding for the training of OSCE election observers. The election was held on 9 September 2001, and Lukashenka was returned to power with 75.7% of the votes cast, according to official figures, although many observers disputed the results. Gancharyk was credited with 15.7% of the votes (however, the opposition claimed that Lukashenka had received only 47% of the votes, and Gancharyk 41%, which would have forced a second round of voting). The USA refused to recognize the results of the election, and there were widespread allegations of serious electoral malpractice; members of the opposition demanded Lukashenka's resignation. Despite concerns over the results of the election, the EU stated that diplomatic isolation would neither benefit the Belarusian people, nor contribute to the strengthening of democratic development, and announced that Western Governments needed to reassess their policies towards Belarus. A new premier, Genadz Navitsky, was appointed on 1 October. After the election, Lukashenka moved quickly to punish organizations and individuals that had supported the opposition. Gancharyk was forced to resign as Chairman of the Federation of Trade Unions of Belarus, and the Government banned the automatic deduction and payment of union dues from salaries.

In March 2003 Lukashenka received considerable support in local government elections, when only a few dozen of the 24,012 local council seats were won by opposition supporters. (However, the seats were contested by only 25,805 candidates, of whom just 1,138 were opposition candidates.) The rate of participation by the electorate was 73.4%, and was highest in rural areas. According to opinion polls, however, support for Lukashenka had declined since 2001, particularly among pensioners and farmers, traditionally some of his main supporters. None the less, Lukashenka remained a consummate politician, and continued to distinguish between the 'Government' and his presidency. For example, in 2002 the Government sharply increased the prices for electricity and heating, subsequently attracting criticism from Lukashenka, who ordered a price 'freeze', despite the need to raise prices further in preparation for currency union with Russia (see below).

Although there is no formal law on censorship, the Lukashenka regime created a number of tools for controlling the media, closing non-governmental organizations (NGOs) and restricting religious freedom. The Government officially recognizes 26 religious denominations, not all of which have the right to practice on a nation-wide basis. It provides financial support for the Russian Orthodox Church (to which about 80% of believers are affiliated—although more than one-half of the population identifies itself as atheist), and in June 2003

signed a co-operation agreement with the Church. Religious affairs are managed by a Committee on Religious Affairs and Nationalities of the Cabinet of Ministers. Recognized denominations must register to receive recognition, and to do so they must have a legal place of worship that can serve as an address. In 2000, following the adoption of a new housing code in 1999, religious groups were required to register or re-register their properties with local authorities. Several denominations and congregations that had been practising for years were subsequently refused registration. In late 2002 both houses of the legislature passed a new law on religion, which restricted the spread of unapproved and non-traditional denominations, and strongly favoured the Russian Orthodox Church.

The media and NGOs are controlled by a series of nebulous laws. One such law forbids defamation of the President, a term that is broadly defined. (In 2003, for example, a newspaper editor was fined for satirizing the 2001 presidential election campaign.) Those found guilty can be sentenced to up to six years' imprisonment. Under Article 57 of the Civil Code, NGOs and organizations can be shut down after a single violation of the law, including a violation of their charter. In April 2003 the Chamber of Representatives passed new legislation on demonstrations, which allows the authorities to close down any political party or NGO that fails to ensure the maintenance of law and order during a demonstration causing large-scale damage (which can include simply disruption to traffic). After his re-election, Lukashenka further tightened his hold over the country's cultural and political institutions. In early 2002 he replaced the editors of leading literary magazines with government-approved editors, and he also ordered history textbooks to be rewritten. In early 2003 three Russian radio stations broadcasting in Belarus lost their transmitter facilities, as the rebroadcasting facilities of Russian television stations were restricted. In late March Lukashenka suggested that all industrial enterprises with at least 300 employees, and all agricultural companies employing at least 150 people should appoint deputy directors for ideological work. He has also increased presidential control over education; in June 2003, for example, a Western-style school, teaching in Belarusian, was closed.

## CHORNOBYL AND PUBLIC HEALTH

The Chornobyl incident has had a lasting impact on Belarus. By December 2000 some 135,000 people had been resettled, and a further 7,000 were still awaiting resettlement. After the accident, the Government had to build 64,836 new housing units, and provide 44,072 new places in schools and 18,470 new places in kindergartens. Many villages were provided with gas to obviate the need to use contaminated peat or firewood, which required the laying of thousands of kilometres of gas pipelines.

Some 70,371 people were involved in the initial remediation programme in 1986–87, and 37,949 were involved between 1988 and 1989. As a result of the incident, 9,343 people were classified as invalids, and some 1,571,000 were classified as living on contaminated land; 282 rural settlements were closed. The total number of affected people, about 1,800,000, represented almost 20% of the country's population. The worst-affected regions were Gomel and Mogilev oblasts. Within Gomel oblast, the population declined from 1,677,500 in 1986 to 1,535,000 in 2000. The impact was felt mainly in rural areas of the oblast, where the population declined from 653,600 to 475,200, whereas the urban population, in fact, increased slightly. In some areas of the oblast, the decline in population has been even more dramatic. The total population of the Khoiniki district declined from 45,850 to 25,900, and the district's rural population declined from 29,450 to just 11,100, a reduction of almost two-thirds.

Some 43,500 sq km of Belarusian land has been classified as contaminated. There are five categories of contaminated land: an exclusion zone exists nearest to the Chornobyl power station; slightly less severely affected are the highly contaminated zones of priority resettlement, in which several tens of thousands of people continued to reside in the early 2000s; a zone of secondary resettlement is identified as an area where radiation poses a risk to particular groups, such as those reliant on subsistence farming and hunting, and where average individual doses of radiation may exceed legal limits; the final two zones are subject to the right to resettle, or to periodic radiation monitoring. (In some areas of Europe, natural radiation levels exceed the threshold for the latter zone.) In general, policy has been such that the Government has aimed to resettle all but those in the zone with the lowest level of contamination. Owing to the natural decay of radioactivity, it is estimated that radiation in affected areas will decline by about 55% by 2046, and by 90% in the most severely affected areas. The issue of the resettlement and redevelopment of formerly polluted areas, as radiation levels decline, is only gradually being addressed.

The main risk to health comes from eating or drinking radioactive food, and in some cases the cumulative dose of radiation is high, and growing. Privately cultivated food, particularly that grown for subsistence purposes, was less likely to be checked for radiation, and more likely to suffer from contamination. Increased poverty and growing reliance on subsistence plots increased exposure among large sections of the population. Initially, cases of leukaemia were expected to increase sharply. Although this did not occur, the incidence of thyroid cancer grew substantially. By 1998 1,800 cases of childhood thyroid cancer had been diagnosed in the areas affected by fall-out (which included areas in Russia and Ukraine—about 600 cases were in Belarus), which, usually rare in children, appeared to be directly linked to Chornobyl. Although generally treatable, treatment is costly, and within Belarus foreign assistance paid for the treatment of up to 30% of cases. A major need was the reduction of endemic iodine deficiency, which leads to the enhanced uptake of iodine in foodstuffs, since, in the affected areas, radioactive iodine is still present in the food chain.

Compensation programmes were established for those affected by the accident. There are several different categories of those eligible for aid, including those who took part in the initial remediation activities; those who succumbed to radiation sickness; those who continue to live in contaminated areas; and those who were evacuated, resettled, or who left affected areas. Despite this, the proportion of the national budget devoted to Chornobyl expenses declined from 19.9% in 1992 to just 5.3% in 2001.

The problems of Chornobyl notwithstanding, the health situation in the country overall deteriorated after 1991, and the population declined from a peak of 10,244,000 in 1993 to an estimated 9,899,000 at the beginning of 2002, mainly owing to the effects of a decreasing birth rate, reduced life expectancy and higher infant mortality. Net immigration in 1992–2002 accounted for more than 53,000 people, but many skilled workers and educated personnel had chosen to leave Belarus over the same period.

## FOREIGN AND DEFENCE POLICY

### Foreign Policy

Belarus was a founding member of the UN in 1945, but had no independent foreign policy until 1991. By late 1992 it had been recognized by over 100 countries, but had done relatively little to develop contacts beyond its immediate neighbours and the CIS. In many countries Belarus continued to be represented diplomatically under the aegis of Russia. Belarus improved relations with Poland, and in June 1992 the two countries signed a treaty guaranteeing the inviolability of the Polish–Belarusian border. Poland also offered assistance in establishing Belarusian fishing and merchant fleets.

From 1991 the main focus of Belarusian foreign policy was the member states of the CIS and, above all, Russia. Belarus and Russia established diplomatic relations in June 1992, and in July 1993 the Prime Ministers of Belarus, the Russian Federation and Ukraine signed a declaration on economic integration; in April 1994 Belarus and Russia concluded an agreement on an eventual currency union. However, the aim of creating a 'common economic space' failed, and in May 1995 Belarus introduced its own currency, the Belarusian rouble. On 2 April 1996 Belarus and Russia signed a Treaty on the Formation of a Community of Sovereign Republics (CSR), which provided for extensive military, economic and political co-operation. However, Russian caution ensured that most practical developments were confined to border and military matters. On 2 April 1997 President Lukashenka and the Russian President, Boris Yeltsin, signed a further Treaty of Union. They also initialled a Charter of the Union, which detailed the procedures and institutions that would lead the CSR towards the development of a common infrastructure, single currency and a joint defence policy, with the eventual aim of 'voluntary unification of the member states'. The Charter was signed on 23 May and ratified by the respective legislatures the following month. Shortly afterwards the Union's Parliamentary Assembly, comprising 36 members from the legislature of each country, convened in official session for the first time.

Declarations of Union seemed to become an annual occurrence. In late December 1998 an outline union accord was signed. An agreement creating a more formal union structure, officially known as the Union of the Russian Federation and Belarus, was signed on 8 December 1999, confirmed by the Russian State Duma (the lower chamber of parliament) one week later, and ratified in January 2000. The agreement, said to be modelled on the EU's Treaty on European Union (the Maastricht Treaty), committed the two countries to unify customs, tariffs and taxes, and currency union was planned by the end of 2005. A two-chamber supranational legislature was to be created; the upper chamber was to comprise 36 representatives from each republic, and the lower chamber was to comprise 25 representatives from Belarus and 75 from Russia. It was unlikely, however, to become a substantive decision-making body, since Belarus, with just over 10m. citizens, was vastly over-represented in comparison with Russia, which had approximately 147m. Neither country could withdraw from the Union unless a referendum on withdrawal was held and approved. The opposition responded by claiming that the Union agreement breached the Belarusian Constitution. Supporters of the agreement argued that it would provide a guaranteed export market for Belarusian goods and ensure cheaper supplies of energy. In late January 2000 Pavel Borodin, a former aide to President Yeltsin, was appointed State Secretary of the new Union. However, he was arrested in New York, USA, in January 2001, in connection with a bribery scandal, and replaced, in an acting capacity, by one of his deputies, Igor Selivanov. (In March 2002 a Swiss court found Borodin guilty of money 'laundering'—the processing of illegitimately obtained funds through legitimate accounts—and he was fined some US $180,000.)

A number of common institutions were established to co-ordinate progress towards the Union, including a Supreme State Council, comprising the Presidents, Prime Ministers and heads of the legislatures of both countries, and an executive organ, the Union Council of Ministers, which was made up of the cabinets of the two countries. Meetings of the two Councils were prepared by a third body, the Standing Committee of the Union Government. Finally, an Interbank Currency Council was established to represent both countries' central banks during the preparations for monetary union. However, these institutions had few powers, and were mainly consultative. The main objective seemed to be economic integration. In 2000 a timetable was developed, establishing a range of deadlines for different components of the move towards Union. Price regulations were to be harmonized by the end of 2001, followed by the two countries' tax codes by the end of 2002.

By 2005 work on two other broad areas was to be completed: first, the alignment of the foreign trade and customs regimes of the two countries; and, second, that of transport, energy and telecommunications. Progress has been made slowly in these areas. In April 2002 three agreements standardizing economic issues between the two countries were signed, but problems remain over subsidies and transfer payments, over the timing and conditions of the proposed currency union, and over the powers of future union institutions. Belarus was to adopt the Russian rouble at the beginning of 2005; further plans anticipated the creation of a 'union rouble' by 2008. Monetary union is perhaps the most difficult task confronting Belarus, and is the area in which progress has been slowest. Russia's economy is far more open and less structured than that of Belarus, and monetary union would require Belarus to compromise its 'socially-orientated market economy', which is, in effect, a 'command and control' system, with administered prices and wages. By mid-2003 there were doubts that the initial stage of currency union—the linking of the Belarusian rouble to the Russian rouble at a fixed rate of exchange—would be ready to proceed by the beginning of 2004, and doubts were expressed that actual currency union would take place at the beginning of 2005. Although detailed negotiations on monetary union were supposed to begin in September 2002, they did not get under way until April 2003. By June it had been agreed that Belarus would have limited control over monetary emission, and that the rouble would be monitored by the Interbank Council, consisting of eight or nine Russians and one Belarusian. The two countries were to retain their central banks, although from 1 January 2005 the Russian central bank would supply Belarus with bank notes. However, in mid-June, in an apparently contradictory statement, Lukashenka announced that Belarus would adopt the Russian rouble only if it would lead to further economic progress and raise living standards, adding that monetary union would take place only after all other union agreements had been implemented.

Russian President Vladimir Putin appeared somewhat less committed to the Union than had Yeltsin. In June 2002 Putin rejected the creation of a supranational body, as indicated by the union agreements signed with Yeltsin, and equally rejected the idea of reviving any association akin to the USSR, proposing, instead, that the Union proceed on the basis of a unified federal state, according to which Belarus would, in effect, be incorporated into the Russian Federation; Putin emphasized the fact that the size of the Belarusian economy was only 3% that of Russia. He later stated that a Union with supranational institutions could undermine the integrity of the Russian state. Further negotiations took place in Moscow in mid-August 2002, at which Putin suggested that a referendum be held in May 2003, followed by common parliamentary and presidential elections in 2003–04, and adoption of the rouble as the Union's common currency at the beginning of 2004, rather than 2005. Lukashenka, however, denounced the plan as unacceptable, and as constituting a threat to Belarusian sovereignty. In May 2003 Putin failed to mention Belarus or plans for the creation of the Union in his annual message to the Russian parliament, leading to suggestions that relations between the two Presidents had collapsed,

owing to Belarus's failure to fulfil its economic commitments; none of Belarus's three main television stations made reference to the speech. Moreover, by late 2002 Belarus owed the union budget some 1,000m. Russian roubles. From early 2002 Lukashenka also appeared increasingly uncertain about his support for the Union, while under Putin Russia had rapidly implemented reform, drawing further apart from Belarus.

Eventually, at the end of March 2003 a draft constitution for the union state was finalized. The Union was to comprise two sovereign states, with executive powers vested in the governing body, the Supreme State Council. The union state would not levy its own taxes, but was to rely on transfers from the member countries. The lower chamber of the union legislature would be able to pass legislation only if more than three-quarters of its members voted in favour, and would be consulted on the appointment of a union prime minister. By late 2002 opinion polls suggested that support for the Union was generally strong among both Russian and Belarusian citizens (although Russians tended to support the creation of a single state, whereas Belarusians favoured a union of states).

In March 1995 Belarus signed a preliminary partnership and co-operation agreement with the EU. However, as the Lukashenka regime became progressively autocratic, relations with the EU deteriorated. Following the referendum of November 1996 and the abolition of the Supreme Soviet, the EU suspended the partnership agreement and continued to recognize the deputies of the old assembly as the legitimate legislature. The EU, in co-operation with the Council of Europe, attempted to mediate a settlement between the deputies of the old and new legislatures, but the efforts were abandoned in September 1997. In June 1998 a diplomatic compound in Drozhdy, outside Minsk, where 22 diplomats had homes, was closed to them after the Belarusian Government announced that the compound needed urgent repairs. The ambassadors from the EU and the USA left the country, as did ambassadors from Bulgaria, Japan and Poland. In July Belarus informed diplomats that if furniture was not removed from the compound, the Government would seize the buildings. In mid-July the EU and the USA responded by banning Lukashenka and government ministers and officials from visiting their countries. Eventually, in mid-January 1999 ambassadors from five EU countries—France, Germany, Greece, Italy and the United Kingdom—returned to the country, and by September all ambassadors had returned to Minsk, although relations between Belarus and Western governments remained uneasy.

The actions of the Lukashenka Government drew severe criticism from many official and many non-governmental bodies, including the European Parliament, the International Helsinki Foundation for Human Rights (based in Finland) and the OSCE, for the apparent disregard for the democratic process and for the observance of human rights. In February 1998 the OSCE opened an advice and monitoring mission in Belarus, in order to promote democratization and monitor human rights in the country. The mission was initially tolerated by the Government, but from 2000 relations steadily deteriorated. In April 2002 the acting head of the mission was compelled to leave the country, after the authorities refused to renew his visa, and in October the last remaining foreign member of the organization's staff left the country. In response to the effective closure of the mission, all the EU member states (with the exception of Portugal), together with Norway and the USA imposed a travel ban on President Lukashenka and seven other high-ranking government officials, and in November Lukashenka was also refused a visa to travel to the Czech Republic to participate in a meeting of the North Atlantic Treaty Organization's (NATO) Euro-Atlantic Partnership Council. However, in December Belarus agreed to permit the OSCE establish a new mission office in Belarus, and in April 2003 the travel bans were lifted.

In early 2000 the Government announced plans to establish and improve relations with Arab and Middle Eastern states, focusing particularly on Iran and Iraq. By 2002 there were persistent allegations that Belarus had supplied Iraq with anti-missile components and had trained Iraqi technicians, in violation of UN sanctions, prompting concern from US government officials.

### Defence

In mid-1992 Belarus assumed nominal control of former Soviet troops still on its territory, although these troops remained under joint CIS/Russian command, and it was announced that Belarus was to form its own armed forces. However, Belarusians constituted only 20% of the staff at the Ministry of Defence and fewer than 30% of officers in the Belarusian armed forces, the remainder being mainly ethnic Russians. Moreover, the 1992 agreement on co-operation between Russia and Belarus ceded effective control over the country's military technology and production to Russia. Under Soviet rule, Belarus had one of the highest concentrations of military personnel in the former USSR—one per 43 civilians. Forces totalled 250,000 personnel, of which as many as one-third were officers. Plans were announced to reduce the officer corps by 20,000, to 22,000 men; to reduce the General Staff by 40%; and to reduce the number of troops to about 90,000 men. In June 1995 forces totalled over 150,000, of which 98,400 were officers and enlisted men, and the remainder were support staff. By August 2001 the total number of officers and enlisted men had been reduced to 82,900, and was to be further reduced to 65,000 personnel by 2006. In March 2003 Lukashenka announced that the air and air-defence forces were to be re-equipped within six to 12 years.

Belarus' adherence to the Treaty on Collective Security (the so-called Tashkent Agreement), signed by six CIS states in May 1992, initially provoked controversy, some claiming that it contradicted the Constitution, but in April 1993 the Supreme Council voted to authorize its Chairman, Stanislau Shushkevich, to sign the Agreement, after imposing conditions on Belarusian inclusion in the pact. The most notable of these was the stipulation that Belarusian troops were not to serve outside the country and that no foreign troops were to be stationed in Belarus without the consent of the Government. The proposal was opposed by Shushkevich and the BPF on the grounds that it would commit Belarus to participate in armed conflicts in Russia and elsewhere in the CIS and violate the 1990 declaration of state sovereignty, which committed Belarus to neutrality. Shushkevich initially refused to sign the Tashkent Agreement, but eventually yielded in December 1993, thereby losing BFP support and eventually, his post.

As one of four nuclear powers created by the collapse of the USSR, in May 1992 Belarus signed the Lisbon Protocol to the Treaty on the Non-Proliferation of Nuclear Weapons, which committed it to transfer its nuclear weapons to Russia by 1999. The country inherited nearly 2,500 tanks, 3,000 armoured personnel carriers and 340 aircraft. The Supreme Council ratified the Treaty on Conventional Forces in Europe (CFE) on 4 February 1993, and the following day adhered to the Treaty on the Non-Proliferation of Nuclear Weapons.

Ratification was accompanied by US $65m. in aid from the USA, plus $10m. to help Belarus dismantle its nuclear weapons. Belarus' commitment to the CFE agreement required it to destroy 2,171 tanks, 1,420 armoured carriers and 167 aircraft. The arms-destruction programme was impeded by lack of funds and was halted several times as a result. However, by March 1996 the last combat aircraft had been destroyed, and the last remaining nuclear warhead was transferred to Russia in November of that year. In February 1999 Lukashenka announced that Belarus had made a mistake in surrendering its nuclear arsenal, although in February 2000 he declared there to be no need for Russian nuclear weapons to be stationed in Belarus.

In connection with the proposed Union with Russia (see above), in February 2000 Lukashenka announced that Belarus and Russia were to create a new military grouping of several hundred thousand troops, in response to the eastward expansion of NATO. In January it had also been announced that the Governments of Belarus and Russia were to establish a joint defence-financial-industrial group. The Russian Government approved a plan to develop the group, 'Defence Systems', consisting of the Russian financial-industrial group of the same name and some Belarusian enterprises. Military co-operation subsequently intensified, with Russia completing an early-warning radar system along the country's western border, manned by Russian personnel. There were also plans to integrate the Belarusian and Russian air defence systems into one combined, regional system.

## CONCLUSION

After independence was formally declared in 1991, the process of state-building faltered in Belarus, partly because of the low level of national consciousness. Relations with Russia dominated the political agenda from 1991. Economic and constitutional reform was repeatedly delayed, initially by the Supreme Council, and later by President Lukashenka, and from 1996 the country reacquired many of the features of a command economy. The legal system had lost its independence, and freedom of speech had been eliminated. The Government exercised tight control over the media, cultural organizations, non-governmental organizations, political parties and religious groups. The European Bank for Reconstruction and Development characterized commercial and financial regulations as weak, and the human rights organization Freedom House noted that human rights in Belarus were only slightly better observed than those in Turkmenistan (which had perhaps the worst human rights record in the CIS). The accession of Poland to NATO in 1999, and to the EU in 2004, along with the anticipated accession of Latvia and Lithuania to both organizations in 2004, left Belarus increasingly geopolitically isolated. Consequently, economic survival depended largely on close co-operation with Russia, with inevitable political consequences; however, both Putin and Lukashenka have appeared to waver on their commitment to Union, while support for Lukashenka appeared to be diminishing. According to the existing Constitution, Lukashenka was due to stand down in 2004, but it was possible that he might hold a referendum in an attempt to enable him to seek a third term in office. The opposition continues to represent little threat, and remains fragmented and marginalized.

# The Economy

## Dr ANDREW RYDER

### INTRODUCTION

Belarus has few natural resources. At the beginning of the 1990s its industrial base was heavily dependent on the former Soviet military-industrial complex and its agricultural sector suffered from structural defects and the after-effects of the 1986 Chornobyl (Chernobyl) disaster in Ukraine. Nevertheless, following the dissolution of the USSR at the end of 1991, restructuring occurred more slowly than in some other former Soviet republics, largely as a result of the leadership's reluctance to embark on a programme of transition to a market economy. Instead, from 1994 the Government attempted to create what it termed a 'socially-orientated market economy', with state-controlled prices, a very limited private sector, extensive directed subsidies, artificially low unemployment, and a dominant, essentially unreformed state sector.

Within the former USSR, Belarus was a high-income Union Republic. With 3.6% of the total population of the USSR, Belarus accounted for 4.1% of industrial output and 4.0% of industrial employment. Industrial output per head was 14.5% greater than the all-Union average, and throughout the 1980s the rate of increase in inward investment was substantially higher than the USSR average, showing the highest rate of increase of any Soviet republic in 1986–88. In the 1970s and 1980s rates of return on investment also appeared to be substantially higher (18%–19%) than the all-Union average, and rates of increase of labour productivity were consistently the highest in the USSR throughout the 1980s. Within the former USSR, the economy of Belarus had relatively low energy intensity, when measured per unit of gross domestic product (GDP) and energy per head, but the republic was highly dependent on energy imports. At the end of Soviet rule, the republic had a positive trade balance with the rest of the USSR. Its main trading partners within the USSR were Russia (accounting for 58% of exports and 63% of imports) and Ukraine (18% of exports, 19% of imports).

It is difficult to gauge Belarus' economic performance under Soviet rule, and equally difficult to gauge it after independence. The lack of a responsive pricing mechanism, Soviet accounting practices, and the Soviet method of deriving measures of national income (national income produced and net material product—NMP) obscured economic reality. A difficulty for the leaders of the newly independent Belarus was coming to terms with adjusted measures of economic performance, which showed Belarus to be less prosperous than had been imagined. This difficulty was evident in changing assessments of per-head GNP in terms of purchasing-power parity. In contrast to the 1991 estimate of US $3,110, in 1994 it was estimated at $5,010, not far behind Russia and Latvia, and in 1995 at $4,220. Estimates by the World Bank, calculated by the more conventional method of using exchange rates as a conversion factor, showed that GNP per head was $2,160 in 1994 and $2,070 in 1995. The difficulty in determining GNP could be seen in the relative changes in industrial producer prices between 1991 and 1995. Taking 1991 as 100, energy prices reached 127, fuel reached 185 and chemicals reached 123. Ferrous metals declined to 86, glass to 30, textiles to 53 and food to 62. These prices reflected both changing demand and changing factor costs. They also indicated the slow pace of reform and the income and profit problems of firms trapped in the reform process. During the same period energy prices in Russia rose by 222%. Overall, it was estimated that GNP per head declined at an annual average rate of 3.7% in 1990–98.

Total GNP, measured at 1996–98 prices, was estimated at $22,332m. in 1998, equivalent to $2,180 per head. By 2000 GNP, measured at average 1998–2000 prices, was $29,959m., equivalent to $2,990 per head (or $7,550 per head in terms of purchasing-power parity), according to World Bank estimates.

Changing trade relations among the countries of the former USSR and a partial shift to world market prices substantially altered the republic's terms of trade after 1991, and from 1993 Belarus had a persistent trade deficit. According to the IMF, the visible trade deficit was US $570m. in 1999, $884m. in 2000, and $807m. in 2001. The deficit was largely a result of trading relations within the Commonwealth of Independent States (CIS), particularly with Russia in the energy sector. The republic accumulated a high debt for energy imports from Russia. The debt was periodically cancelled, after Belarus made a series of concessions to Russia (see Mining and Energy below). Barter agreements were also implemented, and the Russian Government agreed to sell energy to Belarus at a reduced price. In 1999 Belarus also owed a substantial amount of money to Lithuania for electricity, but by early 2000 it was announced that 50% of the debt had been repaid through the exchange of goods.

From 1991 high rates of inflation, the retention of state control of prices and wages and the existence of several different exchange rates made it difficult to measure economic performance. Officially, Belarus successfully weathered the adjustment to a post-Soviet economy, but the calculation of official GDP was unreliable. Moreover, GDP declined sharply, and by the end of 1995, when it contracted by an annual average of 10.2%, in real terms, it had fallen to 51% of the 1989 level, according to some estimates. In 1996 GDP increased by 2.7%, and this recovery accelerated in 1997, when GDP increased by 11.5%. Annual growth declined to 8.3% in 1998, however, owing to the currency crisis in March of that year and the Russian currency crisis in August, and was achieved only through high inflation and a declining exchange rate. Unemployment remained low, at approximately 2.3%, partly owing to the contraction of the labour force, which declined by more than 5% over a five-year period. Low unemployment also reflected the slow reform process, which could be discerned from the accumulation of unsold industrial inventories in the country, which slowly increased to 65.3% of monthly output by the end of 2002. In 1999 GDP growth slowed to 3.4%, but it reached 5.8% in 2000, 4.1% in 2001, and (year-on-year) more than 4.7% in 2002. However, the measurement of growth is complicated by controlled prices, high inflation, and barter trade.

The proportion of loss-making firms showed a steady upward trend from 1992, when they accounted for just 5% of the total. By November 1995 they were estimated to represent 17.9% of all enterprises in Belarus, and by the end of 2002 4,082 firms (34.9%) of the country's approximately 11,700 enterprises were registering losses. Wage arrears accounted for some 10% of the wage fund at August 2000, and continued to increase thereafter.

### ECONOMIC POLICY

#### Privatization and Reform

Before 1995 privatization was erratic. It was impeded by the opposition of part of the parliamentary leadership and, subsequently, by President Alyaksandr Lukashenka and members of the Supreme Council. Even before Lukashenka came to power, the prevailing policy appeared to be to minimize economic disruption at any cost, and to postpone reform in favour of maintaining social stability. The institution of a socially-orientated market economy from 1994 caused economic policy to become an explicitly political instrument, and the Government introduced a return to the 'command and control' economy, with fixed prices and wages. A main aim of government policy was that of preserving and protecting large Soviet-era enterprises and farms.

In April 1994 the Government began to implement a voucher privatization programme, the first auctions for which were to be held in July. One-half of the shares in enterprises to be privatized were to be distributed to voucher holders, and the remainder were to be sold. However, few of those eligible applied for vouchers. When he took office in July Lukashenka suspended the programme, on the grounds of corruption. Later that year it was reorganized, with greater emphasis placed on investment funds and actual sales; the first voucher auctions were to be held in early 1995. The President approved the programme in March, but at the same time he halted the activities of private investment funds and suspended their licences to deal in privatization vouchers. By early 1995 private companies accounted for 19.3% of enterprises, collectives for 47.5%, state enterprises for 18.8%, co-operatives for 4.6% and joint ventures for approximately 2%. However, fully private and co-operative enterprises accounted for only 6.6% of total employment. The privatization of smaller enterprises was suspended in March 1996, and in February all private enterprises were required to re-register with the authorities. At the same time Lukashenka advocated the nationalization of the country's six largest commercial banks. In addition, severe restrictions existed on foreign ownership. There were further delays to the voucher privatization scheme, owing to both official obstacles and public indifference, which could be attributed in part to the poor economic performance of state-owned businesses. By mid-1999 only 40% of local government-owned enterprises had been privatized—this figure had reached only 45% by the end of 2002—and only 10% of large republican-owned firms. Only one in 10 of the firms selected for privatization in 1993 had actually been privatized, and only 40% of vouchers had been redeemed for shares.

The Government subsequently identified 960 large-scale enterprises that were not to be privatized, on the grounds of national interest. The privatization of large 'town-forming' enterprises requires the approval of the workers' collective, generally ensuring that privatization will not occur. Normally, privatization can only be commenced if the process is initiated by the labour force. If the labour force and the authorities are unable to reach an agreement, it is the responsibility of either the President (in the case of firms with more than 4,000 employees), the Cabinet of Ministers (firms with 2,000–4,000 employees), or the relevant ministry (firms with fewer than 2,000). Voucher privatization was still officially under way at the beginning of the 2000s, but the supply of shares in the firms being privatized was inadequate. Small-scale privatization had also stalled; only about one-half of all eligible communally operated small and medium-sized enterprises had been privatized by the end of 2000.

Reflecting the Government's negative bias towards the private sector, in September 1998 another registration process for private businesses was introduced, on the grounds that 17% of those registered were idle or had been formed primarily to avoid the payment of taxes. This process came into force in March 1999. All private firms had to complete the registration process by the beginning of 2001. Privatization through sale to foreign firms was hindered by a law stip-

ulating that no more than 50% of a state-owned industrial enterprise could be sold to private-sector owners, and any sale of stock worth US $40,000 or more had to be approved by the President. Price controls were extended to the private sector in October 1999 (it had previously been exempt). Private companies were also required to pay salaries that conformed to government guide-lines. At the end of January 2003 officially almost 50% of GDP was produced in the private sector, including some 1,500 large enterprises corporatized since 1991, but remaining under state ownership. Moreover, all enterprises in which the Government retained as little as one share were subject to the 'golden share' regulation, which allowed the President to issue a decree giving the Government effective control of the firm, even if this had not been anticipated when the firm was initially privatized; as a result, privatization was, effectively, a meaningless process.

By 1997 only an estimated 13% of GDP was produced by the private sector (actually a small decline compared with the figure recorded two years earlier). Although its contribution had increased to 20% by 1998, the level remained unchanged in 2000. However, this figure was in doubt, since many firms classified as private were in fact wholly owned by state-owned enterprises. Only 18.6% of employment was in the private sector, compared with some 22% in 1993. Despite this, privatization has advanced, albeit slowly: by the end of 2002 941 large (republican) firms had been privatized, an increase from 623 in 1997, and 2,716 small (communal) firms had been transferred to private ownership, compared with 1,943 in 1997.

In 2002 the Government announced plans to auction a 43% stake in each of four petrochemical companies in the following year: the Naftan petroleum refinery; the Polymir polymer plant; Grodno Azot, a fertilizer plant in Grodno; and a chemical-fibre firm, Khimvolokno. The shares were to be transferred to the winning bidder in three tranches: 20% in 2003, 10% in 2004 and the remainder in 2005. This was in large part owing to a need to liquidate outstanding energy debts, and increase foreign-currency reserves. However, the sale prices were extremely high, and the Government could still invoke the 'golden share' clause, leading many to conclude that it was unlikely that the shares would be divested successfully. In June 2002 the Governments of Russia and Belarus agreed to implement a joint action plan (JAP) prior to the introduction of a single currency in 2005. In order to make commercial conditions more equitable for both Russian and Belarusian firms, Belarus agreed to abandon many preferential taxes for domestic enterprises (but continued to direct credit, employ differential interest rates, and tolerate arrears to support key sectors and firms). In addition, Belarus promised to convert Beltransgaz, the national gas supplier, into a joint-stock company, as a first step towards creating a Russian-Belarusian gas consortium, sharing ownership with Gazprom, the Russian monopoly provider (see below). In 2001–03 Belarus also received a stabilization loan of US $4,500m. Russian roubles, delivered in three equal tranches. Originally designed to last for just one year, the loan could be utilized in subsequent years, subject to satisfactory progress in fulfilling the JAP. The plan also provided for a $40m. export credit from Russia, granted in December 2002, for the purchase of Russian products (mainly gas) on the condition that Belarus maintain its budget deficit at less than 1.5% of GDP, reform the bank system, and raise export duties on petroleum and petroleum products to Russian levels. The JAP also demanded further harmonization of tax and budgetary legislation with that of Russia; the elimination of all industrial subsidies; the consolidation of extra-budgetary funds into the state budget; the elimination of direct central bank credits to the budget; the creation of a joint venture to manage gas transport across Belarus; and numerous other legislative provisions.

## Employment and Social Affairs

In mid-1995 31.0% of the labour force was employed in industry, 19.9% in agriculture and just 12.8% in the services sector (including transport and communications). A further 8.9% were employed in education, and 7.7% in construction. According to official figures, in 2002 27.3% of the work-force were engaged in industry, 12.7% in agriculture, 12.4% in trade and services, 10.4% in education, 7.5% in health care, 7.4% in transport and communications, 7.2% in construction and some 15% in other sectors. After independence, unemployment increased slowly, reaching only 96,000 by mid-1993, which amounted to approximately 1.0%–1.5% of the total labour force. According to IMF sources, the rate of unemployment rose to a peak of 3.9% in the last quarter of 1996, but declined thereafter; it was only 2.3% in 1999, but reached 3.0% in 2002 and 3.2% in the first six months of 2003. The IMF estimated that up to 10% of the labour force were underemployed. Low unemployment was partly the result of a government policy of subsidizing faltering industries at the expense of more profitable ones, with a predictable effect on the budgetary deficit. It also reflected the contraction of the labour force, which decreased in size, by 16%, between 1989 and 1996, and recovered to only 83.2% of its 1989 level by the end of 2002. Labour-force participation rates were higher for women than for men, and most of those unemployed were women. (From the mid-1990s, the number of unemployed females was around 1.5 times the number of unemployed males.) Although unemployment figures were based on the number of people applying for unemployment benefits, benefits were so low that many people did not apply for them. In late 2000 the Ministry of Labour estimated that the rate of unemployment was actually between 5% and 8%, and in 2002 IMF and others estimated that unemployment was at least 8% higher than officially recorded. The situation was compounded by the widespread late payment of wages and by the practice of granting furlough to employees, without pay or with reduced pay. This situation worsened after the Russian currency crisis, with wage arrears reaching approximately 10% of the total wage bill by August 1999. Wage arrears persisted in the early 2000s, and were concentrated mainly in the agricultural sector, although in 2002 industrial arrears increased as a result of government-mandated wage increases.

Wage rates are regulated by the Government, and two main reference points are used in determining wages and pensions. The first is the so-called minimum wage, which is used in calculating social-assistance payments and pensions. The second is the wage 'grid', specifically the first-grade wage. The grid has 28 increments or grades, all defined as a multiple of the first-grade wage; the maximum wage grade is 8.39 times the first grade. The wage grid covers about 1m. workers, 700,000 of whom work for central and local government, mainly in the social and cultural sphere. From 1 March 2001 those working in the so-called 'power ministries'—in defence, security, the police-force, or as border guards—and workers in the state administration were excluded from the grid. The Government defined a subsistence level of income, which was equivalent to 3.5 times the first-grade wage, or seven times the minimum wage, at July 2001.

Wages are supposed to be increased regularly, according to a formula codified in the Law on Indexation of Wages, passed in 1991. The basis for wage indexation is subsistence income, 50% of which is index-linked to inflation, whenever the monthly rate of inflation has exceeded 5%. If inflation is below that level, no wage increase takes place; therefore, between January 2001 and July 2002 there were no automatic adjustments. However, the Government increasingly relied on discretionary adjustments to wages, and these increases had become the most important component of the adjustment system. Public employees receive bonuses and associated benefits in recognition of years of service and work performed. Some benefits are universal, such as long-service allowances and performance bonuses. Professional allowances are also given, as are other special bonuses. In mid-2001, at the mid-level of the wage grid, benefits exceeded basic wages by 65%–75%. State-owned enterprises are excluded from the wage grid. None the less, wage increases tend to occur at the same time as those covered by the grid. Consequently, excessive wage increases have damaged enterprise balance sheets. Wages have increased as profits have fallen, and such enterprises are not able to make workers redundant.

High inflation and foreign-exchange and price controls have enabled the Government periodically to increase wages sharply, in real terms, and then allow their value to erode, leaving the population poorer. In US dollar terms, in Russia labour costs decreased by 20% between 1993 and 2000, but rose by 130% in Belarus, or by over 230%, according to the official exchange rate. In dollar terms, wages increased in 2001 and 2002 by a further 15%, while productivity increased by just 11.2%. Between 1993 and 2000, unit labour costs increased by 20%—among the highest rates of increase in any transition country.

During the presidential campaign for re-election in 2001, Lukashenka promised to increase the average wage to US $100 per month by the end of 2001, to $125 by the end of 2002, and to $250 by the end of 2005. In the months preceding the election wages were increased in all sectors of the economy, enabling the President to claim to have fulfilled his promise. However, devaluation meant that wages declined, in dollar terms, at the beginning of 2002, although they had recovered to over $100 per month by the end of the year. The minimum wage and the first grade of the wage grid were raised successively in 2000–02. In rouble terms, the minimum wage increased at five-monthly intervals, and was raised from 2,600 roubles per month on 1 May 2000, to 7,500 roubles per month on 1 July 2001, and to 20,300 roubles by the end of 2002. In dollar terms, the minimum wage increased from $2.70 per month at the beginning of May 2000 to $6.50 per month by December 2001, and to $10.59 one year later. The first grade of the wage grid was also increased successively, from 5,200 roubles per month on 1 May 2000, to 14,500 roubles on 1 July 2001, and 19,500 roubles on 1 December 2001 (or from an initial rate of $5.40 to $12.70). By September the average, public-sector monthly wage had reached $88, while the average monthly wage for the economy as a whole had reached $97. Employees in the 'power ministries' and the state administration received a separate series of wage increases. According to official statistics, wages increased by 30.3%, in real terms, during 2001, and pensions increased by 35.7%, the highest increases to be recorded in almost a decade, although it appeared to be unsustainable.

In the first half of 2002 the social protection fund, responsible for providing pensions, ran into deficit, prompting suggestions that the pension system be reformed. As well as providing pensions, the fund also provides child support and other social benefits. In theory, the pension element of the fund is self-supporting, but indications suggest that in the future it will have to rely on budget transfers from the central Government. At present, pensions increase in synchronization with wages, and pensions have increased sharply, from the equivalent of 32.5% of average wage and salary income in 1994 to almost 44% in 2002; this figure was expected to increase to 45% in 2003. This caused a deficit in the pension system, exacerbated by a sharp decline in the number of employed persons per pensioner, from an average of 2.2 in 1990 to just under 1.8 in 2002. During a period in which employment has declined by over 16%, the number of pensioners has risen by 11%. Consequently, the pensions bill increased from 18.1% of the estimated salary bill in 1994 to 27.1% in 2002. There were delays in payments of pensions throughout 2002, and the fund was eventually assisted by central government funding.

Higher wages resulted in increased wage arrears, particularly in the agricultural sector, and there was a sharp rise in the number of unprofitable firms. Moreover, wage increases were not accompanied by increased productivity. Between the beginning of 2001 and the beginning of 2003 wages increased by 41.7%, but productivity rose by only 11.2%. Furthermore, between September 2001 and the end of January 2003, the real exchange rate of the rouble had grown by 10%, or by 20% against the US dollar and by 6% against the Russian rouble, making Belarusian firms still less competitive. By mid-2002 inflation, resulting in part from the raising of government-controlled prices, had eroded many of the benefits of the wage increases, leaving the economy far less competitive. Thus, taking December 2000 prices as 100, in real terms, rents increased to 376, heating to 353, water and sewage tariffs to 195, hot water to 354, natural gas to 271, electricity to 165, and urban transport costs to 228. In rouble terms, the appreciation was much steeper. For example, rents increased by 7.4 times, natural gas prices by 5.4 times and urban transport fares by 4.5 times. Despite these price increases, cost coverage of most services was low: at the end of 2002 it was only 31.5% for rents, 75.3% for heat, 50.8% for water, 53.8% for sewage, and 42.5% for hot water.

Rapid wage growth complicated government finance: in 2000 the wage bill was equivalent to 6% of GDP, and it was expected to reach 9% in 2001. Belarus, therefore, had one of the largest government wage bills in the CIS. To compensate for increased wages, the Government reduced spending in other areas, including capital expenditure. Despite this, in mid-2000 the IMF estimated that about one-third of the population was living in poverty, a percentage that had increased in comparison with previous years. However, the Government announced that the basic wage would reach subsistence level by the end of 2005.

An additional problem facing the labour force is the *propiska* system, a legacy from the days of the USSR. People have to register with the authorities in order to live in most towns and cities, and without being registered they are unable to obtain housing or work; however, without a job it is often difficult to register. Consequently, it is not easy to migrate elsewhere in search of work. In July 2003 the Organization for Security and Co-operation in Europe (OSCE) announced that it was to help the Government reform the system.

There is no overall programme in place to address poverty. Instead, the Government has continued to implement a series of untargeted benefits, such as price controls, child support and subsidies for housing and agriculture. There is also a state pension, but its value, although increased in recent years, is low. In order to focus support on those in need, in May 2000 a plan for targeted social-security benefits was adopted by the Government, which was to become operational at the beginning of 2001. To qualify, recipients had to have an income that was less than one-half of the subsistence level. In addition, aid was to be directed at specific groups, including single pensioners, single parents with children under 16 years old, families with three or more children, and families with disabled members. The Government aimed to accompany the introduction of targeted assistance with reductions in subsidies for communal services and housing.

In addition to social security, the country maintained a fund for victims of the Chornobyl disaster, initially funded by a 12% payroll levy, although the value of compensation payments was eroded by inflation. The Government was also committed to undertaking environmental protection and reconstruction in areas affected by Chornobyl. Within the former USSR, Belarus was the region most damaged by the disaster. Fallout was particularly severe in four areas: an area north and west of the nuclear power plant, extending as far north as Pinsk and to within 100 km of Brest; a central region, to the west and north-west of Minsk (Miensk); an eastern region, covering the eastern part of Mogilev Oblast; and a south-eastern region, including much of Gomel (Homiel) Oblast. In addition, concentrations of radioactive incidence were scattered throughout the country, and radioactive deposits were spread by droughts and forest fires.

### Finance

In late 1991 Belarus assumed 4.13% of the total debt of the former USSR, which it later transferred to Russia in exchange for Belarus' share of Soviet assets. In early 1992 shortages of currency led to a requirement that substantial payments be made by cheque, rather than cash, and the Government introduced currency coupons for use in state stores. The coupons (officially denominated as roubles, but popularly known as *zaichiki*) were given a value of 10 Russian roubles, and 10%–15% of salaries were paid in coupons. In November 1992 the state halted the sale of food, tobacco and alcohol for ordinary (Russian) roubles and announced that these goods could only be purchased with coupons (Belarusian roubles). The decision was apparently prompted by mass purchases of these (still subsidized) items by buyers from Lithuania and Ukraine.

After much discussion between 1992 and 1995, a new Belarusian currency was introduced. This was supported by pro-independence politicians and deplored by those keen to re-create a 'common economic space' with Russia. Although the National Bank of Belarus supported the introduction of a national currency, an agreement with Russia, from September 1993, to create a joint monetary system, seemed to preclude a separate currency. However, a Belarusian proposal for monetary union with Russia was rejected in early 1995, because the proposed conversion undervalued the Russian rouble and threatened Russian economic reforms. Consequently, in May Belarus introduced the Belarusian rouble (rubel), which became the country's sole legal tender, although estimates suggested that between 30% and 40% of all transactions may actually have taken place in US dollars. The introduction of the national rouble, and stronger exercise of authority by the central bank, led to a sharp reduction in the rate of inflation.

In 1995 Lukashenka nationalized the country's leading private currency exchange and transferred supervision of the central bank from the legislature to his office. In March 1998, with the collapse in the value of the currency, exchange-rate controls were imposed and the central bank lost its vestigial independence. Such responses to the country's problems prompted warnings from the World Bank and the IMF, and both institutions suspended lending to Belarus in the mid-1990s, insisting that significant economic reform would have to come first. However, in April 2001 the IMF restored its relations with Belarus, and subsequently produced monitoring reports on the economy and economic performance.

By 2000 official policy aimed to restore the economy to its 1990 levels and government intervention continued to play a key role in economic management. Wage and price controls, reintroduced in 1996, and the expansion of the monetary supply were leading aspects of the economic policies of the Lukashenka regime. The main indicators used in shaping economic policy were the rate of growth of GDP and the unemployment level. According to official statistics, GDP grew steadily after 1996, and had recovered to 93% of its 1989 level by the end of 2002. However, given the high rate of inflation, the increase in barter trade, and tax and wage arrears in a growing number of enterprises, GDP figures were unreliable.

In October 1999 wage and price controls were extended to the private sector, which had previously been exempt. However, monetary policy remained largely unreformed and reform of banking and of non-bank financial institutions was non-existent. An indication of this could be seen in the declining share it contributed to GDP, falling from 9.1% in 1993 to just 3.3% in 1997.

Prices are regulated by the Government through the Price Committee of the Ministry of the Economy. By late 2000 controls existed for 30% of producer goods sold, and prices for the remaining 70% were set by manufacturers, within government limits. Until 2001 the Government regularly set mandatory maximum price increases on a monthly and quarterly basis. These varied, depending on the product and on the prevailing rate of inflation. If a firm wanted to increase prices it had to apply at least 15 days in advance; requests were generally refused, but if a firm increased prices without permission it had to pay fines equal to three times the difference in revenue. A consequence has been that many firms fail to make a profit, although government-sponsored loans compensate for this to some extent. A second consequence is that many firms are driven into the so-called 'grey' (unofficial) economy, which was estimated to equal between 20% and 25% of GDP in the 1990s; in the case of small and medium-sized enterprises operating in the private sector, it was estimated to equal as much as 60%.

By late 1999 Belarus had exchange rates that comprised official cash and non-cash rates, a market-cash rate, a 'black market' rate and a parallel inter-bank market rate. The official rate was set by the central bank, and the market-cash rate was subject to a currency maximum limited, as of September 1999, to 1,000 foreign currency units. The Russian currency devaluation of August 1998 compounded the problems of the Belarusian currency, which was forced to devalue even earlier in the year. In 1999 the Government instituted a 'sliding peg' devaluation of the official rate, whereby the exchange rate moves in response to supply and demand conditions, but by a restricted amount each month. Also, in late 1999 the proportion of foreign currency that exporters, commercial banks and domestic retailers were required to surrender was set at 40%, later reduced to 30%, where it remained in 2003. From the beginning of 2000 a redenominated currency began to be introduced, with one new rouble being equivalent to 1,000 old roubles. By April 2000 the exchange rate to the dollar was some 475,000 new roubles (or 475 redenominated roubles), although on the open market the currency was worth approximately 40% of the official rate. The existence of different exchange rates and subsidized prices encouraged the growth of a cross-border 'black' (illegal) market trade with Latvia, Lithuania and Poland. In September the National Bank introduced a single rouble exchange rate.

Since independence, inflation has been a persistent feature of the economy, and it remains a key element of fiscal policy. It peaked at an annual rate of 2,219% in 1994, before declining to 27.5% in 1995. However, after 1996 it increased again, reaching an annual rate of 293.8% in 1998, then declining gradually to reach 42% in 2002. Despite declining inflation rates, from 1998 Belarus had the highest rate of consumer-price inflation in the CIS, and in 2001–02 the rate was almost three times that of Russia. In addition, as inflation declined, the role of administered price increases in total inflation increased, and in 2002 the IMF estimated that they were responsible for about one-third of total inflation (12% out of 35%, year-on-year, in December 2002), although the main cause of inflation remained the expansion of the monetary supply.

Inflation and the depreciation of the currency led to the 'dollarization' of the economy. Deposits in US dollars are permitted, and even encouraged, and between 1995 and the end of 1999 the share of dollar deposits increased from 39% to 53% of total deposits, although this was owing, in part, to the depreciation of the rouble against the dollar. However, the trend continued thereafter: by the end of 2002 60.5% of deposits in the banking system, and 57.4% of domestic loans, were in foreign currency.

Foreign remittances remained an important source of foreign income, accounting for over US $120m. in 1998 and $60m. in 1999. In order to discourage dollar 'flight', the authorities introduced a number of measures, including a 1998 decree guaranteeing foreign-currency household deposits and exempting interest on foreign-currency deposits from tax. By June 1998 there was $151m. in deposits in the formal banking system, but it was estimated that a further $2,000m. was held by the Belarusian population, and another $2,000m. was banked abroad. Banking-sector assets amounted to 15% of GDP in mid-2000, the lowest level of all the CIS countries, and even that level may be overstated, owing to inflation.

Strong state control and frequent state intervention, plus the view that banks should fulfil a set of social obligations, led to widespread lending to state-owned enterprises and farms that were and are not creditworthy. Loans were also extended to priority sectors, including housing and agriculture, at nominal rates, far below the prevailing rate of inflation. Moreover, although a deposit insurance system exists, the maximum payout under the scheme is US $1,000 in foreign currency, or the equivalent value in roubles, calculated at the official rate. Although lending limits exist, they do not appear to be enforced. Banking losses are likely to be great if serious restructuring ever takes place. Based on existing rules for loss provisions, problem loans equalled 48% of bank system equity at the end of 2000, but this category included only loans that had been made to already liquidated entities and similar situations, and did not take into account those enterprises that were technically insolvent.

The banking system is unreformed. In 2003 there were 28 banks, with a total of 485 branches: five were completely foreign-owned and another seven were more than 50% foreign-owned; eight banks had been founded since the beginning of 2000. Of the six largest banks, five were state-owned. Over 50% of the shares in one, Priorbank, were sold to the Raiffeisen Bank of Austria in 2001, and at the end of January 2003 Raiffeisen Bank acquired the remainder. At the end of 2002 the six largest banks accounted for 88.4% of total bank assets, and 448 branches. The Government compelled banks to lend to specific sectors and enterprises designated by the state, regardless of their solvency. Consequently, the quality of their assets was uncertain, and the Government had to provide periodic injections of capital. Despite a 2001 agreement with the IMF to end directed lending, in the second half of 2002 banks were required to lend to agricultural enterprises, and to finance the clearance of wages arrears and foreign energy debts. At the end of 2001 non-performing loans accounted for 14.1% of total lending. The authorities claimed that in 2002 the proportion had fallen to just 8.3%, but the IMF suggested that the situation might, in fact, have worsened. Reserves were also insufficient, particularly in terms of foreign currency. Although a substantial proportion of deposits were in foreign currency, foreign asset cover is low, and at the end of 2002 central bank foreign-currency reserves were equal to just 0.8 months of import spending.

Subsidies are a prominent feature of economic management. The IMF estimated that exchange-rate subsidies amounted to between 6% and 8% of GDP at their peak in 1998. The unification of foreign-exchange rates subsequently reduced subsidies. In 2000 the IMF estimated that direct and indirect subsidies were, together, equivalent to about 10% of

GDP, although this understated the total, since it excluded tax arrears and other liabilities. Direct subsidies, provided by the state budget, equalled about 2% of GDP, while indirect and extrabudgetary subsidies were equivalent to some 8%. Direct subsidies included aid to state enterprises and government organizations, as well as assistance to social programmes and sectors such as agriculture and housing. Non-budgetary subsidies included tax concessions, the free provision of communal services, and exemptions from customs duties for selected firms or sectors. One of the largest single subsidies was for energy, particularly natural gas.

Consumer subsidies, which allow consumers to purchase goods at below cost price, operated through price controls, the under-pricing of rents and utilities, and various types of cross-subsidy. From April 2001, in response to pressure from the IMF, the Government reduced the number of categories of 'socially important' goods, subject to price controls, from 48 to 13, and then to nine, and removed limits on permissible maximum monthly price increases. Goods that subsequently remained subject to price controls included the 13 categories of socially important goods, goods produced by 25 'strategic' enterprises, and goods that, for one reason or another, were under ministerial control. The share of controlled prices in the consumer price index subsequently fell to 20%–22% by the end of 2001, compared with 50% at the end of 1998.

Enterprises paid surcharges to offset consumer subsidies, but benefited from subsidies of their own, which included tax preferences, tax exemptions and exemptions from customs duties. Agriculture benefited from free fuel during harvest times, and indirect subsidies on fertilizers and other inputs. Interest subsidies were also granted to key sectors, including agriculture, housing and selected manufacturing enterprises. Commercial banks had been under instruction to provide subsidized loans to priority sectors, especially agriculture, although by 2001 this practice was supposed to have been halted.

Arrears on wage, tax and energy payments were substantial, and constituted a further subsidy. In 2001 agricultural enterprises accounted for the largest proportion of energy arrears, followed by housing and communal services, construction enterprises and education, although by 2002 industry had risen to first place, and was responsible for about one-half of all energy arrears. Wage arrears also increased substantially, mainly owing to the Government's initiative to raise monthly wages (see above). Unprofitable firms were also subsidized. At the end of 1999 the IMF found that inter-enterprise arrears amounted to the equivalent of 37.5% of GDP, and, as mentioned above, a high percentage of the country's enterprises operated at a loss. Overdue payables were equivalent to 18.1% of GDP in 2002, and the stock of expenditure arrears increased sharply in rouble terms from 1999. Tax arrears also increased sharply between 1999 and 2002.

## AGRICULTURE

Until the early 1970s the Belarusian economy had a largely agricultural base. In 1990 agriculture accounted for 29.3% of NMP, although this decreased to 16.7% by 1994. In terms of GDP, the contribution of agriculture was estimated at 24.0% in 1990 and was 12.7% in 2002, according to official statistics; however, according to the IMF, agriculture and forestry accounted for just 10.9% of GDP. Some 16.4% of the workforce was still employed in agriculture in 1998, although by the end of 2002 the total had declined sharply, to just 11.8% or 513,000, a loss of some 133,000. About two-thirds of those employed in the sector worked on collective farms. Since much of the land was poor and the climate was severely continental, animal husbandry and hardier crops predominated. Major products included flax, accounting for 27% of total production

in the USSR at the time of its dissolution, potatoes (15% of Soviet production), buckwheat, rye, meat and dairy products, and, from the early 1980s, sugar beet. Other important crops included barley and animal fodder. Oats, millet, hay and tobacco were also grown in small amounts.

Agriculture in Belarus was devastated by the spread of radioactive 'fall-out' from the accident at the Chornobyl nuclear power station in Ukraine in 1986. Official estimates claimed that about 20% of Belarusian territory suffered contamination, in particular the regions of Gomel and Mogilev (Mahiloŭ). This was the main agricultural region of Belarus and contained some 2.2m. people. By 1992 257,000 hectares (ha) of agricultural land, just over 4% of the country's total, had been removed from use, as had 1,340,000 ha of forests, about 15% of the total. Unfortunately, after 1986 the authorities were slow to recognize the extent of the disaster and were impeded by a lack of information and poor access to sites. In the early 1990s poisoned soil continued to be dislodged by ploughing, and contaminated food products were still being sold. In 1990, for example, 784,000 metric tons of meat (not much less than the total level of consumption within the republic and over 65% of Belarus' total production) were reported to have come from contaminated zones and to have been marketed in Belarus and elsewhere in the USSR. The problems caused by the Chornobyl disaster ensured that agricultural production began to decline in the late 1980s, and the collapse of the USSR in late 1991 led to the loss of markets, and further declines in output.

In the early 2000s the agricultural sector remained unreformed, and assistance to the agricultural sector had profoundly destabilized the national economy. The sector accounted for the bulk of wage arrears (about 90% of the total in 2001). Overall profitability in the sector declined from 12.8% in 1997 to 6.2% in 2000, –5.3% in 2001 and –0.3% in 2002. The depreciation of fixed assets increased dramatically between 1997 and 2000, from 58.2% to 80.6% of nominal value, and the sector remained starved of investment capital. As a solution to the sector's problems, Lukashenka suggested that existing collective and co-operative farms be merged to form larger agro-combines, a proposal first suggested in the late 1970s, under Soviet rule. However, the rural population accounted for a substantial proportion of Lukashenka's support and, as part of his social contract, he implicitly guaranteed to preserve the sector in its existing form and to protect workers from massive economic upheavals. The sector benefited from a special tax, and a resolution, adopted in March 2000 and aimed at aiding state and collective farms, requested that all government agencies, banks and state-owned enterprises 'adopt' a farm. Loans continue to be made at a notional rate of interest, despite high inflation, and helped to raise the country's fiscal deficit by several percentage points. Aid to agriculture destabilized the economy in several ways; for example, at the beginning of the 2000s banks were asked to provide 35,000m. roubles in lending, by selling foreign-exchange reserves to the central bank. Banks were still compelled to extend loans to agricultural enterprises, although the practice was formally halted at the beginning of 2001. In 2002 the tax for agriculture accounted for about 2% of government revenue (down from 3.3% in 2000), and from the beginning of 2001 there was a special tax for agriculture and roads of 2% of the sales of goods, labour and services, or, in the case of banks and non-bank financial organizations, net income. Income from this tax was divided evenly between support for roads and agriculture.

Despite these subsidies, rural poverty remained widespread, and farm workers' wages were well below those of the general population. Many agricultural workers were paid in goods instead of money, and virtually all relied on household plots. From the late 1990s the Government attempted to raise rural incomes by increasing the purchasing price of output more rapidly than the rate of inflation, but in January 2002 Lukashenka announced that the state was only to raise purchase prices for farm products to compensate for the rate of inflation. He implied that the sector would encounter declining demand, owing, seemingly, to declining real incomes for the population at large. He added that the sector needed to reduce production costs by 25% by means of better organization and work discipline.

Production of grain and other crops declined sharply from the early 1990s, owing to environmental factors, such as drought and widespread flooding in the south of the country. Animal husbandry suffered too, and meat production declined by 46% between 1990 and 2002. According to the UN's Food and Agriculture Organization (FAO), the number of cattle declined from 7,270,000 head in 1989 to 4,220,500 in 2001, the number of pigs decreased from 5,134,000 to 3,430,700, and that of sheep decreased from 570,400 to 89,000. According to official statistics, measured in constant prices, by the end of 2002 total output in the sector had declined to 61.6% of the 1989 level. The decline in output partly reflected the loss of markets in the former USSR, particularly the Baltic states and the St Petersburg region of Russia, but also reflected declining living standards. This was indicated by the fact that the contribution of food to retail turnover had increased from 44.9% in 1990 to 64.1% by 2002.

Overall, agricultural GDP declined by an annual average of 3.0% in 1990–2001, declining by 8.3% in 1999, owing to poor harvests in 1998–99, before registering growth of 9.3% in 2000, the first year of growth since 1996, and by 1.8% in 2001. Output increased by 1.5% in 2002.

Decreasing production levels were partly attributable to the structural defects of the collective-farm system, but from 1993 sectoral reform was largely abandoned. At the beginning of the 1990s some private farms were created, however. In addition, household plots, initially up to 0.5 ha but, from 1999, up to 1 ha in size, could be privately owned. From the mid-1990s the private sector dominated production of a number of commodities, including 95% of fruit, 85% of potatoes and 75% of vegetables. Household plots accounted for about 15.5% of agricultural land, but produced about 40% of gross agricultural output. Private land had to be used for its initial purpose after privatization, and owners of household plots were permitted to lease another 2 ha of land for subsistence farming, while private farmers were permitted to lease up to 100 ha. Although the number of private farms increased from 1992 (when there were 792, accounting for just 0.2% of agricultural land), by 2000 there were fewer than 3,000 privately owned family farms.

At the beginning of the 1990s Belarus had about 2,500 state and collective farms; by the beginning of the 2000s most remained essentially unchanged. Agriculture is still managed centrally; there are district and regional production targets for farms, all farms are required to make deliveries to state procurement agencies, and there are fixed price-procurement quotas for all the major crops and livestock products. Moreover, profits are strictly controlled. Consequently, in the case of some products, commercial sales do not take place, owing to the need to fulfil production quotas. In late 1999 publicly owned farms sold about 85% of their output to the state or to state-owned processing firms, and private farms nearly two-thirds. According to the IMF, at the end of 1999 even household plots sold 20% of their output to state purchasers and processors, and another 35% to local collective farms. State agencies supply nearly all fertilizer, farm machinery, construction materials and fuel, and prices are controlled for fertilizers, pesticides, leasing machinery, drainage and veterinary medicines.

Throughout the 1990s state support amounted to about US $250m.–$300m. per year. In 1999 it was equivalent to about 3% of GDP, and equalled about 20% of sectoral output, although it declined slightly thereafter, and was just 2.2% of GDP in 2002, equivalent to 8.7% of output, and accounted for 6.4% of total government spending. About one-third of all investment in agriculture came from the state. Support came directly from the budget but, as has been noted, also includes central bank credits, directed through commercial banks, state-sponsored support from enterprises, and indirect subsidies, including cheap foreign exchange and fuel. This led to unpaid debts at banks, and helped to maintain an essentially unreformed system of agriculture. Despite the costs to the economy and the risks to the banking system, the policy of farm subsidies remained popular, although the subsidy was a major political and economic issue. However, even with government support, throughout the 1990s wages in agriculture were among the lowest of all sectors, and at just 57.8% of the average wage in 2002, remain so. Despite subsidies, agriculture is in an increasingly parlous state. Observers claimed that at the end of 2002 the cost of food was higher in Belarus than in neighbouring Lithuania and Poland. By the end of 2002 1,500 of the country's 2,500 agricultural enterprises were loss-making, and more than one-third were bankrupt. The average debt of each was 800m. roubles (about $400,000). In late 2002 the Government announced plans to reform the sector. It was expected that farms would be able to sell their produce freely, and that regulations on the trade and sale of agricultural produce would be lifted or simplified. Bankrupt enterprises were to be denied state aid, and the state was to refuse to purchase from them. Collective farms were to be transformed into co-operatives, although their basic organization would be essentially unchanged. However, the status of the reforms remained in doubt, and in mid-2003 the most popular type of reform seemed to involve merging collective farms with industrial enterprises, so that farm losses could be covered.

## MINING AND ENERGY

Peat was traditionally used locally to produce electricity and for domestic heating, particularly in rural areas. However, after the Chornobyl disaster contaminated peat could not be burned to produce electric power, as the dispersal of contaminated ash could cause further long-term problems. Small deposits of petroleum and natural gas had been found and exploited, although output declined from the 1970s; annual petroleum production stabilized in the late 1980s at approximately 2.0m. barrels per year and annual production of natural gas remained at between 200m. and 300m. cu m in the mid-1990s. Belarus was an important producer of potassium salts, producing about one-half of the total output of the former USSR. Although there were some deposits of brown coal (lignite) and other minerals, few were commercially exploitable. The republic imported the bulk of its raw materials and fuels.

Two important petroleum pipelines run through the country, both built during the Soviet period: the Druzhba (Friendship) pipeline along the southern border; and the Soyuz (Union) pipeline along the northern border. To complement the pipelines, two refineries were built. One was located at Mozyr (Mazyr), where the Druzhba pipeline split into two sections (one going towards Hungary and Slovakia, and the other towards Poland and Germany). The second refinery was sited at Polotsk (Polacak), where the Soyuz pipeline also split into two (one line going to Poland, and the second to Ventspils in Latvia). As a result, until 1990 Belarus was an important supplier of refined petroleum products. However, declining output in Russia, problems of supply, and Russia's need to sell petroleum on the world market to obtain convertible currency, contributed to a decline in supplies to Belarus.

Belarus is heavily dependent on energy imports, which are the main cause of the trade deficit. Imports of petroleum, natural gas, and electricity, and accumulated energy debts caused regular trade crises, which led to interruptions in energy supplies throughout the 1990s and early 2000s. In 2001 25% of domestic electricity consumption was met through imports, although in 2002 imports supplied just 20% of electricity needs. In 2002 the cost of electricity imports was US $136.2m., or about 15% of the total trade deficit. Industry consumes almost one-half of all electricity: 47.3% in 2002. Despite problems in paying for electricity imports the transmission system suffers high losses—almost 12.3% of total output in 2001—and consumption of electricity has generally increased since the mid-1990s.

The situation with natural gas is even more precarious. Gas is used for both heating and generating electricity. In the 1980s many power stations were converted to use natural gas, as the USSR was unable to consume its domestic gas output. In 2002, for example, 80% of natural gas consumption was used in electricity generation. Since 1993 Belarus has repeatedly fallen behind in its energy payments, and defaulted several times on payments for gas, although after the proclamation of the Union Treaty, the country benefited from subsidized energy prices. However, in exchange for low prices, the authorities were compelled to cede control over key assets. Thus, after Belarus defaulted on gas payments in 1993, a 30% share in the Mozyr petroleum refinery was transferred to Russia, in exchange for a 10.8% stake in the petroleum firm Slavneft, leading to liquidation of the debt. After arrears accrued again in 1996–99, the Belarusian and Russian Governments concluded agreements that allowed the repayment of debts by barter, using food, technical resources and manufactured goods. However, by the end of January 2000 Belarus's gas debt to Russia still stood at a little over US $200m. The Belarusian authorities demanded that energy be sold by Russia at a reduced price, and in January Gazprom announced that the price of gas (already reduced from $50 per 1,000 cu m to $30 per 1,000 cu m in March 1999) was to be further reduced, by 10%, a concession related to the Union Treaty. In 2002, in connection with the JAP for currency union, the Russian Government announced that Belarus was to receive gas and transportation services at domestic Russian prices, leading to a reduction in the prices for both gas and electricity imports from Russia. (Belarus was to pay the same price for gas as Russia's so-called 'fifth energy belt'—the Smolensk region.) Thus the price of gas was reduced to $24 per 1,000 cu m; however, the agreement only covered 10,600m. cu m of gas, or 59.8% of domestic consumption in that year. The deal also committed Belarus to establishing a joint venture with Russia to transport natural gas through Belarus, by divesting part of the national gas pipeline monopoly, Beltransgaz. In June 2002 the privately owned Russian trader Itera halted supplies to the republic, after it accumulated debts of $24m. By late October Gazprom was also threatening to terminate supplies to Belarus, and after inter-governmental negotiations Belarus announced that it was to buy additional gas supplies, but at the much higher price of $36. (Even at this higher price, however, Itera was losing money, as it was buying gas from Turkmenistan at $44 per 1,000 cu m. Gas was sold by Russia to Ukraine for about $60 per 1,000 cu m, to Lithuania and Poland for about $80 and to Western European consumers for over $100 per 1,000 cu m.) In December the Belarusian Government sold its stake in Slavneft.

The gas debt crisis was partly resolved by a disbursement of US $40m. from the Russian authorities to be used to buy Russian products, although it was dependent on additional

economic reforms. Despite lower gas prices, by the beginning of January 2003 Belarus owed $208.7m. for gas, $129.4m. of which was owed to Gazprom ($282m. if penalties and past debts were included). However, according to the IMF, overall gas debts declined by $73m. in 2002. The Belarusian authorities resolved to privatize Beltransgaz by mid-2003, and to create a new joint venture with Gazprom; in preparation for this, it transformed Beltransgaz into a joint-stock company in April 2003. (This required a legislative amendment, since the firm was one of several designated for state ownership.) However, the value of the organization was disputed, with the Belarusian authorities proposing $3,000m., and the Russian side considerably less, prompting Lukashenka to express doubts about the planned privatization. In addition, there were questions about what form the purchase would take: shares for debt or shares for cash, and over which side would have overall control of the firm. In 2003 Belarus was promised 10,200m. cu m of gas (of a total of 18,500m. cu m) at Russian domestic prices. However, in September the Russian Government announced that Gazprom was to halt its subsidized gas exports to Belarus from 2004.

As was the case with electricity, Belarus made few efforts to restrict energy consumption or to promote energy conservation. Gas consumption rose steadily from 1997, and government projections anticipated further rises. As electricity consumption grew, gas consumption registered a corresponding increase. Despite subsidized prices, industry remained the main energy debtor, accounting for 54.5% of total energy debts, distributed fairly evenly between gas and electricity. None the less, energy tariffs remain relatively low, although energy prices were increased substantially in 2000–02.

Although energy subsidies to Belarus were costly for the Russian Government, the country remained a more reliable agent than Ukraine, through which another major gas pipeline passes to the West. Belarus was expected to become more important to Russia's energy industry when the Yamal gas pipeline opened in 2003. Work commenced in 2000, and a 575 km segment of the pipeline, crossing Belarusian territory, had been completed by July 2003. Once the entire pipeline was finished, the amount of gas shipped across Belarus was expected to increase three-fold, dramatically reducing Russia's dependence on Ukraine as a gas transit route.

In the mid-1990s construction of nuclear power stations was postponed, although more recently it has been suggested that, despite the experience of Chornobyl, new nuclear power stations should be built, in order to reduce Belarus's dependence on energy imports.

## INDUSTRY

Industry (including transport and construction) contributed some 44% of total NMP in 1990 and 26.6% by 1994. In terms of GDP, industry contributed 28.9% in that year (when transport and construction are excluded), and by the end of 2001 contributed just 27.7%. Construction accounted for an additional 5.3% of GDP, and transport and communications for 11.3%. According to the IMF, in 1990 industry employed 30.9% of the labour force (or 26.0%, according to the state statistical office).

Until the early 1970s Belarus specialized in light industry, based on the processing of agricultural products. By the late 1980s the chemicals and machine-building industries were well developed, although light industry remained important. Minsk became one of the most important centres of the Soviet microelectronics and computer industry. As a rule, major industrial enterprises were concentrated in large cities, but smaller enterprises, processing agricultural and timber products, were distributed fairly evenly throughout the country. Since independence, light industry has declined sharply in terms of output and profitability. By the end of 2002 inventories of unsold goods were highest in this sub-sector, equivalent to 130.2% of monthly output, or twice the national average.

Belarus was a leading producer of consumer durables within the USSR, including radio receivers, television sets, furniture and shoes, production of which far exceeded domestic demand. It was responsible for some 20% of Soviet motorcycle production and was the world's third largest producer of tractors in the 1980s. Large lorries and trucks were also manufactured, although production only accounted for a small fraction of that of the former USSR. Two factories, one producing self-propelled fodder harvesters in Gomel, and another producing the important chemical, di-methyl terephthalate, in Mogilev, dominated production of their respective products in the former USSR (accounting for 91% and 93% of total Soviet output, respectively, by the beginning of the 1990s). However, Belarus depended on other parts of the former USSR for most basic products.

At independence Belarus had a small steel industry: annual production of crude steel remained at an average of 1m. metric tons during the 1980s, and annual production of finished steel products remained fairly constant at some 700,000 tons. This industry was entirely dependent on imported raw materials, and was able to satisfy only a small proportion of domestic demand. Despite this, steel production declined after 1991. However, in 1996 the iron and steel industry recorded an increase in production of 23.2%, and production continued to expand dramatically. By the late 1990s over one-half of the sector's output was exported and, of that, more than one-half was sold outside the CIS. In 2002 ferrous and non-ferrous metallurgy remained among the most successful branches of industry in the country.

A large number of enterprises in Belarus were involved in production for the Soviet armed forces. With the collapse of the USSR, military orders almost halted, and attempts to convert to civil production were largely unsuccessful, partly because of a lack of available investment. In 1992 there were an estimated 120 large enterprises in Belarus dependent on military orders for survival, employing 370,000 people. Their closure would have had a severe impact on unemployment, hence the enthusiasm among many of the directors of such companies for an economic union with Russia, which would allow factories to regain at least some of their pre-independence markets. From the mid-1990s the factories were partly sustained by the growing barter trade between Belarus and Russia, and in late January 2000 it was announced that the Belarusian and Russian Governments were to set up 'Defence Systems', a joint defence-financial-industrial group, comprising the Russian company of the same name and some Belarusian enterprises. This plan was the product of earlier proposals, announced in April 1999, to co-ordinate the development and production of weapons, to stimulate co-operation in border protection and to co-ordinate security strategies.

Industrial production declined at an annual average rate of 0.8% in 1990–2001, according to the World Bank, although production began to increase from 1996. Official statistics suggested that output recovered from its lowest level of 60.3% of the 1989 level in 1995, to 82.3% in 1998, and to just over 100% by the end of 2002. Industrial production expanded by 10.3% in 1999, by 7.8% in 2000, by 5.9% in 2001 and by 4.3% in 2002. Although growth has been maintained, the rate of increase has slowed, and despite IMF concerns about a tendency to overstate the value of industrial output, figures from previous years are regularly revised upwards. Moreover, prices of inputs are subsidized, product prices are controlled by the state, and a substantial proportion of exports are bartered for other goods. Therefore, real market prices of goods are uncertain and, at the very least, output values are overstated.

Investment also declined after 1991, decreasing by 18% annually in 1992 and 1993, by 24% in 1994 and by 28% in 1995. With some signs of economic recovery in 1996 and 1997, however, a certain amount of foreign investment was forthcoming, encouraged by political stability (despite misgivings in other quarters about the manner in which this was achieved) and the customs union with Russia. In 1995 foreign investment totalled US $15m. (compared with a total of over $1,134m. in neighbouring Poland). Since 2000, partly owing to pressure from the Russian Government, and partly to a need to liquidate energy debts, sales of state-owned firms to foreign investors have increased. However, in comparison with other transition countries, foreign direct investment (FDI) remains low, and domestic investment also remains insufficient. Although industry accounted for 32% of capital investment nation-wide in 2002, capital investment levels were just 59.5% of the 1990 level, and had remained below 60% throughout the 1990s.

As discussed above, government policy has protected unprofitable firms, and although the average monthly salary increased, wage arrears also increased, to represent one-eighth of the total wage bill. For industry as a whole, profitability in the sector decreased from 15.8% in 2000 to 10.8% in 2001. (It should be noted that the calculation of profitability does not include such factors as depreciation.)

After the 2001 presidential election, the Government took a two-fold approach to industry. One of these was making the case that industrial mismanagement (rather than government policy) was responsible for any economic difficulties experienced by the country. Lukashenka arrested a number of prominent managers, and pledged to imprison at least 15 business leaders accused of sabotaging the country's economy. Those arrested included the Director of the country's largest refrigerator plant, Leanid Kaluhin, and the head of Belarusian State Railways, Viktor Rakhmanko, who was also a member of the upper house of the legislature. In early January 2002 Mikhail Lyavonaw, the Director of the Minsk Tractor Plant, the country's largest factory, was arrested on suspicion of abuse of power and negligence, and accused of being responsible for fiscal losses amounting to some US $4m. However, foreign and domestic observers argued that the main reason for the prevailing economic situation was the fact that manufacturing costs often exceeded the price at which goods were sold abroad. Thus, by the end of 2002 32.9% of industrial firms were loss-making, and unsold inventories in industrial enterprises averaged 65.3% of monthly output, compared with 55.9% five years previously.

In January 2002 the Government announced that six subsidiaries of Belneftkhim were to be converted into joint-stock companies prior to their sale. It appeared that the likely buyers would be Russian petroleum and gas firms, and it was suggested that privatization would take one of two forms: firms would be re-organized and stocks sold to investors, or investors would buy a share of the firm, in exchange for a stock holding. Some suggested that the removal of the managers of other large enterprises was a precursor to their privatization by foreign, probably Russian, interests.

## TRADE

Under Soviet rule, Belarus depended heavily on inter-republican trade, which accounted for 44.6% of GDP in 1989, and it remained dependent on external trade, which equalled between 110% and 125% of GDP annually, by the beginning of the 2000s. The economic reality of trade was obscured by the Soviet pricing system, which undervalued the prices of raw materials (in comparison with world prices) in which the republic was deficient, but tended to overvalue those for machinery, in which Belarus specialized. In terms of domestic prices, Belarus had a positive inter-republican trade balance, even in 1989, of some 3,476m. roubles. However, when partial estimates of world market prices were used to calculate the trade balance (according to the World Bank), the republic recorded a deficit in its trade balance with other Union Republics, of 812m. roubles in 1989. The main factor in this disparity was the difference between the domestic price of petroleum, produced in Russia, and the world market price. Since Belarus depended on Russia for supplies of petroleum, it was evident that any transfer of Belarus' trade with Russia to world prices would cause either a severe balance-of-payments crisis or an energy crisis. This unattractive choice was with Belarus' leaders from independence. In the mid-1990s the World Bank estimated that, depending on the mix of exports and imports in any given year, the shift to world market prices could cause GDP to decline by 4%–7%.

Before 1991, in foreign (extra-Soviet) trade, Belarus appeared to have a negative balance. In 1989 the foreign-trade deficit was 2,522m. roubles at domestic prices (at foreign prices it was only 668m. roubles, there being less distortion), and in that year extra-Soviet trade accounted for 23.3% of all imports and 9.8% of total exports. In the same year the republic was responsible for some 4% of the foreign trade of the USSR, and total foreign trade accounted for 7.4% of GDP. The foreign-trade deficit increased to 7,040m. roubles in 1991. After 1991 the trade balance with non-CIS countries became positive, although trade returned to deficit by the mid-1990s.

In 1991 the republic's authorities asserted control over foreign trade, management of which was previously the preserve of the all-Union authorities in Moscow. However, erratic progress towards a unified exchange rate, a unified import tariff system and the removal of impediments to exports was commenced only in mid-1993. Belarus soon accumulated large debts with Russia for purchases of petroleum and gas. This led to an intermittent supply throughout the 1990s and early 2000s, and remains a persistent irritant in relations between the two countries. Despite this, the country's trade remained concentrated in the CIS: in 2002 the CIS accounted for 62.5% of total trade turnover, 55.1% of total exports and 69.2% of imports. Russia consistently accounted for the bulk of CIS trade, representing 91.3% in 2001 and about 97.5% in 2002, largely accounted for by energy. Below market prices for imports of petroleum and gas mean that the dominance of the CIS and particularly Russia, in trade, is understated. This dependence has resulted in a persistent trade deficit with Russia, which amounted to US $1,193.0m. in 2001 and $1,788.6m. in 2002, despite subsidized prices. The balance of trade with the rest of the world was positive. Despite the growing dependence on Russia as a source of imports, Belarus had slowly managed to diversify the direction of its exports, so that, for example, between 2001 and 2002 the proportion of exports going to the CIS declined from 60.7% to 55.1%. However, this may have been implemented at some cost. In mid-2003, for example, it was reported that the Belarusian authorities were felling trees in the historic Bielovezhskaya Pushcha National Park, one of the oldest and most well-preserved forests in Europe, in order to sell the timber abroad. Continued dependence on the CIS market, continued trade deficits and a lack of restructuring had also resulted in the growth of barter trade. In July 1999 a tax on barter (excluding certain goods and strategic companies) was introduced, of 15% for general transactions and 5% for raw materials and intermediaries; the tax was suspended in August 2000. Barter trade accounted for 38% of imports and 34% of exports in the first five months of 1999, and for 28% and 22%, respectively, during the same period in 2000. About one-quarter of barter transactions were imports of natural gas from Russia, in exchange for industrial products. Although barter trade subsequently declined, in the first half of 2001 it accounted for 15% of imports and 20% of exports. In 2000 barter trade,

including domestic trade, reached an estimated equivalent of 43.8% of GDP, although by the end of 2002 it had declined to 36.2%.

Trading patterns remained volatile. In 2002 Latvia was the leading non-CIS purchaser of Belarusian goods (accounting for 6.4%), followed by the United Kingdom (6.1%). All together, the eight accession countries of Central and South-Eastern Europe scheduled to join the EU in May 2004 accounted for about 15% of total exports from Belarus in 2002, which could have implications for future export prospects. Of the CIS countries, Russia accounted for 50.1% of total Belarusian exports in 2002, and 65.1% of imports. In the same year the leading non-CIS sources of imports was Germany (accounting for 7.7%).

By late 1995 the Belarusian legal system and practice of law enforcement, particularly as related to FDI and private entrepreneurs, were described as flawed by the European Bank for Reconstruction and Development (EBRD) and, since then, according to transition indicators published by the EBRD, Belarus had regressed in terms of reform. Although there were no major obstacles to inward investment or to repatriating profits, legal statutes were said still to be in need of significant improvement, and their effectiveness was weak. Laws were unclear and contradictory, independent legal advice was limited, courts were not independent and the administration of law was substantially deficient. Belarus generally remained unattractive to foreign investment (in 1997 the World Bank rated the country 115th, on a list of 135, in terms of business attraction), and the country remains among the least attractive of the transition countries for investment and business. Per-head investment between 1989 and 2000 was only US $123, a rate exceeded by all but six other transition countries. At late 2000 Germany was the leading investor in Belarus, accounting for about 12% of FDI, and Russia was in fifth place. Gas-pipeline construction has expanded Russian FDI: in 1999 investment increased by about $80m., owing to the financing of a gas pipeline project designed to replace the existing link between Russia and Western Europe, which passes through Ukraine, as have purchases of state-owned firms, the JAP, and creative solutions to energy debts. In 2002 FDI equalled $434m. or about $43 per head, and by the end of 2002 per head FDI had reached $179, owing to the privatization of several large state-owned firms, but the country still lagged behind most transition countries. However, by the beginning of 2001 only about 2% of the work-force and 9% of industrial output were accounted for by foreign-owned firms.

### PROSPECTS

In 2003 Belarus remained the only 'command and control' economy among the European transition states, and was described by the EBRD as remaining in the early stages of transition, an assessment unchanged since 1996. It was characterized as having a weak institutional environment for small and medium-sized enterprises, and underdeveloped legal institutions and safeguards for investment. Government opposition to reform intensified, even after the financial crisis of 1998. The banking sector faced extensive liabilities, owing to the provision of forced loans to enterprises and farms that were technically insolvent. Domestic and international trade were characterized by a high reliance on barter, and the prospect of union with Russia remained uncertain.

Although an improvement in NATO-Russian relations may have reduced the strategic importance of Belarus, it remained significant. Belarus was the main transit route between metropolitan Russia and the Russian exclave of Kaliningrad, and for Russian petroleum and gas deliveries to Western Europe. Until 1998 Russian politicians were content to encourage the prospect of a Russia-Belarus union as a means of appealing to

Russian voters, nostalgic for the Soviet past. It was often intimated that such a union could be the first stage towards the creation of a broader union, which could, in some ways, act as a reconstituted USSR. In a disorganized Russia, the strong, authoritarian Government in Belarus secured stability on its western flank, and guaranteed access to the West. Apparent stability under Lukashenka, and the apparent preservation of living standards, made him an appealing figure to many in Russia.

Following the election of Vladimir Putin as Russia's President in March 2000, the economic and political situation changed. One decade previously, it was uncertain whether Belarus would re-orientate itself towards Western Europe or the CIS. By the early 2000s Russia was the republic's principal trading partner. The prospect of EU membership for Latvia, Lithuania and Poland from 2004 meant that the Belarusian border would become part of the new EU border. The EU had already compelled prospective members to strengthen their borders prior to EU membership, which had economic repercussions for border region economies in Belarus. It might be that Belarus will turn increasingly towards Russia and the rest of the CIS for its trade and economic relations, and Belarus may eventually become an economic protectorate of the Russian Federation.

Despite his authoritarian rule, allegations of electoral fraud, and the preservation of a command-style economy, Lukashenka remained popular and firmly in control, although by mid-2003 his popularity had declined. There were suggestions that he might schedule a referendum, in an attempt to secure support for a third term of office. Belarusians had witnessed the breakdown of government and local economies in the Russian Federation, and had experienced rapid growth in unemployment, and a decline in living standards, in the border regions of Poland, Latvia and Lithuania. Ironically,

given the underlying rate of unemployment, and the general decline in living standards and investment, Belarusians had experienced many of the same privations, but the rate of decline has been slower and more controlled. Russia was likely to continue to subsidize the Belarusian economy through the sale of cheap petroleum and gas, and continued barter trade, but, as evidenced by recent privatizations, economic dependence on Russia, particularly for imports of energy, made Belarus increasingly vulnerable to Russian political influence and economic penetration. Belarus was one of the few transition countries to reverse the reform process, retreating from privatization and the use of market forces in economic management. Economic union with Russia has been threatened by Belarus's refusal to embrace economic reform, and political union was increasingly uncertain as the Russian Government began to focus on the economic costs. As the deadline for union approaches, Lukashenka may be forced to abandon some of his principal economic policies, including his reluctance to embrace market forces, in order to retain Russian support. This could lead to a sharper real decline in living standards, and to a loss of state control over the economy.

Lukashenka was likely to remain in power, however, unless Russia should decide to support interest groups opposed to the Government. Lukashenka had no party organization to maintain his support. Instead, he was a charismatic leader, supported by the security services. Political opposition was diffuse and unco-ordinated. The press was tightly controlled, and the courts and the security services were under the control of the President. If Lukashenka were to lose the support of the security services, the end of his regime could leave a chaotic vacuum in his place. This was, perhaps, the main reason for continued Russian support, and appeared to guarantee the continuation of the existing regime and its policies in the short to medium term.

# Statistical Survey

Source: mainly Ministry of Statistics and Analysis, 220070 Minsk, pr. Partizanski 12; tel. (17) 249-42-78; fax (17) 249-22-04; e-mail minstat@mail.belpak .by; internet www.president.gov.by/Minstat/en/main.html.

## Area and Population

### AREA, POPULATION AND DENSITY

| | |
|---|---:|
| Area (sq km) . . . . . . . . . . | 207,595* |
| Population (census results)† | |
|   12 January 1989 . . . . . . . . | 10,151,806 |
|   16 February 1999 | |
|     Males . . . . . . . . . . | 4,717,621 |
|     Females . . . . . . . . . . | 5,327,616 |
|     Total . . . . . . . . . . | 10,045,237 |
| Population (official estimates at 1 January) | |
|   2000 . . . . . . . . . . | 9,990,435 |
|   2001 . . . . . . . . . . | 9,950,900 |
|   2002 . . . . . . . . . . | 9,899,000 |
| Density (per sq km) at 1 January 2002 . . . . . | 47.7 |

\* 80,153 sq miles.
† Figures refer to the *de jure* population. The *de facto* total was 10,199,709 in 1989.

### POPULATION BY NATIONALITY
(1999 census)

| | % |
|---|---:|
| Belarusian . . . . . . . . . . . . | 81 |
| Russian . . . . . . . . . . . . | 11 |
| Polish . . . . . . . . . . . . | 4 |
| Ukrainian . . . . . . . . . . . . | 2 |
| Others . . . . . . . . . . . . | 2 |
| **Total** . . . . . . . . . . . . | **100** |

### PRINCIPAL TOWNS*
(estimated population at 1 January 2001)

| | | | | |
|---|---:|---|---|---:|
| Minsk (Miensk, capital) | 1,699,100 | | Borisov (Barysau) . | 150,900 |
| Gomel (Homiel) . . | 480,000 | | Pinsk . . . . . | 131,100 |
| Mogilev (Mahiloŭ) . . | 360,600 | | Orsha (Vorsha) . . | 124,000 |
| Vitebsk (Viciebsk) . . | 341,500 | | Mozyr (Mazyr) . . | 110,700 |
| Grodno (Horadnia) . . | 307,100 | | Novopolotsk . . . | 102,100 |
| Brest (Bieraście)† . . | 291,400 | | Soligorsk . . . . | 101,900 |
| Bobruysk (Babrujsk) . | 221,400 | | Lida . . . . . | 100,000 |
| Baranovichi | | | | |
|   (Baranavichy) . . . | 168,800 | | | |

\* The Belarusian names of towns, in Latin transliteration, are given in parentheses after the more widely used Russian names.
† Formerly Brest-Litovsk.

## BIRTHS, MARRIAGES AND DEATHS

| | Registered live births | | Registered marriages | | Registered deaths | |
|---|---|---|---|---|---|---|
| | Number | Rate (per 1,000) | Number | Rate (per 1,000) | Number | Rate (per 1,000) |
| 1994 . . | 110,599 | 10.7 | 75,540 | 7.3 | 130,003 | 12.6 |
| 1995 . . | 101,144 | 9.8 | 77,027 | 7.5 | 133,775 | 13.0 |
| 1996 . . | 95,798 | 9.3 | 63,677 | 6.2 | 133,422 | 13.0 |
| 1997 . . | 89,586 | 8.8 | 69,735 | 6.8 | 136,653 | 13.4 |
| 1998 . . | 92,645 | 9.1 | 71,354 | 7.0 | 137,296 | 13.5 |
| 1999 . . | 92,975 | 9.3 | 72,994 | 7.3 | 142,027 | 14.2 |
| 2000 . . | 93,691 | 9.4 | 62,485 | 6.2 | 134,867 | 13.5 |
| 2001* . . | 91,700 | 9.2 | 68,700 | 6.9 | 140,300 | 14.1 |

* Figures are provisional.

**Expectation of life** (WHO estimates, years at birth): 68.5 (males 62.9; females 74.2) in 2001.

## EMPLOYMENT
(annual averages, '000 persons)

| | 1998 | 1999 | 2000 |
|---|---|---|---|
| Agriculture . . . . . . | 695.3 | 659.5 | 625.1 |
| Forestry . . . . . . | 28.7 | 29.7 | 32.5 |
| Industry* . . . . . | 1,221.0 | 1,231.0 | 1,226.7 |
| Construction . . . . . | 329.5 | 330.5 | 312.3 |
| Trade and communications . . | 321.4 | 323.5 | 318.3 |
| Trade and public catering† . . | 483.2 | 493.3 | 532.3 |
| Housing, public utilities and personal services . . . . | 193.4 | 202.5 | 208.1 |
| Health care . . . . . | 262.0 | 266.1 | 269.9 |
| Physical culture and social security | 51.6 | 56.3 | 56.2 |
| Education . . . . . . | 454.5 | 460.6 | 463.7 |
| Culture and arts . . . . | 73.9 | 77.0 | 80.2 |
| Science. . . . . . | 43.7 | 43.9 | 42.2 |
| Credit and insurance . . . | 53.2 | 55.7 | 58.4 |
| Other activities . . . . | 205.2 | 212.4 | 215.1 |
| **Total** . . . . . . | 4,416.6 | 4,442.0 | 4,441.0 |
| Males . . . . . . | 2,146.5 | 2,127.8 | 2,113.9 |
| Females . . . . . | 2,270.1 | 2,314.2 | 2,327.1 |

* Comprising manufacturing (except printing and publishing), mining and quarrying, electricity, gas, logging and fishing.
† Including material and technical supply and procurement.

**Unemployment** ('000 persons registered at December): 95.8 (males 37.6, females 58.2) in 2000; 102.9 (males 40.8, females 62.1) in 2001; 130.5 (males 47.8, females 82.7) in 2002.

**2002** ('000 persons): Total labour force (annual average) 4,500.3 (males 2,103.8, females 2,396.5).

# Health and Welfare

## KEY INDICATORS

| | |
|---|---|
| Total fertility rate (children per woman, 2001) . . . . | 1.2 |
| Under-5 mortality rate (per 1,000 live births, 2001) . . . | 20 |
| HIV/AIDS (% of persons aged 15–49, 2001) . . . . . | 0.27 |
| Physicians (per 1,000 head, 1998) . . . . . . | 4.43 |
| Hospital beds (per 1,000 head, 1996) . . . . . | 12.23 |
| Health expenditure (2000): US $ per head (PPP) . . . | 430 |
| Health expenditure (2000): % of GDP . . . . . | 5.7 |
| Health expenditure (2000): public (% of total) . . . . | 82.8 |
| Access to water (% of persons, 2000). . . . . . | 100 |
| Human Development Index (2001): ranking . . . . | 53 |
| Human Development Index (2001): value . . . . . | 0.804 |

For sources and definitions, see explanatory note on p. vi.

# Agriculture

## PRINCIPAL CROPS
('000 metric tons)

| | 1999 | 2000 | 2001 |
|---|---|---|---|
| Wheat . . . . . . . . | 711.4 | 949.0* | 1,050.0* |
| Barley . . . . . . . | 1,180.7 | 1,574.0* | 1,750.0* |
| Maize . . . . . . . | 9.9 | 13.0* | 15.7* |
| Rye. . . . . . . . | 928.9 | 1,239.0* | 1,300.0* |
| Oats . . . . . . . | 368.5 | 491.0* | 600.0* |
| Buckwheat . . . . . . | 8.8 | 12.0* | 12.0* |
| Triticale (wheat-rye hybrid) . . | 203.6 | 270.0* | 198.0* |
| Potatoes . . . . . . | 7,491.0 | 8,717.8 | 7,767.6 |
| Sugar beet. . . . . . | 1,186.5 | 1,473.6 | 1,682.1 |
| Dry beans* . . . . . | 101 | 135 | 100 |
| Dry peas* . . . . . . | 130 | 173 | 127 |
| Walnuts† . . . . . . | 12 | 12 | 12 |
| Sunflower seed† . . . . . | 19 | 22 | 18 |
| Rapeseed . . . . . . | 57.2 | 68.0† | 58.0† |
| Linseed . . . . . . | 12.6 | 22.0† | 18.0† |
| Cabbages . . . . . . | 446.3 | 525.0* | 538.0* |
| Tomatoes . . . . . . | 76.6 | 125.0* | 130.0* |
| Cucumbers and gherkins . . | 178.5 | 128.0* | 150.0* |
| Dry onions . . . . . . | 63.5 | 66.1* | 70.0* |
| Carrots . . . . . . | 200.2 | 185.0* | 171.0* |
| Other vegetables† . . . . | 207 | 177 | 229 |
| Apples . . . . . . . | 123* | 144† | 160† |
| Pears . . . . . . . | 8* | 10† | 16† |
| Plums . . . . . . . | 28* | 32† | 43† |
| Sour cherries . . . . . | 17* | 18† | 30† |
| Cherries . . . . . . | 10* | 12† | 16† |
| Other fruits and berries† . . | 6 | 8 | 6 |
| Flax fibre . . . . . . | 20.9 | 37.2 | 31.5 |

* Unofficial figure(s).
† FAO estimate(s).

Source: FAO.

## LIVESTOCK
('000 head at 1 January)

| | 1999 | 2000 | 2001 |
|---|---|---|---|
| Horses . . . . . . . | 229 | 221 | 217 |
| Cattle . . . . . . . | 4,686 | 4,326 | 4,221 |
| Pigs . . . . . . . | 3,698 | 3,556 | 3,431 |
| Sheep . . . . . . . | 106 | 92 | 89 |
| Goats . . . . . . . | 56 | 58 | 61* |
| Chickens . . . . . . | 30,000* | 30,000* | 32,000† |

* Unofficial figure.
† FAO estimate.

Source: FAO.

## LIVESTOCK PRODUCTS
('000 metric tons)

| | 1999 | 2000 | 2001 |
|---|---|---|---|
| Beef and veal . . . . . | 262.1 | 269.4* | 283.0* |
| Mutton and lamb* . . . . | 3.0 | 2.6 | 2.7 |
| Pig meat . . . . . . | 311.0 | 256.0* | 270.0* |
| Poultry meat . . . . . | 70.0 | 65.0* | 68.0* |
| Other meat . . . . . | 6.2 | 6.2† | 6.0 |
| Cows' milk . . . . . | 4,740.8 | 4,489.6 | 4,834.1 |
| Cheese. . . . . . . | 56.8 | 56.6 | 62.5 |
| Butter . . . . . . . | 62.6 | 65.1 | 65.9 |
| Hen eggs* . . . . . . | 188.3 | 182.3 | 174.0 |
| Honey . . . . . . . | 3.2 | 2.4† | 3.2† |
| Cattle hides (fresh)† . . . . | 29.4 | 29.7 | 31.2 |
| Sheepskins (fresh)† . . . . | 95.7 | 83.2 | 86.4 |

* Unofficial figure(s).
† FAO estimate(s).

Source: FAO.

# Forestry

**ROUNDWOOD REMOVALS**
('000 cubic metres, excl. bark)

|  | 1999 | 2000 | 2001 |
|---|---|---|---|
| Sawlogs, veneer logs and logs for sleepers | 2,995 | 3,168 | 3,202 |
| Pulpwood | 893 | 991 | 1,114 |
| Other industrial wood | 1,530 | 1,049 | 1,035 |
| Fuel wood | 1,144 | 928 | 923 |
| **Total** | 6,561 | 6,136 | 6,274 |

Source: FAO.

**SAWNWOOD PRODUCTION**
('000 cubic metres, incl. railway sleepers)

|  | 1999 | 2000 | 2001 |
|---|---|---|---|
| Coniferous (softwood) | 1,457 | 1,211 | 1,153 |
| Broadleaved (hardwood) | 718 | 597 | 568 |
| **Total** | 2,175 | 1,808 | 1,721 |

Source: FAO.

# Fishing

(metric tons, live weight)

|  | 1998 | 1999 | 2000 |
|---|---|---|---|
| Capture | 457 | 514 | 553 |
| Aquaculture | 4,727 | 5,289 | 6,716 |
| Common carp | 3,254 | 4,088 | 5,867 |
| Crucian carp | 410 | 354 | 396 |
| Silver carp | 1 | 125 | 358 |
| Northern pike | 1,062 | 477 | 40 |
| **Total catch** | 5,184 | 5,809 | 7,269 |

Source: FAO, *Yearbook of Fishery Statistics*.

# Mining

('000 metric tons, unless otherwise indicated)

|  | 1998 | 1999 | 2000 |
|---|---|---|---|
| Crude petroleum | 1,830 | 1,840 | 1,841 |
| Natural gas (million cu metres) | 252 | 256 | 257 |
| Chalk | 79 | 78 | 114 |
| Gypsum (crude) | 17 | 27 | 30 |
| Peat: for fuel | 2,035 | 3,090 | 2,023 |
| Peat: for agriculture | 107 | 308 | 188 |

# Industry

**SELECTED PRODUCTS**
('000 metric tons, unless otherwise indicated)

|  | 1998 | 1999 | 2000 |
|---|---|---|---|
| Refined sugar | 476 | 501 | 565 |
| Margarine | 15.0 | 22.4 | 20.8 |
| Wheat flour | 1,153 | 1,134 | 924 |
| Ethyl alcohol ('000 hectolitres) | 1,046 | 982 | 1,035 |
| Wine ('000 hectolitres) | 5,832 | 5,467 | 6,917 |
| Beer ('000 hectolitres) | 2,603.7 | 2,728.4 | 2,370.6 |
| Mineral water ('000 hectolitres) | 1,082.5 | 1,453.4 | 1,532.5 |
| Soft drinks ('000 hectolitres) | 2,196.3 | 1,870.3 | 1,861.4 |
| Cigarettes (million) | 7,296 | 9,259 | 10,356 |
| Cotton yarn (pure and mixed) | 18.6 | 15.1 | 16.8 |
| Flax yarn | 17.4 | 16.6 | 10.2 |
| Wool yarn (pure and mixed) | 16.3 | 16.4 | 15.7 |
| Woven cotton fabrics (million sq metres) | 67.1 | 50.6 | 66.6 |
| Woven woollen fabrics (million sq metres) | 9.5 | 9.3 | 9.3 |
| Linen fabrics (million sq metres) | 50.1 | 49.4 | 33.1 |
| Woven fabrics of cellulosic fibres (million sq metres) | 77.2 | 71.5 | 62.4 |
| Carpets ('000 sq metres) | 8,145 | 9,155 | 8,744 |
| Footwear (excluding rubber, '000 pairs) | 16,223 | 16,538 | 15,388 |
| Plywood ('000 cu metres) | 139 | 140 | 126 |
| Paper | 45 | 53 | 44 |
| Paperboard | 150 | 162 | 176 |
| Benzene (Benzol) | 16.7 | 23.4 | 51.7 |
| Ethylene (Ethene) | 108.1 | 115.4 | 114.7 |
| Propylene (Propene) | 70.5 | 74.2 | 70.7 |
| Xylenes (Xylol) | — | 7.5 | 38.0 |
| Sulphuric acid (100%) | 640 | 614 | 584 |
| Nitrogenous fertilizers (a)[1] | 559 | 615 | 597 |
| Phosphate fertilizers (b)[1] | 130 | 120 | 87 |
| Potash fertilizers (c)[1] | 3,451 | 3,613 | 3,372 |
| Non-cellulosic continuous fibres | 66.2 | 66.8 | 72.7 |
| Cellulosic continuous filaments | 14.3 | 13.0 | 11.7 |
| Soap | 26.3 | 33.7 | 38.6 |
| Rubber tyres ('000)[2] | 2,324 | 2,263 | 2,440 |
| Rubber footwear ('000 pairs) | 5,036 | 4,797 | 3,348 |
| Quicklime | 684 | 663 | 586 |
| Cement | 2,035 | 1,998 | 1,847 |
| Concrete blocks ('000 cu metres) | 2,130 | 1,759 | 1,752 |
| Crude steel | 1,412 | 1,449 | 1,623 |
| Tractors ('000) | 26.9 | 27.4 | 22.5 |
| Refrigerators ('000) | 802 | 802 | 812 |
| Domestic washing machines ('000) | 90.8 | 92.2 | 88.1 |
| Television receivers ('000) | 468 | 516 | 532 |
| Radio receivers ('000) | 114 | 195 | 101 |
| Lorries (number) | 12,799 | 13,370 | 14,656 |
| Motorcycles ('000) | 20.4 | 24.4 | 36.6 |
| Bicycles ('000) | 452 | 508 | 586 |
| Cameras ('000) | 5 | 8 | 4 |
| Watches ('000) | 4,848 | 5,218 | 5,602 |
| Electric energy (million kWh) | 23,492 | 26,516 | 26,095 |

[1] Production in terms of (a) nitrogen; (b) phosphoric acid; or (c) potassium oxide.

[2] For lorries and farm vehicles.

**2001** ('000 metric tons, unless otherwise indicated): Paper 51; Cement 1,803; Tractors ('000) 22.7; Electric energy (million kWh) 25,100.

**2002** ('000 metric tons, unless otherwise indicated): Paper 52; Cement 2,171; Tractors ('000) 24.3; Electric energy (million kWh) 26,400.

# Finance

## CURRENCY AND EXCHANGE RATES

**Monetary Units**

100 kopeks = 1 readjusted Belarusian rouble (rubel).

**Sterling, Dollar and Euro Equivalents** (31 January 2003)

£1 sterling = 3,219.3 readjusted roubles;

US $1 = 1,950.0 readjusted roubles;

€1 = 1,803.0 readjusted roubles;

10,000 readjusted Belarusian roubles = £3.106 = $5.128 = €5.546.

**Average Exchange Rate** (readjusted Belarusian roubles per US $)

2000    876.750

2001    1,390.000

2002    1,790.920

Note: The Belarusian rouble was introduced in May 1992, initially as a coupon currency, to circulate alongside (and at par with) the Russian (formerly Soviet) rouble. The parity between Belarusian and Russian currencies was subsequently ended, and the Belarusian rouble was devalued. In August 1994 a new Belarusian rouble, equivalent to 10 old roubles, was introduced. On 1 January 1995 the Belarusian rouble became the sole national currency, while the circulation of Russian roubles ceased. On 1 January 2000 a readjusted Belarusian rouble, equivalent to 1,000 of the former units, was introduced. Some of the figures in this survey are still in terms of new roubles prior to redenomination.

## STATE BUDGET

('000 million roubles)*

| Revenue | 1999 | 2000 | 2001 |
|---|---|---|---|
| Tax revenue . . . . . . . | 802.38 | 2,447.22 | 4,568.97 |
| Taxes on income, profits and | | | |
| capital gains . . . . . | 93.15 | 287.01 | 468.62 |
| Social security contributions . . | 297.86 | 928.75 | 1,863.39 |
| Payroll taxes . . . . . . | 23.93 | 73.10 | 154.54 |
| Domestic taxes on goods and | | | |
| services . . . . . . . | 329.42 | 1,016.56 | 1,782.42 |
| General sales, turnover or | | | |
| value-added taxes . . . | 176.79 | 544.30 | 936.15 |
| Excises . . . . . . . | 66.44 | 183.40 | 323.06 |
| Taxes on international trade and | | | |
| transactions . . . . . | 58.01 | 141.80 | 300.00 |
| Other current revenue . . . | 66.46 | 172.47 | 321.30 |
| Capital revenue . . . . . | 7.39 | 26.33 | 47.93 |
| **Total** . . . . . . . | 876.23 | 2,646.02 | 4,938.20 |

| Expenditure† | 1999 | 2000 | 2001 |
|---|---|---|---|
| General public services . . . . | 43.71 | 121.25 | 228.04 |
| Defence . . . . . . . | 37.96 | 113.06 | 229.93 |
| Public order and safety . . . . | 35.25 | 111.12 | 228.59 |
| Education . . . . . . . . | 32.16 | 102.17 | 201.60 |
| Health . . . . . . . . | 32.64 | 92.77 | 178.76 |
| Social security and welfare . . . | 311.38 | 1,008.17 | 2,233.09 |
| Recreation, cultural and religious | | | |
| affairs and services . . . . | 12.14 | 40.95 | 74.68 |
| Economic affairs and services . . | 135.42 | 399.28 | 711.79 |
| Agriculture, forestry, fishing and | | | |
| hunting . . . . . . . | 64.61 | 219.53 | 344.89 |
| Transport and communications . | 34.08 | 89.50 | 247.57 |
| Other purposes . . . . . . | 291.93 | 650.60 | 992.95 |
| **Total** (incl. others) . . . . | 933.88 | 2,639.80 | 5,080.21 |
| Current expenditure . . . . | 723.35 | 2,197.84 | 4,440.63 |
| Capital expenditure . . . . | 210.53 | 441.96 | 639.58 |

* Figures are in terms of the readjusted rouble, introduced on 1 January 2000 and equivalent to 1,000 of the former units. The data represent a consolidation of the operations of central government bodies.

† Excluding lending minus repayments ('000 million roubles) : 2.58 in 1999; −0.99 in 2000; 93.67 in 2001.

Source: IMF, *Government Finance Statistics Yearbook*.

## INTERNATIONAL RESERVES

(US $ million at 31 December)

| | 2000 | 2001 | 2002 |
|---|---|---|---|
| IMF special drawing rights . . . | 0.18 | 0.40 | 0.26 |
| Reserve position in IMF . . . . | 0.03 | 0.03 | 0.03 |
| Foreign exchange . . . . . . | 350.29 | 390.26 | 618.52 |
| **Total** . . . . . . . . | 350.50 | 390.68 | 618.81 |

Source: IMF, *International Financial Statistics*.

## MONEY SUPPLY

(million roubles at 31 December)*

| | 2000 | 2001 | 2002 |
|---|---|---|---|
| Currency outside banks . . . . | 238,796 | 512,211 | 650,020 |
| Demand deposits at deposit money | | | |
| banks . . . . . . . . | 259,602 | 376,038 | 714,285 |
| **Total money** (incl. others) . . . | 508,432 | 889,553 | 1,365,668 |

* Figures are in terms of the readjusted rouble, introduced on 1 January 2000 and equivalent to 1,000 of the former units.

Source: IMF, *International Financial Statistics*.

## COST OF LIVING

(Consumer price index; base: 1992 = 100)

| | 1999 | 2000 | 2001 |
|---|---|---|---|
| Food (incl. beverages) . . . . | 5,264.1 | 13,945.7 | 21,871.1 |
| Fuel and light . . . . . | 4,297.4 | 22,462.4 | 60,457.4 |
| Clothing (incl. footwear) . . . . | 1,508.6 | 3,369.5 | 4,939.0 |
| Rent . . . . . . . . | 10,789.0 | 41,576.4 | 85,797.1 |
| **All items** (incl. others) . . . . | 4,130.5 | 11,094.6 | 17,877.8 |

Source: partly ILO.

## NATIONAL ACCOUNTS

**Expenditure on the Gross Domestic Product**

('000 million roubles at current prices)*

| | 2000 | 2001 | 2002 |
|---|---|---|---|
| Government final consumption | | | |
| expenditure . . . . . . | 1,779.1 | 3,701.3 | 5,398.0 |
| Private final consumption | | | |
| expenditure . . . . . . | 5,198.1 | 9,895.9 | 15,665.0 |
| Increase in stocks . . . . . | 18.0 | 187.5 | 197.8 |
| Gross fixed capital formation . . | 2,301.9 | 3,893.0 | 5,411.6 |
| **Total domestic expenditure** . . | 9,297.1 | 17,677.7 | 26,672.4 |
| Exports of goods and services . . | 6,321.6 | 11,462.7 | 16,617.7 |
| *Less* Imports of goods and services | 6,612.7 | 12,072.3 | 17,731.8 |
| Statistical discrepancy . . . . | 127.8 | 105.1 | −39.9 |
| **GDP in purchasers' values** . . | 9,133.8 | 17,173,2 | 25,518.4 |

* Figures are in terms of the readjusted rouble, introduced on 1 January 2000 and equivalent to 1,000 of the former units.

Source: IMF, *International Financial Statistics*.

**Gross Domestic Product by Economic Activity**
('000 million new roubles at current prices)

| | 1998 | 1999 | 2000* |
|---|---|---|---|
| Agriculture | 80,461.9 | 368,551.9 | 1,155.6 |
| Forestry | 4,231.5 | 15,775.3 | 41.9 |
| Industry† | 203,708.6 | 836,333.3 | 2,354.9 |
| Construction | 40,921.5 | 175,733.9 | 516.3 |
| Transport | 59,348.5 | 297,289.2 | 938.6 |
| Communications | 10,125.9 | 48,595.9 | 139.5 |
| Trade and catering | 66,148.3 | 289,678.5 | 844.1 |
| Material supply | 8,739.3 | 41,175.1 | 123.2 |
| Procurement | 1,683.9 | 7,271.9 | 20.6 |
| Housing | 27,644.0 | 82,626.4 | 273.6 |
| Public utilities | 10,340.0 | 45,131.2 | 153.4 |
| Health care | 21,678.4 | 93,608.3 | 294.4 |
| Education | 30,758.2 | 131,271.8 | 388.7 |
| Culture and science | 6,883.7 | 34,391.4 | 86.0 |
| Banks and insurance | 14,433.0 | 81,497.4 | 226.7 |
| Public administration and defence | 22,438.4 | 87,552.6 | 276.2 |
| Other services | 11,294.0 | 51,210.1 | 162.5 |
| **Sub-total** | 620,839.1 | 2,687,694.2 | 7,996.2 |
| *Less* Imputed bank service charge | 10,314.9 | 62,885.3 | 177.3 |
| **GDP at factor cost** | 610,524.2 | 2,624,808.9 | 7,818.9 |
| Indirect taxes, *less* subsidies | 91,636.9 | 401,254.8 | 1,306.7 |
| **GDP in purchasers' values** | 702,161.1 | 3,026,063.7 | 9,125.6 |

* Preliminary figures, in terms of the readjusted rouble.
† Principally mining, manufacturing, electricity, gas and water.

**BALANCE OF PAYMENTS**
(US $ million)

| | 1999 | 2000 | 2001 |
|---|---|---|---|
| Exports of goods f.o.b. | 5,646.4 | 6,640.5 | 7,256.2 |
| Imports of goods f.o.b. | −6,216.4 | −7,524.6 | −8,063.1 |
| **Trade balance** | −570.0 | −884.1 | −806.9 |
| Exports of services | 753.3 | 1,015.6 | 1,013.1 |
| Imports of services | −438.8 | −562.6 | −602.7 |
| **Balance on goods and services** | −255.5 | −431.1 | −396.5 |
| Other income received | 20.8 | 25.7 | 27.0 |
| Other income paid | −62.8 | −72.4 | −69.8 |
| **Balance on goods, services and income** | −297.5 | −477.8 | −439.3 |
| Current transfers received | 137.0 | 177.1 | 202.6 |
| Current transfers paid | −33.2 | −22.4 | −48.5 |
| **Current balance** | −193.7 | −323.1 | −285.2 |
| Capital account (net) | 60.4 | 69.4 | 56.3 |
| Direct investment abroad | −0.8 | −0.2 | −0.3 |
| Direct investment from abroad | 444.0 | 118.8 | 95.8 |
| Portfolio investment assets | −15.4 | −5.7 | 10.5 |
| Portfolio investment liabilities | −5.2 | 50.1 | −45.4 |
| Other investment assets | −36.7 | 41.7 | −139.2 |
| Other investment liabilities | 13.6 | −64.6 | 328.6 |
| Net errors and omissions | −246.3 | 238.9 | −99.6 |
| **Overall balance** | 19.9 | 125.3 | −78.5 |

Source: IMF, *International Financial Statistics*.

# External Trade

**PRINCIPAL COMMODITIES**
('000 million new roubles at domestic prices*)

| Imports | 1998 | 1999 | 2000† |
|---|---|---|---|
| Industrial products | 414,175 | 1,682,403 | 5,772 |
| Petroleum and gas | 86,540 | 361,776 | 1,784 |
| Metallurgy | 53,195 | 240,737 | 719 |
| Chemical and petroleum products | 65,749 | 262,317 | 814 |
| Machinery and metalworking | 112,650 | 419,624 | 1,233 |
| Wood and paper products | 12,756 | 53,590 | 194 |
| Light industry | 21,889 | 96,514 | 307 |
| Food and beverages | 39,081 | 166,818 | 474 |
| Agricultural products (unprocessed) | 11,565 | 73,858 | 255 |
| **Total** (incl. others) | 431,447 | 1,779,247 | 6,117 |
| USSR (former)‡ | 277,518 | 1,146,268 | 4,380 |
| Other countries | 153,929 | 632,979 | 1,738 |

| Exports | 1998 | 1999 | 2000† |
|---|---|---|---|
| Industrial products | 358,398 | 1,535,208 | 5,176 |
| Petroleum and gas | 27,761 | 142,750 | 1,047 |
| Metallurgy | 27,371 | 104,504 | 306 |
| Chemical and petroleum products | 78,228 | 350,334 | 1,010 |
| Machinery and metalworking | 118,053 | 536,793 | 1,532 |
| Wood and paper products | 24,517 | 102,658 | 320 |
| Construction materials | 9,967 | 33,164 | 125 |
| Light industry | 36,364 | 147,838 | 460 |
| Food and beverages | 34,900 | 110,083 | 350 |
| **Total** (incl. others) | 367,897 | 1,574,700 | 5,360 |
| USSR (former)‡ | 259,282 | 968,077 | 3,272 |
| Other countries | 108,615 | 606,623 | 2,088 |

* Figures relating to trade with Russia are compiled from enterprise surveys, while data on trade with other countries are calculated on the basis of customs declarations.
† Figures in terms of the readjusted rouble.
‡ Excluding trade with Estonia, Latvia and Lithuania.

**PRINCIPAL TRADING PARTNERS**
(US $ million)

| Imports c.i.f. | 2000 | 2001 | 2002 |
|---|---|---|---|
| Brazil | n.a. | n.a. | 104.5 |
| Germany | 587.6 | 589.2 | 692.7 |
| Italy | 162.6 | 163.9 | 215.2 |
| Lithuania | n.a. | 107.3 | 109.4 |
| Netherlands | 79.5 | 79.3 | 84.0 |
| Poland | 215.8 | 199.5 | 219.6 |
| Russia | 5,549.7 | 5,230.6 | 5,842.5 |
| Ukraine | 340.6 | 277.4 | 290.7 |
| United Kingdom | 106.3 | 61.3 | 67.7 |
| USA | 138.7 | 131.3 | 103.1 |
| **Total** (incl. others) | 8,646.0 | 8,046.0* | 8,980.0* |

| Exports f.o.b. | 2000 | 2001 | 2002 |
|---|---|---|---|
| Brazil | n.a. | 76.7 | 89.4 |
| China, People's Republic | 148.4 | 143.1 | 217.4 |
| Estonia | 147.4 | 129.2 | 63.4 |
| Germany | 231.7 | 241.0 | 348.0 |
| Hungary | n.a. | 75.4 | 70.8 |
| Italy | n.a. | 85.4 | 130.1 |
| Latvia | 467.3 | 492.3 | 520.1 |
| Lithuania | 348.8 | 275.8 | 256.7 |
| Netherlands | 130.3 | 125.8 | 279.0 |
| Poland | 276.8 | 248.0 | 273.3 |
| Russia | 3,715.7 | 4,037.6 | 4,053.9 |
| Ukraine | 559.7 | 421.8 | 271.6 |
| United Kingdom | 95.9 | 222.9 | 493.7 |
| USA | 97.0 | 77.1 | 91.3 |
| **Total** (incl. others) | 7,326.0 | 7,525.0* | 8,098.0* |

* Figure rounded.

**2001** (US $ million, revised figures): Total imports c.i.f. 8,178; Total exports f.o.b. 7,448.

# Transport

**RAILWAYS**
(traffic)

|                              | 2000   | 2001   | 2002   |
| ---------------------------- | ------ | ------ | ------ |
| Passenger-km (million) . . . | 17,722 | 15,264 | 14,349 |
| Freight ton-km (million) . . . | 31,425 | 29,727 | 34,169 |

**ROAD TRAFFIC**
(motor vehicles in use at 31 December)

|                              | 1998      | 1999      | 2000      |
| ---------------------------- | --------- | --------- | --------- |
| Passenger cars . . . . . | 1,279,208 | 1,356,611 | 1,448,491 |
| Buses and coaches . . . . | 8,768 | 8,452 | 8,273 |
| Motorcycles and mopeds . . . | 558,251 | 533,658 | 523,613 |

Source: partly IRF, *World Road Statistics*.

**CIVIL AVIATION**
(traffic on scheduled services)

|                              | 2000 | 2001 | 2002 |
| ---------------------------- | ---- | ---- | ---- |
| Passengers carried ('000) . . . | 216 | n.a. | n.a. |
| Passenger-km (million) . . . . | 513 | 546 | 553 |
| Total ton-km (million) . . . . | 18 | 28 | 37 |

# Tourism

**FOREIGN TOURIST ARRIVALS**

| Country of Nationality | 1999   | 2000   | 2001   |
| ---------------------- | ------ | ------ | ------ |
| Cyprus . . . . . . . . | 1,887 | 1,101 | 1,375 |
| Germany . . . . . . . | 5,354 | 5,669 | 4,952 |
| Israel . . . . . . . . | 4,724 | 3,723 | 882 |
| Italy . . . . . . . . | 1,812 | 1,463 | 1,642 |
| Latvia . . . . . . . . | 9,020 | 6,364 | 7,603 |
| Lithuania . . . . . . | 3,437 | 1,949 | 2,744 |
| Poland . . . . . . . . | 19,122 | 13,464 | 11,755 |
| Russia . . . . . . . . | 17,657 | 11,257 | 9,929 |
| Ukraine . . . . . . . | 1,624 | 449 | 540 |
| United Kingdom . . . . | 3,983 | 6,197 | 8,915 |
| USA . . . . . . . . . | 2,223 | 2,881 | 4,768 |
| **Total** (incl. others) . . . . . | 75,440 | 59,676 | 61,033 |

**Tourism receipts** (US $ million): 55 in 1996; 23 in 1997; 22 in 1998; 13 in 1999; 17 in 2000.

Sources: World Tourism Organization, *Yearbook of Tourism Statistics*, and World Bank.

# Communications Media

|                              | 1998    | 1999    | 2000    |
| ---------------------------- | ------- | ------- | ------- |
| Television receivers ('000 in use) . | 3,300 | 3,400 | 3,500 |
| Telephones ('000 main lines in use) | 2,489.9 | 2,638.5 | 2,751.9 |
| Facsimile machines (number in use) . | 19,472 | 23,847 | 26,925 |
| Mobile cellular telephones (subscribers) . . . . . | 12,155 | 23,457 | 49,353 |
| Internet users ('000) . . . . . | 7.5 | 50.0 | 180.0 |
| Book production (incl. pamphlets): | | | |
| titles . . . . . . . . | 6,073 | 6,064 | 7,686 |
| copies ('000) . . . . . | 60,022 | 63,305 | 61,627 |
| Daily newspapers: | | | |
| number . . . . . . | 20 | 12 | 10 |
| average circulation ('000) . . | 1,559 | 1,094 | 1,101 |
| Non-daily newspapers: | | | |
| number . . . . . . | 560 | 578 | 600 |
| average circulation ('000) . . | 8,973 | 10,094 | 10,339 |
| Other periodicals: | | | |
| number . . . . . . | 318 | 331 | 354 |
| average circulation ('000) . . | 1,687 | 1,498 | 1,381 |

**Radio receivers** ('000 in use): 3,020 in 1997 (Source: UNESCO, *Statistical Yearbook*).

**2001:** Telephones ('000 main lines in use) 2,857.9; Mobile cellular telephones ('000 subscribers) 138.3; Internet users ('000) 422.2.

**2002:** Telephones ('000 main lines in use) 2,967.2; Mobile cellular telephones ('000 subscribers) 465.2; Internet users ('000) 808.7.

Source: partly International Telecommunication Union.

# Education

(2001/02)

|                              | Institutions | Teachers | Students  |
| ---------------------------- | ------------ | -------- | --------- |
| Pre-primary . . . . . . | 4,423 | 52,524 | 390,812 |
| Primary (Grades 1–4) . . . . } | 4,709 | 138,744 | 1,473,950 |
| Secondary (Grades 5–11) . . . } | | | |
| Vocational and technical . . . | 248 | 14,772 | 138,593 |
| Specialized secondary . . . . | 156 | 12,748 | 155,352 |
| Higher . . . . . . . . | 58 | 21,684 | 301,753 |
| Institutions offering post-graduate studies . . . . . | 377 | 9,000 | 570,000 |

Source: Ministry of Education, Minsk.

**Adult literacy rate** (UNESCO estimates): 99.7% (males 99.8%; females 99.6%) in 2001 (Source: UN Development Programme, *Human Development Report*).

# Directory

## The Constitution

A new Constitution came into effect on 30 March 1994. An amended version of the 1994 Constitution became effective on 27 November 1996, following a referendum held on 24 November. The following is a summary of its main provisions:

### PRINCIPLES OF THE CONSTITUTIONAL SYSTEM

The Republic of Belarus is a unitary, democratic, social state based on the rule of law. The people are the sole source of state power and the repository of sovereignty in the Republic of Belarus. The people shall exercise their power directly through representative and other bodies in the forms and within the bounds specified by the Constitution. Democracy in the Republic of Belarus is exercised on the basis of diversity of political institutions, ideologies and opinions. State power in the Republic of Belarus is exercised on the principle of division of powers between the legislature, executive and judiciary, which are independent of one another. The Republic of Belarus is bound by the principle of supremacy of law; it recognizes the supremacy of the universally acknowledged principles of international law and ensures that its laws comply with such principles.

Property may be the ownership of the State or private. The mineral wealth, waters and forests are the sole and exclusive property of the State. Land for agricultural use is the property of the State. All religions and creeds are equal before the law. The official languages of the Republic of Belarus are Belarusian and Russian. The Republic of Belarus aims to make its territory a neutral, nuclear-free state. The capital is Minsk.

### THE INDIVIDUAL, SOCIETY AND THE STATE

All persons are equal before the law and entitled without discrimination to equal protection of their rights and legitimate interests. Every person has the right to life. Until its abolition, the death penalty may be applied in accordance with the verdict of a court of law as an exceptional penalty for especially grave crimes. The State ensures the freedom, inviolability and dignity of the individual. No person may be subjected to torture or cruel, inhuman or humiliating treatment or punishment. Freedom of movement is guaranteed. Every person is guaranteed freedom of opinion and beliefs and their free expression. The right to assemble publicly is guaranteed, as is the right to form public associations, including trade unions. Citizens of the Republic of Belarus have the right to participate in the solution of state matters, both directly and through freely elected representatives; the right to vote freely and to be elected to state bodies on the basis of universal, equal, direct or indirect suffrage by secret ballot. The State shall create the conditions necessary for full employment. The right to health care is guaranteed, as is the right to social security in old age, in the event of illness, disability and in other instances. Each person has the right to housing and to education. Everyone has the right to preserve his or her ethnic affiliation, to use his or her native language and to choose the language of communication. Payment of statutory taxes and other levies is obligatory. Every person is guaranteed the protection of his or her rights and freedom by a competent, independent and impartial court of law, and every person has the right to legal assistance.

## THE ELECTORAL SYSTEM AND REFERENDUMS

Elections and referendums are conducted by means of universal, free, equal and secret ballot. Citizens of the Republic of Belarus who have reached the age of 18 years are eligible to vote. Deputies are elected by direct ballot. Referendums may be held to resolve the most important issues of the State and society. National referendums may be called by the President of the Republic of Belarus, by the National Assembly or by no fewer than 450,000 citizens eligible to vote. Local referendums may be called by local representative bodies or on the recommendation of no less than 10% of the citizens who are eligible to vote and resident in the area concerned. Decisions adopted by referendum may be reversed or amended only by means of another referendum.

## THE PRESIDENT

The President of the Republic of Belarus is Head of State, the guarantor of the Constitution of the Republic of Belarus, and of the rights and freedoms of its citizens. The President is elected for a term of five years by universal, free, equal, direct and secret ballot for no more than two terms.

The President calls national referendums; calls elections to the National Assembly and local representative bodies; dissolves the chambers of the National Assembly, as determined by the Constitution; appoints six members to the Central Electoral Commission; forms, dissolves and reorganizes the Administration of the President, as well as other bodies of state administration; appoints the Chairman of the Cabinet of Ministers (Prime Minister) of the Republic of Belarus with the consent of the House of Representatives; determines the structure of the Government, appoints and dismisses Ministers and other members of the Government, and considers the resignation of the Government; appoints, with the consent of the Council of the Republic, the Chairman of the Constitutional, Supreme and Economic Courts, the judges of the Supreme and Economic Courts, the Chairman of the Central Electoral Commission, the Procurator General, the Chairman and members of the board of the National Bank, and dismisses the aforementioned, having notified the Council of the Republic; appoints six members of the Constitutional Court, and other judges of the Republic of Belarus; appoints and dismisses the Chairman of the State Supervisory Committee; reports to the people of the Republic of Belarus on the state of the nation and on domestic and foreign policy; may chair meetings of the Government of the Republic of Belarus; conducts negotiations and signs international treaties, appoints and recalls diplomatic representatives of the Republic of Belarus; in the event of a natural disaster, a catastrophe or unrest involving violence or the threat of violence that may endanger people's lives or jeopardize the territorial integrity of the State, declares a state of emergency; has the right to abolish acts of the Government and to suspend decisions of local councils of deputies; forms and heads the Security Council of the Republic of Belarus, and appoints and dismisses the Supreme State Secretary of the Security Council; is the Commander-in-Chief of the Armed Forces and appoints and dismisses the Supreme Command of the Armed Forces; imposes, in the event of military threat or attack, martial law in the Republic of Belarus; issues decrees and orders which are mandatory in the Republic of Belarus. In instances determined by the Constitution, the President may issue decrees which have the force of law. The President may be removed from office for acts of state treason and other grave crimes, by a decision of the National Assembly.

## THE NATIONAL ASSEMBLY

The National Assembly is a representative and legislative body of the Republic of Belarus, consisting of two chambers: the House of Representatives and the Council of the Republic. The term of the National Assembly is four years. The House of Representatives comprises 110 deputies. Deputies are elected by universal, equal, free, direct suffrage and by secret ballot. The Council of the Republic is a chamber of territorial representation with 64 members, consisting of eight deputies from every region and from Minsk, elected by deputies of local councils. Eight members of the Council of the Republic are appointed by the President. Any citizen who has reached the age of 21 years may become a deputy of the House of Representatives. Any citizen who has reached the age of 30 years, and who has been resident in the corresponding region for no less than five years, may become a member of the Council of the Republic. The chambers of the National Assembly elect their Chairmen.

The House of Representatives considers draft laws concerning amendments and alterations to the Constitution; domestic and foreign policy; the military doctrine; ratification and denunciation of international treaties; the approval of the republican budget; the introduction of national taxes and levies; local self-government; the administration of justice; the declaration of war and the conclusion of peace; martial law and a state of emergency; and the interpretation of laws. The House of Representatives calls elections for the presidency; grants consent to the President concerning the appointment of the Chairman of the Cabinet of Ministers; accepts the resignation of the President; together with the Council of the Republic, takes the decision to remove the President from office.

The Council of the Republic approves or rejects draft laws adopted by the House of Representatives; consents to appointments made by the President; elects six judges of the Constitutional Court and six members of the Central Electoral Commission; considers charges of treason against the President; takes the decision to remove the President from office; considers presidential decrees on the introduction of a state of emergency, martial law, and general or partial mobilization.

Any proposed legislation is considered initially in the House of Representatives and then in the Council of the Republic. On the proposal of the President, the House of Representatives and the Council of the Republic may adopt a law, delegating to him legislative powers to issue decrees which have the power of a law. However, he may not issue decrees making alterations or addenda to the Constitution or to policy laws.

## THE GOVERNMENT

Executive power in the Republic of Belarus is exercised by the Cabinet of Ministers. The Government is accountable to the President and responsible to the National Assembly. The Chairman of the Cabinet of Ministers is appointed by the President with the consent of the House of Representatives. The Government of the Republic of Belarus formulates and implements domestic and foreign policy; submits the draft national budget to the President; and issues acts that have binding force.

## THE JUDICIARY

Judicial authority in the Republic of Belarus is exercised by the courts. Justice is administered on the basis of adversarial proceedings and equality of the parties involved in the trial. Supervision of the constitutionality of enforceable enactments of the State is exercised by the Constitutional Court, which comprises 12 judges (six of whom are appointed by the President and six are elected by the Council of the Republic).

## LOCAL GOVERNMENT AND SELF-GOVERNMENT

Citizens exercise local and self-government through local councils of deputies, executive and administrative bodies and other forms of direct participation in state and public affairs. Local councils of deputies are elected by citizens for a four-year term, and the heads of local executive and administrative bodies are appointed and dismissed by the President of the Republic of Belarus.

## THE PROCURATOR'S OFFICE AND THE STATE SUPERVISORY COMMITTEE

The Procurator's office exercises supervision over the implementation of the law. The Procurator General is appointed by the President with the consent of the Council of the Republic, and is accountable to the President. The Supervisory Authority monitors the implementation of the national budget and the use of public property. The State Supervisory Committee is formed by the President, who appoints the Chairman.

## APPLICATION OF THE CONSTITUTION AND THE PROCEDURE FOR AMENDING THE CONSTITUTION

The Constitution has supreme legal force. Amendments and supplements to the Constitution are considered by the chambers of the National Assembly on the initiative of the President, or of no fewer than 150,000 citizens of the Republic of Belarus who are eligible to vote. The Constitution may be amended or supplemented via a referendum.

# The Government

## HEAD OF STATE

**President:** ALYAKSANDR R. LUKASHENKA (elected 10 July 1994; inaugurated 20 July; re-elected 9 September 2001; inaugurated 20 September).

## CABINET OF MINISTERS
(October 2003)

**Prime Minister:** SYARHEY S. SIDORSKY (acting).

**Deputy Prime Minister and Minister of the Economy:** ANDREY U. KABYAKOW.

**Deputy Prime Ministers:** ULADZIMIR N. DRAZHYN, RAMAN UNUCHKA, ANATOL D. TSYUTSYUNOW.

**Minister of Agriculture and Food:** ZYANON LOMATS.

**Minister of Architecture and Construction:** GENADZ F. KURACHKIN.

**Minister of Culture:** LEANID N. HULYAKA.

**Minister of Defence:** Col-Gen. LEANID S. MALTSAW.

**Minister of Education:** ALYAKSANDR RADZKOU.

**Minister for Emergency Situations:** VALERY P. ASTAPOU.

**Minister of Energy:** ULADZIMIR SYMASHKA.

**Minister of Finance:** NIKOLAY P. KORBUT.

**Minister of Foreign Affairs:** SYARHEY MARTYNOW.

**Minister of Health Care:** LYDMILA A. PASTAYALKA.

**Minister of Housing and Municipal Services:** ALYAKSANDR A. MILKOTA.

**Minister of Industry:** ANATOL D. KHARLAP.

**Minister of Information:** ULADZIMIR RUSAKEVICH.

**Minister of Internal Affairs:** ULADZIMIR U. NAUMAU.

**Minister of Justice:** VIKTAR G. GOLOVANOU.

**Minister of Labour and Social Protection:** ANTONINA P. MOROVA.

**Minister for Natural Resources and Environmental Protection:** LYAVONTSY I. KHAROUZHYK.

**Minister of Posts and Telecommunications:** ULADZIMIR I. GANCHARENKO.

**Minister of Revenue and Taxes:** KONSTANTIN A. SUMAR.

**Minister of Sports and Tourism:** YURIY SIVAKOW.

**Minister of Statistics and Analysis:** ULADZIMIR I. ZINOVSKY.

**Minister of Trade:** ALYAKSANDR M. KULICHKOW.

**Minister of Transport and Communications:** MIKHAIL I. BOROVOY.

**Head of the Presidential Administration:** URAL R. LATYPAW.

## MINISTRIES

**Office of the President:** 220016 Minsk, vul. K. Marksa 38, Dom Urada; tel. (17) 222-60-06; internet www.president.gov.by.

**Office of the Prime Minister and Deputy Prime Ministers:** 220010 Minsk, vul. Savetskaya 11; tel. (17) 222-61-05; fax (17) 222-66-65.

**Cabinet of Ministers of the Republic of Belarus:** 220010 Minsk, pl. Nezalezhnasti, Dom Pravitelstva; tel. (17) 222-69-05; fax (17) 222-66-65; e-mail cm@mail.belpak.by; internet www.president.gov .by.

**Ministry of Agriculture and Food:** 220050 Minsk, vul. Kirava 15; tel. (17) 227-37-51; fax (17) 227-42-96; e-mail kanc@mshp.minsk.by; internet mshp.minsk.by.

**Ministry of Architecture and Construction:** 220050 Minsk, vul. Myasnikova 39; tel. (17) 227-26-42; fax (17) 220-74-24.

**Ministry of Culture:** 220004 Minsk, pr. Masherava 11; tel. (17) 223-75-74; fax (17) 223-90-45.

**Ministry of Defence:** 220034 Minsk, vul. Kamunistychnaya 1; tel. (17) 239-23-79; fax (17) 289-19-74; internet www.mod.mil.by.

**Ministry of the Economy:** 220050 Minsk, vul. Stankevicha 14; tel. (17) 222-60-48; fax (17) 220-37-77; e-mail gen@plan.minsk.by.

**Ministry of Education:** 220010 Minsk, vul. Savetskaya 9; tel. (17) 227-47-36; fax (17) 220-84-83; e-mail root@minedu.unibel.by; internet www.minedu.unibel.by.

**Ministry for Emergency Situations:** 220050 Minsk, vul. Revolutsionnaya 5; tel. (17) 206-54-25; fax (17) 206-51-91; e-mail mcs@ infonet.by; internet www.rescue01.gov.by.

**Ministry of Energy:** 220050 Minsk, vul. K. Marksa 14; tel. (17) 229-83-59; fax (17) 229-84-68.

**Ministry of Finance:** 220010 Minsk, vul. Savetskaya 7; tel. (17) 222-61-37; fax (17) 222-66-40; e-mail mofb@office.un.minsk.by; internet www.ncpi.gov.by/minfin.

**Ministry of Foreign Affairs:** 220030 Minsk, vul. Lenina 19; tel. (17) 227-29-22; fax (17) 227-45-21; internet www.mfa.gov.by.

**Ministry of Health Care:** 220095 Minsk, vul. Myasnikova 39; tel. (17) 222-60-33; fax (17) 222-62-97.

**Ministry of Housing and Municipal Services:** 220050 Minsk, vul. Bersana 16; tel. (17) 220-15-45; fax (17) 220-38-94.

**Ministry of Industry:** 220033 Minsk, pr. Partizansky 2, kor. 4; tel. (17) 224-59-95; fax (17) 224-87-84; e-mail minproml@ntc.niievm .minsk.by; internet www.niievm.minsk.by/minprom/minprom.htm.

**Ministry of Information:** 220048 Minsk, pr. Masherava 11; tel. (17) 223-92-31; fax (17) 223-34-35.

**Ministry of Internal Affairs:** 220050 Minsk, Gorodskoy Val 4; tel. (17) 229-78-08; fax (17) 226-12-47; internet mvd.belarus.nsys.by.

**Ministry of Justice:** 220004 Minsk, vul. Kalektarnaya 10; tel. (17) 220-97-55; fax (17) 220-86-94; e-mail dep07@minjust.belpak.minsk .by; internet www.ncpi.gov.by/minjust.

**Ministry of Labour and Social Protection:** 220004 Minsk, pr. Masherava 23, kor. 2; tel. (17) 206-37-97; fax (17) 206-38-84; e-mail mintrud@mail.belpak.by; internet www.ssf.gov.by.

**Ministry for Natural Resources and Environmental Protection:** 220048 Minsk, vul. Kalektarnaya 10; tel. (17) 220-66-91; fax (17) 220-55-83; e-mail minproos@mail.belpak.by; internet www .president.gov.by/minpriroda.

**Ministry of Posts and Telecommunications:** 220050 Minsk, pr. F. Skaryny 10; tel. (17) 227-21-57; fax (17) 226-08-48; e-mail mpt@ belpak.by; internet www.mpt.gov.by.

**Ministry of Revenue and Taxes:** 220010 Minsk, vul. Savetskaya 9; tel. (17) 222-68-90; fax (17) 222-64-50; internet www.nalog.by.

**Ministry of Sports and Tourism:** 220600 Minsk, vul. Kirava 8, kor. 2; tel. (17) 227-72-37; fax (17) 227-30-31; e-mail inter.sport@solo .by; internet www.mst.by.

**Ministry of Statistics and Analysis:** 220033 Minsk, pr. Partizansky 12; tel. (17) 249-52-00; fax (17) 249-22-04; e-mail minstat@ mail.belpak.by; internet www.president.gov.by/Minstat/en/main .html.

**Ministry of Trade:** 220050 Minsk, vul. Kirava 8, kor. 1; tel. (17) 227-08-97; fax (17) 227-24-80.

**Ministry of Transport and Communications:** 220029 Minsk, vul. Chicherina 21; tel. (17) 234-11-52; fax (17) 239-42-26; e-mail mail@mintrans.by; internet www.mintrans.by.

# President and Legislature

## PRESIDENT

**Presidential Election, 9 September 2001**

| Candidates | Votes | % |
| --- | --- | --- |
| Alyaksandr Lukashenka . . . . . . . | 4,666,680 | 75.65 |
| Uladzimir Gancharyk . . . . . . . | 965,261 | 15.65 |
| Syarhey Gaydukevich . . . . . . . | 153,199 | 2.48 |
| Invalid votes . . . . . . . . . . | 383,947 | 6.22 |
| **Total** . . . . . . . . . . . | 6,169,087 | 100.00 |

## NATIONAL ASSEMBLY*

### Council of the Republic

**Chairman:** GENADZ V. NAVITSKY.

The Council of the Republic is the upper chamber of the legislature and comprises 64 deputies. Of the total, 56 deputies are elected by regional councils and eight deputies are appointed by the President.

### House of Representatives

**Chairman:** VADZIM PAPOW.

**Deputy Chairman:** ULADZIMIR KANAPLYOW.

The House of Representatives is the lower chamber of the legislature and comprises 110 deputies elected by universal, equal, free, direct electoral suffrage and by secret ballot. In the first round of voting in the legislative election of 15 October 2000, 41 seats were filled and 13 constituencies were declared invalid. A second round of voting for the remaining 56 seats took place on 29 October. Owing to the high incidence of electoral violations, however, repeat elections in the invalid constituencies took place on 18 March and 1 April 2001.

* The National Assembly was formed following a referendum held on 24 November 1996. Deputies who had been elected to the Supreme Council at the general election held in late 1995 were invited to participate in the new legislative body. However, many deputies regarded the new National Assembly as unconstitutional and declared themselves to be the legitimate legislature. A form of 'shadow' cabinet, the Public Coalition Government—National Economic Council, chaired by Genadz Karpenka, was established in January 1997 by opposition deputies. Following Karpenka's death in April 1999, the chairmanship of the Council was assumed by Mechislau Gryb (he was officially elected to the post in November).

# Local Government

Belarus was divided into six regions (oblasts or vobłaśćs) and the capital city of Minsk (Miensk). The six regions, which were divided into districts (rayons), were based around the cities of Minsk, Grodno (Horadnia), Brest (Bieraście), Vitebsk (Viciebsk), Mogilev (Mahiloŭ;) and Gomel (Homiel).

Local self-government was exercised by popularly elected councils, with four-year terms of office. The head of local executive and administrative bodies, the chairman of the regional executive committee (governor), was appointed by the President. Local elections took place in March 2003.

## OBLASTS

**Brest:** Regional Executive Committee, Brest, vul. Lenina 11; tel. (16) 226-23-32; fax (16) 223-51-82; Chair. of Council LEANID LEME-SHEVSKY (tel. 223-53-44); Gov. VASILY DOLGOLEV.

**Gomel:** Regional Council, Gomel, vul. Lenina 2; tel. (23) 253-06-24; internet www.region.gomel.by; Chair. VALERI SELITSKY; Gov. ALYAK-SANDR YAKOBSON (tel. 253-41-65; fax 253-51-19).

**Grodno:** Regional Council, Grodno, vul. Ozheshko 3; tel. (15) 244-35-95; internet www.region.grodno.by; Chair. ARKADI KAPUTS; Gov. ULADZIMIR SAVCHENKA (tel. 244-20-29; fax 272-02-32).

**Minsk:** Regional Council, Minsk, vul. Engelsa 4; tel. (17) 227-24-15; Chair. ALPHONS TSISHKEVICH; Gov. PETR PETUKH (tel. 227-50-81; fax 227-24-15).

**Minsk City:** City Council, Minsk, pr. F. Skaryny 8; tel. (17) 227-28-98; Chair. VLADIMIR PAPKOVSKY; Gov. MIKHAIL PAWLAW (tel. 227-44-33; fax 227-68-84).

**Mogilev:** Regional Council, Mogilev, Dom Sovietov; tel. (22) 231-00-97; internet www.region.mogilev.by; Chair. NICK ZHUK; Gov. BORIS BATURA (tel. 232-67-44; fax 222-05-11).

**Vitebsk:** Regional Council, Vitebsk, vul. Gogolya 6; tel. (21) 235-40-07; Chair. VLADIMIR KULAKOV; Gov. VLADIMIR ANDREICHENKO (tel. 225-41-77; fax 236-30-84).

# Political Organizations

Following the Government's imposition of stringent measures for re-registration in January 1999, in September of that year there were only 17 political parties officially registered with the Ministry of Justice (28 had previously been registered).

**Agrarian Party (AP)** (Agrarnaya Partya): 220050 Minsk, vul. Kazintsa 86–2; tel. (17) 220-38-29; fax (17) 249-50-18; f. 1992; Leader SYAMYON SHARETSKY.

**Belarusian Christian-Democratic Party** (Belaruskaya Khryst-siyanska-Demakratnaya Partya): Minsk, vul. Bagdanovicha 7A; f. 1994; Leader MIKALAI KRUKOUSKY.

**Belarusian Christian-Democratic Union** (Belaruskaya Khryst-siyanska-Demakratnaya Zluchnasts): 220065 Minsk, vul. Ava-kyana 38–59; tel. and fax (17) 229-67-56; f. 1991; nationalist, reformist; Leader PETR SILKO.

**Belarusian Ecological Green Party:** Minsk; tel. (17) 220-11-16; fax (17) 256-82-72; f. 1998 by the merger of the Belarusian Ecological Party (f. 1993) and the Green Party of Belarus (f. 1992).

**Belarusian Green Party** (Belaruskaya Partya Zyaleny): 246023 Gomel, vul. Brestkaya 6; tel. (23) 247-08-08; fax (23) 247-96-96; f. 1994 as Belarusian Greenpeace Party, present name adopted 1999; Leaders OLEG GROMYKA, NICK LEKUNOVICH.

**Belarusian National Party** (Belaruskaya Natsiyanalnaya Partya): 220094 Minsk, vul. Plekhanava 32–198; tel. (17) 227-43-76; f. 1994; Leader ANATOL ASTAPENKA.

**Belarusian Party of Labour** (Belaruskaya Partya Pratsy): 220126 Minsk, pr. Masherava 21; tel. (17) 223-82-04; fax (17) 223-97-92; e-mail acmbel2@mail.belpak.by; f. 1993; Leader LEANID LEMYA-SHONAK.

**Belarusian Party of Women 'Hope'** (Belaruskaya Partya Zhan-chyn 'Nadzeya'): 220126 Minsk, pr. Masherov 21; tel. (17) 223-89-57; fax (17) 223-90-40; e-mail zmn@sfpb.belpak.minsk.by; internet www.nadzeya.org; f. 1994; Pres. VALENTINA POLEVIKOVA.

**Belarusian Patriotic Party** (Belaruskaya Patryatychnaya Partya): Minsk; tel. (17) 220-27-57; f. 1994; Leader ANATOL BAR-ANKEVICH.

**Belarusian Peasant Party** (Belaruskaya Syalyanskaya Partya): 220068 Minsk, vul. Gaya 38-1; tel. (17) 277-19-05; fax (17) 277-96-51; f. 1991; advocates agricultural reforms; 7,000 mems; Leader YAUGEN M. LUGIN.

**Belarusian People's Patriotic Union:** Minsk; f. 1998; a pro-Lukashenka alliance supportive of further integration with Russia, comprising 30 left-wing and centrist organizations, incl. the CPB, the Belarusian Patriotic Party, the Liberal Democratic Party of Belarus, the White Rus Slavonic Council and the Union of Reserve Officers; Exec. Sec. VIKTAR CHYKIN.

**Belarusian Popular Party** (Belaruskaya Narodnaya Partya): 220050 Minsk, vul. K. Marksa 18; tel. (17) 227-89-52; fax (17) 227-13-30; e-mail imi@imibel.belpak.minsk.by; f. 1994; Leader VIKTAR TERESCHENKO.

**Belarusian Republican Party** (Belaruskaya Respublikanskaya Partya): 220100 Minsk, vul. Kulman 13–71; tel. (17) 234-07-49; f. 1994; Leaders VALERY ARTYSHEUSKY, ULADZIMIR RAMANAU.

**Belarusian Social Democratic Assembly** (Belaruskaya Satsyal-demakratychnaya Hramada): 220035 Minsk, vul. Drozda 8–52; tel. and fax (17) 226-74-37; e-mail bsdggramada@tut.by; f. 1998; Leader STANISLAU SHUSHKEVICH.

**Belarusian Social Democratic Party:** Minsk; f. 2001 by defectors from the Belarusian Social Democratic Party (National Assembly); Leader ALYAKSEY KAROL.

**Belarusian Social Democratic Party (National Assembly)** (Belaruskaya Satsyal-demakratychnaya Partya—Narodnaya Hra-mada): 220114 Minsk, pr. F. Skaryny 153/2/107; tel. and fax (17) 263-37-48; e-mail bsdp@infonet.by; f. 1903, re-established 1991; merged with Party of People's Accord (f. 1992) in 1996; centrist; Leader MIKALAI STATKEVICH; c. 2,500 mems.

**Belarusian Socialist Party** (Belaruskaya Satsyalistychnaya Partya): Minsk; tel. (17) 229-37-38; f. 1994; aims for a civilized society, where rights and freedoms are guaranteed for all; Leader MIKHAIL PADGAINY.

**BPF—'Revival'** (BPF—'Adradzhennye'): 220005 Minsk, vul. Var-vasheni 8; tel. (17) 231-48-93; fax (17) 233-50-12; e-mail bpf@bpf.minsk.by; internet pages.prodigy.net/dr_fission/bpf; fmrly the Belarusian Popular Front, name changed as above Dec. 1999; f. 1988; anti-communist movement campaigning for democracy, gen-uine independence for Belarus and national and cultural revival; Chair. VINTSUK VYACHORKA; Exec. Sec. ANATOL KRYVAROT.

**Christian-Democratic Choice** (Khrystsiyanska-Demakratychny Vybar): 220050 Minsk, vul. Leningradskaya 3–1; tel. (17) 237-28-86; f. 1995; Leader VALERY SAROKA.

**Communist Party of Belarus (CPB)** (Kamunistychnaya Partya Belarusi): 220007 Minsk, vul. Varanyanskaga 52; tel. (17) 226-64-22; fax (17) 232-31-23; Leader VIKTAR CHYKIN.

**Conservative Christian Party of the BPF:** Minsk; f. 1999 as a breakaway faction of the BPF; Chair. ZYANON PAZNYAK; Dep. Chair. MIKALAI ANTSIPOVICH, YURIY BELENKI, SYARHEY PAPKOW, ULADZIMIR STARCHANKA.

**Liberal Democratic Party of Belarus** (Liberalna-Demakratych-naya Partya Belarusi): 220071 Minsk, vul. Platonava 22, 12th Floor; tel. and fax (17) 231-63-31; e-mail ldpb@infonet.by; f. 1994; advo-cates continued independence of Belarus, increased co-operation with other European countries and eventual membership of the European Union, and expansion of the private sector; Leader SYARHEY GAYDUKEVICH; over 45,000 mems (2002).

**National Democratic Party of Belarus** (Natsyanalna-Demakra-tychnaya Partya Belarusi): Minsk, vul. Labanka 97–140; tel. (17) 271-95-16; fax (17) 236-99-72; f. 1990; Leader VIKTAR NAVUMENKA.

**Party of Common Sense** (Partya Zdarovaga Sensu): 220094 Minsk, pr. Rakasouskaga 37–40; tel. (17) 247-08-68; f. 1994; Leader IVAN KARAVAYCHYK.

**Party of Communists of Belarus** (Partya Kamunistau Belar-uskaya): 220005 Minsk, POB 194; tel. (17) 284-16-08; fax (17) 231-80-36; e-mail ck_pkb@anitex.by; f. 1991; Leader SYARHEY KALYAKIN.

**Republican Party** (Respublikanskaya Partya): 220000 Minsk, vul. Pershamayskaya 18; tel. (17) 236-50-71; fax (17) 236-32-14; f. 1994; aims to build a neutral, independent Belarus; Leader ULADZIMIR BELAZOR.

**Republican Party of Labour and Justice** (Respublikanskaya Partya Pratsy i Spravyadlivasti): 220004 Minsk, vul. Amuratarskaya 7; tel. (17) 223-93-21; fax (17) 223-86-41; f. 1993; Leader ANATOL NYATYLKIN.

**Social-Democratic Party of Popular Accord** (Satsiyal-Demakratychnaya Partya Narodnay Zgody): 220050 Minsk, vul. K. Marksa 10; tel. (17) 286-35-65; f. 1992; Leader SYARHEY ERMAK.

**United Civic Party of Belarus (UCP)** (Abyadnanaya Hramadzyanskaya Partya Belarusi): 220050 Minsk, vul. Kamsamolskaya 11, Office 216; tel. (17) 227-75-49; fax (17) 211-02-79; e-mail ucpb@ ucpb.org; internet www.ucpb.org; f. 1990; liberal-conservative; Chair. ANATOL U. LIABEDZKA; Hon. Chair. STANISLAU A. BAHDANKEVICH; Dep. Chair. PAVEL DANEIKA, ALYAKSANDR A. DABRAVOLSKY, JAROSLAU ROMANCHUK, VASILY SHLYNDZIKAV.

**White Rus Slavonic Council** (Slavyansky Sabor 'Belaya Rus'): 220088 Minsk, vul. Pershamayskaya 24/1/80; tel. (17) 239-52-32; fax (17) 270-09-28; f. 1992; Leader MIKALAY SYARHEY.

# Diplomatic Representation

## EMBASSIES IN BELARUS

**Armenia:** 220050 Minsk, vul. Kirava 17; tel. and fax (17) 227-09-36; Ambassador SUREN HAROUTUNIAN.

**Bulgaria:** 220030 Minsk, pl. Svabody 11, 1st Floor; tel. (17) 206-65-58; fax (17) 206-65-59; Chargé d'affaires a.i. BOYKO KOSEV BOEV.

**China, People's Republic:** 220071 Minsk, vul. Berestyanskaya 22; tel. (17) 285-36-82; fax (17) 285-36-83; e-mail zbesg@telecom.by; Ambassador YU ZHENQI.

**Cuba:** 220071 Minsk, vul. Krasnozviozdnaya 13; tel. (17) 220-03-83; fax (17) 220-23-45; e-mail embacuba@belsonet.net; Ambassador FÉLIX LEÓN CARBALLO.

**Czech Republic:** 220030 Minsk, Muzykalny per. 1/2; tel. (17) 226-52-43; fax (17) 211-01-37; Chargé d'affaires a.i. ALES FOJTIK.

**France:** 220030 Minsk, pl. Svabody 11; tel. (17) 210-28-68; fax (17) 210-25-48; Ambassador STÉPHANE CHMELEWSKY.

**Germany:** 220034 Minsk, vul. Zakharava 26; tel. (17) 288-17-52; fax (17) 236-85-52; e-mail germanembassy@mail.belpak.by; internet www.germanembassy.org.by; Ambassador HELMUT FRICK.

**Greece:** 220030 Minsk, vul. Engelsa 13, Hotel Oktyabrskaya, Room 515; tel. (17) 227-27-60; fax (17) 226-08-05; Ambassador PANAYOTIS GOUMAS.

**Holy See:** Minsk, vul. Valadarskaga 6, 3rd Floor; tel. (17) 289-15-84; fax (17) 289-15-17; Apostolic Nuncio IVAN JURKOVIČ (Archbishop of Corbavia).

**India:** 220090 Minsk, vul. Kaltsova 4, kor. 5; tel. (17) 262-93-99; fax (17) 262-97-99; e-mail indembminsk@indiatimes.com; Ambassador BHARATH RAJ MUTHU KUMAR.

**Iran:** 220049 Minsk, vul. Suvorava 2; tel. (17) 207-66-99; fax (17) 207-61-99; Ambassador MUHAMMAD MOUSSA HASHEMI GOLPAYEGANI.

**Iraq:** Minsk, tr. Smorgovsky 68B; tel. (17) 213-44-99; fax (17) 213-38-99; Ambassador SALMAN ZEIDAN.

**Israel:** 220033 Minsk, pr. Partizansky 6A; tel. (17) 230-44-44; fax (17) 210-52-70; Ambassador MARTIN PELED-FLAX.

**Italy:** 220030 Minsk, vul. K. Marksa 37; tel. (17) 229-29-69; fax (17) 234-30-46; e-mail ambitminsk@belsonet.net; Ambassador STEFANO BENAZZO.

**Japan:** 220004 Minsk, pr. Masherova 23, kor. 1, 8th Floor; tel. (17) 223-60-37; fax (17) 210-41-80; Chargé d'affaires a.i. NAOTAKE YAMASHITA.

**Kazakhstan:** 220029 Minsk, vul. Kuibysheva 12; tel. (17) 213-30-26; fax (17) 234-96-50; e-mail tem@kazemb.belpak.minsk.by; Ambassador GAZIZ ALDAMZHAROV.

**Kyrgyzstan:** 220002 Minsk, vul. Staravilenskaya 57; tel. (17) 234-91-17; fax (17) 234-16-02; e-mail manas@nsys.minsk.by; Ambassador RYSBEK KACHKEYEV.

**Latvia:** 220013 Minsk, vul. Doroshevicha 6A; tel. (17) 284-93-93; fax (17) 284-73-34; e-mail daile@belsonet.net; Ambassador EGONS NEIMANIS.

**Libya:** Minsk, vul. Nyajdanavay 41; tel. (17) 268-66-01; fax (17) 234-70-88; Chargé d'affaires a.i. ABDALLA AL MAGRAVI.

**Lithuania:** 220088 Minsk, vul. Zakharova 68; tel. (17) 285-24-48; fax (17) 285-33-37; e-mail lt.embassy@belsonet.net; Ambassador JONAS PASLAUSKAS.

**Moldova:** 220030 Minsk, vul. Belaruskaya 2; tel. (17) 289-14-41; fax (17) 289-11-47; Ambassador ILIE VANCEA.

**Peru:** 220082 Minsk, vul. Pritytskogo 34; tel. and fax (17) 216-91-14.

**Poland:** 220034 Minsk, vul. Rumyantsava 6; tel. (17) 288-23-13; fax (17) 236-49-92; e-mail ambminsk@nsys.by; internet embassypoland .nsys.by; Ambassador TADEUSZ PAWŁAK.

**Romania:** 220035 Minsk, per. Moskvina 4; tel. (17) 223-77-26; fax (17) 210-40-85; Chargé d'affaires a.i. MIHAI PUYU.

**Russia:** 220002 Minsk, vul. Staravilenskaya 48; tel. (17) 234-54-97; fax (17) 250-36-64; e-mail karp@rusamb.belpak.minsk.by; Ambassador ALEKSANDR BLOKHIN.

**Serbia and Montenegro:** 220012 Minsk, vul. Surganova 28A; tel. (17) 239-39-90; fax (17) 232-51-54; e-mail embassies@smip.sv.gov .yu; Ambassador NIKOLA PEJAKOVICH.

**Slovakia:** 220050 Minsk, vul. Valadarskaga 6; tel. (17) 206-57-78; fax (17) 206-57-76; Chargé d'affaires a.i. JOSEF BOZHEK.

**Tajikistan:** 220050 Minsk, vul. Kirava 17; tel. (17) 222-37-98; fax (17) 227-76-13; Chargé d'affaires OLIM RAKHIMOV.

**Turkey:** 220050 Minsk, vul. Valadarskaga 6, 4th Floor; tel. (17) 227-13-83; fax (17) 227-27-46; e-mail dtmin@comco.belpak.minsk.by; Ambassador ALI VURAL ÖKTEM.

**Turkmenistan:** 220050 Minsk, vul. Kirava 17; tel. (17) 222-34-27; fax (17) 222-33-67; Ambassador ILYA VELDJANOV.

**Ukraine:** 220002 Minsk, vul. Staravilenskaya 51; tel. (17) 283-19-90; fax (17) 283-19-80; e-mail slavutych@anitex.by; Ambassador PETRO SHAPOVAL.

**United Kingdom:** 220030 Minsk, vul. K. Marksa 37; tel. (17) 210-59-20; fax (17) 229-23-06; e-mail pia@bepost.belpak.minsk.by; Ambassador BRIAN BENNETT.

**USA:** 220002 Minsk, vul. Staravilenskaya 46; tel. (17) 210-12-83; fax (17) 234-78-53; e-mail webmaster@usembassy.minsk.by; internet www.usembassy.minsk.by; Ambassador GEORGE KROL.

# Judicial System

In May 1999 there were 154 courts in Belarus, employing some 200 judges.

**Supreme Court:** 220030 Minsk, vul. Lenina 28; tel. (17) 226-12-06; fax (17) 227-12-25; Chair. VALENTIN SUKALO; Dep. Chair. ALYAKSANDR FEDARTSOW.

**Supreme Economic Court:** 220050 Minsk, vul. Valadarskaga 8; tel. and fax (17) 227-16-41; fax (17) 229-20-85; e-mail bxc@court.by; internet www.court.by; Chair. VIKTAR KAMYANKOW.

**Procuracy:** 220050 Minsk, vul. Internatsionalnaya 22; tel. (17) 226-43-57; fax (17) 226-42-52; Procurator General VIKTAR SHEYMAN.

**Constitutional Court:** 220016 Minsk, vul. K. Marksa 32; tel. and fax (17) 227-80-12; e-mail ksrb@user.unibel.by; f. 1994; 12 mem. judges; Chair. RYHOR VASILEVICH; Dep. Chair. ALYAKSANDR MARYSKYN.

# Religion

## CHRISTIANITY

The major denomination is the Eastern Orthodox Church, but there are also an estimated 1.1m. adherents of the Roman Catholic Church. Of these, some 25% are ethnic Poles and there is a significant number of Uniates or 'Greek Catholics'. There is also a growing number of Baptist churches.

### The Eastern Orthodox Church

In 1990 Belarus was designated an exarchate of the Russian Orthodox Church, thus creating the Belarusian Orthodox Church.

**Belarusian Orthodox Church:** 220004 Minsk, vul. Osvobozhdeniya 10; tel. and fax (17) 223-25-05; e-mail orthobel@gin.by; f. 922; Metropolitan of Minsk and Slutsk, Patriarchal Exarch of All Belarus His Eminence FILARET.

### The Roman Catholic Church

Although five Roman Catholic dioceses, embracing 455 parishes, had officially existed since the Second World War, none of them had a bishop. In 1989 a major reorganization of the structure of the Roman Catholic Church in Belarus took place. The dioceses of Minsk and Mogilev (Mahilou) were merged, to create an archdiocese, and two new dioceses were formed, in Grodno (Horadnia) and Pinsk. The

Eastern-rite, or Uniate, Church was abolished in Belarus in 1839, but was re-established in the early 1990s. At 31 December 2001 the Roman Catholic Church had an estimated 1,037,000m. adherents in Belarus (about 10.0% of the population).

Latin Rite

**Archdiocese of Minsk and Mogilev:** 220030 Minsk, pl. Svabody 9; tel. (17) 223-65-41; fax (17) 226-90-92; e-mail archdioces@catholic .by; Archbishop Cardinal KAZIMIERZ ŚWIĄTEK.

Byzantine Rite

**Belarusian Greek Catholic (Uniate) Church:** 224014 Brest, vul. Dvornikova 63; tel. and fax (16) 224-74-82; e-mail bgkc_carkva@tut .by; Dean Protopresbyter VIKTAR DANILAU.

### Protestant Churches

**Union of Evangelical Christian Baptists of Belarus:** 220093 Minsk, POB 108; tel. (17) 253-92-67; fax (17) 253-82-49; e-mail beluecb@belsonet.net; internet www.gospel-web.org.

### ISLAM

There are small communities of Azeris and Tatars, who are adherents of Islam. In 1994 the supreme administration of Muslims in Belarus, which had been abolished in 1939, was reconstituted. In mid-1998 there were some 4,000 Muslims and four mosques.

**Muslim Society:** 220004 Minsk, vul. Zaslavskaya 11, kor. 1, kv. 113; tel. (17) 226-86-43; f. 1991; Chair. ALI HALEMBEK.

### JUDAISM

Before Belarus was occupied by Nazi German forces, in 1941–44, there was a large Jewish community, notably in Minsk. There were some 142,000 Jews at the census of 1989, but many have since emigrated.

**Jewish Religious Society:** 220030 Minsk, pr. F. Skaryny 44A.

# The Press

According to official figures, in 2002 there were 740 newspapers, 351 magazines and other periodicals and four information agencies in Belarus; 12 titles were published in a language other than Belarusian or Russian (primarily English, Polish or Ukrainian). Most daily newspapers are government-owned.

### PRINCIPAL DAILIES

In Russian, except where otherwise stated. The Russian-based newspapers *Argumenty i Fakty* and *Komsomolskaya Pravda v Belorusii* also maintain a high rate of circulation in the country.

**Belaruskaya Niva** (Belarusian Cornfield): 220013 Minsk, vul. B. Hmyalnitskaga 10A; tel. (17) 268-26-20; fax (17) 268-26-43; e-mail belniva@yandex.ru; internet belniva.chat.ru; f. 1921; 5 a week; organ of the Cabinet of Ministers; in Belarusian and Russian; Editor E. SEMASHKO; circ. 65,000 (2000).

**Belorusskaya Delovaya Gazeta (BDG):** 220039 Minsk, vul. Chekalova, d. 12, et. 4; tel. (17) 216–25–85; e-mail edit@bdg.unibel.by; internet www.bdg.by; f. 1992; 4 a week; business affairs; in Russian; suspended for three months in May 2003; subsequently printed in Smolensk, Russia; leading independent newspaper; Editor-in-Chief SVYATLANA KALINKINA; circ. 70,000.

**Narodnaya Hazeta** (The People's Newspaper): 220013 Minsk, vul. B. Hmyalnitskaga 10A; tel. (17) 268-28-70; fax (17) 268-25-29; e-mail info@ng.press.net.by; f. 1990; 5–6 a week; in Belarusian and Russian; Editor-in-Chief M. SHIMANSKY; circ. 90,000 (2000).

**Narodnaya Volya:** Minsk; f. 1995; daily; independent; 5 a week; in Belarusian and Russian; Editor-in-Chief IOSIF SEREDICH; circ. 55,000.

**Respublika** (Republic): 220013 Minsk, vul. B. Hmyalnitskaga 10A; tel. (17) 268-26-15; fax (17) 268-26-12; e-mail info@respublika.info; internet www.respublika.info; 5 a week; in Belarusian; Editor ANATOLI LEMIASHONAK; circ. 120,000 (2002).

**Sovetskaya Belorussiya** (Soviet Belorussia): 220013 Minsk, vul. B. Hmyalnitskaga 10A; tel. and fax (17) 232-14-32; e-mail admin@sb .press.net.by; internet sb.press.net.by; 5 a week; Editor-in-Chief PAVEL YAKUBOVICH; circ. 435,000 (2000).

**Vechernii Minsk** (Evening Minsk): 220805 Minsk, pr. F. Skaryny 44; tel. (17) 284-50-44; fax (17) 213-48-35; e-mail vm@nsys.by; internet newsvm.com; f. 1967; Editor S. SVERKUNOU; circ. 93,000 (2000).

**Znamya Yunosti** (Banner of Youth): 220013 Minsk, vul. B. Hmyalnitskaga 10A; tel. and fax (17) 268-26-84; f. 1938; 5 a week; organ of the Cabinet of Ministers; Editor-in-Chief ELENA PHILIPTCHIK; circ. 9,000 (2000).

**Zvyazda** (Star): 220013 Minsk, vul. B. Hmyalnitskaga 10A; tel. (17) 268-29-19; fax (17) 268-27-79; f. 1917 as Zvezda; 5 a week; organ of the Cabinet of Ministers; in Belarusian; Editor ULADZIMIR B. NARKEVICH; circ. 90,000 (1998).

### PRINCIPAL PERIODICALS

In Belarusian, except where otherwise stated.

**Advertisements Weekly:** 220805 Minsk, pr. F. Skaryny 44; tel. and fax (17) 213-45-25; e-mail omp@bm.belpak.minsk.by; Editor T. ANANENKO; circ. 21,500 (1997).

**Alesya:** 220013 Minsk, pr. F. Skaryny 77; tel. and fax (17) 232-20-51; e-mail magalesya@mail.ru; f. 1924; monthly; Editor TAMARA BUNTO; circ. 10,500 (2003).

**Belarus:** 220005 Minsk, vul. Zakharava 19; tel. (17) 284-80-01; f. 1930; monthly; publ. by the State Publishing House; journal of the Union of Writers of Belarus and the Belarusian Society of Friendship and Cultural Links with Foreign Countries; fiction and political essays; in Belarusian, English and Russian; Editor-in-Chief A. A. SHABALIN.

**Belaruskaya Krinitsa:** 220065 Minsk, vul. Avakyana 38–59; tel. and fax (17) 229-67-56; f. 1991; monthly; journal of the Belarusian Institute of Social Development and Co-operation; Editor-in-Chief MIKHAIL MALKO; circ. 5,000.

**Byarozka** (Birch Tree): 220013 Minsk, pr. F. Skaryny 77; tel. (17) 232-94-66; f. 1924; monthly; fiction; illustrated; for 10–15-year-olds; Editor-in-Chief UL. I. JAGOUDZIK.

**Chyrvonaya Zmena** (Red Rising Generation): 220013 Minsk, vul. B. Hmyalnitskaga 10A; tel. and fax (17) 232-21-03; e-mail czm@mail .ru; internet czm.press.net.by; f. 1921; weekly; Editor A. KARLUKIEVICH; circ. 5,000 (2000).

**Gramadzyanin:** Minsk; tel. (17) 229-08-34; fax (17) 272-95-05; publ. by the United Civic Party of Belarus.

**Holas Radzimy** (Voice of the Motherland): 220005 Minsk, pr. F. Skaryny 44; tel. (17) 288-17-82; fax (17) 288-11-97; e-mail golas_radzimy@tut.by; f. 1955; weekly; articles of interest to Belarusians in other countries; Editor-in-Chief NATALIA SALUK.

**Krynitsa** (Spring): 220807 Minsk, vul. Kiseleva 11; tel. (17) 236-60-71; fax (17) 236-61-42; e-mail www.krynitsa@open.by; f. 1988; monthly; publ. by the state media holding, Literatura i Mastatstva; literary and cultural; in Belarusian; Editor ALA KANAPELKA; circ. 2,100 (2001).

**Litaratura i Mastatstva** (Literature and Arts): 220005 Minsk, vul. Zakharava 19; tel. (17) 284-84-61; f. 1932; weekly; publ. by the state media holding, Literatura i Mastatstva; Editor ALYAKSANDR PISMENKOV; circ. 5,000 (1998).

**Maladosts** (Youth): 220013 Minsk, vul. B. Hmyalnitskaga 10A; tel. (17) 268-27-54; f. 1953; monthly; publ. by the state media holding, Literatura i Mastatstva; novels, short stories, essays, translations, etc., for young people; Editor-in-Chief G. DALIDOVICH.

**Mastatstva** (Art): 220029 Minsk, vul. Chicherina 1; tel. (17) 289-34-67; fax (17) 276-94-67; e-mail masta@ibamedia.com; internet www .ibamedia.com; monthly; illustrated; Editor-in-Chief ALYAKSEY DUDARAU; circ. 1,000–1,200 (2001).

**Narodnaya Asveta** (People's Education): 220023 Minsk, vul. Makaenka 12; tel. (17) 264-62-68; f. 1924; publ. by the Ministry of Education; Editor-in-Chief N. I. KALESNIK.

**Navinki:** Minsk; private; weekly; satirical; publication suspended for three months in June 2003; Editor-in-Chief PAVLYUK KANAVALCHYK; circ. 3,000.

**Neman** (The River Nieman): 220005 Minsk, pr. F. Skaryny 39; tel. (17) 213-40-72; fax (17) 213-44-61; f. 1945; monthly; publ. by the state media holding, Literatura i Mastatstva; literary; fiction; in Russian; Editor-in-Chief A. ZHOUK.

**Polymya** (Flame): 220005 Minsk, vul. Zakharava 19; tel. (17) 284-80-12; f. 1922; monthly; publ. by the state media holding, Literatura i Mastatstva; literary; fiction; Editor-in-Chief S. I. ZAKONNIKOU.

**Tovarisch:** 220005 Minsk, pr. F. Skaryny 46A; tel. (17) 202-08-14; fax (17) 231-80-36; e-mail ck_pkb@anitex.by; internet pkb.promedia .minsk.by; f. 1994; weekly newspaper of the Party of Communists of Belarus; Editor-in-Chief SYARGEY. V. VOZNYAK; circ. 6,000 (2001).

**Vozhyk** (Hedgehog): 220013 Minsk, pr. F. Skaryny 77; tel. and fax (17) 232-12-40; f. 1941; fortnightly; satirical; Editor-in-Chief MIKHAIL POZDNYAKOV; circ. 12,000 (1998).

**Vyaselka** (Rainbow): 220617 Minsk, vul. Kalektarnaya 10; tel. (17) 220-92-61; fax (17) 236-62-67; f. 1957; monthly; popular; for 5–10-year-olds; Editor-in-Chief V. S. LIPSKY; circ. 30,000 (1999).

## PRESS ASSOCIATIONS

**Belarusian Association of Journalists:** Minsk; tel. (17) 227-05-58; internet www.baj.unibel.by; f. 1995; Pres. ZHANNA LITVINA.

**Belarusian Union of Journalists:** 220005 Minsk, vul. Rumyantsava 3; tel. and fax (17) 236-51-95; 3,000 mems; Pres. L. EKEL.

## NEWS AGENCIES

**BelaPAN:** tel. (17) 232-55-01; fax (17) 232-56-57; e-mail mail@belapan.com; internet www.belapan.com; in Belarusian, English and Russian; independent, commercial information company.

**BelTa** (Belarusian News Agency): 220030 Minsk, vul. Kirava 26; tel. (17) 227-19-92; fax (17) 227-13-46; e-mail coper@belta.minsk.by; internet www.belta.minsk.by; f. 1921; Dir DMITRIY ZHUK.

### Foreign Bureaux

**Interfax Zapad:** Minsk; tel. (17) 222-42-75; fax (17) 222-42-76; e-mail market@interfax.minsk.by; internet interfax.minsk.by.

# Publishers

In 2000 there were 7,686 titles published in Belarus (62m. copies).

**Belarus:** 220600 Minsk, pr. F. Skaryny 79; tel. (17) 223-87-42; fax (17) 223-87-31; f. 1921; social, political, technical, medical and musical literature, fiction, children's, reference books, art reproductions, etc.; Dir MIKHALAY KAVALEVSKY; Editor-in-Chief ELENA ZAKONNIKOVA.

**Belaruskaya Entsiklopediya** (Belarusian Encyclopedia): 220072 Minsk, vul. Akademicheskaya 15A; tel. (17) 284-17-67; fax (17) 284-09-83; f. 1967; encyclopedias, dictionaries, directories and scientific books; Editor-in-Chief G. P. PASHKOV.

**Belaruskaya Navuka** (Science and Technology Publishing House): 220067 Minsk, vul. Zhodinskaya 18; tel. (17) 263-76-18; f. 1924; scientific, technical, reference books, educational literature and fiction in Belarusian and Russian; Dir LUDMILA PIETROVA.

**Belarusky Dom Druku** (Belarusian House of Printing): 220013 Minsk, pr. F. Skaryny 79; tel. (17) 268-27-03; fax (17) 231-67-74; e-mail dom.pechati@bdp.minsk.by; f. 1917; social, political, children's and fiction in Belarusian, Russian and other European languages; Dir ROMAN OLEINIK.

**Belblankavyd:** 220035 Minsk, vul. Timirazeva 2; tel. (17) 226-71-22; reference books in Belarusian and Russian; Dir VALENTINA MILOVANOVA.

**Mastatskaya Litaratura** (Art Publishing House): 220600 Minsk, pr. Masherava 11; tel. (17) 223-48-09; f. 1972; fiction in Belarusian and Russian; Dir GEORGE MARCHUK.

**Narodnaya Asveta** (People's Education Publishing House): 220600 Minsk, pr. Masherava 11; tel. and fax (17) 223-61-84; e-mail igpna@asveta.belpak.minsk.by; f. 1951; scientific, educational, reference literature and fiction in Belarusian, Russian and other European languages; Dir IGAR N. LAPTSYONAK.

**Polymya** (Flame Publishing House): 220004 Minsk, pr. Masherava 11; tel. and fax (17) 223-52-85; f. 1950; social, political, scientific, technical, religious, children's and fiction; Dir MIKHAIL A. IVANOVICH.

**Uradzhay** (Harvest Publishing House): 220048 Minsk, pr. Masherava 11; tel. (17) 223-64-94; fax (17) 223-80-23; f. 1961; scientific, technical, educational, books and booklets on agriculture; in Belarusian and Russian; Dir YAUGEN MALASHEVICH.

**Vysheyshaya Shkola** (Higher School Publishing House): 220048 Minsk, pr. Masherava 11; tel. and fax (17) 223-54-15; e-mail vsh@solo.by; internet www.vsh.h1.ru; f. 1954; textbooks and science books for higher educational institutions; in Belarusian, Russian and other European languages; absorbed the Universitetskae publishing house in 2002; Dir ANATOL A. ZHADAN; Editor-in-Chief T. K. MAIBORODA.

**Yunatstva** (Youth Publishing House): 220600 Minsk, pr. Masherava 11; tel. (17) 223-24-30; fax (17) 223-31-16; f. 1981; fiction and children's books; Dir ALYAKSANDR KOMAROVSKY; Vice-Dir MIKHAIL POZDNIAKOV.

# Broadcasting and Communications

## TELECOMMUNICATIONS

**BelCel:** 22005 Minsk, vul. Zolotaya Gorka 5; tel. (17) 276-01-00; fax (17) 276-03-33; e-mail belcel@belcel.by; internet www.belcel.com.by; f. 1993; 50% owned by Cable and Wireless (United Kingdom); mobile telecommunications services; Gen. Dir ARTEM H. ORANDZH.

**Beltelecom:** 220030 Minsk, vul. Engelsa 6; tel. (17) 217-10-05; fax (17) 227-44-22; e-mail info@main.beltelecom.by; internet www.beltelecom.by; f. 1995; national telecommunications operator; Dir-Gen. NIKOLAY KRUKOVSKY.

## BROADCASTING

At the beginning of 2003 there were 183 radio and television companies registered in Belarus; however, all such companies were required to re-register by mid-2003.

**National State Television and Radio Company of Belarus:** 220807 Minsk, vul. A. Makayenka 9; tel. (17) 263-13-20; fax (17) 264-81-82; internet www.tvr.by; f. 1925; Chair. EGOR RYBAKOV.

**Belarusian Television:** 220807 Minsk, vul. A. Makayenka 9; tel. (17) 233-45-01; fax (17) 264-81-82; f. 1956; Pres. A. R. SITYLAROU.

**Belarusian Radio:** 220807 Minsk, vul. Chyrvonaya 4; tel. (17) 239-58-30; fax (17) 284-85-74; e-mail radio-minsk@tvr.by; internet www.tvr.by; Gen. Dir A. P. SALAMAHA.

### Television

The Russian channels NTV—Independent Television, ORT—Public Russian Television (later Pervyi Kanal—First Channel and RTR–TV (later Telekanal—Rossiya) had been widely viewed in Belarus; however, their transmitter facilities were reallocated by the Government to regional television channels in early 2003. In July the Minsk bureau of NTV was ordered to close by the Belarusian Government.

**Television Broadcasting Network (TBN):** 220072 Minsk, pr. F. Skaryny 15A; tel. (17) 284-10-86; fax (17) 284-10-86; e-mail tbn@promedia.by; internet www.data.minsk.by/tbn; f. 1995; comprises 16 private television cos in Belarus's largest cities and an advertising co.

**Minsk Television Company:** Minsk; private; broadcasts to the CIS, Western Europe and North America.

**ONT:** Minsk; e-mail info@ont.by; internet www.ont.by; f. 2002; 51% state-owned; the country's second nation-wide television channel; Chair. GRIGORIY L. KISEL.

# Finance

(cap. = capital; dep. = deposits; res = reserves; m. = million; brs = branches; amounts in readjusted Belarusian roubles, unless otherwise indicated)

## BANKING

At January 2003 there were 28 commercial banks registered in Belarus.

### Central Bank

**National Bank of Belarus:** 220008 Minsk, pr. F. Skaryny 20; tel. (17) 219-23-03; fax (17) 227-48-79; e-mail k.badulin@nbrb.by; internet www.nbrb.by; f. 1990; cap. 60,000,000m. roubles, res 170,835,052m., dep. 296,807,809m. (Dec. 2001); Chair. PYOTR P. PRAKAPOVICH.

### Commercial Banks

**Absolutbank CJSC:** 220023 Minsk, pr. F. Skaryny 95, POB 9; tel. (17) 237-07-02; fax (17) 264-24-43; e-mail root@absolutbank.by; f. 1993; cap. 10,000m. (Oct. 2003); total assets 6,865m. (June 2001); Chair. BORIS G. CHEREDNIK; 2 br.

**Bank Poisk:** 220090 Minsk, vul. Gamarnik 9/4; tel. (17) 228-32-49; fax (17) 228-32-48; e-mail t_lyahnovich@mail.ru; f. 1974 (as a regional branch of Gosbank of the USSR); renamed Housing and Communal Bank (ZhilSotsBank) in 1989; present name adopted in 1992; 74.42% owned by the National Bank of Belarus; cap. 672m., res 535m., dep. 14,184m. (Dec. 2000); Chair. ALGERDAS TABATADZE; 4 brs.

**BELAGROPROMBANK:** 220073 Minsk, vul. Olshevskaga 24; tel. (17) 228-55-13; fax (17) 228-53-19; e-mail bapb@bapb.minsk.by; internet www.belapb.com; f. 1991; 98.74% state-owned; cap. 89,730m., res 67,284m., dep. 315,187m. (Dec. 2001); Chair. ALYAKSANDR A. GAVRUSHEV; 132 brs.

**Belarusbank:** 220050 Minsk, vul. Myasnikova 32; tel. (17) 220-18-31; fax (17) 226-47-50; e-mail info@belarusbank.minsk.by; internet www.belarusbank.minsk.by; f. 1995 following merger with Sberbank (Savings Bank; f. 1922); cap. 100,695m., res 71,958m., dep. 1,473,323m. (Dec. 2001); Chair. NADEZHDA A. YERMAKOVA; 146 brs.

**Belarusian Industrial Bank:** 220004 Minsk, vul. Melnikaite 8; tel. (17) 223-95-78; fax (17) 209-42-06; e-mail bib@bib.by; internet www.bib.by; f. 1991 as Profbank; name changed as above in 1999; cap. 2,481.8m., res 3,658.4m., dep. 8,219.9m. (Dec. 2001); Chair. of Bd PAVEL DIK; 5 brs.

**Belarusian Joint-Stock Commercial Bank for Industry and Construction (BELPROMSTROIBANK):** 220071 Minsk, Blvd Lunacharskogo 6; tel. (17) 210-13-14; fax (17) 210-03-42; e-mail teletype@bpsb.by; internet www.bpsb.by; f. 1991; provides credit to enterprises undergoing privatization and conversion to civil production; 28% privately owned; cap. 10,901m., dep. 237,140m. (Dec. 2001); Gen. Dir GALINA P. KUKHARENKO; 59 brs.

**Belarusky Narodnyi Bank:** 220004 Minsk, vul. Tankovaya 1A; tel. and fax and fax (17) 223-84-57; e-mail bnb@bnb.by; internet www.bnb.by; f. 1992; cap. 593.4m., res 3,610.1m., dep. 7,663.9m. (Dec. 2001); Chair. of Bd ANDREY S. TARATUKHIN; 1 br.

**Belgazprombank:** 220121 Minsk, vul. Pritytsky 60/2; tel. (17) 259-40-24; fax (17) 259-45-25; e-mail telecom@bgpb.minsk.by; internet www.belgazprombank.by; f. 1990; cap. 17,415.2m., dep. 27,321.4m. (Aug. 2002); Chair. of Bd VIKTAR D. BABARIKO; 7 brs.

**Belinvestbank JSC:** 220002 Minsk, vul. Varvasheniy 81; tel. (17) 289-35-42; fax (17) 289-36-70; e-mail corr@belinvestbank.by; internet www.belinvestbank.by; f. 2001, by merger of Belbusinessbank JSC and the Belarusian Bank of Development; cap. US $40.0m. (Jan. 2003); Chair. of Bd ALYAKSANDR E. RUTKOVSKY; 52 brs.

**OJSC Belvnesheconombank:** 220050 Minsk, vul. Myasnikova 32; tel. (17) 238-12-15; fax (17) 226-48-09; e-mail office@bveb.minsk.by; internet www.bveb.by; f. 1991; merged with Belkoopbank in March 2001; 51.8% privately owned; cap. 17,158.0m., res 1,983.6m., dep. 220,948.2m. (Jan. 2002); Chair. of Bd GEORGIY YEGOROV; 28 brs.

**Djembank:** 220012 Minsk, vul. Surganava 28; tel. (17) 219-84-44; fax (17) 219-84-90; e-mail main@djem.com.by; internet www.djem.com.by; f. 1991; cap. 20,390.9m. (Jan. 2003); Gen. Dir ALYAKSANDR V. TATARINTSEV.

**Foreign Bank Moskva-Minsk:** 220002 Minsk, vul. Kommunisticheskaya 49; tel. (17) 288-63-01; fax (17) 288-63-02; e-mail mmb@mmbank.by; f. 2000; wholly owned by Moscow Municipal Bank—Bank of Moscow (Russia); cap. US $1.8m., res $1.9m., dep. $9.1m. (Dec. 2001); Dir ALYAKSANDR RAKOVETS.

**Golden Taler Bank** (Bank Zolotoy Taler): 220035 Minsk, vul. Tatarskaya 3; tel. (17) 206-44-26; fax (17) 210-55-32; e-mail office@gtbank.gtp.by; internet www.gtbank.gtp.by; f. 1994; cap. 801.4m., res 2,472.2m., dep. 14,571.8m. (Jan. 2003); Chair. of Bd ALYAKSANDR A. ZHILINSKY.

**Infobank:** 220035 Minsk, vul. Ignatenka 11; tel. and fax (17) 250-43-88; e-mail root@infobank.by; f. 1994; cap. 6,748m., res 6,664m., dep. 17,255m. (Dec. 2001); Chair. VIKTOR SHEVTSOV; 4 brs.

**ITI Bank** (International Trade and Investment Bank): 220030 Minsk, vul. Sovetskaya 12; tel. (17) 220-68-80; fax (17) 220-17-00; e-mail iti_bank@tut.by; f. 1999; cap. 30,820m., dep. 178,190m. (Dec. 2002); Chair. GENNADY ALEINIKOV.

**MinskComplexBank:** 220050 Minsk, vul. Miasnikova 40; tel. (17) 217-84-42; fax (17) 217-83-55; e-mail welcome@minskcomplexbank.com; internet www.minskcomplexbank.com; f. 1994; cap. US $4.5m., res $4.2m., dep. $27.7m. (Dec. 2001); Chair. of Council YURIY PREDCA.

**Minski Tranzitnyi Bank** (JSC Minsk Transit Bank): 220033 Minsk, pr. Partizansky 6A; tel. (17) 213-29-00; fax (17) 213-29-09; e-mail cor@mtb.minsk.by; f. 1994; 90.29% owned by Nachalo Veka, Minsk; cap. US $10.2m., res $0.6m., dep. $3.2m. (Jan. 2003); Chair. of Bd TAMARA I. ZHEVNYAK; 5 brs.

**Priorbank JSC:** 220002 Minsk, vul. V. Khoruzhey 31A; tel. (17) 269-09-64; fax (17) 234-15-54; e-mail root@priorbank.by; internet www.priorbank.by; f. 1989, present name since 1992; 27% owned by the European Bank for Reconstruction and Development; cap. US $26,137m. (July 2002), res 2,432m., dep. 256,023m. (Dec. 2001); Pres. SYARHEY A. KOSTYUCHENKA.

**Slavneftebank:** 220007 Minsk, vul. Fabritsius 8; tel. (17) 222-07-09; fax (17) 222-07-52; e-mail snb@snbank.by; internet www.snbank.by; f. 1996; 31.93% owned by Belneftechim, Minsk; 26.25% owned by Slavneft-M CJSC, Minsk; cap. 10,258.1m., res 5,718.6m., dep. 91,837.8m. (Dec. 2002); Pres. IVAN BAMBIZA; Chair. of Bd ULADZIMIR V. IVANOV; 6 brs.

**Technobank:** 220002 Minsk, vul. Krapotkina 44; tel. (17) 283-27-27; fax (17) 283-15-10; e-mail info@technobank.com.by; internet www.technobank.com.by; f. 1994; total assets 27,086m. (June 2001); Chair. of Bd VIKTAR I. KHLOPITSKY; 2 brs.

**Trade and Industrial Bank SA** (Torgovo-Promishlenny Bank): 220141 Minsk, vul. Russiyanov 8; tel. and fax (17) 268-03-45; e-mail tib_sa@anitex.by; f. 1994 as Novokom; cap. 1,141,435m. new roubles (Nov. 1999); Chair. FELIKS I. CHERNYAVSKY.

## BANKING ASSOCIATION

**Association of Belarusian Banks:** 220071 Minsk, vul. Smolyachkova 9; tel. (17) 227-78-90; fax (17) 227-58-41; e-mail root@abbank.minsk.by; Chair. NIKOLAY POZNIAK.

## COMMODITY AND STOCK EXCHANGES

**Belagroprambirzha** (Belarusian Agro-Industrial Trade and Stock Exchange): 220108 Minsk, vul. Kazintsa 86, kor. 2; tel. (17) 277-07-26; fax (17) 277-01-37; f. 1991; trade in agricultural products, industrial goods, shares; 900 mems; Pres. ANATOL TIBOGANOU; Chair. of Bd ALYAKSANDR P. DECHTYAR.

**Belarusian Currency and Stock Exchange:** 220004 Minsk, vul. Melnikaite 2; tel. (17) 276-91-21; fax (17) 229-25-66; f. 1991; Gen. Dir VYACHESLAV A. KASAK.

**Belarusian Universal Exchange (BUE):** 220099 Minsk, vul. Kazintsa 4; tel. (17) 278-11-21; fax (17) 278-85-16; f. 1991; Pres. ULADZIMIR SHEPEL.

**Gomel Regional Commodity and Raw Materials Exchange (GCME):** 246000 Gomel, vul. Savetskaya 16; tel. (232) 55-73-28; fax (232) 55-70-07; f. 1991; Gen. Man. ANATOL KUZILEVICH.

## INSURANCE

**Belarusian Insurance Co:** 220141 Minsk, vul. Zhodinskaya 1–4; tel. (17) 263-38-57; fax (17) 268-80-17; e-mail reklama@belinscosc.belpak.minsk.by; f. 1992; Dir-Gen. LEANID M. STATKEVICH.

**Belgosstrakh** (Belarusian Republican Unitary Insurance Co): 220036 Minsk, vul. K. Libknekht 70; tel. (17) 259-10-21; fax (17) 213-08-05; e-mail bgs@belsonet.net; internet www.belgosstrakh.by; Dir-Gen. VIKTAR I. SHOUST; 145 brs.

**Belingosstrakh:** 220050 Minsk, pr. Myasnikova 40; tel. (17) 223-58-78; fax (17) 217-84-19; e-mail bigs1@msil.belpak.by; internet www.belingosstrakh.by; f. 1977; non-life, property, vehicle and cargo insurance; Dir-Gen. YURI A. GAVRILOV.

**GARIS:** 220600 Minsk, vul. Myasnikova 32; tel. (17) 220-37-01.

**Polis:** 220087 Minsk, pr. Partizansky 81; tel. (17) 245-02-91; Dir DANUTA I. VORONOVICH.

**SNAMI:** 220040 Minsk, vul. Nekrasova 40A; tel. and fax (17) 231-63-86; f. 1991; Dir S. N. SHABALA.

# Trade and Industry

## CHAMBERS OF COMMERCE

**Belarusian Chamber of Commerce and Industry:** 220035 Minsk, pr. Masherava 14; tel. (17) 226-91-27; fax (17) 226-98-60; e-mail mbox@cci.by; internet www.cci.by; f. 1952; brs in Brest, Gomel, Grodno, Mogilev and Vitebsk; Pres. ULADZIMIR N. BOBROV.

**Minsk Branch:** 220113 Minsk, vul. Kolasa 65; tel. (17) 266-04-73; fax (17) 266-26-04; Man. Dir P. A. YUSHKEVICH.

## EMPLOYERS' ORGANIZATION

**Belarusian Union of Industrialists and Entrepreneurs:** 220004 Minsk, vul. Kalvaryskaya 1-608; tel. (17) 222-47-96; fax (17) 222-47-94; e-mail buee@nsys.by; internet vyales.nysys.by; f. 1990; business association; Pres. GEORGY BADEY.

## UTILITIES

### Electricity

In November 1999 an agreement was signed on the unification of Russia's and Belarus' energy systems (including a power-grid merger).

**Institute of Nuclear Energy:** 223061 Minsk, Sosny Settlement; tel. (17) 246-77-12.

### Gas

**Belnaftagaz:** Minsk; tel. (17) 233-06-75.

**Beltopgaz:** distributes natural gas to end-users.

**Beltransgaz:** legislation enabling its privatization approved in Nov. 2002; imports natural gas; acts as holding co for regional transmission and storage enterprises.

## MAJOR COMPANIES

### Chemicals

**Belaruskali Production Amalgamation:** 223710 Soligorsk, vul. Korzha 5; tel. (17) 103-72-83; fax (17) 103-71-65; e-mail mep@kali

.belpak.minsk.by; internet www.Belarus.net/kali; f. 1970; produces potassium chloride and potash; Dir Pyotr Kalugin; 20,000 employees.

**Caprolactam Industrial Group:** Gorkovskaya obl., 606000 Dzerzhinsk; tel. (17) 59-31-15; fax (17) 54-37-92; f. 1939; production and sale of chemical products; Man. Dir A. A. Mukhanov; 14,000 employees.

**Dolomit Joint Stock Co:** 211321 Vitebsk, Tsentralnaya 23; tel. (21) 291-52-36; fax (21) 291-52-81; produces dolomite fertilizer; Gen. Dir G. P. Mitrofanov; 1,500 employees.

**Minsk Chemical Plant:** 220024 Minsk, Serova 8; tel. (17) 277-19-14; fax (17) 278-01-07; produces a wide range of chemicals; Gen. Dir N. R. Sikalyuk.

**Polymir Production Association:** 211440 Vitebsk, Polotsky ray., Novopolotsk 5; tel. (21) 457-74-00; fax (21) 457-78-82; e-mail market@polymir.vitebsk.by; internet www.polymir-pa.com; f. 1968; chemical products; sales US $200m. (2001); Dir Alyaksandr V. Borovsky; 6,000 employees.

### Electrical Goods

**Atlant Incorporated Refrigerator Production (Minsk Refrigerator Plant):** 220711 Minsk, pr. Masherava 61; tel. (17) 223-67-19; fax (17) 223-62-47; internet www.belarus.net/atlant/refng_1.htm; f. 1959; production and export of household appliances and industrial equipment; 6,000 employees.

**Brest Electric Lamp Plant (BELP):** Brest, vul. Moskovskaya 204; tel. (16) 242-45-93; fax (16) 242-60-78; f. 1966; manufactures electric incandescent lamps for automobiles, medical use and general application; Dir G. S. Teleshouk; 3,500 employees.

**Brestgazoapparat Joint-Stock Co:** 224016 Brest, Ordzhonikidze 22; tel. (16) 22-29-07; fax (16) 222-19-06; e-mail gefest@sigma.belpak.brest.by; f. 1951; design and manufacture of domestic gas and electrical appliances; Gen. Dir Mikhail F. Ioffe; 3,080 employees.

**Elektrodvigatel Plant:** 212649 Mogilev, vul. Koroleva 8; tel. (222) 23-43-50; fax (222) 23-43-52; manufactures electrical motors; Dir Svyatoslav A. Titov; 2,250 employees.

**Elektromodule Joint-Stock Co:** 222310 Minsk, Molodechno, vul. Velikiy Gostinets 143; tel. (17) 736-08-77; fax (17) 735-26-87; f. 1970; manufactures electric and electronic equipment; Gen. Dir I. I. Dragun; 2,000 employees.

**Integral Research and Production Corpn:** 220064 Minsk, pl. Kazintsa; tel. (17) 277-30-51; fax (17) 278-79-80; e-mail dzum@intergral.minsk.by; internet www.integral.by; f. 1963; manufactures semi-conductors, integrated circuits, telephones, counters; Pres. Viktar Emelyanow; 15,000 employees.

**Izmeritel Measuring Instrument Plant:** 211440 Polotsky ray., Novopolotsk, vul. Molodezhnaya 166; tel. (21) 442-28-36; fax (21) 442-02-55; e-mail izmeritel@vitebsk@by; internet www.izmeritel.boom.ru; f. 1979; state-owned; manufactures electronic and communications equipment; Gen. Dir Y. P. Reshko; 2,200 employees.

**Kalibr Production Co:** 220815 Minsk, vul. Fabritsiusa 8; tel. (17) 222-23-67; fax (17) 222-07-28; e-mail kalibr@brm.by; state-owned; manufactures batteries, halogen lamps and televisions; Gen. Dir Nikolai P. Oltushchets; 1,500 employees.

**Kamerton Plant:** 225710 Pinsk, vul. Brestskaya 137; tel. (16) 534-15-80; fax (16) 534-18-84; e-mail box@camert.belpak.brest.by; f. 1979; state-owned; manufactures electronic wristwatches and pedometers; Gen. Dir Vasiliy Mikhailovich Ogiyevich; 1,000 employees.

**Kozlov Electrical Plant:** 220692 Minsk, vul. Uralskaya 4; tel. (17) 253-54-03; manufactures transformers; Dir Alyaksandr Kozlov; 3,600 employees.

### Foodstuffs

**Meat and Dairy Industry Regional Production Association:** 210024 Vitebsk, pr. Generala Beloborodova 2; tel. (21) 236-42-22; fax (21) 236-09-13; manufactures dairy products and processes meat; Pres. and Gen. Dir Nikolai Vasilevich Savinov; 9,000 employees.

**Myasomolprom Industrial Group:** 224621 Brest, vul. Karbysheva 119; tel. (162) 20-05-23; fax (162) 20-50-48; f. 1975; state-owned; processes and produces meat and dairy products; Dir Dmitriy Y. Tarasyuk; 7,500 employees.

### Metal-processing

**Gomel Casting Enterprise:** 246010 Gomel, vul. Mogilevskaya 16; tel. (23) 254-44-66; fax (23) 256-22-28; state-owned; produces and exports hardware; Man. Dir A. I. Kamko; 6,000 employees.

**RUE Gomel Foundry Tsentrolit:** 246647 Gomel, vul. Barykina 240; tel. (23) 249-32-60; fax (23) 241-45-95; e-mail centrlit@mail.ru; f. 1963; manufacture of grey and ductile cast iron for industry; Dir Mikhail A. Saikov; 2,000 employees.

**Gomel Machine Tool Production Group:**

**Special Designing Bureau of Machining Centres (SDBMC):** 246640 Gomel, vul. Internatsionalnaya 10A; tel. (23) 253-15-89; fax (23) 253-93-71; f. 1987; design and production of specialized metal-cutting machine tools; Man. N. A. Starovoitov; 107 employees.

**Stanko-Gomel:** 246640 Gomel, Internatsionalnaya 10; tel. (23) 253-15-43; fax (23) 253-04-98; e-mail axel99@mail.ru; internet www.belarus-online.com/kirov/index_ru.html; f. 1885; state-owned; production of metal-cutting machine tools; sales 1,909m. new roubles (1999); Gen. Dir A. Shevko; 2,000 employees.

**Kirov Cutting Machinery Plant:** 220030 Minsk, vul. Krasnoarmeyskaya 21; tel. and fax (17) 227-14-44; state-owned; manufactures machine tools; Dir Gennadiy Mikhailovich Kolesnikov; 2,500 employees.

**Minsk Automatic Lines Plant:** 220038 Minsk, vul. Dolgobrodskaya 18; tel. (17) 238-13-00; fax (17) 230-32-51; state-owned; produces iron castings and machine tools; Dir A. A. Potapchuk; 2,400 employees.

**Minsk Bearing Plant:** 220026 Minsk, vul. Zhilunovich 2; tel. (17) 245-15-18; fax (17) 245-20-72; e-mail ft@mpz.com.by; internet www.mpz.com.by; f. 1950, joint-stock co from 1992; state-owned; production of ball- and roller-bearings; Man. Valery N. Penza; 6,500 employees.

**VISTAN Vitebsk Machine-Tool Plant:** 210627 Vitebsk, vul. Dmitrova 36/7; tel. (21) 237-66-30; fax (21) 237-09-34; state-owned; manufactures metal-cutting machine tools; Dir Uladzimir Pavlovich Turavinov; 2,000 employees.

**Vizas:** 210602 Vitebsk, pr. Frunze 83; tel. (21) 224-02-36; fax (21) 224-05-17; f. 1897; state-owned; manufactures tool and cutter grinders, special-purpose grinders, woodworking machinery, optical lens grinders, etc.; Dir-Gen. Yevgeny O. Kiselev; 1,700 employees.

### Motor Vehicles and Components

**AMKODOR-UDARNIK Joint Stock Co:** 220013 Minsk, vul. P. Brovki 8; tel. (17) 288-15-58; fax (17) 288-20-85; e-mail marketing@amkodor.by; f. 1991; manufactures road-construction machinery, including front loaders and road rollers; Gen. Dir Vladimir Kluchnikov; 3,200 employees.

**Avtogidrousilitel Plant:** 222120 Borisov, vul. Chapaeva 56; tel. (17) 773-14-19; fax (17) 773-15-44; f. 1968; state-owned; manufactures hydraulic steering systems and components for motor vehicles; Gen. Dir Alyaksandr A. Pukhovoy; 6,000 employees.

**Belarusian Autoworks (BELAZ):** 222160 Zhodino, vul. Oktyabrya 40; tel. (17) 753-37-37; fax (17) 757-01-37; e-mail reklama@belaz.minsk.by; f. 1958; state-owned; manufactures heavy-load and off-road vehicles and consumer goods; Dir Pavel L. Mariev; 8,000 employees.

**Belshina OJSC** (Belarus Tyre Works): 213824 Bobruisk, Minskoye shosse; tel. (22) 514-63-66; fax (22) 513-50-68; e-mail belshinaexport@yahoo.com; internet www.beltyre.com; f. 1972; manufactures tyres for domestic and industrial use; Dir Dmitriy A. Sivitsky; 14,000 employees.

**JSC Borisov Auto and Tractor Electrical Plant:** 222120 Borisov, vul. Daumana 95; tel. (17) 773-42-43; fax (17) 773-14-21; e-mail admin@bate.belpak.minsk.by; f. 1957; manufactures starter-motors; Gen. Dir Valentin Petrovich Moroz; 4,765 employees.

**Minsk Automobile Plant (MAZ):** 220831 Minsk, vul. Sotsialisticheskaya 2; tel. (17) 216-96-98; fax (17) 246-07-33; e-mail maz@ads.belpak.minsk.by; internet www.maz.com.by:8000/maz/mazmain.nsf; f. 1948; manufacture of trucks, trailers, buses, specialized vehicles and parts; sales US $300m. (Dec. 1999); Dir Valentin A. Gurinovich; 21,500 employees.

**Minsk Motor Plant Production Corpn:** 220829 Minsk, vul. Vaupshasov 4; tel. (17) 238-73-29; fax (17) 230-31-88; internet www.po-mmz.minsk.by; f. 1962; state-owned; design and manufacture of diesel engines; sales US $100m. (Dec. 2000); Gen. Dir Nikolai I. Lobach; 8,000 employees.

**Minsk Tractor Plant (MTZ):** 220668 Minsk, vul. Dolgobrodskaya 29; tel. (17) 230-50-01; fax (17) 230-85-48; e-mail sales@tractors.com.by; internet www.tractors.com.by; f. 1946; state-owned; manufacture, sale and export of tractors and parts, production of sheet steel; Dir Alyaksandr Pukhavy; 20,000 employees.

**MogilevAutomobile Plant S. M. Kirov (MoAZ):** 212601 Mogilev, pr. Vitebsky 5; tel. (22) 242-39-62; fax (22) 242-28-98; e-mail moaz@mail.spbnd.ru; f. 1935; manufactures items and equipment for road construction, specialized vehicles and consumer goods; Dir Nickanor Georgiyevich Mikhailovich; 4,500 employees.

**Mogilevtransmash Transport Engineering Plant:** 212030 Mogilev, vul. Krupskaya 232; tel. and fax (22) 224-36-01; e-mail info@mztm.belpak.mogilev.by; f. 1982; state-owned; production and export of refrigerators, front-end loaders, trailers and truck-mounted cranes; Dir VALERY CHERTKOV; 4,000 employees.

**Motovelo Corpn:** 220765 Minsk, pr. Partizansky 8; tel. (17) 221-69-05; fax (17) 221-68-06; e-mail info@motovelo.com; internet www .motovelo.com; f. 1945; design and manufacture of small motorcycles and a range of bicycles; Gen. Dir ANATOLY S. YAZVINSKY; 4,000 employees.

### Natural Gas and Petroleum

**Belarusneft Production Association:** 246003 Gomel, vul. Roga-chevskaya 9; tel. (23) 252-66-32; fax (23) 255-08-14; e-mail reception@beloil.gomel.by; internet www.beliol.gomel.by; f. 1964; civil and industrial engineering, oilfield development, production of natural gas and consumer goods; Dir ULADZIMIR VITALEVICH MULYAK; 7,900 employees.

**Belneftekhim** (Belarusian State Oil and Chemical Concern): 220116 Minsk, pr. Dzherzhinskaya 73; tel. (17) 271-79-01; fax (17) 271-94-10; internet www.belneftekhim.by; petrochemical complex comprising 84 cos; largest state-owned company; six largest sub-sidiaries, incl. Naftan (q.v.), Azot, Belshina (see Motor Vehicles and Components), Khimvolokno and Polymir (see Chemicals) were transformed into jt-stock cos in 2003, prior to privatization; Pres. IVAN BAMBIZA; 100,000 employees.

**Naftan Industrial Group:** 211440 Vitebsk, Polotsky ray., Novo-polotsk; tel. (21) 447-82-57; fax (17) 226-15-74; e-mail com@naftan .belpak.vitebsk.by; internet www.naftan.vitebsk.by; f. 1963; state-owned; petroleum refining; sales US $840m. (1998); Dir K. CHES-NOVITSKY; 4,500 employees.

**Mozyr Refinery:** 247760 Mozyr, POB 11; tel. (23) 513-07-77; fax (23) 513-05-43; f. 1975; refines and produces asphalt, diesel fuel, gasoline, jet fuel and liquid paraffin; sales of US $187m. (1999); Dir ANATOLI A KUPRIYANOV; 3,800 employees.

**Neftegazsystema:** 246050 Gomel, POB 309; tel. and fax (23) 272-12-78; e-mail igorm@ogs.gomel.by; internet www.ogs.gomel.by; development and implementation of automated systems for pipeline operation; Dir VITALY ANTONOVICH NASHCHUBSKY.

### Pharmaceuticals

**Belmedpreparaty:** 220001 Minsk, vul. Fabritsiusa 30; tel. (17) 229-37-42; fax (17) 222-76-17; internet belmedpreparaty.com; f. 1929; medical and pharmaceutical products; sales 958,000m. new roubles (1997); Gen. Dir V. M. TSARENKOV; 2,700 employees.

### Textiles and Clothing

**Baranovichi Cotton Production Amalgamation:** 225320 Bar-anovichi, vul. Fabrichnaya 7; tel. (17) 210-32-00; fax (16) 347-55-61; e-mail bcpa@mail.ru; internet bcpa.lpb.ru; f. 1963; produces cotton fabrics (grey, bleached, dyed, printed), yarns, bed linen and non-woven materials; Gen. Dir ALYAKSANDR SELIFONTOV; 4,493 employees.

**Kalinka Joint-Stock Co:** 223710 Minsk, Soligorsk, vul. Mira 32; tel. (17) 105-39-26; fax (17) 105-33-23; e-mail soligorsk@kalinka.by .com; internet www.kalinka.by.com; f. 1981; manufactures clothing; Gen. Dir GALINA KALITSENA; 1,500 employees.

**RUE Khimvolokno Grodno Production Association:** 230026 Grodno, vul. Slavinskogo 4; tel. (15) 226-69-03; fax (15) 274-33-80; e-mail khim_grodno@mail.ru; internet www.khimvolokno.com.by; f. 1978; produces nylon goods, carpets, yarns, fibres and polyamide; Gen. Dir VIKTAR M. PINCHUK; 4,500 employees.

**Kim Vitebsk Joint-Stock Co:** 210012 Vitebsk, vul. Gorkogo 42; tel. (21) 233-25-23; fax (21) 233-10-24; e-mail kim@vitebsk.net; internet www.vitebsk.by/kim; f. 1931; production and export of clothing; Pres. YURIY I. GALIKIN; Gen. Dir ALYAKSANDR N. BELYAKOV; 3,149 employees.

**Milavitsa Joint-Stock Co:** 220053 Minsk, vul. Novovilenskaya 28; tel. (17) 288-07-70; fax (17) 210-13-03; e-mail west_sales@milavitsa .com.by; internet www.milavitsa.by; produces lingerie; sales US $35m. (2000); Dir D. A. DITCHKOVSKY; 2,000 employees.

**Minsk Worsted Combine:** 220028 Minsk, vul. Mayakovskogo 176; tel. (17) 221-14-18; fax (17) 221-75-75; e-mail kamvol@usa.net; internet thor.prohosting.com/kamvol; f. 1953; produces wool and cloth; Gen. Dir NIKOLAY I. KOVALEV; 2,400 employees.

**Mogilev Textile Factory:** 212781 Mogilev, vul. Grishina 87; tel. (22) 223-13-12; fax (22) 223-16-93; e-mail market@mogotex.belpak .mogilev.by; produces a wide range of textiles; Gen. Dir ULADZIMIR DEMIDOV; 5,400 employees.

**Mogotex:** 212023 Mogilev, vul. Grishina 87; tel. (22) 223-13-12; fax (22) 223-16-93; f. 1973; produces silk fabrics and garments; Dir VASILIY FEDOSEYEV; 5,400 employees.

**Orsha Linen Mill:** 211030 Orsha, vul. Molodezhnaya 3; tel. (21) 613-21-38; fax (21) 613-01-77; e-mail flax@linen.belpak.vitebsk.by; f.

1930; produces linen fabrics and products; Dir V. SHATKOV; 8,000 employees.

**Polese Industrial and Trading Amalgamation:** Brest Obl., 225710 Pinsk, Pervomaiskaya 159; tel. (16) 533-07-26; fax (16) 533-09-05; f. 1968; knitted products, wool and acrylic yarn; Gen. Dir A. P. GULEVICH; 6,500 employees.

**Slavyanka Industrial Commercial Co:** 213826 Bobruisk, vul. Sotsialisticheskaya 84; tel. (22) 512-98-50; fax (22) 512-97-76; e-mail slavyanka@mail.ru; internet www.slavyanka.com; f. 1930; designs and manufactures clothing; Dir TEYMURAZ N. BOCHORISHVILI; 2,000 employees.

**Slonim Worsted and Spinning Factory, JSC:** 231800 Slonim, vul. Brestskaya 42; tel. (15) 622-35-83; fax (15) 622-16-99; e-mail alex@skpf.belpak.grodno.by; internet www.yarn.by; f. 1977; pro-duces wool knitting yarns; sales US $15m. (2000); Pres. VIKTAR POZHARSKY; Dir PAVEL KORNEIKOV; 2,100 employees.

**Sukno Public Joint-Stock Co:** 220121 Minsk, vul. Matusevicha 33; tel. (17) 253-83-83; fax (17) 253-99-55; e-mail sukno@sukno .belpak.minsk.by; produces fine-cloth fabrics; Dir N. V. KUZMENKO; 2,000 employees.

### Wood Products

**Bobruyskdrev Plant:** 213802 Bobruisk, vul. Lenina 95; tel. (22) 517-05-67; fax (22) 517-05-67; e-mail agromash@bobruisk.net; internet www.bobruisk.net/agromash; state-owned; wood products; Dir YEVGENIY POLIKARPOVICH PAKHILKO; 3,528 employees.

**Borisovdrev:** 222120 Borisov, vul. 30 Let, VLKSM 18; tel. and fax (17) 773-16-45; f. 1990; wood products; Gen. Dir NIKOLAI LUKICH SERGEYEV; 1,850 employees.

**Pinsk Drev Industrial Woodworking Company:** Brest Obl., 225710 Pinsk, vul. Chuklaya 1; tel. and fax (16) 535-66-34; fax (16) 535-01-63; e-mail box@pres.belpak.brest.by; f. 1880; collective enter-prise; produces industrial and domestic furniture and matches; Gen. Dir LORAN S. ARINICH; 4,500 employees.

### Miscellaneous

**Belarusrezinotekhnika Joint-Stock Co:** 213829 Bobruisk, Min-skoye shosse 102; tel. (22) 513-14-17; fax (22) 513-15-28; f. 1952; produces rubber products for industrial uses; Dir V. A. MOROZ; 2,500 employees.

**Belcoopvneshtorg of Belcoopsoyuz:** 220611 Minsk, pr. Masherava 17; tel. (17) 226-95-89; fax (17) 223-09-69; import and export; Dir ULADZIMIR GAPANOVICH.

**Belomo-Belarussian Optical-Mechanical Production Associ-ation:** 220836 Minsk, Makayenka 23; tel. (17) 263-55-47; fax (17) 263-75-57; e-mail market@belomo.minsk.by; internet www.lemt .minsk.by; f. 1957; manufactures guidance and observation equip-ment; sales US $15m. (1999); Pres. V. A. BURSKY; 4,500 employees.

**Bobruiskagromash RUPE:** 213822 Bobruisk, vul. Shinnaya 5; tel. (22) 513-45-52; fax (22) 513-86-80; e-mail agromash@bobruisk.by; internet www.bobruisk.by/agromash; f. 1974; produces agricultural machinery; Gen. Man. YEVGENIY P. PAKHILKO; 2,340 employees.

**Borisov Lead Crystal Plant:** 222120 Borisov, vul. Tolstikova 2; tel. (17) 776-22-72; fax (17) 776-22-73; sales US $8m. (2001); Dir V. N. IVANOV; 2,500 employees.

**Minsk Electromechanical Plant:** 220023 Minsk, vul. Volgog-radskaya 6; tel. (17) 264-60-80; fax (17) 264-23-22; state-owned; manufactures heating equipment, household driers, electric meters and metal fittings for furniture; 5,000 employees.

**Minsk Watch Plant Joint-Stock Co:** 220043 Minsk, pr. F. Skoryna 95; tel. (17) 266-19-30; fax (17) 266-45-21; internet www .belarus.net/mwp; f. 1954; production and sale of mechanical and quartz watches and watch movements; Pres. ULADZIMIR V. ABRAM-CHIK; 5,575 employees.

**Minskpromstroy:** 220102 Minsk, vul. Partizansky 144; tel. (17) 242-72-58; fax (17) 243-55-50; civil engineering and industrial con-struction; Dir V. P. NABOKO; 3,000 employees.

**Mogilevliftmash-Lift Producing Plant:** 212798 Mogilev, pr. Mira 42; tel. (22) 223-15-12; fax (22) 223-16-55; Dir ULADZIMIR POLY-AKOV; 4,000 employees.

**Monolit Corpn:** 210604 Vitebsk, vul. Gorkogo 145; tel. (21) 233-31-76; fax (21) 233-75-02; e-mail com@mono.belpak.vitebsk.by; f. 1958; state-owned; manufactures ceramic capacitators, ferrite inductors and varistors; Pres. NIKOLAI M. DUBROVSKY; 3,000 employees.

**RUE Polotsk Production Association Steklovolokno:** 211400 Polotsk, Promuzel Ksty; tel. (21) 443-19-91; fax (21) 443-02-89; e-mail root@steklo.vitebsk.belpak.by; internet www.polotsk-psv.by; f. 1958; manufacture of glass-fibre materials; Dir B. P. SIVIY; 4,500 employees.

**Shchuchin Avtoprovod Joint-Stock Co:** 231510 Shchuchin, vul. Sovetskaya 15; tel. (15) 142-16-60; fax (15) 142-11-90; f. 1958; state-owned; production of cables and wires; sales 3,877m. new roubles (Dec. 1999); Pres. A. I. SIMONOVICH; 832 employees.

**Strommashina Mogilev Plant:** 212648 Mogilev, vul. Pervomay-skaya 77; tel. (22) 222-09-16; fax (22) 222-29-45; e-mail strommashina@hotbox.ru; internet strommashina.narod.ru; f. 1913; produces automated machinery for manufacturing building materials, bricks, pipes, tiles, etc.; Dir ULADZIMIR YAKOVLEVICH SAKHANKO; 2,400 employees.

### TRADE UNIONS

**Belarusian Congress of Democratic Trade Unions:** 220005 Minsk, vul. Zaharova 24; tel. (17) 233-31-82; fax (17) 210-15-00; f. 1993; alliance of four independent trade unions; Pres. ALYAKSANDR YARASHUK; 18,000 mems.

**Free Trade Union of Belarus:** 220005 Minsk, vul. Zakharova 24; tel. (17) 284-31-82; fax (17) 284-59-94; e-mail spb@user.unibel .by; internet www.praca.by; f. 1992; Chair. GENADZ BYKOU; Vice-Chair. NIKOLAY KANAH; 6,000 mems.

**Independent Trade Union of Belarus:** 223710 Soligorsk, vul. Lenina 42; tel. and fax (17) 102-00-59; e-mail sol_sn@inbox.ru; f. 1991; Chair. VIKTAR BABAYED; Sec. NIKOLAY ZIMIN; 10,000 mems.

**Belarusian Organization of Working Women:** 220030 Minsk, pl. Svabody 23; tel. (17) 227-57-78; fax (17) 227-13-16; f. 1992; 7,000 mems.

**Belarusian Peasants' Union** (Syalansky Sayuz): 220199 Minsk, vul. Brestskaya 64-327; tel. (17) 277-99-93; Chair. KASTUS YARMOLENKA.

**Trade Union Federation of Belarus:** Minsk; Chair. LEANID KOZIK.

**Belarusian Union of Industrial Workers:** f. 2003 by merger of nine principal state-organized industrial trade unions.

**Union of Electronic Industry Workers:** Minsk; Leader ANATOL FEDYNICH.

**Union of Motor Car and Agricultural Machinery Construction Workers:** Minsk; largest industrial trade union in Belarus; Leader ALYAKSANDR I. BUKHVOSTOU; 200,000 mems.

**Union of Small Ventures:** 220010 Minsk, vul. Sukhaya 7; tel. (17) 220-23-41; fax (17) 220-93-41; f. 1990; legal, business; Gen. Dir VIKTAR F. DROZD.

## Transport

### RAILWAYS

In 2000 the total length of railway lines in use was 5,512 km. Minsk is a major railway junction, situated on the east–west line between Moscow and Warsaw, and north–south lines linking the Baltic countries and Ukraine. There is an underground railway in Minsk, the Minsk Metro, which has two lines (total length 23 km), with 19 stations.

**Belarusian State Railways:** 220745 Minsk, vul. Lenina 17; tel. (17) 225-44-00; fax (17) 227-56-48; internet www.rw.by; f. 1992, following the dissolution of the former Soviet Railways; Pres. VASIL I. HAPEYEV.

### ROADS

At 31 December 2000 the total length of roads in Belarus was 74,385 km (including 15,345 km of main roads and 59,040 km of secondary roads). Some 89.0% of the total network was hard-surfaced. In September 1999 it was estimated that more than 28,000 km of Belarus' road network was in need of repair.

### CIVIL AVIATION

Minsk has two airports, one largely for international flights and one for domestic connections.

**Belair Belarussian Airlines:** Minsk; tel. (17) 222-57-02; fax (17) 222-75-09; f. 1991; operates regional and domestic charter services.

**Belavia:** 220004 Minsk, vul. Nemiga 14; tel. (17) 229-24-24; fax (17) 229-23-83; e-mail info@belavia.by; internet www.belavia.by; f. 1993 from former Aeroflot division of the USSR; became state national carrier in 1996; operates services in Europe and selected destinations in Asia, the CIS and the Middle East; Gen. Dir ANATOLY GUSAROV.

**Gomel Air Detachment:** 246011 Gomel, Gomel Airport; tel. (23) 251-14-07; fax (23) 253-14-15; f. 1944; Chief Exec. VALERY N. KULAKOUSKY.

## Tourism

**BELINTOURIST:** 220004 Minsk, pr. Masherava 19; tel. (17) 226-98-40; fax (17) 223-11-43; e-mail office@belintourist.by; internet www.belintourist.by; f. 1992; leading tourist org. in Belarus; Dir-Gen. ULADZIMIR S. KHOMICH.

## Culture

### NATIONAL ORGANIZATION

**Ministry of Culture:** see section on The Government (Ministries).

### CULTURAL HERITAGE

**Belarusian Humanities Centre:** 220050 Minsk, vul. Karala 16A; f. 1990; promotes the study of Belarusian culture and language.

**Grodno State Historical Museum:** Grodno, vul. Zamkovaya 22; 90,000 exhibits; Dir E. A. SOLOVYOVA.

**National Art Museum of the Republic of Belarus:** 220600 Minsk, vul. Internatsionalnaya 33A; tel. and fax (17) 227-71-63; internet natlib.org.by/web/art_museum/eng/home.htm; f. 1939; 22,431 exhibits; 8 brs; Dir ULADZIMIR I. PROKOPTSOV.

**National Library of Belarus:** 220636 Minsk, vul. Chyrvonarmeskaya 9; tel. (17) 227-54-63; fax (17) 229-24-94; e-mail sol@natbibl .org.by; internet natlib.org.by; f. 1922; over 7.5 m. vols; Dir G. M. ALEJNIK.

**National Museum of the History and Culture of Belarus:** 220050 Minsk, vul. K. Marksa 12; tel. and fax (17) 227-36-65; internet natlib.org.by/web/hist_cult_museum/home.htm; f. 1957; over 250,000 exhibits on the history of the Belarusian people; library.

### SPORTING ORGANIZATIONS

**Ministry of Sports and Tourism:** see section on the Government (Ministries).

**National Olympic Committee of the Republic of Belarus:** 220050 Minsk, vul. K. Marksa 10; tel. (17) 227-87-91; fax (17) 227-61-84; e-mail noc-rb@belsonet.net; Pres. ALYAKSANDR R. LUKASHENKA; Gen. Sec. ANATOLIY IVANOV.

### PERFORMING ARTS

**Belarusian Academy of Arts:** 220012 Minsk, pr. F. Skaryny 81; tel. (17) 232-15-42; fax (17) 232-20-41; f. 1945; fmrly the State Theatrical and Arts Institute; training in drama, arts and applied arts; library of 92,394 vols (1996); Rector Prof. V. P. SHARANGOVICH.

**Belarusian State Philharmonic Society:** 220012 Minsk; tel. (17) 233-49-74; fax (17) 231-90-50; f. 1936; Dir ULADZIMIR P. RATOBYLSKY.

**Belarusian State Puppet Theatre:** 220030 Minsk, vul. Engelsa 20; tel. and fax (17) 227-13-65; f. 1938; Artistic Dir ALEKSEY LELLAVSKY; Man. YEVGENIY KLIMAKOV.

**National Academic Bolshoy Ballet Theatre of Belarus:** 220029 Minsk, vul. E. Pashkevich 23; tel. (17) 234-05-84; internet natlib.org .by/web/balet/index.htm; f. 1939; Artistic Dir VALENTIN YELIZARIEV.

**National Academic Opera Theatre of Belarus:** 220029 Minsk, Parizhskaya Kommuna pl. 1; tel. and fax (17) 234-05-84; e-mail belopera@mail.belpak.by; internet naebibl.org.by; f. 1933; restructured in 1996; Gen. and Artistic Dir SYARGEY KORTES.

**State Russian Drama Theatre of Belarus:** 220050 Minsk, vul. Volodarskaya 5; tel. (17) 220-38-25; f. 1932.

**Yanka Kupala National Academic Theatre:** 220030 Minsk, vul. Engelsa 7; tel. (17) 227-60-81; e-mail teatr_kupala@infonet.by; internet www.kupala-theatre.by; f. 1920; Dir GENNADIY DAVIDKO.

### ASSOCIATIONS

**Belarusian Cultural Fund:** 220029 Minsk, 6B Kommunalnaya nab.; tel. (17) 283-28-26; fax (17) 234-42-03; Pres. ULADZIMIR GILEP.

**Belarusian Rerykhau Fund:** 220050 Minsk, POB 177; tel. (172) 23-07-40.

**Belarusian Union of Designers:** 220039 Minsk, vul. Brilevskaya 14; tel. (17) 229-33-98; fax (17) 222-77-80; e-mail uni_dis@mail.ru; f. 1988; asscn of professionals in graphic and industrial design, clothes design, interiors and advertising; Pres. DMITRIY SURSKII; 406 mems.

**Belarusian World Association—Batskaushchyna (Fatherland):** 220048 Minsk, vul. Sukhaya 4; tel. (17) 223-66-21; develops contacts with the Belarusian diaspora.

**Frantishak Skaryna Belarusian Language Society:** 220005 Minsk, vul. Rumyantcava 13; tel. and fax (17) 284-25-11; e-mail tbm@tbm.lingvo.minsk.by; internet tbm.iatp.by; f. 1989; publishes two weekly newspapers (*Nasa Slova*, circ. 5,300, and *Novy Chas*, circ. 2,300); Chair. ALIEH TRUSAU.

**Society for Friendship and Cultural Links with Foreign Countries:** 220034 Minsk, vul. Zakharova 28; tel. (17) 233-18-21.

**Society of Independent Cinematographers:** 220005 Minsk, vul. Frunze 3; tel. (17) 233-51-94.

**Theatrical Union of Belarus:** 220029 Minsk, vul. Kisyalova 13/6; tel. (17) 236-69-82; Chair. MIKHAIL YAROMENKA.

**Union of Artists of Belarus:** 220050 Minsk, vul. K. Marksa 8; tel. (17) 227-37-23; fax (17) 227-71-01; f. 1938; Chair. GENADZ BURALKIN.

**Union of Belarusian Writers (SBP):** 220034 Minsk, vul. Frunze 5; tel. (17) 236-00-12; Chair. ALYAKSANDR (ALES) PASHKEVICH.

**Union of Cinematographers:** 220050 Minsk, vul. K. Marksa 5; tel. (17) 227-14-13.

**Union of Composers:** 220030 Minsk, pl. Svabody 5; tel. (17) 223-45-47; Chair. IHAR LUCHANOK.

**Union of Journalists:** 220005 Minsk, vul. Rumyantsava 3; tel. and fax (17) 236-51-95; 3,000 mems; Chair. ZHANNA LITVINA.

**Union of Musicians of Belarus:** 220030 Minsk, vul. Yanki Kupaly 17/30; tel. and fax (17) 227-26-55; f. 1991; Chair. MIKHAIL DRINEVSKI.

# Education

In response to public demand, in the early 1990s the Government began to introduce greater provision for education in the Belarusian language and more emphasis on Belarusian, rather than Soviet or Russian, history and literature. In 2001/02 27.7% of all pupils were taught in Belarusian, and 72.2% were taught in Russian (0.1% were taught in Polish). In 2001 the total enrolment at pre-primary level was equivalent to 70.8% of children in the relevant age-group. Enrolment at primary level in that year was equivalent to 91.5% (males 91.8%; females 91.2%). Education is officially compulsory for nine years, but usually lasts for 11 years, between the ages of six and 17 years. Secondary education, beginning at the age of 10, lasts for seven years (Grades 5–11), comprising a first cycle of five years and a second of two years. In 2001 enrolment at Grades 5–9 was equivalent to 93.9% of those in the relevant age group (males 93.9%; females 93.9%). Enrolment at Grades 10–11 was equivalent to 54.6% of those aged 16–17 years, and a further 21% were enrolled at vocational schools. In 1998 a programme of education reform was initiated. The programme, which was scheduled for completion in 2010, was to introduce compulsory education for 10 years and a general education lasting 12 years. In 2001/02 some 301,753 students were studying at higher education institutions, comprising 26 universities, nine academies, 15 institutes, five higher colleges, one higher technical school, and two theological seminaries. In 1999 enrolment at tertiary level was equivalent to 44% of people in the relevant age group (males 38.8%; females 49.3%). Research was co-ordinated by the National Academy of Sciences of Belarus (see section on The Environment). Budgetary expenditure on education by all levels of government was 201,600m. readjusted roubles (equivalent to 2.1% of GDP) in 2001.

## UNIVERSITIES

**Belarusian State Agricultural and Industrial University:** 220023 Minsk, pr. F. Skaryny 99; tel. (17) 264-47-71; fax (17) 264-41-16; e-mail oms@batu.unibel.by; f. 1954; fmrly Belarusian Institute of Mechanization of Agricultural; 4 faculties; 413 teachers; 4,900 students; Rector Prof. L. S. GERASIMOVICH.

**Belarusian State Economic University:** 220672 Minsk, pr. Partizansky 26; tel. (17) 249-30-68; fax (17) 249-51-06; f. 1932; fmrly Belarusian State Institute of Nat. Economy; 10 faculties; 737 teachers; 10,000 students; library of 174,000 vols; Rector R. M. KARSEKO.

**Belarusian State Technological University:** 220050 Minsk, vul. Sverdlova 13A; tel. (17) 226-14-32; fax (17) 227-62-17; e-mail root@bstu.unibel.by; internet www.bstu.unibel.by; f. 1930; 9 faculties; 590 teachers; 9,000 students; Rector I. M. ZHARSKY.

**Belarusian State University:** 220050 Minsk, pr. F. Skaryny 4; tel. (17) 209-52-03; fax (17) 209-54-47; e-mail ava@bsu.by; internet www.bsu.by; f. 1921; 15 faculties, 5 institutes; 7,600 teachers; 16,500 students; Rector Prof. A. V. KOZULIN.

**Francisk Skorina Gomel State University:** 246699 Gomel, vul. Sovetskaya 104; tel. (23) 256-73-71; fax (23) 257-81-11; e-mail selkin@gsu.unibel.by; f. 1930; 12 faculties; 600 teachers; 7,500 students; Rector Prof. Dr M. SELKIN.

**Yanka Kupala State University of Grodno:** 230023 Grodno, vul. Ozheshko 22; tel. (15) 244-85-78; fax (17) 210-85-99; e-mail root@grsu.by; internet www.grsu.by; f. 1940; 11 faculties; 612 teachers; 9,556 students; Rector Prof. SYARGEY MASKEVICH.

**Minsk State Linguistic University:** 220662 Minsk, vul. Zakharova 21; tel. (17) 213-35-44; fax (17) 236-75-04; e-mail mslu@user.unibel.by; internet www.mslu.unibel.by; f. 1948; teacher and interpreter training in 14 languages; international relations, public relations, cultural and management studies; 9 faculties; 665 teachers; 5,120 students; library of 1m. books and periodicals; Rector NATALYA P. BARANOVA.

**Polotsk State University:** 211440 Novopolotsk, vul. Blokhina 29; tel. (21) 455-63-40; fax (21) 445-42-63; e-mail admin4@psu.unibel.by; f. 1968; 9 faculties; 500 teachers; 4,000 students; library of over 450,000 vols; Rector Prof. ERNST M. BABENKO.

# Social Welfare

From 1993 the social-security system was financed by two principal funds: the Social Security Fund (covering family allowances, pensions and sickness and disability benefits) and the Employment Fund (directing employment schemes, retraining projects and unemployment benefits). There were some 2,498m. pensioners in 2003. In 2001 government expenditure on social security and welfare was 2,233,090m. readjusted roubles (equivalent to 44.0% of total spending). In addition, local authorities subsidize housing and communal services for low-income families and individuals. In 2002, according to official statistics, wages declined by 17.7%%, in real terms, although they had increased by 30.3% in 2001 and by 12.7% in 2000. Real pensions also declined, by 22.6%, in 2002, after increasing by 35.7% in 2001 and by 27.0% in 2000.

A variety of benefits, financed through the Chornobyl tax, are paid to victims of the accident at the Chornobyl (Chernobyl) power station in Ukraine in April 1986, and in May 2002 the World Bank announced that it was to provide funds of US $50m. to support those living in contaminated areas. According to the World Health Organization (WHO), there were 124.2 hospital beds per 10,000 inhabitants in 1998. There were 44,800 doctors in 2002 (equivalent to 45.3 per 10,000 inhabitants), according to official statistics. Government expenditure on health from the state budget was 178,760m. readjusted roubles in 2001 (equivalent to 3.5% of total expenditure).

## GOVERNMENT AGENCIES

**Belarusian Children's Fund:** Minsk, Kamunistychnaya 2; tel. (17) 226-12-60; Chair. ULADZIMIR LIPSKY.

**Ministry of Health Care:** see section on The Government (Ministries).

**Ministry of Labour and Social Protection:** see section on The Government (Ministries).

**Social Security Fund:** 220029 Minsk, vul. Chicherina 21; tel. and fax (17) 234-30-61; internet www.ssf.gov.by; f. 1993; on the basis of the Pension Fund and the Social Insurance Fund; Gov. LYUDMILA TIMOFEYEVNA BACHILO.

## HEALTH AND WELFARE ORGANIZATIONS

**Belarusian Charitable Fund for the Children of Chernobyl:** 220029 Minsk, vul. Staravilenskaya 14; tel. (17) 234-21-53; fax (17) 234-34-58; e-mail childr@user.unibel.by; f. 1989; charitable fund to aid the victims of the Chornobyl disaster; Chair. Prof. GENNADIY GRUSHEVOY.

**Belarusian Red Cross (Republican Committee):** 220030 Minsk, vul. K. Marksa 35; tel. and fax (17) 227-26-20; e-mail redcross@un.minsk.by; Sec.-Gen. Dr ANTON A. ROMANOVSKI.

**Belarusian Society for Blind Invalids:** 220004 Minsk, vul. Amuratorskaya 7; tel. (17) 223-05-31; fax (17) 223-86-41; Pres. ANATOLIY I. NETUILKIN.

**Belarusian Society of the Handicapped:** 220012 Minsk, vul. Kalinina 7; tel. (17) 266-96-84; fax (17) 266-00-96; Chair. IGOR V. KURGANOVICH.

**Republic of Belarus Organization of Veterans:** 220030 Minsk, vul. Ya. Kupali; tel. (17) 226-12-60; Pres. ANATOLIY N. NOVIKOV.

**Society of the Deaf:** 220050 Minsk, vul. Volodarskaha 12; tel. (17) 220-37-02; fax (17) 226-55-75; Pres. SYARGEY PETROVICH SAPUTO.

# The Environment

In 1990 Belarus declared itself an ecological disaster area and claimed that 2.2m. people lived in areas contaminated by radioactive matter, released as a result of the Chornobyl disaster. The Chornobyl nuclear power-station is situated in Ukraine, very close to the Belarusian border. When an explosion occurred in April 1986, the radioactive discharge was carried by the prevailing winds across southern and western Belarus. The worst affected areas were Gomel and Mogilev oblasts, in the south and south-east of the country, comprising some 20% of Belarus' territory. The peaty soils and wetlands in these regions were particularly prone to contamination, since they easily absorbed radioactive particles. Later analyses suggested that the area contaminated was even greater than originally believed, including parts of Grodno and Vitebsk oblasts, and covering perhaps as much as 40% of the country.

### GOVERNMENT ORGANIZATIONS

**Ministry for Emergency Situations:** formerly the Ministry for Emergency Situations and the Protection of the Population from the Aftermath of the Chernobyl Nuclear Power Station Disaster; see section on The Government (Ministries).

**Ministry for Natural Resources and Environmental Protection:** see section on The Government (Ministries).

### ACADEMIC INSTITUTES

**National Academy of Sciences of Belarus:** 220072 Minsk, pr. F. Skaryny 66; tel. (17) 284-18-01; fax (17) 239-31-63; e-mail academia@mserv.bas-net.by; internet www.ac.by; f. 1929; Pres. MIKHAIL MYASNIKOVICH; institutes incl.:

**'Ecomir' National Scientific-Technical Centre for Remote Environmental Diagnostics:** 220012 Minsk, vul. Surganava 2; tel. and fax (17) 284-00-47; e-mail ecomir@ecomir.belpak.minsk.by; f. 1990; Dir A. A. KOVALYEV.

**Institute of Forestry:** 246654 Gomel, vul. Praletarskaya 71; tel. (23) 253-14-23; fax (23) 253-53-89; f. 1992; Dir VIKTOR A. IPATYEV.

**Institute of the Problems of the Use of Natural Resources and Ecology:** 220114 Minsk, Staroborisovsky trakt 10; tel. (17) 264-26-31; fax (17) 264-24-13; e-mail ipnrue@ns.ecology.ac.by; internet ns.ecology.ac.by; f. 1932; in the Dept of Chemical and Geological Sciences; environmental research; Dir I. I. LISHTVAN.

**Ecology Department, Belarusian Polytechnical Academy:** 220027 Minsk, pr. F. Skaryny 65; tel. (17) 239-91-29; fax (17) 231-30-49; environmental education and training; Dir Dr SYARGEY DOROZHKO.

**Bureau on Environmental Consultancy (BURENCO):** tel. (17) 231-30-52; fax (17) 231-30-49; e-mail ecology_zone8@infra.belpak.minsk.by; f. 1996; implementation of Environmental Management Systems for industrial enterprises in Minsk; advice to government on environmental policy; EcoTeam project addresses the potential for energy saving in households; environmental education and teacher training; Dir ULADZIMIR KOLTUNOV.

**Students National Ecocenter of Belarus (RECU):** 220023 Minsk, vul. Makaenka 8; tel. (17) 264-11-68; e-mail root@swta.minsk.by; f. 1930; environmental forums and education; Dir Dr LIDIA A. KURGANOVA.

### NON-GOVERNMENTAL ORGANIZATIONS

**Association of Professional Ecologists:** 220004 Minsk, Oboinyi per. 4; tel. (17) 226-71-06.

**Belarusian Ecological Green Party:** see section on Political Organizations.

**Belarusian Ecological Union:** 220030 Minsk, Lenina 15A; tel. (17) 227-87-96; unites various groups concerned with environmental issues.

**Belarusian Green Party** (Belaruskaya Partya Zyaleny): see section on Political Organizations.

**Belovezhskaya Pushcha National Park Museum:** 225063 Brest Obl., Belovezhskaya Pushcha Game Preserve; tel. (16) 315-62-67; fax (16) 312-12-83; e-mail box@hpbprom.belpak.brest.by; f. 1960; works to preserve the almost extinct European bison, and other flora and fauna; Dir N. N. BAMBIZA.

**Chernobyl Socio-Ecological Union:** 220000 Minsk, vul. Myasnikob 39; tel. (17) 220-39-04; fax (17) 271-58-19; e-mail sasha@by.glas.apc.org; f. 1990; concerned with social welfare of victims of the Chornobyl disaster and environmental remediation; campaigns on ecological issues; Pres. VASILY YAKAVENKA; Vice-Pres. YURIY VORONZHTSEV.

**'Green Class' Belarusian National Association:** 246028 Gomel, vul. Sovetskaya 106, ku. 65; tel. (23) 256-99-17; fax (23) 24423-52; e-mail greenway@karopa.belpak.gomel.by; internet www.friends-partners.org/ccsi/nisorgs/belarus/grnclass.htm; f. 1993 to disseminate environmental information; Pres. GENNADIY N. KAROPA.

# Defence

In August 2002 the total strength of Belarus' armed forces was an estimated 79,800, comprising ground forces of 29,300, an air force of 22,000 (including an air defence forces of 10,200), as well as 28,500 in centrally controlled units and Ministry of Defence staff. There is also a border guard numbering 12,000, which is controlled by the Ministry of Internal Affairs. Military service is compulsory and lasts for between nine and 12 months. In late 2001 it was reported that the armed forces were to be reduced to 65,000 personnel, including 50,000 servicemen, by 2006. In 2001 defence expenditure was 229,930m. readjusted roubles. The defence budget for 2002 was projected at 321,300m. readjusted roubles. Belarus joined the North Atlantic Treaty Organization's 'Partnership for Peace' programme of military co-operation in January 1995.

**Chief of the General Staff:** Lt-Gen. SYARHEY HURULYOW.

# Bibliography

Balmaceda, M. M., et al (Eds). *Independent Belarus: Domestic Determinants, Regional Dynamics, and Implications for the West*. Cambridge, MA, Harvard University Press, 2002.

Butler, W. E. *Civil Code of the Republic of Belarus*. The Hague, London and New York, NY, Kluwer Law International, 2000.

British Helsinki Human Rights Group. *Belarus*. Helsinki, British Helsinki Human Rights Group, 1995.

Feder, H. *Belarus and Moldova: Country Studies*. Washington, DC, Library of Congress (Federal Research Division), 1995.

Feus, K. *The EU and Belarus*. London, Kogan Page, 2002.

Garnett, S. W., et al (Eds). *Belarus at the Crossroad*. Washington, DC, Carnegie Endowment for International Peace, 2000.

Glantz, D. M. (Ed.). *Belorussia 1944: The Soviet General Staff Study*. London, Frank Cass, 2001.

Gross, J. *Revolution from Abroad: The Soviet Conquest of Poland's Western Ukraine and Western Belorussia*. Princeton, NJ, Princeton University Press, 2001 (revised edn).

International Business Publications USA. *Belarus Business and Investment Opportunities Yearbook*. International Business Publications USA, 2002.

Kipel, V., and Kipel, Z. *Byelorussian Statehood: Reader and Bibliography*. New York, NY, Belarusian Institute of Arts and Sciences, 1988.

Korosteleva, E., et al (Eds). *Contemporary Belarus: Between Democracy and Dictatorship*. London, Routledge, 2003.

Loftus, J. *The Belarus Secret*. St Paul, MN, Paragon House Publishers, 1998.

Lubachko, I. S. *Belorussia under Soviet Rule, 1917–1957*. Lexington, KY, University of Kentucky Press, 1972.

Marples, D. R. 'Post-Soviet Belarus and the Impact of Chernobyl', in *Post-Soviet Geography*. Vol. 33, No. 7 (Sept.). 1992.

'Environment, Economy, and Public Health Problems in Belarus', in *Post-Soviet Geography*. Vol. 33, No. 7. 1994.

'Belarus Ten Years After Chernobyl', in *Post-Soviet Geography*. Vol. 36, No. 6. 1995.

*Belarus: From Soviet Rule to Nuclear Catastrophe*. London, Macmillan, 1996.

*Belarus: A Denationalized Nation*. Amsterdam, Harwood Academic, 1999.

Martel, R. *Les Blancs-russes: Etude Historique, Geographique, Politique et Economique*. Paris, André Delpeuch, 1929.

Mienski, J. 'The Establishment of the Belorussian SSR', in *Belorussian Review*. No. 1. 1955.

Urban, M. *An Algebra of Soviet Power: Elite Circulation in the Belorussian Republic, 1966–86*. Cambridge, Cambridge University Press, 1989.

Vakar N. *Belorussia: The Making of a Nation.* Cambridge, MA, Harvard University Press, 1956.

World Bank. *Belarus: Prices, Markets, and Enterprise Reform.* Washington, DC, World Bank, 1997.

Zaprudnik, J. *Belarus: At a Crossroads in History.* Boulder, CO, Westview Press, 1993.

   *Historical Dictionary of Belarus.* Lanham, MD, Scarecrow Press, 1998.

See also the Select Bibliography in Part Four.

# GEORGIA

## Geography

### PHYSICAL FEATURES

Georgia (formerly the Republic of Georgia and, prior to that, the Georgian Soviet Socialist Republic, a part of the USSR) is situated in west and central Transcaucasia, on the southern foothills of the Greater Caucasus mountain range. There is a short frontier with Turkey to the south-west and a western coastline on the Black Sea. The northern border with the Russian Federation follows the axis of the Greater Caucasus, and includes borders with the autonomous republics of Dagestan, Chechnya, Ingushetiya, North Osetiya (Ossetia), Kabardino-Balkariya and Karachayevo-Cherkessiya. To the south lies Armenia, and to the south-east, Azerbaijan. Georgia includes two Autonomous Republics (Abkhazia and Ajaria) and the former Autonomous Oblast of South Ossetia. The status of Abkhazia and South Ossetia remained in dispute. Georgia has an area of 69,700 sq km (26,911 sq miles), of which Abkhazia totals 8,600 sq km, Ajaria 3,000 sq km and South Ossetia 3,900 sq km.

Geographically, Georgia is divided by the Suram mountain range, which runs from north to south between the Lesser and Greater Caucasus mountains. To the west of the Surams lie the Rion plains and the Black Sea littoral; to the east lies the more mountainous Kura basin. The Rion, flowing westwards into the Black Sea, and the Kura, flowing eastwards through Azerbaijan into the Caspian Sea, are the country's main rivers.

### CLIMATE

The Black Sea coast and the Rion plains have a warm, humid, subtropical climate, with over 2,000 mm of rain annually and average temperatures of 6°C (42°F) in January and 23°C (73°F) in July. Eastern Georgia has a more continental climate, with cold winters and hot, dry summers.

### POPULATION

At the 1989 census, when the total *de facto* population was 5,443,359, 68.8% of the population were Georgians, 9.0% Armenians, 7.4% Russians, 5.1% Azeris, 3.2% Ossetians (or Ossetes), 1.9% Greeks and 1.7% Abkhazians. Other ethnic groups included Ukrainians (52,443), Kurds (33,331), Georgian Jews (14,314) and European Jews (10,312). After 1989 some non-Georgians emigrated as a result of inter-ethnic violence, notably Ossetians seeking refuge in North Osetiya, on the other side of the Caucasus, and many Pontian Greeks. During the period of conflict in Abkhazia in 1992 and 1993, more than 200,000 ethnic Georgians and others left the region. Some 50,000 refugees were resettled from 1996, but renewed hostilities in mid-1998 resulted in the departure of many of these; refugees began to return once again from March 1999. Ajarians, ethnic Georgians who converted to

Islam under Turkish rule, were not counted separately in Soviet censuses from 1926, when they accounted for less than 4% of the population. Until 1944 there were also some 200,000 Meskhetian Turks in Georgia, who were of mixed Turkish and Georgian descent and predominantly Muslim. In November 1944 they were deported *en masse* to Central Asia and, although they were rehabilitated and granted the right to return to Georgia in 1968, few were actually permitted to leave. Many were forced to flee Central Asia following inter-ethnic violence in 1989, but were refused permission by the Georgian authorities to resettle in their homelands.

Most of the population are adherents of Christianity; the principal denomination is the Georgian Orthodox Church. Islam is professed by Abkhazians, Ajarians, Azeris, Kurds and some Ossetians. Most Ossetians in Georgia are Eastern Orthodox Christians, although their co-nationals in North Osetiya are largely Sunni Muslim. There are also other Christian groups, and a small number of adherents of the Jewish faith (both European and Georgian Jews). The official language is Georgian, a non-Indo-European language, which is written in the Georgian script.

At mid-2002, according to UN estimates, the total population numbered 5,177,000 (compared with 5,400,841 at the census of 12 January 1989), and the average population density was 74.3 persons per sq km. The capital of Georgia is Tbilisi, which is situated in the south-east of the country, on the River Kura. At the census of 17 January 2002 it had an estimated population of 1,181,700, according to preliminary figures. Other important towns include the ports of Batumi (the capital of the Ajarian Autonomous Republic, with an estimated population of 121,800 in 2002) and Sukhumi (capital of the Abkhazian Autonomous Republic, with an estimated population of 112,000 in 1994). The main town of western Georgia, however, is Kutaisi, on the Rioni plains, with an estimated population of some 186,000 at the census of 2002. Rustavi, with a population of approximately 116,400 in 2002, is an important industrial centre near Tbilisi.

## Chronology

***c*. 299 BC–234 BC:** Parnavaz (Farnavazi, Pharnabazus), traditionally the first king of an identifiably 'Georgian' state, reigned over eastern Georgia (anciently known as Iberia); his realm was centred on the province of Kartli, but he also came to dominate the kingdom in western Georgia (Egrisi—the area known as Colchis by the ancient Greeks).

**64:** The Roman general, Pompei, incorporated Colchis, part of the just-defeated kingdom of Pontus, into the Empire and secured hegemony in Kartli-Iberia and Armenia; the Persian (Parthian—Iranian) Empire soon disputed this.

**c. AD 328:** The 'Apostle of the Georgians', St Nino (according to tradition a Cappadocian slave woman), began the evangelization of the Georgians; the king of Kartli-Iberia, Mirian III (Meribanes, 284–361), adopted Christianity in 334.

**5th century:** The first known inscriptions in the Georgian alphabet (*mrglovani*) were created, at a time when the Georgian Church was attempting to resist Persian cultural dominance and the advance of Zoroastrianism.

**523:** Tsete, the ruler of Lazica (established in Egrisi, Roman Colchis, in the previous century), accepted Orthodox Christianity; the territory soon returned to dependence on the Eastern Roman ('Byzantine') Empire.

**580:** The Persians abolished the Kartli-Iberian monarchy, upon the death of Bakur III; the Georgian aristocracy acquiesced in the effective partition of the kingdom, between the Byzantines (based at the old capital of Mtskheta) and the Sasanian Persians (located at the new capital a short distance away, Tbilisi).

**645:** Tbilisi fell to the Arabs; the presiding prince of Kartli-Iberia was forced to acknowledge the Muslim Caliph as overlord.

**888:** The monarchy of Kartli-Iberia was restored by the Armenians, both kingdoms being ruled by branches of the Bagration family; there was also a kingdom in western Georgia (Egrisi), known as Abasgia (Abkhazia) or Abkhazeti.

**1008:** Bagrat III, King of Abkhazia, inherited the kingdom of Kartli-Iberia upon the death of his father, uniting Egrisi and Kartli into a single Georgian kingdom ('Sakartvelo', the land of the Kartvelians or Georgians), with his capital at Kutaisi.

**1089–1125:** Reign of King David IV (the 'Restorer' or 'Builder'), who created a powerful kingdom and gained control of the remaining Georgian lands: the process began when he renounced the tribute to the Seljuq Turkish sultanate (1096); it was secured by the defeat of the Muslims at the Battle of Didgori (12 August 1121); and was symbolized by the final capture of Muslim Tbilisi, which became the royal capital (1122).

**1184–1212:** Reign of Queen Tamar; this marked the apogee of the independent, medieval Georgian kingdom, which witnessed the work of the 'national bard', Shota Rustaveli, repulsed the Muslims and helped establish the Byzantine 'Empire' of Trebizond.

**1223–45:** Reign of Queen Rusudan, under whom Georgia was devastated by Mongol and Khwarazem raiders; the power of the monarchy was destroyed, the kingdom was fractured and the Georgians became tributary to the Mongol rulers of the Persian Empire.

**1314:** Georgia was briefly reunited by Giorgi V (the 'Brilliant'), until the invasion of the Mongol leader, Timur 'the Lame' (Tamerlane, 1370–1405).

**1554:** The Russians captured the Caspian port of Astrakhan; the Georgians, divided into several kingdoms and principalities (the main ones being Imereti, in the west, and Kartli and Kakheti, in the east) disputed by the rival Persian and Turkish Ottoman Empires, could begin to expect help from these Orthodox co-religionists.

**1783:** King Irakli (Erekle) II, of a reunited Kartli-Kakheti (1762–98), concluded the Treaty of Georgievsk with Russia, whereby his eastern kingdom surrendered responsibility for defence and foreign affairs, but retained internal autonomy.

**18 December 1800:** Tsar Paul I (Pavel) of Russia declared Kartli-Kakheti annexed outright to the Russian Empire, although the question of the continuance of the Bagration dynasty was left in abeyance—however, Giorgi XII, the last king of eastern Georgia, died before tsarist troops entered Tbilisi (henceforth known as Tiflis, until 1936).

**12 September 1801:** The new Tsar, Alexander (Aleksandr) I, decreed the abolition of the kingdom of Kartli-Kakheti.

**December 1803:** Moving westwards, the Russians placed Samgrelo (Mingrelia) under the formal protection of the Empire.

**1804:** The last reigning Bagration, King Solomon II of Imereti (the main principality of western Georgia, based at Kutaisi), was forced to accept Russian sovereignty; he, and his title, died in 1810.

**1809:** Safar bey Sharvashedze placed his principality of Abkhazia under Russian protection.

**1811:** Mamia Gurieli placed the principality of Guria (western Georgia, on the Black Sea coast) under the protection of the Tsar; the Russians had also seized Sukhum-Kale and other cities from the Turks. In the same year the autocephaly of the eastern Georgian Orthodox Church was ended; a new exarchate was imposed on the western Georgian Church. Varlam Eristavi was appointed as the first Exarchos.

**1828:** The Treaty of Turkmanchai concluded the war between Russia and Persia, confirming Russian rule over the Georgians.

**1864–65:** Emancipation of the serfs, first in Tiflis province, then in Guria and Imereti (Kutaisi province).

**1892:** The first radical Marxist group, Mesami Dasi (Third Company), was formed; Iosif Dzhugashvili (Ioseb Jughashvili, when transliterated from the Georgian—later known as Stalin) became a member.

**1899:** The first Tiflis committee of the All-Russian Social Democratic Labour Party (RSDLP) was formed, dominated by the Menshevik wing—the Bolsheviks of the main, Russian RSDLP were to include many prominent Georgians, notably Stalin and 'Sergo' Ordzhonikidze (Orjonikidze).

**1 August 1914:** Russia entered the First World War against Austria-Hungary, Germany and Ottoman Turkey.

**1917:** The autocephaly of the Georgian Orthodox Church was restored under Patriarch Kirion (Sadzaglishvili).

**2 March (New Style 15 March) 1917:** Following the abdication of Tsar Nicholas (Nikolai) II, the Provisional Government nominated an executive in Transcaucasia, although its power was dependent upon the soviets (councils) established in Tiflis and Baku (Azerbaijan).

**November 1917:** The Georgian Mensheviks and the Armenian leaderships in Georgia and Armenia denied the legitimacy of the new, Bolshevik, central Government and established a Transcaucasian Commissariat to assume temporary authority (an assembly, or Seim, convened in January 1918).

**22 April 1918:** The Transcaucasian Seim declared the independence of the Democratic Federative Republic of Transcaucasia.

**26 May 1918:** The Georgian leadership, realizing that the new Transcaucasian state was untenable, declared an independent Georgian state, allied to Germany.

**July 1920:** The British withdrew the last of their forces from Batumi, refusing to aid the Transcaucasian states militarily against Russia.

**1921:** The first Georgian Constitution was adopted.

**25 February 1921:** The Menshevik Government fled Tiflis, which was occupied by the Red Army, under Ordzhonikidze; Georgia, the last of the Transcaucasian states to fall to the Bolsheviks, was subsequently declared a Soviet Socialist Republic (SSR).

**10 December 1922:** The Federal Union of SSRs of Transcaucasia (formed 12 March) was transformed into a single republic, the Transcaucasian Soviet Federative Socialist Republic (TSFSR); the TSFSR became a founder member of the Union of Soviet Socialist Republics (USSR) on 30 December.

**28 August 1924:** A widespread revolt, led by a coalition of opposition parties known as the Parity Committee, commenced; it failed and was followed by severe repression.

**5 December 1936:** Under the second Constitution of the USSR, the TSFSR was dissolved and the Georgian, Armenian and Azerbaijani SSRs became full Union Republics.

**1937:** The leader of Georgia, Lavrenti Beria, assured Stalin, the Soviet leader, of his loyalty by conducting among the most severe of the Stalinist purges.

**1938:** A new Abkhazian alphabet, based on the Georgian script (33 characters the same and six unique ones), was introduced.

**8 December 1938:** Beria was succeeded by Kandid Charkviani.

**1941–45:** The German–Soviet struggle during the Second World War had a severe effect on Georgia, although there was no fighting on its territory; the population declined from 3.5m. in 1939 to 3.2m. by 1945.

**March 1953:** Death of Stalin; most members of the Georgian leadership were subsequently dismissed.

**March 1956:** The anniversary of the death of Stalin (whose memory remained popular in Georgia) occasioned the first 'nationalist' demonstration since the 1920s, resulting in harsh suppression; there was great opposition that year to perceived 'russification'.

**29 September 1972:** Eduard Shevardnadze became head of the Communist Party of Georgia (CPG—serving until 1985, when he became Soviet Minister of Foreign Affairs), and subsequently launched an anti-corruption campaign.

**14 April 1978:** A public demonstration unexpectedly led to a constitutional amendment restoring Georgian as a state language.

**9 April 1989:** A number of people were killed in Tbilisi when soldiers dispersed a demonstration opposing Abkhazian secessionism and supporting Georgian independence.

**July 1989:** Several people were killed at Sukhumi University during fighting; a state of emergency and curfew were imposed in the Abkhazian capital.

**November 1989:** The Supreme Soviet of Georgia declared the supremacy of Georgian over all-Union (USSR) laws; the article in the Constitution safeguarding the CPG's monopoly on power was abolished.

**December 1989:** There were violent confrontations in South Ossetia, between Ossetians and Georgians, after demands that South Ossetia be made an autonomous republic and, eventually, be reunified with North Ossetia (part of the Russian Federation) were refused.

**February 1990:** The Georgian Supreme Soviet declared Georgia an 'annexed and occupied country'.

**March 1990:** The Supreme Soviet revoked the communist ban on opposition parties, at the behest of which the republican parliamentary elections were postponed.

**25 August 1990:** The Abkhazian Supreme Soviet voted to declare independence from Georgia and adopt the status of a full union republic; this declaration was pronounced invalid by the Georgian Supreme Soviet and Georgian deputies in the Abkhazian legislature succeeded in reversing the declaration.

**20 September 1990:** The South Ossetian Supreme Soviet proclaimed the region's independence and state sovereignty within the USSR; this was declared unconstitutional by the Georgian Supreme Soviet.

**30 September 1990:** The more radical opposition parties rejected all Soviet institutions and conducted elections to a National Congress, in which only 51% of the electorate participated.

**28 October 1990:** In the first round of elections to the Georgian Supreme Soviet the Round Table-Free Georgia coalition of pro-independence parties won some 64% of the votes cast (after the second round of voting, on 11 November, the coalition held 155 seats).

**14 November 1990:** Zviad Gamsakhurdia, leader of the Georgian Helsinki Union and of the victorious coalition, was elected Chairman of the Supreme Soviet; the state was renamed the Republic of Georgia.

**11 December 1990:** The Georgian parliament abolished South Ossetia's autonomous status, resulting in renewed violence in the region. The Soviet leadership annulled this decision in the following month.

**31 March 1991:** Having boycotted the all-Union referendum on continued federation (although polling stations were opened in South Ossetia and Abkhazia) and the negotiations on a new union treaty, the Georgian authorities conducted a republican referendum on independence, which was overwhelmingly supported.

**9 April 1991:** Georgia became the first republic to secede from the USSR, when the Supreme Soviet (Supreme Council) approved a decree formally restoring Georgian independence; six days later Gamsakhurdia was appointed to the new post of executive President of the Republic.

**26 May 1991:** Gamsakhurdia was directly elected to the presidency, with 85.6% of the votes cast.

**September 1991:** Following criticism of his reaction to the failed Soviet coup of August, and accusations of authoritarian rule, opposition parties united to demand Gamsakhurdia's resignation.

**December 1991:** The South Ossetian Supreme Soviet declared a state of emergency, following the dispatch of Georgian troops to the region; a second declaration of independence was adopted, as was a resolution, endorsed by a referendum held in January 1992, in favour of integration into the Russian Federation.

**21 December 1991:** Georgia sent observers to a meeting in Almaty (Alma-Ata), Kazakhstan, where the leaders of 11 former Union Republics of the USSR signed a protocol on the formation of the new Commonwealth of Independent States (CIS).

**2 January 1992:** President Gamsakhurdia was declared deposed by the opposition; he fled to Armenia four days later, and subsequently Chechnya, Russia. A Military Council was formed, headed by Tengiz Kitovani and Jaba Ioseliani; this subsequently appointed Tengiz Sigua as premier.

**10 March 1992:** Shevardnadze was appointed Chairman of the State Council, which had recently replaced the Military Council.

**24 June 1992:** Shevardnadze and President Yeltsin of Russia reached an agreement for the cessation of hostilities in South Ossetia; however, no political settlement was reached.

**July 1992:** Civil disturbance increased in violence, following repeated attempts by Gamsakhurdia and his supporters ('Zviadists') to regain control. In South Ossetia, where conflict was continuing, a cease-fire agreement was signed and peacekeeping monitors deployed. The Abkhazian legislature proclaimed the region's sovereignty as the 'Republic of Abkhazia'.

**31 July 1992:** Georgia became the last former Soviet Republic to be admitted to the UN.

**11 August 1992:** Zviadists kidnapped the Georgian Minister of Internal Affairs and other senior officials, who had been sent to western Georgia (Mingrelia) to negotiate the release of a deputy premier, taken hostage the previous month.

**14 August 1992:** Three thousand National Guard members arrived in Abkhazia, allegedly in an attempt to release the hostages; Abkhazian troops responded with a series of attacks, but the Georgian forces succeeded in capturing Sukhumi.

**September 1992:** Abkhazian forces launched a counter-offensive and gained control of all of northern Abkhazia; Shevardnadze claimed that secessionist forces were receiving military aid from Russia.

**11 October 1992:** Elections to the Supreme Council were participated in by an estimated 75% of the electorate; Shevardnadze was elected Chairman, in direct elections held simultaneously, with 96% of the votes cast. The new parliament convened for the first time on 6 November.

**6 August 1993:** Sigua and the Council of Ministers resigned, after parliament rejected their proposed budget.

**10 September 1993:** A two-month state of emergency was declared (it ended on 20 February 1994) and a new, smaller Cabinet of Ministers, under Otar Patsatsia, was appointed. Shevardnadze forced parliament to accept these measures after offering his resignation (which was refused). The state of emergency ended on 20 February 1994.

**15 September 1993:** Forces loyal to deposed President Gamsakhurdia began an offensive to the west of Samtredia.

**16 September 1993:** Abkhazian forces launched numerous surprise attacks, breaking the UN cease-fire agreement of 27 July; Sukhumi was taken and government troops defeated after 11 days of fighting.

**30 September 1993:** The last government troops were driven from Abkhazia (with the exception of the Kodori Gorge) and the region was officially declared liberated from Georgia; there were reports of ethnic Georgians being expelled and killed by victorious troops.

**2 October 1993:** Zviadist forces captured the port of Poti and gained control of the railway line to Tbilisi, thereby blocking all rail traffic to the capital.

**20 October 1993:** The Supreme Council agreed that Georgia should join the CIS, which Shevardnadze had proposed a few days earlier. The next day Russian troops and supplies arrived in Georgia and government forces were able to reopen supply lines, while Poti and other towns were soon recaptured. Georgia was formally admitted to the CIS on 3 December.

**8 November 1993:** Gamsakhurdia and his supporters fled to Abkhazia, after being defeated at their main base, the town of Zugdidi, by Georgian troops.

**1 December 1993:** Georgian officials and Abkhazian separatists signed a UN-mediated eight-point peace 'memorandum'.

**23 December 1993:** South Ossetia adopted a new Constitution.

**31 December 1993:** Gamsakhurdia was killed, reportedly by his own hand, after being surrounded by government troops in western Georgia.

**March 1994:** Georgia joined the 'Partnership for Peace' programme of the North Atlantic Treaty Organization (NATO).

**14 May 1994:** The Georgian and Abkhazian Governments declared a full cease-fire agreement, under which a contingent of some 3,000 CIS (mainly Russian) peace-keepers were deployed in the region from June; this was in addition to the UN observer forces already in place. Nevertheless, hostilities recommenced.

**26 November 1994:** The Abkhazian legislature adopted a new Constitution, which declared the region to be a sovereign state; the speaker of the legislature, Vladislav Ardzinba, was appointed President—the Georgian Government suspended peace negotiations.

**March 1995:** Georgia and Russia signed an agreement on the establishment of four Russian military bases in Georgia, for a period of 25 years; however, it was not ratified.

**July 1995:** Discussions on a political settlement in South Ossetia began, under the supervision of the Organization for Security and Co-operation in Europe (OSCE).

**24 August 1995:** The Supreme Council finally adopted Georgia's new Constitution, the drafting of which had been prepared by a special commission appointed in 1992; the new Constitution provided for a strong executive presidency and a 235-member, unicameral Georgian Parliament (Sakartvelos Parlamenti).

**29 August 1995:** Shevardnadze survived an assassination attempt, sustaining only minor injuries. In early October the Minister of State Security, Igor Giorgadze, was named as the chief instigator of the plot, and warrants were issued for his arrest. In May 1996 Ioseliani, leader of the Rescue Corps (as the paramilitary Mkhedrioni, or Horsemen, had been renamed in February 1994), was convicted of complicity in the assassination attempt.

**25 September 1995:** The Government introduced a new currency, the lari, which replaced the interim currency coupons introduced in April 1993. The lari became the sole legal tender on 2 October.

**5 November 1995:** In the election to the restored post of President, Shevardnadze won 74.9% of the votes cast. In the parliamentary election, held simultaneously, Shevardnadze's Citizens' Union of Georgia (CUG) won 90 of the 150 seats filled by proportional representation and 17 of the 85 seats filled on a single-mandate basis.

**11 December 1995:** A new Council of Ministers was announced; the post of Minister of State replaced that of prime minister.

**19 January 1996:** At a meeting of CIS leaders in Moscow, Russia, it was agreed to impose an economic blockade of Abkhazia until it agreed to accept Georgian sovereignty.

**10 November 1996:** South Ossetia having introduced a presidential system of government, an election to the post was won by Ludvig Chibirov, who obtained some 65% of the votes cast; the election was criticized by Shevardnadze.

**23 November 1996:** Elections to the Abkhazian People's Assembly were held, despite condemnation by the UN and the OSCE; the Georgian legislature declared them invalid.

**9 July 1997:** Violent clashes occurred in the Kodori Gorge region of Abkhazia, and 20 people were reportedly killed.

**14 August 1997:** The President of Abkhazia, Vladislav Ardzinba, visited Georgia proper for the first time since 1992.

**11 November 1997:** Parliament formally abolished capital punishment.

**17–19 November 1997:** In UN-sponsored talks, it was decided to establish a joint co-ordinating council, comprising representatives of Georgia and Abkhazia, as well as delegates from Russia, the UN and the EU, to resolve the issues in Abkhazia.

**December 1997:** The South Ossetian parliament voted in favour of an independent South Ossetian republic within the CIS; negotiations scheduled to take place under Russian and OSCE supervision were cancelled.

**9 February 1998:** Shevardnadze survived a second assassination attempt when grenades were fired at his motorcade; Zviadists were blamed for the attack and in March Guram Absandze, a former finance minister, was extradited from Russia to stand trial. In August 2001 Absandze was sentenced to 17 years' imprisonment for his role in the failed attempt on

Shevardnadze's life; seven other men also received prison sentences. However, Absandze was pardoned in April 2002.

**25 May 1998:** A cease-fire agreement was signed, following violent clashes in the Gali district of Abkhazia, a supposedly neutral zone, where many refugees had been resettled; some 30,000 refugees left the region once more.

**16 July 1998:** With the removal of Russian patrols, Georgia began independently to patrol its territorial waters (Abkhazia began patrols of its waters on 7 September); a phased withdrawal of Russian troops from the land borders was also planned.

**26 July 1998:** Following criticism of the Government over the economy and the issue of Abkhazia, Nikoloz Lekishvili resigned as Minister of State. The entire cabinet subsequently resigned, with one exception; Vazha Lortkipanidze was confirmed as Minister of State the following month.

**8 September 1998:** Together with 11 other countries of Central Asia, the Caucasus and the Black Sea region, Georgia signed an agreement to re-create the ancient 'Silk Road' trade route between the People's Republic of China and Europe.

**27 April 1999:** Georgia was admitted to the Council of Europe.

**May 1999:** Seventeen people were arrested following the discovery of a new conspiracy to overthrow the President. All were reported to have connections with Igor Giorgadze, who was accused of involvement in the attempted assassination of Shevardnadze in 1995. Also in May, Georgia refused to sign the Collective Security Treaty of the CIS on its expiry, claiming that it was not relevant to its particular problems.

**12 May 1999:** Legislative elections were held in South Ossetia, in which the Communist Party secured some 39% of the votes cast. The results were not recognized by the Georgian Government and the OSCE.

**3 October 1999:** Ardzinba was re-elected as President of the Republic of Abkhazia, with 99% of the votes cast; the participation rate was 87.7%. A simultaneous referendum upheld the 1994 Constitution, and a State Independence Act was passed by the legislature shortly afterwards.

**14 November 1999:** A second round of legislative elections was held (the first had taken place on 31 October), in which the ruling CUG secured 41.9% of the votes cast and 130 seats (85 were filled by proportional representation and 45 were filled on a single-mandate basis). The Union for the Revival of Georgia bloc, comprising parties loyal to former President Gamsakhurdia, and the Industry will Save Georgia bloc won 58 seats (51 proportional, 7 single-mandate) and 15 seats (14 proportional, 1 single-mandate), respectively. Of the remaining seats, 17 were obtained by independents and two by the Georgian Labour Party. One seat remained unfilled, and the mandates of 12 Abkhazian candidates were renewed, following the region's boycott of the election.

**18–19 November 1999:** At a summit meeting of the OSCE held in İstanbul, Turkey, Russia agreed to vacate two of its four military bases in Georgia by 1 July 2001 (negotiations on the closure of the two remaining bases were ongoing in 2003). Agreement was also reached by the Presidents of Azerbaijan, Georgia, Kazakhstan, Turkey and Turkmenistan on the construction of a pipeline to carry petroleum from Baku, Azerbaijan, to Ceyhan, Turkey, via Tbilisi.

**9 April 2000:** Eduard Shevardnadze was re-elected as President for a further five-year term, with 79.8% of the votes cast; he was sworn in on 30 April. The OSCE expressed concern over violations in voting procedures and demanded an investigation; the Parliamentary Assembly of the Council of Europe, however, witnessed no major violations.

**11 May 2000:** Parliament endorsed the appointment of Gia Arsenishvili as the new Minister of State, replacing Vazha Lortkipanidze.

**14 June 2000:** Georgia joined the World Trade Organization (WTO).

**16 March 2001:** At the conclusion of a UN-sponsored meeting in Yalta, Ukraine, delegations from Georgia and Abkhazia signed an agreement renouncing violence and permitting the safe return of refugees.

**8 April 2001:** The new South Ossetian Constitution, which designated Russian and Ossetian as the state languages, was approved in a referendum; the Georgian community in Ossetia boycotted the poll.

**3 July 2001:** The Government complained to Russia following the failure of its troops to vacate the Gudauta military base in Abkhazia by the agreed deadline of 1 July; Russia claimed the troops' continued presence to be necessary, since Georgia was unable to guarantee security at the base. Shevardnadze subsequently protested to the OSCE.

**17 September 2001:** President Shevardnadze announced his resignation from the post of Chairman of the CUG; the President's decision to retain the chairmanship while serving as President had long been regarded by critics as a violation of the Constitution.

**8 October 2001:** A helicopter carrying members of the UN Observer Mission in Georgia (UNOMIG) was shot down by unidentified attackers in Abkhazia, killing all nine people on board, including UNOMIG's Deputy Chief Military Observer, Col László Toeroerk. Violence subsequently escalated in the region and aerial bomb attacks took place, attributed by Abkhazia to Georgian forces, and by Georgia to Russian forces.

**1 November 2001:** Shevardnadze dismissed the entire Government, following large-scale public demonstrations against the investigation by security officials of the independent television station, Rustavi 2, which had been widely interpreted as an attack on the freedom of the media.

**6 December 2001:** Following a second round of voting, Eduard Kokoyev, a Russian citizen, was confirmed as the new South Ossetian President, having secured 55% of the votes cast.

**27 December 2001:** The composition of a new Government, to which many ministers had been re-appointed, was approved by Parliament; Avtandil Dzhorbenadze was the new Minister of State.

**1 March 2002:** During a CIS summit meeting, held in Almaty, President Shevardnadze and the Russian President, Vladimir Putin, agreed to amend the mandate of the CIS peace-keeping forces stationed in Abkhazia, to satisfy Georgian demands that they withdraw to a more northerly position, undertake policing duties, and include soldiers from CIS countries other than Russia. The troops had been operating in the region without a valid mandate since January.

**2 March 2002:** Parliamentary elections took place in the unrecognized Republic of Abkhazia, which were boycotted by the opposition and condemned by the Georgian Government.

**2 April 2002:** The Constitutional Court ruled that the Constitutions of the separatist regions of Abkhazia and South Ossetia contravened Georgian basic law.

**24 May 2002:** The Supreme Court ruled that the faction of the CUG that supported Shevardnadze was the group rightfully entitled to use the party's name, rather than an opposing 'reformist' faction, established by the former parliamentary Chairman, Zurab Zhvania. Zhvania set up a new party, the United Democrats, in the following month.

**27 May 2002:** The USA's Georgia Train and Equip programme was formally inaugurated; military instructors, the majority of whom had arrived in Georgia on 19 May, were to enhance the country's counter-terrorism capabilities and address the unstable situation in the increasingly lawless Pankisi Gorge region, close to the border with Chechnya, which was believed to have been infiltrated by Chechen rebels and militants with connections to international terrorist networks.

**2 June 2002:** Municipal elections took place, resulting in a serious reverse for the CUG, which failed to win any seats on Tbilisi City Council; the New Right Party won more seats throughout Georgia than did any other party.

**29 June 2002:** At a party congress, Dzhorbenadze was elected Chairman of the CUG, and Shevardnadze Honorary Chairman.

**14 June 2002:** The OSCE confirmed Russia's withdrawal from the Gudauta base, in Abkhazia, one year later than had been agreed at the İstanbul summit meeting in 1999.

**23 August 2002:** Georgia accused Russia of an overt act of aggression, and announced that it would be prepared to utilize 'all possible means' to repel subsequent attacks, after one person died following the aerial bombardment of the Pankisi Gorge region by unmarked aircraft; Russia refused to accept responsibility for the attack.

**25 August 2002:** Some 1,000 government troops entered the Pankisi Gorge as part of an operation to reassert control over the area.

**3 October 2002:** Georgia extradited five suspected Chechen militants to Russia, prompting demonstrations from Chechen refugees in the Pankisi Gorge region, owing to fears that the suspects would be executed without trial. The European Court of Human Rights subsequently appealed to Georgia to halt the extraditions.

**6 October 2002:** At a CIS summit meeting in Chişinău, Moldova, Presidents Shevardnadze and Putin reached an agreement, according to which the two countries were to resume joint patrols of their common border, and seek to resolve border issues by diplomatic means. On 7 March 2003 the Presidents released a further statement, according to which they agreed to expedite the repatriation of displaced persons to Abkhazia, and extend indefinitely the mandate of the CIS peace-keeping forces, until either Georgia or Abkhazia demanded their withdrawal.

**14 October 2002:** A constitutional agreement, regulating relations between the state and the Georgian Orthodox Church, was signed by Shevardnadze and Catholicos-Patriarch Ilia II. Some observers expressed concern that the agreement could threaten religious freedom in Georgia.

**21–22 November 2002:** Georgia formally applied for membership of NATO at a summit meeting of the Alliance, held in Prague, Czech Republic.

**23 May 2003:** Construction work on the Georgian part of the Baku–Tbilisi–Ceyhan petroleum pipeline commenced.

**2 November 2003:** A legislative election took place, amid reports of widespread electoral irregularities.

# History

## GEORGE TARKHAN-MOURAVI

### EARLY HISTORY

**Introduction**

The early archaeological cultures of the South Caucasus (the Kura-Arax and the Trialeti) demonstrate a high degree of sophistication, and from early ancient times Georgia occupied a place in occidental and oriental historiography, folklore and mythology. Parallel to the kingdom of western Georgia (Egrisi, or Colchis to the ancient Greeks), situated along the Black Sea coast, in southern and eastern Georgia another state of Kartli (what was anciently known as Iberia) united tribes speaking the Kartvelian language. Georgian historic tradition dates the first attempt to unite the country under King Parnavaz (Farnavazi, Pharanbazus) of Kartli at the beginning of the 3rd century BC. Georgia became a battlefield for the continuous rivalry of Persia (Iran) and the Eastern Roman (later 'Byzantine') Empire. Christianity was adopted in Georgia in 334 AD, when King Mirian III of Kartli-Iberia (Meribanes, 284–361) followed the instruction of St Nino of Cappadocia; the Georgian alphabet was created for translating holy texts. The first Georgian inscriptions appeared in Jerusalem (Israel) in the 5th century, followed soon after by the first known literary text, the 'Martyrdom of St Shushanik'. At about the same time King Vakhtang Gorgasali founded the future capital city of Tbilisi, and managed briefly to unite east and west Georgia.

In 645 Tbilisi fell to the Arabs, who dominated the area for two centuries, before being replaced by the Byzantines, and later by the Seljuq Turkish sultanate, in the 11th century. A new dynasty, the Bagration family, gained control of Inner Kartli and the city of Uplistsikhe, and in 978 King Bagrat III Bagration became the first king of both Kartli and Abkhazia,

that is to say of both eastern and western Georgia. The ascent to the throne of David IV (the 'Restorer' or 'Builder', 1089–1125) was marked by victory over the Muslim coalitions at the Battle of Didgori in 1121 and the recapture of Tbilisi. Under the reign of Queen Tamar (1178–1212) Georgia's statehood reached its peak, but it also developed the first signs of weakness. It fell to the invasions of Jelal-ed-Din in 1225–27, which were followed by a Mongol raid in 1235. Only in 1314 was Giorgi V (the 'Brilliant') able to reunite Georgia but, soon after, the invasions of the Mongol leader, Timur 'the Lame' (Tamerlane, 1370–1405) finally broke Georgia's resistance. With the fall of the Byzantine capital, Constantinople, in 1453, Georgia remained the only Christian stronghold in the region, surrounded by Muslim kingdoms, which relentlessly invaded the country. Georgia fragmented into a number of kingdoms and principalities (among the most important of which were Imereti, in the west, and Kartli and Kakheti, in the east). In despair, in 1783 King Irakli (Erekle) II of the reunified Kartli-Kakheti (1762–98) signed the Treaty of Georgievsk, under the terms of which the kingdom became a Russian protectorate. Nevertheless, when the Persians invaded Tbilisi in 1795, Russia showed no willingness to help. Irakli II's successor, Giorgi XII, continued to negotiate with Tsar Paul (Pavel) I of Russia, but, upon his death in December 1800 the Tsar immediately declared the annexation of eastern Georgia. The decree of his successor, Tsar Alexander (Aleksandr) I, of 12 September 1801, finalized the issue, abolishing the kingdom.

**Under the Russian Empire (1801–1917)**

Having annexed Kartli-Kakheti, the Russian Government exiled the heir, David, and the royal family to Russia, and continued expansion. In 1804 King Solomon II of Imereti (the main principality of western Georgia) was forced to accept Russian sovereignty; subsequently, in 1810, he was captured and deposed, and he died in exile, in Turkey, in 1815. The leaders of other, smaller principalities showed little resistance to Russian conquest. Subsequently, the autocephaly of the Georgian Orthodox Church was abolished and the Russian exarchate was imposed, instead. Successful wars with Turkey and Persia confirmed Russian rule over Transcaucasia. Between 1811 and 1877 the Russian army captured Sukhum-Kale, Poti, Akhalkalaki, Akhaltsikhe and Batumi. None the less, frequent mishandling of sensitive issues and local traditions by the Russian administration caused uprisings throughout the 19th century. Forceful Russian expansion caused the Muslim peoples of the North Caucasus to resort to military resistance. Russian forces, supported by Georgian militia, finally won the Great Caucasian War, which ended in 1864–65. Many Caucasian Muslims (*muhajirs*), Abkhazians, among others, left for the Turkish Ottoman Empire, dramatically altering the demographic balance. Muslims from Akhaltsikhe (Meskheti) and Ajaria also emigrated.

With the appointment of the first viceroy, Mikhail Vorontsov (1845–54), Georgia integrated more rapidly into the Russian Empire. At the same time, a political movement emerged, aimed at protecting national identity and headed by the prominent poet, Ilia Chavchavadze. The 1860s were marked by the emancipation of the serfs in Georgia. This caused further social differentiation and economic disaster for the majority of peasants. The politicization of society increased, creating a favourable environment for the development of socialist ideas. The first radical Marxist group, Mesami Dasi (Third Company), was created in 1892. Seven years later the Tiflis committee of the All-Russian Social Democratic Labour Party was formed, dominated by a Menshevik, legalist wing, led by Noe Jordania. It was opposed by the Bolsheviks, among whom Stalin (Iosif Dzhugashvili, or Ioseb Jughashvili, when transliterated from the Georgian) gradually acquired a leading position. On 1 August 1914 Russia entered the First World War, and the Russian Army proceeded deep into Turkey, occupying Kars, Ardahan and Eastern Anatolia. Following the abdication of Tsar Nicholas (Nikolai) II in March 1917, the Provisional Government nominated an executive in Transcaucasia, the Special Transcaucasian Committee (Ozakom), its power restricted by soviets (councils), which were controlled by Mensheviks. While the latter supported central Russian government and the prolongation of the war, the Bolsheviks demanded peace at any price, demobilization and revolution. When, in November, the Bolsheviks seized power in Petrograd (now St Petersburg), the Georgian Mensheviks, the Armenian Dashnaks and the Azeri Musavatists immediately responded by creating an executive body, the Transcaucasian Commissariat, and, later, the Seim (the legislature). Following the signature of the Brest-Litovsk Treaty on 3 March 1918, the Bolsheviks ceded the districts of Akhaltsikhe, Akhalkalaki, Ardahan, Batumi and Kars to Turkey, and the Russian-Caucasian army withdrew. Transcaucasia had no means to resist Turkish advancement, and an armistice was negotiated. Under Turkish pressure, an independent Federative Republic of Transcaucasia was proclaimed. Disagreements between Armenians, Azeris and Georgians put an end to the federation only five weeks later. On 26 May the Georgian Democratic Republic declared its independence.

### First Republic (1918–21)

In June 1918 the soviet was dissolved and Noe Jordania became the Prime Minister of a social-democratic cabinet. The Government implemented limited land reform and nationalized mines and railroads. After a Georgian Government was created, a special agreement was signed with the German

General, Otto von Lossow, establishing a German protectorate. Shortly after that, another agreement was signed, with Turkey, which recognized the loss of Akhalkalaki and Akhaltsikhe. When, in November, Germany ultimately lost the War, Georgia's pro-German orientation became a definite disadvantage, as the British emerged as the dominant power in the region. The dissatisfaction of the peasants and Bolshevik propaganda also caused several uprisings, until, in 1919–20, peasants were given full land-ownership rights, although the nobility retained significant amounts of land. Still, ethnocentric policies continued to feed tensions among the non-Georgian population. In December 1918, owing to a territorial dispute, the Armenian army moved into Georgia, which retaliated, following early Armenian successes. Further fighting on the Armenian border was halted by British forces. Later, the British decided to limit their presence in Baku (Azerbaijan) and Batumi. The British Foreign Office supported Georgia's independence at the Paris Peace Conference in January 1919, where Georgia received *de facto* recognition by the Allied Powers. In the mean time, a serious military threat was presented by the Volunteer Army of Gen. Denikin, which attacked Georgian forces in the Sochi region in February.

During 1920 the geopolitical situation changed dramatically. Civil war in Russia came to an end, and Soviet authority in the Caucasus, the Caucasian Bureau (Kavburo), was formally established by Russia, under the leadership of 'Sergo' Ordzhonikidze (Orjonikidze). When the Bolsheviks organized uprisings in South Ossetia (Osetiya) and Abkhazia, the People's Guard responded with violence. In April the Red Army occupied Azerbaijan and proclaimed it a Soviet Republic, and the Soviet Republic of Armenia was declared in December. Georgia was left undefended against Soviet expansion when, in July, the British withdrew their forces. Russia signed a peace treaty with Georgia on 7 May. Nevertheless, Ordzhonikidze and his unyielding supporters in Baku continued to insist on invasion and, with the assistance of Sergei Kirov, then the ambassador to Georgia, they prepared the Bolshevik network for the inevitable takeover. On 16 February a Revolutionary Committee was formed by Bolsheviks in Georgia. The 11th Red Army entered Georgia from the east, and other troops moved in from Armenia and from Sochi. The Georgian Republic was officially recognized by the Western powers at the beginning of 1921, and on 25 February the Georgian ambassador plenipotentiary presented his credentials in Paris, France; on the same day, however, Russian troops, led by Ordzhonikidze, entered Tbilisi, and Georgia's brief period of independence came to an end.

### SOVIET GEORGIA

With the fall of Tbilisi, the Menshevik Government retreated to Batumi without any serious resistance, finally fleeing to Europe on 16 March 1921. On 21 May Georgia's Bolshevik Government signed a treaty with the Russian Soviet Federative Socialist Republic (RSFSR), and Georgia became a Soviet Socialist Republic (SSR). Officially dismissed, most of the leading members of the Menshevik Party who remained in the country were arrested in January 1922. The opposition began preparing an anti-communist revolt, the Mensheviks, in alliance with the other opposition parties, forming the so-called Parity Committee, in order to co-ordinate their efforts. Uprisings in Guria, Kakheti and Svaneti in 1922–23 were brutally suppressed. The Georgian Church was also persecuted, and its head, Patriarch Ambrosi (Khelaia), was arrested and imprisoned. In February 1923 the internal police (Cheka) arrested and shot leading conspirators. Nevertheless, a rebellion started on 28 August, but initial success was short-lived, and was followed by widespread executions.

A number of autonomies were created. Turkey's interests were taken into account when the Autonomous SSR of Ajaria, populated mainly by Muslim Georgians, was established along religious lines in June 1921. Although a provisional Abkhazian SSR was declared in May, on 16 December a special contract of alliance was signed between Georgia and Abkhazia, which defined Abkhazia's somewhat ambiguous status as the 'Contractual' SSR of Abkhazia; however, this was subsequently abolished in 1931, and Abkhazia became an autonomous republic within Georgia. The South Ossetian (Osetiyan) Autonomous Oblast (region), with its capital at Tskhinvali, was created on 20 April 1922. The external borders of Georgia were also changed, and certain territories passed to Armenia, Azerbaijan and Russia. The economic structures of Armenia, Azerbaijan and Georgia were integrated, and in March of that year the three republics merged into a Federal Union of SSRs of Transcaucasia. Later, in December, it was further transformed into a single republic, the Transcaucasian Soviet Federative Socialist Republic (TSFSR), with Tbilisi as its capital. Georgia entered the USSR as part of the TSFSR on 30 December.

During 1925–26 the pressure temporarily eased. Growth, both in agriculture and industry, was discernible. However, in 1927 the Soviet leadership, disappointed by the New Economic Policy, shifted from individual farming to collectivization, and ordered severe measures to suppress resistance. Repression in Georgia increased after 1931, when Lavrenti Beria became the First Secretary of the Transcaucasian Committee of the Communist Party. On 5 December 1936 the new Soviet Constitution (the 'Stalin' Constitution) was adopted. The TSFSR was dissolved, and Georgia became a 'sovereign' Union Republic, in its own right. Mass repression continued, progressively applied to different sectors of the population. Many Abkhazians experienced subjugation, and inhabitants of the Georgian mountains were forcibly moved to Abkhazia to colonize depopulated land.

In 1941 Adolf Hitler, the German leader, ordered an invasion of the USSR. Although the Germans did reach the North Caucasus, Georgia was spared from the fighting. Shortly after achieving his first military successes, Stalin ordered the deportation of entire peoples for alleged treason. In late 1944, for example, some 90,000 Muslims from Meskheti were deported to Central Asia, overnight, in cattle wagons. Georgian losses in the war were also enormous. Up to 600,000 Georgians fought in the war, and more than one-half that number perished. Georgian prisoners-of-war passed by the Allied Forces to the Soviet security police (People's Commissariat for Internal Affairs—NKVD) found themselves in even worse conditions in Soviet concentration camps. A new wave of purges followed in 1947–53. Stalin's death in March 1953, however, changed the distribution of power in the Kremlin.

### After Stalin (1953–85)

With the death of Stalin, the Georgian leadership was immediately reshuffled by Beria, now the leading political figure. However, he soon fell victim to a conspiracy led by Nikita Khrushchev, part of the new collective leadership of the USSR, and further personnel changes followed. At a closed session of the 20th Congress of the Communist Party of the Soviet Union (CPSU), held on 25 February 1956, Khrushchev devoted his speech to uncovering the crimes of Stalin and the 'cult of personality'. Many Georgians, however, were unhappy with the defamation of Stalin, who had been an ethnic Georgian; in March students celebrating the anniversary of Stalin's birth were brutally dispersed, causing numerous casualties.

The economic reform carried out by Khrushchev brought privation and disaster to Georgia. His arrest was ordered, and Leonid Brezhnev replaced him as General Secretary of the CPSU. However, little changed while Vasilii Mzhavanadze continued in power as the First Secretary of the Communist Party of Georgia (CPG). His uninterrupted 19-year rule was

characterized by the development of an extensive parallel economy and the criminalization of society. In 1972 the republican Minister of Internal Affairs, Eduard Shevardnadze, presented evidence to the Soviet leadership in Moscow (Russia) of widespread corruption at all levels of the Georgian party and state bureaucracy. On 29 September Shevardnadze succeeded Mzhavanadze as the leader of the CPG, and proceeded to launch unrelenting campaigns against so-called 'negative phenomena'.

As was the case elsewhere in the USSR, the dissident movement started in Georgia with the dissemination of 'samizdat' literature. In April 1977 a young philologist, Zviad Gamsakhurdia, the son of one of Georgia's leading novelists, was arrested and accused of carrying out anti-Soviet activities. Prior to closed legal proceedings, a recording of Gamsakhurdia's recantation was broadcast on television, representing an important victory for the secret services, and a reverse for emerging Georgian dissent. After a new Soviet Constitution was adopted in October 1977, the Supreme Soviet of Georgia considered a draft republican constitution; in contrast to the Constitution of 1936, however, Georgian was no longer declared to be the state language. Following a demonstration of protest during the parliamentary session of 14 April 1978, Shevardnadze contacted the central authorities and obtained permission to amend the Constitution. However, events in Tbilisi triggered tensions in Abkhazia, and frustrated Abkhazians, suspicious of emerging Georgian nationalism, demanded that their autonomy be transferred to Russia. Subsequently, a number of changes were introduced, instead: the pedagogical institute, for example, was transformed into a university, and television broadcasts in Abkhazian commenced.

In 1982 Leonid Brezhnev died. The one-year rule of his successor, the former head of the Committee for State Security (KGB), Yuri Andropov, was characterized by the launch of campaigns against corruption and alcoholism, and damage to the Georgian economy, which was strongly dependent upon the production of wine and alcoholic liquors, was great. The subsequent death of the elderly Konstantin Chernenko, who succeeded Andropov, opened the way for the dramatic metamorphosis of *perestroika* (restructuring).

### THE NATIONALIST MOVEMENT

With the ascent to power of the new Soviet leader, Mikhail Gorbachev, in 1985, the first steps of his policies of *glasnost* (openness) and *perestroika*, as his programme of gradual political and economic reform came to be known, brought immediate changes to the distribution of power in Georgia. At the beginning of July Shevardnadze was appointed Soviet Minister of Foreign Affairs and his former deputy, Dzhumber Patiashvili, became First Secretary of the CPG.

Ideas of dissent and liberalism became combined with those of nationalism in the following years. One particularly sensitive area was the environment, which, being ideologically relatively safe, rapidly attracted the attention of the emerging political opposition. The most debated issues were proposed projects to construct a railway tunnel through the Caucasian range to link Vladikavkaz, in Russia, with Tbilisi, and to build the Khudoni hydroelectric power station on the Enguri river, although both were soon abandoned, partly owing to insufficient resources. Zviad Gamsakhurdia, a political outsider since his recantation, gained unprecedented popularity, owing to his overtly anti-communist rhetoric and nationalist slogans. Dangerous tensions emerged inside Georgia, as nationalism was considered a growing threat by ethnic minorities. Abkhazians and Ossetians linked their hopes to support from Russia and the prolongation of the USSR, and demanded their incorporation into the Russian Federation, causing protests among ethnic Georgians. At the end of March and the beginning of April 1989 a number of demonstrations took place, initially directed against Abkhazian secessionism, but later extending to general demands for Georgian independence. On 9 April armed forces were used to disperse a group of protesters, as a result of which some 20 people died. National passions intensified, and in mid-1989 there were new, violent clashes in Sukhumi, and many casualties.

The actions of communist leaders radicalized the national movement, already fully dominated by Gamsakhurdia. Elections to the Supreme Soviet of Georgia took place on 28 October and 11 November 1990, and brought victory to the nationalist, anti-communist Round Table-Free Georgia bloc, led by Gamsakhurdia, with 64% of the votes cast, while the CPG took 29% of the votes (legislation to permit full multi-party elections had been adopted in August). Meanwhile, in September the South Ossetian Supreme Soviet had issued a unilateral declaration of sovereignty. South Ossetia boycotted the all-Georgian parliamentary elections and, instead, parliamentary elections were held in that region on 9 December. The new parliament immediately subordinated itself to the direct control of the all-Union authorities in Moscow; the Georgian parliament responded by abolishing the region's autonomy. Clashes began in the region's capital, Tskhinvali, and Gamsakhurdia, by that time Chairman of the Supreme Soviet, introduced a state of emergency. Fighting, with sporadic cease-fires, continued throughout 1991 and the continuous shelling of Tskhinvali and neighbouring Ossetian and Georgian villages, accompanied by a disastrous earthquake, left large areas in ruin.

When, in March 1991, a referendum on Gorbachev's concept of a renewed union treaty took place, Georgia refused to participate and, instead, held its own referendum on independence. Subsequently, the Georgian Supreme Soviet declared the country's independence on 9 April, thereby becoming the first republic to secede from the USSR. A few weeks later, on 26 May, Gamsakhurdia became the elected President of Georgia, with 86.5% of the votes cast.

## INDEPENDENT GEORGIA

Although Gamsakhurdia secured the full support of the ethnic Georgian population, his nationalist rhetoric alienated him from both non-Georgians and the intelligentsia. His lack of managerial skills and haphazard personnel policies created enemies even among those who had been friends, such as the former Prime Minister, Tengiz Sigua, and the Defence Minister, Tengiz Kitovani. His economic policies were even less successful, and the country gradually moved towards financial catastrophe. At the same time, most of the Soviet organizational legacy was preserved, and even the *kolhozs* (collective farms) were retained under the euphemistic title of 'people's enterprises'. In August 1991 the attempted *coup d'état* against Gorbachev in Moscow demonstrated Gamsakhurdia's lack of strength and unwillingness to adopt a clear position, provoking severe criticism from all sides. The opposition demanded Gamsakhurdia's resignation and accused him of authoritarian rule. Anti-Gamsakhurdia sentiments mounted after violence was applied to disperse a demonstration by the National Democratic Party. The Government gradually lost control of the military, and mass arrests of members of the opposition 'Mkhedrioni' (Horsemen) militia, led by Jaba Ioseliani, only prolonged the crisis. Gamsakhurdia's rhetoric, together with a general reluctance among Western powers to provoke Russia, caused full international isolation.

Georgia sent observers to a meeting held in Almaty, Kazakhstan, on 21 December 1991, at which the leaders of 11 former Union Republics of the USSR agreed to form the Commonwealth of Independent States (CIS). Georgia, however, refused to join the new structure. The same day, the Georgian opposition, led by Sigua and Kitovani, began concentrating tanks and other weaponry, received or purchased from the Soviet army, around the presidential residence in the centre of Tbilisi. On 22 December armed conflict began, causing significant casualties and severely damaging the surrounding area, and Gamsakhurdia and his Government sought refuge in the basement of the building. Jaba Ioseliani was released from prison, and the Mkhedrioni joined forces with Kitovani's troops. After 10 days of fluctuating success, the opposition succeeded in acquiring a significant amount of weaponry from Russia, and consequently tightened the siege. On 2 January 1992 Gamsakhurdia was declared deposed by the opposition. He fled first to Armenia, and then to Chechnya, in Russia. A Military Council was formed to replace the Government, headed by Tengiz Kitovani and Jaba Ioseliani, with Tengiz Sigua acting as premier.

## POLITICAL DEVELOPMENTS

The Military Council encountered great difficulties in managing the country and Gamsakhurdia's supporters (or 'Zviadists') organized armed resistance in western Georgia. In an attempt to increase their legitimacy, the former Soviet Minister of Foreign Affairs, Eduard Shevardnadze, was invited to Georgia as Chairman of the State Council, a structure created in March to replace the Military Council in legislative and executive matters. Shevardnadze's international renown put an end to Georgia's international isolation. In October he was elected Chairman of the Supreme Council (as the Supreme Soviet was now known) and Head of State, as indisputably as Gamsakhurdia had been one year previously. However, leading Georgia towards stability was a difficult task, when real control was held by the military leadership. Moreover, the country's integrity was threatened by civil war, and separatist conflicts in Abkhazia and South Ossetia. Former President Gamsakhurdia launched an offensive when, in September 1993, Georgian forces were defeated by Abkhazian units supported by the Russian army and North Caucasian volunteers. To prevent the partition of Georgia, in October Shevardnadze was forced to accept the assistance of Russian troops and to commit Georgia to entering the CIS. In early November Gamsakhurdia and his supporters fled to the mountains, after being defeated at their main base, Zugdidi, and Gamsakhurdia died shortly afterwards, reportedly committing suicide. On 3 February 1994 Georgia and Russia signed a 10-year Treaty on Friendship, Good-Neighbourliness and Co-operation. One year later, a further agreement provided for the establishment of four Russian military bases in Georgia. Thus, Russia's dominant role in the region was acknowledged, although neither treaty was ratified.

On 24 August 1995 the Supreme Council adopted Georgia's new Constitution, providing for a strong executive presidency and a 235-seat, unicameral Parliament. Five days later, Shevardnadze survived an assassination attempt. In early October the Minister of State Security, Igor Giorgadze, was named as the principle instigator of the plot, and he subsequently escaped to Russia by military aircraft. In May 1996 Ioseliani, the leader of the Mkhedrioni, was convicted of complicity in the assassination attempt. On 5 November 1995 Shevardnadze won 75% of the votes cast in a presidential election, and his Citizens' Union of Georgia (CUG) secured a decisive majority in Parliament. He immediately assumed full control, and attempted a new reorientation towards the West. This represented a turning point in Georgian politics. Along with political stabilization, an economic revival began, and the rate of growth was over 10%, annually, in 1996–97. However, the Russian economic crisis of 1998 also had dire consequences for the Georgian economy, causing growth to decelerate to a virtual standstill.

A new Government was announced in December 1995, with Nikoloz Lekishvili as Minister of State, a post that replaced that of Prime Minister; following his resignation in July 1998, he was replaced by Vazha Lortkipanidze. On 9 February of that year Shevardnadze survived a further assassination attempt. On this occasion, Gamsakhurdia's followers were blamed for the attack and Guram Absandze, a former Minister of Finance, was extradited from Russia to stand trial. In May 1999 17 people were detained, following the discovery of a plot to overthrow Shevardnadze. All of those arrested were reported to have links with Giorgadze, and the group included both former and existing state officials. Despite this, the parliamentary elections of October and November, in which 68% of the electorate participated, and the presidential election of 9 April 2000, although far from fully democratic, demonstrated once more the strength of Shevardnadze's position against the fragmented opposition, which was mostly concentrated around the Chairman of the Ajarian Supreme Council and the leader of the Union for the Revival of Georgia, Aslan Abashidze. The CUG obtained 41.9% of the votes cast in the legislative elections, securing 130 of the 235 seats available in Parliament, and Shevardnadze was re-elected as president with 79.8% of the votes cast. A government reshuffle subsequently took place, and Lortkipanidze was replaced as Minister of State by Giorgi (Gia) Arsenishvili.

None the less, a significant problem for the Shevardnadze Government remained that of achieving a settlement of the conflict in Abkhazia, and returning to their homes the hundreds of thousands of people displaced as a result of it. Even more urgent was the need to improve the country's overall economic performance and to combat the overwhelming corruption that was destroying economic confidence. The President's family was widely believed to control the larger part of Georgia's scarce economic resources, and Shevardnadze's popularity declined significantly after 2000, as did that of the ruling party, the CUG, in which divisions increased between the older generation of redressed communist functionaries, and the younger and more energetic 'reformist' wing. As a result, the President resigned from the party's chairmanship. He also reshuffled the Government, ridding it of a number of reformists, and finally dismissed the entire cabinet at the beginning of November 2001. At the same time, the opposition was again closing ranks around Aslan Abashidze, although it lacked both unity and popularity, and Abashidze showed little activity.

Severe crises in both the Government and the governing political party were followed by significant changes to all branches of power. Nino Burdzhanadze replaced Zurab Zhvania as parliamentary speaker in November 2001, and Zhvania gave open support to the opposition, resulting in a split within the CUG. In June 2002 the Minister of State appointed in December 2001, Avtandil Dzhorbenadze, was elected Chairman of the embattled CUG, but events had already served to demonstrate the party's dramatic loss of support. The local government elections, held in early June 2002, were considered to represent the final preparations before the anticipated struggle for a successor to Shevardnadze; hence, they were vested with great symbolic importance, demonstrating crucial changes to the political environment. The CUG was unable to surpass the 4% threshold required to secure seats on Tbilisi City Council, partly owing to the passivity of the urban electorate. Overall, despite numerous electoral violations (in particular, in the cities of Rustavi and Zugdidi), the elections demonstrated a shift in public sympathy towards the pro-US New Rights Party, which had been established in 2000 by former members of the CUG, Levan Gachechiladze and David Gamkrelidze, and which represented business interests; the populist, leftist Georgian Labour Party, led by Shalva Natelashvili; and other reformist

descendants of the CUG, led by the former Minister of Justice, Mikheil Saakashvili, and the former parliamentary Chairman, Zurab Zhvania, who established, respectively, the radical, nationalist National Movement and the more moderate, centrist United Democrats, both of which were strongly pro-Western. As a result of an agreement between Natelashvili and Saakashvili, the latter was elected to the position of Chairman of the Tbilisi City Council in November 2002, and he hoped to use this position to erode support for pro-presidential representatives, including the City Mayor, Vano Zodelava. However, any expectation that he might use the post to increase his popularity was largely undermined by his unsettled relations with Natelashvili, and a lack of control over funds, which made many of his pre-electoral promises irrelevant.

The parliamentary and presidential elections, scheduled to take place in November 2003 and in 2005, respectively, posed a clear challenge to the opportunistic, post-communist Government of the ageing Shevardnadze, and his hold on power. In particular, throughout 2002–03 preparations for the general election increasingly influenced the political climate of Georgia. The pro-Shevardnadze CUG, under the leadership of Dzhorbenadze, began to consolidate support in order to improve its performance, even if its chance of overall victory remained low. The CUG became the core of the new political bloc, For a New Georgia, which attempted to use its administrative leverage to unite those opposition elements that had declined in popularity over the preceding months, such as the Socialist Party of Georgia and the National Democratic Party of Georgia. There were political battles over voting arrangements, such as composition of the Central Electoral Commission and the creation of voters' lists. In early June 2003 the main opposition parties, in an attempt to pressurize the Government, organized political rallies on electoral issues, while student associations mounted anti-Government actions, under the slogan *Kmara* (Enough), and allegedly with prominent international support, at which demands were made for Shevardnadze's resignation. Meanwhile, the popular Chairman of Parliament, Nino Burdzhanadze, appealed to the US Government to ensure that free and fair elections took place.

In a separate development, in mid-October 2002 Shevardnadze and the Catholicos-Patriarch of the Georgian Orthodox Church, Ilia II, signed a constitutional agreement between the state and the Church, which was intended to regulate the legal relationship between the two sides and, in particular, provided for compensation for the moral and material damage experienced by the Church under Soviet rule. None the less, religious life in the country was far from harmonious. Although the majority of the population are adherents of the Orthodox Church, violence by extremist groups of orthodox zealots toward confessional minorities marred the tradition of religious tolerance in the country, and drew protests from international human rights and religious freedom organizations.

## CONFLICT

Inter-ethnic conflict dominated the internal politics of Georgia throughout the first half of the 1990s. Ajaria was the least troubled of Georgia's self-governing regions. However, discontent increased in the early 1990s, as a result of proposals to abolish Ajarian autonomy and convert the Muslim population to Christianity, and relations between Aslan Abashidze and Eduard Shevardnadze continued to worsen.

In South Ossetia, although in the majority (Ossetians comprised approximately 70% of the inhabitants, and over 100,000 lived elsewhere in Georgia), the Ossetians, an Indo-European people, were considered to be relatively recent immigrants, and their autonomy to be artificially created by

Soviet power. Inter-ethnic relations deteriorated in 1989, as a result of Ossetian demands for reunification with North Ose-tiya and autonomy within the Russian Federation. Renewed violence began when the South Ossetian Supreme Soviet declared itself the Soviet Republic of South Ossetia in December 1990, provoking legal conflict and, subsequently, the dispatch of Georgian police and paramilitary troops. Fighting continued until 24 June 1992, when Shevardnadze and the Russian President, Boris Yeltsin, reached agreement on ending the conflict and introducing a trilateral peace-keeping force (comprising Georgians, Ossetians and Rus-sians). A tense peace was established and no significant military action took place subsequently, although the issue of the future status of South Ossetia, active mediation by the Organization for Security and Co-operation in Europe (OSCE) notwithstanding, remained unresolved. In December 1997 the South Ossetian parliament voted, once again, in favour of independent status for the region, within the CIS. Never-theless, economic relations between the two sides were devel-oping, refugees had begun to return to their homes, people travelled more freely, and the prospects for a political solution continued to improve.

The Abkhazians (an ethnic group related to the Circassians, a neighbouring people in the north-west Caucasus), having been decimated by migration to Turkey in the 1860s, con-stituted, before the outbreak of conflict, no more than 19% of the total population of Abkhazia, whereas Georgians made up approximately 46%. Following outbreaks of violence in the region from 1989, the violence intensified on 14 August 1992, when Georgian troops, ostensibly for the purpose of releasing hostages and protecting rail communications, entered Ab-khazia and captured the capital, Sukhumi, forcing the Ab-khazian leadership to evacuate. One month later Abkhazian forces, reputedly assisted by volunteers from Russia, launched a counter-offensive and occupied northern Ab-khazia. In July 1993 Russia and the UN brokered a trilateral agreement providing for a cease-fire and demilitarization. However, in September Abkhazian forces launched an unex-pected attack, taking Sukhumi and defeating the Georgian forces after 11 days of fighting. Georgian troops were driven from most parts of Abkhazia, excluding the Kodori Gorge, and large numbers of the Georgian population fled. On 14 May 1994 a cease-fire agreement was declared, providing for about 1,300 CIS (predominantly Russian) peace-keepers to be deployed in the border zone, in addition to UN military observers. Meanwhile, the Abkhazian legislature adopted a Constitution, declared sovereignty and appointed Vladislav Ardzinba as *de facto* President. Under Georgian pressure, CIS leaders, meeting in Moscow in January 1996, imposed an economic blockade of Abkhazia. Relations improved slightly thereafter, but in May 1998 hostilities were resumed in the Gali district, where the Georgian population had begun to resettle, demonstrating the fragility of the peace. Negoti-ations continued, but the most sensitive issues, concerning Georgian refugees and the future status of Abkhazia, proved complex to resolve. An additional concern was the activity of Georgian guerrillas, presumably supported by the Govern-ment, in Gali and the Kodori valley, which presented a per-manent threat to both the Abkhazian population and author-ities. The revival of civil conflict in Chechnya, from late 1999, significantly altered the disposition of forces and interests in the region. While negotiations were proceeding at a slow pace, the fragility of peace in Abkhazia was demonstrated in August–September 2001 when, in addition to Georgian guer-rillas, between 500 and 900 Chechen rebels, allegedly under the command of Ruslan Gelayev, were reported to have gath-ered in the Kodori Gorge to fight against the same Abkhazians that they had supported so ardently eight years previously. In early October 2001 a helicopter carrying members of the UN's

Observer Mission in Georgia (UNOMIG) was shot down after taking off from Sukhumi, killing all nine passengers on board. Clashes between Abkhazian forces and guerrillas followed throughout October, and military aircraft, apparently of Rus-sian origin, bombed the Kodori Gorge region on 9 October (although Russia denied its involvement). There remained no clear explanation of the motives of the Chechen militants, and it was not known whether their actions had been provoked by the global anti-terrorism efforts declared after the large-scale suicide attacks on the USA on 11 September.

In February 2002 the UN submitted a draft document on principles for the 'Distribution of Competences between Tbi-lisi and Sukhumi', which had been agreed between members of the UN Secretary-General's Group of Friends on Georgia (comprising France, Germany, Russia, the United Kingdom and the USA), and which was to have served as a basis for negotiations. However, the Abkhaz side, under the 'hardline' *de facto* Prime Minister, Anri Dzhergenia, refused officially to receive the document. On 29 November Dzhergenia was dis-missed by Ardzinba; none the less, the attitude toward the UN document did not change considerably. Meanwhile, Russia augmented its contacts with Abkhazia, issuing Russian pass-ports and unilaterally resuming, on 25 December, railway connections from the Russian Black Sea port of Sochi to Tbilisi, via Sukhumi, thereby causing additional tensions in relations with Georgia. However, during a meeting between President Vladimir Putin of Russia and Shevardnadze, held on 7 March 2003 in Sochi, with the participation of Gagulia, it was agreed to co-ordinate the restoration of the railway con-nection through Abkhazia with the parallel return of inter-nally displaced persons to Gali, Ochamchire and other regions of Abkhazia. The participants also decided to carry out several projects aimed at increasing energy production, through the rehabilitation of the Inguri hydroelectric power station and the construction of several new energy complexes. The Geor-gian Government was ready to compromise, in order to achieve at least symbolic progress in negotiations with the Abkhaz side, prior to the forthcoming parliamentary elec-tions. As a result, by mid-2003 progress was already evident in negotiations over the return of refugees to Gali region, and the overall situation appeared more positive.

From its inception, the conflict in Chechnya (1994–96 and 1999–) represented a serious threat to stability in Georgia. In August 1999 Yeltsin requested consent to fly military mis-sions to Chechnya from Russian bases in Georgia. Although this request was firmly rejected, Russia made further attempts to secure Georgian support in the conflict. Sig-nificant numbers of Chechen refugees moved across the Geor-gian–Russian border to the Pankisi Gorge, which was tradi-tionally home to an ethnic Chechen population. The Pankisi region became a permanent concern for the Georgian Govern-ment, owing to its limited control of the area and the increasing instability there, characterized by frequent kid-nappings and drugs-trafficking. Accusations by Russia that Pankisi had become a base and training site for Chechen rebels were not initially formally substantiated by OSCE observers, but Georgia subsequently admitted the presence of Chechen militants there. According to official Georgian esti-mates, there were about 800 militants in the region in 1999–2002 (prior to the launch, in August–September 2002, of an operation to reassert control over the area—see below). Indeed, in July incursions into Georgia by Chechen militants brought Russia and Georgia to the brink of war.

From 2000 there were cases of the accidental shelling of Georgian villages by Russian aircraft, and there were fears that, following the suicide attacks of 11 September 2001, the emerging internationalization of the fight against terrorism might serve as a pretext for the Russian military to attack Pankisi and thus further aggravate the situation there.

Finally, following repeated accusations by the Russian side of the presence in the Pankisi Gorge of militants linked to the al-Qa'ida (Base) organization (held responsible for the attacks on the USA), in February–March 2002 the US Government resolved to assist the Georgian military in consolidating its capacity to undertake counter-terrorist operations, through the implementation of a special Train and Equip programme, with the allocation of US $64m. The principal group of US military instructors arrived in Georgia in May, and trained several detachments of Georgian élite security forces, with a special focus on anti-terrorist operations. Nevertheless, Russian pressure on Georgia was mounting, and air raids and bombings of Georgian territory became increasingly frequent. Between 29 July and 23 August five violations of Georgian airspace were recorded in the region adjacent to Chechnya and in Abkhazia's Kodori Gorge, and on at least three occasions Russian aircraft opened fire, finally prompting a strong rebuke from the US Government. Meanwhile, on the ground, there were reports of an unauthorized Russian military presence in the Kodori Gorge and South Ossetia, although they were denied by Russia.

Tension increased further after Georgian border guards captured 15 Chechen militants trespassing on the Chechen–Georgian border, and refused to extradite all of them. As the result of increased external pressure, and in an attempt to subdue continued lawlessness in the Pankisi Gorge, at the end of August 2002 the Georgian authorities dispatched around 1,000 servicemen of the Ministries of Internal Affairs and of State Security to the Gorge, establishing check-points throughout the area, while the 'anti-criminal operation' was supported by a 1,500-strong army unit. The troops re-established control over the Gorge and arrested several suspects, although the majority of Chechen militants were believed to have left the area in advance. Although the situation had begun to stabilize, on 11 September (symbolically linking the situation with the anniversary of the suicide attacks on the USA) Putin issued an ultimatum, stating that if Georgia did not implement immediate measures to improve the Pankisi security situation, Russian forces might consider unilateral military action. The resulting international criticism led Russia to moderate its position, while the success of the Georgian Government's security operation led to a gradual improvement in Russian-Georgian relations.

### FOREIGN AFFAIRS

Although Georgia declared its independence in 1991, initially it had difficulty in securing international recognition. When Shevardnadze returned to Georgia in March 1992, however, the situation changed. In April Germany opened an embassy in Tbilisi, soon followed by the USA, Turkey and Russia. Georgia also started actively to seek participation in international organizations. After joining the Conference on Security and Co-operation in Europe (now the OSCE) in March 1992 and the Black Sea Economic Co-operation (now the Organization of the Black Sea Economic Co-operation), it finally become a member of the UN, the IMF and the World Bank in May–July 1992.

While trying to establish bilateral relations with all the newly independent states, Georgia avoided joining the CIS until the disastrous situation that resulted from defeat in Abkhazia obliged Shevardnadze to request membership in October 1993. Russia preserved four military bases in Georgia and participated in peace-keeping operations in both Abkhazia and South Ossetia, prompting Georgian politicians to accuse the Russian leadership of supporting secessionist forces and misusing military bases to destabilize its domestic situation. The Russian political élite, too, was dissatisfied with Georgia's gradual reorientation towards the West, its emerging role as an alternative transportation route for Cas-

pian petroleum and, especially, with Georgia's unwillingness to become involved in the Russian–Chechen conflict. Moreover, although a bilateral Treaty on Friendship, Good-Neighbourliness and Co-operation was signed with Russia in February 1994, it was never ratified.

In the late 1990s Georgia increasingly sought to develop stronger relations with the West and the USA provided significant assistance to Georgia at critical times. In March 1998 Georgia and the USA signed an agreement on military and security co-operation, reflecting the US commitment to the provision of special assistance to Georgia. Cordial relations were also established with the European Union (EU), as expressed by an agreement on partnership and co-operation, which was signed in April 1996. In April 1999 Georgia became a member of the Council of Europe and two months later, at a celebration in Luxembourg to mark the initiation of a partnership and co-operation treaty between the EU and the three South Caucasian states, Shevardnadze officially declared Georgia's intention to join that organization.

Although Georgia refused to renew its participation in the CIS Collective Security Treaty, it became an associate member of the North Atlantic Treaty Organization (NATO) Parliamentary Assembly. In July 1997, moreover, Shevardnadze attended a NATO summit meeting, held in Madrid, Spain, and participated in the work of the Euro-Atlantic Partnership Council (EAPC), and the Georgian Government openly expressed its willingness further to integrate into NATO. In November 2002 Georgia formally applied for membership of the Alliance.

In 1997 Georgia, together with Azerbaijan, Moldova and Ukraine, created a new sub-regional structure known as GUAM (Uzbekistan's subsequent accession changed the name to GUUAM), which aimed to promote political and economic co-operation and to complement alternative alliances within the CIS. The participating states adopted the organization's charter in June 2001. Members of GUUAM tend to have Western-orientated policies, and are united by a mutual distrust of Russia and by a willingness to use the organization to counterbalance the Moscow-dominated CIS security structure. A summit meeting held in Yalta, Ukraine, on 6–7 June 2001, gave the organization new impetus, when the Yalta Charter was signed by the countries' five Presidents, marking progress towards closer co-operation. The USA's reinvigorated interest and support for the grouping also increased GUUAM's future prospects, and in December 2002 it was invited to attend a session of the OSCE Ministerial Council, held in Porto, Portugal, as an independent organization.

Co-operation with neighbouring countries Azerbaijan and Turkey increased in the 1990s, linked to common interests in both security and the construction of a pipeline to carry petroleum from the Caspian Sea to the Turkish port of Ceyhan. A pipeline to transport petroleum from Baku to Supsa began to operate in April 1999, and a project to construct two larger petroleum and natural gas pipelines, extending from the Caspian to Turkey, was under way. In late May 2003 construction work on the Georgian stretch of the vast Baku–Tbilisi–Ceyhan petroleum pipeline commenced, to be followed shortly by work on the Baku–Erzurum (Turkey) gas pipeline. It was anticipated that their completion might help Georgia to escape its dependence on Russian energy supplies, a situation that had often been used to gain political leverage. Although ecologists expressed strong concern that the pipelines would traverse the Borjomi-Kharagauli National Park and endanger the environment, this controversy did not prevent public support for their construction. Overall, much of Georgia's future development appeared to be linked to international transportation projects, including the EU-sponsored Transport Corridor Europe–Caucasus–Asia

(TRACECA—the 'Silk Road') agreement, which aimed to develop an East–West trade route.

At an OSCE summit meeting, held in İstanbul, Turkey, in November 1999, several important agreements were signed, including an agreement on the gradual removal of Russia's military bases from Georgia, preparing the way for the introduction of new security arrangements. Technically, the agreement was a modification and clarification of the Conventional Forces in Europe (CFE) Treaty, setting limits on Russian troops in the Caucasus. The İstanbul protocol provided for the closure by July 2001 of two of the four Russian bases in Georgia: the Gudauta base, in Abkhazia, and the Vaziani base, near Tbilisi; withdrawal from the former was only completed in 2002. The protocol also provided for negotiations on the closures of the remaining two—in Akhalkalaki, in the majority ethnic Armenian-populated south-eastern region of Samtskhe-Javakheti, and in the autonomous province of Ajaria, in south-west Georgia, both regions that are only weakly controlled by the central Government. Russia continued to request at least an 11-year transition period for the closure of the last two bases, owing to a lack of necessary funds, but Georgia demanded their closure within four years. Although negotiations had reached an impasse, the EU and the USA had expressed willingness to facilitate, and possibly even finance, the withdrawal, while the OSCE and the Parliamentary Assembly of the Council of Europe urged Russia to meet its obligations under the 1999 agreement.

As discussed above, the war in Chechnya was an important factor in Georgia's deteriorating relations with Russia, which accused it of supporting the Chechen militants' struggle for independence. Both political and economic pressure was applied, when Russia unilaterally introduced a visa regime with Georgia in December 2000, and also used its control of gas supplies as a political instrument. Although Georgian–Russian relations reached their nadir in September 2002, when Putin openly threatened Georgia with military action, Georgia had begun to benefit from US support following the arrival of US military advisers in early 2002. Relations between Georgia and Russia also began to improve from October, following a meeting between Shevardnadze and Putin, in the Moldovan capital, Chişinău, and subsequent meetings in Kiev and Sochi. In addition to positive developments over the issue of Abkhazia, the two sides also registered progress in the preparation of a comprehensive framework agreement, partly owing to US pressure on both countries. In the early 2000s Georgia's orientation toward the West, and especially towards the USA, strengthened, and US influence increased greatly. For example, in January 2003 Georgia initially refused to extend the mandate of the Russian peacekeepers in Abkhazia, but Shevardnadze relented following an appeal by the US Department of State. Georgia fully supported the US-led military action to remove the regime of Saddam Hussain in Iraq in early 2003, and it subsequently agreed to dispatch some 70 service-men to that country. Moreover, in March Parliament ratified an agreement granting members of the US military the right to enter Georgia without a visa and to diplomatic immunity (prompting strong protests from the Russian State Duma). Overall, international affairs remained the most developed area of Georgia's politics.

# The Economy
## VERONICA SCHNEIDER

### INTRODUCTION

Since the ancient times of the Silk Road, Georgia's geopolitical location between the Caucasus mountains and the Black Sea, at the junction of most of the trade routes connecting Asia and Europe, has been of great strategic and trade importance. Georgian agriculture is quite diversified, owing to its climate, which ranges from subtropical to montane. Georgia was the leading tourist resort in the USSR, and it has retained significant potential for tourism. The country also developed a considerable industrial base during the Soviet era. Standards of living in Georgia were higher than those in the other Soviet republics, not only as a result of the natural advantages of geography and climate, but also as a result of its 'shadow' (unofficial) activities. After the collapse of the USSR, Georgia experienced a difficult transition.

During the early years of independence (1991–94), Georgia experienced regional conflicts in both South Ossetia and Abkhazia. Georgia's greatest economic asset is its potential to become a major transit point for transporting energy resources, such as petroleum from Azerbaijan and natural gas from Central Asia, to Europe. However, the unsettled political situation, together with the conflict in the neighbouring Republic of Chechnya (Russia), have presented obstacles to the exploitation of this economic potential. The construction of the so-called BTC pipeline, to transport petroleum from Baku (Azerbaijan) to Ceyhan (Turkey), via Tbilisi (Georgia), which began in April 2003, and the construction of a natural gas pipeline from the Shah Deniz field in Azerbaijan through Georgia to Turkey, could lead to a dramatic increase in foreign direct investment.

Macroeconomic stability was swiftly achieved at the beginning of 1994, following the implementation of the IMF's Structural Adjustment Programme. A number of important measures were undertaken to achieve this stability: the National Bank of Georgia established strict control over the issuance of credits to the Government and commercial banks, and the state budgetary accounts of the Ministry of Finance were transferred to its control, as were domestic and international reserves. In order for the commercial banking system to become credible and strong, and in order to protect the interests of bank clients, the privatization of state-owned banks was commenced; certification and licensing rules became stricter, and action against problematic banks was taken through liquidation and mergers. The National Bank requested that commercial banks increase their authorized capital to at least 5m. lari before the end of 2000.

To facilitate the improvement of the fiscal process, new laws were adopted and tax legislation was developed. In order to centralize state revenue and expenditure, a State Treasury Department was established. However, despite these positive trends, the comprehensive effectiveness of the budgetary process, its transparency and the fair distribution of resources were not achieved, and more efficient measures continued to be required.

In the absence of structural reforms and improvements in budgetary-revenue collection, macroeconomic stability has been ensured by the continued tight monetary position of the National Bank of Georgia. Thus, inflation has been brought under control and the pressure on the exchange rate reduced. As a result of the implementation of economic stabilization measures, economic performance improved strongly in 1995–

97, when the average annual rate of increase in gross domestic product (GDP) was around 8%. The problem of 'hyperinflation' was overcome, with an average annual inflation rate of only 7.1% in 1997, compared with more than 15,607% in 1994. No significant progress, however, was achieved in strengthening state finances, and the contribution of budgetary tax revenue to GDP was low. Moreover, chronic fiscal deficits reflected the activities of the shadow economy.

Budgetary problems, which emerged from 1998, were aggravated by the financial crisis in Russia, Georgia's principal trading partner, and resulted in a declining balance of trade. These events brought about a significant deterioration in the country's macroeconomic and financial situation. Growth in GDP decreased, and it constituted only 2.9% in 1998, compared with 10.7% in 1997. Owing to the worsening balance-of-payments situation, domestic financial markets lacked foreign-exchange supplies, and in December 1998 the National Bank ceased its intervention in the financial market.

In 1999 the Government attempted to minimize the consequences of the crisis and to re-establish macroeconomic stability. In that year the rate of economic growth was 2.9%, and the rate of increase in consumer-price inflation was 19.2%. An increase in GDP, of 1.9%, was recorded in 2000, although a severe drought in that year caused significant damage to the agricultural sector, altering the structure of GDP, and obstructing overall growth. In other sectors of the economy, the rate of GDP growth was around 6.6% in 2000, while the overall annual rate of inflation was 4.0%.

In 2001 a recovery in agriculture, together with growth in the transport sector and in retail trade, was reflected by GDP growth of 4.5%, in real terms. However, the industrial sector continued to contract, partly owing to energy-supply problems early in the year. The annual rate of inflation was 4.7% in 2001, and the exchange rate depreciated modestly, reflecting economic problems in Turkey and the dismissal of the Georgian Government at the beginning of November. The fiscal deficit, on a commitments basis, declined from the equivalent of 4% of GDP in 2000, to 2% in 2001. Meanwhile, international reserves increased from US $106m. at the end of 2000, to $156m. at the end of 2001, equivalent to around 1.5 months of imports of goods and services. The balance of payments was negatively affected by weak demand from Turkey and the downturn in the world economy, while broad money increased by 18.5%, as the process of remonetization continued. The trade deficit widened in 2001, reflecting a decline in exports, and foreign direct investment was substantially lower than in the previous year. In March 2001 the 'Paris Club' of official creditors agreed to reschedule bilateral debts due in 2001 and 2002 over 20 years, with a three-year grace period and a graduated repayment schedule. However, further rescheduling was jeopardized by the suspension of IMF activities (see below).

The rate of inflation was 5.4% in 2002, and the exchange rate appreciated in minimal terms, by just over 1%, year-on-year, against the US dollar, in February 2002. The state budget deficit reached 226.7m. lari (US $103m.), or 3.1% of GDP in 2002. Gross international reserves amounted to US $198m. in 2002, an increase of 24%, year-on-year, and equivalent to 1.8 months of imports. The current-account deficit widened, to $258.3m. (equivalent to some 7.8% of GDP) in 2002, compared with $211.7m. (6.7% of GDP) in 2001, reflecting a deterioration in the income and transfers balance. In 2002 real GDP increased by 5.4% (the highest rate recorded since the Russian economic crisis of 1998), compared with 4.7% in 2001. Economic growth was stimulated by domestic demand and a considerable expansion in industry. The fastest-growing sector was construction, owing largely to petroleum transit related construction work.

## ECONOMIC POLICY

In 1994 Georgia began to co-operate with the IMF under its Structural Adjustment Programme, and macroeconomic stability began to be achieved shortly afterwards. However, the country's persistent failure to meet fiscal targets for revenue collection and deficit reduction caused the international financial institutions to suspend their support programmes in 1999; negotiations were only resumed in October 2000. The IMF renewed assistance to Georgia in January 2001 under a three-year Poverty Reduction and Growth Facility (PRGF) worth SDR 108m. (US $144m.). By mid-2002 Georgia had drawn SDR 27m. (about $36m.). In July 2002 the IMF Executive Board completed its second review of Georgia's economic performance under the programme supported by the PRGF, and approved, in principle, the disbursement of $30m. The decision of the Board became effective after the World Bank's review of progress on the development of Georgia's Poverty Reduction Strategy Paper (PRSP).

Of the IMF programme in operation from 2001, four tranches were transferred to the National Bank of Georgia to replenish international reserves and support the balance of payments. However, after the final instalment was paid in July 2002, further payments were suspended, since the Government failed to comply with the Fund's requirements. Under the recommendations, Georgia was required to reduce the 2003 budget by US $65m.; to amend the tax code (see below), in order to allow the collection of an extra $17m. in tax revenues; to draw up a plan to pay several years of accumulated wages and pensions arrears; and to issue treasury bonds maturing in 2006. Parliament failed to reach agreement on the IMF's demands prior to the expiry of an IMF-imposed deadline of mid-August 2003.

The Government, with the support of the international financial organizations, elaborated an Economic Growth and Poverty Reduction Programme (EGPRP), which was approved by President Eduard Shevardnadze in June 2003. The main objectives of the EGPRP, endorsed by the donor community, were: the elimination of poverty; support for economic growth; improvement of social conditions; an increase in the living standards of the population; and the participation of poor citizens in the country's development process. Combating corruption and legalizing the large-scale shadow economy were also among the Government's priorities. Work was implemented to develop a new tax code to stimulate tax compliance and improve tax collection, owing to the failure of the Tax Code adopted in 1997, and its subsequent amendments, to improve the functioning and transparency of the system. In March 2003 Parliament passed the new tax code in its first reading.

Structural-reform policies were carried out with the support of the World Bank and were assisted financially by its three Structural Adjustment Credits (SACs). The Structural Adjustment Programme included measures to harmonize existing legislation with international standards and norms, in order to enhance the business environment. Parliament adopted laws on state procurement and the licensing of business activities, as well as normative acts to simplify the registration procedure for entrepreneurial activities.

Important measures were also implemented to develop the land market. Mechanisms for leasing state-owned land were elaborated, and appropriate laws and normative acts were adopted. The process of land registration began, with support from international organizations and donor countries. Owing to land-market development, tangible results were achieved in buying, selling and mortgaging the land in order to receive credits from banks.

Within the framework of this programme, special attention had to be paid to the privatization process. By January 2003 14,017 small enterprises had been approved for privatization, and 16,810 had been privatized since 1993, when small-scale privatization began. The law on privatization of state property was amended to permit the privatization of the energy, communications and transport sectors. Telasi (the electricity distribution company of the capital, Tbilisi) was privatized in 1999 and Tbilsresi (the main power plant supplying the capital with electricity) was partially privatized in early 2000. (Some electricity distribution and generation assets had already undergone privatization.) A tender for the management of the energy transmission and dispatch companies was completed in 2001. There was no progress in privatizing the assets of the energy sector in 2002 and in the first half of 2003, and the planned privatization of hydroelectric generation companies was halted. An electricity distribution company created by the Ministry of State Property Management, in co-operation with the International Finance Corporation (IFC), on the basis of the grouping of state regional electricity distribution companies, was to be transferred to private management for five years; a tender was announced, and eight companies expressed interest in managing the distribution company. However, little success had been achieved in privatizing the large gas-distribution companies and the privatization of telecommunications assets had stalled. In December 2002 the Ministry of State Property Management, in co-operation with the National Securities Commission, for the first time offered shares in a number of state-owned enterprises through the Georgian Stock Exchange trading system. Among the enterprises to be offered were a gas operating company, tea and wine factories and an electrical wagon repair factory. A tender to transfer the Tbilisi Water Utility to private management was announced in 2001, although only one company submitted a proposal. A majority shareholding in the joint-stock company Azot (producing fertilizers) was sold, and the Tbilaviamsheni aircraft works was transferred to management in early 2003. In addition, 51% of the shares in the Zestafoni Ferro-Alloy Plant were transferred to private ownership. According to the conditions of SAC III, at least 20 of the 29 large-scale enterprises identified as initial priorities had to be privatized or liquidated prior to the disbursement of the second tranche of funding. By April 2003 19 such enterprises had been privatized, and bankruptcy procedures had been initiated against a further nine, thus fulfilling conditions for the release of the credit. In order to receive the third tranche of funding all the enterprises on the first priority list had to be privatized or liquidated. With regard to the second priority list of large-scale enterprises, 26 of a total of 29 had been privatized.

## AGRICULTURE

The development of the agricultural sector was important to economic growth, as it was significant both in terms of size and in terms of the number of people it employed. Agriculture and agro-business remained the major source of subsistence for many households, especially low-income families. The agricultural sector accounted for 18.3% of GDP and, according to the State Department for Statistics, employed up to 60% of the labour force at the end of 2002. The primary food crops produced are citrus fruits, nuts, tea, wheat and wine, as well as barley, maize, potatoes and sugar beet. The primary meat products are beef and veal, chicken, lamb and pork.

The liberalization of prices and the creation of a progressive environment for trade were some of the most important goals in the early stages of the country's reforms. In this respect, significant progress was quickly achieved in the agricultural sector. State intervention in the goods market was eliminated, and a liberal trade regime was successfully created. Georgia's accession to the World Trade Organization (WTO) in June 2000 was also an important step forward towards the further implementation of reforms.

Efficient measures were undertaken for the privatization of state-owned assets in the agricultural sector, including the privatization of agricultural lands and agro-processing enterprises. Land reform began in 1992 and was followed by a land-leasing programme in 1996. As a result of these two measures, 31% of agricultural land was under private ownership by mid-2001, and about the same proportion of land was being leased from the state by private entrepreneurs. Privatization of state-owned enterprises was under way, and by mid-2001 60% of agro-processing industries were already privately owned.

Despite the privatization of the majority of agro-business enterprises, production volume did not increase significantly, owing to the lack of necessary investment to develop modern management systems and to conquer new markets. Also related to the above-mentioned problems was the country's inability to utilize fully its existing export potential. Foreign investment was deemed to be the major means of resolving these issues; therefore, the creation of a favourable investment climate was crucial for improving the situation. The promotion and implementation of scientific innovations and the training of farmers were also considered important. The implementation of reforms would foster economic growth in the agricultural sector and, therefore, in the economy as a whole, being an essential prerequisite for the improvement of living standards and the alleviation of poverty. The process of privatizing agricultural land and restructuring it as small plots raised the issue of infrastructural and institutional changes to the management of irrigation and drainage systems. In March 2002 the World Bank initiated an Irrigation and Drainage Community Development Project, aimed at the establishment of water-consumer communities and the rehabilitation of water-supply networks. The first five-year phase involves the allocation of US $32m., of which $27m. is in the form of an International Development Association Credit.

The poor performance of the agricultural sector, largely owing to unfavourable weather conditions, restrained economic growth in 2002. The slight contraction in output of the agrarian sector in 2002 and the persistence of adverse weather conditions in early 2003 was expected negatively to affect the food-processing industry in 2003. Among the other problems contributing to economic deceleration in the sector were lack of credit, lack of modern machinery and lack of high-quality fertilizers. Although most agricultural land was privately owned, raising investment funds remained a problem for farmers. A draft law on privatizing remaining state-owned agricultural land was under development by the Association for the Protection of Landowners Rights and the State Department for Land Management.

The agricultural and food sector, characterized by high levels of (largely low-efficiency) employment, was expected to retain its important position in the national economy, although its role had to be strictly defined. In addition, measures directed towards alleviating the sector's vulnerability to climatic fluctuations, and thereby improving stability, had to be taken into account. In order to achieve this, primary objectives should be the development of rural infrastructure and the re-equiping of enterprises.

## ENERGY

After the collapse of the USSR, Georgia lost the cheap energy resources supplied under the centralized economy. This caused a number of problems in the energy sector, and presented a heavy burden to the overall population, as well as to businesses. The weakness of the power sector was one of the major obstacles to economic growth. Interruptions to power supplies were frequent, especially during the winter months, hindering the normal development of enterprises and reducing the living conditions of the population. Georgia continued to import electricity, although it had considerable potential for the generation of hydroelectric power. Only 10%–20% of Georgia's total capacity, however, was actually produced. Reform of the energy sector, therefore, was an integral part of the overall economic reforms being implemented in Georgia. The sector was undergoing a restructuring process aimed at attracting investment through privatization (supported by the World Bank's Energy Sector Adjustment Credit—ESAC). As a result of this restructuring, regulatory functions were separated from commercial activities, monopoly power was regulated, and a competitive environment was created. The independent Wholesale Electricity Market and the National Energy Regulatory Commission were established, and measures were implemented to improve tariff policy on electricity and gas.

Existing energy tariffs were a heavy burden for poorer families. Between 1997 and 2002 the energy tariff increased by more than two-fold and, according to the State Department for Statistics, typical household expenditure on electricity consumption was equivalent to approximately 21.5% of the average monthly salary.

The privatization of some distribution companies was accomplished successfully; substantial amounts of foreign investment were attracted and a significant improvement in energy distribution was achieved. One of the largest distribution companies, Telasi, for example, was purchased, at the end of 1998, by a US company, AES, leading to significant investment and increased revenue from electricity usage (it was subsequently transferred to Russian ownership in 2003). Although AES introduced increased electricity tariffs in late 2002, they were reduced by the National Energy Regulatory Commission in March 2003. The Commission was expected to review its decision, based on consumer and producer interests, following investors' claims that the tariffs made the operation of energy plants and companies unviable. Despite progress towards private management of the energy sector, its overall financial situation had not improved. Substantial arrears (of US $1,817.7m. at 31 May 2003) were accumulated, as a result of poor collection rates, and the inefficient management and corruption that dominated the sector. These problems, however, could only be solved by means of a continued and more enhanced reform process.

Georgia's importance to global energy markets stemmed from its location as a centre for the transit of Caspian petroleum and natural gas from Azerbaijan and Kazakhstan. Georgia forms part of the Transport Corridor Europe–Caucasus–Asia (TRACECA), which was to carry petroleum, gas and other products from the Caspian and Caucasus region to Europe. The proximity of the unstable regions of South Ossetia and Abkhazia posed certain risks, although TRACECA transit routes did not pass through them directly.

## INDUSTRY

The progress achieved in the industrial sector in 2000, compared with previous years, was positive. In 2001, however, the overall trend was reversed, and industrial production recorded negative growth, of 0.4%. Despite real GDP growth of 5.4% in 2002, growth remained uneven: about 75% of value-added was accounted for by just three sectors: transport, construction and financial services. Construction growth increased by 28.2% in 2002, mainly owing to construction work on the new petroleum pipeline and the petroleum shipment terminal at Poti port. The contribution of this sector to GDP increased to 4.5% in 2002, compared with 3.9% in 2001.

Although Georgia has some small refineries, it imports petroleum products via Poti. Plans were made to add a tanker terminal and additional storage facilities to the port, to increase capacity. Georgia also planned to build a new terminal in the Khobi region. This situation was likely to change

with the completion of the BTC pipeline, which was expected to become operational in the first quarter of 2005.

Production was also unevenly distributed between industries, with about 50 industrial enterprises (out of 2,800) accounting for around 75% of registered industrial output. The greatest progress was made in the fields of metallurgy, mining and fertilizers. However, this also demonstrated the low level of diversification within various industries. Another negative factor was the volume of unofficial production. Georgia's shadow economy was estimated to account for more than one-third of the economy's output and one-third of its trade; this was one of the major reasons for the chronic fiscal deficit, and caused damage to the competitive environment. However, it also indicated significant potential in the industrial sector. Therefore, the industrial situation could be deemed to be unstable, since it was very much dependent on the performance of certain large industries, the success or failure of which could have an enormous impact on the whole sector.

Taking into consideration the ongoing privatization and reform process, the fact that 42.9% of total industrial production continued to be produced by state-owned enterprises seemed unsatisfactory. The low level of diversification within the sector indicated that the most important and productive enterprises remained state-owned. This could not contribute to the development of the sector, and nor could it promote the establishment and rapid development of market relations.

## TRANSPORT AND COMMUNICATIONS

In contrast to other sectors, the development of the transport sector was relatively stable. The strong performance of the transport sector reflected the country's favourable geopolitical situation, which allowed it to serve as a transport corridor for the region. The Baku–Supsa pipeline was inaugurated in April 1999, and the construction of the larger BTC pipeline commenced in 2003. The pipeline was expected to become operational in the first quarter of 2005, and have an annual capacity of 50m. metric tons. The South Caucasus Gas Pipeline Project (SCP), envisaging the construction of a gas export pipeline from the Shah Deniz gasfield in Azerbaijan to Erzurum, Turkey, via Georgia, was approved in March 2003; the SCP pipeline was to be laid parallel with the BTC pipeline, in an attempt to reduce costs.

Georgia's transit function, however, was not limited only to petroleum and gas transportation—it was essential for it to build modern motorways, in accordance with international standards. For this purpose, a presidential decree was issued in 1996, under which a programme for the rehabilitation and modernization of the road system was adopted. The implementation of this programme was declared to be a priority for the economic development of Georgia.

Substantial increases in the international transportation of cargo contributed to increased turnover at Georgian railways and sea ports. In 2002 turnover of rail cargo increased by 12.9%, and Georgian Railways transported 10.4m. metric tons of petroleum and petroleum products. The ports at Batumi and Poti processed 13.5m. tons of cargo (14.1% more than in 2001). The discharging of ships loaded with the equipment intended for the construction of the Georgian section of the BTC pipeline commenced in January 2003. The possibility of transporting humanitarian shipments to Afghanistan through Georgia also represented an opportunity to raise transit volumes in the near future.

In 2001 there were approximately 30 telephone lines per 100 citizens in urban areas (10 telephone lines per 100 in rural areas). There was also substantial expansion of the cellular communications network. Mobile telecommunications has been one of the fastest growing and most dynamic sectors in the Georgian economy. There is considerable growth potential in the sector; however, long-term growth is likely to be restricted, owing to the limited size of the address-able market, the main reason for which is low income per head. The number of mobile telephone consumers increased by 71% in 2001, when there were 295,000 subscribers, equivalent to some 5.6% of the population. The number of mobile telephone subscribers increased by a further 70.7% in 2002, to 503,600. Of the three providers of mobile telecommunications services in Georgia, the two principal companies are Magti and Geocell. The liberalization of the communications sector promoted competition, as a result of which it became possible to introduce lower prices and to provide greater choice for the population. Data transmission and internet resources were still in the process of development. However, there too positive progress was registered, and by 2002 there were some 73,500 internet users in Georgia, a number that was increasing constantly.

## TRADE

After proclaiming independence, the volume of trade declined dramatically, causing substantial growth in the deficit on the balance of trade. However, Georgia managed to re-establish its trade relations, and Russia and some other former Soviet states remained among its principal trading partners. Georgia later expanded its trade relations, however, and by the early 2000s it also counted Turkey and member countries of the European Union (EU) among its main trading partners. The EU has become Georgia's second largest trading partner, after the member countries of the Commonwealth of Independent States (CIS). Important export commodities are chemicals and fertilizers, fruit and vegetables, manganese, steel, mineral water, tea, nuts, and wine and other alcoholic beverages. The main items imported are consumer goods, electricity, food products, grains, petroleum and natural gas, fuel, tobacco products and medicines.

Foreign trade plays an important role in the stability of the Georgian economy, and its integration into the global economy was essential. Georgia applied for full membership of the WTO in 1996, and acceded in mid-2000. In late December the USA extended non-discriminatory treatment—normal trade relations—to Georgian products, thereby permitting it to deal with Georgia according to standard WTO rules. In November 2001, for the first time as a WTO member country, Georgia sent a delegation to the WTO Ministerial Conference, held in Doha, Qatar. At the Conference, Georgia succeeded in establishing a coalition of eight recently acceded states (the others were Albania, Croatia, Jordan, Kyrgyzstan, Lithuania, Moldova and Oman).

Georgia, as a WTO member state, has the right to initiate formal bilateral and multilateral negotiations with countries in the process of accession to the WTO. Georgia has completed bilateral negotiations with Ukraine, and is undertaking negotiations focusing on market access for trade in industrial goods and services with Russia and with other CIS countries that are not members of the WTO.

Further progress has been made in the field of bilateral trade relations, which should improve market access for Georgian exports. In June 2001 US President George W. Bush designated Georgia a GSP (Generalized System of Preferences) beneficiary developing country. This provided more than 4,650 Georgian products with preferential, duty-free access to the US market, thus encouraging the stimulation of Georgia's foreign economic relations. Following a request by the Georgian Government, Poland granted Georgia GSP beneficiary country status, which entered into force in January 2002, and Estonia granted Georgia GSP beneficiary status in the same year. Thus, at mid-2003 Georgia was the beneficiary of GSP schemes with the USA, the EU, and with Canada, the Czech Republic, Estonia Japan, Poland, Slovakia, Turkey, Poland and Switzerland. GSP status positively influenced the growth of Georgia's export trade in general, and in particular with the EU. Moreover, in July 2002, during a meeting of the heads of state of the members of GUUAM (Georgia-Ukraine-Uzbekistan-Azerbaijan-Moldova), in Yalta, Ukraine, a multilateral agreement was signed, establishing a free-trade zone between those states. In December 2002 Parliament ratified the GUUAM free-trade agreement. A resolution on forming a free-trade zone within the CIS was also ratified in December, and Parliament also adopted changes to the law on customs tariffs. These changes were made according to the obligations taken by Georgia on joining the WTO, and Georgia has adopted material obligations in the sphere of standardization and certification. The list of the goods subject to mandatory certification has been revised and shortened, and the Minister of State issued an order on the adoption of a strategy for the development of the conformity system in Georgia. The negative trade balance increased slightly in 2002, compared with previous years. Recorded external trade turnover amounted to some US $1,045m., of which exports accounted for $325m. and imports $720m.

The contribution of Georgia's 10 principal trading partners to total registered trade turnover remained essentially unchanged, at some 74% in 2002. The main partners in that year, as in previous years, were Russia, Turkey, Azerbaijan, Ukraine and Germany, which together accounted for about 46% of Georgia's total registered trade turnover. The neighbouring countries of Turkey and Russia remained the main markets for Georgian exports, although Turkmenistan, the United Kingdom and Switzerland were also among the major export markets, and exports to EU countries as a whole had also increased. The main market for Georgian exports remained the CIS, although the EU accounted for some 17% of exports and Turkey for 15%. EU market access remains problematic for Georgian companies, owing to differences in standards and technical regulations. In 2001 the Georgian Parliament, in an attempt to curb smuggling, imposed a temporary ban on the export of non-ferrous scrap metals, which, together with significant growth in the exports of military aircraft, altered the structure of exports in that year. In July 2002 the ban was revoked, resulting in a rapid recovery in the growth of revenues, despite a slump in metal prices. In 2002 ferrous scrap and ferro-alloys together accounted for 10.3% of all exports. Other major export products were aircrafts and parts thereof (14.9%), wine (10.3%), natural and mineral waters (5.7%) and mineral fuels (4.7%); unwrought and semi-manufactured gold had also became an important export item (8.1%). Other main export items are sugar, copper ores and concentrates, and mineral or chemical fertilizers. Ten product groups accounted for more than 67% of all registered exports in 2002. In that year the CIS and the EU accounted for 66% of registered imports; Turkey accounted for a further 12%. Georgia's dependence on foreign energy supplies continued, and in 2002 mineral products continued to dominate imports. However the import structure was changing gradually. The largest imported product groups, which together constituted about 45% of total imports in 2002, included petroleum, oils and gases (18.3%), medicines (6.2%), sugar (4.7%), motor cars (3.0%) and tobacco (2.6%). However, figures for registered trade probably differed from the real picture, as a significant proportion of trade was unrecorded.

## LABOUR MARKET AND SOCIAL POLICY

The complicated labour market situation, prevalent among transition economies, persisted in Georgia, reflecting the complexities of the economic situation as a whole. New, stable jobs were rarely created, unemployment, especially 'hidden' unemployment and underemployment, was widespread, and the majority of those in employment were underpaid.

According to the State Department for Statistics, the rate of participation in economic activity was relatively high, at 65.5% at the end of 2002, but it had experienced a year-on-year decline from 1998, and it appeared likely that this trend would be maintained, at least in the short term. The national unemployment rate, calculated according to the International Labour Organization's (ILO) 'strict' methodology, was 11.9% at the end of 2002 (or 15%, according to its 'loose' methodology). The national unemployment rate was highly influenced by the figures for rural areas, which served to create the impression of a reduced overall national unemployment rate and a higher participation rate.

The labour market was largely dominated by the self-employed, and the latter by self-employment in the agricultural sector. The share of the self-employed in the labour force and in total employment increased to account for as much as 57% of the former, and 64% of the latter by the end of 2002. Underemployment was also a widespread phenomenon, with the majority of those employed being engaged in low-paid and insecure segments of the labour market.

Social-policy reform, aimed at introducing a sustainable pensions system, was among the country's main priorities. Fundamental restructuring of the state social-protection system was essential for the creation of economically viable and equitable social-security provisions. Social reforms were acknowledged by the Government to be a long-term strategic objective. As mentioned above, the main objectives of the EGPRP, approved by President in June 2003, were: the elimination of poverty by supporting economic growth, thereby leading to the creation of new jobs; raising the living standards of the population; and ensuring the participation of all citizens in the country's development process. According to the EGPRP, it was necessary to develop targeted social-protection mechanisms to cover as many unprotected people as possible. Under the existing 'pay-as-you-go' system, pensions were financed by means of the Pension Fund (United State Social Insurance Fund), providing fixed-rate old-age pensions to the majority of pensioners. However, the pensions system had long proven to be both unsustainable and insolvent, and it continued to accumulate arrears. Reform of the system was, therefore, a matter of urgency, and a far-reaching, programme to introduce a 'multi-pillar' pension system, to be implemented in stages, was drawn up in 2001, as part of the EGPRP. The programme aimed to establish a financially sustainable, modern pension system, suited to the changing demands of a transition economy and, where possible, tailored to suit local conditions. The first private pensions insurance company in Georgia was founded in May 2001, and was to offer, in addition to the existing, universal scheme, voluntary, non-state pensions insurance to the population. Reform of the pensions system had begun by 2003, and in July Parliament passed a number of laws, providing the necessary legal framework for introducing changes to the social insurance system and introducing a new pension system based on insurance principles.

## PROSPECTS

Georgia's economic recovery was impeded by the separatist conflict in Abkhazia and South Ossetia, a persistently weak economic infrastructure, resistance to reform on the part of certain corrupt and reactionary factions, and the Russian economic crisis of 1998. Despite the difficulties experienced during the transition period, the Government had, none the less, managed to achieve certain objectives, such as curbing inflation, meeting IMF targets and qualifying for SACs, introducing a stable national currency (the lari), introducing free market prices for bread products, joining the WTO, signing agreements that allowed for the development of the pipeline to transport Caspian petroleum across Georgia, and passing laws on commercial banking, land and tax reform. There had been strong progress towards structural reform. Prices and the majority of trade had been liberalized, reform of the legal framework was under way, and large-scale reductions in government bureaucracy had been implemented.

One of the major objectives of the Government in the 2000s was the targeted reduction of the budgetary deficit as a proportion of GDP. While a gradual reduction in the deficit would be achieved by the improved balancing of revenue and expenditure, in order to achieve growth in state revenue the introduction of improvements to tax policy and its administration was also important. Structural reforms to the state customs and tax departments were planned, and a revision of the tax code was approved, in order to revise the tax base and optimize existing tax rates, and improve tax-administration mechanisms. Tax policy was also to be adapted to promote the attraction of investment and the development of small businesses.

Moderately strict monetary policy was to be continued, in order to maintain price stability, the provision of credits to the Government was to be reduced to a minimum, and the growth of reserves was to be achieved, primarily, by accumulating the international assets of the National Bank of Georgia. In order to balance the lari exchange rate with inflows of foreign exchange, and to weaken the influence of external factors, foreign-exchange policy needed to be based on a 'floating' (freely convertible) exchange rate. If cash existing outside the banking system (both in terms of the national currency and foreign exchange) could be channelled into the system, then the economy would be supplied with adequate money supplies. To develop financial markets, emphasis was to be given to reducing the internal state debt, which would release additional resources, creating a favourable background for reducing interest rates, and broaden facilities for granting credits to the private sector.

Real GDP growth is likely to accelerate in the short to medium term, owing to a rapid rise in investment relating to the construction of the BTC pipeline and the SCP, which is likely to result in a revival in domestic demand, owing to higher disposable income. Such growth will also stimulate moderate inflation, as employment and wages grow. Pipeline construction and operation is likely to boost related sectors, such as transport and telecommunications. However, industrial-sector growth is likely to remain limited to a small number of sectors, and the development of the manufacturing sector is likely to be hampered by limited investment and a lack of restructuring activities, which will, in turn, limit export growth. The lari is expected to remain stable as a result of continuing tight control over the growth of the money supply. Increased import costs, resulting from pipeline construction, are likely to contribute to growth in the current-account deficit, and growth in export revenue is expected to be constrained by the poor agricultural harvest in recent years.

In order to achieve long-term economic growth and poverty reduction, as set out in the EGPRP, the following objectives were critical: maintaining a stable macroeconomic environment, supported by a prudent monetary policy, including a build-up of official reserves, and further fiscal consolidation; raising fiscal revenue by accelerating administrative reforms in the areas of tax and customs, as well as through tax policy measures; making further progress in improving management of budgetary expenditure; concluding bilateral debt-rescheduling agreements; strengthening the financial system; accelerating structural reforms, in particular in the energy sector; improving the business environment by making progress in combating corruption; and finalizing a full poverty-reduction strategy paper (PRSP), focused on growth-enhancing strategies and appropriate social-sector reforms.

A Partnership and Co-operation Agreement (PCA), signed between Georgia and the EU in April 1996, finally came into force on 1 July 1999, following its ratification. The agreement aimed to establish a partnership, the objectives of which were the development of political relations, the consolidation of democracy, economic development, and the completion of the transition to a market economy, as well as the promotion of trade and investment. Moreover, it was to provide a basis for legislative, economic, social, financial, civil, scientific, technological and cultural co-operation. Strong emphasis was attached to support and development, in the light of the

values inherent to Europe, which would enable Georgia to participate in, and integrate with, the structures common to the European states, in particular the member countries of the EU. Thus, the PCA, together with Georgia's accession to the Council of Europe in April 1999, and its membership of the WTO from mid-2000, formed part of Georgia's endeavours to integrate with the international community. Work on the elaboration of a National Programme of Harmonization of Georgian Legislation with that of the EU, pursuant to the PCA, was under way in the early 2000s.

# Statistical Survey

Source (unless otherwise indicated): State Department for Statistics, 380085 Tbilisi, K. Gamsakhurdia 4; tel. (32) 33-14-50; fax (32) 93-89-36; e-mail ngabunia@statistics.gov.ge; internet georgia-gateway.org/SDS.

## Area and Population

### AREA, POPULATION AND DENSITY

| | |
|---|---|
| Area (sq km) . . . . . . . . . . | 69,700* |
| Population (census results)† | |
| 17 January 1979 . . . . . . . . | 4,993,182 |
| 12 January 1989 | |
| Males . . . . . . . . | 2,562,040 |
| Females . . . . . . . . | 2,838,801 |
| Total . . . . . . . | 5,400,841 |
| Population (UN estimates at mid-year)‡ | |
| 2000 . . . . . . . . . . | 5,262,000 |
| 2001 . . . . . . . . . . | 5,224,000 |
| 2002 . . . . . . . . . . | 5,177,000 |
| Density (per sq km) at mid-2001 . . . . . . . | 74.3 |

\* 26,911 sq miles.
† Population is *de jure*. The *de facto* total at the 1989 census was 5,443,359.
‡ Source: UN, *World Population Prospects: The 2002 Revision*.

### POPULATION BY NATIONALITY
(1989 census result)

| | % |
|---|---|
| Georgian . . . . . . . . . . . . . . | 68.8 |
| Armenian . . . . . . . . . . . . . | 9.0 |
| Russian . . . . . . . . . . . . . | 7.4 |
| Azerbaijani . . . . . . . . . . . . | 5.1 |
| Ossetian . . . . . . . . . . . . . | 3.2 |
| Greek . . . . . . . . . . . . . . | 1.9 |
| Abkhazian . . . . . . . . . . . . | 1.7 |
| Others . . . . . . . . . . . . . | 2.9 |
| **Total** . . . . . . . . . . . . . | 100.0 |

### PRINCIPAL TOWNS
(census of 17 January 2002, preliminary figures)

| | | | | |
|---|---|---|---|---|
| Tbilisi (capital) . . | 1,081,700 | Rustavi . . . | 116,400 |
| Kutaisi . . . . | 186,000 | Sukhumi . . . | 112,000* |
| Batumi . . . . | 121,800 | Gori . . . . . | 66,500† |

\* 1 January 1994.
† Estimate at 1 January 2002.

Source: Thomas Brinkhoff, *City Population* (www.citypopulation.de).

### BIRTHS, MARRIAGES AND DEATHS

| | Registered live births | | Registered marriages | | Registered deaths | |
|---|---|---|---|---|---|---|
| | Number | Rate (per 1,000) | Number | Rate (per 1,000) | Number | Rate (per 1,000) |
| 1993 . . | 61,594 | 11.3 | 24,105 | 4.4 | 48,938 | 9.0 |
| 1994 . . | 57,311 | 10.6 | 21,908 | 4.0 | 41,596 | 7.7 |
| 1995 . . | 56,341 | 10.4 | 21,481 | 4.0 | 37,874 | 7.0 |
| 1996 . . | 53,669 | 9.9 | 19,253 | 3.6 | 34,414 | 6.4 |
| 1997 . . | 52,020 | 9.8 | 17,100* | 3.2*. | 37,679 | 7.1 |
| 1998* . . | 57,300 | 10.8 | 15,343 | 2.9 | 41,600 | 7.9 |

\* Provisional data.

Sources: mainly UN, *Demographic Yearbook*; Caucasus Health International Forum.

**2000:** Births 40,392 (number), 8.2 (rate); Deaths 41,320 (number), 8.4 (rate) (Source: UN, *Population and Vital Statistics Report*).

**Expectation of life** (WHO estimates, years at birth): 68.9 (males 65.4; females 72.4) in 2001 (Source: WHO, *World Health Report*).

## EMPLOYMENT
(annual averages, '000 persons)*

| | 1999 | 2000 | 2001 |
|---|---|---|---|
| Agriculture, hunting and forestry | 903.2 | 910.4 | 989.9 |
| Fishing | 1.2 | 0.8 | 0.5 |
| Mining and quarrying . . . | 6.1 | 6.3 | 7.3 |
| Manufacturing . . . . . | 111.5 | 103.9 | 102.4 |
| Electricity, gas and water supply | 21.0 | 29.1 | 29.2 |
| Construction . . . . . . | 24.9 | 32.0 | 35.3 |
| Wholesale and retail trade; repair of motor vehicles and personal and household goods . . . | 153.2 | 174.8 | 181.5 |
| Hotels and restaurants . . . | 15.4 | 15.0 | 16.0 |
| Transport, storage and communications . . . . | 68.5 | 71.9 | 83.1 |
| Financial intermediation . . . | 10.9 | 9.0 | 10.2 |
| Real estate, renting and business activities | 40.3 | 37.7 | 38.7 |
| Public administration and defence; compulsory social security . . | 106.5 | 105.8 | 105.6 |
| Education . . . . . . | 138.5 | 114.2 | 138.7 |
| Health and social work . . . | 77.9 | 85.2 | 85.3 |
| Other community, social and personal service activities . . | 42.5 | 45.3 | 46.5 |
| Private households with employed persons . . . . . . | 6.9 | 3.2 | 4.1 |
| Extra-territorial organizations and bodies . . . . . . | 1.9 | 1.9 | 2.0 |
| Activities not adequately defined | 0.7 | 2.3 | 1.3 |
| **Total employed** . . . . . | 1,731.5 | 1,748.8 | 1,877.6 |
| Unemployed . . . . . | 277.5 | 212.2 | 235.6 |
| **Total labour force** . . . . | 2,009.1 | 1,961.2 | 2,113.0 |
| Males . . . . . . | 1,044.3 | 1,051.6 | 1,093.5 |
| Females . . . . . . | 964.8 | 909.6 | 1,019.5 |

* Figures exclude employment in the informal sector, estimated to total about 750,000 persons at the end of 1997.

Source: ILO.

# Health and Welfare

## KEY INDICATORS

| | |
|---|---|
| Total fertility rate (children per woman, 2001) . . . . | 1.4 |
| Under-5 mortality rate (per 1,000 live births, 2001) . . | 29 |
| HIV/AIDS (% of persons aged 15–49, 2001) . . . . | <0.10 |
| Physicians (per 1,000 head, 1998) . . . . | 4.36 |
| Hospital beds (per 1,000 head, 1996) . . . . | 4.81 |
| Health expenditure (2000): US $ per head (PPP) . . . | 199 |
| Health expenditure (2000): % of GDP . . . | 7.1 |
| Health expenditure (2000): public (% of total) . . . | 10.5 |
| Human Development Index (2001): ranking . . . . | 88 |
| Human Development Index (2001): value . . . . | 0.746 |

For sources and definitions, see explanatory note on p. vi.

# Agriculture

## PRINCIPAL CROPS
('000 metric tons)

| | 1999 | 2000 | 2001 |
|---|---|---|---|
| Wheat . . . . . . . | 226.1 | 89.4 | 306.0 |
| Barley . . . . . . | 50.8 | 30.1 | 98.4 |
| Maize . . . . . . | 490.5 | 295.9 | 288.6 |
| Potatoes . . . . . | 443.3 | 302.0 | 415.0 |
| Sugar beet* . . . . . | 23.1 | 23.0 | 23.0 |
| Nuts* . . . . . . | 50.9 | 44.7 | 36.2 |
| Sunflower seed . . . . | 40.5 | 2.6 | 3.0 |
| Cabbages . . . . . | 102† | 125 | 76.7† |
| Tomatoes† . . . . . | 210 | 155 | 202.6 |
| Cucumbers and gherkins† . . . | 42.0 | 30.2 | 27.6 |
| Dry onions† . . . . | 45 | 31 | 33.2 |
| Other vegetables† . . . . | 18 | 13 | 9.9 |
| Oranges . . . . . | 56.0 | 40.0 | 32.0† |
| Apples . . . . . . | 98.2 | 83.0 | 66.2 |
| Pears . . . . . . | 40.5 | 34.2 | 27.5† |
| Sour cherries† . . . . | 27.0 | 24.0 | 19.5 |
| Peaches and nectarines . . . | 15.2 | 12.8 | 10.2† |
| Plums . . . . . | 22.6 | 19.1 | 15.4† |
| Grapes . . . . . | 220.0 | 210.0 | 180.0† |
| Watermelons . . . . | 108.2 | 80.0 | 70.0* |
| Other fruit* . . . . | 43.3 | 36.5 | 29.2 |
| Tea (made) . . . . | 60.3 | 24.0 | 30.0* |
| Tobacco (leaves) . . . . | 1.9 | 1.9 | 2.1* |

* FAO estimate(s).
† Unofficial figure(s).

Source: FAO.

## LIVESTOCK
('000 head at 1 January)

| | 1999 | 2000 | 2001 |
|---|---|---|---|
| Horses . . . . . . . | 34.1 | 35.2 | 38.5 |
| Cattle . . . . . . | 1,122 | 1,177 | 1,180 |
| Buffaloes . . . . . | 33 | 35 | 33 |
| Pigs . . . . . . | 411 | 443 | 445 |
| Sheep . . . . . . | 553 | 540* | 560* |
| Goats . . . . . . | 80 | 88* | 99* |
| Chickens . . . . . | 8,473 | 7,826 | 8,495 |
| Turkeys† . . . . . . | 405 | 400 | 405 |

* Unofficial figure.
† FAO estimates.

Source: FAO.

## LIVESTOCK PRODUCTS
('000 metric tons)

| | 1999 | 2000 | 2001 |
|---|---|---|---|
| Beef and veal . . . . . | 41.3 | 48.3 | 47.0 |
| Mutton and lamb . . . . | 6.9 | 8.9 | 7.6 |
| Pig meat . . . . . | 40.8 | 36.9 | 34.7 |
| Poultry meat . . . . | 11.3 | 13.7 | 12.8 |
| Cows' milk . . . . . | 660.3 | 618.9 | 690.4 |
| Hen eggs* . . . . . . | 21.7 | 20.7 | 21.9 |

* Unofficial figures.

Source: FAO.

# Fishing

(metric tons, live weight)

|  | 1998 | 1999 | 2000 |
|---|---|---|---|
| Capture | 3,001 | 1,680 | 2,450 |
| Rainbow trout | — | 80 | 100 |
| Whiting | 53 | 41 | 40* |
| European sprat | 24 | 42 | 42* |
| European anchovy | 2,346 | 1,264 | 2,080 |
| Sharks, rays and skates | 550 | 18 | 21 |
| Aquaculture | 96 | 83 | 86 |
| Common carp | 42 | 34 | 35 |
| **Total catch** | **3,097** | **1,763** | **2,536** |

\* FAO estimates.

Source: FAO, *Yearbook of Fishery Statistics*.

# Mining

('000 metric tons, unless otherwise indicated)

|  | 1998 | 1999 | 2000 |
|---|---|---|---|
| Coal | 14.7 | 12.0 | 7.0 |
| Crude petroleum | 119.2 | 91.3 | 109.5 |
| Natural gas (million cu m) | — | — | 100.0 |
| Manganese ore | 50.0 | 47.9 | 59.1 |

Source: US Geological Survey.

# Industry*

**SELECTED PRODUCTS**

('000 metric tons, unless otherwise indicated)

|  | 1998 | 1999 | 2000 |
|---|---|---|---|
| Refined sugar | — | 20.0 | 35.3 |
| Canned foodstuffs | 1.9 | 6.6 | 4.6 |
| Wine ('000 hectolitres) | 218 | 194 | 182 |
| Beer ('000 hectolitres) | 74 | 126 | 235 |
| Vodka and liqueurs ('000 hectolitres) | 31 | 46 | 43 |
| Soft drinks ('000 hectolitres) | 290 | 220 | 290 |
| Mineral water ('000 hectolitres) | 291 | 245 | 362 |
| Cigarettes (million) | 600 | 1,300 | 300 |
| Textile fabrics (million sq metres) | 0.2 | 0.2 | — |
| Mineral fertilizers | 55.4 | 95.1 | 100.2 |
| Synthetic ammonia | 77.5 | 126.6 | 136.2 |
| Motor spirit (petrol) | 2.4 | 3.6 | 1.8 |
| Distillate fuel oil (diesel fuel) | 4.7 | 22.3 | 8.8 |
| Building bricks (million) | 13.1 | 7.7 | 4.7 |
| Steel | 56.4 | 7 | — |
| Steel pipes | 8.8 | 0.1 | 0.2 |
| Electric energy (million kWh) | 8,100 | 8,100 | 7,400 |

\* Data for South Ossetia and Abkhazia are not included.

# Finance

**CURRENCY AND EXCHANGE RATES**

**Monetary Units**
100 tetri = 1 lari.

**Sterling, Dollar and Euro Equivalents** (30 May 2003)
£1 sterling = 3.538 lari;
US $1 = 2.148 lari;
€1 = 2.539 lari;
100 lari = £28.26 = $46.57 = €39.39.

**Average Exchange Rate** (lari per US $)
| | |
|---|---|
| 2000 | 1.9762 |
| 2001 | 2.0730 |
| 2002 | 2.1957 |

Note: On 25 September 1995 Georgia introduced the lari, replacing interim currency coupons at the rate of 1 lari = 1,000,000 coupons. From April 1993 the National Bank of Georgia had issued coupons in various denominations, to circulate alongside (and initially at par with) the Russian (formerly Soviet) rouble. From August 1993 coupons became Georgia's sole legal tender, but their value rapidly depreciated. The transfer from coupons to the lari lasted one week, and from 2 October 1995 the lari became the only permitted currency in Georgia.

**BUDGET**
(million lari)*

| Revenue† | 1998 | 1999 | 2000 |
|---|---|---|---|
| Tax revenue | 526.1 | 649.2 | 706.6 |
| Taxes on income | 87.8 | 104.8 | 108.2 |
| Taxes on profits | 50.5 | 55.6 | 79.7 |
| Value-added tax | 219.7 | 248.1 | 289.8 |
| Customs duties | 67.0 | 33.7 | 53.1 |
| Other current revenue | 97.1 | 42.8 | 45.6 |
| Extrabudgetary revenue‡ | 117.5 | 133.1 | 144.8 |
| **Total** | **740.8** | **825.1** | **897.1** |

| Expenditure§ | 1998 | 1999 | 2000 |
|---|---|---|---|
| Current expenditure | 997.3 | 1,132.5 | 1,094.2 |
| Wages and salaries | 176.7 | 190.8 | 180.1 |
| Other goods and services‖ | 202.4 | 190.9 | 132.2 |
| Subsidies and transfers | 119.3 | 142.2 | 166.7 |
| Interest payments | 114.8 | 159.0 | 178.4 |
| Extrabudgetary expenditure¶ | 212.5 | 211.7 | 203.7 |
| Local government expenditure | 171.7 | 237.9 | 233.1 |
| Capital expenditure | 65.5 | 48.7 | 30.2 |
| **Total** | **1,062.8** | **1,181.2** | **1,124.4** |

\* Figures represent a consolidation of the State Budget (covering the central Government and local administrations) and extrabudgetary funds.
† Excluding grants received (million lari): 45.7 in 1998; 48.2 in 1999; 16.2 in 2000.
‡ Comprising the revenues of the Social Security Fund, the Employment Fund, the Privatization Fund and the Road Fund (established in October 1995).
§ Excluding net lending (million lari): 33.6 in 1998; 71.7 in 1999; 31.6 in 2000.
‖ Comprising other goods and services, other current expenditure and unclassified expenditure.
¶ Including the payment of pensions and unemployment benefit.

**INTERNATIONAL RESERVES**
(US $ million at 31 December)

|  | 2000 | 2001 | 2002 |
|---|---|---|---|
| IMF special drawing rights | 3.27 | 3.96 | 2.89 |
| Reserve position in the IMF | 0.01 | 0.01 | 0.01 |
| Foreign exchange | 106.13 | 155.40 | 194.64 |
| **Total** | **109.41** | **159.37** | **197.55** |

Source: IMF, *International Financial Statistics*.

## MONEY SUPPLY
(million lari at 31 December)

| | 2000 | 2001 | 2002 |
|---|---|---|---|
| Currency outside banks . . . . | 315.18 | 348.85 | 390.79 |
| Demand deposits . . . . . | 53.20 | 45.33 | 62.01 |
| **Total money** (incl. others) . . . | 368.38 | 394.23 | 452.84 |

Source: IMF, *International Financial Statistics.*

## COST OF LIVING
(Consumer price index for five cities; base: 1995 = 100)

| | 1999 | 2000 | 2001 |
|---|---|---|---|
| Food, beverages and tobacco . . | 171.4 | 173.7 | 185.2 |
| Fuel and light . . . . . | 305.6 | 373.5 | 394.8 |
| Clothing (incl. footwear). . . . | 168.4 | 168.0 | 169.4 |
| Rent . . . . . . . . | 129.3 | 136.0 | 140.1 |
| **All items** (incl. others) . . . . | 184.3 | 191.7 | 200.7 |

Source: ILO.

## NATIONAL ACCOUNTS
### Gross Domestic Product
(million lari at current prices)

| | 1998 | 1999 | 2000 |
|---|---|---|---|
| Government final consumption expenditure. . . . . . | 556.6 | 581.2 | 504.7 |
| Private final consumption expenditure. . . . . . | 4,350.5 | 4,760.0 | 5,073.3 |
| Increase in stocks . . . . | 57.5 | 65.4 | 75.6 |
| Gross fixed capital formation . . | 561.2 | 1,024.9 | 944.6 |
| **Total domestic expenditure**. . | 5,525.8 | 6,431.5 | 6,598.2 |
| Exports of goods and services . . | 826.6 | 1,080.2 | 1,389.6 |
| *Less* Imports of goods and services | 1,863.6 | 2,159.6 | 2,397.1 |
| **Sub-total** . . . . . . . | 4,488.8 | 5,352.3 | 5,590.6 |
| Statistical discrepancy . . . . | 551.8 | 313.7 | 380.0 |
| **GDP in purchasers' values** . . | 5,040.6 | 5,666.0 | 5,970.6 |

### Gross Domestic Product by Economic Activity
(% of total)

| | 1998 | 1999 | 2000 |
|---|---|---|---|
| Agriculture, forestry and fishing | 26.7 | 24.7 | 20.0 |
| Industry* . . . . . . . | 12.3 | 13.0 | 14.0 |
| Construction . . . . . . | 4.6 | 3.7 | 3.8 |
| Trade . . . . . . . | 10.4 | 11.5 | 12.7 |
| Hotels and restaurants . . . | 1.9 | 2.4 | 2.4 |
| Transport and communications . | 10.9 | 11.9 | 14.4 |
| Financial intermediation . . | 1.2 | 1.6 | 1.7 |
| General administration and defence . . . . . . . | 3.9 | 3.5 | 3.2 |
| Education . . . . . . . | 2.8 | 3.3 | 3.6 |
| Health . . . . . . . | 4.5 | 4.3 | 5.1 |
| Other services . . . . . | 20.7 | 20.1 | 19.2 |
| **Total** . . . . . . . . | 100.0 | 100.0 | 100.0 |

* Principally mining, manufacturing, electricity, gas and water.

## BALANCE OF PAYMENTS
(US $ million)

| | 2000 | 2001 | 2002 |
|---|---|---|---|
| Exports of goods f.o.b. . . . . | 459.0 | 496.1 | 578.7 |
| Imports of goods f.o.b. . . . . | −970.5 | −1,045.6 | −1,030.9 |
| **Trade balance** . . . . . | −511.5 | −549.5 | −452.2 |
| Exports of services . . . . | 206.4 | 314.1 | 353.4 |
| Imports of services . . . . | −216.3 | −236.9 | −260.5 |
| **Balance on goods and services**. | −521.4 | −472.3 | −359.3 |
| Other income received . . . . | 178.6 | 97.7 | 93.2 |
| Other income paid . . . . | −61.1 | −65.4 | −148.3 |
| **Balance on goods, services and income**. . . . . . . | −403.9 | −440.0 | −414.4 |
| Current transfers received . . . | 163.2 | 246.4 | 181.0 |
| Current transfers paid . . . . | −28.3 | −18.1 | −24.9 |
| **Current balance** . . . . . | −269.0 | −211.7 | −258.3 |
| Capital account (net) . . . . | −4.8 | −5.2 | 66.6 |
| Direct investment abroad . . . | 0.5 | 0.1 | −0.1 |
| Direct investment from abroad . | 131.1 | 109.8 | 145.8 |
| Portfolio investment assets . . | 2.7 | −0.1 | — |
| Portfolio investment liabilities . . | — | n.a. | n.a. |
| Other investment assets . . . | −7.7 | −24.6 | −28.9 |
| Other investment liabilities . . | −33.8 | 124.5 | 101.8 |
| Net errors and omissions . . . | 187.4 | 34.9 | 10.8 |
| **Overall balance** . . . . . | 6.4 | 27.7 | 37.7 |

Source: IMF, *International Financial Statistics.*

# External Trade

## PRINCIPAL COMMODITIES
(US $ million)

| Imports f.o.b. | 2000 | 2001 | 2002 |
|---|---|---|---|
| Crude petroleum and petroleum products . . . | 71.9 | 87.7 | 87.3 |
| Petroleum gases and other gaseous hydrocarbons . . | 48.6 | 47.1 | 45.6 |
| Sugar . . . . . . . | 24.6 | 24.1 | 37.1 |
| Cigars and cigarettes . . . | 29.4 | 18.7 | 18.1 |
| Wheat . . . . . . . | 21.9 | 11.2 | 13.8 |
| Flour . . . . . . . | 20.3 | 14.8 | n.a. |
| Medicines . . . . . . | 33.9 | 38.3 | 45.8 |
| Automobiles . . . . . | 15.2 | 12.4 | 21.8 |
| **Total** (incl. others) . . . . | 650.7 | 678.7 | 720.0 |

| Exports f.o.b. | 2000 | 2001 | 2002 |
|---|---|---|---|
| Iron and steel scrap . . . . | 39.0 | 32.9 | 31.5 |
| Ferro-alloys . . . . . . | 13.6 | 17.5 | 14.5 |
| Aluminium waste and scrap . | 12.9 | 15.4 | n.a. |
| Gold (unwrought or semi-manufactured). . . . . | n.a. | 12.5 | 28.5 |
| Aircraft . . . . . . . | 7.1 | 35.7 | 44.5 |
| Crude petroleum and natural gas . . . . . . . . | 12.8 | n.a. | n.a. |
| Petroleum products . . . . | 6.4 | n.a. | n.a. |
| Tea . . . . . . . | 6.1 | n.a. | n.a. |
| Fertilizers . . . . . . | 16.2 | 4.9 | 11.0 |
| Nuts . . . . . . . | 19.3 | 9.8 | n.a. |
| Copper ore . . . . . . | 9.8 | 9.6 | n.a. |
| Wine and related products . . | 29.0 | 32.2 | 26.2 |
| Mineral water . . . . . | 9.5 | 11.7 | 15.3 |
| Electricity . . . . . . | 7.2 | 11.1 | n.a. |
| **Total** (incl. others) . . . . | 329.9 | 320.0 | 325.0 |

## PRINCIPAL TRADING PARTNERS
(US $ million)

| Imports c.i.f. | 2000 | 2001 |
|---|---|---|
| Armenia | 13.5 | n.a. |
| Azerbaijan | 55.4 | 73.2 |
| Germany | 50.2 | 69.1 |
| Italy | 17.3 | 25.5 |
| Russia | 91.9 | 91.3 |
| Switzerland | 22.7 | 14.0 |
| Turkey | 104.0 | 105.0 |
| Ukraine | 35.4 | 49.5 |
| United Kingdom | 23.0 | 25.1 |
| USA | 35.7 | 27.8 |
| **Total** (incl. others) | 449.0 | 498.2 |

| Exports f.o.b. | 2000 | 2001 |
|---|---|---|
| Armenia | 13.7 | n.a. |
| Azerbaijan | 21.3 | 10.6 |
| Germany | 34.3 | 7.9 |
| Italy | 12.4 | 8.6 |
| Russia | 69.6 | 73.5 |
| Switzerland | 13.4 | 15.6 |
| Turkey | 74.8 | 68.7 |
| Turkmenistan | n.a. | 28.9 |
| Ukraine | 11.0 | 11.7 |
| United Kingdom | 10.3 | 22.9 |
| USA | 7.3 | 9.5 |
| **Total** (incl. others) | 268.0 | 257.8 |

Source: partly National Bank of Georgia.

## Transport

### RAILWAYS
(traffic)

| | 1998 | 1999 | 2000 |
|---|---|---|---|
| Passenger-km (million) | 397 | 349 | 450 |
| Freight net ton-km (million) | 2,574 | 3,139 | 3,910 |

Source: UN, *Statistical Yearbook for Asia and the Pacific.*

### ROAD TRAFFIC
('000 motor vehicles in use)

| | 1998* | 1999 | 2000 |
|---|---|---|---|
| Passenger cars | 260.4 | 247.9 | 244.8 |
| Buses | 14.8 | 18.9 | 19.8 |
| Lorries and vans | 56.2 | 50.0 | 47.0 |

* Estimates.

Source: International Road Federation, *World Road Statistics.*

### SHIPPING

**Merchant Fleet**
(registered at 31 December)

| | 2000 | 2001 | 2002 |
|---|---|---|---|
| Number of vessels | 118 | 201 | 261 |
| Total displacement ('000 grt) | 118.6 | 276.6 | 569.3 |

Source: Lloyd's Register-Fairplay, *World Fleet Statistics.*

## CIVIL AVIATION
(traffic on scheduled services)

| | 1997 | 1998 | 1999 |
|---|---|---|---|
| Kilometres flown (million) | 3 | 5 | 5 |
| Passengers carried ('000) | 110 | 175 | 159 |
| Passenger-km (million) | 206 | 340 | 307 |
| Total ton-km (million) | 20 | 34 | 30 |

Source: UN, *Statistical Yearbook.*

## Tourism

### FOREIGN TOURIST ARRIVALS

| Country of residence | 1999 | 2000 | 2001 |
|---|---|---|---|
| CIS countries* | 219,318 | 220,327 | 184,057 |
| Turkey | 100,955 | 84,170 | 57,005 |
| USA | 7,846 | 9,308 | 6,536 |
| **Total** (incl. others) | 383,817 | 387,258 | 302,215 |

* Comprising Armenia, Azerbaijan, Belarus, Kazakhstan, Kyrgyzstan, Moldova, Russia, Tajikistan, Turkmenistan, Ukraine and Uzbekistan.

**Tourism receipts** (US $ million): 423 in 1998; 400 in 1999.

Source: World Tourism Organization, *Yearbook of Tourism Statistics.*

## Communications Media

| | 2000 | 2001 | 2002 |
|---|---|---|---|
| Television receivers ('000 in use) | 2,590 | n.a. | n.a. |
| Telephones ('000 main lines in use) | 757.5 | 867.6 | 648.5 |
| Mobile cellular telephones ('000 subscribers) | 185.5 | 295.0 | 503.6 |
| Internet users ('000) | 23.0 | 25.0 | 73.5 |
| Personal computers (in use, '000) | n.a. | n.a. | 156 |
| Newspapers: titles | 184 | n.a. | n.a. |
| Newspapers: circulation | 600,000 | n.a. | n.a. |

**Radio receivers:** 3,005 in 1995; 3,010 in 1996; 3,020 in 1997.

**Facsimile machines:** 500 in 1996.

**Book production** (including pamphlets): 581 titles in 1996 (834,000 copies); 697 titles in 1999.

Sources: UN, *Statistical Yearbook*; UNESCO, *Statistical Yearbook*; and International Telecommunication Union.

## Education
(2000/01)

| | Institutions | Students† |
|---|---|---|
| Pre-primary schools | 1,195 | 72,700 |
| General education: Day schools (primary)* | 1,505 | 105,700 |
| General education: Day schools (secondary) | 1,652 | 591,700 |
| General education: Day schools (special) | 18 | 2,000 |
| General education: Evening schools | 26 | 5,100 |
| State secondary specialized schools | 85 | 27,400 |
| Private secondary specialized schools | 55 | 5,100 |
| Vocational/technical schools | 82 | 14,300 |
| State higher schools (incl. universities) | 26 | 105,800 |
| Private higher schools (incl. universities) | 145 | 33,100 |

* Including primary schools covering part of the secondary syllabus.
† Figures are rounded.

**Teachers** (1998/99): Total in general day schools 71,700 (excl. teachers in special schools); Total in institutes of higher education 11,166.

**Adult literacy rate** (UNESCO estimates): 99.5% (males 99.7%; females 99.4%) in 1995 (Source: UNESCO, *Statistical Yearbook*).

# Directory

## The Constitution

A new Constitution was approved by the Georgian legislature on 24 August 1995; it entered into force on 17 October. The Constitution replaced the Decree on State Power of November 1992 (which had functioned as an interim basic law). The following is a summary of the Constitution's main provisions:

### GENERAL PROVISIONS

Georgia is an independent, united and undivided state, as confirmed by the referendum conducted throughout the entire territory of the country (including Abkhazia and South Ossetia) on 31 March 1991, and in accordance with the Act on the Restoration of the State Independence of Georgia of 9 April. The Georgian state is a democratic republic. Its territorial integrity and the inviolability of its state borders are confirmed by the republic's Constitution and laws.

All state power belongs to the people, who exercise this power through referendums, other forms of direct democracy, and through their elected representatives. The State recognizes and defends universally recognized human rights and freedoms. The official state language is Georgian; in Abkhazia both Georgian and Abkhazian are recognized as state languages. While the State recognizes the exceptional role played by the Georgian Orthodox Church in Georgian history, it declares the complete freedom of faith and religion as well as the independence of the Church from the State. The capital is Tbilisi.

### FUNDAMENTAL HUMAN RIGHTS AND FREEDOMS

Georgian citizenship is acquired by birth and naturalization. A Georgian citizen may not concurrently be a citizen of another state. Every person is free by birth and equal before the law, irrespective of race, colour, language, sex, religion, political and other views, national, ethnic and social affiliation, origin and place of residence. Every person has the inviolable right to life, which is protected by law. No one may be subjected to torture or inhuman, cruel or humiliating treatment or punishment.

Freedom of speech, thought, conscience and faith are guaranteed. The mass media are free. Censorship is prohibited. The right to assemble publicly is guaranteed, as is the right to form public associations, including trade unions and political parties. Every citizen who has attained the age of 18 years has the right to participate in referendums and elections of state and local administrative bodies.

### THE GEORGIAN PARLIAMENT

The Georgian Parliament is the supreme representative body, implementing legislation and determining the basis of the country's domestic and foreign policies. It controls the activities of the Government, within the limits prescribed by the Constitution, and has other powers of implementation.

Parliament is elected on the basis of universal, equal and direct suffrage by secret ballot, for a term of four years. It is composed of 235 members: 150 elected by proportional representation (with a minimum requirement of 7% of the votes cast to secure parliamentary representation) and 85 by majority vote in single-member constituencies. Any citizen who has attained the age of 25 years and has the right to vote may be elected a member of Parliament. The instigation of criminal proceedings against a member of Parliament, and his/her detention or arrest, are only permitted upon approval by Parliament. A member of Parliament may not hold any position in state service or engage in entrepreneurial activities.

Parliament elects a Chairman and Deputy Chairmen (including one Deputy Chairman each from deputies elected in Abkhazia and Ajaria), for the length of its term of office. Members of Parliament may unite to form parliamentary factions. A faction must have no fewer than 10 members.

Following the creation of the appropriate conditions throughout the territory of Georgia and the formation of bodies of local self-government, the Georgian Parliament will be composed of two chambers: the Council of the Republic and the Senate. The Council of the Republic will be composed of deputies elected according to the proportional system. The Senate will be composed of deputies elected in Abkhazia, Ajaria and other territorial units of Georgia, and five members appointed by the President of Georgia.

### THE PRESIDENT OF GEORGIA AND THE GOVERNMENT

The President of Georgia is Head of State and the head of executive power. The President directs and implements domestic and foreign policy, ensures the unity and territorial integrity of the country, and supervises the activities of state bodies in accordance with the Constitution. The President is the supreme representative of Georgia in foreign relations. He/she is elected on the basis of universal, equal and direct suffrage by secret ballot, for a period of five years. The President may not be elected for more than two consecutive terms. Any citizen of Georgia who has the right to vote and who has attained the age of 35 years and lived in Georgia for no less than 15 years, is eligible to be elected President.

The President of Georgia concludes international treaties and agreements and conducts negotiations with foreign states; with the consent of Parliament, appoints and dismisses Georgian ambassadors and other diplomatic representatives; receives the credentials of ambassadors and other diplomatic representatives of foreign states and international organizations; with the consent of Parliament, appoints members of the Government and Ministers; is empowered to remove Ministers from their posts; submits to Parliament the draft state budget, after agreeing upon its basic content with parliamentary committees; in the event of an armed attack on Georgia, declares a state of war, and concludes peace; during war or mass disorders, when the country's territorial integrity is threatened, or in the event of a *coup d'état* or an armed uprising, an ecological catastrophe or epidemic, or in other instances when the bodies of state power cannot implement their constitutional powers normally, declares a state of emergency; with the consent of Parliament, has the right to halt the activities of representative bodies of self-government or territorial units (if their activities create a threat to the sovereignty and territorial integrity of the country) as well as to halt state bodies in the exercise of their constitutional powers; signs and promulgates laws; decides questions of citizenship and the granting of political asylum; grants pardons; schedules elections to Parliament and other representative bodies; has the right to revoke acts of subordinate executive bodies; is the Commander-in-Chief of the Armed Forces; and appoints members of the National Security Council, chairs its meetings, and appoints and dismisses military commanders.

The President enjoys immunity. During his/her period in office, he/she may not be arrested, and no criminal proceedings may be instigated against him/her. In the event that the President violates the Constitution, betrays the State or commits other crimes, Parliament may remove him/her from office (with the approval of the Constitutional Court or the Supreme Court).

Members of the Government are accountable to the President. They do not have the right to hold other posts (except party posts), to engage in entrepreneurial activities or to receive a wage or any other permanent remuneration for any other activities. Members of the Government may be removed from their posts by an edict of the President or by Parliament. Ministries perform state management in specific spheres of state and public life. Each Ministry is headed by a Minister, who independently adopts decisions on questions within his/her sphere of jurisdiction.

### JUDICIAL POWER

Judicial power is independent and is implemented only by the courts. Judges are independent in their activities and are subordinate only to the Constitution and the law. Court proceedings are held in public (except for certain specified instances). The decision of the court is delivered in public. Judges enjoy immunity. It is prohibited to instigate criminal proceedings against a judge or to detain or arrest him/her, without the consent of the Chairman of the Supreme Court.

The Constitutional Court is the legal body of constitutional control. It is composed of nine judges, three of whom are appointed by the President, three elected by Parliament, and three appointed by the Supreme Court. The term of office of members of the Constitutional Court is 10 years.

The Supreme Court supervises legal proceedings in general courts according to the established judicial procedure and, as the court of first instance, examines cases determined by law. On the recommendation of the President of Georgia, the Chairman and judges of the Supreme Court are elected by Parliament for a period of at least 10 years.

The Procurator's Office is an institution of judicial power, which carries out criminal prosecution, supervises the preliminary investigation and the execution of a punishment, and supports the state prosecution. On the recommendation of the President of Georgia, the Procurator-General is appointed by Parliament for a term of five years. Lower-ranking procurators are appointed by the Procurator-General.

## DEFENCE OF THE STATE

Georgia has armed forces to protect the independence, sovereignty and territorial integrity of the country, and also to fulfil international obligations. The President of Georgia approves the structure of the armed forces and Parliament ratifies their numerical strength, on the recommendation of the National Security Council. The National Security Council, which is headed by the President of Georgia, carries out military organizational development and the defence of the country.

# The Government

## HEAD OF STATE

**President of Georgia:** EDUARD SHEVARDNADZE (elected by direct popular vote 5 November 1995; re-elected 9 April 2000).

## GOVERNMENT
(October 2003)

**Minister of State and Head of the State Chancellery:** AVTANDIL DZHORBENADZE.

**Minister of Agriculture and Produce:** DAVIT KIRVALIDZE.

**Minister of Culture:** SESILI GOGIBERIDZE.

**Minister of Defence:** Gen. DAVIT TEVZADZE.

**Minister of Economics, Industry and Trade:** GIORGI GACHECHILADZE.

**Minister of Education:** ALEKSANDZRE KARTOZIA.

**Minister of Environmental Protection and Natural Resources:** NINO CHKHOBADZE.

**Minister of Finance:** MIRIAN GOGIASHVILI.

**Minister of Foreign Affairs:** IRAKLI MENAGHARISHVILI.

**Minister of Fuel and Energy:** MAMUKA NIKOLEISHVILI (designate).

**Minister of Labour, Health and Social Welfare:** AMIRAN GAMKRELIDZE.

**Minister of Internal Affairs:** KOBA NARCHEMASHVILI.

**Minister of Justice:** MARIAM TSATSANASHVILI.

**Minister of Refugees and Resettlement:** VALERIAN VASHAKIDZE.

**Minister of State Property Management:** SOLOMON PAVLIASHVILI.

**Minister of State Security:** VALERIAN KHABURDZHANIA.

**Minister of Transport and Communications:** Dr MERAB ADEISHVILI.

**Minister of Construction and Urban Planning:** GIORGI ISAKADZE.

**Minister of Emergency Affairs:** MALKHAZ KAKABADZE.

## MINISTRIES

**Office of the President:** 300002 Tbilisi, Rustaveli 29; tel. (32) 99-74-75; fax (32) 99-96-30; e-mail office@presidpress.gov.ge.

**Office of the Government:** 380018 Tbilisi, Ingorovka 7; tel. (32) 93-59-07; fax (32) 98-23-54.

**Ministry of Agriculture and Produce:** 380023 Tbilisi, Kostava 41; tel. (32) 99-02-72; fax (32) 99-94-44.

**Ministry of Construction and Urban Planning:** 380060 Tbilisi, Vazha Pshavela 16; tel. (32) 37-42-76; fax (32) 22-05-41.

**Ministry of Culture:** 380008 Tbilisi, Rustaveli 37; tel. (32) 93-22-55; fax (32) 99-90-37; e-mail info@mc.gov.ge; internet www.mc.gov.ge.

**Ministry of Defence:** 380007 Tbilisi, Universitetis 2A; tel. (32) 98-39-30; fax (32) 98-39-29.

**Ministry of Economics, Industry and Trade:** 380008 Tbilisi, Chanturia 12; tel. (32) 93-33-61; fax (32) 93-15-35.

**Ministry of Education:** 380002 Tbilisi, Uznadze 52; tel. (32) 95-88-86; fax (32) 77-00-73; internet www.parliament.ge/education.

**Ministry of Emergency Affairs:** Tbilisi, Leonidze 2; tel. (32) 92-18-91; e-mail msa@gol.ge; internet msa.gol.ge.

**Ministry of Environmental Protection and Natural Resources:** 380015 Tbilisi, Kostava 68A; tel. (32) 23-06-64; fax (32) 94-34-20; e-mail irisi@gmep.kneta.ge; internet www.parliament.ge/governance/gov/enviro/parliament/ministry.htm.

**Ministry of Finance:** 380062 Tbilisi, Abashidze 70; tel. (32) 22-68-05; fax (32) 93-19-22; e-mail minister@mof.ge; internet www.mof.ge.

**Ministry of Foreign Affairs:** 380018 Tbilisi, 9 April 4; tel. (32) 98-93-77; fax (32) 99-72-48; internet www.mfa.gov.ge.

**Ministry of Fuel and Energy:** 380007 Tbilisi, Lermontov 10; tel. (32) 99-60-98; fax (32) 93-35-42; internet www.minenergy.ge.

**Ministry of Internal Affairs:** 380014 Tbilisi, Didikheivani 10; tel. (32) 99-62-96; fax (32) 98-65-32.

**Ministry of Justice:** 380008 Tbilisi, Griboedov 19; tel. (32) 93-27-21; fax (32) 93-02-25.

**Ministry of Labour, Health and Social Welfare:** 380060 Tbilisi, K. Gamsakhurdia 30; tel. (32) 38-70-71; fax (32) 37-00-86.

**Ministry of Refugees and Resettlement:** 380008 Tbilisi, Dadiani 30; tel. (32) 94-16-11; fax (32) 92-14-27.

**Ministry of State Property Management:** 380062 Tbilisi, Chavchavadze 64; tel. (32) 29-48-75; fax (32) 22-52-09; internet web.sanet.ge/mospm.

**Ministry of State Security:** 380018 Tbilisi, 9 April 4; tel. (32) 92-23-15; fax (32) 93-27-91.

**Ministry of Transport and Communications:** 380060 Tbilisi, Rustaveli 12; tel. (32) 93-28-46; fax (32) 77-00-17; e-mail mtc@iberiapac.ge; internet www.mtc.gov.ge.

# President and Legislature

## PRESIDENT

### Presidential Election, 9 April 2000

| Candidates | Votes | % |
|---|---|---|
| Eduard Shevardnadze | 1,870,311 | 79.82 |
| Dzhumber Patiashvili | 390,486 | 16.66 |
| Kartlos Gharibashvili | 7,863 | 0.34 |
| Avtandil Joglidze | 5,942 | 0.25 |
| Vazha Zhghenti | 3,363 | 0.14 |
| Tengiz Asanidze | 2,793 | 0.12 |
| **Total*** | **2,343,176** | **100.00** |

* Including 62,418 spoilt voting papers (2.66% of the total).

## GEORGIAN PARLIAMENT

### Sakartvelos Parlamenti

380028 Tbilisi, Rustaveli 8; tel. (32) 93-61-70; fax (32) 99-93-86; internet www.parliament.ge.

**Chairman:** NINO BURDZHANADZE.

**Deputy Chairmen:** GIORGI TSERETELI, ROSTOM DZHAPARIDZE, VAKHTANG KOLBAYA, VAKHTANG RCHEULISHVILI, ELDAR SHENGELAIA, MERAB SAMADASHVILI.

### General Election, 31 October and 14 November 1999

| Parties and blocs | Party lists | | Single-member constituency seats | Total seats |
|---|---|---|---|---|
| | % of votes* | Seats | | |
| Citizens' Union of Georgia | 41.9 | 85 | 45 | 130 |
| Union for the Revival of Georgia bloc | 25.7 | 51 | 7 | 58 |
| Industry Will Save Georgia bloc | 7.8 | 14 | 1 | 15 |
| Georgian Labour Party | 6.7 | 0 | 2 | 2 |
| Abkhazian deputies† | — | — | 12 | 12 |
| Independent candidates | — | — | 17 | 17 |
| **Total** (incl. others) | **100.0** | **150** | **84** | **234‡** |

* In order to win seats, parties needed to obtain at least 7% of the total votes cast.

† Owing to the electoral boycott in the secessionist region of Abkhazia, the mandates of 12 deputies from Abkhazia (elected to the legislature in 1992) were renewed.

‡ One of the single-member constituency seats remained unfilled.

According to the Constitution of August 1995, the unicameral Georgian Parliament would be transformed into a bicameral body following the eventual restoration of Georgia's territorial integrity. The future Parliament would comprise a Council of the Republic and a Senate (the latter representing the various territorial units of the country).

# Local Government

Georgia contains three autonomous territories: the Autonomous Republic of Ajaria; and Abkhazia and South Ossetia. The status of the latter two were both disputed (see p. 208), although some settlement involving a degree of autonomy was provided for by the 1995 Constitution. The rest of the country is divided into nine regions (oblasts) headed by governors appointed by the central Government. Local elections, originally scheduled to take place on 4 November 2001, were held on 2 June 2002.

### OBLASTS

**Guria:** Central Administration, Ozurgety; tel. (296) 99-66-75; Governor KARLO GUJABIDZE.

**Imereti:** Central Administration, Kutaisi; tel. (331) 43-135; Governor TEMUR SHASHIASHVILI.

**Kakheti:** Central Administration, Telavi; tel. (350) 99-67-03; Governor BIDZINA SONGHULASHVILI.

**Kvemo Kartli:** Central Administration, Rustavi; tel. (34) 93-60-35; Governor LEVAN MAMALADZE.

**Mtskheta Mtianeti:** Central Administration, Mtskheta; tel. (225) 99-90-40; Governor ARMAZ SHAMANAURI.

**Ragha-Lechkumi and Kvemo Svaneti:** Central Administration, Ambrolauri; tel. (203) 5-61; Governor IRAKLI PRUIDZE.

**Samegrelo-Zemo Svaneti:** Central Administration, Zugdidi; tel. (215) 94-13-36; Governor BONDO JIKIA.

**Samtskhe-Javakheti:** Central Administration, Akhaltsikhe; tel. (265) 99-32-39; Governor GELA KVARATSKHELIA.

**Shida Kartli:** Central Administration, Gori; tel. (270) 93-32-39; Governor DAVIT KOBLIANIDZE.

# Political Organizations

More than 40 parties and alliances contested the legislative election of 31 October 1999. The following are among the most prominent parties in Georgia:

**Agrarian Party of Georgia:** Tbilisi; f. 1994; Chair. ROIN LIPARTELIANI.

**All Georgian Union of Revival:** Batumi, Gogebashvili 7; tel. (222) 76-500; f. 1992; 200,000 mems; Chair. ASLAN ABASHIDZE.

**Christian Democratic Union of Georgia:** 380060 Tbilisi, Kazbegi 19; tel. (32) 37-25-34; fax (32) 37-47-44; f. 1990; centre-right; formed part of the For a New Georgia bloc in 2003; Leader VAZHA LORTKIPANIDZE.

**Citizens' Union of Georgia (CUG)** (SMK): Tbilisi, Chavchavadze 55; tel. (32) 99-94-79; fax (32) 93-15-84; e-mail cug@access.sanet.ge; f. 1993; formed part of the For a New Georgia bloc in 2003; 300,000 mems; Chair. AVTANDIL DZHORBENADZE; Exec. Sec. GELA KVARATSKELIA.

**Communist Party of Georgia:** Tbilisi; tel. (32) 53-25-17; f. 1992; Chair. IVANE TSIKLAURI.

**Conservative Party of Georgia:** Tbilisi, Sabaduri 32; tel. (32) 72-44-73; f. 1995; legal successor to the Liberal–Conservative Party; separated from the Monarchist Party; Chair. GIORGI KARTOZIA.

**Georgian Labour Party:** Tbilisi, Javakhishvili 48; tel. (32) 94-39-22; fax (32) 96-60-46; f. 1997; main aim is the social protection of the population; Chair. SHALVA NATELASHVILI; 64,000 mems.

**Georgian People's Party:** Tbilisi; f. 1996 by dissident members of the National Democratic Party of Georgia.

**Georgian Social Democratic Party:** 380018 Tbilisi, 9 April 2; tel. (32) 99-95-50; fax (32) 98-73-89; f. 1893; ruling party 1918–21; re-established 1990; formed part of the Dzhumber Patiashvili-Unity bloc in 2003; Chair. Prof. JEMAL KAKHNIASHVILI.

**Georgian Social-Realistic Party:** f. 1999; centrist party aimed at building united democratic Georgian state; Chair. Dr GURAM BEROZASHVILI.

**Georgian Union of Reformers and Agrarians:** Tbilisi; f. 1999; merger of Reformers' Union of Georgia and the Agrarian Union.

**Industry Will Save Georgia:** Tbilisi, Marjvena Sanapiro 7; tel. (32) 94-09-81; f. 1999; opposition alliance; formed electoral bloc with Sporting Georgia in 2003; Chair. GIORGI TOPADZE.

**Liberal Democratic Party:** Tbilisi; Chair. MIKHEIL NANEISHVILI.

**Motherland Political Alliance** (Samshoblo): Tbilisi; left-wing alliance, which included the Georgian Conservative-Monarchist Party to contest the 2003 general election; renamed in 2003 (fmrly the All-Georgian Patriotic Alliance, which included the People's Patriotic Union); Co-Chair. IGOR GIORGADZE, TEMUR ZHORZHOLIANI.

**Mtsvanta Partia** (Green Party of Georgia): 380012 Tbilisi, Davit Aghmashenebeli 182; tel. (32) 95-20-33; fax (32) 35-16-74; e-mail party@access.sanet.ge; internet www.greensparty.ge; f. 1990; formed part of the For a New Georgia bloc in 2003; Chair. GIORGI GACHECHILADZE.

**National Democratic Party of Georgia:** 380008 Tbilisi, Rustaveli 21; tel. (32) 98-35-36; fax (32) 93-19-78; e-mail ndpfc@parliament.ge; f. 1981; centre-right; formed part of the For a New Georgia bloc in 2003; Leader IRINA SHARISHVILI-CHANTURIA.

**National Independence Party:** 380007 Tbilisi, Machabeli 8; tel. (32) 98-27-70; f. 1988; Chair. IRAKLI TSERETELI.

**National Movement:** 380018 Tbilisi, Vukol Beridze 9; tel. (32) 93-89-69; fax (32) 92-12-31; f. 2001; formed an electoral bloc, the National Movement-Democratic Front in 2002; Co-Chair. MIKHEIL SAAKASHVILI, LEVAN BERDZENISHVILI.

**Nationalist Party:** Tbilisi; tel. (32) 95-14-85; f. 1993; Chair. ZAZA VASHAKMADZE.

**New Rights Party:** 380014 Tbilisi, Bevreti 3; tel. (32) 92-03-13; fax (32) 92-38-58; e-mail newrights@kheta.ge; internet www.newrights .com; f. 2000 as the New Faction by former members of the Citizens' Union of Georgia and other political parties; name changed as above in 2001; won majority of seats in the municipal elections held in June 2002; formed New Right bloc for the 2003 election; Chair. DAVIT GAMKRELIDZE.

**Party for Liberation of Abkhazia:** Tbilisi; advocates the restoration of the jurisdiction of Georgia and constitutional order in Abkhazia; f. 1998; formed part of the For a New Georgia bloc for the 2003 legislative election; Chair. TAMAZ NADAREISHVILI.

**People's Party—Didgori:** Tbilisi, Uznadze 56; tel. (32) 96-03-69; fax (32) 93-57-98; e-mail pppess@parliament.ge; f. 1996; Chair. MAMUKA GIORGIADZE.

**Republican Party of Georgia:** Tbilisi, Antoneli 31/2; tel. and fax (32) 93-25-36; e-mail cdc@access.sanet.ge; internet www.repblic.org .ge; f. 1995; absorbed Georgian Popular Front (f. 1989); Chair. DAVIT BERDZENISHVILI.

**Rightist Alternative Alliance:** Tbilisi; f. 2000; alliance between the Union of Georgian Traditionalists and the Liberal Economic Party.

**Round Table—Free Georgia:** Tbilisi, Dgebuadze 4; tel. (32) 95-48-20; f. 1990; opposition party uniting supporters of former President Zviad Gamsakhurdia; Chair. SOSO DZHADZHANIDZE.

**Socialist Party of Georgia:** Tbilisi, Leselidze 41; tel. (32) 93-10—21; fax (32) 93-27-09; e-mail spg@geo-plus.net; internet www .geo-plus.net/spg; f. 1995; formed part of the For a New Georgia bloc for the 2003 general election; Chair. VAKHTANG RCHEULISHVILI.

**Union for the Revival of Georgia:** Batumi, Ninoshvili 5; tel. (222) 76-500; fax (222) 76-510; principal opposition alliance including parties loyal to the former President, Zviad Gamsakhurdia (the All-Georgian Union of Revival, the Socialist Party of Georgia, the Union of Traditionalists, the People's Party and the 21st Century bloc); Chair. ASLAN ABASHIDZE.

**Union of Georgian Realists:** f. 1997; aims to achieve political and economic stability in a united Georgia.

**Union of Georgian Traditionalists:** Tbilisi, Arsena 10; f. 1990; formed part of the Burdzhanadze-Democrats bloc for the 2003 general election; Chair. AKAKI ASATIANI.

**Union of National Concord and Justice:** Tbilisi; f. 2002; formed part of the National Accord-Iberian Revival bloc for the 2003 legislative election; Leader GURAM ABSANDZE.

**United Communist Party of Georgia:** Tbilisi; tel. (32) 38-41-65; f. 1994; 87,000 mems (2000); First Sec. PANTELEIMON GIORGADZE.

**United Democrats:** Tbilisi, Marshal Gelovani 4A; tel. (32) 95-98-23; f. 2002; radical centrist; formed from the reformist faction of CUG; formed part of the Burdzhanadze-Democrats bloc for the 2003 legislative election; Chair. ZURAB ZHVANIA.

**Unity Alliance** (Ertoba): Tbilisi, Svobodi pl.; tel. (32) 92-30-65; fax (32) 93-46-94; e-mail ertoba@post.com; internet www.ertoba.ge; f. 2001; social-democratic; formed part of the Dzhumber Patiashvili-Unity bloc for the 2003 general election; Co-Chair. DZHUMBER PATIASHVILI, ALEXANDER CHACHIA.

# Diplomatic Representation

### EMBASSIES IN GEORGIA

**Armenia:** 380002 Tbilisi, Tetelashvili 4; tel. (32) 95-94-43; fax (32) 99-01-26; Ambassador GEORGE KHOSROEV.

**Azerbaijan:** 380079 Tbilisi, Mukhadze 4; tel. and fax (32) 23-40-37; Ambassador HAJAN HAJIYEV.

**China, People's Republic:** 380008 Tbilisi, Barnov 52; POB 224; tel. (32) 99-80-11; fax (32) 93-12-76; e-mail gzj@access.sanet.ge; Ambassador XU JIANGUO.

**Czech Republic:** 380054 Tbilisi, Tsereteli 57; tel. (32) 95-44-37; fax (32) 95-40-92; e-mail tbilisi@embassy.mzv.cz; Ambassador JIŘI NEK-VASIL.

**France:** 380008 Tbilisi, Gogebashvili 15; tel. (32) 932-28-51; fax (32) 98-71-15; Ambassador SALOMÉ ZOURABICHVILI (designate).

**Germany:** 380012 Tbilisi, Davit Aghmashenebeli 166; tel. (32) 95-09-36; fax (32) 95-89-10; e-mail deut.bot.tbilissi@access.sanet.ge; Ambassador UWE SCHRAMM.

**Greece:** 380079 Tbilisi, Arakishvili 5; tel. and fax (32) 93-89-81; fax (32) 00-10-39; e-mail grembgeo@access.sanet.ge; Ambassador CONSTANTINA MAVROSKELIDOU.

**Holy See:** 380086 Tbilisi, Dzhgenti 40, Nutsubidze Plateau II; tel. (32) 94-13-05; fax (32) 29-39-44; e-mail nuntius@access.sanet.ge; Apostolic Nuncio Most Rev. CLAUDIO GUGEROTTI (Titular Archbishop of Ravello).

**Iran:** 380060 Tbilisi, Zovreti 16; tel. (32) 98-69-90; fax (32) 98-69-93; Ambassador HOSSEIN AMIAN TUSIMI.

**Israel:** 380012 Tbilisi, Davit Aghmashenebeli 61; tel. (32) 96-02-13; fax (32) 95-17-09; Ambassador EHUD EITAM.

**Italy:** 380008 Tbilisi, Chitadze 3A; tel. (32) 99-64-18; fax (32) 99-64-15; e-mail ambita.tbilisi@access.sanet.ge; Ambassador FABRIZIO ROMANO.

**Korea, Republic:** Tbilisi; Ambassador YI CHONG-PIN.

**Poland:** Tbilisi, Zubalashvili 19; tel. (32) 92-03-98; fax (32) 92-03-97; e-mail ambpolgruzja@access.sanet.ge; Chargé d'affaires JACEK MULTANOWSKI.

**Romania:** Tbilisi, Lvov 7; tel. (32) 25-00-98; fax (32) 25-00-97; e-mail ambasada@caucasus.net; Ambassador CONSTANTIN GIRBEA.

**Russia:** 380002 Tbilisi, Tsinamdzgvrishvili 90; tel. (32) 95-59-11; fax (32) 95-52-33; Ambassador VLADIMIR CHKHIKVISHVILI.

**Turkey:** 380002 Tbilisi, Davit Aghmashenebeli 61; tel. (32) 95-20-14; fax (32) 95-18-10; e-mail tiblisbe@mfa.gov.tr; Ambassador DICLE KOPUZ.

**Ukraine:** 380060 Tbilisi, Oniashvili 75; tel. (32) 98-93-62; fax (32) 23-71-45; e-mail emb_ge@mfa.gov.ua; internet www.uaembingeorgia.gov.ua; Ambassador MYKOLA SPYS.

**United Kingdom:** 380003 Tbilisi, Sheraton Palace Hotel; tel. (32) 95-54-97; fax (32) 00-10-65; e-mail british.embassy@caucasus.net; internet www.britishembassy.org.ge; Ambassador (vacant).

**USA:** 380026 Tbilisi, Atoneli 25; tel. (32) 98-99-67; fax (32) 93-37-59; internet web.sanet.ge/usembassy; Ambassador RICHARD MILES.

## Judicial System

**Constitutional Court:** Tbilisi, Rustaveli 29; e-mail court@const.gov.ge; internet www.constcourt.gov.ge; Chair. DZHONI KHETSURIANI.

### Supreme Court

380010 Tbilisi, Zubalashvili 32; tel. (32) 93-12-62; fax (32) 92-08-76; e-mail reception@supremecourt.ge; internet www.supremecourt.ge. Chair. LADO CHANTURIA.

**Procurator-General:** NUGZAR GABRICHIDZE.

**First Deputy Procurator-General:** BADRI BITSADZE.

**Council of Justice:** Tbilisi, Davit Aghmashenebeli 80; tel. and fax (32) 95-86-77; e-mail justice@caucasus.net; f. 1997; 12-member council that co-ordinates the appointment of judges and their activities; four mems nominated by the President, four by Parliament and four by the Supreme Court; Exec. Sec. ZURAB ABASHIDZE.

## Religion

### CHRISTIANITY

#### The Georgian Orthodox Church

The Georgian Orthodox Church is divided into 27 dioceses, and includes not only Georgian parishes, but also several Russian, Greek and Armenian Orthodox communities, which are under the jurisdiction of the Primate of the Georgian Orthodox Church. There are 40 monasteries and convents, two theological academies and four seminaries.

**Patriarchate:** 380005 Tbilisi, King Erekle II Sq. 1; tel. (32) 99-03-78; fax (32) 98-71-14; e-mail ecclesia@access.sanet.ge; internet www.orthodox-patriarchate-of-georgia.org.ge; Catholicos-Patriarch of All Georgia ILIA II.

#### The Roman Catholic Church

The Apostolic Administrator of the Caucasus is the Apostolic Nuncio to Georgia, Armenia and Azerbaijan, who is resident in Tbilisi (see Diplomatic Representation).

### ISLAM

There are Islamic communities among the Ajarians, Abkhazians, Azerbaijanis, Kurds and some Ossetians. The country falls under the jurisdiction of the Muslim Board of Transcaucasia, based in Baku (Azerbaijan).

## The Press

**Department of the Press:** 380008 Tbilisi, Jorjiashvili 12; tel. (32) 98-70-08; govt regulatory body; Dir V. RTSKHILADZE.

### PRINCIPAL NEWSPAPERS

In 2000 184 newspaper titles were printed. Those listed below appear in Georgian, except where otherwise stated.

**Akhalgazrda Iverieli** (Young Iberian): Tbilisi, Kostava 14; tel. (32) 93-31-49; 3 a week; organ of the Georgian Parliament; Editor MERAB BALARJISHVILI.

**Akhali Taoba** (New Generation): Tbilisi, Davit Aghmashenebeli 89/24; tel. (32) 95-25-89; fax (32) 94-06-91; e-mail akhtao@geo.net.ge; internet www.opentext.org.ge/akhalitaoba; f. 1993; in Georgian; Editor SOSO GONIASHVILI.

**Dilis Gazeti** (Morning Newspaper): Tbilisi, Marjanishvili 5; tel. (32) 96-91-88; fax (32) 96-91-81; e-mail dilgazet@access.sanet.ge; internet www.opentext.ge/dilisgazeti; Editor MANANA KARTOZIA.

**Droni** (Times): Tbilisi, Kostava 14; tel. (32) 99-56-54; e-mail newspdroni@usa.net; internet www.opentext.org.ge/droni/; 2 a week; Editor-in-Chief SOSO SIMONISHVILI.

**Eri** (Nation): Tbilisi; weekly; organ of the Georgian Parliament; Editor A. SILAGADZE.

**Ertoba:** Tbilisi; f. 1918; weekly; organ of the Georgian Social Democratic Party.

**Georgian Messenger:** Tbilisi, Chavchavadze 55; tel. and fax (32) 22-76-21; e-mail gtze@messenger.com.ge; internet www.messenger.com.ge; f. 1919; daily; in English; Editor-in-Chief ZAZA GACHECHILADZE.

**Georgian Times:** Tbilisi, Gorgasali 37; tel. (32) 93-10-25; fax (32) 99-60-97; e-mail times@gtze.com.ge; internet www.georgiantimes.ge; f. 1993; weekly; in English, Georgian and Russian; Editor-in-Chief ZVIAD POCHKHUA; circ. 2,000.

**Iberia Spektri** (Iberian Spectrum): Tbilisi, Machabeli 11; tel. (32) 98-73-87; fax (32) 98-73-88; internet www.opentext.org.ge/iberia-spectri/; Editor IRAKLI GOTSIRIDZE.

**Literaturuli Sakartvelo** (Literary Georgia): Tbilisi, Gudiashvili Sq. 2; tel. (32) 99-84-04; internet www.opentext.org.ge/literaturulisakartvelo/; weekly; organ of the Union of Writers of Georgia; Editor TAMAZ TSIVTSIVADZE.

**Mamuli** (Native Land): Tbilisi; fortnightly; organ of the Rustaveli Society; Editor T. CHANTURIA.

**Respublika** (Republic): 380096 Tbilisi, Kostava 14; tel. and fax (32) 93-43-91; f. 1990; weekly; independent; Editor J. NINUA; circ. 40,000.

**Rezonansi:** Tbilisi, Davit Aghmashenebeli 89–24; tel. (32) 95-69-38; fax (32) 96-92-60; e-mail n1001@geo.net.ge; internet www.resonancedaily.com.ge; f. 1992; daily; Editor-in-Chief LASHA TUGUSHI; circ. 10,000.

**Sakartvelo** (Georgia): 380096 Tbilisi, Kostava 14; tel. (32) 99-92-26; internet www.opentext.org.ge/sakartvelo/; 5 a week; organ of the Georgian Parliament; Editor SERGO DZHANASHIA.

**Shvidi Dghe** (Seven Days): Tbilisi, Krilov 5; tel. (32) 94-35-52; fax (32) 95-40-76; e-mail dge7@caucasus.net; internet www.opentext.org.ge_7dge; f. 1991; weekly; Dir GELA GURGENIDZE; Editor KOBA AKHALBEDASHVILI; circ. 3,000.

**Svobodnaya Gruziya** (Free Georgia): Tbilisi, Rustaveli 42; tel. (32) 93-13-54; fax (32) 93-17-06; e-mail new@caucasus.net; internet www.svobodnaya-gruzia.com; f. 1922 as *Zanya Vostoka*, name changed as above in 1991; socio-political; in Russian; Editor-in-Chief TATO LASCHISHVILI; circ. 5,000.

**Tavisupali Sakartvelo** (Free Georgia): 380008 Tbilisi, POB W227; tel. (32) 95-48-20; weekly; organ of Round Table—Free Georgia party.

**Tbilisi Times:** 380007 Tbilisi, Kostava 20; tel. (32) 98-76-13; fax (32) 99-63-24; e-mail david@tbilisitimes.com; internet www .tbilisitimes.com; in English and Georgian; independent, non-profit; Dirs DAVID DZIDZIKASHVILI, SHAVLEG SHAVERDASHVILI.

**Vestnik Gruzii** (Georgian Herald): Tbilisi; 5 a week; organ of the Georgian Parliament; in Russian; Editor V. KESHELAVA.

**Weekly Post:** 380002 Tbilisi, POB 85; tel. and fax (32) 94-07-07; e-mail weekpost@iberiapac.ge; f. 1991; Editor BESIK KHARANAULI.

## PRINCIPAL PERIODICALS

**Alashara:** 394981 Sukhumi, Govt House, kor. 1; tel. (122) 2-35-40; organ of the Abkhazian Writers' Organization of the Union of Writers of Georgia; in Abkhazian.

**Dila** (Morning): 380096 Tbilisi, Kostava 14; tel. (32) 93-41-30; f. 1904; fortnightly; illustrated; for 5–12 year-olds; Editor-in-Chief DODO TSIVTSIVADZE; circ. 4,500.

**Drosha** (Banner): Tbilisi; f. 1923; monthly; politics and fiction; Editor O. KINKLADZE.

**Fidiyag:** Tskhinvali; tel. (344) 2-22-65; organ of the South Ossetian Writers' Organization of the Union of Writers of Georgia; in Ossetian.

**Khelovneba** (Art): Tbilisi; f. 1953, fmrly Sabchota Khelovneba (Soviet Art); monthly; journal of the Ministry of Culture; Editor N. GURABANIDZE.

**Kritika** (Criticism): 380008 Tbilisi, Rustaveli 42; tel. (32) 93-22-85; f. 1972; every 2 months; publ. by Merani Publishing House; journal of the Union of Writers of Georgia; literature, miscellaneous; Editor V. KHARCHILAVA.

**Kurieri:** Tbilisi, Kostava 14; tel. (32) 99-00-49; Editor IRAKLI TSINTSADZE.

**Literaturnaya Gruziya** (Literary Georgia): 380008 Tbilisi, Kostava 5; tel. (32) 99-06-59; fax (32) 22-47-37; e-mail abzianidze@ hotmail.com; f. 1957; quarterly journal; politics, art and fiction; in Russian; Editor Prof. ZAZA ABZIANIDZE.

**Metsniereba da Tekhnika** (Science and Technology): 380060 Tbilisi; f. 1949; monthly; publ. by the Metsniereba Publishing House; journal of the Georgian Academy of Sciences; popular; Editor Z. TSILOSANI.

**Mnatobi** (Luminary): 380008 Tbilisi, Rustaveli 28; tel. (32) 99-51-56; f. 1924; monthly; journal of the Union of Writers of Georgia; fiction, poetry and arts; Editor T. CHILADZE.

**Nakaduli** (Stream): Tbilisi, Kostava 14; tel. (32) 93-31-81; f. 1926; fmrly *Pioneri*; monthly; journal of the Ministry of Education; illustrated; for 10–15-year-olds; Editor MANANA GELASHVILI; circ. 5,000.

**Niangi** (Crocodile): 380096 Tbilisi, Kostava 14; f. 1923; fortnightly; satirical; Editor Z. BOLKVADZE.

**Politika** (Politics): Tbilisi; theoretical, political, social sciences; Editor M. GOGUADZE.

**Sakartvelos Kali** (Georgian Woman): 380096 Tbilisi, Kostava 14; tel. (32) 99-98-71; f. 1957; popular, socio-political and literary; Editor-in-Chief NARGIZA MGELADZE; circ. 3,000.

**Sakartvelos Metsnierebata Akedemiis Matsne** (Herald of the Georgian Academy of Sciences, Biological Series): Tbilisi; f. 1975; 6 a year; in Georgian, English and Russian; Editor-in-Chief VAZHA OKUJAVA.

**Sakartvelos Metsnierebata Akedemiis Matsne** (Herald of the Georgian Academy of Sciences, Chemical Series): Tbilisi; f. 1975; quarterly; in Georgian, English and Russian; Editor-in-Chief TEIMURAZ ANDRONIKASHVILI.

**Sakartvelos Metsnierebata Akademiis Moambe** (Bulletin of Georgian Academy of Sciences): 380008 Tbilisi, Rustaveli 52; tel. (32) 99-75-93; fax (32) 99-88-23; e-mail bulletin@presid.achet.ge; f. 1940; 6 a year; in Georgian and English; Editor-in-Chief ALBERT TAVKHELIDZE.

**Sarke:** Tbilisi, Chubinashvili 50; tel. (32) 96-75-43; Editor MEDEA SANAIA.

**Saunje** (Treasure): 380007 Tbilisi, Dadiani 2; tel. (32) 72-47-31; f. 1974; 6 a year; organ of the Union of Writers of Georgia; foreign literature in translation; Editor S. NISHNIANIDZE.

**Tsiskari** (Dawn): 380007 Tbilisi, Khidis 1/29; tel. (32) 99-85-81; f. 1957; monthly; organ of the Union of Writers of Georgia; fiction; Editor ZAUR KALANDIA.

## NEWS AGENCIES

**Black Sea Press:** Tbilisi, Rustaveli 42; tel. (32) 98-94-69; fax (32) 93-17-49; Dir DAVIT IMEDASHVILI.

**Iberia:** Tbilisi, Marjanishvili 5; tel. (32) 93-64-22; Dir KAKHA GAGLOSHVILI.

**Iprinda:** Tbilisi, Rustaveli 19; tel. (32) 99-03-77; fax (32) 98-73-65; Dir KETEVAN BOKHUA.

**Kontakt:** Tbilisi, Kostava 68; tel. (32) 36-04-79; fax (32) 22-18-45; Dir DIMITRI KIKVADZE.

**Prime News Agency:** Tbilisi, Kutateladze 5; tel. (32) 92-32-12; fax (32) 92-32-02; e-mail pna@pna.com.ge; internet www.prime-news .com.ge; f. 1997 after dissolution of BGI news agency.

**Sakinform:** 380008 Tbilisi, Rustaveli 42; tel. (32) 93-19-20; fax (32) 99-92-00; e-mail gha@lberiapac.ge; internet www.sakinform.ge; f. 1921; state information agency; Dir KAKHA IMNADZE.

**Sarke Information Agency:** 380002 Tbilisi, Davit Aghmashenebeli 63; tel. (32) 95-06-59; fax (32) 95-08-37; e-mail info@sarke.com; internet www.sarke.com; f. 1992; economic and business news from Georgia and the Caucasus; Dir VALERIAN KHUKHUNASHVILI; Editor-in-Chief VICTORIA GUJELASHVILI.

### JOURNALISTS' ASSOCIATION

**Independent Association of Georgian Journalists:** 380002 Tbilisi, Marjanishvili 5, Rm 230; tel. and fax (32) 95-68-50; e-mail iagj@ gol.ge; internet www.iagj.gol.ge; f. 2000; Pres. ZVIAD POCHKHUA.

**Journalists' Federation of Georgia:** 380005 Tbilisi, Erekles 6; tel. (32) 98-24-47; Chair. AKAKI SIKHARULIDZE.

# Publishers

**Ganatleba** (Education): 380064 Tbilisi, Chubinashvili 50; tel. (32) 95-50-97; f. 1957; educational, literature; Dir L. KHUNDADZE.

**Georgian National Universal Encyclopaedia:** Tbilisi, Tsereteli 1; Editor-in-Chief A. SAKVARELIDZE.

**Khelovneba** (Art): 380002 Tbilisi, Davit Aghmashenebeli 179; f. 1947; Dir N. DZHASHI.

**Merani** (Writer): 380008 Tbilisi, Rustaveli 42; tel. (32) 99-64-92; fax (32) 93-46-75; e-mail hmerani@iberiapac.ge; f. 1921; fiction; Dir G. GVERDTSITELI.

**Metsniereba** (Sciences): 380060 Tbilisi, Gamrekeli 19; tel. and fax (32) 37-22-97; e-mail publicat@gw.acnet.ge; f. 1941; Industrial-Publishing Corpn of the Georgian Academy of Sciences; Dir DAVID KOLOTAURI; Editor CISANA KARTOZIA.

**Nakaduli** (Stream): 380094 Tbilisi, Gamsakhurdia 28; tel. (32) 38-69-12; f. 1938; books for children and youth; Dir BAKUR SULAKAURI.

**Publishing House of Tbilisi State University:** 380079 Tbilisi, Chavchavadze 14; f. 1933; scientific and educational literature; Editor V. GAMKRELIDZE.

**Sakartvelo** (Georgia): 380002 Tbilisi, Marjanishvili 5; tel. (32) 95-42-01; f. 1921; fmrly *Sabchota Sakartvelo* (Soviet Georgia); political, scientific and fiction; Dir DZHANSUL GVINJILIA.

# Broadcasting and Communications

## TELECOMMUNICATIONS

**National Regulatory Authority:** Tbilisi; Chair. VAKHTANG ABASHIDZE.

**Telecom Georgia Ltd:** 380058 Tbilisi, Rustaveli 31; tel. (32) 99-91-97; fax (32) 00-11-11; e-mail isonishvili@telecom.ge; internet www .telecom.ge; f. 1994; provides telecommunications services; 51% state-owned, 30% owned by International Telecell Inc. (USA), 19% owned by Bulcom (Cyprus); Pres. G. KHMALADZE; Dir N. KAKHELI.

**Geocell:** 380102 Tbilisi, POB 48; tel. (32) 77-01-00; fax (32) 77-01-01; e-mail cc@geocell.com.ge; internet www.geocell.com.ge; f. 1996; Global System for Mobile Communications (GSM) operator; merged with GT Mobile in 2001.

**Magti GSM:** 380186 Tbilisi, Jikia 5; tel. (32) 32-23-31; fax (32) 32-28-83; e-mail office@magtigsm.ge; internet www.magticom.ge; f. 1997.

## BROADCASTING

**State Department of Television and Radio:** Tbilisi, Kostava 68; tel. (32) 36-81-66; e-mail gtvr@iberiapac.ge; Chair. (vacant).

## Television

**Ajaria TV:** 384500 Batumi, Memed Abashidze 41; tel. (222) 74-370; fax (222) 74-371; e-mail ajaratv@ajaratv.com; internet www.ajaratv .com; Chief Exec. TAMAZ BAKURIDZE; Dir VAKHTANG TODUA.

**Channel 7:** Tbilisi; tel. (32) 94-31-65; fax (32) 33-12-33; e-mail channel@macrocom.ge; internet www.macrocom.com.ge; f. 2000; cable television, 15 channels.

**Georgian Television and Radio Broadcasting:** 380071 Tbilisi, Kostava 68; tel. and fax (32) 29-42-54; e-mail office@geotvr.ge; internet www.geotvr.ge; f. 1956; two stations; relays from Russian television; Chair. ZAZA SHENGELIA.

**Rustavi 2:** 380077 Tbilisi, Vazha-Pshavela 45; tel. (32) 32-22-71; fax (32) 25-00-31; e-mail tv@rustavi2.com; internet www.rustavi2.com; f. 1994; independent; Gen. Dir NIKA TABATADZE.

## Radio

**Georgian Radio:** 380071 Tbilisi, Kostava 68; tel. (32) 36-83-62; fax (32) 36-86-65; f. 1956; govt-controlled; broadcasts in Georgian and Russian, with regional services for Abkhazia, Ajaria and South Ossetia; foreign service in English and German; two stations; Dir VAKHTANG NANITASHVILI.

# Finance

(cap. = capital; res = reserves; dep. = deposits; m. = million; brs = branches; amounts in lari, unless otherwise indicated)

## BANKING

In August 1991 the Georgian Supreme Soviet adopted legislation which nationalized all branches of all-Union (USSR) banks in Georgia. Georgian branches of the USSR State Bank (Gosbank) were transferred to the National Bank of Georgia.

In 1995 more than 50% of the commercial banks in Georgia (then numbering almost 230) were closed down, as many banks did not satisify general legal provisions and only five properly complied with the paid-in captial requirement. In 1996 the authorized capital requirement was raised to 5m. lari. At March 2003 there were 27 commercial banks operating in Georgia.

### Central Bank

**National Bank of Georgia:** 380005 Tbilisi, Leonidze 3–5; tel. (32) 99-65-05; fax (32) 99-93-46; e-mail nbg@access.sunet.ge; internet www.nbg.gov.ge; f. 1991; cap. 5.0m., res 76.8m., dep. 98.7m. (Dec. 2001); Pres. and Chair. of Bd IRAKLI MANAGADZE; 9 brs.

### Other Banks

**Agro-Business Bank:** Tbilisi, Budapeshti 10; tel. (32) 25-08-20; fax (32) 93-28-80; internet www.abg.com.ge; f. 2000; cap. 6.9m., dep. 4.1m. (Dec. 2001); wholly owned by the European Commission; Chair. MIKHEIL MGALOBLISHVILI; 61 brs.

**Bank of Georgia:** 380005 Tbilisi, Pushkin 3; tel. (32) 44-41-05; fax (32) 44-41-82; e-mail welcome@bog.ge; internet www.bog.ge; f. 1991 as Zhilsotsbank—Social Development Bank, one of five specialized state commercial banks; renamed as above 1994; universal joint-stock commercial bank; cap. 44.9m., dep. 98.7m. (Dec. 2002); Pres. VLADIMER PATEISHVILI; Gen. Dir ELGUJA SILAGADZE; 25 brs.

**Bank Republic:** 380079 Tbilisi, Abashidze 2; tel. (32) 29-45-98; fax (32) 22-75-66; e-mail info@republic.com.ge; internet www.republic .ge; f. 1991; cap. 5.8m., res 1.9m., dep. 37.9m. (Dec. 2001); Pres. LASHA PAPASHVILI.

**Cartu Bank JSC:** 380062 Tbilisi, Chavchavadze 39A; tel. (32) 23-00-21; fax (32) 23-03-83; e-mail cartubank@cartubank.ge; internet www.cartubank.ge; f. 1996 name changed as above Sept. 1998; cap. 12.5m., res 1.9m., dep. 3.7m. (Dec. 2000); Chair. of Bd G. CHRDILELI; 4 brs.

**Cavcasioni:** 380062 Tbilisi, Chubinishvili 41; tel. (32) 95-14-44; fax (32) 95-93-93; e-mail caucasioni@iberiapac.ge; f. 1992; cap. 3.0m., res 0.1m., dep. 0.4m. (Dec. 1999); Pres. BESO MAGRADZE; Chair. ZAZIA PANKVELASHVILI.

**Georgian Capital Bank:** 384517 Batumi, Gogebashvili 60; tel. (222) 7-65-82; fax (222) 7-60-01; e-mail inter@gmb-batumi.com; f. 1993; cap. 3.6m., res 0.3m., dep. 13m. (Dec. 1998); Chair. NUGZAR MIKELADZE; 4 brs.

**Georgian Post Bank JSC:** 380064 Tbilisi, Rustaveli 12; tel. (32) 99-01-10; fax (32) 956-82-69; e-mail info@postbank.ge; internet www .postbank.ge; f. 1995; 35 brs.

**Intellectbank:** 380064 Tbilisi, Davit Aghmashenebeli 127; tel. (32) 23-71-64; fax (32) 95-09-31; e-mail info@intellect.ge; internet www

.intellectbank.com; f. 1993; cap. 5.0m., dep. 35.5m. (Dec. 2001); Pres. DEVI VEPKHAVADZE; Gen. Dir VLADIMER CHANISHVILI; 13 brs.

**TBC Bank:** 380079 Tbilisi, Chavchavadze 11; tel. (32) 22-06-61; fax (32) 22-04-06; e-mail info@tbcbank.com.ge; internet www.tbcbank .com.ge; f. 1992; cap. 5.0m., res 24.9m., dep. 134.4m. (2002); Pres. VAKHTANG BUTSKHRIKIDZE; 9 brs.

**TbilCreditBank:** 380008 Tbilisi, Rustaveli 27; tel. (32) 98-60-10; fax (32) 98-27-83; e-mail tbilcred@caucasus.net; internet www .tbilcreditbank.com; f. 1994; cap. 5.5m., dep. 7m. (Dec. 1999); Chair. and Chief Exec. DAVIT BUADZE.

**Tbiluniversalbank Ltd:** 380071 Tbilisi, Kostava 70; tel. (32) 99-82-92; fax (32) 99-82-92; e-mail info@tub.ge; internet www .tbiluniversalbank.com; f. 1994 as Superbank; name changed as above 1995; cap. 5.9m., dep. 17.2m. (Dec. 2003); Chair. of Bd of Dirs VASIL DZOTSENIDZE; Deputy Chair. SULKHAN GVALIA; 3 brs.

**United Georgian Bank:** 380002 Tbilisi, Uznadze 37; tel. (32) 95-60-85; fax (32) 99-91-39; e-mail admin@ugb.com.ge; internet www .ugb.com.ge; f. 1995 by merger of three specialized state commercial banks; cap. 21.0m., res 3.2m., dep. 72.9m. (2002); Chair. of Supervisory Bd IVANE CHKARTISHVILI; Gen. Dir IRAKLI KOVZANADZE; 18 brs.

## STOCK EXCHANGE

**Georgian Stock Exchange:** 380062 Tbilisi, Chavchavadze 74A; tel. (32) 22-07-18; fax (32) 25-18-76; e-mail info@gse.ge; internet www .gse.ge; f. 1999; Chair. of Supervisory Bd GEORGE LOLADZE; Gen. Dir VAKHTANG SVANADZE.

## CURRENCY EXCHANGE

**Tbilisi Interbank Currency Exchange (TICEX):** 380005 Tbilisi, Galaktion Tabidze 4; tel. (32) 92-34-43; fax (32) 92-23-01; Gen. Dir DAVIT KLDIASHVILI.

## INSURANCE

**Aldagi Insurance Co:** 380179 Tbilisi, Melikishvili 16; tel. (32) 92-44-11; fax (32) 29-49-05; e-mail aldagi@aldagi.com.ge; internet www .aldagi.com; f. 1990; Chair. GURAM ASSATHIANY; Gen. Dir EVA IASHVILI.

**Anglo-Georgian Insurance Co (AGIC):** 380030 Tbilisi, I. Abashidze 29; tel. (32) 25-03-51; fax (32) 25-03-50; e-mail post@ agic.com.ge; internet www.agic.com.ge; f. 1998 as a joint-stock co; all types of insurance; Gen. Dir FRANCIS MATHEW.

**Central Insurance Co:** 380019 Tbilisi, Tsereteli 126; tel. (32) 98-87-18; Gen. Dir NIKOLAI A. DVALADZE.

**Georgian Pension and Insurance Holding Co:** Tbilisi, Chavchavadze 1, Bldg 5; tel. (32) 92-01-20; internet www.gpih.ge; Gen. Dir PAATA GADZADZE.

**Georgian International Insurance Ltd:** Tbilisi; tel. (32) 983-94-80; fax (32) 98-94-79; f. 1993; Pres. V. KIZIKURASHVILI; Dir IGOR KARPOVICH.

# Trade and Industry

## GOVERNMENT AGENCIES

**Georgian Investment Centre:** 380077 Tbilisi, Kazbegi 42; tel. (32) 23-41-34; fax (32) 92-18-40; e-mail gic@access.sanet.ge; internet www.gic.ge; f. 1996 to promote foreign and domestic investment; Dir SABA SARISHVILI.

**State Property Management Agency:** Tbilisi; responsible for divestment of state-owned enterprises.

## CHAMBER OF COMMERCE

**Georgian Chamber of Commerce and Industry:** 380079 Tbilisi, Chavchavadze 11; tel. (32) 23-00-45; fax (32) 23-57-60; e-mail gcci@ access.sanet.ge; internet www.gcci.org.ge; f. 1963; brs in Sukhumi and Batumi; Chair. GURAM D. AKHVLEDIANI.

## TRADE ASSOCIATION

**Georgian Import Export (Geoimpex):** 380008 Tbilisi, Giorgiashvili 12; tel. (32) 99-70-90; fax (32) 98-25-41; Gen. Dir T. A. GOGOBERIDZE.

## UTILITIES

### Regulatory Authorities

**Georgian National Energy Regulation Committe:** 380077 Tbilisi, Kazbegi Ave 45; tel. (32) 25-33-98; fax (32) 25-36-91; e-mail gnerc@caucasus.net; f. 1997; Dir E. ERISTAVI.

State Agency for the Regulation of Oil and Gas Resources of
Georgia: 380077 Tbilisi, Kazbegi Ave 45; tel. (32) 25-33-11; f. 1999;
Dir G. Itonishvili.

### Electricity

**Department of Power Supply:** Tbilisi, V. Vekua 1; tel. (32) 98-05-
65; attached to the Ministry of Fuel and Energy.

**Georgian United Distribution Co (GUDC):** f. 2002; from an
amalgamation of the majority of regional electricity cos, excluding
the regions of Tbilisi, Ajaria and Kakheti; 5,000 employees.

**Sakenergo:** 380005 Tbilisi, V. Vekua 1; tel. (32) 98-98-14; fax (32)
98-31-97; formerly state-owned energy supplier; in 1996 restructured into three cos (generation, transmission and distribution);
responsible for dispatch and sales; Gen. Dir Vazha Metreveli.

**Sakenergogeneratsia:** 38005 Tbilisi, V. Vekua 1; tel. and fax (32)
98-98-13; f. 1996; state power-generating co; Gen. Dir G. Badur-
ashvili.

**Telasi:** 380054 Tbilisi, Vani 3; tel. (32) 25-52-11; fax (32) 77-99-78;
internet www.AES-TELASI.com; privatized in 1999; 75% bought
from AES Silk Road BV, a subsidiary of AES Corpn (USA) by Unified
Energy Systems (Russia) in 2003; Tbilisi distribution grid; Dir
Dangiras Mikalajunas.

### Gas

**Georgian Gas International Corpn (GIC):** 380044 Tbilisi, 300
Aragveli 24; tel. (32) 92-29-55; fax (32) 92-32-29; joint-stock co;
Chair. Aleksandr Gotsiridze.

**Sakgazi:** Tbilisi; gas distribution; five distribution centres;
majority-owned by Itera (Russia).

**Saktransgasmretsvi:** 380077 Tbilisi, Delisi III 22; tel. (32) 93-22-
04; fax (32) 99-66-83; e-mail transgas@access.sanet.ge; f. 1962; state-
owned; operates main gas pipelines; Chair. of Bd Ivane Zazashvili.

**Tbilgazi Ltd:** 380007 Tbilisi, Mitsskevichi 18; tel. (32) 38-76-25; fax
(32) 37-56-51; gas-distribution co for the Tbilisi region; management
contract pending; Chair. Vakhtang Tsaava.

### Water

**Tbilisi Water Utility** (Tbiltskalkanali LLC): Tbilisi; scheduled for
privatization; water supply and sewerage system.

## MAJOR COMPANIES

Economic reforms from 1994 encouraged the development of the
private sector. In early 1998 almost all small-scale enterprises were
under private control and the privatization of medium and large-
scale enterprises was in progress. By the end of 1998 72% of
medium-sized and large enterprises had been privatized.

### Chemicals

**AZOTI JSC (Rustavi Chemical Industrial Complex):** 383040
Rustavi, Mshvidobis 2; tel. (34) 15-14-73; fax (34) 15-05-43; e-mail
grazot@access.anet.ge; f. 1956; produces ammonium nitrate and
other fertilizers, oxygen and cosmetics; Gen. Dir George Gogoladze;
3,400 employees.

**Chemcombinat:** 383040 Rustavi, Mshvidobis 2; tel. (34) 15-28-82;
fax (34) 15-05-43; f. 1956; produces ammonia products; Dir-Gen.
Zurab Lobjanidze; 3,800 employees.

**Chiaturmanganumi JSC:** 383950 Chiatura, Tsereteli 1; tel. (379)
5-25-35; fax (379) 55-023; f. 1880; privately owned extraction and
enrichment of manganese ore; production of peroxide and manganese concentrates; Gen. Dir Roland Gotsadze; 2,500 employees.

**Khimvolokno Rustavi Industrial Group:** 383040 Rustavi, Mira
12; tel. (34) 12-12-32; production of chemical fibres and resins.

### Electrical Goods

**Control Computers Plant:** 380086 Tbilisi, Gikia 5; tel. (32) 31-44-
89; manufacture of computers and computer and electronic equipment; Gen. Dir Nodar E. Chkadua; 1,510 employees.

**Ekrani Joint Stock Company:** 380014 Tbilisi, Didi Kheivani 3;
tel. (32) 75-59-99; fax (32) 75-58-88; e-mail ekrani@caucasus.net; f.
1993; manufactures television sets and domestic electrical appliances; Man. Dir Revaz Tsulaia.

**Elektroapparat Industrial Association:** 380021 Tbilisi, Tornike
Eristavi 8; tel. (32) 66-80-36; fax (32) 66-72-20; f. 1971; produces a
wide range of low-voltage electrical equipment and goods for general
use; Gen. Dir Bugan A. Egenala; 3,500 employees.

**Electrovozostroitel:** 380092 Tbilisi, Guramushvili 24; tel. (32) 62-
81-31; f. 1948; manufactures direct-current long-haul industrial
electric locomotives; Principal Officer Giorgi Zgudadze; 2,450
employees.

**Orbi:** 380019 Tbilisi, Tsereteli 117; tel. (32) 34-88-49; fax (32) 34-72-
95; f. 1956; manufacture of communications equipment; state-
owned; Dir Dzhimsher Akhobadze; 500 employees.

### Food and Beverages

**Agrom:** 384694 Poti, Kokaya Alley 1; tel. (393) 5-59-10; production
of tea.

**Aromaproduct Ltd:** 380092 Tbilisi, Guramishvili 17; tel. (32) 61-
42-91; fax (32) 39-98-02; e-mail info@aroma.ge; internet www.aroma
.ge; f. 1958; production of fruit products, food flavourings, etc.,
beverages, and additives for medicines and cosmetics; state-owned;
Gen. Dir Vladimir Gugushvili; 1,042 employees.

### Metals

**Rustavi Iron and Steel Works:** 3704 Rustavi, Gagarina 12; tel.
and fax (34) 19-20-10; e-mail metalurg@gol.ge; f. 1956; seamless pipe
manufacturer; 51% owned by Metallurggasoilinvest; Gen. Dir
Nodari Gvamberia; 3,500 employees.

### Petroleum and Natural Gas

**Batumi Oil Refinery:** 384051 Batumi, Tamaris Dasaxleba; tel.
(222) 3-21-55; Gen. Dir I. R. Abashidze.

**Georgia International Oil Corporation (GIOC):** 380026 Tbilisi,
Sanapiro 4; tel. (32) 92-02-48; fax (32) 93-56-94; in charge of the
construction of Tbilisi–Supsa and Tbilisi–Kazakh (Azerbaijan) pipelines; Pres. Giorgi Chanturia.

**Georgia Pipeline Company:** Tbilisi; in charge of construction of
Baku (Azerbaijan)–Bapu petroleum pipeline; Vice-Pres. and Man.
Robert Moore.

**Gruzneft (Georgian State Oil Co):** 380015 Tbilisi, Kostava 65;
tel. (32) 136-16-42; fax (32) 133-30-32; f. 1930; petroleum and gas
exploration; petroleum production and refining; Gen. Dir Giorgi
Chanturia; 6,000 employees.

**Saknavtobi:** Tbilisi; state-owned; petroleum producer.

### Textiles and Clothing

**Gori Cotton and Sewing Industrial Association:** 383507 Gori,
Moskorskaya; tel. (370) 2-37-70; f. 1951; Principal Officer Merab
Nizharadze; 3,545 employees.

**Kambovolnarti:** 380092 Tbilisi, Peikrebi 12; tel. (32) 61-31-24; fax
(32) 61-89-11; f. 1963; transformed into a joint-stock co in 1993;
produces silk and worsted woollen yarn, bedding and mattresses;
Dir Omari Janjalia; 270 employees.

### Miscellaneous

**Delita:** 380094 Tbilisi, Saburtalo 32; tel. (32) 38-20-06; fax (32) 38-
20-39; f. 1956; manufacture of metal-cutting and wood-processing
machinery; operates a supermarket chain; Pres. Shota Maniashvili;
Gen. Dir Temuri Kharebava; 500 employees.

**Egrisi:** 380086 Tbilisi, Jikia 16; tel. (32) 32-52-52; fax (32) 00-11-22;
e-mail egrisi@caucasus.net; internet www.egrisi.caucasus.net;
design, installation and maintenance of long-distance and international telecommunications services, digital television channels
and data transmission systems; Pres. Fridon Injia; Gen. Dir Avtandil
Iashvili.

**Georgian Glass and Mineral Water Co N.V.:** Tbilisi, Chavchavadze 26; tel. (32) 94-16-22; fax (32) 22-36-68; e-mail ggmw@borjomi
.com.ge; internet www.borjomi.com.ge; f. 1997; joint Georgian-
Dutch-French venture; water-bottling and bottle-making facilities;
Man. Dir Jacques Fleury.

**Gruzimpex** (Georgian Import-Export): 380008 Tbilisi, Chanturia
12; tel. (32) 99-70-90; fax (32) 99-73-13; f. 1987; foreign-trade org.;
Gen. Dir Tengiz A. Gogoberidze.

**Kakheti Gruzpomkombinat:** 380098 Tbilisi, Yumasheva 17; tel.
(32) 41-51-51; fax (32) 41-06-57; production of cardboard products
and brochures; Dir Nugzar Shalvovich Robitashvili; 350 employees.

**Kutaisi Automobile Factory:** 384009 Kutaisi, Avtomashenebeli
88; tel. (331) 7-26-95; fax (331) 0-10-81; e-mail autoplant@sanet.knet
.ge; f. 1945; manufactures freight containers and trailers, incl.
Kamaz lorries; Principal Officer Tengiz Shubladze; 1,300 employees.

**Poti Hydraulic Machine Plant:** 384694 Poti, Khobskaya 7; tel.
(39) 35-56-85; manufactures hydraulic dredging machinery.

**Poti Shipyard:** 384696 Poti, Davitaya 1; tel. and fax (39) 32-17-00;
f. 1941; shipbuilding and ship repairs; provides port services; 99%
state-owned, 1% owned by employees; Gen. Dir Dmitrii Chitanava;
550 employees.

**Tbilaviamsheni JSC:** 380036 Tbilisi, Khmelnitskogo 181; tel. (32)
70-84-12; fax (32) 70-88-38; e-mail tordia@gol.ge; internet www.tam
.ge; f. 1941; nine facilities, including metallurgical, mechanical,

engraving, aircraft assembly and flight-testing; produces aircraft, agricultural equipment, bicycles and metal containers; name changed from Tbilisi Aircraft Factory in 2002; Pres. PANTIKO TORDIA; Gen. Dir NODAR BERIDZE; 2,000 employees.

**Tbilisi Instrumental Production Amalgamation:** 380094 Tbilisi, Saburtalo 32; tel. (32) 38-14-69; fax (32) 38-20-07; manufactures metal-cutting and wood-processing machinery; Gen. Dir SHUKURI A. KOIAVA; 622 employees.

**Tbilisi Lathe-Manufacturing Industrial Association:** 380092 Tbilisi, T. Eristavil; tel. (32) 66-22-78; f. 1934; Principal Officer ANZAR SHAUTUDZE; 1,107 employees.

### TRADE UNIONS

**Amalgamation of Trade Unions of Georgia (GTUA):** 380122 Tbilisi, Shartava 7; tel. (32) 38-29-95; fax (32) 22-46-63; e-mail gtua@geo.net.ge; f. 1995 as Confederation of Trade Unions of Georgia, name changed as above in 2000; comprises branch unions with a total membership of approx. 800,000; Chair. IRAKLI TUGUSHI.

**Free Trade Union of Journalists:** Tbilisi, Vazha Pshavela pr. 43; f. 2000; over 100 mems; Chair. BEZHAN MESKHI.

# Transport

### RAILWAYS

In 1997 Georgia's rail network (including the sections within the secessionist republic of Abkhazia) totalled approximately 1,600 km. However, some 500 km of track was reported to be in a poor state of repair, as a result of which the capacity of some sections of the network had decreased by more than 75% since 1990. The main rail links are with Russia, along the Black Sea coast, with Azerbaijan, with Armenia and with Iran. The Georgian–Armenian railway continues into eastern Turkey. Civil conflict in the mid-1990s disrupted sections of the railway network. The separatist war in Abkhazia resulted in the severance of Georgia's rail connection with Russia. However, services to the Russian capital, Moscow, resumed in mid-1997, following a four-year interruption. In mid-1998 it was announced that the European Bank for Reconstruction and Development was to assist with the refurbishment of the railways.

The first section of the Tbilisi Metro was opened in 1966; by 1999 the system comprised two lines with 20 stations, totalling 23 km in length, and three extensions, totalling 15 km, were under construction.

**Georgian Railways Ltd:** 380012 Tbilisi, Tamara Mepe 15; tel. (32) 94-20-60; fax (32) 95-25-27; e-mail a.chkhaidze@georail.org.ge; internet www.railway.ge; f. 1872, following the dissolution of the former Soviet Railways, became a Ltd co in 1998; Chair. AKAKI CHKHAIDZE.

**Tbilisi Metropolitena:** 380012 Tbilisi, Pl. Vokzalnaya 2; tel. (32) 95-15-78; fax (32) 93-41-86; e-mail almer@iberiapac.ge; f. 1966; Gen. Man. GURAM GABUNIA.

### ROADS

In 2000 the total length of roads in use was an estimated 20,362 km (including 15,562 km of secondary roads). In the same year 93.5% of roads were paved. Under a presidential decree issued in 1996, a plan to modernize and develop the road system in Georgia was to be implemented.

### SHIPPING

There are international shipping services with Black Sea and Mediterranean ports. The main ports are at Batumi, Poti and Sukhumi.

#### Shipowning Company

**Georgian Shipping Company:** 384517 Batumi, Gogebashvili 60; tel. (222) 14-02-312; fax (222) 73-91-114; Pres. Capt. B. VARSHANIDZE.

#### Port Authorities

**Port of Batumi:** 384500 Batumi, Gogebashvili 20; tel. (222) 76-261; fax (222) 76-830; e-mail bsport@batumi.net; internet www.batport.batumi.net; operates cargo port; Gen. Dir DZHAMBUL NINIDZE; 1,413 employees.

**Port of Poti:** 384694 Poti, David Agmashenebeli 52; tel. (393) 20-660; fax (393) 20-688; e-mail ptp@iberiapac.ge; internet www.potiport.com; operation of cargo port; Gen. Dir DZHEMAL INAISHVILI.

### CIVIL AVIATION

**Air Georgia:** 380062 Tbilisi, I. Chavchavadze 49A; tel. (32) 29-40-53; fax (32) 23-34-23; e-mail airgeo@caucasus.net; internet www

.airgeorgia.com; national and international transport of passengers and freight; Dir ELGOUDZHA DVALI.

**Iveria:** Tbilisi; f. 1998 as a joint-stock co following merger.

**Orbi** (Georgian Airlines): 380058 Tbilisi, Tbilisi Airport; tel. (32) 98-73-28; fax (32) 49-51-51; successor to the former Aeroflot division in Georgia; charter and scheduled services to destinations in the CIS and the Middle East; Chief Exec. VASILI S. DZHAMILBAZISHVILI.

**Sakaeronavigatsia:** 380058 Tbilisi, Tbilisi Airport; tel. (32) 94-76-96; fax (32) 94-75-83; e-mail office@airnav.com.ge; internet www.airnav.com.ge; f. 1993; state-owned; provides airspace and aerodrome control service.

**Sukhumi United Aviation Detachment (Taifun—Adjal Avia):** 384962 Sukhumi, Babushara Airport; tel. (122) 22021; domestic scheduled and chartered flights; Commdr ZAUR K. KHAINDRAVA.

# Tourism

Prior to the disintegration of the USSR, Georgia attracted some 1.5m. tourists annually (mainly from other parts of the USSR), owing to its location on the Black Sea and its favourable climate. However, following the outbreak of civil conflict in the early 1990s in South Ossetia and Abkhazia, there was an almost complete cessation in tourism. Efforts to regenerate the sector were made in the late 1990s, with the historic buildings of Tbilisi and the surrounding area one of the primary attractions. The ski resort at Gudauri also remained popular with foreign tourists in the winter months. Other attractions included the mineral spas in the Borzhomi Gorge, and Mount Kazbek. In 1999 receipts from tourism totalled US $400m. and, according to the World Tourism Organization, there were 302,215 tourist arrivals in 2001, compared with 387,258 in 2000.

**Department of Tourism:** 380074 Tbilisi, Chavchavadze 80; tel. (32) 22-61-25; fax (32) 29-40-52; Chair. KONSTANTINE SALIA.

# Culture

### NATIONAL ORGANIZATION

**Ministry of Culture:** see section on The Government (Ministries).

**Ministry of Culture of the Autonomous Republic of Abkhazia:** Tbilisi; tel. (32) 93-17-20; Minister SVETLANA KETSBA.

### CULTURAL HERITAGE

In 1998 there were 97 museums in Georgia.

**Georgian Cultural Heritage Information Centre (GCHIC):** 380030 Tbilisi, Chavchavadze 62, Kv. 49; e-mail info@heritage.ge; internet www.heritage.ge; non-governmental org.; Exec. Dir Dr NICHOLAS VACHEISHVILI.

**Georgian State Art Museum:** 380003 Tbilisi, Gudiashvili 1; tel. (32) 99-66-35; f. 1920 as the National Gallery of Georgia; 135,952 exhibits; Dir NODAR LOMOURI.

**Georgian State Museum of Oriental Art:** Tbilisi, Azizbekova 3; large collection of Georgian art, carpets, fabrics, etc.; Dir G. M. GVISHIANI.

**Modern Art Museum—National Picture Gallery:** 380003 Tbilisi, Rustaveli 11; tel. (32) 93-16-52; f. 1920; 25,000 items; Dir TEIMURAZ GOTSADZE.

**National Library of Georgia:** 380003 Tbilisi, Gudiashvili 5; tel. (32) 99-80-95; fax (32) 99-80-95; f. 1846; 16m. vols; Dir LEVAN BERDZENISHVILI.

**Kutaisi State Museum of History and Ethnography:** 384000 Kutaisi, Tbilisi 4; tel. (331) 4-56-91; f. 1922; attached to Georgian Academy of Sciences; 190,000 items; Dir M. V. NIKOLEISHVILI.

**State Museum of Folklore and Applied Arts of Georgia:** 380003 Tbilisi, Sololaki Lane 11; tel. (32) 99-61-52; f. 1899; 10,000 exhibits; Dir MICHEIL KIKHNAVELIDZE.

**State Museum of Georgian Literature:** 380003 Tbilisi, Giorgi Chanturia 10; tel. (32) 99-86-67; f. 1929; 19th- and 20th-century Georgian literature; 125,000 exhibits; library of almost 12,000 vols; Dir I. A. ORJONIKIDZE.

**State Museum of the Abkhazian Autonomous Republic:** Sukhumi, Lenina 22; f. 1915; 100,000 exhibits; Dir A. A. ARGUN.

**State Museum of the History of Georgia:** 380003 Tbilisi, Rustaveli 3; tel. (32) 99-80-22; f. 1919; 1.2m. exhibits; library of over 250,000 vols; Dir L. A. CHILASHVILI.

**Tbilisi State Museum of Anthropology and Ethnography:** Tbilisi, Komsomolsk 11; archaeological material; library of over 150,000 vols; Dir A. V. TKESHELASHVILI.

## SPORTING ORGANIZATION

**Georgian National Olympic Committee:** 380002 Tbilisi, Davit Aghmashenebeli 65; tel. (32) 95-30-79; fax (32) 95-38-29; e-mail geonoc@access.sanet.ge; Pres. JANSUG BAGRATIONI; Sec.-Gen. EMZAR ZENAISHVILI.

**Georgian National Sport Foundation:** 380060 Tbilisi, Zh. Shartava 40; tel. (32) 94-07-82; fax (32) 94-02-45.

## PERFORMING ARTS

In 1998 there were 32 theatres in Georgia.

**George Mikeladze Tbilisi State Puppet Theatre:** 380002 Tbilisi, Davit Aghmashenebeli 103; tel. (32) 95-26-71; fax (32) 95-17-13; e-mail puppets@ip.osgf.ge; f. 1934; Dir TEMUR BADRIASHVILI.

**Georgian Folk Theatre:** Tbilisi; tel. (32) 99-90-01; fax (32) 95-59-05; f. 1980.

**Griboedov Russian Drama Theatre:** 380007 Tbilisi, Rustaveli 2; tel. (32) 93-16-24; fax (32) 93-31-15; e-mail theatre@ip.osgf.ge; internet www.griboedovtheatre.org.ge; f. 1845; Dir AVTANDIL VARSI-MASHVILI.

**Marjanishvili State Academic Drama Theatre:** 380002 Tbilisi, Marjanashvili 8; tel. (32) 95-35-82; fax (32) 95-40-01; e-mail eastern@caucasus.net; f. 1928 in Kutaisi; Gen. Man. GAIOZ KANDE-LAKI; Artistic Dir OTAR MEGVINETUKHUTSESI.

**Nicko Sulkhanishvili State Chorus Choir of Georgia:** 380005 Tbilisi, Gorgasali 1; tel. (32) 72-27-25; f. 1947; Dir NATO MOISTSRA-PISHVILI; Artistic Dir GIVI MUNJISHVILI.

**Shota Rustaveli State Academic Drama Theatre:** 380008 Tbilisi, Rustaveli 17; tel. (32) 99-85-87; fax (32) 99-65-20; e-mail rustaveli.theatre@access.sanet.ge; f. 1879; Dir GIA TEVZADZE; Artistic Dir ROBERT STURUA.

**Tbilisi V. Sarajishvili State Conservatoire:** 380004 Tbilisi, Griboedova 8; Dir NODAR GABUNIA.

**Tbilisi State Pantomime Theatre:** 380008 Tbilisi, Rustaveli 37; tel. (32) 98-25-06; f. 1965; Dir AMIRAN SHALIKASHVILI.

**Tbilisi Zakharia Paliashvili Opera and Ballet State Academic Theatre:** 380008 Tbilisi, Rustaveli 25; tel. (32) 99-06-42; fax (32) 98-32-50; e-mail opera@access.sanet.ge; internet www.opera.ge; f. 1851; Gen. Dir ZURAB LOMIDZE.

## ASSOCIATIONS

**Union of Writers of Georgia:** 380000 Tbilisi, Machabeli 13; tel. (32) 99-84-90; includes five regional Writers' Organizations.

**Abkhazian Writers' Organization:** 384000 Sukhumi, Frunze 44; tel. (122) 2-35-34.

**Ajar Writers' Organization:** 384516 Batumi, Engels 21; tel. (222) 3-29-66.

**South-Ossetian Writers' Organization:** 383570 Tskhinvali, Lenin 3; tel. (341) 2-32-63.

# Education

Education is free and compulsory for nine years, between the ages of six and 14. Free secondary education is available for the highest-achieving 30% of primary-school pupils. In 1997 34% of children of the relevant age-group attended pre-primary schools. In 2000/01 the net primary enrolment ratio was 95%; in 1998/99 the secondary enrolment ratio was 73%. In 2000/01 the gross, combined primary, secondary and tertiary enrolment ratio was 69% (females 70%; males 69%). In 1994/95 75.4% of all pupils were taught in Georgian-language schools, while 3.9% were taught in Russianlanguage schools, 3.7% in Armenian-language schools, 6.1% in Azerbaijani-language schools and 9.6% in mixed Georgian- and Russian-language schools. There was also teaching in Abkhazian and Ossetian. In 2000/01 there were 1,505 primary day schools. In that year there were 1,652 secondary day schools, with a total enrolment of 591,700 pupils.

In addition to state institutions, many private institutions of higher education were opened after 1991. In 2000/01 there were 138,900 students enrolled at 171 institutions of higher education (including universities). In 2000 4.0% of total expenditure (26.9m. lari) was allocated to education.

## GOVERNMENT AGENCIES

**Ministry of Education:** see section on The Government (Ministries).

**Ministry of Education of the Autonomous Republic of Abkhazia:** Tbilisi; tel. (32) 95-07-52; Minister JANO JANELIDZE.

## UNIVERSITIES

**Abkhazian A. M. Gorkii State University:** 384900 Sukhumi, Tsereteli 9; tel. (122) 2-25-98; f. 1985; 6 faculties; 3,800 students.

**Georgian Technical University:** 380075 Tbilisi, M. Kostava 77; tel. (32) 29-48-56; fax (32) 94-20-33; internet www.gtu.edu.ge; f. 1922 (as Georgia Polytechnic Institute, renamed 1990); 14 faculties; 2,050 teachers; 16,000 students; Chancellor Prof. R. KHURODZE.

**Ivan Javakhishvili Tbilisi State University:** 380028 Tbilisi, Chavchavadze 1; tel. (32) 22-02-41; e-mail usc@ictsu.tsu.edu.ge; internet www.tsu.edu.ge; f. 1918; language of instruction is Georgian, with a Russian section in some faculties; 19 faculties; 4 institutes; 5,000 teachers; 30,000 students; 5 brs; Rector Prof. ROIN METREVELI.

**Kutaisi Akaki Tsereteli State University:** Kutaisi; tel. (331) 42-173; e-mail ksu@gateway.ge; internet ksu.gateway.ge; f. 1990; 9 faculties; 380 teachers; 5,000 students; Rector AVTANDIL NIKOLEISH-VILI.

**Tbilisi State Medical University:** 380077 Tbilisi, V. Pshavela 33; tel. (32) 39-18-79; fax (32) 94-25-19; e-mail iad@tsmu.edu; internet www.tsmu.edu; f. 1918; 8 faculties; 1,200 teachers; 4,300 students; 3 university hospitals; 29 clinics; Rector R. G. KHETSURIANI.

# Social Welfare

Great pressures were placed on Georgia's social-welfare system as a result of the civil and separatist conflicts in the early 1990s, when large numbers were killed, wounded or displaced.

At the end of 1998 there were 890,000 registered pensioners in Georgia. Under the existing 'pay-as-you-go' system, pensions are financed by the extrabudgetary Pension Fund (United State Social Safety Fund), which provides fixed-rate old-age pensions. However, the pensions system continued to accumulate arrears, and reform of the system was required urgently. In 2001 a plan was drawn up, as part of the country's Poverty Reduction and Economic Growth Programme, for the introduction, over a period of five years, of a programme to introduce a 'multi-pillar' pension system. The country's first private pensions insurance company, Georgian Pension Investment Holding (GPIH), was founded in May 2001, and aimed to offer (in addition to the existing, universal scheme), voluntary, non-state pensions insurance.

There are two further extrabudgetary funds: the Employment Fund, established in 1991, provides unemployment, sickness and maternity benefits; and a Health Fund was established in 1995. The Government aimed to privatize most health care facilities by 1998, although free medical care was to continue to be provided to the neediest sections of the population. In 2000 the Government adopted a state programme for a national health policy and a strategic plan for health-care development in Georgia, according to which government spending on health care was to increase from 4% of GDP by 2005 to 6% of GDP by 2010. In 2000 there were 4.8 hospital beds per 1,000 people, and there were 473.1 doctors for every 100,000 people. The 2000 budget allocated 16.2% of total expenditure (109.3m. lari) to social security, and a further 3.0% (20.5m. lari) to health care.

## GOVERNMENT AGENCIES

**Ministry of Labour, Health and Social Welfare:** see section on The Government (Ministries).

**Ministry of Health of the Autonomous Republic of Abkhazia:** Tbilisi; tel. (32) 38-97-07; Minister ELGUJA BERIA.

**Ministry of Social Protection of the Autonomous Republic of Abkhazia:** Tbilisi; tel. (32) 95-41-08; Minister SHALVA TZULEISKIRI.

**Georgian Social Investment Fund (GSIF):** 380062 Tbilisi, Chavchavadze 39A, 11 floor; 380079, POB 112; tel. (32) 23-07-79; fax (32) 23-01-03; e-mail gsif@gsif.ge; internet www.gsif.ge; f. 1996.

# The Environment

Georgia experienced environmental degradation as a result of conflict in the autonomous territories of Abkhazia and South Ossetia, and as a result of industrial pollution. In 1996 three industrial enterprises were found to be responsible for 63.2% of the country's air emissions. Georgia is a member of the Black Sea environmental programme, which aims to improve the ability of Black Sea countries to manage the environment, to implement environmental legislation, and to promote ecologically-sound investments. The most sensitive ecological issue of the early 2000s concerned the planned construction of a Baku (Azerbaijan)–Tbilisi–Ceyhan (Turkey) petroleum pipeline, which was to pass through the Borjomi valley, close to a national park and its mineral-water-producing springs.

## GOVERNMENT ORGANIZATIONS

**Ministry of Environmental Protection and Natural Resources:** see section on The Government (Ministries).

**State Department of Geology:** 380062 Tbilisi, Mosashvili 24; tel. (32) 25-01-14; fax (32) 22-56-13; e-mail irakli@gw.acnet.ge; f. 1925; Dir TAMAZ V. DJANELIDZE.

**State Department of Environmental Protection and Natural Resources of the Autonomous Republic of Abkhazia:** Tbilisi, Davit Aghmashenebeli 150, Hydrometeorology Bldg; tel. (32) 96-94-75; f. 1975; Chair. LEONID RIGVAVA.

## ACADEMIC INSTITUTES

**Georgian Academy of Sciences:** 380008 Tbilisi, Rustaveli 52; tel. (32) 99-88-91; fax (32) 99-88-23; e-mail frg@gas.hepi.edu.ge; internet www.acnet.ge; Pres. ALBERT N. TAVKHELIDZE.

attached institutes include:

**Commission on Nature Conservation:** Tbilisi, Z. Rukhadze 1; tel. (32) 99-88-91; fax (32) 99-88-23; Chair. L. K. GABUNIA.

**Commission for Studying Productive Forces and Natural Resources:** 380062 Tbilisi, Paliashvili 87; tel. (32) 22-32-16; f. 1978; attached to the Presidium of the Academy; Chair. IRAKLI ZHORDANIA.

**A. Djanelidze Institute of Geology:** 380093 Tbilisi, M. Aleksidze 1; tel. (32) 29-39-41; e-mail root@geology.acnet.ge; f. 1925; Dir MIRIAN TOPCHISHVILI.

**V. Gulisashvili Institute of Mountain Forestry:** 380086 Tbilisi, Mindeli 9; tel. (32) 30-34-66; e-mail postmaster@forest.acnet.ge; Dir GIORGI GIGAURI.

**Institute of Water Management and Engineering Ecology:** 380062 Tbilisi, J. Chavchavadze 60; tel. (32) 22-40-94; fax (32) 22-74-01; e-mail tsotnem@zambeez.ru; f. 1929; Dir TSOTNE E. MIRSKHOULAVA.

**N. Ketskhoveli Institute of Botany:** 380007 Tbilisi, Kodzorskoe; tel. (32) 99-77-46; fax (32) 99-88-23; e-mail giorgi@botany.kheta.ge; f. 1933; also includes the Georgian Botanical Society; Dir GIORGI SH. NAKHUTSRISHVILI.

**Scientific Research Centre for Radiobiology and Radiation Ecology:** 380003 Tbilisi, Telavi 51; tel. (32) 77-54-42; fax (32) 93-35-23; e-mail kiazo@caucasus.net; internet www.acnet.ge/radiobio/; f. 1990; Dir K. S. NADAREISHVILI.

## NON-GOVERNMENTAL ORGANIZATIONS

**Georgian Centre for Environmental Research:** 380007 Tbilisi, Chonkhadze 16; tel. and fax (32) 33-47-29; e-mail geocer@mmc.net.ge; consultants on environment, agriculture and tourism; Dir GRIGORI ABRAMIA.

**Georgian Geoinformation Centre (G-Info):** Tbilisi, Napareuli 14; tel. (32) 22-20-14; e-mail eis@ginfo.kheta.ge; f. 1994; creates geographical information systems and environmental databases.

**Mtsvanta Partia** (Green Party of Georgia): c/o Sakartvelos Mtsvaneta Modzraoba (Georgia Green Movement), 380012 Tbilisi, Davit Aghmashenebeli 182, Green House, Mushthaid Park; tel. (32) 34-80-68; fax (32) 35-16-74; e-mail gagreens@glas.apc.org; f. 1990 by mems of the Georgia Green Movement; ecological party; national branch of Friends of the Earth International; Leader GIORGI GACHECHILADZE.

**Sakartvelos Mtsvaneta Modzraoba—Dedamicis Megobrebi Sakartvelo** (Georgia Green Movement—Friends of the Earth): 380012 Tbilisi, Davit Aghmashenebeli 182, Green House, tel. (32) 35-47-51; fax (32) 35-16-74; e-mail gagreens@access.sanet.ge; f. 1998; activist environmental group; non-political; affiliated with the Green Party of Georgia and the Asscn of Biofarmers of Georgia (ELKANA); Chair. NANA NEMSADZE, NANA NEMSADZE; Exec. Dir RUSUDAN SIMONIDZE.

**Society of Young Ecologists—Green Cross:** Akhalsikhe, Antimoz Iverieli 15; tel. 2-06-68; Leader RAMAZ KORSHIA.

**World Wide Fund for Nature Caucasus Programme Office:** 380093 Tbilisi, M. Aleksidze 11, Academy of Sciences; tel. (32) 33-01-54; fax (32) 33-01-90; e-mail office@wwfgeo.org.ge; f. 1992; conservation of biodiversity; Dir GIORGI SANDIRADZE.

# Defence

Following the dissolution of the USSR in December 1991, Georgia began to create a unified army from the various existing paramilitary and other groups. A National Security Council (headed by the President) was established in early 1996 as a consultative body to co-ordinate issues related to defence and security. Compulsory military service lasts for 18 months. In August 2002 total armed forces numbered some 17,500: 8,620 army, 1,830 navy, 1,250 air force and 5,800 troops attached to the Ministry of Defence. The number of troops had been dramatically reduced since 2000. There were also an estimated 3,000 Russian troops based in Georgia. In addition, an estimated 1,600 CIS peace-keeping forces were present in Abkhazia and 530 in South Ossetia, in addition to 116 UN Observer Mission in Georgia (UNOMIG) personnel. In December 1993 Georgia became a member of the CIS and its collective security system; however Georgia failed to renew its participation in the system upon its expiry in May 1999. In March 1994 Georgia joined the North Atlantic Treaty Organization's 'Partnership for Peace' programme of military co-operation. In June 2002 the Vaziani military base, near Tbilisi, which had been vacated by the Russian military in the previous year, was reopened by the Georgian army, with financial assistance from Turkey. The 2002 budget allocated 70m. lari to defence.

**Commander-in-Chief of the Armed Forces:** President of the Republic.

**Chief of the General Staff:** Lt-Gen. DZHONI PIRTSKHALAISHVILI.

# AUTONOMOUS TERRITORIES

Georgia contains two Autonomous Republics, Abkhazia and Ajaria, and one former Autonomous Oblast, South Ossetia. The status of both Abkhazia and South Ossetia was disputed. President Eduard Shevardnadze attempted to persuade all three regions to enter an 'asymmetric federation', which would give them a large degree of political and economic autonomy, while remaining within Georgia.

# ABKHAZIA

The Autonomous Republic of Abkhazia is situated in the north-west of Georgia and covers an area of 8,600 sq km. In 1989 the total population was 537,000; in that year 17.8% of the population were Abkhazians, with most of the remainder ethnic Georgians (45.7%). During the conflict in 1992 and 1993 more than 200,000 ethnic Georgians and others left the region. Some 50,000 refugees were resettled from 1996, but many subsequently departed, following renewed hostilities. The language of the region is Abkhazian, a member of the North-Western group of Caucasian languages; according to the Constitution of Georgia, Georgian is also a recognized state language. The capital of Abkhazia is Sukhumi, with an estimated population of 122,000 in 1990. Formerly a colony of the Eastern Roman or 'Byzantine' Empire, Abkhazia was an important power in the ninth and 10th centuries, but it was later dominated by Georgian, Turkish and Russian rulers.

**Chairman of the Supreme Council of the Autonomous Republic of Abkhazia:** Tamaz Nadareishvili (resident in Tbilisi); tel. (32) 98-57-48.

**Deputy Chairmen:** Davit Tsanava (resident in Tbilisi); tel. (32) 98-37-57, Elguja Gvazava (resident in Tbilisi); tel. (32) 93-27-34.

**Chairman of the Council of Ministers of the Autonomous Republic of Abkhazia:** Londer Tsaava (resident in Tbilisi); tel. (32) 98-25-57.

**Deputy Chairman:** Loric Marshania (resident in Tbilisi); tel. (32) 98-23-49.

# 'REPUBLIC OF ABKHAZIA'

In 1989 Abkhazians renewed a campaign for secession from the Georgian Soviet Socialist Republic and in July 1992 the Abkhazian legislature proclaimed the 'Republic of Abkhazia'. In late September 1993, following a bloody civil war in which Georgian government troops were defeated, Abkhazian separatist forces officially declared the region liberated from Georgia, although this was not accepted by the central authorities. In May 1994 a full cease-fire agreement was signed, providing for the deployment of Commonwealth of Independent States (CIS) peace-keepers in the region; however, hostilities continued. On 26 November the Abkhazian legislature adopted a new Constitution, declaring the 'Republic of Abkhazia' to be a sovereign state, with an executive presidency. This was condemned by the Georgian Government and protests were also voiced by the USA, Russia and the UN Security Council, all of which reaffirmed their recognition of Georgia's territorial integrity. Peace negotiations were subsequently suspended. Elections to the Abkhazian People's Assembly were held on 23 November 1996 and to local councils on 14 March 1998, both of which were declared invalid by President Shevardnadze. On 3 October 1999 the incumbent President of the Republic, Vladislav Ardzinba, the sole candidate, was re-elected, obtaining 99% of the votes cast; the election was declared illegal by international observers. A referendum was held concurrently, in which 97% of the participants upheld the 1994 Constitution. The Abkhaz legislature subsequently passed the State Independence Act. Despite this, negotiations between Georgia and Abkhazia resumed from 2000.

Local elections, held in Abkhazia on 10 March 2001, prompted condemnation from both the Georgian Government and the UN. None the less, at the conclusion of a UN-sponsored meeting in Yalta, Ukraine, in mid-March, delegations from both Georgia and Abkhazia agreed to renounce violence, and to allow the safe return of refugees. In early October, however, a helicopter carrying members of the UN Observer Mission in Georgia (UNOMIG) was shot down by unidentified attackers, killing all nine people on board. The Abkhazian authorities blamed the Georgian Government for the subsequent escalating violence in the region, accusing it of planning to carry out an assault on the Republic, with the aid of Chechen militants. The authorities also blamed the Georgian Government for subsequent aerial attacks on the Kodori Gorge, which the Georgian side attributed to Russian military aircraft. Georgian troops were dispatched to the region in mid-October, with the declared aim of protecting the Georgian population there; the UN, however, deemed their deployment to be a violation of the 1994 cease-fire agreement. A protocol was signed by the Abkhazian and Georgian sides on 17 January 2002, according to which Georgia was to withdraw its troops by mid-April. Parliamentary elections, scheduled to take place in Abkhazia on 24 November 2001, were postponed until 2 March 2002, owing to the unstable security situation; the elections were once again condemned as illegal by the Georgian Government, and the results were not recognized by international organizations. The Abkhazian *de facto* premier, Anri Dzhergenia, was dismissed in December, and Gennadii Gagulia was appointed as his replacement. In April 2003 a new Government, under Raul Khadzhimba, was appointed.

A state of emergency was declared in areas bordering Georgian territory, following the arrival of US military advisers in Georgia from early 2002. At the beginning of March President Shevardnadze and the Russian President, Vladimir Putin, agreed to amend the mandate of the CIS peace-keepers stationed in Abkhazia, deploying them further north, along the Galidzga River. The amendments were condemned by the Abkhazian authorities. In late March several bombs exploded on a local train and in the port of Ochamchire, killing one person and injuring 15; Abkhazia blamed the attacks on Georgian guerrillas. On 29 July the UN Security Council approved Resolution 1427, which demanded that the region begin negotiations on its progressive reintegration into Georgia, a proposal that was strongly opposed by Abkhazia; however, Russia's failure to employ its power of veto appeared to demonstrate a new tone of conciliation with Georgia. In late January 2003 Georgia refused to renew the mandate of the CIS peace-keepers in Abkhazia until, *inter alia*, the definition of the conflict zone was extended and a recently resumed railway link from the Russian Black Sea port of Sochi to Tbilisi, via Sukhumi, was halted (it was subsequently temporarily halted). On 30 January the UN Security Council adopted Resolution 1462, which welcomed the reduction in tension in the Kodori region, but expressed regret at the lack of progress in reaching a political settlement on the status of Abkhazia. On 7 March Shevardnadze and Putin issued a joint statement, agreeing to expedite the repatriation of displaced persons to Abkhazia, prior to the resumption of the Sochi–Sukhumi–Tbilisi railway service and the renovation of the region's Inguri hydroelectric plant. In addition, they agreed to extend indefinitely the mandate of the CIS peace-keeping forces.

At the beginning of August 2002 the Abkhazian National Assembly adopted amendments to the Constitution, which would enable Abkhazian citizens to hold dual citizenship. Some 60% of the region's population had already acquired Russian passports, following the adoption of amendments to the law on citizenship by the Russian State Duma. A population census was scheduled to take place in Abkhazia in 2003.

It is generally accepted that Russia conducts some trade with Abkhazia (despite sanctions imposed by the CIS, under pressure from Georgia), permitting the import of petroleum, flour and sugar, and the export of citrus fruits, fish, wine and timber. Some revenue is generated by continued Russian tourism, particularly by members of the military. In mid-2002 Georgia condemned as illegal attempts by the Abkhazian authorities to privatize some of its sanatoriums and tourist resorts.

**President of the Republic:** VLADISLAV G. ARDZINBA.

**Deputy President:** VALERII ARSHBA.

**Prime Minister:** RAUL KHADZHIMBA.

**Chairman of the National Assembly of Abkhazia:** NUGZAR ASHUBA.

**Chairman of the Supreme Council:** SOKRAT DZHINDZHOLIA.

# AJARIA

The Autonomous Republic of Ajaria was established on 16 July 1922. It is situated in the south-west of Georgia, on the border with Turkey, and covers an area of 3,000 sq km. In 1989 the population was 393,000. The Ajars are a Georgian people, who adopted Islam while Ajaria was under Ottoman rule. The Ajars have an unwritten language, Ajar, which is closely related to Georgian, but has been strongly influenced by Turkish. The capital of Ajaria is Batumi, with an estimated population of 137,000 in 1990.

In the late 1980s the Georgian nationalist movement questioned the region's autonomous status. In April 1991 Aslan Ibragimovich Abashidze, a senior government official in Tbilisi of noble Ajarian descent, was appointed Chairman of the Ajarian Supreme Soviet. Abashidze's party, the All-Georgian Union of Revival, secured the majority of the parliamentary seats in Ajaria in the November 1995 elections, a victory suspected by many to be in return for Abashidze's support for Shevardnadze in the national presidential election held simultaneously. Elections to the Ajarian Supreme Council were held on 22 September 1996, when the majority of seats (some 83%, according to official results) were won by an alliance of the All-Georgian Union of Revival and Shevardnadze's Citizen's Union of Georgia, amid further allegations of electoral irregularities. Abashidze was re-elected Chairman of the Council. Relations between the region and the central authorities deteriorated somewhat thereafter, as the Ajarians claimed the Georgian Government was attempting to increase its control over the republic. In October 1999 relations deteriorated further, when Ajaria refused to release prisoners pardoned by Shevardnadze under an amnesty. Abashidze also criticized the legislative elections held in Georgia in October and November, and subsequently relinquished his parliamentary man-

date, ostensibly owing to fear of assassination in Tbilisi; his seat was awarded to another member of his party. Abashidze was to have stood as a candidate in the Georgian presidential election of April 2000, but he withdrew his candidacy the day before it took place. On 18 April the Georgian Parliament voted to amend the Constitution, officially to register Ajaria as an Autonomous Republic. In June the Ajarian Supreme Council endorsed amendments to its Constitution, and in July 2001 it voted to rename itself the Parliament of the Autonomous Republic of Ajaria. Following elections in late 2001, a second parliamentary chamber was established. The 35-member Council of the Republic was elected by proportional representation, while seven of the Senate's 10 members were elected by majority vote. Abashidze was directly elected to the new post of Head of the Autonomous Republic (leader of the executive) on 4 November. The region's new bicameral legislature held its inaugural session one month later, following the implementation of amendments to the Constitution. In 2003 Ajaria withheld its tax contribution to Georgia's central budget, claiming that it had not received its share of budgetary spending; this was one of the reasons leading to the suspension of IMF lending in Georgia (see The Economy). In mid-July Abashidze dismissed the Government, owing to its failure to improve the budgetary deficit in the first six months of the year.

**Head of the Autonomous Republic of Ajaria:** ASLAN IBRAGIMOVICH ABASHIDZE.

**Chairman of Parliament:** REVAZ SHAMILISHVILI.

**Speaker of the Council of the Republic:** ALEKSANDRE GOBRONIDZE.

**Deputy Speaker of the Council of the Republic:** OSIKO GVARISHVILI.

# SOUTH OSSETIA

The South Ossetian Autonomous Oblast (region) was established on 20 April 1922. It is situated in the north of Georgia and borders the Russian federal territory of North Ossetia (Osetiya). It covers an area of 3,900 sq km. In 1989 the population was 99,000, although the subsequent conflict resulted in the displacement of as many as 30,000 refugees. In 1979 66.4% of the population were Ossetians and 28.8% Georgians. The Ossetians are an Iranian (Persian) people, some of whom adopted Islam from the Kabardins. The national language is Ossetian, a member of the North-Eastern group of Iranian languages. The capital of the region is Tskhinvali.

The Regional Council (oblast soviet) adopted a declaration of sovereignty on 20 September 1990 and proclaimed the territory the South Ossetian Soviet Democratic Republic. The region's autonomous status was abolished by the Georgian Supreme Soviet on 11 December 1990, and it was merged with adjoining areas to form an administrative region known as Shidi Kartli. Jurisdiction of the region was then disputed, amid continuing conflict. A second declaration of independence was issued in December 1991, supported by a referendum held in the region in January 1992. Following the ousting of President Gamsakhurdia in January the Georgian Military Council released the South Ossetian leader and reformed the system of local government. Tension in the area eased, although South Ossetia persisted in its stated intent to secede. In July a cease-fire agreement was reached and a Russian-led peace-keeping force was deployed in the region. South Ossetia introduced a new Constitution on 23 December 1993 and held elections in April 1994. In July 1995 discussions on a political settlement began, under the aegis of the Organization for Security and Co-operation in Europe (OSCE). South Ossetian and Georgian leaders signed a Memorandum on Security and Mutual Understanding on 16 May 1996. In September a presidential system of government was introduced; a presidential election was held on 10 November and won by Ludvig

Chibirov, who obtained some 65% of the votes cast. In September 1997 and June 1998 agreements providing for economic assistance to the region and the safe return of refugees were signed by President Shevardnadze and Chibirov. The status of the region was to be determined after the return of the refugees; Shevardnadze proposed the creation of a federation of states, including South Ossetia, but the South Ossetian parliament continued to favour the creation of an independent republic within the Commonwealth of Independent States (CIS). In May 1999 legislative elections were held. The Communist Party obtained some 39% of the votes cast, but neither the Georgian authorities nor the OSCE recognized the results. Dimitri Sanakoyev was appointed Prime Minister in mid-June 2001, following the resignation of Merab Chigoyev. Negotiations with the Georgian Government, on reconstruction and the status of the region, were held in September, but no agreement was reached. A presidential election took place on 18 November, and the two leading candidates, Eduard Kokoyev, a Russian-based businessman, and the parliamentary Chairman, Stanislav Kochiyev, subsequently proceeded to a second round of voting. The 'run-off' election finally took place on 6 December, having been postponed when Chibirov's son reportedly led a detachment of police-officers to the parliament building in protest at the first-round results. Kokoyev secured 55% of the votes cast in the second round, and was subsequently confirmed as President. Kokoyev advocated unification with North Osetiya and associate membership of the Russian Federation, following recognition of South Ossetian independence. At the beginning of July 2003 Kokoyev purged his Government (allegedly pre-empting a possible coup), thus undermining both the political power and business connections of several high-ranking figures, and strengthening his own position, which had previously been regarded as tenuous. In September he appointed Igor Sanakoyev, a Russian citizen, as Prime Minister, after dismissing the Government in the previous month for its failure to fulfil the budget, amid allegations of corruption.

**President:** EDUARD KOKOYEV (KOKOITI).

**Prime Minister and Chairman of the Council of Ministers:** IGOR SANAKOYEV.

# Bibliography

Allen, W. E. D. *A History of the Georgian People from the Beginning Down to the Roman Conquest in the Nineteenth Century.* London, Paul, 1932; New York, NY, Barnes and Noble, 1971.

Avalov, Z. *The Annexation of Georgia to Russia.* New York, Chalidze Publications, 1982.

Aves, J. *Path to National Independence in Georgia 1987–1990.* London, London School of Slavonic and East European Studies, 1991.

*Georgia: From Chaos to Stability.* London, Royal Institute of International Affairs, 1996.

Bitov, A. *A Captive of the Caucasus: Journeys in Armenia and Georgia.* (Translated by Susan Brownsberger.) London, Harvill, 1993.

Braund, D. *A History of Colchis and Transcaucasian Iberia.* Oxford, Clarendon Press, 1994.

Chervonnaya, S. *Conflict in the Caucasus: Georgia, Abkhazia and the Russian Shadow.* Glastonbury, Gothic Image Publications, 1995.

Diuk, N., and Karatnycky, A. *New Nations Rising: The Fall of the Soviets and the Challenge of Independence.* New York, NY, and Chichester, John Wiley and Sons, 1993.

Ekedahl, Carolyn M., and Goodman, Melvin A. *The Wars of Eduard Shevardnadze.* London, C. Hurst and Co, 1997.

Gachechiladze, R. *The New Georgia: Space, Society, Politics.* London, University College London Press, 1995.

Hewitt, George. *The Abkhazians: A Handbook.* New York, NY, St Martin's Press, 1999.

Jones, Stephen. 'The Establishment of Soviet Power in Transcaucasia: the Case of Georgia 1921–28' in *Soviet Studies.* Vol. 40, No. 4, 1982.

Kautsky, K. *Georgia, a Social-Democratic Peasant Republic, Impressions and Observations.* London, 1921.

Lang, D. M. *The Last Years of the Georgian Monarchy, 1658–1832.* New York, NY, Columbia University Press, 1957.

*A Modern History of Georgia.* London, Weidenfeld and Nicolson, 1962.

*The Georgians.* London, Thames and Hudson, 1966.

Parsons, R. 'National Integration in Soviet Georgia', in *Soviet Studies.* Vol. 34, No. 4, 1982.

Rayfield, D. *The Literature of Georgia.* Oxford, Clarendon Press, 1995.

Reisner, O. 'The Tergdaleulebi–Founders of the Georgian National Identity', in Löb, L. (Ed.). *Forms of Identity in European History.* Szeged, 1995.

Suny, R. G. *The Making of the Georgian Nation.* London, I. B. Tauris, 1989.

Wyzan, Michael. *First Steps Towards Economic Independence.* Westport, CT, Praeger, 1995.

Also see the Select Bibliography in Part Four.

# KAZAKHSTAN

## Geography

### PHYSICAL FEATURES

The Republic of Kazakhstan (until December 1991, the Kazakh Soviet Socialist Republic) is a landlocked country in Central Asia, the western extremity of which reaches into Europe. It is the second-largest country in the region, extending some 1,900 km (1,200 miles) from the Volga river in the west to the Altai mountains in the east, and about 1,300 km (800 miles) from the Siberian plain in the north to the Central Asian deserts in the south. Western geographers considered Kazakhstan to be the northernmost of five Central Asian republics, but Soviet geographers, for historical reasons, did not include it in their concept of Central Asia. After the dissolution of the USSR, however, Kazakhstan considered itself part of the Central Asian region.

To the south Kazakhstan borders Turkmenistan, Uzbekistan and Kyrgyzstan. To the east there is a 1,700-km frontier with the People's Republic of China. The long northern border is with Russia. In the south-west there is a 2,320-km coastline on the Caspian Sea. The total area is 2,717,300 sq km (1,049,150 sq miles), over four-fifths the size of India (but with only 2% of the population).

The relief is extremely varied. A northern belt dominated by steppes is separated by the hilly uplands of central Kazakhstan from the semi-desert and desert to the south (part of the Kzyl Kum—Red Sands—desert falls within the borders of the country). Lowlands account for more than one-third of the territory, mountainous regions cover nearly one-fifth and hilly plains and plateaux occupy the rest of the country. The western regions are dominated by the lowlands of the Caspian Depression, which is drained by the River Ural. To the east of the western lowlands is the vast Turan Plain, much of which is sparsely inhabited desert. The flat north-central regions are the beginning of the Western Siberian Plain; to the south of the Plain are the hilly uplands of central Kazakhstan. On the eastern and south-eastern borders there are high mountain ranges.

Northern Kazakhstan possesses relatively good water resources, being dominated by numerous lakes and two large river systems. In the west the Ural and the Emba drain into the Caspian Sea. In the centre of the country the Irtysh, which rises in the north-east, and its tributaries flow north, across Siberia, Russia, to empty into the Arctic Ocean. There is a shortage of water in the south, however, the only substantial river in the area being the Syr-Dar'ya, which rises in Kyrgyzstan, in the Tien Shan mountain range, and used to empty into the Aral Sea. The waters of the Syr-Dar'ya were extensively used for irrigation from the 1960s, causing serious desiccation of the Aral Sea, the northern part of which is in Kazakhstan.

The Aral Sea became one of the world's most serious areas of environmental disaster. Without the in-flow from the Syr-Dar'ya and, except in years of exceptionally high rainfall, without that from the Amu-Dar'ya either, the Sea shrank at an ever-increasing rate. By the late 1990s it had lost almost one-half of its original area (to comprise almost 40,000 sq km), the surface level had fallen by 20 m (66 ft) and the volume reduced by over 800 cu km. For many years the favoured solution for alleviating the water shortage in the southern belt and in the southern Central Asian countries, and thereby lessening the demands on the Syr-Dar'ya, was to divert the waters of the rivers that rose in central Kazakhstan (at its most extreme, the scheme aimed at the so-called reversal of

the Siberian rivers; that is, to make them flow southwards rather than northwards). The demise of the USSR seemed to end the likelihood of this scheme being realized. Attempts were then concentrated on stabilizing the level of the Sea, to prevent any further deterioration.

### CLIMATE

The climate is of a strongly continental type, but there are wide variations throughout the territory. Average temperatures in January range from –18°C (0°F) in the north to –3°C (27°F) in the south. Winters are long in the north, lasting from late October to mid-April. In July average temperatures are 19°C (66°F) in the north, although the north-east of the country tends to be slightly warmer, and 28°–30°C (82°–86°F) in the south. Levels of precipitation are equally varied. Average annual rainfall in mountainous regions reaches 1,600 mm (63 ins), whereas in the central desert areas it is less then 100 mm. There are strong winds throughout the year, especially in the north, west and central regions; the dry *sukhovei* is particularly harmful to agriculture.

### POPULATION

According to the census of 1999, at which the total population was 14,953,126, Kazakhs formed the largest ethnic group in the republic, accounting for 53.4% of the population, out-numbering the ethnic Russian population (30.0%—which had formed the majority at the 1979 census, and which had accounted for 37.8% of the population at the 1989 census), owing primarily to increased emigration by ethnic Russians and immigration by ethnic Kazakhs from other, mainly former Soviet, states. Other major ethnic groups were Ukrainians (3.7%), Uzbeks (2.5%) and Germans (2.4%). There were also Tatars and small numbers of Uigurs, Belarusians, Koreans (deported from the Soviet Far East in the late 1930s), Azeris and Turks.

Kazakh, a member of the Central Turkic group of languages, replaced Russian as the official language in September 1989. Since 1940 it has been written in a Cyrillic script of 42 characters. A Latin script was used until 1940, the traditional Arabic script having been replaced in 1928. The predominant religion is Islam, most Kazakhs being Sunni Muslims of the Hanafi school. Other ethnic groups have their own religious communities, notably the (Christian) Eastern Orthodox Church, which is attended mainly by Slavs.

The total population at 31 December 2002 was estimated to be 14,862,500. The large areas of desert accounted for the low population density of 5.5 inhabitants per sq km. In 2001 56.3% of the population lived in urban areas. In November 1997 the city of Akmola was officially declared the capital. The city was located in the centre-north of the country, in the heart of the so-called 'Virgin Lands' (for which, from the 1950s, it was renamed under Soviet rule—Tselinograd). In May 1998 it was renamed Astana ('Capital' in Kazakh), and it was declared open on 10 June; the city's population was estimated at 328,000 in mid-2001. Astana replaced as capital the largest city, Almaty (Alma-Ata), with an estimated population of 1,127,000 at mid-2000, which was situated in the extreme south-east of the country, on a seismic fault. Other important towns included Karaganda, an industrial city in central Kazakhstan (with a population of 436,900 at the census of 1999), and Shymkent (Chimkent —360,100) and Taraz (formerly Dzhambul—330,100) in the south of the country, near the border with Uzbekistan. The main urban centres, however, were in the north-east: Ust-Kamenogorsk (311,000), Pavlodar (300,500) and Semipalatinsk (269,600). The main port on the Caspian Sea was Atyrau (formerly Guriyev—142,500).

# Chronology

**6th century:** Turkic tribes began to settle in the area of modern Kazakhstan, which was on the western borders of their empire.

**1219:** The Mongols conquered the area, destroying the urban culture of the south, which had emerged in the 10th century. The Golden and White Hordes (Tatars) became the dominant powers of the region.

**c. 1511–23:** Kasym Khan established himself as leader of a loose confederation of steppe tribes, the Kazakh Orda (Horde). Some unity continued under his successor, Tahir, but did not persist.

**1645:** Guriyev (Atyrau), on the Caspian Sea, was acquired by the Russian Empire, which by this time bordered the territories of the Kazakh Hordes (the Little, the Middle and the Great).

**1731:** Under pressure from the Oirot Mongols, the Khan of the Little Horde (in the west, near the Caspian) was granted the protection of the Russian Tsar.

**1740:** The Khans of the Middle Horde (in the north and east of modern Kazakhstan) gained Russian protection.

**1742:** Part of the Great Horde, to the south of the other Hordes, secured the protection of the Russian Empire from the Oirot Mongols (although in 1758 the Oirots were to be defeated by the Chinese Manzhou—Manchu Empire, which became the ruler of the rest of the Great Horde).

**1822:** The absorption of the Kazakhs into the Russian Empire began with the territory of the Middle Horde, which was divided into Russian administrative units, while Russian military jurisdiction was imposed for criminal offences and Kazakhs were forbidden to acquire serfs.

**1824:** The same process was implemented in the territory of the Little Horde and, despite some revolts and resistance, was followed by new taxation demands and strictures, such as Kazakhs being denied the right to cultivate land.

**1847:** The Great Horde lost its independence, when it was required to pledge its allegiance to the Russian Empire. The following year the last Khan of the Middle Horde was formally deposed.

**1854:** Foundation of the Russian garrison town of Vernoye (now Almaty).

**1861:** The emancipation of the serfs in the Russian Empire witnessed the first large influx of Slav settlers to Kazakh territory.

**1895:** A Russian commission set aside more land of the nomadic Kazakhs for settlement by Slav cultivators.

**1906–12:** The Stolypin agrarian reforms allowed another large influx of Slav (mainly Russian and Ukrainian) settlers, provoking Kazakh nationalism and resentment.

**1916:** An attempt to impose labour and military service on the non-Russian peoples of the Empire occasioned a widespread revolt by the Kazakhs; the rebellion was savagely crushed by the Governor-General of Turkestan, who resolved to drive the nomads from their lands.

**1917:** With the collapse of tsarist authority in the Russian Revolutions, three Kazakh Conferences were held in Orenburg (now in the Russian Federation), although their narrow nationalism failed to attract widespread support. Kazakhstan became fiercely contested by the Red Army, the 'Whites' and the Kazakh nationalists of the Alash Orda (led by Ali Bukeikhanov and Ahmed Bayturshin).

**26 August 1920:** Following the communist victory in the Civil War, the Russian authorities established a Kyrgyz Autonomous Soviet Socialist Republic (ASSR), in Orenburg (the Russians called the Kazakhs 'Kyrgyz' or 'Kyrgyz-Kazakhs' and knew the Kyrgyz as 'Kara-Kyrgyz').

**1925:** The Kyrgyz ASSR was renamed the Kazakh ASSR.

**1928:** The Arabic script was replaced by a Latin script for the written Kazakh language.

**1929:** The communist authorities decided on the collectivization and the resettlement of nomads in Kazakhstan; this provoked fierce resistance, and subsequent famine.

**1930:** Karakalpakstan was detached from the Kazakh ASSR and made part of Uzbekistan.

**5 December 1936:** The Kazakh ASSR was detached from the Russian Federation and made a constituent partner of the Soviet federation, a Union Republic, the Kazakh Soviet Socialist Republic (SSR).

**1940:** A modified Cyrillic alphabet (with an unusually large number of characters—42) was introduced for the Kazakh language.

**1944:** The Soviet leader, Stalin (Iosif V. Dzhugashvili), ordered the deportation to Kazakhstan and Siberia of many peoples who had attracted his suspicion, including some 400,000 Chechens, 200,000 Crimean Tatars, 75,000 Ingush and 40,000 Balkars. Many of the Volga Germans had already been deported, mainly to Kazakhstan. Despite the rehabilitation of significant numbers of these peoples in 1957, many remained in Kazakhstan.

**1954:** A Kazakh was replaced as First Secretary of the Communist Party of Kazakhstan (CPK) by an ethnic Russian, together with a Russian Second Secretary, Leonid Brezhnev (later Soviet leader, 1964–82), who himself became leader of the CPK in 1955–56. The official encouragement of ploughing 'Virgin Lands' began; the scheme continued to 1960 and Kazakhstan accounted for almost 60% of the extra land farmed throughout the USSR.

**4 October 1957:** The USSR placed the first man-made satellite (Sputnik I) in orbit around the earth; the Soviet space programme was based at the Baikonur space centre, Leninsk (Turatam).

**1961–62:** There was a major influx of Kazakh and Uigur refugees from the People's Republic of China.

**12 April 1961:** The first manned space flight was undertaken, by Maj. Yurii Gagarin, on the Vostok I spacecraft.

**1964:** Dinmukhamed Kunayev, who had briefly succeeded Brezhnev as First Secretary of the CPK in 1956, returned to the post, later becoming the first Kazakh in the Politburo of the all-Union Party.

**1984:** Nursultan Nazarbayev was appointed Chairman of the Council of Ministers, the republican premier.

**16 December 1986:** The first nationalist riots experienced by the new Soviet leader, Mikhail Gorbachev, occurred in Almaty, after Kunayev was dismissed for corruption and replaced by an ethnic Russian, Gennadii Kolbin.

**June 1989:** Nazarbayev was appointed First Secretary of the CPK. The first outbreak of ethnic violence, precipitated by economic deprivation, occurred in the western, petroleum-refining town of Novyi Uzen, when Kazakh youths attacked Lezgins; the violence continued sporadically for the next few months.

**September 1989:** Among other reforms, the Supreme Soviet (parliament) enacted a law making Kazakh the official language of the republic; Russian remained the language of inter-ethnic communication (this law was upheld by the Constitution of January 1993).

**February 1990:** Nazarbayev was elected Chairman of the Supreme Soviet.

**25 March 1990:** Elections to the Supreme Soviet of Kazakhstan took place, with the communists retaining an overwhelming majority in the legislature, despite some political reforms; in the following month parliament elected Nazarbayev to the new post of President.

**September 1990:** An explosion at a factory in Ulba, eastern Kazakhstan, contaminated a large area with toxic gases and led to demonstrations; pollution was a major focus for opposition in the late 1980s and early 1990s, as was protest about the nuclear tests at Semipalatinsk (one of the largest opposition groups was the Nevada-Semipalatinsk movement of Olzhas Suleimenov).

**25 October 1990:** Kazakhstan declared itself to be a sovereign state and attempted to outlaw the storing or testing of nuclear weapons on its territory.

**17 March 1991:** In the referendum on the preservation of the Union, 94.1% of those who voted (88.2% of the electorate) favoured Kazakhstan remaining in the federation.

**18–21 August 1991:** An attempted *coup d'état* in Moscow, Russia (the Soviet capital), failed, signalling the final dismantling of institutionalized communist authority in the USSR; the effective increase of authority for republican leaders enabled President Nazarbayev to ban nuclear testing at Semipalatinsk. In the same month Kazakhstan announced its first programme for the privatization of enterprises.

**October 1991:** Sergei Tereshchenko, an ethnic Ukrainian, was appointed Chairman of the Council of Ministers (Prime Minister).

**1 December 1991:** Nazarbayev was confirmed in office as President of Kazakhstan by direct election; he was the sole candidate and won 98.8% of the votes cast.

**16 December 1991:** The Supreme Soviet (Supreme Kenges) declared the independence of Kazakhstan, the last Union Republic to do so.

**21 December 1991:** At a meeting in Almaty the leaders of 11 Union Republics signed a protocol on the formation of the new Commonwealth, thereby dissolving the USSR.

**March 1992:** Kazakhstan became a member of the UN.

**June 1992:** Some 5,000 opposition supporters demonstrated in Almaty against the continued dominance of government by former communists. Four months later the three main nationalist groups, Azat (Freedom), the Republican Party and the Dzheltoksan (December) National Democratic Party, united to form the Republican Party—Azat.

**28 January 1993:** After public consultations lasting almost one year, the Supreme Kenges enacted a new Constitution.

**15 November 1993:** Amid complaints of being forced out of the 'rouble zone', Kazakhstan introduced its own currency, the tenge, with the support of the IMF.

**December 1993:** The Supreme Kenges announced its imminent dissolution, in preparation for new elections; it then proceeded to grant the President additional powers in the interim and to ratify the Treaty on the Non-Proliferation of Nuclear Weapons. The dissolution had been precipitated by 43 deputies resigning their mandates.

**25 December 1993:** Kazakhstan, unable to afford the maintenance of the space programme alone, agreed that Russia should lease the Baikonur facilities.

**7 March 1994:** A general election to the Supreme Kenges took place.

**May 1994:** Kazakhstan joined the North Atlantic Treaty Organization's (NATO) 'Partnership for Peace' programme of military co-operation.

**October 1994:** The Government tendered its resignation, having been criticized by President Nazarbayev for the slow pace of economic reform. The President subsequently appointed Akezhan Kazhegeldin to chair a new Council of Ministers.

**11 March 1995:** Following the findings of the Constitutional Court, which had ruled in the previous month that the results of the general election of 1994 were null and void, President Nazarbayev dissolved parliament and proceeded to rule by decree. The Council of Ministers tendered its resignation but was later reinstated, with few changes.

**29 April 1995:** A nation-wide referendum was held on the extension of President Nazarbayev's term of office until 1 December 2000. A total of 95.4% of participants, representing 91% of the electorate, voted in favour.

**30 August 1995:** A new Constitution was approved by 89.1% of the electorate in a referendum; it took effect on 6 September, replacing the Supreme Kenges with a bicameral Parliament (comprising a 47-member Senate and a 67-member Majlis or Assembly) and the Constitutional Court with a Constitutional Council.

**September 1995:** A presidential decree confirmed that Akmola (formerly Tselinograd) would become the new capital (agreed by the Supreme Kenges in July 1994).

**5 December 1995:** Elections were held to the upper chamber of the new Parliament, the Senate; 38 of the 40 regionally elected seats were filled.

**9 December 1995:** In elections to the lower chamber of the legislature, the Majlis, candidates obtained the requisite number of votes in only 43 of the 67 constituencies, necessitating further elections in the remaining constituencies on 23 December.

**22 September 1997:** Prime Minister Kazhegeldin departed for medical treatment in Switzerland; despite being exonerated of alleged financial malpractice in August, his reputation had been undermined by earlier Russian media reports that he had admitted involvement with the former Soviet state security service (KGB) in the late 1980s.

**10 October 1997:** Nurlan Balgymbayev, hitherto President of the state hydrocarbons company, KazakhOil, and considered an opponent of privatization, was appointed Prime Minister; he formed a new, smaller Government.

**8 November 1997:** Akmola was inaugurated as the new capital by President Nazarbayev.

**6 May 1998:** A presidential decree was issued, changing the name of the new capital, Akmola, to Astana; it was officially opened on 10 June.

**6 July 1998:** The Presidents of Kazakhstan and Russia signed a treaty agreeing the demarcation of seabed claims in the northern part of the Caspian Sea.

**8 October 1998:** Parliament adopted a number of constitutional amendments and a revised date for the presidential election (originally scheduled for 2000), which was brought forward to January 1999.

**10 January 1999:** Nazarbayev was re-elected as President with 81.0% of the votes cast in an election in which 86.3% of the registered electorate took part. The Organization for Security and Co-operation in Europe (OSCE) refused to monitor the election, judging it to be an unfair contest, owing, in part, to a ruling that had debarred certain candidates, including former Prime Minister Kazhegeldin. President Nazarbayev was sworn in on 20 January and he announced a new government structure two days later, which included six new ministries and seven new agencies, to replace former state committees.

**5 July 1999:** A Russian craft exploded when launching from the Baikonur space centre at Turatam, dispersing potentially toxic debris over central Kazakhstan. A further incident occurred in October, prompting officials to prohibit Russia from using the facilities. In November Russia agreed to pay outstanding rental fees of US $115m., and the restriction was removed in February 2000.

**1 October 1999:** Balgymbayev resigned as Prime Minister and returned to his former position as President of KazakhOil. Kasymzhomart Tokayev was confirmed as his successor on 12 October.

**10 October 1999:** Elections to an expanded, 77-member Majlis (as well as those to municipal and local councils) were held. Further rounds of voting to the Majlis were held on 24 October and 26 December, as a result of which Otan (Fatherland), a pro-presidential coalition, obtained 23 seats. Independent candidates secured 34 seats.

**27 June 2000:** A law was passed granting President Nazarbayev, as the first President of Kazakhstan, certain guarantees and rights, which were to remain in force even after the expiry of his term of office.

**31 January 2001:** New legislation on land ownership came into effect. Land was to remain largely under state ownership, but individuals were allowed to buy small plots or rent large areas of agricultural land; foreigners were prohibited from owning land but could rent large areas.

**26–27 April 2001:** At a meeting of leaders of the Turkic-speaking countries, the Presidents of Azerbaijan, Kazakhstan, Kyrgyzstan, Turkey and Turkmenistan, and the Chairman of Uzbekistan's Oly Majlis (Supreme Assembly) signed an agreement on regional co-operation to combat terrorism and drugs trafficking, the revival of the old 'Silk Road' trade route between China and Europe, and protection of the environment.

**6 September 2001:** Former Prime Minister Kazhegeldin, who had been tried *in absentia* on charges of abuse of power, bribery and the illegal possession of weapons, was sentenced to 10 years' imprisonment, amid allegations that the trial had been politically motivated.

**18 November 2001:** A number of prominent political and business figures, including the Akim (Governor) of Pavlodar oblast, Ghalymzhan Zhakiyanov, and a Deputy Prime Minister, Uraz Dzhandosov, announced the formation of a new, reformist political party, the Democratic Choice of Kazakhstan (DCK). Zhakiyanov and Dzhandosov subsequently left their government posts, following accusations of disloyalty.

**27 November 2001:** A pipeline to carry petroleum from the country's Tengiz oilfield to Novorossiisk, on Russia's Black Sea coast, was inaugurated.

**14 December 2001:** President Nazarbayev signed the Comprehensive Nuclear Test Ban Treaty, following its ratification by both houses of Parliament.

**21 December 2001:** President Nazarbayev made an official visit to the USA, where he had talks with President George W. Bush on counter-terrorism and energy issues. An agreement was consequently signed, committing Kazakhstan to the export of petroleum via a proposed pipeline from Georgia to Turkey, which was strongly supported by the US Government.

**28 January 2002:** Prime Minister Kasymzhomart Tokayev announced the resignation of his Government. Tokayev was succeeded by Imangali Tasmagambetov, and a new Government was formed, to which four new ministers were appointed.

**16 March 2002:** Following divisions with the DCK, the founding congress of a new party, Ak Zhol (Light Road), established by Dzhandosov, took place.

**13 May 2002:** An agreement was signed with Russia on the equal division of three oilfields in the northern Caspian, augmenting the 1998 accord on the delimitation of the Sea. A trilateral agreement was signed between Azerbaijan, Kazakhstan and Russia on 14 May 2003.

**15 July 2002:** President Nazarbayev passed a new law on political parties, amid widespread opposition. The legislation required political parties to have at least 50,000 members, from every region of the country, in order to qualify for registration; all parties were required to re-register by April 2003.

**18 July 2002:** The former Minister of Energy, Industry and Trade, and a leading member of the DCK, Mukhtar Ablyazov, was sentenced to six years' imprisonment, after being found guilty of abuse of office; however, he received a presidential pardon in May 2003, and subsequently announced his withdrawal from politics.

**2 August 2002:** Opposition leader Ghalymzhan Zhakiyanov was sentenced to seven years' imprisonment, following charges of abuse of office and embezzlement. Human rights organizations expressed concern at the severity of the sentence, which the opposition claimed was politically motivated.

**8 October 2002:** Partial elections to the Senate were held.

**28 November 2002:** Aleksandr Lukin, a former Governor of Ust-Kamenogorsk (the administrative centre of the Eastern Kazakhstan oblast), was sentenced to more than three years in prison, after being found guilty of offences relating to his time in office.

**28 January 2003:** Sergei Duvanov, an independent journalist, was sentenced to over three years' imprisonment, after being convicted of rape. Some observers believed his arrest had been politically motivated, as he had been strongly critical of President Nazarbayev, and the sentence was condemned by the European Union and the USA.

**30 March 2003:** A US businessman was indicted under the 1977 US Foreign Corrupt Practices Act (which prohibits US companies or individuals from bribing foreign officials in order to secure an agreement), for allegedly using financial incentives to persuade prominent Kazakhstani politicians to award important contracts to US petroleum companies. Nazarbayev and former Prime Minister Nurlan Balgymbayev were among those alleged to have received money and gifts totalling US \$78m. from James H. Giffen, a former adviser to Nazarbayev.

**28 April 2003:** Representatives from Armenia, Belarus, Kazakhstan, Kyrgyzstan, Russia and Tajikistan formally inaugurated the successor to the Collective Security Treaty, a new regional defence organization known as the Collective Security Treaty Organization (CSTO).

**19 May 2003:** Tasmagambetov's Government won a vote of 'no confidence', over its handling of agrarian reform. None the less, on 11 June Tasmagambetov announced the resignation of his Government, claiming that some votes had been falsified.

**13 June 2003:** Parliament approved the nomination of Daniyal Akhmetov, a former Governor of Pavlodar oblast, as Prime Minister. Several ministers in the previous administration were subsequently re-appointed to the Government.

**20 June 2003:** Parliament adopted a controversial new land code, with amendments proposed by Nazarbayev, providing for the private ownership of land.

**4 July 2003:** Nazarbayev signed a number of laws confirming the delimitation of Kazakhstan's borders with Kyrgyzstan, Turkmenistan and Uzbekistan.

**6–12 August 2003:** Kazakhstan and the People's Republic of China jointly hosted military manoeuvres involving troops from both countries, as well as from Kyrgyzstan, Russia and Tajikistan, under the auspices of the Shanghai Convention on Combating Terrorism, Separatism and Extremism, signed by the five countries in June 2001.

**12 September 2003:** Zautbek Turisbekov was appointed as Minister of Internal Affairs, replacing Col-Gen. Kairbek Suleimenov, following demands by Nazarbayev that the heads of the law-enforcement and security offices be civilian appointments. The following day new Ministers of Culture and of Information were appointed, after the reorganization of the Ministry of Culture, Information and Public Accord.

# History

## Dr SHIRIN AKINER

### THE FORMATION OF KAZAKHSTAN

Kazakhstan, in its modern form as a unified, political entity, came into being after the establishment of Soviet rule. In 1920 the Kyrgyz (that is, Kazakh) Autonomous Soviet Socialist Republic (ASSR) was created, within the jurisdiction of the Russian Federation. The Kazakhs were then known to the Russians as Kyrgyz, or Kyrgyz-Kazakhs, to distinguish them from the unrelated Cossacks. As a result of the 1924–25 National Delimitation of Central Asia, some Kazakh-populated areas were transferred to the jurisdiction of the territory, which, in 1925, was formally renamed the Kazakh ASSR. In 1930 the Karakalpak region (now in Uzbekistan) was detached from the republic. In 1936 Kazakhstan was elevated to the status of a full Union Republic, becoming the Kazakh Soviet Socialist Republic (SSR). Despite some redrawing of the borders, therefore, the main contours of Kazakhstan remained those that had been mapped out in the early Soviet period. With the collapse of the USSR, on 16 December 1991 the territory declared its independence as the Republic of Kazakhstan. It joined 11 other former Union Republics in the Commonwealth of Independent States (CIS), by the Almaty Declaration of 21 December, and was admitted to the UN as a member state in March 1992.

### THE PEOPLES OF KAZAKHSTAN

Independent Kazakhstan was a multi-ethnic, multicultural country. At the beginning of the 1990s the population numbered some 16.5m., encompassing over 100 ethnic groups. The two largest groups were the Kazakhs (39.7% of the total population according to the 1989 census) and the Russians (37.8%). Other groups of significant size included non-indigenous peoples, such as Germans, Ukrainians and Koreans. Within a decade, the population had declined to 14.9m., of which 53.4% were Kazakhs and only 30.0% Russians. This change in the ethnic balance was the result of such factors as the immigration of Kazakhs from other countries (mainly other Soviet successor states, but also including the return of several thousand from Iran and Mongolia, descendants of those who fled the Russian Revolution and Civil War) and the mass emigration of non-Kazakhs, especially Russians.

#### Kazakhs

The Kazakhs are a Turkic people, descendants of nomadic tribes who settled on the territory of present-day Kazakhstan in the sixth century AD, or possibly earlier. The region lay on the ancient transcontinental 'Silk Road', a network of trade routes that linked China, Persia (Iran) and Transoxiana (roughly the area of modern Uzbekistan). During the 10th century a strong urban culture developed in the south, although further to the north nomadic pastoralism remained the dominant way of life. In the early 13th century Kazakhstan was conquered by the Mongols and the cities of the south, such as Otrar and Taraz, were destroyed. Trade links were eventually revived, but the urban centres never fully regained their previous levels of prosperity and sophistication.

The 14th and 15th centuries were marked by power struggles, most of which were centred on the southern belt. Mongol princes from the Golden and White Hordes fought among themselves, and also with Uzbek and Nogai contenders, for control of the region. This strife resulted in migration, as whole tribes changed allegiance and moved from one area to another. There was a period of relative stability in the early 16th century, when one warlord, Kasym Khan, succeeded in uniting the main tribes (such as the Kipchaks, Naimans, Usuns and Dulats) under his rule (from approximately 1511 to 1523). From this time it is possible to speak of a Kazakh nation, despite the fact that after Kasym's death the internecine struggles were renewed as, too, were the campaigns against Central Asian fiefdoms in the south. By the beginning of the 17th century three major groupings had emerged among the Kazakhs, each under the leadership of its own khan (leader): the Great Horde (Ulu Zhuz), the territory of which lay to the south-east, between the Aral Sea and Lake Balkhash; the Middle Horde (Orta Zhuz), which controlled the central zone, further north, between the Irtysh and the Tobol rivers; and the Little Horde (Kishi Zhuz), with territory to the north of the Caspian Sea, between the Emba and the Ural rivers. These Hordes were further divided into tribes and clans. There was a highly developed awareness of genealogy, since lineage determined both place in society and rights to pasture land. This feature of Kazakh society survived the later tsarist and Soviet periods.

The Kazakh aristocracy adopted Islam during the 14th and 15th centuries. Turkestan, a city in the far south, was the home of Ahmad Yasavi (who died in the middle of the 12th century), one of the greatest Sufi mystics. His influence did much to encourage the spread of Islam in the region. By the 14th century his burial place had become a highly revered shrine (three pilgrimages to this site were supposed to equal the Pilgrimage—hajj—to Mecca). In 1397 the Mongol ruler, Timur 'the Lame' (Tamerlane), built a mausoleum over Yasavi's tomb and, later, several of the khans of the Middle and Little Hordes were buried there. The nomadic tribes in the north, however, had little contact with Islam. They were probably not fully converted until the 19th century, when, under the Russian tsarist administration, Tatar Muslim missionaries were sent to the region as part of a policy to tame these unruly subjects. A number of mosques were built during this period, but, although the Kazakhs became, by their own standards, sincere believers, they were not very devout by conventional measures. They incorporated many elements of customary law (adat) and animism into Islam, creating a fusion of different traditions that was uniquely Kazakh.

The Kazakh Hordes came under Russian domination because they were constantly under attack from their neighbours, particularly the Oirot Mongols. Thus, during the 18th century the Kazakhs gradually had recourse to Russian protection: the Little Horde in 1731; the Middle Horde in 1740; and part of the Great Horde in 1742 (the rest of this Horde was to come under Manzhou—Manchu rule and remained part of China). Russian influence in the steppes grew ever stronger until, eventually, the entire region was under Russian control (with the exception of the area that fell within the Chinese Empire). After a gradual policy of limiting the powers of the khans and the introduction of the Russian administrative system under Tsar Alexander I (1801–25), the last Khan of the Middle Horde was deposed in 1848. A Russian garrison named Vernoye (Faithful) was established in the far east of the territory in 1854; this town, renamed Alma-Ata (later Almaty), was to become the capital of the Kazakh SSR and, until 1997, of independent Kazakhstan.

Traditionally, Kazakh culture was rooted in the nomadic way of life, expressed in the crafts and skills of daily life, as well as in the oral epics that encapsulated the history and philosophy of the people. The advent of the Russians opened the way to the ideas and opportunities of a (comparatively) developed European society. The majority of the Kazakh élite was highly responsive and came genuinely to admire Russian culture. A number of Kazakhs received an excellent education in St Petersburg and other Russian cities. A member of one of the princely families, Shokan Valikhanov (1835–65), served as an officer in the imperial army and wrote numerous scholarly works in Russian. The first of several Russian-Kazakh schools was opened in 1841. Scholars such as Ibraj Altynsarin (1841–89) played an active role in the development of the Kazakh literary language (which was written in the Arabic script until 1928), as well as in the general process of educational reform. Likewise, Abay Kunanbayev (1845–1904), a poet and prose writer, is widely considered to be the father of Kazakh literature. It was thanks to the pioneering efforts of this generation that, by the turn of the century, the Kazakhs were better educated and more politically aware than the other peoples of Central Asia.

Nomadism first came under threat in the second half of the 19th century, when large numbers of Russian settlers moved into northern Kazakhstan, took possession of the local population's traditional pasture lands and obstructed the routes of migration. This mass invasion of their territory was the cause of considerable resentment among the Kazakhs. It culminated in the fierce, although unsuccessful, uprising of 1916, which was triggered by the introduction of a draft for labour units, even though the Kazakhs had traditionally been exempt from military service. More than 50,000 tribesmen on the steppes and in the Fergana valley took part in the revolt, which was brutally suppressed.

Soon after, the February 1917 Revolution caused the collapse of tsarist power and, under Ali Bukeikhanov, a semi-independent Kazakh state, known as Alash Orda, was formed. However, the Kazakhs were soon brought under Bolshevik control, initially as part of the Russian Federation, although they were acknowledged as one of the nationalities of the USSR. It was under the communists that the second and decisive onslaught on the nomadic way of life took place. This was the collectivization campaign of the 1930s, as a result of which the remaining nomads were forcibly sedentarized. It has been estimated that just under one-half of the Kazakh population died from starvation and other problems caused by collectivization during this period (by 1959 the Kazakh population had still not recovered from these losses, then numbering some 347,000 fewer than in 1926). Subsequently, however, there was a demographic recovery and by the 1980s the Kazakhs once again became the largest ethnic group in their own republic. In addition to the numerical recovery of the population, Kazakh representation in the republican government and party institutions began to increase as, after the 1950s, a new generation of urbanized, educated Kazakhs emerged. In the 1990s, after independence, there was a revival of interest in the cultural legacy of nomadism, but it was no longer a living tradition. However, the great majority of Kazakhs still lived in rural areas, mostly in the less-developed southern belt. They tended to be conservative and culturally far removed from the highly educated, Europeanized, Russian-speaking Kazakhs of the urban centres.

**Slavs**

Slavs first began to settle in Kazakhstan in large numbers in the second half of the 19th century. The majority were farmers; there was a vast influx of land-hungry peasants after the emancipation of the serfs, in 1861, and the authorities continued to set aside large tracts of land for Russian and Ukrainian settlers, disrupting nomadic life and forcing many Kazakhs eastwards into Chinese territory. However, there were also industrial labourers who came to work in the nascent mining industry, as well as military personnel (including Cossack detachments) and a large civilian infrastructure. By 1926 the Russians already constituted nearly 20% (1.3m.) of the total population of Kazakhstan, and the Ukrainians accounted for a further 13% (860,000). While the Kazakh population was decreasing, the influx of Slavs continued during the 1930s and reached a peak during the Second World War (1939–45), when many industries and academic institutions were relocated to Kazakhstan. The 'Virgin Lands' scheme of Nikita Krushchev (Soviet leader in 1953–64), which aimed to raise grain production by ploughing large areas of the steppe, brought new Slav settlers to the region in the 1950s and early 1960s. By 1970 there were 5.5m. Russians and 933,000 Ukrainians in Kazakhstan. Both groups continued to expand, although at a slower rate than previously, with far less immigration to increase numbers. These population trends were only reversed in the 1990s, owing to the political changes arising from the demise of the USSR. By the 1999 census there were some 4.5m. Russians and 547,000 Ukrainians, compared with 8.0m. Kazakhs.

Post-independence, as in the 19th century, the Slavs remained concentrated in the northern belt, particularly in the eastern corner of the country, where most of the industrial centres were located. They were well represented in parliament (in the early 1990s it was claimed by some Kazakhs that over one-half of the deputies were Slavs) and several of them held key positions in government. The Cossacks and other nationalist groups sometimes demanded autonomy, but, at least in the early years of independence, the majority of the Slav population seemed prepared to remain part of Kazakhstan. For some time, however, the Slav population constituted the most serious potential threat to the integrity of the new state: if they had decided to press for partition, either to form their own state or to seek reunification with Russia, it seemed unlikely that the Kazakhs would be able to resist this pressure. However, many Russians chose to return to Russia and by August 1998 it was estimated that more than 2m. had left Kazakhstan.

### 'Punished Peoples'

On the eve of the Second World War, and during the War itself, many thousands of Volga Germans, Crimean Tatars, Koreans, Greeks, Chechen, Ingush and other peoples believed to be unreliable and anti-Soviet were deported to Kazakhstan from other parts of the Union. In the post-war period they gradually succeeded in gaining acceptance in Kazakhstani society and some came to hold high public office. However, by the beginning of the 1990s a number of these groups were either beginning to return to their pre-deportation homes or seeking repatriation to their original homelands abroad. In 1989 the German population in Kazakhstan numbered just under 1m. (5.8% of the total population), but many subsequently emigrated to Germany, reducing the number to 353,000 by 1999 (2.4% of the total population). The reasons for their departure were varied, but the primary causes were undoubtedly their hope for a more secure economic future in Germany, as well as their concern over what they perceived to be an inherent instability in Kazakhstan. By contrast, the Koreans (numbering just under 100,000 in 1999) seemed determined to stay and were extremely active in business ventures involving partnerships with the Republic of Korea (South Korea). The other, smaller groups of deportees had relatively limited opportunities to leave and there was little discernible reduction in their numbers during the early 1990s.

One of these smaller groups, the Poles, did, however, make an impact on politics in Kazakhstan. The Kazakhstani Poles were the result of successive phases of political exile from 1831, and many of the descendants of the earliest exiles did not, in the 1990s, exhibit much evidence of their Polish identity. Nevertheless, in the early 1990s many of them applied for repatriation to Poland, claiming that they feared persecution on religious grounds, if not immediately, then at some time in the future. Poland, at that time, did not have the welfare resources to devote to the settlement of repatriates, and adopted delaying tactics: a case-by-case approach, and slow processing of applications. The Roman Catholic Church in Poland tacitly supported this approach, and organized fund-raising to build churches for the Kazakhstani Poles. In September 1998 a mutual co-operation agreement was signed between Kazakhstan and the Vatican. The need to reassure the Kazakhstani Poles that their religious future was secure was undoubtedly one of the motives for concluding this agreement.

### THE NATIONALIST MOVEMENT

The revival of Kazakh nationalism began during the period of *glasnost* or *aygilik* (openness), initiated by the Soviet leader, Mikhail Gorbachev (1985–91). Complaints about lack of school instruction in the Kazakh language led to a decree of March 1987, which recommended improvements in the teaching of both Kazakh and Russian—an indication of the authorities' constant awareness of having to balance the demands and anxieties of both the major ethnic groups. In September 1989 the Supreme Soviet declared Kazakh to be the official language, although Russian was to be the language of inter-ethnic communication and all officials dealing with the public were to know both languages. This ruling was later embodied in the new Constitution of January 1993. The issue did seem to cause some increases in inter-ethnic tension, but, generally, it seemed to have been economic hardship that encouraged actual incidents in the Soviet period (notably the 1989 riot in Novyi Uzen). However, the return of many Russians to their homeland in the 1990s was in part attributed to concern for the future of their children, since reductions in Russian tuition in secondary schools made it increasingly difficult for Russian children educated in Kazakhstan to proceed to higher education in Russia. Moreover, even fluent Kazakh-speakers encountered difficulties when using their language for 'official' purposes.

In independent Kazakhstan the Government remained cautious of any nationalist group, discouraging extremists such as the radical party Alash (founded in 1999) or Slav groups, such as Yedinstvo and Lad. Kazakhs were increasingly dominant in the state, however, which fuelled ethnic Russian fears. This was a reversal of the situation in the late 1980s, when many Kazakhs feared that Russians were dominating the state and party apparatus. Under the First Secretary of the Communist Party of Kazakhstan (CPK), Dinmukhamed Kunayev (1956–86), Kazakhs had reached the highest positions of state in the republic, but often as a result of nepotism and corruption. Gorbachev's dismissal of Kunayev and many of his supporters, therefore, as part of his anti-corruption campaign (part of the *perestroika* or *qayta qurilis*, restructuring, initiative), was interpreted by some as anti-Kazakh. In December 1986 there was a violent nationalist protest in Almaty, in reaction to the announcement that the party's new First Secretary was to be an ethnic Russian, Gennadii Kolbin (1986–89). Kolbin continued with his reforms, although he also recommended institutions for ensuring fair ethnic representation in the administration. However, the problem was only really resolved by the appointment of Nursultan Nazarbayev, an ethnic Kazakh, to the CPK leadership, in June 1989.

Nazarbayev was careful to allay the fears of the Slavs and won their confidence partly because of his obvious support for the Union in the last years of the USSR. The Supreme Soviet did make a declaration of sovereignty in October 1990, and Nazarbayev was an advocate of economic sovereignty. However, in the referendum on the continuation of the Union, in March 1991, there was an overwhelming vote in favour of the federation. Although the question asked of voters in Kazakhstan was slightly different to the standard one, 94.1% of the votes cast (88.2% of those eligible voted) supported the renewal of the USSR. Kazakhstan was ready to sign the new Union Treaty in August, but the event was forestalled by the attempted *coup d'état* in Moscow (the Soviet, and Russian, capital). On 20 August Nazarbayev openly condemned the coup and, as it collapsed, he led the communist resignations and ordered the depoliticization of state institutions. Nevertheless, Kazakhstan signed the Treaty of the Economic Community in October and committed itself to a new Union in November. It had still not declared its independence when the leaders of the Slav republics resolved on a CIS and the effective dissolution of the USSR. The Supreme Soviet (Supreme Kenges) declared the independence of the country on 16 December, before it was admitted to the CIS as a founder member by the Almaty Declaration of 21 December.

In 1994 there was sporadic unrest among the Russian minority. The March elections to the Supreme Kenges, in which 59% of successful candidates were ethnic Kazakhs and only 28% ethnic Russians, led to allegations of discrimination against the Slav population (although, in fact, the ratio of

Kazakh–Russian representation in the Supreme Kenges did not deviate very greatly from that in the country as a whole). In March 1995, in an attempt to address the problem of inter-ethnic relations in the country, President Nazarbayev established the Assembly of Peoples of Kazakhstan, a forum with the status of a 'consultative presidential body'. The decision to move Kazakhstan's capital from Almaty to the industrial city of Akmola (formerly Tselinograd and, from May 1998, Astana), in the north of Kazakhstan, was perceived by some observers to be a strategic move to undermine Russian influence in the area, where Russians far outnumbered Kazakhs. President Nazarbayev's policy of maintaining close relations with Russia, however, helped allay Slav anxieties.

## THE POLITICAL STRUCTURES OF INDEPENDENT KAZAKHSTAN

The country has a presidential system of government, with separate executive, legislative and judicial bodies. During the early years of independence the executive branch of government consolidated its pre-eminence. This tendency was echoed in local government, which retained a considerable degree of autonomy, even under the Constitution of 1995. As in Russia, at the local level there was an initial lack of clarity between the functions of the legislative bodies (soviets, councils or maslikhat) and the executive bodies (previously known as the ispolkom, then the akimiyat). The latter grew increasingly powerful in the last years of the Union and the early years of independence, and came to report directly to the President, bypassing both the local councils and the ministries of the central Government.

### Presidential Power

In December 1991 Nursultan Nazarbayev became the first elected President of Kazakhstan, initially for a five-year term, with extensive personal powers, which included the authority to appoint and dismiss officials at all levels and to issue decrees counteracting parliamentary legislation. In 1995 his term of office was extended until 2000, as the result of a referendum, although, in the event, a presidential election was held in 1999 (see below). Nazarbayev had been appointed to the post of Chairman of the Council of Ministers (Head of Government) of Kazakhstan in 1984, then to that of First Secretary of the CPK in 1989. He introduced political and administrative reforms in September 1989, including the introduction of extra executive duties for the Chairman of the Supreme Soviet (the republican legislature). He was duly elected to this post in February 1990 and was, therefore, *de facto*, the republican Head of State. On 1 December 1991 he was the sole candidate in elections to the presidency, in which he obtained 98.8% of the votes cast. He played a prominent role in all-Union politics in the last years of the Soviet regime, and came to be regarded by many as one of the most active and internationally respected of the post-Soviet presidents. Nazarbayev was considered to be an astute negotiator, capable of toughness as well as flexibility. One of his greatest assets was his ability to maintain the political balance between the Russian and Kazakh factions. Thus, although his authoritarian (albeit relatively benign) style of government did not encourage the growth of multi-party democracy, it did act as a stabilizing force in the country and the region.

### The Legislature

The legislative body that Kazakhstan inherited from the Soviet era was the Supreme Kenges (formerly the Supreme Soviet). Elections to the 360-member parliament had been held on 25 March 1990—many candidates were unopposed and the system of reserving seats for CPK-affiliated candidates was still in existence. In December 1993, having enacted a new Constitution on 28 January, parliament declared itself dissolved. It granted President Nazarbayev additional legis-

lative powers until after the general election, which was held on 7 March 1994. Kazakhstan's first free multi-party elections were held amid reports, by international observers, of irregularities, particularly allegations of discrimination against the Russian population (75% of the 754 candidates who registered were ethnic Kazakhs, and it was suggested that ethnic minority candidates had been obstructed from registering). Supporters of Nazarbayev secured a significant majority in the new Supreme Kenges, which was reduced in size to 177 seats.

Like its predecessor, the new Supreme Kenges was critical of the Government, in particular regarding the slow pace of economic reforms. In early 1995 the Supreme Kenges refused to approve the draft budget, this time because of the social hardships that the proposed economic measures would create. In April the impending political impasse was supplanted by a constitutional crisis, however, when the Constitutional Court declared the result of the 1994 elections to be null and void, owing to 'procedural infringements'. Parliament was dissolved and the President effectively ruled by decree pending the introduction of a new Constitution and a general election, which was held in December.

Under the terms of the new Constitution, approved at a referendum held at the end of August 1995, the Supreme Kenges was to be replaced by a bicameral Parliament, with a 47-member upper chamber, the Senate, and a directly elected 67-member lower chamber, the Majlis (Assembly). However, the new constitutional arrangements were, in many ways, inadequate and in some instances unnecessarily cumbersome. President Nazarbayev proposed a number of constitutional changes in his annual 'state of the nation' address to Parliament in September 1998. After initial opposition, Parliament finally accepted the amendments in October, although not entirely as the President had originally proposed. The reforms as enacted included: the extension of the presidential term of office from five to seven years; the extension of the mandates of the Senate (from four to six years) and of the Majlis (from four to five years); the raising of the minimum age for a presidential candidate from 35 to 40 years and the abolition of the upper age limit; and a reduction of the threshold for parties and movements to secure representation in parliamentary elections from 10% to 7% of the votes cast. In addition, the date for the presidential election was brought forward to January 1999.

### Political Parties

Political parties played a very minor role in the politics of Kazakhstan. It was not the President alone, but the whole of society, that preferred consensus to debate. By 2003 the main parties included Otan (Fatherland), a coalition of pro-presidential groupings (established in March 1999); the re-formed CPK (granted legal status in late March 1994); and the Civic Party of Kazakhstan. The Azamat (Citizen) Democratic Party of Kazakhstan, although small, had been regarded by some as the country's only genuine voice of opposition. Founded as an opposition movement in 1996 by a group of intellectuals, it was registered as a political party in 1999; however, it did not apply for re-registration under the new law on political parties that came into effect in 2002 (see below). In November 2001 a new opposition party was launched, called the Democratic Choice of Kazakhstan (DCK), the leaders of which were predominantly of a younger generation than the incumbent leadership. Several held senior positions in the administration, including Uraz Dzhandosov, a Deputy Prime Minister, and Galymzhan Zhakiyanov, Akim (Governor) of Pavlodar oblast. The party's main aim was to combat corruption. However, it was refused registration, and internal divisions soon became evident (see below). In early 2002 Dzhandosov created a separate party, Ak Zhol (literally, 'Light Road'—i.e. Right Way), regarded by some to reflect aspirations similar to those of the pro-presidential Otan party. In July a controversial law on the regulation of political parties was passed by Nazarbayev. It included a requirement that parties seeking re-registration (a necessary precondition for political activity) should have branches in each of the country's regions, and a minimum of 50,000 members, instead of 3,000, as had previously been the case. By the end of the re-registration period in April 2003, only seven parties were registered with the Ministry of Justice. Restrictive pressures on the media were also intensified; this coincided with media allegations that more than US $1,000m. in state funds was being held in Swiss banks in President Nazarbayev's name. Journalists who expressed criticism of the Government were subjected to both official and unofficial harassment, including physical attacks, and arrests for alleged tax violations and other financial irregularities. In October 2002 Sergei Duvanov, a journalist covering human rights issues, was arrested and charged with the rape of a minor; he was sentenced in January 2003. Many commentators believed that the charge was politically motivated.

## THE 1999 ELECTIONS AND POLITICAL DEVELOPMENTS

President Nazarbayev was re-elected, although with a somewhat reduced majority (80.97% of the votes cast), in the election held, as scheduled, on 10 January 1999; he was followed by the CPK candidate, Serikbolsyn Abdildin (with 11.87% of the votes). The election was monitored by over 130 international observers. It was generally agreed that the voting took place without any gross violations, although there were many shortcomings in the pre-electoral procedures. For this reason, the Organization for Security and Co-operation in Europe (OSCE) declined to take part in the official monitoring process. One of the main causes for concern was the debarring of presidential candidates, including the former Prime Minister, Akezhan Kazhegeldin. The only serious rival to the incumbent President, he was disqualified in November 1998 by means of a minor legal technicality. Kazhegeldin left Kazakhstan in 1999, to live in self-imposed exile in Europe. In April 1999 he was charged with tax evasion; further charges were later brought against him. His trial *in absentia* began in August 2001, and in early September the Supreme Court found him guilty of abuse of power, tax evasion and the illegal possession of weapons. He was sentenced to 10 years in prison; in addition, a substantial fine was imposed and his property was confiscated.

Parliamentary elections were held in late 1999, with partial elections to the Senate taking place in September, and elections to the Majlis in October. Of the 77 seats available in the Majlis, 10 were elected by party lists, and the remaining 67 were directly elected. Only 20 seats were filled in the first round of direct elections, and a second round was held later in the month. A third round of voting took place in December, after three results were declared invalid. Otan won 23 seats (securing over 30% of the popular vote); the Civic Party, 13; and the CPK and the Agrarian Party both won three. Pro-Government independents and non-party 'business' groups accounted for 30 of the remaining seats. As in previous elections, there were many reports of irregularities and violations of the electoral law.

In June 2000 a law was passed by both houses of Parliament, granting President Nazarbayev extraordinary powers and privileges, which were to remain in force after the expiry of his existing term of office. The bill prompted criticism from the opposition, some of whom blamed the country's rampant corruption and economic mismanagement on a system of government that focused on one person—the President. Nazarbayev stressed that he did not intend to be a President for life. However, in 2003 he made clear his intention to stand for an additional term of office in the next presidential election, which was scheduled to take place in 2006.

From November 2001 a series of scandals disrupted the Kazakhstani political establishment. The first sign of discord was an open letter to President Nazarbayev, in which a parliamentary deputy, Tolen Toktasynov, accused the President's son-in-law, Rakhat Aliyev, the Deputy Chairman of the National Security Committee (NSC), of abuse of office, corruption and the manipulation of the mass media. The leaders of the newly founded DCK voiced their support for these charges, prompting the Prime Minister, Kasymzhomart Tokayev, to launch a counter-attack, denouncing the opposition members as disloyal. The President appeared to distance himself from the affair. However, although Aliyev resigned from the NSC, he was almost immediately appointed deputy chief of the Presidential Guard. (He was removed from this post in January 2002, becoming ambassador to Austria.) Meanwhile, in late January the Prime Minister suddenly tendered his resignation; Tokayev was subsequently appointed Minister of Foreign Affairs and Secretary of State in the new Government of Imangali Tasmagambetov, a former Deputy Prime Minister. In mid-2002 two leaders of the DCK, Mukhtar Ablayazov and Zhakiyanov, were imprisoned, following charges of financial irregularities and abuse of office. The US Department of State expressed concern at the seven-year sentence received by Zhakiyanov.

On 11 June 2003 Tasmagambetov resigned. According to official sources, he left his post owing to the alleged falsification of the results of a parliamentary vote of confidence linked to the proposed introduction of a new land code, which was to provide for the privatization of agricultural land; it was claimed that Tasmagambetov had been unaware of the fraud. In accordance with the Constitution, the entire Government duly resigned. The new Prime Minister, confirmed in office on 13 June, was Daniyal Akhmetov, former Governor of Pavlodar oblast. Some two-thirds of the members of the previous Government were subsequently reappointed, including the Ministers of Justice, of Labour and Social Security, of Public Health and of Transport and Communications. In terms of policy, economic development was identified as a priority issue for the new Government.

## FOREIGN AFFAIRS

Given the geographic constraints of its location, the future prosperity of Kazakhstan would depend, to a very considerable degree, on the state of its relations with its immediate neighbours, namely Russia, the People's Republic of China, the southern former Soviet Central Asian countries and, across the Caspian Sea, Iran. In the more distant past Kazakhstan was a nodal point in the Eurasian trade networks, a crossroads for the east–west, north–south routes. Later, especially after the region's incorporation into the tsarist empire, the links with Russia assumed ever greater importance until, during the Soviet period, Kazakhstan was virtually sealed off from China and Iran. Even the links with the other Central Asian republics were weaker than had formerly been the case. The relationship with Russia became the central factor in the economic life of the territory, as well as in most other spheres, including politics, defence, communications and transportation.

After the collapse of the USSR there remained a high level of interdependency in trade between Kazakhstan and Russia. Despite Kazakhstan's initial intention to remain in a 'rouble zone', it was obliged to introduce its own currency (the tenge) in November 1993. This caused some tension between the two countries. In 1998 the Presidents of Kazakhstan and Russia concluded a bilateral Treaty of Eternal Friendship and Co-operation. Problems continued to arise, relating to such matters as the terms of Russia's lease of the Baikonur space-launch centre. Although there were indications that Russia would terminate operations at the space centre, largely owing to the high cost of rent (US $115m. per year), it remained active in late 2003.

At an institutional level, economic, as well as cultural and social links were strengthened in March 1996, with the signature of the so-called Quadripartite Treaty, aimed at developing closer integration, and a customs union, between Belarus, Kazakhstan, Kyrgyzstan and Russia; Tajikistan joined the body in 1998. In October 2000, at a summit meeting of heads of state, held in Astana, it was decided to transform the customs union into the Eurasian Economic Community. Although it was emphasized that the aims of the new organization would be mainly economic (see The Economy), it was interpreted by some as a step towards the creation of a 'Eurasian Union', a project first mooted by President Nazarbayev in 1994; political opinion in Uzbekistan was especially critical of this development, warning that it could lead to renewed 'Russian hegemony'. An unrelated initiative that involved the same countries was the decision to create a Rapid Reaction Force, based in Bishkek, Kyrgyzstan, to defend the southern borders of the CIS against external attack; the primary targets were identified as terrorism, drugs smuggling and Islamist fundamentalism. An anti-terrorism centre opened in Bishkek on 1 August 2001.

During the 1990s the Government of Kazakhstan made serious efforts to develop a good working relationship with the People's Republic of China. The interest was reciprocated by the Chinese Government and there were exchanges of high-level official delegations, as well as numerous trade, cultural and scientific missions. Both sides were eager to revive the 'Silk Road' of old, in modern form. At the beginning of the 1990s road, rail and air links, as well as a direct telephone line, already connected Almaty and Urumchi, the capital of Xinjiang Uigur Autonomous Region, a Chinese province with a Kazakh population of over 1m. There were plans to upgrade these links in the near future, so as to facilitate the eventual integration of the Chinese and Central Asian transportation and communications networks. A bilateral agreement to develop 'long-term neighbourly and stable relations' was signed by the leaders of the two countries in late 1995. At the end of July 1996 a source of considerable tension was removed when China announced that it had conducted its last nuclear test explosion. The issue of the demarcation of parts of the China–Kazakhstan border (still unresolved at the time of the collapse of the USSR) was finally settled to the satisfaction of both Governments in 1999. Some progress was also made on reaching agreement regarding the utilization of trans-boundary water resources. China announced plans to draw off some 10% of the flow of the Cherny Irtysh river by 2010 (some 1,000m. cu m of water per year); a joint commission was established in 2000 to monitor the situation. However, experts remained concerned that the Cherny Irtysh–Karamay canal, under construction as part of a plan to develop western China, might have a harmful effect on adjacent areas of Kazakhstan.

China and Kazakhstan were regular participants in summit meetings of the heads of state of the so-called Shanghai Five (known as the Shanghai Forum from mid-2000), other members being Kyrgyzstan, Tajikistan and Russia, which aimed to co-ordinate policies on regional co-operation and security. At a summit meeting, held in Shanghai, China, in mid-June 2001, the body was transformed into the Shanghai Co-operation Organization (SCO); Uzbekistan was also admitted to the Organization. At the meeting the six heads of state signed the Shanghai Convention on Combating Terrorism, Separatism and Extremism, which provided a legal framework for increased regional co-operation in police operations and intelligence information gathering. In order to facilitate these efforts, an anti-terrorism centre was to be created. Bilateral contacts between China and Kazakhstan were strengthened by reciprocal visits by high-level delegations in 2002. The main areas of concern remained the effort to control illegal immigration, religious extremism and terrorism. In August 2003 China and Kazakhstan jointly hosted co-ordinated military exercises of SCO member states.

Kazakhstan's relationship with Iran was far less problematic than that with either the People's Republic of China or Russia. There was little direct contact between the two countries for many years (although there were still a few thousand Kazakhs in Iran, descendants of refugees from Soviet rule). With Kazakhstan an independent state, it was eager to develop transport and communication links to the south, through Turkmenistan, but also across the Caspian Sea. There were plans to build a petroleum pipeline through Iran, but Iran's participation in the construction of a pipeline was obstructed by the US Government, which was keen to bring about that country's economic isolation. However, exchange agreements between the two countries continued to provide a conduit for Kazakhstani petroleum exports. (For more information on the politics of energy, see the article by the same author on energy in the Caspian Sea region in Part One—General Survey.)

Relations with the other Central Asian states were complicated by economic rivalry and competition for foreign aid. Some progress was made in the creation of mechanisms for co-operation in the mid-1990s. In July 1994 Kazakhstan formed a trilateral economic and defence union with Uzbekistan and Kyrgyzstan, the implementation of which was to be supervised by an Interstate Council (established in February 1995). In March 1998 Tajikistan joined this alliance, which was renamed the Central Asian Economic Union in July. The aim was to foster regional co-operation in order to address more effectively issues of joint concern, notably the sharing of water resources, natural disasters, the prevention of arms- and drugs-trafficking and the threat of political and militant Islamism. However, despite good intentions and numerous working meetings at various levels, little real progress was made. In January 2001, in response to outspoken criticism by the Uzbek President, Islam Karimov, the organization was, less ambitiously, renamed the Central Asian Economic Forum. A few months later the name was changed again, to Central Asia Co-operation Organization.

Looking beyond the adjacent countries, the Government of Kazakhstan emphasized its intention to maintain good relations with the international community at large. There was an acute awareness of the need to avoid potentially provocative and divisive alliances. In joining the Economic Co-operation Organization (ECO—founded originally by Iran, Pakistan and Turkey), Kazakhstan made it clear that it was not seeking to create an Islamic bloc, but merely to facilitate mutually beneficial economic activities. Similarly, it was eager to develop relations with Turkey, but on the same basis as with other countries, and not as part of a uniquely Turkic group. President Nazarbayev regularly participated in the Turkic Summits, a series of high-level meetings between Turkey and the former Soviet Turkic states (namely Azerbaijan, Kazakhstan, Kyrgyzstan, Turkmenistan and Uzbekistan). Initiated in 1992, these meetings were held on an almost annual basis, in capitals of the member states. Initially the emphasis was on economic co-operation, particularly in the transport and energy sectors, but later issues such as the fight against terrorism and organized crime attracted increasing attention. In 1994 President Nazarbayev also created an Asian equivalent of the OSCE, named the Conference on Interaction and Confidence-Building Measures in Asia (CICA). This brought together senior representatives of 25 countries from the Middle East, South Asia and South-

East Asia for annual meetings. However, little progress was made towards creating institutions, and in 2001 there was dissatisfaction at the lack of active engagement on the part of some of the member states, notably the People's Republic of China, Pakistan and Uzbekistan. The first CICA summit meeting of Heads of State was held in June 2002.

The West, from which Kazakhstan hoped to receive investment, was attracted by the country's natural resources. It was also concerned about the fate of the nuclear arsenal and in the growth of the trade in illegal drugs (against which Kazakhstan sought aid from the West). After the disintegration of the USSR, Kazakhstan had declared its commitment to becoming a non-nuclear state. In 1992 the country ratified the first Strategic Arms' Reduction Treaty (START 1) and became a signatory to the Treaty on the Non-Proliferation of Nuclear Weapons in December 1993. By April 1995 all nuclear warheads in Kazakhstan had been transferred to Russia; remaining intercontinental ballistic missile units were dismantled by mid-1996. The country's role as a nuclear test-site was not, however, over; in September 1998 the Academy of Sciences of Kazakhstan concluded an agreement with the USA to carry out two underground nuclear explosions, one at Semipalatinsk and the other at the USA's test-site in Nevada, in order to refine the monitoring techniques used to dis-

tinguish between bomb tests and natural seismic events. In July 2000 the Semipalatinsk nuclear facility was finally closed, and in late 2001 Kazakhstan ratified the Comprehensive Nuclear Test Ban Treaty. Following the suicide attacks on the USA on 11 September 2001, Kazakhstan promptly demonstrated its support for the US-led 'war on terrorism' by opening its airspace to US military aircraft. In March 2003 the Kazakhstani Ministry of Defence announced that the USA was to assist in building up Kazakhstan's navy, by supplying military ships for its Caspian Sea fleet. Deliveries of cargo aircraft and helicopters were also envisaged for the future. In July 500 Kazakhstani airborne troops and units of the Kazakhstani peace-keeping battalion Kazbat were joined by British and US troops in operation 'Steppe Eagle 2003', one week of military manoeuvres in Almaty oblast.

Kazakhstan's policy of encouraging international contacts, while maintaining a non-aligned stance, proved to be very effective. By the beginning of the 21st century the country was generally regarded as one of the most stable of the CIS states. It maintained diplomatic links with over 100 countries and was a member of numerous international and regional organizations, reinforced by high-level missions to and from Kazakhstan. Its balanced foreign policy adds to its efficacy as a regional leader.

# The Economy

## Dr SHIRIN AKINER

### INTRODUCTION

Kazakhstan encompassed approximately 20% of the arable land of the former USSR, although it represented only some 12% of the total territory. The country's extensive natural resources provided the base for a relatively diversified economy. However, years of central planning ensured that the economy developed into one that was highly dependent upon other former Soviet republics, notably Russia, for supply lines and markets. With the failure of the Soviet economic system and the advent of full political independence in 1991, Kazakhstan began, cautiously, but with commitment, a programme of reform. The country had significant problems to overcome in the early 1990s, but the long-term prospects seemed secure, particularly with its natural advantages. By the end of the 1990s the main sectors of the economy were agriculture, heavy industry, construction and services. Gross domestic product (GDP) decreased by an annual average of 2.2% in 1990–2001, but registered growth of 13.2% in 2001 and 9.5% in 2002. Official surveys of the country's economic performance were, in general, optimistic, although the statistics had to be treated with some caution, owing not only to the unreliability of much economic data, but to the added distortions of the transformation to a free-market economy.

### ECONOMIC POLICY

Until December 1991 economic planning for Kazakhstan, as for the other Soviet republics, was carried out at Union level, in Moscow, Russia—the Soviet capital. The role of the republican governments was, primarily, to carry out the directives that they received from the centre. Scope for formulating policies within a given republic was extremely limited, because of the highly integrated nature of the Union economy as a whole. Detailed data were collected on a regular basis, but were transmitted to Moscow for full analysis. Several key areas of the economy, such as the military-industrial complexes, transport, communications and major industrial

plants, came directly under the jurisdiction of the all-Union authorities; the republican administrations had little, if any, knowledge as to how they functioned. In Kazakhstan, strategically important facilities such as the nuclear testing site at Semipalatinsk and the Baikonur space centre were run almost exclusively by immigrant Slavs. In effect, they represented extra-territorial enclaves. They contributed virtually nothing to the local economy and existed outside the control of the republican government. However, the activities at Semipalatinsk were suspected of causing environmental and health damage in the republic and, with increased authority for republican government from August 1991, President Nursultan Nazarbayev gained popularity by banning future testing activities. That detailed information on the activities there remained in the Russian archives, however, was indicated by Kazakhstan's need to employ US help in 1997 in an attempt to compile basic mapping data on the site. By contrast, at Baikonur, Kazakhstan acknowledged the inappropriateness and expense of local control, and in March 1994 the Presidents of Kazakhstan and Russia signed an agreement, which granted the latter a 20-year lease for the use of the space centre. This arrangement subsequently proved less than satisfactory (it was almost impossible to compel the Russians to pay what the Kazakhs increasingly considered a far less than adequate rent) and in mid-1998 a new agreement was signed. However, there were continuing problems with payment, and following the accidental explosion of two Proton rockets from the site in 1999, Kazakhstan prohibited the use of the site by Russia until payment was agreed. Nevertheless, in November 2000 Kazakhstan expressed its willingness to extend Russia's lease on the Baikonur space launch facility for a further 10 years. By 2002 Russia indicated that it might terminate the agreement in the near future, owing to the high rent demanded by Kazakhstan (of US \$115m. per year).

After 1991 in Kazakhstan, as elsewhere in the former USSR, the Government was trying to unravel the mysteries of its own economy. Much of the information that was available during the early 1990s was unreliable and partial. Requests for training and technical assistance were addressed to the IMF and other international bodies, as well as to the national governments of interested countries (India, Japan, Turkey, the United Kingdom and the USA). Some training was provided in the fields of central banking, taxation and economic and financial management, but technical capability in all the essential areas of economic planning remained very limited. President Nazarbayev was deeply committed to the process of economic reform, but mechanisms to implement proposed changes were often lacking. Moreover, the officials charged with the responsibility of implementing such programmes were often too conservative to sympathize with the task or too inexperienced to understand the nature of the transformation. Consequently, progress was slow. There were frequent changes in the administrative apparatus, leading to a rapid turnover of personnel.

The first stage of a privatization programme was launched in 1992, but the initial results were disappointing. The plan was overly ambitious, and progress was impeded by the lack of basic technical and professional skills, together with public suspicions. Corruption and organized crime complicated the development of private enterprise, and a high level of bankruptcy further discredited the process. Nevertheless, while only 380 enterprises were privatized in 1992, some 6,000 small enterprises were sold to the private sector during the following year. Official support for privatization remained strong, and the second two-year stage of the programme was duly initiated in 1993. It proved to be more successful than the first. Its objective was to transfer the majority of state enterprises and farms to the private sector by one of three methods: privatization of small-scale enterprises by cash auctions; mass privatization of medium-sized and large enterprises by voucher and coupon auctions; and privatization of some 180 major enterprises via tenders on a case-by-case basis, usually to foreign investors. Of the small-scale enterprises offered for sale about one-half, amounting to over 4,500 enterprises with a combined work-force of over 1m., were sold. These companies belonged mainly to the distribution and catering sectors. By the end of 1995 about 1,000 enterprises with more than 400,000 employees had been sold by mass privatization, which involved 169 Investment Privatization Funds. The establishment of an Enterprise Restructuring Agency in 1994 and a Rehabilitation Bank in 1995, together with the adoption of a new bankruptcy law in early 1995, resulted in substantial progress in enterprise restructuring during that year. The privatization of major enterprises attracted several international companies to the mining and metallurgy sector in the mid-1990s. Of particular significance was the acquisition of the Karmet steelworks near Karaganda by the international steel group, Ispat, in November 1995.

In January 1996 a new phase of privatization began. A law came into effect, which abolished the preferential treatment of workers in the privatization of enterprises, and retained only two privatization methods: direct sales to investors and auctions. The privatization programme for 1996–98 included the auction of remaining state shares and of enterprises scheduled for privatization, but which remained unsold. The principle was that only the natural monopolies (energy, transport, water, etc.) should remain under state ownership. Kazakhstan became a major target for Western (including Japanese) investment, which by 1998 was the highest per head in the Commonwealth of Independent States (CIS). In that year the Government sold its 14.3% stake in a joint venture, the Offshore Kazakhstan International Operating Company, for US $500m. Subsequent large-scale privatizations included the sale in November of a 90% stake in the Eastern Kazakhstan Copper and Chemical Plant to Samsung Deutschland GmbH (a subsidiary of Samsung of the Republic of Korea—

South Korea) for $6.3m. In total, 3,073 state enterprises were privatized in 1998. However, further privatization of selected major state assets was interrupted, owing to unfavourable market conditions. The programme was resumed in 1999, with stakes being offered in the national telecommunications company, Kazakhtelecom, the Ust-Kamenogorsk metallurgy plant, and the petroleum producers, JSC Aktobemunaigaz and JSC Mangistaumunaigaz.

Other economic reforms were also introduced, often in response to situations, rather than as a result of serious planning. In 1991 there were already signs of serious economic dislocation. Essential industrial supplies were disrupted as republics, voluntarily or otherwise, reneged on contracts with partners within the Union. This triggered a negative series of events, with declining production, shortages, rising prices and, in some cases, unemployment. The Kazakhstani Government, although it had begun to advocate local control of republican economies when in the Union, was not eager to introduce economic reforms at this stage, for fear of increasing the hardship that the population was already suffering. However, because of the intimate relationship between the Russian and Kazakhstani economies, once the Russian Government decided on price liberalization, Kazakhstan could only follow suit. Accordingly, on 6 January 1992 the prices of all but some basic foodstuffs and essential services were deregulated. Public anger was such that some degree of control had to be reintroduced almost immediately. Salaries and social benefits were increased, and continued to be increased at regular intervals, but they were unable to keep pace with inflation. The most significant areas affected were fuel, staple foods (bread, milk and meat) and transportation costs (public and private).

President Nazarbayev was a strong supporter of an integrated economic policy for the CIS. He suggested a number of proposals for co-ordinating economic decision-making among the member states and remained firmly committed to the 'rouble zone'. The announcement by the Central Bank of Russia, on 24 July 1993, that pre-1993 banknotes would no longer be legal tender was wholly unexpected. The measure was clearly designed to compel countries such as Kazakhstan either to introduce their own currency or to surrender their fiscal independence to Russia. The Kazakhstani Government was reluctant to adopt the former course in haste. However, the threat to stability from the vast stocks of old roubles in existence and the Russian demands, which proved too compromising for an independent state, required, on 15 November, the introduction of Kazakhstan's own currency, the tenge (which had already been printed, for such an eventuality).

The introduction of the tenge increased international optimism that Kazakhstan would be better able to control its economy and, importantly, its fiscal deficit. Despite extremely high inflation during 1992 (consumer prices increased by an annual average of 1,381%—largely caused by the monetary policies of the Russian central bank), which continued into the mid-1990s (with an average increase of 1,258% in 1994), the Government remained committed to improving the quality of, and its control over, public finances. A stabilization programme, introduced in January 1994 and assisted by a one-year stand-by arrangement from the IMF, initially foundered. Consequently, the exchange rate of the tenge depreciated by almost 600% in the first half of the year, and by June the monthly rate of inflation had reached 46%. In 1995, however, the annual average rate of increase in consumer prices was reduced to 176.2%, largely owing to a tightening of monetary and credit policies. From the late 1990s, the annual rate of inflation slowed considerably, to 17.4% in 1997, and to 13.2% in 2000, 8.4% in 2001 and 6.6% in 2002.

The national debt, meanwhile, continued to grow. According to the National Bank of Kazakhstan, between 1 January 1994 and 1 April 1998 direct national and state-guaranteed foreign debt rose by 89%, from US $1,765.6m. to $3,328.2m., and non-state-guaranteed foreign debt rose from $4,328.2m. to $1,604.1m.; payments due from Kazakhstani enterprises to foreign partners rose from $208.2m. to $1,113m. By the end of 1998 Kazakhstan's total external debt was estimated at $7,543m. Debt-servicing costs for that year were estimated at $539.7m. for direct and state-guaranteed foreign debt, and $1,458.6m. for non-government-guaranteed debt. The balance of payments continued to deteriorate; the current-account deficit increased to $1,201.3m. Domestic finances were, likewise, in disarray: arrears of wages and salaries were estimated at around $550m. The move of the capital from Almaty to Astana had not only been extremely expensive but had also, inevitably, proved disruptive. By mid-June, only a few days after the official opening of that new capital, the economy was openly admitted to be in crisis.

There was serious disagreement over the reason for this state of affairs. The Prime Minister, Nurlan Balgymbayev, blamed it on the decline in world prices for Kazakhstan's main exports, and the effects of the economic collapse in South-East Asia in 1997–98, whereas President Nazarbayev attributed it to domestic incompetence and corruption. All were agreed, however, that urgent measures were necessary and an emergency programme was duly implemented. The collapse of the Russian rouble in August 1998 exacerbated the situation. Various measures refining the emergency programme followed. Thus, in mid-September a presidential decree ordered massive job reductions in the National Security Committee and other internal affairs and law-enforcement services. It was hoped that funds could be diverted to augment the customs service and so, hopefully, to boost the revenue flowing into the budget. Then, at the end of the month, there was announced what amounted to, in effect, a renationalization of bankrupt firms, reversing the existing policy of restricting state ownership to the natural monopolies. The recession persisted in 1999, and in April of that year, following a sharp decline in the value of the tenge against the US dollar, the Kazakhstani currency was 'floated' (made fully convertible) on the foreign-exchange markets. The Government also made a number of proposals to strengthen the economy, such as the further privatization of large enterprise and export promotion. As a result, Kazakhstan's total external debt had declined to an estimated US $6,664m. by the end of 2000, and by April 2000 Nazarbayev was able to state that all outstanding debts owed to the IMF had been repaid seven years ahead of schedule, owing to a strong recovery in regional demand, increased global petroleum prices and careful macroeconomic policy.

Throughout the 1990s Kazakhstan maintained its determination to foster traditional links, and in March 1996 signed an agreement with Belarus and Russia, as well as Kyrgyzstan, on a common market and customs union. Closer economic integration within Central Asia was more actively encouraged, and in January 1994 Kazakhstan and Uzbekistan announced their intention to form a common market by 2000. Kyrgyzstan subsequently announced its support and in July an agreement was reached between the three countries to form a trilateral economic and defence union, to be implemented by an Interstate Council (founded in February 1995). In March 1998 Tajikistan announced its intention to join, and in July of that year the four formally constituted themselves as the Central Asian Economic Union, which became known as the Central Asian Co-operation Organization in 2001.

## AGRICULTURE

Kazakhstan is an important producer and exporter (mostly to other former Soviet territories) of agricultural products. During the Soviet era, agriculture was the second largest sector of the economy. At the time of independence, it accounted for over one-third of GDP. During the 1990s, however, agricultural production declined sharply. This was partly owing to political disruption, and the uncertainties that ensued, but, more significantly, the result of the short-term consequences of economic reform. This could be attributed to shortages of inputs (for example, of fuel, feed and fertilizers), machinery and expertise, but also to adverse weather conditions. There was an urgent need for investment in new technologies, and in storage and transport facilities. In 1990–95 agricultural product declined by an annual average of 18%. The decline slowed to 5.6% in 1996, and to 1.5% in 1997, but increased to 18.9% in 1998. By 2001 agriculture's contribution to GDP had declined to 8.7%. Nevertheless, the percentage of the work-force engaged in the sector remained fairly static, and agriculture employed 35.5% of the employed population in 2002. In 1999 agricultural production recorded an increase for the first time since independence (of 27.3%) and, despite a decline of 2.9% in 2000, continued to increase thereafter. Agricultural GDP increased by 2.1% in 2001 and by 2.7% in 2002.

The shortfall in agricultural production was, to some extent, offset by the collapse of former markets in the USSR. Moreover, the decline in production had some incidental benefits—in particular, the reduced demand for irrigation water from the Syr-Dar'ya facilitated the planned recovery of the northern part of the Aral Sea. The Sea, owing to the overuse of its feeder rivers in the last decades of Soviet power, had shrunk to about one-half of its original surface area, with concurrent decline of some 20 m (66 ft) in its water level. However, the improvement in environmental conditions there was relative, and certainly far from sufficient to restore the Sea's once flourishing fisheries. With assistance from the World Bank, some restocking with fish had begun by the late 1990s. International financial institutions also financed projects to improve water management. In 2000 the Asian Development Bank (ADB) provided US $40m. for irrigation and land improvement, and the World Bank also provided credits for irrigation and drainage projects.

Grain production remained of crucial importance to the Kazakhstani economy. In the early 1990s approximately one-half of the land under cultivation was devoted to wheat, almost entirely under state supervision. This was a legacy of the Soviet 'Virgin Lands' scheme of the 1950s and early 1960s, whereby vast tracts of northern Kazakhstan were brought under the plough. After independence the total area under crop cultivation diminished. In 1999 15.2m. hectares (ha) were sown (a reduction from 18.6m. ha in 1998); of this area, 11.3m. ha were under grain (compared with 16.0m. ha in 1998). The main grain is wheat. Barley, millet and, in the south, rice are also cultivated. In 1992 and 1993 the grain harvest was good, but despite the decline in production thereafter, Kazakhstan remained self-sufficient in this commodity (domestic consumption needs, according to Western estimates, amounted to between 5m. and 7m. metric tons). However, the wheat harvest fell to a disastrous low of 4.7m. tons in 1998 (partly owing to adverse weather conditions); in 1999 the yield was very much better, at some 11.2m. tons, almost equal to that of the early 1990s. None the less, there were further reverses when, in 1999–2000, the country suffered a devastating infestation of locusts. This was largely occasioned by the failure on the part of the Ministry of Agriculture to undertake pesticide spraying at the appropriate time. More than 4m. ha of arable land were damaged. The wheat harvest in 2000 was just over 9m. tons, but it recovered to an estimated 12.5m. tons in 2001. At this time, Kazakhstan accounted for some 1.0% of world grain production, and 1.4% of world grain exports. The main markets for Kazakhstani grain products (wheat accounted for just under 90%) included Belarus, Iran and Uzbekistan.

Sugar beet and tobacco production were less significant, in terms of volume, than grain, but after the dissolution of the USSR they acquired a new significance and value. Inter-republican supplies of these commodities, especially sugar, were severely disrupted. However, Kazakhstan remained without significant timber resources, and continued to rely on imports from Russia. Foreign investors showed a particular interest in the tobacco industry; in 1993 Philip Morris, the US multinational, announced proposals for a joint venture for the production of cigarettes in Kazakhstan and a manufacturing plant was opened in May 2000. A similar deal for a confectionery factory was not carried through, mainly owing to problems with the distribution network to local markets. Cotton was grown mostly on irrigated land in the south. The region was badly affected by the locust infestation of 1999–2000; the yield of seed cotton in 2000 was about 280,000 metric tons, a decline of some 15% per ha compared with the previous year.

Cattle are raised mainly in the north and north-east of the country, sheep and camels in the south, and horses in the east. This sector is mainly orientated towards meat production. There is, however, significant output of milk and dairy products, including dried milk, butter and cheese. Wool (including the valuable astrakhan), camel hair and hides are, likewise, produced in large quantities. Animal husbandry was of major importance during the Soviet period. However, the relative importance of this sector declined after independence. As with grain production, from the early 1990s there was a massive decline in output, with livestock numbers falling to levels comparable to those of the period of collectivization in the early 1930s. Despite a partial recovery, by 2000 livestock breeding had not regained the importance that it had held prior to independence. In the 1990s attempts to restructure the agricultural sector were initiated, including the privatization of the national stock of cattle, horses and poultry. The ADB and the World Bank provided assistance through Farm Restructuring and Development and Agricultural Sector Development Programmes.

## PETROLEUM AND NATURAL GAS

Kazakhstan's proven petroleum and gas reserves are very considerable. During the Soviet period the centre of the petroleum industry was Atyrau (Guriyev), on the north-eastern shore of the Caspian Sea. Petroleum production initially declined after independence. Crude petroleum output amounted to only 19.3m. metric tons in 1993 (it had been 25.5m. tons in 1988). Foreign petroleum and gas companies were increasingly invited to tender for exploration and development rights. Kazakhstan's success in attracting foreign investment in this sector brought about a significant recovery in the mid-1990s, and output had reached 25.9m. tons by 1998. The upward trend continued; 30.6m. tons of petroleum were produced in 2000, and 42.0m. tons in 2002.

A number of production-sharing agreements and joint ventures have been agreed with foreign partners. The most important of these focus on three significant deposits. First, the Tengiz field, located on the northern littoral of the Caspian, is estimated to hold some 6,000m.–9,000m. barrels of recoverable oil. The field had been partially developed in the 1980s, but its full potential had not been realized. In 1990 the US Chevron Corporation began negotiations with the Soviet Government, later continued with the Government of independent Kazakhstan, on the development of this field, and in 1993 the TengizChevroil (TCO) partnership was formed

between Chevron and the Kazakhstani authorities to implement the project. Second, Karachaganak is a huge oil and gas condensate field in western Kazakhstan, discovered in 1979, but not fully developed during the Soviet period. In 1992 British Gas (now BG) and Azienda Generale Italiana Petroli SA (Agip SA of Italy) were awarded exclusive rights to negotiate a contract for the rehabilitation and development of the field, and in November 1997 BG and Agip, in partnership with Texaco (of the USA) and LUKoil (Russia), concluded a production-sharing agreement for the field. Third, and largest of all, is Kashagan. In 1997 a multinational consortium, formed by European, US and Kazakhstani partners, signed an agreement to undertake seismic exploration in the northern Caspian. The Kashagan deposit was discovered in July 2000, some 75 km south of Atyrau. The project operator at that time was the Offshore Kazakhstan International Operating Company (OKIOC), renamed the Agip Kazakhstan North Caspian Operating Company (AgipKCO) in mid-2001.

One of the main obstacles to the export of Kazakhstani hydrocarbons was the limited nature of the routes to world markets. Consequently, the construction of new pipelines became a priority. The Caspian Pipeline Consortium (CPC) was formed in 1993 by the Governments of Kazakhstan and Oman; it was subsequently joined by the Governments of Azerbaijan and Russia, and a number of Western companies. The objective was the construction of a 1,568-km pipeline linking the Tengiz field with the Russian Black Sea port of Novorossiisk, in order to enable exports to reach the European market. After numerous legal and technical difficulties the project finally got under way in the late 1990s, and petroleum began to flow through the pipeline in September 2001 (although it was not formally inaugurated until late November). It had an initial capacity of some 560,000 barrels per day (b/d); this was to be upgraded to 1.34m. b/d by 2015. The Atyrau–Samara pipeline, which connected to the Russian pipeline network, was also upgraded to carry 310,000 b/d. In August 2002 work begun on the construction of of the Kenkiyak–Atyrau pipeline, linking the oilfields of western Kazakhstan with the Samara pipeline to the north, and to the CPC pipeline to the west, as well as to the Kazakhstani port of Aktau. A Kazakhstani company, MunaiTas (owned by KazMunaiGaz), held a 51% stake in the venture, and the remainder was held by a subsidiary of the China National Petroleum Corporation; it was hoped that the pipeline would be the first stage of a transcontinental line joining western Kazakhstan with the People's Republic of China.

Post-independence, Kazakhstan had three main petroleum refineries: at Pavlodar in the east, Shymkent (Chimkent) in the south and Atyrau on the Caspian. The Pavlodar plant received crude petroleum from western Siberian (Russian) oilfields, whereas the other two operated on domestic crude. After the collapse of the USSR, however, all three refineries were underutilized and the Kazakhstani Government sought investment for the renovation of the plants. In 2001 the Marubeni company of Japan embarked on the refurbishment of the Atyrau plant. The centre of the Kazakhstani petroleum industry, the small town was experiencing rapid growth, as numerous foreign businessmen and technical personnel moved in to the region. In August 2002 the European Bank for Reconstruction and Development (EBRD) provided financing for the upgrading of the local airport to international standards. The Shymkent refinery, largely owned by Petrokazakhstan (of Canada), was also scheduled for modernization.

Kazakhstan's natural gas reserves are estimated at 83,000,000m. cu ft. Production declined from 8,112m. cu m in 1992 to about one-half that level in 1994, but increased to 8,114m. cu m by 1997, to 11,542m. cu m in 2000, and to 13,137m. in 2002. The largest deposits, accounting for over 40% of the country's total reserves, are in the vast Karachaganak field located in north-west Kazakhstan. There are estimated reserves of some 1,300,000m. cu m of natural gas and 650m. metric tons of gas condensate. Other major gas fields include the Tengiz, Zhanazhol and Uritau fields. In March 1995 the Russian company, Gazprom, together with British Gas and Agip agreed to invest US $5,000m. in the development of the Karachaganak natural gas field. Gazprom owned a 15% equity stake in the venture, and British Gas and Agip each held a share of 42.5%. As with the petroleum sector, gas production is hindered by the poor pipeline infrastructure. Existing gas pipelines, like oil pipelines, all traverse Russia. The gas from Karachaganak is transported to the Orenburg processing plant in Russia, from where it is exported via the Russian pipeline system. Several projects to construct new gas pipelines were under consideration in 2000, but by 2003 they had not been implemented. In June 2002 a 10-year agreement was signed by the Kazakhstani and Russian Presidents to stimulate co-operation in the gas sector. The agreement included the creation of a joint venture, KazRosGaz, to transport Kazakhstani gas to Europe.

Initially, the development of the hydrocarbon reserves of the Caspian Sea was complicated by the lack of an internationally recognized legal regime. The Caspian, being landlocked, is not automatically covered by the Law of the Sea (which would assign territorial waters and zones of influence to all littoral states). During the Soviet period, its status was covered by two treaties between the USSR and Iran, which effectively treated it as a trans-boundary lake. Russia (the principal 'successor state' of the USSR) and Iran wanted to keep this treaty in force, or to replace it with a similar one in which all resources of the Caspian would be held in common. The three new successor states, Kazakhstan, Azerbaijan and Turkmenistan, wanted the Sea divided. In July 1998 Kazakhstan and Russia signed a pioneering bilateral agreement on the demarcation of their respective zones of the seabed. In May 2002 the leaders of the two countries signed a supplementary protocol setting out the geographic co-ordinates of the modified median line, and a trilateral agreement was signed between Azerbaijan, Kazakhstan and Russia in May 2003. By late 2003 some progress had been made in multilateral negotiations between the five littoral states, and it seemed possible that consensus agreement on a legal regime, based on international principle, might eventually be achieved, leading to a comprehensive demarcation of the Sea (for further information see the essay by the same author on energy in the Caspian Sea region in Part One—General Survey).

From the late 1990s a growing concern for foreign petroleum companies was Kazakhstan's reputation as an 'investor friendly' country, which had been somewhat damaged by the growing propensity of the Government to re-interpret contracts in such a way as to extract more revenue. In 2001 this resulted in a serious contractual dispute between the Kazakhstani authorities and the Tengizchevroil joint venture (TCO). In November 2002 TCO decided not to implement the next phase of development until this matter had been resolved satisfactorily. In the mean time, Kazakhstan imposed a fine of US $70m. on TCO, for alleged damage to the environment, supposedly caused by the way in which it was storing more than 6m. metric tons of sulphur extracted from the petroleum. In January 2003 an uneasy settlement was reached, and TCO announced that it would proceed with the project as planned. However, this was not a unique case. In the Karachaganak oil and gas field, the consortium led by BG and ENI (which incorporated Agip in 1998) came close to suspending production in 2001, owing to the proposed imposition of 'double taxation' on exports of gas condensates from Kazakhstan to Russia. Furthermore, in 2003 the consortium developing the Kashagan field was informed that its exemption on paying

value-added tax had been revoked; in addition, the ruling was backdated to 1999. The consortium regarded this as a violation of the terms of the production-sharing agreement signed in 1997. Further problems arose when the consortium sought to postpone production, which had originally been due to commence in 2005 (to coincide with preparations for the presidential elections in 2006); drilling problems in the north Caspian, where the water is shallow (about three metres deep) and covered with ice for at least three months of the year, made this unfeasible, and the consortium anticipated a delay of one to two years. The Government threatened to impose heavy penalties if there was any interruption of the schedule.

Another problem for investors in Kazakhstan was the high level of corruption. In 2001 and 2002 international surveys placed it well below almost all the CIS countries, with the exception of Azerbaijan. In March 2003 the issue of bribery and corruption attracted attention when, following an extensive investigation, James H. Giffen, a close associate of President Nazarbayev, was arraigned in New York, USA, charged with violating the US Foreign Corrupt Practices Act (which prohibits US companies or individuals from using financial inducements to secure an agreement). He was accused of channelling illegal payments, worth more than US $78m., to the Swiss bank accounts of two senior Kazakhstani officials. The transactions were allegedly connected with the granting of contracts to US petroleum companies. One of the deals under investigation was the acquisition by Mobil (of France— now ExxonMobil) of a stake in the Tengiz oilfield in 1996. Giffen's trial was tentatively scheduled to begin in January 2004.

## COAL AND METALS

Kazakhstan possesses large deposits of coal (it accounted for some 19% of Soviet coal production), petroleum and natural gas, and minerals such as chrome (some 90% of total Soviet reserves were located in Kazakhstan), copper, gold, lead, wolfram (tungsten) and zinc. Most of the industrial base of the country is connected with the extraction and processing of these mineral resources. Industry (excluding construction) accounted for over one-third of GDP in the late 1980s. About one-fifth of the total work-force were employed in industry at that time. Post-independence, the basic infrastructure of industry remained sound, but equipment was generally old, inefficient and environmentally harmful, and there was a high degree of wastage, except in those enterprises that benefited from foreign investment. Overall, industrial production (including petroleum and gas and other, non-mining sectors) recorded an average annual decline of 5.5% in 1990–2001, although the GDP of the sector increased by 15.5% in 2001, and by 9.8% in 2002. Employment in industry declined however, from 1.5m. in 1992 (20.4% of the work-force) to 1.1m. (16.3%) in 2002.

The Karaganda region is the main centre of the coal industry (in 2000 it had 13 mines producing high-quality coking coal); further north, Ekibastuz (the third largest coal basin in the former USSR), is also well developed, as are Turgai and Maikuben. In the Soviet era the republic produced far more coal than was needed for domestic consumption and had long been an exporter, mainly to the Volga region of Russia. Total coal production (hard coal and brown coal) declined from a peak of 143m. metric tons in 1988 to 70.6m. tons in 2002; this decrease in production was mainly the result of reduced demand and excess stocks. The main route for coal exports is by rail from Pavlodar to western Siberia and the Urals (where there are plants designed to use such supplies).

Ferrous and non-ferrous metallurgy are highly developed. By the beginning of the 2000s the country's copper reserves were ranked fourth in the world, its manganese third, its barite, lead and tungsten first, its iron ore seventh and its gold ninth. Important copper, zinc and lead works are located in the north-east of the country. The mining and processing of iron is based in the north, especially in the Kustanai and Karaganda regions. There are copper deposits in the centre of the country and lead and zinc in the south. In the north-east of the country is one of the world's largest gold deposits (with estimated reserves of over 10m. troy ounces—some 310 metric tons), at the low-cost mines near Auezov. Kazakhstan is the largest producer of base metals in the CIS; it is second only to Russia in the production of aluminium and nickel. In 1999 the proportion of metals in the total industrial output of the country was approximately 14%; in the same year metals constituted some 30% of total exports. A Metal Exchange was established in Kazakhstan in 1992.

Post-independence, the Government made positive efforts to privatize the metallurgy sector. By 1999 joint ventures involving the Government and strategic investors had been established in all the main metals enterprises. Substantial investments in new technology were made in 1995–97; there was also radical restructuring of management and production. This resulted in a significant growth in output (in 1997 this amounted to 24% in the non-ferrous sector and 15% in the ferrous sector). A number of foreign mining groups showed interest in Kazakhstan's gold reserves in the mid-1990s. In 1993 the Bakyrchik mine, registered in the United Kingdom, became the first gold-mining enterprise in the CIS to be wholly foreign-owned, and it was quoted on the London Stock Exchange; subsequently, however, there were production difficulties and changes in ownership, particularly in 1995–97. In April 1995 Placer Dome (based in Canada) announced plans to develop the Vasilkovskoye gold property (which had proven extractable reserves of 6.5m. troy ounces), but withdrew from the project in October; this affair, with its associated legal disputes, prompted caution among foreign investors, leading to a degree of stagnation. Total gold production reached 28.2 metric tons in 2000, but gold exploitation was still at an exploratory stage, behind the more buoyant gold sectors in Kyrgyzstan and Uzbekistan.

Apart from the petrochemicals sector, mining and the processing of agricultural products, industry was dominated by heavy engineering works, which produced a broad range of machinery and machine tools, and some light industry, especially the production of textiles. These industries all suffered from the problems experienced throughout the economy of Kazakhstan (and other former Soviet republics), such as increased fuel prices and disruptions to traditional trading partnerships. There were also problems in the supply of raw materials and with the decay of capital equipment and basic infrastructure. Total industrial output during the first nine months of 1994 was some 30% lower than that during the same period of the previous year. By 1995, however, the situation had stabilized, although the sectoral composition of industrial activity had begun to alter. The metals and energy sectors had become increasingly dominant by the end of the 1990s, accounting for over two-thirds of industrial production, while machine-building, construction materials and light industry had contracted.

## OTHER SECTORS

The construction industry, which had been a strong contributor to economic activity under the Soviet system, experienced an initial decline following the final collapse of the USSR. Transfers from the all-Union Government had been important to investment, from which construction benefited. There was an added problem in the early months of independence, when the State Committee (later the Ministry) of the Economy did not assume responsibility for investment from the all-Union authorities (defunct since December 1991) until August 1992. As a proportion of GDP, construction provided only an estimated 5.4% in 2001. Employment in the sector declined after independence, accounting for only 4.0% of the total by 2002. Construction activity tended to be concentrated in small, high-value projects, usually associated with the extractive industries. However, in the late 1990s the Government began to encourage investment, with infrastructure projects for pipelines and communications with countries apart from Russia, and with the building of the new capital Astana (formerly Akmola, earlier still Tselinograd).

The decline in construction activity in the 1990s caused housing and social facilities to deteriorate, along with the country's infrastructure. This last factor was notable, because transport and communications were significant contributors to the economy. Transport and communications accounted for an estimated 10.9% of GDP by 2001, and 7.5% of employment by 2002. There was a well-developed transport system in Kazakhstan, which was important considering the sheer size of the country. However, it was orientated to Russia and often dependent on it and other former Soviet territories for spare parts. Thus, the railway system (the most important of the transport networks), apart from needing substantial basic investment and modernization, required spare parts, equipment and rolling stock from Russia and Ukraine. Likewise, the lorry fleet (numbering some 400,000 in 1992, but little more than 230,000 in 2000), upon which road transport was reliant, was affected by the rising cost and shortages of fuel, and the need for spare parts from Russia and Belarus. The disruption to trade added to the shortages created by the restraint on resources. Investment was important to maintain the transport network, particularly as Kazakhstan could benefit from this, being in a focal position in the heart of Asia. The country participated in the September 1998 treaty designed to reactivate the ancient 'Silk Road', involving countries from Mongolia to the European Black Sea, and benefited from the associated European Union (EU) funds for the Transport Corridor Europe–Caucasus–Asia (TRACECA) project. Kazakhstan's existing facilities, notably its air links with Russia and Europe and with the other, southern Central Asian countries, helped make Almaty the Central Asian city with the largest foreign population during the 1990s.

The services sector, although less state-dominated, remained largely dependent on government expenditure. In 1992 it was estimated that services (mainly education and health) accounted for 26.5% of total employment. In 1994, excluding trade and catering (which involves procurement and material supply), services provided only 19.2% of GDP. Services, however, increased in importance during the course of the 1990s. Private retail outlets increased in number, and the services sector contributed an estimated 53.9% of GDP in 2001, and provided 48.2% of employment in 2002.

With respect to trade, Russia remained Kazakhstan's principal trading partner in 2002 (despite a noticeable decline in the volume of trade in 1998–99), accounting for 39.1% of total imports and 15.7% of exports. However, Western trading partners were increasingly prominent, and included the USA (accounting for 9.8% of imports, but only 1.2% of exports), Germany (8.7% of imports and 2.3% of exports), Italy (3.3% of imports and 9.5% of exports) and Switzerland (0.9% of imports, but 8.1% of exports). Notably, Bermuda purchased 20.7% of Kazakhstani exports in 2002, and a further 10.5% of exports went to the People's Republic of China.

## PROSPECTS

The decline in the economic performance of many sectors, brought about by the disintegration of Soviet infrastructure and inter-republican trade, continued into the mid-1990s. Agriculture, construction and transport and communications, which had been vital contributors to GDP prior to Kazakhstan's independence, all suffered from the political and economic disruptions as the country struggled to make the transition to a market economy. In other areas, the signs were more promising. Extensive interest by foreign investors in the petroleum and natural gas sector, as well as an increase in exports of ferrous and non-ferrous metals, caused output in these commodities to increase. Furthermore, after limited success in 1994, the Government's stabilization programme helped to control inflation and make significant progress in enterprise restructuring. However, from 1997 the decline in world prices for Kazakhstan's principal exports led to major economic difficulties. In September 1998 a new Council on Economic Problems was established by President Nazarbayev, specifically to counter the effects of the global economic crisis. These remedial measures were undermined by the financial crisis in Russia; this led to negative growth of 1.8% in that year. However, real GDP registered increasingly strong growth from 1999. In January 2001 a National Oil Fund was created. The aims were to guard against the adverse impact of sudden declines in petroleum prices, and to manage the country's wealth for the benefit of future generations. By 2002 the Fund had accumulated US $2,000m. None the less, its management attracted criticism, and there were allegations of corruption and the misappropriation of funds. Growing social problems, exacerbated by unemployment and underemployment, heightened popular dissatisfaction. In February 2002 Prime Minister Imangali Tasmagambetov emphasized the need to attract more investment in small and medium-sized businesses. He also called for the greater diversification of the economy and more movement of capital. Another priority was the reduction of poverty. According to World Bank estimates, over 30% of the population of Kazakhstan was living below the poverty line.

However, the country's rich resource base, its sound record on structural reform and its clear commitment to safeguarding macroeconomic stability helped to maintain a relatively benign investment climate, despite the concerns discussed above. More than 130 US companies were operating in Kazakhstan in 2000, and other major business partners included companies from Canada, the People's Republic of China, Germany, Japan, South Korea, Switzerland, Turkey and the United Kingdom. Kazakhstan had succeeded in attracting by far the largest share of foreign direct investment (FDI) in Central Asia (in 2000 net FDI in Kazakhstan amounted to some US $1,350m.; total cumulative investment in 1993–2000 was over $10,000m.). More than one-half of FDI came from the USA, and over 80% of the total was in the petroleum and gas sector. Thus, the economic outlook for Kazakhstan by the early 2000s was, despite a variety of problems, on balance encouraging.

# Statistical Survey

Source (unless otherwise stated): Agency on Statistics of the Republic of Kazakhstan, 480008 Almaty, pr. Abaya 125; tel. (3272) 62-66-45; fax (3272) 42-08-24; e-mail kazstat@mail.banknet.kz; internet www.stat.kz.

## Area and Population

### AREA, POPULATION AND DENSITY

| | |
|---|---|
| Area (sq km) . . . . . . . . . . | 2,717,300* |
| Population (census results) | |
| 12 January 1989† . . . . . . . . | 16,464,464 |
| 25 February–4 March 1999 | |
| Males . . . . . . . . . . | 7,201,785 |
| Females. . . . . . . . . . | 7,751,341 |
| Total . . . . . . . . . | 14,953,126 |
| Population (official estimates at 31 December) | |
| 2000 . . . . . . . . . . . | 14,862,700 |
| 2001 . . . . . . . . . . . | 14,846,000 |
| 2002 . . . . . . . . . . . | 14,862,500 |
| Density (per sq km) at 31 December 2002 . . . . | 5.5 |

* 1,049,150 sq miles.

† Figure refers to the *de jure* population. The *de facto* total was 16,536,511.

### PRINCIPAL ETHNIC GROUPS
(permanent inhabitants, at 1999 census)

| | Number* | % |
|---|---|---|
| Kazakh . . . . . . . . . . | 7,985,000 | 53.4 |
| Russian . . . . . . . . . . | 4,479,600 | 30.0 |
| Ukrainian . . . . . . . . . | 547,100 | 3.7 |
| Uzbek . . . . . . . . . . | 370,700 | 2.5 |
| German . . . . . . . . . . | 353,400 | 2.4 |
| Tatar . . . . . . . . . . | 249,000 | 1.7 |
| Uigur . . . . . . . . . . | 210,400 | 1.4 |
| Belarusian . . . . . . . . | 111,900 | 0.7 |
| Korean . . . . . . . . . . | 99,700 | 0.7 |
| Azeri . . . . . . . . . . | 78,300 | 0.5 |
| Turkish . . . . . . . . . | 75,900 | 0.5 |
| Others. . . . . . . . . . | 392,100 | 2.6 |
| **Total** . . . . . . . . . . | 14,953,100 | 100.0 |

* Figures are rounded to the nearest 100 persons.

### PRINCIPAL TOWNS
(population at 1999 census)

| | | | | |
|---|---|---|---|---|
| Astana* (capital). . | 313,000 | Petropavlovsk . . | 203,500 |
| Almaty (Alma-Ata) . | 1,129,400 | Uralsk. . . . . | 195,500 |
| Karaganda . . . | 436,900 | Temirtau . . . . | 170,500 |
| Shymkent | | | |
| (Chimkent). . . | 360,100 | Kzyl-Orda. . . . | 157,400 |
| Taraz†. . . . . | 330,100 | Aktau§ . . . . | 143,400 |
| Ust-Kamenogorsk . | 311,000 | Atyrau‖ . . . . | 142,500 |
| Pavlodar . . . . | 300,500 | Ekibastuz . . . . | 127,200 |
| Semipalatinsk . . | 269,600 | Kokchetau . . . | 123,400 |
| Aktobe‡ . . . | 253,100 | Rudniy . . . . | 109,500 |
| Kustanai . . . . | 221,400 | | |

* Formerly Akmola.

† Formerly Dzhambul.

‡ Formerly Aktyubinsk.

§ Formerly Shevchenko.

‖ Formerly Guriyev.

**Mid-2000** (UN estimate, incl. suburbs): Almaty (Alma-Ata) 1,127,000 (Source: UN, *World Urbanization Prospects: The 2001 Revision*).

**Mid-2001** (UN estimate, incl. suburbs): Astana 328,000 (Source: UN, *World Urbanization Prospects: The 2001 Revision*).

## BIRTHS, MARRIAGES AND DEATHS

| | Registered live births | | Registered marriages | | Registered deaths | |
|---|---|---|---|---|---|---|
| | Number | Rate (per 1,000) | Number | Rate (per 1,000) | Number | Rate (per 1,000) |
| 1995 . . . | 277,006 | 17.2 | 116,380 | 7.2 | 168,885 | 10.5 |
| 1996 . . . | 253,175 | 16.3 | 102,558 | 6.6 | 166,028 | 10.7 |
| 1997 . . . | 232,356 | 15.2 | 101,874 | 6.6 | 160,138 | 10.4 |
| 1998 . . . | 222,380 | 14.8 | 96,048 | 6.4 | 154,314 | 10.2 |
| 1999 . . . | 209,039 | 14.0 | 85,872 | 5.8 | 144,450 | 9.7 |
| 2000 . . . | 217,379 | 14.6 | 90,873 | 6.1 | 148,834 | 10.0 |
| 2001* . . . | 220,748 | 14.8 | 92,852 | 6.3 | 147,587 | 10.0 |
| 2002 . . . | 227,169 | 15.3 | 98,986 | 6.7 | 148,706 | 10.0 |

* Provisional figures.

Source: partly UN, *Demographic Yearbook* and *Population and Vital Statistics Report*.

**Expectation of life** (years at birth): 63.0 (males 58.8; females 67.2) in 2001 (Source: WHO, *World Health Report*).

## ECONOMICALLY ACTIVE POPULATION

(annual averages, '000 persons)

| | 1997 | 1998 | 1999 |
|---|---|---|---|
| Agriculture, forestry and fishing | 1,542 | 1,360 | 1,342 |
| Industry* . . . . . . . . | 921 | 903 | 904 |
| Construction . . . . . . | 261 | 223 | 211 |
| Trade, restaurants and hotels . . | 1,382 | 1,405 | 1,398 |
| Transport, storage and communications . . . . | 646 | 560 | 576 |
| Financing and insurance . . | 37 | 38 | 36 |
| Community, social and personal services . . . . . . . | 1,387 | 1,639 | 1,638 |
| Activities not adequately defined | 296 | — | — |
| **Total employed** . . . . . . | 6,472 | 6,128 | 6,105 |
| Unemployed . . . . . . | 968 | 925 | 950 |
| **Total labour force** . . . . . | 7,440 | 7,053 | 7,055 |

Source: UN, *Statistical Yearbook for Asia and the Pacific*.

**2000** (annual average, '000 persons aged 15 years and over): Total employed 6,201.0; Unemployed 906.4; Total labour force 7,107.4.

**2001** (annual average, '000 persons aged 15 years and over): Total employed 6,698.8; Unemployed 780.3; Total labour force 7,479.1.

**2002** ('000 persons aged 15 years and over): Agriculture, hunting and forestry 2,366.7; Fishing 13.5; Industry* 824.0; Construction 268.4; Wholesale and retail trade, repair of cars and household appliances 1,007.2; Restaurants and hotels 56.5; Transport, storage and communications 503.7; Financial intermediation 50.1; Real estate, renting and business activities 203.4; Public administration 280.4; Education 589.0; Health and social work 292.6; Other community, social and personal service activities 186.3; Private households with employed persons 66.8; Extra-territorial organizations and bodies 0.3; Total employed 6,708.9; Unemployed 690.7; Total labour force 7,399.7.

* Including mining and quarrying, manufacturing, and electricity, gas and water.

# Health and Welfare

## KEY INDICATORS

| | |
|---|---|
| Total fertility rate (children per woman, 2001) . . . . . | 2.0 |
| Under-5 mortality rate (per 1,000 live births, 2001) . . . | 76 |
| HIV/AIDS (% of persons aged 15–49, 2001) . . . . . . | 0.07 |
| Physicians (per 1,000 head, 2001) . . . . . . . . | 3.46 |
| Hospital beds (per 1,000 head, 2001) . . . . . . | 7.44 |
| Health expenditure (2000): US $ per head (PPP) . . . . | 211 |
| Health expenditure (2000): % of GDP . . . . . . | 3.7 |
| Health expenditure (2000): public (% of total) . . . . . | 73.2 |
| Access to water (% of persons, 2000). . . . . . . | 91 |
| Access to sanitation (% of persons, 2000) . . . . . | 99 |
| Human Development Index (2001): ranking . . . . . | 76 |
| Human Development Index (2001): value . . . . . . | 0.765 |

For sources and definitions, see explanatory note on p. vi.

# Agriculture

## PRINCIPAL CROPS

('000 metric tons)

| | 1999 | 2000 | 2001 |
|---|---|---|---|
| Wheat . . . . . . . . . . | 11,241.9 | 9,073.5 | 12,500.0* |
| Rice (paddy) . . . . . . | 199.3 | 214.3 | 262.2* |
| Barley . . . . . . . . | 2,264.9 | 1,663.6 | 2,287.0* |
| Maize . . . . . . . . | 197.6 | 248.8 | 310.0* |
| Rye . . . . . . . . . | 16.6 | 48.3 | 66.4* |
| Oats . . . . . . . . | 194.2 | 181.8 | 250.0* |
| Millet . . . . . . . . | 43.8 | 62.3 | 85.6* |
| Buckwheat . . . . . . | 16.1 | 28.7 | 40.0* |
| Other cereals . . . . . | 74.0 | 25.6 | 70.0* |
| Potatoes . . . . . . . | 1,694.7 | 1,692.6 | 2,192.0 |
| Sugar beet. . . . . . | 293.9 | 272.7 | 283.0 |
| Dry beans* . . . . . . | 9.0 | 7.4 | 9.2 |
| Dry peas* . . . . . . | 6.6 | 9.2 | 13.6 |
| Sunflower seed . . . . | 104.3 | 104.6 | 149 |
| Safflower seed . . . . | 34.0 | 25.4 | 25.0† |
| Cottonseed . . . . . . | 249.4 | 287.1 | 420.0 |
| Cabbages . . . . . . | 215.4 | 262.7 | 303.5* |
| Tomatoes . . . . . . | 300.6 | 387.0 | 447.2* |
| Cucumbers and gherkins* . . . | 162.0 | 190.6 | 220.2 |
| Aubergines (Eggplants)* . . . | 18.0 | 21.5 | 24.8 |
| Chillies and green peppers* . . | 32 | 34.0 | 39.3 |
| Dry onions* . . . . . | 280.0 | 302.0 | 348.9 |
| Carrots . . . . . . . | 128.2 | 163.6 | 189.1* |
| Other vegetables* . . . . | 285.4 | 316.0 | 214.1 |
| Apples . . . . . . . | 64.0* | 144.6 | 132.4* |
| Pears . . . . . . . | 7.5* | 10.2 | 9.4* |
| Grapes . . . . . . . | 26.8 | 61.6 | 40.0† |
| Watermelons . . . . . | 369.6 | 421.6 | 450.0† |
| Tobacco (leaves) . . . . | 8.0 | 16.2 | 19.0† |
| Cotton (lint) . . . . . | 66.7 | 83.0* | 142.0* |

* Unofficial figure(s).
† FAO estimate.

Source: FAO.

## LIVESTOCK

('000 head, year ending September)

| | 1999 | 2000 | 2001 |
|---|---|---|---|
| Horses . . . . . . . . | 986 | 970 | 976 |
| Asses* . . . . . . . . | 29 | 30 | 30 |
| Cattle . . . . . . . . | 3,958 | 3,998 | 4,107 |
| Buffaloes* . . . . . . | 9 | 9 | 9 |
| Camels . . . . . . . | 96 | 96 | 99† |
| Pigs . . . . . . . . | 892 | 984 | 1,076 |
| Sheep . . . . . . . | 8,691 | 8,725 | 8,939 |
| Goats . . . . . . . | 835 | 931 | 1,042 |
| Chickens . . . . . . | 16,985 | 18,023 | 19,706 |
| Rabbits* . . . . . . | 58,000 | 60,000 | 61,500 |

* FAO estimates.
† Unofficial figure.

Source: FAO.

**LIVESTOCK PRODUCTS**
('000 metric tons)

| | 1999 | 2000 | 2001 |
|---|---|---|---|
| Beef and veal . . . . . . | 343.9 | 306.3 | 358.7* |
| Mutton and lamb* . . . . | 94.7 | 87.2 | 117.5 |
| Goat meat* . . . . . | 4.0 | 3.9 | 5.0 |
| Horse meat . . . . . | 64.8 | 57.9 | 66.6* |
| Pig meat . . . . . . | 97.7 | 133.4 | 81.2* |
| Poultry meat . . . . . | 29.3 | 33.3 | 24.7* |
| Rabbit meat* . . . . . | 0.4 | 0.4 | 0.5 |
| Cows' milk . . . . . | 3,535.2 | 3,730.2 | 3,922.9 |
| Sheeps' milk . . . . . | 31.6* | 34.8* | 35† |
| Goats' milk . . . . . | 9.9 | 9.7 | 10.5† |
| Cheese . . . . . . | 6.3 | 6.8† | 6.7† |
| Butter . . . . . . | 3.2* | 4.4 | 3.9 |
| Hen eggs* . . . . . | 84.0 | 93.8 | 103.0 |
| Wool: greasy . . . . . | 22.3 | 22.9 | 23.6 |
| Wool: scoured . . . . | 13.4 | 13.7 | 14.2 |
| Cattle hides (fresh) . . . . | 37.8 | 34.8 | 39.9† |
| Sheepskins (fresh) . . . . | 10.4 | 9.9 | 13.0† |

* Unofficial figure(s).
† FAO estimate.

Source: FAO.

# Forestry

**ROUNDWOOD REMOVALS**
('000 cubic metres, excl. bark)

| | 1995 | 1996 | 1997 |
|---|---|---|---|
| **Total** (all fuel wood). . . . . | 339 | 315 | 315 |

Source: FAO.

**SAWNWOOD PRODUCTION**
(unofficial figures, '000 cubic metres, incl. railway sleepers)

| | 1999 | 2000 | 2001 |
|---|---|---|---|
| Coniferous (softwood) . . . | 191 | 261 | 261 |
| Broadleaved (hardwood). . . | 146 | 199 | 199 |
| **Total** . . . . . . | 337 | 460 | 460 |

Source: FAO.

# Fishing

('000 metric tons, live weight)

| | 1998 | 1999 | 2000 |
|---|---|---|---|
| Capture | 23.1 | 21.0 | 25.8 |
|   Freshwater bream* . . . . | 9.8 | 8.9 | 10.9 |
|   Crucian carp* . . . . | 2.1 | 1.9 | 2.3 |
|   Roaches* . . . . | 1.3 | 1.2 | 1.4 |
|   Wels (Som) catfish* . . . . | 0.7 | 0.7 | 0.8 |
|   Pike-perch* . . . . | 2.9 | 2.7 | 3.3 |
|   Azov sea sprat* . . . . | 4.8 | 4.4 | 5.4 |
| Aquaculture . . . . | 1.1 | 1.2 | 1.2 |
|   Silver carp . . . . | 1.0 | 1.1 | 1.1 |
| **Total catch** . . . . . | 24.2 | 22.2 | 27.0 |

* FAO estimates.

Source: FAO, *Yearbook of Fishery Statistics*.

# Mining

('000 metric tons, unless otherwise indicated)

| | 1998 | 1999 | 2000 |
|---|---|---|---|
| Hard coal . . . . . | 68,058 ⎱ | 58,378 | 74,872 |
| Brown coal (incl. lignite) . . . | 1,715 ⎰ | | |
| Crude petroleum* . . . . | 25,945 | 26,736 | 30,648 |
| Natural gas (million cu m) . . | 7,948 | 9,946 | 11,542 |
| Iron ore (gross weight) . . . | 8,693 | 9,617 | 13,829 |
| Copper ore (metal content) . . | 339 | 374 | 430 |
| Nickel ore (metal content, metric tons)† . . . . . . . | 6,000 | n.a. | 3,000 |
| Bauxite . . . . . . . | 3,437 | 3,607 | 3,730 |
| Lead ore (metal content) . . . | 30 | 34 | 39 |
| Zinc ore (metal content) . . . | 224 | 270 | 322 |
| Manganese ore . . . . . | 399 | 563 | 720 |
| Chromite . . . . . . | 1,603 | 2,406 | 2,607 |
| Titanium (metric tons) . . . | 12,000 | 8,767 | 8,280 |
| Vanadium (metal content, metric tons)† . . . . . . . | 1,000 | 1,000 | 1,000 |
| Silver ore (metal content, metric tons) . . . . . . . | 726 | 905 | 927 |
| Uranium (metal content, metric tons) . . . . . . . | 1,074 | 1,367 | 1,740 |
| Gold (metal content, kg) . . . | 18,100 | 20,236 | 28,171 |
| Asbestos . . . . . . . | 155 | 139 | 233 |

* Including gas condensate.
† Estimates.

Source: mainly US Geological Survey.

**2001** ('000 metric tons, unless otherwise indicated): Coal 76,455; Crude petroleum 36,060; Natural gas (million cu m) 11,610; Iron ore 29,637; Copper ore 34,872; Lead and zinc ore 5,740.

**2002** ('000 metric tons, unless otherwise indicated): Coal 70,603; Crude petroleum 42,037; Natural gas (million cu m) 13,137; Iron ore 33,520; Copper ore 36,668; Lead and zinc ore 6,214.

# Industry

**SELECTED PRODUCTS**
('000 metric tons, unless otherwise indicated)

| | 1998 | 1999 | 2000 |
|---|---|---|---|
| Wheat flour . . . . . | 1,546 | 1,262 | 1,741 |
| Raw sugar. . . . . . | 230 | 228 | 280 |
| Wine ('000 hectolitres) . . . | 163 | 218 | n.a. |
| Beer ('000 hectolitres) . . . | 8,503 | 8,244 | 13,568 |
| Mineral water ('000 hectolitres) . | 475 | 549 | n.a. |
| Cigarettes (million) . . . . | 21,747 | 18,773 | 19,293 |
| Cotton yarn . . . . . . | 1.9 | 1.8 | 1.0 |
| Woven cotton fabrics (million sq metres) . . . . . . | 10 | 9 | 5 |
| Sulphuric acid . . . . . | 605 | 685 | 635 |
| Motor spirit (petrol) . . . . | 1,732 | 1,298 | 1,255 |
| Kerosene . . . . . . | 229 | 71 | 63 |
| Gas-diesel (distillate fuel) oils . . | 2,495 | 1,830 | 1,954 |
| Residual fuel oils. . . . . | 3,052 | 2,133 | 2,391 |
| Cement . . . . . . | 622 | 838 | 1,175 |
| Pig-iron . . . . . . | 2,594 | 3,438 | 4,010 |
| Crude steel . . . . . . | 3,116 | 4,105 | 4,799 |
| Copper (unrefined) . . . . | 335.0 | 384.2 | n.a. |
| Electric energy (million kWh) . . | 49,145 | 47,498 | 51,635 |

Sources: mainly UN, *Statistical Yearbook for Asia and the Pacific* and *Industrial Commodity Statistics Yearbook*.

**2001** ('000 metric tons, unless otherwise indicated): Raw sugar 347; Wine ('000 litres) 41,032; Cotton (carded and combed) 113; Woven cotton fabrics (million sq metres) 8; Motor spirit (petrol) 1,582; Cement 2,029; Pig-iron 3,907; Steel 4,691; Copper (refined) 426; Electric energy (million kWh) 55,384.

**2002** ('000 metric tons, unless otherwise indicated): Raw sugar 395; Wine ('000 litres) 37,955; Cotton (carded and combed) 146; Woven cotton fabrics (million sq metres) 14; Motor spirit (petrol) 1,691; Cement 2,129; Pig-iron 4,089; Steel 4,868; Copper (refined) 453; Electric energy (million kWh) 58,475.

# Finance

## CURRENCY AND EXCHANGE RATES

**Monetary Units**
    100 tein = 1 tenge.

**Sterling, Dollar and Euro Equivalents** (30 April 2003)
    £1 sterling = 242.21 tenge;
    US $1 = 151.75 tenge;
    €1 = 136.33 tenge;
    1,000 tenge = £4.129 = $6.590 = €7.335.

**Average Exchange Rate** (tenge per US $)
    2000    142.13
    2001    146.74
    2002    153.28

Note: The tenge was introduced on 15 November 1993, replacing the old Russian (formerly Soviet) rouble at an exchange rate of 1 tenge = 500 roubles. On 18 November the rate was adjusted to 250 roubles per tenge. In April 1999 the tenge was allowed to 'float' on foreign exchange markets.

## STATE BUDGET
(million tenge)

| Revenue | 1999 | 2000 | 2001* |
|---|---|---|---|
| Tax revenue | 330,267 | 524,058 | 635,792 |
| Other current revenue | 26,896 | 38,602 | 70,539 |
| Capital revenue | 35,787 | 24,378 | 24,267 |
| Official transfers | 2,629 | 3,169 | 233 |
| Repayment of debt principal | 3,013 | 8,511 | 12,719 |
| **Total** | 398,592 | 598,746 | 743,550† |

| Expenditure‡ | 1999 | 2000 | 2001 |
|---|---|---|---|
| General public services | 28,856 | 35,114 | 47,771 |
| Defence | 17,198 | 20,379 | 32,347 |
| Public order and security | 32,507 | 47,738 | 63,681 |
| Education | 78,491 | 84,668 | 105,024 |
| Health care | 44,825 | 54,323 | 62,238 |
| Social security and social assistance | 159,064 | 171,065 | 186,641 |
| Recreation and cultural activities | 12,237 | 17,487 | 18,076 |
| Housing and communal services | 6,012 | 22,106 | 30,396 |
| Economic affairs and services | 48,794 | 87,761 | 132,188 |
| Agriculture, forestry, water management, fishing and environmental protection | 6,944 | 11,441 | 23,113 |
| Mining and minerals (excl. fuel), manufacturing and construction | 2,867 | 7,191 | 4,558 |
| Transport and communications | 12,865 | 37,804 | 41,651 |
| Other purposes | 19,442 | 35,541 | 37,764 |
| Debt interest | 19,442 | 35,541 | 37,764 |
| **Total** | 447,426 | 576,182 | 716,126 |

* Provisional figures.
† Including adjustment (28 million tenge).
‡ Excluding lending minus repayments (million tenge): 20,997 in 1999; 25,842 in 2000; 32,966 in 2001.

**Revised totals** (million tenge, rounded figures): *Revenue:* 598,700 in 2000; 746,600 in 2001; *Expenditure (excluding lending minus repayments):* 602,000 in 2000; 759,600 in 2001.

**2002** (million tenge, rounded figures): Total revenue 821,200; Total expenditure (excluding lending minus repayments) 834,200.

## INTERNATIONAL RESERVES
(US $ million at 31 December)

| | 2000 | 2001 | 2002 |
|---|---|---|---|
| Gold | 501.5 | 510.7 | 585.6 |
| IMF special drawing rights | — | — | 1.0 |
| Reserve position in IMF | 0.01 | 0.01 | 0.1 |
| Foreign exchange | 1,594.1 | 1,997.2 | 2,549.7 |
| **Total** | 2,095.6 | 2,507.9 | 3,136.3 |

Source: IMF, *International Financial Statistics*.

## MONEY SUPPLY
(million tenge at 31 December)

| | 2000 | 2001 | 2002 |
|---|---|---|---|
| Currency outside banks | 106,428 | 131,175 | 161,701 |
| Demand deposits at commercial banks | 126,124 | 137,014 | 219,423 |
| **Total money** (incl. others) | 236,163 | 270,009 | 381,935 |

Source: IMF, *International Financial Statistics*.

## COST OF LIVING
(Consumer Price Index; base: 1992 = 100)

| | 1997 | 1998 | 1999 |
|---|---|---|---|
| Food | 50,946.3 | 53,208.3 | 57,161.7 |
| Clothing | 27,476.1 | 28,174.6 | 30,263.2 |
| Rent | 49,590.9 | 54,922.6 | 57,014.6 |
| **All items** (incl. others) | 62,775.9 | 67,245.5 | 72,833.6 |

**2000:** Food 66,302.0; All items 82,419.0.

**2001:** Food 73,894.0; All items 89,309.0.

Source: ILO.

## NATIONAL ACCOUNTS
('000 million tenge at current prices)

**Expenditure on the Gross Domestic Product**

| | 1999 | 2000 | 2001* |
|---|---|---|---|
| Government final consumption expenditure | 232.7 | 384.8 | 540.6 |
| Private final consumption expenditure | 1,460.1 | 1,620.2 | 1,926.1 |
| Increase in stocks | 32.2 | 21.3 | 102.4 |
| Gross fixed capital formation | 326.3 | 442.8 | 744.5 |
| **Total domestic expenditure** | 2,051.3 | 2,469.1 | 3,313.6 |
| Exports of goods and services<br>*Less* Imports of goods and services | 47.3 | 246.4 | −77.3 |
| **Sub-total** | 2,098.6 | 2,715.5 | 3,236.3 |
| Statistical discrepancy† | −82.1 | −115.6 | 49.1 |
| **GDP in purchasers' values** | 2,016.5 | 2,600.0 | 3,285.4 |
| **GDP at constant 1993 prices** | 24.4 | 26.7 | 30.2 |

* Provisional figures.
† Referring to the difference between the sum of the expenditure components and official estimates of GDP, compiled from the production approach.

Source: Asian Development Bank, *Key Indicators of Developing Asian and Pacific Countries*.

**Gross Domestic Product by Economic Activity**

| | 1999 | 2000 | 2001* |
|---|---|---|---|
| Agriculture, forestry and fishing | 199.4 | 210.9 | 284.2 |
| Industry† | 569.1 | 864.7 | 1,051.9 |
| Construction | 95.7 | 134.6 | 178.6 |
| Trade, restaurants and hotels | 273.9 | 323.5 | 387.4 |
| Transport, storage and communications | 243.2 | 298.5 | 357.8 |
| Other services<br>Import duties<br>*Less* Imputed bank service charges | 635.2 | 767.8 | 1,025.5 |
| **GDP in purchasers' values** | 2,016.5 | 2,600.0 | 3,285.4 |

* Provisional figures.
† Including mining and quarrying, manufacturing, and electricity, gas and water.

Source: Asian Development Bank, *Key Indicators of Developing Asian and Pacific Countries*.

## BALANCE OF PAYMENTS
(US $ million)

| | 2000 | 2001 | 2002 |
|---|---|---|---|
| Exports of goods f.o.b. . . . . | 9,288.1 | 8,927.9 | 10,066.5 |
| Imports of goods f.o.b. . . . . | −6,848.2 | −7,607.1 | −7,646.4 |
| **Trade balance** . . . . . | 2,439.9 | 1,320.8 | 2,420.1 |
| Exports of services . . . . | 1,133.3 | 1,307.0 | 1,587.1 |
| Imports of services . . . . | −2,004.3 | −2,824.1 | −3,734.3 |
| **Balance on goods and services** | 1,568.9 | −196.3 | 272.9 |
| Other income received . . . . | 138.8 | 229.6 | 272.6 |
| Other income paid . . . . | −1,281.2 | −1,356.6 | −1,254.9 |
| **Balance on goods, services and income** . | 426.5 | −1,323.3 | −709.4 |
| Current transfers received . . . | 352.2 | 394.4 | 425.6 |
| Current transfers paid . . . | −103.2 | −162.6 | −312.2 |
| **Current balance** . . . . | 675.5 | −1,091.5 | −596.0 |
| Capital account (net) . . . . | −290.6 | −197.3 | −132.2 |
| Direct investment abroad . . . | −4.4 | −26.7 | −422.7 |
| Direct investment from abroad. . | 1,282.5 | 2,822.8 | 2,560.6 |
| Portfolio investment assets . . | −85.5 | −1,354.0 | −1,064.3 |
| Portfolio investment liabilities . | 30.7 | 31.7 | −183.1 |
| Other investment assets . . . | 43.6 | 480.1 | −1,089.8 |
| Other investment liabilities . . | 41.2 | 659.8 | 1,594.7 |
| Net errors and omissions . . . | −1,122.7 | −940.0 | −132.0 |
| **Overall balance** . . . . . | 570.3 | 384.9 | 535.2 |

Source: IMF, *International Financial Statistics.*

# External Trade

## PRINCIPAL COMMODITIES
(US $ million)*

| Imports c.i.f. | 1998 | 1999 | 2000 |
|---|---|---|---|
| Crude petroleum (incl. gas condensate). . . . . . . | 146.9 | 21.3 | 79.9 |
| Refined petroleum products . . | 194.3 | 87.9 | 252.9 |
| Electrical and non-electrical machinery . . . . . . | 1,199.9 | 969.3 | 1,391.2 |
| Foodstuffs . . . . . . . | 241.6 | 282.2 | 235.9 |
| Non-food consumer goods . . . | 356.0 | 410.8 | 427.6 |
| Vehicles . . . . . . . | 434.0 | 629.9 | 564.8 |
| **Total** (incl. others) . . . . . | 4,349.6 | 3,682.7 | 5,052.1 |

| Exports f.o.b. | 1998 | 1999 | 2000 |
|---|---|---|---|
| Crude petroleum (incl. gas condensate). . . . . . . | 1,650.5 | 2,040.2 | 4,502.4 |
| Coal . . . . . . . | 323.2 | 152.0 | 168.5 |
| Refined copper . . . . . | 507.9 | 525.6 | 669.1 |
| Unrefined zinc . . . . . | 181.6 | 163.0 | 198.2 |
| Iron ores and concentrates . . . | 177.7 | 38.2 | 51.3 |
| Ferro-alloys . . . . . . | 224.0 | 212.9 | 293.4 |
| Rolled iron and steel . . . . | 515.7 | 599.9 | 764.1 |
| Cereals . . . . . . . | 295.4 | 313.6 | 500.5 |
| **Total** (incl. others) . . . . . | 5,435.8 | 5,592.2 | 9,139.5 |

* Figures refer to trade recorded by the customs authorities. After adjusting for operations excluded from customs statistics, shuttle transactions and, in the case of imports, other corrections (grants received, barter trade and a deduction for freight charges), the value of total trade (in US $ million), on an f.o.b. basis, was: Imports 6,726.1 in 1998, 5,645.0 in 1999, 6,849.8 in 2000; Exports 5,870.6 in 1998, 5,988.5 in 1999, 9,604.0 in 2000.

Source: IMF, *Republic of Kazakhstan: Selected Issues and Statistical Appendix* (March 2002).

**2001** (US $ million): Total imports 5,787.4; Total exports 7,975.6.

## PRINCIPAL TRADING PARTNERS
(US $ million)

| Imports c.i.f. | 2000* | 2001 | 2002 |
|---|---|---|---|
| Belarus . . . . . . . . | 39.9 | 46.1 | 54.4 |
| China, People's Repub. . . . . | 154.0 | 169.2 | 304.8 |
| Finland . . . . . . . | 57.4 | 69.1 | 68.3 |
| France . . . . . . . . | 75.4 | 138.4 | 107.5 |
| Germany . . . . . . . | 333.7 | 471.4 | 565.3 |
| Italy . . . . . . . . | 155.0 | 266.1 | 212.6 |
| Japan . . . . . . . . | 105.5 | 140.2 | 161.6 |
| Korea, Repub. . . . . . | 82.5 | 106.5 | 107.2 |
| Netherlands . . . . . . | 64.7 | 82.4 | 85.6 |
| Poland . . . . . . . . | 58.8 | 59.3 | 72.2 |
| Russia . . . . . . . . | 2,459.8 | 2,890.9 | 2,540.4 |
| Switzerland . . . . . . | 54.3 | 65.8 | 57.1 |
| Turkey . . . . . . . . | 142.6 | 131.3 | 166.8 |
| Ukraine . . . . . . . | 79.8 | 154.9 | 215.6 |
| United Kingdom . . . . . | 219.4 | 246.3 | 255.7 |
| USA . . . . . . . . | 276.9 | 341.6 | 637.7 |
| Uzbekistan . . . . . . | 73.3 | 80.2 | 84.9 |
| **Total** (incl. others) . . . . . | 5,051.7 | 6,363.0 | 6,490.5 |

| Exports f.o.b. | 2000* | 2001 | 2002 |
|---|---|---|---|
| Bermuda . . . . . . . | 1,358.1 | 1,221.2 | 2,011.3 |
| China, People's Repub. . . . . | 670.3 | 655.5 | 1,020.2 |
| Finland . . . . . . . | n.a | 56.1 | 48.6 |
| Germany . . . . . . . | 566.6 | 509.7 | 218.6 |
| Italy . . . . . . . . | 891.9 | 970.9 | 921.6 |
| Korea, Repub. . . . . . | n.a | 45.4 | 49.3 |
| Kyrgyzstan . . . . . . | 58.5 | 87.1 | 107.6 |
| Netherlands . . . . . . | 240.0 | 145.0 | 123.2 |
| Poland . . . . . . . . | 71.2 | 164.2 | 320.4 |
| Russia . . . . . . . . | 1,783.9 | 1,748.4 | 1,524.2 |
| Switzerland . . . . . . | 497.6 | 407.3 | 786.8 |
| Tajikistan . . . . . . . | n.a | 61.3 | 46.0 |
| Turkey . . . . . . . . | n.a | 74.4 | 98.0 |
| Ukraine . . . . . . . | 268.5 | 490.5 | 291.8 |
| United Kingdom . . . . . | 231.0 | 295.0 | 132.9 |
| USA . . . . . . . . | 211.0 | 159.1 | 118.8 |
| Uzbekistan . . . . . . | 139.2 | 148.8 | 103.6 |
| **Total** (incl. others) . . . . . | 9,138.0 | 8,646.9 | 9,709.1 |

* Source: Asian Development Bank, *Key Indicators of Developing Asian and Pacific Countries.*

# Transport

## RAILWAYS
(estimated traffic)

| | 1999 | 2000 | 2001 |
|---|---|---|---|
| Passenger-km (million) . . . . | 8,859 | 10,215 | 10,384 |
| Freight net ton-km (million) . . | 91,700 | 124,983 | 135,653 |

## ROAD TRAFFIC
(motor vehicles in use at 31 December)

| | 1998 | 1999 | 2000 |
|---|---|---|---|
| Passenger cars . . . . . | 971,170 | 987,724 | 1,000,298 |
| Buses and coaches . . . . | 44,295 | 43,421 | 45,666 |
| Lorries and vans . . . . . | 270,198 | 247,693 | 233,045 |
| Motorcycles and mopeds . . . | 200,637 | 155,850 | 112,742 |

Source: International Road Federation, *World Road Statistics.*

## SHIPPING

### Merchant Fleet
(registered at 31 December)

| | 2000 | 2001 | 2002 |
|---|---|---|---|
| Number of vessels . . . . | 20 | 21 | 20 |
| Total displacement (grt) . . . | 11,476 | 13,096 | 11,845 |

Source: Lloyd's Register-Fairplay, *World Fleet Statistics.*

**CIVIL AVIATION**
(traffic on scheduled services)

| | 1999 | 2000 | 2001 |
|---|---|---|---|
| Passengers carried ('000) . . . | 800 | 800 | 900 |
| Passenger-km (million) . . . . | 2,136 | 1,797 | 1,901 |
| Total ton-km (million) . . . . | 64 | 118 | 44 |

**Kilometres flown** (million): 20 in 1996; 20 in 1997; 35 in 1998 (Source: UN, *Statistical Yearbook*).

**Passengers carried** ('000): 1,904 in 2002.

## Communications Media

| | 1998 | 1999 | 2000 |
|---|---|---|---|
| Television receivers ('000 in use) . | 3,890 | 3,900 | 3,910 |
| Telephones ('000 main lines in use) | 1,775.4 | 1,759.8 | 1,834.2 |
| Facsimile machines (number in use) . . . . . . . . . | 1,636 | 2,045 | n.a. |
| Mobile cellular telephones ('000 subscribers). . . . . | 29.7 | 49.5 | 197.3 |
| Internet users ('000) . . . . . | 20.0 | 70.0 | 100.0 |

**Book production** (incl. pamphlets, 1996): Titles 1,226; Copies 21,014,000.

**Daily newspapers** (1996): Titles 3; Average circulation 500,000.

**Radio receivers** ('000 in use, 1997): 6,470.

**2001:** Telephones ('000 main lines in use) 1,834.2; Mobile cellular telephones ('000 subscribers) 582.0; Internet users ('000) 100.0.

**2002:** Telephones ('000 main lines in use) 1,939.6; Mobile cellular telephones ('000 subscribers) 582.0; Internet users ('000) 150.0.

Sources: UNESCO, *Statistical Yearbook*; UN, *Statistical Yearbook*; International Telecommunication Union.

## Education

(1999/2000, unless otherwise indicated)

| | Institu-tions | Teachers | Students |
|---|---|---|---|
| Pre-primary . . . . . | 1,102 | 12,600 | 124,400 |
| Primary . . . . . . | 1,447 | 62,700 | 1,208,300 |
| Secondary: general . . . | 8,309* | 176,900 | 1,913,100 |
| Secondary: vocational . . . | 293* | n.a. | 89,900 |
| Higher: universities, etc. . .⎱ | 170 ⎰ | 27,189†⎱ | 440,700 |
| Higher: other . . . . . .⎰ | ⎱ | 11,998‡⎰ | |

* 2000/01.
† 1994/95.
‡ 1995/96.

Sources: partly Ministry of Education; UNESCO, *Statistical Yearbook*; UN, *Statistical Yearbook for Asia and the Pacific*.

**2002/03:** *Secondary (general):* Institutions 8,334; Students 3,115,000; *Secondary (vocational):* Institutions 335; Students 211,300; *Higher (universities and other):* Institutions 177, Students 597,500.

**Adult literacy rate** (census results): 99.4% (males 99.7%; females 99.2%) in 2001 (Source: UNDP, *Human Development Report*).

# Directory

## The Constitution

The Constitution of the Republic of Kazakhstan was endorsed by 89% of the electorate voting in a national referendum on 30 August 1995, and was officially adopted on 6 September, replacing the Constitution of January 1993. A number of constitutional amendments were adopted on 8 October 1998. The following is a summary of the Constitution's main provisions:

### GENERAL PROVISIONS

The Republic of Kazakhstan is a democratic, secular, law-based, unitary state with a presidential system of rule. The state ensures the integrity, inviolability and inalienability of its territory. State power belongs to the people, who exercise it directly through referendums and free elections, and also delegate the exercise of their power to state bodies. State power is separated into legislative, executive and judicial branches; these interact, with a system of checks and balances being applied.

Ideological and political diversity are recognized. State and private property are recognized and afforded equal protection. The state language is Kazakh. Russian is employed officially in state bodies and local government bodies on a par with Kazakh. The state creates the conditions necessary for the study and development of the languages of the peoples of Kazakhstan.

### HUMAN AND CIVIL RIGHTS AND LIBERTIES

Citizenship of the Republic of Kazakhstan is acquired and terminated in accordance with the law. Citizenship of another state is not recognized for any citizen of Kazakhstan. The rights and liberties of the individual are recognized and guaranteed. No one may be subjected to discrimination on grounds of origin, sex, race, language, religious or other beliefs, or place of residence. No one may be subjected to torture, violence or other treatment or punishment that is cruel or degrading. All are entitled to use their native language and culture. Freedom of speech and creativity are guaranteed.

Censorship is prohibited. Citizens are entitled to assemble and to hold meetings, rallies, demonstrations, marches and picket-lines peacefully and without weapons. Defence of the republic is the sacred duty and obligation of every citizen. Human and civil rights and liberties may be restricted only by law and only to the extent that is necessary to defend the constitutional system and to safeguard public order, and human rights and liberties. Any action capable of disrupting inter-ethnic accord is deemed unconstitutional. Restriction of civil rights and liberties on political grounds is not permitted in any form.

### THE PRESIDENT OF THE REPUBLIC

The President of the Republic is the Head of State and highest official of Kazakhstan, who determines the main directions of the state's domestic and foreign policy and represents Kazakhstan within the country and in international relations. The President is symbol and guarantor of the unity of people and state power, the permanency of the Constitution and of human and civil rights and liberties. The President is elected for a seven-year term by secret ballot on the basis of general, equal and direct suffrage. No person may be elected to the office for more than two consecutive terms. A citizen of the republic by birth, who is at least 40 years of age, has a fluent command of the state language, and has lived in Kazakhstan for no less than 15 years, may be elected President.

The President addresses an annual message to the people; schedules regular and extraordinary elections to Parliament; signs and promulgates laws submitted by the Senate, or returns draft legislation for further discussion; with the consent of Parliament, appoints the Prime Minister and relieves him of office; on the recommendation of the Prime Minister, determines the structure of the Government, appoints its members to office and relieves them of office; presides at sessions of the Government on matters of particular importance; may cancel or suspend acts of the Government and of the akims (heads of regional administrative bodies); with the consent of Parliament, appoints to and relieves of office the

Chairman of the National Bank; with the consent of the Senate, appoints to and relieves of office the Prosecutor-General and the Chairman of the National Security Committee; appoints and recalls the heads of diplomatic missions of the republic; decides on the holding of referendums; negotiates and signs international treaties; is supreme Commander-in-Chief of the armed forces; bestows state awards and confers honours; resolves matters of citizenship and of granting political asylum; in the event of aggression against the republic, imposes martial law or announces a partial or general mobilization; forms the Security Council, the Supreme Judicial Council and other consultative and advisory bodies.

The President may be relieved of office only in the event of his having committed an act of treason or if he exhibits a consistent incapacity to carry out his duties owing to illness. A decision on the President's early dismissal is adopted at a joint sitting of the chambers of Parliament by a majority of no less than three-quarters of the total number of deputies of each chamber. Dismissal of a treason indictment against the President at any stage shall result in the early termination of the powers of the Majlis members who initiated the consideration of the matter. The question of dismissal of the President may not be raised at the same time as he is considering early termination of the authority of Parliament.

## PARLIAMENT

Parliament is the supreme representative body of the republic, exercising legislative functions. It consists of two chambers, the Senate (upper chamber) and the Majlis (assembly, lower chamber). The Senate comprises 47 members, of whom 40 are elected at joint sittings of the deputies of all representative bodies of the regions and the capital, while the remaining seven deputies are appointed by the President. The Majlis consists of 67 deputies elected from single-mandate constituencies by secret ballot on the basis of general, equal and direct suffrage and 10 elected by party lists. The Senate's term is six years, and that of the Majlis is five years. One-half of the elected deputies in the Senate are subject to election every three years.

## THE GOVERNMENT

The Government exercises the executive power of the republic and is responsible to the President. The Government drafts the main areas of the state's socio-economic policy, defence capability, security and public order, and orders their implementation; presents to Parliament the republican budget and the report of its implementation, and ensures that the budget is implemented; submits draft legislation to the Majlis and provides for the implementation of laws; organizes the management of state property; formulates measures for the pursuit of Kazakhstan's foreign policy; directs the activity of Ministries, State Committees and other central and local executive bodies. The Prime Minister organizes and directs the activity of the Government and is personally responsible for its work.

## THE CONSTITUTIONAL COUNCIL

The Constitutional Council consists of seven members whose term of office is six years. Former Presidents of the Republic are by right life members of the Constitutional Council. The Chairman and two members of the Council are appointed by the President of the Republic, two members are appointed by the Chairman of the Senate and two by the Chairman of the Majlis. One-half of the members of the Council are replaced every three years. The Council decides whether to hold a presidential or parliamentary election, or a republican referendum; prior to signature by the President, examines laws passed by Parliament for compliance with the Constitution; prior to ratification, examines international treaties.

## LOCAL STATE ADMINISTRATION AND GOVERNMENT

Local state administration is exercised by local representative and executive bodies, which are responsible for the state of affairs on their own territory. The local representative bodies—the councils (maslikhat)—express the will of the population of the corresponding administrative-territorial units and, bearing in mind the overall state interest, define the measures necessary to realize this will and monitor the ways in which these are implemented. Councils are elected for a four-year term by a secret ballot of the public on the basis of general, equal and direct suffrage. The local executive bodies are part of the unified system of executive bodies of Kazakhstan, and ensure that the general state policy of the executive authority is implemented in co-ordination with the interests and development needs of the corresponding territory. Each local executive body is headed by the akim of the corresponding administrative-territorial unit, who is the representative of the President and the Government of the Republic.

# The Government

## HEAD OF STATE

**President of the Republic of Kazakhstan:** NURSULTAN A. NAZARBAYEV (elected 1 December 1991; re-elected 10 January 1999).

## GOVERNMENT
(October 2003)

**Prime Minister:** DANIYAL AKHMETOV.

**First Deputy Prime Minister:** ALEKSANDR PAVLOV.

**Deputy Prime Ministers:** SAUAT MYNBAYEV, KARIM MASIMOV.

**Deputy Prime Minister and Minister of Agriculture:** AKHMETZHAN YESIMOV.

**Minister of Finance:** YERBOLAT DOSAYEV.

**State Secretary and Minister of Foreign Affairs:** KASYMZHOMART K. TOKAYEV.

**Minister of Internal Affairs:** ZAUTBEK TURISBEKOV.

**Ministry of Economy and Budget Planning:** KEYRAT NEMATOVICH KELIMBETOV.

**Minister of Energy and Mineral Resources:** VLADIMIR S. SHKOLNIK.

**Minister of Defence:** Gen. MUKHTAR ALTYNBAYEV.

**Minister of Industry and Trade:** ADILBEK DZHAKSYBEKOV.

**Minister of Labour and Social Security:** GULZHANA KARAGUSOVA.

**Minister of Education and Science:** ZHAKSYBEK KULEKEYEV.

**Minister of Environmental Protection:** AITKUL B. SAMAKOVA.

**Minister of Justice:** GEORGI KIM.

**Minister of Culture:** DYUSEN KASEINOV.

**Minister of Information:** SAUTBEK ABDRAKHMANOV.

**Minister of Transport and Communications:** KAZHMURAT NAGMANOV.

**Minister of Public Health:** ZHAKSYLYK DOSKALIYEV.

**Mayor of Astana:** TEMIRKHAN DOSMUHAMBETOV.

## HEADS OF GOVERNMENT BODIES

**National Bank:** GRIGORII MARCHENKO.

**National Commission on Family and Women's Affairs:** AITKUL B. SAMAKOVA.

**National Security Council:** BULAT UTEMURATOV.

**State Committee for Affairs of the Commonwealth of Independent States:** ASAN KOZHAKOV.

**State Committee for Aviation and Space:** ALMAS KOSUNOV.

**State Agency for Emergency Situations:** ZAMANBEK NURKADILOV.

**State Committee for Energy Supervision:** MURAT RAMAZANOV.

**State Agency for Financial Police:** BOLATBEK BULGAKBAYEV.

**State Agency for Management of Land Resources:** BAKYT OSPANOV.

**State Agency for Material Reserves:** KABIDOLLA SAREKENOV.

**State Agency for Migration and Demography:** ALTYNSHASH DZHAGANOVA.

**State Agency for the Protection of State Secrets:** SERIK AKHMETOV.

**State Committee for State Property and Privatization:** MAKSUTBEK RAKHANOV.

**State Agency for Statistics:** ALIKHAN SMAILOV.

**State Agency for Tourism and Sports:** DAULET TURLYKHANOV.

## MINISTRIES

In 1998 ministries were relocated to Astana (formerly Akmola) from the former capital, Almaty.

**Office of the President:** 473000 Astana, Mira 11; tel. (3172) 32-13-99; fax (3172) 32-61-72; internet www.president.kz.

**Office of the Prime Minister:** 473000 Astana, Beibitshilik 11; tel. (3172) 32-31-04; fax (3172) 32-40-89.

**Ministry of Agriculture:** 473000 Astana, pr. Abaya 49; tel. (3172) 32-37-63; fax (3172) 32-62-99; internet www.minagri.kz.

**Ministry of Culture:** Astana.

**Ministry of Defence:** 473000 Astana, Beibitshilik 51A; tel. and fax (3172) 33-78-89.

**Ministry of Economy and Budget Planning:** 473000 Astana, Popeda 33; tel. (3172) 71-77-70; fax (3172) 71-77-12; e-mail mineconom@nursat.kz; internet www.geocities.com/economy_kz.

**Ministry of Education and Science:** 473000 Astana, Kenesary 83; tel. (3172) 32-25-40; fax (3172) 32-64-82.

**Ministry of Energy and Mineral Resources:** 473000 Astana, Beibitshilik 37; tel. (3172) 31-71-33; fax (3172) 31-71-64; e-mail ministr@minenergo.kegoc.kz; internet www.minenergo.kz.

**Ministry of Environmental Protection:** 475000 Kokchetau, Marks 81; tel. (31622) 54-265; fax (31622) 50-620.

**Ministry of Finance:** 473000 Astana, pl. Respubliki 60; tel. (3172) 28-00-65; fax (3172) 32-40-89; internet www.minfin.kz.

**Ministry of Foreign Affairs:** 473000 Astana; tel. (3172) 32-76-69; fax (3172) 32-76-67; internet www.mfa.kz.

**Ministry of Industry and Trade:** 473000 Astana.

**Ministry of Information:** Astana.

**Ministry of Internal Affairs:** 473000 Astana, Manasa 4; tel. (3172) 34-36-01; fax (3172) 34-17-38; internet www.mvd.kz.

**Ministry of Justice:** 473000 Astana, Pobeda 45; tel. (3172) 39-12-13; fax (3172) 32-15-54; internet www.minjust.kz.

**Ministry of Labour and Social Security:** 473000 Astana, Manasa 2; tel. (3172) 15-36-02; internet www.enbek.banknet.kz.

**Ministry of Public Health:** Astana.

**Ministry of Transport and Communications:** 473000 Astana, pr. Abaya 49; tel. (3172) 32-62-77; fax (3172) 32-16-96.

## President and Legislature

### Presidential Election, 10 January 1999

| Candidate | % of votes |
| --- | --- |
| Nursultan A. Nazarbayev | 80.97 |
| Serikbolsyn A. Abdildin | 11.87 |
| Gani Kasymov | 4.68 |
| Engels Gabbasov | 0.77 |
| Against all candidates | 1.71 |
| **Total** | 100.00 |

#### PARLIAMENT

Parliament is a bicameral legislative body, comprising the Senate and the Majlis (Assembly). Elections to Parliament were held for the first time in December 1995.

**Parliament:** e-mail www@parlam.kz; internet www.parlam.kz.

#### Senate

**Chairman:** ORALBAI ABDYKARIMOV.

The Senate is the upper chamber of Parliament. It comprises 39 members: 32 elected by special electoral colleges (comprising members of local councils) in Kazakhstan's 14 regions and two cities (the country's third city, Turatam, is effectively governed by Russia), and seven appointed by the President of the Republic. At the first elections to the Senate, held on 5 December 1995, only 38 of the then 40 regionally elected seats were filled, necessitating further voting at a later date for the remaining two seats. The remaining seven Senators were appointed by President Nazarbayev. Elections are held every three years for one-half of the elected seats. Partial elections to the Senate were held on 17 September 1999 and 8 October 2002.

#### Majlis

**Chairman:** ZHARMAKHAN A. TUYAKBAYEV.

The Majlis is the 77-seat lower chamber of Parliament. The first direct elections to a 67-seat Majlis were held on 9 December 1995. Further direct elections to the Majlis were held on 10 October 1999, with the participation of 62.6% of the electorate. For the first time, an additional 10 seats were elected by party lists, bringing the total number of seats to 77. However, the required two-thirds' quorum was not achieved, as candidates succeeded in obtaining the requisite 50% of the votes in only 20 of the 67 single-mandate constituencies. A further round of voting took place in the remaining 47 constituencies on 24 October. Three of these results were subsequently declared to be invalid, thus necessitating a third round of voting in the three constituencies on 26 December.

### General Election, 10 and 24 October and 26 December 1999

| Party | Number of seats | | |
| --- | --- | --- | --- |
| | Single-mandate constituencies | Party lists | Total |
| Independents and others | 34 | — | 34 |
| Otan | 19 | 4 | 23 |
| Civic Party of Kazakhstan | 11 | 2 | 13 |
| Communist Party of Kazakhstan | 1 | 2 | 3 |
| Agrarian Party of Kazakhstan | 1 | 2 | 3 |
| National Co-operative Party of Kazakhstan | 1 | — | 1 |
| **Total** | 67 | 10 | 77 |

## Local Government

For the purposes of local government Kazakhstan is divided into 17 units: 14 regions (oblasts) and three cities. However, the city of Leninsk, now Turatam, serving the Baikonur space centre, was transferred to Russian jurisdiction in August 1995, for a period of 20 years. Each region has an elected council (maslikhat), which is elected for a four-year term by secret ballot. Elections to local maslikhats took place in September–October 2003. In each unit, executive authority is represented by the akimiyat, headed by the akim or governor, who is appointed by the President.

**Aktyubinsk:** Aktobe; tel. (3132) 53-22-65; fax (3172) 57-00-41; Akim YERMAK ZH. IMANTAYEV.

**Almaty City:** Almaty; tel. (3172) 32-30-12; fax (3172) 32-07-32; internet www.mayor-almaty.kz; Mayor SHALBAY KULMAKHANOV.

**Almaty:** Taldykorgan; Akim VIKTOR KHRAPUNOV.

**Astana:** Astana (Akmola, formerly Tselinograd); Akim VITALIY KULAGIN.

**Astana City:** Astana; Mayor TEMIRKHAN DOSMUHAMBETOV.

**Atyrau:** Atyrau; tel. (3122) 25-45-01; fax (3122) 25-45-13; Akim ASLAN MUSIN.

**Dzhambul:** Taraz (formerly Dzhambul); tel. (3262) 23-18-22; fax (3262) 24-46-28; Akim SERIK UMBETOV.

**Eastern Kazakhstan** (Vostochno-Kazakhstan): Ust-Kamenogorsk; tel. (3232) 26-33-10; fax (3232) 26-13-63; Akim TALGATBEK ABAYDILDIN.

**Karaganda:** Karaganda; tel. (3212) 42-10-45; fax (3212)42-10-33; Akim K. B. MUKHAMEDZHANOV.

**Kostanai:** Kostanai; tel. (3142) 58-03-33; fax (3142) 53-03-63; internet www.kostanai.kz; Akim UMIRZAK YE. SHUKEYEV.

**Kzyl-Orda:** Kzyl-Orda; tel. (3242) 26-21-44; fax (3242) 26-12-25.

**Mangystau:** Atyrau (formerly Guriyev); tel. (3292) 33-42-15; fax (3292) 43-01-02; internet www.mangystau.kz; Akim BOLAT PALYMBETOV.

**Northern Kazakhstan** (Severo-Kazakhstan): Petropavlovsk; tel. (3152) 46-41-25; fax (3152) 46-94-78; Akim ANATOLIY SMIRNOV.

**Pavlodar:** Pavlodar; tel. (3182) 32-33-35; fax (3182) 32-33-35; Akim KAIRAT NURPEISOV.

**Southern Kazakhstan** (Yuzhno-Kazakhstan): Shymkent (Chimkent); tel. (3252) 53-74-73; fax (3252) 44-59-73; internet www.uko.kz; Akim BULAT SHILKISHIYEV.

**Western Kazakhstan** (Batys-Kazakhstan): Uralsk; tel. (3112) 22-40-13; fax (3112) 22-06-26; Akim KRYMBEK KUSHERBAYEV.

## Political Organizations

A new law was introduced in July 2002, which required all parties to have a minimum of 50,000 members from among all the country's regions in order to qualify for official registration. At the expiry of the re-registration period in April 2003, the following seven parties were registered with the Ministry of Justice, compared with 19 in January.

**Agrarian Party of Kazakhstan:** Astana, Pobedy 104; tel. (3172) 32-48-06 (Astana); e-mail agro@mail.kz; f. 1999 to support farmers and campaign for the introduction of private land ownership; centrist; Leader ROMIN MADINOV; 45,000 mems.

**Ak Zhol (Light Road) Party:** Almaty; f. 2002 by former members of the Democratic Choice of Kazakhstan; Leader URAZ DZHANDOSOV; c. 65,000 mems.

**Aul (Village) Peasant and Social Democratic Party:** Almaty; f. 2000; Leader GANI KALIYEV.

**Civic Party of Kazakhstan:** Almaty, Zheltoksan 115, pav. 50; tel. (3272) 62-19-16; e-mail civicparty@mail.kz; f. 1998; seeks strengthening of state system and improvements in the provision of social welfare; Leaders AZAT PERUASHEV, DYUSEMBAY DUYSENOV; over 50,000 mems.

**Communist Party of Kazakhstan (CPK):** Almaty, Karasai batyr 85/312; tel. (3272) 65-11-19; suspended Aug. 1991, re-registered March 1994 and March 2003; Chair. SERIKBOLSYN A. ABDILDIN.

**Otan** (Fatherland): Almaty, Furmanov 174B; tel. (3272) 63-29-79; e-mail party_otan@nursat.kz; internet www.otan.nursat.kz; f. 1999 by the People's Unity Party, the Kazakhstan–2030 Movement, the Liberal Movement of Kazakhstan and the Democratic Party of Kazakhstan; pro-presidential republican party; seeks to strengthen the state system and preserve political stability; mergers with the People's Co-operative Party of Kazakhstan and the Republican Labour Party reported in Sept. and Nov. 2002, respectively; Chair. SERGEI TERESHCHENKO; Deputy Chair. KAZBEK KAZKENOV; 126,000 mems.

**Party of Patriots of Kazakhstan (PPK):** Almaty; f. 2000; Leader GANI KASYMOV.

# Diplomatic Representation

## EMBASSIES IN KAZAKHSTAN

**Afghanistan:** Almaty, Khan Tengri; tel. (3272) 55-27-92; Ambassador SAYD ZAHER SHAH AKHBARI.

**Armenia:** 480075 Almaty, Seifullina 579, 7th Floor; tel. and fax (3272) 69-29-08; e-mail akod100@hotmail.com; Ambassador Dr EDUARD SH. KHURSHUDIAN.

**Belarus:** 473000 Astana, pr. Respubliki 17; tel. (3172) 32-18-70; fax (3172) 32-06-65; e-mail kazakhstan@belembassy.org; Ambassador PAKUSH LARISA VLADIMIROVNA.

**Bulgaria:** 480002 Almaty, Makatayeva 13A; tel. (3272) 33-27-55; fax (3272) 30-27-55; e-mail dekov@itte.kz; Chargé d'affaires a.i. DIMITAR DEKOV.

**Canada:** 480100 Almaty, Karasai Batyr 34; tel. (3272) 50-11-51; fax (3272) 58-24-93; e-mail almat@dfait-maeci.gc.ca; internet www .canada.nursat.kz; Ambassador HECTOR COWAN.

**China, People's Republic:** Almaty, Furmanova 137; tel. (3272) 63-49-66; fax (3272) 63-82-09; e-mail chinaemb_kz@mfa.gov.cn; Ambassador ZHOU XIAOPEI.

**Cuba:** 473005 Astana, Samal 10, kv. 1; tel. and fax (3172) 22-14-19; e-mail embacuba@cubakaz.com; internet www.cubakaz.com; Chargé d'affaires a.i. BLÁS NABEL PÉREZ CAMEJO.

**Czech Republic:** 480002 Almaty, Dostyk 212, POB 5; tel. (3272) 64-16-06; fax (3272) 64-49-97; e-mail amaata@embassy.mzv.cz; Ambassador (vacant).

**Egypt:** 480100 Almaty, Zenkova 59; tel. (3272) 60-16-22; fax (3272) 61-10-22; e-mail sphinx_emb@nursat.kz; Ambassador MUHAMMAD NABIL FEDAWI.

**France:** 480110 Almaty, Furmanova 173; tel. (3272) 50-62-36; fax (3272) 50-61-59; e-mail ambafrance@mail.kz; Ambassador GÉRARD PERROLET.

**Georgia:** Almaty, Bayan Aul 7; tel. (3272) 31-09-09; Ambassador TEMUR GOGOLADZE.

**Germany:** 480091 Almaty, Furmanova 173; tel. (3272) 50-61-55; fax (3272) 50-62-76; e-mail german_embassy_almaty@nursat.kz; internet www.deutschebotschaft-almaty.org; Ambassador ANDREAS R. KÖRTING.

**Greece:** 480051 Almaty, pr. Dostyka 216/1, Zavodskaya; tel. (3272) 50-39-61; fax (3272) 50-39-38; e-mail gr_embassy@kaznet.kz; Ambassador NIKOLAS HATOUPIS.

**Holy See:** 473000 Astana, Zelyonaya Alleya 20; tel. (3172) 24-16-03; fax (3172) 24-16-04; e-mail nuntius_kazakhstan@lycos.com; Apostolic Nuncio JÓZEF WESOŁOWSKI.

**Hungary:** 480000 Almaty, ul. Muszabajeva 4; tel. (3272) 55-12-08; fax (3272) 58-18-37; e-mail titkarsagala@mail.online.kz; Ambassador MIKLÓS JACZKOVITS.

**India:** 480091 Almaty, Maulenova 71; tel. (3272) 92-14-11; fax (3272) 92-67-67; e-mail ambind@netel.kz; Ambassador Dr V. S. VERMA.

**Iran:** Almaty, Kabanbai Batyr 119; tel. (3272) 67-78-46; fax (3272) 54-27-54; Ambassador MURTAZA SAFFARI.

**Israel:** Almaty, Zheltoksan 87; tel. (3272) 50-72-15; fax (3272) 50-62-83; e-mail emb_isr_almaty@kaznet.kz; Ambassador MOSHE KIMCHE.

**Italy:** 480100 Almaty, Kazybek bi 20A , 3rd Floor; tel. (3272) 91-00-07; fax (3272) 91-00-53; e-mail ambalma@nursat.kz; Ambassador DIEGO LONGO.

**Japan:** Almaty, Kazybek bi 41, 3rd Floor; tel. (3272) 60-86-00; fax (3272) 60-86-01; internet www.kz.emb-japan.go.jp; Ambassador TOSHIO TSUNOZAKI.

**Korea, Democratic People's Republic:** Almaty, Voronezhskaya 58; tel. (3272) 61-89-98; fax (3272) 25-27-66; Ambassador PAK UI CHUN.

**Korea, Republic:** Almaty, Jarkentskaya 2/77; tel. (3272) 53-26-60; fax (3272) 50-70-59; e-mail kzemb@hanmail.net; Ambassador TAE SUK-WON.

**Kyrgyzstan:** Almaty, Amangeldy 68A; tel. (3272) 63-33-09; fax (3272) 63-33-62; Ambassador AKBAR RYSKULOV.

**Lebanon:** Almaty, Sovkhoz 'Alatau', Naberezhnaya 20; tel. (3272) 48-71-51; Ambassador ASSIF NASSER.

**Libya:** Almaty, Satpaeva 10, kv. 2; tel. (3272) 62-67-17; fax (3272) 62-22-23; Chargé d'affaires a.i. OMAR ALI GEIT.

**Lithuania:** 480099 Almaty, Iskanderova 15; tel. (3272) 65-61-23; fax (3272) 65-14-60; e-mail lrambkaz@nursat.kz; Chargé d'affaires a.i. JONAS VORONAVIČIUS.

**Malaysia:** 480099 Almaty, pr. Al Farabi 36/2; tel. (3272) 53-35-03; fax (3272) 53-35-06; e-mail mwalmaty@nursat.kz; Ambassador TAN SEN SUNG.

**Mongolia:** Almaty, Kazybek bi 18; tel. (3272) 20-08-65; fax (3272) 60-17-23; e-mail monkazel@kazmail.asdc.kz; Ambassador DANDIMZHAVYN DASHNYAM.

**Netherlands:** 480072 Almaty, Nauryzbai Batyr 103; tel. (3272) 50-37-73; fax (3272) 50-37-72; e-mail alm@minbuza.nl; internet www .nlembassy-almaty.org; Ambassador PETER VAN LEEUWEN.

**Pakistan:** 480004 Almaty, Tulebayeva 25; tel. (3272) 73-35-48; fax (3272) 73-13-00; e-mail parepalmaty@hotmail.com; Ambassador DURRAY SHAHWAR KURESHI.

**Poland:** 480099 Almaty, Dzharkentskaya 9–11, POB 228; tel. (3272) 58-15-51; fax (3272) 58-15-50; e-mail ambpol@mail.kz; Ambassador ZDZISŁAW NOWICKI.

**Romania:** 480100 Almaty, Pushkina 97; tel. (3272) 63-57-72; fax (3272) 58-83-17; e-mail ambro@nursat.kz; Ambassador VASILE SOARE.

**Russia:** Almaty, Dzhandosova 4; tel. (3272) 44-64-91; fax (3272) 44-83-23; e-mail rfe@nursat.kz; Ambassador VLADIMIR BABICHEV.

**Saudi Arabia:** Almaty, Gornaya 137; tel. (3272) 65-77-91; fax (3272) 50-28-11; e-mail kzemb@mofa.gov.sa; Ambassador ALI AL-HAMDAN.

**Spain:** Almaty, Baitursinova 102; tel. (3272) 50-09-06; fax (3272) 50-35-30; e-mail embespkz@mail.mae.es; Ambassador FRANCISCO PASCUAL DE LA PARTE.

**Tajikistan:** Almaty, Al Farabi 96; tel. (3272) 93-51-65; fax (3272) 93-51-80; e-mail tajemb-kaz@vitelco.kz; Chargé d'affaires DAVLAT SIPINEROV.

**Turkey:** 480100 Almaty, Tole bi 29; tel. (3272) 61-81-53; fax (3272) 50-62-08; e-mail almatyturk@kaznet.kz; Ambassador KURTULUŞ TAŞKENT.

**Turkmenistan:** 473000 Astana, Otyrar 64; tel. and fax (3172) 28-08-82; e-mail tm_emb@at.kz.

**Ukraine:** Astana, Aezova 57; tel. (3172) 32-60-42; fax (3172) 32-68-11; e-mail embassy_ua@kepter.kz; internet ukrembassy.kepter.kz; Ambassador VASILIY G. TSUBENKO.

**United Kingdom:** 480110 Almaty, Furmanova 173; tel. (3272) 50-61-91; fax (3272) 50-62-60; e-mail british-embassy@nursat.kz; internet www.britishembassy.gov.uk/kazakhstan; Ambassador JAMES LYALL SHARP.

**USA:** 480091 Almaty, Furmanova 97–99A; tel. (3272) 63-39-21; fax (3272) 63-38-83; e-mail usembassy-almaty@freenet.kz; internet www.usembassy-kazakhstan.freenet.kz; Ambassador LARRY NAPPER.

**Uzbekistan:** 480100 Almaty, Baribayeva 36; tel. (3272) 61-02-35; fax (3272) 61-10-55; Ambassador TURDIKUL BUTAYAROV.

# Judicial System

**Chairman of the Constitutional Council:** YURII KHITRIN.

**Chairman of the Supreme Court:** IGOR I. ROGOV.

**Prosecutor-General:** RASHID T. TUSUPBEKOV.

# Religion

The major religion of the Kazakhs is Islam. They are almost exclusively Sunni Muslims of the Hanafi school. The Russian Orthodox Church is the dominant Christian denomination; it is attended mainly by Slavs. There are also Protestant Churches (mainly Baptists), as well as a Roman Catholic (Latin Rite) presence.

## ISLAM

The Kazakhs were converted to Islam only in the early 19th century, and for many years elements of animist practices remained. Over the period 1985–90 the number of mosques in Kazakhstan increased from 25 to 60, 12 of which were newly built. By 1991 there were an estimated 230 Muslim religious communities functioning in Kazakhstan and an Islamic institute had been opened in Almaty. The Islamic revival intensified following Kazakhstan's independence from the USSR, and during 1991–94 some 4,000 mosques were reported to have been opened.

**Mufti of Kazakhstan:** ABSATTAR B. DERBISALIYEV, Almaty.

## CHRISTIANITY

### The Roman Catholic Church

In May 2003 the hierarchy of the Roman Catholic Church in Kazakhstan was restructured. The former apostolic administration of Astana was elevated to the status of archdiocese, with authority over the dioceses of Almaty (formerly an apostolic administration) and Karaganda, and the apostolic administration of Atyrau. Adherents to the Roman Catholic Church totalled an estimated 177,600 at 31 December 2001.

**Archbishop of the Most Holy Virgin Mary in Astana:** Rt Rev. TOMASZ PETA, 473033 Astana, Tashenova 3, POB 622; tel. (3172) 34-29-35; fax (3172) 34-29-27.

### The Russian Orthodox Church (Moscow Patriarchate)

**Metropolitanate of Astana and Alma-Ata:** Almaty; internet www.svet.orthodoxy.ru/epr/epr.htm; f. 2003; three dioceses; Metropolitan MEFODII.

# The Press

At July 2001 an estimated 950 newspaper and 342 periodical titles were published in Kazakhstan. In addition, 15 news agencies were operating in the country.

## REGULATORY AUTHORITY

**National Agency for the Press and Mass Information:** 480013 Almaty, pl. Respubliki 13; tel. (3272) 63-93-97; fax (3272) 63-93-17; f. 1995; Deputy Chair. ALIBEK A. ASKAROV.

## PRINCIPAL DAILY NEWSPAPERS

**Almaty Asia Times:** Almaty, Dzhandosova 60; tel. (3272) 44-74-50; fax (3272) 44-78-40.

**Almaty Herald:** Almaty, pr. Dostyk 85A; tel. and fax (3272) 63-36-55; internet www.herald.asdc.kz.

**Ekspress-K:** 480044 Almaty, Abdullinykh 6; tel. (3272) 59-60-00; fax (3272) 59-60-39; e-mail express-k@nursat.kz; internet www.ek .kz; f. 1922; 5 a week; in Russian; Editor-in-Chief IGOR SHAKHNOVICH; circ. 18,500.

**Kazakhstanskaya Pravda** (Truth of Kazakhstan): 480044 Almaty, Gogolya 39; Astana; tel. (3272) 63-65-65; fax (3272) 50-18-73; tel. (3172) 32-19-44; e-mail kpam@kaznet.kz; internet www .kazpravda.kz; f. 1920; 5 a week; publ. by the Govt; in Russian; Editor-in-Chief V. MIKHAILOV; circ. 34,115.

**Khalyk Kenesi** (Councils of the People): Almaty; tel. (3272) 33-10-85; f. 1990; 5 a week; publ. by Parliament; in Kazakh; Editor-in-Chief ZH. KENZHALIN.

**Vecherniy Almaty** (Evening Almaty): Almaty, Ablai Khan 2; tel. (3272) 33-34-87; fax (3272) 39-64-24.

**Yegemen Kazakhstan** (Sovereign Kazakhstan): 480044 Almaty, Gogolya 39; Astana; tel. and fax (3272) 63-25-46; tel. (3172) 34-16-41; e-mail astegemen@nursat.kz; f. 1919; 6 a week; organ of the Government; in Kazakh; Editor-in-Chief M. SERKHANOV; circ. 31,840.

## OTHER PUBLICATIONS

**Akikat** (Justice): 480044 Almaty, Gogolya 39; tel. (3272) 63-94-33; fax (3272) 63-94-19; f. 1921; monthly; social and political; circ. 1,484.

**Aktsionerny** (Stock Business Guide): 480004 Almaty, Chaikovskogo 11; tel. (3272) 32-96-09; fax (3272) 39-98-95; f. 1990; in Russian; twice a week; Editor-in-Chief VIKTOR SHATSKY.

**Ana Tili** (Native Language): 484044 Almaty, pr. Dostyk 7; tel. (3272) 33-22-21; fax (3272) 33-34-73; f. 1990; weekly; publ. by the Kazakh Tili society; in Kazakh; Editor-in-Chief ZH. BEISENBAY-ULY; circ. 11,073.

**Ara-Shmel** (Bumble-bee): 480044 Almaty, Gogolya 39; tel. (3272) 63-59-46; f. 1956; monthly; satirical; in Kazakh and Russian; Editor-in-Chief S. ZHUMABEKOV; circ. 53,799.

**Arai** (Dawn): Almaty, Furmanova 53; tel. (3272) 32-29-45; f. 1987; every two months; socio-political; Editor-in-Chief S. KUTTYKADAMOV; circ. 7,500.

**Atameken** (Fatherland): 484100 Almaty, pr. Dostyk 85; tel. (3272) 63-58-43; f. 1991; ecological; publ. by Ministry of Environmental Protection; circ. 25,063.

**Aziya Kino** (Asian Cinema): 480100 Almaty, Tole bi 23A; tel. (3272) 61-86-55; f. 1994; monthly; in Russian and Kazakh; Editor-in-Chief G. ABIKEYEVA.

**Baldyrgan** (Sprout): 480044 Almaty, pr. Zhibek zholy 50; tel. (3272) 33-16-73; f. 1958; monthly; illustrated; for pre-school and first grades of school; in Kazakh; Editor-in-Chief T. MOLDAGALIYEV; circ. 150,000.

**Budem:** 480004 Almaty, Chaikovskogo 11; tel. (3272) 39-97-04; f. 1997; monthly; in Russian; Editor-in-Chief R. GARIPOV.

**Business World:** Astana; tel. (3172) 75-17-51; e-mail areket-kz@ hotmail.com; f. 1999; weekly; circ. 10,000.

**Continent:** Almaty; tel. (3272) 50-10-39; fax (3272) 50-10-41; e-mail continent@asdc.kz; f. 1999; policy and society journal; Editor-in-Chief ANDREI KUKUSHKIN; circ. 7,500.

**Delovaya Nedelya** (Business Week): 484044 Almaty, pr. Zhibek zholy 64; tel. (3272) 50-62-72; fax (3272) 33-91-48; e-mail rikki@ kazmail.asdc.kz; f. 1992; weekly; in Russian; Editor-in-Chief O. CHERVINSKII; circ. 16,066.

**Deutsche Allgemeine Zeitung:** 480044 Almaty, pr. Zhibek zholy 50, Office 418; tel. (3272) 73-42-69; fax (3272) 73-92-91; e-mail daz@ ok.kz; f. 1966; weekly; political, economic, cultural, social; in German; Editor-in-Chief IRINA ZIRENTSCHIKOWA; circ. 1,700.

**Ekonomika i Zhizn** (Economics and Life): Almaty; tel. (3272) 63-96-86; f. 1926; monthly; publ. by the Govt; in Russian; Editor-in-Chief MURAT T. SARSENOV; circ. 4,800.

**Globe:** 480009 Almaty, pr. Abaya 155, Rms 13/14; tel. (3272) 50-76-39; fax (3272) 50-63-62; e-mail ipa@mailonline.kz; internet www .globe.kz; f. 1995; twice a week; in English and Russian; Editor-in-Chief NURLAN ABLYAZOV; circ. 5,550.

**Golos Kazakha** (Voice of Kazakhstan): Almaty, Zenkov 75; tel. (3272) 61-79-09; fax (3272) 61-94-47; f. 1989; weekly; organ of the Federation of Trade Unions of Kazakhstan; circ. 30,000.

**Islam Nury** (The Light of Islam): Semipalatinsk; f. 2000; every two weeks; Islamic.

**Kakadu:** 480004 Almaty, Chaikovskogo 11; tel. (3272) 39-97-04; f. 1995; monthly; in Russian; Editor-in-Chief L. GERTZY.

**Karavan:** 480004 Almaty, Chaikovskogo 11; tel. (3272) 32-08-39; fax (3272) 32-97-57; e-mail advertising@caravan.kz; internet www .caravan.kz; f. 1991; 20% of shares were reported to have been sold to a US investment co in 2001; weekly; in Russian; Editor-in-Chief ANDREI SHUKHOV; circ. 250,000.

**Kazakh Adebiety** (Kazakh Literature): 484091 Almaty, pr. Ablaikhana 105; tel. and fax (3272) 69-54-62; f. 1934; weekly; organ of the Union of Writers of Kazakhstan; in Kazakh; Editor-in-Chief A. ZHAKSYBAYEV; circ. 7,874.

**Kazakhstan:** 480044 Almaty, pr. Zhibek zholy 50; tel. (3272) 33-13-56; f. 1992; weekly; economic reform; in English; Editor-in-Chief N. ORAZBEKOV.

**Kazakhstan Aielderi** (Women of Kazakhstan): 480044 Almaty, pr. Zhibek zholy 50; tel. (3272) 33-06-23; fax (3272) 46-15-53; f. 1925; monthly; literary, artistic, social and political; in Kazakh; Editor-in-Chief ALTYNSHASH K. JAGANOVA; circ. 15,200.

**Kazakhstan Business:** 480044 Almaty, pr. Zhibek zholy 50; tel. (3272) 33-42-56; f. 1991; weekly; in Russian; Editor-in-Chief B. SUKHARBEKOV.

**Kazakhstan Mektebi** (Kazakh School): 480004 Almaty, pr. Ablaikhana 34; tel. (3272) 39-76-65; f. 1925; monthly; in Kazakh; Editor-in-Chief S. ABISHEVA; circ. 10,000.

**Kazakhstan Mugalimi** (Kazakh Teacher): 484100 Almaty, Dzhambula 25; tel. (3272) 61-60-58; f. 1935; weekly; in Kazakh; Editor-in-Chief ZH. TEMIRBEKOV; circ. 6,673.

**Kazakhstan Zaman** (Kazakh Time): 480002 Almaty, pr. Dostyk 106G; tel. (3272) 65-07-39; e-mail kazakistanzaman@mail.ru; f. 1992; in Kazakh and Turkish; weekly; publ. by the al-Farabi Foundation; circ. 15,000; Gen. Dir ERSIN DEMIRCI.

**Khalyk Kongresi** (People's Congress): Almaty; tel. (3272) 62-87-86; f. 1993; 3 a week; publ. by the People's Congress Party of Kazakhstan and the Nevada-Semipalatinsk anti-nuclear movement; in Kazakh (also appears in Russian, as *Narodnyi Kongress*); Editor-in-Chief SAYIN MURATBEKOV.

**Korye Ilbo:** 480044 Almaty, pr. Zhibek zholy 50; tel. (3272) 33-90-10; fax (3272) 63-25-46; f. 1923; weekly; in Korean and Russian; Editor-in-Chief YAN WON SIK.

**Medicina** (Medicine): Almaty, pr. Ablaikhana 63; tel. (3272) 33-48-01; fax (3272) 33-16-90; e-mail zdrav_kz@nursat.kz; f. 2000 (fmrly appeared as *Densaulik* ); monthly; in Kazakh; Editor-in-Chief A. SH. SEYSENBAYEV.

**Novoye Pokoleniye** (New Generation): 480091 Almaty, Bogenbai Batyr 139; tel. (3272) 62-31-06; fax (3272) 63-96-45; e-mail np@asdc .kz; f. 1993; weekly; in Russian; Editor-in-Chief OLEG C. CHERVINSKY; circ. 50,000.

**Panorama:** 480013 Almaty, pl. Respubliki 15, Office 647; tel. (3272) 63-28-34; fax (3272) 63-66-16; e-mail panorama@kazmail.asdc.kz; internet www.panorama.kz; f. 1992; weekly; in Russian; Editor-in-Chief LERA TSOY; circ. 18,500.

**Parasat** (Intellect): 480044 Almaty, pr. Zhibek zholy 50; tel. (3272) 33-49-29; fax (3272) 33-64-58; f. 1958; socio-political, literary, illustrated; in Kazakh; Editor-in-Chief BAKKOZHA S. MUKAY; circ. 20,000.

**Petroleum of Kazakhstan:** 480091 Almaty, Bogenbai Batyr 139; tel. (3272) 62-31-06; fax (3272) 63-96-45; e-mail np@asdc.kz; every two months; in Russian and English; Editor-in-Chief OLEG C. CHERVINSKY; circ. 2,000.

**Prostor** (Expanse): 480091 Almaty, pr. Ablaikhana 105; tel. (3272) 69-61-87; e-mail info@prstr.samal.kz; internet prostor.samal.kz; f. 1933; monthly; literary and artistic; in Russian; Editor-in-Chief R. V. PETROV; circ. 1,800.

**Russkii Yazyk i Literatura** (Russian Language and Literature): 480091 Almaty, pr. Ablaikhana 34; tel. (3272) 39-76-68; f. 1962; monthly; in Russian; Editor-in-Chief B. S. MUKANOV; circ. 17,465.

**Shalkar:** 480044 Almaty, pr. Zhibek zholy 50; tel. (3272) 33-86-85; f. 1976; twice a month; in Kazakh (in the Arabic script); Editor-in-Chief A. KAIYRBEKOV; circ. 2,500.

**Soldat:** Almaty; f. 1999; weekly; indepedent, opposition publication; in Kazakh and Russian; Editor-in-Chief (vacant).

**Soviety Kazakhstana** (Councils of Kazakhstan): 480002 Almaty, pr. Zhibek zholy 15; tel. (3272) 34-92-19; f. 1990; weekly; publ. by Parliament; in Russian; Editor-in-Chief YU. GURSKII; circ. 30,000.

**Sport and ks:** 480044 Almaty, pr. Zhibek zholy 50; tel. (3272) 33-92-90; f. 1959; weekly; in Kazakh and Russian; Editor-in-Chief NESIP ZHUNUSBAYEV; circ. 20,000.

**Turkistan:** 484012 Almaty, Bogenbai Batyr 150; tel. (3272) 69-61-54; fax (3272) 62-08-98; f. 1994; weekly; political; in Kazakh; circ. 4,883.

**Uigur Avazi** (The Voice of Uigur): 480044 Almaty, pr. Zhibek zholy 50; tel. (3272) 33-84-59; f. 1957; 2 a week; publ. by the Govt; socio-political; in Uigur; Editor-in-Chief I. AZAMATOV; circ. 9,179.

**Ukraine Novini** (Ukraine News): 473000 Astana, pr. Respubliki 17; tel. (3172) 21-74-62; e-mail un_astana@mail.kz; internet ukrnovini.host.kz; f. 1994; weekly; in Ukrainian; CEO CHERNEGA TARAS; Editor-in-Chief A. GARKAVETS; circ. 1,200.

**Ulan:** 480044 Almaty, pr. Zhibek zholy 50; tel. (3272) 33-80-03; f. 1930; weekly; in Kazakh; Editor-in-Chief S. KALIYEV; circ. 183,014.

**Vremya** (Time): 480060 Almaty, Dzhandosova 60A; tel. (3272) 44-49-03; fax (3272) 45-51-44; internet www.time.kz; f. 1999; weekly; in Russian; Editor-in-Chief IGOR MELTSER; circ. 250,000.

**Zerde** (Intellect): 480044 Almaty, pr. Zhibek zholy 50; tel. (3272) 33-83-81; f. 1960; monthly; popular, scientific, technical; in Kazakh; Editor-in-Chief E. RAUSHAN-ULY; circ. 68,629.

**Zhalyn** (Flame): Almaty; tel. (3272) 33-22-21; f. 1969; monthly; literary, artistic, social and political; in Kazakh; Editor-in-Chief M. KULKENOV; circ. 2,196.

**Zhas Alash** (Young Generation): 480044 Almaty, Makatayeva 22; tel. (3272) 30-60-90; fax (3272) 30-24-69; internet www.zhasalash .kz; f. 1921; publ. by the Kazakhstan Youth Union; in Kazakh; Editor-in-Chief ZHUSIP NURTORE; circ. 133,000.

**Zhuldyz** (Star): 480091 Almaty, pr. Ablai-Khan 105; tel. (3272) 62-51-37; f. 1922; monthly; journal of the Union of Writers of Kazakhstan; literary, artistic, socio-political; in Kazakh; Editor-in-Chief MUKHTAR MAGAUIN; circ. 1,539.

### NEWS AGENCY

**Kazakh Information Agency (KazAAG):** 480091 Almaty, pr. Ablaikhana 75; tel. (3272) 62-61-80; fax (3272) 69-58-39; e-mail arenov@nursat.kz; f. 1997; responsible to the Ministry of Culture; provides information on government activities in Kazakhstan and abroad; Editor-in-Chief ARENOV M. MURAT.

#### Foreign Bureaux

**Agence France-Presse (AFP):** 480100 Almaty, Dostyk 29/31; tel. (3272) 91-06-58; fax (3272) 91-06-58.

**Informatsionnoye Telegrafnoye Agentstvo Rossii—Telegrafnoye Agentstvo Suverennykh Stran (ITAR—TASS)** (Russia): Almaty; Astana; tel. (3272) 33-96-81; tel. (3172) 32-42-02; Correspondent IGOR CHEREPANOV; Correspondent ORAL KAPISHEV.

**Internews Network Agency** (USA): 480091 Almaty, Nauryzbai Batyr 58, 1st Floor; tel. (3272) 50-89-50; fax (3272) 50-89-59; e-mail oleg@internews.kz; internet www.internews.kz.

**Islamic Republic News Agency (IRNA)** (Iran): Almaty; tel. (3272) 68-10-05; e-mail irna@irna.com; internet www.irna.com; Correspondent BAHARVAND ALI RAHMAD.

**Reuters** (United Kingdom): Astana; tel. (3172) 50-94-10.

**Rossiiskoye Informatsionnoye Agentstvo—Novosti (RIA—Novosti)** (Russia): Almaty; tel. (3272) 33-99-50; Correspondent REVMIRA VOSHENKO.

**Xinhua (New China) News Agency** (People's Republic of China): Almaty; tel. (3272) 24-68-68.

## Publishers

**Green Movement Centre (GMC):** Taraz; tel. and fax (3262) 23-14-96; e-mail oasis97@kaznet.kz; f. 1988; education; environment; Chair. ALEX ZAGRIBELNY.

**Gylym** (Science): 480100 Almaty, Pushkina 111–113; tel. (3272) 91-18-77; fax (3272) 61-88-45; f. 1946; books on natural sciences, humanities and scientific research journals; Dir S. G. BAIMENOV.

**Izdatelstvo Kazakhstan** (Kazakhstan Publishing House): 480124 Almaty, pr. Abaya 143; tel. and fax (3272) 42-29-29; f. 1920; political science, economics, medicine, general and social sciences; Dir E. KH. SYZDYKOV; Editors-in-Chief M. D. SITKO, M. A. RASHEV.

**Kainar** (Spring): 480124 Almaty, pr. Abaya 143; tel. (3272) 42-27-96; f. 1962; agriculture, history, culture; Dir ORAZBEK S. SARSENBAYEV; Editor-in-Chief I. I. ISKUZHIN.

**Kazakhskaya Entsiklopediya** (Kazakh Encyclopedia): Almaty; tel. (3272) 62-55-66; f. 1968; Editor-in-Chief R. N. NURGALIYEV.

**Mektep:** 480009 Almaty, pr. Abaya 143; tel. (3272) 42-26-24; fax (3272) 77-85-44; e-mail oao_mektep@nursat.kz; f. 1947; dictionaries, children's textbooks; fiction by young writers; Pres. E. SATYBALDIYEV; Editor-in-Chief SH. GUSAKOVA.

**Oner** (Art): 480124 Almaty, pr. Abaya 143; tel. (3272) 42-08-88; f. 1980; Dir S. S. ORAZALINOV; Editor-in-Chief A. A. ASKAROV.

**Zhazushy** (Writer): 480124 Almaty, pr. Abaya 143; tel. (3272) 42-28-49; f. 1934; literature, literary criticism, essays and poetry; Dir D. I. ISABEKOV; Editor-in-Chief A. T. SARAYEV.

## Broadcasting and Communications

### TELECOMMUNICATIONS

**Beket:** 480002 Almaty, Zhurgeneva 9; tel. (3272) 30-16-33; fax (3272) 30-01-43; mobile telecommunications services.

**Kazakhtelekom:** 480091 Almaty, pr. Abylai Khan 86; tel. (3272) 62-05-41; fax (3272) 63-93-95; internet www.itte.kz; f. 1994; national telecommunications corpn; 60% state-owned, 40% owned by Daewoo Corpn (Republic of Korea); Pres. SERIK BURKITBAYEV.

    **Satel:** 480100 Almaty, Zenkov 22; tel. (3272) 63-64-32; fax (3272) 63-87-69; telecommunications services; joint venture between Telstra Corpn Ltd (Australia) and Kazakhtelecom; Man. Dir JERRY KOLETH.

### BROADCASTING

Private radio and television stations began operating in Kazakhstan in the 1990s. In mid-2001 there were an estimated 124 radio and television stations.

**Kazakh State Television and Radio Broadcasting Corporation:** 480013 Almaty, Zheltoksan 175A; tel. (3272) 63-37-16; f. 1920; Pres. YERMEK TURSUNOV.

## Radio

**Kazakh Radio:** 480013 Almaty, Zheltoksan 175A; tel. (3272) 63-19-68; fax (3272) 65-03-87; e-mail kazradio@astel.kz; internet www.radio.kz; f. 1921; broadcasts in Kazakh, Russian, Uigur, German and other minority languages; Gen. Dir TOREKHAN DANIYAR.

## Television

**Khabar News Agency:** 480013 Almaty, pl. Respubliki 13; tel. (3272) 63-83-69; fax (3272) 50-63-45; e-mail naz@khabar.almaty.kz; internet www.khabar.kz; f. 1959; international broadcasts in Kazakh, Uigur, Russian and German; two television channels; Dir DARIGA NAZARBAYEVA.

**KTK** (Kazakh Commercial Television): Almaty, pl. Respubliki 13; tel. (3272) 63-44-28; fax (3272) 50-66-25; e-mail ktkao@kzaira.com; f. 1990; independent; 20% of shares were reported to have been sold to a US investment co in 2001; Gen. Dir ANDREI SHUKHOV; Pres. SHOKAN LAUULIN.

**NTK** (Association of TV and Radio Broadcasters of Kazakhstan): 480013 Almaty, pl. Respubliki 13, 6th Floor; tel. (3272) 70-01-83; fax (3272) 70-01-85; e-mail kaztvradio@nursat.kz; f. 2000; privately owned; Pres. AIDAR ZHUMABAYEV.

# Finance

(cap. = capital; res = reserves; dep. = deposits; m. = million; brs = branches; amounts in tenge, unless otherwise indicated)

## BANKING

From 1994 the National Bank of Kazakhstan (NBK) effected a series of measures aimed at rationalizing the banking sector, in order to ensure a sound financial infrastructure. Numerous banks had their licences revoked: between 1995 and 1998 the number of commercial banks declined by almost one-half, and it continued to decline thereafter. By July 2003 the banking system comprised 35 banks, including two state banks and 16 with foreign participation. At 1 July 2003 commercial banks in Kazakhstan had aggregate equity of 183,900m. tenge, and aggregate assets of 1,378,600m. tenge.

## Central Bank

**National Bank of Kazakhstan (NBK):** 480090 Almaty, Koktem-3 21; tel. (3272) 50-46-25; fax (3272) 50-60-90; e-mail hq@nationalbank.kz; internet www.nationalbank.kz; f. 1990; cap. 15,465.6m., res 113,099.2m., dep. 145,476.5m. (Dec. 2001); Chair. GRIGORII MARCHENKO; 19 brs.

## Major Commercial Banks

**Abidbank:** 480100 Almaty, pr. Dostyka 85A; tel. and fax (3272) 41-60-67; e-mail herald@mailbox.kz.

**ABN AMRO Bank Kazakhstan CJSC:** 480099 Almaty, Khadji Mukana 45; tel. (3272) 50-73-00; fax (3272) 50-72-98; e-mail abnamro@kaznet.kz; internet www.abnamro.com; f. 1994; 51%-owned by ABN AMRO Bank NV (the Netherlands); cap. 1,800.0m., res 58m., dep. 23,492m. (Dec. 2001); Gen. Man. JAN WILLEM VAN DEN BOSCH; 1 br.

**Alashbank:** 480012 Almaty, Sharipova 84; tel. (3272) 92-60-08; fax (3272) 67-01-44; e-mail alashbnk@online.ru; 1 br.

**Alfa Bank Kazakhstan:** 480012 Almaty, ul. Masanchi 57A, Room 202; tel. (3272) 92-00-12; fax (3272) 50-78-03; e-mail elerkh@alfabank.ru.

**Almaty Commercial Bank:** 480012 Almaty, Amangeldy 70; tel. (3272) 58-82-26; fax (3272) 58-82-25; e-mail acb1@kaznet.kz.

**Astana Bank:** 487010 Turkestan, Aiteke bi 31; tel. (3252) 57-24-39; e-mail astanabnk@shym.kz.

**ATF Bank:** 480091 Almaty, Furmanova 100; tel. (3272) 50-30-40; fax (3272) 50-19-95; e-mail info@amb.kz; internet www.amb.kz; f. 1995 as Almaty Merchant Bank, name changed as above in June 2002; cap. 3,099.1m., res 1,151.8m., dep. 32,866.3m. (Dec. 2001); Chair. YERKEBLAN OKAYEV; 10 brs.

**Bank Caspiyskiy OJSC:** 480012 Almaty, Adi Sharipova 90; tel. (3272) 50-17-20; fax (3272) 50-95-96; e-mail office@bankcaspian.kz; internet www.bankcaspian.kz; f. 1997 by merger of Kazdorbank with Caspiyskiy; cap. 1,427.3m., res 281.4m., dep. 13,109.1m. (Dec. 2001); Chair. IGOR KIM; 17 brs.

**Bank Centercredit OJSC:** 480072 Almaty, Shevchenko 100; tel. (3272) 58-41-58; fax (3272) 69-29-24; e-mail info@centercredit.kz; internet www.centercredit.kz; f. 1988 as Co-op Bank of the Almaty Union of Co-operatives; name changed to Centerbank 1991, to Centercredit 1996, to JS Centercredit 1998 (following merger with Zhilstroi Bank); cap. 2,588m., res 566m., dep. 21,373m. (Jan. 2002);

Chair. of Council BAKHYTBEK R. BAYSEITOV; Chair. of Bd VLADISLAV S. LI; 19 brs.

**Bank of Development of Kazakhstan:** 473000 Astana, Samal 12; tel. (3172) 58-02-60; e-mail info@kdb.kz.

**Bank Turan Alem:** 480099 Almaty, Samal 2, Zholdasbekov 97; tel. (3272) 50-40-70; fax (3272) 50-02-24; e-mail post@bta.kz; internet www.bta.kz; f. 1997 by merger of Turanbank—Kazakh Corpn Bank and Alembank; privatized in 1998; cap. 16,091m., dep. 138,474m. (Dec. 2001); Chair. YERZHAN N. TATISHEV; 23 brs.

**Central Asian Bank of Co-operation and Development:** 480008 Almaty, pr. Abaya 115A; tel. (3272) 42-27-37; fax (3272) 42-27-37; e-mail cab@asdc.kz; f. 1994; Chair. GAMAL K. SOODANBEKOV; 1 br.

**Citibank Kazakhstan:** 480100 Almaty, Kazybek bi 41; tel. (3272) 60-84-00; fax (3272) 60-83-99; e-mail citibank.kazakhstan@citicorp.com; internet www.citibank.com/kazakhstan; f. 1998; cap. US $25m. (1998).

**DanaBank:** 637000 Pavlodar, Lenina 119; tel. (3182) 32-01-20; e-mail dana@kaznet.kz; 4 brs.

**Demir Kazakhstan Bank:** 480091 Almaty, Kurmangazy 61A; tel. (3272) 50-85-50; fax (3272) 50-85-25; e-mail demirbank@demirbank.kz; internet www.demirbank.kz; f. 1997; cap. 1,000.0m., res 262.9m., dep. 697.4m. (Dec. 2001); Chair. IHSAN UGUR.

**Eurasian Bank:** 480002 Almaty, Kunayeva 56; tel. (3272) 50-86-07; fax (3272) 50-86-50; e-mail info@eurasian-bank.kz; internet www.eurasian-bank.kz; f. 1994; cap. 2,889.7m., res 1,377.1m., dep. 13,225.0m. (Dec. 2002); Chair. KIM INESSA; 3 brs.

**Eximbank Kazakhstan (Eximbank):** 480100 Almaty, Pushkina 118; tel. (3272) 63-43-00; fax (3272) 50-75-49; e-mail post_mail@eximbank.kz; f. 1994; fmrly Export–Import Bank of Kazakhstan; state-owned; cap. 6,091m. (March 2000); Chair. BEISENBAY IZTELEUOV.

**Industrial Bank of Kazakhstan:** 480020 Almaty, pr. Dostyka 264; tel. (3272) 93-51-99; fax (3272) 42-96-03; e-mail info@ibk.kz.

**OJSC Kazakhstan International Bank:** 480072 Almaty, Seifullina 597; tel. (3272) 92-99-62; fax (3272) 92-90-74; e-mail kib@kib.almaty.kz; f. 1993; cap. 887.8m., res 8.2m.; Chair. ASKAR B. NASENOV.

**Kazakhstan-Ziraat International Bank (KZI Bank):** 480057 Almaty, Klochkova 132, POB 34; tel. (3272) 50-60-80; fax (3272) 50-60-82; e-mail kzibank@kzibank.com; f. 1993 as Kazkommerts Ziraat International Bank; name changed as above in 1999; cap. 1,058.3m., res 55.6m., dep. 957.6m. (Dec. 2001); Chair. SALIH CANGA; Gen. Man. HALIL TEKPINAR.

**Kazkommertsbank:** 480060 Almaty, Zh. Gagarina 135; tel. (3272) 58-52-81; fax (3272) 58-52-81; e-mail mailbox@kkb.kz; internet www.kkb.kz; f. 1991; assets US $2,450.0m., cap. $203.0m. (July 2003), dep. $735.6m. (June 2002); Chair. NINA A. ZHUSSUPOVA; Man. Dirs ANDRIY TIMCHENKO, DENIS FEDOSENKO; 23 brs.

**Lariba-Bank:** 480060 Almaty, Rozibakiyeva 181A; tel. (3272) 49-14-32; fax (3272) 49-64-21; e-mail lariba@kazmail.asdc.kz; 1 br.

**Neftebank:** 466200 Aktau, Microraion 9/23A; tel. (3292) 43-61-61; fax (3292) 43-61-45; e-mail nb@neftebank.kz; 5 brs.

**OJSC Nurbank:** 465050 Atyrau, Seifullina 5; tel. (3122) 25-41-75; fax (3122) 21-02-49; e-mail bank@nurbank.kz; internet www.nurbank.kz; f. 1992; cap. 3,000.0m., dep. 29,608.8m. (Dec. 2002); Chair. ABILMAZHEN KUANYSHEVICH GILIMOV.

**OJSC Temirbank:** 480008 Almaty, pr. Abaya 68/74; tel. (3272) 58-78-88; fax (3272) 50-67-72; e-mail board@temirbank.kz; internet www.temirbank.kz; f. 1992; cap. 1,382.9m., res 251.1m., dep. 17,724.0m. (Dec. 2001); Chair. OLEG KONONENKO; 18 brs.

**Tsesnabank:** 473000 Astana, Beibitshilik 43; tel. (3172) 31-81-92; fax (3172) 31-82-58; e-mail tsesnabank_uavt@kepter.kz; internet www.tsesnabank.kz; f. 1992; cap. 531.1m., res 227.5m., dep. 4,442.7m.. (Dec. 2001); Chair. SERIK JAKSYBEKOV; 4 brs.

## Savings Bank

**Halyk (People's) Savings Bank of Kazakhstan:** 480046 Almaty, Rozybakiyeva 97; tel. (3272) 59-00-00; fax (3272) 59-02-71; e-mail hsbk@halykbank.kz; internet www.halykbank.kz; f. 1936 as br. of Savings Bank of USSR, reorganized as joint-stock savings bank in 1994; fully privatized in Nov. 2001; cap. 9,683.8m., res 2,615.7m., dep. 172,408.0m. (Dec. 2002); Chair. KAIRAT SATYLGANOV; Man. Dir KAIRAT RAKHMANOV; 611 brs.

## Bankers' Organization

**Commercial Banks' Association of Kazakhstan:** Almaty; Pres. BAKHYTBEK BAISEITOV.

## STOCK AND COMMODITY EXCHANGES

**Kazakhstan Stock Exchange (KASE):** 480091 Almaty, Aiteke bi 67; tel. (3272) 63-98-98; fax (3272) 63-89-80; e-mail info@kase.kz; internet www.kase.kz; f. 1993; Pres. and Chief Exec. AZAMAT M. DZHOLDASBEKOV.

**Ken Dala Central Kazakhstan Commodity Exchange:** 470074 Karaganda, pr. Stroitelei 28; tel. (3212) 74-27-80; fax (3212) 74-43-35; f. 1991; auth. cap. 6m.; Pres. MADEGDA PAK.

Kazakhstan also has a Metal Exchange (f. 1992).

## INSURANCE

At August 2000 there were 41 licensed insurance companies in Kazakhstan.

**Almaty International Insurance Group:** 480091 Almaty, ul. Kabanbay Batyr 112; tel. and fax (3272) 50-12-31; e-mail aiig@world2.almaty.kz; internet www.aiig.escort.kz; f. 1994; Chair. SUREN AMBARTSUMIAN.

**Dynasty Life Insurance Co:** Almaty, Seifullina 410; tel. (3272) 50-73-95; e-mail dynasty@bta.nursat.kz; Chair. SERIK TEMIRGALEYEV.

**Industrial Insurance Group (IIG):** 480046 Almaty, Nauryzbai Batyr 65–69; tel. (3272) 50-96-95; fax (3272) 50-96-98; e-mail iig@kaznet.kz; internet www.iig.kz; f. 1998; Pres. IVAN MIKHAILOV.

**KazAgroPolicy:** 480091 Almaty, Nauryzbai Batyr 49–61; tel. (3272) 32-13-24; fax (3272) 32-13-26; e-mail kazagropolise@mail.banknet.kz; Chair. YERMEK USPANOV.

**Kazakhinstrakh:** Almaty; tel. (3272) 33-73-49; fax (3272) 50-74-37; e-mail kiscentr@nursat.kz; Chair. NURLAN MOLDAKHMETOV.

**Kazkommerts-Policy:** 480013 Almaty, Satpayeva 24; tel. (3272) 58-48-08; fax (3272) 92-73-97; e-mail kkp@mail.kz; internet www.kkp.kz; Chair. SERGEI G. SUKHAREV; Dir TALGAT K. USSENOV.

**MSCA Interteach:** 480091 Almaty, Furmanova 111/48; tel. and fax (3272) 58-23-32; e-mail interteach@kaznet.kaz; internet www.interteachmsca.com; f. 1989; medical and travel insurance, health care, accident and employee liability insurance; 120 employees; 48 brs; Gen. Dir ERNST M. KURLEUTOV.

> **Interteach Assistance:** 480091 Almaty, Kabanbai Batyra 122A; tel. and fax (3272) 69-58-31; e-mail interteach@kaznet.kz; internet www.interteachmsca.com; medical and travel insurance, health care; Gen. Dir ERNST M. KURLEUTOV.

**West-Kazakhstan Insurance Firm:** Uralsk, pr. Lenina 203; tel. (31122) 50-62-94; Chair. BOLAT DJUMAGALIYEV.

# Trade and Industry

## GOVERNMENT AGENCY

**State Committee for Investment:** Astana.

## CHAMBERS OF COMMERCE

**Union of Chambers of Commerce and Industry of Kazakhstan:** 480091 Almaty, Masanchi 26; tel. (3272) 67-78-23; fax (3272) 50-70-29; e-mail tpprkaz@online.ru; internet www.ccikaz.kz; f. 1959; Chair. KHAMIT RAKISHEV.

**Akmola Chamber of Commerce and Industry:** 475000 Kokshatau, Marks 107; tel. (3162) 25-76-68; e-mail tpp@kokc.kz; Chair. TURSUNHAN T. KALIASKAROVA.

**Aktobe Chamber of Commerce and Industry:** 463000 Aktobe, Zhubanova 289/1; tel. (3132) 51-02-20; e-mail akbtpp@nursat.kz; Chair. ELENA A. RUDENKO.

**Almaty Chamber of Commerce:** 488000 Taldykorgan, Taulsizdik 101/37; tel. (3282) 7-20-40; Chair. EMMA V. KIM.

**Almaty City Chamber of Commerce and Industry:** 480091 Almaty, Tole bi 45; tel. (3272) 62-03-01; e-mail alcci@nursat.kz; internet www.atpp.marketcenter.ru; Chair. ZULFIYA K. AKHMETZHANOVA.

**Astana City Chamber of Commerce and Industry:** 473000 Astana, Auezov 66, POB 1966; tel. (3172) 32-38-33; e-mail akmcci@dan.kz; internet www.chamber.kz; Chair. TATYANA I. KONONOVA.

**Atyrau Chamber of Commerce and Industry:** 465050 Atyrau, Satpayev 36/79; tel. (3122) 23-19-97; e-mail torgpal_atr@asdc.kz; Chair. NURZHAMAL ZH. SULTANOVA.

**East Kazakhstan Chamber of Commerce and Industry:** 492000 Ust-Kamenogorsk, Novatorova 3, POB 177; tel. (3232) 26-53-10; fax (3232) 26-72-47; e-mail cci@ustk.kz; Chair. KAJRAT M. MUKEYEV.

**Karaganda Chamber of Commerce and Industry:** 470061 Karaganda, Mir Bulvar 31; tel. (3212) 56-32-32; e-mail ccikr@nursat.kz; f. 1994; Chair. NESIP SEITOVA.

**Kostanai Chamber of Commerce and Industry:** 458000 Kostanai, Taran 165; tel. (3142) 54-66-72; e-mail ko_tpp@mail.kz; Chair. VALENTINA N. TRIBUSHNAYA.

**Kyzylorda Chamber of Commerce and Industry:** 467014 Kyzylorda, Aiteke bi 24; tel. (3242) 26-24-36; Chair. TAMARA V. HRAMTSOVA.

**Mangistau Chamber of Commerce and Industry:** 466200 Aktau, Skr. 6, 26/131; tel. (3292) 51-19-52; e-mail akt_cci@nursat.kz; Chair. NATELLA D. OTELEPKO.

**North Kazakhstan Chamber of Commerce and Industry:** 642015 Petropavlovsk, Mir 112; tel. (3152) 46-05-68; e-mail tpp@petropavl.kz; internet www.tppsko.freenet.kz; Chair. NELLI F. KUKUSHKINA.

**Pavlodar Chamber of Commerce and Industry:** 637002 Pavlodar, Toraigyrova 95/1; tel. (3182) 75-79-69; e-mail pav-cci@kaznet.kz; Chair. RAJHANGUL SATABAYEVA.

**Semipalatinsk Chamber of Commerce and Industry:** 490050 Semipalatinsk, Abaya 92/22; tel. (3222) 62-78-87; e-mail tpp@relcom.kz; Chair. TAMARA SOPOLEVA.

**South Kazakhstan Chamber of Commerce and Industry:** 486050 Shymkent, Tauke Khan 31; tel. (3252) 21-14-05; Chair. SYRLYBAJ ORDABEKOV.

**West Kazakhstan Chamber of Commerce and Industry:** 417000 Uralsk, Kuibyshev 67; tel. (3112) 50-44-40; e-mail zktpp@kaznet.kz; Chair. KAIR A. SYUNTIYEV.

**Zhambyl Chamber of Commerce and Industry:** 484039 Taraz, Karakhana 2; tel. (3262) 43-05-98; Chair. ADILKHAN ZHAPARBEKOV.

## EMPLOYERS' ORGANIZATIONS

**Kazakhstan Petroleum Association:** 480100 Almaty, pr. Dostyk 38, Office 517; tel. (3272) 50-18-16; fax (3272) 50-18-17; e-mail kpa@arna.kz; internet www.kpa.kz; f. 1998; Chair. Dr SAGINDYK K. NURALIYEV; 49 mem. cos.

**Kazakhtrebsoyuz:** Almaty, Komsomolskaya 57; tel. (3272) 62-34-94; union of co-operative entrepreneurs; Chair. UMIRZAK SARSENOV.

**Union of Small Businesses:** Almaty; f. 1991; Pres. CHINGIZ RYSEBEKOV.

## UTILITIES

### Electricity

Privatization of the electric power sector was undertaken from 1996. Many power stations were withdrawn from the national electricity company and transformed into independent joint-stock companies; several power-supply network companies were established in the region. The state had completed the privatization of virtually all electricity producers and local distribution companies by the end of 2001.

**State Committee for Energy Supervision:** Chair. MURAT RAMAZANOV.

**Kazakstanenergo** (National Power System): 480008 Almaty, Shevchenko 162; tel. (3272) 62-62-00; fax (3272) 68-43-08; f. 1992; electricity co; Gen. Dir BERLIK ORAZBAYEV.

**Kazakhstan Electric Grid Operational Company (KEGOC):** Almaty; internet www.kegoc.kz; f. 1997; technical electricity network operator; Vice-Pres. ESBERGEN ABITAYEV (Operations), ALMASADAM SATKALIYEV (Finance).

> **Kazakhstan Energy and Power Market Operating Company (KEPMOC):** Almaty; f. 2000 under a government resolution; electricity broker.

### Water

**Almaty Vodocanal:** Almaty 480057, Jarokova 196; tel. (3272) 44-00-17; fax (3272) 44-84-02; f. 1937; state-owned co; responsible for water supply and sewerage in Almaty and surrounding villages; Gen. Dir SHARIPBEK SHARDARBEKOV.

## STATE HYDROCARBONS COMPANIES

**Aktobemunaigaz:** Aktyubinsk; 25.1% state-owned; 60.3% owned by China National Petroleum Co (CNPC).

**KazMunaiGaz National Co:** Almaty; f. 2002 by merger of KazakhOil and Transneftegas; Chair. UZAKBAI KARABALIN; Vice-Chair. TIMUR KULIBAYEV; Exec. Dir KAIRGELDY KABILDIN.

> **KazTransOil:** transportation of petroleum; Dir-Gen. ASKAR SMANKULOV.

**KazTransGas:** transportation of natural gas; Dir-Gen. Abay Sadykov.

**Munaigaz:** Almaty; tel. (3272) 69-58-00; fax (3272) 69-52-72; f. 1991; petroleum and gas prospecting and producing; Pres. T. A. Khazanov.

**Aktyubinskneft:** 463022 Aktobe, Atynsarin 8; tel. (3132) 22-47-82; fax (3132) 22-93-21; f. 1993; produces petroleum and natural gas; Pres. S. P. Zimin; 10,500 employees.

**JSC Mangistaumunaigaz:** 466200 Mangistauskaya, Aktau, Mikrorayon 1; tel. (3292) 51-45-57; fax (3292) 43-39-19; 60% owned by Central Asian Petroleum (Indonesia), 10% owned by employees; production and transportation of petroleum and natural gas; Gen. Dir V. Miroshnikov.

**Pavlodar Petrochemical Joint Stock Co:** 637043 Pavlodar, Khimkombinatovskaya 1; tel. (3182) 39-65-20; fax (3182) 39-60-98; e-mail bekturov@pnhz.kz; f. 1978; 51% owned by JSC Mangistaumunaigaz; processes petroleum from western Siberia (Russia); produces unleaded petroleum, diesel fuel, petroleum chemical gases, bitumen and petroleum coke; Gen. Dir Yurii Ginatulin; Exec. Dir Rustem Bekturov.

**Tengizchevroil (TCO):** 466440 Atyrau, Atyrau Airport, TCO Interim Office; tel. (312) 30-26-818; fax (312) 30-26-729; e-mail tiny@tengizchevroil.com; f. 1993; joint venture between the Govt (20%), Chevron Corpn (USA—with 50%), ExxonMobil (USA—25%) and LUKArco (a joint venture between LUKoil of the Russian Federation and Atlantic Richfield of the USA—5%); Gen. Dir Ken Godard.

## MAJOR COMPANIES

### Chemicals

**Fosfor Production Association:** 486025 Shymkent, Lengerskoye B/N; tel. (3252) 44-53-54; fax (3252) 50-61-07; f. 1964; f. 1964; production and sale of phosphorus and phosphorus products; Gen. Dir Emil U. Zhomartbayev; 4,500 employees.

**Khimprom-2030 LLC:** 484026 Taraz Industrial Zone 26; tel. (3262) 34-21-80; fax (3262) 34-30-60; e-mail berrimor@rambler.ru; f. 1968; production and export of yellow phosphorus and its products; Pres. N. O. Ualiyev; 4,800 employees.

**Kramds National Joint Stock Co:** 480059 Almaty, Kabanbay Batyr 164; tel. (3272) 50-93-51; fax (3272) 67-18-50; f. 1988; production of petroleum, and organic and inorganic chemicals; Pres. Kanat S. Bakbergenov; Man. Dir Valerii V. Vrublevskii; 15,000 employees.

**Nodfos Joint Stock Co:** 484037 Taraz; tel. (3262) 25-26-19; fax (3262) 25-35-05; f. 1979; produces chemicals; Dir M. A. Akhmedov; 6,000 employees.

**Polipropilen Co:** Atyrau; manufacturer of polypropylene products; Man. Dir Vladimir Pashkin.

### Metals

**Alyumini Kazakhstan:** 637020 Pavlodar; tel. and fax (3172) 46-49-86; f. 1996 by merger; Dir Almaz Ibragimov.

**Ispat Karmet Steel Plant:** 472319 Karagand, Temirtau, pr. Lenina 1; tel. (3213) 56-22–10; fax (3213) 55-46-27; e-mail general.karmet@ispat.com; f. 1995 by Ispat International (United Kingdom); joint-stock co; owns entire assets of Karmet, the world's third largest steelworks; manufacturer of flat-rolled coated and uncoated products; Gen. Dir Malay Mukherjee; 28,600 employees.

**Kazakhmys:** Jezkazagan, Gogolya 5; internet www.kazakhmys.kz; f. 1928; formerly Zhezkazkantsvetmet; sold to Samsung Deutschland (a subsidiary of Samsung of Korea) in 1996; country's largest producer of copper, zinc, gold, silver and electricity; Chair of Bd Vladimir Kim; 65,000 employees.

**Kazchrome TNC:** 480002 Almaty, Kunayev 56; tel. (3272) 60-26-64; fax (3272) 50-78-59; f. 1995; production of ferrous metals and alloys; produces 30% of chrome world-wide and 90% of chrome within the CIS; 15,000 employees.

### Petroleum and Natural Gas

**Agip Kazakhstan North Caspian Operating Company (AgipKCO):** 465002 Atyrau, Dossorskaya 5; tel. (3122) 25-50-91; fax (3122) 25-50-96; e-mail reception@agipkco.kz; internet www.agipkco.com; f. as the Offshore Kazakhstan International Operating Company; name changed as above 2001; operates the Kashagan oilfield, on behalf of a seven-member consortium of international petroleum cos; subsidiary co of the ENI Group (Italy); Regional Dir Andrea Chiura.

**Batystransgas:** 417029 Uralsk, Esenzhanova 42/1; tel. (3112) 22-79-15; fax (3112) 24-76-24; f. 1995; joint-stock co; processing, storage

and transport of natural gas; Pres. Yesset Aserbayev; 8,128 employees.

**BG Kazakhstan:** 473000 Almaty, Samal, Astana Tower Business Centre; tel. (3272) 59-11-11; fax (3272) 59-18-35; e-mail ddskeels@bgalmaty.kz; internet www.bgalmaty.kz; owned by the BG Group (fmrly British Gas); exploration and production of natural gas; Country Rep. David D. Skeels.

**BP Kazakhstan:** Almaty 480100, Dostyk Business Centre, Dostyk 43/412; tel. (3272) 50-32-35; fax (3272) 50-32-40; owned by BP (United Kingdom/USA); extracting and refining of petroleum, exploration and survey work; Dir Erzhan Buzurbayev.

**Karazhanbasmunai JSC:** 466200 Mangistau, Aktau, 15 Mikrorayon 3; tel. (3292) 43-36-00; fax (3292) 43-50-62; e-mail kbm@kbm.kz; internet www.kbm.kz; formerly Karazhanmunaigaz; production of petroleum and natural gas; Pres. Hashim Dhojohadikusumo.

**Kazakhgas State Holding Company:** 417029 Uralsk, Poymennaya 2/4; tel. (3112) 22-79-15; fax (3112) 24-76-24; f. 1991; production, storage and transport of natural gas from Karachaganak; Pres. Dr Erset Azerbayev; 16,000 employees.

**Kazakhoil–Emba Joint Stock Company:** 465002 Atyrau, Valikhanov 1; tel. (3122) 22-29-24; fax (3122) 25-41-27; f. 1911; production of petroleum and natural gas; fmrly Embamunaigas and Tengizmunaigas; Pres. Makhambet Batyrbayev.

**Kaznefteprodukt:** Almaty; tel. (3272) 62-43-50; fax (3272) 62-30-79; f. 1993; wholesale trade in petroleum products and provision of services; Gen. Dir Kaldybay U. Usenov.

**Petrokazakhstan Inc.:** 480009 Almaty, Karasai Batyr 204; tel. (3272) 58-18-48; fax (3272) 58-18-60; e-mail info@petrokazakhstan.com; internet www.petrokazakhstan.com; corporate headquarters in Calgary (Canada); principal Kazakhstan subsidiaries: PetroKazakhstan Kumkol Resources (94%, fmrly Yuzhneftegaz), PetroKazakhstan Oil Products (97%, fmrly Shymkentnefteorgsyntez—Shymkent Petroleum Refinery), Turgai Petroleum (50%), Kazgermunai (50%); gas and petroleum production and sales; Pres. Marlo C. Thomas.

**Shell Kazakhstan Ltd:** 480124 Almaty, pr. Abaya 155, Offices 7 and 8; tel. and fax (3272) 50-63-58; fax (3272) 50-93-04; extraction and refining of petroleum; subsidiary of Shell International Petroleum Co Ltd; Pres. Martin Ferstl; Gen. Dir D. Smethurst.

### Miscellaneous

**Agrocentre-Astana LLC:** Astana, Pobeda 104; tel. (3172) 31-49-03; fax (3172) 31-97-00; e-mail agrocenter@kepter.kz; f. 1997; production and distribution of agricultural products (grain, meat and milk); Gen. Dir Vladimir M. Petrov; 8,000 employees.

**Astanatechnopark:** 473002 Astana, Pushkin 166; tel. (3172) 32-88-25; fax (3172) 32-88-34; e-mail astanatechnopark@nursat.kz; f. 1942; 90% state-owned; fmrly Akmolaselmash JSC; production of agricultural machinery for soil conservation; Pres. Baurzhan N. Baymukhanov; 100 employees.

**Butya Co Ltd:** 480100 Almaty, Bogenbai Batyr 80; tel. (3272) 50-06-00; fax (3272) 50-70-83; internet www.butya.kz; import and export of grain and metal and petroleum products; construction.

**ELMO:** 480128 Almaty, Mate Zalka 7; the country's largest manufacturer of wiring products and provider of wiring services.

**Investconsulting Co Ltd:** 480072 Almaty, Satpayev 9, POB 50; tel. (3272) 47-84-03; fax (3272) 47-82-86; e-mail inco@nursat.kz; f. 1995; consultancy to cos involved in mining, gold-mining, energy, petroleum and gas; Gen. Dir Kadyr Baikenov.

**JSC Borly:** 470051 Karaganda, 40-Let Kazakhstana 13, 4th Floor; tel. (3212) 41-20-65; fax (3212) 41-20-61; f. 1994 on the dissolution of Karaganda Ugol; country's largest coal-mining company.

**Kazkommerts Securities Open Joint-Stock Co:** 480004 Almaty, Furmanov 65, 5th Floor; tel. (3272) 50-90-80; fax (3275) 501-91-62; e-mail enquiry@kazks.kz; internet www.kkb.kz; f. 1995, jt venture between Global Securities Inc. (Turkey) and Kazkommertsbank; formerly Global Kazkommerts Securities Inc.; corporate finance and advisory services, sales and trading, research; Man. Dir Iskander Yerimbetov.

**Kazstroipolimer:** Karaganda; tel. and fax (3212) 46-01-32; f. 1969; production of textiles, linoleum, foam, dyes, plastic consumer goods, crystal.

**Kurylys Holding Co:** 480004 Almaty, Furmanova 65; tel. (3272) 33-01-72; fax (3272) 33-04-24; e-mail nhc_ak@almatykurylys.k; internet www.almatykurylys.kz; construction, reconstruction of dwellings and civil engineering; Pres. Amangeldy D. Yermegiayev; 9,700 employees.

**Merey Furniture Co:** Almaty; one of the first cos in Kazakhstan to be privatized (1991), it became a joint-stock co in 1992; manufactures and exports furniture; Chair. NADJAT KADYROV; 1,500 employees.

**Pivovarennaya Kompaniya IRBIS (Carlsberg/Baltic Beverages Holding):** Almaty, 95B Angarskaya; 76% owned by Baltic Beverages Holding (Denmark/United Kingdom); leading premium beer producer.

**RG Brands OJSC:** 480061 Almaty; tel. (3272) 58-39-56; f. 2003 by merger of RG Brands, PRG Bottlers and Tea Land; producer of non-alcoholic beverages.

**Shymkent Industrial Amalgamation:** 486008 Shymkent, pr. Abaya 28; tel. (3252) 12-29-43; fax (3252) 23-88-40; f. 1942; state-owned co; specializes in the production of press-forging equipment; Pres. VLADIMIR DMITRIEVICH PLYATSUK; 2,000 employees.

**Tagam:** 480012 Almaty, Bogenbai Batyr 148; tel. (3272) 62-03-62; fax (3272) 62-86-52; f. 1989; joint-stock co; production and sale of sugar and alcohol, sale of tobacco products; Pres. T. M. DNISHEV; 40 employees.

**Tenir Group:** 480004 Almaty, Zhibek zholy 76; tel. (3272) 33-98-20; fax (3272) 58-12-93; e-mail tenir@kaznet.kz; internet www.tenir .com; brokerage, corporate financing, underwriting, business and real-estate valuation.

**Terminal LLC:** 480008 Almaty, Manas 22B , 3rd Floor; tel. (3272) 58-42-25; fax (3272) 58-42-27; e-mail terminal-analytics@mail.kz; f. 1992; customs clearance of import cargoes, storage of cargoes in warehouses, certification of import/export cargoes; Pres. O. BRITVIN; Man. Dir S. BORSCHEV; 150 employees.

**Tsesna Corpn:** Astana, Ugolnaya 24; tel. (3172) 31-03-10; fax (3172) 31-01-54; e-mail marketing@tsesnaastyk.kz; f. 1988; prime producer of wheat; sells wheat products; owns subsidiaries in private and commercial construction; mineral and metal exports, fertilizers, etc.; Chair. NIKOLAY I. MERSHERYAKO.

**Ust-Kamenogorsk Capacitor Plant Joint-Stock Co:** 492001 Vostochno-Kazakstan, Ust-Kamenogorsk; tel. (3232) 26-02-91; fax (3232) 26-02-92; e-mail kvar@ukg.kz; internet www.ukkz.com; f. 1959; produces complete capacitor installations, coupling capacitors, water-cooled capacitors, etc.; Pres. VLADIMIR AKSENOV; 477 employees.

**Ust-Kamenogorsk Titanium and Magnesium Combined Plant:** 492017 Ust-Kamenogorsk; tel. (3232) 33-74-50; fax (3232) 33-66-00; f. 1965; 15.5% of shares offered for privatization in 1999; Pres. BAGHDAD M. SCHAYAKHMETOV.

**Zavod Plasticheskih Mass** (Plastics Production Plant): 466200 Aktau, Industrial Zone, Mangistausky Obl.; tel. (3292) 51-45-19; fax (3292) 33-12-10; e-mail stirene2@nursat.kz; internet www .polystirol.ru; f. 1980; fmrly Akpo Incorporated; manufacturer of plastic products; Gen. Dir M. GERASIMOV; 1,500 employees.

### TRADE UNIONS

**Confederation of Free Trade Unions:** f. 1991; fmrly Independent Trade Union Centre of Kazakhstan; 9 regional branches with 2,200 mems; Chair. SERGEI BELKIN.

**Confederation of Free Trade Unions of Coal and Mining Industries:** Almaty; Chair. V. GAIPOV.

**Federation of Trade Unions of Kazakhstan:** 473000 Astana, pr. Abaya 94; tel. (3172) 216-68-14; fax (3172) 21-68-35; e-mail fprkastana@nursat.kz; internet www.trud.org/kazakhstan; 30 affiliated unions with 2,300,000 mems (2001); Chair. SIYAZBEK MUKASHEV.

**National Trade Union of Journalists of Kazakhstan:** Pres. MADRID RYSBEKOV.

**Union of Manufacturers and Businessmen:** Almaty; tel. (3272) 62-23-07; fax (3272) 66-54-90.

# Transport

## RAILWAYS

In 2000 the total length of rail track in use was 13,615 km (3,725 km of which were electrified). The rail network is most concentrated in the north of the country, where it joins the rail lines of Russia. From the former capital, Almaty, lines run north-eastward, to join the Trans-Siberian Railway, and west, to Shymkent, and then north-west along the Syr-Dar'ya river, to Orenburg in European Russia. From Chu lines run to central and northern regions of Kazakhstan, while a main line runs from Shymkent south to Uzbekistan. There is an international line between Druzhba, on the eastern border of Kazakhstan, and Alataw Shankou, in the People's Republic of China. Measures to restructure and privatize Kazakhstan's railways were announced in 1998, although it was stated that the main railway lines would remain under full state control.

In the late 1990s construction was under way of the first line of a new underground railway (metro) in Almaty. It was envisaged that the metro system, when completed, would comprise three lines (35.4 km in length).

**Department of Railways (Ministry of Transport and Communications):** 473000 Astana, pr. Abaya 49; tel. (3172) 32-62-77; fax (3172) 32-16-96; Dir I. P. SEGAL.

**Kazakhstan Temir Zholy CJSC** (Kazakhstan Railways): 473000 Astana, pr. Pobedy 98; tel. (3172) 14-44-00; fax (3172) 32-82-30; e-mail temirzholy@railways.kz; internet www.railways.kz; f. 1991 following break-up of former Soviet Railways (SZD); Gen. Dir A. I. MYRZAKHMETOV.

### ROADS

In 2000 Kazakhstan's total road network was 81,331 km, including 22,063 km of main roads and 59,268 km of secondary roads. Some 94.7% of the network was hard-surfaced. In 1999 the World Bank approved a US $100m. loan to enable Kazakhstan to repair important sections of its main roads, and to improve road maintenance systems. In 2000 the Islamic Development Bank agreed to donate $200m. towards the rehabilitation of the Karaganda–Astana road. Kazakhstan is linked by road with Russia (46 border crossings), Kyrgyzstan (seven), Uzbekistan (seven) and, via Uzbekistan and Turkmenistan, with Iran. There are six road connections with the People's Republic of China (including two international crossings, at Korgas and Bakhty). Government spending on the repair and construction of roads was to increase significantly, to some 42,000m. tenge, in 2002.

**Department of Roads (Ministry of Transport and Communications):** 473000 Astana, pr. Abaya 49; tel. (3172) 32-02-08; fax (3172) 32-16-96; Dir S. LARICHEV.

### INLAND WATERWAYS

Kazakhstan has an inland waterway network extending over some 4,000 km. The main navigable river is the Irtysh, accounting for approximately 80% of cargo transported by river. The Kazakhstan River Fleet Industrial Association (Kazrechmorflot), comprising 11 water companies, administers river traffic.

**Department of Water Transport (Ministry of Transport and Communications):** 473000 Astana, pr. Abaya 49; tel. (3172) 32-03-58; fax (3172) 32-10-58; Dir JENYS M. KASYMBEK.

### SHIPPING

Kazakhstan's ports of Atyrau and Aktau are situated on the eastern shores of the Caspian Sea. In 1997 a project was undertaken to upgrade the port of Aktau, at an estimated cost of US $74m. The first stage of the project was scheduled for completion in 1999, and it was forecast that by 2000 Aktau would handle more than 7.5m. metric tons of petroleum and up to 1m. tons of dry freight annually. In 1998 the port handled some 2m. tons of petroleum. A ferry port was inaugurated at Aktau in September 2001 as part of the Transport Corridor Europa—Caucasus—Asia (TRACECA) programme, with lines to Azerbaijan, Iran and Russia; the port was capable of processing some 10m. tons of petroleum and up to 30m. tons of dry goods per year. At 31 December 2002 Kazakhstan's merchant fleet comprised 20 vessels, with a combined total displacement of 11,845 grt.

**Aktau Commercial Sea Port:** Aktau, Umirzak; tel. (3292) 44-51-26; fax (3292) 44-51-01; e-mail seaport_akt@kaznet.kz; internet www.portaktau.kz; f. 1963; Dir TALGAT B. ABYLGAZIN; 407 employees.

**Atyrauozenporty** (Atyrau Port): tel. (3122) 25-45-63; fax (3122) 25-45-16; e-mail atr_info@asdc.kz.

### CIVIL AVIATION

There are 18 domestic airports and three airports with international services (at Almaty, Aktau and Atyrau). In 1999 the airport at Astana was being upgraded, following that city's inauguration as the new capital in mid-1998. In 2002 plans were announced for the reconstruction of Atyrau airport, with the help of financial assistance from the European Bank for Reconstruction and Development. The national airline, Air Kazakhstan, was registered in January 1997, and replaced Kazakhstan Aue Zholy, which had been declared bankrupt in August 1996. There were over 50 airline companies registered in Kazakhstan in 2000, two-thirds of which were privately owned. In 2002 19 of the country's 56 air companies had their activities suspended and their licences revoked, in the interests of safety; it was envisaged that many of these companies would merge by the end of the year. Almaty airport has scheduled links with cities in Russia and other former Soviet republics, as well as with destinations in Europe, other parts of Asia and the Middle East.

**Department of Aviation (Ministry of Transport and Communications):** 473000 Astana, pr. Abaya 49; tel. (3172) 32-63-16; fax (3172) 32-16-96; Dir S. BURANBAYEV.

**Aeroservice Kazakhstan Aviakompania:** 480028 Almaty, Alga basskaya 2A; tel. (3272) 36-69-26; fax (3272) 52-93-45; f. 1991; provides charter services to Europe, the Middle East, Pakistan and the Republic of Korea.

**Air Astana:** 473000 Astana, POB 1416, Samal Microdistrict 12, Astana Towers Business Centre, 12th Floor; tel. (3172) 58-09-50; fax (3172) 58-09-80; e-mail astana@air-astana.kz; internet www .air-astana.kz; f. 2001 jointly by the Government and BAE Systems (United Kingdom); domestic flights; Pres. LLOYD PAXTON.

**Air Kazakhstan CJSC** (Kazakhstan Airlines): 480079 Almaty, Ogareva 14; tel. (3272) 57-29-82; fax (3272) 57-25-03; e-mail office@ airkaz.com; internet www.airkaz.com; f. 1997, in succession to Kazakhstan Aue Zholy; state-owned; Pres. YERKIN KALIYEV.

**Asiya Servis Aue Zholy** (Asia Service Airlines): Almaty, Zheltoksan 59; tel. (3272) 33-63-49; operates services to Atyrau and Aktau.

**Jana-Arka Air:** 480012 Almaty, Ninogradova 85; tel. (3272) 63-28-74; fax (3272) 63-19-09; privately owned; provides both domestic and regional flights; Pres. YALKEN VALIN.

**Sayakhat Air:** 480091 Almaty, Bogenbai Batyr 124; tel. (3272) 62-26-28; fax (3272) 62-28-70; e-mail sayakhat@nursat.kz; internet www.sayakhat.com; f. 1989 as the country's first privately owned airline; commenced operations in 1991; passenger and cargo services to Africa, Asia and Europe; Pres. and Dir VLADIMIR KOUROPATENKO.

# Tourism

Tourism is not widely developed in Kazakhstan, owing to its Soviet legacy and infrastructural limitations. However, the country possesses mountain ranges, lakes and a number of historical sites, which the Government plans to promote.

**State Agency for Tourism and Sport:** 473000 Astana, Mukhtar Auezov 126; tel. (3172) 39-66-38; fax (3172) 39-64-68; e-mail turlykhanov@kazsport.kz; internet www.kazsport.kz; f. 2000; Chair. DAULET TURLYKHANOV.

# Culture

## NATIONAL ORGANIZATION

**Ministry of Culture:** see section on The Government (Ministries).

## CULTURAL HERITAGE

In 2002 there were 121 museums in Kazakhstan, which were attended by some 4.0m. people, and 3,312 libraries

**Central State Museum of Kazakhstan:** 480099 Almaty, Samal 1, 44; f. 1931; 90,000 exhibits of history and natural history; Dir ALIMBAY NURSAN.

**Kasteyev Kazakhstan State Museum of Arts:** 480090 Almaty, Satpayeva 30A; tel. (3272) 47-82-49; fax (3272) 47-86-69; e-mail kazart@nursat.kz; internet www.art.nursat.kz; f. 1976; 20,000 exhibits; library of 50,000 vols; Kazakh art, folk art, Soviet and European art; Dir BAYTURSUN E. UMORBEKOV; Deputy Dir (Science) A. J. DJADAIBAYEV.

**National Library of Kazakhstan:** 480013 Almaty, pr. Abaya 14; tel. (3272) 62-72-56; fax (3272) 69-65-86; e-mail info@nlrk.kz; internet www.nlrk.kz; f. 1910; over 5.5m. vols; library, science research centre; organizes international seminars; Dir ROZA A. BERDIGALIYEVA.

## SPORTING ORGANIZATION

**State Agency for Tourism and Sport:** see section on Tourism.

**National Olympic Committee of the Republic of Kazakhstan:** 480012 Almaty, pr. Abai 48; tel. (3272) 93-53-35; fax (3272) 58-85-33; e-mail olymp@nursat.kz; f. 1990; Pres. TIMUR DOSSYMBETOV.

## PERFORMING ARTS

In 2002 there were 47 theatres in Kazakhstan (including 24 drama theatres, three musical comedy theatres, three puppet theatres, and two opera and ballet theatres), with an annual attendance of 1.6m.

**Abai Academic Opera and Ballet Theatre:** Almaty, Kabanbai Batyr 110; tel. (3272) 62-84-45; fax (3272) 62-27-42; e-mail gatob2002@mail.ru; f. 1933; Gen. Dir URAZGALIYEV KUANISH.

**Auezov Drama Theatre:** Almaty, pr. Abaya 103; tel. (3272) 67-33-07; f. 1926; Dir T. ZHAMANKULOV.

**Korean Theatre of Musical Comedy:** 480012 Almaty, Nauryyzbai Batyr 83; tel. (3272) 69-60-90; f. 1932 in Vladivostok (Russia); transferred to Kazakhstan in 1937; Dir G. S. KIM.

**Lermontov Academic Russian Drama Theatre:** Almaty, pr. Abaya 43; tel. (3272) 62-82-73; f. 1933; Artistic Dir R. ANDRIASYAN.

**Uigur Theatre of Musical Comedy:** 480012 Almaty, Nauryzbai Batyr 83; tel. (3272) 62-83-42; f. 1934; Dir M. AKHMADIYEV.

## ASSOCIATIONS

**Association of Kazakhstani Authors and Artists:** 480021 Almaty, pr. Dostyk 85; tel. (3272) 063-69-22; e-mail askar@anesmi .almaty.kz; Pres. ASKAR NURMANOV.

**Kazakhstan Composers' Association:** 480091 Almaty, Kupaeva 83, kv. 41; tel. (3272) 62-50-18; fax (3272) 63-69-22; Pres. BALNUR KYDYRBEK.

**Uigur Association:** 480012 Almaty, Nauryzbai Batyr 83; Pres. KAKHARMAN KHOZAMBERDI.

**Union of Writers of Kazakhstan:** Almaty; subsidiary writers' organizations in Astana (formerly Akmola), Shymkent, Karaganda, Semipalatinsk and Uralsk.

# Education

Education is compulsory and fully funded by the state at primary and secondary level. Primary education begins at seven years of age and lasts for four years, while secondary education, beginning at 11 years of age, lasts for a further seven years. In 2000/01 the total enrolment at primary schools was equivalent to 89% of the relevant age group (females 88%), while secondary enrolment was equivalent to 83% of the appropriate age-group (females 82%). In 1995/96 a total of 52.1% of pupils in general schools were taught in Russian, 44.8% in Kazakh, 2.3% in Uzbek, 0.7% in Uigur and 0.1% in Tajik. In 2002/03 there were 8,334 general schools. After completing general education, pupils are able to continue their studies at specialized secondary schools; there were 335 such schools in 2002/03. In 1995/96 some 24.2% of students at specialized schools were instructed in Kazakh; 203 subjects were taught, with the subject of market economics receiving particular attention. From September 2001 48 secondary schools were to introduce a 12-year system of education, which was to be implemented nationally at a later date.

In the early 1990s the number of university-level institutions was considerably increased, particularly with regard to private institutions. By 2002/03 there was a total of 177 higher schools (including universities), attended by 597,500 students. Ethnic Kazakhs formed a greater proportion (64% in 1995/96) of students in higher education than in general education, since many ethnic Russians chose to study at universities outside Kazakhstan. None the less, the majority of higher-education students (approximately 75% in 1997) were instructed in Russian. Government expenditure on education in 2001 was 105,024m. tenge (14.7% of total spending).

## UNIVERSITIES

**Abay Almaty State University:** 480100 Almaty, Dostyk 13.

**Aktau State University:** 466200 Aktau 14, Mangistau; tel. (3292) 33-84-32; fax (3292) 43-27-56; e-mail helen@arnadat.glas.net; Rector AKHETOV ASHIMZHAN.

**Al-Farabi Kazakh National University:** 480078 Almaty, pr. Al-Farabi 71; tel. (3272) 47-16-71; fax (3272) 47-26-09; e-mail a.rector@ kazsu.kz; internet www.kazsu.kz; f. 1934; languages of instruction: Russian and Kazakh; 15 faculties, seven research institutes; 1,500 teachers; 14,500 students; Rector Prof. T. A. KOZHAMKULOV.

**O. A. Baikonyrov Jezkazagan University:** Jezkazagan, Lenina 7.

**A. Baitursynov Kostanay State University:** 458000 Kostanay, Baitursynov 47; tel. and fax (3142) 54-25-94; e-mail ksu47@mail.kz; internet www.ksu.kst.kz.

**Dosmukhamedov Atyrau University:** Atyrau, Pushkina 212.

**Dzhambul University:** 484002 Taraz, Dzhambul 16A.

**East-Kazakhstan State University:** 492000 Ust-Kamenogorsk, 30 Gvardeiskoy Divisii 34B; tel. (3232) 27-29-11; fax (3232) 40-64-07; e-mail vkgu@ukg.kz; f. 1952, current name since 1991; Rector Prof. ABZHAPPAROV ABDUMUTALIP.

**Karaganda State University:** 470074 Karaganda, Universitetskaya 28; tel. (3212) 74-49-50; e-mail root@kargu.krg.kz; internet www.ksu.kz; f. 1972; 14 faculties; 16,631 students; Pres. DZHAMBUL S. AKYLBAYEV.

**Kazakh National Technical University:** 480013 Almaty, Satbayev 22; tel. (3272) 67-69-01; fax (3272) 67-60-25; e-mail allnt@ kazntu.sci.kz; internet www.kazntu.sci.kz; f. 1934 as Kazakh Polytechnic Institute, name changed as above 1996; 6 institutes; 9 faculties; 1,354 teachers; 10,142 students; library of 1,200,000 vols; Rector Prof. E. M. SHAIKHUTDINOV.

**L. N. Gumilev Eurasian University:** 473021 Astana, Tsiolkovsky 6; tel. (3172) 24-32-93; fax (3172) 24-30-90; e-mail root@lceu.ricc.kz; f. 1962 as teacher-training institute, became Akmola University in 1992, name changed as above 1996; 12 faculties; Rector Prof. AMAN-GELDY HUSSAINOVICH HUSSAINOV.

**North-Kazakhstan University:** 642000 Petropavlovsk, Universitetskaya 18; e-mail mail@nkzu.edu; internet www.nkzu.edu.

**S. Toraigyrov Pavlodar State University:** 637003 Pavlodar, Lomova 64; tel. (3182) 45-12-24; fax (3182) 45-11-10; e-mail pgu@psu .pvl.kz; internet www.psu.kz; f. 1960; 683 teachers; 3,300 students; Rector ARBIN E. MUKHTARUDI.

**Ch. Valikhanov Kokshetau University:** Kokshetau, Karl Marxa 76.

**Taraz M. Kh. Dulati State University:** 484039 Taraz, Suleimanov 7; tel. (3262) 24-42-20; fax (3262) 24-97-25; e-mail targu@nursat.kz; internet www.tarsu.kz; f. 1998; 930 teachers; 13,690 students; Rector Prof. VALICHAN KOZYKEYEVICH BISHIMBAYEV.

**I. Zhansugurov Taldykorgan University:** Taldykorgan; I. Zhansugurova 187A.

**Zhubanov Aktobe University:** 463000 Aktobe, Moldagulova 34.

# Social Welfare

Reforms were introduced in the early 1990s with the aim of making the social-security system self-financing. Of the three new funds introduced, the Pension and Social Insurance Funds were to be entirely financed by employer and employee contributions. New pensions legislation enacted in 1996, and due to be fully implemented by 2002, gradually raised the retirement age from 60 to 63 years for men and from 55 to 58 years for women. In January 1998 a new pensions law came into effect introducing private pension funds. A State Employment Fund was established in 1991, owing to the expected increase in unemployment in a free-market economy, and was financed by contributions, which in 1993 amounted to 2% of an employer's wage bill. The Fund's operations were subsequently extended to include the relief and support of ethnic Kazakh immigrants. With the Government reluctant to inflict the full consequences of a transition to a free-market economy on its population too rapidly, other social-security benefits were raised in 1992 and some were partially indexed in 1993. However, the Government then began to target benefits towards those with the greater need. In June 1997 the Government introduced a comprehensive reform of the system of public pensions provision, which involved the dissolution of the Pension Fund and the creation of a funded system from January 1998.

Living standards were relatively high compared with other Central Asian countries. In 2001 there were 74.4 hospital beds per 10,000 inhabitants. In the same year there were 3.46 physicians per 1,000 persons. State budget expenditure for 2001 was 62,238m. tenge for health care, and 186,641m. tenge for social insurance and social security, together representing 34.7% of total spending.

## NATIONAL AGENCIES

**Ministry of Labour and Social Security:** see section on the Government (Ministries).

**Agency for Health Care:** 473000 Astana, Moskovskaya 66; tel. (3172) 33-74-09.

**Social Insurance Fund:** 480003 Almaty, Zheltoksan 37–41; tel. (3272) 62-28-95; f. 1991, after separation from Soviet system; Dir MAKSUT S. NARIKBAYEV.

**State Employment Fund:** Almaty; f. 1991, in the expectation of increasing unemployment in the transfer to a free-market economy; Chair. SAYAT D. BEYSENOV.

## HEALTH AND WELFARE ORGANIZATIONS

**Charity and Health Fund of Kazakhstan:** 480100 Almaty, D. Kunayev 86; tel. (3272) 62-41-62.

**Kazakhstan Children's Fund:** 480064 Almaty, Furmanova 162; tel. (3272) 62-24-02; Chair. KOZHAKHMET B. BALAKHMETOV.

**Kazakhstan Society of Disabled Women with Children:** 4800072 Almaty, Abia 42–44; tel. (3272) 92-90-88; f. 1992; 5,000 members; 12 staff; 14 regional groups; library; Chief BIBIGUL H. IMANGAZINA.

**National Committee of the Red Crescent and Red Cross of Kazakhstan:** 480100 Almaty, D. Kunayev 86; tel. (3272) 61-62-91;

fax (3272) 61-81-72; e-mail kazrc2@yahoo.co.uk; f. 1937; Pres. ERKEBEK KAMBAROVICH ARGYMBAYEV.

**Voluntary Society of Invalids of Kazakhstan (DOUK):** 480100 Almaty, D. Kunayev 122; tel. (3272) 63-75-87; f. 1988; provides assistance and representation for the disabled; Chair. SAYDALIM N. TANEKEYEV.

**Zhan Society for Support of Families with Disabled Children:** 480118 Almaty, Orbita 2, Bldg 17A , No 36; tel. (3272) 29-32-98.

# The Environment

Kazakhstan developed severe environmental problems during the period of Soviet rule, mainly because of the considerable industrialization, but also because of ambitious agricultural projects in the region. The three main concerns of environmentalists, who led the first popular expressions of opposition to the Soviet regime during the 1980s, were: atmospheric and water pollution from industrial toxins and chemical fertilizers; the desiccation of the Aral Sea, owing to irrigation works; and nuclear testing. The shrinking of the Aral Sea, once the world's fourth-largest freshwater lake, is one of the greatest ecological disasters world-wide. An International Fund for Saving the Aral Sea has been established, although little progress has been made. From late 1999 fears were expressed about the threat of anthrax spores, buried on Vozrozhdeniye Island, spreading to the mainland, owing to the decreasing water level. In October 2003 plans were reported for the construction of a large dam to restore the northern part of the Sea. Likewise, the surface area of Lake Balkhash, one of the largest lakes in the world, had shrunk by 2,000 sq km (772 sq miles) by 2000, affecting many species and the surrounding flood plains. Moreover, from May 2000 up to 10,000 seals, unique to the Caspian Sea, died from toxicosis, owing to cadmium and mercury poisoning in the Mangystau region. By mid-2001 numbers of Caspian sturgeon had become so depleted (largely owing to poaching) that Kazakhstan and other littoral states agreed to a temporary, UN-brokered moratorium on sturgeon fishing.

Nuclear testing, which used to be carried out at Semipalatinsk, in the north of the country (and at Lop Nor, in the neighbouring People's Republic of China), was a major focus for opposition to the former communist regime. The legacy of the nuclear industry remained of concern (in 1994 it was estimated that the tests at Semipalatinsk had affected the health of some 500,000 people in Kazakhstan). In July 2000 Kazakhstan's remaining nuclear-testing capabilities at Semipalatinsk were destroyed. However, in May radiation levels in the regions of Eastern and Western Kazakhstan were reported to be twice as high as those at Semipalatinsk, owing to uranium and beryllium production. In March of the same year the Mangyshlak nuclear reactor was decommissioned, with a US $1m. grant from the International Scientific and Technical Centre, based in Russia. In October 2001 it was confirmed that many former oilfields in the Atyrau region were contaminated with radiation.

In February 2001 Kazakhstan began the implementation of a five-year, US $61m. rural water supply and sewage project jointly funded by the Asian Development Bank, the Islamic Development Bank and the Government. The World Bank was to provide more than US $300m. in 2003–05 for seven projects in water and forestry management, and environmental and rural development.

## GOVERNMENT ORGANIZATIONS

**Ministry of Environmental Protection:** see section on the Government (Ministries); comprises the Committee on Environmental Protection; the Committee on Forestry, Fish and Hunting Economy; the Committee on Water Resources; and the Committee on Geological Protection.

**International Fund for Saving the Aral Sea (IFAS):** 480091 Almaty, Bogenbai Batyr 124; tel. (3272) 62-51-96; fax (3272) 50-77-17; e-mail ifas-almaty@alnet.kz; internet www.ifaz-almaty.kz; f. 1993 by the World Bank; finances programmes and projects concerned with the preservation of the Aral Sea and the rehabilitation of the surrounding environment; Exec. Dir ALMABEK NURUSHEV; Dep. Exec. Dir ALTYNBEK MELDEBEKOV.

**Kazekologiya Information Centre:** Gen. Dir AMANGELDY A. SKAKOV.

## ACADEMIC INSTITUTE

**National Academy of Sciences of Kazakhstan:** 480021 Almaty, Shevchenko 28; tel. (3272) 69-55-93; fax (3272) 69-57-09; e-mail daukeev@academset.kz; f. 1947; several attached institutes involved in environmental research; 6 depts; Pres. SERIKBEK DAUKEEV; Academician Sec.-Gen. MURAT MUKHAMEDZHANOV.

## NON-GOVERNMENTAL ORGANIZATIONS

**ACCA:** 480005 Almaty, S. Kovalevskaya 63, kv. 13; tel. (3272) 41-29-91; e-mail kamilya@itte.kz; f. 1997; implements educational programmes, with the involvement of the local population, on resolving ecological and cultural problems, provides environmental consultancy service to local and international organizations; Exec. Dir KAMILYA SADYKOVA.

**Aral-Asia-Kazakhstan International Public Committee:** Almaty, Lenina 7; tel. (3272) 33-14-94; Pres. MUHTAR SHAHANOV.

**Centre for Ecological Legal Initiatives:** Atyrau; Chair. GALINA CHERNOVA.

**Ecofund of Kazakhstan:** 400037 Almaty, Toslonko 31; tel. (3272) 29-55-59; fax (3272) 67-21-24; f. 1988; once one of largest environmental groups in Kazakhstan, subsequently split several times; Co-Chair. LEV IVANOVICH KURLAPOV, VIKTOR ZONAV.

**Ecology and Public Opinion (EKOM)** (Ekologiya i Obshchestvennoye Mneniye): 637046 Pavlodar, Suvarova 12/131; tel. (3182) 72-67-75; f. 1987; oldest registered environmental NGO in Kazakhstan; Chair. NIKOLAI STEPANOVICH SAVUKHIN; Sec. VALERI PAVLOVICH GALENKO.

**Eikos Co Ltd:** 480016 Almaty, Nusupbekov 32; tel. (3272) 30-49-90; fax (3272) 50-71-84; e-mail kz@eikos.ru; internet www.eikos.ru; f. 1990; provides equipment and technology for desalination and disinfection of drinking water, treatment of municipal and industrial waste water; Pres. Dr TATYANA PILAT.

**Fund in Support of Ecological Education:** 480005 Almaty, S. Kovalevskaya 63, kv. 13; tel. (3272) 41-29-91; fax (3272) 63-66-34; f. 1991; environmental education and ecological library; Chair. ZHARAS ABU-ULY TAKENOV; Principal Officers GULMIRA DJAMANOVA, RAUSHAN KRYLDAKOVA.

**Green Movement Socio-Ecological Centre (GMC):** 484006 Taraz, Lunacharskii 42–2; tel. and fax (32622) 3-27-93; e-mail alex@zagribelny.jambyl.kz; f. 1990; opposition to manufacture of phosphorus fertilizers; publishes *Oasis* monthly newspaper, documentary films; Chair. ALEKSANDR ZAGRIBELNYI; Sec. LUBA RAUPOVA.

**Green Salvation Ecological Society** (Zelonoye Spaseniye): 480091 Almaty, Shagabutdinova 58, kv. 28; tel. (3272) 68-33-74; e-mail ecoalmati@nursat.kz; internet www.greensalvation.org; f. 1990; organizes actions for groups throughout the country, provides environmental education and participates in developing environmental legislation; collects data; raises awareness of issues; Chair. SERGEI G. KURATOV.

**International Ecology Centre (Biosphere Club):** 493910 Ridder, Microraion 3, d. 19, kv. 10; Chair. VLADIMIR PAVLOVICH KARAMANOV.

**Kazakh Community for Nature Protection (Central Council):** 480044 Almaty, Zhibek zholy 15; tel. (3272) 61-65-16; Chair. KAMZA B. ZHUMABEKOV.

**Nevada–Semipalatinsk International Anti-nuclear Movement (IAM):** Almaty; tel. (3272) 63-49-02; fax (3272) 50-71-87; f. 1989; environmental group opposed to nuclear testing; developed and implemented the Programme for the Ecological, Economic and Spiritual Regeneration of regions where nuclear testing took place; Pres. S. O. OMAROVICH; Head of Exec. Cttee MIRZAHAN ERIMBETOV.

**Lop-Nor Semipalatinsk Ecological Committee:** Almaty; tel. (3272) 63-04-64; fax (3272) 63-12-07; f. 1992; semi-autonomous dept of Semipalatinsk-Nevada Movement, enjoys widespread popular support and campaigns against nuclear testing in neighbouring parts of China; Chair. AZAT M. AKIMBEK; Deputy Chair. IRKIZ ILEVA.

# Defence

Kazakhstan was one of the four former Union Republics to become a nuclear power in succession to the USSR, but undertook to dismantle its nuclear facilities. Its remaining nuclear-testing capabilities at Semipalatinsk were destroyed in July 2000. Azerbaijan, Russia and Turkmenistan co-operated with Kazakhstan in the operation of the Caspian Sea Flotilla, another former Soviet force, which was based at Astrakhan, Russia; however, in April 1993 Kazakhstan declared its intention to create its own navy and, in February 1994, announced that it would be based near the town of Bautino, on the Caspian. In January 1995 President Nazarbayev announced his intention that a proportion of the Kazakhstan army form a joint military force with Russia. In August 1999 Kazakhstan became a member of the UN Conference on Disarmament. It was announced in 2002 that the duration of military service was to be gradually decreased; in that year the length of military service was two years (one year for those educated at institutes of higher education). In August 2002, according to Western estimates, the country's total armed forces numbered some 60,000, comprising an army of 41,000 and an air force of 19,000. There were also 34,500 paramilitary troops (including some 20,000 internal security troops, under the command of the Ministry of Internal Affairs) and some 12,000 border guards. The defence budget for 2002 was 34,900m. tenge.

**Commander-in-Chief:** President of the Republic.

**Chief of the General Staff:** Gen. MALIK SAPAROV.

# Bibliography

Akiner, S. *The Formation of Kazakh Identity: From Tribe to Nation-State*. London, Royal Institute of International Affairs, 1995.

Alexandrov, M. *Uneasy Alliance: Relations between Russia and Kazakhstan in the Post-Soviet Era, 1992–1997*. Westport, CT, Greenwood, 1999.

Bradley, C. *The Former Soviet States: Kazakhstan*. London, Aladdin Books, 1992.

Cummings, S. *Centre-Periphery Relations in Kazakhstan*. Washington, DC, Brookings Institution, 2000.

Demko, C. *The Russian Colonization of Kazakhstan, 1896–1916*. Bloomington, VA, Mouton, 1969.

Kaser, M. *The Economies of Kazakhstan and Uzbekistan*. Washington, DC, Brookings Institution, 1997.

Kolst, P. (Ed.), Antane, Aina, Holm Hansen, Jorn, and Malkova, Irina. *Nation-building and Ethnic Integration in Post-Soviet Societies: An Investigation of Latvia and Kazakhstan*. Boulder, CO, Westview Press, 1999.

*Narodnoye Khozyaistvo Kazakhstana za 70 let. Statisticheskii sbornik*. Almaty, 1990.

Nazpary, J. *Post-Soviet Chaos: Violence and Dispossession in Kazakhstan*. London, Pluto Press, 2002.

Olcott, M. B. *The Kazakhs*. Stanford, CA, 1987.

*Kazakhstan: Unfulfilled Promise*. Washington, DC, Carnegie Endowment for International Peace, 2002.

*Qazag Sovet Enciklopedeyasi* (10 vols). Almaty, 1972–78.

Thubron, C. *The Lost Heart of Asia*. London, Heinemann, 2000.

Also see the Select Bibliography in Part Four.

# KYRGYZSTAN

## Geography

### PHYSICAL FEATURES

The Kyrgyz Republic (formerly, as a constituent part of the USSR, the Kyrgyz Soviet Socialist Republic and, between December 1990 and May 1993, the Republic of Kyrgyzstan) is a small, land-locked state situated in eastern Central Asia. It has also been known as Kyrgyzia (or Kirghizia). Kazakhstan borders it to the north, Uzbekistan to the west, Tajikistan to the south-west and south, and the People's Republic of China to the south-east. The country's western border is pincer-shaped, with the Uzbekistan part of the Fergana basin abutting into Kyrgyzstan. The country covers an area of 199,900 sq km (77,182 sq miles).

The terrain is largely mountainous, dominated by the western reaches of the Tien Shan range in the north-east and the Pamir-Alay range in the south-west. The highest mountain is Pik Pobeda (Victory Peak or Tomur Feng, 7,439 m—24,406 ft), at the eastern tip of the country, on the border with China. Much of the mountain region is permanently covered with ice and snow, and there are many glaciers. The Fergana mountain range, running from the north-west across the country to the central-southern border region, separates the eastern and central mountain areas from the Fergana valley in the west and south-west. Other lowland areas include the Chui and Talas valleys near the northern border with Kazakhstan. The most important rivers are the Naryn (at 535 km in length—335 miles), which flows through the central regions and eventually joins the Syr-Dar'ya, and the Chui (221 km), which forms part of the northern border with Kazakhstan, into the deserts of which it flows. In the north-east of the country is the world's second largest crater lake, the Issyk-Kul (with an area of 6,236 sq km).

### CLIMATE

The country has an extreme, continental climate, although there are distinct variations between low-lying and high-altitude areas. In the valleys the mean temperature in July is 28°C (82°F), whereas in January it falls to an average of –18°C (–0.5°F). Annual precipitation ranges from 180 mm (7 ins) in the eastern Tien Shan to 750mm–1,000 mm in the Fergana mountains. In the settled valleys the annual average varies between 100 mm and 500 mm.

### POPULATION

At the census of 1999, at which the total resident population was 4,822,938, 64.9% of the population were ethnic Kyrgyz (Kirghiz), 13.8% Uzbeks, 12.5% Russians, 1.1% Dungans, 1.0% Ukrainians and 1.0% Uigurs. There were also small numbers of Tatars (45,438), Kazakhs (42,657), Tajiks (42,636), Turks (33,327), Germans (21,471), Koreans (19,784) and others. Kyrgyz replaced Russian as the official language in September 1989, although the two languages were given equal status in May 2000. Kyrgyz is a member of the Southern Turkic group of languages and is written in the Cyrillic script. According to the census of 1999, 70% of the population were fluent in Kyrgyz, compared with 53% in 1989. The Arabic script was in use until 1928, when it was replaced by a Latin script. The Latin script was, in turn, replaced by Cyrillic in 1941. In 1993 it was agreed that the use of the Latin script would be reintroduced. The major religion is Islam, with ethnic Kyrgyz and Uzbeks traditionally being Sunni Muslims of the Hanafi school. Russians and Ukrainians were usually adherents of Eastern Orthodox Christianity.

According to UN estimates, the total population numbered 5,067,000 at mid-2002; thus, the population density (persons per sq km) was 25.3. There was a relatively low level of urbanization, with 35.3% of the total population living in the major towns in 1999. Bishkek (known as Frunze in 1926–91), the capital, is situated in the Chui valley in the north of the country. It had a population of 736,000 at mid-2001. The only other town of significant size is Osh (208,520 at the 1999 census), in the Fergana valley, near the border with Uzbekistan. Important regional centres include Karakol, Kyzyl-Kiya, Jalal-Abad (Dzhalal-Abad) and Naryn.

## Chronology

**10th century:** The Turkic ancestors of the Kyrgyz began to migrate from the upper reaches of the Yenisei (in the Tyva region of the Russian Federation), towards the Tien Shan.

**13th century:** The rise of the Mongol Empire hastened the southwards migrations, although the ancestors of the Kyrgyz remained dominated by the Eastern Turkic tribes.

**1685:** The Kyrgyz, reckoned to have emerged as a distinct ethnic group within the previous 200 years, came to be ruled by the Oirot Mongols, against whom the Kyrgyz rulers waged a fierce struggle.

**1758:** The Manzhous (Manchus) defeated the Oirots and the Kyrgyz became nominal subjects of the Chinese emperors.

**1863:** The northern Kyrgyz acknowledged the sovereignty of the Russian tsar, thus providing the official date of the 'voluntary' incorporation of Kyrgyzstan into Russia.

**1866:** The Russians defeated the Khanate of Kokand, which had acquired suzerainty over the southern Kyrgyz earlier in the century.

**1876:** The Khanate of Kokand was abolished and the territory formally incorporated into the Russian Empire; however, there were several Kyrgyz uprisings in the following decades.

**1916:** An attempt to impose labour and military service on the non-Russian peoples of the Empire occasioned a widespread revolt in Central Asia; the savage repression of the rebellion caused many Kyrgyz to emigrate to China.

**25 October (New Style 7 November) 1917:** The Bolsheviks, led by Lenin (Vladimir Ilych Ulyanov), staged a *coup d'état* and seized control of government in Petrograd (St Petersburg); the Russian Soviet Federative Socialist Republic (RSFSR or Russian Federation) was proclaimed.

**14 February (Old Style 1 February) 1918:** First day upon which the Gregorian Calendar took effect in Russia.

**30 April 1918:** The Autonomous Soviet Socialist Republic (ASSR) of Turkestan (based in Tashkent, Uzbekistan) was proclaimed, as part of the Russian Federation; this included Kyrgyzstan, although Bolshevik control was not established here until 1919–20, because of fierce resistance to the Red Army from the 'Whites' and from local *basmachi* insurgents.

**1923:** The reform of the Arabic script helped the formation of a vernacular standard language.

**14 October 1924:** The Kara-Kyrgyz Autonomous Oblast was created, as part of the Russian Federation (until the mid-1920s the Russians knew the Kyrgyz as the 'Kara-Kyrgyz', to differentiate them from the Kazakhs who were called 'Kyrgyz').

**1925:** The Kara-Kyrgyz Autonomous Oblast was renamed the Kyrgyz Autonomous Oblast.

**1 February 1926:** Kyrgyzstan (Kyrgyzia or Kirghizia) became an ASSR, still within the Russian Federation. Also during that year, the capital of Bishkek was renamed Frunze.

**1927–28:** The second programme of land reform (there had been some in 1921–22) continued to aim at resettling the nomadic Kyrgyz; this policy, which had a disastrous effect on the herds and resources of the Kyrgyz, was carried out despite the protests of leading local communists ('the Thirty'), who were subsequently purged. The agricultural reforms and, later, collectivization revived the *basmachi* struggle.

**1928:** A Latin script replaced the Arabic, aiding the improvement of literacy.

**5 December 1936:** The second Constitution of the USSR (the 'Stalin' Constitution) was adopted; Kyrgyzstan became a Soviet Socialist Republic (SSR) and, therefore, a full Union Republic in the Soviet federation.

**1941:** A Cyrillic script replaced the Latin.

**1953:** A Soviet campaign against the epic poetry of Central Asia (such as the Kyrgyz saga *Manas*) provoked strong opposition in Kyrgyzstan.

**1980:** The Chairman of the Council of Ministers, Sultan Ibraimov, was murdered.

**November 1985:** Turdakan Usubaliyev, the First Secretary of the Kyrgyz Communist Party (KCP), was replaced by Absamat Masaliyev, who accused his predecessor of corruption and nepotism.

**September 1989:** Kyrgyz replaced Russian as the official language.

**February 1990:** In elections to the republican Supreme Soviet most seats were won, unopposed, by KCP candidates; those opposition candidates who were elected were united in the Kyrgyzstan Democratic Movement (KDM).

**April 1990:** Masaliyev was elected to the post of Chairman of the Supreme Soviet, which was effectively a republican executive Head of State.

**4 June 1990:** Eleven people were killed and 21 injured in local clashes in the Fergana valley region on the border between Kyrgyzstan and Uzbekistan; numerous deaths followed.

**5 June 1990:** More than 300 people were killed when ethnic Kyrgyz attacked Uzbeks in the town of Uzgen, in the Osh region, and three-quarters of the town was destroyed by fire. The state of emergency was partially lifted in November. Upon the restoration of order, official sources gave the death toll as 212, unofficial reports claiming that as many as 1,000 had died during the conflict.

**30 October 1990:** The Kyrgyz SSR, or Kyrgyzia, was declared a sovereign state and renamed the Socialist Republic of Kyrgyzstan. This followed the election by the Supreme Soviet of a compromise candidate, a liberal academic, Askar Akayev, to the new post of executive President of the Republic—the discredited Masaliyev failed to win the post that he had designed for himself.

**15 December 1990:** The country was renamed the Republic of Kyrgyzstan (the capital, Frunze, was renamed Bishkek in the following February). In the same month Masaliyev resigned as Chairman of the Supreme Soviet (now the post of parliamentary speaker).

**January 1991:** The Council of Ministers was replaced by a smaller Cabinet of Ministers, headed by Nasirdin Isanov; in November Isanov died in an automobile accident.

**17 March 1991:** In an all-Union referendum on the issue of the future state of the USSR, 87.7% of those eligible to vote approved the concept of a 'renewed federation'. The next month Masaliyev was replaced as leader of the KCP by Jumgalbek Amanbayev.

**31 August 1991:** Following the failure of the Moscow (Russia—the Soviet capital) coup attempt and the banning of the KCP, the Supreme Soviet of Kyrgyzstan adopted a declaration of independence.

**12 October 1991:** Akayev was confirmed as President in direct elections, winning some 95% of the votes cast.

**13 December 1991:** Leaders of the five Central Asian Republics (Kazakhstan, Kyrgyzstan, Tajikistan, Turkmenistan and Uzbekistan) met in Ashgabat, Turkmenistan, and agreed to join the Commonwealth of Independent States (CIS).

**21 December 1991:** At a meeting in Almaty, Kazakhstan, the leaders of 11 former Union Republics signed a protocol on the formation of the new Commonwealth and, thereby, the effective dissolution of the USSR.

**11 February 1992:** Tursunbek Chyngyshev was appointed Prime Minister of Kyrgyzstan; Akayev subordinated the Government to the presidency and reduced the number of ministries by one-half.

**June 1992:** The communists re-formed as the Party of Communists of Kyrgyzstan (PCK), led by Masaliyev and Amanbayev.

**5 May 1993:** Parliament, to be known as the Zhogorku Kenesh (Supreme Council), enacted and promulgated the new Constitution of the renamed Kyrgyz Republic.

**10 May 1993:** Kyrgyzstan introduced its own currency, the som; Kazakhstan and Uzbekistan immediately suspended trading relations and the latter introduced what amounted to economic sanctions for a short time.

**10 December 1993:** The Vice-President, Feliks Kulov, resigned (he was later appointed to head the administration of Chui Oblast), following continuing accusations of corruption against the Government by the Zhogorku Kenesh.

**13 December 1993:** Although a parliamentary vote of confidence was inconclusive, President Akayev dismissed the Chyngyshev Government in the hope of securing political stability.

**21 December 1993:** Apas Jumagulov, who had been Chairman of the Council of Ministers in 1986–91, returned as premier, heading a Government that included members of the PCK.

**30 January 1994:** Some 96% of those who voted in a national referendum (with a 96% rate of participation) supported the continued presidency of Akayev; this was interpreted as a mandate for further radicalizing the economic-reform programme.

**22 October 1994:** The results of a referendum approved the introduction of a bicameral parliament, with a 70-seat People's Assembly (upper chamber) to represent regional interests at twice-yearly sessions, and a permanent 35-seat Legislative Assembly (lower chamber) representing the whole country.

**19 February 1995:** A general election to the new Zhogorku Kenesh was contested by more than 1,000 candidates; 89 of the 105 seats were filled after a second round of voting (the first had been held on 5 February). Jumagulov was confirmed as premier in April.

**24 December 1995:** Akayev received 71.6% of the votes cast in the presidential election; the other two candidates were Masaliyev, who had recently been reinstated as the leader of the KCP, and who obtained 24.4% of the votes cast, and Sherimkulov, the former parliamentary speaker, who secured only 1.7%.

**10 February 1996:** A referendum sanctioned enhanced powers for the presidency, prompting the resignation of the Government, to permit restructuring. A new Government, led by Jumagulov, was appointed in the following month.

**24 March 1998:** The Prime Minister, Jumagulov, announced his retirement. He was replaced the next day by Kuvachbek Jumaliyev, the former head of the presidential administration, and a new Government was formed.

**8 September 1998:** Kyrgyzstan signed an agreement with other European and Asian countries aimed at recreating the 'Silk Road' trade route between China and Europe.

**17 October 1998:** Some 90% of those voting in a referendum approved a number of constitutional amendments proposed by President Akayev, including the legalization of private land ownership; an increase in the number of deputies in the lower house of parliament from 35 to 60; and restrictions on parliamentary immunity.

**20 December 1998:** Kyrgyzstan became the first CIS member country to join the World Trade Organization (WTO).

**23 December 1998:** President Akayev dissolved the Government, on the grounds that it had failed to address the country's economic problems. Five days later Jumabek Ibraimov was appointed Prime Minister, with extended powers, which gave him the right to appoint and dismiss ministers.

**21 April 1999:** Amangeldy Muraliyev, a former regional governor, was approved as the new Prime Minister, following the death of Ibraimov.

**May 1999:** A new electoral law was introduced, whereby 15 of the seats in the Legislative Assembly were, henceforth, to be allocated on a proportional basis for those parties that secured at least 5% of the votes. The following month legislation banning those political parties considered to threaten the country's stability was introduced.

**6–13 August 1999:** Four Kyrgyz officials were held hostage by a group of armed fighters, believed to be ethnic Uzbeks and Arabs belonging to an Islamist fundamentalist organization, who had entered the country from Tajikistan.

**22–23 August 1999:** A rebel group, thought to comprise members of the Islamist Movement of Uzbekistan, captured three villages near the Tajik border. The group took hostage a

senior Kyrgyz military commander, among others, prompting Kyrgyz troops to engage in large-scale military action throughout September. The hostages were reported to have been released in October.

**12 March 2000:** As the result of a second round of parliamentary elections (the first had been held on 20 February), the KCP obtained 27.7% of the votes cast, securing five seats, and the Union of Democratic Forces electoral alliance secured 18.6% of the votes, winning four seats.

**25 May 2000:** Parliament approved the use of Russian as a second official language; this was confirmed by a constitutional amendment adopted on 24 December 2001.

**11 August 2000:** From this date Islamist rebels made a series of incursions into Kyrgyzstan from Tajikistan, leading to armed conflict with government forces. Although the Government stated that all rebel forces had left Kyrgyzstan by the end of October, renewed attacks on Kyrgyz territory were reported from mid-2001.

**29 October 2000:** Askar Akayev was re-elected President, with 74.5% of the votes cast, although international observers declared that the voting arrangements had violated international standards.

**2 January 2001:** President Akayev announced the members of his new cabinet. Several ministers from southern Kyrgyzstan, including Prime Minister Kurmanbek Bakiyev (appointed on 21 December 2000), were included among the appointees, in what was believed to be an attempt to appease dissatisfaction at the perceived lack of government representation in the southern oblasts.

**22 January 2001:** Former Vice-President Feliks Kulov, the leader of the Ar-Namys (Dignity) Party, who had been accused of abusing his official position while serving as Minister of National Security in 1997–98, was convicted of abuse of office and sentenced to seven years' imprisonment. Supporters subsequently demonstrated in Bishkek, to demand his release from prison, but the Supreme Court upheld Kulov's sentence in July (although one charge of abuse of office was dismissed); the Prosecutor-General filed further charges, of embezzlement, against Kulov in the same month.

**21 May 2001:** Bakiyev announced the discovery of approximately 10m. metric tons of petroleum in an oilfield in the Jalal-Abad (Dzhalal-Abad) region. It was estimated that the reserves could meet Kyrgyzstan's petroleum requirements for 20 years.

**20 August 2001:** The leader of the Erkindik opposition party, Topchubek Turgunaliyev, who had been sentenced to 16 years' imprisonment in September 2000, on charges—widely held to be politically motivated—of conspiring to assassinate the President, was released, following intense domestic and international pressure.

**25 September 2001:** President Akayev announced that he would be prepared to open Kyrgyz airspace to US military aircraft for the aerial bombardment of Afghanistan, which was harbouring the Islamist fundamentalist, Osama bin Laden, held responsible for co-ordinating the suicide attack of 11 September on the US cities of New York and Washington, DC. In late November the Government agreed to give the US-led anti-terrorism coalition access to its military bases and, later, its main airport.

**5 January 2002:** Azimbek Beknazarov, an opposition deputy and the former Chairman of a parliamentary committee on court reforms and legality, was arrested, owing to allegations that he had misused his powers while investigating a murder case in 1995.

**17–18 March 2002:** During protests in Jalal-Abad against the detention of Beknazarov (which was widely believed to have been politically motivated), six people were reportedly killed and more than 60 injured, after members of the security forces clashed violently with demonstrators.

**8 May 2002:** Having been found guilty of embezzlement, Feliks Kulov was sentenced to an additional 10 years' imprisonment, to be served simultaneously with the sentence received in January 2001. Following an appeal, in October the 10-year sentence was reduced by one-third.

**10 May 2002:** The Legislative Assembly ratified the controversial Sino-Kyrgyz border treaty, signed in 1999, which ceded some 95,000 ha of territory to the People's Republic of China. The treaty was ratified by the People's Assembly one week later, despite demands for its rescission; protesters claimed the agreement to be illegal, since Akayev had initially signed it without the consent of the legislature.

**22 May 2002:** Following a series of country-wide anti-Government protests, Bakiyev tendered his resignation as Prime Minister, prompting, under the terms of the Constitution, the resignation of the entire Government. The First Deputy Prime Minister, Nikolai Tanayev, was appointed as acting Prime Minister, and confirmed as Prime Minister eight days later. Meanwhile, on 28 May Akayev signed into law the Sino-Kyrgyz border treaty.

**19 June 2002:** Tanayev announced the formation of a new Government.

**28 June 2002:** A law approving an amnesty for those involved in the unrest of mid-March was passed by the Legislative Assembly, leading to criticism from opposition politicians. On the same day Beknazarov's one-year, suspended prison sentence, received one month earlier, was annulled.

**2 February 2003:** A referendum was held on proposed constitutional amendments, and the extension of President Akayev's term of office. Despite international concern about both the scheduling of the referendum and alleged procedural violations, 86.7% of the electorate reportedly participated, with 76.6% of voters approving the constitutional amendments, and 78.7% supporting President Akayev's remaining in office until 2005. One of the principal constitutional amendments provided for the reorganization of the Zhogorku Kenesh as a unicameral legislature from 2005.

**28 April 2003:** Representatives from Armenia, Belarus, Kazakhstan, Kyrgyzstan, Russia and Tajikistan formally inaugurated the successor to the Collective Security Treaty, a new regional defence organization known as the Collective Security Treaty Organization (CSTO).

**23 October 2003:** A Russian airbase opened in Kant, some 30 km from the US-led coalition's airbase at Manas.

# History

## DR JOHN ANDERSON

### EARLY HISTORY

The ancestors of the Kyrgyz, a people of mixed Turkic, Mongol and Kipchak descent, probably originated from the area around the upper reaches of the Yenisei, in what is now the Tyva region of Russia. Southwards migration, towards the Tien Shan mountain range, began in the 10th–11th centuries, by which time tribal groups in the area appear to have described themselves as Kyrgyz, although the designation only became common around the 15th century. At various times they were ruled by the Turkic and Chinese empires, before coming under the authority of the Khanate of Kokand at the beginning of the 19th century. In the mid-19th century the Khans of Kokand struggled to gain control of the territory now known as Kyrgyzstan. The mountainous terrain, which had defeated other would-be conquerors, proved particularly problematic and, for a brief period around 1870, the Khanate faced a systematic revolt led by Kurmanja-datka, the widow of a Kyrgyz tribal leader. The loose tribal structures and nomadic life styles of the Kyrgyz, however, did ensure them some degree of independence.

When Russia began to encroach on Central Asia in the mid-19th century, some Kyrgyz tribes sought its support for their resistance to the Khanate and when the latter was formally incorporated into the Russian Empire in 1876 the Kyrgyz effectively found themselves ruled from St Petersburg, the tsarist capital. Various revolts followed, of which the most significant was the 1916 rebellion, which spread across Central Asia when Russia sought to mobilize the local population to support its First World War campaign. The harsh suppression of that revolt caused many Kyrgyz to emigrate to China.

### SOVIET KYRGYZSTAN

During 1917 revolutionary activity in the region was largely confined to the Russian settlers, although there were sponta-

neous rebellions by Kyrgyz groups seeking to take advantage of the collapse of tsarist authority. Despite the efforts of those Kyrgyz who joined *basmachi* groups of Muslim and nationalist resistance fighters, in 1918 the territory formally became part of a Turkestan Autonomous Soviet Socialist Republic (ASSR). This was, in turn, incorporated into the Russian Soviet Federative Socialist Republic (RSFSR), although Soviet control over the territory was not clearly established until the early 1920s. The administrative territory of the Kyrgyz underwent various changes in the mid-1920s, firstly to the Kara-Kyrgyz Autonomous Oblast within the RSFSR in 1924 (the Russians used the term Kara-Kyrgyz for the Kyrgyz until the mid-1920s, to distinguish them from the Kazakhs, who were, at the time, known to the Russians as Kyrgyz), then to the Kyrgyz Autonomous Oblast in 1925 and the Kyrgyz ASSR in 1926; the status of full Union Republic was finally achieved in December 1936.

During the Soviet period Kyrgyzstan shared many of the experiences of its Central Asian neighbours, with land reform, collectivization and the attempt to settle a largely nomadic population leading to thousands of deaths and the dramatic reduction of livestock levels. Those local communists who had sought to give socialism a nationalist content were purged during the 1930s, and some effort was made to rewrite the nation's past in ways that were not deemed threatening to Soviet rule. Although there is considerable evidence to suggest that traditional Kyrgyz culture and lifestyles survived during the communist period, especially in rural areas, through most of the post-Stalinist era the Kyrgyz Soviet Socialist Republic appeared to be among the most loyal of Soviet regions. This was, in part, owing to the First Secretary of the Kyrgyz Communist Party (KCP), Turdakan Usubaliyev, under whose guidance the republic's officials praised the Soviet leadership and promoted the use of the Russian language. At the same time, however, Usubaliyev encouraged the further development of Kyrgyz-dominated patronage networks, which effectively ran the political and economic life of the republic.

## THE NATIONALIST MOVEMENT

In November 1985, soon after Mikhail Gorbachev was appointed to head the Communist Party of the Soviet Union (CPSU), Usubaliyev resigned and was replaced by Absamat Masaliyev, who immediately levelled charges of corruption and general misrule against his predecessor. Although Masaliyev resisted opening Kyrgyzstan to genuine political freedom, by 1989 signs of popular resistance were beginning to appear. Some elements of the media cautiously adopted a more critical tone towards the Government and a number of informal political groups emerged. A particular focus for dissent was the acute housing crisis; in 1989 homeless Kyrgyz began to seize vacant land around the capital, Frunze (Bishkek) and to build houses on it. Conflicts also developed in the southern Osh Duban (Oblast), where local Kyrgyz, supported by an organization known as Osh Aymaghi, took similar actions to acquire land for housing, in a region traditionally dominated by Uzbeks. Masaliyev and his colleagues chose to ignore the various reports from Osh suggesting that violence was imminent. In June 1990 serious intercommunal fighting broke out between Uzbeks and Kyrgyz, leaving several hundred dead and many more injured. A state of emergency was declared (which was partially lifted in November, but only fully ended in 1995), and it took at least two more months to restore some semblance of order and central control.

In February 1990 elections were held to the republic's Supreme Soviet, but these were largely manipulated by the Communist Party so as to prevent any real parliamentary opposition emerging. In April Masaliyev was elected to the post of Chairman of the Supreme Soviet (a post that he held until December); he sought to follow Gorbachev's example and create an executive presidency but, discredited by the violence in Osh, and under attack from a more vocal opposition group in parliament, which had united as the Kyrgyzstan Democratic Movement, Masaliyev failed to win election. Eventually a compromise candidate, Askar Akayev, the President of the Kyrgyz Academy of Sciences and a known liberal, who had worked only briefly within the party apparatus, was elected to the presidency.

During the attempted coup in the USSR, in August 1991, Akayev was the first republican leader to denounce the conspirators and offer support to Boris Yeltsin, the President of the RSFSR, or Russian Federation. Akayev also resisted attempts by conservative communists against his own presidency; within days he announced his resignation from the CPSU and issued a decree prohibiting party involvement in state and military bodies. By the end of August the Kyrgyz Supreme Soviet had voted for independence from the USSR, a status eventually achieved with the *de facto* dissolution of the Union by the end of the year. In October Akayev reinforced his own position by standing for direct election to the presidency, albeit unopposed, and received 95% of the votes cast.

## INDEPENDENT KYRGYZSTAN

Askar Akayev's early speeches as President of newly independent Kyrgyzstan placed much emphasis on the need to develop a liberal democracy, based upon a developed civil society and a market economy. This commitment earned him considerable praise abroad, as well as financial aid from the IMF and some Western countries, but gave rise to less enthusiasm at home. Nationalist and liberal critics increasingly claimed that democratization was more a slogan than reality, and in the communist-led parliament Akayev faced criticism for replacing dominance by Russia with that by international

financial institutions. Despite these attacks, the first year of independence witnessed the emergence of an embryonic civil society with a thriving press, which proved to be the most open and critical in Central Asia. Political parties also began to develop, although, as in much of the former USSR, many of these were ephemeral, subject to constant fragmentation and grouped around leaders prominent in specific regions of the country.

Amid continuous confrontation with the Uluk Kenesh (as the parliament was by this time known) the President sought the adoption of a new constitution, which would create a smaller and more professional parliament. The document eventually accepted on 5 May 1993 provided for a parliamentary form of government, with legislative power vested in a 105-seat assembly, or Zhogorku Kenesh, after elections that were due to be held by 1995. However, the President retained considerable authority, having the power to appoint the Prime Minister, initiate legislation and dissolve parliament. At the same time the document gave parliament broader rights than in other former Soviet states, with key presidential appointments requiring parliamentary approval, and the deputies given the possibility to override presidential vetoes of legislation.

Although the Constitution established formal political rules, much of Kyrgyzstan's political life took place at a level beneath the institutional surface. Many politicians had their roots not in parties or legislative bodies, but in regionally based clan and tribal networks; in particular, there was a strong distinction between northern and southern groups. At the senior level this was apparent in the tensions between President Akayev, who came from the northern Chui Duban, and the former KCP First Secretary, Masaliyev, from the southern Osh Duban. This phenomenon also made it difficult for the central authorities to assert their influence in some parts of the country. For example, on one occasion President Akayev removed the head of the Jalal-Abad (Dzhalal-Abad) regional administration because of his opposition to central policies. He was replaced by a member of an alternative regional political family, who proved to be only marginally more loyal to the centre.

President Akayev also had to respond to the needs of the non-Kyrgyz population, especially the Slavs and Germans, who feared for their future in the new Kyrgyzstan. Although citizenship was open to all resident on Kyrgyz territory at the time of independence, many felt that the rise of nationalist groups, the increasing use of national criteria in the selection of leading personnel and the gradual imposition of language laws that might exclude Slavs from education and key appointments, made their position within Kyrgyzstan untenable. The name of the country was changed by the 1993 Constitution from the Republic of Kyrgyzstan to the less ethnically neutral Kyrgyz Republic. By the end of 1994 about 40% of Germans and nearly 20% of Russians who had been resident in Soviet Kyrgyzstan had left the country, many of them skilled professionals. Considerable efforts were made to persuade them to stay: the creation of a Slavic university in the capital Bishkek, in September 1993; the postponement of the implementation of the law establishing Kyrgyz as the state language, first from 1995 to 2000, and later to 2005; and, in early 1996, an agreement on the continued use of Russian as an official language in areas predominantly populated by Russian speakers. In May 2000 Russian was finally accorded the status of an official language, but, none the less, at the end of July President Akayev expressed concern at the increasing numbers of ethnic Slavs leaving Kyrgyzstan and in 2001 some 25,000 left the country. In December 2001 a constitutional amendment was adopted, describing Russian as an official language in the republic. According to the 1999 census, 65% of the population was ethnic Kyrgyz, compared with 52% in 1989.

In mid-1993 tensions were also present in the south, where some Uzbeks agitated openly for union with neighbouring Uzbekistan, although, in general, such efforts were confined to a minority and did not initially seem to have been encouraged by Uzbekistan's President, Islam Karimov. Members of the non-Kyrgyz population continued to fear exclusion from politics, and in July 1998 a group of Uzbek deputies and Russian activists in the southern Jalal-Abad region formed a new political party, with the principal aim of ensuring minority representation in the next parliamentary elections.

In addition to pressure from the nationalist constituency, President Akayev also experienced communist-led criticism of economic reforms, which were blamed for the deteriorating economic situation, and was accused of betraying Kyrgyz interests to foreign investors. A series of allegations of corruption culminated in a vote of 'no confidence' in the Prime Minister, Tursunbek Chyngyshev, and his Government in the Uluk Kenesh in December 1993. Although the necessary two-thirds' majority was not obtained, President Akayev responded by dismissing the entire Government. He appointed Apas Jumagulov (who had been the last premier of Soviet Kyrgyzstan) Prime Minister, while bringing the leader of the KCP, Jumgalbek Amanbayev, into the Government, as a Deputy Prime Minister. Simultaneously, he arranged a referendum for 30 January 1994, in which 96% of those voting expressed their confidence in the course being followed by the President, and supported Akayev remaining in office until the end of his allotted term (scheduled, at that time, to expire in late 1996). Following the dissolution of parliament, a further referendum was held on 22 October 1994 to approve proposed constitutional amendments, including the transformation of the Zhogorku Kenesh into a bicameral parliament (with a 70-member People's Assembly, the upper chamber, to represent regional interests, and a 35-member lower chamber, the Legislative Assembly, to represent the population as a whole).

In the general election to the Zhogorku Kenesh held on 5 February 1995, only 16 deputies were elected in the first round of voting—two to the 35-seat permanent Legislative Assembly and 14 to the People's Assembly. Following a second round of voting two weeks later, the total number of deputies elected reached 89, but, as voting did not take place in some constituencies, further elections were required before the new parliamentary chambers were filled. Of those elected, the vast majority were Kyrgyz, and only five were women. Just under 40 were nominated by political parties, but the allegiance of many was weak and only one party, the Social Democratic Party of Kyrgyzstan, the members of which were predominantly businessmen and regional administrators, acquired more than four seats. President Akayev complained that the system had largely favoured representatives of the old order, but vowed to work closely with the new parliament. The new Zhogorku Kenesh's early months, however, were spent disputing the relative powers and jurisdiction of each chamber, something unforeseen in a Constitution drafted in terms of a single-chamber parliament.

A presidential election was scheduled for 24 December 1995, in which Akayev sought a renewal of his mandate. The election was contested by Akayev, Absamat Masaliyev, who had recently been reinstated as leader of the KCP, and Medetkan Sherimkulov. During the campaign the media overwhelmingly supported Akayev, and there were complaints about the harassment of opposition supporters in many areas. The results provided, as expected, a victory for Akayev, with 71.6% of the votes cast (the participation rate was 86.2%). Yet, in some areas, notably Masaliyev's home region of Osh, Akayev received as little as 50.0% of the votes cast, with 46.5% going to Masaliyev; critics alleged that even this narrow

majority was falsified. Akayev followed the election with a referendum on 10 February 1996, in which 94.3% of those participating voted in favour of constitutional amendments that greatly increased his formal powers. Even these enhanced powers did not guarantee implementation of his will, however. The Government resigned in late February, and in March Akayev reinstated Jumagulov as Prime Minister and appointed a new Government.

## POLITICAL DEVELOPMENTS

Following the referendum of February 1996, President Akayev was accused of moving Kyrgyzstan from the path of democratization and true reform. Pressures on the media persisted throughout the late 1990s, as members of the élite became impatient with journalistic criticism, although attacks on newspapers were often justified by reference to their breach of the law. Thus, both the Kyrgyz language paper *Asaba* and the respected *Vechernii Bishkek* were subjected to pressures from the tax authorities, although their real offence appeared, to many observers, to be their unwillingness to succumb to political demands. In addition, the increasingly restrictive regime made it harder for social organizations with a more critical stance to gain legal recognition. In particular, the Kyrgyz Committee for Human Rights, the pensioners' movement and the homeless persons' organization, *Yntymak*, found themselves subjected to persistent official harassment in 1998–99.

At the formal level of government the period following the 1996 referendum witnessed considerable turnover in government ministries, as well as a continual rotation of regional leaders. In March 1998 the Prime Minister, Apas Jumagulov, announced his retirement, and was replaced by a young 'technocrat', Kuvachbek Jumaliyev. The Government's main concerns were to maintain the process of macroeconomic stabilization, to combat corruption and to guarantee social stability. The need to improve living conditions and to provide an adequate social-welfare system was much debated, but, in practice, the Government found it extremely difficult to confront such fundamental structural problems. In December 1998, as a result of the financial crisis that affected Russia and other countries in that year, Jumaliyev was replaced as Prime Minister by Jumabek Ibraimov. However, he died in April 1999, and was replaced by Amangeldy Muraliyev, the former Governor of Osh Duban.

Of growing political and social importance in the late 1990s was the issue of religion. From the state's perspective, the primary concern was the threat of Islamist fundamentalism. The advances of the militant Islamist grouping, the Taliban, in Afghanistan, in the second half of the 1990s, and the discovery of alleged religious extremists (described as Wahhabis, a conservative interpretation of Islam originating in Saudi Arabia) in southern Kyrgyzstan and neighbouring Uzbekistan, increased these fears. In consequence, the authorities adopted various measures aimed at monitoring the life of Muslim communities within the country. Although the State Commissioner for Religious Affairs was originally sceptical about the threat posed by Islamists to Kyrgyz security, the religious question resurfaced in August 1999, when a group of Islamist activists, believed to be members of the Islamist Movement of Uzbekistan (IMU), seized four Japanese geologists and several local officials in the southern Batken Duban. Following large-scale military intervention by Kyrgyz troops, with Uzbek military support, the situation was resolved in October, and in early 2000 the Kyrgyz authorities arrested and tried a number of alleged Islamists. However, in August there were further armed incursions into Batken Duban, and it took several months to repel the militants. Such incursions appeared likely to pose a persistent threat in future years, and the Kyrgyz authorities also suggested that a growing number of young people in the south were being attracted by the Islamist teachings of the Hizb-ut Tahrir organization. Economic problems appeared to have created a marginal class of under- or unemployed young people, who found Islamist criticism of the socio-economic and political situation convincing both in terms of analysis, and as guide to action, and the continuing failure of the state to meet the needs of many sections of the population helped to create a fertile recruiting ground for radical organizations. The suicide attacks on the US cities of New York and Washington, DC, on 11 September 2001, attributed to the al-Qa'ida (Base) organization of Osama bin Laden, the Saudi-born Islamist harboured by the Taliban regime, focused international attention on the potential threat posed by organizations such as the IMU, which had continued its armed incursions into Kyrgyzstan in mid-2001. Kyrgyzstan undertook joint exercises with US troops in February 2002, which aimed to facilitate attempts to counter insurgency in the country's mountainous regions. During 2002 and the first half of 2003 dozens of Hizb-ut Tahrir activists were arrested and tried in Kyrgyzstan, and the Minister of Internal Affairs claimed that this hitherto peaceful organization was on the verge of turning to violence. At the same time officials claimed that the revitalized IMU (reportedly renamed the Islamist Movement of Turkestan in 2001) had been responsible for explosions in Bishkek and Osh during 2002–03. Other observers were more sceptical, arguing that the Islamist threat was being inflated by a Government that was keen to divert attention from its own domestic problems.

The other significant political issue confronting the country as it entered the 2000s was the question of elections and succession. A parliamentary election was held on 20 February 2000, the preparations for which were characterized by substantial state efforts to eliminate opposition candidates from the poll. In the event, the Central Electoral Commission reported that some 64% of the electorate participated in the election, and six parties obtained over 5% of the votes cast and thus acquired representation for election by party lists. However, the overall results took some time to finalize. The Commission claimed that the delay resulted from the great distances ballot boxes had to travel, in order to reach the capital for counting, although this problem had not been reported during previous elections or referendums. Indeed, opposition candidates claimed that the delay stemmed from the need to find ways to exclude popular politicians and, in fact, in the individual single-member constituencies few candidates managed to achieve the necessary majority. A second round of voting was held two weeks later, on 12 March. Among those who were elected in the first round of voting were the former communist leader, Turdakun Usubaliyev, and President Akayev's brother, Asankul Akayev. International monitors from the Organization for Security and Co-operation in Europe (OSCE) described the election as not having met the expected electoral standards. During the following weeks there was renewed pressure on those opposition candidates entitled to contest the 'run-off' election, some of whom were successfully eliminated from the ballot. As a result of the second round of voting, the KCP secured 27.7% of the votes cast, the pro-Government Union of Democratic Forces obtained 18.6%, the Women's Democratic Party of Kyrgyzstan obtained 12.7%, the Party of Veterans of the War in Afghanistan and of Participation in other Local Conflicts obtained 8.0%, the Ata-Meken (Fatherland) Socialist Party obtained 6.5%, and the My Country Party of Action won 5.0%. However, a prominent critic of the Government, Daniyar Usenov, was excluded from the poll, allegedly for returning a false statement of his income, and Feliks Kulov, a potential presidential challenger, was defeated in the election, despite entering the second round with a substantial majority. In late March,

moreover, he was arrested and charged with abuse of office during his time as Minister of National Security in 1997–98, although he was acquitted in August.

This pattern of intimidation and exclusion was repeated in the presidential election of October 2000. Prior to the election, opposition candidates were subject to harassment, and particular controversy was aroused by an electoral rule that required candidates to appear before a linguistic commission to prove their ability to communicate in Kyrgyz. In consequence, Akayev's only effective challenger, Feliks Kulov, was barred from standing. At the election, held on 29 October, there were further irregularities, as campaign workers for opposition candidates were arrested, ballot boxes in some areas were found to contain pro-Akayev votes before polling had begun, and there were reports of votes being cast in the names of thousands of deceased voters who remained on the electoral register. According to official reports, some 75% of the population participated in the election, and Akayev was duly re-elected as President with the support of 74.5% of the votes cast. His closest challenger was Omurbek Tekebayev, the leader of the Ata-Meken (Fatherland) Socialist Party, who obtained 13.9% of the votes. Although Akayev would probably have secured the majority of the votes without any external manipulation, there could be little doubt that his majority was inflated considerably by the efforts of the authorities and media to obstruct the campaigns of credible opponents.

The first consequence of the election was a change in government, as Muraliyev was replaced as Prime Minister, in late December 2000, by Kurmanbek Bakiyev, who subsequently introduced a number of new ministers to the cabinet. It also quickly became apparent that Akayev's faith in democracy was severely limited, as several political opponents were subjected to repression. In January 2001 Kulov was sentenced to seven years' imprisonment, on charges of abuse of office; an appeal was rejected in March, and the Supreme Court upheld Kulov's sentence in July (although one charge of abuse of office was dismissed). Kulov was found guilty of further charges, of embezzlement, in May 2002.

The harassment of opposition newspapers and activists also continued during 2001–02, and in May 2001 Tekebayev stood down as Deputy Chairman of the Legislative Assembly, owing to his involvement in a number of protests against incipient authoritarianism. Meanwhile, in February 2001, and on several occasions thereafter, *Res Publica*, was forced to halt publication, owing to unpaid debts. In early 2002 *Res Publica* was made liable for additional fines, and publication of the newspaper was suspended from January until May. The publication of *Asaba* had also been suspended between March and October 2001, after the newspaper lost a number of libel actions. Several other, new newspapers were issued with libel actions during 2001, and in June the Government annulled the registration of newly established newspapers, postponing their registration first until September, and then until the beginning of October. Despite occasional periods of respite, these pressures continued, and several government ministers and other officials sought to sue critical media outlets forcing, for example, the closure of *Moya Stolitsa* in June 2003. International organizations expressed concern at the apparent efforts of the authorities to undermine the independence of the media in Kyrgyzstan.

In January 2002 the arrest of an opposition deputy and a former Chairman of a parliamentary committee on court reforms and legality, Azimbek Beknazarov, on charges of abuse of power, prompted protesters to demand his release and to denounce his detention as politically motivated. Nevertheless, Beknazarov's trial commenced in February (although it was adjourned until the following month). On 17–18 March large-scale protests took place in Jalal-Abad against the ongoing trial; six people were reported to have died, following clashes with security forces. Although the trial was subsequently suspended and Beknazarov was temporarily released, the Government accused the opposition of instigating the riots in an attempt to stage a *coup d'état* and maintained that the security forces had acted in self-defence. On his release, Beknazarov announced that he held the authorities responsible for the violence; witnesses supported his claims, alleging that security officials had shot at unarmed demonstrators without provocation or warning. The People's Congress demanded the resignations of both the President and the Government.

On 10 May 2002 the Legislative Assembly ratified the controversial Sino-Kyrgyz border treaty (see Foreign Affairs), prompting two weeks of anti-Government demonstrations, hunger strikes and acts of civil disobedience. Protesters demanded that the Government accept responsibility for the violence of mid-March; rescind the ratification of the border treaty (which they claimed was signed illegally by President Akayev, since he had agreed to cede land to the People's Republic of China without the consent of the legislature); and close the criminal case against Beknazarov. Nevertheless, the border treaty was ratified by the People's Assembly in mid-May, and subsequently signed into law by the President. Meanwhile, a state commission established to investigate the protests in Jalal-Abad issued a report, in which it criticized all levels of government and the law-enforcement bodies for not having recognized the instability of the political situation and the rising levels of popular discontent in the region during Beknazarov's trial. The commission also stated that the security forces' use of weapons to control the demonstrators had been illegal.

Meanwhile, on 22 May 2002, as a result of increasing opposition, Prime Minister Bakiyev tendered his resignation; the entire Government duly resigned, in accordance with the Constitution. The Chief of the Presidential Administration also resigned, together with a senior prosecutor, and several senior police-officers were dismissed. The First Deputy Prime Minister, Nikolai Tanayev, was subsequently appointed Prime Minister and in early June a new Government was announced. In the same month Tanayev proposed an amnesty for those involved in the disturbances of mid-March. Tanayev stated that he would release the remaining detainees if the organizers of the rallies agreed to a number of conditions, including the cessation of protests against the Sino-Kyrgyz treaty. The draft amnesty proposals were approved by the Legislative Assembly in late June. None the less, in late August the Prosecutor-General's Office announced that charges of abuse of power were to be filed against six officials, including prosecutors and police-officers, accused of mishandling the March protests.

In mid-2002 President Akayev announced his intention to introduce constitutional amendments that would provide a more appropriate balance of presidential and parliamentary authority. Over subsequent months there was considerable debate, although some interpreted this as an attempt to distract attention from growing opposition, or as a means for Akayev to justify maintaining his dominance beyond the end of his presidential term in 2005. A referendum held on 2 February 2003 asked whether the amendments (providing, *inter alia*, for the introduction of a unicameral legislature) should be adopted, and whether the President should serve until 2005. Perhaps inevitably, more than 75% of those voting supported the Government on both questions, although international bodies expressed doubts about some aspects of the referendum process. As a consequence, Akayev's position vis-à-vis the opposition was strengthened, as he was able to argue that he had a fresh mandate from the people, while new clauses on immunity and impeachment made it far harder to remove him from power. In addition, the elimination of the

party-list system of parliamentary election was expected to strengthen the power of regional leaders in controlling the electoral process in their own oblasts, and thus reduce chances for the development of political parties.

## FOREIGN AFFAIRS

In an attempt to strengthen its independence, Kyrgyzstan sought international partners from a variety of quarters, with economic relations being of primary concern. President Akayev turned, in particular, to the IMF and the USA for support, with his early commitment to democracy and market reform attracting substantial aid and credits. This support continued into the late 1990s, and in October 1998 Kyrgyzstan became the first member country of the Commonwealth of Independent States (CIS) to become a member of the World Trade Organization (WTO).

At the same time Kyrgyzstan also looked towards the Middle East and Asia, and the People's Republic of China quickly became an important partner. Despite their very different approaches to politics, the Kyrgyz and Chinese Governments developed good relations, and agreements were signed on water and trade, and a number of Free Economic Zones were established in the country. From early 1997, however, Kyrgyzstan expressed concerns about unrest on its borders with China, owing to activity by an organization known as For a Free Eastern Turkestan, which sought to create an Islamic state on the territory of China's Xinjiang Uygur (Uigur) Autonomous Region.

Kyrgyzstan also cultivated relations with its former Soviet neighbours, especially Kazakhstan and Uzbekistan. These connections were not without problems, in part because of the great disparity in size. Kyrgyzstan was highly dependent on both for energy, and sometimes had to suffer direct interference in its internal affairs by its larger neighbours, as when Uzbek security officials arrested opponents of the President of Uzbekistan, Islam Karimov, who were active in Kyrgyzstan. Relations worsened for a brief period in mid-1993, following Kyrgyzstan's decision to issue its own currency, rather than to continue with the vagaries of the 'rouble zone'. Produced hastily and without consultation, this development prompted a temporary break in economic relations with Kazakhstan and Uzbekistan, and ended with an apology. By the end of 1994 good relations had been resumed, although tensions remained. When Uzbekistan demanded overdue payments for supplies of natural gas, Kyrgyzstan retaliated by suggesting that Uzbekistan pay for the free water supplies it received from Kyrgyz reservoirs. Negotiations over the issue began in late 1997, but little progress was made. Tensions increased again in 1999, when Uzbekistan criticized Kyrgyzstan's handling of the hostage crisis (see above), and Karimov made unfavourable remarks about Akayev. There were also reports in 1999 that Uzbekistan had unilaterally taken control of parts of the republic's southern territory and established border positions within Kyrgyz territory. Tensions subsequently flared when Uzbekistan created border posts and laid landmines in part of the contested territory, leading to the deaths of at least 10 Kyrgyz farmers, in addition to many injuries. An intergovernmental commission met periodically through 2002 and the first half of 2003, and in August it was announced that, following negotiations between the Kyrgyz and Uzbek Prime Ministers, a treaty was expected to be signed by both sides, delineating their common border.

Equally, if not more important was Kyrgyzstan's relationship with Russia. As the country's most significant trading partner it could not be ignored and, in the light of the civil war in the 1990s in neighbouring Tajikistan, President Akayev recognized the need for some guarantor of his nation's security. Yet this was a highly unbalanced relationship, with Kyrgyzstan also dependent on Russia for many manufactured goods. In early 1996, moreover, Kyrgyzstan was forced to cede Russia shares in certain vital industries, in order to repay existing debts. In late March the continuing reliance on Russia was given further emphasis when Akayev joined the Presidents of Belarus, Kazakhstan and Russia in signing a formal treaty committing the countries to closer economic integration. Kyrgyzstan was able to offer some support to Russia in helping to mediate the conflict in Tajikistan. It was under Kyrgyz auspices that the Tajik Government and opposition leaders met in Bishkek in May 1997 and established some of the basic principles underlying the peace agreement concluded in June.

There was concern in Kyrgyzstan, however, at increased instances of drugs-trafficking across the border with Tajikistan, and in April 1997 the country signed an agreement with the People's Republic of China, Kazakhstan, Russia and Tajikistan (together constituting the Shanghai Five, later known as the Shanghai Forum), aimed at improving joint border security. In August 2000 Kyrgyzstan and Russia signed a declaration on friendship, alliance and partnership. Despite all these signs of co-operation, however, the continued close ties with Russia had negative consequences, most notably following the economic crisis of late 1998, which caused the Kyrgyz currency to depreciate rapidly.

Thus, some tensions continued to persist between Kyrgyzstan and the other members of the Shanghai Forum, which some critics considered to be dominated by the People's Republic of China. There was criticism of the Government's perceived willingness to accept a Chinese agenda with regard to the Uigurs, in return for that country's support against Islamist rebels, who staged repeated armed incursions into Kyrgyz territory. Tensions also surrounded the further delimitation of the Chinese–Kyrgyz border, and some parliamentary deputies claimed that China had gained excessively from successive deals arranged during the 1990s. The ratification in May 2002 of a border treaty signed in 1999, which ceded almost 95,000 ha of disputed territory to China, prompted widespread protests in Kyrgyzstan (see above). In mid-2001 the Shanghai Forum was renamed the Shanghai Co-operation Organization (SCO), following the accession of Uzbekistan, and the Presidents of the Organization's member countries signed the so-called Shanghai Convention on Combating Terrorism, Separatism and Extremism, under the auspices of which in August 2003 Kyrgyz forces participated in major anti-terrorist manoeuvres, hosted by China and Kazakhstan.

Following the suicide attacks on the USA on 11 September 2001, President Akayev announced that he was prepared to allow US military aircraft to have access to Kyrgyz airspace for the aerial bombardment of al-Qa'ida militants, and their Taliban hosts in Afghanistan. In late November the Government agreed to give the US-led anti-terrorism coalition access to its military bases and, later, its main airport, and in December US aircraft launched attacks on Afghanistan from the former USSR bomber base at Manas; a US military presence remained at the airbase in 2003. In September 2002 Akayev met the US President, George W. Bush, and the US Secretary of State, Colin Powell, in Washington, where they discussed Kyrgyzstan's human rights record, the USA's declared 'war on terrorism', and economic issues. However, the stationing of US troops outside Bishkek led to political tensions, as some observers believed that Akayev's son-in-law had exploited his role in supplying the airbase, and others felt that Kyrgyzstan should not be involved in conflicts on the territory of other Muslim countries. None the less, Akayev used the improved relations with the USA to recreate ties with Russia, and in late 2002 an agreement was signed permitting President Vladimir Putin of Russia to base Russian forces in Kyrgyzstan once again. A Russian airbase at Kant (some 30 km from Manas) opened in October 2003.

## CONCLUSION

At the end of 1991 Kyrgyzstan, under Akayev, seemed to have the best prospect of any former Soviet Central Asian country for the development of a market economy and a democratic polity. Although it lacked the huge potential energy resources of some of its neighbours, the political will to reform was much stronger. More than 10 years after independence the future appeared less clear. The economy was relatively stable, although meeting the social consequences of economic reform had proved difficult, as government revenues were too low to promote adequate welfare provision. In political terms, the country was still more liberal than its neighbours, but full democratization remained distant. Akayev appeared determined to remain in office and, although invested with considerable powers by the Constitution, he still had to renegotiate constantly his relationship with powerful political figures, especially in the regions, where patronage networks retained a high level of control over public life. Parliamentary and presidential elections in 2000, accompanied by numerous violations of electoral practice and the elimination of opposition deputies from parliament, suggested that Kyrgyzstan's democratic image was open to question. Popular opposition to Akayev's presidency became increasingly manifest in the early 2000s, and the apparent undermining of the independent media during 2001, combined with the violent suppression of protests in March 2002 and the flawed referendum of early 2003, indicated an increase in authoritarian trends within the Kyrgyz polity. President Akayev had, in some ways, been bolstered by the US-led war on terrorism, which allowed him to place the country at the disposal of both US and Russian forces, thus disposing their Governments to pay limited attention to internal political developments. It remained to be seen whether Akayev would manage to remain as President after 2005, despite the constitutional ban on standing for a third term of office.

# The Economy

## Dr JOHN ANDERSON

### INTRODUCTION

Prior to independence, Kyrgyzstan remained one of the poorer Soviet republics, heavily reliant on agriculture and dependent for many manufactured goods on other regions of the USSR. At the time of gaining independence in 1991, the country's gross national product (GNP) per head was around US $1,500, and it possessed a rapidly increasing rural population that encountered severe underemployment and an economy that relied heavily on transfers from central funds. Under Askar Akayev, elected President in October 1990, the political élite frequently proclaimed its commitment to a market economy, based upon a variety of forms of ownership, and the country moved more rapidly to implement this vision than did most of its neighbours. In May 1993 Kyrgyzstan was the first regional state to adopt its own currency, and by 1998 the rate of inflation had been reduced to 10.5%, although it rose to 35.9%

in 1999, before continuing to decline, reaching 6.9% in 2001 and less than 3% in 2002. However, as was the case in other member countries of the Commonwealth of Independent States (CIS), economic reform brought with it many problems, some of which originated from the technical difficulties associated with attempts to introduce a capitalist economic system in a country with little prior experience. Equally importantly, problems resulted from the social changes that followed reform, and, in particular, the fact that although a small minority of the population appeared to have benefited, the vast majority struggled to survive in a new context, in which incomes declined dramatically and social-welfare provision decreased.

## ECONOMIC POLICY

From the outset, Akayev was committed to creating a market-dominated economy, in which private enterprise played a central role. Progress towards this objective began in early 1992, when most price controls were removed, although subsidies were maintained on a few essential goods and on utilities. Simultaneously, the Government implemented an austerity programme and declared its intention to privatize state industry. Not everyone was happy with this programme, and both communists and nationalists expressed unease that Western models were being adopted, regardless of local circumstances. The principal problem facing the country in the first two years of independence was the acceleration of inflation levels, from around 200% in 1991 to 900% in 1992. The situation was made worse by the fact that Kyrgyzstan was tied to the 'rouble zone' and subject to its high rates of inflation and to the impact of other countries, which were pursuing a variety of economic policies. In response to this, in May 1993 the Government decided to introduce a national currency, the som, although little thought was given to the likely consequences for either neighbouring states or for Kyrgyz businesses. Following its introduction, Uzbekistan immediately suspended energy deliveries and demanded payment in US dollars, and suppliers in other CIS states refused to accept payment in soms. Yet, although inadequate preparations had been made for the currency's introduction, substantial financial support from the IMF helped to bring a degree of macroeconomic stability to the country and, in the long term, to reduce substantially inflation rates.

A second aspect of Kyrgyzstan's shift to the market economy was its privatization programme. In the initial phase, this entailed selling around one-third of state enterprises and two-thirds of housing stock, within a two-year period. The process took various forms, such as selling to individuals, collective buyouts by the company's management and work-force, and the creation of joint-stock companies. In the first stage, the intention was to reduce state holdings in small enterprises and light industry, as well as in the services sector and in catering. The subsequent objective was to turn to larger industrial units, although certain sectors, including utilities, mineral resources, defence industries and transport, were initially destined to remain under state ownership. In early 1994 vouchers were issued to all citizens, which enabled them to buy shares in various categories of interest, and by the end of 1996 nearly two-thirds of state enterprises were privately owned. At the same time, plans were being developed for the privatization of heavy industry, and even some of those sectors that had previously been excluded, notably the energy and transportation sectors. In the new sales, foreign investors were to be allowed to buy majority shareholdings for the first time, although most potential investors proved to be wary of purchasing, when they knew so little about the Kyrgyz market or the real value of the businesses on offer. Despite a number of scandals, which revolved around the sale of state-owned enterprises at considerably less than their market value, by the end of 1999 at least 75% of former state enterprises were privately owned. However, most observers noted little change in business strategy, and not until the end of the decade did bankruptcy legislation begin to put pressure on the new owners to find ways of operating that were consonant with market principles.

Among the firms that were to be offered for tender in 1999–2000 were the power company, Kyrgyzenergo, the gas provider, Kyrgyzgas, the telecommunications company, Kyrgyztelekom, and the national airline. In practice, however, the privatization of a number of enterprises proved to be politically sensitive, and members of the Zhogorku Kenesh (Supreme Council—the legislature) were especially reluctant to allow land and energy resources to be removed from state control. In February 2001 the Zhogorku Kenesh created a special commission to oversee the privatization of Kyrgyzenergo, and deputies argued for a delay in the privatization process, to allow time for further discussion, in order to ensure that proper control was maintained over the sale of national assets. During 2002 the Government reported the privatization of more than 40 medium-sized enterprises, resulting in just under 60m. soms for the treasury, although the sale of major sections of the energy sector remained politically controversial.

One consequence of these developments was the need to develop a banking and financial system capable of handling the sort of transactions that were central to a market economy. The National Bank was formed shortly after independence, and given broad responsibility for monetary and exchange-rate policy. It also adopted the strict monetary policy demanded by international financial institutions, thereby ensuring the continued approval of the IMF and other agencies. The National Bank also adopted a supervisory role in relation to the rest of the banking sector. A number of private banks were established in the mid-1990s, and by 1998 there were at least 20, although several struggled to survive the consequences of that year's economic crisis in the Far East and in Russia, and there were closures in 1999. From 1994 the central bank took a more active role in regulating the banking sector and it instituted a stricter regulatory framework. In practice, however, this only began to be effective from the beginning of 1997, when the National Bank started to require international accounting procedures to be adopted and to insist on minimum capital requirements. In addition to the National Bank, a number of larger banks secured substantial international shareholdings, and banks based in Europe, Hong Kong (China) and the USA held a controlling interest in some Kyrgyz banks. In addition, there were a number of specialist banks, concentrated, for example, on the rural sector, although such banks tended to attract excessive numbers of unpaid loans. By the early 2000s there were too many banks, and too little capital to sustain their operations.

The creation of a functional stock exchange proved more difficult, as many Kyrgyz businessmen had little understanding of the role of capital and security markets. The Kyrgyz Stock Exchange opened in the same month as that in which the som was issued, but during the first two years of operation the level of trading was very low. In 1997–98 the volume of trading on the stock market increased considerably, with its value rising from around 3m. soms in 1996 to 46m. soms in 1998, and the number of companies listed on the stock exchange rose to 50. However, many informed observers noted a reluctance to 'float' companies, and only around 10% of those companies that possessed the capacity to enter the market were represented. These problems persisted: by the end of 2000 the number of companies listed on the Kyrgyz Stock Exchange had not yet exceeded 1,000, although there was a gradual increase over the next two years.

## AGRICULTURE

Agriculture was the mainstay of the Kyrgyz economy, and by 2002 it provided 38.6% of gross domestic product (GDP). In 2000 the agricultural sector employed just over 50% of the adult population. Traditionally nomadic people, the enforced settlement encouraged first by Russian and then by Soviet rulers had not ended the country's concentration on cattle-herding and related activities. The Kyrgyz farmers also produced a range of crops, including cereals, sugar beet, tobacco, silk, cotton, fruit and vegetables and, more controversially, wild cannabis and opium. Within this sector there was a degree of regional and ethnic differentiation. Ethnic Kyrgyz tended to focus on livestock, especially in the northern and eastern regions. The inhabitants of the south, however, where there were sizeable ethnic Uzbek minorities, were more inclined to settled agriculture, revolving around grain, fruit and vegetables. It was also the case that much agricultural produce was produced in private plots, which, even during the 1970s, were responsible for the production of about 50% of vegetables and 28% of meat.

Following independence, the agricultural sector experienced a series of crises, recording a major decline in output in the first half of the 1990s. According to the IMF, output fell by around 9% in 1990, by 19% in 1992, by 10% in 1993 and by 15% in 1994. Particularly notable was the decline in livestock production in the first half of the decade, as a shortage of fodder and the loss of some export markets led farmers to slaughter their cattle. For example, there was a decline in the number of sheep and goats from 8,745,100 in 1993 to 3,774,000 in 2001. Stocks of larger cattle had also decreased, from 1,112,400 in 1993 to 970,000 in 2001. During 2002 meat production registered a slight increase, of 0.6%, while the production of milk and eggs rose by around 5%, but many problems remained in the agricultural sphere. These difficulties were reportedly made more severe by high levels of corruption, and various officials and agricultural organizations were accused of mismanaging credits and funds provided by overseas donors.

None the less, official figures reported an increase in agricultural output of 15.2% in 1996 and of 12.3% in 1997, although there was a subsequent decline. From 2000 agricultural production increased, rising by 6.8% in 2001, and by 3.3% in 2002. In part, the earlier improvement resulted from the contribution of household plots to production, although a severe drought in 2000 reduced harvests of grain and other crops. Others attributed the apparent recovery to the Government's encouragement of private-sector investment, although the issue of land privatization remained politically sensitive. In early 1994 a presidential decree gave individuals or legal entities the right to lease and cultivate plots for 49 years (subsequently extended to 99 years), and allowed the exchange or sale of leases to other Kyrgyz citizens. At the same time, the distribution of land-use shares contributed to the disintegration of many collective and state farms, and their replacement by agricultural co-operatives. In 2000 it was planned to end the recent moratorium on land sales, as a result of the inadequate regulation of such activity, and to eliminate various state monopolies in the agricultural sector, most notably that imposed on seed production. In February Akayev offered farmers further relief, by revoking a government decree that would have increased the level of land taxation two-fold. None the less, although by that time some 80%–90% of farming took place on leased land, the formal position on land ownership remained ambiguous, with urban dwellers and foreign companies denied the possibility of owning agricultural land.

## MINING AND INDUSTRY

Industry arrived late in Kyrgyzstan, and on the eve of the Russian Revolution only around 1,500 people were employed in the industrial sector. The Second World War (1939–45) provided a stimulus to industrial development, as industries threatened by the German advances were shipped from western Russia to Central Asia, often accompanied by Slavic and European personnel. In Kyrgyzstan most were located in the northern regions, leading to the development of defence-related product and engineering works, with particular focus on the production of cars, machine tools, electrical equipment and torpedoes, which were tested in lake Issyk-Kul. The republic lacked, however, many of the energy resources available in neighbouring states, and although it possessed considerable mineral resources, many of these were located in relatively inaccessible and mountainous areas. Finally, Kyrgyzstan was involved in the processing of materials produced elsewhere in the USSR, notably furniture, textiles and footwear, as well as sugar, shipped from Cuba.

After independence, the single most important sector of the economy was mineral exploitation, and, in particular, the development of the Kumtor gold-mine. With reserves estimated at over 500 metric tons and valued at almost US $7,000m., the field remained undeveloped by the Soviets, who were concerned by the inaccessibility of the site, which was located at an altitude of around 4,000 m (13,123 ft), and by the inadequacy of the transport infrastructure in the region. After 1991, however, the site proved attractive to foreign investors, and a consortium led by the Cameco Corporation (of Canada) quickly assembled proposals for the development of the field. In the early stages of the project there were considerable difficulties, as a series of corruption scandals led many to believe that Kyrgyzstan was benefiting little from the project; however, a later deal ensured that the country would receive 70% of the profits. In January 1997 the first gold began to be produced by the mine, and 500,000 troy ounces were extracted by the end of the first year of operation. Productivity continued to increase in subsequent years, reaching 20.0 metric tons in 1999, 22.0 tons in 2000, and 24.6 tons in 2001. Although the project created several hundred jobs in the republic, there was growing criticism of the working conditions of those involved, and a spillage of industrial cyanide at Barskoon, near lake Issyk-Kul, in May 1998, led to further criticism of safety standards. A further accident in July 2002, together with the need to work less ore-rich seams, led to a 30% decline in production in 2002, which seriously undermined industrial growth in the economy as a whole. In 2003 the Government embarked upon negotiations that would transfer full ownership of the mine to Cameco, in return for a greater share of the profits, but there was growing recognition that, although the operation could provide a partial basis for the reconstruction of the economy, its potential was limited by time constraints, as production was scheduled to decline from around 2004, and to be exhausted by 2010. Therefore, the Government was keen to encourage the development of other gold sources, most notably the smaller Jeruy mine, which commenced operations in 2002.

Other projects that utilized foreign funding were created for the development of mineral resources, notably mercury, for which Kyrgyzstan was among the major sources in the former USSR. Foremost was the Khaidarakan Mercury Plant, the productivity of which increased to nearly 700,000 metric tons per year in the late 1990s, and most of the products of which were exported from the country. Another major source of income was the Kara-Balta Mining Plant, which produced uranium and molybdenum. Production of the latter was planned to increase from 450 tons to 700 tons in 2000—perhaps reaching 60% of capacity—and the same company also began to refine gold. Coal also served as an important energy supply, with around 15% of Kyrgyzstan's energy resources coming from this source in the mid-1990s, and coal production reached 477,300 tons in 2001, compared with 417,000 tons in 1999. The country lacked significant petroleum and gas reserves, although deposits discovered at an oilfield in the west of the country in May 2001 were thought to be sufficient to meet the country's domestic energy requirements for a 20-year period. More importantly, however, Kyrgyzstan had potentially limitless supplies of water and, thus, the potential for the major development of hydroelectric energy, which by the end of the 1990s already supplied around one-quarter of the country's energy needs, although in 2002 electricity production declined by 13%. Under Soviet rule the region's energy supplies were integrated into a common system, but as neighbouring states began to increase their charges for energy supplies it was suggested that Kyrgyzstan should charge more for the water that originated in the republic.

Industrial production was more problematic, and most sectors experienced a dramatic decline after 1991. By the end of the 1990s industrial output was about 60% of its level at the time of the collapse of the USSR. In 1992 production was about 75% that of the previous year, and it continued to decline until 1995, at which point it was less than one-half the level it had been at the time of the Soviet collapse. In 1996 the National Statistical Committee reported an increase in production of around 10%, rising to nearly 50% in 1997, and for some time it appeared that the situation might stabilize. The Russian economic crisis of 1998, however, raised fears of a further decline, and output consequently decreased by 4.0% in 1999. The sector appeared to recover thereafter, however, and industrial GDP increased by 8.9% in 2000 and by 7.1% in 2001. If gold output were discounted, however, the figures suggested that there had, in fact, been a decline, and in 2002 the decline in gold production at the Kumtor mine led to a fall of 13.1% in industrial output, although light industry grew by 8.8%.

## FOREIGN AID, TRADE AND INVESTMENT

From the beginning of Kyrgyzstan's experiment with economic reform, it was hoped that its commitment to the market economy would bring substantial rewards, in terms of both aid and investment. In the former, this hope was realized, to some extent, as the country received more aid per head than any other CIS member state. For example, in the mid-1990s the US Agency for International Development (USAID) provided 16 times more aid per head to Kyrgyzstan than to Uzbekistan. In addition, the country received substantial amounts of aid from the IMF and the World Bank. A series of loans and credits from the former organization served to bolster the introduction of a new currency in 1993, and to support economic reform. An Enhanced Structural Adjustment Facility (ESAF) from the IMF, of US $80m., was arranged in 1998, and in February 2000, following delays in policy implementation resulting from the financial crisis of 1998, the IMF approved the last part of this funding, under the Poverty Reduction and Growth Facility (PRGF—the successor to the ESAF). At the end of 2001 the IMF approved a new, three-year PRGF. Institutions that provided additional support included the Asian Development Bank (ADB), which provided key resources to support agricultural reform and the improvement of transport infrastructure, and the EBRD, which supported the National Bank in opening credit lines for small and medium-sized enterprises, contributed towards the upgrading of the electricity transmission networks, and helped to fund a variety of other commercial activities. The World Bank offered a total of five loans worth just under $100m. for use on projects relating to urban transport, irrigation, agricultural

infrastructure, and the modernization of water supplies and sewage networks.

Although Kyrgyzstan was relatively successful in generating financial aid, it found it harder to attract direct investment. To facilitate this, parliament and the Government approved a series of measures simplifying foreign entry into the local market, sought to improve the legal and regulatory framework, and tried, without a great deal of success, to tackle the corruption that pervaded economic relationships in the region. In 1996 a new Civil Code was introduced in two stages, providing for the proper legal regulation of contracts and giving equal status to foreign and domestic companies. In the early 1990s a series of Free Economic Zones were created in various parts of the country, although tax incentives failed to attract as much outside financing as had been anticipated. In 1997 a Law on Foreign Investment promised non-discrimination against foreign companies, but at the same time abolished the previous five-year tax exemption offered to new investors. Although the Government removed this to prevent local businesses forming joint ventures for tax purposes, it helped to reduce the attractiveness of other aspects of the law.

By far the most successful internationally funded venture was the Kumtor gold-mine, developed by Cameco, with support from Chase Manhattan Bank of the USA and the EBRD. In consequence, Canada accounted for almost one-half of foreign direct investment in the republic in the first half of the 1990s, and it was joined in later years by major investors from the People's Republic of China, Germany, Japan, Switzerland, Turkey and the USA. None the less, foreign investment in the country remained low, amounting to around US $382.7m. in 1993–98, around $42m. in 2000 and some $73m. in 2001. In per head terms, foreign direct investment was lower than that in many other CIS states. In 1997, for example, per-head investment in Kyrgyzstan was $18.4, compared with $82.5 in Kazakhstan and $42.4 in Russia. In 2002 the primary source of income arose from the basing of Western military forces in the country, which provided both direct income and opportunities to various Kyrgyz suppliers.

At least one-half of Kyrgyzstan's economic transactions remained with the countries of the former USSR, and Russia, in particular, acquired controlling shares in a number of Kyrgyz businesses, in particular in the sectors of tobacco and hydroelectric power, in lieu of the payment of debts. In 2002 Kyrgyzstan's major trading partners were the People's Republic of China, Germany, Kazakhstan, Russia, Switzerland, the USA and Uzbekistan; Russia was the largest single supplier of imports (accounting for 19.9%). Exports to Germany, which had accounted for 28.7% of total exports in 2000, had declined to negligible levels by 2002, when Switzerland was the main purchaser of Kyrgyz exports (19.9%). Less quantifiable were the informal relations developing in the region, for alongside recorded economic exchanges, the relatively permeable borders with other Central Asian states meant that agricultural goods, in particular, were sold in a burgeoning, but undocumented, private market. From late 1999 Uzbekistan moved to halt this trade, and for periods of time effectively closed its borders with Kyrgyzstan, leaving many Kyrgyz citizens unable to buy even basic foodstuffs. Even harder to evaluate were the economic activities of the numerous Chinese traders who regularly passed through Kyrgyzstan in order to sell their wares throughout the region.

## PROSPECTS

The consequences of the economic changes in Kyrgyzstan were mixed. An embryonic free market was created, albeit one with high levels of corruption, which inhibited foreign investment. However, for the population as a whole the post-independence period was characterized by a growing divide, between a small minority of those who gained from reform, and the large mass of the population that saw its position worsen. Living standards declined, real incomes decreased by at least 50% and unemployment increased. Official figures recorded unemployment of 152,000 in 2001 (7.8%), but most sources suggested that if the rising population, seasonal employment accompanying agricultural production, and the frequent quasi-closures of industrial enterprises were taken into account, the real figure would be much higher. At the same time, the social-welfare infrastructure declined, as falling state revenues made it impossible for the state to ensure the lifelong provision of earlier years. Thus, by the end of 2001 free schooling had disappeared, and the availability of hospital beds declined dramatically by the end of the 1990s. Problems also arose in health care, from the inability of the authorities to maintain basic water and irrigation facilities, which contributed to poor hygiene and the spread of disease. All of this was made worse by the inflationary pressures of the early 1990s, which seriously affected those on fixed incomes, such as pensioners and the disabled. The human impact of this was hard to assess with any accuracy, as households developed a variety of coping strategies, and in rural areas they became increasingly adept at under-reporting produce to official agencies. Despite these developments of the post-Soviet period there was some evidence that the number of those living in poverty had fallen below 50% of the population by 2002, as low rates of inflation and real wage growth improved the economic situation of some.

At the macroeconomic level, 1996–98 witnessed an expansion, albeit from a low base, with declining inflation and increased output. In 1997 GDP grew by 9.8%, and inflation fell to around 23%. The Russian financial crisis, however, caused progress to slow, and Kyrgyzstan remained highly dependent upon Russia in many sectors. In consequence, GDP growth was only 2.1% in 1998 and 3.6% in 1999. Inflation rose to 35.9% in 1999, and the prices of food and services increased by 41% and more than 35%, respectively, in that year. There was some economic recovery thereafter, and annual inflation had declined to less than 3% by 2002, and there was a concurrent slight increase in GDP, which rose by 5.4% in 2000 and by 5.3% in 2001, but declined by some 0.5% overall in 2002, largely owing to the problems at the Kumtor mine.

Kyrgyzstan had made considerable progress in the transition from functioning as part of a centrally planned economy to operating as an independent, market-based state. Virtually all small and medium-sized enterprises had been privatized, and in 2001–02 over 100 companies, including some major state-owned concerns, were divested. The country's economic recovery remains perhaps over-reliant on the Kumtor gold-mine, and it is not always clear that the Government has fully taken into account the fact that the mine's reserves will eventually be exhausted. During 2003–04 some improvement is likely, given rises in world gold prices and assuming that the Government sustains low inflation levels, but without more successful diversification an over-reliance on gold cannot guarantee a prosperous future for the population of Kyrgyzstan.

# Statistical Survey

Source (unless otherwise stated): National Statistical Committee, 720033 Bishkek, Frunze 374; tel. (312) 22-63-63; fax (312) 22-07-59; e-mail zkudabaev@nsc.bishkek.su; internet nsc.bishkek.su.

## Area and Population

### AREA, POPULATION AND DENSITY

| | |
|---|---|
| Area (sq km) . . . . . . . . | 199,900* |
| Population (census results)† | |
| 12 January 1989 . . . . . . . | 4,257,755 |
| 24 March 1999 | |
| Males . . . . . . . . | 2,380,465 |
| Females. . . . . . . . | 2,442,473 |
| Total . . . . . . . . | 4,822,938 |
| Population (UN estimates at mid-year)‡ | |
| 2000 . . . . . . . . | 4,921,000 |
| 2001 . . . . . . . . | 4,995,000 |
| 2002 . . . . . . . . | 5,067,000 |
| Density (per sq km) at mid-2002 . . . . . . | 25.3 |

* 77,182 sq miles.

† The figures refer to *de jure* population. The *de facto* total was 4,290,442 at the 1989 census and 4,850,700 at the 1999 census.

‡ Source: UN, *World Population Prospects: The 2002 Revision*.

### PRINCIPAL ETHNIC GROUPS
(permanent inhabitants, 1999 census)

| | Number | % |
|---|---|---|
| Kyrgyz . . . . . . . . | 3,128,147 | 64.9 |
| Uzbek . . . . . . . . | 664,950 | 13.8 |
| Russian . . . . . . . . | 603,201 | 12.5 |
| Dungan . . . . . . . . | 51,766 | 1.1 |
| Ukrainian . . . . . . . | 50,442 | 1.0 |
| Uigur . . . . . . . . | 46,944 | 1.0 |
| Tatar . . . . . . . . | 45,438 | 0.9 |
| Kazakh . . . . . . . . | 42,657 | 0.9 |
| Tajik . . . . . . . . | 42,636 | 0.9 |
| Turkish . . . . . . . . | 33,327 | 0.7 |
| German . . . . . . . . | 21,471 | 0.4 |
| Korean . . . . . . . . | 19,784 | 0.4 |
| Others. . . . . . . . | 72,175 | 1.5 |
| **Total** . . . . . . . . | **4,822,938** | **100.0** |

### ADMINISTRATIVE DIVISIONS
(1999 census)

| Oblast | Area (sq km) | Population |
|---|---|---|
| Batken . . . . . . . . | 17,000 | 382,426 |
| Chui . . . . . . . . | 20,200 | 770,811 |
| Issyk-Kul . . . . . . . | 43,100 | 413,149 |
| Jalal-Abad . . . . . . . | 33,700 | 869,259 |
| Naryn . . . . . . . . | 45,200 | 249,115 |
| Osh . . . . . . . . | 29,200 | 1,175,998 |
| Talas . . . . . . . . | 11,400 | 199,872 |
| Bishkek City . . . . . . | 100 | 762,308 |
| **Total** . . . . . . . . | **199,900** | **4,822,938** |

## PRINCIPAL TOWNS
(population at census of March 1999)

| | | | | |
|---|---|---|---|---|
| Bishkek (capital)* | 750,327 | Karakol† | . . . | 64,322 |
| Osh . . . . . | 208,520 | Tokmok | . . . | 59,409 |
| Jalal-Abad . . . | 70,401 | Kara-Balta | . . . | 53,887 |

* Known as Frunze between 1926 and 1991.
† Formerly Przhevalsk.

**Mid-2001** (UN estimate, incl. suburbs): Bishkek 736,000 (Source: UN, *World Urbanization Prospects: The 2001 Revision*).

## BIRTHS, MARRIAGES AND DEATHS*

| | Registered live births | | Registered marriages | | Registered deaths | |
|---|---|---|---|---|---|---|
| | Number | Rate (per 1,000) | Number | Rate (per 1,000) | Number | Rate (per 1,000) |
| 1993 . . | 116,795 | 26.1 | 36,874 | 8.2 | 34,513 | 7.7 |
| 1994 . . | 110,113 | 24.6 | 26,097 | 5.8 | 37,109 | 8.3 |
| 1995 . . | 117,340 | 26.0 | 26,866 | 6.0 | 36,915 | 8.2 |
| 1996 . . | 108,007 | 23.4 | 26,188 | 5.7 | 34,562 | 7.6 |
| 1997 . . | 102,050 | 21.8 | 26,588 | 5.7 | 34,540 | 7.4 |
| 1998 . . | 104,183 | 21.9 | 25,726 | 5.4 | 34,596 | 7.2 |
| 1999 . . | 104,068 | 21.5 | 26,033 | 5.4 | 32,850 | 6.8 |
| 2000 . . | 96,770 | 19.8 | n.a. | n.a. | 34,111 | 7.0 |

* Rates have not been revised to take account of the results of the 1999 census.

Source: UN, *Demographic Yearbook* and *Population and Vital Statistics Report*.

**Expectation of life** (WHO estimates, years at birth): 64.1 (males 60.1; females 68.2) in 2001 (Source: WHO, *World Health Report*).

## ECONOMICALLY ACTIVE POPULATION
(annual averages, '000 persons)

| | 1997 | 1998 | 1999 |
|---|---|---|---|
| Agriculture, hunting and forestry | 815.6 | 835.4 | 923.8 |
| Fishing . . . . . . . | n.a. | n.a. | 0.5 |
| Mining and quarrying . . . . | 8.9 | 8.2 | 9.5 |
| Manufacturing . . . . . | 143.7 | 143.3 | 127.0 |
| Electricity, gas and water supply . | 19.0 | 20.3 | 22.1 |
| Construction . . . . . . | 57.0 | 50.7 | 45.2 |
| Wholesale and retail trade; repair of motor vehicles, motor cycles and personal and household goods . . . . . . | 174.7 | 180.2 | 183.7 |
| Hotels and restaurants . . . . | 12.1 | 13.9 | 11.5 |
| Transport, storage and communications . . . . | 79.3 | 75.2 | 65.8 |
| Financial intermediation . . . | 7.2 | 8.1 | 7.1 |
| Real estate, renting and business activities . . . . . . . | 41.3 | 38.9 | 28.7 |
| Public administration and defence; compulsory social security . . | 60.4 | 63.0 | 65.7 |
| Education . . . . . . . | 139.4 | 139.3 | 140.7 |
| Health and social work . . . . | 88.6 | 84.5 | 85.2 |
| Other services . . . . . | 42.1 | 43.9 | 47.8 |
| **Total employed**. . . . . | 1,689.3 | 1,704.9 | 1,764.3 |
| Males . . . . . . . | 907.9 | 918.7 | 971.6 |
| Females . . . . . . . | 781.4 | 786.2 | 792.7 |

**Registered unemployed** ('000 persons): 54.6 in 1997; 55.9 in 1998; 54.7 in 1999.

Source: ILO, *Yearbook of Labour Statistics*.

**Total unemployed** (estimates, '000 persons, incl. unregistered): 103.0 in 1997; 106.4 in 1998; 136.8 in 1999.

**2000** ('000 persons): Total employed 1,767.1; Total unemployed 144.3.

**2001** ('000 persons): Total employed 1,787.0; Total unemployed 152.0.

# Health and Welfare

## KEY INDICATORS

| | |
|---|---|
| Total fertility rate (childrens per woman, 2001) . . . . | 2.0 |
| Under-5 mortality rate (per 1,000 live births, 2001) . . | 61 |
| HIV/AIDS (% of persons aged 15–49, 2001). . . . . . | <0.10 |
| Physicians (per 1,000 head, 2000) . . . . . . . | 2.92 |
| Hospital beds (per 1,000 head, 1999) . . . . . . | 7.9 |
| Health expenditure (2000): US $ per head (PPP) . . . . | 145 |
| Health expenditure (2000): % of GDP . . . . . . | 6.0 |
| Health expenditure (2000): public (% of total) . . . . . | 61.7 |
| Access to water (% of persons, 2000). . . . . . . | 77 |
| Access to sanitation (% of persons, 2000) . . . . . | 100 |
| Human Development Index (2001): ranking . . . . . | 102 |
| Human Development Index (2001): value . . . . . . | 0.727 |

For sources and definitions, see explanatory note on p. vi.

# Agriculture

## PRINCIPAL CROPS
('000 metric tons)

| | 1999 | 2000 | 2001 |
|---|---|---|---|
| Wheat . . . . . . . | 1,109.1 | 1,039.1 | 1,190.6 |
| Rice (paddy) . . . . . | 15.1 | 19.0 | 16.6 |
| Barley . . . . . . | 179.9 | 150.2 | 139.9 |
| Maize . . . . . . | 308.4 | 338.3 | 442.8 |
| Potatoes . . . . . . | 957.2 | 1,046.0 | 1,168.4 |
| Sugar beet. . . . . . | 536.1 | 449.8 | 286.6 |
| Cabbages . . . . . | 89.4 | 100.5 | 119.1 |
| Tomatoes . . . . . | 138.4 | 155.6 | 165.5 |
| Cucumbers and gherkins* . . . | 117 | 127 | 187 |
| Dry onions . . . . . | 175.6 | 147.4 | 149.2 |
| Carrots . . . . . | 105.4 | 109.4 | 112.5 |
| Other vegetables* . . . . | 94.0 | 107.0 | 90.0 |
| Apples . . . . . | 82.6 | 102.9* | 101.0* |
| Apricots* . . . . . . | 10.0 | 12.6 | 12.3 |
| Grapes . . . . . . | 18.1 | 26.5 | 27.4 |
| Watermelons† . . . . . | 62.8 | 65.3 | 83.5 |
| Cotton (lint) . . . . . | 28* | 19 | 23* |
| Cottonseed . . . . . | 87.0 | 87.9 | 96.2 |
| Tobacco (leaves) . . . . | 29.8 | 34.6 | 24.0 |

* Unofficial figure(s).
† Including melons, pumpkins and squash.

Source: FAO.

## LIVESTOCK
('000 head at 1 January)

| | 1999 | 2000 | 2001 |
|---|---|---|---|
| Horses* . . . . . . . | 336 | 350 | 346 |
| Asses* . . . . . . . | 8 | 8 | 7 |
| Cattle . . . . . . | 911 | 947 | 970 |
| Camels* . . . . . . | 47 | 47 | 46 |
| Pigs . . . . . . | 105 | 101 | 87 |
| Sheep . . . . . . | 3,620† | 3,198 | 3,104 |
| Goats . . . . . . | 191† | 601 | 640 |
| Chickens . . . . . | 2,600† | 3,064 | 3,254 |
| Turkeys . . . . . . | 128† | 140† | 125* |

* FAO estimate(s).
† Unofficial figure.

Source: FAO.

## LIVESTOCK PRODUCTS

('000 metric tons)

| | 1999 | 2000 | 2001 |
|---|---|---|---|
| Beef and veal . . . . . . | 95.1 | 100.6 | 100.1 |
| Mutton and lamb. . . . . | 43.3 | 39.4 | 40.0 |
| Goat meat . . . . . . . | 3.3 | 3.7 | 3.8 |
| Pig meat . . . . . . . | 28.6 | 23.8 | 25.7 |
| Horse meat . . . . . . | 20.3 | 24.2 | 24.6* |
| Poultry meat . . . . . . | 4.5 | 4.6 | 4.9 |
| Cows' milk . . . . . . | 1,041.8 | 1,078.7 | 1,110.4 |
| Cheese . . . . . . . | 2.8 | 3.4 | 3.4 |
| Butter . . . . . . . | 1.2 | 1.4 | 1.9 |
| Hen eggs . . . . . . | 10.8 | 11.4 | 12.7* |
| Honey . . . . . . . | 1.5 | 1.3 | 1.4 |
| Wool: greasy . . . . . | 11.7 | 11.3 | 11.1 |
| Wool: scoured . . . . . | 7.0 | 11.3 | 11.1 |
| Cattle hides† . . . . . | 9.3 | 10.0 | 9.8 |
| Sheepskins . . . . . . | 5.9 | 5.9 | 6.2 |

* Unofficial figure.
† FAO estimates.

Source: FAO.

## Forestry

### ROUNDWOOD REMOVALS

('000 cubic metres, excl. bark)

| | 1997 | 2000* | 2001* |
|---|---|---|---|
| Sawlogs, veneer logs and logs for sleepers . . . . . . . . | 7 | 4 | 5 |
| Other industrial wood . . . . | 1 | 1 | 1 |
| Fuel wood . . . . . . . | 30 | 20 | 16 |
| **Total** . . . . . . . . | 38 | 25 | 22 |

* Unofficial figures.

Source: FAO.

**1998–99:** All production 0 (FAO estimates).

### SAWNWOOD PRODUCTION

('000 cubic metres, incl. railway sleepers, unofficial figures)

| | 1999 | 2000 | 2001 |
|---|---|---|---|
| Coniferous (softwood) . . . . | 9 | 2 | 2 |
| Broadleaved (hardwood). . . . | 14 | 4 | 4 |
| **Total** . . . . . . . . | 23 | 6 | 6 |

Source: FAO.

## Fishing

(FAO estimates, metric tons, live weight)

| | 1998 | 1999 | 2000 |
|---|---|---|---|
| Capture . . . . . . | 80 | 48 | 52 |
| Freshwater bream . . . . | 5 | 3 | 3 |
| Common carp . . . . | 15 | 9 | 10 |
| Silver carp . . . . . | 12 | 7 | 8 |
| Other cyprinids . . . . | 18 | 11 | 12 |
| Pike-perch . . . . . | 3 | 2 | 2 |
| Whitefishes . . . . . | 26 | 15 | 16 |
| Aquaculture . . . . . | 97 | 71 | 58 |
| Common carp . . . . | 50 | 31 | 10 |
| Grass carp . . . . . | 10 | 5 | 5 |
| Silver carp . . . . . | 30 | 35 | 43 |
| Trout . . . . . . | 5 | – | – |
| **Total catch** . . . . . . | 177 | 119 | 110 |

Source: FAO, *Yearbook of Fishery Statistics*.

## Mining

| | 1999 | 2000 | 2001 |
|---|---|---|---|
| Coal ('000 metric tons) . . . . | 417.0 | 424.9 | 477.3 |
| Crude petroleum ('000 metric tons) | 77.0 | 77.1 | 75.5 |
| Natural gas (million cu metres) . | 25.1 | 32.2 | 32.7 |
| Cement . . . . . . . | 386.3 | 452.9 | n.a. |
| Gold (metric tons)* . . . . . | 20.0 | 22.0 | 24.6 |

* Source: Gold Fields Mineral Services, *Gold Survey 2002*.
Source: US Geological Survey.

## Industry

### SELECTED PRODUCTS

('000 metric tons, unless otherwise indicated)

| | 2000 | 2001 | 2002 |
|---|---|---|---|
| Vegetable oil . . . . . . | 8.7 | 6.9 | 9.4 |
| Refined sugar . . . . . . | 58.0 | 30.5 | 51.0 |
| Vodka ('000 hectolitres) . . . | 13.6 | 18.2 | 23.9 |
| Beer ('000 hectolitres) . . . | 12.4 | 8.7 | 7.1 |
| Cigarettes (million) . . . . | 3,168.6 | 3,013.4 | 2,927.3 |
| Textile fabrics ('000 sq metres) . | 8,702.7 | 8,013.0 | 8,517.8 |
| Footwear ('000 pairs) . . . . | 136.9 | 188.7 | 170.6 |
| Motor spirit (petrol) . . . . | 61.9 | 47.8 | 37.8 |
| Gas-diesel (distillate fuel) oil . . | 34.0 | 43.4 | 27.0 |
| Cement . . . . . . . | 452.9 | 468.9 | 532.8 |
| Electric energy (million kWh) . . | 14,931.3 | 13,666.9 | 11,901.8 |

## Finance

### CURRENCY AND EXCHANGE RATES

**Monetary Units**
 100 tyiyns = 1 som.

**Sterling, Dollar and Euro Equivalents** (31 March 2003)
 £1 sterling = 72.02 soms;
 US $1 = 45.59 soms;
 €1 = 41.85 soms;
 1,000 soms = £13.89 = $21.94 = €23.90.

**Average Exchange Rate** (soms per US $)
 2000    47.704
 2001    48.378
 2002    46.937

Note: In May 1993 Kyrgyzstan introduced its own currency, the som, replacing the Russian (former Soviet) rouble at an exchange rate of 1 som = 200 roubles.

### BUDGET

(million soms)*

| Revenue† | 2000 | 2001 | 2002 |
|---|---|---|---|
| Taxation . . . . . . . | 7,675.5 | 9,187.9 | 10,474.7 |
| Personal income taxes . . . | 753.8 | 960.9 | 1,083.3 |
| Profit taxes . . . . . . | 572.8 | 993.7 | 967.6 |
| Value-added tax . . . . . | 2,976.2 | 4,221.4 | 4,793.7 |
| Excises . . . . . . | 1,518.4 | 1,102.6 | 1,082.0 |
| Taxes on international trade and transactions . . . . . . | 275.1 | 301.4 | 418.9 |
| Other current revenue . . . . | 1,581.0 | 2,672.6 | 2,983.9 |
| Capital revenue . . . . . | 23.5 | 57.1 | 129.5 |
| **Total** . . . . . . . . | 9,280.1 | 11,917.7 | 13,588.1 |

| Expenditure‡ | 2000 | 2001 | 2002 |
|---|---|---|---|
| Administration, defence and internal security . . . . . | 3,637.1 | 3,837.5 | 4,310.6 |
| Education . . . . . . | 2,293.0 | 2,847.6 | 3,350.4 |
| Health care . . . . . | 1,295.9 | 1,379.0 | 1,527.2 |
| Social insurance and security . . | 1,113.9 | 1,417.1 | 2,340.5 |
| Housing and public utilities . . | 666.5 | 800.9 | 1,131.2 |
| Subsidies to economic sectors . . | 1,342.7 | 1,423.0 | 1,894.7 |
| **Total** (incl. others) . . . . . | 11,308.2 | 12,255.7 | 15,188.6 |

\* Figures represent a consolidation of the budgetary transactions of the central Government and local governments. The operations of extra-budgetary accounts, including the Social Fund (formed in 1994 by an amalgamation of the Pension Fund, the Unemployment Fund and the Social Insurance Fund), are excluded.
† Excluding grants received (million soms): 608.2 in 2000; 622.0 in 2001; 823.6 in 2002.
‡ Including lending minus repayments.

## INTERNATIONAL RESERVES
(US $ million at 31 December)

| | 2000 | 2001 | 2002 |
|---|---|---|---|
| Gold . . . . . . | 22.8 | 23.0 | 28.5 |
| IMF special drawing rights . . . | 0.7 | 1.3 | 0.6 |
| Foreign exchange . . . . . | 238.3 | 262.2 | 288.2 |
| **Total** . . . . . . | 261.8 | 286.5 | 317.3 |

Source: IMF, *International Financial Statistics*.

## MONEY SUPPLY
(million soms at 31 December)

| | 2000 | 2001 | 2002 |
|---|---|---|---|
| Currency outside banks . . . . | 4,102 | 5,016 | 6,866 |
| Demand deposits at banking institutions . . . . . | 504 | 542 | 811 |
| **Total money** . . . . . . | 4,606 | 5,558 | 7,677 |

Source: IMF, *International Financial Statistics*.

## COST OF LIVING
(Retail price index; base: 1992 = 100)

| | 1999 | 2000 | 2001 |
|---|---|---|---|
| Food . . . . . . | 10,604.7 | 12,679.3 | 13,407.1 |
| Fuel and light . . . . . | 6,040.1 | 8,018.7 | 10,285.1 |
| Clothing . . . . . | 4,748.3 | 5,121.8 | 5,064.4 |
| Rent . . . . . . | 278,485.7 | 255,000.0 | 389,892.9 |
| **All items** (incl. others) . . . . | 11,678.3 | 13,862.4 | 14,821.9 |

Source: ILO.

## NATIONAL ACCOUNTS
(million soms at current prices)

### Expenditure on the Gross Domestic Product

| | 2000 | 2001 | 2002* |
|---|---|---|---|
| Government final consumption expenditure . . . . . . | 13,098.6 | 12,911.7 | 13,578.3 |
| Private final consumption expenditure . . . . . . | 42,929.6 | 47,893.1 | 50,837.8 |
| Increase in stocks . . . . | 1,136.0 | 724.3 | 769.5 |
| Gross fixed capital formation . . | 11,942.1 | 12,574.2 | 13,153.0 |
| Statistical discrepancy . . . . | — | — | −503.6 |
| **Total domestic expenditure** . . | 69,106.3 | 74,103.3 | 77,835.0 |
| Exports of goods and services . . | 27,350.8 | 27,133.4 | 29,562.7 |
| *Less* Imports of goods and services | 31,099.2 | 27,353.4 | 32,157.3 |
| **GDP in purchasers' values** . . | 65,357.9 | 73,883.3 | 75,240.4 |

### Gross Domestic Product by Economic Activity

| | 2000 | 2001 | 2002* |
|---|---|---|---|
| Agriculture . . . . . . | 22,336.0 | 25,518.4 | 26,759.5 |
| Forestry . . . . . . | 37.0 | 36.2 | 38.8 |
| Industry† . . . . . . | 15,261.0 | 16,596.4 | 15,248.9 |
| Construction . . . . . | 2,492.8 | 2,793.8 | 2,931.7 |
| Trade and catering‡ . . . . . | 7,842.5 | 9,118.0 | 9,875.6 |
| Transport and communications . | 2,495.3 | 3,230.5 | n.a. |
| Housing and communal services . | 1,502.4 | 1,848.9 | n.a. |
| Health care, social security, physical culture and sports . . | 1,306.8 | 1,356.4 | n.a. |
| Education . . . . . . | 1,891.5 | 2,219.1 | n.a. |
| Financing and insurance . . . | 286.3 | 806.7 | n.a. |
| General administration, defence and internal security . . . | 4,070.4 | 3,729.1 | n.a. |
| Other branches of material production and services . . . | 1,495.8 | 1,790.0 | n.a. |
| **Sub-total** . . . . . . | 61,017.8 | 69,043.5 | n.a. |
| *Less* Imputed bank service charge | 215.3 | 516.5 | n.a. |
| **GDP at basic prices** . . . . | 60,802.5 | 68,527.0 | 69,390.9 |
| Taxes on products . . . . | 5,001.6 | 5,930.5 | 5,849.5 |
| *Less* Subsidies on products . . . | 446.2 | 574.2 | — |
| **GDP in purchasers' values** . . | 65,357.9 | 73,883.3 | 75,240.4 |

\* Preliminary data.
† Comprising manufacturing (except printing and publishing), mining and quarrying, electricity, gas, water, logging and fishing.
‡ Including material and technical supply.

## BALANCE OF PAYMENTS
(US $ million)

| | 2000 | 2001 | 2002 |
|---|---|---|---|
| Exports of goods f.o.b. . . . . | 510.9 | 480.3 | 498.1 |
| Imports of goods f.o.b. . . . . | −506.9 | −440.4 | −552.1 |
| **Trade balance** . . . . . | 4.0 | 39.9 | −54.0 |
| Exports of services . . . . | 61.8 | 80.3 | 138.4 |
| Imports of services . . . . | −148.8 | −124.7 | −145.5 |
| **Balance on goods and services** | −83 | −4.5 | −61.1 |
| Income (net) . . . . . . | −83.9 | −65.5 | −59.7 |
| **Balance on goods, services and income** . . . . . . | −166.9 | −70.0 | −120.8 |
| Current transfers (net) . . . | 87.4 | 51.1 | 86.1 |
| **Current balance** . . . . . | −79.5 | −18.9 | −34.7 |
| Capital account (net) . . . . | −11.3 | −32.0 | −27.9 |
| Direct investment (net) . . . . | −6.9 | −1.1 | 4.8 |
| Portfolio investment (net) . . . | −1.3 | 1.2 | −12.0 |
| Financial derivatives assets . . | 25.8 | 17.6 | −5.1 |
| Other investment (net) . . . | 46.7 | 14.0 | 83.3 |
| Statistical discrepancy . . . . | 10.3 | 18.6 | 20.8 |
| **Overall balance** . . . . . | −16.2 | −0.6 | 29.2 |

# External Trade

## PRINCIPAL COMMODITIES
(US $ million)

| Imports c.i.f. | 1999 | 2000 | 2001 |
|---|---|---|---|
| Industrial products . . . . . | 568.3 | 513.2 | 453.1 |
| Petroleum and gas . . . . | 118.7 | 120.8 | 111.0 |
| Non-ferrous metallurgy . . . | 22.9 | 13.1 | 24.9 |
| Chemicals . . . . . | 24.5 | 30.5 | 31.0 |
| Fuel . . . . . . | 14.2 | 17.7 | 13.6 |
| Machinery and metalworking . | 202.4 | 150.6 | 103.4 |
| Timber, wood and paper . . . | 19.1 | 25.6 | 20.9 |
| Light industry . . . . . | 38.6 | 38.8 | 32.1 |
| Food and beverages . . . . | 54.2 | 46.9 | 54.7 |
| Medical products . . . . | 42.3 | 28.1 | 26.6 |
| Agricultural products (unprocessed) . . . . | 31.4 | 40.9 | 14.2 |
| **Total** . . . . . . . | 599.7 | 554.1 | 467.2 |

| Exports f.o.b. | 2000 | 2001 | 2002 |
|---|---|---|---|
| Industrial products . . . . | 457.5 | 430.8 | 429.2 |
| Electricity . . . . . | 79.8 | 46.8 | 22.0 |
| Non-ferrous metallurgy . . . | 234.4 | 247.1 | 197.6 |
| Machinery and metalworking . | 53.7 | 59.1 | 55.5 |
| Construction materials . . . | 8.4 | 8.4 | 12.7 |
| Light industry . . . . | 43.9 | 32.1 | 64.9 |
| Food and beverages . . . | 13.5 | 12.4 | 16.9 |
| Agricultural products (unprocessed) . . . . | 46.9 | 45.3 | 56.1 |
| **Total** (incl. others) . . . . . | 504.5 | 476.2 | 485.5 |

## PRINCIPAL TRADING PARTNERS
(US $ million)

| Imports c.i.f. | 2000 | 2001 | 2002 |
|---|---|---|---|
| Belarus . . . . . . . | 3.9 | 6.0 | 5.1 |
| Belgium . . . . . . | 10.7 | 8.4 | 1.6 |
| Canada . . . . . . | 11.3 | 1.9 | 9.0 |
| China, People's Republic . . | 36.9 | 48.5 | 59.1 |
| Finland . . . . . . | 1.9 | 1.4 | 4.5 |
| France . . . . . . . | 5.7 | 4.4 | 5.2 |
| Germany . . . . . . | 25.2 | 24.3 | 31.4 |
| India . . . . . . . | 2.9 | 4.3 | 2.9 |
| Iran . . . . . . . | 8.7 | 6.7 | 4.3 |
| Italy . . . . . . . | 3.8 | 3.0 | 3.6 |
| Japan . . . . . . . | 10.3 | 5.8 | 6.4 |
| Kazakhstan . . . . . | 57.4 | 81.8 | 12.4 |
| Korea, Republic . . . . | 6.8 | 7.8 | 7.0 |
| Netherlands . . . . | 4.8 | 4.0 | 1.6 |
| Russia . . . . . . | 132.6 | 85.1 | 116.7 |
| Sweden . . . . . . | 2.7 | 0.9 | 7.4 |
| Turkey . . . . . . | 26.8 | 15.8 | 17.0 |
| Turkmenistan . . . . | 18.7 | 9.0 | 1.7 |
| Ukraine . . . . . . | 7.0 | 6.2 | 7.8 |
| United Arab Emirates . . . | 7.0 | 6.8 | 7.3 |
| United Kingdom . . . . | 5.6 | 4.8 | 2.8 |
| USA . . . . . . . | 53.8 | 26.8 | 47.4 |
| Uzbekistan . . . . . | 74.6 | 66.7 | 60.1 |
| **Total** (incl. others) . . . . | 554.1 | 467.2 | 586.8 |

| Exports f.o.b. | 2000 | 2001 | 2002 |
|---|---|---|---|
| Afghanistan . . . . . | 4.5 | 1.6 | 4.4 |
| Belarus . . . . . | 3.0 | 3.2 | 1.3 |
| Belgium . . . . . | 0.7 | 0.8 | 3.2 |
| China, People's Republic . . | 44.1 | 19.4 | 41.1 |
| Czech Republic . . . . | 2.7 | 2.1 | 1.9 |
| France . . . . . . | 3.3 | 1.8 | 5.6 |
| Germany . . . . . . | 144.6 | 94.4 | 1.8 |
| India . . . . . . | 0.8 | 1.4 | 6.1 |
| Iran . . . . . . | 6.7 | 8.2 | 4.7 |
| Kazakhstan . . . . . | 33.4 | 39.0 | 36.8 |
| Latvia . . . . . . | 10.5 | 3.4 | 8.7 |
| Mongolia . . . . . | 2.5 | 1.2 | 1.1 |
| Romania . . . . . | 1.2 | 1.3 | 2.6 |
| Russia . . . . . . | 65.1 | 64.5 | 80.0 |
| Switzerland . . . . | 34.1 | 124.2 | 96.4 |
| Tajikistan . . . . . | 7.5 | 6.7 | 10.2 |
| Turkey . . . . . . | 7.2 | 13.8 | 16.4 |
| United Kingdom . . . . | 18.8 | 14.1 | 0.9 |
| USA . . . . . . | 2.8 | 7.1 | 36.1 |
| Uzbekistan . . . . . | 89.4 | 48.0 | 27.8 |
| **Total** (incl. others) . . . . | 504.5 | 476.2 | 485.5 |

## Transport

### RAILWAYS
(traffic)

| | 1998 | 1999 | 2000 |
|---|---|---|---|
| Passenger-km (million) . . . | 59 | 31 | 44 |
| Freight net ton-km (million) . . | 466 | 354 | 348 |

Source: UN, *Statistical Yearbook*.

**ROAD TRAFFIC**
(vehicles in use at 31 December)

| | 1997 | 1998 | 1999 |
|---|---|---|---|
| Passenger cars . . . . . | 176,075 | 187,734 | 187,322 |
| Motorcycles and mopeds . . . | 26,634 | 23,909 | 20,789 |

Source: International Road Federation, *World Road Statistics*.

**CIVIL AVIATION**
(traffic on scheduled services)

| | 1997 | 1998 | 1999 |
|---|---|---|---|
| Kilometres flown (million) . . . | 8 | 9 | 9 |
| Passengers carried ('000) . . . | 423 | 427 | 312 |
| Passenger-km (million) . . . . | 531 | 519 | 532 |
| Total ton-km (million) . . . . | 52 | 60 | 56 |

Source: UN, *Statistical Yearbook*.

## Tourism

**FOREIGN TOURIST ARRIVALS**

| Country of Residence | 1998 | 1999 |
|---|---|---|
| China, People's Republic. . . . . . . . | 6,088 | 6,237 |
| CIS countries* . . . . . . . . . . | 42,027 | 31,158 |
| Germany . . . . . . . . . . . | 822 | 1,695 |
| India . . . . . . . . . . . . | 1,360 | 1,870 |
| Turkey . . . . . . . . . . . | 2,467 | 2,882 |
| USA . . . . . . . . . . . | 696 | 2,868 |
| **Total** (incl. others) . . . . . . . . . | 59,363 | 68,863 |

* Comprising Armenia, Azerbaijan, Belarus, Georgia, Kazakhstan, Moldova, the Russian Federation, Tajikistan, Turkmenistan, Ukraine and Uzbekistan.

**2001** (total arrivals): 69,000.

**Tourism receipts** (US $ million): 8 in 1998; 8 in 2000; 15 in 2001.

Sources: World Tourism Organization, *Yearbook of Tourism Statistics*; World Bank, *World Development Indicators*.

## Communications Media

| | 2000 | 2001 | 2002 |
|---|---|---|---|
| Telephones ('000 main lines in use) . . | 376.1 | 376.1 | 394.8 |
| Mobile cellular telephones ('000 subscribers) . . . . . . . | 9.0 | 27.0 | 53.1 |
| Internet users ('000) . . . . . . | 51.6 | 51.6 | 152.0 |

**Radio receivers** ('000 in use): 520 in 1997.

**Daily newspapers:** 3 (average circulation 67,000) in 1996.

**Non-daily newspapers:** 146 (average circulation 896,000) in 1996.

**Book production:** 351 titles (1,980,000 copies) in 1996.

**Television receivers** ('000 in use): 240 in 2000.

Sources: International Telecommunication Union; UNESCO, *Statistical Yearbook*.

## Education

(1999/2000)

| | Institutions | Teachers | Students |
|---|---|---|---|
| Pre-primary . . . . . . . | 420 | 2,500 | 45,000 |
| Primary . . . . . . . | 1,985 | 19,200 | 466,200 |
| Secondary: general . . . . | n.a. | 36,600 | 633,900 |
| Secondary: vocational . . . | n.a. | 5,100 | 52,200 |
| Higher (all institutions) . . . . | n.a. | 8,400 | 159,200 |

Source: UN, *Statistical Yearbook for Asia and the Pacific*.

**Adult literacy rate** (1999 census): 98.7%.

# Directory

## The Constitution

A new Constitution was proclaimed on 5 May 1993. The following is a summary of its main provisions (including amendments endorsed in referendums held on 22 October 1994, 10 February 1996, 17 October 1998 and 2 February 2003, and other modifications approved by the Constitutional Court):

### GENERAL PROVISIONS

The Kyrgyz Republic (Kyrgyzstan) is a sovereign, unitary, democratic republic founded on the principle of lawful, secular government. All state power belongs to the people, who exercise this power through the state bodies, on the basis of the Constitution and laws of the republic, and through the bodies of self-governance. Matters of legislation and other issues pertaining to the state may be decided by the people by referendum. The President of the Republic, the deputies of the Zhogorku Kenesh (Supreme Council), and representatives of local administrative bodies are all elected directly by the people. Elections are held on the basis of universal, equal and direct suffrage by secret ballot. All citizens of 18 years and over are eligible to vote.

The territory of the Kyrgyz Republic is integral and inviolable. The state languages are Kyrgyz and Russian. The equality and free use of other languages are guaranteed. The rights and freedoms of citizens may not be restricted on account of ignorance of the state language.

### THE PRESIDENT

The President of the Kyrgyz Republic is Head of State and Commander-in-Chief of the Armed Forces, and represents Kyrgyzstan both within the country and internationally. Any citizen of the republic between the ages of 35 and 65, who has a fluent command of the state language, may stand for election. The President's term of office is five years; he/she may not serve more than two consecutive terms. The President is directly elected by the people.

The President appoints and dismisses (subject to approval by the legislature) the Prime Minister; appoints the other members of the Government, as well as heads of administrative offices and other leading state posts; presents draft legislation to the Zhogorku Kenesh on his/her own initiative; signs legislation approved by the Zhogorku Kenesh or returns it for further scrutiny; signs international agreements; may call referendums on issues of state; may dissolve the legislature (should a referendum demand this) and call fresh elections; announces a general or partial mobilization; and declares a state of war in the event of an invasion by a foreign power.

### ZHOGORKU KENESH
#### (SUPREME COUNCIL)

Supreme legislative power is vested in the 105-member Zhogorku Kenesh, which comprises two chambers: the 45-member Legislative Assembly (lower chamber), which is a permanent chamber, and the 60-member People's Assembly (upper chamber), which sits twice yearly and represents regional interests. Members of both chambers are elected for a term of five years on the basis of universal, equal and direct suffrage by secret ballot.

The Zhogorku Kenesh approves amendments and additions to the Constitution; enacts legislation; confirms the republican budget and supervises its execution; determines questions pertaining to the administrative and territorial structure of the republic; designates presidential elections; approves the appointment of the Prime Minister, as nominated by the President; approves the appointment of the Procurator-General, the Chairman of the Supreme Court and the Chairman of the National Bank, as nominated by the President; ratifies or abrogates international agreements, and decides questions of war and peace; and organizes referendums on issues of state.

From 2005 the Zhogorku Kenesh was to be transformed into a unicameral assembly, with one member (rather than two) from each electoral district.

### THE GOVERNMENT

The Government of the Kyrgyz Republic is the highest organ of executive power in Kyrgyzstan. The Prime Minister heads the Government, which also comprises Deputy Prime Ministers and Ministers. The members of the Government are appointed by the President; however, the President's appointment of the Prime Minister depends upon approval by the Zhogorku Kenesh. The President supervises the work of the Government and has the right to chair its sessions. The Prime Minister must deliver an annual report to the Zhogorku Kenesh on the work of the Government.

The Government determines all questions of state administration, other than those ascribed to the Constitution or to the competence of the President and the Zhogorku Kenesh; drafts the republican budget and submits it to the Zhogorku Kenesh for approval; co-ordinates budgetary, financial, fiscal and monetary policy; administers state property; takes measures to defend the country and state security; executes foreign policy; and strives to guarantee the rights and freedoms of the citizens and to protect property and social order.

### JUDICIAL SYSTEM

The judicial system comprises the Constitutional Court, the Supreme Court, the Higher Court of Arbitration and regional courts. Judges of the Constitutional Court are appointed by the Zhogorku Kenesh, on the recommendation of the President, for a term of 15 years, while those of the Supreme Court and the Higher Court of Arbitration are appointed by the Zhogorku Kenesh, on the recommendation of the President, for ten years. The Constitutional Court is the supreme judicial body protecting constitutionality. It comprises the Chairman/woman, his/her deputies and seven judges. The Supreme Court is the highest organ of judicial power in the sphere of civil, criminal and administrative justice.

## The Government

### HEAD OF STATE

**President of the Kyrgyz Republic:** ASKAR AKAYEV (elected 28 October 1990; re-elected, by direct popular vote, 12 October 1991, 24 December 1995 and 29 October 2000).

### GOVERNMENT
(October 2003)

**Prime Minister:** NIKOLAI TANAYEV.

**First Deputy Prime Minister and Minister of Justice:** KURMANBEK OSMONOV.

**Deputy Prime Minister:** BAZARBAY MAMBETOV.

**Deputy Prime Minister and Minister of Economic Development and Investments:** DZHOOMART OTORBAYEV.

**Deputy Prime Minister and Minister of Transport and Communications:** KUBANYCHBEK ZHUMALIYEV.

**Minister of Foreign Trade and Industry:** SADRIDDIN DZHIYENBEKOV.

**Minister of Agriculture, Water Resources and Processing Industry:** ALEKSANDR KOSTYUK.

**Minister of Foreign Affairs:** ASKAR AITMATOV.

**Minister of Education and Culture:** ISHENKUL BOLDZHUROVA.

**Minister of Health:** MITALIP MAMYTOV.

**Minister of Finance:** BOLOT ABILDAYEV.

**Minister of Labour and Social Welfare:** ROZA AKNAZAROVA.

**Minister of Internal Affairs:** BAKIRDIN SUBANBEKOV.

**Minister of Defence:** Maj.-Gen. ESEN TOPOYEV.

**Minister of Local Self-Government and Regional Development Affairs:** TOLOBEK OMURALIYEV.

**Minister of Ecology and Emergency Situations:** SATYVALDY CHYRMASHEV.

**Chief of Presidential Administration:** BEKBOLOT TALGARBEKOV.

### HEADS OF GOVERNMENT BODIES

**National Bank:** ULAN SARBANOV.

**National Security Service:** KALYK IMANKULOV.

**State Secretary:** OSMONAKUN IBRAIMOV.

**State Committee for Management of State Property and Attraction of Direct Investment:** RAVSHAN ZHEYENBEKOV.

**State Agency for Registration of Real Estate Rights:** TOLOBEK OMURALIYEV.

**State Agency for Tourism, Sport and Youth Policy:** OKMOTBEK ALMAKUCHUKOV.

**State Agency for Science and Intellectual Property:** ROMAN OMOROV.

**State Agency for Standardization and Meteorology:** BATYRBEK DAVLESOV.

**State Agency for Geology and Mineral Resources:** SHEISHENALY MURZAGAZIYEV.

**State Agency for Power Engineering:** ULARBEK MATEYEV.

**State Border Service:** KALMURAT SADIYEV.

**State Commission for Anti-monopoly Policy:** EMILBEK UZAKBAYEV.

**State Commission for Architecture and Construction:** ANVAR TURSONOV.

**State Commission for Business Development:** KAMILA KENENBAYEVA.

**State Commission for Drugs Control:** KURMANBEK KUBATBEKOV.

**State Commission for Religious Affairs:** OMURZAK MAMAYUSUPOV.

**State Commission for Standards, Financial Accounts and Auditing:** KANATBEK SAGYNOV.

**State Securities Commission:** URAN ABDYNASYROV.

**State Communications Agency:** ANDREI TITOV.

### MINISTRIES

**Office of the President:** 720003 Bishkek, Govt House, Dom Pravitelstva; tel. (312) 21-24-66; fax (312) 21-86-27; e-mail office@mail.gov.kg; internet www.president.kg.

**Office of the Prime Minister:** 720003 Bishkek, Govt House; tel. (312) 22-56-56; fax (312) 21-86-27; internet www.gov.kg/prime.htm.

**Office of the First Deputy Prime Minister:** 720003 Bishkek, Govt House; tel. (312) 21-89-35 (Economic Policy Dept); tel. 21-16-52 (Social Policy Dept); fax (312) 21-86-27 (Agriculture Dept); internet www.gov.kg/vicep.htm.

**Ministry of Agriculture, Water Resources and Processing Industry:** 720040 Bishkek, Kievskaya 96A; tel. (312) 62-36-33; fax (312) 62-36-32; e-mail mawr@bishkek.gov.kg.

**Ministry of Defence:** 720001 Bishkek, Logvinenko 26; tel. (312) 22-78-79; e-mail ud@bishkek.gov.kg.

**Ministry of Ecology and Emergency Situations:** 720055 Bishkek, Aliyaskara Toktonaliyeva 2/1; e-mail admin@mecd.bishkek.gov.kg.

**Ministry of Economic Development and Investments:** Bishkek.

**Ministry of Education and Culture:** 720040 Bishkek, Tynystanova 257; tel. (312) 26-31-52; fax (312) 22-86-04; e-mail monk@monk.bishkek.gov.kg.

**Ministry of Finance:** 720040 Bishkek, pr. Erkindik 58; tel. (312) 22-89-22; fax (312) 22-74-04; e-mail postmaster@mf.bishkek.gov.kg; internet www.minfin.kg.

**Ministry of Foreign Affairs:** 720050 Bishkek, Razzakova 59; tel. (312) 22-05-45; fax (312) 26-36-39; e-mail postmaster@mfa.bishkek.gov.kg.

**Ministry of Foreign Trade and Industry:** 720002 Bishkek, pr. Chui 106; tel. (312) 22-38-66; fax (312) 22-07-93; e-mail postmaster@mvtp.bishkek.gov.kg; internet mvtp.bishkek.gov.kg.

**Ministry of Health:** 720040 Bishkek, Moskovskaya 148; tel. (312) 22-86-97; fax (312) 22-84-24; e-mail minzdrav@minzdrav.bishkek.gov.kg; internet www.med.kg.

**Ministry of Internal Affairs:** 720040 Bishkek, Frunze 469; tel. (312) 22-38-66; fax (312) 22-32-78; e-mail mail@mvd.bishkek.gov.kg.

**Ministry of Justice:** 720321 Bishkek, Orozbekova 37; tel. (312) 22-84-89; fax (312) 26-11-15; e-mail minjust@bishkek.gov.kg; internet www.minjust.bishkek.gov.kg.

**Ministry of Labour and Social Welfare:** 720041 Bishkek, Tynystanova 215; tel. (312) 26-42-50; e-mail mlsp@mlsp.kg; internet mlsp.bishkek.gov.kg.

**Ministry of Local Self-Government and Regional Development Affairs:** 720040 Bishkek, Orozbekova 44; e-mail gosreg@bishkek.gov.kg.

**Ministry of Transport and Communications:** 720017 Bishkek, Isanova 42; tel. (312) 61-04-72; fax (312) 66-47-81; e-mail mtk@mtk.bishkek.gov.kg; internet www.mtk.bishkek.gov.kg.

# President and Legislature

## PRESIDENT

### Presidential Election, 29 October 2000

| Candidates | % of votes |
|---|---|
| Askar Akayev | 74.5 |
| Omurbek Tekebayev | 13.9 |
| Almazbek Atambayev | 6.0 |
| Melis Eshimkanov | 1.1 |
| Bakir Ulu Tursunbay | 1.0 |
| Tursunbek Akunov | 0.4 |
| Blank or spoiled | 3.1 |
| **Total** | **100.0** |

### ZHOGORKU KENESH
### (SUPREME COUNCIL)

The Zhogorku Kenesh is a bicameral legislative body, comprising the People's Assembly and the Legislative Assembly.

**People's Assembly and Legislative Assembly:** 720003 Bishkek, Kirova 205; tel. (312) 22-55-23; fax (312) 22-24-04; e-mail postmaster@kenesh.gov.kg; internet kenesh.bishkek.gov.kg.

**Chairman (Speaker) of People's Assembly:** ALTAI BORUBAYEV.

**Chairman (Speaker) of Legislative Assembly:** ABDYGANY ERKEBAYEV.

Elections were held to both chambers of the Zhogorku Kenesh on 20 February 2000, with a second round of voting ('run-off' elections) held on 12 March.

### General Election, 20 February and 12 March 2000*

| Parties and blocs | Party-list seats | Single-mandate constituency seats | Total seats |
|---|---|---|---|
| Union of Democratic Forces | 4 | 8 | 12 |
| Party of Communists of Kyrgyzstan | 5 | 1 | 6 |
| My Country Party of Action | 1 | 3 | 4 |
| Ata-Meken Socialist Party | 1 | 1 | 2 |
| Democratic Women's Party of Kyrgyzstan† | 2 | — | 2 |
| Party of Veterans of the War in Afghanistan | 2 | — | 2 |
| Poor and Unprotected People's Party | — | 2 | 2 |
| Agrarian Labour Party of Kyrgyzstan | — | 1 | 1 |
| Erkin Kyrgyzstan Progressive and Democratic Party | — | 1 | 1 |
| Independents | — | 73 | 73 |
| **Total** | **15** | **90** | **105** |

*Election results include both the People's Assembly (the 45-member upper chamber) and the Legislative Assembly (the 60-member lower chamber).

† In August 2000 it was reported that the two seats gained by representatives of the Democratic Women's Party of Kyrgyzstan had been withdrawn, owing to the violation of regulations during the nomination process.

# Local Government

In March 1996 the heads of local administrations, who represent main executive authority, were given extended powers and renamed akims (governors). In April a resolution in the legislature made provision for the reorganization of regional soviets into regional governments, with governors to be appointed locally. For the purposes of local government, Kyrgyzstan is divided into seven dubans (oblasts) and the metropolitan region of Bishkek. Local elections took place in two rounds in December 2001.

**Batken Duban:** 722720 Batken, ul. Lenina 1; tel. (325) 42-30-20; fax (325) 42-36-85; Akim MAMAT M. AYBALAYEV.

**Bishkek City:** Bishkek; tel. (312) 21-72-34; internet www.bishkek.kg.

**Chui Duban:** 722003 Bishkek, ul. Abdymomunov 205; tel. (312) 22-65-20; fax (312) 22-54-93; Akim TOYCHUBEK K. KASIMOV.

**Issyk-Kul Duban:** 722360 Karakol, ul. 3 Internatsionala 105; tel. (392) 22-32-20; fax (392) 22-22-27; Akim EMILBEK ANAPIYEYEV.

**Jalal-Abad Duban:** 715600 Jalal-Abad (Dzhalal-Abad), Erkindik 11; tel. (372) 25-00-01; fax (372) 25-51-96; e-mail djalal-abad@bishkek.gov.kg; internet djalal-abad.gov.kg; Akim JUSUPBEK SHARIPOV.

**Naryn Duban:** 722600 Naryn, ul. Lenina 76; tel. (352) 25-00-15; fax (352) 25-08-78; Akim ASKAR M. SALYMBEKOV.

**Osh Duban:** 714018 Osh, ul. Lenina 221; tel. (322) 25-55-55; fax (322) 25-92-00; e-mail governor@osh.gov.kg; internet www.osh.gov.kg; Akim NAKEN K. KASIYEV.

**Talas Duban:** 722720 Talas, ul. Frunze 287; tel. (342) 25-30-94; fax (342) 25-29-53; Akim KENESH K. KANACHALOV.

## Political Organizations

**Adilettuuluk (Justice):** Cholpon-Ata; f. 1999 to campaign for the rights of national minorities; Leader MARAT SULTANOV; Dep. Leader BOLOT KARABALAYEV.

**Agrarian Labour Party of Kyrgyzstan:** Bishkek, Kievskaya 120; tel. (312) 26-58-13; f. 1994; Chair. U. S. SYDYKOV.

**Agrarian Party of Kyrgyzstan:** Bishkek, Kievskaya 96; tel. (312) 22-68-52; f. 1993; represents farmers' interests; Chair. E. ALIYEV.

**Ar-Namys (Dignity) Party:** Bishkek, Isanova 60; e-mail info@ar-namys.org; internet www.ar-namys.org; f. 1999; moderate opposition party; Chair. FELIKS KULOV (imprisoned); Leader EMIL ALIYEV (acting).

**Asaba (Banner) Party of National Revival:** Bishkek, pr. Chui 26; tel. (312) 43-04-45; fax (312) 28-53-64; f. 1991; nationalist party; Chair. CHAPRASHTY BAZARBAYEV.

**Ashar:** Bishkek, pr. Molodoi Gvardii 132; tel. (312) 25-71-88; f. 1989; socio-political movement concerned with development of a parliamentary state and with the revival of national architecture; Chair. ZHUMAGAZY USUP-CHONAIU.

**Ata-Meken (Fatherland) Socialist Party:** Bishkek, bul. Erkindik 38; tel. (312) 27-17-79; f. 1992; nationalist; Leader ONURBEK TEKEBAYEV.

**Birimdik Party:** 720040 Bishkek, Tynystanova 249; tel. (312) 66-38-12; fax (312) 66-29-50; e-mail birimdik_party@mail.ru; f. 1994; seeks to unite people within a democratic movement; Chair. KARYPBEK ALYMKULOV.

**Communist Party of Kyrgyzstan (CPK):** Bishkek, Panfilov 242/12; tel. (312) 22-25-80; f. 1999, following split from the Party of Communists of Kyrgyzstan; Chair. KLARA ADZHIBEKOVA.

**Democratic Movement of Kyrgyzstan (DMK):** Bishkek, Abdymomunova 205; tel. (312) 27-14-95; f. 1990; registered as a political party in 1993; campaigns for civil liberties; Pres. DZHYPAR DZHEKSHEYEV.

**Democratic Party of Economic Unity:** Bishkek, Popova 4; f. 1994; Chair. A. D. TASHTANBEKOV.

**Economic Revival Party:** Chui Duban, Sokuluk raion, vil. Voenno-Antonovka; f. 1998; Leader VALERII KHON.

**El (Beibecharalai) Partiyasy:** Bishkek, Moskovskaya 172; tel. (312) 21-59-64; f. 1995; Chair. DANIYAR USENOV.

**Emgekchil (Working People) el Partiyasy:** Bishkek, Microdistrict 5/43; tel. (312) 66-56-95; f. 1997; supports the democratic movement and private ownership; Chair. E. O. OMURAKUNOV.

**Erkin (Free) Kyrgyzstan Progressive-Democratic Party (ERK):** Bishkek, Abdymomunova 207; tel. (312) 22-49-57; fax (312) 22-60-35; f. 1991; social-democratic party; Chair. BAKIR ULU TURSUNBAY.

**Erkindik (Liberty):** Bishkek; f. 2000 following a split from the ERK; Chair. TOPCHUBEK TURGUNALIYEV.

**Islamic Democratic Party:** Bishkek; f. 2002; Leader NARKAS MULLADZHANOV.

**Kayran El (Poor Nation) Party:** Bishkek, 8 Microdistrict 29/12; registered in 1999; nationalist; Leader TOKTOBAY MULKUBATOV.

**Kok-Zhar Sociopolitical Organization:** Bishkek, Mikroraion 7-34-64; f. 1992; seeks to provide housing for the underprivileged; Chair. ZH. ISAYEV.

**Kyrgyz Committee for Human Rights:** Bishkek, Kievskaya 96; e-mail chrights@imfiko.bishkek.su; internet www.kchr.elcat.kg; banned by the Ministry of Justice in Oct. 1998, re-registered in Aug. 1999 following international pressure; Chair. BOLOT TYNALIYEV.

**Manas:** Bishkek; f. 2000; electoral bloc formed prior to Feb. 2000 parliamentary election; composed of the Republican Popular Party and the Party for the Protection of the Interests of Industrial Workers, Farmers and Poor Families.

**My Country Party of Action:** 720040 Bishkek, Tynystanova 110; tel. (312) 22-75-81; e-mail mstrana@hotmail.com; internet www.strana.kg; f. 1998; 670 mems; Chair. DZHOOMART OTARBAYEV; Leader ALMAZBEK ISMANKULOV.

**National Unity Democratic Movement:** Bishkek, bul. Erkindik 41-17; tel. (312) 22-50-84; f. 1991; seeks to unite different ethnic groups; Chair. YU. RAZGULYAYEV.

**Party of Communists of Kyrgyzstan (KCP):** Bishkek, bul. Chui, rm 414; tel. (312) 22-56-20; formerly known as the Communist Party; disbanded 1991, re-established 1992; 25,000 mems; Chair. ABSAMAT M. MASALIYEV.

**Party for the Protection of the Interests of Industrial Workers, Farmers and Poor Families:** Bishkek, pr. Mira 1; tel. (312) 21-58-42; f. 1996; promotes social and economic reforms; Chair. AKBARALY AITIKEYEV.

**Party for Destitute People:** Bishkek, Turusbekov 172, 4th Floor; tel. (312) 21-59-64; registered in 1995; reform of government and the judiciary; Leader DANIYAR USENOV.

**Party of Veterans of the War in Afghanistan and of Participants in Other Local Conflicts:** Bishkek, bul. Chui A; tel. (312) 53-02-15; registered in 1994; Leader AKBOKON TASHTANBEKOV.

**Patriotic Party of Kyrgyzstan:** Bishkek; f. 1998; not registered with the Ministry of Justice; Leader NAZARBEK NYSHANOV.

**People's Congress:** Bishkek; f. 2001 as an opposition alliance; Chair. FELIKS KULOV (imprisoned).

**People's Mother:** Bishkek; f. 2000 to encourage women from all social backgrounds to take part in politics.

**People's Patriotic Movement:** Bishkek; f. 2001; alliance of the Agrarian Labour Party, the Ar-Namys (Dignity) Party, the Ata-Meken (Fatherland) Socialist Party, the Communist Party of Kyrgyzstan, Erkindik, Kairan-El, the Party of Communists of Kyrgyzstan, the People's Party and the Republican Party; aims to defend democracy and human rights.

**Republican Movement for the Union and Brotherhood of Nations:** Bishkek, pr. Chui 114; tel. (312) 22-16-49; Chair. K. AJIBEKOVA.

**Republican Party of Kyrgyzstan (RPK):** tel. (312) 22-14-16; registered in 1999; advocates parliamentary republicanism; Chair. GIYAZ TOKOMBAYEV; Leader ZAMIRA SIDIKOVA.

**Republican Party of Kyrgystan (Adilet):** Bishkek, Bokonbayev 109; tel. (312) 66-48-17; fax (312) 66-50-84; f. 1999; campaigns for economic reform, modernization and investment; Chair. CHINGIZ T. AITMATOV.

**Republican People's Party:** Bishkek, Kievskaya 77; tel. (312) 22-25-65; f. 1992 by prominent scientists and academics; centrist; Chair. ZH. TENTIYEV.

**Slavic Association Soglasiye (Accord):** Bishkek; f. 1994 to eliminate causes of Russian emigration and to preserve Russian community in Kyrgyzstan; Vice-Pres. ANATOLII BULGAKOV.

**Social Democratic Party of Kyrgyzstan:** Bishkek, Alma-Atinskaya 4B/203; tel. (312) 43-15-07; f. 1994; Leader ABDYGANY ERKEBAYEV.

**Union of Democratic Forces:** Bishkek; f. 1999; pro-Government electoral alliance formed prior to Feb. 2000 parliamentary election; composed of the Social Democratic Party of Kyrgyzstan, the Economic Revival Party and the Birimdik Party.

**Unity Party of Kyrgyzstan:** Bishkek, Tynystanova 249; tel. (312) 22-88-62; fax (312) 22-87-65; f. 1994; anti-nationalist; Leader AMANGELDY MURALIEV.

**Women's Democratic Party of Kyrgyzstan:** Bishkek, Abdymomunova 207; tel. (312) 27-16-81; f. 1994 to encourage the participation of women in politics; Chair. TOKON ASANOVNA SHAILIYEVA.

**Youth Party of Kyrgyzstan:** Bishkek; Leader AIDAR BAKIYEV.

## Diplomatic Representation

### EMBASSIES IN KYRGYZSTAN

**Afghanistan:** Bishkek, Aini 4; tel. (312) 42-63-72; fax (312) 54-34-28; Ambassador ABDULKADYR DOSTUM.

**Belarus:** Bishkek, Moskovskaya 210; tel. (312) 24-29-43; Ambassador ALYAKSANDR KOZYR.

**China, People's Republic:** Bishkek, Toktogula 196; tel. (312) 22-24-23; Ambassador ZHANG YANNIAN.

**Egypt:** Bishkek; Ambassador MUHAMMAD NABIL ABDEL AZI FEDAUI.

**France:** Bishkek, Manas 43; tel. (312) 66-00-53; Ambassador SERGE SMESSOW.

**Germany:** 720040 Bishkek, Razzakova 28; tel. (312) 66-66-24; fax (312) 66-66-30; e-mail gerembi@elcat.kg; internet www .deutschebotschaft.bishkek.kg; Ambassador KLAUS ACHENBACH.

**India:** Bishkek, pr. Chui 164A , Hotel Bishkek; tel. (312) 21-08-63; fax (312) 66-07-08; e-mail india@elcat.kg; Ambassador APPUNNI RAMESH.

**Iran:** Bishkek, Razzakova 36; tel. (312) 22-69-64; Ambassador JAVAD HAJ-SAYYED-JAVADI.

**Japan:** Bishkek; Ambassador TOSHIO TSUNOZAKI.

**Kazakhstan:** Bishkek, Togolok Moldo 10; tel. (312) 22-54-63; Ambassador UMARZAK UZBEKOV.

**Myanmar:** Bishkek.

**Pakistan:** Bishkek, Serova-Bailonova 37; tel. (312) 22-72-09; fax (312) 66-15-50; e-mail parepbishkek@exnet.kg; internet www .pakemb.com.kg; Ambassador MOHAMMAD ALAM BRAHIM.

**Russia:** Bishkek, Razzakova 17; tel. (312) 22-16-91; fax (312) 22-18-23; e-mail rusemb@imfiko.bishkek.su; Ambassador YEVGENII SHMAGIN.

**Turkey:** 720001 Bishkek, Moskovskaya 89; tel. (312) 22-78-82; fax (312) 26-88-35; Ambassador MUSTAFA EROKTEM.

**Ukraine:** 720000 Bishkek, bul. Pushkina 70; tel. (312) 66-55-90; e-mail emb_kg@mfa.gov.ua; Ambassador (vacant).

**USA:** 720016 Bishkek, pr. Mira 171; tel. (312) 55-12-41; fax (312) 55-12-64; e-mail mukambaevaibx@state.gov; Ambassador STEPHEN YOUNG.

**Uzbekistan:** 720040 Bishkek, Tynistanova 213; tel. (312) 66-20-65; fax (312) 66-44-03; e-mail uzbembish@infotel.kg; Ambassador ALISHER SALAHITDINOV.

# Judicial System

(see under Constitution, above)

**Chairman of the Constitutional Court:** CHOLPON BAYEKOVA.

**Chairman of the Supreme Court:** NELYA BEYSHENALIYEVA.

**Prosecutor-General:** MYKTYBEK ABDYLDAYEV.

# Religion

**State Commission for Religious Affairs:** 720040 Bishkek, Kievskaya 90; e-mail mail@religion.bishkek.gov.kg; Chair. OMURZAK MAMAYUSUPOV.

## ISLAM

The majority of Kyrgyz are Sunni Muslims (Hanafi school), as are some other groups living in the republic, such as Uzbeks and Tajiks. Muslims in Kyrgyzstan are officially under the jurisdiction of the Muslim Board of Central Asia, based in Uzbekistan. The Board is represented in the country by a kazi.

**Kazi of Muslims of Kyrgyzstan:** Mullah ABDYSATAR.

**Mufti of the Spiritual Directorate of Kyrgyzstan Muslims:** Haji MURTALY AJI JUMANOV.

**Islamic Centre of Kyrgyzstan:** Osh; Pres. Haji SADYKZHAN KAMALOV.

## CHRISTIANITY

### Roman Catholic Church

The Church is represented in Kyrgyzstan by a Mission, established in December 1997. There were an estimated 300 adherents at 31 December 2001.

**Superior:** Rev. Fr ALEKSANDR KAN, 720072 Bishkek, Vasilyeva 203; tel. and fax (312) 21-78-32; e-mail church@freenet.kg.

# The Press

In 1996 there were 146 non-daily newspapers published in Kyrgyzstan, and the average circulation per issue was 896,000 copies. There were three daily newspapers published in that year, with an average circulation of 67,000 copies.

## PRINCIPAL NEWSPAPERS

**Asaba** (The Standard): Bishkek; tel. (312) 26-47-39; weekly; Kyrgyz; publication resumed in Oct. 2001, after having been suspended for seven months; Editor JUMABEK MEDERALIYEV; circ. 10,000.

**Bishkek Observer:** 720000 Bishkek, Ibraimora 105; tel. (312) 29-28-21; e-mail observer@elcat.kg; independent; Russian and English; Editor AVTAR SINGH.

**Bishkek Shamy** (Bishkek Evening Newspaper): Bishkek, Pravdi 24; tel. (312) 72-57-80; f. 1989; daily; official organ of the Bishkek City Council; Kyrgyz; Editor ABDIDJAPAR SOOTBEKOV; circ. 10,000.

**Char Tarap** (Echo of Events): Bishkek; tel. (312) 28-94-63; f. 1994; weekly; Kyrgyz; Editor KALEN SYDYKOVA; circ. 5,000; parallel edition in Russian, *Ekho Sobytii*; Editor MURSURKUL KABYLBEKOV.

**Chui Baayni:** Bishkek, Ibraimova 24; tel. (312) 42-83-31; weekly; Kyrgyz; Editor KURMANBEK RAMATOV.

**Chuskye Izvestiya** (Chui News): Bishkek, pr. Erkindik 45; tel. (312) 42-83-31; weekly; Russian; Editor D. PARCHUKOV.

**Delo No** (Case Number): Bishkek; tel. (312) 22-84-62; fax (312) 66-36-03; e-mail delo@transfer.kg; internet delo.to.kg; f. 1991; weekly; Russian; opposition; Editor VIKTOR ZAPOLSKII; circ. 50,000.

**Erkin Too:** Bishkek, Ibraimova 24; tel. (312) 42-03-15; 3 a week; Kyrgyz; Editor MELIS AYDAPKYLOV.

**Kyrgyz Madaniyaty** (Kyrgyz Culture): 720301 Bishkek, Bokonbayeva 99; tel. (312) 26-14-58; f. 1967; weekly; organ of the Union of Writers; Editor NURALY KAPAROV; circ. 15,940.

**Kyrgyz Tuusu:** Bishkek, Abdymomunova 193; tel. (312) 22-45-09; f. 1924; daily; organ of the Government; Kyrgyz; Editor A. MATISAKOV.

**Kyrgyzstan Chronicle:** Bishkek; tel. (312) 22-48-32; f. 1993; weekly; independent; English; Editor BAYAN SARYGULOV; circ. 5,000.

**Limon:** Bishkek, ul. Moskovskaya 189; tel. (312) 65-03-03; fax (312) 65-02-04; e-mail limon@akipress.org; internet www.akipress.org; f. 1994; Russian; independent; Dir VENERA DJAMANKULOVA.

**Res Publica** (Republic): Bishkek, Belinskogo 28; tel. (312) 21-97-33; e-mail repub@kyrnet.kg; internet www.respublica.elcat.kg; f. 1992; 2 a week; independent; Russian and English; publication suspended Jan.–May 2002; Editor ZAMIRA SIDIKOVA.

**Slovo Kyrgyzstana** (Word of Kyrgyzstan): Bishkek, Abdymomunova 193; tel. (312) 22-53-92; e-mail slovo@infotel.kg; internet www .sk.kg; f. 1925; daily; organ of the Government; Russian; Editor ALEKSANDR I. MALEVANY.

**Svobodniye Gori** (The Free Mountains): Bishkek, Razzakova 63, POB 1450; tel. (312) 26-34-22; 3 a week; Russian; Editor L. DJOLMYKHAMEDOVA.

**The Times of Central Asia:** 720000 Bishkek, pr. Chui 155; tel. (312) 68-05-67; fax (312) 68-07-69; e-mail edittimes@infotel.kg; internet www.times.kg; f. 1995; weekly; English; also distributed in Kazakhstan, Turkmenistan and Uzbekistan; subscribers in Canada, Europe, Malaysia, Turkey and the USA; Editor LYDIA SAVINA.

**Vechernii Bishkek** (Bishkek Evening Newspaper): Bishkek, pr. Usenbayev 2; tel. (312) 28-45-97; fax (312) 68-02-68; e-mail webmaster@vb.kg; internet www.vb.kg; f. 1974; daily; independent; Russian; Editor KHASAN YA. MUSTAFAYEV; circ. (Mon.–Thur.) 20,000, (Fri.) 50,000.

**Yuzhnyi Kurier** (Southern Courier): Bishkek; tel. (312) 26-10-53; f. 1993; weekly; independent; Russian; Editor ALEKSANDR KNYAZYEV; circ. 10,000.

**Zaman Kyrgyzstan** (Kyrgyzstan Herald): Bishkek, Frunze 390; tel. (312) 21-35-66; fax (312) 21-57-29; e-mail zamankrg@asiainfo .kg; f. 1992; weekly; independent; Kyrgyz, Turkish and English; Editor HÜSEYIN DINLEMEZ; circ. 15,000.

## PRINCIPAL PERIODICALS

Monthly, unless otherwise indicated.

**Ala Too** (Ala Too Mountains): Bishkek; tel. (312) 26-55-12; f. 1931; organ of the Union of Writers; politics, novels, short stories, plays, poems of Kyrgyz authors and translations into Kyrgyz; Kyrgyz; Editor KENESH JUSUPOV; circ. 3,000.

**Chalkan** (Stinging Nettle): Bishkek; tel. (312) 42-16-38; f. 1955; satirical; Kyrgyz; Editor B. AZIZOV; circ. 7,600.

**Den-sooluk** (Health): Bishkek; tel. (312) 22-46-37; f. 1960; weekly; journal of the Ministry of Health; popular science; Kyrgyz; Editor MAR ALIYEV; circ. 20,000.

**Korporativnyi Vestnik** (Corporate Bulletin): Bishkek, pr. Chui 106; tel. (312) 22-45-07; fax (312) 66-16-64; e-mail info@cdc.kg; internet www.kv.cdc.kg; bulletin of the govt-controlled Corporate Development Centre; Dir B. KARTANBAYEV.

**Kyrgyz Analytical Magazine:** Bishkek, ul. Moskovskaya 189; tel. (312) 65-02-02; fax (312) 65-02-04; e-mail aki@inftel.kg; internet www.akipress.kg; f. 1993; Russian; independent; Dir MARAT TAZABEKOV.

**Kyrgyzstan Ayaldary** (Women of Kyrgyzstan): Bishkek; tel. (312) 42-12-26; f. 1951; popular; Kyrgyz; Editor S. AKMATBEKOVA; circ. 500.

**Literaturnyi Kyrgyzstan** (Literary Kyrgyzstan): 720301 Bishkek, Pushkina 70; tel. (312) 26-14-63; e-mail lk@users.kyrnet.kg; internet lk.kyrnet.kg; f. 1955; journal of the Union of Writers; fiction, literary criticism, journalism; Russian; Editor-in-Chief A. I. IVANOV; circ. 3,000.

**Zdravookhraneniye Kyrgyzstana** (Public Health System of Kyrgyzstan): 720005 Bishkek, Sovetskaya 34; tel. (312) 44-41-39; f. 1938; 4 a year; publ. by the Ministry of Health; experimental medical work; Russian; Editor-in-Chief N. K. KASIYEV; circ. 3,000.

### NEWS AGENCIES

**AKIpress:** Bishkek, ul. Moskovskaya 189; tel. (312) 61-03-96; fax (312) 65-02-04; e-mail post@akipress.org; internet www.akipress.org; f. 2000; Russian and English; independent; Dir MARAT TAZABEKOV.

**Belyi Parokhod:** 720011 Bishkek, Pushkina 50; tel. (312) 26-45-23; e-mail parokhod@infotel.kg; internet www.kg/parokhod; f. 1997; independent.

**KABAR** (Kyrgyz News Agency): 720337 Bishkek, Sovetskaya 175; tel. (312) 22-67-39; fax (312) 66-14-67; e-mail mlkabar@infotel.kg; internet www.kyrgpress.org.kg; fmrly KyrgyzTag until 1992, and Kyrgyzkabar until 1995; Pres. KOUBANYCHBEK TAABALDIYEV; Editor-in-Chief DJUMAKAN SARIYEV.

#### Foreign Bureaux

**Informatsionnoye Telegrafnoye Agentstvo Rossii– Telegrafnoye Agentstvo Suverennykh Stran (ITAR—TASS)** (Russia): Bishkek, Sovetskaya 175; tel. (312) 26-59-20; Correspondent BORIS M. MAINAYEV.

**Interfax** (Russia): Bishkek, Toktogula 97, Rm 6; tel. and fax (312) 26-72-87; Bureau Chief BERMET MALIKOVA.

**Reuters** (United Kingdom): Bishkek; tel. (312) 54-52-01.

## Publishers

**Akyl:** 720000 Bishkek, Sovetskaya 170; tel. (312) 22-47-57; f. 1994; science, politics, economics, culture, literature; Chair. AMANBEK KARYPKULOV.

**Ilim** (Science): 720071 Bishkek, pr. Chui 265A; tel. (312) 25-53-60; e-mail ilimph@hotmail.kg; internet ilim.aknet.kg; scientific and science fiction; Dir L. V. TARASOVA.

**Kyrgyzskaya Entsiklopediya** (Kyrgyz Encyclopedia): 720040 Bishkek, bul. Erkindik 56; tel. (312) 22-77-57; dictionaries and encyclopedias; Dir BAKTYGUL KALDYBAYEVA; Editor-in-Chief AMANBEK KARYPKULOV.

**Kyrgyzstan** (Kyrgyzstan Publishing House): Bishkek; tel. (312) 26-48-54; politics, science, economics, literature; Dir BERIK N. CHALAGYZOV.

**Uchkun:** Bishkek; state-owned.

## Broadcasting and Communications

**State Communications Agency:** 720005 Bishkek, Sovetskaya 76; e-mail postmaster@nca.bishkek.gov.kg; Dir ANDREI TITOV.

### TELECOMMUNICATIONS

**Kyrgyztelekom:** 720000 Bishkek, pr. Chui 96; tel. (312) 68-16-16; fax (312) 66-24-24; e-mail info@kt.kg; internet www.kt.kg; f. 1994, transformed into public co in 1997; state telecommunications co; undergoing privatization in 2002; Pres. NASIRDIN TURDALIYEV; Vice-Pres. BURKAN JUMABAYEV, ISKENDER KOLBAYEV.

### BROADCASTING

#### Radio

**State National Television and Radio Broadcasting Corpn:** Chair. AMANBEK KARYPLULOV.

**Kyrgyz Radio:** 720010 Bishkek, Molodoi Gvardii 59; tel. (312) 25-79-36; fax (312) 65-10-64; f. 1931; broadcasts in Kyrgyz, Russian, English, German, Ukrainian, Uzbek, Dungan and Uigur; Vice-Pres. BAYMA SUTENOVA; Pres. MOLDOSEIT MAMBETAKUNOV.

**Dom Radio:** 720885 Bishkek, Molodoi Gvardii 63.

**Radio Azattyk:** Bishkek; tel. (312) 66-88-17; fax (312) 66-68-14; e-mail kiyas@liberty.elcat.kg; internet www.azattyk.org; Kyrgyz language news broadcasts by Radio Free Europe/Radio Liberty (USA—based in the Czech Republic); Dir TYNTCHTYKBEK TCHOROEV; Bureau Chief KYIAS MOLDOKASYMOV.

**Radio Pyramid:** 720300 Bishkek, Molodoi Gvardii 59; tel. (312) 28-28-28; fax (312) 52-61-65; e-mail pyramid@mail.elcat.kg; internet www.pyramid.elcat.kg; f. 1992; privately owned; broadcasts to Bishkek and neighbouring regions.

**Sodruzhestvo:** Osh; f. 1996; broadcasts to Kazakhstan, Kyrgyzstan, Tajikistan and Uzbekistan; established by ethnic Russian groups.

There are several other private radio stations operating in Kyrgyzstan.

#### Television

#### State National Television and Radio Broadcasting Corpn.

**Kyrgyz Television:** 720300 Bishkek, pr. Molodoi Gvardii 63; tel. (312) 25-79-36; fax (312) 25-79-30; Gen. Dir TUGELBAY KAZAKOV.

**TV Pyramid:** 720005 Bishkek; tel. and fax (312) 41-01-31; e-mail pyramid@ss5-22.kyrnet.kg; internet www.pyramid.elcat.kg/tv; f. 1991; privately owned; broadcasts to Bishkek and neighbouring regions.

Russian Public Television broadcasts for six hours daily in some regions of Kyrgyzstan. Relays from Kazakhstan, Turkey and Uzbekistan are also broadcast.

## Finance

(cap. = capital; res = reserves; m. = million; brs = branches; amounts in soms, unless otherwise indicated)

### BANKING

#### Central Bank

**National Bank of the Kyrgyz Republic:** 720040 Bishkek, Umetaliyeva 101; tel. (312) 66-90-11; fax (312) 61-07-30; e-mail mail@nbkr.kg; internet www.nbkr.kg; f. 1991, name changed in 1992, and as above in 1993; cap. 50m., res 660.3m., dep. 4,933.7m. (Dec. 2001); Chair. ULAN K. SARBANOV.

#### Other Banks

In early 2001 there were 22 commercial banks in operation in Kyrgyzstan.

**Amanbank:** 720400 Bishkek, Tynistanova 249; tel. (312) 22-23-11; fax (312) 66-24-39; e-mail amanbank@transfer.kg; f. 1995; cap. 55m., dep. 58.9m. (Aug. 2002); Chair. SHATKUL I. KUDABAYEVA.

**AsiaUniversalBank JSC:** 720001 Bishkek, Toktogula 187; tel. (312) 62-02-52; fax (312) 62-02-50; e-mail reception@aub.bg; internet www.aub.kg; f. 1997 as International Business Bank, changed name as above 2000; cap. 200.0m., dep. 4,012.0m. (Oct. 2003); Pres. NURDIN ABDRAZAKOV; 2 brs.

**Bank Bakai:** 720001 Bishkek, Isanov 75; tel. (312) 66-06-10; fax (312) 66-06-12; e-mail bank@bakai.kg; internet www.bakai.kg; f. 1998; cap. 38.0m., dep. 167.3m. (Dec. 2002); Chair. MARAT ALAPAYEV; Pres. MUHAMED IBRAGIMOV.

**Energobank JSC:** 720070 Bishkek, Jibek-Jolu 493; tel. and fax (312) 67-04-71; e-mail energykg@elcat.kg; internet www.energobank.kg; f. 1992 as Kyrgyzenergobank, changed name as above 2000; cap. US $72m., dep. $8m. (Sept. 2002); Pres. BAKIRDIN E. SARTKAZIYEV; Chair. MAKSAT ISHENBAYEV.

**Investment Export-Import Bank:** 720001 Bishkek, K. Akiyev 57; tel. (312) 65-06-10; fax (312) 62-06-54; e-mail ineximbank@infotel.kg; internet www.ineximbank.com; f. 1996 as Eridan Bank, name changed 2001; cap. 100.0m., res 4.1m., dep. 44.8m. (Aug. 2002); Chair. PETROS SHAGINYAN; 1 br.

**JSCB Kyrgyzstan Bank:** 720001 Bishkek, Togolok Moldo 54; tel. (312) 21-95-98; fax (312) 21-02-20; e-mail akb@bankkg.kg; internet www.bankkg.kg; f. 1991; cap. 127.0m., res 36.4m., dep. 280.7m. (Jan. 2002); Pres. SHARIPA S. SADYBAKASOVA; 29 brs.

**JSCB Tolubay Bank:** 720010 Bishkek, Toktogula 247; tel. (312) 24-02-46; fax (312) 25-63-14; e-mail tolubay@infotel.kg; f. 1996; cap. 26m., res 1.5m., dep. 69.0m. (Dec. 2002); Pres. JENISHBEK S. BAIGUTTIYEV; 1 br.

**Kairat Bank:** 720033 Bishkek, Frunze 390; tel. (312) 21-89-32; fax (312) 21-89-55; e-mail kairat@kairatbank.kg; internet www.kairatbank.kg; f. 1999 to replace Maksat Bank (f. 1991); cap.

170.0m., res 0.0m., dep. 237.9m.; Chair. Mamytova Kastoru Kasymbe-kovna; 5 brs.

**Kazkommertsbank Kyrgyzstan:** 720017 Bishkek, Isanova 42; tel. (312) 66-46-46; fax (312) 66-07-04; e-mail bishkek@kkb.kz; internet kg.kkb.kz; f. 1991, changed name as above in 2002; cap. 25.6m., dep. 101.2m. (Dec. 2001); Chair. Kanat Mamakeyev; 6 brs.

**OJSC Kyrgyzpromstroibank:** 720040 Bishkek, pr. Chui 168; tel. (312) 61-07-43; fax (312) 21-84-45; e-mail kirgpasb@transfer.kz; f. 1991; cap. 100m. (Jan. 2001), dep. 43.3m. (Jan. 2000); Pres. Mur-atbek O. Mukashev; 26 brs.

### Foreign Banks

**Demir Kyrgyz International Bank (DKIB):** 720001 Bishkek, pr. Chui 245; tel. (312) 61-06-10; fax (312) 61-04-45; e-mail dkib@demirbank.kg; internet www.demirbank.kg; f. 1997; cap. 54.1m., dep. 524.1m. (Dec. 2002); Chair. Halit Cingillioglu; Gen. Man. Ahmet Kamil Parmaksiz.

**Ecobank:** 720031 Bishkek, Geologicheskii per. 17; tel. (312) 54-35-82; fax (312) 54-35-80; e-mail ecobank@totel.kg; internet www .ecobank.kg; f. 1996 as Bank Rossiiskii Kredit; name changed 1998; joint-stock commercial bank; cap. 61.0m., dep. 88.8m. (Feb. 2001); Chair. Anvar K. Abdrayev; Dep. Chair. Cholpon Z. Isayeva.

**National Bank of Pakistan:** 720017 Bishkek, pr. Manas 9; tel. (312) 66-11-32; fax (312) 66-33-32; Gen. Man. Shujaul Mulk.

### COMMODITY EXCHANGE

**Kyrgyzstan Commodity and Raw Materials Exchange:** 720001 Bishkek, Belinskaya 40; tel. (312) 22-13-75; fax (312) 22-27-44; f. 1990; Gen. Dir Temir Sariyev.

### STOCK EXCHANGE

**Kyrgyz Stock Exchange:** 720010 Bishkek, Moskovskaya 172; tel. (312) 66-50-59; fax (312) 66-15-95; e-mail kse@kse.kg; internet www .kse.kg; Pres. Amangeldy M. Muraliyev; Chair. Chinarbek Otun-chiyev.

### INSURANCE

**Kyrgyzinstrakh:** 72001 Bishkek, pr. Chui 219; tel. (312) 21-95-54; fax (312) 61-00-98; e-mail kinstrakh@infotel.kg; internet kyrgyzinstrakh.online.kg; f. 1996 by the Russian joint-stock insurance company Investstrakh, Kyrgyz insurance companies and the Kyrgyz Government to insure foreign investors.

# Trade and Industry

## GOVERNMENT AGENCIES

**State Agency for Geology and Mineral Resources:** 720739 Bishkek, pr. Erkindik 2; tel. (312) 66-49-01; fax (312) 66-03-91; e-mail mail@geoagency.bishkek.gov.kg; internet www.kgs.bishkek .gov.kg; Chair. Sheishenaly Murzagaziyev.

**State Agency for Power Engineering:** 720055 Bishkek, Akhun-bayeva 119; e-mail postmaster@gae.bishkek.gov.kg; Dir Ularbek Mateyev.

**State Agency for Registration of Real Estate Rights:** 720040 Bishkek, Orozbekova 44; e-mail gosreg@bishkek.gov.kg; Chair. Tol-obek Omuraliyev.

**State Agency for Science and Intellectual Property:** 720021 Bishkek, Moskovskaya 62; tel. (312) 68-08-19; fax (312) 68-17-03; e-mail kyrgyzpatent@infotel.kg; internet www.kyrgyzpatent.kg; Dir Roman Omorov.

**State Agency for Standardization and Metrology (Kyrgyz-standard):** 720040 Bishkek, Panfilova 197; tel. (312) 22-78-84; fax (312) 66-13-67; e-mail gost@kmc.bishkek.gov.kg; internet www.kmc .bishkek.gov.kg; f. 1927; certification, control and testing of products and services; Dir Batyrbek Davlesov.

**State Commission for Anti-monopoly Policy:** 720040 Bishkek, pr. Chui 114; Chair. Emilbek Uzakbayev.

**State Commission for Architecture and Construction:** 720026 Bishkek, pr. Manasa 28; e-mail mail@gosstroy.bishkek.gov.kg; Chair. Anvar Tursunov.

**State Commission for Business Development:** 720002 Bishkek, Tynystanova 120; e-mail gkprp@bishkek.gov.kg; Chair. Kamila Kenenbayeva.

**State Commission for Drugs Control:** 720010 Bishkek, Razza-kova 63; e-mail gkkn@bishkek.gov.kg; Chair. Kurmanbek Kubat-bekov.

**State Commission for Standards, Financial Accounts and Auditing:** 720040 Bishkek, pr. Chui 106; e-mail scaas@intranet.kg; Chair. Kanatbek Sagynov.

**State Committee for Management of State Property and Attraction of Direct Investment:** 720002 Bishkek, pr. Erkindik 57; tel. (312) 22-77-06; fax (312) 66-02-36; e-mail spf@intranet.kg; internet spf.gov.kg; f. 1991; responsible for the privatization of state-owned enterprises and deals with bankruptcies; Chair. Ravshan Zheyenbekov.

**State Securities Commission:** 720040 Bishkek, pr. Chui 114; tel. (312) 62-44-60; fax (312) 66-26-53; e-mail nsc@nsc.kg; internet www .nsc.kg; Chair. Jurii N. Svistov.

### CHAMBER OF COMMERCE

**Chamber of Commerce and Industry of the Kyrgyz Republic:** 720001 Bishkek, Kievskaya 107; tel. (312) 21-05-65; fax (312) 21-05-75; e-mail cci-kr@totel.kg; internet www.chamber.kg; f. 1959; supports foreign economic relations and the development of small and medium-sized enterprises; Pres. Boris V. Perfiliyev.

### TRADE ASSOCIATION

**Kyrgyzvneshtorg Ltd:** 720033 Bishkek, Abdymomunova 276; tel. (312) 21-39-78; fax (312) 66-08-36; e-mail kvt@infotel.kg; f. 1992; export-import org.; Gen. Dir K. K. Kaliyev.

### UTILITIES

#### Electricity

**JSC National Electric Grid of Kyrgyzstan:** 720070 Bishkek, Jibek Jolu 326; tel. (312) 66-10-00; fax (312) 66-06-56; e-mail aoke@infotel.kg; divided into seven companies in 2001; undergoing privatization in 2003; Gen. Dir Bakirgin Saratkaziyev.

#### Gas

**Kyrgyzazmunayzat:** 720000 Bishkek, L. Tolstogo 114; tel. (312) 24-53-80; fax (312) 24-53-93; state-owned joint-stock co; f. 1997 through merger; Dir-Gen. Bakirdin Subanbekov.

**Kyrgyzgaz:** 720661 Bishkek, Gorkogo 22; tel. (312) 53-00-45; fax (312) 43-09-80; state-owned joint-stock co; scheduled for privatization; Dir-Gen. Avtandil Sydykov.

### MAJOR COMPANIES

#### Electrical Goods

**Issyk-Kul Electrical Engineering Plant:** 722452 Kadzhi-Sai, Tonskogo Raion; f. 1963; produces semiconductors and low voltage equipment; Gen. Dir Dushenbayev Dushenbayevich Ishentur; 2,000 employees.

**Dastan JSC Transnational Corpn:** 720005 Bishkek, Baitik Baatyr 36; tel. (312) 42-66-52; fax (312) 54-45-96; e-mail tnkdastan@elcat.kg; internet freewww.elcat.kg/tnkdasta; f. 1993; manufactures industrial electronic equipment, medical equipment and consumer goods; Pres. Soultanbek Tabaldyev; Vice-Pres. Oscar Daminov; Gen. Dir U. Z. Ormonov.

#### Metals

**Kadamjai Antimony Plant:** Kadamjai, Zavodskaya 12; tel. (325) 52-28-10; fax (325) 52-28-38; f. 1936; owned by Kyrgyzaltyn (q.v.); produces antimony; Gen. Dir Mamat Aybalayev; 2,000 employees.

**Kara-Balta Mining Processing Plant:** 722130 Kara-Balta, Truda 1a; tel. (313) 37-21-89; fax (313) 62-06-84; f. 1952; owned by Kyrgy-zaltyn (q.v.); ore refining, production of gold ingots, rolled aluminium, silver, uranium oxide; Pres. N. J. Kojomatov; 1,500 employees.

**Khaidarakan Mercury Plant:** Khaidarakan.

**Kumtor Operating Company:** 720300 Bishkek, Ibraimov 24; tel. (312) 42-22-82; fax (312) 54-08-50; f. 1992; development of Kumtor gold deposit, one of the largest in the world; joint venture with Cameco Corpn (Canada), with support from Chase Manhattan Bank (USA) and the EBRD; Pres. Terry Rogers; 1,500 employees.

**Kyrgyzaltyn JSC:** 720040 Bishkek, Abdumamunov 195; tel. (312) 66-76-70; fax (312) 66-67-00; internet www.kyrgyzaltyn.kg; f. 1992; state-owned; mining and processing of rare and precious metals, incl. gold and antimony; Pres. Kamchybek K. Kudaibergenov.

#### Textiles

**Avgul:** 720343 Bishkek, pr. Chui 147; tel. (312) 28-18-64; fax (312) 28-18-76; joint-stock co; manufacturers of woollen and semi-woollen clothing; Pres. Satarov; 2,000 employees.

**BAKAI:** 722030 Kara-Balta, Otorbayeva 1; tel. (233) 2-13-46; fax (233) 2-37-72; produces sugar, spirits; Dir IBRAGIMOV MUHAMED TURGU-NOVICH.

**Ilbirs Joint Stock Company:** 720393 Bishkek, Kievskaya 77; tel. (312) 21-26-35; fax (312) 22-07-91; f. 1992; manufactures of cotton and woollen clothing; Gen. Dir D. A. TENTIYEV.

**Jibek:** 714003 Osh, Gagarina 108; tel. (322) 22-15-69; fax (322) 22-84-163; joint-stock co; produces silk fabric; Dir SHEPELEV BALERY EVGENEVICH.

**Kasiet Commercial-Production Company:** 722213 Tokmak, Frunze 1; tel. (314) 54-12-31; fax (314) 54-11-05; f. 1977; produces semi-woollen and pure wool yarn; Exec. Dir RADY L. TEN; 1,957 employees.

**Kyrgyz Worsted Woollens Factory (KWWF):** 720022 Bishkek, pr. Chui 4; tel. (312) 28-15-74; fax (312) 53-10-21; e-mail kamvol@elcaf.kg; internet www.cde.kg/kksk/; f. 1963; privately owned joint-stock co; produces and sells blankets and worsted, woollen and semi-woollen fabrics for garments; sales of US $1.37m. (2000); Gen. Dir CHORDOROV MEDERBEK; 1,000 employees.

**Textilshic:** 714024 Osh, Kasymbekova 8A; tel. (3322) 23-03-34; fax (3322) 52-67-46; joint-stock co; produces fabric; Dir SATIBALDIYEV KAKHROMON.

### Miscellaneous

**Ak-Maral Trading:** 720300 Bishkek, ul. Alma-Atinskaya 6; tel. (312) 43-29-97; fax (312) 53-00-20; e-mail ak_maral@infotel.kg; internet www.ak-maral.com.kg; f. 1993; produces cable and satellite television sets, home appliances, telecommunications apparatus, fluorescent lamps, textiles; lathe operator; owns hotel complex on lake Issyk-Kul; Chair. MARAT D. SHARSHEKEYEV; 450 employees.

**Bishkek Agricultural Machinery Plant:** 720008 Bishkek, Intergelpo 1; tel. (312) 25-31-50; fax (312) 24-48-10; manufactures agricultural machinery and equipment; Man. Dir MIKHAIL IVANOVICH BARISHKURA.

**Eridan Group:** 72000 Bishkek, Orozbekov 133; tel. (312) 27-25-58; fax (312) 27-08-65; e-mail eridan1@elcat.kg; internet eridan.online .kg; f. 1993; agriculture, banking, construction, freight forwarding, furniture, medical supplies and equipment, packaging, security, wood processing; Pres. ELDIYAR T. USSENOV; 1,100 employees.

**Kant Cement and Slate Combine:** Chui Duban, 722140 Kant, Promzona; tel. (232) 2-22-80; fax (232) 24-57-50; produces cement and slates; Dir BEZSMERTNY ILYA SEMENOVICH.

**Kyrgyzavtomash Industrial Group:** 720031 Bishkek, Matrosova 1; tel. (312) 43-91-13; joint-stock co; manufactures motor-vehicle parts, machine tools and metal forgings; Gen. Dir VLADIMIR I. CHU-MAKOV; 2,750 employees.

**Avtomash-Radiator Ltd:** 720031 Bishkek, Matrosova 1; tel. (312) 43-91-13; fax (312) 53-00-09; e-mail radiator@mail.kg; f. 2001; produces automobile cooling radiators; Gen. Dir BAYAZITOV MARSEL.

**Krygyzhaberdashery:** 720661 Bishkek, Matrosova 5; tel. (312) 44-45-65; fax (312) 42-89-13; haberdashery products; Pres. ANARALI MATENOVICH SADIKOV.

**Kyrgyzkilem—Kara-Balta Carpet Factory:** 722030 Kara-Balta, P. Tolyatti 1; tel. (313) 32-36-61; fax (313) 32-00-47; f. 1983; produces carpets; 3,200 employees.

**Kyrgyzneftegaz JSC:** 715622 Kochkor-Ata, Lenina 44; tel. and fax (312) 66-12-66; state-owned petroleum and natural gas co; Pres. KASIM ISMANOV.

**Mayluu-Suu Electric Lamp Plant JSC:** 715420 Mayluu Suu, Lenina 210; tel. (324) 42-11-50; fax (324) 42-12-90; e-mail msel@infotel.kg; internet www.msel.kg; f. 1964; produces incandescent lamps; Dir MELKER NIKOLAI ADOLFOVICH; 3,700 employees.

**OKKO:** 720015 Bishkek, Hvoinaja 64; tel. (312) 27-08-41; fax (312) 27-29-30; joint-stock co; manufactures leather accessories; Dir GELNOV NIKOLAI.

**Tash-Kumyr Semiline Materials Plant:** 715430 Tash-Kumyr, Promzona 1; tel. (33542) 28-95-10; fax (33542) 62-04-40; produces semiline materials; Dir DJUMAGULOV SAGYNBEK.

### TRADE UNIONS

**Kyrgyzstan Federation of Trade Unions:** 720032 Bishkek, Chui 207; tel. (312) 21-49-30; fax (312) 21-76-87; Chair. S. BOZBUNBAYEV.

# Transport

## RAILWAYS

Owing to the country's mountainous terrain, the railway network consists of only one main line (340 km) in northern Kyrgyzstan, which connects the republic, via Kazakhstan, with the railway system of Russia. Osh, Jalal-Abad and four other towns in regions of Kyrgyzstan bordering Uzbekistan are linked to that country by short lengths of railway track. In mid-1998 work began on a US $2,500m. project to construct a railway line connecting eastern Uzbekistan with southern Kyrgyzstan. In June 2001 the Governments of Kyrgyzstan and the People's Republic of China signed a memorandum on the construction of a rail link from Kashgar (China) to Bishkek.

**Kyrgyz Railway Administration:** 720009 Bishkek, L. Tolstogo 83; tel. (312) 25-30-54; fax (312) 24-56-11; f. 1924; Pres. I. S. OMUR-KULOV; Dir SADYKBEK A. ABLESOV.

## ROADS

In 1999 Kyrgyzstan's road network totalled an estimated 18,500 km, including 140 km of motorway; in 1996 there were 3,200 km of main roads and 6,380 km of secondary roads. About 91% of roads were paved. Many of the best road links are with neighbouring countries—mainly with Kazakhstan in the north, with Uzbekistan in the west and with China in the south-east. A main road linking the cities of Bishkek and Osh was under reconstruction in the early 2000s. The International Development Bank allocated US $37m. towards the $60m. cost of repairing the Taras–Talas–Susamyr road by 2002.

## CIVIL AVIATION

There are three international airports at Bishkek (Manas Airport), Osh and Tamchy (in the Issyk-Kul region—inaugurated in August 2003). At early 2001 there were 13 privately owned airlines in Kyrgyzstan.

**Asian Star:** 720000 Bishkek, Tynystanova 120; tel. (312) 26-34-55; fax (312) 64-04-05; regional charter passenger services; Pres. BORIS ROLNIK.

**Kyrgyzstan Airlines** (Kyrgyzstan Aba Zholdoru): 720026 Bishkek, Manas Airport; tel. and fax (312) 31-30-84; internet www .minartravels.com/kyrgyzair; f. 1992; operates scheduled and charter flights to destinations in Azerbaijan, the People's Republic of China, Germany, India, Kazakhstan, Pakistan, Russia and Uzbekistan; scheduled for privatization; Pres. ORUSKUL KUTTUBAYEV.

# Tourism

There was little tourism in Kyrgyzstan during the Soviet period. In the first years of independence tourist facilities remained very limited, and foreign visitors tended to be mountaineers. However, the Government hoped that the country's spectacular and largely unspoilt mountain scenery, as well as the great crater lake of Issyk-Kul, might attract foreign tourists and investment. By the late 1990s the number of tourists visiting Kyrgyzstan was increasing, and there were some 69,000 tourist arrivals in 2001, compared with around 59,000 in 1998. The Government's promotion strategy centred on the country's position on the ancient 'Silk Road' trade route, and its potential as a destination for nature tourism and adventure holidays. There were also plans to develop Kyrgyzstan's ski resorts.

**State Agency for Tourism, Sport and Youth Policy:** 720033 Bishkek, Togolok Moldo 17; tel. (312) 22-06-57; fax (312) 21-28-45; e-mail gatiskr@bishkek.gov.kg; Chair. OKMOTBEK ALMAKUCHUKOV.

# Culture

The Kyrgyz tradition is a nomadic one, and that influence is apparent in modern, urban expressions of Kyrgyz culture. Kyrgyz was not a written language until the period of Russian rule, but there was a rich oral canon, the most notable work being the epic poem *Manas*, which is claimed to be the longest work of literature. According to legend, Talas in western Kyrgyzstan was the birthplace of the Kyrgyz folk hero, Manas. The *Manas* contains stories about the hero and the whole of Kyrgyz history. Until relatively recent years the poem was performed by travelling bards known as *manaschi*. In 1995 the Manas Millennium was held in Talas.

## NATIONAL ORGANIZATION

**Ministry of Education and Culture:** see section on The Government (Ministries).

## CULTURAL HERITAGE

**Bishkek Historical Museum:** Bishkek; formerly the Lenin Museum.

**National Library of the Kyrgyz Republic:** Bishkek, Sovetskaya 208; tel. (312) 66-20-90; internet nlkr.org.kg; f. 1934; re-named as above 1993; over 6m. vols; Dir ANARA CHYNYBAYEVA.

**State Historical Museum of Kyrgyzstan:** Bishkek, Krasnooktyabrskaya 236; f. 1925; 80,000 items; Dir N. M. SEITKAZIYEVA.

**State Museum of Fine Art of Kyrgyzstan:** Bishkek, Pervomaiskaya 90; 4,000 modern exhibits; Dir K. N. UZUBALIYEVA.

## SPORTING ORGANIZATIONS

**State Agency for Tourism, Sport and Youth Policy:** 720033 Bishkek, Togolok Moldo 17; tel. (312) 22-06-57; fax (312) 21-28-45; Dir SHERALY SYDYKOV.

**National Olympic Committee of the Republic of Kyrgyzstan:** 720040 Bishkek, ul. Frunze 503; tel. (312) 21-06-83; fax (312) 21-06-72; e-mail noc_kr@hotbox.ru; f. 1991; Pres. M. ECHIM KOUTMANALIYEV; Gen. Sec. M. PYOTR PAVLOVICH TSAPLYA.

## PERFORMING ARTS

**State Drama Theatre:** Bishkek, Panfilova 273.

**State Opera and Ballet Theatre:** Bishkek, Sovetskaya 167.

**State Philharmonia:** Bishkek, Lenina.

## ASSOCIATION

**Union of Writers of Kyrgyzstan:** 720301 Bishkek, Pushkina 70; tel. (312) 22-26-53.

# Education

Education is compulsory for nine years, comprising four years of primary education (for those aged between seven and 10 years) and five years of lower secondary school (ages 11 to 15). Pupils may then attend upper secondary schools (for two years), specialized secondary schools (for between two and four years) or technical and vocational schools (from the age of 15 years). In 2000/01 total enrolment at primary schools was equivalent to 89% of the relevant age group; enrolment at secondary schools was equivalent to 83% of the school-age population. In 1993/94 63.6% of primary and secondary schools used Kyrgyz as the sole language of instruction, 23.4% Russian, 12.7% Uzbek and 0.3% Tajik. Russian, however, was the principal language of instruction in higher educational establishments. A decree signed in December 2001 abolished free schooling. In April 2001, as part of a policy to combat Islamist extremism, the Government banned religious education in state schools and decreed that specialist religious schools would require a licence. At April 2002 there were 44 higher educational establishments in Kyrgyzstan, with courses lasting between four and six years. In 1995/96 enrolment at institutes of higher education was equivalent to 12.2% of the relevant age-group (males 11.6%, females 12.8%). Government budgetary expenditure on education in 2002 was 3,350.4m. soms (22.1% of total spending).

## UNIVERSITIES

**Bishkek Humanities University:** 720044 Bishkek, pr. Tynchtyk 27; tel. and fax (312) 48-40-35; e-mail rectorat@bgupub.freenet.bishkek.su; internet bhu.freenet.kg; f. 1979; seven faculties; Rector Prof. ISHENGUL S. BOLJUROVA.

**International University of Kyrgyzstan:** 720001 Bishkek, pr. Chui 255; tel. (312) 21-83-35; fax (312) 21-96-15; e-mail webmaster@iuk.kg; internet www.iuk.kg; Pres. ASILBEK A. AYDARALIYEV.

**Jalal-Abad University:** 715600 Jalal-Abad, Lenina 57; tel. (3372) 73-22-06; fax (3372) 23-39-72; internet www.freenet.kg/jalal_abad/jala_e.html; f. 1993; 5 faculties; 4,300 students; Pres. TURSUNBEK BEKBOLOTOV; Vice-Pres. NURMAT JAILOBAYEV.

**Kyrgyz-Russian Slavonic University:** 720000 Bishkek, Kievskaya 44; tel. (312) 22-06-95; fax (312) 28-27-76; e-mail krsu@krsu.edu.kg; internet www.krsu.edu.kg; f. 1993; 6 faculties; Rector VLADIMIR NIFADIYEV.

**Kyrgyz State National University:** 720024 Bishkek, Frunze 537; tel. (312) 26-26-34; internet www.ksnu.it.kg; f. 1951; renamed as above in 1993; 12 faculties; 600 teachers; 13,000 students; Rector M. Z. ZAKIROV.

**Kyrgyz Technical University:** 720044 Bishkek, pr. Mira 66; tel. (312) 54-51-25; fax (312) 54-51-51; e-mail root@ktu.bishkek.su; internet ktu.freenet.kg; f. 1954; renamed as above in 1992; 8 facul-

ties; 2 research institutes; 530 teachers; 8,730 students; Pres. UTAN BRIMKULOV.

**Kyrgyz-Turkish University:** 720000 Bishkek, Manasa 56; tel. (312) 54-19-42; fax (312) 54-19-43; e-mail webmaster@manas.kg; internet www.manas.kg; f. 1995; Rectors Prof. Dr ARIF CHAGLAR, Prof. Dr KARYBEK MOLDOBAYEV.

**Osh State University:** 714000 Osh, Lenina 331; tel. (3322) 22-22-73; fax (3322) 22-46-05; e-mail tvs@osupub.freenet.bishkek.su; internet freenet.bishkek.su/institut/osh; f. 1992; 9 faculties; 6,642 students (1994/95); Rector BAKYT BESHIMOV.

# Social Welfare

Even before the dissolution of the USSR, reforms aimed to make the social-security system self-financing, rather than being dependent upon transfers from the all-Union budget. In 1990 a Pension Fund and an Employment Fund were established in Kyrgyzstan, and they began operations in 1991. A social-security (payroll) tax was paid directly into the Pension Fund (in 1991 the tax was 37% of the wage bill of enterprises and 26% for collectives and state farms, as well as a 1% tax on salaries and grants from the central Government). Just over one-third of the revenue was allocated to trade unions for social insurance. In the early 1990s there were some 600,000 pensioners to support, mostly retired people, but also social pensioners. The Employment Fund was intended to provide for those affected by the expected increase in unemployment. It was also responsible for retraining, public-works projects and job centres. Most of its revenue was to come from a 1% levy on enterprise wage bills. In 1994 the Pension Fund, the Employment Fund and the country's third extra-budgetary fund, the Social Insurance Fund, were consolidated into one Social Fund, as was a Medical Insurance Fund, established in 1997. In early 1998 778,010 people were in receipt of benefits from the Social Fund. A comprehensive reform of the pensions system was undertaken in 1998–2000, and the retirement age was to increase by three years by 2007, from 60 years for men and 55 years for women. At October 2002 the average monthly pension amounted to some 559 soms.

By the mid-1990s there had been a general decline in the standard of living in Kyrgyzstan. According to World Bank figures, in 1999 49.1% of the population lived in conditions of extreme poverty. In 2000 there were 2.92 physicians per 1,000 people, and in 1999 there were 126 people per hospital bed. According to official figures, there were 988 non-state and 205 private medical establishments in 2001. Of total current budgetary expenditure in 2002, 1,527.2m. soms (10.1%) was for health, and 2,340.5m. soms (15.4%) for social insurance and security.

## NATIONAL AGENCIES

**Ministry of Health:** see section on The Government (Ministries).

**Ministry of Labour and Social Welfare:** see section on The Government (Ministries).

**Social Fund:** 720300 Bishkek, pr. Chui 106; tel. (3312) 26-48-00; fax (3312) 26-55-37; f. 1994 by merger of the Pension Fund, Employment Fund and Social Insurance Fund; responsible for social protection, training and retraining of the unemployed, all social benefits; Chair. A. KYPCHAKBAYEVA.

## HEALTH AND WELFARE ORGANIZATIONS

**Mercy and Health Fund of Kyrgyzstan:** 720040 Bishkek, pr. Erkindik 10; tel. (312) 26-26-70; fax (312) 26-26-55; provides medical assistance to those in need.

**Red Crescent Society of Kyrgyzstan:** 720040 Bishkek, pr. Erkindik 10; tel. (312) 22-24-14; fax (312) 66-21-81; e-mail redcross@imfiko.bishkek.su; f. 1926; provides medical and social assistance to the elderly, assistance in emergencies and to refugees, youth activities; Pres. RAISA B. IBRAIMOVA; Vice-Pres. RAVZA B. SHYAIAHMETOVA.

# The Environment

As a result of its low level of industrialization and its distance from the ecological problems of the Aral Sea, Kyrgyzstan was less affected than some of its neighbouring countries by environmental problems. Nevertheless, the climate of the entire Central Asian region was affected by the climatic changes engendered by the desiccation of the Aral Sea. In January 1994, together with the other Central Asian states, Kyrgyzstan agreed to contribute to an international Aral Sea fund and that there should be a limit on the amount of water taken from the upper reaches of the Syr-Dar'ya (which has its sources in Kyrgyzstan) and the Amu-Dar'ya rivers. The issue of water resources generally prompted a number of agreements between

Kyrgyzstan and its neighbours. Local environmentalists were mainly concerned with the protection of the country's extensive mountain environment and the large lake of Issyk-Kul; it was also hoped that both would attract tourist visitors. At the end of the 1990s there was concern that waste materials from Kyrgyzstan's mines, situated in areas susceptible to earthquakes and snow- and mud-slides, could cause environmental damage. The southern town of Mayluu Suu, bordering Uzbekistan, which had 23 radioactive waste sites, caused particular environmental concern, and a project to investigate the impact of the waste was inititated in 2001, with European Union funding.

## GOVERNMENT ORGANIZATIONS

**Ministry of Ecology and Emergency Situations:** see section on The Government (Ministries).

**State Agency for Geology and Mineral Resources:** see section on Trade and Industry (Government Agencies).

**State Enterprise on Hydrometeorology:** 720403 Bishkek, Karasuiskaya 1; tel. and fax (312) 21-44-22; e-mail kgmeteo@kyrgyzmeteo.elcat.kg; f. 1926; Gen. Dir MOURATBEK BAKANOV.

**State Forestry Committee:** 720033 Bishkek, Abdymomunov 276; tel. and fax (312) 21-36-79; e-mail mail@forestagency.bishkek.gov .kg; Dir JANYSH RUSTENBEKOV.

## ACADEMIC INSTITUTES

**National Academy of Sciences of the Kyrgyz Republic:** 720071 Bishkek, pr. Chui 265A; tel. (312) 61-00-93; fax (312) 24-36-07; e-mail interdep@aknet.kg; internet academ.aknet.kg; f. 1954; several attached institutes involved in environmental research; collaboration with foreign academies of science, research centres and universities; conferences; publications; Pres. JANYBEK JEENBAYEV.

**Institute of Water Problems and Hydropower Engineering:** 720033 Bishkek, Frunze 533; tel. (312) 21-45-72; e-mail mamatkanov@sdnp.kyrnet.kg; Dir DUISHEN MAMATKANOV.

**Noosphere Organizational Bureau of the Open Scientific Association (OSA):** Bishkek, Panfilova 237, kv. 303; tel. and fax (312) 22-51-76; e-mail sgi@imfiko.bishkek.su; development, organization and implementation of scientific, commercial and intergovernmental ecological development projects; Chair. VIKTOR ALEKSANDROVICH BOBROV.

## NON-GOVERNMENTAL ORGANIZATIONS

**Asian Ecological Group:** 720033 Bishkek, Isanov 131; tel. (312) 61-04-11; e-mail azamat@sdnp.kyrnet.kg; Head AZAMAT HUDAIBERGENOV.

**'Aleyne' Movement for Environmental Protection in Kyrgyzstan:** 720071 Bishkek, POB 50; tel. (312) 66-26-09; e-mail emil@aleyne.bishkek.su; Chair. EMIL SHUKUROV.

**'BIOM' Youth Ecological Movement:** 720001 Bishkek, Abdymomunova 328, Kyrgyz State Scientific University, Faculty of Biology, Rm 105; tel. (312) 25-18-78; e-mail biom@infotel.kg; Head NATALIA KRAVZOVA.

**Bishkek-ECO:** Bishkek; tel. (312) 42-25-00; Head BAKYT DUISHEMBAYEV.

**Committee for the Defence of Lake Issyk-Kul:** 720023 Bishkek, 10 Micro-rayon 32–31; tel. (312) 22-19-68; f. 1990; Pres. OMOR SULTANOV.

**Consortium of Ecological NGOs:** 720033 Bishkek, Isanov 131, Rm 403; tel. (312) 21-26-28; e-mail ecocons@cango.net.kg; Co-ordinator CHINARA SYDYKOVA.

**Ecological Movement of Kyrgyzstan:** Bishkek; tel. (312) 26-55-28; f. 1994; Chair. T. CHODURAYEV.

**Environmental Protection Fund of Kazakhstan:** 720071 Bishkek, pr. Chui 265A, Rm 139; tel. and fax (312) 24-36-61; e-mail eco@kyrnet.kg; Chair. KAZIMIR KARIMOV.

**Green Women Information and Educational Centre:** 720040 Bishkek, Togolok Moldo 21/3; tel. (312) 21-01-48; e-mail putalova@elcat.kg; Dir YELENA PUTALOVA.

**Independent Ecologists' Association:** 720025 Bishkek, POB 702; tel. (312) 29-99-35; Head PAVEL GREBER.

**International Physicians for the Prevention of Nuclear War:** 720040 Bishkek, Togolok Moldo 3; tel. (312) 66-15-16; fax (312) 66-03-87; concerned with radiation levels in the country and with the effects of radiation on the mountain population; Chair. NURLAN NURGAZIEVICH BRIMKULOV; Pres. Prof. MIRSAID MIRHAMIDOVICH MIRRAKHIMOV.

**International Science Centre (ISC):** 720017 Bishkek, pr. Manas 22A; tel. and fax (312) 21-36-48; e-mail isc@freenet.kg; internet www .isc.freenet.kg; f. 1994; Dir AZAMAT TYNYBECOV.

**Lop Nor-Kyrgyz Anti-Nuclear Movement:** Bishkek; f. 1994; seeks the total banning of nuclear testing at Lop Nor (People's Republic of China) and other sites; Chair. A. K. KARIMOV.

**Public Centre of Ecological Information:** 720020 Bishkek, Suerkulova 6A –11; tel. and fax (312) 42-60-26; e-mail pcei@usa.net; Dir STANISLAV ZOPOV.

**Tabiyat** (Kyrgyzstan Environmental Movement): 720044 Bishkek, pr. Manas 27; tel. and fax (312) 48-48-35; e-mail rectorat@bgurub .freenet.bishkek.su; f. 1994; Head TEMIRBEK CHODURAYEV.

**Women's Asscn of the Kyrgyz Republic for Ecological Safety and a Nuclear-free World:** 720017 Bishkek, Koenkozova 8/54; tel. (312) 48-65-68; Head DYIKANOVA CHOLPON.

# Defence

Kyrgyzstan reorganized its armed forces in mid-1993, creating a General Staff in August. Military service is compulsory, and lasts for 18 months, although there were plans to reduce it to one year. In August 2002 Kyrgyzstan's total armed forces numbered 10,900, comprising an army of 8,500 and an air force of 2,400. There were also an estimated 5,000 paramilitary forces. The Government's defence budget for 2002 was some 1,100m. soms (US $23.5m.).

**Commander-in-Chief:** President of the Republic.

**Chief of the General Staff:** Col-Gen. ALIK MAMYRKULOV.

# Bibliography

Anderson, J. *Kyrgyzstan: Central Asia's Island of Democracy?* Reading, Harwood Academic Publishers, 1998.

'The Politics of Civil Society in Kyrgyzstan' in *RIIA Briefing*, No 18, May 1999.

Hetmanek, A. 'Kirgizstan and the Kirgiz', in *Handbook of Major Soviet Nationalities*. New York, NY, Free Press, 1975.

Huskey, E. 'Kyrgyzstan: the Politics of Demographic and Economic Frustration', in *New States, New Politics: Building the Post-Soviet Nations*. Cambridge, Cambridge University Press, 1997.

*Istoriya Kirgizskoi*. Frunze (Bishkek), Kyrgyzstan, 1984.

*Kirgizskaya SSR. Entsiklopediya*. Frunze (Bishkek), Glavnaya Redatktsiya KSE, 1982.

Thubron, C. *The Lost Heart of Asia*. London, Heinemann, 2000.

Also see the Select Bibliography in Part Four.

# MOLDOVA

## Geography

### PHYSICAL FEATURES

The Republic of Moldova (formerly the Moldovan Soviet Socialist Republic, a constituent Union Republic of the USSR), is situated in south-eastern Europe. It includes only a small proportion of the historical territories of Moldova (Moldavia), most of which are in Romania, while others (southern Bessarabia and Northern Bucovina—Bukovyna) are in Ukraine. The country is bounded to the north, east and south by Ukraine. To the west there is a frontier with Romania. Moldova covers an area of 33,800 sq km (13,050 sq miles).

Moldova is a fertile plain with small areas of hill country in the centre and north of the country. The main rivers are the Dniester (Dnestr or Nistru), which flows through the eastern regions into the Black Sea, and the Prut (Prutul), which marks the western border with Romania. The Prut joins the Dunărea (Danube) at the southern tip of Moldova.

### CLIMATE

The climate is very favourable for agriculture, with long, warm summers and relatively mild winters. Average temperatures in Chişinău (Kishinev) range from 21°C (70°F) in July to –4°C (24°F) in January.

### POPULATION

At the census of 1989, at which the total population was 4,335,360, 64.5% of the population were Moldovans (ethnic Romanians), 13.8% Ukrainians, 13.0% Russians, 3.5% Gagauz, 2.0% Jews and 1.5% Bulgarians. The ethnic Moldovans speak a dialect of Romanian, a Romance language, which replaced Russian as the official language in 1989. It is now mostly written in the Latin alphabet; in 1941 the Cyrillic script had been introduced and the language referred to as Moldovan. Ethnic minorities continue to use their own languages; only some 12% of them are fluent in Romanian, whereas most speak Russian. The Gagauz speak a Turkic language, written in the Cyrillic script, but 71% of them claim fluency in Russian; only 4.4% are fluent in Romanian.

Most of the inhabitants of Moldova profess Christianity, the largest denomination being the Eastern Orthodox Church. The Gagauz, despite their Turkish origins, are adherents of Orthodox Christianity. The Russian Orthodox Church

(Moscow Patriarchate) has jurisdiction in Moldova, but there are Romanian and Turkish liturgies.

The total population at 1 January 2002 was an estimated 3,627,812. The population density at that time was 107.3 per sq km. The capital is Chişinău, which is situated in the central region of the country. It had an estimated population of 662,400 at 1 January 2003. Other important centres are the northern town of Bălţi (Beltsy—with an estimated population of 150,600 in 2003) and Tiraspol (187,000 in January 1996), which is situated on the east bank of the Dniester (in Transnistria or Transdnestria), where a majority of the population are ethnic Slavs. The Gagauz mostly inhabit the southern districts, especially the region around the town of Comrat (Komrat).

## Chronology

**106:** Emperor Trajan made Dacia a province of the Roman Empire (by 118 Rome had secured its hegemony over an area including much of modern Moldova).

**270:** Rome abandoned Dacia to Visigothic invaders, the first of many incursions by peoples from the north and east.

**c. 1359:** According to tradition, a Transylvanian prince, Dragoş, became the first lord, or domn, of the region between the Carpathians and the Dnestr (a region that takes its name from the river Molda). Other independent principalities emerged at this time, on the borders of Hungarian territory—the dominant peoples of these Moldovan (Moldavian) and Wallachian lands were Orthodox Christians speaking a Latinate tongue.

**1457:** Ştefan III ('the Great') came to power in Moldova, ruling until his death in 1504; under Ştefan, Moldova reached the height of its political and military power, and gained control of the lands stretching from the Carpathians to the Dnestr (Nistru) and the Black Sea.

**1512:** Moldova became a dependency of the Turkish Ottoman Empire.

**1612:** The Ottomans regained control of Moldova from Sigismund III of Poland.

**1711:** Following periodic uprisings by local nobles (boieri) in Moldova, the territory's autonomous status within the Ottoman Empire was revoked, and directly appointed Turkish administrators, Phanariots, were introduced; these Phanariots made Greek the official language and the Romanian Orthodox Church fell under Hellenic influence.

**1768–74:** The first Russian–Turkish war took place; the Ottomans were assisted by the Habsburg Empire in resisting a Russian attempt to occupy Moldova and Wallachia.

**1806–12:** In another Russian–Turkish conflict, Russian forces gained control of the lands between the Prut and the Dnestr rivers; the war was ended by the Treaty of Bucharest, under which Moldova was divided; the part west of the Prut remained in the Ottoman Empire, while the eastern territory of Bessarabia (between the Prut and the Dnestr, extending to the Black Sea) became an autonomous region within the Russian Empire.

**1815:** The annexation of Bessarabia by Tsar Alexander I (1801–25) was approved by the Congress of Vienna.

**1828:** Bessarabia's autonomy was abolished and it became an imperial district (oblast); the use of the Romanian language in public pronouncements was suspended.

**1854:** Russian was made the official language of Bessarabia.

**1871:** Bessarabia became a province (guberniya) of the Russian Empire, by which time western Moldova (Moldavia) and Wallachia had been united in a single Romanian state (the Ottomans recognized its independence in 1878).

**1905:** The first Romanian-language publications appeared in Bessarabia, during a revolutionary threat to tsarist authority.

**1917:** With the collapse of tsarist authority in the 1917 Revolutions, revolutionary committees of soldiers and peasants quickly established a parliament (Sfatul Ţării) in the Bessarabian capital, Chişinău (Kishinev), and declared a Bessarabian Democratic Moldovan Republic.

**27 March 1918:** The Sfatul Ţării, having declared Bessarabia's independence on 24 January, voted for union with Romania (to counter threats from Bolshevik, 'White' Russian and Ukrainian interests).

**1 December 1918:** The unification of Romania was declared, after Transylvania and Northern Bucovina had also voted to join the Romanian kingdom.

**28 October 1920:** The union of Bessarabia with Romania was recognized in the Treaty of Paris.

**1924:** A Moldovan Autonomous Soviet Socialist Republic (ASSR) was established in Soviet Ukraine, in territory to the east of the Dnestr river; the USSR claimed that the Romanians, in occupying Bessarabia, had violated Moldova's right to self-rule.

**23 August 1939:** The Treaty of Non-Aggression (the Nazi-Soviet or Molotov-Ribbentrop Pact), which was signed by the USSR and Germany, included the 'Secret Protocols', sanctioning territorial gains for the USSR in Bessarabia.

**28 June 1940:** The Soviet Red Army entered Bessarabia.

**2 August 1940:** Bessarabia officially became part of the USSR; parts of annexed Moldova were united with the existing ASSR, and the resulting Moldovan Soviet Socialist Republic (SSR) was declared a Union Republic of the USSR; two Bessarabian counties on the Black Sea, one county in the north and more than one-half of the counties of the former Moldovan ASSR were apportioned to Ukraine.

**1941–44:** The introduction of a Cyrillic alphabet for the 'Moldovan' language was interrupted by the Romanian occupation of Bessarabia, following the German invasion of the USSR; the Romanians were expelled towards the end of the Second World War.

**1950–52:** Leonid Brezhnev (Soviet leader 1964–82) was First Secretary of the Communist Party of Moldova (CPM).

**1961:** Ivan Ivanovich Bodiul became First Secretary of the CPM.

**1982:** Bodiul was succeeded as Moldovan leader by Semion Kuzmich Grossu, who held the post for seven years.

**May 1989:** The pro-Romanian Popular Front of Moldova (PFM) was established; among its aims were the abolition of the use of the Cyrillic script and the return to a Latin one, and the acceptance of Romanian as the country's state language.

**31 August 1989:** The Moldovan Supreme Soviet adopted laws that returned Moldovan to the Latin script, made it the state language of the republic and recognized its unity with the Romanian language. After protests by the Slav population, Russian was to be retained as the language of inter-ethnic communication.

**November 1989:** Grossu, a conservative, was finally replaced as First Secretary of the CPM by the more reformist Petru Lucinschi, an ethnic Romanian, following rioting in Chişinău.

**25 February 1990:** Elections to the Moldovan Supreme Soviet were held; the PFM won the largest number of seats.

**April 1990:** The new Moldovan Supreme Soviet convened; Mircea Snegur, a CPM member supported by the PFM, was re-elected Chairman of the Supreme Soviet. The legislature later adopted a modified version of the Romanian tricolour as Moldova's national flag.

**May 1990:** Petr Paskar's Government resigned after losing a vote of 'no confidence'; Mircea Druc was appointed Chairman of a Council of Ministers (Prime Minister) dominated by radical reformers; the new Government immediately undertook a series of political reforms, including revoking the CPM's constitutional monopoly of power.

**23 June 1990:** The Moldovan Supreme Soviet adopted a declaration of sovereignty, which asserted the supremacy of Moldova's Constitution and laws throughout the republic; the 1940 annexation of Bessarabia by the USSR was declared to have been illegal and, on the following day, thousands of Moldovans and Romanians assembled at the border in commemoration of the 50th anniversary of the occupation. The Supreme Soviet also specified the name of the Republic to be 'Moldova', rather than the russified 'Moldavia'.

**19 August 1990:** Five counties (raione) in southern Moldova, largely populated by ethnic Gagauz (Orthodox Christian Turks), declared a separate 'Gagauz SSR' (Gagauzia).

**2 September 1990:** Slavs in the territory east of the Dnestr river proclaimed their secession from Moldova and the establishment of a 'Dnestr SSR', which was based at Tiraspol.

**September 1990:** Snegur was elected by the Supreme Soviet to the newly instituted post of President of the Republic.

**25 October 1990:** Elections to a 'Republic of Gagauzia' Supreme Soviet were held, despite the opposition of some 50,000 armed Moldovan nationalists, who were prevented from violence only by Soviet troops.

**February 1991:** The Moldovan Supreme Soviet resolved not to conduct the all-Union referendum on the future of the USSR, but to endorse proposals for a confederation of states without central control.

**May 1991:** Mircea Druc was replaced as Prime Minister by Valeriu Muravschi, having lost support in the legislature, which later renamed the state the Republic of Moldova; the Supreme Soviet was renamed the Moldovan Parliament.

**27 August 1991:** Following the attempted coup in the Soviet capital of Moscow, Russia, Moldova declared its independence from the USSR and the CPM was banned. Romania recognized Moldova's independence and diplomatic relations between the two countries were established.

**8 December 1991:** The first popular presidential elections in Moldova took place; Snegur, the only candidate, received 98.2% of the votes cast.

**21 December 1991:** Moldova, as well as 10 other former Union Republics, signed the Almaty (Alma-Ata) Declaration, by which was formed the Commonwealth of Independent States (CIS). In the same month armed conflict broke out in the Transnistria (Transdnestr) region between the Slavic 'Dnestr Guards' and government troops.

**February 1992:** The PFM re-formed as the Christian Democratic Popular Front (CDPF).

**June 1992:** The CDPF-dominated Government resigned; Andrei Sangheli was appointed Prime Minister and, over the following two months, negotiated a new coalition administration. The pro-Romanian minority in Parliament (including the CDPF) remained able to prevent the enactment of basic or constitutional legislation (which required a two-thirds' majority).

**21 July 1992:** A peace agreement accorded Transnistria 'special status' within Moldova; Russian, Moldovan and Dnestrian peace-keeping forces were deployed in the region to monitor the cease-fire.

**January 1993:** Alexandru Moşanu was replaced as Chairman of the Moldovan Parliament by Lucinschi, the former First Secretary and now leader of the Agrarian Democratic Party (ADP), which dominated the Government and enjoyed strong support in mainly rural Moldova.

**August 1993:** The Moldovan Parliament failed to secure the necessary majority for ratification of the Almaty Declaration and to formalize the country's entry into the CIS. Nevertheless, President Snegur continued to sign CIS documents, including a treaty on economic union in September.

**January 1994:** The President of the 'Dnestr Republic' (the 'Transdnestrian Moldovan Soviet Socialist Republic'), Igor Smirnov, declared a state of emergency in Transnistria, until 1 March, in an attempt to prevent the inhabitants of the region from participating in the forthcoming Moldovan general election.

**27 February 1994:** Multi-party elections to the new, 104-member, unicameral Moldovan Parliament took place; the ADP emerged as the largest party (winning 43.2% of the votes cast and 56 seats), followed by the Slav-dominated former communists, the Socialist Party, in alliance with the Yedinstvo (Unity) movement (28 seats). Pro-unification groups shared the remaining 20 seats: the Peasants' Party of Moldova/Congress of Intelligentsia alliance (11) and the CDPF alliance (nine).

**March 1994:** In a national referendum on Moldova's statehood, more than 95% of those who voted were in favour of the country's continuing independence. Andrei Sangheli and Petru Lucinschi were re-elected Prime Minister and Chairman of Parliament, respectively.

**April 1994:** The Moldovan Parliament finally ratified membership of the CIS by 76 votes to 18. Later in the month Sangheli appointed a new Council of Ministers, consisting solely of members of the ADP.

**28 July 1994:** Parliament adopted a new Constitution, which described Moldova as a sovereign, independent, unitary and indivisible state. The official state language was described as 'Moldovan', although that was acknowledged to be identical to Romanian. The Constitution proclaimed the country's neutrality and provided for a 'special autonomous status' for Transnistria and Gagauzia within Moldova (the exact terms of which were to be determined at a later date).

**December 1994:** The Moldovan Parliament adopted legislation on the special status of Gagauz-Eri (Gagauzia): the region was to enjoy a considerable degree of autonomy; Gagauz was to be one of three official languages; and legislative power was to be vested in a regional assembly, the Halk Toplusu, while a directly elected baskan was to hold a quasi-

presidential position. This law entered into force in February 1995.

**March–April 1995:** Local elections in the 'Transdnestrian Moldovan Soviet Socialist Republic' confirmed the popularity of the Union of Patriotic Forces, which had led the self-proclaimed republic for the previous four years. In a referendum, some 91% of those who voted were against the agreed withdrawal from the region of the 14th Army. President Snegur declared both the elections and the referendum illegal.

**June 1995:** In response to the rejection by Parliament of his proposal to make Romanian (rather than Moldovan) the country's official language, Snegur resigned his membership of the ADP and established, in the following month, the Party of Revival and Conciliation (PRC), with the support of 11 rebel ADP deputies.

**24 December 1995:** A new bicameral legislature was elected in Transnistria. At the same time, two referendums were held in the region; 82.7% of the electorate endorsed a new Constitution, which proclaimed Transnistria's independence, while 89.7% voted for the region to become a member of the CIS as a sovereign state.

**21 July 1996:** Officials from the Moldovan and Transnistrian legislatures initialled a memorandum on the principles for a peace settlement, which envisaged Transnistria as having 'special status' within a Moldovan confederation; Snegur declared his opposition to the memorandum and announced that any decision on the issue be postponed until after the presidential election.

**17 November 1996:** In the first round of the presidential election, Snegur received 38.7% of the votes cast, while his closest rival, the parliamentary speaker, Lucinschi, obtained 27.7%; the Moldovan Party of Communists (MPC—the former CPM) candidate, Vladimir Voronin, won 10.2% of the ballot.

**1 December 1996:** As no candidate in the presidential election had received more than one-half of the votes cast, the two leading candidates contested a second round of voting: Lucinschi obtained 54.1% of the ballot, compared with Snegur's 45.9%.

**10 January 1997:** Smirnov, who had been re-elected for a second term as President of the 'Dnestr Republic' in December 1996, with more than 70% of the votes cast, was formally inaugurated.

**15 January 1997:** Lucinschi was inaugurated as President of Moldova. The next day he nominated Ion Ciubuc, Chairman of the State Accounting Chamber, as Prime Minister; Ciubuc was confirmed as premier later in the month.

**8 May 1997:** A memorandum of understanding on the normalization of relations between Moldova and Transnistria was signed by President Lucinschi and Smirnov in Moscow, Russia; the memorandum committed both sides to further negotiations on the status of the region; Russia, which was willing to withdraw troops from Transnistria, and Ukraine were guarantors of the agreement.

**10 November 1997:** Ciubuc and Smirnov signed a document designed to foster economic and social co-operation between Moldova and the 'Dnestr Republic'.

**17 February 1998:** At a meeting sponsored by the Organization for Security and Co-operation in Europe (OSCE), President Lucinschi and Smirnov signed protocols on economic co-operation in Tiraspol; following the meeting President Lucinschi declared that the 'Dnestr Republic' remained an integral part of Moldova, but Smirnov stressed the partnership of two equal states.

**20 March 1998:** At a meeting in Odessa, Ukraine, representatives of Moldova, the 'Dnestr Republic', Russia and Ukraine agreed a reduction in Moldovan and Transnistrian peace-keeping forces; Russian troops were to remain in Transnistria until a final political settlement had been reached (according to an agreement signed on 21 October 1994, troops of the Soviet 14th Army, under Russian jurisdiction, were orginally to have been withdrawn from Moldova within three years).

**22 March 1998:** In a general election the MPC won the largest number of seats (40) in the 104-seat Parliament, while the Democratic Convention of Moldova (CDM), an alliance that included the PRC and the CDPF, obtained 26 seats and the pro-Lucinschi Movement for a Democratic and Prosperous Moldova (MDPM) came third with 24 seats; the Moldovan Party of Democratic Forces won 11 seats.

**21 April 1998:** The CDM, the MDPM and the Party of Democratic Forces agreed to form a parliamentary alliance, led by former President Snegur; the MPC, therefore, was excluded from all major parliamentary and government posts. Two days later Diacov of the MDPM was elected speaker of the legislature.

**21 May 1998:** Parliament approved a new Government, again led by Ciubuc, a member of the CDM; the cabinet included other members of the CDM and its parliamentary allies.

**4 August 1998:** Moldova and Ukraine agreed a border delineation so as to facilitate Moldova's construction of a petroleum terminal on the Danube; the two countries also agreed to draft a 10-year economic co-operation treaty.

**1 February 1999:** Prime Minister Ion Ciubuc resigned, as, subsequently, did the parliamentary leader, Snegur, when his candidate for the premiership was rejected. Ion Sturza was confirmed as premier on 12 March.

**23 May 1999:** A referendum on increasing presidential powers was held. The Constitutional Court later deemed it to be valid (despite the rate of participation being below the stipulated threshold of 60%), but not binding.

**May 1999:** Following local elections in Moldova, both Transnistria and Gagauzia were to be designated autonomous entities, responsible for supporting themselves financially.

**10 November 1999:** Ion Sturza's Government was dismissed following a vote of 'no confidence' by Parliament.

**18–19 November 1999:** At a summit meeting of the OSCE, held in İstanbul, Turkey, Russia agreed to withdraw it troops from Moldova by the end of 2002. In December 2002, however, the deadline was extended by one year, to 31 December 2003.

**20 December 1999:** Parliament approved a new Government under Dumitru Braghiş, ending six weeks of political crisis, in which two previous nominees had failed to attract a sufficient number of votes.

**March 2000:** An agreement was signed between the 'Transdnestrian Supreme Soviet' and the Moldovan Parliament, to the effect that Transnistrian deputies would, henceforth, participate in the work of international parliamentary organizations as part of the Moldovan delegation.

**22 June 2000:** The 'Transdnestrian Supreme Soviet' was converted to a unicameral parliament, and reduced in number from 67 to 43 deputies.

**21 July 2000:** Parliament overturned a veto imposed by the President on a law that introduced parliamentary rule to Moldova, by permitting Parliament to elect the head of state; Lucinschi had favoured a national constitutional referendum on the issue. Meanwhile, the President of the 'Dnestr Republic', Igor Smirnov, dismissed his Government the next day, and introduced a form of presidential rule.

**28 July 2000:** Constitutional amendments transforming Moldova into a parliamentary state were enacted.

**4 December 2000:** The first election for the presidency to be held under new legislation took place, following the annulment of the ballot held three days previously, owing to proce-

dural irregularities. The MPC candidate, Vladimir Voronin, was supported by 50 of the 101 parliamentary deputies, and his opponent, the Chairman of the Constitutional Court, Pavel Barbalat, received 35 votes. Neither of the candidates reached the level of support required to be elected (three-fifths of the votes). A second inconclusive round of voting took place two days later.

**10 December 2000:** Parliamentary elections were held in Transnistria. Of the 43 seats, 25 were won by independent candidates; the Yedinstvo (Unity) movement emerged as the largest single party, with nine seats.

**21 December 2000:** A further round of voting for the presidency, between Voronin and Barbalat, proved inconclusive after a number of centre-right deputies boycotted the parliamentary session. After consulting the Constitutional Court, 10 days later Lucinschi dissolved Parliament, with effect from 12 January 2001, and set a parliamentary election for 25 February.

**25 February 2001:** In the parliamentary election, the MPC won 71 of 101 seats, the centrist Braghiş Alliance won 19 seats, and the Christian Democratic People's Party (CDPP— as the CDPF was known by this time) won 11 seats.

**20 March 2001:** The outgoing Government of Dumitru Braghiş tendered its resignation. On the same day Eugenia Ostapciuc was elected Chairwoman of Parliament, obtaining 72 of the 98 votes cast.

**4 April 2001:** Another presidential election took place, at which Voronin was finally elected President, securing 71 of the 89 votes cast by the deputies of the new Parliament; Braghiş received 15 votes, and another communist candidate, Valerian Christea, received three; the 11 deputies of the CDPP abstained from voting.

**19 April 2001:** A new cabinet was approved, with Vasile Tarlev as Prime Minister.

**27 July 2001:** Moldova became a full member of the World Trade Organization.

**9 December 2001:** A presidential election was held in Transnistria. Igor Smirnov was re-elected President, with some 82% of the votes cast.

**9 January 2002:** A demonstration, organized by the CDPP and attended by an estimated 3,000 people, took place in Chişinău, in protest at proposals to introduce the compulsory teaching of Russian language to the national curriculum. Daily protests, attended by up to 60,000 people, continued thereafter.

**6 February 2002:** The reformist Minister of Finance, Mihai Manole, resigned. His resignation, which followed that of the Deputy Prime Minister and Minister of the Economy, Andrei Cucu, prompted international concern that the loss of the only two non-MPC members of the Council of Ministers would hinder the implementation of economic reforms.

**26 February 2002:** The continuing domestic crisis led to the dismissal of the Minister of Education, Ilie Vancea. The Minister of the Interior, Vasile Draganel, resigned the following day, amid reports that he had been unwilling forcibly to dispel protesters.

**21 March 2002:** Vlad Cubreacov, a Deputy Chairman of the CDPP and a co-ordinator of the ongoing protests, disappeared in suspicious circumstances, prompting opposition claims of government involvement. However, on 25 May Cubreacov was discovered alive near the Transnistrian border; his kidnappers remained unidentified.

**24 April 2002:** The Parliamentary Assembly of the Council of Europe (PACE) adopted a resolution demanding that a moratorium be placed on the introduction of compulsory Russian language lessons in schools, and the cessation of the continuing anti-Government demonstrations. The CDPP agreed to end its protests five days later, but stated that failure by the Government to comply with Council of Europe recommendations calling for, *inter alia*, judicial reform, the granting of independence to the state-owned media, and the registration of the Bessarabian Metropolitan Church would lead to renewed protests.

**25 June 2002:** Dumitru Croitor announced his resignation as Baskan of Gagauzia, following months of conflict with the region's legislature. On 20 October Gheorghe Tabunscic, who had held the post of Baskan in 1995–99, was elected to succeed him.

**3 July 2002:** Mediators from Russia, Ukraine and the OSCE submitted a new draft agreement, under the terms of which Moldova would become a federal state, in which autonomous territories would maintain their own legislature and constitution; Smirnov permitted participation in negotiations on the proposals, but insisted that recognition of Transnistria's independence would be a fundamental prerequisite in negotiations.

**12 January 2003:** The Government approved legislation reintroducing a Soviet-style administrative structure to Moldova, comprising 33 districts and one municipality (Chişinău).

Local elections were held on 25 May and 8 June, in which the MPC secured the majority of the votes cast.

**27 February 2003:** The countries of the European Union (EU) and the USA (and subsequently other countries), imposed travel restrictions on 17 Transnistrian officials, including Smirnov, considered to be 'primarily responsible for a lack of co-operation in promoting a political settlement'; in retaliation, in March the Transnistrian authorities declared 14 Moldovan officials *persona non grata* in the region. Also in March the Transnistrian authorities sanctioned unconditionally the withdrawal of Russian military equipment from the region.

**28 February 2003:** After two days of negotiations, the Moldovan and Transnistrian authorities reached a preliminary agreement on proposals by Voronin for the joint drafting of a new constitution for a federal Moldovan state, which would be subject to approval by a nation-wide referendum by February 2004.

**25 July 2003:** Parliament approved a constitutional amendment, officially recognizing the autonomous status of Gagauzia and granting the Gagauz Popular Assembly the right to self-determination and the initiation of legislation.

# History

## Dr STEVEN D. ROPER

### EARLY HISTORY

Contemporary Moldova is a land-locked country located between Romania and Ukraine. According to the last census, taken in 1989, Moldova's ethnic population is approximately 64% Moldovan, 14% Ukrainian, 13% Russian, 4% Gagauz and 2% Bulgarian. The country consists of 33 districts and one municipality, the capital Chişinău (Kishinev), covering the regions of Bessarabia to the west and Transnistria (Transdnestria) to the east. The Prut river forms a natural border between Romania and Moldova, while the Dnestr (Nistru) river, which rises in Ukraine, generally forms the border between Bessarabia and Transnistria. A Moldovan principality was first established during the mid-14th century. This principality covered areas in contemporary Moldova and Romania (in the region known as Moldavia). During the 15th century, the region prospered under two important princes, Alexandru cel Bun ('the Good') and Ştefan cel Mare ('the Great'), who promoted the principality and defended Moldovan interests against the Hungarians, the Poles and the Ottoman Turks. Because of the length of their reigns (32 years and 47 years, respectively), Moldova was able to protect its territory. However, by the 1530s Moldova became a tributary state to the Ottoman Porte (Empire). Although Moldova was part of the Empire, local princes ruled the region. This situation changed in 1711, with the appointment of Turkish nobles, or Phanariots, to administer the principality.

Also by the 18th century, the increasing power of Russia and Austria was challenging Ottoman pre-eminence in the region. In 1774 Russia was awarded the right to represent Moldova at the Ottoman Sultanate, and in 1775 Austria annexed Bucovina, the northern portion of Moldova. By 1792 the territory of present-day Transnistria was ceded by the Ottoman Turks to Russia. Following the Russo–Turkish war of 1806–12, the eastern area of Moldova, between the Prut and Dnestr rivers, was formally known as Bessarabia. Following the Russian annexation of Bessarabia in 1812, the region enjoyed considerable autonomy within the Russian Empire. However, by the mid-19th century local government

control had been rescinded, and in 1854 the Moldovan (Romanian) language was supplanted by the Russian language in all legal proceedings. An influx of Russians and other ethnic groups decreased the percentage of Moldovans in the population to less than one-half. Meanwhile, in 1859 the principalities of Western Moldova (eastern Romania to the Prut) and Wallachia (southern Romania) each elected Alexandru Ioan Cuza as Prince, thereby creating a *de facto* union. Following the Berlin Congress in 1878, the principalities achieved independence, and in 1881 they were recognized as the Kingdom of Romania.

The First World War (1914–18) and the Russian Revolution (1917) provided Bessarabia's pan-Romanian nationalists with an opportunity to press their claims for Romanian integration. On the request of the Bessarabian national assembly (Sfatul Ţării), Romanian troops entered Chişinău in January 1918 and, in the same month, the Sfatul Ţării voted to form an independent Moldovan Democratic Republic of Bessarabia. Two months later, on 27 March, the Sfatul Ţării voted to unite with Romania, and by the end of 1918 Bucovina and Transylvania had joined Bessarabia to form 'Greater Romania'. Prior to the Second World War (1939–45), Bessarabia was an integral part of Romania. Of all Romania's regions, Bessarabia had one of the lowest concentrations of ethnic Romanians. So, during the interwar period, the Romanian Government undertook linguistic and educational reform to increase Romanian language literacy rates and promote Romanian culture. At the same time the Soviet authorities constructed a competing political region, the Moldovan (Moldavian) Autonomous Soviet Socialist Republic (ASSR), on the left bank of the Dnestr, in present day Transnistria.

### SOVIET MOLDOVA

In August 1939 Germany and the USSR signed the Molotov-Ribbentrop or Nazi-Soviet Pact (also known as the Treaty of Non-Aggression). The agreement included the 'Secret Protocols', which conceded the USSR's interest in Bessarabia. On 26 June 1940 the USSR issued an ultimatum to Romania, demanding the immediate cession of Bessarabia and Northern Bucovina, and by 3 July both territories were under Soviet control, as the Moldovan Soviet Socialist Republic (SSR). The SSR of Moldova was formed by joining Bessarabia with six counties that had formed part of the ASSR; a significant amount of territory was also awarded to Ukraine. Moldova inherited a large Russian-speaking community, and immigration, particularly of ethnic Russian industrial workers, caused the majority population of many cities to become heavily russified. The percentage of ethnic Russians in Moldova increased almost two-fold from 6.7% in 1941 to 13.0% by 1989. Throughout this period, the Soviet leadership encouraged the creation of a distinct Moldovan nation. As part of the policy of russification, the alphabet for the Moldovan language was changed from Latin to Cyrillic, and Russian once again became the language of inter-ethnic communication, higher education and public life.

As occurred elsewhere, reforms introduced by the Soviet leader, Mikhail Gorbachev, in the mid-1980s (*glasnost*—openness and *perestroika*—restructuring) created conditions in which long-standing resentment against Soviet ethnic policies could be expressed. In 1987 Moldovan intellectuals organized informal discussion groups that focused on promoting the use of the Romanian language. Within a year these groups had become formally organized around the issue of linguistic and cultural freedom. By mid-1988 Moldovan intellectuals and the pro-Romanian opposition had formed the Democratic Movement in Support of Restructuring (later renamed the Popular Front or PF) to advocate democratization and redress for discriminatory practices imposed upon the majority population. The prospect of ethnic Moldovans gaining political power provoked an immediate response from Russian-speaking minorities. Many non-ethnic Moldovans supported Yedinstvo, the Internationalist Movement for Unity, a pro-Russian movement, for which the strongest base of support existed in Transnistria.

By 1989 the PF had become the leading Moldovan opposition force, proposing a strong Romanian and unionist agenda. Interestingly, several leading PF members were also senior Communist Party members. In August the Moldovan Supreme Soviet (parliament) proclaimed Moldovan (using the Latin alphabet) as the state language. Moldova's last Soviet-era parliament was elected in March 1990. Unlike earlier elections to the Supreme Soviet, the 1990 election was generally fair. Following the election, the PF entered into a parliamentary coalition with several other parties, and held over 66% of the seats. Alexandru Moşanu of the PF was named parliamentary Chairman (speaker), and parliament confirmed a Government composed almost entirely of ethnic Moldovans. Moreover, the Chairman of the Council of Ministers (Prime Minister) appointed in May, Mircea Druc, was a strong advocate of union with Romania. Parliament also re-elected Mircea Snegur as Chairman of the Supreme Soviet and, subsequently, President of the Republic (he was popularly elected in 1991). During this period PF members of parliament and the Druc Government pursued a pro-Romanian and pro-unionist agenda that alienated the Russian minority.

### INDEPENDENT MOLDOVA

The early actions of the legislature and the Government had an immediate negative consequence. Ethnic minorities, including ethnic Russians, Ukrainians and Gagauz, felt that they were being marginalized by the pro-Romanian nationalists. Inside Parliament (as the Supreme Soviet was renamed in May 1991), anti-reformists organized themselves into a legislative faction called Soviet Moldavia and, on the streets of Chişinău, Moldovan demonstrators became increasingly hostile towards members of Parliament from ethnic minorities.

On 27 August Moldova proclaimed its independence, which escalated demands for independence by Transnistria. The resulting civil conflict and the cease-fire agreement of mid-1992 marked the turning point in the political fortunes of the PF. The party was perceived as responsible for the war with Transnistria, and in August 1992 several PF members defected and formed an alliance to remove the party's leadership. By early 1993 the PF, re-formed as the Christian Democratic Popular Front (CDPF), was in total disarray. The party's voting strength in Parliament was reduced to a mere 25 deputies. The Prime Minister, Valeriu Muravschi, who had replaced Mircea Druc in May 1991, was, in turn, replaced by Andrei Sangheli in June 1992, and in January 1993 the Chairman of Parliament, Alexandru Mosanu, was replaced by Petru Lucinschi. However, these changes only increased tensions. The reformist communists and the less nationalistic forces, which comprised the core support for the Sangheli Government, dominated Parliament, and this led to a legislative impasse. Finally, Parliament was dissolved and new parliamentary elections were held in February 1994.

An electoral law changed several features of Parliament and the electoral system, including a reduction in the number of members of Parliament from 380 to 104, the introduction of a 4% electoral threshold, and the creation of a single national electoral district. Reformist communist groupings, such as the Socialist Party and the Agrarian Democratic Party (ADP), demanded a much more cautious approach towards economic issues. These parties favoured full participation in the structures of the Commonwealth of Independent States (CIS) and a conciliatory approach to the Transnistrian and Gagauz separatists. The result of this first entirely post-communist election marked a sharp reversal from the politics of the early transition period. Nationalist and pro-Romanian forces were overwhelmingly rejected, in favour of those supporting Moldovan independence and accommodation with ethnic minorities. The ADP won 43% of the votes cast and received 56 of the 104 seats in Parliament. Another 28 seats were won by the socialist bloc, which received 22% of the votes. The pro-Romanian parties suffered a severe reverse. The PF, which two years earlier led the coalition Government, received only 7.5% of the votes cast and nine seats. Members of the ADP controlled all of Parliament's leadership positions, and Lucinschi was renamed speaker. President Snegur joined the party in February 1994.

The ADP was a coalition of diverse ideological views, and although the party held a majority of seats, it later suffered several key defections. Several members of Parliament left the party in 1995, among them Snegur, who left in June. The parliamentary defections forced the ADP to rely increasingly on the socialists. By the time of the November 1996 presidential election, the ADP was losing its influence. In the first round of presidential elections, none of the top three candidates were ADP members. In the 'run-off' election on 1 December Lucinschi received 54% of the votes cast, defeating Snegur. Shortly thereafter, Prime Minister Sangheli resigned and was replaced by Ion Ciubuc. Lucinschi's victory did not create a major reorientation of Moldovan foreign or domestic policy; while he emphasized relations with other CIS countries, Lucinschi continued the country's existing foreign policy with Romania and the Russian Federation.

By the time of the parliamentary election of March 1998 the party formations and alliances within Moldova had changed. Snegur's party, the Party of Revival and Conciliation (PRC), merged with other rightist parties, including the Popular Front, to form the Democratic Convention of Moldova (CDM). In addition, the pro-Lucinschi Movement For a Democratic and Prosperous Moldova (MDPM) was established in February 1997. Economic issues dominated the election campaign, and because of the dissatisfaction that many Moldovans felt about the economy, the Moldovan Party of Communists (MPC) received 30% of the votes cast and approximately 40% of parliamentary seats. However, the remaining three parties in Parliament, the Party of Democratic Forces, the CDM and the MDPM, formed a parliamentary coalition called the Alliance for Democratic Reform (ADR), and confirmed Ion Ciubuc as Prime Minister, once again. In February 1999 tensions in the coalition prompted the resignation of Ciubuc, and in March Ion Sturza was confirmed as Prime Minister. His Government was considered much more pro-reform than the previous two Ciubuc Governments and enjoyed real popular support. Perhaps because of his popularity, conflict with Lucinschi and Parliament resulted in Sturza's removal from office in November. In December Dumitru Braghiş was confirmed as Prime Minister.

The conflict between Sturza and Lucinschi formed part of a larger conflict between the legislature and the President. In May 1999 Lucinschi held a consultative referendum proposing constitutional changes to increase his presidential powers. Although the referendum was to have no judicial effect, Lucinschi proposed a controversial draft law to provide the President with sole authority to appoint and remove cabinet ministers. However, Lucinschi lacked a parliamentary majority, and conflict with Parliament increased as, by mid-2000, the ADR had fragmented, and even the pro-presidential MDPM, which changed its name to the Democratic Party of Moldova (PDM) in April, began openly to criticize the President. In early July Parliament approved a series of constitutional amendments, allowing the President to be elected and dismissed by Parliament; Lucinschi vetoed the proposed changes, but Parliament overturned his decision in late July.

Although Parliament was united in its opposition to Lucinschi, the process of voting for a new president demonstrated significant differences between party factions. It was necessary to hold a presidential election by 1 January 2001, as Lucinschi's term of office was due to expire on 15 January. Two inconclusive rounds of voting took place in early December 2000, after an initial round was annulled. Several parties subsequently boycotted a fourth round of voting, preventing it from taking place, and permitting Lucinschi to dissolve Parliament and announce an early general election, which took place on 25 February 2001.

In the legislative election, the MPC received 50% of the votes cast and 71 seats in Parliament. The only other parties to obtain seats were the Braghiş Alliance (formed by Dumitru Braghiş) and the Christian Democratic Popular Party (CDPP, the former CDPF), as fewer parties qualified for entry into Parliament following the increase of the electoral threshold to 6%. On 4 April 2001 Vladimir Voronin, the First Secretary of the MPC, was finally elected to the presidency, securing 71 votes. Following his inauguration on 7 April, Voronin nominated Vasile Tarlev as Prime Minister.

The MPC-dominated Government, and particularly the Ministry of Education, attempted to enact several of the electoral pledges made by President Voronin and the MPC. At the end of 2001 the Government proposed replacing the study of the history of Romania with that of Moldova, and making the teaching of Russian language compulsory. The education reform plans were criticized by several noted scientists and educators, and the CDPP undertook a series of protests in Chişinău from January 2002, in an attempt to block the proposed changes, and to demand the resignations of both the Government and the Parliament. The almost daily protests were held on the main street of the capital, with attendance ranging from several hundred to several thousand; a demonstration held at the end of March was the largest, attended by more than 50,000 people. Although the CDPP was motivated by pan-Romanian concerns, many demonstrators were pro-

testing at the country's deteriorating economy. Meanwhile, Vlad Cubreacov, the Deputy Chairman of the CDPP, was reported missing in March. The scandal surrounding Cubreacov's mysterious disappearance, together with the ongoing protests, compelled the Government to cancel the proposed amendments to the education system. However, the political crisis failed to unseat the ruling party; although most Moldovans were dissatisfied with the economy, the CDPP was not viewed as a credible alternative to the MPC. Cubreacov was discovered alive in late May, and by mid-2002 the protests had ended and the MPC maintained its dominance over central institutions.

Following the demonstrations, the first real test of the political strength of the MPC occurred during the local elections of May–June 2003, for mayors and county and city councils. Although the MPC won more than 54% of the seats on the county and city councils and more than 40% of the mayoralties, it did not win the important mayoral election for the city of Chişinău. Moreover, for the first time, the Organization for Security and Co-operation in Europe's (OSCE) electoral observation mission was critical of the state's interference in the local elections, in particular its manipulation of the state media.

### TRANSNISTRIA

Transnistria's ethnic composition is unlike that of the rest of Moldova. In Transnistria approximately 55% of the population are ethnic Ukrainians and Russians, and the region, excluding the city of Tighina (Bender) and a few villages, was never part of Romania. Therefore, pan-Romanian appeals by the PF in the early 1990s were especially resented in Transnistria. The Transnistrians refused to acknowledge the 1989 language law, and in early May 1990, the city governments of Tiraspol and Tighina refused to accept any of the measures passed by the Moldovan Parliament. Following the formation of the Transnistrian Moldovan SSR in September 1990, relations with the separatists emerged as the dominant issue for the Moldovan Government.

After the declaration of Moldovan independence in August 1991, the future President of Transnistria, Igor Smirnov, and other Transnistrian officials negotiated for the creation of a confederal government. During 1991 and 1992, several clashes occurred between the Moldovan military and Transnistrian paramilitary units. The Transnistrian paramilitary greatly benefited from equipment and personnel provided by the Russian 14th Army located in Tiraspol. As the Transnistrian separatists consolidated their position, nationalists inside the Moldovan Parliament became increasingly militant. This brought intense pressure on President Snegur to undertake decisive action to resolve the conflict. In late March 1992 a state of emergency was declared and an effort was made to disarm units of the separatist militia by force. This attempt met with violent resistance, and by May the conflict had escalated into a full-scale civil war. The heaviest fighting occurred close to the Moldovan and Transnistrian border, particularly in the cities of Dubasari and Tighina. There are various estimates of the number of casualties, but perhaps as many as 1,000 died during this period. The violence in Tighina compelled the Russian Government to intervene actively in the conflict. In July the Russian President, Boris Yeltsin, and Snegur signed a cease-fire agreement that established a Joint Control Committee to observe the military forces in the security zone and maintain order.

From July 1992 the relationship between Moldova and Transnistria did not change fundamentally. There were periods of negotiation, followed by months of inactivity. In July 1996 a memorandum on the settlement of the conflict was endorsed by Moldovan and Transnistrian officials. The memorandum recognized Transnistria's right to maintain international contacts and to develop relations in the framework of a 'common state'. President Snegur refused to sign the memorandum, and it was hoped that Lucinschi's election would represent a turning point in the relationship. Many believed that his relations within the former Communist Party would enable him to resolve the conflict. However, after taking office, President Lucinschi did not achieve any significant progress in the negotiation process. Initially, he too refused to sign the memorandum, but, finally, in May 1997, he and Smirnov signed the document in Moscow. From then, there were a number of high-level meetings in Odessa and Kiev (both in Ukraine), but the negotiating positions generally remained unchanged, and little substantive progress was made. Transnistria asserted that the concept of a common state be defined as an equal partnership between two states, but the Moldovan Government rejected this definition, as did international bodies, including the OSCE. According to a document signed at an OSCE summit, held in İstanbul, Turkey, in November 1999, Russia was to withdraw its military presence from Transnistria in three stages, with all hardware to be removed by the end of 2001 and troops by 2002. Although three convoys, carrying limited weaponry and non-combat material, were dispatched immediately, only one convoy left Transnistria in 2000, and the first destruction of equipment did not begin until July 2001. In late 2001 several more trains departed from Transnistria, and by the end of the year Russia claimed to have met its obligations under the agreement reached in 1999. However, at mid-2002 Russia had still to withdraw some 2,600 troops from Transnistria. Meanwhile, the Transnistrian leadership continued to oppose the planned withdrawal, and demanded some form of financial compensation. Following an agreement by Russia to cancel part of Transnistria's US $100m. gas debt, Russia withdrew a substantial quantity of ammunition and weapons in the first half of 2003, but progress continued to be hampered by the Transnistrian authorities. In an attempt to ensure that the full evacuation of ammunition was completed by the end of 2003, the USA eventually offered to provide financial aid to Transnistria.

Following the election of President Voronin in early 2001, there was a great deal of optimism that a conclusive status could be negotiated for Transnistria. During the parliamentary election campaign, the MPC had proposed the elevation of Russian to a second state language and Moldovan membership of the Russia-Belarus Union. Although these policies were not immediately implemented, it was hoped that the support of the Moldovan leadership for such issues would satisfy Transnistria. The negotiations between Voronin and Smirnov were initially successful: in May Transnistria released the Romanian-Moldovan nationalist, Ilie Ilascu, from a Transnistrian gaol, following his imprisonment on charges of terrorism in 1992. The release of Ilascu (his colleagues remained imprisoned) had been a long-standing demand of the Moldovan Government, and Voronin and Smirnov met on subsequent occasions to negotiate a wide range of issues. However, by late 2001 Voronin had concluded that Smirnov had no real interest in ending the status quo and, therefore, the negotiations had produced no lasting agreement on resolving the conflict.

In July 2002 the first signs of possible progress in the negotiating process were finally discernible. Mediators from Russia, Ukraine and the OSCE submitted a new draft agreement to the Moldovan and Transnistrian sides, which constituted the most detailed and far-reaching proposals thus far. Fundamentally, the 'Kiev agreement' envisioned the federalization of Moldova, with state-territorial formations (specifically Transnistria) to exercise local power over a range of issues, subordinate to the Moldovan central administration. The proposals included plans for the creation of a bicameral

parliament, the upper house of which would represent the territorial formations. Although the proposal was well-received by President Voronin and leading members of the MPC, opposition parties were more critical. There were concerns that the proposal did not specify the number of territorial formations to be created and that it failed to provide a mechanism for constitutional revision.

The Kiev agreement continued to serve as a basis of discussion between Moldovan and Transnistrian officials throughout 2003. In February Voronin proposed that a new constitution be adopted, based on the federal principles of the Kiev agreement. Voronin established a Constitutional Commission, charged with drafting a new constitution (in collaboration with Transnistrian representatives), which was to be submitted to the population at a referendum and which, if passed, would result in new elections to all nation-wide offices. Although the OSCE, the European Union (EU) and Western countries, such as the USA, were in favour of the federalization of the country, most opposition parties remained firmly opposed to both the principle of federalization and the Kiev agreement. From the opposition perspective, the proposed federalization of the country represented a 'Russian view', which would end the sovereign integrity of the country. However, international organizations, such as the OSCE, argued that federalization was the only basis for ending the long-standing conflict. Throughout mid-2003 the Constitutional Commission met to finalize the draft, which was subsequently to be sent to the Moldovan and Transnistrian leaderships and international mediators for examination.

## GAGAUZIA

The Gagauz constitute approximately 3.5% of the Moldovan population and are concentrated in the south. They are a Turkic language-speaking people of Orthodox Christian faith who originated in Bulgaria, and they have inhabited the area of southern Moldova for centuries. The Gagauz were highly russified during the Soviet period and, even by the beginning of the 2000s, Russian remained their primary language of commerce and education. The Gagauz initially participated in the meetings of the PF, as they had formed an organization called the Gagauz Halki (Gagauz People), which co-operated with the Front. However, as the PF transformed from a reformist to a pan-Romanian organization, the Gagauz Halki demanded Gagauz independence. In August 1990 the Gagauz announced the formation of a republic with Comrat (Komrat) as the capital; national symbols were adopted and a local defence force was organized. Also during this time, Gagauz and Transnistrians began to co-operate in several areas. However, the formation of a Gagauz state never achieved the same degree of development as it did in Transnistria. The industrial base, significant ethnic Russian population and the presence of the 14th Army provided Transnistria with several advantages that the Gagauz never possessed.

In October 1990 the Gagauz conducted a parliamentary election to a Supreme Soviet. As in Transnistria, Gagauz élites supported the August 1991 coup, and the Moldovan declaration of independence only hardened the Gagauz position. In December Stepan Topol was elected President of Gagauzia. At the time, the Moldovan Government was unable to exercise authority over the area, and Gagauzia was essentially independent of Moldova. However, the Transnistrian civil war convinced the Moldovan leadership that moderation was the best approach to conflict resolution. This, combined with a change in the Moldovan leadership, made negotiations much easier. After the February 1994 parliamentary election and the passage of the Constitution in July, the Moldovan Government entered into the final phase of negotiations with the Gagauz élite. The legislation creating Gagauz-Eri

(Gagauz Land) recognized Gagauzia as an autonomous territorial unit with a special status of self-determination. The Gagauz were to elect a governor (baskan) and a Popular Assembly. Elections for the post of baskan and the Popular Assembly were held in 1995, and again in 1999. The Moldovan Government hoped that the special status of Gagauzia would serve as an example for Transnistria. However, paradoxically, many Transnistrians were unwilling to accept territorial autonomy, precisely because of the example of Gagauzia from 1995. Most Transnistrians and, indeed, almost all Gagauz, believed that Gagauzia did not enjoy a truly autonomous status within Moldova and, instead, considered there to have been a devolution of power from Comrat to Chişinău. The Gagauz leadership began to make increasing demands for greater local autonomy towards the end of the 1990s, and Baskan Dumitru Croitor campaigned for authority over local taxation, as well as the power to undertake territorial-administrative reorganization.

In February 2002 deputies in the Popular Assembly who were sympathetic to the MPC supported a motion of 'no confidence' in Croitor's governorship, and the scheduling of a referendum on the issue, following allegations of the misuse of budgetary funds. The MPC attempted to consolidate local power, and even demanded that a new local election be held in April. Ultimately, the referendum failed, as supporters of Croitor claimed that it had not been approved by the required majority, and Croitor remained in office, despite his deteriorating relationship with both the central Government and the MPC. In March President Voronin visited the region, and also made demands for Croitor's resignation. Finally, in July both Croitor and the Chairman of the Popular Assembly resigned. At an election to the post of baskan, held in October, Gheorghe Tabunscic secured the highest proportion of the votes cast; however, Croitor had been barred from participating in the election by the electoral commission, owing to a legal technicality.

On 25 July 2003 the Moldovan Parliament approved a constitutional amendment, officially recognizing the autonomous status of Gagauzia and granting the Popular Assembly the right to self-determination and the initiation of legislation.

### RELATIONS WITH ROMANIA SINCE 1991

After Moldova proclaimed its independence, the Romanian Government adopted an ambivalent policy. On the one hand, Romania was the first country to recognize Moldova's independence; on the other, Romanian politicians articulated a policy of eventual reunification. The Romanian Government always maintained that reunification should be a Moldovan decision. In 1991 and 1992 President Snegur maintained a policy of 'one people, two states'. Throughout this period, Snegur resisted calls for reunification and, at the same time, the pro-Front majority became a minority by 1994. The Moldovan public's zeal for reunification had clearly waned, and in March 1994 a non-binding referendum was held on the question of statehood. An overwhelming 95% of the electorate voted for the continuation of Moldovan statehood. This result was not surprising considering that even in 1992, fewer than 15% of ethnic Moldovans had favoured reunification. By the mid-1990s Snegur had changed his position somewhat. He attempted to change the Constitution and rename the state language as Romanian, while maintaining a pro-independence stance. During the 1996 presidential election Snegur and his chief opponent, Lucinschi, both articulated a pro-independence position. Following Lucinschi's election, relations between the two countries generally remained cordial, if sometimes distant, although Romania's relationship with the EU caused tensions. Following the election of a communist Government in Moldova in early 2001, there were concerns that Moldova would pursue ties with Russia, at the expense of those with Romania.

Many Moldovans feared that Romania's application for full EU membership might eventually force the country to close its Moldovan border. From mid-2001 Moldovans entering Romania were required to carry a passport (as opposed to a Moldovan identity card), although Romania agreed to provide financial assistance to Moldova to facilitate the issuing of passports.

Meanwhile, after the electoral victory of the MPC in 2001, Moldovan-Romanian relations began to show severe strain. The Moldovan and Romanian Governments diverged on several issues, including proposals for the registration in Moldova of a pro-Romanian Orthodox Church (which eventually took place at the end of July 2002); the language to be used in the long-delayed bilateral friendship treaty; and the enrolment of Moldovan students in Romanian educational institutions. As an indication of the deteriorating relations, in March the Moldovan Government expelled the Romanian military attaché from Chişinău; the Romanian Government immediately retaliated by expelling a Moldovan diplomat. By mid-2003 relations had improved marginally. In May the Moldovan Parliament passed legislative amendments allowing dual citizenship. The law came into effect in July, and more than 5,000 Moldovans had applied for Romanian citizenship by August. However, the Romanian Government continued to refuse to enter into negotiations over a basic treaty between the two countries, and the Moldovan Government took several actions that limited the ability of Moldovan students to study in Romania.

# The Economy

## Dr STEVEN D. ROPER

### INTRODUCTION

Throughout the mid-1990s Moldova was regarded by international financial organizations such as the World Bank and the IMF as one of the success stories of the former USSR. Because of its pursuit of a strict monetary policy, the Moldovan currency, the leu, was one of the most stable in the region. Although the country experienced 'hyperinflation' in the early 1990s, the Government was able to reduce annual inflation to 11.8% by 1997. However, in 1998 the collapse of the Russian economy and the loss of its markets contributed to a 6.5% decrease in gross domestic product (GDP). By the first quarter of 1999 GDP had declined significantly in comparison with the first quarter of 1998. Although the Government attempted to enact economic reforms, the economy continued to decline throughout 1999 and, overall, GDP declined by 4.4% in that year. Between September 1998 and September 1999, the leu lost one-half of its value against the US dollar, and the annual rate of inflation increased from 4% in August 1998 to 50% in August 1999. The annual inflation rate for 1999 was 39.3%, which was the highest level recorded over the previous five years.

Although the economic picture was bleak, the Government of Prime Minister Ion Sturza (March–November 1999) undertook several reforms that eventually led to a stronger economy. These reforms were cautiously continued by his successor, Dumitru Braghiş (December 1999–March 2001), and GDP increased by some 1.9% in 2000, while the annual rate of inflation decreased to 31.3%. Despite significant political turmoil in 2001, the economy continued to improve. The rate of GDP growth in that year was a remarkable 6.1%, and the rate of inflation continued to decline. By 2002 annual GDP growth had reached its highest recorded level (7.2%) and the annual rate of consumer-price inflation was 5.5%. However, even with these improvements in the economy, Moldova continued to amass an enormous level of foreign debt, including substantial energy debts. By the end of 2001 total external debt was valued at US $1,214m. (including a sizeable energy debt to Russia). The accumulation of debt coincided with a decline in export earnings, making it difficult for the country to service its debt; Moldova resorted to new borrowing simply to service debt obligations. In 2001 the cost of external debt-servicing amounted to 19.4% of the value of exports of goods and services. This situation became more critical as international institutions, such as the IMF, suspended sovereign lending in 2003.

Trade and energy issues became increasingly important in the discussions between the Moldovan Government and the Transnistrian authorities. Transnistria (Transdnestria) is a region situated on the left bank of Moldova's Nistru (Dnestr) river. Following civil conflict in May 1992, this region remained *de facto* independent of Moldova (see History). The Government in Chişinău (Kishinev), the Moldovan capital, carried out negotiations with the Transnistrian leadership from 1992, but several political and economic issues separated the two sides. The loss of Transnistria was particularly difficult, because most light industries and energy facilities are located in the region. Moreover, as the Moldovan Government attempted to negotiate a new, federalized constitution with Transnistria in 2003, one of the major issues of concern was whether the central Government or the local Transnistrian authorities would be responsible for the large Transnistrian debt.

The difficult economic situation also caused a social crisis. Some of the problems facing Moldova in the social sector included hidden unemployment (often inherent in reduced working hours), salary arrears (in 1998 over US $70m. was owed by the Government to workers and pensioners) and an increase in the number of people living in poverty. Moreover, as state-owned enterprises were privatized, the level of unemployment increased. The financing of social provisions, distributed between the central and local government budgets (health, education and cash compensation) and the Social Fund (pensions, short-term sickness and maternity benefits), was severely overstretched.

Perhaps because of privatization efforts, employment in industry decreased sharply. However, industrial employment was not reduced as significantly as that in the agricultural sector. Part of the difficulty in determining the level of unemployment in Moldova is that the country's definition of unemployment is different to that in the West, as it does not include workers who give notice voluntarily; only workers who are dismissed are eligible to register as unemployed. Based on a Western definition of unemployment, the World Bank calculated that between 10% and 20% of the labour force was not working at any one time. According to the UN Development Programme (UNDP), at the end of the 1990s between 240,000 and 250,000 individuals were unemployed. Owing to salary arrears, even those who are employed have difficulty maintaining their existence. There has been substantial emigration from the country precisely because of these economic difficulties, and it is estimated that at least 10% of the population emigrated after 1991.

## ECONOMIC POLICY

### Currency and Foreign Investment

The Moldovan leu was introduced in November 1993. Before that time the Russian rouble and a Moldovan coupon were the recognized currencies. Once the leu was issued, all Soviet and Russian money issued between 1961 and 1992, and all Moldovan coupons, had to be exchanged for the new currency by December. There were many reasons why Moldova left the so-called 'rouble zone'. First, there was a shortage of roubles in Moldova because of the early restrictive monetary policy of the Russian Central Bank. Second, Moldova did not want to be dependent on Russia for monetary policy, since this made it difficult for the Moldovan Government to implement its own domestic stabilization programme. Third, the leu was an obvious sign of sovereignty. For some observers, the naming of the leu was controversial. Romania's currency is also called the leu, and the Government's decision to adopt this name for its currency was used by certain political parties and authorities in Transnistria as evidence that it intended to reunify with Romania.

The law on foreign investment was passed in April 1992. The Government realized that restructuring the economy would require foreign capital. Moreover, the privatization process required certain state-owned enterprises to be purchased with 'hard' (convertible) currency by foreign investors. The foreign investment law recognized various forms of investment: joint-enterprise ownership, intellectual property, buildings and other areas of construction. However, initially, foreign investors were not allowed to purchase land. In 1992 and 1993 many companies were reluctant to invest in Moldova, because they were concerned that the Transnistrian civil war would spread to other regions, especially the area of southern Moldova, known as Gagauzia. Therefore, during 1990–92 only 257 enterprises with foreign investment were registered. In October 1993 foreign investment reached US $52m. in 170 joint ventures. By 1998 annual foreign direct investment had reached almost $75m., and by 2000 foreign investment totalled $125m. In 2001 the privatization of various energy enterprises resulted in the highest-ever level of annual foreign direct investment, amounting to approximately $300m. However, in 2002 foreign direct investment was a mere $37m. This reflected concerns expressed by many companies over the worsening business environment in Moldova, particularly after the Spanish company Unión Eléctrica Fenosa, a strategic investor and owner of three power distribution networks in Moldova, had repeated difficulties dealing with both the central and local Government.

### Trade and International Organizations

The Moldovan economy has always been orientated towards agriculture, as this is where Moldova enjoys a comparative advantage over most of the other former Soviet republics. During the Soviet period, Moldova was the sixth largest agricultural producer of the 15 republics and the most productive in relative terms. Commerce with the countries of the Commonwealth of Independent States (CIS) still accounted for over 70% of Moldovan trade at the beginning of the 2000s. Although there was a reorientation towards Western markets (non-CIS exports totalled US $300m. in 1996, and accounted for 45% of export trade in 2000), Moldova had a growing trade deficit with the West. For example, in 1997 the Western trade deficit was $343m., of which $340m. was the result of trade with the European Union (EU).

After achieving independence in 1991, economic policy worked towards securing Moldova's membership of international economic organizations. Within one year of proclaiming independence, Moldova became a member of the European Bank for Reconstruction and Development (EBRD). In early July 1992 the USA granted Moldova most-favoured nation trade status, and in mid-August Moldova joined both the IMF and the World Bank. By 2000 the World Bank had granted Moldova credits worth over US $200m. However, in 1996 the World Bank encountered strong criticism from the Parliament, when, as part of the terms for the receipt of a Structural Adjustment Loan, the Government was required to increase tariffs for electricity, reduce the budgetary deficit and reform the pensions system. The World Bank and the IMF demanded an increase in the retirement age for men to 65 years (from 60 years) and for women to 60 years (from 55 years). Parliament refused to enact many of these measures, and the communists, in particular, protested against raising the retirement age. In 1999 the World Bank suspended the disbursement of further lending until concessions were finally enacted by Parliament in late 2000.

The first use of IMF resources in Moldova occurred in 1993, when the IMF granted a US $19m. credit to defray the cost of cereal imports, under the Compensatory and Contingency Financing Facility. In mid-September Moldova received a further loan of $32m., under the Fund's Systemic Transformation Facility, in order to assist the Government's reform programme until 30 June 1994. In 1995 the IMF's Executive Board described Moldova's performance under the three-year extended arrangement (1993–95) as highly satisfactory. The IMF was particularly pleased with the ability of the Moldovan Government to reduce inflation and maintain the strength of its currency. In May 1996 the IMF approved an $185m. Extended Fund Facility (EFF). However, after that time the IMF, like the World Bank, encountered opposition to its orthodox monetary policies from Parliament. By November 1997 the IMF refused to release the fourth tranche of the EFF, because of continuing budgetary deficits and the refusal of Parliament to implement pensions reform.

Following the general election of March 1998, IMF officials stated that there were grounds for optimism concerning Moldovan economic reform, but in February 1999, less than one year after taking office, Prime Minister Ion Ciubuc resigned his post. In March Ion Sturza was confirmed as Prime Minister. He was generally regarded as much more pro-Western and pro-reform than previous prime ministers. By August his Government had negotiated a new IMF loan and the release of a tranche of an earlier World Bank loan, but conflict with President Petru Lucinschi and with Parliament prompted Sturza's removal from office in November. After two failed nominations, Dumitru Braghiş was confirmed as Prime Minister in December. However, by this time Moldova's relationship with the international lending organizations had deteriorated significantly. The IMF had halted lending, and it was only after commitments from Sturza that necessary reforms would occur, that financing resumed. The removal of Sturza and the failure of Parliament to privatize large state-owned enterprises compelled the IMF to suspend the disbursement of further lending. In March 2000 Parliament began debating the year's budget. Although the IMF and the World Bank had urged the privatization of the tobacco and the wine industries, the communists voted overwhelmingly not to include the sale of these enterprises in the new budget. Braghiş warned that such a budget would prevent Moldova from signing a new agreement with the IMF. Credits were subsequently suspended until further concessions by the Government were made in late 2000, when the IMF approved a new, three-year

loan. However, disbursement of the third tranche of this loan was, once again, suspended, following the parliamentary election of February 2001, as the new communist Government of Prime Minister Vasile Tarlev refused to abide by the previous IMF and World Bank agreements. Moldova desperately needed the continuing financial support of both organizations in order to repay its foreign debt. In mid-2001 Moldova joined both the World Trade Organization (WTO) and the Stability Pact for South Eastern Europe, from which it hoped to benefit economically. Subsequently, following repeated negotiations with the Tarlev Government, both the IMF and the World Bank began to resume limited financing to Moldova in mid-2002, although lending was suspended once again in 2003.

### The Budget

As in many former Soviet republics, Moldova's foreign debt continued to rise, placing severe pressure on the budget. In 1990 it recorded a budgetary surplus, and in 1991 the budget was balanced. However, by 1992 Moldova began to generate budgetary deficits. For example, in 1994 the budgetary deficit, as a percentage of GDP, reached 8.1%. In 1998 the country paid over US $120m. towards debt-servicing, and by 2001 debt-servicing comprised almost 30% of the budget. Although the 2002 budget deficit was equivalent to approximately 1% of GDP, some 75% of the budget was devoted to debt-servicing. By 2002 President Vladimir Voronin acknowledged that unless external debt was restructured, the country would have to default on its repayments. The Government was successful in renegotiating its Eurobonds, and urged the 'Paris Club' of international creditors to renegotiate some $300m. of debt. As a consequence of the prospect of default, rating agencies downgraded the country's foreign liabilities and investment rating.

There are a number of reasons why foreign debt and the budgetary deficit have become such intractable problems in Moldova. First, the industrial sector, which, of all the economic sectors, had the greatest potential for generating capital, is inefficient, and, moreover, many of the most productive industries are located in Transnistria. Moldova's industrial sector is superior to its agricultural sector in its capacity for economic production. In fact, in the past, Moldovan industry was responsible for between 60% and 70% of the country's budgetary revenue. However, because of the uncertain status of Transnistria, budgetary revenue from industry declined. In the early 2000s almost 25% of industrial production was located in Transnistria, and 87% of Moldova's electricity and all of its large electric-machinery output came from this region. However, in 2000 industrial output finally registered an increase, of 2.8%, after years of decline, and in 2002 industrial output contributed approximately 19% of GDP.

Although the industrial sector is an important source of revenue, the agricultural sector, and especially the agro-industrial sector, are important contributors to the budgetary deficit. Using the old Soviet-style accounting procedures, agriculture in the early 1990s accounted for 40% of net material product (NMP). An additional 20% (or one-half of the industrial sector share of NMP) came from the agro-industrial sector (mainly food-processing). While output from the agricultural sector diminished because of severe floods and droughts in 1993 and 1994 and an extremely harsh winter in 1997, if the figures are analyzed, the evidence indicates that the state collective farms were primarily responsible for the negative performance of agriculture. In 1993 the production level of private farms was almost double the 1989 production level. One of the problems with the agro-industrial sector is that the food-processing plants are not located in proximity to the produce. For example, 65% of the agro-industrial capacity for fruits and vegetables is located in the south-east, whereas produce is located in the northern and central regions. This problem reflects a significant resource problem throughout the former Soviet republics. None the less, agriculture continues to be an important economic sector. In 2002 the sector accounted for 21% of GDP and for 75% of exports, despite the adverse effects of severe weather problems.

## AGRICULTURAL PRIVATIZATION

The political debate surrounding agricultural privatization was much more heated in Moldova than that concerning industrial privatization (see below). This is not surprising given the relative political importance of the old-style Soviet farm system and the significance of the agricultural sector. The issue was also more politically sensitive, because there was no overwhelming support for agricultural privatization. Although industrial privatization was supported by a large segment of Moldovan society, surveys conducted in 1994 found that only 51% of respondents believed that there should be a programme to allow citizens to become landowners. Owing to the sensitivity surrounding agricultural privatization, a very different approach was used to privatize state farms. Although there were two types of farm during the Soviet era (*sovkhozy* and *kolkhozy*), the actual difference between the farms was minimal. *Sovkhozy* were state farms in which workers received a monthly wage, and *kolkhozy* were the collective farms, in which assets were shared by the collective, and members were paid according to the profits generated, together with a minimum living wage. However, the fixed component of income, for those working on a *kolkhoz*, was raised at the expense of the variable one, so that the difference between the two kinds of farm became nominal. Agricultural assets could be privatized or converted into municipal property. Each year after 1 April, the mayor's office decided which land plots would be transferred to landowners. National patrimonial bonds could not be used to acquire land; however, employees of collective farms or enterprises residing in rural areas, and veterans of the Second World War or the Transnistrian civil war could obtain free land. Article 82 of the Land Code entitled all citizens living in a rural area to receive a plot of land near their home; individuals in urban areas could also obtain land plots under certain circumstances. Land privatization involved two components: small-scale privatization, that is the privatization of land near home (domestic land), and large-scale privatization of land for production purposes.

In 1993 the land to be privatized for production purposes was assessed at 1.9m. hectares (ha), or 63% of the total, while 1.1m. ha remained under state control. Once individuals received land from the state, they had two options. They could continue in either type of farm system and use their share of land within the farm as a shareholder, or they could use their plot of land as a private farm (in essence leaving the farm system). One of the problems with leaving the *kolkhozy* was that most fixed assets (such as tractors and trucks) were not physically divided, so those that left the collective farm would no longer have access to these assets. Moreover, owing to the structure of these agro-industrial farms, the incentive structure typical of a Soviet *kolkhoz* remained largely in place.

One of the critical issues surrounding land privatization was accurately defining land boundaries. In 1997 the World Bank proposed a US $16m. loan to provide for the first national cadastre project, that is, a public register of land for fiscal purposes; however, Parliament rejected the draft law. Finally, in February 1998 Parliament passed a law that established a system for the registration of property and rights and this assisted in accelerating the process of land privatization. The land privatization programme known as *pamint* began in late October and completed its first phase in October 2000; approximately 1m. individuals received land titles under the programme.

## INDUSTRIAL PRIVATIZATION

The privatization programme in Moldova borrowed heavily from the Czech, Romanian and Russian experiences but was, none the less, uniquely Moldovan. The programme had two major objectives. First, the Government hoped to maximize revenue from the sale of state-owned enterprises, the proceeds of which were distributed to the local and the national Government at a 20%–80% basis. Second, the Government wanted privatization to spread ownership widely throughout society. The privatization programme occurred in two stages. Initially, there was privatization based on national patrimonial bonds and privatization for cash, or indexed savings only. The first stage was scheduled to take place between 1993 and 1994, and the second stage was to be conducted in 1995–96 (however, many important state-owned enterprises had yet to be privatized by the early 2000s). Privatization was accomplished through two types of auction. Small and medium-sized state-owned enterprises were sold at regional, open auctions for enterprises valued up to 100,000 lei. These auctions involved enterprises sold almost exclusively for national patrimonial bonds. The second type of auction involved subscriptions for shares. These were national auctions for enterprises valued at over 100,000 lei that took two weeks to complete. The Government had first wanted all auctions to be open; however, it became clear that this would be impractical for medium-sized and large enterprises and the subscription-for-shares model was adopted.

The distribution of national patrimonial bonds began in September 1993 and lasted until mid-September 1995. Bonds were distributed to all citizens born before 15 September 1993, along with a number of coupons, each of which had a different face value. This was unlike the system adopted in the Czech Republic, Romania or Russia, where every bond had the same value. Each Moldovan received a bond based on the number of years worked, including military service, postgraduate studies, higher and trade schools and disablement periods. As a result, pensioners as a group had as much purchasing power as the rest of the population. Those who had never worked, and children, were granted a minimum of five working years. The bond itself was not tradeable; shares could only be traded once invested. However, the bond could be transferred without proxy to immediate family members. The stocks purchased with the bond could be sold both to Moldovans and foreigners, and it could be used to purchase shares in state commercial enterprises or housing units. Despite the fact that over 90% of Moldovans had received their national patrimonial bonds by 1994, there were problems with the distribution system. The initial problem with the privatization programme was the structure of the bond itself. The fact that the coupons had arbitrary denominations unrelated to share price increased the number of transactions and made the system unnecessarily complex.

The fact that the bonds were not tradeable was another problem. The international auditors found that this normally resulted in delays before vouchers could be used to buy shares, resulting in frustration and sometimes cynicism on the part of the population. However, the Government felt that freely tradeable vouchers might create a parallel, uncontrolled currency with inflationary consequences. The Government also believed that the poorest members of society would be the first to sell their bonds. This would deprive those that ultimately needed them most from enjoying ownership rights.

During 1993–94 citizens received 3,646,000 bonds, worth 1,900m. monetary units. The objective at this stage of the process was to privatize 1,500 small, medium-sized and large-scale state-owned enterprises. By 1 February 1994 372 medium-sized and large, and 265 small enterprises had been privatized. However, most officials did not regard the first stage of privatization as successful; the number of enterprises privatized was far less than had been anticipated and the process was much slower than expected. In addition, illegal or so-called 'spontaneous' privatization began to occur. In September 1994 the Government announced that the 1993–94 programme target had not been realized.

By the second stage of privatization, the programme had gathered pace. There were 61,400 economic entities registered for privatization by 1 January 1995. Because privatization based on national patrimonial bonds did not immediately contribute to the strength of an individual enterprise or the economy, it was felt that many enterprises needed an influx of capital. This is why the second stage was based on cash or indexed savings (which, in essence, replaced the bonds after 15 September 1995). The 1995–96 privatization law stated that the objective was to begin mass privatization for cash upon completion of the national patrimonial bond phase. In addition, as of 1 January 1995, the value of state-owned enterprises for open and share-subscription auctions was raised from 100,000 to 200,000 lei for open, and to over 200,000 lei for share subscriptions. This confirmed the criticism made by individuals that the Government had increased the starting bid price and supported the claim that the bonds had been devalued.

In 1997 the Ministry of Privatization announced that 77m. lei of state property had been privatized. However, after 85 auctions offering 636 assets, only 90 objects had been privatized. The Russian economic crisis in 1998 further slowed the pace of privatization. None the less, in 1999 approximately 360 enterprises were privatized, for US $34m. although most of the country's strategic companies remained under state control. The rate of privatization increased in 2000–01. In 2000 three of the country's five energy grids were sold to Unión Eléctrica Fenosa for $26m. However, owing to disputes between the city Government of Chişinău and Unión Eléctrica Fenosa, the company was discouraged from purchasing the remaining energy grids (prompting it to consider international arbitration). By 2003 Moldova had still to privatize Moldtelecom (the national telecommunications company), although a 51% stake was expected to be divested to a Russian telecommunications company; however, previous attempts to sell the enterprise had foundered. Moreover, some of the companies that had been privatized were subject to speculation about possible renationalization. For example, the Government had sold 49% of its interest in Air Moldova to a German consortium in mid-2000, only to announce plans for the possible repossession of the shares in 2002.

### PROSPECTS

By 2003 there were encouraging signs that the Moldovan economy was recovering, after years of declining growth. Growth of GDP had been positive in 2000 and 2001, and reached one of its highest levels in 2002, while the rate of inflation continued to decline. Although the Moldovan Party of Communists controlled the presidency, the Government and the Parliament, reforms were enacted and privatization plans proceeded. Despite the dismissal of some important, reform-minded individuals, the Tarlev Government negotiated successfully with the IMF, the World Bank and Eurobond holders. However, the economy remained very fragile. In 2003 the Government failed to fulfil its obligations under an IMF package, and lending was suspended in July. The IMF refused to provide any additional borrowing in 2003, which meant that Moldova would have to service its debt without external assistance. The country's failure to reach an agreement with the IMF also meant that the country would not benefit from any debt rescheduling by the members of the Paris Club. Therefore, although the economic situation in 2003 was better than during the late 1990s, the country was still experiencing severe economic problems, which required immediate reform.

# Statistical Survey

Principal sources (unless otherwise indicated): State Department for Statistics and Sociology, 2028 Chişinău, şos. Hînceşti 53D; tel. (2) 73-37-74; fax (2) 22-61-46; e-mail dass@statistica.md; internet www.statistica.md.

Note: Most of the figures for 1993–2003 exclude the Transnistria (Transdnestr) region of eastern Moldova, i.e. the area on the left bank of the Dniester (Dnestr or Nistru) river.

## Area and Population

### AREA, POPULATION AND DENSITY

| | |
|---|---|
| Area (sq km) . . . . . . . . . . | 33,800* |
| Population (census results)† | |
| 17 January 1979 . . . . . . . | 3,949,756 |
| 12 January 1989 | |
| Males . . . . . . . . . . . | 2,063,192 |
| Females . . . . . . . . . . | 2,272,168 |
| Total . . . . . . . . . . . | 4,335,360 |
| Population (official estimates at 1 January) | |
| 2000 . . . . . . . . . . . | 4,281,500 |
| 2001 . . . . . . . . . . . | 4,264,300 |
| 2002 . . . . . . . . . . . | 3,627,812 |
| Density (per sq km) at January 2002 . . . . . . | 107.3 |

\* 13,050 sq miles.

† Figures refer to the *de jure* population. The *de facto* total at the 1989 census was 4,337,592 (males 2,058,160; females 2,279,432).

### POPULATION BY ETHNIC GROUP
(permanent inhabitants, 1989 census)

| | Number | % |
|---|---|---|
| Moldovan . . . . . . . . . . . | 2,794,749 | 64.5 |
| Ukrainian . . . . . . . . . . | 600,366 | 13.8 |
| Russian . . . . . . . . . . . | 562,069 | 13.0 |
| Gagauz . . . . . . . . . . . | 153,458 | 3.5 |
| Bulgarian . . . . . . . . . . | 88,419 | 2.0 |
| Jewish . . . . . . . . . . . | 65,672 | 1.5 |
| Others and unknown . . . . . . | 70,627 | 1.7 |
| **Total** . . . . . . . . . . . | **4,335,360** | **100.0** |

### PRINCIPAL TOWNS
(estimated population at 1 January 1996)

| | | | | |
|---|---|---|---|---|
| Chişinău (Kishinev) | | | | |
| (capital) . . . | 655,000 | Tighina (Bender) . | 128,000 |
| Tiraspol . . . | 187,000 | Râbnita (Rybnitsa) . | 62,900 |
| Bălţi (Beltsy) . . | 153,500 | | |

**2003** (estimate, 1 January): Chişinău 662,400; Bălţi 150,600.

## ADMINISTRATIVE DIVISIONS

(estimated population at 1 January 2003)

| | | | |
|---|---|---|---|
| Bălți . . . . | 500,900 | Taraclia . . . | 465,600 |
| Cahul . . . . | 190,800 | Tighina . . . | 169,000 |
| Chișinău . . . | 1,161,800 | Ungheni . . . | 260,300 |
| Edinet . . . . | 279,100 | *Autonomous territory* | |
| | | *of Gagauzia* . . | 158,900 |
| Lapusna . . . . | 2776,300 | *Transnistria and* | |
| | | *Tighina (Bender)\** . | 629,800 |
| Orhei . . . . | 300,400 | **Total** . . . . | 3,617,700 |
| Soroco . . . . | 274,600 | | |

\* 2001 figure.

## BIRTHS, MARRIAGES AND DEATHS

| | Registered live births | | Registered marriages | | Registered deaths | |
|---|---|---|---|---|---|---|
| | Number | Rate (per 1,000) | Number | Rate (per 1,000) | Number | Rate (per 1,000) |
| 1994 . . . | 62,085 | 14.3 | 33,742 | 7.8 | 51,514 | 11.8 |
| 1995 . . . | 56,411 | 13.0 | 32,775 | 7.5 | 52,969 | 12.2 |
| 1996 . . . | 51,865 | 12.0 | 26,089 | 6.0 | 49,748 | 11.5 |
| 1997 . . . | 51,286 | 11.9 | 26,305 | 6.1* | 51,138 | 11.9 |
| 1998 . . . | 46,755 | 10.9 | 25,793 | 6.0* | 47,691 | 11.1 |
| 1999† . . | 38,501 | 9.0 | 23,524 | 5.5 | 41,315 | 9.6 |
| 2000† . . | 36,939 | 8.7 | 21,684 | 5.1 | 41,224 | 9.7 |
| 2001 . . . | 36,448 | 10.0 | 21,200‡ | 5.8 | 40,100‡ | 11.0 |

\* Estimate.
† Numbers exclude, but rates include, Transnistria.
‡ Rounded figures.

Sources: partly UN, *Population and Vital Statistics Report;* **Moldovan Economic Trends**.

**Expectation of life** (WHO estimates, years at birth): 68.0 (males 64.2; females 71.7) in 2001 (Source: WHO, *World Health Report*).

## ECONOMICALLY ACTIVE POPULATION

('000 persons)

| | 1999 | 2000 | 2001 |
|---|---|---|---|
| Agriculture, hunting and forestry | 730 | 769.0 | 763.4 |
| Fishing . . . . . . . | 1 | 1.4 | 1.4 |
| Mining and quarrying . . . . | 3 | 1.7 | 2.0 |
| Manufacturing . . . . . | 135 | 135.8 | 136.8 |
| Electricity, gas and water supply . | 22 | 28.5 | 26.4 |
| Construction . . . . . . | 44 | 44.4 | 43.2 |
| Wholesale and retail trade; repair of motor vehicles, motorcycles and personal and household goods | 135 | 147.3 | 144.5 |
| Hotels and restaurants . . . . | 15 | 18.0 | 19.3 |
| Transport, storage and communications | 70 | 63.9 | 64.3 |
| Financial intermediation . . . | 10 | 8.1 | 9.2 |
| Real estate, renting and business activities . . . . . . | 35 | 19.5 | 19.5 |
| Public administration and defence; compulsory social security . . | 49 | 64.5 | 65.8 |
| Education . . . . . . | 137 | 101.5 | 100.9 |
| Health and social work . . . . | 80 | 74.2 | 70.7 |
| Other community, social and personal service activities . . | 29 | 28.2 | 28.2 |
| Private households with employed persons . . . . . . . | — | 8.6 | 3.1 |
| **Total employed** . . . . . | 1,495 | 1,514.6 | 1,499.0 |
| Unemployed . . . . . . | 187 | 140.1 | 117.7 |
| **Total labour force** . . . . . | 1,682 | 1,654.6 | 1,616.7 |
| Males . . . . . . . . | 853 | 828.0 | 806.6 |
| Females . . . . . . . | 829 | 826.6 | 810.1 |

Source: ILO.

# Health and Welfare

## KEY INDICATORS

| | |
|---|---|
| Total fertility rate (children per woman, 2001) . . . . . . | 1.5 |
| Under-5 mortality rate (per 1,000 live births, 2001) . . . . | 32 |
| HIV/AIDS (% of persons aged 15–49, 2001) . . . . . . | 0.24 |
| Physicians (per 1,000 head, 1998) . . . . . . . | 3.5 |
| Hospital beds (per 1,000 head, 1996) . . . . . . . | 12.12 |
| Health expenditure (2000): US $ per head (PPP) . . . . | 64 |
| Health expenditure (2000): % of GDP . . . . . . . | 3.5 |
| Health expenditure (2000): public (% of total) . . . . . | 82.4 |
| Access to water (% of persons, 2000) . . . . . . . | 100 |
| Human Development Index (2001): ranking . . . . . | 108 |
| Human Development Index (2001): value . . . . . . | 0.700 |

For sources and definitions, see explanatory note on p. vi.

# Agriculture

## PRINCIPAL CROPS

('000 metric tons)

| | 1999 | 2000 | 2001 |
|---|---|---|---|
| Wheat . . . . . . . . . | 800.4 | 725.0 | 1,180.0 |
| Barley . . . . . . . . | 182.6 | 133.0 | 232.8 |
| Maize . . . . . . . . | 1,140.3 | 1,031.0 | 1,116.5 |
| Potatoes . . . . . . . | 329.5 | 330.0 | 384.0 |
| Sugar beet . . . . . . . | 1,008.8 | 943.4 | 1,193.6 |
| Dry peas . . . . . . . | 34.3 | 15.0 | 37.8 |
| Sunflower seed . . . . . . | 285.6 | 268.4 | 278.0 |
| Cabbages . . . . . . . | 50.3 | 45.0 | 51.5 |
| Tomatoes . . . . . . . | 167.2 | 104.0 | 105.0 |
| Cucumbers and gherkins . . . | 32.1 | 26.0* | 32.0* |
| Chillies and green peppers* . . | 38 | 33 | 38 |
| Dry onions . . . . . . | 69.3 | 62.0 | 74.4 |
| Carrots . . . . . . . | 19.8 | 20.0 | 20.7 |
| Other vegetables* . . . . . | 50.7 | 50.0 | 51.2 |
| Apples . . . . . . . . | 56.1 | 162.4 | 186.9 |
| Plums . . . . . . . . | 38.1 | 41.2 | 59.2 |
| Grapes . . . . . . . . | 464.9 | 700.1 | 503.0 |
| Watermelons . . . . . . | 22.0† | 28.0 | 27.0 |
| Other fruits* . . . . . . | 41.7 | 62.3 | 71.0 |
| Tobacco (leaves) . . . . . | 22.4 | 23.5 | 15.1 |

\* Unofficial figure(s).
† FAO estimate.

Source: FAO.

## LIVESTOCK

('000 head at 1 January)

| | 1999 | 2000 | 2001 |
|---|---|---|---|
| Horses* . . . . . . . | 68 | 68 | 68 |
| Cattle . . . . . . . . | 452 | 416 | 402 |
| Pigs . . . . . . . . | 807 | 683 | 447 |
| Sheep† . . . . . . . | 1,008 | 830 | 819 |
| Goats . . . . . . . . | 97† | 100 | 109 |
| Chickens . . . . . . . | 13,800† | 12,575 | 13,041 |

\* FAO estimates.
† Unofficial figure(s).

Source: FAO.

## LIVESTOCK PRODUCTS
('000 metric tons)

|  | 1999 | 2000 | 2001 |
|---|---|---|---|
| Beef and veal . | 23.5 | 21.0* | 12.1 |
| Mutton and lamb. | 3.6 | 3.4* | 3.1* |
| Pig meat . | 60.8 | 59.8 | 57.2 |
| Poultry meat . | 15.8 | 21.5 | 26.3 |
| Cows' milk . | 569.0 | 554.8 | 560.6 |
| Sheep's milk . | 16.1 | 14.3* | 14.4* |
| Goats' milk . | 4.3 | 4.7* | 4.5* |
| Butter . | 1.9 | 2.5 | 3.0 |
| Cheese . | 5.1 | 4.6 | 4.9 |
| Hen eggs . | 19.1 | 32.1* | 34.5 |
| Honey . | 2.0 | 1.8† | 2.0† |
| Wool: greasy . | 2.3 | 2.1 | 2.1 |
| Cattle hides (fresh)† . | 3.1 | 1.5 | 1.6 |

* Unofficial figure.

† FAO estimate(s).

Source: partly FAO.

# Forestry

## ROUNDWOOD REMOVALS
('000 cubic metres, excl. bark)

|  | 1998 | 1999 | 2000 |
|---|---|---|---|
| Sawlogs, veneer logs and logs for sleepers . | 10 | 3 | 5 |
| Other industrial wood . | 7 | 9 | 24 |
| Fuel wood . | 356 | 36 | 30 |
| **Total** . | 373 | 49 | 58 |

Source: FAO.

## SAWNWOOD PRODUCTION
('000 cubic metres, incl. railway sleepers)

|  | 1998 | 1999 | 2000 |
|---|---|---|---|
| Coniferous (softwood) . | 25 | — | — |
| Broadleaved (hardwood). | 5 | 6 | 5 |
| **Total** . | 30 | 6 | 5 |

Source: FAO.

# Fishing

(metric tons, live weight)

|  | 1998 | 1999 | 2000 |
|---|---|---|---|
| Capture . | 491 | 129 | 151 |
| Common carp . | 280 | n.a. | n.a. |
| Crucian carp . | 159 | 104 | 132 |
| Aquaculture . | 1,129 | 1,007 | 1,168 |
| Common carp . | 91 | 299 | 351 |
| Crucian carp . | 139 | 105 | 110 |
| Grass carp (White amur) . | 87 | 92 | 99 |
| Silver carp . | 812 | 511 | 608 |
| **Total catch** . | 1,620 | 1,136 | 1,319 |

Source: FAO, *Yearbook of Fishery Statistics.*

# Mining

('000 metric tons)

|  | 1998 | 1999 | 2000 |
|---|---|---|---|
| Gypsum . | 19.8 | 18.5 | 32.1 |
| Peat* . | 475 | 475 | 475 |

* Estimated production.

Source: US Geological Survey.

# Industry

## SELECTED PRODUCTS
('000 metric tons, unless otherwise indicated)

|  | 1998 | 1999 | 2000 |
|---|---|---|---|
| Vegetable oil . | 18 | 17 | 22 |
| Flour . | 229 | 159 | 145 |
| Raw sugar. | 187 | 99 | 102 |
| Wine ('000 hectolitres) . | 1,196 | 668 | 1,150 |
| Mineral water ('000 hectolitres) . | 176 | 242 | 290 |
| Soft drinks ('000 hectolitres) . | 295 | 142 | 206 |
| Cigarettes (million) . | 7,512 | 8,731 | 9,262 |
| Carpets (million sq m) . | 0.7 | 0.5 | 0.4 |
| Footwear ('000 pairs) . | 739 | 705 | 1,003 |
| Cement . | 74 | 50 | 222 |
| Washing machines ('000 units). | 43 | 18 | 25 |
| Television receivers ('000 units) . | 10 | 3 | 2 |
| Tractors ('000 units) . | 0.7 | 0.0 | 0.2 |
| Electric energy (million kWh) . | 4,584 | 3,814 | n.a. |

Source: UN, *Industrial Commodity Statistics Yearbook.*

# Finance

## CURRENCY AND EXCHANGE RATES

**Monetary Units**

100 bani (singular: ban) = 1 Moldovan leu (plural: lei).

**Sterling, Dollar and Euro Equivalents** (30 May 2003)

£1 sterling = 23.324 lei;

US $1 = 14.157 lei;

€1 = 16.735 lei;

1,000 Moldovan lei = £42.87 = $70.64 = €59.75.

**Average Exchange Rate** (Moldovan lei per US$)

2000    12.4342

2001    12.8651

2002    13.5705

Note: The Moldovan leu was introduced (except in the Transnistria region) on 29 November 1993, replacing the Moldovan rouble at a rate of 1 leu = 1,000 roubles. The Moldovan rouble had been introduced in June 1992, as a temporary coupon currency, and was initially at par with the Russian (formerly Soviet) rouble.

## STATE BUDGET
(million lei)*

| Revenue† | 1999 | 2000 | 2001 |
|---|---|---|---|
| Tax revenue . | 3,050 | 3,973 | 4,644 |
| Taxes on profits . | 233 | 275 | 350 |
| Taxes on personal incomes . | 220 | 265 | 348 |
| Value-added tax . | 940 | 1,333 | 1,498 |
| Excises . | 444 | 658 | 681 |
| Taxes on international trade. | 231 | 222 | 234 |
| Social Fund contributions . | 783 | 994 | 1,304 |
| Other taxes . | 199 | 227 | 231 |
| Non-tax revenue . | 535 | 806 | 749 |
| **Total** . | 3,745 | 4,780 | 5,393 |

| Expenditure‡ | 1999 | 2000 | 2001 |
|---|---|---|---|
| Current budgetary expenditure . | 3,176 | 2,922 | 2,890 |
| National economy . | 287 | 331 | 298 |
| Social sphere . | 1,340 | 1,570 | 1,795 |
| Education . | 575 | 719 | 924 |
| Health care . | 335 | 464 | 542 |
| Interest payments . | 906 | 1,021 | 797 |
| Capital budgetary expenditure. . | 103 | 175 | 206 |
| Social Fund expenditure . | 889 | 1,328 | 1,373 |
| Project loan spending . | 368 | 212 | 245 |
| Other expenditure . | 643 | 776 | 946 |
| **Total** . | 4,535 | 5,413 | 5,661 |

* Figures refer to a consolidation of the operations of central (republican) and local governments, including the Social Fund.

† Excluding grants received (million lei): 132 in 1999; 147 in 2000.

‡ Excluding net lending (million lei): −44 in 1999; −32 in 2000; −17 in 2001.

Source: IMF, *Republic of Moldova: 2002 Article IV Consultation* (August 2002).

## INTERNATIONAL RESERVES
(US $ million at 31 December)

|  | 2000 | 2001 | 2002 |
|---|---|---|---|
| IMF special drawing rights . . . | 0.34 | 0.74 | 0.27 |
| Reserve position in IMF . . . . | 0.01 | 0.01 | 0.01 |
| Foreign exchange . . . . . . | 229.80 | 228.29 | 268.46 |
| **Total** (excl. gold) . . . . . | 230.15 | 229.04 | 268.74 |

Source: IMF, *International Financial Statistics*.

## MONEY SUPPLY
(million lei at 31 December)

|  | 2000 | 2001 | 2002 |
|---|---|---|---|
| Currency outside banks . . . . | 1,469.26 | 1,834.20 | 2,288.56 |
| Demand deposits at commercial banks . . . . . . . | 553.75 | 665.76 | 1,271.14 |
| **Total money** (incl. others) . . . | 2,032.22 | 2,500.00 | 3,559.80 |

Source: IMF, *International Financial Statistics*.

## COST OF LIVING
(Consumer Price Index; base: Dec. 1994 = 100)

|  | 2000 | 2001 | 2002 |
|---|---|---|---|
| Food . . . . . . . . | 268.8 | 297.6 | 310.4 |
| Non-food goods . . . . . | 238.5 | 260.6 | 281.0 |
| Services . . . . . . | 629.8 | 668.0 | 700.0 |
| **All items** . . . . . . | 298.7 | 327.8 | 345.8 |

Source: Moldovan Economic Trends.

## NATIONAL ACCOUNTS
(million lei at current prices, excl. Transnistria)

**Expenditure on the Gross Domestic Product**

|  | 2000 | 2001 | 2002* |
|---|---|---|---|
| Government final consumption expenditure† . . . . . | 2,471.8 | 2,878.0 | 3,985.7 |
| Private final consumption expenditure . . . . . | 14,030.9 | 16,384.7 | 18,640.2 |
| Changes in inventories . . . | 1,363.7 | 1,245.7 | 1,350.6 |
| Gross fixed capital formation . . | 2,472.5 | 3,190.0 | 3,653.3 |
| **Total domestic expenditure** . . | 20,338.9 | 23,698.4 | 27,629.8 |
| Exports of goods and services . . | 7,945.7 | 9,536.3 | 12,238.1 |
| *Less* Imports of goods and services | 12,265.1 | 14,183.0 | 17,827.5 |
| **GDP in purchasers' values** . . | 16,019.6 | 19,051.5 | 22,040.4 |

* Preliminary figures.
† Including non-profit institutions.

Source: *Moldovan Economic Trends*.

**Gross Domestic Product by Economic Activity**

|  | 1998 | 1999 | 2000 |
|---|---|---|---|
| Agriculture, hunting, forestry and fishing . . . . . . . | 2,351 | 3,066 | 3,919 |
| Mining and quarrying . . . . | 17 | 24 | 23 |
| Manufacturing . . . . . | 1,276 | 1,613 | 2,423 |
| Electricity, gas and water supply | 229 | 456 | 358 |
| Construction . . . . . . | 289 | 409 | 423 |
| Wholesale and retail trade; repair of motor vehicles, motorcycles and personal and household goods . . . . . . | 941 | 1,885 | 2,135 |
| Transport, storage and communications . . . . | 671 | 1,013 | 1,434 |
| Other services . . . . . | 2,381 | 3,226 | 4,248 |
| **Sub-total** . . . . . . | 8,155 | 11,692 | 14,963 |
| Taxes (less subsidies) on products and imports . . . . . | 1,403 | 1,323 | 1,976 |
| *Less* Financial intermediation services indirectly measured . . | 436 | 693 | 959 |
| **GDP in purchasers' values** . . | 9,122 | 12,322 | 15,980 |

## BALANCE OF PAYMENTS
(US $ million)

|  | 2000 | 2001 | 2002 |
|---|---|---|---|
| Exports of goods f.o.b. . . . . | 476.8 | 567.3 | 659.8 |
| Imports of goods f.o.b. . . . . | −770.5 | −878.6 | −1,038.1 |
| **Trade balance** . . . . . | −293.6 | −311.3 | −378.3 |
| Exports of services . . . . | 164.7 | 167.9 | 210.0 |
| Imports of services . . . . | −203.8 | −211.3 | −248.8 |
| **Balance on goods and services** | −332.7 | −354.7 | −417.1 |
| Other income received . . . . | 173.1 | 235.2 | 276.5 |
| Other income paid . . . . | −99.1 | −133.6 | −117.2 |
| **Balance on goods, services and income** . . . . . . | −258.7 | −253.1 | −257.8 |
| Current transfers received . . . | 160.9 | 159.5 | 163.9 |
| Current transfers paid . . . . | −9.1 | −11.7 | −14.8 |
| **Current balance** . . . . | −106.8 | −105.3 | −108.6 |
| Capital account (net) . . . . | 1.9 | −2.0 | 0.3 |
| Direct investment abroad . . . | −0.1 | −0.1 | −0.4 |
| Direct investment from abroad . | 129.1 | 100.0 | 110.8 |
| Portfolio investment assets . . | — | −3.2 | −1.0 |
| Portfolio investment liabilities . . | 2.5 | 3.6 | −20.3 |
| Other investment assets . . . | −37.2 | −25.9 | −66.8 |
| Other investment liabilities . . | 45.9 | −14.9 | 2.4 |
| Net errors and omissions . . . | −10.6 | 12.2 | 21.9 |
| **Overall balance** . . . . | 24.5 | −35.5 | −61.6 |

Source: IMF, *International Financial Statistics*.

# External Trade

## PRINCIPAL COMMODITIES
(US $ million)

| Imports | 1999 | 2000 | 2001 |
|---|---|---|---|
| **Food and live animals** . . . | 22.1 | 40.0 | 69.3 |
| **Beverages and tobacco** . . . | 11.1 | 58.1 | 49.2 |
| Cigarettes . . . . . . . | 2.8 | 48.0 | 33.9 |
| **Crude materials, inedible, except fuels** . . . . . | 14.7 | 23.5 | 34.4 |
| **Mineral products** . . . . | 228.0 | 252.1 | 237.5 |
| Petroleum petroleum products etc. | 69.9 | 108.5 | 111.7 |
| Gas, natural and manufactured . | 102.7 | 92.8 | 101.3 |
| **Products of chemical or allied industries** . . . . . | 51.9 | 84.4 | 97.2 |
| Medicinal and pharmaceutical products . . . . . . | 21.9 | 41.9 | 31.5 |
| **Basic manufactures** . . . . | 117.3 | 146.6 | 197.3 |
| Textiles and textile articles . . . | 51.0 | 62.7 | 78.6 |
| **Machinery and transport equipment** . . . . . . | 88.0 | 109.6 | 144.6 |
| **Total** (incl. others) . . . . | 586.6 | 777.0 | 896.6 |

| Exports f.o.b. | 1999 | 2000 | 2001 |
|---|---|---|---|
| **Food and live animals** . . . | 134.5 | 100.8 | 117.2 |
| Meat and preparations . . . | 22.9 | 15.7 | 11.1 |
| Cereals and preparations . . | 30.1 | 15.9 | 20.8 |
| Vegetables and fruit . . . . | 59.1 | 52.5 | 61.4 |
| Edible nuts . . . . . | 17.0 | 17.0 | 18.3 |
| Fruit or vegetable juices . . | 17.3 | 15.0 | 24.0 |
| **Beverages and tobacco** . . . | 143.2 | 158.2 | 198.7 |
| Wine of fresh grapes . . . . | 100.5 | 114.2 | 156.4 |
| **Crude materials, inedible** . . | 38.4 | 42.3 | 44.8 |
| **Basic manufactures** . . . . | 22.7 | 34.1 | 38.6 |
| **Machinery and equipment** . . | 34.3 | 29.3 | 39.2 |
| **Miscellaneous manufactures** . . | 73.6 | 92.7 | 113.8 |
| Apparel and clothing . . . . | 57.4 | 75.7 | 92.7 |
| **Total** (incl. others) . . . . | 464.1 | 471.6 | 570.2 |

Source: UN, *International Trade Statistics Yearbook*.

## PRINCIPAL TRADING PARTNERS
(US $ million)

| Imports c.i.f. | 1999 | 2000 | 2001 |
|---|---|---|---|
| Belarus . . . . . . . . | 22.7 | 31.9 | 38.9 |
| Bulgaria . . . . . . . | 9.4 | 13.6 | 20.7 |
| France . . . . . . . . | 12.6 | 20.0 | 25.9 |
| Germany . . . . . . . | 61.4 | 87.7 | 85.4 |
| Greece . . . . . . . . | 8.4 | 15.1 | 5.3 |
| Hungary . . . . . . . | 6.9 | 13.0 | 18.2 |
| Italy . . . . . . . . | 38.2 | 48.9 | 65.4 |
| Netherlands . . . . . . | 9.4 | 8.7 | 12.8 |
| Poland . . . . . . . . | 8.3 | 15.5 | 18.0 |
| Romania . . . . . . . | 81.6 | 119.3 | 93.3 |
| Russia . . . . . . . . | 138.7 | 119.6 | 144.1 |
| Turkey . . . . . . . . | 11.8 | 18.2 | 19.7 |
| Ukraine . . . . . . . | 79.2 | 105.6 | 152.6 |
| United Kingdom . . . . | 8.2 | 9.7 | 11.7 |
| USA . . . . . . . . | 22.2 | 48.2 | 28.1 |
| **Total** (incl. others) . . . . | 586.7 | 777.0 | 896.6 |

| Exports f.o.b. | 1999 | 2000 | 2001 |
|---|---|---|---|
| Austria . . . . . . . | 10.0 | 5.6 | 8.5 |
| Belarus . . . . . . . | 21.8 | 21.8 | 30.2 |
| Bulgaria . . . . . . . | 5.3 | 3.6 | 3.7 |
| Canada . . . . . . . | 3.3 | 2.1 | 2.3 |
| France . . . . . . . . | 6.4 | 7.9 | 8.4 |
| Germany . . . . . . . | 33.5 | 36.3 | 40.8 |
| Greece . . . . . . . . | 5.8 | 2.4 | 2.7 |
| Hungary . . . . . . . | 16.3 | 4.6 | 7.2 |
| Italy . . . . . . . . | 25.6 | 36.4 | 46.0 |
| Kazakhstan . . . . . . | 3.4 | 4.7 | 4.5 |
| Poland . . . . . . . . | 5.0 | 2.0 | 1.7 |
| Romania . . . . . . . | 41.3 | 37.6 | 38.0 |
| Russia . . . . . . . . | 191.2 | 209.5 | 248.7 |
| Ukraine . . . . . . . | 32.9 | 35.5 | 40.8 |
| United Kingdom . . . . | 3.9 | 5.4 | 5.6 |
| USA . . . . . . . . | 14.5 | 15.6 | 25.7 |
| **Total** (incl. others) . . . . | 464.2 | 471.4 | 570.2 |

Source: UN, *International Trade Statistics Yearbook*.

# Transport

## RAILWAYS
(traffic)

| | 1998 | 1999 | 2000 |
|---|---|---|---|
| Passenger journeys (million) . . | 9.4 | 5.4 | 4.8 |
| Passenger-km (million) . . . . | 656 | 343 | 315 |
| Freight transported (million metric tons) . . . . . . . . . | 11.1 | 6.6 | 8.2 |
| Freight ton-km (million) . . . | 2,575 | 1,191 | 1,513 |

## ROAD TRAFFIC
(motor vehicles in use)

| | 1997 | 1998 | 1999 |
|---|---|---|---|
| Passenger cars . . . . . . | 205,973 | 222,769 | 232,278 |
| Buses and coaches . . . . | 11,169 | 12,917 | 13,582 |
| Lorries and vans . . . . . | 56,924 | 57,404 | 52,430 |

Source: IRF, *World Road Statistics*.

## INLAND WATERWAYS
(traffic)

| | 1998 | 1999 | 2000 |
|---|---|---|---|
| Freight transported ('000 metric tons) . . . . . . . . . | 13.1 | 15.9 | 8.7 |

## CIVIL AVIATION
(traffic)

| | 1996 | 1997 | 1998 |
|---|---|---|---|
| Kilometres flown (million) . . . | 5 | 2 | 4 |
| Passengers carried ('000) . . . | 190 | 46 | 118 |
| Passenger-km (million) . . . . | 240 | 61 | 146 |
| Total ton-km (million) . . . . | 23 | 6 | 14 |

Source: UN, *Statistical Yearbook*.

**1999:** Passengers carried ('000) 200; Passenger-km (million) 240; Freight transported ('000 metric tons) 1.3; Freight ton-km (million) 3.3.

**2000:** Passengers carried ('000) 220; Passenger-km (million) 253; Freight transported ('000 metric tons) 1.4; Freight ton-km (million) 4.1.

# Tourism

## FOREIGN VISITOR ARRIVALS
(incl. excursionists)

| Country of origin | 1999 | 2000 | 2001 |
|---|---|---|---|
| Belarus . . . . . . . . | 550 | 546 | 509 |
| Bulgaria . . . . . . . | 458 | 528 | 295 |
| Germany . . . . . . . | 277 | 537 | 558 |
| Italy . . . . . . . . | 409 | 594 | 572 |
| Romania . . . . . . . | 2,087 | 2,341 | 2,076 |
| Russia . . . . . . . . | 2,595 | 5,146 | 2,361 |
| Turkey . . . . . . . . | 1,612 | 2,548 | 2,405 |
| Ukraine . . . . . . . | 1,944 | 1,969 | 2,261 |
| United Kingdom . . . . | 615 | 327 | 163 |
| USA . . . . . . . . | 889 | 1,030 | 1,072 |
| **Total** (incl. others) . . . . | 14,088 | 18,964 | 15,690 |

**2002:** 20,161 tourist arrivals.

**Receipts from tourism** (US $ million): 4 in 1998; 2 in 1999; 4 in 2000.

Sources: World Tourism Organization, *Yearbook of Tourism Statistics*; and World Bank, *World Development Indicators*.

# Communications Media

|  | 1999 | 2000 | 2001 |
|---|---|---|---|
| Television receivers ('000 in use) . | 1,300 | 1,300 | n.a. |
| Telephones ('000 main lines in use) | 555.3 | 583.8 | 639.2 |
| Facsimile machines (number in use) . . . . . . . . | 716 | n.a. | n.a. |
| Mobile cellular telephones ('000 subscribers). . . . . . . | 18.0 | 132.3 | 225.0 |
| Personal computers ('000 in use) . | 35 | 64 | 70 |
| Internet users ('000) . . . . . | 25 | 53 | 60 |

**Radio receivers** ('000 in use): 3,220 in 1997.

**Book production** (including pamphlets): 921 titles (2,779,000 copies) in 1996.

**Daily newspapers:** 4 (average circulation 261,000) in 1996.

**Non-daily newspapers:** 206 (estimated average circulation 1,350,000) in 1996.

**Other periodicals:** 76 (average circulation 196,000) in 1994.

Sources: UNESCO, *Statistical Yearbook*; International Telecommunication Union.

# Education

(2002/03)

|  | Institutions | Teachers* | Students |
|---|---|---|---|
| Primary . . . . . . . | 120 ⎫ | 42,300 | 19,200 |
| Secondary: general. . . . . | 1,460 ⎭ |  | 523,400 |
| Secondary: vocational . . . . | 83 | 2,300 | 22,600 |
| Higher: colleges* . . . . . | 60 | 1,900 | 19,900 |
| Higher: universities . . . . | 45 | 5,300 | 95,039 |

* 2000/01 figures.

**Adult literacy rate** (UNESCO estimates): 99.0% (males 99.6%; females 98.4%) in 2001 (Source: UN Development Programme, *Human Development Report*).

# Directory

## The Constitution

The Constitution of the Republic of Moldova, summarized below, was adopted by the Moldovan Parliament on 28 July 1994 and entered into force on 27 August. On 28 July 2000 amendments to the Constitution were enacted, which transformed Moldova into a parliamentary republic. Following alterations to the law on presidential election procedure, approved on 22 September, the President of the Republic was, henceforth, to be elected by the legislature, rather than directly.

### GENERAL PRINCIPLES

The Republic of Moldova is a sovereign, independent, unitary and indivisible state. The rule of law, the dignity, rights and freedoms of the people, and the development of human personality, justice and political pluralism are guaranteed. The Constitution is the supreme law. The Constitution upholds principles such as human rights and freedoms, democracy and political pluralism, the separation and co-operation of the legislative, executive and judicial powers of the State, respect for international law and treaties, fundamental principles regarding property, free economic initiative and the right to national identity. The national language of the republic is Moldovan and its writing is based on the Latin alphabet, although the State acknowledges the right to use other languages spoken within the country.

### FUNDAMENTAL RIGHTS, FREEDOMS AND DUTIES

The Constitution grants Moldovan citizens their rights and freedoms and lays down their duties. All citizens are equal before the law; they should have free access to justice, are presumed innocent until proven guilty and have a right to an acknowledged legal status.

The State guarantees fundamental human rights, such as the right to life and to physical and mental integrity, the freedoms of movement, conscience, expression, assembly and political association, and the enfranchisement of Moldovan citizens aged over 18 years. Moldovan citizens have the right of access to information and education, of health security, of establishing and joining a trade union, of working and of striking. The family, orphaned children and the disabled enjoy the protection of the State. Obligations of the citizenry include the payment of taxes and the defence of the motherland.

### PARLIAMENT

Parliament is the supreme legislative body and sole legislative authority of Moldova. It consists of 101 members, directly elected for a four-year term. The Chairman of Parliament is elected by members, also for a four-year term. Parliament holds two ordinary sessions per year. The Parliament's basic powers include: the enactment of laws, the holding of referendums, the provision of legislative unity throughout the country, the approval of state policy, the approval or suspension of international treaties, the election of state officials, the mobilization of the armed forces and the declaration of the states of national emergency, martial law and war.

### THE PRESIDENT OF THE REPUBLIC

The President of the Republic is the Head of State and is elected by the legislature for a four-year term. A candidate must be aged no less than 40 years, be a Moldovan citizen and a speaker of the official language. The candidate must be in good health and, with his or her application, must submit the written support of a minimum of 15 parliamentarians. A decision on the holding of a presidential election is taken by parliamentary resolution, and the election must be held no fewer than 45 days before the expiry of the outgoing President's term of office. To be elected President, a candidate must obtain the support of three-fifths of the parliamentary quorum. If necessary, further ballots must then be conducted, contested by the two candidates who received the most votes. The candidate who receives more votes becomes President. The post of President may be held by the same person for not more than two consecutive terms.

The President's main responsibilities include the promulgation of laws, the issue of decrees, the scheduling of referendums, the conclusion of international treaties and the dissolution of the Parliament. The President is allowed to participate in parliamentary proceedings. The President, after consultation with the parliamentary majority, is responsible for nominating a Prime Minister-designate and a Government. The President can preside over government meetings and can consult the Government on matters of special importance and urgency. On proposals submitted by the Prime Minister, the President may revoke or renominate members of the Government in cases of vacancies or the reallocation of portfolios. The President is Commander-in-Chief of the armed forces.

If the President has committed a criminal or constitutional offence, the votes of two-thirds of the members of Parliament are required to remove the President from office; the removal must be confirmed by the Supreme Court of Justice, for a criminal offence, and by a national referendum, for a constitutional offence.

### THE COUNCIL OF MINISTERS

The principal organ of executive government is the Council of Ministers, which supervises state policy and public administration of the country. The Council of Ministers is headed by a Prime Minister, who co-ordinates the activities of the Government. The Council of Ministers must resign if the Parliament votes in favour of a motion of 'no confidence' in the Council.

### LOCAL ADMINISTRATION

For administrative purposes, the Republic of Moldova is divided into districts, towns and villages, in which local self-government is practised. At village and town level, elected local councils and mayors operate as autonomous administrative authorities. At district level, an elected council co-ordinates the activities of village and town councils.

The area on the left bank of the Dniester (Dnestr or Nistru) river, as well as certain other places in the south of the republic (i.e. Gagauzia) may be granted special autonomous status, according to special statutory provisions of organic law*.

## JUDICIAL AUTHORITY

Every citizen has the right to free access to justice. Justice shall be administered by the Supreme Court of Justice, the Court of Appeal, tribunals and the courts of law. Judges sitting in the courts of law and the Supreme Court of Justice are appointed by the President following proposals by the Higher Magistrates' Council. They are elected for a five-year term, and subsequently for a 10-year term, after which their term of office expires on reaching the age limit. The Higher Magistrates' Council is composed of 11 magistrates, who are appointed for a five-year term. It is responsible for the appointment, transfer and promotion of judges, as well as disciplinary action against them.

The Prosecutor-General, who is appointed by Parliament, exercises control over the enactment of law, as well as defending the legal order and the rights and freedoms of citizens.

## THE CONSTITUTIONAL COURT

The Constitutional Court is the sole authority of constitutional judicature in Moldova. It is composed of six judges, who are appointed for a six-year term. The Constitutional Court's powers include: the enforcement of constitutionality control over laws, decrees and governmental decisions, as well as international treaties endorsed by the republic; the confirmation of the results of elections and referendums; the explanation and clarification of the Constitution; and decisions over matters of the constitutionality of parties. The decisions of the Constitutional Court are final and are not subject to appeal.

## CONSTITUTIONAL REVISIONS

A revision of the Constitution may be initiated by one of the following: a petition signed by at least 200,000 citizens from at least one-half of the country's districts and municipalities; no less than one-third of the members of Parliament; the President of the Republic; the Government. Provisions regarding the sovereignty, independence, unity and neutrality of the State may be revised only by referendum.

*In July 2003 a constitutional amendment was approved by Parliament, officially recognizing the autonomous status of Gagauzia.

# The Government

## HEAD OF STATE

**President:** VLADIMIR VORONIN (elected 4 April 2001).

## COUNCIL OF MINISTERS
(October 2003)

**Prime Minister:** VASILE TARLEV.

**First Deputy Prime Minister:** VASILE IOVV.

**Deputy Prime Minister:** VALERIAN CRISTEA.

**Deputy Prime Minister and Minister of Agriculture and the Food Industry:** DUMITRU TODOROGLO.

**Minister of the Economy:** MARIAN LUPU.

**Minister of Finance:** ZINAIDA GRECÎANII.

**Minister of Industry:** MIHAI GARŞTEA.

**Minister of Energy:** IACOB TIMCIUC.

**Minister of Transport and Telecommunications:** VASILE ZGARDAN.

**Minister of Ecology, Construction and Territorial Development:** GHEORGHE DUCA.

**Minister of Education:** VALENTIN BENIUC.

**Minister of Health:** ANDREI GHERMAN.

**Minister of Labour and Social Protection:** VALERIAN REVENCO.

**Minister of Culture:** VEACESLAV MADAN.

**Minister of Justice:** VASILE DOLGHIERU.

**Minister of Foreign Affairs:** NICOLAE DUDĂU.

**Minister of Internal Affairs:** GHEORGHE PAPUC.

**Minister of Defence:** Brig.-Gen. VICTOR GAICIUC.

**Minister of Reintegration:** VASILE SOVA.

**Baskan (Leader) of Gagauzia:** GHEORGHE TABUNSCIC.

## STATE DEPARTMENTS

**Chairman of the State Department for Civil Defence and Emergencies:** (vacant).

**Chairman of the State Department for Fuel and Energy:** VALERIU ICONNICOV.

**Chairman of the State Department for Inter-Ethnic Relations and Languages:** (vacant).

**Chairman of the State Department for Privatization and State Property Administration:** NICOLAE GUMENII.

**Chairman of the State Department for Statistical and Sociological Analysis:** ANA CUCUREAVI.

**Chairman of the State Department for Technical Supervision, Standardization and Metrology:** (vacant).

## MINISTRIES

**Office of the President:** Chişinău, bd Ştefan cel Mare 154; tel. (2) 23-47-93.

**Office of the Council of Ministers:** 2033 Chişinău, Piaţa Marii Adunări Naţionale 1; tel. (2) 23-30-92.

**Ministry of Agriculture and the Food Industry:** 2012 Chişinău, bd Ştefan cel Mare 162; tel. (2) 23-34-27; fax (2) 23-23-68.

**Ministry of Culture:** 2033 Chişinău, Piaţa Marii Adunări Naţionale 1; tel. (2) 23-39-56; fax (2) 23-23-88.

**Ministry of Defence:** 2028 Chişinău, şos. Hînceşti 84; tel. (2) 79-94-89; fax (2) 23-45-35.

**Ministry of Ecology, Construction and Territorial Development:** 2005 Chişinău, str. Cosmonauţilor 9; tel. (2) 22-16-68; fax (2) 22-07-48; e-mail capcelea@moldova.md.

**Ministry of the Economy:** 2033 Chişinău, Piaţa Marii Adunări Naţionale 1; tel. (2) 23-74-48; fax (2) 23-40-64; e-mail minecon@moldova.md.

**Ministry of Education:** 2033 Chişinău, Piaţa Marii Adunări Naţionale 1; tel. (2) 23-35-15; fax (2) 23-34-74; e-mail tiron@minedu.moldnet.md.

**Ministry of Energy:** 2012 Chişinău, str. V. Alecsandri 78; tel. (2) 22-22-64; fax (2) 25-33-42; e-mail mdepen@rambler.ru.

**Ministry of Finance:** 2005 Chişinău, str. Cosmonauţilor 7; tel. (2) 23-35-75; fax (2) 22-13-07; e-mail protocol@minfin.moldova.md; internet www.moldova.md.

**Ministry of Foreign Affairs:** 2012 Chişinău, str. 31 August 1989 80; tel. (2) 23-39-40; fax (2) 23-23-02; e-mail massmedi@mfa.un.md; internet www.moldova.md/ro/government/oll/FOREIGN/en/index _en.html.

**Ministry of Health:** 2009 Chişinău, str. V. Alecsandri 1; tel. (2) 72-98-60; fax (2) 73-87-81; e-mail sdomente@mednet.md.

**Ministry of Industry:** 2012 Chişinău, bd Ştefan cel Mare 69; tel. (2) 27-80-59; fax (2) 27-80-00.

**Ministry of Internal Affairs:** 2012 Chişinău, bd Ştefan cel Mare 75; tel. (2) 22-45-47; fax (2) 22-27-43; e-mail mai@mai.md; internet www.mai.md.

**Ministry of Justice:** 2012 Chişinău, str. 31 August 1989 82; tel. (2) 23-47-95; fax (2) 23-47-97; e-mail dagri@cni.md.

**Ministry of Labour and Social Protection:** 2009 Chişinău, str. V. Alecsandri 1; tel. (2) 73-75-72; fax (2) 72-30-00; e-mail mmpsf@cni .md.

**Ministry of Transport and Communications:** 2012 Chişinău, bd Ştefan cel Mare 134; tel. (2) 22-10-01; fax (2) 24-15-53; e-mail secretary@mci.gov.md; internet mci.gov.md.

## STATE DEPARTMENTS

**State Department for Civil Defence and Emergencies:** Chişinău, str. Gh. Asachi 69; tel. (2) 73-85-01; fax (2) 23-34-30.

**State Department for Fuel and Energy:** see Ministry of Energy.

**State Department for Inter-Ethnic Relations and Languages:** Chişinău.

**State Department of Privatization and State Property Administration:** 2012 Chişinău, str. Puşkin 26; tel. (2) 23-43-50; fax (2) 23-43-36; e-mail dep.priv@moldtelecom.md.

**State Department for Statistics and Sociology:** 2028 Chişinău, şos. Hînceşti 53D; tel. (2) 73-37-74; fax (2) 22-61-46; e-mail dass@statistica.md; internet www.statistica.md.

**State Department for Technical Supervision, Standardization and Metrology:** 2069 Chişinău, str. E. Coca 28; tel. (2) 74-85-88; fax (2) 75-05-81; e-mail moldovastandard@standart.mldnet.com.

# President and Legislature

## PRESIDENT

The Moldovan Parliament failed to elect a President in four rounds of voting in December 2000. Therefore, under the terms of the Constitution, Parliament had to be dissolved and legislative elections held before a fresh presidential election could take place. Three candidates contested the presidential election of 4 April 2001. Vladimir Voronin was elected President with 71 votes; Dumitru Braghiş received 15 votes and Valerian Cristea received three votes. The 11 deputies of the Christian Democratic People's Party abstained from voting.

## PARLIAMENT

### Parlamentul
### (Parliament)

2073 Chişinău, bd Ştefan cel Mare 105; tel. (2) 23-33-52; fax (2) 23-30-12; e-mail info@parlament.md; internet www.parlament.md.

**Chairman:** EUGENIA OSTAPCIUC.

**Deputy Chairmen:** VADIM MISIN, MIHAIL CAMERZAN.

**General Election, 25 February 2001**

| Parties and alliances | % of votes | Seats |
|---|---|---|
| Moldovan Party of Communists . . . . | 49.93 | 71 |
| Braghiş Alliance . . . . . . . . . | 13.40 | 19 |
| Christian Democratic People's Party . . . . | 8.31 | 11 |
| Other parties, alliances and independents* . . | 28.36 | — |
| **Total** . . . . . . . . . . . | 100.00 | 101 |

*Including the Party of Revival and Conciliation, the Democratic Party of Moldova, the National Liberal Party, the Social Democratic Party of the Republic of Moldova and the National Peasants' Christian Democratic Party.

# Local Government

In January 2003 the Government approved legislation reintroducing a Soviet-style administrative structure to Moldova, comprising 33 districts (raions) and one municipality (Chişinău). In March legislation was passed by Parliament confirming the direct election of mayors, and abolishing the position of prefect. Local elections were held on 25 May and 8 June, in which the Moldovan Party of Communists secured the majority of the votes cast.

Not all territories acknowledged the authority of the central government. In 1991 the region east of the Dniester river (Transnistria), which was dominated by ethnic Russians, declared the independence of a 'Transdnestrian Moldovan Soviet Socialist Republic', based in Tiraspol. In the south of Moldova, five districts dominated by the Gagauz (Turkish Christians) declared a 'Gagauz Soviet Socialist Republic', based in Comrat (Komrat). Under the terms of the Constitution that came into force in August 1994, provision was made for Transnistria and Gagauzia to be granted special autonomous status.

In December 1994 the Moldovan Parliament adopted legislation on the special status of Gagauzia, which allowed the region broad self-administrative powers. Legislative power was vested in a 34-seat regional assembly, the Halk Toplusu, presided over by a baskan or governor. Local officials were given wider administrative powers. Elections to the Halk Toplusu were held in May 1995 and August 1999, and elections to the post of Baskan were held in June 1995, August–September 1999 and October 2002. In July 2003 a constitutional amendment was approved by Parliament, officially recognizing the autonomous status of Gagauzia.

Elections were held in Transnistria in March–April 1995, in which the Union of Patriotic Forces received more than 90% of the votes cast; the elections were declared illegal by the Moldovan authorities. In December an unofficial bicameral legislature was elected in Transnistria. In December 1996 Igor Smirnov was re-elected 'President' of Transnistria, with more than 70% of the votes cast. In July 2000 a unicameral legislature was reinstalled, under a system of presidential governance, and elections were held on 10 December, in which the majority of seats were won by independents; the Yedinstvo (Unity) movement emerged as the largest single party, with nine seats. On 13 December 2001 Smirnov was re-elected for a third term of office, receiving some 82% of the votes cast.

### GAGAUZ-ERI
### (GAGAUZIA)

**Baskan of Gagauz-Eri:** GHEORGHE TABUNSCIC.

**Chairman of the Popular Assembly:** IVAN KRISTIOGLU.

### TRANSNISTRIA
### (TRANSDNESTRIA)

**Co-Chairmen of the Joint Moldovan-Transdnestrian Monitoring Commission:** GHEORGHE ROMAN (Moldovan Govt), VLADIMIR BODNAR (Govt of 'Transdnestrian Moldovan SSR').

### 'Transdnestrian Moldovan Soviet Socialist Republic'

**President of the 'Transdnestrian Moldovan Soviet Socialist Republic':** IGOR N. SMIRNOV.

# Political Organizations

In December 2002 Parliament approved new legislation, which required political organizations to re-register with the Ministry of Justice each year, and provide evidence that their membership numbered at least 5,000 people, from among at least one-half of Moldova's districts. At March 2003 26 political parties were registered with the Ministry of Justice.

**Agrarian Democratic Party (ADP)** (Partidul Democrat Agrar din Moldova): Chişinău; tel. (2) 22-42-74; fax (2) 22-23-63; f. 1991 by moderates from both the Popular Front of Moldova and the Communist Party of Moldova; supports Moldovan independence, and economic and agricultural reform; Chair. ANATOL POPUŞOI.

**Christian Democratic People's Party (CDPP)** (Partidul Popular Creştin Democrat—PPCD): 2009 Chişinău, str. Nicolae Iorga 5; tel. (2) 23-33-56; fax (2) 23-86-66; e-mail magic@cni.md; internet inima .dnt.md; f. 1989 as the Popular Front of Moldova, renamed 1992, and as above 1999; advocates Moldova's entry into the European Union and NATO; Chair. IURIE ROŞCA.

**Civic Dignity Party of Moldova** (Particul Demnităţii Civice din Moldova—PDCM): Chişinău, str. M. Costin 7; tel. (2) 49-84-73; f. 1999; Pres. ION LIPCIU.

**Democratic Labour Party of Moldova:** Chişinău; f. 1993; Pres. ALECSANDRU ARSENI.

**Democratic Party of Moldova (PDM)** (Partidul Democrat din Moldova): 2001 Chişinău, str. Tighina 32; tel. (2) 27-82-89; fax (2) 27-82-30; e-mail mpmdp@moldova.md; internet www.pdm.md; f. 1997; centrist; formerly Movement for a Democratic and Prosperous Moldova, name changed in April 2000; formed bloc with the Party of Progressive Forces in Sept. 2001; Chair. DUMITRU DIACOV.

**Democratic Unity Party:** Chişinău; f. 2001; pro-European, concerned with social issues; Leader SERGIU MOCIANU.

**'Green Alliance' Ecological Party of Moldova** (Alianţa Verde—PEM-AVE): 2012 Chişinău, str. Şciusev 63; tel. and fax (2) 72-16-43; e-mail iondediu@yahoo.com; f. 1992; represents political ecology and sustainable development; Pres. Prof. ION DEDIU; 10,000 mems.

**Moldova Noastra Social Liberal Alliance:** Chişinău, str. Puskin 62A; tel. (2) 54-85-38; e-mail vitalia@ch.moldpac.md; f. 2003 by merger of the Alliance for Independent Moldova, the Moldovan Liberal Party and the Social Democratic Alliance of Moldova; supports Moldova's integration into Europe, a market economy and inter-ethnic harmony; Chair. DUMITRU BRAGHIŞ, SERAFIM URECHEAN, VEACESLAV UNTILĂ; c. 100,000 mems.

**Moldovan Centrist Union:** Chişinău; f. 2000; splinter group of former Movement for a Democratic and Prosperous Moldova; Chair. MIHAI PETRACHE.

**Moldovan Democratic Forum:** Chişinău; f. 2001 by the merger of six right-wing parties: the National Liberal Party, the Moldovan Party of Democratic Forces, the National Peasants' Christian Democratic Party, the Party of Social Justice and Order, the New National Moldovan Party and the Party of Civil Dignity.

**Moldovan Party of Communists (MPC)** (Partidul Comunistilor din Republica Moldova): 2012 Chişinău, str. N. Iorga 11; tel. (2) 23-46-14; fax (2) 23-36-73; e-mail info@pcrm.md; internet www.pcrm .md; fmrly the Communist Party of Moldova (banned Aug. 1991); revived as above 1994; formed a 10-party Left–Centre Union for the 2003 local election; First Sec. VLADIMIR VORONIN.

**National Salvation Movement (NSM):** Chişinău; f. 2000; break-away faction from the National Liberal Party.

**Popular Democratic Party of Moldova (PDPM):** Chişinău, str. Kogălniceanu 87; tel. (2) 24-91-10; Pres. MIHAI CEBAN.

**Reform Party (PRM):** Chişinău, str. Bucureşti 87; tel. (2) 23-26-89; fax (2) 22-80-97; f. 1993; centre-right Christian-Democratic party, which seeks to represent middle-class interests; Leader MIHAI GIMPU; Chair. ŞTEFAN GORDA; 12,000 mems.

**Republican Party of Moldova (PRM):** Chişinău, str. A. Vlahuţă 11/4; tel. (2) 22-83-18; f. 1999; Pres. VALERI EFREMOV.

**Social Liberal Party:** Chişinău, str. Bulgară 24в; tel. (2) 27-66-20; fax (2) 22-25-03; e-mail secretariat@psl.md; internet www.psl.md; f. 1999; absorbed the Christian Democratic League of Women and the National Youth League of Moldova; merged with the Party of Democratic Forces in December 2002; Leader OLEG SEREBREAN; Deputy Chair. VALERIU MATEI.

**Socialist Party of Moldova** (Partidul Socialist din Moldova): Chişinău, str. Calea Ieşilor 61/1, ap. 15; tel. (2) 75-87-62; successor to the former Communist Party of Moldova; favours socialist economic and social policies, defends the rights of Russian and other minorities and advocates CIS membership; Pres. VICTOR MOREV.

**Yedinstvo (Unity) Movement:** 2009 Chişinău, str. Hînceşti 35; tel. (2) 23-79-52; f. 1989; represents interests of ethnic minorities in Moldova; 35,000 mems; Pres. PETR SHORNIKOV.

Parties and organizations in Transnistria include: the Union of Patriotic Forces (Tiraspol; radical socialist; Leader VASILII YAKOVLEV); the Movement for the Development of Dnestr (Tiraspol; moderate); the United Council of Workers' Collectives (Tiraspol; radical); 'For Accord and Stability' (Tiraspol; moderate); and 'Position' (Tiraspol; moderate; Leader SVETLANA MIGULEA); Russia's Unity—Yedinstvo Party established a branch in Tiraspol in 2000 (founded by the local Union of Industrialists, Agriculturalists and Entrepreneurs).

Parties and organizations in Gagauzia include: the Vatan (Motherland) Party (Comrat; Leader ANDREI CHESHMEJI) and Gagauz Halky (Gagauz People—Comrat; Leader KONSTANTIN TAUSHANDJI).

# Diplomatic Representation

## EMBASSIES IN MOLDOVA

**Belarus:** 2009 Chişinău, str. Mateevici 35; tel. (2) 23-83-02; fax (2) 23-83-00; Ambassador VASILY SAKOVICH.

**Bulgaria:** Chişinău, str. 31 August 1989 125, Hotel Codru; tel. (2) 23-79-83; fax (2) 23-79-08; e-mail amb_bg@mdl.net; Ambassador EVGENII EKHOV.

**China, People's Republic:** Chişinău, str. Mitropolit Dosoftei 124; tel. (2) 24-85-51; fax (2) 24-75-46; e-mail root@chinam.mldnet.com; Ambassador XU ZHONGKAI.

**France:** Chişinău, str. 31 August 1989 101A; tel. (2) 22-82-04; fax (2) 22-82-24; e-mail amb-fr@cni.md; internet www.ambafrance.md; Ambassador EDMOND PAMBOUKJIAN.

**Germany:** 2012 Chişinău, str. Maria Cibotari 35, Hotel Jolly Alon; tel. (2) 20-06-00; fax (2) 23-46-80; e-mail de-botschaft@riscom.md; internet ambasada-germana.org.md; Ambassador Dr MICHAEL ZICK-ERICK.

**Hungary:** 2004 Chişinău, bd Ştefan cel Mare 131; tel. (2) 22-34-04; fax (2) 22-45-13; e-mail huembkiv1@meganet.md; Ambassador Dr SÁNDOR RÓBEL.

**Poland:** Chişinău, str. Plamadeala 3; tel. (2) 23-85-51; fax (2) 23-85-52; e-mail ambpolsk@ch.moldpac.md; f. 1994; Ambassador PIOTR MARCINIAK.

**Romania:** Chişinău, str. Bucureşti 66/1; tel. (2) 22-30-37; fax (2) 22-81-29; e-mail ambrom@ch.moldpac.md; Ambassador FILIP TEODOR-ESCU.

**Russia:** 2004 Chişinău, bd Ştefan cel Mare 153; tel. (2) 23-49-43; fax (2) 54-51-07; e-mail domino@mdl.net; internet www.moldova.mid .ru; Ambassador YURII ZUBAKOV.

**Turkey:** Chişinău, str. Mateevici 57; tel. (2) 24-26-08; fax (2) 22-55-28; e-mail tremb@moldova.md; Ambassador OGUZ OZGE.

**Ukraine:** 2004 Chişinău, str. Sfatul Ţării 55; tel. (2) 58-21-51; fax (2) 58-51-08; e-mail emb_md@mfa.gov.ua; Ambassador PETRO CHALYI.

**USA:** 2009 Chişinău, str. Mateevici 103; tel. (2) 23-37-72; fax (2) 23-30-44; e-mail rosenquist@chisinaub.us-state.gov; internet www .usembassy.md; Ambassador HEATHER HODGES.

# Judicial System

**Supreme Court:** Chişinău; Chair. VALERIA STERBET.

## Constitutional Court

2004 Chişinău, str. A. Lapusneanu 28; tel. (2) 24-05-49; fax (2) 24-52-23; e-mail curtea@constit.mldnet.com; internet www.ccrm.rol.md.

Chair. VICTOR PUSCAS.

**Prosecutor-General:** VASILE RUSU.

# Religion

The majority of the inhabitants of Moldova profess Christianity, the largest denomination being the Eastern Orthodox Church. The Gagauz, although of Turkic descent, are also adherents of Orthodox Christianity. The Russian Orthodox Church (Moscow Patriarchy) has jurisdiction in Moldova, but there are Romanian and Turkish liturgies.

### Eastern Orthodox Church

In December 1992 the Patriarch of Moscow and All Russia issued a decree altering the status of the Eparchy of Chişinău and Moldova to that of a Metropolitan See. The Government accepted this decree, thus tacitly rejecting the claims of the Metropolitan of Bessarabia (based in Romania). However, at the end of July 2002 the Government agreed to register the Bessarabian Metropolitan Church, following international pressure.

**Archbishop of Chişinău and Moldova:** VLADIMIR, 2012 Chişinău, str. Mitropolit Dosoftei 85; tel. (2) 22-34-70; fax (2) 22-52-10; e-mail administ@apost.modpac.md.

### Roman Catholic Church

In October 2001 the diocese of Chişinău, covering the whole country, was established. At 31 December 2001 there were an estimated 20,000 Catholics in Moldova.

**Bishop of Chişinău:** Rt Rev. ANTON COŞA, 2012 Chişinău, str. Mitropo lit Dosoftei 85; tel. (2) 22-34-70; fax (2) 22-52-10; e-mail administ@apost.moldpac.md; internet catholic.dnt.md.

# The Press

In 1996 there were four daily newspapers published in Moldova (with a combined circulation averaging 261,000 copies). In that year 206 non-daily newspapers were published (with an estimated circulation of 1,350,000). In 1994 there were 76 other periodicals (31 for the general public and 45 for specific readership, with a total circulation of 196,000).

The publications listed below are in Romanian (or Moldovan, as it is officially termed), except where otherwise indicated.

## PRINCIPAL NEWSPAPERS

**Accente:** Chişinău, str. Vlaicu Pîrcălab 45, 405; internet www .accente.com.md; weekly; Editor-in-Chief SERGIU AFANASIU.

**Dnestrovskaya Pravda** (Dnestr Truth): Tiraspol, str. 25 October 101; tel. and fax (33) 3-46-86; f. 1941; 3 a week; Russian; Editor TATYANA M. RUDENKO; circ. 7,000.

**Ekonomicheskoye Obozrenie** (Economic Review): Chişinău, bd Ştefan cel Mare 180; tel. (2) 24-69-52; fax (2) 24-69-50; e-mail red@ logos.press.md; internet logos.press.md; f. 1990; weekly; Editor-in-Chief SERGEI MIŞIN.

**GP Flux:** Chişinău, str. Corobceanu 17; tel. (2) 23-22-14; fax (2) 24-75-29; e-mail secretar@flux.press.md; internet flux.press.md; daily; Editor-in-Chief IGOR BURCIU.

**Glasul Naţiunii** (Voice of the Nation): Chişinău, str. 31 August 15; tel. and fax (2) 54-31-37; 2 a month; Editors VASILE NESTASE, LEONID LARI.

**Jurnal de Chişinău:** Chişinău, str. Puşkin 22, 446; tel. (2) 23-40-41; fax (2) 23-42-30; e-mail jurnal@chisinau.moldline.net; internet jurnal.press.md; Editor-in-Chief VAL BUTNARU.

**Kishinevskiye Obozrevatel** (Chişinău Correspondent): Chişinău, bd Ştefan cel Mare 162, 604/7; tel. (2) 21-02-34; fax (2) 21-02-64; e-mail oboz@molodvacc.md; internet www.ko.md; weekly; Russian; Editor-in-Chief IRINA ASTAHOVA.

**Kishinevskiye Novosti** (Chişinău News): Chişinău, str. Puşkin 22; tel. (2) 23-39-18; fax (2) 23-42-40; e-mail kn@mdl.net; weekly; Russian; Editor-in-Chief SERGEI DROBOT.

**Kommersant Moldovy:** Chişinău, str. Puşkin 22, 601; tel. (2) 23-36-94; e-mail vartem@commert.press.md; internet www.km.riscom .net; weekly; Russian; Editor-in-Chief ARTEM VARENIŢA.

**Komsomolskaye Pravda Moldova:** Chişinău, str. Vlaicu Pîrcălab 45; tel. (2) 22-07-13; fax (2) 22-12-74; e-mail ser@kp.md; internet www.kp.md; daily; Russian; Editor-in-Chief SERGEI CIURICOV.

**Moldavskie Vedomosti** (Moldovan Gazette): Chişinău, str. Banulescu-Bodoni 21; tel. and fax (2) 23-86-18; e-mail editor@mv.net.md; internet vedomosti.md; weekly; Russian; Editor-in-Chief DMITRII CIUBASENKO.

**Moldova Suverană** (Sovereign Moldova): 2012 Chişinău, str. Puşkin 22, et. 3; tel. (2) 23-35-38; fax (2) 23-31-96; e-mail cotidian@

suverana.press.md; internet www.moldova-suverana.md; f. 1924; daily; organ of the Govt; Editor Ion Berlinschi; circ. 105,000.

**Nezavisimaya Moldova** (Independent Moldova): 2012 Chişinău, str. Puşkin 22, 303; tel. (2) 23-36-05; fax (2) 23-31-41; e-mail admin@ nm.mldnet.com; internet www.nmmd; f. 1925; daily; organ of the Govt; Russian; Editor Iurii Tiscenco; circ. 60,692.

**Tinerimya Moldovei/Molodezh Moldovy** (Youth of Moldova): Chişinău; f. 1928; 3 a week; editions in Romanian (circ. 12,212) and Russian (circ. 4,274); Editor V. Botnaru.

**Trudovoi Tiraspol** (Working Tiraspol): Tiraspol, str. 25 October 101; tel. (33) 3-04-12; f. 1989; main newspaper of the east-bank Slavs; Russian; Editor Dima Kondratovich.

**Viaţă Satului** (Life of the Village): 2612 Chişinău, str. Puşkin 22, Casa presei, 4th Floor; tel. (2) 23-03-68; f. 1945; weekly; govt publ.; Editor V. S. Spiney.

## PRINCIPAL PERIODICALS

**Basarabia** (Bessarabia): Chişinău; f. 1931; fmrly *Nistru*; monthly; journal of the Union of Writers of Moldova; fiction; Editor-in-Chief D. Matkovsky.

**Chipăruş** (Peppercorn): 2612 Chişinău, str. Puşkin 22; tel. (2) 23-38-16; f. 1958; fortnightly; satirical; Editor-in-Chief Ion Vikol.

**Femeia Moldovei** (Moldovan Woman): 2470 Chişinău, str. 28 June 45; tel. (2) 23-31-64; f. 1951; monthly; popular, for women.

**Lanterna Magică** (Magic Lantern): Chişinău, str. Puşkin 24, 49; tel. (2) 74-86-43; fax (2) 23-23-88; e-mail lung_ro@yahoo.com; internet www.iatp.md/lanternamagica; f. 1990; publ. by the Ministry of Culture; 6 a year; art, culture.

**Literatură şi Artă:** 2009 Chişinău, str. Sfatul Ţării 2; tel. (2) 23-82-12; fax (2) 23-82-17; e-mail literatura@moldnet.md; f. 1954; weekly; organ of the Union of Writers of Moldova; literary; Editor Nicolae Dabija.

**Moldova si Lumea** (Moldova and the World): 2012 Chişinău, str. Puşkin 22, 510; tel. (2) 23-75-81; fax (2) 23-40-32; f. 1991; monthly; state-owned; international socio-political review; Editor Boris Stratulat.

**Noi** (Us): Chişinău; tel. (2) 23-31-10; f. 1930; fmrly *Scînteia Leninista*; monthly; fiction; for 10–15-year-olds; Man. Valeriu Volontir.

**Pămint şi Oameni** (Land and People): Chişinău; tel. (2) 22-33-87; organ of the Agrarian Democratic Party; weekly.

**Politica:** 2033 Chişinău, bd Ştefan cel Mare 105; tel. (2) 23-74-03; fax (2) 23-32-10; e-mail vppm@cni.md; f. 1991; monthly; political issues.

**Săptămína:** Chişinău, str. 31 August 107; tel. (2) 22-44-61; fax (2) 21-37-07; e-mail saptamin@mom.mldnet.com; internet www.net .md/saptamina/; weekly magazine; Editor-in-Chief Viorel Mihail.

**Sud-Est** (South-East): Chişinău, str. Maria Cibotaru 16; tel. (2) 23-26-05; fax (2) 23-22-42; internet www.sud-est.md; f. 1990; publ. by the Ministry of Culture; quarterly; art, culture; Editor-in-Chief Valentina Taslauana.

## NEWS AGENCIES

**AP Flux Press Agency:** Chişinău, str. Corobceanu 17; tel. (2) 24-92-72; fax (2) 24-91-51; e-mail flux@cni.md; internet flux.press.md; f. 1995; Dir Nadine Gogu.

**BASA-press—Moldovan Information and Advertising Agency:** 2012 Chişinău, str. Vasile Alecsandri 72; tel. (2) 22-03-90; fax (2) 22-13-96; e-mail basa@basa.md; internet www.basa.md; f. 1992; independent; co-operates with Deutsche Presse-Agentur (Germany); Gen. Dir Valeriu Renita.

**DECA Press Agency:** Bălţi, str. Independentei 33; tel. (31) 61-385; fax (31) 607-44; e-mail info@deca-press.net; internet www .deca-press.net; f. 1996; local news; non-profit; Dir Vitalie Cazacu.

**InfoMarket.MD (Denimax Grup):** tel. (2) 27-76-26; e-mail editor@ infomarket.md; internet www.infomarket.md; on-line business news; Editor Alecsandru Burdeinii.

**Infotag News Agency:** 2014 Chişinău, str. Kogâlniceanu 76; tel. (2) 23-49-30; fax (2) 23-49-33; e-mail office@infotag.net.md; internet www.infotag.md; f. 1993; leading private news agency; Dir Alexandru Tanas.

**Interlic News Agency:** 2012 Chişinău, str. M. Cibotari 37, Of. 306; tel. and fax (2) 25-16-49; fax (2) 23-20-67; e-mail red@interlic.md; internet www.interlic.md; f. 1995; independent; Dir Ivan Sveatcenko.

**State Information Agency—Moldpres:** 2012 Chişinău, str. Puşkin 22; tel. (2) 23-26-69; fax (2) 23-43-71; e-mail director@ moldpres.md; internet www.moldpres.md; f. 1990 as Moldovapres, reorganized 1994; Dir-Gen. (vacant).

## PRESS ASSOCIATIONS

**Independent Journalism Centre (IJC):** 2012 Chişinău, str. Sciusev 53; tel. (2) 21-36-52; fax (2) 22-66-81; e-mail ijcnews@ijc.iatp .md; internet ijc.iatp.md; f. 1994; non-governmental org.

**Independent Press Association (API):** Chişinău, str. Corobceanu 15; tel. (2) 21-06-02; fax (2) 20-36-86; e-mail api@ moldtelecom.md; internet api.iatp.md; f. 1997; Pres. Ion Ciumeica.

**Mass Media Association of Moldova:** Chişinău; internet www .media.ist.md; f. 2000.

**Union of Journalists of Moldova:** 2012 Chişinău, str. Puşkin 22; tel. and fax (2) 23-34-19; e-mail ujm@moldnet.md; internet www .iatp.md/ujm; f. 1957; Chair. Valeriu Saharneanu.

# Publishers

In 1996 there were 921 titles (books and pamphlets) published in Moldova (2.8m. copies).

**Editura Cartea Moldovei:** 2004 Chişinău, bd Ştefan cel Mare 180; tel. (2) 24-65-10; fax (2) 24-64-11; f. 1977; fiction, non-fiction, poetry, art books; Dir Dumitru Furdui; Editor-in-Chief Raisa Suveica.

**Editura Hyperion:** 2004 Chişinău, bd Ştefan cel Mare 180; tel. (2) 24-40-22; f. 1976; fiction, literature, arts; Dir Valeriu Matei.

**Editura Lumina** (Light): 2004 Chişinău, bd Ştefan cel Mare 180; tel. (2) 24-63-95; f. 1966; educational textbooks; Dir Victor Stratan; Editor-in-Chief Anatol Malev.

**Editura Ştiinţa** (Science): 2028 Chişinău, str. Academiei 3; tel. (2) 73-96-16; fax (2) 73-96-27; e-mail prini@stiinta.asm.md; f. 1959; textbooks, encyclopaedias, dictionaries, children's books and fiction in various languages; Dir Gheorghe Prini.

**Izdatelstvo Kartia Moldoveniaske:** 2004 Chişinău, bd Ştefan cel Mare; tel. (2) 24-40-22; f. 1924; political and literature; Dir N. N. Mumzhi; Editor-in-Chief I. A. Tsurkanu.

# Broadcasting and Communications

## TELECOMMUNICATIONS

### Regulatory Authority

**Ministry of Transport and Telecommunications:** see section on the Government.

### Telecommunications Company

**Moldcell SA:** 2060 Chişinău, str. Belgrad 3; tel. (2) 20-62-06; fax (2) 20-62-07; e-mail moldcell@moldcell.md; internet www.moldcell.md; f. 1999; mobile-telecommunications; owned by Fintur Holdings b.v. (Netherlands).

**Moldtelecom SA:** 2001 Chişinău, bd Ştefan cel Mare 10; tel. (2) 54-87-97; fax (2) 54-64-19; e-mail office@moldtelecom.md; internet www .moldtelecom.md; f. 1993; telephone communication and internet service provider; scheduled for partial privatization; Gen. Dir Stela Şcola.

## BROADCASTING

### Regulatory Authorities

**National Regulatory Agency in Telecommunications and Informatics (ANRTI):** 2012 Chişinău, bd Ştefan cel Mare 134; tel. (2) 25-13-17; fax (2) 22-28-85; e-mail office@anrti.md; internet www .anrti.md; Dir Yu. Tabirţa.

**Radio and Television Co-ordinating Council** (Consiliul Coordonator al Audiovizualului): 2012 Chişinău, str. Mihai Eminescu 28; tel. (2) 27-75-51; fax (2) 27-74-71; e-mail cca_moldova@mdl.net; internet www.cca.md; regulatory and licensing body; Chair. Ion Mihailo.

**State Communication Inspectorate** (Inspectoratul de Stat al Comunicatiilor): 2021 Chişinău, str. Drumul Viilor 28-2; tel. (2) 73-53-64; fax (2) 73-39-41; e-mail ciclicci@isc.net.md; f. 1993; responsible for frequency allocations and monitoring, certification of post and communications equipment and services; Dir Teodor Ciclicci.

### Radio

**State Radio and Television Company of Moldova (Teleradio)** (Televiziunea de Stat a Republicii Moldova): 2028 Chişinău, str. Miorița 1; tel. (2) 72-10-77; fax (2) 72-33-52; e-mail info@trm.md; internet www.trm.md; f. 1994; Dir Artur Efremoy.

**Radio Moldova:** 2028 Chişinău, str. Miorița 1; tel. (2) 72-13-88; fax (2) 72-35-37; f. 1930; broadcasts in Romanian, Russian, Ukrainian, Gagauz and Yiddish; Dir-Gen. Ilie Telesco.

### Television

**State Radio and Television Company of Moldova (Teleradio)** (Televiziunea de Stat a Republicii Moldova): see Radio.

**TV Moldova** (Televiziunea Nationala Moldova): f. 1958; Dir-Gen. Sergiu Prodan.

**Chişinău Television:** 2028 Chişinău, str. Hînceşti 64; tel. (2) 73-91-94; fax (2) 72-35-37; f. 1958; Dir-Gen. Arcadie Gherasim.

# Finance

(cap. = capital; res = reserves; dep. = deposits; m. = million; brs = branches; amounts in Moldovan lei, unless otherwise stated)

## BANKING

Restructuring of Moldova's banking system was begun in 1991 with the establishment of a central bank, the National Bank of Moldova (NBM), which was formerly a branch of the USSR Gosbank (state bank). The NBM is independent of the Government (but responsible to Parliament) and has the power to regulate monetary policy and the financial system. The lack of a stringent regulatory framework and the consequent proliferation of small commercial banks led the Government to introduce, in January 1996, new legislation on financial institutions. All commercial banks were subsequently inspected and a more effective banking supervision was implemented. At mid-2000 there were 21 commercial banks in operation.

### Central Bank

**National Bank of Moldova** (Banca Națională a Moldovei): 2006 Chişinău, bd Renaşterii 7; tel. (2) 22-50-52; fax (2) 22-05-91; e-mail official@bnm.org; internet www.bnm.org; f. 1991; cap. 100.0m., res 257.0m., dep. 638.8m. (Dec. 2001); Gov. Leonid Talmaci; Dep. Gov. Dumitru Ursu.

### Commercial Banks

**Banca de Finanțe şi Comerț** (FinComBank—Bank of Finance and Commerce): 2012 Chişinău, str. Puşkin 26; tel. (2) 22-74-35; fax (2) 22-82-53; e-mail office@fincombank.com; internet www.fincombank.com; f. 1993; cap 77.0m., dep. 184.2m., total assets 302.5m. (Dec. 2002); Chair. Victor Hvorostovschi; 5 brs.

**Banca Socială:** 2006 Chişinău, str. Bănulescu-Bodoni 61; tel. (2) 22-14-94; fax (2) 22-42-30; e-mail office@socbank.md; internet www.socbank.md; f. 1991; joint-stock commercial bank; cap. 57.6m., res 8.6m., dep. 451.0m. (Feb. 2002); Pres. Vladimir Suetnov; Chair. Valentin Kunev; 18 brs.

**BC 'Eximbank' SA** (Eximbank Joint-Stock Commercial Bank): 2001 Chişinău, bd Ştefan cel Mare 6; tel. (2) 27-25-83; fax (2) 54-62-34; e-mail info@eximbank.com; internet www.eximbank.com; Chair. Marcel Chircă.

**BC Unibank SA:** 2012 Chişinău, str. G. Bănulescu Bodoni 45; tel. (2) 22-55-86; fax (2) 22-05-30; e-mail welcome@unibank.md; internet www.unibank.md; f. 1993; joint-stock commercial bank; cap. 88.6m., res 5.7m., dep. 200.0m. (Oct. 2003); Pres. Claudia Melnic; 5 brs.

**CB Businessbank SA:** 2012 Chişinău, str. Alecsandru cel Bun 97; tel. (2) 20-56-10; fax (2) 22-23-70; e-mail bank@busbank.mldnet.com; internet www.businessbank.md; f. 1997; cap. 72.1m., res 1.1m., dep. 81.1m. (Jan. 2003); Chair.of Bd Sergiu N. Brinzila.

**CB Comerțbank JSC:** 2001 Chişinău, str. Hînceşti 38a; tel. (2) 73-99-91; fax (2) 73-99-81; e-mail comertbank@mdl.net; internet www.comertbank.md; f. 1991; cap. 96.0m., total assets 149.9m. (Jan. 2003); Chair. Natalia Uliyanova.

**Energbank:** 2012 Chişinău, str. Vasile Alecsandri 78; tel. (2) 54-43-77; fax (2) 25-34-09; e-mail office@energbank.com; internet www.energbank.com; f. 1997; cap. 58.3m. (2002), dep. 146.3m., total assets 239.4m. (Jan. 2003); Chair. Mihail Ogorodnicov; 31 brs.

**EuroCreditBank JSC:** 2001 Chişinău, str. Ismail 33; tel. (2) 50-01-01; fax (2) 54-88-27; e-mail info@ecb.md; internet www.ecb.md; f. 2002 to replace Petrolbank; commercial investment bank; cap. 40.1m., res 14.2m., dep. 115.7m. (Dec. 2000); Pres. Aleksandr Zholondkovskii; Pres. Dumitru Lupan; 2 brs.

**Guinea:** 2068 Chişinău, str. Alecu Russo 1; tel. (2) 43-05-11; fax (2) 44-41-40; cap. 10.4m., total assets 59.1m. (Jan. 1998); Chair. Iurii Stasiev.

**IBID-MB** (International Bank for Investment and Development): 2067 Chişinău, bd Moscow 21; tel. (2) 34-62-49; fax (2) 34-62-31; cap. 9.6m., total assets 24.7m. (Jan. 1998); Chair. Gheorghe Nechit.

**Investprivatbank SA:** 2001 Chişinău, str. Sciusev 34; tel. (2) 27-43-86; fax (2) 54-05-10; e-mail ipb.md@ipb.md; f. 1994; cap. 67.9m., total assets 171.4m. (Dec. 2002); Chair. Ivan Chirpalov.

**CB Mobiasbanca JSC:** 2012 Chişinău, bd Ştefan cel Mare 81; tel. and fax (2) 54-19-74; e-mail info@mobiasbank.com; internet www.mobiasbank.com; f. 1990; acquired Bank-coop in 2001; commercial bank; cap. US $8.9m., res US $0.8m., dep. US $14.8m. (Jan. 2003); Pres. Victor Popusoi; Chair. of Bd Nicolae Dorin; 8 brs.

**Moldindconbank SA** (Moldovan Bank for Industry and Construction): 2012 Chişinău, str. Armeneasca 38; tel. (2) 22-55-21; fax (2) 24-91-95; e-mail info@micb.net.md; internet www.moldindconbank.com; f. 1991; joint-stock commercial bank; cap. 30.1m., res 7.2m., dep. 540.1m. (Dec. 2001); Chair. of Bd Valerian Mirzac; 23 brs.

**Moldova Agroindbank SA:** 2005 Chişinău, str. Cosmonauților 9; tel. (2) 21-28-28; fax (2) 22-80-58; e-mail aib@maib.md; internet www.maib.md; f. 1991; joint-stock commercial bank; Chair. Victor Miculet; Pres. Natalia Vrabie; 45 brs.

**Oguzbank:** 2004 Chişinău, str. Toma Ciorba 24/1; tel. (2) 24-98-40; fax (2) 24-91-00; f. 1991; cap. 17.5m., total assets 53.5m. (Jan. 1998); Chair. Dumitru Sarov.

**Universalbank:** 2004 Chişinău, bd Ştefan cel Mare 180, et. 4; tel. (2) 24-64-06; fax (2) 24-64-89; e-mail ub@mail.universalbank.md; internet www.universalbank.md; f. 1994; cap. 67.4m., res 6.8m., dep. 92.7m., total assets 205.5m. (Jan. 2002); Chair.of Bd Irina Drozd; Gen. Man. Victoria Tofan.

**Vias:** 2002 Chişinău; tel. (2) 54-14-10; fax (2) 54-14-20; cap. 10.3m., total assets 18.1m. (Jan. 1998); Chair. Nicolae Dede.

**Victoriabank:** 2004 Chişinău, str. 31 August 141; tel. (2) 23-30-65; fax (2) 23-39-33; e-mail mail@victoriabank.md; internet www.victoriabank.md; f. 1989; cap. 146.0m., total assets 767.5m. (Dec. 2001); Chair. Victor Țurcanu; 12 brs.

### Savings Bank

**Banca de Economii a Moldovei:** 2012 Chişinău, str. Columna 115; tel. (2) 24-47-22; fax (2) 24-47-31; e-mail bem@bem.md; internet www.bem.md; f. 1992; cap. 100.0m., dep. 396.0m.. (Dec. 2001); Pres. Raisa Cantemir; 30 brs.

## STOCK EXCHANGE

**Moldovan Stock Exchange** (Bursa de Valori a Moldovei SA): 2001 Chişinău, bd Ştefan cel Mare 73; tel. (2) 27-75-94; fax (2) 27-73-56; e-mail dodu@moldse.md; internet www.moldse.md; f. 1994; Chair. Dr Corneliu Dodu.

## INSURANCE

**QBE Asito SA:** 2005 Chişinău, str. Mitropolit Bănulescu-Bodoni 57/1; tel. and fax (2) 22-62-12; fax (2) 22-11-79; e-mail asito@qbe-asito.com; internet www.qbe-asito.com; f. 1991; 74% owned by QBE Insurance Group (based in Australia); leading insurance co, with 40% market share; Gen. Man. Eugen Shlopak; 1,100 employees.

# Trade and Industry

## GOVERNMENT AGENCY

**State Department of Privatization and State Property Administration:** 2012 Chişinău, str. Pushkin 26; tel. (2) 22-54-78; fax (2) 23-43-50; e-mail privatization@mop.mldnet.com; internet www.privatization.md/; Gen. Dir Nicolae Gumenii.

**Moldovan Export Promotion Organization (MEPO):** 2009 Chişinău, str. Mateevici 65; tel. (2) 27-36-54; fax (2) 22-43-10; e-mail mepo@mepo.net; internet www.mepo.net; f. 1999; assists enterprises in increasing exports and improving business environment; Gen. Dir Valeriu Canna.

## CHAMBER OF COMMERCE

**Chamber of Commerce and Industry of the Republic of Moldova:** 2012 Chişinău, str. M. Eminescu 28; tel. (2) 22-15-52; fax (2) 24-14-53; e-mail inform@chamber.md; internet www.chamber.md; f. 1969; Chair. Gheorghe Cucu.

## UTILITIES

### Regulatory Authority

**National Energy Regulatory Agency (ANRE):** 2012 Chişinău, str. Columna 90; tel. (2) 54-13-84; fax (2) 22-46-98; e-mail anre@moldova.md; internet www.anre.moldpac.md; f. 1997; autonomous public institution; Dirs Marin Profir, Vasile Carafizi; Gen. Dir Nicolae Triboi.

## Electricity

**IS Moldtranselectro:** 2012 Chişinău, str. Vasile Alecsandri 78; tel. (2) 25-33-50; fax (2) 25-31-41; e-mail disp@mtenerg.mldnet.com; f. 2000; state-owned operator of electricity transmission system; in 2000 plans to reorganize the co into four independent state-owned enterprises were announced; Dir-Gen. VASILE PLESHCAN.

**Retelele Electrice de Distributie Nord SA:** 3121 Bălţi, bd Ştefan cel Mare 180A; tel. (31) 2-20-00; fax (31) 2-33-12; e-mail red-nord@mdl.net; f. 1997; state-owned; electricity distribution and transmission.

**Retelele Electrice ale Raoinul Rîbnîta:** 5501 Rîbnîta, str. Gvardeiskaia 25; tel. (55) 4-12-80; f. 1980; state-owned; electricity transmission and distribution.

**Retelele Electrice Sud-Est IS:** 3300 Tiraspol, str. Ukrainskaia 5; tel. (33) 3-44-23; fax (33) 3-55-87; f. 1974; state-owned; electricity transmission and distribution.

## Gas

**MoldovaGaz SA:** 2005 Chişinău, str. Albisoara 38; tel. (2) 22-32-70; fax (2) 24-00-14; f. May 1999; national gas pipeline and distribution networks; 51% owned by Gazprom (Russia), 35% owned by Moldova and 14% held by Transnistria; Gen. Dir GHENADII ABASCIN (acting).

**Moldovatransgas SRL:** 5233 Drochia, şos. Tarigrad, POB 24; tel. (52) 24-452; fax (52) 26-238; f. 1986; natural gas transportation, supply and equipment service.

## MAJOR COMPANIES

### Electrical Products

**Alfa Production Association:** 2071 Chişinău, str. Alba Yuliya 75; tel. (2) 75-37-18; fax (2) 74-15-20; e-mail ctc_alfa@mdl.net; f. 1995; household appliances and repairs.

**Bender Mechanical Engineering Factory:** 2100 Tighina, Benderskogo vosstaniya 5; tel. (32) 2-68-43; fax (32) 22-24-73; f. 1972; specialized electronic aviation equipment.

**Chişinău Refrigerator Plant:** 2036 Chişinău, str. M. Manole 9; tel. (2) 47-42-71; fax (2) 47-16-17; f. 1964; manufactures refrigerators and freezers; Dir V. S. USATYI; 1,000 employees.

**Compecs Factory:** 2075 Chişinău, str. Mikhay Cadovyany 20/2; tel. (2) 33-36-34; fax (2) 33-36-76; f. 1986; computers, radio-electronic equipment, electronic components, washing machines.

**Elcas-Market SRL:** 2005 Chişinău, str. P. Rares 77; tel. (2) 22-00-30; fax (2) 22-04-19; f. 1998; construction materials and home appliances.

**Electroapparatura Plant:** 3215 Tighina, str. Tiraspol 3; tel. (32) 24-351; fax (32) 24-117; f. 1959; electrical equipment for cranes, manual drilling machines.

**Elektromash SA:** 3300 Tiraspol, str. Sakrieru 1; tel. (33) 3-3-2-53; fax (33) 5-19-70; f. 1959; electric motors, diesel generators, transformers, synchronized electric motors.

**Raut SA:** 3101 Bălţi, str. Decebal 13; tel. (31) 2-30-90; fax (31) 2-71-30; e-mail raut99@mdl.net; internet www.beltsy.md/reut; underwater sonar navigation and research equipment, telephones, electric toasters, umbrellas, thermal cabinets.

**Revel Computers SRL:** 2004 Chişinău, bd Ştefan cel Mare 202, et. 1; tel. (2) 22-13-52; fax (2) 22-23-47; e-mail comp@revel.moldova.su; internet www.revel.moldova.com; f. 1994; network equipment, installation and services; Pres. and Dir ALECSANDRU KOPANSKIY.

**Semnal Joint-Stock Venture:** 2032 Chişinău, str. Zelinschi 11; tel. (2) 52-80-65; fax (2) 55-30-87; radios, home computers, consumer goods.

**Sigma SA:** 2038 Chişinău, bd Decebal 99; tel. and fax (2) 76-57-82; e-mail schiotmash@hotbox.ru; internet www.qp.sa.md/sigma.htm; f. 1963; plastic casting, radio receivers, power metres; Dir ANDREI NITSOU.

**Tiraspol Electrical Equipment Plant Joint-Stock Co:** 3300 Tiraspol, str. Ilyin 33; tel. (33) 3-43-59; fax (33) 3-51-87; e-mail tez@idknet.com; internet www.tez.idknet.com; f. 1958; development and manufacturing of automatic switches up to 63 amps; Dir N. ARLAKOV.

### Pharmaceuticals

**Farmaco SA:** 2023 Chişinău, str. Vadul-lui-Voda 2; tel. (2) 47-33-50; fax (2) 47-20-74; e-mail farmaco@ch.moldpac.md; f. 1929; produces pharmaceutical goods; Chief Exec. DORIN UNGUREANU; 400 employees.

### Textiles

**Floare-Carpet SA:** 2062 Chişinău, str. Grădina Botanică 15; tel. (2) 55-80-57; fax (2) 52-20-00; e-mail floare@carpet.midnet.com;

internet www.floare-carpet.md; f. 1978; mfr of carpets; sales US $5.2m. (2001); Gen. Man RABIL NICOLAE; 900 employees.

**Ionel SA:** 2001 Chişinău, str. Bulgară 47; tel. (2) 57-88-11; fax (2) 57-88-00; e-mail partners@ionel.mldnet.com; f. 1945; woollen and cotton clothing; Gen. Dir AGLAYA OSTROVSKAYA; 1,500 employees.

**Pielart SA:** 2069 Chişinău, str. Calea Iesilor 10; tel. (2) 22-13-23; fax (2) 74-03-64; e-mail pielart@mnc.md; internet www.pielart.md; f. 1957; artificial leather, rubber and thermoelastoplastic articles; Gen. Dir S. V. CHEIBOS.

**Vestra:** 3200 Tighina, str. Lazo 16; tel. (32) 2-05-03; fax (32) 2-33-60; e-mail vestra@bendery.md; f. 1944; manufactures clothing for women and children; Man. Dir TAMARA IVANOVA POLOZ; 1,083 employees.

### Miscellaneous

**Agromashina SA:** 2023 Chişinău, str. Uzinelor 21; tel. (2) 47-12-16; fax (2) 47-22-00; f. 1949; machines for cultivation, sowing and processing, for use in horticulture, viniculture, arboriculture and fruit-growing; Gen. Dir NICOLAE PAVLENKO; 150 employees.

**Alimentarmash SA:** 2044 Chişinău, str. Mesterul Manole 12; tel. (2) 47-43-20; fax (2) 47-13-36; e-mail almash@mdl.net; internet www.almash.net.md; f. 1945; industrial equipment for use in the food-processing industry; Pres. Z. H. SULEIMANOV; 271 employees (2003).

**Chişinău Glass Factory:** 2036 Chişinău, str. Transnistria 20; tel. (2) 47-34-30; fax (2) 37-38-70; e-mail moldova@glassf.midnet.com; f. 1970; mfr of glass and glassware; sales US $20m. (2000); Man. TROFIM YU PROFIR; 1,140 employees.

**Chişinău Refrigerator Plant:** 2036 Chişinău, str. Mesterul Manole 9; tel. (2) 47-34-34; fax (2) 47-16-17; mfr of refrigerators and freezers; Dir VYACHESLAV USATLI; 1,000 employees.

**Floarea-Soarelui Joint Stock Co:** 3101 Bălţi, str. 31 August 6; tel. (31) 22-280; fax (31) 25-414; e-mail florea@beltsy.md; f. 1922; produces sunflower and soya oil and associated products, incl. butter and soap; Pres. VASILIY KIRTOKA; Gen. Dir EMIL BUTU; 611 employees.

**Gloden Sugar Refinery:** 4900 Gloden, str. Stefan cel Mare 48; tel. (49) 23-383; fax (49) 24-590; f. 1977; processing of sugar beet and raw sugar; sales US $10m. (2001); 850 employees.

**Hidropompa SA:** 2001 Chişinău, bd Gagarin 2; tel. (2) 27-02-69; fax (2) 27-03-56; e-mail ovs@hidropompa.company.md; internet www.mgm-wdc.com/web/hidro; f. 1984; production of submersible pumps; Dir IVAN IVANOVICH MARTYA.

**Incon Joint Stock Co SA:** 2004 Chişinău, str. Lapusneanu 16; tel. (2) 23-29-42; fax (2) 23-39-89; e-mail incongroup@mold.net; f. 1992; export of apple juice concentrates, canned fruits and vegetables, tomato paste and jams; sales US $10m. (2000); Chair. ION ZGARCHI-BABA.

**Kirov Litmash Plant:** 3300 Tiraspol, str. Sacrieru 2v; tel. (33) 3-43-61; fax (33) 3-40-97; e-mail mark@litmash.com; internet www.litmash.com; f. 1924; injection-moulding machines and equipment; sales US $1.7m. (2000); Man. Dir V. A. GLUSHKOV; 600 employees.

**Mobila-Grup:** 2001 Chişinău, bd Ştefan cel Mare 69/1; tel. (2) 27-81-01; fax (2) 27-80-52; e-mail info@mobilagrup.md; f. 1992; financing industrial gp; manufactures furniture and paper products; sales US $4.9m. (1999); Pres. NICOLAE DORIN; Gen. Dir PETRU TISHACOV; 2,056 employees.

**Moldagrotehnica SA:** 3100 Bălţi, str. Industrială 4; tel. (31) 2-01-02; fax (31) 4-36-65; e-mail agroteh@mdl.net; internet www.moldagrotehnica.md; f. 1944; agricultural equipment; Dir PETRU T. FRUNZA; 456 employees.

**Moldavizolit SATI:** 3300 Tiraspol, str. Sevcenko 90; tel. (33) 3-42-28; fax (33) 3-51-33; e-mail moldavizolit@tirastel.md; internet www.izolit.tirastel.md; f. 1960; foil-clad paper-based laminate, insulation plastics; 1,410 employees.

**Molddata IS:** 2012 Chişinău, str. Armeneasca 37/1; tel. and fax (2) 54-52-66; e-mail info@moldova.md; internet www.melodata.md; f. 1993; state-owned; service provider, software, registration of domain names, computer technology and training.

**Moldimpex:** 2018 Chişinău, str. Botanicheskaia 15; tel. (2) 55-70-36; foreign-trade org.; Gen. Dir V. D. VOLODIN.

**Moldova Steel Works:** 5500 Rîbnita, str. Industrialnaya 1; tel. (55) 3-08-38; fax (55) 3-87-63; e-mail mark@aommz.com; internet www.aommz.com; f. 1985; owned by Itera Group; Gen. Dir ANATOLIY K. BELICHENKO; 4,000 employees.

**Moldovahidromash SA:** 2023 Chişinău, str. Mesterul Manole 7; tel. (2) 47-37-68; fax (2) 47-40-69; e-mail mold@hidromas.mldnet.com; internet www.moldhidromash.nm.ru; f. 1953; centrifugal leak-proof electric pumps of various types; Chair. MIKHAIL VLAS; 700 employees.

**Moldovcable Plant:** 3200 Bendery, str. Industrialnaya 10; tel. (32) 2-41-16; fax (32) 2-15-29; e-mail yunis@moldavcable.com; internet www.moldavcable.com; f. 1958; production of enammelled wires, magnet wires and lighting fittings; sales US $17m. (2001); Gen. Dir ALECSANDRU Z. ZYMAN; 1,200 employees.

**Pribor Plant:** 3215 Tighina, str. 28 Iunie 1; tel. (32) 2-84-63; fax (32) 2-11-76; f. 1971; technological equipment and tools; 600 employees.

**Rif-Acvaaparat Research Institute Joint-Stock Company:** 3121 Bălți, str. Decebal 9; tel. (31) 2-11-47; fax (31) 2-64-41; e-mail rifacva@beltsy.md; f. 1957; navigation equipment for river- and sea-vessels, sonar equipment; Dir VLADIMIR BOGORAD; 179 employees.

**Terminal:** construction of Danube petroleum terminal in Giurgiulesti; Tirex-petrol owns 41%, Technovax of Greece 39% and the EBRD 20%.

**Tirex-Petrol SA:** 2012 Chișinău, str. Columna 90; tel. (2) 23-30-78; fax (2) 24-05-09; f. 1940; joint-stock co; Mabanaft of Germany won the tender for 82% of state shares in July 2000; a consortium of Romanian companies were also allocated shares in exchange for debt-cancellation; Pres. M. CIORNII.

**Topaz Plant SA:** 2004 Chișinău, pl. D. Cantemir 1; tel. (2) 74-16-50; fax (2) 74-17-20; e-mail topaz@cni.md; internet moldova.cc/uzina-topaz; f. 1978; injection and press moulds for plastic items, circuit boards and non-standard metal constructions, including machines for the alimentary industry; Gen. Man. VALERIU BUTSANU; 265 employees.

**Tractor Factory Production Association:** 2004 Chișinău, Kontemira 170; tel. (2) 63-29-33; fax (2) 22-24-73; f. 1961; caterpillar tractors, stone-cutting machines, heating equipment.

**Vibroapparat:** 2001 Chișinău, bd Gagarin 10; tel. (2) 26-95-15; fax (2) 26-02-83; gas equipment and optics.

**Zorile SA:** 2069 Chișinău, str. Calea Iesilor 8; tel. (2) 75-86-33; fax (2) 74-08-42; f. 1945; manufacturing and sale of footwear; Gen. Dir T. IACOVLENCO; 1,250 employees.

### TRADE UNIONS

**Confederation of Trade Unions of Moldova:** 2012 Chișinău, str. 31 August 129; tel. (2) 23-76-74; fax (2) 23-76-98; e-mail cfsind@cni.md; internet www.csrm.md; f. 1990; Pres. PETRU CHIRIAC.

### CONSUMER ORGANIZATION

**Central Union of Consumers' Co-operatives of Moldova** (Uniunea Centrală a Cooperativelor de Consum din Republica Moldova —MOLDCOOP): 2001 Chișinău, bd Ștefan cel Mare 67; tel. (2) 27-15-95; fax (2) 27-41-50; f. 1925; Chair. PAVEL G. DUBALARI.

## Transport

### RAILWAYS

Plans for the construction of a new rail link, connecting Chișinău wth Iași, Romania, were announced in mid-2002.

**Moldovan Railways:** 2012 Chișinău, str. Vlaicu Pîrcălab 48; tel. (2) 25-44-08; fax (2) 22-13-80; e-mail secr@railway.md; internet www.railway.md; f. 1992 following the dissolution of the former Soviet Railways (SZhD) organization; total network 1,326 km; Dir-Gen. MIRON GAGAUZ.

### ROADS

At 1 January 1999 Moldova's network of roads totalled 12,657 km (87.0% of which was hard-surfaced), including 2,813 km of main roads and 6,588 km of regional roads. In 1999 there was a total of 298,290 passenger cars, buses and goods vehicles in use.

### INLAND WATERWAYS

In 1997 the total length of navigable waterways in Moldova was 424 km. The main river ports are at Tighina (Bender, Bendery), Rîbnița and Reni. The construction of a maritime port (petroleum terminal) on the River Danube was under way.

### SHIPPING

**Neptun-M SA:** 2064 Chișinău, str. V. Belinski 101; tel. (2) 74-95-51; fax (2) 74-09-01; f. 1992; Gen. Dir VICTOR ANDRUȘCA.

### CIVIL AVIATION

Chișinău International Airport and the air-traffic-control operator, Moldatsa, were re-opened in June 2000, after refurbishment funded by the European Bank for Reconstruction and Development (EBRD). Moldova has three civilian airports, in Chișinău, Tiraspol and Bălți.

In 2003 proposals were announced to transform the country's only military airbase, in Marculesti, into a fourth civilian airport.

**Civil Aviation Administration:** 2026 Chișinău, Aeroportul Chișinău; tel. (2) 52-40-64; fax (2) 52-91-18; e-mail info@caa.md; internet www.caa.md; f. 1993; Dir VLADIMIR PETRAȘ.

**Compania Aeriana Moldova Ltd:** 2026 Chișinău, Aeroportul Chișinău; tel. (2) 52-51-62; fax (2) 52-40-40; formerly Air Moldova; Unistar Ventures GmbH (Germany) purchased a stake in June 2000; 51% retained by the state; scheduled and charter passenger and cargo flights to destinations in Europe and the CIS; Dir-Gen. PETER CHEBAN.

**Air Moldova International:** 2026 Chișinău, Aeroportul Chișinău, 4th Floor; tel. (2) 52-97-91; fax (2) 52-64-14; e-mail info@ami.md; internet www.ami.md; scheduled and charter flights to destinations in Europe and the CIS; Dir-Gen. DORIN TIMCIUC.

**Moldavian Airlines SA:** 2026 Chișinău, Aeroportul Chișinău; tel. (2) 52-93-56; fax (2) 52-50-64; e-mail sales@mdv.md; internet www.mdv.md; f. 1994; scheduled and charter passenger and cargo flights to destinations in Europe, the Middle East and North Africa; Pres. and Chief Exec. NICOLAE PETROV.

**Moldtransavia SRL:** 2026 Chișinău, Aeroportul Chișinău; tel. (2) 52-59-71; fax (2) 52-63-99; e-mail mold@travia.mldnet.com; air freight and passenger transportation.

## Tourism

In 2001 15,690 tourists visited Moldova, 15.3% of whom were from Turkey, and 15.0% from Russia.

**Federation of Sport and Tourism of the Republic of Moldova:** Chișinău; tel. (2) 44-51-81; e-mail ftsmd@narod.ru; internet www.ftsmd.narod.ru; Pres. IVAN D. ZABUNOV.

**Moldova-Tur SA:** 2001 Chișinău, bd Ștefan cel Mare 4; tel. (2) 54-03-01; fax (2) 54-04-94; e-mail moldovatur@travers.md; internet www.jpm.md/mtur; f. 1959.

## Culture

### NATIONAL ORGANIZATION

**Ministry of Culture:** see section on The Government (Ministries).

### CULTURAL HERITAGE

**Institute of Ethnography and Folklore:** 2012 Chișinău, bd Ștefan cel Mare 1; tel. (2) 26-45-14; f. 1991; attached to the Academy of Sciences of Moldova; Dir N. A. DEMCENCO.

**Institute of the History and Theory of Art:** Chișinău, bd Ștefan cel Mare 1; tel. (2) 26-06-02; fax (2) 22-33-48; f. 1991; attached to the Academy of Sciences of Moldova; Dir L. M. CEMORTAN.

**Moldovan National State Art Museum:** 2012 Chișinău, str. 31 August 1989 115; tel. (2) 24-17-30; f. 1940; 22,000 exhibits; Dir V. J. NEGRUȚĂ.

**National Museum of Plastic Arts:** 2012 Chișinău, str. 31 August 1989 115; e-mail mnap@muzeu.dnt.md.

**National Library of the Republic of Moldova:** 2012 Chișinău, str. 31 Augusta 1989 78A; tel. and fax (2) 22-14-75; e-mail bnrm@ns.moldova.md; internet www.iatp.md/bnrm; f. 1832; 3.0m. vols; Dir ALECSE A. RĂU.

**National Museum of Ethnography and Natural History:** 2009 Chișinău, str. M. Kogalniceanu 82; tel. (2) 24-40-02; fax (2) 23-88-48; e-mail ursu@etno.museum.dnt.md; f. 1989; 135,000 exhibits; Dir MIHAI URSU.

**National Museum of the History of Moldova:** 2012 Chișinău, str. 31 August 1989 121A; tel. (2) 24-15-61; fax (2) 24-36-77; e-mail museum@mnc.md; f. 1983; 190,000 exhibits; Dir NICOLAE RAILEANU.

### SPORTING ORGANIZATIONS

**Federation of Sport and Tourism of the Republic of Moldova:** Chișinău; tel. (2) 44-51-81; e-mail ftsmd@narod.ru; internet www.ftsmd.narod.ru; Pres. IVAN D. ZABUNOV.

**Moldovan Olympic Committee:** 2012 Chișinău, bd Ștefan cel Mare 77; tel. (2) 22-81-96; fax (2) 24-80-48; f. 1991; Pres. EFIM JOSANU.

### PERFORMING ARTS

**Chekhov Russian Drama Theatre:** Chișinău, str. Vlaicu Pîrcâlab 75; tel. and fax (2) 22-33-62; f. 1934; plays and concerts; Dir MADAN VYACHESLAV.

**Likurich Puppet Theatre:** 2012 Chişinău, str. Bucureşti 68; tel. (2) 24-47-25; fax (2) 24-30-46; e-mail licurici@moldnet.md; f. 1945; Artistic Dir TITUS JUCOV.

**Moldova National Philharmonic:** 277012 Chişinău, str. Metropolit Varlaam 78; tel. (2) 22-40-16; fax (2) 23-23-88; e-mail somnph@ch.moldpac.md; f. 1940; Dir TEODOR COTICI; Dep. Dir VALENTIN GOGA.

**National Mihai Eminescu Theatre:** 2012 Chişinău, bd Ştefan cel Mare 79; tel. (2) 22-64-27; fax (2) 22-27-93; e-mail tnme@eminescu.md; internet www.eminescu.md; Dir VITALIE CARAUS.

**National Theatre of Opera and Ballet:** Chişinău, bd Ştefan cel Mare 152; tel. (2) 24-50-88.

**Vasile Alecsandri National Theatre:** Bălţi, Piaţa Vasile Alecsandri 1; tel. (31) 2-00-05; f. 1990; Gen. Dir ANATOL RECILA.

### ASSOCIATIONS

**PEN Centre of Moldova:** 2068 Chişinău, Apt 24, bd Miron Costin 21; tel. (2) 44-35-40; f. 1991; Pres. SPIRIDON VANGHELI; 25 mems.

**Nistru (Dniester) Writers' Union:** f. 2003; publishes *Nistru* in Romanian and Russian; Chair. NIKOLAI SAVOSTIN.

**Union of Writers of Moldova:** 2612 Chişinău, str. Kievskaya 98; tel. (2) 22-73-73.

# Education

Until the late 1980s the system of education was an integral part of the Soviet system, with most education in the Russian language. In 1990 and 1991 there were extensive changes to the education system, with Romanian literature and history added to the curriculum. Many Russian-language schools were closed in the early 1990s. Primary education begins at seven years of age and lasts for four years. Secondary education, beginning at 11, lasts for a maximum of seven years, comprising a first cycle of five years and a second of two years. In 1996 total enrolment at primary and secondary schools was equivalent to 87% of the school-age population (86% of males; 87% of females). Primary enrolment in 2000/01 was equivalent to 78% of children in the relevant age group, while the comparable ratio for secondary enrolment in that year was 68%. In 2001 budgetary expenditure on education amounted to 924m. lei (16.3% of total spending).

### UNIVERSITIES

**Free International University of Moldova:** 2012 Chişinău, str. Vlaicu Pâzcâlab 52; tel. (2) 22-00-29; fax (2) 22-00-28; e-mail agalben@ulim.moldnet.md; internet ulim.moldnet.md; f. 1992; five faculties; 600 teachers; 5,000 students; Rector ANDREI GALBEN.

**Moldova State University:** 2009 Chişinău, str. A. Mateevici 60; tel. (2) 57-74-00; fax (2) 24-06-55; e-mail stahi@usm.md; internet www.usm.md; languages of instruction: Romanian and Russian; f. 1946; 12 faculties; 800 teachers; 10,000 students; Rector GHEORGHE RUSNAC.

**Slavonic University of Moldova:** 2045 Chişinău, str. Florilor 28/1; tel. (2) 43-03-80; fax (2) 43-03-81; f. 1997; three faculties; Rector VIKTOR N. KOSTETSKII.

**State University of Medicine and Pharmacy 'Nicolae Testemitsanu':** 2004 Chişinău, bd Ştefan cel Mare 165; tel. (2) 24-34-08; fax (2) 24-34-44; e-mail nicolae@mededu.moldline.net; internet www.usmf.md; five faculties; 900 teachers; 5,000 students; Rector ION ABABII.

**Technical University of Moldova:** 2004 Chişinău, bd Ştefan cel Mare 168; tel. (2) 24-92-05; fax (2) 24-90-28; e-mail amariei@mail.utm.md; internet www.utm.md; languages of instruction: Romanian and Russian; f. 1964; nine faculties; 750 teachers; 8,740 students; Rector Dr S. ION BOSTAN.

**University of Applied Sciences of Moldova:** 2069 Chişinău, str. Iablochkin 2; tel. (2) 24-72-75; fax (2) 24-72-56; e-mail edu@usam.md; internet www.usam.md; f. 1992; Rector NICOLAE PELIN.

# Social Welfare

The social-security and health systems provided a comprehensive service. In 1991 a Social Fund was established in order to dispense a system of social benefits, including family benefits and allowances, pensions and social insurance. Social security provided allowances for families, especially those with low incomes, pensioners and invalids. Women aged 55 who have worked for at least 20 years, and men who are 60 and who have worked for at least 25 years, were eligible for a pension. In 1996 an estimated 752,000 people were in receipt of pensions. In the previous year expenditure on pensions

and other allowances totalled the equivalent of US $143.6m. Social Fund outlay accounted for 24.3% of total government expenditure in 2001.

In 2000 there were 76 hospital beds and 36 doctors per 10,000 inhabitants. A number of measures were introduced in 1999, in an attempt to reduce spending on health care, including the closure of several village hospitals and the loss of 7,000 hospital beds. In 2001 the state budget allocated 542m. lei (9.6% of total expenditure) to health care.

### NATIONAL AGENCIES

**Ministry of Health:** see section on The Government (Ministries).

**Ministry of Labour and Social Protection:** see section on The Government (Ministries).

**National Office of Social Insurance:** 2028 Chişinău, str. Gh. Tudor 3; tel. (2) 72-57-97; fax (2) 73-51-81; f. 1990; comprises Dept of the State Social Insurance Budget, Dept of Pensions and Allowances and Dept of Medical Examinations; Pres. TAMARA SHUMSCAIA.

### HEALTH AND WELFARE ORGANIZATIONS

**Clipa Siderala Charitable Children's Foundation:** Chişinău; tel. (2) 43-46-06; fax (2) 43-04-30; e-mail clipasiderala@mdl.net; internet www.clipa.md; f. 1996; support and integration of orphans; Chair. SERGHEI MOCAN.

**Moldovan Charity and Health Fund:** 2012 Chişinău, str. Vasile Alecsandri 1; tel. (2) 72-96-89; fax (2) 73-53-22; f. 1988; provides social, moral, medical and material assistance for pensioners, invalids, families with many children and other needy people; Pres. ION P. CUZUIOC.

**National Society of Invalids:** 2009 Chişinău, str. Hînceşti 1; tel. (2) 73-57-31; fax (2) 73-57-51; Pres. VASILE NECULCE.

**Organization of the Red Cross in Moldova:** Chişinău; tel. (2) 72-97-00; Pres. ION P. DUMITRAŞ.

# The Environment

In October 1995 the Russian news agency, ITAR—TASS, reported that the Moldovan Ministry of Health had stated that the country had the highest rate of illness in Europe, with evidence suggesting that seven out of every 10 Moldovans suffered from some kind of ill health. Experts believed that the poor level of health was, in part, a consequence of harmful industrial emissions and the over-intensive use of chemicals in agriculture. In September 2000 the Government passed a 10-year plan to protect the environment, as it was claimed that 50% of all wild animals and plants in Moldova were facing extinction.

### GOVERNMENT ORGANIZATIONS

**Ministry of Ecology, Construction and Territorial Development:** see section on The Government (Ministries).

**Environment Protection Information Centre:** f. 2001; funded by the Danish Environment Protection Agency.

### ACADEMIC INSTITUTES

**Academy of Sciences of Moldova:** 2001 Chişinău, bd Ştefan cel Mare 1; tel. (2) 27-14-78; fax (2) 27-27-38; e-mail presidiu@academy.as.md; internet www.asm.md; f. 1946; Pres. A. ANDRIEŞ; attached institutes incl.:

**Commission on Nature Conservation:** 2612 Chişinău, bd Ştefan cel Mare 1; tel. (2) 26-14-78; fax (2) 22-33-48; e-mail presidiu@academy.moldova.su; attached to the Presidium of the Academy; Chair. S. I. TOMA.

**Institute of Botany:** 2002 Chişinău, str. Pădurii 18, Botanical Garden; tel. (2) 55-04-43; fax (2) 52-38-98; e-mail fnfm@rnoldnet.md; f. 1950; over 10,000 species of plant; Dir Prof. ALECSANDRU CIUBOTARU.

**National Institute of Ecology:** 2060 Chişinău, bd Dacia 58; tel. (2) 77-04-33; fax (2) 22-07-48; e-mail relint@moldova.md; Exec. Dir Dr DUMITRU DRUMEA.

**Republic of Moldova Committee on the UNESCO 'Man and Biosphere' Programme:** 2001 Chişinău, bd Ştefan cel Mare 1; tel. (2) 24-75-93; e-mail unesco@moldova.md; attached to the Presidium of the Academy; Chair. M. F. LUPAŞCU.

**Research Institute for Plant Protection:** 2060 Chişinău, bd. Dacia 58; tel. (2) 77-04-66; fax (2) 77-96-41; e-mail slipbp@cc.acad.md; f. 1969; Dir I. N. BOUBATRAN.

## NON-GOVERNMENTAL ORGANIZATIONS

**BIOTICA Ecological Society:** 2043 Chişinău, POB 1451; tel. and fax (2) 24-32-74; e-mail biotica@biotica-moldova.org; internet www .biotica-moldova.org; f. 1993; environmental law, biodiversity conservation and environmental education, development of civil society; Bd ALECSEI ANDREEV, PIOTR GORBUNENKO, ILYA TROMBITSKY.

**Ecological Movement of Moldova (EMM):** 2004 Chişinău, str. Serghei Lazo 13; tel. (2) 23-24-08; fax (2) 23-71-57; e-mail renitsa@ eco.moldnet.md; internet www.iatp.md/emm; f. 1990; local green movement and political party; environmental education and legislation development; mem. of the World Conservation Union for Nature; founded Natura newspaper; Pres. ALECU RENIŢA; 17 brs.

**Ecosfera** (Asociatia de Informare si Educatie Ecologica): 2028 Chişinău, str. Schinoasa Deal 78/4; tel. (2) 32-30-42; fax (2) 22-27-71; e-mail ecosfera@mail.md; internet ecosfera.ournet.md; f. 1997; produces electronic magazine; also includes the Young Ecologists' Club; Contact CORNELIU MARZA.

**Environmental Movement of Moldova:** 2009 Chişinău, str. Mihai Eminescu 1; tel. (2) 22-15-16; fax (2) 22-27-71; e-mail chbemm@moldnet.md; internet www.chbemm.ngo.md; f. 1990; information, education, activities, environmental consulting and auditing; Chief Officer VLADIMIR GARABA.

**Grupul Fauna:** 2004 Chişinău, POB 409; tel. (2) 57-78-09; e-mail gfauna@excite.com; internet www.fauna.ngo.md; f. 1994; research, conservation and education in biodiversity; non-profit ecological org.; Pres. SERGIU ANDREEV.

**Moldovan Society of Animal Protection:** Chişinău, Apt 6, str. Serghei Lazo 17; tel. (2) 24-75-99; environmental education, co-operates with government agencies and non-governmental organizations with interests in animal welfare and the environment; Pres. Prof. P. I. NESTEROV.

**Regional Environmental Centre—Moldova:** 2005 Chişinău, str. Bănulescu-Bodon1 57/1; tel. (2) 23-86-85; fax (2) 23-86-86; e-mail recmd@moldova.md; internet www.rec.moldova.md; f. 1998; international, non-commercial, non-political org.; Chair. TOM GARVEY.

**SalvaEco:** 2009 Chişinău, str. Mihai Eminescu 1; tel. (2) 29-18-17; fax (2) 22-77-71; e-mail salvaeco@salvaeco.org; internet www .salvaeco.org; f. 1999; independent, non-profit ecological org.

**Terra Nostra Public Organization for Environmental Education and Information:** 2009 Chişinău, 60 str. Mateevici, B. 4, t. 3; tel. and fax (2) 57-75-57; e-mail tnostra@mrda.md; internet www .terra_nostra.org.md; environmental research, education and ecological tourism and expeditions; Pres. Prof. MARIA DUCA; Dir VIORICA GLADCHI.

# Defence

Following independence from the USSR (declared in August 1991), the Moldovan Government initiated the creation of national armed forces. In August 2002, according to Western estimates, these numbered 7,210, including an army of 5,560 and an air force of 1,400. There are paramilitary forces attached to the Ministry of the Interior, numbering 3,400 (2,500 internal troops and 900 riot police). Military service is compulsory and lasts for up to 18 months. A military-reform plan was launched in 2002. A law was passed in July, which reduced the length of military service to 12 months (graduates of higher education were to serve only three months), and the armed forces was to be reduced in size. Legislation was passed in 2003 that further reduced the size of the armed forces by some 400 officers and 100 civilian staff. In that year proposals were also announced to convert Moldova's only military airbase, in Marculesti, into a civilian airport. Under an agreement concluded by the Moldovan and Russian Governments in late 1994, the former Soviet 14th Army (under Russian jurisdiction) was to have been withdrawn from the separatist Transnistria (Transdnestr) region within three years, but in March 1998 it was agreed that Russian forces would remain in Transnistria until a political settlement for the region was reached. In November 1999, however, it was agreed to withdraw the Russian military presence from Transnistria in three stages, with all hardware to be removed by the end of 2001 and all troops to be removed by the end of 2002; the deadline was subsequently extended until December 2003. In early 1994 Moldova joined NATO's 'Partnership for Peace' programme of military co-operation. In 2002 the defence budget was an estimated 95m. lei.

**Commander-in-Chief of the Armed Forces:** (President of the Republic).

**Chief of General Staff and Commander of the Ground Force:** Brig.-Gen. ION COROPCEAN.

**Commander of the Air Force:** Col OLEG COROI.

# Bibliography

Argunsah, M., and Gungor, H. *The Gagauz.* London, Caucasus World, 2001.

Brezianu, A. *Historical Dictionary of the Republic of Moldova.* European Historical Series, No 37. Maryland, MD, Scarecrow Press, 2000.

Dailey, E., Laber, J., and Whitman, L. *Human Rights in Moldova: The Turbulent Dniester.* New York, NY, Helsinki Watch, 1993.

Dima, N. *Moldova and the Transdnestr Republic.* New York, NY, Columbia University Press, 2001.

Hill, R. J. *Soviet Political Élites: The Case of Tiraspol.* London, Martin Robertson, 1977.

King, C. *The Moldovans: Romania, Russia, and the Politics of Culture.* Stanford, CA, Hoover Institute Press, 1999.

Manoliu-Manea, M. (Ed.). *The Tragic Plight of a Border Area: Bessarabia and Bucovina.* Humboldt, CA, Humboldt State University Press, 1983.

Mitrasca, M. *Moldova: A Romanian Province.* New York, NY, Algora Publishing, 2002.

Stoilik, G. *Moldavia.* Moscow, Novosti Press Agency Publishing House, 1987.

Waters, T. *The 'Moldovan Syndrome' & The Re-russification of Moldova: Forward into the Past!* Camberley, Conflict Studies Research Centre, 2002.

See also the Select Bibliography in Part Four.

# RUSSIAN FEDERATION

## Geography

### PHYSICAL FEATURES

The Russian Federation (formerly the Russian Soviet Federative Socialist Republic of the USSR) is bounded to the west by Norway (in the far north-west), Finland, Estonia and Latvia. Belarus and Ukraine lie to the south-west of European Russia, the southern borders of which are with the Transcaucasian states of Georgia and Azerbaijan, and with Kazakhstan. There is a short coastline in the north-west, near St Petersburg (Petrograd 1914–24, Leningrad 1924–91), where the country has access to the Baltic Sea via the Gulf of Finland. In the south, towards the Caucasus, European Russia has a coastline on the Black Sea and the Sea of Azov in the south-west, with the Caspian Sea to the east. Beyond the Ural Mountains, the Siberian and Far Eastern regions have southern frontiers with Kazakhstan, the People's Republic of China, Mongolia and, in the south-east, there is a short frontier with the Democratic People's Republic of Korea (North Korea). The eastern coastline is on the Sea of Japan, the Sea of Okhotsk, the Pacific Ocean and the Barents Sea. The northern coastline is on the Arctic Ocean. The region around Kaliningrad (formerly Königsberg in East Prussia), on the Baltic Sea, became part of the Russian Federation in 1945. It is separated from the rest of Russia by Lithuania and Belarus. It borders Poland to the south, Lithuania to the north and east and has a coastline on the Baltic Sea. Russia covers a total area of 17,075,400 sq km (6,592,850 sq miles), making it by far the largest country in the world. Its territory consists of 89 federal units, including the cities of Moscow (Moskva), the capital, and St Petersburg (Sankt-Peterburg, the old tsarist capital).

The territory includes a wide variety of physical features. European Russia (traditionally meaning that part of Russia to the west of the Urals) and western Siberia form a vast plain, interrupted only by occasional outbreaks of hill country and wide river valleys. In the south, between the Black and Caspian Seas, the territory is more undulating, until it reaches the foothills of the Caucasus (Kavkaz) mountain range in the far south. The Ural Mountains provide only a symbolic barrier between Siberia and European Russia, their mean altitude being just 500 m (1,640 ft). Beyond them the Western Siberian Plain extends for some 2,000 km, before reaching the Central Siberian Plateau and high mountain ranges on the southern border with Mongolia. The territory of eastern Siberia and the Far East is dominated by several mountain ranges (notably the Verkhoyansk, Cherskii and Anadyr mountains), which extend off shore in a series of islands and peninsulas. The Kamchatka Peninsula, which extends 1,200 km south to the northernmost of the Kurile (Kuril) Islands, has 100 active volcanoes, the highest being Klyuchevskaya Sopka, at an altitude of 4,800 m. Only the basins of the Amur and Ussuri rivers in the south of the Far Eastern region can support any significant population. The northern regions of both Asian and European Russia are inhospitable areas, much of the territory being covered by permafrost.

### CLIMATE

The climate of Russia is extremely varied. The central regions experience the climatic conditions characteristic of Central and Eastern Europe, although in a more extreme form. There are wide temperature differences between summer and winter, and there is considerable snow in winter. The average temperature in Moscow in July is 19°C (66°F); the average for January is –9°C (15°F). Average annual precipitation in the capital is 575 mm. Further south the climate is more temperate, especially along the Black Sea coastline. Average temperatures in Rostov-on-Don (Rostov-na-Donu) range from –5.3°C (22.5°F) in January to 23.5°C (74.3°F) in July. In the northern areas of Russia and in much of Siberia the climate is severe, with Arctic winters and short, hot summers. Only the northern fringe is under the polar ice-cap; the zone of permafrost is, however, extensive. Average temperatures in the southern Siberian town of Irkutsk range from –20.8°C (–5.4°F) in January to 17.9°C (64.2°F) in July. Average annual rainfall is 458 mm, most of which falls in the summer months. In Verkhoyansk, in the far north of Siberia, the average January temperature is –46.8°C (–52.2°F). The Far Eastern region combines the extreme temperatures of Siberia with monsoon-type conditions common elsewhere in Asia, although they are not so pronounced, owing to the protection of mountain ranges on the Pacific coast. The mean temperature in January in the eastern port of Vladivostok is –14°C (7°F); in August the average is 21°C (70°F).

### POPULATION

At the 1989 census, Russians formed the largest ethnic group in the Federation, accounting for 81.5% of the population. Other important ethnic groups included Tatars (3.8%), Ukrainians (3.0%) and Chuvash (1.2%). There were also significant communities of Bashkirs, Belarusians, Mordovians, Chechens, Germans, Udmurts, Mari, Kazakhs, Avar, Jews and Armenians. Religious adherence was equally varied, with many religions closely connected with particular ethnic groups. Christianity was the major religion, mostly adhered to by ethnic Russians and other Slavs. The Russian Orthodox Church (Moscow Patriarchate) was the largest denomination. The main concentrations of Muslims were among Volga Tatars, Chuvash and Bashkirs, and the peoples of the North Caucasus, including the Chechen, Ingush, Kabardins and the peoples of Dagestan. Buddhism was the main religion of the Buryats, the Tyvans and the Kalmyks. The large pre-1917 Jewish population was depleted by war and emigration, but there remained some 400,000 Jews in Russia in the late 1990s.

The official language is Russian, but a large number of other languages are in daily use. The majority of the population lives in European Russia, the population of Siberia and the Far East being only some 32m. in 1989, approximately 22% of the total. In 1998 it was estimated that some 73% of the population lived in urban areas, although there were substantial regional differences, with 83% of the inhabitants of central Russia living in towns in the early 1990s, compared with only 57% in the North Caucasus region.

The estimated total population of Russia at 1 January 2002 was 143,954,400, and the population density was, therefore, 8.4 per sq km. The capital of Russia is Moscow, which had an estimated population of 8,304,600 in January 2001. The second city is St Petersburg, with a population of 4,627,800. Other important regional centres are Nizhnii Novgorod (formerly Gorkii—1,343,300), Samara (formerly Kuibyshev—1,146,400), Kazan (1,090,200), the Siberian cities of Novosibirsk (1,393,200) and Omsk (1,138,400), and the industrialized Ural towns of Yekaterinburg (formerly Sverdlovsk—

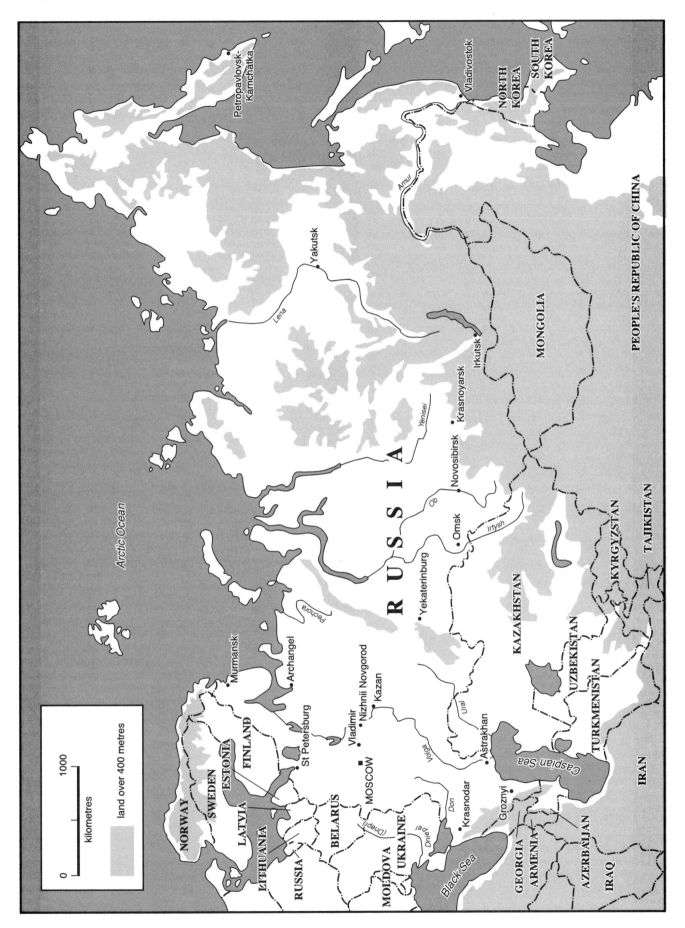

1,256,900), Ufa (1,088,800), Chelyabinsk (1,081,100) and Perm (1,004,800).

Many ethnic Russians lived beyond the borders of the Russian Federation, in the other countries of the former USSR. They formed significant minorities in the neighbouring countries of Estonia, Latvia, Belarus, Ukraine and Kazakh-stan. Large Russian communities were also present in Moldova and the Central Asian countries. In addition, there were a number of minor boundary disagreements with other Soviet successor states and various border disputes inherited from the USSR, notably with Japan over the northern Kurile Islands (annexed by the USSR in 1945).

# Chronology

## RUSSIA AND THE RUSSIAN EMPIRE

**c. 878:** Kievan Rus, the first unified state of the Eastern Slavs, was founded, with Kiev (Kyiv) as its capital.

**c. 988:** Vladimir (Volodymyr) I—'the Great', ruler of Kievan Rus, converted to Orthodox Christianity.

**1237–40:** The Rus principalities were invaded and conquered by the Mongol Tatars.

**1462–1505:** Reign of Ivan III of Muscovy (Moscow), who consolidated the independent Rus domains into a centralized state.

**1480:** Renunciation of Tatar suzerainty.

**1533–84:** Reign of Ivan IV—'the Terrible', who began the eastern expansion of Russian territory.

**1547:** Ivan IV was crowned 'Tsar of Muscovy and all Russia'.

**1552:** Subjugation of the Khanate of Kazan.

**1556:** Subjugation of the Khanate of Astrakhan.

**1581:** The Russian adventurer, Yermak Timofeyev, led an expedition to Siberia, pioneering Russian expansion beyond the Ural Mountains.

**1645:** A Russian settlement was established on the Sea of Okhotsk, on the coast of eastern Asia.

**1654:** Eastern and central Ukraine came under Muscovite rule as a result of the Treaty of Pereyaslavl.

**1679:** Russian pioneers reached the Kamchatka Peninsula and the Pacific Ocean.

**1682–1725:** Reign of Peter (Petr) I—'the Great', who established Russia as a European Power, expanded its Empire, and modernized the civil and military institutions of the state.

**1703:** St Petersburg was founded at the mouth of the River Neva, in north-west Russia.

**1721:** The Treaty of Nystad with Sweden ended the Great Northern War and brought Estonia and Livonia (now Latvia and parts of Estonia) under Russian rule. Peter I, who was declared the 'Tsar of all the Russias', proclaimed the Russian Empire.

**1762–96:** Reign of Catherine (Yekaterina) II—'the Great'.

**1772:** Parts of Belarus were incorporated into the Russian Empire at the First Partition of Poland.

**1774:** As a result of the Treaty of Kuçuk Kainavci with the Turks, the Black Sea port of Azov was annexed and Russia became protector of Orthodox Christians in the Balkans.

**1783:** Annexation of the Khanate of Crimea.

**1793:** Second Partition of Poland; acquisition of western Ukraine and Belarus.

**1795:** Third Partition of Poland.

**1801–25:** Reign of Alexander (Aleksandr) I.

**1801:** Annexation of Georgia.

**1809:** Finland became a possession of the Russian Crown.

**1812:** Bessarabia (now mostly in the Republic of Moldova) was acquired from the Turks. Napoleon I of France invaded Russia.

**1815:** The Congress of Vienna established 'Congress Poland' as a Russian dependency (annexed 1831).

**1825:** On the death of Alexander I, a group of young officers, the 'Decembrists', attempted to seize power; the attempted *coup d'état* was suppressed by troops loyal to the new Tsar, Nicholas (Nikolai) I.

**1825–55:** Reign of Nicholas I.

**1853–56:** The Crimean War was fought, in which the United Kingdom and France aided Turkey against Russia, after the latter had invaded the Ottoman tributaries of Moldavia and Wallachia; the War was concluded by the Congress of Paris.

**1855–81:** Reign of Alexander II, who introduced economic and legal reforms.

**1859:** The conquest of the Caucasus was completed, following the surrender of rebel forces.

**1860:** Acquisition of provinces on the Sea of Japan from China and the establishment of Vladivostok.

**1861:** Emancipation of the serfs.

**1867:** The North American territory of Alaska was sold to the USA for US $7m.

**1868:** Subjugation of the Khanates of Samarkand and Bukhara.

**1873:** Annexation of the Khanate of Khiva.

**1875:** Acquisition of Sakhalin from Japan in exchange for the Kurile Islands.

**1876:** Subjugation of the Khanate of Kokand.

**1881:** Assassination of Alexander II.

**1881–94:** Reign of Alexander III, who re-established autocratic principles of government.

**1891:** Construction of the Trans-Siberian Railway was begun.

**1894–1917:** Reign of Nicholas II, the last Tsar.

**1898:** The All-Russian Social Democratic Labour Party (RSDLP), a Marxist party, held a founding congress in Minsk (now in Belarus). In 1903, at the Second Congress in London, United Kingdom, the party divided into 'Bolsheviks' (led by Lenin—Vladimir Ilych Ulyanov) and 'Mensheviks'.

## WAR AND REVOLUTION

**1904–05:** Russia was defeated in the Russo–Japanese War.

**22 January 1905:** Some 150 demonstrators were killed by the Tsar's troops, in what came to be known as 'Bloody Sunday'.

**17 October 1905:** Strikes and demonstrations in the capital, St Petersburg, and other cities forced the Tsar to introduce limited political reforms, including the holding of elections to a Duma (parliament).

**January 1912:** At the Sixth Congress of the RSDLP the Bolsheviks formally established a separate party, the RSDLP (Bolsheviks).

**1 August 1914:** Russia entered the First World War against Austria-Hungary, Germany and the Ottoman Empire (the Central Powers).

**2 March (New Style 15 March) 1917:** Abdication of Tsar Nicholas II after demonstrations and strikes in Petrograd (as St Petersburg was renamed in 1914); a Provisional Government, led by Prince Lvov, took power.

**9 July (22 July) 1917:** In response to widespread public disorder, Prince Lvov resigned; he was replaced as Prime Minister by Aleksandr Kerenskii, a moderate socialist.

**25 October (7 November) 1917:** The Bolsheviks, led by Lenin, staged a *coup d'état* and overthrew Kerenskii's Provisional Government; the Russian Soviet Federative Socialist Republic (RSFSR or Russian Federation) was proclaimed.

**6 January (19 January) 1918:** The Constituent Assembly, which had been elected in November 1917, was dissolved on Lenin's orders. A civil war between the Bolshevik Red Army and various anti-Communist leaders (the 'Whites'), who received support from German and from Entente or Allied forces, was by now under way and lasted until 1921.

**14 February (Old Style 1 February) 1918:** Adoption of the Gregorian Calendar by the Russian civil authorities.

**3 March 1918:** Treaty of Brest-Litovsk: the Bolsheviks ceded large areas of western territory to Germany, including the Baltic regions, and recognized the independence of Finland and Ukraine. Belarus, Georgia, Armenia and Azerbaijan subsequently proclaimed their independence.

**6–8 March 1918:** The RSDLP (Bolsheviks) was renamed the Russian Communist Party (Bolsheviks)—RCP (B).

**9 March 1918:** The capital of Russia was moved from Petrograd (renamed Leningrad in 1924) to Moscow.

**10 July 1918:** The first Constitution of the RSFSR was adopted by the Fifth All-Russian Congress of Soviets.

**18 July 1918:** Tsar Nicholas II and his family were murdered in Yekaterinburg (Sverdlovsk, 1924–91) by Bolshevik troops.

**11 November 1918:** The Allied Armistice with Germany (which was denied its gains at Brest-Litovsk) ended the First World War.

**8–16 March 1921:** At the 10th Party Congress of the RCP (B), the harsh policy of 'War Communism' was replaced by the New Economic Policy (NEP), which allowed peasants and traders some economic freedom.

**18 March 1921:** A rebellion by Russian sailors in the island garrison of Kronstadt (near St Petersburg) was suppressed by the Red Army. Signature of the Treaty of Rīga between Russia, Ukraine and Poland, which formally concluded the Soviet–Polish War of 1919–20, with territorial gains for Poland.

**3 April 1922:** Stalin (Iosif V. Dzhugashvili) was elected General Secretary of the RCP (B).

**18 April 1922:** The Soviet-German Treaty of Rapallo was signed, which established diplomatic relations between the two powers.

### THE UNION OF SOVIET SOCIALIST REPUBLICS

**30 December 1922:** The Union of Soviet Socialist Republics (USSR) was formed at the 10th All-Russian (first All-Union) Congress of Soviets by the RSFSR, the Transcaucasian Soviet Federative Socialist Republic (TSFSR), the Ukrainian SSR (Soviet Socialist Republic), the Belarusian SSR, and the Central Asian states of the Khorezm People's Socialist Republic and the People's Soviet Republic of Bukhara.

**6 July 1923:** Promulgation of the first Constitution of the USSR (the Constitution was ratified by the Second All-Union Congress of Soviets in January 1924).

**21 January 1924:** Death of Lenin.

**October 1927:** Expulsion of Trotskii (Lev Bronstein) and other opponents of Stalin from the Communist Party.

**1928:** The NEP was abandoned; beginning of the First Five-Year Plan and forced collectivization of agriculture, which resulted in widespread famine, particularly in Ukraine.

**November 1933:** Recognition of the USSR by the USA.

**18 September 1934:** The USSR was admitted to the League of Nations.

**1 December 1934:** Sergei Kirov, a leading member of the Political Bureau (Politburo) of the Communist Party, was shot and killed in Leningrad; following the shooting, Stalin initiated a new campaign of repression.

**25 November 1936:** The anti-Comintern (Third Communist International—established in 1919) Pact was signed between imperial Japan and Nazi Germany.

**26 September 1936:** Nikolai Yezhov was appointed head of the security police, the People's Commissariat for Internal Affairs (NKVD); a series of mass arrests and executions, which came to be known as the 'Great Purge' or the 'Yezhovshchina', began.

**5 December 1936:** The second Constitution of the USSR (the 'Stalin' Constitution) was adopted; two new Union Republics (the Kyrgyz and Kazakh SSRs) were created, and the TSFSR was dissolved into the Georgian, Armenian and Azerbaijani SSRs.

**March 1938:** Nikolai Bukharin, Aleksei Rykov and other prominent Bolsheviks were sentenced to death at the Moscow 'Show' Trials.

**23 August 1939:** Signing of the Treaty of Non-Aggression with Germany (the Nazi-Soviet Pact), including the 'Secret Protocols', which sanctioned territorial gains for the USSR in eastern Poland, the Baltic states (Estonia, Latvia and Lithuania) and Bessarabia.

**17 September 1939:** Soviet forces invaded eastern Poland.

**28 September 1939:** The Treaty on Friendship and Existing Borders was signed by Germany and the USSR, by which the two powers agreed that the USSR should annex Lithuania.

**30 November 1939:** The USSR invaded Finland.

**14 December 1939:** The USSR was expelled from the League of Nations.

**June 1940:** The Baltic states and Bessarabia were annexed by the USSR.

**22 June 1941:** Germany invaded the USSR in Operation Barbarossa.

**2 February 1943:** German forces surrendered at Stalingrad (now Volgograd), marking the first reverse for the German Army. Soviet forces began to regain territory.

**8 May 1945:** German forces surrendered to the USSR in Berlin, and Germany subsequently capitulated; most of Eastern and Central Europe had come under Soviet control.

**26 June 1945:** The USSR, the USA, the United Kingdom, China and 46 other countries, including the Belarusian and Ukrainian SSRs, signed the Charter of the United Nations (UN).

**8 August 1945:** The USSR declared war on Japan and occupied Sakhalin and the Kurile Islands.

**September 1947:** The Communist Information Bureau (Cominform) was established, to control and co-ordinate Communist Parties that were allied to the USSR (the Comintern had been dissolved in 1943; Cominform was abolished in April 1956).

**25 January 1949:** The Council for Mutual Economic Assistance (CMEA or Comecon) was established, as an economic alliance between the USSR and its Eastern European allies.

**14 July 1949:** The USSR exploded its first atomic bomb.

**5 March 1953:** Death of Stalin; he was replaced by a collective leadership, which included Georgii Malenkov and Nikita Khrushchev.

**September 1953:** Khrushchev was elected First Secretary of the Central Committee of the Communist Party of the Soviet Union (CPSU).

**14 May 1955:** The Warsaw Treaty of Friendship, Co-operation and Mutual Assistance was signed by Albania, Bulgaria, Czechoslovakia, the German Democratic Republic (GDR—'East' Germany), Hungary, Poland, Romania and the USSR. The Treaty established a military alliance between these countries, known as the Warsaw Treaty Organization (or the Warsaw Pact).

**14–25 February 1956:** At the 20th Party Congress, Khrushchev denounced Stalin in the 'secret speech'.

**26 August 1956:** The first Soviet inter-continental ballistic missile (ICBM) was launched.

**4 November 1956:** Soviet forces invaded Hungary to overthrow Imre Nagy's reformist Government.

**June 1957:** Malenkov, Vyacheslav Molotov and Lazar Kaganovich (the so-called 'Anti-Party' group) were expelled from the CPSU leadership after attempting to depose Khrushchev.

**4 October 1957:** The USSR placed the first man-made satellite (Sputnik I) in orbit around the earth.

**March 1958:** Khrushchev consolidated his position in the leadership by being elected Chairman of the Council of Ministers (premier), while retaining the office of CPSU First Secretary.

**October 1961:** Stalin's body was removed from its place of honour in the mausoleum in Red Square, in Moscow.

**18–28 October 1962:** The discovery of Soviet nuclear missiles in Cuba by the USA led to the 'Cuban Missile Crisis'; tension eased when Khrushchev announced the withdrawal of the missiles, following a US blockade of the island.

**5 August 1963:** The USSR signed the Partial Nuclear Test Ban Treaty.

**13–14 October 1964:** Khrushchev was deposed from the leadership of the CPSU and the USSR and replaced as First Secretary by Leonid Brezhnev and as premier by Aleksei Kosygin.

**20–21 August 1968:** Soviet and other Warsaw Pact forces invaded Czechoslovakia to overthrow the reformist Government of Alexander Dubček.

**12 August 1970:** A non-aggression treaty was signed with the Federal Republic of Germany (FRG—'West' Germany).

**May 1972:** The US President, Richard Nixon, visited Moscow, thus marking a relaxation in US-Soviet relations, a process which came to be known as *détente*.

**1 August 1975:** Signing of the Helsinki Final Act by 32 European countries, plus the USA and Canada, committing all signatories to approve the post-1945 frontiers in Europe and to respect basic human rights.

**16 June 1977:** Brezhnev became Chairman of the Presidium of the Supreme Soviet (titular head of state).

**7 October 1977:** The third Constitution of the USSR was adopted.

**24 December 1979:** Soviet forces invaded Afghanistan (troops were withdrawn between July 1986 and February 1989).

**October 1980:** Kosygin was replaced as premier by Nikolai Tikhonov.

**10 November 1982:** Death of Brezhnev; Yurii Andropov, former head of the Committee for State Security (KGB), succeeded him as General Secretary of the CPSU.

**9 February 1984:** Death of Andropov; Konstantin Chernenko succeeded him as General Secretary.

## THE GORBACHEV ERA AND THE END OF THE USSR

**10 March 1985:** Death of Chernenko; he was succeeded as General Secretary by Mikhail Gorbachev.

**2 July 1985:** Andrei Gromyko was replaced as Minister of Foreign Affairs by Eduard Shevardnadze; Gromyko became Chairman of the Presidium of the Supreme Soviet.

**27 September 1985:** Nikolai Ryzhkov replaced Tikhonov as Chairman of the Council of Ministers.

**24 February–6 March 1986:** At the 27th Congress of the CPSU, Gorbachev proposed radical economic and political reforms and 'new thinking' in foreign policy; emergence of the policy of *glasnost* (openness).

**26 April 1986:** An explosion occurred at a nuclear reactor in Chernobyl (Chornobyl), Ukraine, which resulted in discharges of radioactive material.

**October 1986:** A summit took place in Reykjavík, Iceland, attended by Gorbachev and the US President, Ronald Reagan, at which the issue of nuclear disarmament was discussed.

**January 1987:** At a meeting of the CPSU Central Committee, Gorbachev proposed plans for the restructuring of the economy and some democratization of local government and the CPSU (*perestroika*).

**21 June 1987:** At local elections, the CPSU nominated more than one candidate in some constituencies.

**21 October 1987:** Boris Yeltsin, who had been appointed First Secretary of the Moscow City Party Committee in 1985, resigned from the Politburo.

**8 December 1987:** In Washington, DC, USA, Gorbachev and President Reagan signed a treaty to eliminate all intermediate-range nuclear forces in Europe.

**1 October 1988:** As the pace of reform quickened, Andrei Gromyko resigned as Chairman of the Presidium of the Supreme Soviet, to be replaced by Gorbachev.

**1 December 1988:** The all-Union Supreme Soviet approved constitutional amendments creating a new legislative system, consisting of the Congress of People's Deputies and a full-time Supreme Soviet (a number of wide-ranging reforms, including partly free elections, had been agreed by the Party earlier in the year).

**6 December 1988:** In a speech at the UN, Gorbachev announced troop withdrawals from Eastern Europe.

**25 March 1989:** Multi-party elections to the Congress of People's Deputies took place; several prominent 'hardliners' were defeated by radical candidates.

**25 May 1989:** The Congress of People's Deputies convened for the first time; Gorbachev was elected to the new post of Chairman of the USSR Supreme Soviet (executive President).

**27 May 1989:** Congress elected an all-Union Supreme Soviet, which would act as a full-time legislature, in which only a few radicals managed to secure seats.

**6 December 1989:** After issuing declarations of political and economic sovereignty in May, the Supreme Soviet of Lithuania abolished the Communist Party's constitutional right to power, thus establishing the first multi-party system in the USSR. Lithuanian independence was declared on 11 March 1990.

**4 February 1990:** Some 150,000 people joined a pro-reform march in the centre of Moscow. Three days later the CPSU Central Committee approved draft proposals to abolish Article 6 of the Constitution, which had guaranteed the CPSU's monopoly of power.

**4 March 1990:** Elections took place to the local and republican soviets of the Russian Federation; reformists made substantial gains in the larger cities, notably Moscow and Leningrad (elections to the Supreme Soviets of Belarus, Estonia, Kazakhstan, Kyrgyzstan, Latvia, Lithuania, Moldova, Tajikistan, Ukraine and Uzbekistan also took place in February–March, producing overtly nationalist majorities in the Baltic republics and Moldova).

**15 March 1990:** Congress approved the establishment of the post of President of the USSR and elected Mikhail Gorbachev to that office.

**29 May 1990:** Boris Yeltsin was elected as Chairman of the Supreme Soviet of the Russian Federation. On 12 June Congress adopted a declaration of Russian sovereignty within the USSR.

**5 June 1990:** More than 500 people were killed in inter-ethnic violence in Kyrgyzstan, as protests increased throughout the USSR.

**16 July 1990:** The Supreme Soviet of Ukraine declared Ukraine to be a sovereign state, with the right to maintain its own armed forces. In the following month Turkmenistan and Tajikistan made similar declarations.

**3 September 1990:** Boris Yeltsin announced a 500-day programme of economic reform to the Supreme Soviet of the Russian Federation.

**October 1990:** Legislation allowing freedom of conscience and the existence of other political parties, apart from the CPSU, was adopted by the all-Union Supreme Soviet. It also approved a reform programme designed to establish a market economy. In Georgia pro-independence parties won an overall majority in the Supreme Soviet.

**25 October 1990:** Kazakhstan declared itself to be a sovereign state, and outlawed the storing or testing of nuclear weapons on its territory; Kyrgyzstan declared its sovereignty five days later.

**December 1990:** Despite further constitutional changes and proposals for a new Union Treaty, Eduard Shevardnadze resigned as Minister of Foreign Affairs, claiming that the country was moving towards dictatorship. Congress subsequently granted Gorbachev extended presidential powers. Ryzhkov was succeeded as Soviet premier by Valentin Pavlov, while Gennadii Yanayev was eventually endorsed as Vice-President.

**13 January 1991:** Thirteen people died when Soviet troops occupied radio and broadcasting buildings in Vilnius, Lithuania. One week later four people died in Rīga, Latvia, when Soviet troops occupied government buildings.

**22 February 1991:** Some 400,000 people demonstrated in Moscow, in support of Boris Yeltsin, who had demanded Gorbachev's resignation, and reform.

**17 March 1991:** In an all-Union referendum on the issue of the future state of the USSR, some 75% of participants approved Gorbachev's concept of a 'renewed federation' (several republics did not participate).

**23 April 1991:** Gorbachev and the leaders of nine Union Republics, including Yeltsin, signed the 'Nine-Plus-One Agreement'.

**12 June 1991:** Yeltsin was elected President of the Russian Federation in direct elections, with Aleksandr Rutskoi as Vice-President; residents of Leningrad voted to change the city's name back to St Petersburg.

**1 July 1991:** The USSR and the other member countries of the Warsaw Pact signed a protocol, formalizing the dissolution of the alliance.

**31 July 1991:** The USSR and the USA signed the first Strategic Arms' Reduction Treaty (START 1).

**18–21 August 1991:** With Gorbachev placed under house arrest in his summer residence in Crimea, Ukraine, a 'hardline' State Committee for the State of Emergency in the USSR (SCSE), under Vice-President Yanayev, attempted to seize power in a *coup d'état*. Thousands of people demonstrated against the coup in St Petersburg and in Moscow. Yeltsin demanded the restoration of Gorbachev to power and, amid increasing institutional opposition, the coup collapsed and Gorbachev was reinstated. Estonia declared independence on 20 August and Latvia the next day.

**23 August 1991:** Gorbachev replaced supporters of the coup attempt, in the Council of Ministers and in the KGB. Yeltsin suspended the activities of the Russian Communist Party (RCP) and the publication of six CPSU newspapers (the RCP was formally banned in November).

**24 August 1991:** Gorbachev resigned as General Secretary of the CPSU, nationalized the party's property, demanded the dissolution of the Central Committee and banned party cells in the Armed Forces, the KGB and the police. The Supreme Soviet of Ukraine adopted a declaration of independence, pending approval by referendum on 1 December (90% of the participating voters were to approve the decision).

**25 August 1991:** Gorbachev established an interim government, headed by Ivan Silayev. The Supreme Soviet of Belarus adopted a declaration of independence. Later that month the Supreme Soviets of Moldova, Azerbaijan, Uzbekistan and Kyrgyzstan also adopted declarations of independence.

**6 September 1991:** The newly formed State Council, which comprised the supreme officials of the Union Republics, recognized the independence of Estonia, Latvia and Lithuania.

**9 September 1991:** The Supreme Soviet of Tajikistan adopted a declaration of independence. Two weeks later, following a referendum, Armenia also declared its independence.

**27 September 1991:** Ivan Silayev officially resigned as Prime Minister of the Russian Federation, following his appointment as Soviet Prime Minister; he was one of a number of reformers promoted by Gorbachev.

**5 October 1991:** The USSR was officially admitted as an associate member of the IMF.

**18 October 1991:** A treaty, which established an Economic Community between its signatories, was signed by representatives of the Russian Federation and Armenia, Belarus, Kazakhstan, Kyrgyzstan, Tajikistan, Turkmenistan and Uzbekistan; four other republics had earlier agreed to some form of economic co-operation.

**21 October 1991:** The first session of the newly established all-Union Supreme Soviet was attended by delegates of the Russian Federation, Belarus, Kazakhstan, Kyrgyzstan, Tajikistan, Turkmenistan and Uzbekistan. Representatives of Azerbaijan and Ukraine attended as observers.

**27 October 1991:** Following a referendum, Turkmenistan declared its independence. An election was held in the Checheno-Ingush Autonomous Republic to the presidency of the self-proclaimed 'Chechen Republic' (Chechnya) and was won by Gen. Dzhokhar Dudayev.

**November 1991:** President Yeltsin announced the formation of a new Russian Government, with himself as Chairman (Prime Minister).

**8 December 1991:** The leaders of the Russian Federation, Belarus and Ukraine, meeting at Belovezhskaya Pushcha, Belarus, agreed to form a Commonwealth of Independent States (CIS) to replace the USSR, as stated in the so-called Minsk Agreement.

**16 December 1991:** Kazakhstan declared its independence, following a decision by it and the four other Central Asian republics to join a Commonwealth.

**21 December 1991:** At a meeting in Almaty, the leaders of 11 former Union Republics of the USSR signed a protocol on the formation of the new CIS. Georgia did not sign, but sent observers to the meeting.

**25 December 1991:** Mikhail Gorbachev formally resigned as President of the USSR, thereby confirming the effective dissolution of the Union.

**30 December 1991:** The 11 members of the CIS agreed, in Minsk, Belarus, to establish a joint command for armed forces (this arrangement was formally ended in 1993); use of nuclear weapons was to be under the control of the Russian Federation's President, after consultation with other Commonwealth leaders and the agreement of the presidents of Belarus, Kazakhstan and Ukraine.

## POST-SOVIET RUSSIA

**2 January 1992:** A radical economic reform programme was introduced, under which most consumer prices were liberalized.

**31 March 1992:** Eighteen of the 21 autonomous republics of the Russian Federation, the leaders of the Russian administrative regions and the mayors of Moscow and St Petersburg signed the Russian Federation Treaty; representatives from the 'Chechen Republic' and Tatarstan did not participate.

**15 May 1992:** At a meeting of the CIS Heads of State in Tashkent, Uzbekistan, a Five-Year Collective Security Agreement was signed by Armenia, Kazakhstan, Russia, Tajikistan, Turkmenistan and Uzbekistan.

**1 October 1992:** The Government's voucher privatization programme was initiated.

**9 December 1992:** The Congress rejected Yeltsin's nomination of a supporter of radical economic reform, Yegor Gaidar, as Prime Minister (Gaidar had been serving as premier, in an acting capacity, since mid-June); Yeltsin subsequently appointed Viktor Chernomyrdin to the post.

**3 January 1993:** President Yeltsin and the US President, George Bush, signed START 2, which envisaged a reduction in the strategic nuclear weapons of both powers. It was ratified by the Russian legislature on 14 April 2000, and signed into law on 4 May.

**11 March 1993:** Congress granted itself the right to suspend any presidential decrees that contravened the Constitution, pending a ruling by the Constitutional Court.

**20 March 1993:** Following the rejection by Congress of his proposal to hold a referendum on the issue of the respective powers of the presidency and the legislature, Yeltsin announced his intention to rule Russia by decree until such a referendum could take place.

**25 April 1993:** Some 65.7% of the registered electorate participated in a referendum, of which 57.4% endorsed President Yeltsin and 70.6% voted in favour of early elections to the Congress of People's Deputies.

**12 July 1993:** The Constitutional Conference approved a proposed compromise text.

**31 August 1993:** The heads of administration from 58 constituent parts of the Russian Federation and 45 heads of regional legislative bodies approved Yeltsin's proposal for the establishment of a Federation Council, which convened in mid-September.

**21 September 1993:** Yeltsin issued a decree 'On Gradual Constitutional Reform' (Decree 1,400), which suspended the powers of the legislature with immediate effect and scheduled elections to a new bicameral legislature, the Federal Assembly. An emergency session of the Supreme Soviet appointed Rutskoi acting President, although the Constitutional Court ruled against this.

**23 September 1993:** As the institutional crisis continued, an emergency session of the Congress of People's Deputies was convened.

**24 September 1993:** At a meeting of the CIS Council of Heads of State, in Moscow, an agreement was reached on a framework for economic union, including the gradual removal of tariffs and a currency union; nine states signed the agreement, and Turkmenistan and Ukraine agreed to be associate members of such a union.

**26 September 1993:** Some 10,000 demonstrators attended a rally outside the White House, the seat of the Supreme Soviet, in support of the legislators.

**28 September 1993:** An unarmed militia-man was killed in disturbances in the centre of Moscow, as a crowd of several thousand supporters of Ruslan Khasbulatov (the parliamentary Chairman and one of Yeltsin's leading opponents) and Rutskoi attempted to break through the police cordon around the White House.

**3 October 1993:** Negotiations between the Government and parliament, mediated by the Moscow Patriarchate, broke down. A state of emergency was declared in Moscow after a group of anti-Yeltsin demonstrators stormed the office of the Mayor of Moscow and the Ostankino television building. Rutskoi was formally dismissed.

**4 October 1993:** The White House was shelled by government forces and severely damaged by fire, and over 140 people were killed. Later that day Khasbulatov and Rutskoi surrendered and the perpetrators of the violence were arrested.

**7 October 1993:** The Constitutional Court was suspended, pending the adoption of a new constitution and the election of new judges.

**15 October 1993:** The Constitutional Convention opened. Yeltsin decreed that a nation-wide plebiscite be held on the draft constitution. The leaders of the anti-Government insurrection were charged with incitement to riot.

**12 December 1993:** The proposed new Constitution was approved by 58.4% of participating voters in a referendum. On the same day elections to the new Federal Assembly (comprising the Federation Council and the State Duma) were held, producing an unexpected number of votes (22.8% of the total) for Vladimir Zhirinovskii's nationalist Liberal Democratic Party of Russia (LPDR) and for the Communist Party (12.4%).

**January 1994:** Parliamentary representatives of the Communist Party established a conservative bloc with the Democratic Party and the Agrarian Party; this bloc controlled 115 seats out of a total of 450 in the State Duma, while the liberal bloc occupied some 196 seats and the LDPR 64 seats.

**February 1994:** The State Duma granted an amnesty to the members of the SCSE of the 1991 coup attempt and to the organizers of the parliamentary resistance of September–October 1993.

**22 June 1994:** Russia became a signatory to the 'Partnership for Peace' co-operation programme drawn up by the North Atlantic Treaty Organization (NATO). A broader accord with NATO also came into effect.

**30 July 1994:** Against a background of armed raids by rebel Chechens on Russian towns, Yeltsin declared his support for an 'Interim Council' in Chechnya. The Council, headed by Umar Avturkhanov, had proclaimed itself the rightful Government of Chechnya, in opposition to the administration of President Dudayev, which, within two weeks, ordered mobilization in Chechnya.

**3 September 1994:** Armed conflict broke out in Argun, east of Groznyi, the capital of Chechnya, between supporters of Dudayev and opposition troops.

**11 October 1994:** The rouble collapsed, losing almost one-quarter of its value against the US dollar and resulting in the resignation of several ministers and the Chairman of the Central Bank, Viktor Gerashchenko.

**26 November 1994:** Groznyi was attacked by warplanes, allegedly operating from a federal airbase. Opposition forces had attacked the city earlier in the month with Russian tanks.

**11 December 1994:** Following the collapse of peace negotiations, Yeltsin ordered the invasion of Chechnya by some 40,000 ground troops.

**19 January 1995:** After a bitterly fought resistance, Dudayev fled Groznyi and established his headquarters outside the city.

**March 1995:** The Russian Government installed a 'Government of National Revival' in Chechnya, chaired by Salambek Khadzhiyev; this existed alongside the Interim Council, by this time largely discredited, but was replaced in November by a new Government, under Doku Zavgayev.

**14 June 1995:** The militant Chechen leader, Shamil Basayev, took over 1,000 people hostage in a hospital in Budennovsk (Stavropol Krai). After a few days, to secure the release of the captives, the Prime Minister, Chernomyrdin, intervened in the negotiations and agreed to resume peace talks with the Chechen rebels. More than 100 people died during the hostage-taking, and, particularly, during the operations to end the siege.

**21 June 1995:** A vote of 'no confidence' in the Government was overwhelmingly approved by the State Duma.

**12 July 1995:** An impeachment motion against the President was defeated, largely owing to the fact that Yeltsin was hospitalized at the time, having suffered a heart attack.

**30 July 1995:** A military accord was signed on the gradual disarmament of the Chechen rebels, in return for the partial withdrawal of federal troops from Chechnya; it remained in effect until October.

**17 December 1995:** In elections to the State Duma, in which an estimated 64.4% of eligible voters participated, the Communist Party of the Russian Federation (CPRF) achieved the greatest success, winning 22.7% of the votes cast; the LDPR won 11.2% of the votes, Our Home is Russia (a centre-right electoral bloc headed by Viktor Chernomyrdin) 10.1% and Yabloko (headed by the liberal, Grigorii Yavlinskii) 6.9%.

**9 January 1996:** Chechen rebels, led by Salman Raduyev, held some 2,000 civilians captive in the town of Kizlyar, Dagestan. Some hostages were later released, while others were taken in convoy to the nearby village of Pervomaiskoye. The village was bombarded for several days by federal air and ground troops, resulting in the release of the captives at the expense of many casualties.

**25 January 1996:** Russia was admitted to the Council of Europe.

**15 March 1996:** The Communist-dominated State Duma declared the Minsk Agreement null and void, although this motion was not endorsed by any other state bodies and officials stated that there was no implicit threat to the sovereignty of other former Soviet states.

**2 April 1996:** The Russian President signed a treaty with President Lukashenka of Belarus establishing a 'Community of Sovereign Republics'. The treaty envisaged closer integration, with a view to the eventual creation of a confederation.

**21 April 1996:** Dzhokhar Dudayev, the Chechen rebel leader, was killed in a Russian missile attack. He was succeeded by his erstwhile Deputy President, Zemlikhan Yandarbiyev.

**27 May 1996:** A cease-fire agreement was concluded between Yeltsin and Yandarbiyev (in effect from 1 June).

**16 June 1996:** Eleven candidates contested the presidential election; Yeltsin secured the greatest number of votes (35%), followed by the leader of the CPRF, Gennadii Zyuganov (32%); Lt-Gen. (retd) Aleksandr Lebed won an unexpectedly high level of support, with 15% of the votes cast, and was later appointed as Secretary of the National Security Council.

**3 July 1996:** Amid increasing speculation about his health, Boris Yeltsin won the second round of voting in the presidential election, with 53.8% of the votes cast. Yeltsin was inaugurated as President on 9 August.

**31 August 1996:** Following a successful attack by Chechen forces on Groznyi, Lebed negotiated a cease-fire agreement (the Khasavyurt Accords) with the rebel chief of staff, Col Khalid 'Aslan' Maskhadov; the basic principles of the agreement included postponing a solution to the issue of Chechen sovereignty until 2001. Despite the peace deal, Lebed was dismissed in mid-October.

**1 January 1997:** Maskhadov was elected as President of the Chechen Republic (which subsequently renamed itself 'the Chechen Republic of Ichkeriya', defeating Basayev.

**2 April 1997:** A Treaty of Union was signed by the Presidents of Russia and Belarus, without consultation with their respective legislatures; the following month a Charter of the Union of Belarus and Russia was concluded, committing the two countries to closer integration.

**27 May 1997:** At a NATO summit meeting in Paris, France, a Founding Act on Mutual Relations, Co-operation and Security between NATO and the Russian Federation was signed, which provided Russia with equal status with the Alliance in peace-keeping operations and enhanced its consultative rights.

**28 May 1997:** The Russian–Ukrainian dispute over ownership of the Soviet Black Sea Fleet was finally resolved: Russia would lease part of the naval base at the port of Sevastopol for 20 years and provide financial compensation for ships and equipment received from Ukraine; a few days later a Treaty on Friendship, Co-operation and Partnership was signed by the Presidents of the two countries.

**November 1997:** During a visit by President Yeltsin to the People's Republic of China, it was agreed to end a long-running border dispute and allow for the implementation of a 1991 accord demarcating the entire 4,300-km frontier.

**1 December 1997:** A Partnership and Co-operation Agreement reached between Russia and the European Union (EU) in 1994 took effect.

**27 March 1998:** Following the dismissal of Chernomyrdin and his Government a few days before, Sergei Kiriyenko, hitherto Minister of Fuel and Energy, was nominated as premier; a new Government was gradually appointed over the following month. Kiriyenko was confirmed as premier by the State Duma on 24 April, his nomination having been rejected twice earlier in the month.

**17 July 1998:** Following the approval, four days earlier, of an IMF loan of US $22,600m., the State Duma rejected two of the main tax proposals in the government programme of emergency fiscal measures demanded by the Fund.

**17 August 1998:** Following an escalating financial crisis, and in a complete reversal of its monetary policies, the Government announced a series of emergency measures, which included the effective devaluation of the rouble.

**21 August 1998:** The State Duma reconvened for an extraordinary plenary session to debate the financial and economic crisis in Russia; a resolution was passed urging the voluntary resignation of President Yeltsin. Two days later President Yeltsin dismissed the Government and reappointed Chernomyrdin premier.

**11 September 1998:** Following the State Duma's second overwhelming rejection of Chernomyrdin's nomination as Prime Minister, the foreign minister, Yevgenii Primakov, was confirmed as premier by the State Duma. On the same day Viktor Gerashchenko was reappointed as Chairman of the Central Bank, following the resignation of Sergei Dubinin.

**5 November 1998:** The Constitutional Court ruled that Boris Yeltsin was ineligible to seek a third presidential term in 2000.

**4 March 1999:** Boris Yeltsin dismissed Boris Berezovskii as Executive Secretary of the CIS, prompting protests that the decision had not been approved by the Commonwealth's Council of Heads of State.

**24 March 1999:** Russia condemned NATO airstrikes against Yugoslav targets, initiated in response to the repression of ethnic Albanians in the Serbian province of Kosovo and Metohija (Kosovo), and suspended relations with the Organization.

**16 April 1999:** The Duma voted overwhelmingly in favour of the admission of the Federal Republic of Yugoslavia (now Serbia and Montenegro) to the Union of Russia and Belarus. Political leaders assessed the measure to be of solely symbolic significance.

**12 May 1999:** Yeltsin dismissed Primakov, and appointed Sergei Stepashin, hitherto First Deputy Prime Minister and Minister of the Interior, as acting premier; he was approved by the State Duma one week later.

**15 May 1999:** An attempt by the State Duma to impeach the President failed, as none of the five counts, including that of bringing about 'genocide' through economic reforms that resulted in a lower birth-rate and a reduced life expectancy, succeeded in securing the necessary majority support of two-thirds of the chamber's membership.

**12 June 1999:** Russian troops entered Kosovo, ahead of NATO forces. The Serbs had capitulated three days earlier, aided by the mediation efforts of Russia's special envoy to the Balkans conflict, the former Prime Minister, Viktor Chernomyrdin. International negotiations took place throughout the month on the role to be undertaken in the region by Russian peace-keeping forces.

**28 July 1999:** The Executive Board of the IMF approved a US $4,500m. stand-by credit, to be released in instalments. The disbursement of the funds, which were designated for existing debt repayments, was suspended in February 2000, owing to concerns about the extent of economic reform in Russia.

**7 August 1999:** Armed Chechen guerrillas invaded neighbouring Dagestan and seized control of two villages. Federal troops retaliated and claimed, by the end of the month, to have quelled the rebel action.

**9 August 1999:** Stepashin was dismissed by Yeltsin, and replaced as premier by Vladimir Putin, hitherto the Secretary of the Security Council and head of the Federal Security Service (Federalnaya sluzhba bezopasnosti—FSB), one of the successor bodies to the KGB.

**9 and 13 September 1999:** Two bomb attacks, which targeted apartment blocks in Moscow, killing almost 200 people, were attributed by the federal authorities to Chechen rebels. In August a bomb explosion at a Moscow shopping centre had injured more than 30 people, and further bombings in southern Russian, against both civilian and military targets, took place in mid-September.

**23 September 1999:** Russia initiated major airstrikes against Chechnya, officially in retaliation for the bombings, and as part of a declared 'anti-terrorism' campaign.

**6 December 1999:** Following the full-scale invasion of Chechnya at the beginning of November, Russian forces warned residents of the capital, Groznyi, to evacuate the city by 11 December, resulting in strong international disapproval. A ground offensive against the city subsequently commenced.

**8 December 1999:** The signature of the Union Treaty of Russia and Belarus took place in Moscow. The Treaty entered into force on 26 January 2000, following its ratification by the Russian executive.

**19 December 1999:** A total of 29 parties and blocs contested the election to the State Duma, in which 62% of the electorate participated. The CPRF secured the most seats, winning 113. Unity, formed by 31 leaders of Russia's regions, took 72 seats, and the Fatherland—All Russia bloc obtained 67 seats. The pro-market Union of Rightist Forces, led by Sergei Kiriyenko, obtained 29 seats, Yabloko took 21, and the Zhirinovskii bloc (contesting the election in place of the Liberal Democratic Party of Russia) won 17.

**31 December 1999:** Boris Yeltsin unexpectedly resigned as President. Putin assumed the role in an acting capacity, and a presidential election, under the terms of the Constitution required within three months of Yeltsin's resignation, was scheduled for 26 March 2000.

**14 January 2000:** A new national security concept was published, which lowered the threshold for the use of nuclear weapons, in an attempt to contain the threat from the West's perceived attempts to achieve global domination.

**18 January 2000:** The Duma reconvened, and the CPRF and Unity factions formed an alliance. In protest at the move, the Fatherland—All Russia, Yabloko and Union of Rightist Forces factions, together with the newly formed Russia's Regions group of deputies, agreed to a boycott, although the situation was resolved after eight days, following Putin's intervention.

**9 February 2000:** A Treaty of Friendship, Neighbourliness and Co-operation was signed between Russia and the Democratic People's Republic of Korea (North Korea), replacing a 1961 agreement, which had been abolished following the establishment of diplomatic relations between the then USSR and the Republic of Korea (South Korea) in 1990.

### THE PUTIN PRESIDENCY

**26 March 2000:** Vladimir Putin achieved a clear victory in the first round of the presidential election, with 52.9% of the votes cast. Gennadii Zyuganov was the second-placed candidate, with 29.2% of the votes cast.

**6 April 2000:** The Parliamentary Assembly of the Council of Europe voted to suspend Russia's membership unless progress was made to end human-rights abuses in Chechnya.

**5 May 2000:** Putin decreed that, henceforth, Chechnya was to come under direct federal, rather than direct presidential, rule. Maskhadov was no longer to be recognized as President of the Republic, and on 19 June a new administrative leader for Chechnya, Akhmed haji Kadyrov, was inaugurated.

**7 May 2000:** Vladimir Putin was inaugurated as President of the Russian Federation. He subsequently relinquished the post of premier and formed a new Government headed by the former First Deputy Prime Minister, Mikhail Kasyanov.

**13 May 2000:** The President issued a decree dividing Russia's 89 constituent regions and republics between seven federal districts (okrugs). Each district was to come under the control of a presidential envoy, who was to oversee local regions' compliance with federal legislation. Of the new presidential envoys, five were senior officers of the security services or the military.

**31 May 2000:** Three pieces of legislation, proposed by Putin to extend the powers of the President and curtail those of the regional governors, were passed by the State Duma. The first proposed that regional governors should lose their seats in the Federation Council, and be replaced by representatives elected from regional legislatures; following its ratification by the Federation Council in July, all existing Council members were to be replaced by the beginning of 2002. The second bill accorded the President the right to dismiss regional governors, and the third allowed governors to remove from office elected officials who were subordinate to them.

**8 August 2000:** A bomb, attributed to Chechen extremists, exploded in central Moscow, resulting in 11 deaths and some 90 injuries.

**12 August 2000:** The Russian nuclear submarine, *Kursk*, sank after an explosion, during exercises in the Barents Sea. The Russian authorities attracted criticism, owing to delays in responding to the crisis; all 118 sailors on board the vessel perished.

**September 2000:** The General Staff issued an order specifying a reduction of some 350,000 in the strength of the Russian armed forces; the reductions were expected to take place in 2001–03. On 9 November the Security Council voted to reduce the overall strength of the armed forces by 600,000 (approximately one-fifth of the 2000 level) by 2005.

**20 September 2000:** The Minister for the Press, Broadcasting and Mass Media, Mikhail Lesin, admitted that he had approved a document stating that criminal charges against Vladimir Gusinskii, the Chairman of the Mediya-MOST holding company, would be dropped in return for the sale of Gusinskii's media interests to the partially state-owned gas monopoly, Gazprom.

**10 October 2000:** President Putin and the Presidents of Belarus, Kazakhstan, Kyrgyzstan and Tajikistan signed a treaty creating a new customs union, to be known as the Eurasian Economic Community.

**23 November 2000:** The State Council, a body comprising the President and the territorial governors and formed as part of the reforms of the Federation Council in May, convened for the first time.

**30 November 2000:** The Presidents of Russia and Belarus signed an agreement on the introduction of a common currency unit for the two countries by 2008.

**13 December 2000:** Following the issuance of a federal arrest warrant on charges of fraud, Gusinskii, who had lost control of Mediya-MOST in the previous month, was arrested in Spain. Spain refused to extradite Gusinskii to Russia, however, and he travelled to Israel (where he held dual citizenship) in April 2001, purportedly to complicate conditions for his extradition. Another 'oligarch', the former Executive Secretary of the CIS, Berezovskii, had entered self-imposed exile, after corruption charges were brought against him in November.

**22 January 2001:** Putin signed a decree transferring control of operations in Chechnya from the defence ministry to the FSB.

**7 March 2001:** The State Duma approved the introduction of a new national anthem, which combined the tune of the former Soviet Anthem, abandoned in 1990, with new words, written by the composer of the original lyrics, Sergei Mikhalkov.

**28 March 2001:** Putin announced a ministerial reshuffle, in which, notably, Sergei Ivanov was appointed as Minister of Defence.

**12 July 2001:** New conditions for the registration of political parties were introduced, which were intended to facilitate the consolidation of national parties.

**1 September 2001:** Following condemnation by Sergei Ivanov of the reported appointment of the Islamist extremist, Osama bin Laden, as Commander-in-Chief of the Taliban's defence forces in Afghanistan, the military districts of Russia were reformed; the former Volga and Urals regions were combined in a new, strengthened Trans-Volga region, in response to a perceived heightened security threat from the Central Asian region.

**1 December 2001:** The founding congress of the Unity and Fatherland—United Russia party, uniting two hitherto separate centrist movements, Fatherland–All Russia and Unity, took place.

**16 January 2002:** A new session of the Federation Council opened; for the first time, the Council comprised the full-time appointees of both regional governors and the chairmen of regional legislative assemblies. Sergei Mironov, an ally of Putin, had replaced Yegor Stroyev as Chairman of the Council in the previous month.

**18 February 2002:** Ilya Klebanov, who had been responsible for carrying out an investigation into the sinking of the *Kursk* nuclear submarine in August 2000, was dismissed from the position of Deputy Chairman of the Government, although he retained his post as Minister of Industry, Science and Technology.

**20 March 2002:** The State Duma voted to remove the deciding vote in the governing body of the chamber, the Duma Council, from the Chairman, CPRF deputy Gennadii Seleznev. (Seleznev was subsequently expelled from the CPRF and founded his own political movement, which was registered as the Party of the Rebirth of Russia in October.) On the same day the Duma accepted the resignation of Viktor Gerashchenko from the chairmanship of the Central Bank, and approved the appointment of Sergei Ignatiyev in his place.

**3 April 2002:** The Duma voted to revoke seven of the nine committee chairmanships held by the CPRF, leading that party to assume a more aggressively oppositional role than had hitherto been the case.

**25 April 2002:** Federal sources reported that the rebel Islamist leader, al-Khattab, who had led a faction in the war in Chechnya, had been killed, a report that was subsequently confirmed by rebel sources.

**9 May 2002:** During Victory Day processions in Kaspiisk, Dagestan, 45 people were killed, and more than 130 others injured as the result of a bomb attack attributed to Chechen militants.

**24 May 2002:** President Putin and the US President, George W. Bush, signed an agreement, in accordance with which Russia and the USA were each to reduce their stocks of strategic nuclear warheads by more than one-half over a period of 10 years. This development followed an announcement by the USA in late 2001 that it was to withdraw from the Anti-Ballistic Missiles (ABM) Treaty, signed between the USA and the USSR in 1972, with effect from June 2002. On 13 June Russia withdrew from the START 2 Treaty, which had been superseded by the new nuclear arms reduction agreement.

**28 May 2002:** The new NATO-Russia Council, which made Russia a full partner of NATO in discussions on a number of issues, including counter-terrorism, non-proliferation and emergency planning, was inaugurated at a NATO conference in Rome, Italy.

**25 July 2002:** President Putin approved legislation permitting the sale and purchase of agricultural land; however, the sale of farmland to foreign purchasers or to foreign-controlled enterprises remained prohibited. The law came into effect in January 2003.

**19 August 2002:** In the single largest loss of life since the recommencement of military operations in Chechnya in 1999, some 118 federal troops were killed when rebels shot down a military helicopter.

**23 September 2002:** The Presidents of Russia and Azerbaijan signed a bilateral agreement on the delimitation of the Caspian Sea, based on the principle that the surface be used in common, but the seabed be divided into national sectors, corresponding to each country's coastline, along a median line; a similar agreement had already been signed between Russia and Kazakhstan. A trilateral agreement was signed on 14 May 2003.

**6 October 2002:** Following months of escalating tension between Georgia and Russia, the latter accusing Georgia of allowing Chechen rebels to operate from bases within its territory, the two countries agreed to undertake joint patrols of their common border.

**23 October 2002:** Some 50 heavily armed Chechen rebels took more than 700 people hostage in a Moscow theatre, demanding the immediate withdrawal of federal troops from Chechnya. On 26 October élite Russian troops stormed the theatre, killing the rebels in an operation that also resulted in the deaths of some 129 hostages. It rapidly emerged that the vast majority of these deaths had resulted from the use of an incapacitating gas by the federal troops.

**5 November 2002:** The Russian authorities requested the extradition of Berezovskii from the United Kingdom (where he had taken up residence), but he was granted political asylum in September 2003.

**7 November 2002:** In a move that was generally regarded as a promotion, Stanislav Ilyasov, hitherto Chairman of the Government of Chechnya, was appointed to the federal Government, as Minister without Portfolio, responsible for the Social and Economic Development of Chechnya. Capt (retd) Mikhail Babich was appointed as the new premier of Chechnya. (Babich resigned in January 2003; he was replaced, in the following month, by Anatolii Popov, hitherto the deputy Chairman of the State Commission for the Reconstruction of Chechnya).

**27 December 2002:** At least 83 people died, and more than 150 others were injured, when suicide bombers detonated bombs in two vehicles stationed outside the headquarters of the Chechen republican Government in Groznyi.

**11 March 2003:** Putin removed Valentina Matviyenko from her post as Deputy Chairman of the Government, responsible for Social Affairs, appointing her as Presidential Representative in the North-Western Federal District, based in St Petersburg. On the same date several presidential decrees provided for a reorganization of the federal security agencies, as a result of which the powers of the FSB were expanded.

**23 March 2003:** A referendum was held in Chechnya on the draft republican constitution, which described the region as an integral part of the Russian Federation. According to the official results, some 88.4% of the electorate participated in the plebiscite, of whom 96.0% voted in favour. Two further questions, on the method of electing the president and the parliament of the republic, were also approved, receiving the support of 95.4% and 96.1% of the votes cast, respectively.

**28 April 2003:** Representatives from Armenia, Belarus, Kazakhstan, Kyrgyzstan, Russia and Tajikistan formally inaugurated the successor to the Collective Security Treaty, a new regional defence organization known as the Collective Security Treaty Organization (CSTO).

**24 March 2003:** Two additional Deputy Chairmen were appointed to the Government, including Galina Karelova, who assumed the position vacated by Matviyenko in the previous month.

**12 May 2003:** At least 59 people were killed when suicide bombers attacked offices of the Chechen Government in Znamenskoye, in the north of the republic. Two days later another suicide bombing in Chechnya, at a religious festival attended by Kadyrov, resulted in at least 14 deaths.

**16 June 2003:** Vladimir Yakovlev, hitherto Governor of St Petersburg, was appointed to the federal Government as a Deputy Chairman, with particular responsibility for housing and utilities.

**18 June 2003:** A vote of 'no confidence' in the Government, presented to the State Duma by the liberal Yabloko and the CPRF factions, was defeated.

**21 June 2003:** An interim legislative body in Chechnya, the State Council, was inaugurated.

**22 June 2003:** The national independent television channel, TVS, was forced to cease operations, ostensibly for financial reasons.

**6 July 2003:** Fifteen people were killed as a result of a suicide bombing, attributed to Chechen militants, at a music festival outside Moscow.

**21 August 2003:** Gusinskii was arrested in Greece, on an international arrest warrant issued in 2001, following his return from Israel. He was released on bail later in the month and ordered to remain in Greece (on 14 October a Greek court rejected Russia's request for his extradition).

**1 September 2003:** The overall command for military operations in Chechnya was transferred from the FSB to the Ministry of Internal Affairs. Moreover, the Minister of Internal Affairs, Boris Gryzlov, stated that such operations were no longer regarded as having an 'anti-terrorist' character, but were rather, henceforth, to form part of an 'operation to protect law and constitutional order'.

**5 October 2003:** At a second round of voting, Matviyenko was elected as Governor of St Petersburg, having received the support of Putin. On the same day Kadyrov was elected as President of Chechnya, with 88% of the votes cast, according to official figures. However, many observers were critical of the conduct of voting in Chechnya, citing a heightened military presence at polling stations, and noting that several of Kadyrov's principal rivals had withdrawn, or been obliged to withdraw, their candidacies.

**26 October 2003:** Mikhail Khodorkovskii, the Chairman of Yukos Oil Co, and a prominent supporter of the pro-market Union of Rightist Forces and the liberal Yabloko party, was arrested and detained, reportedly following his failure to attend a court hearing at which various charges of fraudulent practice by the company were being investigated. Khodorkovskii, who was the third senior executive of the company to be arrested since July, was subsequently charged with tax evasion and fraud.

# History

## ANGUS ROXBURGH

### EARLY HISTORY

The Russians are Eastern Slavs, inhabitants of the huge Eurasian land mass, which is a territory with no great natural frontiers. This fact has made the Russians throughout history both vulnerable to invaders and themselves inclined to migration and expansion. Their first state was established towards the end of the ninth century, around Kiev (Kyiv—now in Ukraine). Kievan Rus (forerunner not only of the 'Great' Russians, but also of the Belarusians or 'White Russians' and the Ukrainians or 'Little Russians') was a slave-holding society, which was officially Christianized in 988. The state did not exist for long, however. Much of its population, tired of constant enemy attacks from the south and west, gradually migrated to the north and east. By the late 12th century the early Russians were scattered over a large area in what is now western Russia, Belarus and Ukraine. Their territory was fragmented among a large number of (usually warring) principalities, the most powerful centred on the town of Vladimir.

The disintegration of the Russian nation was halted, ironically, by outsiders. In 1237 ferocious invaders from the east, the Mongol Tatars, led by Batu (a descendant of Chinghiz or Genghis Khan), crossed the River Volga and imposed almost 250 years of subjugation on the Russian people. Mongol rule established in Russia a social, political, administrative and military system quite unlike that of Western Europe. It was based on the unquestioning submission of all individuals to the group and to the absolute power of the ultimate ruler, the Khan. Russia's feuding princes all became vassals of the Golden Horde, as the Khan and his entourage were known. One of the smallest principalities, Muscovy (based in the town of Moscow—Moskva), rose to prominence, largely as a reward for its devotion to the Khan and its position as chief tax-collector for the Golden Horde.

From the late 14th century the Mongol empire began to disintegrate into smaller khanates. In 1480 a new Russian state finally emerged, when the Muscovite prince, Ivan III, proclaimed complete independence from the Tatars. Moreover, with the fall of Constantinople (İstanbul) to the Turks in 1453, Moscow could lay claim to being the 'Third Rome', the capital of the most pre-eminent Orthodox Christian state. The new state retained many features of the Mongol system, including the supremacy of the state over the individual and the principle of universal compulsory service to the state. The Russian historian, Nikolai Berdyayev, described Muscovite Russia as a 'Christianized Tatar kingdom'. Ivan IV ('the Terrible') was the first of many a Russian Tsar (Caesar or Emperor) to use his unquestioned rights as supreme ruler to establish a despotic regime in which terror was, effectively, an instrument of state policy. His *oprichniki*, a secret police force, were used to suppress dissent, whether real or imagined, in barbaric fashion. Ivan IV annexed the Mongol Khanates of Kazan and Astrakhan to Moscow and began to colonize the middle and upper reaches of the Volga. This led to a mass migration of peasants to these more fertile areas. It was under Ivan's rule that the Cossack leader, Yermak Timofeyev, began Russia's expansion eastwards beyond the Ural Mountains into Siberia, where villages, forts and trading posts were soon established. For the first time the Russian Empire extended into two continents. In 1645, under the first Tsar of the Romanov dynasty, Muscovite rule reached the Sea of Okhotsk, and the port town of Okhotsk was founded.

Over subsequent centuries, Russia's development was marked by almost continuous expansionism and by arguments over whether to follow a 'Western', European model of civilization, or to create a peculiarly Russian one. Peter (Petr) I ('the Great') combined despotic methods with a determination to modernize Russia and establish it as a great European Power. To symbolize this, in 1712 he moved the capital from Moscow to a newly built city on the Baltic coast, St Petersburg (Sankt-Peterburg), which he called his 'window on the West'. Under Catherine (Yekaterina) II ('the Great') the Russian Empire was expanded south to the Black Sea and west into Poland. The Tsars Alexander (Aleksandr) I (1801–25), Nicholas (Nikolai) I (1825–55) and Alexander II (1855–81) extended the Russian frontiers into the Caucasus and parts of Central Asia. In 1885 the Turkmen became the last of the Muslim peoples of Central Asia to be incorporated into the Empire. During this period, new territories were also claimed in the Far East, reaching Vladivostok in 1860. Politically, 19th-century Russia alternated between reactionary Tsars, such as Nicholas I, and enlightened ones, such as Alexander II (whose most famous act was the emancipation of the serfs in 1861). European liberal and revolutionary ideas constantly threatened the political stability and the last Tsar, Nicholas II, was obliged to introduce elements of parliamentary democracy, with the establishment of a legislative assembly, the Duma, in 1906.

In 1917 the pressures of defeats in the First World War and growing economic and social chaos in the country at large brought two revolutions. The first, which occurred in March, overthrew the Tsar and established a Provisional Government, which, however, soon found itself sharing power with new workers' councils known as soviets. The second, the Bolshevik Revolution, on 7 November (25 October under the old style calendar, which remained in use by the civil authorities until 1918), brought the communists, under Vladimir Lenin (Ulyanov), to power in the capital (renamed Petrograd in 1914) and, after three years of civil war, throughout most of the territory of the Russian Empire.

### SOVIET RUSSIA

In the new Union of Soviet Socialist Republics (USSR—established in 1922), Russia (the Russian Soviet Federative Socialist Republic or RSFSR) became just one of (eventually) 15 national republics. In 1918 Moscow again became the capital city of Russia, and subsequently of the USSR. Under Stalin (Iosif V. Dzhugashvili, 1924–53), especially after a surge of Russian nationalism during the Second World War, which the USSR entered in 1941, the accepted dogma was that the Soviet nations would not merely 'come together' (*sblizheniye*), but eventually 'merge' (*sliyaniye*—which most understood to mean the subjugation of the other nations by the Russian people). Even after Stalin, Russians remained the *de facto* colonial masters, their Empire simply renamed the USSR. Many of the characteristics of pre-Soviet Russia came to dominate the political culture of the USSR. The communist regime was highly centralized. It encouraged and relied upon traditions of collectivism in the population. The three basic principles of tsarism: orthodoxy, autocracy and nationality (*pravoslaviye*, *samoderzhaviye* and *narodnost*), were transmuted into the communist doctrines of Marxism-Leninism, Communist Party dictatorship and the idealization of the People (*narod*). Russia ensured the loyalty of non-Russian parts of the Soviet empire by the appointment of Russian second secretaries in all republican Communist Party organizations, by establishing Russian as the language of the Soviet state and by making the republics' economies dependent on each other and on the all-Union Government in Moscow. Russian migration to the other republics was encouraged. Additionally, the RSFSR lacked the republican institutions granted to the other national republics in the USSR, thereby encouraging the assimilation of Russian national identity to that of the entire Union. Until Mikhail Gorbachev's policy of *glasnost* (openness) in the late 1980s, the colonized Soviet nations rarely protested in public, although the suppression of certain non-Russian nationalities caused bitter resentment throughout the Soviet period, and became a major focus of political protest from the late 1980s.

Soviet rule transformed Russia from a largely peasant, illiterate society into an industrialized, urbanized and educated one, but this was achieved at the cost of untold human suffering. Tens of millions of people lost their lives in a series of man-made disasters: the civil war of 1918–21, the enforced collectivization of agriculture and resultant famines in the early 1930s, Stalin's purges from 1936, and the Second World War. For most of the 74 years of communist rule, political freedoms were stifled and dissidents were incarcerated in labour camps. Even during Nikita Khrushchev's 'thaw' (when he was First Secretary of the Communist Party of the Soviet Union—CPSU, 1953–64), as part of which he denounced Stalin's 'cult of personality', the one-party state remained intact.

Under Leonid Brezhnev, who served as First Secretary of the CPSU's Central Committee from 1964 until his death in 1982, the USSR developed into a military 'superpower', competing with the USA to build up supplies of nuclear armaments, a policy that was to prove devastating for the economy. The Soviet authorities sponsored governments sympathetic to communism and 'national liberation movements' throughout the world, and its forces invaded Afghanistan in 1979, in an attempt to establish and uphold a client regime. Domestically, political dissent was not tolerated, and the centrally run economy entered what was later termed a 'period of stagnation', unable to meet the requirements of the populace.

## *PERESTROIKA* AND THE END OF THE USSR

Between 1985 and 1991 Mikhail Gorbachev, as Communist Party leader and later President of the USSR, attempted to reform the Soviet system from within. His economic reforms, known as *perestroika* (restructuring), were uneven and unsuccessful, but his political reforms unleashed unofficial, 'grassroots' activity, which led, ultimately, to the collapse of the communist system and the beginnings of a civil society. Throughout his years in power, Gorbachev tried to steer a course between 'hardline' communist leaders, who opposed the CPSU's decision, in 1990, to relinquish its constitutionally guaranteed monopoly of power, and reformists such as Boris Yeltsin, the leader of the Moscow Party Committee, who demanded faster reforms and an end to the privileged status of the CPSU.

Post-Soviet Russia emerged from the USSR almost by default. Under Gorbachev other Union Republics (especially the Baltic states—Estonia, Latvia and Lithuania) led the way in fighting for greater autonomy from the all-Union Government. Russia was a latecomer to the 'national movement'; from mid-1990 its newly elected parliament (a 1,068-member Congress of People's Deputies, which elected a standing parliament, or Supreme Soviet, of 274 members, both then chaired by Boris Yeltsin) began to oppose 'Soviet' centralism and demand greater financial autonomy. These rights were inscribed in a Declaration of Sovereignty approved by the RSFSR Congress of People's Deputies (then a minor body

compared with the USSR Congress elected one year earlier) on 12 June 1990, a date subsequently commemorated as the Day of Sovereignty of the Russian Federation. One year later Yeltsin became Russia's first directly elected executive President, with 57.3% of the votes cast, and, from then on, Russia's political power matched, or even outweighed, that of the Soviet central authorities. Unlike the Soviet President, Mikhail Gorbachev, who had never experienced a popular election, Yeltsin had a real mandate for reform. Confronted by 15 republics all demanding autonomy, Gorbachev tried to negotiate a Union Treaty that would preserve the USSR, at least as some kind of confederation.

However, the signing of the Treaty, scheduled for 20 August 1991, was pre-empted by an attempted *coup d'état*, led by conservative communists determined to maintain the old Union. Their plan had unforeseen consequences, for when Gorbachev returned to Moscow, having been briefly held under house arrest in Crimea, Yeltsin led an invigorated crusade against both central Soviet power and communist rule. On 23 August he suspended the activities of the Russian Communist Party (which had been active within the RSFSR). One day later Gorbachev resigned as General Secretary of the CPSU, demanded that the Central Committee disband itself, and nationalized the Party's assets and property. Henceforth, the Communist Party was no longer capable of running the country. In the months that followed, the Russian Supreme Soviet adopted numerous decrees that removed the all-Union Government's control over key economic and financial apparatus.

On 7–8 December 1991 the leaders of the RSFSR and the Ukrainian and Belarusian Soviet Socialist Republics met at Belovezhskaya Pushcha, Belarus, and signed a treaty, according to which the USSR ceased to exist and was replaced by a new Commonwealth of Independent States (CIS). Apart from the three Baltic states, all of the former Soviet republics eventually joined the CIS; the founding declaration, was signed in Almaty (Alma-Ata), Kazakhstan, by representatives of 11 republics on 21 December, and on 25 December Gorbachev accepted that he should resign. His resignation signified the end of the USSR. Above the Kremlin, the red Soviet flag was replaced by the white, blue and red tricolour of Russia (which was formally renamed the Russian Federation on the same day). When Yeltsin moved into the former General Secretary's office in the Kremlin, he was the first Russian leader for centuries to rule over such a truncated territory. The population of the Russian Federation was less than 150m., compared with the 290m. of the USSR. It remained, however, the largest country in the world.

## THE BIRTH OF DEMOCRACY

President Yeltsin had two principal aims as Russia emerged as a new state. First, to transform the country into a genuine democracy, something it had never been. Second, to abandon the centrally planned economy and create a capitalist economy, based on a free market and private ownership. A far-reaching economic reform programme, termed 'shock therapy', was introduced from January 1992, initially under the guidance of a radical young economist, Yegor Gaidar. It comprised two phases: the liberalization of prices; and the privatization of state industries. The immediate effect, for most people, was a dramatic decline in living standards and, in many cases, extreme poverty. In April Western nations announced a US $24,000m. aid package, intended to bolster the reforms and alleviate poverty. The reforms were fiercely opposed by a loose 'red-brown' coalition of neo-communists and Russian nationalists, who accused the Government of humiliating Russia: by losing its empire; by abandoning 25m. Russians to live in countries of what was now termed 'the near abroad'; and by 'betraying' ordinary citizens by promising them prosperity, yet turning them into paupers. Under the influence of the coalition, parliament (the Congress of People's Deputies and the Supreme Soviet, both elected during the communist era) obliged Yeltsin to moderate his policies. In December the seventh Congress refused to endorse Gaidar as Prime Minister and forced Yeltsin to nominate a centrist figure, Viktor Chernomyrdin, whose premiership signalled a deceleration of the reform process.

By March 1993 more serious problems began to occur for President Yeltsin. The eighth Congress of People's Deputies imposed a series of obstacles to his programme, revoking emergency powers, granted to the President in April 1992, to introduce reforms by decree. On 20 March 1993 Yeltsin introduced emergency rule, effectively bypassing parliament. One week later an emergency session of the Congress attempted to impeach Yeltsin for violating the Constitution, but narrowly failed to achieve the required two-thirds' majority. None the less, a national vote of confidence in Yeltsin was arranged. The referendum, held on 25 April, included four questions: on confidence in Yeltsin as President; on support for his economic reforms; and on whether to hold early presidential and parliamentary elections. The result confounded the President's enemies. Not only did he win 57.4% in the personal vote of confidence, but a majority even endorsed his economic policies.

In September 1993 the tension between the legislative and the executive branches of power turned into serious confrontation. On 21 September, in defiance of the Constitution, Yeltsin dissolved parliament and announced that elections would be held to a new, bicameral legislature, the Federal Assembly. The Supreme Soviet responded by summoning an emergency session of the Congress of People's Deputies. About 180 parliamentary deputies barricaded themselves inside the parliament building, known as the White House. Yeltsin had power supplies to the building suspended, and surrounded it with barbed wire and riot police. On 3–4 October armed hostilities occurred between supporters of the defiant deputies and the army and interior ministry troops. On 3 October the Ostankino television station was attacked by anti-Yeltsin demonstrators. The following day Yeltsin persuaded his army generals to bring tanks right up to the White House. Troops bombarded the building and overcame the resistance. Some 146 people were reported to have died in the conflict, and more than 1,000 were purportedly injured. The organizers of the resistance, among them the Chairman of the Supreme Soviet, Ruslan Khasbulatov, and the Russian Vice-President, Aleksandr Rutskoi, were arrested, and later imprisoned.

Having suppressed the rebellion, Yeltsin sought to finalize a draft constitution. On 10 November 1993 a Constitutional Convention agreed upon a text that was put to a nation-wide vote in a referendum on 12 December. Some 54.8% of registered voters in Russia participated in the plebiscite, and 58.4% of them endorsed the Constitution, which provided for a strong presidency, with few legislative checks on its power. Anticipating the outcome of the referendum, elections were held on the same day to the Federal Assembly—the legislature provided for by the, as yet, unapproved Constitution. The Assembly was to consist of a lower chamber, the State Duma (comprising 450 deputies), and an upper chamber, the Federation Council (consisting of a total of 178 members, two for each of the 89 constituent units of the Russian Federation). In the State Duma 225 deputies were elected in single-member constituencies (a 'first-past-the-post' system), and the remaining 225 seats were contested by proportional representation on the basis of party lists.

Results in the proportional voting amounted to a serious indictment of Yeltsin's policies (and, probably, of his violent attack on the White House): only 15.4% voted for Russia's Choice, the coalition of radical reformers led by Yegor Gaidar.

By contrast, the Liberal Democratic Party of Russia (LDPR), an uncompromising, anti-Western, nationalist party led by Vladimir Zhirinovskii won an unexpectedly large proportion of the votes cast (some 22.8%). Once members elected to individual constituencies were added, Russia's Choice had 76 seats, the LDPR 63, the re-legalized Communist Party of the Russian Federation (CPRF) 32, and their allies, the Agrarian Party, 21 seats. In the event, the lower chamber of the new legislature was at least as conservative as its predecessor. Less than two months after the opening of its first session, the State Duma voted to end criminal proceedings against both the August 1991 coup plotters and the perpetrators of the anti-Yeltsin uprising of October 1993. All were amnestied and released from gaol.

### THE NEW ORDER 1994–99

The new State Duma was a noisy and, at times, disorderly body. Its powers were highly restricted by the new Constitution: apart from endorsing the President's nomination for prime minister, its influence on policy-making was largely limited to minor corrections to the budget. It served, however, as a public forum for opposition politicians, particularly for Zhirinovskii and the leader of the CPRF, Gennadii Zyuganov.

Yeltsin responded to the December 1993 election result by replacing some of his more reformist ministers. Prime Minister Chernomyrdin appointed conservative, Soviet-era managers to key positions. The champions of 'shock therapy', including Gaidar, resigned. Only Yeltsin's Chairman of the State Committee for Property Management, Anatolii Chubais, who was appointed as first deputy premier, kept the reformers' hopes alive.

Chernomyrdin found himself caught between his own conservative instincts and the need for reform, driven both by Yeltsin and by Russia's need to satisfy the demands of the IMF and Western governments, in order to continue to receive economic aid. The impetus for reform was never completely lost, and measures to establish improved financial discipline were established in late 1994. A second stage of privatization was initiated in 1995 and the IMF was sufficiently convinced of the Government's intentions to release, in stages, a loan of US $6,800m.

As Yeltsin struggled to accommodate his critics, however, he lost many of his original, pro-democracy supporters. Gaidar's Russia's Choice group effectively moved into opposition, and in early 1995 a new pro-Government 'party of power', Our Home is Russia (OHR), was founded by Prime Minister Chernomyrdin. This was a centrist grouping, more compatible with the President's new political stance. Meanwhile, evidence of Yeltsin's decline in physical fitness (he suffered two heart attacks during 1995) and increasing signs of his weakness for alcohol, resulted in doubts concerning the President's capacity for office.

Confirmation of Yeltsin's shift to the political centre ground came in December 1994, with Russia's military intervention in the self-styled 'Chechen Republic of Ichkeriya' (Chechnya), designed to put an end to the southern region's three-year-old bid for independence. This had been proclaimed in October 1991, after the election of Gen. Dzhokhar Dudayev to the republican presidency. The most vociferous opponents of the war were Yeltsin's erstwhile liberal supporters: Yegor Gaidar led anti-war rallies, and a fellow democrat, Sergei Kovalev, the President's own human rights commissioner, devoted himself to publicizing Russian human rights abuses against the civilian population in Chechnya. Thus, the Chechen war became one of Russia's most acute political issues.

Meanwhile, the CPRF had experienced an impressive revival, becoming effectively the chief focus for criticism of government policies and of economic liberalism. The state's inability to pay wages and pensions to millions of people gave rise to further criticism. Opinion polls at times during 1995 showed Zyuganov to be the most popular Russian politician, whereas Yeltsin's popularity rating declined to less than 10%.

The findings of the opinion polls were borne out by the results of the election of 17 December 1995 to a new State Duma, elected this time for four years. The CPRF became the largest party, winning 22.7% of the popular vote and 157 out of 450 seats. Another 30 directly elected single-member seats went to the allied Agrarian Party and other left-wing groupings. Zhirinovskii's LDPR came second, with 11.2% of the votes cast and 51 seats. Only 10.1% of the votes cast were won by OHR, but, owing to its success in directly elected constituencies, it represented the second-largest grouping in the Duma, with 55 seats. Yeltsin's Government was, thus, isolated in parliament, and it became clear that if the CPRF followed its victory with similar success in the June 1996 presidential election, it would be able to effect a significant change in Russia's future policies.

In the six months between the legislative and the presidential elections Yeltsin became increasingly populist, adopting policies that were almost indistinguishable from those of the CPRF. In January 1996 he dismissed the remaining liberal reformists in his administration (including the First Deputy Chairman with responsibility for the economy, Anatolii Chubais). None the less, the majority of Russians, although they remained disillusioned with Yeltsin, began to regard him as the only candidate with a chance of preventing a communist return to power and, as a result, his opinion-poll ratings rose dramatically during the first half of 1996.

In the presidential election of 16 June 1996 Yeltsin secured 35% of the votes cast and Zyuganov 32%. As neither had obtained the required overall majority, a second round of voting was scheduled for 3 July. During the interim period, Yeltsin formed an alliance with the third-placed candidate, Lt-Gen. (retd) Aleksandr Lebed, whom Yeltsin appointed as Secretary of the Security Council. Lebed had attained public prominence as commander of the Russian 14th Army in the separatist Transnistria region of Moldova in 1992–95, and had obtained some 15% of the votes cast, largely owing to his outspoken criticism of Russia's crime and corruption problems and of the war in Chechnya. Yeltsin's obvious absence from public life during the last week of June gave rise to renewed concern over his state of health. Nevertheless, on 3 July he won 53.8% of the votes cast (compared with 40.3% for Zyuganov) and became independent Russia's first directly elected head of state.

By the time of Yeltsin's inauguration on 9 August 1996 the President had already moderated some of his more populist positions of the previous months and had dismissed the most anti-democratic members of his administration. Moreover, some reformists, among them Chubais, reappeared in office. Gen. Lebed, a plain-speaking populist, quickly moved to establish himself. He won respect by negotiating an end to the conflict in Chechnya, which was increasingly proving unwinnable for the federal Government. It was agreed that the federal troops would withdraw, and the question of Chechnya's ultimate status would be deferred for five years. In December the troops pulled out, and in January 1997 the Chechen military commander, Khalid 'Aslan' Maskhadov, was elected President of the republic. The war had cost tens of thousands of lives and left the republic almost entirely in ruins, but heading for *de facto* independence.

Lebed was removed from office in October 1996, following his public criticism of President Yeltsin. Shortly after his dismissal, a prominent business executive, Boris Berezovskii, was appointed Deputy Secretary of the Security Council. His political influence with Chernomyrdin and Yeltsin grew rapidly, making him the first of a group of so-called 'oligarchs'—

powerful business tycoons or plutocrats—who came to shape Russian politics in the latter half of the 1990s. Berezovskii bought a major stake in the former state-owned television channel, ORT, and several newspapers. Using a variety of what were often considered dubious business practices, a number of 'oligarchs', including the head of Oneximbank, Vladimir Potanin (who became Deputy Prime Minister), and the banking and industrial magnates, Mikhail Khodorkovskii and Roman Abramovich, built up massive fortunes, much of it contained in foreign bank accounts. Between them, the 'oligarchs' controlled much of the country's natural resources, including its petroleum and gas reserves, which were sold off in the mid-1990s, and they came to exercise great influence over the Government, the economy and the media. Berezovskii's support, for example, was believed by many to have been critical in securing Yeltsin's election victory.

The 'oligarchs' were only the most visible part of a huge clandestine and, often, criminal system that gained a hold over the Russian economy. Many businesses paid as much to 'mafia' (mafiya) gangs for 'protection' (krysha—literally meaning 'roof') as they did to the tax authorities. Organized crime, in addition to complex and ever-changing taxation rules, served as a deterrent to all but the most audacious foreign companies contemplating investing in the new Russia. (Organized crime is discussed in more detail in an article in Part One—General Survey.)

President Yeltsin, his health so weakened that he had to undergo major heart bypass surgery in November 1996, appeared for several months to have little control over events, and retreated further and further from public life. At times, the 'oligarchs' held sway; at others, reformists such as Chubais and Boris Nemtsov, a pioneering young reformist and Governor of Nizhnii Novgorod, both of whom became first deputy premiers in 1997.

At the beginning of 1998 Yeltsin returned to his duties with more vigour and embarked on the first of two years of constant government reshuffles, intended, apparently, not only to improve the economy, but also to identify a possible successor. In March the President's unexpected dismissal of Chernomyrdin and the entire Government was widely interpreted as an attempt to reassert his authority. Chernomyrdin was replaced by a relatively unknown figure, the Minister of Fuel and Energy, Sergei Kiriyenko, who was immediately presented with the threat of economic collapse in Russia, largely owing to the combined effects of a decline in world petroleum prices and the Asian financial crisis that year. Kiriyenko introduced austerity measures designed to reduce government spending by around 25%, and in July Western governments responded by granting a total of US $22,600m. in aid, on condition that certain political requirements were met.

This failed to quell a widespread lack of confidence in the Russian currency, however, and on 17 August 1998, despite assurances by President Yeltsin to the contrary, the rouble was effectively devalued, precipitating a major financial crisis. (At the beginning of January a new rouble, equivalent to 1,000 old roubles, had already been introduced.) The market was paralyzed by liquidity shortages, share prices plunged, and Russia defaulted on its foreign loans. Six days later Yeltsin dismissed Kiriyenko and reinstated Chernomyrdin as acting premier. Far from being perceived as a reliable figure who would bring about economic stability, however, Chernomyrdin was held largely responsible for the crisis, and his appointment was twice rejected by the Duma. A compromise candidate, the hitherto Minister of Foreign Affairs, and a former foreign-intelligence chief, Yevgenii Primakov, was finally agreed upon and endorsed as Prime Minister in mid-September.

The following year saw some improvement in the performance of the Russian economy, owing to three factors: Primakov's steady leadership, a sharp increase in the world price for petroleum (Russia's prime export) and the devaluation of the rouble, which made imports much more expensive and, thus, encouraged domestic production. As a result, substantially more domestically produced merchandise began to appear on the market. None the less, in May 1999 Primakov, too, was abruptly dismissed by Yeltsin. His successor, Sergei Stepashin, hitherto the Minister of Internal Affairs, remained in office for less than three months. In August Yeltsin dismissed Stepashin and appointed the relatively unknown head of the Federal Security Service (FSB), Vladimir Putin, to the post. The move shocked everyone, but was evidently linked to Yeltsin's quest for a successor: nominating Putin, Yeltsin immediately declared that he eventually wanted Putin to take over from him as President.

Putin was aided in this ambition by a surge of Chechen rebel activity, which he brutally suppressed, with the enthusiastic approval of most Russians. Chechnya had, effectively, been independent since 1997, but even sympathetic Russians were horrified by what had happened there: elements of *Shari'a* (Islamic religious law) had been introduced, and hostage-taking and, on occasion, the murder of foreign aid workers, journalists and others had led the separatist republic to become widely regarded as a focus for terrorism and organized crime. In August 1999 a group of Islamist militants based in Chechnya invaded the neighbouring republic of Dagestan (Daghestan); Putin responded vigorously and had them driven out. Moreover, in late August and September more than 300 people were killed in a series of bomb explosions in Moscow (where two entire apartment blocks were destroyed), in Dagestan, and in Volgodonsk, in Rostov Oblast, southern Russia, all of which Putin attributed to Chechen militant groups. The attacks provided the pretext for Putin to launch a second war, on 23 September, to bring the separatist republic back under the jurisdiction of the Russian Federation—although he always termed the campaign an 'anti-terrorist operation', rather than a war.

Despite the brutality of the campaign, the conflict, unlike the previous one, proved popular among Russians, and Putin's opinion-poll ratings soared. A new party, Unity, was formed to contest the election to the State Duma, which was to be held on 19 December 1999. It was led by Sergei Shoigu, the Minister of Civil Defence, Emergencies and Clean-up Operations, but was, effectively, Putin's political vehicle (although the Prime Minister was not a member of any political party). The party won 72 seats, and the Government also enjoyed the support of the other major groupings represented, in particular, Fatherland—All Russia, an alliance formed by the Mayor of Moscow, Yurii Luzhkov, a grouping of regional governors and the former Prime Minister, Yevgenii Primakov (with 67 seats). The CPRF won 113 seats, compared with the 157 it had previously held. On the basis of these results, Unity quickly negotiated with the CPRF, to share the control of parliamentary committees, so as to ensure a period of co-operation between the Government and the Duma.

Putin was by this time well placed to stand for the presidency, but no one could have anticipated how soon that would happen. On 31 December 1999, unpredictable to the last, Yeltsin suddenly made a televised announcement of his resignation. Putin was to become acting President forthwith, pending an election, which was to be brought forward from July 2000 to 26 March. Thus, the Yeltsin years came to an end. They had seen Russia grow, through a turbulent period of violent political struggle, into a democracy, which, although flawed, seemed strong enough to rule out any return to totalitarianism. Political parties scarcely existed: instead, *ad hoc* groupings came and went, built around one or two strong individuals. However, democratic institutions had taken root, and Yeltsin made no attempt to prolong his period in office.

The economy was still in a lamentable state, and the 'system' was an ugly hybrid of communist leftovers, capitalist excesses and organized crime. Moreover, the uncertainties and hardships had brought about an unprecedented demographic crisis: from 1992 Russia's population began to decline by some 400,000 per year, to around only 146m. at the end of the 1990s; had it not been for the influx of ethnic Russians from other former Soviet republics, this figure would have been even lower. Nevertheless, for all his faults, Boris Yeltsin was likely to be remembered as the man who dragged Russia into a new era.

## THE PUTIN PRESIDENCY

Vladimir Putin had risen from almost total obscurity and remained a mystery to most, even when he assumed power. He had spent almost his entire career in the Committee for State Security (the KGB) and one of its post-Soviet successor organizations, the FSB. In 1990 he returned to Russia from what was then the German Democratic Republic (GDR or 'East' Germany), where he had been working as a foreign agent, and became deputy to the reformist Mayor of St Petersburg, Anatolii Sobchak, before moving to Moscow to work in the Kremlin administration. In 1998 President Yeltsin appointed Putin as head of the FSB, and then as Chairman of the Council of Ministers in August 1999.

Given that few Russians had heard of Putin only one year earlier, and given that he had shown no ambition to become a political leader, his popularity was astounding. It was a result, not only of his apparent determination to resolve the Chechen question, but also of the image he cultivated of strength and directness. He spoke of restoring Russia's status as a world power, of rebuilding a strong state and of reintegrating Russia's regions into a more centralized administration. As acting President, the first decrees he signed generally concerned the security system and armed forces. He undertook to rebuild an army that had been demoralized and underfunded over the previous decade, and increased spending on arms procurement by 50%. In January 2000 he signed a new Concept on National Security, which lowered the threshold at which Russia might use nuclear weapons—not, as previously, 'in the case of a threat to the very existence of the Russian Federation as a sovereign state', but 'to repel armed aggression if all other means of resolving a crisis situation have been exhausted or prove to be ineffective'.

Putin secured victory in the first round of the presidential election on 26 March 2000. He won 53% of the votes cast, defeating his nearest rival, Gennadii Zyuganov (with 29%), and nine other contenders. His election slogan was 'Dictatorship of the Law', appealing to the longing of many Russians for a strong hand to re-establish the rule of law and combat crime. Putin's first year as President, however, seemed to be beset by misfortune. In early August the *Kursk* nuclear submarine sank in the Barents Sea, with the loss of 118 lives. The President's initial response—he refused to return from his holiday, and declined Western offers of help, which it was thought might have saved lives—was judged by many Russians to be callous, and his popularity declined. Later in the month, a huge fire partly destroyed the Ostankino television tower in Moscow, a symbol of Soviet achievement. For many, the two events symbolized the scale of the legacy that Putin had inherited, as Soviet-era accomplishments neared the end of their viability.

Serious concerns were raised by what was widely regarded as a concerted attempt to impose control on the critical mass media, in particular those companies owned by Vladimir Gusinskii's Mediya-MOST group and those associated with Berezovskii, following Putin's election as President. In April 2001 the only independent national television station, NTV, was taken over by the state-controlled natural gas monopoly,

Gazprom, and its senior journalists were dismissed. This was followed by the editorial take-over of Gusinskii's other outlets—the influential daily newspaper, *Segodnya* (Today), and the weekly news magazine, *Itogi* (Results)—both of which had, hitherto, been fiercely independent and critical of the Government. These measures were considered to be a demonstration of Putin's stated determination to limit the powers of the 'oligarchs'. Ultimately, both Gusinskii and Berezovskii (whose financial assistance had contributed to Putin's election victory) left the country, after warrants were issued for their arrest, on corruption charges, in Russia. However, media sources that represented a vocal source of opposition to government policies encountered further pressure, which resulted in, *inter alia*, the closure in 2002, purportedly on financial grounds, of the TV station TV6, to which many of the former journalists of NTV had transferred. Its successor, TVS, was, in turn, compelled to cease broadcasting in June 2003, and was replaced by a sports channel. The loss of Russia's last privately owned national television network, again officially because of financial and management difficulties, was regarded by many as a reverse for press diversity. All the remaining national stations were, to a greater or lesser degree, pro-Government in their coverage. New media laws, introduced in mid-2003, introduced strict regulations relating to the coverage of election campaigns, although it remained unclear how, or whether, these regulations would be implemented in practice, prior to the elections to the State Duma due to be held in December 2003, and the elections to the federal presidency in March 2004.

Politically, Putin tried to tackle the centrifugal forces that had threatened to tear Russia apart under Yeltsin's rule. In mid-2000 Putin announced the establishment of seven federal districts (okrugs), each headed by a presidential representative (five of whom had been recruited from the military and security services), whose task was to co-ordinate federal and regional laws and restore a measure of central control. The governors of the Federation's 89 members lost their *ex officio* seats in the upper chamber of parliament, the Federation Council, and had their power further reduced by the reallocation of tax revenues, which awarded a larger proportion to the centre and less to the regions. A major overhaul of the judicial system was initiated, and new criminal and administrative law codes came into effect at the beginning of July 2002. These codes envisaged the introduction of trials by jury (provided for by the 1993 Constitution, but never fully implemented); removed some powers from prosecutors, including the authority to order arrests; and strengthened the independence of judges. (It was expected that the vast majority of Russia's 89 administrative regions would introduce trials by jury, albeit in many cases only for the most serious crimes, in 2003.) It was hoped that corruption would be reduced by changing the system used for selecting judges, by raising their salaries and by ending their lifetime tenure.

The issue of restoring peace and federal order in Chechnya appeared certain to remain a long-term problem, however, as federal forces struggled to impose their control over a severely war-damaged region and a largely hostile population, while under constant attack from rebel fighters. Meanwhile, bomb attacks across Russia, primarily in southern regions and in Moscow, attributed to Chechen militants, which had occurred intermittently since the late 1990s, became more widespread and devastating, with the increasing use of suicide attacks in the early 2000s. Putin, in particular, became increasingly outspoken about the purported links of Chechen rebels with international Islamist militant groups, frequently seeking to portray the military operations in Chechnya as part of the US-led international 'war on terrorism'. In the most audacious attack to date, in October 2002 a group of heavily armed militants, led by the Chechen rebel Movsar Barayev, held some 800 people hostage in a theatre in Moscow. After three days, élite special forces stormed the theatre, killing all 41 rebels; some 129 theatre-goers also died, the vast majority apparently from exposure to an incapacitating gas used by the special forces. However, despite ongoing insecurity in the republic, the Government insisted that it sought a political settlement in Chechnya. On 23 March 2003 a referendum was held in Chechnya, with three questions, on the introduction of a new constitution for the republic, and on the eventual holding of elections to the republican presidency and legislature. With participation in the plebiscite officially reported at almost 90%, and with a positive response in excess of 95% reported to each of the three questions, the Government expressed satisfaction with the outcome of its policies in the republic. None the less, international observers cast doubt on the referendum's legitimacy and value. Meanwhile, alleged human rights violations by Russian troops, and attacks by Chechen rebels continued. Suicide bombers destroyed the republican government headquarters in the Chechen capital, Groznyi, in December 2002, and 15 people were killed in a suicide attack at a music festival outside Moscow in July 2003. None the less, at the end of August control of paramilitary operations in Chechnya was formally transferred from the Federal Security Service (FSB) to the Ministry of Internal Affairs, and it was announced that such operations were no longer regarded as counter-terrorist activities, but rather as a means 'to protect law and constitutional order'. On 5 October 2003 Akhmed haji Kadyrov, a former rebel leader and mufti, who had been appointed to head the republican administration by Putin in mid-2000, won the presidential election held in the republic by a substantial majority, although several candidates regarded as his principal rivals had withdrawn, or had been obliged to withdraw from the contest. In this context it remained uncertain as to whether Kadyrov's presidency would be regarded as legitimate within the republic, and some commentators expressed concern that an intra-Chechen conflict could evolve.

Meanwhile, the economy, under the guidance of Prime Minister Mikhail Kasyanov, made steady progress. Tax reform, aimed at bolstering the state's finances by reducing tax evasion, introduced a fixed, uniform rate of personal income tax (of 13%) from the beginning of January 2001. Helped by the 1998 devaluation of the rouble and, in particular, by high world petroleum prices, steady economic growth was recorded in 2000–02. With the CPRF increasingly marginalized in the Duma, largely as the result of enhanced co-operation between the two centrist, pro-presidential factions, Fatherland-All Russia and Unity (which merged in 2002 to form a new party, Unity and Fatherland—United Russia), the Government was able to revive or renew economic reforms originally envisaged under the radical programme begun in 1991, and still welcomed by foreign investors. A new Labour Code, introduced in February 2002, gave recognition to private employment, and a reformed Land Code, approved by the Duma in September 2001, permitted the sale and purchase of urban plots of land for the first time since the 1920s. In June 2002 these provisions were extended to include agricultural land, finally ending the era of communist collectivization—although foreign ownership of farmland remained proscribed. In the same month, with around 70% of the economy estimated to be in the private sector, the European Union and the US Department of Commerce officially designated Russia a 'market economy'. More and more ordinary Russians were exposed to the rigours of the market in 2003, thanks to a 'communal reform', which encouraged local authorities to reduce subsidies for domestic power, heating and building maintenance.

Abroad, Putin was widely regarded as determined to reintegrate Russia into the world's political and economic system, but few—including his own advisers—expected the apparently radical reversal of Russian foreign policy that followed the suicide attacks of 11 September 2001 on the US cities of New York and Washington, DC. Putin immediately declared Russia's full support for the US-led 'anti-terrorist' coalition formed in the aftermath of the attacks (attributed to the Islamist al-Qa'ida—Base—organization of Osama bin Laden), and offered logistical support and intelligence to the USA when military operations against Afghanistan (the Taliban regime of which was harbouring al-Qa'ida militants) commenced in October. Putin gave tacit approval to the stationing of US and allied troops at former Soviet bases in Central Asia and, in mid-2002, to the dispatch of US military instructors to Georgia. The *rapprochement* with the USA went further. Putin abandoned his opposition to plans by the US President, George W. Bush, to abrogate the 1972 Anti-Ballistic Missiles (ABM) Treaty, in order to develop a space-based anti-missile shield. (None the less, Putin stated that he would have preferred to renegotiate the Treaty, from which the USA formally withdrew in June 2002.) Putin also appeared to override widespread domestic objections to the eastward expansion of the North Atlantic Treaty Organization (NATO), and in late May he signed an historic treaty in Rome, Italy, which established a new NATO-Russia Council, and awarded Russia equal influence with the 19 full members of NATO, on a range of issues, such as counter-terrorism, peace-keeping and arms control, and replaced the more limited Permanent Joint Council that had been established in 1997. There were limits, however, to Putin's acquiescence to US foreign policy. In January 2002 Bush controversially identified Iran, Iraq and the Democratic People's Republic of Korea (North Korea) as forming an 'axis of evil', said to sponsor terrorism and to be involved in the development and proliferation of weapons of mass destruction. Despite this, Russia continued to assist Iran with the construction of a nuclear power plant, and played host to the North Korean leader, Kim Jong Il. Subsequently, as the crisis over Iraq's alleged refusal to rid itself of weapons of mass destruction intensified in 2002, and the USA and the United Kingdom prepared to launch military action in Iraq, with the aim of removing from power the regime of Iraqi President Saddam Hussain, Russia supported other European anti-war states, notably France and Germany. Russia's defiance of US policy in Iraq appeared to reflect Putin's unease over increasing US domination of world affairs, as well as his need to retain the support of the public at home, the vast majority of whom were opposed to the conflict.

Even the rift over Iraq failed to cause serious damage to US-Russian relations, however, and Putin's first three-and-a-half years in office brought Russia considerably closer to the West. At a meeting of the Group of Eight (G-8) nations (comprising the seven leading industrial economies, plus Russia), in Kananaskis, Canada, in June 2002, Russia was asked to host the summit meeting due to be held in 2006—an indication of formal recognition of Russia's full participation in the Group. It appeared that most Western Governments regarded Putin as a confident and competent politician, who had brought relative stability to the country and made significant progress towards sealing its place in the world. New legislative elections were to be held in December 2003, and presidential elections were to take place in March 2004. By mid-2003, and in the absence of any credible challenger, opinion polls suggested that Putin could expect to be re-elected, with a comfortable majority, for a further four-year term as President.

# The Economy

## Prof. PHILIP HANSON

### INTRODUCTION

Since the last years of communism the Russian economy has experienced periods of both deep decline and steady growth. Production fell precipitously for the 10 years from 1989, before reviving strongly in the early 2000s. The decline in economic activity in Russia during the 1990s was one of the most dramatic economic collapses ever experienced by a large country. The Russian State Committee of Statistics series for gross domestic product (GDP) at constant prices showed a decline in 1989–98 of about 45%. This collapse in output in the 1990s was, in reality, somewhat less dramatic than the official data reported. Nevertheless, output and income certainly declined, while the attempt to change the Russian economic system from centrally administered socialism to market capitalism was implemented in a confused and confusing fashion.

It was important politically that the true decline in the population's economic welfare during the decade was less than the GDP figures implied. First, state-enterprise managers had previously overstated their output in order to qualify for plan-fulfilment bonuses. This incentive to exaggerate output figures disappeared with the abandonment of central planning. Second, some of the output actually produced before the changes was an unwanted side-effect of the planning system, the loss of which caused no reduction in welfare. Third, some of the loss of output was a loss of military production, which made no contribution to consumption or the growth of capital stock. Fourth, there was a far greater decline in investment than in consumption; although potentially damaging for future prosperity, this entailed no immediate loss to the population. Fifth, the movement of prices towards market equilibrium levels meant a reduction in shortages and, therefore, in time spent queuing—a welfare gain not reflected in output figures. Finally, the private sector's output was inadequately reported in the official statistics and was more dynamic than that of the state sector. The new, private firms were increasing output rapidly, albeit from very low levels. Other important, long-established private-sector activities, such as household production of food (which was extensive among the urban as well as the rural population), had always been important and under-represented; such production declined only slightly, or even increased.

For these reasons, the decline in officially measured output suggested a more desperate situation than actually prevailed. Substantial numbers of people who started their own businesses, or were employed in the private sector, or who had other new opportunities created by the changes, actually benefited. At the same time, however, economic conditions became more uncertain for everyone, and some sections of the population, particularly large families with low incomes, experienced a significant deterioration in their standard of living. Moreover, many of Russia's 'entrepreneurs' were members of criminal gangs, which operated an illegal ('black') market with a level of violence hitherto unknown in Russian cities.

In any event, Russian society somehow coped with drastic and disturbing economic change until the financial crisis of August 1998, after which the economy began a recovery that lasted into 2003. In 1999–2002 annual GDP growth averaged more than 6%. By 2003, although a slightly lower rate of growth, of 5%, was projected, the upturn in economic activity could no longer be discounted as merely a brief respite in an inexorable decline. On the contrary, the recovery was beginning to look sustainable. Business confidence in Russia was strong.

The Government could take some of the credit for this recovery, although other factors proved more significant. It began as an unintended consequence of the forced devaluation of the rouble in mid-1998. In a society more resistant to radical economic reforms than those of the former communist states of Central Europe or the Baltic states, in the 1990s Russian policy-makers struggled to implement coherent transformation measures such as the liberalization of markets, the implementation of monetary and fiscal austerity and privatization. By 1998 Russia's economic system had been radically altered, but many problems remained. Around 70% of output was credited to the private sector; however, privatization had been mainly to 'insiders', foreign direct investment remained limited and informal state intervention continued to be pervasive. Moreover, the banks and stock markets were underdeveloped and, although inflation had been reduced, the public-finance budget was consistently in deficit. It was these failures of fiscal policy that were significant factors in creating the financial crisis of 1998. Additionally, the Government effectively maintained a large and thinly disguised subsidy to all sectors of the economy, and in particular manufacturing, by ensuring that the domestic prices of petroleum products and fuels were kept artificially low. In consequence, overall, competition did not operate freely in either product or capital markets.

Thus, for much of the 1990s the real economy was not adjusting successfully to the financial pressures of monetary stabilization. Loss-making state and privatized enterprises remained open even when the prospect of their recovery was minimal. They did this, in part, by simply not paying employees, suppliers and taxes and, in part, by using barter deals and money surrogates to 'settle' some of their debts. Arrears of payment to electricity companies and by them, in turn, to the monopoly supplier of natural gas, Gazprom—both groups of creditors were partly state-owned—accounted for a large part of the total. Gazprom and the regional electricity companies, therefore, also fell behind in their tax payments. Federal and regional governments conspired to prolong this dangerous situation by allowing tax arrears to accumulate and failing to establish effective procedures for bankruptcy. Two main groups of immediate losers emerged from this state of affairs: workers with wage arrears; and the public provision of health, education and other services, which were under pressure from chronic budget problems, as well as the adverse consequences of the widespread non-payment of wages in these sectors.

In 1997–98 Russia's precarious 'virtual' economy began to feel the effects of the financial crisis in Asia. The IMF had persuaded the Russian Government to open debt markets (chiefly for treasury bills) to foreign investors. With problems in other emerging markets, these investors began to pay more attention to the fragile state of Russian public finances, and to fear a rouble devaluation. This meant that the interest rate on rouble-denominated Russian debt, having been reduced to 20%–25%, began to increase again, raising debt-servicing costs still further and threatening the 1998 budget. Eventually, in July 1998 Western governments, acting chiefly through the IMF, agreed to an emergency loan amounting to US $22,600m. (although this included money from previous loans that had not been disbursed). This agreement helped to stabilize the markets for a while, although it failed to guarantee the resolution of fundamental problems within the

economy. Such efforts, however, were overtaken by the financial crisis of August.

The financial crisis forced an unforeseen and unintended major devaluation of the rouble, which declined dramatically in value against the US dollar; prior to the crisis, from mid-1995, the rouble exchange rate had been maintained in a 'corridor', which shifted downwards only slowly. Many feared that the huge devaluation would trigger a resurgence of the high levels of inflation that had characterized the economy in the early 1990s. In fact, however, the devaluation served to benefit the manufacturing sector. Previously unable to compete with imported food, clothing and engineering goods, Russian producers suddenly found that their foreign competitors had been priced out of the Russian market.

The revival of production was startling. In 1999 the economy received further encouragement from an increase in world petroleum prices, leading to official GDP growth of 10.0% in 2000. Although the rate of growth declined to 5.0% in 2001—a rate that President Vladimir Putin described as inadequate—it appeared that the economy was not lapsing into stagnation. Although growth might not have meant catching up with the developed world as rapidly as an ambitious leader would have liked, there were, none the less, indications that the economy was moving in the right direction. By 2001 the sustained economic recovery could no longer be ascribed simply to the devaluation or regarded as an adjunct of high petroleum prices. Although these factors had undoubtedly played their part in initiating the recovery, domestic demand had subsequently become the driving force behind this growth. In 2001, although the balance of trade declined, total demand continued to rise, fuelled by strong increases in household consumption and domestic investment. Remarkably, fixed investment, which had plummeted for most of the 1990s, rose by some 13% in 2000 and by almost 10.3% in 2001.

As economic performance improved, so did the implementation of economic reforms. From 2000, when he took office, President Putin and his Government displayed, with increasing clarity, a determination to advance reform, aided by a more compliant parliament than those with which President Boris Yeltsin's governments had contended in the 1990s. Legislation that sought to simplify the tax system and reduce the official tax burden on companies and individuals (while simultaneously intending to reduce the high rate of tax evasion) was approved in 2001–03. This led to the introduction of a uniform tax rate (of 13%) on all personal incomes above a certain threshold, a reduction in profit tax from 35% to 24%, and a reduction in value-added tax (VAT—to take effect from the beginning of 2004) to 18%. Another innovation was the introduction, in 2001–02, of laws that, for the first time in more than 70 years, permitted the sale and purchase of land. Bankruptcy law was revised, after earlier legislation was exploited to obtain assets at artificially low prices. The difficult process of reforming the monopolies in electricity and, to a lesser extent, in gas, was embarked upon, and radical reform of the judicial system was initiated. However, the transfer to majority private ownership of the petroleum company, Slavneft, in late 2002, which raised some US $1,700m., prompted fresh concerns over the degree of transparency in the privatization process; six bidders were disqualified or forced to withdraw from the auction in conditions that remained largely opaque, while the proceeds of the sale were substantially below the Audit Chamber of the State Duma's estimate of the company's value, of $3,000m. From the beginning of Putin's term as President, regional governors were subject to closer monitoring by the presidential administration, as part of measures to reassert central political control and enhance what Putin described as 'vertical power'. Given that much state interference in business in Russia since the 1990s had originated at sub-national levels of administration, it appeared that any weakening of those regional authorities was potentially beneficial for the economy. Although these pieces of legislation contained no guarantees of economic success and, moreover, required effective implementation, many observers suggested that the Russian business environment was improving in the early 2000s.

Meanwhile Russian economic liberals, including the former Minister of the Economy, Yevgenii Yasin, and President Putin's adviser, Andrei Illarionov, continued to stress the urgency of further reform, arguing that economic growth could be sustained at an annual rate of around 8% if the burden of the state on the economy were systematically reduced. In particular, they wanted government taxation and spending to be reduced from around 37% of GDP to around 30%, government regulation of business to be reduced, remaining state stakes in enterprises to be diminished, housing subsidies reduced, the military and the bureaucracy reformed, and the ongoing reforms of the electricity and gas sectors to be accelerated and made more systematic.

## GROSS DOMESTIC PRODUCT

In addition to the statistical problems already noted in the post-communist period, the statistical reporting system that existed was generally rather weak. An extremely rapid increase in consumer prices, as well as substantial changes in the composition of output, presented that system with challenges that would have proved difficult to meet for more advanced statistical offices. The figures that are quoted here must, therefore, be treated with some caution.

At current prices, GDP amounted to 10,863,400m. roubles in 2002. Services, rather than goods, constituted more than one-half of that figure (54%), representing a substantial change from the Soviet era. Distribution of GDP by end-use did not change so dramatically in the early post-communist period, although investment began to account for somewhat less of the total than in Soviet times. In 2002 household consumption was estimated at 50% of total GDP, and gross fixed investment was estimated at 18%. Government spending on goods and services (but excluding social benefits) was about 17%. Changes in inventories and net exports made up the balance. In real terms (that is, adjusting for inflation), gross fixed investment had declined particularly steeply (by about 76% in 1991–98). This decline in gross investment (i.e. including depreciation), at a time when much of the Russian capital stock was becoming obsolete, meant that the capital stock was decreasing—only slightly, according to the official data; quite substantially, according to one alternative estimate. The subsequent recovery of investment was, therefore, from a dangerously low level; for sustained rapid economic growth, it was widely agreed, the share of fixed investment in GDP needed to substantially exceed its recent average of around 18%.

## AGRICULTURE

State and collective farms had played their part in the downfall of the Soviet regime. The stagnation of Soviet agricultural output after 1978 (after a period of substantial growth) was a significant factor in the general deterioration of morale in the USSR towards the end of Leonid Brezhnev's rule. This, together with a new readiness to import grain when domestic supplies were low, had allowed a general improvement in the diet of Soviet citizens, although labour productivity remained pitifully low by Western European standards. The end of that improvement, during the early 1980s resulted in an absolute decline in food consumption per head. Retail food prices were kept artificially low, while costs rose and availability in many cities fell. Local food rationing was widespread in 1981–84.

Despite the severity of the problem, the Soviet approach to agricultural reform was notoriously more cautious and less effective than in the People's Republic of China. In communist China, from the late 1970s agricultural land was effectively re-privatized and peasant farming was allowed, even encouraged, to flourish. In the USSR, however, reform, when it came, was focused on industry, rather than agriculture. In the countryside very little changed.

The reasons for the lack of reform in agriculture seem to have been political. The Communist Party apparatus in the countryside was especially resistant to change. So too, and less predictably, was the rural population. Opinion surveys around 1989–90 tended to find that the privatization of farmland was supported by a majority of city-dwellers, but not by a majority of rural residents. That, in turn, may have been connected with the characteristics of the Soviet farm labour force. For many years the agricultural sector had been given low priority. The social infrastructure in rural areas was weaker than in the cities. Pay and working conditions in most regions were less favourable, and young and enterprising people had left the land in large numbers over several generations. As a result, the farm labour force was comprised disproportionately of older people and women. Their expectations were, typically, low and their scepticism about any government reforms was profound.

Following the appointment of Mikhail Gorbachev as General Secretary of the Communist Party of the Soviet Union in 1985, and the introduction of the reforms known as *perestroika* (restructuring), there was a relaxation of the restrictions on the subsidiary household plots that most rural and many urban households possessed. However, the prime constituent of the agricultural sector, the giant state and collective farms, was barely affected, and tentative attempts to give greater independence to workers over particular areas of land had no discernible effect.

The Russian Federation inherited about 26,000 Soviet state and collective farms. Some 11m. people were employed on them, an average of more than 400 per farm. Under Gorbachev, some experiments had shown that a few peasant families, working on their own and appropriately motivated, could easily outperform these giant farms in the livestock sector. So far as crop production was concerned, the advantage of a much smaller size was less obvious, but there was little doubt that efficient large farms would employ far fewer people than were working on Russian state and collective farms.

The Russian Government's policy, announced in December 1991, was to require all state and collective farms to hold meetings of their employees in early 1992, at which decisions would be taken on the future form of organization of the farm. In this way, the most radical and politically provocative option, namely, enforcing the disbanding of these 'socialized' farms, was avoided. By the end of the year more than three-quarters of the farms had taken their decision and been re-registered. About one-third of these, some 7,000 farms, had opted to retain their previous status as a collective or a state farm. Another 9,000 had elected to be registered as companies and 1,700 as farm co-operatives. In practice, very little changed in the organization of these farms.

It was officially reported that only one in five peasants in the re-registered farms had proceeded to transform their 'share' in the original collective into an independent peasant farm. The reallocation of land to facilitate the creation of private farms was the responsibility either of the former state- or collective-farm management or of the local council. Both were usually traditionalist in orientation and did little to help the new independent farmers. For similar reasons, supplies of machinery, fertilizer, seed, etc., for the new private sector were problematic.

A hard-fought struggle ensued between reformers and traditionalists over the crucial question of property rights in land. Land in agricultural use tended to be treated in legislation as a category separate from other land, such as urban real estate, and was an area of particular contention. In the new Russian Constitution of December 1993, President Yeltsin managed to have an article inserted that made individual ownership of land a basic right of Russian citizens. To give legislative effect to the intention behind this, however, additional laws and regulations were needed, concerning such matters as the acquisition of private plots of land from existing farms and the sale and purchase of land. These were contested successfully in the Russian parliament over the following eight years. A reform to the land code, approved by the Duma in September 2001, finally permitted the sale and purchase of urban real estate across the Federation. In June 2002 similar legislation was passed approving the sale of agricultural land, although restrictions on foreign ownership remained in place.

In early 1993 there were 184,000 peasant farms, occupying some 3%–4% of Russian farmland. Thereafter, many private farming ventures were abandoned, as financial circumstances in the sector continued to worsen. Nevertheless, the scale of the new, private sector continued, on balance, to increase, albeit slowly. At the same time, the long-established household subsidiary plots were being increased in size and various pre-existing 'kitchen garden' associations in urban areas were also being encouraged. By 1997 these two sources of private food production occupied only around 10% of farmland but, according to official statistics, accounted for 91% of the country's production of potatoes, 76% of green vegetables, 55% of meat and 67% of milk. By 1998 the private sector accounted for almost 60% of farm output. This combination of private farming and horticulture was devoted mainly to subsistence production for the extended families of the households that worked the plots of land in question. In the late 1990s private agricultural businesses began to develop, often under the guise, for tax purposes, of a group of apparently separate household plots. In 2000–03 some large Russian businesses began to buy farmland, prior to the implementation of the new land code, although it was uncertain whether these purchases were chiefly made for speculative purposes or for the development of agro-businesses.

In the short term, the administrative problems encountered by the private farms and household plots were less important than the deteriorating 'terms of trade' that confronted the sector. It could be roughly estimated that in 1989–97 farm prices rose so much less than non-farm prices that the terms of trade between the farm sector and the rest of the economy declined by about 72%. Thus, farmers and farm-workers saw their ability to buy both consumer goods and farm inputs of machinery, fertilizers, fuel, etc., decline sharply. This led to a fall in industrial inputs, with a negative impact on farm output, and a growth in farm debt. State subsidies to the farm sector did little to offset this. In 1992 farm subsidies totalled 3.6% of GDP. From 1995 policy-makers made a concerted effort to resist the traditional pressure for budgetary subsidies for the farms at sowing and harvesting seasons (much of the money went missing), and by 2001 explicit farm subsidies from the federal budget were equivalent to only 0.5% of GDP. Some support continued from regional and local budgets, but not enough to counter the decline in federal subsidies.

The level of farm subsidies emerged as one of the main negotiating points in Russia's bid to join the World Trade Organization (WTO). Russian negotiators emphasized that the European Union (EU) and the USA subsidized their farmers far more heavily than did Russia. Russia sought approval, in principle, for the right to increase such subsidies in the future, without jeopardizing the likelihood of accession to the WTO, although such measures were, at least initially, resisted by both the EU and the USA. None the less, in June 2002 the EU and the US Department of Commerce finally approved the official designation of Russia as a 'market economy'.

Despite these complications, officially recorded agricultural output declined no more severely in 1989–98 than did industrial production or GDP as a whole—by about 45%. The reduction in agricultural output was concentrated in the livestock sector. The decline in many households' purchasing power produced a shift in the composition of retail food, with greater emphasis on bread and potatoes, and less on meat and milk. When the economy began to grow again after 1998, so did farm production, and at roughly the same rate.

In general, the farming sector in Russia was full of anomalies. By 2003 a market in farmland had still to develop, even though the legislative basis was in place. The sector had been impoverished by the relative movement of agricultural and non-agricultural prices. Subsidies were disappearing. At the same time, farm output had proved to be relatively resilient and, in practice, the private production and distribution of food grew in importance.

## INDUSTRY

Industrial output declined, officially, by about one-half between 1989 and 1998. Within that total, electricity generation fell by only 23% (surprisingly, given the general recorded decline in economic activity); the fuel sector (petroleum, natural gas and coal) by just over one-third; and the chemicals sector, steel and non-ferrous metals by about three-fifths. After 1995 recorded output in the fuel sector remained relatively stable. Steel and non-ferrous metals production, increasingly linked to exports, stabilized and, in 1997 and 1999, slightly increased. The very largest declines were in light industry (footwear, clothing and textiles) and in the engineering sector. Light-industrial output in 1998 was down to about one-eighth of its 1989 level. By 1998 engineering production had declined by more than 70%, but showed signs of recovery in 1999. Broadly, the pattern of change reflected the particularly steep decline in demand for investment goods and the impact of heightened import competition (the latter particularly in light industry).

Those output declines, combined with substantial changes in relative producer prices for different branches of industry, produced a significant change in the composition of industrial output by branch in current prices. In particular, the weight of the fuel and energy sub-sector, plus steel and non-ferrous metals, rose substantially. When Russian critics of the changes spoke of a 'de-industrialization' of Russia, they referred to both the lesser role of industry, as a whole, in the economy and the reduced importance of manufacturing, especially processing, as distinct from extractive industry. The decline in engineering output was particularly emphasized. The underlying problem was that much Russian manufacturing was uncompetitive. At least some of it was 'value-subtracting'—i.e. was unable to be sold as finished output on competitive markets for as much as could be made by selling the materials and energy that had gone into it. This pattern changed somewhat during the post-1998 recovery, as branches of industry hitherto in decline began to revive.

Even the more resilient branches of industry, however, were in trouble in the 1990s. Crude petroleum output in 1999, amounting to about 6.8m. barrels per day (b/d), was little more than one-half of its highest level in 1987. Thereafter, it began to recover, reaching 7.3m. b/d in 2002. Natural gas output, which had earlier risen continuously, albeit at an increasingly slow rate, declined slightly after 1991, and then fluctuated. As a result of the difficulties experienced in the agricultural sector (see above), the agricultural-machinery industry encountered an especially steep decline in demand, although some recovery was apparent in 2001–02.

At the beginning of the transformation process, in 1992–93, Russian production units, still mostly state-owned, did not adapt output to demand as a matter of course. A tendency to continue producing for stock was widely observed. So, too, was a practice of delivering output even to customers likely to be insolvent, and billing them through the banking system in the old way. The implicit assumption in many cases was that either customer or payee would receive assistance from the state. In this way, arrears among enterprises increased sharply, especially in early 1992.

By 1994–95, however, as monetary policy became stricter, privatization proceeded and expectations of direct state financial assistance began to fade, the behaviour of enterprises began to change, but not in a particularly healthy way. Payment arrears remained a substantial problem, especially arrears of payments to the energy sector. It appeared, however, that many manufacturing companies, even after privatization, found ways of surviving that were not part of prescribed economic and business practice. The use of barter increased substantially; by late 1997, according to some surveys, it accounted for as much as 50% of recorded industrial sales. Money surrogates also were increasingly used, especially so-called *veksels* (bills of exchange, used extensively to clear payments along a chain of suppliers, in the absence of bank credit) and tax offsets. Russian producers were also able to accumulate mounting tax arrears and significant arrears in their payment of wages. In 1999–2003 the economy became substantially more monetized. The role of barter, tax offsets and *veksels* declined, although it did not disappear entirely.

Before 1999 many, if not most, industrial enterprises were subject to declines in real demand and the need to make major changes to the quality and range of their products if they were to survive in the long term. None the less, the process of privatization developed fairly rapidly in the industrial sector. In Russia, as in other former communist countries, industrial privatization entailed substantially greater difficulties than the privatization of small-scale non-agricultural concerns, such as shops, cafés, road-haulage businesses and local housing construction. Small-scale, or 'petty', privatization could be carried out by auction sales of the assets to individuals or small partnerships. Many people could raise the money required and, moreover, in such cases the value of the assets was not subject to very great uncertainties, which was frequently not the case in the industrial sector.

The privatization of state industrial enterprises or other large concerns was much more difficult. To begin with, the average industrial enterprise in Russia was very much larger (and encompassed a wider range of social responsibilities) than the average Western industrial plant; small-scale industrial production scarcely existed and it was seldom easy to divide large state enterprises into small units for separate sale. The valuation of such assets was also somewhat vulnerable to uncertainties about prices and government policies. Moreover, the near-absence of bankruptcies in Russia meant that new firms were seldom able to develop by acquiring assets from insolvent enterprises, as happened quite widely in Poland and elsewhere in the former Soviet bloc during the transition to a market economy in the 1990s.

Privatization policy in the Russian Federation was developed mainly by the deputy premier responsible for privatization in 1992–94, Anatolii Chubais. His aim was to achieve rapid, large-scale privatization on the basis of the free issue of privatization vouchers to the entire population. He argued that this would finally detach the enterprises concerned from state control and protection and help to create a new property-owning class that would resist any moves in the direction of the old order. Chubais was well aware of the risks of worker ownership, but saw no politically feasible alternative for securing a rapid change in ownership across a large section of the economy. He contended that disposal mainly to workers and managers at the outset could be followed by a rapid restructuring of ownership through subsequent share-trading, and that any attempt by the Government to dispose of shares to 'outsiders' would be resisted by management and workers alike. Of the options available in Russia's mass 'voucher privatization', the variant that gave at least a 51% 'insider' stake was chosen by the great majority of the enterprises. A further share of 30% of the equity could be sold, albeit on unfavourable terms, at auction.

The phase of voucher privatization of large enterprises continued until mid-1994. By that time almost all vouchers had been used to acquire former state assets, and 15,052 large and medium-sized state enterprises had been privatized, accounting for more than 80% of industrial employment. Meanwhile, small-scale privatization was proceeding, as was the creation of new private firms. By mid-1995 some 100,000 small businesses, many of them shops and cafés, had been privatized. The growth in numbers of new, small firms seemed, however, to slow down after 1995, both in the industrial sector and more widely, and the small-firm sector appeared to be severely restricted.

In general, therefore, formal privatization in Russia developed quite rapidly. There were, however, considerable doubts about the nature of the privatization process in the industrial sector. In particular, it did not appear to be changing enterprise behaviour patterns or leading to a purposeful reorganization of the internal structure of the enterprises concerned. One reason for this was that state enterprises had not undergone a phase of commercialization beforehand, in which they would have had to adjust to strict ('hard') budgetary constraints. Instead, they had been operating in what was still a 'soft' financial environment, i.e. one in which subsidies could still be obtained, and pressures to adapt to competition and customers' choices were weak. In most cases, the management wanted to preserve this situation. The second reason was that the preferential arrangements for workers and managers to gain control of their own enterprises gave them the chance to avoid real change. Studies of enterprises undergoing privatization found that the main force in 'insider' privatization was the desire to defend the 'collective' against other owners, who might reduce the size of the work-force and impose tougher terms on both staff and management. In 1995 it was found that, on average, around 70% of large privatized enterprises were controlled by a combination of worker and manager shareholders. Scope for outside investors to acquire equity was limited, although some banks and individual entrepreneurs were beginning to seek, and in some cases to gain, controlling equity stakes.

From 1995 there was an attempt by the Government to revitalize the privatization process in its second, or 'cash privatization', phase. This involved selling some concerns that were not yet privatized and some of the remaining state equity stakes in others, but for cash, not vouchers. In late 1995 the Government set up a 'shares-for-loans' scheme, under which banks or other lenders would lend to the state, taking state-equity holdings as collateral and obtaining the right to manage that stake for a three-year period. Several shares-for-loans auctions went ahead. The Government and, particularly, the state property committee, was subsequently criticized, however, for allowing several deals to take place, in which certain banks gained valuable equity stakes in petroleum and metals companies at unrealistically low prices, allegedly on an insider basis. The Government did not repay the loans, so that these deals amounted to bargain sales.

In 1997, when further 'cash-privatization' deals were made, the criticism was rather different. In the case at least of the major telecommunications company, Svyazinvest, the sale of a large government-equity stake was competitive, and the eventual price was well above the reserve set before the auction. The groups that lost that and other bids, however, claimed unfair treatment. The Government's group of favoured banks, hitherto united in backing the reformers, now began to dispute among themselves and, in some cases, to attack the Government. In the first half of 1998, in an atmosphere of impending financial crisis, two attempts to sell a large government stake in the one remaining large, state-owned petroleum company, Rosneft, failed to find buyers. This was partly owing to the decline in world petroleum prices, but even a substantial reduction in the reserve price and in the investment conditions attached to the sale failed to produce a buyer.

Thus, in the industrial sector at least, the actual results of privatization were less impressive than the speed with which the first, voucher phase was implemented. Restructuring of enterprises after privatization remained the exception rather than the rule. One indicator of this was the very small number of enforced redundancies, even though voluntary job-changing remained quite high. Equally, there was slow progress in the establishment of an internal structure for industrial firms more appropriate to a market economy, such as the creation of finance and marketing departments.

One reason for the slow pace of restructuring was a dearth of investment funds. There was little bank lending to industry, and almost no new issues on the embryonic stock market. Another reason was that managers, who typically held less than 20% of equity between them, feared that any attempt they might make to reduce the work-force would turn the workers (who, on average, possessed around 40% of the stock) from 'sleeping partners' into active and resentful controllers of the firm. Similarly, the management was typically reluctant to admit major new outside investors.

Some industrial restructuring was beginning to occur, however, by the mid-1990s. There were three main ways in which this tended to happen. One was the active involvement of leading Russian banks. Having made large profits during a time of very high inflation, chiefly from foreign-exchange, inter-bank and treasury-bill markets, the leading banks were looking for other spheres of activity as inflation slowed. Several began to develop industrial and commercial groups. A second channel through which restructuring occurred was the development of new private firms. By October 1997 there were about 130,000 small firms in the industrial sector. They accounted for around one-third of the number of industrial firms (still a low proportion by international standards), and employed about 1.4m. people. The third channel was the acquisition of assets by foreign companies and, in a few cases, their creation of completely new concerns. Foreign-investor involvement was strongly resisted in the petroleum and gas sectors. Here existing insiders knew that they held extremely valuable assets, and chose to believe that they would do better without foreign partners. Foreign investment was, however, beginning to play an important part in a number of other sectors, including the tobacco industry.

From 1999 the reshaping of Russian industry entered a new phase. Most commercial banks were severely affected by the financial crisis of 1998. Bank lending to producers was even more limited than before, and bank-led industrial groups tended to fade, as those affiliated to energy and natural-resource firms, such as Gazprom, LUKoil and Yukos appeared in the ascendancy. Two factors combined to accelerate restructuring. First, higher international prices for petroleum products, natural gas and metals served to increase the profits of Russia's large natural-resource exporting firms. Second, the

recovery of sectors such as clothing, food-processing and engineering, following the devaluation, made their assets more attractive than had hitherto been the case. As the large natural-resource-based industrial groups began to purchase 'downstream' assets in the manufacturing sector, the previous owners began to lose control: one study found that such 'insiders' owned less than one-half of industrial equity by 2000. Potentially, this development could have extremely important consequences for the Russian economy: if the wealthy natural-resource businesses develop sufficiently their recently acquired manufacturing businesses, a substantial flow of resources into these previously debilitated sectors could ensue. While effective capital markets continue to be absent in Russia, such acquisitions may prove the most effective means of permitting finance to flow between different industrial sectors. At the same time, however, bank lending to producers was beginning to develop, albeit from very low levels. At 1 April 2003 bank lending to firms and households had increased by 17%, in real terms, compared with one year earlier.

## FOREIGN TRADE AND PAYMENTS

For Russia, the meaning of the term 'foreign trade' became ambiguous when the USSR disintegrated at the end of 1991. After that, by convention, only Russia's trade outside the former USSR was treated as 'foreign', while transactions with other former Soviet republics of the so-called 'near abroad' were treated, for a time, as a special category. This was reasonable at first, when the former Soviet states were still sharing a single currency. From the second half of 1992, however, it was a questionable practice. The two external markets began to be treated together in the statistics, but payments continued to be handled differently. Ukraine, for example, accumulated large unpaid bills for Russian natural gas deliveries, while also incurring the wrath of Gazprom through its unauthorized 'siphoning' of gas in transit across Ukrainian territory to Central and Western European markets.

In July 1993 Russia effectively ended the rouble zone by the withdrawal of pre-1993 currency and by setting credit limits for each of the other former Soviet countries in their trade with Russia. Separate currencies were eventually established in all the successor states of the USSR. All the Commonwealth of Independent States (CIS) countries, however, were economically distressed, to varying degrees. Russian trade was increasingly redirected to markets beyond the former USSR.

Russia's foreign trade declined sharply in 1990–95, before showing signs of recovery. Merchandise exports to all non-Soviet partners amounted to US $81,000m. in 1990, $64,300m. in 1995, and $69,500m. in 1997. Imports decreased to an even greater extent in 1996, and then declined precipitously following devaluation in August 1998, causing the merchandise balance to change from a deficit of $2,000m. in 1990 to a surplus (in trade with all partners) of $36,100m. in 1999, which increased to $60,200m. in 2000, and then narrowed to $48,100m. in 2001 and to $46,300m. in 2002.

This change in trade balance suggested a strengthening of Russia's external finances, albeit at a high cost in domestic supplies of goods forgone. In fact, the external financial position remained weak. The overall trade surplus (with CIS as well as non-CIS countries) was partly offset by a net outflow of payments on services and interest. In 2001 the current-account balance was less than the merchandise trade surplus alone, although still very large, at some US $35,000m., and it was $31,100m. in 2002. The capital account of the balance of payments, as required by accounting conventions, balanced this, but not in a very healthy way. Inward foreign investment of a commercial nature languished at low levels. By the end of the 1990s the inflow consisted almost entirely of foreign direct investment. The earlier (late 1996–early 1998) surge of inward foreign portfolio investment was concentrated on short-term government debt (treasury bills); this money could (and in 1998 did) flow out again rather quickly, making Russia's external finances more unstable for a time. Meanwhile, capital-account inflows also included continued borrowing from international financial institutions, such as the IMF, and payment delays. These inflows, together with the current-account surplus, covered outflows that could be construed as capital 'flight' (the export of funds for legitimate investment reasons, as well as tax avoidance). In other words, Russian traders, financiers and individual citizens contrived, by mainly illegal means, to transfer substantial funds out of Russia for reasons that could be summed up as a lack of confidence in the rouble, in Russian banks, in Russian economic prospects and in the security of personal wealth in Russia. The outflow averaged about $20,000m. per year in the late 1990s. However, in 2000–03 capital flight, although continuing, stabilized or declined somewhat, while domestic investment grew quite strongly. Moreover, some of the capital outflow that had been recorded from Russia in the 1990s returned to the country. Indeed, in the second quarter of 2002, according to preliminary estimates, the inflow of capital to Russia exceeded the outflow—a significant development. Net private-sector capital outflows continued thereafter, but were much reduced, at close to zero in the first quarter of 2003.

By the early 2000s the overall Russian balance of payments was comparatively healthy. In late June 2003 gold and foreign-exchange reserves totalled some US $64,900m., equivalent to about one year's merchandise imports. Government external debt was not only being serviced, but there was little new borrowing, with the effect that total sovereign external debt was being reduced. At 1 January 2003 Russia's sovereign external debt stood at $118,000m., equivalent to only 34% of GDP in 2002. The Government calculated that even a modest decline in petroleum prices would not prevent Russia servicing its debt, without being obliged to undertake new borrowing. Moreover, if petroleum prices were to decline steeply (which appeared unlikely), the IMF had announced its readiness to recommence lending to Russia. Although this positive state of affairs had only been achieved after two generous restructurings of the inherited, Soviet-era debt to Western banks, one restructuring of Soviet-era debt to Western governments and a fortuitous rise in the price of petroleum, the end result was that the Russian Government was no longer dependent on the external support of the IMF or other creditors. The budget plan for 2004 included a further reduction of external public debt, with some increase in domestic borrowing.

There was still a lack of the kind of inward foreign investment that would raise productivity without adding to the volatility of the country's external finances. Legal ambiguities, a lack of information on company finances and a weak supporting structure of share registration, share custody and settlement procedures were all deterrents to portfolio equity investment by outsiders. At the same time political and tax uncertainties, and the resistance of Russian insiders to foreign participation in the most obviously lucrative areas (petroleum, natural gas and some metals) created barriers to foreign direct investment. Nevertheless, many Western senior executives continued to believe that the sheer size of the Russian market and natural resources, together with the existence of an educated labour force, with average wages of around US $156 per month (in February 2003), required them to seek entry to some sector of the Russian economy. The most usual approach was to attempt to become established in the Russian market without committing large amounts of money to a venture, and then, in time, perhaps invest more heavily. At first, such direct and portfolio investment was heavily

concentrated in Moscow. Later, however, with the decline of centralized control in Russia, Western equity investors moved away from the capital. St Petersburg was one favoured location; others included Samara, the emerging commercial centre on the River Volga; Nizhnii Novgorod and Yekaterinburg, in the Urals; and Novosibirsk, in Siberia. In the late 1990s and early 2000s offshore petroleum and natural gas development made the Pacific island of Sakhalin one of the regions most attractive for foreign direct investment.

In 2002–03 there were three main developments insofar as the private sector's financial relations with the rest of the world were concerned. Russian companies greatly expanded their foreign borrowings, usually in the form of bond issues and bank loans. Russian households reduced their holdings of cash US dollars, shifting partly into euros, as the dollar weakened, and partly into roubles, as their confidence in their own currency increased. Moreover, one very large direct investment deal challenged the established pattern of foreign direct investment into Russia—the agreement, worth some $6,150m., finalized by British Petroleum (of the United Kingdom) with the Tyumen Oil Company (TNK) and Sidanco in June 2003, to form a joint venture, NewCo, which was to trade as TNK-BP. The new company would control current output of about 1m. b/d of petroleum, as well as substantial reserves of both petroleum and natural gas in Russia. This deal alone was equivalent to almost three times the previous annual rate of foreign direct investment in Russia, and was the first instance of a major Western energy company acquiring a major stake in Russian petroleum production. (Paradoxically, the deal might not be recorded in the official figures as foreign investment, because it was between BP and a Russian-controlled 'offshore' company, but in practical terms that was what it was.) Speculation persisted that foreign interests were considering making a bid for the combined company that was expected to be formed in late 2003 by the merger of two principal Russian-owned petroleum companies, Yukos and Sibneft.

Russian trade was increasingly being conducted with the market economies of the West—only 16.9% of its merchandise trade turnover was conducted with the other countries of the CIS in 2002. With regard to the commodity composition of trade, there was somewhat more continuity with the Soviet era. Russia remained dependent on fuel, raw materials and semi-processed products as staple export earners. In 2002 nearly 69% of Russian exports consisted of petroleum, gas and metals, while more than one-third of imports were of machinery and equipment. Arms exports declined sharply in 1992, and subsequently remained below the USSR's late-1980s levels. However, from the late 1990s considerable official effort was put into re-organizing and promoting Russian arms export trade. According to some estimates, in 2002 Russia was the world's largest exporter of weapons, in terms of their military value; however, in terms of actual revenues received from arms sales, Russia was well behind the USA, the United Kingdom and France, in fourth place—but a significant competitor in the world arms market, none the less. New strategic export-control machinery was introduced, as Russia moved to co-operate more closely with the West in matters of security. It was reckoned by specialists, however, that the arrangements introduced in Russia to monitor arms sales and prevent deliveries to some 'pariah' states, such as Iraq, lacked effective enforcement.

Deregulation of Russia's trade was a slow and fitful process. Export licensing, quotas and taxes were at first widely used. The fact that the Government sought to limit exports was a reflection of the continued shortages arising from domestic price controls. In particular, owing to the control of domestic energy prices in the early 1990s, it was vastly more profitable for producers to export petroleum products than to supply the domestic market: in early 2003 the domestic wholesale price of petroleum in Russia was only about one-third of the world price, while for natural gas the ratio was even lower, at about one-sixth.

Pressures for the liberalization of foreign trade and investment came from international organizations. In 2000–03 Russia was in intensive negotiations over accession to the WTO, although it appeared unlikely that Putin's stated intention to join the Organization before parliamentary and presidential elections were held in 2003–04 would be fulfilled. In order to comply with the demands of WTO member states, a number of reforms that may prove unpopular in Russia would have to be implemented: among the most significant of these were the liberalization of domestic energy prices; the opening of the domestic aviation and vehicle markets to heightened foreign access and competition; the imposition of severe restrictions on agricultural subsidies; and the possibility of permitting greater participation by foreign firms in Russia's financial-services and energy sectors.

There was also the question of money 'laundering' (the processing of illicit or illegally obtained funds into legitimate accounts). In mid-2000 Russia was named as a 'non-co-operative' financial centre by the Financial Action Task Force (FATF), a body established by the Group of Seven (G-7) industrialized nations, and was consequently threatened with possible economic sanctions by member states of the Organisation for Economic Co-operation and Development (OECD). In August 2001, however, President Putin finally signed into law measures to combat money laundering, designed to bring Russia into greater conformity with international norms and standards. As a consequence, FATF sanctions were suspended, and in October 2002 Russia was removed from its list of non-co-operative countries.

Meanwhile, informal control of petroleum exports continued to be exercised through the Government's regulation of access to export pipelines. However, domestic pressures of a kind more familiar in the West, for protection against import competition, increased substantially, particularly in relation to food imports. It was difficult to make a free-trade case against such protection when Western countries were 'dumping' (exporting at below their marginal cost) surpluses of subsidized farm produce on Russian (and Eastern European) markets, but that did not prevent the US administration and the Commission of the EU from protesting about such measures.

More generally, imports were severely restricted by the decline in Russian output and incomes, and by the country's limited ability to pay, especially after the August 1998 devaluation. Machinery imports retained their volume surprisingly well, in view of the significant decline in investment. When investment revived (from 1999) they grew substantially. In 2002 imports of machinery were 25% higher than in the previous year, an encouraging indication that domestic production facilities were being upgraded. In the 1990s imports of automobiles, clothing and food products (as distinct from grain) increased substantially, mainly encouraged by the demand of the relatively prosperous segments of the Russian population. The previously high levels of grain imports declined dramatically, as even the unreformed Russian farm sector was forced to operate in a more efficient way. The import of grain to feed Russian livestock was curtailed, partly because lower average incomes resulted in a reduced demand for livestock products, and partly because it was more cost-effective simply to import meat. In 2001 and 2002, however, for the first time in several decades, Russia was a net exporter of grain. It promptly encountered import restrictions imposed by the EU.

From 1992 the rouble declined in value against Western currencies. The Russian currency was at first endowed with a limited internal convertibility by the merging of the Central Bank and black-market exchange rates in July 1992. The rate of exchange was left to 'float' (was made freely convertible), with the Moscow Inter-bank Currency Exchange providing the main market. This was a very limited market, on which the exchange rate bore no relationship to the domestic purchasing power of the rouble, except that both decreased rapidly.

From mid-1992 to mid-1995 the rouble's exchange rate against the US dollar declined steeply. None the less, the rouble appreciated in real terms against the dollar. As domestic inflation slowed, the Russian monetary authorities sought to control the decline of the rouble and keep it in conformity with relative inflation rates—in other words, to keep the real exchange rate approximately constant. To this end, the rouble 'corridor' ensured that the exchange rate remained within a periodically adjusted band, varying from around 4.4 roubles to the dollar in mid-1995 to 6.1 roubles to the dollar in August 1998, prior to the abolition of this arrangement and the rapid decline of the exchange rate, to around 24 roubles to the dollar, in the immediate aftermath of the financial crisis. Subsequently, a more gradual decline ensued, with the effect that in 2002 an average exchange rate of 31.35 roubles to the dollar was recorded. The effect of these measures was to erode somewhat the competitive advantage that had been gained by Russian manufacturers from the initial devaluation. Although the trade surplus narrowed in 2001–02, Russian producers probably continued to be slightly better able to compete with foreign firms in the Russian market than had been in the case prior to August 1998.

## BUDGET AND FINANCES

Austere fiscal and monetary policies are the banal but unavoidable prescription for dealing with a rise in consumer prices. In 1991–94 Russian policy-makers failed to follow this rule. This failure in stabilization, although neither complete nor irredeemable, was of the greatest significance. The control of inflation is desirable in all circumstances. When a government and a whole population are trying to make the transition from a centrally administered to a market economy, however, it is vital.

In 1991–95 Russia avoided 'hyperinflation', but the rate of growth of consumer prices remained high. The immediate causes of this, themselves closely related, were a large budgetary deficit and an excessive expansion of credit. The struggle to reduce inflation to manageable proportions was the most controversial issue of the transition, reflecting a history of state financial support for all sanctioned economic activities. Once it became clear to members of the communist-era élite that they had a good chance of profiting from privatization and from freer links with the outside world, the removal of a state 'safety net' for their economic ventures came to be seen as the greatest threat posed by the reformers.

A 'reform team' remained in place in the Government from 1991 until 1998, but with frequent changes of personnel. These successive teams of young reformers fought tenaciously to contain government spending and reduce the rate of growth of the money supply. There were three other campaigns that were part of the stabilization effort: developing government securities and markets so that any government deficit would not have to be financed entirely by increasing the money supply; seeking external financial assistance as another less inflationary way of financing the deficit; and reconstructing and consolidating the Government's revenue base. 'Post-reform' governments in 1998–99, led by Yevgenii Primakov and Sergei Stepashin, did not, in the event, reverse the policies of the reformers. When Vladimir Putin became acting President at the end of 1999 and, after the March 2000 election, President, reform policies were strengthened. However, by 2003 only limited reform of the financial system had been undertaken, and the banking sector continued to be dominated by state-owned banks. None the less, financial stabilization was maintained and annual inflation rates were kept below 25%, largely as a result of maintaining tight controls on public spending, while recovering economic activity led, simultaneously, to an increase in government revenue. One result was federal budgetary surpluses in 2000–02, equivalent in 2002 to 1.8% of GDP (after payment of interest), which enabled the Government to set aside funds for the repayment of its principal debts as they became due.

Until 1997 the reformers had faced resistance within the Government itself, often from the Ministry of Economics, which had inherited most of the old State Planning Committee apparatus. From mid-1992 until late 1994 they also faced resistance from what in any other country would have been an unlikely source—the Central Bank, headed by Viktor Gerashchenko, a former head of the USSR State Bank and an opponent of large reductions in government subsidies to producers.

The money supply was brought under control in 1995. Conflict by this time revolved mainly around the budget. Loans from the IMF were conditional on the reduction of the government deficit, and on its being financed by credit (chiefly treasury bills), not by printing money. The deficit was indeed reduced, but slowly, and it was somewhat illusory. For example, cash spending was diminished by the simple device of not paying government suppliers and employees when funds were short. Explicit subsidies to producers were also reduced, but state and privatized enterprises were allowed to withhold taxes, which amounted to much the same thing.

The budgetary struggle was compounded by the fluidity and disorganization of relations between the federal Government and the 89 'federal subjects' or constituent units of the Russian Federation. There was no well-defined and widely accepted formula for redistributing public money among the country's federal units, which differed enormously in wealth. The politically weak centre tended, for the most part, to cede revenue to the regions, but in no clear and consistent way. It also handed down spending responsibilities without the accompanying revenue transfers or assignment of tax bases to the regions and municipalities. Finally, poor information and a lack of openness aggravated the problem. A number of extra-budgetary funds existed alongside the acknowledged budget, and information about them, especially at the regional level, was scant. Moreover, until 1996 the Russian Government reported expenditure and the resulting general government balance in ways that departed from standard international practice.

Gradually, however, the 'fiscal federal' problem began to come under rather more control. In 1999–2002 some limited improvements were made in the separation of the federal from the sub-national tax bases and the clarification of criteria for federal transfers to regional budgets. Above all, under Putin, and with a growing economy, the central Government began to control a larger share of revenue—a process made less difficult politically by the rising volume of total state revenue.

Altogether, the stabilization process proved to be extremely difficult. Overall public finances (federal plus sub-national budgets) did not move into surplus until 2000, and by 2002 the rate of consumer-price inflation was 15%, and was decelerating only gradually. In 2002 Gerashchenko was replaced as head of the Central Bank by Sergei Ignatiyev, who was expected to co-operate more harmoniously with a reformist Government. None the less, the money supply remained, to a large extent, beyond the control of the Central Bank, not least because so much of Russia's money supply consisted of dollars, rather than roubles. Moreover, the 1998 crisis had almost destroyed the government bond market, so that should budg-

etary deficits return, non-inflationary means of financing them would prove difficult to find. In addition, the budget remained vulnerable to variations in international petroleum prices. Despite this financial fragility, the Russian economy was growing, and the rate of inflation was manifestly not incompatible with such growth.

## PROSPECTS

By mid-2003 the Russian economy had been growing for four-and-a-half years. President Putin was vigorously promoting economic liberalization. The Russian business community was showing signs of a major shift from 'asset-stripping' to ensuring the longer-term growth of their businesses. All of these factors were encouraging for the future, while a simple extrapolation of recent rates of change would present a reasonably positive overview, showing Russia's economy to remain far behind those of Western Europe and North America, but to be, however, growing somewhat faster, with manageable inflation, strong reserves and a debt burden that was gradually being reduced. In such circumstances, most Russian citizens could expect their material circumstances to improve steadily, if not dramatically.

These prospects were not, however, secure, being vulnerable to an international downturn in growth, and any consequent sharp fall in the petroleum price. Moreover, the basis of Russia's recent economic successes had the effect of transforming the country into a quasi-'petro-state', which did not necessarily provide a sound basis for sustained or balanced economic growth over a long period. Moreover, many of the basic institutions of a well-functioning market economy remained underdeveloped or lacking in the early 2000s, and further reforms remained necessary in many areas, including banking, accounting, public administration and the legal system, in order to ensure that the progress achieved in recent years would be repeated and extended. Additionally, recently established, smaller firms, a source of dynamism in any economy, appeared to be chronically underdeveloped in Russia, accounting for only around 20% of employment in 2000, compared with 40%–60% in much of Central and Western Europe. This lagging development appeared to be connected with the particularly oppressive character of local bureaucracy in Russia, where licensing and certification processes are cumbersome and commonly corrupt. Although Putin and his Government attempted to resolve these problems through various 'de-bureaucratization' measures, and there was some evidence of a reduction in the regulatory burden, it remained unclear just how much direct impact these measures would make.

Underlying these phenomena was the dominance of informal networking and the casual interpretation of rules. Few formal institutions—from shareholders' meetings to tax payment and contract enforcement—worked according to the official rules. Accordingly, the cost of doing business outside a small circle of known partners was high. It was argued that much the same could be said of several highly successful economies, such as those of the People's Republic of China and the Republic of Korea. International business perceptions of the degree of corruption, investigated by Transparency International, suggested, however, that the problem might be greater in Russia than in almost any Asian economy: in 2003 the organization rated Russia 86th equal out of 133 countries in terms of perceived corruption, well below the Republic of Korea, China and Thailand. The countries that were positioned, like Russia, in the bottom one-third of this table, were also languishing economically: examples include Tanzania, Ukraine, Nigeria and Bangladesh. This pervasive lack of trust was one reason why investment in Russia was still so modest and why so much capital had been placed offshore.

A different measure, the 'business environment ranking' of the London (United Kingdom)-based Economist Intelligence Unit, placed Russia 50th out of 60 nations in projections for 2001–05. If, as World Bank economists argued, the key requirement for Russia in the early 2000s is very rapid investment growth, this assessment was not encouraging. Should it indeed be the case that Russia has what some economic historians call 'poor institutional quality', the historical evidence suggests that this is not something that readily changes even over extended periods of time. For all these reasons, many economists, both Russian and Western, doubted that Russia could, in the foreseeable future, exhibit sustained growth at above the average for the industrialized member countries of the OECD.

All these doubts, however, were a matter for speculation. It might also prove to be the case that in a world in which the speed of communications is unprecedented and in which there are very close international links, through trade and investment, the possibilities for a rapid improvement in a country's economic institutions are greater. Just as Central European states have moved rapidly to assimilate the EU's economic conventions, the Russian leadership is pressing hard to make the Russian economy more open and competitive, in order to join the WTO. If the increased confidence of the Russian business community, stimulating higher investment, and Putin's liberalizing zeal are both sustained, Russia's prospects for growth in the first decade of the 2000s might be rather better than the annual rates of 3%–4% forecast by many analysts at the beginning of the decade.

# Statistical Survey

Sources (unless otherwise indicated): State Committee of Statistics of the USSR; State Committee of Statistics of the Russian Federation, 103450 Moscow, ul. Myasnitskaya 39; tel. (095) 207-49-41; fax (095) 207-42-80; internet www.gks.ru.

## Area and Population

### AREA, POPULATION AND DENSITY

| | |
|---|---|
| Area (sq km) . . . . . . . . . | 17,075,400* |
| Population (census results)† | |
| 17 January 1979 . . . . . . . | 137,409,921 |
| 12 January 1989 | |
| Males . . . . . . . . | 68,713,869 |
| Females . . . . . . . | 78,308,000 |
| Total . . . . . . . . | 147,021,869 |
| Population (official estimates at 1 January) | |
| 2000 . . . . . . . . | 145,559,200 |
| 2001 . . . . . . . . | 144,819,100 |
| 2002 . . . . . . . . | 143,954,400 |
| Density (per sq km) at 1 January 2002 . . . . . | 8.4 |

* 6,592,850 sq miles.
† Figures refer to *de jure* population. The *de facto* total at the 1989 census was 147,400,537.

### POPULATION BY ETHNIC GROUP*
(census of 12 January 1989)

| | '000 | % |
|---|---|---|
| Russian . . . . . . . . . . . | 119,865.9 | 81.5 |
| Tatar† . . . . . . . . . . | 5,522.1 | 3.8 |
| Ukrainian . . . . . . . . | 4,362.9 | 3.0 |
| Chuvash . . . . . . . . . | 1,773.6 | 1.2 |
| Bashkir . . . . . . . . . | 1,345.4 | 0.9 |
| Belarusian . . . . . . . . | 1,206.2 | 0.8 |
| Mordovian . . . . . . . . | 1,072.9 | 0.7 |
| Chechen . . . . . . . . . | 899.0 | 0.6 |
| German . . . . . . . . . | 842.3 | 0.6 |
| Udmurt . . . . . . . . . | 714.5 | 0.5 |
| Mari . . . . . . . . . . | 643.7 | 0.4 |
| Kazakh . . . . . . . . . | 635.9 | 0.4 |
| Avar . . . . . . . . . . | 544.0 | 0.4 |
| Jewish‡ . . . . . . . . . | 536.8 | 0.4 |
| Armenian . . . . . . . . . | 532.4 | 0.4 |
| Others . . . . . . . . . | 6,524.4 | 4.4 |
| **Total** . . . . . . . . . . | 147,021.9 | 100.0 |

* According to official declaration of nationality.
† Excluding Crimean Tatars, numbering 21,275.
‡ Excluding Mountain Jews, numbering 11,282.

### REPUBLICS WITHIN THE FEDERATION
(estimates, 1 January 2002, except where otherwise indicated)

| Republic | Area (sq km) | Population ('000) | Capital (with population, '000)* |
|---|---|---|---|
| Adygeya . . . . . | 7,600 | 444.9 | Maikop (167.0) |
| Altai . . . . . | 92,600 | 204.9 | Gorno-Altaisk (52.7) |
| Bashkortostan . . . | 143,600 | 4,090.6 | Ufa (1,086.8) |
| Buryatiya . . . . | 351,300 | 1,019.4 | Ulan-Ude (368.9) |
| Chechnya† . . . . | n.a. | 624.6 | Groznyi (182.7‡) |
| Chuvashiya . . . . | 18,300 | 1,346.3 | Cheboksary (461.2) |
| Dagestan . . . . | 50,300 | 2,179.5 | Makhachkala (327.6) |
| Ingushetiya† . . . . | n.a. | 466.3 | Magas (0.1)§ |
| Kabardino-Balkariya . | 12,500 | 782.0 | Nalchik (228.4) |
| Kalmykiya . . . . | 76,100 | 305.6 | Elista (107.8) |
| Karachayevo- | | | |
| Cherkessiya . . . . | 14,100 | 428.6 | Cherkessk (120.7) |
| Kareliya . . . . | 172,400 | 756.4 | Petrozavodsk (282.9) |
| Khakasiya . . . . | 61,900 | 575.4 | Abakan (167.9) |
| Komi . . . . . | 415,900 | 1,117.2 | Syktyvkar (227.7) |
| Marii-El . . . . | 23,200 | 750.3 | Yoshkar-Ola (248.5) |
| Mordoviya . . . . | 26,200 | 910.0 | Saransk (313.2) |
| North Osetiya (Alaniya) | 8,000 | 678.2 | Vladikavkaz (310.6) |
| Sakha (Yakutiya) . . | 3,103,200 | 982.9 | Yakutsk (197.8) |
| Tatarstan . . . . | 68,000 | 3,768.2 | Kazan (1,090.2) |
| Tyva . . . . . | 170,500 | 310.3 | Kyzyl (101.5) |
| Udmurtiya . . . . | 42,100 | 1,616.2 | Izhevsk (650.3) |

* Estimated population at 1 January 2001.
† Until 1992 the territories of the Republic of Chechnya and the Republic of Ingushetiya were combined in the Checheno-Ingush Autonomous Republic (area 19,300 sq km).
‡ Estimated population at 1 January 1995.
§ In October 1998 Magas replaced Nazran (estimated population 113,400 at 1 January 2001) as the capital.

## PRINCIPAL TOWNS
(estimated population at 1 January 2001)

| | | | | |
|---|---:|---|---|---:|
| Moskva (Moscow, the capital) . . . | 8,304,600 | Orenburg . . . . | | 516,600 |
| Sankt Peterburg (St Petersburg)* . | 4,627,800 | Tyumen . . . . | | 500,200 |
| | | Tula . . . . . | | 495,500 |
| Novosibirsk . . | 1,393,200 | Kemerovo. . . . | | 487,200 |
| Nizhnii Novgorod* . | 1,343,300 | Tomsk . . . . | | 483,100 |
| Yekaterinburg* . | 1,256,900 | Astrakhan . . . | | 479,700 |
| Samara* . . . . | 1,146,400 | Kirov (Vyatka) . . | | 466,300 |
| Omsk . . . . | 1,138,400 | Cheboksary . . . | | 461,200 |
| Kazan . . . . | 1,090,200 | Ivanovo . . . . | | 452,100 |
| Ufa. . . . . | 1,088,800 | Bryansk . . . . | | 450,600 |
| Chelyabinsk . . | 1,081,100 | Tver* . . . . | | 447,100 |
| Perm . . . . | 1,004,800 | Kursk . . . . | | 437,400 |
| Rostov-na-Donu | | Magnitogorsk. . . | | 427,100 |
| (Rostov-on-Don) . | 997,800 | Kaliningrad . . . | | 421,000 |
| Volgograd . . . | 982,900 | Nizhnii Tagil . . | | 386,900 |
| Voronezh . . . | 901,800 | Murmansk . . . | | 370,700 |
| Saratov . . . | 864,400 | Ulan-Ude . . . | | 368,900 |
| Krasnoyarsk . . | 758,700 | Kurgan . . . . | | 359,700 |
| Tolyatti . . . | 724,300 | Arkhangelsk | | |
| Ulyanovsk | | (Archangel). . | | 358,500 |
| (Simbirsk) . . | 662,100 | Smolensk . . . . | | 347,600 |
| Izhevsk* . . . | 650,300 | Belgorod . . . . | | 342,000 |
| Krasnodar . . | 634,700 | Stavropol . . . | | 339,500 |
| Yaroslavl . . . | 608,800 | Orel . . . . | | 338,800 |
| Khabarovsk . . | 603,500 | Kaluga . . . . | | 335,300 |
| Vladivostok . . | 596,600 | Sochi . . . . | | 332,900 |
| Irkutsk . . . | 587,200 | Vladimir . . . | | 331,700 |
| Barnaul . . . | 573,300 | Makhachkala . . . | | 327,600 |
| Novokuznetsk . | 564,500 | Cherepovets . . | | 323,300 |
| Penza . . . . | 524,900 | Saransk . . . . | | 313,200 |
| Ryazan . . . | 523,400 | Vladikavkaz* . . | | 310,600 |
| Lipetsk . . . | 519,200 | Tambov . . . . | | 308,000 |
| Naberezhnye | | Chita . . . . | | 303,300 |
| Chelny*. . . . | 518,300 | | | |

* Some towns that were renamed during the Soviet period have reverted to their former names: St Petersburg (Leningrad); Nizhnii Novgorod (Gorkii); Yekaterinburg (Sverdlovsk); Samara (Kuibyshev); Izhevsk (Ustinov); Naberezhnye Chelny (Brezhnev); Tver (Kalinin); Vladikavkaz (Ordzhonikidze).

## BIRTHS, MARRIAGES AND DEATHS

| | Registered live births | | Registered marriages | | Registered deaths | |
|---|---:|---:|---:|---:|---:|---:|
| | Number | Rate (per 1,000) | Number | Rate (per 1,000) | Number | Rate (per 1,000) |
| 1994 . . | 1,408,159 | 9.5 | 1,080,600 | 7.3 | 2,301,366 | 15.6 |
| 1995 . . | 1,363,806 | 9.2 | 1,075,219 | 7.3 | 2,203,811 | 14.9 |
| 1996 . . | 1,304,638 | 8.8 | 866,651 | 5.9 | 2,082,249 | 14.1 |
| 1997 . . | 1,259,943 | 8.6 | 928,411 | 6.3 | 2,015,779 | 13.7 |
| 1998 . . | 1,283,292 | 8.8 | 848,691 | 5.8 | 1,988,744 | 13.6 |
| 1999 . . | 1,214,689 | 8.3 | 911,162 | 6.2 | 2,143,174 | 14.7 |
| 2000 . . | 1,266,789 | 8.7 | 789,999 | 5.4 | 2,225,332 | 15.3 |
| 2001 . . | 1,308,596 | 9.1 | 1,001,100* | 6.9* | 2,251,814 | 15.6 |

* Provisional figure.

Sources: mainly Council of Europe, *Demographic Year Book*; UN, *Population and Vital Statistics Report*.

**Expectation of life** (WHO estimates, years at birth): 65.2 (males 58.9; females 72.3) in 2001 (Source: WHO, *World Health Report*).

## EMPLOYMENT
(sample surveys, '000 persons aged 15 to 72 years, at October)

| | 1998 | 1999* | 2000 |
|---|---:|---:|---:|
| Agriculture, hunting and forestry | 8,978.7 | 9,076.7 | 8,911.7 |
| Mining and quarrying . . . . | 1,409.6 | 1,071.8 | 1,086.0 |
| Manufacturing . . . . . | 11,524.6 | 11,714.3 | 11,911.2 |
| Electricity, gas and water supply . | 1,370.1 | 1,400.9 | 1,505.4 |
| Construction . . . . . . | 4,643.9 | 4,649.0 | 4,590.7 |
| Wholesale and retail trade, restaurants and hotels . . . | 9,634.0 | 9,621.5 | 9,761.6 |
| Transport, storage and communications . . . . . | 4,848.1 | 4,928.1 | 5,035.2 |
| Financial intermediation, real estate, renting and business activities . . . . . . | 5,297.1 | 5,128.0 | 5,074.6 |
| Public administration and defence; compulsory social security . . | 2,894.2 | 3,001.6 | 3,061.3 |
| Education . . . . . . | 5,772.3 | 5,816.4 | 5,742.1 |
| Health and social work . . . . | 4,295.3 | 4,341.4 | 4,355.8 |
| Other community, social and personal service activities . . | 3,055.0 | 3,178.9 | 3,271.6 |
| **Total employed** (including others) | 63,812.0 | 63,963.4 | 64,327.0 |
| Unemployed . . . . . . | 8,876.0 | 9,094.0 | 6,999.0 |
| **Total labour force** . . . . . | 72,688 | 73,057.4 | 71,326.0 |

* Sample survey conducted in November.

Source: UN, *Statistical Yearbook for Asia and the Pacific*.

**2001** (sample survey, '000 persons, November): Total employed 64,664; Unemployed 6,303; Total labour force 70,968 (males 36,846, females 34,122).

# Health and Welfare

## KEY INDICATORS

| | |
|---|---:|
| Total fertility rate (children per woman, 2001) . . . . | 1.2 |
| Under-5 mortality rate (per 1,000 live births, 2001) . . . | 21 |
| HIV/AIDS (% of persons aged 15–49, 2001) . . . . . | 0.90 |
| Physicians (per 1,000 head, 1998) . . . . . . . | 4.21 |
| Hospital beds (per 1,000 head, 1997) . . . . . . | 12.1 |
| Health expenditure (2000): US $ per head (PPP) . . . | 405 |
| Health expenditure (2000): % of GDP . . . . . | 5.3 |
| Health expenditure (2000): public (% of total) . . . . | 72.5 |
| Access to water (% of persons, 1999) . . . . . . | 99 |
| Human Development Index (2001): ranking . . . . . | 63 |
| Human Development Index (2001): value . . . . . . | 0.779 |

For sources and definitions, see explanatory note on p. vi.

# Agriculture

**PRINCIPAL CROPS**
('000 metric tons)

|  | 1999 | 2000 | 2001 |
|---|---|---|---|
| Wheat | 30,995.2 | 34,500.0 | 46,871.0 |
| Rice (paddy) | 444.0 | 586.0 | 497.0 |
| Barley | 10,602.6 | 14,100.0 | 19,500.0 |
| Maize | 1,069.2 | 1,500.0 | 831.0 |
| Rye | 4,782. | 5,400.0 | 6,600.0 |
| Oats | 4,396.9 | 6,000.0 | 7,700.0 |
| Millet | 924.8 | 1,122.0 | 600.0 |
| Sorghum | 31.8 | 116.0 | 12.5* |
| Buckwheat | 578.8 | 998.0 | 574.0 |
| Potatoes | 31,343.9 | 34,000.0 | 35,000.0 |
| Sugar beet | 15,227.2 | 14,040.8 | 14,539.0 |
| Dry peas | 598.1 | 800.0 | 1,300.0 |
| Soybeans (Soya beans) | 334.5 | 342.0 | 350.0 |
| Sunflower seed | 4,149.6 | 3,900.0 | 2,700.0 |
| Rapeseed | 135.1 | 197.8 | 115.7 |
| Cabbages | 3,940.1 | 4,000.0* | 4,300.0* |
| Tomatoes | 1,696.4 | 1,750.0* | 1,850.0* |
| Cucumbers and gherkins* | 555.0 | 593.0 | 625.0 |
| Dry onions | 1,129.8 | 1,150.0* | 1,200.0* |
| Garlic | 180.7 | 198.0* | 202.0* |
| Carrots | 1,372.2 | 1,405.0* | 1,480.0* |
| Other vegetables* | 3,427.9 | 3,408.0 | 3,647.0 |
| Apples | 1,060 | 1,832* | 1,643* |
| Cherries (incl. sour cherries)* | 174 | 255 | 253 |
| Plums* | 100 | 135 | 125 |
| Strawberries | 115* | 128* | 125† |
| Raspberries* | 100 | 102 | 90 |
| Currants | 206 | 220* | 203* |
| Watermelons†‡ | 540 | 475 | 435 |
| Grapes | 248.4 | 279.0 | 280.0† |
| Other fruits* | 351 | 450 | 362 |

\* Unofficial figure(s).
† FAO estimate(s).
‡ Including melons, pumpkins and squash.

Source: FAO.

**LIVESTOCK**
('000 head at 1 January, unless otherwise indicated)

|  | 1999 | 2000 | 2001 |
|---|---|---|---|
| Horses | 1,800 | 1,750* | 1,750* |
| Cattle | 28,480 | 28,000 | 27,294 |
| Pigs | 17,248 | 18,271 | 15,708 |
| Sheep | 13,413 | 12,715† | 12,734† |
| Goats | 2,144 | 2,036† | 2,309† |
| Chickens | 350,168 | 341,400† | 332,500† |
| Turkeys* | 2,500 | 2,400 | 2,500 |
| Geese* | 3,200 | 3,000 | 3,000 |

\* FAO estimate(s).
† Unofficial figure.

Source: FAO.

**LIVESTOCK PRODUCTS**
('000 metric tons)

|  | 1999 | 2000 | 2001 |
|---|---|---|---|
| Beef and veal | 1,868.0 | 1,895.0 | 1,837.0 |
| Mutton and lamb | 123.6 | 123.0* | 120.0* |
| Pig meat | 1,485.4 | 1,569.0 | 1,547.0 |
| Poultry meat | 748.0 | 766.0 | 871.0 |
| Other meat* | 99.3 | 51.0 | 99.0 |
| Cows' milk | 32,000.6 | 31,977.0* | 32,571.0* |
| Goats' milk | 299.0 | 322.5* | 328.5* |
| Cheese | 364.6 | 390.7 | 433.0 |
| Butter | 261.7 | 267.0 | 269.0 |
| Hen eggs | 1,846.4 | 1,894.6 | 1,950.0* |
| Honey | 51.0 | 53.9 | 54.0† |
| Wool: greasy | 40.2 | 40.0 | 40.0† |
| Wool: scoured | 24.2 | 20.0 | 20.0† |
| Cattle hides | 229.3 | 232.6† | 228.0† |

\* Unofficial figure(s).
† FAO estimate.

Source: FAO.

# Forestry

**ROUNDWOOD REMOVALS**
('000 cubic metres, excl. bark)

|  | 1999 | 2000 | 2001 |
|---|---|---|---|
| Sawlogs, veneer logs and logs for sleepers | 46,500 | 49,700 | 63,360 |
| Pulpwood | 39,200 | 46,400 | 42,300 |
| Other industrial wood | 8,900 | 9,700 | 12,300 |
| Fuel wood | 49,000 | 52,300 | 44,340 |
| **Total** | 143,600 | 158,100 | 162,300 |

Source: FAO.

**SAWNWOOD PRODUCTION**
('000 cubic metres, incl. railway sleepers)

|  | 1999 | 2000 | 2001 |
|---|---|---|---|
| Coniferous (softwood) | 16,635 | 17,460 | 17,500 |
| Broadleaved (hardwood) | 2,465 | 2,540 | 2,500 |
| **Total** | 19,100 | 20,000 | 20,000 |

Source: FAO.

# Fishing*

('000 metric tons, live weight)

|  | 1998 | 1999 | 2000 |
|---|---|---|---|
| Capture | 4,454.8 | 4,141.2 | 3,973.5 |
| Pink (humpback) salmon | 191.4 | 187.1 | 157.1 |
| Azov sea sprat | 116.4 | 152.9 | 122.8 |
| Atlantic cod | 248.7 | 215.6 | 171.0 |
| Alaska (Walleye) pollock | 1,930.7 | 1,500.5 | 1,215.1 |
| Blue whiting (Poutassou) | 130.0 | 182.6 | 241.9 |
| Atlantic herring | 139.6 | 170.6 | 174.2 |
| Pacific herring | 395.6 | 359.2 | 361.2 |
| Aquaculture | 63.2 | 68.6 | 74.1 |
| **Total catch** | 4,518.0 | 4,209.8 | 4,047.7 |

Source: FAO, *Yearbook of Fishery Statistics*.
\* Figures exclude seaweeds and other aquatic plants ('000 metric tons): 30.3 in 1998; 25.7 in 1999; 53.7 in 2000. Also excluded are aquatic mammals (whales, seals, etc.).

# Mining

('000 metric tons, unless otherwise indicated)

| | 1998 | 1999 | 2000 |
|---|---|---|---|
| Hard coal . . . . . . . | 153,100 | 165,700 | 173,110 |
| Lignite . . . . . . . | 78,800 | 83,400 | 83,740 |
| Crude petroleum . . . . . | 303,300 | 305,000* | 325,000* |
| Natural gas (million cu metres) . | 591,400 | 591,641 | 538,878 |
| Iron ore: gross weight . . . | 72,343 | 81,311 | 86,630 |
| Iron ore: metal content . . . . | 41,700 | 46,900 | 50,000 |
| Copper ore† . . . . . . | 500 | 530* | 570* |
| Nickel ore*† . . . . . | 250 | 260 | 270 |
| Bauxite* . . . . . | 3,450 | 3,750 | 4,200 |
| Lead ore† . . . . . . | 13 | 13* | 13* |
| Zinc ore† . . . . . . | 115* | 132* | 136 |
| Tin (metric tons)*† . . . . | 4,500 | 4,500 | 5,000 |
| Manganese ore*† . . . . | 21 | 22 | 23 |
| Chromium ore* . . . . . | 130 | 100 | 100 |
| Tungsten concentrates (metric tons)*† . . . . . . | 3,000 | 3,500 | 3,500 |
| Molybdenum (metric tons)* . | 2,000 | 2,400 | 2,400 |
| Antimony ore (metric tons)*† . . | 4,000 | 4,000 | 4,500 |
| Cobalt ore (metric tons)*† . . | 3,200 | 3,300 | 3,600 |
| Mercury (metric tons)* . . . | 50 | 50 | 50 |
| Silver (metric tons)*† . . . | 350 | 375 | 370 |
| Uranium concentrate (metric tons)*† . . . . . . | 2,000 | 2,000 | 2,500 |
| Gold (metric tons)† . . . . | 114.9 | 125.9 | 143.0 |
| Platinum (metric tons)* . . . | 30 | 32 | 35 |
| Palladium (metric tons)* . . | 70 | 75 | 84 |
| Kaolin (concentrate) . . . . | 50 | 41 | 45* |
| Magnesite . . . . . . | 852 | 900* | 1,000* |
| Phosphate rock (Apatite)‡ . . | 3,735 | 4,161 | 4,150 |
| Potash*§ . . . . . . | 3,500 | 4,200 | 3,700 |
| Native sulphur* . . . . . | 50 | 50 | 50 |
| Fluorspar (concentrate)* . . . | 120.2 | 153.8 | 187.6 |
| Barite (Barytes)* . . . . | 60 | 60 | 60 |
| Salt (unrefined) . . . . . | 2,200 | 3,200 | 3,200* |
| Diamonds: gems ('000 metric carats): | | | |
| gem* . . . . . . | 11,600 | 11,500 | 11,600 |
| industrial* . . . . . | 11,600 | 11,500 | 11,600 |
| Gypsum (crude) . . . . . | 609 | 650 | 700* |
| Graphite* . . . . . . | 6 | 6 | 6 |
| Asbestos . . . . . | 600* | 675 | 752 |
| Mica* . . . . . . | 100 | 100 | 100 |
| Talc . . . . . . | 79 | 90* | 100* |
| Feldspar* . . . . . . | 40 | 45 | 45 |
| Peat (fuel use) . . . . . | 1,700 | 2,000 | 2,000* |

* Estimated production.

† Figures refer to the metal content of ores.

‡ Figures refer to the phosphoric acid content. The data exclude sedimentary rock (estimates, '000 metric tons): 300 per year in 1998–2000.

§ Figures refer to the potassium oxide content.

Source: mainly US Geological Survey.

# Industry

**SELECTED PRODUCTS**

('000 metric tons, unless otherwise indicated)

| | 1997 | 1998 | 1999 |
|---|---|---|---|
| Margarine . . . . . . | 222.3 | 238.7 | 379.4 |
| Wheat flour . . . . . | 10,400 | 10,112 | 10,789 |
| Raw sugar . . . . . . | 3,777.7 | 4,744.6 | 6,807.6 |
| Vodka and other spirits (million hectolitres) . . . . . . | 8.3 | 8.7 | 13.4 |
| Wine ('000 hectolitres) . . . . | 1,230 | 1,260 | 1,830 |
| Beer ('000 hectolitres) . . . | 26,100 | 33,600 | 44,500 |
| Cigarettes (million) . . . . | 140,077 | 198,506 | 266,031 |
| Wool yarn (pure and mixed) . . | 27.7 | 23.5 | 29.2 |
| Cotton yarn (pure and mixed) . . | 175.1 | 149.1 | 191.4 |
| Flax, ramie and hemp yarn . . | 31.6 | 17.1 | 20.1 |
| Cotton fabrics (million sq metres) . | 1,374 | 1,241 | 1,455 |
| Woollen fabrics (million sq metres) | 62.6 | 51.8 | 61.1 |
| Linen fabrics (million sq metres) . | 106.4 | 61.2 | 74.9 |
| Leather footwear ('000 pairs) . . | 34,541 | 24,998 | 30,821 |
| Plywood ('000 cubic metres) . . | 943.0 | 1,101.8 | 1,324.0 |
| Particle board ('000 cubic metres) . | 1,490 | 1,568 | 1,969 |
| Mechanical wood pulp . . . . | 899 | 981 | 1,160 |
| Chemical and semi-chemical wood pulp . . . . . . . | 2,851 | 3,010 | 3,922 |
| Newsprint . . . . . . | 1,195 | 1,395 | 1,620 |
| Other printing and writing paper . | 441 | 474 | 569 |
| Other paper and paperboard . . | 1,983 | 2,222 | 3,184 |
| Sulphuric acid . . . . . | 6,247 | 5,840 | 7,148 |
| Caustic soda (sodium hydroxide) . | 946 | 847 | 1,036 |
| Soda ash (sodium carbonate) . . | 1,652 | 1,538 | 1,918 |
| Nitrogenous fertilizers (a)* . . | 4,272 | 4,082 | 5,159 |
| Phosphate fertilizers (b)* . . . | 1,787 | 1,703 | 2,044 |
| Potassic fertilizers (c)* . . . | 3,487 | 3,596 | 4,294 |
| Synthetic rubber . . . . . | 703.9 | 621.7 | 736.3 |
| Aviation gasoline . . . . . | 39 | 31† | n.a. |
| Jet fuels . . . . . . | 9,189 | 9,189† | n.a. |
| Motor spirit (petrol) . . . . | 27,178 | 25,923† | 26,300 |
| Kerosene . . . . . . | 107 | 51† | n.a. |
| Gas-diesel (distillate fuel) oils . . | 47,226 | 45,102† | 46,800 |
| Residual fuel oils . . . . . | 63,887 | 56,701† | 50,100 |
| Lubricating oils . . . . . | 2,145 | 1,885† | n.a. |
| Petroleum wax (paraffin) . . . | 70 | 157† | n.a. |
| Petroleum coke . . . . . | 794 | 997† | n.a. |
| Petroleum bitumen (asphalt) . . | 3,139 | 4,294† | n.a. |
| Liquefied petroleum gas . . . | 5,041 | 4,808† | n.a. |
| Coke . . . . . . | 21,879 | 19,772† | n.a. |
| Rubber tyres ('000)‡ . . . . | 22,954 | 22,008 | 26,155 |
| Rubber footwear ('000 pairs) . . | 20,447 | 20,687 | 20,085 |
| Cement . . . . . . | 26,688 | 26,018 | 28,529 |
| Pig-iron: foundry . . . . . | 890 | 1,061 | 1,032 |
| Pig-iron: steel-making . . . . | 36,387 | 33,521 | 39,663 |

| — continued | 1997 | 1998 | 1999 |
|---|---|---|---|
| Crude steel: for castings. . . . | 2,758 | 2,459 | 3,125 |
| Crude steel: ingots . . . . . | 45,744 | 41,214 | 48,392 |
| Copper (refined, unwrought)† . . | 600 | 620 | 750 |
| Aluminium (unwrought): primary | 2,906 | 3,005 | 3,146 |
| Tractors (number)§ . . . . . | 12,438 | 9,771 | 15,417 |
| Domestic refrigerators ('000) . . | 1,186.2 | 1,042.7 | 1,172.7 |
| Domestic washing machines ('000) | 799.7 | 862.4 | 998.5 |
| Television receivers ('000) . . . | 327.2 | 329.0 | 280.7 |
| Radio receivers ('000) . . . . | 342 | 235 | 332 |
| Passenger motor cars ('000). . . | 986.2 | 840.1 | 954.5 |
| Buses and motor coaches ('000) . | 46.0 | 45.7 | 50.0 |
| Lorries ('000) . . . . . . | 145.9 | 141.5 | 174.6 |
| Cameras: photographic ('000) . . | 143 | 60 | 81 |
| Watches ('000) . . . . . . | 4,983 | 3,763 | 6,304 |
| Electric energy (million kWh) . . | 834,100 | 827,200 | 846,200 |

* Production in terms of (a) nitrogen; (b) phosphoric acid; or (c) potassium oxide.
† Provisional or estimated figure(s).
‡ Tyres for road motor vehicles, excluding bicycles and motorcycles.
§ Tractors of 10 horse-power and over, excluding industrial tractors and tractors for tractor-trailer combinations.

Source: mainly UN, *Industrial Commodity Statistics Yearbook*.

**Raw sugar** ('000 metric tons): 6,076.6 in 2000.

**Vodka and other spirits** (million hectolitres): 12.3 in 2000.

**Wine** ('000 hectolitres): 2,410 in 2000.

**Beer** ('000 hectolitres): 51,600 in 2000.

**Plywood** ('000 cubic metres): 1,484.4 in 2000.

**Motor spirit (petrol)** ('000 metric tons): 27,200 in 2000; 27,500 in 2001.

**Gas-diesel (distillate fuel) oils** ('000 metric tons): 49,200 in 2000; 50,200 in 2001.

**Residual fuel oils** ('000 metric tons): 48,200 in 2000; 50,200 in 2001.

**Rubber tyres** ('000): 27,819 in 2000; 31,100 in 2001.

**Cement** ('000 metric tons): 32,389 in 2000; 35,100 in 2001.

**Crude steel** ('000 metric tons): 59,150 in 2000.

**Tractors** (number): 19,200 in 2000; 15,200 in 2001.

**Domestic refrigerators** ('000): 1,326.8 in 2000; 1,714.0 in 2001.

**Domestic washing machines** ('000): 953.9 in 2000.

**Television receivers** ('000): 1,115.5 in 2000; 1,004.0 in 2001.

**Passenger motor cars** ('000): 969.2 in 2000; 1,022.0 in 2001.

**Electric energy** (million kWh): 877,800 in 2000; 888,000 in 2001.

Source: mainly Ministry of Economic Development and Trade, Moscow.

# Finance

## CURRENCY AND EXCHANGE RATES

**Monetary Units**
100 kopeks = 1 Russian rubl (ruble or rouble).

**Sterling, Dollar and Euro Equivalents** (30 May 2003)
£1 sterling = 50.60 roubles;
US $1 = 30.71 roubles;
€1 = 36.30 roubles;
1,000 roubles = £19.76 = $32.56 = €27.55.

**Average Exchange Rate** (roubles per US dollar)
2000    28.1292
2001    29.1685
2002    31.3485

Note: On 1 January 1998 a new rouble, equivalent to 1,000 of the former units, was introduced. Figures in this Survey are expressed in terms of new roubles, unless otherwise indicated.

## FEDERAL BUDGET
(million roubles)

| Revenue | 1999 | 2000 | 2001 |
|---|---|---|---|
| Tax revenue . . . . . . . | 509,507.2 | 964,782.2 | 1,460,398.0 |
| Taxes on corporate profit and capital gains . . . . . | 101,129.2 | 205,650.2 | 217,366.0 |
| Taxes on goods and services . . | 307,383.5 | 504,931.6 | 845,546.5 |
| Taxes on the use of natural resources . . . . . . . | 10,496.0 | 18,569.0 | 49,692.9 |
| Taxes on international trade and transactions . . . . . . | 86,261.8 | 229,224.2 | 331,340.4 |
| Other current revenue . . . . | 43,105.3 | 74,104.4 | 119,068.5 |
| Income from state property and activities . . . . . . | 6,773.0 | 31,274.4 | 56,990.6 |
| Income from external economic activity . . . . . . | 31,047.1 | 37,406.3 | 51,506.4 |
| Special budgetary funds. . . . | 55,183.4 | 92,115.3 | 14,511.5 |
| **Total** (incl. others) . . . . . | 611,709.6 | 1,131,801.8 | 1,593,978.1 |

| Expenditure | 1999 | 2000 | 2001 |
|---|---|---|---|
| State administration. . . . . | 14,832.4 | 25,003.6 | 41,971.4 |
| International organizations, etc. . | 58,080.3 | 10,342.8 | 23,765.9 |
| National defence . . . . . . | 116,127.5 | 191,727.6 | 247,703.0 |
| Public order and safety . . . . | 55,445.5 | 105,393.1 | 148,909.4 |
| Scientific and technical research . | 11,196.8 | 17,396.4 | 23,687.7 |
| Industry, energy and construction | 16,921.3 | 35,099.1 | 44,153.2 |
| Agriculture and fisheries . . . | 9,068.0 | 13,392.5 | 23,712.1 |
| Transport, communications and information technology . . . | 941.6 | 1,852.2 | 37,122.4 |
| Education . . . . . . . . | 20,945.4 | 38,127.6 | 54,498.8 |
| Health and sport . . . . . . | 10,141.0 | 16,879.3 | 23,085.1 |
| Social security and welfare . . . | 49,096.0 | 67,991.8 | 112,285.4 |
| Servicing of government debt . . | 162,582.7 | 248,656.4 | 231,104.1 |
| Federal transfers. . . . . . | 62,145.0 | 101,208.2 | 230,007.0 |
| Special budgetary funds. . . . | 55,275.3 | 97,679.8 | 14,526.7 |
| **Total** (incl. others) . . . . . | 664,673.8 | 1,019,116.8 | 1,321,902.7 |

Source: Ministry of Finance, Moscow.

## INTERNATIONAL RESERVES
(US $ million at 31 December)

| | 2000 | 2001 | 2002 |
|---|---|---|---|
| Gold* . . . . . . . . . | 3,707.8 | 4,079.8 | 3,739.3 |
| IMF special drawing rights . . | 0.5 | 2.9 | 1.2 |
| Reserve position in IMF . . . | 1.2 | 1.4 | 1.6 |
| Foreign exchange. . . . . . | 24,262.6 | 32,538.1 | 44,050.8 |
| **Total** . . . . . . . . | 27,972.1 | 36,622.2 | 79,792.9 |

* Valued at US $300 per troy ounce.

Source: IMF, *International Financial Statistics*.

## MONEY SUPPLY
(million roubles at 31 December)

| | 2000 | 2001 | 2002 |
|---|---|---|---|
| Currency outside banks . . . . | 419,261 | 584,328 | 764,406 |
| Demand deposits at banks . . . | 443,021 | 585,469 | 706,240 |
| **Total money** (incl. others) . . . | 879,309 | 1,192,627 | 1,499,165 |

Source: IMF, *International Financial Statistics*.

## COST OF LIVING
(Consumer Price Index; base: 1991 = 100)

| | 1998 | 1999 | 2000 |
|---|---|---|---|
| Food . . . . . . . . . . | 412,043.8 | 810,254.3 | 952,103.8 |
| **All items** . . . . . . . . | 416,814.0 | 773,814.0 | 934,450.5 |

Source: ILO.

**2001** (rounded figures): Food 1,148,070; All items 1,135,160 (Source: UN, *Monthly Bulletin of Statistics*).

## NATIONAL ACCOUNTS
('000 million roubles at current prices)

### Expenditure on the Gross Domestic Product

| | 2000 | 2001 | 2002 |
|---|---|---|---|
| Final consumption expenditure . | 4,476.8 | 5,896.8 | 7,402.0 |
| Households . . . . . | 3,295.2 | 4,321.1 | 5,421.9 |
| Non-profit institutions serving households . . . . . | 79.1 | 99.9 | 143.2 |
| General government . . . | 1,102.5 | 1,475.8 | 1,836.9 |
| Gross capital formation . . | 1,365.8 | 1,993.8 | 2,287.3 |
| Gross fixed capital formation . | 1,232.0 | 1,685.8 | 1,947.7 |
| Changes in inventories . . ⎫ | | | |
| Aquisitions, less disposals, of valuables . . . . . ⎬ | 133.8 | 308.0 | 339.6 |
| **Total domestic expenditure** . | 5,842.6 | 7,890.6 | 9,689.3 |
| Exports of goods and services (net) . . . . . . | 1,463.1 | 1,150.0 | 1,148.5 |
| **Sub-total** . . . . . | 7,305.7 | 9,040.7 | 10,837.8 |
| Statistical discrepancy* . . . | — | — | 25.6 |
| **GDP in market prices** . . . | 7,305.7 | 9,040.7 | 10,863.4 |

* Referring to the difference between the sum of the expenditure components and official estimates of GDP, compiled from the production approach.

### Gross Domestic Product by Economic Activity

| | 2000 | 2001 | 2002* |
|---|---|---|---|
| Agriculture and forestry . . . | 420.3 | 526.9 | 565.5 |
| Industry† . . . . . . . | 2,049.2 | 2,271.7 | 2,605.1 |
| Construction . . . . . . | 428.8 | 604.4 | 713.5 |
| Other production sectors . . . | 41.4 | 61.8 | 79.0 |
| Market services . . . . . | 3,041.3 | 3,872.5 | 4,912.0 |
| Transport and communications . | 586.4 | 749.1 | 977.7 |
| Trade and catering . . . | 1,545.5 | 1,811.8 | 2,238.5 |
| Non-market services . . . . | 549.5 | 738.4 | 957.2 |
| **GDP at factor cost** . . . . | 6,530.5 | 8,075.7 | 9,832.3 |
| Indirect taxes, *less* subsidies . . | 775.2 | 965.0 | 1,031.1 |
| **GDP at market prices** . . . | 7,305.7 | 9,040.7 | 10,863.4 |

* Provisional figures.
† Comprising manufacturing (except printing and publishing), mining and quarrying, electricity, gas, water, logging and fishing.

## BALANCE OF PAYMENTS
(US $ million)

| | 2000 | 2001 | 2002 |
|---|---|---|---|
| Exports of goods f.o.b. . . . . | 105,034 | 101,884 | 107,247 |
| Imports of goods f.o.b. . . . . | −44,862 | −53,764 | −60,966 |
| **Trade balance** . . . . . | 60,172 | 48,121 | 46,281 |
| Exports of services . . . . | 9,565 | 10,785 | 13,042 |
| Imports of services . . . . | −16,229 | −19,229 | −22,111 |
| **Balance on goods and services** | 53,508 | 39,677 | 37,212 |
| Other income received . . . | 4,752 | 6,800 | 5,655 |
| Other income paid . . . . | −11,491 | −10,759 | −11,772 |
| **Balance on goods, services and income** . . . . . . | 46,769 | 35,718 | 31,095 |
| Current transfers received . . . | 808 | 381 | 1,600 |
| Current transfers paid . . . . | −737 | −1,140 | −1,605 |
| **Current balance** . . . . | 46,840 | 34,959 | 31,091 |
| Capital account (net) . . . . | 10,675 | −9,378 | −12,396 |
| Direct investment abroad . . . | −3,177 | −2,533 | −3,284 |
| Direct investment from abroad . . | 2,713 | 2,469 | 2,956 |
| Portfolio investment assets . . . | −411 | 77 | −796 |
| Portfolio investment liabilities . . | −12,809 | −730 | 3,295 |
| Other investment assets . . . | −17,662 | 80 | 2,879 |
| Other investment liabilities . . | −3,089 | −3,444 | −3,676 |
| Net errors and omissions . . . | −9,158 | −18,443 | −19,883 |
| **Overall balance** . . . . | 13,922 | 3,058 | 186 |

Source: IMF, *International Financial Statistics*.

# External Trade

## PRINCIPAL COMMODITIES
(distribution by SITC, US $ million)*

| Imports c.i.f. | 1999 | 2000 | 2001 |
|---|---|---|---|
| **Food and live animals** . . . | 5,846.5 | 5,287.1 | 6,704.8 |
| Meat and meat preparations . . | 1,244.0 | 1,050.4 | 1,755.9 |
| Fresh, chilled or frozen meat and edible offal . . . . . | 1,168.6 | 985.0 | 1,690.4 |
| Sugar, sugar preparations and honey . . . . . . . | 1,260.1 | 895.3 | 1,362.3 |
| Sugar and honey . . . . | 1,194.3 | 790.2 | 1,266.2 |
| **Beverages and tobacco** . . . | 1,108.5 | 1,129.4 | 1,273.2 |
| **Crude materials (inedible) except fuels** . . . . . | 1,911.5 | 2,451.8 | 2,334.3 |
| Metalliferous ores and metal scrap | 1,133.7 | 1,554.0 | 1,461.6 |
| **Mineral fuels, lubricants, etc.** . | 796.0 | 1,508.1 | 1,013.1 |
| **Chemicals and related products** . . . . . . | 2,920.0 | 3,715.8 | 5,022.8 |
| Medicinal and pharmaceutical products . . . . . . . | 917.5 | 1,325.4 | 1,867.0 |
| Medicaments (incl. veterinary medicaments) . . . . | 772.3 | 1,109.1 | 1,579.0 |
| **Basic manufactures** . . . . | 3,956.5 | 4,778.3 | 5,585.7 |
| Iron and steel . . . . . | 1,087.4 | 1,424.4 | 1,471.4 |
| **Machinery and transport equipment** . . . . . . | 7,566.4 | 7,698.3 | 11,410.2 |
| Machinery specialized for particular industries . . . . | 1,602.8 | 1,677.0 | 1,894.0 |
| General industrial machinery, equipment and parts . . . . | 1,755.3 | 1,762.9 | 2,466.8 |
| Telecommunications, sound recording and reproducing equipment . . . . . . | 776.7 | 866.4 | 1,432.7 |
| Electrical machinery, apparatus and appliances, etc . . . . | 1,088.6 | 1,119.7 | 1,795.0 |
| Road vehicles . . . . . . | 766.1 | 1,003.3 | 1,869.3 |
| **Miscellaneous manufactured articles** . . . . . . | 1,973.2 | 2,452.1 | 3,533.6 |
| **Total** (incl. others)† . . . . | 40,429.0 | 45,452.8 | 41,527.9 |

| Exports f.o.b. | 1999 | 2000 | 2001 |
|---|---|---|---|
| **Crude materials (inedible) except fuels** . . . . . | 4,437.3 | 4,670.9 | 4,100.6 |
| **Mineral fuels, lubricants, etc.** . | 31,192.0 | 52,846.0 | 53,477.7 |
| Petroleum, petroleum products, etc. . . . . . . . . | 18,905.7 | 34,500.4 | 34,071.7 |
| Crude petroleum oils, etc. . | 13,466.8 | 23,644.3 | 24,562.6 |
| Refined petroleum products . | 5,364.5 | 10,717.5 | 9,412.5 |
| Natural and manufactured gas . | 11,531.8 | 16,990.7 | 17,881.6 |
| Petroleum gases, etc., in the gaseous state . . . . | 11,446.4 | 16,823.7 | 17,766.0 |
| **Chemicals and related products** . . . . . . | 3,894.0 | 4,966.1 | 4,802.4 |
| **Basic manufactures** . . . . | 14,853.6 | 18,367.0 | 15,648.9 |
| Iron and steel . . . . . | 4,759.1 | 6,166.5 | 5,582.0 |
| Ingots and other primary forms | 2,409.5 | 3,099.0 | 2,577.2 |
| Non-ferrous metals . . . . . | 6,826.1 | 8,140.8 | 6,764.9 |
| Aluminium . . . . . . | 4,156.8 | 4,777.4 | 4,267.0 |
| Aluminium and aluminium alloys, unwrought . . . | 3,612.9 | 4,141.8 | 3,632.4 |
| **Machinery and transport equipment** . . . . . . | 5,096.8 | 6,033.3 | 6,234.9 |
| **Total** (incl. others)† . . . . . | 74,663.0 | 103,008.2 | 99,197.5 |

* Figures are provisional. Including adjustments (e.g. for barter trade), the revised totals (in US $ million) are: Imports c.i.f. 43,588 in 1999, 49,125 in 2000, 58,992 in 2001; Exports f.o.b. 75,665 in 1999, 105,565 in 2000, 103,139 in 2001 (Source: IMF, *International Financial Statistics*).
† Including commodities not classified according to kind (US $ million): Imports 13,822.9 in 1999, 15,975.4 in 2000, 4,165.7 in 2001; Exports 9,389.8 in 1998, 12,348.7 in 1999, 12,574.2 in 2000, 11,553.8 in 2001.

Source: UN, *International Trade Statistics Yearbook*.

## PRINCIPAL TRADING PARTNERS
(US $ million)*

| Imports | 1999 | 2000 | 2001 |
|---|---|---|---|
| Austria | 402.4 | 419.2 | 540.1 |
| Belarus | 3,236.0 | 3,764.2 | n.a. |
| Belgium | 447.7 | 481.1 | 642.7 |
| Brazil | 717.4 | 387.6 | 920.6 |
| China, People's Republic | 893.5 | 948.7 | 1,616.9 |
| Cuba | 365.5 | 304.5 | 434.8 |
| Czech Republic | 343.6 | 366.4 | 463.0 |
| Denmark | 359.1 | 345.7 | 496.0 |
| Finland | 947.5 | 958.0 | 1,273.8 |
| France (incl. Monaco) | 1,233.3 | 1,187.8 | 1,520.6 |
| Germany | 4,201.6 | 3,895.9 | 5,753.6 |
| Hungary | 313.3 | 403.5 | 443.5 |
| India | 677.2 | 556.2 | 542.3 |
| Italy | 1,160.1 | 1,211.3 | 1,691.1 |
| Japan | 455.7 | 571.8 | 814.5 |
| Kazakhstan | 1,397.5 | 2,199.7 | 1,815.6 |
| Korea, Republic | 316.7 | 358.6 | 788.9 |
| Netherlands | 688.6 | 739.2 | 846.8 |
| Poland | 602.7 | 716.2 | 952.3 |
| Spain | 246.6 | 313.1 | 488.3 |
| Sweden | 477.2 | 465.4 | 713.6 |
| Turkey | 312.6 | 349.4 | 512.4 |
| Ukraine | 2,528.4 | 3,650.2 | 3,779.4 |
| United Kingdom | 676.2 | 860.7 | 984.2 |
| USA | 2,389.5 | 2,703.2 | 3,208.0 |
| Uzbekistan | 467.6 | 662.6 | 581.3 |
| **Total** (incl. others) | 40,429.0 | 45,452.8 | 41,527.9 |

| Exports | 1999 | 2000 | 2001 |
|---|---|---|---|
| Belarus | 3,759.3 | 5,535.2 | n.a. |
| British Virgin Islands | 1,751.8 | 3,324.1 | 3,006.9 |
| China, People's Republic | 3,526.8 | 5,234.7 | 3,878.3 |
| Cyprus | 170.5 | 1,720.2 | 1,397.1 |
| Czech Republic | 1,325.0 | 1,744.5 | 1,586.7 |
| Estonia | 691.7 | 1,234.8 | 1,251.1 |
| Finland | 2,414.0 | 3,104.5 | 3,164.9 |
| France (incl. Monaco) | 1,218.1 | 1,913.7 | 1,995.0 |
| Germany | 6,202.3 | 9,230.9 | 8,375.6 |
| Hungary | 1,549.0 | 2,405.5 | 2,203.4 |
| India | 1,177.3 | 1,081.7 | 704.4 |
| Italy | 3,755.0 | 7,255.4 | 6,972.6 |
| Japan | 2,124.7 | 2,763.3 | 2,020.7 |
| Kazakhstan | 1,225.6 | 2,247.1 | 2,671.5 |
| Korea, Republic | 826.2 | 972.1 | 733.8 |
| Latvia | 981.4 | 1,625.7 | 970.7 |
| Lithuania | 1,163.0 | 2,065.4 | 1,782.7 |
| Netherlands | 3,673.3 | 4,341.0 | 4,469.6 |
| Poland | 2,607.8 | 4,451.9 | 4,106.0 |
| Slovakia | 1,428.3 | 2,121.2 | 2,092.7 |
| Spain | 501.5 | 1,067.4 | 890.7 |
| Sweden | 1,190.4 | 1,729.4 | 1,623.6 |
| Switzerland-Liechtenstein | 3,479.1 | 3,976.3 | 1,473.1 |
| Turkey | 1,630.8 | 3,098.2 | 3,027.5 |
| Ukraine | 4,792.4 | 5,024.5 | 6,853.6 |
| United Kingdom | 2,885.7 | 4,668.9 | 3,115.3 |
| USA | 4,714.0 | 4,647.8 | 2,876.3 |
| **Total** (incl. others) | 74,663.0 | 103,008.2 | 99,197.5 |

* The figures are compiled on the basis of reporting by Russia's trading partners. Adjusted totals (in US $ million) are: Imports c.i.f. 43,588 in 1999, 49,125 in 2000, 58,992 in 2001; Exports f.o.b. 75,665 in 1999, 105,565 in 2000, 103,139 in 2001(Source: IMF, *International Financial Statistics*).

Source: UN, *International Trade Statistics Yearbook*.

**2002** (US $ million): Total imports c.i.f. 66,243; Total exports f.o.b. 107,110 (Source: IMF, *International Financial Statistics*).

# Transport

## RAILWAYS
(traffic)

| | 1998 | 1999 | 2000 |
|---|---|---|---|
| Paying passengers ('000 journeys) | 1,471,306 | 1,337,509 | 1,418,780 |
| Freight carried ('000 metric tons) | 834,800 | 947,400 | 1,046,800 |
| Passenger-km (million) | 152,900 | 141,000 | 167,100 |
| Freight ton-km (million) | 1,019,500 | 1,204,500 | 1,373,000 |

## ROAD TRAFFIC
(motor vehicles in use)

| | 1998 | 1999 | 2000 |
|---|---|---|---|
| Passenger cars | 18,819,600 | 19,717,800 | 20,353,000 |
| Buses and coaches | 627,500 | 633,200 | 640,100 |
| Lorries and vans | 4,260,000 | 4,387,800 | 4,400,600 |
| Motorcycles and mopeds | 7,165,900 | 6,328,600 | n.a. |

Source: IRF, *World Road Statistics*.

## SHIPPING

**Merchant Fleet**
(registered at 31 December)

| | 2000 | 2001 | 2002 |
|---|---|---|---|
| Number of vessels | 4,755 | 4,727 | 4,943 |
| Total displacement ('000 grt) | 10,485.1 | 10,247.8 | 10,380.0 |

Source: Lloyd's Register-Fairplay, *World Fleet Statistics*.

**International Sea-borne Freight Traffic**
('000 metric tons)

| | 1999 | 2000 | 2001 |
|---|---|---|---|
| Goods loaded | 7,092 | 8,280 | 8,976 |
| Goods unloaded | 744 | 840 | 660 |

Source: UN, *Monthly Bulletin of Statistics*.

## CIVIL AVIATION
(traffic on scheduled services)

| | 1997 | 1998 | 1999 |
|---|---|---|---|
| Kilometres flown (million) | 609 | 581 | 550 |
| Passengers carried ('000) | 20,419 | 18,685 | 18,600 |
| Passenger-km (million) | 49,278 | 46,158 | 45,863 |
| Total ton-km (million) | 5,269 | 4,931 | 5,036 |

Source: UN, *Statistical Yearbook*.

**Passenger-km** (million): 42,948 in 2000; 73,812 in 2001 (Source: UN, *Monthly Bulletin of Statistics*).

# Tourism

**FOREIGN VISITOR ARRIVALS**
('000, incl. excursionists)

| Country of nationality | 1998 | 1999 | 2000 |
|---|---|---|---|
| Armenia | 259.6 | 185.8 | 234.9 |
| Azerbaijan | 601.5 | 930.5 | 1,074.1 |
| Belarus | 218.7 | 190.0 | 243.7 |
| China, People's Republic | 464.2 | 445.9 | 493.8 |
| Estonia | 271.1 | 463.9 | 418.4 |
| Finland | 1,260.3 | 1,406.7 | 1,453.5 |
| Georgia | 924.7 | 1,044.4 | 948.0 |
| Germany | 316.5 | 361.4 | 363.2 |
| Kazakhstan | 203.3 | 358.8 | 2,189.4 |
| Latvia | 209.4 | 259.8 | 329.9 |
| Lithuania | 752.1 | 980.4 | 1,048.8 |
| Moldova | 663.1 | 493.7 | 599.9 |
| Poland | 803.6 | 958.7 | 947.9 |
| Tajikistan | 101.9 | 156.1 | 314.1 |
| Ukraine | 6,412.8 | 7,757.1 | 7,391.7 |
| USA | 212.9 | 184.0 | 198.8 |
| Uzbekistan | 155.9 | 223.9 | 489.3 |
| **Total** (incl. others) | 15,805.2 | 18,493.0 | 21,169.1 |

**Tourism receipts** (US $ million): 6,508 in 1998; 7,510 in 1999.

Source: World Tourism Organization, *Yearbook of Tourism Statistics*.

# Communications Media

| | 1999 | 2000 | 2001 |
|---|---|---|---|
| Television receivers ('000 in use) | 74,000 | 79,000 | n.a. |
| Telephones ('000 main lines in use) | 30,949 | 32,070 | 35,700 |
| Mobile cellular telephones ('000 subscribers) | 1,370.6 | 3,263.2 | 5,560.0 |
| Personal computers ('000 in use) | 5,500 | 6,300 | 7,300 |
| Internet users ('000) | 1,500 | 3,100 | 4,300 |

Source: International Telecommunication Union.

**Radio receivers** ('000 in use): 61,500 in 1997.

**Facsimile machines** (number in use): 52,900 in 1998.

**Book production** (including pamphlets): 36,237 titles in 1996 (421,387,000 copies).

**Daily newspapers:** 285 in 1996 (average circulation 15,517,000 copies).

**Non-daily newspapers:** 4,596 in 1996 (average circulation 98,558,000 copies).

**Other periodicals:** 2,751 in 1996 (average circulation 387,832,000 copies).

Sources: UNESCO, *Statistical Yearbook*; and UN, *Statistical Yearbook*.

# Education

(2000/01)

| | Institu-tions | Teachers | Students |
|---|---|---|---|
| Pre-primary | 51,329 | 608,700 | 4,263,000 |
| Primary | | 330,200 | 5,911,800 |
| Secondary: | 67,063 | | |
| general | | 1,350,200 | 15,837,600 |
| vocational | 3,893 | | 1,679,300 |
| Higher | 965 | n.a | 4,741,400* |

* Excluding foreign students registered at Russian institutions.

Source: partly UN, *Statistical Yearbook for Asia and the Pacific*.

**Adult literacy rate** (UNESCO estimates): 99.6% (males 99.7%; females 99.4%) in 2001 (Source: UN Development Programme, *Human Development Report*).

# Directory

## The Constitution

The current Constitution of the Russian Federation came into force on 12 December 1993, following its approval by a majority of participants in a nation-wide plebiscite. It replaced the Constitution originally adopted on 12 April 1978, but amended many times after 1990.

### THE PRINCIPLES OF THE CONSTITUTIONAL SYSTEM

Chapter One of Section One declares that the Russian Federation (Russia) is a democratic, federative, law-based state with a republican form of government. Its multi-ethnic people bear its sovereignty and are the sole source of authority. State power in the Russian Federation is divided between the legislative, executive and judicial branches, which are independent of one another. Ideological pluralism and a multi-party political system are recognized. The Russian Federation is a secular state and all religious associations are equal before the law. All laws are made public and in accordance with universally acknowledged principles and with international law.

### HUMAN AND CIVIL RIGHTS AND FREEDOMS

Chapter Two states that the basic human rights and freedoms of the Russian citizen are guaranteed regardless of sex, race, nationality or religion. It declares the right to life and to freedom and personal inviolability. The principles of freedom of movement, freedom of expression and freedom of conscience are upheld. Censorship is prohibited. Citizens are guaranteed the right to vote and stand in state and local elections and to participate in referendums. Individuals are to have equal access to state employment, and the establishment of trade unions and public associations is permitted. The Constitution commits the State to protection of motherhood and

childhood and to granting social security, state pensions and social benefits. Each person has the right to housing. Health care and education are free of charge. Basic general education is compulsory. Citizens are guaranteed the right to receive qualified legal assistance. Payment of statutory taxes and levies is obligatory, as is military service.

### THE ORGANIZATION OF THE FEDERATION

Chapter Three names the 89 members (federal territorial units) of the Russian Federation. Russian is declared the state language, but all peoples of the Russian Federation are guaranteed the right to preserve their native tongue. The state flag, emblem and anthem of the Russian Federation are to be established by a federal constitutional law. The Constitution defines the separate roles of the authority of the Russian Federation, as distinct from that of the joint authority of the Russian Federation and the members of the Russian Federation. It also establishes the relationship between federal laws, federal constitutional laws and the laws and other normative legal acts of the subjects of the Russian Federation. The powers of the federal executive bodies and the executive bodies of the members of the Russian Federation are defined.

### THE PRESIDENT OF THE RUSSIAN FEDERATION

Chapter Four describes the powers and responsibilities of the Head of State, the President of the Russian Federation. The President is elected to office for a term of four years by universal, direct suffrage. The same individual may be elected to the office of President for no more than two consecutive terms. The President may appoint the Chairman of the Government (Prime Minister) of the Russian Federation, with the approval of the State Duma, and may dismiss the Deputy Chairmen and the federal ministers from office. The President is entitled to chair sessions of the Government. The President's responsibilities include scheduling referendums and elections to the State Duma, dissolving the State Duma, submitting legislative proposals to the State Duma and promulgating federal laws. The President is responsible for the foreign policy of the Russian Federation. The President is Commander-in-Chief of the Armed Forces and may introduce martial law or a state of emergency under certain conditions.

If the President is unable to carry out the presidential duties, these will be assumed by the Chairman of the Government. The acting President, however, will not possess the full powers of the President, such as the right to dissolve the State Duma or to order a referendum. The President may only be removed from office by the Federation Council on the grounds of a serious accusation by the State Duma.

### THE FEDERAL ASSEMBLY

Chapter Five concerns the Federal Assembly, which is the highest representative and legislative body in the Russian Federation. It consists of two chambers: the Federation Council (upper chamber) and the State Duma (lower chamber). The Federation Council comprises two representatives from each member of the Russian Federation, one appointed by its legislative and one by its executive body (178 senators in total). The State Duma, which is composed of 450 deputies, is elected for a term of four years. The procedures for forming the Federation Council and for electing the State Duma are to be determined by federal legislation. The deputies of the Russian Federation must be over 21 years of age and may not hold government office or any other paid job. The Federal Assembly is a permanent working body.

Both chambers of the Federal Assembly may elect their Chairman and Deputy Chairmen, who preside over parliamentary sessions and supervise the observance of their regulations. Each chamber adopts its code of procedure. The powers of the Federation Council include the approval of the President's decrees on martial law and a state of emergency, the scheduling of presidential elections and the impeachment of the President. The State Duma has the power to approve the President's nominee to the office of Chairman of the Government. Both chambers of the Federal Assembly adopt resolutions by a majority vote of the total number of members. All federal and federal constitutional laws are adopted by the State Duma and submitted for approval first to the Federation Council and then to the President. If the Federation Council or the President reject proposed legislation it is submitted for repeat consideration to one or both chambers of the Federal Assembly.

The State Duma may be dissolved by the President if it rejects all three candidates to the office of Chairman of the Government or adopts a second vote of 'no confidence' in the Government. However, it may not be dissolved during a period of martial law or a state of emergency or in the case of charges being lodged against the President. A newly elected State Duma should be convened no later than four months after dissolution of the previous parliament.

### THE GOVERNMENT OF THE RUSSIAN FEDERATION

The executive authority of the Russian Federation is vested in the Government, which is comprised of the Chairman, the Deputy Chairmen and federal ministers. The Chairman is appointed by the President and his nomination approved by the State Duma. If the State Duma rejects three candidates to the office of Chairman, the President will appoint the Chairman, dissolve the State Duma and order new elections. The Government's responsibilities are to submit the federal budget to the State Duma and to supervise its execution, to guarantee the implementation of a uniform state policy, to carry out foreign policy and to ensure the country's defence and state security. Its duties also include the maintenance of law and order.

Regulations for the activity of the Government are to be determined by a federal constitutional law. The Government can adopt resolutions and directives, which may be vetoed by the President. The Government must submit its resignation to a newly elected President of the Russian Federation, which the President may accept or reject. A vote of 'no confidence' in the Government may be adopted by the State Duma. The President can reject this decision or demand the Government's resignation. If the State Duma adopts a second vote of 'no confidence' within three months, the President will announce the Government's resignation or dissolve the State Duma.

### JUDICIAL POWER

Justice is administered by means of constitutional, civil, administrative and criminal judicial proceedings. Judges in the Russian Federation must be aged 25 or over, have a higher legal education and have a record of work in the legal profession of no less than five years. Judges are independent, irremovable and inviolable. Proceedings in judicial courts are open. No criminal case shall be considered in the absence of a defendant. Judicial proceedings may be conducted with the participation of a jury.

The Constitutional Court comprises 19 judges. The Court decides cases regarding the compliance of federal laws and enactments, the constitutions, statutes, laws and other enactments of the members of the Russian Federation, state treaties and international treaties that have not yet come into force. The Constitutional Court settles disputes about competence among state bodies. Enactments or their individual provisions that have been judged unconstitutional by the Court are invalid. At the request of the Federation Council, the Court will pronounce its judgment on bringing an accusation against the President of the Russian Federation.

The Supreme Court is the highest judicial authority on civil, criminal, administrative and other cases within the jurisdiction of the common plea courts. The Supreme Arbitration Court is the highest authority in settling economic and other disputes within the jurisdiction of the courts of arbitration.

The judges of the three higher courts are appointed by the Federation Council on the recommendation of the President. Judges of other federal courts are appointed by the President.

The Prosecutor's Office is a single centralized system. The Prosecutor-General is appointed and dismissed by the Federation Council on the recommendation of the President. All other prosecutors are appointed by the Prosecutor-General.

### LOCAL SELF-GOVERNMENT

Chapter Eight provides for the exercise of local self-government through referendums, elections and through elected and other bodies. The responsibilities of local self-government bodies include: independently managing municipal property; forming, approving and executing the local budget; establishing local taxes and levies; and maintaining law and order.

### CONSTITUTIONAL AMENDMENTS AND REVISION OF THE CONSTITUTION

Chapter Nine states that no provision contained in Chapters One, Two and Nine of the Constitution is to be reviewed by the Federal Assembly, while amendments to the remaining Chapters may be passed in accordance with the procedure for a federal constitutional law. If a proposal for a review of the provisions of Chapters One, Two and Nine wins a three-fifths majority in both chambers, a Constitutional Assembly will be convened.

### CONCLUDING AND TRANSITIONAL PROVISIONS

Section Two states that the Constitution came into force on the day of the nation-wide vote, 12 December 1993. Should the provisions of a federal treaty contravene those of the Constitution, the constitutional provisions will apply. All laws and other legal acts enforced before the Constitution came into effect will remain valid unless they fail to comply with the Constitution. The President of the Russian Federation will carry out the presidential duties established by the Constitution until the expiry of his term of office. The Council of Ministers will acquire the rights, duties and responsibility of the Government of the Russian Federation established by the Constitution and henceforth be named the Government of the Russian Federation. The courts will administer justice in accordance with their powers established by the Constitution and retain their powers until the expiry of their term.

# The Government

### HEAD OF STATE

**President of the Russian Federation:** VLADIMIR V. PUTIN (elected 26 March 2000; inaugurated 7 May).

### THE GOVERNMENT
(October 2003)

**Chairman (Prime Minister):** MIKHAIL M. KASYANOV.

**Deputy Chairman and Minister of Agriculture and Foodstuffs:** ALEKSEI V. GORDEYEV.

**Deputy Chairman and Minister of Finance:** ALEKSEI L. KUDRIN.

**Deputy Chairman, responsible for Industrial Policy:** BORIS S. ALESHIN.

**Deputy Chairman, responsible for Social Affairs:** GALINA N. KARELOVA.

**Deputy Chairmen:** VIKTOR B. KHRISTENKO, VLADIMIR A. YAKOVLEV.

**Minister for Antimonopoly Policy and Support for Entrepreneurship:** ILYA A. YUZHANOV.

**Minister of Atomic Energy:** ALEKSANDR YU. RUMYANTSEV.

**Minister of Civil Defence, Emergencies and Clean-up Operations:** Lt-Gen. SERGEI K. SHOIGU.

**Minister of Communications and Information Technology:** LEONID D. REIMAN.

**Minister of Culture:** MIKHAIL YE. SHVYDKOI.

**Minister of Defence:** SERGEI B. IVANOV.

**Minister of Economic Development and Trade:** GERMAN O. GREF.

**Minister of Education and Vocational Training:** VLADIMIR M. FILIPPOV.

**Minister of Energy:** IGOR KH. YUSUFOV.

**Minister of Foreign Affairs:** IGOR S. IVANOV.

**Minister of Health:** YURII L. SHEVCHENKO.

**Minister of Industry, Science and Technology:** ILYA I. KLEBANOV.

**Minister of Internal Affairs:** BORIS V. GRYZLOV.

**Minister of Justice:** YURII YA. CHAIKA.

**Minister of Labour and Social Development:** ALEKSANDR P. POCHINOK.

**Minister of Natural Resources:** VITALII G. ARTYUKHOV.

**Minister of the Press, Broadcasting and Mass Media:** MIKHAIL YU. LESIN.

**Minister of Railways:** VADIM N. MOROZOV.

**Minister of State Property:** FARIT R. GAZIZULLIN.

**Minister of Transport:** SERGEI O. FRANK.

**Minister of Taxes and Levies:** GENNADII I. BUKAYEV.

**Head of the Presidential Administration and Minister Without Portfolio:** KONSTANTIN E. MERZLIKIN.

**Minister without Portfolio, responsible for the Social and Economic Development of Chechnya:** STANISLAV V. ILYASOV.

**Minister without Portfolio, responsible for Nationalities Policy:** VLADIMIR YU. ZORIN.

**Minister without Portfolio:** VLADIMIR V. YELAGIN.

## MINISTRIES

**Office of the President:** 103073 Moscow, Kremlin; tel. (095) 925-35-81; fax (095) 206-51-73; e-mail president@gov.ru; internet president.kremlin.ru.

**Office of the Government:** 103274 Moscow, Krasnopresnenskaya nab. 2; tel. (095) 205-57-35; fax (095) 205-42-19; internet www.government.ru.

**Ministry of Agriculture and Foodstuffs:** 107139 Moscow, Orlikov per. 1/11; tel. (095) 207-83-86; fax (095) 207-95-80; e-mail info@aris.ru; internet www.aris.ru.

**Ministry for Antimonopoly Policy and Support for Entrepreneurship:** 123231 Moscow, ul. Sadovaya-Kudrinskaya 11; tel. (095) 254-74-45; fax (095) 254-75-21; e-mail gak1@infpres.ru; internet www.maprf.ru.

**Ministry of Atomic Energy:** 109017 Moscow, ul. B. Ordynka 24/26; tel. (095) 239-45-45; fax (095) 230-24-20; e-mail info@minatom.ru; internet www.minatom.ru.

**Ministry of Civil Defence, Emergencies and Clean-up Operations:** 103012 Moscow, Teatralnyi proyezd 3; tel. (095) 926-39-01; fax (095) 924-19-46; e-mail pressa@emercom.gov.ru; internet www.emercom.gov.ru.

**Ministry of Communications and Information Technology:** 103375 Moscow, ul. Tverskaya 7; tel. (095) 292-71-44; fax (095) 292-74-55; internet www.minsvyaz.ru.

**Ministry of Culture:** 103074 Moscow, Kitaigorodskii proyezd 7; tel. (095) 925-11-95; fax (095) 928-17-91; e-mail root@mincult.isf.ru; internet www.mincultrf.ru.

**Ministry of Defence:** 105175 Moscow, ul. Myasnitskaya 37; tel. (095) 293-38-54; fax (095) 296-84-36; internet www.mil.ru.

**Ministry of Economic Development and Trade:** 125993 Moscow, ul. Tverskaya-Yamskaya 1/3; tel. (095) 200-03-53; e-mail presscenter@economy.gov.ru; internet www.economy.gov.ru.

**Ministry of Education and Vocational Training:** 113833 Moscow, ul. Lyusinovskaya 51; tel. (095) 237-61-55; fax (095) 237-83-81; e-mail mail@ministry.ru; internet www.ed.gov.ru.

**Ministry of Energy:** 103074 Moscow, Kitaigorodskii proyezd 7/191; tel. (095) 220-51-33; fax (095) 220-56-56; e-mail abs@cdu.oilnet.ru; internet www.mte.gov.ru.

**Ministry of Finance:** 103097 Moscow, ul. Ilinka 9; tel. (095) 298-91-01; fax (095) 925-08-89; internet www.minfin.ru.

**Ministry of Foreign Affairs:** 121200 Moscow, Smolenskaya–Sennaya pl. 32/34; tel. (095) 244-16-06; fax (095) 230-21-30; e-mail ministry@mid.ru; internet www.mid.ru.

**Ministry of Health:** 101431 Moscow, ul. Neglinnaya 25; tel. (095) 927-28-48; fax (095) 928-58-15; e-mail press-center@minzdrav-rf.ru; internet www.minzdrav-rf.ru.

**Ministry of Industry, Science and Technology:** 125889 Moscow, pl. Miusskaya 3; tel. (095) 972-70-51; fax (095) 229-55-49; e-mail info@mpnt.gov.ru; internet www.mptn.gov.ru.

**Ministry of Internal Affairs:** 117049 Moscow, ul. Zhitnaya 16; tel. (095) 237-754-85; fax (095) 293-59-98; e-mail uimvd@mvdinform.ru; internet www.mvdinform.ru.

**Ministry of Justice:** 109830 Moscow, ul. Vorontsovo Pole 4A; tel. (095) 206-05-54; fax (095) 916-29-03; internet www.minjust.ru.

**Ministry of Labour and Social Development:** 101999 Moscow, Birzhevaya pl. 1; tel. (095) 298-88-88; fax (095) 230-24-07; e-mail press_mt@zanas.ru; internet www.mintrud.ru.

**Ministry of Natural Resources:** 123812 Moscow, ul. B. Gruzinskaya 4/6; tel. (095) 254-48-00; fax (095) 254-43-10; e-mail admin@mnr.gov.ru; internet www.mnr.gov.ru.

**Ministry of the Press, Broadcasting and Mass Media:** 127994 Moscow, Strastnoi bulv. 5; tel. (095) 229-66-93; fax (095) 200-22-81; internet www.mptr.ru.

**Ministry of Railways:** 107174 Moscow, ul. Novobasmannaya 2; tel. (095) 262-10-02; e-mail info@mps.ru; internet www.mps.ru.

**Ministry of State Property:** 103685 Moscow, Nikolskii per. 9; tel. (095) 298-75-62; fax (095) 206-11-19; e-mail mgi1@ftcenter.ru; internet www.mgi.ru.

**Ministry of Taxes and Levies:** 103381 Moscow, ul. Neglinnaya 23; tel. (095) 200-38-48; fax (095) 200-11-78; e-mail mns@nalog.ru; internet www.nalog.ru.

**Ministry of Transport:** 109012 Moscow, ul. Rozhdestvenka 1/1; tel. (095) 926-10-00; fax (095) 200-33-56; e-mail mcc@morflot.ru; internet www.mintrans.ru.

# President and Legislature

## PRESIDENT

**Presidential Election, 26 March 2000**

| Candidates | Votes | % |
|---|---|---|
| Vladimir V. Putin | 39,740,434 | 52.9 |
| Gennadii A. Zyuganov | 21,928,471 | 29.2 |
| Grigorii A. Yavlinskii | 4,351,452 | 5.8 |
| Aman M. Tuleyev | 2,217,361 | 3.0 |
| Vladimir V. Zhirinovskii | 2,026,513 | 2.7 |
| Konstantin A. Titov | 1,107,269 | 1.5 |
| Ella A. Pamfilova | 758,966 | 1.0 |
| Others | 824,659 | 1.1 |
| Against all candidates | 1,414,648 | 1.9 |
| Invalid votes | 701,003 | 0.9 |
| **Total** | 75,070,776 | 100.0 |

### FEDERAL ASSEMBLY

The Federal Assembly is a bicameral legislative body, comprising the Federation Council and the State Duma.

#### Federation Council

103426 Moscow, ul. B. Dmitrovka 26; tel. (095) 203-90-74; fax (095) 203-46-17; e-mail post_sf@gov.ru; internet www.council.gov.ru.

The Federation Council is the upper chamber of the Federal Assembly. It comprises 178 deputies, two appointed from each of the constituent members (federal territorial units) of the Russian Federation, representing the legislative and executive branches of power in each republic and region.

**Chairman:** SERGEI M. MIRONOV.

**First Deputy Chairman:** VALERII P. GOREGLYAD.

**Deputy Chairmen:** ANDREI A. VIKHARYEV, MIKHAIL YE. NIKOLAYEV, ALEKSANDR P. TORSHIN.

#### State Duma

103265 Moscow, Okhotnyi ryad 1; tel. (095) 292-83-10; fax (095) 292-94-64; e-mail info@duma.ru; internet www.duma.ru.

The State Duma is the 450-seat lower chamber of the Federal Assembly, members of which are elected for a term of four years. Elections to the State Duma were held on 19 December 1999.

**Chairman:** GENNADII N. SELEZNEV.

**First Deputy Chairman:** LYUBOV K. SLISKA.

**Deputy Chairmen:** Vladimir A. Averchenko, Georgii V. Boos, Vladimir V. Zhirinovskii, Vladimir P. Lukin, Petr V. Romanov, Gennadii Yu. Semigin, Irina M. Khakamada, Artur N. Chilingarov.

### General Election, 19 December 1999

| Parties and blocs | Federal party lists | | |
|---|---|---|---|
| | % of votes | Seats | Total seats* |
| Communist Party of the Russian Federation . . . . . . . | 24.29 | 67 | 113 |
| Unity . . . . . . . | 23.32 | 64 | 72 |
| Fatherland—All Russia . . . | 13.33 | 37 | 67 |
| Union of Rightist Forces . . . | 8.52 | 24 | 29 |
| Zhirinovskii bloc . . . . . . | 5.98 | 17 | 17 |
| Yabloko. . . . . . | 5.93 | 16 | 21 |
| Our Home is Russia. . . . | 1.19 | — | 7 |
| Pensioners' Party . . . . | 1.95 | — | 1 |
| Communists and Workers of Russia—for the Soviet Union . | 2.22 | — | — |
| Women of Russia . . . . | 2.04 | — | — |
| Others . . . . . . . | 5.99 | — | 8 |
| Independents . . . . . . | — | — | 106 |
| Against all lists . . . . . | 3.30 | — | — |
| **Total** . . . . . . . | **100.00‡** | **225** | **441§** |

* Including seats filled by voting in single-member constituencies, totalling 225.

† There were 16 other groups, of which six obtained representation in the Duma.

‡ Including spoilt ballot papers (1.95% of the total).

§ Repeat elections were held in March 2000 in eight constituencies where the electorate had voted against all candidates. The remaining constituency, Chechnya, was to remain vacant, owing to the impossibility of holding elections while the conflict in the republic continued.

### THE STATE COUNCIL

The State Council is a consultative body, established in September 2000, and intended to improve co-ordination between federal and regional government, and to strengthen federal control in the regions. The membership of the Council comprises the leaders of the 89 federal subjects and the President of the Russian Federation, who chairs the Council. The President appoints a presidium, comprising seven-members of the Council, who serve for a period of six months.

# Local Government

The Russian Federation comprises 89 federal territorial units (subjects—for details, see p. 369). The basic divisions of local government are autonomous republics, oblasts (regions), krais (provinces), autonomous okrugs (districts), cities, raions (boroughs), and municipal and village authorities.

The Federation Treaty, which was signed on 31 March 1992, provided for a Russian Federation composed of 20 republics (16 of which were autonomous republics under the previous system of local government, and four of which were autonomous oblasts), one autonomous oblast and six krais (provinces). There are also 10 autonomous okrugs (districts), of which nine are under the jurisdiction of the oblast or krai within which they are situated. A further republic, Ingushetiya, was created in June 1992. Two cities, Moscow and St Petersburg, subsequently assumed the status of federal cities. In May 2000 a presidential decree grouped the 89 administrative entities into seven federal districts. Under the new arrangement, the republic of Chechnya was to be governed federally. On 23 March 2003 a referendum on a draft constitution for Chechnya, describing the region as an integral part of Russia, and providing for strengthened powers for the republican president (governor) was held; according to official results the constitution was supported by 96.0% of the participating electorate.

# Political Organizations

In 1999 numerous political parties and movements were formed, in anticipation of the election to the State Duma in December of that year, for which the Central Electoral Commission approved a list of 29 electoral associations and blocs. Each electoral association was based on one registered political party or movement, and each electoral bloc represented an alliance of two or more parties or movements. All 29 presented federal lists of candidates. In accordance with a law signed by President Putin in July 2001, a political party must have at least 10,000 members, including no fewer than 100 members in at least 50 of the 89 subjects of the Russian Federation, in order to register and to function legally.

By July 2003 some 51 parties had registered with the Ministry of Justice, in accordance with the conditions imposed by the legislation signed in July 2001; by early September 44 of those parties registered complied with the conditions of eligibility to participate in the State Duma elections scheduled to be held on 7 December, of which the following were among the most significant. Additionally, 20 'public associations' were eligible to partipate in legislative elections, subject to the condition that they affiliated themselves to electoral blocs.

**Agrarian Party of Russia (APR)** (Agrarnaya partiya Rossii): 107045 Moscow, per. B. Golovin 20/1; tel. (095) 207-99-51; fax (095) 207-99-01; e-mail apr@hotbox.ru; internet www.agroparty.ru; f. 1993; left-wing, supports the agricultural sector; member of the Fatherland-All Russia alliance in 1999–2002; Leader Mikhail I. Lapshin; 41,477 mems (2002).

**Communist Party of the Russian Federation (CPRF)** (Kommunisticheskaya partiya Rossiiskoi Federatsii—KPRF): 103051 Moscow, per. M. Sukharevskii 3/1; tel. (095) 928-71-29; fax (095) 292-90-50; e-mail cprf2000@mail.ru; internet www.kprf.ru; f. 1993; claims succession to the Russian Communist Party, which was banned in 1991; mem. of the People's Patriotic Union of Russia (Narodno-patrioticheskii soyuz Rossii—NPSR); Chair. of Central Committee Gennadii A. Zyuganov; 19,013 mems (2002).

**Congress of Russian Communities** (Kongress russkikh obshchin—KRO): 119270 Moscow, Frunzenskaya nab. 46; tel. (095) 292-71-78; e-mail congress-kro@mail.ru; internet www.congress-kro.ru; f. 1994; concerned with Russian communities resident outside the Russian Federation, particularly in Ukraine, Kazakhstan and Israel, and the relations of Russia with the states of the 'near abroad'; left-wing, 'national-patriotic', party; affiliated to the Motherland (Rodina) electoral bloc registered in Sept. 2003; Chair. Sergei Yu. Glazyev.

**Democratic Party of Russia** (Demokraticheskaya Partiya Rossiya): 103287 Moscow, ul. Poltavskaya 18; tel. (095) 214-39-91; fax (095) 213-11-08; e-mail demparty@fromru.com; internet www .demparty.ru; f. 1990; liberal-conservative; Chair. Mikhail M. Prusak; 12,086 mems (2001).

**Eurasia Political Party of Russia** (Politicheskaya Partiya 'Yevraziya'): 117418 Moscow, ul. Novocheremushkinskaya 69; tel. (095) 310-51-72; promotes the re-integration of the Russian Federation with the countries of the CIS; supports the restoration and maintenance of military parity between Russia and the USA; Leader Aleksandr G. Dugin; 10,794 mems (2002).

**Liberal Democratic Party of Russia (LDPR)** (Liberalno-demokraticheskaya partiya Rossii): 103045 Moscow, Lukov per. 9; tel. (095) 925-07-15; fax (095) 924-08-69; e-mail pressldpr@duma.gov .ru; internet www.ldpr.ru; f. 1988; nationalist; contested 1999 general election as Zhirinovskii bloc; Chair. Vladimir V. Zhirinovskii; 19,098 mems (2002).

**Liberal Russia** (Liberalnaya Rossiya): 103064 Moscow, ul. Zemlyanoi val 4; tel. and fax and fax (095) 722-53-08; e-mail info@ librussia.ru; internet librussia.ru; f. 2001; co-founded by fmr Deputy Secretary of the Security Council, and Executive Secretary of the Commonwealth of Independent States, Boris Berezovskii; registered in Oct. 2002, following expulsion of Berezovskii (in exile); a faction of the party voted to re-admit Berezovskii as its leader in Dec. 2002, and to expel the party's co-chairmen, although this vote was not officially recognized by the party or by the Ministry of Justice; that faction of the party loyal to Berezovskii chose Ivan Rybkin as its leader in July 2003; officially recognized section affiliated to New Course-Automotive Russia electoral bloc formed in late 2003; Co-Chair. Viktor Pokhmelkin, Boris Zolotukhin; 13,000 mems (2003).

**Party of the Rebirth of Russia** (Partiya vozrozhdeniya Rossii): c/o 103625 Moscow, Okhotnyi ryad 1, State Duma; internet seleznev.on .ru/party; f. 2002 on the basis of the Russia (Rossiya) movement; socialist, aims to re-establish Russia as a great power; formed electoral bloc with Russian Party of Life in advance of Dec. 2003 legislative elections; Leader Gennadii N. Seleznev; 20,282 mems (2002).

**People's Party of the Russian Federation (NPRF)** (Narodnaya Partiya Rossiiskoi Federatsii): 109017 Moscow, Klimentovskii per. 9/1; tel. (095) 292-29-34; fax (095) 292-29-32; e-mail info@ narod-party.ru; internet www.narod-party.ru; f. 2001 on the basis of the People's Deputy movement; supports nationalization of natural monopolies and a centrally planned economy; Chair. Gennadii N. Raikov; 39,293 mems (2002).

**People's Will** (Narodnaya volya): 105064 Moscow, Yakovoapostolskii per. 6/3; tel. (095) 917-71-88; fax (095) 917-50-21; e-mail realist@caravan.ru; internet www.narodnayavolya.ru; f. 2002 on basis of Russia All People's Union; left-wing, nationalist, statist;

affiliated to the Motherland (Rodina) electoral bloc registered in Sept. 2003; Chair. SERGEI N. BABURIN; 10,728 mems (2002).

**Russian Democratic Party—Yabloko** (Rossiiskaya Demokraticheskaya Partiya—Yabloko): 119034 Moscow, per. M. Levshinskii 7/3; tel. (095) 201-43-79; fax (095) 292-34-50; e-mail admin@yabloko.ru; internet www.yabloko.ru; f. 1993 on the basis of the Yavlinskii-Boldyrev-Lukin electoral bloc; democratic-centrist; Chair. GRIGORII A. YAVLINSKII; 26,500 mems (2003).

**Russian Ecological Party—Greens** (Rossiiskaya Ekologicheskaya Partiya—Zelenye): 103045 Moscow, per. Poslednyi 26; Chair. ANATOLII A. PANFILOV; 13,195 mems (2002).

**Russian Party of Life** (Rossiiskaya partiya zhizni): 103012 Moscow, Novaya pl. 10; tel. (095) 787-85-15; e-mail info@rpvita.ru; internet www.rpvita.ru; f. 2002; supports the restoration of Russia as a Great Power, and to prolong and improve the quality of life of its citizens; supports presidency of Vladimir Putin; formed electoral bloc with Party of the Rebirth of Russia in advance of Dec. 2003 legislative elections; Chair. SERGEI M. MIRONOV; 11,642 mems (2002).

**Russian Pensioners' Party** (Rossiiskaya Partiya Pensionerov): 101000 Moscow, Sretenskii bulv. 6/1/57; tel. (095) 923-09-42; f. 1998; aims to achieve prosperity, health protection and respect for pensioners; Leader SERGEI P. ATROSHENKO; 18,415 mems (2002).

**Slon (The Elephant)—Union of People for Education and Science** (Partiya 'Slon'—Soyuz lyudei za obrazovaniye i nauku): Moscow; tel. (095) 232-26-43; e-mail press@slon-party.ru ; internet www.slon-party.ru; f. 2002 by fmr mems of Yabloko (q.v.); politically liberal; concerned with protecting the national interests of Russia, the development of the intellectual potential of its people and the strengthening of the state as a means of guaranteeing stability, security, and protection of human rights; Chair. VYACHESLAV V. IGRUNOV.

**Social-Democratic Party of Russia** (Sotsial-Demokraticheskaya Partiya Rossii): 107066 Moscow, per. Tokmakov 23/1; tel. (095) 921-91-04; fax (095) 923-65-56; f. 2001 by merger; Co-Chair. MIKHAIL S. GORBACHEV, KONSTANTIN A. TITOV; 12,671 mems (2002).

**Union of Rightist Forces (URF)** (Soyuz Pravikh Sil—SPS): 109544 Moscow, ul. M. Andronyevskaya 15; tel. (095) 232-04-06; fax (095) 201-26-15; e-mail edit@sps.ru; internet www.sps.ru; f. 1998 as alliance of nine movements, which merged to form one party in 2001; supports moderate pro-market reform; Chair. of the Federal Political Council BORIS YE. NEMTSOV; 14,647 mems (2002).

**Unity and Fatherland-United Russia (UF-UR)** (Yedinstvo i Otechestvo-Yedinaya Rossiya—YeO-YeR): 129110 Moscow, Bannyi per. 3A; tel. (095) 786-86-78; fax (095) 975-30-78; internet www.edinros.ru; f. 2001 on the basis of Unity (Yedinstvo—f. 1999, incorporating Our Home is Russia—Nash Dom-Rossiya), Fatherland (Otechestvo—f. 1999, and led by Mayor of Moscow Yurii Luzhkov) and the All Russia (Vsya Rossiya) grouping of regional governors; centrist, reformist; supports Govt of Pres. Putin; Chair. of Supreme Council YURII VOLKOV; Chair. of Gen. Council VALERII BOGOMOLOV; 19,579 mems (2001).

# Diplomatic Representation

## EMBASSIES IN RUSSIA

**Afghanistan:** 101000 Moscow, Sverchkov per. 3/2; tel. (095) 928-72-78; fax (095) 924-04-78; e-mail afghanem@online.ru; Ambassador AHMAD ZIA MASUD.

**Albania:** 117049 Moscow, ul. Mytnaya 3/23; tel. (095) 230-77-32; fax (095) 230-76-35; e-mail embassy@cnt.ru; Chargé d'affaires a.i. ALBERT JERASI.

**Algeria:** 103051 Moscow, Krapivinskii per. 1A; tel. (095) 200-66-42; fax (095) 200-22-22; Ambassador AMAR ABBA.

**Angola:** 119590 Moscow, ul. U. Palme 6; tel. (095) 923-02-98; fax (095) 956-18-80; e-mail angomosc@garnet.ru; Ambassador ROBERTO LEAL RAMOS MONTEIRO.

**Argentina:** 119017 Moscow, ul. B. Ordynka 72; tel. (095) 502-10-20; fax (095) 502-10-21; e-mail efrus@co.ru; Ambassador JUAN CARLOS SÁNCHEZ ARNAU.

**Armenia:** 101000 Moscow, Armyanskii per. 2; tel. (095) 924-12-69; fax (095) 924-45-35; e-mail armembru@df.ru; internet www.armenianembassy.ru; Ambassador ARMEN SMBATIAN.

**Australia:** 119034 Moscow, Kropotkinskii per. 13; tel. (095) 956-60-70; fax (095) 956-61-70; e-mail austem@comail.ru; internet www.australianembassy.ru; Ambassador LESLIE A. ROWE.

**Austria:** 119034 Moscow, Starokonyushennyi per. 1; tel. (095) 201-73-79; fax (095) 937-42-69; e-mail moscau-ob@bmaa.qv.at; Ambassador Dr FRANZ CEDE.

**Azerbaijan:** 103009 Moscow, Leontyevskii per. 16; tel. (095) 229-16-49; fax (095) 202-50-72; e-mail incoming@azembassy.msk.ru; internet azembassy.msk.ru; Ambassador RAMIZ G. RIZAYEV.

**Bahrain:** 109017 Moscow, ul. B. Ordynka 18/1; tel. (095) 203-00-13; fax (095) 230-24-01; Ambassador TAWFEEQ AHMED KHALIL ALMANSOOR.

**Bangladesh:** 119121 Moscow, Zemledelcheskii per. 6; tel. (095) 246-79-00; fax (095) 248-31-85; e-mail moscow.bangla@com2com.ru; Ambassador S. K. SHARJIL HASSAN.

**Belarus:** 101000 Moscow, ul. Maroseika 17/6; tel. (095) 777-66-44; fax (095) 777-66-33; e-mail mail@embassybel.ru; internet www.embassybel.ru; Ambassador VLADIMIR V. GRIGORYEV.

**Belgium:** 121069 Moscow, ul. M. Molchanovka 7; tel. (095) 937-80-40; fax (095) 937-80-38; e-mail ambabelmos@co.ru; Ambassador ANDRÉ MERNIER.

**Benin:** 103006 Moscow, Uspenskii per. 7; tel. (095) 299-23-60; fax (095) 200-02-26; e-mail ambabeninmoscou@hotmail.com; Ambassador HUBERT SYLVESTRE DÉGUÉNON.

**Bolivia:** 119034 Moscow, Lopukhinskii per. 5; tel. (095) 201-25-13; fax (095) 201-25-08; e-mail embolivia-moscu@rree.gov.bo; Chargé d'affaires a.i. RUBÉN VIDAURRE ANDRADE.

**Bosnia and Herzegovina:** 119590 Moscow, ul. Mosfilmovskaya 50/1/484; tel. (095) 147-64-88; fax (095) 147-64-89; e-mail embassybih@mail.cnt.ru; Ambassador GORDAN MILINIĆ.

**Brazil:** 121069 Moscow, ul. B. Nikitskaya 54; tel. (095) 363-03-66; fax (095) 363-03-67; e-mail brasrus@brasemb.ru; internet www.brasemb.ru; Ambassador JOSÉ VIEGAS FILHO.

**Brunei:** 121059 Moscow, Berezhkovskaya nab. 2, Radisson-Slavyanskaya Hotel, kom. 440–441; tel. (095) 941-82-16; fax (095) 941-82-14; e-mail brumos@mosbusiness.ru; Ambassador Dato PADUKA MAHADI bin Haji WASLI.

**Bulgaria:** 119590 Moscow, ul. Mosfilmovskaya 66; tel. (095) 143-90-22; fax (095) 232-33-02; e-mail bulemrus@bolgaria.ru; internet www.bolgaria.ru; Ambassador ILIYAN VASILEV.

**Burundi:** 117049 Moscow, Kaluzhskaya pl. 1/226–227; tel. (095) 230-25-64; fax (095) 230-20-09; e-mail bdiam@mail.cnt.ru; Ambassador GERMAIN NKESHIMANA.

**Cambodia:** 121002 Moscow, Starokonyushennyi per. 16; tel. (095) 201-24-03; fax (095) 956-65-73; e-mail cambodia@mail.cnt.ru; Ambassador ROS KONG.

**Cameroon:** 121069 Moscow, ul. Povarskaya 40, BP 136; tel. (095) 290-65-49; fax (095) 290-61-16; Ambassador ANDRÉ NGONGANG OUANDJI.

**Canada:** 121002 Moscow, Starokonyushennyi per. 23; tel. (095) 105-60-00; fax (095) 105-60-25; e-mail mosco@dfait-maeci.gc.ca; Ambassador RODNEY IRWIN.

**Cape Verde:** 121615 Moscow, Rublevskoye shosse 26/180–181; tel. (095) 415-45-04; fax (095) 415-45-05; e-mail pts287@ipc.ru; Chargé d'affaires HÉRCULES DO NASCIMENTO CRUZ.

**Central African Republic:** 117571 Moscow, ul. 26-i Bakinskikh Kommissarov 9/124–125; tel. (095) 434-45-20; Ambassador CLAUDE BERNARD BELOUM.

**Chad:** 121615 Moscow, Rublevskoye shosse 26/1/20–21; tel. (095) 415-41-39; fax (095) 415-29-41; Ambassador DJIBRINE ABDOUL.

**Chile:** 121002 Moscow, Denezhnii per. 7/1; tel. (095) 241-01-45; fax (095) 241-68-67; e-mail echileru@aha.ru; Ambassador PABLO CABRERA GAETE.

**China, People's Republic:** 117330 Moscow, ul. Druzhby 6; tel. (095) 938-20-06; fax (095) 938-21-32; e-mail chinaembassy_ru@fmprc.gov.cn; internet www.chinaembassy.ru; Ambassador ZHANG DEGUANG.

**Colombia:** 119121 Moscow, ul. Burdenko 20/2; tel. (095) 248-30-42; fax (095) 248-30-25; e-mail emoscu@minrelaxt.gov.co; Ambassador MIGUEL SANTAMARIA DAVILA.

**Congo, Democratic Republic:** 113556 Moscow, Simferopolskii bulv. 7A/ 49–50; tel. and fax (095) 113-83-48; Chargé d'affaires a.i. SOPHIE MUIKA BAKENGE.

**Congo, Republic:** 117049 Moscow, ul. Donskaya 18/7; tel. (095) 236-33-68; fax (095) 236-41-16; Ambassador JEAN-PIERRE LOUYEBO.

**Costa Rica:** 121615 Moscow, Rublevskoye shosse 26/1/23; tel. (095) 415-40-42; fax (095) 415-40-14; e-mail embaric2@rol.ru; Ambassador PLUTARCO HERNÁNDEZ SANCHO.

**Côte d'Ivoire:** 119034 Moscow, Korobeinikov per. 14/9; tel. (095) 201-24-00; fax (095) 201-20-45; e-mail ambacimow@hotmail.com; Ambassador JEAN-CLAUDE KALOU-DJÈ.

**Croatia:** 119034 Moscow, per. Korobeinikov 16/10; tel. (095) 201-38-68; fax (095) 201-46-24; e-mail admin@croemba.msk.ru; Chargé d'affaires a.i. MIRKO VLASTELICA.

**Cuba:** 103009 Moscow, Leontiyevskii per. 9; tel. (095) 290-28-82; fax (095) 202-53-92; e-mail embacuba@online.ru; Ambassador CARLOS PALMAROLA CORDERO.

**Cyprus:** 121069 Moscow, ul. B. Nikitskaya 51; tel. (095) 290-21-54; fax (095) 200-12-54; e-mail piocypmos@col.ru; Ambassador CHARALOMBOS G. IOANNIDES.

**Czech Republic:** 123056 Moscow, ul. Yu. Fuchika 12/14; tel. (095) 251-05-40; fax (095) 250-15-23; e-mail moscow@embassy.mzv.cz; internet www.mfa.cz/moscow; Ambassador JAROSLAV BAŠTA.

**Denmark:** 119034 Moscow, Prechistenskii per. 9; tel. (095) 201-78-68; fax (095) 201-53-57; e-mail mowamb@mowamb.um.dk; internet www.danishembassy.ru; Ambassador LARS VISSING.

**Ecuador:** 103064 Moscow, Gorokhovskii per. 12; tel. (095) 261-55-44; fax (095) 267-70-79; e-mail mosecua@online.ru; Ambassador XIMENA MARTÍNEZ DE PÉREZ.

**Egypt:** 121069 Moscow, Kropotkinskii per. 12; tel. (095) 246-30-96; fax (095) 246-10-64; Ambassador RAOUF SAAD.

**Equatorial Guinea:** 109017 Moscow, Pogorelskii per. 7/1; tel. (095) 953-27-66; fax (095) 953-20-84; Ambassador LUIS OBIANG MENGUE.

**Eritrea:** 129090 Moscow, ul. Meshchanskaya 17; tel. (095) 971-06-20; fax (095) 971-37-67; Ambassador NAIZGHI KEFLU BAHTA.

**Estonia:** 103009 Moscow, M. Kislovskii per. 5; tel. (095) 737-36-40; fax (095) 737-36-46; e-mail embassy@estemb.ru; internet www.estemb.ru; Ambassador KARIN YAANI.

**Ethiopia:** 129041 Moscow, Orlovo-Davydovskii per. 6; tel. (095) 280-16-16; fax (095) 280-66-08; e-mail eth-emb@col.ru; Ambassador ASAMINEW BEDANIE AREGGIE.

**Finland:** 119034 Moscow, Kropotkinskii per. 15/17; tel. (095) 787-41-74; fax (095) 247-33-80; e-mail sanomat.mos@formin.fi; internet www.finemb-moscow.fi; Ambassador RENÉ NYBERG.

**France:** 117049 Moscow, ul. B. Yakimanka 45; tel. (095) 937-15-00; fax (095) 937-14-30; e-mail amba@ambafrance.ru; internet www.ambafrance.ru; Ambassador CLAUDE BLANCHEMAISON.

**Gabon:** 121002 Moscow, Denezhnyi per. 16; tel. (095) 241-00-80; fax (095) 244-06-94; Ambassador BENJAMIN LÉGNONGO-NDUMBA.

**Georgia:** 121069 Moscow, M. Rzhevskii per. 6; tel. (095) 290-46-57; fax (095) 291-21-36; e-mail ineza@got.mmtel.ru; Ambassador ZURAB I. ABASHIDZE.

**Germany:** 119285 Moscow, ul. Mosfilmovskaya 56; tel. (095) 937-95-00; fax (095) 938-23-54; e-mail germanmo@aha.ru; internet www.deutschebotschaft-moskau.ru; Ambassador Dr HANS-FRIEDRICH VON PLOETZ.

**Ghana:** 121069 Moscow, Skatertnyi per. 14; tel. (095) 202-18-71; fax (095) 202-29-41; e-mail embghmos@astelit.ru; Ambassador Maj.-Gen. FRANCIS YAHAYA MAHAMA.

**Greece:** 103009 Moscow, Leontiyevskii per. 4; tel. (095) 290-14-46; fax (095) 771-65-10; e-mail gremb.mow@mfa.gr; internet www.hellas.ru; Ambassador DIMITRIOS PARASKEVOPOULOS.

**Guatemala:** 117049 Moscow, ul. Korovyi val 7/92; tel. (095) 238-59-14; fax (095) 238-22-14; e-mail embguarus@online.ru; Ambassador ALFONSO MATTA FAHSEN.

**Guinea:** 119034 Moscow, Pomerantsev per. 6; tel. (095) 201-36-01; fax (502) 220-21-38; Ambassador Lt-Col AMARA BANGOURA.

**Guinea-Bissau:** 113556 Moscow, Simferopolskii bulv. 7A /183; tel. and fax (095) 317-95-82; Ambassador ROGERIO ARAUGO ADOLPHO HERBERT.

**Holy See:** 127055 Moscow, Vadkovskii per. 7/37 (Apostolic Nunciature); tel. (095) 726-59-30; fax (095) 726-59-32; e-mail nuntius@cityline.ru; Apostolic Nuncio Most Rev. ANTONIO MENNINI (Titular Archbishop of Ferrento).

**Hungary:** 119590 Moscow, ul. Mosfilmovskaya 62; tel. (095) 796-93-70; fax (095) 796-93-80; e-mail email@huembmow.macomnet.ru; internet www.huembmow.macomnet.ru; Ambassador Dr FERENC KONTRA.

**Iceland:** 101000 Moscow, Khlebnyi per. 28; tel. (095) 956-76-05; fax (095) 956-76-12; e-mail icemb.moscow@utn.stjr.is; Ambassador BENEDIKT JÓNSSON.

**India:** 101000 Moscow, ul. Vorontsovo Polye 6/8; tel. (095) 917-40-44; fax (095) 917-42-09; e-mail indianembas@pol.ru; internet www.indianembassy.ru; Ambassador KRISHNAN RAGHUNATH.

**Indonesia:** 109017 Moscow, ul. Novokuznetskaya 12/14; tel. (095) 951-95-50; fax (095) 230-64-31; e-mail kbrimos@online.ru; Ambassador Prof. JOHN ARIO KATILI.

**Iran:** 117292 Moscow, Pokrovskii bulv. 7; tel. (095) 917-72-82; fax (095) 230-28-97; Ambassador GHOLMREZA SHAFEHEE.

**Iraq:** 110121 Moscow, ul. Pogodinskaya 12; tel. (095) 246-55-08; fax (095) 230-33-93; e-mail iraqimoscow@yahoo.com; Ambassador ABBAS KHALAF KUNFUD.

**Ireland:** 129010 Moscow, Grokholskii per. 5; tel. (095) 937-59-11; fax (095) 975-20-66; e-mail ireland@col.ru; Ambassador JUSTIN. HARMAN.

**Israel:** 113095 Moscow, ul. B. Ordynka 56; tel. (095) 230-67-00; fax (095) 238-13-46; e-mail moscow@israel.org; Ambassador ARKADII MELMAN.

**Italy:** 121002 Moscow, Denezhnyi per. 5; tel. (095) 796-96-91; fax (095) 253-92-89; e-mail embitaly@ambmosca.ru; internet www.ambmosca.ru; Ambassador GIANFRANCO FACCO BONETTI.

**Japan:** 103009 Moscow, Kalashnyi per. 12; tel. (095) 291-85-00; fax (095) 200-12-40; e-mail embjapan@mail.cnt.ru; internet www.embjapan.ru; Ambassador ISSEI NOMURA.

**Jordan:** 103001 Moscow, Mamonovskii per. 3; tel. (095) 299-43-44; fax (095) 299-43-54; Ambassador AHMAD ALI AL-MUBAYDEEN.

**Kazakhstan:** 101000 Moscow, Chistoprudnyi bulv. 3A; tel. (095) 927-17-15; fax (095) 208-26-50; e-mail kazembassy@kazembassy.ru; internet www.kazembassy.ru; Ambassador ALTYNBEK SARSENBAIULY.

**Kenya:** 101000 Moscow, ul. B. Ordynka 70; tel. (095) 237-47-02; fax (095) 230-23-40; e-mail kenya@cityline.ru; Ambassador Dr MESHAK G. NYAMBATI.

**Korea, Democratic People's Republic:** 107140 Moscow, ul. Mosfilmovskaya 72; tel. (095) 143-62-49; fax (095) 143-63-12; Ambassador PAK HIU CHUN.

**Korea, Republic:** 131000 Moscow, ul. Spiridonovka 14; tel. (095) 956-14-74; fax (095) 956-24-34; e-mail info@koreamb.ru; Ambassador CHONG TAE-IK.

**Kuwait:** 119285 Moscow, ul. Mosfilmovskaya 44; tel. (095) 147-00-40; fax (095) 956-60-32; Ambassador MOHAMMED SAAD UDAHA AL-SALLAL.

**Kyrgyzstan:** 109017 Moscow, ul. B. Ordynka 64; tel. (095) 237-48-82; fax (095) 237-44-52; Ambassador KEMELBEK NANAYEV.

**Laos:** 131940 Moscow, ul. M. Nikitskaya 18; tel. (095) 290-25-60; fax (095) 290-49-24; Chargé d'affaires a.i. SODOM PHETRASY.

**Latvia:** 103062 Moscow, ul. Chaplygina 3; tel. (095) 925-27-07; fax (095) 923-92-95; e-mail embassy.russia@mfa.gov.lv; Ambassador NORMANS PENKE.

**Lebanon:** 103051 Moscow, ul. Sadovaya-Samotechnaya 14; tel. (095) 200-00-22; fax (095) 200-32-22; Ambassador BOUTROS ASSAKER.

**Libya:** 131940 Moscow, ul. Mosfilmovskaya 38; tel. (095) 143-03-54; fax (095) 938-21-62; Secretary of Peoples' Bureau (Ambassador) SALLEH ABDALLAH SALLEH.

**Lithuania:** 121069 Moscow, Borisoglebskii per. 10; tel. (095) 785-86-05; fax (095) 785-86-00; e-mail ltemb@ltembassy.ru; internet amb.urm.lt/rusija; Ambassador RIMANTAS ŠIDLAUSKAS.

**Luxembourg:** 119034 Moscow, Khrushchevskii per. 3; tel. (095) 202-53-81; fax (095) 200-52-43; e-mail amb.amluxru@lbg.ru; Ambassador CAMILLE WEIS.

**Macedonia, former Yugoslav republic:** 117292 Moscow, ul. D. Ulyanova 16/2/509–510; tel. (095) 124-33-57; fax (095) 124-33-59; e-mail mkambmos@mail.tascom.ru; Ambassador DIMITAR DIMITROV.

**Madagascar:** 119034 Moscow, Kursovoi per. 5; tel. (095) 290-02-14; fax (095) 202-34-53; Ambassador ELOI MAXIME DOVO.

**Malaysia:** 117192 Moscow, ul. Mosfilmovskaya 50; tel. (095) 147-15-14; fax (095) 937-96-02; e-mail mwmoscow@co.ru; Ambassador Dato KAMARUDDIN MUSTAFA.

**Mali:** 113184 Moscow, ul. Novokuznetskaya 11; tel. (095) 951-06-55; fax (095) 230-28-89; e-mail amalirus@orc.ru; Ambassador (vacant).

**Malta:** 117049 Moscow, ul. Korovyi val 7/219; tel. (095) 237-19-39; fax (095) 237-21-58; e-mail maltamsk@online.ru; Ambassador Dr JOSEPH CASSAR.

**Mauritania:** 109017 Moscow, ul. B. Ordynka 66; tel. (095) 237-37-92; fax (095) 237-28-61; e-mail embarim@hotmail.com; Ambassador MOHAMMAD MAHMOUD OULD MOHAMMAD VALL.

**Mexico:** 119034 Moscow, B. Levshinskii per. 4; tel. (095) 201-48-48; fax (095) 230-20-42; e-mail embmxru@online.ru; Ambassador LUCIANO EDUARDO JOUBLANC MONTAÑO.

**Moldova:** 103031 Moscow, ul. Kuznetskii most 18; tel. (095) 924-53-53; fax (095) 924-95-90; e-mail moldemb@online.ru; internet www.moldova.ru; Ambassador VLADIMIR TSURCAN.

**Mongolia:** 121069 Moscow, Borisoglebskii per. 11; tel. (095) 290-67-92; fax (095) 291-46-36; e-mail mongolia@online.ru; Ambassador SANJAA BAYAR.

**Morocco:** 119034 Moscow, Prechistenskii per. 8; tel. (095) 201-73-51; fax (095) 230-20-67; e-mail sifmamos@df.ru; Ambassador ABDEL-MALEK EL-JEDDAOUI.

**Mozambique:** 129090 Moscow, ul. Gilyarovskogo 20; tel. (095) 284-40-07; fax (095) 200-42-35; e-mail embamocru@netscape.ru; Ambassador GREGÓRIO ELTON PAULO LINGANDE.

**Myanmar:** 121069 Moscow, ul. B. Nikitskaya 41; tel. (095) 291-05-34; fax (095) 956-31-86; e-mail mofa.aung@mptmail.net.mm; Ambassador U TIN SOE.

**Namibia:** 113096 Moscow, 2-i Kazachii per. 7; tel. (095) 230-01-13; fax (095) 230-22-74; e-mail namibembrf@glasnet.ru; Ambassador MARTEN N. KAPEWASHA.

**Nepal:** 119121 Moscow, 2-i Neopalimovskii per. 14/7; tel. (095) 244-02-15; fax (095) 244-00-00; e-mail nepal@orc.ru; Ambassador LILA PRASAD SHARMA.

**Netherlands:** 103009 Moscow, Kalashnyi per. 6; tel. (095) 797-29-00; fax (095) 797-29-04; e-mail nederl@sovintel.ru; internet www.netherlands.ru; Ambassador TIDDO P. HOFSTEE.

**New Zealand:** 121069 Moscow, ul. Povarskaya 44; tel. (095) 956-35-79; fax (095) 956-35-83; e-mail nzembmos@online.ru; internet www.nzembassy.msk.ru; Ambassador GEOFF K. WARD.

**Nicaragua:** 117192 Moscow, ul. Mosfilmovskaya 50/1; tel. (095) 938-20-82; fax (095) 938-27-01; e-mail embanic_moscu@mail.ru; Ambassador CARLOS IVÁN OTERO CASTAÑEDA.

**Nigeria:** 121069 Moscow, ul. M. Nikitskaya 13; tel. (095) 290-37-83; fax (095) 956-28-25; e-mail nigeriamosco@glasnet.ru; internet www.nigerianembassy-moscow.ru/; Ambassador Maj.-Gen. (retd) ABDUL-LAHI SARKI MUKHTAR.

**Norway:** 131940 Moscow, ul. Povarskaya 7; tel. (095) 933-14-10; fax (095) 933-14-11; e-mail emb.moscow@mfa.no; internet www.norvegia.ru; Ambassador ØYVIND NORDSLETTEN.

**Oman:** 109180 Moscow, Staromonetnii per. 14/1; tel. (095) 230-15-87; fax (095) 230-15-44; e-mail amoman@ipc.ru; Ambassador MUHAMMAD BIN SAID BIN MUHAMMAD AL-LAWATI.

**Pakistan:** 103001 Moscow, ul. Sadovaya-Kudrinskaya 17; tel. (095) 254-97-91; fax (095) 956-90-97; e-mail chancery@interanet.ru; Ambassador S. IFTIKHAR MURSHED.

**Panama:** 119590 Moscow, ul. Mosfilmovskaya 50/1; tel. (095) 956-07-29; fax (095) 956-07-30; e-mail empanrus@aha.ru; Ambassador HARRY ALBERTO DÍAZ STRUNZ.

**Peru:** 121002 Moscow, Smolenskii bulv. 22/14/15; tel. (095) 248-77-38; fax (095) 230-20-00; e-mail leprumoscu@mtu-net.ru; Ambassador Dr PABLO HUGO PORTUGAL RODRIGUEZ.

**Philippines:** 121099 Moscow, Karmanitskii per. 6; tel. (095) 241-05-63; fax (095) 241-26-30; e-mail moscowpe@co.ru; internet phil_embassy_moscow.tripod.com; Ambassador ERNESTO LLAMA.

**Poland:** 123557 Moscow, ul. Klimashkina 4; tel. (095) 231-15-00; fax (095) 231-15-15; e-mail pol.amb@g23.relcom.ru; Ambassador STEFAN MELLER.

**Portugal:** 129010 Moscow, Botanicheskii per. 1; tel. (095) 280-62-68; fax (095) 280-92-03; e-mail embptrus@deltacom.ru; Ambassador JOÃO DIOGO NUNES BARATA.

**Qatar:** 117049 Moscow, ul. Korovyi val 7/196–198; tel. (095) 230-15-77; fax (095) 230-22-40; e-mail moscow@mofa.gov.qa; Ambassador SHAMLAN MARZOUQ AL-SHAMLAM.

**Romania:** 101000 Moscow, ul. Mosfilmovskaya 64; tel. (095) 143-04-24; fax (095) 143-04-49; e-mail bucur@dol.ru; Ambassador AUREL CONSTANTIN ILIE.

**Saudi Arabia:** 119121 Moscow, 3-i Neopalimovskii per. 3; tel. (095) 245-39-70; fax (095) 246-94-71; Ambassador MOHAMED H. ABDULWALI.

**Serbia and Montenegro:** 119285 Moscow, ul. Mosfilmovskaya 46; tel. (095) 147-41-06; fax (095) 147-41-04; e-mail ambasada@co.ru; Ambassador MILAN ROCEN.

**Sierra Leone:** 121615 Moscow, Rublevskoye shosse 26/1/58–59; tel. (095) 415-41-66; fax (095) 415-29-85; Ambassador MELROSE BEYON KAI-BANYA.

**Singapore:** 121099 Moscow, per. Kamennoi Slobody 5; tel. (095) 241-37-02; fax (095) 241-78-95; e-mail sinemb@online.ru; Chargé d'affaires a.i. CHRISTOPHER CHEANG.

**Slovakia:** 123056 Moscow, ul. Yu. Fuchika 17/19; tel. (095) 250-10-70; fax (095) 973-20-81; e-mail skem@col.ru; Ambassador IGOR FURDIK.

**Slovenia:** 103006 Moscow, ul. M. Dmitrovka 14/1; tel. (095) 209-02-03; fax (095) 200-15-68; e-mail vmo@mzz-dkp.sigov.si; internet www.gov.si/mzz/vmo; Ambassador Dr FRANCI DEMŠAR.

**Somalia:** 121248 Moscow, Simferopolskii bulv. 7A /145; tel. and fax (095) 317-06-22; Chargé d'affaires a.i. MAYE MAO DERE.

**South Africa:** 113054 Moscow, B. Strochenovskii per. 22/25; tel. (095) 230-68-69; fax (095) 230-68-65; e-mail info@saembassy.ru; internet saembassy.ru; Ambassador Dr MOCHUBELA JACOB SEEKOE.

**Spain:** 121069 Moscow, ul. B. Nikitskaya 50/8; tel. (095) 202-21-61; fax (095) 291-91-71; e-mail ispan@aha.ru; internet www.ispania.aha.ru; Ambassador JOSÉ MARIA ROBLES FRAGA.

**Sri Lanka:** 129090 Moscow, ul. Shchepkina 24; tel. (095) 288-16-20; fax (095) 288-17-57; e-mail lankaemb@com2com.ru; Ambassador N. SIKKANDER.

**Sudan:** 103006 Moscow, Uspenskii per. 9; tel. (095) 290-33-13; fax (095) 290-39-85; e-mail sudy@com2com.ru; Ambassador Dr IBRAHIM AL-BASHIR OSMAN AL-KABASHI.

**Sweden:** 119590 Moscow, ul. Mosfilmovskaya 60; tel. (095) 937-92-00; fax (095) 937-92-02; e-mail sweden@aha.ru; internet www.sweden.ru; Ambassador SVEN HIRDMAN.

**Switzerland:** 100100 Moscow, per. Ogorodnoi Slobody 2/5; tel. (095) 258-38-30; fax (095) 200-17-28; e-mail swiss.embassy@g23.relcom.ru; internet www.eda.admin.ch/moscow_emb/e/home.html; Ambassador WALTER FETSCHERIN.

**Syria:** 119034 Moscow, Mansurovskii per. 4; tel. (095) 203-15-21; fax (095) 956-31-91; Ambassador WAHIB AL-FADEL.

**Tajikistan:** 103001 Moscow, Granatnyi per. 13; tel. (095) 290-38-46; fax (095) 291-89-98; e-mail tajikistan@tajikistan.ru; internet www.tajikistan.ru; Ambassador SAFAR G. SAFAROV.

**Tanzania:** 109017 Moscow, ul. Pyatnitskaya 33; tel. (095) 953-82-21; fax (095) 956-61-30; e-mail tzmos@wm.west.call.com; Ambassador EVA LILIAN NZARO.

**Thailand:** 129090 Moscow, ul. B. Spasskaya 9; tel. (095) 208-08-17; fax (095) 207-53-43; e-mail thaiemb@nnt.ru; Ambassador SORAYOUTH PROMPOJ.

**Tunisia:** 113105 Moscow, ul. M. Nikitskaya 28/1; tel. (095) 291-28-58; fax (095) 291-75-88; Ambassador KHALIFA EL HAFDHI.

**Turkey:** 119121 Moscow, 7-i Rostovskii per. 12; tel. (095) 246-00-09; fax (095) 245-63-48; e-mail turemb@dol.ru; internet www.turkishline.ru/embassy; Ambassador KURTULUS TASKENT.

**Turkmenistan:** 121019 Moscow, Filippovskii per. 22; tel. (095) 291-66-36; fax (095) 291-09-35; Ambassador KHALNAZAR A. AGAKHANOV.

**Ukraine:** 103009 Moscow, Leontiyevskii per. 18; tel. (095) 229-10-79; fax (095) 924-84-69; e-mail ukremb@online.ru; Ambassador MYKOLA P. BILOBLOTSKIY.

**United Arab Emirates:** 101000 Moscow, ul. U. Palme 4; tel. (095) 147-00-66; fax (095) 234-40-70; e-mail uae@mail.cnt.ru; Ambassador TARIQ AHMED AL-HAIDAN.

**United Kingdom:** 121099 Moscow, Smolenskaya nab. 10; tel. (095) 956-72-00; fax (095) 956-72-01; e-mail moscow@britishembassy.ru; internet www.britemb.msk.ru; Ambassador Sir RODERIC LYNE.

**USA:** 121099 Moscow, B. Devyatinskii per. 8; tel. (095) 728-50-00; fax (095) 728-50-90; e-mail pamoscow@pd.state.gov; internet www.usembassy.ru; Ambassador ALEXANDER R. VERSHBOW.

**Uruguay:** 117330 Moscow, Lomonosovskii pr. 38; tel. (095) 143-04-01; fax (095) 938-20-45; e-mail ururus.embajada@mtu-net.ru; Ambassador ALBERTO LEOPOLDO FAJARDO KLAPPENBACH.

**Uzbekistan:** 109017 Moscow, Pogorelskii per. 12; tel. (095) 230-75-52; fax (095) 238-89-18; Ambassador SHAKASYM I. SHAISLAMOV.

**Venezuela:** 103051 Moscow, B. Karetnyi per. 13/15; tel. (095) 299-40-42; fax (095) 956-61-08; e-mail karakas@mail.cnt.ru; Ambassador PAULINO PARADES.

**Viet Nam:** 119021 Moscow, ul. B. Pirogovskaya 13; tel. (095) 247-02-12; fax (095) 245-10-92; e-mail dsqvn@com2com.ru; Ambassador NYUGEN VAN NGANG.

**Yemen:** 119121 Moscow, 2-i Neopalimovskii per. 6; tel. (095) 246-15-40; fax (095) 230-23-05; Ambassador ABDO ALI ABDULRAHMAN.

**Zambia:** 129041 Moscow, pr. Mira 52A; tel. (095) 288-50-01; fax (095) 975-20-56; Ambassador Prof. LYSON POTIPHER TEMBO.

**Zimbabwe:** 119121 Moscow, per. Serpov 6; tel. (095) 248-43-67; fax (095) 230-24-97; e-mail zimbabwe@rinet.ru; Ambassador Brig. (retd) AGRIPPAH MUTAMBARA.

# Judicial System

In January 1995 the first section of a new code of civil law came into effect. It included new rules on commercial and financial operations, and on ownership issues. The second part of the code was published in January 1996. The Constitutional Court rules on the conformity of government policies, federal laws, international treaties and presidential enactments with the Constitution. Following its suspension in October 1993, the Court was reinstated, with a new membership of 19 judges, in April 1995. The Supreme Arbitration Court rules on disputes between commercial bodies. The Supreme Court overseas all criminal and civil law, and is the final court of appeal from lower courts. A system of Justices of the Peace, to deal with certain civil cases, and with criminal cases punishable by a maximum of two years' imprisonment, was established in 1998. In December 2001 President Putin approved several reforms to the judicial system, including the introduction of trials by jury across the Russian Federation, and procedures to guarantee the independence of judges. Some 70 of the 89 administrative regions of Russia were expected to introduce jury trials, in many cases only for the most serious crimes, during 2003.

**Constitutional Court of the Russian Federation:** 103132 Moscow, ul. Ilinka 21; tel. (095) 206-16-72; fax (095) 206-19-78; e-mail ksrf@ksmail.rfnet.ru; internet ks.rfnet.ru; f. 1991; Chair. VALERII D. ZORKIN; Dep. Chair. VLADIMIR G. STREKOZOV; Sec.-Gen. YURII V. KUDZYAVTSEV.

**Office of the Prosecutor-General:** 103793 Moscow, ul. B. Dmitrovka 15A; tel. (095) 292-88-69; fax (095) 292-88-48; Prosecutor-General VLADIMIR V. USTINOV; Dep. Prosecutor-General VLADIMIR KOLESNIKOV.

**Supreme Arbitration Court of the Russian Federation:** 101000 Moscow, M. Kharitonevskii per. 12; tel. (095) 208-11-19; fax (095) 208-11-62; internet www.arbitr.ru; f. 1993; Chair. VENYAMIN F. YAKOVLEV.

**Supreme Court of the Russian Federation:** 103289 Moscow, ul. Ilinka 7/3; tel. (095) 924-23-47; fax (095) 202-71-18; e-mail gastello@ilinka.supcourt.ru; internet www.supcourt.ru; Chair. VYACHESLAV M. LEBEDEV.

# Religion

The majority of the population of the Russian Federation are adherents of Christianity, but there are significant Islamic, Buddhist and Jewish minorities.

In September 1997 legislation concerning the regulation of religious organizations was approved, whereby only those religious groups able to prove that they had been established in Russia for a minimum of 15 years were to be permitted to operate. Russian Orthodoxy, Islam, Buddhism and Judaism, together with some other Christian denominations, were deemed to comply with the legislation. Religious organizations failing to satisfy this requirement were, henceforth, obliged to register annually for 15 years, before being permitted to publish literature, hold public services or invite foreign preachers into Russia. Moreover, foreign religious groups were additionally obliged to affiliate themselves to Russian organizations. An extension of this law, announced in August 1998, decreed that foreign religious workers were permitted to remain in Russia for a maximum of three months per visit. In March 2000 President Putin signed a decree that required all non-registered religious groups to be dissolved by the end of the year; however neither this decree nor the legislation passed in 1997 was applied consistently across the Russian Federation, and some constituent regions introduced legislation that was more restrictive than the 1997 law.

## CHRISTIANITY

### The Russian Orthodox Church (Moscow Patriarchate)

The Russian Orthodox Church (Moscow Patriarchate) is the dominant religious organization in the Russian Federation, with an estimated 75m. adherents. In 2003 there were 131 dioceses, 16,195 parishes, 295 monasteries and 319 convents operating under the auspices of the Patriarchate in Russia. In 1988–2001 more than 12,000 churches were established or returned to religious use. The Patriarchate's jurisdiction is mainly challenged by the Russian Orthodox Church Abroad (operating in Russia as the Free Russian Orthodox Church, which itself split with the overseas hierarchy and established the Russian Autonomous Orthodox Church in 1998), the jurisdiction of which was established in 1921 in Yugoslavia and which primarily operated in the USA, rejecting the canonical legitimacy of the Moscow Patriarchate. It re-established operations in Russia after 1988.

The Russian Orthodox Church (Moscow Patriarchate) is governed by the Holy Synod, consisting of six bishops (permanent members), the Patriarch, and several temporary member bishops. The supreme ruling organ of the Church is the Local Synod, which comprises representatives of bishops, clergy, monks and laity and convenes once every five years.

**Moscow Patriarchate:** 115191 Moscow, Danilov Monastery, ul. Danilovskii val 22; tel. (095) 230-24-39; fax (095) 230-26-19; e-mail commserv@mospat.dol.ru; internet www.russian-orthodox-church.org.ru; Patriarch of Moscow and all Rus ALEKSEI II (RIDIGER).

### The Roman Catholic Church

At 31 December 2001 there were an estimated 786,015 Roman Catholics in the Russian Federation. In 1991 administrative structures of the Roman Catholic Church in Russia were restored, with the establishment of two apostolic administratures for European Russia and Siberia, respectively. In 1999 each administrature was sub-divided, establishing two additional administratures. In February 2002 the administratures were replaced by four dioceses, the Diocese of the Mother of God at Moscow, of St Clement at Saratov, of the Transfiguration at Novosibirsk, and of St Joseph at Irkutsk.

### Bishops' Conference

Conference of Catholic Bishops of the Russian Federation, 101031 Moscow, ul. Petrovka 19/5/35; tel. and fax (095) 923-16-97; e-mail ostastop@glasnet.ru; internet www.catholic.ru.

f. 1999; Pres. Most. Rev. TADEUSZ KONDRUSIEWICZ (Archbishop of the Diocese of the Mother of God at Moscow).

**Archbishop of the Diocese of the Mother of God at Moscow:** Most Rev. TADEUSZ KONDRUSIEWICZ, 107078 Moscow, POB 116, ul. N. Basmannaya 16/31; tel. and fax (095) 261-67-14; e-mail cathmos@dol.ru.

### Protestant Churches

In 2001 there were more than 3,000 religious organizations registered with the Ministry of Justice. Among these were 1,323 Pentecostal groups, 975 Baptist groups, 784 other evangelical or charismatic organizations, 563 Seventh Day Adventist groups, 213 Lutheran churches, 192 Presbyterian churches and 330 branches of the Jehovah's Witnesses. There were also a small number of groups registered representing sects which had broken away from the Russian Orthodox Church, including the Old Believers (with a total of 278 organizations), the Molokane ('Milk-drinkers'—19 organizations) and Dubkhovory ('Spirit-wrestlers'—one organization). Some of these are regarded as having similar doctrines and practices to churches of the Western reformed traditions.

**Euro-Asiatic Federation of the Union of Evangelical Christians-Baptists:** 109028 Moscow, Trekhsvyatitelnyi per. 3; tel. (095) 227-39-90; fax (095) 975-23-67; e-mail moderator@baptist.org.ru; internet baptist.org.ru; 231 communities, 16,530 adherents in the Russian Federation and other former republics of the USSR (2000); Pres. GRIGORII I. KOMENDANT.

**Russian Union of Evangelical Christians-Baptists:** 109028 Moscow, ul. M. Trekhsvyatitelskii 3; tel. (095) 985-13-36; fax (095) 954-92-31; e-mail ecb@hotbox.ru; internet ecb.hotbox.ru; 1,380 communities and 85,000 adherents (2001); Pres. PETR B. KONOVALCHIK.

**Russian Union of Christians of the Evangelical Faith—Pentecostalists ('Pyatidesyatnikov'):** 123363 Moscow, ul. Fabritsiusa 31A; tel. and fax (095) 493-15-41; e-mail pentecostalunion@mtu-net.ru; internet www.pentecostalunion.ru; f. 1907, re-established 1990; 1,350 parishes and more than 300,000 adherents in 2001; Chair. Dr PAVEL N. OKARA.

### Other Christian Churches

**Armenian Apostolic Church:** 123022 Moscow, ul. S. Makeyeva 10; tel. (095) 255-50-19.

**Old Believers** (The Old Ritualists): 109052 Moscow, ul. Rogozhskii pos. 29; tel. (095) 361-51-92; e-mail tarasburnos@mail.ru; internet www.staroobryad.narod.ru; f. 1652 by separation from the Moscow Patriarchate; total of 278 groups registered in 2001; divided into two main branches: the *popovtsi* (which have priests) and the *bespopovtsi* (which reject the notion of ordained priests and the use of all sacraments, other than that of baptism). Both branches are further divided into various groupings. The largest group of *popovtsi* are those of the Belokrinitskii Concord, under the Metropolitan of Moscow and All-Rus ALIMPYI (ALEKSANDR K. GUSEV); c. 120 parishes, four bishops in Russia, Ukraine and Moldova; a further significant group of *popovtsi* Old Believers are those of the Beglopopovtsyi Concord, under the Archbishop of Novozybkov, Moscow and All Rus (AFANASII KALININ).

**Russian Autonomous Orthodox Church:** 125212 Moscow, Church of the New Martyrs and Confessors of Russia, Golovinskoye shosse 13A; tel. (095) 152-50-76; formally established in 1990 as the Free Russian Orthodox Church; re-registered in 1998 under above name following opposition by local, 'catacomb' priests to moves of reconciliation between the Russian Orthodox Church Abroad and the Moscow Patriarchate; 100 parishes in 2001; First Hierarch Metropolitan of Suzdal and Vladimir VALENTIN (Rusantsov).

## ISLAM

Most Muslims in the Russian Federation are adherents of the Sunni sect. Islam is the predominant religion among many peoples of the North Caucasus, such as the Chechens, the Ingush and many smaller groups, and also in the Central Volga region, among them the Tatars, Chuvash and Bashkirs. In 2000 there were some 7,000 mosques in Russia, and there were estimated to be between 19m. and 20m. Muslims in Russia in 2001. There were 3,048 Islamic religious organizations registered with the Ministry of Justice in January 2001.

**Central Muslim Spiritual Board for Russia and European Countries of the CIS:** 450057 Bashkortostan, Ufa, ul. Tukaya 50; tel. (3472) 50-80-86; e-mail rdumpo@permonline.ru; internet muslim-board.narod.ru; f. 1789; 27 regional branches in the Russian Federation, and one branch in Ukraine; Chair. Mufti Sheikh-ul Islam TALGAT-KHOZRAT TADZHUDDIN.

**Council of Muftis of Russia:** 129090 Moscow, per. Vypolzov 7; tel. and fax (095) 281-49-04; Chair. Mufti Sheikh RAVIL KHAZRAT GAINUTDIN.

## JUDAISM

At the beginning of the 20th century approximately one-half of the world's Jews lived in the Russian Empire (primarily in those regions that form part of present-day Ukraine, Belarus, Moldova and Lithuania). Although many Jews emigrated from the USSR in the 1970s and 1980s, there is still a significant Jewish population (400,000 at the end of 1998) in the Russian Federation, particularly in the larger cities. In January 2001 there were 197 Jewish religious organizations registered with the Ministry of Justice, of which 176 were Orthodox and 21 Reform.

**Congress of Jewish Religious Communities and Organizations of Russia:** 101000 Moscow, B. Spaso Glinishevskii per. 8, Moscow Choral Synagogue; tel. (095) 924-24-24; fax (095) 956-75-40; e-mail synrus@corbina.ru; f. 1996; co-ordinates activities of 120 Jewish communities throughout Russia; Chief Rabbi ADOLF SHAYEVICH; Dir ZINOVY KOGAN.

**Federation of the Jewish Communities of the CIS:** 103055 Moscow, ul. 2-i Vysheslaytzev per. 5A; tel. (095) 281-45-23; fax (095) 281-26-72; e-mail office@fjc.ru; internet www.jewish.ru/fjcnews.asp; f. 1999; Exec. Dir AVRAHAM BERKOVITZ; Chair. LEV LEVIYEV.

**Federation of the Jewish Communities of Russia:** 103055 Moscow, ul. 2-i Vysheslaytzev per. 5A; tel. (095) 281-45-23; fax (095) 281-26-72; e-mail russia@fjc.ru; internet www.fjc.ru/russiafr.htm; unites 130 communities in Russia; Chief Rabbi of Russia, Chair. of Rabbinical Alliance of Russia and the CIS BEREL LAZAR.

**Russian Jewish Congress:** 121265 Moscow, ul. Novyi Arbat 36; tel. (095) 290-81-02; fax (095) 290-80-47; e-mail rjc@rjc.ru; internet www.rjc.ru; Pres. YEVGENII SATANOVSKII.

## BUDDHISM

Buddhism (established as an official religion in Russia in 1741) is most widespread in the Republic of Buryatia, where the Central Spiritual Department of Buddhists of Russia has its seat, the Republics of Kalmykiya and Tyva and in the Irkutsk and Chita Oblasts. There are also newly established communities in Moscow and St Petersburg. Before 1917 there were more than 40 datsans (monasteries) in Buryatia, but in 1990 only two of these remained in use. By December 1999 19 datsans had been built or restored. There were believed to be 1m. Buddhists in Russia in 1997. There were 193 Buddhist organizations registered with the Ministry of Justice in January 2001.

**Central Spiritual Department of Buddhists:** 670000 Buryatia, Ulan-Ude, Ivolginskii datsan; Chair. Lama NIMAZHAP ILYUKHINOV.

**Representative of the Central Spiritual Department of Buddhists:** 119034 Moscow, ul. Ostozhenka 49; tel. (095) 245-09-39.

## BAHÁ'Í FAITH

**National Office of the Bahá'ís of Russia:** 129515 Moscow, POB 55; tel. (095) 956-24-96; e-mail secretariat@bahai.ru; internet www.bahai.ru; over 3,500 adherents in more than 400 locations; 19 registered orgs in January 2001.

# The Press

In 1999 there were 15,836 officially registered newspaper titles published in the Russian Federation. There were also 7,577 periodicals. Almost all newspapers and periodicals suffered a sharp decrease in circulation in the early 1990s. Despite having lost over 25m. subscribers, *Argumenty i Fakty* remained the best-selling Russian weekly newspaper in 1998, while in 2001 *Moskovskii Komsomolets* and *Komsomolskaya Pravda* were the most popular dailies.

**Russian Federation Press Committee:** 101409 Moscow, Strastnoi bulv. 5; tel. (095) 229-33-53; fax (095) 200-22-81; e-mail komitet@presscom.ru; f. 1993 to replace the Ministry of Press and Information and the Federal Information Centre of Russia; central organ of federal executive power; Chair. IVAN D. LAPTEV.

## PRINCIPAL NEWSPAPERS

### Moscow

**Argumenty i Fakty** (Arguments and Facts): 101000 Moscow, ul. Myasnitskaya 42; tel. (095) 923-35-41; fax (095) 925-61-82; e-mail n-boris@aif.ru; internet www.aif.ru; f. 1978; weekly; Editor VLADISLAV A. STARKOV; circ. 2,880,000 (2000).

**Gudok** (The Horn): 105066 Moscow, ul. Staraya Basmannaya 38/2/3; tel. (095) 262-26-53; fax (095) 262-45-74; e-mail admin@gudok.info; internet www.gudok.ru; f. 1917 as newspaper of railway workers; daily; Editor-in-Chief IGOR T. YANIN.

**Izvestiya** (News): 101999 Moscow, ul. Tverskaya 18/1. POB 9; tel. (095) 209-05-81; fax (095) 209-36-20; e-mail info@izvestia.ru; internet www.izvestia.ru; f. 1917; owned by Prof-Mediya; Editor-in-Chief RAF SHAKIROV; circ. 263,250 (2001).

**Kommersant** (Businessman): 125080 Moscow, ul. Vrubelya 4/1; tel. (095) 943-97-71; fax (095) 195-96-36; e-mail kommersant@kommersant.ru; internet www.kommersant.ru; f. 1989; daily; Editor ANDREI VASILIYEV; circ. 117,340 (2002).

**Komsomolskaya Pravda** (Young Communist League Truth): 125866 Moscow, ul. Pravdy 24, POB A-137; tel. (095) 257-51-39; fax (095) 200-22-93; e-mail kp@kp.ru; internet www.kp.ru; f. 1925; fmrly organ of the Lenin Young Communist League (Komsomol); independent; weekly supplements *KP-Tolstushka* (KP-Fat volume), *KP-Ponedelnik* (KP-Monday); managed by Prof-Mediya; Editor VLADIMIR SUNGORKIN; circ.785,000 (2001).

**Konservator** (The Conservative): 109240 Moscow, ul. Goncharnaya 1; tel. (095) 915-28-07; fax (095) 915-70-40; e-mail egk@egk.ru; internet www.egk.ru; f. 2002 to replace *Obshchaya Gazeta*; weekly; Pres.and Editor-in-Chief VYACHESLAV LEIBMAN.

**Krasnaya Zvezda** (Red Star): 123007 Moscow, Khoroshevskoye shosse 38; tel. (095) 941-21-58; fax (095) 941-40-66; e-mail redstar@mail.cnt.ru; internet www.redstar.ru; f. 1924; organ of the Ministry of Defence; Editor N. N. YEFIMOV; circ. 80,000 (2000).

**Krestyanskaya Rossiya** (Peasant Russia): 123022 Moscow, ul. 1905 Goda 7; tel. and fax (095) 259-41-49; weekly; f. 1906; Editor-in-Chief KONSTANTIN LYSENKO; circ. 94,000 (2000).

**Megapolis-Ekspress** (Megalopolis-Express): 113184 Moscow, ul. B. Tatarskaya 29; tel. (095) 953-50-40; fax (095) 959-08-61; e-mail megapol@megapolis.garnet.ru; f. 1990; weekly; popular; Editor LEV KULAKOV; circ. 500,000.

**Moskovskaya Pravda** (The Moscow Truth): 123846 Moscow, ul. 1905 Goda 7, POB D-22; tel. (095) 259-82-33; fax (095) 259-63-60; e-mail newspaper@mospravda.ru; internet www.mospravda.ru; f. 1918; fmrly organ of the Moscow city committee of the CPSU and the Moscow City Council; 5 a week; independent; Editor SHOD S. MULADZHANOV; circ. 325,000 (2000).

**Moskovskii Komsomolets** (The Moscow Young Communist): 123995 Moscow, ul. 1905 Goda 7; tel. (095) 259-50-36; fax (095) 259-46-39; e-mail letters@mk.ru; internet www.mk.ru; f. 1919; 6 a week; independent; Editor-in-Chief PAVEL GUSEV; circ. 800,000 (2001), the largest circulation of any daily newspaper in Russia; also *MK-Voskresenye* (Sundays); Editor-in-Chief PAVEL GUSEV.

**Moskovskiye Novosti** (The Moscow News): 125009 Moscow, ul. Tverskaya 16/2; tel. (095) 200-07-67; fax (095) 209-17-28; e-mail info@mn.ru; internet www.mn.ru; f. 1930; weekly; in English and in Russian; independent; democratic, liberal; Editor-in-Chief YEVGENII KISELEV; circ. 118,000 in Russian, 40,000 in English (2000).

**Moscow Times:** 125212 Moscow, ul. Vyborgskaya 16/4; tel. (095) 937-33-99; fax (095) 937-33-93; e-mail webeditor@imedia.ru; internet www.themoscowtimes.com; f. 1992; daily; in English; independent; Publr STEPHAN GROOTENBOER; Editor LYNN BERRY.

**Nezavisimaya Gazeta (NG)** (The Independent): 101000 Moscow, ul. Myasnitskaya 13; tel. (095) 928-48-50; fax (095) 975-23-46; e-mail info@ng.ru; internet www.ng.ru; f. 1990; 5 a week; regular supplements include *NG-Nauka* (NG-Science), *NG-Regiony* (NG-Regions), *NG-Politekonomiya* (NG-Political Economy), *NG-Dipkuryer* (NG-Diplomatic Courier); Gen. Man. RUSTAM NARZIKULOV; Editor-in-Chief TATIANA KOSHKAREVA; circ. 50,000 (2001).

**Novaya Gazeta** (New Newspaper): 101000 Moscow, Potapovskii per. 3; tel. (095) 921-57-39; fax (095) 923-68-88; e-mail gazeta@novayagazeta.ru; internet www.novayagazeta.ru; f. 1993; weekly; Editor DMITRII A. MURATOV; circ. 670,000 (2001).

**Novye Izvestiya** (New News): 125315 Moscow, Leningradskii pr. 68; tel. (095) 783-06-36; fax (095) 783-06-37; e-mail webmaster@newizv.ru; internet www.newizv.ru; f. 2003 following the closure of the fmr *Novye Izvestiya* (f. 1997); daily; Editor-in-Chief VALERII YAKOV.

**Parlamentskaya Gazeta** (Parliamentary Newspaper): 125190 Moscow, ul. Pravdy 24; tel. (095) 257-50-90; fax (095) 257-50-82; e-mail pg@pnp.ru; internet www.pnp.ru; f. 1998; 5 a week; organ of the Federal Assembly of the Russian Federation; Editor-in-Chief (vacant); circ. 55,000 (2001).

**Pravda** (Truth): 125867 Moscow, ul. Pravdy 24; tel. (095) 257-31-00; fax (095) 251-26-97; e-mail pravda@cnt.ru; internet www.gazeta-pravda.ru; f. 1912; fmrly organ of the Cen. Cttee of the CPSU; independent; communist; Editor-in-Chief ALEKSANDR ILYIN; circ. 70,200 (2001).

**Pravda.ru:** Moscow; e-mail post@pravda.ru; internet pravda.ru; f. 1999; online only, in Russian, English and Portuguese; has no asscn with the newspaper *Pravda*; Editor-in-Chief VADIM V. GORSHENIN.

**Rossiiskaya Gazeta** (Russian Newspaper): 125881 Moscow, ul. Pravdy 24; tel. (095) 257-52-52; fax (095) 973-22-56; e-mail www@rg.ru; internet www.rg.ru; f. 1990; organ of the Russian Govt; 5 a week; Gen. Man. ALEKSANDR N. GORBENKO; Editor-in-Chief VLADISLAV A. FRONIN; circ. 482,700 (2002).

**Rossiiskiye Vesti** (Russian News): 127006 Moscow, ul. M. Dmitrovka 3/10; tel. and fax (095) 937-64-36; fax (095) 937-64-25; e-mail mail@rosvesty.ru; internet www.rosvesty.ru; f. 1991; weekly; Editor-in-Chief ALEKSEI TITKOV; circ. 50,000 (2000).

**Rossiya** (Russia): 103811 Moscow, Kostyanskii per. 13; e-mail agalakov@rgz.ru; internet www.rgz.ru; f. 2000; controlled by Sistema Mass-Mediya; weekly supplement *Gubernskaya Rossiya—Regions of Russia* (Mondays), of news from the territories of the Russian Federation; circ. 50,000 (2001).

**Selskaya Zhizn** (Country Life): 125869 Moscow, ul. Pravdy 24, POB 137; tel. (095) 257-51-51; fax (095) 257-58-39; e-mail sg@sgazeta.ru; internet www.sgazeta.ru; f. 1918 as *Bednota* (Poverty), present name adopted in 1960; 2 a week; fmrly organ of the Cen. Cttee of the CPSU; independent; Editor-in-Chief and Gen. Man. SHAMUN M. KAGERMANOV; circ. 102,000 (2002).

**Sovetskaya Rossiya** (Soviet Russia): 125868 Moscow, ul. Pravdy 24; tel. (095) 257-53-00; fax (095) 200-22-90; e-mail sovross@aha.ru; internet www.rednews.ru; f. 1956; fmrly organ of the Cen. Cttee of the CPSU and the Russian Federation Supreme Soviet and Council of Ministers; 3 a week; reflects views of left-wing of Communist Party; Editor VIKTOR CHIKIN; circ. 300,000 (2002).

**Stolichnaya** (Capital City News): 113184 Moscow, ul. Pyatnitskaya 55/25/4; tel. (095) 411-63-91; fax (095) 411-64-01; e-mail mail@stog.ru; internet www.stog.ru; f. 2003; daily, evenings; publ. by New Media Publishing Group; Editor-in-Chief KIRILL KHARATYAN.

**Tribuna** (Tribune): 125993 Moscow, ul. Pravdy 24, POB A-40; tel. (095) 257-59-13; fax (095) 973-20-02; e-mail tribuna@adi.ru; internet www.tribuna.ru; f. 1969; national industrial daily; Editor-in-Chief VIKTOR ANDRIYANOV; circ. 201,943 (2000).

**Trud** (Labour): 103792 Moscow, Nastasinskii per. 4; tel. (095) 299-39-06; fax (095) 299-47-40; e-mail letter@trud.ru; internet www.trud.ru; f. 1921; 5 a week; Editor ALEKSANDR S. POTAPOV; circ. 1,700,000 (2001).

**Vechernyaya Moskva** (Evening Moscow): 123849 Moscow, ul. 1905 Goda 7; tel. (095) 256-20-11; fax (095) 259-05-26; e-mail post@vm.ru; internet www.vm.ru; f. 1923; independent; Editor-in-Chief VALERII YEVSEYEV; circ. 300,000 (2001).

**Vedomosti** (Gazette): 125212 Moscow, ul. Vyborgskaya 16; tel. (095) 232-32-00; fax (095) 956-07-16; e-mail vedomosti@media.ru; internet www.vedomosti.ru; f. 1999; independent business newspaper, publ. jointly with the *Financial Times* (United Kingdom) and the *Wall Street Journal* (USA); Editor LEONID BERSHIDSKII; circ. 42,000 (2001).

**Vremya-MN** (Time-Moscow News): 103829 Moscow, ul. Tverskaya 16/2; tel. (095) 209-05-20; fax (095) 209-17-28; e-mail vremya@mn.ru; internet www.vremyamn.ru; f. 1995; Pres. ALEKSANDR VAINSHTEIN; Editor VLADIMIR V. UMNOV; circ. 54,000 (2001).

**Vremya Novosti** (Time News): 113326 Moscow, ul. Pyatniyskaya 25; tel. (095) 231-18-17; fax (095) 959-33-40; e-mail info@vremya.ru; internet www.vremya.ru; f. 2000; 5 a week; Editor-in-Chief VLADIMIR GUREVICH; circ. 51,000.

**Zhizn** (Life): 101970 Moscow, ul. Maroseika 13/3; tel. (095) 206-88-56; fax (095) 206-85-48; e-mail info@zhizn.ru; weekly; Editor-in-Chief VLADIMIR TOPORKOV; circ. 1,068,000 (2002).

## St Petersburg

**Peterburgskii Chas Pik** (Petersburg Rush Hour): 191040 St Petersburg, Nevskii pr. 81; tel. (812) 279-25-65; fax (812) 279-19-12; e-mail nabor2@chaspik.spb.ru; internet www.chaspik.spb.ru; f. 1990; weekly; Editor-in-Chief NATALIYA CHAPLINA; circ. 33,000 (2002).

**Novosti Peterburga** (Petersburg News): St Petersburg; tel. and fax (812) 312-35-66; e-mail press@neva.spb.ru; f. 1997; Editor-in-Chief ALEKSANDR V. MARKOV; circ. 25,000 (2001).

**Sankt-Peterburgskiye Vedomosti** (St Petersburg Gazette): 191023 St Petersburg, ul. Fontanka 59; tel. (812) 327-22-00; fax (812) 310-51-41; e-mail post@spbvedomosti.ru; internet www.spbvedomosti.ru; f. 1728; re-established 1991; Editor OLEG KUZIN; circ. 90,000 (2002).

**Smena** (The Rising Generation): 191119 St Petersburg, ul. Marata 69; tel. (812) 315-04-76; fax (812) 315-03-53; e-mail info@smena.ru; internet www.smena.ru; f. 1919; 6 a week, controlled by Sistema Mass-Mediya; Editor-in-Chief LEONID DAVYDOV; circ. 80,000 (2002).

**The St Petersburg Times:** 190000 St Petersburg, Isaakevskaya pl. 4; tel. and fax (812) 325-60-80; e-mail letters@sptimesrussia.com; internet www.sptimes.ru; f. 1993; 2 a week; in English; independent; Publr TATYANA SHALYGINA; Man. Dir SERGEI PODOINTITSIN; Editor THOMAS RYMER.

**Vechernii Peterburg** (Evening Petersburg): 191023 St Petersburg, ul. Fontanka 59; tel. (812) 311-88-75; fax (812) 314-31-05; e-mail gazeta@vspb.spb.ru; f. 1992; Editor VLADIMIR GRONSKII; circ. 20,000 (2001).

## PRINCIPAL PERIODICALS

### Agriculture, Forestry, etc.

**Agrarnyi Zhurnal** (Agrarian Journal): Moscow; tel. (095) 204-49-80; fax (095) 207-44-78; e-mail mobilecenter@mtu-net.ru; f. 2000; monthly; Editor-in-Chief ALEKSANDR MORGACHEV.

**Agrokhimiya** (Agricultural Chemistry): 119991 Moscow, Maronovskii per. 26; tel. (095) 238-24-00; e-mail ovpes@mail.ru; f. 1964; monthly; journal of the Russian Academy of Sciences; results of theoretical and experimental research work; Editor V. N. KUDEYAROV; circ. 400 (2002).

**Doklady Rossiiskoi Akademii Selskokhozyaistvennykh Nauk** (Reports of the Russian Academy of Agricultural Sciences): 117218 Moscow, ul. Krzhizhanovskii 15, POB B-2; tel. and fax (095) 207-76-60; f. 1936; 6 a year; developments in agriculture; Editor-in-Chief N. S. MARKOVA; circ. 1,000.

**Ekologiya i Promlyshlennost Rossii** (The Ecology and Industry of Russia): 119911 Moscow, Leninskii pr. 4; tel. (095) 247-23-08; fax (095) 955-00-58; e-mail ecip@online.ru; internet ecip.newmail.ru; f. 1996; monthly; environmental protection, forestry, wood and paper products, nature conservation; Editor-in-Chief V. D. KALNER.

**Ekonomika Selskokhozyaistvennykh i Pererabatyvayushchikh Predpriyatii** (Economics of Agricultural and Processing Enterprises): 107996 Moscow, ul. Sadovaya-Spasskaya 18/423; tel. (095) 207-15-80; fax (095) 207-18-56; internet www.reason.ru/economy; f. 1926; monthly; publ. by Ministry of Agriculture and Foodstuffs; Editor S. K. DEVIN; circ. 4,500 (1998).

**Lesnaya Promyshlennost** (Forest Industry): 101934 Moscow, Arkhangelskii per. 1/234; tel. (095) 207-91-53; f. 1926; 3 a week; publ. by the state forest industrial company, Roslesprom; Editor V. G. ZAYEDINOV; circ. 250,000.

**Mezhdunarodnyi Selskokhozyaistvennyi Zhurnal** (International Agricultural Journal): 107996 Moscow, ul. Sadovaya-Spasskaya 18; tel. and fax (095) 207-23-11; f. 1957; 6 a year; Editor-in-Chief VIKTOR P. KOROVKIN; circ. 4,000.

**Molochnoye i Myasnoye Skotovodstvo** (Dairy and Meat Cattle Breeding): 107996 Moscow, ul. Sadovaya-Spasskaya 18; tel. (095) 207-19-46; f. 1956; 6 a year; Editor V. V. KORGENEVSKII; circ. 791 (1996).

**Selskokhozyaistvennaya Biologiya** (Agricultural Biology): 117218 Moscow, ul. Krzhizhanovskogo 15; tel. (095) 921-93-88; f. 1966; 6 a year; publ. by the Russian Academy of Agricultural Sciences; Editor E. M. BORISOVA; circ. 1,000.

**Tekhnika v Selskom Khozyaistve** (Agricultural Technology): 117218 Moscow, ul. Krzhizhanovskogo 15/2; tel. (095) 207-37-62; fax (095) 207-28-70; e-mail jurali@mail.ru; internet www.tehnvsh.by.ru; f. 1941; 6 a year; journal of the Ministry of Agriculture and Foodstuffs and the Russian Academy of Agricultural Sciences; Editor-in-Chief PETR S. POPOV; circ. 2,000 (1998).

**Veterinariya** (Veterinary Science): 107996 Moscow, ul. Sadovaya-Spasskaya 18; tel. (095) 207-10-60; fax (095) 207-28-12; f. 1924; monthly; Editor V. A. GARKAVTSEV; circ. 4,860 (2000).

**Zashchita i Karantin Rastenii** (The Protection and Quarantine of Plants): 107996 Moscow, ul. Sadovaya-Spasskaya 18, POB 6; tel. (095) 207-21-30; fax (095) 207-21-40; e-mail fitopress@ropnet.ru; f. 1932; monthly; Editor V. E. SAVZDARG; circ. 5,200 (2000).

**Zemledeliye** (Farming): 107996 Moscow, ul. Sadovaya-Spasskaya 18; tel. (095) 207-24-66; fax (095) 207-28-70; f. 1939; 6 a year; publ. by Ministry of Agriculture and Foodstuffs, Russian Academy of Agricultural Sciences, Russian Scientific Research Institute of Farming; Editor V. IVANOV; circ. 4,000 (1998).

### For Children

**Koster** (Campfire): 193024 St Petersburg, ul. Mytninskaya 1/20; tel. (812) 274-15-72; fax (812) 274-46-26; e-mail root@kostyor.spb.org; internet www.kostyor.ru; f. 1936; monthly; journal of the International Union of Children's Organizations (UPO-FCO); fiction, poetry, sport, reports and popular science; for ages 10–14 years; Editor-in-Chief N. B. KHARLAMPIYEV; circ. 7,500 (2000).

**Murzilka:** 125015 Moscow, ul. Novodmitrovskaya 5A; tel. and fax (095) 285-18-81; e-mail documents@mtu-net.ru; internet www .murzilka.km.ru; f. 1924; monthly; illustrated; for first grades of school; Editor TATYANA ANDROSENKO; circ. 115,000 (2000).

**Pioner** (Pioneer): 101459 Moscow, Bumazhnyi proyezd 14; tel. (095) 257-34-27; f. 1924; monthly; fmrly journal of the Cen. Cttee of the Lenin Young Communist League (Komsomol); fiction; illustrated; for children of fourth–eighth grades; Editor A. S. MOROZ; circ. 7,000 (2000).

**Pionerskaya Pravda** (Pioneers' Truth): 127994 Moscow, ul. Sushchevskaya 21; tel. (095) 972-22-38; fax (095) 972-10-28; e-mail pionerka@hotmail.ru; f. 1925; 3 a week; fmrly organ of the Union of Pioneer Organizations (Federation of Children's Organizations) of the USSR; Editor O. I. GREKOVA; circ. 60,000 (2000).

**Veselye Kartinki** (Merry Pictures): 107076 Moscow, Stromynskii per. 4; tel. (095) 269-52-96; fax (095) 268-49-68; e-mail merrypictures@mtu-net.ru; internet vkids.km.ru/subjects .asp?id_sect=5&id_subj=4; f. 1956; monthly; publ. by the Molodaya Gvardiya (Young Guard) Publishing House; humorous; for preschool and first grades; Editor R. A. VARSHAMOV; circ. 140,000 (1999).

**Yunyi Naturalist** (Young Naturalist): 125015 Moscow, ul. Novodmitrovskaya 5A; tel. (095) 285-89-67; f. 1928; monthly; fmrly journal of the Union of Pioneer Organizations (Federation of Children's Organizations) of the USSR; popular science for children of fourth–10th grades, who are interested in biology; Editor B. A. CHASHCHARIN; circ. 16,350 (2000).

**Yunyi Tekhnik** (Young Technician): 125015 Moscow, ul. Novodmitrovskaya 5A; tel. (095) 285-44-80; e-mail yt@got.mmtel.ru; f. 1956; monthly; publ. by the Molodaya Gvardiya (Young Guard) Publishing House; popular science for children and youth; Editor BORIS CHEREMISINOV; circ. 13,050 (2000).

### Culture and Arts

**7 Dnei** (7 Days): 125871 Moscow, Leningradskoye shosse 5A; tel. (095) 195-92-76; fax (095) 753-41-32; e-mail 7days@7days.ru; internet www.7days.ru; f. 1967; celebrity news and television listings magazine; Editor V. V. ORLOVA; circ. 937,000 (2000).

**Dekorativnoye Iskusstvo** (Decorative Art): 103009 Moscow, ul. Tverskaya 9; tel. (095) 229-19-10; fax (095) 229-68-75; f. 1957; 4 a year; all aspects of visual art; illustrated; Editor A. KURCHI; circ. 1,500 (1999).

**Iskusstvo Kino** (The Art of the Cinema): 125319 Moscow, ul. Usievicha 9; tel. (095) 151-56-51; fax (095) 151-02-72; e-mail kino@ kinoart.ru; internet www.kinoart.ru/main.html; f. 1931; monthly; journal of the Russian Film-makers' Union; Editor DANIIL DONDUREI; circ. 5,000 (1998).

**Knizhnoye Obozreniye** (Book Review): 129272 Moscow, ul. Sushchevskii val 64; tel. and fax (095) 281-62-66; f. 1966; weekly; summaries of newly published books; Editor S. V. YATSENKO; circ. 15,280 (1999).

**Kultura** (Culture): 127055 Moscow, ul. Novoslobodskaya 73; tel. (095) 285-06-40; fax (095) 200-32-25; e-mail kultura@dol.ru; internet www.kulturagz.ru; f. 1929; controlled by Sistema Mass-Mediya; weekly; Editor YURII I. BELYAVSKII; circ. 29,200 (2002).

**Literaturnaya Gazeta** (Literary Newspaper): 103811 Moscow, Kostyanskii per. 13; tel. (095) 208-96-60; fax (095) 206-62-25; e-mail litera@nettaxi.com; internet www.lgz.ru; f. 1831; publ. restored 1929; weekly; literature, politics, society; controlled by Sistema Mass-Mediya; Editor-in-Chief LEV GUSHIN; circ. 57,000 (2002).

**Literaturnaya Rossiya** (Literary Russia): 103051 Moscow, Tsvetnoi bulv. 30; tel. (095) 200-50-10; fax (095) 921-40-00; f. 1958; weekly; essays, verse, literary criticism, political reviews; Editor VLADIMIR V. YEREMENKO; circ. 24,000 (2000).

**Muzykalnaya Akademiya** (Musical Academy): 103006 Moscow, ul. Sadovaya-Triumfalnaya 14/12; tel. (095) 209-23-84; f. 1933; quarterly; publ. by the Kompozitor (Composer) Publishing House; journal of the Union of Composers of the Russian Federation and the Ministry of Culture; Editor YU. S. KOREV; circ. 1,000 (1998).

**Muzykalnaya Zhizn** (Musical Life): 103006 Moscow, ul. Sadovaya-Triumfalnaya 14/12; tel. (095) 209-75-24; f. 1957; fortnightly; publ. by the Kompozitor (Composer) Publishing House; journal of the Union of Composers of the Russian Federation and the Ministry of Culture; development of music; Editor J. PLATEK; circ. 10,000 (2000).

**Neva** (The River Neva): 191186 St Petersburg, Nevskii pr. 3; tel. and fax (812) 312-65-37; fax (812) 312-65-37; e-mail office@nevajournal .spb.ru; internet www.nevajournal.spb.ru; f. 1955; monthly; journal of the St Petersburg Writers' Organization; fiction, poetry, literary criticism; Editor B. N. NIKOLSKII; circ. 4,000 (2000).

**Oktyabr** (October): 125040 Moscow, ul. Pravdy 11/13; tel. (095) 214-62-05; fax (095) 214-50-29; internet magazines.russ.ru/october; f. 1924; monthly; independent literary journal; new fiction and essays by Russian and foreign writers; Editor-in-Chief IRINA N. BARMETOVA; circ. 4,500 (2002).

**Teatr** (Theatre): 121835 Moscow, ul. Arbat 35; tel. and fax (095) 248-07-45; monthly; publ. by the Izvestiya (News) Publishing House; journal of the Theatrical Workers' Union and the Russian Federation Union of Writers; new plays by Russian and foreign playwrights; Editor V. SEMENOVSKI; circ. 5,000 (2000).

**Znamya** (Banner): 103001 Moscow, ul. B. Sadovaya 2/46; tel. (095) 299-52-38; e-mail znamlit@dialup.ptt.ru; internet magazines.russ .ru/znamia; f. 1931; monthly; independent; novels, poetry, essays; Editor-in-Chief SERGEI CHUPRININ; circ. 10,000 (2000).

### Economics, Finance

**Dengi** (Money): 123308 Moscow, Khoroshevskoye shosse 41; tel. (095) 943-91-17; fax (095) 956-18-13; e-mail dengi@kommersant.ru; internet www.kommersant.ru/k-money; weekly; publ. by the Kommersant Publishing House; Editor SERGEI YAKOVLEV; circ. 85,500 (2002).

**Dengi i Kredit** (Money and Credit): 103016 Moscow, ul. Neglinnaya 12; tel. (095) 771-99-87; fax (095) 771-99-85; e-mail ggv@cbr.ru; f. 1927; monthly; publ. by the Central Bank; all aspects of banking and money circulation; Editor Y. G. DMITRIYEV; circ. 5,430 (2002).

**Ekonomika i Matematicheskiye Metody** (Economics and Mathematical Methods): 117418 Moscow, Nakhimovskii pr. 47; tel. (095) 332-46-39; internet www.cemi.rssi.ru/emm; f. 1965; 4 a year; publ. by the Nauka (Science) Publishing House; theoretical and methodological problems of economics, econometrics; Editor V. L. MAKAROV; circ. 796 (2000).

**Ekonomika i Zhizn** (Economics and Life): 101462 Moscow, Bumazhnyi proyezd 14; tel. (095) 257-30-62; fax (095) 250-55-58; e-mail gazeta@ekonomika.ru; f. 1918; weekly; fmrly *Ekonomicheskaya gazeta*; news and information about the economy and business; Editor YURII YAKUTIN; circ. 460,000 (1999).

**Ekspert** (Expert): 125866 Moscow, ul. Pravdy 24, Novyi Gazetnyi kor.; tel. (095) 257-47-27; fax (095) 250-52-09; e-mail ask@expert.ru; internet www.expert.ru; weekly; business and economics; financial and share markets; policy and culture; owned by Prof-Mediya; Editor-in-Chief VALERII FADEYEV; circ. 60,000 (2002).

**Finansy** (Finances): 103009 Moscow, ul. Tverskaya 22B; tel. and fax (095) 299-96-16; e-mail finance@df.ru; internet www.df.ru/~finance; f. 1926; monthly; publ. by the Finansy (Finances) Publishing House; fmrly journal of the Ministry of Finance; theory and information on finances; compilation and execution of the state budget, insurance, lending, taxation etc.; Editor YU. M. ARTEMOV; circ. 10,000 (2002).

**Finansovaya Rossiya** (Financial Russia): 103051 Moscow, B. Sukharevskii per. 19/1; tel. (095) 207-57-55; e-mail fr@fr.ru; internet www.fr.ru; f. 1996; weekly; economics, business, finance, society; Editor-in-Chief ANDREI A. MIROSHNICHENKO; circ. 103,000 (2001).

**Kompaniya** (The Firm): 125047 Moscow, ul. Usachyeva 11; tel. (095) 755-87-88; fax (095) 755-87-21; e-mail info@ko.ru; internet www.ko.ru; f. 1998; weekly; politics, economics, finance; Editor-in-Chief ANDREI GRIGORYEV; circ. 40,000 (2002).

**Mirovaya Ekonomika i Mezhdunarodniye Otnosheniya** (World Economy and International Relations): 117859 Moscow, ul. Profsoyuznaya 23; tel. (095) 128-08-83; fax (095) 310-70-27; e-mail memojour@imemo.ru; f. 1957; monthly; publ. by the Nauka (Science) Publishing House; journal of the Institute of the World Economy and International Relations of the Russian Academy of Sciences; problems of theory and practice of world socio-economic development, international policies, international economic co-operation, the economic and political situation in Russia and different countries of the world, etc.; Editor A. V. RYABOV; circ. 4,000 (2002).

**Profil** (Profile): 109544 Moscow, ul. B. Andronyevskaya 17; tel. (095) 745-94-01; fax (095) 278-72-05; e-mail profil@orc.ru; internet www.profil.orc.ru; f. 1997; weekly; Editor-in-Chief VLADIMIR A. ZMEYUSHCHENKO; circ. 103,000 (2001).

**Rossiiskii Ekonomicheskii Zhurnal** (Russian Economic Journal): 109542 Moscow, Ryazanskii pr. 99; tel. and fax (095) 377-25-56; e-mail rem@mail.magelan.ru; f. 1958; monthly; fmrly *Ekonomicheskiye Nauki* (Economic Sciences); theory and practice of economics and economic reform; Editor A. YU. MELENTEV; circ. 6,074 (2000).

**Vek** (The Age): 125124 Moscow, ul. Pravdy 24, POB 35; tel. (095) 257-30-38; fax (095) 251-72-00; e-mail wek@wek.ru; internet www.wek.ru; f. 1992; Editor-in-Chief ALEKSANDR KOLODNYI.

**Voprosy Ekonomiki** (Questions of Economics): 117218 Moscow, Nakhimovskii pr. 32; tel. and fax (095) 124-52-28; e-mail mail@vopreco.ru; internet www.vopreco.ru; f. 1929; monthly; journal of the Institute of Economics of the Russian Academy of Sciences; theoretical problems of economic development, market relations, social aspects of transition to a market economy, international economics, etc.; Editor L. ABALKIN; circ. 7,000 (2002).

### Education

**Pedagogicheskii Vestnik** (Pedagogical Herald): 117393 Moscow, ul. Profsoyuznaya 62; tel. (095) 125-95-01; weekly; Editor-in-Chief LEONID RUVINSKII; circ. 120,000 (2002).

**Pedagogika** (Pedagogy): 119905 Moscow, ul. Pogodinskaya 8; tel. (095) 248-51-49; f. 1937; monthly; publ. by Academy of Education; Chief Editor V. P. BORISENKOV; circ. 4,550 (2000).

**Semya** (Family): 107996 Moscow, Orlikov per. 5; tel. (095) 975-05-29; fax (095) 975-00-76; e-mail mail@semya.ru; internet www.semya.ru; f. 1988; weekly; fmrly publ. by Soviet Children's Fund; Editor-in-Chief SERGEI A. ABRAMOV; circ. 100,000 (1999).

**Semya i Shkola** (Family and School): 129278 Moscow, ul. P. Korchagina 7; tel. (095) 283-82-21; fax (095) 283-86-14; e-mail semia_i_shkola@mtu-net.ru; f. 1871; monthly; for parents and children; Gen. Man. V. F. SMIRNOV; Editor-in-Chief P. I. GELAZONIYA; circ. 5,000 (2002).

**Shkola i Proizvodstvo** (School and Production): 127254 Moscow, ul. Sh. Rustaveli 10/3; tel. (095) 219-08-40; e-mail marketing@shkolapress.ru; f. 1957; 8 a year; publ. by the Shkola-Press (School-Press) Publishing House; Editor YU. YE. RIVES-KOROBKOV; circ. 14,700 (2000).

**Uchitelskaya Gazeta** (Teachers' Gazette): 109012 Moscow, Vetoshnyi per. 13/15; tel. (095) 928-82-53; fax (095) 924-29-27; e-mail ug@ug.ru; internet www.ug.ru; f. 1924; weekly; independent pedagogical newspaper; distributed throughout the CIS; Editor PETR POLOZHEVETS; circ. 98,500 (2002).

**Vospitaniye Shkolnikov** (The Upbringing of Schoolchildren): 129278 Moscow, ul. P. Korchagina 7; tel. (095) 283-86-96; f. 1966; 6 a year; publ. by Pedagogika (Pedagogics) Publishing House; Editor L. V. KUZNETSOVA; circ. 41,000 (2000).

### International Affairs

**Ekho Planety** (Echo of the Planet): 103860 Moscow, Tverskoi bulv. 10/12; tel. (095) 202-67-48; fax (095) 290-59-11; e-mail echotex@itar-tass.com; internet www.explan.ru; f. 1988; weekly; publ. by ITAR—TASS; international affairs, economic, social and cultural; Editor-in-Chief VALENTIN VASILETS; circ. 29,000 (2002).

**Mezhdunarodnaya Zhizn** (International Life): 103064 Moscow, Gorokhovskii per. 14; tel. (095) 265-37-81; fax (095) 265-37-71; e-mail inter_affairs@mid.ru; f. 1954; monthly; Russian and English; publ. by the Pressa Publishing House; problems of foreign policy and diplomacy of Russia and other countries; Editor B. D. PYADYSHEV; circ. 70,530 (2002).

**Novoye Vremya** (New Times): 127994 Moscow, M. Putinkovskii per. 1/2, POB 4; tel. (095) 229-88-72; fax (095) 200-41-92; e-mail contact@newtimes.ru; internet www.newtimes.ru; f. 1943; weekly; Russian, English; publ. by the Moskovskaya Pravda Publishing House; foreign and Russian affairs; Editor-in-Chief ALEKSANDR PUMPYANSKII; circ. 25,000 (2002).

### Language, Literature

**Ex Libris-NG:** 113935 Moscow, ul. Myasnitskaya 13; tel. (095) 928-48-50; fax (095) 975-23-46; e-mail info@ng.ru; internet exlibris.ng.ru; weekly; literature; Editor-in-Chief IGOR ZOTOV.

**Filologicheskiye Nauki** (Philological Sciences): Moscow; tel. (095) 203-36-23; f. 1958; 6 a year; publ. by the Vysshaya Shkola (Higher School) Publishing House; reports of institutions of higher learning on questions of literary studies and linguistics; Editor P. A. NIKOLAYEV; circ. 900 (1999).

**Knizhnoye Obozreniye** (The Book Review): 129272 Moscow, ul. Sushchevskii val 64; tel. (095) 281-62-66; fax (095) 281-51-45; internet www.knigoboz.ru; f. 1966; weekly; publ. of Ministry of the Press, Broadcasting and Mass Media; Editor-in-Chief ALEKSANDR GAVRILOV; circ. 10,500 (2003).

**Russkaya Literatura** (Russian Literature): 199034 St Petersburg, nab. Makarova 4; tel. (812) 328-16-01; fax (812) 328-11-40; f. 1958; quarterly; journal of the Institute of Russian Literature of the Russian Academy of Sciences; development of Russian literature from its appearance up to the present day; Editor N. N. SKATOV; circ. 1,467 (1999).

**Russkaya Rech** (Russian Speech): 121019 Moscow, ul. Volkhonka 18/2; tel. (095) 290-23-78; f. 1967; 6 a year; publ. by the Nauka (Science) Publishing House; journal of the Institute of Russian Language of the Academy of Sciences; popular; history of the development of the literary Russian language; Editor V. G. KOSTOMAROV; circ. 1,092 (2000).

**Voprosy Literatury** (Questions of Literature): 125009 Moscow, B. Gnezdnikovskii per. 10; tel. (095) 229-49-77; fax (095) 229-64-71; internet magazines.russ.ru/voplit; f. 1957; 6 a year; joint edition of the Institute of World Literature of the Academy of Sciences and the Literary Thought Foundation; theory and history of modern literature and aesthetics; Editor L. I. LAZAREV; circ. 2,400 (2002).

**Voprosy Yazykoznaniya** (Questions of Linguistics): 121019 Moscow, ul. Volkhonka 18/2; tel. (095) 201-25-16; f. 1952; 6 a year; publ. by the Nauka (Science) Publishing House; journal of the Department of Literature and Language of the Russian Academy of Sciences; Editor T. M. NIKOLAYEVA; circ. 1,448 (2000).

### Leisure and Sport

**Afisha** (Poster): 103009 Moscow, per. B. Gnezdnikovskii 7/28/1; tel. (095) 785-17-00; fax (095) 785-17-01; e-mail info@afisha.net; internet www.afisha.ru; f. 1999; every 2 weeks; listings and reviews of events in Moscow; Editor-in-Chief ILYA OSKOLKOV-TSENTSIPER; circ. 82,000 (2003).

**Avtopilot** (Autopilot): 123308 Moscow, Khoroshevskoye shosse 41; tel. (095) 493-91-44; fax (095) 493-91-64; e-mail autopilot@kommersant.ru; internet www.autopilot.ru; cars; publ. by the Kommersant Publishing House; Editor-in-Chief ALEKSANDR FYODOROV; circ. 96,500 (2002).

**Dosug v Moskve** (Leisure in Moscow): 101000 Moscow, Potapovskii per. 3; tel. and fax (095) 924-09-27; internet dosug-v-moskve.chat.ru; weekly; Thursday; listings and reviews of events in Moscow; circ 70,000.

**Filateliya** (Philately): 121069 Moscow, Khlebnyi per. 6; tel. (095) 291-14-32; fax (095) 254-85-84; f. 1966; monthly; journal of the Publishing and Trading Centre 'Marka'; Editor-in-Chief Y. G. BEKHTEREV; circ. 2,900 (2000).

**Fizkultura i Sport** (Exercise and Sport): 125130 Moscow, per. 6-i Novopodmoskovnii 3, POB 198; tel. (095) 786-60-62; fax (095) 786-61-39; e-mail fisemail@mtu-net.ru; f. 1922; monthly; activities and development of Russian sports, health; Editor I. SOSNOVSKII; circ. 37,600 (2001).

**Rossiiskaya Okhotnichya Gazeta** (Russian Hunters' Magazine): 123848 Moscow, ul. 1905 Goda 7; tel. (095) 256-94-74; e-mail rog@mk.ru; internet www.mk.ru/rog.asp; weekly; hunting, shooting, fishing; Editor-in-Chief OLEG MALOV.

**Sport Ekspress** (Sport Express): 123056, Moscow, ul. Krasina 27/2; tel. (095) 254-47-87; fax (095) 733-93-08; e-mail sport@sport-express.ru; internet www.sport-express.ru; f. 1991; daily; sport; Dir-Gen. IVAN RUBIN; Editor-in-Chief VLADIMIR KUCHMII; circ. in Moscow and St Petersburg 176,418 (2003).

**Sovetskii Sport** (Soviet Sport): 101913 Moscow, B. Spasoglinishchevskii per. 8; tel. and fax (095) 925-36-26; e-mail org@sovsport.ru; internet www.sovsport.ru; f. 1924; weekly; owned by Prof-Mediya; Editor-in-Chief ALEKSANDR KOZLOV; circ. 450,215 (2002).

**Teoriya i Praktika Fizicheskoi Kultury** (Theory and Practice of Exercise): 105122 Moscow, Sirenevyi bulv. 4; tel. and fax (095) 166-37-74; e-mail tpfk@infosport.ru; internet www.infosport.ru/press/tpfk; f. 1925; monthly; fmrly journal of the USSR State Committee for Exercise and Sport; Editor L. I. LUBYSHEVA; circ. 1,500 (1999).

**Turist** (Tourist): 107078 Moscow, B. Kharitonevskii per. 14; tel. (095) 923-64-23; fax (095) 959-23-36; f. 1929; every two months; publ. by the Intour Central Council for Tourism; articles, photo-essays, information, recommendations about routes and hotels for tourists, natural, cultural and historical places of interest; Editor BORIS V. MOSKVIN; circ. 3,000 (2000).

**Za Rulem** (Behind The Wheel): 103045 Moscow, per. Selivyerstov 10; tel. (095) 207-23-82; e-mail stas@zr.ru; internet www.zr.ru; f.

1928; monthly; cars and motorsport; Gen. Man. VIKTOR PANYARSKII; Editor-in-Chief PETR S. MENSHIKH; circ. 580,000 (2001).

## Politics and Military Affairs

**Gazeta:** 123242 Moscow, ul. Zoologicheskaya 4; tel. (095) 787-39-99; fax (095) 787-39-98; e-mail info@gzt.ru; internet www.gzt.ru; f. 2001; Editor-in-Chief RAF SHAKIROV; circ. 35,000 (2002).

**Litsa** (People): 121099 Moscow, Smolenskaya pl. 13/21, POB 99; tel. (095) 241-37-92; e-mail litsa@aha.ru; f. 1996; monthly; Editor-in-Chief ARTEM BOROVIK; circ. 100,000 (2002).

**Na Dne** (The Lower Depths): 191025 St Petersburg, POB 110; tel. (812) 310-54-12; fax (812) 310-52-09; e-mail office@nadne.ru; internet www.nadne.ru; f. 1994; current affairs; social issues; 2 a month.

**Nezavisimoye Voyennoye Obozreniye** (Independent Military Review): 101000 Moscow, ul. Myasnitskaya 13; tel. (095) 928-48-50; fax (095) 975-23-46; internet nvo.ng.ru; Editor VADIM SOLOVYEV; circ. 26,998 (2002).

**NZ—Neprikosnovennyi Zapas: Debaty o politike i kulture** (NZ—Reserve Stock: Debates On Politics and Culture): 129626 Moscow, ul. Kostyakova 10, POB 55; tel. (095) 976-47-88; fax (095) 977-08-28; e-mail nz@nlo.magazine.ru; internet www.nz-online.ru; f. 1998; 6 a year; politics, economics, culture and society; Editor-in-Chief IRINA PROKHOROVA.

**Rossiiskaya Federatsiya Segodnya** (The Russian Federation Today): 103800 Moscow, ul. M. Dmitrovka 3/10; tel. (095) 299-40-55; fax (095) 200-30-80; e-mail rfs@rfnet.ru; f. 1994; journal of the State Duma; Editor YURII A. KHRENOV; circ. 50,000 (1999).

**The Russia Journal:** 113054 Moscow, nab. Ozerkovskaya 50/451; e-mail info@russiajournal.com; internet www.russiajournal.com; f. 1998; published by Norasco Publishing Ltd; Editor JON WRIGHT.

**Shchit i Mech** (Shield and Sword): 127434 Moscow, ul. Ivanovskaya 24; tel. (095) 976-66-44; fax (095) 977-21-72; e-mail ormvd@itar-tass.com; f. 1989; weekly; military, security, geopolitical concerns; publ. by the Ministry of Internal Affairs; Editor-in-Chief VALERII KULIK; circ. 45,000 (2002).

**Sovershenno Sekretno** (Top Secret): 121099 Moscow, Smolenskaya pl. 13/21, POB 255; tel. (095) 241-68-73; fax (095) 241-75-55; e-mail topsec@dol.ru; internet www.topsecret.ru; f. 1989; monthly; Editor ARTEM BOROVIK; circ. 2,300,000 (2002).

**Svobodnaya Mysl** (Free Thought): 107140 Moscow, ul. Mosfilmovskaya 40; tel. (095) 788-65-00; f. 1924; fmrly *Kommunist* (Communist); monthly; politics, philosophy, economics; Editor-in-Chief N. B. BIKKENNIN; circ. 4,600 (2002).

**Vlast** (Power): 123308 Moscow, Khoroshevskoye shosse 41; tel. (095) 195-96-36; fax (095) 234-16-60; e-mail vlast@kommersant.ru; internet www.kommersant.ru/k-vlast; f. 1997; weekly; publ. by the Kommersant Publishing House; Editor MAKSIM KOVALSKII; circ. 73,500 (2002).

**Yezhenedelnyi Zhurnal** (Weekly Magazine): 129110 Moscow, Pereyaslavskii per. 4; tel. (095) 785-82-50; fax (095) 785-82-51; e-mail info@ej.ru; internet www.ej.ru; f. 2001; Editor-in-Chief SERGEI PARKHOMENKO.

**Zakon** (Law): 127994 Moscow, ul. Tverskaya 18/1; tel. (095) 209-46-24; fax (095) 209-75-60; e-mail zakon@izvestia.ru; f. 1992; monthly; publ. by the editorial board of Izvestia JSC; publishes thematic legislation and commentaries relating to business and commerce; legal issues for businessmen; Editor-in-Chief NIKOLAI KAPINUS; circ. 8,000 (2002).

**Zavtra** (Tomorrow): 119146 Moscow, Komsomolskii pr. 13; tel. (095) 247-13-37; fax (095) 245-37-10; e-mail zavtra@zavtra.ru; internet zavtra.ru; extreme left, nationalist; Editor-in-Chief ALEKSANDR A. PROGANOV; circ. 100,000 (2002).

## Popular, Fiction and General

**Akh!** (Ah!): 129090 Moscow, ul. Novyi Arbat 21, POB 36; e-mail info@ahmagazine.ru; internet www.ahmagazine.ru; f. 1998; monthly; general; Editor LARISA BORUZDNIA.

**Alfavit** (Alphabet): 129090 Moscow, ul. Novyi Arbat 21, POB 36; e-mail alphabet@alphabet.ru; internet www.alphabet.ru; f. 1998; weekly; general; Editor-in-Chief MIKHAIL POLYACHEK; circ. 25,000 (2002).

**Druzhba Narodov** (The Friendship of Peoples): 121827 Moscow, ul. Povarskaya 52; tel. (095) 291-62-27; fax (095) 291-63-54; e-mail dn@mail.sitek.ru; internet magazines.russ.ru/druzhba; f. 1939; monthly; independent; prose, poetry and literary criticism; Editor A. EBANOIDZE; circ. 7,000 (2002).

**Geo:** 123056 Moscow, per. Krasina 16; tel. (095) 937-60-90; fax (095) 937-60-91; e-mail geo@gjrussia.com; f. 1998; monthly; travel magazine; Editor YEKATERINA SEMINA; circ. 175,000 (2000).

**Inostrannaya Literatura** (Foreign Literature): 109017 Moscow, ul. Pyatnitskaya 41; tel. (095) 953-51-47; fax (095) 953-50-61; e-mail inolit@rinet.ru; internet magazines.russ.ru/inostran; f. 1891; monthly; independent; Russian translations of modern foreign authors and literary criticism; Editor-in-Chief ALEKSEI SLOVESNII; circ. 10,000 (2002).

**Krokodil** (Crocodile): 101455 Moscow, Bumazhnyi proyezd 14; tel. (095) 257-31-14; f. 1922; monthly; publ. by the Pressa Publishing House; satirical; Editor A. S. PYANOV; circ. 40,900 (2000).

**Molotok** (Little Hammer): 125080 Moscow, vul. Vrubelya 4; tel. (095) 209-11-32; fax (095) 200-40-55; e-mail molotok@unity.kommersant.ru; internet www.zabey.ru; f. 2000; weekly; popular culture.

**Moskva** (Moscow): 119002 Moscow, ul. Arbat 20; tel. (095) 291-71-10; fax (095) 291-07-32; e-mail jurmos@cityline.ru; f. 1957; monthly; fiction; Editor LEONID I. BORODIN; circ. 7,100 (2002).

**Nash Sovremennik** (Our Contemporary): 103051 Moscow, Tsvetnoi bulv. 30; tel. (095) 200-24-24; fax (095) 200-23-05; e-mail nashsovr@chat.ru; internet www.friends-partners.org/partners/rpiac/nashsovr/; f. 1956; monthly; publ. by the Union of Writers of Russia; contemporary prose and 'patriotic polemics'; Editor STANISLAV KUNAYEV; circ. 13,000 (1999).

**Novaya Rossiya** (New Russia): 103772 Moscow, Petrovskii per. 8; tel. (095) 229-14-19; fax (095) 232-37-99; f. 1930; monthly; in Russian and English; illustrated; Editor A. N. MISHARIN; circ. 15,000 (1999).

**Novyi Mir** (New World): 103806 Moscow, M. Putinkovskii per. 1/2; tel. and fax (095) 200-08-29; e-mail nmir@aha.ru; internet magazines.russ.ru/novyi_mi; f. 1925; monthly; publ. by the Izvestiya (News) Publishing House; new fiction and essays; Editor ANDREI V. VASILEVSKII; circ. 14,700 (2000).

**Ogonek** (Beacon): 191456 Moscow, Bumazhnyi proyezd 14; tel. (095) 250-22-30; fax (095) 943-00-70; e-mail ogonyok@ropnet.ru; internet www.ropnet.ru/ogonyok; f. 1899; weekly; independent; politics, popular science, economics, literature; Editor VIKTOR LOSHAK; circ. 50,000 (2002).

**Rodina** (The Motherland): 103025 Moscow, ul. Novyi Arbat 19; tel. (095) 203-75-98; fax (095) 203-47-45; e-mail rodina@istrodina.com; f. 1989; monthly; popular historical; supplement *Istochnik* (Source), every two months, documents state archives; Editor V. DOLMATOV; circ. 20,000 (2002).

**Roman Gazeta** (Novels): 107078 Moscow, ul. Novobasmannaya 19; tel. 261-95-87; fax (095) 261-11-63; f. 1927; fortnightly; contemporary fiction including translations into Russian; Editor VICTOR MENSHIKOV; circ. 15,000 (2000).

**Rossiiskii Kto Yest Kto** (Russian Who's Who): 117335 Moscow, POB 81; tel. (095) 234-46-92; e-mail zhurnal@whoiswho.ru; internet www.whoiswho.ru; f. a year; biographical and directory material; Editor-in-Chief SVYATOSLAV RYBAS; circ. 10,000.

**Sobesednik** (Interlocutor): 101484 Moscow, ul. Novoslobodskaya 73, POB 4; tel. (095) 285-56-65; fax (095) 973-20-54; e-mail info@sobesednik.ru; internet www.sobesednik.ru; f. 1984; weekly; Editor-in-Chief YURII PILIPENKO; circ. 227,500 (2002).

**SPID-Info:** 125284 Moscow, POB 42; tel. (095) 255-02-99; fax (095) 252-09-20; e-mail mail@si.ru; internet www.s-info.ru; f. 1991; monthly; satirical; Editor-in-Chief ANDREI MANN; circ. 2,910,000.

**Vokrug Sveta** (Around the World): 125015 Moscow, ul. Argunovskaya 12/1/6A; tel. and fax (095) 215-01-65; e-mail vokrugsveta_g@onlin.ptt.ru; f. 1861; monthly; geographical, travel and adventure; illustrated; Editor A. DMITRII ZAKHAROV; circ. 145,000 (2002).

**Zvezda** (Star): 191028 St Petersburg, ul. Mokhovaya 20; tel. (812) 272-89-48; fax (812) 273-52-56; e-mail arjev@zvezda.spb.su; internet magazines.russ.ru/zvezda; f. 1923; monthly; publ. by the Zvezda Publishing House; novels, short stories, poetry and literary criticism; Editors A. YU. ARYEV, YA. A. GORDIN; circ. 10,000 (2003).

## Popular Scientific

**Meditsinskaya Gazeta** (Medical Gazette): 129090 Moscow, B. Sukharevskaya pl. 1/2; tel. (095) 208-86-95; fax (095) 208-69-80; e-mail mggazeta@online.ru; internet www.medgazeta.rusmedserv.com; f. 1938; 2 a week; professional international periodical; Editor ANDREI POLTORAK; circ. 52,000 (2002).

**Modelist-Konstruktor** (Modelmaker-Designer): 125015 Moscow, ul. Novodmitrovskaya 5A; tel. (095) 285-80-46; fax (095) 285-27-57; f. 1962; monthly; information about amateur cars, planes, cross-country vehicles; designs of cars, planes, ships, tanks, garden furniture etc.; Editor A. RAGUZIN; circ. 22,000 (1999).

**Nauka i Zhizn** (Science and Life): 101990 Moscow, ul. Myasnitskaya 24; tel. (095) 924-18-35; fax (095) 200-22-59; e-mail mail@nauka.relis.ru; internet nauka.relis.ru; f. 1890, resumed 1934;

monthly; recent developments in all branches of science and technology; Chief Editor I. K. Lagovskii; circ. 49,800 (2002).

**PC Week:** 109047 Moscow, ul. Marksistskaya 34/10; tel. (095) 974-22-60; fax (095) 974-22-63; e-mail editorial@pcweek.ru; internet www.pcweek.ru; f. 1995; 48 a year; Editor-in-Chief Eduard Proydakov; circ. 35,000 (2000).

**Priroda** (Nature): 117810 Moscow, Maronovskii per. 26; tel. (095) 238-24-56; fax (095) 238-26-33; f. 1912; monthly; publ. by the Nauka (Science) Publishing House; journal of the Presidium of the Academy of Sciences; natural sciences; Editor A. F. Andreyev; circ. 2,500 (1999).

**Radio:** 103045 Moscow, per. Seliverstov 10; tel. (095) 207-31-18; fax (095) 208-77-13; f. 1924; monthly; audio, video, communications, practical electronics, computers; Editor Y. I. Krylov; circ. 70,000 (2000).

**Tekhnika-Molodezhi** (Engineering—For Youth): 125015 Moscow, ul. Novodmitrovskaya 5A; tel. (095) 285-16-87; fax (095) 234-16-78; f. 1933; monthly; engineering and science; Editor A. N. Perevozchikov; circ. 50,000 (1999).

**Vrach** (Physician): 119881 Moscow, ul. B. Pirogovskaya 2/6; tel. (095) 248-57-27; fax (095) 248-02-14; f. 1990; monthly; medical, scientific and socio-political; illustrated; Editor-in-Chief Mikhail A. Paltsev; circ. 6,000 (1999).

**Zdorovye** (Health): 127994 Moscow, Bumazhnyi proyezd 14; tel. (095) 250-58-28; fax (095) 257-32-51; e-mail zdorovie@zdr.ru; internet zdorovie.ad.ru; f. 1955; monthly; medicine and hygiene; Editor T. Yefimova; circ. 195,000 (2002).

**Zemlya i Vselennaya** (The Earth and The Universe): 117810 Moscow, Maronovskii per. 26; tel. (095) 238-42-32; f. 1965; 6 a year; publ. by the Nauka (Science) Publishing House; jt edition of the Academy of Sciences and the Society of Astronomy and Geodesy; current hypotheses of the origin and development of the earth and the universe; astronomy, geophysics and space research; Chief Editor V. K. Abalakin; circ. 1,000 (2000).

### The Press, Printing and Bibliography

**Bibliografiya** (Bibliography): 119019 Moscow, Kremlevskaya nab. 1/9; tel. and fax (095) 298-25-82; e-mail bookch@postman.ru; f. 1929; 6 a year; publ. by the Book Chamber International Publishing House; theoretical, practical and historical aspects of bibliography; Editor G. A. Alekseyeva; circ. 2,200 (2002).

**Poligrafist i Izdatel** (Printer and Publisher): 129272 Moscow, ul. Suchevskii val 64/105; tel. (095) 288-93-17; fax (095) 288-94-44; e-mail pub@online.ru; f. 1994; monthly; Editor A. I. Ovsyannikov; circ. 5,000 (2000).

**Poligrafiya** (Printing): 129272 Moscow, ul. Sushchevskii val 64; tel. (095) 281-74-81; fax (095) 288-97-66; e-mail polimag@aha.ru; internet www.aha.ru/~polimag; f. 1924; 6 a year; equipment and technology of the printing industry; Dir N. N. Kondratiyeva; circ. 5,000 (1999).

**Slovo** (Word): 121069 Moscow, ul. Povarskaya 11/2; tel. and fax (095) 202-50-51; f. 1936; monthly; fmrly *V Mire Knig* (In the World of Books); reviews of new books, theoretical problems of literature, historical and religious; Editor A. V. Larionov; circ. 4,000 (1999).

**Vitrina Chitayushchei Rossii** (Through the Window of Reading Russia): 127550 Moscow, Listvennichnaya alleya 2A; tel. (095) 921-11-56; fax (095) 977-12-11; e-mail vitrina@souzpechat.ru; internet www.souzpechat.ru/vitrina; f. 1994; monthly; Editor Marina Dmitrieva.

**Zhurnalist** (Journalist): 101453 Moscow, Bumazhnyi proyezd 14; tel. (095) 257-30-58; fax (095) 257-31-27; f. 1920; monthly; publ. by Ekonomicheskaya Gazeta Publishing House; Editor G. P. Maltsev; circ. 6,200 (2002).

### Religion

**Bratskii Vestnik** (Herald of the Brethren): 109028 Moscow, M. Vuzovskii per. 3; tel. (095) 917-96-26; f. 1945; 6 a year; organ of the Russian Union of Evangelical Christians-Baptists; Chief Editor Yu. Agapov; circ. 10,000 (1998).

**Istina I Zhizn** (Truth and Life): 105215 Moscow, POB 38; tel. (095) 965-00-07; e-mail istina@aha.ru; inter-confessional Christian magazine; Editor Fr Aleksandr Khmelnitskii.

**Mezhdunarodnaya Yevreyskaya Gazeta** (International Jewish Newspaper): 107005 Moscow, Pleteshkovskii per. 3A; tel. and fax (095) 265-08-69; e-mail tankred@aha.ru; internet www.jig.nm.ru; f. 1989; weekly; Editor-in-Chief Nikolai Propirnyi; circ. 15,000 (2002).

**NG-Religii** (The Independent-Religions): 101000 Moscow, ul. Myasnitskaya 13; tel. (095) 923-42-40; fax (095) 921-58-47; e-mail ngr@ng .ru; internet religion.ng.ru; f. 1997; analysis of religious affairs and their social and political implications both within Russia and world-

wide; 2 a month; Editor-in-Chief Maksim Shevchenko; circ. 50,000 (2002).

**Russkii Yevrey** (Russian Jew): 107005 Moscow, Pleteshkovskii per. 3A; tel. and fax (095) 265-08-69; f. 1879; re-established 1996; quarterly.

**Zhurnal Moskovskoi Patriarkhii** (Journal of the Moscow Patriarchate): 119435 Moscow, ul. Pogodinskaya 20/2; tel. (095) 246-98-48; fax (095) 246-21-41; e-mail pressmp@jmp.ru; internet www.jmp .ru; f. 1934; monthly; Editor Archpriest Vladimir (Silovyev); circ. 6,000 (1999).

### Trade, Trade Unions, Labour and Social Security

**Chelovek i Trud** (Man and Labour): 103064 Moscow, Yakovoapostolskii per. 6/3; tel. and fax (095) 916-10-00; monthly; employment issues and problems of unemployment; Editor-in-Chief G. L. Podvoiskii; circ. 20,000 (1999).

**Profsoyuzy** (Trade Unions): 101000 Moscow, ul. Myasnitskaya 13/18/231; tel. (095) 924-57-40; fax (095) 975-23-29; e-mail iidprof@ cityline.ru; f. 1917; monthly; fmrly publ. by the General Confederation of Trade Unions of the USSR; Editor Y. I. Korobko; circ. 3,200 (1999).

**Vneshnyaya Torgovlya** (External Trade): 121108 Moscow, ul. Minskaya 11; tel. (095) 145-68-94; fax (095) 145-51-92; e-mail vneshtorg@mtu-net.ru; internet www.trade-point.ru/vt; f. 1921; monthly; Russian and English; organ of the Ministry of Economic Development and Trade; Editor-in-Chief Yurii Deomidov; circ. 7,000 (1999).

### Transport and Communication

**Grazhdanskaya Aviyatsiya** (Civil Aviation): 125836 Moscow, Leningradskii pr. 37; tel. and fax (095) 155-59-23; f. 1931; monthly; journal of the Union of Civil Aviation Workers; development of air transport; utilization of aviation in construction, agriculture and forestry; Editor A. M. Troshin; circ. 10,000 (1999).

**Radiotekhnika** (Radio Engineering): 103031 Moscow, Kuznetskii most 20/6/31; tel. (095) 921-48-37; fax (095) 925-92-41; e-mail iprzhr@online.ru; internet www.webcenter.ru/~iprzhr/; f. 1937; monthly; publ. by the Svyaz (Communication) Publishing House; journal of the A. S. Popov Scientific and Technical Society of Radio Engineering, Electronics and Electrical Communication; theoretical and technical problems of radio engineering; other publications include *Advances in Radio Science*, *Radio Systems* and *Antennae*; Editor Yu. V. Gulyayev; circ. 1,500 (1999).

**Radiotekhnika i Elektronika** (Radio Engineering and Electronics): 103907 Moscow, ul. Mokhovaya 11; tel. (095) 203-47-89; f. 1956; monthly; journal of the Russian Academy of Sciences; theory of radio engineering; Editor Y. V. Gulyayev; circ. 468 (2000).

**Vestnik Svyazi** (Herald of Communication): 101000 Moscow, Krivokolennyi per. 14/1; tel. (095) 925-42-57; fax (095) 921-27-97; e-mail irais@vestnik-sviazy.ru; internet www.vestnik-sviazy.ru; f. 1917; monthly; publ. by the IRIAS Agency; telecommunications; Editor E. B. Konstantinov; circ. 10,000 (2002).

### For Women

**Domovoi** (House-Sprite): 113035 Moscow, ul. B. Ordynka 16; tel. (095) 956-77-02; fax (095) 956-22-09; e-mail info@domovoy.ru; internet www.domovoy.ru; monthly; Editor-in-Chief Kseniya Makhnenko; circ. 105,000 (2000).

**Elle:** 101959 Moscow, ul. Myasnitskaya 35; tel. (095) 204-17-77; fax (095) 795-08-15; e-mail elle@hfm.ru; f. 1996; monthly; fashion; Editor-in-Chief Yelena Sotnikova; circ. 180,000 (1998).

**Krestyanka** (Peasant Woman): 127994 Moscow, Bumazhnyi proyezd 14; tel. (095) 257-39-39; fax (095) 257-39-63; e-mail mail@ krestyanka.ru; internet www.krestyanka.ru; f. 1922; monthly; publ. by the Krestyanka Publishing House; popular; supplements *Khozyayushka* (Dear Hostess), *On i ona* (He and She), *Moda v dome* (Fashion at Home), *Samochuvstvie* (Health), *Nasha Usadba* (Our Garden), *Pyatnashki* (Game of Tag); Pres and Editor-in-Chief Anastasiya V. Kupriyanova; circ.100,000 (2003).

**Mir Zhenshchiny** (Woman's World): 101999 Moscow, Glinitchevskii per. 6; tel. and fax (095) 209-95-33; f. 1945; monthly; fmrly *Zhenshchina* (Woman); in Russian, Chinese, English, French, German and Spanish; fmrly publ. by the Soviet Women's Committee and the General Confederation of Trade Unions; popular; illustrated; Editor-in-Chief V. I. Fedotova; circ. 50,000 (2000).

**Modeli Sezona** (Models of the Season): 103031 Moscow, Kuznetskii most 7/9; tel. (095) 921-73-93; fax (095) 928-77-93; f. 1957; 4 a year; Editor-in-Chief N. A. Kasatkina; circ. 45,000 (1999).

**Rabotnitsa** (Working Woman): 101458 Moscow, Bumazhnyi proyezd 14; tel. (095) 257-36-49; fax (095) 956-90-94; e-mail webmaster@rabotnitsa.ru; internet www.rabotnitsa.ru; f. 1914;

monthly; publ. by the Pressa Publishing House; popular; Editor ZOYA P KRYLOVA; circ. 223,000 (2000).

**Zhurnal Mod** (Fashion Journal): 103031 Moscow, Kuznetskii most 7/9; tel. (095) 921-73-93; f. 1945; 4 a year; illustrated; Editor-in-Chief N. A. KASATKINA; circ. 45,000 (1999).

### Youth

**Molodaya Gvardiya** (Young Guard): 125015 Moscow, ul. Novodmitrovskaya 5A; tel. (095) 285-88-29; fax (095) 285-56-90; f. 1922; monthly; fiction, poetry, criticism, popular science; Editor Y. YUSHIN; circ. 6,000 (2000).

**Rovesnik** (Contemporary): 125015 Moscow, ul. Novodmitrovskaya 5A; tel. (095) 285-89-20; fax (095) 285-06-27; e-mail rovesnik@rovesnik.ru; f. 1962; publ. by the Molodaya Gvardiya (Young Guard) Publishing House; fmrly journal of the Cen. Cttee of the Leninist Young Communist League; popular illustrated monthly of fiction, music, cinema, sport and other aspects of youth culture; Editor I. A. CHERNYSHKOV; circ. 100,000 (2000).

**Selskaya Molodezh** (Rural Youth): 125015 Moscow, ul. Novodmitrovskaya 5A; tel. (095) 285-80-04; fax (095) 285-08-30; f. 1925; monthly; publ. by the Molodaya Gvardiya (Young Guard) Publishing House; supplements *Podvigi* (Heroic Deeds) and *Detektivy selskoy molodezhi* (Rural Youth Detective Stories); popular illustrated, fiction, verses, problems of rural youth; Editor-in-Chief MICHAEL MASSUR; circ. 10,000 (1999).

**Smena** (The Rising Generation): 101457 Moscow, Bumazhnyi proyezd 14; tel. (095) 212-15-07; fax (095) 250-59-28; e-mail smena@garnet.ru; internet www.smena-id.ru; f. 1924; monthly; publ. by the Pressa Publishing House; popular illustrated, short stories, essays and problems of youth; Editor-in-Chief M. G. KIZILOV; circ. 50,000 (2001).

**Yunost** (Youth): 101524 Moscow, ul. Tverskaya-Yamskaya 8/1; tel. (095) 251-31-22; fax (095) 251-74-60; f. 1955; monthly; novels, short stories, essays and poems by beginners; Editor V. LIPATOV; circ. 15,000 (2000).

## NEWS AGENCIES

**ANI** (News and Information Agency): 103009 Moscow, Kalashnyi per. 10, bldg 2; tel. (095) 202-37-06; fax (095) 202-54-03; e-mail ani@ani.ru; internet www.ani.ru; f. 1991; Editor-in-Chief MARIANNA MEDOVAYA.

**Federal News Service (FNS):** 119992 Moscow, per. Obolenskyi 10; tel. (095) 245-58-00; fax 245-58-23; e-mail commerce@fednews.ru; internet www.fednews.ru; f. 1992; Bureau Chief VYACHESLAV NEMODRUK.

**Interfax:** 103006 Moscow, ul. 1-aya Tverskaya-Yamskaya 2; tel. (095) 250-92-03; fax (095) 250-89-94; e-mail webmaster@interfax.ru; internet www.interfax.ru; f. 1989; independent news agency; Gen. Dir M. KOMISSAR.

**ITAR—TASS** (Information Telegraphic Agency of Russia—Telegraphic Agency of the Sovereign Countries): 103009 Moscow, Tverskoi bulv. 10/12; tel. (095) 292-36-14; fax (095) 291-83-72; e-mail dms@itar-tass.com; internet www.itar-tass.com; f. 1904; state information agency; 74 bureaux in Russia and the states of the former USSR, 65 foreign bureaux outside the former USSR; Dir-Gen. VITALII N. IGNATENKO.

**Prima Human Rights News Agency:** 111399 Moscow, POB 5; tel. and fax (095) 455-30-11; e-mail prima@prima-news.ru; internet www.prima-news.ru; f. 2000; Editor-in-Chief ALEKSANDR PODRABINEK.

**RIA—Novosti** (Russian Information Agency—News): 103786 Moscow, Zubovskii bulv. 4; tel. (095) 201-82-09; fax (095) 201-45-45; e-mail marketing@rian.ru; internet www.rian.ru; f. 1961; collaborates by arrangement with foreign press and publishing organizations in 110 countries; provider of Russian news features and photographs; Chair. SVETLANA MIRONYUK.

**RosBalt Information Agency:** 190000 St Petersburg, Konnogvardeiskii bulv. 7; tel. (812) 320-50-30; fax (812) 320-50-31; e-mail rosbalt@rosbalt.ru; internet www.rosbalt.ru; news coverage of European Russia and other countries in northern Europe; bureau in Moscow; Chair. NATALIYA CHERKESOVA; Gen. Man. ALEKSANDR KADYROV.

**Rossiiskoye Informatsionnoye Agentstvo 'Oreanda'** (RIA 'Oreanda'): 117342 Moscow, POB 21; tel. (095) 330-98-50; fax (095) 23-04-39; e-mail info@oreanda.ru; internet www.oreanda.ru; f. 1994.

**Strana-Ru** (Country-Russia): 119021 Moscow, Zubovskii bulv. 4, podyezd 8; tel. (095) 201-81-34; fax (095) 201-41-17; e-mail mail@strana.ru; internet www.strana.ru; f. 2000; news agency; central bureau in Moscow, regional bureaux in each of the 7 Federal Okrugs, and in Groznyi, Chechnya; controlled by the All-Russian State Television and Radio Broadcasting Company (VGTRK) from 2002; Gen Man. MARINA A. LITVINOVICH.

### Foreign Bureaux

**Agence France-Presse (AFP):** 103006 Moscow, ul. Dolgorukovskaya 18/3; tel. (095) 926-59-69; fax (095) 931-95-85; e-mail desk .moscou@afp.com; internet www.afp.com; Dir BERNARD ESTRADE.

**Agencia EFE** (Spain): 103051 Moscow, ul. Sadovaya-Samotechnaya 12/24/23; tel. (095) 200-15-32; fax (095) 956-37-38; e-mail efemos@co.ru; internet www.efe.es; Bureau Chief MANUEL VELASCO.

**Agenzia Nazionale Stampa Associata (ANSA)** (Italy): 121248 Moscow, Kutuzovskii pr. 9/1/12–14; tel. (095) 243-73-93; fax (095) 243-06-37; e-mail ansamos@online.ru; internet www.ansa.it; Bureau Chief GIULIO GELIBTER.

**Anatolian News Agency** (Turkey): 121552 Moscow, Rublevskoye shosse 26/1/279; tel. (095) 415-44-19; e-mail roonni@hotmail.com; Correspondent REMZI ONER OZKAN.

**Associated Press (AP)** (USA): 121248 Moscow, Kutuzovskii pr. 7/4, kor. 5, kv. 33; tel. (095) 234-43-53; fax (095) 974-18-45; e-mail mosed@ap.org; internet www.ap.org; Bureau Chief DEBORAH SEWARD.

**Athens News Agency** (Greece): 121148 Moscow, Kutuzovskii pr. 13/91; tel. and fax (095) 243-73-73; internet www.ana.gr; Correspondent DIMITRIOS KONSTANTA KOPOULOS.

**Baltic News Service** (Estonia, Latvia and Lithuania): 121069 Moscow, ul. Povarskaya 24/15; tel. and fax (095) 202-38-05; e-mail juri@bns.ee; internet www.bns.ee; f. 1990; Bureau Chief JÜRI MALOVERJAN; also maintains bureau in Kaliningrad.

**Česká tisková kancelář (ČTK)** (Czech Republic): 125047 Moscow, ul. 3-aya Tverskaya-Yamskaya 31-35/5/106; tel. and fax (095) 251-71-63; e-mail bwanamar@glas.apc.org; internet www.ctk.cz; Correspondent ALEXANDRA MALACHOVSKA.

**Deutsche Presse-Agentur (dpa)** (Germany): 121248 Moscow, Kutuzovskii pr. 7/4/210; tel. (095) 243-97-90; fax (095) 243-14-46; internet www.dpa.de; Bureau Chief GÜNTHER CHALUPA.

**Iraqi News Agency:** 119121 Moscow, ul. Pogodinskaya 12; tel. (095) 316-99-75; fax (095) 246-77-76; Correspondent MUHAMMAD ABDEL MUTTALIB.

**Islamic Republic News Agency (IRNA)** (Iran): 121609 Moscow, Rublevskoye shosse 36/2/264; tel. (095) 415-43-62; fax (095) 415-42-88; e-mail irna@garnet.ru; Bureau Chief MAHMOUD HIDAJI.

**Jiji Tsushin (Jiji Press)** (Japan): 117049 Moscow, ul. Korovyi val 7/35; tel. (095) 564-81-02; fax (095) 564-81-13; Bureau Chief KITAGATA KAZUYA.

**Korea Central News Agency (KCNA)** (Democratic People's Republic of Korea): 119590 Moscow, ul. Mosfilmovskaya 72; tel. (095) 143-62-31; fax (095) 143-63-12; Bureau Chief KAN CHU MIN.

**Kuwait News Agency (KUNA):** 117049 Moscow, ul. Korovyi val 7/52; tel. (095) 230-25-10; fax (095) 956-99-06; Correspondent ADIB AL-SAYYED.

**Kyodo News** (Japan): 121059 Moscow, B. Dorogomilovskaya 12; tel. (095) 956-60-22; fax (095) 956-60-26; Bureau Chief YOSHIDA SHIGEYUKI.

**Magyar Távirati Iroda (MTI)** (Hungary): 129010 Moscow, ul. B. Spasskaya 12/46; tel. (095) 280-04-25; fax (095) 280-04-21; Bureau Chief SÁNDOR TAMASSY.

**Middle East News Agency (MENA)** (Egypt): 107113 Moscow, ul. Sokolnicheskii val 24/2/176; tel. (095) 264-82-76; fax (095) 269-60-93; Correspondent Dr MAMDOUH MUSTAFA.

**Mongol Tsahilgaan Medeeniy Agentlag (Montsame)** (Mongolia): 117333 Moscow, ul. Vavilova 79/52; tel. (095) 950-55-16; fax (095) 229-98-83; Bureau Chief SHAGDAR.

**News Agencies of Sweden, Norway, Denmark and Finland:** 121248 Moscow, Kutuzovskii pr. 7/4/5/30; tel. (095) 956-60-50; fax (095) 974-81-52; Correspondent THOMAS HAMBERG.

**Notimex News Agency** (Mexico): 123182 Moscow, ul. Akademika Bochvara 5/2/30–1; tel. and fax (095) 196-47-75; Correspondent FERNANDO OROZCO LLOREDA.

**Polska Agencja Prasowa (PAP)** (Poland): 117334 Moscow, Leninskii pr. 45/411; tel. and fax (095) 135-11-06; e-mail papmos@online .ru; Chief Correspondent ANDRZEJ LOMANOWSKI.

**Prensa Latina** (Cuba): 123182 Moscow, ul. Akademika Bochvara 5/2/30–1; tel. and fax (095) 196-47-75; Chief Correspondent ANTONIO RONDÓN.

**Press Trust of India:** 129041 Moscow, ul. B. Pereyaslavskaya 7/133–134; tel. and fax (095) 437-43-60; Correspondent VINAY KUMAR SHUKLA.

**Reuters** (United Kingdom): 121059 Moscow, Radisson-Slavyanskaya Hotel, Berezhkovskaya nab. 2; tel. (095) 941-85-20; fax (095) 941-88-01; Man. MICHAL BRONIATOWSKI.

**Rompres** (Romania): Moscow, 121248 Kutuzovskii pr. 14/21; tel. (095) 243-67-96; Bureau Chief NICOLAE CRETU.

**Schweizerische Depeschenagentur** (Switzerland): 121059 Moscow, B. Dorogomilovskaya 8/19; tel. and fax (095) 240-90-78; Bureau Chief CHRISTOPH GÜDEL.

**Syrian Arab News Agency (SANA):** 121248 Moscow, Kutuzovskii pr. 7/4/184–185; tel. (095) 243-13-00; fax (095) 243-75-12; Dir FAHED KAMNAKESH.

**Tlačová agentúra Slovenskej republiky (TASR)** (Slovakia): 123056 Moscow, ul. Yu. Fuchika 17–19/43; tel. and fax (095) 250-24-89; Correspondent BLAZEJ PÁNIK.

**United Press International (UPI)** (USA): 119334 Moscow, Leninskii pr. 45/426; tel. (095) 135-32-55; fax (095) 564-86-61; e-mail newsdesk@unitedpress.ru; internet www.upi.com; Bureau Chief ANTHONY LOUIS.

**Viet Nam News Agency (VNA):** 117334 Moscow, Leninskii pr. 45/326–327; tel. (095) 135-11-08; fax (095) 137-38-67; e-mail pxmoscow@online.ru; Bureau Chief NGO GIA SON.

**Xinhua (New China) News Agency** (People's Republic of China): 109029 Moscow, ul. M. Kalitnikovskaya 9A; tel. (095) 270-47-41; fax (095) 270-44-85; Dir WEI ZHENGQIANG.

**Yonhap (United) News Agency** (Republic of Korea): 103009 Moscow, Tverskoi bulv. 10/425; tel. and fax (095) 290-65-75; Correspondent CHI IL-WOO.

### PRESS ASSOCIATIONS

**Russian Guild of Publishers of Periodical Press:** 125047 Moscow, ul. Sesnaya 20/6-211; tel. and fax (095) 978-41-89.

**Union of Journalists of Russia:** 119021 Moscow, Zubovskii bulv. 4; tel. (095) 201-51-01; fax (095) 201-35-47; f. 1991; Sec.-Gen. IGOR YAKOVENKO.

# Publishers

**Ad Marginem-Ad Patres:** 119034 Moscow, Kropotkinskii per. 23; tel. and fax (095) 201-52-62; e-mail robot@rosd.org.ru; internet ad-marginem.pp.ru; f. 1994; fiction, philosophy, artistic and literary criticism; Dir SERGEI DATSYUK.

**AST:** 129085 Moscow, Zvezdnyi bulv. 21; tel. (095) 215-01-01; fax (095) 215-51-10; e-mail astpub@aha.ru; internet www.ast.ru; original and translated fiction and non-fiction, children's and school-books.

**Avrora** (Aurora): 191186 St Petersburg, Nevskii pr. 7/9; tel. (812) 312-37-53; fax (812) 312-54-60; f. 1969; fine arts; published in foreign languages; Dir ZENOBIUS SPETCHINSKII.

**Bolshaya Rossiiskaya Entsiklopediya** (The Great Russian Encyclopedia): 109028 Moscow, Pokrovskii bulv. 8; tel. (095) 917-94-86; fax (095) 917-71-39; e-mail gnibre2000@mail.ru; f. 1925; universal and specific encyclopedias; Dir A. P. GORKIN.

**Detskaya Entsiklopediya** (Children's Encyclopedia): 107042 Moscow, ul. Bakuninskaya 55; tel. (095) 269-52-76; f. 1933; science fiction, literature, poetry, biographical and historical novels.

**Detskaya Literatura** (Children's Literature): 103720 Moscow, M. Cherkasskii per. 1; tel. (095) 928-08-03; e-mail detlit@detlit.ru; f. 1933; State Publishing House of Children's Literature (other than school books); Dir E. A. NORTSOVA.

**Drofa:** 127018 Moscow, ul. Sushchevskii val. 49; tel. (095) 795-05-50; fax (095) 795-05-44; e-mail info@drofa.ru; internet www.drofa .ru; f. 1991; school textbooks, children's fiction; Dir-Gen. KONSTANTIN M. DRAGAN.

**Ekonomika** (Economy): 121864 Moscow, Berezhkovskaya nab. 6; tel. (095) 240-48-77; fax (095) 240-58-28; f. 1963; various aspects of economics, management and marketing; Dir G. I. MAZIN.

**Eksmo:** 125190 Moscow, Leningradskii pr. 80/16/3; tel. and fax (095) 956-24-11; e-mail osipova.eg@eksmo.ru; internet www.eksmo .ru; f. 1991; popular fiction; Gen. Dir OLEG YE. NOVIKOV.

**Energoatomizdat** (Atomic Energy Press): 113114 Moscow, Shluzovaya nab. 10; tel. (095) 925-99-93; f. 1981; different kinds of energy, nuclear science and technology; Dir A. P. ALESHKIN.

**Finansy i Statistika** (Finance and Statistics): 101000 Moscow, ul. Pokrovka 7; tel. (095) 925-47-08; fax (095) 925-09-57; e-mail mail@ finstat.ru; internet www.finstat.ru; f. 1924; education, economics, science, finance, statistics, banking, insurance, accounting, computer science; Dir Dr A. N. ZVONOVA.

**Fizkultura i Sport** (Exercise and Sport): 101421 Moscow, ul. Dolgorukovskaya 27; tel. (095) 978-26-90; fax (095) 200-12-17; f.

1923; books and periodicals relating to all forms of sport, chess and draughts, etc.; Gen. Dir T. BALYAN.

**Forum:** 101831 Moscow, Kolpachnyi per. 9A; tel. and fax (095) 925-01-97; e-mail forum-books@mail.ru; internet www.infra-m.ru/forum .htm; f. 2001; general and professional educational textbooks; Gen. Man. IRINA S. MONAKHOVA.

**GALART:** 125319 Moscow, ul. Chernyakhovskogo 4; tel. (095) 151-25-02; fax (095) 151-37-61; f. 1969; fmrly *Sovetskii Khudozhnik* (Soviet Artist); art reproduction, art history and criticism; Gen. Dir V. V. GORYAINOV.

**Gorodets:** 117419 Moscow, 2-i Roshchinskii pr. 8/7/1201; tel. (095) 955-71-28; fax (095) 234-39-67; e-mail info@gorodets.com; internet www.gorodets.com; law, politics, international relations, economics.

**INFRA-M:** 127214 Moscow, Dmitrovskoye shosse 107; tel. (095) 485-70-77; fax (095) 485-53-17; e-mail office@infra-m.ru; internet www.infra-m.ru; f. 1992; economics, law, computing, history, reference works, encyclopaedias; Gen. Man. YELENA V. MELCHUK.

**Iskusstvo** (Art): 103009 Moscow, M. Kislovskii per. 3; tel. (095) 203-58-72; f. 1936; fine arts, architecture, cinema, photography, television and radio, theatre; Dir O. A. MAKAROV.

**Izobrazitelnoye Iskusstvo** (Fine Art): 129272 Moscow, ul. Sushchevskii val 64; tel. (095) 281-65-48; fax (095) 281-41-11; reproductions of pictures, pictorial art, books on art, albums, calendars, postcards; Dir V. S. KUZYAKOV.

**Khimiya** (Chemistry): 107976 Moscow, ul. Strominka 21/2; tel. (095) 268-29-76; f. 1963; chemistry and the chemical industry; Dir BORIS S. KRASNOPEVTSEV.

**Khudozhestvennaya Literatura** (Fiction): 107078 Moscow, ul. Novobasmannaya 19; tel. (095) 261-88-65; fax (095) 261-83-00; fiction and works of literary criticism, history of literature, etc.; Dir A. N. PETROV; Editor-in-Chief V. S. MODESTOV.

**Kniga and Business Ltd** (Books and Business): 125047 Moscow, ul. 1-aya TverskayaYamskaya 22; tel. (095) 251-60-03; fax (095) 250-04-89; fiction, biographies, history, commerce, general; Dir VIKTOR N. ADAMOV.

**Kolos** (Ear of Corn): 107807 Moscow, ul. Sadovaya-Spasskaya 18; tel. (095) 207-29-92; fax (095) 207-28-70; f. 1918; all aspects of agricultural production; Dir ANATOLII M. ULYANOV.

**Kompozitor** (Composer): 103006 Moscow, ul. Sadovaya-Triumfalnaya 12–14; tel. (095) 209-41-05; fax (095) 209-54-98; e-mail music@ spica-eng.ru; f. 1957; established by the Union of Composers of the USSR; music and music criticism; Dir GRIGORII A. VORONOV.

**Malysh** (Dear Little One): 121352 Moscow, ul. Davydkovskaya 5; tel. (095) 443-06-54; fax (095) 443-06-55; f. 1958; books, booklets and posters for children aged three to 10 years; Dir V. A. RYBIN.

**Meditsina** (Medicine): 101838 Moscow, Petroverigskii per. 6/8; tel. (095) 924-87-85; fax (095) 928-60-03; e-mail meditsina@iname.com; internet www.medlit.ru; f. 1918; state-owned; imprint of Association for Medical Literature; books and journals on medicine and health; Dir A. M. STOCHIK; Editor-in-Chief Prof. NIKOLAI R. PALEYEV.

**Metallurgiya** (Metallurgy): 119034 Moscow, 2-i Obydenskii per. 14; tel. (095) 202-55-32; f. 1939; metallurgical literature; Dir A. G. BELIKOV.

**Mezhdunarodnye Otnosheniya** (International Relations): 107078 Moscow, ul. Sadovaya-Spasskaya 20; tel. (095) 207-67-93; fax (095) 200-22-04; f. 1957; international relations, economics and politics of foreign countries, foreign trade, international law, foreign language textbooks and dictionaries, translations and publications for the UN and other international organizations; Dir B. P. LIKHACHEV.

**Mir** (The World): 107996 Moscow, l-i Rizhskii per. 2; tel. (095) 286-17-83; fax (095) 288-95-22; e-mail akhp@mir-publishers.net; internet www.mir-publishers.net; f. 1946; Russian translations of foreign scientific, technical and science fiction books; translations of Russian books on science and technology into foreign languages; Dir KHABIB P. ABDULLAYEV.

**Molodaya Gvardiya** (The Young Guard): 103030 Moscow, ul. Sushchevskaya 21; tel. (095) 972-05-46; fax (095) 972-05-82; f. 1922; fmrly publishing and printing combine of the Lenin Young Communist League (Komsomol); joint-stock co; books and magazines, newspaper for children and for adolescents; Gen. Dir V. F. YURKIN.

**Moscow University Press:** 119899 Moscow, ul. Khokhlova 11; tel. and fax (095) 939-33-23; e-mail kd_mgu@df.ru; f. 1756; more than 200 titles of scientific, educational and reference literature annually, 19 scientific journals; Dir N. S. TIMOFEYEV.

**Moskovskii Rabochii** (Moscow Worker): 101854 Moscow, Chistoprudnyi bulv. 8; tel. (095) 921-07-35; f. 1922; publishing house of the Moscow city and regional soviets; all types of work, including fiction; Dir D. V. YEVDOKIMOV.

**Muzyka** (Music): 103031 Moscow, ul. Neglinnaya 14; tel. (095) 921-51-70; fax (095) 928-33-04; f. 1861; sheet music, music scores and related literature; Dir Igor P. Savintsev.

**Mysl** (Thought): 119071 Moscow, Leninskii pr. 15; tel. (095) 952-42-48; fax (095) 955-04-58; f. 1963; science, popular science, economics, philosophy, demography, history, political science, geography; Editor-in-Chief I. V. Ushakov.

**Nauka** (Science): 117997 Moscow, ul. Profsoyuznaya 90; tel. (095) 336-02-66; fax (095) 420-22-20; e-mail secret@naukaran.ru; f. 1964; publishing house of the Academy of Sciences; general and social science, mathematics, physics, chemistry, biology, earth sciences, oriental studies, books in foreign languages, university textbooks, scientific journals, translation, export, distribution, typesetting and printing services; Dir-Gen. V. Vasiliyev.

**Nauka i Tekhnologiya** (Science and Technology): 107076 Moscow, Stromynskii per. 4; tel. (095) 269-51-96; fax (095) 269-49-96; e-mail admin@nauka-technologiy.ru; f. 2000; journals on chemistry, electronics and telecommunications; Gen. Dir Maksim A. Kovalevskii.

**Nedra Biznestsentr** (Natural Resources Business Centre): 125047 Moscow, Tverskaya zastava 3; tel. (095) 251-31-77; fax (095) 250-27-72; e-mail business@nedrainform.ru; internet www.nedrainform.ru; f. 1964; geology, natural resources, mining and coal industry, petroleum and gas industry; Dir V. D. Menshikov.

**Norma** (The Norm): 101831 Moscow, Kolpachnyi per. 9a; tel. and fax (095) 925-45-05; e-mail norma@norma-verlag.com; internet www.infra-m.ru/norma.htm; f. 1995; law and jurisprudence, philosophy, psychology, sociology, economics; Gen. Man. Eduard I. Machulskii.

**Novosti** (News): 105082 Moscow, ul. B. Pochtovaya 7; tel. (095) 265-63-35; fax (095) 975-20-65; f. 1964; politics, economics, fiction, translated literature; Dir Aleksandr Yeidinov.

**Olma Press:** 129075 Moscow, Zvezdnyi bulv. 23/12; tel. (095) 784-67-74; fax (095) 215-80-53; e-mail info@olmapress.ru; internet www.olmapress.ru; f. 1991; fiction, history, reference; children's books, popular science; general; Pres. Vladimir I. Uzun; Gen. Man. Oleg P. Tkach.

**Pedagogika Press** (Pedagogy Press): 119034 Moscow, Smolenskii bulv. 4; tel. and fax (095) 246-59-69; f. 1969; scientific and popular books on pedagogics, didactics, psychology, developmental physiology; young people's encyclopaedia, dictionaries; Dir I. Kolesnikova.

**Planeta** (Planet): 103779 Moscow, ul. Petrovka 8/11; tel. (095) 923-04-70; fax (095) 200-52-46; f. 1969; postcards, calendars, guidebooks, brochures, illustrated books; co-editions with foreign partners; Dir V. G. Seredin.

**Pressa** (The Press): 125865 Moscow, ul. Pravdy 24; tel. (095) 257-46-21; fax (095) 250-52-05; f. 1934 as Pravda (Truth) Publishing House; publishes booklets, books and many newspapers and periodicals; Dir V. P. Leontev.

**Profizdat** (Professional Publishers): 101000 Moscow, ul. Myasnitskaya 13/18; tel. (095) 924-57-40; fax (095) 975-23-29; e-mail profizdat@profizdat.ru; f. 1930; books and magazines; Gen. Dir Vladimir Soloviev.

**Progress** (Progress): 119992 Moscow, Zubovskii bulv. 17; tel. (095) 246-90-32; fax (095) 230-24-03; e-mail progress@mcn.ru; f. 1931; translations of Russian language books into foreign languages and of foreign language books into Russian; political and scientific, fiction, literature for children and youth; encyclopedias; Dir-Gen. Sarkis V. Oganian.

**Prosveshcheniye** (Enlightenment): 127521 Moscow, 3-i proyezd M. Roshchi 41; tel. (095) 789-30-40; fax (095) 789-30-41; e-mail prosv@prosv.ru; internet www.prosv.ru; f. 1930; school textbooks, fiction; Dir A. P. Sudakov.

**Radio i Svyaz** (Radio and Communication): 103473 Moscow, 2-i Shchemilovskii per.4/5; tel. (095) 978-54-10; fax (095) 978-53-51; f. 1981; radio engineering, electronics, communications, computer science; Dir Ye. N. Salnikov; Editor-in-Chief I. K. Kalugin.

**Raduga** (Rainbow): 121839 Moscow, per. Sivtsev Vrazhek 43; tel. (095) 241-68-15; fax (095) 241-63-53; e-mail raduga@pol.ru; f. 1982; translations of Russian fiction into foreign languages and of foreign authors into Russian; Dir Tanyana Zimina.

**Respublika** (Republic): 125811 Moscow, Miusskaya pl. 7; tel. (095) 251-42-44; fax (095) 200-22-54; e-mail respublik@dataforce.net; f. 1918; fmrly *Politizdat* (Political Publishing House); dictionaries, books on politics, human rights, philosophy, history, economics, religion, fiction, arts, reference; Dir Aleksandr P. Polyakov.

**Russkaya Kniga** (Russian Book): 123557 Moscow, Tishinskii per. 38; tel. (095) 205-33-77; fax (095) 205-34-27; f. 1957 as Sovetskaya Rossiya; fiction, politics, history, social sciences, health, do-it-yourself, children's; Dir M. F. Nenashev.

**Russkii Yazyk** (Russian Language): 117303 Moscow, ul. M. Yushunski 1; tel. (095) 319-83-14; fax (095) 319-83-12; e-mail russlang@mtu-net.ru; f. 1974; textbooks, reference, dictionaries; Dir Irina Kainarskaya.

**Sovremennyi Pisatel** (The Contemporary Writer): 121069 Moscow, ul. Povarskaya 11; tel. (095) 202-50-51; f. 1934; fiction and literary criticism, history, biography; publ. house of the International Confederation of Writers' Unions and the Union of Russian Writers; Dir A. N. Zhukov.

**Stroyizdat** (Construction Publishing House): 101442 Moscow, ul. Kalyayevskaya 23a; tel. (095) 251-69-67; f. 1932; building, architecture, environmental protection, fire protection and building materials; Dir V. A. Kasatkin.

**Sudostroyeniye** (Shipbuilding): 191186 St Petersburg, ul. M. Morskaya 8; tel. (812) 312-44-79; fax (812) 312-08-21; f. 1940; shipbuilding, ship design, navigation, marine research, underwater exploration, international marine exhibitions; Dir and Editor-in-Chief A. A. Andreyev.

**Transport** (Transport): 103064 Moscow, Basmannyi tupik 6a; tel. (095) 262-67-73; fax (095) 261-13-22; f. 1923; publishes works on all forms of transport; Dir V. G. Peshkov.

**Vagrius:** 129090 Moscow, ul. Troitskaya 7/1; tel. (095) 785-09-62; fax (095) 785-09-69; e-mail vagrius@vagrius.com; internet www.vagrius.com; f. 1992; fiction, politics, history; Pres. and Dir-Gen. Gleb Uspenskii.

**Ves Mir** (The Whole World): 101831 Moscow, Kolpachnyi per. 9a; tel. (095) 923-68-39; fax (095) 925-42-69; e-mail info@vesmirbooks.ru; internet www.vesmirbooks.ru; f. 1994; university textbooks, scholarly works, history, encyclopaedias, in Russian and European languages; Dir Dr Oleg Zimarin; Editor-in-Chief Tatyana Komarova.

**Vneshtorgizdat** (External Trade Printing and Publishing Association): 125047 Moscow, ul. Fadeyev 1; tel. (095) 250-51-62; fax (095) 253-97-94; f. 1925; publishes foreign technical material translated into Russian, and information on export goods, import and export firms, joint ventures; in several foreign languages; Dir-Gen. V. I. Prokopov.

**Voyenizdat** (Military Publishing House): 103160 Moscow, ul. Zorgye 1; tel. (095) 195-25-95; fax (095) 195-24-54; military theory and history, general fiction; Dir Yurii I. Stadnyuk.

**Vysshaya Shkola** (Higher School): 101439 Moscow, ul. Neglinnaya 29/14; tel. (095) 200-04-56; fax (095) 973-21-80; f. 1939; textbooks for higher-education institutions; Dir Mikhail I. Kiselev.

**Yuridicheskaya Literatura** (Legal Literature): 121069 Moscow, ul. M. Nikitskaya 14; tel. (095) 203-83-84; fax (095) 291-98-83; f. 1917; law subjects; official publishers of enactments of the Russian President and Govt; Dir I. A. Bunin.

**Znaniye** (Knowledge): 101835 Moscow, proyezd Serova 4; tel. (095) 928-15-31; f. 1951; popular books and brochures on politics and science; Dir V. K. Belyakov.

# Broadcasting and Communications

## TELECOMMUNICATIONS

**Delta Telecom:** 191014 St Petersburg, per. Manezhnyi 14; tel. (812) 314-61-26; fax (812) 275-01-30; e-mail delta@deltatel.ru; internet www.deltatelecom.net; f. 1991; provides mobile cellular telecommunications services in St Petersburg, Kareliya, and Leningrad, Novgorod and Pskov Oblasts; Man. Dir Sergei Soldatenkov.

**Megafon:** 119435 Moscow, Savvinskaya nab. 15; tel. (095) 504-50-20; fax (095) 504-50-21; e-mail aklimov@megafon.ru; internet www.megafon.ru; f. 2002 by merger; operates mobile cellular communications networks across the territory of the Russian Federation; 6 regional cos; 5.0m. subscribers (Sept. 2003).

**Petersburg Telephone Network (PTS):** 119186 St Petersburg, ul. B. Morskaya 24; tel. (812) 314-15-50; fax (812) 110-68-34; e-mail office@ptn.ru; internet www.ptn.ru; f. 1993; subsidiary of Severo-Zapadnyi Telekom (North-Western Telecom); Dir Igor N. Samylin.

**Rostelekom:** 125047 Moscow, ul.1-aya Tverskaya-Yamskaya 14; tel. (095) 787-28-49; fax (095) 787-28-50; e-mail info@rostelecom.ru; internet www.rt.ru; 50.7% owned by Svyazinvest; dominant long-distance and international telecommunications service provider; seven regional subsidiary cos based in St Petersburg, Samara, Novosibirsk, Yekaterinburg, Khabarovsk, Moscow and Rostov-on-Don; Dir Aleksei Ye. Shevchenko.

**Sistema Telecom:** 125047 Moscow, ul. 1-aya Tverskaya-Yamskaya 5; tel. (095) 105-74-21; fax (095) 105-74-58; e-mail info@sistel.ru; internet www.sistel.ru; subsidiary of Sistema; Pres. Aleksandr Goncharuk.

**Mobile TeleSystems (MTS):** 109147 Moscow, ul. Marksistskaya 4; tel. (095) 766-01-77; e-mail info@mts.ru; internet www.mts.ru;

f. 1993; 776,000 subscribers (Dec. 2000); provides mobile cellular telecommunications services in 25 regions of Russia; majority-owned by Sistema Telecom; 35.1% owned by Deutsche Telekom (Germany); Pres. M. A. SMIRNOV; 9.5m. subscribers (March 2003).

**Moscow City Telephone Network (MGTS):** 127994 Moscow, Petrovskii bulv. 12/3; tel. (095) 950-00-00; fax (095) 950-06-18; e-mail mgts@mgts.ru; internet www.mgts.ru; f. 1882; provides telecommunications services to over 4.2m. subscribers (2001) in Moscow City; 56% owned by Sistema Telecom; Gen. Man. VLADIMIR S. LAGUTIN.

**Svyazinvest:** 119121 Moscow, ul. Plyushchikha 55/2; tel. (095) 248-24-71; fax 248-24-53; e-mail dms@svyazinvest.ru; internet www .sinvest.ru; f. 1995; 51%-state-owned telecommunications co; holds controlling stakes in 75 regional telecommunications operators, 2 inter-city and international telephone exchanges, and non-controlling stakes in 5 regional and city telecommunications cos; Gen. Dir VALERII N. YASHIN.

**Teleross:** 111250 Moscow, ul. Krasnokazarmennaya 12; tel. (095) 787-10-00; fax (095) 787-10-10; e-mail info@goldentelecom.ru; internet www.teleross.ru; f. 1994; operates mobile cellular telecommunications network in 16 cities in the Russian Federation, and in Almaty (Kazakhstan) and Kiev (Ukraine); subsidiary of the Golden TeleSystems Group (USA); Dir-Gen. STAN ABBELOOS.

**Vympelcom-Beeline:** 125083 Moscow, ul. 8 Marta 10/14; tel. and fax (095) 725-07-00; e-mail info@beeline.ru; internet www.beeline .ru; operates mobile cellular telecommunications networks in Moscow City and Moscow Oblast, and in Yaroslavl, Nizhnii Novgorod, Novosibirsk, Omsk, Ufa, Rostov-on-Don and Volgograd; 25% owned by Telenor (Norway), 25% owned by Alfa-Bank; 1,800,000 subscribers (Nov. 2001); Chief Exec. JO LUNDER; Pres. DMITRII B. ZIMIN.

## BROADCASTING

In 1995 there was extensive reorganization of Russian broadcasting, and a new organization, Public Russian Television (ORT), was formed to take over the broadcasting responsibilities of the Ostankino Russian State Television and Radio Broadcasting Company. Pervyi Kanal (First Channel), as ORT's Channel 1 was renamed in 2002, is received throughout Russia and many parts of the CIS. The All-Russian State Television Company (VGTRK) broadcasts Telekanal 'Rossiya', which reaches some 92% of the Russian population. In 1997 it began broadcasting Telekanal 'Kultura', founded for the purpose of broadcasting Russian-made programmes. In mid-2003 the VGTRK also began broadcasting a new channel, Telekanal 'Sport', on the frequency vacated by the independent channel, TVS, which had recently ceased operations. In addition to the nation-wide television channels, there are local channels, and the Independent Television (NTV) channel (65% owned by the gas utility, Gazprom, in which the Government holds a majority stake) is broadcast in most of central Russia. In the regions, part of Rossiya's programming is devoted to local affairs, with broadcasts in minority languages. In late 2001 there were some 550 television stations in the Russian Federation, of which approximately 150 were state-owned.

**Association of Regional State Television and Radio Broadcasters:** 113326 Moscow, ul. Pyatnitskaya 25/226; tel. and fax (095) 950-60-28; e-mail fstratyv@rzn.rosmail.com; Chair. of Bd ALEKSANDR N. LEVCHENKO.

### Regulatory Authority

**Russian Television and Radio Broadcasting Network:** 113326 Moscow, ul. Pyatnitskaya 25; tel. (095) 233-66-03; fax (095) 233-28-93; f. 2001; Gen. Man. GENNADII I. SKLYAR.

### Radio

**All-Russian State Television and Radio Broadcasting Company (VGTRK):** 125124 Moscow, ul. 5-aya Yamskogo Polya 19/21; tel. (095) 214-42-58; fax (095) 975-26-11; e-mail info@vesti-rtr.com; internet www.tvradio.ru; f. 1991; broadcasts 'Rossiya' and 'Kultura' television channels, 89 regional television and radio cos, and national radio stations 'Radio Rossiya', 'Radio Mayak', 'Radio Orfei' and 'Radio Nostalzhi'; Chair. OLGA DOBRODEYEVA.

**Radio Mayak** (Radio Beacon): 113326 Moscow, ul. Pyatnitskaya 25; tel. (095) 950-67-67; fax (095) 959-42-04; e-mail inform@ radiomayak.ru; internet www.radiomayak.ru; f. 1964; state-owned; Chair. IRINA A. GERASIMOVA.

**Radio Nostalzhi** (Radio Nostalgia): 113162 Moscow, ul. Shabolovka 37; tel. (095) 955-84-00; e-mail nostalgie@vimain.vitpc.ru; f. 1993; Gen. Man. IRINA A. GERASIMOVA.

**Radio Orfei** (Radio Orpheus): 121069 Moscow, ul. M. Nikitskaya 24; tel. and fax (095) 290-19-16; e-mail orphei@dol.ru; internet www.mmv.ru/orphei; f. 1991; broadcasts classical music; Gen. Dir OLGA A. GROMOVA.

**Radio Rossiya** (Radio Russia): 125040 Moscow, ul. 5-aya Yamskogo Polya 19/21; tel. (095) 234-85-94; fax (095) 730-42-77; e-mail direction@radiorus.ru; internet www.radiorus.ru; f. 1990; broadcasts information, social, political, musical, literary and investigate progamming; Dir-Gen. ALEKSEI V. ABAKUMOV.

**Ekho Moskvy** (Moscow Echo): 119992 Moscow, ul. Novyi Arbat 11; tel. (095) 202-92-29; e-mail info@echo.msk.ru; internet www.echo .msk.ru; f. 1990; stations in Moscow, St Petersburg, Rostov-on-Don and Vologda; also broadcasts from Moscow to Chelyabinsk, Krasnoyarsk, Novosibirsk, Omsk, Perm, Saratov and Yekaterinburg; 66% -owned by Gazprom-Mediya, 34% staff-owned; Gen. Man. YURII FEDUTINKOV.

**Golos Rossii** (The Voice of Russia): 113326 Moscow, ul. Pyatnitskaya 25; tel. (095) 950-64-40; fax (095) 230-28-28; e-mail letters@ vor.ru; internet www.vor.ru; fmrly Radio Moscow International; international broadcasts in 31 languages; Man. Dir ARMEN G. OGANESIAN.

**Radio Arsenal:** 119992 Moscow, ul. Novyi Arbat 11; tel. (095) 202-92-29; e-mail info@radioarsenal.ru; internet www.echo.msk.ru/ headings/arsenal.html; f. 2002 by the former staff of Ekho Moskvy (Moscow Echo—q.v.); broadcasts news, interviews and conversation; Dir ALEKSEI VENEDIKTOV.

**Yevropa Plyus** (Europa Plus): 127427 Moscow, ul. Akademika Koroleva 19; tel. (095) 217-82-57; fax (095) 956-35-08; e-mail main@ europaplus.ru; internet www.europaplus.ru; FM station, broadcasting music, entertainment and information programmes to 500 cities; Pres. ZHORZH POLINSKI; Gen. Man. ALEKSANDR POLESITSKII.

### Television

**All-Russian State Television and Radio Broadcasting Company (VGTRK):** see Radio.

**Telekanal 'Kultura'** (Television Channel 'Culture'): 123995 Moscow, ul. M. Nikitskaya 24; e-mail kultura@tvkultura.ru; internet www.tvkultura.ru; f. 1997; Gen. Dir ALEKSANDR S. PONOMAREV.

**Telekanal 'Rossiya'** (Television Channel 'Russia'): 115162 Moscow, ul. Shabolovka 37; tel. (095) 924-63-74; fax (095) 234-87-71; e-mail info@rutv.ru; internet www.rutv.ru; fmrly RTR-TV; name changed as above in 2002; Dir-Gen. ALEKSANDR S. PONAMAREV.

**Telekanal 'Sport'** (Television Channel 'Sport'): Moscow; e-mail info@rtr-sport.ru; internet www.rtr-sport.ru; f. 2003 to assume broadcasting frequencies of TVS; Dir-Gen. VASILII KIKNADZE.

**NTV—Independent Television:** 127000 Moscow, ul. Akademika Koroleva 12; tel. (095) 217-51-03; fax (095) 217-92-74; e-mail info@ ntv-tv.ru; internet www.ntv-tv.ru; f. 1993; 65% owned by Gazprom-Mediya; also NTV International, broadcasting to Russian communities in Israel, Western Europe and the USA; Chief Exec. ALEKSANDR DYBAL; Dir-Gen. NIKOLAI YU. SENKEVICH.

**Pervyi Kanal—First Channel:** 127000 Moscow, ul. Akademika Koroleva 12; tel. (095) 215-82-47; fax (095) 215-82-47; e-mail ort_int@ortv.ru; internet www.1tv.ru; f. 1995; fmrly ORT—Public Russian Television; name changed as above in 2002; 51% state-owned; 49% owned by private shareholders; broadcasts Russia's main television channel; Chair. VITALII IGNATENKO; Dir-Gen. KONSTANTIN ERNST.

**Ren-TV Network:** 119843 Moscow, Zubovskii bulv. 17/510; tel. (095) 246-25-06; fax (095) 245-09-98; e-mail site@rentv.dol.ru; internet www.ren-tv.com; f. 1991; network of more than 100 television stations in the Russian Federation and 60 stations in republics of the CIS; fmrly 70% owned by Unified Energy Systems of Russia; Pres. IRENA LESNEVSKAYA; Gen. Man. DMITRII A. LESNEVSKII.

**STS—Network of Television Stations:** 123298 Moscow, ul. 3-aya Khoroshevskaya 12; tel. (095) 797-41-73; fax (095) 797-41-01; e-mail www@ctc-tv.ru; internet www.ctc-tv.ru; f. 1996; owned by StoryFirst Communications (USA); broadcasts programmes of popular entertainment to 350 cities in Russia; Dir-Gen. ALEKSANDR YE. RODNYANSKII.

**TNT—Territory of Our Viewers—TV Network:** 127427 Moscow, ul. Akademika Koroleva 19; tel. (095) 217-81-88; fax (095) 748-14-90; e-mail info@tnt-tv.ru; internet www.tnt-tv.ru; f. 1997; cable television network broadcasting to 582 cities in Russia; Chief Exec. ALEKSANDR DYBAL; Dir-Gen. ROMAN PETRENKO.

**TV-Tsentr (TVTs—TV-Centre):** 113184 Moscow, ul. B. Tatarskaya 33/1; tel. (095) 959-39-87; fax (095) 959-39-66; e-mail info@tvc.ru; internet www.tvc.ru; f. 1997; broadcasting consortium for terrestrial cable and satellite television; Pres. OLEG M. POPTSOV; Dir PAVEL V. KASPAROV.

# Finance

(cap. = capital; res = reserves; dep. = deposits; m. = million;
brs = branches; amounts in new roubles, unless otherwise stated)

## BANKING

Following the dissolution of the USSR in 1991, the majority of state-owned banks were privatized and the establishment of private banks was permitted. The Central Bank of the Russian Federation, founded in 1991, replaced the Gosbank (State Bank). Under the 1993 Constitution, responsibility for bank licensing, regulation and supervision was accorded to the Central Bank.

The number of commercial banks increased considerably in the early 1990s, reaching more than 2,500 in 1994. Consolidation of the banking sector, begun in 1995, meant that there were some 1,641 private banks registered in April 1998; by 1 January 2001 there were reported to be 1,311 credit institutions in Russia.

### Central Bank

**Bank Rossii—Central Bank of the Russian Federation:** 103016 Moscow, ul. Neglinnaya 12; tel. (095) 771-40-46; fax (095) 921-91-47; e-mail webmaster@www.cbr.ru; internet www.cbr.ru; f. 1990; cap. 166,048m., res 192,532m., dep. 201,460m. (Dec. 2001); Chair. SERGEI M. IGNATIYEV; 78 brs.

### State-owned Bank

**Vneshtorgbank** (Bank for Foreign Trade): 103778 Moscow, Kuznetskii most 16; tel. (095) 101-18-80; fax (095) 258-47-81; e-mail info@vtb.ru; internet www.vtb.ru; f. 1990; cap. US $2,153m., res –$318m., dep. $2,885m. (Dec. 2001); Chair. and Chief Exec. ANDREI L. KOSTIN; 39 brs.

### Major Commercial and Co-operative Banks

**AK BARS Bank:** 420066 Tatarstan, Kazan, ul. Dekabristov 1; tel. (8432) 19-39-00; fax (8432) 57-83-76; e-mail kanc@akbars.ru; internet www.akbars.ru; f. 1993; cap. 2,015.4m., res 810.2m., dep. 9,421.0m. (Dec. 2001); Chair. and Chief Exec. MOUDARIS IDRISSOV.

**Alfa-Bank:** 107078 Moscow, ul. M. Poryvayevoi 9; tel. (095) 974-25-15; fax (095) 207-61-36; e-mail mail@alfabank.ru; internet www.alfabank.ru; f. 1991; cap. US $112.8m., res $165.2m., dep. $2,272.9m. (Dec. 2001); Chair. of Bd LEONID VID; Chief Exec. ALEKSANDR KNASTR; 45 brs.

**Avtobank:** 127055 Moscow, ul. Lesnaya 41; tel. (095) 723-77-77; fax (095) 918-66-23; e-mail info@avtobank.ru; internet www.avtobank.ru; f. 1988; 22.7% owned by Ingosstrakh Insurance Co Ltd; cap. US $43m., res $0.9m., dep. $240m. (Sept. 2002); Chair. LYUDMILA A. SHABALKINA; 25 brs.

**Bank MENATEP St Petersburg** (MENATEP SPb): 191186 St Petersburg, Nevskii pr. 1; tel. (812) 320-45-14; fax (812) 326-39-11; e-mail finance@menatepspb.com; internet www.menatepspb.com; f. 1995; cap. 2,896.4m., res 425.0m., dep. 34,587.8m. (Dec. 2002); Pres. VITALII SAVELIYEV; Chair. of Bd DMITRII LEBEDEV; 58 brs.

**Bank of Khanty-Mansiisk:** 628012 Khanty-Mansii AOk—Yugra, Khanty-Mansiisk, ul. Mira 13; tel. (34671) 302-10; fax (34671) 302-19; e-mail admin@khmb.ru; internet www.khmb.ru; f. 1992; cap. 1,000.0m., res 199.3m., dep. 7,026.9m. (Dec. 2001); Pres. DMITRII MIZGULIN; 7 brs.

**Bank Petrocommerce:** 103051 Moscow, ul. Petrovka 24; tel. (095) 200-00-51; fax (095) 923-36-07; e-mail welcome@petrocommerce.ru; internet www.petrocommerce.ru; f. 1992; 77.9% owned by LUKoil; cap. 4,500.0m., res 334.2m., dep. 16,953.8m. (Dec. 2001); Pres. VLADIMIR N. NIKITENKO.

**Bank ZENIT:** 129100 Moscow, Bannyi per. 9; tel. (095) 937-07-37; fax (095) 937-07-36; e-mail info@zenit.ru; internet www.zenit.ru; f. 1994; 50% owned by Tatneft, 20% owned by Novolipetsk MetKom (New Lipetsk Metallurgical Group); cap. 2,000.0m., res 202.9m., dep. 12,842.9m. (Dec. 2001); Chair. of Bd ALEKSEI A SOKOLOV; 4 brs.

**BIN Bank:** 121471 Moscow, ul Grodnenskaya 5A; tel. (095) 755-50-60; fax (095) 440-09-75; e-mail binbank@binbank.ru; internet www.binbank.ru; f. 1993; cap. 2,040.0m., res 1,005.8m., dep. 20,919.9m. (Dec. 2001); Chair. of Bd SERGEI YE. YEGOREV; Pres. and Chief Exec. MIKHAIL O. SHISHKHANOV; 19 brs.

**Commercial Bank for the Development of Business Activities—Guta Bank LLC:** 107078 Moscow, Orlikov per. 5/3; tel. (095) 975-63-00; fax (095) 975-63-33; e-mail post@guta.ru; internet www.guta.ru; f. 1991; wholly state-owned; cap. 6,573.3m., res –1,035.5m., dep. 11,571.6m. (Dec. 2001); Pres. ALEKSANDR PETROV; 30 brs.

**Doveritelnyi i Investitsionnyi Bank** (Trust and Investment Bank): 113035 Moscow, ul. Sadovnicheskaya 84/3/7; tel. (095) 247-25-83; fax (095) 956-99-65; e-mail office@tibank.ru; internet www.tibank.ru; f. 1994; cap. US $86.4m., res $55.8m., dep. $1,030.6m. (Dec. 2001); Chair. and Chief Exec. ILYA YUROV.

**Evrofinance:** 121099 Moscow, ul. Novyi Arbat 29; tel. (095) 967-81-82; fax (095) 967-81-33; e-mail info@evrofinance.ru; internet www.evrofinance.ru; f. 1990; 58% owned by Banque Commerciale pour l'Europe du Nord (Eurobank—France); cap. 1,312,0m., res 2,541.6m., dep. 15,142.5m. (Dec. 2001); Pres. and Chair. of Bd VLADIMIR M. STOLYARENKO; 6 brs.

**Gazprombank:** 117420 Moscow, ul. Nametkina 16/1; tel. (095) 719-17-63; fax (095) 913-73-19; e-mail mailbox@gazprombank.ru; internet www.gazprombank.ru; f. 1990; 87.5% owned by Gazprom; cap. US $872.9m., res $-158.9m., dep. $3,024.5m. (Dec. 2001); Chair. of Bd of Dirs ALEKSEI B. MILLER; Chair. of Man. Bd YURII I. LVOV.

**Globex Commercial Bank (GlobexBank):** 121069 Moscow, ul. B. Nikitskaya 60/1; tel. (095) 202-24-82; fax (095) 290-56-08; e-mail post@globexbank.ru; internet www.globexbank.ru; f. 1992; cap. 10,084.4m., res –5.3m., dep. 2,114.1m. (Dec. 2001); Chair. ANDREI F. DUNAYEV; Pres. ANATOLII L. MOTYLEV.

**IMPEXBANK (JSC Import-Export Bank IMPEXBANK):** 125252 Moscow, ul. Novopeschanaya 20/10/1a; tel. and fax (095) 752-52-52; e-mail mail@impexbank.ru; internet www.impexbank.ru; f. 1993; cap. US $83.4m., dep. US $357.7m., total assets US $442.5m. (Dec. 2002); Chair. of Bd DMITRII P. YEROPKIN; 180 brs and sub-brs (2002).

**Industry and Construction Bank (ICB)** (Promyshlenno-Stroitelnyi Bank): 191014 St Petersburg, ul. Kovesnkii 17–18; tel. (812) 329-84-51; fax (812) 310-61-73; e-mail lider@icbank.ru; internet www.icbank.ru; f. 1870 as Volga-Kama Bank; present name adopted 1990; cap. 383.8m., res 4,155.8m., dep. 38,455.3m. (Dec. 2002); Chair. ALEKSANDR PUSTOVALOV; 48 brs, 21 sub-brs.

**International Moscow Bank:** 119034 Moscow, Prechistenskaya nab. 9; tel. (095) 258-72-58; fax (095) 258-72-72; e-mail imbank@imbank.ru; internet www.imb.ru; f. 1989; 43.2% owned by Bayerische Hypo- und Vereinsbank AG (Germany), 21.6% by Nordea Bank Finland plc, 20% by Banque Commerciale pour l'Europe du Nord—EUROBANK (France); finances joint ventures, investments and projects of domestic and foreign customers and international trade deals; absorbed Bank Austria Creditanstalt (Russia ZAO) in 2001; cap. US $139.6m., res $16.6m., dep. $2,233.8m. (Sep. 2003); Chair. of Bd of Dirs PETER O. KOELLE; Chair. of Bd of Management SALONEN ILKKA; 15 brs.

**Mezhdunarodnyi Promyshlennyi Bank** (International Industrial Bank): 103009 Moscow, ul. B. Dmitrovka 23–8/1–2; tel. (095) 926-44-46; fax (095) 292-82-84; e-mail mail@iib.ru; f. 1992; cap. 25,000m., res 923.4m., dep. 74,582.3m. (Dec. 2001); Pres. SERGEI A. VEREMEYENKO; 5 brs.

**Moscow Business World Bank (MDM Bank)** (Bank Moskovskii Delovoi Mir): 113035 Moscow, ul. Sadovnicheskaya 3; tel. (095) 797-95-00; fax (095) 797-95-01; e-mail info@mdm.ru; internet www.mdmbank.com; f. 1993; cap. 152.1m., res 2,514.3m., dep. 7,150.0m. (Dec. 1999); total assets US $1,520.7m. (Dec. 2001); Chief Exec. VLADIMIR RASHEVSKII; 70 brs and sub-brs.

**Moscow Municipal Bank—Bank of Moscow:** 107996 Moscow, ul. Rozhdestvenka 8/15/3; tel. (095) 745-80-00; fax (095) 795-26-00; e-mail info@mmbank.ru; internet www.mmbank.ru; f. 1995; 62.7% owned by Govt of Moscow Federal City; cap. 3,000m., res 905.9m., dep. 62,800m. (Jan. 2002); Pres. and Chief Exec. ANDREI BORODIN; 40 brs.

**NIKoil IBG Bank:** 119048 Moscow, ul. Yefryemova 8; tel. (095) 705-90-39; fax (095) 705-90-60; e-mail pr@nikoil.ru; internet www.nikoil.ru; f. 1990 as Rodina Joint-Stock Bank; present name adopted 1998; cap. 2,945.2m., res 369.9m., dep. 9,197.0m. (Dec. 2001); Pres. NIKOLAI TSVETKOV; 6 brs.

**Novaya Moskva (NOMOS-BANK):** 109240 Moscow, ul. V. Radishchevskaya 3/1; tel. (095) 797-32-45; fax (095) 797-32-50; e-mail nmosmail@online.ru; internet www.nomos.ru; f. 1992; cap. 1,185.0m., res 1,768.8m., dep. 10,026.2m. (Dec. 2001); Pres. IGOR FINOGENOV.

**Promsvyazbank** (Industry and Communications Bank): 109052 Moscow, ul. Smirnovskaya 10/2–3/22; tel. (095) 733-96-20; fax (095) 777-10-21; e-mail postmaster@psbank.ru; internet www.psbank.ru; f. 1995; owned by a consortium of communications cos; cap. 2,684.3m., dep. 12,282.4m. (June 2002); Chair. of Bd DMITRII N. ANANIEV; Pres. ALEKSANDR A. LEVKOVSKII; 11 brs.

**Rosbank:** 107078 Moscow, ul. M. Poryvayevoi 11, POB 208; tel. (095) 725-05-95; fax (095) 725-05-11; e-mail mailbox@rosbank.ru; internet www.rosbank.ru; f. 1998 by merger of Menatep, Most-Bank and Oneximbank, merged with UNEXIMbank in 2000; owned by Interros; cap. 3,405.3m., res 4,190.3m., dep. 58,410.5m. (Dec. 2001); Chair. of Exec. Bd YEVGENII IVANOV; 11 brs.

**Sberbank Rossii—Savings Bank of the Russian Federation (Sberbank):** 117997 Moscow, ul. Vavilova 19; tel. (095) 957-57-58; fax (095) 957-57-31; e-mail sbrf@sbrf.ru; internet www.sbrf.ru; f. 1841 as a deposit-taking institution, reorganized as a joint-stock commercial bank in 1991; 60.6% owned by Bank Rossii—Central Bank of the Russian Federation; cap. 1,000m., res 23,167m., dep. 645,145m. (Jan. 2002); Chair. of Bd and Chief Exec. ANDREI I. KAZMIN; 1,233 brs and 18,831 sub-brs.

**Sobinbank:** 121248 Moscow, pr. Kutuzovskii 17; tel. (095) 725-25-25; fax (095) 777-25-45; e-mail mail@sobin.ru; internet www .sobinbank.ru; f. 1990; cap. 500.0m., res 75.0m., dep. 4,054.5m. (Jan. 2002); Chair. of Bd SERGEI A KIRILENKO; 17 brs.

**Surgutneftegazbank (SNGB):** 628400 Tyumen obl., Khanty-Mansii AOk—Yugra, Surgut, ul. Kukuyevitskogo 19; tel. (3462) 39-86-10; fax (3462) 39-87-11; e-mail telex@sngb.ru; internet www.sngb .ru; f. 1965 as a br. of Promstroibank; reorganized as a commercial bank in 1990; 81.2% owned by Surgutneftegaz (SNG) Oil Co; cap. 633.0m., res 30.5m., dep. 59,927.6m. (Dec. 2000); Pres. VLADIMIR BOGDANOV; Chair. of Bd YEVGENIYA NEPOMNYASHIKHA.

**TransKreditBank:** 121099 Moscow, Novinskii bulv. 3/1; tel. (095) 788-08-80; fax (095) 788-08-79; internet www.tkb.ru; f. 1992; cap. 2,931.0m., res –910.4m., dep. 8,202.2m. (Dec. 2001); Pres. ALEKSANDR B. MASALSKII.

**UralSib** (Uralo-Siberian Bank): 450000 Bashkortostan, Ufa, ul. Revolutsionnaya 41; tel. (3472) 51-94-85; fax (3472) 51-94-88; e-mail ufa@uralsibbank.ru; internet www.uralsibbank.ru; f. 1993 as Bash-CreditBank, present name adopted 2001; 75% owned by the Government of the Republic of Bashkortostan; cap. 9,583.3m., res –4,855.6m., dep. 20,600.8m. (Dec. 2001); Pres. and Chief Exec. AZAT T. KURMANAYEV; Chair. RAFAEL I. BAIDAVLETOV.

**Vneshekonombank** (Bank for Foreign Economic Affairs): 103810 Moscow, pr. Sakharova 9; tel. (095) 207-10-37; fax (095) 975-21-43; e-mail postmaster@veb.ru; internet www.veb.ru; f. 1924; total assets US $3,826m. (Dec. 2001); Chair. VLADIMIR A. CHERNUKHIN.

**Vozrozhdeniye—V-Bank** (Rebirth—Moscow Joint Stock Commercial Bank Vozrozdeniye): 101999 Moscow, per. Luchnikov 7/4/1, POB 9; tel. (095) 929-18-88; fax (095) 929-19-99; e-mail vbank@co.voz.ru; internet www.vbank.ru; f. 1991; cap. 145.4m., res 1,374.0m., dep. 12,727.9m. (July 2002); Pres. DMITRII L. ORLOV; 60 brs.

### Foreign Banks

**ABN AMRO Bank AO** (Netherlands): 103009 Moscow, ul. B. Nikitskaya 17/1; tel. (095) 931-91-41; fax (095) 931-91-40; internet www.abnamro.com; Dir M. SCHWARZ.

**Crédit Lyonnais Rusbank** (France): 191186 St Petersburg, Nevsky pr. 12, POB 139; tel. (812) 313-31-00; fax (812) 313-33-90; f. 1991; present name adopted 1997; cap. 20.0m., res 1,150.5m., dep. 6,885.4m. (Dec. 2000); Chair. BERNARD MIGNUCCI.

**Crédit Suisse First Boston AO** (Switzerland): 103009 Moscow, Nikitskii per. 5; tel. (095) 967-82-00; fax (095) 967-82-10; investment bank; cap. 460.0m., res 586.1m., dep. 5,040.0m. (Dec. 2000); Pres. NICHOLAS GORDON-SMITH.

**Deutsche Bank Ltd** (Germany): 129090 Moscow, ul. Shepkina 4; tel. (095) 797-50-00; fax (095) 797-50-17; f. 1998; cap. 1,237.5m., res 891.4m., dep. 3,378.1m. (Dec. 2000); Chief. Exec. HUBERT ALBERT PANDZA.

**Dresdner Bank ZAO** (Germany): 190000 St Petersburg, ul. M. Morskaya 23; tel. (812) 118-51-51; fax (812) 324-32-81; e-mail zao@dresdner-bank.com; internet www.dresdner-bank.ru; f. 1993 as BNP-Dresdner Bank (ZAO); present name adopted 2001; cap. 727.3m., res 830.5m., dep. 3,853.8m. (Dec. 2001); Pres. WARNIG MATTHIAS.

**ING Bank (Eurasia) ZAO—ING Bank** (Netherlands): 123022 Moscow, ul. Krasnaya Presnya 31; tel. (095) 755-54-00; fax (095) 755-54-99; internet www.ing.ru; f. 1993; present name adopted 1997; cap. US $6.6m., res $84.6m., dep. $228.5m. (Dec. 2000); Pres and Dir-Gen. HENDRICK WILLEM TEN BOSCH.

**Raiffeisenbank Austria ZAO:** 129090 Moscow, ul. Troitskaya 17/1; tel. (095) 721-99-00; fax (095) 721-99-01; e-mail common@ raiffeisen.ru; internet www.raiffeisen.ru; f. 1996; cap. 6.175.4m., res –3,475.4m., dep. 21,668.6m. (Dec. 2001); Chair. of Man. Bd MICHEL P. PERHIRIN; 7 brs and sub-brs.

### Bankers' Association

**Association of Russian Banks:** 121069 Moscow, Skatertnyi per. 20/1; tel. and fax (095) 291-80-98; e-mail arb@arb.ru; internet www .arb.ru; f. 1991; unites some 500 private banks; Pres. GAREGIN A. TOSUNYAN.

## INSURANCE

**Department of Insurance Supervision:** 109097 Moscow, ul. Ilinka 9; tel. (095) 748-45-10; fax (095) 748-45-11; e-mail d2400@ minfin.ru; Dir KONSTANTIN I. PYLOV.

**Agroinvest Insurance Co:** 127422 Moscow, ul. Timiryazevskaya 26; tel. (095) 976-94-56; fax (095) 977-05-88; health, life and general insurance services; Pres. YURII I. MORDVINTSEV.

**AIG Russia:** 103009 Moscow, ul. Tverskaya 16/2; tel. (095) 935-89-50; fax (095) 935-89-52; e-mail aig.russia@aig.com; internet www .aigrussia.ru; f. 1994; mem. of the American International Group-Inc.; personal and business property insurance, also marine, life, financial etc.; Pres. GARY COLEMAN.

**Ingosstrakh Insurance Co Ltd:** 115998 Moscow, ul. Pyatnitskaya 12/2; tel. (095) 232-32-11; fax (095) 959-45-18; e-mail ingos@ingos .ru; internet www.ingos.ru; f. 1947; undertakes all kinds of insurance and reinsurance; Chair. NATALIYA A. RAYEVSKAYA; Gen. Dir YEVGENII TUMANOV.

**Medstrakh—Medical Insurance Fund of the Russian Federation:** 107076 Moscow, pl. Preobrazhenskaya 7A /1; tel. (095) 964-84-27; fax (095) 964-84-21; e-mail mz@mcramn.ru; internet www .medstrah.ru; f. 1991; health, life, property, travel, liability; also provides compulsory medical insurance; Pres. PETR KUZNETSOV.

**Ost-West Allianz Insurance Co:** 127473 Moscow, 3-i Samotechnii per. 3; tel. (095) 937-69-96; fax (095) 937-69-80; e-mail allianz@ allianz.ru; internet www.allianz.ru; engineering, professional liability, life, medical, property, marine and private; Man. Dir ERHARD JOERCHEL.

**RESO-Garantiya Insurance Co:** 125047 Moscow, ul. Gasheka 12/1; tel. (095) 234-18-00; fax (095) 956-25-85; e-mail reso@orc.ru; internet www.reso.ru; f. 1991; Dir-Gen. SERGEI E. SARKISOV.

**Rosgosstrakh—Russian State Insurance:** 127994 Moscow, ul. Novoslobodskaya 23; tel. (095) 781-24-00; fax (095) 978-27-64; e-mail admin@rgs.ru; internet www.gosstrah.ru; majority state-owned; 49% stake transferred to private ownership in 2001; undertakes domestic insurance; subsidiary cos in 80 federal subjects (territorial units) of the Russian Federation; Chair. VLADISLAV REZNIK; Gen. Dir RUBEN VARDANIAN.

**ROSNO—Russian National Society Insurance Co:** 115184 Moscow, Ozerkovskaya nab. 30; tel. (095) 232-33-33; fax (095) 232-00-14; e-mail info@rosno.ru; internet www.rosno.ru; f. 1992; offices in 70 regions of Russia; owned by Sistema; Gen. Man. YEVGENII A. KURGIN.

**Russkie Strakhovye Traditsii** (Russian Traditions Insurance Co): 129366 Moscow, Raketnyi bulv. 13/2; tel. (095) 283-88-03; fax (095) 283-88-05; e-mail info@rustrad.ru; internet www.rustrad.ru; f. 1992; Pres. IVAN I. DAVYDOV.

**SOGAZ—Insurance Co of the Gas Industry:** 117997 Moscow, ul. Nametkina 16; tel. (095) 782-09-17; fax (095) 432-90-05; e-mail sogaz@sogaz.ru; internet www.sogaz.ru; f. 1993; owned by gas industry interests; Chair. of Bd of Dirs SERGEI A. LUKASH.

**Soglasiye (Agreement) Insurance Co:** 109017 Moscow, M. Tolmachevskii per. 8–11/3; tel. and fax (095) 959-46-32; e-mail official@soglasie.ru; internet www.soglasie.ru; f. 1993 as Interros-Soglasiye; owned by Interros; Gen. Man. IGOR ZHUK.

## STOCK EXCHANGES

**Moscow Stock Exchange (MSE):** 125047 Moscow, Miusskaya pl. 2/2; tel. (095) 250-20-10; fax (095) 250-17-34; e-mail mse@mse.ru; internet www.mse.ru; f. 1997; Pres. ROMAN N. MYLTSEV.

**Moscow International Stock Exchange:** 103045 Moscow, Prosvirin per. 4; tel. and fax (095) 923-33-39; f. 1990; Pres. VIKTOR SAKHAROV.

**Siberian Stock Exchange:** 630104 Novosibirsk, ul. Frunze 5, POB 233; tel. (3832) 21-60-67; fax (3832) 21-06-90; e-mail sibex@sibex.nsk .su; f. 1991; Pres. ALEKSANDR V. NOVIKOV.

## COMMODITY EXCHANGES

**Asiatic Commodity Exchange:** 670000 Buryatiya, Ulan-Ude, ul. Sovetskaya 23/37; tel. and fax (30122) 2-26-81; f. 1991; Chair. ANDREI FIRSOV.

**European-Asian Exchange (EAE):** 101000 Moscow, ul. Myasnitskaya 26; tel. and fax (095) 787-58-93; e-mail info@eae.ru; internet www.eae.ru; f. 2000; Chair. of Council TATYANA S. SOKOLOVA; Gen. Man. ALEKSANDR B. YEREMIN.

**Khabarovsk Commodity Exchange (KhCE):** 680037 Khabarovsk, ul. K. Marksa 66; tel. and fax (4212) 33-65-60; f. 1991; Pres. YEVGENII V. PANASENKO.

**Komi Commodity Exchange (KoCE):** 167610 Komi, Syktyvkar, Oktyabrskii pr. 16; tel. (82122) 2-32-86; fax (82122) 3-84-43; f. 1991; Pres. PETR S. LUCHENKOV.

**Kuzbass Commodity and Raw Materials Exchange (KECME):** 650090 Kemerovo, ul. Novgradskaya 19; tel. (3842) 23-45-40; fax (3842) 23-49-56; f. 1991; Gen. Man. FEDOR MASENKOV.

**Moscow Commodity Exchange (MCE):** 129223 Moscow, pr. Mira, Russian Exhibition Centre, Pavilion 69 (4); tel. (095) 187-86-14; fax (095) 187-88-76; f. 1990; organization of exchange trading (cash, stock and futures market); Pres. and Chair. of Bd YURII MILYUKOV.

**Petrozavodsk Commodity Exchange (PCE):** 185028 Kareliya, Petrozavodsk, ul. Krasnaya 31; tel. and fax (8142) 7-80-57; f. 1991; Gen. Man. VALERII SAKHAROV.

**Russian Exchange (RE):** 101000 Moscow, ul. Myasnitskaya 26; tel. (095) 787-84-34; fax (095) 262-57-57; e-mail ic@ci.re.ru; internet www.re.ru; f. 1990; Pres. PAVEL PANOV.

**Russian Commodity Exchange of the Agro-Industrial Complex (RosAgroBirzha):** 125080 Moscow, Volokolamskoye shosse 11; tel. (095) 209-52-25; f. 1990; Chair. of Exchange Cttee ALEKSANDR VASILIYEV.

**St Petersburg Exchange:** 199026 St Petersburg, Vasilyevskii Ostrov, 26-aya liniya 15; tel. (812) 322-44-11; fax (812) 322-73-90; e-mail spbex@spbex.ru; internet www.spbex.ru; f. 1991; Pres. and Chief Exec. VIKTOR V. NIKOLAYEV.

**Surgut Commodity and Raw Materials Exchange (SCME):** 626400 Tyumen obl., Khanty-Mansii AOk—Yugra, Surgut, ul. 30 let Pobedy 32; tel. (34561) 2-05-69; f. 1991.

**Udmurt Commodity Universal Exchange (UCUE):** 426075 Udmurtiya, Izhevsk, ul. Soyuznaya 107; tel. (3412) 37-08-88; fax (3412) 37-16-57; e-mail iger@udmnet.ru; f. 1991; Pres. N. F. LAZAREV.

**Yekaterinburg Commodity Exchange (UCE):** 620012 Sverdlovsk obl., Yekaterinburg, pr. Kosmonavtov 23; tel. (3432) 34-43-01; fax (3432) 51-53-64; f. 1991; Chair. of Exchange Cttee KONSTANTIN ZHUZHLOV.

# Trade and Industry

## GOVERNMENT AGENCY

**Russian Federal Property Fund:** 119049 Moscow, Leninskii pr. 9; tel. (095) 236-71-15; fax (095) 956-27-80; e-mail rffi@dol.ru; internet www.fpf.ru; f. 1992 to ensure consistency in the privatization process and to implement privatization legislation; Chair. VLADIMIR V. MALIN.

## NATIONAL CHAMBER OF COMMERCE

**Chamber of Commerce and Industry of the Russian Federation:** 109012 Moscow, ul. Ilinka 6; tel. (095) 929-00-09; fax (095) 929-03-60; e-mail dios-inform@tpprf.ru; internet www.tpprf.ru; f. 1991; Pres. YEVGENII M. PRIMAKOV.

## REGIONAL CHAMBERS OF COMMERCE

In early 2002 there were a total of 148 regional chambers of commerce in the Russian Federation.

**Astrakhan Chamber of Commerce:** 414040 Astrakhan, ul. Zhelyabova 50; tel. (8512) 25-58-44; fax (8512) 28-14-42; e-mail cci@mail.astrakhan.ru; internet astrcci.astrakhan.ru; f. 1992; Pres. ALEKSEI D. KANTEMIROV.

**Bashkortostan Chamber of Commerce:** 450008 Bashkortostan, Ufa, ul. Vorovskogo 22; tel. (3472) 23-23-80; fax (3472) 51-70-79; e-mail tpp@bashnet.ru; internet www.tpprb.ru; f. 1990; Chair. ZINNAT KH. KHAIRULLIN.

**Bryansk Chamber of Commerce:** 241035 Bryansk, ul. Komsomolskaya 11; tel. (0832) 56-68-06; fax (0832) 56-44-24; e-mail tpp@online.bryansk.ru; internet www.bryansk.ru/btpp; Pres. TATYANA F. SUVOROVA.

**Buryat Chamber of Commerce:** 670047 Buryatiya, Ulan-Ude, ul. Sakhyanovoi 5, POB 4284; tel. (3012) 37-56-26; fax (3012) 37-34-34; e-mail tpprb@buryatia.ru; f. 1993; Pres. GENNADII M. BERBIDAYEV; 85 mems.

**Central-Siberian Chamber of Commerce:** 660049 Krasnoyarsk, ul. Kirova 26; tel. (3912) 23-96-13; fax (3912) 23-96-83; e-mail cstp@krasmail.ru; internet www.cstpp.ru; f. 1985; Chair. VALERII A. KOSTIN.

**Dagestan Chamber of Commerce:** 367012 Dagestan, Makhachkala, pl. Lenina 2; tel. (8722) 67-04-61; fax (8722) 67-87-96; e-mail tpprd@dagestan.ru; f. 1991; Pres. SAID G. GAZIYEV.

**Eastern Siberian Chamber of Commerce:** 664003 Irkutsk, ul. Sukhe-Batora 16; tel. (3952) 33-50-60; fax (3952) 33-50-66; e-mail info@ccies.ru; internet www.ccies.ru; f. 1974; Pres. KONSTANTIN S. SHAVRIN.

**Far East Chamber of Commerce:** 680670 Khabarovsk, ul. Sheronova 113; tel. (4210) 30-47-70; fax (4210) 30-54-58; e-mail dvtpp@fecci.khv.ru; f. 1970; Pres. MIKHAIL V. KRUGLIKOV.

**Kaliningrad Chamber of Commerce:** 236010 Kaliningrad, ul. Vatutina 20; tel. (0112) 55-58-81; fax (0112) 21-87-15; e-mail kaliningrad_cci@baltnet.ru; internet www.kaliningrad-cci.ru; f. 1990; Pres. IGOR V. TSARKOV.

**Kamchatka Chamber of Commerce:** 683000 Kamchatka obl., Petropavlovsk-Kamchatskii, ul. Leninskaya 38/208; tel. and fax (4152) 12-35-10; e-mail kamtpp@iks.ru; Pres. ALLA V. PARKHOMCHUK.

**Krasnodar Chamber of Commerce:** 350063 Krasnodar, ul. Kommunarov 8; tel. and fax (8612) 68-22-13; e-mail tppkk@tppkuban.ru; internet www.tppkuban.ru; f. 1969; Chair. YURII N. TKACHENKO.

**Kursk Chamber of Commerce:** 305000 Kursk, ul. Kirova 7; tel. (0712) 56-24-69; fax (0712) 56-24-69; e-mail info@kcci.ru; internet www.kcci.ru; f. 1994; Pres. VALENTINA G. ORDYNETS.

**Kuzbass Chamber of Commerce:** 650099 Kemerovo, pr. Sovetskii 63/407; tel. and fax (3842) 58-77-64; e-mail ktpp@mail.kuzbass.net; internet city.info.kuzbass.net/ktpp; f. 1991; Pres. TATYANA O. IVLEVA.

**Lipetsk Chamber of Commerce:** 398019 Lipetsk, ul. Skorokhodova 2; tel. (0742) 45-60-04; fax (0742) 72-05-04; e-mail cci@cci.lipetsk.su; internet lcci.lipetsk.ru; f. 1992; Pres. LILIYA D. POGUDINA.

**Magnitogorsk Chamber of Commerce:** 455002 Chelyabinsk obl., Magnitogorsk, ul. Kirova 70; tel. (3519) 24-82-16; fax (3519) 24-82-17; e-mail mtpp@mdv.ru; Pres. GERMAN I. ZAPYANTSEV.

**Maritime (Primorskii) Krai Chamber of Commerce:** 690600 Maritime Krai, Vladivostok, Okeanskii pr. 13A; tel. (4232) 26-96-30; fax (4232) 22-72-26; e-mail palata@online.vladivostok.ru; internet www.ptpp.com.ru; f. 1964; Pres. VLADIMIR B. BREZHNEV.

**Moscow Chamber of Commerce:** 117393 Moscow, ul. Akademika Pilyugina 22; tel. (095) 132-75-10; fax (095) 132-00-29; e-mail mtpp@mtpp.org; internet www.mtpp.org; f. 1991; Chair. YURII I. KOTOV; Pres. LEONID V. GOVOROV.

**Naberezhnye Chelny Chamber of Commerce:** 423826 Tatarstan, Naberezhnye Chelny, ul. Sh. Usmanova 122; tel. (8552) 54-79-08; fax (8552) 54-76-31; e-mail tpp@tpp.chelny.ru; f. 1994; Pres. VALERII P. SOTSKII.

**Nizhnii Novgorod Chamber of Commerce:** 603005 Nizhnii Novgorod, pl. Oktyabrskaya 1; tel. (8312) 19-42-10; fax (8312) 19-40-09; e-mail tpp@rda.nnov.ru; internet www.tpp.nnov.ru; f. 1990; Pres. GENNADII M. KHODYRYEV.

**North Osetiya—Alaniya Chamber of Commerce:** 362002 North Osetiya—Alaniya, Vladikavkaz, ul. Avgustovskikh sobytii 10; tel. (8672) 53-15-84; fax (8672) 54-21-61; e-mail tpprso-a@osetia.ru; f. 1993; Pres. KAZBEK KH. TUGANOV.

**Northern Chamber of Commerce:** 183766 Murmansk, per. Rusanova 10; tel. (8152) 47-29-99; fax (8152) 47-39-78; e-mail ncci@online.ru; internet www.ncci.ru; f. 1990; Chair. ANATOLII M. GLUSHKOV.

**Novgorod Chamber of Commerce:** 173002 Velikii Novgorod, ul. Germana 1A; tel. (8162) 13-69-00; fax (8162) 13-20-46; e-mail ncci@ncci.novline.ru; internet nbp.natm.ru/~ncci; Pres. VIKTOR A. BYKOV.

**Novosibirsk Chamber of Commerce:** 630064 Novosibirsk, pr. K. Marksa 1; tel. and fax (3832) 46-41-50; e-mail main@sbcnet.ru; internet www.sbcnet.ru; f. 1991; Chair. BORIS V. BRUSILOVSKII; 315 mems (2002).

**Omsk Chamber of Commerce:** 644099 Omsk, ul. Krasnyi Put 18; tel. (3812) 23-05-23; fax (3812) 23-52-48; e-mail omtpp@omsknet.ru; internet www.omsknet.ru/cci; f. 1992; Pres. TATYANA A. KHOROSHAVINA.

**Orenburg Chamber of Commerce:** 460356 Orenburg, Parkovyi pr. 6; tel. and fax (3532) 77-73-29; e-mail cci@orenburg-cci.ru; internet www.orenburg-cci.ru; f. 1995; Pres. VIKTOR A. SYTYEZHEV.

**Perm Chamber of Commerce:** 614000 Perm, ul. Sovetskaya 24B; tel. (3422) 12-28-11; fax (3422) 12-41-12; e-mail permtpp@permttp.ru; internet www.permtpp.ru; f. 1991; Pres. VIKTOR A. ZAMARAYEV.

**Rostov Chamber of Commerce:** 344022 Rostov-on-Don, ul. Pushkinskaya 176; tel. and fax (8362) 64-45-47; e-mail tpp@rost.ru; internet www.tpp.tis.ru; f. 1992; Pres. NIKOLAI I. PRISYAZHNYUK.

**Ryazan Chamber of Commerce:** 390023 Ryazan, ul. Gorkovo 14; tel. (0912) 77-20-67; fax (0912) 28-99-02; e-mail ryazancci@rtpp.ryazan.su; f. 1993; Pres. TATYANA V. GUSEVA; 44 mems.

**Sakha (Yakutiya) Chamber of Commerce:** 677000 Sakha (Yakutiya), Yakutsk, ul. Lenina 22/214; tel. (4112) 26-64-96; e-mail palata91@mail.ru; f. 1991; Chair. SERGEI G. BAKULIN.

**Samara Chamber of Commerce:** 443034 Samara, ul. A. Tolstogo 6; tel. (8462) 32-11-59; fax (8462) 70-48-96; e-mail ccisr@samara.ru; internet www.cci.samara.ru; f. 1989; Pres. BORIS V. ARDALIN.

**Saratov Gubernskaya Chamber of Commerce:** 410600 Saratov, ul. B. Kazachya 30; tel. (8452) 24-76-10; fax (8452) 24-72-31; e-mail iao@sgtpp.renet..ru; internet www.sgtpp.renet.ru; f. 1986; Pres. VLADIMIR V. DAVYDOV.

**Smolensk Chamber of Commerce:** 214000 Smolensk, ul. K. Marksa 12; tel. (0812) 55-41-42; fax (08122) 3-74-50; e-mail smolcci@keytown.com; internet www.keytown.com/users/Torgpal/ f. 1993; Pres. OLEG V. LUKIRICH.

**South Urals Chamber of Commerce:** 454080 Chelyabinsk, ul. Vasenko 63; tel. (3512) 66-52-18; fax (3512) 66-52-32; e-mail mail@tpp.chelreg.ru; internet www.tpp.chelreg.ru; f. 1992; Pres. FEDOR L. DEGTYAREV; 365 mems.

**St Petersburg Chamber of Commerce:** 191194 St Petersburg, ul. Chaikovskogo 46–48; tel. (812) 273-48-96; fax (812) 272-64-06; e-mail spbcci@spbcci.ru; internet www.spbcci.ru; f. 1921; Pres. TATYANA S. AVETIKYAN (acting).

**Stavropol Chamber of Commerce:** 355034 Stavropol, ul. Lenina 384; tel. (8652) 94-53-34; fax (8652) 34-05-10; e-mail infostcci@yandex.ru; internet www.ccistavropol.best-business.biz; f. 1991; Pres. VITALII S. NABATNIKOV.

**Tatarstan Chamber of Commerce:** 420503 Tatarstan, Kazan, ul. Pushkina 18; tel. (8432) 38-24-76; fax (8432) 36-09-66; e-mail tpp@radiotelcom.ru; f. 1992; Gen. Dir SHAMIL R. AGEYEV; 160 mems.

**Tolyatti Chamber of Commerce:** 445009 Samara obl., Tolyatti, ul. Pobedy 19A; tel. (8482) 22-46-21; fax (8482) 22-47-45; e-mail tpp@infopac.ru; internet www.ccitogliatti.ru; Pres. VLADIMIR A. ZHUKOV.

**Tula Chamber of Commerce:** 300600 Tula, Krasnoarmeiskii pr. 25/1001–1007; tel. (0872) 31-17-28; fax (0872) 36-02-16; e-mail tulacci@tula.net; internet www.ccitula.ru; f. 1993; Pres. YURII M. AGAFONOV.

**Udmurtiya Chamber of Commerce:** 426034 Udmurtiya, Izhevsk, ul. Udmurtskaya 251A; tel. (3412) 43-82-81; fax (3412) 43-11-76; e-mail postmaster@izhtpp.udm.ru; internet izhtpp.udmweb.ru; f. 1993; Pres. YEVGENII YU. VYLYEGZHANIN.

**Ulyanovsk Chamber of Commerce:** 432600 Ulyanovsk, ul. Engelsa 19; tel. (8422) 31-45-23; fax (8422) 32-93-73; e-mail ultpp@mv.ru; f. 1992; Pres. YEVGENII S. BALANDIN.

**Urals Chamber of Commerce:** 620027 Sverdlovsk obl., Yekaterinburg, ul. Vostochnaya 6, POB 822; tel. (3432) 53-04-49; fax (3432) 53-58-63; e-mail ucci@dialup.mplik.ru; internet ucci.ur.ru; f. 1959; Pres. YURII P. MATUSHKIN.

**Volgograd Chamber of Commerce:** 400005 Volgograd, ul. 7-aya Gvardeiskaya 2; tel. (8442) 34-41-78; fax (8442) 34-22-02; e-mail cci@volgogradcci.ru; internet www.volgogradcci.ru; f. 1990; Pres. ALEKSANDR D. BELITSKII.

**Vologda Chamber of Commerce and Industry:** 160600 Vologda, ul. Lermontova 15; tel. (8172) 72-14-80; fax (8172) 72-32-58; e-mail grant@vologda.ru; f. 1992; Pres. GALINA D. TELEGINA.

**Voronezh Chamber of Commerce:** 394030 Voronezh, 'Voronezhvnesh-servis', POB 63; tel. and fax (0732) 52-49-38; e-mail mail@ootpp.vm.ru; f. 1991; fmrly Central-Black Earth Chamber of Commerce and Industry; Pres. VYACHESLAV A. KONDRATYEV.

**Vyatka (Kirov) Chamber of Commerce:** 610000 Kirov, ul. Gertsena 37; tel. and fax (8332) 67-93-43; e-mail iac@vtpp.kirov.ru; internet www.vtpp.kirov.ru; f. 1993; Pres. NIKOLAI M. LIPATNIKOV.

**Yaroslavl Chamber of Commerce:** 150000 Yaroslavl, Sovetskaya pl. 1/19; tel. (0852) 32-87-98; fax (0852) 32-88-85; e-mail tpp@adm.yar.ru; internet yartpp.ru; f. 1992; Pres. VALERII A. LAVROV.

## EMPLOYERS' ORGANIZATIONS

**Co-ordinating Council of Employers' Unions of Russia** (Koordinatsionnyi Sovet Obyedinenii Rabotodatelei Rossii—KSORR): 109017 Moscow, per. M. Tolmachevskii 8–11; tel. (095) 232-55-77; fax (095) 232-39-13; e-mail official@ksorr.ru; internet www.ksorr.ru; f. 1994; co-ordinates and represents employers in relations with government bodies and trade unions; Chair. ARKADII I. VOLSKII; Gen. Dir OLEG V. YEREMEYEV; unites 31 major employers' unions, including the following:

> **Agro-Industrial Union of Russia:** 107139 Moscow, B-139; tel. (095) 204-41-04; fax (095) 207-83-62; e-mail sva@gvs.aris.ru; internet www.aris.ru/GALLERY/ROS/INF/AGROSZ; Pres. VASILII A. STARODUBTSEV.

> **Russian Union of Industrialists and Entrepreneurs (Employers) (RSPPR):** 103070 Moscow, Staraya pl. 10/4; tel. (095) 748-42-37; fax (095) 206-11-29; e-mail info@rsppr.ru; internet www.rsppr.ru; f. 1991; Pres. ARKADII I. VOLSKII.

**Union of Russian Shipowners (SOROSS):** 121002 Moscow, per. Sivtsev brazhek 44/28/10; tel. (095) 241-56-75; fax (095) 248-29-66; e-mail murashovaiv@morflot.ru; internet www.morflot.ru/info/soross.asp; Pres. MIKHAIL A. ROMANOVSKII.

## UTILITIES

### Electricity

**Federal Energy Commission:** 103074 Moscow, Kitaigorodskii proyezd 7; tel. (095) 220-40-15; fax (095) 206-81-08; e-mail fecrf@orc.ru; regulatory authority for natural energy monopolies; sole responsibility for establishing tariff rates for energy, transportation, shipping, postal and telecommunications industries in the Russian Federation from Sept. 2001; Chair. ANDREI ZADERNYUK.

**Irkutskenergo—Irkutsk Energy Co:** 664000 Irkutsk, ul. Sukhe-Batora 3; tel. (3952) 21-73-00; fax (3952) 21-78-89; e-mail web@irkutskenergo.ru; internet www.irkutskenergo.ru; f. 1954; generation and transmission of electrical and thermal energy; Dir-Gen. VLADIMIR V. KOLMOGOROV.

**Mosenergo** (Moscow Energy Co): 113035 Moscow, Raushskaya nab. 8; tel. (095) 957-35-30; fax (095) 957-34-70; e-mail press-centre@mosenergo.ru; internet www.mosenergo.ru; f. 1887; power generator and distributor; Gen. Man. ARKADII V. YEVSTAFYEV.

**Rosenergoatom** (Russian Atomic Energy Concern): 101000 Moscow, POB 912; tel. (095) 239-47-40; fax (095) 239-27-24; e-mail info@rosatom.ru; internet www.rosatom.ru; f. 1992; electricity generating co; Pres. OLEG SARAYEV.

**Sverdlovenergo** (Sverdlovsk Energy Co): 620219 Sverdlovsk obl., Yekaterinburg, pr. Lenina 38; tel. (3432) 59-13-99; fax (3432) 59-12-22; e-mail post@energo.pssr.ru; internet www.po.pssr.ru; f. 1942; Chair. of Bd MIKHAIL A. ABYZOV; Gen. Man. VALERII N. RODIN.

**Unified Energy System of Russia** (RAO EES Rossii): 109526 Moscow, pr. Vernadskogo 101/3; tel. (095) 220-40-01; fax (095) 927-30-07; e-mail rao@elektra.ru; internet www.rao-ees.ru; f. 1992; operates national electricity grid; 52% state-owned; controls about 43,220 km of transmission lines, 32 power plants and majority stakes in 72 regional power cos, including Mosenergo and Lenenergo, accounting for more than 80% of Russia's electricity output; restructuring pending in 2003; Chair. ALEKSANDR S. VOLOSHIN; Chief Exec. ANATOLII B. CHUBAIS.

**Uralenergo** (Ural Energy): 620219 Yekaterinburg, ul. Tomalcheva 5; tel. (3432) 59-89-22; fax (3432) 56-36-30; manages 22 joint-stock cos; oversees 55 thermal power stations and 6 hydroelectric stations; total installed capacity of over 28,500m. kW.

### Gas

**Gazprom:** 117997 Moscow, ul. Nametkina 16; tel. (095) 719-30-01; fax (095) 719-83-33; e-mail webmaster@gazprom.ru; internet www.gazprom.ru; f. 1989 from assets of Soviet Ministry of Oil and Gas; became independent joint-stock co in 1992, privatized in 1994; 51% state-owned from March 2003; Russia's biggest co and world's largest natural gas producer, owning 30% of global natural gas reserves (14,000m. barrels); Chair. ALEKSEI B. MILLER.

**Mezhregiongaz** (Inter-Regional Gas Co): 113324 Moscow, ul. Sadovnicheskaya 46/1; tel. and fax (095) 953-08-24; internet www.mrg.ru; f. 1997; gas marketing co, founded by Gazprom; brs in more than 60 federal subjects; Dir-Gen. NIKOLAI GORNOVSKII.

### Water

**MosVodoKanal:** 107005 Moscow, per. Pleteshkovskii 2; tel. (095) 742-96-96; e-mail webmaster@mosvodokanal.ru; internet www.mosvodokanal.ru; provides water and sewerage services to Moscow and the surrounding region; Gen. Man. STANISLAV KHRAMENKOV.

**Vodokanal:** 193015 St Petersburg, ul. Kavalergardskaya 42; tel. (812) 326-51-44; fax (812) 274-13-61; e-mail office@vodokanal.spb.ru; internet www.vodokanal.spb.ru; water and sewerage utility; Gen. Man. FELIKS V. KARMAZINOV.

## MAJOR COMPANIES

### Bearings

**Bearings Factory No 6 OOO** (Podshipnikovyi zavod No 6): 620075 Sverdlovsk obl., Yekaterinburg, ul. Shartashskaya 13; tel. (3432) 78-74-95; fax (3432) 78-74-90; e-mail sale@rolik.ru; f. 1941; fmrly Urals Bearing Factory No 6, present name adopted 2002; manufactures roller bearings; Gen. Dir KONSTANTIN V. FEDETOV; 500 employees (2002).

**Desyatyi (10th) Bearings Plant OAO (10–GPZ)** (10–i podshipnikovkyi zavod): 344091 Rostov-on-Don, ul. Peskova 1; tel. (8632) 22-56-72; fax (8632) 22-14-84; e-mail gpz-10@aaanet.ru; internet www.gpz-10.aaanet.ru; manufacture of machine tools, industrial trucks and tractors and anti-friction bearings; Gen. Dir GEORGII A. MELNIK; 3,000 employees.

**European Bearing Corpn (EPK)** (Yevropeyskaya podshipnikovaya korporatsiya): 115088 Moscow, ul. Sharikopodshipnikovskaya 13; tel. (095) 775-81-30; fax (095) 775-81-33; e-mail dir_td@ebcorp .ru; internet www.ebcorp.ru; f. 2001 by merger of Moscow Bearing JSC (fmrly 1st State Bearing Plant) with Volga and Stepnogorsk Bearing Plants; design, manufacture and sale of over 2,000 types of bearings; brs in St Petersburg, Omsk, Chelyabinsk, Ulyanovsk, Volzhskii (Volgograd Obl.), and in Astana (Kazakhstan) and Kiev (Ukraine); Pres. OLEG. V. SAVCHENKO; Gen. Dir NIKOLAI V. PLESHAKOV.

**Roltom OAO:** 634006 Tomsk, Severnyi Gorodok 9; tel. (3822) 75-15-01; fax (3822) 75-31-25; internet www.roltom.ru; fmrly Tomsk Bearing Plant; produces all types of bearings; Gen. Dir YURII GALVAS; Dir VALERII UGRUMOV; 6,500 employees.

**Samara Bearing Plant AO** (Samarskii podshipnikovyi zavod ): 443008 Samara, ul. Kalinina 1; tel. (8462) 58-06-44; fax (8462) 58-04-81; f. 1942; manufacture and export of single, double and four-row tapered and cylindrical roller bearings, bearing parts, forgings and cast parts; Gen. Dir IGOR A. SHVIDAK; 6,500 employees.

**Vologda Bearing Factory ZAO (VBF)** (Vologodskii podshipnikovyi zavod): 160028 Vologda, Okruzhnoye shosse 13; tel. (8172) 23-37-26; fax (8172) 21-07-79; e-mail okid@vbf.vologda.ru; internet vbf .ru; f. 1967; manufactures ball-bearings; Chair. ALEKSANDR I. ELPERIN; Gen. Dir ALEKSANDR L. MELNIKOV; 7,300 employees (2002).

### Chemicals

**Acron OAO** (Akron): 173012 Velikii Novgorod, ul. Mochenkova 17; tel. (8162) 19-61-09; fax (8162) 13-19-40; e-mail root@acron.natm.ru; internet www.acron.ru; f. 1967; fmrly Azot JSC; produces mineral fertilizers, synthetic ammonia, methanol, formalin, glues and other chemical products; owns factories in Velikii Novgorod, Verkhnedneprovskii (Smolensk Obl.) and People's Republic of China; Chair. of Bd IVAN N. ANTONOV; Chair. and Dir-Gen. VALERII A. IVANOV; 10,200 employees (2003).

**Apatit OAO:** 184257 Murmansk obl., Kirovsk, ul. Leningradskaya 1; tel. (81531) 1-25-91; e-mail a.alexandrov@apatit.com; production of apatite concentrate and nepheline concentrate; Dir-Gen. ALEKSEI GRIGORYEV; 15,000 employees.

**Kaprolaktam OAO:** 606003 Nizhnii Novgorod obl., Dzerzhinsk; tel. (8313) 27-56-05; fax (8313) 33-59-87; e-mail gup@capr.nnov.ru; internet www.kis.ru/~comsrv; f. 1939; produces caustic soda, mineral fertilizers, synthetic resins and plastics; Gen. Man. ILYA P. VASYANIN; 11,960 employees.

**Middle Volga Chemical Plant—Samkhimprom** (Srednevolzhskii zavod khimikatov—Samkhimprom): 446102 Samara obl., Chapayevsk, ul. Ordzhonikidze 1; tel. and fax (84639) 2-40-21; e-mail komc@mail.samtel.ru; internet www.samtel.ru/svzh/index.html; f. 1912; manufactures chemical products; Dir SERGEI V. TROPANOV; 4,000 employees.

**Nizhnekamsk Oil and Chemical Plant (Nizhnekamskneftekhim) OAO:** 423570 Tatarstan, Nizhnekamsk; tel. (8555) 37-53-81; fax (095) 255-38-21; e-mail nknh@nknh.ru; internet www.nknk.ru; f. 1967; manufactures chemical products; Gen. Man. VLADIMIR M. BUSYGIN.

**Russian Scientific Centre of Applied Chemistry** (Rossiiskii nauchnyi tsentr 'Prikladnaya khimiya'): 197198 St Petersburg, pr. Dobrolyubova 14; tel. (812) 325-66-45; fax (812) 325-66-48; e-mail rscac@rscac.spb.ru; internet www.rscac.spb.ru; f. 1919; research and development of chemical products, etc.; Dir-Gen. ANATOLII G. BAZANOV; 4,500 employees.

### Coal

**Gukovugol (Gukovo Coal) OAO:** 347879 Rostov obl., Gukovo-9, ul. Komsomolskaya 31; tel. (86361) 3-36-46; fax (86361) 5-20-30; e-mail office@hq.gukov.ugol.ru; internet www.gukov.ugol.ru; coal production; exports to Bulgaria, Greece, Turkey, etc.; Dir-Gen. A. V. GALANTSEV.

**Kuzbassrazrezugol (Kuzbass Open-Cast Coal Mines):** 650054 Kemerovo, Pionerskii bulv. 4A; tel. (3842) 52-38-00; fax (3842) 52-34-29; e-mail office@kru.ru; internet www.kru.ru; f. 1964; coal-mining at 13 sites in Kemerovo Oblast.; Dir-Gen. ANATOLII G. PRISTAVKA.

**Kuzbassugol (Kuzbass Coal) OAO:** 650002 Kemerovo, pr. Shakhterov 14A; tel. (3842) 64-18-00; fax (3842) 64-22-89; e-mail company@ kuzcoal.ru; internet www.kuzcoal.ru; f. 1999 on basis of fmr co Severokuzbassugol (Northern Kuzbass Coal); coal-mining at 13 sites in Kemerovo Oblast; Gen. Dir MAKSIM D. BASOV.

**Rosugol—Rossiiskii ugol (Russian Coal) ZAO:** 121910 Moscow, ul. Novyi Arbat 15/1; tel. (095) 202-03-90; e-mail zir@cnet.rosugol.ru; internet www.rosugol.ru; f. 1994; state-owned coal co; Gen. Dir YURII MALYSHEV.

**Siberian Coal Energy Co (SUEK)** (Sibirskaya ugolnaya energeticheskaya kompaniya): 115035 Moscow, Kadashevskaya nab. 32/2/5; tel. (3952) 21-80-42; fax (3952) 21-81-12; e-mail vsu@aovsu .ru; internet www.aovsu.ru; f. 2001 by merger of Vostsiburgol (East Siberia Coal) and Chita Coal Co; operates 82 enterprises in six administrative regions of Russia; produces coal; Pres. OLEG A. MISERVA; 40,000 employees (2003).

**Southern Kuzbass (Yuzhnyi Kuzbass) OAO:** 652870 Kemerovo obl., Mezhdurechensk, ul. Yunosti 6A; tel. (38475) 2-40-93; fax (38475) 2-23-26; e-mail priem@kuz.rikt.ru; internet www.rusotalc .ru/~kuz/index.htm; f. 1993; coal-mining at four sites in Kemerovo Oblast; Gen. Dir V. A. BEKKER; 7,500 employees.

**Tulaugol (Tula Coal) OAO IVTs:** 300028 Tula, ul. 9 Maya 1; tel. (0872) 35-23-24; fax (0872) 254-59-81; e-mail root@coalnet.ru; internet tula.coalnet.ru; production of fuel; Dir-Gen. VLADIMIR YE. SAVCHENKOV; 37,605 employees.

### Electrical Goods

**Astrakhan Progress Machine-Construction Factory OAO** (Astrakhanskii mashinostroitelnyi zavod 'Progress'): 414056 Astrakhan, ul. Savushkina 61A; tel. (8512) 25-44-54; household appliances, computers, lighting equipment; Dir VIKTOR A. KARCHENKO; 1,240 employees (2002).

**Elektropribor (Electrical Appliances) OAO:** 428000 Chuvashiya, Cheboksary, pr. I. Yakovleva 3; tel. (8352) 21-99-12; fax (8352) 21-25-62; e-mail rosa@chtts.ru; internet www.elpribor.ru; f. 1960; produces electronic measuring instruments and microprocessor controllers; Dir-Gen. GENNADII V. MEDVEDEV; 1,400 employees.

**Elektrovypryamitel (Electrical Rectifiers) OAO:** 420001 Mordoviya, Saransk, ul. Proletarskaya 126; tel. (8342) 24-23-96; fax (8342) 47-18-31; e-mail info@elvpr.ru; internet www.elvpr.ru; f. 1941; manufactures conversion equipment and semi-conductor devices; Chair. of Bd LEV A. ROZHKOV; Dir-Gen. VLADIMIR V. CHIBIRKIN; 4,500 employees.

**ELORG (Elektronorgtekhnika) VAO:** 121099 Moscow, Novinskii bulv. 11A.1; tel. (095) 205-38-76; fax (095) 205-39-01; research and development of original Hi- tech products for application in such areas as microelectronics, computer software, fire-fighting systems, heating elements, etc.; legal protection of intellectual property for domestic and foreign markets; Dir-Gen. YURII V. TRIFONOV.

**Kaskad (Cascade) Central Scientific Production Assn** (Tsentralnoye nauchno-proizvodstvennoye obyedineniye 'Kaskad'): 105120 Moscow, per. Khlebnikov 8/2/1; tel. (095) 278-40-11; fax (095) 918-15-01; internet www.kaskad.ru; f. 1997; non-profit organization; research, design, development and manufacture of electronic, telecommunications and cybernetic systems; union of 46 enterprises; Chair. of Bd ADOLF P. KAZNACHEYEV; Dir-Gen. IVAN I. KONOPLICH; 40,000 employees.

**Kvant Industrial Assn (FGUP PO 'Kvant'):** 173001 Velikii Novgorod, ul. B. Sankt-Peterburgskaya 73/1; tel. (81622) 2-36-17; fax (81622) 2-43-33; e-mail sadkotv@mail.natm.ru; internet www.kvant .natm.ru; f. 1958; manufacture of 'Sadko' televisions, radio communication complexes, satellite television systems, microwave ovens, laser equipment; 3,500 employees; Dir-Gen. G. KAPRALOV.

**Moscow Rubin Television Factory OAO** (Moskovskii televizionnyi zavod 'Rubin'): 121087 Moscow, Bagrationovskii proyezd 7/1; tel. (095) 737-59-59; fax (095) 145-69-29; e-mail info@rubin.ru; internet www.rubin.ru; f. 1956; transferred to private ownership 1993; manufactures 'Rubin' televisions; Dir ANATOLII LASHKEVICH; 3,000 employees.

**Petrovsk Molot (Hammer) Electro-Mechanical Factory GUP** (Molot, Petrovskii elektromekhanicheskii zavod): 412520 Saratov Obl., Petrovsk, ul. Gogolya 40; tel. (84555) 3-37-01; fax (84555) 2-94-72; f. 1938; state-owned ; auto-steering devices, 'Liliya' washing-machines; 6,000 employees; Dir VLADIMIR V. ZAKHAROV.

**Schetmash (Calculating Machines) OAO:** 305901 Kursk, ul. Republikanskaya 6; tel. and fax (71) 6-15-22; e-mail serv@kursknet .ru; internet www.schetmash.ru; f. 1948; production of personal computers, cash registers, printers, typewriters and other consumer goods; Dir-Gen. ALEKSEI B. FORTOV; 5,000 employees.

**Ufa Svet (Light) Electric Lamp Factory OAO (UELZ–Svet)** (Ufimskii elektrolampovyi zavod 'Svet'): 450029 Bashkortostan, Ufa, ul. Yubileinaya 1; tel. (3472) 42-52-13; fax (3472) 42-52-30; e-mail uelz@ufanet.ru; internet svet.ufanet.ru; produces electric light bulbs and lamps; Dir-Gen. RIF T. SAIFULLIN; 2,300 employees (2002).

### Export and Import

**AtomStroiEksport (Atomic Construction Export) ZAO (ASE):** 115184 Moscow, ul. M. Ordynka 35/3; tel. (095) 737-90-37; fax (095) 232-37-25; e-mail post@atomstroyexport.ru; internet www .atomstroyexport.ru; f. 1998 by merger of Atomenergoeksport (Atomic Energy Export) and Zarubezhatomenergostroi (Foreign

Atomic Energy Construction); export and import of equipment for nuclear-power generation and research; undertakes projects and services in the field of nuclear science and technology; Dir-Gen. VIKTOR V. KOZLOV.

**Aviaeksport (Aviation Export) VO:** 127018 Moscow, ul. Obraztsova 21A; tel. (095) 737-31-50; fax (095) 737-31-11; e-mail info@aviaexport.com; internet www.aviaexport.ru; f. 1961; export sales and product support of aircraft, air navigational aids and other civil aviation equipment; Dir-Gen. FELIKS N. MYASNIKOV; 1,300 employees.

**Dalintorg (Far East Trade) Foreign Economic Assen GUP VO:** 692904 Maritime Krai, Nakhodka, Nakhodkinskii pr. 16A; tel. (4326) 64-39-70; fax (4326) 64-48-93; e-mail general@dalintorg.ru; internet www.dalintorg.ru; f. 1964; Eastern Siberian and Far Eastern import and export trade with Japan, Australia, the People's Republic of China and 'North' and 'South' Korea, also wood processing and maritime commercial fishery; Dir GENNADII N. MURZAYEV; 160 employees (2002).

**Eksportkhleb (Bread Export) VAO:** 119002 Moscow, per. Sivtsev Brazhek 25/9/1; tel. (095) 244-47-01; fax (095) 253-90-69; e-mail info@extr.ru; internet www.extr.ru; f. 1923; tranferred to private ownership 1991; involved in the export and import of wheat, rye, barley, oats, maize, rice, pulses, flour, oil seeds and other grain and fodder products; also engaged in barter, futures operations, consulting and joint ventures involving these products; chartering, transportation, insurance, analyses and quality certification of grain; Pres. ALEKSANDR N. BELIK.

**Eksportles (Forestry Export) ZAO:** 101986 Moscow, Archangelskii per. 1; tel. (095) 728-40-40; fax (095) 728-40-50; e-mail info@exportles.ru; internet www.exportles.ru; f. 1926; exports and imports sawn and round timber, wooden articles, wood pulp, paper and cardboard; imports machines and equipment for timber enterprises, consumer goods and foodstuffs; sets up joint ventures, carries out import and export operations under compensation agreements, conducts market research and consulting services; Dir-Gen. ALEKSANDR I. KRYLOV; 200 employees.

**Energomasheksport (Energy Machinery Export Co) (EME):** 129090 Moscow, Protopopovskii per. 25A; tel. (095) 725-27-63; fax (095) 725-27-42; e-mail mail@power-m.ru; internet www.energomachexport.ru; f. 1966; owned by Power Machinery (Silovy Mashiny); exports equipment for thermal, hydroelectric, gas-powered and nuclear power stations, transmission and distribution equipment, transport and railway equipment; Dir-Gen. YEVGENII YAKOVLEV.

**Gammakhim:** 107078 Moscow, Orlikov per. 5; tel. (095) 975-00-23; fax (095) 281-86-63; e-mail gammachim@glasnet.ru; f. 1990 to replace Soyuzkhimeksport (Union of Chemical Exporters); exports and imports soaps, plant oils, animal fats, petroleum and chemical products; sales US $70m. (2002); Pres. YEVGENII GONCHARENKO.

**Litintern OAO:** 121108 Moscow, ul. Minskaya 11; tel. (095) 145-10-10; fax (095) 142-59-02; f. 1994; foreign-trade and agency activities; Dir-Gen IGOR V. MALYSHEV.

**Litsenzintorg (Licensed International Trade) GPVO:** 113093 Moscow, Podoliskoye shosse 8/5; tel. (095) 797-63-60; fax (095) 958-09-83; e-mail info@licenz.ru; internet www.licenz.ru; f. 1962; foreign economic and commercial activities; Chair. ALEKSANDR V. ZEMSKOV.

**Mashinoimport (Machine Import) GPVO:** 109017 Moscow, ul. B. Ordinka 40/37/1; tel. (095) 244-33-09; fax (095) 244-38-07; e-mail general@machin.ru; internet www.machim.ru; f. 1933; exports services associated with the construction of pipelines, coal mines, etc.; imports power engineering and pumps, compressors, hoisting and conveying equipment, extracting equipment for the petroleum and natural-gas industries, industrial fittings; Chair. OLGA M. VDOVICHENKO; 180 employees.

**Novoeksport (New Export) GUP VO:** 117393 Moscow, ul. Arkhitektora Vlasova 13; tel. (095) 128-09-54; fax (095) 128-16-12; e-mail novoexport@tsr.ru; imports and exports textile fibres, yarn, fabrics, petroleum products, raw materials, ferrous and non-ferrous metals and products, porcelainware; Chair. VLADIMIR A. KRUZHKOV; 30 employees.

**Soveksportfilm (Soviet Film Export Co):** 103009 Moscow, Kalashnyi per. 14; tel. (095) 290-50-09; fax (095) 200-12-56; e-mail info@socexp.msk.ru; f. 1924; imports and exports films; joint film production; co-operation in television and video productions; organization of annual international film festivals in Moscow and Sochi; Gen. Dir GRIGORII GEVORKYAN; 61 employees.

**Soyuzpromexport (Union of Industrial Exports) GPVO** (Industrial Exports Union): 103009 Moscow, ul. B. Nikitskaya 24/5; tel. (095) 244-19-73; fax (095) 244-37-93; e-mail spprom@integrum.ru; f. 1930; imports and exports coal and coal by-products, manganese, chrome and iron ore, asbestos and other mineral and semi-finished products; provides intermediary, legal and consultancy

services to Russian and foreign partners; Chair. VALERII V. IGNATOV; 90 employees.

**Soyuzpushnina OAO VO** (Furs Union): 117393 Moscow, ul. Arkhitektora Vlasova 33; tel. (095) 128-68-59; fax (095) 933-50-31; e-mail sojuzpushnina@sojuzpushnina.ru; internet www.sojuzpushnina.ru; f. 1996; opened to private ownership in 1999; exports and imports furs, bristles, animal hair, hides, skins and casings, oils, etc.; organizes international fur auctions in St Petersburg, concludes long-term agreements for deliveries of fur goods to foreign firms; Chair. V. M. IVANOV.

**Soyuztransit (SOTRA)** (Transit Union): 121200 Moscow, Smolenskaya-Sennaya pl. 32/34; tel. (095) 244-22-55; fax (095) 230-28-50; e-mail sotra@col.ru; internet www.col.ru/sotra; f. 1963; handles transit of goods through the territory of Russia and the neighbouring states, incl. the Trans-Siberian Container Service and combined transport of cargoes to and from Europe, Iran, the Far East and other locations; effects transport-forwarding operations and storage of transit and bilateral trade cargoes, etc.; Pres. SERGEI G. MELNIK; Man. Dir Dz. E. PUCHKOV; 140 employees.

**SoyuzVneshTrans OOO (SVT)** (Internal Transit Union): 121013 Moscow, Gogolevskii bulv. 17; tel. (095) 201-95-95; fax (095) 200-02-90; e-mail svt@svt.ru; internet www.svt.ru; f. 1962; handles transport and forwarding of imports, exports and transit goods; Pres. ANATOLII N. NAZAROV; 100 employees.

**Sudoeksport (Maritime Export) GVP:** 123242 Moscow, ul. Sadovaya-Kudrinskaya 11; tel. (095) 252-11-83; fax (095) 200-22-50; e-mail sudoexp@cityline.ru; internet www.user.cityline.ru/~sudoexp; f. 1988; exports ships, ships' equipment and equipment for ship-building; repairs of ships and equipment; foreign-trade services; import of services and delivery of goods, etc.; Dir-Gen. VLADIMIR A. CHMYR.

**Sudoimport (Maritime Import) GVP:** 103006 Moscow, Uspenskii per. 10; tel. (095) 299-02-14; fax (095) 755-57-17; e-mail sudoim@dol.ru; f. 1954; exports and imports all kinds of ships, marine equipment and spare parts, licences and allied consultancy services; provides maintenance and repairs of ships and marine equipment; Chair. BORIS A. YAKIMOV; 80 employees.

**Tekhsnabeksport (Technical Supplies and Export) OAO (TENEX):** 119180 Moscow, Staromonetnyi per. 26; tel. (095) 239-26-83; fax (095) 230-26-38; e-mail tenex@online.ru; internet www.tenex.ru; f. 1963; export and import of isotopes, ionizing radiation sources; export of heat-producing elements for various types of atomic reactors, components and parts for nuclear-power stations, rare and rare-earth metals, nuclear physics equipment, laboratory and medical facilities; Dir-Gen. VLADIMIR A. SMIRNOV; 180 employees.

**Traktoroexport (Tractor Export) OAO:** 117997 Moscow, 2-i Verkhnii Mikhailovskii pr. 9; tel. (095) 955-75-65; fax (095) 952-31-89; e-mail tx@mail.ru; internet trex.webzone.ru; f. 1961; import and export of tractors and agricultural and road construction machinery; cap. 100,000 roubles (2002); sales US $7.5m. (2001); Gen. Dir MIKHAIL S. LEVITIN; 85 employees (2002).

**Vneshintorg:** 109147 Moscow, Marksistskaya ul. 5; tel. (095) 911-90-12; fax (095) 274-01-02; f. 1992 by merger of Vneshposyltorg and Vostokintorg; exports and imports foodstuffs, consumer goods and raw materials; participates in joint-venture operations and wholesale and retail trade; Gen. Dir NAZAR BELYAYEV; 320 employees.

### Food, Beverages and Tobacco

**Baltika Brewery OAO** (Pivovarennaya kompaniya Baltika): 194292 St Petersburg, 6-oi Verkhnii per. 3; tel. (812) 329-91-38; fax (812) 329-78-78; e-mail post@baltika.ru; internet www.baltika.ru; f. 1990; production of beer and soft drinks; Dir-Gen. TEYMURAZ K. BOLLOYEV.

**Donskoi Tabak (Don Tobacco) OAO:** 344000 Rostov-on-Don, ul. Krasnoarmeiskaya 170; tel. (8632) 50-58-14; fax (8632) 40-29-34; e-mail info@dontabak.ru; internet www.dontabak.ru; 1992 on basis of Don State Tobacco Factory; manufactures cigarettes; Dir-Gen. IVAN I. SAVVIDII; 1,346 employees.

**Krasnyi Oktyabr (Red October) Moscow Confectionery Factory OAO** (Moskovskaya konditerskaya fabrika 'Krasnyi Oktyabr'): 109072 Moscow, Bersenevskaya nab. 6; tel. (095) 230-07-33; fax (095) 230-08-66; internet www.konfetki.ru; f. 1867; affiliated to Obyedinennye konditery (United Confectioners) Holdings within the Guta-Gruppa; manufacture of confectionery; Chair. MIKHAIL YU. CHEBOTAREV; Pres. ANATOLII N. DAURSKII; 3,200 employees.

**Murmansk Fish (Murmanrybprom) OAO:** 183001 Murmansk, ul. Tralovaya 38; tel. (8152) 28-62-39; fax (8152) 47-67-25; manufacture and sale of fish and fish-food products; Dir-Gen. ALEKSEI I. KOLESOV.

**Nestlé Food Rossiya OOO:** 115054 Moscow, ul. Valovaya 1/1; tel. (095) 725-70-00; fax (095) 725-70-70; e-mail consumer.services@ru.nestle.com; internet www.nestle.ru; f. 1995; manufacture and distribution of confectionery, coffee and various foodstuffs; Dir JENNIFER GALENKAMP.

**Obyedinennye Konditery (United Confectioners) Holding:** 101990 Moscow, ul. Myasitskaya 35; tel. (095) 933-22-22; f. 2002; member of the Guta-Gruppa; holding co for 17 confectionery factories and cos; Pres. SERGEI NOSENKO.

**Prodintorg GUP VO:** 103084 Moscow, ul. Myasnitskaya 47; tel. (095) 244-20-60; fax (095) 244-26-29; e-mail pit@ropnet.ru; f. 1952; exports and imports meat, sugar, milk powder, butter, tobacco and tobacco products, vegetable oil, other oils; equipment for food industry; Pres. LEONID V. TIKHOMIROV; 50 employees.

**Rot-Front OAO:** 115184 Moscow, 2-i Novokuznetskii per. 13/15; tel. (095) 951-84-78; fax (095) 953-91-63; e-mail info@rotfront.ru; internet www.rotfront.ru; f. 1826; production of confectionery, sweets and chocolate products; affilated to Obyedinennye konditery (United Confectioners) Holdings within the Gruppa-Guta; Gen. Dir VALERII I. PYSHNYAK; 2,500 employees.

**Soyuzplodimport (Union of Food Imports) VO OOO:** 103030 Moscow, ul. Dolgorukovskaya 34/2; tel. (095) 973-23-08; fax (095) 973-21-00; e-mail pr@spi.ru; internet www.spi.ru; affiliated to the SPI Group; manufactures and exports vodka; Dir-Gen. ANDREI SKURIKHIN.

**Soyuzplodoimport (Union of Food Imports) FKP:** 109180 Moscow, Starometnyi per. 12; tel. (095) 780-90-61; fax (095) 780-90-62; internet www.spimport.ru; state-owned; export and import of alcoholic and soft drinks, fresh and processed fruit and vegetables, teas, coffees and spices; Dir-Gen. VLADIMIR G. LOGINOV.

**Tulaspirt (Tula Spirit) OAO:** 300600 Tula, pr. Lenina 85; tel. (0872) 30-88-33; fax (0872) 31-23-90; e-mail tulaspirt@tula.net; internet www.tulaspirt.com; f. 1901; manufacture of alcohol, liquor and vodka products; sales US $70m. (2000); 2,000 employees (2002).

**Vimm-Bill-Dann Produkty Pitaniya (Wimm-Bill-Dann Food Products) OAO:** 109028 Moscow, ul. Solyanka 13/2; tel. (095) 105-58-05; fax (095) 105-58-00; e-mail info@wbd.ru; internet www.wbd .ru; f. 1992; dairy products and fruit juices; 40 factories nation-wide, and in Ukraine and Kyrgyzstan; Chair. DAVID M. YAKOBASHVILI; Chief Exec. SERGEI A. PLASTININ.

### Machinery and Precision Equipment

**ALNAS OAO:** 423461 Tatarstan, Almetyevsk-11; tel. (8553) 39-34-64; fax (8553) 25-87-80; e-mail alnas@alnas.ru; internet www.alnas .ru; f. 1993 on basis of Almetyevsk Electrical Submersible Pumps Plant; principal producer of electrical pumps for crude petroleum production and water extraction from artesian wells in Russia; Dir-Gen. A. V. LUKIN.

**Donetsk Excavator (Donetskii Ekscavator) OAO:** 346338 Rostov obl., Donetsk, ul. Lenina 30; tel. (86368) 2-24-18; fax (86368) 2-10-09; e-mail donex@stroydormash.ru; internet www.donex .stroydormash.ru; f. 1968; produces excavators for use in contruction and road-building, etc.; Gen. Dir BORIS I. GLUSHKO; 1,337 employees (2002).

**Energomashkorporatsiya (Energy Machines Corpn) OAO:** 119034 Moscow, per. Butikovskii 14/5; tel. (095) 792-39-51; e-mail corp@energomash.ru; internet www.energomash.ru; owns 9 cos producing machinery and precision equipment in Russia; Chair. of Bd ALEKSANDR YU. STEPANOV.

**Gidromash (Hydraulic Machinery) NPO:** 129662 Moscow, 2-aya Mytishchinskaya ul. 2; tel. (095) 287-78-20; fax (095) 287-17-12; e-mail npo-gidromash@mtu-net.ru; internet www.mtu-net.ru/npo-gidromash; development and manufacture of pumps and other products; Dir-Gen. BORIS V. POKROVSKII; 21,000 employees.

**Kaliningrad Elektrosvarka (Electric Welding) OAO:** 236012 Kaliningrad, ul. Dzerzhinskogo 136; tel. (0112) 49-57-03; fax (0112) 49-57-51; e-mail esva@kaliningrad.ru; manufactures electric welding equipment and ballast rheostats; Dir-Gen. STANISLAV G. SOKOLOV; 731 employees.

**Kaluga Turbine Works OAO (KTZ)** (Kaluzhskii turbinnyi zavod): 248010 Kaluga, ul. Moskovskaya 241; tel. (0842) 56-30-56; fax (0842) 56-22-90; e-mail ktz_market@kaluga.ru; internet www.ktz.kaluga .ru; produces steam and geothermal turbines, turbo-generators, heat exchangers, separators and centrifuges; wholly owned by Power Machinery; Dir YURII A. MAKSIMOV; 5,500 employees (2002).

**Krasnyi Proletarii (Red Proletarian) OAO:** 117342 Moscow, ul. Butlerova 17; tel. (095) 424-28-33; fax (095) 424-30-55; e-mail sergeev@aokp.ru; internet www.aokp.ru; f. 1857; privatized in 1992; manufactures lathes, and wood-working and brick-making machinery; Dir-Gen. YURII I. KIRILLOV; 955 employees.

**Leningrad Metal Plant OAO (LMZ)** (Leningradskii metalliche-skii zavod): 195009 St Petersburg, Sverdlovskaya nab. 18; tel. (812) 326-71-11; fax (812) 326-70-00; e-mail lmz@lmz.ru; internet www .lmz.ru; f. 1857; wholly owned by Power Machinery; produces steam,

gas and hydraulic turbines and locksmithing and woodworking tools; Dir-Gen. VIKTOR S. SHEVCHENKO; 6,500 employees.

**Power Machinery** (Silovye mashiny): 129090 Moscow, Protopopovskii per. 25A; tel. (095) 725-27-63; fax (095) 725-27-42; e-mail mail@power-m.ru; internet www.power-m.ru; f. 2000; owned by Interros; Dir-Gen. YEVGENII K. YAKOVLEV.

**Pressmash (Press Machinery) OAO:** 347947 Rostov obl., Taganrog, Polyakovskoye shosse 16; tel. (86344) 4-46-44; fax (86344) 4-71-13; e-mail pressmash@itt.net.ru; internet www.pressmash.sdt .ru; f. 1958; manufacture of sheet stamping presses, press forging equipment and smelting machinery; Dir-Gen. VLADIMIR G. SUVORIN; 860 employees.

**Proletarskii Zavod (Proletarian Factory) OAO:** 193029 St Petersburg, ul. Dudko 3; tel. (812) 567-17-56; fax (812) 567-37-33; e-mail proletarskyzavod@peterlink.ru; internet proletarsky.ru; f. 1826; manufacture of marine, power engineering and general engineering machinery; Dir-Gen. IGOR A. PASHKEVICH; 4,000 employees.

**Pskov Electro-machine Construction Plant) OAO (PEMZ)** (Pskovskii elektromashinostroitelnyi zavod): 180600 Pskov, Oktyabrskii pr. 27; tel. (8112) 16-82-53; fax (81122) 3-96-82; e-mail sales@pemz.ru; internet www.pemz.ru; f. 1895; manufactures DC generators, low-capacity electric motors, low-voltage units, outboard engines; Gen. Dir VASILII A. IGNATIYEV; 1,500 employees.

**Sibagromash (Siberian Agricultural Machines) FPG:** 658205 Altai Krai, Rubtsovsk, ul. Krasnaya 100; tel. (38557) 4-26-25; fax (38557) 2-30-00; e-mail altaiselmash@mail.ru; f. 1941; transferred to private ownership 1992; fmrly Altaiselmash (Altai Farming Machines); design and manufacture of all types of agricultural machinery and hand tools; Dir-Gen. VIKTOR K. TOLSTOV; 5,500 employees.

**Sibenergomash (Siberia Energy Machines) OAO:** 656037 Altai Krai, Barnaul, pr. Kalinina 26; tel. (3852) 77-85-40; fax (3852) 77-81-77; e-mail par@energomash.ru; internet www.sibenergomash.ru; f. 1942; subsidiary of Energomashkorporatsiya; forging and pressing machines, automatic machines and semi-automatic machine-tools; Dir-Gen. IVAN V. KONEV; 5,402 employees.

**Taganrog Metallurgical Plant OAO (TagMet)** (Taganrogskii metallurgicheskii zavod): 347928 Rostov obl., Taganrog, ul. Zavod-skaya 1; tel. (8634) 38-70-61; fax (86344) 5-03-49; e-mail general@ tagmet.ru; internet www.tagmet.ru; f. 1896; 57% owned by Rinako-MDM; production of steel tubing, boring equipment; Dir-Gen. ANA-TOLII BROVKO.

**Tulamashzavod—Tula Machine Plant OAO:** 300002 Tula, ul. Mosina 2; tel. (0872) 36-24-65; fax (0872) 27-26-20; e-mail reclama@ tulamash.ru; internet www.tulamash.ru; f. 1939; manufactures equipment and machinery for mining and the petroleum and gas industry, motorcycles, laser tools, woodworking machinery and sewing machines; Dir-Gen. YEVGENII A. DRONOV; 1,500 employees.

**Tyazhmash (Heavy Machinery) OAO:** 446101 Samara obl., Syzran, ul. Gidroturbinnaya 13; tel. (84643) 2-33-57; fax (8464) 99-06-10; e-mail ztm-serv@tyazhmash.com; internet www.tyazhmash .com; f. 1941; heavy turbines and conveyor belts; equipment for hydroelectric power stations; Dir-Gen. VLADIMIR A. PANTELEYEV.

**United Machinery Plants OAO (OMZ)** (Obyedinennye mashinostroitelnye zavody): 123379 Moscow, Yermolayevskii per. 25/1; tel. (095) 974-60-21; fax (095) 974-60-22; e-mail mail@omz.ru; internet www.omz.ru; undertakes research and development, and manufacture of heavy industrial engineering equipment; sales US $435m. (2002); Dir-Gen. KAKHA A. BENDUKIDZE.

**Ust-Ilimsk Timber Industry Complex OAO** (Ust-Ilimskii leso-promyshlennyi kompleks): 665770 Irkutsk obl., Ust-Ilimsk-10, POB 316; tel. (39535) 9-29-58; fax (39535) 7-61-32; f. 1976; owned by Ilim Pulp Enterprize Timber Industry Corpn; produces industrial machinery for the timber trade; Dir-Gen. VLADIMIR VATISHCHEV; 900 employees.

**Volgatsemmash (Volga Cement Machines) OAO:** 445009 Samara obl., Tolyatti, ul. M. Gorkogo 96; tel. (8482) 29-53-31; fax (8482) 22-28-59; f. 1956; manufactures equipment for building-materials and ore-mining industries, autoclaves, steel, iron and bronze castings, vessels and tanks for chemical industry, steel forgings and steel-machined forgings, welded metal-working; Gen. Dir ANATOLII V. KOMIN; 6,000 employees.

**Yaroslavl Electric-Machine Construction Plant (ELDIN)** (Yaroslavskii Elektromashinostroitelnyi Zavod): 150040 Yaroslavl, pr. Oktyabrya 74; tel. (852) 27-02-21; fax (852) 25-49-03; e-mail eldin@yaroslavl.ru; internet www.eldin.yaroslavl.ru; Dir-Gen. TURSUN A. AKHUNOV.

### Metals

**Chelyabinsk Metallurgical Group OAO (Mechel)** (Chelyabin-skii metallurgicheskii kombinat): 454047 Chelyabinsk, ul. 2-aya

Paveletskaya 4; tel. (3512) 24-06-44; fax (3512) 24-16-83; e-mail www@mechel.ru; internet www.mechel.ru; f. 1943; iron and steel; Commercial Dir Ivan S. Boyarchuk.

**Cherepovets Steel-Rolling Plant OAO (ChSPZ)** (Cherepovetskii StaleProkatnyi Zavod): 162600 Volodga obl., Cherepovets, ul. 50-letiya Oktyabrya 1/33; tel. (8202) 53-91-91; fax (8202) 53-85-20; e-mail person@chspz.ru; internet www.chspz.ru; f. 1966; hardware, steel wire, wire nails, meshes, electrodes, fasteners, wire ropes, reinforcing steel, steel bars; Chair. of Bd Vadim A. Shvetsov; Dir-Gen. Olga V. Naumova; 5,500 employees.

**Kamensk-Uralskii Metallurgical Works OAO (KUMZ)** (Kamensk-Uralskii metallurgicheskii zavod): 623405 Sverdlovsk obl., Kamensk-Uralskii, ul. Zavodskaya 5; tel. (34378) 9-53-00; fax (34378) 9-55-12; e-mail any@kumz.uralnet.ru; internet www.kumz .ru; f. 1944; produces alloys and semi-finished and rolled product types from copper, bronze, brass, nickel and zinc; Dir Nikolai T. Tikhonov.

**Krasnoyarsk Metallurgical Plant (KraMZ)** (Krasnoyarskii metallurgicheskii zavod): 660111 Krasnoyarsk, Prombaza; tel. (3912) 24-34-43; fax (3912) 24-32-89; 41.7% state-owned, 28% owned by Russian Aluminium (RusAl); public joint-stock co; manufacture and sale of rolled, extruded, drawn and forged aluminium products; Dir-Gen. Yurii Volchenko; 5,580 employees.

**Kuznetsk-Stal (Kuznetsk Steel) ZAO:** 654000 Kemerovo obl., Novokuznetsk, ul. Druzby 39; tel. and fax (3843) 45-82-24; e-mail met@kuzstal.ru; internet www.kuzstal.ru; joint-stock co; steel manufacturing; Gen. Dir Aleksei Kuznetsov; Man. Dir Nikolai Fomin; 22,000 employees.

**Magnitogorsk Metallurgical Plant OAO (MMK)** (Magnitogorskii metallurgicheskii kombinat): 455002 Chelyabinsk obl., Magnitogorsk, ul. Kirova 93; tel. (3519) 24-30-04; fax (3519) 24-75-55; internet www.mmk.ru; f. 1932; largest producer of steel in Russia; Gen. Dir Viktor F. Rashnikov.

**Nizhnii Tagil Iron and Steel Plant OAO (NTMK)** (Nizhnetagilskii metallurgicheskii kombinat): 622025 Sverdlovsk obl., Nizhnii Tagil, ul. Industrialnaya 80; tel. (3435) 29-21-94; fax (3435) 29-26-94; e-mail post@ntmk.ru; internet www.ntmk.ru; f. 1940; owned by YevrazKholding; mining; prodution of coke-chemical, refractory, blast, smelted-steel and rolled products; Chair. of Bd Aleksandr T. Shamrin; 27,000 employees.

**Norilsk Nickel OAO GMK** (Norilskii Nikel): 125009 Moscow, per. Voznesenskii 22; tel. (095) 787-76-67; fax (095) 797-86-13; e-mail agk@nornik.ru; internet www.nornik.ru; f. 1994; produces 20% of world's output of nickel and 42% of its platinum-group metals from Norilsk, Krasnoyarsk Krai; owned by Interros; sole owner of five subsidiary cos; Chair. of Bd Andrei A. Klishas; Dir-Gen. Mikhail D. Prokhorov.

**NOSTA—Orsko-Khalilovskii Metal Works OAO (NOSTA—OKhMK)** (NOSTA—Orsko-Khalilovskii metallurgicheskii kombinat): 462352 Orenburg obl., Novotroitsk, ul. Zavodskaya 1; tel. (35376) 6-23-33; fax (35376) 6-27-89; e-mail oxmk@nosta.ru; internet www.nosta.ru; f. 1955; manufacture of rolled ferrous metals, cast iron, coke, benzine and resin; Gen. Man. Sergei V. Filippov; 16,500 employees.

**Novolipetsk (New Lipetsk) Metallurgical Group OAO** (Novolipetskii metallurgicheskii kombinat): 398040 Lipetsk, pl. Metallurgov 2; tel. (0742) 44-40-06; fax (0742) 43-25-41; e-mail info@nlmk .ru; internet www.nlmk.ru; f. 1931; transferred to private ownership 1992; production of cast-iron, rolled stock, dynamo steel, transformer steel, etc.; Chair. of Bd Vladimir S. Lisin; Gen. Dir Ivan V. Frantsenyuk; 37,776 employees.

**ORMETO YuUMZ Machine-Building Concern** (Ormeto-YuUMZ Mashinostroitelnyi Kontsern): 462403 Orenburg obl., Orsk, pr. Mira 12; tel. (3537) 25-89-24; fax (3537) 25-83-94; e-mail yumz@ email.orgus.ru; internet www.ormeto-yumz.ru; f. 1942; fmrly South Urals Machine Plant (Yuzhno-uralmash—YuUMZ); production, export, erection, installation, commissioning, maintenance and servicing of full-range equipment for ferrous and non-ferrous metallurgy and steel-making; Pres. Sergei V. Shevtsov; 6,442 employees.

**Pervouralskii Tube Manufacturing Plant OAO** (Pervouralskii novotrubnyi zavod): 623112 Sverdlovsk obl., Pervouralsk, ul. Torgovaya 1; tel. (34392) 7-77-77; fax (34392) 7-77-78; e-mail mail@pntz .com; internet www.pntz.com; f. 1934; production of steel piping and steel cylinders; Chair. of Bd M. A. Gresko; 22,000 employees.

**Russian Aluminium (RusAl):** 109240 Moscow, ul. Nikoloyamskaya 13/1; tel. (095) 720-51-70; fax (095) 728-49-12; e-mail press-center@rusal.ru; internet www.rusal.ru; f. 2000 by merger; the country's second-largest aluminium producer; Gen. Dir and Chief Exec. Oleg V. Deripaska.

**Severovostokzoloto (North-Eastern Gold) OAO:** 685005 Magadan, ul. Proletarskaya 12; tel. (41322) 2-38-21; fax (41322) 2-38-65;

e-mail postmaster@svz.magadan.su; production of gold, silver, tin and mining equipment; Gen. Dir Aleksandr V. Polyakov.

**Severstal (Northern Steel) OAO:** 162600 Vologda obl., Cherepovets, ul. Mira 30; tel. (8202) 56-80-09; fax (8202) 57-12-76; internet www.stal.ru; f. 1951; Chair. of Bd Aleksei A. Mordashov; Dir-Gen. Anatolii N. Kurchinin.

**Steel Construction Concern—CONCEST OAO** (Kontsern Stalkonstruktsiya—CONCEST): 123001 Moscow, ul. Sadovaya-Kudrinskaya 8–12; tel. (095) 291-08-05; fax (095) 291-50-89; e-mail concest@bsim.ru; internet www.concest.ru; f. 1989 on basis of Stalmost (Steel Bridge Co—f. 1938); manufacture and erection of steel structures; owns 13 factories and 22 assembly plants; Pres. Viktor K. Vorobiev; 33,500 employees.

**Volgograd Krasnyi Oktyabr (Red October) Metallurgical Plant OAO** (Volgogradskii metallurgicheskii zavod 'Krasnyi Oktyabr'): 400007 Volgograd, pr. Lenina 110; tel. (8442) 78-38-45; fax (8442) 71-59-36; e-mail ved@vmzko.ru; internet www.vmzko.ru; f. 1898; transferred to private ownership 1999; manufacture of grade steels, round rolled products, rolled wire, hexahedron, drilling hollow rolled sheets, ingots, cableware; Dir-Gen. Pavel Ye. Malinovskii; 15,000 employees.

**YevrazKholding (Eurasian Holding):** 103006 Moscow, ul. Dolgorukovskaya 15/4–5; tel. (095) 234-46-31; fax (095) 234-46-30; e-mail evrazholding@eam.ru; internet www.evraznet.ru; f. 1999; owns 3 metallurgical plants; Pres. Aleksandr G. Abramov.

**Zapsib—West Siberian Metal Works OAO** (Zapsib—Zapadno-Sibirskii metallurgicheskii kombinat): 654043 Kemerovo obl., Novokuznetsk, Zapsibmetkombinat; tel. (3843) 59-59-00; fax (3843) 59-43-43; internet www.zsmk.ru; f. 1964; owned by YevrazKholding; manufacture and sale of pig iron and products in carbon and alloy steel; Gen. Dir Sergei K. Nosov; 35,000 employees.

### Motor Vehicles and Components

**Altai Tractor OAO** (Altaiskii traktor): 658212 Altai Krai, Rubtsovsk, ul. Traktornaya 17; tel. (38557) 3-28-90; fax (38557) 3-68-92; e-mail alttrak@rubtsovsk.ru; internet alttrak.rubtsovsk.ru; f. 1942; design and production of T-4A01, T-40201, T-404, TT-4M, MT-8 and MT-16 tractors; sales (2001) US $44.5m.; Gen. Dir Artur A Derfler; 10,500 employees (2002).

**Avtoeksport (Automobile Export) ZAO:** 119034 Moscow, Gagarinskii per. 3; tel. (095) 203-06-62; fax (095) 202-60-75; e-mail avtoex@ dol.ru; internet avtoexport.netcat.ru; f. 1956; subsidiary of Avtotraktoroeksport; renders services on publicity and promotion of sales, engineering, marketing and after-sale servicing of motor vehicles and equipment; 4 subsidiary cos; Pres. and Chair. of Bd Yevgenii N. Lyubinskii; Dir-Gen. Yurii V. Konyushko.

**Avtoframos OAO:** 109147 Moscow, ul. Vorontsovskaya 35; tel. (095) 775-48-08; fax (095) 775-40-05; e-mail fleet.sales-avtoframos@ renault.com; internet www.renault.ru/about; f. 1998; jt venture between Moscow City Govt and Renault (France); manufactures 'Renault' automobiles; also sole authorized importer of Renault automobiles to Russia; Dir-Gen. Guy Bara.

**Avtotraktoroeksport (Automobile and Tractor Export) OAO (ATEKS):** 103031 Moscow, ul. Kuznetskii Most 21/5; tel. (095) 924-38-26; fax (095) 928-56-10; f. 1990; engaged in economic, financial and investment activities in the Russian Federation and abroad; Pres. and Chair. of Bd Yevgenii N. Lyubinskii; Dir-Gen. Igor K. Terentyev.

**AvtoUAZ (Ulyanovsk Automobile Plant) OAO (UAZ)** (Ulyanovskii avtomobilnyi zavod): 432008 Ulyanovsk, Moskovskoye shosse 8; tel. (8422) 36-73-53; fax (8422) 36-77-58; e-mail press@uaz .ru; internet www.uaz.ru; f. 1941; manufacture of enhanced cross-country capability vehicles; Man. Dir B. I. Kuperman.

**AvtoVAZ (Volga Automobile Plant) OAO:** 445633 Samara Obl., Tolyatti, Yuzhnoye shosse 36/49; tel. (8482) 73-82-43; fax (8482) 73-71-71; e-mail press@vaz.ru; internet www.vaz.ru; f. 1966; manufactures the Lada brand of cars; in 2002 began to manufacture Chevrolet Niva automobiles and sports-utility vehicles as part of a jt venture with General Motors (USA); Chair. of Bd Vladimir V. Kadannikov.

**Carburettor Plant OAO—Pekar** (Karbyuratornyi zavod—Pekar): 192102 St Petersburg, ul. Samoilovoi 5; tel. (812) 166-48-08; fax (812) 166-63-13; e-mail commserv@pecar.spb.su; f. 1929; fmrly V. V. Kuibyshev Carburettor Plant; design, development and manufacture of carburettors for automobiles; Dir Gennadii B. Orlov; 3,400 employees.

**Chelyabinsk Uraltrak (Ural Tractors) Tractor Plant** (ChTZ—Uraltrak) (Chelyabinskii traktornyi zavod 'Uraltrak'): 454007 Chelyabinsk, pr. Lenina 3; tel. (3512) 75-17-60; fax (3512) 72-95-83; e-mail tractor@chtz.chel.su; internet chtz.chelyabinsk.ru; f. 1933; caterpillar tractors; Gen. Dir Valerii M. Platonov; 35,000 employees.

**GAZ (Gorkii Automobile Plant) OAO:** 603004 Nizhnii Novgorod, pr. Lenina 88; tel. (8312) 56-12-25; fax (8312) 53-98-42; e-mail general@atom.gaz.ru; internet www.gaz.ru; f. 1932; manufactures trucks, cars, spare parts, motor vehicles, components and consumer goods; Dir-Gen. ALEKSEI G. BARANTSEV; 77,000 employees (2002).

**Kaluga Factory of Auto-Electro Equipment—KZAE** (Kaluzhskii zavod avtoelektro oborudovaniya): 248631 Kaluga, ul. Azarovskaya 18; tel. and fax (0842) 53-10-44; e-mail kzame@kaluga.ru; internet www.kzae.ru; f. 1941; design and manufacture of a wide range of electronic motors and control units for the automobile industry; Chair. of Bd VYACHESLAV M. MALEYEV; Gen. Dir ANATOLII N. FAYEROVICH; 7,500 employees.

**KamAZ (Kama Automobile Plant) OAO:** 423808 Tatarstan, Naberezhnye Chelny, pr. M. Dzhalilya 29; tel. (8552) 37-68-40; fax (8552) 53-37-98; e-mail amz@kamaz.net; internet www.kamaz.net; f. 1971; manufactures and distributes heavy trucks, diesel engines, spare parts and tools; Chair. of Bd ILYA I. KLEBANOV; Dir-Gen. SERGEI A. KOGOGIN.

**Kostroma Motor Parts Plant OAO—Motordetal** (Kostromskii zavod 'Motordetal'): 156001 Kostroma, ul. Moskovskaya 105; tel. (0942) 53-13-31; fax (0942) 53-27-21; e-mail info@motordetal.ru; internet www.motordetal.ru; f. 1967; manufactures pistons and other automobile spare parts; Dir-Gen. YURII YELISEYEV; 4,681 employees (2003).

**I. A. Likhachev Automobile Plant OAO (ZiL)** (Avtomobilnyi zavod im. Likhacheva): 109280 Moscow, ul. Avtozavodskaya 23; tel. (095) 275-33-28; fax (095) 274-00-78; e-mail crp@amozil.ru; internet www.amozil.ru; f. 1916; manufactures ZIL trucks, engines, industrial ovens and washing machines; also automobiles, particularly luxury limousines; Gen. Dir VALERII T. SALKIN.

**Lipetsk Tractor Plant OAO** (Lipetskii traktornyi zavod): 398006 Lipetsk, ul. Krasnozavodskaya 1; tel. (0742) 73-35-82; fax (0742) 73-2£-46; e-mail ltz@lipetsk.ru; internet www.ltz.lipetsk.ru; f. 1944; manufactures tractors; Dir-Gen. GENNADII M. PISHCHULIN; 9,500 employees.

**Moskvich OAO:** 117607 Moscow, Volgogradskii pr. 42; tel. (095) 911-09-91; fax (095) 179-02-09; e-mail mail@azlk.ru; internet www .azlk.ru; f. 1930; design, manufacture and assembly of automobiles; Dir-Gen. RUBEN S. ASATRJAN; 7,500 employees.

**Pavlovo Bus OAO (PAZ)** (Pavlovskii avtobus): 606108 Nizhnii Novgorod obl., Pavlovo, ul. Suvorova 1; tel. (83171) 6-81-14; fax (83171) 6-03-18; e-mail bereg@paz.nnov.ru; internet www.paz.nnov .ru; f. 1932; manufactures buses; Dir-Gen. ANDREI V. VASILYEV; 9,000 employees.

**Promtraktor (Industrial Tractor) OAO:** Chuvashiya, 428028 Cheboksary, pr. Traktorostroitelei 101; tel. (8352) 62-52-62; fax (8352) 62-22-67; e-mail marketing@promtractor.ru; internet www .promtractor.ru; f. 1974; transferred to private ownership 1993; production, maintenance and repair of heavy-duty crawler tractors and associated parts; manufacture of plastic and metal children's toys, garden accessories and tools; wood-working, etc.; Chair. of Bd MIKHAIL G. BOLOTIN; Dir-Gen. SEMEN G. MLODIK; 14,500 employees.

**SibmashKholding (Siberian Machine Holding) OAO (SMKh):** 660049 Krasnoyarsk, ul. Profsoyuzov 3; tel. (3912) 59-56-05; fax (3912) 59-56-85; e-mail info@smh.ru; internet www.smh.ru; fmrly Krasselmash Production Technological Complex; production of 'Yenisei' combine harvesters,parts, and diesel motors; Pres. YURII I. KOROPACHINSKII; 12,000 employees.

**Staryi Oskol Automobile and Tractor Equipment Plant ZAO (SOATE)** (Starooskolskii zavod avtotraktronogo oborudovaniya): 309507 Belgorod obl., Staryi Oskol, ul. Vatutina 54; tel. (0725) 22-09-65; fax (0725) 24-10-15; e-mail soate@belgtts.ru; internet www.soate .com; f. 1959; produces spare and assembly parts for tractor, automobiles and household goods; Dir-Gen. ANATOLII M. MAMONOV; 3,500 employees.

**Traktoroeksport (Tractor Export) OAO:** 117419 Moscow, 2-i Verknii Mikhailovskii pr. 9; tel. (095) 955-75-65; fax (095) 952-31-89; e-mail tx@mail.ru; internet www.trex.webzone.ru; f. 1961; subsidiary of Avtotraktoroeksport; publicity and promotion of sales, engineering, marketing and after-sale service of tractors and equipment; Chair. of Bd YEVGENII N. LYUBINSKII; Dir-Gen. MIKHAIL S. LEVITIN.

**Tyumen Automobile and Tractor Electrical Equipment ZAO (TATE)** (Tyumenskii zavod avtotraktornogo elektrooborudovaniya ZAO): 625002 Tyumen, ul. Tsiolkovskogo 1; tel. (3452) 24-12-34; fax (3452) 24-15-32; e-mail marktate@sbtx.tmn.ru; produces coil distributors, plugs, electric stoves, electric immersion heaters; Plant Dir VLADISLAV P. ZAGVAZDIN; 2,500 employees.

**Vladimir Tractor Plant OAO (VTZ)** (Vladimirskii traktornyi zavod): 600000 Vladimir, ul. Traktornaya 43; tel. and fax (0922) 23-18-31; fax (0922) 35-52-55; e-mail vladtp@vtsnet.ru; internet www .vladtp.ru; f. 1945; design and manufacture of diesel air-cooled engines and tractors; Dir-Gen. DMITRII G. KUPRYUNIN; 4,450 employees.

**Volgograd Tractor Plant OAO (VgTZ)** (Volgogradskii traktornyi zavod): 400061 Volgograd, pl. Dzerzhinskogo; tel. (8442) 74-61-20; fax (8442) 71-14-55; e-mail chief@vgtz.com; internet www.vgtz.com; f. 1930; produces caterpillar tractors and other agricultural and military machinery, equipment; Dir-Gen. VALERII F. KHVATOV.

### Paper and Pulp

**Archangel Pulp and Paper Mill OAO (ARKhBUM)** (Arkhangelskii tsellyulozno-bumazhnyi kombinat): 164900 Archangel obl., Novodvinsk, ul. Melnikova 1; tel. (81852) 6-31-23; fax (81852) 6-32-79; e-mail info@appm.ru; internet www.appm.ru; f. 1940; joint-stock co since in 1992; manufactures pulp and paper; annual capacity of 900,000 metric tons; sales US $199m. (2002); Chair. of Bd VLADIMIR KRUPCHAK; Dir-Gen. VLADIMIR BELOGLAZOV; 7,000 employees (2003).

**Ilim Pulp Enterprize Timber Industry Corpn ZAO** (Ilim Palp Enterpraiz Lesopromyshlennaya korporatsiya): 191025 St Petersburg, ul. Marata 17; tel. (812) 118-60-50; fax (812) 118-60-06; e-mail office@ilimpulp.ru; internet www.ilimpulp.ru; f. 1992; owns 42 enterprises involved with forestry and paper-manufacturing; Chair. of Bd ZAKHAR D. SMUSHKIN; Dir-Gen. SERGEI S. KOSTYLEV; 49,000 employees (2002).

**Segezha Pulp and Paper Mill OAO—Segezhabumprom (STsBK)** (Segezhskii tsellyulozno-bumazhnyi kombinat): 186420 Kareliya, Segezha, ul. Zavodskaya 1; tel. (81431) 2-33-11; fax (81431) 2-26-63; e-mail office@scbk.ru; internet www.scbk.ru; f. 1939; paper-sack and kraft-paper manufacturer; pulp producer; controlling stake owned by AssiDomän (Sweden); Gen. Dir VASILII F. PREMENIN; 5,000 employees.

### Petroleum, Petrochemicals and Natural Gas

**Astrakhangazprom OOO:** 416154 Astrakhan obl., Krasnoyarsk raion, pos. Aksaraisk, ul. Babushkina 9; tel. (8512) 31-41-84; fax (8512) 39-11-33; e-mail adm@astrakhan.gazprom.ru; subsidiary of Gazprom; production of gasoline, liquefied gas and diesel oil; Dir-Gen. VITALII A. ZAKHAROV; 13,597 employees.

**Komi Oil ZAO (KNK)** (Komi neftyanaya kompaniya): 169400 Komi, Ukhta, ul. Oktyabrskaya 13; tel. (82147) 6-26-12; fax (82147) 6-18-08; f. 2000 by merger; exploration and development of petroleum and natural-gas fields and associated activities in the Republic of Komi and Archangel Oblast; Pres. VASILII V. DEVYATOV; 22,000 employees.

**LUKoil OAO:** 101000 Moscow, Sretenskii bulv. 11; tel. (095) 927-44-44; fax (095) 928-98-41; e-mail pr@lukoil.com; internet www.lukoil .com; extraction, refining and distribution of petroleum; f. 1991 by merger; five principal production subsidiary cos, four principal refining subsidiary cos, three principal national marketing and distribution subsidiary cos, 14 regional marketing and distribution subsidiary cos, two subsidiary cos conducting international operations (refining, marketing, distribution, exploration and production); Chair. of Bd VALERII I. GRAIFER; Pres. VAGIT YU. ALEKPEROV; 114,000 employees.

**Rosneft Oil OAO NK** (Neftyanaya kompaniya 'Rosneft'): 115998 Moscow, Sofiiskaya nab. 26/1; tel. (095) 777-44-22; fax (095) 777-44-44; e-mail postman@rosneft.ru; internet www.rosneft.ru; f. 1995; petroleum exploration and production; 40 subsidiary operations in the North Caucausus, Northern Russia, Sakhalin and Western Siberia; Chair. of Bd IGOR KH. YUSUFOV; Pres. SERGEI M. BOGDANCHIKOV; 69,880 employees.

**Samaraneftegaz (Samara Oil and Gas) OAO:** 443010 Samara, ul. Kuibysheva 145; tel. (8462) 33-02-32; fax (8462) 33-45-08; internet www.yukos.ru/121.shtml; f. 1936; production of petroleum, gas and sulphur; subsidiary of Yukos (q.v.); Gen. Dir PAVEL A. ANISIMOV.

**Siberian–Ural Petrochemical and Gas OAO—SIBUR (AKSIBUR)** (Sibirsko-Uralskaya neftegazokhimicheskaya kompaniya): 117218 Moscow, ul. Krzhizhanovskogo 16/1; tel. (095) 127-90-15; fax (095) 129-60-97; e-mail info@sibur.ru; internet www.sibur.ru; Pres. ALEKSANDR DYUKOV.

**Sibneft (Siberian Oil) OAO** (Sibirskaya neftyanaya kompaniya 'Sibneft'): 113035 Moscow, ul. Sadovnicheskaya 4; tel. (095) 777-31-52; fax (095) 777-31-51; e-mail alexeyf@sibneft.ru; internet www .sibneft.ru; f. 1995 by presidential decree; petroleum co, five subsidiary production cos; merger with Yukos Oil Co approved in 2003; 55,000 employees.

**Slavneft (Slavonic Oil) OAO** (Neftegazovaya kompaniya 'Slavneft'): 115054 Moscow, ul. Pyatnitskaya 69; tel. (095) 787-82-06; fax (095) 777-73-17; e-mail slavneft@slavneft.ru; internet www.slavneft .ru; f. 1994; transferred to private ownership in 2002; 48.75% owned by Sberbank—Savings Bank of the Russian Federation, 26.21% by

Citibank (USA), 13.18% by ING Bank—Eurasia, 10.83% by Deutsche Bank (Germany); Pres. and Chair. of Bd YURII YE. SUKHANOV.

**Stroitransgaz (Gas Transit Construction) OAO:** 117418 Moscow, ul. Novocheremushkinskaya 65; tel. (095) 332-79-41; fax (095) 363-94-95; e-mail stg@stroytransgaz.com; internet www .stroytransgaz.com; f. 1990; 25% owned by Gazprom; pipeline design and construction; involved in the 'Blue Stream' project for the transportation of petroleum from Russia to Turkey, under the Black Sea; Chair. of Bd ERNEST T. ERVALD; Pres. VIKTOR YA. LORENZ.

**Surgutneftegaz (Surgut Oil and Gas) OAO (SNG):** 628400 Tyumen obl., Khanty-Mansii AOk—Yugra, Surgut, ul. Kukuyevitskogo 1; tel. (3462) 42-61-33; fax (3462) 42-63-63; e-mail secret_b@ surgutneftegas.ru; internet www.surgutneftegas.ru; f. 1993; petroleum and natural-gas production; Chair. of Bd ALEKSANDR V. USOLTSEV; Dir-Gen. VLADIMIR L. BOGDANOV; 84,500 employees.

**Tatneft (Tatar Oil) OAO:** 423400 Tatarstan, Almetyevsk, ul. Lenina 75; tel. (8533) 25-58-56; fax (8553) 25-68-65; e-mail tnr@ tatneft.ru; internet www.tatneft.ru; f. 1950; transferred to private ownership 1990; petroleum survey and exploration; petroleum drilling; production and export; civil and industrial construction; manufacture of plastic coated metal pipes, cable and wire products and petroleum production equipment and tools; Chair. of Bd RUSTAM N. MINNIKHANOV; Gen. Dir SHAFAGAT F. TAKHAUTDINOV; 65,489 employees.

**TNK-BP:** 115093 Moscow, ul. Schipok 18/2; tel. (095) 787-89-50; fax (095) 787-96-68; e-mail web-master@tnk.ru; internet www.tnk-bp .ru; f. 2003 by merger of Sidanco, Tyumen Oil Co (TNK) and the Russian interests of British Petroleum (BP—United Kingdom); 50% owned by Alfa-Group and Access/Renova, 50% owned by BP; 15 subsidiary cos involved in extraction, 5 subsidiary cos in refining, 11 subsidiary cos in marketing and distribution; Pres. and Chief Exec. ROBERT DUDLEY.

**Yukos Oil Co:** 115054 Moscow, ul. Dubininskaya 31A; tel. (095) 232-31-61; fax (095) 232-31-60; e-mail info@yukos.ru; internet www .yukos.ru; f. 1993; petroleum co operating in Khanty-Mansii Autonomous Okrug (Tyumen Oblast, Western Siberia); 40% of shares owned by Menatep, 45% owned by Govt; merger with Sibneft approved in 2003; 120,000 employees.

**Yuganskneftegaz (Nefteyugansk Oil and Gas) OAO (YuNG):** 628309 Tyumen obl., Khanty-Mansii AOk—Yugra, Nefteyugansk, ul. Lenina 26; tel. (34612) 3-52-01; fax (34612) 2-89-51; internet www.yukos.ru/120.shtml; f. 1977; subsidiary of Yukos; production of crude petroleum; provision of oil and gasfield services; Gen. Man SERGEI I. KUDRYASHOV; 8,824 employees.

### Miscellaneous

**Agrovod (Agricultural Irrigation) AOZD:** 107078 Moscow, ul. N. Basmannaya 10; tel. (095) 265-95-14; fax (095) 213-02-56; design and construction of irrigation systems, roads, dams and agricultural equipment; Pres. GEORGII G. GULYUK.

**ALROSA (Almazy Rossii-Sakha) Diamonds of Russia—Sakha AK (Alrosa):** 678170 Sakha (Yakutiya), Mirnyi, ul. Lenina 6; tel. (41136) 3-01-80; fax (41136) 2-44-51; e-mail info@alrosa.ru; internet www.alrosa.ru; f. 1957; joint stock co since 1992; 37% owned by the Federal Govt, 32% by the Govt of the Republic of Sakha (Yakutiya); world's second largest producer of rough diamonds, commerical diamond mining, manufacturing of polished diamonds, trade in rough and polished diamonds, development of diamondiferous deposits, construction, transportation; cap. 34,841.2m. roubles (2001), sales (2001) US $1,901.3m. 55,461.0m. roubles; Pres. VLADIMIR T. KALITIN; 40,996 employees (2007).

**Altaidizel (Altai Diesel) OAO:** 656023 Altai Krai, Barnaul, pr. Kosmonavtov 8; tel. (3852) 77-37-86; fax (3852) 75-16-43; internet www.altdiesel.ru; f. 1992 on basis of Altai Motor Plant; owned by Sibmashkholding; manufactures diesel engines, fuel pumps, etc.; Gen. Dir VLADIMIR M. ZAKHAROV; 3,800 employees.

**Aviastar Ulyanovsk Aviation Industrial Complex OAO** (Ulyanovskii Aviyatsionnyi Promyshlennyi Kompleks 'Aviyastar'): 432072 Ulyanovsk, pr. Antonova 1; tel. (8422) 20-25-75; fax (8422) 20-35-06; internet www.aviastar.info; f. 1977; established asa joint stock co 1992; 75% plus 1 share owned by the Russian Govt, 25% less one share owned by Sirocco Aerospace International (Egypt); production and export of TU-204 and AN-124 aircraft; Chair. of Bd DENIS V. MANTUROV; Dir-Gen. VIKTOR MIKHAILOV; 35,000 employees.

**Interros:** 119180 Moscow, ul. B. Yakimanka 9; tel. (095) 785-63-63; fax (095) 785-63-64; e-mail info@interros.ru; internet www.interros .ru; holding co for energy, financial and media cos, including Norilsk Nickel (q.v.), Power Machinery (q.v.), Prof-Mediya and Rosbank (q.v.); Pres. VLADIMIR POTANIN; Dir-Gen. and Chair. ANDREI KLISHAS.

**Kama-Volga Rubber Products ZAO—QUART** (Kamsko-Volzhskoye AO rezinotekhniki—KVART): 420054 Tatarstan, Kazan, ul. Tekhnicheskaya 25; tel. (8432) 78-48-91; fax (8432) 37-75-62; e-mail

kvart@bancorp.ru; internet kvart.knet.ru; f. 1942; transferred to private ownership 1992; manufactures rubber products; Dir-Gen. VENIAMIN D. GRIGORYEV; 5,000 employees.

**S. P. Korolev Energiya Space-Rocket Corpn** (Raketno-kosmicheskaya korporatsiya 'Energiya' im. S. P. Koroleva): 141700 Moscow obl., Korolev, ul. Lenina 4A; tel. (095) 513-72-48; fax (095) 187-98-77; e-mail mail@rsre.ru; internet www.energia.ru; f. 1946; development and operation of manned space technology, special-purpose satellite complexes ; development and production of non-space products based on space technologies, including prosphetic and orthopedic prodcuts, consumer goods, automatic ecological monitoring stations, power facilities; operates the Mir space station; involved, with Boeing (USA), Kvaerner (United Kingdom/Norway) and Pivdenne Yuzhnoye MK Yangel NPO (Ukraine), in the Sea Launch programme, which aims to launch communications satellites from the Pacific Ocean; cap. 1,100m. roubles. sales (2001) 3,400m. roubles,; Pres. Prof. YURII P. SEMYONOV; 17,000 employees (incl. subsidary cos—2002).

**Maritime Satellite Communications (Morsvyazsputnik) GP:** 115230 Moscow, Varshavskoye shosse 42; tel. (095) 795-32-08; fax (095) 967-18-34; e-mail root@marsat.glasnet.ru; internet www .marsat.ru; communications and navigational aids; Pres. VALERII A. BOGDANOV; 75 employees.

**Rosoboroneksport (Russian Defence Export) FGUP:** 107076 Moscow, ul. Stromynka 27/3; tel. (095) 964-61-83; fax (095) 963-26-13; internet www.rusarm.ru; state-owned; manufacture and export of weapons; f. 2001 by merger of Rosvooruzheniye (Russian Weapons Co) and Promeksport (Industrial Export Co); Dir-Gen. ANDREI YU. BELYANINOV.

**Selkhozpromeksport (Agro-Industrial Export) FGUP VVO:** 113324 Moscow, Ovchinnikovskaya nab. 18/1; tel. (095) 950-16-92; fax (095) 921-93-64; e-mail agiro@4unet.ru; internet www.shpex.ru; f. 1964; assists in construction of hydrotechnical and irrigation facilities, storage plants and other agricultural projects; also involved in the fishing industry, petroleum extraction and the timber, microbiological and confectionary industries; Chair. VLADIMIR P. MORGUTOV; 120 employees.

**Slava (Glory)—Second Moscow Watch and Clock Factory OAO** (Slava—Vtoroi moskovskii chasovoi zavod): 125040 Moscow, Leningradskii pr. 8; tel. (095) 251-29-37; fax (095) 257-15-02; e-mail info@slava.ru; internet www.slava-moscow.ru; f. 1924; produces 'Slava' mechanical and electronic watches and clocks; Dir-Gen. VLADIMIR M. KOROLEV; 10,000 employees.

**Sukhoi Aviation Military and Industrial Complex GUP** (Aviatsionnyi voyenno-promyshlennyi kompleks 'Sukhoi'): 125284 Moscow, ul. Polikarpova 23A; tel. (095) 941-01-30; fax (095) 945-55-70; internet www.sukhoi.org; the country's leading manufacturer of military aircraft; also manufactures civilian aircraft; Gen. Dir MIKHAIL A. POGOSYAN.

**Tekhnopromeksport (Techno-Industry Export) FGUP VO:** 113324 Moscow, Ovchinnikovskaya nab. 18/1; tel. (095) 950-15-23; fax (095) 953-33-73; e-mail inform@tpe.ru; internet www.tpe.ru; f. 1955; power equipment and materials; construction of power projects on a turn-key basis; mediatory and consultancy services on foreign economic activities in Russia and abroad; Chair. VALENTIN A. KUZNETSOV; 250 employees.

**Tekhnopromimport (Techno-Industry Import) VO** ( Co): 129085 Moscow, pr. Mira 101; tel. (095) 287-85-31; fax (095) 287-04-21; e-mail tpi-admin@mtu-net.ru; f. 1930; assists in petroleum production; construction of industrial plants, pharmaceutical plants, hospitals, schools; Chair. VITALII. I. BOIKO; 70 employees.

**Terekalmaz—Terek Diamond Tool Factory OAO** (Terskii zavod almaznogo instrumenta 'Terekalmaz'): 361200 Kabardino–Balkariya, Terek, ul. Yubileinaya 1; tel. (86632) 9-11-76; fax (86632) 9-37-10; e-mail mail@terekalmaz.ru; internet www.terekalmaz.ru; f. 1961; produces diamond-boring tools, diamond drills, etc; Gen. Dir ARKADII K. KARAZHEV; 2,000 employees.

**Tyazhpromeksport (Heavy Industry Export) GPVO:** 113324 Moscow, Ovchinnikovskaya nab. 18/1; tel. (095) 950-16-10; fax (095) 230-22-03; e-mail tyazh@dol.ru; f. 1957; assists construction and extension of integrated iron and steel mining complexes and hardware plants; Chair. NIKOLAI V. ULYANOV; 171 employees.

**Vneshstroiimport (External Construction Import—Sovstrim) GVPO:** 125009 Moscow, Tverskoi bulv. 6; tel. (095) 200-32-04; fax (095) 291-35-60; e-mail info@sovstrim.ru; internet www .sovstrim.ru; f. 1974; arranges joint construction projects with foreign firms; engineering, construction and investment consulting; Chair. VALERII A. AINBUND; 150 employees.

**Vologda Timber—Industry OOO** (Kholdingovaya kompaniya vologodskiye lesopromyshlenniki): 160604 Vologda, ul. Blagoveshchenskaya 47; tel. and fax (8172) 72-88-14; e-mail mail@volwood.ru;

internet www.volwood.ru; f. 1997; produces birch and coniferous sawn timber, plywood, etc.; Dir-Gen. ALEKSANDR N. CHUPKIN.

**Yantar (Amber) Baltic Shipyard OAO** (Pribaltiiskii sudostroitelnyi zavod 'Yantar'): 236005 Kaliningrad, Transportnyi tupik 10; tel. (112) 47-22-40; fax (112) 47-22-43; e-mail marketing@ shipyard-yantar.ru; internet www.shipyard-yantar.ru; shipbuilding, ship repair, mechanical engineering; Dir-Gen. NIKOLAI F. VOLOV.

## TRADE UNIONS

In 1990, in response to the growing independent labour movement, several branch unions of the All-Union Central Council of Trade Unions (ACCTU) established the Federation of Independent Trade Unions of the Russian Federation (FITUR), which took control of part of the property and other assets of the ACCTU. The ACCTU was re-formed as the General Confederation of Trade Unions of the USSR, which was, in turn, renamed the General Confederation of Trade Unions—International Organization in 1992. In November of that year, in an attempt to challenge the influence of the FITUR, the ITUM and several other independent trade unions established a consultative council to co-ordinate their activities.

**All-Russian Labour Confederation:** 103031 Moscow, ul. Rozhdestvenka 5/7; tel. (095) 785-21-30; fax (095) 915-83-67; e-mail vktrussia@online.ru; internet www.trud.org/guide/VKT.htm; f. 1995; unites five national trade unions and 40 regional orgs with 1,270,900 mems; Pres. ALEKSANDR N. BUGAYEV.

**General Confederation of Trade Unions (VKP):** 117119 Moscow, Leninskii pr. 42; tel. (095) 938-82-22; fax (095) 938-21-55; e-mail mail@vkp.ru; internet www.vkp.ru; f. 1992; fmrly the General Confederation of Trade Unions of the USSR; co-ordinating body for trade unions in CIS member states; unites nine national trade unions and 47 regional orgs with 85m. mems; publishes *Profsoyuzy* (Trade Unions), weekly, *Vestnik profsoyuzov* (Herald of the Trade Unions), every two weeks, and *Inform-Contact*, in English and French, quarterly; Pres. VLADIMIR P. SHCHERBAKOV.

**Federation of Independent Trade Unions of the Russian Federation (FITUR):** 117119 Moscow, Leninskii pr. 42; tel. (095) 938-73-12; fax (095) 137-06-94; e-mail korneev@fnpr.ru; internet www.fnpr.ru; f. 1990; Gen. Sec. MIKHAIL V. SHMAKOV.

FITUR unites 48 national trade unions and 78 regional orgs (with c. 40m. mems), including the following:

**All-Russian 'Electroprofsoyuz':** 117119 Moscow, Leninskii pr. 42, kor. 3; tel. (095) 938-83-78; fax (095) 930-98-62; f. 1990; electrical workers; Pres. VALERII P. KUZICHEV.

**Automobile and Farm Machinery Construction Industries Workers' Union:** 117119 Moscow, Leninskii pr. 42/3; tel. (095) 938-76-13; fax (095) 938-86-15; Pres. YULII G. NOVIKOV.

**Automobile Transport and Road Workers' Union of the Russian Federation:** 117218 Moscow, ul. Krzhizhanovskogo 20/30/5; tel. (095) 125-23-30; fax (095) 125-07-98; f. 1990; Pres. VIKTOR I. MOKHNACHEV.

**Civil Aviation Workers' Union:** 117218 Moscow, ul. Krzhizhanovskogo 20/30/5; tel. and fax (095) 125-18-39; Pres. BORIS A. KREMNEV.

**Communication Workers' Union of Russia:** 117119 Moscow, Leninskii pr. 42/3; tel. (095) 938-72-06; fax (095) 930-22-86; f. 1905; Pres. ANATOLII G. NAZEIKIN.

**Construction and Building Materials Industry Workers' Union of the Russian Federation:** 117119 Moscow, Leninskii pr. 42/1; tel. (095) 930-71-74; fax (095) 952-55-47; f. 1991; Pres. BORIS A. SOSHENKO.

**Timber Industry Workers' Union of the Russian Federation:** 117119 Moscow, Leninskii pr. 42/1; tel. (095) 938-89-03; fax (095) 137-06-81; Pres. VALERII N. OCHEKUROV.

**Geological, Survey and Cartographical Workers' Union of the Russian Federation:** 117119 Moscow, Leninskii pr. 42/5; tel. (095) 938-87-20; Pres. NIKOLAI K. POPKOV.

**Health Workers' Union of the Russian Federation:** 117119 Moscow, Leninskii pr. 42/3; tel. (095) 938-84-43; fax (095) 938-81-34; e-mail ckprz@online.ru; f. 1990; Chair. MIKHAIL M. KUZMENKO.

**Moscow Federation of Trade Unions:** 121205 Moscow, ul. Novyi Arbat 36; tel. (095) 290-82-62; fax (095) 202-92-70; e-mail mfpmskru@cityline.ru; f. 1990; largest regional branch of FITUR; Chair. MIKHAIL D. NAGAITSEV; 3.2m. mems.

**National Educational and Scientific Workers' Union of the Russian Federation:** 117119 Moscow, Leninskii pr. 42/3; tel. (095) 938-87-77; fax (095) 930-68-15; f. 1990; Pres. VLADIMIR M. YAKOVLEV.

**Oil, Gas and Construction Workers' Union:** 119119 Moscow, Leninskii pr. 42/4; tel. (095) 930-69-74; fax (095) 930-11-24; e-mail rogwu@rogwu.ru; internet www.rogwu.ru; f. 1990; Pres. LEV A. MIRONOV.

**Russian Chemical Industry Workers' Union:** 117119 Moscow, Leninskii pr. 42/ 3; tel. (095) 930-99-18; fax (095) 938-21-55; f. 1990; Pres. BORIS S. POPENKO (acting).

**Russian Fishing Industry Workers' Union:** 117119 Moscow, Leninskii pr. 42/3; tel. (095) 938-77-82; fax (095) 930-77-26; e-mail bfish@fnpr.ru; f. 1991; Pres. YURII V. SHALONIN.

**Russian Independent Trade Union of Coal-industry Workers:** 109004 Moscow, ul. Zemlyanoi val 64/1; tel. (095) 915-28-52; fax (095) 915-01-02; Chair. IVAN I. MOKHNACHUK.

**Russian Radio and Electronics Industry Workers Union:** 109180 Moscow, 1-i Golutvinskii per. 3; tel. (095) 238-08-02; fax (095) 238-17-31; Pres. VALERII YE. MARKOV.

**Russian Textiles and Light Industry Workers' Union:** 117119 Moscow, Leninskii pr. 42/3; tel. (095) 938-78-24; fax (095) 938-84-05; f. 1990; Pres. TATYANA I. SOSNINA.

**Russian Trade Union of Railwaymen and Transport Construction Workers (Rosprofzhel):** 103064 Moscow, ul. Staraya Basmannaya 11; tel. (095) 262-58-73; fax (095) 923-88-31; e-mail iturr@orc.ru; Pres. ANATOLII B. VASILIYEV.

**Russian Union of Aviation Engineering Workers:** Moscow; tel. and fax (095) 938-81-07; f. 1934; Pres. ANATOLII F. BREUSOV.

**Russian Union of Cultural Workers:** 109004 Moscow, ul. Zemlyanoi val 64/1; tel. (095) 915-06-30; fax (095) 915-09-43; Pres. GENNADII P. PAROSHIN.

**Russian Union of Workers in Small and Entrepreneurial Enterprises:** 117119 Moscow, Leninskii pr. 42/1; tel. (095) 930-67-71; fax (095) 938-75-85; Pres. VLADIMIR I. KUZNETSOV.

**Shipbuilding Workers' Union:** 117119 Moscow, Leninskii pr. 42/5; tel. (095) 938-88-72; fax (095) 938-84-74; Pres. VLADIMIR YE. MAKAVCHIK.

**Union of Agro-industrial Workers of the Russian Federation:** 117119 Moscow, Leninskii pr. 42/3; tel. (095) 938-77-35; fax (095) 930-68-27; f. 1919; Pres. ALEKSANDR S. DAVYDOV; 37m. mems.

**Union of Engineering Workers of the Russian Federation:** 127486 Moscow, ul. Deguninskaya 1/2; tel. (095) 487-3507; fax (095) 487-56-37; Pres. YURII S. SPICHENOK.

**Union of Food Industry and Production Co-operative Workers of the Russian Federation:** 117119 Moscow, Leninskii pr. 42/3; tel. (095) 938-75-03; fax (095) 930-10-56; Pres. VALERII K. ZHOVTERIK.

**Union of Security Services Workers of the Russian Federation:** 101000 Moscow-Tsentr, ul. Malaya Lubyanka 5/12; tel. (095) 928-99-76; fax (095) 923-72-36; Pres. YURII N. SIRESHCHIKOV.

**Union of State and Community Service Workers of the Russian Federation:** 117119 Moscow, Leninskii pr. 42/2; tel. (095) 938-74-44; fax (095) 952-56-24; Pres. VLADIMIR P. SAVCHENKO.

**Union of Workers in Enterprises with Foreign Investment of the Russian Federation:** 117119 Moscow, Leninskii pr. 42/1; tel. (095) 938-84-62; fax (095) 938-81-95; Pres. VLADIMIR F. BAZAYEV.

### Independent Trade Unions

**Federation of Air Traffic Controllers' Unions of Russia (FPAR):** 125993 Moscow, Leningradskii pr. 37/472, POB 3; tel. (095) 155-57-01; fax (095) 155-59-17; e-mail postmaster@fatcurus.ru; internet www.fatcurus.ru; f. 1989; Pres. SERGEI A. KOVALEV.

**Metallurgical Industry Workers' Union:** Moscow, ul. Pushkinskaya 5/6; left the FITUR in 1992 to form independent organization; Pres. BORIS MISNIK.

# Transport

## RAILWAYS

In 2000 the total length of railway track in use was 86,660 km, of which 40,800 km were electrified. The railway network is of great importance in the Russian Federation, owing to the poor road system, and the relatively few private vehicles outside the major cities. The Trans-Siberian Railway, the electrification of which began in 1998, provides the main route connecting European Russia with Siberia and the Far East. A new joint-stock company, Russian

Railways, was formed in September 2003 to assume the management of the railways network from the Ministry of Railways; it was anticipated that the Ministry would subsequently be abolished.

**Russian Railways OAO (RZD)** (Rossiiskiye zheleznyye dorogi): 107174 Moscow, ul. Novobasmannaya 2; tel. (095) 262-16-28; fax (095) 975-24-11; e-mail info@rzd.ru; internet www.rzd.ru; f. 2003; Pres. Gennadii Fadayev.

### City Underground Railways

**Moscow Metro:** 129110 Moscow, pr. Mira 41/2; tel. (095) 222-10-01; fax (095) 971-37-44; e-mail info@mosmetro.ru; f. 1935; 11 lines (266 km) with 165 stations; suburban light railway extension scheduled to open in late 2003; Gen. Man. Dmitrii V. Gayev.

**Nizhnii Novgorod Metro:** 603002 Nizhnii Novgorod, pl. Revolutsii 7; tel. (8312) 44-17-60; fax (8312) 44-20-86; e-mail metro@sandy.ru; f. 1985; 15 km with 13 stations; Gen. Man. A. Kuzmin.

**Novosibirsk Metro:** 630099 Novosibirsk, ul. Serebrennikovskaya 34; tel. (3832) 90-81-10; fax (3832) 46-56-82; e-mail nsk@metro.snt.su; internet www.nsk.su/~metro/; f. 1986; 2 lines (13.2 km) with 11 stations, and a further 6 km under construction; Gen. Man. V. I. Demin.

**St Petersburg Metro:** 198013 St Petersburg, Moskovskii pr. 28; tel. (812) 251-66-68; fax (812) 316-14-41; f. 1955; 4 lines (103 km) with 58 stations; Gen. Man. V. A. Garyugin.

Short underground railways began to operate in Samara and Yekaterinburg in 1987 and 1991, respectively. In 2002 construction of underground railways was under way in Chelyabinsk, Kazan, Krasnoyarsk and Omsk.

### ROADS

In 2000 the total length of roads was 532,393 km (45,978 km of highways and 486,415 km of other roads); 67.4% of roads were paved in 1999. In Siberia and the Far East there are few roads, and they are often impassable in winter, while the *rasputitsa*, or spring thaw, notoriously impedes rural road traffic, even in European Russia. In 1999 the World Bank granted Russia a loan of US $400m. to finance the construction and repair of roads in Siberia and the Far East of Russia. A new highway, linking Vladivostok with St Petersburg, was due for completion in 2004. In August 2003 proposals were announced by the Government of Moscow Oblast for the construction of the first toll-motorway in Russia.

### SHIPPING

The seaports of the Russian Federation provide access to the Pacific Ocean, in the east, the Baltic Sea and the Atlantic Ocean, in the west, and the Black Sea, in the south. Major eastern ports are at Vladivostok, Nakhodka, Vostochnyi, Magadan and Petropavlovsk. In the west St Petersburg and Kaliningrad provide access to the Baltic Sea, and the northern ports of Murmansk and Archangel (Arkhangelsk) have access to the Atlantic Ocean, via the Barents Sea. Novorossiisk and Sochi are the principal Russian ports on the Black Sea.

### Principal Shipowning Companies

**Baltic Shipping Co:** 198035 St Petersburg, Mezhevoi kanal 5; tel. (812) 251-33-97; fax (812) 186-85-44; freight and passenger services; Chair. Mikhail A. Romanovskii.

**Baltic Transport Systems:** 199106 St Petersburg, pl. Morskoi Slavy 1; tel. (812) 303-99-14; fax (812) 380-34-76; e-mail bts@baltics.ru; internet www.baltics.ru; f. 1994; freight and passenger services; Gen. Dir Aleksei E. Shukletsov.

**Far Eastern Shipping Co:** 690019 Maritime (Primorskii) Krai, Vladivostok, ul. Aleutskaya 15; tel. (4232) 41-14-32; fax (4232) 52-15-51; e-mail 41401@fesco.ru; internet www.fesco.ru; f. 1880; Gen. Man. Yevgenii N. Ambrosov.

**Kamchatka Shipping Co:** 683600 Kamchatka obl., Petropavlovsk-Kamchatskii, ul. Radiosvyazi 65; tel. (41522) 2-82-21; fax (41522) 2-19-60; f. 1949; freight services; Pres. Nikolai M. Zablotskii.

**Murmansk Shipping Co:** 183038 Murmansk, ul. Kominterna 15; tel. (8152) 48-10-48; fax (8152) 48-11-48; e-mail postmaster@msco.ru; f. 1939; shipping and icebreaking services; Gen. Dir Vyacheslav Ruksha.

**Novorossiisk Shipping Co:** 353900 Krasnodar Krai, Novorossiisk, ul. Svobody 1; tel. (8617) 25-31-26; fax (8617) 25-11-43; e-mail novoship@novoship.ru; internet www.novoship.ru; f. 1992; Chair. V. I. Yakunin.

**NSC Northern Maritime Steamships-Arkhangelsk:** 163000 Archangel, nab. Sev. Dviny 36; tel. (8182) 63-71-06; fax (8182) 65-53-09; e-mail pan@ansc.ru; internet www.ansc.ru; f. 1870; dry cargo shipping, liner services; Gen. Dir Vladimir G. Uroshnikov.

**Primorsk Shipping Corpn:** 692904 Maritime (Primorskii) Krai, Nakhodka, Administrativnyi Gorodok; tel. (4236) 69-45-05; fax (4236) 69-45-75; e-mail psc@prisco.ru; internet www.prisco.ru; f. 1972, tanker shipowner; Dir-Gen. Aleksandr D. Kirilichev.

**Sakhalin Shipping Co:** 694620 Sakhalin obl., Kholmsk, ul. Pobedy 16; tel. (42433) 6-62-07; fax (42433) 6-60-66; Pres. Yakub Zh. Ale-gedpinov.

**Sovfrakht JSC:** 127944 Moscow, Rakhmanovskii per. 4, Morskoi Dom; tel. (095) 258-27-41; fax (095) 230-26-40; e-mail general@sovfracht.ru; internet www.sovfracht.ru; f. 1929; chartering and broking of tanker, cargo and other ships; forwarding and booking agency; ship management; Dir-Gen. A. I. Koltypin; 60 employees.

**White Sea and Onega Shipping Co:** 185005 Kareliya, Petrozavodsk, ul. Rigachina 7; tel. (8142) 71-12-33; fax (8142) 71-12-67; e-mail dir@bpo.onego.ru; f. 1940; cargo shipping, cargo-ship construction and repair; Gen. Dir Nikolai Grachov.

### CIVIL AVIATION

Until 1991 Aeroflot—Soviet Airlines was the only airline operating on domestic routes in the former USSR. In 1992–94 some 300 different independent airlines emerged on the basis of Aeroflot's former regional directorates. Several small private airlines were also established. In 1992 Aeroflot—Soviet Airlines became a joint-stock company, Aeroflot—Russian Airlines. The Government retained 51% of the shares, and company personnel own 49%. A reorganization of Russia's civil aviation industry was proposed in 1998. By 2003 there were 451 airports in Russia, compared with 1,302 in 1992.

**Aeroflot—Russian Airlines:** 125167 Moscow, Leningradskii pr. 37/9; tel. and fax (095) 155-66-43; internet www.aeroflot.ru; f. 1923; 51% state-owned; operates flights to 108 destinations in 54 countries, and to 26 destinations in Russia; Gen. Dir Valerii M. Okulov.

**Bashkir Airlines (BAL):** 450056 Bashkortostan, Ufa, Ufa Airport; tel. (3472) 22-75-12; fax (3472) 23-37-36; e-mail interdep@airbal.ufanet.ru; internet www.bal.ufanet.ru; f. 1933; flights between Ufa and 24 destinations in Russia, and to the countries of the CIS and Turkey; Dir-Gen. Viner V. Shakirov.

**Domodedova Airlines:** 142045 Moscow, Domodedova Airport; tel. (095) 504-03-00; fax (095) 787-86-18; e-mail ak_e3@tch.ru; internet www.dmo.tch.ru; f. 1964; scheduled passenger flights to domestic and CIS destinations; chartered passenger and freight flights to domestic, CIS and international destinations; Gen. Dir Andrei Maslov.

**Pulkovo Airlines:** 196210 St Petersburg, ul. Pilotov 18/4; tel. (812) 324-36-34; fax (812) 104-37-02; internet www.pulkovo.ru; operates regular, direct flights from St Petersburg to 26 destinations in Russia and 10 further destinations in the CIS, as well as destinations in the Middle East; Gen. Dir B. G. Demchenko.

**Sibir Airlines:** 633104 Novosibirsk obl., gorod Ob; tel. (3832) 59-90-11; fax (3832) 59-90-64; e-mail pr@s7.ru; internet www.s7.ru; scheduled and charter flights to domestic, CIS, Asian, European and Middle Eastern destinations; Gen. Dir Vladislav Filev.

**Transaero Airlines:** 121099 Moscow, 2-i Smolenskii per. 3/4; tel. (095) 937-84-77; fax (095) 578-86-88; e-mail info@transaero.ru; internet www.transaero.ru; f. 1991; Russia's largest privately owned airline; operates scheduled and charter passenger services to the CIS, Europe and Central Asia; Chief Exec. Aleksandr Pleshakov.

**Tsentr-Avia:** 140150 Moscow obl., pos. Bykovo, ul. Sovetskaya 19; tel. (095) 558-44-07; fax (095) 501-13-66; e-mail pr@centreavia.ru; internet www.centreavia.ru; f. 1999; flights from Moscow to domestic destinations, and to Austria and Germany.

**Ural Airlines:** 620910 Sverdlovsk obl., Yekaterinburg, ul. Sputnikov 6; tel. and fax (3432) 26-64-16; e-mail sale@uralairlines.ru; internet www.uralairlines.ru; f. 1993; flights from Yekaterinburg to 17 destinations in Russia, and to destinations in the CIS, Europe and the Middle East.

**Vladivostok Avia:** 692800 Maritime (Primorskii) Krai, Artem, ul. Portovaya 41, Vladivostok Airport; tel. (4232) 30-71-46; fax (4232) 30-77-00; e-mail support@vladavia.ru; internet www.vladavia.ru; f. 1994; freight and scheduled passenger services to 10 destinations in Russia, and to the People's Republic of China, Japan and the Republic of Korea; Gen. Dir Vladimir Saibel.

# Tourism

In 2000 there were 21,169,100 tourist arrivals in Russia, and in 1999 receipts from tourism totalled US $7,510m.

**Intourist Holding Co:** 127015 Moscow, ul. Vyatskaya 70; tel. and fax (095) 234-55-49; e-mail intourholding@mtu-net.ru; f. 1992; travel and tourism investment co; owns tour-operating subsidiary; publishing; Gen. Man. SERGEI I. KRUCHEK.

**Intourist:** 101990 Moscow, Milyutinskii per. 13/1; tel. (095) 956-44-99; fax (095) 956-42-02; e-mail info@intourist.ru; internet www .intourist.ru; f. 1929; brs throughout Russia and abroad; Pres. ABBAS ALIYEV.

# Culture

## NATIONAL ORGANIZATIONS

**Ministry of Culture:** see section on The Government (Ministries).

**Council for Culture and Arts:** Office of the President, 103073 Moscow, Kremlin; f. 2001 to promote the discussion of cultural affairs.

**Russian Association for International Co-operation** (Rossiiskaya assotsiatsiya mezhdunarodnogo sotrudnichestva): 121009 Moscow, ul. Vozdvizhenka 14; tel. (095) 203-03-72; fax (095) 200-12-20; f. 1992; unites more than 80 societies of cultural relations with foreign countries; Pres. VALENTINA V. TERESHKOVA.

**Russian Cultural Foundation** (Rossiiskii fond kultury): 121019 Moscow, 6/7/1 Gogolevskii bul.; tel. (095) 202-69-84; fax (095) 291-71-80; e-mail info@culture.ru; internet www.culture.ru; f. 1986 as Cultural Foundation of the USSR; encourages interest in, and study of, cultural heritage at Russian and abroad, especially architecture, literature, music and education.

## CULTURAL HERITAGE

### Moscow

**All-Russian Museum of Decorative, Applied and Folk Art** (Vserossiiskii muzei dekorativno-prikladnogo i narodnogo iskusstva): 127473 Moscow, ul. Delegatskaya 3; tel. (095) 923-77-25; fax (095) 923-06-20; e-mail m276@mail.museum.ru; internet www .museum.ru/M276; f. 1981; decorative art from the 16th to the late 20th centuries; Dir VLADIMIR A. GULYAYEV.

**S. T. Morozov Folk-Art Museum** (Narodnogo isskusstva muzei im. S. T. Morozova): 103009 Moscow, Leontyevskii per. 7; tel. (095) 290-21-14; e-mail rosizo@sovintel.ru; f. 1885; handicrafts connected with peasant life, applied arts, and experimental decorative applied art; about 800,000 exhibits; Dir G. A. YAKOVLEVA.

**Central A. A. Bakhrushin State Theatrical Museum** (Gosudarstvennyi tsentralnyi teatralnyi muzei im. A. A. Bakhrushina): 113054 Moscow, ul. Bakhrushina 31/12; tel. (095) 953-48-70; fax (095) 953-54-48; e-mail gctm@ncport.ru; internet www.gertstein .org/bakhrushin/index.htm; f. 1894; materials on history and theory of theatre, including archives of original MSS of Ostrovskii, Stanislavskii, etc; 1.3m. exhibits; library of 120,000 vols; Dir VALERII V. GUBIN.

**Central M. I. Glinka State Museum of Musical Culture** (Muzikalnoi kultury gosudarstvennyi tsentralnty muzei im. M. I. Glinki): 125047 Moscow, ul. Fadeyeva 4; tel. (095) 972-32-37; fax (095) 972-32-55; e-mail glinka@cityline.ru; internet www.museum.ru/glinka; f. 1943; 800,000 items, including archives, manuscripts and memorabilia, musical instruments, records and tape recordings, etc.; Dir ANATOLII D. PANYUSHKIN.

**Central S. V. Obraztsov State Puppet Theatre Museum** (Muzei teatralnykh kukol muzei GATsTK im. S. V. Obraztsova): 103473 Moscow, ul. Sadovo-Samotechnaya 3; tel. and fax (095) 299-89-10; e-mail gactk@mail.ru; internet www.puppet.ru/museum; f. 1937; 3,500 puppets from 60 countries; library of 15,000 vols; Dir Dr BORIS P. GOLDOVSKII.

**Central Andrei Rublev Museum of Ancient Russian Art and Culture** (Drevnerusskoi kulturi i iskusstva tsentralnyi muzei im. Andreya Rubleva): 107120 Moscow, Andronyevskaya pl. 10; tel. (095) 278-14-89; fax (095) 278-50-55; e-mail rublevmu@aha.ru; f. 1947; collection of Russian icons dating from 14th to 19th Centuries, located in former Spaso-Andronikov Monastery; library of 23,000 vols; Dir GENNADII V. POPOV.

**Matryoshka Museum** (Muzei matreshki): 103009 Moscow, Leontyevskii per. 7; e-mail streltsof@mtu-net.ru; internet www .russiandolls.narod.ru; f. 2001.

**Moscow Kremlin State Historic-Cultural Museum-Reserve** (Gosudarstvennyi istoriko-kulturnyi muzei-zapovednik 'Moskovskii kreml'): 103073 Moscow, Kremlin; tel. (095) 924-55-03; fax (095) 921-63-23; e-mail head@kremlin.museum.ru; internet www.kreml.ru; includes the Armoury (f. 1857; 100,000 items; weapons, arms and jewels from the 12th century to 1917) and the Kremlin Cathedrals (including Cathedral of the Assumption—f. 1479, icons of the 14th–

17th centuries, throne of Ivan the Terrible); Dir YELENA YU. GAGARINA.

**Russian State Arts Library** (Rossiiskaya gosudarstvennaya biblioteka po iskusstvu): 103031 Moscow, ul. B. Dmitrovka 8/1; tel. (095) 292-06-9253; fax (095) 292-06-53; e-mail bisk@liart.ru; internet www.liart.ru; f. 1922; over 1.7m. items (books, periodicals, press cuttings, engravings, sketches, postcards, photographs, posters); Dir ADA A. KOLGANOVA.

**Russian State Library** (Rossiiskaya gosudarstvennaya biblioteka): 10100 Moscow, ul. Vozdvizhenka. 3/5; tel. (095) 202-35-65; fax (095) 913-69-33; e-mail mbs@rsl.ru; internet www.rsl.ru; f. 1852 as the Rumyantsev Library, reorganized 1925; fmrly Lenin State Library of the USSR; 42.7m. books, periodicals and serials, newspapers in all 91 languages of the former USSR and 156 foreign languages, 480,600 manuscripts, 860 archival collections, etc.; Dir VIKTOR V. FEDOROV.

**A. V. Shchusev State Scientific-Research Museum of Architecture (MUAR)** (Gosudarstvennyi naucho-issledovatelskii muzei arkhitektury im. A. V. Shchuseva): 121019 Moscow, UL. Vozdvizhenka 5/25; tel. and fax (095) 291-21-09; e-mail schusev@muar.ru; internet /www.muar.ru; f. 1934; exhibitions and research in the field of architectural history; over 70,000 sheets of architectural drawings and prints; over 300,000 negatives and 400,000 photographs of architectural monuments; architectural materials; painting, sculpture, furniture and clothing from the 16th to the 21st centuries; library of 50,000 vols; Dir DAVID A. SARKISYAN.

**State Archives of the Russian Federation** (Gosudarstvennyi arkhiv Rossiiskoi Federatsii): 119817 Moscow, ul. B. Pirogovskaya 17; fax (095) 245-12-87; e-mail garf@online.ru; internet garf.narod .ru; f. 1920; more than 5.5m. items; Dir SERGEI V. MIRONENKO.

**State Historical Museum** (Gosudarstvennyi istoricheskii muzei): 103012 Moscow, Krasnaya pl. 1/2; tel. (095) 924-45-29; fax (095) 925-95-27; e-mail shkurko@shm.ru; internet www.shm.ru; f. 1872; 4.5m. exhibits on Russian history; library of 100,000 vols, 29,000 manuscripts, collection of birch-bark writings; 7 branch museums; Dir-Gen. ALEKSANDR I. SHKURKO.

**Novodevichii Convent Museum** (Muzei 'Novodevichii monastyr'): 119435 Moscow, Novodevichii proyezd 1; tel. (095) 246-22-01; fax (095) 246-85-26; e-mail m337@mail.museum.ru; internet www.shm.ru/filials/novodev/fil_nov.htm; Russian fine and decorative art of the 16th and 17th centuries, situated in a late 17th-century convent including the Smolensk Cathedral (1624), converted into a museum in 1922; Dir IRINA G. BORISENKO.

**State Literature Museum** (Gosudarstvennyi literaturnyi muzei): 103051 Moscow, ul. Petrovka 28; tel. (095) 921-38-57; fax (095) 923-30-22; e-mail litmuz@orc.ru; internet www.museum.ru/M289; f. 1934; library of 250,000 vols; 11 branch museums; Dir NATALIYA V. SHAKHALOVA.

**State Museum of Ceramics and the 18th Century Kuskovo Estate** (Gosudarstvennyi muzei keramiki i usadba Kuskovo XVIII veka): 111402 Moscow, ul. Yunosti. 2; tel. (095) 370-01-50; fax (095) 918-65-40; e-mail kuskovo@kuskovo.ru; internet www.kuskovo.ru; large collection of Russian and foreign art, ceramics and glass, located in fmr country residence of the Counts Sheremetevo; Dir YELENA S. YERITSYAN.

**State Museum of Oriental Art** (Gosudarstvennyi muzei iskusstva narodov vostoka): 1190190 Moscow, Nikitskii bulv. 12A; tel. (095) 291-03-41; fax (095) 202-48-46; e-mail info@orientalart.ru; internet www.orientalart.ru; f. 1918; large collection of art of the Middle and Far East, and of the fmr Soviet Central Asian Republics and Transcaucasia, carpets, fabrics, ceramics; Dir-Gen. VLADIMIR A. NABATCHIKOV.

**State A. S. Pushkin Museum of Fine Arts** (Gosudarstvennyi muzei izobrazitelnykh iskusstv im. A. S. Pushkina): 121019 Moscow, ul. Volkhonka 12; tel. (095) 203-95-78; fax (095) 203-46-74; e-mail finearts@gmii.museum.ru; internet www.museum.ru/gmii; f. 1912; some 558,000 items of ancient Eastern, Graeco-Roman, Byzantine, European and American art; library of 200,000 vols; Dir IRINA A. ANTONOVA.

**State L. N. Tolstoi Museum** (Gosudarstvennyi muzei L. N. Tolstogo): 119034 Moscow, ul. Prechistenka 11; tel. (095) 202-93-38; fax (095) 201-58-11; e-mail m299@museum.ru; internet www.museum .ru/M299; f. 1911; contains 170,000 sheets of Tolstoi's writings and some 600,000 manuscripts and archive material; library of 76.000 works by or about Lev Tolstoi; some 87,000 newspaper cuttings, and over 42,000 exhibits in the form of painting, sculpture, photographs, etc; Dir VITALII B. REMIZOV.

**State Tretyakov Gallery** (Gosudarstvennaya Tretyakovskaya Galereya): 109017 Moscow, Lavrushinskii per. 10; tel. (095) 230-77-88; fax (095) 231-10-51; e-mail tretyakov@tretyakov.ru; internet www.tretyakov.ru; f. 1856; collection of 40,000 Russian icons and works of Russian and Soviet painters, sculptors and graphic artists; 7 branch museums; Dir VALENTIN A. RODIONOV.

### St Petersburg

**All-Russian A. S. Pushkin Museum** (Vserossiiskii muzei A. S. Pushkina): 191186 St Petersburg, nab. Moiki 12; tel. (812) 311-38-01; e-mail vmp@mail.admiral.ru; internet www.museumpushkin .ru; f. 1879; 200,000 exhibits illustrating the life and work of Pushkin and his epoch; Dir S. M. NEKRASOV; 4 brs in St Petersburg and 2 brs in Tsarskoye Selo (fmrly Pushkin, Leningrad Oblast).

**Central Music Library, attached to the Mariinskii Theatre** (Tsentralnaya muzykalnaya biblioteka Mariinskogo teatra): 191000 St Petersburg, ul. Zodchego Rossi 2; tel. (812) 312-35-73; fax (812) 314-17-44; e-mail cml@mariinsky.ru; contains one of the largest collections in the world of Russian music; Dir MARIYA N. SHCHERBA-KOVA.

**F. M. Dostoyevskii Literary-Memorial Museum** (Literaturno-memorialnyi muzei F. M. Dostoyevskogo): 191002 St Petersburg, Kuznechnyi per. 5/2; tel. (812) 311-40-31; e-mail museum@md.spb .ru; internet www.md.spb.ru; f. 1971; fmr residence of author F. M. Dostoyevskii in 1878–81; manuscripts, documentary material; library of 23,000 vols; Dir NATALIYA I. ASHIMBAYEVA.

**Literary Museum of the Institute of Russian Literature—Pushkin House** (Literaturnyi muzei instituta russkoi literatury—Pushkinskii dom): 199034 St Petersburg, nab. Makarova 4; tel. (812) 328-19-01; fax (812) 328-11-40; e-mail irliran@mail.ru; internet www.pushkinhouse.spb.ru; 95,000 exhibits and over 120,000 items of reference material on 18th–20th-century Russian classical literature; based on the material of the Pushkin Anniversary Exhibition of 1899; seven halls containing permanent exhibitions devoted to Radishchev, Lermontov, Gogol, Dostoevskii, I. S. Turgenev, and other Russian writers; Dir TATYANA A. KOMAROVA.

**Peter the Great Museum of Anthropology and Ethnography (Kunstkamera)** (Muzei antropologii i etnografii im. Petra Velikogo): 199034 St Petersburg, Universitetskaya nab. 3; tel. (812) 328-14-12; fax (812) 328-08-11; e-mail info@kunstkamera.ru; internet www.kunstkamera.ru; f. 1714; attached to Russian Acad. of Sciences; 900,000 items of ethnographical, archaeological and anthropological material on the native peoples of Africa, North and South America, Australasia, the Middle East, Central and Eastern Asia, Russia and Europe; Dir Prof. Dr YURII K. CHISTOV.

**Peterhof (Petrodvorets) State Museum Reserve** (Gosudarstvennyi muzei-zapovednik Petergof—Petrodvorets): 198516 St Petersburg, Petrodvorets, ul. Razvodnaya 2; tel. (812) 427-74-25; fax (812) 427-93-30; e-mail admin@peterhof.org; internet www.peterhof .org; f. 1918; 18th–20th century architecture, paintings and landscape gardening, library of 21,000 vols; Dir VADIM V. ZNAMENOV.

**Russian Ethnographical Museum** (Rossiiskii etnograficheskii muzei): 191011 St Petersburg, ul. Inzhenernaya 4/1; tel. (812) 210-47-68; fax (812) 315-85-02; e-mail rme@infopro.spb.ru; internet www .ethnomuseum.ru; f. 1992; 600,000 exhibits; 150,000 photographs; library of 112,000 vols; Dir VLADIMIR M. GRUSMAN.

**St Petersburg State Museum of Theatre and Music** (Sankt-Peterburgskii Gosudarstvennyi musei teatralnogo i muzykalnogo iskusstva): 191011 St Petersburg, pl. Ostrovskogo 6; tel. (812) 315-52-43; fax (812) 31477-46; e-mail theatre@museums.org.ru; internet www.theatremuseum.ru; f. 1918; over 440,000 exhibits depicting the history of Russian ,Soviet and foreign theatre; library of 5,000 vols; 4 brs; Dir IRINA V. YEVSTIGNEYEVA.

**State Anna Akhmatova Literary-Memorial Museum in Fountain House** (Literaturno-memorialnyi muzei Anny Akhmatovoi v Fontannom Dome): 191104 St Petersburg, nab. reky Fontanki 34; tel. (812) 272-22-11; fax (812) 272-20-34; e-mail all@anna-museum .spb.ru; internet www.akhmatova.spb.ru/ru/; f. 1989; former residence of the poet Anna Akhmatova in 1925–52; manuscripts and documentary material relating to the literary life of Leningrad under Stalin (Iosif V. Dzhugashvili) in 1924–53; 46,300 exhibits; Dir NINA I. POPOVA.

**State Hermitage Museum** (Gosudarstvennyi Ermitazh): 190000 St Petersburg, Dvortsovaya nab. 34; tel. (812) 110-34-20; e-mail chancery@hermitage.ru; internet www.hermitagemuseum.org; f. 1764 as a court museum, opened to the public in 1852; richest collection in the fmr USSR of the art of prehistoric, ancient Eastern, Graeco-Roman and medieval times; also has a large Western European collection; Dir MIKHAIL B. PIOTROVSKII.

**State Russian Museum** (Gosudarstvennyi Russkii Muzei): 191011 St Petersburg, ul. Inzhenernaya 2; tel. (812) 318-46-91; e-mail info@ rusmuseum.ru; internet www.rusmuseum.ru; f. 1895; over 400,000 exhibits of Russian and Soviet art, ranging from icons to the avant-garde; 5 brs; Dir VLADIMIR A. GUSEV.

**Summer Garden (Letnii sad) and Summer Palace-Museum of Peter the Great** (Letnii sad i Letnii dvorets-muzei Petra I): 191041

St Petersburg, Letnii Sad, nab. Kutuzova 2; tel. (812) 312-77-15; fax (812) 312-96-66; e-mail m126@mail.museum.ru; f. 1934; 18th-century architecture and sculpture; Dir TATYANA D. KOZLOVA.

### Other Regions

**Mordovian Republic S. D. Erzi Museum of Fine Arts** (Mordovskii respublikanskii muzei izobrazitelnykh iskusstv im. S. D. Erzi): 430000 Mordoviya, Saransk, ul. Kommunisticheskaya 61; tel. (8342) 17-56-38; fax (8342) 17-56-38; e-mail m1451@mail.museum.ru; internet www.museum.ru/M1451; f. 1960; 8,977 exhibits; painting, sculpture, prints, decorative arts; library of 10,000 vols; Dir MARGARITA N. BARANOVA.

**National Museum of the Republic of Tatarstan** (Natsionalnyi muzei Respubliki Tatarstana): 420111 Tatarstan, Kazan, ul. Kremlevskaya 2; tel. (8432) 92-71-62; fax (8432) 92-14-84; e-mail tatar_museum@mail.ru; internet www.tatar.museum.ru; f. 1895; fmrly State United Museum of the Republic of Tatarstan; history, archaeology, ethnography, natural resources and decorative applied art of Tatarstan, Russia and other countries; over 500,000 exhibits; library of 12,000 vols; 6 brs in Kazan; Dir-Gen. GENNADII S. MUKHANOV.

**North Osetiyan K. L. Khetagurov Memorial Museum** (Khudozhestvennyi muzei im. M. S. Tuganova): 362040 North Osetiya–Alaniya, Vladikavkaz, ul. Butyrina 19; tel. (8672) 53-62-22; collection of materials on Caucasian poetry and literature; Dir E. A. KESAYEVA.

**Novocherkassk Museum of the History of the Don Cossacks** (Muzei istorii Donskogo kasachestva): 346430 Rostov obl., Novocherkassk, ul. Atamanskaya 38; tel. (86352) 2-84-70; e-mail m838@mail .museum.ru; internet www.museum.ru/M838; f. 1899; collections of porcelain and painting; library of 17,000 vols; Dir SVETLANA A. SEDINKO.

**'Perm-36' Memorial Centre of the History of Political Repressions** (Memorialnyi tsentr istorii politicheskii repressii 'Perm-36'): 614000 Perm, ul. Siberskaya 17A/36, Muzei 'Perm-36'; tel. (3422) 12-00-30; fax (3422) 12-37-18; e-mail muzeum@permnet.ru; internet www.perm36.ru; f. 1992; museum on site of fmr corrective labour camp for political prisoners; seeks to record the abuses of the oppressions undertaken during the USSR, particularly during the Stalin and Brezhnev eras, the workings of the GULAG system, and to provide a memorial to the victims thereof; Dir VIKTOR SHMYROV.

**Sergiyev Posad State Historical-Artistic Museum-Reserve** (Sergiyevo-Posadskii Gosudarstvennyi Istoricho-khudozhestvennyi Muzei-zapovednik): 141300 Moscow obl., Sergiyev Posad, pr. Krasnoi Armii 144; tel. and fax (9654) 4-13-58; e-mail sergiev@divo .ru; internet www.musobl.divo.ru; f. 1920; 120,000 items dealing with the development of Russian art and religion (particularly tapestries and liturgical art) from the 14th century to the present; in monastery founded in 1340, including Troitskii (Trinity) Cathedral (15th century) and the Uspenskii (Dormition) Cathedral (16th century); library of 17,000 vols; Dir FELIKS KH. MAKOYEV.

**S. Stalskii Literary Memorial Museum** (Literaturno-memorialnyi dom muzei Suleimana Stalskogo): 368765 Dagestan, Suleiman-Stalskii raion, selo Ashaga-stalsk; tel. (87200) 7-53-85; e-mail m1802@museum.ru; internet www.museum.ru/M1802; f. 1950; exhibits on the history of the literature of the peoples of Dagestan, in fmr home (1934–37) of poet Suleiman Stalskii; library of 20,000 vols; Dir LIDIYA M. STALSKAYA.

**State Artistic-Architectural Palace and Park Museum-Reserve of Pavlovsk** (Gosudarstvennyi khudozhestvenno-arkhitekturnyi dvortsovo-parkovyi muzei-zapovednik 'Pavlosk': 196621 Leningrad obl., Pavlovsk, ul. Revolyutsii 20; tel. (812) 470-21-55; fax (812) 465-11-04; e-mail pavlovsk@mail.ru; internet www .pavlovskart.spb.ru; f. 1918; many examples of Russian garden architecture; sculpture by 18th-century Italian and French masters; European paintings of the 16th–19th centuries; Russian portraits of the 18th century; Russian decorative art of the 18th and 19th centuries; furniture, porcelain, bronzes and textiles; library of 17,000 vols; Dir NIKOLAI S. TRETYAKOV.

**State Artistic-Architectural Palace and Park Museum-Reserve of Tsarskoye Selo** (Gosudarstvennyi muzei-zapovednik Tsarskoye Selo): 189690 Leningrad obl., Tsarskoye Selo, ul. Sadovaya 7; tel. (812) 466-66-69; fax (812) 465-21-96; e-mail tzar@cityline .spb.ru; internet www.tzar.ru; f. 1918; Russian garden architecture, sculpture by Italian and French masters of the 18th and 19th centuries; palace of Catherine (Yekaterina) II ('the Great'), collection of the costumes of the Imperial Family; library of 6,800 vols; Dir. IVAN P. SAUTOV.

**State Museum of Palekh Art** (Gosudarstvennyi muzei palekhskogo iskusstva): 155620 Ivanovo obl., Palekh, ul. Bakanova 50; tel. (9334) 2-20-54; fax (9334) 2-26-41; e-mail m1571@mail.museum.ru; internet www.museum.ru/M1571; more than 6,000 items of Palekh art, including more than 2,000 miniature varnished Palekh boxes, and also icons and manuscripts; Dir ALEVTINA G. STRAKHOVA.

**State Union of the Museums of the Artistic Culture of the Russian North** (Gosudarstvennoye muzeinoye obyedineniye 'Khudozhestvennaya kultura Russkogo Severa'): 163061 Archangel, pl. Lenina 2; tel. (818) 3-26-73; e-mail m1444@mail.museum.ru; internet www.museum.ru/M1444; incorporates Archangel Oblast Museum of Fine Arts (f. 1737); 150,000 items featuring the history of the north-coast area of Russia, dating back to ancient times; library of 30,000 vols; Dir MAIYA V. MITKEVICH.

**Yaroslavl State Historical, Architectural and Art Museum-Reserve** (Yaroslavskii gosudarstvennyi istoriko-arkhitekturnyi muzei-zapovednik): 150000 Yaroslavl, pl. Bogoyavlenskaya pl. 25; tel. (0852) 30-56-30; fax (0852) 30-57-55; e-mail mp@yarmp.yar.ru; internet www.yarmp.yar.ru; f. 1865; over 370,000 exhibits on the history of the Russian people from ancient times to the present; library of 42,000 vols; Dir YELENA A. ANKUDINOVA.

**Yasnaya Polyana—State Memorial and Natural Reserve-Museum and Estate of L. N. Tolstoi** (Yasnaya Polyana—Gosudarstvennyi memorialnyi i prirodnyi zapovednik muzei-usadba L. N. Tolstogo): 301214 Tula obl., Shchekinskii raion, Yasnaya Polyana; tel. and fax (0872) 38-67-10; e-mail yaspol@tula.net; internet www.yasnayapolyana.ru; f. 1921; former house and estate of the author Lev N. Tolstoi; literary museum, estate with park grounds and forest; Dir VLADIMIR I. TOLSTOI.

## SPORTING ORGANIZATIONS

**'Rossiya' (Russia) Trade Unions' Physical Culture and Sports Society** (Fizkulturno-sportivnoye obshchestvo profsoyuzov 'Rossiya'): 109004 Moscow, ul. Vorontsovskaya 6/1; tel. and fax (095) 911-73-37; f. 1991; principal organization for professional and amateur participants in sports in Russia; unites 64 regional societies and 32,000 teams and clubs (Jan. 2002); supported by Federation of Independent Trade Unions of the Russian Federation; owns 50,200 sporting establishments including 30,100 sports fields, 7,920 sports halls, 2,980 sports-health clubs, 1,795 ski centres, 1,190 shooting ranges, 1,046 stadiums, 798 swimming pools (Jan. 2002); owns 517 youth sports schools, employing 6,980 coaches and catering for some 250,000 children and youths; Pres. of Central Council GENNADII N. SHIBAYEV.

**Russian Olympic Committee** (Olimpiiskii komitet Rossii): 119270 Moscow, Luzhnetskaya nab. 8; tel. (095) 248-00-44; fax (095) 248-23-09; e-mail pr@olympic.ru; internet www.roc.ru; f. 1989; Pres. LEONID V. TYAGACHEV; Gen. Sec. LEONID A. MIROSHNICHENKO.

**Russian Paralympic Committee** (Paralimpiiskii komitet Rossii): 119415 Moscow, ul. Udaltsova 11; tel. (095) 935-00-64; fax (095) 936-13-00; e-mail id.voi@relkom.ru; public, non-profit organization, associated with the All-Russian Society of Invalids (q.v.); Pres. VLADIMIR LUKIN; Gen. Sec. FLYUR NURLYGAYANOV.

**State Committee for Exercise and Sport** (Goskomsport): 103064 Moscow, ul. Kazakova 18; tel. (095) 263-08-40; fax (095) 263-07-61; e-mail info@goskomsport.ru; internet www.goskomsport.ru; Chair. VYACHESLAV A. FETISOV.

## PERFORMING ARTS

**Helikon Opera State Musical Theatre** (Gelikon Opera gosudarstvennyi muzykalnyi teatr): 125009 Moscow, ul. B. Nikitskaya 19; tel. (095) 290-09-71; fax (095) 291-13-23; e-mail helikon@helikon.ru; internet www.helikon.ru; f. 1990; traditional and avant-garde productions of classical operas; Dir DMITRII BERTMAN.

**International A. P. Chekhov Theatre Festival** (Mezhdunarodnyi teatralnyi festival im. A. P. Chekhov): 103009 Moscow, Leontievskii per. 21/1; tel. (095) 929-70-27; fax (095) 742-09-33; e-mail olympic@cf.mos.ru; internet www.chekhovfest.ru; f. 1992; Dir-Gen. VALERII SHADRIN.

**Lenkom Moscow State Theatre** (Lenkom Moskovskii gosudarstvennyi teatr): 103006 Moscow, ul. M. Dmitrovka 6; tel. (095) 299-12-61; e-mail nimfa@lenkom.ru; internet www.lenkom.ru; f. 1927 as Moscow Young Workers' Theatre; Artistic Dir MARK A. ZAKHAROV.

**Malyi Drama Theatre—Theatre de l'Europe (St Petersburg) (MDT)** (Malyi dramaticheskii teatr—teatr yevropy): 191002 St Petersburg, ul. Rubinshteina 18; tel. (812) 113-20-15; fax (812) 113-33-66; e-mail levdodin@mdt.sp.ru; internet www.mdt-dodin.ru; Artistic Dir LEV A. DODIN.

**Mariinskii Theatre:** 190000 St Petersburg, Teatralnaya pl. 1; tel. (812) 114-12-11; fax (812) 314-17-44; e-mail post@mariinsky.ru; internet www.mariinsky.ru; f. 1874; fmrly Kirov Theatre; ballet, opera, orchestral music; also organizes the arts festival, *Stars of the White Nights* (Zvezdy Belykh Nochei) annually, usually in May–June, in and around St Petersburg; Artistic Dir VALERII A. GERGIYEV.

**Moscow A. P. Chekhov Art and Academic Theatre (MKhAT im. Chekhova)** (Moskovskii khudozhestvennii akademicheskii teatr im. A. P. Chekhova): 103009 Moscow, Kamergerskii per. 3; tel. (095) 229-67-48; fax (095) 975-21-96; e-mail mxat@theatre.ru; internet www.mxat.ru; f. 1897; Dir MARIYA YE. REVYAKINA; Artistic Dir OLEG P. TABAKOV.

**Moscow V. Mayakovskii Academic Theatre** (Moskovskii akademicheskii teatr im. Vl. Mayakovskogo): 103009 Moscow, ul. B. Nikitskaya 19; tel. (095) 290-27-25; e-mail mayak_teatr@mail.ru; internet www.mayakovsky.ru; f. 1922; Dir MIKHAIL P. ZAITSEV; Artistic Dir SERGEI N. ARTSIBASHEV.

**Moscow Taganka Comedy and Drama Theatre** (Moskovskii teatr dramy i komedii na Taganke): 109004 Moscow, ul. Zemlyanoi val 76/21; tel. and fax (095) 915-11-48; e-mail taganka@krls.ru; internet www.taganka.org; f. 1964; Dir YURII LYUBIMOV.

**Rudolph Nuriyev International Festival of Classical Ballet** (Mezhdunarodnyi festival klassicheskogo baleta im. Rudolfa Nuriyeva): 420015 Tatarstan, Kazan, pl. Svobody, Tatar Musa Dzhalil Academic Theatre of Opera and Ballet; tel. (8432) 38-45-58; f. 1987; held annually, in May.

**Sovremennik (Contemporary) Moscow Theatre** (Moskovskii teatr 'Sovremennik'): 101000 Moscow, Chistoprudnyi bulv. 19a; tel. (095) 921-17-90; fax (095) 921-66-29; e-mail teatr@sovremennik.ru; internet www.sovremennik.ru; f. 1956; Artistic Dir GALINA VOLCHEK.

**State Academic Bolshoi Theatre** (Gosudarstvennyi akademicheskii Bolshoi teatr): 103009 Moscow, Teatralnaya pl. 1; tel. (095) 292-08-18; fax (095) 292-33-67; e-mail pr@bolshoi.ru; internet www.bolshoi.ru; f. 1776; opera and ballet company; Dir-Gen. ANATOLII IKSANOV.

**State Academic Malyi Drama Theatre (Moscow)** (Gosudarstvennyi akademicheskii Malyi teatr): 103009 Moscow, Teatralnaya pl. 1/6; tel. (095) 925-98-68; fax (095) 921-03-50; e-mail theatre@maly.ru; internet www.maly.ru; f. 1824; Artistic Dir YURII M. SOLOMIN; Dir VIKTOR I. KORSHUNOV.

**P. I. Tchaikovsky Moscow State Conservatoire** (Moskovskaya Gosudarstvennaya Konservatoriya im. P. I. Chaikovskogo): 125009 Moscow, ul. B. Nikitskaya 13; tel. (095) 229-20-60; fax (095) 290-22-73; e-mail economy@mosconsv.ru; internet www.mosconsv.ru; Rector ALEKSANDR S. SOKOLOV; Artistic Dirs BORIS TEVLIN, VLADIMIR TARNOPOLSKII.

**Yugo-Zapandnyi (South-Western) Studio-Theatre:** 117526 Moscow, pr. Vernadskogo 125; tel. (095) 433-11-91; internet www.teatr-uz.ru; f. 1977; Dir VALERII R. BELYAKOVICH.

## ASSOCIATIONS

**All-Russia Music Society (VMO)** (Vserossiiskoye Muzykalnoye Obshchestvo): 103009 Moscow, M. Kislovskii per. 9; tel. (095) 290-40-54; fax (095) 290-56-49; internet www.vmo.ru; f. 1859; promotes music throughout Russia, especially among young people; organizes competitions, festivals, etc.; supports music groups; Chair. Prof. NIKOLAI KALININ.

**International Arts Fund** (Mezhdunarodnyi khudozhestvennyi fond): 119034 Moscow, B. Levshinskii per. 8/1; tel. (095) 202-74-77; fax (095) 201-52-55; e-mail mail@artfund.ru; internet www.artfund.ru; f. 1992; 10 regional brs; Pres. ROMAN N. VASILYEV; Dir-Gen. LARISA A. KOMAROVA.

**International Organization of Writers—Russian PEN Centre** (Russkii PEN-Tsentr): 103031 Moscow, ul. Neglinnaya 18/1/2; tel. (095) 209-45-89; fax (095) 200-02-93; e-mail penrus@aha.ru; internet www.penrussia.org; f. 1989; defends the rights of authors; Pres. ANDREI BITOV; Gen. Sec. ALEKSANDR TKACHENKO; 226 mems (2002).

**Russian Union of Composers** (Soyuz kompozitorov Rossii): 103878 Moscow, Bryusov per. 8/10/2; tel. and fax (095) 229-52-18; f. 1960; Chair. VLADISLAV I. KAZENIN; 1,450 mems.

> **Musical Foundation of the Russian Federation:** 103006 Moscow, ul. Sadovaya-Triumfalnaya 14/12; tel. (095) 200-19-14.

> **St Petersburg Cultural Foundation:** 191011 St Petersburg, Nevskii pr. 31; tel. (812) 311-83-49; fax (812) 315-17-01.

**Theatre Union of the Russian Federation** (Soyuz teatralnykh deyatelei RF): 103031 Moscow, Strastnoi bulv. 10; tel. (095) 209-28-46; fax (095) 230-22-58; e-mail std@theatre.ru; internet std.theatre.ru; f. 1986 to replace All-Russian Theatrical Society; 76 regional orgs; library of 500,000 vols; Chair. ALEKSANDR A. KALYAGIN; 24,000 mems.

> **Theatrical Foundation of the Russian Federation (TEA-FOND):** 103031 Moscow, Strastnoi bulv. 10; tel. (095) 200-13-56; e-mail stdrf@rc.ru; internet www.museum.ru/stdrf/tfstdrf.htm; f. 1973.

**Union of Architects of Russia** (Soyuz arkhitektorov Rossii): 103001 Moscow, Granatnyi per. 22; tel. (095) 291-55-78; fax (095)

202-81-01; e-mail sarrus@rambler.ru; internet www.uar.ru; f. 1932; public, non-commercial organization; Pres. YURII P. GNEDOVSKII; 12,000 mems.

**Union of Artists of Russia** (Soyuz khdozhnikov Rossii): 103062 Moscow, ul. Pokrovka 37; tel. (095) 917-56-52; fax (095) 917-40-89; Chair. VALENTIN M. SIDOROV.

**Union of Film-makers of the Russian Federation** (Soyuz kinematografistgov Rossiiskoi Federatsii): 123056 Moscow, ul. Vasilyevskaya 13; tel. (095) 251-53-70; internet www.unikino.ru; f. 1990; 51 regional brs; Chair. NIKITA S. MIKHALKOV.

**Union of Writers of Russia:** 119087 Moscow, Komsomolskii pr. 13; tel. (095) 246-43-50; internet www.voskres.ru/sp; Chair. YURII BONDAREV.

**United Nations Educational, Scientific and Cultural Organization (UNESCO)—Moscow Office:** 119034 Moscow, B. Levshinskii per. 15/28/2; tel. (095) 202-80-97; fax (095) 202-05-68; e-mail moscow@unesco.ru; internet www.unesco.ru; responsible for the work of UNESCO in Azerbaijan, Armenia, Belarus, Georgia, the Republic of Moldova and the Russian Federation; Dir PHILIPPE QUÉAU.

**Znaniye (Knowledge) Society of Russia** (Obshchestvo ZNANIYE Rossii): 101990 Moscow, Novaya pl. 3/4/4; tel. (095) 921-90-58; fax (095) 925-42-49; e-mail znanie@znanie.org; internet www.znanie.org; f. 1947; independent public educational organization; Pres. GURII I. MARCHUK.

# Education

Education in the Russian Federation is compulsory for nine years, to be undertaken between the ages of six and 15 years. State primary and secondary education is generally provided free of charge, although in 1992 some higher education establishments began charging tuition fees. Primary education usually begins at seven years of age and lasts for three years, but some pupils begin at the age of six and have one additional year of primary schooling. Secondary education, beginning at 10 years of age, lasts for seven years, comprising a first cycle of five years and a second of two years. In 1997 the total enrolment at primary schools was equivalent to 99.9% of the school-age population; secondary enrolment in that year was equivalent to 87.6%.

Following the disintegration of the USSR, there were extensive changes to the curriculum, with particular emphasis on changes in the approach to Soviet history, and the introduction of the study of literary works that had previously been banned. At this time a number of private schools and colleges were introduced. In 1997/98 there were some 600 independent schools and 244 independent higher education institutions.

The level of education in the Russian Federation is relatively high, and 4.7m. Russian students were enrolled at institutes of higher education in 2000/01. Although Russian is the principal language used in educational establishments, a number of local languages are also in use. Budgetary expenditure on education in 2000 was an estimated 54,498.8m. roubles (representing 4.1% of total federal spending).

## UNIVERSITIES

**Altai State University:** 656099 Altai Krai, Barnaul, pr. Lenina 61; tel. (3852) 66-75-84; fax (3852) 66-76-26; e-mail rector@asu.ru; internet www.asu.ru; f. 1973; 15 faculties; 681 teachers; 15,000 students; Chancellor YURII KIRUSHIN.

**Amur State University:** 675027 Amur obl., Blagoveshchensk, Ignatevskoye shosse 21; tel. (4162) 35-06-87; fax (4162) 35-03-77; e-mail master@amursu.ru; internet www.amursu.ru; f. 1975; 9 faculties; 528 teachers; 5,315 students; Rector ANDREI D. PLUTENKO.

**Bashkir State University:** 450074 Bashkortostan, Ufa, ul. Frunze 32; tel. (3472) 22-63-70; fax (3472) 22-61-05; e-mail interdpt@bsu.bashedu.ru; internet www.bashedu.ru; f. 1957; 10 faculties; 525 teachers; 8,300 students; Rector MUKHAMET KH. KHARASOV.

**Chechen State University:** 364907 Chechnya, Groznyi, ul. Sheripova 32; tel. (8712) 23-40-89; 11 faculties; 620 teachers; 10,000 students; Rector ADNAN D. KHAMZAYEV.

**Chelyabinsk State University:** 454021 Chelyabinsk, ul. Br. Kashirinykh 129; tel. (3512) 42-05-31; fax (3512) 42-09-25; e-mail odou@cgu.ru; internet www.csu.ru; f. 1976; 14 faculties; 578 teachers; 7,800 students (full time), 6,569 students (by correspondence); Rector Prof. VALENTIN D. BATUKHTIN.

**Chuvash I. N. Ulyanov State University:** 428015 Chuvashiya, Cheboksary, Moskovskii pr. 15; tel. (8352) 24-03-79; fax (8352) 42-80-90; e-mail oper@chuvsu.ru; internet www.chuvsu.ru; f. 1967; 24 faculties; 940 teachers; 10,600 students; Rector Prof. Dr LEV P. KURAKOV.

**Dagestan State University:** 367025 Dagestan, Makhachkala, ul. Gadzhiyeva 43A; tel. (8722) 68-23-26; fax (8722) 67-06-33; e-mail dgu@dgu.ru; internet www.dgu.ru; f. 1931; 16 faculties; 1,000 teachers; 20,000 students; Rector Prof OMAR A. OMAROV.

**Dubna State International University of Nature, Society and Man:** 141980 Moscow obl., Dubna, ul. Universitetskaya 19; tel. (09621) 2-20-71; fax (09621) 2-24-64; e-mail rector@uni-dubna.ru; internet www.uni-dubna.ru; f. 1994; 13 faculties; Pres. V. G. KADYSHEVSKII; Rector O. L. KUZNETSOV.

**Far Eastern State University:** 690600 Maritime Krai, Vladivostok, ul. Sukhanova 8; tel. (4232) 26-12-80; fax (4232) 25-72-00; e-mail office@dip.dvgu.ru; internet www.dvgu.ru; f. 1899; 27 faculties; 7 institutes; 1 college; 993 teachers; 16,000 students; Rector Prof. VLADIMIR I. KURILOV.

**Irkutsk State University:** 664003 Irkutsk, ul. K. Marksa 1; tel. (3952) 24-34-53; fax (3952) 24-22-38; e-mail rector@isu.ru; internet www.isu.ru; f. 1918; 13 faculties; 7 institutes; 853 teachers; 12,230 students; Rector Prof. ALEKSANDR I. SMIRNOV.

**Ivanovo State University:** 153377 Ivanovo, ul. Yermaka 39; tel. (0932) 32-62-10; fax (0932) 32-46-77; e-mail rector@ivanovo.ac.ru; internet www.ivanovo.ac.ru; f. 1974; 9 faculties; 9,500 students; Rector VLADIMIR N YEGOROV.

**Kabardino-Balkar State University:** 360004 Kabardino-Balkariya, Nalchik, ul. Chernyshevskogo 173; tel. and fax (095) 337-99-55; e-mail bsk@ns.kbsu.ru; internet www.kbsu.ru; f. 1932; 13 faculties; 790 teachers; 10,120 students; Rector BARASBI S. KARAMURZOV.

**Kaliningrad State University:** 236041 Kaliningrad, ul. A. Nevskogo 14; tel. (0112) 46-59-17; fax (0112) 46-58-13; e-mail rector@admin.albertina.ru; internet www.albertina.ru; f. 1967; 9 faculties; 807 teachers; 10,821 students; Rector Dr A. P. KLEMESHEV.

**Kalmyk State University:** 358000 Kalmykiya, Elista, ul. Pushkina 11; tel. (84722) 5-34-31; fax (84722) 5-37-29; e-mail uni@kalmsu.ru; internet kalmsu.ru; f. 1970; 8 faculties; 5,000 students; Rector GERMAN M. MANDZHIYEVICH.

**Kazan State University:** 420008 Tatarstan, Kazan, ul. Kremlevskaya 18; tel. (8432) 38-70-69; fax (8432) 38-74-18; e-mail public.mail@ksu.ru; internet www.kcn.ru/tat_en/university/index.php3; f. 1804; 16 faculties; 2 research institutes; 1,075 teachers; 10,151 students; Rector M. SALAKHOV.

**Kemerovo State University:** 650043 Kemerovo, Krasnaya ul. 6; tel. (3842) 23-12-26; fax (3842) 23-30-34; e-mail rector@kemsu.ru; internet www.kemsu.ru; f. 1974; 11 faculties; 780 teachers; 8,834 students; Rector YU. A. ZAKHAROV.

**Krasnoyarsk State University:** 660041 Krasnoyarsk, pr. Svobodnyi 79; tel. (3912) 44-82-13; fax (3912) 44-86-25; e-mail kgu@krasu.ru; internet www.krasu.ru; f. 1969; 719 teachers; 9,600 students; Rector Prof. A. S. PROVOROV.

**Kuban State University:** 350040 Krasnodar, ul. Stavropolskaya 149; tel. (8612) 69-95-02; fax (8612) 69-95-17; e-mail rector@kubsu.ru; internet www.kubsu.ru; f. 1924; 15 faculties; 12 research institutes; 1,500 teachers; 23,000 students; Rector V. A. BABESHKO.

**Mari State University:** 424001 Marii-El, Yoshkar-Ola, pl. Lenina 1; tel. (8362) 42-59-20; fax (8362) 45-45-81; e-mail postmaster@marsu.ru; f. 1972; 9 faculties; 384 teachers; 4,055 students; Rector Dr V. I. MAKAROV.

**Mordoviyan N. P. Ogarev State University:** 430000 Mordoviya, Saransk, ul. Bolshevistskaya 68; tel. (83422) 4-17-77; fax (8342) 32-75-27; e-mail rectorat@mrsu.ru; internet www.mrsu.ru; f. 1957; 10 faculties; 5 institutes; 1,400 teachers; 18,500 students; Rector Prof. NIKOLAI P. MAKARKIN.

**Moscow M. V. Lomonosov State University (MGU):** 111992 Moscow, Vorobyovy gory; tel. (095) 939-10-00; fax (095) 938-01-26; e-mail rector@rector.msu.ru; internet www.msu.ru; f. 1755; 28 faculties; 8 institutes; 9,800 teachers; 40,000 students; Rector VIKTOR A. SADOVNICHII.

**Nizhnii Novgorod N. I. Lobachevskii State University:** 603950 Nizhnii Novgorod, pr. Gagarina 23; tel. (8312) 65-84-90; fax (8312) 65-85-92; e-mail rector@unn.ac.ru; internet www.unn.ac.ru; f. 1916; 14 faculties; 1,250 teachers; 25,000 students; Rector Prof. ALEKSANDR F. KHOKHLOV.

**North-Osetiyan K. L. Khetagurov State University:** 362025 North Osetiya—Alaniya, Vladikavkaz, ul. Vatutina 46; tel. and fax (8672) 74-31-91; e-mail indep@nosu.ru; internet www.nosu.ru; f. 1969; 15 faculties; 700 teachers; 10,500 students; Chancellor AKHURBEK M. MAGOMETOV.

**Novgorod Yarolslavl the Wise State University (NovSU):** 173003 Velikii Novgorod, ul. B. St Peterburgskaya 41; tel. (816) 222-37-07; fax (816) 222-41-10; e-mail tel@novsu.ac.ru; internet www.novsu.ac.ru; f. 1993; 22 faculties; 990 lecturers; 21,000 students; Pres. ANATOLII L. GAVRIKOV.

**Novosibirsk State University:** 630090 Novosibirsk, ul. Pirogova 2; tel. (3832) 30-32-44; fax (3832) 39-71-01; e-mail rector@nsu.ru; internet www.nsu.ru; f. 1959; 10 faculties; 700 teachers; 5,000 students; Rector Prof. NIKOLAI S. DIKANSKII.

**Omsk State University:** 644077 Omsk, pr. Mira 55A; tel. (3812) 26-84-22; fax (3812) 28-55-81; e-mail gering@omsu.omskreg.ru; internet www.omsu.omskreg.ru; f. 1974; 12 faculties; 640 teachers; 10,000 students; Rector Dr GENNADII I. GERING.

**Perm State University:** 614600 Perm, ul. Bukireva 15; tel. (3422) 33-61-83; fax (3422) 33-39-83; e-mail info@psu.ru; internet www.psu.ru; f. 1916; 11 faculties; 4 attached research institutes; 756 teachers; 11,869 students; Rector VLADIMIR V. MALANIN.

**Petrozavodsk State University:** 185640 Kareliya, Petrozavodsk, pr. Lenina 33; tel. (8142) 78-51-40; fax (8142) 71-10-00; e-mail rector@mainpgu.karelia.ru; internet petrsu.karelia.ru; f. 1940; 13 faculties; 740 teachers; 14,800 students; Rector VIKTOR N. VASILYEV.

**Rostov State University:** 344006 Rostov-on-Don, ul. Bolshaya Sadovaya 105; tel. (8632) 64-84-66; fax (8632) 64-52-55; e-mail rectorat@mis.rsu.ru; internet www.rsu.ru; f. 1915; 14 faculties; 11 attached institutes; 1,918 teachers; 12,000 students; Rector Prof. Dr A. V. BELOKON.

**Russian Friendship of Peoples' University:** 117198 Moscow, ul. Miklukho-Maklaya 6; tel. (095) 434-66-41; fax (095) 433-15-11; e-mail lomakin@pfu.ru; f. 1960 as Patrice Lumumba Friendship of Peoples' University, to train students from Africa, Asia and Latin America; 10 faculties; 1,800 teachers; 18,000 students; Rector Prof. D. P. BILIBIN.

**St Petersburg State University:** 199034 St Petersburg, Universitetskaya nab. 7/9; tel. (812) 328-20-00; fax (812) 328-13-46; e-mail office@inform.pu.ru; internet www.spbu.ru; f. 1724; 19 faculties; 2,954 teachers; 22,680 students; Rector L. A. VERBITSKAYA.

**Samara State University:** 443011 Samara, ul. Akademika Pavlova 1; tel. (8462) 34-54-02; fax (8462) 34-54-17; e-mail avn@ssu.samara.ru; internet www.ssu.samara.ru; f. 1969; 9 faculties; 442 teachers; 6,782 students; Rector G. P. YAROVOI.

**Saratov N. G. Chernyshevskii State University:** 410026 Saratov, ul. Astrakhanskaya 83; tel. (8452) 24-16-46; fax (8452) 24-04-46; e-mail rector@sgu.ssu.runnet.ru; internet www.ssu.runnet.ru; f. 1909; 13 faculties; Rector Prof. DMITRII I. TRUBETSKOV.

**Southern Ural State University:** 454080 Chelyabinsk, pr. Lenina 76; tel. (3512) 65-65-04; fax (3512) 34-74-08; e-mail dgsh@inter.tu-chel.ac.ru; internet www.tu-chel.ac.ru; f. 1943, fmrly Chelyabinsk State Technical University; 15 faculties; 1,500 teachers; 20,000 students; Rector Dr GERMAN P. VYATKIN.

**Syktyvkar State University:** 167001 Komi, Syktyvkar, Oktyabrskii pr. 55; tel. and fax (8212) 43-72-86; e-mail intdep@ssu.komi.com; internet www.ssu.komi.com; f. 1972; 10 faculties; 370 teachers; 4,700 students; Chancellor VASILII N. ZADOROZHNII.

**Tomsk State University:** 634050 Tomsk, pr. Lenina 36; tel. (3822) 23-44-65; fax (3822) 41-55-85; e-mail rector@tsu.ru; internet www.tsu.ru; f. 1878; 18 faculties; 1,410 teachers; 14,000 students; Rector Prof. G. MAYER.

**Tver State University:** 170000 Tver, ul. Zhelyabova 33; tel. (0822) 33-15-50; fax (0822) 33-12-74; e-mail uni@tversu.ru; internet university.tversu.ru; f. 1971; 18 faculties; Rector ALEKSEI N. KUDINOV.

**Tyumen State University:** 625003 Tyumen, ul. Semakova 10; tel. (3452) 46-19-30; fax (3452) 46-17-98; e-mail international@utmn.ru; internet www.utmn.ru; f. 1930; 10 faculties; 3 institutes; 26,000 students; Rector GENNADII F. KUTSEV.

**Udmurt State University:** 426034 Udmurtiya, Izhevsk, ul. Universitetskaya 1; tel. (3412) 75-16-10; fax (3412) 78-15-92; e-mail inter@uni.udm.ru; internet www.uni.udm.ru; f. 1931; 22 faculties; 1 research centre; 959 teachers; 28,157 students; Rector VITALII A. ZHURAVLEV.

**Urals A. M. Gorkii State University:** 620083 Sverdlovsk obl., Yekaterinburg, pr. Lenina 51; tel. (3432) 55-74-20; fax (3432) 55-59-64; e-mail vladimir.tretyakov@usu.ru; internet www.usu.ru; f. 1920; 12 faculties; 4 research institutes; 900 teachers; 12,400 students; Rector Prof. VLADIMIR E. TRETYAKOV.

**Volgograd State University:** 400062 Volgograd, 2-aya Prodolnaya ul. 30; tel. and fax (8442) 43-81-24; e-mail oms@volsu.ru; internet www.volsu.ru; f. 1980; 11 faculties; 612 teachers; 11,409 students; Rector OLEG V. INSHAKOV.

**Voronezh State University:** 394006 Voronezh, pl. Universitetskaya 1; tel. (0732) 55-29-83; fax (0732) 78-97-55; e-mail office@main.vsu.ru; internet www.vsu.ru; f. 1918; 17 faculties; 4 research institutes, 8 museums; 300 teachers; 18,500 students; library of 3m. volumes (2002); Rector Prof. IVAN. I. BORISOV.

**Yakutsk State University:** 677000 Sakha (Yakutiya), Yakutsk, ul. Belinskogo 58; tel. (4112) 26-33-44; fax (4112) 26-14-53; e-mail oip@sitc.ru; f. 1956; languages of instruction: Russian and Yakut; 2 brs; 8 faculties; 8 institutes; 950 teachers; 10,000 students; Chancellor Prof. ANATOLII N. ALEKSEYEV.

**Yaroslavl State University:** 150000 Yaroslavl, ul. Sovetskaya 14; tel. (0852) 72-51-38; fax (0852) 30-75-15; e-mail depint@uniyar.ac.ru; internet www.uniyar.ac.ru; f. 1970; 9 faculties; 530 teachers; 6,500 students; Rector Prof. GERMAN S. MIRONOV.

# Social Welfare

A basic social-security and health system exists in the Russian Federation. The Social Insurance Fund provides maternity benefit (which is payable for up to 18 weeks), payments for the loss of earnings owing to ill-health and, in certain instances, child allowance. Old-age pensions are provided from a Pension Fund (financed largely by employer contributions, but also including contributions from workers, and with a budgetary transfer to pay for family benefits). Women over the age of 55 years and men over the age of 60 are entitled to receive old-age pensions if they have worked for at least 20 years (women) or 25 years (men). A social pension, equivalent to two-thirds of the minimum pension, may be paid to citizens who have worked a maximum of five years less than the qualifying period. Disability benefits are also payable from the Pension Fund. According to official figures, at the end of 1996 the number of pensioners in Russia stood at 38m. (including 29m. on account of old age, and 3.8m. for reasons of disability). A new pension system was expected to be introduced in the early 2000s, which was to consist of a basic state pension financed by the budget, a state pension based on contributions by employees and employers and private pension schemes.

Unemployment benefit was introduced in Russia in 1991, with the establishment of the Federal Employment Fund (financed by employer contributions and government funds), and is paid to those who have been without employment for a period of more than three months (for the first three months the previous employer is obliged to continue paying the former employee's salary). In March 1998 the Government approved a federal special-purpose programme of employment assistance for 1998–2000, which aimed largely to alleviate the social consequences of the acceleration of redundancies during the mid-1990s. In 2001 federal budgetary expenditure on social security and welfare amounted to 112,285.4m. roubles (8.5% of the total).

A basic health service is provided for all citizens. All health care in the Russian Federation was previously financed by the state. In 1993, however, a health-insurance scheme, the Medical Insurance Fund, was introduced, funded by employers' contributions. Very few private medical facilities were in existence at this time. In 1999 there were 213.8 members of the population per physician, and 87.3 per hospital bed.

In 2000 federal budgetary expenditure on health care (including sport) was 23,085.1m. roubles (1.7% of the total). In the early and mid-1990s wages in the health sector declined, in real terms, and there was a severe shortage of medical supplies. As in most other former Soviet republics, medical production in Russia effectively collapsed as most newly privatized pharmacies became unprofitable. The difficulties experienced by the health-care system were reflected by a serious deterioration in the health of the population. The reasons cited for this were unsatisfactory environmental conditions, a decline in immunity, a shortage of vitamins and medicine and insufficient inoculations. Average life expectancy for males had decreased from 64 years in 1990 to 59 years by 2001. Female life expectancy was 72 years in 2001. In April 2002 the Ministry of Health initiated an eight-month, nation-wide programme to offer free medical examinations to children, owing to evidence of an accelerating decline in children's health. By the early 2000s the spread of HIV/AIDS had become a serious problem in Russia; in 2001 0.9% of the population were infected, compared with 0.2% in 1999. Widespread alcohol misuse was also a matter for concern.

The number of migrants in Russia increased rapidly during the mid-1990s, largely owing to the armed conflict in the Republics of Chechnya, Ingushetiya and North Osetiya—Alaniya, and inter-ethnic tensions in other former republics of the USSR, particularly those in Central Asia. According to the Federal Migration Service, at 1 October 1995 some 915,000 people were registered as refugees and displaced persons. In that year a total of 45,000m. roubles was spent on maintaining temporary holding centres for some 25,000 refugees.

### GOVERNMENT AGENCIES

**Ministry of Health:** see section on The Government (Ministries).

**Ministry of Labour and Social Development:** see section on The Government (Ministries).

**Commission for the Affairs of Women, the Family and Demography:** 103132 Moscow, Ipatyevskii per. 4/10; tel. (095) 206-06-55; f. 1996; Chair. YEKATERINA F. LAKOVA.

**Commission for Improving the Status of Women:** 103706 Moscow, Krasnopresnenskaya nab. 2; tel. (095) 220-92-55; fax (095) 230-24-07.

**Commission for the Rehabilitation of Victims of Political Repression:** 103132 Moscow, Staraya pl. 4; tel. (095) 206-34-53; f. 1991; Chair. ALEKSANDR N. YAKOVLEV.

**Federal Employment Service:** 107078 Moscow, 1-i Basmannyi per. 3; tel. (095) 261-64-64; fax (095) 261-20-21.

**Federal Migration Service (FMS)** (Federalnoi migratsionnoi sluzhby): 107078 Moscow, Boyarskii per. 4; tel. (095) 928-98-48; Chair. ALEKSANDR A. CHEKALIN.

**Federal Scientific-Methodogical Centre for the Prevention of and Combat of AIDS** (Federalnyi nauchno-metodicheskii tsentr po profilaktike i borbe so SPID): 111123 Moscow, ul. Novogireyevskaya 3A/11; tel. (095) 105-05-43; fax (095) 305-54-23; e-mail info@pcr.ru; internet www.pcr.ru; affiliated to the Central Scientific—Research Institute of Epidemiology of the Ministry of Health; Head VADIM POKROVSKII.

**Medstrakh—Medical Insurance Fund of the Russian Federation:** see section on Insurance.

**Pension Fund of the Russian Federation** (Pensionnyi fond RF): 117049 Moscow, ul. Shabolovka 4; tel. (095) 230-92-45; fax (095) 959-83-53; f. 1991; financed by contributions from employers and employees; Chair. of Bd MIKHAIL ZURABOV.

**Social Insurance Fund of the Russian Federation** (Fond sotsialnogo strakhovaniya RF): 107139 Moscow, per. Orlikov 3A; tel. (095) 797-92-77; e-mail mail@ca.fss.ru; internet www.fss.ru; f. 1991; financed by employers on behalf of their workers by means of tax inspectorate; administered by the federal Government; Chair. YURII A. KOSAREV.

**State Inspectorate of Non-State Pension Funds** (Inspektsiya negosudarstvennykh pensionnykh fondov pri MTSR RF): 109074 Moscow, Slavyanskaya pl. 4/1; tel. and fax (095) 925-85-00; e-mail npfinsp@dol.ru; internet npfinsp2.narod.ru; supervizes operations of private sector and non-state pension funds; Dir-Gen. VYACHESLAV V. BATAYEV.

## HEALTH AND WELFARE ORGANIZATIONS

**All-Russian Association of the Blind** (Vserossiiskoye obshchestvo slepykh): 101999 Moscow, Novaya pl. 14; tel. (095) 928-13-74; fax (095) 923-76-00; e-mail info@vos.org.ru; internet www.vos.org.ru; f. 1925; social rehabilitation, training of guide dogs, leisure and sports; Chair. ALEKSANDR. YA. NEUMYVAKIN.

**All-Russian Society of the Deaf (VOG)** (Vserossiiskoye obshchestvo glukhikh): 123022 Moscow, ul. 1905 goda 10A; tel. (095) 255-67-04; fax (095) 253-28-12; e-mail centrog@mail.ru; f. 1926; 150,000 mems; Pres. KHALIL M. KILMAYEV (acting).

**All-Russian Society of Invalids (VOI)** (Vserossiiskoye obshchestvo invalidov): 117415 Moscow, ul. Udaltsova 11; tel. (095) 935-00-12; fax (095) 936-13-00; e-mail id.voi@relcom.ru; f. 1988; non-profit, non-governmental organization; concerned with the protection of the rights and interests of disabled people and the integration of the disabled into Russian society; Chair. ALEKSANDR V. LOMAKHIN.

**Baikal Foundation:** 665718 Irkutsk obl., Bratsk, POB 52; tel. (095) 292-65-11; founded to promote voluntary work in the Russian Federation; organizes work camps to increase international participation in community development projects.

**Federal Caritas of Russia:** 127434 Moscow, Dmitrovskoye shosse 5/1/136, POB 93; tel. (095) 956-05-85; fax (095) 956-05-84; e-mail fcr@carit.msk.su; Roman Catholic charitable organization; Pres. Most Rev. TADEUSZ KONDRUSIEWICZ (Archbishop of the Diocese of the Mother of God at Moscow); Dir Deacon ANTONIO SANTI.

**Caritas of European Russia:** 127437 Moscow, Dmitrovskoye shosse 5/1/136, POB 93; e-mail secretary@caritas.ru; internet www.caritas.ru; tel. (095) 956-05-85; fax (095) 976-24-38.

**Caritas of Asian Russia:** 630099 Novosibirsk, ul. Gorkogo 100.

**Foundation for Help and Assistance to Women Victims of Stalinist Repressions (MARIYA):** 101458 Moscow, Bumazhnyi proyezd 14; tel. (095) 257-32-30; fax (095) 956-90-94; f. 1990; provides support and assistance to women who suffered human-rights abuses under Stalin's (Iosif V. Dzhugashvili's) leadership of the USSR (1924–53); Pres. ZOYA KRYLOVA.

**Help to Orphans of St Petersburg:** 193015 St Petersburg, ul. Ochakovskaya 3; tel. and fax (812) 110-04-64.

**International Charity and Health Fund** (Mezhdunarodnyi obshchestvennyi blagotvoritelnyi fond miloserdiya i zdrovya): 101990 Moscow, ul. Pokrovka. 22; tel. (095) 917-79-05; fax (095) 916-23-22; f. 1988 as Soviet Charity and Health Fund, renamed 1992; provides humanitarian aid to the elderly, disabled and chronically ill; operates in the territories of the former USSR in the fields of medicine, health and social welfare; organizes conferences, programmes and training courses; provides grants to institutions and individuals; Chair. VLADIMIR MUDRAK.

**Memorial Human Rights Centre:** 103051 Russia, M. Karetnyi per. 12; tel. (095) 973-20-94; fax (095) 976-03-43; e-mail info@memo.ru; internet www.memo.ru; researches into and provides support for victims of Stalinist repression; campaigns for the observance of human rights; Chair. SERGEI A. KOVALYEV.

**Moscow Charity House:** 121099 Moscow, ul. Novyi Arbat 11/1728–1735; tel. (095) 291-14-73; fax (095) 291-20-04; f. 1991.

**Russian Association of Medico Social Aid:** 103715 Moscow, Slavyanskaya pl. 4, kom. 590; tel. (095) 220-97-43; fax (095) 208-56-70.

**Russian Charity and Health Foundation (RFMZ)** (Rossiiskii fond miloserdiya i zdorovya): 101971 Moscow, ul. Pokrovka 22; tel. (095) 916-18-88; fax (095) 975-22-45; f. 1989; brs in 78 regions; operates through scholarships and fellowships, conferences, international training courses and publications; Pres. OLEG FILIPPOV.

**Russian Children's Foundation** (Rossiiskii Detskii Fond): 101000 Moscow, per. Armyanskii 11/2A; tel. (095) 925-82-00; fax (095) 200-22-76; e-mail madf@online.ru; Chair. ALBERT A. LIKHANOV.

**Russian Foundation of Disabled Afghanistan War Veterans:** 603011 Nizhnii Novgorod, ul. Magistratskaya 11, POB 66; tel. (8312) 33-03-72; fax (8312) 33-82-05.

**Russian Society of the International Committee of the Red Cross and the Red Cresent:** 117036 Moscow, Cheremushinskii proyezd 5; tel. (095) 126-67-70; fax (095) 230-28-67; e-mail redcross@dataforce.net; internet www.icrc.ru; f. 1867; Chair. TATYANA NIKO-LAYENKO.

**St Petersburg Health-Care Trust:** 199161 St Petersburg, Vasilevskii Ostrov, 12-aya liniya 51; tel. (812) 234-63-51; fax (812) 312-41-28.

**Voluntary Service of the Urals:** 614000 Perm, ul. Siberskaya 8; tel. and fax (3422) 12-97-36; e-mail vsu@pi.cci.ru; f. 1995; voluntary youth work in spheres of culture, ecology, education, organizes international work camps; Chair. SERGEI BRITVIN.

**Women's Union of Russia** (Soyuz zhenshchin Rossii): 103832 Moscow, Glinishchevskii per. 6; tel. (095) 229-32-23; fax (095) 200-02-74; e-mail wur@newmail.ru; f. 1990; Chair. ALEVTINA V. FEDULOVA.

# The Environment

Serious environmental problems developed in the Russian Federation during the Soviet period. In December 1993, according to an official environmental report, some 15% of Russian territory was an 'ecological disaster zone' and only one-half of the country's arable land was suitable for agriculture. Although there was a marked improvement during the 1990s in the ability of the Russian authorities to implement environmental legislation, there were an estimated 250,000 violations of such laws in 1997.

During the Soviet period weapons-grade material production sites were located in closed cities near Tomsk, Yekaterinburg and Krasnoyarsk. Prolonged nuclear testing at the testing-range in Semipalatinsk, Kazakhstan, caused substantial damage in the neighbouring Altai Krai. The accident at the Chernobyl (Chornobyl) nuclear power station in Ukraine in 1986 resulted in widespread contamination, in particular of the Bryansk, Orel and Tula Oblasts. In January 1996 the Russian Government adopted a programme of rehabilitation of the area affected by the disaster and agreed to pay some 11,700m. roubles in compensation to the victims; at that time an estimated 2.9m. people were living in contaminated areas. Accidents connected with outdated, Soviet-designed nuclear reactors continued to occur: in April 1993, an explosion at the closed city of Tomsk-7 in Siberia contaminated an area of 40 sq km, and in February 1996, at Dimitrovgrad on the River Volga, an accident involving one of seven nuclear reactors caused 1.2 metric tons of radioactive gas to be released into the atmosphere. Three months later it was announced that a huge nuclear disaster could occur at the Mayak nuclear reprocessing plant, near Chelyabinsk, in the Urals, if urgent measures were not taken to stabilize the installation.

The issue of disposing of radioactive waste at sea, which the USSR had done for over 30 years, was also an important environmental issue at this time. In 1993 the Barents Council was created by the Governments of Russia, Finland, Norway and Sweden to formalize co-operation with regard to the widespread pollution of the Kola Peninsula. The Peninsula was home to Russia's ageing Northern

Fleet, and to 182 working nuclear reactors, 135 reactors no longer in operation and 15 waste storage sites on land and at sea. Of particular urgency was the safe disposal of the nuclear warheads and reactors contained in the Northern Fleet's nuclear storage ships and submarines.

Russia initially agreed to destroy its stockpile of Soviet nuclear, biological and chemical weapons by 2007, although in the early 2000s it sought to extend this deadline until 2012. In June 2002 the leaders of the Group of Seven (G-7) industrialized nations agreed to provide some US $20,000m. to Russia, over a 10-year period, to assist in the protection and decommissioning of existing nuclear materials and weaponry, partly owing to international fears that terrorist organizations might gain access to dangerous substances.

Pollution of Russia's water supplies is considered to be of particular concern to the country's population. In October 1994 thousands of metric tons of petroleum were spilled near the Arctic town of Usinsk (Komi Republic). An inefficient clean-up operation caused the spill to spread to the northern reaches of the Pechora river, where some 100 km of shoreline were affected by 1996. In 1997 the industrial town of Dzerzhinsk, located around 400 km east of Moscow, was named by Greenpeace, the international environmental organization, as the site of Russia's worst chemical pollution and its nearby lake was identified as the world's most poisonous.

Following the abolition, in May 2000, of the State Committee for Environmental Protection, the functions of which were assumed by the Ministry of Natural Resources, there was concern from environmental activists that the handling of environmental issues would be affected by partiality. In July President Vladimir Putin instructed the Ministry to develop a proposal for the creation of an independent commission to assess the ecological impact. In July 2001 President Putin signed into law measures to permit the import of spent nuclear fuel from abroad for permanent storage in Russia, prompting protests from environmental groups, which argued that the country did not have the infrastructure required safely to transport and store large quantities of such fuel. In September 2002 the Chairman of the Government (Prime Minister), Mikhail Kasyanov, approved a new national environmental doctrine, with a view to encouraging greater concern for environmental matters in government departments and commercial organizations. In November an official report indicated that some 60% of Russians lived in an environment that was detrimental to health.

## GOVERNMENT ORGANIZATIONS

**Ministry of Natural Resources:** see section on The Government (Ministries).

**Arctic and Antarctic Research Unit:** 199397 St Petersburg, ul. Beringa 38; tel. (812) 352-00-96; fax (812) 352-26-88; f. 1920; research into ecology of the Arctic and Antarctic; responsible for the Russian Antarctic Expedition; Dir I. YE. FROLOV.

**Federal Authority of Russia for Nuclear and Radiation Safety** (Federalnyi nadzor Rossii po yadernoi i radiatsionnoi bezopasnosti): 109147 Moscow, ul. Taganskaya 34; tel. (095) 912-39-11; fax (095) 912-40-41; e-mail bla@gan.ru; internet www.gan.ru; Chair. ANDREI B. MALYSHEV.

**Interdepartmental Commission for Ecological Security** (Mezhvedomstvennaya komissiya po ekologicheskoi bezopastnosti): 103070 Moscow, Staraya pl. 6; f. 1993; commission of the Security Council; Chair. ALEKSEI V. YABLOKOV.

**International Science and Technology Centre (ISTC)** (Mezhdunarodnyi nauchno-tekhnicheskii tsentr—MNTT): 115516 Moscow, ul. Luganskaya 9; tel. (095) 797-60-10; fax (095) 797-60-47; e-mail istcinfo@istc.ru; internet www.istc.ru; f. 1992 under an intergovernmental agreement between the Russian Federation, the European Union, Japan and the USA; carries out research in the fields of nuclear safety and environmental protection and utilizes the skills of former weapons scientists and engineers with a view to ensuring nuclear non-proliferation; Exec. Dir M. KRÖNING.

**Russian Federal Hydrometeorology and Environmental Monitoring Service:** 195196 St Petersburg, pr. Malookhtinskii 98; tel. (812) 444-25-96; fax (812) 444-6090; affiliated to the Russian State Hydrometeorological University.

**State Committee for Social Protection of Citizens and the Rehabilitation of Territories Affected by Chernobyl and Other Radiation Accidents:** 103132 Moscow, Staraya pl. 8/2/3; tel. (095) 206-48-81; Chair. VASSILII VOZNYAK.

## RUSSIAN ACADEMY OF SCIENCES

**Russian Academy of Sciences:** 119991 Moscow, Leninskii pr. 14; tel. (095) 954-29-05; fax (095) 954-33-20; e-mail uvs@pran.ru; internet www.pran.ru; f. 1724; renamed Academy of Sciences of the USSR 1925; original name reinstated 1991; 12 depts; Pres. YURII S. OSIPOV; a Commission on Questions of Ecology is attached to the Presidium of the Academy; the principal sections and institutes involved in environmental matters incl.:

**All-Russia Research Institute for Nature Conservation:** 113628 Moscow, ul. Znamenskoye Sadki; tel. (095) 423-03-22; fax (095) 423-23-22; f. 1981; research, general methodology, environmental protection strategy domestically and internationally; five departments; major repository of research material; Dir B. L. SAMOILOV.

### Section of Chemical, Technological and Biological Sciences

**Institute of the Ecology of the Volga River Basin:** 445003 Samara obl., Tolyatti, ul. Komzina 10; tel. and fax (8469) 48-95-04; f. 1983; attached to the Dept of Biological Sciences; monitors the environment of the Volga; Dir Prof. G. S. ROZENBURG.

**Institute of Soil Science and Photosynthesis:** 142260 Moscow obl., Pushchino; tel. (095) 923-35-58; fax (0967) 79-05-32; attached to the Dept of Biochemistry, Biophysics and Physiological Chemistry; research incl. soil conservation and land reclamation; Dir V. I. KEFELYA.

**I.D. Papanin Institute of the Biology of Inland Waters (IBVV RAN):** 152742 Yaroslavl obl., Nekouzskii raion, pos. Borok; tel. and fax (08547) 2-40-42; e-mail adm@ibiw.yaroslavl.ru; internet www.ibiw.yaroslavl.ru; attached to the Dept of Biological Sciences; incl. Commission on the Conservation of Natural Waters; publishes journal, *Biology of Inland Waters*, quarterly; Dir Dr SERGEI I. GENKAL.

**A. N. Severtsov Institute of Ecology and Evolution:** 119071 Moscow, Leninskii pr. 33; tel. (095) 952-20-88; fax (095) 954-55-34; e-mail sevin@orc.ru; f. 1934; attached to the Dept of Biological Sciences; research of general ecology, morphology, ecology and ethology of animals, animal evolution, problems of biodiversity and nature conservation; Dir D. S. PAVLOV.

### Section of Earth Sciences

**Institute of Water Problems:** 107078 Moscow, ul. Novaya Basmannaya 10, POB 231; tel. (095) 265-97-57; fax (095) 265-18-87; e-mail iwapr@iwapr.msk.su; f. 1968; complex evaluation of water resources; development of scientific substantiation for their rational use and protection; Dir M. G. KHUBLARYAN.

**Laboratory for the Monitoring of the Environment and Climate:** c/o Dept of Oceanology, Atmospheric Physics and Geography, 117901 Moscow, Leninskii pr. 14; tel. (095) 234-14-24; Dir (vacant).

The Section of Earth Sciences also includes the Institute of Lake Conservation and the Scientific Council on Study of the Caspian Sea.

### Section of Social Sciences

**Centre for Environmental Legal Studies, Institute of State and Law:** 119841 Moscow, ul. Znamenka 10; tel. (095) 291-38-27; fax (095) 291-85-74; e-mail isl_ran@rinet.ru; f. 1972; research into Russian, comparative and international environmental law; Dir Prof. MIKHAIL M. BRINCHUK.

### Regional Divisions

**Siberian Division:** 630090 Novosibirsk, pr. Akademika Lavrenteva 17; tel. (3832) 30-05-67; Chair. N. L. DOBRETSOV; institutes involved in environmental matters incl.:

**Chita Institute of Natural Resources:** 672014 Chita, ul. Nedorezova 16; tel. and fax (302) 221-25-82; e-mail root@cinr.chita.su; f. 1981; scientific research into the region's ecosystems; Dir A. B. PTITSYN; Scientific Sec. G. Z. ZYBEKMITOVA.

**Limnological Institute:** 664033 Irkutsk, ul. Ulan-Batorskaya 3; tel. (3952) 46-05-04; fax (3952) 420-21-06; e-mail root@lin.irkutsk.su; studies the ecology of lakes; particularly concerned with the conservation programme in Lake Baikal; Dir M. A. GRACHEV.

**Institute of Water and Ecological Problems:** 656099 Altai Krai, Barnaul, ul. Papanintsev 105; tel. (3852) 36-78-56; fax (3852) 24-03-96; e-mail iwep@iwep.secna.ru; f. 1987; research into water-resource use, land reclamation and environmental protection in Siberia; experimental and mathematical methods for analysis of hydrophysical, hydrochemical and other natural processes in the aquatic environment; environmental assessment of large-scale engineering projects; development of information- and modelling systems for specific research projects and management resources; decision support systems; Dir Prof. YURII I. VINOKUROV.

**Far Eastern Division:** 690600 Maritime Krai, Vladivostok, ul. Svetlanskaya 50; tel. (4232) 22-25-28; Chair. G. B. YELYAKOV; attached institutes incl.:

**Institute of Biological Problems of the North:** 685000 Magadan, ul. K. Marksa 24; tel. (41322) 2-47-30; fax (41322) 2-01-66; f. 1972; Dir F. B. CHERNYAVSKII.

**Institute of Water and Ecological Problems:** 680063 Khabarovsk, ul. Kim Yu Chena 65; tel. (4212) 22-75-73; fax (4212) 22-70-85; e-mail dmitry@ivep.khv.ru; f. 1968; research into Far Eastern ecosystems and their biodiversity and the sustainable use of natural resources; Dir B. A. VORONOV.

**Urals Division:** 620219 Sverdlovsk obl., Yekaterinburg, ul. Pervomaiskaya 91; tel. (343) 74-02-23; Chair. V. A. CHERESHNEV; attached institutes incl.:

**Institute of Industrial Ecology:** 620219 Sverdlovsk obl., Yekaterinburg, ul. Sophy Kovalevskoi 20A; tel. and fax (3432) 74-37-71; e-mail chukanov@ecko.uran.ru; f. 1992; environmental research; research into health, socio-economics, demographic consequences of environmental contamination, risk assessment and radioecology; Dir Prof. V. N. CHUKANOV.

**Institute of Plant and Animal Ecology:** 620144 Sverdlovsk obl., Yekaterinburg, ul. 8-go Marta 202; tel. (3432) 22-05-70; fax (3432) 29-41-61; e-mail common@ipae.uran.ru; internet www.ipae .uran.ru; f. 1944; environmental research; Dir V. N. BOLSHAKOV.

### NON-GOVERNMENTAL ORGANIZATIONS

**All-Russian Society for Nature Conservation (VOOP)** (Vserossiiskoye obshchestvo okhrany prirody): 103012 Moscow, Bogoyavlenskii per. 3/3; tel. (095) 924-77-65; fax (095) 921-78-12; f. 1924; promotes environmental education and the implementation of environmental law; 34 regional brs; Dir-Gen. IVAN F. BARISHPOL.

**Association for Environmental Education (AsEkO)** (Assotsiatsiya 'Ekologicheskoye obrazovaniye'): 249020 Kaluga obl., Obninsk-9, POB 9081; tel. (095) 497-88-42; e-mail web@online.ru; internet www.aseko.org; f. 1991; educational programmes and projects; initiation of environmental education at all levels and promotion of sustainable development; support for teachers; development of a network for information exchange; training seminars and conferences; produces regular journal and e-mail bulletin; Chair. V. SHELEGED.

**Ekoline:** 125047 Moscow, POB 7; tel. and fax (095) 978-90-61; e-mail ecoline@ecoline.ru; internet www.ecoline.ru; f. 1995; promotes environmental management.

**Ekozashchita!—Ecodefense!:** 236000 Kaliningrad, POB 1477; tel. (0112) 43-72-86; fax (0112) 75-71-06; e-mail ecodefense@ecodefense .ru; internet www.ecodefense.ru; f. 1990; nation-wide environmental asscn; promotes environmental education, brs in Kaliningrad, Moscow and Voronezh.

**Green World Environmental Association** (Zelenyi Mir): 197371 St Petersburg, Komendantskii pr. 29/1/307; tel. and fax (812) 306-40-37; e-mail greenworld@spb.org.ru; internet www.greenworld.org .ru; f. 1988; applied research institute; Chair. OLEG BODROV.

**Greenpeace Russia:** 127994 Moscow, ul. N. Bashilovka 6, POB 4; tel. (095) 257-41-16; fax (095) 257-41-10; e-mail gprussia@diala .greenpeace.org; internet www.greenpeace.ru; f. 1992; national office of Greenpeace International; activities include a campaign for the protection of Lake Baikal; Exec. Dir SERGEI TSYPLENKOV; Campaign Co-ordinator IVAN BLOKOV.

**International Public Foundation for the Survival and Development of Humanity** (Mezhdunarodnyi fond 'Za vyzhivaniye i razvitiye chelovechestva'): 121002 Moscow, Denezhnyi per. 9/5/22; tel. (095) 241-82-55; fax (095) 230-26-08; e-mail gcinfo@space.ru; f. 1988 to identify opportunities for global change and to promote solutions to global problems; Pres. RUSTEM I. KHAIROV.

**Laboratory for Radiation Control:** 650070 Kemerovo, Kemerovo State University, ul. Tukhachevskaya 33; tel. and fax (3842) 31-14-98; e-mail nl@irk.da.ru; f. 1994; concerned with control of radiation, environmental monitoring; Head of Laboratory NADEZHDA ALUKER.

**Moscow Ecological Federation:** 121019 Moscow, per. Bogoyavlenskii 3/3; tel. (095) 924-77-65; e-mail ecology-mef@narod.ru; internet ecology-mef.narod.ru; concerned with Moscow's ecological problems; provides environmental information; assists with urban development plans; Chair. TATYANA ZAKHARCHENKO.

**Moscow Society of Naturalists (MOIP)** (Moskovskoye obshchestvo ispytatelei prirody): 103009 Moscow, ul. B. Nikitskaya 6; tel. (095) 203-67-04; internet www.seminarium.narod.ru/moip/ moip.htm; f. 1805; 2,500 mems; library of 522,000 vols; Chair. V. A. SADOVNICHII.

**Movement for a Nuclear-Free North:** 183038 Murmansk; advocates demilitarization of the Kola Peninsula and an end to nuclear testing on Novaya Zemlya.

**Rostov Regional Ecological Centre:** 344007 Rostov-on-Don, ul. Stanislavskogo 114/1; tel. (863) 32-33-70; f. 1988; urban ecology and geochemistry, research into atmospheric, soil, surface- and ground-water pollution; environmental rehabilitation programmes; Pres. Dr VALERII PRIVALENKO.

**Russian Ecological Party—Greens:** see section on Political Organizations.

**Socio-Ecological Union International (SoES)** (Sotsialno-ekologicheskii soyuz): 117312 Moscow, ul. Vavilova 41; tel. and fax (095) 124-79-34; e-mail soceco@seu.ru; internet www.seu.ru; f. 1987; co-ordinates 250 environmental committees, clubs and societies in all countries of the CIS, as well as Estonia, Norway and the USA; international co-operation; campaigns on issues of the environment, human rights, biodiversity protection, energy efficiency, nuclear energy and radioactive pollution; environmental education; Sec. N. I. ZABELIN.

# Defence

In May 1992 the Russian Federation established its own armed forces, on the basis of former Soviet forces on the territory of the Russian Federation and those former Soviet forces outside Russian territory that were not subordinate to other former republics of the USSR. In August 2002 the total active armed forces in Russia numbered some 988,100 (this figure included an estimated 330,000 conscripts, 200,000 staff of the Ministry of Defence and an estimated 149,000 permanent members of the Strategic Deterrent Forces). Military service is compulsory for men over 18 years of age and lasts for a term of 18–24 months, although the rate of conscription evasion is, reportedly, high. In late 2001 proposals were announced to gradually eliminate conscription in 2004–10, subject to parliamentary approval, and experiments with various forms of alternative, civilian service, were under way in several regions in 2002. Ground forces in the Russian army consisted of some 321,000 troops, including 190,000 conscripts. There was a navy of 171,500, including 16,000 conscripts and an air force of an estimated 184,600 (following its merger with the air defence troops). There were a further estimated 409,100 paramilitary troops active. In November 2000 it was announced that the armed forces were to be reduced in size by some 600,000 in 2005. Projected budgetary expenditure on defence for 2002 was 262,900m. roubles.

By late 2000 most member states of the CIS had formed national armies. The formation of a joint CIS military force, which had initially won much support from the organization's members, became increasingly less popular. None the less, in April 2003 the Government announced that citizens of other CIS countries were to be eligible to serve in the Russian armed forces, for a period of up to three years, after which time they were to become eligible to apply for Russian citizenship.

**Commander-in-Chief of the Armed Forces of the Russian Federation:** President of the Federation.

**Chief of the General Staff:** Gen. ANATOLII KVASHNIN.

**Internal Troops Chief of Staff:** Col-Gen. MIKHAIL PANKOV.

**Navy Commander-in-Chief:** Adm. VLADIMIR KUROYEDOV.

**Air Force Chief of Staff:** Gen. VLADIMIR MIKHAILOV.

# MEMBERS OF THE RUSSIAN FEDERATION

There are 89 members (federal subjects or territorial units) of the Russian Federation. According to the Constitution of December 1993, these consist of 21 republics, six krais (provinces), 49 oblasts (regions), two cities of federal status, one autonomous oblast and 10 autonomous okrugs (districts). Their status had begun to be regularized by the Federation Treaty of 31 March 1992, which had provided for a union of 20 republics (16 of which had been Autonomous Soviet Socialist Republics—ASSRs under the old regime, and four of which were autonomous oblasts), six krais and one autonomous oblast. The 10 autonomous okrugs remained under the jurisdiction of the krai or oblast within which they were located (a situation that largely continued thereafter) but, as federal units, were raised to the same status as oblasts and krais. The former republic of Chechno-Ingushetiya was divided into two republics in June 1992, by the formal recognition of a republic of Ingushetiya. Moscow and St Petersburg subsequently assumed the status of federal cities. Under the terms of the Treaty, republics were granted far wider-reaching powers than the other federal units, specifically over the use of natural resources and land. They consequently represent quasi-autonomous states within the Russian Federation, as opposed to being merely administrative units of a unitary state. Autonomous republics, autonomous okrugs and the autonomous oblast are (sometimes nominally) ethnically defined, while krais and oblasts are defined on territorial grounds. One of Vladimir Putin's earliest actions after his election as federal President in March 2000 was to group the federal subjects into seven large Federal Okrugs (districts). These seven Federal Okrugs are the Central Federal Okrug (based in the capital, Moscow), the North-Western Federal Okrug (St Petersburg), the Southern Federal Okrug (Rostov-on-Don), the Volga Federal Okrug (Nizhnii Novgorod), the Urals Federal Okrug (Yekaterinburg), the Siberian Federal Okrug (Novosibirsk) and the Far Eastern Federal Okrug (Khabarovsk). Additionally, the federal subjects are grouped into 11 economic areas, which, with the exception of that in the Far East, differ from the newer Federal Okrugs of the same name. These are the Central Economic Area, the Central Chernozem (Black Earth) Economic Area, the East Siberian Economic Area, the Far Eastern Economic Area, the North Caucasus Economic Area, the North-Western Economic Area, the Northern Economic Area, the Urals Economic Area, the Volga Economic Area, the Volga-Vyatka Economic Area and the West Siberian Economic Area.

Of the 89 members of the Russian Federation, the 21 republics are each administered by a president and/or prime minister. The republics each have their own governments and ministries. The remaining federal units are governed by a local administration, the head (governor) of which is the highest official in the territory, and a representative assembly. Governors are able to veto regional legislation, although their vetoes may be overridden by a two-thirds' parliamentary majority. The federal Supreme Soviet (legislature), which created the post of governor in August 1991, intended that the official be elected by popular vote, but the federal President, Boris Yeltsin, secured an agreement with the Congress of People's Deputies that the governors be appointed. In many regions conflict subsequently arose between the executive and legislative bodies, as the presidential appointees encountered much resistance from the communist-dominated assemblies. In those cases where a vote of 'no confidence' was passed in the governor, elections were permitted. (This occurred in seven oblasts and one krai in December 1992.) Following President Yeltsin's dissolution of the Russian legislature in September 1993, and parliament's violent resistance, it was announced that all heads of local administrations would, henceforth, be appointed and dismissed by presidential decree. However, this ruling was relaxed in December 1995, when gubernatorial elections were held in one krai and 11 oblasts. From the late 1990s elected governors became the norm in all of the federal subjects, as initial terms of office expired, and Vladimir Putin (who was elected as Federal President in early 2000) made no use of presidential decrees to appoint or dismiss regional governors during his first three years in office.

As Russian President, before the disintegration of the USSR Yeltsin strongly advocated decentralization within the Russian Fed-eration, and hence increasing political and economic diversity among the 89 federal units. From 1995 the undertaking of bilateral treaties to delineate powers between federal Government and the regional authorities became increasingly commonplace. This resulted in the establishment, in March 1996, of the precise terms of the delimitation of jurisdiction and powers between federal and regional authorities. Any treaties on the delimitation of powers could not change the status of a federal unit, threaten the territorial integrity of the Russian Federation or violate the terms of the federal Constitution. Fears that the country was being transformed from a constitution-based to a treaty-based federation became more widespread as these power-sharing agreements were signed by a majority of federal subjects.

Attempts to regulate the subsequent peripheral–central tensions in the governance of Russia took a variety of forms, particularly after the election of Vladimir Putin to the presidency In particular, the establishment of the Federal Okrugs, each of which was headed by a presidential appointee, was considered by many to be a device to ensure closer central supervision of regional activity. The federal President also assumed the right to dismiss governors at will, extending such a right over local officials to regional governors themselves, hence encouraging a more efficient form of government, with a clearer hierarchy, which Putin referred to as 'vertical power'. In the event, however, these powers were seldom used in the three years following their introduction. Instead, a series of presidential decrees in 2000–01 ruled that laws specific to certain regions were unconstitutional and must be amended. The federal republics, which had the greatest degree of autonomy to lose under the new arrangements, were most severely affected; by April 2002 28 of the 42 'power-sharing treaties' signed between the regional and federal authorities had been annulled, and many of those which remained had been amended, in order to bring regional legislation into conformity with the federal norm. A new body, the State Council of the Russian Federation, was created by presidential decree in September 2000, the members of which were the heads of the 89 constituent parts of the Russian Federation. The organization's presidium was chaired by the Russian President, and was to be formed on a rotational basis every six months. Since the Russian Constitution remained unchanged, the State Council's functions were consultative, and participation in it was voluntary. According to its founding decree, the body was to advise the President mainly on issues concerning the relationship between the central administration and Russia's regions.

**Presidential Representative in the Central Federal Okrug:** Lt-Gen. GEORGII S. POLTAVCHENKO; 103132 Moscow, Nikolskii per. 6; tel. (095) 206-12-76; e-mail malakhov_dm@gov.ru; internet www .cfopolpred.ru.

**Presidential Representative in the Far Eastern Federal Okrug:** Lt-Gen. KONSTANTIN B. PULIKOVSKII; 680030 Khabarovsk, ul. Sheronova 22; tel. (4212) 31-39-78; fax (4212) 31-38-04; internet www.dfo.ru.

**Presidential Representative in the North-Western Federal Okrug:** (vacant); 193015 St Petersburg, ul. Shpalernaya 47; tel. (812) 346-20-09; fax (812) 326-64-84.

**Presidential Representative in the Siberian Federal Okrug:** LEONID V. DRACHEVSKII; 630091 Novosibirsk, ul. Derzhavina 18/120; tel. (3832) 20-17-56; fax (3832) 20-13-90; e-mail sibokrug@online .sinor.ru; internet www.sfo.nsk.su.

**Presidential Representative in the Southern Federal Okrug:** Col-Gen. VIKTOR G. KAZANTSEV; 344006 Rostov-on-Don, ul. B. Sadovaya 73; tel. (8632) 44-16-16; fax (8632) 40-39-40; e-mail polpred@ polpred-ug.donpac.ru.

**Presidential Representative in the Urals Federal Okrug:** SERGEI V. KIRIYENKO; 620031 Sverdlovsk obl., Yekaterinburg, pl. Oktyabrskaya 3; tel. (3432) 77-18-96; e-mail support@uralfo.ru; internet www.uralfo.ru.

**Presidential Representative in the Volga Federal Okrug:** Col-Gen. PETR M. LATYSHEV; 603082 Nizhnii Novgorod, Kreml, kor. 1; tel. (8312) 31-46-07; fax (8312) 31-47-51; internet www.pfo.ru.

# AUTONOMOUS REPUBLICS

## Republic of Adygeya

The Republic of Adygeya (Adygheya) is situated in the foothills of the Greater Caucasus, a land-locked region in the basin of the Kuban river, within Krasnodar Krai. The Republic is in the Southern Federal Okrug and the North Caucasus Economic Area. The territory of the Republic, of which some two-fifths is forested, is characterized by open grassland, fertile soil and numerous rivers. The Republic has an area of 7,600 sq km (2,930 sq miles) and is comprised of seven administrative districts and two cities. At 1 January 2002 it was estimated to have 444,900 inhabitants, giving a population density per sq km of 58.5. In January 2001 54.0% of the population of the Republic were urban. In 1989 of the total republican population some 68% were ethnic Russian and 22% Adyges (Lower Circassians or Kiakhs). Of the Adyge population, an estimated 95% speak the national tongue, Adyge—part of the Abkhazo-Adyge group of Caucasian languages—as their native language, although some 82% are also fluent in Russian. The dominant religion in the Republic, owing to the preponderance of Russian inhabitants, is Orthodox Christianity, but the traditional religion of the Adyges is Islam. The administrative centre of Adygeya is the only large city, Maikop, which had a total of 167,000 inhabitants at 1 January 2001.

## History

The Adyges were traditionally renowned for their unrivalled horsemanship and marksmanship. They emerged as a distinct ethnic group among the Circassians in the 13th century, when they inhabited much of the area between the Don river and the Caucasus, and the Black Sea and the Stavropol plateau. They were conquered by the Mongol Empire in the 13th century. In the 1550s the Adyges entered into an alliance with the Russian Empire, as protection against the Tatar Khanate of Crimea and against Turkic groups such as the Karachai, the Kumyks and the Nogai, which had retreated into the Caucasus from the Mongol forces of Temujin (Chinghiz or Ghengis Khan). Russian settlers subsequently moved into the Don and Kuban regions, causing unrest among the Adyges and other Circassian peoples, many of whom supported the Ottoman Empire against Russia in the Crimean War of 1853–56. The Circassians were finally defeated by the Russians in 1864. Most were forced either to emigrate or to move to the plains that were under Russian control. A Kuban-Black Sea Soviet Republic was established in 1918, but the region was soon occupied by anti-communist forces ('Whites'). The Adygeya Autonomous Oblast was established on 27 July 1922. From 24 August 1922 until 13 August 1928 it was known as the Adygeya (Circassian) Autonomous Oblast. The Oblast subsequently formed part of Stavropol Krai, which was constituted in 1937.

Following the emergence of the policy of *glasnost* (openness) in the USSR, under Mikhail Gorbachev, the Adyge-Khase Movement was formed. This group, which demanded the formation of a national legislative council or khase, began to raise the issues of nationalism and independence in the Autonomous Oblast. Adygeya officially declared its sovereignty on 28 June 1991 and from the following year entered into co-operative agreements with several other federal subjects; an inter-parliamentary council was subsequently formed to include Adygeya and the other Circassian Republics (Kabardino-Balkariya and Karachayevo-Cherkessiya). A Constitution, which formally provided for the recognition of Adygeya as an autonomous republic, separate from the surrounding Krai, was adopted on 10 March 1995, confirming a decision of the Supreme Soviet of the RSFSR of 3 June 1991. The new Constitution provided for the institution of a bicameral legislature, the Khase (State Council), comprising a Council of Representatives and a Council of the Republic. Although during the late 1990s the Republic remained strongly supportive of the Communist Party of the Russian Federation, the Adyge President, Aslan Dzharimov, was among those instrumental in forming the All-Russia parliamentary bloc in 1999. In an election held on 13 January 2002 Dzharimov was conclusively defeated, receiving only around 10% of the votes cast; he was succeeded by Khazrat Sovmen, the owner of a gold-mining co-operative. Following the death of Gen. (retd) Aleksandr Lebed, the Governor of Krasnoyarsk Krai, in April 2002, his former deputy, Gennadii Mikichura, who was reported to be a business associate of Sovmen, was approved by the legislature as Prime Minister of Adygeya. In August 2003 Mikichura resigned, and was replaced later in the month by Khazret Khuade, a former head of the republican customs service.

## Economy

Agriculture is, traditionally, the principal economic activity of Adygeya. In 1999 the territory's gross regional product was 5,110.2m. roubles, or 11,373.7 roubles per head. The territory's major industrial centres are at the cities of Maikop and Kamennomostskii. At 2000 there were 148 km (92 miles) of railway track on its territory, and 1,537 km of paved roads.

Agricultural production consists mainly of grain, sunflowers, sugar beet, tobacco and vegetables, cucurbit (gourds and melons) cultivation and viniculture. The Republic produced over 17% of the Federation's output of grape wine in the first half of 2000. The entire sector employed some 22.1% of the working population in 2000. The decline in overall agricultural production in the Republic slowed during the mid-1990s, although animal husbandry decreased to less than one-half of its 1991 level by 1998. By 2000 the value of agricultural output was 2,240m. roubles, compared with 995m. roubles in 1998. A severe drought in mid-2003 was expected to result in a marked decrease in agricultural output in that year. There is some extraction of natural gas. In industry, food-processing is particularly important, accounting for almost one-half of industrial production. Timber-processing, mechanical engineering, pharmaceuticals and metal-working are also significant. Adygeya lies along the routes of the 'Blue Stream' pipeline, completed in 2002, which delivers gas to Turkey, and planned petroleum pipelines from the Transcaucasus and Dagestan to the Black Sea ports of Novorossiisk and Tuapse. Some 18.5% of the working population were engaged in industry in 2000. Industrial production declined during the early 1990s, but began to increase from 1999. In 2000 the value of industrial production was 2,795m. roubles, compared with 1,018m. roubles in 1998.

In 2000 the economically active population in Adygeya amounted to 200,200, and some 14.1% of the labour force were unemployed, one of the highest rates in the Federation at that time. The average monthly wage was 2,625.9 roubles in mid-2002. In 2000 there was a budgetary deficit of 84.9m. roubles. In that year the Republic's external trade amounted to a value of US $10.4m., of which $7.9m. was accounted for by imports and $2.5m. by exports. Adygeya's main trading partners, in the mid-1990s, in terms of exports, were Belarus, France, Kazakhstan, Poland, Turkey and Ukraine. Exports consisted mainly of food products, machine-tools and petroleum and chemical products. There was relatively little foreign investment in the Republic: in 2000 it amounted to just $719,000. At 31 December 2000 there were 2,200 small businesses registered on Adygeya's territory.

## Directory

**President:** Khazrat M. Sovmen; 352700 Adygeya, Maikop, ul. Zhukovskogo 22; tel. (87722) 7-19-01; fax (87722) 2-59-58; internet www.adygheya.ru.

**Prime Minister:** Khazret Khuade; 352700 Adygeya, Maikop, ul. Pionerskaya 199; tel. (87722) 7-02-22; fax (87722) 2-59-58.

**Chairman of the Council of Representatives of the Khase (State Council):** Tatyana M. Petrova, 352700 Adygeya, Maikop, ul. Zhukovskogo 22; tel. (87722) 2-12-61; e-mail apparat@parlament.adygheya.ru; internet www.parlament.adygheya.ru.

**Chairman of the Council of the Republic of the Khase (State Council):** Anatolii G. Ivanov; 385000 Adygeya, Maikop, ul. Zhukovskogo 22; tel. (87722) 2-19-02; fax (87722) 2-19-04; e-mail apparat@parlament.adygheya.ru; internet www.parlament.adygheya.ru.

**Chief Representative of the Republic of Adygeya in the Russian Federation:** Ruslan Yu. Gusaruk; 115184 Moscow, per. Staryi Tolmachevskii 6; tel. (095) 230-34-01; fax (095) 230-07-48.

**Head of Maikop City Administration:** N. M. Pivovarov; 352700 Adygeya, Maikop, ul. Krasnooktyabrskaya 21; tel. (87722) 2-27-61; fax (87722) 2-63-19; e-mail priemn@admins.maykop.ru; internet www.admins.maykop.ru.

## Republic of Altai

The Republic of Altai (Gornyi Altai—Mountainous Altai) is situated in the Altai Mountains, in the basin of the Ob river. The Republic forms part of the Siberian Federal Okrug and the West Siberian Economic Area. It has international borders with Kazakhstan in the south-west, a short border with the People's Republic of China to the south, and with Mongolia to the south-east. Kemerovo Oblast lies to the north, the Republics of Khakasiya and Tyva to the east, and the Altai Krai, of which the Republic formerly constituted a part, to the north-west. The Republic includes the highest peak in Siberia, Belukha, at 4,506 m (14,783 feet), and about one-quarter of its territory is forested. Its major rivers are the Katyn and the Biya, and it has one lake, Teletskoye. It contains one of Russia's major national parks, Altai State National Park, covering an area of some 9,000 sq km (3,475 sq miles). The Republic occupies 92,600 sq km and comprises 10 administrative districts and one city. Its climate is continental, with short summers and long, cold winters. At 1 January 2002 it was estimated to have a population of 204,900 and a population density, therefore, of only 2.2 per sq km. Of its inhabitants, 25.7% resided in urban areas in January 2001. The census of 1989 put the number of Russians at some 60% of the total and of ethnic Altai at 31%, while some 5.6% of the population were Kazakh. The Altai people can be divided into two distinct groups: the Northern Altai, or Chernnevye Tatars, consisting of the Tubalars, the Chelkans or Leberdin and the Kumandins; and the Southern Altai, comprising the Altai Kizhi, the Telengit, the Telesy and the Teleut. The language spoken by both groups is from the Turkish branch of the Uralo-Altaic family: that of the Northern Altais is from the Old Uigur group, while the language of the Southern Altais is close to the Kyrgyz language and is part of the Kipchak group. Over 84% of Altais speak one or other language as their native tongue, and some 62% of the Altai population is fluent in Russian. Although the traditional religion of the Altai was animist, many were converted to Christianity, so the dominant religion in the Republic is Russian Orthodoxy. The Republic's administrative centre is at Gorno-Altaisk, which had a population of 52,700 at 1 January 2001.

## History

From the 11th century the Altai peoples inhabited Dzungaria (Sungaria—now mainly in the north-west of the People's Republic of China). The region was under Mongol control until 1389, when it was conquered by the Tatar forces of Tamerlane (Tamberlane or Timur 'the Lame'); it subsequently became a Kalmyk confederation. In the first half of the 18th century many Altais moved westwards, invading Kazakh territory and progressing almost as far as the Urals. In 1758, however, most of Dzungaria was incorporated into Xinjiang (Sinkiang), a province of the Chinese Empire. China embarked on a war aimed at exterminating the Altai peoples. Only a few thousand survived, finding refuge in the Altai Mountains. In the 19th century Russia began to assert its control over the region, which was finally annexed in 1866. In the early 1900s Burkhanism or White Faith, a nationalist religious movement, emerged. The movement was led by Oirot Khan, who claimed to be a descendant of Chinghiz (Genghis) Khan and promised to liberate the Altais from Russian control. However, in February 1918 it was a secular nationalist leader, B. I. Anuchin, who convened a Constituent Congress of the High Altai and demanded the establishment of an Oirot Republic—to include the Altai, the Khakassians and the Tyvans. In partial recognition of such demands, on 1 July 1922 the Soviet Government established an Oirot Autonomous Oblast in Altai Krai. In 1948 the region was renamed the Gorno-Altai Autonomous Oblast, in an effort to suppress nationalist sentiment.

In the late 1980s nationalism re-emerged in response to Mikhail Gorbachev's policy of *glasnost* (openness). Renamed the Altai Republic, the region became an autonomous republic, independent of Altai Krai, at the signing of the Russian Federation Treaty in March 1992, having adopted its State Sovereignty Declaration on 25 October 1990. A resolution adopted on 14 October 1993 provided for the establishment of a State Assembly (El Kurultai), which comprised 27 deputies and represented the highest body of power in the Republic. The Altai Republic was one of only four subjects of the Russian Federation to award the communist candidate, Gennadii Zyuganov, a higher proportion of the votes than Vladimir Putin in the presidential election of 26 March 2000. In February 2001 several amendments to the republican Constitution were approved by the El Kurultai, to bring them into conformity with the fundamental laws of the Russian Federation, as had been demanded by the federal Constitutional Court. A provision that had forbidden persons of the same nationality from simultaneously occupying the posts of chairman of the republican government and parliamentary speaker was one of those to be removed. Following an inconclusive first round of voting in the election to the post of chairman of the government held in the Republic on 16 December, the incumbent, Semen Zubakin, and Mikhail Lapshin, the leader of the Agrarian Party of Russia (APR), progressed to a second round, held on 20 January 2002. On that occasion Lapshin decisively defeated Zubakin, receiving 68% of the votes cast, according to preliminary results. Notably, Lapshin received the support of the pro-Government Unity and Fatherland-United Russia party in the second round, in addition to that of the Communist Party of the Russian Federation. Legislative elections were held in the Republic in December. In the

early 2000s proposals for the re-unification of the Altai Republic with Altai Krai were led by the Krai's legislative Chairman, Aleksandr Nazarchuk. Despite the close political allegiances of Lapshin and Nazarchuk (was was also a prominent member of the APR), the authorities in the Republic reportedly opposed any merger, fearing that such a measure would result in the former Autonomous Oblast returning to a subordinate status within the Krai.

## Economy

The Republic of Altai is predominantly an agricultural region. Its gross regional product amounted to 2,568.1m. roubles in 1999, or 12,570.4 roubles per head. The main industrial centre in the Republic is at its capital, Gorno-Altaisk. Owing to its mountainous terrain, in 2000 it contained just 2,774 km (1,724 miles) of paved roads, including a section of the major Novorossiisk–Biisk–Tashanta highway. There are no railways or airports. In March 1996 the Russian Government allocated some 1,800m. old roubles to alleviate the effects in the Republic of the nuclear tests conducted at Semipalatinsk, Kazakhstan, in 1949–62. However, in the early 2000s further concern was expressed about the negative effect of frequent rocket launches from the Baikonaur Cosmodrome in Kazakhstan on both the health of the residents of the Republic and the surrounding environment.

Agriculture in the Republic of Altai, which employed 31.4% of the working population in 2000, consists mainly of livestock-breeding (largely horses, deer, sheep and goats, amounting to 60% of agricultural activity in the late 1990s), bee-keeping, grain production and hunting. The export of the antlers of Siberian maral and sika deer, primarily to South-East Asia, is an important source of convertible currency to the Republic. In 2000 the total value of agricultural output was 1,479m. roubles. The Republic's mountainous terrain often prevents the easy extraction or transport of minerals, but there are important reserves of manganese, iron, silver, lead and wolfram (tungsten), as well as timber. Stone, lime, salt, sandstone, gold, mercury and non-ferrous metals are also produced. There are food-processing, light, chemicals, metal-working and machine-tool industries, as well as factories assembling tractors, automobiles, radios, televisions, engines, boilers and electrical appliances. Industry employed just 8.2% of the working population in 2000, and the value of industrial production amounted to 361m. roubles.

In 2000 a total of 91,000 of the Republic's inhabitants were economically active, and some 17.5% of the labour force were unemployed. The average monthly wage was 3,160.6 roubles in mid-2002. The territory suffered severe financial difficulties in the late 1990s, and there was a budgetary deficit of 47.9m. roubles in 2000. In that year the value of the Republic's exports was US $51.8m., and its imports were equivalent to around $68.5m. The level of foreign investment was very low, amounting to just $99,000 in 2000. At December 2000 there were approximately 1,400 small businesses registered in the Republic.

## Directory

**Chairman of the Government:** MIKHAIL I. LAPSHIN; 659700 Altai Republic, Gorno-Altaisk, ul. Kirova 16; tel. (38822) 2-26-30; e-mail root@apra.gorny.ru; internet www.altai-republic.com.

**Chairman of the El Kurultai (State Assembly):** IGOR E. YAIMOV; 659700 Altai Republic, Gorno-Altaisk, ul. Erkemena Palkina 1; tel. (38822) 2-26-18; fax (38822) 9-51-65; e-mail root@altek.gorny.ru.

**Chief Representative of the Altai Republic in the Russian Federation:** SERGEI D. KONCHAKOVSKII; 103795 Moscow, ul. M. Dmitrovka 3/221; tel. (095) 299-41-94; fax (095) 299-81-97.

**Head of Gorno-Altaisk City Administration:** VIKTOR A. OBLOGIN; 659700 Altai Republic, Gorno-Altaisk, pr. Kommunicheskii 18; tel. (38822) 2-23-40; fax (38822) 2-25-59.

# Republic of Bashkortostan

The Republic of Bashkortostan (Bashkiriya) is situated on the slopes of the Southern Urals. It forms part of the Volga Federal Okrug and the Urals Economic Area. Orenburg Oblast lies to the south and south-west of Bashkortostan, and the Republics of Tatarstan and Udmurtiya lie to the north and north-west, respectively. There are borders with Perm and Sverdlovsk Oblasts to the north and Chelyabinsk to the east. The north of the Republic (more than one-third of its land area) is forested, while the southern part is steppe. The Republic occupies an area of 143,600 sq km (55,440 sq miles) and comprises 54 administrative districts and 21 cities. At 1 January 2002 Bashkortostan had an estimated population of 4,090,600, giving a population density of 28.5 per sq km. In January 2001 some 65.3% of the Republic's population inhabited urban areas. The most numerous ethnic group was Russian (39% in 1989). Tatars made up

28% of the population, while Bashkirs only constituted 22%. Of the ethnic Bashkir inhabitants, some 72% spoke Bashkir as their native tongue. Bashkir is a Kipchak language closely related to that spoken by the Tatars. There are two distinct Bashkir dialects: Kuvakan is spoken in the north of the Republic, while Yurmatin (Yurmatyn) is current in the south. The majority of Bashkirs and Tatars are Sunni Muslims of the Hanafi school, although some Bashkirs, the Nagaibak (Noghaibaq or Nogaibak), were converted to Orthodox Christianity. The Republic's administrative centre is at Ufa, which had a population of 1,088,800 in 2001. Its other major cities, with populations in excess of 100,000, are Sterlitamak, Salavat, Nefte-kamsk and Oktyabrskii.

## History

The Bashkirs were thought to have originated as a distinct ethnic group during the 16th century, out of the Tatar, Mongol, Volga, Bulgar, Oguz, Pecheneg and Kipchak peoples. They were tradition-ally a pastoral people renowned for their bee-keeping abilities. The territory of Bashkiriya was annexed by Russia in 1557, during the reign of Ivan IV—'the Terrible', and many Bashkirs subsequently lost their land and wealth and were forced into servitude. Rebellions against Russian control, most notably by Salavat Yulai in 1773, were unsuccessful, and the identity and survival of the Bashkir com-munity came under increasing threat. A large migration of ethnic Russians to the region in the late 19th century resulted in their outnumbering the Bashkir population. A Bashkir ASSR was formed on 23 March 1919. Bashkir resistance to the collectivization policy of Stalin (Iosif V. Dzhugashvili) caused many to be relocated to other regions in the USSR. It was this, combined with losses during the civil wars of the revolutionary period, which resulted in the Bashkirs becoming outnumbered by the Tatar population in the Republic.

The Bashkir Autonomous Republic declared its sovereignty on 11 October 1990. On 12 December 1993, the same day that Murtaza Rakhimov was elected to the new post of President, a republican majority voted against acceptance of the new federal Constitution. On 24 December the republican Supreme Soviet adopted a new Constitution, which stated that its own laws had supremacy over federal laws. The name of Bashkortostan was adopted, and a bicam-eral legislature, the Kurultai, established. The Republic's constitu-tional position was regularized and further autonomy granted under a treaty signed on 3 August 1994. By this, the federal authorities granted Bashkortostan greater independence in economic and legis-lative matters; the administration of the Republic, however, remained highly centralized, with the republican executive retaining extensive controls over both local government and industry, particularly the petroleum sector. A further bilateral treaty was signed in 1995. A presidential election, held on 14 June 1998, returned Rakhimov to office, his candidacy having been endorsed publicly by the Russian President, Boris Yeltsin. In the State Duma elections of December 1999, the candidates of Rakhi-mov's favoured grouping, Fatherland—All Russia, were successful in the Republic; prior to the election Rakhimov was rebuked by the federal Prime Minister, Vladimir Putin, for blocking the trans-mission of two television channels opposed to the grouping. Com-mentators also observed the absence of any opposition press in Bashkortostan, and the removal from electoral lists of most of Rakhimov's opponents, owing to alleged electoral violations. In the federal presidential election of 26 March 2000, Bashkortostan returned 62% of votes in favour of Vladimir Putin, well above the national average.

In May 2000 Putin ordered that Bashkortostan's Constitution be altered to conform with Russia's basic law. A new republican Con-stitution was introduced in November, although several articles continued to contradict federal norms. In January 2001 one of the most significant contradictions, the statement that republican legis-lation should take precedence over federal law, was rescinded, and several powers formerly attributed to the republican prime minister were transferred to the republican president. In June 2002 the federal Supreme Court ruled that some 37 articles of Bashkorto-stan's new Constitution failed to comply with federal law, and the redaction of a further new Constitution commenced. Rakhimov declared that he wished to introduce a parliamentary system of government, and to abolish the republican presidency; in mid-November, however, this measure was rejected by the legislature, which expressed concern that the introduction of a directly elected prime minister would effectively result in the maintenance of a presidential system.

On 3 December 2002 a new Constitution was adopted, which, notably, combined the posts of President and Prime Minister, while maintaining a presidential system of Government. The new docu-ment removed all references to the 'sovereignty' of Bashkortostan found in its predecessors, although reference was made to the 'statehood' of the Republic. None the less, the text was widely regarded as broadly conforming with federal laws, although the future of the bilateral treaties signed between the republican and federal authorities in 1994 and 1995 remained unclear. The new

Constitution also introduced a unicameral legislative assembly, which retained the name of its bicameral predecessor, the Kurultai. This new body was to have a term of five years, compared with the four-year term enjoyed by its predecessor. One of the final decisions made by the outgoing legislature, in early March 2003, was to extend Rakhimov's term of office from mid-June, when it had been due to expire, until December, in order that the republican presidential elections would be held concurrently with those to the federal State Duma.

At elections to the new Kurultai, held on 16 March 2003, the pro-Government Unity and Fatherland-United Russia (UF-UR) party obtained control of 91 of the 120 seats. Notably, Ural Rakhimov, the son of the President, who also held senior positions at three petro-leum-sector companies owned by the republican Government, was elected to the Kurultai as a deputy of UF-UR. In July the federal Constitutional Court ruled that it was the sole body with the authority to determine whether the constitutions of federal subjects were in conformity with federal law; one consequence of this ruling appeared to be that a number of challenges to the former Con-stitutions of Bashkortostan from other bodies (such as the repub-lican Supreme Court) were thereby effectively invalidated, and it appeared likely that measures to rewrite the new Constitution, so as to reintroduce the notion of republican sovereignty, would ensue.

## Economy

Bashkortostan's economy is dominated by its fuel and energy and agro-industrial complexes. The Republic is one of Russia's key petroleum-producing areas and the centre of its petroleum-refining industry. It produced 4% of Russia's total petroleum output in the first six months of 2000 and accounted for around 15% of its petroleum refining. However, the quantity of petroleum both pro-duced and refined in the Republic declined significantly during the 1990s. In 1999 the territory's gross regional product stood at 114,145.1m. roubles, or 27,722.6 roubles per head. Amid concerns that the federal Government was seeking to gain increased control over the natural resources of the Republic, at the expense of the republican authorities, republican President Rakhimov announced, in August 2002, that several of the republican petroleum companies were to be transferred to private ownership. Bashkortostan's major industrial centres are at Ufa (at which the Republic's petroleum refineries are based), Sterlitamak, Salavat and Ishimbai. In 2000 there were 1,475 km (917 miles) of railways on its territory, and 21,869 km of paved roads. Bashkir Airlines (BAL) operates air services between Ufa and major centres within Russia and else-where within the Commonwealth of Independent States from the Republic's international airport.

Bashkortostan's agricultural production, the value of which amounted to 27,918m. roubles in 2000, ranks among the highest in the Russian Federation. Its main agricultural activities are grain, sugar beet, sunflower and vegetable production, animal husbandry, poultry-farming and bee-keeping. Some 19.8% of the Republic's work-force were employed in agriculture in 2000. As well as its petroleum resources (of which the deposits amount to 400m. metric tons), Bashkortostan contains deposits of natural gas (55m. tons), brown coal—lignite (250m. tons), iron ore, copper, gold (with reserves amounting to 32 tons in 1997, sufficient for 19 years of production), zinc, aluminium, chromium, salt (2,270m. tons), man-ganese, gypsum and limestone. The Republic's other industries include processing of agricultural and forestry products, mechanical engineering, metal-working, metallurgy, electricity generation, pro-duction of mining and petroleum-exploration equipment, automo-biles, geophysical instruments, cables and electrical equipment and building materials. In 2000 industry employed 24.1% of the Repub-lic's working population. Total industrial output was worth 141,792m. roubles in that year.

In 2000 the economically active population in the Republic amounted to 1,928,000, and 11.5% of the labour force were unem-ployed. The average monthly wage was 3,780.0 roubles in mid-2002. In 2000 there was a budgetary surplus of 1,425.7m. roubles. In the same year the Republic's external trade totalled US $2,910m., of which exports, largely comprising petroleum products and pet-rochemical goods, accounted for $2,668.6m. Bashkortostan's prin-cipal trading partner is Germany. Foreign investment in the Republic in 2000 amounted to some $10.4m. At the end of the year there were 14,300 small businesses registered on the Republic's territory.

## Directory

**President and Prime Minister:** Murtaza G. Rakhimov; 450101 Bashkortostan, Ufa, ul. Tukayeva 46; tel. (3472) 50-27-24; fax (3472) 50-02-81; e-mail aprbinfo@admbashkortostan.ru; internet www .bashkortostan.ru.

**Chairman of the State Assembly (Kurultai):** Konstantin B. Tolkachev; 450101 Bashkortostan, Ufa, ul. Tukayeva 46; tel. (3472)

50-19-15; fax (3472) 50-08-86; e-mail pred@kurultai.rb.ru; internet www.gs.rb.ru.

**Chief Representative of the Republic of Bashkortostan in the Russian Federation:** IREK YU. ABLAYEV; 103045 Moscow, Sretenskii bulv. 9/2; tel. (095) 208-46-62; fax (095) 208-39-25.

**Head of Ufa City Administration (Mayor):** PAVEL R. KACHKAYEV; 450098 Bashkortostan, Ufa, pr. Oktyabrya 120; tel. (3472) 79-05-79; fax (3472) 33-18-73; e-mail cityadmin@ufacity.info; internet www .ufacity.info.

# Republic of Buryatiya

The Republic of Buryatiya is situated in the Eastern Sayan Mountains of southern Siberia and forms part of the Siberian Federal Okrug and the East Siberian Economic Area. It lies mainly in the Transbaikal region to the east of Lake Baikal, although it also extends westwards along the international boundary with Mongolia in the south, to create a short border with the Russian federal territory of Tyva in the extreme south-west. Irkutsk Oblast lies to the north and west, and Chita Oblast to the east. Buryatiya's rivers mainly drain into Lake Baikal, the largest being the Selenga, the Barguzin and the upper Angara, but some, such as the Vitim, flow northwards into the Siberian plains. The Republic's one lake, Baikal, forms part of the western border of the Republic. Baikal is the oldest and deepest lake in the world, possessing over 80% of Russia's freshwater resources and 20% of the world's total. Considered holy by the Buryats, until the 1950s it was famed for the purity of its waters and its unique ecosystem. Intensive industrialization along its shores threatened Baikal's environment, and only in the 1990s were serious efforts made to safeguard the lake. Some 70% of Buryatiya's territory, including its low mountains, is forested, and its valleys are open steppe. The Republic's territory covers 351,300 sq km (135,640 sq miles) and comprises a total of 21 administrative districts and six cities. The winter is protracted but sees little snow, with the average temperature in January falling to –27.1°C; the average temperature in July is 16.0°C. Buryatiya had an estimated population of 1,019,400 at 1 January 2002, and a population density of 2.9 per sq km. Around 59.9% of the population inhabited urban areas in January 2001. In 1989 some 70% of the inhabitants were ethnic Russians and 24% Buryats. The industrial areas of the Republic are mainly inhabited by ethnic Russians. The Buryats are a native Siberian people of Mongol descent. The majority of those inhabiting the Republic are Transbaikal Buryats, as distinct from the Irkutsk Buryats, who live west of Lake Baikal. The Buryats' native tongue is a Mongol dialect. Some Buryats are Orthodox Christians, but others still practise Lamaism (Tibetan Buddhism), which has been syncretized with the region's traditional animistic shamanism. The Pandito Hambo Lama, a Buddhist spiritual leader, resides in Buryatiya's capital, Ulan-Ude, which had a population of 368,900 in January 2001 and is paired, for the purpose of commercial, cultural and social exchanges, with Taipei in Taiwan.

## History

Buryatiya was regarded as strategically important from the earliest years of the Muscovite Russian state, as it lay on the Mongol border. Russian influence reached the region in the 17th century and Transbaikal was formally incorporated into the Russian Empire by the Treaties of Nerchinsk and Kyakhta in 1689 and 1728, respectively. The latter agreement ended a dispute over the territory between the Russian and the Chinese Manzhou (Manchu) Empires. Many ethnic Russians subsequently settled in the region, often inhabiting land confiscated from the Buryats, many of whom were 'russified'. Other Buryats, however, strove to protect their culture, and there was a resurgence of nationalist feeling in the 19th century. Jamtsarano, a prominent nationalist, following a series of congresses in 1905 demanding Buryat self-government and the use of the Buryat language in schools, led a movement that recognized the affinity of Buryat culture to that of the Mongolians. Russia's fears about the Buryats' growing allegiance to its eastern neighbour were allayed, however, after a formal treaty signed with Japan in 1912 recognized Outer Mongolia (Mongolia) as a Russian sphere of influence.

With the dissolution of the Far Eastern Republic (based at Chita), a Buryat-Mongol ASSR was established on 30 May 1923. In the early 1930s, following Stalin—Iosif V. Dzhugashvili's policy of collectivization, many Buryats fled the country or were found guilty of treason and executed. In 1937 the Soviet Government considerably reduced the territory of the Republic, transferring the eastern section to Chita Oblast and a westerly region to Irkutsk Oblast. Furthermore, the Buryat language's Mongolian script was replaced with a Cyrillic one. In 1958 the Buryat-Mongol ASSR was renamed the Buryat ASSR, amid suspicions of increasing co-operation between the Mongolian People's Republic (Mongolia) and the People's Republic of

China. The territory declared its sovereignty on 10 October 1990, and was renamed the Republic of Buryatiya in 1992. In March 1994 the republican legislature, the Supreme Soviet, adopted a Constitution, providing for an executive presidency. The hitherto Chairman of the Supreme Soviet, Leonid Potapov, became the Republic's first President, and the legislature was redesignated the People's Khural. A bilateral treaty on the division of powers was signed with the Federation Government in 1995. On 21 June 1998 presidential and legislative elections were held in the Republic, and Potapov was re-elected President. In October 2000 the People's Khural approved several amendments to Buryatiya's Constitution, but rejected the implementation of several proposed amendments required by federal legislation, including, notably, the abolition of the requirement that presidential candidates know both state languages, Russian and Buryat. In early 2002 Potapov resigned from the Communist Party of the Russian Federation. In April he threatened to dissolve the Khural if it opposed the cancellation of the declaration of sovereignty issued in 1990; the declaration of sovereignty was consequently rescinded. On 23 June Potapov was re-elected for a third term as President of the Republic, receiving 68% of the votes cast. The pro-Government Unity and Fatherland–United Russia party (UF-UR) chose to support Potapov, in preference to his closest electoral opponent, Bato Semenov, a representative of the UF-UR in the State Duma. Notably, in the period preceding the election, three of the four independent radio stations in Ulan-Ude had their operations suspended by the republican State Communications Inspectorate.

## Economy

In 1999 Buryatiya's gross regional product amounted to 18,085.0m. roubles, equivalent to 17,424.6 roubles per head. Its major industrial centre is at Ulan-Ude, which is on the route of the Trans-Siberian Railway. In 2000 there were 1,199 km (745 miles) of railways on Buryatiya's territory, and 6,226 km of paved roads.

The Republic's agriculture, which employed around 14.3% of the work-force in 2000, consists mainly of animal husbandry (livestock and fur-animal breeding), grain production and hunting. Total agricultural production in 2000 was worth 4,829m. roubles. The Republic is rich in mineral resources, including gold, uranium, coal, wolfram (tungsten), molybdenum, brown coal, graphite and apatites. Its main gold-mining enterprise, Buryatzoloto, operates two mines near Lake Baikal. In 1996 its reserves were estimated at 3.2m. troy ounces (almost 100 metric tons). Apart from ore-mining and the extraction of minerals, its main industries are mechanical engineering, metal-working, food-processing, timber production and wood-working. The Republic is also a major producer of electrical energy. The industrial sector employed 19.1% of the Republic's work-force in 2000, and its total output in that year was worth 11,570m. roubles. The services sector with the most potential is tourism, owing to the attractions of Lake Baikal.

Buryatiya's economically active population totalled 491,000 in 2000, and some 19.1% of the Republic's labour force were unemployed. The average monthly wage in the Republic was 4.088.4 roubles in mid-2002. In 2000 there was a budgetary deficit of 1,151.7m. roubles. Foreign trade in that year comprised US $116.5m. in exports and $29.7m. in imports; the Republic had over 50 trading partners, although in 1999 over one-half of its international trade was with the People's Republic of China. Foreign investment in Buryatiya amounted to just $291,000 in 2000. At 31 December 2000 there were 4,100 small businesses registered in the Republic.

## Directory

**President and Chairman of the Government:** LEONID V. POTAPOV; 670001 Buryatiya, Ulan-Ude, ul. Sukhe-Batora 9; tel. (3012) 21-51-86; fax (3012) 21-28-22; e-mail pres_rb@icm.buryatia .ru; internet president.buryatia.ru.

**Chairman of the People's Khural:** ALEKSANDR G. LUBSANOV; 670001 Buratiya, Ulan-Ude, ul. Sukhe-Batora 9; tel. (3012) 21-31-57; fax (3012) 21-49-61; e-mail kontup01@icm.buryatia.ru; internet chairman.buryatia.ru.

**Chief Representative of the Republic of Buryatiya in the Russian Federation:** INNOKENTII N. YEGOROV; 107108 Moscow, ul. Myasnitskaya 43/2; tel. (095) 925-95-00; fax (095) 923-60-46.

**Head of Ulan-Ude City Administration (Mayor):** GENNADII A. AYDAYEV; 670000 Buryatiya, Ulan-Ude, ul. Lenina 54; tel. (3012) 21-57-05; fax (3012) 26-32-44; internet www.ulan-ude.ru.

# Chechen (Nokchi) Republic— Chechnya

The Chechen (Nokchi) Republic is located on the northern slopes of the Caucasus. It forms part of the Southern Federal Okrug and the North Caucasus Economic Area. To the east, Chechnya abuts into the Republic of Dagestan. Stavropol Krai lies to the north-west and the Republics of North Osetiya—Alaniya (Ossetia) and Ingushetiya to the west. There is an international boundary with Georgia (South Osetiya) to the south-west. The exact delimitation of the western boundary remained uncertain, awaiting final agreement between Chechnya and Ingushetiya on the division of the territory of the former Chechen-Ingush ASSR. The Republic comprises three cities and 18 administrative districts. The Republic comprises lowlands along the principal waterway, the River Terek, and around the capital, Groznyi, in the north; mixed fields, pastures and forests in the Chechen plain; and high mountains and glaciers in the south. The former Checheno-Ingush ASSR had an area of some 19,300 sq km (7,450 sq miles), most of which was allotted to the Chechens. At 1 January 2002 the Republic had an estimated population of 624,600, compared with an estimated population of 780,500 in January 1999. Some 26.0% of the total population lived in urban areas in 2001. The Chechens, who refer to themselves as Nokchi, are closely related to the Ingush (both of whom are known collectively as Vainakhs). They are Sunni Muslims, and their language is one of the Nakh dialects of the Caucasian linguistic family. Founded as Groznyi in 1818, the capital had a population of 405,000 in 1989, but an estimated 182,700 inhabitants in 1995. The Republic's other major towns are Urus-Martan, Gudermes (the oldest town in the territory, founded in the mid-18th century), Shali and Argun.

## History

In the 18th century the Russian, Ottoman and Persian (Iranian) Empires fought for control of the Caucasus region. The Chechens violently resisted the Russian forces with the uprising of Sheikh Mansur in 1785 and throughout the Caucasian War of 1817–64. Chechnya was finally conquered by Russia in 1858 after the resistance led by the ethnic Avar, Imam Shamil ended. Many Chechens were exiled to the Ottoman Empire in 1865. Subsequently, ethnic Russians began to settle in the lowlands, particularly after petroleum reserves were discovered around Groznyi in 1893. Upon the dissolution of the Mountain (Gorskaya) People's Republic in 1922, Chechen and Ingush Autonomous Oblasts were established; they merged in 1934 and became the Checheno-Ingush ASSR in 1936. This was dissolved in 1944, when both peoples were deported en masse to Central Asia and Siberia. On 9 January 1957 the ASSR was reconstituted, but with limited provisions made for the restoration of property to the dispossessed Chechens and Ingush.

During 1991 an All-National Congress of the Chechen People seized effective power in the Checheno-Ingush ASSR and agreed the division of the territory with Ingush leaders. Exact borders were to be decided by future negotiation, but by far the largest proportion of the territory was to constitute a Chechen Republic. Elections to the presidency of this new polity, the Chechen Republic (Chechnya), which claimed independence from Russia, were held on 27 October, and were won by Gen. Dzhokhar Dudayev. In 1993 the territory refused to participate in the Russian general election and rejected the new federal Constitution. Dudayev's policies provoked the Chechen opposition into violent conflict from August 1994. In December federal troops entered Chechnya and, by January 1995, had taken control of the city, including the presidential palace, although fierce resistance continued throughout the Republic. In an effort to end hostilities, the federal President, Boris Yeltsin, signed an accord with the Chechen premier granting the Republic special status, including its own consulate and foreign-trade missions. None the less, in April more than 100 civilians were reported to have been killed by federal troops in a so-called 'cleansing' operation (*zachistka*) in the village of Samashki. Subsequently, in June the federal premier, Viktor Chernomyrdin, intervened in negotiations to end a siege by militants associated with the rebel Chechen leader, Shamil Basayev, who took hostage around 1,000 people in a hospital in Budennovsk, Stavropol Krai. (None the less, more than 100 people were killed during the siege, which Basayev described as an act of revenge for an attack by federal troops on the village of Vedeno in the previous month, in which 11 of his relatives had been killed.) A further large-scale hostage-taking incident conducted by Chechen militants took place in Kizlyar, Dagestan, in January 1996, increasing demands across Russia for the Government to find a settlement to the Chechen conflict; other incidences of hostage-taking attributed to supporters of Chechen independence took place in Chechnya, in other regions of Russia and, less frequently, internationally during the late 1990s and early 2000s.

In April 1996 Dudayev was killed in a Russian missile attack; he was succeeded by Zelimkhan Yandarbiyev. In May the rebel and federal authorities signed a peace agreement. However, the truce ended following Yeltsin's re-election as federal President in July. In August Chechen rebel forces led a successful assault on Groznyi, prompting the negotiation of a cease-fire by Lt-Gen. Aleksandr Lebed, the recently appointed Secretary of the Security Council. An agreement, the Khasavyurt Accords, was signed in Dagestan on 31 August. The proposed peace settlement incorporated a moratorium on discussion of Chechnya's status for five years, until 2001. An agreement on the withdrawal of all federal troops by January 1997 was signed in November 1996, signalling the end of a war that had claimed up to 100,000 lives. A formal Treaty of Peace and Principles of Relations was signed on 12 May 1997 and ratified by the Chechen Parliament the following day.

On 1 January 1997 a presidential election was held in the Republic (which subsequently renamed itself 'the Chechen Republic of Ichkeriya'), at which Khalid 'Aslan' Maskhadov, a former Chechen rebel chief of staff, obtained 64.8% of the votes cast, defeating Basayev. The main issues to dominate politics were the increasing lawlessness in the Republic and the growth of Islamist groupings, both of which served to destabilize neighbouring polities, particularly the Republic of Dagestan (q.v.). Moreover, the population of Chechnya decreased markedly following the establishment of *de facto* independence, as civilians—particularly ethnic Russians—migrated to other regions of Russia. During 1998 two dramatic incidents drew attention to the disorderly state of Chechen society: Valentin Vlasov, the federal presidential representative in Chechnya, was kidnapped in May and held hostage for six months; later in the year four engineers from the United Kingdom and New Zealand were captured, and subsequently killed. By the end of the year Groznyi was no longer secure for the Government and Maskhadov was mainly based on the outskirts of the city.

The resurgence of Chechen nationalism in the 1990s was accompanied by a renaissance for Islam. In 1997 the republican authorities announced their intention to introduce Islamic *Shari'a* law over a three-year period from 1999, in contravention of the federal Constitution. Hostilities between armed groupings in Gudermes in July 1998 resulted in the outlawing of oppositionist Islamist groups, which the federal authorities referred to as representatives of the austere Wahhabi Islamic sect, in the Republic.

In August–September 1999 Islamist factions associated with Basayev launched a series of attacks on Dagestan from Chechnya, in particular, with the aim of protecting and extending the jurisdiction of a 'separate Islamic territory' in Dagestan, over which rebels had obtained control in the previous year. (The territory was returned to federal rule in mid-September.) A series of bomb explosions in August and September in Moscow, Dagestan and Volgodonsk (Rostov Oblast), including two that destroyed entire apartment blocks, officially attributed by the Government to Chechen separatists, killed almost 300 people, prompting the redeployment of federal armed forces in the Republic from late September; the recently inaugurated premier, Vladimir Putin, presented the deployment as an 'anti-terrorist operation'. The federal regime declined requests from Maskhadov for the negotiation of a settlement, stating that it recognized only the Moscow-based State Council of the Chechen Republic, which had been recently formed by former members of the republican legislature. (None the less, prior to the redeployment of federal troops, Putin apparently arranged a meeting between the Head of State of Dagestan, Magomedali Magomedov, as the *de facto* representative of the federal authorities, and Maskhadov, in Khasavyurt, Dagestan. However, the meeting was prevented from taking place by crowds of demonstrators, who apparently objected to any negotiations taking place with the Chechen authorities.)

In February 2000 federal forces took control of Groznyi and proceeded to destroy much of the city; many republican and federal administrative bodies were relocated to Gudermes. In May 2000 Putin, by this time the elected President of the Russian Federation, decreed that Chechnya would, henceforth, be ruled federally. Akhmad haji Kadyrov, a former senior mufti and a former ally of Maskhadov, was inaugurated as the Head of the Republican Administration on 20 June. Kadyrov was to be directly responsible to the federal presidential administration. In October it was announced that all Chechen ministries and government departments were to be relocated from Gudermes to Groznyi, with effect from November.

In January 2001 Putin transferred control of military operations in Chechnya from the Ministry of Defence to the Federal Security Service (FSB). The majority of troops in the region were to be withdrawn, leaving a 15,000-strong infantry division and 7,000 interior ministry troops. The FSB was to strengthen its presence in Chechnya, however, in order to combat insurgency. The local administration in Chechnya was restructured to allow it greater autonomy, and Stanislav Ilyasov, a former Governor of Stavropol Krai, was appointed as Chechen premier. Despite claims that federal military operations had effectively ended, guerrilla attacks showed no sign of abating, and concern escalated among international human rights organizations about the conduct of cleansing operations by federal troops, in which entire towns or areas were searched for rebels; the discovery of a number of mass graves, in 2001–02, containing severely mutilated corpses, prompted outrage. In August 2001 Kadyrov criticized the federal defence forces for abusing the human rights of civilians; he subsequently criticized the activities of federal troops in the Republic on several occasions.

In late September 2001, encountering increasing demands for a political solution to the Chechen conflict, Putin announced a 72-hour amnesty, during which rebels could surrender weapons without charge. Although only a negligible quantity of weapons were surrendered, the first official, direct negotiations to take place since the renewal of hostilities in 1999 commenced in Moscow, on 18 November, between the Presidential Representative in the Southern Federal Okrug, Col-Gen. Viktor Kazantsev, and Akhmed Zakayev, deputy premier in the Maskhadov regime. The meeting, however, reached no substantive agreement, and no further high-level negotiations occured. Putin, meanwhile, repeatedly described the conflict in Chechnya as an integral part of the 'war on terrorism' announced by US President George W. Bush in the aftermath of the suicide attacks against the US cities of New York and Washington, DC, on 11 September, and attributed to Osama bin Laden's mlitant Islamist al-Qa'ida (Base) network. In mid-October Kadyrov reformed the Chechen administration; although Ilyasov (who remained resident in Stavropol) was maintained as republican Prime Minister, a new, more senior position, the Chief of Staff of the Chechen Administration, was assigned to Lt-Gen. Yakov (Yan) Sergunin, hitherto responsible for the judicial system in Chechnya.

In March 2002 further progress towards a negotiated settlement of the conflict was reported. A newly established 'Chechen Consultative Council', comprising both Chechens supportive of, and opposed to, the independence of the Republic held its first meeting in the building of the Federal Assembly in Moscow. In April a leading Islamist commander in the conflict, who was believed to be of Jordanian or Saudi Arabian origin, Emir ibn al-Khattab, was killed by federal forces. However, rebel activity increased markedly in the months that followed; although the political authority of Maskhadov, who remained in hiding, had dwindled, his military leadership, of what was known as the State Defence Committee, becaming increasingly prominent as a focus for resistance to the federal troops. In July it was reported that Basayev had been appointed to a senior position on the Committee, although the exact relationship between Maskhadov and Basayev remained obscure. In mid-August federal forces experienced their single largest loss of life since the commencement of operations in 1999, when a military helicopter was shot down by rebels in Groznyi, killing 118 troops. At the end of September 2002 rebels, led by Ruslan Gelayev, staged incursions into Ingushetiya; at least 17 deaths were reported in fighting near the village of Galashki (including two crew members of a helicopter that was shot down by rebels), in what was described as one of the largest battles in the conflict to date. A further military helicopter was shot down in Chechnya in late October. In mid-October 22 police-officers were killed, following the detonation of a bomb at a police station in Groznyi.

On 23–26 October 2002 over 40 heavily armed rebels, led by Movsar Barayev, the cousin of a Chechen rebel leader who had been killed by federal troops in 2001, held captive more than 800 people in a Moscow theatre, and demanded the withdrawal of federal troops from the Republic. The rebels described themselves as members of a 'suicide batallion' and, notably, included several women (referred to by the Russian authorities as 'black widows'), armed with explosive devices. The siege ended when ?lite federal forces stormed the theatre, having initially filled the building with an incapacitating gas. The rebels were killed, and it subsequently emerged that at least 129 hostages had also died, in almost all cases owing to the toxic effects of the gas. Maskhadov issued a statement condemning the rebels' use of terrorist methods, but, despite denials by the Maskhadov-led authorities of their involvement in the incident, Zakayev was arrested on 29 October, on the orders of the federal Government, while attending a World Chechen Congress in Copenhagen, Denmark. (In early November Basayev announced that groups linked to him had perpetrated the hostage-taking in Moscow, and stated that Maskhadov had not known of the incident.) In early December Denmark formally rejected demands for Zakayev's extradition, and he was released. However, he was subsequently detained on arrival in the United Kingdom, as a result of new charges by the Russian Government, before being released on bail. Meanwhile, in the aftermath of the theatre siege the federal Minister of Defence, Sergei Ivanov, announced that the Government was to intensify its military offensive in Chechnya, and that the previously planned withdrawal of troops had been cancelled. Representative offices of the 'Chechen Republic of Ichkeriya' were closed in several countries, including Azerbaijan, Georgia and Turkey, in November, as the result of pressure from the Russian Government.

In mid-November 2002 Ilyasov was removed from his position as Prime Minister of Chechnya and, in what was widely perceived as a promotion, appointed as Minister without Portfolio in the federal

Government, responsible for the Social and Economic Development of Chechnya; Ilyasov was succeeded as republican premier by Capt. (retd) Mikhail Babich, who had previously held senior positions in the regional administrations of Ivanovo and Moscow Oblasts. On his appointment, Babich announced measures intended to facilitate the economic development of the Republic, and encouraged Chechens who had left the Republic during the 1990s to return. In late November Ilyasov announced that a referendum on a new draft Chechen constitution, which would, *inter alia*, determine the status of the Republic within the Russian Federation, was to be held in March 2003; this measure was confirmed by Putin in mid-December 2002. In late December at least 83 people died, and more than 150 others were injured, when suicide bombers detonated bombs in two vehicles stationed outside the headquarters of the republican Government in Groznyi; no senior officials were killed. (Basayev subsequently claimed personal responsibility for, and involvement in, the attack.) By late December 2002 federal losses during the campaign, according to official figures, were put at 4,572 dead and 15,549 wounded, with 29 missing, although Chechen estimates were considerably higher. (It was also estimated that more than 14,000 rebel fighters had been killed since September 1999.) In early January 2003 Babich was appointed to head a committee that was to organize the planned referendum on the future administration of Chechnya. However, on 23 January Babich resigned as premier, reportedly following a disagreement with Kadyrov regarding the appointment of a republican Minister of Finance. On 10 February Anatolii Popov, the hitherto deputy chairman of the state commission for the reconstruction of Chechnya, was appointed as the new republican premier.

The referendum on the draft constitution for Chechnya, describing the republic (referred to as the Chechen—Nokchi Republic) as both a sovereign entity, with its own citizenship, and as an integral part of the Russian Federation proceeded, as scheduled, on 23 March 2003, despite concerns that the instability of the Republic would prevent the poll from being free and fair. The draft constitution also provided for the holding of fresh elections to a strengthened republican presidency and legislature. According to the official results, some 88.4% of the electorate participated in the plebiscite, of whom 96.0% supported the draft constitution. Two further questions, on the method of electing the president and the parliament of the Republic of Chechnya, were supported by 95.4% and 96.1% of participants, respectively. However, independent observers challenged the results, reporting that the rate of participation by the electorate had been much lower than officially reported. (According to official results, an identical number of valid votes had been cast in response to all three questions, while it was reported that the total number of votes cast had, in fact, been in excess of the registered electorate.)

Political violence, however, continued to dominate Chechen affairs in the period after the referendum; in early April 2003 at least 22 people were killed in two separate incidents when their vehicles detonated landmines. In early May 2003 at least 59 people were killed when suicide bombers attacked government offices in Znamenskoye, in the north of Chechnya. Two days later another suicide bombing at a religious festival attended by Kadyrov (in his new capacity as acting President) near Gudermes resulted in at least 14 deaths, although Kadyrov escaped unhurt; Basayev claimed responsibility for the organization of both attacks. In mid-May Putin presented draft legislation to parliament, providing for an amnesty for rebels in the Republic who surrendered their weapons; the proposed amnesty was also to apply to federal soldiers accused of abuses committed in Chechnya; the amnesty, which took effect from 7 June, was to continue until 1 September, and was, notably, to exclude several prominent rebel leaders. (However, by September only 145 rebels and 226 members of the federal forces had been granted amnesty.)

In early June 2003 Kadyrov, using the new powers that he had been granted following the constitutional referendum, dismissed the majority of the republican Government, and the heads of every regional administration in the Republic; the vast majority were reappointed shortly afterwards, although a new Mayor was appointed in Groznyi. On 21 June Kadyrov inaugurated an interim legislative body, the 42-member State Council, comprising the head of, and an appointed representative of, each administrative district; Khusein Isayev, hitherto head of the apparatus of the Ministry of State Property in Chechnya, was elected as Chairman of the Council, defeating the candidate of the pro-Government Unity and Fatherland-United Russia candidate, Ruslan Yamadayev. In early July Putin announced that the presidential elections in Chechnya were to be held on 5 October. On 5 August Popov assumed the post of acting President, in order to permit Kadyrov to commence his electoral campaign; however, on 20 August, following a ruling by the republican electoral commission, Kadyrov was permitted to resume his former duties until 5 September.

From 1 September 2003 control of military operations in Chechnya was assumed by the federal Ministry of Internal Affairs from the FSB; it was announced that such operations were no longer regarded as having an 'anti-terrorist' character but were, rather, to form part of an 'operation to protect law and constitutional order'. Meanwhile, campaigning for the presidential elections commenced: by 20 August, when the deadline for submitting candidacies for the presidential election expired, 11 valid applications had been made. However, by mid-September the three candidacies regarded as most likely to pose a credible challenge to Kadyrov had withdrawn, or been forced to withdraw from the contest. In particular, the withdrawal of Aslanbek Aslakhanov, a representative of the Republic in the State Duma, and the debarring of a business executive, Malik Saidullayev, both of which occured on 11 September, effectively removed any major challenges to Kadyrov's candidacy. As expected, on 5 October Kadyrov was elected as President, receiving 87.7% of votes cast, according to official figures. The rate of participation in the polls was stated to be 82.6%. In this context it remained uncertain whether Kadyrov's presidency would be regarded as legitimate within the Republic, and some commentators expressed concern that an intra-Chechen conflict could evolve. Kadyrov subsequently re-appointed Popov as premier. Legislative elections were due to be held in the Republic in January 2004.

## Economy

Prior to the outbreak of armed hostilities in the region in 1994–95 Groznyi was the principal industrial centre in Chechnya. In 2000 there were 304 km (189 miles) of railways and 3,057 km of paved roads on the Republic's territory. Its agriculture consisted mainly of horticulture, production of grain and sugar beet and animal husbandry. Its main industrial activities were production of petroleum and petrochemicals, petroleum refining, power engineering, manufacture of machinery and the processing of forestry and agricultural products. Conflict in 1994–96, and again from 1999, seriously damaged the economic infrastructure and disrupted both agricultural and industrial activity. At April 1998 around four-fifths of the Republic's population were unemployed, and the 1998 budget showed a deficit of 68m. roubles. However, future developments depended on greater stability in the territory. Another asset that could be sabotaged by, or displaced because of, violence was one of Russia's major petroleum pipelines that crossed Chechnya (transit fees from Caspian hydrocarbons could be a major source of revenue). In mid-1999 the Chechen section of a petroleum pipeline from Baku, Azerbaijan, to Novorossiisk, was closed, owing to the lack of security in the region. However, attempts were being made to restore industry in the Republic, and a sugar refinery and a brickworks were in operation there in 2001. The principal petroleum company operating the Republic in the early 2000s was Grozneftegaz, which was 51%-owned by Rosneft, and 49% by the republican Government. Output of petroleum in 2002 was estimated at approximately 1.5m. metric tons. A new polypropylene-fabric factory was constructed in Groznyi in 2002. In November 2002 it was reported that the federal budget for 2003 was to allocate some 3,500m. roubles to the Republic, under a programme that aimed to promote economic and social recovery.

## Directory

**President and Head of the Administration:** AKHMED A. haji KADYROV; 364000 Chechnya, Groznyi, ul. Garazhnaya 10A; tel. and fax (095) 777-92-28; e-mail info@chechnya.gov.ru; internet www .chechnya.gov.ru.

**Chairman of the Republican Government (Prime Minister and First Deputy Head of the Administration):** ANATOLII A. POPOV; 364000 Chechnya, Groznyi, ul. Garazhnaya 10A; tel. (095) 777-92-14.

**Chairman of the State Council:** KHUSEIN ISAYEV; 364000 Chechnya, Groznyi, ul. Garazhnaya 10A.

**Chief Representative of the Chechen (Nokchi) Republic in the Russian Federation:** ADLAN MAGOMADOV; 127025 Moscow, ul. Novyi Arbat 19; tel. (095) 203-91-45; fax (095) 203-63-52.

**Head of Groznyi City Administration (Mayor):** KHOZH-AHMED ARSANOV; tel. (8712) 22-01-42.

# Chuvash Republic (Chuvashiya)

The Chuvash Republic is situated in the north-west of European Russia. It forms part of the Volga Federal Okrug and the Volga-Vyatka Economic Area. The Republic lies on the Eastern European Plain on the middle reaches of the Volga. Ulyanovsk Oblast neighbours it to the south, the Republic of Mordoviya to the south-west, Nizhnii Novgorod Oblast to the west and the Republics of Marii-El and Tatarstan to the north and the east, respectively. The Republic's major rivers are the Volga and the Sura, and one-third of its territory is covered by forest. It occupies 18,300 sq km (7,070 sq miles) and comprises 21 administrative districts and nine cities. The territory measures 190 km (118 miles) from south to north and 160 km from west to east. At 1 January 2002 the Republic had an estimated total population of 1,346,300 and a relatively high population density of 73.6 per sq km. Some 61.2% of the population lived in towns in January 2001. In contrast to the native peoples in the majority of autonomous republics, the Chuvash outnumber ethnic Russians in Chuvashiya: at the census of 1989, 67.8% of inhabitants were Chuvash and 26.7% Russian. The native tongue of the Republic is Chuvash, which has its origins in the Bulgar group of the Western Hunnic group of Turkic languages and is related to ancient Bulgar and Khazar. It is spoken as a first language by an estimated 76.5% of Chuvash. The dominant religions in Chuvashiya are Islam and Orthodox Christianity. Chuvashiya's capital is at Cheboksary (Shupashkar—with a population of 461,200 in 2001). Its other major town is Novocheboksarsk, with 124,200 inhabitants.

## History

The Chuvash, traditionally a semi-nomadic people, were conquered by the Mongol-Tatars in the 13th century. Their territory subsequently became part of the dominion of the Golden Horde and many were converted to Islam. From the late 1430s the Chuvash were ruled by the Kazan Khanate. In 1551 Chuvashiya became a part of the Russian Empire. Despite intense Christianization and 'russification' on the part of the Russian state, the Chuvash acquired their own national and cultural identity, which had Suvar-Bulgar and Finno-Ugric components, by the end of the 15th century. The Chuvash capital was founded at Cheboksary in 1551, at the site of a settlement first mentioned in Russian chronicles in 1469. The construction of other towns and forts, intended to encourage migration into the area, followed. After 1917 the Chuvash people made vociferous demands for autonomy to the Soviet Government. A Chuvash Autonomous Oblast was established on 24 June 1920, which was upgraded to the status of an ASSR on 21 April 1925.

Chuvash nationalism re-emerged in the early 1990s: the Chuvash ASSR declared its sovereignty on 27 October 1990. It adopted the name of the Chuvash (Chavash) Republic in March 1992. In December 1993 the Republic voted against acceptance of the federal Constitution. In May 1996 the Chuvash Government signed a treaty with the Russian President, Boris Yeltsin, on the delimitation of powers. It granted the Republic greater freedom to determine policy in political, economic and social areas. Elections to the 87-seat republican legislature, the State Council, were held on 13 July 1998, with further elections for 23 unfilled seats on 1 November. In October 2001 the Chairman of the republican Council of Ministers, Enver Ablyakimov, resigned; republican President Nikolai Fedorov appointed himself to the position, announcing that combining the roles of republican president and prime minister would increase the Government's accountability. Fedorov was re-elected, with some 41% of the votes, in the presidential election held in Chuvashiya on 16 December. However, immediately following his re-election as Governor, Fedorov announced that he was to rescind his position as Chairman of the Council of Ministers (Prime Minister); Nataliya Partasova assumed this position. Elections to the republican legislature were held on 21 June 2002. In March 2003 the State Council voted to extend the term of office of deputies from four to five years.

## Economy

In 1999 the Republic's gross regional product amounted to 18,372.1m. roubles, equivalent to 13,526.8 roubles per head. Chuvashiya's major industrial centres are at Cheboksary, Novocheboksarsk, Kanash and Alatyr. In 2000 there were 396 km of railways and 4,474 km of paved roads on the Republic's territory.

Its agriculture, which employed 25.3% of the work-force in 2000, consists mainly of grain, potato, vegetable, hop, hemp and makhorka-tobacco production, horticulture and animal husbandry. The value of total agricultural output in that year amounted to 8,563m. roubles. The Republic contains deposits of peat, sand, limestone and dolomite. Its main industries are mechanical engineering, metal-working, electricity generation, production of chemicals, light industry, wood-working, manufacture of building materials and food-processing. The industrial sector employed 24.4% of the working population in 2000 and generated 19,531m. roubles in income.

The economically active population in Chuvashiya amounted to 686,000 in 2000; 9.1% of the Republic's labour force were unemployed, one of the lowest levels in the Federation. The average monthly wage in the territory was 2,435.3 roubles in mid-2002. In 2000 there was a budgetary surplus of 35.7m. roubles. In that year exports from the Republic amounted to US $62.0m., and imports to the Republic to $55.7m. Chuvashiya's major trading partners are the People's Republic of China, Finland, Germany, Italy, the Netherlands, Poland, Ukraine and the USA. Foreign investment in 2000 was worth $1.7m. At 31 December 2000 there were 4,000 small businesses operating in Chuvashiya.

# Directory

**President:** NIKOLAI V. FEDOROV; 428004 Chuvashiya, Cheboksary, pl. Respubliki 1; tel. (8352) 62-46-87; fax (8352) 62-17-99; e-mail president@cap.ru; internet www.cap.ru.

**Chairman of the Cabinet of Ministers (Prime Minister):** NATALIYA YU. PARTASOVA; 428004 Chuvashiya, Cheboksary, pl. Respubliki 1; tel. (8352) 62-01-76; fax (8352) 62-31-84; e-mail partasova@chuvashia.com.

**Chairman of the State Council (Parliament):** MIKHAIL A. MIKHAILOVSKII; 428004 Chuvashiya, Cheboksary, pl. Respubliki 1; tel. (8352) 62-22-72; fax (8352) 62-23-15; e-mail gs@cap.ru; internet www.gs.chuvashia.com.

**Chief Representative of the Chuvash Republic in the Russian Federation:** GENNADII S. FEDOROV; 119017 Moscow, ul. B. Ordynka 46/1; tel. and fax (095) 953-21-59.

**Head of Cheboksary City Administration:** NIKOLAI I. YEMELYANOV; 428004 Chuvashiya, Cheboksary, ul. K. Marksa 36; tel. (8352) 62-35-76; fax (8352) 62-40-50; e-mail gcheb@cap.ru; internet www.gcheb.cap.ru.

# Republic of Dagestan

The Republic of Dagestan (Daghestan) is situated in the North Caucasus on the Caspian Sea. Dagestan forms part of the Southern Federal Okrug and the North Caucasus Economic Area. It has international borders with Azerbaijan to the south and Georgia to the south-west. The Republic of Chechnya and Stavropol Krai lie to the west and the Republic of Kalmykiya to the north. Its largest rivers are the Terek, the Sulak and the Samur. It occupies an area of 50,300 sq km (19,420 sq miles) and measures some 400 km (250 miles) from south to north. Its Caspian Sea coastline, to the east, is 530 km long. The north of the Republic is flat, while in the south are the foothills and peaks of the Greater Caucasus. The Republic's lowest-lying area is the Caspian lowlands, at 28 m (92 feet) below sea level, while its highest peak is over 4,000 m high. Dagestan is made up of 41 administrative districts and 10 cities. The climate in its mountainous areas is continental and dry, while in coastal areas it is subtropical, with strong winds. Dagestan had an estimated population of 2,179,500 at 1 January 2002, and a population density of 43.3 per sq km. In January 2001 some 39.9% of the Republic's population inhabited urban areas. In 1989, according to the census, some 27.5% of the population of Dagestan were Avars, 15.6% Dargins, 12.9% Kumyks, 11.3% Lezgins, 5.1% Laks, 4.3% Tabasarans, 1.6% Nogai, 0.8% Rutuls, 0.8% Aguls and 0.3% Tsakhurs, while ethnic Russians formed the fifth-largest nationality, accounting for 9.2%. (However, preliminary results of the 2002 census suggested that up to one-third of those previously categorized as Avars regarded themselves as belonging to some 15 other ethnic groups.) Dagestan's capital is at Makhachkala, which had 327,600 inhabitants in 2001. The city lies on the Caspian Sea and is the Republic's main port. Other major cities are Derbent (93,200), Khasavyurt (85,300), Kaspiisk (69,500) and Buinaksk (55,400).

## History

Dagestan formally came under Russian rule in 1723, when the various Muslim khanates on its territory were annexed from Persia (Iran). The Dagestani peoples conducted a series of rebellions against Russian control, including the Murid Uprising of 1828–59, before Russian control could be established. A Dagestan ASSR was established on 20 January 1920.

The Republic of Dagestan acceded to the Federation Treaty in March 1992 and officially declared its sovereignty in May 1993. The Republic voted against the new federal Constitution in December and adopted a new republican Constitution on 26 July 1994. On 21 March 1996 the powers of the Dagestani State Council, the supreme executive body, which comprised a representative of each of the 14 largest ethnic groups in the Republic, were prolonged by a further two years. When this extra term had elapsed, the republican legislature convened as a Constituent Assembly and, on 26 June 1998, confirmed Magomedali Magomedov as the Chairman of the State Council. Parliamentary elections, for a new People's Assembly, were held on 7 March 1999, concurrently with a referendum to decide whether to institute an executive presidency in Dagestan; the proposal was rejected for a third time. The republican Government was widely regarded as the federal Government's closest ally, and the most active supporter of Russian territorial integrity, among the North Caucasian republics. A constitutional change of March 1998, which permitted Magomedov to serve a further term, also removed the nationality requirements for senior republican positions; this was thought to unsettle the fragile balance of power between the different ethnic groups in the Republic.

Concern was expressed at a growth in support for militant Islamist groups in Dagestan in the late 1990s, which, however, appeared to have abated somewhat by the early 2000s. In February 1998 Islamist militants seized three villages in Buinaksk district as 'a separate Islamic territory'. In May a group of 200–300 fighters belonging to the Union of Russian Muslims, a political party represented in the republican parliament and led by Nadirshakh Khachilayev, the brother of the head of the ethnic Lak community in Dagestan, occupied a government building in Makhachkala; simultaneously, 2,000 demonstrators gathered in the main city square to demand the resignation of the republican Government. (Khachilayev was assassinated in August 2003.) Meanwhile, there was increasing evidence of close ties between militant groups in Dagestan and those operating abroad, particularly in Arab countries. In 1996–97 Ayman al-Zawahiri, the leader of the militant Egyptian Islamic Jihad and a close ally of the Saudi-born leader of the Islamist al-Qa'ida (Base) organization, Osama bin Laden, was imprisoned for six months in Dagestan, after having been found guilty of entering Russia illegally.

Chechen militants, aided by Dagestani militant Islamists, invaded Dagestan on 2 August 1999, and again on 5 September; fighting ceased on 16 September, when federal troops additionally regained control over the separate Islamic territory declared in February 1998. On the same day the republican legislature approved a law prohibiting the austere Wahhabi Islamic sect. Later in the month, when the re-commencement of military operations by federal troops in Chechnya appeared imminent, crowds of demonstrators, who blocked approach roads to the city of Khasavyurt, prevented a planned meeting there, which had been reportedly instigated by the federal Chairman of the Government, Vladimir Putin, between Magomedov, as the *de facto* representative of the federal Government, and the President of the 'Chechen Republic of Ichkeriya', Khalid Maskhadov; it was reported that the demonstrators objected to any negotiations taking place with the Chechen authorities, who they held responsible for the increasing lawlessness, and in particular the widespread incidence of hostage-taking, in Dagestan in 1996–99, including, most notoriously, an incident in January 1996, when some 2,000 hostages had been seized in the town of Kizlyar. Indeed, such was the hostility towards the rebel Chechen movement in Dagestan that the federal authorities agreed to a request from officials of the Dagestani Government that no refugees from Chechnya be accommodated in Dagestan, in contrast with most of the neighbouring territories under Russian control.

In late September 1999, following the re-commencement of military operations in Chechnya, an explosion in Buinaksk, outside accommodation used by federal troops, killed about 60 people; a larger bomb nearby was defused. In 2001–03 a number of explosions in Dagestan were attributed to supporters of Chechen separatism. On 9 May 2002 , during a Victory Day parade in Kaspiisk, 45 people were killed and more than 130 injured in an explosion; it was reported in June 2003 that the alleged instigator of the bombing, Rappani Khalilov, a supporter of Chechen separatism, had been killed by federal troops.

On 25 June 2002 the Constitutional Assembly voted by an overwhelming majority for Magomedov to serve for a third term as Chairman of the State Council. Elections to the State Council took place on 16 March 2003, at which Magomedov was re-elected as Chairman of the State Council, and, hence, of the Government. On 10 July the republican Constitutional Assembly unanimously approved the introduction of a new republican Constitution, which implemented wide-ranging reforms to the structure of government. (The new Constitution came into effect on 26 July.) Notably, a directly elected Presidency was to be established, to replace the State Council, which would be abolished following the end of its term of office, in 2006; moreover, the number of parliamentary deputies was also to be reduced from 121 to 72. Meanwhile, it was reported that at least eight parliamentary deputies had been assassinated in Dagestan in 1992–2003. On 28 August 2003 the republican Minister for National Policy, Information and Foreign Affairs, Magomedsalikh Gusayev, was killed when a bomb was detonated by his car; Gusayev had played a particularly prominent role in combating Islamist militancy in Dagestan.

## Economy

In 1999 gross regional product in the Republic of Dagestan amounted to 13,043.6m. roubles, or 6,110.3 roubles per head—one of the lowest figures among the federal units. The economic situation in the Republic suffered greatly from the wars in Chechnya, mainly as a result of the transport blockade, the energy shortage and the influx of refugees. The Republic's major industrial centres are at Makhachkala, Derbent, Kaspiisk, Izberbash, Khasavyurt, Kizlyar, Kizilyurt and Buinaksk. In 2000 there were 516 of km railways and 4,474 km of paved roads in the Republic. There are fishing and trading ports in Makhachkala, which is a major junction for trading routes by rail, land and sea. The major railway line between Rostov-on-Don and Baku, Azerbaijan, runs across the territory, as does the federal Caucasus highway and the petroleum pipeline between Groznyi (Dzhokhar Gala) and Baku. There is an airport some 15 km from Makhachkala. In September 1997 the federal Government announced that a new section of the petroleum pipeline from Baku would traverse the southern part of Dagestan, rather than run through Chechnya. However, the section was closed indefinitely in June 1999, following an explosion, caused by insurgents.

Owing to its mountainous terrain, Dagestan's economy is largely based on animal husbandry, particularly sheep-breeding. Its agriculture also consists of grain production, viniculture, horticulture and fishing. The agricultural sector employed around 33.6% of the Republic's work-force in 2000 (when just 14.3% worked in industry) and total output in that year amounted to a value of 8,199m. roubles. Its main industries are petroleum and natural gas production, electricity generation, mechanical engineering, metal-working, food-processing, the production of building materials, and handicrafts (especially chiselling and carpet-making). Industrial production in 2000 was worth 5,715m. roubles. The Republic's large defence-sector enterprises, such as the Dagdizel Caspian Plant, the Mogomed Gadzhiyev Plant, Aviagregat and the Dagestan Plant of Electro-thermal Equipment, were operating below capacity by the mid-1990s.

Dagestan's economically active population comprised 830,000 inhabitants in 2000. In that year over one-quarter of the Republic's labour force (25.6%) were unemployed. In mid-2002 the average monthly wage was 2,188.6 roubles, the lowest in the Federation. There was a budgetary surplus of 307.3m. roubles in 2000. Foreign investment in the territory was minimal (amounting to just US \$53,000 in 1998), owing to Dagestan's proximity to Chechnya and its own incidences of insurgency and unrest. In August 1999 the federal Government approved funds of 100m. roubles in reconstruction assistance and a further 12m. roubles to aid displaced persons. There were 2,000 small businesses in Dagestan at the end of 2000.

## Directory

**Chairman of the State Council (Head of the Republic):** MAGO-MEDALI M. MAGOMEDOV; 367005 Dagestan, Makhachkala, pl. Lenina 1; tel. (8722) 67-30-59; fax (8722) 67-30-60; e-mail info@dagestan.ru; internet www.magomedov.ru.

**Chairman of the Government:** KHIZRI I. SHIKHSAIDOV; 367005 Dagestan, Makhachkala, pl. Lenina; tel. (8722) 67-20-17; internet www.diap.ru.

**Chairman of the People's Assembly:** MUKHU G. ALIYEV; 367005 Dagestan, Makhachkala, pl. Lenina; tel. (8722) 67-30-55; fax (8722) 67-30-66; internet www.rd.dgu.ru.

**Chief Representative of the Republic of Dagestan in the Russian Federation:** Ramazan Sh. MAMEDOV GAMZAYEV; 105062 Moscow, ul. Pokrovka 28; tel. (095) 916-15-36; fax (095) 928-41-12.

**Head of Makhachkala City Administration:** SAID D. AMIROV; 367025 Dagestan, Makhachkala, pl. Lenina 2; tel. (8722) 67-21-57; e-mail z999@km.ru; internet www.makhachkala.dgu.ru.

# Republic of Ingushetiya

The Republic of Ingushetiya (formerly part of the Checheno-Ingush ASSR) is situated on the northern slopes of the Greater Caucasus, in the centre of the Northern Caucasus mountain ridge. It forms part of the Southern Federal Okrug and the North Caucasus Economic Area. The Republic of Chechnya borders Ingushetiya on its eastern and northern sides and the Republic of North Osetiya—Alaniya lies to the west. In the southern mountains there is an international border with Georgia. The Terek, which forms part of the northern border of Ingushetiya, the Assa and the Sunzha are the territory's main rivers. The Republic is extremely mountainous, with some peaks over 3,000 m high. The territory of the Republic occupies about 3,600 sq km (1,400 sq miles) and includes four cities. However, the border with Chechnya is not exactly determined, and the Ingush were also in dispute with North Osetiya. There were thought to be around 35,000 displaced persons from the Prigorodnyi raion of North Osetiya—Alaniya in the Republic. The number of refugees from Chechnya has fluctuated with the conflict; estimated figures in October 1999 were in the region of 155,000, but one year later the establishment of large-scale refugee camps in the Republic brought the total to around 210,000, although the number had declined to 69,000 by late November 2002, following the commencement of measures by the federal authorities to facilitate the return of refugees to Chechnya; in August 2003 the acting President of Chechnya, Anatolii Popov, announced that all Chechen refugee camps in Ingushetiya would be closed by October of that year. At 1 January 2002 the estimated population of the Republic had increased to 466,300, giving a population density of some 129.5 per sq km. In 2001 some

42.2% of the population lived in urban areas. The Ingush are a Muslim people closely related to the Chechens (collectively they are known as Vainakhs). They are indigenous to the Caucasus Mountains and have been known historically as Galgai, Lamur, Mountaineers and Kist. Like the Chechen language, their native tongue is a dialect of the Nakh group of the Caucasian language family. Ingushetiya's administrative centre is at Magas, a new city, opened officially in October 1998, which was named after the medieval Alanic capital believed to have been situated thereabouts. Initially the city consisted solely of a gold-domed presidential palace and government buildings, and by January 2001 its population was only about 100. The former capital of Nazran, approximately 15 miles from Magas, remained the largest city in the Republic, with a population of 113,400 at January 2001.

## History

The Ingush are descended from the western Nakh people, whose different reaction to Russian colonization of the Caucasus region in the 1860s distinguished them from their eastern counterparts (subsequently known as the Chechens). The Chechens resisted the invaders violently and were driven into the mountains, while the Ingush reacted more passively and settled on the plains. Despite this, the Ingush suffered severely under Soviet rule. In 1920 their territory was temporarily integrated into the Mountain (Gorskaya) People's Republic, but became the Ingush Autonomous Oblast on 7 July 1924. In 1934 the region was joined to the Checheno-Ingush Autonomous Oblast, which was upgraded to the status of a Republic in 1936. At this time, many leading Ingush intellectuals became victims of 'purges' and the Ingush literary language was banned. In February 1944 the entire Ingush population (74,000, according to the 1939 census) was deported to Soviet Central Asia, owing to its alleged collaboration with Nazi Germany. The territory was subsequently handed over to the Osetiyans. On their return after rehabilitation in 1957 the Ingush were forced to purchase the property from Osetiyan settlers.

With the ascendancy in the ASSR of the All-National Congress of the Chechen People in 1991, a *de facto* separation between Chechen and Ingush territories was achieved. In June 1992 the Supreme Soviet of the Russian Federation formalized Ingushetiya's existence as an separate republic within the Federation, although the borders between the two new units were not delineated. In addition, the Ingush Republic claimed the eastern regions of North Osetiya and part of the North Osetiyan capital, Vladikavkaz (which had been shared until the 1930s.) Prigorodnyi raion (district), with a majority of Ingush inhabitants, was at the centre of the dispute. (A federal law passed in April 1991 established the right for deported peoples to repossess their territory.) Armed hostilities between the two Republics ensued from October 1992, until a peace agreement was signed in 1994, although subsequent relations remained strained.

On 27 February 1994, alongside simultaneous parliamentary and presidential elections in the Republic, 97% of the electorate voted in favour of a draft republican constitution, which took immediate effect. At the republican presidential election, held in March 1998, Ruslan Aushev was re-elected. His popular mandate emboldened him to seek to amend federal law to conform more closely to what he termed 'national traditions', but which also incorporated aspects of *Shari'a*, or Islamic law. Following a declaration by federal President Boris Yeltsin that a planned referendum, which sought, in particular, to pardon those charged with crimes such as revenge killings, was unconstitutional, in February 1999 Aushev signed a power-sharing agreement with the federal Government. In July Aushev issued a decree, permitting men up to four wives, in breach of the Russian Federation's family code.

The population of Ingushetiya remained generally supportive of the federal authorities, but strongly opposed federal military intervention in Chechnya—Aushev was a prominent critic of the military operations. This apparent inconsistency was reflected in the outcome of the federal presidential election of 26 March 2000; despite his leading role in recommencing armed hostilities in Chechnya, Ingushetiya awarded Vladimir Putin the largest proportion of the votes (85.4%) cast for any candidate in any federal subject. The successful implementation of a settlement between Ingushetiya and North Osetiya, signed in March 2001, according to which the Ingush could return to their former homes in Prigorodnyi and Vladikavkaz, was inhibited by logistical difficulties and protests. In November 2001 the People's Assembly voted to shorten the republican presidential term by one year, to four years, and scheduled presidential elections for March 2002. However, in December 2001 the republican Supreme Court declared these measures to be unconstitutional. In late December Aushev resigned, having announced that he would not seek re-election; in January 2002 he was appointed as Ingushetiya's representative in the Federation Council, the upper chamber of the Russian Federal Assembly. Aushev resigned from this position in April, following the disqualification of his preferred candidate for the republican presidency. After an inconclusive first round of voting on 7 April, Murat Zyazikov, the Deputy Presidential

Representative in the Southern Federal Okrug (and a general in the Federal Security Service—FSB), and Alikhan Amirkhanov, a State Duma deputy, progressed to a second round. On 28 April Zyazikov was elected President, receiving 53.1% of the votes cast. In late September up to 70 deaths were reported near the village of Galashki, as Chechen rebels, who were reported to have entered the territory from the Pankisi Gorge in Georgia, clashed with federal forces; notably, rebels shot down a helicopter gunship, killing two people. In October Ingushetiya and North Osetiya signed an 'Agreement on the Development of Co-operation and Good Neighbourly Relations', which committed both sides to adopting measures to resolve their remaining differences. On 2 June 2003 Zyazikov dismissed the republican Government; on 19 June the hitherto Deputy chairman of the republican Government and a petroleum-industry business executive, Timur Mogushkov, was appointed as Chairman (Prime Minister). At the end of July five federal troops died after their vehicles struck a landmine near Galashki. In mid-September an explosive device, assembled outside the residence of Zyazikov, was successfully disabled. Later in the month three people were killed, and another 31 injured, when a truck bomb was detonated by two suicide bombers outside the offices of the FSB in Magas. At the end of September renewed clashes, apparently involving several hundred rebel fighters, in which at least 17 deaths were reported, broke out between Chechen rebels and troops and police near Galashki, although the rebels subsequently fled, allegedly returning to Chechnya.

## Economy

In 1999 the gross regional product of the Republic totalled 2,030.7m. roubles, or just 5,040.1 roubles per head. Essentially agricultural, Ingushetiya had hoped to benefit from the transit of Caspian hydrocarbons from the beginning of the 2000s, although continuing instability in neighbouring Chechnya and Dagestan appeared to reduce its prospects in the short term. In 2000 there were 39 km (24 miles) of railways and 804 km of paved roads in the Republic.

In the early 1990s Ingushetiya's economy was largely agricultural (the sector employed only 6.6% of the Republic's work-force in 2000, compared with 28.5% in 1995), its primary activity being cattle-breeding. The serious decline in agricultural production led to intervention by the republican Government; unprofitable collective farms were converted into private enterprises and joint-stock companies. By 1 January 1997 there were over 1,000 private farms and 20 joint-stock companies in the Republic. In 2000 the value of its agricultural output was 826m. roubles. Ingushetiya's industry, which employed just 8.1% of the working population in 2000, consists of electricity production, petroleum-refining and food-processing. The major petroleum company, LUKoil, was a participant in the construction of the Caspian pipeline running through the territory. Total industrial production amounted to a value of 895m. roubles in 2000. From the mid-1990s the services sector had also made a contribution to the economy, with the local economy receiving substantial benefits from registration fees paid by companies operating in the so-called 'offshore' tax haven that was in operation in 1994–97. At that time, the resources of this zone accounted for some 70% of the Republic's capital investments, but it was terminated following criticism by the IMF. In 2000 the economic sectors providing the largest share of employment in Ingushetiya were trade and commerce (19.4% of the total) and construction (17.2%).

In 2000 the economically active population of Ingushetiya numbered 112,000, and in that year some 32.0% of the Republic's labour force were unemployed, by far the highest level of any federal subject (excluding Chechnya, for which no figures were available). None the less, this represented a considerable improvement compared with preceding years; in 1997 as many as 58.2% of Ingushetiya's labour force were out of work, and the rate of unemployment remained in excess of 50% in 1998 and 1999. In 2002 the average monthly wage in the Republic was 3,518.8 roubles. In 2000 the regional budget showed a surplus of 25.7m. roubles. In that year the value of the Republic's foreign trade amounted to US $72.6m. in exports and $91.6m. in imports. In 2000 there were approximately 300 small businesses in the Republic.

## Directory

**President:** MURAT M. ZYAZIKOV; 366720 Ingushetiya, Magas, Dom Pravitelstva; tel. and fax (87345) 5-11-55; e-mail murad@ingushetia.ru; internet ingushetia.ru.

**Chairman of the Government (Prime Minister):** TIMUR A. MOGUSHKOV; 366720 Ingushetiya, Magas, Dom Pravitelstva; tel. (87322) 2-56-80.

**Chairman of the People's Assembly:** RUSLAN S. PLIYEV; 366720 Ingushetiya, Magas, Narodnoye Sobraniye; tel. (87322) 2-61-81; fax (87322) 2-56-80.

**Chief Representative of the Republic of Ingushetiya in the Russian Federation:** KHAMZAT M. BELKHAROYEV; 109044 Moscow, ul. Vorontsovskaya 22/2; tel. (095) 912-93-09; fax (095) 912-92-75.

**Head of Magas City Administration:** ILEZ M. MIZIYEV; tel. (87322) 6-10-81.

# Kabardino-Balkar Republic (Kabardino-Balkariya)

The Kabardino-Balkar Republic is situated on the northern slopes of the Greater Caucasus and on the Kabardin Flatlands. It forms part of the Southern Federal Okrug and the North Caucasus Economic Area. The Republic of North Osetiya—Alaniya (Ossetia) lies to the east and there is an international border with Georgia in the southwest. Stavropol Krai lies to the north, with the Republic of Karachayevo-Cherkessiya to the west. Kabardino-Balkariya's major rivers are the Terek, the Malka and the Baskan. The territory of the Republic occupies an area of 12,500 sq km (4,800 sq miles), of which one-half is mountainous. The highest peak in Europe, twin-peaked Elbrus, at a height of 5,642 m (18,517 feet), is situated in Kabardino-Balkariya. The Republic consists of nine administrative districts and eight cities. At 1 January 2002 the estimated population of the Republic was 782,000, giving a population density of 62.6 per sq km, one of the highest in the Russian Federation. In January 2001 57.0% of the Republic's population lived in urban areas. Figures from the census of 1989 indicate that at that time some 48.2% of inhabitants were Kabardins, 9.4% were Balkars and 32.0% were Russian. Both the Kabardins and the Balkars are Sunni Muslims. The Kabardins' native language belongs to the Abkhazo-Adyge group of Caucasian languages. The Balkars speak a language closely related to Karachai, part of the Kipchak group of the Turkic branch of the Uralo-Altaic family. Both peoples almost exclusively speak their native tongue as a first language, but many are fluent in the official language, Russian. The capital of the Republic is at Nalchik, which had a population of 228,400 at 1 January 2001.

## History

The Turkic Kabardins, a Muslim people of the North Caucasus, are believed to be descended from the Adyges. They settled on the banks of the Terek river, mixed with the local Alan people, and became a distinct ethnic group in the 15th century. The Kabardins were converted to Islam by the Tatar Khanate of Crimea in the early 16th century, but in 1561 appealed to Tsar Ivan IV for protection against Tatar rule. The Ottoman Turks and the Persians (Iranians) also had interests in the region and in 1739 Kabardiya was established as a neutral state between the Ottoman and Russian Empires. In 1774, however, the region once again became Russian territory under the terms of the Treaty of Kuçuk Kainavci. Although the Kabardins were never openly hostile to the Russian authorities, in the 1860s many of them migrated to the Ottoman Empire. The Balkars were pastoral nomads until the mid-18th century, when they were forced by threats from marauding tribes to retreat further into the Northern Caucasus Mountains and settle there as farmers and livestock breeders. They were converted to Islam by Crimean Tatars, followed by the Nogai from the Kuban basin, although their faith retained strong elements of their animist traditions. Balkariya came under Russian control in 1827, when it was dominated by the Kabardins. Many ethnic Russians migrated to the region during the 19th century. In 1921 autonomous Balkar and Kabardin Okrugs were created within the Mountain (Gorskaya) People's Republic (which also included present-day Chechnya, Ingushetiya, Karachayevo-Cherkessiya and North Osetiya). In January 1922 the two former Okrugs (which had been recently separated from the Mountain Republic and reconstituted as Autonomous Oblasts) were merged into a Kabardino-Balkar Autonomous Okrug, although the progress of integrating the two polities proved difficult, and was achieved in defiance of widespread hostility from representatives of both peoples. The Kabardino-Balkar ASSR was established on 5 December 1936. In 1943 the Balkars were deported to Kazakhstan and Central Asia, in response to their alleged collaboration with German forces, and the Balkar administrative district within the Republic (which was thereby renamed the Kabardin ASSR) was disbanded. The Balkars were not rehabilitated until 1956, when they were allowed to return to the Caucasus region; in 1957 the Republic reverted to its previous name.

Thus, although greatly outnumbered by Kabardins and Russians, the Balkars had developed a strong sense of ethnic identity. In 1991 they joined the Assembly of Turkic Peoples and on 18 November 1996 the first congress of the National Council of the Balkar People declared the sovereignty of Balkariya and the formation of a 'Republic of Balkariya' within the Russian Federation; this declaration, which reportedly had little support among the Balkar population, was, however, rescinded later in the month. Kabardino-Balkariya declared its sovereignty on 31 December 1991, and signed a bilateral treaty with the federal authorities during 1995. The Republic also developed links with its neighbours: on 21 February 1996 its President, Valerii Kokov, declared that Kabardino-Balkariya would not abide by the Commonwealth of Independent States' decision to impose sanctions on Abkhazia, Georgia, as that would run counter to a treaty between the two polities. In May 1998, at the second session of an interparliamentary council with the Republics of Adygeya and Karachayevo-Cherkessiya, a programme was adopted on the co-ordination of legislative, economic, environmental and legal activities.

Kabardino-Balkariya has an executive presidency and a bicameral Legislative Assembly or Parliament, which comprises an upper chamber, the Council of the Republic, and a lower chamber, the Council of Representatives. In the 1990s the old *nomenklatura* class remained firmly in control, although its allegiance was divided between the federal Government and the Communist Party. The republican leadership took a pragmatic approach to reform and encouraged foreign investment. A new republican Constitution was adopted in July 2001, which prevented the Republic from existing independently of the Russian Federation. In August it was reported that an attempt to stage a *coup d'état* in the Republic, and in neighbouring Karachayevo-Cherkessiya, had been prevented, and that the alleged leader of the plot, Khysyr Sallagarov, had been arrested, along with his accomplices. On 13 January 2002 the incumbent republican President, Valerii Kokov, was elected to serve a third term of office, receiving 87% of the votes cast. Revisions to the republican Constitution, implemented in mid-2002, appeared to have the effect of increasing the protection of political and civil rights in the Republic; henceforth, the ability of the republican authorities to prohibit public demonstrations, rallies and meetings was to be significantly reduced.

## Economy

Gross regional product in Kabardino-Balkariya amounted to 10,529.8m. roubles in 1999, equivalent to 13,295.2 roubles per head. The Republic's main industrial centres are at Nalchik, Tyrnyauz and Prokhladnyi. In 2000 there were 133 km (83 miles) of railways and 2,887 km of roads in the Republic. Prokhladnyi is an important junction on the North Caucasus Railway. There is an international airport at Nalchik, from which there are regular flights to the Middle East, as well as to other cities within the Russian Federation.

Karbardino-Balkariya's main agricultural products are maize and sunflowers. Animal husbandry, horticulture and viniculture are also important. By 1997 there were over 600 private agricultural enterprises in the Republic, covering some 5,500 ha. In 2000 around 26.6% of the Republic's work-force was engaged in the agricultural sector, the output of which was worth a total of 8,110m. roubles. Like the rest of the North Caucasus region, the Republic is rich in minerals, with reserves of petroleum, natural gas, gold, iron ore, garnet, talc and barytes. The Republic's main industries, which employed some 23.1% of the work-force in 2000, are mechanical engineering, metal-working, non-ferrous metallurgy, food-processing and light industry, the production of electricity, manufacture of building materials and the production and processing of tungsten-molybdenum ores. Total industrial output in 2000 was worth 6,033m. roubles.

In 2000 the economically active population of Kabardino-Balkariya numbered 353,000, and some 16.6% of the Republic's labour force were unemployed. In mid-2002 those in employment were earning an average of 2,375.0 roubles per month. In 2000 there was a budgetary deficit of 211.2m. roubles. External trade is minimal, amounting to only US $23.2m. in 2000. Most of the Republic's exports (of which raw materials comprise some 70%) are to Finland, Germany, the Netherlands, Turkey and the USA. Some four-fifths of its imports are from Europe. Foreign investment in the Republic in 2000 amounted to just $244,000. At 31 December 2000 there was a total of 2,200 small businesses in operation.

## Directory

**President:** VALERII M. KOKOV; 360028 Kabardino-Balkariya, Nalchik, pr. Lenina 27; tel. (8662) 40-41-42; fax (8662) 47-61-74; internet www.nalnet.ru.

**Prime Minister:** KHUSEIN D. CHECHENOV; 360028 Kabardino-Balkariya, Nalchik, pr. Lenina 27; tel. (8662) 40-29-70; fax (8662) 47-61-83.

**Chairman of the Council of the Republic of the Legislative Assembly (Parliament):** ZAURBI A. NAKHUSHEV; 360028 Kabardino-Balkariya, Nalchik, pr. Lenina 55; tel. (8662) 47-13-65; fax (8662) 47-27-13.

**Chairman of the Council of Representatives in the Legislative Assembly:** MURADIN KH. TUMENOV; 360028 Kabardino-Bal-

kariya, Nalchik, pr. Lenina 55; tel. (86622) 40-55-79; fax (86622) 76-27-13.

**Chief Representative of the Kabardino-Balkar Republic in the Russian Federation:** ANATOLII M. CHERKESOV; 109004 Moscow, ul. B. Kommunisticheskaya 4; tel. (095) 911-18-52; fax (095) 912-40-53.

**Head of Nalchik City Administration:** MUKHAMED M. SHOGENOV; 360000 Kabardino-Balkariya, Nalchik, ul. Sovetskaya 70; tel. (86622) 2-20-04.

# Republic of Kalmykiya

The Republic of Kalmykiya (known as the Republic of Kalmykiya-Khalmg Tangch in 1992–96) is situated in the north-western part of the Caspian Sea lowlands. It forms part of the Southern Federal Okrug and the Volga Economic Area. The south-eastern part of the Republic lies on the Caspian Sea. It has a southern border with the Republic of Dagestan and a south-western border with Stavropol Krai, while Rostov, Volgograd and Astrakhan Oblasts lie to the west, north-west and north-east, respectively. The Republic occupies an area of 75,900 sq km (29,300 sq miles), one-half of which is desert, and comprises 13 administrative districts and three cities. At 1 January 2002 it had an estimated population of 305,600, giving a population density of 4.0 per sq km. In January 2001 42.3% of the Republic's population lived in urban areas. In 1989, according to the census, some 45.4% of the total population were Kalmyks and 37.7% Russians. Unusually for Europe, the dominant religion among the Kalmyks is Lamaism (Tibetan Buddhism). Their native language is from the Mongol division of the Uralo-Altaic family and is spoken as a first language by some 90% of the indigenous population. The capital of Kalmykiya is at Elista, which had 107,800 inhabitants at 1 January 2001.

## History

The Kalmyks (also known as the Kalmuks, Kalmucks, and Khalmgs) originated in Eastern Turkestan (Central Asia—Dzungaria or Sungaria, mostly now part of the province of Xinjiang, People's Republic of China) and were a semi-nomadic Mongol-speaking people. Displaced by the Han Chinese, some 100,000 Kalmyks migrated westwards, in 1608 reaching the Volga basin, an area between the Don and Ural rivers, which had been under Russian control since the subjugation of the Astrakhan Khanate in 1556. The region, extending from Stavropol in the west to Astrakhan in the east, became the Kalmyk Khanate, which was dissolved by Russia in 1771. By this time the Kalmyk community was severely depleted, the majority having been slaughtered during a mass migration eastwards to protect the Oirots from persecution by the Chinese. Those that remained were dispersed: some settled along the Ural, Terek and Kuma rivers, some were moved to Siberia, while others became Don Cossacks. Many ethnic Russians and Germans invited by Catherine (Yekaterina) II (the 'Great') settled in Kalmykiya during the 18th century. In 1806 the Kalmyks' pasture lands were greatly reduced by the tsarist Government, forcing many to abandon their nomadic lifestyle and find work as fishermen and salt miners. A Kalmyk Autonomous Oblast was established by the Soviet Government on 4 November 1920 and the Kalmyks living in other regions of Russia were resettled there. Its status was upgraded to that of an ASSR in 1935. In 1943 the Republic was dissolved as retribution for the Kalmyks' alleged collaboration with German forces. The Kalmyks were deported to Central Asia, where they lived until their *de facto* rehabilitation in 1956. A Kalmyk Autonomous Oblast was reconstituted in 1957 and an ASSR in 1958. (The Kalmyks were not, however, formally rehabilitated until 1993.) In the late 1990s territorial disputes between Kalmykiya and Astrakhan Oblast over a particularly fertile area known as the 'Black Lands' resurfaced, with Kalmykiya claiming three districts that had been part of the pre-1943 Kalmyk Republic. These territories were of particular significance, because they stood on the route of a pipeline being constructed from Tengiz, Kazakhstan, to Novorossiisk, in Krasnodar Krai.

During the late 1980s a growing Kalmyk nationalist movement began protesting against the treatment of the Kalmyks under Stalin (Iosif V. Dzhugashvili) and demanding local control of the region's mineral resources. A declaration of sovereignty by the Republic was adopted on 18 October 1990. In April 1993 a business executive, Kirsan Ilyumzhinov, was elected as President of Kalmykiya. In March 1994 Ilyumzhinov abrogated the republican Constitution and decreed that from 25 March only the Russian basic law would be valid in the Republic. However, a new republican Constitution, known as the Steppe Legislation, was adopted on 5 April 1994. The new Constitution provided for a presidential form of government, with a presidential term of seven years, and for a unicameral legislature, the People's Khural, to which deputies were to be elected for terms of four years.

In October 1995 Ilyumzhinov (who was also elected head of the International Chess Federation—FIDE in that year) was the sole, unopposed candidate in the presidential election, in contravention of federal legislation. There was little serious challenge to his rule in the second half of the decade, although he attracted an increasing degree of controversy. In early 1998 he issued a decree abolishing the republican Government, in order to reduce public spending and bureaucracy. There were repeated reports of financial irregularities on the part of the republican authorities—the federal legislature instructed the Audit Chamber to investigate the legitimacy of federal budget spending in 1996–98. Reforms to the republican Constitution, approved in mid-2002, appeared to place greater restrictions upon the Kalmyk authorities than had hitherto existed; notably, elected local councils were to be established, and heads of local and city administrations to be reinstated. The presidential term of office was to be reduced to five years. In the first round of presidential elections, held on 21 October, Ilyumzhinov obtained 47.3% of the votes cast. In the second round, held on 27 October, Ilyumzhinov was re-elected as President for a further seven-year term, receiving around 57% of the votes cast and defeating a banking executive, Baatyr Shondzhiyev. In April 2003 Timofei Sasykov, the republican Minister of Internal Affairs and a close ally of Ilyumzhinov, was dismissed at the instigation of the Federal Ministry of Internal Affairs; in the following month he was arrested and detained on suspicions of abuse of office. He was released in mid-July, pending further investigations by the office of the Prosecutor-General of the Southern Federal Okrug.

## Economy

The Republic's gross regional product amounted to 2,127.1m. roubles, or 6,733.3 roubles per head in 1999. Kalmykiya is primarily an agricultural territory. In the 1990s much of its agricultural land suffered from desertification, a consequence of its irresponsible exploitation by the Soviet authorities during the 1950s, when the fragile black topsoil on the steppe was ploughed up or grazed all year round by sheep and cattle. Kalmykiya's major industrial centres are at Elista and Kaspiisk. In 2000 there were 154 km (96 miles) of railway lines and 2,367 km of paved roads in the Republic; 65% of the road network was paved in 1998. The Republic is intersected by the Astrakhan–Kizlyar railway line. The Republic has serious problems with its water supply, with a deficit of fresh water affecting almost all regions.

Kalmykiya's agriculture consists mainly of grain production and animal husbandry. Although agricultural output declined sharply, in real terms, throughout much of the 1990s, by 2000 the sector continued to employ 28.4% of the Republic's work-force, and it generated 1,281m. roubles in that year, compared with 465m. roubles in 1998. The Republic's industry, which engaged just 7.9% of the working population in 2000, consists mainly of electricity production, the manufacture of building materials, food-processing and the production of petroleum and natural gas. In 2000 industrial output was equivalent to 1,546m. roubles. The Republic has major hydrocarbons reserves, the more efficient exploitation of which was named a primary objective of Aleksandr Dordzhdeyev, the premier appointed in August 1999, who aimed to increase petroleum output in the Republic to between 1.5m. and 2.0m. metric tons each year. In August 1995 Kalmykiya began negotiations with several foreign countries to build a petroleum refinery in Elista with an annual capacity of 500,000 tons of petroleum products. The Oman Oil Company and LUKoil (a Russian company) showed interest in exploiting the Republic's petroleum and natural gas deposits, as part of a wider programme of exploitation across the Northern Caspian region. In September 2000 discussions began on the establishment of a Kalmyk-Belarusian joint venture to extract and process crude petroleum. Despite its potential, Kalmykiya is a net importer of energy.

The economically active population in the Republic amounted to 145,000 in 2000, when some 20.1% of the Republic's labour force were unemployed. The average monthly wage in mid-2002 was 2,564.4 roubles. The cost of a minimum 'consumer basket' of foodstuffs in Elista, purchased in August 2002, was the second cheapest in the Russian Federation. There was a budgetary deficit of 26.0m. roubles in 2000. Measures introduced by President Ilyumzhinov to encourage investment in the Republic (including, notably, the abolition of local taxes for companies, and their replacement with a single fee of US $300, which marked the creation of a 'special economic zone' in 1995), appeared to have little impact on improving either living standards or the republican infrastructure. In 1995 there was some US $1.64m. of foreign investment in the Republic. At the end of 2000 the Republic had 900 small businesses.

## Directory

**President and Chairman of the Government:** KIRSAN N. ILYUMZHINOV; 358000 Kalmykiya, Elista, pl. Lenina, Dom Pravitelstva; tel. (84722) 6-13-88; fax (84722) 6-28-80; e-mail aris_rk@cityline.ru; internet kalm.ru.

**Chairman of the People's Khural (Parliament):** VYACHESLAV A. BEMBETOV; 358000 Kalmykiya, Elista, pl. Lenina, Dom Pravitelstva; tel. (84722) 5-27-32; fax (84722) 5-03-02.

**Chief Representative of the Republic of Kalmykiya in the Russian Federation:** ALEKSEI M. ORLOV; 121170 Moscow, ul. Poklonnaya 12/2; tel. (095) 291-56-72; fax (095) 249-87-41; e-mail fund@elec.ru; internet www.kalmykembassy.ru.

**Head of Elista City Administration (Mayor):** RADII N. BURULOV; 358000 Kalmykiya, Elista, ul. Lenina 249; tel. (84722) 5-35-81; fax (84722) 5-42-56.

# Republic of Karachayevo-Cherkessiya

The Republic of Karachayevo-Cherkessiya is situated on the northern slopes of the Greater Caucasus. It forms part of the Southern Federal Okrug and the North Caucasus Economic Area. Krasnodar Krai borders it to the north-west, Stavropol Krai to the north-east and the Republic of Kabardino-Balkariya to the east. There is an international boundary with Georgia (mainly with Abkhazia) to the south. Its major river is the Kuban. The total area of the Republic occupies some 14,100 sq km (5,440 sq miles). The territory measures 140 km (87 miles) from north to south and 160 km from west to east. Karachayevo-Cherkessiya consists of eight administrative districts and four cities. It had an estimated population of 428,600 at 1 January 2002, giving a population density of 30.4 per sq km. In 2001 some 44.1% of the Republic's population inhabited urban areas and the capital city, Cherkessk, had a population of 120,700. Figures from the 1989 census showed that the Karachai accounted for 31.2% of the Republic's population, the Cherkess (Circassians) for 9.7% and ethnic Russians for 42.4%. Both the Karachai and the Cherkess are Sunni Muslims of the Hanafi school. The Cherkess speak a language close to Kabardin, from the Abkhazo-Adyge group of Caucasian languages, while the Karachais' native tongue, from the Kipchak group, is the same as that of the Balkars.

## History

The Karachai, a transhumant group descended from Kipchak tribes, were driven into the highlands of the North Caucasus by marauding Mongol tribes in the 13th century. Their territory was annexed by the Russian Empire in 1828, although, like their neighbouring North Caucasian peoples, they continued to resist Russian rule throughout the 19th century. In the 1860s and 1870s many Karachai migrated to the Ottoman Empire to escape oppression by the tsarist regime. Many of the Cherkess, a Circassian people descended from the Adyges who inhabited the region between the lower Don and Kuban rivers, also fled across the Russo–Turkish border at this time. They had come under Russian control in the 1550s, having sought protection from the Crimean Tatars and some Turkic tribes, including the Karachai. Relations between the Cherkess and Russia deteriorated as many Russians began to settle in Cherkess territory. Following the Treaty of Adrianople in 1829, by which the Ottomans abandoned their claim to the Caucasus region, a series of rebellions by the Circassians and reprisals by the Russian authorities occurred. In 1864 Russia completed its conquest of the region and many Cherkess fled.

The Cherkess Autonomous Oblast was established in 1928 and was subsequently merged with the Karachai Autonomous Oblast to form the Karachayevo-Cherkess Autonomous Oblast. This represented part of Stalin—Iosif V. Dzhugashvili's policy of 'divide and conquer', by which administrative units were formed from ethnically unrelated groups (the same applied to the Kabardino-Balkar ASSR). The Karachai were deported to Central Asia in late 1943, but the Cherkess remained in the region, which was renamed the Cherkess Autonomous Oblast, until the Karachai were rehabilitated and permitted to return in 1957. Ethnic separatism in the territory, which was upgraded to republican status, and separated from Stavropol Krai, under the terms of the 1992 Federation Treaty, was, however, relatively minimal. On 6 March 1996 a new constitutional system was adopted in the Republic, based on the results of a referendum on a republican presidency. The Republic had already, in the previous year, agreed on a division of responsibilities by treaty with the Russian Federation. The Communist Party of the Russian Federation remained the predominant party, winning 40% of the republican vote in federal parliamentary elections in late 1995. In May 1998, at the second session of an interparliamentary council with the Republics of Adygeya and Kabardino-Balkariya, a programme was adopted on the co-ordination of the Republics' legislative, economic, environmental and legal activities. The Republic's first presidential election, in 1999, provoked violence and ethnic unrest, when a second round of voting, in May, reversed the positions achieved by the 'run-off' candidates, Stanislav Derev, an ethnic Cherkess (who secured 40% of the votes in the first round and 12% in the second), and Gen. Vladimir Semonov, an ethnic Karachai and a former Commander-in-Chief of the Russian Ground Troops (who secured 18% of the votes in the first round and 85% in the second). Semonov was confirmed as the winning candidate in August and sworn in on 14 September. Derev's supporters continued to protest at the decision, and in mid-September a congress of the Republic's Cherkess and Abazin groups voted to pursue reintegration into the former Cherkess Autonomous Oblast in neighbouring Stavropol Krai. In August 2001 it was reported that an attempt to stage a *coup d'état* in the Republic, and in neighbouring Kabardino-Balkariya, had been prevented, and that the alleged leader of the plot, Khysyr Sallagarov, and his accomplices had been arrested. In the first round of presidential elections, held on 17 August 2003, and in which all five candidates were ethnic Karachais, the largest proportion of the votes cast (41.7%) was awarded to Mustafa Batdyyev, hitherto director of the republican bank; Semonov was the second-placed candidate, with 36.9%. In the run-off election, held on 31 August, Batdyyev, with 48.0% of the votes cast, narrowly defeated Semonov, with 46.4%. The rate of participation in the second round was notably high, at some 67.5%.

## Economy

In 1999 gross regional product in Karachayevo-Cherkessiya totalled 4,317.5m. roubles, or 9,916.2 roubles per head. The predominant sector within the economy, in terms of volume of output and number of employees, is industry. The Republic's major industrial centres are at Cherkessk, Karachayevsk and Zelenchukskaya. In 2000 it contained 51 km of railway track and 1,887 km of paved roads, including the Stavropol–Sukhumi (Georgia) highway.

Karachayevo-Cherkessiya's agriculture, which employed some 19.0% of the working population in 2000, consists mainly of animal husbandry. At 1 January 1999 there were some 133,000 cattle, 11,700 pigs and 362,800 sheep and goats in the Republic. The production of grain, sunflower seeds, sugar beet and vegetables is also important. In 2000 total agricultural production amounted to a value of 3,106m. roubles. The Republic's main industries are petrochemicals, chemicals, mechanical engineering and metal-working, although the manufacture of building materials, food-processing and coal production are also important. In 2000 the total output of the industrial sector was equivalent to 2,834m. roubles, and it employed around 19.5% of the work-force.

In 2000 the economically active population of the Republic numbered 145,000, and 20.7% of the Republic's labour force were unemployed. The average wage was 2,596.6 roubles per month in mid-2002. In 2000 there was a budgetary surplus of 31.0m. roubles. International trade was minimal in comparison with other areas in the Federation, amounting to only US $9.6m. in 2000, and foreign investment in the Republic in that year amounted to just $65,000. At the end of that year there were 1,800 small businesses registered in the Republic.

## Directory

**President and Head of the Republic:** Mustafa Batdyyev; 357100 Karachayevo-Cherkessiya, Cherkessk, ul. Krasnoarmeiskaya 54; tel. (87822) 5-40-11; fax (87822) 5-29-80.

**Chairman of the Government:** Ruslan A. Kazanokov; 357100 Karachayevo-Cherkessiya, Cherkessk, ul. Krasnoarmeiskaya 54; tel. (87822) 5-40-08; fax (87822) 5-40-20.

**Chairman of the People's Assembly:** (vacant).

**Chief Representative of the Republic of Karachayevo-Cherkessiya in the Russian Federation:** Emma M. Kardanova; Moscow; tel. (095) 959-55-15.

**Head of Cherkessk City Administration (Mayor):** Mikhail M. Yakush; 357100 Karachayevo-Cherkessiya, Cherkessk, pr. Lenina 54 a; tel. (87822) 5-37-23; fax (87822) 5-78-43.

# Republic of Kareliya

The Republic of Kareliya (Karelia) is situated in the north-west of Russia, on the edge of the Eastern European Plain. The Republic forms part of the North-Western Federal Okrug and the Northern Economic Area. It is bordered by Finland to the west. The White Sea lies to the north-east, Murmansk Oblast to the north and Vologda and Archangel Oblasts to the south. It contains some 83,000 km (51,540 miles) of waterways, including its major rivers, the Kem and the Vyg, and its numerous lakes (the Ladoga—Ladozhskoye, and the Onega—Onezhskoye, being the largest and second largest lakes in Europe). A canal system 225 km long, the Belomorkanal (White Sea Canal), connects the Kareliyan port of Belomorsk to St Petersburg. One-half of its territory is forested and much of the area on the White Sea coast is marshland. It lies, on average, 300 m–400 m above sea level. Kareliya measures some 600 km south–north and 400 km west–east and occupies an area of 172,400 sq km (66,560 sq miles). It comprises 16 administrative districts and 13 cities. At 1 January 2002 it had an estimated population of 756,400, giving a population density of 4.4 per sq km. In January 2001 some 74.0% of the Republic's population inhabited urban areas. In 1989 some 10.0% of the population were Kareliyans (Finnish—also known as Karjala or Karyala, Korela and Karyalainen) and 73.6% Russians. The dominant religion among Kareliyans, and in the Republic as a whole, is Orthodox Christianity. The Kareliyan language consists of three dialects of Finnish (Livvi, Karjala and Lyydiki), which are all strongly influenced by Russian. In 1989, however, more than one-half of the ethnically Kareliyan population spoke Russian as their first language. The capital of Kareliya is at Petrozavodsk, with a population of 282,900 at 1 January 2001.

## History

Kareliya was an independent, Finnish-dominated state in medieval times. In common with much of present-day Finland, in the 16th century the area came under Swedish hegemony, before being annexed by Russia in 1721. A Kareliyan Labour Commune was formed on 8 June 1920 and became an autonomous republic within the USSR in July 1923. A Karelo-Finnish SSR (Union Republic), including territory annexed from Finland, was created in 1940. However, part of its territory was ceded to the Russian Federation in 1946; in 1956 Kareliya subsequently resumed the status of an ASSR within the Russian Federation. The Republic declared sovereignty on 9 August 1990, and was renamed the Republic of Kareliya in November 1991: a republican Constitution was adopted in January 1994. In April elections took place to a new bicameral legislature, the Legislative Assembly (comprising a Chamber of the Republic and a Chamber of Representatives). The premier, Viktor Stepanov, who was vested with a quasi-presidential status as the republican head, was prominent in urging greater decentralization in the Russian Federation. On 17 May 1998 Stepanov was narrowly defeated in the second round of direct elections to the premiership by the former Mayor of Petrozavodsk, Sergei Katanandov. In December 2001 Stepanov (who had hitherto been widely regarded as the most popular potential challenger to the incumbent President in the forthcoming elections) was appointed as the Republic's representative to the Federation Council, the upper chamber of the Russian Federal Assembly. Katanandov was re-elected for a third term of office on 28 April 2002, receiving 54% of the votes cast. Non-partisan candidates were elected to a majority of seats in the concurrent legislative elections.

## Economy

The economy of Kareliya is largely based on its timber industry. In 1999 its gross regional product was 20,382.3m. roubles, equivalent to 26,491.2 roubles per head. Its major industrial centres include those at Petrozavodsk, Sortavala and Kem. In 2000 there were 2,105 km of railway lines and 6,567 km of paved roads in the Republic. In the mid-1990s Russia's first privately operated railway was constructed on Kareliya's territory. The Republic is at an important strategic point on Russia's roadways, linking the industrially developed regions of Russia with the major northern port of Murmansk. Its main port is at Petrozavodsk.

Kareliya's agriculture, which employed just 6.1% of the work-force in 2000, consists mainly of animal husbandry, fur farming and fishing. In that year total production within the sector was equivalent to a value of 1,705m. roubles. The Republic has important mineral reserves, and ranks among the leading producers of rosin and turpentine in the Russian Federation. An important agreement with the city of Moscow, which had need for construction materials, promised an increase in natural-stone production from some 3,000 cu m in 1998 to 20,000 cu m by 2002. Kareliya's main industries, apart from the processing of forestry products, are mechanical engineering, metallurgy and the extraction of iron ore and muscovite (mica). Industry engaged some 25.5% of the Republic's labour force in 2000, when total output within the sector was worth 25,305m. roubles. The Republic's major enterprise, Segezhabumprom, is one of the world's largest pulp and paper manufacturers; it was reorganized as a joint-stock company in 1999. In the first quarter of 2000, Kareliya produced over 50% of the paper bags, over 30% of newsprint, and over 22% of all paper in the Russian Federation. It was suggested that new duties on forestry products, introduced in

December 1999, might threaten the fulfilment of existing contracts with Western customers.

The economically active population amounted to 394,000 in 2000, when 11.5% of the labour force were unemployed. The average monthly wage in the Republic was 4,613.8 roubles in mid-2002. The republican budget showed a surplus of 185.6m. roubles in 2000. In that year international exports from the Republic were worth US $538.8m., and the value of imports from abroad was $157.8m. Foreign investment in Kareliya at that time amounted to $22.2m. There were 79 foreign joint enterprises in Kareliya in 2000, of which 39 had Finnish partners. At 31 December 2000 there were some 4,000 small businesses operating in the Republic.

## Directory

**Chairman of the Government (Head of the Republic):** SERGEI L. KATANANDOV; 185028 Kareliya, Petrozavodsk, pr. Lenina 19; tel. (8142) 76-41-41; fax (8142) 76-41-48; e-mail government@karelia.ru; internet www.gov.karelia.ru.

**Chairman of the Chamber of Representatives of the Legislative Assembly:** NIKOLAI I. LEVIN, 185610 Kareliya, Petrozavodsk, ul. Kuibysheva 5; tel. (8142) 78-02-95; fax (8142) 78-28-27; e-mail parl@karelia.ru; internet www.gov.karelia.ru/gov/LA.

**Chairman of the Chamber of the Republic of the Legislative Assembly:** VLADIMIR V. SHILNIKOV, 185610 Kareliya, Petrozavodsk, ul. Kuibysheva 5; tel. (8142) 77-27-48; fax (8142) 78-28-27; e-mail parl@karelia.ru; internet www.gov.karelia.ru/gov/LA.

**Chief Representative of the Republic of Kareliya in the Russian Federation:** ANATOLII A. MARKOV; 101934 Moscow, per. Arkhangelskii 1; tel. (095) 207-87-24; fax (095) 208-03-18.

**Head of Petrozavodsk City Administration:** VIKTOR N. MASLYAKOV; 185630 Kareliya, Petrozavodsk, pr. Lenina 2/501; tel. (8142) 78-35-70; fax (8142) 78-47-53; e-mail admcity@karelia.ru.

# Republic of Khakasiya

The Republic of Khakasiya is situated in the western area of the Minusinsk hollow, on the left bank of the River Yenisei, which flows northwards towards, ultimately, the Arctic Ocean. In the heart of Eurasia, it lies on the eastern slopes of the Kuznetsk Alatau and the northern slopes of the Western Sayan Mountains. It comprises part of the Siberian Federal Okrug and the East Siberian Economic Area. The Republic of Tyva lies to the south-east and the Republic of Altai to the south-west. To the west is Kemerovo Oblast, while Krasnoyarsk Krai lies to the north and east. Its major rivers are the Yenisei and the Abakan. Khakasiya occupies 61,900 sq km (23,900 sq miles) and comprises eight administrative regions and five cities. At 1 January 2002 it had an estimated population of 575,400 and a population density, therefore, of 9.3 per sq km. In 2001 some 71.0% of the population lived in urban areas. In 1989 ethnic Khakasiyans were found to number 11.1% of the population, and Russians 79.5%. However, at that time over 76% of the Khakass spoke the national language, primarily derived from the Uigur group of Eastern Hunnic languages of the Turkic family, as their native tongue. Khakasiya's capital is at Abakan, with 167,900 inhabitants in 2001.

## History

The Khakasiyans were traditionally known as the Minusinsk (Minusa), the Turki, the Yenisei Tatars or the Abakan Tatars. They were semi-nomadic hunters, fishermen and livestock-breeders. Khakasiya was a powerful state in Siberia, owing to its trading links with Central Asia and the Chinese Empire. Russian settlers began to arrive in the region in the 17th century and their presence was perceived as valuable protection against Mongol invasion. The annexation of Khakasiyan territory by the Russians was eventually completed during the reign of Peter (Petr) I—'the Great', with the construction of a fort on the River Abakan. The Russians subsequently imposed heavy taxes, seized the best land and imposed Orthodox Christianity on the Khakasiyans. After the construction of the Trans-Siberian Railway in the 1890s the Khakasiyans were heavily outnumbered. Following the Bolshevik Revolution a Khakass National Uezd (district) was established in 1923, becoming an Okrug in 1925, and the Khakass Autonomous Oblast on 20 October 1930, within Krasnoyarsk Krai. In 1992 it was upgraded to the status of an Autonomous Republic under the terms of the Federation Treaty, having declared its sovereignty on 3 July 1991.

The Communist Party remained the most popular political grouping in the Republic in the early 1990s, and the nationalist ideas of Vladimir Zhirinovskii (leader of the Liberal Democratic Party of Russia) also enjoyed significant support. On 25 May 1995 the Republic adopted its Constitution. Aleksei Lebed, an independent candidate and younger brother of the politician and former general, Aleksandr Lebed (Governor of Krasnoyarsk Krai from May 1998 until his death in 2002), was elected to the presidency of the Republic in December 1996, when elections were also held for a new republican legislature. A former representative of the Republic in the State Duma, Aleksei Lebed had based his electoral campaign on the issues of administrative, budgetary, social and economic reform. Lebed was re-elected as Chairman of the Government, receiving 72% of the votes cast, in December 2000.

## Economy

Khakasiya's gross regional product amounted to 14,317.2m. roubles in 1999, or 24,591.3 roubles per head. Khakasiya's major industrial centres are at Abakan, Sorsk, Sayanogorsk, Chernogorsk and Balyksa. In 2000 there were 642 km (399 miles) of railway lines and 2,485 km of paved roads in the Republic.

The Republic's agriculture, which employed around 12.1% of the working population in 2000, consists mainly of grain production and animal husbandry. Total agricultural production in 2000 was worth 3,377m. roubles. The Republic's main industries are ore-mining, electricity production, light manufacturing, mechanical engineering, non-ferrous metallurgy and the processing of agricultural products. A major element of industrial activity was the processing of natural resources. In 1997 Khakasiya was estimated to have reserves of 36,000m. metric tons of coal and 1,500m. tons of iron ore. Other mineral reserves included molybdenum, lead, zinc, barytes, aluminium and clay. There was also the potential for extraction of petroleum and natural gas. In 2000 the Republic's industrial output amounted to a value of 14,114m. roubles, and the industrial sector employed 24.6% of the work-force.

The Republic's economically active population numbered 267,000 in 2000, when 12.3% of the labour force were unemployed. The average monthly wage stood at 4,146.5 roubles in mid-2002. The republican budget for 2000 showed a deficit of 30.7m. roubles. Foreign investment in Khakasiya was minimal. Throughout the 1990s the highest level recorded was US $2.3m., in 1996, and such investment totalled just $24,000 in 2000. However, external trade was been somewhat more substantial; in 2000 exports amounted to a value of $380.0m., of which some 91% were with countries outside the Commonwealth of Independent States, and imports amounted to $187.2m. At 31 December 2000 there were 1,500 small businesses registered in the Republic.

## Directory

**Chairman of the Government:** ALEKSEI I. LEBED; 655019 Khakasiya, Abakan, pr. Lenina 67; tel. (39022) 6-33-22; fax (39022) 6-50-96; e-mail pressa@khakasnet.ru; internet www.gov.khakassia.ru.

**Chairman of the Supreme Council:** VLADIMIR N. SHTYGASHEV; 655019 Khakasiya, pr. Lenina 67; tel. (39022) 6-74-00; fax (39022) 6-82-81; e-mail info@vskhakasia.ru; internet www.vskhakasia.ru.

**Chief Representative of the Republic of Khakasiya in the Russian Federation:** VIKTOR K. BABAKHIN; 127025 Moscow, ul. Novyi Arbat 19/830; tel. (095) 203-83-41; fax (095) 203-83-45.

**Head of Abakan City Administration:** NIKOLAI G. BULAKIN; 655000 Khakasiya, Abakan, ul. Shchetinkina 10A/6, POB 6; tel. and fax (39022) 6-37-91; internet meria.abakan.ru.

# Republic of Komi

The Republic of Komi is situated in the north-east of European Russia. Its northern border lies some 50 km within the Arctic Circle. It forms part of the North-Western Federal Okrug and the Northern Economic Area. Mountains of the Northern, Circumpolar and Polar Urals occupy the eastern part of the Republic. Its major rivers are the Pechora, the Vychegda and the Mezen. Komi is bordered to the west by Archangel Oblast, to the north by the Nenets Autonomous Okrug, and to the east by the Tyumen Oblast (both the Oblast proper and the two Autonomous Okrugs, Khanty-Mansii—Yugra and Yamal-Nenets). To the south Komi borders Kirov Oblast, Perm Oblast (including the Komi-Permyak Autonomous Okrug) and Sverdlovsk Oblast. Some 90% of its territory is taiga (forested marshland), while the extreme north-east of the Republic lies within the Arctic tundra zone. The Republic occupies an area of 415,900 sq km (160,580 sq miles). It comprises 12 administrative districts and 10 cities and had an estimated population of 1,117,200 at 1 January 2002, and a population density, therefore, of 2.7 per sq km. In 2001 some 74.2% of the population lived in urban areas. In 1989 some 23.3% of the Republic's inhabitants were Komi and 57.7% were ethnic Russians. The predominant religion in the region is Orthodox Christianity, although among the Komi this faith is combined with strong animist traditions. Their language, spoken as a native tongue by some 74% of the Komi population, belongs to the Finnic branch of the Uralo-Altaic family. Komi's capital is at Syktyvkar, which had a population of 227,700 in 2001. The Republic's other major cities are Ukhta (98,700) and Vorkuta (87,400).

## History

The Komi (known historically as the Zyryans or the Permyaks) are descended from inhabitants of the river basins of the Volga, the Kama, the Pechora and the Vychegda. From the 12th century Russian settlers began to inhabit territory along the Vychegda, and later the Vym, rivers. The Vym subsequently acquired a strategic significance as the main route along which Russian colonists advanced to Siberia, and Ust-Sysolsk (now Syktyvar), the territory's oldest city, was founded in 1586. The number of Slavs increased after the territory was annexed by Russia in 1478. The region soon acquired importance as the centre of mining and metallurgy, following the discovery of copper and silver ores in 1491. In 1697 petroleum was discovered in the territory; the first refinery was built by F. Pryadunov in 1745. The Komi were renowned as shrewd commercial traders and exploited important trade routes between Archangel and Siberia, via the Vyatka-Kama basin. Trade in fish, furs and game animals developed in the 17th century, while coal, timber, iron ore and paper became significant in the years prior to the Russian Revolution. The Komi Autonomous Oblast was established on 22 August 1921 and became an ASSR in 1931.

The Komi Republic declared its sovereignty on 30 August 1990. A new republican Constitution was adopted on 17 February 1994, establishing a quasi-presidential premier at the head of government and a State Council as the legislature; the territory became known as the Republic of Komi. In March 1996 the republican and federal Governments signed a power-sharing treaty. The Republic repudiated its declaration of sovereignty in September 2001, following a ruling of the federal Supreme Court, which stated that over one-half of the provision's declarations were in contravention of federal law. The republican presidential election, held on 16 December, was won by Vladimir Torlopov, hitherto Chairman of the republican State Council, who received 40% of the votes cast, while the incumbent, Yurii Spiridonov, received 35%. Torlopov received the support of the liberal Yabloko party, whereas Spiridonov's supporters included the pro-Government Unity and Fatherland-United Russia party. In May 2002 Torlopov signed an agreement with federal President Vladimir Putin, annulling the power-sharing treaty signed with Komi in 1996. Following legislative elections, held on 2 March 2003, repeat elections were required in six of the 30 electoral districts, in which votes 'against all candidates' had received the greatest share of votes cast. (The overall rate of participation by the electorate was 44.1%, and 27% of the votes cast were 'against all candidates'.) Only six of the incumbent legislators were returned to office. It was reported that the new State Council was dominated by representatives of business interests, particularly the energy industry; in all, some 15 corporate executives were believed to have been elected to the legislature. In April 2003 the recently appointed Presidential Representative in the North-Western Federal Okrug, Valentina Matviyenko, stated that the recent election results should serve as an indicator to the republican authorities of the need for change, stating that the economic and social situation in the republic was a great cause of concern.

## Economy

The Republic of Komi is Russia's second largest fuel and energy base. Apart from a wealth of natural resources, it is strategically placed close to many of Russia's major industrial centres and has a well-developed transport network. It also contains Europe's largest area of virgin forest—approximately one-third of its massive forest stock (amounting to 2,800m. cu m) has never been cut. In the 1990s Komi had a high ranking within the Federation in terms of gross domestic product per head and it possessed a wealth of natural resources. However, in order to fulfil its economic potential the Republic needed to improve its export performance and diversify its economy into higher value-added activities. In 1999 gross regional product in the Republic amounted to 50,914m. roubles, equivalent to 44,587.4 roubles per head—one of the highest figures in Russia. Komi's major industrial centres are at Syktyvkar, Ukhta and Sosnogorsk. In 2000 the Republic contained 1,692 km (1,051 miles) of railway lines and 5,253 km of paved roads.

Komi's agriculture, which employed 4.8% of the work-force in 2000, consists mainly of animal husbandry, especially reindeer-breeding. Total production within the sector amounted to a value of 2,715m. roubles in 2000. Ore-mining was developing from the mid-1990s: the Republic contained the country's largest reserves of bauxite, titanium, manganese and chromium ore. It also accounted for around one-half of northern Europe's petroleum stock and one-third of its natural gas reserves. Total output from industry, which was based on the processing of forestry products, the production of coal and the production and processing of petroleum and natural

gas, was worth 53,362m. roubles in 2000, when the sector employed 24.3% of the work-force.

In 2000 the economically active population numbered 594,000, and 12.1% of the labour force were unemployed. In mid-2002 the average monthly wage in the Republic was relatively high, at 6,274.0 roubles. In 2000 there was a budgetary surplus of 149.5m. roubles. Foreign trade was encouraged, with, for example, an agreement being reached with Iran in December 1998. In 2000 exports from the Republic amounted to US $1,121.5m., compared with $73.3m. of imports to the Republic. Foreign investment in Komi was substantial in the late 1990s, amounting to $218.1m. in 1998, although the level of investment had declined, to $54.0m., by 2000. In the mid-1990s a number of joint ventures were established in Komi, with investment from France, the United Kingdom and the USA. These included Komi Arctic Oil, Sever TEK and Northern Lights. At 31 December 2000 there were 4,000 small businesses in operation.

## Directory

**Chairman of the Government (Head of the Republic):** VLADIMIR A. TORLOPOV; 167010 Komi, Syktyvkar, ul. Kommunisticheskaya 9; tel. (8212) 28-51-05; fax (8212) 28-52-52; internet www.rkomi.ru.

**Chairman of the State Council:** IVAN YE. KULAKOV; 167000 Komi, Syktyvkar, ul. Kommunisticheskaya 9; tel. (8212) 28-55-08; fax (8212) 42-44-90; internet www.rkomi.ru/gossov/gossovet/gs_rk .html.

**Chief Representative of the Republic of Komi in the Russian Federation:** NIKOLAI N. KOCHURIN; 125367 Moscow, Volokolamskoye shosse 62; tel. and fax (095) 490-10-80.

**Head of Syktyvkar City Administration:** SERGEI M. KATUNIN; 167000 Komi, Syktyvkar, ul. Babushkina 22; tel. (8212) 29-44-70.

# Republic of Marii-El

The Republic of Marii-El is situated in the east of the Eastern European Plain in the middle reaches of the River Volga. It forms part of the Volga Federal Okrug and the Volga-Vyatka Economic Area. Tatarstan and Chuvashiya neighbour it to the south-east and to the south, respectively. Nizhnii Novgorod Oblast lies to the west and Kirov Oblast to the north and north-east. Its major rivers are the Volga and the Vetluga and about one-half of its territory is forested. Marii-El measures 150 km (over 90 miles) from south to north and 275 km from west to east. It occupies an area of 23,200 sq km (9,000 sq miles) and consists of 14 administrative districts and four cities. At 1 January 2002 the estimated population was 750,300, and the population density approximately 32.3 per sq km. In 2001 some 61.6% of the population inhabited urban areas. In 1989 some 43.3% of the Republic's inhabitants were Mari (also known as Cheremiss) and 47.5% ethnic Russians. Orthodox Christianity is the predominant religion in Marii-El, although many Mari have remained faithful to aspects of their traditional animistic religion. Their native language belongs to the Finnic branch of the Uralo-Altaic family. The capital of the Republic is at Yoshkar-Ola, with a population of 248,500 at 1 January 2001.

## History

The Mari emerged as a distinct ethnic group in the sixth century. In the eighth century they came under the influence of the Khazar empire, but from the mid-ninth to the mid-12th century they were ruled by the Volga Bulgars. In the 1230s Mari territory was conquered by the Mongol Tatars and remained under the control of the Khazar Khanate until its annexation by Russia in 1552. Nationalist feeling on the part of the Mari did not become evident until the 1870s, when a religious movement, the Kugu Sorta (Great Candle), attacked the authority of the Orthodox Church in the region. A Mari Autonomous Oblast was established in 1920. On 5 December 1936 the territory became the Mari ASSR.

The Republic declared its sovereignty on 22 October 1990. A presidential election was held on 14 December 1991. In December 1993 elections were held to a new 300-seat parliament, the State Assembly, which was dominated by the Communist Party. The new legislature adopted the republican Constitution in June 1995, when the territory became known as the Republic of Marii-El. A power-sharing agreement between the Republic and the federal Government was signed in May 1998. At parliamentary elections held in the Republic in October 2000, left-wing and communist candidates secured the highest proportion of the votes cast. At gubernatorial elections in December the incumbent, Vyacheslav Kislitsyn, was defeated by Leonid Markelov, who represented the nationalist Liberal Democratic Party of Vladimir Zhirinovskii.

## Economy

In 1999 the Republic's gross regional product amounted to 10,467.7m. roubles, equivalent to 13,771.5 roubles per head. Its major industrial centres are at Yoshkar-Ola and Volzhsk. In 2000 there were 204 km of railway lines and 3,233 km of paved roads on the Republic's territory.

Marii-El's agriculture, which in 2000 employed 20.0% of the work-force, consists mainly of animal husbandry and flax and grain production. Total agricultural output in 2000 was worth 5,847m. roubles. The Republic's main industries are mechanical engineering, metal-working, electricity production and the processing of forestry and food products. The total value of production within the industrial sector (which employed 24.4% of the work-force) was 8,585m. roubles in 2000.

In 2000 the economically active population in the Republic numbered 370,000, and 11.3% of the labour force were unemployed; in mid-2002 those in employment earned an average of 2,358.6 roubles per month. In 2000 there was a budgetary deficit of 36.2m. roubles. In that year the value of external trade with the Republic amounted to just US $45.2m. (of which exports accounted for $32.6m.). Exports primarily comprised raw materials (peat), machine parts and medical supplies, and its major trading partners were Belarus, Finland, France, Germany, Ireland, Italy, Kazakhstan, the Netherlands, Ukraine, the United Kingdom and the USA. Foreign investment in Marii-El was minimal, amounting to just $140,000 in 2000. At 31 December 2000 there were 4,100 small businesses registered in the Republic.

## Directory

**President and Head of the Government:** LEONID I. MARKELOV; 424001 Marii-El, Yoshkar-Ola, Leninskii pr. 29; tel. (8362) 64-15-25; fax (8362) 64-19-21; e-mail president@gov.mari.ru; internet gov .mari.ru.

**Chairman of the State Assembly:** YURII A. MINAKOV; 424001 Marii-El, Yoshkar-Ola, Leninskii pr. 29; tel. (8362) 64-14-13; e-mail parliament@gov.mari.ru; internet parliament.mari.ru.

**Chief Representative of the Republic of Marii-El in the Russian Federation:** VIKTOR P. RASSONOV; 119019 Moscow, ul. Novyi Arbat 21; tel. (095) 291-48-38; fax (095) 291-46-32.

**Head of Yoshkar-Ola City Administration (Mayor):** VLADIMIR V. TARKOV; 424001 Marii-El, Yoshkar-Ola, Leninskii pr. 27; tel. (8362) 55-64-01; fax (8362) 55-64-22; internet capital.mari-el.ru:8101.

# Republic of Mordoviya

The Republic of Mordoviya is situated in the Eastern European Plain, in the Volga river basin. The north-west of the Republic occupies a section of the Oka-Don plain and the south-east lies in the Volga Highlands. The region forms part of the Volga Federal Okrug and the Volga-Vyatka Economic Area. The Republic of Chuvashiya lies to the north-east of Mordoviya. The neighbouring oblasts are Ulyanovsk to the east, Penza to the south, Ryazan to the west and Nizhnii Novgorod to the north. The major rivers in Mordoviya are the Moksha, the Sura and the Insar; one-quarter of its land area is forested. The territory of Mordoviya straddles the two major natural regions in Russia, forest and steppe, and occupies an area of 26,200 sq km (10,110 sq miles). The Republic consists of 22 administrative districts and seven cities. Its climate is continental, but with unpredictable levels of precipitation. At 1 January 2002 the Republic had a population of 910,000 and a population density, therefore, of approximately 34.7 per sq km. In 2001 some 59.8% of the Republic's population inhabited urban areas. In 1989 some 32.5% of the total population were Mordovians and 60.8% Russians. The majority of Mordovians inhabited the agricultural regions of the west and north-east. The capital, Saransk, is a major rail junction and the Moscow–Samara highway passes through the south-west of the Republic. The dominant religion among the Republic's inhabitants is Orthodox Christianity. The native tongue of the Mordovians belongs to the Finnic group of the Uralo-Altaic family, although this is spoken as a first language by less than two-thirds of the ethnic group. Mordoviya's capital is at Saransk, which lies on the River Insar and had a population of 313,200 at 1 January 2001.

## History

The Mordovians (Mordvinians) first appear in historical records of the sixth century, when they inhabited the area between the Oka and the middle Volga rivers. Their territory's capital was, possibly, on the site of Nizhnii Novgorod, before it was conquered by the Russians in 1172. In the late 12th and early 13th centuries a feudal society began to form in Mordoviya. One of its most famous fiefdoms

was Purgasov Volost, headed by Prince Purgas, which was recorded in the Russian chronicles. The Mordovians came under the control of the Mongols and Tatars between the 13th and the 15th centuries and, at the fall of the Khanate of Kazan in 1552, they were voluntarily incorporated into the Russian state. Many thousands of Mordovians fled Russian rule in the late 16th and early 17th centuries to settle in the Ural Mountains and in southern Siberia, while those that remained were outnumbered by ethnic Russian settlers. The region was predominantly agricultural until the completion of the Moscow–Kazan railway in the 1890s, when it became more commercial and its industry developed.

Although Mordovians had become increasingly assimilated into Russian life from the late 19th century, a Mordovian Autonomous Okrug was created in 1928, which was upgraded to an Autonomous Oblast in 1930, and to an ASSR in 1934. It declared its sovereignty on 8 December 1990. A conservative region, the territory was only renamed the Republic of Mordoviya (dispensing with the words Soviet and Socialist from the title) in January 1994. Its Constitution was adopted on 21 September 1995, establishing an executive presidency and a State Assembly as the legislature. In February 1998 President Nikolai Merkushkin was re-elected, with 96.6% of the votes cast, owing to a legislative device that disqualified all opponents other than the director of a local pasta factory, who had frequently announced his support for Merkushkin's policies. On 16 February 2003 Merkushkin was elected to a further term of office, receiving 87.3% of the votes cast in an election contested by five candidates; the rate of participation by the registered electorate was measured at 83.2%.

## Economy

In 1999 the gross regional product of Mordoviya was 14,075.5m. roubles, or 15,075.0 roubles per head. The territory's major industrial centres are at Saransk and Ruzayevka. In 2000 there were 546 km (339 miles) of railway lines and 4,205 km of paved roads on the Republic's territory.

The principal crops in Mordoviya are grain, sugar beet, potatoes and vegetables. Animal husbandry (especially cattle) and bee-keeping are also important. Agriculture employed 18.1% of the working population in 2000, when total agricultural production was worth 8,688m. roubles. Industry is the dominant sector of the economy, with output amounting to a value of 14,977m. roubles in 2000. The main industries are mechanical engineering and metal-working. There is also some production of electricity, production of chemicals and construction materials, and food-processing. Total employment in industry was equal to 24.4% of the Republic's work-force in 2000. Mordoviya is the centre of the Russian lighting-equipment industry and contains the Rossiiskii Svet (Russian Light) association. In December 1995 the federal Government approved a programme for the economic and social development of Mordoviya, to be implemented in 1996–2000 at a cost of around US $10,000m. The regional President, Nikolai Merkushkin, established close links and trading relationships with Moscow City under Mayor Yurii Luzhkov; the capital purchased over one-half of the Republic's output.

In 2000 the economically active population was 445,000, and 10.7% of the labour force were unemployed. The average monthly wage in the Republic was 2,346.6 roubles in mid-2002 (one of the lowest wages in the Federation). In 2000 there was a budgetary deficit of 38.7m. roubles. External trade was relatively low, earning US $19.7m. in exports and $25.8m. in imports in that year. In 2000 foreign investment in the Republic amounted to $8.6m. At 31 December 2000 there were some 2,300 small businesses in the Republic.

## Directory

**President:** NIKOLAI I. MERKUSHKIN; 430002 Mordoviya, Saransk, ul. Sovetskaya 35; tel. (8342) 17-54-71; fax (8342) 17-45-26; e-mail radm@whrm.moris.ru; internet whrm.moris.ru.

**Chairman of the Government (Prime Minister):** VLADIMIR D. VOLKOV; 430002 Mordoviya, Saransk, ul. Sovetskaya 35; tel. (8342) 32-74-69; fax (8342) 17-36-28; e-mail pred@whrm.moris.ru.

**Chairman of the State Assembly:** VALERII A. KECHKIN; 430002 Mordoviya, Saransk, ul. Sovetskaya 26; tel. (8342) 32-79-50; fax (8342) 17-04-95; e-mail gsprot@whrm.moris.ru.

**Chief Representative of the Republic of Mordoviya in the Russian Federation:** VIKTOR I. CHINDYASKIN; 127018 Moscow, ul. Obraztsova 29; tel. (095) 219-40-49; fax (095) 218-01-42.

**Head of Saransk City Administration:** IVAN YA. NENYUKOV; 430002 Mordoviya, Saransk, ul. Sovetskaya 34; tel. (8342) 17-64-16; fax (8342) 17-67-70; e-mail saransk@moris.ru.

# Republic of North Osetiya— Alaniya

The Republic of North Osetiya (Severnaya Osetiya), Alaniya, is situated on the northern slopes of the Greater Caucasus and forms part of the Southern Federal Okrug and the North Caucasus Economic Area. Of the other federal subjects, Kabardino-Balkariya lies to the west, Stavropol Krai to the north and Ingushetiya to the east. There is an international boundary with Georgia (specifically South Ossetia or Osetiya) in the south. Its major river is the Terek. In the north of the Republic are the steppelands of the Mozdok and Osetiyan Plains, while further south in the foothills are mixed pasture and beechwood forest (about one-fifth of the territory of the Republic is forested). Narrow river valleys lie in the southernmost, mountainous region. The territory of North Osetiya covers a total of 8,000 sq km (3,090 sq miles) and comprises eight administrative districts and six cities. It had an estimated population of 678,200 at 1 January 2002, giving a population density of 84.8 per sq km. In 2001 some 67.1% of the Republic's population inhabited urban areas. In 1989 some 53.0% of the population were Osetiyans and 29.9% ethnic Russians, although around one-quarter of Russians were thought to have left North Osetiya between 1989 and 1999, largely owing to the decline of the military-industrial complex in the Republic, which had been their major employer. The Osetiyans speak an Indo-European language of the Persian (Iranian) group. In January 2001 310,600 of the region's inhabitants lived in the capital, Vladikavkaz (Ordzhonikidze 1932–44, 1954–90), situated in the east of the Republic. At the end of 1999 there were approximately 37,000 registered refugees from the armed hostilities between South Ossetian and Georgian government forces, although around 1,500 others had returned to Georgia from 1997, as conditions there improved and the economy of North Osetiya deteriorated further. By the end of 1999 about 35,000 Ingush had been displaced from the Prigorodnyi raion of North Osetiya, most of whom were living in Ingushetiya.

## History

The Osetiyans (Ossetins, Oselty) are descended from the Alans, a tribe of the Samartian people. The Alans were driven into the foothills of the Caucasus by the Huns in the fourth century and their descendants (Ossetes) were forced further into the mountains by Tatar and Mongol invaders. Although the Osetiyans had been converted to Orthodox Christianity in the 12th and 13th centuries by the Georgians, a sub-group, the Digors, adopted Islam from the Kabardins in the 17th and 18th centuries. Perpetual conflict with the Kabardins forced the Osetiyans to seek the protection of the Russian Empire, and their territory was eventually ceded to Russia by the Ottoman Turks at the Treaty of Kuçuk Kainavci in 1774 and confirmed by the Treaty of Iaşi (Jassy) in 1792. (Transcaucasian Osetiya, or South Ossetia—Osetiya, subsequently became part of Georgia.) The Russians fostered good relations with the Osetiyans, as they represented the principal Christian group among the Muslim peoples of the North Caucasus. Furthermore, both ends of the strategic Darial pass were situated in the region. The completion of the Georgian Military Road in 1799 facilitated the Russian conquest of Georgia (Kartli-Kakheti) in 1801.

After the Bolshevik Revolution, and having briefly been part of the Mountain (Gorskaya) People's Autonomous Republic, North Osetiya was established as an Autonomous Oblast on 7 July 1924, and as an ASSR in 1936. The Osetians were rewarded for their loyalty to the Soviet Government during the Second World War: in 1944 their territory was expanded by the inclusion of former Ingush territories to the east and of part of Stavropol Krai to the north. Furthermore, for 10 years the capital, renamed Ordzhonikidze in 1932, was known as Dzaudzhikau, the Osetian form of Vladikavkaz. The Digors, however, were deported to Central Asia, along with other Muslim peoples, in 1944.

The Republic declared sovereignty in mid-1990. From 1991 there was considerable debate about some form of unification with South Ossetia (which had, however, been deprived of its autonomous status and merged with adjoining regions by the Georgian Supreme Soviet in December 1990.) This resulted in armed hostilities between the South Ossetians and Georgian troops, during which thousands of refugees fled to North Osetiya. Meanwhile, the Republic's administration refused to recognize claims by the Ingush to the territory they were deprived of in 1944 (the Prigorodnyi raion), which led to the onset of violence in October 1992 and the imposition of a state of emergency in the affected areas (see Ingushetiya). Despite a peace settlement in 1994, the region remained unstable. Under the terms of its Constitution, adopted on 7 December 1994, the Republic's name was amended to North Osetiya—Alaniya. A power-sharing agreement was signed with the federal authorities in 1995. The territory was a redoubt of the Communist Party of the Russian Federation during the late 1990s, although in the 2000

presidential election Vladimir Putin received the highest share of the votes cast for any candidate in the region. In January 1998 Aleksandr Dzasokhov, a former member of the Communist Party of the Soviet Union Politburo, and the Chairman of the Russian delegation to the Parliamentary Assembly of the Council of Europe, was elected as republican President, with 75% of the votes cast. Relations with Ingushetiya remained strained, and in July 1999 the President of Ingushetiya, Ruslan Aushev, announced the suspension of all negotiations with North Osetiya and proposed that direct federal rule be imposed on Prigorodnyi; in March 2000, however, Putin rejected the proposal as unconstitutional. Instability in North Osetiya, as elsewhere in the North Caucasus, increased during 1999, as insurgency became increasingly widespread. A bomb exploded in Vladikavkaz in March, killing 42, and three further bombs exploded in military residences in May. In March 2001 three simultaneous explosions, which killed over 20, were attributed to Chechen separatists. (The trial of two Ingush residents of Prigorodnyi, on charges of perpetrating bombings in Vladikavkaz in 1999–2002, and of maintaining contacts with Chechen rebels led by Ruslan Gelayev commenced at the Supreme Court of North Osetiya—Alaniya in April 2003.) On 27 January 2002 Dzasokhov was re-elected as President, receiving 56.0% of the votes cast. Notably, 10 days before the election the republican Supreme Court had invalidated the candidacy of the former republican premier, Sergei Khetagurov; this decision was subsequently confirmed by the Federal Supreme Court. In September the power-sharing agreement of 1995 was dissolved, and in October North Osetiya and Ingushetiya signed an 'Agreement on the Development of Co-operation and Good Neighbourly Relations', which committed both sides to adopting measures to resolve remaining differences. Legislative elections were held on 11 May 2003, although repeat elections were required in 31 of the 75 electoral districts on 1 June. Of the 44 deputies elected on 11 May, some 41 were reported to be members or supporters of the pro-Government Unity and Fatherland-United Russia party, giving that party a working majority in the chamber. In early June a suicide bomber detonated explosives close to a bus carrying federal air force personnel, near Mozdok, killing 17 people; later in the month 13 police-officers were killed when their vehicle hit a landmine in the Republic. On 1 August more than 50 people were killed, and at least 100 others injured, following a suicide bombing outside a military hospital at Mozdok; both the commander of the hospital and of the military garrison were subsequently suspended by the federal Ministry of Defence, for permitting a breach of security to occur.

## Economy

In 1999 gross regional product in North Osetiya—Alaniya totalled 7,572.3m. roubles, equivalent to 11,318.8 roubles per head. Its major industrial centres are at Vladikavkaz, Mozdok and Beslan. In 2000 the Republic contained 144 km (89 miles) of railway track, including a section of the North Caucasus Railway. There were 2,309 km of paved roads, and one of the two principal road routes from Russia to the Transcaucasus; this route, the Transcaucasian Highwaywas being upgraded in 2003 at the initiative of the North Osetiyan authorities. There is an international airport at Vladikavkaz.

Agriculture in North Osetiya, which employed 14.5% of the labour force in 2000, consists mainly of vegetable and grain production, horticulture, viniculture and animal husbandry. The rate of reform in agriculture during the 1990s was slow. In 2000 agricultural production amounted to a value of 2,803m. roubles. In the same year industrial output was worth 4,466m. roubles, and the sector employed 17.1% of the working population. The Republic's main industries are radio-electronics (until the 1990s largely used for defence purposes), non-ferrous metallurgy, mechanical engineering, wood-working, light industry, chemicals, glass-making and food-processing. There are also five hydroelectric power stations, with an average capacity of around 80 MWh. By the mid-1990s some 70% of industrial production within the defence sector had been converted to civilian use.

The economically active population totalled 328,000 in 2000, when some 28.5% of the labour force were unemployed. Those in employment earned an average wage of 2,522.4 roubles per month in mid-2002. The republican budget showed a surplus of 16.5m. roubles in 2000. In 2000 export trade amounted to US $67.1m., and imports to $67.4m. Foreign investment remained deterred by the instability endemic to much of the North Caucasus region. At 31 December 2000 there were some 3,700 small businesses in operation in North Osetiya.

## Directory

**President of the Republic:** ALEKSANDR S. DZASOKHOV; 362038 North Osetiya—Alaniya, Vladikavkaz, pl. Svobody 1, Dom Pravitelstva; tel. (8672) 53-35-24; fax (8672) 74-92-48; internet president.osetia.ru.

**Chairman of the Government:** MIKHAIL M. SHATALOV; 362038 North Osetiya—Alaniya, Vladikavkaz, pl. Svobody 1, Dom Pravitelstva; tel. (8672) 53-35-56; fax (8672) 75-87-30.

**Chairman of the Parliament:** TAIMURAZ D. MAMSUROV; 362038 North Osetiya—Alaniya, Vladikavkaz, pl. Svobody 1; tel. (8672) 53-81-01; fax (8672) 53-93-46; e-mail parliament@rno-a.ru; internet parliament.rno-a.ru.

**Chief Representative of the Republic of North Osetiya—Alaniya in the Russian Federation:** ERIK R. BUGULOV; 109028 Moscow, per. Durasovskii 1/9; tel. (095) 916-21-47; fax (095) 916-25-22.

**Head of Vladikavkaz City Administration (Mayor):** MIKHAIL M. SHATALOV; 362040 North Osetiya—Alaniya, Vladikavkaz, pl. Shtyba 1; fax (8672) 75-34-35.

# Republic of Sakha (Yakutiya)

The Republic of Sakha (Yakutiya) is situated in eastern Siberia on the Laptev and Eastern Siberian Seas. Some two-fifths of the Republic's territory lies within the Arctic Circle. It forms part of the Far Eastern Federal Okrug and the Far Eastern Economic Area. To the west it borders Krasnoyarsk Krai (the Taimyr and Evenk AOks), while Irkutsk and Chita Oblasts lie in the south-west, Amur Oblast to the south and Khabarovsk Krai and Magadan Oblast in the south-east. In the north-eastern corner of the territory there is a border with the Chukot AOk. Its main river is the Lena, which drains into the Laptev Sea via a large swampy delta; other important rivers are the Lena's tributaries, the Aldan, the Viliyuy, the Olenek, the Yana, the Indigirka and the Kolyma. Apart from the Central Yakut Plain, the region's territory is mountainous and four-fifths is taiga (forested marshland). Yakutiya is the largest federal unit in Russia, occupying an area of 3,103,200 sq km (1,198,150 sq miles), making it larger than Kazakhstan, itself the second largest country, after Russia, in Europe or the former USSR. The Republic consists of 33 administrative districts and 13 cities. Its climate, owing to its size, is varied: the north lies within the arctic zone whereas the south has a more temperate climate. The average temperature in January is as low as −35.6°C, and the average temperature in July is around 13.3°C. At 1 January 2002 the Republic had an estimated population of just 982,900, and a population density, therefore, of 0.3 per sq km. Some 64.3% of the population inhabited urban areas in 2001. In the late 1990s and early 2000s there was a continuous outflow of population from the Republic. In 1989 33.4% of the total population were the indigenous Yakuts (who represent the largest ethnic group in Siberia, apart from Russians) and 50.3% Russians. Orthodox Christianity is the dominant religion in the region. The Yakuts' native tongue, spoken as a first language by over 93% of the indigenous population, is part of the North-Eastern branch of the Turkic family, although it is considerably influenced by Mongolian. The capital is at Yakutsk, which had a population of 197,800 at 1 January 2001.

## History

The Yakuts (Iakuts), also known as the Sakha (Saka), were historically known as the Tungus, Jekos and the Urangkhai Sakha. They are believed to be descended from various peoples from the Lake Baikal area, Turkish tribes from the steppe and the Altai Mountains, and indigenous Siberian peoples, including the Evenks. They were traditionally a semi-nomadic people, with those in the north of the region occupied with hunting, fishing and reindeer-breeding, while those in the south were pastoralists who bred horses and cattle and were also skilled blacksmiths. Their territory, briefly united by the toion (chief), Tygyn, came under Russian rule in the 1620s and a fur tax was introduced. This led to violent opposition from the Yakuts between 1634 and 1642, although all rebellions were crushed. Increasing numbers of Russians began to settle in the region, as the result of the completion of a mail route to the Far East, the construction of camps for political opponents to the tsars and the discovery of gold in 1846. The territory became commercialized after the construction of the Trans-Siberian Railway in the 1880s and 1890s and the development of commercial shipping on the River Lena. The economic resources of the territory enabled the Yakut to secure a measure of autonomy as an ASSR in 1922. Collectivization and the purges of the 1930s greatly reduced the Yakut population, and the region was rapidly industrialized, largely involving the extraction of gold, coal and timber.

Nationalist feeling re-emerged during the period of *glasnost* (openness) in the late 1980s. Cultural, ecological and economic concerns led to the proclamation of a Yakut-Sakha SSR on 27 April 1990. The republican Supreme Soviet declared a Yakut Republic on 15 August 1991, and demanded republican control over the reserves of gold, diamonds, timber, coal, petroleum and tin located on its territory.

On 22 December elections for an executive presidency were held, and were won by the former Chairman of the Supreme Soviet, Mikhail Nikolayev. The Republic was renamed the Republic of Sakha (Yakutiya) in March 1992 and a new Constitution was promulgated on 27 April. On 12 October 1993 the Supreme Soviet dissolved itself and set elections to a 60-seat bicameral legislature for 12 December. On 26 January 1994 the new parliament named itself the State Assembly; it comprised an upper Chamber of the Republic and a lower Chamber of Representatives. Although support for the Communist Party of the Russian Federation was relatively high in Sakha, the federal Government's willingness to concede a significant degree of local control over natural resources ensured that it too enjoyed some confidence. Native languages were designated official in certain areas and attempts to protect traditional lifestyles even involved the restoration of land. Thus, a Yeven-Bytantai Okrug was established on traditional Yeven territory in the mid-1990s. In June 1997 the Republic was honoured at a UN special session on the environment held in New York, the USA, for its commitment to preserving its natural heritage (around one-quarter of its territory had been set aside as protected areas). Meanwhile, in December 1996 Nikolayev was re-elected President by an overwhelming majority and continued his efforts to win greater autonomy from the centre, including the maintenance (in breach of federal law) of gold and hard-currency reserves and, from August 1998, a ban on the sale of gold outside the republican government. A power-sharing agreement with the federal Government in June 1995 was followed, in March 1998, by a framework agreement on co-operation for five years, which provided for collaboration on a series of mining and energy projects. In May 2001 over 5,000 people were adversely affected by particularly severe flooding in the Republic. In December the federal Audit Chamber announced that an investigation was to take place into the alleged misspending by the republican Government of funds allocated for restoration work. In the same month Nikolayev withdrew his candidacy from the forthcoming gubernatorial election, and urged voters to transfer their support to Vyacheslav Shtyrov, the President of the local diamond-producing joint-stock company, Almazy Rossii-Sakha—Alrosa, who was the candidate of the pro-presidential Unity and Fatherland-United Russia party. In the first round of voting, held on 23 December, Shtyrov received 45% of the votes cast, more than any other candidate, but fewer than the 50% required to secure an outright victory. Shtyrov subsequently received 59% of the votes in the second round, held on 13 January 2002, defeating businessman Fedot Tumusov. The election, in particular the second round, was characterized by widespread allegations of malpractice. Meanwhile, controversy ensued with regard to discrepancies between the republican and federal Constitutions; in March the approval by the republican legislature of amendments to 11 articles of Sakha's Constitution was reportedly regarded as insufficiently rigorous by the federal authorities, and it was reported that the Republic's Chief Prosecutor was to recommend that President Shtyrov dissolve the legislature. Elections to the new, unicameral, 70-member legislature, were held on 29 December; some 33 business executives were among the deputies elected, while 14 employees of Alrosa and its subsidiaries were elected.

## Economy

Owing to the Republic's wealth of mineral reserves, its gross regional product in 1999 was 64,688.0m. roubles, equivalent to 65,846.9 roubles per head, the second highest figure in the Russian Federation, after the city of Moscow. The Republic's major industrial centres are at Yakutsk, Mirnyi, Neryungra, Aldan and Lensk. Its main port is Tiksi. In 2000 there were 165 km (103 miles) of railways in the Republic, and during the 1990s the extent of paved roads increased over two-fold, to reach some 7,292 km by 2000.

Sakha (Yakutiya)'s agriculture, in which 10.3% of the working population was engaged in 2000, consists mainly of animal husbandry (livestock- and reindeer-breeding), hunting and fishing. Grain and vegetable production tends to be on a small scale. Total agricultural output in 2000 was worth 5,793m. roubles (compared with a figure of 64,898m. roubles for the industrial sector). Industry employed 16.2% of the Republic's working population in 2000: its main industries are ore-mining (gold—Sakha produced approximately 25% of the Russian Federation's output in the first half of the 1990s, diamonds—of which Sakha is the second largest producer and exporter in the world, tin, muscovite—mica, antimony and coal), the production of electricity, food-processing and natural gas production. Both industrial output and foreign trade in Sakha (Yakutiya) increased throughout the 1990s. In September 1997 Alrosa signed a preliminary one-year trade accord with the South African diamond producer, De Beers. The accord was subsequently extended until 2001, and De Beers was to purchase US $550m. worth of raw diamonds during this period. Alrosa also diversified its operations into polishing and selling its gems. A new, five-year agreement was signed with De Beers in December 2001.

The economically active population of the Republic amounted to 497,000 in 2000, and some 11.3% of the labour force were unemployed. The social situation in Yakutiya from the mid-1990s was typical of the northern regions of the Russian Federation. Growth in the cost of goods and services was compounded by a weak economic structure, poorly developed social services and inappropriate conditions for people to grow their own food. In 1999, in terms of a 'consumer basket', the Republic was one of the most expensive regions in the country. The average monthly wage was 8,357.8 roubles in mid-2002 (considerably higher than the national average, but offset by the high cost of living). During the late 1990s the Republic maintained consistently large budgetary deficits; in 1998 the deficit amounted to 2,238m. roubles. However, in 2000 the republican budget recorded a surplus of 649.7m. roubles. In the same year the value of export trade amounted to some US $1,089.5m., compared with imports of $39.0m. Foreign investment in Sakha (Yakutiya) amounted to $159.6m in 2000. At 31 December 2000 there were 2,700 small businesses registered on its territory.

## Directory

**President:** VYACHESLAV A. SHTYROV; 677012 Sakha (Yakutiya), Yakutsk, ul. Kirova 11; tel. (4112) 43-50-50; fax (4112) 24-06-24; internet www.sakha.gov.ru.

**Chairman of the Government:** YEGOR A. BORISOV; 677000 Sakha (Yakutiya), Yakutsk, ul. Kirova 11; tel. (4112) 43-55-55; fax (4112) 24-06-07; internet www.sakha.gov.ru/main.asp?c=1476.

**Chairman of the State Assembly (Il Tumen):** NIKOLAI I. SOLOMOV; 677022 Sakha (Yakutiya), Yakutsk, ul. Yaroslavskogo 24/1; tel. (4112) 43-53-88; internet www.sakha.gov.ru/main.asp?c=10.

**Chief Representative of the Republic of Sakha (Yakutiya) in the Russian Federation:** ANDREI V. KRIVOSHAPKIN; 107078 Moscow, Myasnitskii pr. 3/26; tel. (095) 925-52-81; fax (095) 928-42-21.

**Head of Yakutsk City Administration (Mayor):** ILYA F. MIKHAL-CHUK; 677000 Sakha (Yakutiya), Yakutsk, ul. Kirova 11; tel. (4112) 42-30-20; fax (4112) 42-48-80; e-mail erb@yacc.yakutia.su.

# Republic of Tatarstan

The Republic of Tatarstan is situated in the east of European Russia and forms part of the Volga Federal Okrug and the Volga Economic Area. It neighbours several other Republics: Bashkortostan to the east; Udmurtiya to the north; Marii-El to the north-west; and Chuvashiya to the west. The Oblasts of Ulyanovsk, Samara and Orenburg lie to the south, and that of Kirov to the north. Its major rivers are the Volga and the Kama, and one-fifth of its total territory of 67,836 sq km (26,260 sq miles) is forested. It measures 290 km (180 miles) from south to north and 460 km from west to east. The Republic is divided into 43 administrative districts and 20 cities. At 1 January 2002 it had an estimated population of 3,768,200 and, therefore, a population density of 55.4 per sq km. In 2001 some 73.9% of the Republic's population inhabited urban areas. In 1989 some 48.5% of the total population were Tatars and 43.3% ethnic Russians. Tatarstan's capital is Kazan, which lies on the River Volga and had a population of 1,090,200 in 2001. Other major cities include Naberezhnye Chelny (formerly Brezhnev—with a population of 518,300), Nizhnekamsk (226,100), Almetevsk (141,600) and Zelenodolsk (100,500).

## History

After the dissolution of the Mongol Empire the region became the Khanate of Kazan, the territory of the Golden Horde. Kazan was conquered by Russian troops, led by Tsar Ivan IV—'the Terrible' in 1552. Some of the Muslim Tatars succumbed to Russian pressures to convert to Orthodox Christianity (the Staro-Kryashens—'Old-Baptized' still exist, using Tatar as their spoken and liturgical tongue), but most did not. A modernist school of thought in Islam, Jadidism, originated among the Volga Tatars, who attained an exceptionally high cultural level in the 19th-century Russian Empire. A Tatar ASSR was established on 27 May 1920.

On 31 August 1990 the Chairman of the republican Supreme Soviet, Mintimer Shamiyev, declared Tatarstan a sovereign republic. In 1991 Shamiyev was elected as republican President. Apart from secessionist Chechnya, Tatarstan was the only Republic to reject the Federation Treaty and adopt its own Constitution on 6 November 1992, which provided for a presidential republic with a bicameral legislature, the State Council. In February 1994 Shamiyev won important concessions from Russia's central Government by signing a treaty that ceded extensive powers to Tatarstan, including full ownership rights over its petroleum reserves and industrial companies, the right to retain most of its tax revenue and the right to pursue its own foreign-trade policy. This was the first agreement of its kind in the Federation and, despite significant contradictions and weaknesses, it became a model for other federal

subjects seeking to determine their relations with the federal centre. The division of responsibilities was confirmed by treaty with the Federation in 1995.

In a republican presidential election, held on 24 March 1996, Shamiyev was re-elected, winning some 93% of the votes cast. During 1999 Shamiyev was one of the regional governors most active in the creation of the new All Russia political bloc. Republican parliamentary by-elections in March gave the President's supporters a clear majority in the legislature.

In 2000 federal President Vladimir Putin offered Shamiyev the post of presidential envoy to the new Volga Federal Okrug, which he declined, amid constitutional uncertainty regarding the legitimacy of Shamiyev's intention to contest a third term of office as Governor. In the event, Shamiyev was permitted to compete in the election in March 2001, when he obtained some 80% of the votes cast, becoming the first Governor of any federal subject in the Russian Federation to be elected three times to that post.

As Putin's administration, from mid-2000, sought to harmonize federal legislation with that of the constituent units of the Russian Federation, Tatarstan (along with neighbouring Bashkortostan) became one of the principal regions in which the republican authorities demonstrated sustained resistance to these measures. In May 2001 the federal Supreme Court declared that some 42 articles of the Republic's Constitution were at variance with federal law (a ruling by the republican Supreme Court confirmed these findings in October). Despite federal government demands that the inconsistencies be removed, in July Shamiyev signed an agreement with the Presidential Representative to the Volga Federal Okrug, Sergei Kiriyenko, which permitted the continued operation of various practices that contradicted federal practice; in particular, a highly centralized system of local governance was to be retained in Tatarstan. The text of a new Constitution, which was intended to comply with federal law, was none the less approved by the republican State Council in late February 2002; the new Constitution took effect from 19 April. Although the new document referred to Tatarstan being subject to the Constitution and laws of the Russian Federation, it continued to declare the 'limited' and 'residual' sovereignty of the Republic of Tatarstan and preserved the notion of Tatar citizenship. Consequently, in June the office of the federal Prosecutor-General demanded that several articles of the Constitution be amended, issuing a complaint to both the republican legislature and republican Supreme Court. However, in mid-September the State Council rejected any notion that the constitutional text was in breach of federal law, and instead referred the matter to both the republican and federal Constitutional Courts. Eventually the threat of the office of the Prosecutor-General to disband the State Council was rescinded, but the tensions between the federal and republican authorities remained largely unresolved. (These tensions were further heightened by federal legislation, approved by Putin in November 2002, that demanded that all state languages of federal subjects be written in Cyrillic on official documents—the republican authorities had, in 2000, begun to implement a programme to reintroduce the Latin script for the Tatar language.) In July 2003 the federal Constitutional Court ruled that it was the sole body with authority to determine whether the constitutions of federal subjects were in conformity with federal law; one consequence of this ruling appeared to be that a number of challenges to the Constitution of Tatarstan from other bodies (including the federal Supreme Court) were declared invalid.

## Economy

In 1999 the Republic's gross regional product stood at 123,671.8m. roubles, or 32,723.5 roubles per head. The territory is one of the most developed economic regions of the Russian Federation and has vast agricultural and industrial potential. Its main industrial centres are Kazan, Naberezhnye Chelny, Zelenodolsk, Nizhnekamsk, Almetyevsk, Chistopol and Bugulma. Kazan is the most important port on the Volga and a junction in the national rail, road and air transport systems. Russia's second primary petroleum export pipeline to Europe starts in Almetyevsk. In 2000 there were 878 km of railway lines and 12,508 km of paved roads on the Republic's territory.

Tatarstan's agriculture, in which some 14.9% of the work-force were engaged in 2000, consists mainly of grain production, animal husbandry, horticulture and bee-keeping. Total output in this sector amounted to a value of 31,049m. roubles in 2000. Mineral natural resources are more important, and the Republic has significant reserves of hydrocarbons reserves. The region is an important industrial centre (industry accounted for 25.3% of employment in 2000): its capital, Kazan, and the neighbouring towns of Zelendolsk and Vasilyevo are centres for light industry, the manufacture of petrochemicals and building materials, and mechanical engineering. The automobile and petroleum industries are major employers in the region. Kazanorgsintez, a petrochemicals giant, is the largest polyethylene producer in Russia. Industries connected with the extraction, processing and use of petroleum represent around one-half of the Republic's total industrial production, which was worth

191,300m. roubles in 2000. In the mid-1990s the US automobile company, General Motors, signed a contract to manufacture 50,000 automobiles per year at the Yelabuga plant, which later became the centre of a zone offering special tax incentives. In April 1996 a programme, drafted with French and US assistance, which envisaged the transformation of Tatarstan's economy from a military to a socially orientated system, was adopted by the Council of Ministers.

The economically active population in the Republic amounted to 1,845,000 in 2000, when 8.0% of the labour force were unemployed, one of the lowest levels in the Russian Federation. The average monthly wage was 3,866.4 roubles in mid-2002. The 2000 budget recorded a surplus of 914.5m. roubles. Tatarstan also fared well in terms of trade; the value of exports amounted to US $2,990.2m. in 2000, and imports to $363.1m. In the same year foreign investment in the Republic amounted to $143.0m. In 2000 there were 93 foreign joint-stock enterprises in Tatarstan, 20 of which received financing from the USA, while 13 received financing from Germany, 10 from the United Kingdom and seven from Cyprus. By the beginning of 1997 over 1,000 large and medium-sized enterprises in Tatarstan had been privatized; at 1 December 2000 there were some 16,100 small businesses.

## Directory

**President:** MINTIMER SH. SHAIMIYEV; 420014 Tatarstan, Kazan, Kreml; tel. (8432) 92-74-66; fax (8432) 91-78-66; e-mail secretariat@tatar.ru; internet www.tatar.ru.

**Prime Minister:** RUSTAM N. MINNIKHANOV; 420060 Tatarstan, Kazan, pl. Svobody 1; tel. (8432) 64-15-51; fax (8432) 36-28-24.

**Chairman of the State Council:** FARID KH. MUKHAMETSHIN; 420060 Tatarstan, Kazan, pl. Svobody 1; tel. (8432) 64-15-00; fax (8432) 36-88-45; e-mail gossov@kabmin.tatarstan.ru; internet www.gossov.tatarstan.ru.

**Chief Representative of the Republic of Tatarstan in the Russian Federation:** NAZIF M. MIRIKHANOV; 107813Moscow, per. 3-i Kotelnicheskii 13–15/1; tel. (095) 915-05-02; fax (095) 915-06-10; e-mail adm@msk.tatarstan.ru.

**Head of Kazan City Administration:** KAMIL SH. ISKHAKOV; 420014 Tatarstan, Kazan, ul. Kremlevskaya 1; tel. (8432) 92-38-38; fax (8432) 92-76-72; e-mail kanc@kazan.gov.tatarstan.ru; internet www.kazan.org.ru.

# Republic of Tyva

The Republic of Tyva (Tuva) is situated in the south of eastern Siberia in the Sayan Mountains. It forms part of the Siberian Federal Okrug and the East Siberian Economic Area. Tyva has an international border with Mongolia to the south. The Republic of Altai lies to the west, the Republic of Khakasiya to the north-west and Krasnoyarsk Krai to the north, Irkutsk Oblast lies to the northeast and the Republic of Buryatiya forms part of the eastern border. Its major river is the Yenisei, which rises in the Eastern Sayan mountain range. The territory of the Republic consists of a series of high mountain valleys. One-half of its area is forested. The Republic has numerous waterways, including over 12,000 rivers and 8,400 freshwater lakes. Tyva occupies 170,500 sq km (65,830 sq miles) and consists of 16 administrative districts and five cities. At 1 January 2002 it had an estimated population of 310,300 and a population density of only 1.8 per sq km. Some 48.4% of the population lived in urban areas in 2001. In 1989 some 64.3% of inhabitants were Tyvans (Tuvinians) and 32.0% Russians. Lamaism (Tibetan Buddhism) is the predominant religion in the Republic. The Tyvan language belongs to the Old Uigur group of the Turkic branch of the Uralo-Altaic linguistic family. The capital of Tyva is at Kyzyl, which had a population of 101,500 at 1 January 2001.

## History

The Tyvans (known at various times as Soyons, Soyots and Uriankhais) emerged as an identifiable ethnic group in the early 18th century. The territory of what is now Tyva was occupied in turn between the sixth and the ninth centuries by the Turkish Khanate, the Chinese, the Uigurs and the Yenisei Kyrgyz. The Mongols controlled the region from 1207 to 1368. In the second half of the 17th century the Dzungarians (Sungarians) seized the area from the Altyn Khans. In 1758 the Manzhous (Manchus) annexed Dzungaria and the territory thus became part of the Chinese Empire. Russian influence dates from the Treaty of Peking (Beijing) of 1860, after which trade links were developed and a number of Russians settled there. One year after the Chinese Revolution of 1911 Tyva declared its independence. In 1914, however, Russia established a protectorate over the territory, which became the Tannu-Tuva People's Republic. This was a nominally independent state until October 1944, when it was incorporated into the USSR as the Tuvinian Autonomous Oblast. It became an ASSR on 10 October 1961, within the Russian Federation.

The Republic declared sovereignty on 11 December 1990 and renamed itself the Republic of Tuva in August 1991. On 21 October 1993 the Tyvan Supreme Soviet resolved that the Republic's name was Tyva (as opposed to the russified Tuva) and adopted a new Constitution. The Constitution provided for a legislature, the Supreme Khural, and a supreme constitutional body, the Grand Khural. The new parliament was elected on 12 December. On the same day the new Constitution was approved by 62.2% of registered voters in Tyva. Only 32.7%, however, voted in favour of the Russian Constitution. The victory of a nationalist Liberal Democratic candidate, Aleksandr Kashin, in the April 1998 mayoral elections in Kyzyl was, perhaps, a sign of intolerance with the reformism of the federal Government (particularly among the predominantly ethnic Russian population of the city). Apathy was also a likely cause, as a low rate of participation in the general election of the same month meant that only 21 of the 38 seats in the Supreme Khural were filled. Further rounds later in the year failed to resolve the situation and, indeed, for two months in 1998–99 the parliament was rendered inquorate by the death of a deputy. In 2000 the Grand Khural was obliged to make 26 amendments to the republican Constitution, in order to comply with the All-Russian Constitution. A new Constitution, which removed Tyva's right to self-determination and to secede from the Federation, was approved by referendum in May 2001; in early March 2002 various amendments to this Constitution were approved, in order to bring it more closely into compliance with federal norms. Notably, the Supreme Khural was reconstituted as a bicameral legislature, comprising an upper chamber, the 130-member Chamber of Representatives, and a lower chamber, the 32-member Legislative Chamber. On 17 March the incumbent President, Sherig-ool Oorzhak, was elected to serve a third term of office, receiving 53% of the votes cast. Elections to the bicameral legislature were held on 2 June; the overall rate of participation by the electorate was 52%, although repeat elections were to be required to elect 40 members of the Chamber of Representatives and nine members of the Legislative Chamber.

## Economy

Tyva's economy is largely agriculture-based. In 1999 its gross regional product stood at 2,616.3m. roubles, or 8,404.4 roubles per head. The Republic's main industrial centres are at Kyzyl and Ak-Dovurak. There are road and rail links with other regions, although the distance from Kyzyl to the nearest railway station is over 400 km (250 miles). In 2000 there were 2,473 km of paved roads in the Republic.

The Republic's agriculture, which employed 16.1% of the workforce in 2000, consists mainly of animal husbandry, although forestry and hunting are also important. Total agricultural production in 2000 amounted to a value of 1,285m. roubles. At 1 January 1999 there were some 670,400 sheep and goats, 140,100 cattle and 19,200 pigs in the Republic. Gold extraction was developed from the mid-1990s: in 1996 it amounted to almost one metric ton. Tyva's main industries were ore-mining (asbestos, coal, cobalt and mercury), production of electricity, the processing of agricultural and forestry products, light manufacturing, manufacture of building materials and metal-working. In 2000 industry employed 8.6% of the working population and total production within the sector was worth just 692m. roubles.

The economically active population of Tyva totalled 115,000 in 2000, when 22.9% of the labour force were unemployed. In mid-2002 the average monthly wage in the Republic was 3,870.5 roubles, somewhat lower than the national average. However, in the late 1990s the Republic was one of the areas of the Russian Federation worst affected by wage arrears and most dependent on federal transfers. In September 2000 the federal Government arranged to pay wage arrears amounting to 216.7m. roubles in Tyva, in addition to providing for improvements to educational and medical services in the Republic. The 2000 budget showed a surplus of 100.9m. roubles. Foreign investment in the Republic was minimal, and amounted to just US $381,000 in 2000. At 31 December 2000 a total of 700 small businesses were registered in the Republic.

## Directory

**President (Chairman of the Government):** SHERIG-OOL D. OORZHAK; 667000 Tyva, Kyzyl, ul. Chulduma 18, Dom Pravitelstva; tel. (39422) 1-12-77; fax (39422) 3-74-59; e-mail tuva@tuva.ru; internet gov.tuva.ru.

**President of the Chamber of Representatives of the Supreme Khural:** DANDYR-OOL K.-KH. OORZHAK; 667000 Tyva, Kyzyl, ul. Lenina 32; tel. (39422) 1-31-79; fax (39422) 3-33-71; e-mail parliament@tuva.ru; internet gov.tuva.ru/gosvo/predct_p.htm.

**President of the Legislative Chamber of the Supreme Khural:** Vasilii M. Oyun; 667000 Tyva, Kyzyl, ul. Lenina 32; tel. (39422) 3-74-78; fax (39422) 1-16-32; e-mail parliament@tuva.ru; internet gov.tuva.ru/gosvo/zakdat_p.htm.

**Chief Representative of the Republic of Tyva in the Russian Federation:** Orlan O. Cholbenei; 119049 Moscow, ul. Donskaya 8/2; tel. (095) 236-48-01; fax (095) 236-45-53.

**Head of Kyzyl City Administration (Mayor):** Dmitrii K. Dongak; 667000 Tyva, Kyzyl, ul. Lenina 32; tel. (39422) 3-50-55.

# Udmurt Republic (Udmurtiya)

The Udmurt Republic occupies part of the Upper Kama Highlands. It forms part of the Volga Federal Okrug and the Urals Economic Area. Tatarstan lies to the south, Bashkortostan to the south-east, Perm to the east and Kirov to the north and west. Its major river is the Kama, dominating the southern and eastern borderlands, while the Vyatka skirts the territory in the west. About one-half of its territory is forested. Its total area covers some 42,100 sq km (16,250 sq miles). The Republic consists of 25 administrative districts and six cities. At 1 January 2002 Udmurtiya had an estimated population of 1,616,200, and a population density, therefore, of 38.4 per sq km. In 2001 some 69.4% of the population inhabited urban areas. In 1989 some 30.9% of the total population were Udmurts and 58.9% ethnic Russians. The dominant religion in the Republic is Orthodox Christianity. The 1989 census showed that some 70% of Udmurts spoke their native tongue, from the Permian group of the Finnic branch of the Uralo-Altaic family, as their first language. The capital of Udmurtiya is at Izhevsk (formerly Ustinov), which had a population of 650,300 in 2001. Other major towns in the region are Glazov (106,800), Sarapul (104,200) and Votkinsk (101,700).

## History

The first appearance of the Votyaks (the former name for Udmurts) as a distinct ethnic group occurred in the sixth century. The territories inhabited by Votyaks were conquered by the Khazars in the eighth century, although Khazar influence gave way to that of the Volga Bulgars in the mid-ninth century. In the 13th century the Mongol Tatars occupied the region, but were gradually displaced by the Russians from the mid-15th century. By 1558 all Votyaks were under Russian rule. A Votyak Autonomous Oblast was established on 4 November 1920. On 1 January 1932 it was renamed the Udmurt Autonomous Oblast, which became an ASSR on 28 December 1934.

The Republic declared sovereignty on 21 September 1990, although a new republican Constitution was not adopted until 7 December 1994. The Chairman of the legislature, the State Council, remained head of the Republic, and a premier chaired the Government. In 1996 the Udmurt parliament was accused of having virtually eliminated local government in the Republic, in contravention of federal law. Measures to introduce a presidential system of regional government in Udmurtiya, in common with most other Republics within the Russian Federation, were endorsed by a referendum held on 26 March 2000. In June the Udmurt State Council adopted a number of draft laws transferring the Republic to presidential rule. Aleksandr Volkov, hitherto the parliamentary speaker, was elected President on 15 October. The Republic's Prime Minister, Nikolai Ganza, who was supported by the Unity party, was the third-placed candidate; he resigned three days later. From the 1990s the disposal of chemical weapons on the territory of Udmurtiya proved to be a serious social and ecological problem—the Republic was thought to contain around one-quarter of Russia's entire arsenal of such weapons.

## Economy

In 1999 the Republic's gross regional product amounted to 37,501.6m. roubles, equivalent to 22,948.0 roubles per head. Udmurtiya possesses significant hydrocarbons reserves and is an important arms-producing region. Its major industrial centres are at Izhevsk, Sarapul and Glazov. Its main river-ports are at Sarapul and Kambarka. In 2000 there were 768 km (477 miles) of railway track and 5,487 km of paved roads on its territory. In 1998 there were 178 km of navigable waterways. Twelve major gas pipelines and two petroleum pipelines pass through the Udmurt Republic.

Udmurtiya's agriculture employed 15.4% of the working population in 2000 and consists mainly of livestock-breeding, grain production and flax-growing. Total agricultural production in 2000 was worth 10,100m. roubles. There are substantial reserves of coal and of petroleum (prospected resources are estimated at 379,543m. metric tons), which in the late 1990s the Republic hoped to exploit with the aid of foreign investment. In 2000 some 27.8% of its working population was engaged in industry. The main industries in Udmurtiya, apart from the manufacture of weapons, are mechanical engineering (in the first half of 2000 the Republic produced some 89% of all the motorcycles manufactured in Russia), metal-working, metallurgy, processing of forestry and agricultural products, petroleum production, glass-making and the production of peat. Total industrial output in 2000 amounted to a value of 54,804m. roubles.

In 2000 the economically active population amounted to 820,000, and 9.3% of the labour force were unemployed; in mid-2002 those in employment earned an average monthly wage of 3,475.8 roubles. The republican budget recorded a surplus of 334.5m. roubles in 2000, when there was US $10.6m. of foreign investment in the Republic. External trade in 2000 amounted to $1,037.2m., of which exports accounted for $959.6m. The principal exports are metallurgical products, engines and machinery, and rifles. In the late 1990s the Republic had particularly active trade links with Germany. At 31 December 2000 there were approximately 8,000 small businesses registered in the Republic.

## Directory

**President:** Aleksandr A. Volkov; 426074 Udmurtiya, Izhevsk, pl. 50 let Oktyabrya 15; tel. and fax (3412) 49-70-10; e-mail president@udmurt.ru.

**Chairman of the Government:** Yurii S. Pitkeyvich; 426007 Udmurtiya, Izhevsk, ul. Pushkinskaya. 214; tel. (3412) 25-50-89; fax (3412) 25-50-17; e-mail premier@udmurt.ru.

**Chairman of the State Council (Legislature):** Igor N. Semenov; 426074 Udmurtiya, Izhevsk, ul. 50 let Oktyabrya 15; tel. (3412) 75-34-98; fax (3412) 75-29-87; e-mail premier@udmurt.ru.

**Chief Representative of the Udmurt Republic in the Russian Federation:** Andrei V. Sakovich; 127025 Moscow, ul. Novyi Arbat 19; tel. (095) 203-53-52; fax (095) 203-91-47.

**Head of Izhevsk City Administration (Mayor):** Viktor V. Balakin; 426070 Udmurtiya, Izhevsk, ul. Pushkinskaya 276; tel. (3412) 22-45-90; fax (3412) 22-84-94; e-mail izhevsk@izh.ru; internet www.izh.ru.

# KRAIS (PROVINCES)

## Altai Krai

Most of Altai Krai lies within the Western Siberian Plain. Part of the Siberian Federal Okrug and the West Siberian Economic Area, it has international boundaries to the south with Kazakhstan, the People's Republic of China and Mongolia. To the north lie the federal subjects of Novosibirsk Oblast, Kemerovo Oblast and the Republic of Khakasiya, while the Republic of Altai (formerly the Gorno-Altai Autonomous Oblast, then a constituent part of the Krai) and the Republic of Tyva lie to the east. Its major river is the Ob, which has numerous tributaries (there are altogether some 17,000 rivers within the territory). It has one main lake, the Teletskoye, although there are a total of 13,000 lakes, one-half of which are fresh water. About one-third of its total area is forested. In the east of the Krai are mountains, in the west steppe. The Krai occupies an area of 169,100 sq km (65,290 sq miles). It is divided into 60 administrative districts and 12 cities. It had an estimated population of 2,621,000 at 1 January 2002, giving a population density of 15.5 per sq km. In 2001 some 52.3% of the population lived in urban areas. In 1996 ethnic Russians comprised an estimated 90.3% of the population, Germans 4.8%, Ukrainians 2.4% and Altais just 0.1%. The Krai's administrative centre is at Barnaul, which had a population of 573,300 at 1 January 2001. Other major cities are Biisk (223,500) and Rubtsovsk (161,800).

### History

The territory of Altai Krai was annexed by Russia in 1738. The region was heavily industrialized during the Soviet period, particularly in 1926–40. Altai Krai was formed on 28 September 1937. On 13 March 1994, in accordance with a federal presidential decree of October 1993, a new provincial legislature, the Legislative Assembly, was elected, in place of the Provincial Soviet. The new legislature was bicameral, comprising a lower chamber of 25 deputies and an upper chamber of 72 deputies (one from each district in the Krai). The Chairman of the Provincial Council of People's Deputies, Aleksandr Surikov, a communist, defeated the incumbent Governor, Lev Korshunov, in the gubernatorial election of November 1996. Surikov retained his post in the election of 26 March 2000, obtaining 77% of the votes cast. In the early 2000s proposals for the reunification of Altai Krai with the Altai Republic became increasingly popular, with the most prominent proponent of reunification being the Krai's legislative Chairman, Aleksandr Nazarchuk, who repeatedly called for a referendum to be held concerning the proposed merger. However, despite the close political allegiances of Nazarchuk and the Governor of the Republic of Altai elected in December 2001, Mikhail Lapshin (both of whom were prominent members of the Agrarian Party of Russia), the authorities in the Republic reportedly opposed any merger, fearing that such a measure would result in the former Autonomous Oblast returning to a subordinate status within the Krai.

### Economy

Altai Krai's gross regional product in 1999 totalled 34,837.7m. roubles, equivalent to 13,103.8 roubles per head. Its main industrial centres are at Barnaul, Biisk, Rubtsovsk, Novoaltaisk and Slavgorod. There are major river-ports at Barnaul and Biisk. It has well-developed transport networks—1,803 km (1,067 miles) of railway lines in 2000, and 14,441 km of paved roads. About one-quarter of its territory is served by water transport, which operates along a network of some 1,000 km of navigable waterways. There are five airports, including an international airport at Barnaul, with a service to Düsseldorf, Germany. The Krai is bisected by the main natural gas pipeline running from Tyumen to Barnaul via Novosibirsk.

The Krai's principal crops are grain, flax, sunflowers and sugar beet. Horticulture, animal husbandry and fur-animal breeding are also important. In 2000 some 25.7% of its work-force was engaged in agriculture, while total production in the sector amounted to 24,428m. roubles. The Krai contains substantial mineral resources, including salt, iron ore, soda and precious stones, most of which are not industrially exploited. Its main industries are mechanical engineering (including tractor-manufacturing, primarily by the Rubtsovsk tractor plant), food-processing (the Krai's agro-industrial complex is one of the largest in the country), electricity production, metallurgy, chemicals and petrochemicals, and the manufacture of building materials. In addition, Barnaul contains one of the largest textiles enterprises in Russia, producing cotton fibre and yarn for cloth. Industry employed 20.0% of the population in 2000, when total production in the sector amounted to a value of 30,357m. roubles.

In 2000 the economically active population in Altai Krai totalled 1,260,000, and 11.5% of the Krai's labour force were unemployed. The average monthly wage was 2,558.8 roubles in mid-2002. Living costs are low in the region: in August 2002 a 'consumer basket' of basic foodstuffs purchased in Barnaul was found to be the lowest-priced in the Russian Federation. In 2000 the local budget showed a deficit of 121.5m. roubles. External trade amounted to a value of US $206.6m. in exports and $114.0m. in imports; the majority of trade was conducted with other member countries of the Commonwealth of Independent States. Foreign investment in the territory in 2000 totalled $6.5m. At 31 December 2000 there were 12,100 small businesses registered in the Krai.

### Directory

**Head of the Provincial Administration (Governor):** ALEKSANDR A. SURIKOV; 656035 Altai Krai, Barnaul, pr. Lenina 59; tel. (3852) 35-69-35; e-mail glava@alregn.ru; internet www.altairegion.ru.

**Chairman of the Provincial Council of People's Deputies:** ALEKSANDR G. NAZARCHUK; 656035 Altai Krai, Barnaul, pr. Lenina 59; tel. (3852) 35-69-86; fax (3852) 22-85-42; e-mail press@alregn.ru.

**Chief Representative of Altai Krai in the Russian Federation:** TEIMURAZ S. BABLUMYAN; 109017 Moscow, per. B. Tolmachevskii 5/9; tel. (095) 953-36-83; fax (095) 953-01-84; e-mail altaypred@mail.ru.

**Head of Barnaul City Administration:** VLADIMIR N. KOLGANOV; 656099 Altai Krai, Barnaul, pr. Lenina 18/16; tel. (3852) 39-32-72; e-mail info@bar.alt.ru; internet barnaul.altai.ru.

## Khabarovsk Krai

Khabarovsk Krai is situated in the Far East, on the Sea of Okhotsk and the Tatar Strait. The region forms part of the Far Eastern Federal Okrug and the Far Eastern Economic Area. Maritime Krai lies to the south, the Jewish Autonomous Oblast (Birobidzhan—part of the Krai until 1991) is to the south-west, Amur Oblast lies to the west, the Republic of Sakha (Yakutiya) to the north-west and, in the north of the province, Magadan Oblast lies to the east. The island of Sakhalin (part of Sakhalin Oblast) lies offshore to the east, across the Tatar Strait. There is a short international border with the People's Republic of China in the south-west. Its main river is the Amur, which rises near the Russo–Chinese border and flows into the Tatar Strait at the town of Nikolayevsk-on-Amur (Nikolayevsk-na-Amure). More than one-half of the Krai's total area of 788,600 sq km (304,400 sq miles) is forested and almost three-quarters comprises mountains or plateaux. The territory, one of the largest in the Federation, measures 1,780 km (1,105 miles) south to north and 7,000 km west to east. Its coastline is 2,500 km long. It is divided into 17 administrative districts and seven cities. The climate is monsoon-like in character, with hot, humid summers. Annual average precipitation in mountain areas can be as much as 1,000 mm (40 inches), while in the north it averages 500 mm. The total population in Khabarovsk Krai at 1 January 2002 was an estimated 1,485,800; the population density was 1.9 per sq km. In 2001 80.8% of the population lived in urban areas. Khabarovsk Krai's administrative centre is at Khabarovsk, which had a population of 603,500 in 2001. The Krais' second largest city is Komsomolsk-on-Amur (Komsomolsk-na-Amure—289,500).

### History

Khabarovsk city was established as a military outpost in 1858. It was named after Yerofei Khabarov, a Cossack, who in 1650 led an expedition to the region. The region prospered significantly with the construction of the Trans-Siberian Railway, which reached Khabarovsk in 1905. The Krai was formally created on 20 September 1938. The area was industrialized in 1946–80. Elections to a new, provincial legislature, the Legislative Duma, were held in March 1994. In April 1996 the federal President, Boris Yeltsin, and the head of the provincial administration, Viktor Ishayev, signed an agreement on the division of powers between the provincial and federal governments. Ishayev also headed the Far East-Transbaikal Association of Economic Interaction, which sought to promote a coherent programme of economic development across the Russian Far East. Ishayev was re-elected as Governor on 10 December 2000, obtaining 88% of the votes cast. Legislative elections were held on 9 December

2001. Ishayev was elected to the Supreme Council of the pro-Government Unity and Fatherland-United Russia party in March 2003.

## Economy

The Krai's principal land use is forestry. In 1999 its gross regional product totalled 49,534.8m. roubles, or 32,467.0 roubles per head. Its main industrial centres are at Khabarovsk, Komsomolsk-on-Amur, Sovetskaya Gavan, Nikolayevsk-on-Amur and Amursk. Its principal ports are Vanino (the port of the city of Sovetskaya Gavan), Okhotsk and Nikolayevsk-on-Amur. It is traversed by two major railways, the Trans-Siberian and the Far Eastern (Baikal–Amur). In 2000 there were 2,307 km of railway lines and 4,492 km of paved roads in the territory. In the early 2000s the construction of the final stages of the Chita–Khabarovsk highway was under way; the road was expected to be completed by late 2003. A ferry service runs between the Krai and Sakhalin Oblast. The Krai is the most important Far Eastern territory in terms of its national and international air services, which connect Moscow and other European cities with Japan.

Agriculture, which employed just 4.0% of the working population in 2000 and generated 3,841m. roubles, consists mainly of grain production, animal husbandry, bee-keeping, fishing and hunting. Hunting is practised on about 97.5% of the Krai's territory. The Krai's main industries are mechanical engineering, electricity production, metal-working, non-ferrous and ferrous metallurgy, food-processing, the processing of forestry products, extraction of coal (2.0m. metric tons of which were mined in 2000), ores and non-ferrous metals, shipbuilding (including oil rigs) and petroleum-refining. Some 21.6% of the territory's work-force was engaged in industry in 2000, when total industrial output amounted to a value of 59,898m. roubles.

Khabarovsk Krai's economically active population was 792,000 in 2000, when 11.6% of the labour force were unemployed. In mid-2002 the average monthly wage was some 5,639.5 roubles. In 2000 the provincial administration recorded a budgetary deficit of 868.1m. roubles. In the 1990s the territory began to develop its trade links with 'Pacific Rim' nations apart from Japan (with which it had a long trading history), such as Canada, the People's Republic of China, the Democratic People's Republic of Korea (North Korea) and the Republic of Korea (South Korea), Australia, New Zealand, Singapore and the USA. Its exports largely consisted of raw materials (timber, petroleum products, fish and metals). External trade amounted to a value of some US $1,308.2m. in exports and $122.2m. in imports in 2000, when 99.3% of such trade was conducted with countries outside the Commonwealth of Independent States. In common with other regions of the Russian Far East, economic activity was disrupted in early 2003 by the outbreak of Severe Acute Respiratory Syndrome (SARS) in China and other countries of the Far East, and border crossings were temporarily closed in May–June. In 2000 total foreign investment amounted to $27.2m. According to the regional foreign investment promotion agency, in January 2000 731 joint ventures were registered in the territory. At 31 December there were 8,300 small businesses in operation.

## Directory

**Head of the Provincial Administration (Governor):** VIKTOR I. ISHAYEV; 680000 Khabarovsk, ul. K. Marksa 56; tel. (4212) 33-55-40; fax (4212) 33-87-56; internet www.adm.khv.ru.

**Chairman of the Provincial Legislative Duma:** YURII I. ONO-PRIYENKO; 680002 Khabarovsk, ul. Muravyeva-Amurskogo 19; tel. (4212) 32-52-19; fax (4212) 32-44-57; e-mail duma@duma.khv.ru; internet www.duma.khv.ru.

**Chief Representative of Khabarovsk Krai in the Russian Federation:** ANDREI B. CHIRKIN; 127025 Moscow, ul. Novyi Arbat 19; tel. (095) 203-41-28; fax (095) 203-83-25; e-mail khab.rep@g23 .relcom.ru; internet www.khabrep.ru.

**Head of Khabarovsk City Administration (Mayor):** ALEKSANDR N. SOKOLOV; 680000 Khabarovsk, ul. K. Marksa 66; tel. (4212) 23-58-67; fax (4212) 33-53-46; internet www.khabarovsk.kht.ru.

## Krasnodar Krai

Krasnodar Krai, often known as the Kuban, is situated in the south of European Russia, in the north-western region of the Greater Caucasus and Kuban-Azov lowlands. The Krai forms part of the Southern Federal Okrug and the North Caucasus Economic Area. It has a short international border with Georgia (Abkhazia) in the south, while Karachayevo-Cherkessiya and Stavropol Krai lie to the east and Rostov Oblast to the north-east. The Krai's territory encloses the Republic of Adygeya (formerly an Autonomous Oblast within Krasnodar Krai). The Krai lies on the Black Sea (on the shores of which is sited the resort town of Sochi) in the south-west and on the Sea of Azov in the north-west. The narrow Kerch Gulf, in places only 10 km (six miles) wide, separates the western tip of the province from Crimea (under Ukrainian jurisdiction since 1954). Its major river is the Kuban. The territory of Krasnodar Krai covers 76,000 sq km (29,340 sq miles) and measures 372 km south to north and 380 km west to east. The region is divided into 38 administrative districts and 26 cities. It had an estimated population of 4,987,600 at 1 January 2002. Its population density at that time was 65.6 per sq km, a considerably higher figure than the national average. In 2001 some 53.0% of the population lived in urban areas. Krasnodar, the Krai's administrative centre, had a population of 634,700 in 2001.

## History

Krasnodar city (known as Yekaterinodar until 1920) was founded as a military base in 1793, during the campaign of Catherine (Yekaterina) II–'the Great' to win control of the Black Sea region for the Russian Empire, which was eventually achieved in 1796. Dominated by the 'Whites' in the civil wars that followed the collapse of the tsarist regime, in post-Soviet Russia the area became a stronghold of the Communist Party of the Russian Federation (CPRF). The Krai had been formed on 13 September 1937. In September 1993 the Krasnodar Provincial Soviet condemned President Boris Yeltsin's dissolution of the federal legislature. In October the Soviet refused to dissolve itself, but announced that elections would be held to a new, 32-member, provincial legislative assembly in March 1994, although this poll was subsequently postponed. CPRF leadership of the new Provincial Legislative Assembly was not seriously challenged by other forces, and the party also fared well in federal parliamentary and presidential elections in the province in 1995–96.

During 1996 the incumbent Governor, Nikolai Yegorov, attempted to use the regional courts to postpone the gubernatorial election scheduled for December. He failed, however, and Nikolai Kondratenko, a communist, and the former Chairman of the Provincial Soviet, was elected Governor by a large majority. Supporters of Kondratenko retained control of the provincial legislative assembly at elections held in November 1998. Kondratenko consistently attracted national notoriety by making overtly anti-Semitic remarks and promoting hostility towards other minority groups. Kondratenko was aided in this latter point by the establishment of a voluntary Cossack militia in the region, which was accused of persecuting minority groups. (Notably, however, more than 100,000 migrants from other regions of Russia arrived in the Krai in 1995–2000.) Following a gubernatorial election, held on 3 December 2000, Kondratenko was replaced as Governor by Aleksandr Tkachev, who obtained 82% of the votes cast. Kondratenko did not stand as a candidate in the election, citing ill health. (However, in advance of elections to the federal State Duma in December 2003, the CPRF chose Kondratenko as its second-placed candidate on its federal party list, behind the party leader, Gennadii Zyuganov.) Tkachev also became noted for his xenophobic remarks, on occasion urging various groups of non-ethnic Russians to leave the region. In March 2002, in violation of federal law, the Krai authorities declared the implementation of a 5-km 'border zone' between the Krai and Abkhazia, Georgia, with special permits required for those wishing to enter, leave, reside or work in the zone. In September the Presidential Representative in the Southern Federal Okrug, Col-Gen. Viktor Kazantsev, dismissed the deputy head of the provincial administration, Leonid Baklitskii, following his implication in the misuse of budgetary funds, although concern at the reputed prevelance of corruption in the Krai continued to be reported. At a legislative election, held in the Krai on 24 November 2002, Kondratenko's 'Fatherland' movement (unconnected with the pro-Government Unity and Fatherland-United Russia party) won 32 of the 50 seats, with the CRPF receiving a further 13 seats. In the late 1990s and early 2000s the presence of up to 21,000 Meshketian Turks—who had been exiled to the region from Georgia under Stalin (Iosif V. Dzhugashvili–1924–53), or who sought refuge in the Krai following the outbreak of inter-ethnic violence in the Fergana valley (in Kyrgyzstan, Tajikistan and Uzbekistan) in 1989 (the majority of whom were stateless), and of several thousand Armenians in the Krai, were exploited by the chauvinist 'Fatherland' movement. In 2002 the Krai implemented legislation that restricted the granting of permanent residency permits to migrants, and also restricted access to housing and education to those without permanent residency. A new immigration service was established in the Krai in July 2003, initially on an experimental basis, in an attempt to combat the problem of illegal migration to the region. None the less, in October of that year the US mission to the Organization for Security and Co-operation in Europe (OSCE) issued a statement which, *inter alia*, criticized the treatment of Meshketian Turks by the provincial authorities, and which urged the Russian federal authorities to intervene to ensure that full civil rights were granted to the stateless Meshketian Turks resident in Krasnodar Krai.

## Economy

In 1999 gross regional product in Krasnodar Krai amounted to 109,100.8m. roubles, or 21,524.8 roubles per head. Krasnodar is one of the Krai's main industrial centres, as are Armavir, Novorossiisk, Kropotkin, Tikhoretsk and Yeisk. Novorossiisk, Tuapse, Yeisk, Temryuk and Port Kavkaz are important sea-ports. In 2000 the Krai had 2,174 km of railway track and 10,397 km of paved roads.

The Krai's principal crops are grain, sugar beet, rice, tobacco, essential-oil plants, tea and hemp. Horticulture, viniculture and animal husbandry are also important. Agricultural output was worth 48,056m. roubles in 2000, when some 23.9% of the working population was engaged in agriculture. The agricultural sector of the Krai was affected by prolonged drought conditions in 2002, resulting in the loss of some 300,000 hectares of crops. Widespread, severe flooding in the previous year, in which more than 100 people died, damaged both the agricultural sector and broader infrastructure and industry of the province. There are important reserves of petroleum and natural gas in Krasnodar Krai. In 2000 around 1.7m. metric tons of petroleum were extracted, and 4.3m. tons were refined on the Krai's territory in 1996. Its main industries are food-processing (which comprised 42.8% of industrial output in 2000), electricity generation, fuel extraction, mechanical engineering and building materials. Total production in the sector (which employed 16.4% of the work-force) amounted to a value of 57,293m. roubles in 2000. The tourism sector is also important: the Kuban region's climate, scenery and mineral and mud springs attracted around 6m. visitors annually in the mid-1990s, when some 400,000 people were employed in tourism. The Krai contains the resort towns of Sochi, Anapa and Tuapse. The transportation and refinery of Caspian Sea hydrocarbons reserves (particularly in Novorossiisk, the terminus of a major petroleum pipeline from Baku, Azerbaijan) brought economic benefits to the region from the late 1990s.

In 2000 the economically active population numbered 2,335,000, and 12.5% of the labour force were unemployed. The average monthly wage was 3,483.8 roubles in mid-2002. In 2000 there was a budgetary surplus of 287.7m. roubles. In that year international trade comprised exports amounting to US $995.7m., and imports of $571.7m. The recommencement, in January 2003, of passenger rail services between Sochi and Sukhumi, in Abkhazia, for the first time since the initiation of the Abkhaz–Georgian conflict in 1992, was expected to facilitate increased international trade with the seperatist region. Foreign investment amounted to $979.5m., more than 60 times greater than the figure recorded in 1997. At 31 December 2000 there were 20,500 small businesses in operation in the Krai.

## Directory

**Head of the Provincial Administration:** ALEKSANDR N. TKACHEV; 350014 Krasnodar, ul. Krasnaya 35; tel. (8612) 62-57-16; fax (8612) 68-25-40; e-mail registry@kuban.ru; internet admkrai.kuban.ru.

**Chairman of the Legislative Assembly:** VLADIMIR A. BEKETOV; 350014 Krasnodar, ul. Krasnaya 3; tel. (8612) 68-50-07; fax (8612) 68-37-41.

**Representation of Krasnodar Krai in the Russian Federation:** 119180 Moscow, per. 2-i Kazachii 6; tel. (095) 238-20-28.

**Head of Krasnodar City Administration (Mayor):** NIKOLAI V. PRIZ; 350000 Krasnodar, ul. Krasnaya 122; tel. (8612) 55-43-48; fax (8612) 55-01-56; e-mail post@krd.ru; internet www.krd.ru.

# Krasnoyarsk Krai

Krasnoyarsk Krai occupies the central part of Siberia and extends from the Arctic Ocean coast in the north to the western Sayan Mountains in the south. The Krai forms part of the Siberian Federal Okrug and the East Siberian Economic Area. It is bordered by the Republic of Sakha (Yakutiya) and Irkutsk Oblast to the east and the Republic of Tyva to the south. To the west lie the Republic of Khakasiya, the Oblasts of Kemerovo and Tomsk, as well as Tyumen Oblast's Khanty-Mansii and Yamal-Nenets AOks. Its major river is the Yenisei, one of the longest in Russia, measuring 4,102 km (2,549 miles). Most of its area is covered by taiga (forested marshland). The Krai, including its two autonomous okrugs (Evenk and Taimyr—Dolgan-Nenets), covers a total area of 2,339,000 sq km (902,850 sq miles), the second largest federal unit in Russia, or 710,000 sq km (274,133 sq miles) when they are excluded. Krasnoyarsk Krai measures almost 3,000 km from south to north. In the Krai proper there are 42 administrative districts and 24 cities. The Krai lies within three climatic zones—arctic, sub-arctic and continental. It had an estimated total population of 3,015,300 at 1 January 2002, and a population density of 1.3 per sq km. Some 74.6% of the population inhabited urban areas in 2001. The Krai's administrative centre is at Krasnoyarsk, which had a population of 758,700 in 2001. Other major cities include Norilsk (143,100—which is considered an integral part of the Krai, and not part of the Taimyr—Dolgano-Nenets AOk, which surrounds it), Achinsk (120,400), Kansk (108,100) and Zheleznogorsk (95,300).

## History

The city of Krasnoyarsk was founded in 1628 by Cossack forces as an ostrog (military transit camp) during the period of Russian expansion across Siberia (1582–1639). The region gained importance after the discovery of gold, and with the construction of the Trans-Siberian Railway. The Krai was formed on 7 December 1934. During the Soviet era the region was closed to foreigners, owing to its nuclear-reactor and defence establishments.

A gubernatorial election in December 1992 was won by Valerii Zubov (the incumbent, a supporter of federal President Boris Yeltsin), and elections to a new parliament, the Legislative Assembly, were held on 6 March 1994. In the mid-1990s Zubov's regime proved to be increasingly ineffectual, and by 1997 the region had one of the worst records for wage arrears in the country. This largely contributed to the victory in the 1998 gubernatorial election of Gen. (retd) Aleksandr Lebed, the former secretary of the National Security Council, who was perceived by many as a suitably strong leader to rule a region of such economic and political significance. Lebed died in a helicopter crash on 28 April 2002. An election to appoint a successor, held on 8 September, and contested by 14 candidates, proved inconclusive; the Chairman of the provincial legislature, Aleksandr Uss, whose campaign was supported by the company Russian Aluminium (RusAl), received 27.6% of the votes cast, closely followed by the Governor of Taimyr AOk and the former General Director of Norilsk Nickel, Aleksandr Khlopanin, with 25.2%; these two candidates proceeded to a second round. In third place, with an unexpected 21.4%, was Sergei Glazyev, who was supported by the Communist Party of the Russian Federation (CPRF), but who had served as Minister of External Economic Relations in the 'reform' Government of 1992–93. In the 'run off' election, held on 22 September, Khlopanin was the first-placed candidate, winning 48.1% of the votes cast, compared with the 41.8% of the votes received by Uss. However, at the end of September the Krai's electoral commission annulled the results of the election, citing irregularities in the conduct of Khlopanin's campaign, and announced that new polls were to be held. Khlopanin declared that he was to appeal against the commission's decision. On 1 October a court in Krasnoyarsk overturned the decision of the commission, and two days later federal President Vladimir Putin appointed Khlopanin to serve as acting Governor, pending a decision by the Supreme Court; on the following day the central electoral commission confirmed Khlopanin as elected Governor, and Khlopanin was inaugurated shortly afterwards. The Supreme Court confirmed the validity of the election results in November, and at the end of January 2003 a provincial court agreed to the request of central electoral commission that the Krai's electoral commision be disbanded. (Following his inauguration as Governor of Krasnoyarsk Krai, Khlopanin was thereby obliged to resign as Governor of the Taimyr AOk.) Although Khlopanin emphasized that he did not intend to transfer officials from the AOk administration to the Krai, his success appeared to heighten speculation that the two federal subjects (and potentially the third constituent part of the Krai, the Evenk AOk) would eventually merge to form a single unit. (A proposed referendum on such a merger had been cancelled in 2002, following the death of Lebed.) In February 2003 the Governors of Krasnoyarsk Krai and the two AOks signed a protocol of intent to establish a Council of Governors, to facilitate joint decision-making in social, economic and cultural areas of policy; a council of the legislative assemblies of the three entities was subsequently established, although it was emphasized that there would be no expedited measures towards the merging of the territories. At the end of March Khlopanin was elected to the Supreme Council of the pro-Government Unity and Fatherland-United Russia party, although he was not formally a member of the party. A new electoral commission in the Krai, which contained no members of the disbanded former commission, was inaugurated in mid-May.

## Economy

Krasnoyarsk Krai is potentially one of Russia's richest regions, containing vast deposits of minerals, gold and petroleum, although, particularly since the late 1990s, it has experienced serious economic problems, many of them typical of northern regions. All of the figures included in this survey include figures for the two autonomous okrugs, which are also considered separately. In 1999 the Krai's gross regional product amounted to 129,456.9m. roubles, equivalent to 42,429.6 roubles per head. The Krai's major industrial centres are at Krasnoyarsk, Norilsk, Achinsk, Kansk and Minusinsk. In 2000 there were 2,068 km of railway track and 12,842 km of paved roads on the Krai's territory.

The principal crops are grain, flax, and hemp. Animal husbandry, fur farming and hunting are also important. The agricultural sector employed 10.2% of the working population in 2000, when total output within the sector was worth 20,347m. roubles. The Krai's main industries are non-ferrous metallurgy, electricity production, mechanical engineering, metal-working, ore-mining (particularly bauxite, for aluminium), chemicals, forestry and food-processing. Industry employed 25.1% of the work-force in 2000, when the industrial output of Krasnoyarsk Krai amounted to a value of 199,618m. roubles. The Krai contains the world's second largest aluminium smelter, Krasnoyarsk Aluminium, which forms part of the Krasnoyarsk Metallurgical Plant (KraMZ), was 28% owned by RusAl in 2003.

In 2000 the territory's economically active population totalled 1,556,000, and 11.9% of the Krai's labour force were unemployed. The average monthly wage in the Krai was 5,971.7 roubles in mid-2002, somewhat in excess of the national average. In 2000 the local budget showed a surplus of 1,118.2m. roubles. In that year export trade amounted to US $3,632.9m., and imports to $649.6m. Foreign investment totalled $64.3m. in 2000. At the end of the year there were 14,000 small businesses in Krasnoyarsk Krai.

## Directory

**Head of the Provincial Administration (Governor):** ALEKSANDR G. KHLOPANIN; 660009 Krasnoyarsk, pr. Mira 110; tel. (3912) 22-22-63; fax (3912) 22-11-63; e-mail klimik@krskstate.ru; internet www.krskstate.ru.

**Chairman of the Legislative Assembly:** ALEKSANDR V. USS; 660009 Krasnoyarsk, pr. Mira 110; tel. (3912) 22-33-87; fax (3912) 22-22-24; internet www.legis.krsn.ru.

**Representation of Krasnoyarsk Krai in the Russian Federation:** 107996 Moscow, ul. Gilyarovskogo 31/2; tel. (095) 284-86-56; fax (095) 284-82-41.

**Head of Krasnoyarsk City Administration (Mayor):** PETR I. PIMASHKOV; 660049 Krasnoyarsk, ul. K. Marksa 93; tel. (3912) 22-22-31; fax (3912) 22-25-12; e-mail webmaster@admkrsk.ru; internet www.admkrsk.ru.

# Maritime (Primorskii) Krai

Maritime (Primorskii) Krai—Primorye is situated in the extreme south-east of Russia, on the Tatar Strait and the Sea of Japan. The province is part of the Far Eastern Federal Okrug and the Far Eastern Economic Area. Its only border with another federal subject is with Khabarovsk Krai to the north. There is an international border with the People's Republic of China to the west and a short border with the Democratic People's Republic of Korea (North Korea) in the south-west. Its major river is the Ussuri. The territory occupies 165,900 sq km (64,060 sq miles), more than two-thirds of which is forested. It is divided into 24 administrative districts and 12 cities. At 1 January 2002 the total number of inhabitants in the territory was estimated at 2,124,700 and the population density was, therefore, 12.8 per sq km. In 2001 some 78.1% of the population lived in urban areas. Maritime Krai's administrative centre is at Vladivostok, which had 598,600 inhabitants. Other major cities are Ussuriisk (formerly Voroshilov—156,600) and Nakhodka (155,600).

## History

The territories of the Maritime Krai were recognized as Chinese possessions by Russia in the Treaty of Nerchinsk in 1687. They became part of the Russian Empire in 1860, however, being ceded by China under the terms of the Treaty of Peking (Beijing), and the port of Vladivostok was founded. Along with other Transbaikal and Pacific regions of the former Russian Empire, the territory was part of the Far Eastern Republic until its reintegration into Russia under Soviet rule in 1922. Maritime Krai was created on 20 October 1938.

The territory declared itself a republic in mid-1993, but was not recognized as such by the federal authorities. In 28 October 1993 the provincial Governor disbanded the Soviet. Elections for a provincial Governor, set for October 1994, were cancelled by presidential decree, after alleged improprieties by the incumbent, Yevgenii Nazdratenko, during his election campaign. Nazdratenko was elected, however, in December 1995, with 76% of the votes cast, and was re-elected by a similar majority in December 1999. His populist style of government and control of the local media reinforced his position.

The Governor's disputes with the central Government continued after his election—in October 1996 the head of the Presidential Administration, Anatolii Chubais publicly blamed Nazdratenko for the serious energy crisis in the region, citing his failure to introduce market reforms. An ongoing energy crisis in the region, owing to non-payment of bills, finally forced the resignation of Nazdratenko

(officially on health grounds), in February 2001, whereupon he was appointed as Chairman of the federal State Committee for Fisheries. (He was suspended in February 2002, following a dispute over regional quotas, and dismissed in April, whereupon he was appointed as Deputy Secretary of the Security Council.) In gubernatorial elections held in May–June 2001, Sergei Darkin, a local businessman, who was intitially regarded as Nazdratenko's preferred successor, was elected Governor in the second round of voting, with 40% of the votes cast, defeating Gennadii Apanasenko, the deputy presidential representative to the region; Viktor Cherepkov, the former Mayor of Vladivostok, who had taken second place in the first round of voting, behind Darkin, was barred from standing as a candidate in the second round of the elections by the provincial court, which cited irregularities in his campaign. Cherepkov encouraged his supporters to vote against all candidates in the 'run off' election, and 33.7% of voters did so. Regional legislative elections, held in December 2001, were declared invalid for 18 of the 39 seats, as the rate of voter participation was lower than the 25% required to legitimize the results, particularly in the large cities. Repeat elections, in which the majority of votes were cast by supporters of Nazdratenko, were held in June 2002; although the rate of participation by the electorate was just 18%, the elections were declared valid, as the 25% threshold had been abolished. Between mid-2001 and late 2002 there were reported to have been more than 30 contract killings, mostly of businessmen, in the region; consequently the security services of the Krai were placed under special federal supervision.

## Economy

Maritime Krai's gross regional product totalled 54,791.9m. roubles in 1999, equivalent to 25,070.7 roubles per head. Its major industrial centres are at Vladivostok, the terminus of the Trans-Siberian Railway, Ussuriisk, Nakhodka, Dalnegorsk and Lesozavodsk. The Krai's most important ports are at Vladivostok, Nakhodka and Vostochnyi (formerly Vrangel). Vessels based in these ports comprise around four-fifths of maritime transport services in the Far East. Maritime Krai has rail links with Khabarovsk Krai and, hence, other regions, as well as international transport links with North Korea and the Republic of Korea (South Korea). In 2000 there were 1,553 km (965 miles) of railway lines and 7,057 km of paved roads on the Krai's territory.

The Krai's agricultural sector, which employed 9.0% of the labour force in 2000, consists mainly of grain and soya production, animal husbandry, fur farming, bee-keeping and fishing. Total agricultural output in 2000 amounted to a value of 5,317m. roubles. Illicit agricultural activities were also thought to include the cultivation of marijuana, particularly in the Khankai district. The Krai contains some 1,200m. metric tons of coal reserves. The hydroelectric-energy potential of the region's rivers is estimated at 25,000m. kWh, and timber reserves are estimated at 1,500m.–1,800m. cu m. Its main industries are food-processing (which accounted for 46.7% of industrial production in 2000), fuel and electrical energy production, non-ferrous metallurgy, ore-mining, the processing of fish and forestry products, mechanical engineering and ship repairs, metal-working, building materials and chemicals. Total industrial production was worth 40,618m. roubles in 2000, when the sector employed 21.1% of the working population. Energy production in the Krai was hindered by political mismanagement from the mid-1990s. Dalenergo, its electricity-generation monopoly, was notorious as one of the worst-performing utilities in the country, unable to collect accounts, service debts or pay for fuel, which led to fuel shortages and frequent strikes by its workers. The territory is ideally placed, in terms of its proximity to the Pacific nations, for international trade, although the perception of widespread corruption restrained its development. A new railway crossing into the People's Republic of China at Makhalino-Hunchun, which was expected to carry an eventual 3m. tons of cargo annually, opened in August 1998. The construction of a cross-border trade and economic centre, uniting the city of Pogranichnyi, in the Krai, with Suifenhe, in China, commenced in early 2003, and was due for completion in 2005. In common with other areas of the Russian Far East, restrictions on cross-border travel were implemented in May–June 2003, during the outbreak of Severe Acute Respiratory Syndrome (SARS) in China and other countries of the region.

The economically active population of Maritime Krai numbered 1,166,000 in 2000, when 11.9% of the labour force were unemployed. The average monthly wage was 4,573.2 roubles in mid-2002. In 2000 there was a budgetary deficit of 639.7m. roubles. External export trade amounted to US $612.4m. in that year, when imports totalled $329.3m. According to the European Bank for Reconstruction and Development, the Krai had huge investment potential; foreign investment totalled $78.1m. in 2000. In August 1997 Hyundai (of South Korea), opened a $100m. hotel and business centre in Vladivostok. South Korea also planned to create an industrial park for high-technology industries over an 11-year period in the free economic zone of Nakhodka, although some analysts doubted the practicality of the project. At 31 December 2000 there were 16,100 small businesses registered in the territory.

## Directory

**Head of the Provincial Administration (Governor):** SERGEI M. DARKIN; 690110 Maritime Krai, Vladivostok, ul. Svetlanskaya 22; tel. (4232) 22-38-00; fax (4232) 22-52-77; e-mail gubernator@primorsky.ru; internet www.primorsky.ru.

**Chairman of the Provincial Duma:** SERGEI A. SOPCHUK; 690110 Maritime Krai, 690110 Vladivostok, ul. Svetlanskaya 22; tel. (4232) 22-35-70; fax (4232) 26-90-32; e-mail predsedatel@duma.primorsky.ru; internet www.primorsky.ru/prim/duma.

**Chief Representative of Maritime (Primorskii) Krai in the Russian Federation:** MIKHAIL N. MALGINOV; 123100 Moscow, pr. 1-i Krasnogvardeiskii 9/22/315; tel. (095) 255-82-14; fax (095) 255-82-13.

**Head of the Vladivostok City Administration (Mayor):** YURII M. KOPYLOV; 690600 Maritime Krai, Vladivostok, Okeanskii pr. 20; tel. (4232) 22-30-16; fax (4232) 22-68-40.

# Stavropol Krai

Stavropol Krai is situated in the central Caucasus region and extends from the Caspian lowlands in the east to the foothills of the Greater Caucasus Mountains in the south-west. It is part of the Southern Federal Okrug and the North Caucasus Economic Area. Krasnodar Krai lies to the west, there is a short border with Rostov Oblast in the north-west of the Krai and it shares longer borders with Kalmykiya to the north-east and Dagestan to the east. Chechnya, Ingushetiya, North Osetiya (Ossetia)—Alaniya and Kabardino-Balkariya lie to the south, and Karachayevo-Cherkessiya to the south-west. The Krai's major rivers are the Kuban, the Kuma and the Yegorlyk. Much of its territory is steppe. Its total area is 66,500 sq km (25,670 sq miles), and it is divided into 26 administrative districts and 19 cities. The population of Stavropol Krai numbered 2,642,600 at 1 January 2002. The Krai's population density, therefore, was 39.7 per sq km. In 2001 some 55.1% of the population lived in urban areas. The Krai's administrative centre is at Stavropol, which had a population of 339,500 in 2001. Other major cities are Nevinnomyssk (131,800), Pyatigorsk (126,800) and Kislovodsk (111,900).

## History

Stavropol city was founded in 1777 as part of the consolidation of Russian rule in the Caucasus. The territory was created on 13 February 1924, although it was originally known as South-Eastern Oblast (when it also incorporated territories of Krasnodar Krai) and, subsequently, the North Caucasus Krai. It was named Ordzhonikidze Krai in 1937–43, before adopting its current title. The former Karachai and Cherkess Autonomous Oblasts, which were reconstituted as the Republic of Karachayevo-Cherkessiya upon the adoption of the 1992 Federation Treaty, previously formed part of the Krai.

In March 1994 elections were held to a new representative body, the State Duma. In June 1995 the town of Budennovsk, situated about 150 km north of the Chechen border, was the scene of a large-scale hostage-taking operation at a hospital by rebel Chechen forces; over 1,000 civilians were seized, but they were released after a few days, although more than 100 people were killed during the siege. In the gubernatorial elections of November 1996 the Communist Party

candidate, Aleksandr Chernogorov, defeated the government-supported incumbent. In October 2000 four people died, and more than 100 people were wounded, as a result of three simultaneous bomb explosions in Pyatigorsk and Nevinomyssk. There was a series of further attacks, including bombings and the hijacking of a bus, in the Krai during 2001–03, which official sources attributed to Chechen separatists, and in which more than 25 people died. In an attempt to calm the disorder in the region, Chernogorov demanded that the Krai to be granted special territorial status, and demanded the implementation of stricter immigration controls within the Krai, although these appeals were rejected by the State Duma. Chernogorov was re-elected for a further term as Governor in a second round of voting in December 2000. Elections to the State Duma took place in December 2001. In June 2002, following the introduction of similar legislation in neighbouring Krasnodar Krai, the regional legislature approved legislation, which, in contravention of federal requirements, sought to place restrictions on the number of immigrants permitted to settle in specific regions of the Krai.

## Economy

In 1999 Stavropol Krai's gross regional product was 43,440.1m. roubles, or 16,148.1 roubles per head. Its main industrial centres are at Stavropol, Nevinnomyssk, Georgiyevsk and Budennovsk. In 2000 there were 944 km (587 miles) of railway lines and 7,497 km of paved roads on the Krai's territory. In September 1997 the federal Government announced that a new section of a petroleum pipeline from Baku, Azerbaijan, would cross Stavropol Krai, rather than run through Chechnya.

The Krai contains extremely fertile soil. Its agricultural production, which amounted to a value of 20,678m. roubles in 2000, consists mainly of grain, sunflower seeds, sugar beet and vegetables. Horticulture, viniculture and animal husbandry are also important. The sector employed 24.4% of the working population in 2000. However, the 2003 harvest was expected to be significantly lower than usual, as a result of a prolonged drought in the region. The Krai's main industries are food-processing, mechanical engineering, production of building materials, chemicals and the production of natural gas, petroleum, non-ferrous metal ores and coal, and electrical energy. Around 15.9% of the labour force worked in industry in 2000, when total industrial output was worth 28,416m. roubles.

The economically active population in Stavropol Krai was 1,237,000 in 2000, when 13.8% of the region's labour force were unemployed, compared with 18.5% in the previous year. The average wage was 3,015.6 roubles per month in mid-2002. In 2000 there was a budgetary surplus of 387.1m. roubles. In that year the value of exports from the Krai amounted to US $271.6m., and imports were worth $97.3m. Foreign investment in the territory amounted to $34.2m. At 31 December 2000 there were 7,100 small businesses in operation.

## Directory

**Head of the Provincial Administration (Governor):** ALEKSANDR L. CHERNOGOROV; 355025 Stavropol, pl. Lenina 1; tel. (8652) 35-22-52; fax (8652) 35-03-30; e-mail stavadm@stavropol.net.

**Chairman of the State Duma:** YURII A. GONTAR; 355025 Stavropol, pl. Lenina 1; tel. (8652) 34-82-55; fax (8652) 35-14-55.

**Representation of Stavropol Krai in the Russian Federation:** 127025 Moscow, ul. Novyi Arbat 19/1713; tel. (095) 203-55-36; fax (095) 203-55-39.

**Head of Stavropol City Administration (Mayor):** DMITRII S. KUZMIN; 355000 Stavropol, pr. K. Marksa 96/307; tel. (8652) 26-78-06; fax (8652) 26-28-23; e-mail goradm@smtn.stavropol.ru; internet www.stavropol.stavkray.ru.

# OBLASTS (REGIONS)

## Amur Oblast

Amur Oblast is situated in the south-east of the Russian Federation, to the west of Khabarovsk Krai. It forms part of the Far Eastern Federal Okrug and the Far Eastern Economic Area. The Jewish Autonomous Oblast lies to the south-east, Chita Oblast to the west and the Republic of Sakha (Yakutiya) to the north. Southwards it has an international border with the People's Republic of China. The Oblast's main river is the Amur, which is 2,900 km (1,800 miles) long. A large reservoir, the Zeya, is situated in the north of the region. A little under three-quarters of the Oblast's territory is forested. Its total area occupies 363,700 sq km (140,430 sq miles) and measures 750 km south to north and 1,150 km south-east to north-west. It is divided into 20 administrative districts and nine cities. The territory's inhabitants numbered some 982,200 at 1 January 2002 and the population density was, therefore, 2.7 per sq km. In 2001 most people (65.7%) lived in urban areas. Amur Oblast's administrative centre is at Blagoveshchensk, near the Chinese border, which had a population of 220,600 in 2001.

### History

The Amur region was first discovered by European Russians in 1639 and came under Russian control in the late 1850s. Part of the pro-Bolshevik Far Eastern Republic (based in Chita) until its reintegration into Russia in 1922, Amur Oblast was formed on 20 October 1932.

In the first year of post-Soviet Russian independence, the federal President, Boris Yeltsin, called for a gubernatorial election to be held in the region in December 1992. However, his appointed head of the administration was defeated. In July 1993 Amur Oblast declared itself a republic, a measure that was not recognized by the federal authorities. The Governor was subsequently dismissed and the Regional Soviet dissolved. In January 1996 the Regional Administration brought action against the Regional Assembly for adopting a Charter, a republican constitution, some of the clauses of which ran counter to federal laws and presidential decrees. In the same month, in accordance with the Charter, the Assembly changed its name to the Council of People's Deputies. In elections to the new legislature, held in March, Communist Party of the Russian Federation (CPRF) candidates won up to 40% of the votes cast. In June President Yeltsin again dismissed the Governor, and appointed Yurii Lyashko, formerly the chief executive of Blagoveshchensk city, in his place. A further gubernatorial election was held on 22 September. It was won by the CPRF candidate, Anatolii Belonogov, by a narrow margin, but the results were subsequently annulled because of alleged irregularities. Belonogov succeeded in securing a clear majority in the repeat election held in March 1997. In gubernatorial elections held in two rounds in March–April 2001 Belonogov was defeated by Leonid Korotkov, hitherto a deputy in the State Duma, and a member of the CPRF until 1999. Legislative elections were held on 25 March 2001. In May–June 2003, in response to the outbreak of Severe Acute Respiratory Syndrome (SARS) in the People's Republic of China and other countries in the Far East, border crossings between the Oblast and China were temporarily closed, causing particular short-term economic disruption to the Oblast. It was also reported in May by the federal Ministry of Health that a hospital patient in Blagoveshchensk had been diagnosed with the disease. Meanwhile, in June Amur Oblast was named by the federal First Deputy Minister of Finance as one of the three federal subjects worst affected by public-sector wage arrears, with delays of more than half a month reported.

### Economy

Amur Oblast's gross regional product was 22,773.0m. roubles in 1999, equivalent to 22,534.1 roubles per head. Its main industrial centres are at Blagoveshchensk, Belogorsk, Raichikhinsk, Zeya, Shimanovsk and Svobodnyi. In 2000 there were 6,915 km of paved roads in the Oblast. There were 3,002 km of railway track, including sections of two major railways, the Trans-Siberian and the Far Eastern (Baikal–Amur). There are five river-ports, at Blagoveshchensk, Svobodnensk, Poyarkovsk, Amursk (all of which transport cargo to and from the People's Republic of China) and Zeisk. There is an international airport at Blagoveshchensk, which serves flights to Japan, the Democratic People's Republic of Korea (North Korea) and the Republic of Korea (South Korea), and (on a charter basis) to Turkey.

Agriculture in Amur Oblast, which employed 13.0% of its work-force in 2000, significantly less than in 1995, consists mainly of grain and vegetable production, animal husbandry and bee-keeping. The soil in the south of the region is particularly fertile—in 1998 Amur Oblast contained 57% of the arable land in the Russian Far East and produced 30% of its agricultural output. In 2000 agricultural output in Amur Oblast amounted to 6,637m. roubles. In 1998 timber reserves were estimated at 2,000m. cu m. The region is rich in mineral resources, but by the end of the 1990s it was estimated that only around 5% of these resources were being exploited. None the less, the mining sector produced around 15% of gross regional product in the late 1990s. In the late 1990s around 10–12 metric tons of gold were extracted annually, making the Oblast the third largest producer of gold in Russia. The eventual liberalization of the artisanal sector, which was reported to be supported by the regional authorities in the early 2000s, subject to the approval of the federal parliament, could be expected to increase the output of gold appreciably. Other raw-material deposits in the Oblast include bituminous coal, lignite (brown coal) and kaolin. There are also substantial reserves of iron, titanium, silver and gold ores. In addition, coal-mining is important, as are mechanical engineering, electricity generation, electro-technical industry and the processing of agricultural and forestry products. In 2000 14.6% of the Oblast's work-force were employed in industry, and total output in the sector amounted to a value of 8,878m. roubles. The region contains the Amur Ship-building Plant. In 1997 the plant was contracted to build a 111-sq km steel platform for a foreign consortium, intended to exploit the petroleum and natural gas fields of Sakhalin Oblast, and produces nuclear-powered submarines. There is a hydroelectric power plant at Zeya, with a reservoir of 2,400 sq km. Another power station was under construction at Bureya, the first part of which was expected to commence operations in 2003.

Amur's economically active population numbered 520,000 in 2000, when 13.4% of the region's labour force were unemployed. Those in employment earned, on average, 4,882.6 roubles per month in mid-2002. There was a budgetary deficit of 634m. roubles in 2000. In that year export trade amounted to a value of US $58.4m., and import trade totalled $17.1m. The Oblast's main trading partners were the People's Republic of China, Japan and North Korea. Foreign investment totalled $4.5m. in 2000. At 31 December 2000 there were 3,800 small businesses registered in the Oblast.

### Directory

**Head of the Regional Administration:** Leonid V. Korotkov; 675023 Amur obl., Blagoveshchensk, ul. Lenina 135; tel. (4162) 44-03-22; fax (4162) 44-62-01; e-mail glava@amurobl.ru; internet www.amurobl.ru.

**Chairman of the Regional Council of People's Deputies (Regional Council):** Stanislav I. Goryanskii; 675023 Amur obl., Blagoveshchensk, ul. Lenina 135; tel. (4162) 42-46-75; fax (4162) 44-38-58.

**Representation of Amur Oblast in the Russian Federation:** 127006 Moscow, ul. M. Dmitrovka 3; tel. (095) 299-38-63; fax (095) 299-42-02.

**Head of Blagoveshchensk City Administration (Mayor):** Aleksandr M. Kolyagin; 675023 Amur obl., Blagoveshchensk, ul. Lenina 133; tel. (4162) 42-49-85.

## Archangel Oblast

Archangel (Arkhangelsk) Oblast is situated in the north of the Eastern European Plain. It lies on the White, Barents and Kara Seas (parts of the Arctic Ocean) and includes the northern archipelago of Zemlya Frantsa-Iosifa and the Novaya Zemlya islands. The Oblast forms part of the North-Western Federal Okrug and the Northern Economic Area. In the north-east the Nenets Autonomous Okrug, a constituent part of the Oblast, runs eastwards along the coast to end in a short border with the Yamal-Nenets AOk (within Tyumen Oblast). The Republic of Komi lies to the south of the Nenets AOk and to the east of Archangel proper. Kirov and, mainly, Vologda Oblasts form the southern border and the Republic of Kareliya lies to the west. The Oblast contains several large rivers (the Severnaya Dvina, the Onega, the Mezen, the Pinega, the Vaga and the Pechora) and some 2,500 lakes. Some two-fifths of its entire area is forested—much of the north-west of the territory is taiga (forested marshland). The Oblast, including the autonomous okrug, occupies an area of 587,400 sq km (226,800 sq miles) and is divided into 20 administrative districts and 14 cities. It spans three climatic zones—arctic, sub-arctic and continental. The total population at 1 January 2002 was an estimated 1,428,900 and its population density, therefore, stood at 2.4 per sq km. In 2001 some 74.5% of the population lived in urban areas. Archangel Oblast's administrative centre is at Archangel (Arkhangelsk), which had 358,500 inhabitants in 2001. The Oblast's second city is Severodvinsk (232,800).

## History

The city of Archangel was founded in the 16th century, to further Muscovite trade. It was the first Russian seaport and the country's main one until the building of St Petersburg in 1703. The port played a major role in the attack by the Entente fleet (British and French navies) against the Red Army in 1918, and was an important route for supplies from the Allied Powers during the Second World War. Archangel Oblast was founded on 23 September 1937.

On 13 October 1993 the Archangel Regional Soviet transferred its responsibilities to the Regional Administration. Communist candidates initially formed the largest single group elected to the legislative chamber of the Regional Assembly of Deputies, although supporters of the federal Government and liberal reformists also enjoyed respectable levels of support in the cities. In March 1996 the unpopular head of the regional administration, Pavel Pozdeyev, a federal appointee nominated only one month previously, was forced to leave his position. Anatolii Yefremov's position as Governor was confirmed by his popular election to the post in December 1997, and by his re-election in December 2000. Legislative elections were held on 18 June 2000.

## Economy

All figures in this survey incorporate data for the Nenets AOk, which is also treated separately. Archangel Oblast's gross regional product totalled 38,994.1m. roubles in 1999, equivalent to 26,541.0 roubles per head. The Oblast's main industrial centres are at Archangel, Kotlas, Severodvinsk and Novodvinsk. In 2000 there were 1,764 km (1,096 miles) of railways and 7,118 km of paved roads on the Oblast's territory. Its main ports are Archangel, Onega, Mezen and Naryan Mar (sea- and river-ports).

The Oblast's agriculture, which employed just 5.8% of the labour force in 2000, consists mainly of grain and vegetable production, animal husbandry (livestock and reindeer) and hunting. Total agricultural output in the Oblast amounted to a value of 5,129m. roubles in 2000. Its industry, which employed 27.2% of the working population in that year, is based on timber and timber-processing (which accounted for 50.9% of industrial production in 2000), the extraction of minerals (in particular, bauxite), petroleum and natural gas, mechanical engineering and food-processing. Industrial output across the Oblast was worth 42,821m. roubles in 2000. In July 1998 it was announced that the federal Ministry of Finance was to allocate credit worth US $30m. for development of a diamond field in the Oblast, one of Russia's largest, run by Severoalmaz (Northern Diamonds) as part of a multinational consortium, although repeated licensing problems delayed progress.

The Oblast's economically active population amounted to 761,000 in 2000, when 12.2% of the region's labour force were unemployed. The average monthly wage was 5,094.2 roubles in mid-2002. In 2000 the Oblast recorded a budgetary surplus of 357.2m. roubles. External trade in that year amounted to US $873.6m., of which $769.6m. were exports, and $104.0m. were imports. Total foreign investment totalled $39.0m. in 2000. At 31 December 2000 there were 4,800 small businesses registered on the Oblast's territory.

## Directory

**Head of the Regional Administration (Governor):** ANATOLII A. YEFREMOV; 163004 Archangel, pr. Troitskii 49; tel. (8182) 43-21-12; fax (8182) 64-65-11; internet www.arkhadm.gov.ru.

**Chairman of the Regional Assembly of Deputies:** VITALII S. FORTYGIN; 163061 Archangel, pl. Lenina 1; tel. (8182) 64-66-81; fax (8182) 64-66-30; e-mail ac@aosd.ru.

**Chief Representative of Archangel Oblast in the Russian Federation:** BORIS A. GAGARIN; 127006 Moscow, ul. M. Dmitrovka 3/10; tel. (095) 299-44-12.

**Head of Archangel City Administration:** OLEG V. NILOV; 163061 Archangel, pl. Lenina 5; tel. (8182) 65-64-84; fax (8182) 65-20-71; e-mail webmaster@arhcity.ru; internet www.arhcity.ru.

# Astrakhan Oblast

Astrakhan Oblast is situated in the Caspian lowlands and forms part of the Southern Federal Okrug and the Volga Economic Area. Lying between the Russian federal subject of Kalmykiya to the south

and the former Soviet state of Kazakhstan to the east, Astrakhan is a long, relatively thin territory, which flanks the River Volga as it flows out of Volgograd Oblast in the north-west towards the Caspian Sea to the south-east, via a delta at Astrakhan. The delta is one of the largest in the world and occupies more than 24,000 sq km (9,260 sq miles) of the Caspian lowlands. It gives the Oblast some 200 km (over 120 miles) of coastline. It has one lake, the Baskunchak, measuring 115 sq km. Astrakhan occupies some 44,100 sq km (17,000 sq miles) and is divided into 11 administrative districts and six cities. At 1 January 2002 its total population was an estimated 1,008,700 and its population density, therefore, was 22.9 per sq km. In 2001 some 66.2% of the population lived in urban areas. The Oblast's administrative centre is at Astrakhan (formerly Khadzhi-Tarkhan), which had a population of 479,700 in January 2001. The city lies at 22 m (72 feet) below sea level and is protected from the waters of the Volga delta by 75 km of dykes. Other major cities are Akhtubinsk (47,200) and Znamensk (37,000).

## History

The Khanate of Astrakhan, which was formed in 1446, following the dissolution of the Golden Horde, was conquered by the Russians in 1556. The region subsequently became an important centre for trading in timber, grain, fish and petroleum. Astrakhan Oblast was founded on 27 December 1943.

There was considerable hardship in the region with the dissolution of the USSR and the economic reforms of the early 1990s. Dissatisfaction was indicated by the relatively high level of support for the nationalist Liberal Democrats in the 1995 State Duma elections, and by the continued pre-eminence of the Communist Party of the Russian Federation in the Oblast. The Governor, Anatolii Guzhvin, initially a federal appointee, retained his post at elections in 1997, and was re-elected for a further term of office in December 2000, receiving 81% of the votes cast. Elections to the regional legislature, the Representative Assembly, were held on 28 October 2001; in the following month the Assembly voted to rename itself the State Duma. The region continued to suffer from severe social difficulties in the early 2000s; it was reported that the operations of the Oblast's police force had been subject to criticism in a report commissioned in late 2002 by the federal Ministry of Internal Affairs. Moreover, Astrakhan was reputed to have the highest crime rate of any federal subject in the Southern Federal Okrug. Meanwhile, the municipal authorities in Akhtubinsk, the second city of the Oblast, were reported to have commenced a scheme, in accordance with which free housing was to be provided to married women who, subject to certain conditions, would agree to bear three children over the course of five years, in an attempt to combat the declining birth rate in the region.

## Economy

Astrakhan Oblast's gross regional product was 18,942.9m. roubles in 1999, equivalent to 18,479.1 roubles per head. The Oblast's main industrial centres are at Astrakhan and Akhtubinsk. In 2000 there were 567 km of railways and 2,635 km of paved roads on the Oblast's territory. The rise in the level of the Caspian Sea (by some 2.6 m between the late 1970s and the late 1990s) and the resulting erosion of the Volga delta caused serious environmental problems in the region. These were exacerbated by the pollution of the water by petroleum products, copper, nitrates and other substances, which frequently contributed to the death of a significant proportion of fish reserves.

The Oblast remains a major producer of vegetables and cucurbits (gourds and melons). Grain production and animal husbandry are also important. Total agricultural production amounted to a value of 3,094m. roubles in 2000, when the sector employed 14.7% of the working population. The Oblast is rich in natural resources, including gas and gas condensate, sulphur, petroleum and salt. Its main industries are the production of petroleum and natural gas, food-processing, mechanical engineering, and electricity production. It was hoped that the former activity would improve the economic fortunes of the region, as the exploitation of Caspian hydrocarbons reserves increased. Industrial output in 2000 was worth 18,423m. roubles, and the sector employed 16.4% of the Oblast's labour force. Regional trade was also important to the economy of Astrakhan. The Lakor freight company established important shipping links with Iran, handling around 940,000 metric tons of cargo in 1996, and in early 2000 announced plans to develop a trade route with India. In September 1997 the company, with an Iranian group, Khazar Shipping, registered the Astrakhan–Nowshahr joint shipping line. Astrakhan's exports to Iran mainly comprised paper, metals, timber, mechanical equipment, fertilizers and chemical products.

Astrakhan Oblast's economically active population numbered 502,000 in 2000, when 11.5% of the region's labour force were unemployed. The average monthly wage was 3,708.2 roubles in mid-2002. In 2000 there was a budgetary surplus of 107.7m. roubles. In that year export trade totalled US $249.7m., and the value of imports amounted to $53.0m. Foreign investment in the territory amounted to $0.4m., compared with $7.6m. in 1998. At 31 December 2000 there were 3,600 small businesses in operation.

## Directory

**Head of the Regional Administration (Governor):** ANATOLII P. GUZHVIN; 414000 Astrakhan, ul. Sovetskaya 14–15; tel. (8512) 22-85-19; fax (8512) 22-95-14; e-mail ves@astrakhan.ru; internet www.gov .astrakhan-region.ru.

**Chairman of the State Duma:** PAVEL P. ANISIMOV; 414000 Astrakhan, ul. Volodarskogo 15; tel. (8512) 22-96-44; fax (8512) 22-22-48; e-mail ootsops@astranet.ru; internet duma.astranet.ru.

**Representation of Astrakhan Oblast in the Russian Federation:** 125407 Moscow, ul. 3-aya Tveskaya-Yamskaya 58/5; tel. (095) 251-07-19; fax (095) 251-06-96.

**Head of Astrakhan City Administration (Mayor):** IGOR A. BEZRUKAVNIKOV; 414000 Astrakhan, ul. Chernyshevskogo 6; tel. (8512) 22-55-88; fax (8512) 24-71-76; e-mail munic@astranet.ru; internet astrakhan.astranet.ru.

# Belgorod Oblast

Belgorod Oblast is situated in the south-west of the Central Russian Highlands. It forms part of the Central Federal Okrug and the Central Chernozem Economic Area. The Oblast lies on the international border with Ukraine, with the Oblasts of Kursk to the north and Voronezh to the east. Its main rivers are the Severnii Donets, the Vorskla and the Oskol. The territory occupies 27,100 sq km (10,460 sq miles) and measures around 260 km (160 miles) from west to east. It is divided into 21 administrative districts and 10 cities. It had an estimated population of 1,498,000 at 1 January 2002, giving a population density of 55.3 per sq km. In 2001 some 65.8% of the population inhabited urban areas. According to the 1989 census, 92.9% of the Oblast's inhabitants were ethnic Russians. The Oblast's administrative centre is at Belgorod, which had 342,000 inhabitants in 2001. A further major city is Staryi Oskol (215,200).

## History

Belgorod was established as a bishopric during the early days of Orthodox Christianity. The region was part of Lithuania until 1503, when it was annexed by the Muscovite state. The new city of Belgorod was founded in 1593. Belgorod Oblast was formally established on 6 January 1954.

In late 1993 President Boris Yeltsin dismissed the region's Governor and arranged for elections to a new Regional Duma to be held in 1994. The communists enjoyed a majority in this body, too, and there was constant conflict with the administration, the head of which, however, also enjoyed popular support. For this reason, the Oblast was one of only 12 areas in the Federation to be permitted gubernatorial elections in December 1995. The incumbent, Yevgenii Savchenko was duly elected. Savchenko was re-elected in May 1999, with the leader of the Liberal Democratic Party of Russia, Vladimir Zhirinovskii, coming third in the poll, as part of his unsuccessful campaign to become a regional governor. In 2001 a treaty was signed between the Russian and Ukrainian authorities, initially on an experimental basis, which provided for a simplification of the customs and border formalities for residents of the Oblasts of Belgorod (in Russia) and Kharkhiv (Kharkov—in Ukraine), with a view to facilitating increased cross-border trade. This measure was widely regarded as a success, and by early 2003 annual trade between the two regions was estimated at US $800m. Savchenko was elected to a further term of office, as an independent candidate, on 25 May 2003, receiving 61.2% of votes cast in a poll contested by three candidates.

## Economy

In 1999 Belgorod Oblast's gross regional product amounted to 34,526.3m. roubles, or 23,097.6 roubles per head. The main industrial centres in the territory are situated at Belgorod, Shebekino and Alekseyevka. In 2000 there were 690 km of railway lines and 6,410 km of paved roads on the Oblast's territory.

Belgorod Oblast's principal crops are grain, sugar beet, sunflower seeds and essential-oil plants. Horticulture and animal husbandry are also important. In 2000 24.3% of the region's working population were engaged in the agricultural sector, which generated a total of 16,759m. roubles. There are substantial reserves of bauxite, iron ore and apatites. The Oblast's main industries are ore-mining (iron ores), the production of electricity, mechanical engineering, metalworking, chemicals, the manufacture of building materials and food-

processing. Industry employed 21.5% of the work-force in 2000, and total industrial production was worth 41,426m. roubles.

The economically active population in Belgorod Oblast numbered 725,000 in 2000, when 5.8% of the region's labour force were unemployed. In mid-2002 the average monthly salary was 4,599.6 roubles. There was a budgetary surplus of 192.9m. in 2000. In that year export trade totalled US $536.4m., while import trade amounted to $576.8m. Foreign investment in the Oblast totalled $35.4m. in 2000, compared with $156.1m. in 1998. In 2000 there were 4,600 small businesses in the Oblast.

## Directory

**Head of the Regional Administration (Governor):** YEVGENII S. SAVCHENKO; 308005 Belgorod, pl. Revolyutsii 4; tel. (0722) 22-42-47; fax (0722) 22-33-43; e-mail admin@regadm.bel.ru; internet beladm .bel.ru.

**Chairman of the Regional Duma:** ANATOLII YA. ZELIKOV; 308005 Belgorod, pl. Revolyutsii 4; tel. (0722) 32-24-37; fax (0722) 27-65-88; e-mail duma@bel.ru; internet duma.bel.ru.

**Chief Representative of Belgorod Oblast in the Russian Federation:** ALEKSANDR G. MATSEPURO; 113052 Moscow, Zagorodnoye shosse 5/21; tel. (095) 952-02-03; fax (095) 952-28-36; e-mail moscow@ bel.ru.

**Head of Belgorod City Administration:** VASILII N. POTRYASAYEV; 308800 Belgorod, ul. Lenina 38; tel. (0722) 27-72-06.

# Bryansk Oblast

Bryansk Oblast is situated in the central part of the Central Russian Highlands and is in the Central Federal Okrug and the Central Economic Area. It has international borders to the west (Belarus) and south (Ukraine), with Kursk and Orel Oblasts to the east, Kaluga to the north-east and Smolensk to the north-west. Bryansk's main river is the Desna, a tributary of the Dnepr (Dnieper), and just under one-third of its area is forested. The Oblast occupies 34,900 sq km (13,480 sq miles) of territory and measures 245 km (152 miles) from south to north and 270 km from west to east. It is divided into 27 administrative districts and 16 cities. At 1 January 2002 the region's estimated population was 1,410,300, giving a population density of 40.4 per sq km. In 2001 some 68.8% of the population inhabited urban areas. Bryansk, with a population of 450,600 at 1 January 2001, is the Oblast's administrative centre.

## History

The ancient Russian city of Bryansk was part of the independent principality of Novgorod-Serversk until 1356. It was an early Orthodox Christian bishopric. The Muscovite state acquired the city from Lithuania in the 16th century. Bryansk Oblast was founded on 5 July 1944.

In the 1990s and early 2000s the region was considered part of the communist-dominated 'red belt'. Bryansk was one of the eight federal territories permitted gubernatorial elections in December 1992. The incumbent, a supporter of the federal President, Boris Yeltsin, was defeated by the communist-backed candidate, Yurii Lodkin. After the constitutional crisis of September–October 1993 Lodkin was dismissed and the Soviet disbanded, and a Regional Duma formed. The Communist Party secured about 35% of the votes cast in the region for the State Duma in December 1995. After a series of scandals involving successive, short-lived (and non-communist) governors, Lodkin returned to the post of governor, following elections in December 1996. Relations with the federal centre improved after the signature of a power-sharing agreement in July 1997, although the Communist Party dominated the local elections held in the previous month and maintained its influence in the federal presidential election of March 2000. Lodkin was re-elected as Governor in December 2000, although he obtained only 29% of the votes cast. In the early 2000s concerns were expressed regarding the regulation of the media by the Oblast authorities; notably, in September 2003 the Oblast electoral commission formally warned three newspapers that had violated recently introduced federal legislation concerning the coverage of election campaigns, representing the first application of the legislation. In early October the federal Minister of the Press, Broadcasting and Mass Media, Mikhail Lesin, stated that actions such as those taken by the Bryansk electoral commission could have the effect of reducing informed political coverage in the press, and of thereby encouraging electoral abstention.

## Economy

Bryansk Oblast is one of the Russian Federation's major industrial regions. The territory's gross regional product was 18,554.3m. roubles in 1999, equivalent to 12,802.2 roubles per head. Its main industrial centres are at Bryansk and Klintsy. In 2000 there were 1,019 km of railway track on its territory, and 6,215 km of paved roads.

The Oblast's agriculture, which employed 19.1% of its work-force in 2000, consists mainly of grain and vegetable production and animal husbandry. Around one-half of its area is used for agricultural purposes. In 2000 total production in the sector was worth 10,256m. roubles. The Oblast's main industries are mechanical engineering, food-processing, electrical energy, the manufacture of building materials and timber-working. Industry employed 20.9% of the work-force in 2000 and generated 14,509m. roubles.

In 2000 the economically active population of Bryansk Oblast numbered 664,000, and some 13.1% of the region's labour force (more than in any other region in the Central Federal Okrug) were unemployed. In mid-2002 the average monthly wage was 2,641.7 roubles. There was a regional government budgetary surplus of 25.7m. roubles in 2000. In that year international trade comprised US $80.7m. of exports and $131.0m. of imports. Foreign investment amounted to $6.3m. At 31 December 2000 there were 3,800 small businesses registered in the region.

## Directory

**Head of the Regional Administration (Governor):** Yurii Ye. Lodkin; 241002 Bryansk, pr. Lenina 33; tel. (0832) 46-26-11; fax (0832) 41-38-95; e-mail press@admin.debryansk.ru; internet www.bryanskobl.ru.

**Chairman of the Regional Duma:** Stepan N. Ponasov; 241000 Bryansk, pl. K. Marksa 2; tel. (0832) 43-36-91; fax (0832) 74-31-95.

**Chief Representative of Bryansk Oblast in the Russian Federation:** Nikolai I. Moskin; 103025 Moscow, ul. Novyi Arbat 19; tel. and fax (095) 203-50-52.

**Head of Bryansk City Administration (Mayor):** Valerii Polyakov; 241002 Bryansk, pr. Lenina 35; tel. (0832) 74-30-13; fax (0832) 74-47-30; e-mail postmaster@comimm.bryansk.su.

# Chelyabinsk Oblast

Chelyabinsk Oblast is situated in the Southern Urals, in the Transural (Asian Russia). It forms part of the Urals Federal Okrug and the Urals Economic Area. Orenburg Oblast lies to the south, the Republic of Bashkortostan to the west, Sverdlovsk Oblast to the north and Kurgan Oblast to the east. There is an international border with Kazakhstan in the south-east. Much of the region lies on the eastern slopes of the southern Ural Mountains. The major rivers in the Oblast are the Ural and the Miass. It has over 1,000 lakes, the largest of which are the Uvildy and the Turgoyak. The Oblast covers an area of 87,900 sq km (34,940 sq miles) and is divided into 24 administrative districts and 30 cities. Chelyabinsk had an estimated population of 3,268,700 at 1 January 2002, giving a population density of 37.2 per sq km. In 2001 some 81.3% of the population inhabited urban areas. The Oblast's administrative centre is at Chelyabinsk, which had a population of 1,081,100 in 2001. Other major cities are Magnitogorsk (427,100), Zlatoust (195,900) and Miass (164,300).

## History

Chelyabinsk city was established as a Russian frontier post in 1736, but was deep within Russian territory by the 19th century. The Oblast was created on 17 January 1934. The region was heavily industrialized during the Soviet period and remained dominated by communist cadres following the disintegration of the USSR. In December 1992, at elections for the head of the regional administration, the incumbent Governor, a supporter of Boris Yeltsin, the Russian President, was defeated. President Yeltsin re-established his authority in late 1993 and required the election of a Duma during 1994. Both in this body, and in the local results of the general election of 1995, pro-Yeltsin and reformist forces obtained significant levels of support. In the gubernatorial election of late 1996, however, Petr Sumin was returned to power. Sumin, a communist, had been removed as head of the regional administration following the attempted coup of August 1991. Sumin's pro-communist movement also won an absolute majority of seats in the legislature in the local elections held in December 1997. Sumin was re-elected as Governor in December 2000.

## Economy

In 1999 the gross regional product of the Oblast amounted to 84,579.6m. roubles, equivalent to 22,996.1 roubles per head. The region's major industrial centres are at Chelyabinsk, Magnitogorsk,

Miass, Zlatoust and Kopeisk. Although output declined by one-half between 1989 and 1997, Magnitogorsk remains well-known as the city that produced the steel for over one-half of the tanks used by Soviet troops in the Second World War, and as the largest iron and steel production complex in the world. The Oblast is a major junction of the Trans-Siberian Railway. In 2000 there were 1,793 km (1,114 miles) of railway track in the Oblast and 8,065 km of paved roads.

The Oblast's agriculture, which employed 9.9% of the working population in 2000, consists mainly of animal husbandry, horticulture and the production of grain and vegetables. Total agricultural output in 2000 was worth 12,071m. roubles. The Oblast is one of the most polluted in the Federation; in particular, high rates of disease and environmental despoliation resulted from the Kyshtym nuclear accident of 1957, in the north of the region, when up to three times the levels of radiation emitted at the Chornobyl (Chernobyl) disaster in Ukraine in 1986 were released into the surrounding area. Approximately 180 sq km of agricultural land remained out of use because of radioactivity, and water supplies in many parts of the region were also unsafe. Chelyabinsk Oblast became one of the most industrialized territories of the Russian Federation, following the reconstruction of plants moved there from further west during the Second World War. In 2000 industry employed some 30.9% of the economically active population. The Oblast's main industries are ferrous and non-ferrous metallurgy (which accounted for a total of 64.4% of industrial activity in 2000), ore-mining, mechanical engineering, metal-working, fuel and energy production, food-processing and the manufacture of building materials. In the north-west, the closed city of Ozersk (formerly Chelyabinsk-40) is a major plutonium-processing and -storage site, while in the west are centres for weapons manufacturing and space technology. The conversion of former military plants to civilian use in the 1990s meant that the former tank factory at Magnitogorsk began to produce tractors, and the Mayak nuclear armament plant (the location of the 1957 disaster) sought to become a recycling plant for foreign nuclear waste. In 2000 the industrial sector generated 146,116m. roubles.

The economically active population numbered 1,817,000 in 2000, when 8.1% of the labour force were unemployed. At mid-2002 those in employment earned an average wage of 3,953.7 roubles per month. The 2000 budget recorded a deficit of 422.3m. roubles. Export trade amounted to US $1,861.0m. in 2000, when imports were worth $586.9m. Attempts to attract foreign investment in the Oblast from the mid-1990s were largely successful: foreign capital amounted to $595.7m. by 2000, compared with $59.1m. in 1998. In 2000 there were some 119 enterprises with foreign capital in the Oblast. At 31 December 2000 there were 19,100 small businesses registered on the Oblast's territory.

## Directory

**Governor:** Petr I. Sumin; 454009 Chelyabinsk, ul. Tsvillinga 28; tel. (3512) 63-92-41; fax (3512) 63-12-83; internet www.ural-chel.ru.

**Chairman of the Legislative Assembly:** Viktor F. Davydov; 454009 Chelyabinsk, ul. Kirova 114; tel. (3512) 65-78-26; fax (3512) 63-63-79; e-mail zscr@chel.surnet.ru; internet www.ural-chel.ru/gubern/zaksob/index.html.

**Chief Representative of Chelyabinsk Oblast in the Russian Federation:** Oleg N. Andreyev; 127422 Moscow, Dmitrovskii pr. 4a; tel. (095) 210-88-59; fax (095) 977-08-35.

**Head of Chelyabinsk City Administration (Mayor):** Vyacheslav M. Tarasov; 454113 Chelyabinsk, pl. Revolyutsii 2; tel. (3512) 33-38-05; fax (3512) 33-38-55.

# Chita Oblast

Chita Oblast is situated in Transbaikal, and forms part of the Siberian Federal Okrug and the East Siberian Economic Area. Buryatiya lies to the west, Irkutsk Oblast to the north, Sakha (Yakutiya) and Amur to the east. To the south there are international borders with the People's Republic of China and Mongolia. The Aga-Buryat Autonomous Okrug (AOk) lies within the Oblast, in the south. The western part of the region is situated in the Yablonovii Khrebet mountain range. Chita Oblast's major rivers are those in the Selenga, the Lena and the Amur basins. More than one-half of the Oblast's territory is forested. Excluding the AOk, the Oblast covers an area of 412,500 sq km (159,300 sq miles) and is divided into 28 districts and 10 cities. The population of the Oblast, excluding the AOk, was estimated at 1,157,600 at 1 January 2002, and its population density was 2.8 per sq km (less than one-third of the national average). In 2001 some 62.1% of the region's inhabitants lived in urban areas. The Oblast's administrative centre is at Chita, which had a population of 303,300 at that time. The region's other cities include Krasnokamensk (56,000) and Balei (renowned as the birthplace of Temujin—Chinghiz or Genghis Khan).

# History

The city of Chita was established by the Cossacks in 1653, at the confluence of the Chita and Ingoda rivers. It was named Ingodinskoye Zirnove for a time. Chita was pronounced the capital of the independent, pro-Bolshevik Far Eastern Republic upon its establishment in April 1920. It united the regions of Irkutsk, Transbaikal, Amur and the Pacific coast (Maritime Krai, Khabarovsk Krai, Magadan and Kamchatka), but merged with Soviet Russia in November 1922. Chita Oblast was founded on 26 September 1937.

A new Regional Duma was elected in 1994. The communists and the nationalist liberal democrats were the most popular parties in the mid- and late 1990s. In a gubernatorial election held on 29 October 2001 the incumbent Governor, Ravil Genialutin, was re-elected with 57.4% of the votes cast. Elections to the regional legislature were held concurrently. In July 2003 one of the Oblast's vice-governors, Aleksandr Shapnevskii, was murdered, in what was suspected to be a contract killing.

# Economy

All figures in this survey incorporate data for the Aga-Buryat AOk, which is also treated separately. Chita Oblast's gross regional product amounted to 22,160.9m. roubles in 1999, equivalent to 17,535.2 roubles per head. The region's main industrial centres are at Chita, Nerchinsk, Darasun, Olovyannaya and Tarbagatai. In 2000 there were some 2,399 km (1,490 miles) of railway track in the territory, including sections of the Trans-Siberian and the Far Eastern (Baikal–Amur) Railways. There were also 9,680 km of paved roads, and in 1998 there were 1,000 km of navigable waterways. The Chita–Khabarovsk highway (which was to form part of a direct route between Moscow and Vladivostok) was under construction in the late 1990s.

Chita Oblast's agriculture, which employed some 15.2% of its working population in 2000, consists mainly of animal husbandry (livestock- and reindeer-breeding) and fur-animal hunting. In that year total agricultural output amounted to a value of 6,062m. roubles. The region's major industries are non-ferrous metallurgy, electrical energy, mechanical engineering, fuel extraction (including uranium), processing of forestry and agricultural products, the manufacture of building materials and ore-mining. Industry employed some 14.4% of the work-force in 2000, when total industrial production was worth 9,316m. roubles. Coal-mining in the Oblast was centred around the Vostochnaya mine; gold- and tin-mining were based at Sherlovaya Govra; and lead- and zinc-ore mines are situated at Hapcheranga, 200 km south-east of Yakutsk. In 1992 it was revealed that thorium and uranium had been mined until the mid-1970s at locations just outside Balei. The resulting high levels of radiation had serious consequences among the town's population, with abnormally high incidences of miscarriages and congenital defects in children. The regional Government lacked sufficient funds to relocate Balei's inhabitants and reduce radiation in the area. In 1997, however, the Australian mining company, Armada Gold, announced that it planned to seal the abandoned mines and exploit the nearby gold deposits. A 'Chinese market' in Chita city reflects the importance of the People's Republic of China as a major trading partner of the Oblast, in particular as a source of imports. In common with other regions neighbouring China, Chita suffered short-term economic disruption in May–June 2003, when cross-border travel was restricted, as a result of the outbreak of Severe Acute Respiratory Syndrome (SARS) in China and elsewhere in the Far East.

The territory had an economically active population of 565,000 in 2000, when 13.9% of the labour force were unemployed; the average monthly wage was 4,378.4 roubles in mid-2002. In 2000 the budget showed a deficit of 143.6m. roubles. In that year the Oblast's exports, largely comprising timber, metals and radioactive chemicals, amounted to US $103.6m., and imports amounted to $59.9m. For much of the 1990s foreign investment in the Oblast remained low, and it totalled just $414,000 in 2000. At 31 December 2000 a total of 3,100 small businesses were in operation in Chita Oblast.

# Directory

**Head of the Regional Administration (Governor):** RAVIL F. GENIALUTIN; 672021 Chita, ul. Chaikovskogo 8; tel. (3022) 23-34-93; fax (3022) 26-33-19; internet www.adm.chita.ru.

**Chairman of the Regional Duma:** ALESKANDR F. EPOV; 67021 Chita, ul. Chaikovskogo 8; tel. (3022) 23-58-59.

**Representation of Chita Oblast in the Russian Federation:** 127025 Moscow, ul. Novyi Arbat 19/2001; tel. (095) 203-33-28; fax (095) 203-45-39.

**Head of Chita City Administration (Mayor):** ANATOLII D. MIKHALEV; 672090 Chita, ul. Butina 39; tel. (3022) 23-24-07; fax (3022) 32-06-85; e-mail info@admin.chita.ru.

# Irkutsk Oblast

Irkutsk Oblast is situated in eastern Siberia in the south-east of the Central Siberian Plateau. The Oblast forms part of the Siberian Federal Okrug and the East Siberian Economic Area. The Republic of Sakha (Yakutiya) lies to the north-east, Krasnoyarsk Krai (including the Evenk AOk) to the north-west and Tyva to the south-west. Most of the long south-eastern border is with Buryatiya and, in the east, Chita. Irkutsk Oblast includes the Ust-Orda Buryat Autonomous Okrug (AOk). Lake Baikal is the deepest in the world, possessing over 80% of Russia's, and 20% of the world's, freshwater resources. The Oblast's main rivers are the Angara (the only river to drain Lake Baikal), the Nizhnyaya Tunguska, the Lena, the Vitim and the Kirenga. More than four-fifths of the region's territory is covered with forest (mainly coniferous). The total area of the Oblast, excluding that of the AOk, is 745,500 sq km (287,838 sq miles) and stretches 1,400 km (850 miles) from south to north and 1,200 km west to east. The Oblast proper is divided into 27 administrative districts and 22 cities. The Oblast's estimated population, excluding the AOk, was 2,570,400 in January 2002, giving a population density of 3.4 per sq km. In 2001 some 79.3% of the total population lived in urban areas. The Oblast's administrative centre is at Irkutsk, which had a population of 587,200 in 2001. Other major cities in the region include Bratsk (278,800), Angarsk (264,000) and Ust-Ilimsk (106,600).

# History

The city of Irkutsk was founded as an ostrog (military transit camp) in 1661, at the confluence of the Irkut and Angara rivers, 66 km to the west of Baikal. Irkutsk became one of the largest economic centres of eastern Siberia. After the collapse of the Russian Empire, the region was part of the independent, pro-Bolshevik Far Eastern Republic (based in Chita), which was established in April 1920 and merged with Soviet Russia in November 1922. On 26 September 1937 an Irkutsk Oblast was formed.

In late 1993, following the federal presidency's forcible dissolution of parliament, the executive branch of government secured the dissolution of the Regional Soviet, and in 1994 a Legislative Assembly was elected in its place. As a 'donor region' to the Russian Federation, central-regional relationships in Irkutsk Oblast were frequently strained. In May 1996 the regional and federal authorities signed a power-sharing agreement. Following the resignation of the Governor, Yurii Nozhikov, in April 1997, the government-supported candidate, Boris Govorin (who also received Nozhikov's endorsement), was elected as his successor, receiving 50.3% of the votes cast. At the gubernatorial election held in August 2001 Govorin was re-elected for a further term of office; however, the relatively high proportion of votes awarded to the Communist Party candidate, Sergei Levchenko, who received 45.4% (compared with the 47.5% received by Govorin), appeared to reflect increasing dissatisfaction with the economic situation in the region. In March 2002 the Chairman of the Legislative Assembly, Viktor Borovskii, who had been regarded as the leading opponent of Govorin in the region, was removed from office, and replaced by a loyalist, Sergei Shishkin. During the early 2000s proposals to unite the Ust-Orda Buryat AOk and Irkutsk Oblast became increasingly popular and appeared to be supported by the authorities in both the AOk and the Oblast; moreover, in September 2002 the Chairman of the Federation Council, Sergei Mironov, stated that the two federal subjects already satisfied the prerequisites for becoming a single unit. However, only very limited progress towards the merging of the two political entities was reported during the course of the following year. In late May 2003 the Legislative Assembly approved legislation providing for the extension of the terms of office of both the regional governor and regional deputies, from four years to five years. In both cases these extensions were to apply from the next elections, scheduled to take place in 2005 and 2004, respectively.

# Economy

Irkutsk Oblast is one of the most economically developed regions in Russia, largely owing to its significant fuel, energy and water resources, minerals and timber, and its location on the Trans-Siberian Railway. All figures in this survey incorporate data for the Usta-Orda Buryat AOk, which is also treated separately. In 1999 the Oblast's gross regional product totalled 85,889.1m. roubles, or 31,163.3 roubles per head. The region's main industrial centres are at Irkutsk, Bratsk, Ust-Ilimsk and Angarsk. The Oblast, which is traversed by the Trans-Siberian and the Far Eastern (Baikal–Amur) Railways, contained 2,479 km of railway track in 2000. There were almost 12,151 km of paved roads in the region, which carry some 40m. metric tons of freight annually in the late 1990s. The Oblast has two international airports, at Irkutsk and Bratsk, from which there are direct and connecting flights to Japan, the People's Republic of China, the Republic of Korea (South Korea), Mongolia and the USA. In the late 1990s approximately one-10th of the region's freight was transported by river—there are two major river-ports on the Lena river at Kirensk and Osetrovo (Ust-Kut). These are used to transport freight to Sakha (Yakutiya) and the northern seaport of Tiksi.

The Oblast's agriculture, which employed just 10.4% of its work-force in 2000, consists mainly of grain production, animal husbandry (fur-animal-, reindeer- and livestock-breeding), hunting and fishing. Total agricultural production in the territory generated 11,090m. roubles in 2000. The region contains the huge Kovytkinskoye oil-field, which was awaiting an international consortium with the resources to construct an export pipeline across the People's Republic of China. In the late 1990s more than 45% of the Oblast's fixed assets were in the industrial sector, which engaged some 24.7% of the working population in 2000. The main industries are non-ferrous metallurgy, the processing of forestry products, mining (coal, iron ore, gold, muscovite or mica, gypsum, talc and salt), mechanical engineering, metal-working, chemicals and petrochemicals, petro-leum-refining, fuel extraction, electricity generation, and food-pro-cessing. In 2000 the total value of manufactured goods in the Oblast was 87,984m. roubles, of which the non-ferrous metallurgy industry contributed 27% and the timber and timber-processing industries 23%.

The economically active population in Irkutsk Oblast totalled 1,406,000 in 2000, when 11.4% of the labour force were unemployed. For those in employment, the average wage amounted to 4,966.2 roubles per month in mid-2002. In 2000 there was a budgetary deficit of 204.8m. roubles. In that year the value of exports from the territory amounted to some US $2,942.2m., while imports were worth $537.3m. Foreign investment in the territory was worth some $82.3m. At 31 December 2000 there were 13,800 small businesses registered in the Oblast.

## Directory

**Governor:** BORIS A. GOVORIN; 664047 Irkutsk, ul. Lenina 1A; tel. (3952) 20-00-15; fax (3952) 24-33-40; internet www.admirk.ru.

**Chairman of the Legislative Assembly:** SERGEI I. SHISHKIN; 664047 Irkutsk, ul. Lenina 1A; tel. (3952) 24-17-60; fax (3952) 20-00-27; internet irk.gov.ru.

**Chief Representative of Irkutsk Oblast in the Russian Federation:** TATYANA I. RYUTINA; 109028 Moscow, per. Durasovskii 3/2; tel. (095) 916-17-08; fax (095) 915-70-58.

**Head of Irkutsk City Administration (Mayor):** VLADIMIR V. YAKUBOVSKII; 664025 Irkutsk, ul. Lenina 14; tel. (3952) 24-37-04.

# Ivanovo Oblast

Ivanovo Oblast is situated in the central part of the Eastern Euro-pean Plain. It forms part of the Central Federal Okrug and the Central Economic Area. It is surrounded by the Oblasts of Kostroma (to the north), Nizhnii Novgorod (east), Vladimir (south) and Yar-oslavl (north-west). Its main river is the Volga and one-half of its territory is forested. The Oblast covers a total area of 21,800 sq km (9,230 sq miles), and includes 21 administrative districts and 17 cities. Its estimated population at 1 January 2002 was 1,191,200, giving a population density of 54.6 per sq km. In 2001 some 82.4% of the population inhabited urban areas. Its administrative centre, Ivanovo, had a population of 452,100 in 2001.

## History

The city of Ivanovo was founded in 1871 and was known as Ivanovo-Voznesensk until 1932. It was an important centre of anti-govern-ment activity during the strikes of 1883 and 1885 and in the 1905 Revolution. Ivanovo Oblast was founded on 20 July 1918.

In the post-Soviet era the region displayed support for political diversity. Although the Communist Party of the Russian Federation (CPRF) and Vladimir Zhirinovskii's nationalist Liberal Democrats both performed well in elections in 1994–95, moderates were suc-cessful in the gubernatorial and regional legislative elections held in 1996, and the elections to the State Duma in 1999. However, in the gubernatorial elections held in two rounds in December 2000, the CPRF candidate, Vladimir Tikhonov, defeated the regional Prime Minister, Vladimir Golovkov. Legislative elections took place in the same month.

## Economy

In 1999 Ivanovo Oblast's gross regional product totalled 12,760.9m. roubles, equivalent to 10,382.3 roubles per head. The region's main industrial centres are at Ivanovo (a major producer of textiles), Kineshma, Shuya, Vichuga, Furmanov, Teikovo and Rodniki. There

are well-developed rail, road and river transport networks in the region and the largest international airport in central Russia. In 2000 there were 341 km (212 miles) of railways and 3,495 km of paved roads on the Oblast's territory.

Ivanovo Oblast was the historic centre of Russia's cotton-milling industry and was known as the 'Russian Manchester' at the begin-ning of the 20th century. Flax production was still an important agricultural activity in the region in the 1990s, as were grain and vegetable production and animal husbandry. However, agriculture employed just 9.6% of its work-force in 2000, and total agricultural production in that year amounted to a value of 4,421m. roubles. The region's main industries were light manufacturing (especially tex-tiles), electrical energy, mechanical engineering, chemicals, food-processing, wood-working, handicrafts (especially lacquerware) and the production of building materials. Some 33.4% of its working population were engaged in the sector, which generated 14,374m. roubles in 2000.

The economically active population amounted to 600,000 in 2000, when 10.1% of the labour force were unemployed, compared with 18.6% in 1998. The average wage was 2,631.5 roubles per month in mid-2002. In 2000 the budget recorded a surplus of 162.4m. roubles. External trade was relatively low in that year, amounting to a value of US $65.7m. in exports and $198.4m. in imports. Although foreign investment amounted to only $120,000 in 1998, this figure had increased to $3.3m. by 2000. However, at that time there were only nine enterprises with foreign capital in the Oblast, fewer than in any other region of the Central Federal Okrug. At 31 December 2000 there were 5,100 small businesses registered in the region.

## Directory

**Head of the Regional Administration (Governor):** VLADIMIR I. TIKHONOV; 153000 Ivanovo, ul. Baturina 5; tel. (0932) 41-77-05; fax (0932) 41-92-31; e-mail 001@adminet.ivanovo.ru; internet ivadm .ivanovo.ru.

**Chairman of the Legislative Assembly:** VLADIMIR S. GRISHIN; 153461 Ivanovo, ul. Pushkina 9; tel. and fax (0932) 41-60-68; e-mail zsio@gov.ivanovo.ru.

**Representation of Ivanovo Oblast in the Russian Federation:** 127025 Moscow, ul. Novyi Arbat 16/1714; tel. (095) 203-41-34; fax (095) 203-93-45.

**Head of Ivanovo City Administration:** ALEKSANDR V. GROSHEV; 153001 Ivanovo, pl. Revolyutsii 6; tel. (0932) 32-70-20; fax (0932) 41-25-12; e-mail info@goradm.ivanovo.ru; internet ivgoradm.ivanovo .ru.

# Kaliningrad Oblast

Kaliningrad Oblast forms the westernmost part of the Russian Federation, being an exclave separated from the rest of the country by Lithuania (which borders it to the north and east) and Belarus. Poland lies to the south. It falls within the North-Western Federal Okrug and is sometimes included in the North-Western Economic Area. The city of Kaliningrad (formerly Königsberg) is sited at the mouth of the River Pregolya (Pregel), where it flows into the Vistula Lagoon, an inlet of the Baltic Sea. The other main river is the Neman (Memel). The Oblast occupies 15,100 sq km (5,830 sq miles), of which only 13,300 sq km are dry land, the rest of its territory comprising the freshwater Kurshskaya (Curonian) Lagoon, in the north-east, and the Vistula Lagoon. The coastline is 140 km (87 miles) long. The Oblast is divided into 13 administrative districts and 22 cities. It had an estimated population of 943,200 at 1 January 2002 and its population density was, therefore, 62.5 per sq km. In 2001 some 76.7% of the population inhabited urban areas. The Oblast's admin-istrative centre is at Kaliningrad, which had a population of 421,000 at 1 January 2001. Other cities in the Oblast are Chernyakhovsk (formerly Insterburg—43,800) and Sovetsk (formerly Tilsit—43,700).

## History

The city of Kaliningrad was founded in 1255, as Königsberg, during German expansion eastwards. The chief city of East Prussia, it was the original royal capital of the Hohenzollerns (from 1871 the German Emperors). After the Second World War it was annexed by the USSR and received its current name (1945). Most of the German population was deported and the city almost completely destroyed and rebuilt. On 7 April 1946 the region became an administrative-political entity within the Russian Federation.

In mid-1993 Kaliningrad requested the status of a republic, a petition refused by the federal authorities. On 15 October the Regional Soviet was disbanded by the head of the regional admin-istration for failing to support the state presidency's struggle against the federal parliament. A regional Duma was later formed. In January 1996 Yurii Matochkin was one of the first oblast governors to sign a power-sharing agreement with the federal Government. Leonid Gorbenko, an independent candidate, was elected as Governor in October.

Despite the establishment of a 'free-trade zone' in the Oblast in 1991, Kaliningrad was bedevilled by particularly high levels of corruption in the 1990s. Relations with the exclave's neighbours were also troubled at times. German groups in Russia (primarily those resident along the River Volga) and Russian ultra-nationalists made unsuccessful demands for increased German influence in the management of the Oblast. In 1998 a proposal that the region be awarded the status of an autonomous Russian Baltic republic within Russia was submitted to the Federation Council. However, Gorbenko opposed plans for greater autonomy, instead supporting the growth of closer ties with Belarus. In gubernatorial elections held in two rounds in November 2000, Gorbenko was defeated by Adm. Vladimir Yegorov, the former Commander of the Baltic Fleet. Yegorov was regarded as a pro-presidential candidate, and was elected largely on the basis of his anti-corruption campaign. In 2002, as the European Union (EU) prepared to admit several Eastern European countries, including Lithuania and Poland, in 2004, the status of Kaliningrad became an increasing source of contention; in particular, Russia initially objected to proposals that residents of Kaliningrad would require visas to travel to metropolitan Russia. In November 2002, at an EU-Russia summit meeting, held in Brussels, Belgium, Russia finally agreed to an EU proposal for simplified visa arrangements. According to the compromise accord, multiple-transit travel documentation would be made available to residents of the exclave travelling by motor vehicle; the new regulations took effect from 1 July 2003. The EU also agreed to undertake a feasibility study on the possibility of allowing high-speed, sealed trains to operate between the exclave and the remainder of the Federation, thus negating the need for transit documents. In August 2003 the oblast prosecutor's office commenced criminal proceedings against former Governor Gorbenko, on charges of abuse of office.

## Economy

Kaliningrad Oblast is noted for containing more than 90% of the world's reserves of amber. Within Russia it is also noted for its reputedly flourishing parallel ('black') market, with federal officials suggesting in January 1999 that the region had become a major transhipment point for illegal drugs. In 1999 its gross regional product totalled 16,157.5m. roubles, or 17,006.1 roubles per head. Its main industrial centres are at Kaliningrad, Gusev and Sovetsk. There are rail services to Lithuania and Poland, and there were 639 km of railways on the Oblast's territory in 2000. In that year Kaliningrad Oblast's road network consisted of 4,577 km of paved roads. Its main ports are at Kaliningrad and Baltiisk.

Kaliningrad Oblast's agricultural sector, which employed 9.3% of its work-force in 2000, consists mainly of animal husbandry, vegetable growing and fishing. Total agricultural output was worth 3,628m. roubles in 2000. The Oblast has substantial reserves of petroleum (around 275m. metric tons), more than 2,500m. cu m in peat deposits and 50m. tons of coal. The industrial sector employed 19.4% of its working population and generated 14,410m. roubles in 2000. The region's main industries are the production of natural gas, mechanical engineering, electro-technical industry, the processing of agricultural and forestry products, light manufacturing and the production and processing of amber. In 2000 some 749,000 tons of petroleum were extracted. A plant to construct German BMW automobiles for the Russian market opened in 1999. The continuing strategic geopolitical situation of Kaliningrad Oblast meant that demilitarization proceeded at a much slower pace than it did elsewhere in the former USSR; in 1998 there were around 200,000 members of military units in the Oblast.

The economically active population numbered 489,000 in 2000, when some 15.4% of the labour force were unemployed, one of the highest levels in European Russia outside the North Caucasus. The average monthly wage was 3,832.1 roubles in mid-2002. The 2000 regional budget recorded a deficit of 22.6m. roubles, and the region is largely dependent on federal subsidies. Foreign investment totalled US $19.1m. in 2000, and there were hopes that the region would be favoured as an entry point to the Russian market. In 2000 export trade amounted to $441.6m., with the fishing industry representing a major source of exports; in that year imports were worth $809.0m. At 31 December 2000 there was a total of 7,600 small businesses registered in the region.

## Directory

**Head of the Regional Administration (Governor):** VLADIMIR G. YEGOROV; 236007 Kaliningrad, ul. D. Donskogo 1; tel. (0112) 46-75-45; fax (0112) 46-38-62; e-mail egorov@gov.kaliningrad.ru; internet www.gov.kaliningrad.ru.

**Chairman of the Regional Duma:** VLADIMIR A. NIKITIN; 236000 Kaliningrad, ul. Kirova 17; tel. (0112) 22-84-39; fax (0112) 22-84-82; e-mail nikitin@duma.kaliningrad.org; internet duma.kaliningrad .org.

**Chief Representative of Kaliningrad Oblast in the Russia Federation:** YEVGENII I. IZOTOV; 114049 Moscow, ul. Zhitnaya 14/3; tel. (095) 258-44-01; e-mail rngs@online.ru.

**Head of Kaliningrad City Administration (Mayor):** YURII A. SAVENKO; 236040 Kaliningrad, ul. Pobedy 1; tel. (0112) 21-14-82; fax (0112) 21-16-77; e-mail cityhall@klgd.ru; internet www.klgd.ru.

# Kaluga Oblast

Kaluga Oblast is situated in the central part of the Eastern European Plain, its administrative centre, Kaluga, being 188 km (177 miles) south-west of Moscow. It forms part of the Central Federal Okrug and the Central Economic Area. Tula and Orel Oblasts lie to the south-east, Bryansk Oblast to the south-west, Moscow Oblast to the north-east and Smolensk Oblast to the north-west. Kaluga's main river is the Oka and some two-fifths of its territory is forested. It occupies 29,900 sq km (11,540 sq miles) and is divided into 24 administrative districts and 19 cities. The Oblast had a population of 1,058,900 in 2002 and a population density, therefore, of 35.4 per sq km. In 2001 some 74.3% of the population inhabited urban areas. Its administrative centre is at Kaluga, a river-port on the Oka river, which had a population of 335,300 in 2001. Other major cities in the Oblast include Obninsk (107,800), the site of the world's first nuclear power station.

## History

The city of Kaluga, first mentioned in the letters of a Lithuanian prince, Olgerd, in 1371, was founded as a Muscovite outpost. The region was the scene of an army mutiny in 1905 and was seized by Bolshevik troops at the end of 1917. Kaluga Oblast was founded on 5 July 1944.

Communist-affiliated managers of industrial and agricultural bodies dominated the new representative body, the Legislative Assembly, elected in March 1994. The Communist Party of the Russian Federation (CPRF) won over one-quarter of the region's votes in the 1995 elections to the State Duma. However, in elections to the Legislative Assembly in 1996 the CPRF failed to win any seats. Valerii Sudarenkov, the Governor from 1996, had previously been the Deputy Prime Minister of the Uzbek Soviet Socialist Republic (SSR—Uzbekistan). Sudarenkov did not stand for re-election in November 2000; his former deputy, Anatolii Artamonov, was elected to succeed him, with 56.7% of the votes cast.

## Economy

In 1999 gross regional product in Kaluga Oblast totalled 17,300.8m. roubles, equivalent to 15,935.1 roubles per head. Apart from Kaluga, the region's main industrial centres are at Lyudinovo, Kirov, Maloyaroslavets and Sukhinichi. In 2000 there were 853 km of railway track in the Oblast, and 4,943 km of paved roads.

Certain areas of the Oblast contain fertile black earth (*chernozem*). Agriculture employed 11.7% of the work-force in 2000, comprising mainly animal husbandry and production of vegetables, grain and flax. Agricultural output amounted to a value of 6,478m. roubles in 2000. The Oblast's main industries are mechanical engineering, food-processing, wood-working, the production of building materials and electrical energy. The industrial sector employed 25.7% of the working population in 2000 and generated 22,148m. roubles.

The economically active population totalled 564,000 in 2000, when 8.2% of the labour force were unemployed. The average monthly wage in Kaluga Oblast was 3,503.4 roubles in mid-2002. In 2000 there was a budgetary surplus of 22.1m. roubles. In that year export trade amounted to a value of US $84.8m.; imports amounted to $127.7m. Total foreign investment totalled $80.7m. in 2000. At the end of 2000 there were 5,900 small businesses registered in the region.

## Directory

**Head of the Regional Administration (Governor):** ANATOLII D. ARTAMONOV; 248661 Kaluga, pl. Staryi Torg 2; tel. (0842) 56-23-57; fax (0842) 53-13-09; e-mail postmaster@admobl.kaluga.su; internet www.admobl.kaluga.ru.

**Chairman of the Legislative Assembly:** VALERII I. KRESTYANINOV; 248600 Kaluga, pl. Staryi Torg 2; tel. (0842) 57-45-00; fax (0842) 59-15-63.

**Chief Representative of Kaluga Oblast in the Russian Federation:** VLADIMIR V. POTEMKIN; 121002 Moscow, per. Glazovskii 8; tel. (095) 203-17-12; fax (095) 229-98-05; e-mail kaluga@orc.ru.

**Head of Kaluga City Administration:** VALERII V. IVANOV; 248600 Kaluga, ul. Lenina 93; tel. (0842) 56-26-46; fax (0842) 24-41-78; e-mail uprava@kaluga.ru; internet users.kaluga.ru/uprava.

# Kamchatka Oblast

Kamchatka Oblast occupies the Kamchatka Peninsula in the easternmost part of Russia and is, therefore, part of the Far Eastern Federal Okrug and the Far Eastern Economic Area. The Peninsula, some 1,600 km (1,000 miles) in length and 130 km (80 miles) in width, separates the Sea of Okhotsk, in the west, from the Bering Sea, in the east. The Oblast also includes the Karaginskiye and Komandorskiye (Commander) Islands and the southernmost part of the Chukhotka Peninsula. In the latter area there are land borders with other Russian federal territories, the Chukchi Autonomous Okrug (AOk) to the north and Magadan Oblast to the west. This part of the Oblast, together with the northern section of the Kamchatka Peninsula, comprises the Koryak AOk. The region is dominated by the Sredinnyi Khrebet mountain range, which is bounded to the west by a broad, poorly drained coastal plain, and to the east by the Kamchatka river valley. The territory's other main river is the Avacha. Two-thirds of its area is mountainous (including the highest point in the Russian Far East, Mt Klyuchevskaya, at 4,685 m—15,961 feet) and it contains many hot springs. Kamchatka Oblast covers an area of 472,300 sq km (182,350 sq miles), including the autonomous okrug, but only 170,800 sq km (65,946 sq miles), excluding the Koryak AOk. The Oblast, excluding the AOk, is divided into seven administrative districts and four cities. There is a high annual rate of precipitation in the region, sometimes as much as 2,000 mm, and temperatures vary considerably according to region. The average temperature for January is –16.4°C, while that for July is 13.0°C. At 1 January 2002 the estimated total population in the region proper was 351,700 and the population density, therefore, was 2.1 per sq km. In 2001 an estimated 81.1% of the region's population inhabited urban areas. The Oblast's administrative centre is at Petropavlovsk-Kamchatskii, in the south-east, which was inhabited by 195,500 people.

## History

The Kamchatka Peninsula was first sighted in 1697 and was annexed by Russia during the 18th century. Petropavlovsk came under Russian control in 1743. After the Soviet Revolution Kamchatka was part of the short-lived Far Eastern Republic. A distinct Kamchatka Oblast was formed on 20 October 1923, but as part of Khabarovsk Krai until 23 January 1956.

Following the dissolution of the USSR in 1991, Kamchatka tended to be supportive of the federal Government. In the general election of December 1995, however, the most successful party was the liberal Yabloko, which obtained 20% of the votes cast in the Oblast (a higher proportion than the reformists obtained even in the great cities). This success was largely because the local candidate, Mikhail Zadornov, was a popular figure, who was subsequently appointed as the federal Minister of Finance in 1997. Yabloko repeated this success in the oblast legislative elections of December 1997, in which it won nine seats, coming second only to the Communist Party of the Russian Federation (CPRF), with 10. However, as the Oblast continued to suffer from economic and social hardship, support for the CPRF and left-wing supporters experienced a resurgence. At the gubernatorial election held in December 2000, the CPRF candidate, Mikhail Mashkovtsev, was elected Governor; the incumbent, Vladimir Biryukov, had declined to stand. A particular source of tension in the region in the early 2000s was the accumulation of debts by Petropavlovsk-Kamchatskii municipality (headed by Mayor Yurii Golenishchev) to energy companies, and the consequent disruption to power supplies in the oblast capital. In December 2002 the regional legislature voted to transfer control of the public utilities in the city from the municipal to the oblast authorities, following a month-long strike by municipality workers. However, it was reported in April 2003 that the oblast legislature was to sue the regional electricity company, following an increase in tariffs.

## Economy

The waters around Kamchatka Oblast (the Sea of Okhotsk, the Bering Sea and the Pacific Ocean) being extremely rich in marine life, fishing, especially of crabs, is the dominant sector of Kamchatka Oblast's economy, accounting for over 90% of its trade in the mid-1990s. The region's fish stocks comprise around one-half of Russia's total. All figures in this survey incorporate data for the Koryak AOk, which is also treated separately. In 1999 the Oblast's gross regional product (GRP) amounted to 15,462.2m. roubles, or 39,984.9 roubles per head. Petropavlovsk is one of two main industrial centres and ports in the territory, the other being Ust-Kamchatka. There is an international airport, Yelizovo, situated 30 km from Petropavlovsk-Kamchatskii. In 2000 there were 1,338 km of paved roads in the Oblast.

Apart from fishing, agriculture in Kamchatka Oblast consists of animal husbandry (livestock, reindeer, mostly in the Koryak AOk, and fur animals), poultry farming and hunting. Just 4.7% of the working population were employed in agriculture in 2000, when agricultural output amounted to 1,677m. roubles. There are deposits of gold, silver, natural gas, sulphur and other minerals in Kamchatka Oblast, which by the early 2000s had been explored and were in the process of development. The relatively limited industrial sector, which employed 26.8% of the work-force in 2000, is based on the processing of agricultural products and coal and electricity production. The first geothermal energy plant in Russia, at Mutnovo, commenced operations in October 2002; by 2003 the plant was expected to produce annual output of 50 MW, representing one quarter of the Oblast's energy requirements. Total industrial output was worth 15,565m. roubles in 2000.

The economically active population of Kamchatka Oblast numbered 226,000 in 2000, when 16.0% of the labour force were unemployed. Those in employment earned an average of 8,177.6 roubles per month in mid-2002, a relatively high wage compared with the rest of the Russian Federation, but one balanced by the high cost of living in the Oblast. (In that year the cost of a 'consumer basket' of foodstuffs in Petropavlovsk-Kamchatskii was the second highest in the federation, behind Anadyr, the capital of the remote Chukot AOk.) Moreover, wages arrears prompted municipal workers in Petropavlovsk-Kamchatskii to observe a widespread strike from late November. There was a budgetary deficit of 267.5m. roubles in 2000. Foreign investment in the Oblast amounted to US $29.4m. in that year, although international trade was limited, amounting to just $122.5m. in exports and $29.6m. in imports. With trade dominated by the fishing industry, one of the Oblast's main foreign markets was Japan. At 31 December 2000 there were 2,000 small businesses registered in the region.

## Directory

**Governor:** MIKHAIL B. MASHKOVTSEV; 683040 Kamchatka obl., Petropavlovsk-Kamchatskii, pl. Lenina 1; tel. (4152) 11-20-96; fax (4152) 11-20-96; e-mail kra@svyaz.kamchatka.su.

**Chairman of the Legislative Assembly:** NIKOLAI YA. TOKOMANTSEV; 683040 Kamchatka obl., Petropavlovsk-Kamchatskii, pl. Lenina 1; tel. (4152) 11-27-61; fax (4152) 11-26-95.

**Chief Representative of Kamchatka Oblast in the Russian Federation:** MIKHAIL M. SITNIKOV; 119002 Moscow, Denezhnyi per. 12/16; tel. (095) 241-03-13; fax (095) 241-35-46.

**Head of Petropavlovsk-Kamchatskii City Administration:** YURII I. GOLENISHCHEV; 683040 Kamchatka obl., Petropavlovsk-Kamchatskii, ul. Leninskaya 14; tel. (41522) 2-49-13; e-mail citiadm@svyaz.kamchatka.su.

# Kemerovo Oblast

Kemerovo Oblast, also known as the Kuzbass, is situated in southern central Russia and forms part of the Siberian Federal Okrug and the West Siberian Economic Area. Krasnoyarsk Krai and the Republic of Khakasiya lie to the east, Tomsk to the north, Novosibirsk to the west and the Altai Krai and the Republic of Altai to the south-west. The region lies in the Kuznetsk basin, the area surrounding its main river, the Tom. The territory of the Oblast occupies 95,500 sq km (36,870 sq miles) and is divided into 19 administrative districts and 20 cities. At 1 January 2002 the total population was 2,940,500 and the population density in the region was 30.8 per sq km. Some 86.7% of the population inhabited urban areas in 2001. The region's administrative centre is at Kemerovo, which had a population of 487,200 at that time. Other major cities are Novokuznetsk (564,500), Prokopevsk (231,200), Leninsk-Kuznetskii (111,600), Kiselevsk (108,200) and Mezhdurechensk (105,300).

## History

Kemerovo (formerly Shcheglovsk) was founded in 1918 and became the administrative centre of the Oblast at its formation on 26 January 1943. The city is at the centre of Russia's principal coal-mining area. In July 1997 the Governor, Mikhail Kislyuk, a former head of the Kuzbass coal workers, was dismissed by President Boris Yeltsin, as the result of a dispute over unpaid pensions arrears. Kislyuk had earned criticism, as had the federal authorities, for refusing to schedule elections to a new Duma (to replace the bicameral Regional Assembly—elected in March 1994, its activities were suspended in 1995).

In the December 1995 federal general election, the Communist Party of the Russian Federation won 48% of the regional votes cast, its second highest proportion in any constituent unit of the Federation. Much of this support was secured because of the popular leadership of Amangeldy Tuleyev, speaker of the suspended local assembly. Tuleyev contested the federal presidency in 1991, 1996 and 2000, and spent 11 months in 1996–97 as the Minister for Co-operation with Members of the CIS. Having been appointed Governor by Yeltsin, following the removal of Kislyuk, Tuleyev's position was confirmed by an overwhelming victory in popular elections to the post in October 1997. (He received 94.6% of the votes cast.) In May 1998 widespread industrial action by coal-miners over wage arrears threatened to bring the regional administration into direct confrontation with the federal Government. The workers blockaded a section of the Trans-Siberian Railway, seriously affecting rail transportation throughout the country, and the strike did not end until late July. At this time Tuleyev's administration signed a framework agreement with the federal Government on the delimitation of powers, and accompanied by 10 accords aimed at strengthening the economy of the region. Despite the economic situation, Tuleyev was widely considered to be Russia's most popular regional leader and, when he stood for the presidency of the Russian Federation in March 2000, Tuleyev received 51.6% of the votes cast in Kemerovo Oblast, more than twice the number of votes cast there for Vladimir Putin. In January 2001 Tuleyev announced his resignation, thus bringing forward the gubernatorial election to April of that year, several months earlier than previously scheduled. His opponents criticized this decision as a tactic to ensure his re-election, as the Governor had widespread popular support at that time. In the election, held on 22 April, Tuleyev received 93.5% of the votes cast. In March 2003 Tuleyev was appointed to the Supreme Council of the generally pro-Government Unity and Fatherland-United Russia party (UF-UR). Supporters of Tuleyev, comprising the oblast organizations of the UF-UR and the People's Party of the Russian Federation, united in the 'I Serve the Kuzbass!' (Sluzhu Kuzbassu!) electoral bloc, won an overwhelming majority in oblast legislative and municipal elections held on 20 April 2003; the bloc obtained 34 seats in the 35-member legislature, and obtained control of 11 of 12 municipalities where elections were held. Moreover, at the end of May federal President Vladimir Putin appointed Tuleyev to serve for a six-month term of office on the rotating presidium of the consultative State Council.

## Economy

The economy of Kemerovo Oblast is based on industry. It is rich in mineral resources and contains the Kuzbass basin, one of the major coal reserves of the world. The region produced over 35% of Russia's coal in the late 1990s, but intensive mining in the Soviet period had resulted in severe environmental degradation. In 1999 Kemerovo's gross regional product amounted to 68,975.4m. roubles, equivalent to 23,011.0 roubles per head. The Oblast's main industrial centres are at Kemerovo, Novokuznetsk, Prokopevsk, Kiselevsk and Leninsk-Kuznetskii. In 2000 the region had 1,728 km (1,074 miles) of railway track and 5,635 km of paved roads on its territory.

Kemerovo Oblast's agriculture, which employed just 5.5% of the work-force in 2000, consists mainly of vegetable production, animal husbandry, bee-keeping and fur-animal hunting. The value of agricultural output in 2000 was 9,614m. roubles. In the mid-1990s reserves of coal to a depth of 1,800 m (5,900 feet) were estimated at 733,400m. metric tons. In the same period deposits of iron ore were estimated at 5,250m. tons. Production of complex ores, ferrous and non-ferrous metallurgy, chemicals, mechanical engineering, metalworking and food-processing are also important industries in the region. The industrial sector as a whole employed 31.7% of the working population in 2000 and generated 103,511m. roubles.

The economically active population numbered 1,475,000 in 2000, when 10.4% of the labour force were unemployed. The average monthly wage was 4,345.0 roubles in mid-2002. The 2000 regional budget registered a surplus of 401.9m. roubles. In that year export trade totalled US $1,854.7m., and imports were worth $169.0m. From the mid-1990s foreign investors showed some interest in exploiting the region's coal reserves. Total foreign investment in the Oblast in 2000 amounted to $5.1m. By 1995 some 61% of employees were working in the private sector. In the late 1990s the regional Government aimed to promote small businesses, of which there were 11,700 registered at 31 December 2000.

## Directory

**Head of the Regional Administration (Governor):** AMANGELDY M. TULEYEV; 650099 Kemerovo, pr. Sovetskii 62; tel. (3842) 36-43-33;

fax (3842) 36-34-09; e-mail postmaster@ako.kemerovo.su; internet www.kemerovo.su.

**Chairman of the Regional Council of People's Deputies:** GENNADII T. DYUDYAYEV; 650099 Kemerovo, pr. Sovetskii 58; tel. (3842) 58-41-42; fax (3842) 58-54-51.

**Chief Representative of Kemerovo Oblast in the Russian Federation:** SERGEI V. SHATIROV; 115184 Moscow, ul. B. Tatarskaya 5/14/9; tel. and fax (095) 953-54-89.

**Head of Kemerovo City Administration (Mayor):** VLADIMIR V. MIKHAILOV; 650099 Kemerovo, pr. Sovetskii 54; tel. (3842) 36-46-10; fax (3842) 58-18-91; e-mail sityadm@kuzbass.net; internet kemerovo.rosemis.ru.

# Kirov Oblast

Kirov Oblast is situated in the east of the Eastern European Plain. It forms part of the Volga Federal Okrug and the Volga-Vyatka Economic Area. It is bordered by Archangel and Komi to the north, the Komi-Permyak AOk (part of Perm Oblast) and Udmurtiya to the east, Tatarstan and Marii-El to the south, and Nizhnii Novgorod, Kostroma and Vologda to the west. Its main rivers are the Kama and the Vyatka; in addition there are almost 20,000 rivers and more than 1,000 lakes on its territory. Kirov occupies a total area of 120,800 sq km (46,640 sq miles) and measures 570 km (354 miles) from south to north and 440 km from west to east. It is divided into 39 administrative districts and 18 cities. The total population at 1 January 2002 was 1,560,000 and the population density was 12.9 per sq km. Around 71.0% of the population inhabited urban areas in 2001. At the census of 1989 ethnic Russians comprised 90.4% of the population. The Oblast's administrative centre is at Kirov (Vyatka), a river-port, which had 466,300 inhabitants in 2001.

## History

The city of Khlynov was founded in 1181 as an outpost of Novgorod, and came under Muscovite rule in 1489. The city was renamed Vyatka in 1780, and Kirov in 1934, when Kirov Oblast was formed. In September 1993 a draft constitution for Kirov Oblast was prepared, which referred to the Oblast as Vyatka Krai and provided for a universally elected governor and a new legislature, a provincial duma. On 18 October the Kirov Regional Soviet voted to disband itself. The federal authorities refused to acknowledge the area's redesignation and during 1994 a Regional Duma was elected. The most popular party in the mid-1990s was that of the nationalist supporters of Vladimir Zhirinovskii, although members of the old communist establishment were well represented in its ranks. The Communist Party of the Russian Federation candidate, Vladimir Sergeyenkov, was elected as Governor, by a narrow margin, in October 1996. In October 1997 Sergeyenkov signed a power-sharing treaty with federal President Boris Yeltsin, with the specific hope that investment in the extraction of raw materials and health care would benefit the region. Sergeyenkov was re-elected, with 58% of the votes cast, on 26 March 2000, in elections that had been brought forward by seven months to coincide with those to the federal presidency. In May 2003 the Oblast was named as one of the three federal subjects with the worst record on wage arrears. In mid-August it was reported that gubernatorial elections were again to be brought forward, to 7 December, concurrently with elections to the federal State Duma.

## Economy

In 1999 the Oblast's gross regional product (GRP) stood at 28,543.1m. roubles, equivalent to 17,886.4 roubles per head. Its main industrial centres are at Kirov, Slobodskoi, Kotelnich, Omutninsk, Kirovo-Chepetsk and Vyatskiye Polyany. In 2000 there were 1,098 km of railway track in the region, 8,915 km of paved roads and over 2,000 km of navigable waterways on the Vyatka river. Owing to the density of rivers in the region its soil is high in mineral salts, reducing its fertility.

The Oblast's agriculture, which employed 17.3% of the working population in 2000, consists mainly of animal husbandry and the production of grain, flax and vegetables. Total output within the sector amounted to 11,752m. roubles in 2000. Kirov Oblast has significant deposits of peat, estimated at 435m. metric tons, and phosphorites, reserves of which amounted to some 2,000m. tons in the mid-1990s. Its main industries are mechanical engineering, the production of electrical energy, metal-working, ferrous and non-ferrous metallurgy, chemicals, the processing of agricultural and forestry products and light manufacturing. In March 1998 the regional administration signed a protocol with the federal ministries of defence and the economy on the restructuring of the Oblast's military-industrial complex, which in 1997 accounted for just one-

10th of the Oblast's GRP, despite owning 58% of its main assets. The region was also renowned for the manufacturing of toys and wood products (especially skis). Industry employed 27.2% of the work-force in 2000 and generated 32,858m. roubles.

The economically active population numbered 844,000 in 2000, when 8.2% of the Oblast's labour force were unemployed, one of the lowest levels recorded in any federal subject. The average monthly wage was 3,105.2 roubles at mid-2002. In 2000 the Oblast recorded a budgetary deficit of 187m. roubles. In the late 1990s exports, the value of which amounted to US $387.8m. in 2000, largely comprised chemical and petrochemical goods, while imports (worth $31.6m. in 2000) were dominated by automobiles and equipment and food products. In 2000 foreign investment amounted to $14.7m. In late 2000 there were 3,900 small businesses registered in Kirov Oblast.

## Directory

**Head of the Regional Administration (Governor):** VLADIMIR N. SERGEYENKOV; 610019 Kirov, ul. K. Libknekhta 69; tel. (8332) 62-95-64; fax (8332) 62-89-58; e-mail region@gov-vyatka.ru; internet gov-vyatka.ru.

**Chairman of the Regional Duma:** ALEKSANDR N. STRELNIKOV; 610019 Kirov, ul. K. Libknekhta 69; tel. and fax (8332) 62-48-00; e-mail assembly@gov-vyatka.ru.

**Representation of Kirov Oblast in the Russian Federation:** 109028 Moscow, ul. Zemlyanoi Val 50/2; tel. (095) 916-69-42; e-mail kirovmos@rol.ru.

**Head of Kirov City Administration:** VASILII A. KISELEV; 610000 Kirov, ul. Vorovskogo 39; tel. (8332) 62-89-40; fax (8332) 67-69-91.

# Kostroma Oblast

Kostroma Oblast is situated in the central part of the Eastern European Plain. It forms part of the Central Federal Okrug and the Central Economic Area. It is bordered by Vologda Oblast to the north, Kirov Oblast to the east, Nizhnii Novgorod and Ivanovo Oblasts to the south and Yaroslavl Oblast to the west. Its main rivers are the Volga, the Kostroma, the Unzha, the Vokhma and the Vetluga. It has two major lakes—the Galichskoye and the Chukh-lomskoye. The total area of Kostroma Oblast is 60,100 sq km (23,200 sq miles), almost three-quarters of which is forested. It is divided into 24 administrative districts and 12 cities. The region had an estimated population of 776,400 at 1 January 2002, giving a pop-ulation density of 12.9 per sq km. In 2001 some 66.1% of the population inhabited urban areas. The Oblast's administrative centre is at Kostroma, a river-port situated on both banks of the Volga, and a popular tourist resort as part of the 'Golden Ring', which had 287,000 inhabitants in 2001.

## History

The city of Kostroma was founded in the 12th century. Kostroma Oblast was formed on 13 August 1944. The region remained loyal to the communist *nomenklatura* in the 1990s—its oblast Soviet sup-ported the federal parliament in its 1993 defiance of the Russian President, Boris Yeltsin, and was replaced by a new representative body, the Duma, in 1994. The Communist Party of the Russian Federation (CPRF) was the predominant party in this body, and the CPRF candidate, Viktor Shershunov, was elected as Governor in December 1996 (although Yeltsin had been the preferred candidate in the Oblast, in the presidential election held earlier that year). Shershunov was re-elected to serve a further term of office in December 2000.

## Economy

In 1999 gross regional product in Kostroma Oblast amounted to 14,286.9m. roubles, or 18,098.5 roubles per head. The Oblast's main industrial centres are at Kostroma, Sharya, Nerekhta, Galich, Bui, Manturovo and Krasnoye-on-Volga (Krasnoye-na-Volge). The region has major road and rail networks—in 2000 there were 640 km (398 miles) of railways in use on its territory and 5,507 km of paved roads. There were 985 km of navigable waterways in 1998.

Agriculture in Kostroma Oblast, which employed 10.4% of the work-force in 2000, consists mainly of production of grain, flax (the region is one of Russia's major producers of linen) and vegetables, and animal husbandry. Total agricultural output in 2000 was worth 5,437m. roubles. Severe weather conditions in mid-2003 caused severe disruption to the regional harvest. The region has an energy surplus, exporting some four-fifths of electrical energy produced. Electricity generation comprised 29.9% of total industrial produc-tion in Kostroma Oblast in 2000. The other main industries in the region are light manufacturing, wood-working, mechanical engi-

neering, food- and timber-processing and handicrafts (especially jewellery). The territory is also an important military centre, with numerous rocket silos, of which 23 had been converted to agricul-tural use by early 1996, with plans to recultivate a further 20. Some 24.2% of the Oblast's working population was engaged in industry in 2000, when industrial production amounted to a value of 13,305m. roubles.

The economically active population numbered 387,000 in 2000, when 8.6% of the labour force of the region were unemployed. The average wage in the Oblast was 3,164.1 roubles per month in mid-2002. There was a budgetary deficit of some 36.2m. roubles in 2000. In that year external trade comprised US $69.8m. of exports and $19.3m. of imports, one of the lowest levels in the Central Federal Okrug. Foreign investment totalled $4.7m. At 31 December 2000 there were 3,200 small businesses registered in the Oblast.

## Directory

**Head of the Regional Administration (Governor):** VIKTOR A. SHERSHUNOV; 156001 Kostroma, ul. Dzerzhinskogo 15; tel. (0942) 31-34-72; fax (0942) 31-33-95; e-mail shershunov@kos-obl.kmtn.ru; internet www.region.kostroma.net.

**Chairman of the Regional Duma:** VALERII P. IZHITSKII; 156000 Kostroma, Sovetskaya pl. 2; tel. (0942) 31-62-52; fax (0942) 31-21-73; e-mail info@kosoblduma.ru; internet www.kosoblduma.ru.

**Chief Representative of Kostroma Oblast in the Russian Federation:** GALINA M. PSHENITSYNA; 127025 Moscow, ul. Novyi Arbat 19/1811; tel. (095) 203-42-44; fax (095) 203-41-69.

**Head of Kostroma City Administration:** (vacant); 156000 Kos-troma, pl. Sovetskaya 1; tel. (0942) 31-44-40; fax (0942) 31-39-32.

# Kurgan Oblast

Kurgan Oblast is situated in the south of the Western Siberian Plain. It forms part of the Urals Federal District and the Urals Economic Area. Chelyabinsk Oblast lies to the west, Sverdlovsk Oblast to the north and Tyumen Oblast to the north-east. There is an international border with Kazakhstan to the south. The main rivers flowing through Kurgan Oblast are the Tobol and the Iset and there are numerous lakes (more than 2,500) in the south-east of the region. The Oblast occupies 71,000 sq km (27,400 sq miles) and measures 290 km (180 miles) from south to north and 430 km from east to west. It is divided into 24 administrative districts and nine cities, and had an estimated population of 1,074,400 at 1 January 2002, giving a population density of 15.1 per sq km. In 2001 some 55.3% of the population inhabited urban areas, the lowest proportion of any region in the Urals Economic Area. Its administrative centre is at Kurgan, which had a population of 359,700 in 2001.

## History

The city of Kurgan was founded as a tax-exempt settlement in 1553, on the edge of Russian territory. Kurgan Oblast was formed on 6 February 1943. The Communist Party of the Russian Federation (CPRF) was the largest party in the Regional Duma elected on 12 December 1993, and remained the most popular party in the Oblast at elections to the State Duma in 1995. The CPRF candidate, Oleg Bogomolov, hitherto speaker of the Regional Duma, was elected as Governor in late 1996, running unopposed in the second round of the election after his opponent stood down. Bogomolov was re-elected in December 2000. The agricultural policies of the federal Government were a focus for political protest in Kurgan in the early 2000s, as a result of the increasing economic difficulties faced by farmers in the Oblast. Concern was also expressed about the economic viability of Kurgan Oblast as a political entity, giving rise to suggestions that the region be merged with one or more of its neighbours, although by mid-2003 no definite proposals had been established to that end.

## Economy

Kurgan Oblast, with its fertile soil and warm, moist climate, is the agricultural base of the Urals area, producing around one-10th of the region's grain, meat and milk. In 1999 its gross regional product amounted to 15,424.2m. roubles, equivalent to 14,016.9 roubles per head. Its main industrial centres are at Kurgan, a river-port in the south-east of the region, and Shadrinsk. In 2000 there were 748 km of railways and 6,393 km of paved roads on the Oblast's territory. The Trans-Siberian Railway passes through the Oblast, as do sev-eral major petroleum and natural gas pipelines.

The Oblast's important agricultural sector employed 28.5% of the work-force in 2000 and consists mainly of grain production and animal husbandry. Total agricultural production in the region was worth 7,896m. roubles in 2000. Its main industries are mechanical engineering, metal-working, chemicals, electricity production, manufacturing of building materials, and food-processing. The industrial sector employed 18.9% of the working population and generated 14,774m. roubles in 2000.

The economically active population numbered 529,000 in 2000. The rate of unemployment increased from the late 1990s, reaching 13.2% of the labour force by 2000. Those in employment earned, on average, 3,030.1 roubles per month in mid-2002. There was a budgetary deficit of 142.7m. roubles in 2000, when foreign investment totalled US $582,000. In 2000 external trade amounted to a value of $183.9m., while imports totalled $68.1m. The economic situation of the region deteriorated markedly from the late 1990s, and in mid-2002 it was reported that up to 60% of the Oblast's budget comprised transfers from the federal Government, and that around 60% of the region's population lived in conditions of, or approaching, poverty. In late 2000 there were 2,900 small businesses registered in the Oblast.

## Directory

**Head of the Regional Administration (Governor):** OLEG A. BOGOMOLOV; 640024 Kurgan, ul. Gogolya 56; tel. (3522) 41-70-30; fax (3522) 41-71-32; e-mail kurgan@admobl.kurgan.ru; internet www.admobl.kurgan.ru.

**Chairman of the Regional Duma:** VALERII Z. PONOMAREV; 640024 Kurgan, ul. Gogolya 56; tel. (3522) 41-72-17; fax (3522) 41-88-91.

**Chief Representative of Kurgan Oblast in the Russian Federation:** OLEG YE. PANTELEYEV; 103798 Moscow, ul. M. Dmitrovka 3; tel. (095) 200-39-78; fax (095) 299-33-67.

**Head of Kurgan City Administration (Mayor):** ANATOLII F. YELCHANINOV; 640000 Kurgan, pl. Lenina; tel. (3522) 46-22-25; fax (3522) 41-70-40; e-mail inform@munic.kurgan.ru; internet www.munic.kurgan.ru.

# Kursk Oblast

Kursk Oblast is situated within the Central Russian Highlands. It forms part of the Central Federal Okrug and the Central Chernozem Economic Area. An international boundary with Ukraine lies to the south-west, with neighbouring Russian federal territories consisting of Bryansk in the north-west, Orel and Lipetsk in the north, Voronezh in the east and Belgorod in the south. Its main river is the Seim. The Oblast measures 171 km (106 miles) from south to north and 305 km from west to east. It occupies 29,800 sq km (11,500 sq miles) and is divided into 28 administrative districts and 10 cities. It had a population of 1,284,500 in 2002, when its population density was 43.1 per sq km. In 2001 some 61.6% of the population inhabited urban areas. The Oblast's administrative centre is at Kursk, which had 437,400 inhabitants at 1 January 2001.

## History

The city of Kursk, one of the most ancient in Russia, was founded in 1032 and became famous for its nightingales and Antonovka apples. The region was the scene of an army mutiny in 1905 and, in 1943, of a decisive battle against German forces during the Second World War. Kursk Oblast was formed on 13 July 1934, and was regarded as part of the communist-supporting 'red belt' in the 1990s and early 2000s. The Communist Party of the Russian Federation (CPRF) dominated the regional assembly, a Duma, elected in 1994, and in its successors, elected in 1996 and 2001. The former federal Vice-President, Aleksandr Rutskoi, a noted opponent of liberal reforms, was elected regional Governor on 20 October 1996. However, he was prevented from standing as a candidate in the election of 22 October 2000, one day before the election, owing to a legal technicality. In a second round of voting on 5 November, the CPRF candidate, Aleksandr Mikhailov, defeated the pro-Government, former Federal Security Service (FSB) General, Viktor Surzhikov. Immediately after being elected, Mikhailov provoked controversy by making a number of anti-Semitic remarks, prompting Rutskoi (who had a Jewish mother) to threaten to take legal action. (Surgikov was elected as Mayor of Kursk city in September 2003.) Following the success of a scheme established by Belgorod Oblast (see above) with Kharkiv (Kharkov) Oblast in Ukraine to promote cross-border trade, in November 2001 the Kursk Oblast authorities signed a trade agreement with the neighbouring Sumy Oblast, in Ukraine; by the following year it was reported that cross-border merchandise trade had increased by 500%. In October 2003 it was reported that the federal Ministry of Internal Affairs was to issue criminal charges against Rutskoi for alleged abuse of office as Governor of Kursk, although Rutskoi denied the accusations.

## Economy

Kursk Oblast's gross regional product stood at 25,351.6m. roubles in 1999, equivalent to 19,182.5 roubles per head. Its main industrial centres are at Kursk and Zheleznogorsk. In 2000 there were 1,067 km of railway lines and 6,055 km of paved roads on the Oblast's territory.

The region's agriculture, which employed 24.6% of the working population in 2000, consists mainly of sugar beet and grain production, horticulture and animal husbandry. Total agricultural production in 2000 amounted to a value of 13,753m. roubles. The territory contains a major iron-ore basin, with significant deposits of Kursk magnetic anomaly. Kursk Oblast's main industries were the production of electricity, production and enrichment of iron ores, mechanical engineering, electro-technical products and chemicals, and timber- and food-processing. Some 21.2% of the work-force were engaged in industry in 2000, when the sector's output was worth 26,109m. roubles.

The economically active population in Kursk Oblast numbered 650,000 in 2000, when 10.4% of the labour force were unemployed, compared with 6.1% in 1995. The average monthly wage in the region was 2,719.0 roubles in mid-2002. In 2000 there was a budgetary deficit of 113.7m. roubles. From the mid-1990s the Oblast's main foreign trading partners were Poland and the Czech Republic, although it also had economic links with other European countries, North America, India and Turkey, and was undertaking measures that would, it was hoped, facilitate greater cross-border trade with Ukraine (see above). Its principal exports comprised iron ore and concentrate, automobiles and machinery. In 2000 the total value of external trade was US $111.1m., of which imports accounted for $179.9m. Foreign investment in that year amounted to $7.5m. At 31 December 2000 some 2,800 small businesses were registered in the Oblast.

## Directory

**Head of the Regional Administration (Governor):** ALEKSANDR N. MIKHAILOV; 305002 Kursk, Krasnaya pl., Dom Sovetov; tel. (07122) 2-62-62; fax (0712) 56-65-73; e-mail intercom@region.kursk.ru; internet www.region.kursk.ru.

**Chairman of the Regional Duma:** ALEKSANDR N. ANPILOV; 305001 Kursk, ul. S. Perovskoi 24; tel. (0712) 56-09-91; fax (0712) 56-20-06; e-mail oblduma@kursknet.ru; internet oblduma.kursknet.ru.

**Representation of Kursk Oblast in the Russian Federation:** Moscow; tel. (095) 917-08-69.

**Head of Kursk City Administration:** VIKTOR SURZHIKOV; 305000 Kursk, ul. Lenina 1; tel. (07122) 2-63-63; fax (07122) 2-43-16; e-mail kursk@pub.sovest.ru; internet www.kurskadmin.ru.

# Leningrad Oblast

Leningrad Oblast is situated in the north-west of the Eastern European Plain. It lies on the Gulf of Finland, an inlet of the Baltic Sea, and forms part of the North-Western Federal Okrug and the North-Western Economic Area. The Republic of Kareliya (Karelia) lies to the north and the oblasts of Volodga to the east and Novgorod and Pskov to the south. There is an international border with Estonia to the west and with Finland to the north-west. Two-thirds of the Oblast is forested and over one-10th is swampland. Its main rivers are the Neva, the Sayas, the Luga and the Vuoksa. Lake Ladoga, the largest lake in Europe, with a surface area of 17,800 sq km, forms a partial border with Kareliya, and the southern tip of Lake Onega (9,700 sq km) also lies within Leningrad Oblast. The Oblast, including St Petersburg city, occupies 85,900 sq km (33,166 sq miles) and is divided into 17 administrative districts and 31 cities. Its total population at 1 January 2002, excluding the St Petersburg city region, was 1,649,600, and in 2001 some 66.0% of the population of the Oblast inhabited urban areas. Its administrative centre is at St Petersburg, now a federal city in its own right. The largest cities within the Oblast proper are Gatchina (population 82,300) and Vyborg (79,200).

## History

The city of St Petersburg (known as Petrograd in 1914–24 and Leningrad until 1991) was built in 1703. Leningrad Oblast, which was formed on 1 August 1927 out of the territories of five regions (Cherepovets, Leningrad, Murmansk, Novgorod and Pskov), was heavily industrialized during the Soviet period, particularly during 1926–40. The region did not change its name when the city reverted to the name of St Petersburg in October 1991.

In mid-1996 an agreement delimiting the division of powers between the federal and regional governments was signed. Later that year gubernatorial elections were held, which were won by an independent candidate, Vladimir Gustov. On 24 September 1998 the federal President, Boris Yeltsin, approved a proposal to merge the Oblast with the federal city of St Petersburg, although any immediate implementation seemed unlikely. Gustov resigned to take up the position of Deputy Prime Minister in September 1998, and his replacement, Valerii Serdyukov, confirmed his position on 5 September 1999, by securing 30% of the votes cast in an election contested by 16 candidates. The power-sharing agreement signed by the federal and regional authorities in 1996 was annulled in April 2002. In February 2003 the regional legislature approved an extension to the gubernatorial term of office from four to five years, to take effect from the forthcoming elections. Serdyukov was re-elected as Governor on 21 September 2003, receiving 56.5% of the votes cast, according to preliminary figures. Gustov was the second-placed candidate, with around 25% of the votes.

Although little formal progress towards the eventual merging of Leningrad Oblast with St Petersburg had been made by 2003, the appointment in that year of Valentina Matviyenko, known to be an enthusiastic supporter of the proposal, as Presidential Representative in the North-Western Federal Okrug, and her subsequent election, in October, as the Governor of St Petersburg, was believed likely to result in a revival of measures intended to result in the practical implementation of the scheme.

## Economy

Leningrad Oblast's gross regional product amounted to 42,604.2m. roubles in 1999, equivalent to 23,395.9 roubles per head. Its main industrial centres are at St Petersburg, Vyborg (both major seaports), Sestroretsk and Kingisepp. A new port opened at Primorsk in December 2001, as part of the country's Baltic Pipeline System, to facilitate the transportation of petroleum. In 2000 the region contained 2,833 km (1,760 miles) of railway track, of which 1,352 km were electrified in 1999. In 2000 there were 10,498 km of paved roads.

The Oblast's agriculture, which employed 11.7% of the working population in 2000, consists mainly of animal husbandry and vegetable production. Total agricultural output was worth 14,857m. roubles in 2000. The region's timber reserves are estimated to cover 6.1m. ha (15m. acres). Its major industries are the processing of forestry and agricultural products, mechanical engineering, nonferrous metallurgy, chemicals and petrochemicals, petroleum-refining, the production of electrical energy, the production of building materials, bauxites, slate and peat. Some 25.4% of the Oblast's work-force was engaged in industry in 2000, when industrial output amounted to a value of 56,951m. roubles.

The economically active population numbered 851,000 in 2000, when 9.7% of the labour force were unemployed—a relatively low figure compared with elsewhere in the Russian Federation, and a marked decrease compared with the figures recorded in 1998 and 1999, which had been in excess of 14%. The average monthly wage was 4,466.0 roubles in mid-2002. In 2000 the budget showed a surplus of 449.0m. roubles. The Oblast enjoys a relatively high level of external trade; in 2000 exports were worth US $2,098.6m., while imports amounted to $460.0m. Foreign investment amounted to $305.6m. in 2000, compared with $190.7m. in 1998. In 2002 the American Chamber of Commerce in Russia, which unites US business interests, named Leningrad Oblast its 'region of the year', and annual growth of some 35.6% was reported in 2002, the highest of any federal subject. At the end of 2000 there were 12,000 small businesses registered in Leningrad Oblast.

## Directory

**Head of the Regional Administration (Governor):** Valerii P. Serdyukov; 193311 St Petersburg, Suvorovskii pr. 67; tel. (812) 274-35-63; fax (812) 274-67-33; internet www.lenobl.ru.

**Chairman of the Regional Legislative Assembly:** Vitalii N. Klimov; 193311 St Petersburg, Suvorovskii pr. 67; tel. (812) 274-68-73; fax (812) 274-85-39; e-mail klimov@assemblylenobl.ru; internet www.assemblylenobl.ru.

**Chief Representative of Leningrad Oblast in the Russian Federation:** Aleksei I. Akulov; 121019 Moscow, ul. Novyi Arbat 15/1/1604; tel. (095) 291-33-55; e-mail plorf@mail.ru.

# Lipetsk Oblast

Lipetsk Oblast is situated within the Central Russian Highlands, some 508 km (315 m) south-east of Moscow. It forms part of the Central Federal Okrug and the Central Chernozem Economic Area. It is bordered by Voronezh and Kursk Oblasts to the south, Orel Oblast to the west, Tula Oblast to the north-west, Ryazan Oblast to the north and Tambov Oblast to the east. Its main rivers are the Don and the Voronezh. The Oblast occupies 24,100 sq km (9,300 sq miles) and is divided into 18 administrative districts and eight cities. It had an estimated population of 1,228,900 at 1 January 2002, when its population density was, therefore, 50.0 per sq km. In 2001 some 64.4% of the Oblast's population inhabited urban areas. Its administrative centre is at Lipetsk, which had a population of 519,200 in 2001. The Oblast's second largest city is Yelets (117,900).

## History

Lipetsk was founded in the 13th century and was later famed for containing one of Russia's oldest mud-bath resorts and spas. In the late tsarist and Soviet period the region became increasingly industrialized. Lipetsk Oblast was formed on 6 January 1954. By the 1990s it was considered part of the 'red belt' of support for the Communist Party of the Russian Federation (CPRF) across central Russia. Thus, in December 1992, when Lipetsk was one of eight territorial units permitted to hold gubernatorial elections (in an attempt to resolve the dispute between the head of the administration and the regional assembly), the incumbent, a supporter of the federal Government, was defeated by the CPRF candidate. In September 1993 both the Regional Soviet and the Governor, therefore, denounced the Russian President's dissolution of the federal parliament. Subsequently, the territory was obliged to comply with the directives of the federal Government. Legislative elections were held in the region on 6 March 1994, but were invalidated, owing to a low level of attendance. Further elections were held later that year. Political apathy also contributed to a relatively low level of support for the CPRF, in comparison to other 'red belt' regions, in the election to the State Duma held in December 1995 (29%). However, in the election to the federal presidency of March 2000, Lipetsk Oblast awarded the CPRF candidate, Gennadii Zyuganov, a higher proportion of the votes (47.4%) than did any other federal subject. On 12 April 1998 the Chairman of the Regional Council of Deputies (legislature), Oleg Korolev, won an overwhelming victory (some 79% of the votes cast) in the gubernatorial election. He was supported primarily by the CPRF, but also by the local branch of Yabloko and other political movements. Korolev, who was regarded as the candidate supported by the federal Government, was re-elected on 14 April 2002, with 73% of the votes cast, after his principal rival withdrew his candidacy.

## Economy

In 1999 Lipetsk Oblast's gross regional product totalled 31,923.6m. roubles, or 25,695.1 roubles per head. Its main industrial centres are at Lipetsk, Yelets, Dankov and Gryazi. In 2000 there were 752 km (467 miles) of railway lines and 5,157 km of paved roads on the Oblast's territory. Yelets and Gryazi contain the region's major railway junctions.

The region's agriculture consists mainly of animal husbandry, horticulture and the production of grain, sugar beet, makhorka tobacco and vegetables. Some 21.6% of the work-force was engaged in agriculture in 2000. Agricultural output in that year amounted to a value of 10,625m. roubles. The Oblast's main industries are ferrous metallurgy (which comprised 65% of the region's total industrial output in 2000), mechanical engineering, metal-working, electrotechnical industry, food-processing and the production of electricity. Novolipetsk MetKom (New Lipetsk Metallurgical Group), based in the region, is one of the country's major industrial companies. In 2000 the industrial sector employed 24.2% of the region's working population and generated 61,245m. roubles.

The economically active population totalled 603,000 in 2000, when 8.5% of the labour force were unemployed. Those in employment earned, on average, 3,475.2 roubles per month in mid-2002. In 2000 the regional budget recorded a surplus of 901.4m. roubles. In that year exports amounted to US $1,053.6m. and imports were worth $161.0m. Foreign investment amounted to $1.4m. in that year. At 31 December 2000 there were around 4,300 small businesses registered in the territory.

## Directory

**Head of the Regional Administration (Governor):** Oleg P. Korolev; 398014 Lipetsk, Sobornaya pl. 1; tel. (0742) 77-65-96; fax (0742) 72-24-26; e-mail office@admlr.lipetsk.ru; internet www.admlr.lipetsk.ru.

**Chairman of the Regional Council of Deputies:** Anatolii I. Savenkov; 398014 Lipetsk, Sobornaya pl. 1; tel. (0742) 74-35-08; fax (0742) 72-24-15.

**Representation of Lipetsk Oblast in the Russian Federation:** Moscow.

**Head of Lipetsk City Administration (Mayor):** MIKHAIL GULEV-SKII; 398600 Lipetsk, ul. Sovetskaya 22; tel. (0742) 77-66-17; fax (0742) 77-44-30.

# Magadan Oblast

Magadan Oblast is situated in the north-east of Russia and forms part of the Far Eastern Federal Okrug and the Far Eastern Economic Area. To the north-east, on the Chukotka Peninsula, lies the Chukot AOk, which, until 1992, formed part of Magadan Oblast. The rest of its border with territory on Chukotka is with the Koryak AOk (Kamchatka Oblast), which lies to the east. Magadan has a coastline on the Sea of Okhotsk in the south-east. Khabarovsk Krai lies to the south-west of the region and the Republic of Sakha (Yakutiya) to the north-west. Its main river is the Kolyma, which flows northwards and drains into the Arctic Ocean by way of Yakutiya. A considerable proportion of the territory of the region is mountainous, while the area around the Anadyr estuary is low marshland. Much of the Oblast is tundra or forest-tundra. The Oblast occupies a total area of 461,400 sq km (178,150 sq miles—much reduced from when it included the Chukot AOk). It is divided into six administrative districts and two cities. The climate in the region is severe, with winters lasting from six to over seven months. The average temperature in January is −29.4°C, while that in July is 14.4°C. The Oblast had an estimated population of 229,200 at 1 January 2002. It is one of the most sparsely populated regions, with a population density of just 0.5 per sq km. The majority of the population (91.1%) inhabited urban areas in 2001. Its administrative centre is at the only large city in the Oblast, Magadan, which had a population of 120,600 in 2001.

## History

Russians first reached the Magadan region in the mid-17th century. At the beginning of the Soviet period it was in the Far Eastern Republic, which in 1922 was reintegrated into Russia. The region held many penal establishments of the GULAG (State Corrective Camp) system established during the regime of Stalin—Iosif Dzhugashvili (1924–53). Magadan Oblast was formed on 3 December 1953, after the death of Stalin, although it then included the Chukot National Okrug. The successful rejection of Magadan's jurisdiction over the Chukot Autonomous Okrug (as it had by then become—acknowledged by the federal authorities in 1992) significantly reduced Magadan's territory. Deteriorating social conditions contributed to local feeling of remoteness and of neglect by the centre in the 1990s. Thus, in the elections to the State Duma held in December 1995, candidates of the nationalist Liberal Democratic Party of Russia secured 22% of the votes cast in the region and remained relatively popular there during the late 1990s. The gubernatorial election of 3 November 1996 was won by a gold-mine proprietor, Valentin Tsvetkov, who was backed by the communist-dominated Popular-Patriotic Union. In May 1999 a special economic zone was created in the Oblast, in the hope that investors would facilitate the exploitation of the region's rich natural resources. Tsvetkov was re-elected as Governor in November 2000; however in mid-October 2002 he was shot and killed in Moscow, in an apparent contract killing. He was succeeded, on an acting basis, by Nikolai Dudov, hitherto First Vice-Governor of the Oblast. Following the first round of gubernatorial elections, held on 2 February 2003 and contested by 12 candidates, Dudov, who received 26.0% of the votes cast, and Nikolai Karpenko, the Mayor of Magadan (who was supported by the pro-Government Unity and Fatherland-United Russia party), with 37.6%, proceeded to a second round, held on 16 February. In this poll Dudov obtained 50.4% of the votes cast, thereby being elected as Governor.

## Economy

Magadan Oblast is Russia's principal gold-producing region. Its gross regional product in 1999 amounted to 11,328.6m. roubles, equivalent to 47,941.5 roubles per head. The Oblast's main industrial centres are at Magadan and Susuman. Magadan and Nagayevo are its most important ports. There are no railways in the territory, but there are 2,231 km (1,386 miles) of paved roads. There is an international airport at Magadan.

The region's primary economic activities are fishing, animal husbandry and hunting. These and other agricultural activities, which employed 4.1% of the region's work-force, generated just 373m. roubles in 2000. Ore-mining is important: apart from gold, the region contains considerable reserves of silver, tin and wolfram (tungsten). It is also rich in peat and timber. In early 1998 the regional Government hired a prospecting company to explore off-shore petroleum deposits in the Sea of Okhotsk, in a zone thought to hold around 5,000m. metric tons of petroleum and natural gas. The

Kolyma river is an important source of hydroelectric energy. In 1997 the Pan American Silver Corporation of Canada purchased a 70% stake in local company ZAO Dukat, to reopen a defunct silver mine in the Oblast, which contained an estimated 477m. troy ounces of silver and 1m. troy ounces of gold. However, licensing and other bureaucratic obstacles delayed operations. Other industry includes food-processing, mechanical engineering and metal-working. In 2000 22.7% of the working population were engaged in industry, and industrial output amounted to 10,728m. roubles. Construction is a significant source of employment, engaging 10.6% of the labour force in 2000.

The economically active population of the Oblast numbered 144,000 in 2000, when 10.8% of the labour force were unemployed, a reduction of almost one-half compared with the previous year. The average monthly wage was some 7,101.1 roubles in mid-2002, one of the highest figures in the Federation, although the region was also among those with the highest cost of living. In 2000 the budget recorded a deficit of 192.3m. roubles, and throughout the 1990s persistent deficit problems, not helped by high wages, led to continuing problems with payment arrears. The value of external trade was relatively low; in 2000 exports were worth only US $3.8m., while imports amounted to $41.3m. Foreign investment in the Oblast amounted to $27.7m. in 2000. At 31 December 2000 there were 2,900 small businesses registered in the Oblast.

## Directory

**Governor:** NIKOLAI N. DUDOV; 685000 Magadan, ul. Gorkogo 6; tel. (41322) 2-31-34; fax (41322) 2-04-25; e-mail info@magadan.ru; internet www.magadan.ru.

**Chairman of the Regional Duma:** STANISLAV A. YELISEIKIN; 685000 Magadan, ul. Gorkogo 6; tel. (41322) 2-31-00; fax (41322) 2-55-12.

**Representation of Magadan Oblast in the Russian Federation:** 103025 Moscow, ul. Novyi Arbat 19; tel. (095) 203-92-74.

**Head of Magadan City Administration (Mayor):** NIKOLAI B. KARPENKO; 685000 Magadan, pl. Gorkogo 1; tel. (41300) 2-50-47; fax (41322) 2-49-40; e-mail admin@cityadm.magadan.ru; internet www.cityadm.magadan.ru.

# Moscow Oblast

Moscow Oblast is situated in the central part of the Eastern European Plain, at the Volga-Oka confluence. It forms part of the Central Federal Okrug and the Central Economic Area. Moscow is surrounded by seven other oblasts: Tver and Yaroslavl to the north, Vladimir and Ryazan to the east, Tula and Kaluga to the south-west and Smolensk to the west. Most of the region is forested and its main rivers are the Moskva and the Oka. The territory of the Oblast (including Moscow City) covers an area of 47,000 sq km (18,147 sq miles) and has 39 administrative districts and 75 cities. Its total population, excluding Moscow City, was estimated at 6,409,700 at 1 January 2002. Inhabitants of urban areas comprised around 80.2% of the region's total population in 2001. The Oblast's administrative centre is in Moscow City. Within the Oblast proper, there are several cities with a population of over 100,000 including (in order of size) Podolsk, Lyubertsy, Mytishchi, Kolomna, Elektrostal, Khimki and Korolyev.

## History

The city of Moscow was established in the mid-12th century and became the centre of a burgeoning Muscovite state. The region soon became an important trade route between the Baltic Sea in the north and the Black and Caspian Seas in the south. It first became industrialized in the early 18th century, with the development of the textiles industry, in particular the production of wool and cotton. The region and the city of Moscow were captured by the troops of Emperor Napoleon I of France in 1812, but the invaders were forced to retreat later that year. German invaders reached the Moscow region (which had been formed as Moscow Oblast on 14 January 1929) in 1941, and the Soviet Government was removed from the city until 1943. Between late 1941 and early 1942 the German forces were driven from the Oblast's territory. Otherwise, the region and the city have benefited from Moscow being the Soviet, and the Russian, capital.

As the seat of government, in the 1990s the federal executive could rely on a reasonable level of support in the Moscow region. The gubernatorial elections of December 1999–January 2000 were closely fought, with Col-Gen. Boris Gromov, an ally of Moscow City Mayor Yurii Luzhkov, and a former State Duma deputy and Deputy Minister of Defence, emerging the victor. Relative prosperity kept discontent to a minimum and the region did not experience the problems of wage arrears to the same extent as elsewhere in the

Federation. In mid-2003 proposals for the construction of the first toll motorway in Russia were announced by the Government of Moscow Oblast. In September it was announced that gubernatorial elections were to be held on 7 December, concurrently with elections to the federal State Duma.

## Economy

In 1999 Moscow Oblast's gross regional product (GRP) amounted to 160,034.6m. roubles, or 24,509.9 roubles per head. The main industrial centres are at Podolsk, Lyubertsy, Kolomna, Mytishchi, Odintsovo, Noginsk, Serpukhov, Orekhovo-Zuyevo, Shchelkovo and Sergiyev Posad (formerly Zagorsk). The latter city is an important centre of Russian Orthodoxy, containing Russia's foremost monastery and two medieval cathedrals. In 2000 there were 2,738 km (1,701 miles) of railways and 16,134 km of paved roads on the Oblast's territory.

Moscow Oblast's agriculture, which employed 8.6% of the region's work-force in 2000, consists mainly of animal husbandry and the production of vegetables and grain. Total agricultural production generated 25,326m. roubles in 2000. The Oblast's industry, in which some 24.3% of the working population were engaged in 2000, mainly comprised heavy industry. The region's major industries are mechanical engineering, radio electronics, chemicals, light manufacturing, textiles, ferrous and non-ferrous metallurgy, metalworking, the manufacture of building materials, wood-working and handicrafts (ceramics, painted and lacquered wooden ornaments). The region's military-industrial complex is also important. Industrial output was worth 137,537m. roubles in 2000.

The economically active population in the Oblast was 3,531,000 in 2000, when 7.4% of the labour force were unemployed. The average monthly wage was 4,741.7 roubles in mid-2002. In 2000 there was a regional budgetary surplus of 2,339.6m. roubles. The Oblast's external trade increased significantly during the late 1990s, and exports amounted to US $2,079.8m. in 2000, when imports were worth $2,109.3m. Total foreign investment in Moscow Oblast amounted to $290.6m. in 2000. In 1997 there was a total of 110 joint enterprises operating in the Oblast, of which 78 had foreign partners, particularly from Germany, Italy and the USA. In 2000 there were some 46,000 small businesses registered in the Oblast.

## Directory

**Governor:** Boris V. Gromov; 103070 Moscow, pl. Staraya 6; tel. (095) 206-60-93; fax (095) 206-61-23; e-mail amo@mosreg.ru; internet www.mosreg.ru.

**Chairman of the Regional Duma:** Viktor A. Akskakov; 103070 Moscow, pl. Staraya 6; tel. (095) 206-61-32; fax (095) 925-17-46.

**Representation of Moscow Oblast in the Russian Federation:** Moscow.

# Murmansk Oblast

Murmansk Oblast occupies the Kola Peninsula, which neighbours the Barents Sea to the north and the White Sea to the east. It forms part of the North-Western Federal Okrug and the Northern Economic Area. It has international borders with Norway and Finland to the west and the Russian federal subject of Kareliya (Karelia) lies to the south. Much of its territory lies within the Arctic Circle. The major rivers in the Oblast are the Ponoi, the Varguza, the Umba, the Kola, the Niva and the Tulona. It has several major lakes, including the Imandra, Umbozero and Lovozero. The territory of the Oblast covers an area of 144,900 sq km (55,930 sq miles), extending some 400 km (250 miles) from south to north and 500 km from west to east. The climate in the Oblast is severe and changeable, influenced by cold fronts from the Arctic and warm, moist weather from the Atlantic. Its total population was estimated at 977,600 at 1 January 2002, when it had a population density of 6.7 per sq km. In 2001 some 91.7% of the population inhabited urban areas. Murmansk Oblast is divided into five administrative districts and 16 cities. Its administrative centre is at the only large city in the region, Murmansk, a major seaport and tourist centre, which had a population of 370,700 in 2001.

## History

Murmansk city was founded in 1916, as a fishing port on the Barents Sea, and was known as Romanov-on-Murman (Romanov-na-Murmane) until the following year. After the Bolshevik Revolution of 1917 Murmansk region was a centre of anti-communist resistance until a peace treaty was signed with the Soviet Government on 13 March 1920. Murmansk Oblast was formed on 28 May 1938.

The development of industry in the region, particularly after the Second World War, resulted in a steady increase in population until the late 1950s. However, heavy industry, particularly the sulphurous emissions from the vast nickel-smelting works on the Kola Peninsula, were accused of causing major environmental damage by the neighbouring Nordic nations (agreement on the monitoring and limiting of this was achieved, to an extent, in mid-1996). The concentration of nuclear reactors on the Kola Peninsula, considered to be the world's most hazardous, is also a major source of concern—in July 2002 the European Union pledged considerable funds to improving atomic safety and environmental degradation in the region.

In the 1990s political allegiances in the Oblast as a whole were fairly evenly balanced, with both the reformist Yabloko movement and the nationalist Liberal Democrats receiving over 10% of the votes cast overall in the 1995 and, more unusually, the 1999 general elections, although disparity by area was immense. Yurii Yevdokimov, a candidate favoured by the former Chairman of the National Security Council, Gen. (retd) Aleksandr Lebed, was elected in the Oblast's first direct poll to the governorship, held in November 1996. A power-sharing agreement was signed between the federal and regional authorities in November 1997. On 26 March 2000 Yevdokimov was re-elected as Governor, at a second round of voting. On 21 March 2002 elections to the regional legislature were held.

## Economy

In 1999 Murmansk Oblast's gross regional product stood at 42,976.7m. roubles, or 43,332.0 roubles per head. The Oblast's principal industrial centres are at Murmansk, Monchegorsk, Kirovsk, Zapolyarnyi and Apatity. In 2000 there were 891 km of railway track in the region, with Murmansk, Apatity, Olenegorsk and Kandalaksha the main railway junctions, and 2,503 km of paved roads. The port at Murmansk is Russia's sole all-weather Northern port, through which some 12m. metric tons of cargo pass every year. This is also the base for the world's only nuclear ice-breaker fleet, the Northern Fleet, and the scene of the 'Kursk' submarine disaster in August 2000. There is an international airport at Murmansk, which operates flights to destinations in Finland, Norway and Sweden.

The Oblast's agricultural sector, which, owing to its extreme climate, employed just 2.0% of the work-force in 2000, consists mainly of fishing (the region produces 45% of the country's fish supplies) and animal husbandry. In 2000 agricultural production generated a total of 1,107m. roubles. The territory is rich in natural resources, including phosphates, iron ore and rare and non-ferrous metals. In 1985 the Shtokmanovsk gas-condensate deposit, the world's largest, was opened on the continental shelf of the Barents Sea. It was hoped that by 2005 the deposit would supply most of the north and north-west of the country. The region produces almost all of Russia's apatites, over 40% of its nickel, some 14% of its refined copper and about 11% of its concentrates of iron. Some 26.9% of the Oblast's working population were engaged in industry in 2000, when the industrial sector generated 48,585m. roubles. Its major industries are the production and enrichment of ores and ferrous metals, ore-mining, ferrous metallurgy, chemicals and petro-chemicals, the production of electricity and food-processing. In 1995 the UN Development Programme approved a project to strengthen the economy of the area and encourage sustainable development. In 1999 LUKoil, the domestic petroleum producer, signed an agreement with Governor Yevdokimov, which made Murmansk a base for exploration of the Barents Sea, in association with the natural gas producer, Gazprom. LUKoil also agreed to accept payment in barter, in addition to money, for supplies of petroleum to the region. In late November 2002 LUKoil and three other large-scale domestic petroleum companies, Tyumen Oil Co (TNK—now TNK-BP), Siberian Oil Co (Sibneft) and Yukos—which merged in late 2003, announced that they were to co-operate in the development of a deep-sea oil terminal in Murmansk, and connecting pipelines, at a projected cost of some US $4,500m., in an attempt to increase exports.

In 2000 the region's economically active population numbered some 583,000. Unemployment declined in the late 1990s, from 21.1% of the labour force in 1998, to 12.8% in 2000. In mid-2002 the average monthly wage in the Oblast was some 7,275.8 roubles, one of the highest in the Federation. The 2000 budget recorded a surplus of 104.6m. roubles. The Oblast's major exports are non-ferrous metals, fish products and apatite concentrate. In 2000 exports amounted to US $592.6m., and imports were worth $130.3m. Foreign investment totalled $44.0m. in 2000. The Kola Centre for Business Development, employing Russian and US specialists, opened in Murmansk in 1997. It holds annual conventions bringing together companies from across and outside the Barents Region. At 31 December 2000 there were 2,900 small businesses registered in the Oblast.

# Directory

**Head of the Regional Administration (Governor):** Yurii A. Yevdokimov; 183006 Murmansk, pr. Lenina 75; tel. (8152) 48-65-01; fax (8152) 45-10-04; e-mail evdokimov@murman.ru; internet gov.murman.ru.

**Chairman of the Regional Duma:** Pavel A. Sazhinov; 183016 Murmansk, ul. S. Perovskoi 2; tel. (8152) 45-36-72; fax (8152) 45-10-35; e-mail murduma@com.mels.ru.

**Chief Representative of Murmansk Oblast in the Russian Federation:** Petr I. Zelenov; 103851 Moscow, ul. B. Nikitskaya 12; tel. (095) 229-69-77; fax (095) 229-53-51.

**Head of Murmansk City Administration:** Gennadii G. Guryanov; 183006 Murmansk, pr. Lenina 75; tel. (8152) 45-81-60.

# Nizhnii Novgorod Oblast

Nizhnii Novgorod Oblast is situated on the middle reaches of the Volga river. It forms part of the Volga Federal Okrug and the Volga-Vyatka Economic Area. Mordoviya and Ryazan lie to the south, Vladimir and Ivanovo to the west, Kostroma to the north-west, Kirov to the north-east and Marii-El and Chuvashiya to the east. Its major rivers are the Volga, the Oka, the Sura and the Vetluga. The terrain in the north of the Oblast is mainly low lying, with numerous forests and extensive swampland. The southern part is characterized by fertile black soil (*chernozem*). The Oblast occupies a total area of 76,900 sq km (29,690 sq miles) and measures some 400 km (250 miles) from south to north and 300 km from east to west. It is divided into 48 administrative districts and 28 cities. At 1 January 2002 it had an estimated total population of 3,598,300 and a population density, therefore, of 46.8 per sq km. Some 78.2% of the Oblast's inhabitants resided in urban areas in 2001. Its administrative centre is at Nizhnii Novgorod (formerly Gorkii), which lies at the confluence of the Volga and Oka rivers. The city is Russia's fourth largest, with a population of 1,343,300 in 2001. Other major cities include Dzerzhinsk (formerly Chernorech—with an estimated population of 274,900 in 2001), Arzamas (109,600), Sarov (formerly Arzamas-16—84,900) and Pavlovo (69,600).

# History

Nizhnii Novgorod city was founded in 1221 on the borders of the Russian principalities. With the decline of Tatar power the city was absorbed by the Muscovite state. The Sarov Monastery, one of Russian Orthodoxy's most sacred sites, was founded in the region. Industrialization took place in the late tsarist period. In 1905 mass unrest occurred among peasants and workers in the region, which was one of the first areas of Russia to be seized by the Bolsheviks in late 1917. Nizhnii Novgorod Oblast was formed on 14 January 1929. In 1932–90 the city and region were named Gorkii, and for much of the time the city was 'closed', owing to the importance of the defence industry.

In 1991 the Russian President, Boris Yeltsin, appointed a leading local reformer, Boris Nemtsov, as Head of the Regional Administration (Governor). Nemtsov instituted a wide-ranging programme of economic reform, which was widely praised by liberals and by the federal Government. Nemtsov secured popular election in December 1995, and was a prominent advocate of democratization and decentralization in the Federation. In June 1996 Nemtsov signed a treaty on the delimitation of powers with the federal Government, giving the Oblast greater budgetary independence and more control over its public property. In April 1997 Nemtsov was appointed to the federal Government; gubernatorial elections were subsequently held, in which the pro-Government candidate, Ivan Sklyarov (former Mayor of Nizhnii Novgorod), defeated Gennadii Khodyrev (who was supported both by the Communist Party of the Russian Federation—CPRF and the nationalist Liberal Democrats) after a 'run-off' vote in July. The Oblast's economic situation subsequently deteriorated somewhat, and the federal Government withheld funds for the continuing conversion of the Oblast's defence industry. At the second round of gubernatorial elections held in July 2001, Khodyrev, by this time a CPRF deputy in the State Duma, was elected Governor, obtaining almost 60% of the votes cast. Following his election, Khodyrev suspended his membership of the CPRF, apparently in response to allegations that the federal Government was to transfer the administrative centre of the Volga Federal Okrug to another city in the event of the election of a communist governor. In mid-September the regional Legislative Assembly voted in favour of a proposal made by Khodyrev that he act both as Governor and as Prime Minister of the Oblast. In 2001 the city of Nizhnii Novgorod became the first area in Russia to implement proposals that permitted objectors to compulsory military service to perform an alternative, civilian service; however, in early 2002 President Putin criticized these measures, and several of those undertaking civilian service were subsequently inducted into the military. Elections to the regional Legislative Assembly in March 2002 resulted in the formation of a centre-right majority in the new chamber, including many representatives of business interests in the Oblast, with Unity and Fatherland-United Russia becoming the single largest party grouping. In April the power-sharing treaty agreed in 1996 was annulled. Khodyrev finally resigned from the CPRF in May 2002, in protest at the expulsion of State Duma Chairman Gennadii Seleznev from the party. (In September 2003 Khodyrev was chosen as the first-placed candidate on the Volga inter-regional list—covering the Republic of Marii-El, the Chuvash Republic and Nizhnii Novgorod—of the pro-Government Unity and Fatherland-United Russia party, in advance of elections to the federal State Duma, scheduled to be held on 7 December.) Meanwhile, considerable controversy arose nationally, as a result of the conduct of mayoral elections in Nizhnii Novgorod, held in two rounds, in September–October 2002; the favoured candidate of both the oblast and federal authorities, Vadim Bulavinov, narrowly won the election, defeating the incumbent, Yurii Lebedev. However, the disqualification of a popular candidate, Andrei Klimentiyev, prior to the first round, was believed to be a determining factor prompting more than 28% of eligible votes, in both rounds of voting, to be cast 'against all candidates'.

# Economy

In 1999 the Oblast's gross regional product amounted to 83,456.2m. roubles, or 22,741.4 roubles per head. Its principal industrial centres are at Nizhnii Novgorod, Dzerzhinsk and Arzamas. Nizhnii Novgorod contains a major river-port, from which it is possible to reach the Baltic, Black, White and Caspian Seas and the Sea of Azov. In 2000 there were 12,978 km of paved roads and 1,214 km of railway track in the region. In 1985 an underground railway system opened in Nizhnii Novgorod and in 1994 an international airport was opened, from which Lufthansa (of Germany) operates flights to the German city of Frankfurt. In late 1996 plans to extend the Second Trans-European Corridor to Nizhnii Novgorod were initiated by the Russian Government and the European Union.

Reform of the farming sector in the 1990s involved extensive privatization and investment in rural infrastructure. Agriculture in the region, which employed 7.7% of the working population in 2000, consists mainly of the production of grain, sugar beet, flax and onions and other vegetables, although the Oblast lacks many areas with the fertile black topsoil typical of the European Plain. Animal husbandry and poultry farming are also important. In 2000 total agricultural output was worth 15,212m. roubles. As one of the three most industrially developed regions in Russia, however, it was the Oblast's industry that provided some 80% of total production (industrial output generated 106,984m. roubles in 2000). The principal industries of the Oblast include the manufacture of automobiles, mechanical engineering, metal-working, ferrous metallurgy, chemicals, petrochemicals, the processing of agricultural and forestry products, the production of electricity and light manufacturing. The Italian automobile company, Fiat, announced a joint venture with the GAZ—Gorkii Automobile plant for the production, sale and servicing of three models of car in Nizhnii Novgorod by 2002. In 2000 some 30.3% of the working population was engaged in industry. During the Soviet period the region was developed as a major military-industrial centre, with the defence sector accounting for around three-quarters of the regional economy, and Gorkii became a 'closed' city. The Oblast also contains the secret city of Arzamas-16 (now Sarov), a centre of nuclear research. In the early 1990s much of Governor Nemtsov's reform programme was aimed at the conversion of as much of the industrial base to civilian use as possible, but this process was made increasingly difficult as federal funds became less readily available. Indeed, defence-industry production in the region increased by 130% in 1999 compared with the previous year, although, overall, the Oblast was among those that dealt most successfully with the transition from military to civilian industry.

The economically active population numbered 1,871,000 in 2000, when 7.5% of the labour force were unemployed. The average monthly wage in the Oblast was 3,403.5 roubles in mid-2002. The 2000 budget recorded a deficit of 1,267.6m. roubles. In 2000 external trade in the Oblast comprised US $861.8m. in exports and $321.2m. in imports. The Oblast exports principally to Belarus, Belgium, France, Kazakhstan, Switzerland and the United Kingdom, and imports goods from Austria, Belarus, the People's Republic of China, Germany, Kazakhstan, the Netherlands, Ukraine and the USA. In 1997 there were 1,153 joint-stock companies in the region, as well as 34 commercial banks and 35 insurance companies. Nizhnii Novgorod Oblast was the first Russian federal subject, other than the two federal cities, to issue Eurobonds, in 1997. In 2000 foreign investment in the region totalled $64.3m. Infrastructure for small-business development had resulted in the emergence of some 13,600 small businesses by the end of 2000.

## Directory

**Head of the Regional Administration (Governor and Prime Minister):** GENNADII M. KHODYREV; 603082 Nizhnii Novgorod, Kreml, kor. 1; tel. (8312) 39-13-30; fax (8312) 39-00-48; e-mail official@kreml.nnov.ru; internet www.government.nnov.ru.

**Chairman of the Legislative Assembly:** YEVGENII B. LYULIN; 603082 Nizhnii Novgorod, Kreml, kor. 2; tel. (8312) 39-05-38; fax (8312) 39-06-29; e-mail nnovg@duma.gov.ru.

**Representation of Nizhnii Novgorod Oblast in the Russian Federation:** Moscow; tel. (095) 203-77-41.

**Head of Nizhnii Novgorod City Administration (Mayor):** VADIM YE. BULAVINOV; 603082 Nizhnii Novgorod, Kreml, kor. 5; tel. (8312) 39-15-06; fax (8312) 39-13-02; e-mail lebedev@admgor.nnov.ru; internet www.admcity.nnov.ru.

# Novgorod Oblast

Novgorod Oblast is situated in the north-west of the Eastern European Plain, some 500 km (just over 300 miles) north-west of Moscow and 180 km south of St Petersburg. It forms part of the North-Western Federal Okrug and the North-Western Economic Area. Tver Oblast lies to the south-east, Pskov Oblast to the south-west and Leningrad and Vologda Oblasts to the north. The territory's major rivers are the Msta, the Lovat and the outlet of Lake Ilmen, the Volkhov. Just over two-fifths of its territory is forested (either taiga—forested marshland—or mixed forest). The region contains the Valdai state national park. Its territory covers an area of 55,300 sq km (21,350 sq miles) and extends 250 km from south to north and 385 km from west to east. It is divided into 21 administrative districts and 10 cities. At 1 January 2002 the population of the Oblast was estimated at 710,900 and its population density, therefore, was 12.9 per sq km. In 2001 the urban population was reckoned at 70.6% of the total. The region's administrative centre is at Great (Velikii) Novgorod, which lies on the River Volkhov, some 6 km from Lake Ilmen (it had a population of some 226,500 in 2001).

## History

One of the oldest Russian cities, Great Novgorod remained a powerful principality after the dissolution of Kievan Rus, and even after the Mongol incursions further to the south-west. In 1478 Ivan III ('the Great'), prince of Muscovy and the first Tsar of All Russia, destroyed the Republic of Novgorod, a polity sometimes used as evidence for the rather spurious claim of a democratic tradition in Russia. Its wealth and importance, based on trade, declined after the foundation of St Petersburg. Novgorod Oblast was formed on 5 July 1944.

In the mid-1990s the region displayed a relatively high level of support for reformists and the centrist supporters of the federal Government of President Boris Yeltsin. The Oblast was permitted gubernatorial elections in December 1995, which were won by the pro-Yeltsin incumbent, Mikhail Prusak. Prusak's administration was characterized by his policy of pragmatic compromise with regard to the economy, spreading the region's economic benefits as widely as possible. Similar policies prevailed in the Duma, the members of which did not bear allegiance to any national political party. Prusak was re-elected for a further term of office on 5 September 1999, with approximately 90% of the votes cast. He combined demands for regional governors to be appointed rather than elected, and even for the end of direct elections to the federal presidency, with support for the purported (historical) 'Novgorod model' of federalism, property rights and subsidiarity. In May 2003 the oblast legislature voted to extend the gubernatorial term from four years to five, to take effect from the election due to be held later that year. Prusak was re-elected as Governor on 7 September, receiving 78.7% of the votes cast in a poll contested by seven candidates.

## Economy

In 1999 Novgorod Oblast's gross regional product amounted to 16,409.7m. roubles, equivalent to 22,417.7 roubles per head. The Oblast's major industrial centres are at Great Novgorod and Staraya Russa (a 19th century resort town famous for its mineral and radon springs and therapeutic mud). The major Moscow–St Petersburg road and rail routes pass through the region. In 2000 there were 1,147 km (713 miles) of railways on the Oblast's territory. The road system, comprising 8,644 km of paved roads in 2000, is its major transport network.

The region's agriculture, which employed 12.1% of the work-force in 2000, consists mainly of flax production and animal husbandry. Its major natural resource is timber: in the late 1990s some 2.5m. cu

m were produced annually, but it was thought that there was potential for this amount to be expanded by four or five times. In 2000 total agricultural production amounted to a value of 4,314m. roubles. The region's major industries include mechanical engineering, chemicals, wood-working, the processing of forestry and agricultural products, ferrous metallurgy and electricity production. The industrial sector employed 24.6% of the working population in 2000, and generated 18,909m. roubles. Great Novgorod city is an important tourist destination, attracting around 1m. visitors annually.

The economically active population totalled 365,000 in 2000, when 7.8% of the labour force were unemployed. Those in employment in mid-2002 earned an average wage of 3,557.5 roubles per month. In 2000 the regional budget showed a surplus of 57.6m. roubles. In that year the external trade of the Oblast comprised US $271.6m. in exports and $64.4m. in imports. Legislative conditions for foreign investors in Novgorod Oblast were considered to be favourable in the 1990s, owing to a foreign company's exemption from all local taxes until its project returned a profit. The multinational company Cadbury's Schweppes invested $150m. in a chocolate factory in the region, which opened in 1996 and was the largest project the company had been involved in, outside the United Kingdom. In 2000 total foreign investment in the region amounted to $49.5m. At 31 December 2000 there were 3,000 small businesses registered in the region.

## Directory

**Head of the Regional Administration (Governor):** MIKHAIL M. PRUSAK; 173005 Velikii Novgorod, Sofiiskaya pl. 1; tel. (8162) 27-47-79; fax (8162) 13-13-30; e-mail infoserv@niac.natm.ru; internet region.adm.nov.ru.

**Chairman of the Regional Duma:** ANATOLII A. BOITSEV; 173005 Velikii Novgorod, Sofiiskaya pl. 1; tel. (8162) 27-47-79; fax (8162) 13-25-14.

**Chief Representative of Novogorod Oblast in the Russian Federation:** VLADIMIR N. PODOPRIGORA; 127006 Moscow, ul. M. Dmitrovka 3/219–220; fax (095) 299-40-04.

**Head of Great (Velikii) Novgorod City Administration (Mayor):** NIKOLAI I. GRAZHDANKIN; 173007 Velikii Novgorod, ul. B. Vasilyevskaya 4; tel. (81622) 7-25-40; fax (8162) 13-25-99; e-mail mayor@adm.nov.ru; internet www.adm.nov.ru.

# Novosibirsk Oblast

Novosibirsk Oblast is situated in the south-east of the Western Siberian Plain, at the Ob-Irtysh confluence. The Oblast forms part of the Siberian Federal Okrug and the West Siberian Economic Area. Its south-western districts lie on the international border with Kazakhstan. The neighbouring federal territories are Omsk Oblast to the west, Tomsk Oblast to the north, Kemerovo Oblast to the east and Altai Krai to the south. The region's major rivers are the Ob and the Om. The Oblast has around 3,000 lakes, the four largest being Chany, Sartlan, Ubinskoye and Uryum. About one-third of its territory is swampland. It occupies a total area of 178,200 sq km (68,800 sq miles) and measures over 400 km (250 miles) from south to north and over 600 km from west to east. It is divided into 30 administrative districts and 14 cities. At 1 January 2002 the Oblast had an estimated population of 2,717,400, and a population density, therefore, of 15.2 per sq km. In 2001 some 73.9% of the population inhabited urban areas. There is a small German community in the Oblast, constituting 2.2% of its population in 1989. Just over one-half of the region's inhabitants live in its administrative centre, Novosibirsk, which had a population of 1,393,200 in 2001. Other major cities included Berdsk (87,100) and Iskitim (68,400).

## History

The city of Novosibirsk (known as Novonikolayevsk until 1925) was founded in 1893, during the construction of the Trans-Siberian Railway. It became prosperous through its proximity to the Kuznetsk coal basin (Kuzbass—see Kemerovo Oblast). The Oblast, which was formed on 28 September 1937, increased in population throughout the Soviet period as it became heavily industrialized, and was a major centre of industrial production during the Second World War.

In October 1993 the Russian President, Boris Yeltsin, dismissed the head of the regional administration, Vitalii Mukha. In 1994 elections were held to a new representative body, which was dominated by the Communist Party of the Russian Federation (CPRF), following elections in 1994 and 1998. It was constantly in dispute with the regional administration, the head of which was a presidential appointment. In an effort to resolve this power struggle, the

President permitted the Oblast a gubernatorial election in December 1995. It was the CPRF candidate, Mukha, who was returned to his former post by the electorate. In January 2000 another politician regarded as a left-wing statist, despite his reported closeness to 'oligarch' Boris Berezovskii, was elected as the new regional Governor. Viktor Tolokonskii, who had previously served as Mayor of Novosibirsk City, defeated Ivan Starikov, the federal deputy Minister of the Economy, by a margin of just 2% in the second round of voting. Support for the CPRF declined somewhat in the regional legislative elections of December 2001, when the party and its ally, the Agrarian Party of Russia, secured just 18 of the 49 seats available, while the remainder were filled by independent candidates. Gubernatorial elections were scheduled to be held on 7 December 2003.

## Economy

In 1999 Novosibirsk Oblast's gross regional product stood at 58,301.8m. roubles, or 21,217.6 roubles per head. Novosibirsk city is a port on the Ob river, and is also the region's principal industrial centre. In 2000 there were 1,530 km of railways and 9,506 km of paved roads on the Oblast's territory. There are four airports in the region, including Tolmachevo, an international airport.

The Oblast's agriculture employed 15.6% of its working population in 2000 and consists mainly of animal husbandry, fur-animal breeding and the production of grain, vegetables, potatoes and flax. Agriculture generated 21,678m. roubles in 2000, compared with a total of 36,487m. roubles contributed by the industrial sector. Extraction industries involved the production of coal, petroleum, natural gas, peat, marble, limestone and clay. Manufacturing industry includes non-ferrous metallurgy, mechanical engineering, metal-working, chemicals, electricity generation, food-processing, light manufacturing, timber production and the manufacture of building materials. Industry employed some 18.6% of the region's work-force in 2000. In the mid-1990s the region's defence industry was largely converted to civilian use—by 1999 only 15% of the output from the former military-industrial complex was for military purposes.

The Oblast's economically active population totalled 1,380,000 in 2000, when 13.4% of the labour force were unemployed. The average monthly wage in the region was 3,892.7 roubles in mid-2002. The 2000 budget showed a deficit of 798.7m. roubles. In 2000 the Oblast's external trade comprised US $463.8m. in exports and $262.2m. in imports. In the same year foreign investment in the Oblast totalled some $157.2m. roubles. At the end of the year there were some 23,700 small businesses registered in the region, one of the largest figures in any federal subject outside Moscow and St Petersburg.

## Directory

**Head of the Regional Administration (Governor):** VIKTOR A. TOLOKONSKII; 630011 Novosibirsk, Krasnyi pr. 18; tel. (3832) 23-08-62; fax (3832) 23-57-00; internet www3.adm.nso.ru.

**Chairman of the Regional Council of Deputies:** VIKTOR V. LEONOV; 630011 Novosibirsk, ul. Kirova 3; tel. (3832) 23-62-52; fax (3832) 23-23-78; internet www.sovet.nso.ru.

**Chief Representative of Novosibirsk Oblast in the Russian Federation:** NINA M. PIRYAZEVA; Moscow; tel. (095) 203-27-20.

**Head of Novosibirsk City Administration (Mayor):** VLADIMIR F. GORODETSKII; 630099 Novosibirsk, Krasnyi pr. 34; tel. (3832) 22-49-32; fax (3832) 22-08-58; e-mail cic@admnsk.ru.

# Omsk Oblast

Omsk Oblast is situated in the south of the Western Siberian Plain on the middle reaches of the Irtysh river. Kazakhstan lies to the south. Other federal subjects that neighbour the Oblast are Tyumen to the north-west and Tomsk and Novosibirsk to the east. Omsk forms part of the Siberian Federal Okrug and the West Siberian Economic Area. Its major rivers are the Irtysh, the Ishim, the Om and the Tara. Much of its territory is marshland and about one-quarter is forested. The total area of Omsk Oblast covers some 139,700 sq km (53,920 sq miles). It measures some 600 km (370 miles) from south to north and 500 km from west to east and is divided into 32 administrative districts and six cities. At 1 January 2002 the region had a total population of 2,127,000 and a population density, therefore, of 15.2 per sq km. Of the Oblast's inhabitants, some 67.2% lived in urban areas in 2001. Its administrative centre is at Omsk, which lies at the confluence of the Ob and Irtysh rivers and had a population of 1,138,400 in 2001.

## History

The city of Omsk was founded as a fortress in 1716. In 1918 it became the seat of Adm. Aleksandr Kolchak's 'all-Russian Government'. However, Omsk fell to the Bolsheviks in 1919 and Kolchak 'abdicated' in January 1920. Omsk Oblast was formed on 7 December 1934.

In the 1990s the region was generally supportive of the Communist Party of the Russian Federation (CPRF), although the nationalist Liberal Democrats also enjoyed a significant level of popularity. The regional Governor, Leonid Polezhayev, although a supporter of the federal state President, Boris Yeltsin, was well respected locally and was re-elected in December 1995. In May 1996 the regional and federal administrations signed a treaty on the delimitation of powers. Legislative elections were held in the Oblast on 22 March 1998, in which the CPRF and other leftist candidates won 30 assembly seats and a majority of seats on Omsk city council. Polezhayev was re-elected in September 1999, defeating the regional leader of the CPRF, Aleksandr Kravets. Nevertheless, Omsk was one of four regions in which the CPRF candidate, Gennadii Zyuganov, received a larger proportion of the votes cast than Vladimir Putin in the federal presidential election of March 2000. The Oblast abolished its power-sharing treaty with the Federal Government in mid-2001. At elections to the Legislative Assembly on 24 March 2002 supporters of Polezhayev, including, notably, members of the Unity and Fatherland-United Russia party, obtained control of the Assembly. Polezhayev was re-elected as Governor on 7 September 2003, receiving 57% of the votes cast.

## Economy

In 1999 Omsk Oblast's gross regional product amounted to 40,591.1m. roubles, equivalent to 18,702.1 roubles per head. Omsk is one of the highest-ranking cities in Russia in terms of industrial output. The region lies on the Trans-Siberian Railway and is a major transport junction. In 2000 it contained 775 km of railway track, 7,662 km of paved roads and over 1,250 km of navigable waterways. There were also some 580 km of pipeline on its territory, carrying petroleum and petroleum products. There are two airports—a third, international airport was under construction in the late 1990s.

The Oblast's soil is the fertile black earth (*chernozem*) characteristic of the region. Its agriculture, which generated a total of 15,827m. roubles in 2000, and employed some 19.0% of the work-force, consists mainly of the production of grain, flax, sunflower seeds and vegetables, and animal husbandry and hunting. The region's mineral reserves include clay, peat and lime. There are also deposits of petroleum and natural gas. Industry employed 18.5% of the work-force in 2000. The Oblast's main industries are electricity generation, fuel, chemical and petrochemical production, mechanical engineering, petroleum-refining and food-processing. Total industrial production amounted to a value of 28,494m. roubles in 2000. The Omsk petroleum refinery, one of Russia's largest and most modern, formed part of Sibneft (Siberian Oil Co), one of the country's newer, vertically integrated petroleum companies. The region's exports primarily comprise chemical, petrochemical and petroleum products. The defence sector is also significant to the economy of the region.

The economically active population numbered 1,040,000 in 2000, when 13.9% of the region's labour force were unemployed, almost twice the rate recorded in 1996. In mid-2002 the average wage in the Oblast was 3,464.0 roubles per month, although it was named as one of the worst regions in Russia for wages arrears. The region was, however, among those with the cheapest prices for foodstuffs in that year. The 2000 budget recorded a surplus of 326.1m. roubles. In that year external trade comprised US $911.2m. in exports and $150.9m. in imports. The Oblast's main trading partners include the People's Republic of China, Cyprus, Germany, Kazakhstan, Spain, Switzerland and the United Kingdom. Foreign investment in the region in 2000 totalled some $791.8m., an increase of 75% compared with 1998. In that year there were some 74 enterprises in the Oblast with foreign capital. At 31 December 2000 there was a total of 10,900 small businesses registered in the region.

## Directory

**Head of the Regional Administration (Governor):** LEONID K. POLEZHAYEV; 644002 Omsk, ul. Krasnyi Put 1; tel. (3812) 24-14-15; fax (3812) 24-23-72; e-mail teleomsk@echo.ru; internet www.omskportal.ru.

**Chairman of the Regional Legislative Assembly:** VLADIMIR A. VARNAVSKII; 640002 Omsk, ul. Krasnyi Put 1; tel. (3812) 24-23-33; fax (3812) 23-24-66; e-mail root@topos.omsk.ru.

**Representation of Omsk Oblast in the Russian Federation:** 107078 Moscow, per. B. Kozlovskii 14–15/1; tel. (095) 921-65-54; fax (095) 921-21-57.

**Head of Omsk City Administration (Mayor):** YEVGENII I. BELOV; 644099 Omsk, ul. Gagarina 34; tel. (3812) 24-30-33; fax (3812) 24-49-34; e-mail media@grad.omsk.ru; internet www.omsk.ru.

# Orel Oblast

Orel Oblast is situated in the central part of the Eastern European Plain within the Central Russian Highlands. The Oblast forms part of the Central Federal Okrug and the Central Economic Area. It is surrounded by five other oblasts: Kursk (to the south), Bryansk (west), Kaluga (north-west), Tula (north-east) and Lipetsk (east). The Ukrainian border lies some 180 km (just over 100 miles) to the south-west. The Oblast's major river is the Oka, the source of which is found in the south-west. There are a total of around 2,000 rivers, with a combined length of 9,100 km, although none are navigable. Just over 7% of the Oblast's area is forested. The territory of Orel Oblast covers an area of 24,700 sq km (9,530 sq miles) and is divided, for administrative purposes, into 24 districts and seven cities. At 1 January 2002 the estimated population of the Oblast was 883,500 and the population density was 35.8 per sq km. Some 62.8% of the inhabitants of the region lived in urban areas in 2001. The Oblast's administrative centre is at Orel, which had 338,800 inhabitants in 2001. Other major cities are Livny (53,600) and Mtsensk (50,300).

## History

Orel was founded as a fortress in 1566. In the 1860s it served as a place of exile for Polish insurgents and was later a detention centre for prisoners on their way to exile in Siberia. Orel Oblast was formed on 27 September 1937. In post-Soviet Russia it formed part of the political 'red belt'. The Communist Party candidate defeated the pro-Government incumbent in elections for a head of the regional administration in December 1992. The victor was eventually dismissed and the regional legislature dissolved by presidential decree, following its criticism of the federal Government during the constitutional crisis of 1993. A 50-seat Regional Duma, elected in March 1994, was dominated by the Communist Party of the Russian Federation (CPRF), which received 45% of the votes cast in the Oblast during the 1995 elections to the State Duma. Despite the loyalty to President Yeltsin shown by the head of the regional administration, Yegor Stroyev (a former cabinet member and the speaker of the upper house of the federal parliament, the Federation Council), the greatest show of support in the presidential election of 1996 was for Gennadii Zyuganov, the CPRF candidate. Although Orel Oblast was Zyuganov's home region, he received 44.6% of the regional votes cast in the federal presidential election of 26 March 2000, which was 1.2% fewer than the number of votes cast in support of Vladimir Putin. Stroyev was re-elected Governor, with more than 97% of the votes cast, in October 1997. He was one of the most consistent opponents of power-sharing agreements between regional and federal government, and in September 2000 he advocated closer co-operation with the People's Republic of China and other Asian countries. Following his re-election as Governor in October 2001, Stroyev resigned from the Federation Council in early December, in order to comply with new legislation that prevented regional governors from holding seats in the Council. In the regional legislative elections held in March 2002 the CPRF retained just three seats. In March 2003 Stroyev was elected to the Supreme Council of the pro-Government Unity and Fatherland-United Russia party.

## Economy

Orel Oblast's gross regional product amounted to 17,928.2m. roubles in 1999, equivalent to 19,884.8 roubles per head. The principal industrial centres in the region are at Orel, Livny and Mtsensk. Orel city lies on the Moscow–Simferopol (Crimea, Ukraine) highway and is an important railway junction. In 2000 there were 590 km of railway track in the Oblast and 4,032 km of paved roads.

Orel Oblast is an important agricultural trade centre. In 2000 around 21.6% of the economically active population were engaged in agriculture. Agricultural production consists mainly of grain, sugar beet, sunflower seeds, potatoes, vegetables, hemp and animal husbandry, and amounted to a value of 9,567m. roubles in 2000. There are some 17.5m. cu m of timber reserves in the Oblast and a major source of iron ore, at Novoyaltinskoye. However, this and reserves of other minerals in the region have generally not been exploited to their full potential. The industrial sector employed around 22.2% of the economically active population in 2000 and generated some 13,805m. roubles in that year. The Oblast's main industries are mechanical engineering, metallurgy, chemicals, light manufacturing, the production of building materials and food-processing. It produces around one-third of its electrical-energy requirements, the remainder being supplied by neighbouring Oblasts (Tula, Kursk and Lipetsk).

The region's economically active population numbered 445,000 in 2000, when 8.5% of the labour force were unemployed. In mid-2002 those in employment earned an average of 3,079.6 roubles per month. There was a budgetary surplus of 53.9m. roubles in 2000. In that year external trade amounted to a value of US $83.3m. in exports, and $121.4m. in imports. Total foreign investment in Orel Oblast amounted to $42.8m. At 31 December 2000 there were some 2,500 small businesses in operation in the region.

## Directory

**Head of the Regional Administration (Governor):** YEGOR S. STROYEV; 302021 Orel, pl. Lenina 1; tel. (0862) 41-63-13; fax (0862) 41-25-30; e-mail post@adm.orel.ru; internet www.adm.orel.ru.

**Chairman of the Regional Council of People's Deputies:** NIKOLAI A. VOLODIN; 302021 Orel, pl. Lenina 1; tel. (0862) 41-58-53; fax (0862) 41-60-22.

**Chief Representative of Orel Oblast in the Russian Federation:** MARINA G. ROGACHEVA; 109240 Moscow, ul. Goncharnaya 12/3; tel. (095) 915-85-51; fax (095) 915-86-14.

**Head of Orel City Administration (Mayor):** VASILII I. UVAROV; 302000 Orel, Proletarskaya gora 1; tel. (0862) 43-33-12; fax (08622) 6-39-44.

# Orenburg Oblast

Orenburg Oblast is situated in the foothills of the Southern Urals. It forms part of the Volga Federal Okrug and the Urals Economic Area. Orenburg sprawls along the international border with Kazakhstan, which lies to the south and east. Samara Oblast lies to the west, and in the north-west of the territory there is a short border with the Republic of Tatarstan. The Republic of Bashkortostan and Chelyabinsk Oblast neighbour the north of the Oblast. Orenburg's major river is the Ural. The region occupies a total area of 124,000 sq km (47,860 sq miles) and is divided into 35 districts and 12 cities. At 1 January 2002 the total population of the Oblast was 2,199,400 and the population density was, therefore, 17.7 per sq km. In 2001 some 56.8% of the population lived in urban areas. The Oblast's administrative centre is at Orenburg, which had 516,600 inhabitants in 2001. Other major cities are Orsk (274,600) and Novotroitsk (109,600).

## History

The city of Orenburg originated as a fortress in 1743. During the revolutionary period Orenburg was a headquarters of 'White' forces and possession of it was fiercely contested with the Bolsheviks. The city was also a centre of Kazakh (then erroneously known as Kyrgyz) nationalists and was the capital of the Kyrgyz ASSR in 1920–25. The region was then separated from the renamed Kazakh ASSR. Orenburg Oblast was formed on 7 December 1934.

The Communist Party of the Russian Federation (CPRF) remained the most popular party into the 1990s, winning 24% of the votes cast in the region at the general election of December 1995. Simultaneous elections to the post of governor, however, were won by the incumbent, Vladimir Yelagin, despite his having expressed support for the federal President, Boris Yeltsin. He was, however, defeated in the gubernatorial elections of December 1999 by the former chair of the State Duma Committee on Agrarian Issues, Aleksei Chernyshev. The region was considered strategically important, owing to its proximity to Kazakhstan, a fact that led to the signature, on 30 January 1996, of an agreement between the regional administration and President Yeltsin. The accord defined the powers and areas of remit of the federal and local authorities. In regional legislative elections held at the end of March 1998 the CPRF maintained its relatively high level of support, but in the election of March 2002 the representation of left-wing deputies declined to just four seats. The power-sharing treaty signed in 1996 was annulled in April 2002. In June 2003 the regional legislature voted to extend the gubernatorial term of office from four years to five; it was anticipated that this measure would take effect following the gubernatorial elections scheduled to be held in December of that year.

## Economy

The Oblast's gross regional product was 56,583.4m. roubles in 1999, or 25,411.3 roubles per head. In 2000 there were 1,652 km (1,027 miles) of railways and 13,032 km of paved roads on the Oblast's territory. Its principal industrial centres are at Orenburg, Orsk, Novotroisk, Mednogorsk, Buzuluk, and Buguruslan. Owing to the region's high degree of industrialization, and that of its neighbours, Chelyabinsk and Bashkortostan, there is a high level of pollution in the atmosphere. Around 1m. metric tons of harmful substances are emitted annually, including almost 700 tons of nickel and one ton of lead. In addition, the intensive exploitation of petroleum and gas deposits have caused serious damage to the land—around 60% of arable land is eroded or in danger of suffering erosion.

Agriculture in Orenburg Oblast, which employed 20.8% of the work-force in 2000, consisted mainly of grain, vegetable and sunflower production and animal husbandry. Agricultural output in the region in 2000 amounted to a value of 20,063m. roubles. The Oblast's major industries are ferrous and non-ferrous metallurgy, mechanical engineering, metal-working, natural gas production, electrical energy, chemicals, food-processing and the production of petroleum, ores, asbestos (the region produces around two-fifths of asbestos produced in Russia) and salt. In 2000 some 21.7% of the working population were engaged in industry, which generated a total of 63,704m. roubles.

The economically active population stood at 1,040,000 in 2000, when some 11.8% of the labour force were unemployed, more than twice the level recorded in 1996. The regional average monthly wage was 3,232.9 roubles in mid-2002. The Oblast's budget for 2000 showed a deficit of 2,716.6m. roubles, and in 2002 the region was named as one of the worst for wage arrears. In 2000 external trade comprised US $1,333.1m. in exports and $601.6m. in imports. Total foreign investment in the region in that year amounted to some $78.8m. At 31 December 2000 there were 7,600 small businesses registered in the Oblast.

## Directory

**Head of the Regional Administration (Governor):** ANDREI A. CHERNYSHEV; 460015 Orenburg, Dom Sovetov; tel. (3532) 77-69-31; fax (3532) 77-38-02; e-mail office@gov.orb.ru; internet www.orb.ru.

**Chairman of the Legislative Assembly:** YURII V. TROFIMOV; 460015 Orenburg, Dom Sovetov; tel. (3532) 77-33-20; fax (3532) 77-42-12; e-mail parlament@gov.orb.ru; internet www.parlament.orb .ru.

**Chief Representative of Orenburg Oblast in the Russian Federation:** VYACHESLAV S. RYABOV; 127025 Moscow, ul. Novyi Arbat 19/2014; tel. (095) 203-85-32; fax (095) 203-59-76.

**Head of Orenburg City Administration (Mayor):** YURII N. MIS-CHERYAKOV; 461300 Orenburg, ul. Sovetskaya 60; tel. (3532) 98-70-10; fax (3532) 77-60-58; e-mail glava@admin.orenburg.ru; internet www .admin.orenburg.ru.

# Penza Oblast

Penza Oblast is situated in the Volga Highlands, to the south of the Republic of Mordoviya. It forms part of the Volga Federal Okrug and the Volga Economic Area and shares borders with Ulyanovsk Oblast to the east, Saratov Oblast to the south, Tambov Oblast to the south-west and touches Ryazan Oblast to the north-west. Penza's major river is the Sura, a tributary of the River Volga. Its territory covers an area of 43,200 sq km (16,750 sq miles) and is divided into 28 districts and 11 cities. At 1 January 2002 the population of the Oblast was estimated to be 1,504,100, giving a population density, therefore, of 34.8 per sq km. In 2001 some 64.4% of the population inhabited urban areas. Its administrative centre, Penza, had a population of 524,900 in 2001.

## History

The city of Penza was founded in 1663 as an outpost on the south-eastern border of the Russian Empire. The region was annexed by Bolshevik forces in late 1917 and remained under the control of the Red Army throughout the period of civil war. Penza Oblast was formed on 4 February 1939. Described as part of the 'red belt' of communist support in the 1990s, in 1992 the Communist Party candidate defeated the pro-Yeltsin Governor in elections to head the regional administration. The communists controlled the Legislative Assembly, elected in 1994 (although the federal presidency replaced the governor), and, almost exactly three years after the gubernatorial elections, obtained some 37% of the local vote in the federal general elections of December 1995. Although the presidentially appointed Governor, Anatolii Kovlyagin, was a member of the pro-Government movement, Our Home is Russia, he failed to give public support to the federal Government's reforms during the mid-1990s. On 12 April 1998 a new Governor, Vasilii Bochkarev, was elected. His campaign promoted effective management and pragmatism, and he contested the election as an independent. Bochkarev was re-elected on 14 April 2002, with the support of the pro-Government Unity and Fatherland-United Russia party. The adoption, in 2002, of a new oblast flag, depicting a Russian Orthodox icon of Jesus Christ, resulted in protests in the region, particularly by representa-

tives of the estimated 100,000-strong Muslim population of the region, and by communists; concern was expressed that the use of an image with religious connotations could breach the separation of religion and state guaranteed by the federal Constitution.

## Economy

In 1999 Penza's gross regional product was 19,686.5m. roubles, or 12,816.7 roubles per head. The Oblast's principal industrial centres are at Penza and Kuznetsk. In 2000 there were 827 km (514 miles) of railway track in the region, which included lines linking the territory to central and southern Russia as well as the Far East and Ukraine and Central Asia. Some 6,239 km of paved roads included several major highways.

Around three-quarters of the agricultural land in the Oblast consists of fertile black earth (*chernozem*). Agricultural activity, which employed 19.7% of the work-force in 2000, consists mainly of the production of grain, sugar beet, potatoes, sunflower seeds and hemp. Animal husbandry is also important. Total agricultural production amounted to a value of 7,883m. roubles in 2000. The main industries are mechanical engineering, the processing of timber and agricultural products, chemicals and the production of electricity. Industry employed some 23.1% of the working population in 2000, and generated 17,895m. roubles.

The economically active population in Penza Oblast numbered 768,000 in 2000, when 11.2% of the labour force were unemployed. Those in employment earned an average of 2,585.0 roubles per month in mid-2002. The 2000 regional budget showed a surplus of 122.8m. roubles. The external trade of the Oblast was relatively low, amounting to US $53.7m. in exports and $34.1m. in imports in 2000. Foreign investment in the Oblast in that year amounted to just $443,000. In 2000 there was a total of 6,100 small businesses registered in the Oblast.

## Directory

**Head of the Regional Administration (Governor):** VASILII K. BOCHKAREV; 440025 Penza, ul. Moskovskaya 75; tel. (8412) 55-04-11; fax (8412) 63-35-75; e-mail pravobl@sura.com.ru; internet www .penza.ru.

**Chairman of the Regional Legislative Assembly:** VIKTOR A. LAZUTKIN; 440025 Penza, pl. Lenina, Dom Sovetov; tel. (8412) 52-22-66; fax (8412) 55-25-95; e-mail zsobl@sura.ru.

**Chief Representative of Penza Oblast in the Russian Federation:** MELS U. NOSINOV; 127025 Moscow, ul. Novyi Arbat 19/1914; tel. (095) 203-10-75; fax (095) 203-48-93.

**Head of Penza City Administration:** ALEKSANDR S. KALASHNIKOV; 440064 Penza, pl. Marshala Zhukova 4, Gorodskaya Duma; tel. (8412) 66-29-85; fax (8412) 6-65-88.

# Perm Oblast

Perm Oblast is situated on the western slopes of the Central and Northern Urals and the eastern edge of the Eastern European Plain. It forms part of the Volga Federal Okrug and the Urals Economic Area. The Komi-Permyak Autonomous Okrug (AOk) forms the north-western part of the Oblast, providing part of the northern border with the Republic of Komi and most of the western border with Kirov Oblast. The Republic of Udmurtiya also lies to the west, the Republic of Bashkortostan to the south and Sverdlovsk Oblast to the east. Apart from the Kama, its major rivers are the Chusovaya, the Kosva and the Vishera. The Kamsk reservoir lies in the centre of the region. Its territory, including that of the AOk, occupies an area of 160,600 sq km (61,990 sq miles) and extends some 600 km (370 miles) from south to north and 400 km from west to east. The Oblast, excluding the AOk, is divided into 29 districts and 24 cities. The region's total population at 1 January 2002 was estimated at 2,923,700, giving a population density of 18.2 per sq km. In 2001 some 75.1% of the population inhabited urban areas. The Oblast's administrative centre is at Perm, which had a population of 1,004,800 in 2001. Other major cities include Berezniki (with a population of 182,200) and Solikamsk (105,400).

## History

Perm city was founded in 1723, with the construction of a copper foundry. Industrial development was such that by the latter part of the 20th century the city extended for some 80 km along the banks of the Kama. Perm Oblast was formed on 3 October 1938. The city was called Molotov in 1940–57 and entry was forbidden to foreigners until 1989. In December 1993 there were regional elections for a new parliament, the Legislative Assembly. On 31 May 1996 the regional administration signed a power-sharing treaty with the Russian

President, Boris Yeltsin. In December the Governor, Genadii Igumnov, retained his post in direct elections, and pro-reform candidates loyal to Igumnov were successful in securing an absolute majority of seats in elections to the regional legislature in December 1997. Following the gubernatorial election held in December 2000, Igumnov was replaced as Governor by Yurii Trutnev, hitherto the Mayor of Perm City. Elections to a new Legislative Assembly were held in December 2001. In July 2002, following visits by the Chairman of the Federation Council, Sergei Mironov, and the Presidential Representative in the Volga Federal Okrug, Sergei Kiriyenko, to Perm and to Kudymkar, the administrative centre of the Komi-Permyak AOk, Trutnev announced that measures to merge the two federal subjects would be instigated in the near future. In September, in what was described as an experimental measure, the (federally controlled) justice services in the two regions were organized into a unified structure, the first instance of such a unification. In February 2003 the legislative organs of both Perm Oblast and the Komi-Permyak AOk voted in favour of the merger. In March the Governors of the two regions met federal President Vladimir Putin, who expressed support for the proposal. In late May the oblast legislature approved legislation to permit the holding of a plebiscite on the merger, and further legislation pertaining to the merger was approved by the parliaments of both the Oblast and the Autonomous Okrug in June. Pending approval of the merger by a referendum (which, it was anticipated, would be held in December 2003), elections to the leadership of the new political entity, to be known as Perm Krai, were expected to take place in December 2005, although the establishment of a single budget for the two regions was not anticipated before 2007.

## Economy

All figures in this survey include data pertaining to the Komi-Permyak AOk, which is also treated separately. In 1999 Perm Oblast's gross regional product amounted to 94,893.9m. roubles, or 31,928.2 roubles per head. Its major industrial centres are at Perm, Berezniki, Solikamsk, Chusovoi and Krasnokamsk. In 2000 there were 1,494 km of railways and 10,143 km of paved roads on the Oblast's territory.

Agriculture in the Oblast, which in 2000 employed just 10.9% of the working population, consists mainly of grain and vegetable production and animal husbandry. In 2000 agricultural production was worth 14,977m. roubles, compared with a total in the industrial sector of 110,377m. roubles. The main industries are coal, petroleum, natural gas, potash and salt production, mechanical engineering, electro-technical industries, chemicals and petrochemicals, petroleum-refining, the processing of forestry and food products, ferrous and non-ferrous metallurgy, and printing. There is also a significant defence sector. Some 25.6% of the working population were engaged in industry in 2000.

The economically active population numbered 1,466,000 in 2000, when 10.4% of the labour force were unemployed. The average wage was above the national average, amounting to 4,375.3 roubles per month in mid-2002. In 2000 there was a budgetary surplus of 323.2m. roubles. In that year external trade amounted to a value of US $2,341.8m. in exports and $265.6m. in imports. The region was named as the eighth-highest in Russia, in terms of investment potential, in late 1999, and in 2000 foreign investment amounted to $96.9m. At 31 December 2000 there were 8,200 small businesses registered in the region.

## Directory

**Governor:** YURII P. TRUTNEV; 614006 Perm, ul. Kuibysheva 14; tel. (3422) 58-70-75; fax (3422) 34-89-52; e-mail home@trutnev.ru; internet www.trutnev.ru.

**Chairman of the Legislative Assembly:** NIKOLAI A. DEVYATKIN; 614006 Perm, ul. Lenina 51; tel. (3422) 58-75-55; fax (3422) 34-27-47; e-mail parliament@perm.ru; internet www.parliament.perm.ru.

**Chief Representative of Perm Oblast in the Russian Federation:** ALEKSANDR A. POTEKHIN; 103795 Moscow, ul. M. Dmitrovka 3; tel. (095) 299-48-36; fax (095) 209-08-97.

**Head of Perm City Administration:** ARKADII L. KAMENEV; 614000 Perm, ul. Lenina 15; tel. (3422) 34-33-02; fax (3422) 34-94-11; e-mail gorodperm@permregion.ru; internet www.gorodperm.ru.

# Pskov Oblast

Pskov Oblast is situated on the Eastern European Plain. The Oblast forms part of the North-Western Federal Okrug and the North-Western Economic Area. It has international borders with Belarus to the south and Latvia and Estonia to the west. During the first half of the 1990s Estonia and Latvia questioned Russia's sovereignty of

parts of Pskov Oblast and by the beginning of the 2000s there had still been no formal ratification of the now accepted border delimitations. Smolensk Oblast lies to the south-east, Tver and Novgorod Oblasts to the east and Leningrad Oblast to the north-east. Pskov's major river is the Velikaya and around two-fifths of its territory is forested. On its border with Estonia lie the Pskovskoye (Pihkva) and Chudskoye (Peipsi) lakes. Pskov Oblast covers an area of 55,300 sq km (21,350 sq miles) and is divided into 24 administrative districts and 14 cities. The population at 1 January 2002 was estimated at 778,000 and the population density was, therefore, 14.1 per sq km. Around 94.3% of the territory's inhabitants were ethnic Russian in 1989, and 66.4% inhabited urban areas in 2001. The Oblast's administrative centre is at Pskov, which had a population of 200,100 in 2001. The second largest city is Velikiye Luki (115,000).

## History

Pskov city was founded in 903, and in 1242 was the the area in which Muscovite Prince Aleksandr Nevskii defeated an army of Teutonic knights, who sought to expand eastwards. The Muscovite state finally acquired the region in 1510. The Oblast was created on 23 August 1944. Some territory to the south of Lake Pskov was transferred from Estonia to Pskov Oblast in 1945, remaining a cause for dispute between newly independent Estonia and Russia in the 1990s. In 1995 Estonia formally renounced any territorial claim, but it remained eager to secure Russian acknowledgement of the 1920 Treaty of Tartu (by which Estonia had been awarded the disputed territory), which would render the Soviet occupation illegal. The Oblast was a traditional bastion of support for the extreme nationalist policies of Vladimir Zhirinovskii; a gubernatorial election was held on 21 October 1996, which was won by Yevgenii Mikhailov, a former Liberal Democrat deputy. The eastward expansion of the North Atlantic Treaty Organization (NATO) was a major issue in the election campaign, as were proposals that the regional Government receive a share of the customs revenue generated by trade with the Baltic States. As Governor, Mikhailov visited both Chechnya and the Serbian province of Kosovo and Metohija in the Federal Republic of Yugoslavia (now Serbia and Montenegro), reflecting the high levels of support for him among the military (accounting for approximately one-10th of the population of Pskov Oblast). Mikhailov was re-elected as Governor in November 2000. Legislative elections were held on 31 March 2002.

## Economy

In 1999 Pskov Oblast's gross regional product amounted to 11,548.8m. roubles, equivalent to 14,312.6 roubles per head. The Oblast's principal industrial centres are at Pskov and Velikiye Luki. In 2000 there were 1,092 km of railway track in the region and 9,954 km of paved roads. There is an airport at Pskov, which was upgraded to international status in the late 1990s.

In 1996–98 a federal programme for the socio-economic development of Pskov Oblast invested some 1,500,000m. old roubles in the improvement of agriculture in the region. Agricultural activity, which employed 21.4% of the work-force in 2000, consists mainly of animal husbandry and the production of grain, potatoes, vegetables and flax. Total output in the sector amounted to a value of 5,428m. roubles in 2000. The region's major industries are the production of electricity, manufacture of building materials, mechanical engineering, light manufacturing, food-processing and wood-working. Industry employed 18.9% of the working population in 2000, and generated 8,306m. roubles. According to local official sources, industry in the Oblast was completely privatized by 1995, although it was severely affected by the 1998 financial crisis, and the proportion of the working population employed in the sector declined by more than one-quarter in 1995–2000. Owing to its three international borders, there are two representatives of foreign consulates, Latvian and Estonian, operating in the region. Pskov's main trading partners are Estonia, Finland and Germany.

Pskov Oblast's economically active population numbered 377,000 in 2000, when 12.6% of the labour force were unemployed. In mid-2002 those in employment earned, on average, 2,954.6 roubles per month, reflecting Pskov's status as one of the poorer areas of the Russian Federation. There was a budgetary deficit of 158m. roubles in 2000. In that year external trade amounted to a value of US $108.2m. in exports and $77.6m. in imports, the lowest figures in the North-Western Federal Okrug. In 2000 foreign investment in the region totalled $1.1m. At 31 December 2000 2,800 small businesses were registered in the Oblast.

## Directory

**Head of the Regional Administration (Governor):** YEVGENII E. MIKHAILOV; 180001 Pskov, ul. Nekrasova 23; tel. (8122) 16-22-03; fax (8122) 16-03-90; e-mail glava@obladmin.pskov.ru; internet www.pskov.ru.

**Chairman of the Regional Assembly of Deputies:** YURII A. SHCHMATOV; 180001 Pskov, ul. Nekrasova 23; tel. (8122) 16-24-44; fax (8122) 16-00-51.

**Chief Representative of Pskov Oblast in the Russian Federation:** IGOR P. NOVOSELOV; Moscow; tel. (095) 928-84-43; fax (095) 928-07-95.

**Head of Pskov City Administration (Mayor):** MIKHAIL YA. KHORONEN; 180000 Pskov, ul. Nekrasova 22; tel. (8122) 16-26-67; internet www.pskov.ellink.ru.

# Rostov Oblast

Rostov Oblast is situated in the south of the Eastern European Plain, in the Southern Federal Okrug and the North Caucasus Economic Area. It lies on the Taganrog Gulf of the Sea of Azov. Krasnodar and Stavropol Krais lie to the south and the Republic of Kalmykiya to the east. Volgograd Oblast lies to the north-east and Voronezh Oblast to the north-west. The region has an international border with Ukraine to the west. Its major rivers are the Don and the Severnyi Donets. The Volga–Don Canal runs through its territory. Rostov Oblast covers an area of 100,800 sq km (38,910 sq miles) and consists of 43 administrative districts and 23 cities. The region is relatively densely populated, having an estimated 4,286,200 inhabitants at 1 January 2002, giving it a population density of 42.5 per sq km. Some 67.5% of the region's inhabitants resided in urban areas in 2001. Its administrative centre is at Rostov-na-Don (Rostov-na-Donu), which had a population of 997,800 in 2001. Other major cities are Taganrog (with a population of 280,900), Shakhty (218,200), Novocherkassk (181,600) and Volgodonsk (179,100).

## History

The city of Rostov-on-Don was established as a Cossack outpost in 1796. It became an important grain-exporting centre in the 19th century, and increased in economic importance after the completion of the Volga–Don Canal. Rostov Oblast was formed in September 1937. The region became heavily industrialized after 1946 and, therefore, considerably increased in population.

In the mid-1990s the liberal Yabloko bloc enjoyed its highest level of support outside the two federal cities and Kamchatka in Rostov, and it managed to obtain over 15% of the votes cast in some parts of the Oblast in elections to the State Duma in December 1999. The regional Government signed a power-sharing treaty with the federal authorities in June 1996. The Oblast directly elected the incumbent, Vladimir Chub, as Governor in September of that year. Chub was re-elected for a further term of office on 23 September 2001, as the candidate of the pro-Government Unity bloc, receiving 78% of the votes cast. (The sole opposition candidate was regarded as an obscure regional official.) Sergei Shilo, the Mayor of Taganrog, the second largest city in the Oblast, and a close ally of Chub, was murdered in October 2002; the killing was believed to be linked with a conflict of business interests. On 29 March 2003, one day before the holding of regional legislative elections, Chub was elected to the Supreme Council of the pro-Government Unity and Fatherland-United Russia (UF-UR) party. In these elections, supporters of UF-UR were successful in 39 districts, although it was reported that many of these candidates had, in fact, concealed their party allegiance; 24 of the 45 deputies elected were business executives. Moreover, the proportion of votes cast 'against all candidates' was reported to be in excess of 20% in several districts. Commentators observed that regional media legislation had resulted in severe restrictions being placed on coverage of candidates' campaigns.

## Economy

In 1999 Rostov Oblast's gross regional product stood at 68,975.9m. roubles, or 15,780.0 roubles per head. The Oblast's main industrial centres are at Rostov-on-Don, Taganrog, Novocherkassk, Shakhty, Kamensk-Shakhtinskii, Novoshakhtinsk and Volgodonsk. In 2000 there were 1,858 km (1,154 miles) of railways and 11,525 km of paved roads on the Oblast's territory. Its ports are Rostov-on-Don (connected by shipping routes to 16 countries) and Ust-Donetskii, both of which are river-ports.

The Oblast is one of the major grain-producing regions in Russia, with agricultural land comprising some 85% of its territory. The production of sunflower seeds, coriander, mustard, vegetables and cucurbits (gourds and melons) is also important, as are viniculture and horticulture. The sector employed some 19.2% of the working population in 2000, when total agricultural output amounted to a value of 27,882m. roubles. The Oblast is situated in the eastern Donbass coal-mining region and contains some 6,500m. metric tons of coal, as well as significant deposits of anthracite. It is also rich in natural gas, reserves of which are estimated at 54,000m. cu m. Its other principal industries are food-processing and mechanical engineering: Rostov-on-Don contained some 50 machine-building plants. In the early 1990s the industrial association, Rostselmash, produced 70% of all grain combines in Russia (although the quantity produced in 1999 was less than one-50th of that achieved 15 years earlier) and Krasnyi Aksai manufactured 50% of all tractor-mounted cultivators (although from 1997 it specialized in the assembly of automobiles for Daewoo of the Republic of Korea); in Novocherkassk, Krasnyi Kotelshchik produced 70% of Russia's electric locomotives, and is now a joint-stock company; and 60% of the country's steam boilers were made in Taganrog, where the largest industrial concern in the Oblast, Taganrog Metallurgical Plant (TagMet), is located. Light manufacturing, chemicals and ferrous and non-ferrous metallurgy are also major economic activities. In 2000 some 20.0% of the Oblast's working population were employed in industry, and industrial production was worth 57,372m. roubles.

The economically active population numbered 2,062,000 in 2000, when 14.9% of the labour force were unemployed. In mid-2002 those in employment earned an average monthly wage of 3,115.2 roubles. The 2000 budget showed a surplus of 95.4m. roubles. In the same year external trade amounted to a value of US $709.2m. in exports and $519.6m. in imports; total foreign investment in the region amounted to $91.1m. At 31 December 2000 there were some 25,000 small businesses registered in the Oblast.

## Directory

**Head of the Regional Administration (Governor):** VLADIMIR F. CHUB; 344050 Rostov-on-Don, ul. Sotsialisticheskaya 112; tel. (8632) 66-18-10; fax (8632) 65-67-43; e-mail pressa_rra@donpac.ru; internet www.donland.ru.

**Chairman of the Legislative Assembly:** ALEKSANDR V. POPOV; 344050 Rostov-on-Don, ul. Sotsialisticheskaya 112; tel. (8632) 40-14-47; fax (8632) 40-55-82; internet www.zsro.ru.

**Chief Representative of Rostov Oblast in the Russian Federation:** VIKTOR P. VODOLATSKII; 127025 Moscow, ul. Novyi Arbat 19/1909; tel. (095) 203-94-71; fax (095) 203-89-58; e-mail info@rostovregion.ru; internet www.rostovregion.ru.

**Head of Rostov-on-Don City Administration (Mayor):** MIKHAIL A. CHERNYSHEV; 344007 Rostov-on-Don, ul. B. Sadovaya 47; tel. (8632) 44-13-23; fax (8632) 66-62-62; e-mail meria@rostov-gorod.ru; internet www.rostov-gorod.ru.

# Ryazan Oblast

Ryazan Oblast is situated in the central part of the Eastern European Plain and forms part of the Central Federal Okrug and the Central Economic Area. Ryazan city lies some 192 km (just under 120 miles) south-east of Moscow. The other neighbouring regions are Vladimir (to the north), Nizhnii Novgorod (north-east), the Republic of Mordoviya (east), Penza (south-east), Tambov and Lipetsk (south), and Tula (west). There are some 2,800 lakes in the region (the largest being the Velikoye and the Dubovoye) and its major rivers are the Oka and the Don and their tributaries. The Oka extends 489 km (304 miles) along the borders with Moscow and Vladimir Oblasts. Its catchment area amounts to over 95% of the region's territory, which occupies an area of 39,600 sq km (15,290 sq miles) and is divided into 25 administrative districts and 12 cities. At 1 January 2002 its population was estimated at 1,255,000, giving a population density of 31.7 per sq km. In 2001 some 68.5% of the population inhabited urban areas. The Oblast's principal city is Ryazan, with a population of 523,400 at 1 January 2001.

## History

Ryazan city was an early Orthodox Christian bishopric. The Oblast was formed on 26 September 1937. In the 1990s it was described as part of the 'red belt' of communist support in Russia. With 31% of the Oblast's participating electorate voting for the Communist Party of the Russian Federation (CPRF) in the general election of December 1995, this party was also able to dominate the Regional Duma. In October 1998 the incumbent Governor was removed by the federal Government; the acting Governor, Igor Ivlev, lost the subsequent election to the CPRF candidate, Vyacheslav Lyubimov. In April 1999, at the time of the aerial bombardment of Serbia and Montenegro, the Federal Republic of Yugoslavia, by North Atlantic Treaty Organization (NATO) forces, Lyubimov was one of the leading supporters in the Federation Council of the expansion of the Russia-Belarus Union to include Yugoslavia. From the late 1990s Ryazan obtained notoriety as a region in which far-right groups, notably Russian National Unity and its successor organization, Russian Rebirth, were able to operate, in particular following an attack on a Jewish Sunday school class by 15 youths in September 2000. Lyubimov was re-elected as Governor in December 2000.

## Economy

In 1999 Ryazan Oblast's gross regional product amounted to 22,789.8m. roubles, or 17,666.5 roubles per head. The Oblast's industrial centres are at Ryazan, Skopin, Kasimov and Sasovo. In 2000 there were 942 km of railways and 6,596 km of paved roads in the region.

The Oblast's warm, moist climate is conducive to agriculture, which consists mainly of grain and vegetable production, horticulture and animal husbandry, and employed 18.1% of the workforce in 2000. Total agricultural production amounted to a value of 10,432m. roubles in that year. There are 162.8m. cu m of timber reserves in the region and substantial reserves of brown coal and peat, estimated at around 302m. metric tons and 222m. tons, respectively. Deposits of peat are concentrated in the north, the east and the south-west of the region. The Oblast's main industries are mechanical engineering, the generation of electrical energy, petroleum-processing, the production of building materials, light manufacturing and food-processing. In 2000 some 24.7% of the working population were engaged in industry, which generated a total of 22,781m. roubles.

The economically active population numbered 613,000 in 2000, when 9.5% of the labour force were unemployed. In mid-2002 those in employment earned, on average, 3,425.3 roubles per month. The 2000 budget showed a surplus of 75.2m. roubles, and foreign investment in the region totalled US $1.3m. in that year. In 2000 external trade amounted to a value of $788.0m. in exports and $64.5m. in imports. At 31 December 2000 there were 6,400 small businesses registered in the Oblast.

## Directory

**Head of the Regional Administration (Governor):** VYACHESLAV N. LYUBIMOV; 390000 Ryazan, ul. Lenina 30; tel. (0912) 27-21-25; fax (0912) 44-25-68; e-mail korn@adm1.ryazan.su; internet www.gov .ryazan.ru.

**Chairman of the Regional Duma:** VLADIMIR N. FEDOTKIN; 390000 Ryazan, ul. Pochtovaya 50/57; tel. (0912) 77-48-82; fax (0912) 21-64-22; e-mail duma@adm.gov.etr.ru.

**Representation of Ryazan Oblast in the Russian Federation:** 127025 Moscow, ul. Novyi Arbat 19/2213; tel. (095) 203-61-78; fax (095) 203-61-85.

**Head of Ryazan City Administration (Mayor):** PAVEL D. MAMATOV; 390000 Ryazan, ul. Radishcheva 28; tel. (0912) 77-34-02; fax (0912) 24-05-70; e-mail glava@cityadmin.ryazan.ru.

# Sakhalin Oblast

Sakhalin Oblast comprises the island of Sakhalin and the Kurile (Kuril) Islands in the Pacific Ocean. It forms part of the Far Eastern Federal Okrug and the Far Eastern Economic Area. The island of Sakhalin lies off the coast of Khabarovsk Krai, separated from the mainland by the Tatar Strait. Eastward lie the Kurile Islands (annexed by the USSR in 1945, but claimed by Japan), which are an archipelago of some 56 islands extending from the Kamchatka Peninsula in the north-east, to Hokkaido Island (Japan) in the south-west. Sakhalin Island is 942 km (just over 580 miles) in length and contains two parallel mountain ranges running north to south and separated by a central valley. The highest peaks on the island, both belonging to the eastern range of mountains, are Lopatin (1,609 m or 5,281 feet) and Nevelskogo (1,397 m). The north-west coast of the island is marshland, and much of its area is forested. The Kurile Islands are actively volcanic and contain many hot springs. There are some 60,000 rivers on Sakhalin Island, the major ones being the Poronai (350 km in length), the Tym (330 km), the Viakhtu (131 km) and the Lyutoga (130 km), all of which are frozen during the winter months, December–April/May. The Kurile Islands contain around 4,000 rivers and streams and the largest waterfall in the Russian Federation, Ilya Muromets. Sakhalin Oblast covers a total area of 87,100 sq km (33,620 sq miles) and is divided into 17 administrative districts and 18 cities. The estimated total population at 1 January 2002 was 584,700, the region's population density being 6.7 per sq km. Some 86.7% of the region's total population resided in urban areas in 2001. The population of the Oblast was reported to have declined by some 110,000, or 15%, between 1991 and 1998, largely reflecting migration from the region as a result of the decline of its industrial base. The Oblast's administrative centre is at Yuzhno-Sakhalinsk, which had 176,200 inhabitants in 2001.

## History

Sakhalin was traditionally known as a place of exile for political opponents to the tsars. It was originally inhabited by the indigenous Gilyak people; Russians first reached the island in 1644, although the region was assumed to be a peninsula until the early 19th century. The island was conquered by the Japanese at the end of the 18th century, but Russia established a military base at Korsakov in 1853. Joint control of the island followed until 1875, when it was granted to Russia in exchange for the Kurile Islands. Karafuto, the southern part of the island, was won by Japan during the Russo–Japanese War (1904–05), but the entire island was ceded to the USSR in 1945. The Kurile Islands, which were discovered for Europeans by the Dutch navigator, Martin de Vries, in 1634, were divided between Japan and Russia in the 18th century and ruled jointly until 1875. Russia occupied the islands in 1945 and assumed full control in 1947. The southern Kuriles remained disputed between Japan and the newly independent Russia. Sakhalin Oblast had been formed on 20 October 1932 as part of Khabarovsk Krai. It became a separate administrative unit in 1947, when the island was united with the Kuriles. The region contained several penal institutions of the GULAG (State Corrective Camps) system established during the regime of Stalin—Iosif V. Dzhugashvili (1924–53), and remained closed to foreigners until 1990.

On 16 October 1993 the head of the regional administration disbanded the Regional Soviet; a Regional Duma was elected in its place. In May 1995 a major earthquake, one of the largest ever to occur in Russia, destroyed the settlement of Neftegorsk in the north of the region, and claimed an estimated 2,000 lives. In May 1996 the Russian President, Boris Yeltsin, signed a power-sharing treaty with the regional Government. The gubernatorial elections of October 1996 and October 2000 were won by the incumbent, Igor Farkhutdinov. In 1998 Russia and Japan agreed to attempt to settle their territorial dispute by 2000. However, in September 2000 President Vladimir Putin rejected continuing Japanese demands for the sovereignty of four of the Southern Kuriles (known as the 'Northern Territory' to Japan), and the continuing dispute meant that the two countries had still to sign a peace treaty officially to mark the end of the Second World War. In December 1998 the Oblast authorities signed a friendship and economic co-operation accord with the Japanese province of Hokkaido, and a further agreement was signed in January 2000. A special economic zone in the Southern Kuriles was established in the late 1990s, in order to encourage foreign investment. Concerns about the high levels of organized crime in the Oblast, and the illicit smuggling of fish and fish produce, notably to Japan, were increasingly expressed from the late 1990s. These concerns were believed to be a factor behind the introduction, by the federal authorities, of restrictions on movement on Sakhalin Island (and other border regions of the Russian Federation) from March 2003; henceforth both foreign citizens and Russian citizens resident outwith the Oblast were required to obtain permits before travelling outside Yuzhno-Sakhalinsk. On 20 August 2003 Farkhutdinov and several senior officials of Sakhalin Oblast were killed in a helicopter crash. Gubernatorial elections were scheduled for 7 December, to be held concurrently with elections to the federal State Duma.

## Economy

In 1999 Sakhalin Oblast's gross regional product amounted to 28,329.3m. roubles, or 46,980.5 roubles per head. The Oblast's principal industrial centres are at Yuzhno-Sakhalinsk, Kholmsk, Okha (the administrative centre of the petroleum-producing region), Nevelsk, Dolinsk and Poronaisk. In 2000 there were 957 km of railways and 1,820 km of paved roads in the Oblast. Its ports are Kholmsk (from where the Kholmsk-Vanino ferry connects Sakhalin Island with the mainland) and Korsakov. There are flights to Moscow, Khabarovsk, Vladivostok, Petropavlovsk-Kamchatskii and Novosibirsk, and international services to Alaska, the USA, the Republic of Korea (South Korea) and Japan.

Agriculture in the region is minimal, owing to its unfavourable climatic conditions—agricultural land occupies only 1% of its territory. It employed just 4.6% of the working population in 2000, and consists mainly of potato and vegetable production, animal husbandry and fur farming. Total agricultural production amounted to a value of 1,865m. roubles in 2000. Annual catches of fish and other marine life amount to around 400,000 metric tons. Fishing and fish-processing is the major traditional industry, accounting for two-fifths of industrial production. The entire industrial sector employed some 24.9% of the region's work-force and generated 30,166m. roubles in 2000. There is some extraction of coal and, increasingly, petroleum and natural gas in, and to the north of, Sakhalin Island. Some petroleum is piped for refining to a plant in Komsomolsk-on-Amur (Khabarovsk Krai), although from 1994 the Oblast had its own refinery, with a capacity of some 200,000 tons per year. Coal was the region's primary source of energy, but in the late 1990s a gradual conversion to gas was initiated. The further development of Sakhalin's rich hydrocarbons reserves was the subject of negotiations between a number of Russian and foreign companies in the mid-1990s. By 1999 four major consortia had been formed. Sakhalin-1, a project to produce petroleum on the continental shelf of Sakhalin

Island, comprised Rosneft (of which Sakhalinmorneftegas is a local subsidiary and which had a 40% stake), Exxon (now ExxonMobil— of the USA) and Sodeco (of Japan), both of which had a 30% stake. Sakhalin-2, two fields containing an estimated 1,000m. barrels of petroleum and 408,000m. cu m of natural gas, was run by Sakhalin Energy Investment, comprising Mitsui and Mitsubishi (of Japan), Marathon (of the USA) and the Anglo-Dutch company, Shell. Sakhalin-3, backed by Mobil (now ExxonMobil) and Texaco (now ChevronTexaco—of the USA), was seeking to develop what was potentially the largest field on the Sakhalin shelf, containing an estimated 320m. tons of recoverable reserves. It was hoped that the proceeds from the ongoing projects would help to alleviate the high level of poverty in the region. In July 1998 the federal premier, Sergei Kiriyenko, signed a resolution extending a federal programme on social and economic development of the Oblast, to be financed by proceeds from Sakhalin-1 and Sakhalin-2, until 2005. In 2001 ExxonMobil was undertaking a project to examine the feasibility of constructing a pipeline to export petroleum and gas from Sakhalin to Japan. In July 2002 it was announced that Rosneft was to undertake the development of a further project, Sakhalin-5, in association with British Petroleum (United Kingdom). In addition, food-processing was a significant industrial sector in the Oblast, accounting for 27% of such activity in 2000.

Sakhalin Oblast's economically active population totalled 324,000 in 2000, when 13.0% of the labour force were unemployed, compared with 20.4% in the previous year. The average monthly wage in the region amounted to some 6,735.7 roubles in mid-2002. The 2000 budget showed a surplus of 147.9m. roubles. In the same year exports from the Oblast were valued at US \$425.3m. and imports to the Oblast were worth \$85.1m.; total foreign investment in the region amounted to some \$250.6m. At 31 December 2000 4,800 small businesses were registered in the Oblast.

## Directory

**Governor:** IVAN MALAKHOV (acting) 693011 Sakhalin obl., Yuzhno-Sakhalinsk, Kommunisticheskii pr. 39; tel. (4242) 72-19-02; fax (4242) 23-60-81; e-mail webmaster@adm.sakhalin.ru; internet www .adm.sakhalin.ru.

**Chairman of the Regional Duma:** VLADIMIR I. YEFREMOV; 693000 Sakhalin obl., Yuzhno-Sakhalinsk, ul. Chekhova 37; tel. (4242) 42-14-89; fax (4242) 72-15-46; e-mail chairman@duma.sakhalin.ru; internet www.duma.sakhalin.ru.

**Chief Representative of Sakhalin Oblast in the Russian Federation:** VLADIMIR I. SHAPOVAL; 103025 Moscow, ul. Novyi Arbat 19/1132; tel. (095) 203-79-09; fax (095) 023-84-56; e-mail prsakh2001@mail.ru.

**Head of Yuzhno-Sakhalinsk City Administration (Mayor):** FEDOR I. SIDORENKO; 693023 Sakhalin obl., Yuzhno-Sakhalinsk, ul. Lenina 173; tel. (4242) 72-25-11; fax (4242) 23-00-06; internet yuzhno.sakh.ru.

# Samara Oblast

Samara Oblast is situated in the south-east of the Eastern European Plain on the middle reaches of the Volga river. It forms part of the Volga Federal Okrug and the Volga Economic Area. Its southernmost tip lies on the border with Kazakhstan. Saratov lies to the south-west, Ulyanovsk to the west, Tatarstan to the north and Orenburg to the east. The Volga snakes through the west of the territory. The Oblast's other major rivers are the Samara, the Sok, the Kunel, the Bolshoi Igruz and the Kondurcha. The region occupies an area of 53,600 sq km (20,690 sq miles). It is divided into 27 districts and 11 cities. Owing to its proximity to the Kazakh desert, the southernmost part of the Oblast is prone to drought. The region is densely populated, with an estimated population of 3,258,700 at 1 January 2002, and a population density, therefore, of 60.8 per sq km. In 2001 some 80.5% of the population inhabited urban areas. The majority of the population, 83.4%, was ethnic Russian. There were also significant communities of Mordovians, Chuvash, Tatars and Ukrainians. The administrative centre is at Samara (formerly Kuibyshev), which had 1,146,400 inhabitants in 2001. The region's second city is Tolyatti (724,300).

## History

Samara city was founded in 1586 as a fortress. It increased in prosperity after the construction of the railways in the late 19th century. Samara Oblast was founded on 14 May 1928, as the Middle Volga Oblast. In 1929 it was upgraded to the status of a krai, which was renamed Kuibyshev Krai in 1935. On 5 December 1936 Kuibyshev Krai became Kuibyshev Oblast, before assuming its current name in 1991. The city became the headquarters of the Soviet

Government between 1941 and 1943, when Moscow was threatened by the German invasion.

The local legislature defied President Boris Yeltsin in the constitutional crisis of 1993, and was dissolved in October and replaced by a Regional Duma. There was more support in the region for the candidacy of Boris Yeltsin in the presidential election of mid-1996 than for his communist rival, Gennadii Zyuganov, owing to the strong leadership of the Governor, Konstantin Titov. In the election held in December Titov, who was regarded as an ambitious economic reformer, was re-elected as Governor. As the informal head of the 'Great Volga' inter-regional association, Titov sought to protect the power and relative independence of governors from the central authorities. He also strongly urged the Regional Duma to approve legislation on land ownership, which was achieved in June 1998. Titov attempted to gain a higher profile in national politics by standing for the presidency of the Russian Federation at the elections of March 2000. However, his performance, even in Samara Oblast, where he obtained only 20% of the votes cast and came third, was disappointing. Consequently, he resigned from the post of Governor in April, but stood as a candidate for re-election in July, in an attempt to confirm his legitimacy; he was re-elected with 53% of the votes cast. In November 2001 Titov, who had hitherto led a small social-democratic party, was elected as Co-chairman of the recently formed Social Democratic Party of Russia, alongside the former General Secretary of the Communist Party of the Soviet Union and executive President of the USSR, Mikhail Gorbachev.

## Economy

In 1999 Samara Oblast's gross regional product amounted to 21,328.4m. roubles, or 36,736.1 roubles per head. The Oblast's major industrial centres are at Samara, Tolyatti, Syzran and Novokuibyshevsk. In 2000 there were 1,382 km (859 miles) of railways and 7,350 km of paved roads in the region.

Agriculture in the Oblast, which employed just 8.7% of the working population in 2000, consists mainly of animal husbandry and the production of grain, sugar beet and sunflower seeds. Total agricultural production in 2000 was worth 16,520m. roubles. There are some reserves of petroleum and natural gas in the region. Its main industries are mechanical engineering, metal-working, petroleum production and refining, food-processing and petrochemicals. The Oblast's principal company is AvtoVAZ (Volga Automobile Plant), manufacturer of the Lada automobile, accounting for over 40% of industrial output in the region, and the largest automobile manufacturer in Russia. In 2002, as part of a joint venture with the US corporation, General Motors, AvtoVAZ also began to manufacture Chevrolet Niva automobiles and sports-utility vehicles. In 2000 some 28.7% of the region's work-force were engaged in industry, which generated 161,001m. roubles.

The economically active population of Samara Oblast numbered 1,692,000 in 2000, when 10.3% of the labour force were unemployed. In mid-2002 those in employment earned an average wage of 4,317.7 roubles per month, well above the national average. In 2000 the regional budget showed a surplus of 557.4m. roubles. In December 2001, however, the Oblast's Governor, Konstantin Titov, issued a decree introducing state control over the finances of Samara city and two rural districts of the Oblast, the debts of which exceeded 10% of their total consolidated budgets. In 2000 total foreign investment in the region amounted to US \$236.3m. By August 1998 some 300 foreign companies, including some of the world's largest, such as Coca-Cola and General Motors of the USA and Nestlé of Switzerland, had invested in the region, attracted by its technologically advanced industrial base, reputation for creditworthiness and well-educated, urbanized labour force. In 2000 the external trade of the region amounted to some \$3,514.6m. in exports and \$626.2m. in imports, representing one of the highest levels of trade in any federal subject. At 31 December 2000 there were some 27,600 small businesses in operation.

## Directory

**Governor:** KONSTANTIN A. TITOV; 443006 Samara, ul. Molodogvardeiskaya 210; tel. (8462) 32-22-68; fax (8462) 32-13-40; e-mail governor@samara.ru; internet www.adm.samara.ru.

**Chairman of the Regional Duma:** VIKTOR F. SAZANOV; 443110 Samara, ul. Molodogvardeiskaya 187; tel. (8462) 32-75-06; fax (8462) 42-38-08; e-mail samgd@duma.sam-reg.ru; internet www.duma .sam-reg.ru.

**Representative of Samara Oblast in the Russian Federation:** VIKTOR B. LEONTYEV; 103030 Moscow, per. Veskovskii 2; tel. (095) 973-19-95; fax (095) 973-05-54; e-mail tradoc@samarapostpred.ru.

**Head of Samara City Administration (Mayor):** GEORGII S. LIMANSKII; 443010 Samara, ul. Kuibysheva 135/137; tel. (8462) 32-20-68; fax (8462) 33-67-41; e-mail city@vis.infotel.ru.

# Saratov Oblast

Saratov Oblast is situated in the south-east of the Eastern European Plain. It forms part of the Volga Federal Okrug and the Volga Economic Area. On the border with Kazakhstan (to the south-east), the federal territories adjacent to Saratov are Volgograd (south), Voronezh and Tambov (west), and Penza, Ulyanovsk and Samara (north). Its main river is the Volga. The west of the Oblast (beyond the left bank of the Volga) is mountainous, the east low-lying. The region's territory occupies an area of 100,200 sq km (38,680 sq miles). It comprises 38 districts and 18 cities. At 1 January 2002 it had an estimated total of 2,676,400 inhabitants, and a population density of 26.7 per sq km. In 2001 some 73.0% of the Oblast's population inhabited urban areas. Its administrative centre is at Saratov, a major river-port on the Volga, with a population of 864,400 in 2001. Other major cities were Balakovo (207,500) and Engels (190,600).

## History

Saratov city was founded in 1590 as a fortress city, to protect against nomad raids on the Volga trade route. Strategically placed on the Trans-Siberian Railway, it was seized by Bolshevik forces in late 1917 and remained under communist control, despite attacks by the 'White' forces under Adm. Aleksandr Kolchak in 1918–19. The Oblast was formed in 1936, having been part of a Saratov Krai from 1934. The region became heavily industrialized in the Soviet period, before the Second World War.

Saratov remained an important centre for the military and for communist support into the 1990s. However, in September 1996 Dmitrii Ayatskov, a presidential appointment, retained his post heading the regional administration, having secured 81.4% of the popular vote to become the first popularly elected regional leader in Russia. He was re-elected for a further term in April 2000, amid accusations of electoral manipulation, which removed all other serious candidates from the contest, and press censorship. As Governor, Ayatskov carried out extensive reform to the region's agro-industrial sector, which culminated, in November 1997, in the passing in the Oblast of the first law in Russia to provide for the purchase and sale of agricultural land. The law greatly diminished the power base of communists and nationalists in the region, and by April 1998 land sales had already generated 3m. roubles for the regional economy. A series of bilateral trade agreements signed with the Mayor of Moscow, Yurii Luzhkov, in August 1996, also benefited the economy of Saratov Oblast. Legislative elections, held in August 2002, were dominated by nominally independent candidates and by supporters of the pro-Government Unity and Fatherland-United Russia. In February 2003 the former oblast Minister of Culture, Yurii Grishchenko, was sentenced to two years' imprisonment by the regional court, on charges of accepting bribes during his tenure as minister, becoming one of the highest-ranking state officials to be subject to such punishment. (The sentence, however, was regarded as relatively mild, and significantly below that which was provided for by law.) Grishchenko was additionally to be prohibited from being employed by any government body for a period of one year after his release.

## Economy

In 1999 Saratov Oblast's gross regional product totalled 48,595.4m. roubles, equivalent to 17,888.3 roubles per head. The region's major industrial centres are at Saratov, Engels and Balakovo. In 2000 there were 2,298 km (1,428 miles) of railways and 10,169 km of paved roads on the Oblast's territory. It was the major Soviet/Russian arsenal for chemical weapons, provoking some local concern. In January 1996 it was announced that chemical weapons stored near the village of Gornyi would be destroyed, in accordance with international agreements. A new chemicals-weapons processing plant, at Gornyi, commenced operations in December 2002.

Its agriculture, which employed some 19.7% of the working population in 2000, consists primarily of animal husbandry and the production of grain (the Oblast is one of Russia's major producers of wheat), sunflower seeds and sugar beet. In 2000 total agricultural production amounted to a value of 19,733m. roubles. The Oblast's main industries are mechanical engineering, the production of electricity, petroleum-refining, chemicals, the manufacture of building materials, food-processing and the production of petroleum and natural gas. In the late 1990s the region produced over 30% of the cement and 20% of the mineral fertilizer produced in the Volga Economic Area. Total industrial production was worth 41,878m. roubles in 2000, and some 20.3% of the work-force was engaged in industry at that time.

The region's economically active population numbered 1,321,000 in 2000, when 9.5% of the labour force were unemployed. In mid-2002 the average wage in the Oblast was 2,796.3 roubles per month. The regional budget for 2000 showed a deficit of 101.2m. roubles. In

that year the value of external trade amounted to US $511.3m. in exports and $147.2m. in imports. Foreign investment amounted to $5.5m. in 2000, when 48 joint enterprises were registered in the region; of these, 10 involved partners from Cyprus, and nine involved partners from Germany. At 31 December 2000 there were 10,800 small businesses registered in the region.

## Directory

**Head of the Regional Administration (Governor):** DMITRII F. AYATSKOV; 410042 Saratov, ul. Moskovskaya 72; tel. (8452) 27-20-86; fax (8452) 72-52-54; e-mail governor@gov.saratov.ru; internet www.gov.saratov.ru.

**Chairman of the Regional Duma:** SERGEI A. SHUVALOV; 411031 Saratov, ul. Radishcheva 24A; tel. (8452) 27-99-80; fax (8452) 27-53-31; e-mail post@srd.ru; internet www.srd.ru.

**Representation of Saratov Oblast in the Russian Federation:** 109028 Moscow, per. Podkopayevskii 7/3; tel. and fax (095) 917-05-19.

**Head of Saratov City Administration (Mayor):** YURII N. AKSENENKO; 410600 Saratov, ul. Pervomaiskaya 78; tel. (8452) 23-77-78; fax (8452) 27-84-44; e-mail mayor@admsaratov.ru; internet www.admsaratov.ru.

# Smolensk Oblast

Smolensk Oblast is situated in the central part of the Eastern European Plain on the upper reaches of the Dnepr (Dnieper). It forms part of the Central Federal Okrug and the Central Economic Area. An international boundary with Belarus lies to the south-west, while Pskov and Tver Oblasts lie to the north, Moscow to the north-east and Kaluga and Bryansk to the south-east. The Oblast covers an area of 49,800 sq km (19,220 sq miles) and extends for some 280 km (175 miles) from south to north and 250 km from west to east. It is divided into 25 administrative districts and 15 cities. The estimated population was 1,098,300 at 1 January 2002, and the population density 22.1 per sq km. Some 70.5% of the region's inhabitants lived in urban areas in 2001. Its administrative centre is at Smolensk, a river-port on the Dnepr, with 347,600 inhabitants in 2001.

## History

Smolensk city was first documented in 863, as the chief settlement of the Krivichi, a Slavic tribe. It became an Orthodox Christian bishopric in 1128. It achieved prosperity during the 14th and 15th centuries as it was situated on one of the Hanseatic trade routes. Smolensk was the site of a major battle in 1812, between the Russian imperial army and the forces of Emperor Napoleon I of France, who subsequently went on to occupy the city of Moscow for a time. It was seized by the Bolsheviks in late 1917 and remained under their control for the duration of the civil war. Smolensk Oblast was formed on 27 September 1937.

The communist establishment remained in control of the region in the early years of Russia's restored independence. The Communist Party of the Russian Federation (CPRF) won the most seats in the Regional Duma elected in 1994 and secured the highest proportion of the votes of any party in elections to the State Duma in both 1995 and 1999. In the gubernatorial election of April–May 1998, after a second round of voting, the CPRF candidate and Mayor of Smolensk, Aleksandr Prokhorov, defeated the incumbent. However, support for the CPRF declined significantly in the regional legislative elections held in May 2002. In the same month Viktor Maslov, a general in the Federal Security Service (FSB) was elected as the new Governor of Smolensk Oblast, receiving 41.6% of the votes cast, compared with the 35.3% received by Prokhorov. Maslov's campaign had concentrated on issues of law and order, and concern about, in particular, organized crime, which was subsequently heightened, following the assassination of Vladimir Prokhorov, the First Deputy Governor and Maslov's campaign manager, in early August.

## Economy

In 1999 Smolensk Oblast's gross regional product amounted to 21,729.0m. roubles, or 19,057.2 roubles per head. Its major industrial centres are at Smolensk, Roslavl, Safonovo, Vyazma, and Yartsevo. In 2000 there were 1,258 km of railway lines and 8,862 km of paved roads in the Oblast.

Agriculture in Smolensk Oblast, which employed 17.3% of the work-force in 2000, mainly consists of animal husbandry and the production of grain, sugar beet and sunflower seeds. Total agricultural output was worth 6,273m. roubles in 2000. Its main industries are textiles, mechanical engineering, chemicals, light manufacturing, food-processing, electrical-energy production and the production of building materials. In 2000 23.7% of the work-force were engaged in industry. Total industrial production in that year amounted to a value of 27,037m. roubles.

The region's economically active population numbered 565,000 in 2000, when 12.2% of the labour force were unemployed. The average wage in the Oblast stood at 3,305.6 roubles per month in mid-2002. The 2000 budget showed a deficit of 9.4m. roubles. In 2000 the value of external trade amounted to US $412.3m. in exports and $107.3m. in imports. Total foreign investment in the region amounted to $10.9m. in that year. At 31 December 2000 there were 2,600 small businesses in operation.

## Directory

**Head of the Regional Administration (Governor):** Viktor N. Maslov; 214008 Smolensk, pl. Lenina 1; tel. (08122) 3-65-71; fax (08122) 3-68-51; e-mail maslov@admin.smolensk.ru; internet admin.smolensk.ru.

**Chairman of the Regional Duma:** Vladimir I. Anisimov; 214008 Smolensk, pl. Lenina 1; tel. (08122) 3-67-00; fax (08122) 3-71-85; e-mail duma@admin.smolensk.ru; internet admin.smolensk.ru/~duma.

**Representation of Smolensk Oblast in the Russian Federation:** Moscow.

**Head of Smolensk City Administration:** Vladislav N. Khaletskii; 214000 Smolensk, ul. Oktyabrskoi Revolyutsii 1/2; tel. and fax (08100) 3-11-81; e-mail smol@admin.smolensk.ru; internet www.admcity.smolensk.ru.

# Sverdlovsk Oblast

Sverdlovsk Oblast is situated on the eastern, and partly on the western, slopes of the Central and Northern Urals and in the Western Siberian Plain. It forms part of the Urals Federal Okrug and the Urals Economic Area. Tyumen Oblast lies to the east (with its constituent Khanty-Mansii AOk to the north-west), there is a short border with the Republic of Komi in the north-west and Perm Oblast lies to the west. To the south are Bashkortostan, Chelyabinsk and Kurgan. The region's major rivers are those of the Ob and Kama basins. The west of the region is mountainous, while much of the eastern part is taiga (forested marshland). The territory of the Oblast covers an area of 194,800 sq km (75,190 sq miles) and is divided into 30 administrative districts and 47 cities. At 1 January 2001 the estimated population totalled 4,572,800, and the population density was 23.5 per sq km. As many as 87.5% of the region's inhabitants lived in urban areas in 2001. The Oblast's administrative centre is at Yekaterinburg (formerly Sverdlovsk), which had a population of 1,256,900 in 2001. Other major cities are Nizhnii Tagil (386,900), Kamensk-Uralskii (188,300) and Pervouralsk (135,000).

## History

Yekaterinburg city was founded in 1821 as a military stronghold and trading centre. Like the Oblast (formed on 17 January 1934) it was named Sverdlovsk in 1924 but, unlike the Oblast, reverted to the name of Yekaterinburg in 1991. The city was infamous as the location where the last Tsar, Nicholas II, and his family were assassinated in 1918. The region became a major industrial centre after the Second World War.

Following the disintegration of the USSR, Sverdlovsk Oblast was among the most forthright in demanding the devolution of powers from the centre. In September 1993 the Regional Soviet adopted a draft constitution for a 'Ural Republic', which was officially proclaimed on 27 October by the Regional Soviet and the head of the regional administration, Eduard Rossel. The 'Ural Republic' was dissolved by presidential decree, however, and Rossel was dismissed on 9 November. In 1994 elections were held to a Regional Duma. In August 1995 Rossel was reinstated as Governor, having won the direct election to head the regional administration. His popularity enabled him to establish an independent 'Transformation of the Urals Movement' that eclipsed support for the national parties in the region in the federal elections of December 1995.

As Governor, Rossel continued to strive for more autonomy for the Oblast, one of the most powerful and potentially most prosperous regions in the Federation. In January 1996 Rossel signed an agreement on the division of powers and spheres of competence between federal and regional institutions. This accord was the first of its kind to be signed with a federal territory that did not have republican status. In April elections were held to the oblast Legislative Assembly, one of the few bicameral legislatures among the Oblasts of the Russian Federation, and also one of the few regional legis-

latures that makes no provision for the formation of groupings of deputies. Less than one-third of the electorate participated, but some 35% voted for Rossel's Transformation bloc. Subsequently, however, the Governor's popularity began to decline: in April 1998 the Transformation bloc won just 9.3% of the votes to the regional legislature and claimed just two seats in the lower house, the Regional Duma (where it had previously held a majority). Rossel was re-elected as Governor of Sverdlovsk Oblast on 12 September 1999. It was subsequently claimed that Urals Federal Okrug, formed in mid-2000 by President Vladimir Putin, incorporated several regions traditionally regarded as part of Siberia, while excluding other regions that were included in the Urals Economic Area, so as to inhibit any revival of an appeal for a 'Ural Republic'. Rossel subsequently adopted a less oppositional stance towards the federal authorities, and became a member of the pro-Government Unity and Fatherland-United Russia (UF-UR) party; he was elected to the Supreme Council of the party in March 2003. On 21 September Rossel was re-elected as Governor of the Oblast, receiving 55.5% in a 'run off' election against Anton Bakov, of Gennadii Seleznev's Party of the Rebirth of Russia. Later in the month Rossel was appointed as the leader of the UF-UR list in Sverdlovsk Oblast at the forthcoming elections to the State Duma, scheduled for 7 December.

## Economy

Sverdlovsk Oblast is a leading territory of the Russian Federation in terms of industry; the concentration of industry in the Oblast is around four times the average for a federal unit. In 1999 the territory's gross regional product amounted to 123,408.9m. roubles, equivalent to 26,674.9 roubles per head. Its most important industrial centres are at Yekaterinburg, Nizhnii Tagil, Pervouralsk, Krasnouralsk, Serov, Alapayevsk and Kamensk-Uralskii. In 2000 there were 3,569 km (2,218 miles) of railway lines and 10,457 km of paved roads on the Oblast's territory. There is an international airport, Koltsovo.

The Oblast's agriculture, which employed just 6.6% of its work-force in 2000, consists of grain production and animal husbandry. Total agricultural output in 2000 was worth 16,857m. roubles. There is some extraction of gold and platinum in the Oblast. Its main industries are ferrous and non-ferrous metallurgy, the production of electrical energy, mechanical engineering (the most important plant being the Yekaterinburg-based Uralmash), food-processing and the production of copper and other ores, bauxite, asbestos, petroleum, peat and coal. There is also a significance defence sector. Industry employed some 32.2% of the working population in 2000 and generated 168,220m. roubles. The services sector was also of increasing significance in the regional economy; the Oblast was given approval to issue US $500m.-worth of Eurobonds.

Sverdlovsk's economically active population numbered 2,328,000 in 2000, when 10.0% of the labour force were unemployed. The average monthly wage in the region was 4,731.5 roubles in mid-2002. The 2000 budget showed a surplus of 756.0m. roubles, and total foreign investment in that year was US $163.1m.; international trade amounted to some $2,779.6m. in exports and $578.7m. in imports. At 31 December 2000 there were 21,600 small businesses registered in the region.

## Directory

**Chairman of the Administration (Governor):** Eduard E. Rossel; 620031 Sverdlovsk obl., Yekaterinburg, pl. Oktyabrskaya 1; tel. (3432) 51-13-65; fax (3432) 70-54-72; e-mail press-center@midural.ru; internet www.rossel.ru.

**Chairman of the Government:** Aleksei P. Vorobev; 620031 Sverdlovsk obl., Yekaterinburg, pl. Oktyabrskaya 1; tel. (3432) 71-79-20; fax (3432) 77-17-00; internet www.midural.ru.

**Chairman of the House of Representatives of the Legislative Assembly:** Viktor V. Yakimov; 620031 Sverdlovsk obl., Yekaterinburg, pl. Oktyabrskaya 1; tel. (3432) 78-91-08; fax (3432) 71-80-48; e-mail duma@midural.ru; internet www.duma.midural.ru.

**Chairman of the Regional Duma of the Legislative Assembly:** Nikolai A. Voronin; 620031 Sverdlovsk obl., Yekaterinburg, pl. Oktyabrskaya 1; tel. (3432) 78-91-08; fax (3432) 71-80-48; e-mail duma@midural.ru; internet www.duma.midural.ru.

**Chief Representative of Sverdlovsk Oblast in the Russian Federation:** Vladimir S. Melentiyev; 121019 Moscow, ul. Novyi Arbat 21; tel. and fax (095) 291-90-72.

**Head of Yekaterinburg City Administration (Mayor):** Arkadii M. Chernetskii; 620014 Sverdlovsk obl., Yekaterinburg, pr. Lenina 24; tel. (3432) 56-29-90; fax (3432) 71-79-26; e-mail glava@sov.mplik.ru.

# Tambov Oblast

Tambov Oblast is situated in the central part of the Oka-Don plain. It forms part of the Central Federal Okrug and the Central Chernozem Economic Area. Penza and Saratov Oblasts lie to the east, Voronezh to the south, Lipetsk to the west and Ryazan to the north. Tambov city lies 480 km (298 miles) south-east of Moscow. Its major rivers are the Tsna and the Vorona. Its territory occupies 34,300 sq km (13,240 sq miles) and measures around 250 km from south to north and 200 km from west to east. The Oblast is divided into 23 administrative districts and eight cities. At 1 January 2002 its population was estimated at 1,240,700, giving a population density of 36.2 per sq km. In 2001 some 58.0% of the population inhabited urban areas. The administrative centre is at Tambov, which had a population of 308,000 in 2001. The second largest city in the Oblast is Michurinsk (116,800).

## History

Tambov city was founded in 1636 as a fort to defend Moscow. The region, 'the mystical core of Russia', was the scene of an army mutiny during the anti-tsarist uprising of 1905, and came under Bolshevik control immediately following the October Revolution in 1917. None the less, numerous peasant revolts against the Bolsheviks, which were brutally suppressed by forces led by Marshal Mikhail Tukachevskii, took place in the Oblast in the early 1920s. The Oblast, which was formed on 27 September 1937, was considered part of the 'red belt' of committed Communist Party adherence in the 1990s. The dissolution of the oblast Soviet in October 1993, and its replacement by a Regional Duma, did not ease the tension between the communist-led assembly with the regional administration. Having appointed Oleg Betin, a locally respected Governor, President Boris Yeltsin permitted a gubernatorial election in Tambov in December 1995. However, Betin lost to the Communist Party of the Russian Federation candidate, Aleksandr Ryabov, and was instead appointed as presidential representative to the region. Betin, thus, remained visible in the political life of the Oblast prior to his election as governor in December 1999, with the support of two centrist movements, Fatherland and Unity. In elections held to the Regional Duma in March 1998 (at which the rate of participation was just over 25%), the greatest number of seats was won by a local pro-market party, comprised largely of young directors of firms and enterprises. New elections to the Regional Duma were held in December 2001; the rate of voter participation was unexpectedly high, at some 40%.

## Economy

In 1999 Tambov Oblast's gross regional product amounted to 17,878.8m. roubles, equivalent to 14,016.0 roubles per head. The region's industrial centres are at Tambov, Michurinsk, Morshansk, Kotovsk and Rasskazovo. It is situated on the ancient trading routes from the centre of Russia to the lower Volga and Central Asia and contains several major road and rail routes. In 2000 there were 746 km of railway lines and 5,284 km of paved roads in the region.

The Oblast's agriculture, which employed a relatively high proportion of the work-force (some 28.8% in 2000) consists mainly of the production of grain, sugar beet, sunflower seeds and vegetables. Animal husbandry and horticulture are also important. Total agricultural output was worth 9,658m. roubles in 2000. The principal industries in the Oblast are mechanical engineering, metal-working, chemicals and petrochemicals, the production of electrical energy, light manufacturing and food-processing. In 2000 17.9% of the working population was engaged in industry. Total industrial production in that year amounted to a value of 12,557m. roubles.

The economically active population stood at 583,000 in 2000, when 8.2% of the labour force were unemployed. In mid-2002 the average monthly wage in the Oblast was 3,305.6 roubles. In 2002 the region was among those with the lowest-priced foodstuffs in the Russian Federation. There was a budgetary surplus of 105.3m. roubles in 2000. In that year the value of external trade amounted to only US $32.8m. in exports and $45.4m. in imports; foreign investment in the Oblast stood at $9.5m. At 31 December 2000 3,600 small businesses were registered in the region.

## Directory

**Head of the Regional Administration (Governor):** OLEG I. BETIN; 392017 Tambov, ul. Internatsionalnaya 14; tel. (0752) 72-10-61; fax (0752) 72-25-18; e-mail post@regadm.tambov.ru; internet www.regadm.tambov.ru.

**Chairman of the Regional Duma:** VLADIMIR N. KAREV; 392017 Tambov, ul. Internatsionalnaya 14; tel. (0752) 71-23-70; fax (0752) 71-07-72.

**Representation of Tambov Oblast in the Russian Federation:** Moscow.

**Head of Tambov City Administration (Mayor):** ALEKSEI YU. ILIN; 392000 Tambov, ul. Kommunalnaya 6; tel. (0752) 72-20-30; fax (0752) 72-47-71; e-mail cvc_t@rambler.ru; internet www.cityadm.tambov.ru.

# Tomsk Oblast

Tomsk Oblast is situated in the south-east of the Western Siberian Plain. It forms part of the Siberian Federal Okrug and the West Siberian Economic Area. Kemerovo and Novosibirsk Oblast lie to the south, Omsk to the south-west, the Khanty-Mansii AOk (part of Tyumen Oblast) to the north-west and Krasnoyarsk Krai to the east. Its major rivers are the Ob, the Tom, the Chulym, the Ket, the Tym and the Vasyugan. The Ob flows for about 1,000 km (almost 400 miles) from the south-east to the north-west of the territory. Its largest lake is the Mirnoye. Almost all the Oblast's territory is taiga (forested marshland), and over one-half of its total area is forested. It occupies 316,900 sq km (122,320 sq miles) and is divided into 16 administrative districts and six cities. At 1 January 2002 its total population was 1,060,800, giving a population density of only 3.3 per sq km. In 2001 67.2% of the population inhabited urban areas. Around 88.2% of the population were ethnically Russian at this time, 2.6% were Ukrainian and 2.1% Tatar. The administrative centre of the Oblast is at Tomsk, which had a population of 483,100 in 2001. The other major city in the region is Seversk (119,500).

## History

Tomsk city was founded as a fortress in 1604. It was a major trading centre until the 1890s, when the construction of the Trans-Siberian Railway promoted other centres. Tomsk Oblast was formed on 13 August 1944. In 1993 the Regional Soviet was initially critical of President Boris Yeltsin's forcible dissolution of the federal parliament. It too, therefore, was disbanded and replaced by a Regional Duma. The Communist Party of the Russian Federation remained the most popular party in the region, securing 19% of the votes cast in elections to the State Duma in 1995. However, in a simultaneous gubernatorial election for the Oblast, the pro-Yeltsin incumbent, Viktor Kress, won the popular mandate to head the regional administration. In elections to the regional legislature in January 1998, independent candidates fared well, with the business lobby winning 30 of the 42 seats. Kress, the Chairman of the inter-regional association 'Siberian Accord', and a member of Our Home is Russia, was re-elected with a clear majority at the gubernatorial election of 5 September 1999. In March 2003 the Regional Duma approved a motion condemning the US-led military invasion of Iraq; reports suggested that this measure had, in part, been precipitated by a US-Russian agreement to close two of the three reactors used to produce weapons-grade plutonium in the 'closed' city of Seversk. Kress was re-elected to a further term of office on 21 September, obtaining 71.2% of the votes cast, according to preliminary figures.

## Economy

In 1999 the gross regional product of Tomsk Oblast amounted to 31,166.3m. roubles, equivalent to 29,135.5 roubles per head. The industrial sector plays a dominant role in the economy of the Oblast. Its major industrial centres are at Tomsk, Kopashevo, Asino and Strezhevoi. In 2000 there were 346 km of railways and 3,512 km of paved roads on the Oblast's territory.

The Oblast's agricultural sector, which generated 5,719m. roubles in 2000, consists mainly of animal husbandry, the production of grain, vegetables and flax, fishing, hunting and fur farming. Some 10.7% of the Oblast's working population was engaged in agriculture in 2000. Around 1.4m. ha (3.4m. acres) of the Oblast's territory was used for agricultural purposes, of which one-half was arable land. The Oblast has substantial reserves of coal as well as of petroleum and natural gas (estimated at 333.7m. metric tons and 300,000m. cu m, respectively). Its other main industries are mechanical engineering, metal-working, the electro-technical industry, the processing of agricultural products and chemicals. Industry employed 21.5% of the working population in 2000, and industrial output amounted to a value of 24,393m. roubles in that year.

The economically active population of Tomsk Oblast numbered 532,000 in 2000, when 12.2% of the labour force were unemployed. The average monthly wage was 5,508.4 roubles in mid-2002. There was a budgetary deficit of 108.8m. roubles in 2000. The Oblast's most significant partners in international trade are the USA and the Republic of Korea, with the chemical industry accounting for the majority of this activity. In 2000 the value of external trade amounted to US $719.1m. in exports and $50.8m. in imports. In that year total foreign investment amounted to $25.1m. At 31 December 2000 6,900 small businesses were registered in the region.

## Directory

**Head of the Regional Administration (Governor):** Viktor M. Kress; 634050 Tomsk, pl. Lenina 6; tel. (3822) 51-05-05; fax (3822) 51-03-23; e-mail ato@tomsk.gov.ru; internet www.tomsk.gov.ru.

**Chairman of the Regional Duma:** Boris A. Maltsev; 634050 Tomsk, pl. Lenina 6; tel. (3822) 51-01-47; fax (3822) 51-06-02; e-mail duma@tomsk.gov.ru; internet duma.tomsk.gov.ru.

**Chief Representative of Tomsk Oblast in the Russian Federation:** Aleksandr N. Cherevko; 103030 Moscow, ul. Dolgorukovskaya 38/1/406; tel. (095) 973-31-21; fax (095) 299-37-95; e-mail tomskadm@chat.ru.

**Head of Tomsk City Administration (Mayor):** Aleksandr S. Makarov; 634050 Tomsk, pr. Lenina 73; tel. (3822) 52-68-99; fax (3822) 52-68-60; e-mail pmayor@admin.tomsk.ru; internet admin .tomsk.ru.

# Tula Oblast

Tula Oblast is situated in the central part of the Eastern European Plain in the northern section of the Central Russian Highlands. It forms part of the Central Federal Okrug and the Central Economic Area. Tula Oblast is bordered by the Oblasts of Ryazan to the east, Lipetsk to the south-east, Orel to the south-west, Kaluga to the north-west and Moscow to the north. Tula city is 193 km (about 120 miles) south of Moscow City. The region's major rivers are the Oka, the Upa, the Don and the Osetr. The territory of the Oblast covers an area of 25,700 sq km (9,920 sq miles) and extends for 230 km from south to north and 200 km from west to east. It is divided into 23 administrative districts and 21 cities. It is a highly populated area, with a total population of 1,690,000 at the beginning of 2002, and a population density of 65.8 per sq km. At 1 January 2001 some 81.5% of the Oblast's population inhabited urban areas. The Oblast's administrative centre is at Tula, a military town, which had a population of 495,500 in 2001. Other major cities include Novomoskovsk (with 135,300 inhabitants).

## History

The city of Tula was founded in the 12th century. It became an important economic centre in 1712, with the construction of the Imperial Small Arms Factory. Tula Oblast was founded on 26 September 1937. Tula's armaments industry meant that it was closed to foreigners for most of the Soviet period.

On 7 October 1993 the Tula Regional Soviet refused to disband itself, but was subsequently dissolved and its functions transferred to the Regional Administration. A new representative body, the 48-seat Regional Duma, was later elected and remained dominated by members of the former communist *nomenklatura*. The Communist Party of the Russian Federation (CPRF) remained the most widely supported party in the Oblast throughout the 1990s, receiving the largest proportion of the votes cast for any party in the State Duma elections of both 1995 and 1999. The Oblast also had a high-profile CPRF Governor, following the election of Vasilii Starodubtsev in March 1997. He had previously been known nationally as a participant in the coup organized against the Soviet leader, Mikhail Gorbachev, in August 1991. Starodubtsev's continuing reputation as a radical communist was reflected in his standing as the sole 'red belt' governor to support the candidacy of Gennadii Zyuganov in the presidential election of 26 March 2000. Starodubtsev was also elected as a CPRF member of the State Duma in the legislative election of December 1999, but he refused to take his seat as, to do so, he would have been required to relinquish his position as Oblast Governor. Gubernatorial elections, held in two rounds in April 2001, aroused widespread controversy. One day before the first round of the elections a meeting of the electoral commission, which reportedly had been convened to consider withdrawing the right of one candidate, Andrei Samoshin, to participate in the election, was attacked by a group of men, and fighting ensued; the commission had previously accused Samoshin of misusing electoral funds and violating campaign procedures. In the event, Samoshin was permitted to participate, coming in second place, with 21.0% of the votes cast, behind Starodubtsev, with 49.4%, fewer than the 50% of the votes required for an outright victory. However, Samoshin withdrew his candidacy on 19 April, three days before the 'run-off' election was due to take place, citing his dissatisfaction with the conduct of the electoral commission. Despite his reluctance to participate, the commission ruled that the third-placed candidate, Viktor Sokolovskii, was to stand against Starodubtsev in the 'run-off' election. On 22 April Starodubtsev received over 71% of the votes cast in the second round of voting, for which Sokolovskii had refused to campaign.

## Economy

In 1999 Tula Oblast's gross regional product amounted to 30,286.0m. roubles, or 17,232.4 roubles per head. Its important industrial centres are at Tula, Novomoskovsk, Shchekino, Aleksin, Uzlovaya and Yefremov. In 2000 there were 1,103 km of railway lines and 5,162 km of paved roads in the Oblast.

Around 73.7% of the Oblast's territory is used for agricultural purposes. Agricultural activity, in which some 11.4% of the working population were engaged in 2000, consists primarily of animal husbandry and production of grain, potatoes and sugar beet. Agricultural production was worth 10,449m. roubles in 2000. The Oblast's main industries are mechanical engineering, metalworking, chemicals, ferrous metallurgy, food-processing, the production of brown coal (lignite) and the generation of electricity. Industry employed approximately 28.0% of the working population in 2000, and total industrial production amounted to a value of 45,032m. roubles. Ferrous metallurgy, mechanical engineering and metal-working dominated exports in the region. A tourism sector is encouraged by the city's history and the Yasnaya Polyana country estate of Count Leo Tolstoy (1828–1910), the writer.

The economically active population in the Oblast numbered 831,000 in 2000, when 9.7% of the labour force were unemployed. In mid-2002 those in employment earned an average monthly wage of 3,368.1 roubles; the region was named as one of the worst for wage arrears in that year. The 2000 budget showed a surplus of 233.9m. roubles. The main foreign trading partners of the Oblast are Germany, Italy, the Republic of Korea (South Korea), Switzerland and the USA. In 2000 external trade comprised US $651.5m. of exports and $139.9m. of imports. Total foreign investment amounted to $81.6m. in that year. At 31 December 2000 6,300 small businesses were registered in Tula Oblast.

## Directory

**Head of the Regional Administration (Governor):** Vasilii A. Starodubtsev; 300600 Tula, pl. Lenina 2; tel. (0872) 27-84-36; fax (0872) 20-63-26; e-mail michel@adm.tula.ru.

**Chairman of the Regional Duma:** Oleg D. Lukichev; 300600 Tula, pl. Lenina 2; tel. (0872) 20-50-24; fax (0872) 36-47-66; e-mail oblduma@duma.tula.ru.

**Representation of Tula Oblast in the Russian Federation:** 127030 Moscow, Veskovskii per. 2; tel. (095) 978-14-56; fax (095) 978-06-43.

**Head of Tula City Administration (Mayor):** Sergei I. Kazakov; Tula; tel. (0872) 27-80-85.

# Tver Oblast

Tver Oblast (known as Kalinin from 1931 to 1990) is situated in the central part of the Eastern European Plain. It forms part of the Central Federal Okrug and the Central Economic Area. Moscow and Smolensk Oblasts lie to the south, Pskov to the west, Novgorod and Vologda to the north and Yaroslavl to the east. Its westernmost point lies some 50 km (just over 30 miles) from the border with Belarus. The major rivers in the region are the Volga, which rises within its territory, the Mologa and the Tvertsa. The Zapadnaya Dvina and the Msta rivers also have their sources in the Oblast. It has more than 500 lakes, the largest of which is the Seliger, and contains nine reservoirs. The western part of the territory is mountainous, containing the Valdai Highlands. About one-third of the territory of the Oblast is forested. It occupies 84,100 sq km (32,460 sq miles) and is divided into 36 administrative districts and 23 cities. At 1 January 2001 the region had 1,575,000 inhabitants, and a population density, therefore, of 18.7 per sq km. In 2001 some 73.6% of the population inhabited urban areas. The administrative centre is at Tver (formerly Kalinin), a river-port, which at the beginning of January 2001 had a population of 447,100.

## History

The city of Tver was founded as a fort in 1135. The Oblast was formed in January 1935. In the 1990s the region's relations with the federal Government, led by President Boris Yeltsin, were not always cordial. In October 1993 the Tver Regional Soviet refused to disband itself, but was subsequently obliged to comply with the directives of the federal authorities and a new body, the Legislative Assembly, was elected the following year. This, too, was dominated by members of the Communist Party of the Russian Federation (CPRF) and was obstructive of executive action. President Yeltsin appointed a respected local figure to head the regional administration and decided to permit a gubernatorial election in December 1995. The incumbent was defeated by Vladimir Platov, a member of the CPRF;

in the concurrent election to the State Duma, the CPRF secured some 27% of the regional vote. The federal Government attempted to placate local opinion, therefore, and in June 1996 the regional authorities were granted greater autonomy with the signing of a power-sharing treaty. Platov, by then one of the founders of the pro-Vladimir Putin Unity electoral bloc, won a second term in office in the second round of voting at the gubernatorial election held in January 2000, promising reform and improved living standards. Unity also obtained the largest number of votes cast for any party in elections to the State Duma in the Oblast in the previous month. In late September 2003 criminal charges of abuse of office were formally issued against Platov, relating to the apparent disappearance of 463m. roubles from oblast funds in 2002. (The charges had been prepared earlier in the month, but Platov was reportedly hospitalized before they could be issued.) The emergence of accusations of malpractice, denied by Platov, in the period leading up to gubernatorial elections (scheduled for 7 December 2003), created an atmosphere of political tension in the Oblast in late 2003. Platov (who had previously announced his intention to stand for re-election) accused political rivals of conspiring against him.

## Economy

In 1999 Tver Oblast's gross regional product amounted to 27,887.7m. roubles, equivalent to 17,307.6 roubles per head. Industry is the dominant branch of the Oblast's economy. The principal industrial centres are Tver, Vyshnii Volochek, Rzhev, Torzhok and Kimryi. The region is crossed by road and rail routes between Moscow and Rīga, Latvia, and a highway between Moscow and St Petersburg. In 2000 the total length of railway track in the Oblast was 1,811 km, and the network of paved roads was 14,959 km long. There were 924 km of navigable waterways in the region in 1998, mainly on the Volga. There is an international airport at Tver.

Around 2.4m. ha (5.9m. acres) of the Oblast's territory is used for agricultural purposes, of which two-thirds is arable land. Agriculture in Tver Oblast, which employed around 14.8% of the workforce in 2000, consists mainly of animal husbandry and the production of vegetables, potatoes and flax (the region grows around one-quarter of flax produced in Russia). Total agricultural output amounted to a value of 9,238m. roubles in 2000. The region contains deposits of peat, lime and coal, and is famous for its mineral-water reserves. Its major industries are mechanical engineering, metal-working, electricity generation, light manufacturing, chemicals, wood-working, the processing of forestry and agricultural products, printing and glass-, china- and faience-making. In 2000 some 28.0% of the Oblast's working population were engaged in industry, and total industrial production was worth 28,539m. roubles. In 1998 there were 20 commercial banks and 100 insurance companies and branches in operation on the Oblast's territory.

The region's economically active population numbered 778,000 in 2000, when 9.4% of the labour force were unemployed. The average wage amounted to 3,413.9 roubles per month in mid-2002. The 2000 regional budget showed a deficit of 51.3m. roubles. Tver's main trading partners in the late 1990s were the People's Republic of China, Germany, Switzerland, Turkey and the USA. In 2000 external trade amounted to a value of US $105.0m. in exports and $174.2m. in imports. In 1998 a social and cultural development programme for Tver Oblast (for 1998–2005) was adopted by the federal Government, which gave tax incentives to foreign investors. Total foreign investment in the Oblast amounted to $7.9m. in 2000. In that year 3,600 small businesses were operating in the region, employing 38,000 people.

## Directory

**Head of the Regional Administration (Governor):** Vladimir I. Platov; 170000 Tver, ul. Sovetskaya 44; tel. (0822) 33-10-51; fax (0822) 42-55-08; e-mail tradm@tversa.ru; internet www.region.tver .ru.

**Chairman of the Legislative Assembly:** Mark Zh. Khasainov; 170000 Tver, ul. Sovetskaya 33; tel. (0822) 32-10-11; fax (0822) 48-10-15; e-mail zsto@tdn.ru; internet www.zsto.ru.

**Representation of Tver Oblast in the Russian Federation:** 103246 Moscow, ul. B. Dmitrovka 26; tel. (095) 926-65-19; fax (095) 292-14-85.

**Head of Tver City Administration (Mayor):** Oleg S. Levedev; 170640 Tver, ul. Sovetskaya 11; tel. (0822) 33-01-31; fax (0822) 42-59-39; e-mail info@www.tver.ru; internet www.tver.ru.

# Tyumen Oblast

Tyumen Oblast is situated in the Western Siberian Plain, extending from the Kara Sea in the north to the border with Kazakhstan in the south. It forms part of the Urals Federal Okrug and the West Siberian Economic Area. Much of its territory comprises the Khanty-Mansii—Yugra and Yamal-Nenets Autonomous Okrugs (AOks). To the west (going south to north) lie Kurgan, Sverdlovsk, Komi and the Nenets AOk—part of Archangel Oblast; to the east lie Omsk, Tomsk and Krasnoyarsk—in the far north the border is with Krasnoyarsk's Taimyr AOk. The region has numerous rivers, its major ones being the Ob, the Taz, the Pur and the Nadym. Much of its territory is taiga (forested marshland). The territory of the Oblast, including that of the AOks, occupies an area of 1,435,200 sq km (554,130 sq miles) and is divided into 38 administrative districts and 28 cities. The Oblast, in particular that section within the AOks, is a sparsely populated region: the estimated total population at 1 January 2002 was 3,272,200 and the population density was 2.3 per sq km. When the area of the AOks is excluded, the area of the Oblast is 161,800 sq km, and the population of this area was 1,339,500 in 2002, giving a population density of 8.3 per sq km. The Oblast, excluding the AOks, is divided into 22 administrative districts and five cities. In 2001 some 76.6% of the entire Oblast's inhabitants lived in urban areas. The Oblast's administrative centre is at Tyumen, which then had a population of 500,200. Other major cities outside the AOks are Tobolsk (96,800) and Ishim (60,200).

## History

Tyumen city was founded in 1585 on the site of a Tatar settlement. It subsequently became an important centre for trade with the Chinese Empire. Tyumen Oblast was formed on 14 August 1944. The region became industrialized after the Second World War. On 21 October 1993 the Regional Soviet in Tyumen Oblast repealed its earlier condemnation of government action against the federal parliament but refused to disband itself. Legislative elections were held in the Oblast in March 1994, but the results in several constituencies were declared invalid, owing to a low level of participation. Eventually a new assembly, the Regional Duma, was elected. It remained communist-led, but the pro-Government faction was well represented. During the mid-1990s the exact nature of the relationship between Tyumen Oblast proper and the two AOks, which wished to retain a greater share of the income from their wealth of natural resources, became a source of intra-élite contention, despite the establishment of a co-ordinating administrative council between the three entities in 1995. In 1997 the two AOks (which between them accounted for over 90% of the output and profits in the oblast) had boycotted the gubernatorial elections for the Oblast, while a subsequent Constitutional Court ruling failed to clarify the status of the AOks in relation to the Oblast. However, the AOks did participate in elections to the Regional Duma later in 1997. In 1998 Sergei Korepanov, the former Chairman of the Yamal-Nenets legislature, was elected Chairman of the legislature of Tyumen Oblast. This was widely considered to form part of a plan by representatives of the AOks (who together constituted a majority of seats in the oblast legislature) to remove the Governor of Tyumen, Leonid Roketskii. At the gubernatorial election held on 14 January 2001, Sergei Sobyanin, a former speaker in the legislature of the Khanty-Mansii AOk and the first deputy presidential representative in the Urals Federal Okrug, defeated Roketskii, obtaining more than 51% of the votes cast. Sobyanin consistently stated his opposition to any reabsorption of the two AOks into Tyumen Oblast, emphasizing his belief that a successful balance of powers and distribution of financial resources had been attained between the three political entities.

## Economy

All figures in this survey include data for the two AOks, which are also treated separately. In the mid-1990s Tyumen Oblast was considered to have great economic potential, owing to its vast hydrocarbons and timber reserves (mainly located in the Khanty-Mansii—Yugra and Yamal-Nenets AOks). In 1999 its gross regional product amounted to 356,139.0m. roubles, equivalent to 110,475.2 roubles per head (by far the highest figure in the Russian Federation). Its main industrial centres are at Tyumen, Tobolsk, Surgut, Nizhnevartovsk and Nadym. In 2000 there were 2,451 km (1,523 miles) of railway lines and 9,361 km of paved roads on the Oblast's territory.

The Oblast's agriculture, which employed just 6.1% of its workforce in 2000, consists mainly of animal husbandry (livestock- and reindeer-breeding), fishing, the production of grain, flax and vegetables, fur farming and hunting. In 2000 agricultural production was worth 12,310m. roubles. The production of alcohol beverages, particularly vodka, in the region increased markedly in the early 2000s, and by 2003 the region was one of the seven principal regions active in the sector. In the late 1990s the Oblast's reserves of petroleum, natural gas and peat were estimated at 60%, 90% and 36%, respectively, of Russia's total supply. The Tyumen Oil Company (TNK), formed in 1995 from nine other companies, is among the largest petroleum companies in Russia and produced 156m. barrels of crude petroleum in 1996. From 1997, when the state's share in the company was reduced to less than one-half, TNK became increasingly market-driven. In 2003 TNK merged with Sidanco and the Russian interests of British Petroleum (of the United Kingdom), and was renamed TNK-BP. Overall petroleum output in the region totalled 213m. metric tons in 2000. The Oblast's other major industries are the production of electrical energy, mechanical engineering and metal-working. Industry employed some 18.2% of the Oblast's working population in 2000 and generated a total of 469,374m. roubles, by far the highest level of any federal subject.

The economically active population totalled 1,687,000 in 2000, when 10.3% of the work-force were unemployed, compared with 14.0% in 1998. The average monthly wage was 12,400.9 roubles in mid-2002, among the highest wages in the Federation. The budget for 2000 showed a surplus of 6,323.2m. roubles. Trade figures for 2000 showed the Oblast to have generated some US $15,821.4m. in exports (of which some 92% were destined for non-member countries of the Commonwealth of Independent States) and to have purchased $807.0m. of imports. Total foreign investment in the Oblast amounted to $1,842.6m. in that year. At the end of 2000 12,500 small businesses were registered in the region.

## Directory

**Governor:** Sergei S. Sobyanin; 625004 Tyumen, ul. Volodarskogo 45; tel. (3452) 46-77-20; fax (3452) 46-55-42; internet www.adm.tyumen.ru.

**Chairman of the Regional Duma:** Sergei Ye. Korepanov; 625018 Tyumen, ul. Respubliki 52, Dom Sovetov; tel. (3452) 45-50-81; e-mail tyumduma@tmn.ru; internet www.tmn.ru/~tyumduma.

**Chief Representative of Tyumen Oblast in the Russian Federation:** Vladimir M. Goryunov; 119017 Moscow, ul. Pyatnitskaya 47/2; tel. and fax (095) 291-71-94.

**Head of Tyumen City Administration:** Stepan M. Kirichuk; 625036 Tyumen, ul. Pervomaiskaya 20; tel. (3452) 24-67-42; fax 46-42-72; e-mail ves@tyumen-city.ru; internet www.tyumen-city.ru.

# Ulyanovsk Oblast

Ulyanovsk Oblast is situated in the Volga Highlands. It forms part of the Volga Federal Okrug and the Volga Economic Area. The Republics of Mordoviya and of Chuvashiya and Tatarstan lie to the north-west and to the north, respectively. There are also borders with Samara Oblast in the south-east, Saratov Oblast in the south and Penza Oblast in the south-west. The region's major river is the Volga. The region occupies an area of 37,300 sq km (14,400 sq miles) and is divided into 21 administrative districts and six cities. The estimated total population of the Oblast was 1,439,600 in January 2002, when the population density, therefore, was 38.6 per sq km. In 2001 some 73.2% of the population inhabited urban areas. The administrative centre at Ulyanovsk (formerly Simbirsk) had a population of 662,100 in 2001. The other major city in the region is Dimitrovgrad (136,400).

## History

Simbirsk city was founded in 1648. Lenin (Vladimir Ulyanov) was born there in 1870, and it was his home until 1887. The city assumed his family name following his death in 1924. Ulyanovsk Oblast, which was formed on 19 January 1943, formed part of the 'red belt' of communist support in post-Soviet Russia. Thus, it refused to revert to its old name and also gave the Communist Party of the Russian Federation (CPRF) 37% of the regional votes cast in the 1995 elections to the federal State Duma. In December 1996 the CPRF-backed candidate, Yurii Goryachev, won the election to the governorship of the Oblast. Goryachev, whose support came largely from the Oblast's rural community, banned local privatization and collective-farm reforms, imposed restrictions on imports and exports, and subsidized bread prices until early 1997. Goryachev was defeated in the gubernatorial elections held in December 2000, and replaced by Lt-Gen. Vladimir Shamanov. In June 2002 the national power company, Unified Energy System of Russia (RAO EES Rossii), announced its intention to appeal to the federal authorities for the direct imposition of federal rule over Ulyanovsk Oblast, owing to the region's debts to that company, which had been permitted to accrue in the period prior to Shamanov's election. In early 2003 widespread protests followed the announcement that electricity tariffs in the Oblast were to increase by 43%, in order that the debts be repaid over a period of 15 years. In response to these protests, tariffs were, in the event, increased by 14% in April.

## Economy

In 1999 Ulyanovsk Oblast's gross regional product amounted to 26,050.1m. roubles, or 17,693.5 roubles per head. The Oblast's major

industrial centres are at Ulyanovsk and Melekess. In 2000 there were 716 km (445 miles) of railway lines and 4,621 km of paved roads on the Oblast's territory.

Around 1.5m. ha of its territory is used for agricultural purposes, of which over four-fifths is arable land. Agriculture in the region, which employed some 15.8% of the working population in 2000, consists primarily of animal husbandry and the production of grain, sunflower seeds and sugar beet. Total agricultural production amounted to a value of 7,092m. roubles in 2000. The Oblast's main industries are mechanical engineering and metal-working, food-processing, electrical energy and fuel production, and the manufacture of building materials. The region's major companies included the UAZ automobile plant and the Aviastar aeroplane manufacturer (both of which were working at 50% capacity in the late 1990s). In late 2002 Aviastar signed a contract, reportedly worth US $335m., to construct 25 TU-204-120 jets, following the acquisition of a 25% stake (less one share) in the firm by the Egyptian concern Sirocco Aerospace International; the Chairman of Sirocco, Ibrahim Kamel, expressed the intention of further developing the capacities of the Aviastar plant. Industry employed 28.8% of the working population in 2000, and generated some 28,961m. roubles.

The economically active population numbered 684,000 in 2000, when only 6.4% of the labour force were unemployed, the lowest level in any federal subject other than the two federal cities and the remote Evenk and Taimyr AOks. Those in employment earned an average of 2,907.5 roubles per month in mid-2002. In mid-2003 the region was named as one of the three worst regions for public-sector wage arrears, which were reported to amount to some 125m. roubles. The recently appointed Deputy Chairman of the federal Government, responsible for Social Affairs, Galina Karelova, visited Ulyanovsk in June, and announced that a special commission was to be established to investigate the situation. There was a budgetary deficit of 383.1m. roubles in 2000. In that year external trade constituted US $173.1m. in exports and $52.9m. in imports; total foreign investment in the Oblast amounted to $1.5m. At 31 December 2000 5,000 small businesses were registered in the region.

## Directory

**Head of the Regional Administration (Governor):** Lt-Gen. Vladimir A. Shamanov; 432970 Ulyanovsk, pl. Lenina 1; tel. (8422) 41-38-22; fax (8422) 41-48-12; e-mail admobl@mv.ru; internet www.ulyanovsk-adm.ru.

**Chairman of the Legislative Assembly:** Boris I. Zotov; 432700 Ulyanovsk, ul. Radishcheva 1; tel. and fax (8422) 41-34-52; internet zsuo.ru.

**Representative of Ulyanovsk Oblast in the Russian Federation:** Gennadii V. Savinov; 119002 Moscow, per. Denezhnyi 12; tel. (095) 241-31-42; fax (095) 241-38-99.

**Head of Ulyanovsk City Administration (Mayor):** Pavel Romanenko; 432700 Ulyanovsk, ul. Kuznetsova 7; tel. (8422) 41-45-08; fax (8422) 41-40-20; e-mail meria@mv.ru; internet www.ulmeria.ru.

# Vladimir Oblast

Vladimir Oblast is situated in the central part of the Eastern European Plain. It forms part of the Central Federal Okrug and the Central Economic Area. It shares borders with Ryazan and Moscow to the south-west, Yaroslavl and Ivanovo to the north and Nizhnii Novgorod to the east. The Oblast's main rivers are the Oka and its tributary, the Klyazma. Over one-half of its territory is forested. It occupies a total of 29,000 sq km (11,200 sq miles) and measures around 170 km (106 miles) from south to north and 280 km from west to east. The Oblast is divided into 16 administrative districts and 23 cities. It had an estimated population of 1,573,900 at 1 January 2002, giving a population density of 54.3 per sq km. In 2001 some 80.4% of the population inhabited urban areas. The Oblast's administrative centre is at Vladimir, which had a population of 331,700 in 2001. Other major cities are Kovrov (159,300), Murom (139,500) and Gus-Khrustalnyi (71,500).

## History

Founded in 1108 as a frontier fortress by Prince Vladimir Monomakh, after the disintegration of Kievan Rus, Vladimir city was the seat of the principality of Vladimir-Suzdal and an early Orthodox Christian bishopric. Vladimir fell under the rule of Muscovy in 1364 and was supplanted by Moscow as the seat of the Russian Orthodox patriarch, although Vladimir was chosen for the coronations of several Muscovite princes. It declined in importance from the 15th century. Vladimir Oblast was formed on 14 August 1944.

In the December 1995 parliamentary election, the Communist Party of the Russian Federation (CPRF), the nationalist Liberal

Democrats, and the pro-Government Our Home is Russia all obtained more than 10% of the votes cast, while in the December 1999 election the CPRF obtained only a slightly higher share of the votes cast than the recently formed pro-Government party, Unity. The CPRF, however, secured the election of Nikolai Vinogradov, former Chairman of the Legislative Assembly, to the post of Governor in late 1996. Vinogradov was re-elected as Governor in December 2000, with some 66% of the votes cast, defeating Yurii Glasov, who had held the post in 1991–96.

## Economy

Vladimir Oblast's gross regional product in 1999 totalled 25,577.0m. roubles, or 15,828.3 roubles per head. The Oblast's main industrial centres are at Vladimir, Kovrov, Murom, Aleksandrov, Kolchugino, Vyazniki and Gus-Khrustalnyi. In 2000 there were 929 km of railway track and 5,530 km of paved roads on its territory.

Agriculture in the region, which employed 9.9% of its work-force in 2000, consists mainly of animal husbandry, vegetable production and horticulture. Total agricultural output stood at 7,892m. roubles in 2000. Vladimir is rich in peat deposits and timber reserves, but relies on imports for around 70% of its energy supplies. The Oblast's main industries are mechanical engineering, metal-working, food-processing, the production of electrical energy, light manufacturing, chemicals, glass-making and handicrafts. Industrial output in 2000 was worth 36,010m. roubles. In that year a total of 33.8% of the working population were engaged in industry. Vladimir city's largest employer is the Vladimir Tractor Plant, which struggled to adapt to the new economic conditions from the 1990s.

The economically active population numbered 810,000 in 2000, when 12.2% of the labour force were unemployed. The average monthly wage in the Oblast was 3,128.2 roubles in mid-2002. In 2000 there was a regional surplus of 158.3m. roubles. In that year external trade constituted US $101.1m. in exports and $147.3m. in imports; total foreign investment amounted to some $21.3m. At 31 December 2000 6,900 small businesses were registered in the region.

## Directory

**Head of the Regional Administration (Governor):** Nikolai V. Vinogradov; 600000 Vladimir, pr. Oktyabrskii 21; tel. (0922) 33-15-52; fax (0922) 35-34-45; e-mail post@avo.ru; internet avo.ru.

**Chairman of the Legislative Assembly:** Anatolii V. Bobrov; 600000 Vladimir, Oktyabrskaya pr. 21; tel. (0922) 32-66-53; fax (0922) 23-08-06; internet www.zsvo.ru.

**Representative of Vladimir Oblast in the Russian Federation:** Andrei V. Yarin; Moscow; tel. (095) 299-66-49.

**Head of Vladimir City Administration:** Aleksandr P. Rybakov; 600000 Vladimir, ul. Gorkogo 36; tel. (0922) 23-28-17; fax (0922) 23-85-54; e-mail mayor@vladimir-city.ru; internet www.vladimir-city.ru.

# Volgograd Oblast

Volgograd Oblast is situated in the south-east of the Eastern European Plain. It forms part of the Southern Federal Okrug and the Volga Economic Area. The Oblast has an international border with Kazakhstan to its east. The federal subjects of Astrakhan and Kalmykiya lie to the south-east, Rostov to the south-west, Voronezh to the north-west and Saratov to the north. The Oblast's main rivers are the Volga and the Don. Its terrain varies from fertile black earth (*chernozem*) to semi-desert. Volgograd city is the eastern terminus of the Volga–Don Canal. The region occupies an area of 113,900 sq km (43,980 sq miles) and is divided into 33 administrative districts and 19 cities. At 1 January 2002 it had an estimated total of 2,636,500 inhabitants, and a population density of 23.1 per sq km. In 2001 some 73.9% of the population lived in urban areas. In 1989 around 89% of the population were ethnic Russians, while 3% were Ukrainians, 2% were Kazakhs and 1% were Tatars. In the early 1990s there was an influx of immigrants to the Oblast from more unstable areas of the Caucasus. The Oblast's administrative centre is at Volgograd, which had a population of 982,900 in 2001. Other major cities are Volzhskii (281,700) and Kamyshin (124,100).

## History

The city of Volgograd (known as Tsaritsyn until 1925 and Stalingrad from 1925 until 1961) was founded in the 16th century, to protect the Volga trade route. It was built on the River Volga, at the point where it flows nearest to the Don (the two river systems were later connected by a canal). The Oblast was formed on 10 January 1934. In 1942–43 the city was the scene of a decisive battle between the forces of the USSR and Nazi Germany.

In October 1993 the Regional Soviet in Volgograd Oblast eventually agreed to a reform of the system of government in the Oblast. It decided to hold elections to a new 30-seat Regional Duma, which took place the following year. The Communist Party of the Russian Federation (CPRF) was the largest single party. The continued pre-eminence of the old ruling élite was confirmed by the 27% share of the regional poll secured by the CPRF list in the 1995 election to the State Duma. Furthermore, the December 1996 gubernatorial election was won by Nikolai Maksyuta, a communist and a former Chairman of the regional assembly. In December 1998 CPRF candidates won some 23 of the 32 seats in the regional legislative elections. Maksyuta was re-elected for a second term as Governor on 19 December 1999. On 24 September 1998 the Regional Duma had voted for the principle of restoring the Oblast's previous name of Stalingrad, and this notion remained popular, among both members of the oblast legislature, and the broader populace, in the early 2000s; however, federal President Vladimir Putin expressed his opposition to the proposed renaming during a television broadcast in December 2002.

## Economy

In 1999 Volgograd Oblast's gross regional product amounted to 49,974.2m. roubles, or 18,602.7 roubles per head. Its main industrial centres are at Volgograd, Bolzhskii and Kamyshyn. In 2000 there were 1,619 km (1,006 miles) of railways and 8,701 km of paved roads. In 1996 construction of a road bridge across the Volga river into Volgograd began.

The region's principal agricultural products are grain, sunflower seeds, fruit, vegetables, mustard and cucurbits (gourds and melons). Horticulture and animal husbandry are also important. In 2000 18.8% of the Oblast's work-force were engaged in agriculture. Total agricultural production amounted to a value of 16,724m. roubles in that year. The Oblast's mineral reserves include petroleum, natural gas and phosphorites. The main industries in the Oblast are petroleum-refining, chemicals and petrochemicals, mechanical engineering, metal-working, ferrous and non-ferrous metallurgy, the production of electricity, the manufacture of building materials, light manufacturing, food-processing and the production of petroleum and natural gas. Industry employed 23.7% of the working population in 2000, when total industrial production was worth 56,995m. roubles.

The economically active population of the Oblast numbered 1,295,000 in 2000, when 9.7% of the labour force were unemployed. The average monthly wage was 3,312.7 roubles in mid-2002. In 2000 there was a budgetary deficit of 695.7m. roubles. In that year external trade constituted US $869.8m. in exports and $252.7m. in imports; total foreign investment amounted to $139.5m. In 2000 there were some 94 joint foreign enterprises in the region, including 10 with investment from Cyprus and eight with investment from the United Kingdom. At the end of 2000 13,000 small businesses were registered in the region.

## Directory

**Head of the Regional Administration (Governor):** Nikolai K. Maksyuta; 400098 Volgograd, pr. Lenina 9; tel. (8442) 33-66-88; fax (8442) 93-62-12; e-mail glava@volganet.ru; internet www.volganet.ru.

**Chairman of the Regional Duma:** Roman G. Grebennikov; 400098 Volgograd, pr. Lenina 9; tel. (8442) 36-54-25; fax (8422) 36-44-03; internet duma.volganet.ru.

**Representation of Volgograd Oblast in the Russian Federation:** Moscow; tel. (095) 229-96-73.

**Head of Volgograd City Administration (Mayor):** Yevgenii P. Ishchenko; 400131 Volgograd, ul. Volodarskogo 5; tel. (8442) 33-50-10; fax (8442) 36-64-65; e-mail kancelyaria@volgadmin.ru; internet www.volgadmin.ru.

# Vologda Oblast

Vologda Oblast is situated in the north-west of the Eastern European Plain. It forms part of the North-Western Federal Okrug and the Northern Economic Area. It has a short border, in the north-west, with the Republic of Kareliya, which includes the southern tip of Lake Onega (Onezhskoye). Onega also forms the northern end of a border with Leningrad Oblast, which lies to the west of Vologda. Novgorod Oblast lies to the south-west and Tver, Yaroslavl and Kostroma Oblasts to the south. Kirov Oblast forms an eastern border and Archangel Oblast lies to the north. The region's main rivers are the Sukhona, the Yug, the Sheksna and the Mologa. There are three major lakes, in addition to Lake Onega—Beloye, Bozhe and Kubenskoye. Vologda Oblast occupies 145,700 sq km (56,250 sq miles) and extends for 385 km (240 miles) from south to north and 650 km from west to east. It is divided into 26 administrative districts and 15 cities. The Oblast's population at the beginning of 2002 was estimated at 1,301,100 and the population density was, therefore, 8.9 per sq km. Some 68.3% of the total population inhabited urban areas in 2001. The Oblast's administrative centre is at Vologda, which had a population of 298,200 in 2001. Its other major city is Cherepovets (323,300).

## History

Vologda province was annexed by the state of Muscovy in the 14th century. The city was, for a time, the intended capital of Tsar Ivan IV ('the Terrible', 1533–84). Vologda Oblast was formed on 23 September 1937.

In 1991 the newly elected Russian President, Boris Yeltsin, appointed a new head of administration of Vologda Oblast. In mid-1993 the Vologda Oblast declared itself a republic, but failed to be acknowledged as such by the federal authorities. On 13 October the Regional Soviet transferred its responsibilities to the Regional Administration and elections were later held to a Legislative Assembly. In 1995 ballots implemented the Statutes of Vologda Oblast, according to which the region's Governor would lead the executive. There was a high level of support for the nationalist Liberal Democrats, particularly in the countryside, for much of the 1990s. In June 1996 Boris Yeltsin dismissed the local Governor, who was subsequently arrested and imprisoned on charges of corruption. His successor, Vyacheslav Pozgalev, won 80% of the votes cast in a direct election in late 1996, and was re-elected for a further term of office on 19 December 1999, with 83% of the votes cast. In March 2003 Pozgalev was elected to the Supreme Council of the pro-Government Unity and Fatherland-United Russia party.

## Economy

In 1999 Vologda Oblast's gross regional product amounted to 47,279.0m. roubles, equivalent to 35,591.0 roubles per head. Its main industrial centres are at Vologda, Cherepovets, Velikii Ustyug and Sokol. In 2000 there were 768 km of railway track in general use on its territory, as well as 11,766 km of paved roads. There are some 1,800 km of navigable waterways, including part of the Volga–Baltic route network.

Agriculture in Vologda Oblast, which employed 11.7% of the work-force in 2000, consists mainly of animal husbandry and production of flax and vegetables. The region is famous for its butter. In 2000 total agricultural output was worth 9,878m. roubles. The territory imports around one-half of its electrical energy from other Oblasts (Kostroma, Kirov, Leningrad, Tver and Yaroslavl). Its main industries are ferrous metallurgy (the region produces some 20% of Russia's iron, 19% of its rolled stock and 18% of its steel), chemicals (around 11% of the country's mineral fertilizers are manufactured in Vologda Oblast), the processing of forestry products, mechanical engineering, pharmaceuticals, glass-making, food-processing and handicrafts, such as lace-making. In 2000 29.1% of the region's working population were engaged in industry. Severstal, the largest privately owned steel manufacturer in Russia, based in Cherepovets, is one of the major employers in the Oblast. The industrial sector generated a total of 87,603m. roubles.

The Oblast's economically active population numbered 673,000 in 2000, when the rate of unemployment was 8.0%. Those in employment in mid-2002 earned, on average, 4,525.8 roubles per month. The 2000 budget showed a surplus of 308.3m. roubles. In 2000 export trade constituted US $1,518.2m. in exports and $126.8m. in imports; total foreign investment in the Oblast in that year amounted to $19.9m. In December 2000 6,000 small businesses were registered in the region.

## Directory

**Governor:** Vyacheslav Ye. Pozgalev; 160035 Vologda, ul. Gertsena 2; tel. (8172) 72-07-64; fax (8172) 25-15-54; e-mail governor@vologda-oblast.ru; internet www.vologda-oblast.ru.

**Chairman of the Legislative Assembly:** Nikolai V. Tikhomirov; 160035 Vologda, ul. Pushkinskaya 25; tel. (8172) 72-02-60; fax (8172) 25-11-33; e-mail zsvo@vologda.ru.

**Chief Representative of Vologda Oblast in the Russian Federation:** Vladimir S. Smirnov; Moscow; tel. (095) 201-73-48; fax (095) 201-55-24.

**Head of Vologda City Administration:** Aleksei S. Yakunichev; 160035 Vologda, ul. Kamennyi most 4; tel. (8172) 72-00-42; fax (8172) 72-25-59.

# Voronezh Oblast

Voronezh Oblast is situated in the centre of the Eastern European Plain on the middle reaches of the Volga. It forms part of the Central Federal Okrug and the Central Chernozem Economic Area. There is a short border with Ukraine in the south. Of the neighbouring Russian federal territories, Belgorod and Kursk lie to the west, Lipetsk and Tambov to the north, a short border with Saratov to the north-east, Volgograd to the east and Rostov to the south-east. The west of the territory is situated within the Central Russian Highlands and the east in the Oka-Don Lowlands. Its main rivers are the Don, the Khoper and the Bityug. The Voronezh region occupies an area of 52,400 sq km (20,230 sq miles) and is divided into 32 administrative districts and 15 cities. The Oblast's estimated population at 1 January 2002 was 2,414,700, and its population density was, therefore, 46.1 per sq km. In 2001 some 62.1% of the population lived in urban areas. The region's administrative centre is at Voronezh, which had a population of 901,800 in 2001.

## History

Voronezh city was founded in 1586 as a fortress. Tsar Petr (Peter—'the Great') founded the first units of what became the imperial Russian Navy in Voronezh in 1696. The centre of a fertile region, the city began to industrialize in the tsarist period. Voronezh Oblast was formed in June 1934. In the immediate post-Soviet years the region remained committed to the Communist Party of the Russian Federation (CPRF), which controlled the Regional Duma. The regional legislature is among a minority in post-Soviet Russia in which there is a significant proportion (40%) of paid deputies. A CPRF member and former speaker of the oblast assembly, Ivan Shabonov, was elected Governor in December 1996. At the gubernatorial election held in December 2000 Shabonov received only 15% of the votes cast, and was defeated by Vladimir Kulakov, a general in the Federal Security Service (FSB), who obtained some 60% of the votes. Subsequently, at the regional legislative election held in March 2001 the CPRF reduced its level of representation from 23 seats to just five.

## Economy

In 1999 Voronezh Oblast's gross regional product amounted to 40,710.1m. roubles, equivalent to 16,503.2 roubles per head. The important industrial centres in the Oblast are at Voronezh, Borisoglebsk, Rossosh and Kalach. In 2000 the territory contained some 1,189 km (739 miles) of railway track (of which 60.2% are electrified) and 9,102 km of paved roads. The road network includes sections of major routes, such as the Moscow–Rostov, Moscow–Astrakhan and Kursk–Saratov highways. There are some 640 km of navigable waterways.

Around 4.7m. ha (11.6m. acres—90% of the total) of Voronezh's territory is used for agricultural purposes, of which 3.1m. ha is arable land. In 2000 24.3% of the Oblast's working population were employed in the agricultural sector. The Oblast's agriculture consists mainly of the production of grain, sugar beet, sunflower seeds, fruit and vegetables. Animal husbandry was also important. Total agricultural production amounted to a value of 19,134m. roubles in 2000. Its main industries are mechanical engineering, metal-working, chemicals and petrochemicals, the production of electricity, the manufacture of building materials and food-processing. In 2000 some 19.8% of the work-force were engaged in industry, the output of which was valued at a total of 33,131m. roubles.

The Oblast's economically active population numbered 1,179,000 in 2000, when 10.0% of the labour force were unemployed. In mid-2002 the Oblast's average wage was 2.817.3 roubles per month. There was a budgetary deficit of 275.6m. roubles in 2000. In that year the value of external trade amounted to US $182.4m. in exports and $168.2m. in imports. Foreign investment in the region increased dramatically from the mid-1990s, and in 2000 it amounted to $20.9m., compared with $4.0m. in 1998. In 2000 there were 53 joint- or foreign enterprises, established primarily with funds from Belarus, Cyprus, Germany, the United Kingdom and the USA. At 31 December 2000 there were 11,000 small businesses registered in the region.

## Directory

**Head of the Regional Administration:** Vladimir G. Kulakov; 394018 Voronezh, pl. Lenina 1; tel. (0732) 55-27-37; fax (0732) 53-28-02; internet admin.vrn.ru.

**Chairman of the Regional Duma:** Aleksei M. Nakvasin; 394018 Voronezh, ul. Kirova 2; tel. (0732) 52-21-03; fax (0732) 52-09-22; e-mail voblduma@inbox.ru.

**Chief Representative of Voronezh Oblast in the Russian Federation:** Aleksandr I. Firsov; 127006 Moscow, ul. M. Dmitrovka 3/10/501; tel. (095) 250-98-55; fax (095) 299-90-27.

**Head of Voronezh City Administration (Mayor):** ALEKSANDR YA. KOVALEV; 394067 Voronezh, ul. Plekhanovskaya 10; tel. (0732) 55-34-20; fax (0732) 55-47-16; e-mail admin@city.vrn.ru; internet www .city.vrn.ru.

# Yaroslavl Oblast

Yaroslavl Oblast is situated in the central part of the Eastern European Plain. It forms part of the Central Federal Okrug and the Central Economic Area. Ivanovo Oblast lies to the south-east, Vladimir and Moscow Oblasts to the south, Tver Oblast to the west, Vologda Oblast to the north and Kostroma Oblast to the east. Yaroslavl city, which lies on the Volga, is 282 km (175 miles) north-east of Moscow. The region has 2,500 rivers and lakes, its major two lakes being Nero and Pleshcheyevo, and there is a large reservoir at Rybinsk, formed in 1941, following the completion of a dam and a hydroelectric power plant nearby. The Volga river flows for 340 km through the region. Its territory, just over two-fifths of which is forested, covers a total area of 36,400 sq km (14,050 sq miles) and is divided into 17 administrative districts and 11 cities. The estimated total population in the Oblast at the beginning of 2002 was 1,386,300, giving a population density of 38.1 per sq km. In 2001 some 80.4% of the population inhabited urban areas. The Oblast's administrative centre is at Yaroslavl, which had a population of 608,800 in 2001. The second city in the Oblast is Rybinsk (238,300).

## History

Yaroslavl city is reputed to be the oldest town on the River Volga, having been founded *c.* 1024. The region was acquired by the Muscovite state during the reign of Ivan III (1462–1505). Yaroslavl Oblast was formed in March 1936. In the 1990s the region developed a liberal and diverse political climate. A range of interests was represented in the new, 23-seat Regional Duma elected in February 1994. Thus, in December 1995 the federal President, Boris Yeltsin, permitted his appointed Governor, Anatolii Listisyn, to contest a direct election for the post, which he won. He was re-elected for a further term on 19 December 1999, obtaining 63.9% of the votes cast. In early 2003 Listisyn announced his intention to contest gubernatorial elections scheduled to be held on 7 December, having obtained the support of the pro-Government Unity and Fatherland-United Russia party.

## Economy

In 1999 Yaroslavl Oblast's gross regional product amounted to 37,749.3m. roubles, equivalent to 26,580.3 roubles per head. The major industrial centres in the region are at Yaroslavl itself, Rybinsk, Tutayev, Uglich and Pereslavl-Zalesskii. There are river-ports at Yaroslavl, Rybinsk and Uglich. Its total length of railway track amounted to 650 km in 2000. The Oblast lies on the main Moscow–Yaroslavl–Archangel and Yaroslavl–Kostroma highways. In 2000 the total length of paved roads in the territory was 6,270 km. There are also around 789 km of navigable waterways.

The climate and soil quality in the region is not favourable to agriculture. Agricultural activity, which employed just 10.1% of the working population in 2000, consists primarily of animal husbandry and the production of vegetables, flax and grain. Total agricultural output was worth 7,361m. roubles in 2000. The main industries are mechanical engineering (Rybinsk Motors is Russia's largest manufacturer of aircraft engines), chemicals and petrochemicals, petroleum-refining, peat production, the production of electricity and the processing of agricultural products. In 2000 industrial output in the region amounted to a value of 45,534m. roubles and industry employed some 31.1% of the work-force.

The economically active population numbered 747,000 in 2000, when the region had one of the lowest rates of unemployment (7.3%) in the Federation. The average wage was 3,908.4 roubles per month in mid-2002. In 2000 there was a regional budgetary surplus of 240.8m. roubles. In that year total foreign investment in the region amounted to US $7.7m., and external trade amounted to a value of $869.5m. in exports and $191.9m. in imports. At 31 December 2000 there were 7,300 small businesses registered in the Oblast.

## Directory

**Governor:** ANATOLII I. LISITSYN; 150000 Yarovslavl, pl. Sovetskaya 3; tel. (0852) 72-81-28; fax (0852) 32-84-14; internet www.adm.yar.ru.

**Chairman of the Regional Duma:** ANDREI G. KRUTIKOV; 150000 Yaroslavl, pl. Sovetskaya 5; tel. (0852) 30-50-83; fax (0852) 72-76-45; e-mail duma@adm.yar.ru; internet www.adm.yar.ru/duma/index .asp.

**Representation of Yaroslavl Oblast in the Russian Federation:** Moscow; tel. (095) 253-45-18.

**Head of Yaroslavl City Administration (Mayor):** VIKTOR V. VOLONCHUNAS; 150000 Yaroslavl, ul. Andropova 6; tel. (0852) 30-46-41; fax (0852) 30-52-79; e-mail ird@gw.city.yar.ru; internet www.city .yar.ru.

# FEDERAL CITIES

## Moscow

Moscow (Moskva) is located in the west of European Russia, on the River Moskva, which crosses the city from the north-west to the south-east. It is connected to the Volga river system by the Moscow–Volga Canal. Moscow is included in the Central Federal Okrug and the Central Economic Area. The city's total area is 994 sq km (384 sq miles). Moscow is the largest city in the Russian Federation and had an estimated total population of 8.5m. at 1 January 2002; the population of the city declined by some 460,000 in 1990–2002. In 1999 around 89.7% of the city's population were ethnic Russians, 2.9% were Ukrainians and 2.0% were Jews.

## History

Moscow city was founded in about 1147. In 1325 it became the seat of the Eastern Orthodox Metropolitan of Rus (from 1589–1721 and after 1917 the Patriarch of Moscow and all Rus) and the steadily expanding Muscovite state became the foundation for the Russian Empire. The centre of tsarist government was moved to St Petersburg in 1712, but Moscow was restored as the Russian and Soviet capital in March 1918.

In the 1980s and 1990s reformists enjoyed considerable support in the city. On 12 June 1991 the democrat Gavriril Popov won the first mayoral elections held in the city. However, Popov resigned in 1992 after the economic situation deteriorated to such an extent that food-rationing was introduced, and Yurii Luzhkov, head of the City Government, and also regarded as a reformist, was appointed by federal President Boris Yeltsin in his place. In October 1993 a presidential decree suspended the powers of the City Soviet. Elections to a new 35-member Municipal Duma were held on 12 December. The Duma held its first session on 10 January 1994.

In a mayoral election held simultaneously with the federal presidential election on 16 June 1996 Luzhkov was re-elected with 89.7% of the votes cast. Thereafter Luzhkov became an increasingly high-profile political figure nation-wide. In June 1998 Luzhkov signed a power-sharing treaty with the federal authorities, following a protracted period of negotiation that resulted in the city receiving taxation and budget privileges. By late 1998 the Moscow City Government owned controlling stakes in a television station, a bank, and a range of other businesses; moreover, Luzhkov concluded a number of trade agreements with other regions, and in 1998 founded the nation-wide, centrist, generally anti-Government political movement, Fatherland. Meanwhile, in February 1998 the Russian Constitutional Court ruled Moscow City's strict controls over residence permits to be illegal and the Supreme Court outlawed such permits (*propiski*, a legacy of the Soviet era) that July. However, Luzhkov opposed or ignored his critics, and even the ruling of the Constitutional Court. Indeed, following a number of bomb attacks in the city in late 1999, which killed over 200 people, and which were officially attributed to supporters of Chechen independence, the city's unconstitutional laws were implemented yet more firmly. Although Luzhkov was re-elected as Mayor, with 69.9% of votes cast, on 19 December 1999, in the simultaneous nation-wide elections to the State Duma Fatherland—All Russia (FAR—as Fatherland had become, following its merger with the All Russia union of regional governors) came third, behind the Communist Party of the Russian Federation and the newly formed pro-Government bloc, Unity. Many of FAR's supporters in the regions backed the candidacy of Vladimir Putin in the presidential campaign, and, after a period of neutrality (during which time Luzhkov was reportedly a candidate for the presidency), Luzhkov also announced his support for Putin. (Indeed, in 2001 FAR merged with Unity to form a new bloc, Unity and Fatherland-United Russia—UF-UR.) In elections to the Municipal Duma held in December 2001 the Fatherland and Unity parties each secured seven seats, followed by the pro-market Union of Rightist Forces with six seats, and the liberal Yabloko with four seats. In the early 2000s Luzhkov remained a prominent advocate of more widespread use of identity checking, and of permit-based systems as a means of combating illicit activity, in particular as bombings and other attacks attributed to Chechen militants, including, notably, the armed siege of a theatre, in which 129 hostages died, in October 2002, continued, intermittently, in Moscow. In January 2003 the city court ruled that a provision of the city council permitting the direct election of the Vice Mayor concurrently with that of the Mayor (as had occured in 1999) contradicted federal law; at the end of March this ruling was upheld by the Supreme Court. In advance of mayoral elections, scheduled to be held on 7 December 2003, Luzhkov, who had become increasingly critical of the federal Government's policies (particularly with regard to a perceived re-centralization of various social and economic powers) confirmed that he would seek a further mandate; it was also announced that Luzhkov had been appointed to the third position on the UF-UR federal list in the concurrent elections to the State Duma.

## Economy

In 1999 the city of Moscow's gross regional product amounted to 677,372.2m. roubles, equivalent to 78,487.7 roubles per head. There are nine railway termini in the city and 11 electrified radial lines. The metro system includes 11 lines and 164 stations and extends for 266 km (165 miles); a suburban light railway extension was scheduled to open in late 2003. Its trolleybus and tram routes are 1,700 km long, its bus routes 5,700 km. The public-transport system carries around 6.5m. passengers per day. Moscow's waterways connect with the Baltic, White, Caspian and Black Seas and the Sea of Azov. There are also four airports on the city's territory.

Moscow's industry consists primarily of mechanical engineering, electricity production, production of chemicals, petroleum-refining and food-processing. Industry employed around 13.3% of the city's working population in 2000 (in contrast to the 0.2% engaged in agriculture) and generated 224,765m. roubles, a figure surpassed in the Russian Federation only by Tyumen Oblast, which has the majority of gas and petroleum deposits in the Federation. The Moskvich Inc. Automobile Plant, in which the City Government held a controlling stake from 1998, is one of Moscow's principal companies. There are also significant defence-sector industries in the city. In 2000 some 15.4% of the working population of Moscow City were engaged in the construction sector. The services sector is also significant in the city economy, with the city authorities having successfully consolidated its leading position within Russia during the 1990s: in 2000 some 18.9% of the working population of the city were employed in the services sector. Although the financial crisis of August 1998 led to a restructuring of the banking and financial sector, the city was sufficiently resourced to recover. As the Russian capital, the city is the site of a large number of government offices, as well as the centre for major business and financial companies. Tourism is another important service industry.

The economic problems of the 1990s were less accentuated in Moscow than in the rest of Russia. In 2000 the proportion of the labour force that was unemployed in Moscow City, at 3.8%, was lower than elsewhere in the Russian Federation, with the exception of the remote Evenk Autonomous Okrug. (In 2000 the economically active population of the city stood at 4.28m.) In mid-2002 those in employment earned, on average, 6,845.2 roubles per month, one of the highest rates in the Federation. The 2000 budget showed a substantial surplus, of 22,634.6m. roubles, but the city finances, while undoubtedly healthy, are notoriously lacking in transparency. In 2000 international trade amounted to a value of US $24,593.1m. in exports and $10,882.8m. in imports, by far the highest level of any federal subject. Capital investment in the city represents around one-10th of that in Russia as a whole. In 2000 some 47% of Russian enterprises and organizations involving foreign capital were situated in Moscow City and the surrounding Moscow Oblast; in 2000 there were some 5,849 such enterprises and organizations in the region, of which 632 were joint ventures with partners from the USA, 587 had Cypriot partners, 535 had Chinese, and 512 German. Total foreign investment in the city amounted to $4,037.1m. in 2000. In September 1997 Moscow became the first city in Russia to enter the international capital market and place a Eurobonds issue. Local companies also flourished, in one of the few regions of Russia that could claim significant economic growth during the 1990s. At the end of 2000 there were 180,000 small companies registered in the city.

## Directory

**Mayor and Prime Minister of the Government of Moscow City:** YURII M. LUZHKOV; 103032 Moscow, ul. Tverskaya 13; tel. (095) 229-58-03; fax (095) 232-18-74; internet www.mos.ru.

**Chairman of the Municipal Duma:** VLADIMIR M. PLATONOV; 103051 Moscow, ul. Petrovka 22; tel. (095) 923-50-80; fax (095) 921-92-02; e-mail d29@mcd.mos.ru; internet duma.mos.ru.

**Representation of Moscow City in the Russian Federation:** Moscow.

# St Petersburg

St Petersburg (Sankt-Peterburg) is a seaport at the mouth of the River Neva, which drains into the easternmost part of the Gulf of Finland (part of the Baltic Sea). St Petersburg is included in the North-Western Federal Okrug and the North-Western Economic Area. The city's territory, including a total of 42 islands in the Neva delta, occupies an area of 570 sq km (220 sq miles—making it the smallest of the Russia's federal subjects), of which its waterways comprise around 10%. There are more than 580 bridges in the city and surrounding area, including 20 drawbridges. The population of the city was an estimated 4.60m. at 1 January 2002, making it Russia's second largest city.

## History

St Petersburg was founded by the Tsar, Peter—Petr I ('the Great') in 1703, as a 'window on the West', and was the Russian capital from 1712 to 1918. At the beginning of the First World War, in 1914, the city was renamed Petrograd. Following the fall of the Tsar and the Bolshevik Revolution in 1917, the Russian capital was moved back to Moscow. A revolt at the naval base of Kronstadt, west of mainland Petrograd,in March 1921 presented one of the most serious challenges to the nascent Bolshevik authorities, as the island had hitherto been renowned as a stronghold of support for the Bolsheviks; the rebels, who were protesting against the steady centralization of powers, were quashed by troops led by Trotskii (Lev Bronstein), and several thousand deaths resulted on both sides. In 1924 the city was renamed Leningrad. During the Second World War it was besieged by German troops for 870 days, between November 1941 and January 1944. In June 1991 the citizens of the city voted to restore the name of St Petersburg, which took effect from October.

In June 1991 a supporter of economic reform, Anatolii Sobchak, was elected as Governor. The city Soviet was finally dissolved by presidential decree on 22 December 1993. In 1994–96 the future federal President, Vladimir Putin, was First Deputy Governor of the city Government. On 24 April 1996 Sobchak approved a draft treaty on the delimitation of powers between municipal and federal organs of Government. In May 1996 another liberal, the hitherto first deputy Mayor, Vladimir Yakovlev, was elected as Mayor, defeating Sobchak.

In the mid-1990s the reformist Yabloko bloc was the dominant political force in the city. However, a series of corruption scandals implicating the municipal authorities subsequently damaged support for Yabloko, while Yakovlev (who was elected as leader of the All-Russia grouping of regional governors in August 1999) also campaigned against the movement, notably at the December 1998 municipal legislative elections, when he sponsored his own list of candidates; following a poor performance at these elections, Yabloko went into opposition. The city legislature attracted controversy in 1999, as it attempted to bring forward the date of the gubernatorial election (as, in fact, had also happened in 1996). However, the Supreme Court ruled that attempts to hold the election earlier than originally scheduled, believed to be of benefit to Yakovlev, were invalid. None the less, Yakovlev won the election, held on 14 May 2000, obtaining 72.7% of the votes cast, having secured the support of the Communist Party of the Russian Federation and nationalist elements.

At the municipal legislative election held in December 2002 38 of the 50 incumbent deputies were re-elected to the regional assembly, although the rate of participation in the election was only 29.4%. (Of the 50 deputies in the new assembly, 31 held no party allegiance.) In early April 2003, after several months of speculation as to whether the Governor intended to seek a change to the city Constitution to permit him to contest a third term of office, Yakovlev announced that he would not do so: Yakovlev's political position appeared to have been weakened by the formation of an anti-Governor majority in the new legislature, and, in particular, by the appointment of a close ally of Putin (who was generally regarded as an opponent of Yakovlev), Valentina Matviyenko, as Presidential Representative to the North-Western Federal Okrug in mid-March. In early June, moreover, the Chairman of the Audit Chamber, Sergei Stepashin, announced that he was to submit documents to the Office of the Prosecutor-General that apparently demonstrated the misuse of some 100m. roubles of public funds by the city authorities. However, it became clear that gubernatorial elections in the city were to take place ahead of schedule when, on 16 June, Putin appointed Yakovlev as a Deputy

Chairman of the federal Government, with special responsibility for housing and the reform of utility services; the hitherto Vice-Governor, Aleksandr Beglov, thereby assumed the responsibilties of Governor, in an acting capacity. In mid-June Matviyenko announced her candidacy for the forthcoming gubernatorial elections; she received the support of Putin, to an extent that was unprecedented for a candidate to a regional governorship. In addition, Matviyenko was supported by the liberal Union of Rightist Forces, Yabloko, the pro-Government Unity and Fatherland-United Russia, and the Communist Party of the Russian Federation, and she also received the backing of Yakovlev. In the first round of polling, on 21 September, Matviyenko received 48.7% of votes cast; she progressed, with her nearest rival, Anna Markova, Yakovlev's former Deputy Governor (with 15.8%), to a second round, on 5 October. In the 'run off' election Matviyenko was elected as Governor, receiving around 63% of the votes cast, according to preliminary figures. The rate of participation in both rounds was around 29%.

On 24 September 1998 the federal President, Boris Yeltsin, approved the administrative merger of the city with Leningrad Oblast, although there was no indication when, or if, the unification (which would be subject to a referendum) would actually occur.

## Economy

In 1999 St Petersburg's gross regional product amounted to 161,748.5m. roubles, or 34,333.5 roubles per head, less than one-half of the figure recorded in Moscow.

Industry in St Petersburg, which employed around 20.2% of its work-force in 2000 (compared with the 0.8% engaged in agriculture), consists mainly of mechanical engineering, ferrous and non-ferrous metallurgy, electricity generation, manufacture of chemicals and petrochemicals, rubber production, light manufacturing, the manufacture of building materials, food- and timber-processing, and printing. There is also a significant defence-sector industry. Total industrial production in the city amounted to a value of 126,234m. roubles in 2000. The city is also an important centre for service industries, such as tourism, financial services and leisure activities; in 2000 the services sector employed some 20.2% of the city's work-force. Celebrations of the city's 300th anniversary, in 2003, which were marked by a series of festivals and special events, were expected to stimulate tourist revenues in that year.

The economically active population in St Petersburg amounted to 2.42m. in 2000, when 6.3% of the work-force were unemployed, one of the lowest rates in Russia. In mid-2002 the average wage in St Petersburg was 5,350.0 roubles, somewhat higher than the national average. The 2000 city budget showed a surplus of 1,637.0m. roubles. The city is an important centre of trade: in 2000 external trade comprised some US $2,544.4m. in exports and $2,598.6m. in imports; although this figure was relatively high compared with the majority of federal subjects, it comprised only around 14% of the value of Muscovite trade in that year. In the late 1990s around 30% of Russia's imports and 20% of its exports passed through St Petersburg. In 2000 foreign investment in St Petersburg amounted to $1,159.9m., compared with $413.3m. in 1998. However, by 2002 it was not a strong commercial capital—the number of Western companies it had attracted and the extent of its property development failed to rival those of Moscow. The re-nationalization of the Lomonosov Porcelain Factory, which took place following a court ruling in St Petersburg in October 1999, annulled its privatization six years earlier, and caused some concern to foreign investors. In 2000 there were some 1,943 joint enterprises in St Petersburg and the surrounding Leningrad Oblast, some 378 of which had Finnish partners, mainly in the Vyborg area, while 253 firms had US partners and 225 had German partners. In 2000 there were some 109,200 small businesses registered in the city.

## Directory

**Mayor (Governor and Premier of the City Government):** VALENTINA I. MATVIYENKO; 193060 St Petersburg, Smolnyi; tel. (812) 271-74-13; fax (812) 276-18-17; e-mail gov@gov.spb.ru; internet www.gov.spb.ru.

**Chairman of the Legislative Assembly:** VADIM A. TYULPANOV; 190107 St Petersburg, Isaakiyevskaya pl. 6; tel. (812) 319-99-31; fax (812) 319-90-01; e-mail vtulpanov@assembly.spb.ru; internet www.assembly.spb.ru.

**Representation of St Petersburg City in the Russian Federation:** 123001 Moscow, ul. Spiridonovka 20/1; tel. (095) 290-43-64; fax (095) 203-50-60.

# AUTONOMOUS OBLAST

## Jewish Autonomous Oblast

The Jewish Autonomous Oblast (Yevreiskaya AOb—Birobidzhan) is part of the Amur river basin, and is included in Russia's Far Eastern Federal Okrug and Far Eastern Economic Area. It is situated to the south-west of Khabarovsk Krai, on the international border with the People's Republic of China. There is a border with Amur Oblast in the north-west. Apart from the River Amur, which is frozen for around five months of the year, the region's major river is the Tungusk Forest, which is particularly concentrated in the north-west, covers more than one-third of its territory. Around one-half is mountainous, with the south and east occupying the western edge of the Central Amur Lowlands. It occupies 36,000 sq km (13,900 sq miles) and has five administrative districts and two cities. The Jewish AOb had a population of 195,600 in January 2001, and a population density, therefore, of 5.4 per sq km. Around 67.1% of its population inhabited urban areas in 2001. The census of 1989 found that, according to official declaration of nationality, ethnic Russians accounted for some 83.2% of the AOb's population and Jews for 4.2% (although this figure can be expected to have decreased subsequently; in the early 1950s Jews had constituted around one-quarter of the population of the Oblast). Indeed, in 1990 alone, around 1,000 of the 9,000 resident in the Oblast in the previous year whose nationality was officially registered as Jewish emigrated to Israel. The regional capital is at Birobidzhan, which had a population of 78,400 in January 2001.

## History

The majority of Russian Jews came under Russian control following the Partitions of Poland in 1772–95. Attempts by the Soviet authorities in the 1920s to create nominally Jewish regions in Ukraine and Crimea were largely unsuccessful, because of hostility on the part of the local population in these regions, although some nominally Jewish adminstrative sub-districts existed in southern Ukraine prior to the Nazi German invasion of the USSR in 1941. The Soviet regime established an national Jewish district at Birobidzhan in 1928, but it never became the centre of Soviet (or Russian) Jewry, largely because of its remote location and the absence of any prior Jewish settlement there. (In Imperial Russia between 1835 and 1917, Jews were required to receive special permission to live outside the 'Pale of Settlement' to the south-west of the Empire, which constituted territories largely in present-day Belarus, Lithuania, Poland and Ukraine.) This province received the status of an Autonomous Oblast in May 1934 and formed part of Khabarovsk Krai until 25 March 1991. In the early post-Soviet period the region remained a redoubt of communist support. Despite the advice of the Russian President, Boris Yeltsin, at a session on 14 October 1993 the Regional Soviet announced that it would not disband itself. Subsequently, however, the council was replaced by a new body, the Legislative Assembly, elections to which confirmed Communist Party domination. A gubernatorial election held on 20 October 1996 was won by the incumbent, Nikolai Volkov; he was re-elected with 57% of the votes cast on 26 March 2000.

## Economy

In 1999 the Jewish AOb's gross regional product stood at 2,443.5m. roubles, equivalent to 12,156.7 roubles per head. Birobidzhan is the region's main industrial centre. In 2000 there were 309 km (192 miles) of railway track, including a section of the Trans-Siberian Railway, and 1,609 km of paved roads on the AOb's territory. In February 2000 the opening of a bridge across the Amur river provided improved road and rail links with the city of Khabarovsk and the People's Republic of China. There are around 600 km of navigable waterways in the south of the Jewish AOb.

Agriculture, which employed 13.6% of the region's work-force in 2000, and generated a total of 906m. roubles in that year, consists mainly of grain, soybean, vegetable and potato production, animal husbandry, bee-keeping, hunting and fishing. From the late 1990s the oblast authorities encouraged Chinese farmers to undertake agricultural activity (both arable and livestock) in the region; greater diversity of crops, as well as an improvement in productivity, resulting in part from a higher level of farming technology, were reported as a result, although concern was expressed, in early 2003, about the number of illegal immigrants in the region. There are major deposits of coal, peat, iron ore, manganese, tin, gold, graphite, magnesite and zeolite, although they are largely unexploited. The main industries are mechanical engineering, the manufacture of building materials, the production of electricity, wood-working, light manufacturing and food-processing. Industry employed around 15.3% of the AOb's working population and generated a total of 1,172m. roubles in 2000. In the mid-1990s the region's foreign economic activity was largely concentrated in the Far East, including the People's Republic of China and Japan.

In 2000 the AOb's economically active population numbered 94,000. Although more than one-quarter of the labour force were unemployed in 1997, by 2000 the unemployment rate had declined to 15.2%. In mid-2002 the average monthly wage in the AOb was 4,254.2 roubles. The 2000 budget showed a surplus of 35.3m. roubles. In that year external trade amounted to a value of US $12.1m. in exports and $4.6m. in imports. In 2000 foreign investment amounted to just $58,000; five of the seven foreign- or jointly-owned enterprises operating in the territory had Chinese partners. On 31 December 2000 500 small businesses were registered in the region.

## Directory

**Head of the Regional Administration (Governor and Chairman of the Government):** NIKOLAI M. VOLKOV; 682200 Jewish AOb, Birobidzhan, pr. 60-letiya SSSR 18; tel. and fax (42622) 6-04-89; e-mail gov@eao.ru; internet www.eao.ru.

**Chairman of the Legislative Assembly:** ANATOLII F. TIKHOMIROV; 682200 Jewish AOb, Birobidzhan, pr. 60-letiya SSSR 18; tel. (42622) 6-44-27; fax (42622) 6-04-78; e-mail press-zs@eao.ru; internet www .eao.ru/?p=22.

**Representation of the Jewish Autonomous Oblast in the Russian Federation:** Moscow.

**Head of Birobidzhan City Administration:** ALEKSANDR VINNIKOV; Jewish AOb, 682200 Birobidzhan, ul. Lenina 29; tel. (42622) 6-22-02; fax (42622) 4-04-93.

# AUTONOMOUS OKRUGS (DISTRICTS)

## Aga-Buryat Autonomous Okrug

The Aga-Buryat Autonomus Okrug (AOk) is situated in the south-east of Transbaikal, in the southern part of Chita Oblast. It forms part of the Siberian Federal Okrug and the East Siberian Economic Area. Its major rivers are the Onon and the Ingoda, and about one-third of its territory is forested. Aga settlement is about 550 km (just under 350 miles) to the east of Ulan-Ude, the capital of Buryatiya (which lies to the west of Chita Oblast). The AOk contains varied terrain, ranging from desert to forest-steppe. The Aga-Buryat AOk occupies a total of 19,000 sq km (7,340 sq miles) and extends for about 250 km from south to north and 150 km from west to east. It has three administrative districts and four 'urban-type settlements'. Its climate is severe and annual precipitation is as little as 250mm–380 mm (about 100 inches–150 inches) per year. Its population at 1 January 2002 was estimated at 79,600, giving a population density, therefore, of 4.2 per sq km. In 2001 just 32.3% of the population inhabited urban areas. In 1989 ethnic Buryats were found to make up some 54.9% of the population, and ethnic Russians 40.8%. The Buryats inhabiting the district are Transbaikal Buryats, who are more closely related to their Mongol ancestors than their western counterparts, the Irkutsk Buryats. The administrative centre is at Aginskoye, which had a population of just 9,500 in January 2001.

### History

The Aga-Buryat-Mongol AOk was created on 26 September 1937, as part of Stalin—Iosif Dzhugashvili's policy of dispersing the Buryat population, whom he perceived as a threat because of their ethnic and cultural links with the Mongolian People's Republic (Mongolia). Its formation occurred as part of the division of the East Siberian Oblast into Chita and Irkutsk Oblasts (the former of which it became a part). It assumed its current name on 16 September 1958.

Under the Federation Treaty of March 1992, the AOk was recognized as one of the constituent units of the Russian Federation. The area attracted some notoriety in 1997, when Iosif Kobzon, a popular singer frequently referred to as the 'Russian Frank Sinatra', won a by-election for a seat representing the AOk in the State Duma, obtaining 84% of the votes cast. Kobzon attracted controversy, owing to his reputedly close connections with organized crime both within Russia and in the USA. The incumbent Head of the Okrug Administration, Bair Zhamsuyev, was re-elected in October 2000, obtaining more than 89% of the votes cast.

### Economy

The Autonomous Okrug's transport infrastructure is relatively unsophisticated—in 2000 there were only 71 km of railway track and 900 km of paved roads. The economy of the Aga-Buryat AOk is based on agriculture, which consists mainly of animal husbandry (particularly sheep-rearing), fur-animal farming and grain production. Agricultural production amounted to a value of 605m. roubles in 2000 and employed some 36.9% of the Okrug's work-force. The territory is rich in reserves of wolfram (tungsten) and tantalum. Its main industries are non-ferrous metallurgy, ore-mining, the manufacture of building materials and the processing of agricultural products. Industry employed just 6.5% of the Okrug's work-force in 2000, and produced output worth 127m. roubles. The district's main foreign trading partners are the People's Republic of China and Mongolia. The transport, trade and services sectors were fully privatized by 1995. The Aga-Buryat AOk is one of the most under-developed federal territories in terms of its health and social-security provision and educational establishments.

In 2000 the economically active population of the AOk numbered 32,000, and from the mid-1990s, when separate figures for the AOk began to become available, the district was consistently among those federal subjects with the highest levels of unemployment. In 1998 some 35.2% of the labour force were unemployed, although by 2000 the rate had declined to 25.6%. The average monthly wage was just 2,524.6 roubles in mid-2002. The 2000 district budget showed a surplus of 35.1m. roubles. Some 400 small businesses were registered in the territory at late 2000.

### Directory

**Head of the District Administration:** Bair B. Zhamsuyev; 674460 Chita obl., Aga- Buryat AOk, PGT. Aginskoye, ul. Bazara Rinchino 92; tel. (30239) 3-41-52; fax (30239) 3-46-91; e-mail abao@ aginskchita.ru.

**Chairman of the District Duma:** Dashi Ts. Dugarov; 674460 Chita obl., Aga-Buryat AOk, PGT Aginskoye, ul. Bazara Rinchino 92; tel. (30239) 3-44-81; fax (30239) 3-45-95; e-mail duma@agatel.ru.

**Representation of the Aga-Buryat Autonomous Okrug in Chita Oblast:** Chita.

**Chief Representative of the Aga-Buryat Autonomous Okrug in the Russian Federation:** Vladimir D. Shoizhilzhapov; 103025 Moscow, ul. Novyi Arbat 19; tel. (095) 203-95-09; fax (095) 203-80-14; e-mail postpredstvo@hotmail.ru.

## Chukot Autonomous Okrug

The Chukot Autonomous Okrug (AOk—Chukotka) is situated on the Chukotka Peninsula and an adjacent section of the mainland. The Okrug forms part of the Far Eastern Federal Okrug and the Far Eastern Economic Area. It is the easternmost part of Russia and faces the East Siberian Sea (Arctic Ocean) to the north and the Bering Sea to the south; the Anadyr Gulf, part of the Bering Sea, cuts into the territory from the south-east. The USA (Alaska) lies eastwards across the Bering Straits. The western end of the district borders the Republic of Sakha (Yakutiya) to the west, and Magadan Oblast to the south. Also to the south lies the Koryak AOk (within Kamchatka Oblast). The district's major river is the Anadyr. The Chukot AOk occupies an area of 737,700 sq km (284,830 sq miles), of which approximately one-half lies within the Arctic Circle, and is divided into eight administrative districts and three cities. Its climate is severe; the average temperature in January is –29.2°C, and in July it is 9.4°C. The AOk is a sparsely populated area, with an estimated total of 73,800 inhabitants at 1 January 2002, and a population density of 0.1 per sq km. Approximately 68.3% of the territory's population inhabited urban areas in 2001. Around 80,000 people left the AOk between 1991 and 2002, reducing the population by about one-half. According to the census of 1989, ethnic Russians represented 66.1% of the region's total population, while only 7.3% were Chukchi. The Chukchi speak the Chukotic language as their native tongue, which belongs to the Paleo-Asiatic linguistic family. Until the 20th century the Chukchi (who call themselves the Lyg Oravetlyan, and are also known as the Luoravetlan, Chukcha and Chukot) could be subdivided into several distinct tribal groups. Traditionally they were also divided into two economic groups, the nomadic and semi-nomadic reindeer herders (the Chavchu or Chavchuven), and the coastal dwellers (known as the An Kalyn). The district's administrative centre is at Anadyr, which had a population of 12,000 in 2001, compared with 17,000 in 1989.

### History

Russian settlers first arrived in the territories inhabited by Chukchi tribes in the mid-17th century. Commercial traders, fur trappers and hunters subsequently established contact with the Chukchi and many were forcibly converted to Orthodox Christianity and enserfed. Economic co-operation continued to expand and reached its height in 1905, with the construction of the Trans-Siberian Railway. A Chukot national Okrug was created as part of Magadan Oblast by the Soviet Government on 10 December 1930, as part of its policy to incorporate the peoples of the north of Russia into the social, political and economic body of the USSR. (It acquired nominally autonomous status in 1980). Simultaneously, collectivization was introduced into the district. Throughout the 1950s and 1960s eastern Siberia was rapidly industrialized, resulting in extensive migration of ethnic Russians to the area and a drastic reduction of the territory available to the Chukchi for herding reindeer. Many abandoned their traditional way of life to work in industry.

In March 1990 the Chukchi participated in the creation of the Association of the Peoples of the North. They also campaigned for the ratification of two international conventions, which would affirm their right to the ownership and possession of the lands they traditionally inhabited. In February 1991 the legislature of the Chukot AOk seceded from Magadan Oblast and declared the territory the Chukot Soviet Autonomous Republic (the word 'Soviet' was removed from the district's title following the disintegration of the USSR in December). This measure failed to be recognized by the federal Government, although the district was acknowledged as a constituent member of the Federation by the Treaty of March 1992 and, subsequently, as free from the jurisdiction of Magadan Oblast. At the gubernatorial election held in December 2000, the incumbent Governor, Aleksandr Nazarov, withdrew his candidacy. Roman Abramovich, an 'oligarch' associated with the petroleum company

Sibneft (Siberian Oil Co—which merged with Yukos in late 2003), was elected in his place, receiving 91% of the votes cast. Although Abramovich was generally regarded as a popular Governor in the region, owing largely to improvements to public services and utilities implemented in the Okrug since his election, by 2003 he had made it known that he did not intend to stand for re-election in 2004. Abramovich sought to cultivate closer ties between the region and the nearby US state of Alaska. The first 'Alaska-Chukotka summit' was held in Nome, Alaska, in mid-2001 to that end; it was intended that this summit would henceforth be an annual occurrence. Following the 2002 summit Abramovich and the Governor of Alaska, Tony Knowles, signed a document, which provided for the eventual establishment of regular air services between Nome and Anadyr, and the promotion of co-operation in areas including education, health care, economic development and environmental protection.

## Economy

Alone among the autonomous okrugs, Chukotka is no longer included in a larger territory and there has been, therefore, fuller coverage of it in official statistics. In 1999 the AOk's gross regional product amounted to 3,212.1m. roubles, equivalent to 43,173.5 roubles per head. Although relatively high, this level of regional wealth was highly dependent on federal transfers. In 2000 the territory had 1,279 km (795 miles) of paved roads and a relatively undeveloped infrastructure. Anadyr is one of the district's major ports, the others being Pevek, Providenya, Egvekinot and Beringovskii.

The AOk's agricultural sector, which employed 8.6% of its workforce in 2000, consists mainly of fishing, animal husbandry (especially reindeer-breeding) and hunting. Total agricultural production was worth 86m. roubles in 2000. In 1992 it was estimated that some 500,000 reindeers were raised in state-controlled breeding areas. The region contains reserves of coal and brown coal (lignite), petroleum and natural gas, as well as gold, tin, wolfram (tungsten), copper and other minerals. It is self-sufficient in energy, containing two coal-mines, six producers of electricity and one nuclear power-station. Its main industries are ore-mining and food-processing. Industry employed some 19.3% of the AOk's working population in 2000 and generated 2,332m. roubles.

The AOk's economically active population numbered 48,000 in 2000. The rate of unemployment has been relatively low, compared with other regions in the Far East of Russia; in 2000 10.0% of the labour force were unemployed. Those in employment in mid-2002 earned an average of 12,195.5 roubles per month, well above the national average, although this was counterbalanced by some of the highest living costs in the Federation; in August 2002 a typical 'consumer basket' cost about three times as much in Anadyr as the national average and, indeed, considerably more than elsewhere in the Russian Far East. The 2000 district government budget showed a deficit of 3.0m. roubles, representing a considerable improvement on earlier records; in 1994 and 1995 the deficit had exceeded the entire gross output of the district. The external trade of the district is minimal, and in 2000 exports amounted to only US $0.3m. and imports to $1.9m. At 31 December 2000 there were 100 small businesses registered in the AOk; an extra-budgetary fund was created for the support and development of small business during 1996 and 1997, although little success was evident.

## Directory

**Head of the District Administration (Governor):** ROMAN A. ABRAMOVICH; 689000 Chukot AOk, Anadyr, ul. Beringa 20; tel. (42722) 2-90-13; fax (42722) 4-24-66; internet www.chukotka.org.

**Chairman of the District Duma:** VASILII N. NAZARENKO; 689000 Chukot AOk, Anadyr, ul. Otke 29; tel. (42722) 2-25-24; fax (42722) 2-44-70; e-mail dumachao@mail.ru.

**Chief Representative of the Chukot Autonomous Okrug in the Russian Federation:** ALEKSANDR V. MOSKALENKO; 119034 Moscow, per. Kursovoi 4; tel. (095) 502-97-30; fax (095) 925-82-27.

**Head of Anadyr City Administration:** VIKTOR A. KHVAN; 689000 Chukot AOk, Anadyr, ul. Beringa 45; tel. (41361) 2-04-38; fax (41361) 4-22-16.

# Evenk Autonomous Okrug

The Evenk Autonomous Okrug (AOk) is a land-locked territory situated on the Central Siberian Plateau. It is part of the Siberian Federal Okrug and the East Siberian Economic Area. The district forms the central-eastern part of Krasnoyarsk Krai, with the core territories of the province lying to the west and south and the other autonomous okrug, the Taimyr (Dolgano-Nenets) AOk, to the north. Sakha (Yakutia) adjoins to the east, and Irkutsk to the south-east. It has numerous rivers, the largest being the Nizhnyaya Tunguska

and the Podkammenaya Tunguska, both tributaries of the Yenisei. The Evenk AOk occupies a total area of 767,600 sq km (296,370 sq miles), of which almost three-quarters is forested, and comprises three administrative districts and one 'urban-type settlement'. At 1 January 2002 the population was estimated at 18,200. Its population density, of 0.02 per sq km, was the lowest in the Federation. In 2001 some 28.6% of the population inhabited urban areas. According to the 1989 census, ethnic Russians comprised some 67.5% of the district's population and ethnic Evenks 14.0%. The Evenks' native tongue is part of the Tungusic group of the Tungusic-Manuchu division of the Uralo-Altaic language family. The region's administrative centre is at Tura, which had just 5,300 inhabitants on 1 January 2001.

## History

The Evenks, who are thought to be descended from a mixture of Tungus and Yukagir culture, were first identified as a distinct group in the 14th century. Their first contact with Russians occurred in the early 17th century, as Russian Cossacks and fur trappers advanced eastwards through Siberia. By the mid-1620s many Evenks were forced to pay fur taxes to the Russian state. The Evenks' right to land, pasture, and hunting and fishing preserves was officially guaranteed in 1919 by the Soviet Commissariat of Nationalities, but in 1929 forced collectivization of their economic activities was introduced. On 10 December 1930 the Evenk National Okrug was established and the first Congress of Evenk Soviets was convened.

Nationalist feeling among the Evenks later emerged as a result of environmental damage sustained from the construction of hydro-electric projects and extensive mineral development in the region. In the 1980s there were plans to build a dam across the Nizhnyaya Tunguska river, which would have flooded much of the territory of the AOk (as the National Okrug had become). Following protests by the Evenks, and by the Association of the Peoples of the North (formed in 1990), the project was abandoned. After the forcible dissolution of the federal parliament in 1993, the District Soviet was replaced by a Legislative Assembly or Suglan. The speaker of the Suglan, Aleksandr Bokivkov, became Governor of the AOk in March 1997, after an election held three months earlier was annulled, owing to various irregularities. The relationship of the AOk to Krasnoyarsk Krai, of which it also forms a part, has, on occasion, been a source of difficulties, although to a considerably lesser extent than in the Taimyr (Dolgano-Nenets) AOk (see below). From June 1997 a number of agreements were signed between the Evenk AOk and Krasnoyarsk Krai, regulating specific economic issues and stating that the residents of the Okrug would participate fully in all gubernatorial and legislative elections in the Krai. On 8 April 2001 Boris Zolotarev, a director of the petroleum company, Yukos (which merged with Sibneft in late 2003), was elected Governor of the AOk, receiving 51.8% of the popular vote. A proposed referendum on the merging of Krasnoyarsk Krai with both of its constituent AOks was cancelled, following the death of Krasnoyarsk Krai Governor Aleksandr Lebed in 2002. However, in February 2003 the Governors of Krasnoyarsk Krai and the two AOks signed a protocol of intent to establish a Council of Governors, to facilitate joint decision-making in social, economic and cultural areas of policy; a council of the legislative assemblies of the three entities was subsequently established, although it was emphasized that there would be no expedited measures towards the merging of the territories.

## Economy

Despite its size and, indeed, its potential wealth, the Evenk AOk remains an undeveloped and economically insignificant producer. In 2000 13.6% of its working population were occupied in agriculture, producing total output worth 54m. roubles. The AOk's agriculture consists mainly of fishing, hunting, reindeer-breeding and fur farming. The estimated combined hydroelectric potential of the district's two major rivers is 81,300m. kWh. Its main industries otherwise are the production of petroleum, natural gas, graphite and Iceland spar, and food-processing. In 2000 industry employed 15.3% of the Okrug's work-force, and generated 112m. roubles.

The economically active population of the Okrug numbered 11,000 in 2000, when the rate of unemployment, at 3.2%, was the lowest of any territory in the Russian Federation. The average monthly wage was some 7,898.1 roubles in mid-2002. The 2000 budget showed a deficit of 137.0m. roubles. At 31 December 2000 no small businesses were registered in the AOk.

## Directory

**Head of the District Administration:** BORIS N. ZOLOTAREV; 648000 Krasnoyarsk Krai, Evenk AOk, PGT Tura, ul. Sovetskaya 2; tel. (3912) 63-63-55; fax (3912) 63-63-56; e-mail zolotarevbn@tura.evenkya.ru; internet www.evenkya.ru.

**Chairman of the District Legislative Assembly (Suglan):** ANA-
TOLII YE. AMOSOV; 648000 Krasnoyarsk Krai, Evenk AOk, PGT Tura,
ul. Sovetskaya 2; tel. (39113) 2-29-02; fax (39113) 2-26-31; e-mail
amosovae@tura.evenkya.ru.

**Representation of the Evenk Autonomous Okrug in Kras-
noyarsk Krai:** 660097 Krasnoyarsk, pr. Mira 36/719; tel. and fax
(3912) 26-34-55.

**Chief Representative of the Evenk Autonomous Okrug in the
Russian Federation:** GALINA F. SEMENOVA; 127025 Moscow, ul.
Novyi Arbat 19/1531; tel. (095) 956-19-00; fax (095) 207-75-94.

# Khanty-Mansii Autonomous Okrug—Yugra

The Khanty-Mansii Autonomous Okrug (AOk)—Yugra is situated in
the Western Siberian Plain and the Ob-Irtysh river basin. The
district forms part of the Urals Federal Okrug and the West Siberian
Economic Area, and lies within the territory of Tyumen Oblast. The
other autonomous okrug within Tyumen Oblast, the Yamal-Nenets
AOk, lies to the north, while to the south of the district's centre lies
the region of Tyumen proper. Komi is to the west and Sverdlovsk to
the south-west; to the south-east lies Tomsk and to the east Krasnoyarsk. Apart from the Ob and the Irtysh, the district's other major
rivers are the Konda, the Sosva, the Vakh, the Agan and the Bolshoi
Yugan. It has numerous lakes, and much of its territory is Arctic
tundra (frozen steppe) and taiga (forested marshland). More than
one-third of the territory of the Khanty-Mansii district is forested. It
occupies a total of 523,100 sq km (201,970 sq miles) and measures
about 900 km (560 miles) from south to north and 1,400 km from east
to west. There are nine administrative districts in the AOk and 16
cities. Its estimated total number of inhabitants was 1,423,800 at 1
January 2002, giving a population density of 2.7 per sq km. In 2001
as many as 91.3% of the population lived in urban areas. Ethnic
Khants and Mansi, collectively known as Ob-Ugrian peoples, are
greatly outnumbered by ethnic Russians in the district: the census of
1989 found that some 66.3% of total inhabitants were Russians,
11.6% Ukrainians, 7.6% Tatars, 2.4% Bashirs, 2.2% Belarusians,
compared with just 0.9% Khants and 0.5% Mansi. The Khanty and
the Mansii languages are grouped together as an Ob-Ugrian subdivision of the Ugrian division of the Finno-Ugrian group. The
Autonomous Okrug's administrative centre is at the town of Khanty-
Mansiisk, which had 39,700 inhabitants at 1 January 2001. Other
major, and larger, cities in the Okrug are Surgut (278,900), Nizhnevartovsk (238,100) and Nefteyugansk (99,700).

## History

The Khanty-Mansii region, known as the Yugra region in the 11th–
15th centuries, came under Russian control in the late 16th and
early 17th centuries as Russian fur traders established themselves
in western Siberia. Attempts were made to assimilate the Khants
and Mansi into Russian culture, and many were forcibly converted to
Orthodox Christianity. The territory was created in December 1930,
as the East Vogul (Ostyako-Vogulskii) National Autonomous Okrug
(becoming known as Khanty-Mansii Autonomous Okrug in 1943).

From about the time of the Second World War the district became
heavily industrialized, causing widespread damage to fish catches
and reindeer pastures. In 1996 the okrug authorities appealed to the
Constitutional Court against Tyumen Oblast's attempt to legislate
for district petroleum and natural gas reserves, and a protracted
dispute ensued. As in the neighbouring Yamal-Nenets AOk, the
exact nature of the constitutional relationship between Khanty-
Mansii and Tyumen Oblast remained obscure. This dispute partly
reflected the domination of different interest groups in the two
administrations—the district authorities favoured the federal Government and the energy industry, while the Communist Party of the
Russian Federation retained support in Tyumen Oblast. Aleksandr
Filipenko, the head of the district administration, was returned to
power in the gubernatorial election held in late 1996. He was re-
elected, with 91% of the votes cast, in an election held simultaneously with the federal presidential election of 26 March 2000, in
which he was a vocal supporter of Vladimir Putin's candidacy. The
petroleum company Yukos (which merged with Sibneft in late 2003)
assisted in the construction of housing and leisure facilities, and in
the operation of education facilities in the Okrug in the early 2000s.
Legislative elections were held on 14 January 2001; the district
legislature, notably, incorporated a four-member Assembly of Representatives of Native Small Peoples of the North, with a particular
remit to settle disputes over land use. In February 2003 the district
legislature amended the charter of the AOk, renaming it the

Khanty-Mansii Autonomous Okrug—Yugra; in July federal President Putin signed a decree, in accordance with which the new name
was officially incorporated in the federal Constitution.

## Economy

The AOk's economy is based on industry, particularly on the extraction and refining of petroleum. In the late 1990s it produced around
5% of Russia's entire industrial output and over 50% of its petroleum. Its main industrial centre is at the petroleum-producing town
of Surgut. Its major river-port is at Nizhnevartovsk. In 2000 there
were 1,073 km of railway track in the district and 1,698 km of paved
roads, many of which were constructed during the 1990s. In September 2000 a long-awaited road bridge across the River Ob was
opened.

Agriculture in the Khanty-Mansii AOk, which employed just 1.4%
of the work-force in 2000, consists mainly of fishing, reindeer-
breeding, fur farming, hunting and vegetable production. Total
agricultural output in that year was worth 1,756m. roubles, while
industrial production amounted to a value of some 375,665m. roubles. Industry, which employed some 19.4% of the work-force in
2000, is based on the extraction of petroleum and natural gas and
the production of electricity. Khanty-Mansiisk Oil Company
(KMOC) was formed in 1997 by the merger of Khanty-Mansiisknef-
tegazgeologiya (KMNGG)—a petroleum exploration company in possession of oilfields containing up to 3,000m. barrels of petroleum—
and UPC (of Delaware, USA). KMOC is one of Russia's largest
independent exploration companies. Surgutneftegaz (SNG) Oil Co,
also based in the region, and founded in 1993, is also a significant
producer of petroleum and natural gas, with some 84,500 employees
in the early 2000s.

The economically active population of the Okrug numbered
771,000 in 2000, when 11.2% of the labour force were unemployed.
The average monthly wage was some 15,183.9 roubles in mid-2002.
In 2000 the local budget recorded a surplus of 6,274.3m. roubles.
There was considerable foreign investment in the Okrug from the
late 1990s, and it totalled US $61.3m. in 2000. Data for external
trade, although substantial, are included within the aggregate figures for Tyumen Oblast (q.v.). On 31 December 2000 4,900 small
businesses were registered in the Khanty-Mansii AOk.

## Directory

**Governor (Chairman of the Government):** ALEKSANDR V. FILI-
PENKO; 628007 Tyumen obl., Khanty-Mansii AOk, Khanty-Mansiisk,
ul. Mira 5; tel. (34671) 3-20-95; fax (34671) 3-34-60; e-mail kominf@
hmansy.wsnet.ru; internet www.hmao.wsnet.ru.

**Chairman of the District Duma:** VASILII S. SONDYKOV; 628007
Tyumen obl., Khanty-Mansii AOk, Khanty-Mansiisk, ul. Mira 5; tel.
(34671) 3-06-01; fax (34671) 3-16-84; e-mail dumahmao@hmansy
.wsnet.ru.

**Chief Representative of the Khanty-Mansii Autonomous
Okrug—Yugra in Tyumen Oblast:** NIKOLAI M. DOBRYNIN; 626002
Tyumen, ul. Komsomolskaya 37; tel. (3452) 46-67-79; fax (3452) 46-
00-91; e-mail hmaoda@tmn.ru.

**Chief Representative of the Khanty-Mansii Autonomous
Okrug—Yugra in the Russian Federation:** VLADIMIR A. KHAR-
ITON; 119002 Moscow, Starokonyushennyi per. 10/10/2; tel. (095)
920-42-38; fax (095) 291-17-62; e-mail ugra_msk@dial.cnt.ru.

**Head of Khanty-Mansiisk City Administration (Mayor):**
VALERII M. SUDEIKIN; 626200 Tyumen obl., Khanty-Mansii AOk,
Khanty-Mansiisk, ul. Dzerzhinskogo 6; tel. (34671) 3-20-70; fax
(34671) 3-21-74; e-mail ugo@admhmansy.ru; internet www
.admhmansy.ru.

# Komi-Permyak Autonomous Okrug

The Komi-Permyak Autonomous Okrug (AOk) is situated in the
Urals area on the upper reaches of the Kama river and forms the
north-western part of Perm Oblast. The region is part of the Volga
Federal Okrug and the Urals Economic Area. The other neighbouring federal territories are Komi to the north and north-west and
Kirov to the west. A largely forested territory, it occupies an area of
32,900 sq km (12,700 sq miles) and comprises six administrative
districts and one city. The region's population was estimated at
147,800 at 1 January 2002, and the population density was 4.5 per
sq km. In 2001 26.1% of the population inhabited urban areas.
According to the 1989 census, of the district's total population, some
60.2% were Komi Permyak and 36.1% ethnic Russian. The Komi

Permyaks speak two dialects of the Finnic division of the Uralo-Altaic linguistic family. The district's administrative centre is at Kudymkar, which had a population of 34,300 at 1 January 2001.

## History

The Komi Permyaks became a group distinct from the Komis in around 500, when some Komi (Źyryans) migrated from the upper Kama river region to the Vychegda basin, while the Komi Permyaks remained. The Komi-Permyak national Okrug was established on 26 February 1925, the first political entity of its kind to be established in the USSR. In 1977 the Okrug received the nominal status of an Autonomous Okrug. The area frequently perceived the central authorities to be neglectful of their interests, and economic conditions became increasingly harsh from the late 1990s. In May 1996 the AOk's administration signed a treaty with the federal Government on the delimitation of powers between the two bodies. At a gubernatorial election held in November, the incumbent, Nikolai Poluyanov, retained his position, but was defeated by the deputy president of the audit chamber of Perm Oblast, Gennadii Savelyev, in the gubernatorial election held in December 2000. Elections to the 15-member regional Legislative Assembly took place in December 2001. In July 2002, following visits by the Chairman of the Federation Council, Sergei Mironov, and the Presidential Representative in the Volga Federal Okrug, Sergei Kiriyenko, to Perm and to Kudymkar, the Governor of Perm Oblast, Yurii Trutnev, announced that measures to merge the two federal subjects would be instigated in the near future. In September, in what was described as an experimental measure, the (federally controlled) justice services in the two regions were organized into a unified structure, the first instance of such a unification. In February 2003 the legislative organs of both the Oblast and the AOk voted to support the merger. In March Trutnev and Savelyev met federal President Vladimir Putin, who expressed support for the proposal. In late May the oblast legislature approved legislation to permit the holding of a plebiscite on the merger, and further legislation pertaining to the measure was approved by the parliaments of both administrative entities in June. Pending approval of the merger by a referendum (which, it was anticipated, would be held in December 2003), elections to the leadership of the new political entity, to be known as Perm Krai, were expected to take place in December 2005, although the establishment of a single budget for the two regions was not anticipated before 2007.

## Economy

In 2000 there were 1,488 km (925 miles) of paved roads in the AOk. The agriculture of the Komi Permyak AOk consists mainly of grain production, animal husbandry and hunting. In 2000 it occupied 31.7% of the work-force and produced output to the value of 1,277m. roubles. Its timber reserves are estimated at 322m. cu m. There are significant peat deposits and approximately 12.1m. metric tons of petroleum reserves. Its industry is based on the processing of forestry and agricultural products; the sector generated 693m. roubles in 2000 and employed 15.7% of the Okrug's work-force.

The economically active population numbered 66,000 in 2000, when 8.0% of the labour force were unemployed. The average monthly wage was just 2,535.9 roubles in mid-2002, and the Okrug is one of the most underdeveloped and deprived European regions of Russia. The district budget showed a deficit of 54.3m. roubles in 2000. Figures on the foreign investment in, and external trade with, the Okrug were unavailable, being included with those for the Perm Oblast as a whole, but in late 2000 there were approximately 100 small businesses registered in the Okrug.

## Directory

**Head of the District Administration:** GENNADII P. SAVELYEV; 617240 Perm obl., Komi-Permyak AOk, Kudymkar, ul. 50 let. Oktyabrya 33; tel. (34260) 4-59-03; fax (34260) 4-12-74.

**Chairman of the Legislative Assembly:** VALERII A. VANKOV; 617240 Perm obl., Komi-Permyak AOk, Kudymkar, ul. 50 let. Oktyabrya 33; tel. (32460) 4-24-70; fax (32460) 2-12-74.

**Representation of the Komi-Permyak Autonomous Okrug in Perm Oblast:** Perm.

**Chief Representative of Komi-Permyak Autonomous Okrug in the Russian Federation:** TAMARA A. SYSTEROVA; Moscow; tel. (095) 203-94-08.

**Head of Kudymkar City Administration:** ALEKSANDR A. KLIMOVICH; 617420 Perm obl., Komi-Permyak AOk, Kudymkar, ul. Gorkogo 3; tel. (34260) 2-00-47; e-mail admkud@permonline.ru; internet kudymkar.permonline.ru.

# Koryak Autonomous Okrug

The Koryak Autonomous Okrug (AOk) comprises the northern part of the Kamchatka Peninsula and the adjacent area of mainland. It forms part of the Far Eastern Federal Okrug, the Far Eastern Economic Area, and Kamchatka Oblast. Its eastern coastline lies on the Bering Sea, and its western shores face the Shelekhov Gulf (Sea of Okhotsk). South of the district lies the rest of Kamchatka Oblast. In the north it is bordered by the Chukot AOk and Magadan Oblast, to the north and to the west, respectively. The Koryak AOk occupies 301,500 sq km (116,410 sq miles) and is divided, for administrative purposes, into four districts and two 'urban-type settlements'. At 1 January 2002 its estimated total population was 28,500, and its population density, therefore, stood at just 0.1 per sq km. In 2001 just 25.8% of the population inhabited urban areas. The 1989 census showed that 62.0% of its population were ethnically Russian, 7.2% Ukrainian, 16.4% Koryak, 3.6% Chukchi and 3.0% Itelmeni. The administrative centre of the district is at Palana, which had a population of just 4,100 on 1 January 2001.

## History

The area was established as a territorial unit on 10 December 1930. Like the Chukchi, the Koryaks comprise nomadic and semi-nomadic hunters and more sedentary coastal dwellers. They first encountered ethnic Russians in the 1640s, when Cossacks, commercial traders and fur trappers arrived in the district. The Soviet Government attempted to collectivize the Koryaks' economic activity, beginning with the fishing industry in 1929, and continuing with reindeer hunting in 1932, a measure that was violently opposed by the Koryak community. After the Second World War large numbers of ethnic Russians moved to the area, which was becoming increasingly industrialized. The resultant threat to the Koryaks' traditional way of life, and environmental deterioration, became a source of contention between the local community and the federal Government during the period of *glasnost* (openness) in the late 1980s. In the first years of independence, however, the local élite were sufficiently placated to be generally supportive of both the federal Government and, indeed, of the reformists. An independent candidate, Valentina Bronevich, was elected Governor in late 1996, the first woman to head the administration of a territorial unit in the Russian Federation. On 5 May 1999 Bronevich signed a co-operation agreement with the Governor of Kamchatka Oblast. On 3 December 2000 a local businessman, Vladimir Loginov, defeated Bronevich in a gubernatorial election, receiving 51% of the votes cast. The Okrug Duma is the only legislative body of any federal subject, apart from those of the two cities of federal status, to consist in its entirety of paid deputies.

## Economy

Much economic data on the Koryak AOk is incorporated into the figures for Kamchatka Oblast, although certain indicators are available. Fishing is the most important economic activity in the district, contributing 60% of total industrial output.

The AOk's agriculture, which employed 10.8% of the work-force in 2000, consists mainly of reindeer-breeding, fur farming and hunting. Total agricultural output was worth 61m. roubles in that year. The main industries are the production of non-ferrous metals (primarily palladium and platinum), food-processing, the production of electrical energy and the extraction of brown coal (lignite). Industry employed 21.7% of the work-force and generated a total of 2,939m. roubles in 2000.

The economically active population numbered 17,000 in 2000, when 12.5% of the labour force were unemployed. The average monthly wage was some 8,223.9 roubles in mid-2002. The budget recorded a deficit of 361.9m. roubles in 2000. By the early 2000s the Okrug remained impoverished and dependent on federal subsidies; in 1999 it had been named as being among the federal subjects with the highest rates of inflation and the least promising opportunities for investment, and in 2002 was named as one of the worst regions for wage arrears. In 2000 the region attracted foreign investment worth US $300,000, compared with $7.1m. in 1998. At the end of 2000 100 small businesses were registered in the territory.

## Directory

**Governor of the Koryak Autonomous Okrug:** VLADIMIR A. LOGINOV; 684620 Kamchatka obl., Koryak AOk, PGT Palana, ul. Porotova 22; tel. (41543) 3-13-80; fax (41543) 3-13-70.

**Chairman of the District Duma:** VLADIMIR I. ZUYEV; 684620 Kamchatka obl., Koryak AOk, PGT Palana, ul. Porotova 22; tel. (41543) 3-10-30.

**Representation of the Koryak Autonomous Okrug in Kamchatka Oblast:** Kamchatka obl., Petropavlovsk-Kamchatskii.

# Nenets Autonomous Okrug

The Nenets Autonomous Okrug (AOk) is part of Archangel (Arkhangelsk) Oblast and, hence, the North-Western Federal Okrug and the Northern Economic Area. It is situated in the north-east of European Russia, its coastline lying, from west to east, on the White, Barents and Kara Seas, parts of the Arctic Ocean. Most of the territory lies within the Arctic Circle. Archangel proper lies to the south-west, but most of the Nenets southern border is with the Republic of Komi. At its eastern extremity the district touches the Yamal-Nenets AOk (part of Tyumen Oblast) and, to the north-east, the Novaya Zemlya peninsula, which forms a part of Archangel Oblast proper. The major river is the Pechora, which drains into the Pechora Gulf of the Barents Sea just north of Naryan-Mar. The territory occupies an area of 176,700 sq km (68,200 sq miles) and extends some 300 km (190 miles) from south to north and 1,000 km from west to east. For administrative purposes it is divided into one city and two 'urban-type settlements'. At 1 January 2002 the estimated total population of the Nenets AOk was 44,900 and its population density was 0.3 per sq km. Around 60.4% of the population inhabited urban areas in 2001. At 1 January 1997 estimated figures showed some 70.0% of the region's population were ethnic Russian, while 15.6% were Nenets and 9.5% Komi. The language spoken by the Nenets belongs to the Samoyedic group of Uralian languages, which is part of the Uralo-Altaic linguistic group. The district capital is at Naryan-Mar, which had a population of 18,200 at 1 January 2001.

## History

The Nenets were traditionally concerned with herding and breeding reindeer. A Samoyedic people, they are believed to have broken away from other Finno-Ugrian groups in around 3000 BC and migrated east where, in around 200 BC, they began to mix with Turkish-Altaic people. By the early 17th century their territory had come entirely under the control of the Muscovite state. The Russians established forts in the region, from which they collected fur tax.

The Nenets National Okrug was formed on 15 July 1929; in common with other National Okrugs, it was reconstituted as an Autonomous Okrug in 1977. During the Soviet period, collectivization of the Nenets' economic activity, and the exploitation of petroleum and natural gas (which increased markedly from the mid-1960s) resulted in mass migration of ethnic Russians to the region, posing an increasing threat to the traditional way of life of the indigenous population and to the environment.

In March 1994 the federal President, Boris Yeltsin, suspended a resolution by the District Administration ordering a referendum to be held on the territory of the AOk, concerning the status of the district within the Russian Federation. Despite the President's move, however, the district maintained its style of the 'Nenets Republic'. A district Assembly of Deputies replaced the old legislature, and election results in the mid-1990s indicated continued disaffection with federal policies—there was strong support for the nationalist Liberal Democratic Party of Russia. The December 1996 election to head the district administration was won by an independent candidate and businessman, Vladimir Butov, who was re-elected on 14 January 2001, with some 68% of the votes cast. In June 2002 a warrant was issued for the arrest of Butov on charges of abuse of office, in particular with regard to his dismissal of three successive district prosecutors. Although the warrant was subsequently cancelled, a further federal arrest warrant against Butov was issued in July 2003, after he had allegedly assaulted a police-officer in St Petersburg; it was also reported that Butov had been convicted of two criminal offences prior to his being elected as governor, and that several other cases in which he was involved apparently remained unresolved. Butov also attracted criticism for his reputedly authoritarian style, while concern was repeatedly expressed during the early 2000s that he was frequently absent from the region, sometimes for several months at a time. A prominent source of opposition to Butov was believed to be the petroleum company, LUKoil, which opposed the preferable treatment granted in the Okrug to the Nenets Oil Company (NNK), which Butov controlled.

## Economy

As part of Archangel Oblast, the Nenets AOk is usually subsumed into the region's overall statistics, so few separate details are available. In 2000 the AOk contained 150 km (93 miles) of paved roads. The AOk's major ports are Naryan-Mar and Amderma.

Its agriculture, which employed 11.7% of the work-force and produced goods to a value of 158m. roubles in 2000, consists mainly of reindeer-breeding (around two-thirds of its territory is reindeer pasture), fishing, hunting and fur farming. There are substantial reserves of petroleum, natural gas and gas condensate, which have yet to be fully exploited. In 1997 Exxon Arkhangelsk Ltd, an affiliate of Exxon of the USA (now ExxonMobil), purchased a 50% stake in the development of oilfields in Timan-Pechora, although it was forced to withdraw after problems with tender arrangements. In 1998 Governor Bukov gave support to plans for the construction of a petroleum transportation terminal on the Barents Sea coast, allowing the Okrug to benefit from the potential wealth to be generated by the exploitation of the Timan-Pechora oilfields. Bukov's relations with the major fuel companies Gazprom and LUKoil were reported to be strained during the late 1990s and early 2000s, and petroleum deposits in the region were developed only slowly, a new sea terminal for petroleum transportation was opened at Varandei in August 2000. The annual capacity of this terminal, which was constructed by LUKoil and which was to be served by its fleet of ice-breaking tankers, was over 1m. metric tons, although this was expected to expand. Other sectors of the district's industry included the processing of agricultural products and the generation of electricity. Industry employed 12.6% of the Okrug's work-force in 2000, and produced output worth 6,612m. roubles in that year.

The economically active population numbered 24,000 in 2000, when 10.9% of the labour force were unemployed, compared with 20.0% in 1999. In mid-2002 the average monthly wage of 12,830.1 roubles was among the highest in the Russian Federation. The Nenets government budget recorded a surplus of 256.4m. roubles in 2000. In the late 1990s the Okrug was successful in attracting foreign investment, which totalled US $346.0m. in 1999. In December 2000 there were approximately 200 small businesses registered in the district.

## Directory

# Taimyr (Dolgano-Nenets) Autonomous Okrug

Taimyr (Dolgano-Nenets) Autonomous Okrug (AOk) is situated on the Taimyr Peninsula, which abuts into the Arctic Ocean, separating the Kara and Laptev Seas. The district comprises the northern end of Krasnoyarsk Krai and, in common with its south-eastern neighbour, the Evenk AOk, forms part of the Siberian Federal Okrug and the East Siberian Economic Area. The Yamal-Nenets AOk, in Tyumen Oblast, lies to the west and the Republic of Sakha (Yakutiya) is located to the south-east. The Taimyr district's major rivers are the Yenisei (which drains into the Kara Sea in the west of the region), the Pyasina and the Khatanga. The district is mountainous in the south and in the extreme north and just under one-half of it is forested. It has numerous lakes, the largest being Lake Taimyr. The territory occupies a total area of 862,100 sq km (332,860 sq miles), which is divided into three administrative districts and one city. There are 262 km (163 miles) of paved roads. The climate in the AOk is severe, with snow for an average of 280 days per year. The Taimyr AOk had an estimated population of 44,300 at 1 January 2002. Its population density, therefore, was 0.05 per sq km. Some 63.6% of the total population inhabited urban areas in 2001. In 1989 some 67.1% of the district's inhabitants were ethnic Russians, 8.8% Dolgans, 8.6% Ukrainians and 4.4% Nenets. The AOk's administrative centre is at Dudinka, which had a population of 26,700 in 2001. The city of Norilsk, north-east of Dudinka, which had a population of 143,100 in 2001, does not form part of the Okrug, being considered for administrative purposes a part of Krasnoyarsk Krai proper.

## History

The territory of the Taimyr district was first exploited by Russian settlers in the 17th century. An autonomous okrug was founded on 10 December 1930, as part of Krasnoyarsk Krai. In 1993, following Russian President Boris Yeltsin's forcible dissolution of the Russian parliament, on 18 October the Taimyr District Soviet voted to disband itself and a new District Duma was subsequently elected. The administration was generally supportive of the federal authorities, but there was also significant popular support for the nationalist Liberal Democratic Party. Tensions arose between Taimyr and Krasnoyarsk Krai over the division of authorities between the two federal subjects, the exact relationship of which remained constitutionally obscure. In October 1997 Yeltsin and first deputy premier Boris Nemtsov signed a power-sharing treaty with the leaders of the Taimyr AOk, Krasnoyarsk Krai and the other autonomous okrug within the Krai, the Evenk AOk. The first of its kind, this treaty clearly delineated authority between the national, krai and okrug authorities, and ensured that some of the wealth generated by the local company Norilsk Nickel, the world's largest producer of nickel, went to pay salaries and other benefits within the Okrug. None the less, the attitudes of Taimyr leaders towards the Krai were variable; the Okrug did not participate in elections to the Krai legislature in 1997 or 2000, although it did participate in the gubernatorial election of the Krai in April 1998. The victor in that election, Aleksandr Lebed, unilaterally cancelled the previous power-sharing agreement in October 1999, fuelling suspicions that he wished the Krai to reimpose greater control over the Okrug. At the gubernatorial election held in the AOk on 28 January 2001, Aleksandr Khlopanin, hitherto the General Director of Norilsk Nickel, the major employer in the region, was elected as Governor, with some 63% of the votes cast. Following Khlopanin's election as Governor of Krasnoyarsk Krai (q.v.) in September 2002, he was obliged to resign as Governor of the AOk; his deputy, Sergei Nauman, assumed the governorship in an acting capacity. Gubernatorial elections, held on 26 January 2003, and contested by seven candidates, were won by Oleg Budargin, hitherto the Mayor of Norilsk and a former senior manager at Norilsk Nickel, with 69.1% of the votes cast. Although Budargin had contested the election as an independent, he was regarded as the preferred candidate of both Khlopanin and Norilsk Nickel. In February 2003 the governors of Krasnoyarsk Krai and the two AOks signed a protocol of intent to establish a Council of Governors, to facilitate joint decision-making in social, economic and cultural areas of policy; a council of the legislative assemblies of the three entities was subsequently established, although it was emphasized that there would be no expedited measures towards the merging of the territories. (A proposed referendum on such a merger had been cancelled in 2002, following the death of Lebed.)

## Economy

As with most of the autonomous okrugs, separate economic data on the Taimyr (Dolgano-Nenets) AOk are scarce, the district being part of Krasnoyarsk Krai. The major ports in the AOk are Dudinka, Dikson and Khatanga. There is limited transport—only the Dudinka–Norilsk railway line (89 km, or 55 miles, long) operates throughout the year. The district's roads, which total 262 km in length, are concentrated in its more populous areas.

Agricultural production was valued at just 17m. roubles in 2000, mainly provided by fishing, animal husbandry (livestock- and reindeer-breeding) and fur-animal hunting. In that year agriculture employed just 4.5% of the AOk's work-force. There are extensive mineral reserves, however, including those of petroleum and natural gas. The main industries are ore-mining (coal, copper and nickel) and food-processing. In 2000 industry provided employment to some 21.2% of the work-force and produced an output equivalent to 170m. roubles. Norilsk Nickel accounted for some 20% of the world's, and 80% of Russia's, nickel output in the mid-1990s. The plant also produced 19% of the world's cobalt (70% of Russia's), 42% of the world's platinum (100% of Russia's) and 5% of the world's copper (40% of Russia's). Its activity, however, caused vast environmental damage to its surroundings, in the form of sulphur pollution.

The economically active population numbered 27,000 in 2000, when only 5.7% of the labour force were unemployed. The average monthly wage in the region was some 10,736.2 roubles in mid-2002. The district administrative budget for 2000 showed a surplus of 405.0m. roubles. At the end of 2000 there were no small businesses registered in the Okrug.

## Directory

**Head of the District Administration (Governor):** OLEG M. BUDARGIN; 663210 Krasnoyarsk Krai, Taimyr (Dolgano-Nenets) AOk, Dudinka, ul. Sovetskaya 35; tel. (39111) 2-11-60; fax (39111) 2-33-17; e-mail atao@taimyr.ru; internet www.taimyr.ru.

**Chairman of the District Duma:** VIKTOR V. SITNOV; 647000 Krasnoyarsk Krai, Taimyr (Dolgano-Nenets) AOk, Dudinka, ul. Sovetskaya 35; tel. (39111) 2-37-37; fax (39111) 2-29-39; e-mail dudinka@ dumatao.krasnoyarsk.su; internet www.dumatao.ru.

**Representation of the Taimyr (Dolgano-Nenets) Autonomous Okrug in Krasnoyarsk Krai:** Krasnoyarsk.

**Chief Representative of the Taimyr (Dolgano-Nenets) Autonomous Okrug in the Russian Federation:** OLEG YE. MORGUNOV; Moscow; tel. (095) 120-45-36.

**Head of Dudinka City Administration:** SERGEI M. MOSHKIN; 663210 Krasnoyarsk Krai, Taimyr (Dolgano-Nenets) AOk, Dudinka, ul. Sovetskaya 35; tel. (39111) 2-13-30; fax (39111) 2-55-52.

# Ust-Orda Buryat Autonomous Okrug

The Ust-Orda Buryat Autonomous Okrug (AOk) is situated in the southern part of the Lena-Angara plateau. The district forms part of Irkutsk Oblast and, hence, the Siberian Federal Okrug and the East Siberian Economic Area. It lies to the north of Irkutsk city, west of Lake Baikal. Its major rivers are the Angara and its tributaries, the Osa, the Ida and the Kuda. Most of its terrain is forest-steppe. It occupies an area of 22,400 sq km (8,650 sq miles) and comprises six administrative districts. At 1 January 2002 the estimated population was 142,500 and the population density stood at 6.4 per sq km. In 1992, the last year for which comprehensive demographic statistics were available, just 18.3% of the population of the AOk lived in urban areas. According to the 1989 census, some 56.5% of the population were ethnic Russians and 36.3% were western or Irkutsk Buryats. The capital is at Ust-Ordynskii, which had a population of 13,600 in 2001.

## History

The Buryat-Mongol Autonomous Soviet Socialist Republic (BMASSR), created in 1923, was restructured by Stalin (Iosif Dzhugashvili) in September 1937. Anxious to discourage nationalism and links with Mongolia, Stalin had resolved to divide the Buryat peoples administratively. The Ust-Orda Buryat AOk, which represented the four western counties of the BMASSR, was established on the territory of Irkutsk Oblast. The Communist Party of the Russian Federation remained the most popular party in the Legislative Assembly (which replaced the District Soviet in 1994). In 1996 the federal President, Boris Yeltsin, had signed an agreement with the AOk's administration on the delimitation of powers between the federal and district authorities. Later that year an independent candidate, Valerii Maleyev, was elected Governor. In October 1999 the Governor of Irkutsk Oblast, Boris Govorin, stated that the AOk (70% of the budget of which comprised federal transfers) should be re-incorporated into the Oblast proper, as the Oblast provided fuel and other resources to the AOk and there were concerns that Buryat nationalists might seek to unite the three nominally Buryat federal subjects. Maleyev was re-elected Governor in November 2000. During the early 2000s proposals to unite the Ust-Orda Buryat AOk and Irkutsk Oblast became increasingly popular and appeared to be supported by the authorities in both the AOk and the Oblast; moreover, in September 2002 the Chairman of the Federation Council, Sergei Mironov, stated that the two federal subjects already possessed the necessary preconditions for becoming a single unit. However, only very limited progress towards the merging of the two political entities was reported during the course of the following year.

## Economy

Statistical information for Irkutsk Oblast generally includes data on the Ust-Orda Buryat AOk, so separate figures are limited. In 2000 there were 2,189 km (1,360 miles) of paved roads on the AOk's territory.

The district's agriculture consists mainly of grain production and animal husbandry. In 2000 some 56.5% of the AOk's working population was engaged in agriculture (by far the highest proportion of any federal subject), and production in that year was valued at 2,337m. roubles. Its main industries are the processing of agricultural and forestry products, the production of coal and gypsum, machine-building, metal-working, and the manufacture of building materials. Industry generated 281m. roubles in 2000 and employed just 5.9% of the work-force.

The economically active population numbered 67,000 in 2000, when 8.9% of the labour force were unemployed. In mid-2002 the average monthly wage was just 2,336.7 roubles. There was a budgetary surplus of 24.6m. roubles in 2000. In that year there were around 100 small businesses registered in the Okrug.

## Directory

**Head of the District Administration:** VALERII G. MALEYEV; 666110 Irkutsk obl., Ust-Orda Buryat AOk, pos. Ust-Ordynskii, ul. Lenina 18; tel. (39541) 2-10-62; fax (39541) 2-25-93; e-mail okrug@irmail.ru; internet www.ust-orda.ru.

**Chairman of the District Duma:** ALEKSEI P. KHORINOYEV; 669001 Irkutsk obl., Ust-Orda Buryat AOk, pos. Ust-Ordynskii, ul. Lenina 18; tel. (39541) 2-16-87; fax (39541) 2-26-71.

**Chief Representative of the Ust-Orda Buryat Autonomous Okrug in Irkutsk Oblast:** SERGEI V. DOLGOPOLOV; 626002 Tyumen, ul. Komsomolskaya 37; tel. (3952) 57-17-14.

**Chief Representative of the Ust-Orda Buryat Autonomous Okrug in the Russian Federation:** OLEG B. BATOROV; 127025 Moscow, ul. Novyi Arbat 19; tel. and fax (095) 203-52564; fax (095) 203-64-04.

# Yamal-Nenets Autonomous Okrug

The Yamal-Nenets Autonomous Okrug (AOk) is situated on the Western Siberian Plain on the lower reaches of the Ob river. It forms part of Tyumen Oblast and, therefore, the Urals Federal Okrug and the West Siberian Economic Area. The territory lies on the Asian side of the Ural Mountains and has a deeply indented northern coastline, the western section, the Yamal Peninsula, being separated from the eastern section by the Ob bay. The rest of Tyumen Oblast, including the Khanty-Mansii AOk—Yugra, lies to the south. To the west lie the Nenets AOk (within Archangel Oblast) and the Republic of Komi, to the east Krasnoyarsk Krai (including the Taimyr AOk in the north-west). Apart from the Ob, the Yamal-Nenets district's major rivers are the Nadym, the Taz and the Pur. Around one-10th of its area is forested. The territory of the Yamal-Nenets AOk occupies 750,300 sq km (289,690 sq miles). It comprises seven administrative districts and seven cities. It had an estimated total population (at 1 January 2002) of 508,900 inhabitants, and a population density of 0.7 per sq km. In 2001 some 82.6% of the population inhabited urban areas. In the 1989 census, ethnic Russians represented some 59.3% of the population, Ukrainians 17.2% and Tatars 5.3%, while Nenets represented just 4.2%, although the proportion of Nenets was thought to have increased subsequently. The district administrative centre is at Salekhard, which had a population of 34,100 in January 2001. Its other major cities are Noyabrsk (97,800) and Novyi Urengoi (91,600).

## History

The Nenets were traditionally a nomadic people, who were totally dominated by Russia from the early 17th century. The Yamal-Nenets AOk was formed on 10 December 1930. Environmental concerns provoked protests in the 1980s and 1990s, and prompted the local authorities (comprising an administration and, from 1994, an elected Duma) to seek greater control over natural resources and their exploitation. The main dispute was with the central Tyumen Oblast authorities (more pro-communist than the AOk's own), and the AOk's rejection of oblast legislation on petroleum and natural gas exploitation first reached the Constitutional Court during 1996. Constitutional tensions between the two AOks contained within Tyumen Oblast, and the authorities of the Oblast proper, continued

throughout the 1990s. The economic importance of the fuel industry in Yamal-Nenets was reflected in the AOk's political situation. Viktor Chernomyrdin, the leader of Our Home Is Russia and the former Chairman of the federal Government, was elected to the State Duma as a representative of Yamal-Nenets in 1998, and he retained his seat until his appointment as Russia's ambassador to Ukraine in May 2001. He had previously been head of the domestic gas monopoly, Gazprom, the largest employer in the AOk, and in the Duma became head of an inter-factionary group of deputies, Energiya (Energy). At the gubernatorial election of 26 March 2000 the incumbent, Yurii Neyelov, who was regarded as sympathetic to the interests of Gazprom, was re-elected, securing some 90% of the votes cast.

## Economy

Few statistical indicators are available as distinct from those for Tyumen Oblast in general. Agriculture, which in 2000 employed just 1.4% of the work-force in the Yamal-Nenets AOk consists mainly of fishing, reindeer-breeding (reindeer pasture occupies just under one-third of its territory), fur-farming and fur-animal hunting. Total agricultural production amounted to a value of just 244m. roubles in 2000. The AOk's main industries are the production of natural gas and petroleum and the production of electricity. In 2000 the industrial sector employed 21.8% of the work-force and generated a total of some 75,784m. roubles, a considerably larger amount than that generated by many oblasts or republics in the Russian Federation. The potential wealth of the district generated foreign interest. In January 1997 a loan of US $2,500m. to Gazprom was agreed by the Dresdner Bank group (of Germany), to support construction of the 4,200-km (2,610-mile) Jagal pipeline from the Autonomous Okrug to Frankfurt-an-der-Oder on the German border with Poland. This was to be the world's largest gas-transport project and was expected to be fully operational by 2005.

The economically active population numbered 303,000 in 2000, when 7.9% of the labour force were unemployed. In 2000 the district government budget showed a deficit of 384.7m. roubles. These statistics, like the high average monthly wage of 15,374.2 roubles (the highest in the Russian Federation) in mid-2002, have far more in common with those of the Khanty-Mansii AOk than those of the Tyumen Oblast as a whole. The Okrug has also been successful in attracting foreign investment, receiving US $102.9m. in 2000. No separate details for external trade are available, although it was believed to be substantial. At 31 December 2000 there were 2,600 small businesses registered in the Yamal-Nenets Autonomous Okrug.

## Directory

**Governor:** YURII V. NEYELOV; 626608 Tyumen obl., Yamal-Nenets AOk, Salekhard, ul. Respubliki 72; tel. (34922) 4-46-02; fax (34922) 4-52-89; internet www.yamal.ru.

**Chairman of the District State Duma:** SERGEI N. KHARYUCHI; 629000 Tyumen obl., Yamal-Nenets AOk, Salekhard, ul. Respublika 72; tel. and fax (34591) 4-51-51.

**Chief Representative of Yamal-Nenets Autonomous Okrug in Tyumen Oblast:** FUAT G. SAIFITDINOV; 625048 Tyumen, ul. Kholodilnaya 136/1; tel. (3422) 27-32-11; fax (3422) 40-24-80.

**Chief Representative of Yamal-Nenets Autonomous Okrug in the Russian Federation:** NIKOLAI A. BORODULIN; 101000 Moscow, per. Arkhangelskii 15/3; tel. (095) 924-67-89; fax (095) 925-83-38.

**Head of Salekhard City Administration:** ALEKSANDR M. SPIRIN; 629000 Tyumen obl., Yamal-Nenets AOk, Salekhard, ul. Respubliki 72; tel. (34922) 4-50-67; fax (34922) 4-01-82; e-mail press@ytc.ru.

# Bibliography

Aldis, A., and McDermott, R. (Eds). *Russian Military Reform, 1992—2002*. London, Frank Cass, 2003.

Alekseev, M. A. (Ed.). *Center-Periphery Conflict in Post-Soviet Russia: a Federation Imperilled*. Basingstoke, Macmillan, 1999.

Alexander, J. *Political Culture in Post-Communist Russia: Formlessness and Recreation in a Traumatic Transition*. Basingstoke, Macmillan, 2000.

Andrews, C. M., and Mitrokhin, V. *The Sword and the Shield: The Mitrokhin Archive and the Secret History of the KGB*. New York, NY, Basic Books, 1999.

Ashwin, S. (Ed.). *Gender, State and Society in Soviet and Post-Soviet Russia*. London, Routledge, 2000.

Aslund, A., and Olcott, M. B. (Eds). *Russia after Communism*. Washington, DC, Carnegie Endowment for International Peace, 1997.

Barany, Z., and Moser, R. G. (Eds). *Russian Politics: Challenges of Democratization*. Cambridge, Cambridge University Press, 2001.

Baxendale, J. (Ed.). et al. *The EU & Kaliningrad: Kaliningrad and the Impact of EU Enlargement*. London, Kogan Page, 2000.

Boobbyer, P. *The Stalin Era*. London, Routledge, 2000.

Bowker, M., and Ross, C. (Eds). *Russia after the Cold War*. London, Longman, 2000.

Boyko, M., Shleifer, A., and Vishny, R. *Privatizing Russia*. London, MIT Press, 1995.

Brady, R. *Kapitalizm: Russia's Struggle to Free Its Economy*. New Haven, CT, Yale University Press, 1999.

Braithwaite, R. *Across the Moscow River: The World Turned Upside Down*. New Haven, CT, Yale University Press, 2002.

Carrère d'Encausse, H. *The Russian Syndrome: One Thousand Years of Political Murder*. Hadleigh, Holmes and Meier, 1994.

*La Russe Inachevée*. Paris, Editions Fayard, 2000.

Conquest, R. *The Great Terror: A Reassessment*. London, Pimlico, 1992.

Duncan, P. S. *Russian Messianism: Third Rome, Revolution, Communism and After*. London, Routledge, 2000.

Dunlop, J. B. *Russia Confronts Chechnya: Roots of a Separatist Conflict*. Cambridge, Cambridge University Press, 1998.

Evangelista, M. *The Chechen Wars: Will Russia Go the Way of the Soviet Union?* Washington, DC, Brookings Institution Press, 2002.

Figes, O. *A People's Tragedy: The Russian Revolution 1891–1924*. London, Jonathan Cape, 1996.

*Natasha's Dance: A Cultural History of Russia*. London, Penguin, 2002.

Fitzpatrick, S. *The Russian Revolution*, 2nd edn. Oxford, Oxford University Press, 1994.

Freeland, C. *Sale of the Century: Russia's Wild Ride from Communism to Capitalism*. London, Little, Brown and Co, 2000.

Gaddy, C. G., and Ickes, B. W. *Russia's Virtual Economy*. Washington, DC, Brookings Institution Press, 2002.

Gall, C., and de Waal, T. *Chechnya: Calamity in the Caucasus*. New York, NY, New York University Press, 1998.

Gilbert, M. *The Routledge Atlas of Russian History*. London, Routledge, 1993.

Gill, G. (Ed.). *Elites and Leadership in Russian Politics*. Basingstoke, Macmillan, 1998.

Granville, B., and Oppenheimer, P. (Eds). *Russia's Post-Communist Economy*. Oxford, Oxford University Press, 2001.

Hardt, J. P. (Ed.). *Russia's Uncertain Economic Future*. Armonk, NY, M. E. Sharpe, 2002.

Hedlund, S. *Russia's Market Economy: A Bad Case of Predatory Capitalism*. London, Routledge, 1999.

Herspring, D. R. (Ed.). *Putin's Russia: Past Imperfect, Future Uncertain*. Lanham, MD, Rowman & Littlefield, 2002.

Hoffman, D. *The Oligarchs: Wealth and Power in the New Russia*. New York, NY, Public Affairs, 2002.

Hosking, G. *Russia: People and Empire 1552–1917*. HarperCollins, London, 1997.

*Russia and the Russians*. Harmondsworth, Penguin, 2001.

Hughes, L. *Peter The Great: A Biography*. New Haven, CT, Yale University Press, 2002.

Ivanov, I. *The New Russian Diplomacy*. Washington, DC, Brookings Institution Press, 2002.

Kahn, J. *Federalism, Democratization and the Rule of Law In Russia*. Oxford, Oxford University Press, 2002.

Khasbulatov, R. *The Struggle for Russia: Power and Change in the Democratic Revolution*. London, Routledge, 1993.

Klein, L. R., and Pomer, M. (Eds). *The New Russia: Transition Gone Awry*. Palo Alto, CA, Stanford University Press, 2002.

Krickus, R. J. *The Kaliningrad Question*. Lanham, MD, Rowman and Littlefield, 2002.

Kuchins, A. (Ed.). *Russia After the Fall*. Washington, DC, Carnegie Endowment for International Peace, 2002.

Liebich, A. *From the Other Shore: Russian Social Democracy after 1921*. Cambridge, MA, Harvard University Press, 1997.

Lieven, A. *Chechnya: Tombstone of Russian Power*. New Haven, CT, Yale University Press, 1998.

Lieven, D. *Empire—the Russian Empire and its Rivals*. London, John Murray, 2000.

Lynch, D. *Russian Peacekeeping Strategies towards the CIS*. London, Macmillan, 1999.

McCauley, M. *Who's Who in Russia since 1900*. London, Routledge, 1997.

McFaul, M. *Russia's Unfinished Revolution: Political Change from Gorbachev to Putin*. Ithaca, NY, Cornell University Press, 2001.

March, L. *The Communist Party in Post-Soviet Russia*. Manchester, Manchester University Press, 2002.

Murray, J. *The Russian Press from Brezhnev to Yeltsin*. Cheltenham, Edward Elgar Publishing, 1994.

Neumann, I. B. *Russia and the Idea of Europe: A Study in Identity and International Relations*. London, Routledge, 1994.

Ostrovski, D. *Muscovy and the Mongols: Cross-cultural Influences on the Steppe Frontier, 1304–1589*. Cambridge, Cambridge University Press, 1998.

Pilkington, H. *Migration, Displacement and Identity in Post-Soviet Russia*. London, Routledge, 1998.

Pipes, R. *A Concise History of the Russian Revolution*. London, Harvill, 1995.

*Russia Under the Old Regime*. London, Penguin, 1995.

Pitcher, H. *Witnesses of the Russian Revolution*. London, John Murray, 1994.

Politkovskaya, A. *A Dirty War: A Russian Reporter in Chechnya*. London, Harvill, 2001.

Reese, R. R. *The Soviet Military Experience*. London, Routledge, 1999.

Remnick, D. *Resurrection: The Struggle for a New Russia*. London, Vintage, 1998.

Roberts, G. *The Soviet Union in World Politics*. London, Routledge, 1998.

Robinson, N. (Ed.). *Institutions and Political Change in Russia*. Basingstoke, Macmillan, 2000.

Rose, R., and Munro, N. *Elections without Order: Russia's Challenge to Vladimir Putin*. Cambridge, Cambridge University Press, 2002.

Roxburgh, A. *The Second Russian Revolution*. London, BBC Books, 1991.

Sakwa, R. *Soviet Politics*, 3rd edn. London, Routledge, 2002.

Seely, R. *The Russo-Chechen Conflict 1800–2000*. London, Frank Cass, 2001.

Service, R. A. *A History of Twentieth-Century Russia*. Cambridge, MA, Harvard University Press, 1997.

*Russia: Experiment With a People: From 1991 to the Present*. London, Macmillan, 2002.

Shevtsova, L. *Putin's Russia*. Washington, DC, Carnegie Endowment for International Peace, 2003.

Simes, D. K. *After the Collapse: Russia seeks its Place as a Great Power*. London, Simon and Schuster, 1999.

Smith, A. *Russia and the World Economy: Problems of Integration*. London, Routledge, 1993.

Steen, A., and Gelman, V. (Eds). *Elites and Democratic Development in Russia*. London, Routledge, 2003.

Talbott, S. *The Russia Hand: A Memoir of Presidential Diplomacy*. New York, NY, Random House, 2002.

Taylor, B. D. *Politics and the Russian Army: Civil–Military Relations, 1689–2000*. Cambridge, Cambridge University Press, 2003.

Thornton, J. (Ed.) *Russia's Far East: A Region at Risk*. Seattle, WA, University of Washington Press, 2002.

Tikhomirov, V. *The Political Economy of Post-Soviet Russia*. Basingstoke, Macmillan, 2000.

Tolz, V. *Russia: Inventing the Nation*. London, Edward Arnold, 2001.

Trenin, D. *The End of Eurasia: Russia on the Border Between Geopolitics and Globalization*. Washington, DC, Carnegie Endowment for International Peace, 2002.

Truscott, P. *Kursk: Russia's Lost Pride*. London, Simon and Schuster, 2002.

Varese, F. *The Russian Mafia: Private Protection in a New Market Economy*. Oxford, Oxford University Press, 2001.

Volkov, V. *Violent Entrepreneurs: The Use of Force in the Making of Russian Capitalism*. Ithaca, NY, Cornell University Press, 2002.

Wallender, C A. (Ed.). *Sources of Russian Foreign Policy after the Cold War*. Boulder, CO, Westview Press, 1996.

Weinberg, R. *Stalin's Forgotten Zion: Birobidzhan and the Making of a Soviet Jewish Homeland*. Berkeley, CA, University of California Press, 1998.

Wood, A. *Stalin and Stalinism*, 2nd edn. London, Routledge, 1990.

*The Origins of the Russian Revolution*, 2nd edn. London, Routledge, 1993.

Yakovlev, A. N. *A Century of Violence in Soviet Russia*. New Haven, CT, Yale University Press, 2002.

Also see the Select Bibliography in Part Four.

# TAJIKISTAN

## Geography

### PHYSICAL FEATURES

The Republic of Tajikistan (formerly the Tajik or Tadzhik Soviet Socialist Republic, a constituent partner in the USSR) is situated in the south-east of Central Asia. To the north and west it is bounded by Uzbekistan, and to the north-east by Kyrgyzstan. Its eastern boundary is with the People's Republic of China, while to the south lies Afghanistan. Its territory includes the autonomous region of Gornyi Badakhshan (of which the capital is Khorog), in the east of the country. Tajikistan covers an area of 143,100 sq km (55,250 sq miles).

The terrain is almost entirely mountainous, with more than one-half of the country above 3,000 m. The main agricultural areas are in the lower-lying regions of the south-west (Khatlon Oblast) and the north-west. The latter region, Soghd (formerly Leninabad) Oblast, north of mountains that separate it from the rest of the country and surrounding the city of Khujand (Khodzhent—formerly Leninabad), is part of the prosperous Fergana basin. The major mountain ranges are the western Tien Shan in the north, the southern Tien Shan in the central region and the Pamirs in the south-east. The highest mountains of Tajikistan, and of the former USSR, Lenin Peak (7,134 m or 23,414 ft) and Communism Peak (7,495 m), are situated in the northern Pamirs. There is a dense river network, which is extensively used to provide hydroelectric power. The major rivers are the upper reaches of the Syr-Dar'ya and of the Amu-Dar'ya, which forms the southern border with Afghanistan, as the Pyanj. The Zeravshen river flows through the centre of the country. Most settlement is in the valleys of the south-west and the northern areas around Khujand.

### CLIMATE

The climate varies considerably according to altitude. The average temperature in January in Khujand (lowland) is –0.9°C (30.4°F); in July the average is 27.4°C (81.3°F). In the southern lowlands the temperature variation is somewhat more extreme. Precipitation is low in the valleys, ranging from 150–250 mm per year. In mountain areas winter temperatures can fall below –45°C (–51°F); the average January temperature in Murgab, in the mountains of south-east Gornyi Badakhshan, for example, is –19.6°C (–3.3°F). Levels of rainfall are very low in mountain regions and seldom exceed 60 mm–80 mm per year. Snow and ice, however, can make many parts of the country inaccessible for many months of the year.

### POPULATION

In 1992–93, as a result of the civil conflict, many were killed (estimates range from 20,000 to 50,000 or more) and some 600,000 were reckoned to have become refugees. At the census of January 2000 the population numbered 6,127,493. According to UN estimates, at mid-2002 the population was 6,195,000, thus the population density was 43.3 per sq km. The largest ethnic group is the Tajiks (80.0% of the population at the 2000 census), followed by Uzbeks (15.3%), Russians (1.1%) and Tatars (0.3%). Other ethnic minorities included Kyrgyz, Ukrainians, Germans, Turkmen and Koreans. In 1989 Tajik replaced Russian as the official language of the republic. Tajik belongs to the South-Western Iranian group of languages and is closely related to Farsi (Persian). From 1940 the Cyrillic script was used.

The major religion is Islam. Most Tajiks and Uzbeks follow the Sunni tradition, but the Pamiris are mostly Isma'ilis, members of a Shi'ite sect. There are also representatives of the Russian Orthodox Church and a small minority of Protestant Christian groups. There is a small Jewish community, which, in 1989, included 9,701 European Jews and 4,879 Central Asian Jews.

The capital is Dushanbe (Stalinabad 1929–61), which is situated in the west of the country, and had a population of 575,900 in January 2002. Khujand, to the north, is Tajikistan's second-largest city (147,400). Important regional centres are the towns of Qurgonteppa (Kurgan-Tyube) and Kulob (Kulyab), in Khatlon Oblast to the south of Dushanbe. The level of urbanization was 26%, according to provisional results of the 2000 census.

# Chronology

**7th century:** The Arabs, the latest non-Iranian (Persian) invaders of the area, conquered and converted to Islam the peoples of the great 'Silk Road' cities (notably Samarkand and Bukhara), anciently the provinces of Sogdiana and Bactria.

**8th century:** The Persic, islamicized urban dwellers, began to be identifiable as a distinct Tajik people, distinguished from their Turkic neighbours.

**16th century:** The Turkic Uzbek people were established as the rulers of the previously Tajik cities and were overlords of the Tajik clans of modern Tajikistan; a variety of khanates, notably those based in the cities of Bukhara, Samarkand and Kokand, struggled for control in the following centuries.

**1868:** The Emirate of Bukhara became a Russian protectorate and ceded some of what is northern Tajikistan to the Russian Empire, but retained the central and southern regions.

**1876:** The Khanate of Kokand, conquered by the Russians in 1866, was abolished and parts of northern Tajikistan and the Eastern Pamir were incorporated into the Russian Empire.

**1895:** Russia acquired the Western Pamir, after it and the United Kingdom defined their spheres of influence in Afghanistan.

**November 1917:** Khujand (Khodzhent—later renamed Leninabad until 1991) fell to the Bolsheviks, mainly helped by soviets of Slavs, but there were also Tajik groups such as the Union of Muslim Workers; most of the rest of north and east Tajikistan was under Bolshevik control by the end of the next year.

**September 1920:** The Emir of Bukhara was driven from his city by the Bolsheviks, but his supporters retained control of much of the south and centre of modern Tajikistan for another two years, with the help of fierce *basmachi* resistance, some of which lasted until the 1930s.

**15 March 1925:** A Tajik Autonomous Soviet Socialist Republic (ASSR) was formed, with its capital at Dushanbe (called Stalinabad 1929–61), by uniting parts of the old Turkestan ASSR and eastern territories of the Bukharan People's Soviet Republic.

**1927:** It was decided to replace the Arabic script with a Latin alphabet for the Tajik language.

**16 October 1929:** The Tajik ASSR, now including the territory of Khujand, became a full Union Republic and no longer part of the Uzbek Soviet Socialist Republic (SSR).

**1940:** A Cyrillic script replaced the Latin one.

**1978:** Against a background of increasing Islamic influence, there were reports of anti-Russian riots in Tajikistan.

**1985:** The former republican premier, Rakhmon Nabiyev, was replaced as leader of the Communist Party of Tajikistan (CPT) by Kakhar Makkhamov, who criticized his predecessor and acknowledged the economic problems of Tajikistan (not least brought on by a high birth rate—the population increased by 34% between 1979 and 1989).

**1989:** Increasing nationalism was evidenced by a law making Tajik the state language and by ethnic clashes.

**11 February 1990:** Nationalist violence in Dushanbe led to 22 deaths.

**March 1990:** Elections to the Supreme Soviet produced an overwhelmingly communist legislature; voting took place under a state of emergency prompted by rioting the previous month, after which the leadership became less tolerant of dissent.

**19 March 1990:** The Deputy Chairman of the Council of Ministers and the Minister of Culture were dismissed for their alleged role in an attempt to overthrow the Government in February.

**25 August 1990:** The Tajik Supreme Soviet proclaimed the Republic's independence, suspended all USSR legislation that contravened Tajikistan's sovereign rights, and asserted the Republic's right to secede from the USSR.

**November 1990:** Makkhamov was elected to the new post of President of the Republic by the Supreme Soviet, opposed only by Nabiyev.

**17 March 1991:** In an all-Union referendum on the future of the USSR, 90% of the participating electorate favoured a 'renewed federation'.

**31 August 1991:** Mass demonstrations forced the resignation of President Makkhamov, who had failed to condemn the abortive coup in Moscow. Demonstrations continued into the following month, organized by the opposition: the nationalist Rastokhez (Rebirth) movement; the secular, Westernized Democratic Party of Tajikistan (DPT); and the Islamic Renaissance Party (IRP).

**9 September 1991:** The Supreme Soviet declared the independence of the renamed Republic of Tajikistan.

**22 September 1991:** Conceding the demands of the continuing demonstrations, the Chairman of the Supreme Soviet and acting head of state, Kadriddin Aslonov, banned the CPT and nationalized its assets. The next day the Supreme Soviet rescinded his decree, declared a state of emergency and replaced Aslonov with Nabiyev.

**2 October 1991:** The Supreme Soviet reimposed the ban on the CPT (known as the Socialist Party, September 1991–February 1992), after Nabiyev had conceded to key opposition demands some days previously. The IRP was legalized and the state of emergency ended.

**24 November 1991:** Nabiyev (who had resigned as Head of State on 6 October to contest the presidential elections) won 57% of the votes cast, compared with 30% for his main rival, the opposition-backed liberal Davlat Khudonazarov.

**21 December 1991:** Tajikistan and 10 other former Soviet republics declared the foundation of the Commonwealth of Independent States (CIS), thereby finally dissolving the USSR.

**March 1992:** Opposition demonstrations were provoked by President Nabiyev's dismissal of prominent sympathizers of the opposition, the Islamic and democratic elements of which were co-ordinated into a united front largely through the efforts of the Chief Kazi, Haji Akbar Turajonzoda.

**3 May 1992:** Pro-communist counter-demonstrators engaged in the first armed conflicts with the opposition supporters; this marked the start of the civil war.

**6 May 1992:** Shocked at the violence, Nabiyev and the opposition agreed a new Government of National Reconciliation including eight opposition ministers. Peace was secured in Dushanbe, but there was fighting in the south as pro-communist forces based in Kulyab formed militias to harass the opposition.

**7 September 1992:** Dispossessed, captured and threatened by demonstrators supporting the Islamic-democratic parties, President Nabiyev resigned and his powers were assumed by the Chairman of the Supreme Soviet, Akbarsho Iskandarov. The latter supported the continuing coalition Government, the authority of which was steadily being rejected by the establishment outside the capital, but the premier, Akbar Mirzoyev, resigned and was replaced by a Khujand communist, Abdumalik Abdullojonov.

**25 October 1992:** Safarli Kenjayev, leader of a southern militia, was expelled from Dushanbe, having entered and attempted to proclaim himself head of state. He then placed the city under siege.

**10 November 1992:** With civil war still raging, and having agreed to a session of the Supreme Soviet, Iskandarov and the Government resigned.

**27 November 1992:** Having convened in Khujand, the Supreme Soviet instituted a communist reaction by abolishing the presidency and appointing a Kulyabi, Imamali Rakhmonov, as its Chairman (Head of State) and dismissing all opposition figures from the Government.

**10 December 1992:** The pro-communist Kulyabi militias seized control of the capital; there were allegations of widespread atrocities against supporters of the Islamic-democratic opposition, most of the leaders of which fled into exile or to the eastern mountains.

**22 January 1993:** A collective security treaty signed by Tajikistan, Kazakhstan, Kyrgyzstan, Russia and Uzbekistan marked the end of formal CIS neutrality in the civil war (the new regime received particular support from the last two states).

**23 May 1993:** A bilateral treaty between Tajikistan and Russia re-emphasized the latter's concern for the southern borders, now that the armed Tajikistani opposition had fled to Afghanistan (estimates for the number of civil-war dead ranged between 20,000 and 100,000, while the number of refugees was put at more than 800,000 refugees).

**July 1993:** Russia's concerns at Tajikistani opposition incursions increased after a number of its border troops were killed; both Tajikistan and Afghanistan complained to the UN about border violations.

**December 1993:** Abdullojonov resigned as Prime Minister and was replaced by Abdujalil Samadov.

**5–8 January 1994:** Tajikistan's introduction of the new Russian rouble effectively formalized its economic subjection to Russia, which had insisted that the communist regime (hitherto unable to deal with the escalating economic crisis) introduce political and economic reforms that year.

**15 June 1994:** The deputy Minister of Defence was killed in an ambush by opposition forces; the rebels were based in Afghanistan and allegedly aided by the *mujahidin*, fundamentalist guerrillas. Peace talks in the same month in Tehran, Iran, involved discussion of methods to counter the smuggling of illegal drugs.

**18 September 1994:** Government and rebel negotiators agreed to a temporary cease-fire. The cease-fire was eventually implemented in late October (and extended several times), although it was only sporadically observed.

**6 November 1994:** Rakhmonov won the country's first direct presidential election, securing 58% of the votes cast, against former Prime Minister Abdullojonov. A simultaneous plebiscite approved the new Constitution. In the following month Jamshed Karimov became Chairman of the Council of Ministers.

**26 February 1995:** A majority of pro-Rakhmonov candidates was elected to a new legislature, the Supreme Assembly; despite reports that it had sought legalization, the IRP and the DPT did not contest the elections, to which the Organization for Security and Co-operation in Europe (OSCE) refused to send observers.

**13 April 1995:** In an intensification of border clashes, Russian-made fighter jets were alleged to have killed and injured a great number of people in an Afghan border town suspected as the base of Islamist rebels.

**10 May 1995:** Tajikistan introduced its own currency, the rouble. Later in the month President Rakhmonov met Sayed Abdullo Nuri, the leader of the IRP, in Kabul, Afghanistan (they met again in July in Tehran), although at subsequent negotiations the opposition refused to extend the cease-fire (this was eventually agreed for a further six months in August).

**June 1995:** The DPT leader, Shodman Yusuf, was criticized for accommodation with the Government and declared deposed; a more intransigent faction elected Jumaboy Niyazov as its leader, and he participated in the armed opposition's negotiations with the Government. The Yusuf faction had been permitted to register as the DPT with the justice ministry by 1996.

**September 1995:** Two formerly pro-Government military units were reported to be fighting over control of the cotton trade in Kurgan-Tyube; some 300 people were believed to have been killed by the time government forces regained control of the town.

**21 January 1996:** The Chief Mufti of Tajikistan, Fatkhullo Sharifzoda, was assassinated by unidentified killers; a strong supporter of the Government, his death was blamed on the IRP, which denied responsibility.

**27 January 1996:** Makhmoud Khudoberdiyev, the leader of one of the military brigades involved in the September disturbances, took control of Kurgan-Tyube, claiming loyalty to the President, but alleging government corruption. Likewise, the previous day, in Tursan-Zade, another military commander, Ibodullo Boitmatov, began a revolt that also demanded the resignation of senior government figures.

**7 February 1996:** Under pressure from Khudoberdiyev and Boitmatov, and following the dismissal of three senior government officials, Karimov resigned as Prime Minister; Yakhyo Azimov, a former factory director with little political experience, was appointed to be the new Chairman of the Council of Ministers.

**19 July 1996:** A five-month cease-fire agreement between government and opposition negotiators, mediated by the UN, was signed in Ashgabat, although with little discernible effect on the fighting.

**23 December 1996:** At a meeting in Moscow, President Rakhmonov and Sayed Abdullo Nuri agreed to form a National Reconciliation Council (NRC), to be headed by a representative of the United Tajik Opposition (UTO).

**February 1997:** At peace talks held in Mashad, Iran, under UN auspices, it was agreed that the NRC would have 26 seats divided equally between the Government and the UTO.

**30 April 1997:** President Rakhmonov was wounded when a grenade was thrown at his motorcade in Khujand; the UTO denied any involvement in the assassination attempt.

**27 June 1997:** The five-year civil war was formally ended when the provisions of the December 1996 peace agreement were confirmed by the General Agreement on Peace and National Accord in Tajikistan, signed in Moscow.

**7–10 July 1997:** Nuri was elected Chairman of the NRC at its inaugural session; an amnesty was granted whereby UTO fighters would be permitted to return to Tajikistan.

**August 1997:** The new Chief Mufti of Tajikistan, Amonullo Nematzoda, was kidnapped by Rizvon Sadirov, the brother of a rebel captured by government troops in March; the Mufti was freed when the Government decided to release several of Sadirov's supporters, although he himself was later killed by government forces.

**12 March 1998:** Six people, including the brother of former Prime Minister Abdullojonov, were sentenced to death for their part in the attempted assassination of President Rakhmonov.

**18 April 1998:** President Rakhmonov was elected Chairman of the People's Democratic Party of Tajikistan (PDPT).

**September 1998:** A senior opposition member and former Deputy Prime Minister, Otakhon Latifi, was assassinated, in what was interpreted as an attempt to undermine the peace process.

**8 September 1998:** Tajikistan signed an agreement with a number of other Caucasian, Central Asian and European countries aiming to re-create the 'Silk Road' trade route.

**26 October 1998:** At a meeting of the NRC, Nuri announced that Rakhmonov had agreed to grant the UTO a further 19 senior government positions.

**4–7 November 1998:** Heavy fighting took place around Khujand, in what was considered to be the most violent uprising since the signature of the General Agreement on Peace and National Accord. Forces loyal to Makhmoud Khudoberdiyev seized the police and security headquarters and a nearby airport. An estimated 100–300 people were killed. Criminal proceedings were initiated against the alleged instigators, who included Khudoberdiyev, former Prime Minister Abdulmalik Abdullojonov, his brother and former Mayor of Khujand, Abdughani Abdullojonov, and former Vice-President Narzullo Dustov.

**17 June 1999:** Following the UTO's withdrawal from the NRC late the previous month, President Rakhmonov and Nuri met and agreed a series of deadlines for the resolution of the differences that had prompted the UTO to threaten to suspend its participation in the NRC.

**3 August 1999:** The UTO announced that the integration of its fighters into the regular armed forces had been completed; in response, President Rakhmonov revoked a ban on opposition parties and their media, in force since 1993, in accordance with the agreement made in June.

**26 September 1999:** A national referendum took place on 27 proposed amendments to the 1994 Constitution, including the formation of a bicameral legislature, the extension of the presidential term of office from five years to seven, and the right to form religion-based political parties. Some 92% of the electorate were believed to have participated in the referendum, of whom 72% voted in favour of the amendments.

**October 1999:** Around 1,000 anti-Government rebels entered Tajikistan from Uzbekistan, straining relations between the two countries; however, many had left by November, following mediation by the UTO.

**18 October 1999:** The UTO again suspended its participation in the NRC, alleging that the Government was not acknowledging its demands.

**6 November 1999:** Rakhmonov achieved a decisive victory over his only opponent in the presidential election, obtaining 97% of the votes cast; the participation rate was reportedly 99%. The OSCE refused to send observers to monitor the election, owing to widespread allegations of malpractice.

**20 December 1999:** A new cabinet was installed, headed by Akil Akilov.

**27 February 2000:** An election was held to the new lower chamber of parliament, the Majlisi Namoyandagon (Assembly of Representatives); the PDPT was reported to have won 64.5% of the votes cast and to have secured 45 of the 63 seats available. The CPT took some 20.6% of the votes (13 seats), and the IRP 7.5% (two seats). Both the OSCE and opposition parties claimed that there had been electoral malpractice, and Sayed Nuri complained formally. A further round of voting took place on 12 March for 11 constituencies where a 50%

quorum had not been achieved; and two further seats were filled in April and December.

**23 March 2000:** An election to the Majlisi Milliy (National Assembly) took place for the first time. A government reorganization had already taken place earlier in the month. The NRC was dissolved, having witnessed the elections, thereby fulfilling the final condition of the 1997 peace agreement.

**15 May 2000:** The mandate of the UN Mission of Observers in Tajikistan (UNMOT), approved in December 1994, expired.

**31 May 2000:** President Rakhmonov appealed to the international community for aid in response to the worst drought for 70 years.

**30 October 2000:** The Government introduced a new currency, the somoni, to replace the Tajik rouble, one somoni being equivalent to 1,000 roubles.

**18 April 2001:** The Supreme Court imposed long prison sentences on three people for their role in the attempted coup of 1998.

**2 May 2001:** The IRP (now restyled the Islamic Rebirth Party) claimed that some of its members had been persecuted on the pretext of belonging to a banned religious movement, the Hizb-ut-Tahrir, and had been falsely accused of illegally storing weapons.

**11 June 2001:** The former UTO field commander, Rakhmon Sanginov, took seven police-officers hostage. They had been released by 17 June, following an undertaking by the Government to reassess criminal proceedings against eight of Sanginov's supporters.

**24 July 2001:** Tajikistan was granted observer status with the World Trade Organization (WTO).

**8 September 2001:** The Minister of Culture, Abdurakhim Rakhimov, was assassinated.

**16 September 2001:** Russian troops along the Tajik–Afghan border were put on high alert in anticipation of US-led military strikes against Afghanistan.

**8 October 2001:** The Ministry of Foreign Affairs issued a statement in support of the US-led aerial bombardment of Afghanistan.

**12 December 2001:** It was reported that a court in Khujand had convicted 10 men on charges of treason, terrorism and sedition, relating to the November 1998 insurrection, and sentenced them to between eight and 25 years' imprisonment.

**20 February 2002:** Tajikistan joined NATO's 'Partnership for Peace' programme of military co-operation.

**12 March 2002:** The Agreement on Public Accord in Tajikistan, signed in March 1996 by pro-Government political parties and non-governmental organizations to demonstrate support for the peace process, was extended indefinitely; the accord was signed by a representative of the IRP for the first time.

**17 May 2002:** Tajikistan and the People's Republic of China signed a border agreement, according to which Tajikistan ceded 1,000 sq km of disputed territory to China.

**11 June 2002:** Abdulaziz Khamidov, the former leader of Soghd region and relative of a former Prime Minister, was convicted of embezzlement and involvement in the 1996 assassination attempt on Rakhmonov, and sentenced to 15 years' imprisonment.

**9 September 2002:** The first independent radio station began broadcasting in the Tajik capital.

**Late January 2003:** President Rakhmonov implemented a wide-ranging reshuffle of the Council of Ministers, state agencies, local government, state-owned joint-stock companies and the judiciary. The most notable government change was the dismissal of Deputy Prime Minister Fariddun Mukhiddonov, and his replacement by Asadullo Ghulomov, the former Mayor of Dushanbe. Zarif Aliyev was appointed Chairman of the Constitutional Court.

**28 April 2003:** Representatives from Armenia, Belarus, Kazakhstan, Kyrgyzstan, Russia and Tajikistan formally inaugurated the successor to the Collective Security Treaty, a new regional defence organization known as the Collective Security Treaty Organization (CSTO).

**22 June 2003:** Some 96% of the electorate took part in a referendum on proposed amendments to the Constitution, which were approved by 93% of the voters. The amendments provided, *inter alia*, for the extension of judges' terms of office from five to 10 years, the removal of references to religious parties from the Constitution and the abolition of the right to both free health care and higher education. Significantly, approval of the proposals would also enable President Rakhmonov to stand for two further terms of office when his term expired in 2006.

**6 October 2003:** It was reported that the Deputy Chairman of the IRP, Shamsiddin Shamsiddinov, was to be charged with a number of criminal activities, including treason.

# History

## Dr JOHN ANDERSON

### EARLY HISTORY

The territories of Sogdiana and Bactria, which covered what is now Tajikistan and parts of modern Uzbekistan, were part of the Persian Empire until their conquest by Alexander II ('the Great') of Macedon in the fourth century BC. In subsequent centuries the region was dominated by various nomadic confederations, until coming under Arab control at the end of the seventh century. Under the caliphate, the Western Iranian branch of the Persian (Iranian) language came to dominate, and within one century there had emerged a distinctive urban-based ethnic group known as the Tajiks. The Tajik cities of Samarkand and Bukhara were great centres of Muslim art and learning, although by the 16th century the Turkic-speaking Uzbeks had gained political dominance over the region. From this period onwards Tajik groupings were subordinate to Uzbek rule, exchanging it for that of the Russian tsars in the late 19th century.

### SOVIET TAJIKISTAN

In 1918 the Bolsheviks formally incorporated northern Tajikistan into the Turkestan Autonomous Soviet Socialist Republic (ASSR) within the Russian Federation, but it took until 1921 to establish real control over the region. Moreover, in the south-eastern parts of Tajikistan the imposition of Soviet rule proved much harder, for here were to be found some of the most militant strongholds of the *basmachi*, local guerrilla fighters who resisted the efforts of the Red Army until the mid-1920s. Many of them later fled to Afghanistan. The administrative fate of Tajikistan became entangled with conflicts among Central Asian élites, with the dominant influence of Bukharan revolutionaries leading to the initial formation of a new Tajik ASSR within the Uzbek Soviet Socialist Republic (SSR) in 1925. Four years later the region of Khujand (Khodzhent), later renamed Leninabad, of Uzbekistan was added to Tajikistan, which then acquired its own status as an SSR and full Union Republic of the USSR. Even so, this left the historically Tajik cities of Samarkand and Bukhara outside the republic, as well as a substantial Tajik population in Afghanistan. Conversely, the western parts of the new republic, as well as the old Khujand region, had substantial Uzbek minorities.

Soviet rule initially brought little change to the rural areas of Tajikistan, with the Bolsheviks having considerable trouble in finding local personnel to implement their policies. From the late 1920s, however, the collectivization of agriculture severely disrupted the traditional activity of cattle-breeding, while those described as representatives of the old order were subject to repression. In the cities the small indigenous élite that had opted for co-operation with the Bolsheviks was removed, and ethnic Russians were given many of the main positions.

After the Second World War some changes were made. In the economic sphere this entailed the dramatic increase in the cultivation of cotton in the southern areas. To provide labour for this expansion, the period from the 1940s to the mid-1960s witnessed a series of population resettlements, often forced, as whole villages were shifted from the north and east of the republic to the southern Kulob (Kulyab) and Qurgonteppa (Kurgan-Tyube, or Kurgan Teppe) regions (united as Khatlon Oblast at the end of 1992). This created tensions between the new, dislocated settlers (many from the Garm district), who often found themselves in areas with few amenities, and older residents, many of them Uzbeks, who resented the influx of immigrants from the north. The other change that was to have consequences for the future was the Soviet regime's changing personnel policy. After the Second World War some effort was made to increase the number of ethnic Tajiks in the local Communist Party administration, but in practice this meant that the Tajik leadership came to be dominated by representatives of the northern Leninabad Oblast, a development that fostered resentment in other parts of the country. Whether the appointment of local cadres served to reinforce Soviet control, however, was less clear. There were frequent complaints that, under indigenous élites, central directives were all too often ignored or distorted, especially those that sought to eliminate past cultural traditions. Nowhere was this clearer than in the religious sphere, when the mass closure of mosques under the leadership of Stalin (Iosif V. Dzhugashvili) in the USSR left the officially registered number of mosques in the republic at less than 20. By the time of Leonid Brezhnev as Soviet leader, however, it was well known that every village and district had a functioning place of worship, while thousands of self-appointed imams, often perpetuating a family tradition, operated with the acquiescence of local officials. In the early 1980s, following the Soviet invasion of Afghanistan at the end of 1979, there were repeated reports of growing Islamist sentiment, possibly exaggerated by the state, and also of occasional manifestations of anti-Russian sentiment.

This growing independence was threatened by the accession, as Soviet leader, of Mikhail Gorbachev, who sought to bring Central Asia under much closer central control. The First Secretary of the Communist Party of Tajikistan (CPT), Rakhmon Nabiyev, was accused of corruption and nepotism and replaced by Kakhar Makkhamov. Towards the end of the 1980s there was also some relaxation of censorship, which permitted greater discussion of the cultural heritage of the nation, in particular of its Iranian and Islamic connections. This led to the creation of the cultural organization Rastokhez

(Rebirth). Rastokhez took the lead in agitating for the language law enacted at the end of 1989. This established Tajik as the primary medium of communication in state and educational establishments in the republic. Despite this, Makkhamov and the CPT in general tried to restrain the more exuberant manifestations of *glasnost* (openness) seen in other parts of the USSR.

During February 1990 there was serious rioting in the Tajik capital, Dushanbe (Stalinabad 1929–61), following speculation that Armenian refugees from the Nagornyi Karabakh (Azerbaijan) conflict were to be welcomed in a city with an extreme housing shortage. In March 1990 strictly controlled elections to the republican Supreme Soviet, or legislature, produced a parliamentary body in which 94% of the deputies were communists. Following the example of other Union Republics, Tajikistan declared its sovereignty in August 1990, and towards the end of the year parliament elected Makkhamov as the republic's first executive President, in preference to Rakhmon Nabiyev. During the August 1991 coup attempt in Moscow, the Russian and Soviet capital, Tajikistan's leadership effectively supported the plotters, and with the failure of the *putsch* Makkhamov was forced to resign as President. On 9 September the Supreme Soviet declared the independence of Tajikistan, and two weeks later, against a background of demonstrations in the major cities, the acting Head of State, the Chairman of the parliament, Kadriddin Aslonov, formally banned the Communist Party. Aslonov had not, however, reckoned with the communist-controlled Supreme Soviet, which sought to relegalize the Party and succeeded in replacing him with Nabiyev, who served as the acting President until elections could be held on 24 November. Nabiyev won 57% of the votes cast, compared with the 30% won by the film-maker Davlat Khudonazarov, the candidate supported by the opposition. Although there was some evidence of electoral fraud, Nabiyev took office in early December, and it was under his presidency that Tajikistan acceded to the Commonwealth of Independent States (CIS) on 21 December, thus achieving independence with the final collapse of the USSR before the end of the year.

## INDEPENDENT TAJIKISTAN

### Civil War

Independence failed to bring an end to conflict in Tajikistan. By early 1992 the united opposition, which mobilized Islamists, nationalists and democrats, was able seriously to challenge Nabiyev's regime, bringing thousands of demonstrators on to the streets of the capital. In response, the Government organized counter-rallies, bringing a considerable number of demonstrators from the southern Kulob region to the capital and then issuing them with armaments. The ensuing violence, however, led Nabiyev to seek a compromise, and in May 1992 a coalition administration was formed. The Government of National Reconciliation included eight opposition representatives, but none the less found it hard to assert its authority once the Leninabad and Kulob regional administrations refused to recognize the new regime's legality. In early September the opposition forced the resignation of Nabiyev and effectively took power at the centre. Some attempt was made to conciliate the old establishment, with the interim Head of State (Chairman of the Supreme Soviet), Akbarsho Iskandarov, recruiting the northerner Abdumalik Abdullojonov as Prime Minister (Chairman of the Council of Ministers), but the country rapidly disintegrated into a state of civil war.

The centre of resistance to the new regime came from the Kulob region, where there soon appeared a series of armed militias, the most powerful being that associated with a former criminal, Sangak Safarov. While such forces quickly established a brutal ascendancy in the south, another armed group, led by a former parliamentary speaker, Safarali Kenjayev, attempted an attack on the capital in October 1992. Thereafter, along with other militias, Kenjayev's troops maintained a blockade of Dushanbe. By the end of the year the Government had collapsed and the old order appeared to have been restored, albeit with the balance of power resting firmly with the armed Kulyabis of the south rather than with the traditional cadres of the northern Leninabad region.

Although some of the coalition Government remained, notably the Prime Minister, Abdullojonov, its leading supporters fled abroad before the end of the year. Haji Akbar Turajonzoda, the influential *kazi* (supreme judge) of Tajikistan, who, while sympathetic to the opposition, had sought to exercise a moderating influence during the struggles of the previous year, also went into exile. Some figures identified with the Islamist-democratic opposition chose to remain, but many disappeared during the period of terror that followed. Armed groups ranged around the south and centre of Tajikistan, looting and in many cases killing people whose passports revealed them to be from the 'wrong' parts of the country—that is those associated with the opposition. In February 1993 Turajonzoda was replaced as spiritual leader of Tajikistan's Muslims by Fatkhullo Sharifzoda, who was given the title of *mufti*.

### Explaining the Conflict

The Tajikistan that acquired independence was one in which any sense of national unity was weak, in which the state lacked the capacity to create a sense of common belonging or to resolve conflict, and in which most people identified themselves more strongly with their region or family network than with the new nation state. As a result, in the conflict that broke out in 1992, apparent ideological differences overlaid regional distinctions, while opposition challenges to the regime could, in part, be explained in terms of regional resentments at previous exclusion from power. This was evident in the emergence of political parties in the country.

The northern Leninabad Oblast (the capital of which was again called Khujand) was traditionally the richest and most powerful region. Nearly two-thirds of Tajikistan's output came from there, and its cadres had dominated the republican party apparatus since before the Second World War. Here the influence of the Communist Party remained paramount. In the capital, Dushanbe, were the more critical intellectuals who formed Rastokhez. Further south were the regions of Kulob and Qurgonteppa. Economically poor, dependent largely upon the production of cotton, these regions quickly divided during the civil war. Kulob provided the armed units that were to be decisive during the events of 1992 and the legacy of which was to prove disastrous for the country thereafter. The Qurgonteppa region was more fragmented; the resettled people tended to support the Islamist-democratic opposition, while the substantial Uzbek population of the region feared that these often impoverished settlers might prove the basis of a religious fundamentalist threat. In addition, some Tajiks in the region, notably those around the town of Hissar, traditionally enjoyed a role in the communist administration prior to independence and thus tended to support the old regime. To the east of the capital the opposition remained strong, with the Garm district providing many of the supporters of the Islamic Renaissance Party (IRP, restyled the Islamic Rebirth Party from 1999). Further east still, in Gornyi Badakhshan, the small population of Pamiri mountaineers, followers of the Isma'ili tradition in Shi'ism, felt some degree of hostility towards the old regime, but many remained wary of the increasingly Islamist- and Sunni-dominated opposition.

Although regionalism played a vital role in the conflict, there were ideological tensions at work. The old regime may have used the fundamentalist threat for its own purposes, but there were clearly some among the opposition coalition who favoured giving a greater role to Islam in public life. Prior to the civil war *kazi* Turajonzoda had repeatedly stressed that years of secularization had rendered all thought of an Islamic state impossible for the foreseeable future. Thus, he, along with the IRP, spoke of the need for the creation of a non-confessional state, but one in which Islam was allowed the freedom to reassert its influence. Within the ranks of the IRP not all shared this moderation, and one of the ironies of the civil war was that, as a consequence of the brutal suppression of opposition that followed the triumph of the Kulyabi militias in late 1992, many opposition activists were forced into exile in Afghanistan, where they were increasingly radicalized by their contacts with local *mujahidin*.

### Restoring Political Order

In November 1992 the 'rump' Supreme Soviet, purged of Islamic, democratic and nationalist elements, elected Imamali Rakhmonov, a Kulyabi, as its Chairman and Head of State, and formally abolished the presidency. Under him the new regime began to assert its authority, beginning with the detention of those opposition supporters who remained and continuing with an effort to gain control of those areas of the country still dominated by opponents of the regime. Within the regime tensions quickly emerged between the Khujand and Kulob élites, the former resentful of the loss of political dominance and the continued instability encouraged by the presence of numerous armed militia groups. The priority for the Khujand *nomenklatura* was to bring an end to the war, so that their traditionally wealthy region could begin the task of economic reconstruction. To this end they tended to be more conciliatory in negotiations with the opposition than the newly dominant Kulyabis. These tensions surfaced at the end of 1993, when Abdullojonov resigned as Prime Minister and was dispatched as ambassador to Russia. During early 1994 the Rakhmonov administration attempted to legitimize its position further by introducing a draft constitution, which included a proposal to restore the state presidency. On 6 November the people of Tajikistan went to the polls, where they endorsed the new Constitution and selected a new President. The opposition outside the country had urged a boycott of voting, arguing that without a free press or adequate guarantees of human rights the election would be meaningless. In the event, however, there were two candidates: Rakhmonov and Abdullojonov. Official results reported the rate of participation by voters to be in excess of 90% of the registered electorate, of whom 58.3% voted for Imamali Rakhmonov.

A general election followed on 26 February 1995. Once again, all genuine opposition parties were excluded from the contest, although in the approach to the election Abdullojonov's Party of Popular Unity and Accord (PPUA) was granted registration, as were several other parties that favoured the old ruling élite, if not the Kulyabi-dominated Government itself. As during the presidential election, considerable evidence of abuse was reported and Abdullojonov was himself disallowed registration as a candidate. After two rounds of voting a Supreme Assembly of 181 deputies was formed, most coming from the old economic and state apparatus, although about one-quarter had been commanders in the various armed militias that had ensured Kulyabi successes at the end of 1992 and beginning of 1993. Although Rakhmonov tried to ensure some degree of regional representation in the selection of deputy parliamentary speakers, this could not hide the continued dominance of Tajikistan by the representatives of one region, nor could it hope to provide legitimacy in the absence of all genuine opposition.

### Foreign Involvement and the Search for Peace

The development of the conflict in Tajikistan from 1992 caused increasing alarm among the country's neighbours, with Uzbekistan's President, Islam Karimov, expressing particular concern. With his own Islamist troubles in the Fergana valley area, Karimov feared that unrest might traverse the region and unseat his and other regimes that had not fundamentally changed with independence. For that reason he joined other Central Asian states in seeking to encourage Russia, at the time focusing most of its energies on relations with the West, to take more positive action to prevent the spread of instability. In mid-1992 it became clear that some elements in the Russian 201st Motorized Rifle Division present in Tajikistan had been supplying arms to the Kulyabi militias and often choosing to ignore their atrocities. Towards the end of that year the CIS took the decision to create a peace-keeping force based upon this Division, and at the beginning of 1993 Kazakhstan, Kyrgyzstan, Russia and Uzbekistan formally committed themselves to the defence of Tajikistan's southern borders. None the less, border clashes continued at regular intervals, and on occasions groups from the Islamist-democratic opposition, now trained and armed by elements of the Afghan *mujahidin*, were able to make incursions deep into Tajikistan. This led regional leaders to fear that the chaos that had engulfed Afghanistan, stemming in large part from the lack of a sense of national unity, might gradually extend into Tajikistan and dissolve the country.

During late 1993 Russian foreign minister Kozyrev and other Russian diplomats engaged in intensive 'shuttle' diplomacy in the region, in an effort to find ways of bringing the warring sides together. Eventually, a first round of peace negotiations was held under UN auspices in Moscow during April 1994, followed by further rounds in Islamabad, Pakistan (October 1994) and Moscow (April 1995). In May 1995 the first direct meeting took place between President Imamali Rakhmonov and the IRP and opposition leader Sayed Abdullo Nuri, in Kabul, Afghanistan, at which the latter advocated an interim government made up of neutral personalities and suggested that CIS peace-keepers be supplemented by soldiers from Pakistan and Turkey. These talks, and those in Ashgabat, Turkmenistan, in late 1995 and 1996, resulted in agreement on temporary cease-fires and prisoner exchanges, but no lasting peace settlement.

By late 1994 it was clear that the sponsors of Tajikistan's communist Government in Kazakhstan, Russia and Uzbekistan were losing patience with the Rakhmonov administration. At the Almaty summit of CIS leaders in February 1995, President Karimov of Uzbekistan revealed his disquiet at a closed session of the Heads of State, where he reportedly denounced Rakhmonov for his failure to begin serious negotiations with the armed opposition. Yet it was also becoming clear that the Russian Government was frustrated as much by opposition as by government intransigence. Addressing reporters in December 1995, the Deputy Minister of Foreign Affairs, Albert Chernyshev, criticized the opposition's negotiating position as unrealistic, because it simply required the existing Government to hand it political power.

Meeting in Moscow in December 1996, Rakhmonov and Nuri agreed to form a National Reconciliation Council (NRC). Serious progress on the details of a settlement was not made until a meeting in Bishkek, Kyrgyzstan, in May 1997, and two further sessions in Moscow in June. Following the last summit, a General Agreement on Peace and National Accord in Tajikistan was signed on 27 June. The accord envisaged: the legalization of the opposition political parties; the creation of the NRC (of which Nuri was elected Chairman in July); the granting of 30% of government posts to the opposition; elections to be held before the end of 1998; the exchange of prisoners; and the integration of opposition forces into the national army.

## UNEASY PEACE AND POLITICAL RECONSTRUCTION

The peace accord appeared to be in jeopardy, however, as rival factions within Tajikistan's armed forces fought for supremacy in the streets of Dushanbe. Central to these conflicts was a military commander, Makhmoud Khudoberdiyev, an ethnic Uzbek, who had staged a rebellion in 1996 and who was opposed to the peace agreement and its proposal to integrate opposition forces into the national army. In mid-June 1997 Khudoberdiyev seized control of an army post in a mountain pass close to Dushanbe, ostensibly to prevent the return of armed opposition forces (known as the United Tajik Opposition—UTO) from Afghanistan. The situation remained tense in the second half of the year, and in October responsibility for an attack on the barracks of the presidential guard was attributed to Khudoberdiyev.

In January 1998 the UTO delegation on the NRC refused to attend council meetings, in protest at the slow pace at which the Government was implementing the peace agreement. In February, however, the government portfolios of Labour and Employment, the Economy and Foreign Economic Relations, and Land Reclamation and Water Resources, were formally allocated to UTO members; further appointments followed. Later that month, moreover, Turajonzoda, the deputy leader of the UTO and former *kazi* of Tajikistan, who had made his return from exile conditional upon his appointment as a deputy premier, was appointed First Deputy Prime Minister with responsibility for relations with members of the CIS. In May, however, the legislature adopted a law banning all religious parties from operating in the country. This contravened the terms of the peace agreement and President Rakhmonov was subsequently obliged to veto it.

Although all opposition forces on Tajik territory were said to have sworn allegiance to the Government, many practical problems remained in disarming groups that remained sceptical about the deal, and the central Government encountered persistent small-scale revolts when it attempted to assert its authority outside the capital. Successive amnesties brought most opposition members into conformity, with many units integrated (somewhat uneasily) into the national army during 1999. The issue of political parties remained more problematic, as did the constitutional definition of the republic as a secular state, although this was resolved by amendments to the Constitution approved in a referendum in September 1999. These amendments also provided for the election of a new, two-chamber parliament and the extension of the presidential term of office. None the less, problems continued prior to the presidential election, scheduled for 6 November, as the Central Electoral Commission barred three of the challengers to President Rakhmonov, and then at the last moment gave the IRP candidate, Davlat Usmanov, permission to stand. He, in turn, refused to campaign under such conditions, and when the results were announced it was stated that 97% of the 99% of the electorate who voted had supported Rakhmonov. The incumbent had notably been supported by Turajonzoda, who claimed that the IRP had lost its sense of political direction.

Following the election, preparations were begun for parliamentary elections, scheduled for 27 February and 23 March 2000. In December 1999 six parties were formally registered for the election to the lower chamber of parliament, the Majlisi Namoyandagon (or Assembly of Representatives), including President Rakhmonov's People's Democratic Party of Tajikistan (PDPT), the CPT, the IRP, Adolatkah and the Socialist Party. Campaigning was beset by violence; beatings, kidnappings and murders targeting the political community culminated in the assassination of the Deputy Minister of

Security 11 days before the election. Official election results recorded a participation rate of just over 87%, with 64.5% of the votes secured by the PDPT, 20.6% by the CPT and 7.8% by the IRP, although most observers considered the electoral process to be flawed. The other three parties failed to secure representation under the list system. In the single-member constituencies deputies were elected in 28 areas, leaving the remainder to be selected by means of 'run-off' elections. An election to the upper chamber of parliament, the Majlisi Milliy (National Assembly), followed as scheduled on 23 March 2000. At the end of the month the NRC was dissolved, in accordance with the fulfilment of its mandate.

The holding of elections formally ended the transition period envisaged by the 1997 peace agreement, but only partially resolved the divisions within Tajik society. Elements on both sides remained distrustful of their new political allies, and in reality power remained concentrated among a select group of senior officials of the executive. Many of the newly elected deputies were simultaneously representatives of executive power in the regions and districts of Tajikistan, and thus found it difficult to constitute a democratic parliament that was more than an assembly of regional lobbyists. Although the 30% quota for UTO representatives in all government posts, as provided for in the 1997 accord, had been achieved, by May 2000 President Rakhmonov had already removed the Minister of Economy and Trade, an IRP member.

Violence also remained a problem, as armed groups continued to maintain *de facto* control over some parts of the country. In mid-2000 President Rakhmonov issued orders that off-duty soldiers should not carry weapons, and in the same month the Government announced that contract service in the armed forces would be abolished. Although justified in terms of expense, many considered this a decision aimed at former UTO fighters who had been integrated into the regular army on a higher rate of pay than that granted to conscripts. Consequently, by the end of 2000 there were several thousand men who were unemployed and who refused to return their weapons. Several assassinations of senior officials, including that of the governor of the Garm region in June 2000 and of the First Deputy Minister of Interior Affairs in April 2001, exemplified the persistence of a culture of violence. In March 2002 a public accord agreement, signed in 1996 by pro-Government political parties and non-governmental organizations to express support for the peace process, and renewed in 1999, was extended indefinitely; the accord was signed by a representative of the IRP for the first time.

In 2003 political debate centered on the question of constitutional reform, after Rakhmonov's Government proposed a series of amendments to the existing text. The proposals provided for the abolition of free higher and vocational education and health care, and for judges to serve a 10-year, rather than a five-year term. More controversial was a proposal to remove references to religious parties from the Constitution, which the main opposition party, the IRP, feared might lead to a ban on its activities. However, at the centre of the debate was a proposal to remove the restriction on the number of terms that the President might remain in office, which could enable Rakhmonov to serve for a further 14 years following the presidential election due to take place in 2006. For several months the opposition political parties vehemently opposed the proposed changes, and some urged their members to boycott the referendum, scheduled to take place on 22 June. However, the IRP eventually announced that although it considered the amendments to be unnecessary, it would not strongly oppose the referendum, for fear of undermining the relative stability emerging in the country. Ultimately, the Government claimed that the rate of participation by the electorate was 96%, and that some 93% of votes had approved the proposals, although no international observers monitored the voting, and some commentators suggested than many voters had little real understanding of the referendum's purpose.

## SECURITY ISSUES IN THE 2000s

Drugs-smuggling was a significant problem in Tajikistan in the late 1990s and early 2000s, involving government officials as well as Islamist militants. Indeed, in early August 2002 the former Deputy Minister of Defence, Col Nikolai Kim, was sentenced to 13 years' imprisonment for participating in drugs-trafficking and embezzlement while in office in 1998. Organized crime also remained a problem: in October 2002 a senior police official was sentenced to 25 years' imprisonment on charges of murder, fraud and extortion. Drugs-smuggling from Afghanistan via Tajikistan persisted in 2002, despite the efforts of the new Afghan Transitional Authority to curb opium cultivation. Similarly, the infiltration of large quantities of illegal narcotics from Tajikistan into Uzbekistan continued.

In the early 2000s the problem of insecurity in Tajikistan was exacerbated by the presence of guerrillas from the Islamist Movement of Uzbekistan (IMU). During the Tajik civil war members of the IMU fought alongside UTO militants, but after 1997 relations between the two sides became strained. Representatives of the UTO in the Tajik Government were reluctant to upset relations with Uzbekistan by supporting the IMU; at the same time, however, many members of the IRP were sympathetic to its Islamist agenda. In mid-2000 UTO members within the Government attempted to persuade the Uzbek militants to leave Tajikistan, but following IMU incursions into Kyrgyzstan the Tajik authorities often failed to prevent militants from crossing into their territory. This, in turn, caused relations with Uzbekistan and Kyrgyzstan to deteriorate further, as these two countries raised concerns about renewed IMU incursions into their countries. Uzbekistan's decision to place landmines along the Tajik–Uzbek border to prevent IMU infiltration provoked an angry response from the Tajik Government. By July 2002 55 civilians reportedly had been killed and more than 200 injured by the mines. The death of the leader of the IMU, Juma Namangoniy, reported in November, was expected to reduce the threat of the resurgence of radical Islamism in Tajikistan; however, the IMU remained active. An increasing number of reports in mid-2002 claimed that members of the IMU were attempting to cross the Afghan–Tajik border to regroup in eastern Tajikistan. In mid-July, in response to pressure from other Central Asian states, the Tajik authorities deported several hundred alleged members of the IMU to Afghanistan. In September the Chairman of the Kyrgyz National Security Service reported that the IMU had been transformed into the Islamist Movement of Central Asia, incorporating the IMU, Islamist militants from Tajikistan and the separatist republic of Chechnya and Uygur (Uigur) separatists from the Xinjiang Uygur Autonomous Region of the People's Republic of China, although in the following 12 months there was little evidence of any substantial activity on the part of the group.

Regional authorities also expressed concern about the growing influence of the banned Uzbek fundamentalist Hizb-ut-Tahrir al-Islami (Party of Islamic Liberation). The organization, commonly known as Hizb-ut-Tahrir, was committed to creating an Islamic caliphate in Central Asia, and was attracting growing numbers of young people in the Fergana valley. In early May 2001 the IRP claimed that a number of its members in the northern region of Soghd (formerly Leninabad) had been falsely accused of belonging to Hizb-ut-Tahrir and of illegally storing weapons. There were reports that support for Hizb-ut-Tahrir was increasing in 2002–03, and in the first six months of 2003 there were more than 120 arrests of alleged Hizb-ut-Tahrir activists and a series of trials, in which members were sentenced to terms of imprisonment ranging from three to 18 years.

The situation in neighbouring Afghanistan has long threatened the stability of Tajikistan. The success of the ascetic Taliban regime in reducing the influence of the Tajik-based opposition United Islamic Front for the Salvation of Afghanistan (commonly known as the United Front, or Northern Alliance) in the late 1990s threatened to destabilize the situation in Tajikistan. Some tens of thousands of refugees fled to the Tajik–Afghan border as a result of the civil war. In late November 2000 10,000 Afghan refugees were stranded on marshy islands on the River Pyanj at the border. The UN urged Tajikistan to accept the refugees; however, in early 2001, and on several occasions thereafter, President Rakhmonov announced that Tajikistan would not accept the displaced persons, alleging that armed militants were among the group of refugees. The number of refugees at the border increased to almost 15,000 as heavy fighting in northern Afghanistan continued.

The refugee situation became much more critical, and the threat to Tajikistan's internal as well as to regional stability much greater, in the latter part of 2001, as US-led forces launched retaliatory attacks against the Saudi-born Islamist militant Osama bin Laden and his Taliban hosts in Afghanistan. Bin Laden's al-Qa'ida (Base) organization, associated with the IMU, was held principally responsible by the USA for perpetrating large-scale suicide attacks on New York and Washington, DC, on 11 September. Shortly after the attacks on the USA, the 10,000 Russian border troops along the Tajik–Afghan border were put on high alert. Tajikistan continued to prevent refugees from entering its country, again citing the presence of armed militants and also the strain placed on food supplies by the persistence of severe drought. The United Front's military successes from November, and the subsequent collapse of the Taliban regime, reduced pressure on Tajikistan to allow Afghan refugees to enter the country. Repatriation of Afghan refugees stranded on the Tajik–Afghan border took place in April 2002, and in less than two weeks nearly 9,000 displaced people had returned to northern Afghanistan.

Meanwhile, both Tajikistan and Russia initially ruled out the possibility of Tajikistan's territory being used as a base for US-led military action, although US specialists were permitted to enter the country to oversee the distribution of humanitarian aid to Afghanistan. The Tajik Government declared its support for the aerial bombardment of positions of strategic importance in Afghanistan, which began on 7 October 2001, and some days later officially announced that, if requested, it would assist the United Front in its conflict with the Taliban. In early November it was confirmed that Tajikistan had permitted US and NATO troops to utilize three of its airbases. In January 2002 it was announced that US restrictions on the transfer of defence equipment to Tajikistan, imposed in 1993, had been lifted, as a result of Tajikistan's close co-operation with the US-led coalition against global terrorism. In response to these developments, in April 2003 President Vladimir Putin of Russia paid a visit to the country, and pledged further military support for the Rakhmonov Government. The Tajik Government subsequently stated that the compulsory study of Russian language would be reintroduced to schools from September 2003, and Tajik nationals would again be made available for military service in the Russian army.

Tajikistan was a participant in the Shanghai Co-operation Organization (SCO—comprising Tajikistan, the People's Republic of China, Kazakhstan, Kyrgyzstan, Russia and Uzbekistan), and was a signatory of the 2001 Shanghai Convention on Combating Terrorism, Separatism and Extremism. In August 2003 Kazakhstan and China hosted anti-terrorist manoeuvres involving troops from the SCO countries.

## CONCLUSION

By mid-2003 Tajikistan appeared to have acquired a degree of stability. The majority of armed opposition groups had been integrated into the regular army—although the extent of their loyalty following the abolition of contract arrangements had yet to be tested. National, albeit flawed, elections had reinstated President Rakhmonov and produced a new parliament, and UN peace-keeping forces had left the country, following the expiry of their mandate. Despite these positive indications, however, levels of violence remained unacceptably high and political assassinations, although decreasing, remained a reality. Tensions remained within the Government, and more active members of the Islamist opposition retained only a fairly loose commitment to supporting the regime. This was evident in the ambiguous attitude of some UTO members to the IMU, although most government members remained wary of offending their much more powerful neighbour, Uzbekistan. The increasing popularity of Hizb-ut-Tahrir was partly explained by growing disillusionment with the IRP among Islamists.

The collapse of the Taliban regime in late 2001 and the establishment of an interim administration in Afghanistan had reduced tension in the region to a certain extent. Rakhmonov took advantage of the new peace by dismissing around 15% of the commanders of the border-control forces. Nevertheless, for various reasons, Afghanistan remained one of the factors most likely to destabilize Tajikistan. The drugs trade, for example, contributed a large proportion of Tajikistan's illegal economy; weapons continued to be illegally imported from Afghanistan; furthermore, the threat of fundamentalist Islamism persisted, despite global efforts to combat terrorism. International aid agencies agreed that the most effective way to combat drugs-trafficking was to increase humanitarian assistance to border communities. At the same time, the Tajik Government needed to confront problems of corruption and regionalism.

In order to improve internal stability, a programme of democratization and economic reform was essential. The Government had thus far strengthened its powers at the expense of the legislature, and opposition parties had not been awarded the same rights as the ruling party. Moreover, the results of the referendum of mid-2003 appeared likely to increase further the dominance of political life by the executive. Additionally, in 2003 Rakhmonov initiated a campaign to quell his opponents, in particular seeking to extradite a former Minister of Internal Affairs, Yakub Salimov (who was detained in Moscow in August), and launching an apparent campaign of harassment against the IRP. It was widely agreed that the international community's renewed interest in the region was not sufficient incentive for the Tajik Government to implement much-needed changes to prevent political and economic collapse and social unrest; rather, international financial and technical aid was required to assist reform of the public sector and to support poverty-reduction programmes. In July 2002 Russia donated humanitarian aid to Tajikistan, and in early 2003 it rescheduled some of Tajikistan's external debt. In mid-2003 the USA pledged to increase economic assistance to the country and confirmed plans to train the Tajik military as part of its campaign against terrorism. However, the increased US presence in Tajikistan had not signalled the end of Russian influence and involvement in the country, as had initially been expected in 2002.

# The Economy

## Dr JOHN ANDERSON

## INTRODUCTION

Prior to independence Tajikistan was the poorest of the USSR's Union Republics, constituting 0.6% of the territory and 1.8% of the population at the beginning of 1991. With a rapidly growing population in the rural areas, by the time Mikhail Gorbachev came to power as Soviet leader in the mid-1980s the republic was already experiencing grave problems of land shortages, and unemployment or underemployment was becoming a major, if not fully acknowledged, problem. Moreover, despite a degree of self-sufficiency in agricultural produce, some 44% of Tajikistan's republican state budget was provided by transfers from all-Union funds.

Tajikistan was not only seriously affected by the dissolution of the USSR, effected by the formation of the Commonwealth of Independent States (CIS), but also by its rapid descent into civil conflict. The events of 1992 and after had a devastating impact on the country, with the destruction of much of the economic and social infrastructure in the south. According to UN estimates, more than 50,000 people were killed and many more wounded; some 55,000 children were orphaned; 2,000 or more businesses collapsed; 180 bridges and 1,800 km of roads were destroyed; harvesting was disrupted for several years and as many as 800,000 refugees were created. Alongside those displaced by the fighting, the early 1990s saw the emigration of nearly 400,000 Russian-speakers, many highly skilled professionals, who felt threatened by the rise of violence and the possible 'Islamization' of daily life. All of these factors contributed to a dramatic 29% decline in economic output in 1992, which continued, albeit at a slower pace, through the next five years. The signing of the General Agreement on Peace and National Accord in June 1997 enabled the Government to place more emphasis on Tajikistan's economy. However, the country encountered many problems in its search for economic well-being, and despite positive growth in gross domestic product (GDP) from 1999, reaching 10.2% in 2001 and 9.1% in 2002, Tajikistan remained amongst the poorest of the successor states.

## ECONOMIC POLICY

The collapse of the USSR left Tajikistan with considerable economic problems, even before the civil war broke out. At the end of 1991 subsidies from the all-Union Government came to an end, although Russian petroleum was still sold to the country at below world market prices. The immediate consequence was a huge deficit on the state budget. Exacerbated by internal conflict, at the end of 1992 this had reached the equivalent of 30% of GDP, improving thereafter to 25% in 1993 and, officially, 6% in 1994. The 1996 budget envisaged a deficit of 5.4% of GDP, but the Government had reduced the deficit to just over 3% by 1999 and to about 0.6% in 2000, although it increased to just under 1% in 2002. Apart from the loss of the Soviet subsidy, further difficulties were created as a result of corruption, tax avoidance and under-reporting of production by many enterprises, problems common to most of the CIS economies. The situation was not helped by the fact that in 1992–94, for instance, the Government had been forced to spend up to 50% of its revenue on military and security needs. Moreover, there was considerable unwillingness among international investors to become involved with such an unstable country.

In this situation Tajikistan was forced into almost total reliance on Russia, and during the mid-1990s was effectively managed from Moscow. From January 1994 the country became part of the new 'rouble zone' and was obliged to accept all the conditions that went with this, including control of monetary policy, foreign reserves and government expenditure being placed with the Central Bank of the Russian Federation. Increasingly, however, this became untenable, as Russia refused to allow sufficient quantities of roubles to reach the country and in early 1995 the Government of Tajikistan started to discuss the introduction of a national currency.

The continuation of the civil war deterred most international financial organizations from aiding Tajikistan, although the introduction of the Tajik rouble in May 1995 was accompanied by a number of measures designed to attract IMF support. As elsewhere in the CIS, the currency initially declined dramatically in value against the US dollar, but the accompanying strict monetary policy appeared to be reducing the rate of decline by the beginning of 1996. At the same time the annual rate of inflation, which had been brought down from over 2,000% in 1993 to 341% in 1994, appeared to have been adversely affected by the introduction of the new currency, accompanied as it was by the freeing of many prices: the annual rate was some 635% in 1995.

During and after the negotiation of the peace agreement, however, the IMF, the World Bank and other major financial institutions proved more willing to become involved in the reconstruction of Tajikistan. In 1996 the IMF offered a stand-by arrangement to support government reform plans, followed by the World Bank's offer of substantial credits for restructuring. Following a visit by World Bank experts in June 1998 it was agreed to allocate a US $5m. loan to Tajikistan for the reform of its health-care system, badly damaged by the violence of previous years. This, in turn, formed part of a $50m. credit to assist with structural adjustment programmes, involving mass privatization and reform of the financial sector, and to pay pension arrears.

In March 1998 Kazakhstan, Kyrgyzstan and Uzbekistan agreed to admit Tajikistan into the Central Asian Economic Union (superseded by the Central Asian Co-operation Organization in March 2002). In April 1998 the country was admitted to the CIS Customs Union (already comprising Belarus, Kazakhstan, Kyrgyzstan and Russia), although it was not entirely clear that either of these arrangements made a serious contribution to Tajikistan's economic recovery. Indeed, closeness to Russia was to have negative consequences that year, when the Russian economic crisis in August had a severe impact on Tajikistan's faltering recovery.

From 1999 increasing political stability permitted further support from international agencies. In July the IMF approved a further US $40m. loan to help the country strengthen its balance of payments and improve the prospects for economic growth. In announcing this, the Fund's directors commended the efforts of the Government in bringing inflation under control (it had declined dramatically, to 2.7% in 1998) and maintaining some degree of macroeconomic stability in difficult times. At the same time, they expressed the hope that privatization would be developed further and that some of the basic problems created by a partially non-cash economy would be addressed in the coming years. In October 2000 the IMF approved further funds, worth some $51m., in support of the Government's efforts to structure the economy. In April 2001, however, the Fund urged the Tajik

Government to introduce more measures to strengthen revenue-collection mechanisms and undertake further structural reforms. In July the IMF approved a further $8m. loan. By mid-2001 the European Bank for Reconstruction and Development (EBRD) had contributed more than €15m. to various infrastructure projects, including the upgrading of Dushanbe airport and the modernization of telecommunications. At the same time, the EBRD was also encouraging private-sector activities, opening credit lines for the establishment of a bottled-water plant in Urateppa (Ura-Tyube) and a food-packaging plant in the Khujand (Khodzhent) region. In early 2002 it became evident that the IMF had released funding in 2000–01 on the basis of incorrect information, supplied by the Tajik Government, relating to the country's level of external debt. The Ministry of Finance subsequently agreed to repay $31m., and the IMF was to continue to support the Government's economic programme. Meanwhile, the USA had pledged a total of $125m. in investment and aid to Tajikistan in 2002, and the country was also to benefit from a new initiative, endorsed by the IMF, the World Bank, the Asian Development Bank (ADB) and the EBRD in April, which aimed to reduce poverty and external debt, and stimulate growth in seven CIS states. Further support was promised during a World Bank Tajikistan Consultative Group meeting held in Dushanbe during May 2003, with around $99m. promised over a three-year period, although some of this funding was dependent on further reform of governance procedures and adequate guarantees for proper implementation in the country. Those attending the meeting placed particular emphasis on community-based initiatives and combating corruption.

The international financial institutions were eager to promote the sale of state companies to private investors—a process that accelerated after the introduction of a privatization programme in 1998. Previously the state had registered some 9,500 enterprises, of which approximately two-thirds had been sold by mid-2001. In early 2000 an auction organized by the State Property Committee resulted in the sale of more than 1,000 enterprises, mostly in the catering, agricultural and consumer services sector. By the end of 2000 the vast majority of small businesses had been privatized. Larger organizations, however, were overvalued and were thus proving harder to divest; by November 2001 359 of fewer than 1,500 medium-sized and large state-owned enterprises had been privatized. In 2000 all of the state cotton-processing plants were privatized, thereby allowing an element of competition in the important cotton sector. During 2002–03 there were few further initiatives in the area of privatization, and at the end of 2002 the IMF suggested insufficient effort was being made by the Government to promote the sale of state properties.

A major shift in policy was the introduction in October 2000 of a new currency, the somoni, to replace the Tajik rouble. Although there was some depreciation in the first two months after its introduction, the currency had stabilized by early 2001.

## AGRICULTURE

Agriculture was traditionally the principal sector of Tajikistan's economy, providing 45% of employment and more than 40% of net material product (NMP) prior to independence. In 2002 agriculture contributed 29.3% of GDP, and the sector employed some 66.0% of the total labour force in 2001. The major crop after the Second World War was cotton, over one-half of which was grown in the southern Kulob (Kulyab) and Qurgonteppa (Kurgan-Tyube) regions (Khatlon Oblast). The pressure to produce cotton had various consequences during the late Soviet era, with Communist Party leaders compelled to produce ever greater quantities and eventually resorting to misreporting actual production figures to satisfy central planners. Among the numerous negative outcomes for the region were that often unwilling settlers were brought in from the central and northern parts of the republic, children were forced to miss lengthy periods of schooling to help bring in the harvest, and water resources were depleted.

Cotton sowing and harvesting were severely affected by the violence that swept across the southern regions in 1992. Reliable statistics were hard to obtain, but reported annual production of seed (unginned) cotton declined from some 840,000 metric tons at the beginning of the 1990s to 515,000 tons during the civil war. Production continued to fall in the mid-1990s, reaching 317,707 tons in 1996. Nevertheless, in the late 1990s cotton still provided about one-fifth of total export earnings, and output rose to 383,721 tons in 1998. Official sources recorded a harvest of 313,000 tons in 1999, 335,000 tons in 2000 and 453,000 tons in 2001. Other agricultural products included silk, grains, fruit, vegetables and livestock. Some of these escaped the ravages of civil war, with the World Bank registering a high level of fruit production in 1992. Although fruit production was much reduced after that time, it remained steady throughout the 1990s. During the civil war there were also reported declines in the number of sheep and cattle, as those impoverished by war were forced to sell or consume their animals, thus preventing the reproduction of herds. Any gains that were achieved in the late 1990s were, however, reversed by a serious drought in 2000, which nearly halved grain production and meant that the country could only fulfil about one-quarter of its domestic needs. The continuing drought adversely affected agricultural output in 2001. Despite the devastating effects of torrential rains and floods, wheat and cotton production registered growth in 2002, with the latter harvest rising to over 500,000 tons.

In the mid-1990s the administration of President Imamali Rakhmonov, recognizing that the agricultural sector was the most fundamental part of the economy, sought to introduce a degree of reform. There was much rhetoric about the complete privatization of land by the end of the 20th century, and plans for agricultural privatization were announced in the first half of 1996, although there was much resistance to the notion of private land-ownership. In July 1998 the Government adopted a resolution on the establishment of a centre for the support of farm privatization. In practice, reform measures were slow to take hold, with the state retaining control of both machinery and fertilizer production as well as purchasing, and with local collective farms often unwilling to lease out good quality land. By 2002 there still existed only a limited legal basis for the private ownership of land, although in many cases leased agricultural plots became the property of those who worked them, in all but name. It is also worth noting the considerable regional variations within the country, with the climate of lawlessness in the southern regions enabling powerful individuals simply to acquire large plots of land for themselves. In the impoverished Gornyi-Badakhshan region to the east of the country, traditionally the home of the Isma'ili community, however, the Aga Khan Foundation for Economic Development has provided considerable financial support for the creation of peasant co-operatives and offered practical advice on methods of achieving success in such ventures. In 2002 Tajikistan received US $20m. from the International Development Association (IDA) towards a Farm Privatization Support Project. In 2003 a further $2.3m. was provided by the UN Food and Agriculture Organization (FAO) to deal with the social consequences of recent droughts. In particular, this money was aimed at projects to secure food for families in badly affected areas, to combat the expected outbreak of Moroccan locust

infestation in 2003, and to control the spread of brucellosis amongst livestock.

The peace process allowed international organizations to become involved in the reform of Tajikistan's agricultural sector. In 1996 and 1997 the World Bank committed funds to an agricultural recovery programme, although renewed outbreaks of violence sometimes resulted in these and other international loans being diverted to defence needs. Nevertheless, in many parts of the south the regular cycles of sowing and harvesting were renewed, and from 1998 there was some hope that output of agricultural products would begin to increase. The restructuring of the food-production sector, however, took longer than expected. Meat and dairy production declined, although the Director of the Government's Corporation for Food and Processing Industries claimed that output had risen in 1998 compared with previous years. Diversification of the agricultural sector was as important as ever in the early 2000s, in order to reduce Tajikistan's dependence on cotton and aluminium.

The other major growth area was the illegal drugs trade, with the more remote parts of the country producing their own opium crops and trafficking becoming a major business. The armed opposition exploited the trade to raise money for weaponry, and some made this profitable business their prime occupation. Some of the pro-Government militias were also alleged to be involved in the drugs business. Thus, although the Government was formally committed to combating the trade, enforcement of anti-drugs laws was made problematic by the fact that too many groups had a vested interest in circumventing official policies. During a visit to the UN in June 1998, President Rakhmonov stated that the drugs trade presented a major threat to Tajikistan's stability and was an obstacle in attempts to create a sense of statehood. The problem persisted in the early 2000s, and was compounded by the resumption of poppy cultivation by farmers in Afghanistan following the fall of the Taliban. Despite attempts by the Afghan authorities to eradicate opium cultivation, reports in August 2002 suggested that production had reached a level close to that experienced in the late 1990s, before the Taliban banned cultivation. Periodic shootings involving smugglers from Afghanistan and Tajik border guards indicated that the problem of drugs-trafficking remained far from being resolved, and could increase, as some projections envisaged production in neighbouring Afghanistan rising during 2003.

## MINING, ENERGY AND INDUSTRY

Tajikistan has considerable mineral deposits, including gold, iron, lead, tin, mercury and coal, but extracting many of these has been problematic given the mountainous terrain of much of the country. Production of gold increased in 1998, however, owing to greater foreign investment in the sector. The mountains proved advantageous in providing a river system. By the time of the dissolution of the USSR a huge hydroelectric power (HEP) system, built up over previous decades, met nearly 80% of the republic's electricity needs and made Tajikistan the second-largest producer of hydroelectric energy in the former USSR, after Russia. This system, closely guarded by Russian troops, emerged more or less unscathed from the civil war. Production of electricity amounted to just over 15,000m. kWh in 2002. Tajikistan is dependent on imports for other energy sources, notably gas and petroleum, although in May 2003 the Russian firm Gazprom signed a deal to develop the country's gas fields. Despite the country's extensive hydroelectric potential, Tajikistan has remained energy-deficient. However, construction of the Sangtuda power station, commissioned at the end of the Gorbachev era, has resumed with Russian and Iranian financing, although according to some estimates the project required a further US $300m. of direct investment for completion. In May 2001 Japan granted financial aid to support the country's infrastructure programmes, and in August the People's Republic of China agreed to finance and build the first stage of the Roghun HEP installation. Both the Sangtuda and Roghun power stations should allow Tajikistan to cease importing electricity and to become a major net energy exporter in the region. The lack of investment in the energy sector in the early 2000s, however, led to a decline in the capacity of the existing power plants by 20%–50%. Consequently, in 2002 Tajikistan had to import electricity from Kyrgyzstan, Turkmenistan and Uzbekistan. In October the Aga Khan Fund for Economic Development and the International Finance Corporation (IFC) announced plans to develop a new electricity generation and distribution project in Gornyi Badakhshan. The $26m. project, established with the support of the Tajik and Swiss Governments and the IDA, would address the acute energy shortages in the impoverished region. Meanwhile, attempts to recoup income by raising domestic energy tariffs by over 200% for electricity and 30% for gas in the first three months of 2003 severely affected many families and some enterprises.

The industrial sector (including construction) remains relatively small, employing 9.2% of the country's labour force in 2001 and contributing 28.4% of GDP in 2002. A small number of large enterprises have dominated the economy, with the only heavy industry provided by the hydroelectric sector and a massive aluminium plant at Tursunzade (Tursunzoda), to the west of the capital. Producing some 450,000 metric tons in 1991, production declined steadily after independence to stabilize at 237,000 tons in 1994 and 1995, when the plant was estimated to be producing at about 40% of capacity, and some 198,300 tons in 1996. Aluminium provided 59% of export earnings in 1995. However, the industry was not integrated into the national economy, being very dependent on input imports and with little value added to the product locally. Like the cotton sector, this was a feature of its development as part of the Soviet economic system, these two industries being based in Tajikistan to take advantage of its extensive water resources (for the aluminium industry this meant abundant energy). Despite the conclusion of the civil war, previous levels of aluminium production were not sustained, with production of unwrought aluminium slowing to 196,300 tons in 1998; aluminium provided almost 40% of export earnings in that year. Aluminium production gradually recovered, reaching 289,100 tons in 2001 and 306,700 tons in 2002, and aluminium accounted for 61% of total export earnings in 2001. Consequently, aluminium appeared likely to remain the country's primary export commodity.

Following the political settlement, geological explorations were resumed and various joint ventures with European companies in the mining sector were agreed. Indian companies have become involved in the extraction of silver, British companies in the mining of gold, and Uzbek groups in coalmining. In 1996 industrial output decreased by an estimated 19.8%, but in 1997 it declined by only 2.5%. Some growth was anticipated for 1998, before the Russian economic crisis in August of that year caused expectations to be revised downwards. Despite all the signs of stabilization, in 1999 industrial output in Tajikistan still remained at around one-third of the figure for 1989. In 2000 the country finally reported a substantial 10.3% increase in industrial production, although this was mainly the result of the rise in aluminium output.

Other industries established in Tajikistan included engineering (mostly targeted towards the production of agricultural machinery), textiles, and food-processing, which was concentrated largely on fruit, natural oils and tobacco. Much of the latter has in recent years been traded with Pakistan and the People's Republic of China, rather than exported to the former USSR as before 1991. From 2002 there was considerable growth in the light industry sector, particularly in

textiles and cotton-processing, where growth of over 25% was reported in 2002. The textiles sector was further stimulated in April 2003, when the IFC invested funds in the expansion of the Javoni garment company in the northern town of Khujand.

Industrial production outside the Khujand region was badly affected by the civil war, with the destruction of factories, the obstruction of transport networks and the diversion of many workers from production. At the beginning of 1994 the State Statistical Agency produced a report on economic developments for the year, with a published version expressing optimism and a further account, marked 'not for publication', expressing considerable disquiet at Tajikistan's economic progress. The latter report showed that in the final quarter of 1994 production was down by 44%, compared with the corresponding period in 1993. In addition it noted that the construction of social infrastructure, including hospitals and schools, had ceased. In 1995 the Government published a five-year plan to create a market-based economy by the end of the decade, on the basis of massive privatization in the agricultural and industrial sector, and the gradual freeing of all prices, although these proposals were hindered by the continuation of hostilities until 1997.

Industrial production declined by some 54.4% in 1990–94, owing to the civil conflict. This decline, and the collapse of the transport and construction sectors, provided the main cause for total GDP being only 46% of its 1991 level, in real terms, by 1995. In 1996 GDP decreased, in real terms, by 4.4%. In 1997, however, there was an increase in GDP of 1.7%. In part because of the impact of the Russian crisis of 1998, Tajikistan's economic recovery during 1999 was less pronounced than had been hoped, but in an assessment published in early 2000 the IMF stated that GDP had risen by 3.7% in the previous year. In 2000 GDP was officially stated to have expanded by 8.3% compared with the previous year. This upward trend continued, with growth reaching 10.2% in 2001 and 9.1% in 2002.

## PROSPECTS

By 2003 Tajikistan was still confronted by serious economic problems, caused mainly by political and civil conflict. There were, however, indications that the economic decline of the previous eight years was ending and, according to official statistics, real GDP rose each year after 1998. The figures recorded, however, were only marginal improvements for a weakened economy, and many within the country still endured harsh economic conditions. Political violence and crime remained prevalent in the south, the social infrastructure failed to meet the needs of the country's poorest citizens and, in real terms, unemployment was rising, officially reaching its highest level of 3.1% in May 1998 (although actual unemployment, believed to be around 30% in 1999, was considerably greater than official figures showed). In 2001 an estimated 200,000 people left Tajikistan to seek work abroad and by 2003 around 800,000 Tajiks were working abroad. Although this development had negative consequences for family life and reproduction, it also produced some US $120m. in workers' remittances, or around 10% of GDP. However, in practice, measuring the extent of poverty and unemployment was difficult, as many families adopted a series of coping strategies that generated income and welfare in ways that could not readily be tabulated or measured. According to the ADB, poverty affected over 70% of the population in 2002. The country's external debt amounted to just under $1,000m. in 2002, around one-third of which was owed to Russia, although repayment schedules were renegotiated in 2002. From mid-1999 inflation rose sharply (it reached 30.1% in the 12 months to December of that year and 60.6% in the corresponding period of 2000) and the trade deficit was maintained. The rate of inflation was 38.5% in 2001, but a tight monetary policy promoted by the central bank and limited food price increases helped to reduce the rate to 14.5% in 2002.

The poor economic situation was especially pronounced in the southern regions of the country, where violence continued to disturb everyday life, as opposed to the traditionally richer northern province around Khujand, which had experienced less disruption or destruction of economic assets. Here local élites seemed to have some degree of commitment to economic reform, albeit one which did not challenge their vested interests, and traditional trading habits were re-emerging in the form of a small, enterprising business class. In Dushanbe the city authorities were able to implement an initial privatization programme from 1998, which helped to develop the capital's entrepreneurial sector, but in the country as a whole privatization had only affected a minority of the larger enterprises. Nationally there were a few signs of a fragile recovery: foreign direct investment (FDI) reached US $30m. in 2000, but declined dramatically to $8.1m. in 2001, before rising to $21m. in 2002. The gradual, if halting, emergence of peace encouraged a few foreign companies to invest in Tajikistan;

the single largest investment was offered by the Bermuda-based Nelson Gold Corporation. Moreover, in May 2001 a UN-sponsored meeting of six donor countries and eight international organizations pledged some $430m. over the following two years. Although political security and stability remained an elusive goal, the Government's objectives for 2002–03 were to accelerate the pace of privatization in order to enhance economic stability, sustain economic growth and undertake reform of the banking sector. Rakhmonov introduced a Poverty Reduction Strategy Paper in June in an attempt to address Tajikistan's socio-economic problems. In the aftermath of the US-led military campaign against neighbouring Afghanistan from October 2001, aid organizations and individual countries pledged financial and technical assistance to help Tajikistan to reform and develop its economy. Continued improvements will depend upon the commitment of the government to structural reform and diversification, stability in world prices for core products such as aluminium and cotton, and continued political stability within the country and the region as a whole.

# Statistical Survey

Source (unless otherwise indicated): State Committee for Statistics, 734025 Dushanbe, Bokhtar 17; tel. (372) 27-63-31; fax (372) 21-43-75; e-mail stat@tajikistan.com.

## Area and Population

### AREA, POPULATION AND DENSITY

| | |
|---|---:|
| Area (sq km) . . . . . . . . . | 143,100* |
| Population (census results)† | |
| 12 January 1989 . . . . . . . . . | 5,092,603 |
| 20 January 2000 | |
| Males . . . . . . . . . | 3,069,100 |
| Females . . . . . . . . | 3,058,393 |
| Total . . . . . . . . . | 6,127,493 |
| Population (UN estimates at mid-year)‡ | |
| 2000 . . . . . . . . . . | 6,089,000 |
| 2001 . . . . . . . . . . | 6,144,000 |
| 2002 . . . . . . . . . . | 6,195,000 |
| Density (per sq km) at mid-2002 . . . . . . . . | 43.3 |

* 55,251 sq miles.
† Figures refer to *de jure* population. The *de facto* total at the 1989 census was 5,108,576.
‡ Source: UN, *World Population Prospects: The 2002 Revision.*

### POPULATION BY ETHNIC GROUP
(2000 census)

| | % |
|---|---:|
| Tajik . . . . . . . . . . . . . . . . . | 80.0 |
| Uzbek . . . . . . . . . . . . . . . . | 15.3 |
| Russian . . . . . . . . . . . . . . . | 1.1 |
| Tatar . . . . . . . . . . . . . . . . | 0.3 |
| Others . . . . . . . . . . . . . . . | 3.3 |
| **Total** . . . . . . . . . . . . . . | 100.0 |

### PRINCIPAL TOWNS
(population at 1 January 2002)

| | | | |
|---|---:|---|---:|
| Dushanbe (capital) . | 575,900 | Kanibadam . . . | 45,100 |
| Khujand | | | |
| (Khodzhent)* . . | 147,400 | Kofarnihon‡ . . . | 45,100 |
| Kulob (Kulyab) . . | 79,500 | Tursunzade | |
| | | (Tursunzoda) . . | 38,100 |
| Qurgonteppa | | | |
| (Kurgan-Tyube) . | 61,200 | Isfara . . . . . | 37,300 |
| Istravshan† . . . | 51,700 | Panjakent | |
| | | (Pendzhikent) . . | 33,200 |

* Known as Leninabad between 1936 and 1992.
† Also known as Urateppa (Ura-Tyube).
‡ Formerly Ordzhonikidzeabad.

### BIRTHS, MARRIAGES AND DEATHS

| | Registered live births | | Registered marriages | | Registered deaths | |
|---|---:|---:|---:|---:|---:|---:|
| | Number | Rate (per 1,000) | Number | Rate (per 1,000) | Number | Rate (per 1,000) |
| 1994 . . | 191,596 | 34.2 | 38,820 | 6.8 | 39,943 | 7.1 |
| 1995 . . | 193,182 | 34.1 | 32,078 | 5.7 | 34,274 | 6.0 |
| 1996 . . | 172,341 | 30.0 | 28,019 | 4.8 | 31,610 | 5.5 |
| 1997 . . | 178,127 | 30.6 | 27,250 | 4.7 | 27,888 | 4.8 |
| 1998 . . | 185,733 | 31.3 | 22,276 | 3.8 | 29,261 | 4.9 |
| 1999 . . | 180,888 | 29.8 | 22,536 | 3.9 | 25,384 | 4.2 |
| 2000 . . | 167,246 | 27.0 | 26,257 | 4.2 | 29,387 | 4.7 |
| 2001 . . | 171,623 | 27.2 | 28,827 | 4.6 | 32,015 | 5.1 |

**Expectation of life** (WHO estimates, years at birth): 63.3 (males 59.9; females 66.9) in 2001 (Source: WHO, *World Health Report*).

**ECONOMICALLY ACTIVE POPULATION**
(annual averages, '000 persons)

|  | 1999 | 2000 | 2001 |
|---|---|---|---|
| Activities of the material sphere . | 1,420 | 1,416 | 1,452 |
| Agriculture* . . . . . | 1,118 | 1,135 | 1,167 |
| Industry† . . . . . | 133 | 121 | 131 |
| Construction . . . . | 44 | 36 | 31 |
| Trade and catering‡ . . . . | 70 | 72 | 72 |
| Transport and communications | 44 | 42 | 43 |
| Activities of the non-material sphere . . . . . | 313 | 326 | 316 |
| Housing and municipal services | 24 | 27 | 29 |
| Health care, social security, physical culture and sports . | 75 | 82 | 72 |
| Education, culture and arts . . | 179 | 179 | 178 |
| Science, research and development . . . . . | 5 | 5 | 5 |
| Government and finance . . . | 31 | 34 | 23 |
| **Total employed**. . . . . | **1,737** | **1,745** | **1,769** |
| Unemployed . . . . . | 54 | 49 | 43 |
| **Total labour force** . . . . . | **1,791** | **1,794** | **1,812** |

* Including forestry.
† Comprising manufacturing (except printing and publishing), mining and quarrying, electricity, gas, water, logging and fishing.
‡ Including material and technical supply.

# Health and Welfare

**KEY INDICATORS**

| | |
|---|---|
| Total fertility rate (children per woman, 2001). . . . . | 3.1 |
| Under-5 mortality rate (per 1,000 live births, 2001) . . . | 72 |
| HIV/AIDS (% of persons aged 15–49, 2001). . . . . | <0.10 |
| Physicians (per 1,000 head, 1998) . . . . . . . | 2.01 |
| Hospital beds (per 1,000 head, 1998) . . . . . | 6.8 |
| Health expenditure (2000): US $ per head (PPP) . . . | 29 |
| Health expenditure (2000): % of GDP . . . . . . | 2.5 |
| Health expenditure (2000): public (% of total) . . . . | 80.8 |
| Human Development Index (2001): ranking . . . . | 113 |
| Human Development Index (2001): value . . . . . | 0.667 |

For sources and definitions, see explanatory note on p. vi.

# Agriculture

**PRINCIPAL CROPS**
('000 metric tons)

|  | 1999 | 2000 | 2001 |
|---|---|---|---|
| Wheat . . . . . . . . | 365 | 406 | 388 |
| Rice (paddy) . . . . . . | 47 | 82 | 40 |
| Barley . . . . . . . | 25 | 19 | 16 |
| Maize . . . . . . . | 36 | 38 | 42 |
| Potatoes . . . . . . | 240 | 303 | 318 |
| Cottonseed . . . . . . | 313 | 335 | 453 |
| Cabbages . . . . . . | 16 | 18 | 23 |
| Tomatoes . . . . . . | 133 | 129 | 127 |
| Dry onions . . . . . . | 153 | 110 | 129 |
| Carrots . . . . . . . | 52 | 48 | 69 |
| Other vegetables . . . . . | 31 | 49 | 51 |
| Watermelons* . . . . . . | 84 | 95 | 97 |
| Grapes . . . . . . . | 54 | 110 | 111 |
| Other fruits and berries . . . . | 78 | 170 | 152 |
| Cotton (lint) . . . . . . | 98† | 93† | 96‡ |
| Tobacco (leaves) . . . . . | 7 | 7 | 4 |

* Including melons, pumpkins and squash.
† Unofficial figure.
‡ FAO estimate.
Sources: State Committee for Statistics, Dushanbe; and FAO.

**LIVESTOCK**
('000 head at 1 January)

|  | 1999 | 2000 | 2001 |
|---|---|---|---|
| Horses . . . . . . . | 72 | 72 | 71 |
| Asses* . . . . . . . | 32 | 30 | 32 |
| Cattle . . . . . . . | 1,037 | 1,062 | 1,091 |
| Camels* . . . . . . . | 43 | 43 | 42 |
| Sheep . . . . . . . | 1,472 | 1,478 | 1,490 |
| Goats . . . . . . . | 706 | 744 | 779 |
| Poultry. . . . . . . | 771 | 1,061 | 1,320 |

* FAO estimates.
Sources: State Committee for Statistics, Dushanbe; and FAO.

**LIVESTOCK PRODUCTS**
('000 metric tons)

|  | 1999 | 2000 | 2001 |
|---|---|---|---|
| Beef and veal . . . . . . | 15.0 | 14.8 | 14.8 |
| Mutton, lamb and goat meat . . | 13.2 | 13.0 | 12.8 |
| Poultry meat . . . . . . | 0.1 | 0.1 | 0.4 |
| Cows' milk . . . . . . | 302 | 310 | 316 |
| Goats' milk . . . . . . | 22.0* | 24.5* | 25.0† |
| Cheese . . . . . . . | 6.2 | 6.6 | 6.7 |
| Wool: greasy . . . . . . | 2.1 | 2.1 | 2.2 |
| Sheepskins (fresh) . . . . . | 1.7 | 2.1 | 2.0 |

* Unofficial figure.
† FAO estimate.
Sources: State Committee for Statistics, Dushanbe; and FAO.

# Fishing

(aquaculture only, metric tons, live weight)

|  | 1998 | 1999 | 2000 |
|---|---|---|---|
| Silver carp . . . . . . | 81 | 58 | 55 |
| Common carp. . . . . . | 0 | 8 | 10 |
| Grass carp. . . . . . . | 0 | 8 | 21 |
| **Total catch** (incl. others) . . . | **81** | **74** | **86** |

Source: FAO, *Yearbook of Fishery Statistics.*

# Mining

(metric tons, unless otherwise indicated)

|  | 1998 | 1999 | 2000 |
|---|---|---|---|
| Hard coal . . . . . . . | 18,500 | 19,100 | 22,200 |
| Crude petroleum . . . . . | 19,400 | 18,700 | 18,400 |
| Natural gas (million cu m) . . . | 32.4 | 36.1 | 40.0 |
| Lead concentrate*† . . . . | 800 | 800 | 800‡ |
| Antimony ore*† . . . . . | 1,500 | 1,800 | 2,000‡ |
| Mercury*† . . . . . . | 35 | 35 | 40‡ |
| Silver* . . . . . . . | 5 | 5† | 5‡ |
| Gold (kilograms)* . . . . . | 3,000 | 2,700† | 2,700‡ |
| Gypsum (crude)† . . . . . | 31,700 | 35,000 | 35,000‡ |

* Figures refer to the metal content of ores and concentrates.
† Estimated production.
‡ Provisional figure.
Sources: US Geological Survey and State Committee for Statistics, Dushanbe.

**2001:** Hard coal 10,000 metric tons; Crude petroleum 16,000 metric tons; Natural gas 52 million cu m (source: Asian Development Bank, *Key Indicators of Developing Asian and Pacific Countries*).

**2002:** Hard coal 27,000 metric tons; Crude petroleum 16,000 metric tons; Natural gas 33 million cu m (source: Asian Development Bank, *Key Indicators of Developing Asian and Pacific Countries*).

# Industry

**SELECTED PRODUCTS**
('000 metric tons, unless otherwise indicated)

|  | 1999 | 2000 | 2001 |
|---|---|---|---|
| Cottonseed oil (refined) . . . . | 22 | 23 | 16.3 |
| Wheat flour . . . . . . | 341 | 307 | 312 |
| Ethyl alcohol ('000 hectolitres) . . | 28 | 23 | 27 |
| Wine ('000 hectolitres) . . . . | 51 | 39 | 45 |
| Beer ('000 hectolitres) . . . . | 7 | 4 | 8 |
| Soft drinks ('000 hectolitres) . . | 19 | 49 | 118 |
| Cigarettes (million) . . . . . | 209 | 667 | 1,155 |
| Wool yarn (pure and mixed) . . | 0.8 | 0.5 | 0.6 |
| Cotton yarn (pure and mixed) . . | 14.7 | 15.0 | 14.9 |
| Woven cotton fabrics (million sq metres) . . . . . . . | 11.5 | 10.9 | 13.0 |
| Woven silk fabrics ('000 sq metres) | 386 | 253 | 247 |
| Knotted wool carpets and rugs ('000 sq metres) . . . . . | 1,045 | 341 | 509 |
| Footwear, excl. rubber ('000 pairs). | 72 | 110 | 94 |
| Caustic soda (Sodium hydroxide) . | 0.7 | 3.7 | 3.0 |
| Nitrogenous fertilizers* . . . . | 4.6 | 11.1 | 3.4 |
| Clay building bricks (million) . . | 33 | 30 | 26 |
| Cement . . . . . . . . | 33.2 | 54.8 | 68.9 |
| Aluminium (unwrought): primary | 229.1 | 269.2 | 289.1 |
| Electric energy (million kWh) . . | 15,797 | 14,247 | 14,336 |

* Production in terms of nitrogen.

**2002** ('000 metric tons): Wheat flour 293; Cement 89 (source: Asian Development Bank, *Key Indicators of Developing Asian and Pacific Countries*).

# Finance

**CURRENCY AND EXCHANGE RATES**

**Monetary Units**
100 diram = 1 somoni.

**Sterling, Dollar and Euro Equivalents** (30 May 2003)
£1 sterling = 5.091 somoni;
US $1 = 3.090 somoni;
€1 = 3.653 somoni;
100 somoni = £19.64 = $32.36 = €27.38.

**Average Exchange Rate** (somoni per US $)
2000    2.0763
2001    2.3722
2002    2.7641

Note: The Tajik rouble was introduced in May 1995, replacing the Russian (formerly Soviet) rouble at the rate of 1 Tajik rouble = 100 Russian roubles. A new currency, the somoni (equivalent to 1,000 Tajik roubles), was introduced in October 2000.

**BUDGET**
(million somoni)*

| Revenue† | 2001 | 2002 | 2003‡ |
|---|---|---|---|
| Tax revenue . . . . . . | 353.1 | 491.7 | 627.6 |
| Income and profit tax . . . | 47.1 | 59.9 | 72.5 |
| Payroll taxes . . . . . | 44.8 | 62.9 | 76.2 |
| Property taxes . . . . . | 14.8 | 18.8 | 22.8 |
| Internal taxes on goods and services . . . . . . | 128.5 | 227.9 | 310.7 |
| Value-added tax . . . . | 86.0 | 157.7 | 225.7 |
| International trade and operations tax . . . . | 114.4 | 117.8 | 140.1 |
| Total sales taxes . . . . | 62.8 | 63.2 | 80.0 |
| Import duties . . . . . | 51.6 | 54.6 | 60.1 |
| Other taxes . . . . . . | 3.5 | 4.4 | 5.3 |
| Non-tax revenue . . . . . | 28.8 | 60.1 | 29.6 |
| **Total** . . . . . . . | 381.9 | 551.8 | 657.2 |

| Expenditure | 2001 | 2002 | 2003‡ |
|---|---|---|---|
| General administrative services . | 66 | 91 | 115 |
| Protection services . . . . . | 57 | 71 | 85 |
| Social services . . . . . | 172 | 233 | 295 |
| Education . . . . . . | 63 | 87 | 112 |
| Health . . . . . . . | 24 | 30 | 40 |
| Social security and welfare . . | 47 | 67 | 101 |
| Other . . . . . . . | 38 | 49 | 42 |
| Economic services . . . . . | 58 | 64 | 93 |
| Interest payments . . . . . | 38 | 63 | 88 |
| Other purposes . . . . . . | 17 | 41 | 49 |
| External financing of public investment programme (PIP) . . | 54 | 79 | 121 |
| **Total§** . . . . . . . | 462 | 642 | 847 |
| Current . . . . . . . | 332 | 459 | 594 |
| Capital . . . . . . . . | 127 | 181 | 251 |

* Figures refer to the consolidated operations of the State Budget, comprising the budgets of the central (republican) Government and local authorities, and the Social Security Fund.
† Excluding grants received (million somoni): 0.0 in 2001; 8.0 in 2002; 32.0 in 2003.
‡ Revised forecasts.
§ Including lending minus repayments (million somoni) 3 in 2001; 1 in 2002; 2 in 2003.

Source: IMF, *Republic of Tajikistan: First Review Under the Three-year Arrangement Under the Poverty Reduction and Growth Facility and Request for Modification and Waivers of Performance Criteria* (July 2003).

**MONEY SUPPLY**
('000 somoni at 31 December)

|  | 2000 | 2001 | 2002 |
|---|---|---|---|
| Currency outside banks . . . . | 86,773 | 103,631 | 135,768 |
| Demand deposits . . . . . | 15,709 | 23,792 | 36,329 |
| **Total money** (incl. others) . . | 102,715 | 128,830 | 173,192 |

Source: IMF, *International Financial Statistics*.

**COST OF LIVING**
(Consumer price index for December; base: previous December = 100)

|  | 1998 | 1999 | 2000 |
|---|---|---|---|
| Food . . . . . . . . . | 99.1 | 129.7 | 166.4 |
| Other goods . . . . . . | 119.2 | 136.5 | 144.2 |
| Services . . . . . . . | 132.0 | 147.7 | 133.9 |
| **All items** . . . . . . . | 102.7 | 130.1 | 160.6 |

Source: partly IMF, *Republic of Tajikistan: Statistical Appendix* (January 2003).

**Annual averages** (base: 1990 = 0.1): All items 73,107 in 1998; 92,114 in 1999; 114,222 in 2000 (Source: ILO, *Yearbook of Labour Statistics*).

**NATIONAL ACCOUNTS**
(million somoni at current prices)

**Expenditure on the Gross Domestic Product**

|  | 1999 | 2000 | 2001 |
|---|---|---|---|
| Government final consumption expenditure . . . . . . . | 62.7 | 86.0 | 87.2 |
| Private final consumption expenditure . . . . . . . | 1,021.6 | 1,389.5 | 1,972.6 |
| Increase in stocks . . . . . } Gross fixed capital formation . . } | 233.1 | 209.2 | 419.8 |
| **Total domestic expenditure** | 1,317.4 | 1,684.7 | 2,479.6 |
| Exports of goods and services . . | 913.5 | 1,537.6 | 1,702.9 |
| *Less* Imports of goods and services | 893.6 | 1,353.4 | 1,753.7 |
| **Sub-total** . . . . . . . | 1,337.3 | 1,868.9 | 2,428.8 |
| Statistical discrepancy* . . . . | 7.6 | −62.2 | 100.0 |
| **GDP in purchasers' values** . . | 1,344.9 | 1,806.7 | 2,528.8 |

* Referring to the difference between the sum of the expenditure components and official estimates of GDP, compiled from the production approach.

Source: Asian Development Bank, *Key Indicators of Developing Asian and Pacific Countries*.

## Gross Domestic Product by Economic Activity

| | 2000 | 2001 | 2002 |
|---|---|---|---|
| Agriculture . . . . . . | 488.0 | 670.0 | 882.1 |
| Mining . . . . . .⎫ | | | |
| Manufacturing . . . . .⎬ | 431.7 | 566.8 | 740.7 |
| Electricity, gas and water. . .⎭ | | | |
| Construction . . . . . | 61.1 | 103.7 | 112.8 |
| Transport and communications . . | 88.3 | 112.6 | 119.9 |
| Trade . . . . . . | 330.0 | 483.9 | 676.6 |
| Public administration . . . .⎫ | | | |
| Finance . . . . . .⎬ | 258.1 | 361.5 | 476.4 |
| Others . . . . . .⎭ | | | |
| **GDP at factor cost** . . . . . | 1,657.2 | 2,298.5 | 3,008.5 |
| Indirect taxes . . . .⎫ | 149.7 | 230.3 | 336.6 |
| *Less* Subsidies . . . . .⎭ | | | |
| **GDP in purchasers' values** . . | 1,806.9 | 2,528.8 | 3,345.1 |

Source: Asian Development Bank, *Key Indicators of Developing Asian and Pacific Countries.*

## BALANCE OF PAYMENTS
(US $ million)

| | 2001 | 2002 | 2003* |
|---|---|---|---|
| Exports of goods f.o.b.. . . . | 652 | 699 | 766 |
| Imports of goods c.i.f. . . . . | −773 | −823 | −864 |
| **Trade balance** . . . . | −121 | −124 | −98 |
| Other services (net) . . . . | −7 | −36 | −55 |
| **Balance on goods and services** . . . . | −128 | −160 | −153 |
| Other income (net). . . . . | −77 | −58 | −82 |
| **Balance on goods, services and income** . . . . . | −205 | −218 | −235 |
| Current transfers (net) . . . | 131 | 184 | 169 |
| **Current balance** . . . . | −74 | −34 | −66 |
| Capital transfers (net). . . . | 12 | 5 | 15 |
| Direct investment (net) . . . | 74 | 53 | 41 |
| Other public-sector capital (net) | −18 | 2 | 26 |
| Other capital (net). . . . .⎫ | −3 | −6 | −1 |
| Net errors and omissions . . .⎭ | | | |
| **Overall balance** . . . . . | −9 | 20 | 15 |

* Revised estimates.

Source: IMF, *Republic of Tajikistan: First Review Under the Three-year Arrangement Under the Poverty Reduction and Growth Facility and Request for Modification and Waivers of Performance Criteria* (July 2003).

# External Trade

## PRINCIPAL COMMODITIES
(US $ million)

| Imports c.i.f. | 1999 | 2000 | 2001 |
|---|---|---|---|
| Alumina . . . . . . . | 81 | 198 | 184 |
| Natural gas . . . . . | 36 | 35 | 27 |
| Petroleum products . . . . | 54 | 48 | 78 |
| Electricity. . . . . . | 179 | 119 | 98 |
| Grain and flour . . . . | 46 | 45 | 38 |
| **Total** (incl. others) . . . . . | 663 | 675 | 688 |

| Exports f.o.b. | 1999 | 2000 | 2001 |
|---|---|---|---|
| Aluminium . . . . . . | 309 | 433 | 397 |
| Cotton fibre . . . . . . | 82 | 84 | 62 |
| Electricity. . . . . . | 175 | 92 | 79 |
| **Total** (incl. others) . . . . . | 689 | 784 | 652 |

## PRINCIPAL TRADING PARTNERS
(US $ million)

| Imports c.i.f. | 2000 | 2001 | 2002 |
|---|---|---|---|
| Azerbaijan. . . . . . | 63.1 | 33.5 | 36.4 |
| Iran . . . . . . | 7.6 | 10.0 | 10.6 |
| Kazakhstan . . . . . | 82.4 | 89.1 | 96.7 |
| Romania . . . . . . | 41.0 | 10.9 | 11.8 |
| Russia . . . . . . | 105.1 | 129.4 | 88.0 |
| Switzerland . . . . . | 0.6 | 2.1 | 2.1 |
| Turkmenistan . . . . | 29.3 | 62.3 | 67.6 |
| Ukraine . . . . . . | 0.0 | 63.6 | 69.0 |
| United Kingdom . . . . | 86.9 | 2.5 | 1.2 |
| Uzbekistan . . . . . | 185.6 | 150.7 | 163.6 |
| **Total** (incl. others) . . . . . | 675.0 | 687.5 | 704.5 |

| Exports f.o.b. | 2000 | 2001 | 2002 |
|---|---|---|---|
| Belgium . . . . . . | 5.1 | 6.0 | 5.0 |
| Hungary . . . . . . | 1.0 | 38.8 | 65.8 |
| Iran . . . . . . | 12.5 | 29.9 | 24.8 |
| Italy . . . . . . | 21.4 | 5.8 | 18.9 |
| Latvia . . . . . . | 0.0 | 11.7 | 12.7 |
| Netherlands . . . . . | 178.2 | 194.4 | 2.8 |
| Russia . . . . . . | 258.8 | 104.7 | 64.4 |
| Switzerland . . . . . | 72.2 | 52.2 | 54.1 |
| Turkey. . . . . . | 58.4 | 75.1 | 81.5 |
| Uzbekistan . . . . . | 97.8 | 87.2 | 4.7 |
| **Total** (incl. others) . . . . . | 784.3 | 651.6 | 536.6 |

Source: Asian Development Bank, *Key Indicators of Developing Asian and Pacific Countries.*

# Transport

## RAILWAYS
(traffic)

| | 1999 | 2000 | 2001 |
|---|---|---|---|
| Passenger-km (million) . . . . | 61 | 73 | 32 |
| Freight ton-km (million) . . . | 1,282 | 1,326 | 1,248 |

## CIVIL AVIATION
(estimated traffic on scheduled services)

| | 1997 | 1998 | 1999 |
|---|---|---|---|
| Kilometres flown (million) . . . | 7 | 5 | 4 |
| Passengers carried ('000) . . . | 594 | 217 | 156 |
| Passenger-km (million) . . . | 1,825 | 322 | 229 |
| Freight ton-km (million) . . . | 166 | 32 | 23 |

Source: UN, *Statistical Yearbook.*

# Communications Media

| | 1998 | 1999 | 2000 |
|---|---|---|---|
| Television receivers ('000 in use) . | 1,900 | 2,000 | 2,000 |
| Telephones ('000 main lines in use) | 221.3 | 212.5 | 218.5 |
| Facsimile machines (number in use) . . . . . . . . . | 2,000 | 2,100 | n.a. |
| Mobile cellular telephones ('000 subscribers). . . . . . . | 0.4 | 0.6 | 1.2 |
| Internet users ('000) . . . . . | — | 2.0 | 3.0 |

**Books published:** 132 titles and 997,000 copies in 1996.

**Daily newspapers** (estimates): 2 titles and 120,000 copies (average circulation) in 1996.

**Non-daily newspapers:** 73 titles and 153,000 copies (average circulation) in 1996.

**Other periodicals:** 11 titles and 130,000 copies (average circulation) in 1996.

**Radio receivers** ('000 in use): 850 in 1997.

**2001:** Telephones ('000 main lines in use) 223.0; Mobile cellular telephones ('000 subscribers) 1.6; Internet users ('000) 3.5.

**2002:** Telephones ('000 main lines in use) 232.7; Mobile cellular telephones ('000 subscribers) 13.2; Internet users ('000) 3.5.

Sources: UNESCO, *Statistical Yearbook*; International Telecommunication Union.

# Education

(2001/02, unless otherwise indicated)

| | Institutions | Teachers | Students |
|---|---|---|---|
| Pre-primary . . . . | 501 | 6,615* | 57,812 |
| Primary. . . . . . | 660 | | 33,000 |
| Secondary: | | 100,200 | |
| general . . . . | 2,861 | | 1,487,600 |
| specialist. . . . | 128 | | 39,400 |
| vocational . . . | 55 | n.a. | 29,842† |
| Higher (incl. universities) | 31 | 6,100 | 84,400 |

\* 1996/97.
† 1994/95.

Source: partly UNESCO, *Statistical Yearbook*.

**Adult literacy rate** (UNESCO estimates): 99.3% (males 99.6%; females 98.9%) in 2001 (Source: UN Development Programme, *Human Development Report*).

# Directory

## The Constitution

Tajikistan's Constitution entered into force on 6 November 1994, when it was approved by a majority of voters in a nation-wide plebiscite. It replaced the previous Soviet-style Constitution, adopted in 1978. The following is a summary of its main provisions (including amendments approved by referendum on 26 September 1999 and 22 June 2003):

### PRINCIPLES OF THE CONSTITUTIONAL SYSTEM

The Republic of Tajikistan is a sovereign, democratic, law-governed, secular and unitary state. The state language is Tajik, but Russian is accorded the status of a language of communication between nationalities.

Recognition, observance and protection of human and civil rights and freedoms is the obligation of the State. The people of Tajikistan are the expression of sovereignty and the sole source of power of the State, which they express through their elected representatives.

Tajikistan consists of Gornyi Badakhshan Autonomous Region, regions, towns, districts, settlements and villages. The territory of the State is indivisible and inviolable. Agitation and actions aimed at disunity of the State are prohibited.

No ideology, including religious ideology, may be granted the status of a state ideology.

The Constitution of Tajikistan has supreme legal authority and its norms have direct application. Laws and other legal acts which run counter to the Constitution have no legal validity. The State, its bodies and officials are bound to observe the provisions of the Constitution.

Tajikistan will implement a peaceful policy, respecting the sovereignty and independence of other states of the world and will determine foreign relations on the basis of international norms. Agitation for war is prohibited.

The economy of Tajikistan is based on various forms of ownership. The State guarantees freedom of economic activity, entrepreneurship, equality of rights and the protection of all forms of ownership, including private ownership. Land and natural resources are under state ownership.

### FUNDAMENTAL DUTIES OF INDIVIDUALS AND CITIZENS

The freedoms and rights of individuals are protected by the Constitution, the laws of the republic and international documents to which Tajikistan is a signatory. The State guarantees the rights and freedoms of every person, regardless of nationality, race, sex, language, religious beliefs, political persuasion, social status, knowledge and property. Men and women have the same rights. Every person has the right to life. No one may be subjected to torture, punishment or inhuman treatment. No one may be arrested, kept in custody or exiled without a legal basis, and no one is adjudged guilty of a crime except by the sentence of a court in accordance with the law. Every person has the right freely to choose their place of residence, to leave the republic and return to it. Every person has the right to profess any religion individually or with others, or not to profess any, and to take part in religious ceremonies. Every citizen has the right to take part in political life and state administration; to elect and be elected from the age of 18; to join and leave political parties, trade unions and other associations; to take part in meetings, rallies or demonstrations. Every person is guaranteed freedom of speech. State censorship is prohibited.

Every person has the right: to ownership and inheritance; to work; to housing; to social security in old age, or in the event of sickness or disability. Basic general education is compulsory.

A state of emergency is declared as a temporary measure to ensure the security of citizens and of the State in the instance of a direct threat to the freedom of citizens, the State's independence, its territorial integrity, or natural disasters. The period of a state of emergency is up to three months; it can be prolonged by the President of the Republic.

### PARLIAMENT

Parliament is the highest representative and legislative body of the republic. Its members are elected for a five-year term. Any citizen over the age of 25 may be elected to Parliament.

The powers of Parliament include: enactment and amendment of laws, and their annulment; interpretation of the Constitution and laws; determination of the basic direction of domestic and foreign policy; ratification of presidential decrees on the appointment and dismissal of the Chairman of the National Bank, the Chairman and members of the Constitutional Court, the Supreme Court and the Supreme Economic Court; ratification of the state budget; determining and altering the structure of administrative territorial units; ratification and annulment of international treaties; ratification of presidential decrees on a state of war and a state of emergency.

Laws are adopted by a majority of the deputies of the Parliament. If the President does not agree with the law, he may return it to Parliament. If the Parliament once again approves the law, with at least a two-thirds' majority, the President must sign it.

### THE PRESIDENT OF THE REPUBLIC

The President of the Republic is the Head of State and the head of the executive. The President is elected by the citizens of Tajikistan on the basis of universal, direct and equal suffrage for a seven-year term. Any citizen who knows the state language and has lived on the territory of Tajikistan for the preceding 10 years may be nominated to the post of President of the Republic.

The President has the authority: to represent Tajikistan inside the country and in international relations; to establish or abolish ministries with the approval of the Parliament; to appoint or dismiss the Chairman (Prime Minister) and other members of the Council of Ministers and to propose them for approval to the Parliament; to appoint and dismiss chairmen of regions, towns and districts, and propose new appointments for approval to the relevant assemblies of people's deputies; to appoint and dismiss members of the Constitutional Court, the Supreme Court and the Supreme Economic Court (with the approval of the Parliament); to appoint and dismiss judges of lower courts; to sign laws; to lead the implementation of foreign policy and sign international treaties; to appoint diplomatic representatives abroad; to be Commander-in-Chief of the armed forces of Tajikistan; to declare a state of war or a state of emergency (with the approval of the Parliament).

In the event of the President's death, resignation, removal from office or inability to perform his duties, the duties of the President will be carried out by the Chairman of the Parliament until further presidential elections can be held. New elections must be held within three months of these circumstances. The President may be removed from office in the case of his committing a crime, by the decision of at least two-thirds of deputies of the Parliament, taking into account the decisions of the Constitutional Court.

## THE COUNCIL OF MINISTERS

The Council of Ministers consists of the Chairman (Prime Minister), the First Deputy Chairman, Deputy Chairmen, Ministers and Chairmen of State Committees. The Council of Ministers is responsible for implementation of laws and decrees of the Parliament and decrees and orders of the President. The Council of Ministers leaves office when a new President is elected.

## LOCAL GOVERNMENT

The local representative authority in regions, towns and districts is the assembly of people's deputies. Assemblies are elected for a five-year term. Local executive government is the responsibility of the President's representative: the chairman of the assembly of people's deputies, who is proposed by the President and approved by the relevant assembly. The Parliament may dissolve local representative bodies, if their actions do not conform to the Constitution and the law.

## THE GORNYI BADAKHSHAN AUTONOMOUS REGION

The Gornyi Badakhshan Autonomous Region is an integral and indivisible part of Tajikistan, the territory of which cannot be changed without the consent of the regional assembly of people's deputies.

## JUDICIARY

The judiciary is independent and protects the rights and freedoms of the individual, the interests of the State, organizations and institutions, and legality and justice. Judicial power is implemented by the Constitutional Court, the Supreme Court, the Supreme Economic Court, the Military Court, the Court of Gornyi Badakhshan Autonomous Region, and courts of regions, the city of Dushanbe, towns and districts. The term of judges is 10 years. The creation of emergency courts is not permitted.

Judges are independent and are subordinate only to the Constitution and the law. Interference in their activity is not permitted.

## THE OFFICE OF THE PROCURATOR-GENERAL

The Procurator-General and procurators subordinate to him ensure the control and observance of laws within the framework of their authority in the territory of Tajikistan. The Procurator-General is responsible to the Parliament and the President, and is elected for a five-year term.

## PROCEDURES FOR INTRODUCING AMENDMENTS TO THE CONSTITUTION

Amendments and addenda to the Constitution are made by means of a referendum. A referendum takes place with the support of at least two-thirds of the people's deputies. The President, or at least one-third of the people's deputies, may submit amendments and addenda to the Constitution. The form of public administration, the territorial integrity and the democratic, law-governed and secular nature of the State are irrevocable.

Note: In September 1999 Parliament enacted a number of constitutional amendments, including: the creation of a bicameral legislature, the extension of the President's term of office to seven years, and the legalization of religion-based political parties.

# The Government

## HEAD OF STATE

**President of the Republic of Tajikistan:** Imamali Sharipovich Rakhmonov (elected by popular vote on 6 November 1994; re-elected on 6 November 1999).

## COUNCIL OF MINISTERS
### (October 2003)

**Chairman (Prime Minister) and Minister of Construction:** Akil Akilov.

**First Deputy Chairman:** Haji Akbar Turajonzoda.

**Deputy Chairmen:** Nigina Sharipova, Maj.-Gen. Saidamir Zukhurov, Kozidavlat Koimdodov, Zokir Vazirov.

**Minister of Agriculture:** Tursun Rakhmatov.

**Minister of Culture:** Karomatullo Olimov.

**Minister of Defence:** Maj.-Gen. Sherali Khayrulloyev.

**Minister of the Economy and Foreign Economic Relations:** Khakim Soliyev.

**Minister of Education:** Safarali Rajabov.

**Minister of Emergency Situations and Civil Defence:** Maj.-Gen. Mirzo Ziyoyev.

**Minister of Energy:** Abdullo Yorov.

**Minister of Environmental Protection:** Usmonkul Shokirov.

**Minister of Finance:** Safarali Najmiddinov.

**Minister of Foreign Affairs:** Talbak Nazarov.

**Minister of Grain Products:** Bekmurod Urokov.

**Minister of Health:** Nusratullo Faizulloyev.

**Minister of Industry:** Zaid Saidov.

**Minister of Internal Affairs:** Khomiddin Sharipov.

**Minister of Justice:** Khalifabobo Khamidov.

**Minister of Labour, Employment and Social Welfare:** Rafika Musoyeva.

**Minister of Land Improvement and Water Economy:** Abdukakhir Nazirov.

**Minister of Security:** Khayriddin Abdurakhimov.

**Minister of State Revenues and Tax Collection:** Ghulomjon Boboyev.

**Minister of Transport and Roads:** Abdujalol Salimov.

### Chairmen of State Committees

**Chairman of State Committee for Construction and Architecture:** Ismat Eshmirzoyev.

**Chairman for State Committee on Land Resources and Reclamation:** Davlatsho Gulmakhmadov.

**Chairman of State Committee for Oil and Gas:** Salamsho Mukhabbatov.

**Chairman of State Committee for Religious Affairs:** Said Akhmedov.

**Chairman of State Committee for State Property:** Sherali Gulov.

**Chairman of State Committee for Statistics:** Kholmamed Azimov.

**Chairman of State Committee for Television and Radio:** Ubaydullo Rajabov.

**Deputy Chairman of State Committee for State Border Protection:** Maj.-Gen. Safar Sayfulloyev.

## MINISTRIES

**Office of the President:** 734023 Dushanbe, pr. Rudaki 80; tel. (372) 21-04-18; fax (372) 21-18-37.

**Secretariat of the Prime Minister:** 734023 Dushanbe, pr. Rudaki 80; tel. (372) 21-18-71; fax (372) 21-51-10.

**Ministry of Agriculture:** 734025 Dushanbe, pr. Rudaki 44; tel. (372) 22-31-46; fax (372) 21-57-94.

**Ministry of Construction:** Dushanbe, Kirova 36; tel. (372) 22-61-43; fax (372) 27-86-17.

**Ministry of Culture:** 734025 Dushanbe, N. Karabayeva 17; tel. (372) 21-03-05; fax (372) 21-36-30.

**Ministry of Defence:** 734025 Dushanbe, kuchai Bokhtar 59; tel. (372) 23-19-89; fax (372) 23-19-37.

**Ministry of the Economy and Foreign Economic Relations:** 734002 Dushanbe, pr. Rudaki 42; tel. (372) 23-29-44; fax (372) 21-04-04.

**Ministry of Education:** 734025 Dushanbe, Chekhova 13A; tel. (372) 21-46-05; fax (372) 21-70-41.

**Ministry of Emergency Situations and Civil Defence:** 734025 Dushanbe, kuchai Bokhtar 59; tel. (372) 21-12-42; fax (372) 21-13-31.

**Ministry of Energy:** Dushanbe.

**Ministry of Environmental Protection:** 734025 Dushanbe, kuchai Bokhtar 12; tel. (372) 21-30-39; fax (372) 21-18-39.

**Ministry of Finance:** 734025 Dushanbe, kuchai Akademikov Radjabovii 3; tel. (372) 21-14-17; fax (372) 21-33-29.

**Ministry of Foreign Affairs:** 734051 Dushanbe, pr. Rudaki 42; tel. (372) 21-18-08; fax (372) 21-02-59; e-mail dushanbe@mfaumo.td.silk.org.

**Ministry of Grain Products:** 734025 Dushanbe, pr. Rudaki 42; tel. (372) 27-61-31; fax (372) 27-95-71.

**Ministry of Health:** 734025 Dushanbe, Shevchenko 69; tel. (372) 21-18-35; fax (372) 21-48-71.

**Ministry of Industry:** Dushanbe.

**Ministry of Internal Affairs:** 734025 Dushanbe, Dzerzhinskogo 29; tel. (372) 21-30-53; fax (372) 21-26-05.

**Ministry of Justice:** 734025 Dushanbe, pr. Rudaki 25; tel. (372) 21-44-05; fax (372) 21-80-66.

**Ministry of Labour, Employment and Social Welfare:** 734028 Dushanbe, kuchai Alishepa Navoi 52; tel. (372) 35-18-37; fax (372) 36-24-15.

**Ministry of Land Improvement and Water Economy:** 734001 Dushanbe, pr. Rudaki 78; tel. (372) 21-20-31.

**Ministry of Security:** 734025 Dushanbe, Gorkogo 8; tel. (372) 23-29-12; fax (372) 21-15-65.

**Ministry of State Revenues and Tax Collection:** Dushanbe.

**Ministry of Transport and Roads:** 734042 Dushanbe, kuchai Aini 14; tel. (372) 21-17-13; fax (372) 21-20-03.

### Principal State Committees

**State Committee for Construction and Architecture:** 734025 Dushanbe, Mazayeva 1911; tel. and fax (372) 23-18-82.

**State Committee for Land Resources and Reclamation:** Dushanbe.

**State Committee for Oil and Gas:** Dushanbe.

**State Committee for Religious Affairs:** Dushanbe.

**State Committee for State Border Protection:** Dushanbe.

**State Committee for State Property:** Dushanbe, pr. Rudaki 25; tel. (372) 21-86-59; e-mail privatization@tajikistan.com; internet privatization.tajikistan.com.

**State Committee for Statistics:** 734025 Dushanbe, Bokhtar 17; tel. (372) 27-63-31; fax (372) 21-43-75; e-mail stat@tojikiston.com.

**State Committee for Television and Radio:** Dushanbe, kuchai Chapayeva 31; tel. (372) 27-65-69.

# President and Legislature

## PRESIDENT

A presidential election took place on 6 November 1999. There were two candidates, Davlat Usmon and Imamali Rakhmonov. According to official sources, Rakhmonov obtained an estimated 97% of the votes cast, while Davlat Usmon received about 2%. Rakhmonov was inaugurated as President on 16 November.

## PARLIAMENT

Constitutional amendments approved by a referendum in September 1999 provided for the establishment of a 96-member bicameral legislative body, comprising a 63-member lower chamber, the Majlisi Namoyandagon (Assembly of Representatives), and a 33-member upper chamber, the Majlisi Milliy (National Assembly).

## MAJLISI NAMOYANDAGON

The 63 members of the lower chamber are elected for a five-year term: 22 are elected by proportional representation and 41 in single-mandate constituencies. At the first elections to the Assembly of Representatives, held on 27 February 2000, only 49 of the 63 seats were filled. Invalid results were declared in three constituencies, while in 11 no party achieved the requisite 50% of the vote. This

necessitated a second round of voting on 12 March 2000, at which the 11 seats were filled. Two further seats were filled in April and December, respectively; however, one seat remained vacant.

**President:** SAIDULLO KHAIRULLAYEV.

### Elections, 27 February and 12 March 2000

|  | % of votes | Seats |
|---|---|---|
| People's Democratic Party of Tajikistan (PDPT) | 64.5 | 30 |
| Communist Party of Tajikistan (CPT) | 20.6 | 13 |
| Islamic Rebirth Party of Tajikistan (IRP) | 7.5 | 2 |
| Independents (pro-Government/PDPT) | — | 15 |
| Vacant | — | 3 |
| **Total** (incl. others)* | 100.0 | 63 |

* Other parties to receive votes but not win any seats included the Democratic Party of Tajikistan (3.5%), Adolatkoh (1.4%), and the Socialist Party of Tajikistan (1.2%).

### MAJLISI MILLIY

The 33 members of the upper chamber are indirectly elected for five years: of these, 25 are selected by local deputies, while the remaining eight are appointed by the President. Elections to the National Assembly were held for the first time on 23 March 2000.

**President:** MAKHMADSAID UBAYDULLAYEV.

# Local Government

From February 1991 Tajikistan had a three-tier system of local government, when the highest level of local government consisted of one autonomous oblast (region), three oblasts and the capital city of Dushanbe. In December 1992 the two oblasts to the south of Dushanbe, Qurgonteppa (Kurgan-Tyube or Kurgan Teppe) and Kulob (Kulyab), were merged into a single oblast, Khatlon, which occupies the south-west of Tajikistan. Soghd Oblast lies in the north-west, while the Gornyi Badakhshan Autonomous Oblast consists of the eastern part of the country. The rains (districts) of the central belt of territory were not united in an oblast. In all of Tajikistan there were 52 raions, which were part of the second tier of local government, which also included 21 municipalities and four municipal regions (in Dushanbe). Finally, at the lowest level, there were 340 kishlak or village soviets (councils) and 47 other settlements. Each unit of local government had a soviet and an executive committee (administration).

**Dushanbe City:** 734000 Dushanbe, pr. Rudaki 48; tel. (372) 23-22-14; Mayor MAKHMADSAID UBAYDULLOYEV.

**Khatlon Oblast:** 735140 Qurgonteppa (Kurgan-Tyube), Gogolya 2; tel. (37744) 2-54-35; f. 1992 by union of Qurgonteppa and Kulob Oblasts; Chair. of Exec. Cttee AMIRSHO MIRALIYEV.

**Soghd Oblast:** 735700 Khujand (Khodzhent), Dzerzhinskaya 45; tel. (34) 224-02-44; fax (34) 226-77-55; Gov. KAZIM KAZIMOV.

### AUTONOMOUS OBLAST

#### Gornyi Badakhshan

The Autonomous Oblast of Gornyi Badakhshan is situated in the south-east, consisting of the entire eastern part of Tajikistan. The territory is dominated by the Pamir mountain range. Its chief town is Khorog, in the west of the territory, near the border with Afghanistan (there are also international borders with the People's Republic of China in the east and Kyrgyzstan in the north). The population, in 2000, was 206,000, of which some 28,000 lived in Khorog. In 1993 an estimated 80,000 refugees from other parts of Tajikistan arrived in the region. The local administration consists of seven raions (districts).

Gornyi Badakhshan was dominated by the Pamiri people, distinct from the Tajiks in both language and religion (many were Isma'ilis and spoke one of six Eastern Iranian languages). The territory was only acquired by the Russian Empire at the very end of the 19th century and was long an area of disputed sovereignty. Under Soviet rule it gained a special administrative status, but remained one of the poorest regions in the USSR. During the late 1980s a separatist movement, Lale Badakhshon, emerged, which allied itself with the Islamist and democratic opposition to the communist establishment of Tajikistan. In 1993, however, severely affected by the civil war and with the main road from Dushanbe to Khorog closed until August, the local administration pledged its loyalty to the Tajikistani state and appealed for urgent food and medical aid. Although this ended most conflict in the region, its borders remained vulnerable to penetration by opposition forces, and its territory, both because of the nature of its terrain and the sympathies of its inhabitants, remained a redoubt of rebels during the mid-1990s.

**Chairman of the Oblast Soviet:** GARIBSHO SHABOZOV.

**Chairman of the Oblast Executive Committee:** ALIMAMAD NIYOZMAMADOV.

**Administration Headquarters:** 736000 Khorog, Lenina 26; tel. (3779) 25-22.

## Political Organizations

**Adolatkoh** (Justice): Kanibadam, Mira 44; tel. (3467) 2-58-38; f. 1996; campaigns for the establishment of social justice; banned in Aug. 2001; Leader ABDURAKHMON KARIMOV; c. 10,000 mems.

**Communist Party of Tajikistan (CPT):** Dushanbe, Foteh Niyazi 37; f. 1924; sole registered party until 1991; Chair. SHODI SHABDOLOV; c. 70,000 mems (2001)*.

**Hizb-i-Vahdat** (Unity): Dushanbe; f. 2001.

**Justice and Progress of Tajikistan:** Khujand; f. 1996; moderate opposition party; Chair. KARIM ABDULOV.

**Party of Popular Unity and Accord (PPUA):** Dushanbe; f. 1994; represents interests of northern Tajikistan; Leader ABDUMALIK ABDULLOJONOV.

**People's Democratic Party of Tajikistan (PDPT):** Dushanbe, pr. Rudaki 44/319; tel. (372) 12-14-48; f. 1993; campaigns for a united, democratic, secular and law-based state; joined by the Lale Badakhshon Movement in 2000; Chair. IMAMALI RAKHMONOV; 50,000 mems*.

**Social Democratic Party of Tajikistan (SDPT):** Dushanbe; f. 1999; Chair. RAKHMATULLO ZOIROV*.

**Socialist Party of Tajikistan:** Dushanbe, Shotemur 32/9; f. 1996; campaigns for a socialist, law-based state; Chair. KURBON VOSSE (acting); c. 24,000 mems*.

**Taraqqiyot Party** (Development Party): Dushanbe; f. 2001; Chair. SULTON KUVVATOV; 3,000 mems (2001).

The following parties were formally banned by the Supreme Court in June 1993. The DPT was relegalized in 1996. However, one faction of the DPT (led by Jumaboy Niyazov) continued to oppose any accommodation with the Government. The legalization of opposition parties and their media was a term of the peace agreement concluded in June 1997. It was not, however, granted by the President until August 1999. In March and December of that year the further re-registration of parties was carried out.

**Democratic Party of Tajikistan (DPT):** Dushanbe, pr. Rudaki 81/19; tel. (372) 21-77-87; f. 1990; permitted to re-register 1996 and 1999; secular nationalist and pro-Western, adopted pro-Government stance in 2003; Chair. MUKHAMMADRUZI ISKANDAROV; c. 5,000 mems*.

**Islamic Rebirth Party of Tajikistan (IRP):** Dushanbe, Tolstaya 5; tel. (372) 27-25-30; fax (372) 27-53-93; leadership formerly based in Tehran, Iran; registered in 1991 as the Islamic Renaissance Party of Tajikistan; br. of what was the Soviet IRP; renamed in 1999; formerly a moderate Islamist party; Chair. SAYED ABDULLO NURI; c. 50,000 mems*.

**Rastokhez** (Rebirth): f. 1990; nationalist-religious party favoured by intellectuals; Chair. TAKHIR ABDUZHABBOROV*.

During 1992–97 the supporters of the IRP and other opposition parties maintained guerrilla warfare against the regime, often with the support of the Afghan *mujahidin*. Most paramilitary groups were members of the IRP-led **United Tajik Opposition** (UTO, Leader Sayed Abdullo Nuri; Dep. Leader Muhammadsharif Himmafzoda). In 1997, however, following the conclusion of the peace agreement between the Government and the UTO, a National Reconciliation Council (NRC) was formed, comprising 26 members drawn equally from the UTO and the Government to debate executive and constitutional changes. Nevertheless, some opposition elements continued to perpetrate dissident attacks, in an attempt to disrupt the peace process. Following legislative elections, held in February and March 2000, at the end of March the NRC was dissolved.

* Denotes parties re-registered from December 1999.

## Diplomatic Representation

### EMBASSIES IN TAJIKISTAN

**Afghanistan:** Dushanbe, Pushkina 34; tel. (372) 21-60-72; fax (372) 51-00-96; Ambassador Gen. ASEF DELAWAR.

**China, People's Republic:** 734002 Dushanbe, Parvina 143; tel. (372) 24-41-83; fax 51-00-24; e-mail chinaembassy@tajnet.com; internet www.chinaembassy-tj.org; Ambassador WU HONGBIN.

**France:** Dushanbe; Ambassador PIERRE ANDRIEU.

**Germany:** Dushanbe, Warsobskaja 16; tel. (372) 21-21-89; fax (372) 21-22-45; e-mail deutschebotschaftduschanbe@tajnet.com; Ambassador WOLFGANG NEUEN.

**Holy See:** 734006 Dushanbe, pr. Titova 21/10; tel. (372) 23-42-69; e-mail avila@romecc.td.silk.glas.apc.org; Apostolic Nuncio Most Rev. JÓZEF WESOŁOWSKI (Titular Archbishop of Slebte).

**India:** Dushanbe, Bukhoro 45; tel. (372) 21-23-50; fax (372) 21-24-61; e-mail eoi@netrt.org; Ambassador BONDAL JAISHANKER (designate).

**Iran:** Dushanbe, Tehran 18; tel. (372) 21-12-32; internet www.rayztaj.com; Ambassador NASER SARMADI-PARSA.

**Kazakhstan:** Dushanbe; tel. (372) 27-18-38; fax (372) 21-89-40; e-mail dipmiskz@tajik.net; Ambassador AMANZHOLA ZHANKULIYEV.

**Korea, Democratic People's Republic:** Dushanbe.

**Korea, Republic:** Dushanbe; Ambassador KIM SUNG-HWAN.

**Kyrgyzstan:** Dushanbe, Abu Ali ibn Sina 46; tel. and fax (372) 21-18-31; fax (372) 21-03-66; Ambassador ERIK ASANALIYEV.

**Pakistan:** 734000 Dushanbe, pr. Rudaki 37A; tel. (372) 21-19-65; fax (372) 21-17-29; e-mail parepdushanbe@tajnet.com; Ambassador KHALID AMIRKHAN.

**Russia:** Dushanbe, ul. A. A. Sino 29/31; tel. (372) 21-10-05; fax (372) 21-10-85; e-mail rambtadjik@rambler.ru; internet www.rusembassy.tajnet.ru; Ambassador MAKSIM PESHKOV.

**Turkey:** 734019 Dushanbe, pr. Rudaki 15; tel. (372) 21-00-36; fax (372) 51-00-12; e-mail turkdusa@tajnet.com; Ambassador A. FERIT ÜLKER.

**Turkmenistan:** 734000 Dushanbe, pr. Rudaki 105/1; tel. (372) 21-04-61.

**United Kingdom:** Dushanbe, Lutfi 43; tel. (372) 24-22-21; e-mail dhm@britishembassy-tj.com; internet www.britishembassy.gov.uk/tajikistan; Ambassador MICHAEL FORBES SMITH.

**USA:** 734003 Dushanbe, Pavlova 10; tel. (372) 21-03-50; fax (372) 21-03-62; e-mail reception@amemb.tajik.net; internet usembassy.state.gov/dushanbe; Ambassador FRANKLIN P. HUDDLE.

**Uzbekistan:** Dushanbe; Ambassador BAKHTIYOR URDASHEV.

## Judicial System

**Chairman of the Constitutional Court:** ZARIF ALIYEV.

**Chairman of the Supreme Court:** UBAIDULLO DAVLATOV.

**Procurator-General:** AMIRQUL AZIMOV.

## Religion

### ISLAM

The majority of Tajiks are adherents of Islam and are mainly Sunnis (Hanafi school). Some of the Pamiri peoples, however, are Isma'ilis (followers of the Aga Khan), a Shi'ite sect. Under the Soviet regime the Muslims of Tajikistan were subject to the Muslim Board of Central Asia and a muftiate, both of which were based in Tashkent, Uzbekistan. The senior Muslim cleric in Tajikistan was the *kazi* (supreme judge). In 1992 the incumbent *kazi* fled to Afghanistan, and in 1993 the Government established an independent muftiate.

**Chief Mufti:** AMONULLO NEMATZODA, Dushanbe.

### CHRISTIANITY

Most of the minority Christian population is Slav, the main denomination being the Russian Orthodox Church. There are some Protestant and other groups, notably a Baptist Church in Dushanbe.

### Roman Catholic Church

The Church is represented in Tajikistan by a Mission, established in September 1997. There were an estimated 245 adherents at 31 December 2001.

**Superior:** Rev. CARLOS AVILA, 734006 Dushanbe, pr. Titova 21/10; tel. (372) 27-68-21; e-mail carlosavila@tajnet.com.

## The Press

In 2000 there were four national newspapers. In 1996 two daily newspapers and 73 non-daily newspapers were published in Tajikistan. There were also 11 periodicals published in that year.

## PRINCIPAL NEWSPAPERS

**Adabiyet va sanat** (Literature and Art): 734001 Dushanbe, Ismail Somoni 8; tel. (372) 24-57-39; f. 1959; weekly; organ of Union of Writers of Tajikistan and Ministry of Culture; in Tajik; Editor GULNAZAR KELDI; circ. 4,000.

**Biznes i Politika** (Business and Politics): 734018 Dushanbe, pr. S. Sherozi 16; tel. (372) 33-43-96; f. 1991; weekly; in Russian; Editor-in-Chief V. KRASOTIN; circ. 30,000.

**Djavononi Tochikiston** (Tajikistan Youth): 734018 Dushanbe, pr. S. Sherozi 16; tel. (372) 22-60-07; f. 1930; weekly; organ of the Union of Youth of Tajikistan; in Tajik; Editor DAVLAT NAZRIYEV; circ. 3,000.

**Golos Tajikistana** (Voice of Tajikistan): 734018 Dushanbe, pr. S. Sherozi 16; tel. (372) 33-76-27; f. 1992; weekly; organ of the Communist Party of Tajikistan; in Russian; Editor G. SHCHERBATOV; circ. 2,300.

**Jumhuriyat** (Republic): 734018 Dushanbe, pr. S. Sherozi 16; tel. (372) 33-08-11; f. 1925; organ of the President; 3 a week; in Tajik; Editor-in-Chief SARDABIR MUKHABBATSHOYEV; circ. 8,000.

**Khabar:** 734018 Dushanbe, pr. S. Sherozi 16; tel. (372) 22-33-13; Editorial Dir ZAINIDDIN NASPEDDINOV.

**Khalk ovozi** (People's Voice): 734018 Dushanbe, pr. S. Sherozi 16; tel. (372) 33-05-04; f. 1929; organ of the President; 3 a week; in Uzbek; Editor I. MUKHSINOV; circ. 8,600.

**Kurer Tajikistana** (Tajikistan Courier): 734018 Dushanbe, pr. S. Sherozi 16; tel. (372) 33-08-15; e-mail ttemirov@td.silk.org; weekly; independent; Editor KH. YUSIPOV; circ. 40,000.

**Najot:** Dushanbe Toktogulya 55; tel. (372) 31-47-38; organ of the Islamic Rebirth Party of Tajikistan; weekly.

**Narodnaya Gazeta** (People's Newspaper): 734018 Dushanbe, pr. S. Sherozi 16; tel. (372) 33-08-30; f. 1929; fmrly *Kommunist Tajikistana* (Tajik Communist); organ of the President; 3 a week; in Russian; Editor NIKOLAI NIKOLAIYEVICH; circ. 7,000.

**Nidoi ranchbar** (Call of the Workers): 734018 Dushanbe, pr. S. Sherozi 16; tel. (372) 33-38-50; f. 1992; weekly; organ of the Communist Party of Tajikistan; in Tajik; Editor-in-Chief KH. YOROV; circ. 6,000.

**Omuzgor** (Teacher): Dushanbe, kuchai Aini 45; tel. (372) 27-25-49; f. 1932; weekly; organ of the Ministry of Education; in Tajik; Editor-in-Chief S. SAIFULLOYEV; circ. 3,000.

**Posukh** (Answer): 734018 Dushanbe, N. Karabayeva 17; tel. (372) 33-35-60; f. 1994; organ of the Ministry of Culture and the Union of Journalists; weekly; in Tajik; Editor-in-Chief A. KURBANOV; circ. 3,000.

**Sadoi mardum** (The Voice of the People): 734018 Dushanbe, pr. S. Sherozi 16; tel. (372) 22-42-47; f. 1991; 3 a week; organ of the legislature; in Tajik; Editor MURADULLO SHERALIYEV; circ. 8,000.

**Tojikiston ovozi** (Voice of Tajikistan): 734018 Dushanbe, pr. S. Sherozi 16; tel. (372) 33-06-08; f. 1992; organ of the Central Committee of the Communist Party of Tajikistan; weekly; in Tajik and Russian; Editors SULAYMAN ERMATOV, INOM MUSOYEV; circ. 24,700.

**Vechernii Dushanbe** (Dunshanbe Evening Newspaper): 734018 Dushanbe, pr. S. Sherozi 16; tel. (372) 33-55-59; fax (372) 33-30-25; e-mail vecherka@vd.td; f. 1968; weekly; social and political; in Russian; closed down by the Government in 2001; Editor-in-Chief S. LAGUTOV.

## PRINCIPAL PERIODICALS

Monthly, unless otherwise indicated.

**Adab:** 734025 Dushanbe, ul. Chekhova 13; tel. (372) 23-49-36; organ of the Ministry of Education; in Tajik; Editor SH. SHOKIRZODA; circ. (annual) 24,000.

**Bunyod-i Adab** (Culture Fund): f. 1996 to foster cultural links among the country's Persian-speaking peoples; weekly; Editor ASKAR KHAKIM.

**Djashma** (Spring): 734018 Dushanbe, pr. S. Sherozi 16; tel. (372) 33-08-48; f. 1986; journal of the Ministry of Culture; for children; Editor KAMOL NASRULLO; circ. (annual) 10,000.

**Farkhang** (Culture): 734003 Dushanbe, pr. Rudaki 124; tel. (372) 24-02-39; f. 1991; journal of the Culture Fund and Ministry of Culture; in Tajik; Editor-in-Chief J. AKOBIR; circ. 15,000.

**Firuza:** 734018 Dushanbe, pr. S. Sherozi 16; tel. (372) 33-89-10; f. 1932; organ of the Ministry of Culture; social and literary journal for women; Editor ZULFIYA ATOI; circ. (annual) 29,400.

**Ilm va khayot** (Science and Life): 734025 Dushanbe, pr. Rudaki 34; tel. (372) 27-48-61; f. 1989; organ of the Academy of Sciences; popular science; Editor T. BOIBOBO; circ. (annual) 12,000.

**Istikbol:** 734018 Dushanbe, pr. S. Sherozi 16; tel. (372) 33-14-52; f. 1952; organ of the Ministry of Culture; in Tajik; Editor K. KENJAYEVA; circ. (annual) 7,200.

**Marifat:** 734024 Dushanbe, kuchai Aini 45; tel. (372) 23-42-84; organ of the Ministry of Education; in Tajik; Editor O. BOZOROV; circ. (annual) 40,000.

**Pamir:** 734001 Dushanbe, Ismail Somoni 8; tel. (372) 24-56-56; f. 1949; journal of the Union of Writers of Tajikistan; fiction; in Russian; Editor-in-Chief BORIS PSHENICHNYI.

**Sadoi shark** (Voice of the East): 734001 Dushanbe, Ismail Somoni 8; tel. (372) 24-56-79; f. 1927; journal of the Union of Writers of Tajikistan; fiction; in Tajik; Editor URUN KUKHZOD; circ. 1,600.

**Tochikiston** (Tajikistan): 734018 Dushanbe, pr. S. Sherozi 16; tel. (372) 33-89-89; f. 1938; social and political; in Tajik; Editor-in-Chief D. ASHUROV; circ. (annual) 9,000.

**Zdravookhraneniye Tajikistana** (Tajikistan Public Health): 734026 Dushanbe, Ismail Somoni 59; tel. (372) 36-16-37; f. 1933; 6 a year; journal of the Ministry of Health; medical research; in Russian; Editor-in-Chief AZAM T. PULATOV; circ. (annual) 10,500.

## NEWS AGENCIES

**Asia-Plus:** 734002 Dushanbe, Bokhtar 35/1, 8th floor; tel. (372) 21-78-63; fax (372) 51-01-36; e-mail info@asiaplus.tajik.net; internet www.asiaplus.tajnet.com; independent information and consulting agency; Dir UMED BABAKHANOV; Man. DALER NURKHANOV.

**Khovar** (East): 734025 Dushanbe, pr. Rudaki 37; tel. (372) 21-33-13; fax (372) 21-21-37; e-mail khovar@tojikiston.com; internet khovar.tojikiston.com; f. 1991 to replace TajikTA (Tajik Telegraph Agency); govt information agency; Dir NABI KARIMOV.

**Mizon:** Dushanbe; independent information agency.

**Varorud:** Khujand, Ferdowsi 123; e-mail webmaster@varorud.org; internet www.varorud.org; independent information agency.

### Foreign Bureau

**Rossiiskoye Informatsionnoye Agentstvo—Novosti (RIA—Novosti)** (Russia): 734025 Dushanbe, Putovskogo 73/2; tel. (372) 23-49-06.

### PRESS ASSOCIATION

**National Association of Independent Mass Media:** Dushanbe; e-mail nansmit@tojikiston.com; f. 1999.

# Publishers

**Adib** (Literary Publishing House): Dushanbe, pr. Rudaki 37; tel. (372) 23-27-37; f. 1987; literary fiction; Dir K. MIRZOYEV.

**Irfon** (Light of Knowledge Publishing House): 731018 Dushanbe, N. Karabayeva 17; tel. (372) 33-39-06; f. 1926; politics, social sciences, economics, agriculture, medicine and technology; Dir J. SHARIFOV; Editor-in-Chief A. OLIMOV.

**Maorif** (Education Publishing House): Dushanbe, kuchai Aini 126; tel. (372) 25-10-50; educational, academic; Dir A. GHAFUROV.

**Sarredaksiyai Ilmii Entsiklopediyai Millii Tajik** (Tajik Scientific Encyclopaedia Publishing House): Dushanbe, kuchai Aini 126; tel. (372) 25-18-41; f. 1969; Editor-in-Chief A. QURBONOV.

# Broadcasting and Communications

## TELECOMMUNICATIONS

**Joint Venture 'TajikTel':** 734000 Dushanbe, pr. Rudaki 57; tel. (372) 21-01-45; fax (372) 51-01-25; e-mail office@tajiktel.tajik.net; mobile cellular telephone co; Dir-Gen. ZVI SHWA.

**JSC Tajiktelecom:** 734025 Dushanbe; tel. (372) 23-44-44; fax (372) 21-04-04; e-mail tajiktelekom@netrt.org; internet www.netrt.org; f. 1996; national telecommunications operator; Dir-Gen. FARKHOD S. SHUKUROV.

## BROADCASTING

In February 1994 President Rakhmonov placed the State TV-Radio Broadcasting Co of Tajikistan under the direct operational supervision of the Chairman of the legislature. Transmissions of a rebel opposition group, calling itself Voice of Free Tajikistan, began in 1993. In 1996 a new, Iranian-funded television station, Samaniyan, began broadcasting a selection of Iranian and local programmes. In December 2001 there were some 20 independent television stations.

## Radio

**State TV-Radio Broadcasting Co of Tajikistan:** 734025 Dushanbe, kuchai Chapayev 31; tel. (372) 27-75-27; fax (372) 21-34-95; e-mail soro@ctvrtj.td.silk.org; Chair. MIRBOBO MIRRAKHIMOV; Dep. Chair. G. MAKHMUDOV.

**Asia-Plus Radio:** Dushanbe; country's first independent radio station; broadcasts 14 hours per day in Russian and Tajik; Man. Dir DALER NURKHONOV.

**Tajik Radio:** 734025 Dushanbe, kuchai Chapayev 31; tel. (372) 27-65-69; broadcasts in Russian, Tajik and Uzbek.

**Tiroz:** 735700 Khujand, Mikroraion 27; tel. (342) 25–66–89; e-mail trrktiroz@sugdien.com; internet www.tiroz.sugdien.com; Dir KHURSHED ULMASOV.

### Television

**State TV-Radio Broadcasting Co of Tajikistan:** see Radio.

**Tajik Television (TTV):** 734013 Dushanbe, kuchai Behzod 7; tel. (372) 22-43-57.

**Internews Tajikistan:** 434001 Dushanbe, pr. Rudaki 92, 4th floor, apt 23; tel. (372) 24-54-83; fax (372) 21-43-12; e-mail bahodoor@internews.tj; internet www.internews.tj; f. 1982; non-governmental organization to promote free and independent media; includes the Asia-Plus agency; Man. Dir BAHODOOR KOSIMOV.

**Poitakht:** 734013 Dushanbe, Azizbekova 20; tel. (372) 23-26-29; independent; Dir RAKHMON OSTONOV.

**Samaniyan:** Dushanbe, pr. S. Sherozi 16; tel. (372) 21-65-91; f. 1996; Iranian-funded; Dir GULOMALI KURBONOV.

# Finance

(cap. = capital; res = reserves; dep. = deposits; brs = branches; m. = million; amounts in Tajik roubles, unless otherwise stated)

## BANKING

### Central Bank

**National Bank of the Republic of Tajikistan:** 734025 Dushanbe, pr. Rudaki 23/2; tel. (372) 21-26-28; fax (372) 51-00-68; e-mail root@natbank.tajnet.com; f. 1991; cap. 1,594m. Russian old roubles, res 1,025m. Russian old roubles, dep. 1,334,659m. Russian old roubles (Dec. 1993); Chair. MURODALI ALIMARDONOV; First Dep. Chair. SHARIF RAKHIMOV.

### Other Banks

According to the IMF, the number of commercial banks declined from 28 in 1997 to 14 in 2002, owing to consolidation.

**Agroinvestbank:** 734018 Dushanbe, pr. S. Sherozi 21; tel. (372) 21-03-85; fax (372) 21-12-06; e-mail invest@agrobank.td.silk.org; f. 1991; fmrly Agroprombank; cap. 198,411m., res 22,993m., dep. 3,218m. (Jan. 1998); Chair. MAKSUDJON SALYAMOVICH KADIROV; 64 brs.

**Orienbank:** 734001 Dushanbe, pr. Rudaki 95/1; tel. (372) 21-06-57; fax (372) 21-18-77; e-mail ved@orien.tojikiston.com; f. 1922 as republican office of Industrial Bank; cap. 1.2m. somoni, res 3.2m. somoni, dep. 21.8m. somoni (Dec. 2001); commercial bank; Chair. of Bd KURBONOV SAMIKHON; Chair. of Bank Council MALIKOV SHERMALIK; 28 brs.

**Somonbank:** 734025 Dushanbe, proyezd 1, Tursunzoda 3; tel. (372) 21-94-00; fax (372) 23-45-67; e-mail somonbank@tajnet.com.

**Tajbank:** 734064 Dushanbe, Ismail Somoni 59/1; tel. (372) 27-46-54.

**TajikSberbank** (Savings Bank): 734025 Dushanbe, pr. Rudaki 67; tel. (372) 22-70-81; fax (372) 23-14-53; f. 1991; fmrly br. of USSR Sberbank; licensed by presidential decree and not subject to the same controls as the commercial and trading banks; 58 brs, 480 sub-brs.

**Tajprombank:** 734025 Dushanbe, Kh. Dekhlavi 4; tel. (372) 21-26-42; fax (372) 21-25-85.

**Tajikvneshekonombank** (Bank for Foreign Economic Affairs of the Republic of Tajikistan—also known as Tojiksodirotbonk): 734012 Dushanbe, Dekhlavi 4; tel. (372) 21-47-38; fax (372) 21-59-52; e-mail shamatsob@tojikiston.com; fmrly br. of USSR Vneshekonombank; underwent restructuring in 1999; Chair. I. L. LALBEKOV; 6 brs.

## COMMODITY EXCHANGES

**Tajik Republican Commodity Exchange (NAVRUZ):** 374001 Dushanbe, Orjonikidze 37; tel. (372) 23-48-74; fax (372) 27-03-91; f. 1991; Chair. SULEYMAN CHULEBAYEV.

**Vostok-Mercury Torgovyi Dom:** Dushanbe; tel. and fax (372) 24-60-61; f. 1991; trades in a wide range of goods.

## INSURANCE

**Tajikgosstrakh:** Dushanbe, Akademikov Rajabovykh 3; tel. (372) 27-58-49; state-owned; Dir-Gen. MANSUR OCHILDEV.

# Trade and Industry

## GOVERNMENT AGENCY

**Drug Control Agency:** Dushanbe; f. 1999; documents and curbs regional drugs-trafficking; receives financial and technical assistance from the UN Office for Drug Control and Crime Prevention; Dir RUSTAM NAZAROV.

## CHAMBER OF COMMERCE

**Chamber of Commerce and Industry:** 734012 Dushanbe, Valamatzoda 21; tel. (372) 27-95-19; fax (372) 21-14-80; e-mail chamber@tajik.net; Chair. KAMOL SUFIYEV.

## INDUSTRIAL ASSOCIATION

**Tajikvneshtorg Industrial Association:** 734035 Dushanbe, POB 48, pr. Rudaki 25; tel. (372) 23-29-03; fax (372) 22-81-20; f. 1988; co-ordinates trade with foreign countries in a wide range of goods; Pres. ABDURAKHMON MUKHTASHOV.

## EMPLOYERS' ORGANIZATION

**National Association of Small and Medium-Sized Businesses of Tajikistan:** Dushanbe, Bofanda 9; tel. (372) 27-79-78; fax (372) 21-17-26; f. 1993 with govt support; independent org.; Chair. MATLJUBA ULJABAEVA.

## UTILITIES

### Electricity

**Barqi Tojik** (Tajik Electricity): Dushanbe, kuchai Ismoili Somoni 64; tel. (372) 35-87-66; Chair. NURMUHAMMADOV; First Dep. Chair. ALEKSEI SILANTAYEV.

**Pamir Energy Co (PamirEnergy):** Khorog; f. 2002; jt venture between Governments of Tajikistan and Switzerland, the Aga Khan Fund for Economic Development, International Finance Corpn and the International Development Association to provide electricity to Gornyi Badakhshan.

### Gas

**Dushanbe Gas Co:** supplies gas to Dushanbe region.

## MAJOR COMPANIES

The majority of small-scale state-owned enterprises had been privatized by the end of 2000, and 359 medium or large-scale enterprises had been privatized by November 2001.

**Aluminium Works of Tajikistan (TADAZ):** 735014 Tursan Zade; tel. (37730) 2-23-86; fax (37730) 2-32-57; f. 1975; state-owned enterprise; capacity of 500,000 metric tons per year (operated at 37% of its full capacity); third largest in the world; also producer of aluminium profiles, rolled metal, aluminium discs for car wheels, kitchen utensils; Gen. Dir ERMATOV ABDUKADIR; Chief Engineer SHARIPOV SADRIDIN; over 13,000 employees (1998).

**Aprelevka Joint-Stock Co:** e-mail gulfint@axionet.com; internet www.gulf-intl.com; Tajikistan holds 51% of shares and Gulf International Minerals of Canada holds 49%; work is carried out at nine gold deposits; Pres. ALASTAIR RALSTON-SAUL.

**Bokhtar:** 735140 Dushanbe, Karl Marx 9; tel. (372) 22-31-57; manufactures clothing, footwear, furniture; operates dry-cleaning establishments and vehicle service stations; Gen. Dir SAYIFOV MUKHIDDIN; 2,500 employees.

**Carpets of Kairakkum Open Joint-Stock Co:** Soghd Oblast, 735750 Kairakkum, Kovrovschikov 1; tel. (34) 432-36-01; fax (34) 226-07-93; e-mail kolinho@sugdien.com; internet www.carpets_of_kairakkum.ru; f. 1960, privatized 1994; produces half-woollen, woollen and cotton yarn, carpets, synthetic floor coverings; charter cap. US $1.84m.; Gen. Dir BAKHODUR AZIMOV; Financial Dir VALENTINA ABASKINA; 3,000 employees.

**Darvoz:** joint-venture gold mining co.

**Kolkhozabad Cotton Mill:** Khatlon Oblast, 735200 Kolkhozabad, Zheleznodorozhnaya 36; tel. (3774) 44-38-02; fax (3774) 42-36-64; f. 1966; produces cotton; Gen. Dir Mamadiso Kinzhayev.

**Kanibadam Plant:** Soghd Oblast; cotton-processing plant.

**Somonien Joint-Stock Company:** 734025 Dushanbe, pr. Rudaki 48; tel. (372) 23-29-03; fax (372) 21-81-20; f. 1988; import, export and foreign trade, assists in the development of foreign trading activities, organizes exhibitions, tourism; Pres. Abdurakhman Mukhtashov; 73 employees.

**Tajikles:** Dushanbe, Shotemura 31; tel. (372) 27-68-88; state-owned; wood processing; Dir-Gen. Gaibullo Fazylov.

**Tajikneftprodukt:** Dushanbe, Khuseinzoda 14; tel. (372) 21-59-37; state-owned; Chair. Amonullo Khukumov.

**Tajikneft Production Association:** 734018 Dushanbe, Mushfiki 77; tel. (372) 33-60-96; petroleum and gas exploration and production; Gen. Dir N. Malikov.

**Temurmalik:** Kairakkum, Lenina 10; tel. (34) 434-35-73; state-owned; privatization under way in 2002; processing and sale of flour.

**Umron Joint-Stock Co:** Dushanbe, pr. Rudaki 3A; tel. (372) 21-88-13; Pres. Kim Nazirov.

**Vakhsh Fertilizer Factory:** Khatlon Oblast; producer of nitrogenous fertilizers.

**Vostokredmet Industrial Association:** 735730 Chkalovsk; formerly processed uranium for Soviet nuclear industry, but converted to gold refining in 1993; 35,000 employees (1993).

**Zeravshan Gold Co:** 734003 Dushanbe, pr. Rudaki 137, 4th floor; tel. (372) 21-98-54; fax (372) 51-01-55; internet www.nelsongold .com; f. 1996; joint-venture co; Nelson Gold Ltd (Bermuda-based) holds a 44% stake; mine at Sogdiana, Panjikent.

### TRADE UNIONS

**Federation of Trade Unions:** Dushanbe, pr. Rudaki 20; tel. (372) 23-35-16; Chair. Murodali Salikhov.

# Transport

### RAILWAYS

There are few railways in Tajikistan. In 1999 the total length of the rail network was 482 km. Lines link the major centres of the country with the railway network of Uzbekistan, connecting Khujand (Khodzhent) to the Fergana valley lines, and the cotton-growing centre of Qurgonteppa (Kurgan-Tyube) to Termez. A new line, between the town of Isfara, in Soghd region, and Khavast, in Uzbekistan, was opened in 1995 and in 1997 a passenger route between Dushanbe and Volgograd, Russia, was inaugurated. The first section of a new line, between Qurgonteppa and Kulob (Kulyab) in the south-west of the country, was inaugurated in 1998. In October 2002 a new route from Kulob to Astrakhan, Russia, was opened. The predominantly mountainous terrain makes the construction of a more extensive network unlikely.

**Tajik Railways:** 734012 Dushanbe, Nazarshoyeva 35; tel. (372) 21-88-54; fax (372) 21-83-34; f. 1994; comprises part of the former Soviet Railways' Central Asian network; Pres. M. Khabibov.

### ROADS

In mid-2002 Tajikistan's road network totalled an estimated 30,000 km (13,747 km highways and 8,965 km local roads). The principal highway of Tajikistan is the road that links the northern city of Khujand, across the Anzob Pass (3,372 m), with the capital, Dushanbe, and carries on to the border town of Khorog (Gornyi Badakhshan), before wending through the Pamir Mountains, north, to the Kyrgyz city of Osh, across the Akbaytal Pass (4,655 m). This arterial route exhibits problems common to much of the country's land transport: winter weather is likely to cause the road to be closed by snow for up to eight months of the year. In early 2000 Tajikistan and the Asian Development Bank signed a memorandum of understanding for the rehabilitation of the road linking Dushanbe to the south-western cities of Qurgonteppa and Kulob. In the same year a road linking eastern Tajikistan with the People's Republic of China was completed, giving Tajikistan access to the Karakorum highway, which connects China and Pakistan.

### CIVIL AVIATION

The main international airport is at Dushanbe, although there is also a major airport at Khujand. The country is linked to cities in Russia and other former Soviet republics, and also to a growing number of destinations in Europe and Asia. The reconstruction of

Khujand airport was completed by a joint Tajik-Indian company in late 2000.

**Tajikistan Airlines (TZK):** 734006 Dushanbe, Dushanbe Airport, Titova 31/2; tel. (372) 21-21-95; fax (372) 21-86-85; e-mail tt_gart@ tajnet.com; f. 1990; formerly known as Tajik Air; state-owned; operates flights to Russia, India, Pakistan, Iran, Turkey, Kazakhstan, Kyrgyzstan, Germany, the United Arab Emirates and Uzbekistan; commenced weekly flights to Afghanistan in March 2002; Gen. Dir Mirzo Mastangulov.

# Tourism

There was little tourism in Tajikistan even before the outbreak of civil war. There is some spectacular mountain scenery, hitherto mainly visited by climbers, and, particularly in the Fergana valley, in the north of the country, there are sites of historical interest, notably the city of Khujand.

**Tajikistan Republican Council of Tourism and Excursions:** 734018 Dushanbe, S. Sherozi 11; tel. (372) 33-27-70; fax (372) 33-44-20.

**'Sayoh' National Tourism Company:** 734025 Dushanbe, Pushkinskaya 14; tel. (372) 23-14-01; fax (372) 23-42-33; e-mail gafarov@ td.silk.org; internet www.tajiktour.tajnet.com; Chair. Gafarov Kasim.

# Culture

Tajikistan has a rich cultural heritage. A 14-m statue of a sleeping Buddha, dating from the fifth century, was uncovered by archaeologists in 1966. The region's largest ancient Buddha statue was placed on display in August 2001 in the newly opened Museum of National Antiquities. The museum also houses a fifth-century statue of the Hindu god Shiva, which is believed to be the largest artefact illustrating the spread of Hinduism into the northern part of Central Asia.

### NATIONAL ORGANIZATION

**Ministry of Culture:** see section on The Government (Ministries).

### CULTURAL HERITAGE

**Ethnographic Museum:** Dushanbe; tel. (372) 21-07-64; Dir Zebo Kavrakova.

**Firdousi State Public Library of the Republic of Tajikistan:** 734025 Dushanbe, pr. Rudaki 36; tel. (372) 27-47-26; 2,298,000 vols; Dir S. Mukhiddinov.

**Lohuti Tajik Drama Theatre:** Dushanbe; tel. (372) 21-78-43; Dir Iso Abdurashidov.

**Mayakovskii State Drama Theatre:** Dushanbe, pr. Rudaki 76; tel. (372) 21-31-32; e-mail teatrmayaktj@mail.ru; Dir Sukhrob Mirzoev.

**Museum of National Antiquities:** Dushanbe; includes ancient Islamic, Buddhist, Zoroastrian and Hindu artefacts; Dir Saidmurad Babamulloyev.

**Opera and Ballet Theatre:** Dushanbe; tel. (372) 21-80-47; Dir Nariman Karimov.

**Puppet Theatre:** Dushanbe; tel. (372) 23-15-83; Man. Rustam Akhmadov.

**Republican Museum:** Dushanbe; tel. (372) 23-15-44; Dir Sangin Khafizov.

**Shahidi Museum of Musical Culture:** Dushanbe, Shakhidi 108; tel. (372) 24-23-42; Dir Munira Shahidi.

**State Dance Ensemble 'Lola':** Dushanbe; tel. (372) 21-12-13; Man. Radif Yafaev.

**Tajik State Historical Museum:** 734012 Dushanbe, Ayni 31; tel. (372) 23-15-44; f. 1934; museum and art gallery; 55,000 items; library of over 17,000 vols; Dir Mazbut M. Makhmudov.

**Theatre-Studio 'Akhorun':** Dushanbe; tel. (372) 27-09-68; Chief Dir Farrukh Kosimov.

### SPORTING ORGANIZATION

**National Olympic Committee of the Republic of Tajikistan:** 734025 Dushanbe, Aini 24, POB 2; tel. (372) 21-75-51; fax (372) 51-00-73; e-mail noc@tajik.net; f. 1992; Pres. Gafar Mirsoyev; Sec-Gen. Shirindzhon Mamadsafoyev.

## ASSOCIATIONS

**Scientific Industrial Union of Tajikistan:** Dushanbe, pr. Rudaki 6; tel. (372) 27-23-29; Chair. ABDURAKHMON DADABAEV.

**Union of Artists:** Dushanbe, pr. Rudaki 89; tel. (372) 24-15-71; Chair. SUKHROB KURBONOV.

**Union of Cinematographers:** Dushanbe, Bukhoro 43; tel. (372) 21-75-09; Chair. ANVAR TURAEV.

**Union of Journalists:** Khorog, Ismaelova 46; tel. (3779) 10-24-73; Chair. BURIBEK BURIBEKOV; 65 mems.

**Union of Theatre Workers:** Dushanbe, pr. Rudaki 107; tel. (372) 24-29-68; Chair. ATO MUKHAMADJONOV.

**Union of Writers of Tajikistan:** 734001 Dushanbe, Putovskogo 8; tel. (372) 24-57-37; Chair. ASKAR KHAKIM.

# Education

Education is controlled by the Ministry of Education and was, under the Soviet system, fully funded by the state at all levels. Education is officially compulsory for nine years, to be undertaken between seven and 17 years of age. Primary education begins at seven years of age and lasts for four years. Secondary education, beginning at the age of 11, lasts for as much as seven years, comprising a first cycle of five years and a second of two years. In 1996 the total enrolment at primary schools was equivalent to 95% of the relevant age-group. In 2000/01 total enrolment in secondary education was equivalent to 76% of the relevant age-group.

The majority of pupils received their education in Tajik (66.0% of pupils in general day schools in 1988). Following the adoption of Tajik as the state language, greater emphasis was placed in the curriculum on Tajik language and literature, including classical Persian literature. In May 2003 President Imamali Rakhmonov announced that the compulsory teaching of Russian was to be reintroduced to schools from September of that year.

Constitutional amendments approved by referendum in June 2003 were to provide for the withdrawal of guarantees of free higher education. In 2001/02 there were 84,400 students enrolled at 31 institutes of higher education. Agreement on the establishment of a joint Russian-Tajik Slavonic University in Dushanbe was reached in 1997. In 2000 the Presidents of Kazakhstan, Kyrgyzstan and Tajikistan co-signed a charter of foundation for a new University of Central Asia, which was to be established in Khorog and administered by the Aga Khan Development Network, based in Geneva, Switzerland. Expenditure on education by all levels of government was forecast at 112m. somoni (13.2% of total anticipated government expenditure) in 2003.

## UNIVERSITIES

**Khujand State University:** Khujand, B. Mavlonbekova 1; tel. (34) 226-75-18; fax 224-08-15; e-mail public@edu.khj.td.silk.org; f. 1991; fmrly Khujand Pedagological Institute; 14 faculties; 1 pedagogical college; Rector ABDULLOEV SAIDULLO.

**Russian-Tajik Slavonic University:** Dushanbe.

**Tajik State Agricultural University:** 734017 Dushanbe, pr. Rudaki 146; tel. (372) 24-72-07; f. 1931; languages of instruction: Tajik and Russian; 482 teachers; 6,960 students; Rector Prof. YU. S. NAZYROV.

**Tajik State Medical University:** 734003 Dushanbe, pr. Rudaki 139; f. 1996; fmrly Tajik Abu-Ali Ibn-Cina (Avicenna) State Medical Institute; languages of instruction: Tajik and Russian.

**Tajik State Technical University:** Dushanbe, pr. Acad. Rajabovs 10; tel. (372) 21-35-11; fax (372) 21-71-35; e-mail chief@tecuni2.td.silk.glas.org; f. 1956; fmrly Tajik Academician M. S. Osimi Technical University; comprises a branch at Khujand (mechanical and technological faculties), polytechnic, technical college, technological college; languages of instruction: Tajik and Russian; 450 teachers, 8,000 students; Rector Prof. KHISRAV R. SADIKOV.

**Tajik State National University:** 734025 Dushanbe, pr. Rudaki 17; tel. (372) 22-77-11; fax (372) 21-48-84; e-mail tgnu@mail.ru; internet www.tsnu.tojikiston.com; f. 1948; languages of instruction: Tajik and Russian; 12 faculties; 1,228 teachers; 13,060 students; Rector Prof. KH. S. SAFIYEV.

# Social Welfare

Under the Soviet system there was a fully state-funded health and social-welfare system, largely dependent upon transfers from the all-Union budget. There were reforms aimed at making the social-security system self-financing to a greater degree, notably with the help of employee and employer contributions. At the beginning of 1992 an Employment Fund was established and the Pension Fund and Fund for Social Expenditure (social insurance) were reformed. Even before the problems of the civil war their operations were expected to produce a deficit, and tax avoidance problems had increased significantly by the mid-1990s. In theory, social guarantees consisted of five elements: family allowances (including student grants and compensation for reductions in the bread-price subsidy); Pension Fund provision for old age, disability or social reasons; Employment Fund assistance in training, labour placement and unemployment benefits; social insurance payments for sick pay, remedial health-care services and maternity allowances; and price subsidies. Tajikistan also received a high level of international humanitarian assistance. In 1996 a Public Social Protection Fund was established to address the problem of pension arrears. In May 1998 new benefits were introduced for students, pensioners and disabled people to enable them to meet rising living costs.

The civil war of 1992–93 produced some 600,000 refugees, both internally and in neighbouring countries. Gornyi Badakhshan was largely isolated from supplies from November 1992 until August 1993. By the beginning of 1996 many refugees had been able to return to their homes and the confirmation in June 1997 of the peace agreement of December 1996 provided some stability in the country, although there were further outbreaks of violence. Between July 1997 and January 1998 the last groups of refugees returned from camps in northern Afghanistan, finding their homes in ruins or occupied by others. In 1996 there were 24,160 nurses, 5,231 midwives and 959 dentists. In 1998 there were an estimated 2.0 physicians per 1,000 inhabitants and 676 hospital beds per 100,000 inhabitants. Projected expenditure by the Government on health and social security and welfare amounted to 141m. somoni in 2003 (equivalent to 16.6% of total anticipated expenditure).

## NATIONAL AGENCIES

**Ministry of Health:** see section on The Government (Ministries).

## HEALTH AND WELFARE ORGANIZATIONS

**Society for the Blind:** Dushanbe, Karamova 205; tel. (372) 37-32-31; Chair. TURABEK DAVLATOV.

**Society for the Deaf:** Dushanbe, Khuvaidulloev 270; tel. (372) 36-71-21; Chair. GALINA MALISHEVA.

**Society of Invalids:** Dushanbe, Telmana 4; tel. (372) 21-15-74; Chair. KHAKIM KHAKNAZAROV.

# The Environment

Tajikistan was less affected than other former Soviet Central Asian countries by the consequences of over-irrigation, but not completely immune, and there was some concern at intensive fertilizer use in the southern cotton-growing regions. The country was important as a water source for Turkmenistan, in particular. There was anxiety about the effect on the extensive glaciers of the Pamir mountains of wind-borne pesticides and other chemicals from the Aral region, and concern regarding the reduction of the water level of the Aral Sea basin, owing to over-utilization.

## GOVERNMENT ORGANIZATION

**Ministry of Environmental Protection:** see section on The Government (Ministries).

**Ministry of Land Improvement and Water Economy:** see section on The Government (Ministries).

## ACADEMIC INSTITUTES

**Academy of Sciences of the Republic of Tajikistan:** 734025 Dushanbe, pr. Rudaki 33; tel. (372) 22-50-83; fax (372) 23-49-11; e-mail academy@science.tajik.net; f. 1951; Pres. Dr ULMAS MIRSAIDOV; institutes incl.:

> **Department of Conservation and the Rational Use of Natural Resources:** 734025 Dushanbe, Kommunisticheskaya 42; in the Dept of Biological Sciences; Dir K. A. NASREDDINOV.

## NON-GOVERNMENTAL ORGANIZATIONS

**Dushanbe Environmental Movement:** Dushanbe; e-mail isarata@glas.apc.org; deals with ecotourism and environmental monitoring; Contact MIKHAIL TYUTIN.

**Pamir Ecocentre:** Pamir Biological Institute, Khorog, Michurina 1; tel. (3779) 10-41-82; e-mail ogonazar@td.silk.glas.apc.org; f. 1994; conducts environmental education programmes for youth and works to protect the environment of the Pamir region; 2 brs.

**Scientific Education Centre for Tajik Ecologists:** Dushanbe, Chekhova 13; tel. (372) 21-59-86.

**Tajikistan Socio-Ecological Union:** 734043 Dushanbe, Maya-kovskogo 46/2, kv. 34; tel. (372) 36-86-29; Chair. MUAZAMA ALIKU-LOVNA BURKHANOVA; Sec. HAMID ABDULLAYEVICH ATAKHANOV.

**Union of Ecologists and Specialists of the Climate of the Republic of Tajikistan:** Dushanbe; tel. (372) 34-08-30; Pres. ASLOV SIRADJIDIN.

# Defence

Tajikistan began to form its own national armed forces and border guard during 1993. Many of the personnel were from the pro-communist militias of the civil war, but were to be trained by Russian army officers. In August 2002 there was an army of 6,000. There were also an estimated 1,200 paramilitary border guards, who are responsible to the Ministry of Internal Affairs. In addition, there were some 12,000 Tajik conscripts serving as border guards under the control of the Russian armed forces (of which there were an estimated 7,800). The small army airforce of 800 has no combat aircraft, and only a small number of armed helicopters. In 1998 integration of members of the UTO forces, which numbered some 5,000, into the Tajik armed forces began. There were also an esti-mated 20,000 forces of the CIS based in the country (most of whom were from the Russian army). The budget for 2002 allocated an estimated US \$14.8m. to defence. The President of the Republic, the Commander-in-Chief, formed an advisory Security Council in April 1996. In February 2002 Tajikistan became a member of the North Atlantic Treaty Organization's (NATO) 'Partnership for Peace' pro-gramme of military co-operation.

**Commander-in-Chief:** President of the Republic.

**Commander of the Air Force:** RAKHMONALI DAVLATOVICH SAFAR-ALIYEV.

# Bibliography

Abdullaev, Kamoloudin, and Akbarzadeh, Shahram. *Historical Dictionary of Tajikistan.* Lanham, MD, Rowman and Littlefield, 2002.

Akiner, Shirin. *Islamic People of the Soviet Union: An Historical and Statistical Handbook*, 2nd edn. London and New York, NY, Kegan Paul International, 1987.

*Tajikistan.* Washington, DC, Brookings Institution Press, 1998.

*The Tajik War: A Challenge to Russian Policy.* London, Royal Institute of International Affairs, 1997.

*Tajikistan: Disintegration or Reconciliation?* London, Royal Institute of International Affairs, 2002.

Akiner, Shirin, Djalili, Mohammad Reza, and Grare, Frederic (Eds). *Tajikistan: The Trials of Independence.* New York, NY, St Martin's Press, 1998.

Anderson, John. *The International Politics of Central Asia.* Manchester, Manchester University Press, 1997.

Atkin, Muriel. *The Subtlest Battle: Islam in Soviet Tajikistan (The Philadelphia Papers).* University Press of USA, 1989.

Curtin, Molly. *Environmental Profile of Tajikistan.* Manila, Asian Development Bank, 2001.

Falkingham, Jane. *Women and Gender Relations in Tajikistan.* Manila, Asian Development Bank, 2001.

Jawad, Nassim, and Tadjbakhsh, Shahrbanou. *Tajikistan: a Forgotten Civil War.* London, Minority Rights Group, 1995.

Kosach, G. K. 'Tajikistan: Political Parties in Inchoate National Space', in *Muslim Eurasia—Conflicting Legacies*, Y. Ro'i (Ed.), pp. 123–42. London, Frank Cass, 1995.

Lubin, Nancy, Martin, Keith, and Rubin, Barnett R. *Calming the Ferghana Valley: Development and Dialogue in the Heart of Central Asia.* Washington, DC, Brookings Institution Press, 2000.

Martin, K. 'Tajikistan: Civil War without End?' in *RFE/RL Research Report*, Vol. 2, No. 33. Munich, RFE/RL, 1993.

Nourzhanov, Kirill. *Tajikistan: the History of an Ethnic State.* London, C. Hurst and Co, 2002.

Odling-Smee, John. *Tajikistan.* Washington, DC, IMF, 1994.

Rubin, Barnett R. 'Tajikistan: From Soviet Republic to Russian–Uzbek Protectorate', in *Central Asia and the World*, M. Mandelbaum (Ed.), pp. 207–40. New York, NY, Council on Foreign Relations Press, 1994.

'Russian Hegemony and State Breakdown in the Periphery: Causes and Consequences of the Civil War in Tajikistan', in *Post-Soviet Political Order: Conflict and State Building*, B. Rubin and J. Snyder (Eds), pp. 128–61. London, Routledge, 1998.

Saavalainen, T. *Republic of Tajikistan.* Washington, DC, International Monetary Fund, 2001.

Thubron, Colin. *The Lost Heart of Asia.* London, Heinemann, 2000.

Also see the Select Bibliography in Part Four.

# TURKMENISTAN

## Geography

### PHYSICAL FEATURES

The Republic of Turkmenistan, or Turkmenia (formerly the Turkmen Soviet Socialist Republic, a constituent partner in the USSR), is situated in the south-west of Central Asia. It is bordered on the north by Uzbekistan, on the north-west by Kazakhstan and on the west by the Caspian Sea. To the south lies Iran and, to the south-east, Afghanistan. The country has an area of 488,100 sq km (188,456 sq miles).

The Kara-Kum (Black Sand) desert, one of the largest sand deserts in the world, covers more than four-fifths of Turkmenistan, occupying the entire central region. There are mountainous areas along the southern and north-western borders, including the Kopet-Dag range, along the frontier with Afghanistan, which is prone to earthquakes. The main river is the Amu-Dar'ya (Oxus), which flows through the eastern regions of the country and used to empty into the Aral Sea. The Kara-Kum Canal, which was begun in 1954, carries water from the Amu-Dar'ya to the arid central and western regions of Turkmenistan, where there are no significant natural waterways. However, the existence of this Canal is one of the main factors contributing to the desiccation of the Aral Sea, as the Amu-Dar'ya dries up before reaching it. The other major rivers are the Murgab, which flows south into Afghanistan, and the Tejen, which also flows south and forms part of the border with Iran.

### CLIMATE

The climate is severely continental, with extremely hot summers and cold winters. The average temperature in January is −4°C (25°F), but winter temperatures can fall as low as −33°C (−27°F). In summer temperatures often reach 50°C (122°F) in the south-east Kara-Kum; the average temperature in July is 28°C (82°F). Precipitation is slight throughout much of the region. Average annual rainfall ranges from only 80 mm in the north-west to about 300 mm per year in mountainous regions.

### POPULATION

The largest ethnic group is the Turkmen (77.0% of the population, according to the census of January 1995). Minority groups included Uzbeks (9.2%), Russians (6.7%) and Kazakhs (2.0%). There were small communities of other ethnic groups, such as Tatars (numbering an estimated 39,000 in 1993), Ukrainians (34,000), Azeris (34,000), Armenians (32,000) and Baluchis, an Iranian (Persian) people, most of whom live in Pakistan and Iran (who numbered some 28,000 in 1989). Among the Turkmen there remains a strong sense of tribal loyalty, reinforced by dialect. The largest tribes are the Tekke

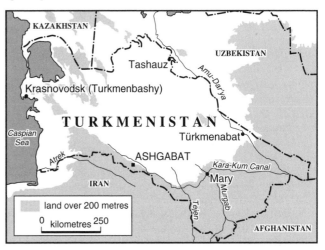

in central Turkmenistan, the Ersary in the south-east and the Yomud in the west of the country. Other Turkmen tribes live in Iran. In 1990 Turkmen was declared the official language of the republic. Russian is also used, but in 1989 only some 25% of Turkmen claimed fluency in Russian. Turkmen is a member of the Southern Turkic group of languages; in 1927 the traditional Arabic script was replaced by a Latin script, which was, in turn, replaced by a Cyrillic script in 1938. In 1993 it was announced that the republic would gradually change to a Latin-based Turkish script. Most of the population are Sunni Muslims. Islam in Turkmenistan traditionally featured elements of Sufi mysticism and shamanism, and pilgrimages to local religious sites were reported to be common.

There are large discrepancies between official and external estimates of the total population. According to the National Institute of State Statistics and Information, the total estimated population at 1 July 2002 was 5,725,200. However, according to UN estimates, the population numbered 4,794,000 at mid-2002, giving a population density of 9.8 per sq km. In 2002, according to official estimates, 46% of the population was urban. Most non-Turkmen live in urban areas: 41% of the population of the capital, Ashgabat (Ashkhabad), were Russian in 1990. Ashgabat is in the south of the country, near the border with Iran. In 2002 it had an estimated population of 743,000. Türkmenabat (formerly Charjew), situated on the Amu-Dar'ya, is the second-largest city (its population was estimated at 203,000 in 1999). Other important centres include Dashkhovuz (Tashauz—165,000 in 1999), Mary (formerly Merv—123,000), Balkanabat (formerly Nebit-Dag—119,000) and the Caspian port of Turkmenbashy (formerly known as Krasnovodsk).

# Chronology

**552–659:** Turkic tribes moved west and settled in the area of modern Turkmenistan.

**644–61:** Southern areas of modern Turkmenistan, including Mary (Merv), were conquered for Islam under Caliphs 'Uthman and 'Ali.

**661–750:** Central and eastern areas of Turkmenistan were taken by Muslims during the Ummayad dynasty.

**10th century:** Turkic Oguz tribes, ancestors of the Turkmen, migrated to Turkmenistan.

**1038–1194:** Southern and eastern areas of Turkmenistan formed part of the territory of the Seljuq Turkic dynasty.

**1219–25:** Mongol forces under Temujin (Chinghiz or Genghis Khan) attacked Khwarezm, formerly a territory owing allegiance to the Abbasid caliphate, conquering the Empire of the Khwarezm Shah.

**1251–65:** Hulagu, a grandson of Chinghiz Khan, established the Empire of the Il-Khans, which included all but the extreme north-west of modern Turkmenistan.

**1353:** The Il-Khans were replaced by a local Turkmen dynasty who established beyliks, administrative areas ruled by beys (princes).

**1370–80:** A Turkmen emir from Transoxania, in modern Uzbekistan, Timur ('the Lame'—Tamerlane), founded the second Mongol Empire, which included the territories of the Turkmen. Timur's empire disintegrated rapidly after his death in 1405 and control of Transoxania passed to the Uzbek tribes.

**17th century:** Southern areas of Turkmenistan, including Mary, were dominated by the Safavid dynasty of Persia (Iran).

**1868–73:** The Uzbek-ruled khanates of Bukhara and Khiva, which had disputed Persia for control of Turkmen territories for more than one century, were made protectorates of the Russian Empire. The Russians also gained control of western areas of Turkmenistan adjacent to the Caspian Sea.

**1881:** After a four-year campaign by the Russians against the tribes of central Turkmenistan, an estimated 14,500 Turkmen were killed at the battle of Gök Tepe (near Ashgabat—Ashkhabad).

**1884:** Persia ceded control of the territories near Mary, which became the southernmost part of the Russian Empire.

**1895:** The United Kingdom and Russia established the southern boundary of modern Turkmenistan, when they demarcated the British and Russian 'spheres of influence'.

**1917:** Following an unsuccessful Bolshevik attempt to gain power, an anti-Bolshevik Russian Provisional Government of Transcaspia and a Turkmen Congress were established.

**30 April 1918:** The Turkestan Autonomous Soviet Socialist Republic, including Transcaspia, was proclaimed after Bolshevik forces had occupied Ashgabat.

**July 1918:** Turkmen nationalists, with limited support from the British, overthrew the Bolshevik regime and created an independent state based in Ashgabat.

**1920:** Following the British withdrawal from the area, Ashgabat was captured by the Red Army and the Turkmen leader, Muhammad Qurban Junaid Khan, joined the *basmachi* resistance (which continued into the mid-1930s).

**27 October 1924:** The Turkmen Soviet Socialist Republic (SSR) was established, becoming a Union Republic of the Soviet federation the following May.

**1927:** The traditional Turkmen Arabic script was replaced by a Latin script.

**1928:** The Soviet authorities began to outlaw religious practices in Turkmenistan and the majority of mosques and other Islamic institutions were closed down.

**1929:** An agricultural collectivization programme was begun, under which nomadic tribes were forced to settle in collective farms.

***c.* 1937:** The execution of Nederbai Aitakov, 'nationalist' Chairman of the Turkmen Supreme Soviet, was the most notable example of the persecution of Turkmen intellectuals, politicians and even communist officials, which was prevalent during the 1930s.

**1938:** The Latin alphabet introduced in 1927 was replaced by a Cyrillic script.

**1954:** Construction work began on the Kara-Kum Canal, which conveys water from the Amu-Dar'ya river (the Oxus of ancient times) on the eastern border of Turkmenistan, to irrigate dry central and western areas of the country; the Canal is a principal cause of the desiccation of the Aral Sea.

**1958:** Babayev, First Secretary of the Communist Party of Turkmenistan (CPT), proposed an increase in the number of ethnic Turkmen in positions of importance, many of which were held by Russians; subsequently Babayev and a large number of his political colleagues were dismissed from office.

**1985:** Saparmyrat Niyazov became First Secretary of the CPT.

**September 1989:** Turkmen intellectuals formed Agzybirlik (Unity), a 'popular-front' organization concerned with cultural, economic and environmental issues; the movement was officially registered in the following month, but was banned in January 1990.

**7 January 1990:** Only the CPT and other approved organizations were allowed to participate in elections to the Supreme Soviet and local councils; consequently the CPT obtained the majority of seats. Niyazov was later elected Chairman of the new Supreme Soviet.

**May 1990:** Turkmenistan followed the example of other Soviet Republics by replacing Russian with the local tongue (Turkmen) as the official language.

**22 August 1990:** The Turkmen Supreme Soviet adopted a declaration of sovereignty, which asserted Turkmenistan's right to secede from the USSR.

**27 October 1990:** Niyazov was unopposed in direct elections for the first executive President of the Republic, receiving 98.3% of the votes cast.

**17 March 1991:** After several months of negotiations for a new Union Treaty, an all-Union referendum was held and 95.7% of the participating electorate in Turkmenistan approved the 'renewal' of the USSR.

**June 1991:** The Turkmen Supreme Soviet adopted a Law on Freedom of Conscience and Religious Organizations.

**18–21 August 1991:** There was little official reaction to the attempted conservative coup in the USSR; however, opposition groups such as Agzybirlik publicly denounced it and attempted to form a coalition, resulting in the arrest of several of their leaders.

**27 October 1991:** The Supreme Soviet declared the country independent the day after 94.1% of voters opted for independence in a national referendum on the issue; the name of the Turkmen SSR was changed to the Republic of Turkmenistan.

**December 1991:** The CPT became known as the Democratic Party of Turkmenistan (DPT), under the chairmanship of Niyazov.

**21 December 1991:** Turkmenistan and 10 other former Union Republics signed the Almaty (Alma-Ata) Declaration establishing the Commonwealth of Independent States (CIS), effectively dissolving the USSR.

**18 May 1992:** A new Constitution was adopted, which increased the powers of the President of the Republic, who became, conjointly, Prime Minister and Supreme Commander-in-Chief of the Armed Forces; the Supreme Soviet was to continue to act as the legislature, the Majlis, until elections were held, after which the body would have 50 members; the Constitution also established the Khalk Maslakhaty (People's Council) as a supervisory national assembly.

**21 June 1992:** Niyazov was re-elected unopposed as President, receiving 99.5% of the votes cast.

**July 1992:** Abdy Kuliyev resigned as Minister of Foreign Affairs, allegedly over Niyazov's growing authoritarianism. Kuliyev subsequently established an opposition grouping based in Moscow, Russia.

**September 1992:** Niyazov was the sole recipient of the country's highest honour, Hero of Turkmenistan (formally conferred in October).

**November 1992:** Elections for the 50 regional representatives to the Khalk Maslakhaty were held (the first session of the Council took place in mid-December).

**January 1993:** Electricity, gas and water supplies were made free to all citizens of Turkmenistan.

**May 1993:** Turkmenistan alone declined to sign a declaration of intent to form a CIS economic union, indicating its preference for securing real independence. The Council of Elders resolved that Niyazov be commemorated in all centres of population.

**October 1993:** The Khalk Maslakhaty conferred the title of Turkmenbashy (Leader of the Turkmen) on President Niyazov.

**1 November 1993:** Turkmenistan introduced its own currency, the manat, and a number of economic reforms.

**23 December 1993:** President Niyazov and the Russian President, Boris Yeltsin, signed an agreement, unique in the former Soviet countries, granting ethnic Russians in Turkmenistan dual nationality with the Russian Federation.

**15 January 1994:** In a referendum proposed by the DPT, 99.9% of the electorate voted to exempt President Niyazov from having to seek re-election in 1997, ostensibly in order to allow the completion of economic reform.

**April 1994:** A council for religious affairs, the Gengesh, was created within the presidential office—it was chaired by the Kazi of Turkmenistan, with the leading Orthodox bishop as his deputy.

**11 December 1994:** Elections to the new, 50-member Majlis were held, with the participation of 99.8% of the electorate; 49 of the deputies were elected unopposed. The Majlis convened later in the month.

**12 July 1995:** Demonstrations took place in Ashgabat and Mary in criticism of Niyazov's leadership and of continuing economic hardship.

**October 1995:** President Niyazov announced the introduction of a six-month probationary period for new ministers. Turkmenistan became the first former Soviet state to become a member of the Non-aligned Movement, at its summit in Cartagena, Colombia—the co-ordinating country.

**12 December 1995:** The UN General Assembly recognized Turkmenistan's neutral status.

**12 July 1996:** A presidential decree introduced electricity charges for domestic consumers.

**January 1997:** A dispute with Azerbaijan over two Caspian oilfields, which were being developed by Azerbaijan and a consortium of international companies, confirmed the need for an agreement on maritime boundaries by the littoral states of the Caspian Sea.

**26 March 1998:** A new Civil Code, providing a legal framework for regulating market relations and property and insurance issues, was enacted by the Majlis.

**5 April 1998:** Elections to the Khalk Maslakhaty were held, with the participation of 99.5% of the electorate.

**7 July 1998:** At a meeting held in Tehran, Iran, President Niyazov supported an equal division of the Caspian Sea by the five littoral states (rather than sharing its resources, according to international custom with transboundary inland waters).

**August 1998:** The US bombing of an alleged terrorist base in Afghanistan caused Unocal, a US company involved in the construction of a gas pipeline from Turkmenistan to Pakistan via Afghanistan, to suspend its involvement in the project (although the Turkmenistani Government insisted that Unocal should honour the contract).

**12 December 1999:** Legislative elections were held to the 50-seat Majlis, with an official participation rate of 98.9%. The DPT was the only party represented.

**27 December 1999:** The Khalk Maslakhaty voted to abolish the death penalty; Turkmenistan thereby became the first Central Asian state to do so. On the following day the new Majlis approved an amendment to the Constitution, permitting Niyazov to remain President indefinitely. Niyazov subsequently announced that no opposition parties would be allowed to be formed until 2010.

**18 April 2000:** The European Bank for Reconstruction and Development (EBRD) announced that it was to suspend public-sector loans to Turkmenistan, in protest at Niyazov's anti-democratic policies.

**7 September 2000:** Turkmenistan became a member of the Asian Development Bank (ADB).

**23 September 2000:** A border treaty defining the 1,867 km border between Turkmenistan and Uzbekistan was signed by the two countries in Almaty, Kazakhstan.

**9 October 2000:** Kazakhstan signed a co-operation agreement with Russia on resolving the legal status of the Caspian Sea; the two Governments urged Azerbaijan, Iran and Turkmenistan to hold a summit meeting to discuss the issue.

**18 February 2001:** President Niyazov declared his intention to resign by 2010.

**4 April 2001:** President Niyazov shut down opera and ballet theatres, denouncing them as 'alien' to Turkmen culture.

**17 April 2001:** The Khalk Maslakhaty announced that a Central Committee for Elections and Consultations would be established.

**26–27 April 2001:** At a meeting of leaders of the Turkic-speaking countries, the Presidents of Azerbaijan, Kazakhstan, Kyrgyzstan, Turkey and Turkmenistan, and the Chairman of Uzbekistan's Oly Majlis (Supreme Assembly) signed an agreement on regional co-operation to combat terrorism and drugs trafficking, the revival of the old 'Silk Road' trade route between the People's Republic of China and Europe, and protection of the environment.

**24 September 2001:** President Niyazov was reported to have given his consent to the use of Turkmenistan's ground and air transport corridors in order to deliver humanitarian aid to Afghanistan in the event of airstrikes against the Taliban and the Islamist fundamentalist, Osama bin Laden. The President refused US troops access to Turkmenistan's military bases.

**19 October 2001:** The Khalk Maslakhaty voted to confer President Niyazov with his fourth Hero of Turkmenistan award and adopted Niyazov's national code of spiritual conduct, the 'Ruhnama'.

**1 November 2001:** A former Minister of Foreign Affairs, Boris Shikhmuradov, who had fled to Moscow in October, publicly declared his opposition to President Niyazov. The Turkmen authorities subsequently filed a number of criminal charges against Shikhmuradov, amid reports that he was intending to instigate a *coup d'état*.

**1 January 2002:** The requirement for those leaving Turkmenistan to obtain an exit visa was abolished for the majority of Turkmen citizens (although it was reinstated in July for those travelling to Iran or Uzbekistan).

**4 January 2002:** Boris Shikhmuradov, who remained in exile, established the opposition People's Democratic Movement of Turkmenistan, and publicly urged Niyazov to resign from office.

**14 March 2002:** In response to increasing opposition activity, Niyazov began a massive purge of high-ranking officials from the security and intelligence agencies. Prominent dismissals included that of the Minister of Defence, Gurbandurdy Begenjev, and the head of the Committee for National Security (KNB), Mukhammed Nazarov.

**6 May 2002:** The Chairman of the Central Bank and Deputy Prime Minister, Seitbay Gandimov, was dismissed from his post for 'professional shortcomings', and replaced by Imamdurdy Gandymov; Gandymov was dismissed in September and replaced by Shakersoltan Mukhammedova.

**30 May 2002:** The Presidents of Turkmenistan, Pakistan and Afghanistan signed a memorandum of understanding to carry out a feasibility study on the construction of the proposed gas pipeline from Turkmenistan to Pakistan, via Afghanistan (suspended since August 1998). A framework agreement on the construction of the pipeline was signed on 27 December.

**June 2002:** The two opposition movements in exile, the People's Democratic Movement and the United Democratic Opposition of Turkmenistan (led by former Minister of For-

eign Affairs Abdy Kuliyev), agreed to work together to promote democracy and the rule of law in Turkmenistan.

**15 June 2002:** The former head of the KNB, Mukhammed Nazarov, received a 20-year prison sentence, having been convicted of crimes including corruption, murder and drugs-trafficking. Gurbandurdy Begenjev had been sentenced to 10 years' imprisonment in May.

**8 August 2002:** Niyazov ordered that the months of the year and the days of the week be known, henceforth, by new Turkmen designations.

**25 November 2002:** An assassination attempt was widely reported to have been made against the presidential motorcade, as it travelled through Ashgabat. At an emergency cabinet meeting, President Niyazov accused the opposition leaders Boris Shikhmuradov and Nurmukhammed Khanamov, founder of the Republican Party of Turkmenistan, of orchestrating a *coup d'état*.

**30 December 2002:** Following a one-day trial, Boris Shikhmuradov was sentenced to 25 years' imprisonment (later increased to a life sentence by the Majlis). In all, more than 50 people received sentences for their involvement in the assassination attempt of November. At the end of December the Uzbekistani ambassador to Turkmenistan was expelled, amid accusations that the Government of Uzbekistan had supported Shikhmuradov's attempted coup, and given him sanctuary in the Uzbekistani embassy in Ashgabat.

**6 April 2003:** Elections to the Khalk Maslakhaty (People's Council) and 5,535 local councils took place, with a reported participation rate of 89.3%.

**10 April 2003:** Niyazov and President Vladimir Putin of Russia signed an agreement, according to which Turkmenistan promised to supply Russia with more than 2,000,000m. cu m of natural gas over the following 25 years.

**15 August 2003:** Constitutional amendments were passed elevating the Khalk Maslakhaty to the status of 'permanently functioning supreme repesentative body of popular authority', and requiring it to remain in continuous session. Niyazov announced his intention to leave office in 2006–07. The constitutional changes also forbade citizens of Turkmenistan from holding dual citizenship, thereby effectively revoking the agreement on dual nationality reached with Russia in December 1993.

# History

## ANNETTE BOHR

### EARLY HISTORY

Although there are various theories about their origin, the Turkmen are widely believed to have descended from the Oguz tribes that migrated from the Altai region north of Mongolia in the latter part of the 10th century. The Turkmen founded the Seljuk dynasty, which had its capital at Merv (now Mary), and the empire of which encapsulated most of the eastern lands of the Islamic world. The largely nomadic Turkmen tribes did not form a national state, and overlordship was divided between the Persian (Iranian) Empire, the Khivan Khanate and the Bukharan Emirate. Over the centuries the Turkmen developed a formidable reputation as caravan raiders and brigands, who were notorious for abducting Persians and, later, Russians and selling them into slavery in the markets of Khiva and Bukhara.

The region comprising modern Turkmenistan was the last Central Asian territory to be brought under the control of

tsarist Russia. The battle for the fortress of Gök Tepe in 1881, at which Russian troops mined and stormed the Turkmen citadel, killing some 14,500 defenders, broke the stubborn Turkmen resistance and decided the fate of the rest of Transcaspia. When tsarist annexation of the Turkmen region was completed in 1884–85, the tribe represented the highest form of political and economic power. A treaty signed in 1895 by the United Kingdom and the Russian Empire, which established an international boundary, and divided the region into British and Russian spheres of influence, left significant numbers of Turkmen outside the borders of what is now Turkmenistan. The Turkmen eventually came under Bolshevik rule following the revolutions of 1917 and the ensuing civil wars. In the first years of Soviet rule Central Asia was divided along national lines, according to Stalin's (Iosif V. Dzhugashvili) four criteria: unity of economy, culture, territory and language. As a result, an autonomous Turkmen region was created in 1921, followed by the establishment of the Turkmen Soviet Socialist Republic (SSR) on 27 October 1924. In the same year the Soviet Turkmen language, which was constructed from the dialects of the Yomud and Tekke tribes, was decreed the official language of the new Union Republic.

## SOVIET TURKMENISTAN

The consolidation of Soviet power in the Turkmen region did not occur without a struggle. Turkmen participated in the *basmachi* guerrilla revolt, which swept Central Asia following the Bolshevik Revolution. Led by Muhammad Qurban Junaid Khan, Turkmen tribes successfully captured Khiva in 1918 and established their leader in power. A Red Army detachment drove him into the desert early in 1920, where he and his followers joined the *basmachi* resistance. The collectivization drive begun in Central Asia in 1929 forced many Turkmen, Kazakh and Kyrgyz nomads to settle and join collective farms. This trauma added impetus to the resistance, and Turkmen fighters waged war in the area of Krasnovodsk (now officially known as Turkmenbashy) and the Kara-Kum desert throughout the early 1930s, until 1936.

A nascent Turkmen intelligentsia was also generally, but peacefully, opposed to Soviet rule. A Provisional Turkmen Congress was established in Ashgabat following the 1917 Bolshevik Revolution. The Congress joined with the 'Whites' (anti-Bolshevik forces) in the latter half of 1918, to form the Government of the Transcaspian Region. This Government, with some British assistance, managed to resist the Bolsheviks for just over one year before succumbing to Soviet rule. It was between 1930 and 1935, however, that the Turkmen intelligentsia was most vocal in its demands for greater political autonomy. The Soviet authorities began purging Turkmen intellectuals on a large scale in 1934, soon widening the purges to include Turkmen government leaders. With the execution of the Chairman of the Supreme Soviet of the Turkmen SSR, Nederbai Aitakov, in 1937–38, the last of a generation of Turkmen nationalists perished.

In 1928 the Soviet authorities began the implementation of an anti-religious policy, with the aim of completely eliminating Islam among the Turkmen. This campaign was perhaps the harshest of the anti-Islamic offensives simultaneously begun in all the republics of Central Asia. Of the approximately 500 mosques that were functioning in Turkmen territory in 1917, only four were still operational in 1979. As in the rest of Central Asia, all Islamic courts of law, *waqf* holdings (religious endowments that formed the basis of clerical economic power) and Muslim primary and secondary schools were liquidated in Turkmenistan by the end of the 1920s. During the Second World War the Soviet leadership temporarily suspended the persecution of Islam, in order to secure greater support for the war effort. An all-Union, official Muslim organization was established in 1942, consisting of four spiritual directorates (Turkmenistan was under the jurisdiction of the Muslim Board of Central Asia and Kazakhstan, based in Tashkent, Uzbekistan). After the War, discrimination against religion was resumed, although the official Islamic establishment remained. Distrust of official Islam among Soviet Muslims and the paucity of officially recognized mosques and clerics, however, forced Islam to establish itself covertly, enabling it to thrive in the post-War period, and especially in the later decades of the 20th century.

Despite two changes in alphabet (the Arabic script was replaced by a Latin script in 1927, and the Latin by a Cyrillic script in 1938), the strongly developed compulsory school system established in the 1920s, together with the mass campaigns against adult illiteracy, caused literacy rates to improve dramatically. According to official statistics, the literacy rate in Turkmenistan rose from 2.3% of the adult population to 99% between 1926 and 1970 (although this

apparently included a large number of people only able to sign their names and spell a few words).

Tsarist Russia had made little attempt at the industrialization of Turkmenistan and it was not until the first years of Soviet rule that this began. Although in the 1920s the central authorities invested sizeable sums in the establishment of industrial enterprises in Turkmenistan and sent a large number of skilled Slavic workers to facilitate the process, industrial development began to decline as early as the 1930s, as the republic became increasingly orientated towards agriculture. At the time of the collapse of the USSR, the industrial enterprises established in Turkmenistan in the 1920s accounted for virtually all light industry in the republic. In the 1990s most heavy industry was geared towards the exploitation of Turkmenistan's large petroleum and natural gas deposits, with the exception of the Kara-Bogaz chemical works.

### The Nationalist Movement

In the mid-1980s, when the twin policies of *glasnost* (openness) and *perestroika* (restructuring) were introduced, Turkmenistan was among the very poorest of the Soviet republics in terms of income per head, and it had the USSR's highest rate of infant mortality, as well as its lowest rate of life expectancy. Encouraged by *glasnost*, members of the intelligentsia and politicians alike began to describe their republic's relationship with the all-Union authorities based in Moscow, Russia, as, in essence, colonialist. In support of their argument, they cited an investment policy aimed at the export of massive amounts of raw cotton and natural gas from their republic, at artificially low prices, while neglecting the development of industry. Concomitantly, a variety of cultural and ecological grievances surfaced, including demands for a reassessment of Turkmen history, the removal of Russian toponyms, the rehabilitation of disgraced Turkmen writers and a halt to environmental damage. In line with the other Soviet republics, in May 1990 Turkmen was made the state language of the republic, and both Russian and Turkmen were declared the languages of inter-ethnic communication. The Constitution adopted in 1992 failed to grant Russian any special status, however, either as a joint state language or as the language of inter-ethnic communication.

Opposition movements, which appeared in Turkmenistan in 1989, played only a limited role before the Government's policy of systematic harassment drove their most active members into exile. Turkmenistan's first and most significant popular movement, Agzybirlik (Unity), the programme of which focused on national revival, organized its first major demonstration on 14 January 1990 at Gök Tepe, the site of the historic last stand of Turkmen resistance to Russian rule. Despite official warnings, nearly 10,000 people gathered to commemorate those who had died in the famous battle. On the following day the Turkmen authorities banned the opposition movement, although it persisted with its founding congress a matter of weeks later.

Turkmenistan's leadership was silent during the attempted conservative coup of August 1991, publicly condemning the actions of the 'hard-line' communists in Moscow only once it had become clear that their State Committee on the State of Emergency was doomed to failure. As the republics of the USSR began declaring their independence in rapid succession following the failure of the August *putsch*, Turkmenistan's leadership decided to put the question of self-rule to a national referendum, which was held in October 1991. Although the population of the Turkmen SSR had voted overwhelmingly in favour of preserving a federation (95.7% of all votes cast) in an all-Union referendum held only seven months before, 94.1% of the electorate cast their votes for independence. Thus, on 27 October 1991—exactly 67 years after the creation of the Turkmen SSR—the independent Republic of Turkmenistan was declared. At its 25th Congress in December the Communist Party of Turkmenistan was renamed the Democratic Party of Turkmenistan (DPT). The leader of the party since December 1985, its First Secretary, Saparmyrat Niyazov, was confirmed in the post of Chairman, and the old communist power structure remained essentially intact. On 21 December, in the capital of Kazakhstan, Turkmenistan became a signatory of the Almaty (Alma-Ata) Declaration, whereby the country became a founder member of the Commonwealth of Independent States (CIS).

## INDEPENDENT TURKMENISTAN

On 18 May 1992 Turkmenistan's parliament adopted a new Constitution, making it the first Central Asian state to enact such a document after the dissolution of the USSR. A direct presidential election was held on 21 June, under the new Constitution, although Niyazov had been popularly elected to the presidency by direct ballot only 20 months previously, in October 1990. According to official results, in 1992 voter participation was 99.8%, with 99.5% of all votes cast in favour of Niyazov. In January 1994 a nation-wide referendum prolonged Niyazov's presidential mandate until 2002, exempting him from another popular election in 1997, as required by the Constitution. Following months of speculation on the introduction of a 'life presidency' at the end of December 1999 the Majlis, taking up the recommendation of the Khalk Maslakhaty, approved amendments to the Constitution, which removed the maximum two-term provision, and thereby enabled Niyazov to remain as President for an unlimited period. Turkmenistan, therefore, became the first CIS country formally to abandon presidential elections. However, President Niyazov stated on several occasions from 2001 that presidential elections would be held before 2010, the year of his 70th birthday. The first parliamentary elections in independent Turkmenistan took place in December 1994, when 49 candidates stood unopposed for seats in the 50-member unicameral legislature, the Majlis (two candidates contested the remaining seat). Parliamentary elections were again held in December 1999, with a declared participation rate of 98.9% of the country's electorate. However, although 104 candidates stood for the 50 parliamentary seats, nearly all of them were members of Niyazov's ruling DPT and served the state in some official capacity. The Organization for Security and Co-operation in Europe (OSCE) declined to send a monitoring mission on the grounds that 'the legislative framework is inadequate for even a minimally democratic election'.

A creation of Niyazov's during the reorganization of political structures in May and June 1992 was the Council of Elders (Yaqshular Maslakhaty), which was proclaimed to be based on national tradition and which brought together nominated elders from all regions of Turkmenistan under the chairmanship of the president. The most original governing body created by President Niyazov, however, was the People's Council (Khalk Maslakhaty). The Khalk Maslakhaty, which is a pseudo-representative organ, is intended to recall the Turkmen 'national tradition' of holding tribal assemblies to solve society's most pressing problems. According to a new constitutional amendment and a constitutional law on the Khalk Maslakhaty, which were passed by that body on 15 August 2003, the Khalk Maslakhaty was elevated to the status of a 'permanently functioning supreme representative body of popular authority'. At the same time, Niyazov was unanimously elected as Chairman of the Khalk Maslakhaty, with a lifetime tenure. Whereas, before August 2003, the law dictated that the Khalk Maslakhaty convene at least once a year, the new law required the Khalk Maslakhaty to remain in continuous session. The 2,507-member body consists of the President, the Majlis deputies, the Chairman of the Supreme Court, the Prosecutor-General, the members of the Council of

Ministers, the hakims (governors) of the five velayats (regions) and the hakim of the city of Ashgabat; people's representatives elected from each district; the chairpersons of parties, the Youth Union, trade unions, and the Women's Union, who are members of the All-national Galkynysh National Revival Movement of Turkmenistan; the chairpersons of public organizations; representatives of the Council of Elders; the hakims of cities that are the administrative centres of the velayats and etraps (districts); and the heads of the local councils (archins) of the cities and villages that are the administrative centres of the districts.

The August 2003 law ascribed to the Khalk Maslakhaty a number of legislative powers, including the passing of constitutional laws, thereby displacing the Majlis as the country's leading legislative body. The official transfer of supreme legislative authority to the Khalk Maslakhaty confirmed that body's hitherto *de facto* status as a fourth branch of power, in addition to the legislature, the executive and judiciary. In reality, however, proposals put forward by Niyazov at sessions of the Khalk Maslakhaty and the Majlis are invariably adopted unanimously by those bodies, which act to validate officially the President's policies.

Local executive power in the five velayats and in the city of Ashgabat is vested in the hakims, who are appointed by the President to execute his instructions. Below the velayats, the President also appoints the executive heads of the cities and districts (shakher hakims and etrap hakims, respectively), purportedly based upon the recommendations of the respective velayat-level hakims. Regarding local legislative organs, the 1992 Constitution provided for the replacement of the local soviets by councils (gengeshes), the members of which are directly elected for five-year terms. The 528 gengeshes are administered by archins, who are elected from among their membership. The President appoints all of the country's judges. A Cabinet of Ministers was formed on 26 June 1992, replacing the Presidential Council, with the President serving as its head. Thus, in 2003 Niyazov continued to hold the posts of President of the Republic (without a term limit), Chairman of the People's Council (without a term limit), Chairman of the Council of Ministers (Prime Minister), Chairman of the Council of Elders, head of the State Security Council, President of the Humanitarian Association of World Turkmen, head of the council for religious affairs, Supreme Commander-in-Chief of the National Armed Forces and Chairman of both the DPT and the National Revival Movement of Turkmenistan. Additionally, decrees issued by the President carried the force of law.

### Authoritarianism and the 'Cult of Personality'

Following more than one decade of independent statehood, the authoritarian regime put in place under President Niyazov remained very firmly entrenched and displayed no signs of impending liberalization. Freedom of speech was severely restricted and official control of the mass media was complete. Censorship was carried out through the Committee for the Preservation of State Secrets, created in February 1991, which was tasked with registering and approving all national and regional newspapers in Turkmenistan, of which Niyazov is the official founder. In July 2002 the Turkmen Government halted the import of Russian newspapers and magazines, and banned cable television (which provided access to Russian channels), thereby eliminating two of the very few sources of alternative information. Satellite dishes were still tolerated in certain urban areas, but were prohibitively expensive for the vast majority of the population. Access to the internet was controlled by the country's sole internet service provider, Turkmen Telecom, which blocked websites critical of government policy. As far as political parties were concerned, by late 2002 there were no parties or movements officially registered in the country other than

Niyazov's DPT and the pro-Government National Revival Movement.

In addition to incorporating elements of populism and despotism, President Niyazov's rule engendered a lavish 'cult of personality'. The honorary title of Turkmenbashy, meaning Leader of the Turkmen, was officially conferred on Niyazov in October 1993. In May of that year the Council of Elders decided to erect monuments to the President in all cities and densely populated areas of the country. By 2002 Niyazov's name or his title of Turkmenbashy (or his nickname, 'Serdar', meaning 'Supreme Chieftain') had been given to at least two cities, several districts and villages, the Kara-Kum Canal, the country's main airport, the Academy of Agricultural Sciences, a military institute, a police academy, sanatoriums, a multitude of schools, farms, mosques, avenues, streets and squares, as well as a cologne and a brand of vodka. His portrait was ubiquitous throughout the state, even appearing on the banknotes of the national currency, the manat. After Niyazov changed his hair colour from grey to black in 1999, a large work-force was reported to have spent weeks incorporating this change into the thousands of presidential portraits and posters throughout the country. Additionally, a 70 m arch commemorating the country's neutrality was completed in 1999 in the centre of the capital, topped by a gold-plated, winged 12 m statue of President Niyazov, which revolved in conjunction with the sun's movements. Study of his multi-volumed writings was introduced as a mandatory subject in all educational establishments. Newspapers, radio and television referred daily to the former Communist Party First Secretary as the 'great thinker and politician of the 20th century', as 'the creator of Turkmenistan' and even, on occasion, as a prophet. All of the country's television stations carried a golden logotype of the President's profile in the upper right-hand corner of the screen. Niyazov's cult of personality was officially extended to include his deceased parents, who were posthumously awarded the highest state titles of 'Hero of Turkmenistan' and 'National Mother and Heroine of Turkmenistan' respectively. In May 2001 the Humanitarian Association of World Turkmen awarded Niyazov the title 'Beik' ('the Great'), thereby amending his official title to 'President Saparmyrat Turkmenbashy the Great'.

## SOCIAL AND POLITICAL DEVELOPMENTS

Independent Turkmenistan was still, in some respects, more of a tribal confederation than a modern nation. In fact, tribal loyalties were stronger there than in any other Muslim area of the CIS. There were some 30 tribes, comprising more than 5,000 clans. The largest tribes were the Tekke in south-central Turkmenistan, the Ersary near the region of the Turkmenistan–Afghanistan border, the Yomud in western and north-eastern Turkmenistan and the Saryks in the southernmost corner of the country, below Mary. Although the tribes steadily lost their economic power from the early Soviet period, tribal loyalties continued to exercise an influence on the Turkmen and were reinforced by rules of endogamy and the persistence of dialects. Virtually all Turkmen had at least a minimal knowledge of their own tribal affiliation, which remains a relatively reliable indicator of birthplace. The exit of the Russian *nomenklatura* (beneficiaries of Soviet patronage) following the collapse of the USSR led to a gradual resurgence of traditionally minded regional élites vying for their economic interests, which, in turn, prompted Niyazov to rely increasingly on a policy of divide and rule with regard to tribal and regional politics. While a sense of national unity and identity was ostensibly being promoted at a higher level (see below), further down hakims tended to be members of the tribe that was dominant in their respective velayat, while a disproportionate number of influential positions in central government tended to go to members of Niyazov's own tribe, the Ahal-Tekke. Niyazov continued to demonstrate a strong preference for his hometown of Gipchak, close to Ashgabat, which had received an inordinate share of investment capital and was the site of a number of ostentatious monuments, including Central Asia's largest mosque (due for completion in 2003).

Over a period of centuries Islam in Turkmenistan has become an unusual blend of orthodox (Sunni), Sufi (mysticism) and shamanistic practices. At the beginning of the 21st century many Turkmen, even among members of the older generation, did not know how to pray. However, worship of ancestors was observed and reverence for members of the six 'holy groups' (the Awlad) was still strong. Pilgrimages to shrines (ziyarat), or the veneration of holy sites, which were generally tombs connected with Sufi saints, mythical characters, pre-eminent scholars or local rulers, continued to play an active role in the preservation of religious feeling among the population. One of the most celebrated holy places in the country was the tomb of Najmuddin Kubra (Sheikh Kebir Ata) in Kunya-Urgench, which was regularly frequented by pilgrims.

Following independence the leadership of Turkmenistan sanctioned the revival of Muslim practices, while simultaneously striving to keep religion within official structures. President Niyazov consequently endorsed the construction of mosques, the teaching of basic Islamic principles in state schools, the refurbishment of holy places and the restoration of Islamic holidays. Yet, while adopting limited measures to promote Islam, at the same time the Turkmen leadership required all religious organizations to obtain legal registration and banned all religious parties. In April 1994 a council for religious affairs, the Gengesh, was created within the presidential apparatus 'to ensure the observance of the law'. In July 2000 a long-serving official in the Gengesh acknowledged that the organization controlled the selection, promotion and dismissal of all clergy in Turkmenistan.

In 1997 the Turkmen leadership initiated the repression of Islamic activity by closing many of the mosques that had been opened only a few years earlier (mostly in the Mary velayat), closing virtually all institutions of Islamic learning, halting the importation of foreign religious literature and tightening restrictions on the legal registration of religious organizations. Turkmenistan had the dubious distinction of being the only country in the CIS where all faiths other than Sunni Islam and Russian Orthodoxy were essentially banned, despite the assurances of religious freedom outlined in the Constitution. The *de facto* ban on minority religious groups was largely the result of a 1997 law, which stipulated that, in order to acquire legal status, religious organizations must demonstrate that they have a minimum of 500 adherents over the age of 18, all living in the same city or town. As a result, Lutherans, Bahá'ís, Jehovah's Witnesses, followers of Hare Krishna and Jews were effectively denied the right legally to meet or distribute religious literature. Some religious minorities faced open persecution: in 1999 the Baptist Churches in Ashgabat, Türkmenabat (formerly Charjew), Mary and Turkmenbashi were raided; the Seventh-Day Adventist Church in Ashgabat and the Hare Krishna Temple in Mary were razed to the ground; and in 2000 the Ashgabat Pentecostal church was confiscated by court order.

From the second half of the 1990s Niyazov's regime dealt several major blows to Turkmenistan's system of education, with the consequence that the majority of children in Turkmenistan no longer had adequate access to education. The 'Ruhnama' (see below) is a compulsory part of school currricula, having even replaced the bulk of teaching in many rural schools. School-children complete their education at the age of 16 years (a circumstance which complicates the entry of

Turkmen students into foreign universities), and only those who have completed two years' work experience after leaving school are allowed to progress to higher education. The length of higher education was reduced to just two years, and all correspondence and evening courses were liquidated. In February 2003 Turkmenistan rescinded a 1993 decree allowing students to freely exchange manats for foreign currency (excepting those studying in countries which have inter-governmental agreements with Turkmenistan), which meant that Turkmen students enrolled in Russian and other foreign universities found it difficult to pay their fees.

Under President Niyazov's 'Ten Years of Prosperity' programme, which aimed to resolve the country's most pressing economic and social problems by 2002, from 1993 the population was supplied with gas, water, electricity and salt free of charge, although amounts were rationed and subject to availability for the vast majority (from August 2001 flour was distributed free to those on low monthly incomes). As the promised economic benefits failed to materialize, however, and living standards declined significantly in the mid-1990s, the name of the programme was discreetly changed to 'Ten Years of Stability'. A plethora of economic and social programmes have been publicized by the Turkmen leadership in the intervening years, with names such as '1,000 days', 'Serdar's Path of Health', 'Grain' and 'New Village'. The 'Ten Years of Stability' programme was effectively superseded in 2000 by the wide-reaching programme 'The Golden Century of the Turkmen Nation', which consists of 10 parts, each covering one decade. Within this programme, the Government's economic strategy for 2000–20 predictably assumes high levels of hard-currency gas export revenues and foreign loans, coupled with optimistic rates of economic development.

### Nation-building

As in other post-Soviet republics, the leadership of Turkmenistan embarked on an extensive process of nation-building in an effort to consolidate the citizenry around a single, national idea and imbue it with patriotic feeling. Hence, President Niyazov introduced an oath of loyalty to the homeland, recited on public occasions, and appearing on the mastheads of the country's newspapers. The glorification of Niyazov as the father of the nation was a major component of the larger nation-building project, and was exemplified by slogans, such as 'Nation, Homeland, Turkmenbashy', prominently displayed throughout the country. Niyazov also sought to revive national customs by creating more than 15 new holidays from 1991, many of which paid homage to an object or tradition closely associated with Turkmen culture, such as Turkmen Carpet Day or Turkmen Melon Day.

From 2000 President Niyazov embarked on a fresh period of nation-building or 'Turkmenization', particularly in the spheres of education, culture and mass media. In October he ordered the destruction of thousands of new history textbooks for 'perverting our glorious past', by purportedly failing to stress sufficiently the Turkmen people's indigenousness and by including descriptions of positive advancements made under Russian and Soviet rule. Universities were encouraged to reject applicants with non-Turkmen surnames, and foreign qualifications were not recognized in Turkmenistan. All teaching in higher educational establishments was carried out exclusively in the Turkmen language. In terms of culture, in April 2001 Niyazov announced the closure of Turkmenistan's only opera and ballet theatre, on the grounds that its repertoire was not 'in conformity with the national mentality'. A national music and drama theatre replaced the opera and ballet theatre, with the aim of increasing the prominence of the works of contemporary Turkmen authors. In the same month three new state television and radio channels were created to broadcast programmes 'with a national flavour'. In August 2002 Niyazov instructed the Khalk Maslakhaty to

redesignate the months of the year and days of the week with Turkmen names, such as 'Turkmenbashy' (for the month of January), 'Ruhnama' (for September) and 'Gurbansoltan Eje' (for April), the latter in honour of the President's mother. Senior state officials must be able to demonstrate ethnic purity by tracing their Turkmen ancestry back several generations. The cornerstone of Niyazov's Turkmenization campaign was the creation and publication of the 'Ruhnama', or national code of spiritual conduct, a final version of which was published in October 2001 to coincide with the country's 10th anniversary of independence. The purported task of the multi-volumed Ruhnama is to record definitively the sources and history of the consolidation of the Turkmen nation, and to depict its fundamental traits and traditions, as well as to provide guidance to the Turkmen people on how 'to live today and in the future'. This 400-page volume, supposedly written by Niyazov, has been accorded the status of a holy book on a par with the Koran and the Bible; Niyazov regularly urged his country's citizens to study and even memorize passages of the Ruhnama.

### Public Purge of the Security Services

Until 2002, Niyazov steadily strengthened the role of the Committee for National Security (KNB)—in September 2002 renamed the Ministry for National Security (MNB)—essentially refashioning it as his personal paramilitary force as well as a counterweight to the armed forces. While the number of personnel in the KNB was increased by over 60% in 2001, the Ministries of Internal Affairs and of Defence were ordered to make significant reductions in personnel. Employees of the KNB were placed in leading positions in all of Turkmenistan's 'power' agencies, including the Ministry of Defence, the Ministry of Foreign Affairs and the Prosecutor-General's office. The Ministry of Internal Affairs, in particular, was restructured as, effectively, a subsidiary of the KNB.

In March 2002, claiming that the organization had expanded uncontrollably and was no longer accountable, Niyazov embarked on a full-scale public purge of the KNB, while also dismissing certain high-ranking officials in Turkmenistan's other security and intelligence agencies. The Minister of Defence, Gurbandurdy Begenjev, was among those dismissed (Begenjev received a 10-year prison sentence in May 2002). More than 60 KNB employees, including 36 senior members of staff, were dismissed, demoted or handed down prison sentences for a multitude of crimes, including abuse of power, bribe-taking, drugs-trafficking, torture and premeditated murder. Most prominent among those given gaol terms was Mukhammed Nazarov, the former Chairman of the KNB, who had concurrently occupied the posts of Adviser to the President on legal issues and Secretary of the State Security Council. Nazarov was sentenced to 20 years' imprisonment in mid-June. In the aftermath of Niyazov's purge, certain functions of the Ministry of Internal Affairs were downgraded, while the Ministry of Defence received a quasi-upgrade: a total of 9,000 employees at the Ministry of Internal Affairs were dismissed in May, in connection with the transfer of several of its key departments (including the traffic police, the fire department and the inter-departmental guard service) to the jurisdiction of the Ministry of Defence.

Niyazov had several likely motives in initiating the extensive overhaul of his security apparatus: first, to prevent high-level security agents from making disclosures that could implicate the President in various crimes and misdemeanours; second, to posit himself as a champion of anti-corruption; third, to carry out a pre-emptive strike against possible plans by security officials to oust the President from power; and fourth, to distance himself from opposition allegations that he had personally overseen a KNB-run international narcotics-smuggling operation from Afghanistan, in co-operation with the ruling (*de facto*) Taliban.

By mid-2003 the KNB, which Niyazov apparently regarded as a potential source of opposition, had not regained the position of authority it held before March 2002. Consequently, Niyazov had devolved greater power to his own personal security administration, the Presidential Guard. The Presidential Guard reportedly consisted of an élite group of some 2,000–3,000 former security agents whose loyalty to the President had been tested over time, and who were charged with numerous functions, ranging from overseeing the personal security of the President to neutralizing all sources of actual or potential oppostion to his rule.

### The Opposition-in-Exile

The appointment of officials in Niyazov's regime was based on their complete loyalty and subservience to the President rather than on a system of merit. Therefore, Turkmen officials were regularly removed from power or transferred to new positions as a means of diminishing their power bases and, hence, their potential ability to become rivals to the President (the official reason given for cadre reshuffling, however, was generally corruption, or simply 'failing in one's duties'). The President's failed economic policies were also ascribed to dismissed officials. Amid this atmosphere of distrust and the continual turnover of personnel, Boris Shikhmuradov, who occupied the post of Minister of Foreign Affairs from 1993, appeared to be a notable survivor, having effectively established himself as the second-most influential person in the state. However, in July 2000 Niyazov removed Shikhmuradov from his position as the country's leading diplomat, reappointing him as presidential envoy for the Caspian Sea region and Afghanistan. Shikhmuradov's subsequent reappointment, in March 2001, as Turkmenistan's ambassador to the People's Republic of China marked the moment of his definitive excommunication from Niyazov's inner circle of advisers. In late October Shikhmuradov was dismissed from his ambassadorial post, and he fled to exile in Moscow. On 1 November Shikhmuradov declared his intention to fight Niyazov's regime and to consolidate the Turkmen opposition. The Turkmen authorities responded the following day by filing criminal charges against Shikhmuradov for his alleged participation in illegal arms deals, the misappropriation of state property, and smuggling operations; they also sent an unsuccessful request to Russia's Prosecutor-General for Shikhmuradov's extradition to Turkmenistan. In January 2002 Shikhmuradov established the People's Democratic Movement of Turkmenistan (PDMT) and launched a website to serve as a general forum for the Turkmen opposition. Following his defection, Shikhmuradov toured foreign capitals, including Washington, DC, USA, in an attempt to attract international support for the overthrow of Niyazov. Meanwhile, Shikhmuradov's decision to join the opposition prompted an unprecedented series of high-level defections between February and May 2002, mainly to Russia. These included Turkmenistan's ambassadors to Turkey and to the United Arab Emirates, as well as a former Chairman of Turkmenistan's Central Bank, a former Deputy Prime Minister and Minister of Water Resources, a former Deputy Chairman of the Majlis and a senior diplomat at the Turkmen embassy in the USA. The opposition was divided into two primary groups, both of which were operating in exile: the United Democratic Opposition of Turkmenistan (the 'old' opposition), led by former Minister of Foreign Affairs Abdy Kuliyev; and the PDMT (the 'oligarchic' opposition), led by Shikhmuradov. Kuliyev, who joined the opposition-in-exile in 1992, criticized Shikhmuradov for having played a key role in establishing Turkmenistan as a closed and corrupt state and for relentlessly persecuting the Turkmen opposition during the latter's long tenure as Deputy Prime Minister and Minister of Foreign Affairs. In June 2002 the two opposition groups publicly agreed to combine their efforts to promote democracy and the rule of law in Turkmenistan, but reports persisted regarding their lack of unity.

### The November 2002 Coup Attempt

According to official reports, on 25 November 2002 President Niyazov's motorcade was fired upon in Ashgabat, as he was travelling to his office from his residence in Arshabil. The Turkmen authorities immediately publicized the attack as a failed assassination and coup attempt co-ordinated by Turkmen oppositionists-in-exile with the aid of foreign mercenaries. President Niyazov was quick to name four of his most prominent rivals as the organizers of the attack: Boris Shikhmuradov; Khudaberdy Orazov, former Deputy Prime Minister and former Chairman of the Central Bank of Turkmenistan; Nurmukhammed Khanamov, former Turkmen ambassador to Turkey; and Saparmyrat Iklymov, former Deputy Minister of Agriculture. The first three were believed to have been living in exile in Russia, while the fourth had been granted political asylum in Sweden. All four suspects identified by Niyazov denied any involvement in the attack. Within a few days of the incident, Orazov fuelled speculation by claiming to a Russian newspaper that Niyazov had staged the attack himself with the aid of his security services in order to provide a pretext for launching the full-scale repression of the opposition. At the end of December it was revealed that Niyazov's most renowned rival among the four official suspects, Shikhmuradov, had clandestinely returned to Turkmenistan from abroad prior to the attack, reportedly in order to organize a series of anti-Government actions inside the country. On 25 December Shikhmuradov was arrested in Ashgabat. In a statement claimed to be written by Shikhmuradov, which was dated 24 December and posted on the website of his opposition group on 26 December, he announced plans to surrender to the Turkmen authorities voluntarily in order to save his relatives from torture and to prevent further arrests. He warned that he could not take responsibility for any statements made after his arrest. Shikhmuradov subsequently made a sensational televised confession, in which he called Niyazov a 'gift given to the people from on high', named his allies in the putative assassination attempt and expressed his deep contrition. Human rights groups and opponents of Niyazov likened the confessions to the Stalinist 'show trials' of the 1930s, asserting that Shikhmuradov made his statement while subjected to torture and under the influence of psychotropic drugs.

A new twist was added to an already complex situation in June 2003 when, in an interview with a German journal, Orazov revealed that Shikhmuradov and his fellow oppositionists had indeed plotted the unsuccessful *coup d'état*, but with no intention of killing Niyazov. According to Orazov, the aim of the coup organizers was to capture the President and take him by force to the parliament building, where he would then be impelled to renounce power in front of television cameras and members of parliament. (Orazov's original account had presumably intended to avoid further incrimination of Shikhmuradov, who was still at large in Turkmenistan at the time.) A new phase of repression was initiated in the aftermath of the armed attack, resulting in the arrests of at least 200 people with purported connections to the opposition. Three of the four opposition leaders accused of co-ordinating the attack were sentenced to 25 years' imprisonment (two of them were convicted *in absentia*). However, following demands by the Khalk Maslakhaty for death sentences, Niyazov proposed that a new maximum penalty of life imprisonment, with no possibility of pardon, amnesty or parole, be introduced for the crime of 'treason', which was very broadly defined as any crime against the state or the President.

## FOREIGN RELATIONS

Central to Turkmenistan's foreign policy was the doctrine of 'permanent neutrality', a concept that was endorsed by the UN in December 1995 and subsequently enshrined in the country's Constitution. To mark the significance of the event, which was hailed in the country as 'the single greatest achievement of the independence period', President Niyazov declared 12 December a national holiday (Neutrality Day) and renamed the country's largest Russian-language newspaper *Neitralnyi Turkmenistan (Neutral Turkmenistan)*. The primary tenets of permanent neutrality proclaimed Turkmenistan's official policy of non-interference and opposition to membership of any 'strongly affiliated' international organizations or military alliances. This included participation in CIS or other peace-keeping forces, which, it was thought, could lead to an infringement of its sovereignty. In early 2000 Turkmenistan addressed a seven-page document to the member states of the UN, in which it elaborated its policy of 'permanent neutrality' for the 21st century.

Although President Niyazov regularly reaffirmed Turkmenistan's official policy of neutrality, he continued to lead his country down a path more closely resembling isolationism. Despite being a member of the Economic Co-operation Organization and the CIS, Turkmenistan stated a clear preference for bilateral relations and rejected the creation of supra-state co-ordinating organs and the delegation of certain powers to them; consequently, it refused to sign more than one-half of all agreements endorsed by the majority of the other CIS member states, including those on collective security and the creation of an inter-state bank. Turkmenistan also declined to join either the Eurasian Economic Community (formerly the CIS Customs Union, now comprising Russia, Belarus, Kazakhstan, Kyrgyzstan and Tajikistan), or the Central Asian Co-operation Organization (formerly the Central Asian Union and later the Central Asian Economic Union, now comprising Uzbekistan, Kazakhstan, Kyrgyzstan and Tajikistan). In June 2001 Uzbekistan joined the Shanghai Forum (already comprising Russia, the People's Republic of China, Kazakhstan, Kyrgyzstan and Tajikistan), which was renamed the Shanghai Co-operation Organization, the primary function of which was to co-ordinate collective measures to counter terrorism and other threats to regional stability. Once again, as had been the case with other CIS or Central Asian regional initiatives, Turkmenistan remained outside this collective grouping.

Pursuing an isolationist course yet further, in June 1999 Turkmenistan became the first country to embark on the establishment of a visa regime inside the territory of the former USSR, by withdrawing from the so-called Bishkek accord, which established visa-free travel for citizens of the CIS. It also required its own citizens to obtain exit visas, often at considerable expense, to travel to foreign states, including neighbouring CIS countries. In mid-2000 the Central Bank received instructions that bank accounts held by Turkmen citizens and organizations abroad should be closed in order to curb the flow of capital outside the country. In another isolationist move, in May of the same year the Turkmen Government rescinded the licences of all the country's independent internet service providers, leaving state-owned Turkmentelekom as the sole remaining company to provide internet access. In June Niyazov approved the creation of a joint Council for the Supervision of Foreigners, which empowered Turkmenistan's security services to monitor the movements of foreigners arriving or temporarily residing in the country. According to a presidential decree issued in June 2001, any foreigner wishing to marry a Turkmen citizen was required not only to own an apartment in the Central Asian state, but also to pay the state US $50,000 to serve as a guarantee of the welfare of any potential offspring in the event of divorce. The

new legislation was ratified by the Majlis in March 2002. In February 2003 a State Service for the Registration of Foreigners was created, which allowed for the imposition of even more restrictive procedures governing the entry, exit and stay of foreign nationals. Although the requirement for Turkmen citizens to obtain exit visas was temporarily suspended amid much publicity in January 2002, it was restored in March 2003 in the aftermath of the November 2002 coup attempt. Citizens were also no longer able to travel freely within the country, and were subject to frequent checks by traffic police and the army.

In the early 2000s Turkmenistan's closest foreign partner remained the Russian Federation, upon which it relied for the bulk of its foreign trade, the export of its natural gas, and its main transportation and communications networks. One of the most important post-independence developments for Turkmenistan was the agreement reached with Russia in December 1991 to allow Turkmenistan to export a limited amount of natural gas to European markets through Russian pipelines, in exchange for convertible ('hard') currency calculated at world prices. Consequently, the Russian decision of November 1993 severely to restrict Turkmenistan's access to its pipeline network deprived the latter state of an outlet to hard-currency markets and forced it to redirect sales of its main commodity to impoverished, unreliable clients, namely Ukraine, which proved unable to pay its debts to Turkmenistan. In March 1997 Turkmenistan halted all its exports through the Russian pipeline network, citing unfavourable conditions imposed by the Russian gas monopoly, Gazprom. Issues at the heart of the dispute were the price at which Russia offered to buy Turkmen gas for resale to other countries, the proportion of payment that was to be made in convertible currency, the transit fees demanded by the Russian side and the transit route itself, all of which, Turkmenistan argued, effectively barred it from profitably exporting through the former Soviet pipeline system. In December 1999, however, despite earlier demands for higher prices, Turkmenistan came to an agreement with Gazprom to deliver 20,000m. cu m of gas from January to September 2000 at a price of US $36 per 1,000 cu m, with 40% of the payments in hard currency and 60% in food and commodities. As a result, gas exports to Russia grew sharply during the first half of 2000, accounting for more than three-quarters of Turkmenistan's total gas exports and greatly boosting that state's economic indicators. From October 2000 Russia purchased relatively small amounts of Turkmen gas on an annual or semi-annual basis, albeit at Turkmenistan's higher asking price. A long-term gas deal with Turkmenistan was vital to Russia in order to free up its own gas for export to the West and to postpone the development of high-cost Arctic and Siberian gas projects.

The failed coup attempt in November 2002 provided Russia with important leverage in its mission to conclude a major, long-term gas agreement with Turkmenistan. Although officials in Russia immediately denied any complicity in the attack (a Turkmen government spokesman had accused politicians in Russia of being 'in connivance' with the organizers), the Russian Government failed publicly to condemn the alleged assassination attempt or even to send a statement of support to Niyazov until January 2003, when Russian Security Council Secretary Vladimir Rushailo and Russian energy ministry officials travelled to Ashgabat to negotiate bilateral security issues and, *inter alia*, a contract for the sale of Turkmen gas to Russia. Rushailo emerged from a meeting with Niyazov to declare the attack a 'manifestation of terrorism' and to sign a protocol on mutual co-operation in the search for and extradition of suspected criminals. Russia's belated condemnation of the November attack, and the simultaneous negotiation of a security agreement and a gas agreement (both of which, together with a protocol ending dual Russian-Turkmen citizenship, were signed when Niyazov and Russian President Vladimir Putin met in Moscow in April 2003) strongly suggested a connection between Russia's preparedness to support Niyazov and the conclusion of a long-term gas contract. Under the terms of the April 2003 agreement, Russia's purchases of Turkmen gas were to increase from 5,000m.–6,000m. cu m in 2004 to 10,000m. cu m in 2006, rising to 60,000m.–70,000m. cu m in 2007 and to 70,000m.–80,000m. cu m from 2009. Russia was contracted to pay US $44 per 1,000 cu m in the first three years, in conformity with the price paid by Ukraine for Turkmen gas. Although this price was considerably higher than Russia's domestic price, which was capped by the Government, it was considerably lower than the $90 to $120 per 1,000 cu m at which Gazprom sold gas to Western Europe. Moreover, unlike Europe, Russia was to pay only half of the price in cash, while half was to be paid in goods and services, which are often of a low quality. Gazprom's purchase price was to be renegotiated in 2007, taking into account the dynamics of international prices, while Turkmenistan retained the right to terminate the contract unilaterally at the end of each five-year period.

In addition to the long-term gas agreement, the Presidents of Russia and Turkmenistan signed a protocol at their meeting in Moscow rescinding the dual citizenship agreement that had been in force between the two countries since 1993. The dual citizenship agreement with Russia had long been a problematic issue for Niyazov, insofar as many of his leading opponents had secured Russian passports in order to ensure their ability to leave the country and, in some cases, to use Russia as a safe haven from Niyazov's regime. On 21 April, less than two weeks after obtaining Putin's agreement to end the dual citizenship arrangement, Niyazov issued a unilateral decree requiring the approximately 95,000 Turkmen-Russian dual passport holders in Turkmenistan to renounce one citizenship or the other within a two-month period, which led to a substantial deterioration in Turkmen-Russian bilateral relations. The Russian Ministry of Foreign Affairs claimed that the protocol on the cancellation of the agreement on dual citizenship signed by Putin and Niyazov was never intended to have retroactive force; moreover, Russian officials maintained that the actions taken by the Turkmen authorities were illegal, since the Russian side had not yet ratified the protocol, until which time it could not come into force. In June 2003, following a joint hearing in the Russian State Duma of three committees responsible for international affairs, security and the CIS, the Russian parliament adopted, by a significant majority, a harsh resolution criticizing the treatment of Russian citizens in Turkmenistan. The Russian Duma expressed particular objections to the requirement that Russian citizens in Turkmenistan obtain an exit visa in order to leave that country. At the end of June, in an unprecedented move, the Russian authorities added Turkmenistan to the list of countries deemed unsafe for Russian citizens. Although the Russian Ministry of Foreign Affairs dispatched a delegation to Ashgabat in June to try to resolve the impasse regarding dual citizenship, the talks failed to result in any substantial progress. At the August session of the Khalk Maslakhaty, a revised constitutional clause forbade citizens of Turkmenistan from holding the citizenship of any other country, which meant that, from the point of view of the Turkmen authorities, dual citizens who had not renounced their Russian citizenship were in breach of the law.

Ukraine signed a major gas sales contract with Turkmenistan in May 2001, consequently becoming that state's biggest customer. According to the agreement, signed by the Turkmen and Ukrainian Presidents, Ukraine was to import 250,000m. cu m of natural gas from Turkmenistan in 2002–06, potentially meeting three-quarters of its gas demand. Ukraine undertook to pay for 50% of the gas in hard currency and 50% in goods, services and inputs into Turkmen investment projects. However, export levels to Ukraine indicated that total deliveries to Ukraine in 2002–06 period would fall short of the agreed amount: in 2002 Ukraine bought 32,000m. cu m of gas, and in 2003 it was due to purchase 36,000m. cu m, bringing exports under the agreement, at mid-2003, to just under 70,000m. cu m. Turkmenistan had suspended gas exports to Ukraine on several occasions owing to an accrual of debt. However, Ukraine improved its payment record in 2003, and began repaying some of its past debt to Turkmenistan.

In the post-independence period Turkmenistan's relations with Iran came to play an increasingly important role in its foreign policy. Given that Turkmenistan shares its longest border with Iran, which is also Turkmenistan's natural choice as a gas export route, a good relationship with its southern neighbour remains vital. In May 1996 a new railway, joining the Turkmen city of Tejen to the northern Iranian city of Mashhad, was inaugurated, giving land-locked Central Asian states access to the Persian (Arabian) Gulf and incorporating the region into the greater railway system that linked Asia from Turkey to the People's Republic of China. Most importantly, in December 1997 President Niyazov and Iran's new President, Muhammad Khatami, officially opened the 200-km gas pipeline linking the Korpedje field in western Turkmenistan to the industrial town of Kord Kuy in northern Iran, which had been built primarily with Iranian financing. Until the opening of the Turkmen–Iranian pipeline, Turkmenistan's sole gas export route had been controlled by Russia. In 2003 Iran was Turkmenistan's third largest gas export market after Ukraine and Russia, although the amounts delivered were relatively small (approximately 5,000m. cu m, which is the minimum amount Turkmenistan agreed to supply Iran annually under the terms of a 25-year contract signed in 1995). In theory Turkmenistan could export gas to Turkey via this southern route; in practice, however, Iran has no real interest in re-exporting Turkmen gas to Turkey, given its own huge reserves located in its southern regions.

In April 2000 Turkmenistan joined forces with Iran amid a bitter dispute for control over the Caspian Sea's petroleum and gas resources, the division of the waters of which had not been formally clarified and had prompted bitter rivalry between the littoral states (see also the essay on the Politics of Energy in the Caspian Sea Region, in Part One). Turkmenistan's leadership declared in August that it would refuse to take part in a decision on the Caspian's status if Iran were excluded and that any solution must be acceptable to its southern neighbour. Iran had announced that it would agree to control 20% of both the seabed and the waters, prompting indignant replies from the other littoral states, given that Iran's coastline entitles it to only about 13%. Turkmenistan also supported Iran in that state's conflict with Azerbaijan over the latter's exploration of oil fields claimed by both countries. This was an expected development, given that Turkmenistan itself remained locked in a dispute with Azerbaijan over the ownership of the Serdar/Kyapaz field in the mid-Caspian, as well as portions of the Azeri and Chirag fields (known as Khazar and Osman, respectively, in Turkmenistan). Turkmenistan's position on the legal status of the Caspian Sea has been ambiguous and subject to change over the years, shifting from an anti-division stance to one advocating the division of the seabed, waters and airspace into national sectors. In 2003 although Turkmenistan appeared to support the idea of 'divided sea floor, common surface waters' in line with Kazakhstan, Russia and Azerbaijan, it also shared the Iranian view that national zones should be relatively large, thereby restricting Russian maritime traffic. While accepting the modified median line principle in general, Turkmenistan's interpretation of the median line is wholly unacceptable to Azerbaijan, leaving as it would disputed oil and gas deposits inside its own sector. In May 2003 officials from Azerbaijan, Kazakhstan and Russia signed an agreement demarcating their respective sectors of the Caspian seabed, under which Kazakhstan received a 29% share and Russia and Azerbaijan each received a 19% share. Turkmenistan's dispute with Azerbaijan over ownership of several oil and gasfields prevented it from joining the Azerbaijan-Kazakhstan-Russia agreement.

Regarding Turkmenistan's relations with its eastern neighbour Uzbekistan, the leaders of those two states signed an agreement on the delimitation of their mutual border in September 2000, yet tensions between them increased as visa regimes were put in place and border controls became stricter. Fortified border regimes in turn increased the frequency of illegal crossings, which were undertaken often for the purpose of carrying out cross-border trade in small-scale contraband, a practice which was supported by the existence of multiple-exchange rates in both countries. Since mid-2001 there have been several reports of localized clashes and shootings on the Turkmen-Uzbek border, resulting in several deaths. Tensions between the two states were also fuelled by disputes over shared resources and by reports of discrimination against Turkmenistan's sizeable ethnic Uzbek minority, which is concentrated in the country's Lebap and Dashkhovuz Provinces, bordering Uzbekistan. Relations between Turkmenistan and Uzbekistan reached an unprecedented low following accusations that Uzbekistan had been complicit in the armed attack on President Niyazov in November 2002. Claiming that Uzbekistan had given shelter to Boris Shikhmuradov at the Uzbek Embassy in Ashgabat, the Turkmen authorities declared Uzbekistan's ambassador *persona non grata* and expelled him from the country at the end of December. In the aftermath of the incident both countries amassed troops on their respective sides of the common border.

In Afghanistan, Turkmenistan had cultivated cordial political and trade relations with the Taliban in the post-independence period, in contrast to Russia and the other Central Asian states. Given that Islam remained relatively unpoliticized in Turkmenistan, President Niyazov did not view the Taliban as a threat, which, it was alleged, allowed Niyazov's regime to engage in systematic drugs-smuggling and to forge ties with poppy producers in Afghanistan. Turkmenistan opened consulates in the Afghan cities of Herat and Mazar-i-Sharif, which were reported to operate as a cover for secret drug deals concluded by Niyazov's regime and the Taliban, the money from which was allegedly 'laundered' in the United Arab Emirates. Turkmenistan was also alleged to have given the leader of the Islamic Movement of Uzbekistan (IMU), Jumaboy (Juma) A. Khojiyev (Namanganiy), and some Taliban fighters permission to transit its territory. Following the large-scale suicide attacks on the USA on 11 September 2001, which were attributed to the al-Qa'ida (Base) network, led by the Saudi-born militant Islamist, Osama bin Laden, Turkmenistan succeeded in maintaining its neutral stance with regard to the conflict in Afghanistan, owing in part to Uzbekistan's willingness to co-operate with the USA in its 'war on terrorism'. Citing the country's neutral status, which Niyazov repeatedly described as inviolate, Turkmenistan was the only Central Asian state that did not offer either its airspace or airfields to US planes for military operations in Afghanistan, or allow foreign troops on its soil (with the exception of a small group of US military personnel who refuelled cargo planes carrying aid to Afghanistan). However, Turkmenistan served as the principal conduit for humanitarian assistance to Afghanistan during the US-led airstrikes against al-Qa'ida and its Taliban hosts from early October, granting extensive ground and air transport 'corridors', and providing the International Security Assistance Force and international relief agencies with landing facilities and secure storage sites for supplies. As a consequence of its limited participation in the anti-terrorism operations, Turkmenistan did not reap the financial rewards or security guarantees that the USA awarded to the other Central Asian states in exchange for their support (although Turkmenistan did receive US technical assistance aimed at improving the security of its borders).

**Pipeline Proposals**

To avoid the undue influence of Russia, from the mid-1990s Turkmenistan pursued a number of different projects for the construction of pipelines to carry its gas to foreign markets, all of which were beset by serious obstacles (with the exception of the Korpedje–Kord Kuy connection described above). The proposed construction of a 1,500-km gas pipeline from Turkmenistan to Pakistan via Afghanistan, an initiative led by the US company Unocal, was suspended indefinitely in 1998, owing to fighting in Taliban-controlled Afghanistan and the lack of an internationally recognized government there. The Niyazov Government has long regarded Afghanistan as a natural 'bridge' between Turkmenistan and the vast markets of the Indian subcontinent. Consequent to the collapse of the Taliban regime in Afghanistan in late 2001, the Turkmen Government's primary interest was in reviving the trans-Afghanistan pipeline project, which would link Turkmenistan's Dauletabad field with Pakistan's gas transport network at Multan, with a possible extension to India. On 27 December 2002 the Presidents of Turkmenistan and Afghanistan and the Prime Minister of Pakistan signed a framework agreement on the construction of the 1,460-km trans-Afghanistan pipeline (TAP). In April 2003 Afghanistan, Pakistan and Turkmenistan formally invited India to participate in the project both as an investor and as a major purchaser of gas. Although India's inclusion in the project would greatly enhance the TAP's viability, that state expressed concern that political tensions with Pakistan could jeopardize its ability to receive gas deliveries. The Asian Development Bank (ADB) agreed to fund a feasibility study for the pipeline project, which was estimated to cost up to US $2,500m. and would take three years to complete. In July, however, the pre-qualification process for the ADB-backed TAP project was postponed while studies were carried out, including a route survey and an estimation of reserves in Turkmenistan's Dauletabad gas fields. Despite the ADB's initial optimistic assessment, serious questions remained regarding virtually all aspects of the pipeline. Major gas and petroleum companies were unlikely to commit themselves to financing the pipeline until concerns about regional stability and the project's viability were allayed. Even if the central Government in Afghanistan was able to secure an internal political consensus, there was no guarantee that individual tribes and warlords would not try to sabotage the pipeline project at a future date. Moreover, sales of Turkmen gas to the Indian subcontinent would be limited by competing projects in Iran as well as by a border dispute that could prevent Pakistan from selling gas to India, making the project economically unviable. Even if political and financing obstacles were ultimately overcome, Turkmenistan's recent large-scale deal with Russia (see above), if fulfilled, would leave little to no gas with which to fill the pipeline for exports to the Indian subcontinent, barring tremendous increases in the country's gas production levels.

As for a Western route to export its hydrocarbon resources, Turkmenistan hoped for the planned construction of a pipeline through Iran to Turkey and, ultimately, to Europe. Although a route through Iran was the most direct and cost-effective way to deliver gas to Turkey, the USA's objections to Iran's inclusion in the pipeline scheme had concomitant repercussions for financing the project. As an alternative route, the US Government strongly promoted the construction of a

2,000-km trans-Caspian pipeline, which would transport gas across the Caspian Sea to Azerbaijan and then to Europe via Georgia and Turkey. Turkish and US representatives reported in Ashgabat in July 1998 that both Turkey and the USA had agreed to support the trans-Caspian pipeline by providing guarantees to investors and offering large government credits. Prospects for the pipeline began to unravel in February 2000, however, when Azerbaijan laid claim to one-half of the pipeline's capacity, after finding a large gas deposit in its Caspian offshore field, much closer to Turkish markets. President Niyazov, in turn, insisted that Azerbaijan's demand would make Turkmenistan's own export plans unprofitable, leaving it with high construction costs and little return. In June the consortium of the US-based Bechtel Corporation and General Electric Capital Services, which had been formed to build the trans-Caspian pipeline, ended its operations in Ashgabat, after the Turkmenistani leadership failed to respond to a final offer for the project. The consortium members explained their withdrawal to be the result of the 'unacceptable conditions' imposed by Turkmenistan's leadership, including the reported demand for an advance payment of several hundred million US dollars by President Niyazov. The Anglo-Dutch firm Royal Dutch/Shell, which owned 50% of the concession to construct the pipeline, remained committed to completing the project. However, by late 2000 it had also proved unable to reach an agreement on terms with the Turkmen leadership, despite having presented new commercial offers on the project to President Niyazov in July.

Of equal significance to the long-term gas sales contract signed by Presidents Niyazov and Putin in April 2003 was a pledge by Russia to modernize Turkmenistan's transport capacities, insofar as the promised volumes of gas would require major investment in pipelines. The agreement envisaged the reconstruction of the Central Asia-Centre gas transport system (the 'northern route'), which could carry only 45,000m.–50,000m. cu m annually, as well as the construction of a new gas pipeline with a capacity comparable to that of the proposed trans-Afghanistan pipeline (approximately 30,000m. cu m annually). Two possible routes for the new pipeline were under examination, the first of which would cross Uzbek and Kazakh territory, and the second of which would run along the Caspian coastline, bypassing Uzbekistan.

### CONCLUSION

Speculation that President Niyazov was steadily losing his grip on power increased significantly from 2001 and was fuelled by a number of factors, including the massive number of rotations and dismissals of senior officials, the full-scale cleansing of the Committee (now Ministry) for National Security, the extensive reorganization of the country's 'power' agencies and an increased level of exile activism. The coup attempt against President Niyazov in November 2002 unleashed a new wave of repression within Turkmenistan, ultimately resulting in hundreds of arrests, draconian restrictions on both internal and foreign travel for Turkmen citizens and the revocation of a dual citizenship agreement with Russia. However, while Niyazov's regime clearly lacked a solid institutional foundation, revenues from gas sales (an easily exploitable natural resource subject to state monopoly)

could continue to support his seemingly unstable rule for a number of years, provided he remained in sufficient health. The Turkmen population remained politically acquiescent, although several rare protest demonstrations did take place in the cities of Ashgabat and Turkmenbashi in mid-2002, some of which were organized by Shikhmuradov's now-defunct People's Democratic Movement. In August 2003 Niyazov declared that he intended to stand down in 2006–07, informing the Khalk Maslakhaty that it should begin preparing for presidential elections as early as 2005–06. Although the Khalk Maslakhaty periodically proposed that Niyazov should hold office until his death, the President stated that he would continue to rule in accordance with the 1999 constitutional amendment that granted him the right to rule without any term limits. The appointment of Niyazov as the Chairman of the Khalk Maslakhaty, with a lifelong tenure, and the concomitant transfer of supreme power to that governing body in August 2003, led to speculation that Niyazov would make good on his pledge to stand down as President, insofar as his relinquishment of the presidency would entail no actual loss of power. Irrespective of external and internal events, Niyazov's history of cardiovascular disease made it far from clear how much longer his health would allow him to remain in power. The lack of a workable political succession mechanism in Turkmenistan made it likely that regime change in Turkmenistan, when it did come, would be accompanied by violence and instability.

In the realm of foreign relations, Turkmenistan had effectively limited its foreign policy to the brokering of gas sales contracts and pipeline feasibility studies. However, in order to meet its export obligations, Turkmenistan will have to greatly increase its levels of gas production and significantly expand its pipeline capacity. Other than Russia's Gazprom, Turkmenistan had three foreign customers for its gas: the Russian gas company Itera, Ukraine and Iran. In April 2003 Turkmenistan signed a 10-year deal with Itera to deliver 10,000m. cu m of gas per year from 2004. Regarding Ukraine, Niyazov planned to renew the current contract, set to expire in 2006, which required Turkmenistan to supply 34,000m.–40,000m. cu m annually to that country. The long-term contract with Gazprom envisioned gas deliveries of 60,000m.–70,000m. cu m in 2007. Given that annual exports to Iran had been set at 5,000m.–8,000m. cu m a year for several years, and domestic consumption accounted for 10,000m.–12,000m. cu m annually, Turkmenistan would have to almost triple its existing levels of gas production by 2007 in order to meet its ambitious export commitments (in 2002 Turkmenistan's output of natural gas was only 54,000m. cu m, a full 25% below its official production target for that year). Even if Turkmenistan somehow managed to achieve this feat, there would be little to no gas left over with which to fill a proposed pipeline crossing Afghanistan. Moreover, both Kazakhstan and Uzbekistan announced plans to significantly increase their own levels of gas production and export, thereby further limiting the extent to which Turkmenistan will be able to use the northern route to increase its export levels. Thus, during the early 2000s it appeared that Turkmenistan's greatest challenge was expanding its gas production and transport capacities, as it sought to preserve its neutrality, while delicately balancing relations with its more powerful neighbours.

# The Economy

## Dr HELEN BOSS

Revised for this edition by the Editorial staff

### INTRODUCTION AND OVERVIEW

In the first decade after it proclaimed independence from the USSR in 1991, the Turkmen economy remained highly dependent on two export commodities, natural gas and cotton. Petroleum, which could be transported by road and rail, was of lesser, if growing, importance. All three industries remained subject to pervasive state influence at the highest level. The official exchange rate was kept grossly overvalued by a variety of non-market measures. Energy and agriculture were exploited by the Government for funds to finance grandiose investment projects. Official policies encouraged output of crops in which the country did not have comparative advantage, and one of the economy's scarcest resources, water, was not rationally used.

Turkmenistan entered the 2000s at the bottom of the league tables for a range of the European Bank for Reconstruction and Development's (EBRD) indicators for countries in transition, including on price and trade liberalization, privatization, and banking and enterprise reform, and it was censured by the Organization for Security and Co-operation in Europe and the EBRD for its record on democratization. It had no agreement with the IMF, only a limited programme with the World Bank, and no plans to institute the reforms needed to qualify for membership of the World Trade Organization. In April 2000 the EBRD suspended its programme of public-sector lending, owing to the undemocratic parliamentary election of December 1999, harassment of opposition politicians and the Government's disinclination to reform the country's distorted foreign-exchange and trade regimes. In September 2000 Turkmenistan joined the Asian Development Bank (ADB). The EBRD adopted a new, two-year strategy for Turkmenistan in September 2002, in which it expressed concern regarding the country's political situation and the slow pace of economic reform. Turkmenistan was expected to sign a strategic partnership agreement with the World Bank later that year. Global institutions, such as the UN, the IMF, the World Bank and the ADB, reported a reticence on the part of the Turkmen authorities to supply up-to-date figures on the economy; there were also concerns regarding official methods of collating statistics.

Although the fate of much-vaunted international pipeline projects was still in doubt, by 2001 the economy was benefiting from the fuller capacity utilization of a gas pipeline to Iran, which opened in late 1997. According to the ADB, gross domestic product (GDP) registered growth of an estimated 17.6% in 2000 and of some 20.5% in 2001, largely owing to the export of natural gas, petroleum and cotton. However, GDP growth slowed in 2002, to 14.9%, according to preliminary official estimates (compared with the ADB's estimate of 8.6%). Gas production increased by some 9.1% in 2001, and by 4.0% in 2002, while petroleum output rose by an estimated 5.0% in 2001 and by 6.6% in 2002. In 2001 cotton yields increased by 6.8%. Turkmenistan's other main economic activity was food production for domestic consumption. Agriculture (including cotton) provided employment for 48.7% of the population in 2002. The former collective farms had to absorb large net additions to the labour force, owing to the country's young age structure and high birth rate. Almost the entire crops of cotton and wheat were subject to obligatory sales to the state at around 50% of world-market prices, resulting in a net transfer out of agriculture of a significant 15% of GDP in 1999. Wheat production rose strongly in the 1990s, owing to the self-sufficiency campaign, and cotton production recovered, but both crops were encouraged without regard for cost or potential gains from trade and at a cost of some 6% of GDP in subsidies, which was clearly an unsustainable situation. Government policy had been detrimental to food production for export, although such potential did exist.

### Overview of the Energy Sector

Turkmenistan's prospects of becoming a major exporter of natural gas to Asia, Europe and Turkey continue to be limited by the lack of an export pipeline infrastructure. Gas extraction in the 1990s languished well below Soviet peak levels of 85,000m. cu m per year, primarily because Russia, by this time a competitor, held a monopoly over access to the Soviet-built Unified Gas Supply System (UGSS) pipeline, serving Western Europe (prior to the completion of the gas pipeline between Turkmenistan and Iran in 1997). Russia, in a dispute over cash payment for transit in March 1997, abrogated the arrangement whereby Turkmenistan supplied gas to the UGSS system, paid Russia for transit in gas, and earned US dollars from Central and Western Europe.

Turkmenistan was left with customers in unconvertible 'soft' currency markets, such as Armenia, Georgia and Ukraine, which frequently paid late, in barter goods of inferior quality, or not at all. Total outstanding rescheduled gas debts owed to Turkmenistan amounted to, for example, some US $1,300m. in early 1998, of which $470m. were due in that year, but only $370m. were paid. Non-payment of debts led Turkmenistan to suspend deliveries to other countries of the former USSR on numerous occasions, for almost the whole of 1998 in the case of Ukraine, which had accounted for some 80% of export volumes earlier in the decade. The Government was, thus, regularly deprived of tax revenue on domestic production and of foreign exchange from the domestically claimed potential exports.

President Saparmyrat Niyazov attempted to raise Western interest in financing alternative pipeline routes to counter the negative revenues on (subsidized) domestic sales and the effects of Russia's monopoly on the UGSS pipeline. However, the President's bargaining was marked by high expectations and an unwillingness to compromise with partners for transit rights, a key element in the equation. It was also affected by the announcement of gas discoveries in Azerbaijan and by Azerbaijan's consequent insistence on a larger share of the volume for itself. Engineering consortium members General Electric Capital Services and Bechtel Enterprises of the USA, and the Anglo-Dutch company Royal Dutch/Shell made financing the proposed Trans-Caspian Gas Pipeline project, for the construction of a 16,000m. cu m underwater gas pipeline, linking Turkmenistan with Turkey, via Azerbaijan and Georgia, contingent on Turkmenistan reaching agreement with other suppliers, such as Azerbaijan and Kazakhstan, on volumes, and with transit countries on fees. Turkmenistan's ongoing dispute with Azerbaijan over ownership of fields in the centre of the Caspian did not aid this negotiation. Seismic work in Azerbaijan and Kazakhstan revealed that sufficient gas volumes were likely to be available closer, geographically and in terms of the number of intervening states, to Turkey. In September 2000 General Electric and Bechtel announced that the consortium was to close its office in Ashgabat and transfer leadership of the project to Royal Dutch/Shell. Russia's rival 'Blue Stream' project, which aimed to construct a gas pipeline under the Black Sea to northern Turkey, also secured financing, and was completed in late 2002. The Trans-Caspian project was postponed indefinitely in March 2003, when Royal Dutch/Shell decided to reduce its activities in Turkmenistan.

After a decade of benefiting from Western support, particularly from the USA, for initiatives designed to help the Central Asian states diversify their economies away from dependence on Russia and towards closer ties with secular Islamic states like Turkey, Western interest in Turkmenistan waned in early 2000. Turkmenistan may have driven too hard a bargain to gain inclusion in the next generation of infrastructure projects, which were to deliver much larger volumes of natural gas to Turkey and Europe, and link the Caspian Sea to the Mediterranean. Turkmenistan appeared to be resigning itself to dependence on traditional markets in Russia and Ukraine in the first instance, with hopes of increasing energy exports to Iran at the margin. Outbreaks of violence in Kyrgyzstan, Tajikistan and Uzbekistan appeared to strengthen Russia's case for playing a greater military role in the region.

Prospects for much larger sales of Turkmen gas to Russia indeed improved in December 1999, when President Niyazov agreed to deliver 20,000m. cu m of gas to Russia in January–September 2000. Another agreement was reached in May, whereby Turkmenistan was to sell an additional 10,000m. cu m to Russia for the next three–four years, until the level of imports reached 50,000m.–60,000m. cu m per year. The reason for Russia's change of heart was apparently the continuing production shortfalls of Gazprom, given rising domestic demand with the industrial recovery in Russia, which impeded Russia's interest in increasing exports to Western and Central Europe and, indeed, to Turkey, when the Blue Stream project was completed. However, in early 2001 Turkmenistan halted its deliveries to Russia, owing to the failure of the two sides to agree on a mutually acceptable price. An agreement was finally reached in February, and was renewed in December. In May Turkmenistan agreed to supply Ukraine with a record 250,000m. cu m of natural gas in 2002–06. This deal made Ukraine the primary export market for Turkmen gas; however, as before, there was no guarantee of payment, particularly since Ukraine already owed Russia for gas imports from that country. In April 2003 Niyazov and President Vladimir Putin of Russia signed an agreement, according to which Turkmenistan agreed to supply Russia with more than 2,000,000m. cu m of natural gas over the next 25 years. In September it was announced that Turkmenistan was expected to sign a 25-year gas-supply agreement with Ukraine in the following month.

### Overview of the Cotton Sector

Turkmenistan's cotton policy, with independence, was eventually to reduce the proportion of raw cotton production in total output, while shifting land, labour and water to food production. Thus, the 1999 'National Programme of the President of Turkmenistan, Saparmyrat Turkmenbashy, Strategy of Socio-Economic Developments in Turkmenistan for the Period up to 2010' aimed to bring about an annual increase in cotton production of 11.2% in the first half of the period, but a rate of growth of only 3.3% in the second half. Cotton output decreased severely in the first years of independence, and in 1998 it was one-half the level recorded in the early 1990s, before recovering in 1999; exports, too, were about one-half the Soviet level. Revenues from cotton-fibre exports displayed sharp fluctuations, in keeping with the vagaries of the world price in the mid-1990s and, indeed, because the country was excluded from global markets for a time, for breach of delivery

contract. Domestic production of textiles greatly increased from a very low base, owing to the import of turn-key mills in joint-ventures with, for example, Gap of the USA.

### ECONOMIC GEOGRAPHY

Turkmenistan's remote, land-locked geographical position remained a principal barrier to development. It borders land-locked Kazakhstan and Uzbekistan to the north and east, Iran and land-locked Afghanistan to the south, and the (land-locked) Caspian Sea to the west. The country was a high-cost exporter to world markets, while its small, impoverished population limited the attractiveness of the internal market. Despite the world-class energy reserves, and its location on the traditional trade routes of medieval Asia, some 80% of its area is part of the Kara-Kum desert. The country's natural aridity was exacerbated by the desiccation of the Aral Sea in the second half of the 20th century, the result of the Soviet leadership's campaign to increase cotton production by taking water from the Amu-Dar'ya river via the Kara-Kum Canal. By the 1970s the level of the Aral Sea had decreased sharply, as had the shallow part of the Caspian. The whole region experienced an increase in soil salinity and chemical pollution, and the Aral Sea is an official disaster area.

The Soviet economic system isolated the Turkic and Mongol peoples of Central Asia from their historic Muslim trading partners to the south and along the 'Silk Road' to the People's Republic of China. Until a rail link with Iran was opened in May 1996, therefore, St Petersburg, Russia, was one of Turkmenistan's nearest rail-linked ports, 3,500 km (2,175 miles) north-west on the Baltic Sea; another was Vladivostok, Russia, on the Pacific, 5,000 km across southern Siberia to the east. The Soviet-built UGSS gas export pipeline went north to Uzbekistan and Russia.

Turkmenistan's proven gas reserves are the fourth-largest in the world, after Russia, the USA and Iran, and the Government claimed that actual reserves were three times the proven figure. At the end of 2002 Turkmenistan's recoverable gas reserves were estimated at 2,010,000m. cu m, and its proven petroleum reserves were assessed at 500m. barrels. There were also smaller reserves of numerous other minerals, such as gold, platinum and sulphur.

Gas production prior to the dissolution of the USSR was over 85,000m. cu m per year. The above-mentioned difficulties with access to cash-paying customers caused output to decline in 1997–98; it was some 12,400m. cu m in 1998, but recovered to an estimated 47,000m. cu m in 2000, 51,270m. cu m in 2001 and 53,339m. cu m in 2002. Petroleum production peaked in the 1970s; production was 8,225,000 metric tons in 2002.

Turkmenistan has two Soviet-era refineries, one in Turkmenbashy (formerly Krasnovodsk) on the Caspian Sea, and the other in Türkmenabat (formerly Charjew) near the Uzbek border, designed to run on Russian petroleum from western Siberia. Both operated in the 1990s at fractions of their capacity and were scheduled for modernization, to cope with the anticipated increase in crude-petroleum output. Turkmenbashy's US $1,400m. upgrade, financed by Japanese and German investors, commenced in 1998 and was scheduled for completion in 2004. An associated petrochemicals complex was under development and was due to become fully operational in late 2002. Construction of a smaller refinery near Atamurat, Lebap Velayat (Oblast), was also in progress.

The population and the labour force increased by one-third in the 1990s, from a low base. Owing to its small and dispersed population (5,725,200 at mid-2002, giving a population density of 11.7 per sq km, according to official estimates—at mid-2002 the UN estimated the total population at 4,794,000, giving a density of 9.8 per sq km), Turkmenistan was of marginal economic importance in the USSR. It was less affected by immigration in the 1930s and 1940s of better-educated Slav and Volga German workers than were Kazakhstan or Kyrgyzstan, although the capital, Ashgabat (with an estimated population of 743,000 in 2002), was still about 40% Caucasian. The country is, however, rather ethnically homogeneous: according to the 1995 census, ethnic Turkmens made up 77.0% of the population, Uzbeks 9.2%, Russians 6.7%, Kazakhs 2.0%, and other nationalities the remainder. Over 35% of the population were estimated to know Russian; ethnic Russians were granted dual citizenship, but continued to emigrate in large numbers; over 150,000 applied to leave in 1999. The departure of Russian-speaking specialists affected sectors such as education and health-delivery.

## THE SOVIET LEGACY

The country was one of the poorest Soviet republics, with recorded GDP of less than 1% of the USSR total in 1988. While Soviet price relativities were in force, Russia claimed it subsidized the Turkmen economy on a scale of 67% of Turkmen GDP (1992) by allocating it machinery, food and raw materials other than natural gas and cotton at below world prices. Even with transfers from the Union centre, Turkmen GDP per head reached only 61% of the former all-Union average.

In 1990 Turkmenistan had the highest infant mortality rate and the lowest life expectancy at birth of the Central Asian republics, although its record on health, literacy and female labour-force participation was vastly better than in other poorer Islamic countries of Western and Southern Asia. The UN Development Programme (UNDP) estimated that the infant mortality rate per 1,000 live births was 99 in 2001. Income losses after independence, the ongoing water pollution from insecticides and fertilizers used in cotton production, and rapid rural population growth kept health indicators at the lowest level among countries in transition, despite an ongoing government commitment to a free national system. Some 40% of the population had no access to safe water or sanitation in the mid-1990s, although, according to the UNDP, 100% of the population was using adequate sanitation facilities. Although the total fertility rate declined in the last two decades of the 20th century, population growth remained very rapid by post-Soviet standards, at 2.5% per year, in part because of low labour demands in the capital-intensive main nationalized industries, which kept the urban population to a modest 46% of the total. The age structure is young, with only 6.5% of the population over 60 years of age. The UN projected that the population would reach some 7.7m. by 2050.

Soviet economic policies reinforced the area's 'colonial' pattern of development. Cotton was the most important crop, and the country was among the 10 highest cotton-producing countries in the world. Despite yearly production of 1.3m.–1.5m. metric tons of seed (unginned) cotton in 1990–95, the country did not possess a significant textiles industry at the time of gaining independence. Turkmenistan produced children's clothing and shoes, but little for adults, so that some 70% of clothing was imported. Almost all consumer durables, medicines, machinery and vehicles came from elsewhere in the former USSR, as did much food; imports from the countries of the former USSR accounted for 34% of consumption in 1991, the highest such rate among those states. However, the import of several turn-key textiles mills resulted in an increase in output in the cotton complex in the 1990s.

After the dissolution of the USSR, there was a sudden repricing of natural resources from under 4% to 50%–80% of world prices. This completely changed the apparent structure of Turkmenistan's GDP. For example, industry comprised 20% of GDP in 1991, but 59% in 1992, while agriculture was 46% of GDP in 1991, but 19% in 1992. Stable labour-force shares implied that this apparent structural change was a function of price movements; industrial employment

remained at about 10% of the total, collective farming (*kolkhoz* agriculture) accounted for about 23% of employment in the early 1990s and plot agriculture for about 16%. In 1991 about one-third of total industrial production was accounted for by 61 textiles enterprises, and a further one-third was contributed by 38 large enterprises in the chemicals, natural gas, petroleum and electricity-generating industries.

The country's dependence on 'soft-budget' trade with Russia and the 'Slavic west' of the former USSR was emphasized by the severe impact of Russia's exclusion of the country from the 'rouble zone' in 1993, a measure that was fiercely resisted by Niyazov. From 1 November 1993 Turkmenistan was no longer allowed to use credits generated in Ashgabat to purchase Russian goods and had to introduce its own currency, the manat. Officials were unprepared for monetary, fiscal and exchange-rate management via the market mechanism, and stabilization proved an ongoing challenge.

### Economic Performance after Independence

Government statistics were incomplete, unreliable and at variance with Western estimates of the same indicators. Until 2000 much government data was unpublished and only incomplete data was provided to the Commonwealth of Independent States (CIS) Statistical Committee. The economy's performance, after accounting for the massive shifts in relative prices, 'hyperinflation' and the widespread resort to non-market mechanisms, remained subject to a wide margin of error.

Industrial production as a whole reflected dependence on the gas sector and showed sharp annual fluctuations in keeping with the export problems of the later 1990s. According to the UN's Economic Commission for Europe, GDP in 1998 stood at 63.8% of the 1989 level, before recovering strongly (by 16%) in 1999. According to the ADB, GDP increased by 17.6% in 2000, by 20.5% in 2001 and by 8.6% in 2002 (official estimated GDP growth in 2002 was 14.9%). According to official forecasts, strong growth was likely to continue. Real gross industrial output in 1998 stood at just over one-half the 1989 level (54%), and increased thereafter. Estimates of growth in industrial GDP of 20.5% in 2002 meant that the sector generally outperformed the rest of the CIS.

## AGRICULTURE

Agriculture in independent Turkmenistan bore the scars of Soviet-era collectivization and misguided protectionist and isolationist policies undertaken by the Niyazov Government. Collective farms were reorganized into farmers' associations, but, as in Soviet times, wheat and cotton were subject to mandatory state orders and quantitative targets, which underpaid farms for these products. The agricultural sector, collectivized under Stalin (Iosif V. Dzhugashvili), and which remained subject to pervasive state intervention, generated about 22.5% of Turkmenistan's GDP in 2002, and employed almost 50% of the labour force. Less than 5% of the total land area was cultivated, and one-half of that was under irrigation. However, the state of the irrigation channels was such that some 50% of the water evaporated without reaching its target, and water use per ha of cotton was some 70% above that in such market economies as Egypt, Greece, Pakistan and Syria. A further legacy of the Soviet era was under-investment in refrigerated storage, so that one-third of the cereal harvest was regularly spoiled by the weather or by vermin.

In 2000 the IMF calculated that an end to the anti-farmer state-order system and freedom to transfer land and water to non-traditional crops, such as sun-dried tomatoes and raisins, could increase farmers' incomes and foreign-exchange earnings by some 7% of GDP. Elimination of subsidies might further benefit the budget by 6% of GDP.

In mid-1995 there were outbreaks of social discontent, including a demonstration in the capital to protest at shortages of water, bread and flour. President Niyazov subsequently dismissed 10 district leaders for failing to meet state orders for wheat supplies. In April 1998 such measures were strengthened, when Niyazov announced that officials in the agricultural sector would be liable to criminal charges if cotton- and grain-production targets were not met. Much bread-quality wheat continued to be imported from Ukraine, for example, as part of barter arrangements. Agricultural production increased by 26.9% in 1999 and by 17.0% in 2000, despite being affected by severe drought. Production increased in 2001, owing to more favourable climatic conditions. In July 2003 Niyazov announced that Turkmenistan would be ready to enter world grain markets by 2010, and predicted that by that time annual grain production would have reached 5m. metric tons.

## FOREIGN TRADE

Like most former states of the USSR, Turkmenistan succeeded in reducing the proportion of its trade with that region and increasing ties with non-traditional partners during the 1990s. However, much of that diversification was not intentional, but rather the effect of the situation on the gas market. Periodic cessations of supply to non-paying former USSR customers, together with Russia's refusal to accept any Turkmen gas between March 1997 and December 1998, seriously affected gas export earnings and made trade appear to be more orientated towards non-traditional partners than it actually was. Gas, delivered almost exclusively to the states of the former USSR in the 1990s, for example, accounted for over 60% of total goods exports in 1996, but for only 12% in 1998. By 2001 the hydrocarbons sector accounted for some 84.7% of total exports, and in 2002 it accounted for 85.7%. Gas export earnings rose by some 21% in 2001, owing to new gas agreements with Russia, Ukraine and Iran. A foreign-trade surplus of US $535m. was recorded in 2001, which increased nearly two-fold, to $1,000m. in 2002, according to the ADB. However, Turkmenistan's highly distorted trade regime and overvalued exchange rate discouraged not only exports, but also imports of consumer goods from traditional partners in Russia and Central Asia, as the state allocated the available foreign exchange for priority imports of machinery and vehicles.

In the immediate post-Soviet period, Turkmenistan diversified almost all of its cotton exports, worth some US $430m., to world markets (mainly in Italy and Turkey), excluding its insolvent former Soviet counterparts. Cotton exports, by volume, to the textiles centres of Belarus, Russia and Ukraine in the first half of 1994 were 14%, 48% and 18%, respectively, of levels in the first half of 1993. In 1996, the last 'normal' year before the severe decline in gas exports, cotton fibre accounted for some 23% of merchandise exports. In the late 1990s Turkmenistan sold large amounts of cotton on futures markets. However, it failed to deliver the goods traded and was debarred by international cotton organizations. The volume of exports rose in 1998, but proceeds were affected by a 20% decline in world market prices during the course of that year. Cotton fibre and yarn accounted for 5% of merchandise exports in 2001.

Depending on the fate of the various pipeline schemes and the course of economic reform, Turkmenistan might, in the future, record increases in the proportion of trade undertaken with world markets and, in addition, derive greater gains from that trade. In 2002 Turkmenistan's main trading partner was Ukraine (which accounted for 17.9% of imports and 16.2 of exports), followed by Russia and other republics of the CIS (in particular, Azerbaijan, Kazakhstan and Tajikistan), Iran, Turkey, Germany and the United Arab Emirates. To the extent that trade was subject to voluntary contract by

firms, the exchange-rate regime was relevant. Turkmenistan's national currency, the manat, was introduced at an official commercial exchange rate of two manats per US dollar. It then traded at multiple rates, controlled by the Government, much against the advice of the IMF, and despite President Niyazov's refusal to use the state bank's reserves, which he personally controlled, to defend the currency via the price mechanism. Official exchange rates and surrender requirements for gas exporters were less generous than the parallel or curb rate; rates for non-gas firms were less confiscatory, but still highly unfavourable.

The country's external competitiveness deteriorated sharply in the second half of the 1990s, as the manat suffered a huge real appreciation (at the officially controlled exchange rate) in relation to the other currencies of the former USSR and the US dollar, owing to ongoing double-digit domestic inflation. Real wages, in dollar terms, increased by 250% between 1995 and mid-1999 (albeit from a low base), whereas they were close to stagnation in Kazakhstan, Russia and Ukraine.

The manat declined sharply in nominal terms between the time of its introduction and 1996, followed by a gentler decline to 5,200 per US dollar in April 1998 (where it remained by the end of 2002).

## FOREIGN INVESTMENT

There is no reliable data on domestic capital formation. However, net investment, compensating for physical depreciation and the economic obsolescence of the country's infrastructure, plants and equipment, was definitely negative in the 1990s. The Soviet-built transportation and communication systems began to break down and wear out. International construction activity mainly involved a few 'prestige' projects, such as the new international airport terminal at Ashgabat, inaugurated in October 1994, a number of new hotels in the capital, the purchase of Boeing aircraft for the national airline, and the construction of a huge national memorial mosque at Gök Tepe. Over 150 construction projects were being carried out under contracts with foreign firms, including the overhaul of the Turkmenbashy refinery. The majority of the projects involved the energy, light-industry and food sectors.

Cumulative foreign direct investment was reported by Western institutions as being in the range of US $780m. in 1992–99. According to EBRD estimates, net foreign direct investment was approximately $100m. in 2000 and was expected to increase to $150m. in 2001. The small scale of the annual inflows may be seen by comparing that stock to the cost estimates of the various large-scale projects that were under consideration, such as the proposed $2,000m.–$2,700m. pipeline from Dauletabad to Pakistan, via Afghanistan, to be constructed by Unocal of the USA and the Central Asian Gas Pipeline (CentGas) Consortium, and a scheme, examined in preliminary fashion by the Japanese company Mitsubishi, for a 6,700-km gas pipeline to run from Turkmenistan through Uzbekistan to Kazakhstan, and then to link up with the internal network of the People's Republic of China. By comparison, Turkmenistan's GDP in 2000, at the official exchange rate, was $4,404m. There is no data available on the flow of capital out of the country, but the frequent attacks on non-repatriation of export proceeds by President Niyazov, and the onerous requirement to convert 50% of proceeds at the unfavourable official rate, testify to the existence of the problem, which is widespread in the former USSR generally, owing to weak stabilization and the rule of law.

A variety of pipeline schemes were at different stages of development. In December 1997 a 200-km gas pipeline was opened, linking the Korpedje field in western Turkmenistan to the town of Kord Kuy (Kurt Kui) in northern Iran. In the first year 1,800m. cu m was exported, although the line's annual capacity was 4,000m. cu m, potentially expandable to 8,000m. cu m. The economic impact of Turkmenistan's first alternative to the Russian route was modest at first, owing to weak demand in Iran and because approximately 65% of the gas went to Iran in the first three years, in payment for the construction. However, the relationship held promise, as it was thought that Iranian demand might increase, owing to the need to inject gas into its oilfields, in order forcibly to expel the petroleum. Nevertheless, Iran was expected to try to increase its own gas output and exports to Turkey, upon development of its South Pars field, so its long-term demand for Turkmen gas was uncertain. However, in February 2001 Iran agreed to double its gas imports to 6,000m. cu m per year, partly owing to Turkmenistan's support during negotiations for control of the Caspian Sea.

The construction of the proposed gas pipeline from Turkmenistan to Pakistan, via Afghanistan was delayed in the late 1990s, owing to political instability in the region. In August 1998 the USA bombed sites in Afghanistan belonging to the Saudi dissident Osama bin Laden and his militant Islamist al-Qa'ida (Base) organization, and Unocal withdrew from the project, citing low world prices and the political situation in the region. However, in May 2002 the Governments of Turkmenistan, Pakistan and Afghanistan signed a memorandum of understanding to carry out a feasibility study for construction of the 1,460-km pipeline, which could eventually have an annual capacity of 15,000m.–30,000m. cu m of gas. In July the ADB formally agreed to provide funding for the project.

Plans for the revival of a new 'Silk Road' rail link for petroleum and goods were discussed at the May 1996 opening of the Tedzhen to Mashhad (Iran) rail track. Some 300-km of new track were laid and a 'free economic zone' was established at Sarakhs, on the border. The railway linked the former USSR network to Iran's Gulf seaports, and promised to reduce journey times between Europe and South-East Asia by up to 10 days. Road transport across Iran to the Gulf also had potential to develop, owing to low Iranian petrol prices. The initial capacity of the rail link was 3m. metric tons of goods per year, which was expected to increase to 8m. tons.

In July 1998 Monument Oil, based in the United Kingdom, which was subsequently taken over by Lasmo Oil, came to an agreement with the National Iranian Oil Company to deliver petroleum from its Burun field offshore to the northern border of Iran and to swap it for petroleum to be exported from the Persian Gulf. The field was considered capable of an increase in output if it were fully developed and if an export route could be regularized. Dragon Oil, based in the United Arab Emirates, also had an exchange deal with Iran, producing about 380,000 metric tons per year near the Cheleken Peninsula. In 1999 the EBRD agreed to provide the Turkmen Government with a loan worth US $75m. for a joint offshore petroleum project with Dragon Oil. The first tranche of $8m. was disbursed in December 2000, which permitted Dragon Oil to commence its drilling programme in January 2001. Production was expected to reach around 80,000 barrels per day. In July 1998 a deal was signed between Western petroleum companies and Turkmenistan's Turkmenneft, to explore and develop oilfields in the Garashsyzlyk area, onshore in western Turkmenistan. Development of Burun and Garashsyzlyk had the potential to yield substantial volumes of petroleum by 2006–07, if a suitable export route were available. Exxon-Mobil (USA) undertook a seismic survey of oil and gas deposits in 2000.

Possible energy links with other countries in Central Asia were the subject of Western feasibility studies, and President Niyazov discussed them on many occasions with various heads of state. A dispute with Azerbaijan over ownership of

the Serdar oil and gasfield, known as Kyapaz by Azerbaijan, continued to prevent development of the field.

In the mid-1990s Mitsubishi was invited to conduct an investigation into a possible 6,700-km gas pipeline from Turkmenistan through Uzbekistan to Kazakhstan, to join with the north-west part of the Chinese internal network, which would be capable of delivering Turkmen gas to the Pacific coast. An extension would involve supplying South-East Asia, either by tanker, or via an underwater pipeline. Subsequent analyses by Western specialists found the basic scheme costs vastly to outweigh the benefits, even without stressing the risks of political instability in East-Central Asia. A preliminary agreement on supplies was drawn up, but no starting date for the project with the China National Petroleum Corporation was mentioned when Chinese President Jiang Zemin visited Ashgabat in July 2000.

## FINANCE AND THE BUDGET

The state budget was subject to numerous fluctuations, owing to the huge swings in revenue from the major exports. A complete picture of state finances was hard to obtain, as many ministerial commitments remained off-budget, and resort to non-cash offsets was widespread. However, it is agreed that the Government's fiscal position weakened markedly during the later 1990s. Deficits were controlled mainly through *ad hoc* compression of expenditure ('sequestration') and changes in subsidies, and revenue was raised via implicit taxes such as the 'price scissors' on agriculture. Confronted with uncertain revenues from gas and cotton exports, the Government reduced budgetary spending by curtailing some expenditure (wages, pensions, stipends and medicines were supposed to be protected), in order to promote fiscal balance. Reported deficits appeared modest, but total commitments were hidden in off-budget accounts, such as those for agricultural supply and procurement. By 1998 the deficit was equivalent to 2.7% of GDP, but closer to 12%–15% of GDP if sectoral commitments were properly accounted for; the official deficit in 1999 was 4%. As a result, credit policy was often expansionary, with directed credits handed out, without great expectations of repayment, to enterprises with soft budget constraints. In 2000 and 2001 Turkmenistan recorded a budgetary surplus, equivalent to 0.9% of GDP in the latter year. The draft budget for 2002, approved in November 2001, envisaged a deficit equivalent to 2% of GDP, although the ADB later reported that the budget deficit was equivalent to just 0.1% of GDP in 2002.

Subsidies that afforded the population free gas and other facilities accounted for one-third of central and local government expenditure in the mid-1990s. Although Turkmenistan was a major importer of flour and wheat in the early 1990s, President Niyazov promised free bread. Such populist promises were anathema to the IMF.

Inflation in the first half of the 1990s was high, if not at hyperinflation levels, and very variable on a monthly basis. Non-market pricing continued to play a large role, as the Government attempted to dictate maximum increases and control profit margins; periodic changes in administered prices generated sharp monthly movements in the consumer price index. According to CIS data, producer prices rose by nearly 1,000% in 1991, by 1,610% in 1992 and by nearly 3,000% in 1996. Consumer prices increased by 1,150% in 1993 and by 1,748% in 1994.

The introduction of a stabilization programme helped to bring inflation below 100% (at 98.8%) in 1996 and to 16.8% in 1997. However, with the serious decrease in gas income and the concomitantly high current-account deficit, improvements ceased, and consumer prices rose by 24.2% in 1999. Owing to high production growth and macroeconomic stability, the inflation rate decreased to only 7.4% in 2000, rising slightly by 2002, to 8.8%, according to the ADB.

## Foreign Debt

From a starting point of essentially zero at independence, total external debt stood at some US $2,015m. at the end of 1999, after extensive borrowing, aimed at mitigating some of the effects of the Russian crisis and the impact of the sharp declines in gas revenue from 1997 on the Government's sectoral-development programme. Agriculture became heavily indebted at commercial rates in the 1990s, and its external debt of $800m. at the end of 1999 was equal to that of the energy sector, and equivalent to 22% of GDP. Loans were spent on the upgrade of the Turkmenbashy refinery and on agricultural machinery, gas infrastructure and textiles plants. There was a sharp rise in actual and projected debt-service ratios. However, owing to high economic growth, the current account moved from a deficit of $527m. in 1999 to a surplus of $20m. in 2000.

## Privatization

The process of privatization in Turkmenistan was extremely slow. In 1999 the country was above only Belarus in the EBRD's ranking of countries in transition. At mid-1999 23 medium-sized enterprises had been privatized, 10 in textiles, seven in food and one electrical-appliance factory; however, the highest price was only US $200,000 and, unusually, all buyers were local. About 24,000 small enterprises had been transferred out of state ownership, but many of the transfers were cosmetic.

Effectively, the entirety of the gas, petroleum and cotton-processing sectors, building materials and food-processing remained owned and regulated by various administrative structures and ministries. The private sector, outside plot agriculture, accounted for less than 10% of GDP. For medium-sized and large enterprises there existed a privatization scheme aiming to sell 280 units over time. In early 1998 President Niyazov approved a procedure whereby 18 large firms were to be valued in preparation for their conversion into joint-stock companies; however, by mid-2001 only nine had been privatized and six had been converted into joint-stock companies. There was little prospect of a rapid divestment of the state from economic activity, because of mercantilist instincts on the part of the presidency, and a poor understanding of the workings of the market. Minimum prices for sales were set too high, the status of the land underneath factory buildings remained uncertain, and winning bidders were required to maintain costly social facilities for workers. According to official figures, the private sector accounted for about 25% of industrial output in 2000.

Collective farms were converted into farmers' associations, but continued to operate under soft budget constraints and remained subject to obligatory deliveries to the state procurement organizations at very unfavourable prices. The Government appeared to be making good progress in land reform.

## Aid

Turkmenistan received a modest amount of international assistance, notably from the European Union's programme of Technical Assistance to the CIS (€8.5m. per year, mainly for consultancy work on the agricultural, telecommunications and energy sectors, a privatization overview and conservation). Much more aid would have been forthcoming had reforms been more to the institution's liking. The EBRD, the US Department of Agriculture and the World Bank provided for some technical assistance in the form of background and feasibility studies for various sectors and projects. However, in May 2000 the EBRD 'froze' all public-sector projects in the country, citing poor progress in privatization and democratization.

## PROSPECTS

Turkmenistan's economic prospects depend on improved exports of its vast gas reserves and, thus, on the construction of transportation networks. Without such networks Turkmenistan will remain limited to selling gas domestically and to Russia, Ukraine and the insolvent Transcaucasian former Soviet states. In the late 1990s Russia tended to exploit its geographical and technological advantages with respect to the land-locked states of Central Asia. For Turkmenistan to finance alternative routes requires Western lenders to provide large amounts of funding to construct new routes across multiple independent, and often quarrelling, competing territories. At the beginning of the 21st century, however, progress was under way towards a revival of Turkmenistan's fuel trade, with the opening of a gas pipeline to northern Iran, some small petroleum-exchange arrangements with Iran, and new contracts to deliver gas to Russia and Ukraine.

Independence opened up new scope for mineral wealth in the sparsely populated country, but the short-term effect was to deal a heavy blow to Turkmenistan's misdeveloped, export-dependent economy. The end of central planning and the demise of the rouble zone led to extremely high inflation, which decimated real and dollar wages, and encouraged rampant corruption, as the energy and cotton barons' fiefs greatly increased in value. Popular discontent was kept in check by state control of the media and highly repressive measures against political expression, but also by populist measures such as free gas for households and ready employment in the public sector.

Despite President Niyazov's declared interest in modernization, the country remained at the bottom of the league tables for the majority of measures of economic, legal and political transition. Foreign investments were few, and foreign borrowing was increased, to the dubious benefit of the population at large. Joint-ventures and production-sharing agreements were checked by the huge risks of doing business in Central Asia. The President was involved in all important economic decisions involving foreign investors and donors. Personal corruption was suspected; Niyazov's insistence, in early 2000, on an upfront payment of some hundreds of millions of dollars was one factor in the curtailment of negotiations with the General Electric-Bechtel consortium over the construction of the Trans-Caspian pipeline. Niyazov bore a good deal of responsibility for his country's failure to undertake the usual macroeconomic and institutional reforms needed to accelerate transition to a more efficient, mixed-market system. The business climate remained non-transparent, and lack of progress caused frustration in the donor community. Many economic basics were poorly understood, such as the social cost of the self-sufficiency in wheat programme, or the cost of maintaining an overly large state apparatus without the tax revenue to finance it in a non-inflationary manner. Directive credits and quantitative output targets continued to be set in Soviet fashion, and ministers dismissed for failure to meet them. The President also shared responsibility for Turkmenistan's less than friendly relations with its most important neighbours, particularly Azerbaijan, but also Russia, at least until early 2000. Unfortunately, these neighbours were in a position to block exports or extract rents in the form of transit fees. The dispute over the dividing line between the Azeri and Turkmen Caspian offshore fields, at issue since independence, was a case in point.

Although Turkmenistan appeared politically stable on the surface, many tensions persisted. The Government's economic policies, particularly in agriculture, were unsustainably costly, both to the budget and to farmers in terms of foregone earnings. Although economic growth was strong from 1999, there were concerns about over-dependence on the hydrocarbons sector. The ADB predicted growth of 7%–8% in 2003–04. In August 2002 President Niyazov reportedly declared his intention to create 500,000 new jobs by 2010. Although the rate of inflation had declined substantially, fears that it could subsequently accelerate remained. Meanwhile, no succession plan was in place for President Niyazov, who had received heart treatment in the West.

Despite the country's vast mineral reserves, and the likelihood that the Caspian region as a whole would experience strong international investment in 2002–15, in order to meet predicted increases in demand, the degree to which Turkmenistan's 5m. impoverished inhabitants would benefit was seen to depend on more rational economic policies, notably the integration of non-budget funds into a more transparent budget, as well as on geopolitical factors outside their control.

# Statistical Survey

Principal sources (unless otherwise stated): IMF, *Turkmenistan, Economic Review, Turkmenistan—Recent Economic Developments* (December 1999); World Bank, *Statistical Handbook: States of the Former USSR.*

## Area and Population

### AREA, POPULATION AND DENSITY

| | |
|---|---|
| Area (sq km) . . . . . . . . | 488,100* |
| Population (census results) | |
| 12 January 1989 . . . . . . . . . | 3,533,925 |
| 10 January 1995 | |
| Males . . . . . . . . . | 2,225,331 |
| Females. . . . . . . . . | 2,257,920 |
| Total . . . . . . . . | 4,483,251 |
| Population (UN estimates at mid-year)† | |
| 2000 . . . . . . . . . | 4,643,000 |
| 2001 . . . . . . . . . | 4,720,000 |
| 2002 . . . . . . . . . | 4,794,000 |
| Density (per sq km) at mid-2002 . . . . . . . | 9.8 |

* 188,456 sq miles.

† Source: UN, *World Population Prospects: The 2002 Revision.*

**Population** (official estimates): 5,369,400 at 1 January 2001; 5,725,200 at 1 July 2002 (Source: National Institute of State Statistics and Information).

### POPULATION BY ETHNIC GROUP

(official estimates at 1 January 1993)

| | Number | % |
|---|---|---|
| Turkmen . . . . . . . . . . . | 3,118,000 | 73.3 |
| Russian . . . . . . . . . | 419,000 | 9.8 |
| Uzbek . . . . . . . . . . | 382,000 | 9.0 |
| Kazakh . . . . . . . . . | 87,000 | 2.0 |
| Tatar . . . . . . . . . . | 39,000 | 0.9 |
| Ukrainian . . . . . . . . | 34,000 | 0.8 |
| Azeri . . . . . . . . . . | 34,000 | 0.8 |
| Armenian . . . . . . . . . | 32,000 | 0.8 |
| Belarusian . . . . . . . . | 9,000 | 0.2 |
| Others . . . . . . . . . . | 100,000 | 2.4 |
| **Total** . . . . . . . . . | 4,254,000 | 100.0 |

### PRINCIPAL TOWNS

(estimated population at 1 January 1999)

| | | | | |
|---|---|---|---|---|
| Ashgabat (capital) . | 605,000 | Türkmenbashi | | |
| | | (Turkmenbashy)‡ . | 70,000 | |
| Türkmenabat* . . | 203,000 | Bayramaly (Bayram- | | |
| | | Ali) . . . . . | 60,000 | |
| Dashkhovuz | | | | |
| (Tashauz) . . | 165,000 | Tejen (Tedzhen) . . | 54,000 | |
| Mari (Mary) . . . | 123,000 | Serdar§ . . . . | 51,000 | |
| Balkanabat† . . . | 119,000 | | | |

* Formerly Charjew (Chardzhou).

† Formerly Nebit-Dag.

‡ Formerly Krasnovodsk.

§ Formerly Gyzylarbat (Kizyl-Arvat).

**1 July 2002** (official estimates): Ashgabat 743,000.

### BIRTHS, MARRIAGES AND DEATHS

| | Registered live births | | Registered marriages | | Registered deaths | |
|---|---|---|---|---|---|---|
| | Number | Rate (per 1,000) | Number | Rate (per 1,000) | Number | Rate (per 1,000) |
| 1987 . . | 126,787 | 37.2 | 31,484 | 9.2 | 26,802 | 7.9 |
| 1988 . . | 125,887 | 36.0 | 33,008 | 9.4 | 27,317 | 7.8 |
| 1989 . . | 124,992 | 34.9 | 34,890 | 9.8 | 27,609 | 7.7 |

**Registered deaths:** 25,755 (death rate 7.0 per 1,000) in 1990; 27,403 (7.3 per 1,000) in 1991; 27,509 (6.8 per 1,000) in 1992; 31,171 (7.2 per 1,000) in 1993; 32,067 (7.3 per 1,000) in 1994.

**1998** (provisional): Live births 98,461 (birth rate 20.3 per 1,000); Marriages 26,361 (marriage rate 5.4 per 1,000); Deaths 29,628 (death rate 6.1 per 1,000).

Source: UN, *Demographic Yearbook.*

**Expectation of life** (WHO estimates, years at birth): 62.5 (males 58.9; females 66.5) in 2001 (Source: WHO, *World Health Report*).

### EMPLOYMENT

('000 persons at 31 December)

| | 1996 | 1997 | 1998* |
|---|---|---|---|
| Agriculture . . . . . . | 769.8 | 778.8 | 890.5 |
| Forestry . . . . . . . | 2.5 | 2.9 | 1.9 |
| Industry† . . . . . . . | 172.0 | 188.1 | 226.8 |
| Construction . . . . . . | 136.2 | 122.8 | 108.2 |
| Trade and catering . . . . . | 91.8 | 101.2 | 115.8 |
| Transport and communications . | 77.7 | 77.9 | 90.7 |
| Information-computing services . | 1.3 | 1.0 | 1.2 |
| Housing and municipal services . | 50.2 | 46.8 | 48.3 |
| Health care and social security . | 97.4 | 100.4 | 89.2 |
| Education, culture and arts. . . | 183.8 | 185.9 | 190.5 |
| Science, research and development | 9.2 | 6.9 | 5.2 |
| General administration . . . . | 24.7 | 25.3 | 28.8 |
| Finance and insurance . . . . | 8.7 | 9.6 | 12.6 |
| Other activities . . . . . | 41.5 | 28.3 | 29.0 |
| **Total** . . . . . . . . | 1,666.8 | 1,675.9 | 1,838.7 |

* Provisional.

† Comprising manufacturing (except printing and publishing), mining and quarrying, electricity, gas, water, logging and fishing.

**2000** ('000 persons at 31 December): Employed 1,908 (Agriculture 908, Industry 248, Other 752); Unemployed 51; Total labour force (incl. those not registered) 2,120 (Source: Asian Development Bank, *Key Indicators of Developing Asian and Pacific Countries*).

**2001** ('000 persons at 31 December): Employed 1,947 (Agriculture 943, Industry 262, Other 742); Unemployed 57; Total labour force (incl. those not registered) 2,179 (Source: Asian Development Bank, *Key Indicators of Developing Asian and Pacific Countries*).

**2002** ('000 persons at 31 December, estimates): Employed 2,013 (Agriculture 980, Industry 285, Other 748); Unemployed 57; Total labour force (incl. those not registered) 2,253 (Source: Asian Development Bank, *Key Indicators of Developing Asian and Pacific Countries*).

# Health and Welfare

## KEY INDICATORS

| | |
|---|---:|
| Total fertility rate (children per woman, 2001). . . . . | 3.3 |
| Under-5 mortality rate (per 1,000 live births, 2001) . | 99 |
| HIV/AIDS (% of persons aged 15–49, 2001). . . . . . | <0.10 |
| Physicians (per 1,000 head, 1998) . . . . . . . | 2.61 |
| Hospital beds (per 1,000 head, 1998) . . . . . . | 11.15 |
| Health expenditure (2000): US $ per head (PPP) . . . | 286 |
| Health expenditure (2000): % of GDP . . . . . . | 5.4 |
| Health expenditure (2000): public (% of total) . . . . | 84.9 |
| Human Development Index (2001): ranking . . . . . | 87 |
| Human Development Index (2001): value . . . . . . | 0.748 |

For sources and definitions, see explanatory note on p. vi.

# Agriculture

## PRINCIPAL CROPS

('000 metric tons)

| | 1999 | 2000 | 2001 |
|---|---:|---:|---:|
| Wheat . . . . . . . . . | 1,506 | 1,150* | 1,760* |
| Rice (paddy) . . . . . . | 33.3 | 27.3 | 39.1* |
| Barley . . . . . . . | 19.5 | 22* | 23* |
| Potatoes . . . . . . . | 28.1 | 29† | 30† |
| Cottonseed . . . . . . | 1,300 | 1,030 | 1,100 |
| Cabbages . . . . . . . | 29.3 | 35† | 32† |
| Tomatoes . . . . . . | 139.0 | 145† | 155† |
| Dry onions . . . . . . | 48.7 | 53† | 49† |
| Carrots . . . . . . | 28.9 | 32† | 36† |
| Other vegetables† . . . . | 32.5 | 31.6 | 31.7 |
| Watermelons‡ . . . . . | 244* | 240† | 235† |
| Grapes . . . . . . . | 145.0 | 140† | 135† |
| Apples . . . . . . . | 20.0 | 19† | 18† |
| Other fruits and berries† . . . | 29.6 | 27 | 26 |
| Cotton (lint) . . . . . . | 234.3 | 232.6 | 187.0* |

* Unofficial figure.
† FAO estimate(s).
‡ Including melons, pumpkins and squash.

Source: FAO.

## LIVESTOCK

(FAO estimates, '000 head at 1 January)

| | 1999 | 2000 | 2001 |
|---|---:|---:|---:|
| Horses . . . . . . . . | 16 | 16 | 17 |
| Asses . . . . . . . | 25 | 24 | 25 |
| Camels. . . . . . . | 41 | 40 | 42 |
| Cattle . . . . . . . | 880 | 850 | 860 |
| Pigs . . . . . . . | 48 | 46 | 45 |
| Sheep . . . . . . . | 5,650 | 5,600 | 6,000 |
| Goats . . . . . . . | 375 | 368 | 375 |
| Chickens . . . . . . | 4,000 | 4,300 | 4,800 |
| Turkeys . . . . . . | 250 | 250 | 200 |

Source: FAO.

## LIVESTOCK PRODUCTS

('000 metric tons)

| | 1999 | 2000 | 2001 |
|---|---:|---:|---:|
| Beef and veal . . . . . . | 63.0 | 65.0* | 67.0* |
| Mutton and lamb. . . . . | 60.0† | 58.5* | 57.0* |
| Goat meat . . . . . . | 3.3† | 3.2* | 3.0* |
| Poultry meat . . . . . | 4.6 | 4.9* | 5.0* |
| Other meat* . . . . . | 2.6 | 2.7 | 2.6 |
| Cows' milk . . . . . | 875.4 | 820.0* | 830.0* |
| Cheese* . . . . . . | 1.6 | 1.5 | 1.6 |
| Butter* . . . . . . | 1.3 | 1.1 | 0.8 |
| Hen eggs . . . . . | 15.9† | 13.0* | 15.0* |
| Honey . . . . . | 9.9 | 8.0* | 8.0* |
| Raw silk (incl. waste) . . . | 5.0* | 4.7† | 5.0* |
| Wool: greasy . . . . . | 21.9 | 20.0* | 21.0* |
| Wool: scoured . . . . . | 13.1 | 12.0* | 12.6* |
| Cattle hides (fresh)* . . . . | 6.7 | 6.8 | 7.0 |
| Sheepskins (fresh)* . . . . | 8.0 | 7.8 | 7.6 |

* FAO estimate(s).
† Unofficial figure.

Source: FAO.

# Fishing

(metric tons, live weight)

| | 1998 | 1999 | 2000 |
|---|---:|---:|---:|
| Capture . . . . . . | 7,010 | 9,058 | 12,228 |
| Azov sea sprat . . . . . | 6,324 | 8,370 | 11,540 |
| Aquaculture . . . . . | 559 | 549 | 547 |
| Silver carp . . . . . . | 445 | 422 | 427 |
| **Total catch** . . . . . . | 7,569 | 9,607 | 12,775 |

Source: FAO, *Yearbook of Fishery Statistics*.

# Mining

('000 metric tons, unless otherwise indicated)

| | 1998 | 1999 | 2000* |
|---|---:|---:|---:|
| Crude petroleum . . . . . . | 6,500† | 7,800† | 7,350 |
| Natural gas (million cu metres) . | 14,000† | 22,800† | 47,000 |
| Bentonite† . . . . . . . | 50 | 50 | 50 |
| Salt (unrefined) . . . . . | 215† | 215† | 215 |
| Gypsum (crude)† . . . . . | 100 | 100 | 100 |

* Preliminary figures.
† Estimated production.

Source: US Geological Survey.

**2001** ('000 metric tons, unless otherwise indicated): Crude petroleum 7,719; Natural gas (million cu metres) 51,270; Salt 218 (Source: Asian Development Bank, *Key Indicators of Developing Asian and Pacific Countries*).

**2002** ('000 metric tons, unless otherwise indicated): Crude petroleum 8,225; Natural gas (million cu metres) 53,339; Salt 221 (Source: Asian Development Bank, *Key Indicators of Developing Asian and Pacific Countries*).

# Industry

**SELECTED PRODUCTS**
('000 metric tons, unless otherwise indicated)

| | 1996 | 1997 | 1998 |
|---|---|---|---|
| Vegetable oil . . . . . . | 36 | 22 | 33 |
| Wheat flour . . . . . . | 329 | 303 | 339 |
| Ethyl alcohol ('000 hectolitres) . . | 2 | 2 | 1 |
| Woven cotton fabrics (million sq metres) . . . . . . . . | 18 | 14 | 15 |
| Woven silk fabrics (million sq metres) . . . . . . | 4,468 | 4,479 | 4,529 |
| Woven woollen fabrics (million sq metres) . . . . . | 2.8 | 3.2 | 2.5 |
| Blankets . . . . . . . | 15 | 19 | 24 |
| Knotted wool carpets and rugs ('000 sq metres) . . . . . . | 417 | 326 | 315 |
| Footwear, excl. rubber ('000 pairs) | 1,546 | 1,108 | 561 |
| Nitric acid (100%) . . . . | 121 | 109 | 145 |
| Ammonia (nitrogen content) . . | 85 | 74 | 93 |
| Nitrogenous fertilizers (a)*† . . | 50 | 49 | 62 |
| Phosphate fertilizers (b)*† . . . | 13 | 5 | 6 |
| Soap . . . . . . . . | 1.7 | 0.4 | 0.7 |
| Motor spirit (petrol) . . . . | 677 | 766 | 693‡ |
| Gas-diesel (distillate fuel) oil . . | 1,253 | 1,520 | 1,575‡ |
| Residual fuel oils . . . . . | 1,301 | 1,600 | 2,214‡ |
| Clay building bricks (million) . . | 371 | 278 | 245 |
| Quicklime . . . . . . . | 21 | 28 | 16 |
| Cement . . . . . . . | 438 | 601 | 750 |
| Electric energy (million kWh) . . | 10,100‡ | 9,498 | 9,416‡ |

\* Production in terms of (a) nitrogen or (b) phosphoric acid.
† Official figures.
‡ Provisional or estimated figure.

Source: mainly UN, *Industrial Commodity Statistics Yearbook*.

**2000** ('000 metric tons, unless otherwise indicated): Wheat flour 545; Nitrogenous fertilizers 89; Gas-diesel (distillate fuel) oil 1,453; Cement 420; Crude steel 341; Electric energy (million kWh) 9,900 (Source: Asian Development Bank, *Key Indicators of Developing Asian and Pacific Countries*).

**2001** ('000 metric tons, unless otherwise indicated): Wheat flour 561; Nitrogenous fertilizers 72; Gas-diesel (distillate fuel) oil 448; Crude steel 356; Electric energy (million kWh) 10,600 (Source: Asian Development Bank, *Key Indicators of Developing Asian and Pacific Countries*).

**2002** ('000 metric tons, unless otherwise indicated): Wheat flour 537; Nitrogenous fertilizers 103; Gas-diesel (distillate fuel) oil 1,509; Cement 487; Crude steel 685; Electric energy (million kWh) 10,700 (Source: Asian Development Bank, *Key Indicators of Developing Asian and Pacific Countries*).

# Finance

**CURRENCY AND EXCHANGE RATES**

**Monetary Units**
100 tenge = 1 Turkmen manat.

**Sterling, Dollar and Euro Equivalents** (30 May 2003)
£1 sterling = 8,567.5 manats;
US $1 = 5,200.0 manats;
€1 = 6,147.3 manats;
10,000 Turkmen manats = £1.167 = $1.923 = €1.627.

Note: The Turkmen manat was introduced on 1 November 1993, replacing the Russian (formerly Soviet) rouble at a rate of 1 manat = 500 roubles. Following the introduction of the Turkmen manat, a multiple exchange rate system was established. The foregoing information refers to the official rate of exchange. This rate was maintained at US $1 = 4,165 manats between May 1997 and April 1998. It was adjusted to $1 = 5,200 manats in April 1998. In addition to the official rate, there was a commercial bank rate of exchange until this market was closed in December 1998. There is also a 'parallel' market rate, which averaged $1 = 6,493 manats in 1998 and reached $1 = 14,200 manats at mid-1999.

**BUDGET**
('000 million manats)

| Revenue* | 1997 | 1998 | 1999† |
|---|---|---|---|
| State budget . . . . . . | 2,067.3 | 1,867.5 | 2,382.3 |
| Personal income tax . . . . | 108.3 | 157.4 | 224.9 |
| Profit tax . . . . . . | 579.6 | 412.0 | 422.0 |
| Value-added tax . . . . . | 797.9 | 714.9 | 946.3 |
| Natural resources tax . . . | 231.2 | 43.1 | 201.1 |
| Excise tax . . . . . . | 92.4 | 221.3 | 377.8 |
| Other receipts* . . . . . . | 257.9 | 318.8 | 210.1 |
| Pension and Social Security Fund | 471.0 | 711.0 | 832.5 |
| Medical Insurance Fund . . . | 32.7 | 8.2 | 0.0 |
| Repayments on rescheduled gas debt . . . . . . . . | 246.6 | 474.1 | 478.3 |
| **Total** . . . . . . . | **2,817.6** | **3,060.8** | **3,693.1** |

| Expenditure | 1997 | 1998 | 1999‡ |
|---|---|---|---|
| National economy . . . . . | 843.9 | 461.1 | 623.3 |
| Agriculture . . . . . | 632.5 | 331.4 | 223.2 |
| Transport and communications | 121.1 | 63.4 | 190.0 |
| Other . . . . . . . | 90.3 | 66.3 | 210.1 |
| Socio-cultural services† . . . . | 975.7 | 1,850.0 | 1,907.9 |
| Education . . . . . | 435.3 | 919.2 | 1,048.7 |
| Health . . . . . . | 443.1 | 493.8 | 550.6 |
| Communal services . . . . | 9.1 | 337.9 | 188.6 |
| Culture, recreation and other | 88.2 | 99.1 | 120.0 |
| Defence§ . . . . . . . | 440.2 | 435.8 | 582.0 |
| Pension and Social Security Fund | 387.8 | 511.5 | 605.9 |
| Interest payments . . . . . | 72.1 | 11.1 | 18.0 |
| Public administration and other purposes . . . . . . . | 94.3 | 153.4 | 157.2 |
| **Total** . . . . . . . | **2,814.0** | **3,422.8** | **3,894.3** |

\* Including grants received and road fund revenues.
† Approved budget.
‡ Excluding expenditure of the Pension and Social Security Fund.
§ Variable coverage, owing to changes in classification.

**2000** ('000 million manats): Revenue 6,682.0; Expenditure 6,604.9 (Source: Asian Development Bank, *Key Indicators of Developing Asian and Pacific Countries*).

**2001** ('000 million manats, estimates): Revenue 5,363.0; Expenditure 5,642.0 (Source: Asian Development Bank, *Key Indicators of Developing Asian and Pacific Countries*).

**INTERNATIONAL RESERVES**
(US $ million at 31 December)

| | 1999 | 2000 | 2001 |
|---|---|---|---|
| **Total** . . . . . . . . . | 1,607.0 | 1,854.0 | 1,935.0 |

Source: Asian Development Bank, *Key Indicators of Developing Asian and Pacific Countries*.

**MONEY SUPPLY**
(million manats at 31 December)

| | 1995 | 1996 | 1997 |
|---|---|---|---|
| Currency in circulation . . . . | 56,629 | 270,248 | 408,000 |
| Demand deposits at banks . . . | 48,475 | 408,000 | 401,000 |

**Currency in circulation** ('000 million manats at 31 December): 1,040.2 in 1998; 1,009.4 in 1999; 1,517.0 in 2000 (Source: Asian Development Bank, *Key Indicators of Developing Asian and Pacific Countries*).

**COST OF LIVING**
(Consumer Price Index; base: previous year = 100)

| | 1995 | 1996 | 1997 |
|---|---|---|---|
| **All items** . . . . . . . . . | 1,105.3 | 1,092.4 | 183.7 |

## NATIONAL ACCOUNTS

### Expenditure on the Gross Domestic Product
('000 million manats, at current prices)

| | 1999 | 2000 | 2001 |
|---|---|---|---|
| Government final consumption expenditure . . . . . | 2,588.4 | 3,595.2 | 4,496.7 |
| Private final consumption expenditure . . . . . | 10,057.7 | 10,578.6 | 15,741.5 |
| Increase in stocks . . . | 392.2 | 453.2 | 1,068.9 |
| Gross fixed capital formation . . | 8,583.6 | 9,598.8 | 12,144.5 |
| **Total domestic expenditure**. . | 21,621.9 | 24,225.8 | 33,451.6 |
| Exports of goods and services . . | 7,337.4 | 13,788.9 | 14,423.9 |
| *Less* Imports of goods and services | 11,004.4 | 12,165.0 | 12,221.3 |
| **Sub-total** . . . . . . | 17,954.9 | 25,849.7 | 35,654.2 |
| Statistical discrepancy . . . . | 2,101.0 | −201.8 | −241.4 |
| **GDP in purchasers' values** . . | 20,055.9 | 25,647.9 | 35,412.8 |

Source: Asian Development Bank, *Key Indicators of Developing Asian and Pacific Countries*.

### Gross Domestic Product by Economic Activity
('000 million manats, at current prices)

| | 2000 | 2001 | 2002* |
|---|---|---|---|
| Agriculture . . . . . | 5,885.9 | 8,327.6 | 9,646.3 |
| Mining and quarrying . . . } | | | |
| Manufacturing . . . . . } | 8,985.5 | 12,996.7 | 15,880.8 |
| Electricity, gas and water . . } | | | |
| Construction . . . . . | 1,736.6 | 2,136.8 | 2,289.4 |
| Trade . . . . . . . | 900.7 | 2,363.9 | 2,056.3 |
| Transport and communications | 1,701.3 | 1,919.2 | 2,094.8 |
| Finance . . . . . . | 353.5 | 422.0 } | |
| Public administration . . . | 735.2 | 912.8 } | 10,887.0 |
| Other activities . . . . | 5,349.2 | 6,333.8 } | |
| **Total** . . . . . . . | 25,647.9 | 35,412.8 | 42,854.6 |

* Estimates.
Source: Asian Development Bank, *Key Indicators of Developing Asian and Pacific Countries*.

## BALANCE OF PAYMENTS
(US $ million)

| | 1996 | 1997 | 1998 |
|---|---|---|---|
| Exports of goods f.o.b. . . . . | 1,692.0 | 774.0 | 614.1 |
| Imports of goods f.o.b. . . . . | −1,388.3 | −1,005.0 | −1,137.1 |
| **Trade balance** . . . . . | 303.7 | −230.9 | −523.0 |
| Services (net) . . . . . . | −323.4 | −402.5 | −471.0 |
| **Balance on goods and services** | −19.7 | −633.5 | −994.0 |
| Other income (net) . . . . | 16.7 | 84.8 | 32.6 |
| **Balance on goods, services and income** . . . . . . . | −3.0 | −548.7 | −961.4 |
| Current transfers (net) . . . . | 4.8 | −31.2 | 26.9 |
| **Current account** . . . . | 1.8 | −579.9 | −934.5 |
| Direct investment . . . . | 108.1 | 102.4 | 64.1 |
| Trade credit (net) . . . . | 60.8 | −266.5 | 56.5 |
| Other (net) . . . . . | −211.6 | 1,035.9 | 749.7 |
| Net errors and omissions . . . | 46.4 | −71.4 | 33.9 |
| **Overall balance** . . . . | 5.4 | 220.6 | −30.3 |

**2000** (US $ million): Exports of goods f.o.b. 2,513.0; Imports of goods f.o.b. −1,723.0; Trade balance 790.0 (Source: Asian Development Bank, *Key Indicators of Developing Asian and Pacific Countries*).

**2001** (US $ million): Exports of goods f.o.b. 2,632.0; Imports of goods f.o.b. −2,097.0; Trade balance 535.0 (Source: Asian Development Bank, *Key Indicators of Developing Asian and Pacific Countries*).

**2002** (US $ million; estimates): Exports of goods f.o.b. 2,866.0; Imports of goods f.o.b. −1,866.0; Trade balance 1,000.0 (Source: Asian Development Bank, *Key Indicators of Developing Asian and Pacific Countries*).

# External Trade

## PRINCIPAL COMMODITIES
(US $ million)

| Imports c.i.f. | 2000 | 2001 | 2002 |
|---|---|---|---|
| Food and live animals . . . . | 180.4 | 129.4 | 114.3 |
| Beverages and tobacco . . . . | 25.2 | 56.8 | 70.1 |
| Mineral fuels, lubricants, etc. . . | 21.3 | 39.1 | 25.7 |
| Chemicals . . . . . . . | 159.0 | 178.6 | 210.8 |
| Basic manufactures . . . . . | 382.4 | 448.7 | 394.2 |
| Machinery and transport equipment . . . . . . | 782.5 | 1,204.7 | 857.6 |
| Miscellaneous manufactured articles . . . . . . | 111.1 | 128.1 | 112.7 |
| **Total** (incl. others) . . . . . | 1,785.0 | 2,348.8 | 2,119.4 |

| Exports f.o.b. | 2000 | 2001 | 2002 |
|---|---|---|---|
| Crude materials (inedible) except fuels . . . . . . . | 257.1 | 123.7 | 83.8 |
| Mineral fuels, lubricants, etc. . . | 2,029.7 | 2,217.2 | 2,447.1 |
| Basic manufactures . . . . . | 107.0 | 141.6 | 150.6 |
| Machinery and transport equipment . . . . . . | 15.5 | 14.5 | 17.1 |
| **Total** (incl. others) . . . . . | 2,506.0 | 2,620.2 | 2,855.6 |

Source: Asian Development Bank, *Key Indicators of Developing Asian and Pacific Countries*.

## PRINCIPAL TRADING PARTNERS
(US $ million)

| Imports | 2000 | 2001 | 2002 |
|---|---|---|---|
| France . . . . . . . . | 75.7 | 50.5 | 67.6 |
| Germany . . . . . . . | 52.6 | 140.6 | 273.9 |
| Iran . . . . . . . | 90.9 | 98.1 | 104.3 |
| Japan . . . . . . . | 144.4 | 35.9 | 6.0 |
| Russia . . . . . . . | 254.5 | 153.4 | 152.3 |
| Turkey . . . . . . . | 253.3 | 115.8 | 125.7 |
| Ukraine . . . . . . | 214.3 | 235.7 | 255.8 |
| United Arab Emirates . . . . | 146.6 | 158.2 | 168.2 |
| USA . . . . . . . | 62.8 | 273.4 | 51.9 |
| Uzbekistan . . . . . . | 35.3 | 38.8 | 42.1 |
| **Total** (incl. others) . . . . . | 1,787.8 | 1,557.5 | 1,432.5 |

| Exports | 2000 | 2001 | 2002 |
|---|---|---|---|
| Afghanistan . . . . . . | 38.0 | 42.0 | 45.5 |
| Azerbaijan . . . . . . | 37.1 | 122.9 | 133.4 |
| Germany . . . . . . | 404.8 | 5.8 | 10.5 |
| Iran . . . . . . . | 242.0 | 241.0 | 199.9 |
| Kazakhstan . . . . . . | 5.3 | 70.5 | 76.5 |
| Russia . . . . . . . | 1,029.3 | 35.5 | 23.4 |
| Switzerland . . . . . . | 91.9 | 0.8 | 0.8 |
| Tajikistan . . . . . . | 29.1 | 56.6 | 61.5 |
| Turkey . . . . . . . | 186.0 | 65.2 | 70.8 |
| Ukraine . . . . . . | 164.9 | 182.1 | 197.6 |
| **Total** (incl. others) . . . . . | 2,505.2 | 1,132.4 | 1,218.9 |

Source: Asian Development Bank, *Key Indicators of Developing Asian and Pacific Countries*.

# Transport

## RAILWAYS
(traffic)

| | 1996 | 1997* | 1999 |
|---|---|---|---|
| Passenger journeys (million) . . | 7.8 | 6.4 | 3.1 |
| Passenger-km (million) . . . . | 2,104 | 958 | 701 |
| Freight transported (million metric tons) . . . . . . . | 15.9 | 18.5 | 17.2 |
| Freight ton-km (million) . . . | 6,779 | 7,445 | 7,337 |

* Data for 1998 not available.
Source: *Railway Directory*.

## SHIPPING

**Merchant Fleet**
(registered at 31 December)

|                               | 2000 | 2001 | 2002 |
|-------------------------------|------|------|------|
| Number of vessels . . . . .   | 40   | 41   | 41   |
| Total displacement ('000 grt) . . | 41.8 | 45.7 | 45.7 |

Source: Lloyd's Register-Fairplay, *World Fleet Statistics*.

## CIVIL AVIATION
(estimated traffic on scheduled services)

|                                 | 1997  | 1998 | 1999 |
|---------------------------------|-------|------|------|
| Kilometres flown (million) . . . | 15    | 11   | 9    |
| Passengers carried ('000) . . . | 523   | 890  | 220  |
| Passenger-kilometres (million) . . | 1,093 | 832  | 640  |
| Total ton-kilometres (million) . . | 101   | 79   | 74   |

Source: UN, *Statistical Yearbook*.

# Tourism

**FOREIGN VISITOR ARRIVALS**
(incl. excursionists)

| Country of nationality        | 1995    | 1996    | 1997    |
|-------------------------------|---------|---------|---------|
| Afghanistan . . . . . . .     | 11,803  | 18,301  | n.a.    |
| Azerbaijan. . . . . . .       | n.a.    | 10,642  | 114     |
| Iran . . . . . . .            | 82,925  | 82,386  | 171,071 |
| Kazakhstan . . . . . .        | n.a.    | 9,466   | 4,971   |
| Kyrgyzstan . . . . . .        | n.a.    | 15,798  | 22,066  |
| Pakistan . . . . . . .        | 7,000   | 5,837   | 3,075   |
| Russia . . . . . . .          | n.a.    | 3,916   | 6,979   |
| Tajikistan . . . . . . .      | n.a.    | 10,623  | 11,310  |
| Turkey. . . . . . .           | 46,414  | 52,230  | 62,915  |
| Uzbekistan . . . . . .        | n.a.    | 45,259  | 31,784  |
| **Total** (incl. others) . . . . . | 232,832 | 281,988 | 332,425 |

Source: World Tourism Organization, *Yearbook of Tourism Statistics*.

**Foreign visitor arrivals:** 300,000 in 1998 (Source: World Tourism Organization).

**Tourism receipts** (US $ million): 66 in 1996; 74 in 1997; 192 in 1998 (Source: World Bank).

# Communications Media

|                                              | 1998  | 1999  | 2000 |
|----------------------------------------------|-------|-------|------|
| Television receivers ('000 in use) .         | 865   | 870   | 875  |
| Telephones ('000 main lines in use)          | 354.0 | 358.9 | 364  |
| Mobile cellular telephones ('000 subscribers). . . . . . . | 3.0 | 4.0 | 9.5 |
| Personal computers ('000 in use) .           | n.a.  | 2.0   | n.a. |
| Internet users ('000) . . . . .              | n.a.  | 2     | 6    |

**1994:** Book production (including pamphlets): 450 titles (5,493,000 copies).

**1997:** Radio receivers in use 1,225,000.

**2001:** Telephones ('000 main lines in use): 387.6; Internet users 8,000.

Sources: International Telecommunication Union; UNESCO, *Statistical Yearbook*.

# Education

(1984/85)

|                                          | Institutions | Students |
|------------------------------------------|--------------|----------|
| Secondary schools . . . . . . . .        | 1,900        | 800,000  |
| Secondary specialized schools . . . . .  | 35           | 36,900   |
| Higher schools (incl. universities). . . | 9            | 38,900   |

**1990/91:** 76,000 students at higher schools (Source: UNESCO, *Statistical Yearbook*).

**Adult literacy rate** (UNESCO estimates): 97.7% (males 98.8%; females 96.6%) at 1989 census (Source: UNESCO, *Statistical Yearbook*).

# Directory

## The Constitution

A new Constitution was adopted on 18 May 1992. The Constitution was organized into eight sections (detailing: fundamentals of the constitutional system; fundamental human and civil rights, freedoms and duties; the system of state governmental bodies; local self-government; the electoral system and provisions for referendum; judicial authority; the office of the prosecutor-general and final provisions), and included the following among its main provisions:

The President of the Republic is directly elected by universal adult suffrage for a five-year term. A President may hold office for a maximum of two terms. The President is not only Head of State, but also head of Government (Prime Minister in the Council of Ministers) and Supreme Commander of the Armed Forces. The President must ratify all parliamentary legislation and in certain circumstances may legislate by decree. The President appoints the Council of Ministers and chairs sessions of the Khalk Maslakhaty (People's Council).

Supreme legislative power resides with the 50-member Majlis, a unicameral parliament which is directly elected for a five-year term. Sovereignty, however, is vested in the people of Turkmenistan, and the supreme representative body of popular power is the Khalk Maslakhaty. This is described as a supervisory organ with no legislative or executive functions, but it is authorized to perform certain duties normally reserved for a legislature or constituent assembly. Not only does it debate and approve measures pertaining to the political and economic situation in the country, but it examines possible changes to the Constitution and may vote to express 'no confidence' in the President of the Republic, on grounds of unconstitutionality. The Khalk Maslakhaty is comprised of all the deputies of the Majlis, a further 50 directly elected and 10 appointed representatives from all districts of the country, the members of the Council of Ministers, the respective Chairmen of the Supreme Court and the Supreme Economic Court, the Prosecutor-General and the heads of local councils.

The Constitution, which defines Turkmenistan as a democratic state, also guarantees the independence of the judiciary and the basic human rights of the individual. The age of majority is 18 years (parliamentary deputies must be aged at least 21). Ethnic minorities are granted equality under the law, although Turkmen is the only official language. A central tenet of Turkmenistan's foreign policy is that of 'permanent neutrality'.

Note: On 15 January 1994 a referendum confirmed President Saparmyrat Niyazov's exemption from the need to be re-elected in 1997. An amendment to the Constitution, approved by the Khalk Maslakhaty in December 1999, extended the term of Niyazov's presidency indefinitely. In February 2001, following Niyazov's announcement that he would retire by 2010, the Khalk Maslakhaty endorsed a resolution to hold open presidential elections in 2008–10, following his retirement. In August 2003 a constitutional law and a constitutional amendment were passed elevating the Khalk Maslakhaty to the status of 'permanently functioning supreme repesentative body of popular authority', and requiring it to remain in continuous session. The constitutional changes ascribed to the Khalk Maslakhaty a number of legislative powers, including the passing of constitutional laws, thereby effectively displacing the Majlis as the country's leading legislative body. The Khalk Maslakhaty was to comprise 2,507 members.

# The Government

## HEAD OF STATE

**President of the Republic:** Gen. SAPARMYRAT A. NIYAZOV (directly elected 27 October 1990; re-elected 21 June 1992—a constitutional amendment of 28 December 1999 extended his term of office indefinitely, although in February 2001 Niyazov announced that he would retire no later than 2010).

## COUNCIL OF MINISTERS
(October 2003)

**Prime Minister:** Gen. SAPARMYRAT A. NIYAZOV.

**Deputy Prime Minister, responsible for Construction, Transport and Communications:** REJEPDURDY ATAYEV.

**Deputy Prime Minister and Minister of Foreign Affairs:** RASHID MEREDOV.

**Deputy Prime Minister and Minister of Health and the Medical Industry:** GURBANGULY BERDYMUKHAMMETOV.

**Deputy Prime Minister and Minister of the Textile Industry:** DORTKULI AYDOGYEV.

**Minister of Agriculture:** BEGENC ATAMRADOV.

**Minister of Construction and Building-materials Production:** MUKHAMMETNAZAR KHUDAYGULYYEV.

**Minister of Culture:** ORAZGELDY AYDOGDIYEV.

**Minister of Defence:** Maj.-Gen. AGAGELDY MAMATGELDIYEV.

**Minister of the Economy and Finance:** YAZGULY KAKALYEV.

**Minister of Education:** MAMEDDURDY SARYKHANOV.

**Minister of Environmental Protection:** MATKARIM RAJAPOV.

**Minister of Internal Affairs:** ASHYR ATAYEV.

**Minister of Justice:** TANGANMURAT GOCHIYEV.

**Minister of National Security:** Gen. BATYR BUSAKOV.

**Minister of Petroleum, Natural Gas and Mineral Resources:** TACHBERDY TAGIYEV.

**Minister of Power Engineering and Industry:** ATAMYRAT BERDIYEV.

**Minister of Railways:** ORAZBERDY HADAYBERDIYEV.

**Minister of Social Security:** ORAZMURAT BEGMURADOV.

**Minister of Trade and Foreign Economic Relations:** CHARYMAMMED GAYIBOV.

**Minister of Water Resources:** GURBANGELDI VELMYRADOV.

### Chairmen of State Committees

**Chairman of the State Committee for the Border Service:** ANNAGELDY. GUMMANOV.

**Chairman of the State Committee for Fisheries:** HUDAJBERDY YAZOVICH YAKATOV.

**Chairman of the State Committee for Hydrometeorology:** SUKHANBERDY BAIRAMOV.

**Chairman of the State Committee for Land Use and Land Reform:** (vacant).

**Chairman of the State Committee for Tourism and Sport:** (vacant).

## MINISTRIES

**Office of the President and the Council of Ministers:** 744000 Ashgabat, ul. 2001 24, Presidential Palace; tel. (12) 35-45-34; fax (12) 35-43-88.

**Ministry of Agriculture:** 744000 Ashgabat, ul. 2011 63; tel. (12) 35-66-91; fax (12) 35-01-18; e-mail minselhoz@online.tm.

**Ministry of Construction and Building-materials Production:** 744000 Ashgabat, ul. 2049; tel. (12) 51-23-59.

**Ministry of Culture:** 744000 Ashgabat, ul. 1984 14; tel. (12) 35-30-61; fax (12) 35-35-60.

**Ministry of Defence:** 744000 Ashgabat, ul. 1995 4; tel. (12) 35-22-59.

**Ministry of the Economy and Finance:** 744000 Ashgabat, ul. 2008 4; tel. (12) 51-05-63; fax (12) 51-18-23.

**Ministry of Education:** 744000 Ashgabat, ul. 2002 2; tel. (12) 35-58-03; fax (12) 39-88-11.

**Ministry of Energy and Industry:** 744000 Ashgabat, ul. 2008 6; tel. (12) 35-38-70; fax (12) 39-06-82; e-mail kuwwat@online.tm.

**Ministry of Environmental Protection:** 744000 Ashgabat, ul. 2011 28; tel. (12) 39-65-12; fax (12) 51-13-97.

**Ministry of Foreign Affairs:** Ashgabat, pr. 2076 83; tel. (12) 26-62-11; fax (12) 25-35-83.

**Ministry of Health and the Medical Industry:** 744000 Ashgabat, pr. 2076 90; tel. (12) 35-60-47; fax (12) 35-50-32.

**Ministry of Internal Affairs:** Ashgabat, pr. 2076 85; tel. (12) 25-13-28.

**Ministry of Justice:** Ashgabat.

**Ministry for National Security:** Ashgabat.

**Ministry of Petroleum, Natural Gas and Mineral Resources:** 744000 Ashgabat, ul. 2002 28; tel. (12) 39-38-27; fax (12) 39-38-21; e-mail ministryoilgas@online.tm.

**Ministry of Social Security:** 744007 Ashgabat, ul. 2003 3; tel. (12) 25-30-03.

**Ministry of the Textile Industry:** 744000 Ashgabat, ul. 2026 52; tel. (12) 51-03-03; fax .

**Ministry of Trade and Foreign Economic Relations:** 744000 Ashgabat, ul. 2002 1; tel. (12) 35-10-47; fax (12) 35-73-24; e-mail mtfer@online.tm.

**Ministry of Water Resources:** 744000 Ashgabat, ul. 2005 1; tel. (12) 39-06-15; fax (12) 39-85-39.

All the principal state committees are also based in Ashgabat.

## KHALK MASLAKHATY
(People's Council)

Under the Constitution of May 1992, the Khalk Maslakhaty is established as the supreme representative body in the country. Formally, it is neither a legislative nor an executive body, although its decisions supersede those of both parliament and presidency. The 2,507-member body consists of the President, the Majlis deputies, the Chairman of the Supreme Court, the Prosecutor-General, the members of the Council of Ministers, the hakims (governors) of the five velayats (regions) and the hakim of the city of Ashgabat; the elected people's representatives of each district; the chairpersons of parties, the Youth Union, trade unions, and the Women's Union, who are members of the All-national Galkynysh National Revival Movement of Turkmenistan; the chairpersons of public organizations; representatives of the Council of Elders; the hakims of cities that are the administrative centres of the velayats and etraps (districts); and the heads of the local councils (archins) of the cities and villages that are the administrative centres of the districts. It is headed by the President of the Republic. Elections for the 50 district representatives were held in November and December 1992; the Council convened for the first time later in December. Fresh elections were held in April 1998 and on 6 April 2003. A constitutional law and constitutional amendment passed in August 2003 elevated the Khalk Maslakhaty to the status of 'permanently functioning supreme repesentative body of popular authority'. The Khalk Maslakhaty was henceforth required to remain in continuous session, and effectively displaced the Majlis as the country's leading legislative body.

# Legislature

## MAJLIS
(Assembly)

Under the Constitution of May 1992, the highest legislative body in Turkmenistan is the 50-member Majlis, directly elected for a term of five years. Until the expiry of its term, the former legislature, the Supreme Soviet, acted as the Majlis. Elections to the Majlis were held on 12 December 1999, officially with the participation of 98.9% of the registered electorate. All contestants were believed to be members of the ruling party, the Democratic Party of Turkmenistan. The new Majlis convened for the first time in late December. Following the December 1999 elections, the new Majlis was granted greater legislative and regulatory powers by the President. The deputies of the Majlis also form part of the Khalk Maslakhaty (see above).

**Chairman:** OVEZGELDY ATAYEV.

# Local Government

Turkmenistan was divided into five velayats (oblasts or regions) for administrative purposes. A lower tier of local government further sub-divided the country into 50 etraps (raions or districts). The President appoints the heads of the local administrations—hakims (governors) in the velayats and, at the next level, the shakher hakims and etrap hakims in the cities and districts, respectively. Each district had an elected soviet or council of elders (gengeshes) with five-year terms, presided over by an archin, who was chosen by the council from among its own number. Local government elections took place in April 1998 and April 2003.

The velayat hakim, or prefect, is based in the main city of the region, which usually bears the same name or the original name.

There are five velayats in Turkmenistan:

**Akhal Velayat:** Akhal, ul. Druzhba narodaw 1; tel. (12) 41-93-53.

**Balkan Velayat:** 745100 Balkanabat (Nebit-Dag), Kvartal 149, bldg 6; tel. (12) 39-16-54.

**Dashkhovuz Velayat:** 746300 Dashkhovuz (Tashauz), ul. Abadanchylyk 9/10; tel. (22) 5-31-95.

**Lebap Velayat:** 7461000 Türkmenabat (Charjew), pr. S. Niyazov 46; tel. (22) 2-36-25.

**Mary Velayat:** 745400 Mary (Merv), ul. Moilanepes 41; tel. (22) 6-06-01.

# Political Organizations

**Agzybirlik:** Ashgabat; internet www.geocities.com/agzybirlik2000; f. 1989; popular front organization; denied official registration except from Oct. 1991 to Jan. 1992; Leader NURBERDY NURMAMEDOV.

**Democratic Party of Turkmenistan:** 744014 Ashgabat 14, ul. 2002 28; tel. (12) 25-12-12; name changed from Communist Party of Turkmenistan in 1991; Chair. Gen. SAPARMYRAT A. NIYAZOV; 116,000 mems (1991).

**National Revival Movement of Turkmenistan (Galkynysh):** Ashgabat; internet www.galkynysh.org; Chair. Gen. SAPARMYRAT A. NIYAZOV.

**Peasants' Justice Party:** Ashgabat; f. 1993 by deputies of the agrarian faction in parliament; still awaited official registration in 2003.

Turkmenistan is effectively a one-party state, with the Democratic Party of Turkmenistan (led by the President of the Republic) dominant in all areas of government. There are, however, several unregistered opposition groups, such as the Islamic Renaissance Party, which had been an all-Union Muslim party in the former USSR, and Agzybirlik. In early 1994 President Niyazov indicated that the Peasants' Justice Party would be permitted registration (although this had apparently not happened by the early 2000s). A Social Democratic Party was reportedly established in Ashgabat in August 1996, upon the merger of several small unofficial groups.

Other opposition elements are based in other republics of the Commonwealth of Independent States, in particular Russia. A leading opposition figure in exile is a former Minister of Foreign Affairs, Abdy Kuliyev, whose United Democratic Opposition of Turkmenistan (ODOT) is based in Moscow. In January 1996 several of the Turkmenistan Fund's leaders left to form the Movement for Democratic Reform (based in Sweden). The Vatan (Motherland) movement (also based in Sweden) comprises Turkmen and other Central Asian oppositionists. In January 2002 a former Minister of Foreign Affairs, Boris Shikhmuradov, established the opposition People's Democratic Movement of Turkmenistan; however, he was imprisoned in December, having been convicted of orchestrating the attempted assasination of President Saparmyrat Nizayov in November. Another opposition leader accused of conspiring with Shikhmuradov was Nurmukhammed Khanamov, founder of the Republican Party of Turkmenistan.

Opposition leaders met in Prague, Czech Republic, at the end of September 2003 and announced the formation of the Union of Democratic Forces of Turkmenistan (UDFT), comprising ODOT, Vatan, Renaissance and the Republican Party of Turkmenistan.

# Diplomatic Representation

## EMBASSIES IN TURKMENISTAN

**Afghanistan:** 744000 Ashgabat, ul. 2002 14; tel. (12) 39-58-21; fax (12) 39-58-20; Ambassador ABDUL KARIM KHADAM.

**Armenia:** 744000 Ashgabat, 2002 14; tel. (12) 35-44-18; fax (12) 39-55-38; e-mail eat@online.tm; Ambassador ARAM GRIGORIAN.

**Azerbaijan:** Ashgabat.

**Belarus:** Ashgabat; Ambassador YURIY MALUMAW.

**China, People's Republic:** 744036 Ashgabat, Berzengi District, Hotel 'Kuwwat'; tel. (12) 51-81-31; fax (12) 51-88-78; e-mail chemb@cat.glasnet; Ambassador LU GUISHENG.

**France:** 744000 Ashgabat, Four Points Ak Altin Hotel, Office Bldg, pr. 2076 141/1; tel. (12) 36-35-50; fax (12) 36-35-46; e-mail alain.couanon@diplomatie.fr; Ambassador JEAN-CLAUDE RICHARD.

**Georgia:** 744000 Ashgabat, ul. 2011 139A; tel. (12) 34-48-38; fax (12) 34-32-48; e-mail georgia@online.tm; Ambassador PETER CHKHEIDZE.

**Germany:** 744000 Ashgabat, Hotel Sheraton 'Four Points Ak Altin', pr. 2076; tel. (12) 36-35-15; fax (12) 36-35-22; e-mail grembtkm@online.tm; Ambassador HANS GÜNTHER MATTERN.

**India:** 744000 Ashgabat, ul. 1993 11, Rm 103, Hotel 'Nogina'; tel. (12) 34-46-31; fax (12) 46-90-30; e-mail ambtm@online.tm; Ambassador GEORGE JOSEPH.

**Iran:** 744000 Ashgabat, Tegeranskaya 3; tel. (12) 35-02-37; fax (12) 35-05-65; e-mail isroiref@online.tm; Ambassador SAYED IBRAHIM DERAZGISOU.

**Kazakhstan:** Ashgabat, ul. 2002 14, 3rd Floor; tel. (12) 39-55-48; fax (12) 39-59-32; e-mail turemb@online.tm; Ambassador AMANGELDY JUMABAYEV.

**Korea, Democratic People's Republic:** Ashgabat; Ambassador SON SONG PHIL.

**Kyrgyzstan:** Ashgabat, ul. 2002 14; tel. (12) 39-20-64; fax (12) 35-55-06; e-mail embassy@meerim.ashgabat.su; Ambassador MARKIL IBRAYEVICH IBRAYEV.

**Libya:** Ashgabat, ul. 2014 15; tel. (12) 35-49-17; fax (12) 39-05-69; Chargé d'affaires a.i. OMAR ELHADI SHIN-SHIN.

**Pakistan:** Ashgabat, ul. 2035 92; tel. (12) 35-00-97; fax (12) 39-76-40; e-mail parepashgabat@online.tm; Ambassador BABAR MALIK.

**Romania:** Ashgabat, ul. 2023 107; tel. (12) 34-67-15; fax (12) 34-76-20; e-mail ambromas@online.tm; Ambassador ION POROJAN.

**Russia:** 744004 Ashgabat, 1966 11; tel. (12) 35-39-57; fax (12) 39-84-66; Ambassador ANDREI MOLOCHKOV.

**Saudi Arabia:** Ashgabat, 1 1951 2/1, Internal Imperial Centre for Business; tel. (12) 45-49-63; fax (12) 45-49-70; e-mail tmemb@mofa.gov.sa.

**Slovenia:** Ashgabat; Ambassador FRANCI DEMSAR.

**Tajikistan:** 744000 Ashgabat, ul. 2002 14; tel. (12) 35-56-96; fax (12) 39-31-74; e-mail embtd@online.tm; Ambassador MARDONY TAJIDDIN NURIDDIN.

**Thailand:** Ashgabat; Ambassador KARUN RUCHUYOTIN.

**Turkey:** 744007 Ashgabat, ul. 2009 9; tel. (12) 35-14-61; fax (12) 39-19-14; e-mail askabat.be@mfa.gov.tr; Ambassador MEHMET BAHATTIN GÜRSÖZ.

**Ukraine:** 744001 Ashgabat, ul. 2011 49; tel. (12) 39-13-73; fax (12) 39-10-28; e-mail ukremb@online.tm; Ambassador VADIM CHUPRUN.

**United Arab Emirates:** Ashgabat; Ambassador HASSAN ABDULLAH AL-AZZAB AL-ZARUUNA.

**United Kingdom:** 744001 Ashgabat, Four Points Ak Altin Hotel, 3rd Floor Office Bldg; tel. (12) 36-34-62; fax (12) 36-34-65; e-mail beasb@online.tm; internet www.britishembassytm.org.uk; Ambassador PAUL BRUMMELL.

**USA:** 744000 Ashgabat, ul. 1984 9; tel. (12) 35-00-45; fax (12) 39-26-14; e-mail irc-ashgabat@iatp.edu.tm; internet www.usemb-ashgabat.rpo.at; Ambassador TRACEY ANN JACOBSON.

**Uzbekistan:** Ashgabat; tel. (12) 34-24-34; fax (12) 34-23-37; e-mail emuzbek@online.tm.

# Judicial System

**Chairman of the Supreme Court:** YAGSHIGELDY ESENOV.

**Vice-Chairman of the Supreme Court:** REJEPNIYAZ CHERKEZOV.

**Prosecutor-General:** GURBANBIBI ATAJANOVA.

# Religion

The majority of the population are adherents of Islam. In June 1991 the Turkmen Supreme Soviet adopted a Law on Freedom of Conscience and Religious Organizations. This law and subsequent amendments have been criticized abroad for the stipulation that religious organizations must have 500 members (of 18 years of age or more) to achieve formal recognition from the Ministry of Justice. In April 1994 a council (Gengesh) for religious affairs was established, within the office of the President; it was chaired by the Kazi of Turkmenistan and his deputy was the head of the Orthodox Church in Turkmenistan.

## ISLAM

Turkmen are traditionally Sunni Muslims, but with elements of Sufism. Islam, the religion of the Turkmen for many centuries, was severely persecuted by the Soviet regime from the late 1920s. Until July 1989 Ashgabat was the only Central Asian capital without a functioning mosque. The Muslims of Turkmenistan are officially under the jurisdiction of the Muslim Board of Central Asia, based in Tashkent, Uzbekistan, but, in practice, the Government permits little external influence in religious affairs. The Board is represented in Turkmenistan by a *kazi*, who is responsible for appointing Muslim clerics in all rural areas.

**Kazi of Turkmenistan:** KAKAGELDY VEPAYEV.

### CHRISTIANITY

#### Roman Catholic Church

The Church is represented in Turkmenistan by a Mission, established in September 1997. There were an estimated 500 adherents at 31 December 2001.

**Superior:** Fr ANDRZEJ MADEJ, 744000 Ashgabat, ul. 2009 20A, POB 98; tel. (12) 39-11-40; fax (12) 35-36-83; e-mail aszomi@online.tm.

# The Press

All publications listed below are in Turkmen, except where otherwise stated.

## PRINCIPAL NEWSPAPERS

**Adalat:** 744000 Ashgabat, ul. Steklozavodskoy 4; tel. (12) 47-84-53; weekly; Editor-in-Chief KHUDAYBERDY GYRBANDURDIYEV; circ. 42,575.

**Ashgabat:** 744004 Ashgabat, ul. 1995 20; tel. (12) 35-16-38; f. 1960; 3 a week; journal of the Union of Writers of Turkmenistan; popular; in Russian and Turkmen; Editor-in-Chief ORAZNAZAR HESHDEKOV; circ. 20,577.

**Edebiyat ve sungat** (Literature and Art): 744604 Ashgabat, ul. 1995 20; tel. (12) 35-30-34; f. 1958; weekly; Editor ANNAMYRAT POLADOV; circ. 1,500.

**Esger:** 744004 Ashgabat, 2038 29; tel. (12) 35-68-09; f. 1993; weekly; organ of the Council of Ministers; Editor-in-Chief GUVANCH MAMMETGELDIYEV (acting); circ. 23,769.

**Galkynysh:** Ashgabat 744604, ul. 1995 20; tel. (12) 46-68-53; weekly; Editor-in-Chief KHUDAYBERDY DIVANGULIYEV; circ. 24,465.

**Habarlar:** 744004 Ashgabat, ul. 1995 20; tel. (12) 46-84-70; weekly; in Russian and Turkmen; business; Editor-in-Chief R. BALABAN; circ. 5,500.

**Khalk sesi** (Voice of the People): 744000 Ashgabat, 1966 13; tel. (12) 25-39-98; f. 1991; weekly; organ of the Federation of Trade Unions of Turkmenistan; Editor P. ALLAGULOV.

**Mugallymlar gazeti** (Teachers' Newspaper): 744004 Ashgabat, ul. 1995 20; tel. (12) 39-59-25; f. 1952; 3 a week; organ of the Ministry of Education; Editor DORTKULI BALAKAYEV; circ. 52,771.

**Neitralnyi Turkmenistan** (Neutral Turkmenistan): 744004 Ashgabat, ul. 1995 20; tel. and fax (12) 46-84-75; e-mail nt@online.tm; internet www.tmpress.gov.tm; f. 1924; 6 a week; organ of the Majlis and the Council of Ministers; in Russian; Editor-in-Chief GOZEL NURALYEVA; circ. 23,000.

**Nesil** (Generation): 744604 Ashgabat, ul. 1995 20; tel. (12) 39-17-64; f. 1922; 3 a week; for young people; Editor GULMURAD MURADOV; circ. 15,386.

**Novosti Turkmenistana** (Turkmenistan News): 744000 Ashgabat, ul. 2002 24A; tel. (12) 39-12-21; fax (12) 51-02-34; f. 1994; weekly; in Russian, English and Turkmen; organ of the Turkmen Dowlet Khabarlar Gullugy news agency; circ. 500.

**Turkmen demiryolchusy** (Turkmen Railwayman): 744007 Ashgabat, 1966 7; tel. (12) 29-17-81; f. 1936; weekly; organ of the Turkmenistan State Railways; Editor BAIRAM SEKHEDOV.

**Turkmenistan:** 744004 Ashgabat, ul. 1995 20; tel. (12) 39-14-55; f. 1920; 6 a week; organ of the Council of Ministers and the Majlis; Editor KAKABAY ILYASOV; circ. 22,500.

**Syyasy sokhbetdesh** (Political Symposium): 744604 Ashgabat, ul. 1995 20; tel. (12) 25-10-84; f. 1992; weekly; organ of the Democratic Party of Turkmenistan; Editor AKBIBI YUSUPOVA; circ. 14,500.

**Vatan** (Motherland): 744604 Ashgabat, ul. 1995 20; tel. (12) 35-43-10; f. 1925; 3 a week; Editor-in-Chief AMANMUHAMMAD REPOV; circ. 23,672.

### PRINCIPAL PERIODICALS

Monthly, unless otherwise indicated.

**Diller duniesi** (World of Languages): 744014 Ashgabat, ul. 1960 22; tel. (12) 29-15-41; f. 1972; 6 a year; publ. by the Ministry of Education; in Russian and Turkmen.

**Diyar:** 744004 Ashgabat, ul. 1995 20; tel. (12) 35-53-97; f. 1992; socio-political and literary magazine; publ. by the President of the Republic and the Council of Ministers; Editor-in-Chief ORAZGELDY AYDOGDIYEV; circ. 3,000.

**Finansovye vesti** (Financial News): 744004 Ashgabat, ul. 1995 20; tel. (12) 29-42-76; f. 1994; in Russian, English and Turkmen; publ. by the Ministry of the Economy and Finance.

**Garagum** (Kara-Kum): 744005 Ashgabat, ul. 1995 20; tel. (12) 46-86-26; f. 1928; cultural; Editor SAPAR OREYEV; circ. 2,000.

**Gunesh:** 744000 Ashgabat, ul. 1997 8; tel. (12) 51-17-83; for children; Editor-in-Chief SHDURDY CHARYGYLLIYEV; circ. 7,415.

**Gurbansoltan Edzhe:** 744604 Ashgabat, ul. 1995 20; tel. (12) 25-20-64; f. 1931 as *Ovadan* (Beautiful) for women; Editor A. B. SEITKULIYEVA.

**Izvestiya Akademii Nauk Turkmenistana** (Academy of Sciences of Turkmenistan News): 744000 Ashgabat, ul. 2011 59; f. 1946; 6 a year; in Russian and Turkmen.

**Politicheskii sobesednik** (Political Symposium): 744604 Ashgabat, ul. 1995 20; tel. (12) 25-10-84; f. 1937; in Russian; publ. by the Democratic Party of Turkmenistan; circ. 2,300.

**Saglyk** (Health): 744000 Ashgabat, ul. 2020 39/57; tel. (12) 39-16-21; f. 1990; 6 a year; publ. by the Ministry of Health and the Pharmaceutical Industry; Editor-in-Chief BAYRAM TYACHMAMEDOV; circ. 13,828.

**Turkmen dili khem edebiyati** (Turkmen Language and Literature): Ashgabat; tel. (12) 41-88-03; f. 1991; 6 a year; publ. by the Ministry of Education.

**Turkmen dunyasi:** 744004 Ashgabat, ul. 2011 20; tel. (12) 47-81-18; organ of the Humanitarian Association of World Turkmen; Editor-in-Chief ANNABERDY AGABAYEV; circ. 11,956.

**Turkmenistanyn oba khozhalygy** (Agriculture of Turkmenistan): 744000 Ashgabat, ul. 2011 63; tel. (12) 35-19-38; f. 1929; Editor BYASHIM TALLYKOV; circ. 3,500.

**Turkmen medeniyeti** (Turkmen Culture): 744007 Ashgabat, ul. 1960 21; tel. (12) 25-37-22; f. 1993; 2 a year; publ. by the Ministry of Culture; Editor GELDYMYRAT NURMUKHAMMEDOV.

**Turkmen sesi** (Voice of the Turkmen): 744007 Ashgabat, ul. 2011 20; tel. (12) 47-81-67; f. 1991; organ of the humanitarian asscn 'Turkmeny Mira'; Editor A. AGABAYEV.

**Vedomosti Majlisa Turkmenistana** (Bulletin of the Majlis of Turkmenistan): 744000 Ashgabat, ul. 2002 17; f. 1960; 4 a year; in Russian and Turkmen.

**Vozrozhdeniye:** 744604 Ashgabat, ul. 1995 20; tel. (12) 35-10-84; in Russian; political; Editor-in-Chief H. DIVANGULYEV; circ. 1,500.

### NEWS AGENCY

**Turkmen Dowlet Khabarlar Gullugy (Turkmen State News Service):** 744000 Ashgabat, ul. 2002 24A; tel. (12) 39-12-21; fax (12) 51-02-34; e-mail tpress@online.tm; f. 1967; Dir JEREN TAIMOVA.

# Publishers

**Magaryf Publishing House:** Ashgabat; Dir N. ATAYEV.

**Turkmenistan State Publishing Service:** 744000 Ashgabat, ul. 1995 20; tel. (12) 46-90-13; f. 1965; politics, science and fiction; Dir A. M. JANMURADOV; Editor-in-Chief A. ALLANAZAROV.

**Ylym Publishing House:** 744000 Ashgabat, ul. 2011 59; tel. (12) 29-04-84; f. 1952; desert development, science; Dir N. I. FAIZULAYEVA.

# Broadcasting and Communications

## TELECOMMUNICATIONS

**Turkmentelekom:** 744000 Ashgabat, ul. 2010 36; tel. (12) 51-12-77; fax (12) 51-02-40; e-mail admin@telecom.tm; internet www.telecom.tm; f. 1993; Dir-Gen. REJEPMURAD M. ATAYEV.

## BROADCASTING

**National Television and Radio Co of Turkmenistan** (Turkmenistanin Milli Teleradiokompaniyasi): 744000 Ashgabat, ul. 2022 5; tel. (12) 35-15-15; fax (12) 36-48-21; Head of Main Directorate Dr GURBANSOLTAN CARYEVNA HANDURDYEVA.

## Radio

**Turkmen Radio:** 744000 Ashgabat, pr. 2076; tel. (12) 25-15-15; fax (12) 25-14-21; broadcasts local programmes and relays from Russia in Turkmen and Russian.

## Television

**Turkmen Television:** see Radio.

# Finance

(cap. = capital; res = reserves; dep. = deposits; m. = million; brs = branches; amounts in Turkmen manats)

## BANKING

Long-standing lack of confidence in the banking sector, together with a regional financial crisis, prompted a restructuring of the sector, in December 1998, by presidential decree. Government ownership of banks was increased, while restrictions on lending by the Central Bank were intensified and the merger of smaller banks was encouraged. By late 2002 there were 12 commercial banks.

### Central Bank

**Central Bank of Turkmenistan:** 744000 Ashgabat, ul. 2002 22; tel. (12) 51-06-73; fax (12) 51-08-12; e-mail treasury_tm@cbtm.net; f. 1991; central monetary authority, issuing bank and supervisory authority; Chair. IMAMDURDY GANDYMOV; 5 brs.

### Other Banks

**Daykhanbank:** Ashgabat, ul. 2067 60; tel. and fax (12) 41-98-68; e-mail daybank@online.tm; f. 1989 as independent bank, Agroprombank, reorganized 1999; specializes in agricultural sector; Chair. of Bd NURBERDY BAYRAMOV; 70 brs.

**Garagum International Joint-Stock Bank:** 744000 Ashgabat, ul. 1960 3; tel. (12) 35-22-01; fax (12) 35-38-54; f. 1993 as International Bank for Reconstruction, Development and Support of Entrepreneurship, name changed 2000; Chair. BEKMAMED SOLTANMEMEDOV.

**Garashsyslyk Bank:** Ashgabat, ul. 2009 30A; tel. (12) 39-01-24; fax (12) 39-78-92; e-mail garash@cbtm.net; f. 1999 following merger of Gas Bank and Ashgabat Bank; Chair. CHARYGELDY BAYGELDIYEV.

**President Bank:** 744000 Ashgabat, ul. 2002 22; tel. (12) 35-79-43; fax (12) 51-08-12; e-mail presidentbank@cbtm.net; f. 2000; cap. US $60m.; Exec. Dir (vacant).

**Savings Bank of Turkmenistan (Sberbank):** 744000 Ashgabat, pr. 2076 86; tel. (12) 35-46-71; fax (12) 35-40-04; f. 1923, reorganized 1989; wholly state-owned; cap. 726m., res 125m., dep. 7,304m. (1997); Chair. BEGENCH BAYMUKHAMEDOV; 120 brs.

**Senagatbank:** 744017 Ashgabat, ul. 1966 42; tel. (12) 51-03-05; fax (12) 35-06-93; e-mail senagat@online.tm; Chair. GELDYMURAD CHAPAYEV.

**State Bank for Foreign Economic Affairs of Turkmenistan (Turkmenvnesheconombank):** 744000 Ashgabat, ul. 2010 22; tel. (12) 35-02-52; fax (12) 39-79-82; e-mail tveb@online.tm; f. 1992 as independent bank, from Soviet Vneshekonombank; wholly state-owned; cap. 100,705m., res 54,181m., dep. 1,487,087m. (Jan. 2001); Chair. GUVANCH B. GEOKLENOV; 5 brs.

**State Commercial Bank 'Turkmenistan' (Turkmenbank):** 744000 Ashgabat, ul. 2002 10A; tel. (12) 51-07-21; fax (12) 39-67-35; e-mail turkmenbank@ctbm.net; f. 1992; Chair. ATAMYRAT REJEPOV.

**Turkmenbashy Bank:** 744000 Ashgabat, ul. 2026 54; tel. (12) 51-24-50; fax (12) 51-11-11; e-mail mail@investbank.org; internet www.turkmenbashi.net; f. 1992 as Investbank, renamed in 2000; Chair. AMANMURAT PAJAYEV; 23 brs.

### Foreign and Joint-Venture Banks

**Bank Saderat Iran:** Ashgabat, pr. 2076 181; tel. (12) 34-67-67; fax (12) 34-20-70; Man. ALI AMOLI.

**Kreditbank:** 744000, pr. Magtymguly 2076; tel. (12) 35-02-22; fax (12) 35-03-09; e-mail kreditbank@online.tm; f. 1995; fmrly Rossiiskii Kredit; jt venture with Russia; Chair. BATYR BAYRIYEV.

**National Bank of Pakistan:** 744000 Ashgabat, ul. 2002 7, Hotel 'Emperyal Grand Turkmen'; tel. (12) 35-35-16; fax (12) 35-04-65; e-mail nbptm@online.tm; Gen. Man. SHAKHZAD JAKHANGIR KHOKAR.

**Turkmen Turkish Commercial Bank:** 744014 Ashgabat, pr. 2076 111/2, POB 15; tel. (12) 51-14-07; fax (12) 51-11-23; e-mail ttcb@online.tm; f. 1993, with 50% Turkish ownership; cap. 26,000m., res 1,942m., dep. 26,497m. (Dec. 2001); Chair. MUSTAFA NAZLIOGLU.

## COMMODITY EXCHANGE

**State Commodity and Raw Materials Exchange of Turkmenistan:** 744000 Ashgabat, pr. 2076 111; tel. (12) 35-43-21; fax (12) 51-03-04; e-mail exchange@cbtm.net; f. 1994; Chair. CHARY GAIBOV.

# Trade and Industry

## GOVERNMENT AGENCIES

**National Institute of State Statistics and Information on Turkmenistan** (Turkmenmillihasabat): 744000 Ashgabat, pr. 2076 72; tel. (12) 39-42-65; fax (12) 35-43-79; e-mail office@natstat.gov.tm; f. 1997; Dir JUMADURDY BAIRAMOV.

**State Agency for Foreign Investment (SAFI):** 744000 Ashgabat, ul. 2011 53; tel. (12) 35-03-18; fax (12) 35-04-13; f. 1996; monitors and regulates all foreign investment in Turkmenistan.

## DEVELOPMENT ORGANIZATION

**Small and Medium Enterprise Development Agency (SMEDA):** 744000 Ashgabat, ul. 2015 8; tel. (12) 34-42-59; fax (12) 34-51-49; e-mail smeda@online.tm; internet www.icctm.org/Smeda; jt venture between Turkmen Govt and EU; Dir SERDAR BABAYEV.

## CHAMBER OF COMMERCE

**Chamber of Commerce of Turkmenistan:** 744000 Ashgabat, ul. 2037 17; tel. (12) 35-64-03; fax (12) 35-13-52; e-mail mission@online.tm; f. 1959; Chair. ARSLAN F. NEPESOV; Dep. Chair. AGAMAMED SAKHATOV.

## UTILITIES

### Electricity

**Kuvvat:** Ashgabat; e-mail kuvvat@online.tm; state electrical power generation co and agency; Chair. DAVYDOV YUSUP.

## STATE HYDROCARBONS COMPANIES

**Turkmengaz:** 744000 Ashgabat, ul. 2003 1; tel. (12) 35-59-59; fax (12) 39–26–00; e-mail tmgas@online.tm; f. 1996; govt agency responsible for natural gas operations, inc. development of system of extraction, processing of gas and gas concentrate and gas transportation; Chair. GUYCHNAZAR TACHNAZAROV.

**Turkmengeologiya:** 744000 Ashgabat, ul. 2023 7/32; tel. (12) 35-13-46; fax (12) 35-50-15; govt agency responsible for natural gas and petroleum exploration; Chair. ORAZMUKHAMMET ATAGELDYEV.

**Turkmenneft:** 745100 Balkanabat, pr. 2076 49; tel. (00243) 2-19-45; govt agency responsible for petroleum operations and production; Pres. SAPARMAMMET VALIYEV; Gen. Dir KHAKIM IMAMOV.

**Turkmenneftegaz:** 744000 Ashgabat, ul. 2002 28; tel. (12) 35-58-94; fax (12) 35-27-28; e-mail tngaz@online.tm; f. 1996; govt trade corpn for petroleum and natural gas marketing; includes Chelekenmorneftegaz (CMNG); Chair. ILYAS CHARIYEV.

> **Turkmenbashy Oil Refinery:** 745000 Balkan, Turkmenbashy, POB 5; tel. (00222) 7-45-45; fax (00222) 7-45-44; production and refining of petroleum; Dir V. I. GUBANOV.

**Turkmenneftegazstroy:** 744000 Ashgabat, ul. 2003 5; tel. (12) 35-58-65; fax (12) 51-08-54; govt agency for construction projects in the hydrocarbons sector; Chair. REJEPDURDY ATAYEV.

## MAJOR COMPANIES

**Barash Communication Technologies Inc:** 744000 Ashgabat, 2038 56; tel. (12) 41-94-92; fax (12) 39-80-40; provides cellular communications and paging services; Pres. ALLA BARASH; Chair. MIKHAIL BARASH.

**Energokhimmashexport:** Ashgabat; f. 1995; main trading dealer for Kuvvat, Turkhmenkhimsenagat and Turkmenmashingurlyshik; exports products from the above companies and imports food, consumer goods and raw materials; 55 employees.

**Kaakhka Cotton Ginning Plant:** 745340 Ashgabat, pos. Kaakhka, Poltoratskogo; tel. (12) 2-13-45; produces cotton and cotton fabrics; Gen. Dir M. ESENOV; 900 employees.

**Mobil Exploration and Producing, Turkmenistan Inc:** 744000 Ashgabat, Hotel Mizan, Mizan Business Centre, ul. Novofiruziskoye; tel. (12) 51-85-23; fax (12) 51-85-24; subsidiary of ExxonMobil Corpn (USA); exploration of, and production from, oil and gas fields; Gen. Man. GREG RENWICK.

**Shell Oil:** 744000 Ashgabat, 202 Office Bldg, Four Points Ak Altyn Hotel, pr. 2033; tel. (12) 51-19-51; fax (12) 51-19-52; produces and distributes petroleum and natural gas; subsidiary of Royal Dutch/Shell (Netherlands/United Kingdom); Dir DIRK VAN DONK.

**Turkmenintorg Foreign Trade Organization:** 744000 Ashgabat, Hivinskaya 1; tel. (12) 39-87-74; fax (12) 39-89-55; f. 1989; develops foreign trade in Turkmenistan by provision of consultancy services for foreign cos; currency transactions; marketing, tourism and organization of exhibitions; exports fibre, cotton seeds, fertilizers and carpets; Gen. Dir SAYED GURBANOVICH BEGIYEV; 60 employees.

**Turkmenkhaly** (Turkmen Carpets): 744000 Ashgabat, pr. 2033 95; tel. (12) 35-39-44; fax (12) 35-43-11; e-mail Turkmenhali@online.tm; internet www.turkmenhali.gov.tm; state joint-stock co; produces and distributes hand-made, pure wool carpets; Chair. GULYA GARAJAYEVA.

**Turkmenkhimsenagat:** Balkan; state-owned chemical production co; supervises the Karabogazsulphate, Balkanabat Iodine Production Plant and Cheleken Chemical Plant enterprises.

**Turkmenmashingurlyshik:** state machine-building production co.

**Turkmenmebel** (Turkmen Furniture Production Society): 744021 Ashgabat, ul. 2015; tel. and fax (12) 33-00-31; state owned.

**Turkmenpagta:** 744000 Ashgabat, ul. Andalib 102; tel. (12) 32-46-01; state-owned cotton corpn; Head AMANMUKHAMMET MUKHADOV.

**Turkmenprod Aktsiyoner** (Turkmen Food Joint-Stock Co): Ashgabat; f. 1994; state-owned; Dir NEDIRMAMMET ALOVOV.

**Wool Primary Processing Factory:** Mary; wool-processing.

### TRADE UNIONS

**Association of Trade Unions of Turkmenistan:** 744000 Ashgabat, 1966 13; tel. (12) 35-62-08; fax (12) 35-21-30; national centre; Chair. ENEBAY G. ATAEVA.

**Committee of Trade Unions of Dashkhovuz Velayat:** 746311 Niyazovsk, Saparmyrat Turkmenbashy shayoly 8; Dir SH. IGAMOV.

**Union of Trade Unions of Akhal Velayat:** Gyaver etrap, Annau; tel. 41-39-19; Dir A. TAGANOV.

## Transport

### RAILWAYS

The main rail line in the country runs from Turkmenbashy (Krasnovodsk), on the Caspian Sea, in the west, via Ashgabat and Mary, to Türkmenabat (Charjew) in the east. From Türkmenabat one line runs further east, to the other Central Asian countries of the former USSR, while another runs north-west, via Uzbekistan and Kazakhstan, to join the rail network of the Russian Federation. In 1998 the total length of rail track in use in Turkmenistan was 2,313 km. A 203-km rail link from Türkmenabat to Atamarut was opened in 1999. In 1996 a rail link was established with Iran (on the route Tejen–Serakhs–Mashhad), thus providing the possibility of rail travel and transportation between Turkmenistan and Istanbul, Turkey, as well as giving access to the Persian (Arabian) Gulf.

**Turkmenistan State Railways:** 744000 Ashgabat, 1966 7; tel. (12) 35-55-45; fax (12) 51-06-32; f. 1992 following the dissolution of the former Soviet Railways (SZhD) organization; 19,200 employees (1998); Chair. BATYR SARJAYEV.

### ROADS

In 1999 there was an estimated total of 24,000 km of roads, of which some 19,500 km were hard-surfaced. In 2000 construction began on a 600-km road linking Ashgabat and Dashoguz.

**Turkmenavtoyollary:** 744000 Ashgabat, ul. 2002 316; tel. (12) 34-84-16; fax (12) 34-52-77; joint-venture co between the state and AML; construction of highway connecting Ashgabat and Kaakha; Chair. BAYMUKHAMMET KELOV.

### SHIPPING

Shipping services link Turkmenbashy (Krasnovodsk) with Baku, Azerbaijan, Makhachkala, Russia, and the major Iranian ports on the Caspian Sea. The Amu-Dar'ya river is an important inland waterway. From 2000 Turkmenbashy port was undergoing an extensive process of modernization.

#### Shipowning Companies

**Neftec Ltd:** Turkmenbashy; tel. (2) 765-81; fax (2) 766-89.

**Turkmen Maritime Steamship Company:** Turkmenbashy, ul. Shagadama 8; tel. (2) 767-34.

**Turkmen Shipping Co:** Turkmenbashy, ul. Shagadama 8; tel. (2) 972-67; fax (2) 767-85.

**Turkmenderyayollary:** Türkmenabat, ul. Gyamichiler 8; tel. (2) 223-12; fax (2) 23–46-88; f. 1992 as Turkmen River Shipping Co; renamed as above in 1998.

**Turkmennefteflot:** Turkmenbashy, Pochtovyi Yashchik 6; tel. (2) 762-62.

### CIVIL AVIATION

Turkmenistan's international airport is at Ashgabat. A new terminal building was completed in late 1994, thus expanding the airport's capacity. A second phase of redevelopment (involving the construction of a new runway and the installation of modern airport systems) was completed in 1998. In 2000 an additional runway was opened at the airport.

**National Civil Aviation Authority of Turkmenistan** (Turkmenhovayollary): 744000 Ashgabat, ul. 2007 3A; tel. (12) 35-10-52; fax (12) 35-44-02; f. 1992; Chief Exec. ILYAE BERDIEV.

**Turkmenistan Airlines:** 744000 Ashgabat, pr. 2033 80; tel. (12) 35-10-52; fax (12) 35-44-02; e-mail info@turkmenistanairline.com; internet www.t5turkmenistan.com; f. 1992; domestic and international scheduled and charter passenger flights, incl. services within Europe, Central and South-East Asia, and the Middle East; operates under three divisions: Akhal Air Co, Khazar Air and Lebap Air Co; Gen. Dir ALEKSEI P. BONDAREV.

## Tourism

Although the tourism sector in Turkmenistan remains relatively undeveloped, owing, in part, to the vast expanse of the Kara-Kum desert (some 80% of the country's total area), the Government has made efforts to improve the standard of visitor accommodation (there are a number of new luxury hotels in Ashgabat) and to improve the capacity and efficiency of the capital's international airport (see Civil Aviation). The scenic Kopet Dagh mountains, the Caspian Sea coast, the archaeological sites and mountain caves of Kugitang and the hot subterranean mineral lake at Kov-Ata are among the country's natural attractions, while the ancient cities of Merv (Mary) and Nisa—former capitals of the Seljuk and Parthian empires, respectively—are of considerable historical interest. In addition, Kunya-Urgench is an important site of Muslim pilgrimage. In 1998, according to the World Tourism Organization, there were approximately 300,000 visitors from abroad, and receipts from tourism totalled US $192m.

**State Committee for Tourism and Sport:** 744000 Ashgabat, ul. 1984 17; tel. (12) 35-47-77; fax (12) 39-67-40; e-mail travel@online.tm; internet www.tourism-sport.gov.tm; f. 2000; Chair. (vacant).

**National Institute of Tourism and Sport:** 744001 Ashgabat, ul. 2038 15A; tel. (12) 36-25-40; fax (12) 36-24-49; f. 1981; Rector ASHIR MOMMADOV.

## Culture

The Turkmen were, by tradition, a nomadic people. Their language was standardized into a national tongue in the Soviet period, based on the dialects of the Tekke and Yomud tribes. The traditional Arabic script was replaced by a Latin one in 1927 and a Cyrillic one in 1938, but, more importantly, under Soviet rule widespread literacy was achieved. This preserved the literary tradition of the Turkmen and, potentially, made it available to the mass of the population, despite the destruction of their traditional nomadic culture and normal means of transmission. National works were, however, subject to bans by the Soviet authorities and it was only with independence that, for example, the religious poems of the 18th century Sufi, Magtymguly (Makhtumkuli), or the national epic of the Oguz Turkmen, *The Book of Gorkut Ata*, could properly be rehabilitated. Traditional Islamic culture also enjoyed cautious official encouragement in the 1990s, notably with the construction of many new mosques, in particular the great memorial mosque at Gök Tepe, which commemorated the great battle of the Turkmen resistance in 1881.

### NATIONAL ORGANIZATIONS

**Ministry of Culture:** see section on The Government (Ministries).

**Directorate for the Protection of Historical and Cultural Monuments and for National Exploration and Restoration:** Ashgabat; financed by the central budget.

**Institute of Culture:** 744000 Ashgabat, ul. 2033 4; tel. (12) 47-39-44.

## CULTURAL HERITAGE

**National Library of Turkmenistan:** 744000 Ashgabat, pl. 2001; tel. (12) 25-32-54; f. 1895; 5.5m. vols; Dir S. A. KURBANOV.

**National Museum of Turkmenistan:** Ashgabat, Novofiryuzinskoe 30; tel. (12) 51-90-20; fax (12) 51-90-22; e-mail vip@online.tm; f. 1998 by merger of the National Museum of History and Ethnograpgy, the State Museum of History and the Turkmen State Museum of Fine Art; eight exhibition halls; Dir OVEZMUHAMMED MAMETNUROV.

**Turkmenistan National Commission for UNESCO:** 744000 Ashgabat, ul. 2002; tel. and fax (12) 35-53-67; e-mail poladov@tm.synapse.tm; Sec.-Gen. Dr K. POLADOV.

## SPORTING ORGANIZATIONS

**Federation of Athletics of Turkmenistan:** Ashgabat; tel. (12) 47-91-26.

**National Institute of Tourism and Sport:** Ashgabat, ul. 2038 15A; tel. (12) 36-25-40; fax (12) 36-24-49; f. 1981; Rector ASHIR MOMMADOV.

**National Olympic Committee of Turkmenistan:** 744001 Ashgabat, ul. 2038 15; tel. (12) 36-13-09; fax (12) 36-33-27; e-mail noctkm@online.tm; f. 1990; Pres. BERDYMURAD REJEPOV; Gen. Sec. ANNAMUHAMED SERHENOV.

**State Committee for Tourism and Sport:** 744000 Ashgabat, ul. 1984 17; tel. (12) 35-47-77; fax (12) 39-67-40; e-mail travel@online.tm; internet www.tourism-sport.gov.tm; f. 2000; Chair. (vacant).

## PERFORMING ARTS

In April 2001 President Niyazov ordered a ban on performances of both opera and ballet, claiming these arts to be 'alien' to Turkmen culture.

**Alp Arslan Young Spectators' Theatre:** Ashgabat; Dir ORAZGELDY AYDOGDIYEV.

**Magtymguly National Music and Drama Theatre:** Ashgabat.

**Turkmen State Mollanepes Academic Drama Theatre:** Ashgabat, 2035 79; tel. (12) 35-69-58; Dir MAMMETVELIYEV TACHMAMMET.

**State Pushkin Russian Drama Theatre:** Ashgabat, ul. 2002 11; tel. (12) 35-11-39; Dir NEPESOV SERDAR KURBANOVICH.

**Turkmen National Conservatory:** Ashgabat, ul. 1984 22; tel. (12) 35-52-19.

**Turkmen State Theatre 'Jan':** tel. (12) 35-10-76.

**Young People's Theatre:** Ashgabat, pr. 2033 115; tel. (12) 35-49-74; Dir AMANGELDIYEV ORAZ.

## ASSOCIATIONS

**Musical Society of Turkmenistan:** 744013 Ashgabat; tel. (12) 25-19-15; Dir ROSA TURAYEVA.

**Union of Architects of Turkmenistan:** 744000 Ashgabat; tel. (12) 47-45-43; Dir A. K. KURBANLIYEV.

**Union of Artists of Turkmenistan:** 744000 Ashgabat, ul. 2010 33; tel. (12) 39-55-43; fax (12) 39-54-39; Dir BABASARY ANNAMURADOV.

**Union of Cinematographers of Turkmenistan:** 744001 Ashgabat, ul. 2023 68; tel. (12) 47-45-43; Dir KHADJAGULLY NARLIYEV.

**Union of Composers of Turkmenistan:** 744000 Ashgabat, ul. 1984 22; tel. (12) 25-46-51; Dir REJEP REJEPOV.

**Union of Designers of Turkmenistan:** 744000 Ashgabat, ul. 1928 12; tel. (12) 47-43-01; Dir O. MAMMETNUROV.

**Union of Journalists of Turkmenistan:** 744500 Ashgabat, ul. 2011 55; tel. (12) 41-33-69; Dir A. MAMEDOV.

**Union of Theatre Artists of Turkmenistan:** 744028 Ashgabat, pr. Khudayberdiyeva 1; tel. (12) 35-45-26; Dir A. BERDIYEV.

**Union of Writers of Turkmenistan:** 744000 Ashgabat; tel. (12) 5-51-78; brs in Mary, Tashauz and Türkmenabat.

# Education

There were few educational establishments in pre-revolutionary Turkmenistan, but a state-funded education system was introduced under Soviet rule. Most school education was conducted in Turkmen, but there were also schools using Russian, Uzbek and Kazakh. It was reported in 2002 that very few schools in Turkmenistan continued to offer Russian-language classes. Until the early 1990s most institutions of higher education used Russian, but there were attempts to increase the provision of Turkmen-language courses. Primary and secondary education lasts for nine years. In 1990 the

total enrolment at higher schools was equivalent to 21.8% of the relevant age-group. The 1999 budget allocated 26.9% of total expenditure (1,048,700m. manats) to education. As part of a programme of educational reform, free education at Turkmenistan's 16 universities was reportedly to be abolished from 2003. Only those who have completed two years' relevant work experience after leaving school are permitted to enroll at institutes of higher education.

## UNIVERSITY

**Turkmen A. M. Gorkii State University:** 744014 Ashgabat, pr. Lenina 31; tel. (12) 5-11-59; f. 1950 as A. M. Gorkii State University; 10 faculties; 11,000 students; Rector MERET ORAZOV.

# Social Welfare

A basic, state-funded health system was introduced under Soviet rule, but the system was of low quality, and underfunded. In 1998 there were 2.61 physicians and 11.2 hospital beds for every 1,000 people. The high levels of disease in Turkmenistan (among adults, as well as children) were attributed to poor overall medical and sanitary conditions, and the critical state of the environment. In 2001 the average life expectancy at birth was 58.9 years for males and 66.5 years for females. The rate of infant mortality reached 99 per 1,000 live births in that year.

In 1991 and the early years of independence the Government of Turkmenistan introduced extensive social protection measures (mostly the responsibility of a Pension Fund), that were relatively more generous than in other former Soviet states. In 1999 397,000 people received pensions or allowances from the Pension and Social Security Fund (of these 284,000 received an old-age pension of 98,000 manats per month). The basic retirement age was 60 years for men and 55 years for women. The Pension and Social Security Fund also distributed allowances to low-income families and to families with children, as well as allocating death, disability and veterans benefits. A new pension system based on voluntary self-funding was being introduced in mid-2000. There are no unemployment benefits.

From the early 1990s electricity, gas and water were made free for all citizens, although in 1996 some charges were introduced for domestic electricity users. Consumer products such as flour, bread, rice, cotton oil and sugar were provided at highly subsidized prices, while salt was available free of charge. The 1999 budget allocated an estimated 14.1% of total spending (550,600m. Turkmen manats) to the health services and 15.6% of spending (605,900m. manats) to the Pension and Social Security Fund (and the Geological Fund).

**Ministry of Health and the Medical Industry:** see section on The Government (Ministries).

**Ministry of Social Security:** see section on The Government (Ministries).

## HEALTH AND WELFARE ORGANIZATIONS

**Association of the Disabled of Turkmenistan:** Ashgabat; tel. (12) 44-97-29.

**Children's Fund of Turkmenistan:** Ashgabat; tel. (12) 29-61-79; Chair. KHULKHANOV DJUMA.

# The Environment

Turkmenistan has experienced severe ecological problems as a result of the desiccation of the lower reaches of the Amu-Dar'ya and the Aral Sea. From the dehydrated seabed of the Aral Sea large amounts of salted dust and sand are blown on to fertile areas in northern Turkmenistan. Excessive use of chemical pesticides and herbicides in cotton-growing areas have also caused severe problems. The chemicals enter the soil and the water supply, and, since only 13% of the population was provided with piped water at the end of the 1980s, most water for domestic use was drawn directly from polluted water channels. In January 1994 Turkmenistan and the four other Central Asian countries agreed to take co-ordinated action against a further deterioration of the Aral Sea ecology and to attempt to reverse some of the damage. Thus, Turkmenistan and Uzbekistan agreed to guarantee a certain minimum level of water reaching the Aral Sea (conditions permitting). On the Caspian Sea, the problem was completely different: in the 1990s there was an increase in the level of the Sea, which caused severe flooding on the Caspian littoral. The Caspian Sea also suffered from 'run-off' phosphate pollution. In June 2001 Turkmenistan, Azerbaijan, Kazakhstan and Russia agreed to attempt to prevent the extinction of the caviar-producing sturgeon by temporarily halting fishing in the Caspian Sea.

## GOVERNMENT ORGANIZATIONS

**Ministry of Environmental Protection:** see section on The Government (Ministries).

**Ministry of Water Resources:** see section on The Government (Ministries).

## ACADEMIC INSTITUTES

**Academy of Sciences of Turkmenistan:** 744000 Ashgabat, Neytralny Turkmenistan 15; tel. (12) 25-44-74; fax (12) 25-53-67; Pres. KHODJAMAMEDOV AGA MAMEDOVICH; Dep. Pres. POLADOV KOUWANDYK; institutes incl.:

**Commission on Nature Conservation:** 744000 Ashgabat, Gogolya 15; attached to the Presidium of the Academy of Sciences; Chair. A. O. TASHILIYEV.

**Desert Research Institute:** 744000 Ashgabat, Neytralny Turkmenistan 15; tel. (12) 29-54-27; fax (12) 25-37-16; f. 1962; programmes incl. research into desert resources and arid environment problems; incl. International Centre for Research and Training in the Problems of Desertification; Dir A. G. BABAYEV; Dep. Dir O. MURADOV.

**Scientific Consultative Ecological Centre (EKOTSENTR):** Ashgabat, ul. 2002 15; Chair. A. G. BABAYEV.

## NON-GOVERNMENTAL ORGANIZATIONS

**Catena Ecology Club:** 744012 Ashgabat, ul. Pavlova 7/2; tel. (12) 35-15-31; fax (12) 35-02-57; e-mail catoffs@cat.glasnet.ru; internet www.ecostan.org/ngo/cathome.html; f. 1994; Co-Chair. ANDREI ARANBAYEV, VAGIF ZEYNALOV.

**Dashkhovuz Ecology Club:** 746301 Dashkhovuz, Micro-raion Ts-1, d. 8, kv. 23; tel. and fax (12) 566-83; e-mail zatoka@glasnet.ru; f.

1992; only registered grass-roots environmental org.; education, public ecological monitoring and control, recycling and protection of biodiversity; Co-Chair. FARID TUKHBATULLIN, ANDREI LVOVICH ZATOKA.

**Ecology Fund of Turkmenistan:** 744000 Ashgabat, ul. 2002 15; tel. (12) 29-42-33; Dir A. BABAYEV.

**Turkmenistan Society for the Conservation of Nature:** 744000 Ashgabat, 2084 62; tel. (12) 29-77-27; Dir A. K. RUSTAMOV.

# Defence

The National Armed Forces of Turkmenistan began to be formed in mid-1992, based on former Soviet forces that had been based in the territory of the republic. By agreement with Russia, these forces were initially under joint Turkmen and Russian command. In August 2002 the national army numbered 14,500; in addition, there was an air force of 3,000. The Government also planned to establish a national navy or coastguard. In 1993–98 Russia and Kazakhstan co-operated with Turkmenistan in the operation of the Caspian Sea Flotilla, another former Soviet force, which was based at Astrakhan, Russia. In September 1993 the country's first military institute opened (formerly a department of Magtymguly University), and in December of that year Turkmenistan agreed that Russian troops should be stationed on its southern borders. In May 1994 Turkmenistan became the first Central Asian republic of the former USSR to join NATO's 'Partnership for Peace' programme. Turkmenistan's policy of neutrality was recognized by the UN General Assembly in December 1995. Defence expenditure in 2003 was forecast at US $173m..

**Supreme Commander-in-Chief of the National Armed Forces:** President of the Republic.

**Chief of the General Staff:** REJEPGELDY NURSHATOV (acting).

# Bibliography

Blackwell, C. *Tradition and Society in Turkmenistan: Gender, Oral Culture and Song*. London, RoutledgeCurzon, 2001.

Pastor, G., and Van Rooden, R. 'Turkmenistan—the Burden of Current Agricultural Policies' in *IMF Working Paper 00/98*, June 2000.

Saray, M. *The Turkmen in the Age of Imperialism: A Study of the Turkmen People and their Incorporation into the Russian Empire*. Ankara, Turkish Historical Society Printing House, 1989.

Thubron, Colin. *The Lost Heart of Asia*. London, Heinemann, 2000.

Turkmenistan Research Group. *Executive Report on Strategies in Turkmenistan, 2000 Edition (Strategic Planning Series)*. San Diego, CA, Icon Group International, 2000.

Also see the Select Bibliography in Part Four.

# UKRAINE

## Geography

### PHYSICAL FEATURES

The Republic of Ukraine (formerly the Ukrainian Soviet Socialist Republic, a constituent part of the USSR) is situated in Eastern Europe. It is bordered by Poland and Slovakia to the west and by Hungary, Romania and Moldova to the south-west. In the western part of the country the northern border is with Belarus, while in eastern Ukraine the northern and eastern borders are with Russia. To the south lie the Black Sea and the Sea of Azov. Ukraine covers an area of 603,700 sq km (233,090 sq miles) and is the largest country entirely within Europe. Its territory includes the Autonomous Republic of Crimea, which lies on a peninsula in the south of the country, almost entirely surrounded by the Sea of Azov, to the east, and by the Black Sea to the south, west and north-west.

The relief consists of a steppe lowland, bordered by uplands to the west and south-west, and by the Crimean mountains in the south, on the Crimean Peninsula. The main rivers are the Dnipro (Dniepr—Dnieper), which drains the central regions of the country and flows into the Black Sea, and the Dniestr (Dniester), which flows through Western Ukraine and Moldova before also entering the Black Sea, near Odesa (Odessa). In the south, to the south-west of Odesa, Ukraine has a short border on the Danube (Dunay) delta.

### CLIMATE

The climate is temperate, especially in the south. The north and north-west share many of the continental climatic features of Poland and Belarus, but the Black Sea coast is noted for its mild winters. Droughts are not infrequent in southern areas. Average temperatures in Kiev range from –6.1°C (21°F) in January to 20.4°C (69°F) in July. Average annual rainfall in Kiev is 615 mm (24 ins).

### POPULATION

According to rounded figures, the total population at the census of 5 December 2001 was 48,457,000. According to official estimates, at 31 December 2002 the population was 48,003,500, giving a population density of 79.5 per sq km. Of permanent inhabitants recorded at the 2001 census, Ukrainians formed the largest ethnic group, comprising 78.1% of the total population, while 17.3% were Russians. There were also significant minorities of Belarusians and Moldovans. Ukraine's traditional Polish, Jewish and German minorities were all considerably reduced after the Second World War. The permanent resident population of Crimean Tatars was enumerated at 248,200; the vast majority of this mostly Muslim people, deported from Crimea in 1944, had returned to the peninsula (prinicipally from Uzbekistan) after 1989.

The increase in the proportion of the population that described itself as Ukrainian following independence from the USSR (from 72.7% of the total in 1989), and concomitant decline in the proportion of the population describing itself as Russian (from 22.1% in 1989), was believed to reflect, in large part, the fluidity of identity between Ukrainian and Russian populations, particularly in eastern and southern regions of Ukraine, as well as changing political circumstances, rather than any significant out-migration of Russians. The official state language is Ukrainian, an Eastern Slavonic language written in the Cyrillic script, although Russian has official status in the Autonomous Republic of Crimea. Many Ukrainians and other minorities were Russian-speaking, particularly in urban areas of the east and south. Most of the population are adherents of Christianity, with the major denominations being the Ukrainian Orthodox Church (both the Kievan Patriarchate and the Moscow Patriarchate, an Exarchate of the Russian Orthodox Church), the Ukrainian Autocephalous Orthodox Church and the Roman Catholic Church (mostly 'Greek' Catholics or 'Uniates', who observe Byzantine Rites). There are also a number of Protestant churches and small communities of Jews and Muslims.

The capital is Kiev (Kyiv), which had a population of 2,611,000 in 2001. It is situated in the north of the country, on the Dnipro river. Other important towns include Kharkiv (Kharkov, population 1,470,000 in 2001), Dnipropetrovsk (Dnepropetrovsk, 1,065,000), the port of Odesa (Odessa, 1,029,000), Donetsk (1,016,000), Zaporizhzhia (Zaporozhe, 815,000), and Lviv (Lvov, 733,000). The capital of Crimea is Simferopol—estimated population 344,000 in 2001, and another important town on the penisula is the port of Sevastopol, which had a population of 342,000 in 2001.

# Chronology

**c. 878:** The Eastern Slavs founded the state of Kievan Rus, with Kiev (Kyiv) as its capital.

**c. 988:** Kievan Rus officially converted to Orthodox Christianity, following the baptism of its ruler, Volodymyr (Vladimir) I ('the Great').

**1237–40:** As a result of internecine feuds over succession, the defenceless Kievan state was captured by invading Mongol Tatars and Kiev burned to the ground.

**1475:** Establishment of the Crimean Khanate of the Tatars.

**1596:** By the Union of Brest a number of Orthodox bishops, mainly in what is modern Western Ukraine and Belarus, acknowledged the primacy of the Roman Catholic spiritual leader, the Pope, to form what became known as the Greek Catholic or 'Uniate' Church.

**1648:** Bohdan Khmelnytsky led a rebellion by Ukrainian Cossacks against their Polish overlords, which resulted in the formation of a Cossack state in eastern Ukraine.

**1654:** Eastern Ukraine came under Muscovite (Russian) rule by the terms of the Treaty of Pereyaslav.

**1667:** Ukraine was divided between the Polish–Lithuanian Commonwealth (which gained the western region) and the Russian Empire (which gained Ukrainian territory east of the Dnipro—Dnieper).

**1709:** Ivan Mazepa, Hetman (ruler) of the Ukrainian Cossack state, supported Charles XII of Sweden in his invasion of Ukraine, having previously pledged allegiance to Russia; the Russian army defeated the Swedes and the Cossack state was incorporated into the Russian Empire.

**1783:** The Crimean Khanate was acquired by Russia.

**1793:** At the Second Partition of Poland the regions of Halychyna (Galicia) and Bukovyna (Bukovina) were acquired by the Habsburgs (who had acquired Transcarpathia—Carpatho-Ruthenia in the 11th century), while the rest of Western Ukraine came under Russian rule.

**1839:** The 'Uniate' Church was suppressed in Russian-controlled Ukraine.

**1861:** Emancipation of the serfs throughout the Russian Empire.

**1876:** The use of the Ukrainian language was banned in the tsarist territories, in reinforcement of a decree of 1863.

**1917:** Following the collapse of the Russian Empire, Ukrainian nationalists formed a Central Rada (council or soviet) in Kiev.

**9 January 1918:** The Rada proclaimed a Ukrainian People's Republic.

**9 February 1918:** The Central Powers (Germany and Austria-Hungary) recognized the independence of the new country in a peace treaty.

**April 1918:** Following the signing of the Treaty of Brest-Litovsk in March, under which the Bolshevik Russian authorities ceded Ukraine to Germany, the Government of the Ukrainian People's Republic was replaced by a pro-German administration, headed by Hetman Pavlo Skoropadsky.

**December 1918:** With the defeat of Germany, Skoropadsky was deposed and a liberal Directorate Government was established in Ukraine.

**January 1919:** The Ukrainian People's Republic was united with the Western Ukrainian People's Republic (formed in Halychyna and Bukovyna after the collapse of the Habsburg Monarchy the previous year).

**December 1920:** A Ukrainian Soviet Socialist Republic (SSR), with its capital in Kharkiv (Kharkov), was proclaimed in eastern Ukraine, following the occupation of the area by the Soviet Red Army; later that month (20 December) the Republic signed a Treaty of Alliance with the Bolshevik administration in Russia.

**18 March 1921:** The Soviet–Polish War was formally ended by the signing of the Treaty of Rīga; the Treaty provided for the division of Western Ukraine according to the provisions of earlier international agreements between Poland (which gained Volhynia and Halychyna), Czechoslovakia (Transcarpathia) and Romania (Bukovyna—Romania had also acquired the previously Russian territory of Bessarabia).

**30 December 1922:** At the 10th All-Russian (first All-Union) Congress of Soviets the Union of Soviet Socialist Republics (USSR) was proclaimed; the Ukrainian SSR was a founding member.

**1928:** The New Economic Policy (NEP), in effect since 1921 and under which Ukraine had thrived, was abandoned by the all-Union Government; it was replaced by a system of forced collectivization of agriculture.

**1929:** The right-wing Organization of Ukrainian Nationalists (OUN) was founded in Halychyna.

**1932–33:** The Great Famine (also known as the Holodomor—'Famine-Genocide'), the direct result of Stalin's (Iosif V. Dzhugashvili) policy of collectivization, resulted in the deaths of an estimated 5m.–7m. Ukrainian peasants.

**1933:** Mykola Skrypnyk, the moderate leader of the Communist Party of Ukraine (CPU), committed suicide; Stalin appointed a close political ally, Lazar Kaganovich, to replace him.

**1936–38:** Large numbers of the Ukrainian cultural and political élite suffered in what came to be known as the 'Great Purge', a series of mass arrests and executions by the Soviet security police, the NKVD (People's Commissariat for Internal Affairs), under the leadership of Nikolai Yezhov.

**June 1941:** The German army invaded Ukraine, as part of 'Operation Barbarossa'. Later in the year, in Lviv (Lvov) the OUN declared the establishment of an independent Ukrainian entity.

**1942:** The Ukrainian Insurgent Army was established by the OUN; the partisans continued to carry out attacks against the Communist Government into the early 1950s.

**9 May 1945:** Following Germany's unconditional surrender, the Second World War ended in Europe; Ukraine had suffered considerable damage during the conflict and some 6m. inhabitants were estimated to have died. The hitherto Czechoslovak region of Transcarpathia subsequently became part of the Ukrainian SSR; southern Bessarabia (a Romanian territory between the World Wars) became part of Ukraine; and some of the territories on the left (East) bank of the Dnistr—Dniestr, taken to form a Moldovan (Moldavian) autonomous region in 1924, were regained. (Northern Bukovyna had become part of the Ukrainian SSR in 1944).

**26 June 1945:** The Ukrainian SSR was one of 50 countries to sign the Charter of the United Nations.

**1954:** The Soviet authorities transferred control of the Black Sea peninsula of Crimea from Russia to Ukraine. Crimea's Tatar population had been deported to Central Asia by Stalin in 1944.

**1963:** Petro Shelest became First Secretary of the CPU; during his time in office a nationalist intellectual movement developed in Ukraine and many independent (*samvydav—samizdat*) publications were produced.

**1972:** Shelest was replaced as CPU leader by Vladimir Shcherbytsky, a politician loyal to the all-Union Government. There was widespread repression of dissidents.

**1976:** The Helsinki Group was founded in Ukraine to monitor the effects in the Republic of the Helsinki Final Act (the human rights final agreement signed by 32 European countries, Canada and the USA in Finland the previous year). The Group was subsequently suppressed, but re-emerged as the Ukrainian Helsinki Union in 1988.

**26 April 1986:** A serious explosion took place at the Chornobyl (Chernobyl) nuclear power station in northern Ukraine; large quantities of radioactive material were discharged, but information concerning the accident was suppressed.

**September 1989:** The Ukrainian People's Movement for Restructuring (Rukh), founded in Kiev in November 1998 and headed by Ivan Drach, held its founding conference. On 28 September Vladimir Shcherbytsky resigned, following his failure to control the opposition movements and the miners' unrest in the Donbas (Donbass) region; Volodymyr Ivashko replaced Shcherbytsky as First Secretary.

**December 1989:** Gorbachev granted official recognition to the Ukrainian Greek Catholic or 'Uniate' Church, after a meeting with Pope John Paul II.

**4 March 1990:** Elections were held to the Ukrainian legislature, the Verkhovna Rada; Rukh, participating as a member of the Democratic Bloc electoral coalition, won 108 of a total of 450 seats.

**June 1990:** Ivashko was elected Chairman of the Verkhovna Rada and subsequently resigned as First Secretary of the CPU. He was succeeded by Stanislav Hurenko.

**16 July 1990:** The Verkhovna Rada adopted a declaration of sovereignty, which asserted the right of Ukraine to possess its own military forces and proclaimed the supremacy of republican law on its territory. In the same month Ivashko was appointed Deputy General Secretary of the Communist Party of the Soviet Union (CPSU). One week later Leonid Kravchuk, formerly Second Secretary of the CPU, was elected Chairman of the Verkhovna Rada.

**17 October 1990:** Vitaliy Masol, Chairman of the Council of Ministers (Prime Minister), resigned, following two weeks of protests by students. Vitold Fokin was elected to replace him the following month.

**20 January 1991:** In a referendum, the inhabitants of Crimea voted to restore to the region the status of an autonomous republic.

**17 March 1991:** In an all-Union referendum on the issue of the future status of the USSR, 70.5% of Ukrainian participants approved Gorbachev's concept of a 'renewed federation'; an additional question on Ukrainian sovereignty secured the support of 80.2% of the electorate; a third question on outright independence, which was held only in parts of Western Ukraine, was supported by 88.4% of voters.

**24 August 1991:** Following an attempted *coup d'état* in Moscow (the Russian and Soviet capital), the Verkhovna Rada adopted a declaration of Ukrainian independence, by 346 votes to one, pending approval by referendum on 1 December. The following week the CPU was proscribed (although it was permitted to re-form in June 1993, and the prohibition was formally rescinded in October 1994).

**1 December 1991:** Presidential elections were held simultaneously with a referendum on Ukraine's declaration of independence, in which 90.3% of participants voted in favour; Leonid Kravchuk was elected to the new post of executive President of the Republic, with 61.3% of the votes cast.

**8 December 1991:** At a meeting in Belarus, the leaders of Ukraine, Belarus and Russia agreed to form a Commonwealth of Independent States (CIS) to replace the USSR. On 21 December a protocol on the formation of the CIS was signed by the leaders of 11 former Soviet republics, meeting in Kazakhstan. Four days later, Gorbachev resigned as President of the USSR, confirming the dissolution of the Union.

**5 May 1992:** The Crimean parliament, the Supreme Council, voted to declare independence from Ukraine. The resolution was annulled the following week by the Verkhovna Rada and rescinded by the Crimean parliament, following threats of an economic blockade and direct rule from Kiev. The following month, however, Ukraine granted Crimea full autonomy.

**30 September 1992:** Fokin's Government resigned, having been defeated in a vote of 'no confidence', as the economic situation deteriorated rapidly.

**13 October 1992:** Leonid Kuchma was approved as Prime Minister by the Verkhovna Rada; several proponents of radical economic reform, and members of Rukh, were appointed to the new Government.

**13 November 1992:** The Soviet currency, the karbovanets (rouble) ceased to be legal tender in Ukraine; it was replaced by a new currency coupon, also known as the karbovanets, or coupon (kupon), intended as a transitional stage to the introduction of a new currency.

**21 November 1992:** The Verkhovna Rada granted Kuchma emergency powers to rule by decree for a period of six months, in order to implement economic reforms.

**16 June 1993:** An emergency committee, headed by Kuchma, was established to deal with the critical political and economic situation in Ukraine, following widespread industrial action in the east.

**9 September 1993:** Kuchma resigned for the third time in four months, in protest at continued parliamentary opposition to his economic programme. The premier's resignation was accepted by the Verkhovna Rada two weeks later, which simultaneously passed a vote of 'no confidence' in the entire Cabinet.

**22 September 1993:** President Kravchuk appointed Yufym Zvyahylsky, a proponent of increased state economic intervention, acting premier. Five days later President Kravchuk assumed direct leadership of the Cabinet of Ministers.

**25 October 1993:** Ukraine agreed with the USA that it would dismantle its ex-Soviet nuclear warheads, in return for US economic aid. Three months later the USA promised further aid and security guarantees in a nuclear-disarmament agreement with Ukraine and Russia, whereby Ukraine would transfer its remaining warheads to Russia. This process was completed in June 1996.

**30 January 1994:** The final round of voting in the first Crimean presidential elections was held; a Russian nationalist, Yurii Meshkov, secured 72.9% of the votes cast.

**8 February 1994:** Ukraine became a signatory to the 'Partnership for Peace' programme of military co-operation, proposed by the North Atlantic Treaty Organization (NATO).

**27 March 1994:** Elections were held to the Verkhovna Rada and the Crimean Supreme Council; in the latter pro-Russian parties won the majority of the seats. At a referendum held concurrently in Crimea, some 70% of voters supported greater autonomous powers for the peninsula.

**April 1994:** Following a second round of voting in elections to the Verkhovna Rada, the CPU won the largest number of seats (86), with its allies, the Peasants' Party of Ukraine and the Socialist Party of Ukraine (SPU), obtaining a further 32 seats; Rukh secured 20 seats. A total of 112 seats remained unfilled; subsequent rounds of voting gradually reduced this number.

**May 1994:** Oleksandr Moroz, the leader of the SPU, was elected Chairman of the Verkhovna Rada. The Crimean Supreme Council voted overwhelmingly to restore the region's Constitution of May 1992, a move that was denounced by the all-Ukrainian Government.

**June 1994:** Vitaliy Masol, who served as Prime Minister between 1987 and 1990, was re-appointed to the post. The first round of voting in the presidential election was contested on 26 June.

**10 July 1994:** The second round of voting in the election to the presidency was contested by the two most successful candidates in the first ballot, President Kravchuk and the former premier, Leonid Kuchma; Kuchma was elected President, securing 52.1% of the votes cast.

**8 August 1994:** President Kuchma placed himself directly in charge of government and subordinated all local councils to the presidency.

**16 November 1994:** The Treaty on the Non-Proliferation of Nuclear Weapons was ratified by the Verkhovna Rada, thus finally enabling the implementation of the first Strategic Arms' Reduction Treaty (START 1), the protocols to which had been signed in May 1992.

**1 March 1995:** Masol resigned as Prime Minister; he was replaced, initially in an acting capacity, by Yevhen Marchuk, who was confirmed as premier in June.

**17 March 1995:** The Verkhovna Rada voted to abolish the Crimean Constitution of May 1992 and the republic's presidency. The following month President Kuchma imposed direct rule in Crimea, which remained in force until 28 August.

**3 July 1995:** President Kuchma appointed a new Government under Marchuk, in which the reformist Viktor Pynzenyk's jurisdiction over economic reform was effectively removed. In the same month Yevhen Suprunyuk, a pro-Ukrainian, was elected Chairman of the Crimean Parliament.

**9 November 1995:** Ukraine was admitted to the Council of Europe.

**27 May 1996:** Marchuk was dismissed, owing to the growing economic crisis; he was succeeded by Pavlo Lazarenko, whose appointment was confirmed by parliament in July. A new Cabinet of Ministers was subsequently formed.

**28 June 1996:** After continuing debate, and following an ultimatum by President Kuchma that included the threat of a referendum, the Verkhovna Rada finally adopted a new Constitution.

**2 September 1996:** A new currency, the hryvnya, was introduced.

**2 April 1997:** Pynzenyk resigned, following months of political obstruction to economic reforms.

**28 May 1997:** An agreement on the division of the Soviet Black Sea Fleet, control over which had been disputed with Russia since 1992, and on the status of the naval base of Sevastopol was signed by President Boris Yeltsin of Russia and President Kuchma. Three days later, in a Treaty of Friendship, Co-operation and Partnership, Russia recognized for the first time the sovereignty of Ukraine; the Treaty was ratified by Ukraine on 14 January 1998.

**16 July 1997:** Valeriy Pustovoytenko, formerly a Minister without Portfolio, was narrowly approved by the legislature as Prime Minister. (Lazarenko had been removed from office by President Kuchma in mid-June).

**22 October 1997:** A new electoral law, providing for a combination of proportionally and directly elected seats was finally approved by President Kuchma.

**19 March 1998:** Criminal proceedings were initiated against the former premier, Lazarenko, on charges of embezzlement. He was subsequently charged with money 'laundering' (the

processing of illegally obtained funds into legitimate holdings) in Switzerland. He sought asylum in the USA, but was detained in that country in February 1999 and indicted on similar charges. In June 2000 Lazarenko was convicted *in absentia* by a Swiss court, which imposed an 18-month suspended prison sentence, and confiscated some US $6.6m. from his Swiss bank accounts.

**29 March 1998:** Of the 30 parties and electoral blocs that contested the general election, eight parties obtained the 4% of the votes necessary for representation in the Verkhovna Rada; the CPU secured 123 seats; of the 225 directly elected seats, the greatest number (136) was won by independent candidates; the results in several constituencies were later declared invalid (repeat elections began in mid-August). In elections to the Crimean Supreme Council, held concurrently at the demand of the Verkhovna Rada, the CPU secured 40 of the 100 seats, to become the largest faction.

**14 May 1998:** Leonid Grach, the leader of the CPU in Crimea, was elected Chairman of the Crimean Supreme Council.

**7 July 1998:** The Verkhovna Rada finally succeeded in electing a speaker, appointing Oleksandr Tkachenko of the Peasants' Party to the position.

**12 January 1999:** A new Crimean Constitution came into effect, codifying relations between the authorities in Kiev and Simferopol, and giving Crimea the right to draft a budget and to manage its own property.

**31 October 1999:** None of the 13 candidates achieved an overall majority in the presidential election, in which 67% of the electorate participated. Kuchma won 36.5% of the votes cast, and the CPU candidate, Petro Symonenko, obtained 22.2%.

**14 November 1999:** Leonid Kuchma won the second round of the presidential elections with 57.7% of the votes cast, and was inaugurated as President on 30 November.

**22 December 1999:** The nomination as Prime Minister of Viktor Yushchenko, hitherto the Chairman of the National Bank of Ukraine, was endorsed by the legislature, following the earlier rejection of the incumbent Prime Minister, Valeriy Pustovoytenko. A new Cabinet of Ministers was subsequently appointed.

**13 January 2000:** A new parliamentary majority faction, formed by deputies from centre-right parties and independents, led by Leonid Kravchuk, petitioned for the removal from office of the Verkhovna Rada Chairman, Oleksandr Tkachenko, and his deputy, Adam Martynyuk. Despite left-wing opposition, eight days later the majority faction voted unanimously to remove the two men from office. In early February it elected Ivan Plyushch, who had held the post in 1994, Chairman.

**22 March 2000:** A law was promulgated, abolishing the death penalty.

**16 April 2000:** Some 81% of the electorate participated in a referendum on constitutional change, of whom 85% were in favour of the dissolution of the Verkhovna Rada for non-approval of the budget within three months of its submission, almost 90% agreed that the number of deputies should be reduced from 450 to 300, some 89% supported limiting deputies' immunity and some 82% voted to introduce a bicameral legislature. There was no indication, however, when or if these reforms would be implemented.

**28 November 2000:** Following the discovery earlier in the same month of a body believed to be that of journalist Georgiy Honhadze, SPU leader Oleksandr Moroz announced that he had taken possession of recordings in which a voice purported to be that of President Kuchma was heard ordering the killing of Honhadze. Controversy surrounded the authenticity of the recordings, and President Kuchma strongly denied the allegations. The presidential administration began legal action against Moroz on 2 December.

**15 December 2000:** The last operational reactor at the Chornobyl site was removed from service.

**19 January 2001:** President Kuchma dismissed the Deputy Prime Minister for Energy Issues, Yuliya Tymoshenko, amid allegations of the illegal smuggling of Russian gas and of tax evasion.

**February 2001:** Following the release of further audio recordings, in which President Kuchma was purportedly heard to order electoral fraud in the presidential election of 1999, and the bribery of energy officials, demonstrations against Kuchma gathered strength, and opposition leaders formed a 'National Salvation Forum' with the aim of unseating the President.

**26 March 2001:** President Kuchma dismissed  Minister of Internal Affairs Yuriy Kravchenko (who had also been implicated in the recently released audio recordings). The following day, former Deputy Prime Minister Yuliya Tymoshenko was released from prison, after having been detained in February, although she was briefly re-arrested at the end of the month.

**26 April 2001:** Prime Minister Viktor Yushchenko lost a vote of 'no confidence' in the Verkhovna Rada, and was thereby removed from office.

**29 May 2001:** Anatoliy Kinakh assumed the post of Prime Minister, having been nominated by President Kuchma, who at the same time created the new position of state secretary in each ministry; the state secretaries were to be appointed for fixed five-year terms.

**23–27 June 2001:** Pope John Paul II made an historic visit to Ukraine, seeking to repair the rift between the Roman Catholic and Orthodox Churches.

**25 July 2001:** Valerii Gorbatov was elected Prime Minister of Crimea, replacing Sergei Kunitsyn.

**3 September 2001:** The Prosecutor-General, Mykhaylo Potebenko, initiated measures to charge former Prime Minister Lazarenko with having arranged the murders of two business figures in 1996 and 1998, respectively.

**11 October 2001:** Following the crash of a Russian passenger aircraft, flying from Tel-Aviv, Israel, to Novosibirsk, Russia, into the Black Sea on 4 October, Ukrainian officials admitted that a surface-to-air missile fired by the Ukrainian Navy during training exercises was the most likely cause of the incident, in which 78 people were killed. (In 2001 a surface-to-air missile fired during similar exercises near to Kiev went astray and demolished an apartment building, killing 20 people.) Col-Gen. Oleksandr Kuzmuk subsequently resigned from his position as Minister of Defence.

**March 2002:** Further audio recordings were released, in which Kuchma was purported to discuss the sale of an advanced anti-aircraft radar system to Iraq, in breach of UN sanctions. During the following months, demonstrations against the President again gathered force, and the allegations served to discredit Kuchma internationally, although the President denied that Ukraine had been involved in any trafficking of military equipment to Iraq.

**31 March 2002:** At elections to the Verkhovna Rada, Viktor Yushchenko's pro-reform Our Ukraine bloc won the largest number of seats of any grouping, with 112 of the 450 elective seats. The For A United Ukraine bloc, which was supportive of President Kuchma, received 101 seats, while the CPU obtained only 66 seats, compared with the 123 held in the outgoing legislature, in which it had been the largest party.

Representatives of seven other parties, and 93 independent candidates, were also elected, meaning that negotiations on the formation of a legislative majority were likely to be protracted. At concurrent elections to the Crimean Supreme Council, the centrist Kunitsyn Team (associated with For a United Ukraine) was the most successful party, obtaining 39 of the 100 seats, defeating the CPU (contesting the elections as the Grach bloc), which secured 28.

**29 April 2002:** Sergei Kunitsyn, was elected as Prime Minister of Crimea. In the opening session of the new Crimean Supreme Council, also in late April, the former Deputy Chairman of the Council, Boris Deich, was elected Chairman, defeating Leonid Grach.

**28 May 2002:** Volodomyr Lytvyn, formerly head of the presidential administration, and the Chairman of the For a United Ukraine electoral bloc, was elected Chairman of the Verkhovna Rada.

**29 July 2002:** At an airshow near Lviv, some 76 people were killed when a military plane crashed into a crowd of spectators. Following a declaration by the Prosecutor-General, Svyatoslav Pyskun, that criminal negligence by pilots and military officials had played a part in the accident, the Chief of the General Staff and the Chief of the Military Air Force resigned, and were replaced by new appointees in August. Although the Minister of Defence, Gen. Volodomyr Shkidchenko, offered to resign, he remained in office.

**October 2002:** In mid-October a senior judge in Kiev, Yuriy Vasylenko, opened a criminal investigation into President Kuchma, who was charged with violating 11 articles of the criminal code. In late October the Supreme Court rejected an appeal declaring the case illegal. However, in early November an ally of Kuchma, Vasyl Malyarenko, was elected as the new Chairman of the Supreme Court, and in late December the court ruled that the investigation into Kuchma had, indeed, been opened illegally.

**16 November 2002:** The hitherto Governor of Donetsk Oblast, Viktor Yanukovych, was appointed as Prime Minister, following the dismissal of Kinakh. A new Government, in which several principal positions remained unchanged, was appointed later in the month.

**17 December 2002:** Serhiy Tyhypko, a former Deputy Prime Minister, responsible for Economic Reform, and leader of the Working Ukraine party, was approved by the Verkhovna Rada as Governor of the National Bank of Ukraine, necessitating his resignation as a parliamentary deputy.

**6 March 2003:** President Kuchma presented proposals for constitutional reform to the Verkhovna Rada, notably including the creation of an appointed Chamber of the Regions as part of a bicameral legislature.

**17 April 2003:** The Verkhovna Rada approved the government programme presented by Prime Minister Yanukovych. In accordance with the Constitution, parliament is prohibited from holding a vote of 'no confidence' in the Government for a period of 12 months from the approval of a government programme. Later that month Yanukovych was elected as Chairman of the Party of the Regions, and Mykola Azarov, First Deputy Prime Minister and Minister of Finance, became Chairman of the party's Political Council.

**26 May 2003:** Kuchma issued a decree abolishing the institution of state secretaries, introduced in May 2001, and re-introducing the arrangements that existed prior to that time, in accordance with which deputy ministers were appointed and dismissed at the will of the President.

# History

## Dr TARAS KUZIO

### EARLY HISTORY

Between the ninth and 13th centuries Ukraine was known as Kievan Rus, with its capital at Kiev (Kyiv), a state that extended into what is now Belarus and parts of European Russia. In 988 its ruler, Volodymyr (Vladimir) I—'the Great' (980–1015) introduced Christianity into his realm from Byzantium. In 1240 Kievan Rus disintegrated, after being attacked and occupied by Mongol Tatars. The successor state of Galicia-Volhynia existed in what is now Western Ukraine, during the 13th and 14th centuries. The Galician-Volhynian kingdom was initially incorporated into the Lithuanian state, which, at the height of its power, stretched from the Baltic to the Black Seas and, after the creation of the Polish-Lithuanian Commonwealth in 1569, the bulk of Ukrainian lands came under Polish rule.

However, in the 16th century a national revival began in Ukraine ('the borderlands'), led by Orthodox Cossacks, who opposed Catholic Polish rule on ethnic, social and religious grounds. Attempts by the Polish authorities to weaken the Ukrainian Orthodox Church led, in 1596, to the creation of the Ukrainian Catholic ('Uniate' or 'Greek') Church, a body that owed its allegiance to the Vatican, but maintained the Orthodox rite. In 1648 a large-scale Ukrainian Cossack rebellion assumed authority over most of the Ukrainian lands and removed Polish control. However, during 1648–54 the creation of a Ukrainian Cossack 'Hetmanate', or quasi-state, left the area vulnerable to military attacks from its neighbours. The Ukrainian Cossack leader, Bohdan Khmelnytsky, attempted to overcome this problem, proposing the transformation of the Polish-Lithuanian Commonwealth through the addition of a third equal partner, Ukraine. Poland's rejection of the proposal led Khmelnytsky to search for allies in Muscovy (Russia), with whom he signed the Treaty of Pereyaslav in 1654. The Treaty, the subject of bitter controversy from then on, was believed by Ukraine to represent the creation of a confederation between two equal states, although for Russia it signified Ukraine's submission to its rule. Promises of Ukrainian autonomy within the Treaty were not honoured, and the Ukrainian Cossacks launched two rebellions, in 1659 at Konotop, and in 1709 at Poltava, but they failed to secure their autonomous status within the expanding Russian Empire.

By the late 18th century the Ukrainian autonomous Cossack Hetmanate had been abolished by Yekaterina (Catherine) II—'the Great' and the region was fully integrated into the Empire as separate provinces. The 'Uniate' Church was forbidden in 1839, and the Ukrainian language was banned from education, the media and the arts by two decrees in 1863 and 1876. Industrialization and urbanization in eastern and southern Ukraine brought many migrant workers from the Russian regions of the Empire and the emerging urban centres increasingly became Russian in culture and language. Meanwhile, with the Partitions of Poland in 1793–95, the Western Ukrainian lands of Galicia, Transcarpathia (Carpatho-Ruthenia) and Bukovyna came under Austrian and Hungarian rule. Unlike the Tsarist regime in eastern Ukraine, the Austrian-Hungarian Empire permitted the growth of cultural, educational and political life for its Ukrainian subjects. The Eastern-rite Catholic Churches were allowed to flourish, thereby becoming identified with Ukrainian national aspirations, since it differentiated them from Latin-rite Catholic Poles and Orthodox Russians. By the eve of the First World War in 1914, therefore, national consciousness was far more developed in western than in eastern Ukraine.

The collapse of the Russian Empire in 1917 led to demands from Ukrainians organized in a central Rada (Council or Soviet) for the Empire to be transformed into a loose federation. The Provisional Government in Petrograd (as St Petersburg had been renamed) refused to accept these moderate proposals, but was itself overthrown by the Bolsheviks in November 1917. Three months later, on 22 January 1918, the Ukrainian People's Republic (UPR) declared independence and was embroiled in military conflict with both the Bolsheviks and the 'White' supporters of the deposed Russian Provisional Government until 1920. In November 1918 the Austrian-Hungarian Empire also collapsed, after the end of the First World War, leading to the declaration of a Western Ukrainian People's Republic (WUPR), centred upon Lviv (Lvov), which united with the UPR in January of the following year. The WUPR was immediately involved in a bitter military conflict with the Poles for control over Galicia, and was finally defeated by 1919. In March 1921 the Treaty of Rīga divided Ukraine between Soviet Russia and Poland. The former created the Ukrainian Soviet Socialist Republic (SSR), with its capital city in Kharkiv (Kharkov), subsequently moved to Kiev in the 1930s. Polish promises to grant autonomy to its large minorities (accounting for one-third of its population) were never honoured, and from 1929 radicals in the integral nationalist Organization of Ukrainian Nationalists (OUN) began a militant campaign against the Polish state.

### SOVIET UKRAINE

Under Soviet rule Ukraine experienced three periods of liberalization, followed by conservativism. In the 1920s, 1960s and the second half of the 1980s liberalization of the Soviet political system led to a reassertion of national communist tendencies in Ukraine, coupled with demands for greater autonomy. The 1920s were the high period of national communism, with a cultural renaissance and widespread indigenization ('Ukrainianization'), in an effort to broaden the ethnic base of the Communist Party to include more ethnic Ukrainians. Ukrainian communist leaders foresaw that industrialization and urbanization would lead to an influx of peasants to urban centres, the infrastructure (such as education and the media) of which would be in the Ukrainian language, and that the modernization of the republic would, therefore, be accompanied by nation-building. After consolidating his power, by the late 1920s Stalin (Iosif V. Dzhugashvili) perceived this as a threat to Soviet rule in Ukraine, believing that nation-building and nationalist sentiment would simply lead to political demands for greater autonomy or even independence. By 1933–34 Stalin had halted nationalist progress, engineered a famine that killed an estimated 5m.–7m. Ukrainians, purged the republic's élites and disbanded the Ukrainian Autocephalous Orthodox Church, which had been established during the period of the UPR as a focus of national identity.

Between 1939 and 1945, during the Second World War, the Western Ukrainian lands of Galicia, Volhynia, Bukovyna, southern Bessarabia and Transcarpathia were incorporated into Ukraine from Poland, Romania and Czechoslovakia (now the Czech and Slovak Republics), bringing into the Ukrainian SSR the majority of ethnic Ukrainians in Eastern Europe (the ethnically non-Ukrainian Crimean region was added in 1954). The OUN, which had led an armed campaign against Polish rule in the inter-war period, turned its attention upon the Soviet regime. In early 1942 the OUN created the 100,000-strong, partisan Ukrainian Insurgent Army (UIA), which fought the Germans until 1943 and the Soviet authorities from 1944 until the early 1950s, primarily in Western Ukraine. At the same time, millions of Ukrainians were drafted into the Soviet army to fight against Germany. Widespread support for the OUN and UIA reflected the high degree of national consciousness that existed in Western Ukraine, as the result of its more liberal treatment under Habsburg rule from the late 18th century until 1918. Its incorporation into Soviet Ukraine reinforced this national consciousness, because ethnic Ukrainians replaced ethnic Poles, who were deported to Poland, and Jews, who were executed by the National Socialist (Nazi) German Workers' Party during the War, in the urban centres of Western Ukraine.

The 1960s again witnessed a period of liberalization prior to the consolidation of power by the Soviet leader, Leonid Brezhnev. In Ukraine, the leader of the Communist Party of Ukraine (CPU) in 1963–72, Petro Shelest, supported moderate attempts to develop national interests and co-operated with the cultural intelligentsia, even ordering a report by Ivan Dziuba, entitled *Internationalism or Russification?*, which was later published in the West, and which lambasted Soviet nationalities policy for its assimilationist strategies concerning Ukrainians. The thaw ended in 1971 and Shelest was replaced in 1972 by Vladimir Shcherbytsky, who led Soviet Ukraine until late 1989 and was instrumental in introducing a widespread campaign of Russification. In 1972 Ukraine's large dissident movement was crushed by arrests, including those of leading cultural figures, such as Dziuba. None the less, the Shcherbytsky era witnessed the growth of a variety of dissident movements.

## THE NATIONALIST MOVEMENT

Although the Soviet leader, Mikhail Gorbachev, launched his policies of *perestroika* (reconstruction) and *glasnost* (openness) in 1985, Shcherbytsky, who remained in power in Ukraine until September 1989, prevented the republic from fully participating in the new era of liberalization. From April 1986 the regime in Ukraine increasingly came under attack from opposition civic groups, following an explosion at the Chornobyl (Chernobyl) nuclear power plant, located north of Kiev, which caused widespread discharges of radioactive material and which was initially hidden by the authorities. In 1987–88 the Soviet Gulag (the system of, in particular, political prisons) was emptied of prisoners of conscience and these activists returned to their respective republics to take up the process of democratization that they had championed since the 1960s. In Ukraine, released dissidents re-founded the Ukrainian Helsinki Group (now renamed the Ukrainian Helsinki Union), which allied itself with the 'cultural intelligentsia' to launch the Ukrainian People's Movement for Restructuring—Rukh. The CPU prevented Rukh from holding its founding congress until September 1989, the same month that Shcherbytsky resigned as communist leader. He died shortly afterwards.

The authorities continued to stifle public initiatives in support of Gorbachev's policies, preventing Rukh from nominating candidates in the USSR's first relatively free elections to the republican parliament in March 1990. Nevertheless, civic groups allied to Rukh obtained one-quarter of the seats in the new Verkhovna Rada (Supreme Soviet or Supreme Council), which gradually rose to one-third with defections from the CPU. The Verkhovna Rada provided Rukh with a public platform from which to criticize the CPU and its opposition to the Gorbachev reformist programme. After the departure of Shcherbytsky the CPU remained in conservative hands, first under Volodymyr Ivashko (September 1989–July 1990) and then under Stanislav Hurenko (July 1990–August 1991). Between July 1990 and December 1991 the chairmanship of the legislature was held by Leonid Kravchuk, who also held a high-ranking position in the CPU, until the CPU was banned by the Verkhovna Rada for supporting the attempted *coup d'état* in Moscow, the Soviet and Russian capital, in August 1991 (see below).

Under Kravchuk's leadership parliament increasingly began to shows signs of supporting state sovereignty, and on 16 July 1990 it overwhelmingly adopted a radical Declaration of Ukrainian Sovereignty, which stressed the pre-eminence of Ukrainian over Soviet legislation in all areas, including economic and security policy. This laid the foundations for legislation adopted during the following year, which increased Ukraine's sovereignty at the expense of the central Soviet authorities. During this same period the conservative, so-called 'Group of 239' communist deputies in the Verkhovna Rada increasingly diverged into two camps. One group, termed 'imperial communists' and led by Stanislav Hurenko, supported only token Ukrainian sovereignty. The second faction was more pragmatic and willing to co-operate with moderates in Rukh (represented in the Verkhovna Rada by the 'democratic bloc' of deputies). This group, led by Kravchuk, increasingly came to be termed 'national' or 'sovereign communists' because they supported a high degree of Ukrainian sovereignty within a USSR transformed into a confederation of states. In March 1991 the 'national communists' added a second question, supporting sovereignty, to the Soviet referendum devised by Gorbachev on a 'renewed federation'. The second question was endorsed by 80.2% of those who participated in the referendum, compared with the 70.5% that voted in favour of the Gorbachev-imposed question. Moreover, an additional question in certain regions of Western Ukraine, which asked voters if they supported a fully independent Ukraine, secured the support of 90% of those voting.

The declining influence of the CPU and the growing authority of the Verkhovna Rada enabled Ukraine to prolong the discussions initiated by Gorbachev on the replacement of the 1922 Union Treaty with a modernized version. However, any attempt at transforming the USSR into a looser entity was anathema to uncompromising members of the Communist Party of the Soviet Union (CPSU), including the CPU and the Hurenko faction in the Verkhovna Rada. On 19 August 1991 conservative communists launched an attempted *coup d'état* in Moscow, which collapsed after only three days. The response of all of the Soviet republics, apart from Russia, to the failure of the coup was to declare independence from the USSR; on 24 August the Ukrainian legislature voted by 346 votes to one to secede from the Union, and six days later it banned the CPU. The vote was supported not only by the Democratic Bloc and national communists, but also by the conservative Hurenko wing of the former CPU, through fear of the anti-communist revolution then sweeping through Moscow under the President of the Supreme Soviet of the Russian Federation, Boris Yeltsin.

On 1 December 1991 the declaration of independence was put to a national referendum. It was endorsed by 90.3% of the participants; since the CPU had been banned, no political forces agitated against a 'yes' vote. On the same day Ukraine held its first presidential election, which Kravchuk, the only candidate from the former communist 'old guard', won with 61.3% of the votes cast, compared with the 23.3% achieved by the second-placed candidate, Vyacheslav Chornovil, a formerly imprisoned dissident and leader of Rukh. On 8 December Kravchuk and the leaders of Belarus and Russia announced the annulment of the 1922 Union Treaty and declared, thereby, that the USSR had ceased to exist; the replacement of the USSR with a less binding Commonwealth of Independent States (CIS) was announced. Although the leaders of all three hitherto Soviet republics represented agreed on the need to dissolve the Union and to remove its non-elected President, Gorbachev, who resigned on 25 December, Russia and Ukraine, in particular, continued to disagree fundamentally on the nature of the CIS.

## INDEPENDENT UKRAINE

In December 1991 Ivan Plyushch replaced Kravchuk as legislative Chairman, following the latter's election to the presidency, and both presided over a Ukraine that increasingly sunk into political and economic stagnation. The election of Kravchuk reflected the inability of nationalist and democratic leaders to obtain majority support from the population, particularly in the Russian-speaking east and south. Kravchuk allied himself with some 'national democrats', although Rukh, under Chornovil, stood in 'constructive opposition' to him. Kravchuk promoted a centrist path of consensus politics that placed greater emphasis upon stability than reform, and he adopted economic and political policies that would not disturb those of his allies among the former Soviet Ukrainian élite who had joined the national communist camp. Fresh elections in 1992 could have brought in a reformist legislature at a time when the CPU was still prohibited. Moreover, no economic reform programme was launched until October 1994 (after Kravchuk had left office) and the President appointed only conservative prime ministers to head the government (the Cabinet of Ministers). The constitutional process persisted through numerous different drafts and, again, was only resolved after Kravchuk had left office, in 1996. In October 1993 a new CPU was registered, which quickly became Ukraine's largest political party. Miners' strikes and regional discontent in eastern Ukraine by the second half of 1993 led the Verkhovna Rada to schedule early presidential elections for the following year.

## POLITICAL DEVELOPMENTS

The two principal candidates in the presidential election of 26 June 1994 were Kravchuk and the former Prime Minister, Leonid Kuchma, who had been responsible for implementing a brief programme of economic reform in 1992–93. Following an inconclusive first round of voting, a second round was held on 10 July, in which Kuchma won 52% of the votes cast. Legislative elections were held in March 1994, March 1998 and March 2002. The legislative elections of 1994 were held using a majority system, whereas in 1998 and 2002 a mixed system was used, whereby one-half of deputies were elected on a majority basis, and the other one-half by a proportional system of voting. Although 30 blocs contested the 1998 elections, only eight managed to exceed the 4% necessary to secure seats in the Verkhovna Rada. Despite the severity of the socio-economic crisis experienced by Ukraine during the 1990s, in both 1994 and 1998 left-wing parties were unable to obtain more than 40% of the votes cast in elections to the Verkhovna Rada. The CPU remained the largest legislative faction, with between 80 and 120 seats, from a total of 450, in both the 1994–98 and 1998–2002 parliaments. However, the left-wing allies of the CPU, comprising representatives of the Socialist Party of Ukraine (SPU), Peasants' Party and the Progressive Socialist Party of Ukraine (PSPU), were unable to unite and, therefore, never succeeded in commanding a majority of votes. Therefore, the combined left-wing groups were unable to dominate parliament, although the Chairmen (speakers) of the legislature were usually members of left-wing parties, as exemplified by Oleksandr Moroz, the leader of the SPU, who held this position in 1994–98, and by Oleksandr Tkachenko of the Peasants' Party, who was Chairman from

March 1998 until January 2000. The domination of the parliamentary leadership by the left-wing from 1994–99 led to conflict with President Kuchma and helped to stall an already faltering reform programme.

The election of Leonid Kuchma, the former director of a missiles factory in Dnipropetrovsk, as President in 1994 shifted the political balance towards eastern Ukraine, which had largely remained passive in the drive to independence prior to 1991, primarily owing to the region's closer ethnic and cultural associations with neighbouring Russia, and consequent lesser sense of Ukrainian identity. A relatively radical programme of economic reform was introduced at Kuchma's behest in October 1994, which brought support from international financial organizations. The programme was, however, plagued by a lack of political will, conflict with a legislature in which the leadership was dominated by the statist left, and prime ministers who were either weak on reform or corrupt, or both. By 1996–97 the reform programme had stalled and Pavlo Lazarenko (Prime Minister in July 1996–July 1997) was accused of widespread corruption; he became the second Prime Minister of independent Ukraine to flee the country, seeking asylum in the USA, apparently so as to hinder investigations into allegations of corruption (Yufym Zviahylsky had fled Ukraine for Israel in 1994 when confronted with similar charges). In June 2000 Lazarenko, then in custody in the USA, was convicted *in absentia* of money 'laundering' (the processing of illegally obtained funds into legitimate accounts) by a court in Switzerland, and given an 18-month suspended prison sentence. A further trial of Lazarenko, who had issued statements implicating other leading Ukrainian politicians, including Kuchma, in various allegedly fraudulent actions, opened in San Francisco, CA, USA, in mid-2002, and at the beginning of that year prosecutors in Ukraine charged Lazarenko, *in absentia*, with ordering the murders of two parliamentary deputies in 1996 and 1998.

The reform programme was only restored after Kuchma's election for a second term as President in November 1999, and the subsequent formation of a reformist majority in parliament. In January 2000 the non-left majority in parliament voted Tkachenko out of office and replaced him with Ivan Plyushch, previously Chairman under Kravchuk, in what was termed a 'Ukrainian velvet revolution'. In addition, the leadership of all of the parliamentary committees was assumed by members of the non-leftist majority. Three leftist factions within the Verkhovna Rada (Hromada—Community, the PSPU and Peasants' Party) disintegrated as members defected, and they were disbanded when their numbers declined to below 14, the minimum number permitted to register a faction. Thereafter, only two leftist factions remained, opposed to the reformist majority—the CPU- and SPU-dominated blocs. Six years of parliamentary–presidential conflict abated when, in early 2000, the reformist majority in parliament outlined its support for President Kuchma and the reform programme of recently appointed Prime Minister Viktor Yushchenko (previously Governor of the National Bank of Ukraine, and, in contrast to many other members of the Ukrainian political élite, a well-respected figure internationally and noted reformist). The failure of the CPU leader, Petro Symonenko, to defeat Kuchma in the second round of the 1999 presidential election and the left wing's loss to the reformist majority of an institutional platform in the legislature signified that the faction was in a defensive position for the first time in many years.

Kuchma had greater success in political, rather than economic, reform. The President had made the adoption of a new Constitution a priority after coming to power. A temporary constitutional agreement was reached between Kuchma and the majority of the Verkhovna Rada in June 1995, which granted the President temporary, and predominately economic, additional powers. The temporary agreement was used as the basis for the adoption of Ukraine's first post-Soviet Constitution, which was finally adopted in June 1996, after Kuchma threatened to put to a referendum his preferred draft, which was largely modelled on the Russian presidential Constitution of December 1993. Although the introduction of this Constitution represented a significant stage in the 'de-Sovietization' of Ukraine, the adopted text was in many ways a compromise, which failed to resolve outstanding questions and unsettled tensions in areas such as the division of responsibilities between government, president and legislature. In April 2000 a referendum called by President Kuchma sought to make significant amendments to the Constitution, by effectively increasing the powers of the President with regard to the legislature. Although all four questions—on the dissolution of the Verkhovna Rada should deputies fail to approve the state budget within three months of its submission; the reduction of the number of deputies from 450 to 300; the establishment of a bicameral legislature; and the placing of limitations on the immunity enjoyed by deputies were approved by the 81% of the electorate that participated, it remained uncertain as to when, or whether, the newly approved proposals would be adopted. Moreover, the Constitution was regularly flouted in several key areas—human rights, the rule of law, socioeconomic policies and the media. By mid-2001 opinion polls showed that only a minority of the population knew and valued the provisions of the Constitution, reflecting a general tendency towards persistent public mistrust of state institutions. Moreover, by as early as 2001 it appeared that the referendum had been all but forgotten, both by the electorate and its representatives, and it seemed that the changes approved by the plebiscite would not be implemented.

From 1997 Kuchma gradually increased his authoritarian control in four areas. First, with regard to the media; international non-governmental organizations (NGOs), such as Reporters without Frontiers and the Committee to Protect Journalists, and, additionally, the Council of Europe accused Ukraine of having one of the worst records of violence against journalists in Europe. Media independent of either executive or 'oligarch' influence were in a minority and state television was tightly controlled. Second, the rule of law, already weak, was corrupted by an executive that was eager to control the courts, the procuracy, and the legal profession as a whole. Third, corruption was endemic to the authoritarian system under Kuchma because it was tied to patronage, and corrupt officials and politicians were prosecuted only if they opposed the executive (as was the case, in the late 1990s and early 2000s, with the sole 'oligarchs' overtly opposed to Kuchma, Pavlo Lazarenko and the former Deputy Prime Minister, responsible for Energy Issues, Yuliya Tymoshenko). The international NGO Transparency International annually ranked Ukraine highly in terms of perceived corruption (it was ranked joint 85th from among 102 countries surveyed in 2002, equal with Georgia, Viet Nam and Venezuela).

Fourth and finally, Kuchma did not abandon attempts to increase executive control over parliament and the Government, something he had failed to do in 1996, when his version of a presidential constitution was not adopted. The April 2000 referendum was sharply criticized by the Council of Europe (which threatened to expel Ukraine from the organization, should it be implemented). Kuchma had hoped that the reformist majority in the legislature would implement the measures approved in the plebiscite, by introducing changes to the Constitution. However, the onset of the scandal surrounding Kuchma from November (see below) ended any possibility that this would happen, as the reformist group disintegrated into pro- and anti-Kuchma factions, the anti-Kuchma faction allying itself with the centre-left Socialists. Following a vote of 'no confidence' in the Yushchenko Govern-

ment on 26 April 2001, Kuchma introduced by a presidential decree (which was subsequently challenged by deputies in the Constitutional Court) new state secretaries, who were to remain in office for a five-year period, regardless of whether there was a change of government. These state secretaries were given control of finances and personnel decisions, and were under the authority of the executive. Commentators remained divided as to whether the introduction of state secretaries would serve primarily to increase the power of the President, or result in the establishment of a greater degree of professionalism and independence within the civil service. However, in late May 2003 Kuchma issued a decree, among the provisions of which was the abolition of state secretaries and the re-introduction of the previous system of deputy ministers and first deputy ministers, who could be appointed and dismissed at will by the President.

The most important domestic event of 2000–01 was what became known as the 'Kuchmagate' scandal. In late November 2000 the SPU leader, Oleksandr Moroz, disclosed tape recordings, alleged to have been made illicitly in Kuchma's office by a former presidential bodyguard, Maj. Mykola Melnychenko, who had subsequently fled abroad (he was granted asylum in the USA in April 2001). The hundreds of hours of recordings, made during 1999–2000, were gradually released over the course of months. Although the authenticity of the tapes remained a controversial issue, the information contained in them was explosive, because it appeared to reveal evidence of high-level corruption, misuse of power, election and referendum fraud, and outright hostility towards the critical media. A particular source of opprobrium arose from the manner in which the tapes linked Kuchma to the disappearance in September 2000 of an oppositionist journalist, Heorhiy Gongadze, whose beheaded body was found near Kiev two months later. These disclosures discredited Kuchma both domestically and internationally, and his credibility was further weakened when additional recordings were released in early 2002, in which Kuchma allegedly discussed the sale of advanced radar equipment to Iraq, in breach of UN sanctions.

The official investigation into the Gongadze murder was widely believed to have been mismanaged, and by July 2002, when a new Prosecutor-General, Svyatoslav Pyskun, was appointed, the case had still not been fully resolved. The Gongadze affair, in addition to the other revelations of executive malpractice, led to the dismissal of both the Chairman of the Security Service, Leonid Derkach, and the Minister of Internal Affairs, Yuriy Kravchenko. International criticism of Kuchma resulted in a cooling of Ukraine's relations with the West, and a consequent improvement in relations with Russia (see below). Kuchma initially claimed that the tapes were forgeries, but, after Melnychenko's existence was proven, claimed the tapes to have been created from misleadingly edited recordings of innocent conversations. Domestically, the discovery of the recordings, in particular those relating to the Gongadze affair, led to the appearance of Ukraine's largest opposition movement since the collapse of the USSR, which coalesced into the 'Ukraine Without Kuchma' civic and 'For Truth' student movements, while high-ranking political leaders established what became known as the National Salvation Forum. At its height, in early 2001 the anti-Kuchma movement mobilized 20,000 demonstrators on the streets of Kiev, although, notably, the CPU, Ukraine's largest political party, refused to join the anti-Kuchma opposition. However, by May Kuchma's position again appeared to be secure, owing to public apathy (although street protests against Kuchma attracted significant support again in mid-2002), and to the continued support for the President of the pro-'oligarch' parties and parliamentary factions, as well as the neutrality of the CPU.

After the dismissal of the Yushchenko Government in April 2001, following a vote of 'no confidence' by the Verkhovna Rada, a long-standing Kuchma loyalist, the Chairman of the Union of Industrialists and Entrepreneurs (later Party of Industrialists and Entrepreneurs of Ukraine—PIEU), Anatoliy Kinakh, was appointed Prime Minister. The main preoccupation of Ukraine's political élite at this time appeared to be the forthcoming parliamentary election in March 2002. Following his dismissal, Yushchenko began attempts to create a centrist, reformist 'Third Force' between the 'oligarchs' and the CPU, known as 'Our Ukraine'. The anti-Kuchma opposition, which Yushchenko refused to join, despite Kuchma's lack of support for his Government, transformed the National Salvation Forum into an election bloc, led by Yuliya Tymoshenko, who became an increasingly vocal opposition figure following her dismissal by Kuchma in January 2001, as she faced investigation into charges of tax evasion and the alleged smuggling of Russian gas. Kuchma's strategy, meanwhile, was to ensure that the parliament elected in 2002 would have a pro-presidential majority, which would finally implement the results of the referendum of April 2000, as well as to determine that he conclude his presidential term in November 2004 with immunity from prosecution.

The outcome of the March 2002 legislative elections appeared to represent a greater potential threat to President Kuchma's authority than those held in 1994 and 1998. Firstly, the former 'sovereign communists', who had taken advantage of 'insider privatizations' over the past decade to establish themselves as 'oligarchs', had far more to lose from the implementation of a programme of sustained reform. Moreover, for the first time in independent Ukraine, the authorities faced a credible and popular non-communist challenger in Yushchenko.

The election campaign was fought between three main groupings. First, the CPU continued to reject both reform and increased Ukrainian statehood, and in the event appeared increasingly out of touch with the Ukrainian electorate, receiving 19.99% of the votes cast for the one-half of the seats elected on a basis of proportional representation, and obtaining 66 of the 450 legislative seats overall, compared with the 123 it had obtained in 1998. A significant section of the CPU's supporters, pensioners, had literally died out, and the party also lost votes because of its failure to present a coherent oppositionist stance to Kuchma, which was now being presented, albeit from a different ideological perspective, by other groupings. Moreover, from 2000, for the first time since independence, Ukraine was experiencing positive economic growth, meaning that wage and pension arrears were being paid, which had frequently not been the case hitherto. The CPU could, therefore, no longer capitalize on socio-economic hardship to obtain popular support.

The second major grouping to contest the elections consisted of pro-Kuchma 'oligarchs', in two main factions, which sought to preserve the status quo and such stability as is provided by an authoritarian, corporatist state, a system that could be further entrenched to resemble the most authoritarian CIS states. The largest of these two factions—For A United Ukraine (FUU), led by Kuchma's close ally, Volodymyr Lytvyn, served as a 'party of power' in the elections, and grouped five major parties on a pro-presidential platform, namely Prime Minister Kinakh's PIEU, the Party of the Regions (PR), the People's Democratic Party and Working Ukraine. None the less, despite support for FUU by the executive, the grouping performed poorly in the election, receiving only 11.78% of the votes on the proportional list. However, the party's success in single-mandate constituencies was sufficient to make it the second-largest grouping in the new parliament, with 101 seats. The second pro-'oligarch' group, the Social-Democratic Party of Ukraine (United)

(SDPU—U), led by Viktor Medvedchuk, obtained 6.28% of the votes on the proportional list and received 24 deputies.

The third grouping in the election were those anti-Kuchma groups that had become radicalized, to varying degrees, and from different standpoints, apparently as a result of the 'Kuchmagate' scandal, among them the SPU and the Yuliya Tymoshenko bloc. Although Yushchenko's Our Ukraine grouping sought not to portray itself as an anti-Kuchma bloc as such, it may be included alongside the SPU (which is more opposed to economic reform) and Tymoshenko bloc in this category because of the common support of the three blocs for increased democratization, and for the revival of Ukraine's national identity, and opposition to the policies favoured by the 'oligarchs'. While the SPU and the Tymoshenko bloc received 14.13% of the proportional votes cast, and won 45 seats between them, Our Ukraine won the largest share of the votes of any party (23.57%) in the proportional lists, although, as a result of its lesser success in single-mandate constituencies, it received only 112 seats, 11 more than FUU, which received around one-half of the proportion of the votes cast obtained by Our Ukraine. Although this degree of representation was insufficient for the immediate formation of a pro-reformist majority in the Verkhovna Rada (or, for that matter, any majority, particularly given the splintering of the FUU faction into a number of regional 'clans'), for the first time in independent Ukraine the CPU had failed to be the most popular party in an election to the legislature, something that may be psychologically important for the further consolidation of Ukrainian statehood. Although the presidential election of 1999 had appeared to indicate that regional divisions in party support had reduced, such divisions re-appeared at the 2002 legislative elections, when the western and central regions expressed greater support for Our Ukraine, the Tymoshenko bloc and the SPU, while eastern and southern regions largely supported pro-'oligarch' parties and the CPU.

In the aftermath of the 2002 elections, and in an attempt to gain advantage in advance of the presidential election scheduled to be held in late 2004, the executive successfully obtained control of all significant state institutions. Lytvyn, a close ally of Kuchma and hitherto head of the presidential administration, was elected Chairman of parliament, and his two Deputy Chairmen were also chosen from among pro-presidential parties. There then began an intensive campaign to organize a pro-presidential parliamentary majority by Lytvyn's successor in his former post, Medvedchuk. Intense pressure was applied by members of the pro-presidential majority to opposition deputies, and some 30 eventually switched allegiance to the pro-presidential grouping, which thereby obtained an absolute, but narrow, majority in the Verkhovna Rada by the end of 2002. The executive also refused to countenance the notion that Our Ukraine, which had obtained the largest number of votes of any of the groupings, should form the government, as such a measure would have been likely to have led to Yushchenko's re-appointment as Prime Minister and provided a basis for his potential campaign for the 2004 presidential election. Instead, in November 2002 Kinakh was replaced as premier by the hitherto Governor of Donetsk Oblast (the Donbas), Viktor Yanukovych, Kuchma's preferred candidate. In his previous position, which he had held since 1997, Yanukovych had developed a close association with Ukraine's wealthiest 'oligarch', Renat Akhmetov, and also enjoyed other important business connections. It appeared that Yanukovych's appointment was intended, at least in part, as a 'reward' for helping to ensure that Our Ukraine had obtained less than 4% of votes cast in the region (the only other administrative regions in which Yushchenko's bloc had obtained such a low level of support were the neighbouring Luhansk Oblast and Sevastopol city). Donetsk Oblast was the only region where FUU came first in the proportional list in the legislative elections, with 36.83% of the votes cast. Moreover, despite initial hostility from the Verkhovna Rada, Serhiy Tihipko, another 'oligarch' and ally of Kuchma, and a leading member of the Working Ukraine grouping, was appointed as chairman of the National Bank in mid-December. Thus, each of the three main pro-presidential 'clans' of 'oligarchs' had obtained control over an important institution—the presidential administration (which was dominated by Medvedchuk's SDPU—U, with its power-base in Kiev), the National Bank (Dnipropetrovsk's Working Ukraine) and the Government (the Donetsk-based PR).

The model of governance that Yanukovych had been associated with during his governorship of Donetsk, which appeared likely to influence the leadership of the national Government, has been described as that of a 'social regulated market economy'; it was, moreover, characterized by political authoritarianism and a tolerance of corrupt practice—a model of governance that has effectively become the norm throughout the CIS, including, most significantly, in Russia. Under this model, ruling élites have come to regard stability as being of paramount importance, while the opposition are marginalized by the authorities, whose refusal to compromise with them seeks to deny them any semblance of legitimacy. The right to protest is condemned as creating instability and threatening the independent state. In Donetsk Oblast the regional 'party of power', the PR, had effectively come to dominate political life by the early 2000s, and following Yanukovych's appointment as Prime Minister, measures that could be interpreted as seeking to extend the party's support beyond its 'home' region were implemented; most notably, in April 2003 the two highest-ranking members of the Government were elected to senior positions within the PR: Yanukovych became the party Chairman, and the First Deputy Prime Minister and Minister of Finance, Mykola Azarov, was elected as the Chairman of the party's Political Council. After the 2002 legislative election, the model of governance apparently favoured by Yanukovych, as demonstrated by his governorship of Donetsk, was even described as liable to lead to the 'Belarusianization of Ukraine', with reference to the authoritarian polity of Belarus under President Alyaksandr Lukashenka.

By late 2003, with presidential elections (which the Constitution barred Kuchma from contesting) due to be held in October–November 2004, it appeared that Yanukovych was being prepared as Kuchma's preferred successor as Head of State. Yanukovych's government programme was approved by the Verkhovna Rada in April 2003; in accordance with the Constitution, the Government may not be subject to a vote of 'no confidence' by the Verkhovna Rada for a period of 12 months following the granting of such approval, thereby encouraging a period of political stability in which the Prime Minister is able to consolidate his authority. A crucial factor in determining the outcome of the presidential election of 2004, presuming that Yanukovych presents himself as a candidate, will be whether he will prove able to consolidate his position sufficiently to defeat the potential challenge from Yushchenko, nation-wide, in a similar fashion to that in which Yushchenko's Our Ukraine bloc was defeated in the Donetsk region at the 2002 legislative elections. A further issue that may be expected to be of significance in the campaigning for the 2004 election, and which could be expected to benefit Yanukovych, may be concerns by Russian-speakers and ethnic Russians that their interests are being marginalized; such an issue had previously been adopted successfully by Kuchma, notably during the 1994 presidential election against the 'nationalist' incumbent, Kravchuk. Moreover, Yanukovych's appointment as Prime Minister, and the successful creation of a pro-presidential majority in the Verkhovna Rada, also seemed to present further difficulties for

Yushchenko's possible candidacy. In particular, the establishment of government control over parliament had blocked proposed changes to the parliamentary election law, supported by opposition parties of the centre-right and centre-left, which would prefer elections to be held under a system of full proportional representation. Centrist, pro-presidential parties and the executive, however, prefer a continuation of the existing arrangements, as such parties have consistently proved themselves more able to be elected in majoritarian constituency elections. Pro-presidential factions also support granting life-long immunity from prosecution for the President and have enthusiastically endorsed the proposals for political reform submitted to the Verkhovna Rada in draft form by Kuchma in March 2003. These reforms, to a large extent, resemble those proposals presented in the 2000 referendum, and, specifically, include the holding of presidential and parliamentary elections in the same year, and the introduction of a bicameral legislature, incorporating an upper chamber, to be known as the Council of the Regions. The introduction of such measures could be expected to result in the extension of Kuchma's term in office, until 2006, when elections to the Verkhovna Rada are scheduled to be held. Second, they would provide a mechanism that could be utilized to grant Kuchma an extension of his immunity from prosecution, as he would be eligible, as a former president, to serve as a senator, in a life-long capacity, in the proposed upper chamber, which, according to the draft proposals, was additionally to comprise two appointed representatives of each administrative region. The Council of Regions would reinforce executive control over parliament as it would be pro-presidential. However, as the major opposition parties were opposed to the reforms, it appeared unlikely that such measures would secure the two-thirds' majority required in the Verkhovna Rada to approve constitutional amendments. In realization of this, Kuchma threatened to submit his proposals to a further referendum.

## FOREIGN AND DEFENCE POLICY

Ukraine and Russia emerged from the USSR with vastly different ideas as to how the CIS should be perceived; as a 'civilized divorce' (Ukraine), or a loose confederation of sovereign states with joint armed forces, dominated by Russia. Security was a key factor in the early stages of the Ukrainian state, and all non-nuclear military assets and personnel were transferred to Ukrainian state control by early 1992. Ukraine failed, however, to gain control of the Black Sea Fleet located largely in Sevastopol, Crimea, and it was not until May 1997, after numerous failed negotiations, that the issue of a 20-year basing agreement for a reduced fleet was finally resolved. The nuclear question also proved to be problematic, as Ukraine had inherited the world's third-largest nuclear force. By May 1992 all tactical nuclear weapons had been removed from Ukrainian soil, but Ukraine continued to demand that it receive security guarantees and financial compensation for the strategic nuclear weapons located on its territory. Negotiations continued until 1994, when the Verkhovna Rada finally ratified the Strategic Arms' Reduction Treaty (START) 1 in February and the Nuclear Non-Proliferation Treaty in November. This change in Ukraine's position only occurred after most Western governments abandoned their 'russocentric' policies towards the former USSR and began to take a greater interest in Ukraine's security. The Trilateral Agreement of January, between Ukraine, Russia and the USA, paved the way for the granting in December of security assurances (but not guarantees) by the world's five declared nuclear powers. The last strategic nuclear weapons left Ukraine in June 1996.

By the beginning of the 2000s Ukraine's foreign policy was defined as 'multi-vector', which meant that it, alone among its neighbours, had opted not to orientate itself in one direction, West or East. This 'multi-vectorism' involved a number of 'strategic partners'—Russia and the other countries of the CIS in the East, and the member countries of the North Atlantic Treaty Organization (NATO), notably the USA and Poland (which was admitted to NATO in 1999), and those of the European Union (EU) in the West. The relative importance of these strategic partners depended on domestic and international events. At the height of the scandal surrounding President Kuchma in 2000–01, for example, when relations with the West deteriorated, Kuchma turned to his only international ally, Russia. Relations with the West cooled further, in 2002, as a result of allegations that Ukraine had sold military equipment illicitly, and in breach of UN sanctions, to Iraq; an investigation into these allegations by representatives of the United Kingdom and the USA was undertaken in October 2002. At more settled times, however, Ukraine's 'multi-vectorism' was orientated, politically and in strategic terms, to the West, while its Eastern orientation was economic and cultural in nature. A significant proportion of Ukraine's élite continued to harbour a strong mistrust of Russia's intentions towards Ukraine and the CIS as a whole, and refused to join the Union of Russia and Belarus, which it perceived to constitute a loss of sovereignty. Ukraine, therefore, regarded NATO, and the USA, in particular, as the guarantor of its independence and territorial integrity. At the same time, as the *de facto* 'second republic' of the USSR, and with broad cultural similarities and family links with Russia, Ukraine preferred to deal with the CIS economically, because this allowed short-term, rapid gain for 'oligarchs', as well as non-transparent practices that were the norm in the majority of CIS countries. An orientation exclusively westwards would require Ukraine's élite to support a transparent, non-corrupt reform programme that would integrate it into 'Europe' (hence the opposition of Kuchma and the 'oligarchs' to Yushchenko's programme of reform). Instead, through 'multi-vectorism', the Ukrainian élite could reap the benefits of political and strategic ties with the West and economic and cultural links with the East.

Russian–Ukrainian relations had remained strained throughout the 1990s, until Presidents Yeltsin and Kuchma signed the long delayed interstate treaty in May 1997, which recognized the Russia–Ukraine borders (a November 1990 Russian–Ukrainian treaty had only recognized their borders within the USSR and the CIS), although they remain undemarcated, in the absence of political will in Russia to give this separation physical form. This was followed by a 10-year economic co-operation agreement in February 1998. Fears over Russian territorial demands were exacerbated by the fact that both chambers of the Russian legislature laid claim to Crimea and its capital city of Sevastopol on a number of occasions between May 1992 and December 1996. The interstate treaty was ratified by both houses of the Russian legislature by February 1999, while the Ukrainian legislature ratified the 20-year agreement on the stationing of the Black Sea Fleet and the introduction of a new Crimean Constitution. Thus, by the time of the presidential elections of October–November 1999, relations with Russia had been normalized and did not feature in the campaign, unlike during the elections of 1994, when Kuchma had accused Kravchuk of weakening links with Russia.

Both Kravchuk and Kuchma restricted Ukraine's involvement in the CIS to that of a participant (rather than that of an active member) and to purely economic questions, preferring bilateral to multilateral ties (indeed, in December 1991, it was Ukraine's reluctance to continue a close union with Russia that was instrumental in the formation of the CIS). Ukraine refused to ratify the CIS Charter (which it regarded as sanctioning the establishment of CIS supra-national institutions),

while supporting the initiative to establish charters for the Black Sea Economic Co-operation Agreement and GUAM (see below). Under Kuchma, Ukraine became less antagonistic towards the CIS, and gradually increased its co-operation, through, for example, membership of the CIS Air Defence Agreement (it held associate membership from 1995), the Inter-Parliamentary Assembly (from 1999), and the establishment of an anti-terrorist centre (from 2000). In January 2001 Ukraine and Russia signed their first large-scale military co-operation agreement. Nevertheless, Ukraine remained frustrated from 1994 by Russia's continued unwillingness to support a CIS free-trade zone and in early 2002 finally decided to become an Observer of the Russian-dominated Eurasian Economic Community (EURASEC). Joining EURASEC also reflected, in part, Ukraine's frustration at being repeatedly rejected by the EU in its attempts to sign an association agreement. In January 2003 Kuchma was elected head of the CIS Council of Heads of State, the first time a non-Russian had ever held the position. In September Kuchma, together with the leaders of Belarus, Kazakhstan and Russia, announced that a CIS Free Trade Area was to be created, confirming proposals that had been outlined earlier in the year. Within Ukraine—to a much greater extent than among the other countries concerned—this move generated contradictory claims as to whether the eventual introduction of such a zone would, or would not, contravene Ukraine's stated objective of seeking EU membership.

In 1997 Ukraine initiated the creation of the GUAM (Georgia-Ukraine-Azerbaijan-Moldova) regional grouping within the CIS, as a security framework and counterweight to Russian attempts at reintegration, and to capitalize on the export of energy from Azerbaijan. (Uzbekistan later acceded to the organization, and it became known as GUUAM.) Although a GUUAM meeting was postponed in March 2001 as a concession to Russia, it took place two months later. At the meeting, GUUAM was structured into a regional organization, a permanent office was established in Yalta, and a charter was drawn up. The organization was expected to receive support from the US Government, as it was regarded as a regional ally of NATO. From 2000, as Ukraine reorientated its foreign policy from East to West, the importance of GUUAM waned. None the less, in November 2002 the Verkhovna Rada ratified an agreement on the creation of a GUUAM free-trade area.

Ukraine continues to be frustrated in its attempts to integrate westwards, and its few successes were its membership of the Council of Europe in 1995 and the Central European Initiative in 1996; the Partnership and Co-operation Agreement signed with the EU in May 1994 did not enter into force until March 1998. At the EU summit meeting held in Helsinki, Finland, in December 1999, a strategic policy document was signed with Ukraine, but it was not included in the 'slow-track' group of future EU members. This was a disappointment to the Ukrainian leadership, which introduced programmes on integration with the EU in June 1998 and July 2000, and which had always sought to join the Union. Enlargement of the EU to Ukraine's western border (which was expected to take effect from May 2004, with the accession of Hungary, Poland and Slovakia) was, therefore, perceived as a security threat, because it would, psychologically, represent the eastern border of 'Europe' and, thereby, signify another dividing line in Europe, similar to that imposed in 1945, at the Yalta Summit, by the leaders of the United Kingdom, the USSR and the USA. At an EU summit held in Copenhagen, Denmark, in July 2002 the EU again refused to consider Ukraine as a future member. Enlargement of the EU in 2004–07, by which time the Union is expected to include most of post-communist Central Europe, will bring it up to all of Ukraine's Western borders, following the proposed accession of Romania. Ukraine's relationship with NATO was more accommodating than that with the EU, and from 1995 Ukraine was the most active member of NATO's 'Partnership for Peace' programme, among the CIS states. This was coupled with growing bilateral security ties with key Western countries, such as the United Kingdom and the USA. Wary of harming relations with Russia, Ukraine did not initially pursue NATO membership but, instead, undertook a policy of co-operation that sought to obscure the differences between membership and non-membership, signing a Charter on Distinctive Partnership in July 1997 and adopting an all-embracing three-year government programme of co-operation in November 1998, which was extended until 2004 in January 2001. Ukraine supported the enlargement of NATO, which it did not consider to pose a threat to its security, unlike the enlargement of the EU. Moreover, the highest governing body of NATO, the North Atlantic Council, held a meeting in Ukraine, its first in a non-NATO country, in early March 2000, on the eve of the Russian presidential elections, in order to demonstrate its continued support for Ukrainian independence.

Following the 'Kuchmagate' scandal, which was revealed in November 2000, President Kuchma was increasingly isolated in the West, and undertook few diplomatic visits abroad. Moreover, in the aftermath of the September 2001 terrorist attacks the USA shifted its priorities in the region from Ukraine to Russia, which was considered an important strategic ally in the US-led 'anti-terrorism' coalition forged to combat radical Islamist groups. Moreover, the acquiescence of the Russian authorities would be required in order to allow proposed large-scale enlargement of NATO to take place. These twin factors and Kuchma's enforced re-orientation towards Russia after the 'Kuchmagate' scandal unfolded presented Ukrainian foreign policy with new dilemmas. In order not to be sidelined further, in late May 2002, as the establishment of a NATO-Russia Council was announced, Ukraine publicly announced for the first time that it would seek eventual membership of NATO, which was confirmed by a presidential decree issued in early July, during the visit to Kiev of the NATO Secretary-General, Lord George Robertson. Ukraine had hoped to establish jointly with NATO a Membership Action Plan (MAP) at the November NATO summit held in Prague, Czech Republic, but succeeded only in obtaining a less specific 'NATO-Ukraine Action Plan'. In particular, as a result of the so-called 'Kolchuga scandal' (in which Kuchma was implicated, according to tape recordings apparently released by his former bodyguard, in the transfer of military radar equipment to Iraq, in defiance of UN sanctions), it had been made clear that Kuchma's presence was not desired at the NATO summit, although he attended, none the less, only to be rebuffed by leaders of the more influential NATO countries. Moreover, a meeting of the NATO-Ukraine Committee was downgraded to take place at the level of Ministers of Foreign Affairs or their equivalents. By 2003 Ukraine hoped to join NATO at its next summit, to be held in 2007, together with Albania, Croatia and the former Yugoslav republic of Macedonia. However, such a measure would be conditional upon Ukraine entering the MAP process (already undertaken by the other three states). Despite an apparent improvement in relations with NATO in 2003, which resulted from the dispatch of a chemical-weapons response unit to Kuwait in March, in advance of the US-led military action to remove the regime of Saddam Hussein in neighbouring Iraq and the approval by the Verkhovna Rada, in June, of the dispatch of some 1,800 Ukrainian troops to Iraq as part of a multi-national peace-keeping force, it appeared likely that Ukraine would not be invited to enter the MAP process until after Kuchma's departure from office. Although Ukraine has been an active participant in UN peace-keeping programmes in the

Kosovo and Metohija province of the union of Serbia and Montenegro (the former Federal Republic of Yugoslavia) and in Sierra Leone, by the early 2000s the credibility of the Ukrainian military had been strained internationally, following a number of incidents in 2000–02 (notably the accidental shooting down of a passenger aircraft *en route* from Israel to Russia in October 2001). In total, more than 200 civilians had been killed as a result of apparent negligence on the part of the military authorities, resulting in the dismissal of senior military staff on two occasions in 2001–02.

## THE AUTONOMOUS REPUBLIC OF CRIMEA

Crimea's autonomous status within the Russian Federation was abolished in 1945, following the deportation en masse of the Crimean Tatars, and the region was transferred to Ukraine in 1954, after nine years as a Russian oblast (province). As the only region within Ukraine with a two-thirds' ethnic Russian majority and a Black Sea Fleet base, the Ukrainian authorities always sought not to inflame ethnic relations that could bring Russia into conflict with Ukraine. In January 1991 the Ukrainian authorities acquiesced in the elevation of the status of the region to that of an autonomous republic within Ukraine, which obtained the support of 93% of participants in a referendum. In May 1992 a potentially serious clash occurred between the Ukrainian authorities and Crimea, when the legislature of the latter declared independence, in a tactical attempt to obtain a greater degree of autonomy.

Further difficulties occurred in 1994–95 when Russian nationalist Yurii Meshkov resoundingly defeated the Ukrainian authorities' preferred choice, Nikolai Bagrov, the Chairman of the Crimean Supreme Council, in Crimean presidential elections. Meshkov wrongly calculated that Kuchma would favour a greater degree of *rapprochement* with Russia and that he would win large-scale support from that country, which was reluctant to be seen to be promoting separatism in Ukraine when it was itself defending its territorial integrity against separatists in Chechnya. Support for Meshkov's Russian nationalism and separatism dramatically declined throughout 1994, as the Ukrainian authorities applied economic and political sanctions against Crimea. In March 1995 the position of Crimean president was abolished and Russian nationalists were replaced by Bagrov's pro-Ukrainian loyalists in the local parliamentary and government leaderships. Crimean-Ukrainian relations settled down after the legislative elections of March 1998, which completely removed Russian nationalists from positions of influence within the peninsula. The local Communist Party took the largest number of seats in the Crimean Supreme Council, and its leader, Leonid Grach, became legislative Chairman. Meanwhile, the pro-Kuchma People's Democratic Party took control of the Government. Both parties remained committed to maintaining Crimea within Ukraine, a factor that helped Crimea to adopt a Constitution in October 1998, which was ratified by the Verkhovna Rada two months later. In March 2002 elections were held to the Crimean legislature, as well as to the Verkhovna Rada. In a similar vein to elections to the national parliament, the CPU, contesting the elections to the Crimean Supreme Council as the Grach bloc, saw its representation reduced from 40 of 100 seats to 28, while the pro-presidential bloc, contesting the elections as the Kunitsyn Team, became the largest faction in the Crimean parliament, with 39 seats and, having been able to form a 67-seat majority faction in association with independent deputies and those of other parties, took control of its leading positions. However, in elections to the Verkhovna Rada, the CPU remained the most popular party in the peninsular. Notably, for the first time, Crimean Tatar deputies were elected to the Verkhovna Rada, within the Our Ukraine bloc. Russian nationalists only successfully captured votes in the Crimean city of Sevastopol.

The adoption of the Crimean Constitution in late 1998 finalized the question of Crimea's autonomous status within Ukraine and ended any speculation that it might eventually return to Russian jurisdiction. Nevertheless, the estimated 270,000 Tatars living in Crimea continued to represent a potential ethnic problem, owing to radical elements among them that opposed any autonomous status for the region that did not define Crimea as a Tatar homeland. The 2001 Ukrainian census showed that the ethnic balance in the Crimea was changing. While Russians are moving out the number of Tatars returning is growing. The proportion of Russians had declined from 65% to 58% since the 1989 Soviet census.

## CONCLUSION

Between 1991 and 1994 a combination of conservative strategies that sought to maintain the status quo domestically, and a foreign policy that sought to establish its presence internationally, while dealing with Russia's inability to come to terms with its independence, left many wondering if the Ukrainian state would survive either at all, or within its Soviet-era borders. Under President Kuchma, the Ukrainian state consolidated itself from 1994 and these fears were largely allayed. Key aspects of this process included the granting of security assurances to Ukraine by the five declared nuclear powers in 1994; membership of the Council of Europe in 1995; the adoption of the Constitution and the introduction of a new currency in 1996; the signature of an inter-state treaty with Russia and a Charter with NATO, and a 20-year Black Sea Fleet agreement in 1997; and the adoption of the Crimean Constitution and ratification of the Ukrainian-Russian treaty by Russia in 1998–99. Moreover, it was thought that the re-election of Kuchma in November 1999, the creation of a reformist majority in the Verkhovna Rada and the election of Ukraine's first seriously reformist Prime Minister might herald a new and decisive stage in Ukraine's state- and nation-building programme. The dismissal of Prime Minister Viktor Yushchenko in April 2001 returned Ukraine to its traditional strategy of balancing domestic and foreign interests through gradual reform and a 'multi-vector' foreign policy. By the 10th anniversary of Ukraine's declaration of independence its independence was no longer in question. The 2002 elections demonstrated that the principal potential domestic threat to independence, the communists, were no longer Ukraine's most popular political grouping, and that, perhaps for the first time for many years, public opinion regarded non-communist groups as the main source of opposition to the executive. By 2002, two years after the economy had begun to grow for the first time since the late 1980s, the proportion of Ukrainians supporting independence had for the first time returned to the high levels recorded in the December 1991 referendum. Nevertheless, the main question that remained unresolved was that of deciding what was to be built in independent Ukraine, something that would appear to rest largely on the outcome of the 2004 presidential elections.

# The Economy

## Dr TARAS KUZIO

Since independence in late 1991, Ukrainian governments can be divided into four groups. The first group—comprising the Governments led by Vitold Fokin in October 1990–September 1992, and by Prime Minister Leonid Kuchma in October 1992–September 1993—did not succeed in establishing a coherent programme of transition from a command administration to a market economy. The second group—the Governments led by Yufym Zvyahylsky (in September 1993–June 1994), Vitaliy Masol (June 1994–March 1995), and Anatoliy Kinakh (May 2001–October 2002) and Viktor Yanukovych (who took office in November 2002)—are best understood as short-term, interim administrations. By mid-2003 it appeared that one of the principal purposes of the Yanukovych administration, which took office as part of the consolidation of pro-presidential powers several months after the 2002 legislative elections (see History) might be to provide Yanukovych with a means to present himself as a presidential candidate, and as Kuchma's chosen successor, at the election scheduled to be held in late 2004. The third group of governments experienced by Ukraine in its first decade of independence were those that implemented radical reform—the administration that immediately followed Kuchma's election as President in 1994–95, and the Government headed by Viktor Yushchenko in December 1999–April 2001. The fourth and final group—the Governments of Yevhen Marchuk (June 1995–May 1996), Pavlo Lazarenko (July 1996–June 1997) and Valeriy Pustovoytenko (July 1997–December 1999) were headed by representatives of the former Soviet Ukrainian *nomenklatura*, who preferred to ensure a 'state-regulated' transition and an evolutionary economic reform. In particular, it was during the period that Ukraine was governed by Lazarenko and Pustovoytenko that the country sunk into deeper economic and political stagnation, accompanied by the rise of a corrupt class of 'oligarchs'.

## ECONOMIC UNCERTAINTY UNDER THE FOKIN GOVERNMENT (1990–92)

Throughout the first year of Ukrainian independence the Government continued to be largely staffed by personnel from the Soviet era, and retained the same outmoded structure. Prime Minister Fokin came to office while the USSR was intact, in October 1990, amid an already crumbling economy and in the aftermath of widespread student protests and demands for greater national sovereignty, all of which had combined to bring down the Government of Vitaliy Masol. The structure of the Fokin Government continued to reflect the Soviet legacy. Committees on prices and production abounded, and the Ministry of Finance lacked the central importance that an equivalent ministry would have had in a Western market economy. There was, as yet, no procedure for establishing a centralized budget and no possibility of the Ministry disciplining the spending of other departments, or the populist parliament that had been elected in March 1990. The newly created National Bank of Ukraine did not, as yet, possess the classic levers of monetary control, such as a system of credit control and fiscal discipline.

A major factor propelling Ukraine to independence in 1990–91 was the view that the republic would benefit economically outside the USSR. When nationalists listed Ukraine's potential economic strengths at the time of independence they tended to enumerate raw materials and Ukraine's historical role as the 'breadbasket of Europe'. This ignored the fact that most of Ukraine's productive capacity dated from the period of reconstruction after the Second World War (1939–45), and that its human and capital resources had no experience of competing in world markets. In addition, Ukraine's economy was a heavy and inefficient consumer of cheap Russian energy. When Russia pushed up energy prices to world levels in 1992–93, Ukraine's economy was severely affected.

The limited reforms initiated in 1990–91 by the Fokin Government were primarily crisis measures designed to secure Ukrainian control over the newly independent country's economy, rather than to introduce a market economy. In any case, prior to independence as much as 95% of economic activity in Ukraine was still controlled by the central Soviet authorities in Moscow. The most important feature of the 'Fokin plan' approved by the Ukrainian Verkhovna Rada (Supreme Soviet—Supreme Council) in late 1990 was the introduction of a protectionist system of the payment of Ukrainian salaries with coupons (also known as karbovanets, the Ukrainian name for the Soviet currency). These then had to be used for the purchase of those consumer goods deemed to be vulnerable to purchase by foreign (primarily Russian) consumers.

In June 1991 the Ukrainian parliament passed a series of resolutions that established a National Bank, which was to introduce a national currency; claimed control over all Union enterprises on Ukrainian territory; and asserted the sole right of the republican Government in Kiev to levy taxes within Ukraine. However, such declarations were not given practical effect until after the declaration of independence on 24 August 1991. The Verkhovna Rada had, rather optimistically in the context of Ukraine's international isolation, approved a 'Law Concerning Foreign Economic Activity' in April 1991, and a 'Law Concerning (Foreign) Investment Activity' in September, but, not surprisingly, no deluge of foreign investment arrived subsequently. (Even as late as 2002, according to the British-based Economist Intelligence Unit, the total sum of foreign investment in Ukraine amounted to only US $4,406m., with the USA being the largest contributor, accounting for $730.9m.) In January 1992 a presidential decree established UkrExImBank—State Export-Import Bank of Ukraine, thus gaining control of the foreign-currency earnings that hitherto went to Russian institutions in Moscow. (However, draconian rates of taxation in both Ukraine and Russia meant that most former Soviet enterprises preferred to keep their earnings outside either country.)

In February 1992 a 'Law on the Limitation of Monopoly and the Promotion of Competition' provided another key prerequisite to the implementation of a free-market economy, although it worked through the limitation of profit margins. For example, a presidential decree issued in January of that year limited the maximum profit margin permitted to most companies to only 25%–40%. Finally, in early 1992 a number of privatization laws were approved, for the most part authored by Volodymyr Lanovyi, then Minister for Privatization and Economic Reform, who was promoted in March 1992 to Deputy Prime Minister. Lanovyi argued that the Ukrainian economy was too weak, and still too interdependent with the other economies of the former USSR, for any rapid establishment of greater economic autonomy to be feasible. In contrast to the economic nationalists (who drew their strength from 'sovereign communists', such as President Leonid Kravchuk, and national-democratic parties, such as the Ukrainian People's Movement for Restructuring—Rukh), Lanovyi argued that a strong national economy would be best built by the reform of basic economic relations, so as to create domestically generated wealth.

On 10 January 1992, following the liberalization of prices eight days earlier in Russia, Ukraine introduced a system of reusable karbovanets (coupons—kupony), to operate as a makeshift currency to operate alongside the former Soviet currency. Above all, the introduction of the kupon should be understood in the context of Ukraine's long-standing desire to introduce its own convertible currency, to be known as the hryvnya, after the currency used by the independent Ukrainian People's Republic of 1917–20. Ukraine regarded the establishment of its own national currency as one of the necessary attributes of state-building. However, Ukraine would only be ready to introduce its own currency once it had gained control of purchasing power and the budgetary deficit, had limited the supply of credits to enterprises, and had implemented structural changes so as to permit the establishment and growth of a market economy. These factors were not in evidence until September 1996, when the hryvnya was successfully introduced by National Bank Chairman Viktor Yushchenko.

The introduction of the kupon essentially served as an interim response by Ukraine to the price and wage reforms that had been implemented in Russia; in contrast to the coupons that had been in use since late 1990, the new kupony were not to act as a parallel currency, but rather as a means to defend the domestic market. Indeed, it became a standard notion among Ukrainian nationalists that Ukraine's more plentiful stores were being 'plundered' of Ukrainian goods by 'foreigners' (in this context, Russians), and such a threat was supposedly magnified by Russia's price reforms. President Kravchuk repeatedly accused the rouble printing presses, located in Russia, of not supplying Ukrainian citizens with enough roubles for Ukraine's needs.

The state budgetary process also remained chaotic. The former Soviet political system had given way to institutional pluralism and a consequent lack of discipline in the process of budget formation and finance (annual budgets did not really exist). Parliament, in particular, was prone to voting for expenditure first and then considering how to fund it at a later date. Moreover, the Minister of Defence Konstyantin Morozov stated that, during the first year of Ukrainian independence, no military budget had been set. Although a national bank existed, the Ukrainian authorities had failed to create an institutional power-base capable of pushing for wholesale reform of the monetary system and acting as a future guardian of a sound currency. The Ministry of Finance had a staff of only 400; there was no tradition of economic forecasting (without which setting and implementing a realistic budget is impossible), and skilled economists were few and far between.

In February–March 1992 the Verkhovna Rada passed three key laws (one each on the Privatization of Large and Small Enterprises, and a Law on Privatization Vouchers). None the less, 'mass privatization' did not begin in Ukraine until almost three years later, in January 1995. According to the laws approved in early 1992, the sale of all Ukrainian enterprises was to begin in the second half of that year, with certain notable exceptions: those that were 'the property of organs of state power'; those that were of national historical or cultural importance; organs of education and science financed from the state budget; those involved in the preparation and manufacture of drugs, arms, explosives and radioactive substances; nuclear power stations; and other items of state property, necessary for the carrying out of state functions. The 'Law On Privatization Vouchers' envisaged that they could be index-linked, if inflation threatened to destroy their value, but could not be exchanged or sold between private citizens.

Ukraine had not adopted the ambitious privatization drive that Russia had adopted earlier, and there was little evidence that President Kravchuk regarded it as a priority. At the same time, individual directors, the former *nomenklatura*, regional governors and various government bureaucrats had begun quietly to take over state enterprises semi-legally, often transforming them into leased companies. This procedure became known, by a pun on the word 'privatization', and the Ukrainian word for 'to grab', as *prykhvatyzatsiya* ('grab-ization').

Kravchuk's relations with the reformer Lanovyi were always poor. Kravchuk was ideologically closer to Oleksandr Yemelianov, head of the economic section of the State Duma (Advisory Council), and an old apparatchik from the Ukrainian State Planning Agency (Gosplan/Derzhplan). As former 'sovereign communists', their enthusiasm for market reform was only tactical, as real reform would have undermined their power-base and damaged their interests. They found it easier to make a common cause with the nationalist opposition than with the liberal reformers in the New Ukraine bloc, as they shared the former's desire to give priority to state-building measures. Consequently, the rival economic programme presented by Yemelianov to a closed session of parliament in late March 1992 differed from Lanovyi's by envisaging a rapid departure from the rouble zone, and by advocating protectionist and retaliatory measures against Russia, in response to measures introduced by Russian Prime Minister Yegor Gaidar in January, including price liberalization and measures towards charging world prices for Russian goods. The main aim of the programme was once again to finalize Ukrainian control over the nation's economy, rather than to establish a market economy. On the basis of radical reformer Lanovyi's alternative economic-reform programme, however, Ukraine was admitted to the IMF in March; Lavonyi's dismissal, in July, reflected Kravchuk's dislike for market economic reform.

The Kravchuk-Yemelianov plan was a dismal failure, leading the economy into further, accentuated, decline. At the end of September 1992 Kravchuk announced Ukraine's withdrawal from the rouble zone. He also outlined plans for the development of market relations, acceleration of privatization and de-monopolization, strengthening of economic independence and liberalization of foreign economic activities, at the same time as enhancing state control over the economy. Kravchuk, like Kuchma's later 'state-regulated transition to a social-market economy', supported a strong role for the state in regulating economic life.

The 'Plan of Actions and Measures on the Deepening of Economic Reform in Ukraine' was composed of 15 sections, divided into three main directions, and based on Yemelianov's protectionist 'Fundamentals of National Economic Policy'. These included reform of budgetary and taxation policy, de-monopolization, attraction of foreign investment, establishment of a system for financing and distributing credits, implementation of monetary reform, stimulation of measures to support enterprises, standardization of the privatization programme and provision for reform of the state administration. It, therefore, represented Kravchuk's preference for an evolutionary 'state-regulated' transition to a market economy.

### 'HYPERINFLATION' UNDER PRIME MINISTER KUCHMA (1992–93)

Although the Kuchma Government, which took office in October 1992, was initially welcomed as a more reformist alternative to the Fokin administration, any analysis of Kuchma's 11 months in office will show that he had little clear vision at that time of what he wanted to accomplish. At different times during his tenure as Prime Minister, Kuchma advocated 'shock therapy', along the lines of Poland, and at other times the 'Chinese model of economic reform'. Of the two, President Kravchuk undoubtedly favoured something closer to the latter—a state-directed transition to a social-market economy. Kravchuk stated on many occasions that if 'shock therapy' were adopted in Ukraine it would lead to mass social unrest; the former 'sovereign communists' placed great emphasis on social 'stability', owing to their fear of such unrest.

The Kuchma Government failed to launch privatization, which would have to wait until he became President one year later. During 1993, gross domestic product (GDP) was 86.3% of its 1992 level, and average monthly wages steadily declined. Inflationary pressures increased, leading to hyperinflation in September–December, at an average monthly rate of 175%. The Government was plagued by a lack of consensus on reform, and by late 1993 was wholly dominated by representatives of the so-called 'red directors' (former members of the communist élite, in particular managers of industrial enterprises, who continued to support an interventionist role for the state in economic affairs), who were primarily interested in 'grab-ization'. The resignation of Deputy Prime Minister Viktor Pynzenyk in August 1993 (who, after the departure of Lanovyi, had been the last proponent of economic reform within the Government) strengthened the hand of those demanding economic union with Russia as a means of avoiding the need to implement economic reforms. After Kuchma's resignation as Prime Minister, in September, he was elected to the post of Chairman of the Union of Industrialists and Entrepreneurs of Ukraine (UIEU) and co-Chairman of the Inter-Regional Bloc of Reforms (MRBR), a newly established social-democratic/liberal electoral bloc based in the predominantly Russian-speaking and industrialized eastern and southern regions of Ukraine. Kuchma became the presidential candidate of these two organizations (UIEU and MRBR) in the following year.

Although Kuchma was granted wide-ranging powers during his tenure as Prime Minister, particularly with regard to the economy, he never fully utilized them, and no radical reforms were forthcoming. Instead, the population became poorer, inflation increased to an unprecedented extent, taxes rose dramatically (including the introduction of excise taxes) and enterprise indebtedness grew, and the value of the karbovanets declined dramatically against the US dollar. Moreover, the Government's unbalanced foreign economic and currency policy generated a large outflow of money and capital from Ukraine.

The June 1993 strikes by 400,000 miners and industrial workers, primarily in eastern Ukraine, was the first indication that the domestic stability that independent Ukraine had enjoyed was over. The strikers had also added political demands, such as local autonomy and a referendum on public confidence in the President and the parliament, to their economic demands. Not only had President Kravchuk lost his support in eastern Ukraine, which had ensured his victory in the December 1991 presidential elections, but the strikers and local leadership also questioned his ability to manage the economy. The regional élite sought greater power within Ukraine, after a period in which they perceived the demands of Ukrainian-speaking and more rural western Ukraine as holding undue influence over the Kravchuk leadership, which resulted in his post-1991 alliance with 'national democrats'. Moreover, bitterness resulted from the fact that, during the Soviet era, Ukraine's ruling élites had traditionally been recruited from the eastern and Russian-speaking Donetsk and Dnipropetrovsk regions, from which Kuchma himself originated, and, indeed, from the mid-1990s, this pattern appeared to be recurring under Kuchma's presidency, when the predominance of a group of state and business executives from Dnipropetrovsk became such that they were widely referred to, somewhat pejoratively, as 'Dnipropetrovtsy'.

### 'CARETAKER' GOVERNMENTS UNDER ZVYAHYLSKY AND MASOL (1993–95)

In October 1993 Yufym Zvyahylsky, a former coal-mine manager and Mayor of Donetsk, assumed the role of acting Prime Minister in a 'caretaker' Government, which remained dominated by representatives from the Donetsk region associated with the Party of Labour and the UIEU. In June 1994 Zvya-hylsky resigned as Ukraine's acting Prime Minister, and soon afterwards fled to Israel, seemingly in order to escape investigation into charges of corruption issued against him. Zvya-hylsky claimed credit for having stabilized the economy after the hyperinflation of 1993 and, although the financial measures that Zvyahylsky's Government had used to stabilize the economy were sharply criticized by the so-called industrial lobby, the programme of stabilization implemented in October 1994–April 1995, after the election of Kuchma as President, was to some extent dependent upon, and benefited from, the policies implemented under Zvyahylsky's Government.

In mid-June 1994, on the eve of presidential elections, Vitaliy Masol (who had led a rather ineffectual Government in June–October 1990) was confirmed as Ukraine's new Prime Minister. Masol's appointment represented an unsuccessful attempt by Kravchuk to secure left-wing support during the June–July 1994 presidential elections, in an attempt to gain the votes of supporters of Kuchma in eastern Ukraine. However, although he remained in office after Kravchuk had lost the presidency to Kuchma, Masol's Government served essentially as an interim administration, with no real interest in implementing market reform.

In October 1994 President Kuchma announced a programme of radical economic reform, stating that private ownership was to be the catalyst for economic growth and development. As proved to be the case when a further programme of radical economic reform was supported by the Government, in 1999–2000 under Prime Minister Viktor Yushchenko, the reform programme of 1994–95 was supported by both centre-right 'national democrats' and by centrist former 'sovereign communists'. The programme aimed rapidly to achieve stabilization in a country that had experienced a decline in living standards of 80% since 1991, and which had high levels of 'hidden' unemployment. In 1992–93 GDP declined at an annual average rate of 15.5%, and in 1994 the rate of decline accelerated further, reaching 22.9%, although in subsequent years the rate of GDP decline began to slow. Masol resigned in March 1995, following disagreements over IMF policy requirements; none the less, the initiation of Ukraine's first post-Soviet economic-reform package, along with the country's decision to relinquish its nuclear weapons, resulted, in April, in the release of the first tranche of IMF funding, which, in this instance, went some way towards covering the large budgetary deficit.

## 'CORRECTED REFORM' UNDER MARCHUK (1995–96)

President Kuchma's task of encouraging parliament to accept his reform programme was greatly aided by the resignation of the Masol Government, following a vote of 'no confidence' in the Verkhovna Rada; thereafter, Kuchma was able to preside over a Government more sympathetic to policies of reform. Nevertheless, opposition to the IMF conditions in the 1995 budget continued to grow, and was not confined solely to the parliamentary left. Particular hostility was generated by reductions in agricultural subsidies and the social expenditure that the new policy necessitated. The 1995 budget envisaged a reduction in the monthly rate of inflation of 1%–2%, and measures implemented to ensure this included the abolition of agricultural and industrial credits, the introduction of a strict incomes policy and increases in utility prices to households. Moreover, subsidies to the coal industry were replaced by inter-industry transfers. In a further measure to accelerate reform and achieve fiscal stabilization, a presidential decree offered shares in restructured joint-stock companies on the Kiev stock exchange. Up to 30% of these shares would be for sale to individual and corporate investors, the proceeds of which would finance the establishment of new voucher auction centres, as well as a national electronic stock exchange. Ukraine also planned to reduce the budgetary deficit in 1995 by some 8%, through the issuance of bonds.

The programme of radical economic reform outlined in October 1994 by President Kuchma largely followed the prescriptions of international financial institutions, in particular the IMF. However, by early 1995 these prescriptions were not only being ignored, but were being denounced openly by the Ukrainian leadership, which now returned to the rhetoric of the Kravchuk era, announcing support for a state-regulated transition to a social-market economy. Ukraine's experiment with radical economic reform had proved to be short-lived, lasting somewhat less than one year and amounting to support for stabilization, but not structural reform.

In his annual address to parliament on 4 April 1995 Kuchma criticized those supporting a 'blind monetarist policy'. Economic reform, he declared, should be 'state-regulated' and provide a social 'safety net'. An immediate casualty of this amendment to Ukraine's economic-reform programme was the radical reformer and former Deputy Prime Minister, responsible for Economic Reform, Viktor Pynzenyk (who had been a leading proponent of reforms in the Government led by Prime Minister Kuchma in 1992–93, and whose resignation from that Government had been regarded as marking the departure of the last serious advocate of economic reform). Kuchma initially did not include Pynzenyk in the new Government created after the June 1995 Constitutional Agreement. However, in October, at the time of a visit by IMF officials to Ukraine to negotiate the next instalment of lending, worth a total of US $1,500m., Pynzenyk was brought back into the Government in an apparent attempt to gain support from international financial institutions.

In June 1995 Kuchma announced a significant amendment to the previously announced economic policy. Henceforth, the IMF-approved inflation target was to be replaced by a higher, 'corrected' monthly target of 4%–5%. The author of the programme of reform introduced in October 1994, Anatoliy Halchynsky, stated the revisions to these targets to reflect the emergence of a 'second stage' of economic reform, with different priorities: whereas the first stage had aimed at financial stabilization, the second sought to combine monetarist methods with increased production. The Government appointed in June 1995, led by Yevhen Marchuk, sought to implement a structural reorganization of the economy, to provide substantial support for domestic producers and to improve living standards and social welfare. However, as it turned out, the Government failed in all of these areas. The Government had failed to create the conditions for sustained economic progress, and targets for privatization were not met. There was, moreover, little public support for a programme of radical economic reform. It appeared, therefore, that the reforms introduced in the October 1994 programme merely reflected the post-election euphoria of an administration that sought to distance itself from its predecessors, and which sought the acceptance of international financial institutions and Western governments.

Although Kuchma had announced his opposition to 'blindly copying the West's economic model' and despite the 'corrections' that had been made to the reform programme during 1995, the President continued to insist that Ukraine had not abandoned economic reform once again. The introduction of the new currency, the hryvnya (which had been printed as early as 1992, in Canada), had been long anticipated. In May 1995 the chairman of the National Bank of Ukraine, Viktor Yushchenko, indicated that a number of factors, among them the stabilization of the karbovanets (which fluctuated against the US dollar in 1995–96, but did not decline markedly in value), a sharp decline in inflation, control of the budgetary deficit and currency emission, as well as large international credits, finally provided an opportunity to introduce the hryvnya. In August 1995 the National Bank of Ukraine announced that it was to be introduced at the beginning of September 1996, at a rate of 100,000 hryvnya to one karbovanets.

## STAGNATION UNDER LAZARENKO AND PUSTOVOYTENKO (1997–99)

In reality, Ukraine would not possess a serious reform programme until Yushchenko was appointed as Prime Minister in December 1999. In particular, the resignation, in April 1997, of Pynzenyk from the position of Deputy Prime Minister, responsible for Economic Reform, for the second time, represented a serious challenge to the implementation of economic reforms. Indeed, the period of so-called 'correction' that lasted from 1995–99, rather than being a period of reform and progress, brought Ukraine close to bankruptcy and, to a much greater extent than in the preceding years, led to the creation of an increasingly powerful group of wealthy and frequently corrupt business executives, widely referred to in Ukraine, as in the equivalent situation in Russia, as 'oligarchs', who in many cases overlapped with the 'red directors' and the 'Dnipropetrovtsy'. Critics of the Marchuk Government pointed to its perilous political balancing act between 'corrected' and 'state-led' economic reform and industrialist lobbies. Kuchma blamed the Pavlo Lazarenko Government (July 1996–July 1997) for its poor performance, its inconsistency, growing wage arrears and the lack of a budget for 1997 (the absence of which delayed further Western assistance). Meanwhile, Kuchma blamed parliament for failing to pass legislation to overcome the economic crisis. However, in appointing Lazarenko as premier, the President had known that he was appointing only a cautious reformer, whose governance would not instil greater momentum to the reform process, but would rather, above all, increase the influence on the Government of the so-called Dnipropetrovtsy, as indeed proved to be the case. Lazarenko's three-year programme for economic recovery was supported by the left because it backed protectionist measures for Ukrainian industry while omitting contentious issues relating to land privatization and agricultural reform. This programme, above all, reflected Lazarenko's willingness to amend his policies, so as to obtain the support of the statist left, while doing little to dispel suspicions about his true commitment to a market economy.

Rumours of Lazarenko's impending dismissal surrounded the Prime Minister throughout his year-long government. Lazarenko faced accusations of permitting wage arrears to reach some US $2,300m. and of inhibiting expedited reform. Kuchma also complained, in his state of the nation speech, of enterprise directors who paid neither salaries nor taxes, as well as widespread corruption. However, the Lazarenko Government, and that led by Valeriy Pustovoytenko, which succeeded it, from July 1997, were increasingly dominated by the so-called Dnipropetrovtsy, who had little interest in radical reform or in the systematic implementation or introduction of anti-corruption measures. Lazarenko granted privileges to the state-controlled Russian energy grid, Unified Energy Systems (RAO EES Rossii), which thus became a *de facto* monopoly importer of Russian gas into Ukraine.

Corruption, including that linked to Lazarenko himself, would have been impossible to undertake without the involvement of other high-ranking state officials, and, at best, a lack of acknowledgement by Kuchma. During his tenure as premier Lazarenko enjoyed good relations with Kuchma and his resignation, in July 1997, came largely in response to criticism of his leadership, particularly in Western countries. Lazarenko's subsequent leadership of the Hromada—Community party, the first and only coherent anti-Kuchma, pro-'oligarch' party in Ukraine, led to his relationship with the

Kuchma administration becoming more ambiguous, however. Lazarenko was permitted to leave Ukraine in 1999, ostensibly for reasons of ill health, and eventually requested political asylum in the USA. His trial on charges of money 'laundering' (the processing of illegally obtained funds into legitimate holdings) began in 2002 in San Francisco, CA, USA.

The appointment of Kuchma loyalist Valeriy Pustovoytenko as premier in 1997 signalled an end to political rivalry between the Prime Minister and the President, although the economy continued to stagnate, and corruption to become increasingly prevalent. Pustovoytenko headed the pro-presidential People's Democratic Party of Ukraine, the 'party of power' in the March 1998 parliamentary elections. Reforms also proved difficult to implement following the election of Oleksandr Tkachenko, of the radical-leftist Peasants' Party, as parliamentary Chairman in July 1998, a position he retained until his removal from office in January 2000.

In May 1998 the Pustovoytenko Government outlined a new economic programme for 1999–2005, which took into account the successes of the 1994 IMF-approved programme. The new programme envisaged a reduction in the budgetary deficit and increased subsidies to industry. However, the initial implementation of the programme failed to stimulate economic growth, although the annual rate of decline in GDP decreased markedly, and was just 0.2% in 1999. In 1998–99 privatization primarily benefited 'oligarchs', rather than the economy. In particular, Viktor Pinchuk—Kuchma's son-in-law—had become the leading steel magnate of Ukraine, owning five major steel-works as part of his company, Interpipe, while Hryhoriy Surkis and Viktor Medvedchuk, the leader of the Social-Democratic Party of Ukraine (United), had, between them, taken control over a majority of regional electricity distribution companies. In November 1998 the Government, with the backing of Kuchma, rejected IMF prescriptions and resorted to Soviet-style actions, such as increasing support to industrial producers and proposing plans to curtail the independence of the National Bank. The reaction of international financial institutions and the European Union was to 'freeze' financial assistance to Ukraine, in consequence of which the financial situation of the country further deteriorated throughout 1999. When Yushchenko became Prime Minister in December 1999, Ukraine was on the verge of bankruptcy.

## RADICAL REFORMER YUSHCHENKO PRESIDES OVER GROWTH (1999–2001)

Viktor Yushchenko claimed that when he was appointed as Prime Minister in December 1999 Ukraine was on the verge of default and that the new Government had inherited US $2,000m. in wage arrears. Ukraine was ranked 87th out of 90 countries on the annual 'corruption perception index' issued by the NGO, Transparency International. The Heritage Foundation's index of economic freedom in 2001 ranked Ukraine 133rd of 161 countries, and the Washington, DC, USA-based, pro-free market CATO Institute's 'Economic Freedom in the World' index also ranked Ukraine poorly. All of these findings reflected the consequences of slow and inconsistent reform that had been thus far applied in post-Soviet Ukraine.

Yushchenko's Government presided over Ukraine's only major experience in the 1990s of radical economic reform, with the exception of the short-lived programme of late 1994–early 1995. The Government reduced corruption through rent-seeking, liberalized supply, curtailed 250 'hidden' subsidies and, by reducing the excessive state regulation of the economy, finally created the circumstances in which the macroeconomic stabilization achieved in 1994–96 could generate positive growth, for the first time since independence. In 2000 GDP increased by 5.9%, and it increased by 9.1% in 2001. Barter trade, which had become widespread in many areas of the Ukrainian economy in the 1990s, was curtailed in the notoriously corrupt energy sector. Yuliya Tymoshenko, an ally of Lazarenko, albeit a greater proponent of reform, was appointed Deputy Prime Minister, responsible for Energy Reform, with a mandate to combat ingrained corruption in this sector. It was estimated that, as a result of anti-corruption measures implemented under Yushchenko, some US $4,000m., equivalent to 13% of GDP, which otherwise would illicitly have benefited the 'oligarchs', was recovered by the state, most of which went to settle wage and pension arrears. A new land code, which permitted the eventual private ownership of land, was also approved in 2001. The reduction in taxation and state regulation helped encourage private small and medium-sized enterprises. As had earlier been the case with Lanovyi and Pynzenyk, Yushchenko was useful to Kuchma in encouraging the impression in the West that reform was still official policy in Ukraine. This, in turn, was persuasive in effecting the resumption of lending by international financial institutions to Ukraine in December 2000, when the IMF announced the release of up to $246m.

The major 'oligarch' groups based in Kiev—Medvedchuk and Surkis's Social-Democratic Party of Ukraine (United), and Oleksandr Volkov's and Ihor Bakai's Democratic Union—and in Dnipropetrovsk (Pinchuk's and Andrei Derkach's Working Ukraine) were financially damaged by the reforms implemented by the Yushchenko Government. The alliance of centre-right reformers and 'oligarch' centrists that had controlled the Verkhovna Rada since early 2000, having staged what had appeared to be a 'velvet revolution', began to disintegrate after the 'Kuchmagate' crisis of November 2000 (see History), and as a result of increasing hostility on the part of the 'oligarchs' to Yushchenko's reforms. Tymoshenko was the first pro-reform minister to be removed from office in February 2001, prior to her arrest, on questionable charges of corruption, later in the year. Following the removal of Yushchenko's Government, by means of a parliamentary vote of 'no confidence', supported primarily by communists and 'oligarchs' supportive of Kuchma, it appeared that the positive consequences of the radical reforms implemented in 2000–01 might prove to be short-lived or limited.

## THE CARETAKER ADMINISTRATIONS OF KINAKH AND YANUKOVYCH (2001–)

Anatoliy Kinakh was a Kuchma loyalist who, like Pustovoytenko and Kuchma himself, had served as Chairman of the UIEU. Although a veteran 'red director', Kinakh's relative 'neutrality', unconnected as he was to any major grouping of 'oligarchs', facilitated Kuchma's continuation of 'divide and rule' tactics amongst the 'oligarchs', so as to prevent any one faction from dominating the economy. Kinakh's candidacy was backed by 'oligarchs', socialists and independents, largely because of the fear that any viable alternative, for example, an allegedly corrupt 'oligarch', such as Serhiy Tihypko of the 'Dnipropetrovtsy', the leader of the Working Ukraine party, would have been far worse. Many ministers in Yushchenko's outgoing Government were, in fact, reappointed to the Kinakh Government, with the notable exception of Tymoshenko, who had become increasingly identified (particularly through her involvement with the National Salvation Forum) as an articulate leader of the anti-Kuchma opposition. Given that Kinakh effectively led a 'caretaker' Government in 2001–02, it appeared unlikely that any major economic reforms, or, conversely, any significant reversion to a more state-driven system, would be implemented under his leadership. Moreover, the appointment of further Kuchma loyalists, following

legislative elections in March 2002, to significant positions in the state and legislative apparatus—notably the selection of Volodymyr Lytvyn as legislative Chairman, and of Medvedchuk as head of the presidential administration—meant that the policies of inertia and intermittent reform, and the tolerance of high-level corruption that characterized the Kuchma presidency, appeared likely to continue until the presidential election.

The dismissal of Kinakh, and his replacement by the hitherto Governor of Donetsk Oblast, Viktor Yanukovych, in November 2002, appeared principally to reflect the political interests of Kuchma: there had been no other evident reason to remove the Kinakh administration from office, as it had not had sufficient time to prove its competence or, conversely, its lack thereof. The appointment of a new Government, however, did appear to result in the formation of a more coherent pro-presidential majority, which thereby could be expected to further accentuate the policy trends that had already become evident under Kinakh. In April 2003 Yanukovych's government programme was approved by 335 votes, including those of most of the non-communist opposition delegates in the Verkhovna Rada, in contrast to only 259 votes for Kinakh's government programme in July 2002. Meanwhile, the return to positive growth, recorded from 2000, also appeared set to continue in the early 2000s, despite the heightening political crisis that affected the country, with GDP growth of 4.8% being recorded in 2002 (compared with growth of 5.8% in 2000, and 9.1% in 2001). Despite the fact that GDP, industrial and agricultural production and monetary income were all significantly less, in real terms, than had been the case in 1991, the return to growth might serve to inhibit demands, at least in the short term, for either more sustained or coherent reform or for a 'reinstallation' of Soviet-style measures. Indeed, an ambitious programme of privatization, which was intended to include eight strategic industries, such as coal-mining, was launched in 2003; following the completion of this programme, in 2008, it was anticipated that privatization would be complete. Meanwhile, by 2003 the privatization of agricultural land was estimated to have created some 6.5m. land-owning farmers, although a significant proportion of the agricultural sector remained under state or collective ownership. In May the Verkhovna Rada approved a uniform income-tax rate of 13% (based on a model that had apparently brought satisfactory results in Russia), to take effect from January 2004, rising to 15% in 2007, with the primary stated intention being to increase the proportion of economic activity taking place outside the parallel economy. (At the time that this measure was approved, income tax bands of 10%, 15%, 20%, 30% and 40% existed, with those who earned more than US $320 per month being placed in the uppermost band.) Despite Yanukovych's strong position, the (largely populist) economic programme of his Government appeared, by mid-2003, to be as unlikely to be fulfilled as that of most of the other government programmes launched in post-Soviet Ukraine. Indeed, the Chairman of the parliamentary budgetary committee, Petro Poroshenko, described the Yanukovych programme as comprising 'political slogans and declarations, rather than concrete steps'. Yanukovych's main concerns, in the period leading up to presidential elections scheduled for 2004, may be reasonably surmised to be political, not economic, particularly given his perceived need to ensure his selection as Kuchma's preferred successor, in preference to other pro-presidential and pro-'oligarch' leaders, such as such as Tyhypko, Chairman of the National Bank of Ukraine, and Medvedchuk, the leader of the Presidential Administration.

# Statistical Survey

Principal sources (unless otherwise stated): State Committee of Statistics of Ukraine, 01023 Kiev, vul. Sh. Rustaveli 3; tel. (44) 226-20-21; fax (44) 235-37-39; e-mail info@ukrstat.gov.ua; internet www.ukrstat.gov.ua; IMF, *Ukraine: Statistical Appendix* (February 2001).

## Area and Population

### AREA, POPULATION AND DENSITY

| | |
|---|---|
| Area (sq km) . . . . . . . . | 603,700* |
| Population (census results) | |
| 12 January 1989 . . . . . . . . . | 51,706,742 |
| 5 December 2001† | |
| Males . . . . . . . . . | 22,441,000 |
| Females. . . . . . . . . | 26,016,000 |
| Total . . . . . . . . | 48,457,000 |
| Population (official estimates at 31 December) | |
| 2002 . . . . . . . . . | 48,003,500 |
| Density (per sq km) at 31 December 2002 . . . . . | 79.5 |

\* 233,090 sq miles.
† Rounded figures.

### POPULATION BY ETHNIC GROUP

(permanent inhabitants, census of 5 December 2001)

| | '000 | % |
|---|---|---|
| Ukrainian . . . . . . . . . . | 37,541.7 | 78.13 |
| Russian . . . . . . . . . | 8,334.1 | 17.34 |
| Belarusian . . . . . . . . | 275.8 | 0.57 |
| Moldovan. . . . . . . . . | 258.6 | 0.54 |
| Crimean Tatar . . . . . . . | 248.2 | 0.52 |
| Bulgarian. . . . . . . . . | 204.6 | 0.43 |
| Hungarian . . . . . . . . | 156.6 | 0.33 |
| Romanian. . . . . . . . . | 151.0 | 0.31 |
| Polish . . . . . . . . . | 144.1 | 0.30 |
| Jewish. . . . . . . . . | 103.6 | 0.22 |
| Armenian. . . . . . . . . | 99.9 | 0.21 |
| Greek . . . . . . . . . | 91.5 | 0.19 |
| Tatar . . . . . . . . . | 73.3 | 0.15 |
| Roma (Gypsy) . . . . . . . | 47.6 | 0.10 |
| Others. . . . . . . . . | 321.7 | 0.67 |
| **Total** . . . . . . . . . . | **48,052.3** | **100.00** |

### ADMINISTRATIVE DIVISIONS

| | Area ('000 sq km) | Population ('000 at 31 Dec. 2002)* | Density (per sq km) |
|---|---|---|---|
| *Regions*† | | | |
| Cherkasy (Cherkassy) . . . . . . | 20.9 | 1,386.6 | 66.3 |
| Chernihiv (Chernigov) . . . . . . | 31.9 | 1,225.2 | 38.4 |
| Chernivtsi (Chernovtsy) . . . . . | 8.1 | 918.5 | 113.4 |
| Dnipropetrovsk (Dnepropetrovsk) . . | 31.9 | 3,532.8 | 110.7 |
| Donetsk . . . . . . . . | 26.5 | 4,774.4 | 180.2 |
| Ivano-Frankivsk (Ivano-Frankovsk) . . | 13.9 | 1,403.7 | 101.0 |
| Kharkiv (Kharkov) . . . . . . | 31.4 | 2,887.9 | 92.0 |
| Kherson . . . . . . . | 28.5 | 1,161.4 | 40.8 |
| Khmelnytskiy (Khmelnitskii) . . . . | 20.6 | 1,414.9 | 68.7 |
| Kirovohrad (Kirovograd) . . . . . | 24.6 | 1,115.7 | 45.4 |
| Kyiv (Kiev) . . . . . . . | 28.1 | 1,808.3 | 64.4 |
| Luhansk (Lugansk) . . . . . . | 26.7 | 2,507.3 | 93.9 |
| Lviv (Lvov) . . . . . . . | 21.8 | 2,611.0 | 119.8 |
| Mykolayiv (Nikolayev) . . . . . | 24.6 | 1,251.5 | 50.9 |
| Odesa (Odessa) . . . . . . | 33.3 | 2,448.2 | 73.5 |
| Poltava . . . . . . . . | 28.8 | 1,609.4 | 55.9 |
| Rivne (Rovno) . . . . . . | 20.1 | 1,168.3 | 58.1 |
| Sumy. . . . . . . . . | 23.8 | 1,279.9 | 53.8 |
| Ternopil (Ternopol). . . . . . | 13.8 | 1,134.2 | 82.2 |
| Transcarpathia . . . . . . | 12.8 | 1,253.9 | 98.3 |
| Vinnytsia (Vinnitsa) . . . . . | 26.5 | 1,753.9 | 66.9 |
| Volyn . . . . . . . . | 20.2 | 1,054.7 | 52.5 |
| Zaporizhzhia (Zaporozhe) . . . . | 27.2 | 1,909.3 | 70.8 |
| Zhytomyr (Zhitomir) . . . . . | 29.9 | 1,373.9 | 46.5 |
| *Cities* | | | |
| Kyiv (Kiev) . . . . . . . | 0.8 | 2,621.7 | 3,277.1 |
| Sevastopol . . . . . . . | 0.9 | 378.5 | 420.6 |
| *Autonomous Republic* | | | |
| Crimea . . . . . . . . | 26.1 | 2,018.4 | 77.8 |
| **Total** . . . . . . . . . | **603.7** | **48,003.5** | **79.5** |

\* Official estimates.
† With the exception of Crimea and Transcarpathia, the names of regions are given in Ukrainian, with alternative Russian versions in brackets where applicable.

## PRINCIPAL TOWNS*
(population at census of 5 December 2001, rounded)

| | | | |
|---|---|---|---|
| Kyiv (Kiev, capital) . | 2,611,000 | Chernihiv | |
| Kharkiv (Kharkov) . | 1,470,000 | (Chernigov). . . | 305,000 |
| Dnipropetrovsk | | Cherkasy | |
| (Dnepropetrovsk) . | 1,065,000 | (Cherkassy) . . | 295,000 |
| Odesa (Odessa) . . | 1,029,000 | Sumy . . . . | 293,000 |
| Donetsk . . . | 1,016,000 | Horlivka (Gorlovka) . | 292,000 |
| Zaporizhzhia | | Zhytomyr (Zhitomir). | 284,000 |
| (Zaporozhe). . . | 815,000 | Dniprodzerzhynsk | |
| Lviv (Lvov) . . | 733,000 | (Dneprodzerzhinsk) | 256,000 |
| Kryvyi Rih (Krivoi | | Khmelnytskiy | |
| Rog). . . . | 669,000 | (Khmelnitskii) . . | 254,000 |
| Mykolayiv | | Kirovohrad | |
| (Nikolayev). . . | 514,000 | (Kirovograd) . . | 254,000 |
| Mariupol† . . . | 492,000 | Rivne (Rovno) . . | 249,000 |
| Luhansk (Lugansk)‡ | 463,000 | Chernivtsi | |
| Makiyivka | | (Chernovtsy) . . | 241,000 |
| (Makayevka) . . | 390,000 | Kremenchuk | |
| Vinnytsia (Vinnitsa). | 357,000 | (Kremenchug) . . | 234,000 |
| Simferopol . . . | 344,000 | Ternopil (Ternopol) . | 228,000 |
| Sevastopol . . . | 342,000 | Ivano-Frankivsk | |
| Kherson . . . | 328,000 | (Ivano-Frankovsk). | 218,000 |
| Poltava . . . | 318,000 | Lutsk . . . . | 209,000 |
| | | Bila Tserkva (Belaya | |
| | | Tserkov) . . . | 200,000 |

\* The names of towns are given in Ukrainian, with alternative Russian versions in brackets where applicable.
† Known as Zhdanov from 1948 to 1989.
‡ Known as Voroshylovhrad (Voroshilovgrad) from 1935 to 1958 and from 1970 to 1989.

## BIRTHS, MARRIAGES AND DEATHS*

| | Registered live births | | Registered marriages | | Registered deaths | |
|---|---|---|---|---|---|---|
| | Number | Rate (per 1,000) | Number | Rate (per 1,000) | Number | Rate (per 1,000) |
| 1995 . . | 492,861 | 9.6 | 431,731 | 8.4 | 792,587 | 15.5 |
| 1996 . . | 467,211 | 9.1 | 307,543 | 6.0 | 776,717 | 15.2 |
| 1997 . . | 442,581 | 8.8 | 345,013 | 6.8 | 754,152 | 15.0 |
| 1998 . . | 419,238 | 8.4 | 310,504 | 6.2 | 719,955 | 14.3 |
| 1999 . . | 389,208 | 7.8 | 344,888 | 6.9 | 739,170 | 14.8 |
| 2000 . . | 385,126 | 7.8 | 274,523 | 5.5 | 758,082 | 15.3 |
| 2001 . . | 376,479 | 7.8 | 309,602 | 6.4 | 745,953 | 15.4 |
| 2002 . . | 390,687 | 8.1 | 317,228 | 6.6 | 754,911 | 15.7 |

\* Rates for 1995–2000 are based on unrevised population estimates.

**Expectation of Life** (WHO estimates, years at birth): 67.7 (males 62.2; females 73.3) in 2001 (Source: WHO, *World Health Report*).

## EMPLOYMENT
(annual averages, '000 employees)

| | 1998 | 1999 | 2000 |
|---|---|---|---|
| Agriculture, hunting, forestry and fishing . . | 5,060 | 4,961 | 4,977 |
| Mining and quarrying . . . . | 687 | 639 | 618 |
| Manufacturing . . . . . . | 3,540 | 3,319 | 2,914 |
| Construction . . . . . . | 1,097 | 974 | 895 |
| Trade, restaurants and hotels . . | 1,514 | 1,604 | 1,406 |
| Transport, storage and communications . . . . . | 1,400 | 1,329 | 1,228 |
| Finance, insurance, real estate and business services . . . . . | 213 | 197 | 196 |
| **Total employed** (incl. others). . | **19,415** | **18,790** | **18,063** |

**Registered unemployed** (annual averages, '000 persons): 1,003.2 in 1998; 1,174.5 in 1999; 1,155.2 in 2000.

**Economically active population** (sample surveys, '000 persons aged 15 years and over, October each year): 22,747.0 (males 11,733.7, females 11,013.3) in 1999; 23,127.4 (males 11,896.6, females 11,230.8) in 2000; 22,755.0 (males 11,678.5, females 11,076.5) in 2001. Figures include unemployed ('000): 2,698.8 in 1999; 2,707.6 in 2000, 2.516.9 in 2001.

Source: ILO.

# Health and Welfare

## KEY INDICATORS

| | |
|---|---|
| Total fertility rate (children per woman, 2001). . . . . | 1.1 |
| Under-5 mortality rate (per 1,000 live births, 2001) . . . | 20 |
| HIV/AIDS (% of persons aged 15–49, 2001). . . . . . | 0.99 |
| Physicians (per 1,000 head, 1998) . . . . . . . | 2.99 |
| Hospital beds (per 1,000 head, 1995) . . . . . . | 11.83 |
| Health expenditure (2000): US $ per head (PPP) . . . . | 152 |
| Health expenditure (2000): % of GDP . . . . . . | 4.1 |
| Health expenditure (2000): public (% of total) . . . . . | 70.1 |
| Human Development Index (2001): ranking . . . . . | 75 |
| Human Development Index (2001): value . . . . . . | 0.766 |

For sources and definitions, see explanatory note on p. vi.

# Agriculture

## PRINCIPAL CROPS
('000 metric tons)

| | 1999 | 2000 | 2001 |
|---|---|---|---|
| Wheat . . . . . . . . . | 13,585.3 | 10,197.0 | 21,348.0 |
| Barley . . . . . . . | 6,424.6 | 6,871.9 | 10,186.0 |
| Maize . . . . . . . | 1,736.9 | 3,848.1 | 3,641.0 |
| Rye . . . . . . . | 918.9 | 968.3 | 1,822.0 |
| Oats . . . . . . | 760.4 | 881.4 | 1,116.0 |
| Millet . . . . . . | 196.0 | 426.1 | 266.0 |
| Buckwheat . . . . . . | 222.1 | 480.6 | 380.0* |
| Potatoes . . . . . . | 12,723 | 19,838 | 17,344 |
| Sugar beet. . . . . . | 14,064.0 | 13,198.8 | 15,575.0 |
| Dry peas . . . . . . | 498 | 499 | 619 |
| Sunflower seed . . . . . | 2,794.0 | 3,457.4 | 2,251.0 |
| Rapeseed . . . . . . | 147.9 | 132.0 | 135.0 |
| Cabbages . . . . . . | 931.7 | 1,104.6 | 1,234.0 |
| Tomatoes . . . . . . | 1,325.0 | 1,126.5 | 1,053.0 |
| Pumpkins, squash and gourds . . | 783.0 | 891.1 | 901.0 |
| Cucumbers and gherkins . . | 641.1 | 709.0 | 467.0 |
| Chillies and green peppers . . . | 108.5 | 108.9 | 120.0 |
| Dry onions . . . . . | 437.8 | 563.0 | 547.0 |
| Garlic . . . . . . . | 89.1 | 127.0 | 127.0 |
| Carrots . . . . . . | 384.7 | 496.5 | 463.0† |
| Other vegetables† . . . . | 146.3 | 321.7 | 344.5 |
| Apples . . . . . . . | 296.8 | 648.2 | 475.0 |
| Pears . . . . . . . | 101.7 | 155.7 | 102.0 |
| Apricots . . . . . . | 57.2 | 102.1 | 44.0 |
| Plums . . . . . . . | 83.4 | 123.0 | 138.0 |
| Grapes . . . . . . . | 306.3 | 513.8 | 336.0 |
| Watermelons . . . . . . | 425.0 | 325.3 | 354.0 |
| Other fruits and berries . . . . | 250.3* | 421.2* | 469.5† |

\* Unofficial figure.
† FAO estimate(s).

Source: FAO.

**LIVESTOCK**

('000 head at 1 January)

|  | 1999 | 2000 | 2001 |
|---|---|---|---|
| Horses | 721 | 698 | 701 |
| Cattle | 11,722 | 10,627 | 9,424 |
| Pigs | 10,083 | 10,073 | 7,652 |
| Sheep | 1,198 | 1,060 | 963 |
| Goats | 828 | 825 | 912 |
| Chickens | 105,000 | 118,000 | 130,000 |

Source: FAO.

**LIVESTOCK PRODUCTS**

('000 metric tons)

|  | 1999 | 2000 | 2001 |
|---|---|---|---|
| Beef and veal | 791.2 | 754.3 | 646.0 |
| Mutton and lamb | 15.0 | 9.2 | 8.0 |
| Pig meat | 656.3 | 675.9 | 591.0 |
| Poultry meat | 204.2 | 193.2 | 239.0 |
| Other meat | 29.1 | 30.2 | 33.0 |
| Cows' milk | 13,140 | 12,436 | 13,169 |
| Sheep's milk | 18 | 17 | 9 |
| Goats' milk | 204 | 257 | 257 |
| Cheese | 64.0 | 80.3 | 110.6 |
| Butter | 108.3 | 135.4 | 151.6 |
| Poultry eggs | 502.0 | 505.3 | 553.8 |
| Hen eggs | 491.5 | 496.6 | 546.4 |
| Honey | 55.5 | 52.4 | 60.0 |
| Cattle hides (fresh)* | 120.5 | 118.5 | 111.6 |

\* FAO estimates.

Source: FAO.

# Forestry

**ROUNDWOOD REMOVALS**

('000 cubic metres, excl. bark)

|  | 1998 | 1999 | 2000 |
|---|---|---|---|
| Sawlogs, veneer logs and logs for sleepers* | 3,290 | 3,379 | 3,379 |
| Other industrial wood* | 953 | 775 | 775 |
| Fuel wood | 1,810* | 1,766* | 4,058† |
| **Total** | 8,453 | 7,920 | 9,859 |

\* FAO estimate(s).

† Unofficial figure.

Source: FAO.

# Fishing

('000 metric tons, live weight)

|  | 1998 | 1999 | 2000 |
|---|---|---|---|
| Capture | 462.3 | 407.9 | 392.7 |
| Blue grenadier | 16.1 | 15.1 | 19.3 |
| Sardinellas | 161.8 | 74.7 | 38.1 |
| European pilchard (sardine) | 12.8 | 49.1 | 40.9 |
| European sprat | 30.3 | 29.2 | 32.7 |
| European anchovy | 3.9 | 5.5 | 16.4 |
| Cape horse mackerel | 18.3 | 4.6 | 13.8 |
| Greenback horse mackerel | 9.3 | 15.3 | 12.2 |
| Chub mackerel | 73.0 | 42.3 | 45.0 |
| Aquaculture | 28.3 | 33.8 | 31.0 |
| Common carp | 18.0 | 20.0 | 20.0 |
| **Total catch** | 490.6 | 441.7 | 423.7 |

Source: FAO, *Yearbook of Fishery Statistics*.

# Mining

('000 metric tons, unless otherwise indicated)

|  | 1998 | 1999 | 2000 |
|---|---|---|---|
| Hard (incl. coking) coal | 74,358 | 80,640 | 79,923 |
| Brown coal (incl. lignite) | 1,409 | 1,184 | 1,067 |
| Crude petroleum | 3,894.8 | 3,797.9 | 3,692.9 |
| Natural gas (million cu m) | 17,967 | 18,092 | 17,847 |
| Iron ore: gross weight | 50,758 | 47,769 | 55,883 |
| Iron ore: metal content* | 28,000 | 26,200 | 30,600 |
| Manganese ore*† | 755 | 675 | 930 |
| Ilmenite concentrate | 507.4 | 536.5 | 576.7 |
| Rutile concentrate | 50.0* | 49.0* | 58.6 |
| Zirconium concentrates* | 65 | 69 | 75 |
| Uranium concentrate (metric tons)† | 500* | 500* | 600 |
| Bentonite* | 300 | 300 | 300 |
| Kaolin | 201.7 | 221.5 | 225.0* |
| Potash salts (crude)*‡ | 35 | 35 | 30 |
| Native sulphur* | 97 | 80 | 80 |
| Salt (unrefined) | 2,500* | 2,185 | 2,287 |
| Graphite (metric tons) | 5,104 | 7,461 | 7,431 |
| Peat* | 1,000 | 1,000 | 1,000 |

\* Estimated production.

† Figures refer to the metal content of ores and concentrates.

‡ Figures refer to potassium oxide content.

Source: US Geological Survey.

# Industry

## SELECTED PRODUCTS
('000 metric tons, unless otherwise indicated)

| | 1997 | 1998 | 1999 |
|---|---|---|---|
| Margarine. | 78 | 90 | 108 |
| Flour | 3,986 | 3,608 | 3,036 |
| Raw sugar* | 2,034 | 1,984 | 1,858 |
| Ethyl alcohol ('000 hectolitres) | 2,461 | 1,576 | 1,360 |
| Wine ('000 hectolitres) | 990 | 771 | 856 |
| Beer ('000 hectolitres) | 6,125 | 6,842 | 8,407 |
| Cigarettes (million) | 54,488 | 59,275 | 54,105 |
| Wool yarn: pure and mixed. | 4.5 | 3.2 | 3.0 |
| Cotton yarn: pure and mixed | 6.4 | 10.6 | 5.4 |
| Flax yarn | 6.5 | 2.9 | 1.7 |
| Woven cotton fabrics (million sq metres) | 28 | 57 | 27 |
| Woven woollen fabrics (million sq metres) | 8.2 | 5.8 | 3.8 |
| Linen fabrics (million sq metres) | 19.7 | 9.9 | 5.5 |
| Footwear, excl. rubber ('000 pairs). | 10,580 | 11,389 | 11,875 |
| Hydrochloric acid. | 107.6 | 81.7 | 47.7 |
| Sulphuric acid | 1,438 | 1,354 | 1,393 |
| Nitric acid. | 17 | 11 | 11 |
| Phosphoric acid | 230.6 | 220.3 | 169.5 |
| Caustic soda (Sodium hydroxide) | 156 | 127 | 99 |
| Soda ash (Sodium carbonate) | 368 | 390 | 456 |
| Nitrogenous fertilizers (a)† | 2,022 | 1,675 | 2,060 |
| Phosphatic fertilizers (b)† | 305 | 240 | 238 |
| Potassic fertilizers (c)† | 49 | 21 | 21 |
| Rubber tyres ('000)‡ | 6,940 | 7,941 | 7,477 |
| Rubber footwear ('000 pairs) | 3,060 | 2,390 | 2,207 |
| Clay building bricks (million) | 1,606 | 1,579 | 1,629 |
| Quicklime. | 3,535 | 3,358 | 3,385 |
| Cement | 5,101 | 5,591 | 5,828 |
| Pig-iron | 21,060 | 21,239 | 23,315 |
| Crude steel: for castings. | 343 | 342 | 480 |
| Crude steel: ingots | 25,629 | 24,447 | 27,393 |
| Tractors (number)§ | 4,645 | 3,248 | 4,984 |
| Household refrigerators ('000) | 382 | 390 | 409 |
| Household washing machines ('000) | 147 | 138 | 127 |
| Radio receivers ('000) | 25 | 10 | 27 |
| Television receivers ('000) | 50 | 93 | 81 |
| Passenger motor cars ('000). | 2 | 26 | 10 |
| Buses and motor coaches (number) | 1,771 | 2,454 | 2,032 |
| Lorries (number). | 3,386 | 4,768 | 7,769 |
| Motorcycles, scooters, etc. ('000) | 1 | — | 1 |
| Bicycles ('000)‖ | 28 | 13 | 31 |
| Electric energy (million kWh) | 181,986 | 172,822¶ | 172,000 |

\* Production from home-grown sugar beet.
† Production of fertilizers is in terms of (a) nitrogen; (b) phosphoric acid; or (c) potassium oxide.
‡ Tyres for road motor vehicles.
§ Tractors of 10 horse-power and over, excluding industrial tractors and road tractors for tractor-trailer combinations.
‖ Excluding children's bicycles.
¶ Estimate.

Source: mainly UN, *Industrial Commodity Statistics Yearbook*.

**Raw sugar** (production from home-grown sugar beet, '000 metric tons): 1,780 in 2000; 1,947 in 2001.

**Footwear, excl. rubber** ('000 pairs): 13,500 in 2000; 14,600 in 2001.

**Cement** ('000 metric tons): 5,300 in 2000; 5,800 in 2001.

**Household refrigerators** ('000): 451 in 2000; 509 in 2001.

**Passenger motor cars** ('000): 32 in 2000; 35 in 2001.

**Electric energy** (million kWh): 171,000 in 2000; 173,000 in 2001.

# Finance

## CURRENCY AND EXCHANGE RATES

### Monetary Units
100 kopiykas = 1 hryvnya.

### Sterling, Dollar and Euro Equivalents (30 May 2003)
£1 sterling = 8.7867 hryvnyas;
US \$1 = 5.3330 hryvnyas;
€1 = 6.3045 hryvnyas;
100 hryvnyas = £11.38 = \$18.75 = €15.86.

### Average Exchange Rate (hryvnyas per US \$)
| | |
|---|---|
| 2000 | 5.4402 |
| 2001 | 5.3722 |
| 2002 | 5.3266 |

Note: Following the dissolution of the USSR in December 1991, Russia and several other former Soviet republics retained the rouble (known as the karbovanets—KRB in Ukraine) as their monetary unit. In November 1992 this currency ceased to be legal tender in Ukraine, and was replaced (initially at par) by a currency coupon, also known as the karbovanets, or kupon, for a transitional period. Following the introduction of the transitional currency, Ukraine operated a system of multiple exchange rates, but in October 1994 the official and auction rates were merged. The unified exchange rate at 31 December 1995 was \$1 = 179,400 KRB. On 2 September 1996 Ukraine introduced a new currency, the hryvnya, at a rate of 100,000 KRB per hryvnya (1.750 hryvnyas per US \$).

## GENERAL BUDGET
(million hryvnyas)*

| Revenue† | 1999 | 2000 | 2001 |
|---|---|---|---|
| Current revenue | 41,120 | 56,709 | 67,761 |
| Tax revenue | 38,959 | 47,810 | 55,982 |
| Taxes on income, profits and capital gains | 11,366 | 14,517 | 17,759 |
| Social security contributions | 9,594 | 11,531 | 15,047 |
| Pension fund | 8,644 | 10,379 | 13,115 |
| Domestic taxes on goods and services | 15,898 | 19,064 | 19,716 |
| General sales tax, turnover tax and value-added tax | 11,369 | 11,898 | 11,308 |
| Value-added tax | 8,409 | 9,441 | 10,348 |
| Excises. | 1,787 | 2,240 | 2,654 |
| Taxes on natural resources | 1,314 | 3,060 | 3,682 |
| Land tax | 1,090 | 1,376 | 1,619 |
| Taxes on international trade and transactions | 1,263 | 1,947 | 2,422 |
| Import duties | 1,236 | 1,555 | 1,938 |
| Other current revenue | 2,161 | 8,899 | 11,779 |
| Entrepreneurial and property income | 859 | 1,280 | 3,428 |
| Gas transit fee | 137 | 236 | 1,943 |
| Administration fees and charges. | 367 | 5,946 | 6,507 |
| Fines and forfeits | 710 | 1,371 | 1,413 |
| Capital revenue | 434 | 65 | 453 |
| **Total** | **41,554** | **56,774** | **68,214** |

| Expenditure and net lending | 1999 | 2000 | 2001 |
|---|---|---|---|
| General public services . . . . | 1,876 | 4,229 | 4,420 |
| Executive and legislative organs | 1,206 | 2,868 | 3,168 |
| Defence . . . . . . . | 1,709 | 2,504 | 3,337 |
| Public order and safety . . . . | 1,527 | 2,637 | 3,717 |
| Law enforcement . . . . . | 1,441 | 2,468 | 3,512 |
| Education . . . . . . . | 3,725 | 5,843 | 7,798 |
| Health . . . . . . . . | 3,250 | 4,251 | 5,403 |
| Social security and welfare . . . | 20,200 | 24,581 | 30,293 |
| Social security . . . . . . | 5,938 | 8,498 | 11,049 |
| Pension fund . . . . . . | 10,841 | 12,678 | 15,547 |
| Housing and community services . | 1,376 | 1,381 | 1,746 |
| Recreational, cultural and religious affairs . . . . . . . | 721 | 1,038 | 1,319 |
| Economic services . . . . | 6,562 | 6,439 | 7,424 |
| Fuel and energy . . . . . | 1,675 | 1,958 | 2,374 |
| Coal mines . . . . . . | 1,100 | 898 | 1,198 |
| Mineral resources extraction. . | 1,377 | 1,291 | 1,442 |
| Transportation and communication . . . . . | 2,023 | 1,883 | 1,778 |
| Road transport . . . . . | 1,742 | 1,534 | 1,174 |
| Interest payments . . . . | 3,010 | 3,845 | 3,931 |
| Foreign . . . . . . . | 1,759 | 1,461 | 2,281 |
| Domestic . . . . . . | 1,251 | 2,384 | 1,650 |
| Other expenditure . . . . | 544 | 1,882 | 924 |
| **Total** . . . . . . . . | **44,500** | **58,630** | **70,312** |

* Figures refer to the consolidated accounts of central government and those of local government.

† Excluding grants received (million hryvynas): 1 in 1999; 0 in 2000; 221 in 2001.

**2002** (million hryvnyas, preliminary figures): Revenue and grants 80,438 (Tax revenue 68,370; Non-tax revenue 11,158, Capital revenue 618; Grants 292); Expenditure and net lending 79,395.

Source: IMF, *Ukraine: Statistical Appendix* (June 2003).

## INTERNATIONAL RESERVES
(US $ million at 31 December)

| | 2000 | 2001 | 2002 |
|---|---|---|---|
| Gold* . . . . . . . . | 123.7 | 134.1 | 175.4 |
| IMF special drawing rights . . . | 249.1 | 251.1 | 28.3 |
| Foreign exchange . . . . . | 1,103.6 | 2,704.3 | 4,213.1 |
| **Total** . . . . . . . . | **1,476.4** | **3,089.5** | **4,416.8** |

* National valuation.

Source: IMF, *International Financial Statistics.*

## MONEY SUPPLY
(million hryvnyas at 31 December)

| | 2000 | 2001 | 2002 |
|---|---|---|---|
| Currency outside banks . . . . | 12,799.0 | 19,464.8 | 26,433.8 |
| Demand deposits at banks . . . | 8,013.5 | 10,301.5 | 13,806.8 |
| **Total money** (incl. others) . . . | **20,825.3** | **29,795.6** | **40,281.1** |

Source: IMF, *International Financial Statistics.*

## COST OF LIVING
(Index of consumer prices; base: 1992 = 100)

| | 1998 | 1999 | 2000 |
|---|---|---|---|
| Food (incl. tobacco) . . . . . | 446,690.4 | 570,891.4 | 767,854.9 |
| **All items** . . . . . . . . | 527,662.7 | 647,356.0 | 829,930.5 |

Source: ILO.

## NATIONAL ACCOUNTS
(million hryvnyas at current prices)

**Expenditure on the Gross Domestic Product**

| | 1998 | 1999 | 2000 |
|---|---|---|---|
| Final consumption expenditure . | 83,569 | 100,481 | 128,901 |
| Household . . . . . . . | 58,323 | 71,310 | 92,406 |
| Non-profit institutions serving households . . . . . . | 3,126 | 3,305 | 3,909 |
| General government . . . . | 22,120 | 25,866 | 32,586 |
| Gross capital formation . . . . | 21,357 | 22,746 | 33,531 |
| Gross fixed capital formation . | 20,096 | 25,131 | 33,427 |
| Changes in inventories . . . | 1,128 | −2,519 | −42 |
| Acquisitions, *less* disposals, of valuables . . . . . . | 133 | 134 | 146 |
| **Total domestic expenditure** . | **104,926** | **126,034** | **162,432** |
| Exports of goods and services . . | 42,974 | 70,884 | 106,200 |
| *Less* Imports of goods and services | 45,307 | 63,669 | 98,562 |
| **GDP in purchasers' values** . . | **102,593** | **130,442** | **170,070** |

Source: UN, *National Accounts Statistics.*

**Gross domestic product** (million hryvnyas at current prices): 130,442 (revised) in 1999; 170,070 in 2000; 201,927 (provisional) in 2001.

**Gross Domestic Product by Economic Activity**

| | 1998 | 1999 | 2000 |
|---|---|---|---|
| Agriculture . . . . . . . | 12,400 | 15,500 | 24,600 |
| Manufacturing* . . . . . . | 27,600 | 37,700 | 47,700 |
| Construction . . . . . . | 4,900 | 5,400 | 6,100 |
| Trade and catering . . . . | 7,600 | 9,300 | 15,200 |
| Transport, storage and communications . . . . . | 12,600 | 15,400 | 19,800 |
| Public adminstration and defence; compulsory social security . . | 4,700 | 5,200 | 6,800 |
| Education; health and social work; other community, social and personal services . . . . . | 13,200 | 14,900 | 17,500 |
| **Sub-total** (incl. others) . . . . | **88,000** | **109,600** | **146,000** |
| *Less* Financial intermediation services, indirectly measured . | 1,000 | 1,200 | 1,700 |
| **Gross value added in basic prices** . . . . . . . | **87,000** | **108,400** | **144,300** |
| Taxes on products . . . . | 17,300 | 24,100 | 27,300 |
| *Less* Subsidies on products . . . | 1,700 | 2,100 | 1,500 |
| **GDP in market prices** . . . | **102,600** | **130,400** | **170,100** |

* Including mining and quarrying, manufacturing (except printing and publishing), electricity, gas and water.

Source: UN, *National Accounts Statistics.*

## BALANCE OF PAYMENTS
(US $ million)

|  | 2000 | 2001 | 2002 |
|---|---|---|---|
| Exports of goods f.o.b. . . . . | 15,722 | 17,091 | 18,669 |
| Imports of goods f.o.b. . . . . | −14,943 | −16,893 | −17,959 |
| **Trade balance** . . . . . | 779 | 198 | 710 |
| Exports of services . . . . | 3,800 | 3,995 | 4,682 |
| Imports of services . . . . | −3,004 | −3,580 | −3,535 |
| **Balance on goods and services** | 1,575 | 613 | 1,857 |
| Other income received . . . | 143 | 167 | 165 |
| Other income paid . . . . | −1,085 | −834 | −769 |
| **Balance on goods, services and** | | | |
| **income** . . . . . | 633 | −54 | 1,253 |
| Current transfers received . . | 967 | 1,516 | 1,967 |
| Current transfers paid . . . | −119 | −60 | −46 |
| **Current balance** . . . . | 1,481 | 1,402 | 3,174 |
| Capital account (net) . . . | −8 | 3 | 17 |
| Direct investment abroad . . . | −1 | −23 | 5 |
| Direct investment from abroad. . | 595 | 792 | 693 |
| Portfolio investment assets. . . | −4 | 1 | 2 |
| Portfolio investment liabilities . . | −197 | −867 | −1,718 |
| Other investment assets . . . | −449 | −1,015 | −781 |
| Other investment liabilities . . | −696 | 921 | 734 |
| Net errors and omissions . . . | −148 | −221 | −895 |
| **Overall balance** . . . . . | 573 | 993 | 1,231 |

Sources: IMF, *International Financial Statistics*.

# External Trade

## PRINCIPAL COMMODITIES
(distribution by SITC, US $ million)

| Imports f.o.b. | 1998 | 1999 | 2000 |
|---|---|---|---|
| **Food and live animals** . . . | 593.8 | 595.3 | 624.0 |
| **Crude materials (inedible)** | | | |
| **except fuels** . . . . . | 669.6 | 628.5 | 824.0 |
| Metalliferous ores and metal scrap | 229.1 | 227.6 | 421.0 |
| **Mineral fuels, lubricants, etc.** | 5,940.7 | 5,213.6 | 5,998.0 |
| **Chemicals and related** | | | |
| **products** . . . . . | 1,338.3 | 1,093.7 | 1,304.0 |
| **Basic manufactures** . . . | 1,851.8 | 1,345.7 | 1,752.0 |
| **Machinery and transport** | | | |
| **equipment**. . . . . | 3,172.1 | 2,078.7 | 2,445.0 |
| Road vehicles . . . . . | 752.7 | 423.3 | 430.0 |
| **Miscellaneous manufactured** | | | |
| **articles**. . . . . | 511.2 | 409.4 | 409.0 |
| **Total** (incl. others) . . . . | 14,675.6 | 11,846.1 | 14,010.8 |

| Exports f.o.b. | 1998 | 1999 | 2000 |
|---|---|---|---|
| **Food and live animals** . . . | 918.0 | 1,073.8 | 815.0 |
| Cereals and cereal preparations | 378.1 | 551.7 | 159.0 |
| **Crude materials (inedible)** | | | |
| **except fuels** . . . . . | 903.9 | 620.9 | 805.0 |
| Metalliferous ores and metal scrap | 502.4 | 355.5 | 465.0 |
| **Mineral fuels, lubricants, etc.** | 520.7 | 701.0 | 808.0 |
| **Chemicals and related** | | | |
| **products** . . . . . | 1,350.8 | 1,134.6 | 1,626.0 |
| Inorganic chemicals . . . . | 508.2 | 443.2 | 630.0 |
| **Basic manufactures** . . . | 6,107.1 | 5,574.0 | 7,383.0 |
| Iron and steel. . . . . | 4,204.4 | 3,888.8 | 5,031.0 |
| Non-ferrous metals . . . | 325.2 | 408.4 | 540.0 |
| **Machinery and transport** | | | |
| **equipment**. . . . . | 1,721.7 | 1,331.4 | 1,797.0 |
| **Miscellaneous manufactured** | | | |
| **articles**. . . . . | 569.6 | 523.1 | 633.0 |
| **Total** (incl. others) . . . . | 12,637.4 | 11,581.6 | 14,579.6 |

Source: UN, *International Trade Statistics Yearbook*.

## PRINCIPAL TRADING PARTNERS
(US $ million)

| Imports f.o.b. | 1999 | 2000 | 2001 |
|---|---|---|---|
| Austria. . . . . . . | 133.4 | 185.1 | 202.1 |
| Belarus . . . . . | 343.5 | 601.9 | 407.1 |
| China, People's Republic . . . | 110.4 | 131.8 | 195.6 |
| Czech Republic . . . . | 131.4 | 162.9 | 203.0 |
| France (incl. Monaco) . . . | 236.9 | 237.4 | 296.0 |
| Germany . . . . . | 942.9 | 1,134.4 | 1,380.2 |
| Hungary . . . . . | 123.6 | 165.4 | 172.1 |
| Italy . . . . . . | 277.0 | 346.6 | 411.9 |
| Japan . . . . . . | 98.7 | 99.1 | 164.7 |
| Kazakhstan . . . . | 164.9 | 412.8 | 666.0 |
| Netherlands . . . . | 133.6 | 146.6 | 177.0 |
| Poland . . . . . . | 258.5 | 312.5 | 450.8 |
| Russia . . . . . . | 5,592.2 | 5,824.9 | 5,813.5 |
| Slovakia . . . . . | 131.6 | 124.4 | 139.9 |
| Sweden . . . . . | 114.5 | 150.4 | 171.5 |
| Switzerland-Liechtenstein . . . | 93.1 | 217.7 | 149.7 |
| Turkey . . . . . . | 142.7 | 159.9 | 138.2 |
| Turkmenistan . . . . | 481.0 | 946.2 | 1,654.1 |
| United Kingdom . . . . | 143.6 | 202.8 | 229.1 |
| USA . . . . . . | 401.7 | 360.5 | 457.9 |
| Uzbekistan . . . . . | 87.3 | 178.0 | 193.0 |
| **Total** (incl. others) . . . . . | 11,846.1 | 14,010.8 | 15,775.1 |

| Exports f.o.b. | 1999 | 2000 | 2001 |
|---|---|---|---|
| Algeria. . . . . . | 184.5 | 235.8 | 173.3 |
| Austria. . . . . . | 139.8 | 163.6 | 174.1 |
| Belarus . . . . . | 345.7 | 272.1 | 244.3 |
| Bulgaria . . . . . | 294.5 | 382.5 | 298.5 |
| China, People's Republic . . . | 730.4 | 628.9 | 542.1 |
| Czech Republic . . . . | 141.4 | 188.9 | 194.4 |
| Egypt . . . . . . | 171.3 | 221.0 | 204.2 |
| Germany . . . . . | 560.1 | 741.4 | 710.9 |
| Hungary . . . . . | 278.2 | 327.3 | 468.5 |
| India . . . . . . | 173.8 | 168.3 | 129.9 |
| Israel . . . . . | 153.8 | 105.9 | 132.6 |
| Italy . . . . . . | 463.6 | 644.2 | 839.7 |
| Latvia . . . . . | 49.1 | 166.5 | 251.2 |
| Moldova . . . . . | 122.8 | 176.3 | 274.4 |
| Netherlands . . . . | 83.6 | 138.0 | 206.6 |
| Pakistan . . . . . | 182.4 | 30.2 | 32.6 |
| Poland . . . . . | 301.4 | 417.9 | 497.4 |
| Romania . . . . . | 75.6 | 164.6 | 266.0 |
| Russia . . . . . . | 2,396.4 | 3,515.6 | 3,679.5 |
| Slovakia . . . . . | 199.2 | 230.9 | 243.1 |
| Spain . . . . . | 105.8 | 162.9 | 245.0 |
| Syria . . . . . . | 122.5 | 160.4 | 177.6 |
| Turkey . . . . . . | 673.4 | 868.5 | 1,009.4 |
| Turkmenistan . . . . | 102.1 | 148.5 | 106.5 |
| United Kingdom . . . . | 108.4 | 137.7 | 368.5 |
| USA . . . . . . | 435.9 | 727.4 | 569.2 |
| **Total** (incl. others) . . . . . | 11,581.6 | 14,579.6 | 16,264.7 |

Source: UN, *International Trade Statistics Yearbook*.

# Transport

## RAILWAYS
(traffic)

|  | 1997 | 1998 | 1999 |
|---|---|---|---|
| Passenger-kilometres (million) . . | 54,540 | 49,938 | 47,600 |
| Freight ton-kilometres (million) . | 160,433 | 158,693 | 156,336 |

Source: UN, *Statistical Yearbook*.

## ROAD TRAFFIC
('000 motor vehicles in use)

|  | 1998 | 1999 | 2000 |
|---|---|---|---|
| Passenger cars . . . . . | 4,877.8 | 5,210.8 | 5,250.1 |

Source: International Road Federation, *World Road Statistics*.

UKRAINE

## SHIPPING

**Merchant Fleet**
(registered at 31 December)

|  | 2000 | 2001 | 2002 |
|---|---|---|---|
| Number of vessels . . . . | 894 | 838 | 828 |
| Total displacement ('000 grt) . . | 1,546.3 | 1,407.7 | 1,349.9 |

Source: Lloyd's Register-Fairplay, *World Fleet Statistics*.

**International Sea-borne Freight Traffic**
('000 metric tons)

|  | 1997 | 1998 | 1999 |
|---|---|---|---|
| Goods loaded . . . . . . | 55,236 | 64,656 | 77,004 |
| Goods unloaded . . . . . | 5,760 | 7,044 | 7,116 |

Source: UN, *Monthly Bulletin of Statistics*.

## CIVIL AVIATION
(traffic on scheduled services)

|  | 1997 | 1998 | 1999 |
|---|---|---|---|
| Kilometres flown (million) . . . | 36 | 37 | 31 |
| Passengers carried ('000) . . . | 1,190 | 1,064 | 891 |
| Passenger-kilometres (million) . . | 1,853 | 1,720 | 1,312 |
| Total ton-kilometres (million) . . | 186 | 188 | 138 |

Source: UN, *Statistical Yearbook*.

## Tourism

**FOREIGN TOURIST ARRIVALS**
('000)

| Country of residence | 1998 | 1999 | 2000 |
|---|---|---|---|
| Belarus . . . . . | 1,238.9 | 548.4 | 530.9 |
| Czech Republic . . . . | 75.6 | 59.9 | 39.9 |
| Germany . . . . . . | 62.5 | 59.3 | 62.4 |
| Hungary . . . . . . | 440.9 | 506.4 | 480.3 |
| Moldova . . . . . . | 1,292.8 | 1,051.7 | 1,199.1 |
| Poland . . . . . . . | 256.0 | 184.7 | 182.2 |
| Russian Federation . . . . | 2,116.8 | 1,222.4 | 1,332.8 |
| Slovakia . . . . . . | 149.0 | 84.5 | 57.7 |
| USA . . . . . . | 46.0 | 54.0 | 52.9 |
| **Total** (incl. others) . . . . . | 6,207.6 | 4,232.4 | 4,405.7 |

**Tourist receipts** (US $ million): 270 in 1997; 315 in 1998; 327 in 1999; 394 in 2000; 573 in 2001.

Sources: World Tourism Organization, *Yearbook of Tourism Statistics*; and National Bank of Ukraine.

## Communications Media

|  | 1999 | 2000 | 2001 |
|---|---|---|---|
| Television receivers ('000 in use) . | 22,000 | 23,000 | n.a. |
| Telephones ('000 main lines in use) | 10,074.0 | 10,417.2 | 10,669.6 |
| Facsimile machines (number in use) . . . . . . . . . | 47,700 | 42,161 | n.a. |
| Mobile cellular telephones ('000 subscribers). . . . . . | 216.6 | 818.5 | 2,224.6 |
| Personal computers ('000 in use) | 800 | 890 | 920 |
| Internet users ('000) . . . . . | 200 | 300 | 600 |

**Radio receivers** ('000 in use): 45,050 in 1997.

**Book production** (incl. pamphlets, 1996): Titles 6,460; Copies ('000) 50,905.

**Daily newspapers** (1996): Number 44; Average circulation ('000) 2,780.

**Periodicals** (1996): Titles 2,162; Average circulation ('000) 19,934.

Sources: UNESCO, *Statistical Yearbook*; International Telecommunication Union.

## Education

(2001/02)

|  | Institutions | Teachers | Students |
|---|---|---|---|
| Pre-primary. . . . . . . | 15,400 | 107,700 | 968,000 |
| Primary . . . . . . . } | 22,200 | 568,000 | 6,601,000 |
| General secondary . . . . . } | | | |
| Specialized secondary: teacher training* . . . . . . . | 38 | n.a. | 21,300 |
| Specialized secondary: vocational | 965 | n.a. | 512,300 |
| Higher† . . . . . . . | 983 | 121,300* | 2,109,300 |

* 1993/94.
† Including evening and correspondence courses.

**Adult literacy rate** (UNESCO estimates): 99.6% (males 99.8%; females 99.5%) in 2001 (Source: UN Development Programme, *Human Development Report*).

# Directory

## Constitution

The Constitution of the Republic of Ukraine, summarized below, was adopted at the Fifth Session of the Verkhovna Rada on 28 June 1996. It replaced the Soviet-era Constitution (Fundamental Law), originally approved on 12 April 1978, but amended several times after Ukraine gained independence in 1991, and entered into force the day of its adoption.

### FUNDAMENTAL PRINCIPLES

The Republic of Ukraine is a sovereign and independent, unitary and law-based state, in which power is exercised directly by the people through the bodies of state power and local self-government. The life, honour, dignity and health of the individual are recognized as the highest social value. The Constitution is the highest legal authority; the power of the State is divided between the legislative, the executive and the judicial branches. The state language is Ukrainian. The use and protection of Russian and other languages of national minorities, and the development of minorities' ethnic and cultural traditions is guaranteed. The State ensures protection of all forms of ownership rights and management, as well as the social orientation of the economy. The state symbols of Ukraine, its flag, coat of arms and anthem, are established.

### THE RIGHTS, FREEDOMS AND DUTIES OF CITIZENS

The rights and freedoms of individuals are declared to be unalienable and inviolable regardless of race, sex, political or religious affiliation, wealth, social origin or other characteristics. Fundamental rights, such as the freedoms of speech and association and the right to private property, are guaranteed. Citizens have the right to engage in political activity and to own private property. All individuals are entitled to work and to join professional unions to protect their employment rights. The Constitution commits the State to the provision of health care, housing, social security and education. All citizens have the right to legal assistance. Obligations of the citizenry include military service and taxes. The age of enfranchisement for Ukrainian citizens is 18 years. Elections to organs of state authority are declared to be free and conducted on the basis of universal, equal and direct suffrage by secret ballot.

## THE VERKHOVNA RADA

The Verkhovna Rada is the sole organ of legislative authority in Ukraine. It consists of 450 members, elected for a four-year term. Only Ukrainian citizens aged over 21 years, who have resided in Ukraine for the five previous years and have not been convicted for a criminal offence, are eligible for election to parliament. The Verkhovna Rada is a permanently acting body, which elects its own Chairman and Deputy Chairmen.

The most important functions of the legislature include: the enactment of laws; the approval of the state budget and other state programmes; the scheduling of presidential elections; the removal (impeachment) of the President; consenting to the President's appointment of the Prime Minister; the declaration of war or conclusion of peace; the foreign deployment of troops; and consenting to international treaty obligations within the time-limit prescribed by law. Within 15 days of a law passed by the Verkhovna Rada being received by the President, the President shall officially promulgate it or return it for repeat consideration by parliament. If, during such consideration, the legislature re-adopts the law by a two-thirds' majority, the President is obliged to sign it and officially promulgate it within 10 days. The President of Ukraine may terminate the authority of the Verkhovna Rada if, within 30 days of a single, regular session a plenary session cannot be convened, except within the last six months of the President's term of office.

Some of the Verkhovna Rada's financial responsibilities, such as the oversight of fiscal resources by the Accounting Chamber on its behalf, are specified in the Constitution. The monetary unit of Ukraine is the hryvnya and providing for the stability of the currency is the primary function of the central state bank, the National Bank of Ukraine.

## THE PRESIDENT OF THE REPUBLIC

The President of the Republic of Ukraine is the Head of State, and is guarantor of state sovereignty and the territorial integrity of Ukraine. The President is directly elected for a period of five years. A presidential candidate must be aged over 35 years and a resident of the country for the 10 years prior to the election. The President may hold office for no more than two consecutive terms.

The President's main responsibilities include: the scheduling of elections and of referendums on constitutional amendments, the conclusion of international treaties; and the promulgation of laws. The President is responsible for appointing a Prime Minister, with the consent of the Verkhovna Rada, and for dismissing the Prime Minister and deciding the issue of his resignation. The President appoints members of the Cabinet of Ministers on the recommendation of the Prime Minister.

The President is the Supreme Commander of the Armed Forces of the Republic of Ukraine and chairs the National Security and Defence Council. The President may be removed from office by the Verkhovna Rada by impeachment, for reasons of state treason or another crime. The decision to remove the President must be approved by at least a three-quarters' majority in the Verkhovna Rada. In the event of the termination of the authority of the President, the Prime Minister executes the duties of the President until the election and entry into office of a new President.

## THE CABINET OF MINISTERS

The principal organ of executive government is the Cabinet of Ministers, which is responsible before the President and accountable to the Verkhovna Rada. The Cabinet supervises the implementation of state policy and the state budget and the maintenance of law and order. The Cabinet of Ministers is headed by the Prime Minister, appointed by the President with the approval of more than one-half of the parliamentary deputies. The duties of the Prime Minister include the submission of proposals to the President on the creation, reorganization and liquidation of ministries and other central bodies of executive authority. The members of the Cabinet, which also include a First Deputy Prime Minister and three Deputy Prime Ministers, are appointed by the President upon the recommendation of the Prime Minister. The Cabinet of Ministers must resign when a new President is elected, or in the event of the adoption of a vote of 'no confidence' by the Verkhovna Rada.

## JUDICIAL POWER

Justice in Ukraine is administered by the Constitutional Court and by courts of general jurisdiction. The Supreme Court of Ukraine is the highest judicial organ of general jurisdiction. Judges hold their position permanently, except for justices of the Constitutional Court and first judicial appointments, which are made by the President for a five-year term. Other judges, with the exception of justices of the Constitutional Court, are elected by the Verkhovna Rada. Judges must be at least 25 years of age, have a higher legal education and at least three years' work experience in the field of law, and have resided in Ukraine for no fewer than 10 years. The Procuracy of Ukraine is headed by the General Procurator, who is appointed with the consent of parliament and dismissed by the President. The term of office of the General Procurator is five years.

A Superior Justice Council, responsible for the submission of proposals regarding the appointment or dismissal of judges, functions in Ukraine. The Council consists of 20 members. The Chairman of the Supreme Court of Ukraine, the Minister of Justice, and the General Procurator are *ex-officio* members of the Superior Justice Council.

## LOCAL SELF-GOVERNMENT

The administrative and territorial division of Ukraine consists of the Autonomous Republic of Crimea, 24 provinces (oblasts), the cities of Kiev and Sevastopol (which possess special status), districts (raions), cities, settlements and villages. Local self-government is the right of territorial communities. The principal organs of territorial communities are the district and provincial councils, which, with their chairmen, are directly elected for a term of four years. The chairmen of district and provincial councils are elected by the relevant council and head their executive structure. Provincial and district councils monitor the implementation of programmes of socio-economic and cultural development of the relevant provinces and districts, and adopt and monitor the implementation of district and provincial budgets, which are derived from the state budget.

## THE AUTONOMOUS REPUBLIC OF CRIMEA

The Autonomous Republic of Crimea is an inseparable, integral part of Ukraine. It has its own Constitution, which is adopted by the Supreme Council of the Autonomous Republic of Crimea (the representative organ of Crimea) and approved by the Verkhovna Rada. Legislation adopted by the Autonomous Republic's Supreme Council and the decisions of its Council of Ministers must not contravene the Constitution and laws of Ukraine. The Chairman of the Council of Ministers is appointed and dismissed by the Supreme Council of the Autonomous Republic of Crimea with the consent of the President of Ukraine. Justice in Crimea is administered by courts belonging to the single court system of Ukraine. An Office of the Representative of the President of Ukraine functions in Crimea.

The jurisdiction of the Autonomous Republic of Crimea includes: organizing and conducting local referendums; implementing the republican budget on the basis of the state policy of Ukraine; ensuring the function and development of the state and national languages and cultures; participating in the development and fulfilment of programmes for the return of deported peoples.

## THE CONSTITUTIONAL COURT

The Constitutional Court consists of 18 justices, six of whom are appointed by the President, six by the Verkhovna Rada and six by the assembly of judges of Ukraine. Candidates must be citizens of Ukraine, who are at least 40 years of age and have resided in Ukraine for the previous 20 years. Justices of the Constitutional Court serve a term of nine years, with no right to reappointment. A Chairman is elected by a secret ballot of the members for a single three-year term.

The Constitutional Court provides binding interpretations of the Constitution. It rules on the constitutionality of: parliamentary legislation; acts of the President and the Cabinet of Ministers; the official interpretation of the Constitution of Ukraine; international agreements; and the impeachment of the President of Ukraine.

## CONSTITUTIONAL AMENDMENTS AND THE ADOPTION OF A NEW CONSTITUTION

A draft law on amending the Constitution may be presented to the Verkhovna Rada by the President or at least one-third of the constitutional composition of the parliament. A draft law on amending the Constitution, which has been given preliminary approval by a majority of the constitutional composition of the Verkhovna Rada, is considered adopted if it receives the support of at least a two-thirds' parliamentary majority. In the case of its approval it is confirmed by a nation-wide referendum designated by the President.

Note: In April 2000 participants in a national referendum approved a number of constitutional amendments permitting: the dissolution of the Verkhovna Rada, should it fail to approve the state budget within a three-month period; the reduction of the number of deputies from 450 to 300; the limitation of deputies' immunity from prosecution; and the introduction of a bicameral legislature.

# The Government

## HEAD OF STATE

**President:** LEONID D. KUCHMA (elected 10 July 1994, re-elected 14 November 1999, re-inaugurated 30 November 1999).

## CABINET OF MINISTERS
(October 2003)

**Prime Minister:** VIKTOR F. YANUKOVYCH.

**First Deputy Prime Minister and Minister of Finance:** MYKOLA YA. AZAROV.

**Deputy Prime Minister:** VITALIY A. HAIDUK.

**Deputy Prime Minister, responsible for the Agro-industrial Complex:** IVAN H. KYRYLENKO.

**Deputy Prime Minister, responsible for Humanitarian Issues:** DMYTRO V. TABACHNYK.

**Minister of Agricultural Policy:** SERHIY M. RYZHUK.

**Minister of Internal Affairs:** MYKOLA V. BILOKON.

**Minister of the Economy and Progress Towards European Integration:** VALERIY I. KHOROSHKOVSKYI.

**Minister of Transport:** HEORHIY M. KIRPA.

**Minister of Defence:** Gen. YEVHEN K. MARCHUK.

**Minister of Ecology and Natural Resources:** SERHIY V. POLYAKOV.

**Minister of Foreign Affairs:** KOSTYANTYN I. HRYSHCHENKO.

**Minister for Emergency Situations and Protection of the Population from the Consequences of the Chornobyl Catastrophe:** HRYHORIY V. REVA.

**Minister of Relations with the Verkhovna Rada:** IVAN I. TKALENKO.

**Minister of Art and Culture:** YURIY P. BOHUTSKYI.

**Minister of Education and Science:** VASYL H. KREMEN.

**Minister of Health Care:** ANDRIY V. PIDAYEV.

**Minister of Fuel and Energy:** SERHIY F. YERMILOV.

**Minister of Labour and Social Policy:** MYKHAILO M. PAPIYEV.

**Minister of Industrial Policy:** ANATOLIY K. MYALYTSYA.

**Minister of Justice:** OLEKSANDR V. LAVRYNOVYCH.

**Minister of the Cabinet of Ministers of Ukraine:** ANATOLIY V. TOLSTOUKHOV.

## MINISTRIES

**Office of the President:** 01220 Kiev, vul. Bankova 11; tel. (44) 291-53-33; fax (44) 293-61-61; e-mail president@adm.gov.ua; internet www.president.gov.ua.

**Cabinet of Ministers:** 01008 Kiev, vul. M. Hrushevskoho 12/2; tel. (44) 293-21-71; fax (44) 293-20-93; e-mail web@kmu.gov.ua; internet www.kmu.gov.ua.

**Ministry of Agricultural Policy:** 01001 Kiev, vul. Khreshchatyk 24; tel. (44) 226-34-66; fax (44) 229-87-56; e-mail ministr@minapk.kiev.ua; internet www.minagro.gov.ua.

**Ministry of Art and Culture:** 01030 Kiev, vul. Ivana Franka 19; tel. (44) 226-26-45; fax (44) 235-32-57; e-mail info@mincult.gov.ua; internet www.mincult.gov.ua.

**Ministry of Defence:** 03168 Kiev, Povitroflotskyi pr. 6; tel. (44) 226-26-56; fax (44) 226-20-15; e-mail pressmou@pressmou.kiev.ua; internet www.mil.gov.ua.

**Ministry of Ecology and Natural Resources:** 01601 Kiev, vul. Khreshchatyk 5; tel. (44) 228-06-44; fax (44) 229-83-83; e-mail menr@menr.gov.ua; internet www.menr.gov.ua.

**Ministry of the Economy and Progress Towards European Integration:** 01008 Kiev, vul. M. Hrushevskoho 12/2; tel. (44) 293-93-94; fax (44) 226-31-81; e-mail meconomy@me.gov.ua; internet www.me.gov.ua.

**Ministry of Education and Science:** 01135 Kiev, pr. Peremohy 10; tel. (44) 226-26-61; fax (44) 274-10-49; e-mail vgk@ministry.edu-ua.net; internet www.mon.gov.ua.

**Ministry for Emergency Situations and Protection of the Population from the Consequences of the Chornobyl Catastrophe:** 01030 Kiev, vul. O. Honchara 55; tel. (44) 247-30-50; e-mail main@mns.gov.ua; internet www.mns.gov.ua.

**Ministry of Finance:** 01008 Kiev, vul. M. Hrushevskoho 12/2; tel. (44) 293-74-66; fax (44) 293-21-78; e-mail infomf@minfin.gov.ua.

**Ministry of Foreign Affairs:** 01018 Kiev, pl. Mykhailivska 1; tel. (44) 21-28-33; fax (44) 226-31-69; internet www.mfa.gov.ua.

**Ministry of Fuel and Energy:** 01601 Kiev, vul. Khreshchatik 30; tel. (44) 221-43-64; fax (44) 462-05-61; e-mail kanc@mintop.energy.gov.ua; internet mpe.energy.gov.ua.

**Ministry of Health Care:** 01021 Kiev, vul. M. Hrushevskoho 7; tel. (44) 253-24-39; fax (44) 253-69-75; internet www.moz.gov.ua.

**Ministry of Industrial Policy:** 03035 Kiev, vul. Surikova 3; tel. (44) 245-47-78; fax (44) 246-32-14.

**Ministry of Internal Affairs:** 01024 Kiev, vul. Akademika Bohomoltsya 10; tel. (44) 291-18-30; fax (44) 291-16-52; e-mail mail@centrmia.gov.ua; internet www.centrmia.gov.ua.

**Ministry of Justice:** 01001 Kiev, vul. Horodetskoho 13; tel. and fax (44) 228-37-23; e-mail themis@minjust.gov.ua; internet www.minjust.gov.ua.

**Ministry of Labour and Social Policy:** 01023 Kiev, vul. Esplanadna 8/10; tel. (44) 220-90-97; fax (44) 220-90-64; e-mail public@subs-mspp.kiev.ua; internet www.minpraci.gov.ua.

**Ministry of Relations with the Verkhovna Rada:** 01008 Kiev, vul. M. Hrushevskoho 12/2.

**Ministry of Transport:** 03680 Kiev, vul. Shchorsa 7/9; tel. (44) 446-30-30; e-mail info@mintrans.gov.ua; internet www.mintrans.kiev.ua.

### State Committees

**State Committee for Archives:** 03110 Kiev, vul. Solomyanska 24; tel. (44) 277-36-55; fax (44) 277-34-44; e-mail mail@archives.gov.ua; internet www.archives.gov.ua; Chair. Prof. HENNADIY V. BORYAK.

**State Committee for Border Control:** 01034 Kiev, vul. Volodymyrska 26; tel. (44) 212-87-77; fax (44) 212-39-80; e-mail dkk@pvu.gov.ua; internet www.pvu.gov.ua; Chair. MYKOLA M. LYTVYN.

**State Committee for Communication and Information:** 01001 Kiev, vul. Khreshchatyk 22; tel. (44) 228-15-00; fax (44) 212-30-74; e-mail l.bychenok@stc.gov.ua; internet www.stc.gov.ua; Chair. MYKOLA V. HONCHAR.

**State Committee for Construction and Architecture:** 03150 Kiev, vul. Dymytrova 24; tel. (44) 226-22-08; fax (44) 227-23-35; e-mail untp@build.gov.ua; internet www.build.gov.ua; Chair. VALERIY I. CHEREP.

**State Committee for Energy Conservation:** 04112 Kiev, vul. Honty 1; tel. (44) 456-81-83; fax (44) 456-80-23; e-mail cenef@elan-ua.net; internet www.cenef.kiev.ua; Chair. YURIY I. SHULGA.

**State Committee for Exercise and Sports:** 01023 Kiev, vul. Esplanadna 42; tel. (44) 220-03-66; fax (44) 220-12-94; e-mail komitet@sport.kiev.ua; internet www.sport.gov.ua; Chair. MARIYA M. BULATOVA.

**State Committee for Family and Youth Affairs:** 01025 Kiev, vul. Desyatynna 14; tel. (44) 229-11-24; fax (44) 228-55-40; e-mail dovzhenko@dksm.gov.ua; Chair. VALENTYNA I. DOVZHENKO.

**State Committee for Forestry:** 01023 Kiev, vul. Sh. Rustaveli 9A; tel. (44) 226-32-53; fax (44) 228-77-94; e-mail dklg@nbi.com.ua; internet www.dklg.kiev.ua; Chair. MYKOLA V. KOLISNYCHENKO.

**State Committee for Housing:** 03150 Kiev, vul. Dymytrova 24; tel. (44) 244-39-82; fax (44) 227-23-35; e-mail iass@ndiasb.kiev.ua; internet www.djkg.gov.ua; Chair. HRIHORIY M. SEMCHUK.

**State Committee for Information Policy, Television and Radio Broadcasting:** 01001 Kiev, vul. Prorizna 2; tel. (44) 228-87-69; fax (44) 229-41-48; e-mail admin@scriptrb.gov.ua; internet www.sciptrb.gov.ua; Chair. IVAN S. CHYZH.

**State Committee for Land Resources:** 01601 Kiev, Muzeinyi provulok 12; tel. (44) 226-21-70; fax (44) 226-21-54; e-mail myland@iatp.kiev.ua; internet myland.org.ua/uk/(main)/790; Chair. ANATOLIY S. DANYLENKO.

**State Committee for Nationalities and Migration:** 01025 Kiev, vul. Volodymyrska 9; tel. (44) 228-17-18; fax (44) 226-23-39; e-mail ksenia@minjust.gov.ua; internet www.scnm.gov.ua; Chair. HENNADIY H. MOSKAL.

**State Committee for Nuclear Regulation:** 01011 Kiev, vul. Arsenalna 9/11; tel. (44) 254-33-47; fax (44) 254-33-11; e-mail pr@hq .snrc .gov.ua; internet www.snrcu.gov.ua; Chair. VADYM V. HRYSH-CHENKO.

**State Committee for Regulatory Policy and the Development of Enterprise:** 04053 Kiev, vul. Sichovykh Striltsiv 73; tel. (44) 246-84-49; fax (44) 246-86-39; internet www.dkrp.gov.ua; Chair. INNA H. BOHOSLOVSKA.

**State Committee for Religions:** 01601 Kiev, vul. Prorizna 15/5; tel. (44) 229-37-16; fax (44) 229-36-43; e-mail dkrelig@iptelecom.net .ua; Chair. VIKTOR D. BONDARENKO.

**State Committee for Statistics:** 01023 Kiev, vul. Sh. Rustaveli 3; tel. (44) 226-20-21; fax (44) 235-37-39; e-mail info@ukrstat.gov.ua; internet www.ukrstat.gov.ua; Chair. OLEKSANDR H. OSAULENKO.

**State Committee for Technical Regulation and Consumption Policy:** 03680 Kiev–150, vul. Antonovycha 174; tel. 226-29-71; fax 226-29-70; e-mail dstu1@dstu.gov.ua; internet www.dssu.gov.ua; Chair. LEONID S. SHKOLNYK.

**State Committee for Veterans:** 04053 Kiev, vul. Lvivska 8/18/1803; tel. (44) 212-51-30; fax (44) 212-02-30; e-mail kiev_veteran@ukrpost.com.ua; internet www.dkusv.cjb.net; Chair. SERHIY V. CHERVONOPYSKYI.

**State Committee for Water Resources:** 01601 Kiev, vul. Vasylkivska 8; tel. (44) 226-26-07; fax (44) 225-31-92; e-mail webmaster@ scwm.gov.ua; internet www.scwm.gov.ua; Chair. VIKTOR M. KHORYEV.

**State Customs Committee:** 04119 Kiev, vul. Degtyarivska 11H; tel. (44) 274-82-83; internet www.customs.gov.ua; Chair. MYKOLA M. KALENSKIY.

# President and Legislature

## PRESIDENT

**Presidential Election, First Ballot, 31 October 1999**

| Candidates | Votes | % |
|---|---|---|
| Leonid D. Kuchma | 9,598,672 | 36.49 |
| Petro M. Symonenko | 5,849,077 | 22.24 |
| Oleksandr O. Moroz | 2,969,896 | 11.29 |
| Nataliya M. Vitrenko | 2,886,972 | 10.97 |
| Yevhen K. Marchuk | 2,138,356 | 8.13 |
| Yuriy I. Kostenko | 570,623 | 2.17 |
| Hennadiy Y. Udovenko | 319,778 | 1.22 |
| Others | 456,021 | 1.73 |
| Against all candidates | 477,019 | 1.81 |
| **Total*** | 26,305,163 | 100.00 |

*Including invalid votes, totalling 1,038,749.

**Second Ballot, 14 November 1999**

| Candidate | Votes | % |
|---|---|---|
| Leonid D. Kuchma | 15,870,722 | 57.70 |
| Petro M. Symonenko | 10,665,420 | 38.77 |
| Against all candidates | 970,181 | 3.52 |
| **Total*** | 27,506,323 | 100.00 |

*Excluding invalid votes, totalling 706,161.

### VERKHOVNA RADA
(Supreme Council)

#### Verkhovna Rada
01008 Kiev, vul. M. Hrushevskoho 5; tel. (44) 226-22-92; fax (44) 293-06-53; e-mail vfsev@rada.gov.ua; internet www.rada.gov.ua.

**Chairman:** VOLODYMYR M. LYTVYN.

**First Deputy Chairman:** HENNADIY A. VASYLYEV.

**Deputy Chairman:** OLEKSANDR O. ZINCHENKO.

**General Election, 31 March 2002**

| Parties and blocs | Federal party lists | | |
|---|---|---|---|
| | % of votes | Seats | Total seats* |
| Our Ukraine | 23.57 | 70 | 112 |
| For A United Ukraine | 11.78 | 35 | 101 |
| Communist Party of Ukraine | 19.99 | 59 | 66 |
| Social-Democratic Party of Ukraine (United) | 6.28 | 19 | 24 |
| Socialist Party of Ukraine | 6.87 | 20 | 23 |
| Yuliya Tymoshenko Bloc | 7.26 | 22 | 22 |
| Democratic Party of Ukraine—Democratic Union | 0.88 | — | 4 |
| Unity | 1.09 | — | 3 |
| Ukrainian Maritime Party | 0.11 | — | 1 |
| Party of National Economic Development of Ukraine | — | — | 1 |
| Nataliya Vitrenko bloc | 3.23 | — | — |
| Women for the Future | 2.11 | — | — |
| Team of the Winter Crop Generation | 2.03 | — | — |
| Communist Party of Ukraine (Renewed) | 1.40 | — | — |
| Green Party of Ukraine | 1.31 | — | — |
| Yabluko | 1.16 | — | — |
| Others† | 4.77 | — | — |
| Independents | — | — | 93 |
| Against all lists | 2.45 | — | — |
| **Total** | 100.00‡ | 225 | 450 |

* Including seats filled by voting in single-member constituencies, totalling 225.
† There were 19 other groups.
‡ Including spoilt ballot papers (3.71% of the total). The total number of votes cast was 25,909,407.

# Local Government

Ukraine is divided for administrative purposes into 24 oblasts (regions), two metropolitan areas (Kyiv—Kiev and Sevastopol) and one Autonomous Republic (Crimea, see p. 539). Each oblast (region) is governed by a directly elected council (rada), and a governor appointed by the President. The 1996 Constitution also guarantees local self-government to boroughs (raions), cities, settlements and villages.

**Government of the Autonomous Republic of Crimea:** 95005 Crimea, Simferopol, pr. Kirova 13; tel. (652) 27-61-65; fax (652) 24-80-20; e-mail prime_minister@tavrida.crimea.ua; internet sovmin .at-crimea.org; Chairman of Council of Ministers (Premier) SERGEI V. KUNITSYN.

**Cherkasy Oblast Administration:** 18001 Cherkasy, bulv. Shevchenka 185; tel. (472) 47-33-33; fax (472) 47-28-40; internet www .oda.ck.ua; Gov. VADYM O. LYOSHENKO.

**Chernihiv Oblast Administration:** 14000 Chernihiv, vul. Shevchenka 7; tel. (462) 75-024; fax (462) 10-12-80; e-mail butko@regadm .cn.ua; internet www.regadm.cn.ua; Gov. VALENTYN V. MELNYCHUK.

**Chernivtsi Oblast Administration:** 58010 Chernivtsi, vul. Hrushevskoho 1; tel. (372) 51-30-10; fax (372) 55-37-76; e-mail inform@leon.bucoda.cv.ua; internet www.bucoda.cv.ua; Gov. MYKHAYLO V. ROMANIV.

**Dnipropetrovsk Oblast Administration:** 49004 Dnipropetrovsk, pr. Kirova 1; tel. (562) 42-83-84; fax (562) 42-89-54; e-mail info@adm .dp.ua; internet www.adm.dp.ua; Gov. VOLODYMYR H. YATSUBA.

**Donetsk Oblast Administration:** 83105 Donetsk, bulv. Pushkina 34; tel. (622) 35-03-89; fax (622) 92-13-62; e-mail info@oda.dn.ua; internet www.oda.dc.dn.ua; Gov. ANATOLIY M. BLYZNYUK.

**Ivano-Frankivsk Oblast Administration:** 76004 Ivano-Frankivsk, vul. Hrushevskoho 21; tel. (3422) 22-291; fax (3422) 25-048; e-mail oda@mail.gov.if.ua; internet www.gov.if.ua; Gov. MYKHAILO V. VYSHYVANYUK.

**Kharkiv Oblast Administration:** 61200 Kharkiv, vul. Sumska 64; tel. (572) 43-21-05; fax (572) 43-22-01; internet www.regionnet .kharkov.ua; Gov. YEVHEN P. KUSHNYARYOV.

**Kherson Oblast Administration:** 73000 Kherson, pl. Svobody 1; tel. (552) 22-30-50; fax (552) 26-36-02; e-mail vd-komp@oda.kherson .ua; internet www.oda.kherson.ua; Gov. ANATOLIY P. YURCHENKO.

**Khmelnytsky Oblast Administration:** 29005 Khmelnytsky, maydan Nezalezhnosti, Budynok Rad; tel. (382) 76-50-25; fax (382)

76-45-02; e-mail rada@khmelnitskiy.com; internet adm.km.ua; Gov.
Viktor M. Lundyshev.

**Kiev (Kyiv) City Administration:** 01044 Kyiv, vul. Kreshchatyk
36; tel. (44) 221-28-01; fax (44) 235-63-48; e-mail kmda012@012
.kyiv-city.gov.ua; internet www.kmv.gov.ua; Mayor Oleksandr O.
Omelchenko.

**Kiev (Kyiv) Oblast Administration:** 01133 Kyiv, pl. L. Ukrainky
1; tel. (44) 226-30-43; fax (44) 296-15-10; internet www.kyiv-obl.gov
.ua; Gov. Anatoliy A. Zasukha.

**Kirovohrad Oblast Administration:** 25022 Kirovohrad, pl.
Kirova 1; tel. (522) 24-03-30; fax (522) 22-35-66; e-mail pres@
obl-admin.kirovograd.ua; internet www.kr-admin.gov.ua; Gov.
Vasyl K. Motsnyi.

**Luhansk Oblast Administration:** 91000 Luhansk, pl. Heroyiv
Velykoyi Vitchyznyanoyi viiny 3; tel. (642) 52-70-19; fax (642) 55-14-
54; e-mail info@oda.lg.ua; internet www.oda.lg.ua; Gov. Oleksandr
S. Yefremov.

**Lviv Oblast Administration:** 79008 Lviv, vul. Vynnychenka 18;
tel. (322) 72-80-93; fax (322) 76-73-99; e-mail admin@oda.lviv.ua;
internet www.loda.gov.ua; Gov. Oleksandr S. Sendega.

**Mykolayiv Oblast Administration:** 54009 Mykolayiv, vul. Admir-
alska 22; tel. (512) 35-40-51; fax (512) 35-12-36; e-mail cancelar@oga
.mk.ua; internet www.oga.mk.ua; Gov. Oleksiy M. Harkusha.

**Odesa Oblast Administration:** 65032 Odesa, pr. Shevchenka 4;
tel. (482) 25-15-47; fax (482) 34-29-71; e-mail webadmin@ogn.odessa
.net; internet www2.ogn.odessa.net; Gov. Serhiy R. Hrynevetskiy.

**Poltava Oblast Administration:** 36014 Poltava, vul. Zhovtenva
45; tel. (532) 56-02-69; fax (532) 56-53-14; e-mail oda@obladmin
.poltava.ua; internet www.obladmin.poltava.ua; Gov. Oleksandr V.
Udovichenko.

**Rivne Oblast Administration:** 33000 Rivne, maydan Prosvity 1;
tel. (362) 69-51-65; fax (362) 26-08-35; e-mail cbc@obladmin.rv.ua;
internet www.rvadmin.net; Gov. Mykola P. Soroka.

**Sevastopol City Administration:** 99011 Sevastopol, vul. Lenina
2; tel. (692) 54-47-73; fax (692) 55-34-01; e-mail gga@stel.sebastopol
.ua; internet www.sebastopol.ua; Gov. Leonid M. Zhunko.

**Sumy Oblast Administration:** 40030 Sumy, pl. Nezalezhnosti 2;
tel. (542) 21-09-80; fax (542) 22-22-63; e-mail mail@state-gov.sumy
.ua; internet www.state-gov.sumy.ua; Gov. Volodymyr P.
Shcherban.

**Ternopil Oblast Administration:** 46021 Ternopil, vul.
M. Hrushevskoho 8; tel. (352) 22-87-81; fax (352) 25-19-59; internet
www.oda.te.gov.ua; Gov. Ivan I. Kurnytskyi.

**Transcarpathian (Zakarpatska) Oblast Administration:**
88008 Transcarpathian obl., Uzhhorod, pl. Narodna 4; tel. (312) 61-
34-19; fax (312) 61-33-56; e-mail admin@carpathia.gov.ua; internet
www.carpathia.gov.ua; Gov. Ivan M. Rizak.

**Vinnytsya Oblast Administration:** 21100 Vinnytsya, vul.
Soborna 70; tel. (432) 32-20-35; fax (432) 32-75-40; e-mail vinoda@
svitonline.com; internet www.vin.gov.ua; Gov. Viktor F. Kotsemyr.

**Volyn Oblast Administration:** 43027 Volyn obl., Lutsk,
pl. Kyivska 9; tel. (332) 72-90-10; fax (332) 72-93-22; e-mail post@
obladmin.lutsk.ua; internet www.voladm.gov.ua; Gov. Anatoliy Y.
Frantsuz.

**Zaporizhzhya Oblast Administration:** 69107 Zaporizhzhya, pr.
Lenina 164; tel. (612) 33-11-91; fax (612) 34-34-83; internet www.oda
.zp.ua; Gov. Volodymyr P. Berezovskyi.

**Zhytomyr Oblast Administration:** 10014 Zhytomyr, maydan Rad
1; tel. (412) 37-24-02; fax (412) 37-04-38; internet www.zhitomiroda
.ic.zt.ua; Gov. Mykola M. Rudchenko.

# Political Organizations

Until 1990 the only legal political party in Ukraine was the Communist Party of Ukraine (CPU), an integral part of the Communist
Party of the Soviet Union. In 1988, however, a Ukrainian People's
Movement for Restructuring (known as Rukh) was established to
support greater democratization and freedom of speech, and several
other political organizations were also founded. In 1990, after the
CPU's constitutional monopoly was abolished, many new political
parties were established. Rukh, which had been the main coalition of
forces opposed to the CPU in 1988–91, became a political party (as
the People's Movement of Ukraine) in 1993. President Leonid
Kuchma, who was elected to that position in 1994, and re-elected in
1999, has been associated with a number of so-called 'parties of
power', including the Inter-regional Bloc for Reform movement
(which was registered as a political party in 1994) and the Party of
Industrialists and Entrepreneurs of Ukraine (founded in 2001),
which contested the parliamentary elections in 2002 as part of the

For A United Ukraine bloc. In December 2001 there were 127
political parties officially registered in Ukraine; the following were
among the most important at early 2003.

**Batkivshchyna** (Fatherland): 01133 Kiev, vul. L. Ukrainky 26/916;
tel. (44) 294-42-21; e-mail info@byti.org.ua; internet www
.tymoshenko.com.ua; f. 1999 by members of Hromada—Community
party; democratic, seeks to combine patriotism, a liberal approach
towards economics and provision of social protection for citizens;
contested 2002 parliamentary elections as Yuliya Tymoshenko Bloc;
Chair. Yuliya V. Tymoshenko; 203,000 mems (2002).

**Christian Democratic Party of Ukraine** (Khrystyyansko-Demo-
kratychna Partija Ukrainy): 01004 Kiev, vul. Baseyna 1/2a; tel. (44)
235-39-96; fax (44) 234-19-49; e-mail info@cdpu.org.ua; internet
cdpu.org.ua; centrist democratic party; Chair. Vitaliy S. Zhuravskiy;
42,000 mems.

**Communist Party of Ukraine (CPU)** (Komunistychna Partiya
Ukrainy): 04070 Kiev, vul. Borysohlibska 7; tel. (44) 416-54-87; fax
(44) 416-31-37; internet www.kpu.kiev.ua; banned 1991–93; advocates state control of economy and confederation with Russia; Sec. of
Cen. Cttee Petro M. Symonenko.

**Communist Party of Ukraine (Renewed) (CPU—R)** (Komunistychna Partiya Ukrainy—Onovlena): 02098 Kiev, pr. Tychyny 10/35;
tel. (44) 554-28-34; f. 2000 by faction of CPU; Leader Mykhaylo M.
Savenko.

**Democratic Party of Ukraine—Democratic Union** (Demokratychna Partiya Ukrainy—Demokratychnyi Soyuz): 04010 Kiev, vul.
Chapayeva 4/4; tel. (44) 235-39-40; e-mail rada@demunion.kiev.ua;
internet www.demunion.kiev.ua; Pres. Volodymyr P. Horbulin.

**For A United Ukraine (FUU)** (Za Yedinu Ukrainu): 04070 Kiev,
vul. Florivska 1; tel. (44) 238-65-16; e-mail info@zaedu.org.ua;
internet www.zaedu.org.ua; electoral bloc formed 2001 to contest
2002 parliamentary elections; supports Govt of President Kuchma;
Chair. Volodymyr M. Lytvyn.

**Agrarian Party of Ukraine** (Agrarna Partiya Ukrainy): 01034
Kiev, vul. Reitarska 6a; tel. (44) 464-01-86; fax (44) 464-05-91;
e-mail webmaster@partiya.net.ua; internet www.apu.org.ua; f.
1996; advocates revival of the Ukrainian countryside; Chair.
Mykhaylo V. Hladiy.

**People's Democratic Party (PDP)** (Narodno-Demokratychna
Partiya—NDP): 03150 Kiev, vul. Antonovicha 107; tel. (44) 252-
84-18; fax (44) 252-87-26; e-mail zagal@s ndp.kiev.ua; internet
ndp.org.ua; f. 1996; centrist; Leader Valeriy P. Pustovoytenko;
242,792 mems (2002).

**Party of Industrialists and Entrepreneurs of Ukraine** (Partiya promyslovtsiv i pidpryyemtsiv Ukrainy): 01023 Kiev, vul.
Baseyna 30/46; tel. (44) 234-37-07; fax (44) 235-82-58; e-mail
pppu@ukr.net; internet pppu.com.ua; f. 2001 by faction of PDPU;
Chair. Anatoliy K. Kinakh.

**Party of the Regions (PR)** (Partiya Regioniv): 04053 Kiev, vul.
Kudryavska 3/5; tel. (44) 212-55-70; fax (44) 212-55-83; e-mail
PressCenter@partyofregions.org.ua; internet www.partyofregions
.org.ua; f. 1997 as Party of Regional Rebirth of Ukraine; present
name adopted 2001; Chair. Viktor F. Yanukovych; 460,000 mems
(Dec. 2001).

**Working Ukraine** (Trudova Ukraina): 01021 Kiev, vul. Shovkovychna 4; tel. (44) 229-89-03; e-mail inform@tu.privat-online
.net; internet www.trud.org.ua; f. 2000; Pres. Serhiy L. Tihipko;
Chair. of Political Committee Andriy Derkach; 20,000 mems
(2002).

**Green Party of Ukraine** (Partiya Zelenykh Ukrainy): 01023 Kiev,
vul. Sh. Rustaveli 38; tel. (44) 220-50-80; fax (44) 220-66-94; e-mail
office@greenparty.org.ua; internet www.greenparty.org.ua; f. 1990
as political wing of environmental organization, Green World
(f. 1987); Pres. Vitaliy M. Kononov.

**Hromada** (Community): 01133 Kiev, Laboratornyi provylok 1; tel.
and fax (44) 252-88-57; e-mail office@hromada.kiev.ua; internet
www.hromada.kiev.ua; f. 1994; social democratic; Leader Pavlo I.
Lazarenko.

**Our Ukraine** (Nasha Ukraina): Kiev; e-mail forum@ua.org.ua;
internet www.razom.org.ua; electoral bloc f. 2001 to contest 2002
parliamentary elections; broadly nationalist and supportive of
greater economic liberalization; Chair. Viktor A. Yushchenko; affiliated parties include.

**Congress of Ukrainian Nationalists** (Kongres Ukrainskykh
Natsionalistiv): 01034 Kiev, vul. Yaroslaviv val 9/4; tel. (44) 224-
70-20; e-mail mkun@ukr.net; f. 1992; Chair. (vacant).

**People's Movement of Ukraine-Rukh (PMU-R)** (Narodnyi
Rukh Ukrainy): 01034 Kiev, vul. O. Honchara 33; tel. (44) 246-47-
67; e-mail nruorg@ukrtel.com; internet www.nru.org.ua; f. 1989
as popular movement (Ukrainian People's Movement for Restruc-

turing); registered as political party in 1993; national democratic party; Chair. BORIS I. TARASYUK.

**Reforms and Order Party** (Reformy i poryadok): 01021 Kiev, vul. Instytutska 28; tel. (44) 201-41-16; fax (44) 201-41-17; e-mail webmaster@reformy.org; internet www.reformy.org; f. 1997; supports economic reform and greater integration of Ukraine with central and western European organizations; Chair. VIKTOR M. PYNZENYK.

**Ukrainian People's Party (UPP)** (Ukrainska Narodna Partiya): 01004 Kiev, vul. Pushkinska 28A; tel. (44) 224-59-17; fax (44) 224-10-30; e-mail org@rukh-unr.org; internet www.rukh-unr.org; f. 1999 as breakaway faction of People's Movement of Ukraine-Rukh by former leader Vyacheslav Chornovil; fmrly Ukrainian People's Movement-Rukh; present name adopted 2003; Chair. YURIY I. KOSTENKO.

**Party of National Economic Development of Ukraine** (Partiya Natsionalno-Ekonoichnoho Ukrainy): 01001 Kiev, vul. Sofiyivska 7; tel. (44) 226-21-63; fax (44) 226-21-08; f. 1996; Leader PAVLO V. MATVIYENKO.

**Progressive Socialist Party of Ukraine** (Prohresyvna Sotsialistychna Partiya Ukrainy): 01032 Kiev, vul. Kominterna 15; tel. (44) 291-74-60; e-mail pspu@aport2000.ru; internet www.vitrenko.org; f. 1996 by members of the Socialist Party of Ukraine; contested parliamentary elections in 2002 as Nataliya Vitrenko bloc; favours extension of Belarus-Russia Union to incorporate Ukraine; opposed to Ukraine seeking membership of NATO; Chair. NATALIYA M. VITRENKO.

**Russian Movement of Ukraine** (Russkoye Dvizheniye Ukrainy): 79008 Lviv, vul. Smolskoho 2/7; tel. and fax (322) 75-80-59; e-mail rdu@rdu.org.ua; internet www.rdu.org.ua; f. 1999; seeks by moderate means to re-establish a political union of Belarus, Russia and Ukraine, and to restore the status of Russian as an official language of Ukraine, alongside Ukrainian; Chair. ALEKSANDR G. SVISTUNOV; affiliated parties include.

**Union** (Soyuz): 95017 Crimea, Simferopol, vul. Krupskoyi 5/9; tel. (652) 24-17-55; fax (652) 24-18-94; f. 1997; Chair. VLADIMIR KLYCHNIKOV.

**Social-Democratic Party of Ukraine (United) (SDPU—U)** (Sotsial-Demokratychna Partiya Ukrainy—Obyednana): 01030 Kiev, vul. Ivano-Franko 18; tel. (44) 536-15-71; fax (44) 536-15-78; e-mail sdpuo@org.ukr.net; internet www.sdpuo.org.ua; f. 1995, by merger of the Social Democratic Party, the Ukrainian Party of Justice and the Party of Human Rights; advocates economic and political reform; social democratic; Chair. VIKTOR V. MEDVEDCHUK; 370,000 mems (2002).

**Socialist Party of Ukraine (SPU)** (Sotsialistychna Partiya Ukrainy): 01054 Kiev, vul. Vorovskoho 45; tel. (44) 216-88-82; fax (44) 244-51-66; e-mail press@socinfo.kiev.ua; internet www.socinfo .kiev.ua; f. 1991; formed as partial successor to CPU; advocates democratic socialism; Leader OLEKSANDR O. MOROZ; c. 69,000 mems.

**Team of the Winter Crop Generation** (Komanda Ozymoho Pokolinnya): Kiev; tel. (44) 254-08-07; e-mail info@zbirna.org.ua; internet zbirna.org.ua; f. 1997; supports economic reform, constitutional democracy and private property; advocates closer links with western Europe; Leader VALERIY I. KHOROSHKOVSKIY.

**Ukrainian Maritime Party** (Ukrainska Morska Partiya): 65000 Odesa, vul. Kanatna 42; represents the interests of sailors; Leader SERHIY V. KIVALOV.

**Unity** (Yednist): 03039 Kiev, vul. Yaroslaviv val 21; tel. (44) 227-55-27; internet www.yednist.org.ua; f. 2000; contested the 2002 parliamentary elections in alliance with Young Ukraine, Social Democratic Union and the Party of Justice–Union of Veterans, Invalids, survivors of the Chernobyl catastrophe and the Soviet–Afghan War; Chair. OLEKSANDR O. OMELCHENKO.

**Women for the Future** (Zhinky za maibutne): 04080 Kiev, vul. Turivska 13; tel. (44) 229-51-08; internet www.woman.org.ua; f. 2001; supports Govt of President Kuchma; Chair. VALENTYNA I. DOVZHENKO.

**Yabluko** (Apple): 01010 Kiev, vul. Moskovska 37/2/1/45; tel. (44) 254-52-88; fax (44) 293-56-71; e-mail yabluko@yabluko.org.ua; internet www.yabluko.org.ua; supports the protection of private property; Chair. MYKHAYLO BRODSKYI.

# Diplomatic Representation

## EMBASSIES IN UKRAINE

**Afghanistan:** 03037 Kiev, pr. Chervonozoryanyi 42; tel. (44) 245-81-04; e-mail afghanem@afghanem.kiev.ua; Chargé d'affaires a.i. MUKHAYEDDIN MASUD.

**Algeria:** 01001 Kiev, vul. B. Khmelnytskoho 64; tel. (44) 216-70-79; fax (44) 216-70-08; e-mail ambkv@ksv.net.ua; Ambassador CHERIF SHIKHI.

**Armenia:** 01901 Kiev, vul. Volodymyrska 45; tel. (44) 224-90-05; fax (44) 224-05-00; e-mail armenia@desp.kiev.ua; Ambassador HRACH H. SILVANYAN.

**Austria:** 01901 Kiev, vul. Ivana Franka 33; tel. (44) 244-39-43; fax (44) 230-23-52; e-mail kiew-ob@bmaa.gv.at; Ambassador KLAUS FABJAN.

**Azerbaijan:** 04050 Kiev, vul. Hlubochytska 24; tel. (44) 461-91-99; fax (44) 461-93-44; e-mail embass@faust.kiev.ua; Ambassador TALYAT MUSEIB OLGY ALIYEV.

**Belarus:** 01010 Kiev, vul. I. Mazepy 6; tel. (44) 290-02-01; fax (44) 290-34-13; e-mail ukraine@belembassy.org; Ambassador VALENTYN V. VELICHKO.

**Belgium:** 01030 Kiev, vul. Leontovicha 4; tel. (44) 238-26-00; fax (44) 238-26-01; e-mail ambbkiev@gu.net; Ambassador PIERRE CLEMENT DUBUISSON.

**Brazil:** 01010 Kiev, bulv. L. Ukrainky 21/17; tel. (44) 290-63-01; fax (44) 290-95-68; e-mail kivbrem@public.ua.net; Ambassador ELDER MARTINS DE MORAES.

**Bulgaria:** 01023 Kiev, vul. Hospitalna 1; tel. (44) 235-52-96; fax (44) 224-99-29; e-mail embbul@carrier.kiev.ua; Ambassador ALEKSANDR DYMYTROV.

**Canada:** 01901 Kiev, vul. Yaroslaviv Val 31; tel. (44) 464-11-44; fax (44) 464-11-33; e-mail kyiv@dfait-maeci.gc.ca; internet www.kyiv.gc .ca; Ambassador ANDREW N. ROBINSON.

**China, People's Republic:** 01901 Kiev, vul. M. Hrushevskoho 32; tel. and fax (44) 253-10-49; fax (44) 253-15-24; e-mail cxjl@ukrpack .net; Ambassador LI GOUBANG.

**Croatia:** 01091 Kiev, vul. Sichovykh Striltsiv 51/50; tel. (44) 216-58-62; fax (44) 224-69-43; e-mail croemb@carrier.kiev.ua; Ambassador Dr MARIO MIKOLIĆ.

**Cuba:** 01901 Kiev, prov. Bekhterevskyi 5; tel. (44) 216-57-43; fax (44) 216-19-07; e-mail embacuba@naverex.kiev.ua; Ambassador JOSÉ DIONISIO PERAZA CHAPEAU.

**Czech Republic:** 01901 Kiev, vul. Yaroslaviv Val 34A; tel. (44) 212-04-31; fax (44) 229-74-69; e-mail kiev@embassy.mzv.cz; Ambassador Dr KAREL ŠTINDL.

**Egypt:** 01901 Kiev, vul. Observatorna 19; tel. (44) 212-13-27; fax (44) 216-94-28; e-mail boustan@egypt-emb.kiev.ua; Ambassador MONA ALY KHASHABA.

**Estonia:** 01901 Kiev, vul. Volodymyrska 61/11; tel. (44) 235-85-82; fax (44) 234-14-03; e-mail embassy@estemb.kiev.ua; internet www .estemb.kiev.ua; Ambassador PAUL LETTENS.

**Finland:** 01901 Kiev, vul. Striletska 14; tel. (44) 228-70-49; fax (44) 228-20-32; e-mail sanomat.kio@formin.fi; Ambassador LAURA REINILÄ.

**France:** 01034 Kiev, vul. Reitarska 39; tel. (44) 228-87-28; fax (44) 229-08-70; e-mail scfr@carrier.kiev.ua; internet www.ambafrance .kiev.ua; Ambassador PHILIPPE DE SUREMAIN.

**Georgia:** 04119 Kiev, vul. Melnikova 83D; tel. (44) 451-43-53; fax (44) 451-43-56; e-mail embassy@geo.kiev.ua; Ambassador GRIGOL SH. KATAMADZE.

**Germany:** 0901 Kiev, vul. B. Khmelnytskoho 25; tel. (44) 247-68-00; fax (44) 247-68-18; e-mail wi@german-embassy.kiev.ua; internet www.deutsche-botschaft.kiev.ua; Ambassador DIETMAR GERHARD STÜDEMANN.

**Greece:** 01901 Kiev, vul. Sofiyisvka 19; tel. (44) 299-57-30; fax (44) 229-13-38; e-mail greece@inec.kiev.ua; Ambassador DIMITRIS KONTOUMAS.

**Holy See:** 01901 Kiev, vul. Turhenyevska 40; tel. (44) 246-95-57; fax (44) 246-95-53; e-mail nunziatura@public.ua.net; Apostolic Nuncio Most Rev. NIKOLA ETEROVIĆ (Titular Archbishop of Sisak).

**Hungary:** 01034 Kiev, vul. Reitarska 33; tel. (44) 238-63-81; fax (44) 212-20-90; e-mail po.box@hunemb.com.ua; Chargé d'affaires a.i. SÁNDOR ALMÁSI.

**India:** 01901 Kiev, vul. Teryokhina 4; tel. (44) 468-66-61; fax (44) 468-66-19; e-mail com@indianembassy.org.ua; internet www .indianembassy.org.ua; Ambassador SHEHKHOLEN KIPGEN.

**Indonesia:** 04107 Kiev, vul. Nahirna 27B; tel. (44) 205-54-46; fax (44) 205-54-40; e-mail kbri@indo.ru.kiev.ua; internet www.kbri.kiev .ua; Ambassador REMY ROMAULI SIAHAAN.

**Iran:** 01901 Kiev, vul. Kruhlouniversytetska 12; tel. (44) 229-44-63; fax (44) 229-32-55; Ambassador AHMAD SADEGH-BONAB.

**Iraq:** 03150 Kiev, vul. A. Barbyusa 49; tel. (44) 268-64-42; fax (44) 269-46-49.

**Israel:** 01901 Kiev, bulv. L. Ukrainky 34; tel. (44) 295-69-36; fax (44) 294-97-48; e-mail embisr@carrier.kiev.ua; Ambassador ANNA AZARI.

**Italy:** 01901 Kiev, vul. Yaroslaviv val 32B; tel. (44) 230-31-00; fax (44) 230-31-03; e-mail ambital.kiev@utel.net.ua; internet www.ambital.kiev.ua; Ambassador JOLANDA BRUNETTI.

**Japan:** 01901 Kiev, Muzeiniy prov. 4; tel. (44) 490-55-00; fax (44) 490-55-02; e-mail jpembua@sovamua.com; internet www.embjapan.com.ua; Ambassador KISHCHINO AMAE.

**Kazakhstan:** 04050 Kiev, vul. Melnykova 26; tel. and fax (44) 213-11-98; e-mail admin@kazemb.kiev.ua; Ambassador RAVIL T. CHERDABAYEV.

**Korea, Republic:** 01034 Kiev, vul. Volodymyrska 43; tel. (44) 246-37-59; fax (44) 246-37-57; e-mail korea@koremb.kiev.ua; Ambassador CHUNG SHIN.

**Kuwait:** 04053 Kiev, vul. Kudryavska 13–19; tel. (44) 238-27-32; fax (44) 238-63-94; Ambassador KHALED MUTLAK ZAED AL-DUWAILAH.

**Kyrgyzstan:** 4053 Kiev, vul. Sichovykh Striltsiv 51/50; tel. (44) 219-13-97; fax (44) 246-88-89; Ambassador ESENGUL K. OMURALIYEV.

**Latvia:** 01901 Kiev, vul. I. Mazepy 6B; tel. (44) 490-70-30; fax (44) 490-70-35; e-mail embassy.ukraine@mfa.gov.lv; Ambassador ANDRIS VILCĀNS.

**Libya:** 04050 Kiev, vul. Ovrutska 6; tel. (44) 238-60-70; fax (44) 238-60-68; Chargé d'affaires a.i. MOHAMED AL-BUAISHI.

**Lithuania:** 01901 Kiev, vul. Buslivska 21; tel. (44) 254-09-20; fax (44) 254-09-28; e-mail embassy@ltembua.org; Ambassador VIKTORAS BAUBLYS.

**Macedonia, former Yugoslav Republic:** 01024 Kiev, vul. Borychiv Tik 28; tel. (44) 238-66-16; fax (44) 238-66-17; e-mail embmac@carrier.kiev.ua; Ambassador VLADO BLAZHEVSKI.

**Moldova:** 01010 Kiev, vul. I. Mazepy 6; tel. (44) 290-77-21; fax (44) 290-77-22; Ambassador NICOLAE CERNOMAZ.

**Netherlands:** 01901 Kiev, pl. Kontraktova 7; tel. (44) 490-82-00; fax (44) 490-82-09; e-mail nlambkie@ukrpack.net; Ambassador M. P. FRANK.

**Nigeria:** 03067 Kiev, bulv. I. Lepse 4, 'Silver-Centre'; tel. (44) 201-44-59; fax (44) 201-44-63; Ambassador ALFRED NANNA.

**Norway:** 01901 Kiev, vul. Striletska 15; tel. (44) 234-00-66; fax (44) 234-06-55; e-mail emb.kiev@mfa.no; Ambassador IOSTEIN BERNHARDSEN.

**Pakistan:** 01015 Kiev, pr. Panfilovtsiv 7; tel. and fax (44) 290-25-77; e-mail parepkiev@mail.kar.net; Ambassador Vice-Adm. (retd) SHAMOON ALAM KHAN.

**Poland:** 01034 Kiev, vul. Yaroslaviv Val 12; tel. (44) 230-07-03; fax (44) 464-13-36; e-mail ambasada@polska.com.ua; Ambassador MAREK ZIOŁKOWSKI.

**Portugal:** 01901 Kiev, vul. V. Vasylkivska 9/2/12; tel. (44) 227-24-42; fax (44) 230-26-25; e-mail embport@ukrpack.net; Ambassador PEDRO MANUEL SARMENTO DE VASCOUCELOS E CASTRO.

**Romania:** 01030 Kiev, vul. M. Kotsyubynskoho 8; tel. (44) 224-52-61; fax (44) 235-20-25; e-mail romania@iptelecom.net.ua; Ambassador ALEXANDRU CORNEA.

**Russia:** 03049 Kiev, Povitroflotskyi pr. 27; tel. (44) 244-09-63; fax (44) 246-34-69; e-mail embrus@public.icyb.kiev.ua; Ambassador VIKTOR S. CHERNOMYRDIN.

**Serbia and Montenegro:** 04070 Kiev, vul. Voloska 4; tel. (44) 416-60-60; fax (44) 416-60-47; e-mail ambayu@svitonline.com; Ambassador (vacant).

**Slovakia:** 01901 Kiev, vul. Yaroslaviv Val 34; tel. (44) 229-79-29; fax (44) 212-32-71; e-mail slovak@i.kiev.ua; Ambassador VASIL GRIVNA.

**South Africa:** 01004 Kiev, vul. V. Vasylkivska 9/2, POB 7; tel. (44) 227-71-72; fax (44) 220-72-06; e-mail saemb@utel.net.ua; Ambassador DELAREY VAN TONDER.

**Spain:** 01901 Kiev, vul. Dekhtyarivska 38–44; tel. (44) 213-04-81; fax (44) 213-00-31; e-mail embespua@mail.mae.es; Ambassador LUIS GÓMEZ DE ARANDA Y VILLÉN.

**Sweden:** 01901 Kiev, vul. Ivana Franka 34/33; tel. (44) 462-05-80; fax (44) 462-05-81; e-mail ambassaden.kiev@foreign.ministry.se; internet www.sweemb.kiev.ua; Ambassador ÅKE PETERSON.

**Switzerland:** 01901 Kiev, vul. I. Fedorova 12/2/111; tel. (44) 220-54-73; fax (44) 246-65-13; e-mail vertretung@kie.rep.admin.ch; Ambassador JEAN-FRANÇOIS KAMMER.

**Turkey:** 01901 Kiev, vul. Arsenalna 18; tel. (44) 294-99-64; fax (44) 295-64-23; e-mail kiev.be@mfa.gov.tr; Ambassador ALI BILGE CANKOREL.

**Turkmenistan:** 01901 Kiev, vul. Pushkinska 6; tel. (44) 229-34-49; fax (44) 229-30-34; e-mail ambturkm@ukrpack.net; Ambassador AMANGELDY O. BAYRAMOV.

**United Kingdom:** 01025 Kiev, vul. Desyatynna 9; tel. (44) 462-00-11; fax (44) 462-00-13; e-mail ukembinf@sovam.com; internet www.britemb-ukraine.net; Ambassador ROBERT BRINKLEY.

**USA:** 01901 Kiev, vul. Yu. Kotsyubynskoho 10; tel. (44) 490-40-00; fax (44) 244-73-50; e-mail press@usinfo.usemb.kiev.ua; internet www.usemb.kiev.ua; Ambassador JOHN HERBST.

**Uzbekistan:** 01901 Kiev, vul. Volodymyrska 16; tel. (44) 228-12-46; fax 229-55-09; Ambassador SHAMANSUR SH. SHAHALILOV.

**Viet Nam:** 01011 Kiev, vul. Lyeskova 5; tel. and fax (44) 295-28-37; fax (44) 294–80–87; Ambassador DOAN DUC.

# Judicial System

**Constitutional Court:** 01033 Kiev, vul. Zhylianska 14; tel. (44) 220-93-98; fax (44) 227-20-01; internet www.ccu.gov.ua; f. 1996; Chair. MYKOLA F. SELIVON; Permanent Rep. of the President at the Constitutional Court VLADYSLAV NOSOV.

**Supreme Court:** 01024 Kiev, vul. P. Orlyka 4; tel. (44) 226-23-04; e-mail interdep@scourt.gov.ua; internet www.scourt.gov.ua; Chair. VASYL MALYARENKO.

**Supreme Arbitration Court:** 01011 Kiev, vul. Kopylenka 6; tel. (44) 536-05-00; fax (44) 536-18-18; e-mail kantselariya@vasu.arbitr.gov.ua; internet www.arbitr.gov.ua; f. 1991; Chief Justice DMYTRO M. PRYTYKA.

**Prosecutor-General:** 01061 Kiev, vul. Riznytska 13/15; tel. (44) 226-20-27; fax (44) 290-26-03; internet www.gpu.gov.ua; Prosecutor-General (vacant); First Deputy Prosecutor-General SERHIY M. VYNOKUROV.

# Religion

## CHRISTIANITY

### The Eastern Orthodox Church

Eastern Orthodoxy is the principal religious affiliation in Ukraine. Until 1990 all legally constituted Orthodox church communities in Ukraine were part of the Ukrainian Exarchate of the Russian Orthodox Church (Moscow Patriarchate). In that year the Russian Orthodox Church in Ukraine was renamed the Ukrainian Orthodox Church (UOC), partly to counter the growing influence of the previously prohibited Ukrainian Autocephalous Orthodox Church (UAOC). In the early 1990s there was considerable tension between the UOC and the UAOC over the issue of church property seized in 1930. A new ecclesiastical organization was formed in June 1992, when Filaret (Denisenko), the disgraced former Metropolitan of Kiev, united with a faction of the UAOC to form the Kievan Patriarchate. The UOC (Kievan Patriarchate) elected a Patriarch, Volodymyr (Romaniuk), in October. Following Volodymyr's death in July 1995, Filaret was elected as Patriarch, prompting some senior clergy to leave the church and join the UAOC, although in the early 2000s the UOC (Kievan Patriarchate) remained the largest church organization in Ukraine.

**Ukrainian Autocephalous Orthodox Church:** 01001 Kiev, vul. Tryokhsvyatytelska 8A; e-mail uapc-ptr@uapc-ptr.kiev.ua; internet www.uaoc.kiev.ua; f. 1921, forcibly incorporated into the Russian Orthodox Church in 1930; continued to operate clandestinely; formally revived in 1990; 1,015 parishes in 2001; Administrator Archbishop IHOR (ISICHENKO).

**Ukrainian Orthodox Church (Moscow Patriarchate):** 01015 Kiev, vul. I. Mazepy 25/49; tel. (44) 290-15-08; internet www.orthodox.org.ua; exarchate of the Russian Orthodox Church (Moscow Patriarchate); 9,049 parishes in 2001; Metropolitan of Kiev VLADIMIR (SABODAN).

**Ukrainian Orthodox Church (Kievan Patriarchate):** 01034 Kiev, vul. Pushkinska 36; tel. (44) 224-10-96; internet www.kievpatr.org.ua; f. 1992 by factions of Ukrainian Orthodox Church and Ukrainian Autocephalous Orthodox Church; 2,781 parishes in 2001; 'Patriarch of Kiev and all Rus-Ukraine' FILARET (DENISENKO).

**Old Believers** (The Old Ritualists): 49017 Dnipropetrovsk, pr. K. Marksa 60/8; tel. (562) 52-17-75; internet www.staroobryad.narod.ru; f. 1652 by separation from the Moscow Patriarchate; 55 parishes in Ukraine in 2001; Leader MARIYA BUZOVSKAYA; Bishop of Kiev and all Ukraine, Savvatiye.

## The Roman Catholic Church

Most Roman Catholics in Ukraine are adherents of the Byzantine Rites, the so-called 'Greek' Catholic Church, which is based principally in Western Ukraine and Transcarpathia. In 2001 there were 3,317 parishes of the Byzantine rites in Ukraine, 807 Roman Catholic parishes of the Latin rite and 15 parishes of the Armenian rite. Ukraine comprises three archdioceses (including one each for Catholics of the Latin, Byzantine and Armenian rites) and 14 dioceses (of which one is directly responsible to the Holy See). At 31 December 2001 there were an estimated 4,436,607 adherents, of which more than 80% followed the Byzantine rites. Adherents of Latin-Rite Catholicism in Ukraine are predominantly ethnic Poles.

**Bishops' Conference:** Bishops' Conference of Ukraine, 79008 Lviv, pl. Katedralna 1; tel. (322) 76-94-15; fax (322) 96–61–14; f. 1992; Pres. Cardinal MARIAN JAWORSKI (Archbishop of Lviv).

### Byzantine Ukrainian Rite

**Archbishop-Major of Lviv:** Cardinal LUBOMYR HUSAR, 79000 Lviv, pl. Sv. Yura 5; tel. (322) 97-11-21; fax (322) 72-25-24; e-mail lv.archeparchy@ugkc.lviv.ua; internet www.ugcc.org.ua; head of Ukrainian Greek Catholic Church; established in 1596 by the Union of Brest, which permitted Orthodox clergymen to retain the Eastern rite, but transferred their allegiance to the Roman Pontiff in 1946, at the self-styled Synod of Lvov (Lviv Sobor); the Catholics of the Byzantine rite were forcibly integrated into the Russian Orthodox Church (Moscow Patriarchate), but continued to function in an 'underground' capacity; re-legalized in 1989.

### Latin Rite

**Metropolitan Archbishop of Lviv:** Cardinal MARIAN JAWORSKI, 79008 Lviv, pl. Katedralna 1; tel. (322) 76-94-15; fax (322) 96-61-14; e-mail k@rkc.lviv.ua; internet www.rkc.lviv.ua.

### Armenian Rite

**Archbishop of Lviv:** (vacant).

### Protestant Churches

There were 6,578 protestant communities registered in Ukraine in 2001. These comprised both those churches that had been repressed and forced to operate clandestinely during the period of Soviet rule, the largest of which were the All-Ukrainian Union of United Evangelical Christians-Baptists, and the All-Ukrainian Union of Christians of the Evangelical Faith—Pentecostalists ('Pyatydesyatnykiv'), and a number of confessions introduced to Ukraine during the 1990s by missionaries, primarily from Europe and North America.

**All-Ukrainian Union of Christians of the Evangelical Faith—Pentecostalists ('Pyatydesyatnykiv'):** 01033 Kiev, vul. Karyerna 44; 1,196 parishes in 2001.

**All-Ukrainian Union of United Churches of Evangelical Christians-Baptists:** 01004 Kiev, vul. L. Tolstoho 3A; tel. (44) 224-04-05; fax (44) 227-74-80; 2,000 parishes, 125,950 adherents in 2001; affiliated to the Euro-Asiatic Federation of the Union of Evangelical Christians-Baptists; Pres. HRIHORIY I. KOMENDANT.

**Ukrainian Lutheran Church:** 01004 Kiev, vul. V. Vasylkivska 14/15; tel. (44) 235-77-21; fax (44) 234-08-00; e-mail vhorpynchuk@yahoo.com0; internet www.ukrlc.org; 30 parishes in 2001; Head of Church Bishop VYACHESLAV HORPYNCHUK.

### ISLAM

In 2001 there were 391 Islamic communities officially registered in Ukraine, of which 293 were located in the Autonomous Republic of Crimea, and an estimated 2m. adherents in total. The return of Crimean Tatars to Crimea from Central Asia, to where they were exiled at Stalin's behest during the Second World War, has had a significant impact upon the growth of Islamic communities in the republic since the early 1990s. An Islamic University was established in Donetsk in 1998.

**Independent Federation of Muslim Social Organizations of Ukraine (Arraid):** 04119 Kiev, vul. Dekhtyarivska 25A; tel. (44) 490-99-00; fax (44) 490-99-22; e-mail office@arraid.org; internet www.arraid.org; f. 1997; brs in Dnipropetrovsk, Donetsk, Kharkiv, Luhansk, Lviv, Odesa, Simferopol, Vinnytsya and Zaporizhzhya; publishes periodical 'Arraid' (*Forward*) in Arabic and Russian and educational material in Russian, Tatar and Ukrainian; undertakes charitable and eductional work; Chair. FAROUK ASHOUR.

**Spiritual Direction of Muslims in Ukraine:** Kiev; f. 1993; Mufti Sheikh TAMIN AHMED MUHAMED MUTAH.

**Mufti of Crimea:** ADZHE NURALI ABLAIYEV, 95000 Crimea, Simferopol, Kebir Çami Mosque.

### JUDAISM

In the mid-1990s there were an estimated 500,000 Jews in Ukraine, despite high levels of emigration from the 1970s. From 1989 there was a considerable revival in the activities of Jewish communities. In 2001 there were 221 Jewish communities in Ukraine, compared with 12 synagogues in 1989. The majority of Jews in Ukraine live in Kiev, Dnipropetrovsk, Kharkiv and Odesa.

**All-Ukrainian Jewish Congress:** 01023 Kiev, vul. Mechnykova 14/1; tel. (44) 235-71-20; fax (44) 235-10-67; e-mail vek@i.kiev.ua; internet www.jewish.kiev.ua; f. 1997; Chief Rabbi of Kiev and All-Ukraine YAAKOV DOV BLEICH; Chair. VADYM RABYNOVYCH.

# The Press

In 1996 there were an estimated 44 daily newspapers and 2,162 periodicals published in Ukraine. In addition to newspapers published in Ukraine, several newspapers and magazines published in the Russian Federation also have a large circulation in Ukraine.

The publications listed below are in Ukrainian, except where otherwise stated.

## PRINCIPAL NEWSPAPERS

**Demokratychna Ukraina** (Democratic Ukraine): 03047 Kiev, pr. Peremohy 50; tel. (44) 441-83-33; f. 1918; fmrly *Radyanska Ukraina* (Soviet Ukraine); 3 a week; independent; Editor OLEKSANDR POBIGAI; circ. 10,000 (2001).

**Den** (The Day): 04212 Kiev, vul Marshala Tymoshenka 2L; tel. (44) 414-40-66; fax (44) 414-49-20; e-mail master@day.kiev.ua; internet www.day.kiev.ua; f. 1998; in Ukrainian and Russian; 5 a week; publ. by the Presa Ukrainy (Press of Ukraine) Publishing House; Editor-in-Chief LARYSA IVSHYNA; circ. 62,500 (2001).

**Fakty i Kommentarii** (Facts and Commentaries): 04116 Kiev, vul. Vandy Vasylevskoy 27–29; tel. (44) 244-57-81; fax (44) 216-85-80; e-mail info@facts.kiev.ua; internet www.facts.kiev.ua; daily; politics, economics, sport, law, culture; in Russian; daily.

**Holos Ukrainy/Golos Ukrainy** (Voice of Ukraine): 03047 Kiev, vul. Nesterova 4; tel. (44) 441-88-11; fax (44) 224-72-54; e-mail mail@golos.com.ua; f. 1991; organ of the Verkhovna Rada; in Ukrainian and Russian; 5 a week; Editor SERHIY M. PRAVDENKO; circ. 150,000 (2002).

**Kievskiye Vedomosti** (Kiev Gazette): 04086 Kiev, vul. Olzhycha 29; tel. (44) 238-28-07; internet www.kv.com.ua; f. 1992; in Russian; national daily; Dir-Gen. VLADIMIR P. DERIKIT; Editor-in-Chief NIKOLAI V. ZAKREVSKII; circ. 138,300 (2002); also weekly edition (Fridays), in Ukrainian, *Kyivski Vidomosti*.

**Kyiv Post:** 01133 Kiev, vul. L. Ukrainky 34/401; tel. (44) 573-83-53; fax (44) 254-31-13; e-mail editor@kppublications.com; internet www.kpnews.com; f. 1995; weekly, in English; Publisher JED SUNDEN; Exec. Editor GREG BLOOM; circ. 25,000 (2002).

**Literaturna Ukraina** (Literary Ukraine): 01061 Kiev, bulv. L. Ukrainky 20; tel. (44) 296-36-39; f. 1927; weekly; organ of Union of Writers of Ukraine; Editor VASYL PLUSHCH; circ. 15,000 (1999).

**Molod Ukrainy** (The Youth of Ukraine): 03047 Kiev, pr. Peremohy 50; tel. (44) 441-83-83; fax (44) 225-31-52; e-mail my@molod.kiev.ua; f. 1994; 3 a week; Editor-in-Chief V. I. BODENCHUK; circ. 37,893 (2001).

**News from Ukraine:** Kiev; tel. and fax (44) 244-58-45; f. 1964; weekly; publ. by the joint-stock co News from Ukraine; in English; readership in 70 countries; Editor VOLODYMYR KANASH; circ. 20,000.

**Pravda Ukrainy** (The Truth of Ukraine): 03047 Kiev, pr. Peremohy 50; tel. (44) 441-85-34; f. 1938; deregistered Jan. 1998, re-registered Jan. 1999; 5 a week; in Russian; Editor-in-Chief OLHA PRONINA; circ. 40,000.

**Robitnycha Hazeta/Rabochaya Gazeta** (Workers' Gazette): 03047 Kiev, pr. Peremohy 50; tel. (44) 441-83-33; fax (44) 446-68-85; f. 1957; 5 a week; publ. by the Cabinet of Ministers and Interregional Association of Manufacturers; editions in Russian and Ukrainian; Editor-in-Chief IVAN G. LITVIN; circ. 113,666 (2001).

**Silski Visti** (Rural News): 03047 Kiev, pr. Peremohy 50; tel. (44) 441-86-32; fax (44) 446-93-71; e-mail silvis@visti.com; internet www.silskivisti.kiev.ua; f. 1920; 3 a week; Editor I. V. SPODARENKO; circ. 572,262 (2002).

**Ukraina Moloda** (Ukraine The Young): 03047 Kiev, pr. Peremohy 50; tel. and fax (44) 454-83-92; e-mail post@umoloda.kiev.ua; 5 a week; independent; opposed to Govt of President Kuchma; Editor MYKHAYLO DOROSHENKO; circ. 103,171 (2002).

**Ukrainska Pravda** (Ukrainian Truth): Kiev; e-mail pravda@svitonline.com; internet www2.pravda.com.ua; online only, in English, Russian and Ukrainian; Editor-in-Chief OLENA PRYTULA.

**Ukrainske Slovo** (The Ukrainian Word): 01010 Kiev, vul. I. Mazepy 6; tel. (44) 290-17-30; fax (44) 290-70-59; e-mail info@

ukrslovo.kiev.ua; internet www.ukrslovo.kiev.ua; f. 1933; weekly; nationalist; Editor-in-Chief BOHDAN CHERVAK.

**Uryadoviy Kuryer** (Official Courier): 01008 Kiev, vul. Sadova 1; tel. (44) 253-12-95; fax (44) 253-39-50; e-mail letter@ukcc.com.ua; internet www.ukcc.com.ua; f. 1990; 5 a week; organ of the Cabinet of Ministers; Editor-in-Chief MYKHAYLO M. SOROKA; circ. 125,000 (2002).

**Vechirniy Kiev** (Evening Kiev): 04136 Kiev, vul. Marshala Hrechka 13; tel. (44) 434-61-09; fax (44) 443-96-09; e-mail office@vecherniykyiv.com; internet www.vecherniykyiv.com; f. 1906; 5 a week; Editor-in-Chief VITALIY KARPENKO; circ. 80,000 (2001).

**Vladi i Polityka/Vlast i Politika** (Power and Politics): 01042 Kiev, vul. P. Lumumby 4v/200; tel. (44) 201-01-28; fax (44) 201-01-29; e-mail vip@vipnews.com.ua; internet www.vipnews.com.ua; f. 2001; weekly; in Ukrainian and Russian; Dir-Gen. ANDRIY V. NAKONECHNYI; Editor-in-Chief YURIY L. UZDEMYR; circ. 22,000 (2002).

**Za Vilnu Ukrainu** (For a Free Ukraine): 79000 Lviv, vul. Voronoho 3; tel. (322) 97-92-49; fax (322) 72-95-27; e-mail zwuky@mail.lviv.ua; f. 1990; 5 a week; independent; Editor-in-Chief MYKHAYLO SIRKIV; circ. 30,058 (2001).

## PRINCIPAL PERIODICALS

**Avto-Tsentr** (Auto-Centre): Kiev-47, POB 2; tel. and fax (44) 441-85-91; e-mail gazeta@avtocentr.kiev.ua; internet www.autocentre.ua; f. 1997; weekly; motoring; in Russian; Editor-in-Chief SERGEI TARNAVSKII; circ. 140,000.

**Barvinok** (Periwinkle): 04119 Kiev, vul. Dekhtyarivska 38–44; tel. (44) 213-99-13; fax (44) 211-04-36; e-mail barvinok@kievweb.com.ua; f. 1928; fortnightly; illustrated popular fiction for school-age children; in Ukrainian and Russian; Editor VASYL VORONOVYCH; circ. 40,000.

**Berezil**: 61002 Kharkiv, vul. Chernyshevskoho 59; tel. (572) 43-41-84; fax (572) 47-61-62; f. 1956; fmrly *Prapor*; monthly; journal of Union of Writers of Ukraine; fiction and socio-political articles; Editor-in-Chief VOLODYMYR NAUMENKO; circ. 5,000.

**Delovaya Stolitsya** (Capital City Business): 01135 Kiev, vul. Pavlovska 29; tel. (44) 461-91-32; fax (44) 461-91-40; e-mail dsnews@dsnews.com.ua; internet www.dsnews.com.ua; f. 2001; weekly; in Russian; Editor-in-Chief INNA KOVTUN; circ. 35,900 (2002).

**Dnipro** (The Dnieper): 04119 Kiev, vul. Dekhtyarivska 38–44; tel. (44) 446-11-42; f. 1927; 2 a month; novels, short stories, essays, poetry; social and political topics; Editor MYKOLA LUKIV.

**Donbas/Donbass**: 83055 Donetsk, vul. Artema 80A; tel. (622) 93-82-26; f. 1923; monthly; journal of Union of Writers of Ukraine; fiction; in Ukrainian and Russian; circ. 20,000 (1991).

**Dzerkalo Tyzhnya/Zerkalo Nedyeli** (Weekly Mirror): 03680 Kiev, vul. Shchorsa 18; tel. (44) 261-82-08; e-mail postmaster@mirror.kiev.ua; internet www.zn.kiev.ua; weekly; politics, economics, the arts; Ukrainian and Russian editions.

**Dzvin** (Bell): 79005 Lviv, vul. Kn. Romana 6; tel. (322) 72-36-20; f. 1940; monthly; journal of Union of Writers of Ukraine; fiction; Editor ROMAN FEDORIV; circ. 152,500.

**Interesna Hazeta** (Interesting Magazine): 03047 Kiev, pr. Peremohy 50; tel. (44) 441-82-59; e-mail postmail@avkpress.kiev.ua; 2 a month; general; circ. 700,000.

**Kiev**: 01025 Kiev, vul. Desyatinna 11; tel. (44) 229-02-80; f. 1983; monthly; journal of the Union of Writers of Ukraine and the Kiev Writers' Organization; fiction; Editor-in-Chief PETRO M. PEREBYJNIS.

**Kompanyon** (Companion): 01103 Kiev, vul. Kykbydze 39; tel. and fax (44) 267-64-07; e-mail komp@maximum.com.ua; internet www.companion.com.ua; f. 1996; weekly; in Russian; economics, politics, business; Editor-in-Chief V. ZUBANYUK; circ. 25,000 (2002).

**Malyatko** (Child): 04119 Kiev, vul. Dekhtyarivska 38–44; tel. and fax (44) 213-98-91; f. 1960; monthly; illustrated; for pre-school children; Editor-in-Chief ANATOLIY GRIGORUK; circ. 25,800 (2002).

**Nataly:** 02156 Kiev, vul. Kyoto 25; tel. (44) 519-34-33; fax (44) 518-77-90; internet www.nataly.com.ua; monthly; women's interest; Editor-in-Chief ZHANNA LAVROVA; circ. 679,115 (2002).

**Natsionalna Bezpeka i Oborona** (National Security and Defence): 01034 Kiev, vul. Volodymyrska 46; tel. (44) 201-11-98; fax (44) 201-11-99; e-mail info@uceps.com.ua; internet www.uceps.com.ua/eng/work/work_journal.shtml; f. 2000; publ. by Oleksandr Razumkov Ukrainian Centre for Political and Economic Research; monthly; politics, economics, international relations; in Ukrainian and English; Pres. ANATOLIY HRYTSENKO.

**Obrazotvorche Mistetstvo** (Fine Arts): 04655 Kiev, vul. Sichovykh Striltsiv 1–5; tel. (44) 212-02-86; fax (44) 212-14-54; e-mail spilka@nbi.com.ua; f. 1933; 4 a year; publ. by the Artists' Union of Ukraine; fine arts; Editor-in-Chief MYKOLA MARYCHEVSKIY; circ. 1,500.

**Perets** (Pepper): 03047 Kiev, pr. Peremohy 50; tel. (44) 441-82-14; fax (44) 441-89-11; f. 1927; fortnightly; publ. by the Presa Ukrainy Publishing House; satirical; Editor YURIY PROKOPENKO; circ. 19,300.

**Politychna Dumka/Politicheskaya Mysl** (Political Thought): 01030 Kiev, vul. Leontovycha 5; tel. and fax (44) 235-02-29; e-mail politdumka@bigmir.net; internet www.politdumka.kiev.ua; f. 1993; current affairs and political analysis; Ukrainian, Russian and English editions; Editor-in-Chief VOLODYMYR POLOKHALO.

**Polityka i Chas/Politics and the Times**: 02160 Kiev, pr. Vozyednanya 15–17; tel. and fax (44) 550-31-44; e-mail times@uct.kiev.ua; f. 1994 to replace *Pid praporom Lenina* (Under the Banner of Lenin); monthly; organ of the Ministry of Foreign Affairs; international relations and foreign affairs; in Ukrainian (monthly) and English (quarterly); Editor-in-Chief LEONID BAIDAK; circ. 6,000 (2003).

**Ukraina** (Ukraine): 03047 Kiev, pr. Peremohy 50; tel. and fax (44) 446-63-16; internet uamedia.visti.net/ukraine/; f. 1941; monthly; social and political life in Ukraine; illustrated; Editor-in-Chief YURIY PERESUNKO; circ. 70,000.

**Ukraina Business** (Ukraine Business): 01004 Kiev, vul. Pushkinska 20/24; tel. and fax (44) 224-25-55; e-mail malva@ukrbus.kiev.ua; f. 1990; weekly; Editor-in-Chief YURIY VASYLCHUK; circ. 22,000 (2001).

**Ukrainskiy Teatr** (Ukrainian Theatre): Kiev; tel. (44) 228-24-74; f. 1936; 6 a year; publ. by the Mistetstvo (Fine Art) Publishing House; journal of the Ministry of Art and Culture, and the Union of Theatrical Workers of Ukraine; Editor-in-Chief YURIY BOHDASHEVSKIY; circ. 4,100.

**Visti z Ukrainy** (News from Ukraine): 01034 Kiev, vul. Zolotovoritska 6; tel. (44) 228-56-42; fax (44) 228-04-28; f. 1960; weekly; aimed at Ukrainian diaspora; Editor VALERIY STETSENKO; circ. 50,000.

**Vitchyzna** (Fatherland): 01021 Kiev, vul. M. Hrushevskoho 34; tel. (44) 253-28-51; f. 1933; 6 a year; Ukrainian prose and poetry; Editor OLEKSANDR HLUSHKO; circ. 50,100.

**Vsesvit** (The Whole World): 01021 Kiev, vul. M. Hrushevskoho 34/1; tel. (44) 293-13-18; fax (44) 253-28-88; e-mail myk@vsesvit-review.kiev.ua; f. 1925; monthly; publ. by the Vsesvit Publishing House; foreign fiction, critical works and reviews of foreign literature and art; Editor-in-Chief OLEH MYKYTENKO; circ. 3,000.

**Yeva** (Eve): 04050 Kiev, vul. Melnykova 12A/8; tel. (44) 568-59-53; e-mail centre@yanko.com.ua; internet www.evamag.kiev.ua; f. 1998; six a year; fashion, design; Editor-in-Chief IRYNA B. DANYLEVSKA; circ. 10,000 (2002).

**Zhinka** (Woman): 03047 Kiev, pr. Peremohy 50; tel. and fax (44) 446-90-34; e-mail zhinka@cki.ipri.kiev.ua; f. 1920; monthly; publ. by Presa Ukrainy Publishing House; social and political subjects; fiction; for women; Editor LIDIYA MAZUR; circ. 250,000.

## NEWS AGENCIES

**Interfax-Ukraina** (Interfax-Ukraine): 01034 Kiev, vul. Reitarska 8/5a; tel. (44) 464-04-65; fax (44) 464-05-69; e-mail news@interfax.kiev.ua; internet www.interfax.kiev.ua; f. 1992; Dir OLEKSANDR MARTYNENKO.

**Respublika Ukrainian Independent Information Agency (UNIAR):** 02005 Kiev, vul. Mechnykova 14/1; tel. (44) 246-46-34; e-mail naboka@uniar.kiev.ua; internet www.uniar.com.ua; independent press agency; Dir S. NABOKA.

**Ukrainian Independent Information and News Agency (UNIAN):** 01001 Kiev, vul. Khreshchatyk 4; tel. (44) 229-33-53; fax (44) 461-91-11; e-mail info@unian.net; internet www.unian.net; press agency and monitoring service; publishes weekly bulletins concerning finance, technology, business, construction; photographic agency; selected services are provided in Ukrainian, Russian and English; Gen. Man. MYKHAYLO I. BATIH; Editor-in-Chief OLEKSANDR KHARCHENKO.

**Ukrainski Novyni Informatsyonnoye Ahentstvo** (Ukrainian News Information Agency): 01033 Kiev, vul. Volodymyrska 61/11/41; tel. (44) 494-31-60; fax (44) 494-31-67; e-mail office@ukranews.com; internet www.ukranews.com; f. 1993; economic and political news; in Ukrainian, Russian and English.

**UkrInform–Ukrainian National Information Agency:** 01001 Kiev, vul. B. Khmelnytskoho 8/16B; tel. (44) 229-22-42; fax (44) 229-81-52; e-mail chiefadm@ukrinform.com; internet www.dinau.com; f. 1918; until 1990 Ukrainian branch of TASS (State Information Agency of the Soviet Union).

### Foreign Bureaux

**Agenzia Nazionale Stampa Associata (ANSA)** (Italy): Kiev, vul. Chitadelna 5–9/45; tel. and fax (44) 290-21-38; internet www.ansa.it; Correspondent ALESSANDRO PARONE.

**Česká tisková kancelář (ČTK)** (Czech Republic): 01042 Kiev, vul. I. Kudri 41/22/49; tel. and fax (44) 295-91-61; internet www.ctk.cz.

**Deutsche Presse-Agentur (dpa)** (Germany): 01001 Kiev, vul. Khreshchatyk 29/32; tel. (44) 225-57-60; internet www.dpa.de.

**Magyar Távirati Iroda (MTI)** (Hungary): 01030 Kiev, vul. Ivana Franka 24A /8; tel. and fax (44) 235-62-04; e-mail mti@gu.kiev.ua; internet www.mti.ua; Correspondent KATALIN BENKONE OZE.

**Reuters Ltd** (United Kingdom): 01001 Kiev, vul. B. Khmelnytskoho 8–16/112; tel. (44) 244-91-50; fax (44) 244-91-53; e-mail kiev .newsroom@reuters.com; internet www.reuters.com; Chief Correspondent T. RODDAM.

**RIA—Novosti** (Russian Information Agency—News) (Russia): 03150 Kiev, vul. V. Vasylivska 134/49; tel. and fax (44) 434-48-45.

# Publishers

In 1996 there were 6,460 book titles (including pamphlets and brochures) published in Ukraine (total circulation 50.9m.).

**Budivelnik** (Builder): 04053 Kiev, vul. Observatorna 25; tel. (44) 212-10-90; f. 1947; books on building and architecture; in Ukrainian and Russian; Dir S. N. BALATSKII.

**Carpaty** (The Carpathians): 88000 Transcarpathian obl., Uzhhorod, Radyanska pl. 3; tel. (312) 23-25-13; fiction and criticism; in Ukrainian and Russian; Dir V. I. DANKANICH.

**Dnipro** (The Dnieper): 01061 Kiev, vul. Volodymyrska 42; tel. (44) 224-31-82; f. 1919; fiction, poetry and critical works; in Ukrainian and Russian; Dir TARAS I. SERGIYCHUK.

**Donbas/Donbass:** 83002 Donetsk, vul. B. Khmelnytskoho 102; tel. (622) 93-25-84; fiction and criticism; in Ukrainian and Russian; Dir B. F. KRAVCHENKO.

**Folio:** Kharkiv; tel. and fax (572) 47-61-25; e-mail foliosp@kharkov .ukrpack.net; internet folio.com.ua; f. 1992; classic and contemporary fiction in Russian, Ukrainian and French; Gen. Man. ALEKSANDR V. KRASOVITSKII.

**Kamenyar** (Stonecrusher): 79000 Lviv, vul. Pidvalna 3; tel. (322) 72-19-49; fax (322) 72-79-22; fiction and criticism; in Ukrainian; Dir DMYTRO I. SAPIGA.

**Konsum:** 61057 Kharkiv, POB 9123; tel. (572) 17-01-19; fax (572) 23-76-75; e-mail book@konsum.kharkov.ua; internet konsum .kharkov.ua; politics, economics, human rights, legal and medical books.

**Lybid** (Swan): 01001 Kiev, vul. Pushkinska 32; tel. (44) 228-10-93; fax (44) 229-11-71; e-mail info@lybid.org.ua; internet www.lybid.org .ua; f. 1835; University of Kiev press; Dir OLENA A. BOIKO.

**Mayak** (Beacon): 65001 Odesa, vul. Zhukovskoho 14; tel. (482) 22-35-95; fiction and criticism; in Ukrainian and Russian; Dir D. A. BUKHANENKO.

**Medytsyna Svitu** (Medicines of the World): 79017 Lviv, vul. Rodyny Krushelnytskykh 14; tel. and fax (322) 75-51-12; e-mail msvitu@mail.lviv.ua; internet www.msvitu.lviv.ua; f. 1997; medical journals and books, books pertaining to history, art and religion; Dirs VOLODYMYR PAVLIUK, ZENON MATCHAK.

**Mistetstvo** (Fine Art): 01034 Kiev, vul. Zolotovoritska 11; tel. (44) 225-53-92; fax (44) 229-05-64; f. 1932; fine art criticism, theatre and screen art, tourism, Ukrainian culture; in Ukrainian, Russian, English, French and German; Dir VALENTIN M. KUZMENKO.

**Molod** (Youth): 04119 Kiev, vul. Dekhtyarivska 38–44; tel. (44) 213-11-60; fax (44) 213-11-92; in Ukrainian; Dir O. I. POLONSKA.

**Muzichna Ukraina** (Music of Ukraine): 01034 Kiev, vul. Pushkinska 32; tel. (44) 225-63-56; fax (44) 224-63-00; f. 1966; books on music; in Ukrainian; Dir N. P. LINNIK; Editor-in-Chief B. R. VERESHCHAGIN.

**Naukova Dumka** (Scientific Thought): 01601 Kiev, vul. Tereshchenkivska 3; tel. (44) 234-40-68; fax (44) 234-70-60; e-mail ndumka@kiev.ua; f. 1922; scientific books and periodicals in all branches of science; research monographs; Ukrainian literature; dictionaries and reference books; in Ukrainian, Russian and English; Dir I. R. ALEKSEYENKO.

**Osvita** (Education): 04053 Kiev, vul. Y. Kotsyubynski 5; tel. and fax (44) 216-54-44; e-mail osvita@kv.ukrtel.net; f. 1920; educational books for schools of all levels; Dir-Gen. IRAYIDA PODOLYUK.

**Prapor** (Flag): 61002 Kharkiv, vul. Chubarya 11; tel. (572) 47-72-52; fax (572) 43-07-21; fmrly named *Berezil*; general; in Ukrainian and Russian; Dir V. S. LEBETS.

**Prosvita** (Enlightenment): 01032 Kiev, bulv. Shevchenka 46; tel. (44) 224-15-86; fax (44) 224-95-23; e-mail office@prosvita.kiev.ua;

internet www.prosvita.kiev.ua; f. 1990; textbooks for all levels from education from pre-school to higher education.

**Rodovid:** 01015 Kiev, vul. I. Mazepy 29; tel. (44) 254-32-37; fax (44) 290-29-31; e-mail rodovid@carrier.kiev.ua; internet www.rodovid .net; history, ethnography, poetry, cultural history.

**Sich** (Camp): 49070 Dnipropetrovsk, pr. K. Marksa 60; tel. (562) 45-22-01; fax (562) 45-44-04; f. 1964; fiction, juvenile, socio-political, criticism; in Ukrainian, English, German, French and Russian; Dir V. A. SIROTA; Editor-in-Chief V. V. LEVCHENKO.

**Tavria:** 95000 Crimea, Simferopol, vul. Gorkogo 5; tel. (652) 27-45-66; fax (652) 27-65-74; fiction, criticism, folklore and geography; in Ukrainian, Russian and Crimean Tatar; Dir Y. IVANICHENKO.

**Tekhnika** (Technologyi): Kiev; tel. (44) 228-22-43; f. 1930; industry and transport books, popular science, posters and booklets; in Ukrainian and Russian; Dir M. G. PISARENKO.

**Tsentr Yevropy** (The Centre of Europe): 79000 Lviv, vul. Kostyushko 18/317; tel. (322) 72-35-66; fax (322) 72-76-71; e-mail centrevtr@is.lviv.ua; internet www.centrevtr@is.lviv.ua; f. 1994; books related to the history and culture of Halychyna; Dir SERHIY E. FRUKHT.

**Ukraina:** 01054 Kiev, vul. Hoholivska 7H; tel. (44) 216-36-02; fax (44) 216-97-35; e-mail ua@alfacom.net; internet www.ua.alfacom .net; f. 1922; humanities, science, reference and literary works; Dir MYKOLA V. STETYUHA; Editor-in-Chief OLEKSANDR P. KOSYUK.

**Ukrainska Ensyklopedia** (Ukrainian Encyclopedia): 01030 Kiev, vul. B. Khmelnytskoho 51; tel. (44) 224-80-85; encyclopedias, dictionaries and reference books; Dir A. V. KUDRITSKIY.

**Ukrainskiy Pysmennyk** (Ukrainian Writer): 01054 Kiev, vul. O. Honshara 52; tel. (44) 216-25-92; f. 1933; publishing house of the Union of Writers of Ukraine; fiction; in Ukrainian; Dir V. P. SKOMAROVSKYI.

**Urozhai** (Harvest): 03035 Kiev, vul. Uritskoho 45; tel. (44) 220-16-26; f. 1925; books and journals about agriculture; Dir V. G. PRIKHODKO.

**Veselka** (Rainbow): 04050 Kiev, vul. Melnikova 63; tel. (44) 213-95-01; fax (44) 213-33-59; e-mail veskiev@iptelecom.net.ua; f. 1934; books for pre-school and school age children; in Ukrainian and foreign languages; Dir YAREMA HOYAN.

**Vyscha Shkola** (High School): 01054 Kiev, vul. Hoholivska 7; tel. and fax (44) 216-33-05; f. 1968; educational, scientific, reference, etc.; Dir V. P. KHOVKHUN; Editor-in-Chief V. V. PIVEN.

**Zdorovya** (Health): 01054 Kiev, vul. O. Honshara 65; tel. (44) 216-89-08; books on medicine, physical fitness and sport; in Ukrainian; Dir A. P. RODZIYEVSKIY.

**Znannya** (Knowledge): 01034 Kiev, vul. Striletska 28; tel. (44) 234-80-43; fax (44) 234-23-36; e-mail znannia@society.kiev.ua; internet www.znannia.com.ua; f. 1948; general non-fiction; Dir VOLODOMYR KARASOV.

# Broadcasting and Communications

## TELECOMMUNICATIONS

### Regulatory Authorities

**RRT:** 04112 Kiev, vul. Dorohozhytska 10; tel. (44) 226-22-60; fax (44) 440-87-22; e-mail vvu@concernbrn.kiev.ua; f. 1970; leases satellite communications channels for radio and television broadcasting and telecommunications; Pres. VOLODYMYR ISHCHUK.

**State Committee for Communication and Information:** see section on The Government.

### Major Service Providers

**Golden Telecom GSM:** 01021 Kiev, vul. Mechnikova 14/1; tel. (44) 247-56-65; internet www.goldentele.com; mobile cellular telephone services; Gen. Man. YURIY BEZBORODIV.

**Ukrainian Mobile Communications (UMC):** 01010 Kiev, vul. Moskovska 21; tel. (44) 311-95-59; fax (44) 314-22-48; e-mail slavik@ umc.com.ua; internet www.umc.com.ua; f. 1991; 51% owned by Ukrtelecom; Deutsche Telekom AG (Germany), TDC Tele Danmark (Denmark) and Royal KPN NV (Netherlands) each own 16.3% of shares; operates mobile cellular telephone network; Gen. Man. MARTIN DIRKS; 1,110,000 subscribers (March 2002).

**UkrTelecom:** 01030 Kiev, bulv. Shevchenka 18; tel. (44) 226-25-41; fax (44) 229-25-06; e-mail ukrtelecom@ukrtel.net; internet www .ukrtel.net; f. 1993; national fixed telecommunications network operator; provides national and international telecommunications services; Gen. Man. P. NETUDYTHATA.

## BROADCASTING

### Regulatory Authorities

**National Council for Television and Radio Broadcasting** (Natsionalna Rada Ukrainy z pytan Telebachennya i Radiomovlennya): 01025 Kiev, vul. Desyatynna 14; tel. (44) 228-74-11; fax (44) 228-75-75; e-mail tvr@i.com.ua; internet www.nradatvr.kiev.ua; f. 1994; monitoring and supervisory functions; issues broadcasting licences; Chair. BORYS KHOLOD.

**State Committee for Information Policy, Television and Radio Broadcasting:** see section on The Government.

### Radio

**Ukrainian State Television and Radio Co** (Derzhavna Teleradiomovna Kompaniya Ukrainy): 01001 Kiev, vul. Khreshchatyk 26; Chair. ZYNOVIY V. KULYK.

**Hromadske—Community Radio:** Kiev, vul. Volodymyrska 61/11/50; tel. (44) 494-40-14; e-mail roman@radio.org.ua; internet www.radio.org.ua; information, news and discussion programmes; Pres. (vacant).

**National Radio Co Ukraine-Ukrainian Radio** (Natsionalna Radiokompaniya Ukrainy-Ukrainske Radio): 01001 Kiev, vul. Khreshchatyk 26; tel. (44) 229-12-85; fax (44) 299-11-70; e-mail vsru@nrcu.gov.ua.

**Radio Ukraine International:** 01001 Kiev, vul. Khreshchatyk 26; tel. (44) 229-45-86; e-mail vsru@nrcu.gov.ua; broadcasts in English, German, Romanian and Ukrainian; Chief Editor VIKTOR I. NABRUSKO.

There were, in addition, several independent radio stations broadcasting to the major cities of Ukraine.

### Television

**Ukrainian State Television and Radio Co** (Derzhavna Teleradiomovna Kompaniya Ukrainy): see Radio (above); Chair. of Television OLEKSANDR M. SAVENKO.

**1+1:** 01023 Kiev, vul. Mechnikova 14/1; tel. (44) 246-46-00; fax (44) 246-45-18; e-mail contact@1plus1.tv; internet www.1plus1.tv; f. 1995; independent; broadcasts for 15 hours daily to 95% of Ukrainian population; Dir-Gen. OLEKSANDR YU. RODNYANSKY.

**Inter:** 01601 Kiev, vul. Dmitriyevska 30; tel. and fax (44) 490-67-65; e-mail pr@inter.ua; internet www.inter.kiev.ua; f. 1996.

**Novy Kanal** (New Channel): 04107 Kiev, vul. Nahorna 24/1; tel. (44) 238-80-28; fax (44) 238-80-20; e-mail post@novy.tv; internet www.novy.tv; f. 1998; broadcasts in Ukrainian and Russian; Chair. OLEKSANDR M. TKACHENKO.

**Pershyi Natsionalnyi** (First National): 04119 Kiev, vul. Melnykova 42; tel. (44) 241-39-09; fax (44) 246-88-48; e-mail office@firstnational.kiev.ua; internet www.fn.com.ua; state-owned.

**STB:** Kiev; e-mail y@stb.ua; internet stb.ua; Dirs VLAD STAROVOYTOV, KYRYL BYSTRYAKOV.

# Finance

(cap. = capital; res = reserves; dep. = deposits; brs = branches; m. = million; amounts in hryvnyas, unless otherwise indicated)

## BANKING

Reform of the banking sector was initiated in 1996, when responsibility for the issuing of licences was transferred to the Committee on Banking Supervision. A division of the National Bank of Ukraine was established to identify those banks in need of restructuring.

In May 1998 there were 217 commercial banks and seven foreign banks in Ukraine. Most of the commercial banks were single-branch banks, operating solely within the region in which they were registered.

### Central Bank

**National Bank of Ukraine:** 01008 Kiev, vul. Institutska 9; tel. (44) 253-44-78; fax (44) 230-20-33; e-mail postmaster@bank.gov.ua; internet www.bank.gov.ua; f. 1991; cap. 10m., res 1,487m. (Jan. 2003), dep. 5,780m. (Dec. 2000); Gov. SERHIY L. TIHIPKO; First Vice-Gov. ARSENIY YATSENYUK.

### Other State Banks

**Republican Bank of Crimea:** 95000 Crimea, Simferopol, ul. Gorkogo; tel. (652) 51-09-46; e-mail webmaster@rbc.crimea.ua.

**UkrExImBank JSC—State Export-Import Bank of Ukraine:** 03150 Kiev, vul. Horkoho 127; tel. (44) 226-27-45; fax (44) 247-80-82; e-mail bank@eximb.com; internet www.eximb.com; f. 1992; fmrly br.

of USSR Vneshekonombank; deals with foreign firms, joint ventures and import-export associations; cap. US $76.6m., res $16.0m., dep. $470.8m. (July 2002); Chair. of Bd OLEKSANDR N. SOROKIN; 28 brs.

### Commercial Banks

**AVAL Bank—JS Postal-Pension Bank Aval:** 01011 Kiev, vul. Leskova 9; tel. (44) 490-88-01; fax (44) 490-87-55; e-mail office@head.aval.kiev.ua; internet www.avalbank.com; f. 1992; 83.86% privately-owned; cap. US $63.8m., dep. $869.7m., total assets $952.8m. (Dec. 2001); Pres. FEDIR I. SHPIG; Chair. of Bd OLEKSANDR DERKACH; 1,230 brs.

**Bank Pekao (Ukraine) Ltd:** 43016 Volyn obl., Lutsk, vul. Halytskoho 14; tel. (332) 77-62-10; fax (332) 72-03-57; e-mail pekao@pekao.com.ua; internet www.pekao.com.ua; f. 1997; present name adopted 2000; 100% owned by Polish interests; cap. 22.5m., res 1.7m., dep. 8.7m. (Dec. 1999); Pres. DARIUSZ KLIMONT.

**Crédit Lyonnais Bank Ukraine (CLBU):** 01034 Kiev, vul. Volodymyrska 23A; tel. (44) 490-14-01; fax (44) 490-14-02; e-mail general@clu.kiev.ua; internet www.creditlyonnais.kiev.ua; f. 1993; cap. 33.6m., res 2.1m., dep. 169.6m. (Dec. 2002); Chair. and Dir-Gen. JACQUES MOUNIER.

**Crimea-Bank:** 95000 Crimea, Simferopol, vul. Krylova 37; tel. (652) 27-04-76; fax (652) 27-04-56.

**EnergoBank:** 01001 Kiev, vul. Lyuteranska 9/9; tel. (44) 201-69-02; fax (44) 228-39-54; e-mail bank@enbank.kiev.ua; internet www.enbank.kiev.ua; f. 1991; cap. 14.4m., res 7.8m., dep. 176.4m. (Dec. 2001); Pres. YEVHEN M. PATRUSHEV.

**Fiatbank:** 29000 Khmelnytsky, vul. Proskurovska 19; tel. (382) 26-47-18; fax (382) 226-91-18; Gen. Dir VALERIY BEZVERKHNIY.

**Finance and Credit Banking Corpn:** 04050 Kiev, vul. Sichovykh Striltsiv 60; tel. (44) 490-68-70; fax (44) 238-24-65; e-mail common@fc.kiev.ua; internet www.fc.kiev.ua; f. 1990; present name adopted 1995; cap. US $13.3m., res $3.3m., dep. $63.7m. (Aug. 2002); Chair. of Bd VADYM PUSHAREV; 11 brs.

**First Ukrainian International Bank/Pershyi Ukrainskyi Mizhnarodnyi Bank (FUIB):** 83000 Donetsk, vul. Universitetska 2A; tel. (623) 32-45-03; fax (623) 32-47-00; e-mail info@fuib.com; internet www.fuib.com; f. 1991; 26.4% owned by AzovStal Iron and Steel Works, 20% by Fortis Bank (Netherlands); cap. US $12.4m., res $52.7m., dep. $144.0m. (Dec. 2001); Chair. of Bd N. P. VINOGRADOV.

**Inko Joint-Stock Bank:** 01021 Kiev, vul. Mechnikova 18; tel. (44) 294-92-19; fax (44) 293-87-90.

**Khreshchatyk Open Joint-Stock Bank:** 01001 Kiev, vul. Khreshchatyk 8A; tel. and fax (44) 464-12-28; e-mail bank@xbank.com.ua; internet www.xcitibank.com.ua; f. 1993 as Zgoda Commercial Bank; 53.3% owned by Central Financial Dept of Kiev City State Administration; present name adopted 2001; cap. 59.9m., res 4.5m., dep. 187.0m. (Dec. 2001); Chair. of Bd DMYTRO M. HRYDZHUK.

**Kredyt Bank (Ukraina):** 79026 Lviv, vul. Sakharova 78; tel. (322) 97-23-20; fax (322) 97-08-37; e-mail office@wucb.lviv.net; internet www.kredytbank.com.ua; f. 1990; fmrly West Ukrainian Commercial Bank—Zakhidno-Ukrainskyi Komertsiinyi Bank; present name adopted 2001; 66.7% owned by Kredyt Bank SA (Poland), 28.25% owned by European Bank for Reconstruction and Development (United Kingdom); cap. 143.4m., res −19.4m., dep. 720.0m. (Dec. 2002); Pres. STEPAN I. KUBIV.

**Kredytprombank:** 01014 Kiev, 38 bulv. Druzhby Naradiv; tel. and fax (44) 244-43-65; e-mail kpb@kreditprombank.com; internet www.kreditprombank.com; f. 1997, as Inkombank-Ukraina; present name adopted 1999; 43.6% owned by Homerton Trading Ltd (Ireland); dep. 415.2m., total assets 595.1m. (Dec. 2001); Chair. of Bd NIKOLAI P. ROZHKO; Chief Exec. LYUDMILA V. RASPUTNA.

**Legbank:** 01033 Kiev, vul. Zhylyanska 27; tel. (44) 227-95-00; fax (44) 227-95-19; e-mail legbank@legbank.kiev.ua; internet www.legbank.kiev.ua; f. 1989; 11 brs.

**Lesbank:** 88000 Uzhhorod, vul. Voloshina 52; tel. (312) 23-31-01; fax (312) 23-25-04; Pres. and Chair. VASYLIY D. SIVULYA.

**Megabank-East Ukrainian Power Bank 'Megabank':** 61002 Kharkiv, vul. Artema 30; tel. (572) 14-33-63; fax (572) 47-20-79; e-mail mega@megabank.net; internet www.megabank.net; f. 1990 as Dobrodiy; present name adopted 1996; cap. US $14.5m., dep. $32.2m., total assets $42.0m. (Dec. 2000); Chair. of Bd VIKTOR H. SUBOTIN; Pres. OLEKSIY LOHVINENKO; 8 brs.

**MRIYA Bank:** 01601 Kiev, vul. Hoholevska 22–24; tel. (44) 239-35-35; e-mail webmaster@mriya.com; internet www.mriya.com; f. 1992; cap. 13.6m., res 4.6m., dep. 315.5m. (Dec. 2001); Chair. of Bd KONSTANTIN VORUSHILIN; 16 brs.

**Nadra Bank:** 04053 Kiev, vul. Sichovykh Striltsiv 15; tel. (44) 238-84-00; fax (44) 246-48-40; e-mail pr@nadrabank.kiev.ua; internet www.nadra.com.ua; f. 1993; cap. 221.1m., res 128.3m. (Jan. 2003); Pres. I. GILENKO; 152 brs.

**JSCB Perkombank—Personal Computer Bank:** 04070 Kiev, vul. P. Sahaidachniy 17; tel. (44) 255-86-23; fax (44) 255-86-54; e-mail bank@percombank.kiev.ua; f. 1990; cap. 20.7m., res 9.6m., dep. 70.8m. (Jan. 2003); Chair. of Bd SERHIY P. BELY; 3 brs.

**Pivdennyi Bank** (Southern Bank): 65044 Odesa, bulv. Frantsuzskyi 10; tel. and fax (482) 34-43-98; e-mail lds@pivdenny.odessa.ua; f. 1993; cap. 42.7m., dep. 484.9m., total assets 551.9m. (Dec. 2001). Chair. of Bd and Dir-Gen. VADYM MOROKHOVSKY; 4 brs.

**Praveks–Bank:** 01021 Kiev, uzviz Klovskiy 9/2; tel. (44) 294-81-80; fax (44) 294-81-03; e-mail bank@pravex.com; internet www.pravex .com; f. 1992; cap. 60.7m., res 69.6m., dep. 470.4m. (Dec. 2001). Chair. of Council LEONID CHERNOVETSKIY; Chair. of Bd ANATOLIY KHIL-CHEVSKIY; 300 brs and sub-brs.

**Premierbank:** 49000 Dnipropetrovsk, vul. Mechnykova 10; tel. (56) 770-44-00; fax (56) 770-02-71; e-mail post@premierbank.dp.ua; internet www.premierbank.dp.ua; f. 1994; present name adopted 1999; cap. 30.0m., res 12.4m., dep. 172.6m. (Dec. 2001); Pres. VOLODYMYR M. HAVRYLOV; Chair. of Bd IGOR N. FOMIN; 5 brs.

**PrivatBank:** 49094 Dnipropetrovsk, nab. Peremohy 50; tel. (562) 39-05-11; fax (56) 778-54-74; e-mail privatbank@pbank.dp.ua; internet www.privatbank.com.ua; cap. 439.3m., dep. 4,271.7m., total assets 4,753.2m. (Dec. 2001); Chair. of Bd A. DOUBILET.

**Prominvestbank** (Industrial-Investment Bank): 01001 Kiev, provulok Shevchenka 12; tel. (44) 201-51-20; fax (44) 229-14-56; e-mail alf@pib.com.ua; internet www.pib.com.ua; f. 1922 as Stroibank, name changed 1992; 90% privately owned; cap. 774.0m., res 302.4m., dep. 2,993.0m. (Jan. 2002); Chair. VOLODYMYR P. MATVYENKO; 600 brs.

**Raiffeisenbank Ukraine:** 01054 Kiev, vul. Vorovskoho 40; tel. (44) 490-05-00; fax (44) 490-05-01; e-mail infobox.rbu@rbu-kiev .raiffeisen.at; internet www.raiffeisenbank.com.ua; f. 1998; 100% owned by Austrian interests; cap. 92.7m., res 23.5m., dep. 814.5m. (Dec. 2001); Chair. of Bd IHOR FRANTSKEVYCH.

**Real Bank:** 61200 Kharkiv, pr. Lenina 60A; tel. (572) 33-27-14; fax (572) 33-31-06; e-mail bank@real.kharkov.ua; internet www.real .kharkov.ua; f. 1990; cap. 26.4m., dep. 81.3m., total assets 148.8m. (Jan. 2002); Chair. YURIY M. SHRAMKO; 4 brs and sub-brs.

**Rostok Bank:** 03067 Kiev, bulv. I. Lepse 4; tel. (44) 484-50-35; fax (44) 488-74-21; e-mail rostok_bank@svitonline.com; internet www .rostok-bank.kiev.ua; f. 1994; cap. US $3.4m., res $0.8m., dep. $2.6m. (Dec. 2002); Pres. IHOR MASOL; Chair. ANATOLIY KOSMIN; 3 brs.

**Skhidno-Yevropeyskiy Bank** (East European Bank): 01042 Kiev, vul. Druzhby Narodiv 17/5; tel. (44) 205-42-70; fax (44) 205-42-78; e-mail eebank@eebank.com.ua; internet www.eebank.com.ua; f. 1993; present name adopted 1998; cap. 20.6m., res 0.7m., dep. 49.6m. (Dec. 2001); Pres. MYKHAYLO HONCHAROV; Dir-Gen. BORYS DOMIN.

**Tavrika Bank:** 99028 Sevastopol, ul. Repina 1; tel. (692) 45-42-01; fax (692) 45-42-02; e-mail bank@ukr.net; internet www.tavrika.com; f. 1991; cap. 41.4m., res 7.0m., dep. 69.6m. (Dec. 2002); Chair. of Bd SERGEI A. BOGATYREV; 7 brs.

**Transbank:** 03150 Kiev, vul. Fizkultury 9; tel. (44) 227-27-83; fax (44) 220-45-88; e-mail common@transbank.kiev.ua; internet www .transbank.kiev.ua; f. 1991; cap. 25.0m., res 3.8m., dep. 35.7m. (Dec. 2002); Pres. ANTON Y. TRETYAKOV; Chair. of Bd VALENTINA V. LASHKEVICH; 3 brs.

**Ukrainian Bank for Trade Co-operation (Bank Torhovoho Spivrobitnytstva):** 61003 Kharkiv, vul. Klochkivska 3; tel. (572) 23-58-68; fax (572) 12-18-52; e-mail bank@ubtc.kharkov.ua; internet www.ubtc.kharkov.ua; f. 1992; cap. 5.0m., res 0.2m., dep. 3.0m. (Jan. 2001); Pres. ZAKHAR BRUK.

**Ukrainian Credit Bank:** 03056 Kiev, pr. Peremohy 37; tel. (44) 236-96-31; fax (44) 230-23-86; e-mail roleg@viaduk.net; internet www.ucb.com.ua; f. 1992; cap. 28.2m., res 29.4m., dep. 501.2m. (Dec. 2002); Pres. VALENTIN A. ZHURSKIY; 1 br.

**Ukrainian Innovation Bank—Ukrinbank:** 04053 Kiev, Voznesenskiy uzviz 10A; tel. (44) 247-20-02; fax (44) 247-21-18; e-mail ukrinbank@ukrinbank.com; internet www.ukrinbank.com; f. 1989; long-term investment credits; commercial and foreign exchange transactions; cap. 40m., res 24m., dep. 293m. (Aug. 2002); Chair. SERHIY MESCHERYAK; 27 brs.

**UkrGazPromBank:** 02098 Kiev, Dniprovska nab. 13; tel. (44) 553-65-45; fax (44) 553-29-39; e-mail ukrgazprombank@ugpb.com; internet www.ugpb.com; f. 1996; cap. 18.2m., res 0.0m., dep. 8.8m. (Dec. 2000); Pres. VOLODYMYR MAKIYINKO; Chair. LEONID STOVBCHATY.

**UkrSibbank:** 61005 Kharkiv, pr. Moskovskyi 60; tel. (572) 21-92-12; fax (572) 28-26-20; e-mail bank@ukrsib.kharkov.ua; internet www.ukrsibbank.com; f. 1990; present name adopted 1992; cap.

90.0m., res 57.9m., dep. 892.0m. (Dec. 2001); Pres. OLEKSANDR YAROSLAVSKIY; 20 brs; 10 sub-brs.

**UkrSotsBank—Joint-Stock Bank for Social Development:** 03150 Kiev, vul. Kovpak 29; tel. (44) 269-08-36; fax (44) 269-13-07; e-mail info@ukrsotsbank.com; internet www.usb.com.ua; f. 1990; cap. 48.6m., res 127.6m., dep. 1,565.4m. (Dec. 2001); Pres. VALERIY MOROSHKOVSKIY; Chair. of Bd BORYS TYMONKYN.

**VA Bank-Vseukrainsky Aktsionerny Bank** (All-Ukrainian Share Bank): 04119 Kiev, vul. Zoolohichna 5; tel. (44) 490-06-09; fax (44) 216-00-33; e-mail bank@vabank.com.ua; internet www.vabank .com.ua; f. 1992; cap. 91.0m., res 25.1m., dep. 201.6m. (Dec. 2002); Pres. SERHIY MAKSIMOV; Chair. YURIY BLASHCHUK; 7 brs.

**Vidrodzhennia** (Rebirth—Kiev Joint Stock Commercial Bank Vidrodzhennia): Kiev; tel. (44) 224-50-12; fax (44) 225-30-42; Gen. Dir ANATOLIY SKOPENKO; 27 brs.

### Savings Bank

**State Oschadny Bank of Ukraine JSC** (Oschadbank): 01023 Kiev, vul. Hospitalna 12H; tel. (44) 247-85-69; fax (44) 247-85-68; internet www.oschadnybank.com; f. 1922; cap. 100m., res 117m., dep. 1,705m. (April 2001); Pres. VIKTOR GRYBKOV.

### Banking Association

**Association of Ukrainian Banks:** Kiev; tel. (44) 516-87-75; fax (44) 516-87-76; e-mail aub@carrier.kiev.ua; fmrly Commercial Bank Asscn; Pres. OLEKSANDR SUHONYAKO.

## COMMODITY EXCHANGES

**Crimea Universal Exchange:** 95050 Crimea, Simferopol, vul. L. Chaikinoy 1/421; tel. (652) 22-04-32; fax (652) 22-12-73; f. 1923 as Simferopol Commodity Exchange; present name adopted 1991; Pres. NATALIYA S. SYUMAK.

**Donetsk Commodity Exchange:** 83086 Donetsk, vul. Pershotravnevska 12; tel. (62) 338-10-93; fax (62) 335-92-91; e-mail oltradex@pub.dn.ua; f. 1991; Gen. Man. PETRO O. VYSHNEVSKYI.

**Kharkiv Commodity Exchange:** 61003 Kharkiv, vul. Universytetska 5; tel. (572) 12-33-21; fax (572) 12-74-95; e-mail ss@htb .kharkov.ua; f. 1993; Pres. IHOR V. ZOTOV.

**Kiev Universal Exchange:** 01103 Kiev, Zaliznychne shose 57; tel. (44) 295-11-29; fax (44) 295-44-36; e-mail nva@iptelecom.net.ua; internet www.kue.kiev.ua; f. 1990; Pres. NIKOLAY DETOCHKA.

**Odesa Commodity Exchange:** 65114 Odesa, vul. Lyustdorfska doroha 140A; tel. (482) 61-89-92; fax (482) 47-72-84; e-mail yuri@oce .odessa.ua; f. 1796; re-established 1990; Gen. Man. MYKOLA O. NIKOLISHEN.

**Transcarpathian Regional Commodity Exchange:** 78200 Ivano-Frankivsk obl., Kolomiya, vul. Vahylevycha 1, POB 210; tel. and fax (343) 32-19-61; f. 1996; Gen. Man. IVAN P. VATUTIN.

**Transdnipro (Pridniprovska) Commodity Exchange:** 49094 Dnipropetrovsk, vul. Nab. Lenina 15A; tel. (562) 35-77-45; fax (56) 744-27-16; e-mail ptb@pce.dp.ua; internet www.pce.dp.ua; originally; f. 1908 as Katerinoslav Commodity Exchange; re-established with present name in 1991; brs in Dniprodzerzhynsk, Kryvyi Rih, Marhanets, Pavlohrad and Synelnykove; Gen. Man. VADYM F. KAMEKO.

**Ukrainian Universal Commodity Exchange:** 03680 Kiev, pr. Akadmika Hlushkova 1, pavillion 6; tel. (44) 261-67-43; fax (44) 251-95-40; e-mail birga@uutb.kiev.ua; internet www.uutb.com.ua; f. 1991; Pres. OLEKSANDR M. BORKOVSKYI.

**Zaporizhzhya Commodity Exchange 'Hileya':** 69037 Zaporizhzhya, vul. 40 rokiv Radyanskoyi Ukrainy 41; tel. (612) 33-32-73; fax (612) 34-76-62; f. 1991; re-established 1996; Gen. Man. ANTON A. KHULAKHSIZ.

## INSURANCE

### State Insurance Companies

**Crimean Insurance Co:** 99011 Crimea, Sevastopol, vul. Butakov 4; tel. (692) 55-30-28; e-mail ksk@stel.sebastopol.ua.

**DASK UkrinMedStrakh:** 01601 Kiev, vul. O. Honshara 65; tel. (44) 216-30-21; fax (44) 216-96-92; e-mail ukrmed@ukrpack.com; f. 1999; provides compulsory medical insurance to foreigners and stateless persons temporarily resident in Ukraine.

**National Joint-Stock Insurance Co (ORANTA):** 01021 Kiev, vul. M. Hrushevskoho 34/1; tel. (44) 293-62-31; fax (44) 253-06-59; e-mail oranta@oranta.ua; internet www.oranta.ua; f. 1921; insurance, reinsurance; Chair. of Bd OLEKSANDR ZAVADA.

### Commercial Insurance Companies

A selection of companies is given below.

**AIG Ukraine:** 01004 Kiev, vul. Shovkovychna 42–44; tel. (44) 490-65-50; fax (44) 490-65-48; e-mail reception@aig.com.ua; internet www.aig.com.ua; affiliated to American International Group (USA); f. 2000; Gen. Man. Ihor Kovalenko.

**AKB Garant Ukrainian-Swiss Joint Stock Insurance Co:** 03062 Kiev, pr. Peremohy 67; tel. (44) 459-52-01; e-mail akb@garant.kiev.ua; internet www.garant.kiev.ua; f. 1994; general insurance services; Gen. Man. Oleksandr I. Dyachenko.

**Alcona Insurance Co:** 03150 Kiev, vul. V. Vasylivska 102; tel. (44) 247-44-77; e-mail alcona@alcona.kiev.ua; internet www.insurance.kiev.ua/alcona; f. 1992; insurance and reinsurance.

**ASKA Insurance Co:** 03186 Kiev, vul. Antonova 5; tel. (44) 241-11-67; e-mail office@aska.com.ua; internet www.aska.com.ua; life and non-life insurance; Chair. Halina N. Tretyakova; Gen. Man. A. Sosys.

**DASK Insurance Co:** 49000 Dnipropetrovsk, vul. K. Libkhnekhta 4d; tel. (562) 32-09-75; fax (562) 32-09-81; e-mail dask@dask.dp.ua; internet www.dask.com.ua; f. 1993; affiliated to DASK Insurance Group; Dir Galina Mazurets.

**DISCO Insurance Co:** 49000 Dnipropetrovsk, vul. K. Lybknekhta 4d; tel. (562) 32-09-78; fax (562) 32-09-81; e-mail disco@disco.dp.ua; internet www.disco.com.ua; f. 1992; affilated to Dask Insurance Group.

**ECCO Insurance Co:** 01034 Kiev, vul. Prorizna 4/23; tel. (44) 228-10-82; e-mail insurance@ecco-alpha.kiev.ua; internet www.ecco-insurance.at; f. 1991; affiliated to ECCO (Austria); life and non-life insurance.

**EnergoPolis Insurance Co:** 03049 Kiev, vul. Bohdanivska 10; tel. (44) 244-02-36; fax (44) 244-05-94; e-mail office@enpolis.viaduk.net; internet www.energopolis.com.ua; Pres. and Gen. Man. Vasyl Makhno.

**Galinstrakh Insurance Co:** 79012 Lviv, vul. Ak. Sakharova 34; tel. (322) 75-70-30; fax (322) 97-10-40; e-mail gis@is.lviv.ua; internet www.gis.com.ua; f. 1991; general insurance services; Chair. of Bd Volodymyr Romanyshyn.

**INPRO Insurance Co:** 03110 Kiev, vul. I. Klymenka 23/219; tel. (44) 227-72-39; fax (44) 240-20-28; e-mail mb@dnister.kiev.ua; internet www.inpro.kiev.ua; f. 1992; life and non-life insurance.

**InterPolis Insurance Co:** 01025 Kiev, vul. Volodymyrska 69; tel. (44) 227-70-96; fax (44) 220-74-45; e-mail inpolis@gu.kiev.ua; internet www.users.gu.net/inpolis; f. 1993.

**Kiev Insurance Co:** 04053 Kiev, vul. Yu. Kotsubynskoho 20; tel. (44) 461-92-41; fax (44) 461-92-43; e-mail info@kic.kiev.ua; internet www.kic.kiev.ua; f. 1998.

**Ostra Insurance Co:** 65026 Odesa, vul. Pushkinska 13; tel. (482) 22-38-87; fax (482) 24-18-37; e-mail main@ostra.com.ua; internet www.ostra.com.ua; f. 1990; non-life insurance; Chair. Khyrach Mahdyev.

**Ostra-Kiev Insurance Co:** 01011 Kiev, vul. Kutuzova 4a; tel. (44) 490-27-44; fax (44) 490-27-48; e-mail office@ostra-kiev.com.ua; internet www.ostra-kiev.com.ua; f. 1994; re-insurance, medical, travel, property and cargo insurance; Chair. of Bd Ihor N. Hordyenko.

**QBE Ukraina Insurance:** 02098 Kiev, Dniprovska nab. 13; tel. (44) 559-82-96; fax (44) 559-28-92; e-mail insurance@qbe-ukraine.com; internet www.qbe-ukraine.com; affiliate of QBE Insurance (New Zealand); f. 1998.

**Skide Insurance Co:** 04050 Kiev, vul. Hlybochytska 72; tel. (44) 417-40-04; fax (44) 228-40-33; e-mail skide@iptelecom.net.ua; f. 1991; Pres. Volodymyr Besarab.

**Skide-West Insurance Co:** 04053 Kiev, vul. Sichovykh Striltsiv 40; tel. (44) 238-62-38; e-mail mail@skide-west.kiev.ua; internet www.skide-west.com.ua; f. 1993; Pres. Andriy Peretyazhko.

**Sun Life Ukraine:** 01032 Kiev, vul. Starovokzalna 17; tel. (44) 235-20-02; fax (44) 235-89-17; e-mail office@sunlife.com.ua; internet www.sunlife.com.ua; f. 1993; life insurance; Pres. Rostyslav B. Talskyi.

**UkrGazPromPolis Insurance Co:** 01034 Kiev, vul. O. Honshara 41; tel. (44) 235-25-00; e-mail office@ugpp.com.ua; internet www.ugpp.com.ua; f. 1996; jointly owned by UkrGazProm, UkrGazPromBank and KievTransGaz; Pres. Konstantyn O. Yefymenko.

### Insurance Association

**League of Insurance Organizations of Ukraine:** 02002 Kiev, vul. M. Raskovoyi 11/523; tel. and fax (44) 516-82-30; e-mail liga@uainsur.com; internet www.uainsur.com; f. 1992; non-profit association to protect the interests of the members and other participants of the insurance services market; Pres. Aleksandr Filonyuk.

# Trade and Industry

## GOVERNMENT AGENCY

**State Property Fund:** 01133 Kiev, vul. Kutuzova 18/9; tel. (44) 295-12-74; fax (44) 296-69-84; e-mail marketing@spfu.kiev.ua; internet www.spfu.gov.ua; Chair. Mykhaylo V. Chechetov.

## NATIONAL CHAMBER OF COMMERCE

**Ukrainian Chamber of Commerce and Industry:** 01601 Kiev, vul. V. Zhytomyrska 33; tel. (44) 212-28-40; fax (44) 212-33-53; e-mail ucci@ucci.org.ua; internet www.ucci.org.ua; f. 1972; Chair. Serhiy Skrypchecnko; 28 brs.

## REGIONAL CHAMBERS OF COMMERCE

Chambers of Commerce are located in every administrative region of Ukraine, including the following.

**Chamber of Commerce of Crimea:** 95013 Crimea, Simferopol, ul. Sevastopolskaya 45; tel. (652) 49-97-31; fax (652) 44-58-13; e-mail cci@cci.crimea.ua; internet www.cci.crimea.ua; 1974; sub-brs in Armyansk, Dzhankoi, Feodosiya, Kerch, Yalta and Yevpatoriya; Pres. Neonila M. Gracheva.

**Dnipropetrovsk Chamber of Commerce:** 49044 Dnipropetrovsk, vul. Shevchenka 4; tel. (562) 36-22-58; fax (562) 36-22-59; e-mail miv@dcci.dp.ua; internet www.dcci.dp.ua; brs at Kryvyi Rih and Dniprodzerzhynsk; Pres. Vytaliy H. Zhmurenko.

**Donetsk Chamber of Commerce:** 83000 Donetsk, pr. Dzherzhynskoho 12; tel. (622) 92-80-60; fax (622) 92-80-48; e-mail dcci@dttp.donetsk.ua; internet www.cci.donbass.com; brs at Artemovsk, Horlivka, Kramatorsk and Mariupol; Gov. Olha H. Pshonka.

**Kharkhiv Chamber of Commerce:** 61012 Kharkiv, vul. Katsarksa 3a; tel. (572) 14-96-90; fax (572) 14-96-82; e-mail info@kcci.kharkov.ua; internet www.kcci.kharkov.ua; Pres. Viktor I. Loboda.

**Kiev Chamber of Commerce:** 01601 Kyiv-54, vul. B. Khmelnytskoho 55; tel. (44) 246-83-01; fax (44) 246-99-66; e-mail info@kiev-chamber.org.ua; internet www.kiev-chamber.org.ua; Pres. Mykola V. Zasulskiy.

**Lviv Chamber of Commerce:** 79011 Lviv, Stryiskiy park 14; tel. (322) 76-46-11; fax (322) 76-79-72; e-mail lcci@cscd.lviv.ua; internet www.lviv.net/tpp; Pres. Oleh M. Khustochka.

**Odesa Chamber of Commerce:** 65011 Odesa, vul. Bazarna 47; tel. (482) 28-66-10; fax (482) 22-48-22; e-mail orcci@orcci.odessa.ua; internet www.orcci.odessa.ua; brs at Illichivsk, Izmayil and Reni; Pres. Serhiy V. Lokarev.

**Sevastopol Chamber of Commerce:** 99011 Crimea, Sevastopol, ul. B. Morskaya 34; tel. (692) 54-35-36; fax (692) 54-06-44; e-mail root@stpp.stel.sebastopol.ua; Pres. Lyudmila I. Vishnya.

**Transcarpathian (Zakarpatska) Chamber of Commerce:** 88015 Transcarpathian obl., Uzhhorod, vul. Hrushevskoho 62; tel. (312) 26-22-14; fax (312) 21-64-77; e-mail tpp@karpaty.uzhgorod.ua; br. at Mukachevo; Pres. Otto O. Kobchar.

**Zaporizhzhya Chamber of Commerce:** 69000 Zaporizhzhya, bulv. Tsentralnyi 4; tel. (612) 13-50-24; fax (612) 33-11-72; e-mail cci@cci.zp.ua; internet www.cci.zp.ua; brs at Berdyansk and Melitopol; Pres. Volodymyr I. Shamylov.

## EMPLOYERS' ORGANIZATION

**Congress of Business Circles of Ukraine:** 01061 Kiev, vul. Prorizna 15; tel. (44) 228-64-81; fax (44) 229-52-84; Pres. Valeriy G. Babich.

## UTILITIES

### Regulatory Bodies

**National Electricity Regulatory Commission of Ukraine:** 03057 Kiev, vul. Smolenska 19; tel. (44) 241-90-01; fax (44) 241-90-47; e-mail box@nerc.gov.ua; f. 1994; promotion of competition and protection of consumer interests; Chair. Yuriy Prodan.

**State Committee for Nuclear Regulation:** see section on The Government.

### Electricity

**EnergoAtom:** 71500 Zaporizhzhya obl., Energodar; tel. (44) 294-48-89; e-mail pr@nae.atom.gov.ua; internet www.energoatom.com.ua; f. 1996; responsible for scientific and technical policy within the nuclear-power industry; manages all five nuclear-power producing installations in Ukraine; Pres. Yuriy Hedashkovskyi.

There are 27 electricity distribution companies in Ukraine, including Dniproenergo (serves Dnipropetrovsk), Kievenergo (serves Kiev) and Zaporizhoblenergo (serves the Zaporizhzhya province). These companies were previously grouped in the Unified Energy Systems of Ukraine. Thirteen regional distribution companies were privatized in 1998–2001; a further 12 companies were scheduled to be transferred to majority private ownership during 2002.

**Kievenergo:** 01001 Kiev, 1 pl. Ivana Franka 5; tel. (44) 201-03-37; fax (44) 201-03-38; e-mail pubrel@me-press.kiev.ua; internet www .kievenergo.com.ua; power generation and distribution; Chair. Ivan Plachkov.

**Zakhidenergo** (West Energy): 79011 Lviv, vul. Sventitskoho 2; tel. (322) 79-89-41; fax (322) 78-90-59; e-mail z_vtv@rdc.west.energy.gov .ua; f. 1995; power generation; Pres. and Gen. Dir Volodymyr Pavlyuk.

### Gas

**Naftogaz Ukrainy JSC** (Oil and Gas of Ukraine): 01001 Kiev, vul. B. Khmelnytskoho 6в; tel. (44) 461-25-37; fax (44) 220-15-26; e-mail ngu@naftogaz.net; internet www.naftogaz.com; f. 1998; production, processing and storage of gas and petroleum; gas- and condensate-processing; Chair. of Bd Yuriy A. Boyko.

## MAJOR COMPANIES

The first full privatizations began in early 1993, after delays in implementing the initial legislation, passed in 1992. Following a suspension in June 1994, the privatization programme was restarted in October, although progress was again slow. In late 1996 the process was accelerated, and by mid-1997 almost all small-scale enterprises were in private ownership. The privatization programme had provided for the transfer of medium- and large-scale concerns to the private sector by 2000. A new programme of privatization was launched in 2003; upon its completion (due in 2008), it was anticipated that the privatization process would be complete.

### Chemicals

**Chemical Reagent Plant:** 18036 Cherkasy; tel. (472) 43-21-63; fax (472) 43-60-70; e-mail react@uch.net; f. 1949; development and manufacture of chemical reagents, production of medicinal substances, pesticides, shampoos, deodorants; sales US $18m. (2000); Dir E. H. Vishnevetskiy; 1,000 employees (2001).

**Cherkasy Nitrogen Production Asscn** (VAT Azot): 18014 Cherkasy, vul. Pershotravnevska 72; tel. (472) 14-29-26; fax (472) 64-03-36; internet www.azot.cherkassy.net; f. 1965; production of nitrogenous and phosphate fertilizers, ammonia, resins and consumer goods; Gen. Man. V. P. Byelyi; 6,285 employees (2001).

**Darnitsa Pharmaceutical JSC:** 02093 Kiev, vul. Borisopolska 13; tel. (44) 566-68-78; fax (44) 568-32-10; e-mail webmaster@darnitsa .kiev.ua; internet www.darnitsa.kiev.ua; f. 1954; manufacture of chemicals, medicines and pharmaceuticals; sales US $40.0m. (2000); Pres. and Gen. Dir Volodymyr A. Zahoriy; 800 employees (2001).

**Lukor ZAO:** 77305 Ivano-Frankivsk obl., Kalush; tel. (3472) 2-26-62; fax (3472) 2-30-21; internet 3980.ukrindustrial.com; f. 1867 as Oriana, name changed as above in 2000; produces vinyl chloride, synthetic resins, caustic soda, and polyethylene; Pres. Ivan I. Bysek; 6,500 employees.

**Slavyansk Soda Plant JSC** (Slavyansk sodovyi zavod OAO): 84104 Donetsk obl., Slavyansk, vul. Chubarya 91; tel. (6262) 3-33-49; fax (6262) 2-99-04; internet 1576.ukrindustrial.com; f. 1896; production of various chemical products, including detergents, fire extinguishing powders, soda products, etc.; Pres. Eduard E. Krech; 4,000 employees (2001).

**Sumykhimprom—Sumy Chemical Industrial Group OAO:** 40012 Sumy, vul. Kharkivska 10; tel. (542) 33-85-13; fax (542) 21-42-14; e-mail info@alphachemical.sumy.ua; internet www.alphachemical .sumy.ua/himpromru.htma; f. 1954; manufacture and distribution of chemicals, fertilizers, pigments, coagulants (water purifiers) and consumer products; Chair. Yevhen V. Lapyn; 6,300 employees (2002).

**Zaporozhabraziv—Zaporizhzhya Abrasive Factory JSC** (Zaporozhabraziv—Zaporozhskii abrazivnyi kombinat OAO): 69084 Zaporizhzhya, vul. Dmitrova 44; tel. (612) 61-72-72; fax (612) 65-09-14; e-mail export@abrasive.comint.net; internet 1175.ukrindustrial .com; f. 1939; manufacture of chemicals and abrasive tools, carbides etc.; Chair. of Bd Anatoliy V. Bereza; 3,000 employees (2002).

### Electrical Goods

**Mayak Kiev (Kiev Beacon) Plant:** 04073 Kiev, pr. Chervonykh Kozakiv 8; tel. (44) 464-49-42; fax (44) 410-26-67; f. 1924; present name adopted 1963; manufacture of audio equipment; Dir Nikolai I. Piven; 1,310 employees (2001).

**Pivelektromash/Yuzhelektromash—Southern Electrical Machinery Co** (Yuzhnyi elektromashinostroitelnyi zavod OAO—Yuzhelektromash): 74900 Kherson obl., Nova Kakhovka, vul. Per-

shotravnevska 35; tel. (5549) 51-959; fax (5549) 53-830; e-mail motor@yuzhelectromash.com; internet www.yuzhelectromash.com; f. 1952; design and manufacture of electric motors; Gen. Dir Anatoliy P. Hurtovoi; 8,000 employees (2001).

**Preobrazovatel (Transformer) Zaporizhzhya Plant JSC** (Preobrazovatel Zaporozhskii zavod OAO): 69069 Zaporizhzhya, Dnipropetrovske shose 9; tel. and fax (612) 52-04-67; e-mail preobr@reis.zp .ua; internet www.reis.zp.ua/preobraz; f. 1967; manufacture of power semi-conductor devices, modules and chips, power-conversion equipment and electrical appliances; Pres. Oleksandr V. Tarasenko; 1,500 employees (2002).

**Ukrelektromash—Kharkhiv Ukrainian Electrical Machinery JSC** (Ukrelektromash—Kharkovskii elektrotekhnicheskii zavod OAO): 61005 Kharkiv, vul. Iskrinska 37; tel. (572) 21-44-72; fax (572) 21-84-92; internet 1134.ukrindustrial.com; produces electric motors, centrifugal pumps and electrical household appliances; Pres. Boris T. Sirota; 2,200 employees.

**Zaporozhtransformator OAO:** 69600 Zaporizhzhya, Dnipropetrovske shose 3; tel. (612) 57-15-44; fax (612) 52-52-03; e-mail room@ ztr.zp.ua; internet www.ztr.zp.ua; f. 1947; manufactures transformers, high-voltage equipment and consumer goods; Chair. of Bd Viktor B. Choban; 5,600 employees.

### Food and Beverages

**Obolon ZAT:** 04655 Kiev, vul. Bohatyrska 3; tel. (44) 412-86-55; fax (44) 412-76-03; e-mail general@obolon.kiev.ua; internet www.obolon .kiev.ua; f. 1974; produces beer and soft drinks; Gen. Man. Oleksandr D. Puchok.

**Rata:** 88000 Transcarpathian obl., Uzhhorod; produces soft drinks; Gen. Man Valeriy Birman.

**Ukrainian Sugar Concern:** 01001 Kiev, vul. B. Hrinchenko 1; tel. (44) 228-11-37; fax (44) 229-65-83; f. 1913; operates sugar factories and refineries; Chair. of Bd Hrihoriy D. Zahorodnyi; Gen. Man. Mykola M. Yarchuk; 210,000 employees (2001).

### Machinery

**Atek JSC** (Atek ZAO): 03062 Kiev, pr. Peremohy 83/2; tel. (44) 443-71-36; fax (44) 443-74-36; internet 1356.ukrindustrial.com; f. 1898; manufacture of excavators, loaders and components, hydraulic loaders and cylinders; Dir Petr Kh. Belous; 4,000 employees (2001).

**Kiev Machine-Tool Building Plant:** 01062 Kiev, pr. Peremohy 67; tel. (44) 442-83-24; fax (44) 449-97-46; e-mail vercon@alfacom .net; production of automatic lathes and other machinery; Pres. Valentin Drozdenko; 2,000 employees.

**Krasnaya Zvezda/Chervona Zorya (Red Star) Plant:** 25050 Kirovohrad, vul. Medvedeva 1; tel. (522) 27-83-09; fax (522) 22-88-66; internet 1099.ukrindustrial.com; f. 1874; production of farm machinery; Gen. Dir Oleskandr D. Saynsus; 2,701 employees.

**NKMZ—New Kramatorsk Machine-Construction Plant** (Novo-Kramatorskii mashinostroitelnyi zavod ZAO): 83905 Donetsk obl., Kramatorsk, vul. Ordzonikidze 5; tel. (6264) 3-70-80; fax (6264) 7-22-49; e-mail ztm@nkmz.donetsk.ua; internet www.nkmz.donetsk .ua; f. 1934; manufactures pressing and forging equipment, rolling mill and smelting machinery, excavators and other industrial machinery; Pres. Heorhiy M. Skudar; Dir-Gen. Viktor A. Pankov; 25,000 employees (2001).

**Yasinovataya Machine-Construction Plant** (Yasinovatskii mashinostroitelnyi zavod OAO): 86000 Donetsk obl., Yasinovataya, vul. Artema 31; tel. (6236) 2-19-01; internet 1060.ukrindustrial.com; f. 1947; manufactures tunnelling machines and related equipment; Gen. Dir Viktor I. Trubchanin; 4,000 employees.

### Metals

**Alchevsk Iron and Steel Works (AMK) JSC** (OAO Alchevskii metallurgicheskii kombinat): 94202 Luhansk obl., Alchevsk, vul. Shmidta 4; tel. (6442) 9-33-01; fax (6422) 9-33-76; e-mail web@amk .al.lg.ua; internet www.amk.al.lg.ua; f. 1896; Dir Taras H. Shevchenko.

**AzovStal Iron and Steel Works** (Metalurhiynyi kombinat AZOV-STAL): 87500 Donetsk obl., Mariupol, vul. Leporskoho 1; tel. (629) 22-69-55; fax (629) 52-70-00; e-mail oao@azovstal.com.ua; internet www.azovstal.com.ua; f. 1933; iron and steel works; Gen. Dir Oleksei P. Bilyi; 25,827 employees (2001).

**Dnipro Dzerzhinskiy Iron and Steel Integrated Works** (Dneprovskii metallurgicheskii kombinat): 51902 Dnipropetrovsk obl., Dniprodzherzhinsk, vul. Kirova 18в; tel. (5692) 3-00-64; fax (5692) 3-30-64; e-mail dmkd@unimetal.dp.ua; internet www.slegmatis.com/ dmkd; f. 1889; manufacture of objects in carbon steel; Chair. Volodomyr Pykhtin; 20,500 employees (2001).

**Dnipro Petrovskiy Iron and Steel Works—Petrovka** (Dnepropetrovskii metallurgicheskii zavod im. Petrovskogo OAO): 49064

Dnipropetrovsk, vul. Mayakovskoho 31; tel. (562) 32-31-00; fax (562) 32-31-02; e-mail afan@fregat.com; internet 2588.ukrindustrial.com; production of pig-iron and steel products, manufacture of carbon-steel, seamless, round and rectangular section tubes; Chair. VOLO-DOMYR KUZNENKO; Gen. Dir VITALIY N. KORNYIVSKIY; 8,000 employees (2001).

**Interpipe:** 49600 Dnipropetrovsk, vul. Pysarzhevskoho 1A; tel. (562) 47-69-69; fax (562) 70-20-01; e-mail office@bipe.dp.ua; internet www.interpipegroup.dp.ua; f. 1990; production of steel pipes; import and export of various metal products; also owns subsidiaries in Belarus, Germany, Kazakhstan, Russia and Uzbekistan; Pres. VIKTOR M. PINCHUK; Gen. Man. MYKHAYLO M. SHCHEHOLEVSKIY.

**Khartsyzsk State Tube Works** (Khartsyzskii trubnyi zavod OAO): 86703 Donetsk obl., Khartsyzsk, vul. Patona 9; tel. (6257) 7-03-01; fax (6257) 4-56-95; e-mail pmt@htz.donetsk.ua; internet 1043 .ukrindustrial.com; f. 1988; production of steel pipes; Pres. FEDOR S. DERMENTLY; 7,500 employees.

**Kryvyi Rih State Steel Works (Kryvorizhstal)** (Krivorozhskii gosudarstvennyi metallurgicheskii kombinat Krivorozhstal): 50095 Dnipropetrovsk obl., Kryvyi Rih, vul. Ordzhonikidze 1; tel. (564) 78-30-09; fax (564) 74-59-96; e-mail kggmk@mg.dp.ua; internet www .slegmatis.com/kggmk; state-owned; Gen. Man. VOLODYMYR A. NECHEPORENKO; 47,127 employees (2002).

**Makiyivka Iron and Steel Combine** (Makeyevskii metallurgiche-skii kombinat OAO): 86101 Donetsk obl., Makiyivka, vul. Metal-urhiyna 47; tel. and fax (62) 332-09–90923-01; e-mail mmk@tr.dn .ua; internet 1442.ukrindustrial.com; f. 1899; production of iron products; 60.86% state-owned, 27.95% by employees; Chair. and Gen. Dir VOLODYMYR R. ZHUKOV; 13,800 employees (2001).

**Mariupol Ilyich Iron and Steel Works** (Mariupolskii metal-lurgicheskii kombinat im. Illicha—MMK im. Illicha—OAO): 87504 Donetsk obl., Mariupol, vul. Levchenko 1; tel. (629) 39-35-09; fax (629) 53-00-60; e-mail kma@ilyich.donetsk.ua; internet 2998 .ukrindustrial.com; f. 1996; production of carbon steel products; Pres. and Dir-Gen. VOLODYMYR S. BOYKO; 30,000 employees (2001).

**Nizhneneprovskiy (Lower Dnipro) Tube-Rolling Plant** (Nizh-nedneprovskii truboprokatnyi zavod): 49081 Dnipropetrovsk, vul. Stoletiya 21; tel. (562) 35-90-25; fax (562) 34-91-06; e-mail ftf@mail .neon.dp.ua; internet www.ntz.com.ua; f. 1891; manufactures tubes and tubular products; owned by Interpipe; Pres. and Gen. Dir A. I. KOZLOVSKIY; 12,000 employees (2001).

**Zaporozhstal—Zaporizhzhya Iron and Steel JSC** (Zaprozh-stal—Zaporozhskii metallurgicheskii kombinat OAO): 69008 Zapor-izhzhya, Pivdenne shose 72; tel. (612) 39-33-01; fax (612) 13-18-58; e-mail zstal@zaporizhstal.com; internet www.zaporizhstal.com; f. 1933; produces and exports metal products for the automotive, tractor, railway, construction and mechanical engineering indus-tries; Chair. of Bd VITALIY A. SATSKIY; 20,000 employees (2002).

### Mining and Mining Equipment

**Azovmash—Azov Machines JSC** (Azovmash OAO): 87535 Donetsk obl., Mariupol, pl. Mashinostroitelei 1; tel. (629) 53-01-26; fax (629) 38-30-81; e-mail ves@azovmash.com.ua; f. 1936; research, development and manufacture of open-cast mining equipment, met-allurgical equipment, cast and forged metal stock and consumer goods; sales US $38.5m. (1999); Chair. and Gen. Dir OLEKSANDR V. SAVCHUK; 15,000 employees (2001).

**Chornomornaftogaz—Black Sea Oil and Gas JSC:** 95000 Crimea, Simferopol, pr. Kirova; tel. (652) 52-34-00; fax (652) 51-11-51; e-mail office@gas.crimea.ua; internet www.blackseagas.com; f. 1979; major producer of petroleum and gas from fields in the Black Sea and the Sea of Azov; Chair. IHOR FRANCHUK.

**Donetsk Mining Machinery (Donetsgormash) JSC:** 83005 Donetsk, vul. I. Tkachenko 189; tel. (622) 61-45-08; fax (622) 66-22-09; e-mail admin@dongormash.donetsk.ua; internet www .dongormash.donetsk.ua; f. 1889; research, design and production of mining equipment; Gen. Dir HEORHIY V. SOKOLOV; 2,200 employees (2001).

**Druzhkivka Machine Construction Plant** (Druzhkovskii mashi-nostroitelnyi zavod OAO): 84205 Donetsk obl., Druzhkivka, vul. Lenina 7; tel. (6267) 4-34-04; fax (6267) 3-09-68; internet 1034 .ukrindustrial.com; f. 1893; production of mining equipment and electrical machinery; Gen. Dir SERHIY V. RYABTSIV; 10,900 employees.

**Marhanets Manganese Plant** (Marganetskii gorno-obogatitelnyi kombinat OAO): 53400 Dnipropetrovsk obl., Marhanets, vul. Radyanska 62; tel. (5665) 2-22-02; fax (5665) 2-30-31; e-mail postmaster@mgok.dp.ua; internet 3002.ukrindustrial.com; f. 1885; produces manganese using underground mining methods; Chair. PAVEL O. KRAVCHENKO; 6,442 employees.

**Poltava Petroleum Company:** 36032 Poltava, vul. Frunze 153; tel. (532) 50-13-04; fax (532) 50-13-14; f. 1994; joint venture with the British Co JKX to increase the output of the Novo-Nikolayevskoye

oil and gasfield near Poltava; Gen. Dir PETER DICKSON; 320 employees.

**UKRTATNAFTA—Ukrainian-Tatar Petroleum JSC** (Ukrtat-nafta AOZT): 39609 Poltava obl., Kremenchuk, vul. Svyshtovska 3; tel. (5366) 4-15-00; fax (5366) 282-20; e-mail pobox@ukrtatnafta .com; internet www.ukrtatnafta.com; f. 1995; petroleum and gas exploration and development, production and sale of petroleum and gas, production and sale of petroleum products; 43.1% owned by State Property Fund of Ukraine, 28.8% by State Property Com-mittee of the Republic of Tatarstan (Russian Federation); Chair. VOLODYMYR M. MATYTSYN; 4,192 employees (2001).

### Motor vehicles and Components

**AvtoZAZ JSC—Zaporizhzhya Automobile Plant (ZAZ):** 69600 Zaporizhzhya, pr. Lenina 8; tel. (612) 13-83-03; fax (612) 13-87-49; e-mail admin@zaz.zp.ua; internet www.avtozaz.com; f. 1863 as man-ufacturer of agricultural equipment, commenced manufacture of automobiles in 1959; re-registered as a joint stock co with foreign investment in 2003; produces passenger cars, engines and tools; Gen. Dir OLEKSANDR SOTNIKOV; 20,000 employees.

**Elektromash JSC:** 73000 Kherson, vul. Ushakova 57; tel. (552) 22-62-68; fax (552) 24-21-25; e-mail hemz@selena.net.ua; internet www .selena.kherson.ua/hemz; f. 1930; produces starter motors and alter-nators for automobile, tractor and motorcycle engines, automobile engine fans, etc.; Dir ZAKHAR I. GORLOVSKIY; 1,300 employees.

**Kharkiv Ordzhonykydze Tractor Plant (KhTZ)** (Kharkovskii traktornyi zavom im. Ordzhonikidze OAO): 61007 Kharkiv, pr. Moskovskyi 275; tel. (572) 95-77-77; fax (572) 94-17-60; e-mail info@ xtz.kharkov.ua; internet www.tractor-plant.kharkov.com; f. 1931; production of all types of tractors; Pres. PETR P. TODOROV.

**Kremenchuk Automobile Plant (KrAZ)** (Kremenchugskii avto-mobilnyi zavod OAO): 39631 Poltava obl., Kremenchuk, vul. Kyivska 62; tel. (5366) 5-92-00; fax (5366) 7-88-01; internet 1440 .ukrindustrial.com; production of heavy trucks; six plants; Gen. Man. VIKTOR M. ZAKHAROV; 20,000 employees.

**ZAO SP Rosava:** 09108 Kiev obl., Bila Tserkva, vul. Levanevskoho 91; tel. (4463) 3-79-23; fax (4463) 3-79-38; e-mail tyres@bcrosava .com.ua; internet www.bcrosava.com.ua; manufactures tyres for automobiles, trucks, etc.; f. 1964; restructured 1998; Chair. ANATOLIY PODOLYAK; 6,046 employees (2002).

**Vinnytsya Tractor Unit Plant JSC** (Vinnitskii zavod traktornykh agregatov OAO): 21001 Vinnytsya, pr. Kotsyubynskoho 4; tel. (432) 27-57-97; fax (432) 27-76-29; internet 2861.ukrindustrial.com; spe-cializes in the production of hydraulic gear pumps and cylinders, and high-pressure hoses; Dir OLEKSANDR P. ZABROTSKYI.

### Miscellaneous

**Dnipropetrovsk Air Aggregates Plant—Raketa JSC** (Dnepro-petrovskii agregatnyi zavod OAO): 49052 Dnipropetrovsk, vul. Shchepkina 53; tel. (562) 37-28-05; fax (562) 42-22-10; e-mail aodaz@ a-teleport.com; internet www.aodaz.com.ua; f. 1926; manufacture and sale of hydraulics, centrifugal pumps and vacuum cleaners; Dir YEVGENIY V. MOROZENKO; 3,500 employees.

**O. K. Antonov Aeronautic Scientific and Technical Complex (ANTK Antonov):** 03062 Kiev, vul. Tupoleva 1; tel. (44) 443-00-18; fax (44) 442-61-24; e-mail office@antonov.kiev.ua; internet www .antonovaircargo.com; f. 1946; designs, modifies, and engineers pro-totype and existing aircraft, trains air crew, and operates charter freight flights; Dir VOLODYMYR N. KAREL.

**Kamyanka Machine Construction Plant—Kammash** (Kamen-skii mashinostrotelnyi zavod OAO): 20800 Cherkasy obl., Kamyanka, vul. Lenina 40; tel. (4732) 2-28-93; fax (4732) 2-14-76; e-mail kammash@kammash.ck.ua; internet 1236.ukrindustrial .com; f. 1936; manufactures industrial pumps, winding machinery, lifting equipment and trucks; Dir. VOLODYMYR I. HETSKO; 730 employees (2001).

**Kherson Shipbuilding Plant** (Khersonskii sudostroitelnyi zavod GP): 73019 Kherson, Karantinyi Ostrov 1; tel. (552) 27-06-09; fax (552) 27-49-22; internet 1294.ukrindustrial.com; f. 1951; constructs ships, tankers, and related facilities; Gen. Dir MYKOLA M. SPYVAK; 5,600 employees (2001).

**Kiev State Aviation Plant:** 03062 Kiev, pr. Peremohy 100/1; tel. (44) 443-72-45; fax (44) 442-43-85; e-mail avtant@carrier.kiev.ua; f. 1920; manufacture of aircraft, aircraft parts and equipment; Gen. Dir VASYL PELYKH; 5,300 employees (2002).

**Ukrimpeks—Ukrainian Import and Export JSC:** 01054 Kiev, vul. Vorovskoho 22; tel. (44) 216-21-74; fax (44) 216-29-96; e-mail info@ukrimpex.com.ua; internet www.ukrimpex.com.ua; f. 1987; foreign-trade org.; imports and exports a wide range of goods; organizes joint ventures, exhibitions; provides consultancy and mar-keting expertise and business services; Chair. STANISLAV I. SOKO-LENKO.

**Ukrspetseksport—Ukainian Special Export Co:** 04119 Kiev, vul. Degtyarivksa 36; tel. (44) 269-20-06; fax (44) 269-10-01; e-mail aira@ukrspetsexport.com; internet www.ukrspetsexport.com; export and import of military and special-purpose goods and services; Dir-Gen. VALERIY SHMAROV.

**Yuzhnoye M.K. Yangel Construction Bureau NPO:** 49008 Dnipropetrovsk, vul. Kryvorozhska 3; tel. (56) 770-04-47; fax (56) 770-01-25; e-mail info@yuzhnoye.com; internet www.yuzhnoye.com; f. 1954; space-rocket systems, missiles and launch vehicles; involved with Boeing (USA), S. P. Korolev Energiya Space-Rocket Corpn (Russia) and Kvaerner (Norway/United Kingdom) in the Sea Launch programme, which aims to launch communications satellites from the Pacific Ocean; Gen. Dir STANISLAV N. KONYUKHOV.

### TRADE UNION FEDERATIONS

**Confederation of Free Trade Unions of Ukraine (CFTUU):** Kiev; independent; Chair. MYKHAYLO VOLYNETS.

**Federation of Trade Unions of Ukraine (FTUU):** 01012 Kiev, maydan Nezalezhnosti 2; tel. (44) 228-87-88; fax (44) 229-80-57; e-mail belova@uprotel.net.ua; f. 1990; fmrly Ukrainian branch of General Confederation of Trade Unions of the USSR; affiliation of 40 trade union brs; Chair. OLEKSANDR M. STOYAN.

# Transport

### RAILWAYS

In 2001 there were 22,218 km of railway track in use, of which more than 9,000 km were electrified. Lines link most towns and cities in the republic. Kiev is connected by rail to all the other republics of the former USSR, and there are direct lines to Vienna (Austria), Warsaw (Poland), Budapest (Hungary), Bucharest (Romania), Bratislava (Slovakia) and Berlin (Germany).

**State Railway Transport Administration—Ukrzaliznytsia:** 03680 Kiev, vul. Tverska 5; tel. (44) 223-00-10; fax (44) 258-80-11; e-mail ci@uz.gov.ua; internet www.uz.gov.ua; Dir-Gen. Minister of Transport; Dir, International Dept IHOR B. MATVIYIV.

**Ukrreftrans:** 03049 Kiev, vul. Furmanova 1/7; tel. (44) 245-47-22; e-mail sekretar@interntrans.com.ua; internet www.intertrans.com.ua; state-owned freight transportation service.

#### City Underground Railways

**Dnipropetrovsk Metro:** 49000 Dnipropetrovsk, vul. Kurchatova 8; tel. (562) 42-37-68; e-mail master@gorod.dp.ua; internet gorod.dp.ua/metro; f. 1995; one line with six stations; total length 8 km; total planned network of 74 km.

**Kharkiv Metro:** 61012 Kharkiv, vul. Engelsa 29; tel. (572) 12-59-83; fax (572) 23-21-41; e-mail metro@tender.kharkov.com; internet www.metro.kharkov.ua; f. 1975; three lines with 26 stations, total length 34 km; Gen. Man. LEONID A. ISAYEV.

**Kiev Metro:** 03055 Kiev, pr. Peremohy 35; tel. (44) 238-44-21; fax (44) 229-18-57; e-mail nto@metro.kiev.ua; internet www.metro.kiev.ua; f. 1960; three lines with 40 stations; Dir MYKOLA M. SHAVLOVSKIY.

### ROADS

At 31 December 2001 there were 169,630 km of roads, of which 96.7% were paved. In December 2000 there were 13,081 km of main or national roads, and 156,410 km of secondary or regional roads. A major new road-building programme was announced in March 1998, under which 3,375 km of roads were to be constructed by 2005.

### INLAND WATERWAYS

The length of navigable inland waterways in Ukraine declined notably during the 1990s, from 4,405 km in 1990 to 2,281 km in 2001. The Dnipro (Dniepr—Dnieper) river, which links Kiev, Cherkasy, Dnipropetrovsk and Zaporizhzhya with the Black Sea, is the most important route for river freight.

### SHIPPING

The main ports are Yalta and Yevpatoriya in Crimea, and Odesa. In addition to long-distance international shipping lines, there are services to the Russian ports of Novorossiisk and Sochi, and Batumi and Sukhumi in Georgia. Although many passenger routes on the Black Sea ceased to operate in the 1990s, there are frequent passenger services from Odesa to Haifa (Israel) and İstanbul (Turkey). In 2001 Ukraine's merchant fleet (838 vessels) had a total displacement of 1.4m. grt.

#### Port Authority

**Port of Odesa Authority:** 65026 Odesa, pl. Mytna 1; tel. (48) 729-35-55; fax (48) 729-36-27; e-mail bev@port.odessa.ua; internet www.port.odessa.ua; cargo handling and storage; Gen. Man. OLEKSANDR S. SOBOROV.

#### Shipping Companies

**Azov Shipping Co:** 87510 Donetsk obl., Mariupol, pr. Admirala Lunina 89; tel. (629) 31-15-00; fax (629) 31-12-25; e-mail admin@c2smtp.azsco.anet.donetsk.ua; f. 1871; Pres. SERHIY V. PRUSIKOV.

**State Black Sea Shipping Co:** 65026 Odesa, vul. Lanzheronovska 1; tel. (482) 25-21-60; fax (482) 60-57-33; Pres. BORIS SCHERBAK.

**Ukrainian Danube Shipping Co:** 68600 Odesa obl., Izmayil, vul. Chervonaflotska 28; tel. (4841) 2-55-50; fax (4841) 2-53-55; e-mail udp_t@udp.izmail.uptel.net; f. 1944; cargo and passenger services; Pres. PETR S. SUVOROV.

**Ukrainian Shipping Co (UkrShip):** 65014 Odesa, vul. Marazlyevska 8; tel. (482) 34-73-50; fax (487) 77-07-00; e-mail admin@ukrship.odessa.ua; f. 1996; Pres. A. SAVITSKIY.

**Ukrrechflot Joint-Stock Shipping Co:** 04071 Kiev, Nizhny val. 51; tel. (44) 416-88-79; fax (44) 417-86-82; Pres. NIKOLAY A. SLAVOV.

**Yugreftransflot JSC:** 99014 Crimea, Sevastopol, ul. Rybakov 5; tel. (692) 41-25-79; fax (692) 42-39-39; Chair. VOLODYMYR ANDREYEV.

### CIVIL AVIATION

Ukraine has air links with cities throughout the former USSR and with major European, North American, Asian and African cities. The principal international airport is at Boryspil (Kiev).

**AeroSvit Airlines:** 01032 Kiev, bulv. Shevchenko 58A; tel. (44) 246-50-70; fax (44) 246-50-46; e-mail av@aswt.kiev.ua; internet www.aerosvit.com; f. 1994; operates scheduled and charter passenger services to domestic and international destinations; Chief Exec. and Dir-Gen. HRIHORIY HURTOVOY.

**Air Urga:** 25005 Kirovograd, vul. Dobrovolskoho 1A; tel. (522) 35-11-25; fax (522) 35-11-52; e-mail office@urga.com.ua; internet www.urga.com.ua; f. 1993; regional and international passenger and cargo flights; Dir-Gen. LEONID SHMAYEVICH.

**Khors Air Company:** 01133 Kiev, vul. L. Ukrainki 34; tel. (44) 294-64-69; fax (44) 573-86-72; e-mail info@khors.com.ua; internet www.khors.com.ua; f. 1990; operates international, regional and domestic cargo and passenger services; Gen. Dir SERHIY SHAMENKO.

**Ukraine International Airlines JSC (Mizhnarodni Avialinyi Ukraini):** 01054 Kiev, ul. B. Khmelnytskogo 63A; tel. (44) 461-56-56; fax (44) 230-88-66; e-mail uia@ps.kiev.ua; internet www.ukraine-international.com; f. 1992; 61.6% state-owned, 22.5% owned jointly by SAir (Switzerland) and Austrian Airlines (Austria); operates domestic services, and international services to domestic, European and Middle Eastern destinations from Kiev, Dnipropetrovsk, Kharkiv, Lviv, Odesa, Simferopol; Pres. VITALIY M. POTEMSKIY.

# Tourism

The Black Sea coast of Ukraine has several popular resorts, including Odesa and Yalta. The Crimean peninsula is a popular tourist centre in both summer and winter, owing to its temperate climate. Kiev, Lviv and Odesa have important historical attractions and there are many archaeological monuments on the Black Sea coast, including the remains of ancient Greek and Ottoman settlements. However, the tourist industry is little developed outside Kiev, Lviv and the Black Sea resorts, with few hotels or other facilities. There were 4.4m. foreign tourist arrivals in Ukraine in 2000, and receipts from tourism totalled US $573m. in 2001, compared with $394m. in the previous year.

**Ministry of Resorts and Tourism of the Autonomous Republic of Crimea:** 95005 Crimea, Sevastopol, pr. Kirova 13; tel. (652) 54-46-68; e-mail ministry@tourism.crimea.ua; internet www.tourism.crimea.ua.

**State Tourism Adminstration of Ukraine:** 01034 Kiev, vul. Yaroslaviv val 36; tel. (44) 212-42-15; e-mail info@tourism.gov.ua; internet www.tourism.gov.ua; f. 1999; Chair. VALERIY I. TSYBUKH.

# Culture

### NATIONAL ORGANIZATION

**Ministry of Art and Culture:** see section on The Government (Ministries).

## CULTURAL HERITAGE

**Bohdan and Varvara Khanenko Museum of Arts:** 01004 Kiev, vul. Tereschenkivska 15–17; tel. (44) 235-02-25; fax (44) 235-02-06; f. 1919; 25,300 items, principally of Western European arts; Dir V. I. VINOHRADOVA.

**Kamyanets-Podilsk State Historical Museum-Reserve:** 32300 Khmelnytsky obl., Kamyanets-Podilsk, vul. Ioano-Predtechenksa 2; tel. (3849) 2-37-84; f. 1890; archaeological collection of 111,000 objects, including artefacts of the Roman and Russian empires, icons, sculptures; Dir L. P. STANISLAVSKA.

**Kiev Holy Dormition Monastery of the Caves** (Svyato-Uspenska Kiyevo-Pecherska Lavra): 01015 Kiev, vul. I. Mazepy 21; tel. (44) 254-22-57; fax (44) 290-46-48; e-mail lavra@lavra.kiev.ua; internet www.lavra.kiev.ua; large collection of icons; operated as a 'state historical-cultural museum-reserve' during Soviet period, returned to ecclesiastical usage from 1988; Gov. PAVEL (Bishop of Vyshhorod).

**Kiev Lesya Ukrainka State Literature Museum:** 01032 Kiev, vul. Saksahanskoho 97; tel. (44) 220-57-52; f. 1962; fmr residence of family of poet Lesya Ukrainka; exhibits on the life of the Ukrainian poets and artists of the 19th and early 20th centuries; library of 5,000 vols; Dir IRINA L. VEREMEYEVA.

**Kiev Museum of Russian Art:** 01004 Kiev, vul. Tereschenkivska 9; tel. (44) 451-40-27; fax (44) 234-61-07; e-mail kmru@uninet.kiev.ua; f. 1922; 17,000 exhibits; library of 19,000 vols; Dir T. N. SOLDATOVA.

**Kiev Taras Shevchenko National University Maksymovych Academic Library:** 01601 Kiev, vul. Volodymyrska 58; tel. and fax (44) 235-70-98; e-mail info@libcc.univ.kiev.ua; internet www.library.univ.kiev.ua; f. 1834; 3,559,000 vols; Dir V. G. NESTERENKO.

**Lviv Historical Museum:** 79008 Lviv, pl. Rynok 4/6/24; tel. (322) 74-33-04; f. 1893; 310,000 exhibits; 2 brs; Dir BORYS. CHAIKOVSKYI.

**Museum of Ukrainian Folk and Decorative Art:** 01015 Kiev, vul. I. Mazepy 21; tel. (44) 254-36-42; f. 1954; more than 54,000 exhibits from 16th century onwards; library of 3,180 vols; Dir V. H. NAHAI.

**National Art Museum of Ukraine:** 01001 Kiev, vul. M. Hrushevskoho 6; tel. (44) 228-13-57; fax (44) 228-74-54; e-mail namu@i.com.ua; f. 1899; 30,000 items including painting, sculpture, engraving and wood-carving dating from the Middle Ages; Dir A. I. MELNIK.

**National Museum of the History of Ukraine:** 01025 Kiev, vul. Volodymyrska 2; tel. (44) 228-65-45; fax (44) 228-43-23; e-mail nmu@ukr.net; f. 1899; history, archaeology, religion, ethnography, numismatics; 2 brs; 600,000 exhibits; Dir SERHIY CHAIKOVSKYI.

**National Taras Shevchenko Museum:** 01032 Kiev, bulv. Shevchenko 12; tel. (44) 224-25-23; f. 1940; 4,000 exhibits on the life and work of the 19th century Ukrainian national poet and political writer, Taras Shevchenko; Dir S. A. HALCHENKO.

**Odesa Archaeological Museum:** 65026 Odesa, vul. Lanzheronovska 4; tel. (482) 22-01-71; e-mail arhaeology@farlep.net; internet www.arhaeology.farlep.odessa.ua; f. 1825; more than 160,000 items, including items from ancient Greece, Egypt and Italy; library of 26,000 vols; Dir V. P. VANCHUHOV.

**St Sophia of Kiev National Architectural Conservation Area:** 01034 Kiev, vul. Volodymyrska 24; tel. (44) 228-26-20; fax (44) 228-67-06; e-mail stsophia@i.kiev.ua; f. 1934; comprises 11th-century St Sophia cathedral, frescoes, mosaics, paintings, applied decorative arts, architectural monuments; Dir and Curator NELYA M. KUKOVALSKA.

**State Committee for Archives:** see section on the Government (State Committees).

**State History Library:** 01015 Kiev, vul. I. Mazepy 21/24; tel. (44) 290-46-17; e-mail shlu@shlu.freenet.kiev.ua; f. 1939; Dir OLENA VINOHRADOVA.

**State Museum of Theatrical, Musical and Cinematographic Art of Ukraine:** 01015 Kiev, vul. I. Mazepy 21/24; tel. (44) 290-51-31; fax (44) 290-51-31; f. 1923; more than 250,000 exhibits; library of 30,000 vols; Dir L. N. MATAT.

**State Parliamentary Library of Ukraine:** 01001 Kiev, vul. M. Hrushevskoho 1; tel. and fax (44) 228-85-12; e-mail nplu@nplu.kiev.ua; internet www.nplu.kiev.ua; f. 1866; 4.0m. vols; Dir ANATOLIY P. KORNIYENKO.

## SPORTING ORGANIZATIONS

**National Olympic Committee of Ukraine:** 01023 Kiev, vul. Esplanadna 42; tel. (44) 246-64-26; fax (44) 246-62-33; e-mail info@noc-ukr.org; internet www.noc-ukr.org; Pres. VIKTOR F. YANUKOVYCH; Gen. Sec. VOLODYMYR HERASHCHENKO.

**National University of Physical Education and Sport of Ukraine:** 03680 Kiev, vul. Fizkulturna 1; tel. (44) 227-54-52; fax (44) 227-61-91; e-mail rectorat@uni-sport.edu.ua; internet www.uni-sport.edu.ua; f. 1930; Faculties of Olympic and Professional Sport, of Physical Rehabilitation and Sports Medicine, of Physical Education, Recreation and Health-Related Physical Culture, of Correspondence Tuition; Rector VOLODYMYR PLATONOV.

## PERFORMING ARTS

**Kharkiv N. V. Lysenko State Academic Opera and Ballet Theatre (KhATOB):** 61057 Kharkiv, vul. Sumska 25; tel. (572) 47-72-16; fax (572) 47-80-64; e-mail th@vl.kharkov.ua; f. 1920; Dir HEORHIY SELIKHOV.

**Kiev State Puppet Theatre:** 01000 Kiev, maydan Nezalezhnosti; tel. (44) 265-23-53.

**Lviv Solomyii Krushelnytskyi State Academic Theatre of Opera and Ballet:** 79000 Lviv, pr. Svobody; tel. (322) 72-85-62; internet www.lvivopera.org; f. 1900; Dir TADEI O. EDER; Artistic Dir MYRON YUSYPOVYCH.

**National Ivan-Franko Academic Drama Theatre:** 01001 Kiev, pl. Ivana Franka 3; tel. (44) 229-58-51; fax (44) 229-59-51; e-mail nadift@gu.kiev.ua; internet www.franko-theatre.kiev.ua; f. 1920; Gen. Dir MYKHAYLO V. ZAKHAREVICH; Artistic Dir BOHDAN S. STUPKA.

**National Lesya Ukrainka Academic Russian Drama Theatre:** 01001 Kiev, vul. B. Khmelnytskoho 5; tel. (44) 235-42-50; fax (44) 235-42-50; e-mail kievrusdram@mail.ru; internet www.rusdram.kiev.ua; f. 1926; Gen. and Artistic Dir MYKHAYLO REZNIKOVICH.

**National Odesa Philharmonic Orchestra:** 65026 Odesa, vul. I. Bunina 15; tel. (482) 25-01-89; e-mail info@odessaphilharmonic.org; internet www.odessaphilharmonic.org; f. 1937; Musical Dir HOBART EARLE.

**National Philharmonia of Ukraine:** 01304 Kiev, 2 Volodymyrskyi uzviz; tel. (44) 229-62-51; fax (44) 228-03-30; e-mail filarmonia@g.com.ua; internet www.filarmonia.com.ua; f. 1863; Gen. Dir DMYTRO I. OSTAPENKO; Artistic Man. VOLODYMYR A. LUKASHEV.

**Odesa State Academic Opera and Ballet Theatre:** 65026 Odesa, prov. Chaikovskoho 1; e-mail opera-ballet@tm.odessa.ua; internet www.opera-ballet.tm.odessa.ua; f. 1810; Dir VASILIY NABROTSKIY.

**National Academic Taras Shevchenko Opera and Ballet Theatre:** 01034 Kiev, vul. Volodymrska 50; tel. (44) 224-71-65; Dir PETR CHUPRYN.

## ASSOCIATION

**Union of Writers of Ukraine:** 01024 Kiev, vul. Bankova 2; tel. and fax (44) 293-45-86; e-mail nspu@i.kiev.ua; internet www.iptelecom.net.ua/~nspu; f. 1934; incl. 26 regional writers' organizations; Chair. YURIY M. MUSHKETYK; approx. 1,600 members.

# Education

The reversal of perceived 'Russification' of the education system was one of the principal demands of the opposition movements that emerged in the late 1980s. After Ukrainian was adopted as the state language, in 1990 policies were adopted to ensure that all pupils were granted the opportunity of tuition in Ukrainian. In the early 1990s there were significant changes to the curriculum, with more emphasis on Ukrainian history and literature. Some religious and private educational institutions were established, including a private university, the Kiev-Mohyla Academy, which had been one of Europe's leading educational establishments before 1917.

In 2001/02 there were 15,400 pre-primary educational establishments in Ukraine, which provided for some 968,000 students. In that year a total of 6,601,000 students attended 22,200 primary and general-secondary institutions. There were approximately 568,000 teachers of primary and general secondary education in that year. In 1998/99 72% of children in the relevant age-group were enrolled in primary education. In 1993 total enrolment at secondary level was 91% (88% of males, 94% of females). A total of 2,109,300 students were enrolled in higher education in 2001/02. Government expenditure on education in 2001 was 7,798m. hryvnyas (11.1% of total budgetary expenditure).

## UNIVERSITIES

**Chernivtsi National University:** 58012 Chernivtsi, vul. Kotsyubinskoho 2; tel. (3722) 2-62-35; fax (372) 25-38-36; e-mail rectro@chnu.cv.ua; internet www.chnu.cv.ua; f. 1875; language of instruction: Ukrainian; 13 faculties; 786 teachers; 7,421 full-time students, 6,682 part-time; Pres. M. V. TKACH.

**Dnipropetrovsk State University:** 32062 Dnipropetrovsk, vul. Naukovy 13; tel. (562) 46-00-95; fax (562) 46-55-23; e-mail admin@

dsu.dp.ua; internet www.dsu.dp.ua; f. 1918; languages of instruction: Ukrainian and Russian; 17 faculties; 1,100 teachers; 11,168 students; Pres. Prof. V. F. PRISNYAKOV.

**Donetsk National University:** 83055 Donetsk, vul. Universytetska 24; tel. (62) 337-19-45; fax (62) 345-21-76; e-mail postmaster@univ.donetsk.ua; internet www.dnu.donetsk.ua; f. 1965; languages of instruction: Ukrainian and Russian; 12 faculties; 815 teachers; 17,300 students; Rector VOLODYMYR P. SHEVCHENKO.

**Ivan Franko National University of Lviv:** 79000 Lviv, vul. Universytetska 1; tel. (322) 74-12-62; fax (322) 72-28-01; e-mail dirlu@franko.lviv.ua; internet www.franko.lviv.ua; language of instruction: Ukrainian; f. 1661; 16 faculties; 1,161 teachers; 22,000 students; Rector BORYS IVAN VAKARCHUK.

**V. N. Karazin Kharkhiv National University:** 61077 Kharkiv, pl. Svobody 4; tel. (57) 705-12-47; fax (57) 705-12-48; e-mail postmaster@univer.kharkov.ua; internet www.univer.kharkov.ua; f. 1804; languages of instruction: Russian and Ukrainian; 18 faculties, 4 research institutes; 2,000 teachers; 12,000 students; Rector V. S. BAKIROV.

**Kiev T. Shevchenko National University:** 01033 Kiev, vul. Volodmymyrska 64; tel. (44) 234-12-88; fax (44) 220-83-91; e-mail office@univ.kiev.ua; internet www.univ.kiev.ua; f. 1834; 21 faculties and academic institutes; 3 research institutes; 2,000 teachers; 20,000 students; Rector Prof. VIKTOR V. SKOPENKO.

**Odesa I. I. Mechnikov National University:** 65026 Odesa, vul. Petra Dvoryanska 2; tel. (482) 23-52-54; fax (482) 23-35-15; e-mail oguint@paco.net; internet odnu.edu.ua; f. 1865; languages of instruction: Russian and Ukrainian; 10 faculties; 3 educational institutes; c. 2,000 teachers; 17,000 students; Rector Prof. Dr VALENTIN A. SMYNTYNA.

**Taurida National University:** 95007 Crimea, Simferopol, ul. Yaltinskaya 4; tel. (652) 23-22-80; fax (652) 23-23-10; e-mail rector@tnu .crimea.ua; internet www.tnu.crimea.edu/tnu; f. 1918; language of instruction: Russian; 14 faculties; 800 teachers; 15,000 students; Rector NIKOLAI V. BAGROV.

**University of Kiev-Mohyla Academy:** 04070 Kiev, vul. Skovorody 2; tel. (44) 416-45-15; fax (44) 417-84-61; e-mail rec@ukma .kiev.ua; internet www.ukma.kiev.ua; f. 1615, abolished 1817; re-founded 1991, acquired status of national university in 1994; languages of instruction: Ukrainian and English; 6 faculties; 713 teachers; 2,675 students; Pres. VYACHESLAV BRYUKHOVETSKIY; Rector SERHIY IVANYUK.

**Uzhhorod State University:** 88000 Transcarpathian obl., Uzhhorod, vul. Pidhirna 46; tel. and fax (3122) 3-33-41; e-mail admin@univ.uzhgorod.ua; internet www.univ.uzhgorod.ua; f. 1945; language of instruction: Ukrainian; 14 faculties; 10,000 students; Rector VOLODYMYR YU. SLYVKA.

**Zaporozhzhya State University:** 69600 Zaporizhzhya, vul. Zhukovskoho 66; tel. (612) 64-45-46; fax (612) 62-71-61; e-mail rektor@zsu.zp.ua; internet www.zsu.edu.ua; f. 1985; languages of instruction: Russian and Ukrainian; 14 faculties; 541 teachers; 8,200 students; Rector Prof. VYACHESLAV A. TOLOK.

# Social Welfare

Until independence in 1991, the Soviet state-funded system of social welfare was in existence in Ukraine. In 1991 three extra-budgetary funds were created: the Pension Fund, the Social Insurance Fund and the Employment Fund, which were intended to administer most of Ukraine's social-security benefits. The Social Insurance Fund is administered by the trade unions and finances health clinics at workplaces, sick leave, and benefits, such as maternity leave and child-birth allowances. The Employment Fund provides unemployment insurance payments to workers for up to one year. A fourth fund, the Chornobyl Fund, was later established, providing a variety of benefits, including social payments, to victims of the Chornobyl nuclear accident. Family benefits, which are means-tested, are also paid by the state.

In 2001 the average life expectancy at birth was 62.2 years for men and 73.3 years for women; the rate of infant mortality was 20 per 1,000 live births. In 2000 there were 3.0 physicians and 9.0 hospital beds for every 1,000 people. The compulsory retirement age in Ukraine is 55 years for women and 60 years for men; the Pension Fund distributed pensions to some 14m. people in 1996. Reform of the pension system was approved by the Government in mid-1997. Three forms of pensions were proposed: a labour pension, comprising contributions from employees' salaries; welfare pensions, paid from the central and local government budgets; and a supplementary pension paid from private pension funds. Further reforms were proposed in April 1998, providing for a phased increase in the

amount received. In 2001 government expenditure on health care amounted to 5,403m. hryvnyas (7.7% of total budgetary expenditure), and expenditure on social security and welfare totalled 30,293m. hryvnyas (43.1% of spending).

**Ministry of Health Care:** see section on The Government (Ministries).

**Ministry of Labour and Social Policy:** see section on The Government (Ministries).

**Chornobyl Fund:** 04053 Kiev, pl. Lvivska 8.

**Employment Fund:** 04053 Kiev, vul. Kudryavska 26–28; f. 1991.

**Pension Fund:** 01014 Kiev, vul. Bastionna 9; tel. (44) 294-42-01; f. 1991; Chair. of Bd BORYS ZAYCHUK.

**Social Insurance Fund:** 04053 Kiev, vul. Kudryavska 26–28; f. 1991.

# The Environment

An explosion at the Chornobyl (Chernobyl) nuclear power station in April 1986 resulted in serious contamination of many areas in Ukraine (an estimated 40,000 sq km of territory), as well as areas in many other European countries. The incident, particularly the secrecy surrounding it and the subsequent decontamination operation, led to the formation of several environmental campaigning and political organizations. It was announced in April 1996 that some 2,500 deaths in Ukraine, caused by cancer, cardiovascular and neurological diseases, may have been the result of the Chornobyl accident. In total some 3.2m. people in the country, including 950,000 children, had been affected by the disaster. In 1998 cracks in the protective cover of the defective reactor were found; measures were swiftly taken to prevent leakage of radioactive material. The last functioning reactor at Chornobyl was finally shut down in December 2000, after the European Bank for Reconstruction and Development (EBRD) agreed to provide funds for the construction of new reactors. The other area of environmental concern was the heavily industrialized Donbas region. The country also participated in efforts to control pollution in the Black Sea.

### GOVERNMENT ORGANIZATIONS

**Ministry of Ecology and Natural Resources:** see section on The Government (Ministries).

**Ministry for Emergency Situations and Protection of the Population from the Consequences of the Chornobyl Catastrophe:** see section on The Government (Ministries).

**Ukrainian Scientific Research Institute for Ecological Problems (USRIEP):** 61166 Kharkov, vul. Bakulina 6; tel. and fax (57) 702-15-92; e-mail griz@kharkov.com; f. 1971; environmental protection, water resource management and treatment, environmental legislation and regulations; Dir YAROSLAV PODOBA.

### ACADEMIC INSTITUTES

**National Academy of Sciences of Ukraine:** 01601 Kiev, vul. Volodmymyrska 54; tel. (44) 225-22-39; fax (44) 224-32-43; e-mail prez@nas.gov.ua; internet www.nas.gov.ua; f. 1918; Pres. B. E. PATON.

attached institutes incl.:

**Ukrainian State Steppe Reservation:** 87172 Donetsk obl., Telmanov raion, Samsonove; tel. (6279) 27-325; associated with the Institute of Biology; has some environmental responsibilities; Dir ANATOLIY P. HENOV.

**Ukrainian Institute of Energy:** 04070 Kiev, vul. Pokrovska 11; tel. and fax (44) 417-01-42; e-mail ie@ienergy.kiev.ua; f. 1997; publishes journal *The Problems of Energy*; Dir of Scientific Activity M. KULIK.

### NON-GOVERNMENTAL ORGANIZATIONS

**Ecological Information Centre (EITs):** 83000 Donetsk, bulv. Pushkina 13; tel. and fax (62) 335-43-09; e-mail webmaster@infoeco .dn.ua; internet www.infoeco.dn.ua; f. 2001.

**EcoPravo-Kharkiv:** 61002 Kharkiv, POB 10479; tel. and fax (572) 19-10-21; e-mail eco@ecopravo.kharkov.ua; internet www.ecopravo .kharkov.ua; f. 1993; environmental law, legal assistance to citizens and non-governmental organizations, developing and promotion of environmental legislation in Ukraine; Dir Prof. OLEKSIY M. SHUMYLO.

**Green Party of Ukraine** (Partiya Zelenykh Ukrainy) (see section on Political Organizations).

**Interecocentre:** 01601 Kiev, vul. Tereschenkivska 2; tel. (44) 235-73-74; fax (44) 235-70-62; e-mail intereco@post.com.ua; internet www.geocities.com/interecocentre; f. 1994; seeks to monitor and protect environment; works with the World Bank, the Govt, industry and unions, etc.; Dir LEONID PROTSENKO.

**Ukrainian Chornobyl Union:** c/o 01655 Kiev, pl. Lvivska 8; f. 1991; represents victims of the Chornobyl disaster; 420,000 members; Pres. YURIY ANDREYEV.

**Zeleniy Svit** (Green World—Ukrainian Environmental Association): 01070 Kiev, pl. Kontraktova 4; tel. (44) 417-02-83; fax (44) 417-43-83; e-mail zsfoe@melp.dp.ua; f. 1988; ecological asscn of various Ukrainian groups; affiliated to Rukh and to the Ukrainian Peace Council's campaign against nuclear power; Chair. YURIY SAMOYLENKO.

## Defence

In December 1991 an independent Ukrainian military was established. At August 2002 there were an estimated 302,300 active personnel in the Ukrainian Armed Forces (excluding Strategic Nuclear Forces and the Black Sea Fleet), including 150,700 ground forces, an air force of 49,100 and a navy of an estimated 13,500. Reserves numbered approximately 1m. There were also paramilitary forces, comprising some 45,000 in the Border Guard, 44,000 serving under the Ministry of Internal Affairs, 14,00 serving in the Coast Guard, and some 9,500 civil defence troops. Military service in Ukraine is compulsory for males over 18 years of age, for a period of 18 months in the ground and air forces, and two years in the navy.

In 1998 proposals to end conscription by 2015 were announced as part of a programme of military reforms.

In 1993–94 a programme of nuclear disarmament was agreed with the USA and Russia, involving the dismantling of ex-Soviet nuclear warheads and, finally, the surrender of the remaining warheads. The transfer of strategic nuclear weapons to Russia for dismantling was funded by the USA and completed in mid-1996. Later that year Ukraine began a programme of destruction or conversion to civilian use of its missile silos. In mid-1998 110 launch silos had been destroyed, and 90 of the 130 ballistic missiles possessed by Ukraine had been neutralized. Ukraine declared itself to be of non-aligned status. In November 1994 the Verkhovna Rada ratified the Treaty on the Non-Proliferation of Nuclear Weapons, which enabled the implementation of the first Strategic Arms' Reduction Treaty (START 1), ratified in February 1994. On 31 May 1997 Ukraine and Russia signed an agreement on the division of the Soviet Black Sea Fleet, on the terms of its deployment and on the status of its base, Sevastopol. Defence spending in 2001 totalled 3,337m. hryvnyas (representing 4.7% of total expenditure).

**Supreme Commander of the Armed Forces of the Republic of Ukraine:** President of the Republic.

**Chief of the General Staff:** Col-Gen. OLEKSANDR ZATYNAYKO.

**Chief of the Air Defence:** Lt-Gen. ANATOLIY YA. TOROPCHYN.

**Chief of the Land Forces:** Col-Gen. PETRO I. SHULYAK.

**Chief of the Military Air Force:** Lt-Gen. YAROSLAV I. SKALKO.

**Commander-in-Chief of the Navy:** Adm. IHOR KNYAZ.

# THE AUTONOMOUS REPUBLIC OF CRIMEA

## Introduction

The Autonomous Republic of Crimea (Krym) is bounded to the south and west by the Black Sea and is separated from mainland Ukraine—Kherson Oblast (to the north) by the Perekop Isthmus and from the Taman Peninsula (situated in the Krasnodar Krai of the Russian Federation, to the east) by the Kerch Strait. The republic covers a total area of 26,100 sq km, a large proportion of which is dry steppeland. It is rich in minerals. The peninsula is divided into 14 administrative districts and 16 cities. The peninsula's main cities are Simferopol, the capital, Sevastopol (which does not, however, form part of the Autonomous Republic, although, from the 2000s, the city increasingly has been included in statistical data pertaining to the Republic) and Kerch. The towns of the south coast, particularly Yalta, are popular tourist resorts. The population of the republic at the census of 5 December 1998, according to rounded figures, was 2,031,000. At the end of 2002 the population of the republic was estimated at 2,018,400, with an additional 378,500 resident in Sevastopol; the population density of the peninsula at that time was, therefore, 88.8 per sq km, or 77.3 per sq km within the republic proper. In January 2001 62.6% of the republic's population inhabited urban areas, a proportion that has remained approximately constant since the early 1960s. According to the census of January 1989, 82.6% of the population of Crimea (including Sevastopol) regarded Russian as their native language, compared with 13.7% who described Ukrainian in this way. (Notably, only 52.6% of those who defined their ethnicity as Ukrainian stated that Ukrainian was their native language.) At that time an estimated 26% of the population of Crimea were ethnically Ukrainian and 67% Russian. Crimea's Tatar population was deported to Central Asia by Stalin (Iosif V. Dzhugashvili) in May 1944; some 100,000, about one-half of the population, died during the deportations. After Stalin's death in 1953 the Tatars were allowed to resettle in Central Asia (principally in Uzbekistan), but were not permitted to return to Crimea. After 1989, however, approximately 270,000 Tatars

returned to the region and, by 2001, constituted some 13% of the population of the peninsula.

### History

The Crimean peninsula was originally colonized by the ancient Greeks in the seventh century BC and subsequently invaded by the Goths (AD250), the Huns (373), the Khazars (eighth century), the Eastern Roman, or 'Byzantine', Greeks (1016), the Kipchaks (1050), the Mongol Tatars (13th century) and the Ottoman Turks (late 15th century). An independent Crimean Khanate was founded by the Tatars in northern and central Crimea in 1475, and survived until the late 18th century, when the Russian Empire made repeated incursions into the peninsula. The Khanate was finally annexed in 1783. The Russians were defeated in the Crimean War (1854–55) by the Western Powers (France, the Kingdom of Sardinia and the United Kingdom) and the Ottoman Turks. Crimea formed part of the short-lived republic of Taurida (Tavria—established in 1918), until 18 October 1921, when the Crimean Autonomous Soviet Socialist Republic (ASSR) was created, within the Russian Soviet Federative Socialist Republic (RSFSR).

The Crimean ASSR was abolished on 30 June 1945, following the deportation of the Tatars, and the peninsula became merely an oblast (region) within the RSFSR. However, purportedly to mark the 300th anniversary of the *de facto* union of Ukraine and Russia in 1654, on 19 February 1954 Crimea was transferred to the control of the Ukrainian Soviet Socialist Republic (Ukrainian SSR). Following a referendum held on the peninsula on 20 January 1991, Crimea claimed the status of an autonomous republic. In February 1992 the Crimean Supreme Council (legislature) voted to transform the region into the self-styled 'Republic of Crimea'. The Ukrainian authorities subsequently offered the region greater powers of self-government, but on 5 May the Crimean Supreme Council declared independence from Ukraine. The decision was annulled by the all-Ukrainian Verkhovna Rada the following week; however, in June the

Ukrainian authorities recognized Crimea as an Autonomous Republic. On 16 January 1994 elections were held to the new presidency of the Crimea, won by Yurii Meshkov, a Russian nationalist and leader of the Republican Party of Crimea.

Elections to the republican legislature of Crimea, held on 27 March 1994, likewise demonstrated a large degree of popular support for pro-Russian parties. Meanwhile, in a concurrently-held referendum, 70% of participants responded in favour of greater autonomy from Ukraine. In May the new Crimean parliament voted to restore the May 1992 Constitution, which effectively represented a declaration of the republic's independence. Compromise with the Ukrainian central authorities was later reached.

The main political concern in Crimea during 1994 was the struggle between the Meshkov presidency and the republican parliament, although both factions remained advocates of increased autonomy. In September the two sides agreed to draft a new basic law. On 17 March 1995 the Verkhovna Rada voted to abolish the May 1992 Crimean Constitution and the post of President of Crimea. Two weeks later the national President, Leonid Kuchma, in an effort to avert a political crisis, assumed direct control of the administration of Crimea and ordered the restoration of Anatolii Franchuk (who had been dismissed by the Crimean Supreme Council one week earlier) as republican premier. Direct presidential administration over the region ended on 28 August 1995.

Ukrainian control over the peninsula was consolidated in mid-1995, when the results of local elections demonstrated a significant decrease in support for pro-Russian parties. The new Crimean Supreme Council elected Yevhen Suprunyuk, thought to be more conciliatory towards the national Government, as its Chairman. In October 1995 the Crimean parliament adopted a new Constitution, which was not recognized by the national authorities until April 1996, when significant amendments were suggested. A fifth draft of this Constitution was approved by the Crimean parliament in October 1998. The Constitution stated that Crimea had the status of an autonomous republic, without sovereignty, and was a part of Ukraine. (Meanwhile, the Constitution of Ukraine, finally adopted on 28 June 1996, described Ukraine as a unitary state, recognizing Crimea as an inseparable, integral part of that state and the Supreme Council of the Autonomous Republic of Crimea as its representative organ.)

In October 1996 Suprunyuk resigned and was replaced by Vasyl Kiselev. In January 1997 the Crimean Supreme Council approved a motion of 'no confidence' in the Council of Ministers, led by Arkadii Demydenko since January 1996. The following month, contrary to Ukrainian law, the parliament approved legislation, whereby the Government was, in the future, to be appointed by the Crimean legislature, rather than by the Ukrainian President. In April the parliament duly appointed Anatolii Franchuk as the new head of the Council of Ministers, a resolution suspended by President Kuchma. However, following a second vote of 'no confidence' in Demydenko, President Kuchma consented to Franchuk's appointment.

On 26 February 1998 President Kuchma signed legislation stating that the Crimean Supreme Council was to comprise 100 deputies, elected on the basis of universal, equal and direct suffrage. The Presidium of the Supreme Council consists of 15 members including a Chairman (speaker). In March elections to the Crimean Supreme Council were held simultaneously with the elections to the national Verkhovna Rada. Of the registered electorate, 63.8% participated in the elections. The Communist Party of Ukraine (CPU) obtained 40 of the 100 seats in the Crimean Supreme Council, by far the largest number gained by a single party. Independent candidates secured 44 seats. Leonid Grach, the leader of the CPU in Crimea, was elected Chairman on 14 May. In April results in a number of constituencies were declared invalid, prompting the need for repeat elections to be held. The Organization for Security and Co-operation in Europe (OSCE) estimated that about one-half of the Tatars resident in Crimea in 1998 did not have Ukrainian citizenship and were, therefore, ineligible to vote (in October of that year the process of naturalization of Tatars was simplified). On 27 May 1998 a new Council of Ministers was appointed, with the centrist, Sergei Kunitsyn, who was also an ally of President Kuchma, as premier. On 12 January 1999 a new Crimean Constitution came into effect, establishing relations between the authorities in Kiev and Simferopol and granting Crimea the right to draft a budget and manage its own property. In February the first Crimean Tatars received Ukrainian citizenship, which was believed to have been extended to some 90% of the Crimean

Tatars resident on the peninsula prior to the holding of legislative elections in March 2002. None the less, in May 2000 some 20,000 Crimean Tatars held a demonstration in Simferopol to demand greater political autonomy.

A political impasse developed from the second half of 2000, apparently as a result of political rivalry between Kunitsyn and Grach, and as a result of alleged corruption within the Crimean Government; in September five ministers and two deputy prime ministers, all of whom were members of the CPU, resigned from the cabinet; Kunitsyn nominated new ministers in their place in December. Tensions between the Crimean parliament and executive continued into mid-2001. In mid-July the Supreme Council dismissed Kunitsyn from the premiership for the third time, appointing Deputy Prime Minister Lentun Bezaziyev as acting premier. Although Kuchma had refused to recognize two previous dismissals, on this occasion the removal of Kunitsyn was accepted, and Kuchma expressed support for the new premier elected by the Crimean Supreme Council, Valerii Gorbatov of the Working Ukraine party. A new Crimean Government was appointed in mid-September; however, continuing tensions between the Government and the parliament resulted in 11 of the 30 ministerial posts remaining vacant in late November.

As campaigning for the concurrent elections to the Verkhovna Rada and the Crimean Supreme Council, to be held on 31 March 2002, got under way, controversy was provoked at the end of February by the invalidation of Grach's candidacy for a seat in the Supreme Council on technical grounds. Shortly after Grach's disqualification, some 30 candidates opposed to Grach were also disqualified, and Grach reportedly threatened to demand a referendum supporting the reversion of Crimea to Russian rule; additionally, supporters of Grach pitched tents in the centre of Simferopol in order to demand that he be permitted to contest the elections. Following the rejection of Grach's appeal by the Crimean Court of Appeal, the case was referred to the Ukrainian Supreme Court, but was not heard until after the elections, in April. Meanwhile, despite his disqualification, Grach's name appeared on ballot papers, and he was re-elected to the Supreme Council in defiance of the Crimean Appeal Court's decision. The elections to the Crimean Supreme Council demonstrated a sizeable shift in support away from the CPU, towards centrists close to Kunitsyn, who, contesting the elections as the Kunitsyn Team, won 39 of 100 seats and, subsequently, were able to organize a majority faction in the legislature. The CPU and their allies, contesting the elections as the Grach bloc, won 28 seats; three other parties gained representation, and 29 independent candidates were elected. In late April the Ukrainian Supreme Court approved Grach's appeal, thereby serving to legitimize his status as a deputy. However, Grach was unsuccessful in his campaign for re-election as speaker of the legislature, being resoundingly defeated by a former deputy speaker, Boris Deich, at the opening session in late April. The new parliament also voted for the dismissal of Gorbatov and the re-appointment of Kunitsyn as Prime Minister, and reformists loyal to Kunitsyn were successful in establishing a majority in the legislature, which eventually became known as the 'Stability' bloc, comprising some 86 of 100 deputies. None the less, in the concurrent elections to the Verkhovna Rada, the CPU remained the most popular party on the peninsula. Notably, for the first time, Crimean Tatar deputies were elected to the Verkhovna Rada, within the Our Ukraine bloc. Russian nationalists only successfully attracted votes in the Crimean city of Sevastopol.

### Economy

Tourism has traditionally been the principal economic activity of the territories that constitute the Autonomous Republic of Crimea, although there is also a significant agro-industrial complex. In 1999 the gross regional product of the republic was 3,350.3m. hryvynas, equivalent to 1,576 hryvynas per head.

Agricultural production consists mainly of fruit, berries and vegetables (particularly of grapes), and of animal husbandry. The Republic produced over 34% of the Ukraine's output of grapes in 2000. At constant 1996 prices, agricultural output in 2000 was equivalent to 924.3m. hryvynas, compared with 1,162.7m. hryvynas in 1995. Agricultural production decreased, in real terms, by 8.3% per year in 1995–99, with meat and dairy production declining by more than one-half in 1990–2000. The production of wool declined rapidly during the late 1990s, from 2,224 metric tons in 1995 to 603 tons in 2000. The collective sector remained important in the agriculture of the Republic in the early 2000s. There are reserves of petroleum and natural gas in the north of Crimea, and in surrounding regions of the Black Sea and the Sea of Azov. In 2000 extraction of petroleum, including gas condensate, amounted to 79,900 metric tons, and extraction of some 764,500 tons of natural gas was recorded. The industrial production of Crimea (including Sevastopol), at current prices, amounted to 2,607.1m. hryvynas in 2000, compared with 1,971.4m. hryvynas (excluding Sevastopol) in 1999. According to preliminary figures, the value of industrial production in the Autonomous Republic in 2000 was equivalent to only 44% of that recorded in 1990, and to 93% of recorded production in 1995. (These figures reflected a steeper decline than had been the case in Ukraine as a whole, where industrial output in 2000 was equivalent to 58% of the level recorded in 1990, and to 110% of that recorded in 1995.) Of the regions of Ukraine bordering the Black Sea, only Kherson Oblast registered a steeper decline in industrial output during either or both of these periods. A major factor in precipitating the rapid decline in industrial output during the 1990s was the failure to convert military production facilities, which were formerly widespread on the peninsula, to civilian use after the collapse of the USSR.

In 2000 the economically active population in Crimea (including Sevastopol) amounted to 1,869,800, of whom some 5.5% were registered as unemployed. Of those in employment in that year, the average monthly wage was 225.2 hryvynas. In 2000 there was a budgetary deficit of 0.4m. hryvynas for Crimea (including Sevastopol). In that year the external merchandise trade of Crimea (including Sevastopol) amounted to a value of US $319.6m., of which $146.2m. was accounted for by imports and $173.4m. by exports. Prinicipal exports included chemicals and chemical products (amounting to 39.6% of the total) and crude metals (14.6%). Principal imports in that year included mechanical equipment and transportation products. There was $147.2m. of foreign investment in the Republic in 2000. In that year there were 9,183 small businesses registered in the Autonomous Republic. In 1999 consumer prices of goods and services within the Republic (excluding Sevastopol) increased by 19.8%, compared with the previous year; in 2000 the consumer price index for Crimea (including Sevastopol), increased by 14.9%. Tourism has long been an important contributor to the Crimean economy, with many holiday resorts and sanatoria, particularly in coastal regions, while the mountain scenery of inland regions also attracts visitors. The vast majority of foreign tourists are citizens of Russia, although there are also considerable numbers of visitors from Belarus, Estonia, Germany, Kazakhstan, Latvia and Lithuania. In the first six months of 2002 tourism and associated industries generated $5.8m. of income from non-Ukrainian citizens, compared with $4.0m. in the corresponding period of 2001. The principal ports of Crimea are located at Yevpatoriya, Yalta, Feodosiya, Kerch and (although not part of the Autonomous Republic) Sevastopol.

# Directory

## The Government

**Chairman of the Presidium of the Supreme Council:** BORIS D. DEICH 95000 Crimea, Simferopol, vul. K. Marksa 18; e-mail webmaster@rada.crimea.ua; internet www.rada.crimea.ua.

**Chairman of the Council of Ministers (Prime Minister):** SERGEI V. KUNITSYN 95005 Crimea, Simferopol, vul. Kirova 13; e-mail letter@ark.gov.ua; internet www.crimea-portal.gov.ua.

**Representative of the President of Ukraine in Crimea:** OLEKSANDR M. DIDENKO 95000 Crimea, Simferopol, vul. Kirova 13.

# Crimean Supreme Council

### General Election, 31 March 2002

| Party | Number of seats |
|---|---|
| Kunitsyn Team* | 39 |
| Grach bloc† | 28 |
| Social-Democratic Party of Ukraine (United) | 2 |
| Democratic Party of Ukraine—Democratic Union | 1 |
| Peasants' Party | 1 |
| Independents | 29 |
| Total | 100 |

* An electoral alliance, led by Sergei Kunitsyn of the People's Democratic Party/For A United Ukraine.

† An electoral alliance, led by Leonid Grach of the Communist Party of Ukraine.

# Crimean Political Organizations

Like its national counterpart, the Communist Party in Crimea was banned in August 1991. In September, however, several local communist unions were established, which merged in June 1992 to form the Union of Communists of Crimea. On 18 June 1993 the Union was renamed the Communist Party of Crimea and was officially registered on 15 September. Several other powerful political interest groups emerged in 1993–94. The 'Russia' bloc consisted of various pro-Russian parties, including the Russian Movement of Crimea, led by Aleksandr Chernomorov, and the Republican Party of Crimea, the former leader of which, Yurii Meshkov, won the Crimean presidential elections in January 1994. Several parties promoting business interests were formed, including the Party for the Economic Renewal of Crimea, and Working Ukraine, which was founded in 2000. The Communist Party of Ukraine (CPU), the People's Democratic Party of Ukraine, the Agrarian Party of Ukraine, and Union (Soyuz), a constituent member of the Russian Movement of Ukraine, which aspires to a peaceful re-unification of Belarus, Russia and Ukraine, and the Socialist Party of Ukraine also attracted support in the March 1998 legislative elections. The dominant political party among the Crimean Tatars was the Organization of the Crimean Tatar Movement (OCTM—f. 1989), which advocates the restoration of Tatar statehood in the Crimea. The OCTM also organized a Crimean Tatar representative body, the Majlis, led by Mustafa Dzhemilev. The National Movement of the Crimean Tatars is a more moderate organization, committed to co-operation with the existing political structures in the Crimea, and in 2002 seven Crimean Tatars were elected to the Crimean Supreme Council, compared with just one in 1998. The National Party (Milli Firka) is a radical nationalist group. In the elections to the Verkhovna Rada held concurrently with elections to the Crimean Supreme Council in March 2002, the CPU was the most popular party, receiving 33.9% of the votes cast, one of the highest proportions in any region in Ukraine, while the Social-Democratic Party of Ukraine (United) also received a markedly higher proportion of the votes cast (12.5%) than was the case nation-wide. Although the Our Ukraine bloc only received 9.8% of the votes cast in Crimea, it was believed to have gained particular support among Crimean Tatars, many of whom were permitted to vote in Ukrainian elections for the first time in 2002, partially because of the inclusion of Mustafa Dzhemiliev and another leader of the Majlis, Refat Chubarov, on the party's list.

# Bibliography

Albright, D. E., and Appatov, S. J. (Eds). *Ukraine and European Security.* London, Macmillan, 1999.

Åslund, A., and De Menil, G. (Eds). *Economic Reform in Ukraine: The Unfinished Agenda.* Armonk, NY, M. E. Sharpe, 2000.

Birch, S. *Elections and Democratization in Ukraine.* Basingstoke, Macmillan, 2000.

Bojcun, M. *Ukraine and Europe. A Difficult Reunion.* London: Kogan Page, 2001.

Bukkvoll, T. *Ukraine and European Security.* London, Royal Institute of International Affairs, 1997.

D'Anieri, P. *Economic Interdependence in Ukrainian-Russian Relations.* New York, New York State University Press, 1999.

D'Anieri, P., and Kuzio, T. (Eds). *State-Led Nation Building in Ukraine.* Westport, CT, Praeger, 2002.

D'Anieri, P., Kravchuk, R., and Kuzio, T. *Politics and Society in Ukraine.* Boulder, CO, Westview, 1999.

*State and Institution Building in Ukraine.* New York, NY, St Martin's Press, 1999.

Drohobycky, M. (Ed.). *Crimea: Dynamics, Challenges and Prospects.* Lanham, MD, Rowman and Littlefield, 1995.

Dyczok, M. *The Grand Alliance and Ukrainian Refugees*. Basingstoke, Macmillan, 2000.

  *Ukraine: Movement Without Change, Change Without Movement*. Reading, Harwood Academic Publishers, 2000.

Garnett, W. *Keystone in the Arch: Ukraine in the Emerging Security Environment of Central and Eastern Europe*. Washington, DC, Carnegie Endowment, 1997.

Harasymiw, B. *Post-Communist Ukraine*. Toronto, Canadian Institute of Ukrainian Studies, 2002.

Jones, S. A. *Whither Ukraine?: Weapons, State Building and International Cooperation*. Aldershot, Ashgate Publishing, 2002.

Kravchuk, R. S. *Ukrainian Political Economy*. Basingstoke, Palgrave Macmillan, 2002.

Kubicek, P. *Unbroken Ties: The State, Interest Associations, and Corporatism in Post-Soviet Ukraine*. Ann Arbor, MI, University of Michigan Press, 2000.

Kuzio, T. *Ukraine: State and Nation Building*. London, Routledge, 1998.

  *Ukraine: Perestroika to Independence*, 2nd edn. London, Macmillan, 2000.

Kuzio, T. (Ed.). *Contemporary Ukraine. Dynamics of Post-Soviet Transformation*. Armonk, NY, M. E. Sharpe, 1998.

Kuzio, T., Molchanov, M., and Moroney, J. D. P. (Eds). *Ukrainian Foreign and Security Policy. Theoretical and Comparative Perspectives*. Westport, CT, Praeger, 2002.

Lewis, A. (Ed.). *The EU and Ukraine: Neighbours, Friends, Partners?* London, Federal Trust for Education and Research, 2002.

Lieven, A. *Ukraine and Russia: A Fraternal Rivalry*. Washington, DC, US Institute of Peace, 1999.

Lutz, H., and Mollers, F. (Eds). *Ukraine on the Road to Europe*. Heidelberg, Physica, 2001.

Magosci, P. R. *A History of Ukraine*. Toronto, University of Toronto Press, 1996.

  *The Roots of Ukrainian Nationalism: Galicia as Ukraine's Piedmont*. Toronto, University of Toronto Press, 2001.

Molchanov, M. A. *Political Culture and National Identity in Russian-Ukrainian Relations*. College Station, TX, Texas A&M University Press, 2002.

Morozov, K. *Above and Beyond: From Soviet General to Ukrainian State-Builder*. Cambridge, MA, Harvard University Press, 2001.

Müller, D., Spillmann, K. R., and Wenger, A. (Eds). *Between Russia and the West: Foreign and Security Policy of Independent Ukraine*. Bern, Peter Lang, 1999.

Nahaylo, B. *The Ukrainian Resurgence*. London, Hurst, 1999.

Plokhy, S. *The Cossacks and Religion in Early Modern Ukraine*. Oxford, Oxford University Press, 2002.

Sanders, D. *Security Cooperation between Russia and Ukraine in the Post-Soviet Era*. New York, Palgrave, 2002.

Satzewich, V. *The Ukrainian Diaspora*. London, Routledge, 2002.

Shandor, V. *Carpatho-Ukraine in the 20th Century: A Political History*. Cambridge, MA, Harvard University Press, 1997.

Simon, G. (Ed.). *Die neue Ukraine. Gesellschaft-Wirtschaft-Politik (1991–2001)*. Köln, Bohlau Verlag, 2002.

Simon, R. *Labour and Political Transformation in Russia and Ukraine*. Aldershot, Ashgate Publishing, 2001.

Skirda, A. *Nestor Makhno: Anarchy's Cossack: The Struggle for Free Soviets in the Ukraine: 1917-1921*. Oakland, CA, AK Press, 2003.

Solchanyk, R. *Ukraine: From Chernobyl to Sovereignty*. London, Macmillan, 1992.

Subtelny, O. *Ukraine: A History*. Toronto, University of Toronto Press, 1988.

Van Zon, H. *The Political Economy of Independent Ukraine*. Basingstoke, Macmillan, 2000.

von Cramon-Taubadel, S., and Akimova, I. *Fostering Sustainable Growth in Ukraine*. Heidelberg, Physica, 2002.

Wanner, C. *Burden of Dreams: History and Identity in Post-Soviet Ukraine*. Philadelphia, PA, Pennsylvania State University Press, 1998.

Williams, B. G. *The Crimean Tatars: The Diaspora Experience and the Forging of a Nation*. Leiden, Brill, 2001.

Wilson, A. *Ukrainian Nationalism in the 1990s: A Minority Faith*. Cambridge, Cambridge University Press, 1997.

  *The Ukrainians: Unexpected Nation*, 2nd edn. New Haven, CT, Yale University Press, 2002.

Wolchik, S. L., and Zviglyanich, V. (Eds). *Ukraine: The Search for a National Identity*. Lanham, MA, Rowman and Littlefield, 2000.

Wolczuk, K. *The Moulding of Ukraine: The Constitutional Politics of State Formation*. Budapest, Central European University Press, 2001.

Wolczuk, R. *Ukraine's Foreign and Security Policy 1991-2000*. London, RoutledgeCurzon, 2002.

Also see the Select Bibliography in Part Four.

# UZBEKISTAN

## Geography

### PHYSICAL FEATURES

The Republic of Uzbekistan (formerly the Uzbek Soviet Socialist Republic, a constituent part of the USSR) is located in the heart of Central Asia. The country lies along a north-west to south-east axis and its eastern extremity, the Fergana valley region, abuts into Kyrgyzstan to the east, with Tajikistan to the south, forming the south-eastern border of the country. Uzbekistan has a short border with Afghanistan in the south, near the town of Termez, and Turkmenistan lies to the south-west. The north-western end of the country consists of the Kara-Kalpak Autonomous Republic (Karakalpakstan), to the west of which is Kazakhstan, which also lies to the north, beyond the Aral Sea, and forms the entire north-eastern border of Uzbekistan. The country covers an area of 447,400 sq km (172,740 sq miles), of which 165,600 sq km constitutes Karakalpakstan.

Much of the land is desert, including the south-western part of the Kyzyl-Kum or Red Sands desert, but the western reaches of the Tien Shan range extend into the south-east of the country. The two main rivers are the Amu-Dar'ya (anciently the Oxus) and the Syr-Dar'ya (Jaxartes), both of which rise in the mountainous regions of the Tien Shan and flow north-westwards, to drain into the Aral Sea. However, severe overuse of these water resources for irrigation (notably the Kara-Kum Canal in Turkmenistan) from the 1950s, caused a dramatic depletion of the waters reaching the Aral Sea. The consequent decline in its water level and the increase in the area of toxic desert (owing to the use of chemical fertilizers) had severe environmental implications for the whole region. The Amu-Dar'ya is the worst affected of the two rivers and usually dries up far short of the Aral Sea, in the region of Nukus. It is the more southerly river and flows through Turkmenistan, parallel to the Uzbek border, before forming that border, until it reaches the oasis towns of Khorezm, where it enters Uzbek territory and heads towards the Aral Sea. The Syr-Dar'ya waters the prosperous Fergana valley region, crosses the Kojand region of Tajikistan, and then cuts north across Uzbekistan before entering Kazakhstan.

### CLIMATE

The climate is marked by extreme temperatures and low levels of precipitation. Summers are long and hot with average temperatures in July of 32°C (90°F); daytime temperatures often exceed 40°C (104°F). During the short winter there are frequent severe frosts and temperatures can fall as low as –38°C (–36°F).

### POPULATION

Uzbeks form the largest ethnic group in the country (71.4% of the total population in 1989); the remainder includes Russians (8.3%), Tajiks (4.7%), Kazakhs (4.1%) and Tatars (2.4%). Other ethnic groups include Karakalpaks (411,878), most of

whom are resident in Karakalpakstan, Crimean Tatars (188,772), who were deported from their homeland in 1944, Koreans (183,140), Kyrgyz (174,907), Ukrainians (153,197), Turkmen (121,578) and Turks (106,302). The population of Karakalpakstan was 6.1% of the total population in 1989, although its area is 37% of the total of the country. According to unofficial figures, there were some 200,000 Arabs in Kaskadarin Oblast in 1990.

Islam is the predominant religion. Most Uzbeks are Sunni Muslims (Hanafi school), but there are small communities of Wahhabis, whose influence is reported to be growing. Some unusual Muslim sects were reported to be represented in the ancient cities of Samarkand and Bukhara. There were Orthodox Christians among the Slavic communities, and some 65,000 European Jews and 28,000 Central Asian Jews. The Roman Catholic Church is also represented. The official language is Uzbek, a member of the Eastern Turkic language group. From the 1940s it was written in Cyrillic (replacing a Latin alphabet introduced in the late 1920s), but in 1993 it was decreed that the country would proceed with the transition to the official use of a Latin script. The language is closely related to modern Uigur. Minority communities continued to use their own languages and Russian was still widely used in business and official circles, although in 1989 only 49% of Uzbeks claimed fluency in Russian.

According to UN estimates, the total population at mid-2002 was 25,705,000, and the population density was 57.5 persons per sq km. In 2000 it was estimated that 37% of the population lived in urban areas. The capital is Tashkent, with an estimated population of 2,157,000 in 2001. Other important urban centres were the historic towns of Samarkand (362,300 in 1999), Bukhara (237,900), Karshi (197,600) and Kokand (192,500), the industrial, Fergana valley towns of Namangan (376,600), Andizhan (323,900) and Fergana itself (182,800), and Nukus (199,000), the capital of Karakalpakstan.

# Chronology

**7th century:** The Arabs conquered and brought Islam to the ancient provinces of Sogdiana and Bactria, notably the 'Silk Road' trading cities of Samarkand (Marakanda) and Bukhara (Bactra or Bacharia, previously the Kushan capital).

**13th century:** Nomadic Mongols settled among the predominantly Turkic population of Central Asia.

**1313–41:** Reign of Uzbeg, a khan of the Golden Horde, after whom the Uzbeks were named.

**1370–1405:** Reign of Timur 'the Lame' (Tamerlane), originally from Transoxania (in modern Uzbekistan), who established a second Mongol Empire, which disintegrated rapidly after his death.

**16th century:** Competing Uzbek khanates had established their dominance in the territory of modern Uzbekistan, especially Bukhara, Khiva, Kokand and Samarkand.

**1866:** The Khanate of Kokand was conquered by Russia, which was expanding southwards. In the following year much of the area that is now Karakalpakstan was annexed by Russia from the Khanate of Khiva.

**1868:** With the fall of Samarkand to the Russians, the Emirate of Bukhara surrendered and became a protectorate of the Russian Empire, following over a century of struggle by the Uzbek khanates with Persia; Samarkand and Tashkent were ceded to Russia.

**1873:** The Khanate of Khiva, which controlled much of what is western Uzbekistan, became a protectorate of the Russian Empire.

**1876:** The Khanate of Kokand was abolished and its territory absorbed into the Russian Empire.

**November 1917:** The Bolsheviks gained control of areas of Uzbekistan.

**30 April 1918:** The Turkestan Autonomous Soviet Socialist Republic (ASSR) was formed, covering an area that included Uzbekistan; Soviet forces withdrew temporarily when confronted by the nationalist *basmachi* movement, supported by British and 'White' (anti-Bolshevik) forces.

**September 1919:** Soviet forces re-established control over much of Uzbek territory.

**February 1920:** Khiva fell to the Red Army and the Khorezm People's Socialist Republic was proclaimed.

**September 1920:** The Emir of Bukhara fled as the city and most of his territory was conquered by the Red Army, although *basmachi* resistance continued in the east for some years. A People's Soviet Republic of Bukhara, also nominally independent, was declared.

**December 1922:** Bukhara and Khorezm were founding states of the Union of Soviet Socialist Republics (USSR).

**27 October 1924:** The Uzbek Soviet Socialist Republic (SSR) was established.

**May 1925:** The Uzbek SSR formally became a constituent Union Republic of the USSR.

**1929:** The Tajik ASSR, formerly part of the Uzbek SSR, became a full Union Republic of the USSR; the Khujand (Leninabad) area of the Uzbek SSR was also incorporated within the Tajik SSR.

**1936:** Karakalpakstan (which included much of the territory of Khiva, to the north and east of the city), to the south-east of the Aral Sea, passed from Kazakhstan (then part of the Russian Federation) to the Uzbek SSR.

**1940:** The Uzbek Latin script imposed in the late 1920s was changed to a Cyrillic script.

**1943:** The Muslim Board of Central Asia was founded in Tashkent as part of the Government's improving attitude towards religion; in the same decade two religious colleges and a small number of mosques were allowed to open in Uzbekistan.

**1954–60:** The 'Virgin Lands' scheme brought more land into agricultural use, particularly for cotton, but the accompanying irrigation works eventually caused the environmental catastrophe of the Aral Sea and its environs.

**1983:** A major fraud was revealed in the cotton industry, involving some 3,000m. roubles—it eventually led to the removal from office of the Uzbek Party leader, Inamzhon Usmankhojayev (January 1988), the Chairman of the Uzbek Supreme Soviet, Akil Salimov, and the Party leaders in Bukhara and Samarkand. Yuri Churbanov (deputy interior minister of Uzbekistan 1980–83), the son-in-law of the late Soviet leader, Leonid Brezhnev, was also accused and convicted of involvement.

**November 1988:** A group of Uzbek intellectuals founded Birlik (Unity), the first significant movement of opposition to the Communist Party of Uzbekistan (CPU). In March 1989 Birlik failed in its attempt to put forward a candidate in elections to the Congress of People's Deputies of the USSR, having previously been refused official registration.

**June 1989:** More than 100 people died in riots resulting from conflict between ethnic Uzbeks and members of the minority Meskhetian Turk community.

**October 1989:** Legislation was adopted, which made Uzbek (rather than Russian) the official state language.

**February 1990:** There were further outbreaks of inter-ethnic conflict in Uzbekistan, culminating in three deaths during confrontations between the police and demonstrators in Parkent, near Tashkent.

**18 February 1990:** Members of Birlik were prevented from standing as candidates in elections to the Uzbek Supreme Soviet; in many constituencies CPU candidates were elected unopposed.

**24 March 1990:** Islam Karimov, First Secretary of the CPU since 1989, was elected to the new position of executive President of the Republic at the first session of the Supreme Soviet; Shakurulla Mirsaidov was elected Chairman of the Council of Ministers (Prime Minister).

**4 June 1990:** Eleven people were killed and 21 injured in local clashes in the Fergana valley region on the border between Kyrgyzstan and Uzbekistan; numerous deaths followed.

**20 June 1990:** The Uzbek Supreme Soviet adopted a declaration on the republic's sovereignty within a renewed Soviet federation.

**November 1990:** The Council of Ministers was abolished and replaced by the Cabinet of Ministers under the leadership of the President of the Republic; the position of Prime Minister ceased to exist and Mirsaidov was appointed to the new position of Vice-President.

**April 1991:** In the month following an all-Union referendum on the issue of the future state of the USSR (an overwhelming majority in Uzbekistan had favoured a 'renewed federation'), Uzbekistan and eight other Union Republics agreed to sign a new Union Treaty.

**19–21 August 1991:** President Karimov did not condemn the attempted conservative coup in Moscow until it became apparent that it had failed.

**31 August 1991:** The Supreme Soviet voted to declare the Uzbek SSR independent and on the following day its name was changed to the Republic of Uzbekistan.

**November 1991:** Having previously voted to sever links with the Communist Party of the Soviet Union, the CPU reorganized itself as the People's Democratic Party of Uzbekistan (PDPU), under the continued leadership of Karimov.

**21 December 1991:** Although it had remained a supporter of a new federation, Uzbekistan agreed to join 10 other former Soviet republics in the capital of Kazakhstan to sign the Almaty Declaration, which established the Commonwealth of Independent States (CIS) and signalled the final dissolution of the USSR.

**29 December 1991:** Karimov was re-elected as President, receiving an estimated 86% of the votes cast in direct popular elections; on the same day 98.2% of voters supported independence in a referendum.

**8 January 1992:** The post of Vice-President was abolished and that of Prime Minister (Chairman of the Cabinet of Ministers) was restored; Abdulkhashim Mutalov was appointed to the latter position. Mirsaidov was appointed State Secretary, but soon resigned, later to be accused of financial improprieties.

**15 May 1992:** Uzbekistan signed the Collective Security Treaty with five other CIS countries, in Tashkent. In August, however, new legislation provided for the establishment of national armed forces.

**8 December 1992:** The Supreme Soviet adopted a new Constitution, which declared Uzbekistan to be a secular, democratic republic and made provision for a Supreme Assembly (Oly Majlis) to replace the Supreme Soviet as the highest legislative body, following elections scheduled for 1994. On the following day the opposition movement, Birlik, which had never been permitted to register as a political party, was banned for its allegedly subversive activities.

**January 1993:** Uzbekistan, the main regional supporter of the new regime in Tajikistan, signed a security agreement with that country, Russia, Kazakhstan and Kyrgyzstan to provide troops for the defence of Tajikistan's southern borders. Uzbek forces were also reported to have acted directly against Tajik rebels.

**June 1993:** Mirsaidov, the former premier and Vice-President, was found guilty of the misuse of state funds, but was pardoned by President Karimov; he was also subjected to physical intimidation.

**6 August 1993:** Uzbekistan agreed to contribute troops to the CIS peace-keeping force to be sent to Tajikistan.

**September 1993:** It was decreed that the Latin script should be used for the Uzbek language, rather than the Cyrillic script; however, the new alphabet was different from the common script agreed upon earlier in the year by representatives from the other Central Asian states.

**1 October 1993:** The Government used technical pretexts to prevent both Birlik and Erk (Freedom), the opposition party established in 1990, from registering with the Ministry of Justice; consequently both organizations were permanently banned. Two days later Erk's newly elected First Secretary, Samad Muratov, was assaulted by anonymous attackers.

**15 November 1993:** Despite earlier intentions to continue participation in the 'rouble zone', Uzbekistan condemned Russia's conditions and introduced a new currency, the sum coupon, announcing that roubles would no longer be legal tender after December; food prices increased when Uzbek citizens attempted to spend their old currency.

**December 1993:** A compulsory re-registration of the mass media excluded all independent publications.

**September 1994:** Vassilya Inoyatova, a leader of the banned opposition group Birlik (Unity), was charged with anti-state activities, after copies of the outlawed newspaper, *Erk* (Freedom), were found in her possession.

**25 December 1994:** Despite indications from the President in May that the parliamentary election could be freely contested by opposition parties, the PDPU and its ally, Progress of the Fatherland (PF), were the only parties to participate (a second round of voting took place in January); of the 83 contested seats, the PDPU obtained 69 and the PF 14. The remaining deputies were nominated by local councils, but most were PDPU members, giving the party overall representation in the Oly Majlis of 193 seats.

**February 1995:** Following Karimov's declaration in the previous month that the Government would welcome more parliamentary blocs, the Adolat (Justice) Social Democratic Party of Uzbekistan was registered; it was believed to command the support of 47 deputies. A further two pro-Government parties were permitted registration in June.

**26 March 1995:** A referendum approved the extension of President Karimov's term of office until 2000.

**October 1995:** A co-ordinating group for the opposition, the Democratic Opposition Co-ordinating Council, was established under the leadership of Mirsaidov; the Council was dissolved in March 1998.

**21 December 1995:** Abdulkhashim Mutalov was dismissed as Prime Minister, to be replaced by Otkir Sultanov, previously the Minister of Foreign Economic Relations.

**21 June 1996:** President Karimov officially resigned as Chairman of the ruling PDPU.

**December 1996:** The Oly Majlis passed a law prohibiting the organization of political parties on a religious or ethnic basis.

**November 1997:** Members of the so-called 'Wahhabi' sect were accused of assassinating the deputy head of the local administration of Namangan region; hundreds of suspected Muslim activists were later arrested.

**1 May 1998:** A law limiting the activities of religious organizations was adopted.

**5 June 1998:** Following the imprisonment of four suspected Islamist militants in May, seven followers of the conservative Wahhabi sect were imprisoned for attempting to destabilize the country and establish an Islamic state. More arrests of Wahhabi activists followed in July, and one member of an Islamist organization was sentenced to death after being found guilty of murder and involvement in the training of Wahhabi militants in Afghanistan.

**8 September 1998:** Uzbekistan signed an agreement with a number of other Caucasian, Central Asian and European countries aiming to re-create the 'Silk Road' trade route.

**9 January 1999:** Five Wahhabi activists were found guilty of attempting to depose the Government and establish an Islamic state.

**16 February 1999:** A series of bomb attacks took place in Tashkent, reportedly killing 15 people and injuring many more. The attacks were blamed on Islamist extremists from the Hezbollah extremist movement. A number of people found guilty of involvement in the attacks received lengthy jail sentences and at the end of June six people were sentenced to death.

**24 April 1999:** A bilateral agreement was signed with Russia on security, following Uzbekistan's departure from the CIS Collective Security Treaty in the previous month.

**12 May 1999:** The Government introduced legislation imposing harsher punishments on those affiliated to 'religious, extremist, separatist and fundamentalist organizations'.

**19 December 1999:** In a second round of voting to the Oly Majlis, the PDPU was reported to have secured the largest representation of any single party in the legislature, with 48 seats. The pro-Karimov Fidokorlar (Self-Sacrificers') National Democratic Party (FNDP), established in December 1998, came second, obtaining 34 seats.

**9 January 2000:** In a presidential election in which an estimated 95% of the registered electorate participated, the incumbent President was reported to have obtained 91.9% of the votes cast. He was inaugurated for a second, five-year term on 22 January.

**12 September 2000:** A number of political parties, religious bodies and social organizations launched a joint programme of action to combat 'international terrorism'.

**14 September 2000:** The remaining members of a group of Islamist rebels, which had made a number of incursions into Uzbekistan from Tajikistan in August, were reported to have been killed by government troops.

**17 November 2000:** Two leaders of the opposition group, the Islamist Movement of Uzbekistan (IMU), were convicted of acts of terrorism and sentenced to death *in absentia* by the Supreme Court.

**26–27 April 2001:** At a meeting of leaders of the Turkic-speaking countries, the Presidents of Azerbaijan, Kazakhstan, Kyrgyzstan, Turkey and Turkmenistan, and the Chairman of Uzbekistan's Oly Majlis (Supreme Assembly) signed an agreement on regional co-operation to combat terrorism and drugs trafficking, the revival of the old 'Silk Road' trade route between China and Europe, and protection of the environment.

**26 June 2001:** Ten Islamist militants were reported to have received prison sentences for attempting to overthrow the Government.

**19 September 2001:** President Karimov confirmed his support for US-led airstrikes against Afghanistan, if it were proven that the suicide attacks of 11 September, on the US cities of New York and Washington, DC, were prepared in that state.

**7 October 2001:** Uzbekistan and the USA signed a co-operation agreement, whereby Uzbekistan agreed to make its airbases available for use in humanitarian and 'search-and-rescue' operations during the US-led aerial bombardment of Afghanistan. The two countries also pledged to improve bilateral relations in order to combat terrorism and ensure long-term regional stability.

**27 January 2002:** At a referendum, a reported 91.8% of participants voted in favour of a constitutional amendment, proposed by President Karimov, which would extend the presidential term of office from five to seven years. In a simultaneous vote, some 93.7% of votes endorsed a proposal to create a second parliamentary chamber representing Uzbekistan's regions.

**30 January 2002:** Four police-officers were found guilty of the torture of suspected Islamist activists, and sentenced to 20 years' imprisonment.

**4 March 2002:** The Independent Human Rights Organization of Uzbekistan was finally registered by the Ministry of Justice.

**4 April 2002:** The Oly Majlis approved a resolution delaying the next presidential elections by two years, until 2007.

**9 September 2002:** At a meeting in the Kazakh capital, Astana, the Presidents of Uzbekistan and Kazakhstan signed a treaty fully demarcating their joint border. An agreement was signed with Tajikistan in the following month, on the demarcation of more than 85% of the Uzbek–Tajik border.

**12 December 2002:** The Oly Majlis adopted legislation on the election of the new, bicameral legislature following the end of the existing legislative session in December 2004.

**20 December 2002:** Turkmenistan declared the Uzbekistani ambassador *persona non grata*, following accusations of Uzbekistan's complicity in an alleged attempt to assassinate the President of Turkmenistan, Saparmyrat Niyazov.

**24 April 2003:** The Oly Majlis approved a number of constitutional amendments permitting the redistribution of authority within the Government, to come into effect from the next legislative election. The prime minister, rather than the president, was to be head of government, and the composition of the government was to be approved by the legislature rather than the Office of the President.

**1 September 2003:** Uzbekistan became a member of the Islamic Development Bank.

**15 October 2003:** The sum was made fully convertible.

# History

## Dr NEIL MELVIN

### EARLY HISTORY

In the 20th century Uzbekistan emerged as home to the most powerful and populous political community in Central Asia. Historically, however, the territory of what is now the Republic of Uzbekistan has been the centre for a wide variety of civilizations, cultures and peoples. The earliest recorded inhabitants of the region were Persian-speakers, who settled in the valleys of the Syr-Dar'ya (Jaxartes) and Amu-Dar'ya (Oxus) rivers. Scythians, as well as Persian-speakers, and smaller groups of nomads largely populated the plains to the north of the Syr-Dar'ya. In the fourth century Alexander III ('the Great') of Macedonia passed through Central Asia on the way to conquer India.

In the seventh century Arabs gained control over important parts of the region, bringing with them Islam and the Arabic script, and adding new cultural patterns to the existing Persian and Turkic ones. In 1219 the Mongols invaded and took control of Central Asia. Later, as Mongol rule weakened, particularly after the reign of Timur or Tamerlane ('the Great'), who established Samarkand as the capital of a revived empire, the name Uzbek first emerged as an important political label. Early in the 16th century Transoxania (the area between the two great rivers of the Oxus and Jaxartes) came under the control of Uzbek tribes moving from the steppe regions of the north and led by Muhammad Sheibani Khan. The Sheibanid invasion accelerated the disintegration and fragmentation of the political arrangements of the Mongol era. The term Uzbek was, thereafter, associated with a number of dynasties claiming descent from Sheibani.

As the Uzbek tribes took control of Transoxania, their nomadic life-style gradually gave way to a sedentary existence. Many settled in the cities and towns of the region and began to mix with the local inhabitants, including other Turkic peoples and Persian-speakers (Tajiks). While retaining their tribal identification, the Uzbeks simultaneously associated themselves with other sedentary peoples under the general label of Sart. Elite-level bilingualism became an important part of the region's identity, with the political life of the court conducted mainly in a Turkic language (Chagatai), while high culture was largely the province of a form of Persian (Farsi).

From the 17th century the previously united Uzbek kingdom began to fragment and was replaced by smaller, highly autonomous kingdoms or khanates. Initially, the two most powerful khanates were Bukhara and Khiva. From the 18th century, however, the Khanate of Kokand, centred on the Fergana valley, began to rival the other two. The near constant state of conflict between these states assisted the Russian conquest of the region.

All three of the khanates fell to the Russian Empire in the latter half of the 19th century. In 1867 the Russian province of Turkestan was established, and as a result of Russian military advances it was steadily expanded to embrace all the former kingdoms. Russian conquest of the region brought important economic and cultural changes. Tashkent, previously a minor town, but which fell to Russia as early as 1865, became the capital of Russian Turkestan and the home of a sizeable ethnic Russian population. Russian language, technology and administration spread rapidly throughout the region. Significant changes in agriculture were also introduced, notably improved irrigation for cotton production. Russian conquest did little, however, to alter fundamentally the way of life for the peoples of the area.

## SOVIET UZBEKISTAN

For much of the Russian Revolution and the civil war that followed, Turkestan was isolated from events in the rest of the former Russian Empire. The Bolsheviks first seized Tashkent in November 1917. The region, however, was subject to control by competing forces during the civil war period—the British, the 'Whites' (anti-Bolsheviks) and the nationalist *basmachi* guerrilla movement—and it was not until September 1919 that Soviet control was re-established. In 1920 Bukhara and Khiva became the capitals of nominally independent Soviet republics, the Bukharan and the Khorezm People's Socialist Republics, which became founder members of the Union of Soviet Socialist Republics (USSR) at the end of 1922. Meanwhile, the *basmachi* movement continued to control some peripheral areas of Turkestan until 1922.

On 27 October 1924 the Uzbek Soviet Socialist Republic (SSR) was created, when most of the territories of the three former khanates of the region were merged. A separate Turkmen SSR was created at the same time. The Tajik Autonomous Soviet Socialist Republic (ASSR) formed part of the Uzbek SSR until 1929, when it was granted the status of a full Union Republic (and the region of Khujand—Leninabad—was detached from the Uzbek SSR and awarded to the new Tajik ASSR). The Karakalpak ASSR (hitherto part of the Russian republic, as it was a region annexed by the tsars from Khiva in advance of the rest of the Khanate) was united with the Uzbek SSR in 1936.

The territorial delimitation of Central Asia in the 1920s and 1930s was conducted on broadly ethno-linguistic lines. Soviet policy-makers intended the Uzbek SSR to become the ethnic homeland for Uzbeks. In the census conducted in the region following the creation of the SSR, small Turkic groups were categorized together with the Uzbeks, although larger minorities, such as Kazakhs, Kyrgyz and Tajiks, continued to enjoy a separate ethnic identity. The formation of the Uzbek SSR was accompanied by the creation of national symbols, most significantly a new popular literary language. Soviet policies in the area also aimed to increase the literacy rate (between 1926 and 1932 literacy rose from 3.8% to 52.5% of the population) and to improve the status of women. At the same time, Soviet anti-religious campaigns resulted in the closure

of Muslim institutions (courts, schools and mosques) and the imprisonment or execution of many of the clergy. Numerous Muslim traditions and rites continued to be observed, especially in rural areas, and the anti-religious campaigns were partially mitigated by the establishment of an Islamic spiritual directorate (Tashkent was the seat of the Muslim Board of Central Asia) during the Second World War.

State-led industrialization formed a key element of the Soviet model of development in Uzbekistan. In the initial decades of Soviet rule there was a steady growth of industrial infrastructure and an expansion of major urban centres, driven primarily by Slavic immigration. Economic growth continued, although at lower levels, after the Second World War, with the help of industry transferred from areas in the USSR threatened by Nazi German invasion. Most Uzbeks, however, continued to live a traditional rural way of life largely untouched by Soviet policies of modernization, except for the dramatic expansion of cotton production initiated by Stalin (Iosif V. Dzhugashvili).

In 1959 Sharaf Rashidov became First Secretary of the Communist Party of Uzbekistan (CPU) and stayed in office until shortly before his death in October 1983. In the 1960s and 1970s there was a strong emphasis on stability, and Rashidov and the Uzbek provincial party chiefs gained extensive powers. The end of the Rashidov era and the accession (in November 1982) of Yurii Andropov as General Secretary of the Soviet Communist Party marked the onset of important changes in Uzbekistan's political order.

## THE NATIONALIST MOVEMENT

Under Andropov, a far-reaching five-year purge of the Uzbek political establishment began (1983–89), initiated by revelations of serious fraud in the cotton industry. Aimed at breaking the local networks of power, which had built up in the course of the previous 25 years, the central authorities' drive to 'de-Rashidovize' the republic also served to bring a new generation of Uzbek leaders to the fore. In June 1989 the bloody ethnic riots in the Fergana valley altered the all-Union Government's policy towards Uzbekistan. The centrally directed purge of cadres was moderated and Islam Karimov was appointed leader, replacing Rafik Nishanov.

Karimov began to rehabilitate the disgraced Rashidov and to consolidate his own position. In March 1990 the new Supreme Soviet of Uzbekistan elected Karimov President of Uzbekistan. A leading member of the Uzbek political élite, Shakurulla Mirsaidov, became Chairman of the Council of Ministers. In November 1990 Mirsaidov was appointed to the newly established post of Vice-President, as President Karimov assumed the chairmanship of the redesignated Cabinet of Ministers.

During the *perestroika* (restructuring) period, mainly associated with Mikhail Gorbachev (Soviet leader in 1985–91), a number of new political groups appeared in Uzbekistan. The desiccation of the Aral Sea and the general deterioration of the environment caused by over-irrigation of land for cotton production served to mobilize ecological groups. As nationalist movements developed in the USSR as a whole, the status of the Uzbek language became an important issue for Uzbekistan's first non-communist political movement, Birlik (Unity). Formed in 1988, Birlik campaigned for a range of political and nationalist goals, but its candidates were denied registration in the February 1990 elections to the Uzbek Supreme Soviet. Later in 1990 the first formal opposition party, Erk (Freedom), was created. Despite the continued institutional pre-eminence of the Communist Party, there were a number of opportunities for potential discontent, if not opposition. Ethnic tension continued to rise in parts of Central Asia and, in June, clashes between Uzbeks and Kyrgyz in the Osh region of Kyrgyzstan threatened the stability of the whole

Fergana valley. A state of emergency was declared on the Uzbekistan side of the border (Andizhan region).

Although Uzbekistan was preparing to sign a new Union Treaty in mid-1991, the August coup attempt by conservatives in Moscow, the Soviet and Russian capital, undermined the agreement. Karimov adopted a neutral position during the *putsch*, but, once the coup collapsed, an extraordinary session of the Supreme Soviet then declared the Uzbek SSR independent and renamed it the Republic of Uzbekistan.

## INDEPENDENT UZBEKISTAN

In November 1991 the CPU was renamed the People's Democratic Party of Uzbekistan (PDPU). In December, following the demise of the USSR, Karimov was re-elected President, but this time by direct popular vote; he was reported to have received some 86% of the votes cast. The only other candidate, the leader of Erk, Muhammad Solikh, received 12% of the votes. On the same day, 98.2% of voters ratified independence in a referendum.

Achieving a popular mandate was merely part of a process of political consolidation for the new President. In January 1992 the post of Vice-President was abolished and Karimov's main potential rival, Mirsaidov, was thereby removed from office (he was initially retained in the post of State Secretary, but soon resigned). Abdulkhashim Mutalov was appointed to the restored premiership. At the same time, in a move to assert central control over the regions, the appointed position of khokim, or regional governor, was established to head the local administrations. The Government also sought to promote the mahallah, or neighbourhood, as the basic element of local government.

The increasingly authoritarian tendency of the Uzbek leadership was officially justified by the activity of the opposition movement. A series of student demonstrations in 1992 and the civil war in neighbouring Tajikistan provided the pretext for the repression of all opposition organizations. Distrust of opposition and of independent religious groups combined in the banning of Islamist parties (see below). The growing political authoritarianism also served to stifle initial attempts at economic reform. The increasing power of the presidency was paralleled by greater repression of opposition groups. Leading dissidents were arrested and on 9 December Birlik was banned, the day after a new Constitution formalized the extensive powers of the President. Throughout 1992–93 a number of opposition leaders disappeared or were assaulted. Many fled into exile. In October 1993 Erk was denied registration as a political party (by the end of the year both it and Birlik were banned organizations), and in December all but the official media were denied registration.

In 1994 and 1995 President Karimov continued to strengthen his position within the establishment, as well as with regard to the opposition. In mid-1994 Mavlon Umurzakov, one of the President's state counsellors, was removed from office. In July a presidential decree dismissed the Mayor of Tashkent, Adkham Fazylbekov, who had been a close associate of Mirsaidov. The previous month, in Almaty, Kazakhstan, two dissidents, Murod Zhorayev and Erkin Ashurov, were seized by an Uzbek security detail and forcibly taken to Uzbekistan to stand trial along with five other dissidents. All seven were sentenced to prison by the Supreme Court in March 1995.

On 22 September 1994 the Supreme Soviet met for the final time. The old parliament was replaced by a smaller, unicameral legislative body, known as the Oly Majlis (Supreme Assembly), elections to which were conducted on 25 December. Of the 250 seats in parliament, 144 went to candidates nominated by regional councils (84 of these were mayors or khokims). Overall, the PDPU took 193 seats, and the remaining 57 were considered to be government sup-

porters, whether nominally independent or members of the only other party permitted registration, Watan Taraqqioti (Progress of the Fatherland). At its first session in February 1995 the new parliament unanimously voted to hold a national referendum to approve an extension of the President's term of office. On 26 March 99.6% of the eligible electorate were reported to have voted to extend President Karimov's term of office by three years, to 2000.

In the wake of the parliamentary elections, in February 1995 a new party, the Adolat (Justice) Social Democratic Party of Uzbekistan, was created and 47 deputies of the PDPU were drafted to provide it with a parliamentary membership. In June two more 'official' parties (organizations known for their pro-Government, non-combative character) were established, the Milli Tiklanish (National Revival) Democratic Party and the Khalk Birliki (People's Unity) Movement. The titles of two of those parties gave rise to accusations that the names of the unregistered opposition, the banned Islamist group, Adolat, and Birlik, were deliberately being exploited. Direct pressure on the opposition continued and in August Rashid Bekjan, the brother of Solikh, leader of Erk, was sentenced to five years in gaol for involvement in the party's youth wing. In October the creation of the Opposition Coordinating Centre in Tashkent, led by Shakurulla Mirsaidov, was announced, which brought together the remnants of Erk, Birlik, Adolat and Mirsaidov's own party; however, the Centre closed in March 1998. Many Uzbek dissidents continued to be active abroad, notably in Russia, Sweden, Turkey and the USA.

On 21 December 1995 the Oly Majlis dismissed the Prime Minister, Mutalov, a decision ostensibly prompted by economic difficulties, notably the decline in value of the national currency, the sum. In February 1996 Mutalov and another deputy premier were removed from the Cabinet. With Mutalov's dismissal, President Karimov had lost most of the core of politicians who had helped him to power, including Mirsaidov, the former Minister of Justice minister and ambassador to the USA, Babur Malikov, and the former Minister of Foreign Affairs, Said-Mukhtar Saidkasimov.

Following the consolidation of his position, in 1996 Karimov briefly promoted a limited pluralism in the country, in part designed to stop the outflow of Slav and Uzbek professionals, but also to placate international criticism. Despite the change in the official tone, international human rights organizations continued to criticize the actions of the Uzbek authorities. At the end of the 1990s all forms of media remained under strict government control and opposition groups were highly restricted and subject to violent repression. Despite the centralized, authoritarian regime, however, Islam continued to be viewed by many in Uzbekistan as a threat to the Karimov regime.

After independence the Government sponsored a revival of Islam and by 1995 there were over 20,000 active mosques. In May President Karimov signed a decree establishing an international Islamic studies centre in Tashkent, at the behest of the state-controlled Muslim Board. Non-official and political Islam, however, endured continued repression from 1992. The Islamic Renaissance Party of Uzbekistan and the conservative Islamist Adolat movement were both banned in 1992 and remained prohibited. Muslim clergy who deviated from officially endorsed 'moderate' Islam were arrested or removed from their positions. On 1 May 1998 the national parliament passed a law on 'freedom of conscience', imposing new restrictions on religious groups. The law required all mosques and religious groups with more than 100 members to be registered and restricted the construction of mosques, the establishment of religious associations and the teaching of theology.

As more conventional, or established, Islam was placed firmly under the Government's control, a variety of groups, the actions of which were particularly undesirable for the Karimov regime, sought to operate independently of the state. From the mid-1990s the Uzbek authorities identified the so-called 'Wahhabi' movement (essentially, any conservative or independent Muslim group) as a major threat to stability in the country and in Central Asia as a whole. President Karimov argued that radical Islamism was poised to penetrate Central Asia and that Wahhabi proselytism from Saudi Arabia (the home of the original Wahhabi sect) was the central threat, together with the Taliban of Afghanistan and the United Opposition in Tajikistan.

Particularly close supervision was exercised in the Fergana valley, the traditional centre for Islam in Central Asia. In this region the Wahhabis' insistence on the total adherence to their interpretation of the Koran earned the movement the description 'fundamentalist'. Muslim leaders and activists from Namangan were gaoled on various charges. Andizhan's main Jami Mosque, built before the 1917 Bolshevik Revolution, was closed in 1995, after its chief cleric, Abdu Alil Mirzayev, allegedly the leader of a Wahhabi group, fell foul of the Government and disappeared on his way to Moscow. In December 1997, in Namangan, a group of masked men killed a highly placed local official. The central authorities responded to the murder by dispatching élite troops to the area. Eventually, the Government accused a group of supposed Islamist militants from Tajikistan of being responsible for the murder. The actions of the Government proved to represent the first stage of a sustained campaign against a range of religious and opposition groups, particularly in the Fergana region. On 1 May 1998, while attending the parliamentary session that passed the new law on freedom of conscience, President Karimov denounced the Wahhabis, whom he accused of seeking to transform Uzbekistan into a second Tajikistan.

In the late 1990s Karimov sought to entice some of the moderate Islamic leaders back to Uzbekistan, but achieved only modest success. The most prominent returnee was Sheikh Mohammad Sodiq, a former mufti, who had spent seven years in exile. Sheikh Sodiq disapproved of the violent tactics of the Islamist movement and worked with the government-sponsored network of officially controlled mosques. In February 1999 the official image of Uzbekistan as a centre of regional stability was challenged by a series of bomb explosions in Tashkent, which killed 15 and injured at least a further 100. The Government blamed radical Islamists and the opposition for the blasts and responded by arresting hundreds of suspects, continuing a series of arrests that had begun in 1998. A number of trials were organized and six of those found guilty were sentenced to death in June.

Despite efforts to eradicate militant Islamism, a series of cross-border attacks were undertaken by the Islamist Movement of Uzbekistan (IMU) in 1999–2001. The IMU, founded in 1999, was banned by the Uzbek Government, and its spiritual leader, Takhir Yoldoshev, and his field commander, Jumaboy Khojiyev (known as Juma Namangoniy), were sentenced to death *in absentia* in November 2000. From mid- to late 1999, Namangoniy organized a series of incursions from bases in Tajikistan. Although unsuccessful militarily, the infiltrations challenged Tashkent's assertions about the lack of support for such organizations in Uzbekistan. Although the IMU was poorly organized, it successfully recruited new members from disaffected groups within Uzbekistan. In June 2001 the IMU reportedly changed its name to the 'Islamic Party of Turkestan', indicating an expansion of the group's political aspirations. In August it was reported that Namangoniy had been appointed Deputy Commander-in-Chief of the Taliban military forces. The militant Islamist movement was further strengthened by the reported appointment of the Saudi-born

leader of the al-Qa'ida (Base) organization, Osama bin Laden, to the post of Commander-in-Chief of the Taliban forces.

Many of Uzbekistan's Slavic population were less alarmed at official intolerance to opposition and religious groups than by the growing significance of Uzbek nationalism and official policies designed to promote an Uzbek national identity. After independence the Uzbek ruling élite fostered Uzbek culture and the writing of a national history, including a cult of Amir (lord) Timur, Tamerlane the Great. The nation-building process also caused internal friction with ethnic minorities such as the Karakalpaks, the Kipchaks of Fergana and the Tajiks in Samarkand and Bukhara. The presence of large numbers of ethnic Uzbeks in neighbouring states (particularly in Tajikistan) helped to ensure that Uzbek nationalism was checked by foreign-policy requirements. To encourage links with the West, as well as re-establish traditional links with Turkey, in 1993 it was decreed that Uzbekistan would adopt a Latin script.

In December 1999 parliamentary elections were held. Five parties, all of which supported the President, and a number of nominally independent candidates contested the elections to the Oly Majlis. As part of the preparations for the elections, Karimov sanctioned the creation of a new political party know as the Fidokorlar (Self-Sacrificers') National Democratic Party. The leading figures of the party were established members of the existing élite, and it secured 34 seats in the legislature, behind the PDPU, with 48 seats. In April 2000 it was announced that Fidokorlar and Watan Taraqqioti were to merge. The new party, to be named Fidokorlar, was to have an estimated combined membership of 50,000, and a total of 54 parliament deputies, representing the second-largest parliamentary faction. Pro-Karimov parties and candidates won the elections for local and provincial assemblies, which were also held in December 1999.

On 9 January 2000 Karimov was re-elected as President. A number of international organizations, including the Organization for Security and Co-operation in Europe (OSCE), refused to send observers to monitor the election and were critical of the entire electoral process. The only alternative candidate was Abdulhafiz Jalolov, a leading member of the PDPU, who had previously worked in the Ideology Department of the CPU. Karimov secured 92% of the votes cast by 95% of the electorate. Jalolov obtained just 4% of the votes cast, and even admitted to having voted for Karimov. Although the President's position appeared secure, Karimov continued to suppress potential challengers by frequently purging rivals and removing regional governors from their posts.

The domestic political situation in Uzbekistan changed following the large-scale suicide attacks on the US cities of New York and Washington, DC, on 11 September 2001 (attributed to al-Qa'ida), and the subsequent US-led military campaign against the Taliban and radical Islamist groups in Afghanistan. In mid-October a large number of IMU members were reported to be fighting alongside Taliban forces there. However, in the course of the campaign, the IMU (which the US Government had already identified as a terrorist threat) was largely destroyed and its leader, Juma Namangoniy, was reportedly killed during fighting in November.

On 27 January 2002 President Karimov initiated a referendum to endorse his proposal to create a second parliamentary chamber, to represent Uzbekistan's regions, a proposal that reportedly received the support of 93.7% of voters. In addition, the referendum was used to extend the presidential term of office from five to seven years, apparently with the support of 91.8% of participants. However, the legitimacy of the referendum was questioned by both the USA and human rights groups. In early April the Oly Majlis approved a resolution delaying the next presidential elections by two years, until 2007. The legislature also endorsed a resolution on the election of the new, bicameral legislature in December 2004.

Under pressure from the USA, the Uzbek authorities undertook a number of measures to liberalize the political system. At the end of January 2002 four police-officers were found guilty of torturing suspected Islamist activists while held in custody, and given 20-year prison terms. In early March the Ministry of Justice finally registered the Independent Human Rights Organization of Uzbekistan, following a five-year struggle for official recognition. Although these changes were symbolically important, many thousands of opposition and Islamist figures continued to be held in custody, and the Government's campaign of repression against Islamist organizations, such as Hizb-ut-Tahrir, continued. The secular opposition and media remained tightly monitored and human rights violations by law-enforcement bodies were widespread. Corruption and poor governance continued to characterize the political order, helping to promote further problems in the country, such as a largely man-made drought in Karakalpakstan in 2002.

The engagement of the USA in Uzbekistan, as a result of the US-led military action in Afghanistan that commenced in late 2001 (see Foreign Relations), was widely regarded as an opportunity for significant change. In Uzbekistan, the US presence was viewed as likely to increase the status of the country and to help address its immediate security threats, particularly from radical Islamist groups based in Afghanistan. There was little sense that the US engagement would necessitate serious domestic reform; instead, the Uzbek authorities put emphasis on a series of possible reform measures, including proposals to introduce a bicameral parliament in 2004 (approved by a referendum held in January 2002) and to alter the Constitution to prevent the President being simultaneously the Head of Government (approved by the Oly Majlis in April 2003). Many observers, however, viewed these changes as cosmetic. Indeed, there was considerable evidence of increasing repression, particularly against the radical Islamist movement Hizb ut-Tahrir, which was identified by the Government as the main threat to the country following the apparent military defeat of the IMU in late 2001. For the international community, the increased US presence in Uzbekistan was interpreted as an opportunity to advance reform in the country. After a request by the UN Secretary-General, accompanied by considerable international pressure, the UN Commissioner on Human Rights visited Uzbekistan in December 2002 to investigate allegations of torture; following his visit, the Commissioner concluded that torture in Uzbekistan was 'systemic'. In 2002–03, the USA and the European Union (EU) became more publicly critical of the human rights situation in Uzbekistan. Heightened international scrutiny appeared to do little, however, to change the Government's repressive practices, particularly with regard to religious adherents. Official harassment of the media also persisted, with the closure of three newspapers in early 2003.

In May 2003 the European Bank for Reconstruction and Development (EBRD) held its annual meeting in Tashkent, at which the opposing views of Uzbekistan's prescribed future development came to the fore. The international community sought to use the meeting as means to induce the authorities in Uzbekistan to launch a variety of political and economic reforms, but President Karimov sought, instead, to use the meeting to convey to his domestic audience international support for his chosen development path. Although the Government did appear to make a number of small concessions following the meeting, notably registering a non-governmental organization, the Ezgulik (Good Deed) Human Rights Society, and allowing the Birlik movement to hold its first public congress since 1992, overall there was little evidence of progress. With growing evidence of social unrest under Karimov's repressive political and economic policies, and a lack of willingness on the part of the Uzbek authorities to countenance the prospect of meaningful reform, Karimov appeared to be confronting a narrowing range of options, a situation that was compounded by the absence of any obvious successor.

## FOREIGN RELATIONS

The central priorities of Uzbekistan's foreign policy have been to ensure stability on its borders, to guarantee the state's sovereignty and independence and to promote regional security. As Uzbekistan is a land-locked country surrounded by land-locked countries, relations with Tajikistan, Turkmenistan, Kyrgyzstan, Afghanistan and Kazakhstan, and leading regional powers, primarily Russia, dominated its foreign-policy agenda.

Ethnic and religious issues were of particular significance in Uzbekistan's relations with other Central Asian states. Of growing importance were its relations with Afghanistan and Tajikistan. The emergence of powerful Islamist groups and the regional instability produced by conflict within these two countries caused considerable alarm in Uzbekistan. In the first years of independence the civil war in Tajikistan posed the greatest challenge. The Uzbek Government was unsympathetic towards the coalition of Islamist and democratic opposition groups in that country in the early 1990s. The situation was considerably complicated by the presence of large numbers of ethnic Uzbeks in the northern Leninabad region of Tajikistan, around the city of Khujand. As fighting flared in 1992, leaders of the Uzbek community reportedly advocated unification with Uzbekistan. In late 1992 Uzbekistan's military became involved in the Tajik conflict, in support of the communist regime. In January 1993 Uzbekistan co-operated with Russia and Kazakhstan in the deployment of troops to secure the southern borders of Tajikistan. Relations with Tajikistan deteriorated in October 1997, however, when the Uzbek authorities were linked to an uprising in western Tajikistan. While becoming a guarantor of the peace process that emerged in Tajikistan in 1997, Uzbekistan remained critical of the inclusion of Islamist representatives in the new Government and advocated the interests of the Leninabad region. Relations were further damaged by the suspicion that Uzbekistan supported an armed rebellion in November 1998, when forces loyal to Col Mahmoud Khudoberdiyev, a Tajik army officer, tried unsuccessfully to raise the province of Leninabad (later renamed Soghd) against the Tajik Government.

The Uzbek Government's concerns regarding the conflict in Tajikistan were exacerbated by developments in Afghanistan in the second half of the 1990s. In the early 1990s Uzbekistan was broadly supportive of the regime in Kabul, the capital of Afghanistan, particularly as the militant Islamist group, the Taliban, grew more powerful. As the Taliban advanced and seized Kabul in late 1996, the Uzbek Government extended considerable political and military support to the ethnic Uzbek warlord, Gen. Abdul Rashid Dostam, in northern Afghanistan, to ensure the creation of a 'buffer' zone between Uzbekistan and the fighting in Afghanistan. Defeat of Dostam's forces and the Taliban's advance to Uzbekistan's southern border prompted a reorientation in official policy, directed towards rebuilding stronger ties with Russia.

The conflicts in Tajikistan and Afghanistan were the main impetuses towards co-operation between Uzbekistan and its neighbours and with Russia. Uzbekistan joined the Commonwealth of Independent States (CIS) at its foundation on 21 December 1991. In August 1993 Uzbekistan agreed to form an economic union with Kazakhstan and Russia, but later introduced its own currency and left the 'rouble zone'. In July 1995 Russia and Uzbekistan agreed on a wide range of bilateral agreements to strengthen economic ties, but President Karimov's Government was increasingly concerned to prevent excessive Russian dominance of the region. During the first decade of independence the country built up strong, independent armed forces, and encouraged military co-operation with the USA.

The rise of the Taliban, the influence of Islamist groups in Tajikistan and the emergence of Wahhabi groups in Uzbekistan prompted a *rapprochement* between Uzbekistan and Russia from 1997. Although Uzbekistan withdrew from the CIS Collective Security Treaty at the end of March 1999 and joined the group of southern states known as GUUAM (Georgia, Ukraine, Uzbekistan, Azerbaijan, Moldova—previously GUAM) in April, bilateral ties with Russia became increasingly important. On a visit to Tashkent, the Russian Prime Minister (and, later, President), Vladimir Putin, praised Uzbekistan's treatment of minorities and indicated that it was Russia's 'strategic partner' in the fight against insurgency, banditry, religious extremism and drugs trafficking in Central Asia. In May 2001 President Karimov agreed to exchange foodstuffs and natural gas for Russian weapons, which were required to combat Islamist insurgents.

Following independence, Uzbekistan also sought closer ties with its neighbours. In mid-January 1994 Uzbekistan agreed to establish an economic union with Kazakhstan and Kyrgyzstan. In July the Presidents of Kazakhstan, Kyrgyzstan and Uzbekistan met in Almaty and signed seven agreements designed to implement this economic partnership. They also committed themselves to the creation of a Central Asian Bank for Co-operation and Development and an International Council, with executive bodies to carry out its decisions. In February 1995 the three countries again resolved to provide greater institutional substance to their 'common economic space' agreement of 1994. In 1998 they were joined by Tajikistan, and the grouping was later renamed the Central Asian Economic Community.

Uzbekistan's co-operation with its neighbours was most successful in the area of water resources and security issues. Considering the calamitous effects of the ecological situation of the Aral Sea on the country, the first issue was of vital significance. In September 1995 the Presidents of Kazakhstan, Kyrgyzstan and Uzbekistan, and a delegation from Turkmenistan, signed the Nukus Declaration on saving the Aral Sea. Subsequently, tensions were generated by suggestions that Kyrgyzstan would introduce water-pricing policies (negotiations on the issue began in 1997), although this was in response to Uzbekistan's complaint over unpaid gas-supply debts. Uzbekistan also co-operated with its neighbours on security issues. In May 1996 it agreed, with Kazakhstan and Kyrgyzstan, on the formation of a common Central Asian peace-keeping force (the Central Asian Peace-keeping Battalion—CENTRASBAT) for use at the behest of the UN. However, although relations with Kazakhstan and Kyrgyzstan were generally good throughout the 1990s, relations with Turkmenistan were noticeably cool.

In 1999 and early 2000 tensions between Uzbekistan and its regional neighbours developed as a result of advances by Uzbekistan to demarcate unilaterally its borders, which, like many in the region, had not been clearly demarcated in the 1920s. In the Fergana valley considerable tension was generated over border questions, particularly following an incursion into Kyrgyzstan from Tajikistan by the IMU in August 1999, to which Uzbekistan responded by bombing parts of the border area; rebels again invaded the country in August 2000. Uzbekistan and Kazakhstan established a joint boundary commission, but Uzbekistan twice sought unilaterally to demarcate the frontier in the first months of 2000. In 2001 similar problems emerged with respect to the demarcation of the border with Kyrgyzstan. A memorandum signed by the

leaders of Uzbekistan and Kyrgyzstan was quickly abandoned, owing to strong criticism. In mid-September it was reported that Uzbekistan had occupied Kyrgyz territory, without the consent of the Kyrgyz Government. In 2001–02 a dispute flared between Uzbekistan and Kazakhstan over a small piece of land along their border. Although the territory was controlled by Uzbekistan, following a border demarcation accord in 2000, the majority of the area's residents were Kazakh. In December 2001 residents of the disputed region of Bagys declared an Independent Kazakh Republic of Bagys, and elected a president and legislature. Uzbek security forces subsequently made a number of arrests, and in April 2002 it was reported that troops had barricaded villages in the region, after virtual martial law had been established there. The village's population was subsequently resettled in Kazakhstan. None the less, in September Uzbekistan and Kazakhstan signed a treaty fully demarcating their joint border, and a border agreement was signed between Uzbekistan and Tajikistan in the following month. There were also some signs of improved co-operation between the Central Asian states in 2002, with the transformation of the Central Asian Economic Community into the Central Asian Co-operation Organization, an institution with a broader remit. Despite this measure, however, ambitions for intensive regional co-operation remained elusive.

From the 1990s the threat posed by the IMU created problems between Uzbekistan and other Central Asian nations. The IMU used bases in Afghanistan and Tajikistan to launch attacks on Uzbekistan, usually crossing Kyrgyz territory en route. The Uzbek Government placed a great deal of pressure on Tajikistan to expel the IMU from its territory; a similar request to the Taliban in Afghanistan was rejected. By mid-2001 the Uzbek, Kyrgyz and Russian Governments were co-ordinating efforts to combat IMU attacks. However, relations were adversely affected when Uzbek government forces laid landmines along the Uzbek–Kyrgyz border, in order to deter IMU incursions, inadvertently killing several Kyrgyz civilians. As a result, the Kyrgyz Legislative Assembly refused to ratify an agreement with Uzbekistan on arms' supplies. Nevertheless, in March 2002 Uzbekistan agreed to supply natural gas to Kyrgyzstan in return for deliveries of water.

Despite the apparent removal of the IMU threat, and thereby one of the main justifications for the militarization of Uzbekistan's borders, relations with Uzbekistan's neighbours showed little sign of improvement in 2002–03. Following the conflict in Afghanistan, Uzbekistan continued to restrict border crossings with Kyrgyzstan and Tajikistan, notably in early 2003, under the pretext that this was necessary to combat the spread of an outbreak of Severe Acute Respiratory Syndrome (SARS) from the People's Republic of China and other countries of the Far East. Deaths and injuries in border regions, caused by Uzbek landmines, also prompted further tensions in relations with Kyrgyzstan and Tajikistan. In late 2002 bilateral relations with Turkmenistan were adversely affected following an assassination attempt against President Saparmyrat Niyazov of Turkmenistan in November. The Turkmenistani authorities accused Uzbekistan of sheltering the Turkmenistani opposition leader and former Minister of Foreign Affairs, Boris Shikhmuradov, the principal suspect in the attempted *coup d'état*, in the Uzbek embassy in Turkmenistan. In late December the Uzbek ambassador to Turkmenistan was expelled and Shikhmuradov was convicted of instigating the coup. These events led to the tightening of controls along the Uzbek–Turkmen border.

Through its involvement in the campaign against militant Islamists in Afghanistan, Uzbekistan's international relations underwent a significant shift. As part of the US-led military campaign in Afghanistan, US troops were deployed in Uzbekistan, fostering a closer relationship with the USA than had previously existed. In the late 1990s US–Uzbek relations had deteriorated, following a period in 1994–96 when ties had been reasonably good. The source of the tension was Uzbekistan's record on human rights and its failure to adopt serious economic reforms. At the same time, Uzbekistan remained strategically important to the USA and, during a visit to the country in April 2000, the US Secretary of State, Madeleine Albright, noted that the USA regarded Uzbekistan as an ally, and was prepared to assist that country in combating the spread of Islamist extremism from Afghanistan or elsewhere in Central Asia. Once it became clear, in late 2001, that the Taliban regime would not surrender Osama bin Laden, held principally responsible by the USA for perpetrating the suicide attacks on its territory, Karimov reiterated his support for retaliatory attacks on Afghanistan. In a co-operation agreement signed with the USA in early October, Uzbekistan confirmed that it would allow access to its airbases for the purpose of undertaking humanitarian or 'search-and-rescue' operations during the US-led aerial bombardment of strategic positions in Afghanistan. In late November Uzbekistan and the USA signed a number of agreements pledging to improve bilateral relations and to increase economic co-operation. The USA agreed to donate more than US $150m. in aid towards improving Uzbekistan's security and economic development. Disagreement over Uzbekistan's pace of democratization, however, remained (see above). Further bilateral agreements on political, economic and military co-operation were signed in early 2002, and in March President Karimov received a warm welcome during a high-level visit to the USA.

The new strategic relationship with the USA produced important changes in Uzbekistan's relationship with Russia. Prior to 1999, Uzbekistan had sought to distance itself from that country and to assume the leading regional role in Central Asia. The rising challenge from radical Islamists led to a *rapprochement* with Russia and, following Russian President Vladimir Putin's declaration of support for the military campaign in Afghanistan, relations improved further. In June 2002 it was announced that Uzbekistan had suspended its membership of GUUAM, which was generally considered to have been designed to counter the Russian-dominated CIS. However, Uzbekistan later withdrew its suspension, following strong US pressure, and in 2003 GUUAM appeared to have been reinvigorated following a summit meeting in Yalta, Ukraine, and indications that the USA supported the grouping.

In the late 1990s the growing importance of regional security, as a result of Islamist insurgency, prompted Uzbekistan to express a desire to join the so-called Shanghai Forum, subsequently known as the Shanghai Co-operation Organization (comprising the People's Republic of China, Russia, Kazakhstan, Kyrgyzstan and Tajikistan). The organization, which was originally concerned with the demilitarization of the border between China and its CIS neighbours, had broadened its focus to include combating international terrorism, separatism and religious extremism. Although Uzbekistan joined the Shanghai Co-operation Organization (SCO) in June 2001, its new relationship with the USA raised the prospect that Uzbekistan might, in fact, not become an active participant in the Shanghai grouping, and Uzbekistan failed to send a representative to the Organization's ministerial meetings in early 2002. Nevertheless, President Karimov did attend the seventh summit meeting of the grouping in June. Furthermore, in 2003, following a summit meeting of SCO Heads of State, held in Moscow, Russia, Karimov indicated that a proposed SCO anti-terrorism centre was to be established in Tashkent, rather than Bishkek, Kyrgyzstan, as had been reported earlier.

Despite the new relationship with the USA, the willingness shown by that country to maintain equally good relations with other Central Asian states prevented Uzbekistan from emerging as the dominant regional power, following the military campaign in Afghanistan. In 2003 the focus of US policy shifted from Afghanistan to the Middle East and weakened Uzbekistan's value as an ally. Despite Uzbekistan's strong support for US-led intervention in Iraq, there were signs of US frustration with Uzbekistan's intransigence on issues of domestic political and economic reform, notably following the EBRD summit meeting held in Uzbekistan (see above). These tensions led to a further *rapprochement* with Russia, as signalled by a visit by President Putin to Uzbekistan in August 2003.

Relations with a range of other international powers were also developed following independence, including countries in Western Europe, in particular Germany, and North America. Western investment in Uzbekistan was regarded as politically, as well as economically, significant. Prior to September 2001, relations with the West were, however, adversely affected by the human rights situation in Uzbekistan, although limited investment also had much to do with the uncertain economic environment in the country. In the second half of the 1990s the souring of relations with the IMF and other international financial institutions, Western criticism of Uzbekistan's internal policies of repression (most notably toward Muslim groups) and the Government's improving links with Russia obscured political relations with the West, although from 1995 trade with Western industrialized countries expanded. Asian countries, particularly the Republic of Korea (South Korea), also contributed important investments to Uzbekistan. Following military action in Afghanistan by Western powers and the stationing of Western military forces in Uzbekistan, relations with that country improved markedly. Levels of aid and investment from the EU increased in 2002.

Relations with Turkey and the countries of the Middle East were also of importance to Uzbekistan. Along with other Central Asian states, the country joined the Economic Co-operation Organization (ECO), originally founded by Iran, Pakistan and Turkey in 1985. Uzbekistan was, however, critical of moves to develop a political role for the organization, and the limited economic resources available to ECO member countries curbed the role that they could play in Uzbekistan. Instead, the Government promoted the role of international bodies, such as the OSCE, which opened a Central Asian office in Tashkent in October 1995, and the UN, which was the principal international forum for the important war against the trafficking of illegal drugs in the region and played an important role in mediating the conflict in Tajikistan.

## CONCLUSION

After 1991 the few democratic institutions in Uzbekistan were eliminated. At the same time there was a steady concentration of power in the state presidency. From the mid-1990s Uzbekistan operated as a highly authoritarian country, based upon the almost unchecked authority of President Karimov. Repression was justified as the only means to avoid ethnic conflict and Islamist militancy, and necessary for binding together a young nation and state. Karimov ensured that there were no plausible internal challengers to his rule, by purging and marginalizing potential rivals. The small and divided secular opposition posed no threat. The only real alternative to the President was the Islamist movement, but this was not a coherent force within Uzbekistan, being divided between radicals and moderates. The emergence of Islamist militant groups based outside the country from 1999 posed a more serious challenge to the Uzbek regime, a threat that was amplified following the suicide attacks on the USA in September 2001. Following the suppression of the Afghanistan-based IMU and its Taliban hosts by the US-led coalition, there were few subsequent signs of serious political and economic liberalization in Uzbekistan. The regime continued to rely upon repression of all dissent, the systematic practice of torture and the abuse of human rights.

In foreign policy, Karimov failed in his original objective of transforming Uzbekistan into the dominant regional power. Former allies in the Tajik Government aligned themselves, instead, with Russia. With signs that the Uzbek economy was faltering, and with growing internal popular dissatisfaction and powerful external challenges, Uzbekistan, too, was forced to rely increasingly on military and political support from the USA and Russia. Relations with the West were damaged by Uzbekistan's very poor record on human rights and its resistance to economic liberalization, although the country's support for US-led military action in Afghanistan produced some improvement in both political and economic relations. More than one decade after the collapse of the USSR, the stability and independence that Karimov had pursued since independence remained as elusive as ever. Instead, Uzbekistan appeared to be attempting to counterbalance the influence of the USA and Russia, while blocking the regional co-operation in Central Asia that was necessary to promote prosperity and long term security.

# The Economy

## Dr NEIL MELVIN

### INTRODUCTION

Historically, the primary economic activities of the regions that constitute contemporary Uzbekistan were agriculture, trade and the production of handicrafts (textiles, jewellery and low-grade domestic goods). During the Soviet era, Uzbekistan's economy underwent a series of fundamental changes, including an extensive reorganization of agriculture, an intensification of production (notably in cotton) and the introduction of new industries. Overall, however, Soviet economic policies left the country poorly prepared for independence. Uzbekistan has an extensive natural resource base (estimated to total US $13,000,000m.), but Soviet planners did little to create indigenous industries capable of exploiting these resources. In the USSR, Uzbekistan functioned primarily as a supplier of raw materials that were processed elsewhere. As a result, official figures identified the Uzbek Soviet Socialist Republic (SSR) as one of the poorer of the republics in the USSR, with only the Tajik SSR having a lower per-head consumption.

The main economic function of the region during the Soviet era was the production of cotton and other agricultural goods. The legacy of this policy was a set of chronic ecological problems, a largely rural work-force and a highly unbalanced economy. The country's population, which was the largest in Central Asia (an estimated 25.7m. at mid-2002), was settled around the major oasis settlements of the region (Tashkent, Samarkand, Bukhara and Khiva) and the fertile region of the Fergana valley. Some 63% of the population lived in rural areas in 2000. According to provisional figures, in 2002 9,333,000 persons were employed, with 32.5% in agriculture, 12.7% in industry and 54.8% in other sectors. In 2002 approximately 35,000 persons (0.4% of the work-force) were registered as unemployed, although the actual figure was believed to be far higher, as the result of 'hidden' unemployment in rural areas. There was also considerable underemployment. In 1999 41.4% of the population was under the age of 16, with the average age being 23.9 years. Population growth slowed to 1.0% by 2001, down from 1.5% in 1999 and the average annual rate of 2.5% during the 1980s, partly owing to large-scale emigration by Slavs, Germans, Greeks and Jews.

A major achievement of the Soviet period was an increase in the human capital of Uzbekistan. With an adult literacy rate of 97.2% in 1993 (which had increased to 99.2% by 2000), the educational level of the population was high. The Soviet regime established a comprehensive educational system, including institutions for higher education. The scientific potential of the country was concentrated in over 350 establishments and well-trained research personnel were engaged in work on a number of areas. The emigration of some of the most skilled members of society in the early years of independence and a decline in education standards, however, damaged the country's scientific and research base.

Uzbekistan's infrastructure was poorly developed during the Soviet years. Although the railway and road networks were built as a connection to the Russian Federation and other republics of the USSR, most routes leading out of Uzbekistan required upgrading if trade and transit traffic were to increase. The European Union (EU) devoted considerable resources to improving east–west communications in the country. The telecommunications system, however, was generally poor and the quality of transmission often very low.

### ECONOMIC POLICY

The main characteristic of economic policy in independent Uzbekistan was the high degree of government direction, designed officially to moderate the social dislocation brought about by the introduction of market-orientated reforms and the preservation of political control. Initially, the Government's attitude to change served to produce a gradualist approach to economic and structural reform in Uzbekistan. The World Bank estimated that there was an average annual decline in real gross domestic product (GDP) of 4.4% in 1990–95, and of 15% between 1992 and 1994 alone. The sectors most affected were construction and industry (the latter declining by an average of 6.6% per year in 1990–95), which faced severe supply problems from other states of the former USSR. Although these figures were high, they fell below the average output decline in the rest of the former USSR. Most of the decline in real GDP was concentrated in 1992, when the IMF gave a figure of 11.0% for the contraction, with the rate slowing to 4.2% in 1994. The IMF conceded that the economic contraction in Uzbekistan was less severe than in other post-Soviet states, but argued that this was achieved despite, rather than as a result of, government policy.

Following independence, 'hyperinflation' quickly took hold of Uzbekistan's economy. At one point in 1992 the annual rate of inflation reached 2,700%. During the year the increase in consumer prices was 818.7%, rising to 1,114.5% in 1993 and 1,515.9% in 1994. In an attempt to bring monetary policy under government control and, thereby, stem inflation, Uzbekistan left the Russian-dominated 'rouble zone' in November 1993 and introduced its own transitional national currency, the sum-coupon. In July 1994 the new national currency, the sum, was introduced. After its introduction the Government gradually raised the official exchange rate of the sum against other currencies, so that the official rate was close to that of the 'black' (unofficial) market rate.

The economy's slow progress during the early years of independence led the President, in 1994, to attempt to accelerate and deepen the reform process. On 21 January President Islam Karimov issued a decree On Measures for Further Deepening Economic Reforms, Providing for the Protection of Private Property and for the Development of Entrepreneurship. This decree bolstered the power of the state to promote economic reform. An inter-ministerial committee on economic reform, entrepreneurship and foreign investment was established, and there was an expansion of the powers of the privatization committee to include aspects of private-sector development. In addition, stock, real-estate and commodity exchanges were to be created, permission for persons to hold foreign-currency accounts was granted, import duties were eliminated for one year and a state insurance company capable of guaranteeing foreign investments was established.

The introduction in 1994 of a comprehensive reform programme supported by the President had important consequences. By the end of 1995 inflation appeared to have declined to around 10% per month. The small amount of data available suggested that the Government was maintaining a restrictive monetary policy, in accordance with IMF demands. The Central Bank reduced interest rates as inflation fell, but ensured that rates remained positive in real terms. Official figures suggested that GDP declined by just 0.9% in 1995, with real industrial output rising by 0.2%.

Despite the changes of 1994, it was only in 1995 that a coherent set of stabilization measures appeared in Uzbekistan. A particular point of criticism was the mixed performance of structural reform. The IMF expressed concern at Uzbekistan's failure to restructure enterprises and the manner in which privatization was conducted. The IMF did, however, praise the widespread withdrawal of state subsidies. In response to Russia's decision to introduce price liberalization on 2 January 1992, prices for basic foodstuffs were limited and subsidies to certain sectors were increased two-fold, in an effort to reduce the impact. The World Bank estimated that consumer subsidies and enterprise credits amounted to at least 21% of GDP in 1993. By mid-1994, however, many of the subsidies that had existed for food, utilities, housing, transport and energy had been removed. Despite supporting the price liberalization, the IMF was critical of the way in which economic policy developed. It questioned the independence of the Central Bank and urged the President to reduce 'administrative interventions' in the economy.

In 1995 the disastrous domestic cotton harvest and low world prices for the commodity led the Uzbek leadership to impose foreign-exchange controls and to begin to print money, thereby encouraging inflation. The actions of the Government led the IMF to suspend a US \$185m. stand-by loan in mid-December 1996, on the grounds that Uzbekistan had missed its inflation targets. The imposition of tight state controls over currency transactions caused severe problems for foreign firms operating in Uzbekistan and foreign investment slowed.

The problems associated with the crisis in state finances represented the end of the limited economic reforms. A strong critic of the more radical economic transitions attempted among the other former Soviet republics, President Karimov effectively suspended market reforms in late 1996, for fear of provoking unrest within the population and opposition among powerful interests in the elite. In 1997–2001 the Uzbek authorities failed to launch significant economic change in the country, as political issues and control over society increasingly became the central policy focus of the authorities.

The Government resisted initiatives to further the restructuring and privatization of enterprises. After 1996 the Government was reluctant to conclude an agreement on a stand-by loan facility with the IMF, owing to conditions that required progress towards currency convertibility. The Uzbek Government was criticized by international financial organizations, including the European Bank for Reconstruction and Development (EBRD), the IMF and the US Department of Commerce, for creating a difficult business environment.

Throughout 1998–2001 the economic situation steadily deteriorated (despite official figures that pointed to growth). The decline in world prices for Uzbekistan's two main exports, cotton and gold, deprived the country of export revenue and produced severe demands on domestic liquidity. With foreign-currency reserves dangerously low, the national currency continued to lose value at both official and black-market rates and inflation fluctuated at around 25%. By 2001 the economic situation had failed to improve significantly, although strong growth in the CIS as a whole for 1999–2000, as a result of recovery from the Russian financial crisis of 1998, assisted Uzbekistan. A severe drought led to another poor cotton harvest in 2000. It remained, therefore, imperative that the Government introduce economic reform. However, the Government showed little willingness to relax exchange-rate controls or to close bankrupt and uncompetitive industries. According to official estimates, GDP grew by 4.0% in 2000, by 4.5% in 2001 and by 4.2% in 2002 (below the target of 5.0%). Consequently, the ADB predicted similar GDP growth figures for the near future, of 3.5% in 2003 and 4.0% in 2004. Moreover, although the rate of inflation for 2002 was officially estimated at 27.6%, the ADB believed this estimate fell short of the true figure, citing concerns about price controls, artificial exchange rates and statistical methodology.

At the end of 2001, a new relationship between Uzbekistan and leading international financial institutions and powerful Western states, principally the USA, created expectations of a shift in economic policy. In the new environment of international goodwill towards Uzbekistan which resulted from that country's co-operation with the US-led 'war on terrorism', initiated after the suicide attacks on the USA in September 2001, Uzbekistan pledged to undertake economic reforms, and contacts were re-established with the IMF (see below). The Uzbek leadership, however, remained extremely cautious about serious economic reform.

## ECONOMIC INSTITUTIONS

Uzbekistan inherited little from the Soviet period in terms of the institutional infrastructure necessary for a market economy. In response to the new demands of macro- and microeconomic management, there was an attempt to create appropriate new structures. However, given the tendency for state intervention in the economy, and the weakly marketized nature of the system, establishing new institutional arrangements was often difficult. Although some progress was made in constructing a reformed and independent financial and economic system, Uzbekistan continued to be characterized by weak institutions, high levels of corruption and extensive state interference.

The President and the Cabinet of Ministers are responsible for major economic decisions. The Ministry of Finance develops the state budget, exercises financial supervision of enterprises and manages all inter-governmental credit agreements and international financial institutions, and oversees foreign-currency loans to enterprises. The Ministry oversees external debt 'servicing' and manages repayments. Although the Central Bank is supposedly subordinated only to parliament, in practice it is controlled by the Government. The ability of the Central Bank to make independent decisions has frequently been doubted, as has its ability to control the banking sector in the country. In 1994 a reform of the banking sector was begun. A two-tier system was established, consisting of the Central Bank and about 30 commercial banks.

The main aim of the reform was to restrict the availability of credit to enterprises, a major source of inflation. The poor supervision of the commercial sector by the Central Bank frequently undermined this aim and the continuing access to cheap credit weakened the process of enterprise privatization.

The failure to foster independent economic institutions ensured that all aspects of the Uzbek economy remained subordinate to the priorities and directives of the President. The lack of autonomous economic institutions meant that it was impossible to talk of a significant private sector in Uzbekistan. The economy lacked autonomous centres for significant economic decision-making and mechanisms for investment driven by economic efficiency. Instead, even the commercial-banking sector was tied to the state system and banks allocated credit to priority sectors as identified by the Government. Commercial banks were also used to maintain the sum at artificially high values. All economic activity remained centred upon the state and key figures in the ruling élite.

## PRIVATIZATION

The Government followed a process of gradual privatization with the law On Denationalization and Privatization, enacted in November 1991, which provided the legal basis for the process. To support privatization, the State Committee for the Management of State Property and Privatization (known by its local acronym of GKI) was established in February 1992. In the first stage of privatization, the GKI undertook the disposal of housing, agriculture and the retail sector. In 1994–95 the second stage began, with over 5,000 enterprises to be privatized.

The pace of privatization accelerated in March 1994, with the decree On the Main Priority Directions for Further Development of Denationalization and Privatization. Karimov announced that the state would no longer finance insolvent enterprises. At the end of 1994 the GKI estimated that there were 67,660 enterprises in Uzbekistan, of which 20,758 were state enterprises and 46,902 private or privatized. In February 1995 President Karimov claimed that 100,000 firms, or 67% of state firms, had been privatized, and that most of the work-force operated in the private sector. In fact, privatization enjoyed only partial success, with most enterprises still under the influence of state or local government to significant degrees.

From the mid-1990s the privatization programme slowed considerably. In 1998 the Government planned to privatize 346 state-owned firms, but in May it announced the postponement of the privatization of the petroleum and gas sectors. Despite privatization, many insolvent firms continued to function, with state support. Critically, the state retained strategic stakes in most enterprises. In 1999 Uzbekistan's need for foreign exchange prompted the Government to develop a list of potential assets for sale. However, even where privatization was carried out, the results were often far from favourable for the new owners, and it proved difficult to attract foreign investors. Revenues from privatization amounted to some 9,100m. sum in 1999. In the first nine months of 2000 income from privatization totalled some 10,954m. sum, and by the end of the year 189 medium-sized and large enterprises had been privatized. In March 2001 the Government listed more than 600 state companies that remained to be sold.

State control over credit facilities, exchange controls, price formation and the activities of various bureaucratic agencies (principally the tax inspectorate) ensured that even nominally private enterprises operated in a tightly state-defined framework. Shareholders have only minor influence over firms. A decree signed in 1998 allowed the Government to block strategic decisions made by majority foreign shareholders if it deemed them not to be in the national interest. Privatization was heavily influenced by contacts with the government and

frequently served as the basis for the construction of networks of political patronage. Associates of the Government and their families staffed the most profitable firms. After President Karimov opted for an autarkic form of economic development in the mid-1990s, there was no significant privatization. Following the revived contacts with the international financial community in late 2001, the Government again pledged to accelerate privatization, although foreign investors remained extremely cautious about the general business environment.

## FINANCES

In 1992 Uzbekistan had a fiscal debt equivalent to 11% of GDP. In 1993 the debt declined to some 9% and in 1994 to 4.8%. In the early years of independence the Government had problems controlling spending, because credit was made available to enterprises and the Government sought to maintain public expenditure in the social and cultural sectors. As Uzbekistan began to abide by IMF conditions, government spending appeared to have been brought under control. In May 1996 it was announced that Uzbekistan had posted a deficit-free budget for the first quarter of the year, but it registered a deficit thereafter. Uzbekistan's external debt was relatively small, as it did not inherit any obligations of the former USSR. However, the economic crisis that afflicted the economy from 1996 placed a significant strain on the debt situation in Uzbekistan. In 1994 Uzbekistan recorded a small trade surplus, and in 1995, according to the Ministry of Foreign Economic Relations, the trade balance was in surplus, at about US $293m., with exports at some $1,890m. and imports at some $1,600m. The heavy reliance on cotton exports (60% of the total in 1992, but later nearer 30%), however, meant that Uzbekistan's trade balance was at the mercy of the world cotton markets.

From 1996 difficulties raising external credit, because of the failure to conclude an agreement with the IMF, led the Uzbek authorities to keep fiscal accounts close to balance by accumulating wage and pension arrears, forcing loans from local banks and retaining a tight grip on local enterprises and their exports. Official estimates put the budget deficit for 2002 at about 0.8% of GDP, but independent estimates put the figure at 2%. Given the poor state of government finances in the late 1990s, the trade situation became critical. The poor cotton harvest and the decline in world prices for cotton in 1995–99 caused acute problems in balancing trade flows. Assessing import and export volume is difficult, owing to inadequate data on trade. Available data for 2000 indicated a trade surplus of US $494m.

The trade deficit was managed by a steadily depreciating national currency, which priced imports out of the local market. Given the problems with government finances, lack of international credit and poor trade figures, the Government was running a significant current-account deficit on the balance of payments by the late 1990s. Some independent estimates placed the deficit at US $329.4m. in 1999, although official figures identified a current-account surplus of $10.6m. According to government estimates, the current account in 2000 registered a surplus of $110m.; however, the ADB estimated a surplus of $184m., while the EBRD estimated a deficit of $19m. The ADB estimated a current-account deficit of 0.5% of GDP in 2001, and a current-account surplus of 0.6% of GDP, or US $47m., in 2002.

The Government appeared to have financed the current-account deficit and industrial investment with foreign debt. External debt, owed largely to bilateral lenders, rose steadily and was estimated by the ADB to total US $4,400m. in 2002 (equivalent to 56% of GDP). Although external debt accumulated quickly in the late 1990s, it did not, by 2003, appear to have reached critical proportions. Despite the considerable potential for investment, Uzbekistan had one of the lowest levels of foreign direct investment in the former communist bloc. The lack of convertibility of the sum was usually identified as the principal factor discouraging foreign companies from investing in the country. However, the sum was made freely convertible from October 2003 (see below).

## AGRICULTURE

Agriculture is fundamental to Uzbekistan's economy and, although arid or semi-arid steppe constitutes 60% of the country, there are also a number of highly fertile regions. The single most important crop in Uzbekistan is cotton, the country being the fourth-largest producer of seed cotton and the second-largest exporter in the world. Uzbekistan is also the largest producer of silk and karakul pelts in the former USSR. Other important products include wheat, rice, jute, tobacco, fruit and vegetables. Despite the large contribution of agriculture to the economy (the agricultural sector, including forestry, constituted 34.6% of GDP in 2002), Uzbekistan is not self-sufficient. A large proportion of foodstuffs is imported, including up to 66% of wheat requirements, 30% of meat, 25% of milk and 50% of potatoes.

The form of agriculture inherited from the Soviet era, with its reliance on the extensive use of land, water and chemicals (fertilizers and pesticides) was particularly damaging to the environment. Uzbekistan has an extensive but inefficient irrigation system to provide water for cotton production, and it is this system that has caused the problems of the Aral Sea and the overuse of water supplies. Irrigating the cotton monoculture depleted water resources in the region, leading to the desiccation of the Aral Sea, which was previously the world's fourth-largest inland lake. By the late 1990s the lake was only one-quarter of its volume in 1960 and the lake was predicted to disappear entirely early in the 21st century unless urgent measures were undertaken. The environmental problems were compounded by salinity, industrial wastes, pesticides and fertilizers, which poisoned the remaining sub-surface and surface waters, land and air in the region.

In an attempt to decrease environmental pollution and ameliorate the problems around the Aral Sea, a policy of shifting production to grain was introduced. This was also intended to reduce Uzbekistan's dependence on the import of foodstuffs and to help redress the balance-of-payments problem. After 1990, the area sown for grain increased from 1.0m. ha to reach a peak of 1.8m. ha in 1997. By 2002 the figure had fallen to 1.2m. ha. In 2002 the harvest was officially reported to total 5.3m. metric tons, up from the average of 3.7m. tons over the previous four years. At the same time, the country continued to import grain, suggesting that official figures for production may be over-estimated.

Cotton production continued to be of critical importance to Uzbekistan. The area devoted to cotton production remained constant, at about 1.5m. ha. Production of seed (unginned) cotton declined steadily after reaching its highest level, of 5m. metric tons, in 1990. From 1995 the cotton crop consistently fell below targets, causing severe problems for the whole economy. The poor harvests and shift of land from cotton to cereal production greatly damaged Uzbekistan's ability to earn 'hard' currency. In 2001 the cotton harvest was 3.3m. tons, and this was followed by a further poor harvest. In 2002 the Government introduced a limited liberalization of the state procurement system to ease pressure on farmers and encourage production. Prospects for the 2003 harvest were far better, with increased production under plastic sheeting expected to raise yields.

Following independence, an important change for agriculture was the abolition of state farms and their conversion to co-operative enterprises. Members of the new collectives did not have the right to sell their shares. Some private farms developed. In 1994 there were 10,408 and the area of land

available for private farming by farm workers rose significantly (from 110,000 ha before 1991 to 630,000 ha in 1994). Land itself was not privatized, although agricultural land could be traded within the mahallah (local neighbourhood or commune), and land attached to an enterprise could be sold with it. Despite the change in the formal structures of ownership, the state continued to dominate agricultural production and maintained a virtual monopoly over the purchase of key crops, notably cotton. In recent years there has, nevertheless, been a growing role for the private sector, in particular the household plot.

A principal problem of the agricultural sector in Uzbekistan was the failure to modernize the food-processing industry to produce better quality goods and provide safe and convenient packaging. In general, processing of primary products had usually taken place elsewhere in the USSR, although after independence Uzbekistan did have some success in upgrading its existing facilities and developing new ones.

## MINING, ENERGY AND INDUSTRY

Uzbekistan has important natural reserves, and soon after independence the Government identified the development of mining and the processing of minerals and metals as a major priority. Metals production in Uzbekistan rose steadily from the mid-1990s, particularly in the gold sector. Uzbekistan has 30 gold deposits and ranks eighth in the world in terms of gold-processing. An average of 70 metric tons of gold was extracted annually in the 1990s, and in 2001 output reached approximately 85.4 tons. Almost all of the gold produced is exported, although data on gold exports had not been released since 1999. Other metals, such as copper, silver and non-ferrous metals, have also been produced in increasing amounts. The export of metals emerged as a critical element of Uzbek trade with the rest of the world, second only to cotton production.

Uzbekistan also has important reserves of hydrocarbons and the Government pursued a policy of becoming self-sufficient in fuel, with some success. There were no significant imports of petroleum after 1995. The refining industry also performed well, raising production in the second half of the 1990s. Petroleum production rose from 2.8m. metric tons in 1991 to 8.1m. tons in 1999, and declined to an estimated 7.2m. tons in 2002. Domestic prices remained low, reflecting the Government's policy of subsidizing the domestic economy. By 2010 annual production was planned to reach 9m. tons per year. Uzbekistan struggled, however, to develop high-grade refining. The practice of controlling energy prices created an important financial incentive to smuggle energy supplies to neighbouring countries.

In terms of natural-gas extraction, Uzbekistan ranks 10th in the world. Gas production also rose during the 1990s, although not at the same pace as that of petroleum. In 1995 about 49,000m. cu m of gas was produced. By 2002 the figure for production reached an estimated 58,000m. cu m. If gas was to be exported in significant volumes, however, investment in infrastructure, including gas pipelines and refineries, would be required. Uzbekistan also experienced serious difficulties in obtaining payment for the gas exported to neighbouring states (3,500m. cu m in 1998). The economic difficulties in Uzbekistan forced the Government to become increasingly assertive in demanding payment for gas from Kazakhstan, Kyrgyzstan and Tajikistan, and supplies to these countries were reduced or suspended, owing to non-payment.

The petroleum and gas sector was attractive to some foreign investors, and France and Japan agreed to provide US $200m. to finance the modernization of the Bukhara refinery being undertaken by Technip of France. Unlike Kazakhstan, Uzbekistan did not plan to become a major exporter of petroleum, but rather to achieve self-sufficiency. Foreign investment was to finance the development of the Mingbulak and Kokdumalak fields as a way to lift total output. Overall, however, the petroleum and gas sector was controlled by the state-owned company, Uzbekneftgaz, and attracted very low levels of foreign direct investment. Stagnating production levels from the early 2000s prompted the Uzbek authorities to seek a closer involvement by Russian companies in domestic production in partnership with Uzbekneftegaz, notably for the development of the Kandym oil and gasfields.

Light industry predominates in the Uzbek economy. Despite the importance of cotton and silk growing, only a small percentage is processed domestically. Uzbekistan relies heavily on textile imports. The development of an indigenous textiles industry was given high priority in the 1990s. The importance of the agricultural sector is reflected in the fact that a significant part of industrial activity is concerned with agro-industrial production—agricultural machinery and fertilizers.

An important new departure for the domestic economy following independence was the production of small trucks and cars, and diesel-engine buses. A number of foreign firms established production facilities in Uzbekistan and the country had ambitions to become a regional centre for the automotive industry. In 1995 Daimler-Benz of Germany expanded vehicle production in Uzbekistan and in March 1996 Daewoo of the Republic of Korea (South Korea) opened a plant in Tashkent. Following the Asian financial crisis of 1998, Daewoo experienced serious domestic financial difficulties and the Uzbek Government was forced to support financially the UzDaewoo Auto plant, although at significantly lower levels of output, when Daewoo went bankrupt in 2000. In 2003 the automotive sector was reported to be performing poorly, with the UzDaewoo Auto plant operating at well below its annual capacity of 200,000 units.

Infrastructural limitations constrained tourism, which has considerable potential in the country because of Uzbekistan's unique historical sites. The lack of an adequate infrastructure of transport, hotels and recreation facilities, however, meant that the sector's potential had yet to be fulfilled. Like almost all sectors of the Uzbek economy, success was dependent on foreign capital. The poor investment climate in the country, however, discouraged extensive developments in the tourist industry. In 1998 Uzbekistan had an estimated 272,000 foreign visitors (including excursionists), and tourism receipts totalled some US $21m.

## INTERNATIONAL FINANCE AND INVESTMENT

A number of Western firms have made sizeable investments in Uzbekistan. Daewoo originally invested nearly US $450m. in its car factories, while BAT Industries (based in the United Kingdom) began production of cigarettes at an existing factory and also constructed new manufacturing facilities. Other important Western firms were active in the mining, energy and telecommunications sectors.

The activity of foreign firms is supported by financial assistance and guarantees provided by foreign governments. The large international organizations supply the final layer of assistance for market reforms and investment, providing finance for individual sectors of the economy and also for macroeconomic projects. In February 1995 the World Bank, the IMF, the Organisation for Economic Co-operation and Development (OECD) and the EBRD announced an international assistance programme to deliver over US $900m. to Uzbekistan over the following two years ($300m. for balance-of-payments support, $45m. for technical assistance and $580m. for financing investments and export loans). Uzbekistan sought to attract other sources of international finance, and in September 1995 it became an official member of the ADB.

From 1996 the change of direction in economic policy undermined the international programmes of assistance. Foreign private investment, already very modest, was also reduced significantly. In early 1998 negotiations with the IMF failed to establish new stabilization measures. Negotiations foundered on Uzbekistan's refusal to reverse its anti-reformist path. In particular, the Government refused to make the sum convertible and, thereby, abandon the system of multiple exchange rates. The Government was also reluctant to commit itself to trade liberalization. Relations with the IMF were, subsequently, difficult, and the Fund published a number of reports critical of government economic policy, and which cast doubt on official statistics. Despite these problems, international institutions, such as the ADB, continued to lend money to Uzbekistan for infrastructure projects, and export-guarantee agencies in Europe and the USA provided loan assistance for the purchase of imports.

At the beginning of 2000 the worsening domestic economic situation and a number of policy statements by President Karimov suggested that the Government was preparing to seek the re-establishment of the IMF stand-by arrangement loan that had previously been suspended. Negotiations, however, were inconclusive and in April 2001 the IMF announced the permanent departure of its representative to Uzbekistan. This measure was interpreted as an implicit criticism of Uzbekistan's economic policies, which were viewed as ineffective, and even counter-productive.

Following Uzbekistan's support for the US-led 'war on terrorism' from late 2001, the country's relationship with international financial organizations, notably the IMF, the World Bank and the EBRD, was reviewed. After a pledge by the USA to secure US $100m. in loans and assistance to Uzbekistan, a team from the IMF visited Uzbekistan in November 2001 and negotiated a Staff Monitored Programme, a crucial element of which was the Government's commitment to make the sum current-account convertible by 1 July 2002. In mid-July President Karimov promised US officials that Uzbekistan would sign an agreement with the IMF by the end of the year, in order to make the sum fully convertible. In 2001 Uzbekistan received assistance from the USA amounting to $161.8m., the highest amount recorded among the Central Asia states. Despite the commitment to reform expressed in 2001, however, reformist measures were not introduced in 2002 or the first half of 2003. In May 2003 the EBRD held its annual meeting in Tashkent, a location that was selected in an attempt to stimulate the long-delayed economic reform in the Uzbekistan. Prior to the meeting, the Uzbek Government repeatedly intimated that it would reach agreement with the IMF on a stabilization programme. In fact, no agreement was achieved, and the IMF indicated that there were no signs of improvement in the general business environment. Government restrictions on trade, the lack of significant reform in the agricultural sector and the failure to establish a single exchange rate were identified by observers as obstructing further IMF engagement. Finally, in mid-October the Deputy Prime Minister and Minister of Macro-economics and Statistics, Rustam Azimov, signed an agreement with the IMF confirming the som's new status as a fully convertible currency.

## CONCLUSION

From 1991 Uzbekistan pursued sporadic economic reform and was reluctant to release data on the performance of the economy. Only in mid-1995 did Uzbekistan finally accede to the demands of the IMF structural adjustment programme. The economy as a whole, however, remained fragile and heavily dependent on agricultural production, in particular cotton. Although economic management and fiscal discipline improved, the state continued to intervene, particularly in areas such as the lucrative foreign-trade sector and the management of enterprises.

The new economic course embarked upon by the Government from 1996 changed significantly the nature and prospects for economic development in the country. Reform stalled and many of the basic structural problems in the economy remained. Given the problems that the Government experienced with international financial institutions, raising international credit proved difficult. Despite these problems, the Government claimed that the Uzbek economy was growing, achieving high levels of investment, modest levels of inflation, and a stable currency. Most independent observers viewed these claims sceptically and, instead, identified growing economic difficulties and a failure to address the key structural impediments to economic progress, and called attention to the

potential for the development of a financial crisis in the country.

The new environment in which Uzbekistan found itself from late 2001, as a result of its support for US-led efforts to combat global terrorism, presented an unexpected opportunity to undertake the significant economic reform that the Government had avoided during the previous decade. Despite considerable pressure from the international community to introduce reforms, the authorities in Tashkent remained, however, reluctant to undertake serious change. Concerns about the ways in which reform could undermine the political dominance of the leadership of the country, which had been established following independence on the basis of state patronage over the economy, appeared to be the principal obstacle to further economic progress.

# Statistical Survey

Principal sources (unless otherwise indicated): IMF, *Republic of Uzbekistan—Recent Economic Developments* (March 2000), IMF, *Uzbekistan, Economic Review*; IMF, *Republic of Uzbekistan—Background Paper and Statistical Appendix*; World Bank, *Statistical Handbook: States of the Former USSR*; World Bank, *Uzbekistan: An Agenda for Economic Reform.*

## Area and Population

### AREA, POPULATION AND DENSITY

| | |
|---|---:|
| Area (sq km) . . . . . . . . . . | 447,400* |
| Population (census results)† | |
| 17 January 1979 . . . . . . . . . . | 15,389,307 |
| 12 January 1989 | |
| Males . . . . . . . . . . | 9,784,156 |
| Females . . . . . . . . . . | 10,025,921 |
| Total . . . . . . . . . . | 19,810,077 |
| Population (UN estimates at mid-year)‡ | |
| 2000 . . . . . . . . . . | 24,913,000 |
| 2001 . . . . . . . . . . | 25,313,000 |
| 2002 . . . . . . . . . . | 25,705,000 |
| Density (per sq km) at mid-2002 . . . . . . . | 57.5 |

* 172,740 sq miles.

† Figures refer to *de jure* population. The *de facto* total at the 1989 census was 19,905,158.

‡ Source: UN, *World Population Prospects: The 2002 Revision.*

### POPULATION BY ETHNIC GROUP

(census of 12 January 1989)

| | % |
|---|---:|
| Uzbek . . . . . . . . . . | 71.4 |
| Russian . . . . . . . . . . | 8.3 |
| Tajik . . . . . . . . . . | 4.7 |
| Kazakh . . . . . . . . . . | 4.1 |
| Tatar . . . . . . . . . . | 2.4 |
| Others* . . . . . . . . . . | 9.1 |
| **Total** . . . . . . . . . . | 100.0 |

* Including Karakalpaks, Crimean Tatars, Koreans, Kyrgyz, Ukrainians, Turkmen and Turks.

### PRINCIPAL TOWNS

(estimated population at 1 January 1999)

| | | | | |
|---|---:|---|---|---:|
| Tashkent (capital) . | 2,142,700 | Chirchik . . . | | 145,600 |
| Namangan . . | 376,600 | Margilan . . . | | 143,600 |
| Samarkand . . | 362,300 | Urgench . . . | | 139,100 |
| Andizhan . . . | 323,900 | Angren . . . | | 128,600 |
| Bukhara . . . | 237,900 | Jizak . . . . | | 126,400 |
| Nukus . . . . | 199,000 | Navoi . . . . | | 117,600 |
| Karshi . . . . | 197,600 | Almalyk . . . | | 115,100 |
| Kokand . . . | 192,500 | Termez . . . | | 111,500 |
| Fergana . . . | 182,800 | | | |

Source: UN, *Demographic Yearbook.*

**Mid-2001** (UN estimate, incl. suburbs): Tashkent 2,157,000 (Source: UN, *World Urbanization Prospects: The 2001 Revision*).

### BIRTHS, MARRIAGES AND DEATHS

| | Registered live births | | Registered marriages | | Registered deaths | |
|---|---:|---:|---:|---:|---:|---:|
| | Number | Rate (per 1,000) | Number | Rate (per 1,000) | Number | Rate (per 1,000) |
| 1994 . . | 657,725 | 29.5 | 176,287 | 7.9 | 148,423 | 6.7 |
| 1995 . . | 677,999 | 29.9 | 170,828 | 7.5 | 145,439 | 6.4 |
| 1996 . . | 634,842 | 27.4 | 171,662 | 7.4 | 144,829 | 6.3 |
| 1997 . . | 602,694 | 25.6 | 181,126 | 7.7 | 137,331 | 5.8 |
| 1999*† . | 553,745 | 23.1 | 170,525 | 7.1 | 140,526 | 5.9 |

* Provisional figures.

† Figures for 1998 are not available.

Source: UN, *Demographic Yearbook.*

**2001** (provisional figures): Registered live births 512,800 (birth rate 20.5 per 1,000); Registered marriages 170,100 (marriage rate 6.8 per 1,000); Registered deaths 131,740 (death rate 5.3 per 1,000) (Sources: UN, *Population and Vital Statistics Report*; Center for Economic Research, Tashkent).

**Expectation of life** (WHO estimates, years at birth): 65.5 (males 62.7; females 68.5) in 2001 (Source: WHO, *World Health Report*).

## EMPLOYMENT
(annual averages, '000 persons)

|  | 1998 | 1999 | 2000 |
|---|---|---|---|
| Agriculture* . . . . . . | 3,467 | 3,213 | 3,083 |
| Industry† . . . . . . . | 1,114 | 1,124 | 1,145 |
| Construction . . . . . | 573 | 640 | 676 |
| Transport and communications . | 362 | 370 | 382 |
| Trade and catering‡ . . . . | 717 | 735 | 754 |
| Other services . . . . . | 1,976 | 2,042 | 2,042 |
| Housing, public utilities and personal services . . . . | 235 | 240 | 246 |
| Health care, social security, physical culture and sports . . | 502 | 538 | 567 |
| Education, culture and art . . . | 1,073 | 1,094 | 1,120 |
| Banking and insurance . . . . | 50 | 48 | 51 |
| General administration . . . . | 111 | 122 | 126 |
| Information and computer services | 5 | — | — |
| **Total** (incl. others) . . . . . | 8,800 | 8,885 | 8,983 |

* Including forestry.

† Comprising manufacturing (except printing and publishing), mining and quarrying, electricity, gas, water, logging and fishing.

‡ Including material and technical supply.

Source: Centre for Economic Research, Tashkent; *Uzbek Economic Trends*.

**2001** ('000 persons): Total employed 9,136 (Agriculture 3,062; Industry 1,160; Other 4,914) (Source: Asian Development Bank, *Key Indicators of Developing Asian and Pacific Countries*).

**2002** ('000 persons): Total employed 9,333 (Agriculture 3,030; Industry 1,186; Other 5,117) (Source: Asian Development Bank, *Key Indicators of Developing Asian and Pacific Countries*).

# Health and Welfare

## KEY INDICATORS

| | |
|---|---|
| Total fertility rate (children per woman, 2001) . . . . . | 2.5 |
| Under-5 mortality rate (per 1,000 live births, 2001) . . . | 68 |
| HIV/AIDS (% of persons aged 15–49, 2001) . . . . . . | <0.10 |
| Physicians (per 1,000 head, 1998) . . . . . . . | 3.09 |
| Hospital beds (per 1,000 head, 1999) . . . . . . | 8.31 |
| Health expenditure (2000): US $ per head (PPP) . . . . | 86 |
| Health expenditure (2000): % of GDP . . . . . | 3.7 |
| Health expenditure (2000): public (% of total) . . . . | 77.5 |
| Access to water (% of persons, 2000) . . . . . . . | 85 |
| Access to sanitation (% of persons, 2000) . . . . | 100 |
| Human Development Index (2001): ranking . . . . . | 101 |
| Human Development Index (2001): value . . . . . | 0.729 |

For sources and definitions, see explanatory note on p. vi.

# Agriculture

## PRINCIPAL CROPS
('000 metric tons)

|  | 1999 | 2000 | 2001 |
|---|---|---|---|
| Wheat . . . . . . . . . | 3,601.8 | 3,521.7 | 3,786.0 |
| Rice (paddy) . . . . . . | 420.8 | 154.8 | 81.6 |
| Barley* . . . . . . . | 84.5 | 80.0 | 58 |
| Maize . . . . . . . . | 167.9 | 131.4 | 100.0* |
| Sorghum* . . . . . . . | 21 | 20 | 15 |
| Potatoes . . . . . . . | 657.8 | 731.1 | 735.5 |
| Sugar beet . . . . . . | 225 | 215* | 104* |
| Dry broad beans* . . . . . | 16 | 14 | 12 |
| Cottonseed . . . . . . | 3,600 | 3,002 | 3,275 |
| Other oilseeds† . . . . . | 22.1 | 41.6 | 35.5 |
| Cabbages* . . . . . . . | 900 | 878 | 921 |
| Tomatoes* . . . . . . . | 1,020 | 994 | 1,040 |
| Cucumbers and gherkins* . . . | 278 | 271 | 284 |
| Dry onions* . . . . . . | 151 | 146 | 154 |
| Garlic* . . . . . . . | 27 | 25 | 26 |
| Carrots* . . . . . . . | 35 | 34 | 40 |
| Other vegetables* . . . . . | 270 | 299 | 313 |
| Apples* . . . . . . | 342 | 549 | 555 |
| Pears* . . . . . . . | 13.9 | 22.3 | 22.6 |
| Apricots* . . . . . . | 11 | 17 | 18 |
| Peaches and nectarines* . . . | 29.0 | 47.0 | 47.5 |
| Plums* . . . . . . . | 62 | 99.5 | 101.0 |
| Grapes . . . . . . . | 344.0 | 624.2 | 573.8 |
| Watermelons‡ . . . . . . | 517.6 | 451.4 | 459.9 |
| Other fruits and berries* . . . | 19 | 32 | 33 |
| Tobacco (leaves)* . . . . . | 19 | 19 | 19 |
| Jute† . . . . . . . . | 21 | 20 | 21 |
| Cotton (lint) . . . . . . | 1,021 | 1,000* | 1,015 |

* Unofficial figure(s).

† FAO estimates.

‡ Including melons, pumpkins and squash.

Source: FAO.

## LIVESTOCK
('000 head at 1 January)

|  | 1999 | 2000 | 2001 |
|---|---|---|---|
| Horses* . . . . . . . | 155 | 155 | 150 |
| Asses* . . . . . . . . | 165 | 160 | 165 |
| Cattle . . . . . . . | 5,225 | 5,268 | 5,344 |
| Camels* . . . . . . . | 28 | 25 | 28 |
| Pigs . . . . . . . . | 80 | 80 | 89 |
| Sheep† . . . . . . . | 7,840 | 8,000 | 8,100 |
| Goats† . . . . . . . | 884 | 886 | 830 |
| Chickens . . . . . . | 13,935 | 14,407 | 14,420 |
| Turkeys* . . . . . . . | 400 | 380 | 380 |
| Rabbits* . . . . . . . | 90,000 | 80,000 | 90,000 |

* FAO estimates.

† Unofficial figure(s).

Source: FAO.

**LIVESTOCK PRODUCTS**
('000 metric tons)

| | 1999 | 2000 | 2001 |
|---|---|---|---|
| Beef and veal* . . . . . | 372 | 390 | 398 |
| Mutton, lamb and goat meat* . . | 73.0 | 79.4 | 81.0 |
| Pig meat* . . . . . . . | 19.8 | 14.6 | 14.7 |
| Poultry meat*. . . . . . | 16.3 | 16.1 | 16.4 |
| Other meat† . . . . . . | 1.4 | 1.9 | 1.9 |
| Cows' milk . . . . . . | 3,543 | 3,633 | 3,667 |
| Sheep's milk* . . . . . . | 20 | 24 | 24 |
| Goats' milk* . . . . . . | 63 | 66 | 63 |
| Cheese† . . . . . . . | 16.1 | 17.1 | 16.8 |
| Butter . . . . . . . . | 3.0† | 2.2 | 3.0† |
| Hen eggs* . . . . . . . | 68.1 | 68.9 | 72.1 |
| Other poultry eggs* . . . . | 1.5 | 1.5 | 1.7 |
| Honey† . . . . . . . . | 2.4 | 2.3 | 2.4 |
| Raw silk (incl. waste) . . . | 0.9* | 1.0† | 1.2† |
| Wool: greasy . . . . . . | 15.7 | 15.8 | 15.9 |
| Wool: scoured . . . . . . | 9.4 | 9.5 | 9.5 |
| Cattle hides (fresh) . . . . | 40.9 | 43.1 | 43.9 |
| Sheepskins (fresh) . . . . | 8.8 | 9.1 | 9.3 |

* Unofficial figure(s).
† FAO estimate(s).

Source: FAO.

# Fishing

(metric tons, live weight)

| | 1998 | 1999 | 2000 |
|---|---|---|---|
| Capture . . . . . . . | 2,799 | 2,871 | 3,387 |
|   Freshwater bream . . . . | 387 | 353 | 335 |
|   Common carp . . . . . . | 804 | 826 | 617 |
|   Goldfish . . . . . . . | 300 | 300 | 400 |
|   Roach . . . . . . . | 392 | 613 | 1,035 |
|   Silver carp . . . . . . | 249 | 322 | 586 |
| Aquaculture . . . . . . | 6,966 | 5,665 | 5,142 |
|   Common carp . . . . . . | 858 | 674 | 592 |
|   Silver carp . . . . . . | 3,570 | 2,899 | 2,576 |
|   Bighead carp . . . . . . | 2,381 | 1,933 | 1,717 |
| **Total catch** . . . . . . | 9,765 | 8,536 | 8,529 |

Source: FAO, *Yearbook of Fishery Statistics*.

# Mining

(metric tons, unless otherwise indicated)

| | 1998 | 1999 | 2000* |
|---|---|---|---|
| Coal ('000 metric tons)† . . . . | 2,950 | 3,033 | 2,556 |
| Crude petroleum ('000 metric tons)‡ . . . . . . . | 8,100 | 8,100 | 7,500 |
| Natural gas (million cu metres) . | 54,800 | 55,600 | 55,600 |
| Copper ore§ . . . . . . | n.a. | 91,600 | 91,800 |
| Tungsten ore§‖ . . . . . | 200 | 0 | 0 |
| Molybdenum ore§‖ . . . . | 350 | 350 | 350 |
| Silver ore (kilograms)§ . . . . | 70,000‖ | 88,700 | 89,900 |
| Uranium ore§ . . . . . . | 2,000 | 2,159 | 2,054 |
| Gold (kilograms)§ . . . . | 80,000 | 66,028 | 62,276 |
| Kaolin ('000 metic tons)‖ . . . | 5,500 | 5,500 | 5,333 |
| Fluorspar . . . . . . . | 80,000‖ | 0 | 0 |
| Feldspar . . . . . . . | n.a. | 300 | 4,300 |

* Preliminary figures.
† Including lignite and brown coal.
‡ Including gas condensate.
§ Figures refer to the metal content of ores.
‖ Estimated production.

Source: mainly US Geological Survey.

**2001** ('000 metric tons, unless otherwise indicated): Coal 2,711; Crude petroleum 7,256; Natural gas (million cu metres) 57,000 (Source: Asian Development Bank, *Key Indicators of Developing Asian and Pacific Countries*).

**2002** ('000 metric tons, unless otherwise indicated): Coal 2,737; Crude petroleum 7,241; Natural gas (million cu metres) 58,000 (Source: Asian Development Bank, *Key Indicators of Developing Asian and Pacific Countries*).

**Gold** (metric tons): 85.4 in 2001 (Source: Gold Fields Mineral Services, *Gold Survey 2002*).

# Industry

## SELECTED PRODUCTS
('000 metric tons, unless otherwise indicated)

| | 1995 | 1996 | 1997 |
|---|---|---|---|
| Ethyl alcohol ('000 hectolitres) . . | 181 | 247 | 357 |
| Wine ('000 hectolitres) . . . . | 801 | 848 | 794 |
| Beer ('000 hectolitres) . . . . | 724 | 677 | 619 |
| Cigarettes (million) . . . . . | 2,742 | 5,172 | 8,521 |
| Wool yarn (pure and mixed) . . | 3.3 | 2.7 | 2.3 |
| Cotton yarn (pure and mixed) . . | 103.2 | 105.2 | 114.3 |
| Woven cotton fabrics (million sq m) | 456 | 445 | 425 |
| Woven silk fabrics ('000 sq m) . | 43,980 | 28,144 | 16,369 |
| Woven jute fabrics ('000 sq m) . . | 4,759 | 447 | 346 |
| Knotted wool carpets and rugs ('000 sq m) . . . . . . . | 1,982 | 1,555 | 1,241 |
| Footwear, excl. rubber ('000 pairs) | 5,654 | 5,591 | 5,547 |
| Sulphuric acid . . . . . . | 1,016 | 984 | 870 |
| Nitric acid . . . . . . . | 10 | 17 | 17 |
| Phosphoric acid . . . . . . | 149.0 | 179.7 | 113.6 |
| Nitrogenous fertilizers (a)* . . . | 775 | 835† | 826† |
| Phosphate fertilizers (b)* . . . | 168 | 194† | 129† |
| Motor spirit (petrol) . . . . | 1,213 | 1,202 | 1,344 |
| Gas-diesel (distillate fuel) oils . . | 2,105 | 1,861 | 2,035 |
| Residual fuel oils . . . . . . | 2,082 | 2,181 | 1,979 |
| Lubricating oils . . . . . . | 208 | 267 | 231 |
| Rubber footwear ('000 pairs) . . | 2,102 | 3,584 | 4,810 |
| Clay building bricks (million) . . | 1,185 | 1,038 | 969 |
| Quicklime . . . . . . . | 241 | 227 | 185 |
| Cement . . . . . . . | 3,419 | 3,277 | 3,286 |
| Domestic refrigerators ('000) . . | 19 | 13 | 13 |
| Domestic washing machines ('000) . | 14 | 4 | 4 |
| Television receivers ('000) . . | 65 | 140 | 269 |
| Electric energy (million kWh) . . | 47,453 | 45,418 | 46,054 |

\* Production in terms of (a) nitrogen; (b) phosphoric acid.
† Official figure.

Source: UN, *Industrial Commodity Statistics Yearbook*.

**1998** ('000 metric tons, unless otherwise indicated): Footwear, excl. rubber ('000 pairs) 5,000; Phosphate fertilizers 141; Motor spirit (petrol) 1,603; Gas-diesel (distillate fuel) oils 2,227; Residual fuel oils 1,977; Lubricating oils 229; Cement 3,358; Domestic refrigerators ('000) 16; Television receivers ('000) 192; Electric energy (million kWh) 45,935.

**1999** ('000 metric tons, unless otherwise indicated): Phosphate fertilizers 171; Motor spirit (petrol) 1,638; Gas-diesel (distillate fuel) oils 2,220; Residual fuel oils 1,750; Lubricating oils 223; Cement 3,331; Electric energy (million kWh) 45,372.

**2000** ('000 metric tons, unless otherwise indicated): Phosphate fertilizers 116; Cement 3,284; Electric energy (million kWh) 46,864.

**2001:** Cement ('000 metric tons) 3,722; Electric energy (million kWh) 47,961.

**2002:** Cement ('000 metric tons) 3,927.

Sources (1998–2002): partly UN, *Industrial Commodity Statistics Yearbook* and Asian Development Bank, *Key Indicators of Developing Asian and Pacific Countries*.

# Finance

## CURRENCY AND EXCHANGE RATES

**Monetary Units**
100 teen = 1 sum.

**Sterling, Dollar and Euro Equivalents** (28 February 2003)
£1 sterling = 1,519.9 sum;
US $1 = 960.3 sum;
€1 = 890.7 sum;
10,000 sum = £6.58 = $10.41 = €11.22.

**Average Exchange Rate** (sum per US $)
1997   66.26
1998   94.48
1999   124.64

Note: Prior to the introduction of the sum (see below), Uzbekistan used a transitional currency, the sum-coupon. This had been introduced in November 1993 to circulate alongside (and initially at par with) the Russian (formerly Soviet) rouble. Following the dissolution of the USSR in December 1991, Russia and several other former Soviet republics retained the rouble as their monetary unit. The Russian rouble ceased to be legal tender in Uzbekistan from 15 April 1994. On 1 July 1994 a permanent currency, the sum, was introduced to replace the sum-coupon at 1 sum per 1,000 coupons. The initial exchange rate was set at US $1 = 7.00 sum. Sum-coupons continued to circulate, but from 15 October 1994 the sum became the sole legal tender. On 15 October 2003 the sum became fully convertible.

## STATE BUDGET
(million sum*)

| Revenue | 1997† | 1998* | 1999‖ |
|---|---|---|---|
| Taxes on income and profits . . | 109,142 | 138,674 | 186,729 |
| Enterprise profit tax . . . | 70,177 | 83,001 | 99,114 |
| Individual income tax . . . | 38,965 | 50,569 | 77,511 |
| Taxes on domestic goods and services . . . . . . . | 132,289 | 216,205 | 306,928 |
| Value-added tax . . . . . | 73,339 | 133,076 | 167,334 |
| Excises . . . . . . . | 58,950 | 83,128 | 139,595 |
| Property, mining and land taxes . | 23,528 | 52,558 | 73,838 |
| Customs duties and export taxes . | 3,104 | 5,519 | 7,489 |
| **Total** (incl. others) . . . . . | 293,676 | 440,140 | 611,897 |

| Expenditure | 1997† | 1998†‡ | 1999‖° |
|---|---|---|---|
| National economy . . . . . | 39,898 | 54,700 | 67,834 |
| Social and cultural services . . . | 111,180 | 167,100 | 240,416 |
| Education . . . . . . . | 69,267 | 107,484 | 171,376 |
| Health and sports . . . . | 31,907 | 44,649 | 53,510 |
| Other subsidies and transfers to population . . . . . . . | 31,064 | 44,990 | 68,500 |
| Services . . . . . . . | 6,121 | 15,003 | 19,345 |
| Allowances . . . . . . | 23,354 | 26,887 | 42,240 |
| Public transfers . . . . . | 1,590 | 3,100 | 4,916 |
| State authority and administration . | 7,951 | 11,000 | 14,457 |
| Other purposes§ . . . . . | 55,087 | 90,268 | 107,065 |
| Investments . . . . . . | 72,170 | 94,600 | 122,347 |
| **Total** . . . . . . . . | 317,350 | 472,244 | 633,085 |

\* Excluding the accounts of extrabudgetary funds.
† Including the former external sector budget.
‡ Excluding net lending (million sum): 16,052 in 1998.
§ Including defence, public order and safety.
‖ IMF estimates.

**2000** (million sum): Total revenue 910,434; Total expenditure 942,379 (Source: Asian Development Bank, *Key Indicators of Developing Asian and Pacific Countries*).

## INTERNATIONAL RESERVES
(US $ million at 31 December)

| | 1998 | 1999 | 2000 |
|---|---|---|---|
| **Total** . . . . . . . . . | 1,168.0 | 1,242.0 | 1,100 |

Source: Asian Development Bank, *Key Indicators of Developing Asian and Pacific Countries*.

## MONEY SUPPLY
(million sum at 31 December)

|  | 1997 | 1998 | 1999 |
|---|---|---|---|
| Currency outside banks . . . . | 71,639 | 101,709 | 137,306 |
| Demand deposits at deposit money banks . . . . . . . | 53,728 | 65,698 | 91,009 |
| **Total money** . . . . . . . | 125,367 | 167,407 | 228,315 |

Source: Asian Development Bank, *Key Indicators of Developing Asian and Pacific Countries.*

## COST OF LIVING
(Consumer Price Index; base: December 1994 = 100)

|  | 1998 | 1999 | 2000 |
|---|---|---|---|
| Food . . . . . . | 492.5 | 619.0 | 737.4 |
| Other goods . . . . . | 372.6 | 493.2 | 667.1 |
| Services . . . . . . | 1,124.2 | 1,615.3 | 2,382.1 |
| **All items** . . . . . . . | 508.3 | 655.9 | 819.6 |

Source: Center for Economic Research, Tashkent, *Uzbek Economic Trends.*

## NATIONAL ACCOUNTS
(million sum at current prices)

### Expenditure on the Gross Domestic Product

|  | 1999 | 2000 | 2001 |
|---|---|---|---|
| Government final consumption expenditure . . . . . | 439,258 | 607,265 | 454,148 |
| Private final consumption expenditure . . . . . . | 1,322,109 | 2,016,386 | 3,485,119 |
| Increase in stocks . . . . | −214,509 | −143,785 | −334,463 |
| Gross fixed capital formation . . | 578,685 | 780,991 | 1,375,378 |
| **Total domestic expenditure** | 2,125,543 | 3,260,857 | 4,980,182 |
| Exports of goods and services . . | 462,693 | 863,987 | 1,517,478 |
| *Less* Imports of goods and services | 459,576 | 869,278 | 1,572,391 |
| **GDP in purchasers' values** . . | 2,128,660 | 3,255,566 | 4,925,269 |

Source: Asian Development Bank, *Key Indicators of Developing Asian and Pacific Countries.*

### Gross Domestic Product by Economic Activity

|  | 2000 | 2001 | 2002 |
|---|---|---|---|
| Agriculture and forestry . . | 978,507 | 1,476,256 | 2,283,751 |
| Mining and quarrying . . . ⎫ | | | |
| Manufacturing . . . . . | 462,423 | 696,229 | 1,052,213 |
| Electricity, gas and water . . ⎭ | | | |
| Construction . . . . . . | 196,180 | 286,489 | 369,588 |
| Trade . . . . . . . | 315,556 | 511,411 | 731,254 |
| Transport and communications | 250,565 | 371,259 | 612,943 |
| Finance . . . . . . | 123,851 | 196,414 ⎫ | |
| Public administration . . . | 96,447 | 164,684 ⎬ | 1,545,962 |
| Other services . . . . | 424,396 | 638,458 ⎭ | |
| **GDP at factor cost** . . . | 2,847,925 | 4,341,200 | 6,595,711 |
| Indirect taxes . . . . . ⎫ | 407,641 | 584,070 | 873,636 |
| *Less* Subsidies . . . . ⎭ | | | |
| **GDP in purchasers' values** . | 3,255,566 | 4,925,270 | 7,469,347 |

Source: Asian Development Bank, *Key Indicators of Developing Asian and Pacific Countries.*

## BALANCE OF PAYMENTS
(US $ million)

|  | 1996 | 1997 | 1998 |
|---|---|---|---|
| Exports of goods f.o.b. . . . . | 3,534 | 3,695 | 2,888 |
| Imports of goods f.o.b. . . . . | −4,240 | −3,767 | −2,717 |
| **Trade balance** . . . . . . | −706 | −72 | 171 |
| Services and other income (net) . | −272 | −540 | −252 |
| **Balance on goods, services and income** . . . . . . . | −978 | −612 | −81 |
| Current transfers (net) . . . . | −2 | 29 | 43 |
| **Current balance** . . . . . | −980 | −584 | −39 |
| Direct investment (net) . . . . | 90 | 167 | 176 |
| Other capital (net) . . . . | 80 | −507 | −802 |
| Net errors and omissions . . . | 296 | −185 | — |
| **Overall balance** . . . . . | −50 | −480 | 1 |

# External Trade

## PRINCIPAL COMMODITIES
(US $ million)

| Imports f.o.b. | 1998 | 1999 | 2000 |
|---|---|---|---|
| Chemicals and plastics . . . . | 407.2 | 363.0 | 399.5 |
| Metals . . . . . . . . | 303.6 | 245.4 | 253.5 |
| Machinery and equipment . . . | 1,553.7 | 1,393.5 | 1,044.1 |
| Food products . . . . . . | 512.2 | 408.1 | 361.1 |
| Energy products . . . . . | 16.3 | 66.6 | 112.7 |
| **Total** (incl. others) . . . . | 3,288.7 | 3,110.7 | 2,696.4 |

| Exports f.o.b. | 1998 | 1999 | 2000 |
|---|---|---|---|
| Cotton fibre . . . . . . | 1,361.0 | 883.7 | 897.1 |
| Chemicals and plastics . . . . | 51.7 | 101.8 | 93.4 |
| Metals . . . . . . . . | 180.7 | 138.9 | 216.7 |
| Machinery and equipment . . . | 146.6 | 103.2 | 111.8 |
| Food products . . . . . . | 111.9 | 206.7 | 176.4 |
| Energy products . . . . . | 277.8 | 371.5 | 335.2 |
| **Total** (incl. others) . . . . | 3,528.2 | 3,235.8 | 3,264.7 |

Source: Center for Economic Research, Tashkent, *Uzbek Economic Trends.*

## PRINCIPAL TRADING PARTNERS
(US $ million)

| Imports | 2000 | 2001 | 2002 |
|---|---|---|---|
| France . . . . . . . . | 73.4 | 118.8 | 42.8 |
| Germany . . . . . . . | 233.3 | 227.2 | 211.4 |
| Kazakhstan . . . . . . | 153.1 | 163.7 | 177.6 |
| Kyrgyzstan . . . . . | 98.3 | 52.7 | 31.5 |
| Korea, Republic . . . . | 253.5 | 380.3 | 412.7 |
| Russia . . . . . . . | 301.9 | 400.2 | 486.9 |
| Tajikistan . . . . . . | 107.6 | 95.9 | 104.1 |
| Turkey . . . . . . . | 90.9 | 98.7 | 107.1 |
| Ukraine . . . . . . | 125.4 | 138.4 | 150.3 |
| USA . . . . . . . | 182.7 | 162.5 | 151.9 |
| **Total** (incl. others) . . . . . | 2,078.1 | 2,303.4 | 2,370.1 |

| Exports | 2000 | 2001 | 2002 |
|---|---|---|---|
| Germany . . . . . . . | 67.6 | 56.4 | 44.2 |
| Italy . . . . . . . | 172.8 | 155.2 | 157.7 |
| Kazakhstan . . . . . . | 66.6 | 72.9 | 79.1 |
| Korea, Republic . . . . | 94.5 | 124.3 | 134.9 |
| Kyrgyzstan . . . . . | 68.4 | 60.7 | 63.6 |
| Poland . . . . . . . | 36.7 | 82.3 | 89.3 |
| Russia . . . . . . . | 602.0 | 527.2 | 327.8 |
| Tajikistan . . . . . . | 168.7 | 137.0 | 148.7 |
| Turkey . . . . . . . | 78.0 | 32.8 | 35.6 |
| Ukraine . . . . . . | 161.8 | 178.0 | 193.2 |
| **Total** (incl. others) . . . . . | 2,135.3 | 2,028.1 | 1,900.0 |

Source: Asian Development Bank, *Key Indicators of Developing Asian and Pacific Countries.*

# Transport

**RAILWAYS**
(traffic)

|  | 1998 | 1999 | 2000 |
|---|---|---|---|
| Passenger-km (million) . . . | 2 | 2 | 2 |
| Freight ton-km (million) . . . | 16 | 14 | 15 |

Source: UN, *Statistical Yearbook*.

**2001:** Passenger journeys (million) 15; Passenger-km (million) 2; Freight transported (million metric tons) 41.5; Freight ton-km (million) 15.7 (Source: Railway Gazette, *Railway Directory*).

**CIVIL AVIATION**
(estimated traffic on scheduled services)

|  | 1997 | 1998 | 1999 |
|---|---|---|---|
| Kilometres flown (million) . . . | 23 | 33 | 37 |
| Passengers carried ('000) . . . | 1,566 | 1,401 | 1,658 |
| Passenger-km (million) . . . | 3,460 | 2,609 | 3,328 |
| Total ton-km (million) . . . | 321 | 284 | 370 |

Source: UN, *Statistical Yearbook*.

# Tourism

**FOREIGN VISITOR ARRIVALS**
('000, incl. excursionists)

|  | 1996 | 1997 | 1998 |
|---|---|---|---|
| **Total** . . . . . . . . . | 174 | 253 | 272 |

**Tourism receipts** (US $ million): 15 in 1996; 19 in 1997; 21 in 1998.

Source: World Tourism Organization.

# Communications Media

|  | 2000 | 2001 | 2002 |
|---|---|---|---|
| Telephones ('000 main lines in use) | 1,655.0 | 1,663.0 | 1,670.0 |
| Mobile cellular telephones ('000 subscribers). . . . . . . | 53.1 | 62.8 | 186.9 |
| Internet users ('000) . . . . . | 120.0 | 150.0 | 275.0 |

Source: International Telecommunication Union.

**Book production:** 1,003 titles and 30,914,000 copies in 1996 (Source: UNESCO, *Statistical Yearbook*).

**Daily newspapers:** 3 titles and 75,000 copies (average circulation) in 1996 (Source: UNESCO, *Statistical Yearbook*).

**Non-daily newspapers:** 350 titles and 1,404,000 copies (average circulation) in 1996 (Source: UNESCO, *Statistical Yearbook*).

**Other periodicals:** 81 titles and 684,000 copies (average circulation) in 1996 (Source: UNESCO, *Statistical Yearbook*).

**Radio receivers** ('000 in use): 10,800 in 1997 (Source: UNESCO, *Statistical Yearbook*).

**Television receivers** ('000 in use): 6,800 in 2000 (Source: International Telecommunication Union).

**Facsimile machines** (number in use): 2,720 in 2000 (Source: International Telecommunication Union).

# Education

(1994/95, unless otherwise indicated)

|  | Institutions | Teachers | Students |
|---|---|---|---|
| Pre-primary . . . . . . | n.a. | 96,100 | 1,071,400 |
| Primary . . . . . . | | 92,400 | 1,905,693 |
| Secondary: | 9,788 | | |
| general . . . . . . . | | 454,400* | 6,076,400* |
| teacher training . . . . | n.a. | 2,464† | 35,411† |
| vocational . . . . . . | 440‡ | 7,900 | 214,500 |
| Higher. . . . . . . . | 61 | 18,400 | 183,600 |

* 2001.
† 1993.
‡ 1992/93.

Sources: UNESCO, *Statistical Yearbook*; and Center for Economic Research, Tashkent.

**Adult literacy rate** (UNESCO estimates): 99.2% (males 99.6%; females 98.9%) in 2001 (Source: UN Development Programme, *Human Development Report*).

# Directory

## The Constitution

A new Constitution was adopted by the Supreme Soviet on 8 December 1992. It declares Uzbekistan to be a secular, democratic and presidential republic. Basic human rights are guaranteed.

The highest legislative body is the Oly Majlis (Supreme Assembly), comprising 250 deputies. It is elected for a term of five years. Parliament may be dissolved by the President (by agreement with the Constitutional Court). The Oly Majlis enacts normal legislation and constitutional legislation, elects its own officials, the judges of the higher courts and the Chairman of the State Committee for Environmental Protection. It confirms the President's appointments to ministerial office, the procuracy-general and the governorship of the Central Bank. It must ratify international treaties, changes to borders and presidential decrees on emergency situations. Legislation may be initiated by the deputies, by the President, by the higher courts, by the Procurator-General and by the Autonomous Republic of Karakalpakstan.

The President of the Republic, who is directly elected by the people for a five-year term, is Head of State and holds supreme executive power. An individual may be elected President for a maximum of two consecutive terms. The President is required to form and supervise the Cabinet of Ministers, appointing the Prime Minister and Ministers, subject to confirmation by the Oly Majlis. The President also nominates the candidates for appointment to the higher courts and

certain offices of state, subject to confirmation by the Oly Majlis. The President appoints the judges of the lower courts and the khokims (governors) of the regions. Legislation may be initiated, reviewed and returned to the Oly Majlis by the President, who must promulgate all laws. The President may dissolve the Oly Majlis. The President is also Commander-in-Chief of the Armed Forces and may declare a state of emergency or a state of war (subject to confirmation by the Oly Majlis within three days).

The Cabinet of Ministers is the Government of the republic; it is subordinate to the President, who appoints its Prime Minister, Deputy Prime Ministers and Ministers, subject to the approval of the legislature. Local government is carried out by elected councils and appointed khokims, the latter having significant personal authority and responsibility.

The exercise of judicial power is independent of government. The higher courts, of which the judges are nominated by the President and confirmed by the Oly Majlis, consist of the Constitutional Court, the Supreme Court and the High Economic Court. There is also a Supreme Court of the Autonomous Republic of Karakalpakstan. Lower courts, including economic courts, are based in the regions, districts and towns. The Procurator-General's office is responsible for supervising the observance of the law.

Note: In accordance with the outcome of a referendum held in January 2002, in April the Oly Majlis approved a resolution to extend immediately the presidential term of office from five years to seven, and adopted a resolution stipulating the procedure for the election in December 2004 of a new, bicameral legislature. It was agreed that the lower legislative chamber would consist of elected deputies; the upper chamber would comprise members of local councils and 16 'widely respected' citizens. Further constitutional amendments were adopted in April 2003.

# The Government

## HEAD OF STATE

**President of the Republic:** ISLAM A. KARIMOV (elected 24 March 1990; re-elected, by direct popular vote, 29 December 1991; term of office extended to 2000, by popular referendum, 27 March 1995; re-elected, by direct popular vote, 9 January 2000).

## CABINET OF MINISTERS
(October 2003)

**Prime Minister:** OTKIR S. SULTANOV.

**First Deputy Prime Minister:** KOZIM N. TULYAGANOV.

**Deputy Prime Minister and Minister of Macroeconomics and Statistics:** RUSTAM S. AZIMOV.

**Deputy Prime Minister and Minister of Agriculture and Water Resources:** ABDUVOHID JORAYEV.

**Deputy Prime Minister and Minister of Energy and Electrification:** VALERII Y. OTAYEV.

**Deputy Prime Minister and Chairman of the State Committee for Women's Affairs:** DILBAR GHULOMOVA.

**Deputy Prime Minister and Minister of Foreign Economic Relations:** ELYOR GANIYEV.

**Deputy Prime Ministers:** ANATOLII N. ISAYEV, KHAMIDULLO S. KARAMATOV, MIRABROR Z. USMONOV, ALISHER A. AZIZKHOJAYEV, UKTAM ISMAILOV, RUSTAM YUNOSOV.

**Minister of Defence:** Maj.-Gen. KHODIR GUFUROVICH GULOMOV.

**Minister of Foreign Affairs:** SODYK SAFAYEV.

**Minister of Justice:** ABDUSAMAD A. POLVONZODA.

**Minister of Labour and Social Security:** OKILJON OBIDOV.

**Minister of Internal Affairs:** ZOKIRJON A. ALMATOV.

**Minister of Finance:** MAMARIZO B. NORMURODOV.

**Minister of Culture:** HAIRULLA JURAYEV.

**Minister of Higher Education and Specialized Secondary Education:** Dr SAIDAHROR GULYAMOV.

**Minister of Health:** FERUZ G. NAZIROV.

**Minister for Emergency Situations:** BAKHTIYOR SUBANOV.

**Minister of Education:** RISBOY HAYDAROVICH JORAYEV.

**Minister of Communications:** FAHTULLAH ABDULLAYEV.

## MINISTRIES

**Office of the President:** 700163 Tashkent, pr. Uzbekistanskii 43; tel. (71) 139-54-04; fax (71) 139-53-25; e-mail presidents_office@press-service.uz; internet www.press-service.uz.

**Office of the Cabinet of Ministers:** 700008 Tashkent, Government House; tel. (71) 139-82-95; fax (71) 139-86-01.

**Ministry of Agriculture and Water Resources:** 700128 Tashkent, ul. Abdulla Qodyri 5A; tel. (712) 41-46-60; fax (712) 41-49-24.

**Ministry of Communications:** Tashkent, ul. Tolstoy 1A; tel. (71) 133-66-45.

**Ministry of Culture:** 700129 Tashkent, ul. Navoi 30; tel. (71) 139-49-57.

**Ministry of Defence:** 700000 Tashkent, ul. Academician Abdullayev 100; tel. (71) 133-66-67; fax (712) 68-48-67.

**Ministry of Education:** 700078 Tashkent, pl. Mustakillik 5; tel. (71) 139-42-14; fax (71) 139-11-73.

**Ministry for Emergency Situations:** Tashkent.

**Ministry of Finance:** 700008 Tashkent, pl. Mustakillik 5; tel. (71) 133-70-73; fax (71) 144-56-43.

**Ministry of Foreign Affairs:** 700029 Tashkent, pr. Uzbekistanskii 9; tel. (71) 133-64-75; fax (71) 139-15-17; e-mail root@relay.tiv.uz; internet www.mfa.uz.

**Ministry of Foreign Economic Relations:** Tashkent, Buyuk Ipak Yuli 75; tel. (712) 68-92-56.

**Ministry of Health:** 700000 Tashkent, ul. Navoi 4; tel. (712) 41-16-80; fax (712) 41-16-41.

**Ministry of Higher and Specialized Secondary Education:** 700078 Tashkent, Mustakillik maidony 5; tel. (71) 139-15-00; fax (71) 139-12-71.

**Ministry of Internal Affairs:** 700029 Tashkent, ul. Yunus Rajaby 1; tel. (71) 133-63-77; fax (71) 133-89-34.

**Ministry of Justice:** 700047 Tashkent, ul. Sailgokh 5; tel. (71) 133-13-05; fax (71) 133-50-39; e-mail adliya@mail.uznet.net; internet www.minjust.uz.

**Ministry of Labour and Social Security:** 700100 Tashkent, ul. Abdulla Avloni 20A; tel. (71) 139-41-24; fax (71) 139-41-56.

**Ministry of Macroeconomics and Statistics:** Tashkent, pr. Uzbekistanii 45A; tel. (71) 139-86-64.

### Principal State Committees

**National Security Service:** Tashkent; tel. (712) 33-56-48; Chair. Col-Gen. RUSTAM INOYATOV.

**Uzbek Association of Utilities Services:** Tashkent; Chair. UKTUR KHOLMUKHAMEDOV.

**State Committee for Architecture and Engineering:** 700011 Tashkent, Abay 6; tel. (71) 144-07-00; fax (71) 144-02-61; e-mail gkas@uzpak.uz; internet www.uzgkas.com; f. 1959; Chair. AZAMAT R. TOHTAYEV.

**State Committee for Border Protection:** Tashkent; Chair. GOFURJON TISHAYEV.

**State Committee for De-monopolization and Competition Development:** 700078 Tashkent, pl. Mustakillik 5; tel. (71) 139-15-42; fax (71) 139-46-70; e-mail devonhona@antimon.uz; internet www.antimon.uz; Chair. AZAMKHON U. BAKHRAMOV.

**State Committee for Forecasting and Statistics:** 700003 Tashkent, pr. Uzbekistanskii 45A; tel. (712) 39-82-16; fax (712) 39-86-39; Chair. RIM A. GINIYATULLIN.

**State Committee for Geology and Mineral Resources:** 700060 Tashkent, ul. Shevchenko 11; tel. (71) 133-46-03; fax (71) 133-18-01; e-mail gicenter@online.ru; f. 1926; Chair. NURMUKHAMMAD AKHMEDOV.

**State Committee for State Property Management and Entrepreneurship Support:** 700003 Tashkent, ul. Uzbekistanskii 55; tel. (71) 139-44-46; fax (71) 139-14-84; e-mail askarov@spc.gov.uz; internet www.spc.gov.uz; f. 1994; Chair. UKTAM K. ISMOILOV; First Dep. Chair. MAKHMUDJON A. ASKAROV.

**State Committee for Nature Protection:** 700128 Tashkent, ul. A. Kadiry 7; tel. (712) 41-04-42; fax (712) 41-39-90; e-mail uznature@gimli.com; Chair. ASKHAT SH. KHABIBULLAYEV.

**State Committee for Precious Metals:** 700019 Tashkent, pr. Turakorgan 26; tel. (712) 48-07-20; fax (712) 44-26-03; Chair. SH. NAZHIMOV.

**State Committee for Science and Technology:** 700017 Tashkent, Hadicha Suleymonova 29; tel. (71) 139-18-43; fax (71) 139-12-43; Chair. POLAT K. HABIBULLAYEV.

**State Committee for Women's Affairs:** Tashkent; Chair. DILBAR GHULOMOVA.

**State Customs Committee:** 700100 Tashkent, ul. Usmon Nasir 62; tel. (71) 136-07-55; fax (712) 53-39-40; Chair. RAVSHAN HAIDAROV.

**State Sports Committee:** Tashkent; Chair. BOKHODIR MAKHSITOV.

**State Statistics Committee:** Tashkent; Chair GHOFURJON QUDRATOV.

**State Taxation Committee:** 700195 Tashkent, ul. Abai 4; tel. (712) 41-78-70; Chair. JAMSHID SAYFIDDINOV.

# Legislature

## OLY MAJLIS
(Supreme Assembly)

### Supreme Assembly

700008 Tashkent, pl. Mustakillik 5; tel. (71) 139-87-49; fax (71) 139-41-51; internet www.gov.uz/oliy.

**Chairman:** ERKIN KH. KHALILOV.

**Deputy Chairmen:** UBBINIYAZ ASHIRBEKOV, BORIS BUGROV, BORITOSH SHODIYEVA, AKMOLZHON KHOSIMOV, MUSA T. ERNIYAZOV.

## General Election, 5 December and 19 December 1999*

| Parties, etc. | Seats |
|---|---|
| People's Democratic Party of Uzbekistan (PDPU) . . | 48 |
| Fidokorlar National Democratic Party . . . . . | 34 |
| Progress of the Fatherland . . . . . . . . | 20 |
| Adolat Social Democratic Party of Uzbekistan . . . | 11 |
| Milli Tiklanish Democratic Party . . . . . . | 10 |
| Citizens' groups . . . . . . . . . . | 16 |
| Local council nominees† . . . . . . . . | 110 |
| Vacant . . . . . . . . . . . . | 1 |
| **Total** . . . . . . . . . . . . | **250** |

* Five parties were permitted to contest the election; however, two opposition parties (Birlik and Erk) were refused permission to put forward candidates.

† The overwhelming majority of local council nominees were members of the PDPU.

# Local Government

Uzbekistan contained one Autonomous Republic (Karakalpakstan) and 13 oblasts (regions). There were further local subdivisions, the basic unit being the mahallah, the neighbourhood or commune. From January 1992 the main figure in local government was the khokim (governor), who was appointed as the chief executive figure in the region by the President of the Republic. There was also a regional soviet (council) of people's deputies.

**Andizhan Oblast:** 710020 Andizhan, ul. A. Fitrata 239; tel. (3742) 22-21-82; fax (74) 22-19-32; e-mail andwork@uzpak.uz; Khokim KOBILDZHON G. OBIDOV.

**Bukhara Oblast:** 705018 Bukhara, ul. I. Muminova 1; tel. (65) 3-55-77; fax (65) 3-03-95; e-mail vhsk@uzpak.uz; internet bukhara .uzpak.uz; Khokim SAMOIDDIN K. KHUSENOV.

**Dzhizak Oblast:** 708000 Dzhizak (Jisak), pr. Sh. Rashidova 63; tel. (72) 6-39-54; fax (72) 6-64-84; Khokim UBAIDULLAH YA. YAMANKULOV.

**Fergana Oblast:** 712083 Fergana, ul. A. Navoii 13; tel. (73) 24-30-63; Khokim ALISHER A. OTOBOYEV.

**Kashkadarin Oblast:** 730000 Karshi, pl. Mustakillik 1; tel. (75) 21-03-81; internet kash.uzpak.uz; Khokim NURIDDIN Z. ZAINIYEV.

**Khorezm Oblast:** 740000 Urgench, ul. Al-Khorezmii 29; tel. (62) 24-31-81; fax (62) 26-44-15.

**Namangan Oblast:** 716000 Namangan, ul. A. Rakhimova 57; tel. (69) 6-60-08; fax (69) 6-57-22; e-mail namangan1@uzpak.uz; internet naman.uzpak.uz; Khokim TULKIN O. ZHABBAROV.

**Navoin Oblast:** 706800 Navoin, ul. Druzhba Narodov 78A; tel. (79) 23-30-10; fax (79) 23-71-25; Khokim BAKHRIDDIN M. RUZIYEV.

**Samarkand Oblast:** 703011 Samarkand, Kuksoroi kuchasi 1; tel. (66) 35-03-42; Khokim SHAVKAT M. MIRZIYEYEV.

**Surkhandarin Oblast:** 732012 Termez, pl. At-Termizii 1; tel. (76) 2-87-58; Khokim TASHMIRZO U. KODIROV.

**Syrdarin Oblast:** 707000 Gulistan, ul. Mustakillik 60; tel. (67) 25-09-39; fax (67) 25-34-31; Khokim RAVSHAN KH. KHAIDAROV.

**Tashkent City Oblast:** 700060 Tashkent, Mirobadskii raion, ul. Movarounnakhr 3; tel. (71) 133-90-69; fax (71) 136-73-00; internet www.tn.uz; Khokim RUSTAM M. SHOABDURAKHMANOV.

**Tashkent Oblast:** 700060 Tashkent, Mirobadskii raion, ul. Movarounnakhr 17; tel. (71) 133-67-16; fax (71) 136-73-00; Khokim UMMAT M. MIRZAKULOV.

### AUTONOMOUS REPUBLIC

Karakalpakstan was ceded to the Russian Empire by the Khanate of Khiva in 1867. It thus formed part of the Bolshevik Russian Federation in the first years of Soviet rule, being an autonomous area within Kazakhstan. The Kara-Kalpak Autonomous Republic became an integral part of Uzbekistan in 1936. Karakalpakstan is the main habitation of the Kara-Kalpak ethnic minority, a Turkic group. The capital is Nukus, on the Amu-Dar'ya river. The territory is among the worst affected by the Aral Sea environmental problems, and was chosen as the site of a commitment to rehabilitation of the Sea by the states of Central Asia in September 1995 (the so-called Nukus Declaration). There is a directly elected President and a legislative Supreme Soviet.

**President of the Kara-Kalpak Autonomous Republic:** D. N. SHAMSHETOV, Karakalpakstan, Nukus.

**Council of Ministers:** 742000 Karakalpakstan, Nukus, Dustlik gazari 96; tel. (61) 22-05-01; Chair. TURSINBAI T. TANIPBERGENOV.

**Permanent Representation in Tashkent:** 70078 Tashkent, pl. Mustakillik 5; tel. (712) 39-40-72; fax (712) 39-48-48.

# Political Organizations

Following Uzbekistan's independence (achieved in August 1991), the ruling People's Democratic Party of Uzbekistan (PDPU) took increasingly repressive measures against opposition and Islamist parties; all religious political parties were banned in 1991, and in 1992 and 1993 the leading opposition groups, Birlik and Erk, were likewise outlawed. In October 1995 several opposition groups, including Birlik, Erk and Adolat, established a joint centre in Tashkent—the Democratic Opposition Co-ordinating Council—in united opposition to the Government (the Council ceased to function in March 1998). A new law on political parties was approved in 1996; among other provisions, the law prohibited the establishment of parties on a religious or ethnic basis and stipulated a minimum membership, per party, of 5,000 people (representing at least eight of the republic's 12 regions). Since independence a number of opposition elements have been based in Russia, in particular in Moscow.

**Adolat (Justice) Social Democratic Party of Uzbekistan:** Tashkent; f. 1995; advocates respect of human rights, improvement of social justice and consolidation of democratic reform; First Sec. ANWAR JURABAYEV; 6,000 mems.

**Birlik** (Unity): c/o Union of Writers of Uzbekistan, 700000 Tashkent, ul. Javakharlara Neru 1; tel. (712) 33-63-74; e-mail webmaster@birlik.net; internet www.birlik.net; f. 1988; leading opposition group, banned in 1992; registered as a social movement; Chair. Prof. ABDURAKHIM PULATOV.

**Erk** (Freedom): Tashkent; e-mail info@uzbekistanerk.org; internet www.uzbekistanerk.org; f. 1990; banned in 1993; Chair. MUHAMMAD SOLIKH (based in Russia); Sec.-Gen. OTANAZAR ORIPOV; 5,000 mems (1991).

**Fidokorlar (Self-Sacrificers') National Democratic Party:** Tashkent; f. 1998; merged with Watan Taraqqioti (Progress of the Fatherland) in Apr. 2000; pro-Government; First Sec. AHTAM TURSUNOV; 30,000 mems.

**Ishtiqlal Yoli** (Independence Path): Tashkent; f. 1994; Leader SHADI KARIMOV.

**Islamic Renaissance Party:** Tashkent; banned in 1991; advocates introduction of a political system based on the tenets of Islam; Leader ABDULLAH UTAYEV.

**Khalk Birliki (People's Unity) Movement:** Tashkent; f. 1995; pro-Government; Chair. TURABEK DOLIMOV.

**Milli Tiklanish (National Revival) Democratic Party:** Tashkent; f. 1995; pro-Government; Chair. AZIZ KAYUMOV.

**People's Democratic Party of Uzbekistan:** 700029 Tashkent, pl. Mustakillik 5/1; tel. (71) 139-83-11; fax (71) 133-59-34; f. 1991; successor of Communist Party of Uzbekistan; Leader ABDULKHAFIZ JALOLOV; c. 570,000 mems (Jan. 2002).

The militant Islamist group **Islamic Movement of Uzbekistan (IMU)** was founded in 1999 and its main leaders were TAKHIR YOLDOSHEV (a former leader of Adolat) and JUMABOY KHOJIYEV (known as Juma Namangoniy). Most active in the Fergana valley, it also operated in Kyrgyzstan and Tajikistan, and was believed to have close links with the al-Qa'ida (Base) organization of the militant Islamist leader Osama Bin Laden. It was banned by the Uzbek Government in 1999 and its leaders sentenced to death *in absentia* in 2000. It reportedly renamed itself the **Islamic Party of Turkestan** in 2001, apparently indicating a widening of its aims. However, Namongoniy was reportedly killed during the US-led military campaign in Afghanistan in late 2001 and the IMU's activities were believed to have been seriously curtailed.

# Diplomatic Representation

### EMBASSIES IN UZBEKISTAN

**Afghanistan:** 700047 Tashkent, ul. Gogolya 73; tel. (712) 34-84-58; fax (712) 34-84-65; e-mail afgemuz@mail.tps.uz; Ambassador ABDUL SAMAD.

**Algeria:** Tashkent, ul. Murtozayeva 6; Ambassador LASKRI KHASEN.

**Bangladesh:** 700015 Tashkent, ul. Kunayeva 17; tel. (71) 152-26-92; fax (71) 120-67-11; e-mail bdoot.tas@online.ru; Ambassador A. B. M. ABDUS SALAM.

**Belarus:** 700090 Tashkent, M. Torobiy Kuchasi 16; tel. (712) 55-69-43; fax (71) 139-82-70; e-mail uzbekistan@belembassy.org; Ambassador Dr NIKOLAI N. DEMCHUK.

**China, People's Republic:** 700047 Tashkent, ul. Yahyo Gulomoy 79; tel. (71) 136–08–51; fax (71) 133-47-35; e-mail chinaemb@bcc.com.uz; internet www.chinaembassy.uz; Ambassador ZHANG ZHIMING.

**Egypt:** 700115 Tashkent, ul. Chilanzarskaya 53; tel. (712) 77-39-91; fax (71) 120-64-52; Ambassador FARGHALI TAHA.

**France:** 700041 Tashkent, ul. Akhunbabayeva 25; tel. (71) 133-53-82; Ambassador JACQUES-ANDRÉ COSTILHES.

**Germany:** 700017 Tashkent, pr. Sharaf-Rashidov 15; tel. (71) 120-84-40; fax (71) 120-66-93; e-mail gerembuz@online.ru; internet www.germanembassy.uz; Ambassador MARTIN HECKER.

**India:** Tashkent, ul. A. Tolstogo 3; tel. (712) 33-82-67; fax (712) 36-19-76; Ambassador M. K. BHADRAKUMAR.

**Indonesia:** 700000 Tashkent, ul. Gogolya 73; tel. (712) 132-02-36; fax (712) 120-65-40; e-mail kbritash@online.ru; Ambassador HASYIM SALIH.

**Iran:** Tashkent, ul. Parkentskaya 20; tel. (712) 68-69-68; fax (712) 68-78-18; Ambassador MUHAMMAD FATHALI.

**Israel:** Tashkent, ul. Abdulla Kakhara 3; tel. (71) 120-58-08; fax (71) 120-58-12; e-mail info@tashkent.mafa.gov.il; Ambassador ZVI COHEN LITANT.

**Italy:** 700031 Tashkent, ul. Yusuf Xos Xojib 40; tel. (71) 152-11-19; fax (71) 120-66-06; e-mail ambital@online.ru; Ambassador ANGELO FERRI PERSIANI.

**Japan:** 700047 Tashkent, ul. Sadyk/Azimov 52/1; tel. (712) 33-51-42; fax (712) 89-15-14; Ambassador KIOKO NAKAYAMA.

**Kazakhstan:** 700015 Tashkent, ul. Chekhov 23; tel. (71) 152-16-54; fax (71) 152-16-50; e-mail kzembuz@silk.org.

**Korea, Democratic People's Republic:** Tashkent; Ambassador RI CHOL GWANG.

**Korea, Republic:** Tashkent, ul. Afrosiab 7; tel. (71) 152-31-51; fax (71) 120-62-48; Ambassador CHOI YOUNG-HA.

**Kyrgyzstan:** Tashkent, ul. Samatova 30; tel. and fax (712) 33-08-93; e-mail krembas@globalnet.uz.

**Latvia:** Tashkent, ul. Murtazayeva 6, Apt 115–17; tel. (712) 234-92-13; fax (71) 120-70-36; e-mail amblatv@bcc.com.uz; Ambassador IGORS APOKINS.

**Malaysia:** Tashkent, Yunus Abad District, ul. Khurshid 6; tel. (71) 137-67-58; fax (71) 137-67-53; e-mail mwtskent@online.ru; Ambassador MUHAMMAD ZAIN ABU BAKR.

**Moldova:** Tashkent; tel. (712) 35-28-52; Ambassador EFIM KILAR.

**Pakistan:** 700115 Tashkent, ul. Abdurakhmonov 15; tel. (712) 48-25-60; fax (71) 144-79-43; Ambassador MOHAMMAD AKHTAR TUFAIL.

**Poland:** 700084 Tashkent, ul. Firdavsiy 66; tel. (71) 120-86-50; fax (71) 120-86-51; e-mail zkuchciak@bcc.com.uz; Ambassador ZENON KUCHCIAK.

**Russia:** 700015 Tashkent, ul. Nukusskaya 83; tel. (71) 152-62-80; fax (71) 152-21-43; e-mail rusemb@albatros.uz; Ambassador DMITRII B. RYURIKOV.

**Sri Lanka:** Tashkent; Ambassador NAGURPITCHAI SIKKANDER.

**Switzerland:** 700070 Tashkent, ul. Usmon Nosyr, Tupik 1/4; tel. (71) 120-67-38; fax (71) 120-62-59; e-mail vertretung@tas.rep.admin.ch; Ambassador WILHELM MEIER.

**Turkey:** Tashkent, ul. Gogolya 87; tel. (71) 133-21-07; fax (71) 136-35-25; e-mail turemb@bcc.com.uz; Ambassador ERDOGAN AYTUN.

**Turkmenistan:** Tashkent; Ambassador SOLTAN PIRMUHAMEDOV.

**Ukraine:** 700000 Tashkent, ul. Gogolya 68; tel. and fax (71) 136-08-12; e-mail emb_uz@mfa.gov.ua; Ambassador ANATOLIY KASIANENKO.

**United Kingdom:** 700000 Tashkent, ul. Gulyamova 67; tel. (71) 120-62-88; fax (71) 120-65-49; e-mail brit@emb.uz; internet www.britain.uz; Ambassador CRAIG MURRAY.

**USA:** 700115 Tashkent, ul. Chilanzarskaya 82; tel. (71) 120-54-50; fax (71) 120-63-35; e-mail consul_tashkent@yahoo.com; internet www.usis.uz; Ambassador JON R. PURNELL.

**Viet Nam:** Tashkent, ul. Rashidova 100; tel. (712) 34-45-36; fax (71) 120-62-65; e-mail dsqvntas@online.ru; Ambassador NGUYEN QUOC BAO.

# Judicial System

**Chairman of the Supreme Court:** FARUHA FAHRUDDINOVA MUHIDDINOVA.

**Judges of the Supreme Court:** KH. B. YODGOROV, N. S. NORMURODOV, H. B. KHOLMIRZAYEV, O. KH. KHOLIQOV, VOKHID NAZAROV, DILBAR SUYUNOVA, DILMIR KHALILOV, BAKHTIYOR DJAMALOV, SOBIR SALIKHOVICH.

**Procurator-General:** RASHIDJON QODIROV.

**Chairman of the Constitutional Court:** BURITOSH MUSTAFAYEV.

**Chairman of the Higher Economic Court:** MIRZOULUGHBEK ABDUSALOMOV.

# Religion

The Constitution of 8 December 1992 stipulates that, while there is freedom of worship and expression, there may be no state religion or ideology. A new law on religion was adopted in May 1998, which severely restricted the activities of religious organizations. The Government stated that the legislation was designed to curb the recent increase in militant Islamist activity (including terrorism) in Uzbekistan.

The most widespread religion in Uzbekistan is Islam; the majority of ethnic Uzbeks are Sunni Muslims (Hanafi school), but the number of Wahhabi communities is increasing. Most ethnic Slavs in Uzbekistan are adherents of Orthodox Christianity. In the early 1990s there were reported to be some 65,000 European Jews and 28,000 Central Asian Jews.

**State Committee for Religious Affairs:** 700028 Tashkent, pl. Mustakillik 5; tel. (71) 139-10-14; fax (71) 139-17-63; e-mail uzreligion@vodiy.com; internet www.uzreligion.vodiy.com; Chair. SHAAZIM SH. MINAVAROV.

## ISLAM

**Muslim Board of Central Asia:** Tashkent, Zarkainar 103; tel. (712) 40-39-33; fax (712) 40-08-31; f. 1943; has spiritual jurisdiction over the Muslims in the Central Asian republics of the former USSR; Chair. ABDURASHID QORI BAKROMOV (Chief Mufti of Mowarounnahr (Central Asia).

## CHRISTIANITY

### Roman Catholic Church

The Church is represented in Uzbekistan by a Mission, established in September 1997. There were an estimated 3,000 adherents at 31 December 2001.

**Superior:** Fr KRZYSZTOF KUKUŁKA, 700015 Tashkent, ul. Vtoraya Sapiyornaya 13; tel. (71) 133-70-35; fax (71) 133-70-25; e-mail misio@silk.org.

# The Press

In 1997, according to official statistics, there were 495 newspapers published in Uzbekistan, including 385 published in Uzbek. The average daily circulation was 1,844,200 copies. There were 113 periodicals published, including 90 in Uzbek. Newspapers and periodicals were also published in Russian, Kazakh, Tajik, Korean, Arabic, English and Karakalpak.

The publications listed below are in Uzbek, unless otherwise stated.

**Uzbek Agency for Press and Information:** 700129 Tashkent, ul. Navoi 30; tel. (71) 144-32-87; fax (71) 144-14-84; Gen. Dir RUSTAM SH. SHAGULYAMOV.

## PRINCIPAL NEWSPAPERS

**Adolat:** Tashkent; f. 1995; organ of the Adolat (Justice) Social Democratic Party of Uzbekistan; Editor TOHTAMUROD TOSHEV; circ. 5,900.

**Biznes-vestnik Vostoka** (Business Bulletin of the East): 700000 Tashkent, ul. Matbuotchilar 32; tel. (71) 133-95-93; e-mail info@bvv.uz; internet www.bvv.uz; f. 1991; weekly; in Russian and Uzbek; economic and financial news; Editor VADIM SIROTIN; circ. 20,000.

**Delovoy Partner:** Tashkent; tel. (71) 139-17-31; internet hamkor.uzpak.uz; f. 1991; in Russian and English; Editor ISMAT HUSHEV; circ. 20,000.

**Fidokor:** Tashkent; tel. (712) 34-87-74; f. 1999; weekly; organ of the Fidokorlar National Democratic Party; Editor JALOLIDDIN SAFAYEV; circ. 32,000.

**Golos uzbekistana:** Tashkent; tel. (71) 133-11-49; f. 1918; in Russian; Editor ANDREI ORLOV; circ. 40,000.

**Hurriyat:** Tashkent; tel. (71) 144-25-06; fax (71) 144-36-16; e-mail amir@uzpac.uz; f. 1996; independent; Editor AMIRKUL KARIMOV; circ. 5,000.

**Khalk suzi** (People's Word): 700000 Tashkent, ul. Matbuotchilar 32; tel. (71) 133-15-22; f. 1991; 5 a week; organ of the Oly Majlis and the Cabinet of Ministers; in Uzbek and Russian; Editor ABBASKHON USMANOV; circ. 41,580 (Uzbek edn), 12,750 (Russian edn).

**Kommercheskiy Vestnik:** Tashkent; f. 1992; in Russian; Editor VALERII NIYAZMATOV; circ. 22,000.

**Ma'rifat** (Enlightenment): 700000 Tashkent, ul. Matbuotchilar 32; tel. (71) 133-50-55; f. 1931; 2 a week; Editor KHALIM SAIDOV; circ. 21,500.

**Menejer** (Manager): 700000 Tashkent, ul. Buyuk Turon 41; tel. (71) 136-58-85; f. 1997; weekly; in Russian and Uzbek; commercial information and advertising; Editor KHOTAM ABDURAIMOV; circ. 15,000.

**Molodiozh Uzbekistana** (Youth of Uzbekistan): 700000 Tashkent, ul. Matbuotchilar 32; tel. (71) 133-72-77; fax (71) 133-41-52; e-mail pressa@online.ru; f. 1926; weekly; in Russian; economic and social news; Editor-in-Chief IVAN N. KASACHEV; circ. 6,000.

**Mulkdor** (Property Owner): 700000 Tashkent, pr. Uzbekistanskii 53; tel. (71) 139-21-96; f. 1994; weekly; Editor MIRODIL ABDURAKHMANOV; circ. 21,000.

**Na postu/Postda:** Tashkent; f. 1930; in Russian and Uzbek; Editor Z. ATAYEV.

**Narodnoye Slovo** (People's Word): 700000 Tashkent, ul. Matbuotchilar 19; tel. (71) 133-15-22; e-mail slovo@uzpak.uz; internet hc.uzpak.uz; f. 1991; govt newspaper; weekly; in Russian and Uzbek; Editor ABBOS USMONOV; circ. 50,000.

**Pravda Vostoka** (Truth of the East): 700000 Tashkent, ul. Matbuotchilar 32; tel. (71) 133-56-33; fax (71) 133-70-98; e-mail pvostok@mail.tps.uz; internet pravdavostoka.intal.uz; f. 1917; 5 a week; organ of the Cabinet of Ministers; in Russian; Editor BAKHTIYOR KHASANOV; circ. 12,000.

**Savdogar:** Tashkent; f. 1992; Editor MUHAMMAD ORAZMETOV; circ. 17,000.

**Soliqlar va Bojhona Habarlari/Nalogovie I Tamojennie Vesti:** Tashkent; f. 1994; Editor MIKHAIL PERPER; circ. 45,000.

**Sport:** Tashkent; f. 1932; Editor HAYDAR AKBAROV; circ. 8,490.

**Tashkentskaya Pravda** (Tashkent Truth): 700000 Tashkent, ul. Matbuotchilar 32; tel. (71) 133-90-82; f. 1954; 2 a week; in Russian; Editor FATKHIDDIN MUKHITDINOV; circ. 6,400.

**Toshkent Khakikati** (Tashkent Truth): 700000 Tashkent, ul. Matbuotchilar 32; tel. (71) 133-64-95; f. 1954; 2 a week; Editor FATKHIDDIN MUKHITDINOV; circ. 19,000.

**Turkiston** (Turkestan): 700000 Tashkent, ul. Matbuotchilar 32; tel. (71) 136-56-58; f. 1925 as *Yash Leninchy* (Young Leninist), renamed as above 1992; 2 a week; organ of the Kamolot Asscn of Young People of Uzbekistan; Editor GAFAR KHATOMOV; circ. 12,580.

**Uzbekiston adabiyoti va san'ati** (Literature and Art of Uzbekistan): 700000 Tashkent, ul. Matbuotchilar 32; tel. (71) 133-52-91; f. 1956; weekly; organ of the Union of Writers of Uzbekistan; Editor AKHMAJON MELIBOYEV; circ. 10,300.

**Uzbekiston ovizi** (Voice of Uzbekistan): 700000 Tashkent, ul. Matbuotchilar 32; tel. (71) 133-65-45; Editor AZIM SUIUK; circ. 40,000.

### PRINCIPAL PERIODICALS

Monthly, unless otherwise indicated.

**Fan va turmush** (Science and Life): 700000 Tashkent, ul. Gulyamova 70; tel. (71) 133-07-05; f. 1933; every 2 months; publ. by the Fan (Science) Publishing House; popular scientific; Editor MURAD SHARIFKHOJAYEV; circ. 28,000.

**Gulistan** (Flourishing Area): 700000 Tashkent, ul. Buyuk Turon 41; tel. (71) 136-78-90; f. 1925; every 2 months; socio-political; Editor TILAB MAKHMUDOV; circ. 4,000.

**Gulkhan** (Bonfire): 700000 Tashkent, ul. Buyuk Turon 41; tel. (71) 136-78-85; f. 1929; illustrated juvenile fiction; Editor SAFAR BARNOYEV; circ. 26,000.

**Guncha** (Small Bud): 700000 Tashkent, ul. Buyuk Turon 41; tel. (71) 136-78-80; f. 1958; illustrated; literary, for pre-school-age children; Editor ERKIN MALIKOV; circ. 35,000.

**Jakhon adabiyoti** (World Literature): 700129 Tashkent, ul. Navoi 30; tel. (71) 144-41-60; f. 1997; Editor OZOD SHARAFIDDINOV; circ. 2,000.

**Mushtum** (Fist): 700000 Tashkent, ul. Buyuk Turon 41; tel. (71) 133-99-72; f. 1923; fortnightly; satirical; Editor ASHURALI JURAYEV; circ. 10,650.

**Obshchestvennye Nauki v Uzbekistane** (Social Sciences in Uzbekistan): 700047 Tashkent, ul. Gulyamova 70; tel. (71) 136-73-29; f. 1957; publ. by the Fan (Science) Publishing House of the Academy of Sciences of Uzbekistan; history, oriental studies, archaeology, economics, ethnology, etc.; in Russian and Uzbek; Editor A. MUKHAMEJANOV; circ. 500.

**Saodat** (Happiness): 700083 Tashkent, ul. Buyuk Turon 41; tel. (71) 133-68-10; f. 1925; twice every 3 months; women's popular; Editor OIDIN KHAJIYEVA; circ. 70,000.

**Sharq yulduzi** (Star of the East): 700000 Tashkent, ul. Buyuk Turon 41; tel. (71) 133-09-18; f. 1932; monthly; journal of the Union of Writers of Uzbekistan; fiction; Editor UTKUR KHASHIMOV; circ. 10,000.

**Sikhat salomatlik** (Health): 700000 Tashkent, ul. Parkentskaya 51; tel. (712) 68-17-54; f. 1990; every 2 months; Editor DAMIN ABDURAKHIMOVICH ASADOV; circ. 36,000.

**Tong yulduzi** (Morning Star): 700129 Tashkent, ul. Navoi 30; tel. (71) 144-62-34; e-mail ijod@uzpak.uz; f. 1929; weekly; children's; Editor UMIDA ABDUAZIMOVA; circ. 60,000.

**Uzbek tili va adabiyoti** (Uzbek Language and Literature): 700000 Tashkent, ul. Muminova 9; tel. (712) 62-42-47; f. 1958; every 2 months; publ. by the Fan (Science) Publishing House; journal of the Academy of Sciences of Uzbekistan; history and modern development of the Uzbek language, folklore, etc.; Editor AZIM KHAJIYEV; circ. 3,700.

**Yoshlik** (Youth): 700000 Tashkent, ul. Buyuk Turon 41; tel. (71) 133-09-18; f. 1932; monthly; literature and arts for young people; Editor SABIR UNAROV; circ. 10,000.

**Zvezda Vostoka** (Star of the East): 700129 Tashkent, ul. Navoi 30; tel. (71) 144-11-49; f. 1932; monthly; journal of the Union of Writers of Uzbekistan; fiction; translations into Russian from Arabic, English, Hindi, Turkish, Japanese, etc.; Editor NIKOLAI KRASILNIKOV; circ. 3,000.

### NEWS AGENCY

**Information Agency of the Ministry of Foreign Affairs of the Republic of Uzbekistan—'Jakhon' ('World'):** 700029 Tashkent, pr. Uzbekistanskii 9; tel. (71) 133-65-91; fax (71) 120-64-43; e-mail jahon@tiv.uz; internet www.jahon.tiv.uz; Dir ABROR GULYAMOV.

**Turkiston Press:** Tashkent; tel. (71) 136-11-45; Dir-Gen. ZAFAR ROZIYEV.

**Uzbekistan National News Agency :** 700047 Tashkent, ul. Musakhanov 38; tel. (71) 133-16-22; fax (71) 133-24-45; internet www.uza.uz; Dir MAMATSKUL KHAZRATSKULOV.

#### Foreign Bureaux

**Agence France-Presse (AFP):** Tashkent; tel. (71) 132-02-93; e-mail galima@bcc.com.uz; Correspondent GALIMA BURHARBAYEVA.

**Associated Press (AP)** (USA): Tashkent; tel. (71) 136-19-58; Correspondent TIMOFEY ZHUKOV.

**Interfax** (Russia): Tashkent; tel. (71) 133-70-69; Correspondent BAKHTIYOR KHASANOV.

**Reuters** (United Kingdom): Tashkent; tel. (71) 120-73-66; e-mail shamil.baygin@reuters.co.uz; Correspondent SHAMIL BAYGIN.

# Publishers

In 1997 there were approximately 1,000 book titles published in Uzbekistan, of which some 70% were in Uzbek.

**Uzbek Agency for Press and Information:** 700129, Tashkent, ul. Navoi 30; tel. (71) 144-32-87; fax (71) 144-14-84; f. 2002; mass media, press and information exchange; printing, publishing and distribution of periodicals; Gen. Dir RUSTAM SH. SHAGULYAMOV.

**Abdulla Kadyri Publishers:** 700129 Tashkent, ul. Navoi 30; tel. (71) 144-61-51; f. 1992; history, culture, literature; Dir D. I. IKRAMOVA.

**Abu Ali ibn Sino Publishers:** Tashkent, ul. Navoi 30; tel. (71) 144-51-72; f. 1958; medical sciences; Dir AKMAL KAMALOV (acting).

**Chulpon** (Morning Star): 700129 Tashkent, ul. Navoi 30; tel. (71) 139-13-75; Dir N. KHOLBUTAYEV.

**Fan** (Science Publishing House): 700047 Tashkent, ul. Gulyamova 70, kv. 102; tel. (71) 133-69-61; scientific books and journals; Dir N. T. KHATAMOV.

**Gafur Gulyam Publishers:** 700129 Tashkent, ul. Navoi 30; tel. (71) 144-22-53; fax (71) 41-35-47; f. 1957; refounded in 2002; fiction, the arts; books in Uzbek, Russian and English; Dir Rikhsitilla N. Khakimov.

**Izdatelstvo Literatury i Iskusstva** (Literature and Art Publishing House): 700129 Tashkent, ul. Navoi 30; tel. (71) 144-51-72; f. 1926; literature, literary criticism and essays; Dir Sh. Z. Usmankhojayev; Editor-in-Chief H. T. Turabekov.

**Izdatelstvo Uzbekistan** (Uzbekistan Publishing House): 700129 Tashkent, ul. Navoi 30; tel. (71) 144-38-10; fax (71) 144-11-35; f. 1924; politics, economics, law, history and art; illustrated; manuals for schools and higher educational institutes; Dir Shukhrat Ya. Akhmedov; Editor-in-Chief Shomukhitdin Sh Mansurov.

**Mekhnat** (Labour): 700129 Tashkent, ul. Navoi 30; tel. (71) 144-22-27; Dir O. I. Mirzayev.

**Sharq Publishing House:** 700000 Tashkent, ul. Buyuk Turon 41; tel. (71) 133-47-86; fax (71) 133-18-58; largest publishing house; govt-owned.

**Ukituvchi** (Teacher): 700129 Tashkent, ul. Navoi 30; tel. (71) 144-23-86; fax (71) 144-30-94; f. 1936; literary textbooks, education manuals, scientific literature, juvenile; Dir M. Ikromova.

**Uzbekiston millii entsiklopediyasi** (Uzbekistan National Encyclopaedia): 700129 Tashkent, ul. Navoi 30; tel. (71) 144-34-38; f. 1997; encyclopedias, dictionaries and reference books; Dir N. Tukhliyev.

**Yozuvchi** (Writer): 700129 Tashkent, ul. Navoi 30; tel. (71) 144-29-97; f. 1990; Dir M. U. Toichiyev.

### WRITERS' UNION

**Union of Journalists of Uzbekistan:** 700129 Tashkent, ul. Navoi 30; tel. and fax (71) 144-19-79; e-mail jorn@online.ru; Pres. Lutfulla Kabirov.

**Union of Writers of Uzbekistan:** 700000 Tashkent, ul. Javakharlara Neru 1; tel. (71) 133-63-74; Chair. Abdulla Aripov.

# Broadcasting and Communications

### TELECOMMUNICATIONS

**Communications and Information Agency of Uzbekistan:** 700000 Tashkent, ul. A. Tolstogo 1; tel. (71) 133-65-03; fax (71) 139-87-82; internet www.uzapt.uzpak.uz; Dir-Gen. Abdulla Aripov.

**Daewoo Unitel:** Tashkent; country's largest provider of global mobile cellular telecommunications services.

**JSC Uzbektelecom:** 700000 Tashkent, ul. Amir Temur 24; tel. (71) 133-42-59; fax (71) 136-01-88; e-mail uztelecom@intal.uz; internet www.uztelecom.uz; f. 2000; comprises 14 regional and four specialized brs; provides local, regional and international telecommunications services; Gen. Dir Kh. A. Mukhitdinov.

**Uzdunrobita:** 700000 Tashkent, ul. Amir Temur 24; tel. (71) 130-01-01; fax (71) 130-01-05; e-mail office@uzdunrobita.com.uz; internet www.uzdunrobita.uz; f. 1991 as an Uzbek-US joint venture; provides mobile cellular telecommunications services; Gen. Dir Bekhzod Akhmedov.

### BROADCASTING

**State Television and Radio Broadcasting Company of Uzbekistan (UZTELERADIO):** 700011 Tashkent, ul. Navoi 69; tel. (71) 133-81-06; fax (71) 144-16-60; e-mail uztrcint@tkt.uz; internet www.teleradio.uz; local broadcasts, as well as relays from Egypt, France, India, Japan, Russia and Turkey; Dir-Gen. Abusaid Kuchimov.

#### Radio

**Uzbek Radio:** 700047 Tashkent, ul. Khorezmskaya 49; tel. (71) 133-89-20; fax (71) 133-60-68; e-mail uzradio@eanetways.com; f. 1947; broadcasts in Uzbek, Russian, English, Urdu, Hindi, Farsi, Dari, Pushtu, Turkish, Tajik, Kazakh, Crimean Tatar, German, Arabic, Chinese and Uigur; Dir Barno Rajabov.

#### Television

**Uzbek Television:** 700011 Tashkent, ul. Navoi 69; tel. (71) 133-81-06; fax (712) 41-39-81; e-mail uzteee@uzpak.uz; four local programmes as well as relays from Russia, Kazakhstan, Egypt, India and Turkey; Chair. Abusaid Kuchimov.

**Kamalak Television:** 700084 Tashkent, ul. Amir Temur 109; tel. (71) 137-51-77; fax (71) 120-62-28; e-mail kam.tv@kamalak.co.uz; f. 1992; joint venture between State Television and Radio Broadcasting Company and a US company; satellite broadcasts; relays from France, Germany, India, Russia, the United Kingdom and the USA; Gen. Dir Pulat Umarov.

# Finance

(cap. = capital; res = reserves; dep. = deposits; m. = million; amounts in Uzbek sum, unless otherwise stated; brs = branches)

### BANKING

A reform of the banking sector was begun in 1994. A two-tier system was introduced, consisting of the Central Bank and about 30 commercial banks. An association of commercial banks was established in 1995 to co-ordinate the role of commercial banks in the national economy. In October 2001 there were reported to be 38 commercial banks, of which 16 were under private ownership.

#### Central Bank

**Central Bank of the Republic of Uzbekistan:** 700001 Tashkent, pr. Uzbekistanskii 6; tel. (71) 133-68-29; fax (71) 140-65-58; e-mail turgun@cbu.gov.uz; internet www.gov.uz/government/cbu/cbu_0e.htm; f. 1991; Chair. of Bd Faizulla M. Mullajonov; Vice-Chair. Shukhrat Toshmurodov.

#### State Commercial Banks

**Asaka—Specialized State Joint-Stock Commercial Bank:** 700015 Tashkent, ul. Nukus 67; tel. (71) 120-81-11; fax (712) 54-06-59; e-mail contact@asakabank.com; internet www.asakabank.com; f. 1995; cap. US $150m., res $4.7m., dep. $99.6m. (Dec. 2001); Chair. Shukhrat M. Tashmuradov; 22 brs.

**National Bank for Foreign Economic Activity of the Republic of Uzbekistan:** 700047 Tashkent, ul. Okhunbabayev 23; tel. (71) 133-62-87; fax (71) 132-01-72; e-mail webmaster@central.nbu.com; internet www.nbu.com; f. 1991; cap. US $400m., res $20m., dep. $1,561m. (Dec. 2001); due to be privatized; Chair. Zainiddin S. Mirkhojayev; 99 brs.

#### State Joint-Stock Commercial Banks

**Halk Bank** (State Commercial People's Bank of the Republic of Uzbekistan ): 700096 Tashkent, Katortol 46; tel. (71) 278-59-44; fax (71) 173-69-13; e-mail farhod_azizov@yahoo.com; internet www.halkbank.uz; f. 1995; fmrly Savings Bank of Uzbekistan; cap. 5,720m., res 519.9m., dep. 43,900m. (Jan. 2003); Chair. Adham Haydarov; 2,849 brs.

**Uzbek State Joint-Stock Housing Savings Bank:** 700000 Tashkent, ul. Pushkina 17; tel. (71) 133-29-57; fax (71) 133-30-89; Chair. Timur S. Azimov.

**Zaminbank:** 700015 Tashkent, ul. Rzhevskaya 3; tel. (712) 55-82-59; fax (712) 55-77-49; e-mail zamin@albatros.uz; internet www.zaminbank.uz; f. 1995; Chair. of Bd Odli O. Mavlanov.

#### Other Joint-Stock Commercial Banks

**Alokabank:** 700000 Tashkent, ul. A. Tolstogo 1; tel. (71) 133-62-54; fax (71) 136-36-22; e-mail alokauz@uzpak.uz; f. 1995; cap. 2,500m., res 429m., dep. 10,182m. (2002); Chair. Fakhriddin T. Yuldashev; 9 brs.

**Avia Bank:** 700015 Tashkent, ul. Nukus 86A; tel. (71) 254-75-75; fax (71) 254-79-53; e-mail aviabank2002@mail.ru; f. 1989; cap. 1,700m., res 732.1m., dep. 3,205.8m. (Jan. 2003); Chair. Shukurullo Imamaliyev.

**Gala Bank:** 700060 Tashkent, ul. Lakhuti 38; tel. and fax (71) 133-42-25; Chair. Yuldashbai E. Ergashev.

**HamkorBank:** 710011 Andizhan, ul. Babura 85; tel. and fax (74) 24-70-39; e-mail hamkorbank@mail.ru; f. 1991; Chair. Ikram Ibragimov; 15 brs.

**Ipak Yuli:** 700135 Tashkent, ul. Farkoda 12; tel. (71) 119-19-91; fax (71) 133-32-00; e-mail ipak@online.ru; f. July 2000 by merger with Namanganbank and Umarbank.

**Pakhta Bank:** 700096 Tashkent, ul. Mukimi 43; tel. (71) 278-21-96; fax (71) 120-88-18; e-mail pahtabnk@sovam.com; internet www.pakhtabank.com; f. 1995; cap. 10,000m., res 13,903.4m., dep. 112,048.6m. (Dec. 2002); Chair. Kobiljon Toshmatov; 184 brs.

**Parvina Bank:** 703001 Samarkand, ul. Uzbekistanskaya 82; tel. (66) 231-05-07; fax (66) 231-02-82; Chair. Dilshod A. Pulatov.

**Sanoatkurilish Bank** (Uzbek Joint-Stock Commercial Industrial Construction Bank 'Uzpromstroibank'): 700000 Tashkent, ul. Abdulla Tukai 3; tel. (71) 133-90-61; fax (71) 133-34-26; f. 1922; cap. 2,438m. Russian roubles, dep. 1,287.1m. Russian roubles (Dec. 1997); Chair. Utkur U. Nigmatov; 46 brs.

**Sarmoyabank:** 700011 Tashkent, ul. Navoi 18; tel. (71) 144-08-84; fax (71) 144-07-83; Chair. KOLMAHON E. KURBONBOYEV.

**Savdogarbank:** 700060 Tashkent, ul. Said Baraka 76; tel. (712) 54-19-91; fax (712) 56-56-71; Chair. MURSURMON N. NURMAMATOV.

**Tadbirkor Bank:** 700047 Tashkent, ul. S. Azimova 52; tel. (71) 133-18-75; fax (71) 136-88-32; Chair. MUZAFFARBEK SABIROV.

**Trustbank:** 700038 Tashkent, ul. Navoi 7; tel. (712) 41-23-43; fax (71) 144-76-25; e-mail magnoliya1974@mail.ru; f. 1994; cap. US $2.6m., res $0.2m., dep. $4.2m.; Chair. VLADISLAV N. PAK; 2 brs.

**Turonbank:** 700011 Tashkent, ul. Navoi 44; tel. (712) 42-27-30; fax (71) 144-33-94; Chair. ATKHAM T. ZIYAYEV.

**Uzlegkombank:** 700031 Tashkent, ul. Baranova 40; tel. and fax (712) 56-05-09; Chair. ZAINUTDIN M. AKROMOV.

**Uzmevasabzavotbank:** 700015 Tashkent, ul. Lakhuti 16A; tel. and fax (71) 133-83-96; Chair. ISLOM T. SALOMOV.

**Uzsayokharinvestbank:** 700047 Tashkent, ul. Khorezmskaya 47; tel. and fax (71) 136-23-30.

### Joint-Venture Banks

**ABN-AMRO Bank NB Uzbekistan AO:** 700000 Tashkent, pl. Khamid Alimzhan (West Side), Business Complex, 4th Entrance; tel. (71) 120-61-41; fax (71) 120-63-67; e-mail aziz.mirjuraev@abnamro.com; internet www.abnamro.com/wholesale/localpresence/uzbekistan.asp; f. 1996 as joint venture between European Bank for Reconstruction and Development, ABN-AMRO (the Netherlands), the World Bank and the Uzbek National Bank for Foreign Economic Relations; universal commercial bank; cap. US $8.5m.; Chair. and Gen. Man. HUGO MINDERHOUD.

**Uzbekistan-Turkish UT Bank:** 700043 Tashkent, ul. Xalger Dostligi 15B; tel. (71) 173-83-25; fax (71) 120-63-62; e-mail utbank@utbk.com; f. 1993; cap. 2,799.3m., res 2.055.9m., dep. 2,379.5m. (Dec. 2002); Chair. MUHAMMADJAN A. SUKURALIYEV.

**UzDaewoo Bank:** 700000 Tashkent, ul. Pushkina; tel. (71) 120-80-00; fax (71) 120-69-70; e-mail office@daewoobank.com; internet www.daewoobank.com; f. 1997; total assets US $20m.; Chair. TAE YOUNG JUAG.

**Uzprivatbank** (Uzbek International Bank): 700003 Tashkent, pr. Uzbekistanskii 51; tel. (71) 120-63-08; fax (71) 120-63-07; e-mail bank@uib.iz; internet www.uzprivatbank.com; f. 1994; cap. US $5.5m.; Chair. A. A. ERGASHEV.

### INSURANCE

**Uzbekinvest National Export–Import Insurance Co:** 700017 Tashkent, ul. Suleimanova 49; tel. (71) 133-05-56; fax (71) 133-07-04; e-mail root@unic.gov.uz; internet www.unic.gov.uz; f. 1994 restructured 1997; joint venture with American International Group (AIG); cap. US $60m.; Dir-Gen. SUNNAT A. UMAROV; Chief Exec. NODIR KALANDAROV.

**Uzbekinvest International Insurance Co:** Tashkent; e-mail nodir.kalandarov@aig.com; f. 1994; Chief Exec. NODIR KALANDAROV.

### COMMODITY EXCHANGE

**Tashkent Commodity Exchange:** 700003 Tashkent, ul. Uzbekistanskii 53; tel. (71) 139-83-77; fax (71) 139-83-85; Chair. of Bd SHUKHRAT MUKHAMEDOV.

### STOCK EXCHANGE

**'Toshkent' Republican Stock Exchange (UZSE):** 700047 Tashkent, ul. Bukhara 10; tel. (71) 136-07-40; fax (71) 133-32-31; e-mail info@uzse.com; internet www.uzse.com; f. 1994; stocks and securities; Chair. BAKHTIYOR RADJABOV.

# Trade and Industry

## GOVERNMENT AGENCIES

**Foreign Investment Agency:** 700011 Tashkent, ul. navoi 16A; tel. (712) 41-55-41; e-mail afi@mail.uznet.net; Gen. Dir SHAZIYATOV SHOAZIZ.

**State Committee for De-monopolization and Competition Development:** 700078 Tashkent, pl. Mustakillik 5; tel. (71) 139-15-42; fax (71) 139-46-70; e-mail devonhona@antimon.uz; internet www.antimon.uz; Chair. AZAMKHON U. BAKHRAMOV.

**State Committee for the Management of State Property and for Privatization:** 700008 Tashkent, pl. Mustakillik 6; tel. (71) 139-82-03; fax (71) 139-46-66; Chair. UKTAM K. ISMOILOV.

## CHAMBER OF COMMERCE

**Chamber of Commodity Producers and Entrepreneurs of Uzbekistan:** 700047 Tashkent, ul. Bukhoro 6; tel. (71) 139-18-83; fax (71) 132-09-03; e-mail info@maroqand.uz; internet www.maroqand.uz; f. 1996; provides assistance, consulting and support for businesses; Chair. MUZAFFARBEK A. SABIROV.

## EMPLOYERS' ORGANIZATIONS

**Employers' Association of Uzbekistan:** 700017 Tashkent, ul. A. Kadiry 2; tel. (712) 34-06-71; fax (712) 34-13-39.

## STATE HYDROCARBONS COMPANY

**Uzbekneftegaz:** 700047 Tashkent, ul. Akhunbabayeva 21; tel. (712) 32-02-10; fax (712) 32-10-62; national petroleum and gas corpn; Chair. IBRAT A. ZAINUTDINOV; 90,000 employees.

## MAJOR COMPANIES

### Cotton and Textiles

**Andizhan Joint-Stock Co:** 711000 Andizhan, Barbur 73; tel. (74) 222-13-53; fax (74) 222-13-52; e-mail aobabur@online.ru; cotton-processing company; possesses spinning, weaving, finishing and sewing plants; Chair. MUYDINOV KAHHOZBEK; 5,000 employees.

**Bukhara Cotton Industrial Group:** 705022 Bukhara, ul. Promyshlennaya 2; tel. (65) 223-06-21; fax (65) 222-65-86; e-mail bphbo@naytov.com; f. 1973; produces cotton cloth and yarns, imports equipment for the textile, knitwear and sewing industries; imports transport equipment; Chair. of Bd SHUKRULLO NOROVICH DAVIROV; 9,237 employees.

**Tashselmash:** 700048 Tashkent, ul. Khamza 2; tel. (71) 136-72-27; fax (71) 136-72-78; manufactures cotton-picking machines.

**Uzhlopkopromsbyt** (Stock Asscn for Cotton-processing and Marketing): 700100 Tashkent, ul. U. Nasir 8A; tel. (712) 56-12-60; fax (712) 56-02-31; produces cotton.

**Uzmashprom Association:** 700047 Tashkent, ul. Nosir 53B; tel. and fax (712) 53-81-51; f. 1994; state-owned; produces machines, equipment and tools for the cotton and textile industries; Chair. T. K. SABIROV; 10,000 employees.

### Furniture

**Almalyk Furniture Works:** Tashkent Obl., Almalyk, ul. Izvestkovaya 14; tel. (71) 614-48-01; fax (71) 614-09-14; manufactures furniture; 1,000 employees.

**Uzbek Furniture:** 700011 Tashkent, ul. Navoi 18; tel. (712) 41-81-18; furniture for the home, offices, nurseries and schools.

### Gases and Chemicals

**Electrokhimprom:** 702108 Tashkent Obl., ul. Tashkentskaya 2, Chirchik 8; tel. (71) 719-32-00; fax (71) 715-12-97; f. 1940; produces mineral fertilizers, synthetic ammonium, nitric acid and liquefied gas; Dir-Gen. MIRZAYEV FATHULLA TURGUNOVICH; Chief Eng. MIGULIN VLADIMIR FEDOSEYEVICH.

**Mubarek Gas Processing Plant:** Kaskadarin Obl., 731000 Mubarek; f. 1971; sulphur production, purification of exhaust gases, etc.; Dir (plant) NURITBIN ZAYNIYEV; 1,900 employees.

**Uzneftegazkurilish:** 700115 Tashkent, ul. Mukimi 98; tel. (712) 53-65-01; fax (712) 53-53-77; f. 1999; construction for the petroleum and gas industry; Gen. Dir B. HAFIZOV.

### Gold and Other Metals

**OJSC 'Almalyk Mining and Metallurgical Complex':** Tashkent Obl., 702400 Almalyk, ul. Amir Timur 14; tel. (71) 614-30-30; fax (71) 613-33-77; e-mail oves_mli@oaoagmk.com; f. 1948; processing of precious and non-ferrous metals; Gen. Dir VITALIY N. SIGEDIN.

**Amantaytau Goldfields:** 700060 Tashkent, ul. Mirabatskaya 11; tel. (71) 56-06-10; fax (71) 120-64-35; f. 1993; joint venture between two state-owned Uzbek cos and British co, Lonhro; gold mining near Zerafshan; started production 1996; Dir DAVID NEWTON.

**Oxus Resources Corporation:** 700031 Tashkent, ul. Kunayev 20; tel. (71) 120-68-64; fax (71) 120-65-64; British co undertaking gold and base-metal mining in Central Asia; Vice-Pres. (new projects) VALERII AXANOV; Vice-Pres. (business devt) ALEKSANDR POLIKASHIN.

**Uzvtortzvetmet Joint-Stock Co:** Tashkent, ul. Shota Rustaveli 45; tel. (712) 58-80-01; fax (712) 55-34-07; aluminium plant, also processes copper scrap, brass, zinc and non-ferrous metals.

**Zerafshan Gold Refinery:** Bukhara Obl., Zerafshan; f. 1967; main gold refinery in country; Dir VALERII NIKOLAYEVICH; 3,000 employees (1993).

## Motor Vehicles

**Tashkent Tractor Plant:** 700142 Tashkent, ul. Bujuk Ipak Yuli 434; tel. (712) 64-17-40; fax (712) 64-06-16; e-mail gaottz@online.ru; internet www.tashkenttractor.com; f. 1942; produces tractors for the cotton industry; Gen. Dir MAKHAMADJON A. AKHMEDJANOV; 7,000 employees.

**Uzavtosanoat Production Asscn:** 700000 Tashkent, ul. Azimov 79; tel. (71) 254-19-24; fax (71) 133-14-29; f. 1994; develops projects for the establishment of the motor industry in Uzbekistan; car, lorry and bus production plants; Dir D. R. PARPIYEV; 14,000 employees.

**Uzselkhozmash-holding:** 700029 Tashkent, pl. Mustakillik 2; tel. (71) 139-48-06; fax (71) 139-49-09; f. 1996; 51% state-owned; produces tractors and agricultural machinery; largest holding co in the country; cap. 7,818,749m. sum (2002); sales 24,353m. (2002); Chair. of Bd Prof. RAFIK D. MATCHANOV; 10,319 employees (2002).

## Miscellaneous

**Central Asia Trans State Joint-Stock Co:** 700077 Tashkent, ul. Bujuk Ipak Yuli 75; tel. (712) 68-76-34; fax (712) 68-72-09; e-mail catrans@online.ru; internet www.catrans.uz; f. 1992 under the Ministry of Foreign Economic Relations; transports and forwards cargo within Central Asia; Chair. KHONDAMIR MAMATOV; 550 employees.

**GUKS** (Main Board for Capital Construction): 700011 Tashkent, pr. Navoi 2A; tel. (712) 41-87-13; fax (712) 289-14-79; contractor to building companies; develops, designs, provides construction sites with equipment and carries out technical supervision and management.

**Innovatsia State Joint-Stock Foreign Trade Co:** 700077 Tashkent, ul. Bujuk Ipak Yuli 75; tel. (712) 68-92-48; fax (712) 68-77-33; e-mail inovac@uzpak.uz; internet www.geocities.com/innovatsia; f. 1991; consulting and mediation services; export of cotton and cotton products; investment projects with Europe, Asia and the USA; Chair. of Bd SHAVKAT P. BARATOV.

**Navoi Mining and Metallurgy Combine (NMMC):** 706800 Navoi-2, ul. Navoi 27; tel. (79) 225-63-50; fax (79) 223-99-51; e-mail ngmkmark@online.ru; f. 1958; mines gold, extracts uranium; produces yarn and knitted goods, manufactures jewellery, produces marble slabs and tiles, manufactures lathes, and produces pipes; Gen. Dir NIKOLAI V. KUCHERSKIY.

**Sovplastital:** 700185 Tashkent, ul. Druzhba Narodova 29A; tel. (712) 76-16-23; fax (71) 120-64-01; e-mail spi@glb.net; internet www .sovplastitalonline.com; f. 1987; Uzbek-Italian joint venture; manufactures plastic goods and handcrafted souvenirs, incl. coloured glass, porcelain and ceramics; Gen. Dir ALEKSANDR MELKUMOV.

**Sredazelektroapparat Joint-Stock Company:** 700005 Tashkent, ul. Manjara 1; tel. (712) 91-29-04; fax (712) 93-09-32; engaged in the production of low-voltage equipment, incl. packet-type switches, cam switches, etc.; Gen. Dir ALIM ABDURAIMOVICH; 7,600 employees.

**Tashkent Industrial Amalgamation:** 700090 Tashkent, Barbur 73; tel. (712) 55-17-23; fax (712) 44-30-43; produces diamond and other grinding wheels, instruments of galvanic binder, etc.; Gen. Man. ANATOLII HEGAY; 1,100 employees.

**Uzbek Refractory and Resistant Metals Integrated Plant:** Tashkent Obl., 702119 Chirchik, ul. Khaydarova 1; tel. (71) 715-57-03; fax (71) 715-57-02; e-mail uzktzhm@chirkom.com; manufactures products from tungsten, molybdenum, rhenium and hard alloys; Gen. Dir FARHAD H. TASHMETOV; 2,000 employees.

**Uzbekistan Metallurgical Plant:** Tashkent Obl., 702902 Bekabad 2; tel. (71) 910-24-23; f. 1944; manufactures carbon steel tubes and bars; Dir-Gen. A. M. ANOKHIN; 10,000 employees.

**Uzbeklegprom:** Tashkent 700100, ul. Babura 45; tel. (71) 139-17-11; fax (71) 139-10-66; state asscn for the development of enterprises, mainly in the textile industry.

**Uzexpocentre:** 700084 Tashkent, ul. Amir Timur 107; tel. (71) 35-09-73; fax (71) 34-54-40; e-mail uzexpoct@globalnet.uz; f. 1992; organization of trade fairs and exhibitions; operation of amusement rides; Dir-Gen. BAKHTIER IRMATOV; 460 employees.

**Uzmarkazimpex State Joint-Stock Co:** 700077 Tashkent, ul. Bujuk Ipak Yuli 75; tel. (712) 68-77-18; fax (712) 68-75-55; foreign-trading company; exports cotton, imports main food products, offers marketing and international trade services.

**Uzmetcombinat:** 702902 Bekabad; tel. (391) 62-24-23; fax (391) 62-25-73; steel-producer, products include metal bars, angles, circular bars and welded pipes.

**Uzplodovoschvinprom** (State Co-operative Asscn for Fruit and Vegetable Growing and Viniculture): 700029 Tashkent, ul. Uzbekistanskii 41; tel. (712) 56-37-54; fax (712) 56-56-48; Chair. NASIROV.

**Uzprommashimpeks State Joint-Stock Co:** 700077 Tashkent, ul. Bujuk Ipak Yuli 75; tel. (712) 68-75-88; fax (71) 120-73-24; e-mail

marketing@upm.uz; internet www.upm.uz; f. 1991; imports machine-building equipment, metallurgical equipment, chemical equipment; exports cotton fibre, cotton yarn, molybdenum, and other domestically produced goods; Chair. SHERZOD A. GUZAIROV; 115 employees.

**Uzstroimaterialy:** 700070 Tashkent, ul. Mirakilova 68A; tel. (71) 152-20-63; fax (712) 55-77-07; e-mail qursan@online.ru; f. 1989; produces more than 100 different building materials; cap. 2,622.2m. sum (2002); sales 50,020m. sum (2002); Chair. AKRAMOV ERKIN MAKSKAMOVICH.

**Uzvneshtrans State Joint-Stock Co:** 700077 Tashkent, ul. Bujuk Ipak Yuli 75; tel. (712) 68-74-76; fax (712) 68-73-37; e-mail transcom@uzvt.gov.uz; f. 1991; foreign trade and transport dispatching company; Gen. Dir ISMAILOV BAHODIR.

## TRADE UNIONS

**Federation of Trade Unions of Uzbekistan:** Tashkent; Chair. of Council KHULKAR DZHAMALOV.

# Transport

## RAILWAYS

Uzbekistan's railway network is connected to those of the neighbouring republics of Kazakhstan, Kyrgyzstan, Tajikistan and Turkmenistan. In 1994 Uzbekiston Temir Yollari (the Uzbekistan State Railway Company) was established on the basis of the existing facilities of its predecessor, the Central Asian Railway. There were 3,986 km of standard-gauge track in 2001, of which 619 km was electrified. Another line, connecting central Uzbekistan with the north-western part of the country, was brought into operation in March 2001.

**Uzbekiston Temir Yollari** (Uzbekistan State Railway Company): 700060 Tashkent, ul. Shevchenko 7; tel. (712) 32-44-00; fax (712) 47-39-58; e-mail uzrailway@uzpak.uz; internet www.uzrailway.uz; f. 1994 to replace the Central Asian Railway's operations in Uzbekistan; state-owned joint-stock co; Pres. ACHILBAY ZH. RAMATOV.

### City Underground Railway

**Tashgorpasstreans** (Tashkent Metro): 700027 Tashkent, pr. Uzbekistanskii 93A; tel. (712) 32-38-52; fax (712) 133-66-81; e-mail metro@sarkor.uz; f. 1977; three lines with total length of 37 km, and fourth line due to open by 2010; Chair. R. FAYZULLAYEV.

## ROADS

In 1997 Uzbekistan's road network totalled 43,463 km, of which 3,237 km were main or national roads, 18,767 km were secondary roads and 21,459 km were other roads. In 1999 the total length of the road network was estimated at 81,600 km, of which approximately 87.3% was paved.

## INLAND WATERWAYS

The extensive use of the waters of the Amu-Dar'ya and Syr-Dar'ya for irrigation lessened the flow of these rivers and caused the desiccation of the Aral Sea. This reduced a valuable transport asset. However, the Amu-Dar'ya Steamship Co still operates important river traffic.

## CIVIL AVIATION

Proposals to construct a new airport, 45 km from Tashkent, first discussed in 1991, were rejected in 1995 in favour of modernizing the capital's existing airport. In 1996 it was announced that the airports at Samarkand, Urgench and Bukhara would be upgraded to stimulate tourism.

**Uzbekistan Airways** (Uzbekiston Havo Yollari): 700061 Tashkent, ul. Proletarskaya 41; tel. (712) 91-14-90; fax (712) 32-73-71; e-mail info@uzbekistan-airways.com; internet www.uzbekistan-airways .com; f. 1992; operates flights to Central Asia, South-East Asia, the USA, the Middle East and Europe; Dir-Gen. RAFIKOV GANIY; Gen. Dir VALERIY TYAN.

# Tourism

Since independence Uzbekistan has sought to promote tourism as an important source of revenue. The republic has more than 4,000 historical monuments, many of which are associated with the ancient 'Silk Route', particularly the cities of Samarkand (Tamerlane's capital), Khiva and Bukhara, as well as other historical sites. Infrastructural limitations, however, have constrained development. In 1998 Uzbekistan received an estimated 272,000 foreign visitors (including excursionists), and tourism receipts totalled some US $21m.

**Uzbektourism:** 700027 Tashkent, ul. Khorezmskaya 47; tel. (71) 133-54-14; fax (71) 136-79-48; f. 1992; Chair. BAKHTIYOR M. HUSAN-BAYEV.

# Culture

Uzbekistan has a rich cultural heritage, particularly in the ancient cities of the 'Silk Road'. Islam, together with Persic (Tajik) and Turkic and Mongol (Uzbek) traditions, provided a varied legacy. Samarkand, the capital and site of the mausoleum of the medieval khan, Timur (known as 'the Lame' or 'the Great'—Tamerlane), was also reviving as a pilgrimage site in the 1990s. The city is the site of the Shah-e-Zinda shrine (formerly a museum), dedicated to Muhammed's nephew, Kussam Ibn Abbas, who, according to tradition, evangelized the area for Islam. In 1996, in celebration of the 660th anniversary of Timur's birth, restoration work began on many of Samarkand's monuments, including Timur's mausoleum and the Bibi Khanym mosque, constructed during his khanate. In February of that year the ancient city of Bukhara was listed by UNESCO as a World Heritage Site. Tashkent, long a centre of Russian influence in the territory, is the base for many cultural activities.

## NATIONAL ORGANIZATIONS

**Ministry of Culture:** see section on The Government (Ministries).

### CULTURAL HERITAGE

**Alisher Navoi National Library of Uzbekistan:** 700078 Tashkent, pl. Mustakillik 5; tel. (71) 139-16-58; fax (71) 133-09-08; e-mail navoi@physic.uzsci.net; f. 1870; 7,500,000 vols; Dir ZUHRIDDIN ISO-MIDDINOV.

**Fine Arts Museum:** Tashkent, ul. Mouveranakhr 16; tel. (712) 36-73-45.

**International Museum of Peace and Solidarity:** 703000 Samarkand, POB 76; tel. (662) 33-17-53; e-mail peacetur@samarkand.uz; internet www.friends-partners.org/~ccsi/nisorgs/uzbek/peacemsm .htm; f. 1986; aims to promote peace through diplomacy, culture and the arts; over 20,000 exhibits, incl. art, literature and memorabilia from over 100 countries; organizes various exhibitions and carries out educational activities; Dir ANATOLY I. IOSENOV.

**Karakalpak Historical Museum:** Karakalpakstan, 742000 Nukus, ul. Rakhmatova 3; contains material on the history of Karakalpakstan and the Uzbek peoples.

**Karakalpakstan Art Museum:** Karakalpakstan, 742000 Nukus, pr. Doslyka 127; tel. (61) 222-25-56; e-mail museum@online.ru; internet www.webcenter.ru/~museum; f. 1966; archaeology of ancient Khorezm, Kara-Kalpak folk art, modern art; library of 8,000 vols; Dir MARINIKA BABANAZAROVA.

**Mukarrama Turgunbayev Museum:** Tashkent, pl. Mustakillik 5; tel. (71) 139-12-96.

**Museum of Applied Arts of Uzbekistan:** 700031 Tashkent, ul. Rokatboshi 15; tel. (712) 56-39-43; fax (71) 52-13-67; e-mail museum@globalnet.uz; national handicrafts, incl. ceramics, embroidery, jewellery and wood-carving.

**Museum of Cinematic Art:** Tashkent, pr. Uzbekistanskii 96; tel. (712) 45-81-61.

**Museum of the History of the Turkestan Military District:** Tashkent, pr. Gorkii; tel. (712) 62-46-46.

**Museum of Literature:** 700011 Tashkent, ul. Navoi 69; tel. (712) 41-02-75; Dir N. S. KHASANOV.

**Museum of Uzbek History:** Tashkent, ul. Sharaf Rashidov 3; tel. (71) 139-10-83; f. 1992 by merger of the Museum of the History of the People of Uzbekistan and the Lenin Central Museum; over 200,000 exhibits; Dir G. R. RASHIDOV.

**Museum of Uzbek History, Culture and Arts:** Samarkand, ul. Sovetskaya 51; f. 1874; over 100,000 items; Dir N. S. SADYKOVA.

**State Museum of Fine Arts:** Tashkent, ul. Proletarskaya 16; tel. (712) 36-73-45; f. 1918; houses the private collection of Grand Duke Nikolai Konstantinovich Romanov; Russian and Uzbek paintings, as well as Oriental and Western art; Dir D. S. RUSIBAYEV.

**Tamara Khanum Museum:** Tashkent, ul. Pushkin Pishpekskaya 1; tel. (712) 67-86-90.

**Ural Tansykbayev Museum:** 700170 Tashkent, ul. Cherdantseva 2; tel. (71) 162-62-30; f. 1981; paintings by late artist Ural Tansykbayev, renowned for his depictions of Uzbek landscapes; Dir TACHOYEV SOLTAN IBRAGIMOVICH.

## SPORTING ORGANIZATION

**National Olympic Committee of Uzbekistan:** 700003 Tashkent, ul. Almazar 15/1; tel. (71) 139-12-95; fax (71) 144-73-29; e-mail olympic@online.ru; f. 1992; Chair. AZIZ NOSIROV; Sec.-Gen. MALIK BABAYEV.

**State Committee for Physical Education and Sport:** 700027 Tashkent, ul. Furkat 1; tel. (712) 38-45-59; fax (712) 45-08-52; Chair. SOBIRJON RUZIYEV.

## PERFORMING ARTS

**Abror Khodoyatov Drama State Theatre:** Tashkent, ul. Uighur 3; tel. (712) 44-11-70.

**Alisher Navoi Opera and Ballet Theatre:** Tashkent, ul. A. Atatürk 28; tel. (712) 33-33-44.

**Khamza Uzbek Drama Theatre:** Tashkent, pr. Navoi 36; tel. (712) 44-35-42.

**Maxim Gorkii Russian Drama Theatre:** Tashkent, ul. Khamza 28; tel. (712) 33-32-05.

**Mukimi Musical Drama and Comedy at the Uzbek State Theatre:** Tashkent, ul. Almazar 187; tel. (712) 45-36-55.

**Republican Puppet Theatre of Uzbekistan:** Tashkent, pr. Kosmonavtov 1; tel. (712) 53-62-46.

**Russian State Musical Drama and Comedy Theatre:** Tashkent, ul Volgogradskii; tel. (712) 77-86-11.

**Uzbek State Philharmonic Society:** Tashkent, pr. Uzbekistanskii 11; tel. (712) 33-46-43.

## ASSOCIATION

**National Association for International Cultural and Humanitarian Relations:** 700003 Tashkent, ul. T. Tula 1; tel. (712) 45-55-54; fax (712) 45-55-53; f. 1992 by merger of Society for Friendship and Cultural Relations with Foreign Countries and Vatan (Motherland) Society for Cultural Relations with Uzbeks Abroad; promotes cultural and educational relations with other countries; Chair. NAIM JA. GAYBOV.

# Education

Until the early 1990s education was based on the Soviet model, but some changes were introduced, including a greater emphasis on Uzbek history and literature, and study of the Arabic script. From 1993 a Latin script was to be introduced. In 1988/89 76.8% of pupils at day schools were educated in Uzbek. Other languages used included Russian (15.0%), Kazakh (2.9%), Kara-Kalpak (2.4%), Tajik (2.3%), Turkmen (0.4%) and Kyrgyz (0.2%). In 2001 the Ministry of Education was reported to have ordered the destruction of a number of books written in the Tajik language. Primary education, beginning at seven years of age, lasts for four years. Secondary education, beginning at 11 years of age, lasts for seven years, comprising a first cycle of five years and a second cycle of two years. According to the Asian Development Bank, in 1999 gross enrolment at primary schools was equivalent to 85% of females and 86% of males in the relevant age-group. The comparable ratio for secondary education in 1994 was 94%. In 2001 6.1m. pupils were enrolled in general secondary schools. Higher education was provided in 61 institutes in 1994/95, with a total enrolment of 183,600 students. In 1993 private educational establishments were banned. In April 1999 the establishment of the Tashkent Islamic University was agreed. In 1999 government expenditure on education was an estimated 171,376m. sum (27.1% of total budgetary expenditure).

## UNIVERSITIES

**Bukhara State University:** 705018 Bukhara, Muhammad Ikbol kuch. 11; tel. (65) 223-23-14; fax (65) 223-12-54; e-mail bukhsu01@ online.ru; internet www.buxdu.narod.ru; 361 teachers; 5,407 students.

**Nukus State University:** Karakalpakstan, 742012 Nukus, ul. Universitetskaya 1; tel. (61) 223-23-72; f. 1979; 11 faculties; 7,000 students; Rector Prof. K. ATANIYAZOV.

**Samarkand State University:** 703004 Samarkand, bul. Universitetskaya 15; tel. and fax (66) 233-68-41; e-mail irosam@samuni.silk .org; internet www.geocities.com/CollegePark/Center/2199; f. 1327; 17 faculties; 1,275 teachers; 16,000 students; Rector Prof. T. M. MUMINOV.

**Tashkent State University:** 700095 Tashkent, Vozgorodok, ul. Universitetskaya 95; tel. (712) 46-02-24; f. 1920; 17 faculties; 1,480 teachers; 19,300 students; Rector Dr S. K. SIRAJINOV.

# Social Welfare

The social-welfare system comprised two funds, the Pension Fund (formerly the Social Insurance Fund) and the Employment Fund, as well as three additional forms of allowance, which were distributed to families on low incomes. The Pension Fund was administered by the Ministry of Social Security and financed by payroll contributions. Benefits included old-age, survivors' and disability pensions. The Employment Fund, supervised by the Ministry of Labour, was also funded by payroll taxes and distributed unemployment benefits and administered employment training schemes.

Subsidies of essential items had also formed part of social protection, but the phasing out of such price-support mechanisms was essential to the process of economic reform, although some still continued after the January 1994 deadline for their elimination. Two new social-security arrangements were then introduced: allowances for low-income families; and compensation payments for a large part of the population. In 1996 there were three main forms of allowance: assistance was distributed to families on low incomes; allowances were paid to families with children under the age of 16 years; and aid was available to mothers with children under two years of age.

Health standards were relatively poor in the country, which was severely affected by environmental problems. Average life expectancy at birth, according to WHO estimates, was 62.7 years for males and 68.5 years for females in 2001. In 1998 there was one physician per 309 inhabitants, and there were 8.31 hospital beds for every 1,000 inhabitants in 1999. The rate of infant mortality was 68 per 1,000 live births in 2001. In 1999 budgetary expenditure on health (including sport) was an estimated 53,510m. sum (or 8.5% of total budgetary expenditure). In September 1998 a US $69.7m. programme to improve health services in Uzbekistan was announced, as part of which the World Bank was to provide a loan of some $30m.

## NATIONAL AGENCIES

**Ministry of Health:** see section on The Government (Ministries).

**Ministry of Labour and Social Security:** see section on The Government (Ministries).

## HEALTH AND WELFARE ORGANIZATIONS

**Central Asian Free Exchange (CAFE):** 700015 Tashkent, ul. Minglar 10; tel. (71) 120-67-57; fax (71) 152-10-87; e-mail cafe@cafengo.org; f. 1991; provides support and technical assistance to govt agencies working in the fields of social-welfare development; Pres. JEFF LIVERMAN.

**Uzbek Institute of Sanitation and Hygiene:** Tashkent, ul. Khamza 85.

# The Environment

Environmental activists were not encouraged by the authorities. Although industrial pollution in Tashkent and the Fergana valley caused disquiet to local groups, the principal environmental concerns in Uzbekistan revolved around water resources and, in particular, the desiccation of the Aral Sea, to which the extensive use of the Syr-Dar'ya and Amu-Dar'ya rivers for irrigation purposes was a major contributing factor (see The Economy). The Sea was once 69 m at its deepest, but in January 1997 it was measured at 37 m. Uzbekistan and other countries of the region again committed themselves to improving the situation by the Nukus Declaration of September 1995, following moves such as the guarantee of a certain level of water input to the Sea. In March 1996, at the meeting of the Inter-State Council on Aral Sea Problems, a new programme to restore the environment of the area was ordered to be drafted and submitted to the ecological commission of the Inter-State Council in July. Measures such as the improvement of irrigation channels, to prevent excessive loss of water, had already been taken. In October 2001 the USA agreed to provide funding of some US $6m. to enable the world's largest known site of buried anthrax, on the island of Vozrozhdeniye (a former location for biological testing), to be destroyed. There were concerns not only that the continued desiccation of the Aral Sea might uncover live anthrax spores, but that insurgents might attempt to obtain the spores in order to perpetrate terrorist attacks.

## GOVERNMENT ORGANIZATION

**Ministry of Agriculture and Water Resources:** see section on The Government (Ministries).

**State Committee for Nature Protection:** see section on The Government (Ministries).

## ACADEMIC INSTITUTES

**Uzbekistan Academy of Sciences (UzAS):** 700000 Tashkent, ul. Acad. Gulamova 70; tel. (71) 133-68-47; fax (71) 133-49-01; e-mail academy@uzsci.net; internet www.academy.uz; f. 1943; 48 attached research institutes, with more than 7,000 members of staff, involved in environmental research covering some 422 sub-disciplines; Pres. Prof. BEKHZAD YULDASHEV.

**Academy of Sciences of Uzbekistan—Karakalpak Branch:** Karakalpakstan, 742000 Nukus, pr. Berdakha 41; tel. (61) 227-72-29; fax (61) 224-06-04; e-mail udasa@uzpak.uz ; f. 1959; scientific research; Chair. TURSUNBAI ESHANOV; Vice-Chair. NAGMET AIMBETOV.

**Institute for Socio-economic Problems of the Aral Sea Region :** Karakalpakstan, 742000 Nukus, ul. Amir Temur 179A; tel. (61) 224-22-09; fax (61) 217-72-28; e-mail udasa@uzpak.uz.

## NON-GOVERNMENTAL ORGANIZATIONS

**Aral SOS Karakalpakstan Republican Society:** Karakalpakstan, 742000 Nukus, ul. Doslik Guzzary 94a; tel. (61) 222-53-42; e-mail artik@silk.glas.apc.org; f. 1994; greening projects in rural areas, programmes for local development, UNDP water supply project, urban environmental rehabilitation; 30 mems.

**Association for an Ecologically Clean Fergana:** 712022 Fergana, ul. Ferganskaya 86; tel. and fax (732) 22-29-17; e-mail ekofergana@vodiy.uz; internet www.cango.net.kg/homepages/uz/CleanFergana; f. 1989; raises ecological awareness; Pres. NITSA POPSPIROVA; 200 mems.

**Bukhara State University Ecology Club:** 705017 Bukhara, Bukhara State University; f. 1993; Chair. MAJDU ARYNOVICH ABDYLGAYEV.

**Committee to Save the Aral Sea:** 700132 Tashkent, Perviya Proen, ul. Sadokat 14; tel. (712) 47-11-95; Chair. PRIMAT SHERMUKHAMEDOV.

**ECOSAN** (International Fund of Ecology and Health): 700000 Tashkent, Shahrisabzkaya 1; tel. (71) 139-83-01; fax (712) 34-24-88; e-mail ecosan@uzpak.uz; internet www.business.uz/ecosan; f. 1992; increases ecological awareness, provides humanitarian aid, attracts foreign investment for realization of ecological projects; Chair. Prof. YUSUFJAN SHADIMETOVICH SHADIMETOV.

**ECOSAN Karakalpakstan:** Karakalpakstan, Nukus, ul. Rashidova 25; tel. (61) 222-17-14; f. 1993; Gen. Dir KHAYRULLA REIPNAZAROV; 17 mems.

**Ecolog Association:** 700105 Tashkent, Gaydara 11A /10; tel. and fax (71) 191-39-35; e-mail tashkent@glasnet.ru; f. 1987; concerned with biodiversity and nature reserves, destruction of the Aral Sea, public health and ecological education; Dirs EUGENE CHERNOGAYEV, ELENA MELNIKOVA, AHTAM SHAYMARDANOV, OLEG IVANOVICH TSARUK; 50 mems.

**Eremurus:** 700048 Tashkent, ul. Botkina 7/47; tel. (712) 68-42-60; e-mail eremurus@hotbox.ru; f. 1982; promotes environmental awareness among the young; Chair. ELENA VLADIMIROVNA MELNIKOVA; 25 mems.

**Green Wave:** Samarkand Obl., Ziadin, Istaklol 20; tel. (66) 403-10-67; f. 1987; environmental protection; 100 mems.

**Lop-Nor Semipalatinsk Ecological Committee (Tashkent):** Tashkent; tel. (712) 46-35-27; f. 1993 as br. of anti-nuclear group based in Kazakhstan; registered as Uigur social org.; Chair. ABDULJAN BARAYEV.

**Union for Defence of the Aral Sea and the Amu-Dar'ya:** Karakalpakstan, 742000 Nukus, pr. Berdakha 41, 8th Floor; tel. and fax (61) 217-72-29; e-mail info@udasa.org; internet www.udasa.org; f. 1989; activities incl. water management in the Aral Sea basin, and the collection of information pertaining to it, energy efficiency, and the publication of a newsletter, *Vdol'Amu (Along Amu)*; Chair. YUSUP SABIROVICH KAMALOV.

# Defence

Military service in Uzbekistan lasts for 18 months. In August 2002 the country possessed total armed forces of an estimated 50,000–55,000. This included an army of 40,000 and an air force of some 10,000–15,000. There were also paramilitary forces numbering an estimated 18,000–20,000 (comprising a 1,000-strong National Guard attached to the Ministry of Defence and about 17,000–19,000 troops attached to the Ministry of Internal Affairs). Although the

Russian Federation was Uzbekistan's main military partner, from the mid-1990s the country increased co-operation with the USA and with the Western military alliance, the North Atlantic Treaty Organization (NATO). Training of a native officer corps was a priority, and one of the main purposes for the country's military academy, the Tashkent Command College. The budget for 2002 allocated an estimated 106m. soms to defence.

**Commander-in-Chief:** President of the Republic.

**Chief of Staff:** Lt-Gen. TOLKIN DZHUMAYEV.

# Bibliography

Allworth, Edward A. *The Modern Uzbeks: From the 14th Century to the Present: a Cultural History*. Stanford, CA, Hoover Institution Press, 1990.

Aminova, R. Kh. *The October Revolution and Women's Liberation in Uzbekistan*. Moscow, Nauka, 1972.

Bohr, A. *Uzbekistan: Politics and Foreign Policy (Central Asian and Caucasian Prospects)*. London, Royal Institute of International Affairs, 1998.

Critchlow, J. *Nationalism in Uzbekistan: A Soviet Republic's Road to Sovereignty*. Boulder, Westview Press, 1991.

Kangas, R. D. *Uzbekistan in the Twentieth Century: Political Development and the Evolution of Power*. New York, NY, St Martin's Press, 1994.

Kalter, Johannes, Pavaloi, Margareta, and Karimov, Islam. *Uzbekistan: Heir to the Silk Road*. London, Thames and Hudson, 1997.

Kaser, Michael. *The Economies of Kazakhstan and Uzbekistan (Former Soviet South Project)*. Washington, DC, Brookings Institution Press, 1997.

Lubin, Nancy, Martin, Keith, and Rubin, Barnett R. *Calming the Ferghana Valley: Development and Dialogue in the Heart of Central Asia*. Washington, DC, Brookings Institution Press, 2000.

Medlin, W. K., Carpenter, F., and Cave, W. M. *Education and Development in Central Asia: A Case Study on Social Change in Uzbekistan*. Leiden, Brill, 1971.

Melvin, N. J. *Uzbekistan: Transition to Authoritarianism on the Silk Road (Post Communist States and Nations)*. London, Routledge, 2000.

Thubron, Colin. *The Lost Heart of Asia*. London, Heinemann, 2000.

Yalcin, R. *Rebirth of Uzbekistan: Politics, Economy and Society in the Post-Soviet Era*. London, Garnet Publishing Ltd, 2002.

Also see the Select Bibliography in Part Four.

PART THREE

# Political Profiles of the Region

# POLITICAL PROFILES

**ABASHIDZE, Aslan Ibragimovich:** Georgian (Ajarian) politician and economist; Chairman of the Supreme Council of the Autonomous Republic of Ajaria; b. 20 June 1938, in Batumi, Ajaria; ethnic Ajar; one s. and one d. *Education:* attended Batumi Pedagogical Institute and Ivan Javakhishvili Tbilisi State University. *Career:* a descendant of the dynasty that ruled Ajaria from 1463 until the late 19th century, he was an economist and philologist for Komsomol (the V. I. Lenin Young Communist League) for three years before becoming an English teacher at Batumi Conservatoire. He was Chairman of the Batumi City Council executive committee (1981–84) and Ajarian Minister of the Civil Service in 1984–86, when he was appointed the First Deputy Minister of the Civil Service of the Georgian SSR. He became Minister in 1990. Between 1990 and 1995 he was Deputy Chairman of the Georgian legislature, the Supreme Soviet (Supreme Council), and in April 1991 he was appointed Chairman of the Supreme Soviet (Supreme Council) of the Autonomous Republic of Ajaria. He managed to maintain civil peace in the region, although he fostered a 'cult of personality'. In 1992 he established the All-Georgia Union of Revival, which obtained a total of 31 seats in the new 235-seat Georgian Parliament in legislative elections in November 1995. Although Abashidze had been an earlier rival to Eduard Shevardnadze (q.v.), nationally his power and popularity were decreasing in the mid-1990s and, after the 1995 elections, he pledged his support for Shevardnadze's presidency, reportedly having been assured that his influence in his native Ajaria would not be challenged. Indeed, in elections to the Ajarian Supreme Council in September 1996, the majority of the seats were won by an alliance of the All-Georgian Union of Revival and President Shevardnadze's Citizens' Union of Georgia; the results were widely considered to have been falsified. Abashidze was re-elected Chairman. However, in the late 1990s relations with Shevardnadze cooled and the opening of another route into Turkey curtailed Ajaria's strategic importance. Abashidze relinquished his parliamentary mandate in November 1999, citing his inability to attend sittings in the Georgian capital, Tbilisi, owing to his fear of assassination, although he had also been vocal in his criticism of the Georgian parliamentary elections held in October–November, in which his Union of Georgian Revival bloc had taken part. He stood as a candidate in the Georgian presidential election of April 2000, but he withdrew his candidacy the day before it took place. In November 2001 Abashidze stood as the sole candidate in the election to the newly created post of Head of the Autonomous Republic (which was to replace the post of Chairman of the Ajarian Supreme Council); in the same month Shevardnadze appointed Abashidze as the President's personal representative for conflict resolution in Abkhazia and South Ossetia, although his failure, at least in the short term, to make meaningful progress in the resolution of the conflict appeared to damage Abashidze's standing in both Georgia and Russia. He became an increasingly harsh critic of Shevardnadze's administration, stating in October 2002 that the President should be impeached. In 2003 he stated that his frustration with the country's political system was such that he would not return to Tbilisi until he was elected President of Georgia. *Address:* Supreme Council of the Republic of Ajaria, 385003 Batumi, ul. Gogebashvili 4/24, Georgia; internet www.adjara-ar.org/eng/head.shtml.htm.

**ABDILDIN, Serikbolsyn Abdildayevich:** Kazakh politician; b. 25 February 1937, in Kyzylkesek, Semipalatinsk; m., with one s. and one d. *Education:* KazGos Agricultural College (1955–60); KazGos Post-Graduate College (1963–66); received a doctorate in economics in 1988. *Career:* he was a member of the Communist Party of the Soviet Union between 1964 and 1991, and a member of the Communist Party of Kazakhstan (CPK) from 1981 until 1991, when it was ordered to cease

activities. The CPK was reformed as the independent Socialist Party of Kazakhstan (SPK), of which Abdildin was a member from 1993. The CPK was permitted to re-register in March 1994, and Abdildin became its First Secretary in April 1996. In January 1999 he contested the presidential election, announcing his support for state ownership of sectors such as electricity and transport, and the imposition of restrictions on foreign investment. He came in second place, behind the incumbent President, Nursultan Nazarbayev (q.v.), with 12.1% of the votes cast. In 2001 Abdildin was subject to criticism from CPK members, who accused him of deviating from communist principles of leadership. Abdildin joined a new opposition movement, the Democratic Choice of Kazakhstan (DCK), in 2001, and was also a vocal member of the opposition as a deputy in the Majlis (Assembly). He remained leader of the CPK, despite criticism directed at him for aligning himself with the DCK (the movement having lost momentum after its founder departed in early 2002). Later in 2002 he survived what he deemed to be an attempt to poison him. *Address:* Communist Party of Kazakhstan, Karasai batyr 85/312, Almaty, Kazakhstan; tel. (3272) 65-11-19.

**ABRAMOVICH, Roman Arkadyevich:** Russian business executive and politician; 24 October 1966, in Saratov; m. 1st Olga Abramovich; one d.; m. 2nd Irina Malandina; one s. and one d. *Education:* Industrial Institute of Ukhta, Komi ASSR, and the Moscow Gubkin Institute of Oil and Gas. *Career:* he is believed to have accrued his initial wealth through the trading of tyres and of other commodities, before concentrating on petroleum products. In 1993–96 he managed the Moscow office of the Swiss petroleum firm Runicom SA and in the mid-1990s was involved in the formation of several hydrocarbons companies, and was a close associate of the prominent business executive, Boris Berezovskii (q.v.). Abramovich amassed a portfolio of investments in some of Russia's biggest companies, most notably in the hydrocarbons group, Sibneft (of which he was made a director in September 1996), the aluminium company, RusAl (Russian Aluminium), and the airline, Aeroflot. In December 1999 he was elected to the State Duma, representing the Chukot Autonomous Okrug (Chukotka), the eastern-most territory in Russia, and in December 2000 he was elected as the territory's Governor. Although he invested large amounts of his own money in Chukotka, improving its infrastructure and amenities, in 2003 Abramovich stated that he did not intend to contest a further term of office as Governor, following the expiry of his first term in 2004. In advance of the merger of Sibneft with Yukos in 2003, Abramovich, who was described as Russia's second-richest man, sought to diversify his interests, and he came to international prominence in mid-2003, when he purchased a British football club, Chelsea. In September it was announced that Abramovich had sold his stake in RusAl. *Address:* 689000 Chukot AOk, Anadyr, ul. Beringa 20, Russia; tel. (42722) 2-90-13; fax (42722) 4-24-66; internet www.chukotka.org.

**AKAYEV, Askar:** President of Kyrgyzstan; b. 10 Nov. 1944, in Kyzyl-Bayzak Keminsky raion; m. Mairam Akayev in 1970, with two s. and two d. *Career:* a mathematics professor, he joined the Communist Party of the Soviet Union (CPSU) in 1981 (resigning from it in 1991). He was a member of the Central Committee of the Kyrgyz Communist Party, President of the Kyrgyz Academy of Sciences and a member of various all-Union committees. A known liberal, he was elected by the republican Supreme Soviet as executive President in October 1990, after the communist leader (for whom the post had been designed) failed to win a majority. Akayev was a compromise candidate, unconnected with the dominant factions, having been in Leningrad (now St Petersburg, Russia) for many years of his academic career. He favoured the introduction of economic reform before political changes, although he also achieved some consensus with the opposition. He ensured that Kyrgyzstan was one of the most ostensibly liberal of the Central Asian states. He condemned the coup attempt against President Mikhail Gorbachev (q.v.) of the USSR, in August 1991, and resigned from the Communist Party, which was subsequently dissolved. In October Akayev was unopposed in a direct presidential election. He resolved to make independent Kyrgyzstan the 'Switzerland of Central Asia', and urged economic reform on an untypically (for Central Asia) critical parliament. During 1993 parliament reduced his powers and he suffered the investigations of political colleagues for corruption. Both the Vice-President, Feliks Kulov (q.v.), and the premier were obliged to resign in December. The President was elected to another term in an election held on 24 December, with some 72% of the votes cast. Sure of his popularity, he then ordered a referendum in February 1996, by which he secured augmented powers vis-à-vis parliament. In 1998 the Constitutional Court approved Akayev's attempt to run for, effectively, a third term in office in 2000, despite the constitutional maximum of two terms. The Court agreed that Akayev's first term pre-dated the Constitution, and should, therefore, not be taken into account. Improved relations with neighbouring states were typified by the marriage in July 1998 of his son to the daughter of President Nursultan Nazarbayev of Kazakhstan (q.v.). A presidential election took place on 29 October 2000, in which Akayev was re-elected with 74.5% of the votes cast, amid allegations of serious irregularities. Subsequently, there were allegations of human rights offences, and reports of the repression of both political opponents and the media. Violent unrest occurred in 2002, following allegations of the politically motivated detention of opposition figures and over the ratification of a controversial border treaty with the People's Republic of China. In February 2003 a new draft constitution, proposed by Akayev, was approved in a referendum (the electorate also supported a proposal that Akayev serve the full term of his presidential mandate, due to expire in December 2005). Speculation emerged that he intended to seek a further presidential term under the provisions of the new Constitution; he swiftly denied that he would be a candidate, although many observers were sceptical. Legislation enacted in June provided for lifelong immunity from prosecution for Akayev upon his departure from office. As the year advanced the future of the presidency became the subject of much conjecture—some newspaper reports suggested that Akayev's wife, Mairam, might seek election (no official comment was made). Following a ruling by the legislature's constitutional affairs commitee in September that he would be eligible for a further term of office Akayev's supporters began campaigning for him to reverse his decision not to stand, but he refused to do so. Unrest among opposition groups continued throughout 2003, as complaints about alleged human rights violations and abuses of the democratic process were frequent. *Address:* Office of the President of the Republic, 720003 Bishkek, Govt House, Dom Pravitelstva, Kyrgyzstan; tel. (312) 21-24-66; fax (312) 21-86-27; e-mail office@mail.gov.kg; internet www .president.kg.

**AKILOV, Akil:** Prime Minister of Tajikistan. *Career:* the former Deputy Governor of Leninabad Oblast, he was appointed Prime Minister on 20 December 1999. His predecessor, Yakhyo Azimov, had resigned in November, in accordance with the Constitution, following the re-election of the incumbent President, Imamali Rakhmonov (q.v.). From 2000 Akilov's cabinet was increasingly composed of members of the United Tajik Opposition (UTO), as demanded by the peace agreement reached in 1997. His main priority was the development of the country's economy. He was a particularly enthusiastic advocate of the development of Tajikistan's hitherto underdeveloped water resources, which were considered capable of providing irrigation and hydroelectric power for much of Central Asia. *Address:* Secretariat of the Prime Minister, 734023 Dushanbe, pr. Rudaki 80, Tajikistan; tel. (372) 21-18-71; fax (372) 21-15-10.

**ALEKSEI II (Ridiger), His Holiness Patriarch:** Russian ecclesiastic; Patriarch of Moscow and all Rus; b. 23 Feb. 1929, in Tallinn, Estonia; of Baltic German and ethnic Russian descent. *Education:* a graduate of the Leningrad (now St

Petersburg) Theological College. *Career:* originally Aleksei M. Ridiger, his early career in the Russian Orthodox Church was in his native Estonia, and he became Bishop of Tallinn and Estonia in 1961. He was appointed Vice-Chairman of the Dept of External Affairs of the Moscow Patriarchate in 1962. In 1964 he became an Archbishop, the Administrative Manager of the Patriarchate and a permanent member of the Holy Synod. In 1968 he became Metropolitan of Tallinn and Estonia and, in 1986, Metropolitan of Leningrad and Novgorod. In 1990 he succeeded Patriarch Pimen as Patriarch of Moscow and All Rus, in which position he was regarded as being theologically conservative. Although there were claims that he had been a collaborator of the Soviet security services, he condemned the attempted *putsch* of August 1991 and mediated between Boris Yeltsin (q.v.) and the Russian parliament in the constitutional crisis of September–October 1993. He also publicly endorsed President Yeltsin's re-election campaign in May 1996. Nevertheless, the role of the Moscow Patriarchate in Russia was a matter of considerable dispute in the 1990s. Patriarch Aleksei publicly declared its neutrality towards the state and forbade priests to participate in elected government, despite having served as a people's deputy himself in 1989–91. Concern persisted over the role of priest-led lay orders, such as the Union of Orthodox Brotherhood, which fostered nationalist sympathies. Moreover, in early 1993 the Patriarch initiated the amendment of a Law on Freedom of Conscience, permitting the Ministry of Justice greater control over foreign missions in Russia. This concern with 'rival' denominations and with other Russian Orthodox jurisdictions in the 'near abroad' (former USSR—particularly in Estonia and in Ukraine) necessitated a certain degree of co-operation with the state. Ecclesiastical concern for former congregations often coincided with state concerns for those of Russian nationality in other countries. This was clearly demonstrated in early 1996, when Russian-Estonian relations deteriorated during a dispute over jurisdictions within Estonia. However, the Moscow Patriarchate's main concern remained the domestic challenge of 'proselytism' by non-Orthodox religious groups; Aleksei II welcomed the restrictive legislation finally introduced by the Russian parliament in September 1997. In April 1999 Aleksei II visited Belgrade, the capital of the Federal Republic of Yugoslavia (now Serbia and Montenegro), and met that country's President, Slobodan Milošević, as part of Russian efforts to mediate a peace settlement during the bombardment of Serbia by North Atlantic Treaty Organization (NATO) forces. On several occasions during the 1990s the Patriarch opposed proposals by Roman Catholic Pope John Paul II to visit Russia, and criticized visits by the Roman pontiff to Kazakhstan and Ukraine in 2001 as impinging upon the Moscow Patriarchate's 'canonical territory'. In 2002, after the Vatican raised the status of its four apostolic administrations in Russia to that of diocese, talks between the Roman Catholic Church and the Moscow Patriarchate were suspended. In 2000 Aleksei II was reported to have signed a co-operation agreement with the state-controlled petroleum company, LUKoil, for the creation of various joint ventures. The Patriarch subsequently appeared in a television advertisement for LUKoil, thanking the company for its support. Aleksei's health deteriorated in late 2002, and he was hospitalized on several occasions in the subsequent months. He maintained his fierce opposition to a visit by the Roman pontiff to Russia and to the expansion of the Roman Catholic Church's activities in the country, and claimed an amount of success in his desire to forge closer links between the Patriarchate and the state. *Address:* Moscow Patriarchate, 115191 Moscow, Danilov Monastery, ul. Danilovskii val 22, Russia; tel. (095) 230-24-39; fax (095) 230-26-19; e-mail commserv@ mospat.dol.ru; internet www.russian-orthodox-church.org.ru.

**ALESKEROV, Murtuz Nadzhaf:** Chairman of the Milli Majlis (parliamentary speaker) of Azerbaijan; b. 20 Sept. 1928, in Gyandzha; m., with two s. and one d. *Education:* Azerbaijan State University and Moscow Institute of State and Law, Russia. *Career:* Formerly the Rector of Azerbaijan State University, he was appointed speaker of the Milli Majlis (legislature) in September 1996, upon the resignation of Rasul Kuliyev. Kuliyev resigned following criticism from President

Heydar Aliyev's (q.v.) New Azerbaijan Party (Yeni Azerbaijan), although the official reason given was ill health. Aleskerov, a staunch supporter of President Aliyev, proved more co-operative, and was trusted to act as interim President on a number of occasions when Aliyev was out of the country or incapacitated. However, the constitutional changes approved in August 2002 made it the responsibility of the Prime Minister, not the speaker, to take on these duties. Aleskerov remained a close ally of the ailing Aliyev, and of his son, Ilham Aliyev (q.v.)., who was elected President in mid-October 2003. *Address:* Milli Majlis, 370152 Baku, Mehti Hussein St 2, Azerbaijan; tel. (12) 92-79-45; fax (12) 98-02-42.

**ALIYEV, Maj.-Gen. Heydar Ali Rza oglu:** former President of Azerbaijan; b. 10 May 1923, in Keleki, Nakhichevan; m. Zarifa Aziz kizy Aliyeva (deceased), with 2 s., incl. Ilham (q.v.). *Education:* Institute of Industry, Baku, and a graduate of Azerbaijan State University (1957). *Career:* already active in the administration of his home territory of Nakhichevan, he joined the Communist Party of the Soviet Union (CPSU) in 1945 and was prominent in the republican apparatus by the 1960s. He became First Secretary of the Communist Party of Azerbaijan, and, thus, leader of the republic, in 1969. In 1982 he was appointed First Deputy Chairman of the USSR Council of Ministers in Moscow, Russia. He was dismissed in October 1987, a victim of Mikhail Gorbachev's (q.v.) drive against corruption. He left the communists in July 1991, and in September was elected Chairman of the Supreme Majlis (parliament) of the Autonomous Republic of Nakhichevan. Aliyev was prevented from contesting the presidential election of June 1992 because he exceeded the maximum age limit of 65 years. In the same year he founded the New Azerbaijan Party (NAP—Yeni Azerbaijan), support for which demonstrated his continuing popularity in the country. In early June 1993, threatened by revolt, President Abulfaz Elchibey summoned Aliyev to Baku and offered him the premiership, which Aliyev refused. On 15 June Aliyev was elected Chairman of the Milli Majlis (National Assembly) and three days later declared that he had appropriated the presidential powers of Elchibey, who had fled to Nakhichevan the previous night. One week later the Milli Majlis granted Aliyev the majority of these powers and on 28 June Col Surat Husseinov, a rebel army commander who had precipitated the crisis, recognized him as acting President. He was elected President by direct popular vote on 3 October, receiving 98.8% of the votes cast. Repeated allegations of planned coup attempts throughout the mid- and late 1990s gave him the excuse further to strengthen his power, with those unsupportive of his regime dismissed from government positions, opponents arrested and some opposition parties suspended. He was re-elected President, with 76.1% of the votes cast, in a single round of voting on 11 October 1998. The main opposition parties refused to participate in the elections, in protest at the undemocratic nature of the contest. President Aliyev strove to improve the country's international relations, particularly with Russia, although the *rapprochement* was a cautious one. Attempts to promote a peace settlement in Nagornyi Karabakh, which had made progress while Levon Ter-Petrossian (q.v.) was President of Armenia (1991–98), faltered when Robert Kocharian (q.v.) was elected to the position in March 1998. Aliyev was a good tactician and recognized the potential of the country's reserves of petroleum. He was widely credited with restoring stability to Azerbaijan and attracting investment in the petroleum sector; however, his critics claimed that insufficient progress had been made towards the repatriation of Azeris who had been forced to leave Nagornyi Karabakh as a result of the conflict in the disputed exclave. Doubts persisted about the state of Aliyev's health from 1999, following heart surgery. None the less, in October 2002 he confirmed that he intended to stand for re-election in 2003, despite a constitutional clause that prohibited a third consecutive presidential term. However, large-scale opposition protests demanding his resignation had commenced in August, raising fears of increased instability, and drawing attention to the lack of an obvious successor. The appointment of his son, Ilham Aliyev (q.v.), to the post of Prime Minister in August 2003, was condemned by opposition groups as an attempt to create a dynastic succession. His health had deteriorated earlier in the year, and he travelled to Turkey shortly afterwards for medical treatment. He returned to Azerbaijan briefly the following month, before departing for further treatment in the USA. Eventually, in early October, less than two weeks before the scheduled presidential election, he announced his withdrawal from the contest. *Address:* New Azerbaijan Party, 370000 Baku, Bul-Bul Ave 13, Azerbaijan.

**ALIYEV, Ilham:** President of Azerbaijan; b. 1961, in Baku; m., with one s. and two d. *Education:* studied at the Moscow State Institute of International Relations, Russia, in 1977–85. *Career:* He taught at the Moscow State Institute of International Relations until 1990, before working as a businessman in both Baku and İstanbul, Turkey. In May 1994 he became First Vice-President of the State Oil Company of the Azerbaijan Republic (SOCAR). On 21 December 1999 he was also elected Deputy Chairman of the New Azerbaijan Party (NAP—Yeni Azerbaijan), chaired by his father, Heydar Aliyev (q.v.), the President of Azerbaijan, and in November 2001 he was elected First Deputy Chairman. This appointment prompted speculation that preparations were being made for him to succeed his father, particularly as uncertainties about the President's health intensified, although some feared that he lacked sufficient authority and political expertise to take on the role. In addition to his political and entrepreneurial positions, Ilham Aliyev was President of the National Olympic Committee of Azerbaijan. He was elected an NAP deputy in the Milli Majlis, following the parliamentary elections of November 2000, but he failed to attract widespread popular support. The President's failing health prompted Ilham Aliyev's appointment as Prime Minister in August 2003, following constitutional amendments approved in the previous year, which provided for power to be transferred to the premier in the event of the President's incapacitation; he resigned his position at SOCAR. Ilham Aliyev took leave of absence from the premiership almost immediately, however, as it was announced that he would contest the presidential election in October, although at this stage his father also remained a candidate, eventually withdrawing from the contest in early October. At the presidential election, held on 15 October, Ilham Aliyev recorded a comfortable victory, obtaining some 79.5% of the votes cast. It remained to be seen whether stability would be maintained in Azerbaijan; in the weeks preceding the election Ilham Aliyev had appeared increasingly uncomfortable when dealing with the inevitable media attention, and was reported to prefer gambling to politics. There were hopes that he could prove himself to be a Western-orientated reformer, but widespread condemnation of the conduct of the election by international observers and opposition groups, together with outbreaks of severe unrest, led many to doubts that this dynastic succession could endure a full term of office. *Address:* Office of the President, 370066 Baku, Istiklal St 19, Azerbaijan; tel. (12) 92-17-26; fax (12) 92-35-43; e-mail office@apparat.gov.az; internet www .president.az.

**BASAYEV, Shamil Salmanovich:** Russian (Chechen) military leader; b. 1965, in Vedeno, Checheno-Ingush ASSR; m. *Education:* Completed secondary education in 1982, reportedly entered Faculty of Law at Moscow M. V. Lomonosov State University—MGU on three occasions, and the Moscow Institute of Land-Construction Engineers, but in all cases failed to complete courses successfully. *Career:* a former computer salesman and Soviet Army fireman, he joined the Confederation of the People of the Caucasus (KNK) in 1991, and in November of that year participated in the hijacking of a plane from Mineralnye Vody (Stavropol Krai) to Turkey, to protest against the introduction of martial law in Chechnya. In August 1992 he participated in fighting in the autonomous Georgian republic of Abkhazia, and in April–July 1994 he received training in Afghanistan. Basayev subsequently fought against Russian troops in Chechnya, following the outbreak of civil conflict in that year. On 14 June 1995 he took some 2,000 people hostage and seized control of a hospital in Budennovsk, in Stavropol Krai, threatening to kill the captives unless federal forces withdrew from Chechnya. A deal was eventually reached with the Russian Prime Minister,

Viktor Chernomyrdin (q.v.), under the terms of which a cease-fire was to come into effect, peace talks were to commence and the Chechen rebels were to be permitted to return to the republic in safety, in return for the release of all hostages. (More than 100 people died in the siege, however.) A fragile cease-fire agreement was implemented in July, but hostilities had resumed by December. In April 1996 Basayev became commander of the self-styled 'Armed Forces of the Chechen Republic'. A peace agreement for Chechnya was eventually reached on 31 August, and Basayev resigned from his army post in December, in order to stand as a candidate in the Republic's forthcoming presidential election. In the election, held on 27 January 1997, he received just 22.7% of the votes cast; the victor was the more moderate candidate, Khalid 'Aslan' Maskhadov (q.v.). Basayev played a prominent role in the renewed civil conflict from August 1999, when Islamist factions from Chechnya launched raids on Dagestan. Despite losing a leg in a landmine accident in early 2000, he was believed to have become Commander-in-Chief of the rebel fighters in July of that year. Basayev was held responsible for organizing suicide attacks in Chechnya in mid-2000 and was dubbed 'public enemy number one' by the federal Government. As the conflict in Chechnya intensified, Basayev was reported, by early 2001, to have established a base in Georgia. In mid-2002 he was allegedly appointed head of a new rebel military committee, the State Defence Committee, with the aim of mounting a further offensive against Russian troops. Frequent reports of his death were refuted, and he continued to move between the numerous rebel bases in the region. Many in Russia believed him to be linked with the group of Chechen separatists which took the audience hostage at a Moscow theatre production in October 2002, and a report by a British journalist who was allowed to speak to the group during the subsequent siege suggested that they considered themselves to be acting on Basayev's orders. The Russian Government later accused Maskhadov and Basayev of ordering the attack. Basayev responded by claiming responsibility, but stated that he had not informed Maskhadov of the plan. Relations between the two separatist leaders subsequently deteriorated, and Maskhadov reportedly severed all links with Basayev in November. Basayev also claimed responsibility for a suicide attack outside the headquarters of the republican Government in the Chechen capital, Groznyi, in late December, in which at least 83 people were killed. Basayev remained in hiding in Chechnya, and continued to claim responsibility for attacks on Russian military and administrative interests there. He and Maskhadov were reported to have been reconciled in June 2003. In August, following a further suicide attack on a military hospital in Mozdok, North Osetiya, the US administration declared Basayev (who had not claimed any responsibility for the attack) a terrorist threat to the USA; Georgia took similar action later in the month. Efforts by Russian forces to detain him increased in mid-2003, and his public pronouncements became less frequent as he endeavoured to avoid capture.

**BEREZOVSKII, Boris Abramovich:** Russian businessman, politician and mathematician, former Executive Secretary of the Commonwealth of Independent States (CIS); b. 23 Jan. 1946, in Moscow; m., with four c. *Education:* Moscow Institute of Wood Technology and Moscow State University. *Career:* a mathematician who joined the car industry, he was a founder and head of the LogoVAZ company during the first half of the 1990s. He accumulated a vast financial, industrial and media empire, and was one of the leading financiers to back the re-election of Boris Yeltsin to the presidency in 1996. In reward, discreet power was translated into an official position, despite an earlier and controversial involvement in the investigation of the murder of a prominent broadcaster. With his influence stemming from his association with Yeltsin's entourage and association with Viktor Chernomyrdin (q.v.), Berezovskii lasted longer in government than other 'oligarchs'. He was appointed Deputy Chairman of the Security Council and served in this position for about one year, until the reformists urged Yeltsin to unravel the administration from association with the 'oligarchs'. Berezovskii remained a power in the hydrocarbons

industry, enjoying influence in Chechnya and in Azerbaijan. His personal relations with President Yeltsin were reported to be tense by the time of his appointment to the ill-defined post of Secretary of the CIS at the end of April 1998. In March 1999 Yeltsin dismissed Berezovskii from his position at the CIS, owing to alleged misconduct and neglect of duties, although Berezovskii insisted that only the Council of Heads of State of the CIS had the authority to remove him from office; several member states also expressed their anger at not having been consulted on the issue. As a result of his dismissal, Berezovskii's diplomatic immunity was revoked; the following month he was charged with money 'laundering' (the processing of illegally obtained funds into legitimate accounts), illegal entrepreneurship and abuse of office. The charges, which Berezovskii insisted were politically motivated, were eventually dropped in November (however, a further warrant for his arrest was issued the following November, when, having left Russia, he failed to return to face questioning on the renewed charges). Berezovskii was elected to the State Duma in December 1999, representing the Republic of Karachayevo-Cherkessiya. He supported the candidacy of Vladimir Putin (q.v.) in the presidential election held in March 2000, but announced his resignation from the State Duma in mid-July, in protest at Putin's perceived autocracy. In December Berezovskii, speaking in New York, the USA, announced the foundation of a non-governmental organization, the International Foundation for Civil Liberties, which was to promote and defend human rights and civil liberties in Russia. In 2001, moreover, Berezovskii co-founded a political party, Liberal Russia, which aimed to promote liberal political and economic policies. (Notably, the party was denied registration on several occasions, following the introduction of stricter controls relating to political parties in July of that year. However, in September 2002 Berezovskii was expelled from the party, after he offered funding to the Communist Party of the Russian Federation, and Liberal Russia was subsequently permitted to register.) In April 2001 a television station, TV-6, which was 70%-owned by Berezovskii, became Russia's leading independent station, following the defection to the channel of several journalists from another independent station, NTV, after that station's majority acquisition by Gazprom-Media, a subsidiary of the state-controlled gas monopoly, Gazprom, from the Media-Most group owned by Vladimir Gusinskii (q.v.). TV-6 became a persistent critic of government policy (as NTV had hitherto been) and in January 2002 it was compelled to cease transmission, following a court case brought by a minority shareholder (and subsidiary of the state-controlled petroleum company, LUKoil), which demanded the company's liquidation on the grounds of insolvency. The ruling prompted protests over free speech and political interference. Although Berezovskii remained outside Russia, in October 2001 a further arrest warrant was issued against him on three charges of financial impropriety. In March 2002 Berezovskii presented a video-recording in London, the United Kingdom (where he had made his home), purporting to demonstrate the involvement of the Federal Security Service (FSB), and the acquiescence of Putin, in the apartment-block bombings of September 1999, which had prompted Russia's renewed offensive in Chechnya. The FSB dismissed the allegations and threatened to challenge Berezovskii over them in court if he returned to Russia. The security service also claimed to hold evidence proving that Berezovskii had financed Chechen separatist fighters—in February 2002 Berezovskii admitted donating funds to the region, but said that they had been intended for a cement factory. In March 2003 Russian authorities issued an extradition warrant for Berezovskii, charging him with fraud relating to his time as head of LogoVAZ. He claimed political asylum in the United Kingdom and appeared in a British court in April, claiming that the charges against him were politically motivated, and that his life would be in danger if he were returned to Russia. He subsequently stated that the killing of a political ally in Russia, the Liberal Russia deputy Sergei Yushchenkov, added weight to his claims (allegations that he had been involved in the murder also surfaced, although the police investigation, concluded in July, found no evidence to support these claims). Also in April Berezovskii claimed that he remained the owner of a stake in the hydro-carbons company Sibneft, which had recently merged with Yukos. A faction of Liberal Russia voted to readmit him to the party, and his prospects of a return to political life, should he ever return to Russia, seemed to improve. In September the British Government reversed an earlier decision and granted asylum to Berezovskii. Although the Russian authorities refused to abandon the extradition case, it had little chance of succeeding and was dismissed a few days later. Russian officials stated that the asylum decision was damaging to Russian-British relations, while Berezovskii pronounced himself delighted at the news. His hopes of returning to Russian political life were quashed later in the month, however, when a court prohibited the faction of Liberal Russia that had voted to readmit Berezovskii as its leader from participating in elections. *Address:* International Foundation for Civil Liberties, 152 West 57th St, 25th Floor, New York, NY 10019, USA; tel. (212) 397-29-74; e-mail info@kolokol.org.

**BRAGHIȘ, Dumitru:** former Prime Minister of Moldova. *Career:* Braghiș, hitherto the Deputy Minister for Economy and Reform, was approved as Prime Minister in December 1999, ending weeks of political crisis, in which both previous nominees had failed to attract a sufficient number of votes. In the parliamentary election of February 2001 the centrist electoral bloc, the Braghiș Alliance, led by the Prime Minister and founded in 2000, won 19 of the 101 seats available. Braghiș' Government tendered its resignation on 20 March on the expiry of its term of office. Braghiș subsequently stood as a candidate in the presidential election held in the following month, but, obtaining only 15 of the 89 votes cast in the legislature, was defeated by the leader of the Communist Party of Moldova, Vladimir Voronin (q.v.). In December 2001 the Braghiș Alliance and the 'Furnica' Social Democratic Party of Moldova formed the Social Democratic Alliance of Moldova, of which Braghiș was elected leader. In April 2002 the Alliance announced a boycott of parliament, pending an agreement by the Government to negotiate with opposition protesters. His opposition to the communist Government remained determined, and he led his group into another boycott of parliament in December, after the Government had refused to allow proposed changes to the country's electoral legislation to be put to a referendum (the boycott ended in April 2003). In July the Alliance merged with two other centrist parties, to form the Moldova Noastra (Our Moldova) Social Liberal Alliance; Braghiș was elected co-leader. He favoured a European orientation for Moldova, seeking greater involvement from Romania and the European Union in the attempts to resolve the conflict in Transnistria. *Address:* Moldova Noastra Social Liberal Alliance, Chișinău, str. Puskin 62A, Moldova; tel. (2) 54-85-38; e-mail vitalia@ch.moldpac.md.

**BURDZHANADZE, Nino:** Georgian academic, lawyer and politician; b. 16 June 1964, in Kutaisi, Imereti Oblast; m. *Education:* graduated from the Faculty of Law of the Ivan Javakhishvili Tbilisi State University in 1986, and in 1990 obtained a doctorate at the Moscow M. V. Lomonosov State University (MGU—Russia) in International Law. *Career:* Professor at the Ivan Javakhishvili Tbilisi State University in the International Relations and International Law Department from 1991, Burdzhanadze subsequently worked as a consultant to the Ministry of Environmental Protection and to the Committee on Foreign Relations at the Georgian Parliament. In 1995 she was elected as a deputy to the Parliament, and was elected Chairman of the Georgian Parliament (Sakartvelos Parlamenti) on 9 November 2001. Controversy about the separation of powers in Georgia arose in December 2001, following the promotion of Burdzhanadze's husband, Badri Bitsadze, to the position of First Deputy Procurator-General. In August 2003 she formed a new electoral bloc, the Burdzhanadze-Democrats, with her predecessor as parliamentary speaker, Zurab Zhvania (q.v.), and a number of other parliamentarians. Although she had previously denied any intention to do so, it was widely believed that she would seek election to the presidency in 2005. A popular figure, she campaigned against the perceived corruption and incompetence of the incumbent Government, and

supported improved relations with Russia. *Address:* Sakartvelos Parlamenti, 380028 Tbilisi, Rustaveli 8, Georgia; tel. (32) 93-61-70; fax (32) 99-93-86; e-mail webmaster@parliament.ge.

**CHERNOMYRDIN, Viktor Stepanovich:** Russian politician, diplomat and former premier; b. 9 April 1938, in Chernyi-Otrog village, Orenburg Oblast; m., with two c. *Education:* Kuibyshev (now Samara) Polytechnic. *Career:* He held various posts in the state and Communist Party bureaucracy, and became involved in the gas industry, before being appointed Soviet Minister of the Gas Industry in 1985. In 1989 he oversaw the formation of the state energy company, Gazprom, of which he was appointed Chairman. He served as Minister of Fuel and Energy in June-December 1992. In December 1992 President Boris Yeltsin (q.v.) nominated him as a Chairman of the Council of Ministers who would be acceptable to the conservative Russian parliament. As premier he was strongly criticized by radical economic reformers, while Western economic institutions were initially suspicious of his policies, mainly owing to his willingness to subsidize inefficient state enterprises. He was particularly protective of the energy industry, the interest group with which he remained most strongly identified. During the mid-1990s, however, Chernomyrdin won a reputation as a proponent of moderate economic reform, following the stabilization of the rouble and a reduction in the rate of inflation. The ill health of the President, and a successful intervention during the Chechen hostage crisis in Budennovsk (Stavropol Krai) in June 1995, also gave Chernomyrdin considerable authority. His support of Yeltsin remained firm and he founded a centrist party, Our Home is Russia (OHR). While adept at mediating between powerful business interests and left-wing factions in parliament, he remained an uninspiring politician; the failure of reform to benefit the population at large helped prompt Yeltsin's unexpected dismissal of him in March 1998. Not long afterwards, however, his successor, Sergei Kiriyenko (q.v.), himself became a victim of the financial crisis of August. Yeltsin turned to Chernomyrdin as a stable influence, although parliament refused to confirm him as premier, sharing the reformers' suspicions that the ground for many of Russia's economic problems had been prepared while he was in government. Yeltsin accepted the State Duma's second rejection of Chernomyrdin in September. In April 1999 Chernomyrdin was appointed by Yeltsin as Russia's special envoy to the Balkans, a position that he held until early August. His appointment was regarded as a challenge to the then Prime Minister, Yevgenii Primakov (q.v.), who had already initiated his own major peace initiative in the region. Chernomyrdin helped to negotiate a peace settlement for the Federal Republic of Yugoslavia in June. At the end of that month he was reappointed Chairman of Gazprom. In elections to the State Duma in December 1999, OHR obtained just seven seats; the party was subsequently absorbed into the Unity movement, which was supportive of the new President, Vladimir Putin (q.v.). In June 2000, at the first board meeting of Gazprom following the election of Putin, Chernomyrdin was ousted as Chairman by Dmitrii Medvedev, an associate of the new President. Reflecting his continuing status in Russian public life, in May 2001 Chernomyrdin was appointed ambassador of the Russian Federation to Ukraine. The appointment of such a well-known public figure was seen by many of the renewed importance given to relations with Ukraine by the Russian authorities. However, there were fears in Ukraine that his high profile and outspoken nature could see Russia attempting to exert greater pressure on Ukraine, particularly in terms of foreign policy. In December 2002 a number of Ukrainian parliamentarians claimed that Chernomyrdin was attempting to do this by urging Ukraine to concentrate on relations with Russia rather than with the West. However, demands for his expulsion were rejected by the Government. *Address:* Embassy of Russia, 03049 Kiev, Povitroflotskyi pr. 27, Ukraine; tel. (44) 244-09-63; fax (44) 244-34-69; e-mail embrus@public.icyb.kiev.ua.

**CHIGIR, Mikhail Nikolayevich:** Belarusian politician and former premier; b. 1948, in Usovo, Minsk; m., with two c. *Education:* a graduate of Belarus State Institute of National

Economics and of Moscow Institute of Finance and Statistics, Russia. *Career:* a member of the Communist Party and an economist, he worked for various banks in Minsk and Moscow, becoming Chairman of the Belarus Agro-industrial Bank (Belagroprombank) in 1991. In July 1994 the new President, Alyaksandr Lukashenka (q.v.), appointed him Prime Minister, leading to a belief that the country would continue on the path of reform and remain non-aligned internationally. The reformist credentials of his Government were, however, challenged by President Lukashenka's subsequent attempts to gain greater control over government policy and led to tensions between the two men. Some opposition deputies accused him of corruption or, at least, of being tolerant of corruption within the establishment. However, Chigir was eventually replaced as premier in November 1996, owing to his implacable opposition to Lukashenka's manipulation of the controversial referendum of that month. In April 1999, one month before the presidential election in which he intended to stand as a candidate, Chigir was accused of abuse of office and embezzlement. The latter charge was abandoned, but Chigir was found guilty of the former, and he received a three-year suspended sentence in May 2000. Although the sentence, which he insisted was politically motivated, was overturned by the Court of Appeal in December, the Court returned his case to the prosecutor's office for further investigation. A new criminal case against Chigir, this time on tax-evasion charges, also opened in September of that year. In 2000 Chigir and other prominent opposition politicians established the Consultative and Co-ordinating Council of Democratic Forces, a body intended to unify the opposition vote in the 2001 presidential election. The Council placed Chigir on the 'short' list of possible candidates (along with four others), but in the event he was not chosen to stand. In July 2002 Chigir was given a three-year, suspended prison sentence following his trial on charges of tax evasion. (In March his son, Alyaksandr Chigir, had been sentenced to seven years in prison, after allegations of theft.) Chigir denounced both trials as politically motivated. An appeal against the tax-evasion charges was rejected in November 2002. In February 2003 a court ruled in favour of a bank which had employed him in the mid-1990s and was seeking compensation for alleged negligence. Chigir was ordered to pay over US $1m. in compensation (he again denounced the decision as political in nature). *Address:* Communist Party of Belarus (Kamunistychnaya Partya Belarusi), 220007 Minsk, vul. Varanyanskaga 52, Belarus; tel. (17) 226-64-22; fax (17) 232-31-23; internet www.chigir.org.

**CHUBAIS, Anatolii Borisovich:** Russian economist, politician and business executive; b. 16 June 1955, in Borizov, Belarus; m., with one s. and one d. *Education:* Leningrad (now St Petersburg) Institute of Technology and Engineering. *Career:* before being appointed to the cabinet in 1991, during the premiership of the radical economic reformer, Yegor Gaidar, he was a member of the Leningrad Municipal Council; he subsequently oversaw the large-scale privatization of Russia's state assets and was promoted to the post of First Deputy Minister responsible for the economy in November 1994. The target of harsh criticism by conservatives, he was dismissed by the President, Boris Yeltsin (q.v.), in January 1996. He was, none the less, appointed to head Yeltsin's re-election campaign team and, following the latter's return to power in July, was rewarded with the post of head of the presidential administration (additionally serving as Minister of Finance for seven months in 1997). He was the focus for much of the public blame over the asset-stripping that attended Yeltsin's return to power. Chubais became the champion of the liberals within government, but attracted controversy for his links with the business 'oligarchs'. Although dismissed in the March 1998 government reorganization, Chubais continued to serve the reformists' agenda with his appointment as head of the giant Unified Energy Systems (RAO EES Rossii) company in April. In August 1999 Chubais' Just Cause party joined the Union of Rightist Forces (URF) electoral bloc, which secured 29 seats in the parliamentary election held in December. A demand by the Communist Party of the Russian Federation for Chubais' resignation as head of RAO EES

Rossii, during a severe energy crisis in the Far East of Russia in early 2001, was dismissed by the State Duma. From 2001 he initiated reforms designed to restructure the company, with the ultimate aim of developing a free market for electricity. However, his reform plans were subject to a series of legislative and administrative delays and, by late 2002, were thought unlikely to gain legislative approval until at least 2004. An energetic modernizer, he had previously announced his intention to enter business management after leaving RAO EES Rossii in 2004, but by early 2003 he was expected to remain until the reforms had been completed, a process which he estimated would take at least three further years (he later signed a contract extending his tenure in the post until April 2008). A motion in the State Duma to order his dismissal from his post at RAO EES Rossii was defeated in September. Earlier, in August, it was announced that he would be a candidate of the URF in the elections to the State Duma scheduled for December. *Address:* Unified Energy Systems (RAO EES Rossii), 103074 Moscow, Kitaigorodskii proyezd 7, Russia; tel. (095) 220-46-46; fax (095) 927-30-07; e-mail uespress@rao.elektra.ru.

**DEMIRCHIAN, Stepan:** Armenian politician; b. 1959, in Yerevan; m., with three d. *Education:* he graduated in technical sciences from Yerevan Polytechnic Institute. *Career:* the son of the Soviet-era head of the Communist Party of Armenia and 1998 presidential candidate, Karen Demirchian, he worked at an electrical engineering plant, and rose to become the director of a company making industrial machinery. He maintained an interest in politics and, upon his father's death in the gun attack on the National Assembly in October 1999, took a more active role. A fierce critic of the incumbent President, Robert Kocharian (q.v.), he was elected acting Chairman of the People's Party of Armenia, in succession to his father, in December. He was confirmed in the post in June 2001, and was identified as the party's candidate in the presidential election scheduled for 2003. He was officially nominated in December 2002, and attracted support from a number of candidates who subsequently abandoned their electoral campaigns. He received 28.2% of the votes cast in the first ballot, held in February 2003, while Kocharian narrowly failed to achieve the 50% of the votes required to be elected. Demirchian received the support of all the eliminated candidates for the second round, but was unable to increase his share of the vote beyond 32.5%, and Kocharian was elected to the presidency. The elections were marred by allegations of irregularities, some of which were acknowledged by Kocharian, and although efforts to have the elections annulled by the courts were unsuccessful, Demirchian emerged with his popular standing enhanced. In March it was announced that the opposition parties would contest the legislative elections scheduled for May as a united Justice (Artarutiun) bloc, with Demirchian at its head. In the event, pro-Kocharian parties emerged from the elections as the largest bloc in the new legislature, Demirchian again complaining of severe electoral irregularities. He had emerged as the figurehead of the opposition to President Kocharian, whose style of leadership was widely seen as becoming increasingly autocratic. *Address:* People's Party of Armenia, Yerevan.

**DZHANDOSOV, Uraz:** Kazakhstani economist and politician; b. 26 October 1961, in Almaty. *Education:* he graduated in economics from Moscow M. V. Lomonosov State University (MGU). *Career:* he worked as an economist, becoming one of the Government's most trusted economic advisers in the early 1990s. Following the definitive collapse of the USSR he was, as First Deputy Minister for the Economy, charged with attracting foreign investment to the country. In 1994 he became Deputy Governor of the Bank of Kazakhstan, becoming Governor two years later. Respected and trusted by the country's President, Nursultan Nazarbayev (q.v.), he left the central bank in 1998 when he was appointed First Deputy Prime Minister. Following a government reorganization in January 1999, he was appointed Deputy Prime Minister and Minister of Finance. It was at this time that observers began to question whether his views on economic reform were compatible with those of the President. He left the Government after the resignation of the Prime Minister in October of that year, and became head of the country's electricity grid operator. However, by the end of 2000 he had returned to a deputy premiership. In what risked being a decisive break from the President, Dzhandosov joined a number of other senior government and business officials in establishing the Democratic Choice of Kazakhstan (DCK), a party favouring political and economic liberalization, in November 2001. The Prime Minister, Kasimzhomart Tokayev, considered this a disloyal act, and threatened to resign if Dzhandosov and two other ministers who had joined the DCK were not dismissed from the Government. The three resigned almost immediately, stating that they could not work with Tokayev, and concentrated on the development of the DCK and an economic consultancy business they had created separately. The DCK soon disintegrated amid internal conflict, but Dzhandosov and the other former ministers established a new reformist party, Ak Zhol (Light Road) in March 2002. Ak Zhol favoured constructive co-operation with President Nazarbayev's regime and many took Dzhandosov's appointment as a presidential adviser in early 2003 to be a sign that this co-operation was working well. Having refused the position of head of the national airline in April 2003, Dzhandosov returned to government service in June as head of the state monopolies and competition agency. *Address:* c/o Ak Zhol, Astana, Kazakhstan.

**DZHORBENADZE, Avtandil (Avto):** Georgian politician, Minister of State (premier) and Head of the State Chancellery; b. 1951, in Chibati, Guria Oblast; m., with two s. *Education:* Tbilisi State Institute of Medicine. *Career:* a medical doctor who became Deputy Head, and subsequently Head, of the Tbilisi City Department of Public Health, Dzhborbenadze was first appointed to the Government in 1992, as Deputy Minister of Public Health and Social Security. In 1993 he became the Minister of Health Care and Social Security, and in 1999 his portfolio was expanded to that of Minister of Labour, Health Care and Social Security. In December 2001, after President Eduard Shevardnadze (q.v.) had dismissed the entire Government, Dzhorbenadze was appointed Minister of State (Prime Minister) and Head of the State Chancellery, to head a new administration. In June 2002 he was elected leader of the Citizens' Union of Georgia. This election in particular gave rise to speculation that Dzhorbenadze, a distant relative of Shevardnadze, was being prepared to succeed the President. In February 2003 it was reported that a number of ministers and government officials had met at Dzhorbenadze's home and discussed a strategy for removing Shevardnadze from power, although Dzhorbenadze vehemently denied this, and he remained a trusted ally of the President. *Address:* Office of the Government, 380018 Tbilisi, Ingorovka 7, Georgia; tel. (32) 93-59-07; fax (32) 98-23-54.

**ERKEBAYEV, Abdygany:** Chairman (speaker) of the Legislative Assembly of Kyrgyzstan; b. 1953, in Kara-Tent, Osh Duban (oblast or region); m., with one d. and two s. *Education:* Kyrgyz State University and Maksim Gorkii Institute of World Literature, Moscow, Russia. *Career:* he worked as a teacher and newspaper editor before being elected to the Supreme Soviet of the Kyrgyz SSR in 1990. In 1991 he was appointed Minister of Press and Information of the newly independent Kyrgyzstan and in 1992 he became Deputy Prime Minister. In 1993 he was appointed head of the Osh regional administration. He returned to national politics in 1995, when he became a member of the People's Assembly (the upper house of parliament), of which he was elected Chairman in 1997. In April 2000 he became the Chairman of the Legislative Assembly (the lower house of parliament). Previously thought of as a staunch supporter of President Askar Akayev (q.v.), he began gradually to distance himself in his new role. He opposed the judicial process against Feliks Kulov (q.v.), instituting an official process against the sentence imposed upon the politiican. A speech he made in late 2002 criticizing the decline in standards in Kyrgyzstan was seen by commentators as a thinly veiled attack on President Akayev, and damaged his relations with the President. He opposed several of the changes specified in the new draft constitution, specifically those that increased the power of the presidential veto,

but stated publicly that he had voted in favour of the document's adoption in the referendum held in February 2003. It was considered likely that he would contest the presidential election scheduled for 2005. *Address:* Office of the Chairman of the Legislative Assembly, 720003 Bishkek, Kirova 205, Kyrgyzstan; tel. (312) 22-55-23; fax (312) 22-24-04; e-mail postmaster@kenesh.gov.kg.

**FILARET (DENISENKO, M. A.):** 'Patriarch of Kiev and all Rus-Ukraine'; b. 1929, in Donetsk Oblast. *Education:* Odesa seminary and Moscow Theological Academy, Russia. *Career:* he was a monk and teacher from 1950, becoming Rector of the Moscow Academy in 1954. He moved to the Saratov Seminary in 1956, and the Kiev Seminary in 1957, before becoming Chancellor of the Ukrainian Exarchate of the Russian Orthodox Church—Moscow Patriarchate. He was appointed Bishop of Luga, in Leningrad (now St Petersburg) diocese, in 1962, and Bishop of Vienna and Austria in November of that year. In December 1964 he became Bishop of Dmitrov in Moscow diocese, and was rector of Moscow's theological schools and Deputy Chairman of the Dept of External Church Relations in 1964-66. He became Archbishop of Kiev and Galicia in 1966 and was appointed Metropolitan of Kiev in 1968. Dismissed as Metropolitan, in disgrace, in May 1992, in the following month Filaret was instrumental, supported by nationalist elements in the Government of Leonid Kravchuk (q.v.), in the formation of a self-styled Patriarchate of Kiev and all Rus-Ukraine. In September 1993 a number of bishops dissatisfied with Filaret's conduct left the Patriarchate and returned to the Ukrainian Autocephalous Orthodox Church (UAOC), which had been revived in 1990. Following the death of Volodomyr (Romaniuk), 'Patriarch of Kiev and all Rus-Ukraine' in July 1995, and violent protests at his funeral in Kiev, Filaret was elected as his successor, prompting further members of the senior clergy to leave the Patriarchate and join the UAOC. An ally of President Leonid Kuchma (q.v.), Filaret remained a controversial figure in Ukrainian public life. In January 2003 he stated that he believed relations with Russia could be harmful for Ukraine if they developed too strongly. In March he revealed his ambition to unite all Ukrainian Orthodox churches, so as to identify a single church more closely with the state. *Address:* Ukrainian Orthodox Church (Kievan Patriarchate), 01034 Kiev, vul. Pushkinska 36, Ukraine; tel. (44) 224-10-96; internet www.kievpatr.org.ua.

**GAMBAR, Isa Yunis oglu:** Azerbaijani politician and historian; b. Feb. 1957, in Baku; m., with two c. *Education:* he studied at Baku State University. *Career:* a former researcher at the Institute of Oriental Studies of the Azerbaijan Academy of Sciences, he became involved in the democratic movement in the late 1980s and was head of the organizational division of the Popular Front of Azerbaijan from 1990 and Deputy Chairman from 1991. He was a member of the Supreme Soviet of Azerbaijan from 1990 and became Chairman of the Milli Majlis in 1992, but resigned in June 1993 in accordance with the demands of the rebel leader, Col Surat Husseinov. From 1992 he was Chairman of Musavat (Equality), which achieved some representation in parliament in November 1995, despite being banned, on allegedly specious grounds, from participating for the proportional representation seats. Gambar joined the (unregistered) Movement for Democratic Elections and Electoral Reform in protest at undemocratic electoral conditions and, therefore, did not participate in the presidential election of October 1998. A proposal by Gambar, to develop a united front for the parliamentary election held on 5 November 2000, was largely ignored by other parties; Musavat subsequently boycotted parliament, as did other opposition parties. In January 2002, however, Musavat joined the United Opposition Alliance, a grouping of some 25 political parties. Gambar contested the presidential election held on October 2003, despite reservations about electoral conditions. He received some 12% of the votes cast, being defeated by Ilham Aliyev (q.v.). *Address:* Musavat (Equality), 37000 Baku, Azerbaijan Ave 37, Azerbaijan; tel. (12) 47-46-56; fax (12) 47-43-75; e-mail ilkin@turgut.baku.az.

**GANCHARYK, Uladzimir (HANCHARYK):** Belarusian politician and former Chairman of the Federation of Trade

Unions of Belarus. *Career:* a former member of the Supreme Council dissolved in 1996, in 2000 Gancharyk and other prominent opposition politicians established the Consultative and Co-ordinating Council of Democratic Forces, a body that intended to unify the opposition vote in the forthcoming presidential election. Gancharyk was placed on the initial 'short' list of possible candidates (along with four others), and was eventually chosen to contest the election. Gancharyk opposed both the Government's retention of a command economy and President Alyaksandr Lukashenka's (q.v.) overt populism, and his campaign focused on plans for economic reform and achieving a balance in relations with Russia and Western Europe. However, in the election, held on 9 September 2001, Gancharyk secured just 16% of the votes cast, according to the official results—although these were widely disputed, and international observers believed the actual percentage may have been significantly higher. At the beginning of October the Supreme Court rejected a request by Gancharyk that a criminal case be opened in connection with the conduct of the presidential election, after he submitted a lengthy complaint, which detailed numerous alleged incidences of electoral malpractice. He resigned the chairmanship of the Federation of Trade Unions of Belarus in December 2001, citing new government directives, which made it more difficult for unions to collect membership dues from their members.

**GHUKASSIAN, Arkadii Arshavirovich:** Azerbaijani (Nagornyi Karabakh) politician and the President of the 'Republic of Nagornyi Karabakh'; b. 21 June 1957, in Stepanakert; ethnic Armenian; m., with one d. *Education:* studied philology at Yerevan State University, Armenia. *Career:* from 1979 he was a reporter for, and from 1981 First Deputy Editor of, the Russian edition of the newspaper *Sovetskii Karabakh (Soviet Karabakh)*. From 1988 he became a prominent figure in the 'Karabakh' movement, against the rule of the central Azerbaijani authorities. In 1992 he was elected as a deputy to the Supreme Soviet (Supreme Council) of Nagornyi Karabakh. He was the self-styled 'Minister of Foreign Affairs of the Republic of Nagornyi Karabakh' from June 1993, and elected 'President' of the entity by popular vote on 1 September 1997, obtaining some 90% of the votes cast. His predecessor, Robert Kocharian (q.v.), who had served as President between December 1995 and March 1997, was appointed Prime Minister of Armenia in March 1997 and, subsequently, President of that country. The premier of Nagornyi Karabakh, Leonard Petrossian, served as acting President of the region from March 1997. Ghukassian was a strong opponent of the peace settlement suggested by the Organization for Security and Co-operation in Europe (OSCE) in 1997, and was committed to the attainment of complete independence for the region. Like Kocharian he favoured resolution of the enclave's status in an initial peace agreement, rather than postponing it in a phased settlement. He was reluctant to abandon Nagornyi Karabakh's military advantage, particularly as petroleum wealth began to accrue in Azerbaijan in the late 1990s. In March 2000 he sustained serious injuries as the result of an assassination attempt by gunmen in Stepanakert. In February 2001 the former Minister of Defence, Samuel Babaian, was convicted of having organized the attack. On 11 August 2002 Ghukassian was elected to a further term of office, obtaining some 88.4% of the votes cast. *Address:* 'Office of the President of the Republic of Nagornyi Karabakh', Stepanakert, Nagornyi Karabakh, Azerbaijan.

**GLAZYEV, Sergei Yuryevich:** Russian politician and economist; b. 1 Jan. 1961, in Zaporzhzhia, Ukraine; m., with three c. *Education:* he trained as an economist at Moscow M. V. Lomonosov State University (MGU), and undertook post-graduate studies at the Central Economic-Mathematical Institute of the Academy of Sciences of the USSR, receiving a doctorate in 1990. In 1999 he was granted the title of Professor, and was a Correspondent-Member of the Russian Academy of Sciences from 2000. *Career:* he worked in economic research before, in 1991, becoming a government adviser on external economic relations. In March 1992 he was appointed a Deputy Minister, then, in December, as a Min-

ister, in the department of External Economic Relations. He was dismissed in September 1993 following his refusal to support Decree 1,400 of President Boris Yeltsin 'On Gradual Constitutional Reform', which dissolved the legislature. In December Glazyev was elected to the newly formed State Duma on the list of the reformist Democratic Party of Russia formed by the Governor of Novgorod Oblast, Mikhail Prusak. In February 1994 he was elected as Chairman of the Duma's economic policy committee. At the elections to the Duma held in December 1995 Glazyev was unsuccessful, having been placed fifth on the federal list of the Congress of Russian Communities (CRC) party of Lt-Gen. (retd) Aleksandr Lebed. He subsequently worked as a manager in the economic administration of the Security Council, and in the apparatus of the upper legislative chamber, the Federation Council. He was, however, re-elected to the Duma in December 1999, when he joined the parliamentary faction of the Communist Party of the Russian Federation (CPRF). In April 2000–April 2002 he was Chairman of the Committee for Economic Policy and Property, and from November 2002 was a member of the State Duma Committee for Credit Organizations and Market Finance. Glazyev came to renewed prominence nation-wide in September 2002, when he contested the gubernatorial election in Krasnoyarsk Krai, in Siberia, following the death of Lebed, who had previously held the position. Although he was only the third-placed candidate, Glazyev received an unexpectedly high proportion of votes cast (21.4%) for a CPRF candidate in that region. Glazyev's relative youth was seen as important in attracting new voters to the CPRF, and his reformist tendencies brought him into repeated conflict with the party's leader, Gennadii Zyuganov (q.v.). Speculation that he would form his own movement abounded in early 2003, and these suspicions were confirmed later in the year, when, in March, he became the leader of the CRC, and subsequently forged links with other left-wing groups; from May he was additionally a co-Chairman of the Party of the Regions of Russia, and also became a co-Chairman of the People's Patriotic Union Russia and the Union of Orthodox Citizens. In September these and other groups announced that they were to contest the forthcoming elections to the State Duma as the Motherland (Rodina) electoral bloc, with Glazyev as the first-placed candidate on their federal list. Glazyev was seen by many as the leading representative of a potentially powerful new force in Russian politics, with the potential to create a new left-wing movement that could, perhaps, eventually win broader appeal than the CPRF. *Address:* State Duma, 103265 Moscow, Okhotnyi ryad 1, Russia; tel. (095) 292-42-60; fax (095) 292-43-22; e-mail glazyev@duma.gov.ru; internet www.glazev.ru.

**GORBACHEV, Mikhail Sergeyevich:** Russian politician and last President of the USSR; b. 2 March 1931, in Privolnoye, Stavropol Krai; m. Raisa Titarenko Gorbacheva in 1953 (deceased), with one d. *Education:* studied law at Moscow M. V. Lomonosov State University (MUG); also studied at Stavropol Agricultural Institute. *Career:* he began his working life as a machine operator, but soon became involved with the Communist Party of the Soviet Union (CPSU) and Komsomol (V. I. Lenin Young Communist League). Although one of the youngest members of the Politburo, which he joined as a full member in October 1980, he became a likely successor to the Soviet leadership during the rule of Yurii Andropov (1982-84). The conservatives were not willing to elect him as Andropov's immediate successor, but in March 1985, following the death of Konstantin Chernenko, he became General Secretary of the CPSU. He was elected to the position of titular head of state (Chairman of the Presidium of the Supreme Soviet of the USSR) in October 1988. In March 1990 he was elected to the new post of executive President of the USSR. He introduced a new style of leadership and dramatic reforms throughout the USSR, with the primary ideas being *glasnost* (openness), *perestroika* (restructuring) and 'new thinking' in foreign policy. He was credited with ending the 'Cold War' and catalysing massive changes in Soviet politics and society; he was awarded the Nobel Peace Prize in the same year. However, he was discredited in his own country by the apparent failure of real reform, his continued faith in the Communist Party and his advocacy of a strong Union. Following an unsuccessful coup attempt in August 1991, he proved unable to maintain the power of the Union in the face of the increasingly assertive republican leaderships. In December the formation of the Commonwealth of Independent States (CIS) marked the end of the USSR and of his post; he resigned on 25 December and the USSR was deemed to have ceased to exist. He announced that he would remain involved in politics and, in January 1992, declared the formation of a social and political research foundation (the Gorbachev Foundation). He subsequently extended his activities to the environmental sphere, with the creation of the International Green Cross/Green Crescent. His dismal performance in the presidential election of 1996 confirmed that too many of the Russian electorate held him responsible for the disintegration of the USSR and the subsequent decline in living standards. In September 2000 Gorbachev launched a new body, which aimed to improve bilateral relations between Russia and the USA. He was co-founder of the Social Democratic Party of Russia in the same year. Travelling widely to conferences and seminars, he has spoken on a variety of issues, including the possibility of Russia joining the European Union. He remained an energetic campaigner, who frequently expressed his bitterness about the manner of his ejection from power. In mid-2003 there was speculation that he would seek election to the State Duma in the elections scheduled for December of that year, but he later announced his decision not to participate. *Address:* The Gorbachev Foundation-International Non-governmental Foundation for Socio-economic and Political Studies, 125167 Moscow, Leningradskii pr. 39/14, Russia; tel. (095) 945-64-99; fax (095) 945-78-99; e-mail gf@gorby.ru; internet www.gorby.ru.

**GUSINSKII, Vladimir Aleksandrovich:** Russian entrepreneur; b. 6 Oct. 1952, in Moscow; m., with three s. *Education:* Moscow Gubhkin Institute of Oil and Chemicals and A. Lunacharskii State Institute of Theatrical Art. *Career:* Gusinskii directed several cultural programmes before founding the co-operative Infex, which later became Holding Most, comprising over 40 enterprises in the fields of construction, property and trade. He served as President of Most-Bank in 1991-97 and in 1997 became President of the Media-Most company, comprising a number of media concerns, including NTV—Independent Television, Russia's only wholly independent national broadcaster. NTV launched a strong campaign for the re-election of Boris Yeltsin (q.v.) to the presidency in 1996, as a result of which it apparently received preferential treatment by the Government. In July 1999, however, NTV became involved in a public dispute with the Government, claiming to have come under pressure from officials following a broadcast critical of the presidential administration. Criticism of the authorities by NTV intensified in 2000, in particular following the inauguration of Vladimir Putin (q.v.) as President in May. Amid growing fears that the Government wished to curtail the powers of the media, the Media-Most offices were raided and a number of charges of fraud were laid against Gusinskii. Attempts were subsequently made by the Government to gain control over Media-Most, culminating, in December 2000, in a demand by the Moscow tax office that the company cease operations, on grounds of insolvency. In mid-2002 the state-controlled Gazprom-Media finally acquired control of NTV and other companies within Media-Most. Gusinskii, who had been placed on Interpol's international wanted list for fraud, at Russia's behest, was arrested in Spain in December 2000. However, Spain refused to extradite him and, following the annulment of all travel restrictions, Gusinskii took up residence in Israel, where he held dual citizenship, in April 2001, purportedly in an attempt to complicate extradition procedures. In mid-2001 Gusinskii was removed from his position as President of the Russian Jewish Congress, which he had held since 1995. Later in 2001 Russia issued a fresh warrant for Gusinskii's arrest, this time on charges of money 'laundering' (the processing of illicitly or illegally obtained funds through legitimate accounts). From his self-imposed 'exile', Gusinskii continued to be highly critical of Putin, whom he accused of favouring an authoritarian style of rule. This stance earned

him a number of allies in the West, where he was portrayed as a proponent of free speech. Speculation that he had returned to Russia in late 2002, following the sale of his media interests, proved groundless, and he remained resident in Israel. In August 2003 Gusinskii was arrested upon his arrival in Athens, Greece, on the basis of an extradition warrant obtained by the Russian authorities. He contested the attempt to extradite him, claiming the charges against him were politically motivated, and was released on bail later in the month. Extradition hearings were postponed until October, to allow for the collection of supporting evidence. Buoyed by his previous success in avoiding extradition from Spain, and by that of Boris Berezovskii (q.v.) in obtaining political asylum in the United Kingdom, Gusinskii began a campaign to publicize what he saw as the personal and political nature of the charges against him. *Address:* RTV—Russian Television International, 110 West 40th St, New York , NY-10018, USA; tel. (212) 944-9899.

**HAROUTUNIAN, Gagik Garushevich:** Chairman of the Constitutional Court of Armenia; b. 1948, in Gekhashen. *Education:* graduated from Yerevan University. *Career:* he was a writer and lecturer at the Yerevan Institute of Industry in 1975-77, and in the Socialist Federal Republic of Yugoslavia in 1977-78. A member of the Central Committee of the Communist Party of Armenia from 1982, he became Head of Department in 1988. He joined the nationalist opposition and from August 1990 was a Deputy Chairman of the Armenian Supreme Soviet (Supreme Council). In October 1991, with the support of President Levon Ter-Petrossian (q.v.), he was elected Vice-President of the Republic. On 22 November he was appointed Chairman of the Council of Ministers (Prime Minister). He was succeeded as Prime Minister by Khosrov Haroutunian in the second half of 1992, but he remained Vice-President until July 1995, when the post was abolished under the terms of the new Constitution. In February 1996 he was appointed Chairman of the newly established Constitutional Court. In November, following much unrest, the Constitutional Court rejected an appeal from opposition candidates that the results of the presidential election of September be declared invalid. The court remained active in Armenia's political life, with the results of the presidential elections of 1998 and 2003 also being challenged. Following the court's approval of the result of the latter election in April 2003 (which the opposition vowed to contest in the European Court of Human Rights) he was accused of undue interference in the political process, when he suggested that a referendum on the continued public confidence in President Robert Kocharian (q.v.) and the Government be held within one year. *Address:* Constitutional Court, 375019 Yerevan, Marshal Baghramian St 10, Armenia; tel. (1) 58-81-40; fax (1) 52-99-91; e-mail armlaw@concourt.am; internet www.concourt.am.

**IGNATIYEV, Sergei Mikhailovich:** Chairman of the Central Bank of the Russian Federation; b. 1948, in Leningrad (now St Petersburg). *Education:* graduated from Moscow M. V. Lomonosov State University (MGU). *Career:* he began his working life as a lecturer in Leningrad, but was asked by Yegor Gaidar, the head of Russia's first post-Soviet Government, to join his administration. He served as deputy head of the Central Bank in the early 1990s, and then held several senior economic policy posts, becoming First Deputy Minister of Finance under President Vladimir Putin (q.v.). He was nominated by Putin as the successor to Vikor Gerashchenko (q.v.), then Chairman of the Central Bank. Gerashchenko resigned before the end of his term in office, in March 2002, after expressing opposition to proposed legislation that aimed to make the Central Bank subordinate to a new, government-led body, the National Banking Council. The legislation, which also contained proposals to accelerate the restructuring of the banking sector, was partly drawn up by Ignatiyev. Despite his hostility to the reforms, which were expected seriously to weaken the independence of the Central Bank, Gerashchenko expressed his confidence in his successor. Overall, policy at the Bank was expected to become more pro-Government under Ignatiyev's leadership. He was expected to initiate investigations into the finances of the business 'oligarchs' and to effect improvements in monetary policy. He announced his intention keep exchange-rate policy unchanged, in the short term. Control of inflation emerged as his greatest priority, with some success, as the monthly rate of inflation, according to official figures, was less than 1% in several months in mid-2003. *Address:* Bank Rossii—Central Bank of the Russian Federation, 107016 Moscow, ul. Neglinnaya 12, Russia; tel. (095) 921-31-16; fax (095) 921-91-47; e-mail webmaster@www.cbr.ru; internet www.cbr.ru.

**ILIA II, Catholicos-Patriarch of All Georgia (IRAKLI SHIOLASHVILI):** Georgian ecclesiastic; b. 4. Dec. 1933, in Sno, Kazbegi Region. *Education:* Moscow Theological Seminary and Moscow Theological Academy, Russia. *Career:* ordained on 10 May 1957 by the late Patriarch Aleksei I of Moscow and All Russia, he became Father-Superior in 1960, and Archimandrite in 1961. He was consecrated as Bishop of Shemokmedi and Vicar to the Georgian Patriarch Ephrem II on 25 August 1963. Between 1963 and 1972 he was Rector of the Georgian Orthodox Theological Seminary and from 1967 he was Bishop of the diocese of Sukhumi and Abkhazia. On 23 December 1977 he was elected primate of the Georgian Orthodox Church, following the death of Catholicos-Patriarch David V, and he was formally enthroned as Catholicos-Patriarch on 25 December. He presided over the signing in October 2002 of a constitutional agreement between the Church and the state, both acknowledging the role of the Orthodox Church in Georgian history and according it special status in the country; this greatly strengthened the power of both himself and the Church, causing concern about the freedom of less well-represented religions. He attracted controversy in September 2003 when he requested the Government not to sign an agreement with the Vatican protecting the rights of Roman Catholics, following riots by Orthodox adherents. Orthodox churches in a number of countries had been concerned at what they considered to be Roman Catholic expansionism, and Ilia believed that any such agreement would be 'perilous for Georgia and its people'. *Address:* Patriarchate of the Georgian Orthodox Church, 380005 Tbilisi, King Erekle II Sq. 1, Georgia; tel. (32) 99-03-78; fax (32) 98-71-14; e-mail ecclesia@access.sanet.ge; internet www.orthodox-patriarchate-of-georgia.org.ge.

**IVANOV, Igor Sergeyevich:** Russian; Minister of Foreign Affairs; b. 23 Sept. 1945, in Moscow; m., with one d. *Education:* Moscow Pedagogical Institute of Foreign Languages. *Career:* initially a researcher, he entered the diplomatic service in 1973. He was posted to Spain until 1983, when he moved to the Ministry of Foreign Affairs, becoming Assistant Minister in 1985 and Chief of Department from 1987 to 1992. He was the Russian ambassador to Spain in 1991–93, but returned to Russia to become First Deputy Minister of Foreign Affairs in 1994 and Minister in 1998. In that year he also became the Co-Chairman of the European Union-Russia Co-operation Council. He opposed the bombardment of the Federal Republic of Yugoslavia by North Atlantic Treaty Organization (NATO) forces from March 1999. In May 2000 Ivanov criticized the work of the UN International Criminal Tribunal for the Former Yugoslavia (ICTY, based at The Hague, Netherlands), declaring that its actions had become political, rather than judicial. In June 1999 Ivanov visited the People's Republic of China, where, following seven years of negotiations, a final agreement was reached on the demarcation of a common border with Russia. In 2001–02 major foreign policy issues concerned the role of Russia in the US-led coalition formed to combat global terrorism and Russia's relations with NATO. Following the large-scale attacks by Islamist radicals on the USA in September 2001, Russia pledged its support for the coalition. In part, however, this seemed designed to allow it to escape international opprobrium for its actions in Chechnya, where Ivanov claimed that international terrorists affiliated to Osama bin Laden's al-Qa'ida (Base) network were operating. In 2002 Ivanov denied that Russia was making too many concessions to the USA and publicly supported the presence of US troops in Central Asia. In early 2002 he announced that participation in the 'anti-terrorism' coalition would continue even in the event of US-led attacks on Iraq (although full support for such attacks remained unforthcoming). In May Ivanov signed an agreement with NATO to set up a new joint body, the NATO-Russia Council, with particular responsibility for countering terrorist and other security threats. The Minister stated that he wished Russia and NATO to co-operate as equals. Ivanov achieved international prominence during the prelude to the US-led military action in Iraq in early 2003, representing Russian opposition to such military action on the international stage. He remained vocal during and after the conflict, consistently urging the USA to permit greater UN participation. *Address:* Ministry of Foreign Affairs, 121200 Moscow, Smolenskaya-Sennaya pl. 32/34, Russia; tel. (095) 244-16-06; fax (095) 230-21-30; e-mail ministry@mid.ru.

**IVANOV, Sergei Borisovich:** Russian; Minister of Defence; b. 31 Jan. 1953, in Leningrad (now St Petersburg); m., with two s. *Education:* Leningrad State University, Committee for State Security (KGB) School of Higher Administration No. 101, Minsk (Belarus). *Career:* he worked within the internal security system, both within the USSR and overseas for 18 years, serving as the head of the Department of Analysis, Forecasting and Strategic Planning of the Federal Security Service (FSB). In August 1998 he was appointed Deputy Director of the FSB, and from November 1999 served as the Secretary of the Security Council of the Russian Federation. In March 2001 Ivanov, a personal ally of President Vladimir Putin (q.v.), was appointed Minister of Defence; he had relinquished his military ranking (of Lt-Gen.) in November 2000, thereby permitting the President to announce this as a civilian appointment. It was hoped that his appointment would aid Russia's complicated defence relationship with the USA, although in public statements he often appeared to contradict the views of President Putin, appearing somewhat less conciliatory towards the interests of the USA and other Western countries. Russia joined the US-led coalition formed to combat global terrorism following the terrorist attacks on the USA in September 2001, but in late 2002 appeared unwilling to support possible US-led military action against Iraq, although Ivanov stated that he supported the return of weapons inspectors to that country. In May 2002 Russia and the USA signed an arms reduction treaty. Relations with the North Atlantic Treaty Organization (NATO) were also an important issue—in March Ivanov said that arrangements for co-operation with the body had, thus far, fallen short of his expectations, although in May the Minister of Foreign Affairs, Igor Ivanov (q.v.), signed an agreement with the Organization to establish a joint NATO-Russia Council. Domestically, the Minister recognized the critical need for reform of the Russian armed forces and pledged to increase pay and improve resources. The continuing conflict in Chechnya and its effects on the morale of the military and on the popularity of the Government proved the most challenging issue for Ivanov during his first years in office. *Address:* Ministry of Defence, 103160 Moscow, ul. Znamenka 19, Russia; tel. (095) 296-84-37; fax (095) 296-84-36; e-mail press@mil.ru.

**JALOLOV, Abdulkhafiz:** Uzbekistani politician; b. 1947. *Career:* he worked in the Ideology Department of the Communist Party of Uzbekistan (CPU), and became Director of the philosophy and law department at the Uzbek Academy of Sciences and leader of the successor to the CPU, the People's Democratic Party of Uzbekistan. He stood as the only other candidate in the presidential election of 9 January 2000, although he was never considered to pose a real threat to the incumbent, Islam Karimov (q.v.). In the event, he obtained just 4.2% of the votes cast, and was even reported to have voted for Karimov. He remained as leader of his party, although its activities were severely restricted. *Address:* People's Democratic Party of Uzbekistan, 700029 Tashkent, pl. Mustakillik 5/1, Uzbekistan; tel. (71) 139-83-11; fax (71) 133-59-34.

**KADYROV, Akhmed haji:** Chechen; President; b. 1954, in Central Asia. *Education:* Mir-i-Arabi Madrassah, Bukhara, and Islamic Institute of Tashkent, Uzbekistan. *Career:* he was deputy imam in Gudermes, Chechnya, and, in 1999, opened the first Islamic institute in the North Caucasus, in the village of Kurchaloy, where he subsequently served as rector. He was appointed Deputy Mufti of Chechnya in 1991 and acting Mufti from September 1994; he was confirmed in the post following an election in 1995. In the 1994–96 Chechen conflict Kadyrov fought against Russian troops, as an ally of Khalid 'Aslan' Maskhadov (q.v.), who was subsequently elected President of the Chechen Republic. After Islamist rebels based in Chechnya staged incursions into neighbouring Dagestan in mid-1999, Kadyrov became an opponent of Maskhadov. On 10 October, two weeks after federal forces had re-entered Chechnya, Kadyrov was dismissed as Mufti of Chechnya by Maskhadov, who described Kadyrov as a 'traitor' and 'an enemy of the Chechen people'. Henceforth, Kadyrov came to be more closely associated with federal forces in the separatist republic, in particular after several of his associates declared three regions of Chechnya as formally 'free of Wahhibism' (as the Russian authorities referred to the brand of militant Islamism that had been adopted by significant factions of the rebels); and after troops led by Kadyrov regained control of the second city of Chechnya, Gudermes, he became a principal figure in attempts by the federal authorities to reassert control over the region. After President Vladimir Putin (q.v.) decreed, in May 2000, that Chechnya was, henceforth, to be ruled federally, Kadyrov was inaugurated as administrative leader (President) of the Republic in June. He was directly responsible to Putin and to the presidential representative to the new Southern Federal Okrug, Viktor Kazantsev. Subsequently, a number of assassination attempts were reportedly made against him. He was unpopular with many Chechens, who resented his abrupt change of sides in the conflict, particularly as he maintained his own private force, commanded by his son, which was accused of numerous atrocities. In January 2001 operational control in Chechnya was transferred from the federal Ministry of Defence to the Federal Security Service (FSB) and the local administration was granted greater autonomy. In August Kadyrov expressed criticism of the abuse of civilians' human rights by federal defence forces searching towns for Chechen rebels, and demanded that senior military commanders face charges. Similarly, in March 2002 he condemned the conduct of 'cleansing' operations carried out near Groznyi by federal troops. However, he remained closely linked to the federal Government. Following the holding of a constitutional referendum in Chechnya in March 2003, Kadyrov assumed the powers of acting President, with the right of appointment over republican ministers and local organs of Government. In early June Kadyrov used these new powers to dismiss the majority of the republican Government, and the heads of every regional administration in the Republic, although the vast majority were re-appointed shortly afterwards. These measures were described by some commentators as a way of ensuring that the 'new' appointees would owe personal loyalty to Kadyrov. On 21 June Kadyrov inaugurated an interim legislative body, the 42-member State Council, comprising the head of, and an appointed representative of, each administrative district. Kadyrov announced his intention to contest the presidential election due to be held in the Republic in early October, although he declined the support that was offered by the republican branches of several national political parties, and contested the election as an independent. Following the withdrawal or debarral of the three candidates regarded as his most serious rivals, Kadyrov was elected with some 87.7% of votes cast, according to official figures. Kadyrov was formally inaugurated as President on 19 October, although continuing insecurity in Chechnya meant that the ceremony was held at a previously unannounced location, in Gudermes. *Address:* President of the Chechen (Nokchi) Republic, 364000 Chechnya, ul. Garazhnaya 10A, Russia; tel. (095) 777-92-28; e-mail info@chechnya.gov.ru; internet www.chechnya.gov.ru.

**KAREKIN II, His Holiness Supreme Patriarch (KTRITCH NARSISSIAN):** Catholicos of All Armenians; Head of the Armenian Apostolic Church; b. 16 Aug 1951, in Etchmiadzin. *Education:* Kevorkian Theological Seminary, the University of Vienna, Austria, and the University of Bonn, Germany. *Career:* He was Assistant Dean at Kevorkian Theological Seminary. He was ordained as a priest in 1972 and worked as a pastor in Germany in 1975. In 1980 he became the assistant to the Vicar-General of Araratian Patriarchal Diocese, before becoming Vicar-General and then Bishop in

1983, and subsequently Archbishop. In 1990 he became a member of the Supreme Spiritual Council of the Catholicosate of All Armenians. On 27 October 1999 he was elected leader of the Armenian Apostolic Church, and on 4 November he was inaugurated as Catholicos Karekin II. *Address:* Residence of the Catholicosate of all Armenians, Vagharshapat, Monastery of St Etchmiadzin, Armenia; tel. (2) 28-57-37; fax (2) 15-10-77; e-mail holysee@etchmiadzin.am; internet www.holyetchmiadzin.com.

**KARIMOV, Islam Abduganiyevich:** President of Uzbekistan; b. 30 Jan. 1938, in Samarkand region; m. Tatyana Karimova, with two d. *Education:* graduated from the Central Asian Polytechnic and Tashkent Economics Institute. *Career:* he worked as a mechanical engineer in aviation construction before moving into economic planning in 1966. He became finance minister of Uzbekistan in 1983. Caught up in the great 'cotton scandal' (the extensive, systematic falsification of cotton-harvest figures and embezzlement of government payments), Karimov became a deputy premier in 1986. A further wave of corruption allegations engulfed his patrons, however, and at the end of the year he was given a regional post. He did not return to republican politics until 1989, when he became Party leader in Uzbekistan, perhaps because an uncompromised candidate was needed, and perhaps because he was neutral in terms of a lack of links with the traditional class of Uzbek politics. From 1989 he was a people's deputy in the all-Union assembly, and in 1990 he became a Communist Party of the Soviet Union (CPSU) Politburo member. He had a reputation as an old-style, conservative communist, but, after the failure of the attempted coup in Moscow, Russia, in 1991, he banned the Communist Party. It was succeeded by the People's Democratic Party of Uzbekistan, with the same personnel. In December he was elected President of the Republic in popular elections. Until January 1992 he also performed the functions previously executed by the Chairman of the Council of Ministers, a position that he had abolished in November 1990. Karimov's leadership became increasingly absolutist, as he consolidated his position of power. He extended his control over the mass media, precluded the spread of opposition movements from neighbouring Tajikistan by giving his full support to the restored communist regime there and prevented domestic opposition movements from registering as political parties. Only two parties were permitted to participate in the legislative elections of December 1994. There were also allegations that Karimov was implicated in the intimidation of opposition leaders, many of whom left Uzbekistan. His stated concern was to ensure political stability, and he particularly discouraged any religious or ethnic-based parties (subsequently outlawed by legislation passed in December 1996). He sought implicitly to identify himself with the state-promoted cult of the national hero, Amir (lord) Timur (Timur 'the lame', Tamerlane). In March 1995 a popular referendum extended his term of office to 2000; parliament declared that this constituted an extension to his first term, and that he would be eligible for re-election in 2000. In June 1996 he resigned from the ruling People's Democratic Party, claiming a wish to be detached from politics. Certainly by then he was attempting to moderate his illiberal image, as Uzbekistan was increasingly viewed as a stabilizing power in the region, by both Russia and the West. Afghanistan's Taliban, a militant, fundamentalist Islamist movement, was perceived by Karimov as the most serious threat to his regime, giving rise to government action against any independent Muslim activity, notably by the conservative 'Wahhabi' sect. In mid-May 1999 further legislation, which imposed harsher punishment for members of 'religious, extremist, separatist and fundamentalist organizations', was introduced. On 9 January 2000 Karimov was re-elected as President, with 91.9% of the votes cast; he was inaugurated for a second, five-year term on 22 January. However, despite frequent international criticism of Uzbekistan's human-rights record, Karimov emerged as perhaps the most important regional ally of the USA in its declared efforts to combat global terrorism, following the large-scale attacks of 11 September 2001, on the US cities of New York and Washington, DC. Karimov confirmed that Uzbekistan would allow

US troops entry to its airbases, for the purpose of undertaking humanitarian or 'search-and-rescue' operations, during the US-led aerial bombardment of strategic positions in Afghanistan, which was harbouring the Saudi-born Islamist fundamentalist, Osama bin Laden, who was believed by the USA to have co-ordinated the terrorist attacks of September. In January 2002 the results of a referendum supported a constitutional amendment, proposed by President Karimov, which was to extend the presidential term of office from five to seven years. His position as the West's key ally in the region appeared assured, even as the country's enhanced profile brought increased attention from human rights groups and more widespread criticism of Karimov's treatment of Islamists and other political opponents. *Address:* Office of the President, 700163 Tashkent, pr. Uzbekistanskii 43, Uzbekistan; tel. (71) 139-54-04; fax (71) 139-53-25; e-mail presidents_office@press-service.uz; internet www.press-service.uz.

**KARIMOVA, Gulnora:** Uzbekistani businesswoman and diplomat; b. 1972; divorced, with one s. and one d. *Education:* she studied in Tashkent, at New York university and at Harvard Business School, USA. *Career:* the daughter of Uzbekistan's President Islam Karimov (q.v.), she married an Uzbek-American and lived in the USA for a number of years, maintaining business interests in Uzbekistan. Following her divorce a US court awarded custody of her children to their father, but she refused to abide by its verdict and returned to Uzbekistan, where a court had ruled in her favour. Risking arrest if she travelled to the West, she remained in Uzbekistan and developed her business interests, which included a mobile cellular telephone operator and numerous industrial companies. She was also employed as an adviser to the Minsitry of Foreign Affairs. As one of the country's most prominent business leaders, and with her links to the President and the Government, she was seen as one of the most powerful figures in Uzbekistan. In September 2003 she accepted a posting at the Uzbekistani embassy in Moscow, Russia. Her ailing father having announced that he would not seek a further term of office, there was speculation that Karimova might seek to succeed him. *Address:* c/o Embassy of Uzbekistan, 109017 Moscow, Pogorelskii per. 12; Russia; tel. (095) 230-00-76; fax (095) 238-89-18.

**KASYANOV, Mikhail Mikhailovich:** Chairman of the Council of Ministers (Prime Minister) of the Russian Federation; b. 8 Dec. 1957, in Solntsevo, Moscow Oblast. *Education:* Moscow Institute of Automobile Transport. *Career:* He worked at the RSFSR State Planning Commission, first as an engineer and then as an economist, and then at the Ministry of Economics in 1981–90. In 1990 he was appointed chief of section for foreign economic relations at the Russian State Committee for Economics. From 1991 he was head of department for foreign economic relations at the Ministry of Finance. He served as head of the Department of Overseas Credits at the Ministry in 1993-95, before becoming Deputy Minister of Finance in 1995-99. Following his appointment as Minister of Finance in May 1999, he negotiated successfully with Russia's international creditors to restructure the repayment of Russia's foreign debt. In that year he also became Deputy Manager for the Russian Federation at the European Bank for Reconstruction and Development (EBRD) and a member of both the Presidium of the Russian Government and of the Security Council. In January 2000 he was appointed a First Deputy Prime Minister in the Government of acting President Vladimir Putin (q.v.). Following Putin's election to the presidency in March, Kasyanov was named acting Prime Minister and, after approval by the State Duma, Prime Minister. He announced his intention to pursue reforms, focusing on the farming and banking sectors, privatization, the military and the fight against corruption, and was regarded as a capable administrator. His background provoked criticism of his policies, to the effect that he was only interested in economics, and that all of his Government's policies were too closely linked to his own economic views. This, in turn, led to an impression of him an an uninspiring politician, and his popularity was never particularly high. Although President Putin repeatedly praised him and his

Government, particularly with reference to economic growth, speculation frequently arose that he would prefer him to be replaced. An opposition motion of 'no confidence' in the Government brought before the State Duma by the Communist Party of the Russian Federation and liberal Yabloko factions in June 2003 was defeated, although it provoked an amount of public debate as to the suitability of Kasyanov's economic policies. *Address:* Office of the Government, 103274 Moscow, Krasnopresnenskaya nab. 2, Russian Federation; tel. (095) 205-57-35; fax (095) 205-42-19; internet www.government.ru.

**KAZHEGELDIN, Akezhan Magzhan-Uly:** Kazakh former premier; b. 27 March 1952, in Georgiyevka, in Semipalatinsk region; m., with two c. *Education:* studied at Kazakh State University and Moscow's Institute of Oriental Studies (Russia). *Career:* he was director of an ore-enriching factory and held various posts in regional government in the 1980s, including being head of Semipalatinsk's regional administration in 1983. From 1991 to 1994 he was the Deputy Governor (Akim) of this region. He was appointed a Deputy Prime Minister in January 1994. However, following criticism of the slow rate of reform in the country, in October the entire Government resigned and Kazhegeldin, himself an economist, was appointed head of a new, more reformist administration. He implemented a series of strict economic measures, which met with opposition in parliament. In early 1995, however, the Constitutional Court declared the parliament illegitimate, necessitating its dissolution and the resignation of the Government. Kazhegeldin and his Government resumed office and the implementation of their programme. A new parliament, elected in December, endorsed Kazhegeldin's premiership. Kazegeldin continued to favour privatization of state-owned industry, and his austerity measures succeeded in bringing inflation under control. In 1997 he was accused of financial malpractice over the arrears in the country's pensions system, and later exonerated. However, Russian media reports suggested that he had admitted involvement with the Soviet security service (KGB) in the 1980s. In October 1997 Kazhegeldin left the country for medical treatment and was replaced as Prime Minister by Nurlan Balgymbayev. Upon his return he criticized the halt to the privatization programme imposed under Balgymbayev's Government. He became increasingly associated with the opposition, and denounced the early presidential election that resulted from the constitutional crisis of October 1998, alleging it to be part of efforts by the élite to perpetuate its hold on power. He was permitted to register as a candidate for the presidential election scheduled for January 1999, but was debarred in November 1998, owing to his presence at an opposition rally. He subsequently established a new political party, the Republican People's Party of Kazakhstan, which was inaugurated in mid-December. In late April 1999 Kazhelgeldin and his wife were charged with tax evasion, and he was arrested at Moscow airport in early September. Kazhelgeldin was released, following criticism of his detention by the Organization for Security and Co-operation in Europe (OSCE). None the less, because of the outstanding charges against him, he was not permitted to stand as a candidate in the parliamentary elections that commenced in October. In February 2000 it was reported that Belgian law-enforcement agencies had brought charges of money 'laundering' (the processing of illegally obtained funds into legitimate accounts) against both himself and his wife; in the same month he was charged with the illegal acquisition and possession of firearms and ammunition. In mid-July he was arrested in Rome, Italy, but he was released after two days. His trial *in absentia* began in mid-August 2001, and in early September the Supreme Court found him guilty of abuse of power, tax evasion and the illegal possession of weapons. He was sentenced to 10 years in prison; in addition, a substantial fine was imposed and his property was confiscated. Allegations persisted that his trial had been politically motivated. Kazhegeldin remained an active critic of the Government from abroad and supported the founding of the reformist Democratic Choice of Kazakhstan in late 2001, but subsequently declined to join its leadership. He constructed a 15-point political plan for Kazakhstan, and speculation about his possible return to the country persisted in 2002; he was regarded as a strong contender for the next presidential election, due to be held in 2006. However, he remained in exile in late 2003.

**KHODORKOVSKII, Mikhail Borisovich:** Russian businessman; b. 26 June 1963, in Moscow; m., with two s. *Education:* Moscow Mendeleyev Institute of Chemistry and Technology, and the G. V. Plekhanov Institute of National Economics. *Career:* he began his career at the USSR State Committee for Science and Technology, heading a division, Menatep, which ostensibly introduced technological innovations to industry but, as the institutions of the USSR decayed, mutated into a trading company, earning substantial sums from the import and sale of goods. Following the collapse of the USSR, Menatep opened a bank, which had great success in the early years of post-Soviet Russia. In 1991 Khodorkovskii was appointed Deputy Minister for Fuel and Energy, but left shortly afterwards to concentrate on business interests. Menatep bought large shares in numerous industrial companies during Russia's privatization programme in the mid-1990s, culminating in the acquisition of some 78% of Yukos, a hitherto state-owned hydrocarbons company with significant reserves, in 1995. Critics claimed that there were irregularities in the purchase, with the company thought to be grossly undervalued and several potential competitors excluded from bidding on questionable grounds. Khodorovskii concentrated on expanding Yukos, disposing of many of his other assets. A merger with Sibneft, controlled by Roman Abramovich (q.v.) in 2003 confirmed the group's position as the largest company in Russia. At this time questions resurfaced as to the propriety of Khodorovskii's conduct, and a number of criminal investigations began. By late 2003 Khodorovskii had instituted Western-style corporate reform at Yukos, in the attempt to banish any suspicion of financial impropriety and boost the company's standing in the global market, and he was one of the world's most significant business figures, described as the richest person in Russia, with a personal fortune estimated at US $8,000m. In common with many of Russia's so-called 'oligarchs', he was thought to harbour political ambitions, and in 2003 announced that he was to fund the pro-market Union of Rightist Forces and the liberal Yabloko party, prior to elections to the State Duma scheduled to be held in December of that year. However, in late October Khodorkovskii was arrested and detained, reportedly following his failure to attend a court hearing at which various cases of fraudulent practice by the company were being investigated; he was subsequently charged with fraud and tax evasion. *Address:* c/o Yukos Oil Co, 115024 Moscow, ul. Dubininskaya 31A, Russia; tel. (095) 232-31-61; fax (095) 232-31-60; e-mail info@yukos.ru;; internet www.yukos.ru.

**KINAKH, Anatoliy Kyryllovych:** politican and former Prime Minister of Ukraine; b. 4 August 1954, in Bratushany, Moldova; m., with three d. *Education:* he graduated from Leningrad (now St Petersburg) Shipbuilding Institute, Russia, in 1978. *Career:* he worked in shipbuilding and repair in Estonia and Ukraine, before his election to the Ukrainian legislature, the Verkhovna Rada, in 1990. From 1992–95 he served as the President's Representative in Mykolayiv Oblast, as head of the regional administration. In 1995–96 he served as a Deputy Prime Minister in charge of industrial policy, and from 1996 as an adviser to the President on industrial policy. Also from that year, Kinakh served as President of the Ukrainian Union of Industrialists and Entrepreneurs, and was widely regarded as one of the leading so-called 'red directors' (former communist officials who had assumed business interests during the 1990s) in Ukraine. He continued to hold a number of industry-related posts after 1997, and served as First Deputy Prime Minister during 1999. On 29 May 2001 President Leonid Kuchma (q.v.) appointed Kinakh as Prime Minister, replacing Viktor Yushchenko (q.v.). Kinakh was widely considered to be less favourably disposed toward rapid economic reform and the advice of international financial institutions than his predecessor. However, at the first meeting of his cabinet he declared his priorities to include: co-operation with the legislature; the implementation of structural changes to the economy, and the creation of an attractive investment environment; legal reform; and freedom of speech. He was criticized for an inability to make progress in key areas, however, particularly regarding social policy, and was eventually dismissed by President Kuchma in November 2002. The following week he stated that he believed his dismissal to be part of the process of political reform in the country. He resumed his duties as leader of the Party of Industrialists and Entrepreneurs—in this capacity he announced, in June 2003, his intention to seek election to the presidency in 2004. *Address:* Party of Industrialists and Entrepreneurs of Ukraine, 01023 Kiev, vul. Baseyna 30/46, Ukraine; tel. (44) 234-37-07; fax (44) 235-82-58; e-mail pppu@ukr.net.

**KIRIYENKO, Sergei Vladilenovich:** Russian politician and former premier; b. 27 July 1962, in Sukhumi, Abkhazia, Georgia; m., with three c. *Education:* Gorkii (now Nizhnii Novgorod) Institute of Water Engineering. *Career:* he had a career in industry and banking, much of it in Nizhnii Novgorod, and acquired a reputation as a protégé of the reformist Governor of that region, Boris Nemtsov (q.v.). He was appointed to the powerful Ministry of Fuel and Oil in 1997, becoming Minister in November, but was still relatively unknown when appointed acting premier in March 1998. The Russian President, Boris Yeltsin (q.v.), secured his endorsement as Prime Minister in a bitter confrontation with parliament, after which he demonstrated his reformist credentials through his nominations to government office. Kiriyenko aimed to pay greater attention to the social problems inherent in the transition to a market economy, but the financial crisis of August 1998 overwhelmed both his social and economic policies. His political future was further undermined by the discrediting of the performance of the reformists as a whole in government, and he was dismissed on 23 August. One year later, Kiriyenko's New Force movement joined the Union of Rightist Forces electoral bloc, of which he became a leader. The bloc won 24 seats in the Duma in the parliamentary election of 19 December. He simultaneously stood as a candidate for mayor of Moscow, obtaining 11.4% of the votes cast, coming in second place behind the incumbent, Yurii Luzhkov (q.v.). In May 2000 Kiriyenko was appointed presidential envoy to the new Volga Federal Okrug, as part of efforts by President Vladimir Putin (q.v.) to strengthen the rule of law in Russia's regions. He was also Chairman of the Russian Chemical Disarmament Commission, in which role he has welcomed external aid to assist in the destruction of chemical weapons. *Address:* Office of the Plenipotentiary Representative of the President of the Russian Federation to the Volga Federal Okrug, 620031 Sverdlovsk obl., Yekaterinburg, pl. Oktyabrskaya 3, Russia; tel. (3432) 77-18-96; e-mail info@kirienko.ru; internet www.pfo.ru.

**KISELEV, Yevgenii Alekseyevich:** Russian journalist, broadcaster and media executive; b. 15 June 1956, in Moscow; m., with one s. *Education:* Institute of African and Asian Studies at Moscow M. V. State University (MGU). *Career:* he taught Farsi at the KGB Higher School in the early 1980s, before joining Radio Moscow, initially as Tehran correspondent and, subsequently, as its chief Middle East correspondent. He returned to Moscow in the late 1980s, becoming a popular host of news and current affairs programmes. In 1993 he was one of the founders of a new, independent TV channel, NTV—Independent Television. The station, owned and financed by Vladimir Gusinskii (q.v.), quickly gained a reputation for quality programming and editorial independence. In the late 1990s and early 2000s the station, in particular its current affairs programmes, presented by Kiselev, became increasingly critical of the Government and of President Vladimir Putin, most notably with regard to the renewed conflict in Chechnya that commenced in September 1999. Kiselev was also the station's chief executive and attracted criticism from government sources on both editorial and administrative grounds. He was eventually dismissed from both roles following the acquisition of a majority share in NTV by the state-owned hydrocarbons company, Gazprom (which had won a legal battle for control of the station with Gusinskii's Mediya-Most group). Kiselev led a campaign by the station's employees to remain independent, but was eventually forced to abandon his posts. He accepted an offer of a similar combined journalistic/executive role at another, smaller station, TV-6, owned by Boris Berezovskii (q.v.), of which he became General Director in May 2001. He employed a number of former NTV journalists and maintained that station's editorial policy. However, TV-6 was declared insolvent, following a court case brought by a minority shareholder, in January 2002. Kiselev and others considered the closure of the company to be politically motivated; the shareholding group that had instigated the court case was a subsidiary of the state-controlled petroleum company LUKoil. In March it was announced that a new non-profit organization, Mediya-Sotsium, headed by the former Prime Minister, Yevgenii Primakov (q.v.), and the Chairman of the Industrialists and Entrepreneurs, Arkadii Volskii, had been awarded the contract to broadcast on the frequencies vacated by TV-6. Many former journalists from that station, including Kiselev, transferred to the new channel, which commenced operations under the name TVS. However, TVS also suffered financial difficulties and was closed down, ostensibly for financial reasons, in June 2003. In September Kiselev was appointed as Editor-in-Chief of the daily newspaper, *Moskovskiye Novosti* (The Moscow News). *Address:* Moskovskiye Novosti, 125009 Moscow, ul. Tverskaya 16/2, Russia; tel. (095) 200-07-67; fax (095) 209-17-28; e-mail info@mn.ru; internet www.mn.ru.

**KOCHARIAN, Robert Sedrakovich:** President of Armenia; b. 31 Aug. 1954, in Stepanakert (Nagornyi Karabakh, Azerbaijan); m., with two s. and one d. *Education:* Yerevan Polytechnic Institute. *Career:* an engineer at the Karabakh Silk Production Factory in Stepanakert for most of the 1980s, he was also an active member of the Communist Party in Nagornyi Karabakh. In the late 1980s he co-founded the movement that demanded Nagornyi Karabakh's transfer from the jurisdiction of Azerbaijan to that of Armenia. With the proclomation of the 'Republic of Nagornyi Karabakh' in late 1991 Kocharian was elected to the rebel enclave's Supreme Soviet (Supreme Council) and, in August of the following year, headed the State Defence Committee, which replaced the Karabakh Government under martial law. His authority was formalized under the new constitutional arrangements of 1995, when he was elected to an executive presidency. On 24 November 1996 he secured an electoral mandate for remaining in the presidency. However, he was obliged to resign the leadership of Nagornyi Karabakh when he was appointed Prime Minister of Armenia itself in March 1997. This appeared to be an attempt by President Levon Ter-Petrossian (q.v.) to mollify opposition parties who were demanding a new presidential election in Armenia. Kocharian successfully implemented several economic reforms. Bringing such a popular, nationalist figure into government, however, was to prove unfortunate for Ter-Petrossian. Although they agreed to some extent on the introduction of economic reforms, with regard to policy on Nagornyi Karabakh Kocharian was far less compromising. He led potent opposition to President Ter-Petrossian's concession that any peace settlement could postpone the question of the enclave's status (which concession Ter-Petrossian accepted in 1997). Kocharian and a number of others in the cabinet favoured a complete settlement, not a phased one, and, eventually, Ter-Petrossian felt obliged to resign as Head of State in February 1998. The parliamentary speaker, Babken Ararktsian, also resigned, so Kocharian assumed the role of acting President until an election was held—on 30 March he was formally elected to the post with a large majority, following a second round of voting. Although the issue of Nagornyi Karabakh had brought him to power, he continued to pursue negotiations. In October 1999 five gunmen besieged the National Assembly, killing eight people, including the Prime Minister, Vazgen Sarkissian, and the Chairman of the National Assembly, Karen Demirchian. Kocharian personally negotiated the release of some 50 hostages and assumed control of the Government. Intermittent protests took place from 2000, demanding Kocharian's resignation, but attempts by the opposition to initiate impeachment proceedings were unsuccessful. The campaign to oust him continued into the early 2000s, but he was re-elected to the presidency in March

2003, narrowly failing to win the required 50% of the votes cast in the first ballot, and obtaining 67.8% of the votes cast in the second round. Opposition candidates alleged widespread electoral irregularities, and Kocharian's second-round opponent, Stepan Demirchian (q.v.), challenged the result in the country's Constitutional Court. Although the result was upheld, Kocharian was angered when the Court's Chairman, Gagik Haroutunian (q.v.), subsequently stated that he believed that a referendum on public confidence in the President should be held within one year. *Address:* Office of the President, 375077 Yerevan, Marshal Baghramian St 26, Armenia; tel. (1) 52-02-04; fax (1) 52-15-51; internet www .president.am.

**KRAVCHUK, Leonid Makarovych:** Ukrainian politician and former President; b. 10 Jan. 1934, in Velykyi Zhytyn, Rivne Oblast; m., with one s. *Education:* Kiev T. Shevchenko State (now National) University and the Academy of Sciences of Moscow, Russia. *Career:* a member of the Communist Party of the Soviet Union (CPSU) from 1958, he was the Second Secretary of the Communist Party of the Ukraine when elected Chairman of the Ukrainian legislature, the Verkhovna Rada in July 1990. Although a communist, he won support for his Ukrainian nationalism and, against a divided opposition, he was elected President of Ukraine, with 63% of the votes cast, on 1 December 1991. On the same day overwhelming support for Ukrainian independence was expressed in a republican referendum. Kravchuk did agree to the formation of the Commonwealth of Independent States (originally with the Russian and Belarusian leaders), but maintained an independent stance against Russian domination of the new association. His relations with parliament were not always easy, particularly during 1993, notably when he made concessions to Russia over the Black Sea Fleet or nuclear disarmament. His defeat in the presidential election of June–July 1994, by his erstwhile Prime Minister, Leonid Kuchma (q.v.), was seen largely to be the result of his failure to formulate a comprehensive economic-reform programme and a resultant decline in the standard of living in Ukraine. He was elected as a deputy to the Verkhovna Rada later that year. In January 2000 a parliamentary majority faction led by Kravchuk (formed by some 240 deputies from 11 centre-right parties, as well as independents) petitioned for the removal from office of the Verkhovna Rada Chairman, Oleksandr Tkachenko, and his deputy, Adam Martynyuk. Despite left-wing opposition, at a separate parliamentary session the majority faction voted unanimously to remove Tkachenko and Martynyuk from office. Although left-wing deputies denied the majority access to the Verkhovna Rada for some days, a number of the Kravchuk faction forcibly gained entry to the building. Kravchuk remained leader of this parliamentary majority grouping until September 2000, when he was replaced by Oleksandr Karpov. Kravchuk was re-elected to the Verkhovna Rada in legislative elections in March 2002, and in June was elected as the head of the parliamentary faction of the Social-Democratic Party of Ukraine (United). He was often viewed as a senior political figure with non-partisan intent rather than as a party leader. He supported proposed changes in Ukraine's Constitution proposed by Kuchma in 2003, which would have the effect of limiting the powers of the presidency and increasing those of parliament, but stated that he thought the necessary conditions for such changes would not be in place until 2006, at the earliest. *Address:* Verkhovna Rada, 01008 Kiev, vul. M. Hrushevskoho 5, Ukraine; tel. (44) 226-22-92; fax (44) 293-06-53; e-mail vfsev@rada.gov.ua; internet www.rada.gov.ua.

**KUCHMA, Leonid Maksimovych:** President of Ukraine; b. 9 Aug. 1938, in Chatikine, Chernihiv Oblast; m., with one d. *Education:* Dnipropetrovsk State University. *Career:* he worked at Yuzmash (Yuzhnoye/Pivdenne M.K. Yangel Construction Bureau NPO), Dnipropetrovsk, the largest missile factory in the world, from 1960 and eventually became its manager. A member of the Communist Party of the Soviet Union (CPSU) in 1960–91, he was appointed to the Central Committee of the Communist Party of Ukraine (CPU) in 1981, where he served for 10 years. He was elected to the Ukrainian legislature, the Verkhovna Rada, in October 1991. On 13

October 1992 his nomination as Prime Minister was approved by the Ukrainian parliament, the Verkhovna Rada. As premier, he energetically pursued a policy of market reform, initially with the support of President Leonid Kravchuk (q.v.). In November he succeeded in persuading the Verkhovna Rada to grant him the power to rule by decree for a period of six months. At the end of this time, however, his powers were not renewed, and after consistent opposition to his economic reforms from the Verkhovna Rada and from the President himself, he eventually resigned. He subsequently became Chairman of the Union of Industrialists and Entrepreneurs until 1994, when he stood in the elections to the presidency. He defeated Kravchuk in the second round of voting, having received massive support in eastern and central Ukraine. As his programme of economic reform, the first of its kind in Ukraine, brought him into conflict with the Verkhovna Rada, he sought to reduce the legislature's authority and, later, to subordinate certain ministries directly to his power. The new Constitution, eventually adopted in June 1996, granted him greater power over government and the power to legislate economic reform by decree—it formalized the situation that had effectively existed under the so-called Constitutional Agreement of June 1995. He managed to achieve a degree of economic stabilization in Ukraine, but substantial reform was hindered by a lack of progress in privatization and by conflict with the Government and legislature, which worsened in the late 1990s. The ability to co-operate with President Kuchma became almost a prerequisite for any position of power in the country, which led to the appointment of allies and friends, in particular so-called 'Dnipropetrovtsy', who shared his origins in the eastern industrial city of Dnipropetrovsk and, partially in consequence of this, corruption became widespread in Ukraine during the late 1990s. In June 1999 campaigning for the presidential election began in earnest, and Kuchma was increasingly attacked by other potential candidates, who accused him of illegally using state funds to finance his campaign and of falsifying the results of parliamentary elections convened to nominate him. In the first round of voting, on 31 October, Kuchma obtained 36.5% of the votes cast. No candidate obtained an overall majority, so a second round of voting took place on 14 November. In the period between the two elections, Kuchma launched an intensive campaign in order to ensure his re-election, dismissing, for example, the Governors of three regions where majority voting had supported other candidates. Despite his unpopularity, Kuchma retained the presidency in the second round, securing 57.7% of the votes cast, defeating the CPU candidate, Petro Symonenko (q.v.). Once re-elected, Kuchma increasingly sought to strengthen his powers, holding a successful referendum that, if implemented, would reduce the powers of the legislature in April 2000. (By late 2003, however, there was no indication that the measures approved in the referendum would be introduced.) From late 2000 Kuchma's popularity, and his reputation internationally, declined substantially, following the release of hundreds of hours of audio recordings made clandestinely by the former presidential security adviser, Maj. Mykola Melnychenko. In particular, Kuchma's position appeared threatened as a result of sections of the recordings that appeared to implicate him in the disappearance, and subsequent murder, of an investigative journalist, Heorhiy Gongadze. As large-scale public protests, which aimed to force Kuchma's resignation, swept across Ukraine in early 2001, Kuchma's hold on the presidency briefly appeared to be in jeopardy, while further recordings appeared to indicate his acquiescence in electoral malpractice and bribery. The President, who blamed the allegations on a plot by 'foreign agents', nevertheless retained his post, and appeared to regain authority following the dismissal of Prime Minister Viktor Yushchenko (q.v.) in April. In early 2002 new revelations from recently released audio recordings, to the effect that Kuchma had, allegedly, personally authorized the sale of advanced radar systems to Iraq, in breach of UN sanctions, further damaged Kuchma's credibility and served to heighten his isolation internationally, and later in the year specialists from the USA and the United Kingdom opened an investigation into the claims. He dismissed the Government led by Anatoliy Kinakh (q.v.) in November 2002, claiming that it had made insufficient progress on social issues. He appointed Viktor Yanukovych (q.v.), whom he had previously appointed as the Governor of Donetsk Oblast, to replace Kinakh. In mid-2003 he proposed changes to the country's Constitution, but withdrew them, following opposition criticisms that they were designed to enable him to serve a third term of office (prohibited under the prevailing Constitution). *Address:* Office of the President, 01220 Kiev, vul. Bankova 11, Ukraine; tel. (44) 291-53-33; fax (44) 293-61-61; e-mail president@adm.gov.ua; internet www.kuchma.gov.ua.

**KULIYEV, Abdy:** Turkmen politician; b. 1936, in Ashgabat. *Education:* gained a doctorate in linguistics at Turkmen State University, later attended the Diplomatic Academy of the USSR. *Career:* he was a researcher at the Institute of Language and Literature of the Turkmen Academy of Sciences, before being a director of Russian language courses at the Soviet Cultural Centre in Yemen in 1960–71. He then served in the Soviet diplomatic service, mainly in the Middle East. In 1990 he was appointed Turkmenistan's Minister of Foreign Affairs. He was a member of the President's Council, but became increasingly resistant to President Saparmyrat Niyazov's (q.v.) authoritarian style of leadership, particularly the 'personality cult' he promoted. It was reportedly this last aspect of Niyazov's leadership that prompted Kuliyev's resignation from the Council of Ministers in July 1992, although the Government claimed that he was avoiding corruption charges. A Russian citizen, he moved to Moscow, Russia, from where he co-ordinated a prominent branch of a growing opposition-in-exile. In April 1998 he returned to Turkmenistan, on a visit timed to coincide with Niyazov's state visit to the USA, in an attempt to draw attention to the repressive treatment of opposition forces in Turkmenistan. However, he was detained on charges of fraud and sedition, and placed under house arrest; after the intercession of the Russian embassy in Ashgabat, he was allowed to return to Moscow. In June 2002 Kuliyev, who had founded a political party, the United Democratic Opposition, agreed to co-operate with the People's Movement of Turkmenistan of Boris Shikhmuradov (q.v.), which was also believed to be based in Moscow. In addition to his political activities, Kuliyev provided commentaries on events in Turkmenistan for Russian and Western media outlets, and asserted that he eventually intended to return to Turkmenistan. In August 2003 he was severely beaten in Moscow, and claimed that his aggressors were agents acting on behalf of President Niyazov (the Turkmen Government denied the allegations).

**KULOV, Feliks:** Kyrgyzstani former politician and administrator; b. 29 Oct. 1948, in Frunze (now Bishkek). *Education:* Osh University. *Career:* he began his political career as Inspector at the Ministry of Internal Affairs, later becoming Chief Inspector, and Head of the Criminal Dept. In December 1978 he was promoted to Vice-Chief of the Internal Affairs Administration of the Talas region, subsequently becoming Vice-Minister of Internal Affairs. A reformist communist, he was a strong supporter of the liberal President elected in 1990, Askar Akayev (q.v.). Minister of Internal Affairs in the Cabinet of Ministers, he resigned his party membership after the August 1991 coup attempt in Moscow. In 1992 he replaced German Kuznetsov as Vice-President of the Republic. However, in March 1993 he was investigated for corruption, although it was also alleged that this was part of a right-wing parliamentary conspiracy to discredit prominent reformers, without directly attacking the popular President. Following the scandals surrounding the 'Seabeco affair', when a naive agreement with a Canadian brokerage company resulted in the apparent loss of a considerable part of the country's gold reserves, on 10 December Kulov resigned, for 'ethical reasons', and urged the Government to do likewise. For Akayev this was a gesture to the parliament, or Zhogorku Kenesh, that he was willing to accommodate them in pursuit of stable government. However, he retained Kulov's services, and demonstrated his confidence in him by appointing him to head the administration of the important Chui region (around the capital) later in December. Kulov remained Akim (Governor) of Chui, but, in September 1996, was criticized by the President for his dubious business connections. In April 1997 he was appointed Minister of National Security. He subsequently became Mayor of Bishkek in April 1998. In July 1999 a new political party, the Ar-Namys (Dignity) Party, was established, with Kulov as its Chairman. However, the party, the country's second largest, was prevented from contesting the parliamentary elections of February 2000 separately, on the grounds of a legal technicality, leading to condemnation from international observers. Kulov was, however, permitted to stand as an independent candidate. He failed to win a seat in the 'run-off' election held on 12 March, prompting demonstrations and allegations that officials had been bribed to ensure his defeat. Later in March Kulov had legal proceedings brought against him for abuse of office during his term as Minister of National Security. A closed military trial commenced in June, prompting criticism by the Russian State Duma, the US Government and international organizations, and allegations that the trial was instigated in order to prevent Kulov from standing as a candidate in the presidential election scheduled to be held in late October. Although Kulov was acquitted by the court in August, he boycotted the language test demanded for registration as a presidential candidate in the following month, and was therefore barred from standing; in the same month Bishkek military court annulled his acquittal, and ordered a retrial. In January 2001 Kulov was sentenced to seven years' imprisonment (one charge of abuse of office was later dismissed and the confiscation of his property reversed). New embezzlement charges were brought against him by the Prosecutor-General in July. In November the four main opposition parties, Ar-Namys, Erkindik (Liberty), Ata-Meken (Fatherland) Socialist and El (Popular), formed a People's Congress (later joined by the Social Democratic Party), with Kulov as its head. In May Kulov was sentenced to a further 10 years' imprisonment (to run concurrently) for the embezzlement charges that had been brought against him; however, an amnesty reduced his sentence by three years in October. Kulov continued to comment on the country's political situation from detention, although the frequency of his public statements declined following his transfer, in April 2003, to a maximum security gaol. In August the Supreme Court rejected final appeals against both conviction and sentence. With all legal recourses now exhausted it appeared likely that Kulov would, for the forseeable future, influence his country's political life only through occasional statements and as a focus for opposition groups' demonstrations and international human rights organizations' concerns. *Address:* c/o Office of the Chairman, Ar-Namys (Dignity) Party, Bishkek, Isanova 60, Kyrgyzstan.

**KVASHNIN, Gen. Anatolii Vasilyevich:** Russian; Chief of General Staff; b. 15 Aug. 1946, in Ufa, Bashkir ASSR (now Bashkortostan—Russian Federation). *Education:* attended Kurgan Machine Construction Institute, the Academy of Armoured Units and the Academy of General Staff. *Career:* he served as Commander of the Allied Group of Armed Forces in the Republic of Chechnya in 1994–95, then as Commander of the Armed Forces of the North Caucasian Command in 1995–97. He served concurrently as First Deputy Minister of Defence of the Russian Federation and as Chief of General Staff of the Armed Forces from 1997. Following renewed hostilities in Chechnya from September 1999, his powers and influence increased. In his role as Chief of General Staff, Kvashnin worked to develop the country's defence relationship with the USA, although he voiced his disapproval of the USA's unilateral exit from the Anti-Ballistic Missiles (ABM) Treaty, announced in late 2001. In mid-2000 a public row erupted with the Minister of Defence, Gen. Igor Sergeyev, who strongly criticized Kvashnin's plans to reduce the strength of Russia's strategic rocket forces. In a clear gesture of support for Kvashnin, Putin dismissed Sergeyev in March 2001. In May 2002 Kvashnin informed Putin that the situation in the defence forces was 'worse than critical', owing to poverty and crime in the ranks, and a pervasive atmosphere of permissiveness. Some observers considered that he had too strong an influence over Putin, urging him strengthen the military at all times and to opt for military solutions where they were not always appropriate—this criticism wsa made with particular relevance to the situation in Chechnya. In 2003 he was

involved in the programme to transform the Russian military from a conscription-based system to one of 'volunteer-contract service'. However, he stated that conscription would not be totally abolished. Later in the year he restated his belief that a budget increase was necessary if the reform of Russia's armed forces was to be successful. *Address:* Ministry of Defence, 103160 Moscow, ul. Znamenka 19, Russia; tel. (095) 296-84-37; fax (095) 296-84-36; e-mail press@mil.ru.

**LAZARENKO, Pavlo Ivanovych:** Ukrainian politician and former premier; b. 23 Jan. 1953, in Karpivka, Dnipropetrovsk Oblast; m., with three c. *Education:* graduated from the Dnipropetrovsk Institute of Agriculture in 1978, received a doctorate in Economics in 1996. *Career:* a former manager of a collective farm, he was a close political ally of President Leonid Kuchma (q.v.). He served as presidential representative in Dnipropetrovsk Oblast from 1992 until his election as a deputy to the Ukrainian legislature, the Verkhovna Rada, in July 1994. After working for eight months as First Deputy Prime Minister he was appointed to the premiership in July 1996. Reformers in parliament criticized the appointment of a 'red director' to the post, while others feared that with little economic experience he would be unable to oversee Ukraine's uneasy transition to a market economy. He survived an assassination attempt in July 1996; the man suspected of this attempt later died in suspicious circumstances. Lazarenko had contacts in many business circles and, by exploiting these, he became one of the richest men in the country, while the economy continued its severe decline. Allegations of corruption increased and in June 1997 President Kuchma removed him from office, ostensibly because of ill-health. However, he retained his parliamentary seat and in late August was elected to lead the centrist Unity faction in the legislature. He remained leader of the Hromada—Community political party, which obtained some 20 seats in the legislative elections of March 1998. The party was permitted to assume positions of responsibility in the government committee charged with combating corruption, which, in effect, allowed the offenders to block investigations. Criminal proceedings began against him in March 1998, on charges of embezzlement. In February 1999 the Verkhovna Rada voted to remove Lazarenko's immunity from prosecution. A warrant was issued for his arrest and he was detained in the USA, officially because of irregularities in his entry visa. Ukraine asked the USA to extradite him, but Lazarenko requested asylum and remained where he was. In January 2000 Lazarenko alleged that large amounts of IMF money loaned to Ukraine had been diverted from the central bank into Ukrainian government securities in December 1997; however, an investigation by the Fund unearthed no evidence of embezzlement. Lazarenko's fortunes deteriorated further in June 2000, when he was convicted *in absentia* of money 'laundering' (the processing of illegally obtained funds into legitimate accounts) by a court in Switzerland, and given an 18-month suspended prison sentence. In September 2001 the Ukrainian Prosecutor-General initiated measures to charge Lazarenko with involvement in the murder of two businessmen in 1996–98. US investigators arrived in Ukraine in May 2003 to collect evidence in preparation for his trial (which was subsequently delayed from October 2003 to February 2004). *Address:* Hromada, 01133 Kiev, Laboratornyi provylok 1, Ukraine; tel. and fax (44) 252-88-57; e-mail office@hromada.kiev.ua; internet www.hromada.kiev.ua.

**LUKASHENKA, Alyaksandr Rygorovich:** President of Belarus; b. 30 Aug. 1954, in Kopys; m. Halyna Rodionovna (estranged), with two s. *Education:* graduated in history from Mogilev Pedagogical Institute and in agricultural economics from the Belarus Agricultural Academy. *Career:* an active member of the Communist Party from an early age, he trained as an economist and held various posts within the party, on collective farms and as a political and ideological instructor in the Soviet army. After four years as a deputy of the Belarusian Supreme Council, he unexpectedly became Belarus' first directly elected President in July 1994, his adversarial, populist style and conservative agenda, based on nostalgia for the certainties of Soviet rule, finding a natural constituency among Belarus' largely rural population. Lukashenka reversed almost all of the advances in the fields of democratic reform and human rights achieved after the collapse of the communist bloc, and established an authoritarian and paternalist regime, becoming known to the Belarusian people as *batka* (little father). Notorious for praising the former German dictator, Adolf Hitler, for his exercise of power, on his accession Lukashenka quickly set about creating what he termed a 'vertical presidency', investing in himself the power to appoint government officials at every level. Lukashenka's disregard for democratic processes and intolerance of opposition involved him in frequent disputes with the Supreme Council (legislature) and Constitutional Court. This culminated in the referendum of November 1996, through which the President amended the Constitution, and effectively removed all barriers to one-man rule, replacing the Supreme Council, extending his term of office and conferring upon himself extensive powers of rule by decree. Confrontations regarding the content and conduct of the referendum led to the dismissal of the Prime Minister and the Chairman of the Central Electoral Commission by Lukashenka, and the subsequent formation of a 'shadow' government, which continued to be recognized internationally as the legitimate legislature, by disenfranchised deputies of the abolished Supreme Council. Lukashenka also restored Russian as a state language and moved Belarus towards closer political and economic relations with Russia. Although the Russian authorities remained suspicious of Lukashenka's maverick behaviour, the integration process was confirmed by the Treaty of Union and Charter of the Union of April 1997, which established confederative structures and envisaged eventual 'voluntary unification'. A framework union accord was signed in December 1998 and a more formal agreement, on the Union of the Russian Federation and Belarus, was signed in December 1999, which committed the two sides to unification of customs, tariffs and taxes, and eventual currency union. However, plans for further links between Belarus and Russia suffered somewhat from a deterioration in relations between Lukashenka and Vladimir Putin (q.v.), the Russian President from 2000. In July 1999, meanwhile, President Lukashenka remained in power, in contravention of the overturned Constitution of 1994, prompting opposition protests. Despite increasingly stern international criticism of the human and civil rights abuses of his administration, however, Lukashenka's hold on power remained firm, amid a fragmented opposition, and observers anticipated the entrenchment of a long-term 'village dictatorship'. A presidential election took place on 9 September 2001, at which Lukashenka was re-elected for a second term of office, with some 76% of the votes cast, although there were reports of serious electoral irregularities. Following his re-election, Lukashenka took steps to further weaken the opposition, dismissing several directors of state enterprises in late 2001, and applying renewed pressure on the independent media. He announced that the priority for his next term of office would be the conclusion of negotiations on union with Russia, although numerous obstacles in the union negotiations led many to suspect initially that he was rather better disposed towards such a union than were the Russian authorities and, subsequently, that the terms proposed by Russia had made him less enthusiastic about such an arrangement. Despite his authoritarian style of rule, and the continued international ostracism of him and his regime, however, Lukashenka continued to attract support inside Belarus, and the opposition remained disorganized and faltering. *Address:* Office of the President, 220016 Minsk, vul. K. Marksa 38, Dom Urada, Belarus; tel. (17) 222-60-06; e-mail contact@president.gov.by; internet www.president.gov.by.

**LUZHKOV, Yurii Mikhailovich:** Russian politician; b. 21 Sept. 1936, in Moscow; m., with two s. and two d. *Education:* studied at the Gubkin Institute of Oil and Gas, Moscow. *Career:* he worked as a researcher and occupied a number of managerial posts in the Soviet Ministry of the Chemical Industry, before becoming First Deputy Chairman of the Moscow City Executive in 1987 and Head of the Moscow Agro-Industrial Committee. His close working relationship with the Mayor of Moscow, Gavriil Popov, led to him running as his deputy in the direct mayoral elections of 1991. When

Popov resigned in June 1992, Luzhkov was appointed by President Boris Yeltsin (q.v.) to replace him. As Mayor, he encouraged financial institutions to support commercial organizations and municipal programmes. He also restarted an ambitious construction programme aimed at solving the city's housing shortage. However, there were allegations of corruption within the municipal government and complaints about Luzhkov's close contacts with local commercial interests. Despite some clashes with both the federal presidency and the federal government, he refused to stand in the presidential election of 1996, declaring himself to be an administrator, rather than a politician. He indicated a preference for Yeltsin's candidature over that of the communist-backed candidate, Gennadii Zyuganov (q.v.). The economic success of the Russian capital city, ostentatiously displayed in the extravagant celebrations of the city's 850th anniversary in 1997, was a powerful advertisement for his interventionist economic policy. It earned him the enmity of the radical pro-free market reformers in the federal Government, but not the explicit condemnation of the President. In November 1998 Luzhkov founded a centrist political movement, Fatherland, which contested the December 1999 State Duma elections as part of the centrist Fatherland-All Russia (FAR) alliance. Luzhkov was re-elected as Mayor by a clear majority on 19 December 1999, while in the simultaneous general election Fatherland-All Russia came third, securing 67 seats. Luzhkov was initially expected to stand as a candidate in the 2000 election for the federal presidency. However, many of his regional supporters backed the candidacy of Vladimir Putin (q.v.) and, after a period of neutrality, Luzhkov and FAR also gave their support to Putin. FAR merged with the pro-Putin Unity party in April 2001, creating a single party, Unity and Fatherland-United Russia (UF-UR). In September 2002 there was disagreement over a proposal by Luzhkov to re-erect a statue of the founder of the Soviet security services, Feliks Dzerzhinskii, in Moscow, which had been removed in 1991. Some thought the proposal represented an attempt on Luzhkov's part to gain favour with Putin, who had himself served in the Service. He was a fierce critic of Russia's so-called 'oligarchs', and disputes with the major hydrocarbons companies recurred throughout his time as Mayor. Luzhkov was a central figure in the authorities' response to the taking hostage of the 800-strong audience at a theatre in the city by Chechen rebels in October 2002; the crisis was thought to have strengthened his relations with Putin. Further 'terrorist acts' in the city during 2003 gave renewed impetus to Luzhkov's plan for the issuing of compulsory permits (*propiski*) for Moscow residents, which he had long supported, despite such measures being forbidden by federal law. In September Luzhkov announced that he would seek election to a third term as Mayor of Moscow in December; he was also appointed to the third position on the UF-UR federal list for the concurrent elections to the State Duma. *Address:* Office of the Mayor and Prime Minister of the Government of Moscow Federal City, 103032 Moscow, ul. Tverskaya 13, Russia; tel. (095) 229-58-03; fax (095) 232-18-74; internet www.mos.ru.

**LYTVYN, Volodymyr Mykhaylovych:** Ukrainian historian and politician; b. 28 April 1956, in Sloboda Romanovska village, Zhytomyr Oblast. *Education:* studied history at Kiev T. Shevchenko State (now National) University. *Career:* From 1978 to 1986 he held a number of academic posts in the Faculty of History at Kiev T. Shevchenko State University, specializing in contemporary Ukrainian history. From 1996 he was appointed to a succession of posts within the presidential administration, where he was regarded as a close ally of President Leonid Kuchma (q.v.). He was appointed as the head of the presidential administration in November 1999, and in the following month was concurrently appointed to the National Security and Defence Council. Prior to the legislative elections held in March 2002 he was instrumental in the formation and leadership of a centrist electoral alliance, For A United Ukraine (FUU), which united several centrist and pro-'oligarch' parties, with the intention of forming a parliamentary majority supportive of Kuchma. Although no workable parliamentary majority was formed by any grouping within several months of the election results, FUU's performance at the election ensured that it obtained 101 of the 450 seats, making it the second largest grouping within the legislature, the Verkhovna Rada. However, it was markedly more successful in winning votes in single-member constituencies than it was on the proportional lists, in which it received only 11.8%, finishing in third place. Although at the polls FUU had, to some extent, served its purpose in acting as a coherent pro-Kuchma electoral bloc, once elected, the faction of FUU deputies rapidly disintegrated into a number of regional groupings, each emphasizing their particular interests. Following the elections, Lytvyn was removed from the position as head of the presidential administration, to enable him to take up the legislative seat to which he had been elected. At the end of May, despite his lack of political experience, Lytvyn was narrowly elected by the new Verkhovna Rada as Chairman (speaker). A speech at the opening session of parliament in September 2003 was widely seen as an attempt to distance himself from President Kuchma and establish himself as a major political figure within Ukraine. He claimed that the Constitution should be amended to grant parliament more powers and that 'the Kuchma era' had 'run its course'. In October he showed his frustrations with the difficulties parliament was experiencing in either accepting or rejecting amendments to the country's electoral legislation, advocating the dissolution of the chamber and the organization of new elections if no agreement could be reached promptly. *Address:* Verkhovna Rada, 01008 Kiev, vul. M. Hrushevskoho 5, Ukraine; tel. (44) 226-22-92; fax (44) 293-06-53; e-mail vfsev@ rada.gov.ua; internet www.rada.gov.ua.

**MAMEDOV, Etibar:** Azerbaijani politician. *Career:* Chairman of the National Independence Party (Istiklal), the party founded in opposition to the Popular Front of Azerbaijan (PFA) in 1992. He was in favour of links with Russia and was an ally of Heydar Aliyev (q.v.), until he was estranged by the appointment of Surat Husseinov as Prime Minister in June 1993. He therefore decided to remain in opposition and was elected to parliament in November 1995. He was one of the few major opposition figures to contest the election to the presidency in October 1998, when he secured 11.6% of the votes cast, the second-highest proportion. He refused to recognize Aliyev's re-election as legitimate and signed a co-operation agreement with Albufaz Elchibey of the PFA to oppose the Government. In November supporters of Mamedov organized a demonstration to protest against alleged electoral irregularities. A new political alliance, formed in April 2000 between Mamedov's NIP and the Democratic Party of Azerbaijan (one of the Chairmen of which was the exiled politician, Rasul Kuliyev), appeared to have the potential to develop into a wider opposition movement. The NIP's consequent lack of success in the legislative election of November led to unsuccessful demands for a repeat election to be held. Mamedov stood for election to the presidency in October 2003, but initial results revealed that he had attracted fewer than 3% of the votes cast. He joined other candidates and opposition leaders in denouncing the election, which was won by Ilham Aliyev (q.v.). *Address:* National Independence Party (NIP—Milli Istiklal), Baku, Azadliq Ave 179, Azerbaijan; internet www.amip .info.

**MARCHUK, Col-Gen. Yevhen Kyrylovych:** Ukrainian politician and security official; Secretary of the National Security and Defence Council; b. 28 January 1941, in Dolynivka, Kirovohrad Oblast. *Education:* Kirovohrad Pedagogical Institute. *Career:* a career security official in the USSR, from 1988 he was head of the State Security Committee (KGB) administration in Poltava Oblast. Following Ukrainian independence, he was appointed Head of the state security service from November 1991, before being appointed First Deputy Prime Minister responsible for security issues in July 1994. In March 1995 he was appointed Prime Minister by President Leonid Kuchma (q.v.), and remained in that post until late May 1996, when he was dismissed for failing to tackle the worsening economy. It was widely considered that Kuchma felt that Marchuk had become too popular and powerful, at the President's expense. Marchuk remained in opposition thereafter, but contested the presidency in October 1999 as the nominally joint candidate of four opposition parties,

coming fifth, with some 8% of the votes cast. In order to gain the backing of Marchuk's supporters, President Kuchma appointed him head of the National Security and Defence Council in November 1999 and was also the President of the Ukrainian Transport Companies Association. In June 2003 he was appointed Minister of Defence, the first civilian to hold the post since independence, and was charged with overseeing the faltering reform of the Ukrainian military. *Address:* Ministry of Defence, 03168 Kiev, Povitroflotskyi per. 6, Ukraine; tel. (44) 226-26-56; fax (44) 226-20-15; e-mail pressmou@ pressmou.kiev.ua; internet www.mil.gov.ua.

**MARKARIAN, Andranik:** Armenian premier; b. 1951, in Yerevan; m., with three c. *Education:* studied at Yerevan Polytechnic Institute in 1967–72. *Career:* a former Soviet dissident, he was sentenced to two years' detention in 1974. He was elected as a National Assembly deputy in 1995. The Chairman of the Republican Party of Armenia, he was appointed Prime Minister on 12 May 2000, following the dismissal of Aram Sarkissian. Upon his appointment, both he and President Robert Kocharian (q.v.) resolved to end the conflict between the presidency, the premiership and the legislature. Markarian also declared that he would seek to undertake constructive reform and tackle corruption, while maintaining the overall economic policy of the previous administration. He had a history of heart problems, and underwent surgery in France in October 2001, but maintained that he was physically capable of remaining Prime Minister. He considered the principal achievement of his first term of office to be Armenia's admission to membership of the World Trade Organization, in December 2002. He remained Prime Minister following the legislative elections held in May 2003. *Address:* Office of the Prime Minister, 375010 Yerevan, Republic Sq. 1, Government House, Armenia; tel. (2) 52-03-60; fax (2) 15-10-35.

**MASKHADOV, Gen. Khalid 'Aslan' Aliyevich:** Chechen rebel leader; b. 1951, in Kazakhstan; m., with one s. and one d. *Education:* Tbilisi Higher Artillery College, Georgia, and Leningrad (now St Petersburg) Kalinin Military Academy. *Career:* he served as a platoon commander in the Far East, and subsequently in Hungary, as a battery commander and a regiment commander. In January 1991 he was among the Soviet troops that occupied radio and television buildings in Vilnius, Lithuania. In 1992–96 Maskhadov served in the Chechen Armed Forces, being promoted to Chief of Staff in December 1993. He became one of the principal negotiators in talks with federal officials in 1995–96. On 31 August 1996, as the result of negotiations with the newly appointed Secretary of the Security Council, Lt-Gen. Aleksandr Lebed, Maskhadov signed the Khasavyurt Agreements, effectively ending the civil conflict in Chechnya. He was Prime Minister of the Chechen coalition Government from October 1996 to January 1997. In this capacity he was a signatory to a further agreement on the principles governing relations between the Russian Federation and the Chechen Republic. Having gained a reputation as a moderate pragmatist, he was elected President of Chechnya on 27 January 1997, securing 64.8% of the votes cast. However, his authority gradually weakened, and was subject to repeated assassination attempts. By 1998 he had full control only over Groznyi, with the rest of the country divided between influential field commanders. In late 1999, following attacks by Chechen rebels in Dagestan and explosions in Moscow and Volgodonsk (Rostov Oblast), Russian forces re-entered Chechnya, and Maskhadov called for resistance. The federal regime declined requests from Maskhadov for the negotiation of a settlement, stating that it recognized only the Moscow-based State Council of the Chechen Republic, which had been formed in October by former members of the republican legislature. In February 2000, after Groznyi had been destroyed by federal forces, Maskhadov stated that the rebels were prepared to engage in a long guerrilla war, and said that the federal army's victory was largely symbolic. Indirect talks with the federal Government were understood to have taken place in early 2000, despite the derecognition of Maskhadov's official status (he was officially replaced as administrative leader by former Mufti Akhmed haji Kadyrov—q.v.—in June), and the federal Government's insistence on his unconditional surrender. Subsequent talks in November 2001 between the federal authorities and a representative of Maskhadov also reached no substantive agreement, and a new rebel offensive was launched the following month. In late December Maskhadov announced the extension of his presidency for an additional year, to January 2003. In June 2002 Maskhadov again offered to suspend hostilities in return for peace talks, but Russia responded by claiming that it had received new information linking him to terrorist activity (an allegation he denied). The USA was subsequently notably less keen to present Maskhadov as a key figure in the future resolution of the conflict. Some suggested that this change of mood was prompted by the allegations of his links to international Islamist groups (which, however, remained largely unproven), others that it was part of a general US effort to maintain Russian support for the US-led 'war on terrorism'. In October Maskhadov condemned a hostage-taking incident in a theatre in Moscow by Chechen rebels. The Russian authorities made clear their view that Maskhadov was primarily responsible for the theatre siege and for other, subsequent terrorist acts by sympathizers of Chechen independence, and it was he that remained the primary target of Russian troops in Chechnya. The planning of many of the acts was attributed to a former associate and rival of Maskhadov's, Shamil Basayev (q.v.), although Basayev stated that Maskhadov had not known, in particular, of the Moscow theatre seige. None the less, it had been reported earlier in 2002 that Basayev had been appointed to a senior position in Maskhadov's military forces, the so-called State Defence Committee. In late 2003 Maskhadov remained at large, with a band of armed fighters estimated to number around 700, although his movements were believed to be restricted to the southern, mountainous regions of Chechnya.

**MATVIYENKO, Valentina Ivanova:** Russian politician and diplomat; Governor of St Petersburg; b. 7 April 1949, in Shepetovka, Khmelnytskiy Oblast, Ukrainian SSR; m., with one s. *Education:* she studied at the Leningrad Institute of Chemistry and Pharmaceuticals, and subsequently at the Academy of Social Sciences of the Central Committee of the Communist Party of the Soviet Union and the Academy of Diplomacy at the Ministry of Foreign Affairs of the USSR. *Career:* she held various posts in the Communist Party of the Soviet Union, and became a people's deputy in 1989. In 1991 she was appointed ambassador of the USSR to Malta. She returned to Moscow in 1994, and in the following year took up a post in the Ministry of Foreign Affairs, before resuming foreign diplomatic service in 1997, as ambassador of the Russian Federation to Greece. The following year she resigned this position and accepted the post of Deputy Chairman of the Government, with responsibility for social issues, the highest office achieved by a woman in post-Soviet Russia. She was a close ally of Vladimir Putin (q.v.), both prior to and after his election as President in 2000, and was widely regarded as a capable politician, with the capacity for higher office. In March 2003 she was appointed as Presidential Representative in the North-Western Federal Okrug, based in St Petersburg. In this capacity she was outspoken in criticizing the management of certain territories that she was responsible for overseeing. Many observers viewed her appointment in this capacity as a prelude to her contesting the governorship of the city, and shortly afterwards the incumbent Governor, Vladimir Yakovlev, announced that he would not seek re-election. In June Yakovlev, in a move that was widely interpreted as facilitating Matviyenko's election as Governor, was appointed as a Deputy Chairman in the federal Government, and the election was brought forward to September. As expected, Matviyenko sought election, and receiving support from President Putin to an extent that was unprecedented for a candidate to a regional governorship, she performed strongly, narrowly failing to be elected in the first round, and comfortably winning in a second round, on 5 October. She was inaugurated later in the month, stating that her main priorities were to improve St Petersburg's infrastructure and economy. There was also speculation that, as Governor, she would seek to merge St Petersburg City with the surrounding Leningrad Oblast, a measure that had been

formally approved by President Boris Yeltsin in 1998. Many commentators thought Matviyenko likely to return to a senior position in the federal administration in the future. *Address:* Office of the Governor, 193060 St Petersburg, Smolnyi; tel. (812) 271-74-13; fax (812) 276-18-27; e-mail gov@gov.spb.ru; internet www.matvienko.info.

**MIRONOV, Sergei Mikhailovich:** Chairman of the Russian Federation Council; b. 14 February 1953, in Leningrad (now St Petersburg); m., with one s. and one d. *Education:* Leningrad Plekhanov Mining Institute and St Petersburg Technical University; further studies in state and municipal administration. *Career:* from 1978 until the early 1990s he worked as a geophysical engineer, including for the Ministry of Geology. In 1993 he began work on securities markets. He served as Executive Director of the 'St Petersburg Revival' Building Corpn in 1994–95. In 1994 he was elected to the St Petersburg Legislative Assembly and, from April 1995, served as First Deputy Chairman of that body. For a brief period, from April–December 1998, he acted as Chairman of the Assembly. In September 2000 he was also elected Chairman of the St Petersburg regional political movement, the 'Will of Petersburg'. In June 2001 Mironov was selected as the representative of the St Petersburg Assembly to the Federation Council (the upper chamber of the Federal Assembly of the Russian Federation). He served as Deputy Chairman of the Federation Council from October, and in December was elected Chairman, replacing the long-serving Yegor Stroyev. As a former colleague of President Vladimir Putin (q.v.), from the latter's days as Deputy Mayor of St Petersburg, Mironov's appointment was expected to strengthen the process of centralization of government. Just two days after assuming the Chairmanship of the Council, in a move that apparently surprised even the presidential administration, he announced that he considered the presidential term to be too short, and hinted at the possibility of constitutional change to amend this. In mid-January 2002 he also expressed support for the direct election of the Federation Council. As Chairman of the Federation Council, Mironov represented Russia at the Parliamentary Assembly of the Council of Europe (PACE). The development of relations with the member states of the European Union was, therefore, of great importance to him, and he became an important figure in Russia's foreign affairs. Obliged by the Constitution to seek re-election to his post on the Federation Council, following his retention of his seat in the St Petersburg Legislative Assembly in elections held in December 2002, he won another term as Chairman the following month. In April 2003 he was elected to the leadership of the Russian Party of Life, a new, pro-Putin political movement. In advance of the State Duma elections scheduled to be held in December, the Russian Party of Life formed an electoral bloc with the the Party of the Rebirth of Russia of Gennadii Seleznev (q.v.). *Address:* Federation Council, 103426 Moscow, ul. B. Dmitrovka 26, Russia; tel. (095) 203-90-74; fax (095) 203-46-17; e-mail postsf@gov.ru; internet www.mironov.ru.

**MOROZ, Oleksandr Oleksandrovych:** Ukrainian politician; b. 29 Feb. 1944, in Buda, Kiev Oblast; m., with two d. *Education:* Ukrainian Agricultural Academy, Kiev. *Career:* he worked as an engineer before being elected as a deputy to the Ukrainian parliament. He co-founded the Socialist Party of Ukraine (SPU) in 1991 and acquired a popular following, as evidenced by his securing of 14% of the votes cast in the presidential election of 1994. He was elected Chairman of the Ukrainian legislature, the Verkhovna Rada, in the same year and played an important role in the conservative-dominated parliament's confrontations with President Leonid Kuchma (q.v.). The Verkhovna Rada contested his unpopular economic reforms and the adoption of a new Constitution (June 1996), which afforded the Verkhovna Rada fewer powers. Moroz remained leader of the SPU, which, in alliance with the Peasants' Party, obtained 29 seats in the Verkhovna Rada in March 1998. Moroz was the third-placed candidate in the first round of the presidential election held on 31 October 1999, obtaining 11.3% of the votes cast. In November 2000 Moroz was instrumental in implicating President Kuchma in the disappearance and murder of an investigative journalist, Heorhiy Honhadze, when he publicly released audio tapes, alleged to contain evidence of the involvement of the President and his advisers in unlawful killing, electoral fraud and bribery. The political survival of President Kuchma represented a severe blow for Moroz, who had staked his reputation on the evidence he provided against him. Moroz was unable to recover significant personal popularity, particularly with policies generally falling between the communists and the centrists, Ukraine's two most popular groupings, and although he was expected to mount a challenge for the presidency in 2004, he was thought unlikely to win. *Address:* Socialist Party of Ukraine, 01054 Kiev, vul. Vorovskoho 45, Ukraine; tel. (44) 216-88-82; fax (44) 244-51-66; e-mail press@socinfo.kiev.ua; internet www.socinfo.kiev.ua.

**MUTALIBOV, Ayaz Niyazi oglu:** former President of Azerbaijan; b. 12 May 1938, in Baku; m., with two s. *Education:* attended the M. Azizbekov Azerbaijani Institute of Oil and Chemistry. *Career:* trained as an engineer, he was director of enterprises manufacturing refrigerators and household equipment in the 1970s. He was a member of the Communist Party of the Soviet Union (CPSU) from 1963, and in 1979 was appointed Minister of Local Industry in Azerbaijan. In January 1990 he was appointed First Secretary of the Azerbaijan Communist Party Central Committee, then a member of the CPSU Politburo and, on 18 May 1990, Chairman of the Supreme Soviet (President) of Azerbaijan. He resigned as communist First Secretary following the Moscow coup attempt of August 1991, although there were reports that he had initially reacted favourably to the news of President Mikhail Gorbachev's (q.v.) deposition. In September there were direct elections to the post of President of the Republic, and Mutalibov was elected unopposed. In March 1992 he was forced to resign over the progress of the war in Nagornyi Karabakh. The Supreme Soviet (Supreme Council) voted to reinstate him in May, but he was deposed by the Popular Front of Azerbaijan (PFA) after one day in office. He was thereafter resident in Moscow, the Russian capital. President Heydar Aliyev (q.v.) repeatedly accused him of organizing attempted coups and in April 1996 he was arrested in Moscow. However, reportedly owing to ill health (he had suffered a heart attack), he was not extradited to Azerbaijan. Suppression of his supporters persisted, as Aliyev continued to allege his involvement in coup attempts. Following much discussion of his desire to return to the country, and demonstrations by his supporters, Mutalibov was elected Chairman of the new Civil Unity Party, founded in support of him, in December 2000, and declared his intention to participate in the presidential election due to take place in 2003. However, his candidature for the presidency was rejected by Azerbaijan's electoral commission in August 2003. *Address:* Cultural-Educational Fund of Ayaz Mutalibov 'For the Progress of Azerbaijan', 101000 Moscow, Pokrovskii bulv. 4/17/23, Russia; tel. (095) 937-71-82; fax (095) 937-71-83; e-mail president@mutalibov.org; internet www.mutalibov.org.

**NAZARBAYEV, Nursultan Abishevich:** President of Kazakhstan; b. 6 July 1940, in Chemolgan; m. Sarah Alplisovna Kounakayeva in 1962, with three d. *Career:* he joined the Communist Party of the Soviet Union (CPSU) in 1962, while working at the Karaganda Metallurgical Combine and, in 1969, began work with the Komsomol (the V. I. Lenin Communist Youth League) in Temirtau. He became the youngest-ever Chairman of the Kazakh Council of Ministers in 1984. In June 1989 he became First Secretary of the Kazakh Communist Party. In April 1990 the Kazakh Supreme Soviet elected him to the new post of executive President. In July he became a member of the all-Union Party Politburo and an increasingly important politician outside Kazakhstan. He supported the Union, Kazakhstan being the last republic to declare independence. He sought to maintain close links with Russia and the Commonwealth of Independent States and, having agreed to lead the new People's Unity Party, retained the support of the country's large ethnic Russian community. Allegations of malpractice and discrimination against ethnic Russians and in favour of members of Nazarbayev's Great Horde kin in the 1994 general election did not significantly affect this policy. Nazarbayev had favoured a

free-market economy, specifically the Far Eastern model, since before independence, and saw political stability as an important element in a successful transition. A referendum held in March extended Nazarbayev's term until 2000, although in October 1998 he agreed to truncate his term of office, parliament voting to hold a presidential election in January 1999 (in which Nazarbayev agreed to be a candidate). The opposition alleged that the 'constitutional crisis' was merely an attempt to extend the terms of the President and the parliamentarians. Another accusation was self-aggrandizement, particularly over the relocation of the capital to Akmola (now Astana) in 1997–98, and the marriage of his daughter to the son of President Akayev of Kyrgyzstan in July 1998. Although a dynast in manner, however, President Nazarbayev's policy remained consistent—his reasons for moving the capital were various, but locating it in the north certainly placated Middle Horde sentiments and would help anchor the Russian-dominated region to the rest of the country (as well as Almaty being too near the vulnerable southern border and prone to seismic disturbance and environmental pollution). In January 1999 Nazarabayev was re-elected for a seven-year term, obtaining 81.0% of the votes cast, although the Organization for Security and Co-operation in Europe (OSCE) refused to monitor the election, owing, in part, to a ruling that had excluded a number of candidates, including the former Prime Minister, Akezhan Kazhegeldin (q.v.). He remained an important influence for stability in both Kazakhstan and the Central Asian region, and in July 2000 legislation was passed, which granted the President certain life-long rights and privileges. From November 2001, however, allegations of nepotism and corruption intensified, amid increasing opposition activity. As the 2000s progressed a number of opposition movements claimed to have suffered unfair treatment by the authorities. In mid-2003 Nazatbayev announced that he intended to seek re-election to the presidency in 2006, stating that he considered he still had 'a decade's worth' of work to do. *Address:* Office of the President, 473000 Astana, Mira 11, Kazakhstan; tel. (3172) 32-13-19; fax (3172) 32-61-72; internet www.president.kz.

**NEMTSOV, Boris Yefimovich:** Russian politician; b. 9 Oct. 1959, in Sochi, Krasnodar Krai; m., with one d. *Education:* Gorkii (now Nizhnii Novgorod) State University. *Career:* he was a researcher in radiophysics before being appointed presidential representative in Nizhnii Novgorod (formerly Gorkii) Oblast in 1991. In 1986, following the explosion at the Chornobyl (Chernobyl) nuclear power station in Ukraine, he successfully campaigned against the construction of a similar facility in Gorkii Oblast. In 1990 he was elected to the Supreme Soviet of the Russian Federation, where he worked on agricultural reform and the liberalization of foreign trade. During the attempted coup of August 1991 he appealed to the regional tank divisions not to oppose the Russian President, Boris Yeltsin (q.v.), in his stand against the *putschists*. He was appointed presidential representative in Nizhnii Novgorod Oblast in late 1991, and later adopted the title of Governor. He rapidly earned a reputation as a successful reformer, particularly in his programme for agricultural privatization, and was confirmed in his post by a direct ballot in December 1995, winning 60% of the votes cast. Although he had been critical of the war in Chechnya, Nemtsov regained favour with the President and was appointed to the federal Government as a deputy premier in March 1997. He forged a strong alliance with the main cabinet reformer, Anatolii Chubais (q.v.), but came into conflict with powerful business interests. Critical of such 'oligarchic' capitalism, he remained one of Russia's most popular politicians, retaining a seat in the cabinet until the August 1998 economic crisis. He resigned soon after the appointment of Viktor Chernomyrdin (q.v.) as acting premier at the end of that month. Nemtsov's Young Russia movement formed part of the Union of Rightist Forces (URF) electoral alliance from August 1999. The alliance obtained 29 seats in the general election held on 19 December and Nemtsov was elected Co-Chairman of the URF in May 2000; when the grouping was reconstituted as a single party in 2001 Nemtsov was chosen as its leader. In mid-2001 he was instrumental in attempts to bring about a negotiated settlement to the conflict in Chechnya, advocating the holding of negotiations with Khalid ('Aslan') Maskhadov (q.v.)—his proposals were initially rejected by President Vladimir Putin (q.v.), but subsequently endorsed, temporarily, in late September 2001. Nemtsov repeatedly spoke out against apparent efforts by the Government to increase its control over the media, claiming that such actions were harmful to democracy. In October 2002 he visited Belarus for a conference held by opposition leaders, but was arrested and deported on arrival, the country's authorities claiming that his visit was one of repeated attempts to interfere in the country's affairs. In mid-2003 he was criticized for cultivating links between the URF and wealthy businessmen; he rebuffed such criticism, stating that all parties attracted such support and that the URF was merely the most transparent. Nemtsov was appointed to lead the URF's list for the elections to the State Duma scheduled for December 2003, and announced in September that the party would contest the elections without forming any alliance; prior to this time it had been anticipated the party might form a joint list with the ideologically similar Yabloko party of Grigorii Yavlinskii (q.v.). A fluent and confident English-speaker, he was frequently sought after by Western media outlets for comments on Russian issues. *Address:* State Duma, 103265 Moscow, Okhotnyi ryad 1, Russia; tel. (095) 292-83-10; fax (095) 292-94-64; e-mail www@duma.ru; internet www.nemtsov.ru.

**NIYAZOV, Gen. Saparmyrat Atayevich:** President and Prime Minister of Turkmenistan; b. 19 Feb. 1940, in Ashgabat; m. Muza Alekseyevna, with one s. and one d. *Education:* at Leningrad (now St Petersburg) Polytechnic Institute (Russia). *Career:* he joined the Communist Party in 1962, heading the Ashgabat organization until 1984, when he went to the central Communist Party of the Soviet Union (CPSU) headquarters in Moscow. In 1985 he returned to Turkmenia (now Turkmenistan) as premier and, subsequently, party leader. He was elected Chairman of the Supreme Soviet (*de facto* head of state) in January 1990, and was returned unopposed as a directly elected President in October. A conservative communist, he neither condemned nor condoned the coup attempt of August 1991, and retained the communists as the ruling party (although the name was changed to the Democratic Party of Turkmenistan). No opposition parties were permitted to register in Turkmenistan, which remained the least reformed of the former Soviet republics and had been the one least interested in independence. Niyazov also became Prime Minister (head of government) and Supreme Commander of the Armed Forces in May 1992, in accordance with the new Turkmen Constitution. In June he was unopposed in presidential elections and, thus, re-elected. In a referendum in January 1994 an official 99.9% of the electorate voted to extend his term of office until 2002. Accused of fostering a 'personality cult', he was awarded the rank of general, the title of Turkmenbashy (Leader of the Turkmen), Turkmenistan's highest honour (uniquely, four times), and had innumerable places named after him, from cities to streets. Under his rule the country did not gain the expected benefits of its hydrocarbons wealth, mainly because of the lack of a secure export route for its natural gas. Any expression of dissatisfaction, however, was dealt with ruthlessly. He was reluctant to allow the pre-eminence of any potential rival within the regime and was accused of promoting tribal rivalries (favouring the Tekke in state appointments) and anti-Russian rhetoric, despite the adverse consequences for the country. In December 1999 the Majlis (Assembly), which had been awarded new legislative and regulatory powers following the legislative election of 12 December, approved an amendment to the Constitution, which extended Niyazov's presidential term indefinitely, although in early 2001 he announced his intention to surrender the presidency in 2010. Speculation that Niyazov was beginning to lose his grip on power intensified from late 2001, and was fuelled by large-scale purges of senior officials, an increased level of exile activism, and allegations of involvement in drugs-smuggling—all of which undermined élite support for his regime—together with increasingly eccentric decrees. However, he stated that his desire to lead the country was as

strong as ever. In November 2002 he alleged that an assassination attempt had been made against him when his motorcade was fired on in Ashgabat. The exiled opposition leader, Boris Shikhmuradov (q.v.), was identified as the prime suspect. He was arrested in December and convicted at the end of the month. The sentence of life imprisonment imposed upon him attracted widespread international criticism, but Niyazov remained undeterred, classifying the alleged assassination attempt as 'a terrorist act'. In August 2003 he stated that he wished to abandon the life-long presidency he had been awarded in 1999, and hold presidential elections in 2006 or 2007. Some days later he was elected Chairman for life of the Khalk Maslakhaty (People's Council). Niyazov remained unperturbed by increasingly fervent international criticism of his regime, and seemed set to remain in almost absolute power in Turkmenistan for as long as he wished. *Address:* Office of the President and the Council of Ministers, Ashgabat, ul. 2001 24, Presidential Palace, Turkmenistan; tel. (12) 35-45-34; fax (12) 35-43-88.

**NURI, Sayed Abdullo:** Tajik politician. *Career:* he was the leader of the Tajik branch of the Islamic Renaissance Party (now renamed the Islamic Rebirth Party of Tajikistan–IRP), a movement that was active on an all-Union basis before the dissolution of the USSR. The party participated in the anti-Government demonstrations of 1992, which led to opposition inclusion in the administration. However, the ensuing civil war saw the Islamic-democratic opposition driven into exile and the IRP formally banned, along with several other parties, in June 1993. Nuri continued to lead the IRP from exile in Afghanistan, and also chaired the association of various Islamic and democratic groups opposed to President Imamali Rakhmonov (q.v.), the United Tajik Opposition (UTO). Having organized armed incursions into Tajikistan, this formal coalition was agreed for the purposes of peace negotiations in 1995. In December 1996 Rakhmonov and Nuri agreed, in principle, to the formation of a National Reconciliation Council (NRC), with membership to be equally divided between government and UTO members. The final peace accord was signed in Moscow, Russia, in June 1997. At the inaugural session of the NRC in July, Nuri was elected Chairman. An amnesty to permit the return from Afghanistan of former UTO fighters was granted. The peace was troubled, with opposition groups accused of attacks on government troops and of involvement in several hostage-taking incidents. Nuri denied UTO participation. The UTO became more supportive of the Government as it granted UTO members increased numbers of official positions, including that of First Deputy Chairman for the former Kazi of Tajikistan, Haji Akbar Turajonzoda (q.v.), although co-operation was regularly suspended. The NRC held its final session on 26 March 2000, following legislative elections to a new, bicameral legislature. Nuri accepted that the mandate of the NRC had been fulfilled, but emphasized that some outstanding issues remained, including the need to repatriate over 100,000 Tajik refugees, fully integrate opposition fighters into the national armed forces and allocate 30% of government posts to opposition politicians. Nuri opposed the constitutional amendments proposed by the President in early 2003, but did not urge his supporters to boycott the referendum on the issue (which approved the changes). He was re-elected to his party's leadership in September. *Address:* Islamic Rebirth Party of Tajikistan, Dushanbe, Tolstaya 5, Tajikistan; tel. (372) 27-25-30; fax (372) 27-53-93.

**PATIASHVILI, Dzhumber Ilich:** Georgian politician; b. 5 Jan. 1940, in Lagodekhi, Kakheti Oblast; m., with two c. *Education:* Tbilisi Agricultural Institute. *Career:* from 1966 worked for the Komsomol (V. I. Lenin Young Communist League), and subsequently for the Communist Party. In 1980–2000 he was director of the Land Institute of Georgia. Patiashvili was appointed First Secretary of the Communist Party of the Georgian SSR in 1985, but resigned his post in April 1989, after a number of demonstrators were killed by Soviet troops in Tbilisi. He stood as a candidate for the presidency in the election of 5 November 1995, obtaining 19% of the votes cast; Eduard Shevardnadze (q.v.) was the victor, with almost 75% of the votes. Patiashvili also contested the presidential election of 9 April 2000, again coming in second place, with 16.7% of the votes cast. In 2001 he founded and led the Unity Alliance (Ertoba) social-democratic political party, which was to contest the general election of November 2003 as part of the Dzhumber Patiashvili-Unity bloc. Patiashvili remained a prominent political figure, and was expected to contest a third presidential election upon the expiry of Shevardnadze's mandate in 2005. *Address:* Unity Alliance (Ertoba), Tbilisi, Svobodi pl., Georgia; tel. (32) 92-30-65; fax (32) 93-46-94; e-mail ertoba@post.com.

**PRIMAKOV, Yevgenii Maksimovich:** Russian politician and former premier; b. 29 Oct. 1929, in Kiev, Ukraine; m., with one d. *Education:* Moscow Institute of Oriental Studies, postgraduate qualification from the Faculty of Economics at Moscow M. V. Lomonosov State University (MGU). *Career:* having joined the Communist Party of the Soviet Union (CPSU) in 1959, he worked as a journalist in 1962–70 for the party newspaper, *Pravda*, initially as a sub-editor for Asian and African affairs, and subsequently, in 1966-70, as the foreign correspondent based in Arab countries. An expert in Middle Eastern affairs, he subsequently held two prestigious academic posts and was appointed to the policy-making Central Committee of the CPSU in 1989. He was the Middle East envoy of the Soviet leader, Mikhail Gorbachev (q.v.), in 1990 and was assigned to attempt to prevent the outbreak of war between Iraq, Russia's traditional ally, and the international community, following the annexation of Kuwait by Iraq in August of that year. Following the attempted coup of August 1991, he supervised the transformation of the foreign-intelligence branch of the Committee for State Security (KGB) into the Russian External Intelligence Service. He earned a reputation for being 'hardline', but his appointment as Minister of Foreign Affairs in January 1996 was not seen as representing a fundamental change in Russia's foreign policy. Primakov commanded wide respect and, when recommended for the premiership by the liberal leader of the Yabloko party, Grigorii Yavlinskii (q.v.), during the constitutional crisis of August–September 1998, he was accepted by most of the factions in the State Duma. Although Primakov managed to stabilize the economy and improve relations between the Government and the State Duma, in mid-May 1999 he was removed from office by President Boris Yeltsin (q.v.). Some observers considered the President's action to have been prompted, at least in part, by his reputation as a possible candidate for the presidency; in addition, a campaign launched by Primakov against the so-called 'oligarchs' was thought to have contributed to his dismissal. In August the party of the Mayor of Moscow (Yurii Luzhkov—q.v.), Fatherland, formed an electoral alliance with the centrist grouping of regional governors, All Russia, to form Fatherland-All Russia (FAR). Primakov accepted the first place on the electoral list of the new bloc, and won a seat in the State Duma in the election of 19 December. He was expected to stand as a candidate in the presidential election of 26 March 2000, but, in February, the FAR bloc announced that it would support the candidacy of Vladimir Putin (q.v.), prompting Primakov to decide against contesting the election. He became head of the Fatherland faction in the Duma later in 2000, and was appointed head of the Russian Commission on Transnistria (Moldova) in the same year. In addition, he became head of the Russian Chamber of Commerce and Industry. In early 2002 Primakov announced that he was prepared to speak in defence of the former Yugoslav President, Slobodan Milošević, at the latter's trial at the International Criminal Tribunal for the former Yugoslavia (ICTY, based at The Hague, Netherlands). Primakov played a prominent diplomatic role during the Kosovo crisis in 1999, famously turning back his plane, en route to the USA, when the bombardment of Yugoslavia (now Serbia and Montenegro) by North Atlantic Treaty Organization (NATO) forces began. In mid-2002 Mediya-Sotsium, a new, non-profit organization co-headed by Primakov, was awarded a contract to broadcast on a channel previously used by the independent television station TV-6, controlled by Boris Berezovskii (q.v.). Many of TV-6's journalists, including, most notably, Yevgenii Kiselev (q.v.), transferred to the channel, which was named TVS. Although Primakov declared

that he would not interfere with the content of the channel, its true independence remained uncertain, even until the time of its closure in mid-2003. Previously, in February of that year, he had been sent by Putin to Iraq, on a 'confidential mission', in support of Putin's efforts to prevent a US-led attack against the regime of Saddam Hussain. International opponents of the prospective action viewed Primakov's visit as a 'last chance' of avoiding conflict, which began some four weeks later. In April it was revealed that Primakov had made a second visit to Iraq in the week before military action started, in an attempt to convince Saddam Hussain to relinquish power and avoid conflict. Despite this flurry of high-profile activity it appeared unlikely that Primakov would return to anything more than a marginal position in Russian political life, as he resumed the writing of his memoirs and his duties with the Chamber of Commerce and Industry. *Address:* State Duma, 103265 Moscow, Okhotnyi ryad 1, Russia; tel. (095) 292-83-10; fax (095) 292-94-64; e-mail www@duma.ru.

**PUSTOVOYTENKO, Valeriy Pavlovych:** Ukrainian politician and former premier; b. 23 February 1947, in Adamivka, Mykolayiv Oblast; m., with 2 c. *Education:* Dnipropetrovsk Institute of Construction Engineering. *Career:* he worked as a mechanical engineer before becoming the head of trusts in Odesa and Dnipropetrovsk in 1965–87. He was a People's Deputy of Ukraine and Chairman of the Dnipropetrovsk City Council in 1987–93. A member of the People's Democratic Party of Ukraine, he headed the successful 1994 presidential election campaign of Leonid Kuchma (q.v.). From July 1994 he served as Minister of the Cabinet (*Chef de Cabinet* or Minister without Portfolio), and was also President of the Ukrainian Soccer Federation, which had strong political links. He served in the same ministerial position in the Government of Yevhen Marchuk (q.v.) appointed in July 1995. He became Mayor of Dnipropetrovsk, the home region of a large majority of those in positions of power. In 1996 he formed and led a centrist political party, the People's Democratic Party, which was perceived as being sympathetic to the interests of the so-called 'red directors' and 'oligarchs'—former communist officials who had benefited from the transfer of state enterprises to private ownership or management in the 1990s. In July 1997 he was narrowly approved by the legislature as Prime Minister, following the dismissal of Pavlo Lazarenko (q.v.). As a long-standing ally of President Leonid Kuchma (q.v.), many suspected that his appointment was not solely based on his abilities, and also feared that he would use his power to benefit the Dnipropetrovsk region at the expense of the country as a whole. He was not renowned for his support of radical reforms and, as a politician, was uncharismatic. Nevertheless, he remained Prime Minister after the general election of March 1998 and Kuchma nominated him to continue in that post, following his inauguration for a second presidential term in November 1999. The Verkhovna Rada, however, rejected his nomination in mid-December. In December 2000 he became an adviser to the President, and in June 2001 was appointed Minister of Transport, although he was removed from this position in mid-2002. He retained his party leadership and in mid-2003 he confirmed that he was in negotiations with a number of other parties about a possible alliance or merger. *Address:* People's Democratic Party, 03150 Kiev, vul. Antonovicha 107, Ukraine; tel. (44) 252-84-18; fax (44) 252-87-26; e-mail zagal@sndp.kiev.ua; internet ndp.org .ua.

**PUTIN, Col Vladimir Vladimirovich:** President of the Russian Federation; b. 7 Oct. 1952, in Leningrad (now St Petersburg); m. Lyudmila, with two d. *Education:* Leningrad (now St Petersburg) State University. *Career:* he was on the staff of the state security service (KGB) of the USSR, with the First Chief Department and in Dresden (the German Democratic Republic—GDR—or 'East' Germany) in 1975–90. In 1990 he was appointed adviser to the Pro-Rector of Leningrad State University, and served as adviser to the Chairman of the Leningrad City Executive Committee in 1990–91. In 1991 he became Chairman of the Committee on Foreign Relations at the St Petersburg Mayor's Office. Between 1994 and 1996 he was First Deputy Chairman (First Deputy Mayor) of the St Petersburg City Government and Chairman of the Committee on Foreign Relations. In 1997–98 he was Deputy Head and then First Deputy Head to the Administration of the Russian Presidency and Head of the Main Control Department. He served as Director of the Federal Security Service (FSB, one of the successor bodies to the KGB) in 1998–99 and as Secretary to the Security Council of Russia from March 1999. In August he was appointed Chairman of the Government (Prime Minister), and was immediately nominated as the preferred successor of President Boris Yeltsin (q.v.). This was in part, some observers believed, owing to his background in the Security Service, which could enable him to protect Yeltsin from the corruption charges mounting against him. Putin's popularity was confirmed in the legislative election of December, in which the Unity movement, which had expressed its support for Putin, performed strongly. Upon the unexpected resignation of Yeltsin on 31 December 1999, Putin became acting President of the Russian Federation. He was subsequently elected President in March 2000, having gained popular respect for his uncompromising approach to the civil conflict in the secessionist republic of Chechnya. In 2001–02 Putin's presidency was marked by a significant move towards greater co-operation with the West and, particularly, the USA. Following the suicide attacks against the USA of 11 September 2001, Putin expressed his support for the US-led coalition against 'global terrorism', against the advice of some senior officials. Moreover, he eased Russian objections to the further expansion of the North Atlantic Treaty Organization (NATO) and offered tacit support for the stationing of US and allied troops in several former Soviet Central Asian states. In return, US criticism of the war in Chechnya, which Putin consistently described as an integral part of US President George W. Bush's 'war on terrorism', became greatly muted, and significant reductions to the two countries' stocks of nuclear warheads were agreed, at a meeting between the two Presidents. Domestically, Putin worked to centralize power, and was accused, in some quarters, of authoritarian tendencies. A 'cult of personality', although apparently not officially endorsed, began to develop around him from 2001, promoted not least by a national youth organization, 'Moving Together'. More worrying, to some observers, was the apparent erosion of the freedom and independence of the media, with several newspapers, as well as two independent television stations, TV-6 and its successor, TVS, being forced to cease operations during Putin's first term of office, in several cases following the bringing of court cases on financial, or fiscal, grounds. The greatest challenge to his presidency came when a group of heavily armed Chechen rebels held hostage some 800 theatre-goers in Moscow in October 2002. The incident immediately became headline news world-wide, and Putin's management of the crisis was closely observed. After several days Putin ordered that the theatre be stormed by élite troops, with the aid of a nerve gas. All the rebels were killed, but most of the 129 hostages who perished died as a result of the gas used in the rescue operation. Putin's resolve to combat terrorism, which he described as the greatest threat to the contemporary world, was intensified by this incident, and his enthusiasm for international co-operation increased, despite some criticisms of his allegedly heavy-handed response. Although he was reluctant to jeopardize improved relations with the USA he considered that its proposed military action against Iraq was unjustified. However, the US Administration did not wish to damage its US-Russian relations any further either, and a reconciliation of sorts took place after the conclusion of combat. Putin was thus considered to be performing well in international affairs, although his domestic policies continued to attract criticism. Media figures complained of state intervention and the conflict in Chechnya continued. However, his promise to investigate alleged wrongdoing by Russia's 'oligarchs' increased his popularity, particularly after police raided the offices of a number of large hydrocarbons firms in late 2003. Putin thus emerged from an extremely difficult period of his presidency with his previous reputation largely intact. Opinion polls suggested that his re-election to the presidency in 2004 was likely. *Address:* Office of the President, 103073 Moscow, Kremlin, Russia; tel. (095) 925-35-81; fax (095) 206-51-73; e-mail president@gov.ru; internet president.kremlin.ru.

**RAKHMONOV, Imamali Sharipovich:** President of Tajikistan; b. 5 Oct. 1952, in Dangar rayon, Kulyab Oblast (now Hatlon Oblast). *Education:* he studied economics at the V.I. Lenin Tajikistan State University, Dushanbe. *Career:* he worked, variously, in positions ranging from an electrician to the director of a collective farm in his native district. He was reportedly a protégé of the main Kulobi militia leader in the 1992–93 civil war, Sangak Safarov. He became head of the Kulob Oblast administration on 2 November 1992, but within a few weeks, on 19 November, was elected Chairman of the Supreme Soviet of Tajikistan (with the abolition of the presidency, therefore Head of State). This was a mark of the importance of the Kulobi militias to the victory of the communist reactionaries, although the traditional ruling élite from Khujand provided the premier. Rakhmonov appointed many fellow Kulobis to high office, although he could not afford to alienate the wealthy Khujandis completely. Their main demand was for him to disarm the militias, but he had limited success at first. Eventually it was decided to achieve this by incorporating the militias into national security services, although the Khujand families were dubious about thus institutionalizing the Kulob military advantage. Progress was made in this process mainly after Safarov's mysterious death in a shooting incident in March 1993. The main military assistance for the Rakhmonov administration, however, came from Russia and Uzbekistan, which favoured a conservative communist regime rather than 'Islamic fundamentalists', as the Islamic-democratic opposition was dubbed. The opposition forces, defeated in the civil war, caused considerable concern to Russia and Tajikistan's Central Asian neighbours with their *mujahidin*-style border raids from Afghanistan. Rakhmonov wished to consolidate his position on a more secure basis and opened talks in April 1994, which continued for the next two years, although with little lasting success. In the presidential election of 6 November Rakhmonov was elected to the presidency, with about 58% of the votes cast, according to official results. Essentially kept in power by Russia and Uzbekistan, he retained close relations with the latter, despite personal animosity with its President, Islam Karimov (q.v.). Uzbekistan was interested in a stable neighbour and increasingly urged a peace settlement with the Islamic-democratic opposition. By 1996, however, Rakhmonov's regime was also suffering the threat of internal fracturing. Based on an alliance of the communist nomenklatura, particularly the northern Khujand economic élite and the mainly Kulobi southern militias, the former group were becoming increasingly dissatisfied with the state of the economy under Rakhmonov. A powerful alliance of prominent Khujandi politicians formed an opposition group in mid-1996. In April 1997 Rakhmonov was wounded in an assassination attempt in Khujand. Soon after, however, in June, Rakhmonov signed a peace treaty with the Islamic-democratic opposition, by now formally grouped in the United Tajikistan Opposition (UTO), officially ending the war. Under the treaty, 30% of government seats were to be granted to the opposition and elections were to be held. Despite some problems, reconciliation with the official opposition had progressed sufficiently to ensure its support during the occupation of Khujand by a mutinous military commander, Makhmoud Khudoberdiyev, in November 1998. Rakhmonov was elected for a second term in the presidential election of 6 November 1999, reputedly securing 97% of the votes cast (the rate of participation in the election was stated to be almost 99%); the presidential term of office had been extended from five to seven years, as the result of constitutional amendments in September. Following elections to a new, bicameral legislature in February and March 2000, the National Reconciliation Council, which had been formed in 1996, was dissolved, in recognition of the fulfilment of its mandate. In June 2003 a number of constitutional amendments proposed by the President were approved in a referendum—the most controversial of these provided for the President to be eligible for two further seven-year terms of office. This measure was criticized by opposition groups as an attempt to preserve power for Rakhmonov himself. *Address:* Office of the President, 734023 Dushanbe, pr. Rudaki 80, Tajikistan; tel. (372) 21-04-18; fax (372) 21-18-37.

**RASIZADE, Artur Tahir oglu:** Azerbaijani politiican; b. 26 Feb. 1935, in Gyanja; m., with one d. *Education:* Azerbaijan Institute of Industry. *Career:* a Communist Party member, he held high government office in Azerbaijan in the Soviet era. He was appointed First Deputy Prime Minister in early 1996 and, following President Heydar Aliyev's (q.v.) dismissal of Fuad Kuliyev in July, he was appointed acting premier, and confirmed in the post in November. Rasizade was not known as a supporter of reform, but government policy encouraging foreign investment in the vital hydrocarbons sector ensured that his administration introduced some economic changes. He was replaced as Prime Minister by the President's son, Ilham Aliyev (q.v.), in August 2003, in a move that was widely criticized as the establishment of a dynastic succession. Rasizade accepted the post of Deputy Prime Minister in the reorganized Government. He resumed the premiership a matter of days later, as the younger Aliyev took leave of absence from his post, in accordance with electoral law, after announcing his candidature for the presidency. *Address:* c/o Office of the Prime Minister, 370066 Baku, Lermontov St 63, Azerbaijan; tel. (12) 92-66-23; fax (12) 92-91-79.

**ROSCA, Iurie:** Moldovan politician; b. 1961. *Education:* trained as a journalist. *Career:* as Chairman of the Christian Democratic Popular Party (CDPP), Rosca was one of the organizers of large-scale protest rallies, from January 2002, against the Government's decision to introduce the compulsory study of Russian language to schools. At the end of the month the Ministry of Justice suspended the CDPP's participation in political activities for a period of one month; however, following intervention by the Council of Europe, the suspension was annulled. Protests continued, and in March the Deputy Chairman of the CDPP, Vlad Cubreacov, went missing; his reappearance, in May, prompted some observers to accuse the CDPP of staging the disappearance, in an attempt to discredit the Government. Rosca led further demonstrations, starting in December 2002, against communists' policy and what he perceived as an attempt to 'russify' Moldovan culture. Rosca, who supported unification with Romania, pledged to lead the protests for as long as was necessary to bring an end to the communist Government. In October 2003 he led a protest outside the Russian embassy, urging Russia to withdraw its forces from Transnistria. *Address:* Christian Democratic People's Party, 2009 Chişinău, str. Nicolae Iorga 5, Moldova; tel. (2) 23-33-56; fax (2) 23-86-66; e-mail magic@cni.md; internet inima.dnt.md.

**SELEZNEV, Gennadii Nikolayevich:** Chairman (speaker) of the State Duma of the Russian Federation; b. 6 Nov. 1947, in Serov, Sverdlovsk Oblast; m., with one d. *Education:* Leningrad (now St Petersburg) University (by correspondence). *Career:* he joined the Communist Party of the Soviet Union (CPSU) in 1979 and pursued a career in journalism. He was Editor-in-Chief of *Pravda*, the leading communist newspaper, in 1993, when it was banned after the violent conclusion to the constitutional crisis of September–October. As a member of the Communist Party of the Russian Federation (CPRF), the successor to the CPSU, he was elected to the State Duma in December, and served briefly as Deputy Chairman, before becoming Chairman (speaker) in 1996. Owing to the considerable powers bestowed on the President by the 1993 Constitution, however, Seleznev and the CPRF (who had gained a substantial majority in the Duma) had little real influence on the direction of policy. Seleznev was re-appointed Chairman of the Duma in January 2000, and in April was elected Chairman of the Parliamentary Assembly of the Union of Russia and Belarus. In mid-March 2002, amid heightened inter-party tensions, the Duma voted to remove the deciding vote in the governing body of the chamber, the Duma Council, from Seleznev. Following a controversial redistribution of committee chairmanships in the following month, the CPRF announced that it would assume a more aggressively oppositional role outside parliament; the leader of the Party, Gennadii Zyuganov (q.v.), demanded that Seleznev resign his position as speaker. Seleznev was reluctant to do so, and the President, Vladimir Putin (q.v.), eventually requested that he remain in his post. Seleznev was expelled from the CPRF in June, along with two other deputies. In September the

founding conference of a new leftist opposition party, the Party of the Rebirth of Russia, based on the Rossiya (Russia) movement established by Seleznev in mid-2000, took place. Seleznev was elected to head the party, which he said would work to promote the strengthening of the rule of law. In April 2003 he announced that he would not seek to remain in his post as Chairman of the State Duma following the elections to the body scheduled for December, preferring to lead his party's faction within the chamber. However, in September he suggested that he might be persuaded to seek the role again. In advance of the elections the Party of the Rebirth of Russia formed an electoral bloc with the Russian Party of Life of Sergei Mironov (q.v.). *Address:* State Duma, 103265 Moscow, Okhotny Ryad 1, Russia; tel. (095) 292-83-10; fax (095) 292-94-64; e-mail www@duma.ru; internet seleznev.on.ru.

**SHARETSKI, Syamyon:** Belarusian politician and former Chairman of the Supreme Council (parliamentary speaker); b. 23 Sept. 1936. *Education:* Goretskaya Agricultural Academy. *Career:* a Supreme Council deputy, he became co-leader of the Agrarian Party (AP), which was formed in 1992 and, by early 1996, had become the second-largest single party in the Supreme Council (after the communists). The AP had a non-reformist, conservative orientation, befitting its rural constituency, and Sharetski became parliamentary speaker in January 1996. Sharetski was a central figure in the hostilities between President Alyaksandr Lukashenka (q.v.) and the Supreme Council regarding the controversial referendum of November 1996, by which Lukashenka sought to acquire quasi-dictatorial powers. Having been a co-signatory, along with the President, of an agreement which declared that the referendum results would be of a recommendatory, rather than obligatory, nature, Sharetski was responsible for reactivating impeachment proceedings against Lukashenka when the agreement was revoked by presidential decree. Following the replacement, under the terms of the referendum, of the Supreme Council, some 50 deputies denounced the referendum and declared themselves the legitimate legislature. Sharetski remained Chairman of the body, leading attempts to negotiate an end to the confrontation with the new legislature, and meeting with international organizations to maintain awareness of the plight of the Belarusian opposition. He was also one of the leading figures in the dissident petition campaign, known as Charter-97 (Khartyya-97), initiated by the opposition in November 1997, with the aim of forcing new elections. In July 1999 Sharetski fled to Lithuania, owing to fears for his safety, following his proclamation by the former Supreme Council as acting President of Belarus (in accordance with the nullified Constitution of 1994, Lukashenka's term of office expired in mid-July 1999). In July 2001 he moved to the USA, from where he hoped to build ties with the Belarusian diaspora, and from where he continued to speak out against Lukashenka's regime.

**SHEVARDNADZE, Eduard Amvrosiyevich:** Georgian; President and former Soviet Minister of Foreign Affairs; b. 25 Jan. 1928, in Mamati village, Guria Oblast; m., one s., one d. *Education:* attended the Communist Party School of the Central Committee (graduated 1951) and the Kutaisi Pedagogical Institute (1957). *Career:* he was a member of Komsomol (the V. I. Lenin Young Communist League), becoming its leader in 1957. In 1961 he joined the hierarchy of the Communist Party of the Soviet Union (CPSU). In 1965 he was appointed as Minister of the Interior of the Georgian SSR, and became First Secretary of the Central Committee of the Communist Party of the Georgian SSR in 1972. He campaigned against corruption, but also gained a reputation for being harsh with dissidents and nationalists. In 1978 he became a candidate (alternating) member of the Communist Party of the Soviet Union (CPSU) Politburo and, in July 1985, a full member (the first Georgian to be so since the death of Stalin—Iosif V. Dzhugashvili). At the same time, as a close colleague of Mikhail Gorbachev (q.v.), he was appointed the Minister of Foreign Affairs of the USSR, in which position he became regarded as one of the leading proponents of the reform policies of *perestroika* (restructuring) and *glasnost* (openness). However, in December 1990 Shevardnadze resigned, warning of the approach of 'dictatorship'. In 1991 he was a founder and leader of an all-Union democratic opposition party and was briefly Minister of Foreign Affairs of the USSR again at the end of the year. His political future was uncertain with the demise of the USSR in December, but in March 1992 he was invited to return to Georgia by the new administration, to which he gave international respectability, and he became Chairman of a State Council. Despite increasing civil unrest, he arranged for elections to a new Supreme Council (legislature) and was himself elected its Chairman (Head of State) in direct popular elections in October 1992. In 1993 his regime seemed in danger of disintegrating with the country, particularly after the fall of Sukhumi (which he had personally committed himself to defend) to Abkhazian rebel forces in September. However, by joining the Commonwealth of Independent States (CIS) later that year (thus securing Russian aid), despite nationalist opposition, and with the death of the former President, Zviad Gamsakhurdia, at the end of December, by 1994 his administration was more secure. In 1993, meanwhile, Shevardnadze formed a political party, the Citizens' Union of Georgia (CUG), of which he was Chairman, and which was to prove extremely influential in Georgian politics. His measures against the militias, the armed political groups, provoked an assassination attempt, in August 1995, which, although it failed, delayed the signing of the new Constitution until October. Under its terms, on 5 November he was elected to the powerful new post of an executive presidency, with almost 75% of the votes cast. He was inaugurated as President on 26 November and enjoyed much popular support. None the less, in February 1998 there was a further assassination attempt upon him, for which supporters of former President Gamsakhurdia were blamed. Relations with Russia deteriorated in 1999, particularly following renewed conflict between the Russian central Government and the separatist republic of Chechnya from August, in which Georgia refused to become involved. In April 2000 Shevardnadze was re-elected as President of Georgia for a second term of office. In September 2001 Shevardnadze resigned the chairmanship of the CUG, possibly in response to long-term assertions that he was violating the Constitution by retaining the post while serving as President. In November despite widespread public demonstrations against perceived state suppression of freedom of speech, he failed to resign. Shevardnadze's position appeared to be less assured in late 2001–02, both as a result of internal tensions, and as a result of heightened criticism from Russia with regard to the alleged presence of Islamist militants in Georgia, particularly in the Kodori Gorge region, near the border with Chechnya. Moreover, the CUG effectively disintegrated into a number of factions following Shevardnadze's resignation as party Chairman, and at postponed local elections, finally held in June 2002, the party obtained fewer than 4% of the votes cast in the capital. A lack of progress on the many problems affecting Georgia, most notably that of the secessionist regions, and his perceived change to a pro-Russian stance in matters of foreign policy, led to a further decline in his popularity in 2003. Shevardnadze declined to nominate a preferred successor (his term of office was due to expire in 2005), although with the allegations of corruption and incompetence surrounding many of his associates, it was doubtful that any such endorsement would be of great electoral value. *Address:* Office of the President, 300002 Tbilisi, Rustaveli 29, Georgia; tel. (32) 99-74-75; fax (32) 99-96-30; e-mail office@ presidpress.gov.ge.

**SHIKHMURADOV, Boris:** Turkmen politician. *Career:* he was Minister of Foreign Affairs for almost a decade until his dismissal in July 2000, when he was reappointed as ambassador to the People's Republic of China. Dismissed from this post in October 2001, he fled into exile in Moscow, Russia, from where, in early November, he issued a statement condemning the rule of President Saparmyrat Niyazov (q.v.). It was subsequently reported that a warrant had been issued for Shikhmuradov's arrest, on charges of misappropriating state property (which he denied). Turkmen officials claimed that his actions were an attempt to avoid prosecution; however, it was widely speculated that Shikhmuradov intended to replace Niyazov by means of a *coup d'état*, possibly with

foreign support. In January 2002 he established the opposition People's Movement of Turkmenistan, with the aim of deposing the President, and in June it was reported that the Movement was to co-operate with the United Democratic Opposition of Abdy Kuliyev (q.v.), which was also believed to be operating from exile in Russia, with the aim of establishing democracy in Turkmenistan. Following an alleged attempt on the life of Niyazov in November, the Turkmen authorities announced that Shikhmuradov was their prime suspect with regard to the organization of the attack, and requested his extradition from Russia. Shikhmuradov was arrested in Turkmenistan in late December; he claimed to have been in the country since September and to have surrendered voluntarily. He subsequently appeared on television and confessed to his involvement in the attack—observers noticed that his speech was slurred and that he had facial injuries. At the end of December he was convicted, and sentenced to 25 years' imprisonment, a sentence subsequently increased to life imprisonment. A representative of the Organization for Security and Co-operation in Europe (OSCE) described the judicial process as 'Stalinist' and 'obscene', and opposition groups attempted to use the conviction to bring the human rights situation in Turkmenistan to the attention of the Western media and governments. In August 2003 Shikhmuradov's sister stated that his health had deteriorated and that he was being denied access to medical treatment.

**SHOIGU, Col-Gen. Sergei Kuzhugetovich:** Russian politician; b. 21 May 1955, in Chadan, Tuva ASSR (now Republic of Tyva), Russia; m., with two d. *Education:* Krasnoyarsk Polytechnical Institute. *Career:* a former engineer and construction-trust manager, he worked for the Communist Party Committee of Abakan City (in the then Khakass Autonomous Oblast, now the Republic of Khakasiya, within Russia) and Krasnoyarsk in 1989–90. In 1990–91 he served as Deputy Chairman of the Russian State Committee on Architecture and Construction. He was subsequently Chairman of the State Committee on Civil Defence, Emergencies and Clean-up Operations from 1991 to 1994 and Minister from 1994, in which role he earned a great deal of respect. In September 1999 he formed the Unity movement, which won 72 seats in the election to the State Duma of 19 December. Between January and May 2000 Shoigu served additionally as a Deputy Prime Minister, and was re-appointed to the post of Minister of Civil Defence, Emergencies and Clean-up Operations under the new Government of Vladimir Putin (q.v.) formed in May 2000. In 2001 Unity merged with the centrist Fatherland—All Russia grouping to form the Unity and Fatherland-United Russia bloc. *Address:* Ministry of Civil Defence, Emergencies and Clean-up Operations, 103012 Moscow, Teatralnyi proyezd 3, Russia; tel. (095) 926-39-01; fax (095) 924-19-46; e-mail pressa@emercom.gov.ru; internet www.emercom.gov.ru.

**SMIRNOV, Igor Nikolayevich:** Moldovan politician; President of the 'Transdnestrian Moldovan Soviet Socialist Republic'; b. 1941, in Petropavlovsk-Kamchatskii, Russia; ethnic Russian; m., with two s. *Education:* attended Zaporozhiye (Zaporizhzhia) Machine Construction Institute in Ukraine. *Career:* he was an engineer, and later manager, at Zaporozhiye Electromash from 1959. In 1963 he joined the Communist Party and in 1989 became Director of the Joint Trade Unions in Tiraspol, in the Moldovan region of Transnistria. The region was the main area of habitation within Moldova of ethnic Slavs, who were increasingly alarmed at the resurgence of Romanian nationalism in the republic. Smirnov was appointed Chairman of Tiraspol City Executive in 1990 and, in the same year, was expelled from the Moldovan Communist Party for his separatist activities. In 1991, with overt hostilities between the separatists and the Moldovan forces, he was declared President of the self-proclaimed 'Republic of Transdnestria'. With the help of the Russian (formerly Soviet) 14th Army, the Transnistrians succeeded in driving government forces from the region by 1992. Direct negotiations with the Moldovan central Government were begun and a mainly Russian peace-keeping force established. Separatist suspicions were allayed by the gradual displacement of pro-Romanian politicians, confirmed by the Moldovan general election results of February 1994. Furthermore, in July a new Constitution provided for a special status for Transnistria and in October the gradual withdrawal of the 14th Army was agreed with Russia. However, Smirnov and his supporters in Transnistria's ruling Union of Patriotic Forces arranged for a number of referendums in 1995 that confirmed the region's aspirations for independence. In December a bicameral legislature was elected in the region and it confirmed Smirnov as President of the 'Transdnestrian Moldovan Soviet Socialist Republic'. The basic principles of a peace settlement were agreed with the Moldovan Government in July 1996. He was re-elected for a second term as President in December and continued to pursue the re-establishment of mutually supportive links with Moldova, while asserting the region's claim for independence. In May 1997 he and the President of Moldova, Petru Lucinschi, signed an agreement on the normalization of relations between Moldova and the separatist region, and protocols on economic and social co-operation followed in November 1997 and February 1998. In July 2000 Smirnov dismissed the Government of the region, after the Constitution was amended to transform it into a presidential republic. Smirnov was re-elected as President in elections held in the region on 9 December 2001, obtaining almost 82% of the votes cast. In December 2002 he was detained briefly by the Austrian authorities upon his arrival in that country, pending the investigation of an alleged passport irregularity. In February 2003 Smirnov reached a preliminary agreement on proposals by Moldovan President Vladimir Voronin (q.v.) for the joint drafting of a new constitution for a federal Moldovan state, which would be subject to approval by a nation-wide referendum. Meanwhile, Smirnov and officials of his Government had been made the subject of travel restrictions imposed by the European Union and the USA, which indentified them as 'primarily responsible for a lack of co-operation in promoting a political settlement'. Talks on a possible federation continued in September, with Smirnov insisting that any future constitutional structure must recognize Moldova and Transnistria as 'equals'. He continued to court Russian support for his secessionist administration and remained closely identified with the very concept of Transnistrian independence. *Address:* Office of the Government of the 'Transdnestrian Moldovan Soviet Socialist Republic', Tiraspol, Moldova; internet www.president-pmr.org.

**SULTANOV, Otkir Tukhtamuradovich:** Prime Minister of Uzbekistan; b. 14 July 1939, in Tashkent; m., with one d. *Education:* Tomsk Polytechnical Institute. *Career:* he was formerly Minister of Foreign Economic Relations (1992–95), where he particularly improved relations with the other former Soviet Central Asian countries—in 1994 Uzbekistan created an economic union with Kazakhstan and Kyrgyzstan—and encouraged economic links with the Russian Federation. In December 1995 President Islam Karimov (q.v.) unexpectedly appointed him Prime Minister, replacing Abdulkhashim Mutalov, formerly a close ally of the President. The premiership had little independent authority, with the Cabinet of Ministers chaired by the President rather than the Prime Minister. He remained in his position in late 2003, although his powers were, by this time, minimal. *Address:* Office of the Cabinet of Ministers, 700008 Tashkent, Government House, Uzbekistan; tel. (17) 139-82-95; fax (17) 139-86-01.

**SYMONENKO, Petro Mykolayovych:** Ukrainian politician; b. 1 August 1952, in Donetsk; m., with two s. *Education:* studied at Donetsk State Polytechnical Institute in 1969–74, and Kiev Institute of Political Science and Social Administration. *Career:* Secretary of the Central Committee of the Communist Party of Ukraine (CPU), Symonenko contested the presidential election of October–November 1999, with the support of the Chairman of the Ukrainian legislature (the Verkhovna Rada), Oleksandr Tkachenko, who withdrew his candidacy. Symonenko was second-placed in the first round of voting, on 31 October, with 22.2% of the votes cast. As no candidate achieved an overall majority, a second round of voting took place on 14 November. The incumbent President, Leonid Kuchma (q.v.), undertook a number of measures in an attempt to ensure his re-election; in early November he

removed three regional Governors from their post, owing to their support of Symonenko or the third-placed candidate, Oleksandr Moroz (q.v.). Following the 'run-off' election, Symonenko had 38.8% of the votes cast, compared with Kuchma's 57.7%; despite retaining the presidency, Kuchma subsequently dismissed other regional governors who had given their support to Symonenko in the second round. The proportion of votes cast in favour of Symonenko was the highest achieved by a communist candidate in the post-Soviet era. None the less, he alleged that electoral malpractice had taken place, an assertion that was confirmed by international observers. He remained leader of the CPU, maintaining his pressure on Kuchma to resign, and was thought almost certain to be its candidate in the presidential election scheduled for 2004. *Address:* Communist Party of Ukraine, 04070 Kiev, vul. Borysohlibska 7, Ukraine; tel. (44) 416-54-87; fax (44) 416-31-37; internet www.kpu.kiev.ua.

**TABUNSCIC, Gheorghe:** Moldovan (Gagauzian) politician and Baskan of Gagauz-Eri; ethnic Gagauz. *Career:* he was an active member of the Moldovan Party of Communists (MPC) in Comrat, in the secessionist territory of Gagauzia, rising to become its First Secretary in the mid-1990s. Following the dissolution of the USSR and Moldova's independence he also became a private businessman. One of the Turkish-speaking, Orthodox-Christian Gagauz minority, he was involved in negotiations with the Moldovan Government over the status of Gagauzia from 1993. He was an advocate of autonomy for Moldova's Gagauz ethnic minority, following the example of Transnistria, although he argued that this must be achieved by peaceful means. This resulted in the constitutional provision of special status in 1994 and a law on the region's autonomy coming into force in February 1995. Following the attainment of autonomy for Gagauzia in February 1995, as leader of the Comrat branch of the MPC, Tabunscic sought election to the quasi-presidential post of 'baskan'. He was elected to that post, following a second round of voting in June. He favoured dialogue and co-operation with the Moldovan authorities, eschewing more aggressive secessionist policies. However, he failed to secure re-election in the elections of September 1999, being defeated in a second round of voting by the Moldovan Deputy Minister of Foreign Affairs, Dumitru Croitor. Following Croitor's resignation in mid-2002, Tabunscic once again sought election as baskan, this time as an independent (but with the endorsement of the MCP). He won 51.0% of the votes cast in the election held in October. He opposed the proposed transformation of Moldova into a federal state, as advocated by many, particularly in Transnistria, as a solution to Moldova's complicated system of government, stating that Gagauzia was content with its status. *Address:* Office of the Baskan, Comrat, Gagauzia, Moldova.

**TANAYEV, Nikolai Timofeyevich:** Kyrgyz Prime Minister; b. 5 Nov. 1945, in Mikhailovka, Russia. *Education:* he received a degree in engineering construction from Jambul Hydroengineering Institute in 1969. *Career:* he was head of the Osh Regional Water Canal Directorate from 1984, and then became head of the Chuipromstroi (Chui Industrial Construction) trust in 1985. In 2000 he was appointed Chairman of the State Agency on Architecture and Construction, and he became First Deputy Prime Minister in 2001. In May 2002 he became acting Prime Minister, following the resignation of Kurmanbek Bakiyev amid civil unrest. Tanayev was approved as Prime Minister at the end of the month, receiving strong parliamentary support. Tanayev, the first Prime Minister of Kyrgyzstan to be an ethnic Russian, pledged administrative reforms. Having assumed office at a time of widespread instability, Tanayev subsequently succeeded in negotiating an amnesty with protesters. In October he and other members of the Government swore an oath of loyalty to the people and the President. He fervently supported the new draft constitution approved by referendum in February 2003, and as his tenure as premier progressed he began to be seen as a loyalist with relatively little political ambition of his own. *Address:* Office of the Prime Minister, 720003 Bishkek, Govt House, Kyrgyzstan; tel. (312) 22-56-56; fax (312) 21-86-27; internet www.gov.kg/prime.htm.

**TARLEV, Vasile:** Prime Minister of Moldova; b. in Bascalia village. *Education:* Polytechnical Institute, Chişinău (1985); he received a doctorate in technical sciences in 1998. *Career:* he served in the Soviet Army from 1981 to 1983. After graduating, he became Chief Mechanic at the Bucuria confectionery factory, and was Chief Engineer from 1991. Two years later he studied international marketing and trade management in the USA, and was elected Chairman of the managing board of Bucuria in 1995. He also became Chairman of the National Association of Producers and a council member of the International Union of Producers. A businessman with no party affiliation, Tarlev was nominated as premier by the newly elected President, Vladimir Voronin (q.v.), on 11 April 2001, and his Government was approved by Parliament eight days later. His administration was criticized by opposition groups for the alleged suppression of demonstrations. In October 2002 he became the subject of personal scrutiny after a newspaper claimed that he had negotiated a higher price for gas purchases from a Russian company, in return for guarantees for a loan he had negotiated with a director of the Bucuria confectionery factory. He vehemently denied any wrongdoing. Despite numerous personnel changes since the Government's appointment (only three portfolios remained with their original ministers in mid-2003) and the continuing opposition protests, Tarlev remained confident that his Government had improved the situation in Moldova and would continue to do so. *Address:* Office of the Council of Ministers: 2033 Chişinău, Piaţa Marii Adunări Naţionale 1, Moldova; tel. (2) 23-30-92.

**TER-PETROSSIAN, Levon Akopovich:** Armenian politician, philologist and former President; b. 9 Jan. 1945, in Aleppo, Syria; m. Lyudmila Pletnitskaya, with one s. *Education:* Yerevan State University and Leningrad (now St Petersburg, Russia) Institute of Orientology. *Career:* his family moved to Armenia in 1946; he was a researcher at the Armenian Institute of Literature in 1972–78 and then Scientific Secretary at the Matenadazan Archive intermittently from 1978 to 1990. A radical nationalist, he was a member of the Karabakh Committee and was in gaol in December 1988–May 1989. He became leader of the Armenian Pan-National Movement (APNM) and, in August 1990, was elected Chairman of the Supreme Soviet (*de facto* Head of State). He was confirmed in office in direct elections for the post of executive President of the Republic in October 1991. The popularity of his regime decreased gradually over the following years, owing to the protracted civil war in Azerbaijan over Nagornyi Karabakh and consequent economic conditions. His pragmatism also brought him into disagreement with more extreme nationalist groups over his policy of improving links with Turkey. However, having retained the support of the domestic electorate and the diaspora, the APNM won a majority in the general election of July 1995. He was re-elected President in September 1996, with a reported 51.8% of the votes cast. It was, however, alleged that the results had been falsified, to avoid a second round against Vazgen Manukian. This claim significantly eroded his political legitimacy, as did accusation of authoritarianism. In October 1997, following pressure from the USA, France and Russia, Ter-Petrossian affirmed his support for a peace settlement in Nagornyi Karabakh and declared that hopes for the enclave's reunification with Armenia were unrealistic. This further increased his political isolation and, with public opinion against him, senior military officials demanded his resignation, which he gave on 3 February 1998. He was replaced by Robert Kocharian (q.v.), the former leader of Nagornyi Karabakh, who he himself had brought into government in Armenia in an attempt to placate nationalist sentiments. He remained President of the APNM. In 2002 he announced that he would not contest the presidential election scheduled to be held early in the following year, stating that the conditions were not right for his return. This was widely interpreted as a belief that the election would not be fair (he had already stated that he regretted ever bringing Kocharian into government). Although a return to active politics remained a possibility in the future, Ter-Petrossian preferred to concentrate on his studies and writings on Armenia's medieval history. *Address:* Armenian Pan-Na-

tional Movement (Haiots Hamazgaien Sharjoum), 375019 Yerevan, Khanjian St 27, Armenia; tel. (2) 57-04-70.

**TIHIPKO, Serhiy Leonidovych:** Ukrainian banker and politician; Governor of the National Bank of Ukraine; b. 13 February 1960; m., with one d. *Education:* Dnipropetrovsk Metallurgical Institute. *Career:* In the late 1980s he held senior positions in the Dnipropetrovsk Oblast V. I. Lenin Young Communist League (Komsomol), and was head of the department of agitation and propaganda. He subsequently worked in banking, and in 1992–97 was Chairman of the Board of Privatbank. He was a close associate of Ukraine's President, Leonid Kuchma (q.v.), and became a Deputy Prime Minister, with responsibility for privatization and economic development, in April 1997. It was widely expected that he would, in due course, become Prime Minister. However, this did not prove to be the case in December 1999, when Viktor Yushchenko (q.v.) was nominated. Tihipko remained in the new Government, as Minister of the Economy. In June 2000 he was elected to the Verkhovna Rada (legislature) in a by election and in November was elected as the leader of the Working Ukraine party, which was widely regarded as representative of business 'oligarch' interests in the eastern Dnipropetrovsk region. In the following month he held the seventh place on the federal list of the pro-Kuchma 'For A United Ukraine' electoral bloc. He refused the offer of a deputy premiership when Anatoliy Kinakh (q.v.) was asked to form a government in May 2001, and left the administration to concentrate on his duties as leader of Working Ukraine. He remained an ally of Kuchma, however, and in December 2002 was appointed Chairman of the National Bank of Ukraine, despite initial hostility to his appointment from the Verkhovna Rada. Although this post was non-political (upon appointment he agreed to resign as leader of Working Ukraine at an appropriate time), it was seen as a base from which to develop his political career, and he was widely expected to contest the country's presidency in 2004. *Address:* National Bank of Ukraine, 01008 Kiev, vul. Institutska 9, Ukraine; tel. (44) 253-44-78; fax (44) 230-20-33; e-mail postmaster@bank.gov.ua; internet www.bank.gov.ua..

**TURAJONZODA, Haji Akbar:** Deputy Prime Minister of Tajikistan; b. 16 Feb. 1954, in Turkobod, Kafarnikhon raion, near Dushanbe; two s. and four d. *Education:* he received religious training in Uzbekistan, at the *madrassah* in Bukhara, then at the Tashkent centre of official Central Asian Islam, before he went to the University of Amman, Jordan. *Career:* he was appointed the Chief Kazi of Tajikistan in 1990. He immediately gained some prominence with his appeals for reconciliation following the February 1990 riots in Dushanbe. Despite gaining the support of radical groupings supportive of the *mujahidin* in Afghanistan, Turajonzoda initially concentrated on political channels and was elected to the republican Supreme Soviet (legislature) later in 1990. He aligned himself with the opposition, although he was careful to reject Islamist fundamentalism or the imposition of any policy against the popular will. The extent of his involvement is indicated by the fact that the headquarters of the united opposition (principally the Islamic Renaissance Party—now the Islamic Rebirth Party of Tajikistan—and the Democratic Party of Tajikistan) was based in the kaziate buildings. Perceived anticlericalism in the establishment led him to abandon his apolitical stance and, effectively, to head the Islamic-democratic opposition. The authorities' attitude was reflected in the opposition of his technical subordinates in the official hierarchy: the mullah of Kulyab (Fatkhullo Sharifov, later appointed Chief Mufti of Tajikistan) rejected his authority as early as 1990; the mullah of Leninabad in 1992. Following the communist reaction to Islamic-democratic gains and the capture of Dushanbe in December 1992 by militias loyal to the new, communist Government, Turajonzoda was denounced as an 'enemy of the people' and obliged to seek exile in Afghanistan. The new Government replaced him as religious leader of Tajikistan in February 1993, by abolishing the kaziate and instituting an independent muftiate. In 1994 he was appointed First Deputy Leader of the Islamic Renaissance Party and was prominent as the leader of the united opposition delegation in negotiations with the

Government, a role later taken by Sayed Abdullo Nuri (q.v.), the party leader. Turajonzoda made his return from exile dependent on his being appointed a deputy premier, and in February 1998 he was invited to be First Deputy Chairman of the Council of Ministers, with responsibility for relations with the Commonwealth of Independent States (CIS). In October 1998 he reiterated his support for the policies of President Rakhmonov during the period of transition, and he supported the candidacy of the incumbent in the presidential election of 6 November 1999. He remained in his post in late 2003, having been closely involved in the negotiations on a possible free-trade area within the CIS. *Address:* Office of the First Deputy Chairman of the Council of Ministers, Dushanbe, pr. Rudaki 80, Tajikistan; tel. (3722) 21-59-56; fax (3722) 21-65-24.

**TYMOSHENKO, Yuliya Volodymyrivna:** Ukrainian politician and business executive; b. 27 November 1960, in Dnipropetrovsk; m., one d. *Education:* Dnipropetrovsk State University. *Career:* in 1991–95 she was the commerical director and general manager of a private company based in Dnipropetrovsk, the Ukrainian Benzine Corporation, and from November 1995 to February 1997 she was President of the state-owned energy utility company, Unified Energy Systems of Ukraine (UESU), in which position she was regarded as a close ally of Prime Minister Pavlo Lazarenko (q.v.). In December 1996 Tymoshenko was elected to the Ukrainian legislature, the Verkhovna Rada, as a representative of Kirovohrad Oblast, and in 1997 she joined the Hromada—Community party of Lazarenko, of which she subsequently became the first deputy leader. She was, however, critical of the perceived autocratic leadership style of Lazarenko, and in January 1999 she left Hromada to form, and lead, a new party, Batkivshchyna—Fatherland. In December 1999, following the dismissal and discrediting of Lazarenko, Tymoshenko was appointed Deputy Prime Minister, with responsibility for energy issues, with the particular objective of tackling corruption and introducing reform in the sector. However, from mid-2000 allegations emerged that she had conspired with officials of the UESU, illegally to transfer over US $100m. to the USA. Her husband Oleksandr, a UESU executive, was arrested in August, on embezzlement charges relating back to the early 1990s. Although Tymoshenko denounced the claims as politically motivated, in January 2001 she was forced to resign, amid accusations of tax evasion and the illegal shipment of Russian gas. Tymoshenko attributed these further allegations to efforts by President Leonid Kuchma (q.v.) to detract attention from the deepening political scandal surrounding his own office. On leaving the Government, Tymoshenko joined the opposition National Salvation Forum, but was arrested in mid-February 2001 on the tax evasion charges. While in prison she described herself as a 'prisoner of conscience', and her indictment of the Kuchma regime was published in the Western press. She was finally released in late March (although briefly re-arrested at the end of the month). On her release she stated that she would intensify her efforts to unseat Kuchma and intimated that she might stand for the presidency. The National Salvation Forum was subsequently reconstituted as an electoral alliance, led by Tymoshenko, who became an increasingly vocal opponent of the Kuchma administration. In August 2001 Russian prosecutors announced that they were bringing bribery charges against Tymoshenko, charges that she again dismissed, stating that they were aimed solely at discrediting the Ukrainian opposition ahead of the parliamentary elections due to take place in March 2002. Tymoshenko's supporters contested the elections under the designation Yuliya Tymoshenko Bloc, which obtained 7.3% of votes cast on the proportional lists, and 22 seats in the Verkhovna Rada. She remained an implacable opponent of Kuchma, and in January 2003 she presented a criminal complaint against him (charges included abuse of office and press censorship), urging the authorities to open an investigation. In April the Supreme Court abandoned all criminal proceedings against Tymoshenko and her husband, although the state prosecutor's office successfully appealed against the ruling later in the month. In September her party began a process towards the potential

impeachment of the President. *Address:* Batkivshchyna (Fatherland), 01133 Kiev, vul. L. Ukrainky 29/916, Ukraine; tel. (44) 294-42-21; e-mail info@byti.org.ua; internet www .tymoshenko.com.ua.

**VORONIN, Vladimir:** President of Moldova; b. 25 May 1941, in Corjova; m., with two c. *Education:* graduated from Technical College in Chişinău in 1961; Union Institute of the Alimentary Industry (1971); Academy of Sciences (1983); Academy of Police, USSR (1991). *Career:* an engineer, economist and lawyer, he began his career in 1961 as the director of a bread factory in Criuleni, and subsequently held a similar role in Dubăsari until 1971. For the following 10 years he was active in regional communist politics, in Dubăsari and Ungheni. In 1980–90 he was a deputy of the Supreme Council of Moldova, and in 1989–90 he served as republican Minister of Internal Affairs. He revived the Communist Party of Moldova (banned in 1991) as the Moldovan Party of Communists in 1994, and was the third-placed candidate in the direct presidential election of 17 November 1996. He subsequently vigorously opposed the reformist Government of President Petru Lucinschi, whose term of office expired in January 2001. After several inconclusive rounds of voting in the presidential elections of December 2000, Voronin was finally elected to the presidency on 4 April 2001, obtaining 71 of the 89 votes cast by the new communist-dominated Parliament (elected in February), thereby becoming the first communist to be elected President since the collapse of the USSR. The early years of his presidency were dominated by opposition protests and by the continuing dispute with the secessionist Transnistria region. Voronin assumed significant personal involvement in the latter issue, and negotiations were ongoing in 2003 on proposals by Voronin for the joint drafting of a new constitution for a federal Moldovan state, which would be subject to approval by a nation-wide referendum. *Address:* Office of the President, Chişinău, by Ştefan cel Mare 154, Moldova; tel. (2) 23-47-93.

**YANUKOVYCH, Viktor Fedorovych:** Ukrainian politician and business executive; Prime Minister of Ukraine; b. 9 July 1950, in Yenakiyevo, Donetsk Oblast; m., with two s. *Education:* Donetsk Polytechnical Institute. *Career:* he worked as a machine engineer in a metallurgical plant, and then as a motor mechanic, before taking up executive positions in the transport industry. During his industrial career he studied for a doctorate in economics. By the mid-1990s he was a prominent figure in the business community of Donetsk; he was working as General Director of the regional road transport company when, in 1996, he was appointed Deputy Governor of Donetsk Oblast. President Leonid Kuchma (q.v.) appointed him as Governor the following year. In 1998 he was elected to the regional legislature, becoming its Chairman in May 1999 (he was obliged to resign this position in March 2001, following a ruling by the national Constitutional Court that a Governor may not hold another public office). As Governor of Donetsk Oblast Yanukovich was a close ally of the President, and was regarded as an active supporter of 'oligarch' business interests in the region. In November 2002, following the dismissal of Anatoliy Kinakh as Prime Minister, Yanukovych was the President's preferred candidate to form a new administration, and was approved by parliament later in the month, stating that his aims were to oversee a sustainable increase in Ukraine's living standards and increase co-operation with the West. Despite some initial successes (he succeeded in convincing the Financial Action Task Force—FATF of the Organisation for Economic Co-operation and Development—OECD to remove sanctions imposed against Ukraine, after the country was deemed to be making insufficient effort to combat money 'laundering'—the processing of illicitly or illegally obtained funds through legitimate accounts), Yanukovich did not achieve widespread popularity. Opposition groups considered him to be merely a client of Kuchma, while popular opinion held him to be a member of an unaccountable business élite. In early 2003 he announced that he was investigating the possibility of contesting the presidential election scheduled for 2004, although opinion polls placed him among the least popular of the potential candidates. He accepted the leadership of the Party of Regions in April 2003, stating that the party would seek alliances so that only one centrist candidate would contest the presidential election. He was heavily criticized after the country experienced a shortage of grain in mid-2003, but stated that the problem was the fault of private business, not the Government. *Address:* Cabinet of Ministers, 01008 Kiev, vul. M. Hrushevskoho 12/2, Ukraine; tel. (44) 293-21-71; fax (44) 293-20-93; e-mail web@kmu.gov .ua; internet www.kmu.gov.ua.

**YAROV, Yurii Fedorovich:** Executive Secretary and Chairman of the Executive Committee of the Commonwealth of Independent States (CIS); b. 2 April 1942, in Mariinsk, Kemerovo Oblast, Russian Federation; m., with one s. and one d. *Education:* he graduated from Leningrad (now St Petersburg) Technical Institute and Leningrad Engineering Economy Institute. *Career:* he worked in various factories, eventually as a Director, and also became active in the Communist Party of the Soviet Union (CPSU). He was Deputy Prime Minister in 1992–96 and subsequently the Russian presidential representative to the Federation Council (the upper chamber of the Federal Assembly of the Russian Federation). In April 1999 he was appointed Executive Secretary of the CIS, following the dismissal of Boris Berezovskii (q.v.). One of his first moves was to reduce the number of CIS executive staff by about one-half. He oversaw negotiations on the creation of a free-trade zone among the countries of the CIS, and while he was frustrated at the slow progress made, he remained confident that an agreement would eventually be reached. He was also prominent as the head of CIS observer missions to elections held in a number of countries. *Address:* c/o Commonwealth of Independent States, 220000 Minsk, vul. Kirava 17, Belarus; tel. (17) 225-35-17; fax (17) 227-23-39; e-mail postmaster@www.cis.minsk.by.

**YAVLINSKII, Grigorii Alekseyevich:** Russian economist and politician; b. 10 April 1952, in Lviv, Ukraine; m., with two s. *Education:* Leningrad (now St Petersburg) Plekhanov Institute of National Economics. *Career:* he originally worked as an electrician, becoming involved in economics in the early 1980s. He was the author of the radical '500-day programme' of economic reform, introduced on 3 September 1990 while he was serving in the Russian Government as a deputy premier (June–November 1990). In 1991 he worked as an economic adviser to the Russian Government and to the Soviet leader, Mikhail Gorbachev (q.v.). In December of that year he became a member of the Economic Council of the President of Kazakhstan. In 1993 he co-founded the liberal Yavlinskii-Boldyrev-Lukin electoral bloc (subsequently known as Yabloko). Yabloko campaigned for more 'conceptual reform' in the Russian parliament and obtained 22 seats in the State Duma in the December elections. He was himself elected as a parliamentary deputy. At this time he also announced his intention to stand in the presidential elections, and was perceived by many democrats as a liberal alternative to President Boris Yeltsin (q.v.). Although he was returned to parliament in December 1995, Yabloko won a total of just 45 seats in the new Duma. In the months prior to the 1996 presidential election Yavlinskii's popularity declined. He was regarded by some as the only remaining 'true democrat' in Russian politics, but was, nevertheless, criticized by some reformers for failing to withdraw from the poll, thereby risking a divided liberal vote. He secured just over 7% of the votes cast in the first round of the election, and refused to endorse Yeltsin explicitly in the second round. Yabloko also refused to join the Government, and remained in 'principled opposition'. Although a supporter of reform, Yavlinskii condemned both the influence of the 'oligarchs' on the administration and the frequent changes of government personnel undertaken by President Yeltsin in 1998 and 1999. In November 1999 Yavlinskii expressed concern that the recently renewed campaign in the secessionist republic of Chechnya amounted to a slow military coup, as senior figures in the federal forces obtained greater policy-making powers. In the election to the State Duma of 19 December Yabloko obtained 21 seats. Following the unexpected resignation of Yeltsin on 31 December, Yavlinskii contested the presidential election held in March 2000. He was the third-placed candidate, with 5.8% of the votes cast. In 2001 Yavlinskii spoke out

against the actions of the winning candidate, Vladimir Putin (q.v.), particularly over what he described as government manipulation of the media. He warned against authoritarianism and described Russia as 'quasi-democratic', with power still retained by the former Soviet élite. In July 2002, however, he announced that Yabloko, which had recently been restyled the Russian Democratic Party—Yabloko, would be prepared to co-operate with the Government on some issues. A number of observers interpreted this as an attempt to reposition both the party and himself in preparation for the next parliamentary and presidential elections. In early 2003 it was thought likely that he would reach an agreement with the Union of Rightist Forces (URF), led by Boris Nemtsov, to form an alliance in order to contest the elections to the State Duma scheduled to be held later in the year. However, in the event, it proved impossible to form any such alliance, despite the ideological similarity of the parties. In June, in an unprecedented move brought about by dissatisfaction with the Government's economic policies, the Yabloko faction in the Duma formed an alliance with that of the Communist Party of the Russian Federation to present a motion of 'no confidence' in the Government of Mikhail Kasyanov (q.v.)—the motion was defeated in the State Duma. Later that year allegations were made of links between certain members of the party's leadership and senior executives of the hydrocarbons company Yukos. Yavlinskii vehemently rejected any description of Yabloko as a pro-'oligarch' party, particularly following the announcement by the Chairman of Yukos, Mikhail Khodorkovskii (q.v.), that he was to fund the party (as well as the URF) in advance of legislative elections scheduled for December. *Address:* Russian Democratic Party—Yabloko, 119034 Moscow, per. M. Levshinskii 7/3, Russia; tel. (095) 201-43-79; fax (095) 292-34-50; e-mail info@yabloko.ru; internet www.yabloko.ru.

**YELTSIN, Boris Nikolayevich:** former President of the Russian Federation; b. 1 Feb. 1931, in Sverdlovsk (now Yekaterinburg); m. Naina Girina, with two d. *Education:* graduated from the Urals Polytechnic Institute. *Career:* after several years working for construction companies, Yeltsin began full-time work for the Communist Party of the Soviet Union (CPSU) in 1968. He was appointed First Secretary in Sverdlovsk Oblast in 1976, with his reputation quickly spreading beyond this region. When Mikhail Gorbachev (q.v.) came to power in 1985, Yeltsin was appointed First Secretary of the Moscow Party Committee. He became increasingly outspoken about the need for reform and to put an end to corruption in the CPSU. His criticism of the slow pace of reform led, in 1987, to his dismissal from his post and from the Politburo and a demotion to a post in the State Construction Committee. In 1989, however, he stood in the elections to the Congress of People's Deputies and won over 90% of the votes in the Moscow constituency. He continued to demand more radical reforms and the dismissal of conservative communists. In 1990 he was elected to the Russian Supreme Soviet and, by a narrow margin, gained the Chairmanship. In early 1991 he was granted executive powers by the Supreme Soviet, pending direct elections to an executive presidency of the Russian Federation in June. He won these elections with a convincing mandate and further secured his authority by his strong leadership during the conservative coup attempt of August 1991. Yeltsin was an original signatory of the Minsk Agreement of December, which established the Commonwealth of Independent States (CIS) and ensured the demise of the USSR. As President of a newly independent Russian Federation, he introduced a radical economic reform programme (termed 'shock therapy') under premier Yegor Gaidar. Confrontation with the legislature culminated in a series of crises in 1993, ending with the forcible suppression of parliamentary revolt and the endorsement of a new Constitution—which provided for a more powerful presidency—by 58.4% of participants in a nation-wide plebiscite on 12 December. Although the new State Duma, and that elected at the end of 1995, remained dominated by hostile elements, the lower house of the new parliament had insufficient authority significantly to hinder Yeltsin's reforms. Yeltsin secured re-election to the presidency in July 1996, obtaining 57% of the votes cast in the second round of voting. By 1998 Yeltsin increasingly displayed the behaviour condemned by his critics, with seemingly arbitrary changes of government enforced in confrontations with the State Duma, and growing evidence of ill health. The financial crisis of mid-1998 exhausted his political credibility and he was forced to accept the appointment of a 'compromise' premier, Yevgenii Primakov (q.v.), to whom he ceded considerable authority. The State Duma's efforts, in August, to impeach the President failed, however. In October he declared that he would not seek re-election, a decision that was confirmed in November, when the Constitutional Court ruled that he was not eligible to stand for a third term. In May 1999 Yeltsin suddenly dismissed Primakov and his Government. Sergei Stepashin formed a short-lived Government before he was, in turn, dismissed, to be replaced by Vladimir Putin (q.v.). On 31 December Yeltsin unexpectedly announced his resignation, which had been due in June 2000, and endorsed Putin as the country's next president, pending elections to be held within three months. His resignation was considered by many to have been timed to allow Putin to gain maximum support in the presidential election, and came amid widespread and increasing allegations of corruption on the part of Yeltsin and his entourage. Upon assuming power, Putin granted Yeltsin and his family permanent immunity from prosecution on criminal and administrative charges. Yeltsin was readmitted to hospital in early 2001, but his health subsequently seemed to improve, and by mid-2002 it was suggested by some analysts that an increasing division between members of the government loyal to Yeltsin, referred to as the 'family', and those loyal to Putin, referred to as 'chekists', was perceptible.

**YUSHCHENKO, Viktor Andriyovich:** former Prime Minister of Ukraine, banker and economist; b. 23 Feb. 1954, in Khoruzhivka, Sumy Oblast; m., with one s. and one d. *Education:* he graduated from Ternopil Institute of Finance and Economy. *Career:* a successful and highly respected banker, in his capacity as Governor of the central bank (from 1993–99), in 1996 he was almost solely responsible for bringing inflation under control and for ensuring the stability of the new currency, the hryvnya. His enemies were to be found on the left-wing and in the industrial lobby, after he halted the provision of unrestrained credits to the agricultural and industrial sectors. On 5 February 1997 he was reappointed Governor for a second term, and continued with a restrictive monetary policy. His popularity in the country was almost unparalleled, with nationalists approving his ardent patrotism and reluctance to speak Russian, and others respecting his attachment to his humble roots in the russified eastern provinces of Ukraine. He was renowned for his overall decency and lack of corruption and, on a personal level, was charismatic and photogenic. Also admired abroad, it was hoped that Western investors would be encouraged by his practices to increase investment in Ukraine. In late 1998 he developed a series of measures designed to protect the economy from the effects of the financial crisis in Russia. Many wished him to run for President in the election scheduled for October 1999, but he refused, it was thought, to protect his family. He was appointed Prime Minister following the rejection of the nomination of the incumbent Valeriy Pustovoytenko (q.v.) in December 1999. In January 2000 Yushchenko denied allegations by the former premier, Pavlo Lazarenko, that large amounts of IMF resources had been diverted from the central bank into Ukrainian government securities in December 1997. In February the IMF initiated an investigation and further lending to Ukraine was suspended. Yushchenko's position was weakened in March, when an audit found the reserves of the central bank to have been exaggerated during his governorship, although there was no evidence of actual embezzlement. As the economy finally began to register growth in 2000, however, Yushchenko was increasingly viewed to be the most competent Prime Minister to hold office in Ukraine, and the guarantor of continued economic reform. None the less, although popular with the public, he became increasingly unpopular with left-wing members of the Verkhovna Rada and with the 'oligarchs', who opposed his anti-corruption efforts. The dismissal and subsequent arrest of the

Deputy Prime Minister for Energy Issues, Yuliya Tymoshenko (q.v.), in early 2001 were viewed as a rebuttal of Yushchenko, who was her close political ally. In late April 2001 the Verkhovna Rada passed a motion of 'no confidence' in Yushchenko, thereby effecting his removal from office, prompting public demonstrations. Prior to the legislative elections of March 2002, Yushchenko established an electoral coalition of reformist and democratic parties, Our Ukraine. This grouping, which emphasized that it was not opposed to the presidency of Leonid Kuchma (q.v.) secured the largest share of votes (23.6%) cast for any party or bloc on the basis of proportional lists, and 112 seats overall. Yushchenko also remained a potential future presidential candidate, with a wide support base that extended from proponents of radical economic reform to elements aligned with Kuchma. By late 2003 he was regarded as a potential winner of the next presidential election, particularly if a number of other candidates were to withdraw in his favour, as had been suggested. *Address:* Our Ukraine, Kiev, Ukraine; e-mail massalsky@ua .org.ua; internet www.razom.org.ua.

**ZHAKIYANOV, Galimzhan:** Kazakh politician; m., with two s. *Career:* the managing director of one of the country's first privatized companies, Zhakiyanov had no party political past when he became the first businessman and youngest-ever Governor to be appointed to the Semipalatinsk region. However, his radical economic-reform policies were opposed by Prime Minister Akezhan Kazhegeldin (q.v.), and he was eventually dismissed from his post for his criticism of the Government. In mid-1997 Zhakiyanov was appointed Chairman of the State Agency for Strategic Resources Control, reporting directly to the President, who subsequently appointed him Governor to the Pavlodar region. In November 2001 Zhakiyanov, together with a Deputy Prime Minister, Uraz Dzhandosov (q.v.), and several other high-profile government and business figures, announced the foundation of a new political movement, the Democratic Choice of Kazakhstan (DCK), which aimed to revive democratic reform. Zhakiyanov and other DCK members were subsequently compelled to resign their official posts. In January 2002 Zhakiyanov was charged with abuse of office, and in March a warrant was issued for his arrest. One month later he was admitted to hospital, following an eight-hour police interrogation. His trial began in July, and in August Zhakiyanov was sentenced to seven years' imprisonment, prompting concern from the USA and international human rights organizations at the severity of the sentence, which was widely denounced as having been politically motivated. In August 2003 the authorities denied that he was suffering from tuberculosis, as had been claimed by his associates. Later that month it was revealed that the Prosecutor-General's office had recommended that he be considered for pardon. However, before an application could be made the recommendation was withdrawn, after the police announced that four new criminal investigations concerning Zhakiyanov had been instituted. These new cases were condemned by his supporters, who claimed that they were little more than a political ruse to prevent his release. In September the authorities released a video-recording, which apparently showed Zhakiyanov agreeing to apply for release, and the abandonment of the new charges, providing he took no active part in politics. His family immediately stated that the recording had been manipulated. The country's opposition movements attracted an amount of international attention to Zhakiyanov's imprisonment, claiming that it was symptomatic of the human rights violations and abuses of the democratic process seen in the country.

**ZHIRINOVSKII, Vladimir Volfovich:** Russian politician; b. 25 April 1946, in Almaty (Alma-Ata), Kazakhstan; m., with two s. *Education:* attended the Institute of Eastern Languages (now the Institute of African and Asian countries), Moscow M. V. Lomonosov State University (MGU) in 1964–70, where he specialized in Turkish language and literature, and the Faculty of Law at MGU in 1972–77. *Career:* he worked for the Ministry of Defence, and was on the General Staff of the Transcaucasian Command, based in Tbilisi, Georgia, in 1970–72. He was employed at the Soviet Committee for Peace of the Soviet Society for Friendship and Cultural Relations in 1973–83, before becoming a legal consultant for Mir Publications between 1983 and 1990. He founded the ultra-nationalist Liberal Democratic Party of the Soviet Union (now of Russia—LDPR) in 1989 and became its flamboyant leader in 1990. A highly intelligent and constantly controversial figure, he stood as a candidate in the presidential election of 1991 and became a member of the State Duma in 1993. The LDPR contested the State Duma election of December 1999 as the Zhirinovskii bloc, after the Party was banned from participating in its own right, owing to the failure of some of its candidates fully to declare their assets; the bloc obtained 17 seats. In January 2000 Zhirinovskii was elected as a vice-speaker (Deputy Chairman) of the State Duma. Although he was originally barred from standing as a candidate for the presidential election of 26 March 2000, owing to the non-disclosure of his assets, in March he was permitted to re-register. He eventually came in fifth place, with 2.7% of the votes cast. In July 2001 Zhirinovskii admitted that his father had been a Jew—his previous anti-Semitic statements had been one of a number of factors that encouraged thousands of Jews to leave Russia, after the success of the LDPR in the 1993 elections. In late 2001 he further renounced his former anti-US stance. He called for the incorporation of Russia into the North Atlantic Treaty Organization (NATO) and advocated increased co-operation with the USA in its declared 'war on terrorism'. He was appointed to head the Russian delegation to NATO's Parliamentary Assembly in February 2002. However, in the same month he appeared to reverse his stance towards the USA once more, warning that it was heading towards catastrophe. In April he proposed the restoration of the Tsarist names of some cities, the redenomination of the rouble and the renaming of the Commonwealth of Independent States (CIS) as the Union of Free Sovereign Republics (which would have the same acronym as the former USSR in Russian). The Duma voted in favour of his proposals, which did not, however, come into effect. A prolific author, he was increasingly viewed by many Russians as an entertainer, rather than a politician of substance; however, other analysts suggested that Zhirinovskii expressed controversial policy proposals, supported by President Vladimir Putin (q.v.), as a means of ascertaining public reaction, prior to their subsequent amendment, adoption or rejection by the administration. In February 2003 there was an unsuccessful attempt to dismiss Zhirinovskii from his post as Deputy Chairman of the State Duma after a television channel showed footage of him, recorded in Iraq, using numerous obscenities while criticizing the prospect of US-led military intervention in the country. He later threatened legal action against the channel. In mid-2003 he announced that, despite his apparently declining support, he would seek election to the presidency in 2004. *Address:* Liberal Democratic Party of Russia, 103045 Moscow, Lukov per. 9; tel. (095) 925-07-15; fax (095) 924-08-69; e-mail pressldpr@duma.gov.ru; internet www.ldpr.ru.

**ZHVANIA, Zurab:** Georgian politician; b. 9 December 1963, in Tbilisi; m. with two c. *Education:* he was educated at Tbilisi Experimental School No. 1, and graduated from the Tbilisi State University, studying in the Department of Biology. *Career:* from 1985 to 1992 he was employed as a senior laboratory assistant and then worked in the Department of Human and Mammal Physiology. He was the founder of the Greenpeace movement in Georgia, and in 1988 became Chairman of the Green Party of Georgia, as well as serving as co-Chairman of the European Union of Greens in 1992–93. A close associate of President Eduard Shevardnadze (q.v.), he was appointed General Secretary of his party, the Citizens' Union of Georgia (CUG), upon its formation in 1993. Following the legislative elections of both 1995 and 1999, in which the CUG secured the largest number of seats, he was appointed Chairman (speaker) of the Georgian Parliament (Sakartvelos Parlamenti). In August 2001 Zhvania sent an open letter to the President, demanding immediate and urgent action to tackle government corruption and initiate reform. Following public protests against the perceived state threat to media freedom, which led to the dismissal of the

Government on 1 November, Zhvania resigned his post (he was replaced by Nino Burzhanadze—q.v.), claiming that Shevardnadze no long understood the needs of the people. None the less, Zhvania (who was widely considered to be a future presidential challenger) believed that Shevardnadze should retain his post, and ensure the implementation of government reform. In 2002, as the CUG fragmented, he formed and led a new 'radical centrist' party, the United Democrats, which had 22 deputies in late 2002. In this position he became increasingly identified as one of the most prominent opposition leaders in Georgia. In August 2003 he allied his party with that of his successor as parliamentary speaker, Burdzhanadze, to form a bloc in order to contest the forthcoming legislative elections. In mid-2003 Zhvania announced his intention to seek election to the presidency at the next election, scheduled for 2005. *Address:* United Democrats, 380059 Tbilisi, Marshal Gelovani 4A, Georgia; tel. (32) 95-98-23.

**ZLENKO, Anatoliy Maksymovych:** Ukrainian politician and foreign-affairs adviser; b. 2 June 1938, in Kiev Oblast; m. with two d. *Education:* he studied at Kiev State University in 1962–67. *Career:* he held a number of diplomatic posts from the late 1960s, working for the UN Educational, Scientific and Cultural Organization (UNESCO) from 1979, and serving as the Permanent Representative of Ukraine to UNESCO from October 1983 until March 1987. He subsequently served as Ukraine's First Deputy Minister of Foreign Affairs until July 1990, when he was promoted to Minister. He retained this post until August 1994, becoming the Permanent Representative of Ukraine to the UN until 1997. In 1997–98 he served as ambassador to France, and from 1998 he was also ambassador to Portugal (although resident in France). In October 2000 Zlenko was re-appointed Minister of Foreign Affairs, replacing Boris Tarasyuk. He was believed to favour warmer relations with Russia, and a 'multi-vectored' foreign policy. He gained domestic and international credit for his handling of US allegations that Ukraine had sold weapons systems to Iraq. He reached the constitutionally imposed retirement age for ministers of 65 years in June 2003 and was replaced in September. The following month he was appointed special presidential adviser on major international issues. *Address:* Ministry of Foreign Affairs, 01018 Kiev, Mykhailivska pl. 1, Ukraine; tel. (44) 21-28-33; fax (44) 226-31-69.

**ZYUGANOV, Gennadii Andreyevich:** Russian politician; b. 26 June 1944, in Mymrino village, Orel Oblast. *Education:* Orel Pedagogical Institute, Academy of Social Sciences of the Central Committee of the Communist Party of the Soviet Union (CPSU). *Career:* he worked as a teacher and a trade-union functionary before becoming active in the CPSU; in 1989–90 he was Deputy Head of the Ideology Division of the CPSU Central Committee. In February 1993 he was elected Chairman of the Central Committee of the Communist Party of the Russian Federation (CPRF) and, in the general election of December, won a seat in the State Duma. Zyuganov, a pragmatist, thereupon began to unite the reactionary Stalinist and social-democratic factions within the CPRF, and managed to increase its popular appeal. The party won a huge majority in the December 1995 parliamentary election. During the election campaign, however, Zyuganov was criticized for appearing to offer one set of promises to Western governments and investors and another to the electorate. He was the main rival to Boris Yeltsin (q.v.) in the presidential election of June–July 1996 and was only narrowly defeated in the second round of voting. It was thought that many voters, although discontented with Yeltsin's administration, were too fearful of a return to a Soviet-style climate of repression to elect a communist as head of state. By the time of the economic crisis of 1998, however, he was demonstrably in charge of the best-organized party in Russia and felt sufficiently confident to challenge the President in refusing to endorse the return of Viktor Chernomyrdin (q.v.) as Prime Minister. Continuing communist influence was demonstrated in the election of December 1999, in which the CPRF secured 113 seats, the largest number obtained by any party. In the presidential election of 26 March 2000, Zyuganov was again the most important rival to the candidate preferred by Yeltsin, obtaining 29.2% of the votes cast. In mid-March 2001 he proposed a motion of 'no confidence' in the Government, which was rejected by the State Duma. In April 2002 a redistribution of Duma committee chairmanships led to seven of the nine positions held by the CPRF being revoked; the party immediately announced that it would assume a more aggressively oppositional role outside parliament. As other communists resigned their government positions, Zyuganov demanded that the speaker of the Duma, Gennadii Seleznev (q.v.), also resign his post. Seleznev refused, however, and in June was expelled from the party, along with two other deputies, considered by many to represent the 'human face' of communism, compared with Zyuganov's uncompromisingly 'hardline' stance; Seleznev subsequently formed his own party, the Party for the Rebirth of Russia. A similar situation occured in 2003, as the youthful economist and politician Sergei Glazyev (q.v.), who had recently come to renewed prominence after he received an unexpectedly high proportion of the votes cast for the CPRF in the gubernatorial election in Krasnoyarsk Krai, switched allegiances from the CPRF to another party, the Congress of Russian Communities after continued disagreements with Zyuganov; many observers had previously expected Glazyev to be given a prominent position on the federal list of the CPRF at the State Duma elections scheduled to be held in December. In June Zyuganov led the CPRF faction in the State Duma with that of the ideologically dissimilar and liberal Yabloko party to bring a motion of 'no confidence' in the Government, although this was defeated. Throughout 2003 the party appeared to become increasingly reactionary, as Zyuganov made openly anti-Semitic statement, and supported the appointment of the outspokenly xenophobic Nikolai Kondratenko, formerly Governor of Krasnodar Krai, to the second position on the party list ahead of the Duma elections. *Address:* Communist Party of the Russian Federation, 103051 Moscow, per. M. Sukharevskii per. 3/1, Russia; tel. (095) 928-71-29; fax (095) 292-90-50; e-mail cprf2000@mail.ru; internet www.kprf.ru.

# PART FOUR
# Regional Information

# REGIONAL ORGANIZATIONS

## THE UNITED NATIONS

**Address:** United Nations, New York, NY 10017, USA.

**Telephone:** (212) 963-1234; **fax:** (212) 963-4879; **internet:** www.un .org.

The United Nations (UN) was founded on 24 October 1945. The organization, which has 191 member states, aims to maintain international peace and security and to develop international co-operation in addressing economic, social, cultural and humanitarian problems. The principal organs of the UN are the General Assembly, the Security Council, the Economic and Social Council (ECOSOC), the International Court of Justice and the Secretariat. The General Assembly, which meets for three months each year, comprises representatives of all UN member states. The Security Council investigates disputes between member countries, and may recommend ways and means of peaceful settlement: it comprises five permanent members (the People's Republic of China, France, Russia, the United Kingdom and the USA) and 10 other members elected by the General Assembly for a two-year period. The Economic and Social Council comprises representatives of 54 member states, elected by the General Assembly for a three-year period: it promotes co-operation on economic, social, cultural and humanitarian matters, acting as a central policy-making body and co-ordinating the activities of the UN's specialized agencies. The International Court of Justice comprises 15 judges of different nationalities, elected for nine-year terms by the General Assembly and the Security Council: it adjudicates in legal disputes between UN member states.

**Secretary-General:** KOFI ANNAN (Ghana) (1997–2006).

### MEMBER STATES IN EASTERN EUROPE, RUSSIA AND CENTRAL ASIA
(with assessments for percentage contributions to the UN budget for 2003, and year of admission)

| | | |
|---|---|---|
| Armenia. | 0.00200 | 1992 |
| Azerbaijan . | 0.01200 | 1992 |
| Belarus[1] . | 0.01900 | 1945 |
| Georgia . | 0.00500 | 1992 |
| Kazakhstan. | 0.02800 | 1992 |
| Kyrgyzstan . | 0.00100 | 1992 |
| Moldova . | 0.00200 | 1992 |
| Russia[2] . | 1.20000 | 1945 |
| Tajikistan . | 0.00100 | 1992 |
| Turkmenistan . | 0.00300 | 1992 |
| Ukraine[1] . | 0.05300 | 1945 |
| Uzbekistan . | 0.01100 | 1992 |

[1] Until December 1991 both Belarus and Ukraine were integral parts of the USSR and not independent countries, but had separate UN membership.

[2] Russia assumed the USSR's seat in the General Assembly and its permanent seat on the Security Council in December 1991, following the USSR's dissolution.

### PERMANENT MISSIONS TO THE UNITED NATIONS
(October 2003)

**Armenia:** 119 East 36th St, New York, NY 10016; tel. (212) 686-9079; fax (212) 686-3934; e-mail armenia@un.int; internet www.un .int/armenia; Permanent Representative ARMEN MARTIROSIAN.

**Azerbaijan:** 866 United Nations Plaza, Suite 560, New York, NY 10017; tel. (212) 371-2559; fax (212) 371-2784; e-mail azerbaijan@un .int; Permanent Representative YASHAR ALIYEV.

**Belarus:** 136 East 67th St, New York, NY 10021; tel. (212) 535-3420; fax (212) 734-4810; e-mail belarus@un.int; internet www.un .int/belarus; Permanent Representative SERGEI LING.

**Georgia:** 1 United Nations Plaza, 26th Floor, New York, NY 10021; tel. (212) 759-1949; fax (212) 759-1832; e-mail georgia@un.int; internet www.un.int/georgia; Permanent Representative REVAZ ADAMIA.

**Kazakhstan:** 866 United Nations Plaza, Suite 586, New York, NY 10017; tel. (212) 230-1900; fax (212) 230-1172; e-mail kazakhstan@ un.int; internet www.un.int/kazakhstan; Permanent Representative YERZHAN KAZYKHANOV.

**Kyrgyzstan:** 866 United Nations Plaza, Suite 477, New York, NY 10017; tel. (212) 486-4214; fax (212) 486-5259; e-mail kyrgyzstan@ un.int; Permanent Representative KAMIL BAIALINOV.

**Moldova:** 573–577 Third Ave, New York, NY 10016; tel. (212) 682-3523; fax (212) 682-6274; e-mail moldova@un.int; internet www.un .int/modova; Permanent Representative VSEVOLOD GRIGORE.

**Russia:** 136 East 67th St, New York, NY 10021; tel. (212) 861-4900; fax (212) 628-0252; e-mail rusun@un.int; internet www.un.int/ russia; Permanent Representative SERGEI V. LAVROV.

**Tajikistan:** 136 East 67th St, New York, NY 10021; tel. (212) 744-2196; fax (212) 472-7645; e-mail tajikistan@un.int; Permanent Representative RASHID ALIMOV.

**Turkmenistan:** 866 United Nations Plaza, Suite 424, New York, NY 10021; tel. (212) 486-8908; fax (212) 486-2521; e-mail turkmenistan@un.int; Permanent Representative AKSOLTAN T. ATAEVA.

**Ukraine:** 220 East 51st St, New York, NY 10022; tel. (212) 759-7003; fax (212) 355-9455; e-mail mail@uamission.org; internet www .uamission.org; Permanent Representative VALERIY P. KUCHINSKY.

**Uzbekistan:** 866 United Nations Plaza, Suite 326, New York, NY 10017; tel. (212) 486-4242; fax (212) 486-7998; e-mail uzbekistan@ un.int; Permanent Representative ALISHER VOHIDOV.

### OBSERVERS

**Asian-African Legal Consultative Organization:** 404 East 66th St, Apt 12C, New York, NY 10021; tel. (212) 734-7608; e-mail aalco@ un.int; Permanent Representative K. BHAGWAT-SINGH (India).

**International Committee of the Red Cross:** 801 Second Ave, 18th Floor, New York, NY 10017; tel. (212) 599-6021; fax (212) 599-6009; e-mail mail@icrc.delnyc.org; Permanent Representative SYLVIE JUNOD.

**International Organization for Migration:** 122 East 42nd St, Suite 1610, New York, NY 10168; tel. (212) 681-7000; fax (212) 867-5887; e-mail unobserver@iom.int; Permanent Representative ROBERT G. PAIVA.

**Organization of the Islamic Conference:** 130 East 40th St, 5th Floor, New York, NY 10016; tel. (212) 883-0140; fax (212) 883-0143; e-mail oic@un.int; internet www.un.int/oic; Permanent Representative MOKHTAR LAMANI.

**World Conservation Union—IUCN:** 406 West 66th St, New York, NY 10021; tel. and fax (212) 734-7608.

The Commonwealth of Independent States, the Council of Europe, the Economic Co-operation Organization and the Organization for Security and Co-operation in Europe are among a number of intergovernmental organizations that have a standing invitation to participate as Observers, but do not maintain permanent offices at the United Nations.

## United Nations Information Centres/Services

**Armenia:** 375001 Yerevan, 14 Karl Libknekht St, 1st Floor; tel. (3741) 560-212; fax (3741) 561-406; e-mail dpi@undpi.am; internet www.undpi.am.

**Azerbaijan:** 370001 Baku, 3 Isteglialiyat St; tel. (12) 98-98-88; fax (12) 98-32-35; e-mail dpi@un.azeri.com; internet www.un-az.org/dpi.

**Belarus:** 220050 Minsk, 17 Kirov St, 6th Floor; tel. 2278149; fax 22260340; e-mail dpi_by@un.dp.org; internet www.un.minsk.by.

**Georgia:** 380079 Tbilisi, Eristavi St 9; tel. (32) 998558; fax (32) 250271; e-mail registry.ge@undp.org; internet www.undp.org.ge.

**Kazakhstan:** 480100 Almaty, Tole bi 67; tel. (3272) 69-53-27; fax (3272) 58-26-54; e-mail registry.kz@undp.org.

**Russia:** 4/16 Glazovsky Per., Moscow; tel. (095) 241-2894; fax (095) 230-2138; e-mail dpi-moscow@unic.ru; internet www.unic.ru.

**Ukraine:** 01021 Kiev-21, Klovsky Uzviz, 1; tel. (44) 253-55-59; fax (44) 253-26-07; e-mail registry@unkiev.ua; internet www.un.kiev .ua.

**Uzbekistan:** 700029 Tashkent, 4 Taras Shevchenko St; tel. (371) 139-09-77; fax (371) 133-69-65; e-mail registry.uz@undp.org; internet www.undp.uz.

# Economic Commission for Europe—ECE

**Address:** Palais des Nations, 1211 Geneva 10, Switzerland.
**Telephone:** (22)-917-44-44; **fax:** (22)-917-05-05; **e-mail:** info.ece@ unece.org; **internet:** www.unece.org.

The UN Economic Commission for Europe was established in 1947. It provides a regional forum for governments from European countries, the USA, Canada, Israel and central Asian republics to study the economic, environmental and technological problems of the region and to recommend courses of action. ECE is also active in the formulation of international legal instruments and the setting of international norms and standards.

## MEMBERS

| | |
|---|---|
| Albania | Liechtenstein |
| Andorra | Lithuania |
| Armenia | Luxembourg |
| Austria | Macedonia, former Yugoslav |
| Azerbaijan | republic |
| Belarus | Malta |
| Belgium | Moldova |
| Bosnia and Herzegovina | Monaco |
| Bulgaria | Netherlands |
| Canada | Norway |
| Croatia | Poland |
| Cyprus | Portugal |
| Czech Republic | Romania |
| Denmark | Russia |
| Estonia | San Marino |
| Finland | Serbia and Montenegro |
| France | Slovakia |
| Georgia | Slovenia |
| Germany | Spain |
| Greece | Sweden |
| Hungary | Switzerland |
| Iceland | Tajikistan |
| Ireland | Turkey |
| Israel | Turkmenistan |
| Italy | Ukraine |
| Kazakhstan | United Kingdom |
| Kyrgyzstan | Uzbekistan |
| Latvia | |

# Organization

(October 2003)

### COMMISSION

ECE, with ECAFE (now ESCAP), was the earliest of the five regional economic commissions set up by the UN Economic and Social Council. The Commission holds an annual plenary session and several informal sessions, and meetings of subsidiary bodies are convened throughout the year.

**Chairman:** CLYDE KULL (Estonia).

### SECRETARIAT

The secretariat services the meetings of the Commission and its subsidiary bodies and publishes periodic surveys and reviews, including a number of specialized statistical bulletins on timber, housing, building, and transport (see list of publications below). It maintains close and regular liaison with the United Nations Secretariat in New York, with the secretariats of the other UN regional commissions and of other UN organizations, including the UN Specialized Agencies, and with other intergovernmental organizations. The Executive Secretary also carries out secretarial functions for the Executive Body of the 1979 Convention on Longrange Transboundary Air Pollution and its protocols. The ECE and UN Secretariats also service the ECOSOC Committee of Experts on the Transport of Dangerous Goods.

**Executive Secretary:** BRIGITA SCHMÖGNEROVÁ (Slovakia).

# Activities

The guiding principle of ECE activities is the promotion of sustainable development. Within this framework, ECE's main objectives are to provide assistance to countries of central and eastern Europe in their transition from centrally-planned to market economies and to achieve the integration of all members into the European and global economies. Environmental protection, transport, statistics, trade facilitation and economic analysis are all principal topics in the ECE work programme, which also includes activities in the fields of timber, energy, trade, industry, and human settlements.

The 52nd plenary session of the ECE, held in April 1997, introduced a programme of reform, reducing the number of principal subsidiary bodies from 14 to seven, in order to concentrate resources on the core areas of work listed below, assisted by sub-committees and groups of experts. The Commission also determined to strengthen economic co-operation within Europe and to enhance co-operation and dialogue with other sub-regional organizations.

**Committee on Environmental Policy:** Provides policy direction for the ECE region and promotes co-operation among member governments in developing and implementing policies for environmental protection, rational use of natural resources, and sustainable development; supports the integration of environmental policy into sectoral policies; seeks solutions to environmental problems, particularly those of a transboundary nature; assists in strengthening environmental management capabilities, particularly in countries in transition; prepares ministerial conferences (normally held every four years—2003: Kiev, Ukraine); develops and promotes the implementation of international agreements on the environment; and assesses national policies and legislation. In April 2003 a committee was established to ensure compliance by governments with the Aarhus Convention on environmental decision-making and information dissemination.

**Committee on Human Settlements:** Reviews trends and policies in the field of human settlements; undertakes studies and organizes seminars; promotes international co-operation in the field of housing and urban and regional research; assists the countries of central and eastern Europe, which are currently in the process of economic transition, in reformulating their policies relating to housing, land management, sustainable human settlements, and planning and development.

**Committee on Sustainable Energy:** Exchanges information on general energy problems; work programme comprises activities including labelling classification systems and related legal and policy frameworks; liberalization of energy markets, pricing policies and supply security; harmonization of energy policies and practices; development of regional sustainable energy strategies for the 21st century; rational use of energy, efficiency and conservation; energy infrastructure including interconnection of electric power and gas networks; coal and thermal power generation in the context of sustainable energy development; Energy Efficiency 21 Project; promotion and development of a market-based Gas Industry in Economies in Transition—Gas Centre programme; and technical assistance and operational activities in energy for the benefit of countries with economies in transition.

**Committee for Trade, Industry and Enterprise Development:** A forum for studying means of expanding and diversifying trade among European countries, as well as with countries in other regions, and for drawing up recommendations on how to achieve these ends. Analyses trends, problems and prospects in intra-European trade; explores means of encouraging the flow of international direct investment into the newly opening economies of central and eastern Europe; promotes new or improved methods of trading by means of marketing, industrial co-operation, contractual guides, and the facilitation of international trade procedures (notably through the Electronic Data Interchange for Administration, Commerce and Transport—UN/EDIFACT, a flexible single international standard).

**Conference of European Statisticians:** Promotes improvement of national statistics and their international comparability in economic, social, demographic and environmental fields; promotes co-ordination of statistical activities of international organizations active in Europe and North America; and responds to the increasing need for international statistical co-operation both within the ECE region and between the region and other regions. Works very closely with FAO, OECD and the EU.

**Inland Transport Committee:** Promotes a coherent, efficient, safe and sustainable transport system through the development of international agreements, conventions and other instruments covering a wide range of questions relating to road, rail, inland water and combined transport, including infrastructure, border-crossing facilitation, road traffic safety, limitation of air pollution and noise, requirements for the construction of road vehicles and other transport regulations, particularly in the fields of transport of dangerous goods and perishable foodstuffs. Also considers transport trends and economics and compiles transport statistics. Assists central and eastern European countries, as well as ECE member states from central Asia, in developing their transport systems and infrastructures.

**Timber Committee:** Regularly reviews markets for forest products; analyses long-term trends and prospects for forestry and timber; keeps under review developments in the forest industries, including environmental and energy-related aspects. Subsidiary bodies run jointly with FAO deal with forest technology, management and training and with forest economics and statistics.

### SUB-REGIONAL PROGRAMMES

**Southeast European Co-operative Initiative—SECI:** initiated in December 1996, in order to encourage co-operation among countries of the sub-region and to facilitate their access to the process of European integration. Nine *ad hoc* Project Groups have been established to undertake preparations for the following selected projects: trade facilitation; transport infrastructure, in particular road and rail networks; financial policies to promote small and medium-sized enterprises; co-operation to combat crime and corruption; energy efficiency demonstration zone networks; interconnection of natural gas networks; co-operation among securities markets; and the recovery programme for rivers, lakes and adjacent seas (with particular emphasis on the Danube River Basin). Activities are overseen by a SECI Agenda Committee and a SECI Business Advisory Council. Participating countries: Albania, Bosnia and Herzegovina, Bulgaria, Croatia, Greece, Hungary, the former Yugoslav republic of Macedonia, Moldova, Romania, Slovenia and Turkey.

**Special Programme for the Economies of Central Asia— SPECA:** initiated in March 1998 as a joint programme of the ECE and ESCAP. Aims to strengthen sub-regional co-operation, in particular in the following areas: the development of transport infrastructure and facilitation of cross-border activities; the rational use of energy and water; regional development and attraction of foreign investment; and development of multiple routes for pipeline transportation of hydrocarbons to global markets. In February 2002 SPECA's Regional Advisory Committee endorsed the terms of reference for the establishment of a Business Advisory Council of SPECA, which aimed to bring together business representatives from participating countries and from their major trading and economic partners. The inaugural session of the Council was held in June, in Almaty, Kazakhstan. Participating countries: Kazakhstan, Kyrgyzstan, Tajikistan, Turkmenistan and Uzbekistan.

## Finance

ECE's budget for the two years 2002–03 was US $40.0m.

## Publications

*ECE Annual Report.*
*Annual Bulletin of Housing and Building Statistics for Europe and North America.*
*Annual Bulletin of Transport Statistics for Europe and North America.*
*ECE Highlights* (3 a year).
*The ECE in the Age of Change.*
*Economic Survey of Europe* (2 a year).
*Statistical Journal of the UNECE* (quarterly).
*Statistical Standards and Studies.*
*Statistics of Road Traffic Accidents in Europe and North America.*
*Timber Bulletin* (6 a year).
*Timber Committee Yearbook* (annually).
*Trends in Europe and North America: Statistical Yearbook of the ECE* (annually).
*UN Manual of Tests and Criteria of Dangerous Goods.*
*UN Recommendations on the Transport of Dangerous Goods.*
*UNECE International Legal Instruments, Norms and Standards.*
*The UNECE Works for Quality and Safety: Norms and Standards.*
*Women and Men in Europe and North America.*
*World Robotics* (annually).

Studies on air pollution, forestry and timber, water, gas, energy; environmental performance reviews; country profiles on the housing sector; transport agreements; customs conventions; maps; trade and investment briefings and guides; reports on fertility and family, gender, migration and population ageing; statistical bulletins; sectoral studies; discussion papers. Reports, proceedings of meetings, technical documents, codes of conduct, codes of practice, guide-lines to governments, etc.

# Economic and Social Commission for Asia and the Pacific—ESCAP

**Address:** United Nations Bldg, Rajdamnern Ave, Bangkok 10200, Thailand.

**Telephone:** (2) 288-1234; **fax:** (2) 288-1000; **e-mail:** unisbkk.unescap@un.org; **internet:** www.unescap.org.

The Commission was founded in 1947 to encourage the economic and social development of Asia and the Far East; it was originally known as the Economic Commission for Asia and the Far East (ECAFE). The title ESCAP, which replaced ECAFE, was adopted after a reorganization in 1974.

### MEMBERS

| | | |
|---|---|---|
| Afghanistan | Korea, Democratic People's Republic | Papua New Guinea |
| Armenia | | Philippines |
| Australia | Korea, Republic | Russia |
| Azerbaijan | Kyrgyzstan | Samoa |
| Bangladesh | Laos | Singapore |
| Bhutan | Malaysia | Solomon Islands |
| Brunei | The Maldives | Sri Lanka |
| Cambodia | Marshall Islands | Tajikistan |
| China, People's Republic | Micronesia, Federated States | Thailand |
| Fiji | Mongolia | Tonga |
| France | Myanmar | Turkey |
| Georgia | Nauru | Turkmenistan |
| India | Nepal | Tuvalu |
| Indonesia | Netherlands | United Kingdom |
| Iran | New Zealand | USA |
| Japan | Pakistan | Uzbekistan |
| Kazakhstan | Palau | Vanuatu |
| Kiribati | | Viet Nam |

### ASSOCIATE MEMBERS

| | | |
|---|---|---|
| American Samoa | Hong Kong | Northern Mariana |
| Cook Islands | Macao | Islands |
| French Polynesia | New Caledonia | |
| Guam | Niue | |

## Organization

(October 2003)

### COMMISSION

The Commission meets annually at ministerial level to examine the region's problems, to review progress, to establish priorities and to decide upon the recommendations of the Executive Secretary or the subsidiary bodies of the Commission.

Ministerial and intergovernmental conferences on specific issues may be held on an *ad hoc* basis with the approval of the Commission, although no more than one ministerial conference and five intergovernmental conferences may be held during one year.

### COMMITTEES AND SPECIAL BODIES

The following advise the Commission and help to oversee the work of the Secretariat:

**Committee on the Environment and Natural Resources Development:** meets annually.

**Committee on Regional Economic-Co-operation:** meets every two years; has a high-level Steering Group, which meets annually to discuss and develop policy options.

**Committee on Socio-economic Measures to Alleviate Poverty in Rural and Urban Areas:** meets annually.

**Committee on Statistics:** meets every two years.

**Committee on Transport, Communications, Tourism and Infrastructure Development:** meets annually.

**Special Body on Least-Developed and Land-locked Developing Countries:** meets every two years.

**Special Body on Pacific Island Developing Countries:** meets every two years.

In addition, an Advisory Committee of permanent representatives and other representatives designated by members of the Commission functions as an advisory body.

### SECRETARIAT

The Secretariat operates under the guidance of the Commission and its subsidiary bodies. It consists of two servicing divisions, covering administration and programme management, in addition to the following substantive divisions: Poverty and Development; Statistics; Trade and Investment; Transport and Tourism; Environment and Sustainable Development; Information, Communication and Space Technology; and Emerging Social Issues.

The Secretariat also includes the ESCAP/UNCTAD Joint Unit on Transnational Corporations and the UN information services.

**Executive Secretary:** Kim Hak-Su (Republic of Korea).

### SUB-REGIONAL OFFICE

**ESCAP Pacific Operations Centre—EPOC:** Private Mail Bag 9004, Port Vila, Vanuatu; tel. 23458; fax 23921; e-mail escap@vanuatu.com.vu; f. 1984, to provide effective advisory and technical assistance at a sub-regional level and to identify the needs of island countries; Dir Nikenike Vurobaravu.

# Activities

ESCAP acts as a UN regional centre, providing the only intergovernmental forum for the whole of Asia and the Pacific, and executing a wide range of development programmes through technical assistance, advisory services to governments, research, training and information.

In 1992 ESCAP began to reorganize its programme activities and conference structures in order to reflect and serve the region's evolving development needs. The approach that was adopted focused on regional economic co-operation, poverty alleviation through economic growth and social development, and environmental and sustainable development. From 2000 a series of administrative reforms were implemented to reorganize the Commission's work into three key areas: Reducing Poverty, Managing Globalization, and Addressing Emerging Social Issues.

**Regional economic co-operation:** Provides technical assistance and advisory services. Aims to enhance institutional capacity-building; gives special emphasis to the needs of least developed, land-locked and island developing countries, and to economies in transition in accelerating their industrial and technological advancement, promoting their exports, and furthering their integration into the region's economy; supports the development of electronic commerce and other information technologies in the region; and promotes the intra-regional and inter-subregional exchange of trade, investment and technology through the strengthening of institutional support services such as regional information networks.

**Development research and policy analysis:** Aims to increase the understanding of the economic and social development situation in the region, with particular attention given to sustainable economic growth, poverty alleviation, the integration of environmental concerns into macroeconomic decisions and policy-making processes, and enhancing the position of the region's disadvantaged economies. The sub-programme is responsible for the provision of technical assistance, and the production of relevant documents and publications.

**Social development:** The main objective is to assess and respond to regional trends and challenges in social policy and human resources development, with particular emphasis on the planning and delivery of social services and training programmes for disadvantaged groups, including the poor, youths, women, the disabled, and the elderly. The sub-programme aims to strengthen the capacity of public and non-government institutions to address the problems of such marginalized social groups and to foster partnerships between governments, the private sector, community organizations and all other involved bodies. Implements global and regional mandates, such as the Programme of Action of the World Summit for Social Development and the Jakarta Plan of Action on Human Resources Development. The Biwako Millennium Framework for Action towards an Inclusive, Barrier-free and Rights-based Society for Persons with Disabilities in Asia and the Pacific was adopted by ESCAP as a regional guide-line underpinning the Asian and Pacific Decade of Disabled Persons (2003–12). In 1998 ESCAP initiated a programme of assistance in establishing a regional network of Social Development Management Information Systems (SOMIS). ESCAP collaborated with other agencies towards the adoption, in November 2001, of a Regional Platform on Sustainable Development for Asia and the Pacific. The Commission undertook regional preparations for the World Summit on Sustainable Development, which was held in Johannesburg, South Africa, in August–September 2002.

**Population and rural and urban development:** Aims to assess and strengthen the capabilities of local institutions in rural and urban development, as well as increasing the capacity of governmental and non-governmental organizations to develop new approaches to poverty alleviation and to support food security for rural households. Promotes the correct use of agro-chemicals in order to increase food supply and to achieve sustainable agricultural development and administers the Fertilizer Advisory Development and Information Network for Asia and the Pacific (FADINAP). Rural employment opportunities and the access of the poor to land, credit and other productive assets are also considered by the sub-programme. Undertakes technical co-operation and research in the areas of ageing, female economic migration and reproductive health, and prepares specific publications relating to population. Implements global and regional mandates, such as the Programme of Action of the International Conference on Population and Development. The Secretariat co-ordinates the Asia-Pacific Population Information Network (POPIN). The fifth Asia and Pacific Population Conference, sponsored by ESCAP, was held in Bangkok, Thailand, in December 2002.

**Environment and natural resources development:** Concerned with strengthening national capabilities to achieve environmentally-sound and sustainable development by integrating economic concerns, such as the sustainable management of natural resources, into economic planning and policies. The sub-programme was responsible for implementation of the Regional Action Programme for Environmentally Sound and Sustainable Development for the period 1996–2000. Other activities have included the promotion of integrated water resources development and management, including water quality and a reduction in water-related natural disasters; strengthening the formulation of policies in the sustainable development of land and mineral resources; the consideration of energy resource options, such as rural energy supply, energy conservation and the planning of power networks; and promotion of the use of space technology applications for environmental management, natural disaster monitoring and sustainable development.

**Transport, communications, tourism and infrastructure development:** Aims to develop inter- and intra-regional transport links to enhance trade and tourism, mainly through implementation of an Asian Land Transport Infrastructure Development (ALTID) programme. ALTID projects include the development of the Trans-Asian Railway and of the Asian Highway road network. Other activities are aimed at improving the planning process in developing infrastructure facilities and services, in accordance with the regional action programme of the New Delhi Action Plan on Infrastructure Development in Asia and the Pacific, which was adopted at a ministerial conference held in October 1996, and at enhancing private sector involvement in national infrastructure development through financing, management, operations and risk-sharing. A Ministerial Conference on Infrastructure Development was organized by ESCAP in November 2001. The meeting concluded a memorandum of understanding, initially signed by ESCAP, Kazakhstan, the Republic of Korea, Mongolia and Russia, to facilitate the transport of container goods along the Trans-Asian Railway. The sub-programme aims to reduce the adverse environmental impact of the provision of infrastructure facilities and to promote more equitable and easier access to social amenities. Tourism concerns include the development of human resources, improved policy planning for tourism development, greater investment in the industry, and minimizing the environmental impact of tourism.

**Statistics:** Provides training and advice in priority areas, including national accounts statistics, gender statistics, population censuses and surveys, and the management of statistical systems. Supports co-ordination throughout the region of the development, implementation and revision of selected international statistical standards. Disseminates comparable socio-economic statistics, with increased use of the electronic media, promotes the use of modern information technology in the public sector and trains senior-level officials in the effective management of information technology.

Throughout all the sub-programmes, ESCAP aims to focus particular attention on the needs and concerns of least developed, land-locked and island developing nations, and economies in transition in the region.

## CO-OPERATION WITH THE ASIAN DEVELOPMENT BANK

In July 1993 a memorandum of understanding was signed by ESCAP and the Asian Development Bank, outlining priority areas of co-operation between the two organizations. These were: regional and sub-regional co-operation; issues concerning the least-developed, land-locked and island developing member countries; poverty alleviation; women in development; population; human resource development; the environment and natural resource management; statistics and data bases; economic analysis; transport and communications; and industrial restructuring and privatization. The two organizations were to co-operate in organizing workshops, seminars and conferences, in implementing joint projects, and in exchanging information and data on a regular basis.

## ASSOCIATED BODIES

**Asian and Pacific Centre for Transfer of Technology:** APCTT Bldg, POB 4575, New Delhi 110 016, India; tel. (11) 26966509; fax (11) 26856274; e-mail infocentre@apctt.org; internet www.apctt.org; f. 1977 to assist countries of the ESCAP region by strengthening their capacity to develop, transfer and adopt technologies relevant to the region, and to identify and to promote regional technology development and transfer; Dir Dr JÜRGEN H. BISCHOFF; publs *Asia Pacific Tech Monitor*, *VATIS Updates on Biotechnology, Food Processing, Ozone Layer Protection, Non-Conventional Energy*, and *Waste Technology* (each every 2 months), *International Technology and Business Opportunities: Catalogue* (quarterly).

**Asian and Pacific Centre for Agricultural Engineering and Machinery—APCAEM:** China International Science & Technology Convention Centre, 12 Yumin Rd, Madian, Deshengmenwai, Chaoyang District, Beijing 100029, People's Republic of China; f. 1977 as Regional Network for Agricultural Engineering and Machinery, elevated to regional centre May 2002; aims to reduce poverty by enhancing technical co-operation throughout the region, and promotes agricultural engineering and machinery and the region's agro-based biotechnologies. Mems: Bangladesh, People's Republic of China, India, Indonesia, Iran, Nepal, Pakistan, Philippines, Republic of Korea, Sri Lanka, Thailand, Viet Nam; Dir TAPIO JUOKSLAHTI.

**ESCAP/WMO Typhoon Committee:** c/o UNDP, POB 7285, ADC, Pasay City, Metro Manila, Philippines; tel. (632) 3733443; fax (2) 3733419; e-mail tcs@philonline.com; f. 1968; an intergovernmental body sponsored by ESCAP and WMO for mitigation of typhoon damage. It aims at establishing efficient typhoon and flood warning systems through improved meteorological and telecommunication facilities. Other activities include promotion of disaster preparedness, training of personnel and co-ordination of research. The committee's programme is supported from national resources and also by UNDP and other international and bilateral assistance. Mems: Cambodia, People's Republic of China, Hong Kong, Japan, Democratic People's Republic of Korea, Republic of Korea, Laos, Macao, Malaysia, Philippines, Singapore, Thailand, USA, Viet Nam; Co-ordinator of Secretariat Dr ROMAN L. KINTANAR.

**Regional Co-ordination Centre for Research and Development of Coarse Grains, Pulses, Roots and Tuber Crops in the Humid Tropics of Asia and the Pacific (CGPRT Centre):** Jalan Merdeka 145, Bogor 16111, Indonesia; tel. (251) 343277; fax (251) 336290; e-mail cgprt@cbn.net.id; internet www.cgprt.org.sg; f. 1981; initiates and promotes research, training and publications on the production, marketing and use of these crops; Dir Dr NOBUYOSHI MAENO; publs *Palawija News* (quarterly), working paper series, monograph series and statistical profiles.

**Statistical Institute for Asia and the Pacific:** JETRO-IDE Building, 2-2 Wakaba 3-chome, Mihama-ku, Chiba-shi, Chiba 2618787, Japan; tel. (43) 2999782; fax (43) 2999780; e-mail staff@ unsiap.or.jp; internet www.unsiap.or.jp; f. 1970; trains government statisticians; prepares teaching materials, provides facilities for special studies and research of a statistical nature, assists in the development of training on official statistics in national and subregional centres; Dir TOMAS P. AFRICA (Philippines).

**WMO/ESCAP Panel on Tropical Cyclones:** Technical Support Unit, c/o Pakistan Meteorological Dept, POB 1214, H-8, Islamabad, Pakistan; tel. (51) 9257314; fax (51) 432588; e-mail tsupmd@hotmail .com; f. 1973 to mitigate damage caused by tropical cyclones in the Bay of Bengal and the Arabian Sea; mems: Bangladesh, India, the Maldives, Myanmar, Pakistan, Sri Lanka, Thailand; Co-ordinator of Secretariat Dr QAMAR-UZ-ZAMAN CHAUDHRY.

# Finance

For the two-year period 2002–03 ESCAP's regular budget, an appropriation from the UN budget, was US $58.8m. The regular budget is supplemented annually by funds from various sources for technical assistance.

# Publications

*Annual Report.*
*Agro-chemicals News in Brief* (quarterly).
*Asia-Pacific Development Journal* (2 a year).
*Asia-Pacific in Figures* (annually).
*Asia-Pacific Population Journal* (quarterly).
*Asia-Pacific Remote Sensing and GIS Journal* (2 a year).
*Atlas of Mineral Resources of the ESCAP Region.*
*Bulletin on Asia-Pacific Perspectives* (annually).
*Confluence* (water resources newsletter, 2 a year).
*Economic and Social Survey of Asia and the Pacific* (annually).
*Environmental News Briefing* (every 2 months).
*ESCAP Energy News* (2 a year).
*ESCAP Human Resources Development Newsletter* (2 a year).
*ESCAP Population Data Sheet* (annually).
*ESCAP Tourism Newsletter* (2 a year).
*Fertilizer Trade Information Monthly Bulletin.*
*Foreign Trade Statistics of Asia and the Pacific* (annually).
*Government Computerization Newsletter* (irregular).
*Industry and Technology Development News for Asia and the Pacific* (annually).
*Poverty Alleviation Initiatives* (quarterly).
*Regional Network for Agricultural Machinery Newsletter* (3 a year).
*Small Industry Bulletin for Asia and the Pacific* (annually).
*Social Development Newsletter* (2 a year).
*Space Technology Applications Newsletter* (quarterly).
*Statistical Indicators for Asia and the Pacific* (quarterly).
*Statistical Newsletter* (quarterly).
*Statistical Yearbook for Asia and the Pacific.*
*Trade and Investment Information Bulletin* (monthly).
*Transport and Communications Bulletin for Asia and the Pacific* (annually).
*Water Resources Journal* (quarterly).

Bibliographies; country and trade profiles; commodity prices; statistics.

# United Nations Children's Fund—UNICEF

**Address:** 3 United Nations Plaza, New York, NY 10017, USA.

**Telephone:** (212) 326-7000; **fax:** (212) 887-7465; **e-mail:** info@unicef.org; **internet:** www.unicef.org.

UNICEF was established in 1946 by the UN General Assembly as the UN International Children's Emergency Fund, to meet the emergency needs of children in post-war Europe and China. In 1950 its mandate was changed to respond to the needs of children in developing countries. In 1953 the General Assembly decided that UNICEF should continue its work, as a permanent arm of the UN system, with an emphasis on programmes giving long-term benefits to children everywhere, particularly those in developing countries. In 1965 UNICEF was awarded the Nobel Peace Prize.

## Organization

(October 2003)

### EXECUTIVE BOARD

The Executive Board, as the governing body of UNICEF, comprises 36 member governments from all regions, elected in rotation for a three-year term by ECOSOC. The Board establishes policy, reviews programmes and approves expenditure. It reports to the General Assembly through ECOSOC.

### SECRETARIAT

The Executive Director of UNICEF is appointed by the UN Secretary-General in consultation with the Executive Board. The administration of UNICEF and the appointment and direction of staff are the responsibility of the Executive Director, under policy directives laid down by the Executive Board, and under a broad authority delegated to the Executive Director by the Secretary-General. In December 2001 there were some 5,600 UNICEF staff positions, of which about 85% were in the field.

**Executive Director:** CAROL BELLAMY (USA).

### REGIONAL OFFICE

UNICEF has a network of eight regional and 126 field offices serving 162 countries and territories. Its offices in Tokyo, Japan, and Brussels, Belgium, support fund-raising activities; UNICEF's supply division is administered from the office in Copenhagen, Denmark. A research centre concerned with child development is based in Florence, Italy.

**Central and Eastern Europe, Commonwealth of Independent States and Baltic States:** Palais des Nations, 1211 Geneva, Switzerland; tel. (22) 9095600; fax (22) 9095909; e-mail ceecisro@unicef.ch.

### NATIONAL COMMITTEES

UNICEF is supported by 37 National Committees, mostly in industrialized countries, whose volunteer members, numbering more than 100,000, raise money through various activities, including the sale of greetings cards. The Committees also undertake advocacy and awareness campaigns on a number of issues and provide an important link with the general public.

## Activities

UNICEF is dedicated to the well-being of children, adolescents and women and works for the realization and protection of their rights within the frameworks of the Convention on the Rights of the Child, which was adopted by the UN General Assembly in 1989 and by 2003 was almost universally ratified, and of the Convention on the Elimination of All Forms of Discrimination Against Women, adopted by the UN General Assembly in 1979. Promoting the full implementation of the Conventions, UNICEF aims to ensure that children world-wide are given the best possible start in life and attain a good level of basic education, and that adolescents are given every opportunity to develop their capabilities and participate successfully in society. The Fund also continues to provide relief and rehabilitation assistance in emergencies. Through its extensive field network in some 162 developing countries and territories, UNICEF undertakes, in co-ordination with governments, local communities and other aid organizations, programmes in health, nutrition, education, water and sanitation, the environment, gender issues and development, and other fields of importance to children. Emphasis is placed on low-cost, community-based programmes. UNICEF programmes are increasingly focused on supporting children and women during critical periods of their life, when intervention can make a lasting difference, i.e. early childhood, the primary school years, adolescence and the reproductive years. Priorities include early years development, immunization strategies, girls' education, combating the spread and impact of HIV/AIDS, and strengthening the protection of children against violence, exploitation and abuse.

UNICEF was instrumental in organizing the World Summit for Children, held in September 1990 and attended by representatives from more than 150 countries, including 71 heads of state or government. The Summit produced a Plan of Action which recognized the rights of the young to 'first call' on their countries' resources and formulated objectives for the year 2000, including: (i) a reduction of the 1990 mortality rates for infants and children under five years by one-third, or to 50–70 per 1,000 live births, whichever is lower; (ii) a reduction of the 1990 maternal mortality rate by one-half; (iii) a reduction by one-half of the 1990 rate for severe malnutrition among children under the age of five; (iv) universal access to safe drinking water and to sanitary means of excreta disposal; and (v) universal access to basic education and completion of primary education by at least 80% of children. UNICEF supported the efforts of governments to achieve progress towards these objectives. The Fund played a leading role in helping governments and other partners prepare for the UN General Assembly special session on Children, which was held in May 2002 to assess the outcome of the 1990 summit and to determine a set of actions and objectives for the next 10 years. At the session the General Assembly adopted a document entitled 'A World Fit for Children', reaffirming its commitment to the agenda of the 1990 summit, and outlining a plan of action for the attainment of new goals and targets in the areas of education, health and the protection of children. A database of economic and social indicators is available at www.unicef.org/information/databases.

The UNICEF Regional Monitoring Project (MONEE) was initiated in 1992 to monitor the effects of economic and social transition on children in Central and South-Eastern Europe and the former USSR. UNICEF publishes on an annual basis a report entitled *Young People in Changing Societies,* assessing the situation of young adults (aged from 15–24 years) residing in Eastern European and Central Asian states with economies in transition. In May 2001 UNICEF supported a conference of high-level representatives of European and Central Asian countries, convened under the auspices of the Governments of Bosnia and Herzegovina and Germany, in Berlin, Germany, to formulate a communal agenda concerning the welfare of children in the region over the coming decade.

In 2000 UNICEF launched a new initiative, the Global Movement for Children—comprising governments, private- and public-sector bodies, and individuals—which aimed to rally world-wide support to improve the lives of all children and adolescents. In April 2001 a 'Say Yes for Children' campaign was adopted by the Global Movement, identifying 10 critical actions required to further its objectives. These were: eliminating all forms of discrimination and exclusion; putting children first; ensuring a caring environment for every child; fighting HIV/AIDS; eradicating violence against and abuse and exploitation of children; listening to children's views; universal education; protecting children from war; safeguarding the earth for children; and combating poverty. UNICEF was to co-ordinate the campaign.

UNICEF, in co-operation with other UN agencies, promotes universal access to and completion of basic and good quality education. The Fund, with UNESCO, UNDP, UNFPA and the World Bank, co-sponsored the World Conference on Education for All, held in Thailand in March 1990, and undertook efforts to achieve the objectives formulated by the conference, which included the elimination of disparities in education between boys and girls. UNICEF participated in and fully supports the objectives and framework for action adopted by the follow-up World Education Forum in Dakar, Senegal, in April 2000. The Fund supports education projects in sub-Saharan Africa, South Asia and countries in the Middle East and North Africa, and implements a Girls' Education Programme in more than 60 developing countries, which aims to increase the enrolment of girls in primary schools. More than 120m. children world-wide, of whom nearly 53% are girls, remain deprived of basic education. In December 2002 UNICEF initiated the '25 by 2005' initiative, which aimed to eliminate gender disparities in education in 25, mainly African and Asian, countries by 2005.

Through UNICEF's efforts the needs and interests of children were incorporated into Agenda 21, which was adopted as a plan of action for sustainable development at the UN Conference on Environment and Development, held in June 1992. In mid-1997, at the UN General Assembly's Special Session on Sustainable Development, UNICEF highlighted the need to improve safe water supply, sanitation and hygiene, and thereby reduce the risk of diarrhoea and other water-borne diseases, as fundamental to fulfilment of child rights. The Fund has supported initiatives to provide the benefits of safe water, sanitation and hygiene education to communities in developing countries. UNICEF also works with UNEP to promote environment issues of common concern and with the World Wide Fund for Nature to support the conservation of local ecosystems.

UNICEF aims to break the cycle of poverty by advocating for the provision of increased development aid to developing countries, and aims to help poor countries obtain debt relief and to ensure access to basic social services. To this end it supports NetAid, an internet-based strategy to promote sustainable development and combat extreme poverty. UNICEF is the leading agency in promoting the 20/20 initiative, which was endorsed at the World Summit for Social Development, held in Copenhagen, Denmark, in March 1995. The initiative encourages developing and donor countries to allocate at least 20% of their domestic budgets and official development aid respectively, to health care, primary education and low-cost safe water and sanitation.

UNICEF estimates that the births of some 50m. children annually are not officially registered, and urges universal registration in order to prevent the abuse of children without proof of age and nationality, for example through trafficking, forced labour, early marriage and military recruitment. The Fund, which vigorously opposes the exploitation of children as a violation of their basic human rights, works with ILO and other partners to promote an end to exploitative and hazardous child labour, and supports special projects to provide education, counselling and care for the estimated 250m. children between the ages of five and 14 years working in developing countries. UNICEF played a major role at the World Congress against Commercial Sexual Exploitation of Children, held in Stockholm, Sweden, in 1996, which adopted a Declaration and Agenda for Action to end the sexual exploitation of children. UNICEF also actively participated in the International Conference on Child Labour held in Oslo, Norway, in November 1997. The Conference adopted an Agenda for Action to eliminate the worst forms of child labour, including slavery-like practices, forced labour, commercial sexual exploitation and the use of children in drugs-trafficking and other hazardous forms of work. UNICEF supports the 1999 ILO Worst Forms of Child Labour Convention, which aims at the prohibition and elimination of the worst forms of child labour. In 1999 UNICEF launched a global initiative, Education as a Preventive Strategy Against Child Labour, with the aim of providing education to children forced to miss school because of work. The Fund helped to draft and promotes full ratification and implementation of an Optional Protocol to the Convention of the Rights of the Child concerning the sale of children, child prostitution and pornography, which was adopted in May 2000 and entered into force in January 2002. UNICEF co-sponsored and actively participated in the Second Congress Against Commercial Sexual Exploitation of Children held in Yokohama, Japan, in December 2001.

Child health is UNICEF's largest programme sector, accounting for some 40% of programme expenditure in 2000. UNICEF estimates that around 10m. children under five years of age die each year, mainly in developing countries, and the majority from largely preventable causes. UNICEF has worked with WHO and other partners to increase global immunization coverage against the following six diseases: measles, poliomyelitis, tuberculosis, diphtheria, whooping cough and tetanus. In 2000 UNICEF, in partnership with WHO, governments and other partners, helped to immunize 550m. children under five years of age in 53 countries against polio. In 1999 UNICEF, WHO, the World Bank and a number of public- and private-sector partners launched the Global Alliance for Vaccines and Immunization (GAVI), which aimed to protect children of all nationalities and socio-economic groups against vaccine-preventable diseases. GAVI's strategy included improving access to sustainable immunization services, expanding the use of existing vaccines, accelerating the development and introduction of new vaccines and technologies and promoting immunization coverage as a focus of international development efforts. UNICEF and WHO also work in conjunction on the Integrated Management of Childhood Illness programme to control diarrhoeal dehydration, a major cause of death among children under five years of age in the developing world. UNICEF-assisted programmes for the control of diarrhoeal diseases promote the low-cost manufacture and distribution of pre-packaged salts or home-made solutions. The use of 'oral rehydration therapy' has risen significantly in recent years, and is believed to prevent more than 1m. child deaths annually. During 1990–2000 diarrhoea-related deaths were reduced by one-half. UNICEF also promotes the need to improve sanitation and access to safe water supplies in developing nations in order to reduce the risk of diarrhoea and other water-borne diseases (see 20/20 initiative, above). To control acute respiratory infections, another leading cause of death in children under five in developing countries, UNICEF works with WHO in training health workers to diagnose and treat the associated diseases. As a result, the level of child deaths from pneumonia and other respiratory infections has been reduced by one-half since 1990. Around 1m. children die from malaria every year, mainly in sub-Saharan Africa. In October 1998 UNICEF, together with WHO, UNDP and the World Bank, inaugurated a new

global campaign, Roll Back Malaria, to fight the disease. UNICEF supports control programmes in more than 30 countries.

According to UNICEF estimates, around 27% of children under five years of age are underweight, while each year malnutrition contributes to about one-half of the child deaths in that age group and leaves millions of others with physical and mental disabilities. More than 2,000m. people world-wide (mainly women and children in developing countries) are estimated to be deficient in one or more essential vitamins and minerals, such as vitamin A, iodine and iron. UNICEF supports national efforts to reduce malnutrition, for example, fortifying staple foods with micronutrients, widening women's access to education, improving household food security and basic health services, and promoting sound child-care and feeding practices. Since 1991 more than 15,000 hospitals in at least 136 countries have been designated 'baby-friendly', having implemented a set of UNICEF and WHO recommendations entitled '10 steps to successful breast-feeding'. In 1996 UNICEF expressed its concern at the impact of international economic embargoes on child health, citing as an example the extensive levels of child malnutrition recorded in Iraq. UNICEF remains actively concerned at the levels of child malnutrition and accompanying diseases in Iraq and in the Democratic People's Republic of Korea, which has also suffered severe food shortages centres.

UNICEF estimates that almost 515,000 women die every year during pregnancy or childbirth, largely because of inadequate maternal health care. For every maternal death, approximately 30 further women suffer permanent injuries or chronic disabilities as a result of complications during pregnancy or childbirth. With its partners in the Safe Motherhood Initiative—UNFPA, WHO, the World Bank, the International Planned Parenthood Federation, the Population Council, and Family Care International—UNICEF promotes measures to reduce maternal mortality and morbidity, including improving access to quality reproductive health services, educating communities about safe motherhood and the rights of women, training midwives, and expanding access to family planning services.

UNICEF is concerned at the danger posed by HIV/AIDS to the realization of children's rights. It is estimated that one-half of all new HIV infections occur in young people. At the end of 2002 3.2m. children under 15 were living with HIV/AIDS. Some 800,000 children under 15 were newly infected during that year, while 610,000 died as a result of AIDS. It was estimated that about one-half of all new HIV infections during 2002 occurred in young people, aged 15–24. It is estimated that more than 13m. children worldwide have lost one or both parents to AIDS since the start of the epidemic. UNICEF's priorities in this area include prevention of infection among young people, reduction in mother-to-child transmission, care and protection of orphans and other vulnerable children, and care and support for children, young people and parents living with HIV/AIDS. UNICEF works closely in this field with governments and co-operates with other UN agencies in the Joint UN Programme on HIV/AIDS (UNAIDS), which became operational on 1 January 1996. In July 2002 UNICEF, UNAIDS and WHO jointly produced a study entitled *Young People and HIV/AIDS: Opportunity in Crisis*, examining young people's sexual behaviour patterns and knowledge of HIV/AIDS.

At December 2001 it was estimated that 85,000 females aged from 15–24 and 340,000 males in that age group were living with HIV/AIDS in Central Europe, South-Eastern Europe and the CIS.

UNICEF provides emergency relief assistance, supports education, health, mine-awareness and psychosocial activities and helps to demobilize and rehabilitate child soldiers in countries and territories affected by violence and social disintegration. It assists children orphaned or separated from their parents and made homeless through armed conflict. In recent years several such emergency operations have been undertaken, including in Afghanistan, Angola, Burundi, Kosovo, Liberia, Sierra Leone and Sudan. In 1999 UNICEF adopted a Peace and Security Agenda to help guide international efforts in this field. Emergency education assistance includes the provision of 'Edukits' in refugee camps and the reconstruction of school buildings. In the area of health the Fund co-operates with WHO to arrange 'days of tranquility' in order to facilitate the immunization of children in conflict zones. Psychosocial assistance activities include special programmes to assist traumatized children and help unaccompanied children to be reunited with parents or extended families.

UNICEF has provided medical supplies, basic educational materials and other items to aid those displaced by the insecurity that has prevailed in the North Caucasus region since late 1999. UNICEF has condemned the killing of women and children there.

An estimated 300,000 children are involved in armed conflicts as soldiers, porters and forced labourers. UNICEF encourages ratification of the Optional Protocol to the Convention on the Rights of the Child on the involvement of children in armed conflict, which was adopted by the General Assembly in May 2000 and entered into force in February 2002, and bans the compulsory recruitment of combatants below 18 years. The Fund also urges states to make unequivocal statements endorsing 18 as the minimum age of voluntary recruitment to the armed forces. UNICEF was an active participant in the so-called 'Ottawa' process (supported by the Canadian Government) to negotiate an international ban on anti-personnel land-mines which, it was estimated, killed and maimed between 8,000 and 10,000 children every year. The Convention on the Prohibition of the Use, Stockpiling, Production and Transfer of Anti-Personnel Mines and on their Destruction was adopted in December 1997 and entered into force in March 1999. By January 2003 the Convention had been ratified by 131 countries. UNICEF is committed to campaigning for its universal ratification and full implementation, and also supports mine-awareness campaigns.

## Finance

UNICEF is funded by voluntary contributions from governments and non-governmental and private-sector sources. Total income in 2000 amounted to US $1,139m., of which 64% was from governments and intergovernmental organizations. Total expenditure in 2000 amounted to $1,111m.

UNICEF's income is divided into contributions for 'regular resources' (used for country programmes of co-operation approved by the Executive Board, programme support, and management and administration costs) and contributions for 'other resources' (for special purposes, including expanding the outreach of country programmes of co-operation and ensuring capacity to deliver critical assistance to women and children for example during humanitarian crises). In 2000 contributions for 'regular resources' totalled US $563m. and those for 'other resources' amounted to $576m.

## Publications

*Facts and Figures* (in English, French and Spanish).

*The State of the World's Children* (annually, in Arabic, English, French, Russian and Spanish and about 30 other national languages).

*UNICEF Annual Report* (in English, French and Spanish).

*UNICEF at a Glance* (annually, in English, French and Spanish).

Reports; series on children and women; nutrition; education; children's rights; children in wars and disasters; working children; water; sanitation and the environment; analyses of the situation of children and women in individual developing countries.

# United Nations Development Programme—UNDP

**Address:** One United Nations Plaza, New York, NY 10017, USA.

**Telephone:** (212) 906-5295; **fax:** (212) 906-5364; **e-mail:** hq@undp .org; **internet:** www.undp.org.

The Programme was established in 1965 by the UN General Assembly. Its central mission is to help countries to eradicate poverty and achieve a sustainable level of human development, an approach to economic growth that encompasses individual well-being and choice, equitable distribution of the benefits of development, and conservation of the environment. UNDP advocates for a more inclusive global economy.

## Organization

(October 2003)

UNDP is responsible to the UN General Assembly, to which it reports through ECOSOC.

### EXECUTIVE BOARD

The Executive Board is responsible for providing intergovernmental support to, and supervision of, the activities of UNDP and the UN Population Fund (UNFPA). It comprises 36 members: eight from Africa, seven from Asia, four from eastern Europe, five from Latin America and the Caribbean and 12 from western Europe and other countries.

### SECRETARIAT

In recent years UNDP has implemented a process aimed at restructuring and improving the efficiency of its administration. Offices and divisions at the Secretariat include: an Operations Support Group; Offices of the United Nations Development Group, the Human Development Report, Audit and Performance Review, and Communications; and Bureaux for Crisis Prevention and Recovery, Resources and Strategic Partnerships, Development Policy, and Management. Five regional bureaux, all headed by an assistant administrator, cover: Africa; Asia and the Pacific; the Arab states; Latin America and the Caribbean; and Europe and the Commonwealth of Independent States. There is also a Division for Global and Interregional Programmes.

**Administrator:** MARK MALLOCH BROWN (United Kingdom).

**Associate Administrator:** Dr ZÉPHIRIN DIABRÉ (Burkina Faso).

**Assistant Administrator and Director, Regional Bureau for Europe and the CIS:** KALMAN MIZSEI (Hungary).

### COUNTRY OFFICES

In almost every country receiving UNDP assistance there is an office, headed by the UNDP Resident Representative, who usually also serves as UN Resident Co-ordinator, responsible for the co-ordination of all UN technical assistance and operational development activities, advising the Government on formulating the country programme, ensuring that field activities are undertaken,

and acting as the leader of the UN team of experts working in the country. The offices function as the primary presence of the UN in most developing countries.

### OFFICES OF UNDP REPRESENTATIVES IN EASTERN EUROPE, RUSSIA AND CENTRAL ASIA

**Armenia:** 375010 Yerevan, Karl Liebknecht St 14; tel. (1) 56-60-73; fax (1) 54-38-11; e-mail registry.am@undp.am; internet www.undp .am; Rep. LISE GRANDE.

**Azerbaijan:** Baku 1001, UN 50th Anniversary St 3; tel. (12) 98-98-88; fax (12) 98-32-35; e-mail registry.az@undp.org; internet www .un-az.org/undp; Rep. MARCO BORSOTTI.

**Belarus:** 220050 Minsk, vul. Kirov 17, 6th Floor; tel. (172) 27-48-76; fax (172) 26-03-40; e-mail fo.blr@undp.org; internet www.un.minsk .by; Rep. FLAVIA BUSTREO.

**Georgia:** 380079 Tbilisi, Eristavi 9, UN House; tel. (32) 25-11-26; fax (32) 25-02-71; e-mail registry.ge@undp.org; internet www.undp .org.ge; Rep. LANCE CLARK.

**Kazakhstan:** 480091 Almaty, Tole bi 67; tel. (3272) 58-26-43; fax (3272) 58-26-45; e-mail registry.kz@undp.org; internet www.undp .kz; Rep. FIKRET AKCURA.

**Kyrgyzstan:** 720040 Bishkek, pr. Chui 160; tel. (312) 61-12-13; fax (312) 61-12-17; e-mail office@undp.kg; internet www.undp.kg; Rep. JERZY SKURATOWICZ.

**Moldova:** 277012 Chişinău-2012, str. 31 August 131; tel. (2) 22-00-45; fax (2) 22-00-41; e-mail registry.md@undp.org; internet www .undp.md; Rep. SOREN TEJNO.

**Russian Federation:** 119034 Moscow, ul. Ostozhenka 28; tel. (095) 787-21-00; fax (095) 787-21-01; e-mail office@undp.ru; internet www .undp.ru; Rep. STEFAN VASSILEV.

**Tajikistan:** Dushanbe 734024, kuchai Aini 39; tel. (372) 21-06-70; fax (372) 51-00-21; e-mail registry.tj@undp.org; internet www.untj .org/undp; Rep. MATTHEW KAHANE.

**Turkmenistan:** 744000 Ashgabat, ul. Atabayeva 40; tel. (12) 41-01-77; fax (12) 41-31-56; e-mail registry.tm@undp.org; internet www .untuk.org; Rep. KHALED PHILBY.

**Ukraine:** 01021 Kiev, Klovsky Uzviz 1; tel. (44) 253-93-63; fax (44) 253-26-07; e-mail registry.ua@undp.org; internet www.un.kiev.ua; Rep. DOUGLAS GARDNER.

**Uzbekistan:** 700029 Tashkent, ul. Taras Shevchenko 4, Rm 601–604; tel. (71) 120-61-67; fax (71) 139-69-65; e-mail registry.uz@undp .org; internet www.undp.uz; Rep. RICHARD CONROY.

## Activities

As the world's largest source of grant-funded technical assistance for developing countries, UNDP provides advisory and support services to governments and UN teams. Assistance is mostly non-monetary, comprising the provision of experts' services, consultancies, equipment and training for local workers, including fellowships for advanced study abroad. UNDP supports programme countries in attracting aid and utilizing it efficiently. The Programme is committed to allocating some 88% of its regular resources to low-income developing countries. Developing countries themselves contribute significantly to the total project costs in terms of personnel, facilities, equipment and supplies.

Since the mid-1990s UNDP has strengthened its focus on results, streamlining its management practices and promoting clearly defined objectives for the advancement of sustainable human development. Under 'UNDP 2001', an extensive internal process of reform initiated during the late 1990s, UNDP placed increased emphasis on its activities in the field and on performance and accountability, focusing on the following priority areas: democratic governance; poverty reduction; crisis prevention and recovery; energy and environment; promotion of information and communications technology; and combating HIV/AIDS. In 2001 UNDP established six Thematic Trust Funds, covering each of these areas, to enable increased support of thematic programme activities. Gender equality and the provision of country-level and co-ordination services are also important focus areas. In accordance with the more results-oriented approach developed under the 'UNDP 2001' process the Programme introduced a new Multi-Year Funding Framework (MYFF), the first phase of which covered the period 2000–03. The MYFF outlines the country-driven goals around which funding is to be mobilized, integrating programme objectives, resources, budget and outcomes. It provides the basis for the Administrator's Business Plans for the same duration and enables policy coherence in the implementation of programmes at country, regional and global levels. A Results-Oriented Annual Report (ROAR) was produced for the first time in 2000 from data compiled by country offices and regional programmes. It was hoped that UNDP's greater focus on performance would generate increased voluntary contributions from donors, thereby strengthening the Programme's core resource base. In September 2000 the first ever Ministerial Meeting of ministers of development co-operation and foreign affairs and other senior officials from donor and programme countries, convened in New York, USA, endorsed UNDP's shift to a results-based orientation.

From the mid-1990s UNDP also determined to assume a more active and integrative role within the UN system-wide development framework. UNDP Resident Representatives—usually also serving as UN Resident Co-ordinators, with responsibility for managing inter-agency co-operation on sustainable human development initiatives at country level—were to play a focal role in implementing this approach. In order to promote its co-ordinating function UNDP allocated increased resources to training and skill-sharing programmes. In late 1997 the UNDP Administrator was appointed to chair the UN Development Group (UNDG), which was established as part of a series of structural reform measures initiated by the UN Secretary-General, with the aim of strengthening collaboration between all UN funds, programmes and bodies concerned with development. The UNDG promotes coherent policy at country level through the system of UN Resident Co-ordinators (see above), the Common Country Assessment mechanism (CCA, a country-based process for evaluating national development situations), and the UN Development Assistance Framework (UNDAF, the foundation for planning and co-ordinating development operations at country level, based on the CCA). Within the framework of the Administrator's Business Plans for 2000–03 a new Bureau for Resources and Strategic Partnerships was established to build and strengthen working partnerships with other UN bodies, donor and programme countries, international financial institutions and development banks, civil society organizations and the private sector. The Bureau was also to serve UNDP's regional bureaux and country offices through the exchange of information and promotion of partnership strategies.

UNDP has a catalyst and co-ordinating function as the focus of UN system-wide efforts to achieve the so-called Millennium Development Goals (MDGs), pledged by governments attending a summit meeting of the UN General Assembly in September 2000. The objectives included a reduction by 50% in the number of people with income of less than US $1 a day and those suffering from hunger and lack of safe drinking water by 2015. Other commitments made concerned equal access to education for girls and boys, the provision of universal primary education, the reduction of maternal mortality by 75%, and the reversal of the spread of HIV/AIDS and other diseases. UNDP plays a leading role in efforts to integrate the MDGs into all aspects of the UN activities at country level. The Programme supports the formulation of MDG Reports for all developing countries.

UNDP aims to help governments to reassess their development priorities and to design initiatives for sustainable human development. UNDP country offices support the formulation of national human development reports (NHDRs), which aim to facilitate activities such as policy-making, the allocation of resources and monitoring progress towards poverty eradication and sustainable development. In addition, the preparation of Advisory Notes and Country

Co-operation Frameworks by UNDP officials helps to high-light country-specific aspects of poverty eradiction and national strategic priorities. In January 1998 the Executive Board adopted eight guiding principles relating to sustainable human development that were to be implemented by all country offices, in order to ensure a focus to UNDP activities. A network of nine Sub-regional Resource Facilities (SURFs) has been established to strengthen and co-ordinate UNDP's technical assistance services. Since 1990 UNDP has published an annual *Human Development Report*, incorporating a Human Development Index, which ranks countries in terms of human development, using three key indicators: life expectancy, adult literacy and basic income required for a decent standard of living. In 1997 a Human Poverty Index and a Gender-related Development Index, which assesses gender equality on the basis of life expectancy, education and income, were introduced into the Report for the first time.

UNDP's activities to facilitate poverty eradication include support for capacity-building programmes and initiatives to generate sustainable livelihoods, for example by improving access to credit, land and technologies, and the promotion of strategies to improve education and health provision for the poorest elements of populations (with a focus on women and girls). In 1996 UNDP launched the Poverty Strategies Initiative (PSI) to strengthen national capacities to assess and monitor the extent of poverty and to combat the problem. All PSI projects were to involve representatives of governments, the private sector, social organizations and research institutions in policy debate and formulation. In early 1997 a UNDP scheme to support private-sector and community-based initiatives to generate employment opportunities, MicroStart, became operational. With the World Bank, UNDP helps governments of developing countries applying for international debt relief to draft Poverty Reduction Stategy Papers.

Approximately one-quarter of all UNDP programme resources support national efforts to ensure efficient and accountable governance and to build effective relations between the state, the private sector and civil society, which are essential to achieving sustainable development. UNDP undertakes assessment missions to help ensure free and fair elections and works to promote human rights, a transparent and competent public sector, a competent judicial system and decentralized government and decision-making. Within the context of the UN System-wide Special Initiative on Africa, UNDP supports the Africa Governance Forum which convenes annually to consider aspects of governance and development. In July 1997 UNDP organized an International Conference on Governance for Sustainable Growth and Equity, which was held in New York, USA. At the World Conference on Governance held in Manila, the Philippines, in May/June 1999, UNDP sponsored a series of meetings held on the subject of Building Capacities for Governance. In April of that year UNDP and the Office of the High Commissioner for Human Rights launched a joint programme to strengthen capacity-building in order to promote the integration of human rights issues into activities concerned with sustainable human development.

In 1997 the Regional Bureau for Europe and the CIS (RBEC) initiated a programme to provide technical support to countries making the transition towards democratic institutions and free-market economies. The programme aimed to focus on public sector reform; decentralization, including strengthening local governments; support for parliaments; establishment of ombudsman institutions; participation and strengthening of civil society; and supreme audit and evaluation capacity, in order to promote transparency, accountability and effective management.

UNDP plays a role in developing the agenda for international cooperation on environmental and energy issues, focusing on the relationship between energy policies, environmental protection, poverty and development. UNDP supports the development of national programmes that emphasize the sustainable management of natural resources, for example through its Sustainable Energy Initiative, which promotes more efficient use of energy resources and the introduction of renewable alternatives to conventional fuels. UNDP is also concerned with forest management, the aquatic environment and sustainable agriculture and food security. Within UNDP's framework of urban development activities the Local Initiative Facility for Urban Environment (LIFE) undertakes small-scale environmental projects in low-income communities, in collaboration with local authorities and community-based groups. Other initiatives include the Urban Management Programme and the Public–Private Partnerships Programme for the Urban Environment, which aimed to generate funds, promote research and support new technologies to enhance sustainable environments in urban areas. In 1996 UNDP initiated a process of collaboration between city authorities world-wide to promote implementation of the commitments made at the 1995 Copenhagen summit for social development (see below) and to help to combat aspects of poverty and other urban problems, such as poor housing, transport, the management of waste disposal, water supply and sanitation. The first Forum of the so-called World Alliance of Cities Against Poverty was convened in October 1998, in Lyon, France. The second Forum took place in

April 2000 in Geneva, Switzerland, and the third Forum was held in April 2002 in Huy, Belgium.

In September 2001 UNDP, with the World Bank, UNEP and Global Environment Facility, approved a new fund, comprising resources of some US $100m., in support of a strategic partnership to reduce nutrient emissions and toxic contamination of the Danube/Black Sea Basin. UNDP was to focus on legal and policy reform at national level, monitoring systems, the development of environmental indicators and promoting public participation.

UNDP collaborates with other UN agencies in countries in crisis and with special circumstances to promote relief and development efforts, in order to secure the foundations for sustainable human development and thereby increase national capabilities to prevent or pre-empt future crises. In particular, UNDP is concerned to achieve reconciliation, reintegration and reconstruction in affected countries, as well as to support emergency interventions and management and delivery of programme aid. In 1995 the Executive Board decided that 5% of total UNDP regular resources be allocated to countries in 'special development situations', i.e. urgently requiring major, integrated external support. Special development initiatives include the demobilization of former combatants, rehabilitation of communities for the sustainable reintegration of returning populations, the restoration and strengthening of democratic institutions, and clearance of anti-personnel landmines. UNDP has established a mine action unit within its Bureau for Crisis Prevention and Recovery in order to strengthen national de-mining capabilities. In December 1996 UNDP launched the Civilian Reconstruction Teams programme, creating some 5,000 jobs for former combatants in Liberia to work on the rehabilitation of that country's infrastructure. UNDP is the focal point within the UN system for strengthening national capacities for natural disaster reduction (prevention, preparedness and mitigation relating to natural, environmental and technological hazards). UNDP's Disaster Management Programme oversees the system-wide Disaster Management Training Programme.

UNDP supports the Tumen River Area Development Programme, under which Russia, the People's Republic of China, the Democratic People's Republic of Korea, the Republic of Korea and Mongolia collaborate to study the feasibility of joint development activity. In December 1995 the Governments agreed to pursue more formal arrangements for promoting economic and technical co-operation in the Tumen River Economic Development Area. A Secretariat, to administer an intergovernmental Consultation Commission and a Co-ordination Committee, was subsequently established in Beijing, People's Republic of China.

UNDP is a co-sponsor, jointly with WHO, the World Bank, UNICEF, UNESCO, UNDCP, ILO, UNFPA and WFP, of the Joint UN Programme on HIV/AIDS (UNAIDS), which became operational on 1 January 1996. UNAIDS co-ordinates UNDP's HIV and Development Programme. UNDP regards the HIV/AIDS pandemic as a major challenge to development, and advocates for making HIV/AIDS a focus of national planning; supports decentralized action against HIV/AIDS at community level; helps to strengthen national capacities at all levels to combat the disease; and aims to link support for prevention activities, education and treatment with broader development planning and responses. UNDP places a particular focus on combating the spread of HIV/AIDS through the promotion of women's rights. Within the UN system UNDP also has responsibility for co-ordinating activities following global UN conferences. In March 1995 government representatives attending the World Summit for Social Development, which was held in Copenhagen, Denmark, approved initiatives to promote the eradication of poverty, to increase and reallocate official development assistance to basic social programmes and to promote equal access to education. The Programme of Action adopted at the meeting advocated that UNDP support the implementation of social development programmes, co-ordinate these efforts through its field offices and organize efforts on the part of the UN system to stimulate capacity-building at local, national and regional levels. The PSI (see above) was introduced following the summit. A special session of the General Assembly to review the implementation of the summit's objectives was convened in June 2000. Following the UN Fourth World Conference on Women, held in Beijing, People's Republic of China, in September 1995, UNDP led inter-agency efforts to ensure the full participation of women in all economic, political and professional activities, and assisted with further situation analysis and training activities. (UNDP also created a Gender in Development Office to ensure that women participate more fully in UNDP-sponsored activities.) In June 2000 a special session of the General Assembly (Beijing + 5) was convened to review the conference. UNDP played an important role, at both national and international levels, in preparing for the second UN Conference on Human Settlements (Habitat II), which was held in İstanbul, Turkey, in June 1996 (see UN Human Settlements Programme). At the conference UNDP announced the establishment of a new facility, which was designed to promote private-sector investment in urban infrastructure. A special session of the UN General Assembly, entitled

İstanbul + 5, was held in June 2001 to report on the implementation of the recommendations of the Habitat II conference.

UNDP aims to ensure that, rather than creating an ever-widening 'digital divide', ongoing rapid advancements in information technology are harnessed by poorer countries to accelerate progress in achieving sustainable human development. UNDP advises governments on technology policy, promotes digital entrepreneurship in programme countries and works with private-sector partners to provide reliable and affordable communications networks. The Bureau for Development Policy operates the Information and Communication Technologies for Development Programme, which aims to promote sustainable human development through increased utilization of information and communications technologies globally. The Programme aims to establish technology access centres in developing countries. A Sustainable Development Networking Programme focuses on expanding internet connectivity in poorer countries through building national capacities and supporting local internet sites. UNDP has used mobile internet units to train people even in isolated rural areas. In 1999 UNDP, in collaboration with an international communications company, Cisco Systems, and other partners, launched NetAid, an internet-based forum (accessible at www.netaid.org) for mobilizing and co-ordinating fundraising and other activities aimed at alleviating poverty and promoting sustainable human development in the developing world. With Cisco Systems and other partners, UNDP has worked to establish academies of information technology to support training and capacity-building in developing countries. By September 2003 88 academies had been established. UNDP and the World Bank jointly host the secretariat of the Digital Opportunity Task Force, a partnership between industrialized and developing countries, business and non-governmental organizations that was established in 2000. UNDP is a partner in the Global Digital Technology Initiative, launched in 2002 to strengthen the role of information and communications technologies in achieving the development goals of developing countries.

In 1996 UNDP implemented its first corporate communications and advocacy strategy, which aimed to generate public awareness of the activities of the UN system, to promote debate on development issues and to mobilize resources by increasing public and donor appreciation of UNDP. UNDP sponsors the International Day for the Eradication of Poverty, held annually on 17 October.

## Finance

UNDP and its various funds and programmes are financed by the voluntary contributions of members of the United Nations and the Programme's participating agencies, as well as through cost-sharing by recipient governments and third-party donors. In 2002 total voluntary contributions amounted to an estimated US $2,830m., of which $670m. was for regular (core) resources. Third-party co-financing amounted to $935m. in 2002 and thematic trust fund income totalled $64m., while cost-sharing by programme country governments amounted to more than $1,000m. In 2002 some $744m. was allocated to governance (40.2% of total programme expenditure), $493m. (26.7%) to poverty reduction and gender, $315m. (17.0%) to crisis prevention and recovery, and $298m. (16.1%) to energy and environment.

## Publications

*Annual Report of the Administrator.*

*Choices* (quarterly).

*Global Public Goods: International Co-operation in the 21st Century.*

*Human Development Report* (annually, also available on CD-ROM).

*Poverty Report* (annually).

*Results-Oriented Annual Report.*

## Associated Funds and Programmes

UNDP is the central funding, planning and co-ordinating body for technical co-operation within the UN system. A number of associated funds and programmes, financed separately by means of voluntary contributions, provide specific services through the UNDP network. UNDP manages a trust fund to promote economic and technical co-operation among developing countries.

### GLOBAL ENVIRONMENT FACILITY—GEF

The GEF, which is managed jointly by UNDP, the World Bank and UNEP, began operations in 1991 and was restructured in 1994. Its aim is to support projects concerning climate change, the conservation of biological diversity, the protection of international waters, reducing the depletion of the ozone layer in the atmosphere, and (since October 2002) arresting land degradation and addressing the issue of persistent organic pollutants. The GEF acts as the financial mechanism for the Convention on Biological Diversity and the UN Framework Convention on Climate Change. UNDP is responsible for capacity-building, targeted research, pre-investment activities and technical assistance. UNDP also administers the Small Grants Programme of the GEF, which supports community-based activities by local non-governmental organizations, and the Country Dialogue Workshop Programme, which promotes dialogue on national priorities with regard to the GEF. In August 2002 32 donor countries pledged $2,920m. for the third periodic replenishment of GEF funds (GEF-3), covering the period 2002–06. During 1991–2002 the GEF allocated $4,000m. in grants and raised $12,000m. in co-financing from other sources in support of more than 1,000 projects in more than 140 developing nations.

**Chair. and CEO:** Dr LEONARD GOOD (Canada).

## MONTREAL PROTOCOL

UNDP assists countries to eliminate the use of ozone-depleting substances (ODS), in accordance with the Montreal Protocol to the Vienna Convention for the Protection of the Ozone Layer, through the design, monitoring and evaluation of ODS phase-out projects and programmes. In particular, UNDP provides technical assistance and training, national capacity-building and demonstration projects and technology transfer investment projects. By mid-2001, through the Executive Committee of the Montreal Protocol, UNDP had completed 822 projects and activities concerned with eliminating ozone-depleting substances.

## UNDP DRYLANDS DEVELOPMENT CENTRE—DDC

The Centre, based in Nairobi, Kenya, was established in February 2002, superseding the former UN Office to Combat Desertification and Drought (UNSO). (UNSO had been established following the conclusion, in October 1994, of the UN Convention to Combat Desertification in Those Countries Experiencing Serious Drought and/or Desertification, Particularly in Africa; in turn, UNSO had replaced the former UN Sudano-Sahelian Office.) The DDC was to focus on the following areas: ensuring that national development planning takes account of the needs of dryland communities, particularly in poverty reduction strategies; helping countries to cope with the effects of climate variability, especially drought, and to prepare for future climate change; and addressing local issues affecting the utilization of resources.

**Director:** PHILIP DOBIE.

## UNITED NATIONS DEVELOPMENT FUND FOR WOMEN— UNIFEM

UNIFEM is the UN's lead agency in addressing the issues relating to women in development and promoting the rights of women worldwide. The Fund provides direct financial and technical support to enable low-income women in developing countries to increase earnings, gain access to labour-saving technologies and otherwise improve the quality of their lives. It also funds activities that include women in decision-making related to mainstream development projects. In 2001 UNIFEM approved 67 new projects and continued to support some 204 ongoing programmes world-wide. In that year UNIFEM's Trust Fund in Support of Actions to Eliminate Violence Against Women (established in 1996) provided grants to 21 national and regional programmes. During 1996–2001 the Trust Fund awarded grants totalling US $5.3m. in support of 127 initiatives in more than 70 countries. UNIFEM has supported the preparation of national reports in 30 countries and used the priorities identified in these reports and in other regional initiatives to formulate a Women's Development Agenda for the 21st century. Through these efforts, UNIFEM played an active role in the preparation for the UN Fourth World Conference on Women, which was held in Beijing, People's Republic of China, in September 1995. UNIFEM participated at a special session of the General Assembly convened in June 2000 to review the conference, entitled Women 2000: Gender Equality, Development and Peace for the 21st Century (Beijing + 5). In March 2001 UNIFEM, in collaboration with International Alert, launched a Millennium Peace Prize for Women. In January 2002 UNIFEM appealed for US $12m. to support women's leadership in the ongoing peace-building and reconstruction process in Afghanistan. UNIFEM maintains that the empowerment of women is a key to combating the HIV/AIDS pandemic, in view of the fact that women and adolescent girls are often culturally, biologically and economically more vulnerable to infection and more likely to bear responsibility for caring for the sick. In March 2002 UNIFEM launched a three-year programme aimed at making the gender and human rights dimensions of the pandemic central to policy-making in ten countries. A new online resource (www.genderandaids.org) on the gender dimensions of HIV/AIDS was launched in February 2003. UNIFEM was a co-founder of WomenWatch (accessible online at www.un.org/womenwatch), a UN system-wide resource for the advancement of gender equality. Programme expenditure in 2001 totalled $25.4m.

### Headquarters

304 East 45th St, 15th Floor, New York, NY 10017, USA; tel. (212) 906-6400; fax (212) 906-6705; e-mail unifem@undp.org; internet www.unifem.org.

**Director:** NOELEEN HEYZER (Singapore).

## UNITED NATIONS VOLUNTEERS—UNV

The United Nations Volunteers is an important source of middle-level skills for the UN development system supplied at modest cost, particularly in the least-developed countries. Volunteers expand the scope of UNDP project activities by supplementing the work of international and host-country experts and by extending the influence of projects to local community levels. UNV also supports technical co-operation within and among the developing countries by encouraging volunteers from the countries themselves and by forming regional exchange teams comprising such volunteers. UNV is involved in areas such as peace-building, elections, human rights, humanitarian relief and community-based environmental programmes, in addition to development activities.

The UN International Short-term Advisory (UNISTAR) Programme, which is the private-sector development arm of UNV, has increasingly focused its attention on countries in the process of economic transition. Since 1994 UNV has administered UNDP's Transfer of Knowledge Through Expatriate Nationals (TOKTEN) programme, which was initiated in 1977 to enable specialists and professionals from developing countries to contribute to development efforts in their countries of origin through short-term technical assignments.

At September 2003 3,395 UNVs were serving in 132 countries. At that time the total number of people who had served under the initiative amounted to more than 30,000 in some 140 countries.

### Headquarters

POB 260111, 53153 Bonn, Germany; tel. (228) 8152000; fax (228) 8152001; e-mail information@unvolunteers.org; internet www.unvolunteers.org.

**Executive Co-ordinator:** (vacant).

# United Nations Environment Programme—UNEP

**Address:** POB 30552, Nairobi, Kenya.

**Telephone:** (20) 621234; **fax:** (20) 624489; **e-mail:** cpiinfo@unep.org; **internet:** www.unep.org.

The United Nations Environment Programme was established in 1972 by the UN General Assembly, following recommendations of the 1972 UN Conference on the Human Environment, in Stockholm, Sweden, to encourage international co-operation in matters relating to the human environment.

## Organization

(October 2003)

### GOVERNING COUNCIL

The main functions of the Governing Council, which meets every two years, are to promote international co-operation in the field of the environment and to provide general policy guidance for the direction and co-ordination of environmental programmes within the UN system. It comprises representatives of 58 states, elected by the UN General Assembly, for four-year terms, on a regional basis. The Council is assisted in its work by a Committee of Permanent Representatives.

### HIGH-LEVEL COMMITTEE OF MINISTERS AND OFFICIALS IN CHARGE OF THE ENVIRONMENT

The Committee was established by the Governing Council in 1997, with a mandate to consider the international environmental agenda and to make recommendations to the Council on reform and policy issues. In addition, the Committee, comprising 36 elected members, was to provide guidance and advice to the Executive Director, to enhance UNEP's collaboration and co-operation with other multilateral bodies and to help to mobilize financial resources for UNEP.

### SECRETARIAT

Offices and divisions at UNEP headquarters include the Office of the Executive Director; the Secretariat for Governing Bodies: Offices for Evaluation and Oversight, Programme Co-ordination and Management, and Resource Mobilization; and divisions of communications and public information, early warning and assessment, policy development and law, policy implementation, technology and industry and economics, regional co-operation and representation, environmental conventions, and Global Environment Facility co-ordination.

**Executive Director:** Dr KLAUS TÖPFER (Germany).

### REGIONAL OFFICE

**Europe:** 11–13 chemin des Anémones, 1219 Châtelaine, Geneva, Switzerland; tel. (22) 9178279; fax (22) 9178024; e-mail roe@unep.ch; internet www.unep.ch/roe.

### OTHER OFFICES

**Convention on International Trade in Endangered Species of Wild Fauna and Flora— CITES:** 15 chemin des Anémones, 1219 Châtelaine, Geneva, Switzerland; tel. (22) 9178139; fax (22) 7973417; e-mail cites@unep.ch; internet www.cites.org; Sec.-Gen. WILLEM WOUTER WIJNSTEKERS (Netherlands).

**Global Programme of Action for the Protection of the Marine Environment from Land-based Activities:** POB 16227, 2500 The Hague, Netherlands; tel. (70) 3114460; fax (70) 3456648; e-mail gpa@unep.nl; internet www.gpa.unep.org; Co-ordinator Dr VEERLE VANDEWEERD.

**Secretariat of the Basel Convention:** CP 356, 13–15 chemin des Anémones, 1219 Châtelaine, Geneva, Switzerland; tel. (22) 9178218; fax (22) 7973454; e-mail sbc@unep.ch; internet www.basel.int; Exec. Sec. SACHIKO KUWABARA-YAMAMOTO.

**Secretariat of the Convention on Biological Diversity:** World Trade Centre, 393 St Jacques St West, Suite 300, Montréal, QC, Canada H2Y 1N9; tel. (514) 288-2220; fax (514) 288-6588; e-mail secretariat@biodiv.org; internet www.biodiv.org; Exec. Sec. HAMDALLAH ZEDAN.

**Secretariat of the Multilateral Fund for the Implementation of the Montreal Protocol:** 1800 McGill College Ave, 27th Floor, Montréal, QC, Canada H3A 3J6; tel. (514) 282-1122; fax (514) 282-0068; e-mail secretariat@unmfs.org; internet www.unmfs.org; Chief Dr OMAR EL-ARINI.

**Secretariat of the UN Framework Convention on Climate Change:** Haus Carstanjen, Martin-Luther-King-Str. 8, 53175 Bonn, Germany; tel. (228) 815-1000; fax (228) 815-1999; e-mail secretariat@unfccc.de; internet www.unfccc.de; Exec. Sec. JOKE WALLER-HUNTER.

**UNEP/CMS (Convention on the Conservation of Migratory Species of Wild Animals) Secretariat:** Martin-Luther-King-Str. 8, 53175 Bonn, Germany; tel. (228) 8152401; fax (228) 8152449; e-mail cms@unep.de; internet www.wcmc.org.uk/cms; Exec. Sec. ARNULF MÜLLER-HELMBRECHT.

**UNEP Chemicals:** International Environment House, 11–13 chemin des Anémones, 1219 Châtelaine, Geneva, Switzerland; tel. (22) 9171234; fax (22) 7973460; e-mail chemicals@unep.ch; internet www.chem.unep.ch; Dir JAMES B. WILLIS.

**UNEP Division of Technology, Industry and Economics:** Tour Mirabeau, 39–43, Quai André Citroën, 75739 Paris Cédex 15, France; tel. 1-44-37-14-41; fax 1-44-37-14-74; e-mail unep.tie@unep.fr; internet www.uneptie.org/; Officer-in-Charge PER BAKKEN.

**UNEP International Environmental Technology Centre— IETC:** 2–110 Ryokuchi koen, Tsurumi-ku, Osaka 538-0036, Japan; tel. (6) 6915-4581; fax (6) 6915-0304; e-mail ietc@unep.or.jp; internet www.unep.or.jp; Dir STEVE HALLS.

**UNEP Ozone Secretariat:** POB 30552, Nairobi, Kenya; tel. (20) 623850; fax (20) 623913; e-mail ozoneinfo@unep.org; internet www.unep.org/ozone/; Officer-in-Charge MICHAEL GRABER.

**UNEP Secretariat for the UN Scientific Committee on the Effects of Atomic Radiation:** Vienna International Centre, Wagramerstrasse 5, POB 500, 1400 Vienna, Austria; tel. (1) 26060-4330; fax (1) 26060-5902; e-mail norman.gentner@unvienna.org; internet www.unscear.org; Sec. Dr NORMAN GENTNER.

## Activities

UNEP serves as a focal point for environmental action within the UN system. It aims to maintain a constant watch on the changing state of the environment; to analyse the trends; to assess the problems using a wide range of data and techniques; and to promote projects leading to environmentally sound development. It plays a catalytic and co-ordinating role within and beyond the UN system. Many UNEP projects are implemented in co-operation with other UN agencies, particularly UNDP, the World Bank group, FAO, UNESCO and WHO. About 45 intergovernmental organizations outside the UN system and 60 international non-governmental organizations have official observer status on UNEP's Governing Council, and, through the Environment Liaison Centre in Nairobi, UNEP is linked to more than 6,000 non-governmental bodies concerned with the environment. UNEP also sponsors international conferences, programmes, plans and agreements regarding all aspects of the environment.

In February 1997 the Governing Council, at its 19th session, adopted a ministerial declaration (the Nairobi Declaration) on UNEP's future role and mandate, which recognized the organization as the principal UN body working in the field of the environment and as the leading global environmental authority, setting and overseeing the international environmental agenda. In June a special session of the UN General Assembly, referred to as the 'Rio + 5', was convened to review the state of the environment and progress achieved in implementing the objectives of the UN Conference on Environment and Development (UNCED), held in Rio de Janeiro, Brazil, in June 1992. The meeting adopted a Programme for Further Implementation of Agenda 21 (a programme of activities to promote sustainable development, adopted by UNCED) in order to intensify efforts in areas such as energy, freshwater resources and technology transfer. The meeting confirmed UNEP's essential role in advancing the Programme and as a global authority promoting a coherent legal and political approach to the environmental challenges of sustainable development. An extensive process of restructuring and realignment of functions was subsequently initiated by UNEP, and a new organizational structure reflecting the decisions of the Nairobi Declaration was implemented during 1999. UNEP played a leading role in preparing for the World Summit on Sustainable Development (WSSD), held in August–September 2002 in Johannesburg, South Africa, to assess strategies for strengthening the implementation of Agenda 21. Governments participating in the conference adopted the Johannesburg Declaration and WSSD Plan of Implementation, in which they strongly reaffirmed commitment to the principles underlying Agenda 21 and also pledged support to all internationally-agreed development goals, including the UN Millennium Development Goals adopted by governments attending a summit meeting of the UN General Assembly in September 2000. Participating governments made concrete commitments to attaining several specific objectives in the areas of water, energy, health, agriculture and fisheries, and biodiversity. These included a reduction by one-half in the proportion of people world-wide lacking access to clean water or good sanitation by 2015, the restocking of depleted fisheries by 2015, a reduction in the ongoing loss in biodiversity by 2010, and the production and utilization of chemicals without causing harm to human beings and the environment by 2020. Participants determined to increase usage of renewable energy sources and to develop by 2005 integrated water resources management and water efficiency plans. A large number of partnerships between governments, private sector interests and civil society groups were announced at the conference.

In May 2000 UNEP sponsored the first annual Global Ministerial Environment Forum (GMEF), held in Malmö, Sweden, and attended by environment ministers and other government delegates from more than 130 countries. Participants reviewed policy issues in the field of the environment and addressed issues such as the impact on the environment of population growth, the depletion of earth's natural resources, climate change and the need for fresh water supplies. The Forum issued the Malmö Declaration, which identified the effective implementation of international agreements on environmental matters at national level as the most pressing challenge for policy-makers. The Declaration emphasized the importance of mobilizing domestic and international resources and urged increased co-operation from civil society and the private sector in achieving sustainable development. The second GMEF, held in Nairobi in February 2001, addressed means of strengthening international environmental governance, establishing an Open-Ended Intergovernmental Group of Ministers or Their Representatives (IGM) to prepare a report on possible reforms. GMEF-3, held in Cartagena, Colombia, in February 2002, considered UNEP's participation in the forthcoming WSSD, with a focus on environmental guidance issues.

## ENVIRONMENTAL ASSESSMENT AND EARLY WARNING

The Nairobi Declaration resolved that the strengthening of UNEP's information, monitoring and assessment capabilities was a crucial element of the organization's restructuring, in order to help establish priorities for international, national and regional action, and to ensure the efficient and accurate dissemination of emerging environmental trends and emergencies.

In 1995 UNEP launched the Global Environment Outlook (GEO) process of environmental assessment. UNEP is assisted in its analysis of the state of the global environment by an extensive network of collaborating centres. Reports on the process are issued every two–three years. (The first *Global Environment Outlook, GEO-I,* was published in January 1997, and the second, *GEO 2000,* in September 1999, and *GEO-3* in May 2002.) The following regional and national *GEO* reports have been produced: *Africa Environment Outlook* (2002), *Brazil Environment Outlook* (2002), *Latin America and the Caribbean—Environment Outlook 2000, North America's Environment* (2002), *Pacific Islands Environment Outlook* (1999), and *Western Indian Ocean Environment Outlook* (1999). UNEP is leading a major Global International Waters Assessment (GIWA) to consider all aspects of the world's water-related issues, in particular problems of shared transboundary waters, and of future sustainable management of water resources. UNEP is also a sponsoring agency of the Joint Group of Experts on the Scientific Aspects of Marine Environmental Pollution and contributes to the preparation of reports on the state of the marine environment and on the impact of land-based activities on that environment. In November 1995 UNEP published a Global Biodiversity Assessment, which was the first comprehensive study of biological resources throughout the world. The UNEP—World Conservation Monitoring Centre (UNEP—WCMC), established in June 2000, provides biodiversity-related assessment. UNEP is a partner in the International Coral Reef Action Network—ICRAN, which was established in 2000 to manage and protect coral reefs world-wide. In June 2001 UNEP launched the Millennium Ecosystems Assessment, which is expected to be completed in 2004. Other major assessments under way in 2002 included GIWA (see above); the Assessment of Impact and Adaptation to Climate Change; the Solar and Wind Energy Resource Assessment; the Regionally-Based Assessment of Persistent Toxic Substances; the Land Degradation Assessment in Drylands; and the Global Methodology for Mapping Human Impacts on the Biosphere (GLOBIO) project.

UNEP's environmental information network includes the Global Resource Information Database (GRID), which converts collected data into information usable by decision-makers. The UNEP-INFOTERRA programme facilitates the exchange of environmental information through an extensive network of national 'focal points'. By late 2003 177 countries were participating in the network. Through UNEP-INFOTERRA UNEP promotes public access to environmental information, as well as participation in environmental concerns. UNEP aims to establish in every developing region an Environment and Natural Resource Information Network (ENRIN)

in order to make available technical advice and manage environmental information and data for improved decision-making and action-planning in countries most in need of assistance. UNEP aims to integrate its information resources in order to improve access to information and to promote its international exchange. This has been pursued through UNEPnet, an internet-based interactive environmental information- and data-sharing facility, and Mercure, a telecommunications service using satellite technology to link a network of 16 earth stations throughout the world.

UNEP's information, monitoring and assessment structures also serve to enhance early-warning capabilities and to provide accurate information during an environmental emergency.

## POLICY DEVELOPMENT AND LAW

UNEP aims to promote the development of policy tools and guidelines in order to achieve the sustainable management of the world environment. At a national level it assists governments to develop and implement appropriate environmental instruments and aims to co-ordinate policy initiatives. Training workshops in various aspects of environmental law and its applications are conducted. UNEP supports the development of new legal, economic and other policy instruments to improve the effectiveness of existing environmental agreements.

UNEP was instrumental in the drafting of a Convention on Biological Diversity (CBD) to preserve the immense variety of plant and animal species, in particular those threatened with extinction. The Convention entered into force at the end of 1993; by December 2002 187 countries and the European Community were parties to the CBD. The CBD's Cartagena Protocol on Biosafety (so called as it had been addressed at an extraordinary session of parties to the CBD convened in Cartagena, Colombia, in February 1999) was adopted at a meeting of parties to the CBD held in Montréal, Canada, in January 2000, and entered into force in September 2003, having been ratified by 57 states and the European Community. The Protocol regulates the transboundary movement and use of living modified organisms resulting from biotechnology in order to reduce any potential adverse effects on biodiversity and human health. It establishes an Advanced Informed Agreement procedure to govern the import of such organisms. In January 2002 UNEP launched a major project aimed at supporting developing countries with assessing the potential health and environmental risks and benefits of genetically-modified (GM) crops, in preparation for the Protocol's entry into force. In February the parties to the CBD and other partners convened a conference, in Montréal, to address ways in which the traditional knowledge and practices of local communities could be preserved and used to conserve highly-threatened species and ecosystems. The sixth conference of parties to the CBD, held in April 2002, adopted detailed voluntary guide-lines concerning access to genetic resources and sharing the benefits attained from such resources with the countries and local communities where they originate; a global work programme on forests; and a set of guiding principles for combating alien invasive species. UNEP supports co-operation for biodiversity assessment and management in selected developing regions and for the development of strategies for the conservation and sustainable exploitation of individual threatened species (e.g. the Global Tiger Action Plan). It also provides assistance for the preparation of individual country studies and strategies to strengthen national biodiversity management and research. UNEP administers the Convention on International Trade in Endangered Species of Wild Flora and Fauna (CITES), which entered into force in 1975.

In October 1994 87 countries, meeting under UN auspices, signed a Convention to Combat Desertification (see UNDP Drylands Development Centre), which aimed to provide a legal framework to counter the degradation of drylands. An estimated 75% of all drylands have suffered some land degradation, affecting approximately 1,000m. people in 110 countries. UNEP continues to support the implementation of the Convention, as part of its efforts to protect land resources. UNEP also aims to improve the assessment of dryland degradation and desertification in co-operation with governments and other international bodies, as well as identifying the causes of degradation and measures to overcome these.

UNEP is the lead UN agency for promoting environmentally sustainable water management. It regards the unsustainable use of water as the most urgent environmental and sustainable development issue, and estimates that two-thirds of the world's population will suffer chronic water shortages by 2025, owing to rising demand for drinking water as a result of growing populations, decreasing quality of water because of pollution, and increasing requirements of industries and agriculture. In 2000 UNEP adopted a new water policy and strategy, comprising assessment, management and co-ordination components. The Global International Waters Assessment (see above) is the primary framework for the assessment component. The management component includes the Global Programme of Action (GPA) for the Protection of the Marine Environment from Land-based Activities (adopted in November 1995), and

UNEP's freshwater programme and regional seas programme. The GPA for the Protection of the Marine Environment for Land-based Activities focuses on the effects of activities such as pollution on freshwater resources, marine biodiversity and the coastal ecosystems of small-island developing states. UNEP aims to develop a similar global instrument to ensure the integrated management of freshwater resources. It promotes international co-operation in the management of river basins and coastal areas and for the development of tools and guide-lines to achieve the sustainable management of freshwater and coastal resources. UNEP provides scientific, technical and administrative support to facilitate the implementation and co-ordination of 14 regional seas conventions and 13 regional plans of action, and is developing a strategy to strengthen collaboration in their implementation. The new water policy and strategy emphasizes the need for improved co-ordination of existing activities. UNEP aims to play an enhanced role within relevant co-ordination mechanisms, such as the UN open-ended informal consultation process on oceans and the law of the sea.

In 1996 UNEP, in collaboration with FAO, began to work towards promoting and formulating a legally binding international convention on prior informed consent (PIC) for hazardous chemicals and pesticides in international trade, extending a voluntary PIC procedure of information exchange undertaken by more than 100 governments since 1991. The Convention was adopted at a conference held in Rotterdam, Netherlands, in September 1998, and was to enter into force on being ratified by 50 signatory states. It aimed to reduce risks to human health and the environment by restricting the production, export and use of hazardous substances and enhancing information exchange procedures. By March 2003 the Convention had been ratified by 41 signatory states.

In conjunction with UN-Habitat, UNDP, the World Bank and other organizations and institutions, UNEP promotes environmental concerns in urban planning and management through the Sustainable Cities Programme, as well as regional workshops concerned with urban pollution and the impact of transportation systems. In 1994 UNEP inaugurated an International Environmental Technology Centre (IETC), with offices in Osaka and Shiga, Japan, in order to strengthen the capabilities of developing countries and countries with economies in transition to promote environmentally-sound management of cities and freshwater reservoirs through technology co-operation and partnerships.

UNEP has played a key role in global efforts to combat risks to the ozone layer, resultant climatic changes and atmospheric pollution. UNEP worked in collaboration with the World Meteorological Organization to formulate the UN Framework Convention on Climate Change (UNFCCC), with the aim of reducing the emission of gases that have a warming effect on the atmosphere, and has remained an active participant in the ongoing process to review and enforce the implementation of the Convention and of its Kyoto Protocol. UNEP was the lead agency in formulating the 1987 Montreal Protocol to the Vienna Convention for the Protection of the Ozone Layer (1985), which provided for a 50% reduction in the production of chlorofluorocarbons (CFCs) by 2000. An amendment to the Protocol was adopted in 1990, which required complete cessation of the production of CFCs by 2000 in industrialized countries and by 2010 in developing countries; these deadlines were advanced to 1996 and 2006, respectively, in November 1992. In 1997 the ninth Conference of the Parties (COP) to the Vienna Convention adopted a further amendment which aimed to introduce a licensing system for all controlled substances. The eleventh COP, meeting in Beijing, People's Republic of China, in November–December 1999, adopted the Beijing Amendment, which imposed tighter controls on the import and export of hydrochlorofluorocarbons, and on the production and consumption of bromochloromethane (Halon-1011, an industrial solvent and fire extinguisher). The Beijing Amendment entered into force in December 2001. A Multilateral Fund for the Implementation of the Montreal Protocol was established in June 1990 to promote the use of suitable technologies and the transfer of technologies to developing countries. UNEP, UNDP, the World Bank and UNIDO are the sponsors of the Fund, which by July 2001 had approved financing for some 3,850 projects in 124 developing countries at a cost of US $1,200m. Commitments of $440m. were made to the fourth replenishment of the Fund, covering the three-year period 2000–02.

## POLICY IMPLEMENTATION

UNEP's Division of Environmental Policy Implementation incorporates two main functions: technical co-operation and response to environmental emergencies.

With the UN Office for the Co-ordination of Humanitarian Assistance (OCHA), UNEP has established a joint Environment Unit to mobilize and co-ordinate international assistance and expertise for countries facing environmental emergencies and natural disasters. In mid-1999 UNEP and UN-Habitat jointly established a Balkan Task Force (subsequently renamed UNEP Balkans Unit) to assess the environmental impact of NATO's aerial offensive against the Federal Republic of Yugoslavia (now Serbia and Montenegro). In November 2000 the Unit led a field assessment to evaluate reports of environmental contamination by debris from NATO ammunition containing depleted uranium. A final report, issued by UNEP in March 2001, concluded that there was no evidence of widespread contamination of the ground surface by depleted uranium and that the radiological and toxicological risk to the local population was negligible. It stated, however, that considerable scientific uncertainties remained, for example as to the safety of groundwater and the longer-term behaviour of depleted uranium in the environment, and recommended precautionary action. In December 2001 UNEP established a new Post-conflict Assessment Unit, which replaced, and extended the scope of, the Balkans Unit. In 2003 the Post-conflict Assessment Unit was undertaking activities in Afghanistan as well as the Balkans, and was compiling desk assessments of the state of the environment in Iraq and the Palestinian territories.

UNEP, together with UNDP and the World Bank, is an implementing agency of the Global Environment Facility (GEF), which was established in 1991 as a mechanism for international co-operation in projects concerned with biological diversity, climate change, international waters and depletion of the ozone layer. UNEP services the Scientific and Technical Advisory Panel, which provides expert advice on GEF programmes and operational strategies.

Through the GEF UNEP supports the Caspian Environment Program (CEP, accessible at www.caspianenvironment.org), which was founded in 1995 by the Governments of Azerbaijan, Iran, Kazakhstan, Russia and Turkmenistan, and aims to reduce pollution in and to promote the sustainable management of the bioresources of the Caspian Sea.

## TECHNOLOGY, INDUSTRY AND ECONOMICS

The use of inappropriate industrial technologies and the widespread adoption of unsustainable production and consumption patterns have been identified as being inefficient in the use of renewable resources and wasteful, in particular in the use of energy and water. UNEP aims to encourage governments and the private sector to develop and adopt policies and practices that are cleaner and safer, make efficient use of natural resources, incorporate environmental costs, ensure the environmentally sound management of chemicals, and reduce pollution and risks to human health and the environment. In collaboration with other organizations and agencies UNEP works to define and formulate international guide-lines and agreements to address these issues. UNEP also promotes the transfer of appropriate technologies and organizes conferences and training workshops to provide sustainable production practices. Relevant information is disseminated through the International Cleaner Production Information Clearing House. UNEP, together with UNIDO, has established eight National Cleaner Production Centres to promote a preventive approach to industrial pollution control. In October 1998 UNEP adopted an International Declaration on Cleaner Production, with a commitment to implement cleaner and more sustainable production methods and to monitor results; the Declaration had 267 signatories at December 2001, including representatives of 45 governments. In 1997 UNEP and the Coalition for Environmentally Responsible Economies initiated the Global Reporting Initiative, which, with participation by corporations, business associations and other organizations and stakeholders, develops guide-lines for voluntary reporting by companies on their economic, environmental and social performance. In April 2002 UNEP launched the 'Life-Cycle Initiative', which aims to assist governments, businesses and other consumers with adopting environmentally-sound policies and practice, in view the upward trend in global consumption patterns.

UNEP provides institutional servicing to the Basel Convention on the Control of Transboundary Movements of Hazardous Wastes and their Disposal, which was adopted in 1989 with the aim of preventing the disposal of wastes from industrialized countries in countries that have no processing facilities. In March 1994 the second meeting of parties to the Convention determined to ban the exportation of hazardous wastes between industrialized and developing countries. The third meeting of parties to the Convention, held in 1995, proposed that the ban should be incorporated into the Convention as an amendment. The resulting so-called Ban Amendment (prohibiting exports of hazardous wastes for final disposal and recycling from states parties also belonging to OECD and, or, the European Union, and from Liechtenstein, to any other state party to the Convention) required ratification by three-quarters of the 62 signatory states present at the time of adoption before it could enter into effect; by February 2003 the Ban Amendment had been ratified by 36 parties. In 1998 the technical working group of the Convention agreed a new procedure for clarifying the classification and characterization of specific hazardous wastes. The fifth full meeting of parties to the Convention, held in December 1999, adopted the Basel Declaration outlining an agenda for the period 2000–10, with a particular focus on minimizing the production of hazardous wastes. At February 2003 the number of parties to the Convention totalled

155. In December 1999 132 states adopted a Protocol to the Convention to address issues relating to liability and compensation for damages from waste exports. The governments also agreed to establish a multilateral fund to finance immediate clean-up operations following any environmental accident.

The UNEP Chemicals office was established to promote the sound management of hazardous substances, central to which has been the International Register of Potentially Toxic Chemicals (IRPTC). UNEP aims to facilitate access to data on chemicals and hazardous wastes, in order to assess and control health and environmental risks, by using the IRPTC as a clearing house facility of relevant information and by publishing information and technical reports on the impact of the use of chemicals.

The UNEP Chemicals office and the Russian Centre for International Projects (CIP) together run the CIP Project on Strengthening of National Chemicals Management in the CIS Countries. In 2003 work was progressing towards the introduction of Pollutant Release and Transfer Registers (PRTRs), for collecting and disseminating data on toxic emissions, in Armenia, Azerbaijan, Belarus, Georgia, Kazakhstan, Moldova, the Russian Federation, Tajikistan, Ukraine and Uzbekistan.

UNEP's OzonAction Programme works to promote information exchange, training and technological awareness. Its objective is to strengthen the capacity of governments and industry in developing countries to undertake measures towards the cost-effective phasing-out of ozone-depleting substances. UNEP also encourages the development of alternative and renewable sources of energy. To achieve this, UNEP is supporting the establishment of a network of centres to research and exchange information of environmentally-sound energy technology resources.

### REGIONAL CO-OPERATION AND REPRESENTATION

UNEP maintains six regional offices. These work to initiate and promote UNEP objectives and to ensure that all programme formulation and delivery meets the specific needs of countries and regions. They also provide a focal point for building national, subregional and regional partnership and enhancing local participation in UNEP initiatives. Following UNEP's reorganization a co-ordination office was established at headquarters to promote regional policy integration, to co-ordinate programme planning, and to provide necessary services to the regional offices.

UNEP provides administrative support to several regional conventions, for example the Lusaka Agreement on Co-operative Enforcement Operations Directed at Illegal Trade in Wild Flora and Fauna, which entered into force in December 1996 having been concluded under UNEP auspices in order to strengthen the implementation of the CBD and CITES in Eastern and Central Africa. UNEP also organizes conferences, workshops and seminars at national and regional levels, and may extend advisory services or technical assistance to individual governments.

### CONVENTIONS

UNEP aims to develop and promote international environmental legislation in order to pursue an integrated response to global environmental issues, to enhance collaboration among existing convention secetariats, and to co-ordinate support to implement the work programmes of international instruments.

UNEP has been an active participant in the formulation of several major conventions (see above). The Division of Environmental Conventions is mandated to assist the Division of Policy Development and Law in the formulation of new agreements or protocols to existing conventions. Following the successful adoption of the Rotterdam Convention in September 1998, UNEP played a leading role in formulating a multilateral agreement to reduce and ultimately eliminate the manufacture and use of Persistent Organic Pollutants (POPs), which are considered to be a major global environmental hazard. The agreement on POPs, concluded in December 2000 at a conference sponsored by UNEP in Johannesburg, South Africa, was adopted by 127 countries in May 2001.

UNEP has been designated to provide secretariat functions to a number of global and regional environmental conventions (see above for list of offices).

UNEP is the secretariat for the Pan-European Biological and Landscape Diversity Strategy. UNEP also supports the preparation of an additional Protocol on Water and Health to the ECE Convention on Transboundary Waters, and a European Charter on Transport, Environment and Health.

### COMMUNICATIONS AND PUBLIC INFORMATION

UNEP's public education campaigns and outreach programmes promote community involvement in environmental issues. Further communication of environmental concerns is undertaken through the media, an information centre service and special promotional events, including World Environment Day, photograph competitions, and the awarding of the Sasakawa Prize (to recognize distinguished service to the environment by individuals and groups) and of the Global 500 Award for Environmental Achievement. In 1996 UNEP initiated a Global Environment Citizenship Programme to promote acknowledgment of the environmental responsibilities of all sectors of society.

# Finance

UNEP derives its finances from the regular budget of the United Nations and from voluntary contributions to the Environment Fund. A budget of US $119.9m. was authorized for the two-year period 2002–03, of which $100m. was for programme activities, $14.9m. for management and administration, and $5m. for fund programme reserves.

# Publications

*Annual Report.*

*APELL Newsletter* (2 a year).

*Cleaner Production Newsletter* (2 a year).

*Climate Change Bulletin* (quarterly).

*Connect* (UNESCO-UNEP newsletter on environmental degradation, quarterly).

*Earth Views* (quarterly).

*Environment Forum* (quarterly).

*Environmental Law Bulletin* (2 a year).

*Financial Services Initiative* (2 a year).

*GEF News* (quarterly).

*Global Environment Outlook* (every 2–3 years).

*Global Water Review.*

*GPA Newsletter.*

*IETC Insight* (3 a year).

*Industry and Environment Review* (quarterly).

*Leave it to Us* (children's magazine, 2 a year).

*Managing Hazardous Waste* (2 a year).

*Our Planet* (quarterly).

*OzonAction Newsletter* (quarterly).

*Tierramerica* (weekly).

*Tourism Focus* (2 a year).

*UNEP Chemicals Newsletter* (2 a year).

*UNEP Update* (monthly).

*World Atlas of Coral Reefs.*

*World Atlas of Biodiversity.*

*World Atlas of Desertification.*

Studies, reports, legal texts, technical guide-lines, etc.

# United Nations High Commissioner for Refugees— UNHCR

**Address:** CP 2500, 1211 Geneva 2 dépôt, Switzerland.
**Telephone:** (22) 7398111; **fax:** (22) 7397312; **e-mail:** unhcr@unhcr
.ch; **internet:** www.unhcr.ch.

The Office of the High Commissioner was established in 1951 to provide international protection for refugees and to seek durable solutions to their problems.

## Organization

(October 2003)

### HIGH COMMISSIONER

The High Commissioner is elected by the United Nations General Assembly on the nomination of the Secretary-General, and is responsible to the General Assembly and to the UN Economic and Social Council (ECOSOC).

**High Commissioner:** RUUD LUBBERS (Netherlands).
**Deputy High Commissioner:** MARY ANN WYRSCH (USA).

### EXECUTIVE COMMITTEE

The Executive Committee of the High Commissioner's Programme (ExCom), established by ECOSOC, gives the High Commissioner policy directives in respect of material assistance programmes and advice in the field of international protection. In addition, it oversees UNHCR's general policies and use of funds. ExCom, which comprises representatives of 57 states, both members and non-members of the UN, meets once a year.

### ADMINISTRATION

Headquarters include the Executive Office, comprising the offices of the High Commissioner, the Deputy High Commissioner and the Assistant High Commissioner. There are separate offices for the Inspector General, the Special Envoy in the former Yugoslavia, and the Director of the UNHCR liaison office in New York. The other principal administrative units are the Division of Communication and Information, the Department of International Protection, the Division of Resource Management, and the Department of Operations, which is responsible for the five regional bureaux covering Africa; Asia and the Pacific; Europe; the Americas and the Caribbean; and Central Asia, South-West Asia, North Africa and the Middle East. At July 2002 there were 268 UNHCR field offices in 114 countries. At that time UNHCR employed 5,523 people, including short-term staff, of whom 4,654 (or 84%) were working in the field.

## Activities

The competence of the High Commissioner extends to any person who, owing to well-founded fear of being persecuted for reasons of race, religion, nationality or political opinion, is outside the country of his or her nationality and is unable or, owing to such fear or for reasons other than personal convenience, remains unwilling to accept the protection of that country; or who, not having a nationality and being outside the country of his or her former habitual residence, is unable or, owing to such fear or for reasons other than personal convenience, is unwilling to return to it. This competence may be extended, by resolutions of the UN General Assembly and decisions of ExCom, to cover certain other 'persons of concern', in addition to refugees meeting these criteria. Refugees who are assisted by other UN agencies, or who have the same rights or obligations as nationals of their country of residence, are outside the mandate of UNHCR.

In recent years there has been a significant shift in UNHCR's focus of activities. Increasingly UNHCR has been called upon to support people who have been displaced within their own country (i.e. with similar needs to those of refugees but who have not crossed an international border) or those threatened with displacement as a result of armed conflict. In addition, greater support has been given to refugees who have returned to their country of origin, to assist their reintegration, and UNHCR is working to enable local communities to support the returnees, frequently through the implementation of Quick Impact Projects (QIPs).

At December 2002 the refugee population world-wide provisionally totalled 10.4m. and UNHCR was also concerned with more than 1m. asylum-seekers, 2.4m. recently returned refugees and 6.7m.

others (of whom an estimated 4.6m. were internally displaced persons—IDPs).

World Refugee Day, sponsored by UNHCR, is held annually on 20 June.

### INTERNATIONAL PROTECTION

As laid down in the Statute of the Office, UNHCR's primary function is to extend international protection to refugees and its second function is to seek durable solutions to their problems. In the exercise of its mandate UNHCR seeks to ensure that refugees and asylum-seekers are protected against *refoulement* (forcible return), that they receive asylum, and that they are treated according to internationally recognized standards. UNHCR pursues these objectives by a variety of means that include promoting the conclusion and ratification by states of international conventions for the protection of refugees. UNHCR promotes the adoption of liberal practices of asylum by states, so that refugees and asylum-seekers are granted admission, at least on a temporary basis.

The most comprehensive instrument concerning refugees that has been elaborated at the international level is the 1951 United Nations Convention relating to the Status of Refugees. This Convention, the scope of which was extended by a Protocol adopted in 1967, defines the rights and duties of refugees and contains provisions dealing with a variety of matters which affect the day-to-day lives of refugees. The application of the Convention and its Protocol is supervised by UNHCR. Important provisions for the treatment of refugees are also contained in a number of instruments adopted at the regional level. These include the 1969 Convention Governing the Specific Aspects of Refugee Problems adopted by OAU (now AU) member states in 1969, the European Agreement on the Abolition of Visas for Refugees, and the 1969 American Convention on Human Rights.

UNHCR has actively encouraged states to accede to the 1951 United Nations Refugee Convention and the 1967 Protocol: 145 states had acceded to either or both of these basic refugee instruments by December 2002. An increasing number of states have also adopted domestic legislation and/or administrative measures to implement the international instruments, particularly in the field of procedures for the determination of refugee status. UNHCR has sought to address the specific needs of refugee women and children, and has also attempted to deal with the problem of military attacks on refugee camps, by adopting and encouraging the acceptance of a set of principles to ensure the safety of refugees. In recent years it has formulated a strategy designed to address the fundamental causes of refugee flows. In 2001, in response to widespread concern about perceived high numbers of asylum-seekers and large-scale international economic migration and human trafficking, UNHCR initiated a series of Global Consultations on International Protection with the signatories to the 1951 Convention and 1967 Protocol, and other interested parties, with a view to strengthening both the application and scope of international refugee legislation. A consultation of 156 Governments, convened in Geneva, in December, reaffirmed commitment to the central role played by the Convention and Protocol. The final consultation, held in May 2002, focused on durable solutions and the protection of refugee women and children. Subsequently, based on the findings of the Global Consultations process, UNHCR developed an Agenda on Protection with six main objectives: strengthening the implementation of the 1951 Convention and 1967 Protocol; the protection of refugees within broader migration movements; more equitable sharing of burdens and responsibilities and building of capacities to receive and protect refugees; addressing more effectively security-related concerns; increasing efforts to find durable solutions; and meeting the protection needs of refugee women and children. The Agenda was endorsed by the Executive Council in October 2002.

### ASSISTANCE ACTIVITIES

The first phase of an assistance operation uses UNHCR's capacity of emergency preparedness and response. This enables UNHCR to address the immediate needs of refugees at short notice, for example, by employing specially trained emergency teams and maintaining stockpiles of basic equipment, medical aid and materials. A significant proportion of UNHCR expenditure is allocated to the next phase of an operation, providing 'care and maintenance' in stable refugee circumstances. This assistance can take various forms, including the provision of food, shelter, medical care and essential supplies. Also covered in many instances are basic services, including education and counselling.

As far as possible, assistance is geared towards the identification and implementation of durable solutions to refugee problems—this being the second statutory responsibility of UNHCR. Such solutions generally take one of three forms: voluntary repatriation, local integration or resettlement in another country. Voluntary repatriation is increasingly the preferred solution, given the easing of political tension in many regions from which refugees have fled. Where voluntary repatriation is feasible, the Office assists refugees to overcome obstacles preventing their return to their country of origin. This may be done through negotiations with governments involved, or by providing funds either for the physical movement of refugees or for the rehabilitation of returnees once back in their own country.

When voluntary repatriation is not an option, efforts are made to assist refugees to integrate locally and to become self-supporting in their countries of asylum. This may be done either by granting loans to refugees, or by assisting them, through vocational training or in other ways, to learn a skill and to establish themselves in gainful occupations. One major form of assistance to help refugees reestablish themselves outside camps is the provision of housing. In cases where resettlement through emigration is the only viable solution to a refugee problem, UNHCR negotiates with governments in an endeavour to obtain suitable resettlement opportunities, to encourage liberalization of admission criteria and to draw up special immigration schemes. During 2000 an estimated 39,500 refugees were resettled under UNHCR auspices.

In the early 1990s UNHCR aimed to consolidate efforts to integrate certain priorities into its programme planning and implementation, as a standard discipline in all phases of assistance. The considerations include awareness of specific problems confronting refugee women, the needs of refugee children, the environmental impact of refugee programmes and long-term development objectives. In an effort to improve the effectiveness of its programmes, UNHCR has initiated a process of delegating authority, as well as responsibility for operational budgets, to its regional and field representatives, increasing flexibility and accountability. An Evaluation and Policy Analysis Unit reviews systematically UNHCR's operational effectiveness.

## CENTRAL ASIA

In late 1992 people began to flee civil conflict in Tajikistan and to seek refuge in Afghanistan. During 1993 an emergency UNHCR operation established a reception camp to provide the 60,000 Tajik refugees with basic assistance, and began to move them away from the border area to safety. In December a tripartite agreement was concluded by UNHCR and the Tajik and Afghan Governments regarding the security of refugees returning to Tajikistan. UNHCR monitored the repatriation process and provided materials for the construction of almost 20,000 homes. The operation was concluded by the end of 1997. Nevertheless, at the end of 2000, there were still nearly 60,000 Tajik refugees remaining in other countries of the former USSR, of whom 14,120 were receiving assistance from UNHCR. During 2000–02 an initiative was being implemented to integrate locally some 10,000 Tajik refugees of Kyrgyz ethnic origin in Kyrgyzstan and 12,500 Tajik refugees of Turkmen origin in Turkmenistan. Some 2,500 Tajik refugees were expected to return to Tajikistan in 2002. From late 2001 about 9,000 Afghan refugees repatriated from Tajikistan under the auspices of UNHCR and the International Organization for Migration. UNHCR expressed concern following the adoption by the Tajikistan authorities in May 2002 of refugee legislation that reportedly contravened the 1951 Convention relating to the Status of Refugees and its 1967 Protocol.

## EASTERN EUROPE

In December 1992 UNHCR dispatched teams to establish offices in both Armenia and Azerbaijan to assist people displaced as a result of the war between the two countries and to provide immediate relief. A cease-fire agreement was signed between the two sides in May 1994, although violations of the accord were subsequently reported and relations between the two countries remained tense. At the end of 2002 the region was still supporting a massive displaced population, including 247,538 Azerbaijani refugees in Armenia and 577,179 IDPs of concern to UNHCR in Azerbaijan. UNHCR's humanitarian activities have focused on improving shelter, in particular for the most vulnerable among the refugee population, and promoting economic self-sufficiency and stability.

In Georgia, where almost 300,000 people left their homes as a result of civil conflict from 1991, UNHCR has attempted to encourage income-generating activities among the displaced population, to increase the Georgian Government's capacity to support those people and to assist the rehabilitation of people returning to their areas of origin. In late 1999 an estimated 7,000 refugees fleeing insecurity in Chechnya (see below) entered Georgia. By 31 December 2002 more than 4,000 Chechen refugees remained in Georgia. There were also 261,583 Georgian IDPs (affected by the ongoing conflicts in Abkhazia and South Ossetia). UNHCR has delivered food to the Chechen refugees and the host families with whom some 80% are staying, and has also assisted the refugees through shelter renovation, psychosocial support and the provision of child-care facilities and health and community development support, as well as monitoring refugee-host family relations. From 1994 UNHCR pursued a process to establish a comprehensive approach to the problems of refugees, returnees, IDPs and migrants in the Commonwealth of Independent States (CIS). A regional conference convened in Geneva, Switzerland, in May 1996, endorsed a framework of activities aimed at managing migratory flows and at developing institutional capacities to prevent mass population displacements. At that time it was estimated that more than 9m. former citizens of the USSR had relocated since its disintegration as a result of conflict, economic pressures and ecological disasters. By June 2002 (with the accession of Ukraine) all CIS member states excepting Uzbekistan had acceded to the 1951 Convention.

In March 1995 UNHCR initiated an assistance programme for people displaced as a result of conflict in the separatist republic of Chechnya (the Chechen Republic of Ichkeriya), the Russian Federation, as part of a UN inter-agency relief effort, in collaboration with the International Committee of the Red Cross (ICRC). UNHCR continued its activities in 1996, at the request of the Russian Government, at which time the displaced population within Chechnya and in the surrounding republics totalled 490,000. During 1997 UNHCR provided reintegration assistance to 25,000 people who returned to Chechnya, despite reports of sporadic violence. The security situation in the region deteriorated sharply in mid-1999, following a series of border clashes and incursions by Chechen separatist forces into the neighbouring republic of Dagestan. In September Russian military aircraft began an aerial offensive against suspected rebel targets in Chechnya, and at the end of the month ground troops moved into the republic. By November an estimated 225,000 Chechens had fled to neighbouring Ingushetiya. UNHCR dispatched food supplies to assist the IDPs and, from February 2000, periodically sent relief convoys into Chechnya, where there was still a substantial displaced population; the poor security situation, however, prevented other UNHCR deployment within Chechnya. In late 2000 UNHCR assisted with the construction of the first tented camp to provide adequate winter shelter for Chechens in Ingushetiya; many others were being sheltered in local homes. About 110,000 Chechens remained in Ingushetiya at the end of 2002. Four tented refugee camps were operational in Ingushetiya at October 2003.

## CO-OPERATION WITH OTHER ORGANIZATIONS

UNHCR works closely with other UN agencies, intergovernmental organizations and non-governmental organizations (NGOs) to increase the scope and effectiveness of its operations. Within the UN system UNHCR co-operates, principally, with the World Food Programme in the distribution of food aid, UNICEF and the World Health Organization in the provision of family welfare and child immunization programmes, OCHA in the delivery of emergency humanitarian relief, UNDP in development-related activities and the preparation of guide-lines for the continuum of emergency assistance to development programmes, and the Office of the UN High Commissioner for Human Rights. UNHCR also has close working relationships with the International Committee of the Red Cross and the International Organization for Migration. In 2002 UNHCR worked with 510 NGOs as 'implementing partners', enabling UNHCR to broaden the use of its resources while maintaining a co-ordinating role in the provision of assistance.

## TRAINING

UNHCR organizes training programmes and workshops to enhance the capabilities of field workers and non-UNHCR staff, in the following areas: the identification and registration of refugees; people-orientated planning; resettlement procedures and policies; emergency response and management; security awareness; stress management; and the dissemination of information through the electronic media.

# Finance

The United Nations' regular budget finances a proportion of UNHCR's administrative expenditure. The majority of UNHCR's programme expenditure (about 98%) is funded by voluntary contributions, mainly from governments. The Private Sector and Public Affairs Service, established in 2001, aims to increase funding from non-governmental donor sources, for example by developing partnerships with foundations and corporations. Following approval of the Unified Annual Programme Budget any subsequently-identified requirements are managed in the form of Supplementary Programmes, financed by separate appeals. The Unified Annual Programme Budget for 2003 amounted to US $836.3m.

## Publications

*Refugees* (quarterly, in English, French, German, Italian, Japanese and Spanish).

*Refugee Resettlement: An International Handbook to Guide Reception and Integration.*

*Refugee Survey Quarterly.*

*The State of the World's Refugees* (every 2 years).

*UNHCR Handbook for Emergencies.*

Press releases, reports.

## Statistics

**PERSONS OF CONCERN TO UNHCR IN EASTERN EUROPE, RUSSIA AND CENTRAL ASIA**
('000 persons, at 31 December 2002*)

|  | Refugees | Asylum-seekers | Returned refugees | Others of concern† |
|---|---|---|---|---|
| Armenia . . . | 247.6 | 0.0 | — | — |
| Azerbaijan . . | 0.5 | 8.1 | — | 579.6 |
| Belarus . . . | 0.6 | 0.3 | — | 16.9 |
| Georgia . . . | 4.2 | — | 0.1 | 261.6 |
| Kazakhstan . . | 20.6 | 0.0 | — | 83.2 |
| Russian Federation | 15.0 | 0.6 | 0.0 | 956.3 |
| Turkmenistan . . | 13.7 | 0.0 | — | — |
| Ukraine . . . | 3.0 | 0.4 | — | 14.3 |
| Uzbekistan . . . | 44.9 | 1.1 | — | — |

* Figures are provided mostly by governments, based on their own records and methods of estimation. Countries with fewer than 10,000 persons of concern to the UNHCR are not listed.
† Mainly internally displaced person (IDPs) or recently returned IDPs.

# United Nations Peace-keeping

**Address:** Department of Peace-keeping Operations, Room S-3727-B, United Nations, New York, NY 10017, USA.
**Telephone:** (212) 963-8077; **fax:** (212) 963-9222; **internet:** www.un .org/Depts/dpko/.

United Nations peace-keeping operations have been conceived as instruments of conflict control. The UN has used these operations in various conflicts, with the consent of the parties involved, to maintain international peace and security, without prejudice to the positions or claims of parties, in order to facilitate the search for political settlements through peaceful means such as mediation and the good offices of the Secretary-General. Each operation is established with a specific mandate, which requires periodic review by the Security Council. United Nations peace-keeping operations fall into two categories: peace-keeping forces and observer missions.

Peace-keeping forces are composed of contingents of military and civilian personnel, made available by member states. These forces assist in preventing the recurrence of fighting, restoring and maintaining peace, and promoting a return to normal conditions. To this end, peace-keeping forces are authorized as necessary to undertake negotiations, persuasion, observation and fact-finding. They conduct patrols and interpose physically between the opposing parties. Peace-keeping forces are permitted to use their weapons only in self-defence.

Military observer missions are composed of officers (usually unarmed), who are made available, on the Secretary-General's request, by member states. A mission's function is to observe and report to the Secretary-General (who, in turn, informs the UN Security Council) on the maintenance of a cease-fire, to investigate violations and to do what it can to improve the situation.

The UN's peace-keeping forces and observer missions are financed in most cases by assessed contributions from member states of the organization. In recent years a significant expansion in the UN's peace-keeping activities has been accompanied by a perpetual financial crisis within the organization, as a result of the increased financial burden and some member states' delaying payment. At October 2003 outstanding assessed contributions to the peace-keeping budget amounted to some US $1,560m.

## UNITED NATIONS OBSERVER MISSION IN GEORGIA—UNOMIG

**Address:** Headquarters: Sukhumi, Georgia.

**Special Representative of the UN Secretary-General and Head of Mission:** HEIDI TAGLIAVINI (Switzerland).

**Chief Military Observer:** Maj.-Gen. KAZI ASHFAQ AHMED (Bangladesh).

UNOMIG was established in August 1993 to verify compliance with a cease-fire agreement, signed in July between the Government of Georgia and the Abkhazian separatist movement. The mission was the UN's first undertaking in the former USSR. In October the UN Secretary-General stated that a breakdown in the cease-fire agreement had invalidated UNOMIG's mandate. He proposed, however, to maintain, for information purposes, the eight-strong UNOMIG team in the city of Sukhumi, which had been seized by Abkhazian forces in late September. In late December the Security Council authorized the deployment of additional military observers in response to the signing of a memorandum of understanding by the conflicting parties earlier that month. Further peace negotiations, which were conducted in January–March 1994 under the authority of the UN Secretary-General's Special Envoy, achieved no political consensus. In July the Security Council endorsed the establishment of a Commonwealth of Independent States (CIS) peace-keeping force to verify a cease-fire agreement that had been signed in May. At the same time the Security Council increased UNOMIG's authorized strength and expanded the mission's mandate to incorporate the following tasks: to monitor and verify the implementation of the agreement and to investigate reported violations; to observe the operation of the CIS peace-keeping force; to verify that troops and heavy military equipment remain outside the security zone and the restricted weapons zone; to monitor the storage of the military equipment withdrawn from the restricted zones; to monitor the withdrawal of Georgian troops from the Kodori Gorge region to locations beyond the Abkhazian frontiers; and to patrol regularly the Kodori Gorge. Peace negotiations were pursued in 1995, despite periodic outbreaks of violence in Abkhazia. In July 1996 the Security Council urged the Abkhazian side to accelerate significantly the process of voluntary return of Georgian refugees and displaced persons to Abkhazia. In October the Council decided to establish a human rights office as part of UNOMIG. In May 1997 the Security Council issued a Presidential Statement urging greater efforts towards achieving a peaceful solution to the dispute. The Statement endorsed a proposal of the UN Secretary-General to strengthen the political element of UNOMIG to enable the mission to assume a more active role in furthering a negotiated settlement. In July direct discussions between representatives of the Georgian and Abkhazian authorities, the first in more than two years, were held under UN auspices. In early 1998 the security situation in Abkhazia deteriorated. Following an outbreak of violence in May the conflicting parties signed a cease-fire accord, which incorporated an agreement that UNOMIG and CIS forces would continue to work to create a secure environment to allow for the return of displaced persons to the Gali region of Abkhazia. In addition, the UN Security Council urged both parties to establish a protection unit to ensure the safety of UN military observers. In December 2000, following a series of detentions and hostage-takings of Mission personnel in the Kodori Gorge during late 1999 and 2000, UNOMIG suspended patrols of that area. Reviewing the operation in January 2001 the UN Secretary-General expressed concern at the recent recurrent abductions and urged the Abkhazian side to cease imposing restrictions on the mission's freedom of movement. Although contacts between the Georgian and Abkhazian authorities continued in 2001, progress towards the conclusion of a durable political settlement remained stalled by an *impasse* between the two sides regarding the future political status of Abkhazia. A Programme of Action on confidence-building measures was concluded in March; however, the negotiation process was interrupted from April, owing to increasing insecurity in the conflict zone and the ongoing activities of illegal armed groups. In October a UNOMIG helicopter was shot down in the Kodori Gorge, resulting in the deaths of nine people. UNOMIG suspended its patrols of the area. In January 2002 a protocol was signed between the conflicting parties providing for the withdrawal of Georgian troops from the upper Kodori valley and the resumption of UN ground patrols. Further discussion on implementation of the protocol resulted in the first joint patrol being conducted in late March. In early April a protocol was concluded by both sides for a final withdrawal of Georgian troops and the resumption of regular UNOMIG/CIS patrols. Renewed diplomatic efforts to secure a political agreement initially focused on a paper of Basic Principles for the Distribution of Competences between Tbilisi and Sukhumi, which had been prepared by the Special Representative of the UN Secretary-General. The document was rejected as a basis for negotiations by the Abkhazian leadership; however, discussions were held between the leadership of the two sides to consider measures to stabilize further the situation in the Kodori Gorge. Both sides agreed to resolve all outstanding issues by peaceful means. A UN-sponsored 'brainstorming' session on the conflict, held in Geneva, Switzerland, in February 2003, identified co-operation in economic and security matters and the return of refugees and internally-displaced persons as being of key importance for the advancement of the peace process.

However, no further progress towards the commencement of negotiations had been achieved by October. UNOMIG co-operates closely with the CIS peace-keeping force, and a joint UNOMIG-CIS fact-finding team undertakes investigations of violent incidents. UNOMIG's mandate was most recently extended until 31 January 2004.

At 31 August 2003 UNOMIG comprised 115 military observers, supported by 273 international and local civilian personnel. The General Assembly budget appropriation for the mission for the period 1 July 2003–30 June 2004 amounted to US $32.1m.

## CENTRAL ASIAN PEACE-KEEPING BATTALION—CENTRASBAT

CENTRASBAT is a regional security organization formed under UN auspices in 1996 by Kazakhstan, Kyrgyzstan and Uzbekistan, in order to undertake training and other related activities in preparation for participation in UN-sponsored multinational peace-keeping and humanitarian efforts. Since September 1997 joint peace-keeping exercises have been conducted annually in Central Asian territory, led by US troops, and with participation by forces from Azerbaijan, Georgia, Mongolia, the Russian Federation, Turkey and the United Kingdom.

# World Food Programme—WFP

**Address:** Via Cesare Giulio Viola 68, Parco dei Medici, 00148 Rome, Italy.
**Telephone:** (06) 6513-1; **fax:** (06) 6513-2840; **e-mail:** wfpinfo@wfp.org; **internet:** www.wfp.org.

WFP, the principal food aid organization of the United Nations, became operational in 1963. It aims to alleviate acute hunger by providing emergency relief following natural or man-made humanitarian disasters, and supplies food aid to people in developing countries to eradicate chronic undernourishment, to support social development and to promote self-reliant communities.

## Organization

(October 2003)

### EXECUTIVE BOARD

The governing body of WFP is the Executive Board, comprising 36 members, 18 of whom are elected by the UN Economic and Social Council (ECOSOC) and 18 by the Council of the Food and Agriculture Organization (FAO). The Board meets four times each year at WFP headquarters.

### SECRETARIAT

WFP's Executive Director is appointed jointly by the UN Secretary-General and the Director-General of FAO and is responsible for the management and administration of the Programme. In 2002 there were 2,684 permanent staff members, of whom more than 75% were working in the field. WFP administers some 87 country offices, in order to provide operational, financial and management support at a more local level, and has established seven regional bureaux, located in Bangkok, Thailand (for Asia), Cairo, Egypt (for the Middle East, Central Asia and the Mediterranean), Rome, Italy (for Eastern Europe), Managua, Nicaragua (for Latin America and the Caribbean), Yaoundé, Cameroon (for Central Africa), Kampala, Uganda (for Eastern and Southern Africa), and Dakar, Senegal (for West Africa).

**Executive Director:** JAMES T. MORRIS (USA).

## Activities

WFP is the only multilateral organization with a mandate to use food aid as a resource. It is the second largest source of assistance in the UN, after the World Bank group, in terms of actual transfers of resources, and the largest source of grant aid in the UN system. WFP handles more than one-third of the world's food aid. WFP is also the largest contributor to South–South trade within the UN system, through the purchase of food and services from developing countries. WFP's mission is to provide food aid to save lives in refugee and other emergency situations, to improve the nutrition and quality of

life of vulnerable groups and to help to develop assets and promote the self-reliance of poor families and communities. WFP aims to focus its efforts on the world's poorest countries and to provide at least 90% of its total assistance to those designated as 'low-income food-deficit'. At the World Food Summit, held in November 1996, WFP endorsed the commitment to reduce by 50% the number of undernourished people, no later than 2015. During 2002 WFP food assistance benefited some 72m. people world-wide, of whom 14m. received aid through development projects, 44m. through emergency operations, and 14m. through rehabilitation programmes. Total food deliveries amounted to 3.7m. metric tons in 82 countries.

WFP aims to address the causes of chronic malnourishment, which it identifies as poverty and lack of opportunity. It emphasizes the role played by women in combating hunger, and endeavours to address the specific nutritional needs of women, to increase their access to food and development resources, and to promote girls' education. It also focuses resources on supporting the food security of households and communities affected by HIV/AIDS and on promoting food security as a means of mitigating extreme poverty and vulnerability and thereby combating the spread of HIV/AIDS. In February 2003 WFP and the Joint UN Programme on HIV/AIDS (UNAIDS) concluded an agreement to address jointly the relationship between HIV/AIDS, regional food shortages and chronic hunger, with a particular focus on Africa, South-East Asia and the Caribbean. In October 2003 WFP became the ninth co-sponsor of UNAIDS, the others being WHO, the World Bank, UNICEF, UNESCO, UNDCP, ILO and UNFPA.

In the early 1990s there was a substantial shift in the balance between emergency relief and development assistance provided by WFP, owing to the growing needs of victims of drought and other natural disasters, refugees and displaced persons. By 1994 two-thirds of all food aid was for relief assistance and one-third for development, representing a direct reversal of the allocations five years previously. In addition, there was a noticeable increase in aid given to those in need as a result of civil war, compared with commitments for victims of natural disasters. Accordingly, WFP has developed a range of mechanisms to enhance its preparedness for emergency situations and to improve its capacity for responding effectively to situations as they arise. A new programme of emergency response training was inaugurated in 2000, while security concerns for personnel was incorporated as a new element into all general planning and training activities. Through its Vulnerability Analysis and Mapping (VAM) project, WFP aims to identify potentially vulnerable groups by providing information on food security and the capacity of different groups for coping with shortages, and to enhance emergency contingency-planning and long-term assistance objectives. In 2003 VAM field units were operational in more than 50 countries. WFP also co-operates with other UN agencies including FAO (undertaking joint activities in 24 countries in 2001), IFAD (conducting joint activities in 14 countries in that year) and UNHCR. The key elements of WFP's emergency response capacity are its strategic stores of food and logistics equipment, stand-by arrangements to enable the rapid deployment of personnel, communications and other essential equipment, and the Augmented Logistics Intervention Team for Emergencies (ALITE), which undertakes capacity assessments and contingency-planning. During 2000 WFP led efforts, undertaken with other UN humanitarian agencies, for the design and application of local UN Joint Logistics Centre facilities, which aimed to co-ordinate resources in an emergency situation. In 2001 a new UN Humanitarian Response Depot was opened in Brindisi, Italy, under the direction of WFP experts, for the storage of essential rapid response equipment. In that year the Programme published a set of guide-lines on contingency planning.

Through its development activities, WFP aims to alleviate poverty in developing countries by promoting self-reliant families and communities. Food is supplied, for example, as an incentive in development self-help schemes and as part-wages in labour-intensive projects of many kinds. In all its projects WFP aims to assist the most vulnerable groups and to ensure that beneficiaries have an adequate and balanced diet. Activities supported by the Programme include the settlement and resettlement of groups and communities; land reclamation and improvement; irrigation; the development of forestry and dairy farming; road construction; training of hospital staff; community development; and human resources development such as feeding expectant or nursing mothers and schoolchildren, and support for education, training and health programmes. In 2002 WFP supported development projects in 55 countries, which benefited some 14m. people. During 2001 WFP initiated a new Global School Feeding Campaign to strengthen international co-operation to expand educational opportunities for poor children and to improve the quality of the teaching environment; school feeding projects benefited 15m. children in that year.

Following a comprehensive evaluation of its activities, WFP is increasingly focused on linking its relief and development activities to provide a continuum between short-term relief and longer-term rehabilitation and development. In order to achieve this objective, WFP aims to integrate elements that strengthen disaster mitigation into development projects, including soil conservation, reafforestation, irrigation infrastructure, and transport construction and rehabilitation; and to promote capacity-building elements within relief operations, e.g. training, income-generating activities and environmental protection measures. In 1999 WFP adopted a new Food Aid and Development policy, which aims to use food assistance both to cover immediate requirements and to create conditions conducive to enhancing the long-term food security of vulnerable populations. During that year WFP began implementing Protracted Relief and Recovery Operations (PRROs), where the emphasis is on fostering stability, rehabilitation and long-term development for victims of natural disasters, displaced persons and refugees. PRROs are introduced no later than 18 months after the initial emergency operation and last no more than three years. When undertaken in collaboration with UNHCR and other international agencies, WFP has responsibility for mobilizing basic food commodities and for related transport, handling and storage costs. PRROs undertaken in 2002 involved the provision of 918,435 metric tons of food.

In 2002 WFP operational expenditure in Europe and the CIS amounted to US $86.8m. (5% of total operational expenditure in that year), including $52.7m. for emergency relief operations and $33.6m. for PRROs.

## Finance

The Programme is funded by voluntary contributions from donor countries and intergovernmental bodies such as the European Union. Contributions are made in the form of commodities, finance and services (particularly shipping). Commitments to the International Emergency Food Reserve (IEFR), from which WFP provides the majority of its food supplies, and to the Immediate Response Account of the IEFR (IRA), are also made on a voluntary basis by donors. In 2001 contributions by donors provided 83% of WFP's food requirements. WFP's operational expenditure in that year amounted to some US $1,744m., while administrative costs totalled $244.7m. for the two-year period 2000–01.

## Publications

*Annual Report.*
*Food and Nutrition Handbook.*
*School Feeding Handbook.*

# Food and Agriculture Organization of the United Nations —FAO

**Address:** Viale delle Terme di Caracalla, 00100 Rome, Italy.
**Telephone:** (06) 5705-1; **fax:** (06) 5705-3152; **e-mail:** fao.hq@fao.org; **internet:** www.fao.org.

FAO, the first specialized agency of the UN to be founded after the Second World War, aims to alleviate malnutrition and hunger, and serves as a co-ordinating agency for development programmes in the whole range of food and agriculture, including forestry and fisheries. It helps developing countries to promote educational and training facilities and the creation of appropriate institutions.

## Organization

(October 2003)

### CONFERENCE

The governing body is the FAO Conference of member nations. It meets every two years, formulates policy, determines the Organization's programme and budget on a biennial basis, and elects new members. It also elects the Director-General of the Secretariat and the Independent Chairman of the Council. Every other year, FAO also holds conferences in each of its five regions (Africa, Asia and the Pacific, Europe, Latin America and the Caribbean, and the Near East).

### COUNCIL

The FAO Council is composed of representatives of 49 member nations, elected by the Conference for staggered three-year terms. It is the interim governing body of FAO between sessions of the Conference. The most important standing Committees of the Council are: the Finance and Programme Committees, the Committee on Commodity Problems, the Committee on Fisheries, the Committee on Agriculture and the Committee on Forestry.

### SECRETARIAT

The total number of FAO staff in May 2002 was 3,700, of whom 1,500 were professional staff and 2,200 general service staff. About one-half of the Organization's staff were based at headquarters. Work is supervised by the following Departments: Administration and Finance; General Affairs and Information; Economic and Social Policy; Agriculture; Forestry; Fisheries; Sustainable Development; and Technical Co-operation.

**Director-General:** Jacques Diouf (Senegal).

### REGIONAL AND SUB-REGIONAL OFFICES

**Regional Office for Europe:** Viale delle Terme di Caracalla, Room A-304, 00100 Rome, Italy; tel. (06) 57051; fax (06) 5705 3152; internet www.fao.org/regional/europe; Regional Rep. Claude Forthomme.

**Sub-regional Office for Central and Eastern Europe:** 1068 Budapest, Benczur u. 34, Hungary; tel. (1) 461-2000; fax (1) 351-7029; e-mail fao-seur@fao.org; Sub-regional Rep. Peter Rosenegger.

### JOINT DIVISION AND LIAISON OFFICE

**Joint FAO/IAEA Division of Nuclear Techniques in Food and Agriculture:** Wagramerstrasse 5, 1400 Vienna, Austria; tel. (1) 20600; fax (1) 20607.

**United Nations:** Suite DC1-1125, 1 United Nations Plaza, New York, NY 10017, USA; tel. (212) 963-6036; fax (212) 963-5425; e-mail fao-lony@field.fao.org; Dir Howard W. Hjort.

## Activities

FAO aims to raise levels of nutrition and standards of living by improving the production and distribution of food and other commodities derived from farms, fisheries and forests. FAO's ultimate objective is the achievement of world food security, 'Food for All'. The organization provides technical information, advice and assistance by disseminating information; acting as a neutral forum for discussion of food and agricultural issues; advising governments on policy and planning; and developing capacity directly in the field.

In November 1996 FAO hosted the World Food Summit, which was held in Rome and was attended by heads of state and senior government representatives of 186 countries. Participants approved the Rome Declaration on World Food Security and the World Food Summit Plan of Action, with the aim of halving the number of people afflicted by undernutrition, at that time estimated to total 828m. world-wide, by no later than 2015. A review conference to assess progress in achieving the goals of the summit, entitled World Food Summit: Five Years Later, held in June 2002, reaffirmed commitment to this objective. During that month FAO announced the formulation of a global 'Anti-Hunger Programme', which aimed to promote investment in the agricultural sector and rural development, with a particular focus on small farmers, and to enhance food access for those most in need, for example through the provision of school meals, schemes to feed pregnant and nursing mothers and food-for-work programmes. In late 2002 FAO reported that an estimated 840m. people were undernourished during the period 1998–2000; of these 799m. resided in developing countries, 30m. in states with economies in transition and 11m. in industrialized countries.

In November 1999 the FAO Conference approved a long-term Strategic Framework for the period 2000–15, which emphasized national and international co-operation in pursuing the goals of the 1996 World Food Summit. The Framework promoted interdisciplinarity and partnership, and defined three main global objectives: constant access by all people to sufficient nutritionally adequate and safe food to ensure that levels of undernourishment were reduced by 50% by 2015 (see above); the continued contribution of sustainable agriculture and rural development to economic and social progress and well-being; and the conservation, improvement and sustainable use of natural resources. It identified five corporate strategies (each supported by several strategic objectives), covering the following areas: reducing food insecurity and rural poverty; ensuring enabling policy and regulatory frameworks for food, agriculture, fisheries and forestry; creating sustainable increases in the supply and availability of agricultural, fisheries and forestry products; conserving and enhancing sustainable use of the natural resource base; and generating knowledge. The November 2001 the FAO Conference adopted a medium-term plan covering 2002–07 and a work programme for 2000–03, both on the basis of the Strategic Framework.

FAO organizes an annual series of fund-raising events, 'TeleFood', some of which are broadcast on television and the internet, in order to raise public awareness of the problems of hunger and malnutrition. Since its inception in 1997 public donations to TeleFood have exceeded US $10m., financing more than 1,000 'grass-roots' projects in more than 100 countries. The projects have provided tools, seeds and other essential supplies directly to small-scale farmers, and have been especially aimed at helping women.

In 1999 FAO signed a memorandum of understanding with UNAIDS on strengthening co-operation. In December 2001 FAO, IFAD and WFP determined to strengthen inter-agency collaboration in developing strategies to combat the threat posed by the HIV/AIDS epidemic to food security, nutrition and rural livelihoods. During that month experts from those organizations and UNAIDS held a technical consultation on means of mitigating the impact of HIV/AIDS on agriculture and rural communities in affected areas.

The Technical Co-operation Department has responsibility for FAO's operational activities, including policy development assistance to member countries; investment support; and the management of activities associated with the development and implementation of country, sub-regional and regional programmes. The Department manages the technical co-operation programme (TCP, which funds 13% of FAO's field programme expenditures), and mobilizes resources.

### AGRICULTURE

FAO's most important area of activity is crop production, accounting annually for about one-quarter of total field programme expenditure. FAO assists developing countries in increasing agricultural production, by means of a number of methods, including improved seeds and fertilizer use, soil conservation and reforestation, better water resource management techniques, upgrading storage facilities, and improvements in processing and marketing. FAO places special emphasis on the cultivation of under-exploited traditional food crops, such as cassava, sweet potato and plantains.

In 1985 the FAO Conference approved an International Code of Conduct on the Distribution and Use of Pesticides, and in 1989 the Conference adopted an additional clause concerning 'Prior Informed Consent' (PIC), whereby international shipments of newly banned or restricted pesticides should not proceed without the agreement of importing countries. Under the clause, FAO aims to inform govern-

ments about the hazards of toxic chemicals and to urge them to take proper measures to curb trade in highly toxic agrochemicals while keeping the pesticides industry informed of control actions. In 1996 FAO, in collaboration with UNEP, publicized a new initiative which aimed to increase awareness of, and to promote international action on, obsolete and hazardous stocks of pesticides remaining throughout the world (estimated in 2001 to total some 500,000 metric tons). In September 1998 a new legally-binding treaty on trade in hazardous chemicals and pesticides was adopted at an international conference held in Rotterdam, Netherlands. The so-called Rotterdam Convention required that hazardous chemicals and pesticides banned or severely restricted in at least two countries should not be exported unless explicitly agreed by the importing country. It also identified certain pesticide formulations as too dangerous to be used by farmers in developing countries, and incorporated an obligation that countries halt national production of those hazardous compounds. The treaty was to enter into force on being ratified by 50 signatory states. FAO was co-operating with UNEP to provide an interim secretariat for the Convention. In July 1999 a conference on the Rotterdam Convention, held in Rome, established an Interim Chemical Review Committee with responsibility for recommending the inclusion of chemicals or pesticide formulations in the PIC procedure. As part of its continued efforts to reduce the environmental risks posed by over-reliance on pesticides, FAO has extended to other regions its Integrated Pest Management (IPM) programme in Asia and the Pacific on the use of safer and more effective methods of pest control, such as biological control methods and natural predators (including spiders and wasps), to avert pests. In February 2001 FAO warned that some 30% of pesticides sold in developing countries did not meet internationally accepted quality standards. A revised International Code of Conduct on the Distribution and Use of Pesticides, adopted in November 2002, aimed to reduce the inappropriate distribution and use of pesticides and other toxic compounds, particularly in developing countries.

FAO's Joint Division with the International Atomic Energy Agency (IAEA) tests controlled-release formulas of pesticides and herbicides that gradually free their substances and can limit the amount of agrochemicals needed to protect crops. The Joint FAO/IAEA Division is engaged in exploring biotechnologies and in developing non-toxic fertilizers (especially those that are locally available) and improved strains of food crops (especially from indigenous varieties). In the area of animal production and health, the Joint Division has developed progesterone-measuring and disease diagnostic kits, of which thousands have been delivered to developing countries. FAO's plant nutrition activities aim to promote nutrient management, such as the Integrated Plant Nutritions Systems (IPNS), which are based on the recycling of nutrients through crop production and the efficient use of mineral fertilizers.

The conservation and sustainable use of plant and animal genetic resources are promoted by FAO's Global System for Plant Genetic Resources, which includes five databases, and the Global Strategy on the Management of Farm Animal Genetic Resources. An FAO programme supports the establishment of gene banks, designed to maintain the world's biological diversity by preserving animal and plant species threatened with extinction. FAO, jointly with UNEP, has published a document listing the current state of global livestock genetic diversity. In June 1996 representatives of more than 150 governments convened in Leipzig, Germany, at a meeting organized by FAO (and hosted by the German Government) to consider the use and conservation of plant genetic resources as an essential means of enhancing food security. The meeting adopted a Global Plan of Action, which included measures to strengthen the development of plant varieties and to promote the use and availability of local varieties and locally-adapted crops to farmers, in particular following a natural disaster, war or civil conflict. In November 2001 the FAO Conference adopted the International Treaty on Plant Genetic Resources for Food and Agriculture, which was to provide a framework to ensure access to plant genetic resources and to related knowledge, technologies and funding. The Treaty was to enter into force once it had been ratified by 40 signatory states; at October 2003 it had been ratified by 32 states.

An Emergency Prevention System for Transboundary Animal and Plant Pests and Diseases (EMPRES) was established in 1994 to strengthen FAO's activities in the prevention, early warning of, control and, where possible, eradication of pests and highly contagious livestock diseases (which the system categorizes as epidemic diseases of strategic importance, such as rinderpest or foot-and-mouth; diseases requiring tactical attention at international or regional level, e.g. Rift Valley fever; and emerging diseases, e.g. bovine spongiform encephalopathy—BSE). EMPRES has a desert locust component, and has published guide-lines on all aspects of desert locust monitoring. FAO has assumed responsibility for technical leadership and co-ordination of the Global Rinderpest Eradication Programme (GREP), which has the objective of eliminating the disease by 2010. Following technical consultations in late 1998, an Intensified GREP was launched. In November 1997 FAO initiated a Programme Against African Trypanosomiasis, which aimed to counter the disease affecting cattle in almost one-third of Africa. EMPRES promotes Good Emergency Management Practices (GEMP) in animal health. The system is guided by the annual meeting of the EMPRES Expert Consultation.

FAO's organic agriculture programme provides technical assistance and policy advice on the production, certification and trade of organic produce. In July 2001 the FAO/WHO Codex Alimentarius Commission adopted guide-lines on organic livestock production, covering organic breeding methods, the elimination of growth hormones and certain chemicals in veterinary medicines, and the use of good quality organic feed with no meat or bone meal content.

## ENVIRONMENT

At the UN Conference on Environment and Development (UNCED), held in Rio de Janeiro, Brazil, in June 1992, FAO participated in several working parties and supported the adoption of Agenda 21, a programme of activities to promote sustainable development. FAO is responsible for the chapters of Agenda 21 concerning water resources, forests, fragile mountain ecosystems and sustainable agriculture and rural development. FAO was designated by the UN General Assembly as the lead agency for co-ordinating the International Year of Mountains (2002), which aimed to raise awareness of mountain ecosystems and to promote the conservation and sustainable development of mountainous regions.

## FISHERIES

FAO's Fisheries Department consists of a multi-disciplinary body of experts who are involved in every aspect of fisheries development from coastal surveys, conservation management and use of aquatic genetic resources, improvement of production, processing and storage, to the compilation and analysis of statistics, development of computer databases, improvement of fishing gear, institution-building and training. In November 1993 the FAO Conference adopted an agreement to improve the monitoring and control of fishing vessels operating on the high seas that are registered under 'flags of convenience', in order to ensure their compliance with internationally accepted marine conservation and management measures. In March 1995 a ministerial meeting of fisheries adopted the Rome Consensus on World Fisheries, which identified a need for immediate action to eliminate overfishing and to rebuild and enhance depleting fish stocks. In November the FAO Conference adopted a Code of Conduct for Responsible Fishing, which incorporated many global fisheries and aquaculture issues (including fisheries resource conservation and development, fish catches, seafood and fish processing, commercialization, trade and research) to promote the sustainable development of the sector. In February 1999 the FAO Committee on Fisheries adopted new international measures, within the framework of the Code of Conduct, in order to reduce over-exploitation of the world's fish resources, as well as plans of action for the conservation and management of sharks and the reduction in the incidental catch of seabirds in longline fisheries. The voluntary measures were endorsed at a ministerial meeting, held in March and attended by representatives of some 126 countries, which issued a declaration to promote the implementation of the Code of Conduct and to achieve sustainable management of fisheries and aquaculture. In March 2001 FAO adopted an international plan of action to address the continuing problem of so-called illegal, unreported and unregulated fishing (IUU). In that year FAO estimated that about one-half of major marine fish stocks were fully exploited, one-quarter under-exploited, at least 15% over-exploited, and 10% depleted or recovering from depletion. IUU was estimated to account for up to 30% of total catches in certain fisheries. In October FAO and the Icelandic Government jointly organized the Reykjavik Conference on Responsible Fisheries in the Marine Ecosystem, which adopted a declaration on pursuing responsible and sustainable fishing activities in the context of ecosystem-based fisheries management (EBFM). EBFM involves determining the boundaries of individual marine ecosystems, and maintaining or rebuilding the habitats and biodiversity of each of these so that all species will be supported at levels of maximum production. FAO promotes aquaculture (which contributes almost one-third of annual global fish landings) as a valuable source of animal protein and income-generating activity for rural communities. In February 2000 FAO and the Network of Aquaculture Centres in Asia and the Pacific (NACA) jointly convened a Conference on Aquaculture in the Third Millennium, which was held in Bangkok, Thailand, and attended by participants representing more than 200 governmental and non-governmental organizations. The Conference debated global trends in aquaculture and future policy measures to ensure the sustainable development of the sector. It adopted the Bangkok Declaration and Strategy for Aquaculture Beyond 2000. In December 2001 FAO issued a report based on the technical proceedings of the conference.

## FORESTRY

FAO focuses on the contribution of forestry to food security, on effective and responsible forest management and on maintaining a balance between the economic, ecological and social benefits of forest resources. The Organization has helped to develop national forestry programmes and to promote the sustainable development of all types of forest. FAO administers the global Forests, Trees and People Programme, which promotes the sustainable management of tree and forest resources, based on local knowledge and management practices, in order to improve the livelihoods of rural people in developing countries. FAO's Strategic Plan for Forestry was approved in March 1999; its main objectives were to maintain the environmental diversity of forests, to realize the economic potential of forests and trees within a sustainable framework, and to expand access to information on forestry.

## NUTRITION

The International Conference on Nutrition, sponsored by FAO and WHO, took place in Rome in December 1992. It approved a World Declaration on Nutrition and a Plan of Action, aimed at promoting efforts to combat malnutrition as a development priority. Since the conference, more than 100 countries have formulated national plans of action for nutrition, many of which were based on existing development plans such as comprehensive food security initiatives, national poverty alleviation programmes and action plans to attain the targets set by the World Summit for Children in September 1990. In October 1996 FAO, WHO and other partners jointly organized the first World Congress on Calcium and Vitamin D in Human Life, held in Rome. In January 2001 a joint team of FAO and WHO experts issued a report concerning the allergenicity of foods derived from biotechnology (i.e. genetically modified—GM—foods). In July the Codex Alimentarius Commission agreed the first global principles for assessing the safety of GM foods, and approved a series of maximum levels of environmental contaminants in food. FAO and WHO jointly convened a Global Forum of Food Safety Regulators in Marrakesh, Morocco, in January 2002. In April the two organizations announce a joint review of their food standards operations, including the activities of the Codex Alimentarius Commission.

## PROCESSING AND MARKETING

An estimated 20% of all food harvested is lost before it can be consumed, and in some developing countries the proportion is much higher. FAO helps reduce immediate post-harvest losses, with the introduction of improved processing methods and storage systems. It also advises on the distribution and marketing of agricultural produce and on the selection and preparation of foods for optimum nutrition. Many of these activities form part of wider rural development projects. Many developing countries rely on agricultural products as their main source of foreign earnings, but the terms under which they are traded are usually more favourable to the industrialized countries. FAO continues to favour the elimination of export subsidies and related discriminatory practices, such as protectionist measures that hamper international trade in agricultural commodities. FAO has organized regional workshops and national projects in order to help member states to implement World Trade Organization regulations, in particular with regard to agricultural policy, intellectual property rights, sanitary and phytosanitary measures, technical barriers to trade and the international standards of the Codex Alimentarius. FAO evaluates new market trends and helps to develop improved plant and animal quarantine procedures. In November 1997 the FAO Conference adopted new guide-lines on surveillance and on export certification systems in order to harmonize plant quarantine standards. FAO participates in PhAction, a forum of 12 agencies that was established in 1999 to promote post-harvest research and the development of effective post-harvest services and infrastructure.

## FOOD SECURITY

FAO's policy on food security aims to encourage the production of adequate food supplies, to maximize stability in the flow of supplies, and to ensure access on the part of those who need them. In 1994 FAO initiated the Special Programme for Food Security (SPFS), designed to assist low-income countries with a food deficit to increase food production and productivity as rapidly as possible, primarily through the widespread adoption by farmers of improved production technologies, with emphasis on areas of high potential. FAO was actively involved in the formulation of the Plan of Action on food security that was adopted at the World Food Summit in November 1996, and was to be responsible for monitoring and promoting its implementation. In March 1999 FAO signed agreements with IFAD and WFP that aimed to increase co-operation within the framework of the SPFS. A budget of US $10.5m. was allocated to the SPFS for the two-year period 2002–03. In early 2003 the SPFS was operational in 74 countries categorized as 'low-income food-deficit', of which 42 were in Africa. The Programme promotes South-South co-operation to improve food security and the exchange of knowledge and experience. By September 2003 28 bilateral co-operation agreements were in force, for example, between Egypt and Cameroon and Viet Nam and Benin.

FAO's Global Information and Early Warning System (GIEWS), which become operational in 1975, maintains a database on and monitors the crop and food outlook at global, regional, national and sub-national levels in order to detect emerging food supply difficulties and disasters and to ensure rapid intervention in countries experiencing food supply shortages. It publishes regular reports on the weather conditions and crop prospects in sub-Saharan Africa and in the Sahel region, issues special alerts which describe the situation in countries or sub-regions experiencing food difficulties, and recommends an appropriate international response. FAO's annual publication *State of Food Insecurity in the World* is based on data compiled by the Organization's Food Insecurity and Vulnerability Information and Mapping Systems programme.

In August 2002 GIEWS issued a special report on the food production situation in Tajikistan. A report on the situation in Moldova was published in July 2003.

### FAO INVESTMENT CENTRE

The Investment Centre was established in 1964 to help countries to prepare viable investment projects that will attract external financing. The Centre focuses its evaluation of projects on two fundamental concerns: the promotion of sustainable activities for land management, forestry development and environmental protection, and the alleviation of rural poverty. In 2000–01 90 projects were approved, representing a total investment of some US $4,670m.

### EMERGENCY RELIEF

FAO works to rehabilitate agricultural production following natural and man-made disasters by providing emergency seed, tools, and technical and other assistance. Jointly with the United Nations, FAO is responsible for WFP, which provides emergency food supplies and food aid in support of development projects. FAO's Division for Emergency Operations and Rehabilitation was responsible for preparing the emergency agricultural relief component of the 2002 UN inter-agency appeals for 17 countries and regions.

New projects approved by the Division for Emergency Operations and Rehabilitation in 2001 included the emergency supply of locally-produced seed potatoes to drought-affected farmers in Armenia; emergency supply of seed potatoes, maize seed and fertilizer to drought-affected farmers in Georgia; emergency procurement and distribution of vegetable seedlings and maize seeds to drought-affected farmers in Moldova; and assistance to the seed potato fund, supply of agricultural inputs to poor rural households and returnees, irrigation rehabilitation and support to animal health services in Tajikistan. FAO was responsible for preparing the emergency agricultural relief component of the 2002 UN inter-agency appeals for the northern Caucasus (concerning support for displaced and host farming families aiming to resume cultivation in Chechnya and Ingushetiya) and for Tajikistan (entailing emergency agricultural assistance to drought-affected rural households, assistance to small farmers in improving their seed multiplication capacity, the development of food security monitoring, and the delivery of sustainable veterinary services).

### INFORMATION

FAO collects, analyses, interprets and disseminates information through various media, including an extensive internet site. It issues regular statistical reports, commodity studies, and technical manuals in local languages (see list of publications below). Other materials produced by the FAO include information booklets, reference papers, reports of meetings, training manuals and audio-visuals.

FAO's internet-based interactive World Agricultural Information Centre (WAICENT) offers access to agricultural publications, technical documentation, codes of conduct, data, statistics and multimedia resources. FAO compiles and co-ordinates an extensive range of international databases on agriculture, fisheries, forestry, food and statistics, the most important of these being AGRIS (the International Information System for the Agricultural Sciences and Technology) and CARIS (the Current Agricultural Research Information System). Statistical databases include the GLOBEFISH databank and electronic library, FISHDAB (the Fisheries Statistical Database), FORIS (Forest Resources Information System), and GIS (the Geographic Information System). In addition, FAOSTAT provides access to updated figures in 10 agriculture-related topics.

In June 2000 FAO organized a high-level Consultation on Agricultural Information Management (COAIM), which aimed to increase access to and use of agricultural information by policy-makers and others. The second COAIM was held in September 2002.

World Food Day, commemorating the foundation of FAO, is held annually on 16 October.

# FAO Councils and Commissions

(Based at the Rome headquarters unless otherwise indicated)

**European Commission on Agriculture:** f. 1949 to encourage and facilitate action and co-operation in technological agricultural problems among member states and between international organizations concerned with agricultural technology in Europe.

**European Commission for the Control of Foot-and-Mouth Disease:** internet www.fao.org/ag/againfo/commissions/en/eufmd/eufmd.html; f. 1953 to promote national and international action for the control of the disease in Europe and its final eradication.

**European Forestry Commission:** f. 1947 to advise on the formulation of forest policy and to review and co-ordinate its implementation on a regional level to exchange information and to make recommendations; 27 member states.

**European Inland Fisheries Advisory Commission:** internet www.fao.org/fi/body/eifac/eifac.asp; f. 1957 to promote improvements in inland fisheries and to advise member governments and FAO on inland fishery matters; 34 mems.

**FAO/WHO Codex Alimentarius Commission:** internet www.codexalimentarius.net; f. 1962 to make proposals for the co-ordination of all international food standards work and to publish a code of international food standards; established Intergovernmental Task Force on Foods Derived from Biotechnology in 1999; 165 member states.

# Finance

FAO's Regular Programme, which is financed by contributions from member governments, covers the cost of FAO's Secretariat, its Technical Co-operation Programme (TCP) and part of the cost of several special action programmes. The proposed budget for the two years 2002–03 totalled US $651.8m. Much of FAO's technical assistance programme is funded from extra-budgetary sources, predominantly by trust funds that come mainly from donor countries and international financing institutions. The single largest contributor is the United Nations Development Programme (UNDP). In 2001 total field programme expenditure amounted to $367m.

# Publications

*Animal Health Yearbook.*
*Commodity Review and Outlook* (annually).
*Environment and Energy Bulletin.*
*Ethical Issues in Food and Agriculture.*
*Fertilizer Yearbook.*
*Food Crops and Shortages* (6 a year).
*Food Outlook* (5 a year).
*Food Safety and Quality Update* (monthly; electronic bulletin).
*Forest Resources Assessment.*
*Plant Protection Bulletin* (quarterly).
*Production Yearbook.*
*Quarterly Bulletin of Statistics.*
*The State of Food and Agriculture* (annually).
*The State of Food Insecurity in the World* (annually).
*The State of World Fisheries and Aquaculture* (every two years).
*The State of the World's Forests* (every 2 years).
*Trade Yearbook.*
*Unasylva* (quarterly).
*Yearbook of Fishery Statistics.*
*Yearbook of Forest Products.*
*World Animal Review* (quarterly).
*World Watch List for Domestic Animal Diversity.*
Commodity reviews; studies, manuals.

# International Atomic Energy Agency—IAEA

**Address:** POB 100, Wagramerstrasse 5, 1400 Vienna, Austria.

**Telephone:** (1) 26000; **fax:** (1) 26007; **e-mail:** official.mail@iaea.org; **internet:** www.iaea.org/worldatom.

The International Atomic Energy Agency (IAEA) is an intergovernmental organization, established in 1957 in accordance with a decision of the General Assembly of the United Nations. Although it is autonomous, the IAEA is administratively a member of the United Nations, and reports on its activities once a year to the UN General Assembly. Its main objectives are to enlarge the contribution of atomic energy to peace, health and prosperity throughout the world and to ensure, so far as it is able, that assistance provided by it or at its request or under its supervision or control is not used in such a way as to further any military purpose.

## Organization

### (October 2003)

#### GENERAL CONFERENCE

The Conference, comprising representatives of all member states, convenes each year for general debate on the Agency's policy, budget and programme. It elects members to the Board of Governors, and approves the appointment of the Director-General; it admits new member states.

#### BOARD OF GOVERNORS

The Board of Governors consists of 35 member states: 22 elected by the General Conference for two-year periods and 13 designated by the Board from among member states which are advanced in nuclear technology. It is the principal policy-making body of the Agency and is responsible to the General Conference. Under its own authority, the Board approves all safeguards agreements, important projects and safety standards. In 1999 the General Conference adopted a resolution on expanding the Board's membership to 43, to include 18 states designated as the most advanced in nuclear technology. The resolution required ratification by two-thirds of member states to come into effect.

#### SECRETARIAT

The Secretariat, comprising about 2,200 staff, is headed by the Director-General, who is assisted by six Deputy Directors-General. The Secretariat is divided into six departments: Technical Co-operation; Nuclear Energy; Nuclear Safety; Nuclear Sciences and Applications; Safeguards; Management. A Standing Advisory Group on Safeguards Implementation advises the Director-General on technical aspects of safeguards.

**Director-General:** Dr Mohammad el-Baradei (Egypt).

## Activities

In recent years the IAEA has implemented several reforms of its management structure and operations. The Agency's functions can be divided into the following categories: technology (assisting research on and practical application of atomic energy for peaceful uses), and safety and verification (ensuring that special fissionable and other materials, services, equipment and information made available by the Agency or at its request or under its supervision are not used for any non-peaceful purpose).

#### TECHNICAL CO-OPERATION AND TRAINING

The IAEA provides assistance in the form of experts, training and equipment to technical co-operation projects and applications worldwide, with an emphasis on radiation protection and safety-related activities. Training is provided to scientists, and experts and lecturers are assigned to provide specialized help on specific nuclear applications.

#### FOOD AND AGRICULTURE

In co-operation with FAO, the Agency conducts programmes of applied research on the use of radiation and isotopes in fields including: efficiency in the use of water and fertilizers; improvement of food crops by induced mutations; eradication or control of destructive insects by the introduction of sterilized insects (radiation-based Sterile Insect Technique); improvement of livestock nutrition and health; studies on improving efficacy and reducing residues of pesticides, and increasing utilization of agricultural wastes; and food preservation by irradiation. The programmes are implemented by the Joint FAO/IAEA Division of Nuclear Techniques in Food and Agriculture and by the FAO/IAEA Agriculture and Biotechnology Laboratory, based at IAEA's laboratory complex in Seibersdorf, Austria. A new Training and Reference Centre for Food and Pesticide Control opened at Seibersdorf in 1999. The Centre was to support the implementation of national legislation and trade agreements ensuring the quality and safety of food products in international trade.

#### LIFE SCIENCES

In co-operation with the World Health Organization (WHO), the IAEA promotes the use of nuclear techniques in medicine, biology and health-related environmental research, provides training, and conducts research on techniques for improving the accuracy of radiation dosimetry.

In 2001 the IAEA/WHO Network of Secondary Standard Dosimetry Laboratories (SSDLs) comprised 80 laboratories in 62 member states. The Agency's Dosimetry Laboratory in Seibersdorf performs dose inter-comparisons for both SSDLs and radiotherapy centres. The IAEA undertakes maintenance plans for nuclear laboratories; national programmes of quality control for nuclear medicine instruments; quality control of radioimmunoassay techniques; radiation sterilization of medical supplies; and improvement of cancer therapy.

#### PHYSICAL AND CHEMICAL SCIENCES

The Agency's programme in physical sciences includes industrial applications of isotopes and radiation technology; application of nuclear techniques to mineral exploration and exploitation; radiopharmaceuticals; and hydrology, involving the use of isotope techniques for assessment of water resources. Nuclear data services are provided, and training is given for nuclear scientists from developing countries. The Physics, Chemistry and Instrumentation Laboratory at Seibersdorf supports the Agency's research in human health, industry, water resources and environment.

#### NUCLEAR POWER

At the end of 2001 there were 438 nuclear power plants in operation throughout the world, providing about 16% of total electrical energy generated during the year. There were also 32 reactors under construction. The Agency helps developing member states to introduce nuclear-powered electricity-generating plants through assistance with planning, feasibility studies, surveys of manpower and infrastructure, and safety measures. It publishes books on numerous aspects of nuclear power, and provides training courses on safety in nuclear power plants and other topics. An energy data bank collects and disseminates information on nuclear technology, and a power-reactor information system monitors the technical performance of nuclear power plants. There is increasing interest in the use of nuclear reactors for seawater desalination and radiation hydrology techniques to provide potable water. In July 1992 the EC, Japan, Russia and the USA signed an agreement to co-operate in the engineering design of an International Thermonuclear Experimental Reactor (ITER). The project aimed to demonstrate the scientific and technological feasibility of fusion energy, with the aim of providing a source of clean, abundant energy in the 21st century. An Extension Agreement, signed in 1998, provided for the continuation of the project. In November 2000 the International Project on Innovative Nuclear Reactors and Fuel Cycles (INPRO) was inaugurated. INPRO aimed to promote nuclear energy as a means of meeting future sustainable energy requirements and to facilitate the exchange of information by member states to advance innovations in nuclear technology.

#### RADIOACTIVE WASTE MANAGEMENT

The Agency provides practical help to member states in the management of radioactive waste. The Waste Management Advisory Programme (WAMAP) was established in 1987, and undertakes advisory missions in member states. A code of practice to prevent the illegal dumping of radioactive waste was drafted in 1989, and another on the international trans-boundary movement of waste was drafted in 1990. A ban on the dumping of radioactive waste at sea came into effect in February 1994, under the Convention on the Prevention of Marine Pollution by Dumping of Wastes and Other Matters (see IMO). The IAEA was to determine radioactive levels, for purposes of the Convention, and provide assistance to countries for the safe disposal of radioactive wastes. The Agency has issued modal regulations for the air, sea and land transportation of all radioactive materials.

In September 1997 the IAEA adopted a Joint Convention on the Safety of Spent Fuel Management and on the Safety of Radioactive Waste Management. The first internationally-binding legal device to address such issues, the Convention was to ensure the safe storage and disposal of nuclear and radioactive waste, during both the construction and operation of a nuclear power plant, as well as following its closure. The Convention entered into force in June 2001, and had been ratified by 30 parties at November 2002.

## NUCLEAR SAFETY

The IAEA's nuclear safety programme encourages international co-operation in the exchange of information, promoting implementation of its safety standards and providing advisory safety services. It includes the IAEA International Nuclear Event Scale; the Incident Reporting System; an emergency preparedness programme (which maintains an Emergency Response Centre); operational safety review teams; the 15-member International Nuclear Safety Advisory Group (INSAG); the Radiation Protection Advisory Team; and a safety research co-ordination programme. The safety review teams provide member states with advice on achieving and maintaining a high level of safety in the operation of nuclear power plants, while research programmes establish risk criteria for the nuclear fuel cycle and identify cost-effective means to reduce risks in energy systems. By the end of 1998 53 member states had agreed to report all nuclear events, incidents and accidents according to the International Nuclear Event Scale. In May the Director-General initiated a review of the Agency's nuclear strategy, proposing the development of national safety profiles, more active promotion of safety services and improved co-operation at governmental and non-governmental levels.

The revised edition of the Basic Safety Standards for Radiation Protection (IAEA Safety Series No. 9) was approved in 1994. The Nuclear Safety Standards programme, initiated in 1974 with five codes of practice and more than 60 safety guides, was revised in 1987 and again in 1995.

Following a serious accident at the Chornobyl (Chernobyl) nuclear power plant in Ukraine (then part of the USSR) in April 1986, two conventions were formulated by the IAEA and entered into force in October. The first, the Convention on Early Notification of a Nuclear Accident, commits parties to provide information about nuclear accidents with possible trans-boundary effects at the earliest opportunity (it had 87 parties by March 2003); and the second commits parties to endeavour to provide assistance in the event of a nuclear accident or radiological emergency (this had 84 parties by March 2003). During 1990 the IAEA organized an assessment of the consequences of the Chernobyl accident, undertaken by an international team of experts, who reported to an international conference on the effects of the accident, convened at the IAEA headquarters in Vienna in May 1991. In February 1993 INSAG published an updated report on the Chernobyl incident, which emphasized the role of design factors in the accident, and the need to implement safety measures in the RBMK-type reactor. In March 1994 an IAEA expert mission visited Chernobyl and reported continuing serious deficiencies in safety at the defunct reactor and the units remaining in operation. An international conference reviewing the radiological consequences of the accident, 10 years after the event, was held in April 1996, co-sponsored by the IAEA, WHO and the European Commission. The last of the Chernobyl plant's three operating units was officially closed in December 2000. The IAEA was to offer a wide range of assistance during Chernobyl's decommissioning period, the first stage of which was expected to have a duration of five years.

In September 1999 the IAEA activated its Emergency Response Centre, following a serious incident at a fuel conversion facility in Tokaimura, Japan. The Centre was used to process information from the Japanese authorities and to ensure accurate reporting of the event. In October a three-member IAEA team of experts visited the site to undertake a preliminary investigation into the causes and consequences of the accident.

An International Convention on Nuclear Safety was adopted at an IAEA conference in June 1994. The Convention applies to land-based civil nuclear power plants: adherents commit themselves to fundamental principles of safety, and maintain legislative frameworks governing nuclear safety. The Convention entered into force in October 1996. The first Review Meeting of Contracting Parties to the Convention was held in April 1999. By October 2002 54 states had ratified the Convention.

In September 1997 more than 80 member states adopted a protocol to revise the 1963 Vienna Convention on Civil Liability for Nuclear Damage, fixing the minimum limit of liability for the operator of a nuclear reactor at 300m. Special Drawing Rights (SDRs, the accounting units of the IMF) in the event of an accident. The amended protocol also extended the length of time during which claims may be brought for loss of life or injury. The amended protocol had been signed by 15 countries and ratified by four at February 2003. A Convention on Supplementary Compensation for Nuclear Damage established a further compensatory fund to provide for the payment of damages following an accident; contributions to the Fund were to be calculated on the basis of the nuclear capacity of each member state. The Convention had 13 signatories and three contracting states by February 2003.

In July 1996 the IAEA co-ordinated a study on the radiological situation at the Mururoa and Fangatauta atolls, following the French nuclear test programmes in the South Pacific. Results published in May 1998 concluded there was no radiological health risk and that neither remedial action nor continued environmental monitoring was necessary.

The IAEA is developing a training course on measurement methods and risk analysis relating to the presence of depleted uranium (which can be used in ammunition) in post-conflict areas. In November 2000 IAEA specialists participated in a fact-finding mission organized by UNEP in Kosovo and Metohija, which aimed to assess the environmental and health consequences of the use of depleted uranium in ammunition by NATO during its aerial offensive against the Federal Republic of Yugoslavia (now Serbia and Montenegro) in 1999. (A report on the situation was published by UNEP in March 2001.)

In May 2001 the IAEA convened an international conference to address the protection of nuclear material and radioactive sources from illegal trafficking. In September, in view of the perpetration of major terrorist attacks against targets in the USA during that month, the IAEA General Conference addressed the potential for nuclear-related terrorism. It adopted a resolution that emphasized the importance of the physical protection of nuclear material in preventing its illicit use or the sabotage of nuclear facilities and nuclear materials. Three main potential threats were identified: the acquisition by a terrorist group of a nuclear weapon; acquisition of nuclear material to construct a nuclear weapon or cause a radiological hazard; and violent acts against nuclear facilities to cause a radiological hazard. In March 2002 the Board of Governors approved in principle an action plan to improve global protection against acts of terrorism involving nuclear and other radioactive materials. The plan addressed the physical protection of nuclear materials and facilities; the detection of malicious activities involving radioactive materials; strengthening national control systems; the security of radioactive sources; evaluation of security and safety at nuclear facilities; emergency response to malicious acts or threats involving radioactive materials; ensuring adherence to international guidelines and agreements; and improvement of programme co-ordination and information management. It was estimated that the Agency's upgraded nuclear security activities would require significant additional annual funding. In March 2003 the IAEA organized an International Conference on Security of Radioactive Sources, held in Vienna.

## DISSEMINATION OF INFORMATION

The International Nuclear Information System (INIS), which was established in 1970, provides a computerized indexing and abstracting service. Information on the peaceful uses of atomic energy is collected by member states and international organizations and sent to the IAEA for processing and dissemination (see list of publications below). The IAEA also co-operates with FAO in an information system for agriculture (AGRIS) and with the World Federation of Nuclear Medicine and Biology, and the non-profit Cochrane Collaboration, in maintaining an electronic database of best practice in nuclear medicine. The IAEA Nuclear Data Section provides cost-free data centre services and co-operates with other national and regional nuclear and atomic data centres in the systematic world-wide collection, compilation, dissemination and exchange of nuclear reaction data, nuclear structure and decay data, and atomic and molecular data for fusion.

## SAFEGUARDS

The Treaty on the Non-Proliferation of Nuclear Weapons (known also as the Non-Proliferation Treaty or NPT), which entered into force in 1970, requires each 'non-nuclear-weapon state' (one which had not manufactured and exploded a nuclear weapon or other nuclear explosive device prior to 1 January 1967) which is a party to the Treaty to conclude a safeguards agreement with the IAEA. Under such an agreement, the state undertakes to accept IAEA safeguards on all nuclear material in all its peaceful nuclear activities for the purpose of verifying that such material is not diverted to nuclear weapons or other nuclear explosive devices. In May 1995 the Review and Extension Conference of parties to the NPT agreed to extend the NPT indefinitely, and reaffirmed support for the IAEA's role in verification and the transfer of peaceful nuclear technologies. At the next review conference, held in April/May 2000, the five 'nuclear-weapon states'— the People's Republic of China, France, Russia, the United Kingdom and the USA—issued a joint statement pledging their commitment to the ultimate goal of complete nuclear disarmament under effective international controls. By March 2003 181 non-nuclear-weapon states and the five nuclear-weapon states were parties to the Treaty, but a number of non-nuclear-weapon states had not complied, within the prescribed time-limit, with their obligations under the Treaty regarding the conclusion of the relevant safeguards agreement with the Agency. The Democratic Republic of Korea (DPRK), which had acceded to the NPT in December 1985, announced its immediate withdrawal from the Treaty in January 2003 (see below).

The five nuclear-weapon states have concluded safeguards agreements with the Agency that permit the application of IAEA safeguards to all their nuclear activities, excluding those with 'direct national significance'. A Comprehensive Nuclear Test Ban Treaty (CTBT) was opened for signature in September 1996, having been adopted by the UN General Assembly. The Treaty was to enter into international law upon ratification by all 44 nations with known nuclear capabilities. A separate verification organization was to be established, based in Vienna. A Preparatory Commission for the treaty organization became operational in 1997. By March 2003 166 countries had signed the CTBT and 98 had ratified it, including 31 of the 44 states with nuclear capabilities. However, the US Senate rejected ratification of the CTBT in October 1999.

Several regional nuclear weapons treaties require their member states to conclude comprehensive safeguards agreements with the IAEA. By December 2001 31 of the 32 states party to the Treaty for the prohibition of Nuclear Weapons in Latin America (Tlatelolco Treaty) had concluded safeguards agreements with the Agency, as had all 11 signatories of the South Pacific Nuclear-Free Zone Treaty (Rarotonga Treaty). The IAEA also aims to administer full applications of safeguards with the ten states party to the Treaty in the South-East Asia Nuclear-Weapon Free Zone (Treaty of Bangkok, adopted in 1995) and the states party to the African Nuclear-Weapon Free Zone Treaty (Pelindaba Treaty, adopted in 1996). In September 2002 experts from Kazakhstan, Kyrgyzstan, Tajikistan, Turkmenistan and Uzbekistan, meeting in Samarkand, Uzbekistan, approved the draft text of a treaty on establishing a Central Asian Nuclear Weapon Free Zone. At the end of 2001 a total of 225 IAEA safeguards agreements were in force with 142 states. Of these, 71 states had declared significant nuclear activities and were under inspection. At the end of the same year there were 908 nuclear installations and locations containing nuclear material subject to IAEA safeguards. A total of 2,487 inspections were conducted in that year. Expenditure on the Safeguards Regular Budget for 2001 was US \$70.0m; extra-budgetary programme expenditure amounted to \$15.2m. During 2000 the IAEA established an imagery database of nuclear sites; digital image surveillance systems had been installed in 24 countries by the end of the year.

In April 1992 the DPRK ratified a safeguards agreement with the IAEA. In late 1992 and early 1993, however, the IAEA unsuccessfully requested access to two non-declared sites in the DPRK, where it was suspected that material capable of being used for the manufacture of nuclear weapons was stored. In March 1993 the DPRK announced its intention of withdrawing from the NPT: it suspended its withdrawal in June, but continued to refuse full access to its nuclear facilities for IAEA inspectors. In May 1994 the DPRK began to refuel an experimental nuclear power reactor at Yongbyon, but refused to allow the IAEA to analyse the spent fuel rods in order to ascertain whether plutonium had been obtained from the reactor for possible military use. In June the IAEA Board of Governors halted IAEA technical assistance to the DPRK (except medical assistance) because of continuous violation of the NPT safeguards agreements. In the same month the DPRK withdrew from the IAEA (though not from the NPT); however, it allowed IAEA inspectors to remain at the Yongbyon site to conduct safeguards activities. In October the Governments of the DPRK and the USA concluded an agreement whereby the former agreed to halt construction of two new nuclear reactors, on condition that it received international aid for the construction of two 'light water' reactors (which could not produce materials for the manufacture of nuclear weapons). The DPRK also agreed to allow IAEA inspections of all its nuclear sites, but only after the installation of one of the 'light water' reactors had been completed (entailing a significant time lapse). In November IAEA inspectors visited the DPRK to initiate verification of the suspension of the country's nuclear programme, in accordance with the agreement concluded in the previous month. From 1995 the IAEA pursued technical discussions with the DPRK authorities as part of the Agency's efforts to achieve the full compliance of the DPRK with the IAEA safeguards agreement. By the end of 1999 the canning of spent fuel rods from the Yongbyon nuclear power reactor was completed. However, little overall progress had been achieved, owing to the obstruction of inspectors by the authorities in that country, including their refusal to provide samples for analysis. The IAEA was unable to verify the suspension of the nuclear programme and declared that the DPRK continued to be in non-compliance with its NPT safeguards agreement. In accordance with a decision of the General Conference in September 2001, IAEA inspectors subsequently resumed a continuous presence in the DPRK. The DPRK authorities permitted low-level inspections of the Yongbyon site by an IAEA technical team in January and May 2002. It was envisaged at that time that the new 'light water' reactors would become operational by 2008. However, in December 2002 the DPRK authorities disabled IAEA safeguards surveillance equipment placed at

three facilities in Yongbyon and took measures to restart reprocessing capabilities at the site, requesting the immediate withdrawal of the Agency's inspectors. (The inspectors were withdrawn at the end of the month.) In early January 2003 the IAEA Board of Governors adopted a resolution deploring the DPRK's non-co-operation and urging its immediate and full compliance with the Agency. Shortly afterwards, however, the DPRK announced its withdrawal from the NPT, stating that it would limit its nuclear activities to peaceful purposes. In late February the IAEA condemned the reported successful reactivation of the Yongbyon reactor.

In April 1991 the UN Security Council requested the IAEA to conduct investigations into Iraq's capacity to produce nuclear weapons, following the end of the war between Iraq and the UN-authorized, US-led multinational force. The IAEA was to work closely with a UN Special Commission of experts (UNSCOM), established by the Security Council, whose task was to inspect and dismantle Iraq's weapons of mass destruction (including chemical and biological weapons). In July the IAEA declared that Iraq had violated its safeguards agreement with the IAEA by not submitting nuclear material and relevant facilities in its uranium-enrichment programme to the Agency's inspection. This was the first time that a state party to the NPT had been condemned for concealing a programme of this nature. In October the sixth inspection team, composed of UNSCOM and representatives of the IAEA, was reported to have obtained conclusive documentary evidence that Iraq had a programme for developing nuclear weapons. By February 1994 all declared stocks of nuclear-weapons-grade material had been removed from Iraq. Subsequently, the IAEA pursued a programme of long-term surveillance of nuclear activity in Iraq, under a mandate issued by the UN Security Council. In September 1996 Iraq submitted to the IAEA a 'full, final and complete' declaration of its nuclear activities. However, in September-October 1997 the IAEA recommended that Iraq disclose further equipment, materials and information relating to its nuclear programme. In April 1998 IAEA technical experts were part of a special group that entered eight presidential sites in Iraq to collect baseline data, in accordance with a Memorandum of Understanding concluded between the UN Secretary-General and the Iraqi authorities in February. The accord aimed to ensure full Iraqi co-operation with UNSCOM and IAEA personnel. In August, however, Iraq suspended co-operation with UN inspectors, which prevented IAEA from implementing its programme of ongoing monitoring and verification (OMV) activities. Iraq's action was condemned by the IAEA General Conference in September. In October IAEA reported that while there was no evidence of Iraq having produced nuclear weapons or having retained or obtained a capability for the production of nuclear weapons, the Agency was unable to guarantee that all items had been found. All IAEA inspectors were temporarily relocated from Iraq to Bahrain in November, in accordance with a decision to withdraw UNSCOM personnel owing to Iraq's failure to agree to resume co-operation. In March 2000 UNSCOM was replaced by a new arms inspection body, the UN Monitoring, Verification and Inspection Commission (UNMOVIC). Although the IAEA carried out inventory verifications of nuclear material in Iraq in January 2000, January 2001 and January 2002, pursuant to Iraq's NPT safeguards agreement, full inspection activities in conjunction with UNMOVIC remained suspended. In September 2002 the US President expressed concern that Iraq was challenging international security owing to its non-compliance with successive UN resolutions relating to the elimination of weapons of mass destruction. In November the UN Security Council adopted Resolution 1441 providing for an enhanced inspection mission and a detailed timetable according to which Iraq would have a final opportunity to comply with its disarmament obligations. Following Iraq's acceptance of the resolution, experts from the IAEA's so-called Iraq Nuclear Verification Office and UNMOVIC resumed inspections on 27 November, with Council authorization to have unrestricted access to all areas and the right to interview Iraqi scientists and weapons experts. In early December Iraq submitted a declaration of all aspects of its weapons programmes, as required under Resolution 1441. In January 2003 Dr Mohammad el-Baradei, the IAEA Director-General, requested an ongoing mandate for his inspectors to clarify the situation regarding nuclear weapons. In mid-March el-Baradei reported that no evidence had been found of nuclear weapons programme activities in Iraq. At that time, however, IAEA and UNMOVIC personnel were withdrawn from Iraq owing to the unilateral initiation of military action against the Iraqi regime by US and allied forces.

In late 1997 the IAEA began inspections in the USA to verify the conversion for peaceful uses of nuclear material released from the military sector. In 1998 the United Kingdom announced that substantial quantities of nuclear material previously in its military programme would become available for verification under its voluntary offer safeguards agreement.

In June 1995 the Board of Governors approved measures to strengthen the safeguards system, including allowing inspection teams greater access to suspected nuclear sites and to information on nuclear activities in member states, reducing the notice time for inspections by removing visa requirements for inspectors and using environmental monitoring (i.e. soil, water and air samples) to test for signs of radioactivity. In April 1996 the IAEA initiated a programme to prevent and combat illicit trafficking of nuclear weapons, and in May 1998 the IAEA and the World Customs Organization signed a Memorandum of Understanding to enhance co-operation in the prevention of illicit nuclear trafficking. In May 1997 the Board of Governors adopted a model additional protocol approving measures to strengthen safeguards further, in order to ensure the compliance of non-nuclear-weapon states with IAEA commitments. The new protocol compelled member states to provide inspection teams with improved access to information concerning existing and planned nuclear activities, and to allow access to locations other than known nuclear sites within that country's territory. By March 2003 29 states had ratified additional protocols to their safeguards agreements.

IAEA's Safeguards Analytical Laboratory analyses nuclear fuel-cycle samples collected by IAEA safeguards inspectors. The Agency's Marine Environment Laboratory, in Monaco, studies radionuclides and other ocean pollutants.

### NUCLEAR FUEL CYCLE

The Agency promotes the exchange of information between member states on technical, safety, environmental, and economic aspects of nuclear fuel cycle technology, including uranium prospecting and the treatment and disposal of radioactive waste; it provides assistance to member states in the planning, implementation and operation of nuclear fuel cycle facilities and assists in the development of advanced nuclear fuel cycle technology. Every two years, in collaboration with OECD, the Agency prepares estimates of world uranium resources, demand and production.

## Finance

The Agency is financed by regular and voluntary contributions from member states. Expenditure approved under the regular budget for 2003 amounted to some US $249m., and the target for voluntary contributions to finance the IAEA technical assistance and co-operation programme in that (and the following) year was $75m.

## Publications

*Annual Report.*

*IAEA Bulletin* (quarterly).

*IAEA Newsbriefs* (every 2 months).

*IAEA Yearbook.*

*INIS Atomindex* (bibliography, 2 a month).

*INIS Reference Series.*

*INSAG Series.*

*Legal Series.*

*Meetings on Atomic Energy* (quarterly).

*The Nuclear Fuel Cycle Information System: A Directory of Nuclear Fuel Cycle Facilities.*

*Nuclear Fusion* (monthly).

*Nuclear Safety Review* (annually).

*Panel Proceedings Series.*

*Publications Catalogue* (annually).

*Safety Series.*

*Technical Directories.*

*Technical Reports Series.*

# International Bank for Reconstruction and Development—IBRD (World Bank)

**Address:** 1818 H St, NW, Washington, DC 20433, USA.

**Telephone:** (202) 477-1234; **fax:** (202) 477-6391; **e-mail:** pic@worldbank.org; **internet:** www.worldbank.org.

The IBRD was established in December 1945. Initially it was concerned with post-war reconstruction in Europe; since then its aim has been to assist the economic development of member nations by making loans where private capital is not available on reasonable terms to finance productive investments. Loans are made either directly to governments, or to private enterprises with the guarantee of their governments. The World Bank, as it is commonly known, comprises the IBRD and the International Development Association (IDA). The affiliated group of institutions, comprising the IBRD, the IDA, the International Finance Corporation (IFC), the Multilateral Investment Guarantee Agency (MIGA) and the International Centre for Settlement of Investment Disputes (ICSID, see below), is now referred to as the World Bank Group.

## Organization

(October 2003)

Officers and staff of the IBRD serve concurrently as officers and staff in the IDA. The World Bank has offices in New York, Brussels, Paris (for Europe), Frankfurt, London, Geneva and Tokyo, as well as in more than 100 countries of operation. Country Directors are located in some 28 country offices.

### BOARD OF GOVERNORS

The Board of Governors consists of one Governor appointed by each member nation. Typically, a Governor is the country's finance minister, central bank governor, or a minister or an official of comparable rank. The Board normally meets once a year.

### EXECUTIVE DIRECTORS

The general operations of the Bank are conducted by a Board of 24 Executive Directors. Five Directors are appointed by the five members having the largest number of shares of capital stock, and the rest are elected by the Governors representing the other members. The President of the Bank is Chairman of the Board.

### PRINCIPAL OFFICERS

The principal officers of the Bank are the President of the Bank, four Managing Directors, two Senior Vice-Presidents and 23 Vice-Presidents.

**President and Chairman of Executive Directors:** JAMES D. WOLFENSOHN (USA).

**Vice-President, Europe and Central Asia:** JOHANNES F. LINN.

## Activities

### FINANCIAL OPERATIONS

IBRD capital is derived from members' subscriptions to capital shares, the calculation of which is based on their quotas in the International Monetary Fund. At 30 June 2002 the total subscribed capital of the IBRD was US $189,505m., of which the paid-in portion was $11,476m. (6.1%); the remainder is subject to call if required. Most of the IBRD's lendable funds come from its borrowing, on commercial terms, in world capital markets, and also from its retained earnings and the flow of repayments on its loans. IBRD loans carry a variable interest rate, rather than a rate fixed at the time of borrowing.

IBRD loans usually have a 'grace period' of five years and are repayable over 15 years or fewer. Loans are made to governments, or must be guaranteed by the government concerned, and are normally made for projects likely to offer a commercially viable rate of return. In 1980 the World Bank introduced structural adjustment lending, which (instead of financing specific projects) supports programmes and changes necessary to modify the structure of an economy so that it can restore or maintain its growth and viability in its balance of payments over the medium term.

The IBRD and IDA together made 229 new lending and investment commitments totalling US $19,519.4m. during the year ending 30 June 2002, compared with 225 (amounting to $17,250.6m.) in the previous year. During 2001/02 the IBRD alone approved commitments totalling $11,451.8m. (compared with $10,487.1m. in the previous year), of which $4,894.7m. (43%) was allocated to Europe and Central Asia. Disbursements by the IBRD in the year ending 30 June 2002 amounted to $11,256m.

IBRD operations are supported by medium- and long-term borrowings in international capital markets. During the year ending 30 June 2002 the IBRD's net income amounted to US $2,778m.

The World Bank's primary objectives are the achievement of sustainable economic growth and the reduction of poverty in developing countries. In the context of stimulating economic growth the Bank promotes both private-sector development and human resource development and has attempted to respond to the growing demands by developing countries for assistance in these areas. In March 1997 the Board of Executive Directors endorsed a 'Strategic Compact', providing for a programme of reforms, to be implemented over a period of 30 months, to increase the effectiveness of the Bank in achieving its central objective of poverty reduction. The reforms included greater decentralization of decision-making, and investment in front-line operations, enhancing the administration of loans, and improving access to information and co-ordination of Bank activities through a knowledge management system comprising four thematic networks: the Human Development Network; the Environmentally and Socially Sustainable Development Network; the Finance, Private Sector and Infrastructure Development Network; and the Poverty Reduction and Economic Management Network. In 2000/01 the Bank adopted a new two-year Strategic Framework which emphasized two essential approaches for Bank support: strengthening the investment climate and prospects for sustainable development in a country, and supporting investment in the poor. In September 2001 the Bank announced that it was to join the UN as a full partner in implementing the so-called Millennium Development Goals, and was to make them central to its development agenda. The objectives, which were approved by governments attending a special session of the UN General Assembly in September 2000, included a reduction by 50% in the number of people with an income of less than US $1 a day and those suffering from hunger and lack of safe drinking water by 2015. The Bank was closely involved in preparations for the International Conference on Financing for Development, which was held in Monterrey, Mexico, in March 2002. The meeting adopted the Monterrey Consensus, which outlined measures to support national development efforts and to achieve the Millennium Development Goals.

The Bank's efforts to reduce poverty include the compilation of country-specific assessments and the formulation of country assistance strategies (CASs) to review and guide the Bank's country programmes. Since August 1998 the Bank has published CASs, with the approval of the government concerned. In 1998/99 the Bank's Executive Directors endorsed a Comprehensive Development Framework (CDF) to effect a new approach to development assistance based on partnerships and country responsibility, with an emphasis on the interdependence of the social, structural, human, governmental, economic and environmental elements of development. The Framework, which aimed to enhance the overall effectiveness of development assistance, was formulated after a series of consultative meetings organized by the Bank and attended by representatives of governments, donor agencies, financial institutions, non-governmental organizations, the private sector and academics.

In December 1999 the Bank introduced a new approach to implement the principles of the CDF, as part of its strategy to enhance the debt relief scheme for heavily indebted poor countries (see below). Applicant countries were requested to formulate a national strategy to reduce poverty, to be presented in the form of a Poverty Reduction Strategy Papers (PRSP). In cases where there might be some delay in issuing a full PRSP, it was permissible for a country to submit a less detailed 'interim' PRSP (I-PRSP) in order to secure the preliminary qualification for debt relief. During 2001/02 seven countries completed PRSPs and nine countries issued interim papers. In 2000/01 the Bank introduced a new Poverty Reduction Support Credit to help low-income countries to implement the policy and institutional reforms outlined in their PRSP. The first credits were approved for Uganda and Viet Nam in May and June respectively. In January 2002 a PRSP public review conference, attended by more than 200 representatives of donor agencies, civil society groups, and developing country organizations was held as part of an ongoing review of the scheme by the Bank and the IMF.

In September 1996 the World Bank/IMF Development Committee endorsed a joint initiative to assist heavily indebted poor countries (HIPCs) to reduce their debt burden to a sustainable level, in order to make more resources available for poverty reduction and economic growth. A new Trust Fund was established by the World Bank in November to finance the initiative. The Fund, consisting of an initial allocation of US $500m. from the IBRD surplus and other contributions from multilateral creditors, was to be administered by IDA. In early 1999 the World Bank and IMF initiated a comprehensive review of the HIPC initiative. In June the G-7 and Russia, meeting in Cologne, Germany, agreed to increase contributions to the HIPC Trust Fund and to cancel substantial amounts of outstanding debt, and proposed more flexible terms for eligibility. In September the Bank and IMF reached an agreement on an enhanced HIPC scheme, with further revenue to be generated through the revaluation of a percentage of IMF gold reserves. It was agreed that,

in order to qualify for debt relief and additional concessional lending, countries were to formulate a PRSP, and should demonstrate prudent financial management in the implementation of the strategy for at least one year. Those countries still deemed to have an unsustainable level of debt at the pivotal 'decision point' of the process were to qualify for assistance. In the majority of cases a sustainable level of debt was targeted at 150% of the net present value (NPV) of the debt in relation to total annual exports (compared with 200%–250% under the original HIPC scheme). Other countries with a lower debt-to-export ratio were to be eligible for assistance under the initiative, providing that their export earnings were at least 30% of GDP (lowered from 40%) and government revenue at least 15% of GDP (reduced from 20%).

In addition to providing financial services, the Bank also undertakes analytical and advisory services, and supports learning and capacity-building, in particular through the World Bank Institute (see below), the Staff Exchange Programme and knowledge-sharing initiatives. The Bank has supported efforts, such as the Global Development Gateway, to disseminate information on development issues and programmes.

### TECHNICAL ASSISTANCE

The provision of technical assistance to member countries has become a major component of World Bank activities. The economic and sector work (ESW) undertaken by the Bank is the vehicle for considerable technical assistance. In addition, project loans and credits may include funds earmarked specifically for feasibility studies, resource surveys, management or planning advice, and training. The Economic Development Institute has become one of the most important of the Bank's activities in technical assistance. It provides training in national economic management and project analysis for government officials at the middle and upper levels of responsibility. It also runs overseas courses aiming to build up local training capability, and administers a graduate scholarship programme.

The Bank serves as an executing agency for projects financed by the UN Development Programme. It also administers projects financed by various trust funds.

Technical assistance (usually reimbursable) is also extended to countries that do not need Bank financial support, e.g. for training and transfer of technology. The Bank encourages the use of local consultants to assist with projects and stimulate institutional capability.

The Project Preparation Facility (PPF) was established in 1975 to provide cash advances to prepare projects that may be financed by the Bank. In December 1994 the PPF's commitment authority was increased from US $220m. to $250m. In 1992 the Bank established an Institutional Development Fund (IDF), which became operational on 1 July; the purpose of the Fund was to provide rapid, small-scale financial assistance, to a maximum value of $500,000, for capacity-building proposals.

### ECONOMIC RESEARCH AND STUDIES

In the 1990s the World Bank's research, conducted by its own research staff, was increasingly concerned with providing information to reinforce the Bank's expanding advisory role to developing countries and to improve policy in the Bank's borrowing countries. The principal areas of current research focus on issues such as maintaining sustainable growth while protecting the environment and the poorest sectors of society, encouraging the development of the private sector, and reducing and decentralizing government activities.

The Bank chairs the Consultative Group on International Agricultural Research (CGIAR), which was founded in 1971 to raise financial support for international agricultural research work for improving crops and animal production in the developing countries; it supports 16 research centres.

### CO-OPERATION WITH OTHER ORGANIZATIONS

The World Bank co-operates closely with other UN bodies, at the project level, particularly in the design of social funds and social action programmes. It collaborates with the IMF in implementing economic adjustment programmes in developing countries. The Bank holds regular consultations with the European Union and OECD on development issues, and the Bank-NGO Committee provides an annual forum for discussion with non-governmental organizations (NGOs). In September 1995 the Bank initiated the Information for Development Programme (InfoDev) with the aim of fostering partnerships between governments, multilateral institutions and private-sector experts in order to promote reform and investment in developing countries through improved access to information technology. Strengthening co-operation with external partners was a fundamental element of the Comprehensive Development Framework, which was adopted in 1998/99 (see above). In 2001/02 a Partnership Approval and Tracking System was implemented to provide information on the Bank's regional and global partnerships.

In June 1995 the World Bank joined other international donors (including regional development banks, other UN bodies, Canada, France, the Netherlands and the USA) in establishing a Consultative Group to Assist the Poorest (CGAP), which was to channel funds to the most needy through grass-roots agencies. An initial credit of approximately US \$200m. was committed by the donors. The Bank manages the CGAP Secretariat, which is responsible for the administration of external funding and for the evaluation and approval of project financing. The CGAP provides technical assistance, training and strategic advice to microfinance institutions and other relevant bodies. As an implementing agency of the Global Environment Facility (GEF) the Bank assists countries to prepare and supervise GEF projects relating to biological diversity, climate change and other environmental protection measures.

In 1997 a Partnerships Group was established to strengthen the Bank's work with development institutions, representatives of civil society and the private sector. The Group established a new Development Grant Facility, which became operational in October, to support partnership initiatives and to co-ordinate all of the Bank's grant-making activities. Also in 1997 the Bank, in partnership with the IMF, UNCTAD, UNDP, the World Trade Organization (WTO) and International Trade Commission, established an Integrated Framework for Trade-related Assistance to Least Developed Countries, at the request of the WTO, to assist those countries to integrate into the global trading system and improve basic trading capabilities.

In December 1998 the Bank convened a special donor conference to assist the countries most severely affected by the Russian economic crisis, which had led to the devaluation of that country's currency, the rouble, in August. The conference raised some US \$200m. in additional balance-of-payments support for Armenia, Azerbaijan, Georgia, Kyrgyzstan, Moldova and Tajikistan. In 1997 a Partnerships Group was established to strengthen the Bank's work with development institutions, representatives of civil society and the private sector. The Group established a Development Grant Facility to support partnership initiatives in key areas of concern and to co-ordinate all of the Bank's grant-making activities.

The Bank conducts co-financing and aid co-ordination projects with official aid agencies, export credit institutions, and commercial banks. During the year ending 30 June 2002 a total of 109 IBRD and IDA projects involved co-financers' contributions amounting to US \$4,700m., or 26% of total bank lending.

### EVALUATION

The Operations Evaluation Department is an independent unit within the World Bank, which studies and publishes the results of projects after a loan has been fully disbursed, so as to identify problems and possible improvements in future activities. In 1996 a Quality Assurance Group was established to monitor the effectiveness of the Bank's operations and performance.

In September 1993 the Bank's Board of Executive Directors agreed to establish an independent Inspection Panel, consistent with the Bank's objective of improving project implementation and accountability. The panel, which became operational in September 1994, was to conduct independent investigations and report on complaints concerning the design, appraisal and implementation of development projects supported by the Bank. By mid-2002 the panel had received 26 formal requests for inspection.

### IBRD INSTITUTIONS

**World Bank Institute (WBI):** founded in March 1999 by merger of the Bank's Learning and Leadership Centre, previously responsible for internal staff training, and the Economic Development Institute (EDI), which had been established in 1955 to train government officials concerned with development programmes and policies. The new Institute aimed to emphasize the Bank's priority areas through the provision of training courses and seminars relating to poverty, crisis response, good governance and anti-corruption strategies. The Institute co-ordinated a process of consultation and dialogue with researchers and other representatives of civil society to examine poverty for the 2000/01 *World Development Report*. During 1999/2000 the WBI expanded its programmes through distance learning, global knowledge networks, and use of new technologies. Under the EDI a World Links for Development programme was initiated to connect schools in developing countries with partner establishments in industrialized nations via the internet. A new initiative, Global Development Learning Network (GDLN), aimed to expand access to information and learning opportunities through the internet, videoconferences and organized exchanges. At mid-2002 37 GDLN distance learning centres were operational and 42

sites were under development; Vice-Pres. FRANNIE LÉAUTIER (Tanzania/France).

**International Centre for Settlement of Investment Disputes (ICSID):** founded in 1966 under the Convention of the Settlement of Investment Disputes between States and Nationals of Other States. The Convention was designed to encourage the growth of private foreign investment for economic development, by creating the possibility, always subject to the consent of both parties, for a Contracting State and a foreign investor who is a national of another Contracting State to settle any legal dispute that might arise out of such an investment by conciliation and/or arbitration before an impartial, international forum. The governing body of the Centre is its Administrative Council, composed of one representative of each Contracting State, all of whom have equal voting power. The President of the World Bank is (*ex officio*) the non-voting Chairman of the Administrative Council. At March 2003 139 countries had signed and ratified the Convention to become ICSID Contracting States. By December 2002 the Centre had considered 68 cases, while 46 were pending; Sec.-Gen. KO-YUNG TUNG (Japan).

# Publications

*Abstracts of Current Studies: The World Bank Research Program* (annually).

*Annual Report on Operations Evaluation.*

*Annual Report on Portfolio Performance.*

*Annual Review of Development Effectiveness.*

*EDI Annual Report.*

*Global Commodity Markets* (quarterly).

*Global Development Finance* (annually, also on CD-Rom and online).

*Global Economic Prospects* (annually).

*ICSID Annual Report.*

*ICSID Review—Foreign Investment Law Journal* (2 a year).

*Joint BIS-IMF-OECD-World Bank Statistics on External Debt* (quarterly, also available on the internet at www.worldbank.org/data/jointdebt.html).

*New Products and Outreach* (EDI, annually).

*News from ICSID* (2 a year).

*Poverty Reduction Strategies Newsletter* (quarterly).

*Research News* (quarterly).

*Staff Working Papers.*

*Transition* (every 2 months).

*World Bank Annual Report.*

*World Bank Atlas* (annually).

*World Bank Economic Review* (3 a year).

*The World Bank and the Environment* (annually).

*World Bank Research Observer.*

*World Development Indicators* (annually, also on CD-Rom and online).

*World Development Report* (annually, also on CD-Rom).

# Statistics

**IBRD Loans Approved in Eastern Europe, Russia and Central Asia, 1 July 2001–30 June 2002**
(US \$ million)

| Country | Purpose | Amount |
|---|---|---|
| Russian Federation . . | Treasury modernization adaptable programme | 231.0 |
| | Fiscal federalism and regional fiscal reform adjustment | 120.0 |
| Ukraine. . . . | Private sector development | 30.0 |
| | Social investment fund | 50.2 |
| | First programmatic adjustment loan | 250.0 |
| Uzbekistan. . . | Rural enterprise support | 36.1 |
| | Bukhara and Samarkand water supply and sanitation investment* | 20.0 |

* Joint IBRD/IDA funded project.

Source: *World Bank Annual Report 2002.*

# International Development Association—IDA

**Address:** 1818 H Street, NW, Washington, DC 20433, USA.

**Telephone:** (202) 477-1234; **fax:** (202) 477-6391; **internet:** www.worldbank.org/ida.

The International Development Association began operations in November 1960. Affiliated to the IBRD, IDA advances capital to the poorer developing member countries on more flexible terms than those offered by the IBRD.

## Organization

(October 2003)

Officers and staff of the IBRD serve concurrently as officers and staff of IDA.

**President and Chairman of Executive Directors:** JAMES D. WOLFENSOHN (*ex officio*).

## Activities

IDA assistance is aimed at the poorer developing countries (i.e. those with an annual GNP per capita of less than US $885 in 2001 dollars qualified for assistance in 2002/03). Under IDA lending conditions, credits can be extended to countries whose balance of payments could not sustain the burden of repayment required for IBRD loans. Terms are more favourable than those provided by the IBRD; credits are for a period of 35 or 40 years, with a 'grace period' of 10 years, and carry no interest charges. At mid-2002 81 countries were eligible for IDA assistance, including several small-island economies with a GNP per head greater than $885, but which would otherwise have little or no access to Bank funds, and 14 so-called 'blend borrowers' (such as India), which are entitled to borrow from both the IDA and IBRD. IDA administers a Trust Fund, which was established in November 1996 as part of a World Bank/IMF initiative to assist heavily indebted poor countries (HIPCs).

IDA's total development resources, consisting of members' subscriptions and supplementary resources (additional subscriptions and contributions), are replenished periodically by contributions from the more affluent member countries. In November 1998 representatives of 39 donor countries agreed to provide US $11,600m. for the 12th replenishment of IDA funds, enabling total lending to amount to an estimated $20,500m. in the period July 1999–June 2002. The new IDA-12 resources were to be directed towards the following objectives: investing in people; promoting good governance; promoting broad-based growth; and protecting the environment. Discussions on the 13th replenishment of IDA funds commenced in February 2001, and for the first time involved representatives of borrowing countries, civil society and other public groups. A final commitment, providing for some US $23,000m. in resources in the period 1 July 2002–30 June 2005, was concluded in early July 2002.

During the year ending 30 June 2002 IDA credits totalling US $8,067.6m. were approved. Some 70% of new lending was for investment projects, in particular for the provision of basic social services and public administration, some 25% was in the form of adjustment credits.

## Publication

*Annual Report.*

## Statistics

**IDA Credits Approved in Eastern Europe, Russia and Central Asia, 1 July 2001–30 June 2002**
(US $ million)

| Country | Purpose | Amount |
|---|---|---|
| Armenia  .  .  . | Natural resources management and poverty reduction project | 8.3 |
| | Foreign investment and export facilitation learning and innovation | 1.0 |
| | Enterprise incubator learning and innovation | 5.0 |
| | Irrigation development project | 24.9 |
| Azerbaijan .  .  . | Second institution-building technical assistance credit | 9.5 |
| | Second structural adjustment credit | 60.0 |
| Georgia .  .  .  . | Health project supplemental credit | 2.7 |
| Kyrgyzstan.  .  . | Rural water supply and sanitation | 15.0 |
| Moldova.  .  .  . | Rural investment and services credit | 10.5 |
| | Third structural adjustment investment credit | 30.0 |
| | Structural adjustment credit—IDA reflow | 5.0 |
| Tajikistan .  .  . | Pamir private power project | 10.0 |
| | Dushanbe water supply investment and maintenance | 17.0 |
| | Second poverty alleviation investment credit | 13.8 |
| Uzbekistan.  .  . | Bukhara and Samarkand water supply and sanitation investment* | 20.0 |

* Joint IBRD/IDA funded project.

Source: *World Bank Annual Report 2002.*

# International Finance Corporation—IFC

**Address:** 2121 Pennsylvania Ave, NW, Washington, DC 20433, USA.

**Telephone:** (202) 473-9331; **fax:** (202) 974-4384; **e-mail:** information@ifc.org; **internet:** www.ifc.org.

IFC was founded in 1956 as a member of the World Bank Group to stimulate economic growth in developing countries by financing private-sector investments, mobilizing capital in international financial markets, and providing technical assistance and advice to governments and businesses.

## Organization

(October 2003)

IFC is a separate legal entity in the World Bank Group. Executive Directors of the World Bank also serve as Directors of IFC. The President of the World Bank is *ex officio* Chairman of the IFC Board of Directors, which has appointed him President of IFC. Subject to his overall supervision, the day-to-day operations of IFC are conducted by its staff under the direction of the Executive Vice-President.

### PRINCIPAL OFFICERS

**President:** JAMES D. WOLFENSOHN (USA).

**Executive Vice-President:** PETER L. WOICKE (Germany).

**Director, Regional Department for Central and Eastern Europe:** EDWARD NASSIM.

**Director, Regional Department for Southern Europe and Central Asia:** KHOSROW ZAMANI.

### OFFICES IN THE REGION

**Armenia:** 375010 Yerevan, V. Sargsyan St 9, Republic Sq.; tel. (2) 54-52-41; fax (2) 59-95-45; Senior Project Officer NERSES KARAMANUKYAN.

**Azerbaijan:** 370004 Baku, Mirza Mansur St 91-95; tel. (12) 92-19-41; fax (12) 92-14-79; Programme Co-ordinator ALIYA NURIYEVA.

**Belarus:** 220033 Minsk, pr. Partizanski 6A, 3rd Floor; tel. (17) 219-78-11; fax (17) 222-74-40; Project Man. IVAN IVANOV.

**Georgia:** 380079 Tbilisi, Chavchavadze Ave 5A First Drive; tel. (32) 91-30-96; fax (32) 91-34-78; Programme Co-ordinator ANNA AKHALKATSI.

**Kazakhstan:** 480100 Almaty, Kazybek bi 41, 4th Floor; tel. (3272) 98-05-80; fax (3272) 98-05-81; Regional Rep. GORTON DE MOND.

**Kyrgyzstan:** 720010 Bishkek, Moskovskaya 214; tel. (312) 61-06-50; fax (312) 61-03-56; Dir GOULNOURA DJOUZENOVA.

**Moldova:** 2012 Chişinău, str. Sciusev 76/6; tel. (2) 23-70-65; fax (2) 23-39-08; Country Man. ROBERTO ALBISETTI.

**Russian Federation:** 103069 Moscow, Bolshaia Molchanovka 36, Bldg 1; tel. (095) 411-75-55; fax (095) 411-75-56; Dir EDWARD NASSIM.

**Tajikistan:** Dushanbe, Rudaki 105; tel. (372) 21-07-56; fax (372) 51-00-42; Investment Officer OLIM KHOMIDOV.

**Ukraine:** 01024 Kiev, vul. Bogomoltsa 4, 5th Floor; tel. (44) 253-05-39; fax (44) 490-58-30; Programme Officer ELENA VOLOSHINA.

**Uzbekistan:** 700048 Tashkent, Amir Temur 107B, Business Center Floor 15C, c/o IBRD (World Bank); tel. (71) 138-59-50; fax (71) 138-59-51; Country Officer ELBEK RIKHSIYEV.

## Activities

IFC aims to promote economic development in developing member countries by assisting the growth of private enterprise and effective capital markets. It finances private sector projects, through loans, the purchase of equity, quasi-equity products, and risk management services, and assists governments to create conditions that stimulate the flow of domestic and foreign private savings and investment. IFC may provide finance for a project that is partly state-owned, provided that there is participation by the private sector and that the project is operated on a commercial basis. IFC also mobilizes additional resources from other financial institutions, in particular through syndicated loans, thus providing access to international capital markets. IFC provides a range of advisory services to help to improve the investment climate in developing countries and offers technical assistance to private enterprises and governments.

To be eligible for financing, projects must be profitable for investors, as well as financially and economically viable, must benefit the economy of the country concerned, and must comply with IFC's environmental and social guide-lines. IFC aims to promote best corporate governance and management methods and sustainable business practices, and encourages partnerships between governments, non-governmental organizations and community groups. In mid-2002 IFC published its first Sustainability Review, reflecting its emphasis on sustainability as a key strategic and corporate priority.

IFC's authorized capital is US $2,450m. At 30 June 2002 paid-in capital was $2,360m. The World Bank was originally the principal source of borrowed funds, but IFC also borrows from private capital markets. IFC's net income amounted to $215m. in 2001/02, compared with $345m. in the previous year.

In the year ending 30 June 2002 project financing approved by IFC amounted to US $5,835m. for 223 projects (compared with $5,357m. for 240 projects in the previous year). Of the total approved, $4,006m. was for IFC's own account, while $1,829m. was in the form of loan syndications and underwriting of securities issues and investment funds by more than 100 participant banks and institutional investors. Generally, the IFC limits its financing to less than 25% of the total cost of a project, but may take up to a 35% stake in a venture (although never as a majority shareholder). Disbursements for IFC's account amounted to $1,498m. in 2001/02 (compared with $1,535m. in the previous year).

Projects approved during 2001/02 were located in 63 countries and regions. The largest proportion of commitments was allocated to Latin America and the Caribbean (41%); East Asia and the Pacific and Europe and Central Asia both received 21%, South Asia and sub-Saharan Africa 7%, and the Middle East and North Africa received 4%. The Corporation invests in a wide variety of business and financial institutions in a broad range of sectors. In 2001/02 more than one-third of total financing committed (34%) was for financial services. Other financing included transportation, warehousing and utilities (17%), information technologies (9%), construction and real estate (8%), and non-metallic mineral product manufacturing (6%).

The dissolution of the USSR in 1991, and the transition to market economies there and in other Central and Eastern European countries, led to an increase in IFC activities in the region during the 1990s. In order to facilitate the privatization process in that region, the IFC has conducted several single-enterprise advisory assignments and has undertaken work to formulate models that can be easily replicated, notably for small-scale privatization and the privatization of agricultural land in Belarus, the Russian Federation and Ukraine. IFC has also been active in supporting and attracting foreign direct investment to exploit business opportunities in the region.

During 2001/02 IFC approved total financing of US $1,365m. for 71 projects in Europe and Central Asia, compared with $1,091m. for 58 projects in the region in the previous year. Projects for which IFC funding was approved in 2002 included support for banks and other parts of the financial sector in Georgia, Kazakhstan, Kyrgyzstan, Moldova, Russia, Ukraine and Uzbekistan; and the promotion of tourism in Armenia, Azerbaijan and Kazakhstan.

In May 2000 IFC established a Private Enterprise Partnership, within the Central and Eastern Europe department, which aimed to work with donors, investors, local businesses and governments in the countries of the former Soviet Union to attract direct investment, stimulate the growth of small and medium-sized enterprises, and to improve the business environment. In 2001 the Partnership established a project to promote sustainable forestry in Russia and advised the governments of Armenia and Russia on means of enhancing the investment environment.

IFC offers risk-management services, assisting institutions to avoid financial risks that arise from changes in interest rates, in exchange rates or in commodity prices. In 2001/02 IFC approved 11 risk-management projects for companies and banks, bringing the total number of projects approved since the introduction of the service in 1990 to 104 in 39 countries.

In 1999/2000 the IFC and World Bank advisory services were integrated into the Private Sector Advisory Services (PSAS). PSAS advises governments and private enterprises on policy, transaction implementation and foreign direct investment. The Foreign Investment Advisory Service (FIAS), established in 1986, provides advice on promoting foreign investment and strengthening the country's investment framework at the request of governments. During 2001/02 FIAS completed 50 advisory projects. Under the Technical Assistance Trust Funds Program (TATF), established in 1988, IFC manages resources contributed by various governments and agencies to provide finance for feasibility studies, project identification studies and other types of technical assistance relating to project preparation.

## Publications

*Annual Report.*

*Emerging Stock Markets Factbook* (annually).

*Impact* (quarterly).

*Lessons of Experience* (series).

*Results on the Ground* (series).

*Review of Small Businesses* (annually).

Discussion papers and technical documents.

# Multilateral Investment Guarantee Agency—MIGA

**Address:** 1818 H Street, NW, Washington, DC 20433, USA.
**Telephone:** (202) 473-6163; **fax:** (202) 522-2630; **internet:** www.miga.org.

MIGA was founded in 1988 as an affiliate of the World Bank. Its mandate is to encourage the flow of foreign direct investment to, and among, developing member countries, through the provision of political risk insurance and investment marketing services to foreign investors and host governments, respectively.

## Organization

(October 2003)

MIGA is legally and financially separate from the World Bank. It is supervised by a Council of Governors (comprising one Governor and one Alternate of each member country) and an elected Board of Directors (of no less than 12 members).

**President:** JAMES D. WOLFENSOHN (USA).

**Executive Vice-President:** MOTOMICHI IKAWA (Japan).

## Activities

The convention establishing MIGA took effect in April 1988. Authorized capital was US $1,082m. In April 1998 the Board of Directors approved an increase in MIGA's capital base. A grant of $150m. was transferred from the IBRD as part of the package, while the capital increase (totalling $700m. callable capital and $150m. paid-in capital) was approved by MIGA's Council of Governors in April 1999. A three-year subscription period then commenced, covering the period April 1999–March 2002. At 30 June 2002 total subscriptions to the capital stock amounted to $1,713m., of which $328m. was paid-in.

MIGA guarantees eligible investments against losses resulting from non-commercial risks, under four main categories:

(i) transfer risk resulting from host government restrictions on currency conversion and transfer;

(ii) risk of loss resulting from legislative or administrative actions of the host government;

(iii) repudiation by the host government of contracts with investors in cases in which the investor has no access to a competent forum;

(iv) the risk of armed conflict and civil unrest.

Before guaranteeing any investment, MIGA must ensure that it is commercially viable, contributes to the development process and is not harmful to the environment. During the fiscal year 1998/99 MIGA and IFC appointed the first Compliance Advisor and Ombudsman to consider the concerns of local communities directly affected by MIGA or IFC sponsored projects. In February 1999 the Board of Directors approved an increase in the amount of political risk insurance available for each project, from US $75m. to $200m.

During the year ending 30 June 2002 MIGA issued 58 investment insurance contracts for 33 projects in 24 countries with a value of US $1,357m., compared with 66 contracts valued at $2,000m. in the previous financial year. The amount of direct investment associated with the contracts in 2001/02 totalled approximately $4,700m. (compared with $5,200m. in 2000/01), bringing the total estimate investment facilitated since 1988 to $45,800m. through 597 contracts.

MIGA also provides policy and advisory services to promote foreign investment in developing countries and in transitional economies, and disseminates information on investment opportunities. In October 1995 MIGA established a new network on investment opportunities, which connected investment promotion agencies (IPAs) throughout the world on an electronic information network. The so-called IPA*net* aimed to encourage further investments among developing countries, to provide access to comprehensive information on investment laws and conditions and to strengthen links between governmental, business and financial associations and investors. A new version of IPA*net* was launched in 1997 (and can be accessed at www.ipanet.net). In June 1998 MIGA initiated a new internet-based facility, 'PrivatizationLink', to provide information on investment opportunities resulting from the privatization of industries in developing economies. In October 2000 a specialized facility within the service was established to facilitate investment in Russia (russia.privatizationlink.com). During 2000/01 an office was established in Paris, France, to promote and co-ordinate European investment in developing countries, in particular in Africa and Eastern Europe. In September 2002 a new regional office was inaugurated in Singapore, in order to facilitate foreign investment in Asia. In April MIGA launched a new service, 'FDIXchange', to provide potential investors, advisors and financial institutions with up-to-date market analysis and information on foreign direct investment opportunities in emerging economies (accessible at www.fdixchange.com).

## Publications

*Annual Report.*
*Investment Promotion Quarterly* (electronic news update).
*MIGA News* (quarterly).

# International Monetary Fund—IMF

**Address:** 700 19th St, NW, Washington, DC 20431, USA.
**Telephone:** (202) 623-7300; **fax:** (202) 623-6220; **e-mail:** publicaffairs@imf.org; **internet:** www.imf.org.

The IMF was established at the same time as the World Bank in December 1945, to promote international monetary co-operation, to facilitate the expansion and balanced growth of international trade and to promote stability in foreign exchange.

## Organization

(October 2003)

**Managing Director:** HORST KÖHLER (Germany).

**First Deputy Managing Director:** ANNE KRUEGER (USA).

**Deputy Managing Directors:** SHIGEMITSU SUGISAKI (Japan), EDUARDO ANINAT (Chile).

**Director, European Department:** MICHAEL C. DEPPLER.

### BOARD OF GOVERNORS

The highest authority of the Fund is exercised by the Board of Governors, on which each member country is represented by a Governor and an Alternate Governor. The Board normally meets annually. The voting power of each country is related to its quota in the Fund. An International Monetary and Financial Committee (IMFC, formerly the Interim Committee) advises and reports to the Board on matters relating to the management and adaptation of the international monetary and financial system, sudden disturbances that might threaten the system and proposals to amend the Articles of Agreement.

### BOARD OF EXECUTIVE DIRECTORS

The 24-member Board of Executive Directors is responsible for the day-to-day operations of the Fund. The USA, the United Kingdom, Germany, France and Japan each appoint one Executive Director. There is also one Executive Director from the People's Republic of China, Russia and Saudi Arabia, while the remainder are elected by groups of the remaining countries.

### REGIONAL OFFICE

**Regional Office for Europe:** 64–66 ave d'Iena, 75116 Paris, France; tel. 1-40-69-30-70; fax 1-47-23-40-89; Dir FLEMMING LARSEN.

## Activities

The purposes of the IMF, as defined in the Articles of Agreement, are:

(i) To promote international monetary co-operation through a permanent institution which provides the machinery for consultation and collaboration on monetary problems;

(ii) To facilitate the expansion and balanced growth of international trade, and to contribute thereby to the promotion and maintenance of high levels of employment and real income and to the development of members' productive resources;

(iii) To promote exchange stability, to maintain orderly exchange arrangements among members, and to avoid competitive exchange depreciation;

(iv) To assist in the establishment of a multilateral system of payments in respect of current transactions between members and in the elimination of foreign exchange restrictions which hamper the growth of trade;

(v) To give confidence to members by making the general resources of the Fund temporarily available to them, under adequate safeguards, thus providing them with the opportunity to correct maladjustments in their balance of payments, without resorting to measures destructive of national or international prosperity;

(vi) In accordance with the above, to shorten the duration of and lessen the degree of disequilibrium in the international balances of payments of members.

In joining the Fund, each country agrees to co-operate with the above objectives. In accordance with its objective of facilitating the expansion of international trade, the IMF encourages its members to accept the obligations of Article VIII, Sections two, three and four, of the Articles of Agreement. Members that accept Article VIII undertake to refrain from imposing restrictions on the making of payments and transfers for current international transactions and from engaging in discriminatory currency arrangements or multiple currency practices without IMF approval. By July 2003 156 members had accepted Article VIII status.

The financial crises of the late 1990s, notably in several Asian countries, Brazil and Russia, contributed to widespread discussions concerning the strengthening of the international monetary system. In April 1998 the Executive Board identified the following fundamental aspects of the debate: reinforcing international and domestic financial systems; strengthening IMF surveillance; promoting greater availability and transparency of information regarding member countries' economic data and policies; emphasizing the central role of the IMF in crisis management; and establishing effective procedures to involve the private sector in forestalling or resolving financial crises. During 1999/2000 the Fund implemented several measures in connection with its ongoing efforts to appraise and reinforce the global financial architecture, including, in March 2000, the adoption by the Executive Board of a strengthened framework to safeguard the use of IMF resources. During 2000 the Fund established the IMF Center, in Washington, DC, which aimed to promote awareness and understanding of its activities. In September the Fund's new Managing Director announced his intention to focus and streamline the principals of conditionality (which links Fund financing with the implementation of specific economic policies by the recipient countries) as part of the wider reform of the international financial system. A comprehensive review was undertaken, during which the issue was considered by public forums and representatives of civil society. New guide-lines on conditionality, which *inter alia* aimed to promote national ownership of policy reforms and to introduce specific criteria for the implementation of conditions given different states' circumstances, were approved by the Executive Board in September 2002. In 2000/01 the Fund established an International Capital Markets Department to improve its understanding of financial markets and a separate Consultative Group on capital markets to serve as a forum for regular dialogue between the Fund and representatives of the private sector.

In early 2002 a position of Director for Special Operations was created to enhance the Fund's ability to respond to critical situations affecting member countries. In February the newly-appointed Director immediately assumed leadership of the staff team working with the authorities in Argentina to help that country to overcome its extreme economic and social difficulties. In September the IMFC approved further detailed consideration of a sovereign debt restructuring mechanism (SDRM), which aimed to establish a procedure to enable countries with an unsustainable level of debt to renegotiate loans more effectively. In January 2003 the IMF hosted a conference for representatives from the financial sector and civil society and other public officials and academics to discuss aspects of the SDRM.

## SURVEILLANCE

Under its Articles of Agreement, the Fund is mandated to oversee the effective functioning of the international monetary system. Accordingly, the Fund aims to exercise firm surveillance over the exchange rate policies of member states and to assess whether a country's economic situation and policies are consistent with the objectives of sustainable development and domestic and external stability. The Fund's main tools of surveillance are regular, bilateral consultations with member countries conducted in accordance with Article IV of the Articles of Agreement, which cover fiscal and monetary policies, balance of payments and external debt developments, as well as policies that affect the economic performance of a country, such as the labour market, social and environmental issues and good governance, and aspects of the country's capital accounts, and finance and banking sectors. In April 1997, in an effort to improve the value of surveillance by means of increased transparency, the Executive Board agreed to the voluntary issue of Press Information Notices (PINs) (on the internet and in *IMF Economic Reviews)*, following each member's Article IV consultation with the Board, to those member countries wishing to make public the Fund's views. Other background papers providing information on and analysis of economic developments in individual countries continued to be made available. In addition, World Economic Outlook discussions are held, normally twice a year, by the Executive Board to assess policy implications from a multilateral perspective and to monitor global developments.

The rapid decline in the value of the Mexican peso in late 1994 and the financial crisis in Asia, which became apparent in mid-1997, focused attention on the importance of IMF surveillance of the economies and financial policies of member states and prompted the Fund to enhance the effectiveness of its surveillance and to encourage the full and timely provision of data by member countries in order to maintain fiscal transparency. In April 1996 the IMF established the Special Data Dissemination Standard (SDDS), which was intended to improve access to reliable economic statistical information for member countries that have, or are seeking, access to international capital markets. In March 1999 the IMF undertook to strengthen the Standard by the introduction of a new reserves data template. By late 2002 52 countries had subscribed to the Standard. In December 1997 the Executive Board approved a new General Data Dissemination System (GDDS), to encourage all member countries to improve the production and dissemination of core economic data. The operational phase of the GDDS commenced in May 2000. The Fund maintains a Dissemination Standards Bulletin Board (accessible at dsbb.imf.org), which aims to ensure that information on SDDS subscribing countries is widely available.

In April 1998 the then Interim Committee adopted a voluntary Code of Good Practices on Fiscal Transparency: Declaration of Principles, which aimed to increase the quality and promptness of official reports on economic indicators, and in September 1999 it adopted a Code of Good Practices on Transparency in Monetary and Financial Policies: Declaration of Principles. The IMF and World Bank jointly established a Financial Sector Assessment Programme (FSAP) in May 1999, initially as a pilot project, which aimed to promote greater global financial security through the preparation of confidential detailed evaluations of the financial sectors of individual countries. Assessments were undertaken of 12 industrialized countries, emerging market economies and developing countries. During 2000 the FSAP was extended to cover a further 24 countries. It remained under regular review by the Boards of Governors of the Fund and World Bank. As part of the FSAP, Fund staff may conclude a Financial System Stability Assessment (FSSA), addressing issues relating to macroeconomic stability and the strength of a country's financial system. A separate component of the FSAP are Reports on the Observance of Standards and Codes (ROSCs), which are compiled after an assessment of a country's implementation and observance of internationally recognized financial standards. In March 2000 the IMF Executive Board adopted a strengthened framework to safeguard the use of IMF resources. All member countries making use of Fund resources were to be required to publish annual central bank statements audited in accordance with internationally accepted standards. It was also agreed that any instance of intentional misreporting of information by a member country should be publicized. In the following month the Executive Board approved the establishment of an Independent Evaluation Office to conduct objective evaluations of IMF policy and operations. In August the Executive Board adopted a Code of Conduct to guide its activities.

In April 2001 the Executive Board agreed on measures to enhance international efforts to counter money-laundering, in particular through the Fund's ongoing financial supervision activities and its programme of assessment of offshore financial centres. In November the IMFC, in response to the terrorist attacks against targets in the USA, which had occurred in September, resolved, *inter alia*, to strengthen the Fund's focus on surveillance, and, in particular, to extend measures to counter money-laundering to include the funds of terrorist organizations. It determined to accelerate efforts to assess offshore centres and to provide technical support to enable poorer countries to meet international financial standards.

## QUOTAS

### MEMBERSHIP AND QUOTAS IN EASTERN EUROPE, RUSSIA AND CENTRAL ASIA
(SDR million*)

| | October 2003 |
|---|---:|
| Armenia . . . . . . . . . . . | 92.0 |
| Azerbaijan . . . . . . . . . | 160.9 |
| Belarus . . . . . . . . . . . | 386.4 |
| Georgia . . . . . . . . . . | 150.3 |
| Kazakhstan . . . . . . . . . | 365.7 |
| Kyrgyzstan . . . . . . . . . | 88.8 |
| Moldova . . . . . . . . . . | 123.2 |
| Russian Federation . . . . . . . | 5,945.4 |
| Tajikistan . . . . . . . . . | 87.0 |
| Turkmenistan . . . . . . . . | 75.2 |
| Ukraine . . . . . . . . . . | 1,372.0 |
| Uzbekistan . . . . . . . . . | 275.6 |

*The Special Drawing Right (SDR) was introduced in 1970 as a substitute for gold in international payments, and was intended eventually to become the principal reserve asset in the international monetary system. Its value (which was US $1.43686 at 10 October 2003 and averaged $1.29484 in 2002) is based on the currencies of the five largest exporting countries. Each member is assigned a quota related to its national income, monetary reserves, trade balance and other economic indicators; the quota approximately determines a member's voting power and the amount of foreign exchange it may purchase from the Fund. A member's subscription is equal to its quota. In January 1998 the Board of Governors adopted a resolution in support of an increase, under the Eleventh General Review, of some 45% in total quotas, subject to approval by member states constituting 85% of total quotas (as at December 1997). Sufficient consent had been granted by January 1999 to enable the overall increase in quotas to enter into effect. All members were then granted until 30 July to consent to the higher quotas. The Twelfth General Review was concluded at the end of January 2003 without an increase in quotas. At 5 September 2003 total quotas in the Fund amounted to SDR 212,794.0m.

### RESOURCES

Members' subscriptions form the basic resource of the IMF. They are supplemented by borrowing. Under the General Arrangements to Borrow (GAB), established in 1962, the 'Group of Ten' industrialized nations (G-10—Belgium, Canada, France, Germany, Italy, Japan, the Netherlands, Sweden, the United Kingdom and the USA) and Switzerland (which became a member of the IMF in May 1992 but which had been a full participant in the GAB from April 1984) undertake to lend the Fund as much as SDR 17,000m. in their own currencies, to assist in fulfilling the balance-of-payments requirements of any member of the group, or in response to requests to the Fund from countries with balance-of-payments problems that could threaten the stability of the international monetary system. In 1983 the Fund entered into an agreement with Saudi Arabia, in association with the GAB, making available SDR 1,500m., and other borrowing arrangements were completed in 1984 with the Bank for International Settlements, the Saudi Arabian Monetary Agency, Belgium and Japan, making available a further SDR 6,000m. In 1986 another borrowing arrangement with Japan made available SDR 3,000m. In May 1996 GAB participants concluded an agreement in principle to expand the resources available for borrowing to SDR 34,000m., by securing the support of 25 countries with the financial capacity to support the international monetary system. The so-called New Arrangements to Borrow (NAB) was approved by the Executive Board in January 1997. It was to enter into force, for an initial five-year period, as soon as the five largest potential creditors participating in NAB had approved the initiative and the total credit arrangement of participants endorsing the scheme had reached at least SDR 28,900m. While the GAB credit arrangement was to remain in effect, the NAB was expected to be the first facility to be activated in the event of the Fund's requiring supplementary resources. In July 1998 the GAB was activated for the first time in more than 20 years in order to provide funds of up to US $6,300m. in support of an IMF emergency assistance package for Russia (the first time the GAB had been used for a non-participant). The NAB became effective in November, and was used for the first time as part of an extensive programme of support for Brazil, which was adopted by the IMF in early December.

### DRAWING ARRANGEMENTS

Exchange transactions within the Fund take the form of members' purchases (i.e. drawings) from the Fund of the currencies of other members for the equivalent amounts of their own currencies. Fund resources are available to eligible members on an essentially short-term and revolving basis to provide members with temporary assis-

tance to contribute to the solution of their payments problems. Before making a purchase, a member must show that its balance of payments or reserve position makes the purchase necessary. Apart from this requirement, reserve tranche purchases (i.e. purchases that do not bring the Fund's holdings of the member's currency to a level above its quota) are permitted unconditionally.

With further purchases, however, the Fund's policy of 'conditionality' means that a member requesting assistance must agree to adjust its economic policies, as stipulated by the IMF. All requests other than for use of the reserve tranche are examined by the Executive Board to determine whether the proposed use would be consistent with the Fund's policies, and a member must discuss its proposed adjustment programme (including fiscal, monetary, exchange and trade policies) with IMF staff. Purchases outside the reserve tranche are made in four credit tranches, each equivalent to 25% of the member's quota; a member must reverse the transaction by repurchasing its own currency (with SDRs or currencies specified by the Fund) within a specified time. A credit tranche purchase is usually made under a 'Stand-by Arrangement' with the Fund, or under the Extended Fund Facility. A Stand-by Arrangement is normally of one or two years' duration, and the amount is made available in instalments, subject to the member's observance of 'performance criteria'; repurchases must be made within three-and-a-quarter to five years. An Extended Arrangement is normally of three years' duration, and the member must submit detailed economic programmes and progress reports for each year; repurchases must be made within four-and-a-half to 10 years. A member whose payments imbalance is large in relation to its quota may make use of temporary facilities established by the Fund using borrowed resources, namely the 'enlarged access policy' established in 1981, which helps to finance Stand-by and Extended Arrangements for such a member, up to a limit of between 90% and 110% of the member's quota annually. Repurchases are made within three-and-a-half to seven years. In October 1994 the Executive Board approved a temporary increase in members' access to IMF resources, on the basis of a recommendation by the then Interim Committee. The annual access limit under IMF regular tranche drawings, Stand-by Arrangements and Extended Fund Facility credits was increased from 68% to 100% of a member's quota, with the cumulative access limit remaining at 300% of quota. The arrangements were extended, on a temporary basis, in November 1997.

In addition, special-purpose arrangements have been introduced, all of which are subject to the member's co-operation with the Fund to find an appropriate solution to its difficulties. During late 1999 the Fund undertook a review of its non-concessional lending facilities. The Buffer Stock Financing Facility (BSFF), established in 1969 in order to enable members to pay their contributions to the buffer stocks which were intended to stabilize markets for primary commodities, was abolished in January 2000, having last been used in 1984. In January 2000 the Executive Board also resolved to eliminate the contingency component of the former Compensatory and Contingency Financing Facility, established in 1988, reforming it as the Compensatory Financing Facility (CCF). The CCF provides compensation to members whose export earnings are reduced as a result of circumstances beyond their control, or which are affected by excess costs of cereal imports. In December 1997 the Executive Board established a new Supplemental Reserve Facility (SRF) to provide short-term assistance to members experiencing exceptional balance-of-payments difficulties resulting from a sudden loss of market confidence. Repayments were to be made within one to one-and-a-half years of the purchase, unless otherwise extended by the Board. The SRF was activated immediately to provide SDR 9,950m. to the Republic of Korea, as part of a Stand-by Arrangement amounting to SDR 15,550m., the largest amount ever committed by the Fund. (With additional financing from governments and international institutions, the total assistance 'package' for the Republic of Korea reached an estimated US $57,000m.) In July 1998 SDR 4,000m. was made available to Russia under the SRF and, in December, some SDR 9,100m. was extended to Brazil under the SRF as part of a new Stand-by Arrangement. In January 2001 some SDR 2,100m. in SRF resources were approved for Argentina as part of an SDR 5,187m. Stand-by Arrangement augmentation. (In January 2002 the Executive Board approved an extension of one year for Argentina's SRF repayments.) In April 1999 an additional facility, the Contingent Credit Lines (CCL), was established to provide short-term financing on similar terms to the SRF in order to prevent more stable economies being affected by adverse international financial developments and to maintain investor confidence. Under the CCL member countries were to have short-term access to up to 500% of their quota, subject to meeting various economic criteria stipulated by the Fund. No funds under the CCL were committed in 2001/02.

In April 1993 the Fund established the Systemic Transformation Facility (STF) to assist countries of the former USSR and other economies in transition. The STF was intended to be a temporary facility to enable member countries to draw on financial assistance for balance-of-payments difficulties resulting from severe disruption of their normal trade and payments arrangements. Access to the facility was limited to not more than 50% of a member's quota, and repayment terms were equal to those for the extended Fund facility. The expiry date for access to resources under this facility was extended by one year from 31 December 1994, to the end of 1995. During the STF's period of operation, purchases amounting to SDR 3,984m. were made by 20 countries, including Azerbaijan, Belarus and Uzbekistan.

In October 1995 the Interim Committee of the Board of Governors endorsed recent decisions of the Executive Board to strengthen IMF financial support to members requiring exceptional assistance. An Emergency Financing Mechanism was established to enable the IMF to respond swiftly to potential or actual financial crises, while additional funds were made available for short-term currency stabilization. (The Mechanism was activated for the first time in July 1997, in response to a request by the Philippines Government to reinforce the country's international reserves, and was subsequently used during that year to assist Thailand, Indonesia and the Republic of Korea, and, in July 1998, Russia.) Emergency assistance was also to be available to countries in a post-conflict situation, in addition to existing arrangements for countries having been affected by natural disasters, to facilitate the rehabilitation of their economies and to improve their eligibility for further IMF concessionary arrangements.

In November 1999 the Fund's existing facility to provide balance-of-payments assistance on concessional terms to low-income member countries, the Enhanced Structural Adjustment Facility, was reformulated as the Poverty Reduction and Growth Facility (PRGF), with greater emphasis on poverty reduction and sustainable development as key elements of growth-orientated economic strategies. Assistance under the PRGF (for which 77 countries were deemed eligible) was to be carefully matched to specific national requirements. Prior to drawing on the facility each recipient country was, in collaboration with representatives of civil society, non-governmental organizations and bilateral and multilateral institutions, to develop a national poverty reduction strategy, which was to be presented in a Poverty Reduction Strategy Paper (PRSP). PRGF loans carry an interest rate of 0.5% per year and are repayable over 10 years, with a five-and-a-half-year grace period; each eligible country is normally permitted to borrow up to 140% of its quota (in exceptional circumstances the maximum access can be raised to 185%). A PGRF Trust replaced the former ESAF Trust.

The PRGF supports, through long-maturity loans and grants, IMF participation in a joint initiative, with the World Bank, to provide exceptional assistance to heavily indebted poor countries (HIPCs), in order to help them to achieve a sustainable level of debt management. The initiative was formally approved at the September 1996 meeting of the Interim Committee, having received the support of the 'Paris Club' of official creditors, which agreed to increase the relief on official debt from 67% to 80%. Resources for the HIPC initiative are channelled through the PRGF Trust. In early 1999 the IMF and World Bank initiated a comprehensive review of the HIPC scheme, in order to consider modifications of the initiative and to strengthen the link between debt relief and poverty reduction. A consensus emerged among the financial institutions and leading industrialized nations to enhance the scheme, in order to make it available to more countries, and to accelerate the process of providing debt relief. In September the IMF Board of Governors expressed its commitment to undertaking an off-market transaction of a percentage of the Fund's gold reserves (i.e. a sale, at market prices, to central banks of member countries with repayment obligations to the Fund, which were then to be made in gold), as part of the funding arrangements of the enhanced HIPC scheme; this was undertaken during the period December 1999–April 2000. Under the enhanced initiative it was agreed that countries seeking debt relief should first formulate, and successfully implement for at least

one year, a national poverty reduction strategy (see above). By November 2002 a total of $25,102m. in NPV terms had been committed, of which the Fund's share was $2,043m.

During 2001/02 the IMF approved funding commitments for new arrangements amounting to SDR 41,219m., compared with SDR 14,333m. in the previous year. Of the total amount, SDR 39,438m. was committed under nine new Stand-by Arrangements and the augmentation of two already in place (for Argentina and Turkey). Nine new PRGF arrangements were approved in 2001/02, amounting to SDR 1,781m., while augmentations of four existing commitments were also approved. During 2001/02 members' purchases from the general resources account amounted to SDR 29,194m., compared with SDR 9,599m. in the previous year, with the main users of IMF resources being Turkey (SDR 16,200m.), Argentina (SDR 5,922m.) and Brazil (SDR 5,277m.). Outstanding IMF credit at 30 April 2002 totalled SDR 58,698m., compared with SDR 48,662m. as at the previous year. In August the Fund approved its largest ever stand-by credit amounting to SDR 22,800m. in support of the Brazilian Government's efforts to secure economic and financial stability.

### TECHNICAL ASSISTANCE

Technical assistance is provided by special missions or resident representatives who advise members on every aspect of economic management, while more specialized assistance is provided by the IMF's various departments. In 2000/01 the IMFC determined that technical assistance should be central to IMF's work in crisis prevention and management, in capacity-building for low-income countries, and in restoring macroeconomic stability in countries following a financial crisis. Technical assistance activities subsequently underwent a process of review and reorganization to align them more closely with IMF policy priorities and other initiatives, for example the Financial Stability Assessment Programme. The majority of technical assistance is provided by the Departments of Monetary and Exchange Affairs, of Fiscal Affairs and of Statistics, and by the IMF Institute. The Institute, founded in 1964, trains officials from member countries in financial analysis and policy, balance-of-payments methodology and public finance; it also gives assistance to national and regional training centres.

# Publications

*Annual Report.*

*Balance of Payments Statistics Yearbook.*

*Direction of Trade Statistics* (quarterly and annually).

*Finance and Development* (quarterly, published jointly with the World Bank).

*Global Financial Stability Report* (quarterly).

*Government Finance Statistics Yearbook.*

*IMF Economic Reviews* (3 a year).

*IMF Research Bulletin* (quarterly).

*IMF Survey* (2 a month).

*International Financial Statistics* (monthly and annually, also on CD-ROM).

*Joint BIS-IMF-OECD-World Bank Statistics on External Debt* (quarterly).

*Staff Papers* (quarterly).

*World Economic Outlook* (2 a year).

Occasional papers, economic and financial surveys, pamphlets, booklets.

# United Nations Educational, Scientific and Cultural Organization—UNESCO

**Address:** 7 place de Fontenoy, 75352 Paris 07 SP, France.

**Telephone:** 1-45-68-10-00; **fax:** 1-45-67-16-90; **e-mail:** scg@unesco .org; **internet:** www.unesco.org.

UNESCO was established in 1946 'for the purpose of advancing, through the educational, scientific and cultural relations of the peoples of the world, the objectives of international peace and the common welfare of mankind'.

# Organization

(October 2003)

### GENERAL CONFERENCE

The supreme governing body of the Organization, the Conference meets in ordinary session once in two years and is composed of representatives of the member states.

## EXECUTIVE BOARD

The Board, comprising 58 members, prepares the programme to be submitted to the Conference and supervises its execution; it meets twice or sometimes three times a year.

## SECRETARIAT

**Director-General:** KOICHIRO MATSUURA (Japan).

## CO-OPERATING BODIES

In accordance with UNESCO's constitution, national Commissions have been set up in most member states. These help to integrate work within the member states and the work of UNESCO.

## REGIONAL OFFICES

**European Centre for Higher Education—CEPES:** Str. Stirbei Vodà 39, 70732 Bucharest, Romania; tel. (1) 3159956; fax (1) 3123567; e-mail cepes@cepes.ro; internet www.cepes.ro; Dir JAN SADLAK.

**Regional Office for Science and Technology for Europe:** Palazzo Loredan degli Ambasciatori, 1262/A Dorsoduro, 30123 Venice, Italy; tel. (041) 522-5535; fax (041) 528-9995; e-mail roste@unesco.org; internet www.unesco.org/venice; Dir Prof. PIERRE LASSERRE.

**UNESCO Institute for Information Technologies in Education:** 8 Kedrova St, 117292 Moscow, Russia; tel. (95) 1292990; fax (95) 1291225; e-mail info@iite.ru; internet www.iite.ru/iite; aims to formulate policies regarding the development of, and to support and monitor the use of, information and communication technologies in education; also conducts research and organizes training programmes; Dir VLADIMIR KINELEV.

**UNESCO Moscow Office:** 119034 Moscow, Bolshoi Levshinskii per. 15/28, bul. 2; tel. (095) 202-81-66; fax (095) 202-05-68; e-mail moscow@unesco.org; internet www.unesco.ru; also covers Armenia, Azerbaijan, Belarus, Georgia and Moldova; Dir WOLFGANG REUTHER.

# Activities

In November 2001 the General Conference approved a medium-term strategy to guide UNESCO during the period 2002–07. The Conference adopted a new unifying theme for the organization: 'UNESCO contributing to peace and human development in an era of globalization through education, the sciences, culture and communication'. UNESCO's central mission as defined under the strategy was to contribute to peace and human development in the globalized world through its four programme domains (Education, Natural and Social and Human Sciences, Culture, and Communication and Information), incorporating the following three principal dimensions: developing universal principles and norms to meet emerging challenges and protect the 'common public good'; promoting pluralism and diversity; and promoting empowerment and participation in the emerging knowledge society through equitable access, capacity-building and knowledge-sharing. Programme activities were to be focused particularly on supporting disadvantaged and excluded groups or geographic regions. The organization aimed to decentralize its operations in order to ensure more country-driven programming. UNESCO's overall work programme for 2002–03 comprised the following major programmes: education; natural sciences; social and human sciences; culture; and communication and information. Basic education; fresh water resources and ecosystems; the ethics of science and technology; diversity, intercultural pluralism and dialogue; and universal access to information, especially in the public domain, were designated as the priority themes. The work programme incorporated two transdisciplinary projects—eradication of poverty, especially extreme poverty; and the contribution of information and communication technologies to the development of education, science and culture and the construction of a knowledge society. UNESCO aims to promote a culture of peace. The UN General Assembly designated UNESCO as the lead agency for co-ordinating the International Decade for a Culture of Peace and Non-Violence for the Children of the World (2001–10), with a focus on education, and the UN Literacy Decade (2003–12). In the implementation of all its activities UNESCO aims to contribute to achieving the UN Millennium Goal of halving levels of extreme poverty by 2015.

## EDUCATION

Since its establishment UNESCO has devoted itself to promoting education in accordance with principles based on democracy and respect for human rights.

In March 1990 UNESCO, with other UN agencies, sponsored the World Conference on Education for All. 'Education for All' was subsequently adopted as a guiding principle of UNESCO's contribution to development. UNESCO advocates 'Literacy for All' as a key component of 'Education for All', regarding literacy as essential to basic education and to social and human development. In April 2000 several UN agencies, including UNESCO and UNICEF, and other partners sponsored the World Education Forum, held in Dakar, Senegal, to assess international progress in achieving the goal of 'Education for All' and to adopt a strategy for further action (the 'Dakar Framework'), with the aim of ensuring universal basic education by 2015. The Forum launched the Global Initiative for Education for All. The Dakar Framework emphasized the role of improved access to education in the reduction of poverty and in diminishing inequalities within and between societies. UNESCO was appointed as the lead agency in the implementation of the Framework. UNESCO's role in pursuing the goals of the Dakar Forum was to focus on co-ordination, advocacy, mobilization of resources, and information-sharing at international, regional and national levels. It was to oversee national policy reforms, with a particular focus on the integration of 'Education for All' objectives into national education plans, which were to be produced by all member countries by 2002. UNESCO's work programme on Education for 2002–03 aimed to promote an effective follow-up to the Forum and comprised the following two main components: Basic Education for All: Meeting the Commitments of the Dakar World Education Forum; and Building Knowledge Societies through Quality Education and a Renewal of Education Systems. 'Basic Education for All', signifying the promotion of access to learning opportunities throughout the lives of all individuals, including the most disadvantaged, was designated as the principal theme of the programme and was deemed to require urgent action. The second part of the strategy was to improve the quality of educational provision and renew and diversify education systems, with a view to ensuring that educational needs at all levels were met. This component included updating curricular programmes in secondary education, strengthening science and technology activities and ensuring equal access to education for girls and women. (UNESCO supports the UN Girls' Education Initiative, established following the Dakar Forum.) The work programme focused on the importance of knowledge, information and communication in the increasingly globalized world, and the significance of education as a means of empowerment for the poor and of enhancing basic quality of life.

Within the UN system, UNESCO is responsible for providing technical assistance and educational services in the context of emergency situations. This includes providing education to refugees and displaced persons, as well as assistance for the rehabilitation of national education systems.

UNESCO is concerned with improving the quality, relevance and efficiency of higher education. It assists member states in reforming their national systems, organizes high-level conferences for Ministers of Education and other decision-makers, and disseminates research papers. A World Conference on Higher Education was convened in October 1998 in Paris, France. The Conference adopted a World Declaration on Higher Education for the 21st Century, incorporating proposals to reform higher education, with emphasis on access to education, and educating for individual development and active participation in society. The Conference also approved a framework for Priority Action for Change and Development of Higher Education, which comprised guide-lines for governments and institutions to meet the objectives of greater accessibility, as well as improved standards and relevancy of higher education.

The April 2000 World Education Forum recognized the global HIV/AIDS pandemic to be a significant challenge to the attainment of 'Education for All'. UNESCO, as a co-sponsor of UNAIDS, takes an active role in promoting formal and non-formal preventive health education.

## NATURAL SCIENCES

In November 1999 the General Conference endorsed a Declaration on Science and the Use of Scientific Knowledge and an agenda for action, which had been adopted at the World Conference on Science, held in June/July 1999, in Budapest, Hungary. UNESCO was to co-ordinate the follow-up to the conference and, in conjunction with the International Council for Science, to promote initiatives in international scientific partnership. The following were identified as priority areas of UNESCO's work programme on Natural Sciences for 2002–03: Science and Technology: Capacity-building and Management; and Sciences, Environment and Sustainable Development. Water Security in the 21st Century was designated as the principal theme, involving addressing threats to water resources and their associated ecosystems. UNESCO was the lead UN agency involved in the preparation of the first *World Water Development Report*, issued in March 2003. UNESCO was a joint co-ordinator of the International Year of Freshwater (2003), which aimed to raise global awareness of the importance of improving the protection and management of fresh water resources. The Science and Technology component of the programme focused on the follow-up of the World Conference on Science, involving the elaboration of national policies on science and technology; strengthening science education;

improving university teaching and enhancing national research capacities; and reinforcing international co-operation in mathematics, physics, chemistry, biology, biotechnology and the engineering sciences. UNESCO aims to contribute to bridging the divide between community-held traditional knowledge and scientific knowledge.

UNESCO aims to improve the level of university teaching of the basic sciences through training courses, establishing national and regional networks and centres of excellence, and fostering co-operative research. In carrying out its mission, UNESCO relies on partnerships with non-governmental organizations and the world scientific communities. With the International Council of Scientific Unions and the Third World Academy of Sciences, UNESCO operates a short-term fellowship programme in the basic sciences and an exchange programme of visiting lecturers. In September 1996 UNESCO initiated a 10-year World Solar Programme, which aimed to promote the application of solar energy and to increase research, development and public awareness of all forms of ecologically-sustainable energy use.

UNESCO has over the years established various forms of intergovernmental co-operation concerned with the environmental sciences and research on natural resources, in order to support the recommendations of the June 1992 UN Conference on Environment and Development and, in particular, the implementation of 'Agenda 21' to promote sustainable development. The International Geological Correlation Programme, undertaken jointly with the International Union of Geological Sciences, aims to improve and facilitate global research of geological processes. In the context of the International Decade for Natural Disaster Reduction (declared in 1990), UNESCO conducted scientific studies of natural hazards and means of mitigating their effects and organized several disaster-related workshops. The International Hydrological Programme considers scientific aspects of water resources assessment and management; and the Intergovernmental Oceanographic Commission focuses on issues relating to oceans, shorelines and marine resources, in particular the role of the ocean in climate and global systems. The IOC has been actively involved in the establishment of a Global Coral Reef Monitoring Network and is developing a Global Ocean Observing System. An initiative on Environment and Development in Coastal Regions and in Small Islands is concerned with ensuring environmentally-sound and sustainable development by strengthening management of the following key areas: freshwater resources; the mitigation of coastline instability; biological diversity; and coastal ecosystem productivity. UNESCO hosts the secretariat of the World Water Assessment Programme on freshwater resources.

UNESCO's Man and the Biosphere Programme supports a worldwide network of biosphere reserves (comprising 425 sites in 95 countries in February 2003), which aim to promote environmental conservation and research, education and training in biodiversity and problems of land use (including the fertility of tropical soils and the cultivation of sacred sites). In October 2002 UNESCO announced that the 138 biospheres in mountainous areas would play a leading role in a new Global Change Monitoring Programme aimed at assessing the impact of global climate changes. Following the signing of the Convention to Combat Desertification in October 1994, UNESCO initiated an International Programme for Arid Land Crops, based on a network of existing institutions, to assist implementation of the Convention.

## SOCIAL AND HUMAN SCIENCES

UNESCO is mandated to contribute to the world-wide development of the social and human sciences and philosophy, which it regards as of great importance in policy-making and maintaining ethical vigilance. The structure of UNESCO's Social and Human Sciences programme takes into account both an ethical and standard-setting dimension, and research, policy-making, action in the field and future-oriented activities. UNESCO's work programme for 2002–03 on Social and Human Sciences comprised three main components: The Ethics of Science and Technology; Promotion of Human Rights, Peace and Democratic Principles; and Improvement of Policies Relating to Social Transformations and Promotion of Anticipation and Prospective Studies. The priority Ethics of Science and Technology element aimed to reinforce UNESCO's role as an intellectual forum for ethical reflection on challenges related to the advance of science and technology; oversee the follow-up of the Universal Declaration on the Human Genome and Human Rights (see below); promote education in science and technology; ensure UNESCO's role in promoting good practices through encouraging the inclusion of ethical guiding principles in policy formulation and reinforcing international networks; and to promote international co-operation in human sciences and philosophy. The Social and Human Sciences programme had the main intellectual and conceptual responsibility for the transdisciplinary theme 'eradication of poverty, especially extreme poverty'.

UNESCO aims to promote and protect human rights and acts as an interdisciplinary, multicultural and pluralistic forum for reflec-

tion on issues relating to the ethical dimension of scientific advances, for example in biogenetics, new technology, and medicine. In May 1997 the International Bioethics Committee, a group of 36 specialists who meet under UNESCO auspices, approved a draft version of a Universal Declaration on the Human Genome and Human Rights, in an attempt to provide ethical guide-lines for developments in human genetics. The Declaration, which identified some 100,000 hereditary genes as 'common heritage', was adopted by the UNESCO General Conference in November and committed states to promoting the dissemination of relevant scientific knowledge and co-operating in genome research. The November Conference also resolved to establish an 18-member World Commission on the Ethics of Scientific Knowledge and Technology (COMEST) to serve as a forum for the exchange of information and ideas and to promote dialogue between scientific communities, decision-makers and the public. UNESCO hosts the secretariat of COMEST. COMEST met for the first time in April 1999 in Oslo, Norway. Its second meeting, which took place in December 2001 in Berlin, Germany, focused on the ethics of energy, fresh water and outer space.

In 1994 UNESCO initiated an international social science research programme, the Management of Social Transformations (MOST), to promote capacity-building in social planning at all levels of decision-making. UNESCO sponsors several research fellowships in the social sciences. In other activities UNESCO promotes the rehabilitation of underprivileged urban areas, the research of sociocultural factors affecting demographic change, and the study of family issues.

UNESCO aims to assist the building and consolidation of peaceful and democratic societies. An international network of institutions and centres involved in research on conflict resolution is being established to support the promotion of peace. Other training, workshop and research activities have been undertaken in countries that have suffered conflict. The Associated Schools Project (ASPnet—comprising 6,483 institutions in 166 countries in early 2003) has, for 50 years, promoted the principles of peace, human rights, democracy and international co-operation through education. An International Youth Clearing House and Information Service (INFOYOUTH) aims to increase and consolidate the information available on the situation of young people in society, and to heighten awareness of their needs, aspirations and potential among public and private decision-makers. UNESCO also focuses on the educational and cultural dimensions of physical education and sport and their capacity to preserve and improve health. Fundamental to UNESCO's mission is the rejection of all forms of discrimination. It disseminates scientific information aimed at combating racial prejudice, works to improve the status of women and their access to education, and promotes equality between men and women.

## CULTURE

In undertaking efforts to preserve the world's cultural and natural heritage UNESCO has attempted to emphasize the link between culture and development. In November 2001 the General Conference adopted the UNESCO Universal Declaration on Cultural Diversity, which affirmed the importance of intercultural dialogue in establishing a climate of peace. The work programme on Culture for 2002–03 included the following interrelated components: Reinforcing Normative Action in the Field of Culture; Protecting Cultural Diversity and Promoting Cultural Pluralism and Intercultural Dialogue; and Strengthening Links between Culture and Development. The focus was to be on all aspects of cultural heritage, and on the encouragement of cultural diversity and dialogue between cultures and civilizations. Under the 2002–03 programme UNESCO aimed to launch the Global Alliance on Cultural Diversity, a six-year initiative to promote partnerships between governments, non-governmental bodies and the private sector, with a view to supporting cultural diversity through the strengthening of cultural industries and the prevention of cultural piracy. UNESCO was designated as the lead agency for co-ordinating the UN Year for Cultural Heritage, celebrated in 2002.

UNESCO's World Heritage Programme, inaugurated in 1978, aims to protect historic sites and natural landmarks of outstanding universal significance, in accordance with the 1972 UNESCO Convention Concerning the Protection of the World Cultural and Natural Heritage, by providing financial aid for restoration, technical assistance, training and management planning. At July 2003 the 'World Heritage List' comprised 754 properties in 129 countries, of which 582 had cultural significance, 149 were natural landmarks, and 23 were of 'mixed' importance. The organization is assisting in the preservation of numerous historical and natural sites in Eastern Europe and Central Asia, including the the Monastery of Haghpat in Armenia, the Bialowieza Forest (Belarus/Poland), Bagrati Cathedral (Georgia), the Kremlin and Red Square in Moscow (Russia), Saint Sophia Cathedral (Ukraine) and the historic centres of Bukhara and Shakhrisyabz, and Samarkand (Uzbekistan). UNESCO also maintains a list of 'World Heritage in Danger', which at July 2003 included the Walled City of Baku (Azerbaijan); the site was damaged by an earthquake in November 2000 and remained endangered by modern urban development.

The formulation of a Declaration against the Intentional Destruction of Cultural Heritage was authorized by the General Conference in November 2001. In addition, the November General Conference adopted the Convention on the Protection of the Underwater Cultural Heritage, covering the protection from commercial exploitation of shipwrecks, submerged historical sites, etc., situated in the territorial waters of signatory states. UNESCO also administers the 1954 Hague Convention on the Protection of Cultural Property in the Event of Armed Conflict and the 1970 Convention on the Means of Prohibiting and Preventing the Illicit Import, Export and Transfer of Ownership of Cultural Property. In 1992 a World Heritage Centre was established to enable rapid mobilization of international technical assistance for the preservation of cultural sites. Through the World Heritage Information Network (WHIN), a world-wide network of more than 800 information providers, UNESCO promotes global awareness and information exchange.

UNESCO supports efforts for the collection and safeguarding of humanity's non-material 'intangible' heritage, including oral traditions, music, dance and medicine. In May 2001 UNESCO awarded the title of 'Masterpieces of the Oral and Intangible Heritage of Humanity' to 19 cultural spaces (i.e. physical or temporal spaces hosting recurrent cultural events) and popular forms of expression deemed to be of outstanding value. UNESCO produces an *Atlas of the World's Languages in Danger of Disappearing*. The most recent edition, issued in February 2002, reported that of some 6,000 languages spoken world-wide, about one-half were endangered.

UNESCO encourages the translation and publication of literary works, publishes albums of art, and produces records, audiovisual programmes and travelling art exhibitions. It supports the development of book publishing and distribution, including the free flow of books and educational material across borders, and the training of editors and managers in publishing. UNESCO is active in preparing and encouraging the enforcement of international legislation on copyright.

In December 1992 UNESCO established the World Commission on Culture and Development, to strengthen links between culture and development and to prepare a report on the issue. The first World Conference on Culture and Development was held in June 1999, in Havana, Cuba. Within the context of the UN's World Decade for Cultural Development (1988–97) UNESCO launched the Silk Roads Project, as a multi-disciplinary study of the interactions among cultures and civilizations along the routes linking Asia and Europe, and established an International Fund for the Promotion of Culture, awarding two annual prizes for music and the promotion of arts. In April 1999 UNESCO celebrated the completion of a major international project, the *General History of Africa*.

### COMMUNICATION AND INFORMATION

In 2001 UNESCO introduced a major programme, 'Information for All', as the principal policy-guiding framework for the Communication and Information sector. The organization works towards establishing an open, non-exclusive knowledge society based on information-sharing and incorporating the socio-cultural and ethical dimensions of sustainable development. It promotes the free flow of, and universal access to information, knowledge, data and best practices, through the development of communications infrastructures, the elimination of impediments to freedom of expression, and the promotion of the right to information; through encouraging international co-operation in maintaining libraries and archives; and through efforts to harness informatics for development purposes and strengthen member states' capacities in this field. Activities include assistance with the development of legislation and training programmes in countries where independent and pluralistic media are emerging; assistance in the monitoring of media independence, pluralism and diversity; promotion of exchange programmes and study tours; and improving access and opportunities for women in the media. UNESCO recognizes that the so-called global 'digital divide', in addition to other developmental differences between countries, generates exclusion and marginalization, and that increased participation in the democratic process can be attained through strengthening national communication and information capacities. UNESCO promotes the upholding of human rights in the use of cyberspace. The organization was to participate in the World Summit on the Information Society, scheduled to take place in Geneva, Switzerland, in December 2003. The work programme on Communication and Information for 2002–03 comprised the fol-

lowing components: Promoting Equitable Access to Information and Knowledge Especially in the Public Domain, and Promoting Freedom of Expression and Strengthening Communication Capacities. During 2002–03 UNESCO was to evaluate its interactive internet-based WebWorld Portal, which aims to provide global communication and information services at all levels of society. UNESCO's Memory of the World project aims to preserve in digital form, and thereby to promote wide access to, the world's documentary heritage.

In regions affected by conflict UNESCO supports efforts to establish and maintain an independent media service. This strategy is largely implemented through an International Programme for the Development of Communication (IPDC, see below). In Cambodia, Haiti and Mozambique UNESCO participated in the restructuring of the media in the context of national reconciliation and in Bosnia and Herzegovina it assisted in the development of independent media. In December 1998 the Israeli-Palestinian Media Forum was established, to foster professional co-operation between Israeli and Palestinian journalists. IPDC provides support to communication and media development projects in the developing world, including the establishment of news agencies and newspapers and training editorial and technical staff. Since its establishment in 1982 IPDC has financed some 1,000 projects in more than 130 countries.

In March 1997 the first International Congress on Ethical, Legal and Societal Aspects of Digital Information ('InfoEthics') was held in Monte Carlo, Monaco. At the second InfoEthics Congress, held in October 1998, experts discussed issues concerning privacy, confidentiality and security in the electronic transfer of information. UNESCO maintains an Observatory on the Information Society, which provides up-to-date information on the development of new information and communications technologies, analyses major trends, and aims to raise awareness of related ethical, legal and societal issues. A UNESCO Institute for Information Technologies in Education was established in Moscow, Russia in 1998. In 2001 the UNESCO Institute for Statistics was established in Montréal, Canada.

# Finance

UNESCO's activities are funded through a regular budget provided by contributions from member states and extrabudgetary funds from other sources, particularly UNDP, the World Bank, regional banks and other bilateral Funds-in-Trust arrangements. UNESCO co-operates with many other UN agencies and international non-governmental organizations.

UNESCO's Regular Programme budget for the two years 2002–03 was US $544.4m., the same as for the previous biennium. Extrabudgetary funds for 2002–03 were estimated at $320m.

# Publications

(mostly in English, French and Spanish editions; Arabic, Chinese and Russian versions are also available in many cases)

*Atlas of the World's Languages in Danger of Disappearing.*

*Copyright Bulletin* (quarterly).

*Encyclopedia of Life Support Systems* (internet-based).

*International Review of Education* (quarterly).

*International Social Science Journal* (quarterly).

*Museum International* (quarterly).

*Nature and Resources* (quarterly).

*Prospects* (quarterly review on education).

*UNESCO Courier* (monthly, in 27 languages).

*UNESCO Sources* (monthly).

*UNESCO Statistical Yearbook.*

*World Communication Report.*

*World Educational Report* (every 2 years).

*World Heritage Review* (quarterly).

*World Information Report.*

*World Science Report* (every 2 years).

Books, databases, video and radio documentaries, statistics, scientific maps and atlases.

# World Health Organization—WHO

**Address:** Ave Appia 20, 1211 Geneva 27, Switzerland.
**Telephone:** (22) 7912111; **fax:** (22) 7913111; **e-mail:** info@who.int; **internet:** www.who.int.

WHO, established in 1948, is the lead agency within the UN system concerned with the protection and improvement of public health.

## Organization

### (October 2003)

#### WORLD HEALTH ASSEMBLY

The Assembly meets in Geneva, once a year; it is responsible for policy making and the biennial programme and budget; appoints the Director-General, admits new members and reviews budget contributions.

#### EXECUTIVE BOARD

The Board is composed of 32 health experts designated by, but not representing, their governments; they serve for three years, and the World Health Assembly elects 10–12 member states each year to the Board. It meets at least twice a year to review the Director-General's programme, which it forwards to the Assembly with any recommendations that seem necessary. It advises on questions referred to it by the Assembly and is responsible for putting into effect the decisions and policies of the Assembly. It is also empowered to take emergency measures in case of epidemics or disasters.

**Chairman:** KYAW MYINT (Myanmar).

#### SECRETARIAT

**Director-General:** Dr JONG-WOOK LEE (Republic of Korea).

**Executive Directors:** Dr ANARFI ASAMOA-BAAH (Ghana) (Health Technology and Pharmaceuticals), MARYAN BAQUEROT (General Management), Dr DAVID L. HEYMANN (USA) (Communicable Diseases), Dr CHRISTOPHER MURRAY (Evidence and Information for Policy), Dr DAVID NABARRO (United Kingdom) (Sustainable Development and Healthy Environments), Dr TOMRIS TÜRMEN (Turkey) (Family and Community Health), Dr DEREK YACH (South Africa) (Non-communicable Diseases and Mental Health), NADIA YOUNES (Egypt) (External Relations and Governing Bodies).

#### REGIONAL OFFICE

**Europe:** 8 Scherfigsvej, 2100 Copenhagen Ø, Denmark; tel. (1) 39-17-17-17; fax (1) 39-17-18-18; e-mail webmaster@who.dk; internet www.who.dk; Dir Dr MARC DANZON (France).

## Activities

WHO's objective is stated in the constitution as 'the attainment by all peoples of the highest possible level of health'. 'Health' is defined as 'a state of complete physical, mental and social well-being and not merely the absence of disease and infirmity'. In November 2001 WHO issued the International Classification of Functioning, Disability and Health (ICF) to act as an international standard and guide-lines for determining health and disability.

WHO acts as the central authority directing international health work, and establishes relations with professional groups and government health authorities on that basis.

It provides, on request from member states, technical and policy assistance in support of programmes to promote health, prevent and control health problems, control or eradicate disease, train health workers best suited to local needs and strengthen national health systems. Aid is provided in emergencies and natural disasters.

A global programme of collaborative research and exchange of scientific information is carried out in co-operation with about 1,200 national institutions. Particular stress is laid on the widespread communicable diseases of the tropics, and the countries directly concerned are assisted in developing their research capabilities.

It keeps diseases and other health problems under constant surveillance, promotes the exchange of prompt and accurate information and of notification of outbreaks of diseases, and administers the International Health Regulations. It sets standards for the quality control of drugs, vaccines and other substances affecting health. It formulates health regulations for international travel.

It collects and disseminates health data and carries out statistical analyses and comparative studies in such diseases as cancer, heart disease and mental illness.

It receives reports on drugs observed to have shown adverse reactions in any country, and transmits the information to other member states.

It promotes improved environmental conditions, including housing, sanitation and working conditions. All available information on effects on human health of the pollutants in the environment is critically reviewed and published.

Co-operation among scientists and professional groups is encouraged. The organization negotiates and sustains national and global partnerships. It may propose international conventions and agreements, and develops and promotes international norms and standards. The organization promotes the development and testing of new technologies, tools and guide-lines. It assists in developing an informed public opinion on matters of health.

#### HEALTH FOR ALL

WHO's first global strategy for pursing 'Health for all' was adopted in May 1981 by the 34th World Health Assembly. The objective of 'Health for all' was identified as the attainment by all citizens of the world of a level of health that would permit them to lead a socially and economically productive life, requiring fair distribution of available resources, universal access to essential health care, and the promotion of preventive health care. In May 1998 the 51st World Health Assembly renewed the initiative, adopting a global strategy in support of 'Health for all in the 21st century', to be effected through regional and national health policies. The new approach was to build on the primary health care approach of the initial strategy, but was to strengthen the emphasis on quality of life, equity in health and access to health services. The following have been identified as minimum requirements of 'Health for All':

Safe water in the home or within 15 minutes' walking distance, and adequate sanitary facilities in the home or immediate vicinity;

Immunization against diphtheria, pertussis (whooping cough), tetanus, poliomyelitis, measles and tuberculosis;

Local health care, including availability of essential drugs, within one hour's travel;

Trained personnel to attend childbirth, and to care for pregnant mothers and children up to at least one year old.

WHO's technical programmes are divided into nine groups, or 'clusters', each headed by an Executive Director, as follows: Communicable Diseases; Non-communicable Diseases and Mental Health; Family and Community Health; Sustainable Development and Healthy Environments; Health Technology and Pharmaceuticals; Evidence and Information for Policy; External affairs and Governing Bodies; General Management; and Office of the Director-General (including audit, oversight and legal activities). In 2000 WHO adopted a new corporate strategy, entailing a stronger focus on performance and programme delivery through standardized plans of action, and increased consistency and efficiency throughout the organization.

The Tenth General Programme of Work, for the period 2002–05, defined a policy framework for pursuing the principal objectives of building healthy populations and combating ill health. The Programme took into account: increasing understanding of the social, economic, political and cultural factors involved in achieving better health and the role played by better health in poverty reduction; the increasing complexity of health systems; the importance of safeguarding health as a component of humanitarian action; and the need for greater co-ordination among development organizations. It incorporated four interrelated strategic directions: lessening excess mortality, morbidity and disability, especially in poor and marginalized populations; promoting healthy lifestyles and reducing risk factors to human health arising from environmental, economic, social and behavioural causes; developing equitable and financially fair health systems; and establishing an enabling policy and an institutional environment for the health sector and promoting an effective health dimension to social, economic, environmental and development policy.

#### COMMUNICABLE DISEASES

WHO identifies infectious and parasitic communicable diseases as a major obstacle to social and economic progress, particularly in developing countries, where, in addition to disabilities and loss of productivity and household earnings, they cause nearly one-half of all deaths. Emerging and re-emerging diseases, those likely to cause epidemics, increasing incidence of zoonoses (diseases passed from animals to humans either directly or by insects) attributable to environmental changes, outbreaks of unknown etiology, and the undermining of some drug therapies by the spread of antimicrobial resistance are main areas of concern. In recent years WHO has noted the global spread of communicable diseases through international travel, voluntary human migration and involuntary population displacement.

WHO's Communicable Diseases group works to reduce the impact of infectious diseases world-wide through surveillance and response; prevention, control and eradication strategies; and research and product development. Combating malaria and tuberculosis (TB) are organization-wide priorities and, as such, are supported not only by their own areas of work but also by activities undertaken in other areas. The group seeks to identify new technologies and tools, and to foster national development through strengthening health services and the better use of existing tools. It aims to strengthen global monitoring of important communicable disease problems. The group advocates a functional approach to disease control. It aims to create consensus and consolidate partnerships around targeted diseases and collaborates with other groups at all stages to provide an integrated response. In April 2000 WHO and several partner institutions in epidemic surveillance established a Global Outbreak Alert and Response Network. Through the Network WHO aims to maintain constant vigilance regarding outbreaks of disease and to link world-wide expertise to provide an immediate response capability. From March 2003 WHO, through the Network, was co-ordinating the international investigation into the global spread of Severe Acute Respiratory Syndrome (SARS), a previously unknown atypical pneumonia. A Global Fund to Fight AIDS, TB and Malaria was established, with WHO participation, in 2001 (see below).

In July 1998 WHO declared the control of malaria a priority concern, and in October the organization formally launched the 'Roll Back Malaria' programme, in conjunction with UNICEF, the World Bank and UNDP, which aimed to halve the prevalence of malaria by 2010. The disease kills an estimated 1m. people each year, and affects a further 300m.–500m. people, some 90% of whom live in sub-Saharan Africa.

In 1995 WHO established a Global Tuberculosis Programme to address the challenges of the TB epidemic, which had been declared a global emergency by the Organization in 1993. According to WHO estimates, one-third of the world's population carries the TB bacillus, and 2m.–3m. people die from the disease each year. WHO provides technical support to all member countries, with special attention given to those with high TB prevalence, to establish effective national tuberculosis control programmes. WHO's strategy for TB control includes the use of DOTS (direct observation treatment, short-course), standardized treatment guide-lines, and result accountability through routine evaluation of treatment outcomes. Simultaneously, WHO is encouraging research with the aim of further disseminating DOTS, adapting DOTS for wider use, developing new tools for prevention, diagnosis and treatment, and containing new threats such as the HIV/TB co-epidemic. In March 1999 WHO announced the launch of a new initiative, 'Stop TB', in partnership with the World Bank, the US Government and a coalition of non-governmental organizations, which aimed to promote DOTS to ensure its use in 85% of detected cases by 2005 (compared with around one-quarter in 1999). The global target for case detection by 2005 was 70%. However, inadequate control of DOTS in some areas, leading to partial and inconsistent treatments, has resulted in the development of drug-resistant and, often, incurable strains of the disease. The incidence of so-called multidrug-resistant TB (MDR-TB) strains, that are unresponsive to the two main anti-TB drugs, has risen in recent years. During 2001 WHO was developing and testing DOTS-Plus, a strategy for controlling the spread of MDR-TB in areas of high prevalence. In 2001 WHO estimated that more than 8m. new cases of TB were occurring world-wide each year, of which the largest concentration was in south-east Asia. It envisaged a substantial increase in new cases by 2005, mainly owing to the severity of the HIV/TB co-epidemic. TB is the principal cause of death for people infected with the HIV virus, an estimated one-third of the 42m. people living with HIV/AIDS globally being co-infected with TB at the end of 2002. In March 2001 the Global TB Drug Facility was launched under the 'Stop TB' initiative; this aimed to increase access to high-quality anti-TB drugs for sufferers in developing countries. In October the 'Stop TB' partnership announced a Global Plan to Stop TB, which envisaged the expansion of access to DOTS; the advancement of MDR-TB prevention measures; the development of anti-TB drugs entailing a shorter treatment period; and the implementation of new strategies for treating people with HIV and TB.

One of WHO's major achievements was the eradication of smallpox. Following a massive international campaign of vaccination and surveillance (begun in 1958 and intensified in 1967), the last case was detected in 1977 and the eradication of the disease was declared in 1980. In May 1996 the World Health Assembly resolved that, pending a final endorsement, all remaining stocks of the smallpox virus were to be destroyed on 30 June 1999, although 500,000 doses of smallpox vaccine were to remain, along with a supply of the smallpox vaccine seed virus, in order to ensure that a further supply of the vaccine could be made available if required. In May 1999, however, the Assembly authorized a temporary retention of stocks of the virus until 2002. In late 2001, in response to fears

that illegally-held virus stocks could be used in acts of biological terrorism (see below), WHO reassembled a team of technical experts on smallpox. In January 2002 the Executive Board determined that stocks of the virus should continue to be retained, to enable research into more effective treatments and vaccines.

In 1988 the World Health Assembly declared its commitment to the eradication of poliomyelitis by the end of 2000 and launched the Global Polio Eradication Initiative. WHO's regional office for Europe declared the continent to be 'polio-free' in June 2002.

WHO is committed to the elimination of leprosy (the reduction of the prevalence of leprosy to less than one case per 10,000 population). The use of a highly effective combination of three drugs (known as multi-drug therapy—MDT) resulted in a reduction in the number of leprosy cases world-wide from 10m.–12m. in 1988 to 597,000 in 2000. The Global Alliance for the Elimination of Leprosy, launched in November 1999 by WHO, in collaboration with governments of affected countries and several private partners, including a major pharmaceutical company, aims to bring about the eradication of the disease by the end of 2005, through the continued use of MDT treatment. Most cases occur in Africa, South America and the Far East.

The objective of providing immunization for all children by 1990 was adopted by the World Health Assembly in 1977. Six diseases (measles, whooping cough, tetanus, poliomyelitis, tuberculosis and diphtheria) became the target of the Expanded Programme on Immunization (EPI), in which WHO, UNICEF and many other organizations collaborated. As a result of massive international and national efforts, the global immunization coverage increased from 20% in the early 1980s to the targeted rate of 80% by the end of 1990. This coverage signified that more than 100m. children in the developing world under the age of one had been successfully vaccinated against the targeted diseases, the lives of about 3m. children had been saved every year, and 500,000 annual cases of paralysis as a result of polio had been prevented. In 1992 the Assembly resolved to reach a new target of 90% immunization coverage with the six EPI vaccines; to introduce hepatitis B as a seventh vaccine (with the aim of an 80% reduction in the incidence of the disease in children by 2001); and to introduce the yellow fever vaccine in areas where it occurs endemically.

In June 2000 WHO released a report entitled 'Overcoming Antimicrobial Resistance', in which it warned that the misuse of antibiotics could render some common infectious illnesses unresponsive to treatment. At that time WHO issued guide-lines which aimed to mitigate the risks associated with the use of antimicrobials in livestock reared for human consumption.

## NON-COMMUNICABLE DISEASES AND MENTAL HEALTH

The Non-communicable Diseases and Mental Health group comprises departments for the surveillance, prevention and management of uninfectious diseases, such as those arising from an unhealthy diet, and departments for health promotion, disability, injury prevention and rehabilitation, mental health and substance abuse. Surveillance, prevention and management of non-communicable diseases, tobacco, and mental health are organization-wide priorities.

Tobacco use, unhealthy diet and physical inactivity are regarded as common, preventable risk factors for the four most prominent non-communicable diseases: cardiovascular diseases, cancer, chronic respiratory disease and diabetes. WHO aims to monitor the global epidemiological situation of non-communicable diseases, to co-ordinate multinational research activities concerned with prevention and care, and to analyse determining factors such as gender and poverty. In mid-1998 the organization adopted a resolution on measures to be taken to combat non-communicable diseases; their prevalence was anticipated to increase, particularly in developing countries, owing to rising life expectancy and changes in lifestyles. For example, between 1995 and 2025 the number of adults affected by diabetes was projected to increase from 135m. to 300m. In 2001 chronic diseases reportedly accounted for about 59% of the estimated 56.5m. total deaths globally and for 46% of the global burden of disease. In February 1999 WHO initiated a new programme, 'Vision 2020: the Right to Sight', which aimed to eliminate avoidable blindness (estimated to be as much as 80% of all cases) by 2020. Blindness was otherwise predicted to increase by as much as twofold, owing to the increased longevity of the global population. In co-operation with the International Association for the Study of Obesity (IASO), WHO has studied obesity-related issues. The International Task Force on Obesity, affiliated to the IASO, aims to encourage the development of new policies for managing obesity. WHO and FAO jointly commissioned an expert report on the relationship of diet, nutrition and physical activity to chronic diseases, which was published in March 2003.

WHO's programmes for diabetes mellitus, chronic rheumatic diseases and asthma assist with the development of national initiatives, based upon goals and targets for the improvement of early detection, care and reduction of long-term complications. WHO's cardiovascular diseases programme aims to prevent and control the major cardiovascular diseases, which are responsible for more than 14m. deaths each year. It is estimated that one-third of these deaths could have been prevented with existing scientific knowledge. The programme on cancer control is concerned with the prevention of cancer, improving its detection and cure and ensuring care of all cancer patients in need. In 1998 a five-year programme to improve cancer care in developing countries was established, sponsored by private enterprises.

The WHO Human Genetics Programme manages genetic approaches for the prevention and control of common hereditary diseases and of those with a genetic predisposition representing a major health importance. The Programme also concentrates on the further development of genetic approaches suitable for incorporation into health care systems, as well as developing a network of international collaborating programmes.

WHO works to assess the impact of injuries, violence and sensory impairments on health, and formulates guide-lines and protocols for the prevention and management of mental problems. The health promotion division promotes decentralized and community-based health programmes and is concerned with developing new approaches to population ageing and encouraging healthy life-styles and self-care. It also seeks to relieve the negative impact of social changes such as urbanization, migration and changes in family structure upon health. WHO advocates a multi-sectoral approach—involving public health, legal and educational systems—to the prevention of injuries, which represent 16% of the global burden of disease. It aims to support governments in developing suitable strategies to prevent and mitigate the consequences of violence, unintentional injury and disability. Several health promotion projects have been undertaken, in collaboration between WHO regional and country offices and other relevant organizations, including: the Global School Health Initiative, to bridge the sectors of health and education and to promote the health of school-age children; the Global Strategy for Occupational Health, to promote the health of the working population and the control of occupational health risks; Community-based Rehabilitation, aimed at providing a more enabling environment for people with disabilities; and a communication strategy to provide training and support for health communications personnel and initiatives. In 2000 WHO, UNESCO, the World Bank and UNICEF adopted the joint Focusing Resources for Effective School Health (FRESH Start) approach to promoting life skills among adolescents.

In July 1997 the fourth International Conference on Health Promotion (ICHP) was held in Jakarta, Indonesia, where a declaration on 'Health Promotion into the 21st Century' was agreed. The fifth ICHP was convened in June 2000, in Mexico City, Mexico.

Mental health problems, which include unipolar and bipolar affective disorders, psychosis, epilepsy, dementia, Parkinson's disease, multiple sclerosis, drug and alcohol dependency, and neuropsychiatric disorders such as post-traumatic stress disorder, obsessive compulsive disorder and panic disorder, have been identified by WHO as significant global health problems. Although, overall, physical health has improved, mental, behavioural and social health problems are increasing, owing to extended life expectancy and improved child mortality rates, and factors such as war and poverty. WHO aims to address mental problems by increasing awareness of mental health issues and promoting improved mental health services and primary care.

The Substance Abuse department is concerned with problems of alcohol, drugs and other substance abuse. Within its Programme on Substance Abuse (PSA), which was established in 1990 in response to the global increase in substance abuse, WHO provides technical support to assist countries in formulating policies with regard to the prevention and reduction of the health and social effects of psychoactive substance abuse. PSA's sphere of activity includes epidemiological surveillance and risk assessment, advocacy and the dissemination of information, strengthening national and regional prevention and health promotion techniques and strategies, the development of cost-effective treatment and rehabilitation approaches, and also encompasses regulatory activities as required under the international drugs-control treaties in force.

The Tobacco or Health Programme aims to reduce the use of tobacco, by educating tobacco-users and preventing young people from adopting the habit. In 1996 WHO published its first report on the tobacco situation world-wide. According to WHO, about one-third of the world's population aged over 15 years smoke tobacco, which causes approximately 3.5m. deaths each year (through lung cancer, heart disease, chronic bronchitis and other effects). In 1998 the 'Tobacco Free Initiative', a major global anti-smoking campaign, was established. In May 1999 the World Health Assembly endorsed the formulation of a Framework Convention on Tobacco Control (FCTC) to help to combat the increase in tobacco use (although a number of tobacco growers expressed concerns about the effect of the convention on their livelihoods). The draft Framework Convention was finalized in March 2003 and was adopted by the World Health Assembly in May. The greatest increase in tobacco use is forecast to occur in developing countries.

## FAMILY AND COMMUNITY HEALTH

WHO's Family and Community Health group addresses the following areas of work: child and adolescent health, research and programme development in reproductive health, making pregnancy safer, women's health, and HIV/AIDS. Making pregnancy safer and HIV/AIDS are organization-wide priorities. The group's aim is to improve access to sustainable health care for all by strengthening health systems and fostering individual, family and community development. Activities include newborn care; child health, including promoting and protecting the health and development of the child through such approaches as promotion of breast-feeding and use of the mother-baby package, as well as care of the sick child, including diarrhoeal and acute respiratory disease control, and support to women and children in difficult circumstances; the promotion of safe motherhood and maternal health; adolescent health, including the promotion and development of young people and the prevention of specific health problems; women, health and development, including addressing issues of gender, sexual violence, and harmful traditional practices; and human reproduction, including research related to contraceptive technologies and effective methods. In addition, WHO aims to provide technical leadership and co-ordination on reproductive health and to support countries in their efforts to ensure that people: experience healthy sexual development and maturation; have the capacity for healthy, equitable and responsible relationships; can achieve their reproductive intentions safely and healthily; avoid illnesses, diseases and injury related to sexuality and reproduction; and receive appropriate counselling, care and rehabilitation for diseases and conditions related to sexuality and reproduction.

In September 1997 WHO, in collaboration with UNICEF, formally launched a programme advocating the Integrated Management of Childhood Illness (IMCI), following successful regional trials in more than 20 developing countries during 1996–97. IMCI recognizes that pneumonia, diarrhoea, measles, malaria and malnutrition cause some 70% of the approximately 11m. childhood deaths each year, and recommends screening sick children for all five conditions, to obtain a more accurate diagnosis than may be achieved from the results of a single assessment. WHO's Division of Diarrhoeal and Acute Respiratory Disease Control encourages national programmes aimed at reducing childhood deaths as a result of diarrhoea, particularly through the use of oral rehydration therapy and preventive measures. The Division is also seeking to reduce deaths from pneumonia in infants through the use of a simple case-management strategy involving the recognition of danger signs and treatment with an appropriate antibiotic.

The HIV/AIDS epidemic represents a major threat to human wellbeing and socio-economic progress. Some 95% of those known to be infected with HIV/AIDS live in developing countries, and AIDS-related illnesses are the leading cause of death in sub-Saharan Africa. At December 2002 an estimated 42m. people world-wide were living with HIV/AIDS (including some 3.2m. children under 15 years); 5m. were newly infected during that year. WHO's Global Programme on AIDS, initiated in 1987, was concluded in December 1995. A Joint UN Programme on HIV/AIDS (UNAIDS) became operational on 1 January 1996, sponsored by WHO, the World Bank, UNICEF, UNDP, UNESCO and UNFPA. (The UN International Drug Control Programme became the seventh sponsoring agency of UNAIDS in 1999, and in 2001 ILO became the eighth sponsor.) The UNAIDS secretariat is based at WHO headquarters. WHO established an Office of HIV/AIDS and Sexually-Transmitted Diseases in order to ensure the continuity of its global response to the problem, which included support for national control and education plans, improving the safety of blood supplies and improving the care and support of AIDS patients. In addition, the Office was to liaise with UNAIDS and to make available WHO's research and technical expertise. HIV/AIDS are an organization-wide priority. Sufferers of HIV/AIDS in developing countries have often failed to receive advanced antiretroviral (ARV) treatments that are widely available in industrialized countries, owing to their high cost. In May 2000 the World Health Assembly adopted a resolution urging WHO member states to improve access to the prevention and treatment of HIV-related illnesses and to increase the availability and affordability of drugs. A WHO-UNAIDS HIV Vaccine Initiative was launched in that year. In July a meeting of the Group of Seven industrialized nations and Russia (G-8), convened in Genoa, Italy, announced the formation of a new Global Fund to Fight AIDS, TB and Malaria (as previously proposed by the UN Secretary-General and recommended by the World Health Assembly). The Fund, a partnership between governments, UN bodies (including WHO) and other agencies, and private-sector interests, aimed in 2004 to disburse US $623m. in grants to prevention and treatment programmes in around 50 countries. In June 2001 governments participating in a special session of the UN General Assembly on HIV/AIDS adopted a

Declaration of Commitment on HIV/AIDS. WHO, with UNAIDS, UNICEF, UNFPA, the World Bank, and major pharmaceutical companies, participates in the 'Accelerating Access' initiative, which aims to expand access to care, support and ARVs for people with HIV/AIDS. In March 2002, under its 'Access to Quality HIV/AIDS Drugs and Diagnostics' programme, WHO published a comprehensive list of HIV-related medicines deemed to meet standards recommended by the Organization. In April WHO issued the first treatment guide-lines for HIV/AIDS cases in poor communities, and endorsed the inclusion of HIV/AIDS drugs in its *Model List of Essential Drugs* (see below) in order to encourage their wider availability. The secretariat of the International HIV Treatment Access Coalition, founded in December of that year by governments, non-governmental organizations, donors and others to facilitate access to ARVs for people in low and middle income countries, is based at WHO headquarters. WHO, jointly with UNAIDS and the Global Fund to Fight AIDS, TB and Malaria (see above), supports the so-called 'three-by-five' target of providing 3m. people in developing countries with ARVs by the end of 2005. WHO supports governments in developing effective health-sector responses to the HIV/AIDS epidemic through enhancing the planning and managerial capabilities, implementation capacity, and resources of health systems. In February 2003 WHO and FAO jointly published a manual on nutritional care for people living with HIV/AIDS.

At December 2002 some 1.2m. people in Eastern Europe and Central Asia were reported to have HIV/AIDS, of whom 250,000 were newly infected during that year. During the period 1997–2000 some 80% of new HIV infections in the Commonwealth of Independent States were reported to have occured in people aged younger than 29. Countries in the region with serious epidemics of HIV/AIDS include the Russian Federation (where the total number of reported HIV infections had exceeded 200,000 by mid-2002, compared with nearly 11,000 at end-1998), Belarus, Kazakhstan, Moldova, Uzbekistan and Ukraine, which has the region's highest national adult HIV prevalence rate (estimated at 1%).

In 1990 the WHO Regional Committee for Europe established the EUROHEALTH programme in Central and Eastern Europe. The programme was to establish reforms in health care and environment, to control communicable and non-communicable diseases, and to improve the health of women and children.

**Joint UN Programme on HIV/AIDS (UNAIDS):** 20 ave Appia, 1211 Geneva 27, Switzerland; tel. (22) 7913666; fax (22) 7914187; e-mail unaids@unaids.org; internet www.unaids.org; established in 1996 to lead, strengthen and support an expanded response to the global HIV/AIDS pandemic; activities focus on prevention, care and support, reducing vulnerability to infection, and alleviating the socioeconomic and human effects of HIV/AIDS; co-sponsors: WHO, UNICEF, UNDP, UNFPA, UNDCP, ILO, UNESCO, the World Bank, WFP; Exec. Dir PETER PIOT (Belgium).

### SUSTAINABLE DEVELOPMENT AND HEALTHY ENVIRONMENTS

The Sustainable Development and Healthy Environments group focuses on the following areas of work: health in sustainable development; nutrition; health and environment; food safety; and emergency preparedness and response. Food safety is an organization-wide priority.

WHO promotes recognition of good health status as one of the most important assets of the poor. The Sustainable Development and Healthy Environment group seeks to monitor the advantages and disadvantages for health, nutrition, environment and development arising from the process of globalization (i.e. increased global flows of capital, goods and services, people, and knowledge); to integrate the issue of health into poverty reduction programmes; and to promote human rights and equality. Adequate and safe food and nutrition is a priority programme area. WHO collaborates with FAO, the World Food Programme, UNICEF and other UN agencies in pursuing its objectives relating to nutrition and food safety. An estimated 780m. people world-wide cannot meet basic needs for energy and protein, more than 2,000m. people lack essential vitamins and minerals, and 170m. children are estimated to be malnourished. In December 1992 WHO and FAO hosted an international conference on nutrition, at which a World Declaration and Plan of Action on Nutrition was adopted to make the fight against malnutrition a development priority. Following the conference, WHO promoted the elaboration and implementation of national plans of action on nutrition. WHO aims to support the enhancement of member states' capabilities in dealing with their nutrition situations, and addressing scientific issues related to preventing, managing and monitoring protein-energy malnutrition; micronutrient malnutrition, including iodine deficiency disorders, vitamin A deficiency, and nutritional anaemia; and diet-related conditions and non-communicable diseases such as obesity (increasingly affecting children, adolescents and adults, mainly in industrialized countries), cancer and heart disease. In 1990 the World Health Assembly resolved to eliminate iodine deficiency (believed to cause mental

retardation); a strategy of universal salt iodization was launched in 1993. In collaboration with other international agencies, WHO is implementing a comprehensive strategy for promoting appropriate infant, young child and maternal nutrition, and for dealing effectively with nutritional emergencies in large populations. Areas of emphasis include promoting health-care practices that enhance successful breast-feeding; appropriate complementary feeding; refining the use and interpretation of body measurements for assessing nutritional status; relevant information, education and training; and action to give effect to the International Code of Marketing of Breast-milk Substitutes. The food safety programme aims to protect human health against risks associated with biological and chemical contaminants and additives in food. With FAO, WHO establishes food standards (through the work of the Codex Alimentarius Commission and its subsidiary committees) and evaluates food additives, pesticide residues and other contaminants and their implications for health. The programme provides expert advice on such issues as food-borne pathogens (e.g. listeria), production methods (e.g. aquaculture) and food biotechnology (e.g. genetic modification). In July 2001 the Codex Alimentarius Commission adopted the first global principles for assessing the safety of genetically-modified (GM) foods. In March 2002 an intergovernmental task force established by the Commission finalized 'principles for the risk analysis of foods derived from biotechnology', which were to provide a framework for assessing the safety of GM foods and plants. In the following month WHO and FAO announced a joint review of their food standards operations. In February 2003 the FAO/WHO Project and Fund for Enhanced Participation in Codex was launched to support the participation of poorer countries in the Commission's activities.

WHO's programme area on environment and health undertakes a wide range of initiatives to tackle the increasing threats to health and well-being from a changing environment, especially in relation to air pollution, water quality, sanitation, protection against radiation, management of hazardous waste, chemical safety and housing hygiene. Some 1,100m. people world-wide have no access to clean drinking water, while a further 2,400m. people are denied suitable sanitation systems. WHO helped launch the Water Supply and Sanitation Council in 1990 and regularly updates its *Guidelines for Drinking Water Quality*. In rural areas, the emphasis continues to be on the provision and maintenance of safe and sufficient water supplies and adequate sanitation, the health aspects of rural housing, vector control in water resource management, and the safe use of agrochemicals. In urban areas, assistance is provided to identify local environmental health priorities and to improve municipal governments' ability to deal with environmental conditions and health problems in an integrated manner; promotion of the 'Healthy City' approach is a major component of the Programme. Other Programme activities include environmental health information development and management, human resources development, environmental health planning methods, research and work on problems relating to global environment change, such as UV-radiation. A report considering the implications of climate change on human health, prepared jointly by WHO, WMO and UNEP, was published in July 1996. The WHO Global Strategy for Health and Environment, developed in response to the WHO Commission on Health and Environment which reported to the UN Conference on Environment and Development in June 1992, provides the framework for programme activities. In December 2001 WHO published a report on the relationship between macroeconomics and health.

WHO's work in the promotion of chemical safety is undertaken in collaboration with ILO and UNEP through the International Programme on Chemical Safety (IPCS), the Central Unit for which is located in WHO. The Programme provides internationally-evaluated scientific information on chemicals, promotes the use of such information in national programmes, assists member states in establishment of their own chemical safety measures and programmes, and helps them strengthen their capabilities in chemical emergency preparedness and response and in chemical risk reduction. In 1995 an Inter-organization Programme for the Social Management of Chemicals was established by UNEP, ILO, FAO, WHO, UNIDO and OECD, in order to strengthen international co-operation in the field of chemical safety. In 1998 WHO led an international assessment of the health risk from bendocine disruptors (chemicals which disrupt hormonal activities).

Following the major terrorist attacks perpetrated against targets in the USA in September 2001, WHO focused renewed attention on the potential deliberate use of infectious diseases, such as anthrax and smallpox, or of chemical agents, in acts of biological or chemical terrorism. In September 2001 WHO issued draft guide-lines entitled 'Health Aspects of Biological and Chemical Weapons'.

Within the UN system, WHO's Department of Emergency and Humanitarian Action co-ordinates the international response to emergencies and natural disasters in the health field, in close co-operation with other agencies and within the framework set out by the UN's Office for the Co-ordination of Humanitarian Affairs. In this context, WHO provides expert advice on epidemiological surveillance, control of communicable diseases, public health information and health emergency training. Its emergency preparedness activities include co-ordination, policy-making and planning, awareness-building, technical advice, training, publication of standards and guide-lines, and research. Its emergency relief activities include organizational support, the provision of emergency drugs and supplies and conducting technical emergency assessment missions. The Division's objective is to strengthen the national capacity of member states to reduce the adverse health consequences of disasters. In responding to emergency situations, WHO always tries to develop projects and activities that will assist the national authorities concerned in rebuilding or strengthening their own capacity to handle the impact of such situations In May 2001 WHO participated with governments and other international agencies in a joint exercise to evaluate national and international procedures for responding to a nuclear emergency.

Since October 1999 WHO has provided emergency humanitarian assistance (including co-ordination activities, strengthening primary care and health care management, improving communicable disease surveillance, TB control, HIV and STD prevention, and psycho-social rehabilitation) for some 500,000 people affected by the civil conflict in the Republic of Chechnya (the Chechen Republic of Ichkeriya, Russian Federation).

### HEALTH TECHNOLOGY AND PHARMACEUTICALS

WHO's Health Technology and Pharmaceuticals group, made up of the departments of essential drugs and other medicines, vaccines and other biologicals, and blood safety and clinical technology, covers the following areas of work: essential medicines—access, quality and rational use; immunization and vaccine development; and world-wide co-operation on blood safety and clinical technology. Blood safety and clinical technology are an organization-wide priority.

In January 1999 the Executive Board adopted a resolution on WHO's Revised Drug Strategy which placed emphasis on the inequalities of access to pharmaceuticals, and also covered specific aspects of drugs policy, quality assurance, drug promotion, drug donation, independent drug information and rational drug use. Plans of action involving co-operation with member states and other international organizations were to be developed to monitor and analyse the pharmaceutical and public health implications of international agreements, including trade agreements. In April 2001 experts from WHO and the World Trade Organization participated in a workshop to address ways of lowering the cost of medicines in less developed countries. In the following month the World Health Assembly adopted a resolution urging member states to promote equitable access to essential drugs, noting that this was denied to about one-third of the world's population. WHO participates with other partners in the 'Accelerating Access' initiative, which aims to expand access to antiretroviral drugs for people with HIV/AIDS (see above).

WHO reports that 2m. children die each year of diseases for which common vaccines exist. In September 1991 the Children's Vaccine Initiative (CVI) was launched, jointly sponsored by the Rockefeller Foundation, UNDP, UNICEF, the World Bank and WHO, to facilitate the development and provision of children's vaccines. The CVI has as its ultimate goal the development of a single oral immunization shortly after birth that will protect against all major childhood diseases. An International Vaccine Institute was established in Seoul, Republic of Korea, as part of the CVI, to provide scientific and technical services for the production of vaccines for developing countries. In September 1996 WHO, jointly with UNICEF, published a comprehensive survey, entitled *State of the World's Vaccines and Immunization*. In 1999 WHO, UNICEF, the World Bank and a number of public- and private-sector partners formed the Global Alliance for Vaccines and Immunization (GAVI), which aimed to expand the provision of existing vaccines and to accelerate the development and introduction of new vaccines and technologies, with the ultimate goal of protecting children of all nations and from all socio-economic backgrounds against vaccine-preventable diseases.

WHO supports states in ensuring access to safe blood, blood products, transfusions, injections, and health-care technologies.

### EVIDENCE AND INFORMATION FOR HEALTH POLICY

The Evidence and Information for Health Policy group addresses the following areas of work: evidence for health policy; health information management and dissemination; and research policy and promotion and organization of health systems. Through the generation and dissemination of evidence the Evidence and Information for Health Policy group aims to assist policy-makers assess health needs, choose intervention strategies, design policy and monitor performance, and thereby improve the performance of national health systems. The group also supports international and national dialogue on health policy.

WHO co-ordinates the Health InterNetwork Access to Research Initiative (HINARI), which was launched in July 2001 to enable relevant authorities in developing countries to access more than 2,000 biomedical journals through the internet at no or greatly reduced cost, in order to improve the world-wide circulation of scientific information; some 28 medical publishers participate in the initiative.

## Finance

WHO's regular budget is provided by assessment of member states and associate members. An additional fund for specific projects is provided by voluntary contributions from members and other sources, including UNDP and UNFPA.

A regular budget of US $842.7m. was proposed for the two years 2002–03, of which some 6.3%, or $52.8m., was provisionally allocated to Europe.

## Publications

*Action against Infection* (newsletter).
*Bulletin of WHO* (monthly).
*Environmental Health Criteria.*
*International Digest of Health Legislation* (quarterly).
*International Classification of Functioning, Disability and Health—ICF.*
*International Statistical Classification of Diseases and Related Health Problems* (Tenth Revision, 1992–1994 (versions in 37 languages)).
*Model List of Essential Drugs* (biennially).
*Weekly Epidemiological Record.*
*WHO Drug Information* (quarterly).
*WHO Model Formulary.*
*World Health Report* (annually).
*World Health Statistics Annual.*

Technical report series; catalogues of specific scientific, technical and medical fields available.

# Other UN Organizations Active in the Region

### OFFICE FOR THE CO-ORDINATION OF HUMANITARIAN AFFAIRS—OCHA

**Address:** United Nations Plaza, New York, NY 10017, USA.

**Telephone:** (212) 963-1234; **fax:** (212) 963-1312; **e-mail:** ochany@un.org; **internet:** www.reliefweb.int/ocha_ol/.

The Office was established in January 1998 as part of the UN Secretariat, with a mandate to co-ordinate international humanitarian assistance and to provide policy and other advice on humanitarian issues. It administers the Humanitarian Early Warning System, as well as Integrated Regional Information Networks (IRIN) to monitor the situation in different countries and a Disaster Response System. A complementary service, Reliefweb, which was launched in 1996, monitors crises and publishes information on the internet.

The IRIN–Central Asia Office, which opened in Islamabad, Pakistan, in August 2000, covers eight countries. A sub-office is based in Bishkek, Kyrgyzstan.

**Under-Secretary-General for Humanitarian Affairs and Emergency Relief Co-ordinator:** JAN EGELAND (Norway).

### OFFICE FOR DRUG CONTROL AND CRIME PREVENTION—ODCCP

**Address:** Vienna International Centre, POB 500, 1400 Vienna, Austria.

**Telephone:** (1) 26060-0; **fax:** (1) 26060-5866; **e-mail:** odccp@odccp.org; **internet:** www.odccp.org.

The Office was established in November 1997 to strengthen the UN's integrated approach to issues relating to drug control, crime prevention and international terrorism. It comprises two principal components: the United Nations International Drug Control Programme (UNDCP) and the Centre for International Crime Prevention, both headed by the ODCCP Executive Director.

**Executive Director:** Antonio Maria Costa (Italy).

## OFFICE OF THE UNITED NATIONS HIGH COMMISSIONER FOR HUMAN RIGHTS—OHCHR

**Address:** Palais Wilson, 52 rue de Paquis, 1201 Geneva, Switzerland.

**Telephone:** (22) 9179290; **fax:** (22) 9179022; **e-mail:** scrt.hchr@unog.ch; **internet:** www.unhchr.ch.

The Office is a body of the UN Secretariat and is the focal point for UN human-rights activities. Since September 1997 it has incorporated the Centre for Human Rights. The High Commissioner is the UN official with principal responsibility for UN human rights activities.

**High Commissioner:** Bertrand Ramcharan (acting).

## UNITED NATIONS HUMAN SETTLEMENTS PROGRAMME—UN-Habitat

**Address:** POB 30030, Nairobi, Kenya.

**Telephone:** (20) 621234; **fax:** (20) 624266; **e-mail:** infohabitat@unhabitat.org; **internet:** www.unhabitat.org.

UN-Habitat was established, as the United Nations Centre for Human Settlements, in October 1978 to service the intergovernmental Commission on Human Settlements. It became a full UN programme on 1 January 2002, serving as the focus for human settlements activities in the UN system.

**Executive Director:** Anna Kajumulo Tibaijuka (Tanzania).

## UNITED NATIONS CONFERENCE ON TRADE AND DEVELOPMENT—UNCTAD

**Address:** Palais des Nations, 1211 Geneva 10, Switzerland.

**Telephone:** (22) 9071234; **fax:** (22) 9070057; **e-mail:** ers@unctad.org; **internet:** www.unctad.org.

UNCTAD was established in 1964. It is the principal organ of the UN General Assembly concerned with trade and development, and is the focal point within the UN system for integrated activities relating to trade, finance, technology, investment and sustainable development. It aims to maximize the trade and development opportunities of developing countries, in particular least-developed countries, and to assist them to adapt to the increasing globalization and liberalization of the world economy. UNCTAD undertakes consensus-building activities, research and policy analysis and technical co-operation.

**Secretary-General:** Rubens Ricúpero (Brazil).

## UNITED NATIONS POPULATION FUND—UNFPA

**Address:** 220 East 42nd St, New York, NY 10017, USA.

**Telephone:** (212) 297-5020; **fax:** (212) 297-4911; **internet:** www.unfpa.org.

Created in 1967 as the Trust Fund for Population Activities, the UN Fund for Population Activities (UNFPA) was established as a Fund of the UN General Assembly in 1972 and was made a subsidiary organ of the UN General Assembly in 1979, with the UNDP Governing Council (now the Executive Board) designated as its governing body. In 1987 UNFPA's name was changed to the United Nations Population Fund (retaining the same acronym).

**Executive Director:** Thoraya A. Obaid (Saudi Arabia).

# UN Specialized Agencies

## INTERNATIONAL CIVIL AVIATION ORGANIZATION—ICAO

**Address:** 999 University St, Montréal, QC H3C 5H7, Canada.

**Telephone:** (514) 854-8219; **fax:** (514) 954-6077; **e-mail:** icaohq@icao.org; **internet:** www.icao.int.

ICAO was founded in 1947, on the basis of the Convention on International Civil Aviation, signed in Chicago, in 1944, to develop the techniques of international air navigation and to help in the planning and improvement of international air transport.

**Secretary-General:** Taïeb Chérif (Algeria).

**Regional Office for Europe and the North Atlantic:** 3 bis, Villa Emile-Bergerat, 92522 Neuilly-sur-Seine Cédex, France; tel. 1-46-41-85-85; fax 1-46-41-85-00; e-mail icaoeurnat@paris.icao.int; internet www.icao.int/eurnat; Dir Chris Eigl (Austria).

## INTERNATIONAL FUND FOR AGRICULTURAL DEVELOPMENT—IFAD

**Address:** Via del Serafico 107, 00142 Rome, Italy.

**Telephone:** (06) 54591; **fax:** (06) 5043463; **e-mail:** ifad@ifad.org; **internet:** www.ifad.org.

IFAD was established in 1977, following a decision by the 1974 UN World Food Conference, with a mandate to combat hunger and eradicate poverty on a sustainable basis in the low-income, food-deficit regions of the world. Funding operations began in January 1978.

**President and Chairman of Executive Board:** Lennart Båge (Sweden).

## INTERNATIONAL LABOUR ORGANIZATION—ILO

**Address:** 4 route des Morillons, 1211 Geneva 22, Switzerland.

**Telephone:** (22) 7996111; **fax:** (22) 7988685; **e-mail:** ilo@ilo.org; **internet:** www.ilo.org.

ILO was founded in 1919 to work for social justice as a basis for lasting peace. It carries out this mandate by promoting decent living standards, satisfactory conditions of work and pay and adequate employment opportunities. Methods of action include the creation of international labour standards; the provision of technical co-operation services; and training, education, research and publishing activities to advance ILO objectives.

**Director-General:** Juan O. Somavía (Chile).

**Regional Office for Europe and Central Asia:** 4 route des Morillons, 1211 Geneva 22, Switzerland; tel. (22) 7996650; fax (22) 7996061; e-mail europe@ilo.org; Dir Friedrich Buttler (Germany).

**Moscow Area Office and East European and Central Asian Multi-disciplinary Team:** 107031 Moscow, ul. Petrovka, Apt 23; tel. (095) 933-08-10; fax (095) 933-08-20; e-mail ouskova@ilo.org; internet www.ilo.ru; Dir Pauline Barrett-Reid.

## INTERNATIONAL MARITIME ORGANIZATION—IMO

**Address:** 4 Albert Embankment, London, SE1 7SR, United Kingdom.

**Telephone:** (20) 7735-7611; **fax:** (20) 7587-3210; **e-mail:** info@imo.org; **internet:** www.imo.org.

The Inter-Governmental Maritime Consultative Organization (IMCO) began operations in 1959, as a specialized agency of the UN to facilitate co-operation among governments on technical matters affecting international shipping. Its main aims are to improve the safety of international shipping, and to prevent pollution caused by ships. IMCO became IMO in 1982.

**Secretary-General:** William A. O'Neil (Canada) (until 31 December 2003), Efthimios Mitropoulos (Greece) (designate).

## INTERNATIONAL TELECOMMUNICATION UNION—ITU

**Address:** Place des Nations, 1211 Geneva 20, Switzerland.

**Telephone:** (22) 7305111; **fax:** (22) 7337256; **e-mail:** itumail@itu.int; **internet:** www.itu.int.

Founded in 1865, ITU became a specialized agency of the UN in 1947. It acts to encourage world co-operation for the improvement and use of telecommunications, to promote technical development, to harmonize national policies in the field, and to promote the extension of telecommunications throughout the world.

**Secretary-General:** Yoshio Utsumi (Japan).

## UNITED NATIONS INDUSTRIAL DEVELOPMENT ORGANIZATION—UNIDO

**Address:** Vienna International Centre, POB 300, 1400 Vienna, Austria.

**Telephone:** (1) 260260; **fax:** (1) 2692669; **e-mail:** unido@unido.org; **internet:** www.unido.org.

UNIDO began operations in 1967 and became a specialized agency in 1985. Its objectives are to promote sustainable and socially equitable industrial development in developing countries and in countries with economies in transition. It aims to assist such countries to integrate fully into global economic system by mobilizing knowledge, skills, information and technology to promote productive employment, competitive economies and sound environment.

**Director-General:** Carlos Alfredo Magariños (Argentina).

## UNIVERSAL POSTAL UNION—UPU

**Address:** Weltpoststr., 3000 Berne 15, Switzerland.

**Telephone:** (31) 3503111; **fax:** (31) 3503110; **e-mail:** info@upu.int; **internet:** www.upu.int.

The General Postal Union was founded by the Treaty of Berne (1874), beginning operations in July 1875. Three years later its name was changed to the Universal Postal Union. In 1948 UPU became a specialized agency of the UN. It aims to develop and unify the international postal service, to study problems and to provide training.

**Director-General:** Thomas E. Leavey (USA).

## WORLD INTELLECTUAL PROPERTY ORGANIZATION— WIPO

**Address:** 34 chemin des Colombettes, 1211 Geneva 20, Switzerland.

**Telephone:** (22) 3389111; **fax:** (22) 7335428; **e-mail:** wipo.mail@ wipo.int; **internet:** www.wipo.int.

WIPO was established in 1970. It became a specialized agency of the UN in 1974 concerned with the protection of intellectual property (e.g. industrial and technical patents and literary copyrights) throughout the world. WIPO formulates and administers treaties embodying international norms and standards of intellectual property, establishes model laws, and facilitates applications for the protection of inventions, trademarks etc. WIPO provides legal and technical assistance to developing countries and countries with economies in transition and advises countries on obligations under the World Trade Organization's agreement on Trade-Related Aspects of Intellectual Property Rights (TRIPS).

**Director-General:** Dr Kamil Idris (Sudan).

## WORLD METEOROLOGICAL ORGANIZATION—WMO

**Address:** 7 bis, ave de la Paix, 1211 Geneva 2, Switzerland.

**Telephone:** (22) 7308111; **fax:** (22) 7308181; **e-mail:** ipa@wmo.ch; **internet:** www.wmo.ch.

WMO was established in 1950 and was recognized as a Specialized Agency of the UN in 1951, aiming to improve the exchange of information in the fields of meteorology, climatology, operational hydrology and related fields, as well as their applications. WMO jointly implements the UN Framework Convention on Climate Change with UNEP.

**Secretary-General:** Prof. G. O. P. Obasi (Nigeria) (until 31 December 2003), Michel Jarraud (France) (designate).

# ASIAN DEVELOPMENT BANK—ADB

**Address:** 6 ADB Ave, Mandaluyong City, 0401 Metro Manila, Philippines; POB 789, 0980 Manila, Philippines.

**Telephone:** (2) 6324444; **fax:** (2) 6362444; **e-mail:** information@adb .org; **internet:** www.adb.org.

The ADB commenced operations in December 1966. The Bank's principal functions are to provide loans and equity investments for the economic and social advancement of its developing member countries, to give technical assistance for the preparation and implementation of development projects and programmes and advisory services, to promote investment of public and private capital for development purposes, and to respond to requests from developing member countries for assistance in the co-ordination of their development policies and plans.

## MEMBERS

There are 44 member countries and territories within the ESCAP region and 17 others (see list of subscriptions below).

## Organization

(October 2003)

### BOARD OF GOVERNORS

All powers of the Bank are vested in the Board, which may delegate its powers to the Board of Directors except in such matters as admission of new members, changes in the Bank's authorized capital stock, election of Directors and President, and amendment of the Charter. One Governor and one Alternate Governor are appointed by each member country. The Board meets at least once a year.

### BOARD OF DIRECTORS

The Board of Directors is responsible for general direction of operations and exercises all powers delegated by the Board of Governors, which elects it. Of the 12 Directors, eight represent constituency groups of member countries within the ESCAP region (with about 65% of the voting power) and four represent the rest of the member countries. Each Director serves for two years and may be re-elected.

Three specialized committees (the Audit Committee, the Budget Review Committee and the Inspection Committee), each comprising six members, assist the Board of Directors in exercising its authority with regard to supervising the Bank's financial statements, approving the administrative budget, and reviewing and approving policy documents and assistance operations.

The President of the Bank, though not a Director, is Chairman of the Board.

**Chairman of Board of Directors and President:** TADAO CHINO (Japan).

**Vice-Presidents:** JOSEPH B. EICHENBERGER (USA), JOHN LINTJER (Netherlands), MYOUNG-HO SHIN (Republic of Korea).

### ADMINISTRATION

The Bank had 2,220 staff at 31 December 2002.

On 1 January 2002 the Bank implemented a new organizational structure. The reorganization aimed to strengthen the Bank's country and sub-regional focus, as well as its capacity for poverty reduction and implementing its long-term strategic framework. Five regional departments cover East and Central Asia, the Mekong, the Pacific, South Asia, and South East Asia. Other departments and offices include Private Sector Operations, Central Operations Services, Regional and Sustainable Development, Strategy and Policy, Cofinancing Operations, and Economics and Research, as well as other administrative units.

There are Bank Resident Missions in Afghanistan, Bangladesh, Cambodia, the People's Republic of China, India, Indonesia, Kazakhstan, Kyrgyzstan, Laos, Mongolia, Nepal, Pakistan, Papua New Guinea, Sri Lanka, Tajikistan, Uzbekistan and Viet Nam, all of which report to the head of the regional department. In addition the Bank has established a country office in the Philippines, an Extended Mission in Gujarat, India, Special Offices in Timor-Leste and Turkmenistan, and a South Pacific Regional Mission, based in Vanuatu. Representative Offices are located in Tokyo, Japan, Frankfurt am Main, Germany (for Europe), and Washington, DC, USA (for North America).

**Secretary:** BINDU N. LOHANI.

**General Counsel:** ARTHUR M. MITCHELL.

## INSTITUTE

**ADB Institute—ADBI:** Kasumigaseki Bldg, 8th Floor, 2–5 Kasumigaseki 3-chome, Chiyoda-ku, Tokyo 100-6008, Japan; tel. (3) 3593-5500; fax (3) 3593-5571; e-mail info@adbi.org; internet www .adbi.org; f. 1997 as a subsidiary body of the ADB to research and analyse long-term development issues and to disseminate development practices through training and other capacity-building activities; Dean Dr PETER MCCAWLEY (Australia).

## FINANCIAL STRUCTURE

The Bank's ordinary capital resources (which are used for loans to the more advanced developing member countries) are held and used entirely separately from its Special Funds resources (see below). A fourth General Capital Increase (GCI IV), amounting to US $26,318m. (or some 100%), was authorized in May 1994. At the final deadline for subscription to GCI IV, on 30 September 1996, 55 member countries had subscribed shares amounting to $24,675.4m.

At 31 December 2002 the position of subscriptions to the capital stock was as follows: authorized US $47,288m.; subscribed $47,234m.

The Bank also borrows funds from the world capital markets. Total borrowings during 2002 amounted to US $6,145m. (compared with $1,607m. in 2001). At 31 December 2002 total outstanding borrowings amounted to $26,324m.

In July 1986 the Bank abolished the system of fixed lending rates, under which ordinary operations loans had carried interest rates fixed at the time of loan commitment for the entire life of the loan. Under the new system the lending rate is adjusted every six months, to take into account changing conditions in international financial markets.

## SPECIAL FUNDS

The Asian Development Fund (ADF) was established in 1974 in order to provide a systematic mechanism for mobilizing and administering resources for the Bank to lend on concessional terms to the least-developed member countries. In 1998 the Bank revised the terms of ADF. Since 1 January 1999 all new project loans are repayable within 32 years, including an eight-year grace period, while quick-disbursing programme loans have a 24-year maturity, also including an eight-year grace period. The previous annual service charge was redesignated as an interest charge, including a portion to cover administrative expenses. The new interest charges on all loans are 1%–1.5% per annum. At 31 December 2002 total ADF loans approved amounted to US $27,392m. for 970 loans, while cumulative disbursements from ADF resources totalled $18,688m.

Successive replenishments of the Fund's resources amounted to US $809m. for the period 1976–78, $2,150m. for 1979–82, $3,214m. for 1983–86, $3,600m. for 1987–90, $4,200m. for 1992–95, and $6,300m. for 1997–2000. In September 2000 25 donor countries pledged $2,910m. towards the ADF's seventh replenishment (ADF VIII), which totalled $5,650m. to provide resources for the period 2001–04; repayments of earlier ADF loans were to provide the remaining $2,740m. ADF VIII became effective in June 2001.

The Bank provides technical assistance grants from its Technical Assistance Special Fund (TASF). By the end of 2002, the Fund's total resources amounted to US $919.6m., of which $851.3m. had been utilized or committed. The Japan Special Fund (JSF) was established in 1988 to provide finance for technical assistance by means of grants, in both the public and private sectors. The JSF aims to help developing member countries restructure their economies, enhance the opportunities for attracting new investment, and recycle funds. The Japanese Government had committed a total of 97,300m. yen (equivalent to some $836.0m.) to the JSF by the end of 2002, of which $751.5m. had been utilized. An Asian Currency Crisis Support Facility (ACCSF) was operational for the three-year period March 1999–March 2002, as an independent component of the JSF to provide additional technical assistance, interest payment assistance and guarantees to countries most affected by financial instability, i.e. Indonesia, Republic of Korea, Malaysia, Philippines and Thailand. At the end of 2002 the Japanese Government, as the sole financier of the fund, had contributed 27,500m. yen (some $241.0m.) to the ACCSF. The Japanese Government funds the Japan Scholarship Program, under which 1,479 scholarships had been awarded to recipients from 34 member countries between 1988 and 2002, and the ADB Institute Special Fund, which was established to finance the ADB Institute's initial operations. By 31 December 2002 cumulative commitments to the Special Fund amounted to 8,700m. yen (or $71.3m.). In May 2000 the Japan Fund for Poverty Reduction was established, with an initial contribution of 10,000m. yen (approximately $92.6m.) from the Japanese Government, to support ADB-financed poverty reduction and social development activities. By the end of 2002 cumulative commitments to the Fund totalled $244m. A Japan Fund for Information and Communication Technology (ICT) was established in July 2001, for a three-year period, to promote the advancement and use of ICT in developing member countries. The Fund was established with an initial contribution of 1,273m. yen (or $10.7m.) from the Japanese Government.

The majority of grant funds in support of the Bank's technical assistance activities are provided by bilateral donors under channel financing arrangements (CFAs). Since 1980, when the first CFA was negotiated, 151 technical assistance grants had been financed under CFAs at the end of 2001, with a total value of $73.7m. CFAs may also be processed as a thematic financing tool, for example concerned with renewable energy, water or poverty reduction, enabling more than one donor to contribute. In 2002 a new multi-donor thematic CFA with a focus on poverty reduction was introduced.

# Activities

Loans by the ADB are usually aimed at specific projects. In responding to requests from member governments for loans, the Bank's staff assesses the financial and economic viability of projects and the way in which they fit into the economic framework and priorities of development of the country concerned. In 1987 the Bank adopted a policy of lending in support of programmes of sectoral adjustment, not limited to specific projects; such loans were not to exceed 15% of total Bank public sector lending. In 1999 the Board of Directors increased the ceiling on programme lending to 20% of the annual total. In 1985 the Bank decided to expand its assistance to the private sector, hitherto comprising loans to development finance institutions, under government guarantee, for lending to small and medium-sized enterprises; a programme was formulated for direct financial assistance, in the form of equity and loans without government guarantee, to private enterprises. In 1992 a Social Dimensions Unit was established as part of the central administrative structure of the Bank, which contributed to the Bank's increasing awareness of the importance of social aspects of development as essential components of sustainable economic growth. During the early 1990s the Bank also aimed to expand its role as project financier by providing assistance for policy formulation and review and promoting regional co-operation, while placing greater emphasis on individual country requirements. In accordance with its medium-term strategy for 1995–98 the Bank resolved to promote sound development management, by integrating into its operations and projects the promotion of governance issues, such as capacity-building, legal frameworks and openness of information. During that period the Bank also introduced a commitment to assess development projects for their impact on the local population and to avoid all involuntary resettlement where possible and established a formal procedure for grievances, under which the Board may authorize an inspection of a project, by an independent panel of experts, at the request of the affected community or group. In 1998 the Bank approved a new anticorruption strategy.

The currency instability and ensuing financial crises affecting many Asian economies in the second half of 1997 and in 1998 prompted the Bank to reflect on its role in the region. The Bank resolved to strengthen its activities as a broad-based development institution, rather than solely as a project financier, through lending policies, dialogue, co-financing and technical assistance. A Task Force on Financial Sector Reform was established to review the causes and effects of the regional financial crisis. The Task Force identified the Bank's initial priorities as being to accelerate banking and capital market reforms in member countries, to promote market efficiency in the financial, trade and industrial sectors, to promote good governance and sound corporate management, and to alleviate the social impact of structural adjustments. In mid-1999 the Bank approved a technical assistance grant to establish an internet-based Asian Recovery Information Centre, within a new Regional Monitoring Unit, which aimed to facilitate access to information regarding the economic and social impact of the Asian financial crisis, analyses of economic needs of countries, reform programmes and monitoring of the economic recovery process. In November the Board of Directors approved a new overall strategy objective of poverty reduction, which was to be the principal consideration for all future Bank lending, project financing and technical assistance. The strategy incorporated key aims of supporting sustainable, grass-roots based economic growth, social development and good governance. The Board also approved a health sector policy, to concentrate resources on basic primary healthcare, and initiated reviews of the Bank's private sector strategy and the efficiency of resident missions. During 2000 the Bank began to refocus its country strategies, projects and lending targets to complement the poverty reduction strategy. In addition, it initiated a process of wide-ranging discussions to formulate a long-term strategic framework for the next 15 years, based on the target of reducing by 50% the incidence of

extreme poverty by 2015. The framework, establishing the operational priorities and principles for reducing poverty, was approved in March 2001. At the same time a medium-term strategy, for the period 2001–05, was approved, which aimed to enhance the development impact of the Bank's assistance and to define the operational priorities within the context of the strategic agenda.

## SUBSCRIPTIONS AND VOTING POWER*
(31 December 2002)

| Country | Subscribed capital (% of total) | Voting power (% of total) |
|---|---|---|
| **Regional:** | | |
| Afghanistan | 0.034 | 0.355 |
| Australia | 5.871 | 5.025 |
| Azerbaijan | 0.451 | 0.689 |
| Bangladesh | 1.036 | 1.157 |
| Bhutan | 0.006 | 0.333 |
| Cambodia | 0.050 | 0.368 |
| China, People's Republic | 6.539 | 5.559 |
| Cook Islands | 0.003 | 0.330 |
| Fiji | 0.069 | 0.383 |
| Hong Kong | 0.553 | 0.770 |
| India | 6.424 | 5.467 |
| Indonesia | 5.526 | 4.749 |
| Japan | 15.836 | 12.997 |
| Kazakhstan | 0.818 | 0.983 |
| Kiribati | 0.004 | 0.331 |
| Korea, Republic | 5.112 | 4.417 |
| Kyrgyzstan | 0.303 | 0.571 |
| Laos | 0.014 | 0.339 |
| Malaysia | 2.763 | 2.538 |
| The Maldives | 0.004 | 0.331 |
| Marshall Islands | 0.003 | 0.330 |
| Micronesia, Federated States | 0.004 | 0.331 |
| Mongolia | 0.015 | 0.340 |
| Myanmar | 0.553 | 0.770 |
| Nauru | 0.004 | 0.331 |
| Nepal | 0.149 | 0.447 |
| New Zealand | 1.558 | 1.575 |
| Pakistan | 2.210 | 2.096 |
| Papua New Guinea | 0.095 | 0.404 |
| Philippines | 2.418 | 2.262 |
| Samoa | 0.003 | 0.331 |
| Singapore | 0.345 | 0.604 |
| Solomon Islands | 0.007 | 0.333 |
| Sri Lanka | 0.588 | 0.799 |
| Taiwan | 1.105 | 1.212 |
| Tajikistan | 0.291 | 0.560 |
| Thailand | 1.382 | 1.433 |
| Timor-Leste | 0.010 | 0.336 |
| Tonga | 0.004 | 0.331 |
| Turkmenistan | 0.257 | 0.533 |
| Tuvalu | 0.001 | 0.329 |
| Uzbekistan | 0.684 | 0.875 |
| Vanuatu | 0.007 | 0.333 |
| Viet Nam | 0.346 | 0.605 |
| **Sub-total** | 63.458 | 65.192 |
| **Non-regional:** | | |
| Austria | 0.345 | 0.604 |
| Belgium | 0.345 | 0.604 |
| Canada | 5.308 | 4.574 |
| Denmark | 0.345 | 0.604 |
| Finland | 0.345 | 0.604 |
| France | 2.362 | 2.217 |
| Germany | 4.390 | 3.840 |
| Italy | 1.834 | 1.795 |
| Netherlands | 1.041 | 1.161 |
| Norway | 0.347 | 0.604 |
| Portugal | 0.345 | 0.604 |
| Spain | 0.345 | 0.604 |
| Sweden | 0.345 | 0.604 |
| Switzerland | 0.592 | 0.802 |
| Turkey | 0.345 | 0.604 |
| United Kingdom | 2.072 | 1.986 |
| USA | 15.836 | 12.997 |
| **Sub-total** | 36.542 | 34.808 |
| **Total** | 100.000 | 100.000 |

*Portugal was admitted as a non-regional member of the Bank in April 2002; Timor-Leste became the Bank's 61st member in July.

In 2002 the Bank approved 89 loans in 71 projects amounting to US $5,675.8m. (compared with $5,339.0m. for 60 projects in 2001). Loans from ordinary capital resources in 2002 totalled $4,042.8m., while loans from the ADF amounted to $1,633.0m. Private-sector operations approved amounted to \$145.0m., which included direct loans without government guarantee of \$60.0m. and equity investments of \$35.5m. The largest proportion of assistance, amounting to some 28% of total lending, was allocated to transport and communications projects. Disbursements of loans during 2002 amounted to \$4,202.1m., bringing cumulative disbursements to \$66,371m.

In 2002 grants approved for technical assistance (e.g. project preparation, consultant services and training) amounted to US \$179.0m. for 324 projects, with \$56.0m. deriving from the Bank's ordinary resources, \$46.7m. from the TASF, \$36.4m. from the JSF, \$9.6m. from the ACCSF, and \$30.3m. from bilateral and multilateral sources. The Bank's Operations Evaluation Office prepares reports on completed projects, in order to assess achievements and problems. In April 2000 the Bank announced that, from 2001, some new loans would be denominated in local currencies, in order to ease the repayment burden on recipient economies.

The Bank co-operates with other international organizations active in the region, particularly the World Bank group, the IMF, UNDP and APEC, and participates in meetings of aid donors for developing member countries. In May 2001 the Bank and UNDP signed a memorandum of understanding (MOU) on strategic partnership, in order to strengthen co-operation in the reduction of poverty, for example the preparation of common country assessments and a common database on poverty and other social indicators. Also in 2001 the Bank signed an MOU with the World Bank on administrative arrangements for co-operation, providing a framework for closer co-operation and more efficient use of resources. In early 2002 the Bank worked with the World Bank and UNDP to assess the preliminary needs of the interim administration in Afghanistan, in preparation for an International Conference on Reconstruction Assistance to Afghanistan, held in late January, in Tokyo. The Bank pledged to work with its member governments to provide highly concessional grants and loans of some US \$500m. over two-and-a-half years, with a particular focus on road reconstruction, basic education, and agricultural irrigation rehabilitation. A new policy concerning co-operation with non-governmental organizations (NGOs) was approved by the Bank in 1998.

# Finance

Internal administrative expenses totalled US \$234.3m. in 2002.

# Publications

*ADB Business Opportunities* (monthly).

*ADB Institute Newsletter.*

*ADB Review* (6 a year).

*Annual Report.*

*Asian Development Outlook* (annually).

*Asian Development Review* (2 a year).

*Basic Statistics* (annually).

*Key Indicators of Developing Asian and Pacific Countries* (annually).

*Law and Policy Reform Bulletin* (annually).

*Loan Disbursement Handbook.*

Studies and technical assistance reports, information brochures, guide-lines, sample bidding documents, staff papers.

# Statistics

## BANK ACTIVITIES BY SECTOR

| Sector | Loan Approvals (US \$ million) 2002 Amount | 2002 % | 1969–2002 % |
|---|---|---|---|
| Agriculture and natural resources . | 492.90 | 8.68 | 17.74 |
| Energy . . . . . . . . | 1,017.60 | 17.93 | 20.70 |
| Finance . . . . . . . | 865.00 | 15.24 | 14.57 |
| Industry and non-fuel minerals . | 85.00 | 1.50 | 3.36 |
| Social infrastructure . . . . | 689.81 | 11.80 | 16.15 |
| Transport and communications. . | 1,612.90 | 28.42 | 20.65 |
| Multi-sector and others . . . . | 932.54 | 16.43 | 6.83 |
| **Total** . . . . . . . . . | 5,675.75 | 100.00 | 100.00 |

## LENDING ACTIVITIES BY COUNTRY (US \$ million)

| Country | Loans approved in 2002 Ordinary Capital | ADF | Total |
|---|---|---|---|
| Afghanistan . . . . . . . | — | 150.00 | 150.00 |
| Bangladesh . . . . . . | 30.20 | 269.57 | 299.77 |
| Cambodia . . . . . . . | — | 100.91 | 100.91 |
| China, People's Republic. . . | 868.48 | — | 868.48 |
| Fiji . . . . . . . . . | 16.80 | — | 16.80 |
| India . . . . . . . . | 1,183.60 | — | 1,183.60 |
| Indonesia . . . . . . . | 636.00 | 131.22 | 767.22 |
| Laos . . . . . . . . | — | 76.00 | 76.00 |
| The Maldives . . . . . | — | 5.0 | 5.0 |
| Marshall Islands . . . . | — | 7.00 | 7.00 |
| Mongolia . . . . . . . | — | 34.10 | 34.10 |
| Nepal . . . . . . . . | — | 60.00 | 60.00 |
| Pakistan . . . . . . . | 865.00 | 276.00 | 1,141.00 |
| Papua New Guinea . . . . | — | 5.70 | 0.10 |
| Philippines . . . . . . | 40.00 | — | 40.00 |
| Sri Lanka . . . . . . . | 76.20 | 160.30 | 256.50 |
| Tajikistan . . . . . . | — | 40.32 | 40.32 |
| Uzbekistan . . . . . . | 166.50 | — | 166.50 |
| Viet Nam . . . . . . . | 90.00 | 225.00 | 225.00 |
| Regional . . . . . . . | 70.00 | 80.00 | 150.00 |
| **Total** . . . . . . . . | 4,042.78 | 1,632.97 | 5,675.75 |

## LENDING ACTIVITIES
(in %)

| Country | 1993–97 Ordinary Capital | 1993–97 ADF | 1998–2002 Ordinary Capital | 1998–2002 ADF |
|---|---|---|---|---|
| Afghanistan . . . . . | — | — | — | 2.3 |
| Bangladesh . . . . . | 0.2 | 21.0 | 1.6 | 16.1 |
| Bhutan. . . . . . | — | 0.3 | — | 0.6 |
| Cambodia . . . . . . | — | 2.5 | — | 5.6 |
| China, People's Republic . | 23.4 | — | 24.8 | — |
| Cook Islands . . . . . | — | 0.2 | — | — |
| Fiji . . . . . . | 0.2 | — | 0.1 | — |
| India . . . . . . | 12.9 | — | 22.5 | — |
| Indonesia . . . . . | 22.2 | 3.6 | 21.6 | 6.0 |
| Kazakhstan . . . . . | 1.6 | 0.8 | — | — |
| Kiribati . . . . . | — | — | — | 0.2 |
| Korea, Republic . . . . | 18.4 | — | — | — |
| Kyrgyzstan . . . . . | — | 3.5 | — | 3.7 |
| Laos . . . . . . | — | 5.8 | — | 3.7 |
| Malaysia . . . . . | 0.9 | — | — | — |
| The Maldives . . . . . | — | 0.2 | — | 0.6 |
| Marshall Islands . . . | — | 0.5 | — | 0.5 |
| Micronesia, Federated States | — | 0.5 | — | 0.3 |
| Mongolia . . . . . | — | 4.8 | — | 2.4 |
| Nepal . . . . . . | 0.2 | 5.1 | — | 7.3 |
| Pakistan . . . . . | 4.1 | 21.2 | 10.6 | 15.0 |
| Papua New Guinea . . . | 0.2 | 0.6 | 0.9 | 0.9 |
| Philippines . . . . . | 6.7 | 3.1 | 7.6 | 0.1 |
| Samoa . . . . . . | — | 0.0 | — | 0.4 |
| Solomon Islands . . . . | — | 0.0 | — | 0.5 |
| Sri Lanka . . . . . . | 0.0 | 7.8 | 1.0 | 11.7 |
| Tajikistan . . . . . | — | — | — | 2.2 |
| Thailand . . . . . | 8.5 | — | 4.8 | — |
| Tonga . . . . . . | — | 0.2 | — | 0.2 |
| Tuvalu . . . . . . | — | — | — | 0.1 |
| Uzbekistan . . . . . | 0.3 | 0.3 | 2.6 | — |
| Vanuatu . . . . . | — | 0.1 | — | 0.3 |
| Viet Nam . . . . . | 0.1 | 18.0 | 0.9 | 15.0 |
| Regional . . . . . | — | — | 1.0 | 4.3 |
| **Total** . . . . . . | 100.0 | 100.0 | 100.0 | 100.0 |
| **Value** (US \$ million) . . | 21,828.8 | 7,209.5 | 20,938.8 | 6,619.4 |

Source: *ADB Annual Report 2002.*

# THE COMMONWEALTH OF INDEPENDENT STATES— CIS

**Address:** 220000 Minsk, Kirava 17, Belarus.

**Telephone:** (172) 22-35-17; **fax:** (172) 27-23-39; **e-mail:** postmaster@www.cis.minsk.by; **internet:** www.cis.minsk.by.

The Commonwealth of Independent States is a voluntary association of 12 (originally 11) states, established at the time of the collapse of the USSR in December 1991.

### MEMBERS

| | |
|---|---|
| Armenia | Moldova |
| Azerbaijan | Russia |
| Belarus | Tajikistan |
| Georgia | Turkmenistan |
| Kazakhstan | Ukraine |
| Kyrgyzstan | Uzbekistan |

Note: Azerbaijan signed the Alma-Ata Declaration (see below), but in October 1992 the Azerbaijan legislature voted against ratification of the foundation documents by which the Commonwealth of Independent States had been established in December 1991. Azerbaijan formally became a member of the CIS in September 1993, after the legislature voted in favour of membership. Georgia was admitted to the CIS in December 1993.

## Organization

### (October 2003)

### COUNCIL OF HEADS OF STATE

This is the supreme body of the CIS, on which all the member states of the Commonwealth are represented at the level of head of state, for discussion of issues relating to the co-ordination of Commonwealth activities and the development of the Minsk Agreement. Decisions of the Council are taken by common consent, with each state having equal voting rights. The Council meets at least twice a year. An extraordinary meeting may be convened on the initiative of the majority of Commonwealth heads of state. From January 2003 the chairmanship of the Council was to be rotated among member states.

### COUNCIL OF HEADS OF GOVERNMENT

This Council convenes for meetings at least once every three months; an extraordinary sitting may be convened on the initiative of a majority of Commonwealth heads of government. The two Councils may discuss and take necessary decisions on important domestic and external issues, and may hold joint sittings.

Working and auxiliary bodies, composed of authorized representatives of the participating states, may be set up on a permanent or interim basis on the decision of the Council of Heads of State and the Council of Heads of Government.

### CIS EXECUTIVE COMMITTEE

The Executive Committee was established by the Council of Heads of State in April 1999 to supersede the existing Secretariat, the Inter-state Economic Committee and other working bodies and committees, in order to improve the efficient functioning of the organization. The Executive Committee co-operates closely with other CIS bodies including the councils of foreign ministers and defence ministers; the Economic Council; Council of Border Troops Commanders; the Collective Security Council; the Secretariat of the Council of the Inter-parliamentary Assembly; and the Inter-state Committee for Statistics.

**Executive Secretary and Chairman of the Executive Committee:** YURII YAROV.

## Activities

On 8 December 1991 the heads of state of Belarus, Russia and Ukraine signed the Minsk Agreement, providing for the establishment of a Commonwealth of Independent States. Formal recognition of the dissolution of the USSR was incorporated in a second treaty (the Alma-Ata Declaration), signed by 11 heads of state in the then Kazakh capital, Alma-Ata (Almaty), later in that month.

In March 1992 a meeting of the CIS Council of Heads of Government decided to establish a commission to examine the resolution that 'all CIS member states are the legal successors of the rights and obligations of the former Soviet Union'. Documents relating to the legal succession of the Soviet Union were signed at a meeting of Heads of State in July. In April an agreement establishing an Inter-parliamentary Assembly (IPA), signed by Armenia, Belarus, Kazakhstan, Kyrgyzstan, Russia, Tajikistan and Uzbekistan, was published. The first Assembly was held in Bishkek, Kyrgyzstan, in September, attended by delegates from all these countries, with the exception of Uzbekistan.

A CIS Charter was formulated at the meeting of the heads of state in Minsk, Belarus, in January 1993. The Charter, providing for a defence alliance, an inter-state court and an economic co-ordination committee, was to serve as a framework for closer co-operation and was signed by all of the members except Moldova, Turkmenistan and Ukraine.

In May 1994 the CIS and UNCTAD signed a co-operation accord. A similar agreement was concluded with the UN Economic Commission for Europe in June 1996. Working contacts have also been established with ILO, UNHCR, WHO and the European Union. In June 1998 the IPA approved a decision to sign the European Social Charter (see Council of Europe); a declaration of co-operation between the Assembly and the OSCE Parliamentary Assembly was also signed.

In November 1995, at the Council of Heads of Government meeting, Russia expressed concern at the level of non-payment of debts by CIS members, which, it said, was hindering further integration. At the meeting of the Council in April 1996 a long-term plan for the integrated development of the CIS, incorporating measures for further socio-economic, military and political co-operation, was approved.

In March 1997 the then Russian President, Boris Yeltsin, admitted that the CIS institutional structure had failed to ameliorate the severe economic situation of certain member states. Nevertheless, support for the CIS as an institution was reaffirmed by the participants during the meeting. At the heads of state meeting held in Chişinău, Moldova, in October, Russia was reportedly criticized by the other country delegations for failing to implement CIS agreements, for hindering development of the organization and for failing to resolve regional conflicts. Russia, for its part, urged all member states to participate more actively in defining, adopting and implementing CIS policies. Meeting in April 1998 heads of state emphasized the necessity of improving the activities of the CIS and of reforming its bureaucratic structure. Reform of the CIS was also the main item on the agenda of the eleventh IPA, held in June. It was agreed that an essentially new institution needed to be created, taking into account the relations between the states in a new way. In the same month the first plenary meeting of a special forum, convened to address issues of restructuring the CIS, was held. Working groups were to be established to co-ordinate proposals and draft documents. However, in October reform proposals drawn up by 'experienced specialists' and presented by the Executive Secretary were unanimously rejected as inadequate by the 12 member states. In March 1999 Boris Yeltsin, acting as Chairman of the Council of Heads of State, dismissed the then Executive Secretary, Boris Berezovskii, owing to alleged misconduct and neglect of duties. The decision was endorsed by the Council of Heads of Government meeting in April. The Council also adopted guide-lines for restructuring the CIS and for the future development of the organization. Economic co-operation was to be a priority area of activity, and in particular, the establishment of a free-trade zone. Vladimir Putin, then acting President of the Russian Federation, was elected as the new Chairman of the Council of Heads of State at a CIS summit held in Moscow in January 2000. Meeting in June, a summit of the Councils of Heads of State and Government issued a declaration concerning the maintenance of strategic stability, approved a plan and schedule for pursuing economic integration, and adopted a programme for combating international terrorism (perceived to be a significant threat in central Asia) during 2000–03. The Council of Heads of Government also approved a programme of action to guide the organization's activities until 2005. An informal CIS 10-year 'jubilee' summit, convened in November 2001, adopted a statement identifying the collective pursuit of stable socio-economic development and integration on a global level as the organization's principal objective. A summit of heads of state convened in January 2003 agreed that the position of Chairman of the Council of Heads of State (hitherto held by consecutive Russian presidents) should be rotated henceforth among member states. Leonid Kuchma, the President of Ukraine, was elected as the new Chairman.

Member states of the CIS have formed alliances of various kinds among themselves, thereby potentially undermining the unity of the Commonwealth. In March 1996 Belarus, Kazakhstan, Kyrgyzstan and the Russian Federation signed the Quadripartite Treaty for greater integration. This envisaged the establishment of a 'New Union', based, initially on a common market and customs union, and was to be open to all CIS members and the Baltic states. Consequently these countries (with Tajikistan) became founding members of the Eurasian Economic Community, inaugurated in October 2001. In April 1996 Belarus and Russia signed the Treaty on the Formation of a Community of Sovereign Republics (CSR), which provided for extensive economic, political and military co-operation. In April 1997 the two countries signed a further Treaty of Union and, in addition, initialled the Charter of the Union, which detailed the procedures and institutions designed to develop a common infrastructure, a single currency and a joint defence policy within the CSR, with the eventual aim of 'voluntary unification of the member states'. The Charter was signed in May and ratified by the respective legislatures the following month. The Union's Parliamentary Assembly, comprising 36 members from the legislature of each country, convened in official session for the first time shortly afterwards. Azerbaijan, Georgia, Moldova and Ukraine co-operated increasingly during the late 1990s as the so-called GUAM Group, which envisaged implementing joint economic and transportation initiatives and establishing a sub-regional free-trade zone. In October 1997 the GUAM countries agreed collectively to establish a Eurasian Trans-Caucasus transportation corridor. Uzbekistan joined in April 1999, creating GUAAM. The group agreed in September 2000 to convene regular annual summits of member countries' heads of state and to organize meetings of ministers of foreign affairs at least twice a year. Russia, Armenia, Azerbaijan and Georgia convene regular meetings as the 'Caucasian Group of Four'.

## ECONOMIC AFFAIRS

At a meeting of the Council of Heads of Government in March 1992 agreement was reached on repayment of the foreign debt of the former USSR. Agreements were also signed on pensions, joint tax policy and the servicing of internal debt. In May an accord on repayment of inter-state debt and the issue of balance-of-payments statements was adopted by the heads of government, meeting in Tashkent, Uzbekistan. In July it was decided to establish an economic court in Minsk.

The CIS Charter, formulated in January 1993 and signed by seven of the 10 member countries, provided for the establishment of an economic co-ordination committee. In February, at a meeting of the heads of foreign economic departments, a foreign economic council was formed. In May all member states, with the exception of Turkmenistan, adopted a declaration of support for increased economic union and, in September, agreement was reached by all states except Ukraine and Turkmenistan on a framework for economic union, including the gradual removal of tariffs and creation of a currency union. Turkmenistan was subsequently admitted as a full member of the economic union in December 1993 and Ukraine as an associate member in April 1994.

At the Council of Heads of Government meeting in September 1994 all member states, except Turkmenistan, agreed to establish an Inter-state Economic Committee to implement economic treaties adopted within the context of an economic union. The establishment of a payments union to improve the settlement of accounts was also agreed. In April 1998 CIS heads of state resolved to incorporate the functions of the Inter-state Economic Committee, along with those of other working bodies and sectional committees, into a new CIS Executive Committee.

In October 1997 seven heads of government signed a document on implementing the 'concept for the integrated economic development of the CIS'. The development of economic co-operation between the member states was a priority task of the special forum on reform held in June 1998. In the same month an economic forum, held in St Petersburg, Russia, acknowledged the severe economic conditions prevailing in certain CIS states.

Guide-lines adopted by the Council of Heads of State in April 1999 concerning the future development of the CIS identified economic co-operation and the establishment of a free-trade zone (see Trade) as priority areas for action. The plan of action for the development of the CIS until 2005, adopted by the Council of Heads of Government in June 2000, outlined medium-term economic co-operation measures, including the formulation of intergovernmental accords to provide the legal basis for the free movement of services, capital, people, etc.; the development of private business and markets; and joint participation in the implementation of major economic projects.

## TRADE

Agreement was reached on the free movement of goods between republics at a meeting of the Council of Heads of State in February 1992, and in April 1994 an agreement on the creation of a CIS free-trade zone (envisaged as the first stage of economic union) was concluded. In July a council of the heads of customs committees, meeting in Moscow, approved a draft framework for customs legislation in CIS countries, to facilitate the establishment of a free-trade zone. The framework was approved by all the participants, with the exception of Turkmenistan. In April 1999 CIS heads of state signed a protocol to the 1994 free-trade area accord, which aimed to accelerate co-operation. In June 2000 the Council of Heads of State adopted a plan and schedule for the implementation of priority measures related to the creation of the free-trade zone, and in early 2003 it was announced that an accord formally establishing the zone could be adopted by CIS heads of state in September.

At the first session of the Inter-state Economic Committee in November 1994 draft legislation regarding a customs union was approved. In March 1998 Russia, Belarus, Kazakhstan and Kyrgyzstan signed an agreement establishing a customs union, which was to be implemented in two stages: firstly, the removal of trade restrictions and the unification of trade and customs regulations; followed by the integration of economic, monetary and trade policies (see above). The development of a customs union and the strengthening of intra-CIS trade were objectives endorsed by all participants, with the exception of Georgia, at the Council of Heads of Government meeting held in March 1997. In February 1999 Tajikistan signed the 1998 agreement to become the fifth member of the customs union. In October 1999 the heads of state of the five member states of the customs union reiterated their political determination to implement the customs union and approved a programme to harmonize national legislation to create a single economic space. In May 2000 the heads of state announced their intention to raise the status of the customs union to that of an inter-state economic organization, and, in October, the leaders signed a treaty establishing the Eurasian Economic Community. Under the new structure member states aimed to formulate a unified foreign economic policy, and collectively to pursue the creation of the planned single economic space. In the following month the five member governments signed an agreement enabling visa-free travel within the new Community. (Earlier in 2000 Russia had withdrawn from a CIS-wide visa-free travel arrangement agreed in 1992.) In December 2000 member states of the Community adopted several documents aimed at facilitating economic co-operation. The Eurasian Economic Community, governed by an inter-state council based in Astana, Kazakhstan, was formally inaugurated in October 2001.

The CIS maintains a 'loose co-ordination' on issues related to applications by member states to join the WTO.

## BANKING AND FINANCE

In February 1992 CIS heads of state agreed to retain the rouble as the common currency for trade between the republics. However, in July 1993, in an attempt to control inflation, notes printed before 1993 were withdrawn from circulation and no new ones were issued until January 1994. Despite various agreements to recreate the 'rouble zone', including a protocol agreement signed in September 1993 by six states, it effectively remained confined to Tajikistan, which joined in January 1994, and Belarus, which joined in April. Both those countries proceeded to introduce national currencies in May 1995. In January 1993, at the signing of the CIS Charter, all 10 member countries endorsed the establishment of an inter-state bank to facilitate payments between the republics and to co-ordinate monetary-credit policy. Russia was to hold 50% of shares in the bank, but decisions were to be made only with a two-thirds majority approval. In December 2000, in accordance with the CSR and Treaty of Union (see above), the Presidents of Belarus and Russia signed an agreement providing for the adoption by Belarus of the Russian currency from 1 January 2005, and for the introduction of a new joint Union currency by 1 January 2008.

## DEFENCE

An Agreement on Armed Forces and Border Troops was concluded on 30 December 1991, at the same time as the Agreement on Strategic Forces. This confirmed the right of member states to set up their own armed forces and appointed Commanders-in-Chief of the Armed Forces and of the Border Troops, who were to elaborate joint security procedures. In February 1992 an agreement was signed stipulating that the commander of the strategic forces was subordinate to the Council of Heads of States. Eight states agreed on a unified command for general-purpose (i.e. non-strategic) armed forces for a transitional period of two years. Azerbaijan, Moldova and Ukraine resolved to establish independent armed forces.

In January 1992 Commissions on the Black Sea Fleet (control of which was disputed by Russia and Ukraine) and the Caspian Flotilla (the former Soviet naval forces on the Caspian Sea) were established. The defence and stability of CIS external borders and the status of strategic and nuclear forces were among topics discussed at the meeting of heads of state and of government, in Bishkek, in October. The formation of a defence alliance was provided for in the CIS Charter formulated in January 1993 and signed by seven of the

10 member countries; a proposal by Russia to assume control of all nuclear weapons in the former USSR was rejected at the same time.

In June 1993 CIS defence ministers agreed to abolish CIS joint military command and to abandon efforts to maintain a unified defence structure. The existing CIS command was to be replaced, on a provisional basis, by a 'joint staff for co-ordinating military co-operation between the states of the Commonwealth'. It was widely reported that Russia had encouraged the decision to abolish the joint command, owing to concerns at the projected cost of a CIS joint military structure and support within Russia's military leadership of bilateral military agreements with the country's neighbours. In December the Council of Defence Ministers agreed to establish a secretariat to co-ordinate military co-operation as a replacement to the joint military command. In November 1995 the Council of Defence Ministers authorized the establishment of a Joint Air Defence System, to be co-ordinated largely by Russia. A CIS combat duty system was to be created in 1999–2005. Russia and Belarus are also developing a joint air-defence unit in the context of the CSR (see above).

In September 1996 the first meeting of the inter-state commission for military economic co-operation was held; a draft agreement on the export of military projects and services to third countries was approved. The basic principles of a programme for greater military and technical co-operation were approved by the Council of Defence Ministers in March 1997. In April 1998 the Council proposed drawing up a draft programme for military and technical co-operation between member countries and also discussed procedures advising on the use and maintenance of armaments and military hardware. The programme was approved by CIS heads of state in October 2002. Draft proposals relating to information security for the military were approved by the Council in December. It was remarked that the inadequate funding of the Council was impeding co-operation. In May 2001 a draft plan for military co-operation until 2005 was agreed.

In August 1996 the Council of Defence Ministers condemned what it described as the political, economic and military threat implied in any expansion of NATO. The statement was not signed by Ukraine. The eighth plenary session of the IPA, held in November, urged NATO countries to abandon plans for the organization's expansion. Strategic co-operation between NATO and CIS member states increased from the mid-1990s, particularly with Russia and Ukraine. In the late 1990s the USA established bilateral military assistance programmes for Azerbaijan, Georgia, and Uzbekistan. Uzbekistan and other central Asian CIS states played a support role in the US-led action initiated in late 2001 against the then Taliban-held areas of Afghanistan (see below).

## REGIONAL SECURITY

At a meeting of heads of government in March 1992 agreements on settling inter-state conflicts were signed by all participating states (except Turkmenistan). At the same meeting an agreement on the status of border troops was signed by five states. In May a five-year Collective Security Agreement was signed. In July further documents were signed on collective security and it was agreed to establish joint peacemaking forces to intervene in CIS disputes. In April 1999 Armenia, Belarus, Kazakhstan, Kyrgyzstan, Russia and Tajikistan signed a protocol to extend the Collective Security Agreement for a further five-year period.

In September 1993 the Council of Heads of State agreed to establish a Bureau of Organized Crime, to be based in Moscow. A meeting of the Council of Border Troop Commanders in January 1994 prepared a report on the issue of illegal migration and drug trade across the external borders of the CIS; Moldova, Georgia and Tajikistan did not attend. A programme to counter organized crime within the CIS was approved by heads of government, meeting in Moscow, in April 1996. In March 2001 CIS interior ministers agreed to strengthen co-operation in combating transnational organized crime, in view of reportedly mounting levels of illicit drugs-trafficking in the region.

In February 1995 a non-binding memorandum on maintaining peace and stability was adopted by heads of state, meeting in Almaty. Signatories were to refrain from applying military, political, economic or other pressure on another member country, to seek the peaceful resolution of border or territorial disputes and not to support or assist separatist movements active in other member countries. In April 1998 the Council of Defence Ministers approved a draft document proposing that coalition forces be provided with technical equipment to enhance collective security.

In June 1998, at a session of the Council of Border Troop Commanders, some 33 documents were signed relating to border co-operation. A framework protocol on the formation and expedient use of a border troops reserve in critical situations was discussed and signed by several participants. A register of work in scientific and engineering research carried out in CIS countries in the interests of border troops was also adopted. A programme aimed at enhancing

co-operation between border troops was adopted by heads of state in October 2002.

In June 1998 CIS interior ministers, meeting in Tashkent, Uzbekistan, adopted a number of co-operation agreements, including a framework for the exchange of information between CIS law-enforcement agencies; it was also decided to maintain contact with Interpol.

An emergency meeting of heads of state in October 1996 discussed the ongoing conflict in nearby Afghanistan and the consequent threat to regional security. The participants requested the UN Security Council to adopt measures to resolve the situation. The IPA subsequently reiterated the call for a cessation of hostilities in that country. In May 2000 the six signatory states to the Collective Security Agreement pledged to strengthen military co-operation in view of the perceived threat to their security from the Taliban regime in Afghanistan. It was reported that a mechanism had been approved that would enable parties to the Agreement to purchase arms from Russia at special rates. In October the parties to the Collective Security Agreement signed an agreement on the Status of Forces and Means of Collective Security Systems, establishing a joint rapid deployment function. The so-called CIS Collective Rapid Reaction Force was to be assembled to combat insurgencies, with particular reference to trans-border terrorism from Afghanistan, and also to deter trans-border illegal drugs trafficking (see above). In June 2001 a CIS anti-terrorism centre was established in Moscow. The centre was to co-ordinate counter-terrorism activities and to compile a database of international terrorist organizations operating in member states. In October, in response to the major terrorist attacks perpetrated in September against targets in the USA—allegedly co-ordinated by Afghanistan-based militant fundamentalist Islamist leader Osama bin Laden—the parties to the Collective Security Treaty adopted a new anti-terrorism plan. In November the head of the co-ordinating Collective Security Council identified combating international terrorism as the main focus of the Collective Security Agreement at that time. In December 2002 the committee of the Collective Security Treaty member countries adopted a protocol on the exchange of expertise and information on terrorist organizations and their activities. The signatory countries to the Collective Security Agreement participate in regular so-called 'CIS Southern Shield' joint military exercises. In October 2002 a central Asian subdivision of the CIS anti-terrorism centre was established in Bishkek, Kyrgyzstan. The formation of a new regional security organization, the Central Asian Co-operation Pact, was announced in February of that year by Kazakhstan, Kyrgyzstan, Tajikistan and Uzbekistan.

The fourth plenary session of the IPA in March 1994 established a commission for the resolution of the conflicts in the secessionist regions of Nagornyi Karabakh (Azerbaijan) and Abkhazia (Georgia) and endorsed the use of CIS peace-keeping forces. In the following month Russia agreed to send peace-keeping forces to Georgia, and the dispatch of peace-keeping forces was approved by the Council of Defence Ministers in October. The subsequent session of the IPA in October adopted a resolution to send groups of military observers to Abkhazia and to Moldova. The inter-parliamentary commission on the conflict between Abkhazia and Georgia proposed initiating direct negotiations with the two sides in order to reach a peaceful settlement.

In December 1994 the Council of Defence Ministers enlarged the mandate of the commander of the CIS collective peace-keeping forces in Tajikistan: when necessary CIS military contingents were permitted to engage in combat operations without the prior consent of individual governments. At the Heads of State meeting in Moscow in January 1996 Georgia's proposal to impose sanctions against Abkhazia was approved, in an attempt to achieve a resolution of the conflict. Provisions on arrangements relating to collective peace-keeping operations were approved at the meeting; the training of military and civilian personnel for these operations was to commence in October. In March 1997 the Council of Defence Ministers agreed to extend the peace-keeping mandates for CIS forces in Tajiskistan and Abkhazia (following much disagreement, the peace-keepers' mandate in Abkhazia was further renewed in October). At a meeting of the Council in January 1998 a request from Georgia that the CIS carry out its decisions to settle the conflict with Abkhazia was added to the agenda. The Council discussed the promotion of military co-operation and the improvement of peace-making activities, and declared that there was progress in the formation of the collective security system, although the situation in the North Caucasus remained tense. In April President Yeltsin requested that the Armenian and Azerbaijani presidents sign a document to end the conflict in Nagornyi Karabakh; the two subsequently issued a statement expressing their support for a political settlement of the conflict. A document proposing a settlement of the conflict in Abkhazia was also drawn up, but the resolutions adopted were not accepted by Abkhazia. Against the wishes of the Abkhazian authorities, the mandate for the CIS troops in the region was extended to cover the whole of the Gali district. The mandate expired in July 1998, but the forces remained in the region while its renewal was debated. In April 1999 the Council of Heads of State agreed to a retrospective extension of the operation's mandate; the mandate has subsequently continued to be renewed at six-monthly intervals. The mandate of the CIS peace-keeping operation in Tajikistan was terminated in June 2000. In February 2001 it was reported that regulations had been drafted for the institution of a CIS Special Envoy for the Settlement of Conflicts.

### LEGISLATIVE CO-OPERATION

An agreement on legislative co-operation was signed at an Inter-Parliamentary Conference in January 1992; joint commissions were established to co-ordinate action on economy, law, pensions, housing, energy and ecology. The CIS Charter, formulated in January 1993, provided for the establishment of an inter-state court. In October 1994 a Convention on the rights of minorities was adopted at the meeting of the Heads of State. In May 1995, at the sixth plenary session of the IPA, several acts to improve co-ordination of legislation were approved, relating to migration of labour, consumer rights, and the rights of prisoners of war.

The creation of a Council of Ministers of Internal Affairs was approved at the Heads of State meeting in January 1996; the Council was to promote co-operation between the law-enforcement bodies of member states. At the 10th plenary session of the IPA in December 1997 14 laws, relating to banking and financial services, education, ecology and charity were adopted. At the IPA session held

in June 1998 10 model laws relating to social issues were approved, including a law on obligatory social insurance against production accidents and occupational diseases, and on the general principles of regulating refugee problems.

### OTHER ACTIVITIES

The CIS has held a number of discussions relating to the environment. In July 1992 agreements were concluded to establish an Inter-state Ecological Council. It was also agreed in that month to establish *Mir*, an inter-state television and radio company. In October 2002 a decision was made by CIS heads of government to enhance mutual understanding and co-operation between members countries through *Mir* radio and television broadcasts. In February 1995 the IPA established a Council of Heads of News Agencies, in order to promote the concept of a single information area.

A Petroleum and Gas Council was created at a Heads of Government meeting in March 1993, to guarantee energy supplies and to invest in the Siberian petroleum industry. The Council was to have a secretariat based in Tyumen, Siberia. In October 2002 the Council of Heads of Government signed a co-operation agreement on energy effectiveness and power supply. In the field of civil aviation, the inter-state economic committee agreed in February 1997 to establish an Aviation Alliance to promote co-operation between the countries' civil aviation industries.

# THE COUNCIL OF EUROPE

**Address:** 67075 Strasbourg Cédex, France.

**Telephone:** 3-88-41-20-00; **fax:** 3-88-41-27-81; **e-mail:** pointi@coe.int; **internet:** www.coe.int.

The Council was founded in May 1949 to achieve a greater unity between its members, to facilitate their social progress and to uphold the principles of parliamentary democracy, respect for human rights and the rule of law. Membership has risen from the original 10 to 44.

### MEMBERS*

| | |
|---|---|
| Albania | Liechtenstein |
| Andorra | Lithuania |
| Armenia | Luxembourg |
| Austria | Macedonia, former Yugoslav |
| Azerbaijan | republic |
| Belgium | Malta |
| Bulgaria | Moldova |
| Bosnia and Herzegovina | Netherlands |
| Croatia | Norway |
| Cyprus | Poland |
| Czech Republic | Portugal |
| Denmark | Romania |
| Estonia | Russia |
| Finland | San Marino |
| France | Slovakia |
| Georgia | Slovenia |
| Germany | Spain |
| Greece | Sweden |
| Hungary | Switzerland |
| Iceland | Turkey |
| Ireland | Ukraine |
| Italy | United Kingdom |
| Latvia | |

* The Holy See, Canada, Japan, Mexico and the USA have observer status with the organization. The Serbia and Montenegro parliament has special 'guest status' at the Parliamentary Assembly, while the parliaments of Canada, Israel and Mexico have observer status with the Assembly.

## Organization

(October 2003)

### COMMITTEE OF MINISTERS

The Committee consists of the ministers of foreign affairs of all member states (or their deputies); it decides with binding effect all matters of internal organization, makes recommendations to governments and draws up conventions and agreements; it also discusses matters of political concern, such as European co-operation, compliance with member states' commitments, in particular con-

cerning the protection of human rights, and considers possible co-ordination with other institutions, such as the European Union (EU) and the Organization for Security and Co-operation in Europe (OSCE). The Committee meets weekly at deputies level and twice a year (usually in May and November) at ministerial level.

### CONFERENCES OF SPECIALIZED MINISTERS

There are 19 Conferences of specialized ministers, meeting regularly for intergovernmental co-operation in various fields.

### PARLIAMENTARY ASSEMBLY

**President:** PETER SCHIEDER (Austria).

**Chairman of the Socialist Group:** TERRY DAVIS (United Kingdom).

**Chairman of the Group of the European People's Party:** RENÉ VAN DER LINDEN (Netherlands).

**Chairman of the European Democratic (Conservative) Group:** DAVID ATKINSON (United Kingdom).

**Chairman of the Liberal Democratic and Reformers' Group:** MÁTYÁS EÖRSI (Hungary).

**Chairman of the Unified European Left Group:** JAAKKO LAAKSO (Finland).

Members are elected or appointed by their national parliaments from among the members thereof; political parties in each delegation follow the proportion of their strength in the national parliament. Members do not represent their governments, speaking on their own behalf. At January 2003 the Assembly had 306 members (and 301 substitutes): 18 each for France, Germany, Italy, Russia and the United Kingdom; 12 each for Poland, Spain, Turkey and Ukraine; 10 for Romania; seven each for Belgium, the Czech Republic, Greece, Hungary, the Netherlands and Portugal; six each for Austria, Azerbaijan, Bulgaria, Sweden and Switzerland; five each for Bosnia and Herzegovina, Croatia, Denmark, Finland, Georgia, Moldova, Norway and Slovakia; four each for Albania, Armenia, Ireland and Lithuania; three each for Cyprus, Estonia, Iceland, Latvia, Luxembourg, the former Yugoslav republic of Macedonia, Malta and Slovenia; and two each for Andorra, Liechtenstein and San Marino. The parliaments of Israel, Canada and Mexico have permanent observer status, while that of Serbia and Montenegro has special 'guest status'. (Belarus's special status was suspended in January 1997.)

The Assembly meets in ordinary session once a year. The session is divided into four parts, generally held in the last full week of January, April, June and September. The Assembly submits Recommendations to the Committee of Ministers, passes Resolutions, and discusses reports on any matters of common European interest. It is also a consultative body to the Committee of Ministers, and elects the Secretary-General, the Deputy Secretary-General, the Secretary-General of the Assembly, the Council's Commissioner for

Human Rights, and the members of the European Court of Human Rights.

**Standing Committee:** represents the Assembly when it is not in session, and may adopt Recommendations to the Committee of Ministers and Resolutions on behalf of the Assembly. Consists of the President, Vice-Presidents, Chairmen of the Political Groups, Chairmen of the Ordinary Committees and Chairmen of national delegations. Meets usually three times a year.

**Ordinary Committees:** political; legal and human rights; economic and development; social, health and family affairs; culture, science and education; environment, agriculture, and local and regional authorities; migration, refugees and demography; rules of procedure and immunities; equal opportunities; honouring of obligations and commitments by member states of the Council of Europe.

## CONGRESS OF LOCAL AND REGIONAL AUTHORITIES OF EUROPE—CLRAE

The Congress was established in 1994, incorporating the former Standing Conference of Local and Regional Authorities, in order to protect and promote the political, administrative and financial autonomy of local and regional European authorities by encouraging central governments to develop effective local democracy. The Congress comprises two chambers—a Chamber of Local Authorities and a Chamber of Regions—with a total membership of 306 elected representatives (and 306 elected substitutes). Annual sessions are mainly concerned with local government matters, regional planning, protection of the environment, town and country planning, and social and cultural affairs. A Standing Committee, drawn from all national delegations, meets between plenary sessions of the Congress. Four Statutory Committees (Institutional; Sustainable Development; Social Cohesion; Culture and Education) meet twice a year in order to prepare texts for adoption by the Congress.

The Congress advises the Council's Committee of Ministers and the Parliamentary Assembly on all aspects of local and regional policy and co-operates with other national and international organizations representing local government. The Congress monitors implementation of the European Charter of Local Self-Government, which was opened for signature in 1985 and provides common standards for effective local democracy. Other legislative guide-lines for the activities of local authorities and the promotion of democracy at local level include the 1980 European Outline Convention on Transfrontier Co-operation, and its Additional Protocol which was opened for signature in 1995, a Convention on the Participation of Foreigners in Public Life at Local Level (1992), and the European Charter for Regional or Minority Languages (1992). In addition, the European Urban Charter defines citizens' rights in European towns and cities, for example in the areas of transport, urban architecture, pollution and security.

**President:** HERWIG VAN STAA (Austria).

### SECRETARIAT

**Secretary-General:** Dr WALTER SCHWIMMER (Austria).

**Deputy Secretary-General:** MAUD DE BOER-BUQUICCHIO (Netherlands).

**Secretary-General of the Parliamentary Assembly:** BRUNO HALLER (France).

# Activities

In an effort to harmonize national laws, to put the citizens of member countries on an equal footing and to pool certain resources and facilities, the Council of Europe has concluded a number of conventions and agreements covering particular aspects of European co-operation. Since 1989 the Council has undertaken to increase co-operation with all countries of the former Eastern bloc and to facilitate their accession to the organization. In October 1997 heads of state or government of member countries convened for only the second time (the first meeting took place in Vienna, in October 1993—see below) with the aim of formulating a new social model to consolidate democracy throughout Europe. The meeting endorsed a Final Declaration and an Action Plan, which established priority areas for future Council activities, including fostering social cohesion; protecting civilian security; promoting human rights; enhancing joint measures to counter cross-border illegal trafficking; and strengthening democracy through education and other cultural activities. In addition, the meeting generated renewed political commitment to the Programme of Action against Corruption, which has become a key element of Council activities.

A Multidisciplinary Group on International Action against Terrorism, established in 2001, has updated the 1977 European Convention on the Suppression of Terrorism. In 2001 the Council's Committee of Ministers adopted a set of 'Guide-lines on Human Rights and the Fight against Terrorism'.

## HUMAN RIGHTS

The promotion and development of human rights is one of the major tasks of the Council of Europe. The European Convention for the Protection of Human Rights and Fundamental Freedoms (European Convention on Human Rights) was opened for signature in 1950. The Steering Committee for Human Rights is responsible for intergovernmental co-operation in the field of human rights and fundamental freedoms; it works to strengthen the effectiveness of systems for protecting human rights, to identify potential threats and challenges to human rights, and to encourage education and provide information on the subject. The Committee has been responsible for the elaboration of several conventions and other legal instruments including Protocol No. 12 of the European Convention on Human Rights, adopted in June 2000, which enforces a general prohibition of discrimination; and Protocol No. 13, adopted in May 2002, which guarantees the abolition of the death penalty in all circumstances (including in time of war).

The Committee was responsible for the preparation of the European Ministerial Conference on Human Rights, held in Rome in November 2000, which commemorated the 50th anniversary of the adoption of the European Convention on Human Rights. The Conference highlighted, in particular, 'the need to reinforce the effective protection of human rights in domestic legal systems as well as at the European level'.

The 1993 Vienna summit meeting also agreed to restructure the control mechanism for the protection of human rights, mainly the procedure for the consideration of cases, in order to reduce the length of time before a case is concluded. As a result, Protocol (No. 11) to the European Convention on Human Rights was opened for signature by member states in May 1994. The then existing institutions (i.e. the European Commission of Human Rights and the European Court of Human Rights) were consequently replaced in November 1998 (when Protocol No. 11 entered into force) by a single Court, working on a full-time basis.

The second summit meeting of the Council's heads of state and government, held in Strasbourg, France, in October 1997, welcomed a proposal to institute a Council of Europe Commissioner for Human Rights to promote respect for human rights in member states; this office was established by a resolution of the Council's Committee of Ministers in May 1999.

The November 2000 European Ministerial Conference on Human Rights commemorated the 50th anniversary of the European Convention on Human Rights and agreed an agenda for the Council's future human rights activities. This included work on a future reform of the control system of the Convention, in order to preserve its effectiveness despite the rising number of individual applications. In November 2002, in this regard, the Committee of Ministers adopted a Declaration on The Court of Human Rights for Europe.

**Commissioner for Human Rights:** ALVARO GIL-ROBLES (Spain).

### European Court of Human Rights

The Court has compulsory jurisdiction and is competent to consider complaints lodged by states party to the European Convention and by individuals, groups of individuals or non-governmental organizations claiming to be victims of breaches of the Convention's guarantees. The Court comprises one judge for each contracting state. The Court sits in three-member Committees, empowered to declare applications inadmissible in the event of unanimity and where no further examination is necessary, seven-member Chambers, and a 17-member Grand Chamber. Chamber judgments become final three months after delivery, during which period parties may request a rehearing before the Grand Chamber, subject to acceptance by a panel of five judges. Grand Chamber judgments are final. The Court's final judgments are binding on respondent states and their execution is supervised at regular intervals by the Committee of Ministers. Execution of judgments includes payment of pecuniary just satisfaction awarded by the Court, adoption of specific individual measures to erase the consequences of the violations found (such as striking out of impugned convictions from criminal records, reopening of judicial proceedings, etc.), and general measures to prevent new similar violations (e.g. constitutional and legislative reforms, changes of domestic case-law and administrative practice, etc.) At January 2002 18,383 applications were pending before the Court.

**President:** LUZIUS WILDHABER (Switzerland).

**Registrar:** PAUL MAHONEY (United Kingdom).

### European Committee for the Prevention of Torture and Inhuman or Degrading Treatment or Punishment—CPT

The Committee was established under the 1987 Convention for the Prevention of Torture as an integral part of the Council of Europe's system for the protection of human rights. The Committee, comprising independent experts, aims to examine the treatment of persons deprived of their liberty with a view to strengthening, if necessary, the protection of such persons from torture and from inhuman or degrading treatment or punishment. It conducts periodic visits to police stations, prisons, detention centres, and all other sites where persons are deprived of their liberty by a public authority, in all states parties to the Convention, and may also undertake *ad hoc* visits when the Committee considers them necessary. By January 2003 the Committee had undertaken 98 periodic visits and 48 *ad hoc* visits. After each visit the Committee drafts a report of its findings and any further advice or recommendations, based on dialogue and co-operation.

**President:** Silvia Casale (United Kingdom).

### European Social Charter

The European Social Charter, in force since 1965, is the counterpart of the European Convention on Human Rights, in the field of protection of economic and social rights. A revised Charter, which amended existing guarantees and incorporated new rights, was opened for signature in May 1996, and entered into force on 1 July 1999. By January 2003 43 of the 44 member states had signed the Charter, some 32 of which had ratified it. Rights guaranteed by the Charter concern all individuals in their daily lives in matters of housing, health, education, employment, social protection, movement of persons and non-discrimination. The European Committee of Social Rights considers reports submitted to it annually by member states. It also considers collective complaints submitted in the framework of an Additional Protocol (1995), providing for a system which entered into force in July 1998, permitting trade unions, employers' organizations and NGOs to lodge complaints on alleged violations of the Charter. The Committee, composed of 13 members (to be expanded to 15 from January 2005), decides on the conformity of national situations with the Charter. When a country does not bring a situation into conformity, the Committee of Ministers may, on the basis of decisions prepared by a Governmental Committee (composed of representatives of each Contracting Party), issue recommendations to the state concerned, inviting it to change its legislation or practice in accordance with the Charter's requirements.

**President of the European Committee of Social Rights:** Jean-Michel Belorgey (France).

### FRAMEWORK CONVENTION FOR THE PROTECTION OF NATIONAL MINORITIES

In 1993 the first summit meeting of Council of Europe heads of state and government, held in Vienna, mandated the Committee of Ministers to draft 'a framework convention specifying the principle that States commit themselves to respect in order to assure the protection of national minorities'. A special committee was established to draft the so-called Framework Convention for the Protection of National Minorities, which was then adopted by the Committee in November 1994. The Convention was opened for signature in February 1995, entering into force in February 1998. Contracting parties (35 States at January 2003) are required to submit reports on the implementation of the treaty at regular intervals to an Advisory Committee composed of 18 independent experts. The Advisory Committee adopts an opinion on the implementation of the Framework Convention by the contracting party, on the basis of which the Committee of Ministers adopts a resolution. At January 2003 23 opinions and 14 resolutions had been adopted.

**President of the Advisory Committee:** Rainer Hofmann.

### RACISM AND INTOLERANCE

In October 1993 heads of state and of government, meeting in Vienna, resolved to reinforce a policy to combat all forms of intolerance, in response to the increasing incidence of racial hostility and intolerance towards minorities in European societies. A European Commission against Racism and Intolerance (ECRI) was established by the summit meeting to analyse and assess the effectiveness of legal, policy and other measures taken by member states to combat these problems. It became operational in March 1996. Members of ECRI are designated by governments on the basis of their recognized expertise in the field, although participate in the Commission in an independent capacity. ECRI undertakes activities in three programme areas: country-by-country approach; work on general themes; and ECRI and civil society. In the first area of activity, ECRI analyses the situation regarding racism and intolerance in each of the member states, in order to advise governments on measures to combat these problems. In December 1998 ECRI completed a first round of reports for all Council members. A follow-up series of reports were prepared during the four-year period 1999–2002. ECRI's work on general themes includes the preparation of policy recommendations and guide-lines on issues of importance to combating racism and intolerance. ECRI also collects and disseminates examples of good practices relating to these issues. Under the third programme area ECRI aims to disseminate information and raise awareness of the problems of racism and intolerance among the general public.

A Committee on the Rehabilitation and Integration of People with Disabilities supports co-operation between member states in this field and undertakes studies in order to promote legislative and administrative action.

### MEDIA AND COMMUNICATIONS

Article 10 of the European Convention on Human Rights (freedom of expression and information) forms the basis for the Council of Europe's mass media activities. Implementation of the Council of Europe's work programme concerning the media is undertaken by the Steering Committee on the Mass Media (CDMM), which comprises senior government officials and representatives of professional organizations, meeting in plenary session twice a year. The CDMM is mandated to devise concerted European policy measures and appropriate legal instruments. Its underlying aims are to further freedom of expression and information in a pluralistic democracy, and to promote the free flow of information and ideas. The CDMM is assisted by various specialist groups and committees. Policy and legal instruments have been developed on subjects including: exclusivity rights; media concentrations and transparency of media ownership; protection of journalists in situations of conflict and tension; independence of public-service broadcasting, protection of rights holders; legal protection of encrypted television services; media and elections; protection of journalists' sources of information; and the independence and functions of broadcasting regulatory authorities. These policy and legal instruments (mainly in the form on non-binding recommendations addressed to member governments) are complemented by the publication of studies, analyses and seminar proceedings on topics of media law and policy. The CDMM has also prepared a number of international binding legal instruments, including the European Convention on Transfrontier Television (adopted in 1989 and ratified by 25 countries by 31 December 2002), the European Convention on the legal protection of services based on or consisting of conditional access (signed by eight countries and ratified by two at the end of 2002), and the European Convention relating to questions on copyright law and other rights in the context of transfrontier broadcasting by satellite (ratified by two countries and signed by seven other member states and the European Community at the end of 2002). CDMM areas of activity in 2002 included: self-regulation of internet services; credibility of information disseminated online; media and privacy; the regulation of digital broadcasting services; and media and terrorism.

### SOCIAL COHESION

In June 1998, the Committee of Ministers established the European Committee for Social Cohesion (CDCS). The CDCS has the following responsibilities: to co-ordinate, guide and stimulate co-operation between member States with a view to promoting social cohesion in Europe, to develop and promote integrated, multidisciplinary responses to social issues, and to promote the social standards embodied in the European Social Charter and other Council of Europe instruments, including the European Code of Social Security. The CDCS is also responsible for executing the terms of reference of the European Code of Social Security, the European Convention on Social Security and the European Agreement on 'au pair' Placement. The CDCS has agreed on policy guide-lines on access to employment, housing and social protection. In November 2002 it adopted a report on *Access to Social Rights in Europe*, and in early 2003 it was drafting a Recommendation on the subject. It also supervises a programme of work on families and children.

The European Code of Social Security and its Protocol entered into force in 1968; by March 2003 the Code and Protocol had been ratified by Belgium, Germany, Luxembourg, the Netherlands, Norway, Portugal and Sweden, while the Code alone had, additionally, been ratified by Cyprus, the Czech Republic, Denmark, France, Greece, Ireland, Italy, Spain, Switzerland, Turkey and the United Kingdom. These instruments set minimum standards for medical care and the following benefits: sickness, old-age, unemployment, employment injury, family, maternity, invalidity and survivor's benefit. A revision of these instruments, aiming to provide higher standards and greater flexibility, was completed for signature in 1990 and had been signed by 14 states at March 2003.

The European Convention on Social Security, in force since 1977, now applies in Austria, Belgium, Italy, Luxembourg, the Netherlands, Portugal, Spain and Turkey; most of the provisions apply automatically, while others are subject to the conclusion of additional multilateral or bilateral agreements. The Convention is concerned with establishing the following four fundamental principles of international law on social security: equality of treatment, unity of applicable legislation, conservation of rights accrued or in course of acquisition, and payment of benefits abroad. In 1994 a Protocol to the Convention, providing for the enlargement of the personal scope of the Convention, was opened for signature. By March 2003 it had been signed by Austria, the Czech Republic, Greece and Luxembourg, and had been ratified by Portugal.

## HEALTH

Through a series of expert committees, the Council aims to ensure constant co-operation in Europe in a variety of health-related fields, with particular emphasis on patients' rights, for example: equity in access to health care, quality assurance, health services for institutionalized populations (prisoners, elderly in homes), discrimination resulting from health status and education for health. These efforts are supplemented by the training of health personnel.

Improvement of blood transfusion safety and availability of blood and blood derivatives has been ensured through European Agreements and guide-lines. Advances in this field and in organ transplantation are continuously assessed by expert committees.

Eighteen states co-operate in a Partial Agreement to protect the consumer from potential health risks connected with commonplace or domestic activities. The committees of experts of the Public Health Committee provide the scientific base for national and international regulations regarding products which have a direct or indirect impact on the human food chain, pesticides, pharmaceuticals and cosmetics.

The 1992 Recommendation on A Coherent Policy for People with Disabilities contains the policy principles for the rehabilitation and integration of people with disabilities. This model programme recommends that governments of all member states develop comprehensive and co-ordinated national disability policies taking account of prevention, diagnosis, treatment education, vocational guidance and training, employment, social integration, social protection, information and research. It has set benchmarks, both nationally and internationally. The 1995 Charter on the Vocational Assessment of People with Disabilities states that a person's vocational abilities and not disabilities should be assessed and related to specific job requirements. The 2001 Resolution on Universal Design aims to improve the accessibility, recommending the inclusion of Universal Design principles in the training for vocations working on the built environment. The 2001 Resolution on New Technologies recommends formulating national strategies to ensure that people with disabilities benefit from new technologies. Current activities include: air travel, community living, disability prevention, and women with disabilities. Tailor-made programmes for Central and Eastern European countries take account of their specific requirements. The Council of Europe designated 2003 as the European Year of People with Disabilities.

In the co-operation group to combat drug abuse and illicit drugs trafficking (Pompidou Group), 34 states work together, through meetings of ministers, officials and experts, to counteract drug abuse. The Group follows a multidisciplinary approach embracing in particular legislation, law enforcement, prevention, treatment, rehabilitation and data collection.

The Convention on the Elaboration of a European Pharmacopoeia (establishing legally binding standards for medicinal substances, auxiliary substances, pharmaceutical preparations, vaccines for human and veterinary use and other articles) entered into force in eight signatory states in May 1974: in January 2003 30 states and the European Union were parties to the Convention. WHO and 16 European and non-European states participate as observers in the sessions of the European Pharmacopoeia Commission. In 1994 a procedure on certification of suitability to the European Pharmacopoeia monographs for manufacturers of substances for pharmaceutical use was established. In 2002 almost 1,100 certificates were granted. A network of official control laboratories for human and veterinary medicines was established in 1995, open to all signatory countries to the Convention and observers at the Pharmacopoeia Commission. The fourth edition of the European Pharmacopoeia, in force since 1 January 2002, is updated three times a year in its electronic version, and includes some 1,800 harmonized European standards, or 'monographs', 300 general methods of analysis and 2,002 reagents.

In April 1997 the first international convention on biomedicine was opened for signature at a meeting of health ministers of member states, in Oviedo, Spain. The so-called Convention for the Protection of Human Rights and the Dignity of Human Beings with Respect to the Applications of Biology and Medicine incorporated provisions on scientific research, the principle of informed patient consent, organ and tissue transplants and the prohibition of financial gain and disposal of a part of the human body. It entered into force on 1 November 1999 (see below).

## POPULATION AND MIGRATION

The European Convention on the Legal Status of Migrant Workers, in force since 1983, has been ratified by France, Italy, the Netherlands, Norway, Portugal, Spain, Sweden and Turkey, and was signed by Moldova in July 2002. The Convention is based on the principle of equality of treatment for migrant workers and the nationals of the host country as to housing, working conditions, and social security. The Convention also upholds the principle of the right to family reunion. An international consultative committee, representing the parties to the Convention, monitors the application of the Convention.

In 1996 the European Committee on Migration concluded work on a project entitled 'The Integration of Immigrants: Towards Equal Opportunities' was concluded and the results were presented at the sixth conference of European ministers responsible for migration affairs, held in Warsaw, Poland. At the conference a new project, entitled 'Tensions and Tolerance: Building better integrated communities across Europe' was initiated; it was concluded in 1999. The Committee was responsible for activities concerning Roma/Gypsies in Europe, in co-ordination with other relevant Council of Europe bodies. The Committee is also jointly responsible, with the *ad hoc* Committee of Experts on the legal aspects of territorial asylum, refugees and stateless persons, for the examination of migration issues arising at the pan-European level.

The European Population Committee, an intergovernmental committee of scientists and government officials responsible for population matters, monitors and analyses population trends throughout Europe and informs governments, research centres and the public of demographic developments and their impact on policy decisions. It compiles an annual statistical review of demographic developments (covering 46 European states) and publishes the results of studies on population issues, such as *Fertility and new types of households and family formation in Europe* (2001), and *Trends in mortality and differential mortality in Europe* (2001). Future publications were to include studies on the demographic characteristics of immigrant populations, the demographic consequences of economic transition in the countries of central and eastern Europe, and social exclusion.

## COUNCIL OF EUROPE DEVELOPMENT BANK

The Council of Europe Development Bank was established in April 1956 by the Committee of Ministers, initially as the Resettlement Fund, and later as the Council of Europe Social Development Fund, and then renamed again in November 1999. It is a multilateral development bank with a social mandate, promoting social development by granting loans for projects with a social purpose. Projects aimed at solving social problems related to the presence of refugees, displaced persons or forced migrants are a priority. In addition, the Bank finances projects in other fields that contribute directly to strengthening social cohesion in Europe: job creation and preservation in small and medium-sized enterprises; social housing; improving urban living conditions; health and education infrastructure, protection of the environment, and rural modernisation; protection and rehabilitation of the historic heritage. At November 2002 the Bank had a subscribed capital of €3,160m. It is currently funding 167 projects in 28 countries. Its lending activities have been increasingly targeted at central and eastern European countries. Since 1995 the Bank has approved 66 projects in 14 transition countries, supported by a cumulative total of €1,800m. worth of loans.

## EQUALITY BETWEEN WOMEN AND MEN

The Steering Committee for Equality between Women and Men (CDEG—an intergovernmental committee of experts) is responsible for encouraging action at both national and Council of Europe level to promote equality of rights and opportunities between the two sexes. Assisted by various specialist groups and committees, the CDEG is mandated to establish analyses, studies and evaluations, to examine national policies and experiences, to work out concerted policy strategies and measures for implementing equality and, as necessary, to prepare appropriate legal and other instruments. It is also responsible for preparing the European Ministerial Conferences on Equality between Women and Men. The main areas of CDEG activities are the comprehensive inclusion of the rights of women (for example, combating violence against women and trafficking in human beings) within the context of human rights; the issue of equality and democracy, including the promotion of the participation of women in political and public life; projects aimed at studying the specific equality problems related to cultural diversity, migration and minorities; positive action in the field of equality between men and women and the mainstreaming of equality into all policies and programmes at all levels of society. In October 1998 the Committee of Ministers adopted a Recommendation to member states on gender mainstreaming; in May 2000 it approved a Recommendation on action against trafficking in human beings for the purpose of sexual exploitation; and in April 2002 it adopted a Recommendation on the protection of women against violence.

## LEGAL MATTERS

The European Committee on Legal Co-operation develops co-operation between member states in the field of law, with the objective of harmonizing and modernizing public and private law, including administrative law and the law relating to the judiciary. The Committee is responsible for expert groups which consider issues relating to administrative law, efficiency of justice, family law, nationality, information technology and data protection.

Numerous conventions and Recommendations have been adopted, and followed up by appropriate committees or groups of experts, on matters which include: efficiency of justice, nationality, legal aid, rights of children, data protection, information technology, children born out of wedlock, animal protection, adoption, information on foreign law, and the legal status of non-governmental organizations. In addition, a new draft Convention on contact concerning children was adopted in May 2002.

In December 1999 the Convention for the Protection of Human Rights and the Dignity of Human Beings with Respect to the Applications of Biology and Medicine: Convention on Human Rights and Biomedicine entered into force, as the first internationally-binding legal text to protect people against the misuse of biological and medical advances. It aims to preserve human dignity and identify, rights and freedoms, through a series of principles and rules. Additional protocols develop the Convention's general provisions by means of specialized texts. A Protocol prohibiting the medical cloning of human beings was approved by Council heads of state and government in October 1997 and entered into force on 1 March 2001. A Protocol on the transplantation of human organs and tissue was opened for signature in January 2002. Work on draft protocols relating to biomedical research, protection of the human embryo and foetus, and genetics is ongoing. A draft Recommendation on xenotransplantation is currently being considered by the Committee of Ministers.

In 2001 an Additional Protocol to the Convention for the protection of individuals with regard to automatic processing of personal data was adopted. The Protocol, which opened for signature in November, concerned supervisory authorities and transborder data flows. By April 2003 it had been signed by 21 states, and ratified by three (Germany, Slovakia and Sweden).

In 2001 the European Committee for Social Cohesion (CDCS) approved three new conventions on contact concerning children, legal aid, and 'Information Society Services'. In 2002 the CDCS approved a Recommendation on mediation on civil matters and a resolution establishing the European Commission for the Efficiency of Justice (CEPEJ). The aims of the CEPEJ are: to improve the efficiency and functioning of the justice system of member states, with a view to ensuring that everyone within their jurisdiction can enforce their legal rights effectively, increasing citizen confidence in the system; and enabling better implementation of the international legal instruments of the Council of Europe concerning efficiency and fairness of justice.

The Consultative Council of European Judges has prepared a framework global action plan for judges in Europe. In addition, it has contributed to the implementation of this programme by the adoption of opinions on standards concerning the independence of the judiciary and the irremovability of judges, and on the funding and management of courts.

A Committee of Legal Advisors on Public and International Law (CAHDI), comprising the legal advisors of ministers of foreign affairs of member states and of several observer states, is authorized by the Committee of Ministers to examine questions of public international law, and to exchange and, if appropriate, to co-ordinate the views of member states. The CAHDI functions as a European observatory of reservations to international treaties. Recent activities of the CAHDI include the preparation of a Recommendation on reactions to inadmissible reservations to international treaties, the publication of a report on state practice with regard to state succession and recognition, and another on expression of consent of states to be bound by a treaty. In 2002 the CAHDI was conducting research into the practice of states with regard to immunities of states and their property.

An *ad hoc* Committee of Experts on the Legal Aspects of Territorial Asylum, Refugees and Stateless Persons (CAHAR) proposes solutions to practical and legal problems relating to its area of expertise and works towards harmonizing rules and practices to be followed in Europe in matters of asylum and refugees. It reviews national and international developments and formulates appropriate legal instruments (mainly Recommendations) for discussion and adoption by the Committee of Ministers. Over the years the Committee has drafted a number of pan-European standards, and in 2002 it prepared a draft recommendation relating to the detention of asylum seekers. The CAHAR has also adopted a series of opinions for the Committee of Ministers on issues relating to refugees and displaced persons in member states. It works closely with other international bodies, in particular UNHCR and the Council's Parliamentary Assembly.

With regard to crime, expert committees and groups operating under the authority of the European Committee on Crime Problems have prepared conventions on such matters as extradition, mutual assistance, recognition and enforcement of foreign judgments, transfer of proceedings, suppression of terrorism, transfer of prisoners, compensation payable to victims of violent crime, money-laundering, confiscation of proceeds from crime, cybercrime and corruption. In 2002 member states concluded an additional Protocol to the 2001 Convention on cybercrime relating to the criminalization of acts of a racist and xenophobic nature committed through computer systems.

The Group of States Against Corruption (GRECO) became operational in 1999 and became a permanent body of the Council in 2002. By the end of that year it had 34 members (33 member states of the Council of Europe and the USA). A monitoring mechanism, based on mutual evaluation and peer pressure, GRECO assesses members' compliance with Council instruments for combating corruption. Its First Round Evaluations were completed by the end of 2002. A Second Round Evaluation commenced in 2003, reviewing Proceeds of Corruption, Public Administration and Corruption, and Legal Persons and Corruption. It was then to cover member states' compliance with, *inter alia*, requirements of the Criminal Law Convention on Corruption, which entered into force in July 2002. The evaluation procedure of GRECO is confidential but it has become practice to make reports public after their adoption.

The select committee of Experts on the Evaluation of Anti-Money laundering Measures (MONEYVAL) became operational in 1998. It is responsible for mutual evaluation of the anti-money laundering measures in place in 25 Council of Europe states that are not members of the Financial Action Task Force (FATF). The MONEYVAL mechanism is based on FATF practices and procedures. States are evaluated against the relevant international standards in the legal, financial and law enforcement sectors. In the legal sector this includes evaluation of states' obligations under the Council of Europe Convention on Laundering, Search Seizure and Confiscation of the Proceeds from Crime. After the terrorist attacks against targets in the USA on 11 September 2001, the Committee of Ministers adopted revised terms of reference, which specifically include the evaluation of measures to combat the financing of terrorism. MONEYVAL completed its first round of onsite visits in 2000 and subsequently adopted all first round reports. Its second round, focusing even more closely on the effectiveness of national systems, began in 2001 and was expected to be completed during 2003. The evaluations of MONEYVAL are confidential, but summaries of adopted reports are made public.

A Criminological Scientific Council, composed of specialists in law, psychology, sociology and related sciences, advises the Committee and organizes criminological research conferences and colloquia. A Council for Penological Co-operation organizes regular high-level conferences of directors of prison administration and is responsible for collating statistical information on detention and community sanctions in Europe. The Council prepared the European Prison Rules in 1987 and the European Rules on Community Sanctions (alternatives to imprisonment) in 1992. A council for police matters was established in 2002.

In May 1990 the Committee of Ministers adopted a Partial Agreement to establish the European Commission for Democracy through Law, to be based in Venice, Italy. The so-called Venice Commission was enlarged in February 2002 and at early 2003 comprised all Council of Europe member states. The Commission is composed of independent legal and political experts, mainly senior academics, supreme or constitutional court judges, members of national parliaments, and senior public officers. Its main activity is constitutional assistance and may supply opinions upon request, made through the Committee of Ministers, by the Parliamentary Assembly, the Secretary-General or any member states of the Commission. Other states and international organizations may request opinions with the consent of the Committee of Ministers. The Commission is active throughout the constitutional domain, and has worked on issues including legislation on constitutional courts and national minorities, electoral law and other legislation with implications for national democratic institutions. The creation of the Council for Democratic elections institutionalized co-operation in the area of elections between the Venice Commission, the Parliamentary Assembly of the Council of Europe, and the Congress of Regional and Local Authorities of Europe. The Commission disseminates its work through the UniDem (University for Democracy) programme of seminars, the CODICES database, and the *Bulletin of Constitutional Case-Law*.

The promotion of local and regional democracy and of transfrontier co-operation constitutes a major aim of the Council's intergovernmental programme of activities. The Steering Committee on Local and Regional Democracy (CDLR) serves as a forum for representatives of member states to exchange information and pursue co-operation in order to promote the decentralization of powers, in accordance with the European Charter on Local Self-Government. The CDLR's principal objective is to improve the legal, institutional and financial framework of local democracy and to encourage citizen participation in local and regional communities. In December 2001 the Committee of Ministers adopted a Recommendation on citizens' participation in public life at local level, drafted on the basis of the work conducted by the CDLR. The CDLR publishes comparative studies and national reports, and aims to identify guide-lines for the effective implementation of the principles of subsidiarity and solidarity. Its work also constitutes a basis for the provision of aid to central and eastern European countries in the field of local democracy. The CDLR is responsible for the preparation and follow-up of Conferences of Ministers responsible for local and regional government.

Intergovernmental co-operation with the CDLR is supplemented by specific activities aimed at providing legislative advice, supporting reform and enhancing management capabilities and democratic participation in European member and non-member countries. These activities are specifically focused on the democratic stability of central and eastern European countries. The programmes for democratic stability in the field of local democracy draw inspiration from the European Charter of Local Self-Government, operating at three levels of government: at intergovernmental level, providing assistance in implementing reforms to reinforce local or regional government, in compliance with the Charter; at local or regional level, co-operating with local and regional authorities to build local government capacity; and at community level, co-operating directly with individual authorities to promote pilot initiatives. Working methods include: awareness-raising conferences; legislative opinion involving written opinions, expert round-tables and working groups; and seminars, workshops and training at home and abroad.

The policy of the Council of Europe on transfrontier co-operation between territorial communities or authorities is implemented through two committees. The Committee of Experts on Transfrontier Co-operation, working under the supervision of the CDLR, aims to monitor the implementation of the European Outline Convention on Transfrontier Co-operation between Territorial Communities or Authorities; to make proposals for the elimination of obstacles, in particular of a legal nature, to transfrontier and interterritorial co-operation; and to compile 'best practice' examples of transfrontier co-operation in various fields of activity. In 2002 the Committee of Ministers adopted a draft recommendation on the mutual aid and assistance between central and local authorities in the event of disasters affecting frontier areas. A Committee of Advisers for the development of transfrontier co-operation in central and eastern Europe is composed of six members appointed or elected by the Secretary-General, the Committee of Ministers and the Congress of Local and Regional Authorities of Europe. Its task is to guide the promotion of transfrontier co-operation in central and eastern European countries, with a view to fostering good neighbourly relations between the frontier populations, especially in particularly sensitive regions. Its programme comprises: conferences and colloquies designed to raise awareness on the Outline Convention; meetings in border regions between representatives of local communities with a view to strengthening mutual trust; and legal assistance to, and restricted meetings with, national and local representatives responsible for preparing the legal texts for ratification and/or implementation of the Outline Convention. The priority areas which had been outlined by the Committee of Advisers include South-East Europe, northern Europe around the Baltic Sea, the external frontiers of an enlarged European Union, and the Caucasus.

### EDUCATION, CULTURE AND HERITAGE

The European Cultural Convention covers education, culture, heritage, sport and youth. Programmes on education, higher education, culture and cultural heritage are managed by four steering committees.

The education programme consists of projects on education for democratic citizenship and human rights, history teaching, the European dimension of education and interreligious dialogue, instruments and policies for plurilingualism, equitable education policies responding to new social, economic and technological realities, and bilateral co-operation for education renewal. Other activities include the partial agreement for the European Centre for Modern Languages located in Graz, Austria, the In Service Educational Staff Training Programme, the Network for School Links and Exchanges, and the European Schools Day competition, organized in co-operation with the European Union. The Council of Europe's main focus in the field of higher education is on the Bologna Process aiming to establish a European Higher Education Area by 2010.

In December 2000 the Committee of Ministers adopted a Declaration on Cultural Diversity, formulated in consultation with other organizations (including the European Union and UNESCO), which created a framework for developing a European approach to valuing cultural diversity. A European Charter for Regional or Minority languages entered into force in 1998, with the aim of protecting regional or minority languages, which are considered to be a threatened aspect of Europe's cultural heritage. It was intended to promote the use in private and public life of languages traditionally used within a state's territory. The Charter provides for a monitoring system enabling states, the Council of Europe and individuals to observe and follow up its implementation.

The Council of Europe's activities related to cultural policy focus on the following priority areas: standard-setting; cultural policy reviews; conflict prevention; comparative studies on cultural diver-

sity, and partnership programmes; archives; the MOSAIC and STAGE projects (co-operation with South-East Europe and the South Caucasus, respectively); and the Action Plan for Russia.

The European Convention for the Protection of Audiovisual Heritage and its Protocol were opened for signature in November 2001. The Eurimages support fund helps to finance co-production of films. The Convention for the Protection of the Architectural Heritage and the Protection of the Archaeological Heritage provide a legal framework for European co-operation in these areas. The European Heritage Network is a being developed to facilitate the work of professionals and state institutions and the dissemination of good practices in more than 30 countries of the states party to the European Cultural Convention.

### YOUTH

In 1972 the Council of Europe established the European Youth Centre (EYC) in Strasbourg. A second residential centre was created in Budapest in 1995. The centres, run with and by international non-governmental youth organizations representing a wide range of interests, provide about 50 residential courses a year (study sessions, training courses, symposia). A notable feature of the EYC is its decision-making structure, by which decisions on its programme and general policy matters are taken by a Programming Committee composed of an equal number of youth organizations and government representatives.

The European Youth Foundation (EYF) aims to provide financial assistance to European activities of non-governmental youth organizations and began operations in 1973. Since that time more than 380 organizations have received financial aid for carrying out international activities, while more than 210,000 young people have participated in meetings supported by the Foundation. The European Steering Committee for Intergovernmental Co-operation in the Youth Field conducts research in youth-related matters and prepares for ministerial conferences.

### SPORT

The Committee for the Development of Sport, founded in November 1977, oversees sports co-operation and development on a pan-European basis, bringing together all the 48 states party to the European Cultural Convention. Its activities focus on the implementation of the European Sport Charter and Code of Sports Ethics (adopted in 1992 and revised in 2002), the role of sport in society, the provision of assistance in sports reform to new member states in central and eastern Europe, and the practice of both recreational and high level sport. A Charter on Sport for Disabled Persons was adopted in 1986. The Committee also prepares the Conferences of European Ministers responsible for Sport and has been responsible for drafting two important conventions to combat negative influences on sport. The European Convention on Spectator Violence and Misbehaviour at Sport Events (1985) provides governments with practical measures to ensure crowd security and safety, particularly at football matches. The Anti-Doping Convention (1989) has been ratified by nearly 40 European countries, and is also open to non-European states.

### ENVIRONMENT AND SUSTAINABLE DEVELOPMENT

In 1995 a pan-European biological and landscape diversity strategy, formulated by the Committee of Ministers, was endorsed at a ministerial conference of the UN Economic Commission for Europe, which was held in Sofia, Bulgaria. The strategy was to be implemented jointly by the Council of Europe and UNEP, in close co-operation with the European Community. In particular, it provided for implementation of the Convention on Biological Diversity.

At March 2002 45 states and the European Community had ratified a Convention on the Conservation of European Wildlife and Natural Habitats, which entered into force in June 1982 and gives total protection to 693 species of plants, 89 mammals, 294 birds, 43 reptiles, 21 amphibians, 115 freshwater fishes, 113 invertebrates and their habitats. The Convention established a network of protected areas known as the 'Emerald Network'. The Council's NATUROPA Centre provides information and documentation on the environment, through periodicals and campaigns. The Council awards the European Diploma for protection of sites of European significance, supervises a network of biogenetic reserves, and co-ordinates conservation action for threatened animals and plants.

Regional disparities constitute a major obstacle to the process of European integration. Conferences of ministers of regional planning are held to discuss these issues. In 2000 they adopted guiding principles for sustainable development of the European continent and, in 2001, a resolution detailing a ten-point programme for greater cohesion among the Regions of Europe.

### EXTERNAL RELATIONS

Agreements providing for co-operation and exchange of documents and observers have been concluded with the United Nations and its agencies, and with most of the European inter-governmental organizations and the Organization of American States. Particularly close relations exist with the EU, OECD, and the OSCE. Relations with non-member states, other organizations and non-governmental organizations are co-ordinated by the Directorate General of Political Affairs.

Israel, Canada and Mexico are represented in the Parliamentary Assembly by observer delegations, and certain European and other non-member countries participate in or send observers to certain meetings of technical committees and specialized conferences at intergovernmental level. Full observer status with the Council was granted to the USA in 1995, to Canada and Japan in 1996 and to Mexico in 1999. The Holy See has had a similar status since 1970.

The European Centre for Global Interdependence and Solidarity (the 'North–South Centre') was established in Lisbon, Portugal, in 1990, in order to provide a framework for European co-operation in this area and to promote pluralist democracy and respect for human rights. The Centre is co-managed by parliamentarians, governments, non-governmental organizations and local and regional authorities. Its activities are divided into three programmes: public information and media relations; education and training for global interdependence; and dialogue for global partnership. The Centre organizes workshops, seminars and training courses on global interdependence and convenes international colloquies on human rights.

During the early 1990s the Council of Europe established a structure of programmes to assist the process of democratic reform in central and eastern European countries that had formerly been under communist rule. In October 1997 the meeting of heads of state or of government of Council members agreed to extend the programmes as the means by which all states are assisted to meet their undertakings as members of the Council. These specific co-operation programmes were mainly concerned with the development of the rule of law; the protection and promotion of human rights; and strengthening local democracy. A scheme of Democratic Leadership Programmes has also been established for the training of political leaders. Within the framework of the co-operation programme 22 information and documentation centres/offices have been established in 17 countries of central and eastern Europe. A secretariat representation to co-ordinate the Council's contribution to the UN operation in Kosovo was established in Priština (the capital of Kosovo and Metohija), in mid-1999.

## Finance

The budget is financed by contributions from members on a proportional scale of assessment (using population and gross domestic product as common indicators). The 2003 budget totalled €175.5m.

## Publications

*The Council of Europe: 800 million Europeans* (introductory booklet).
*Activities Report* (in English and French).
*The Bulletin* (newsletter of the CLRAE, 3 a year).
*The Europeans* (electronic bulletin of the Parliamentary Assembly).
*Naturopa* (3 a year, in 15 languages).
*Bulletin On Constitutional Case-Law* (3–4 times a year, in English and French).
*The Pompidou Group Newsletter* (3 a year).
*Penological Information Bulletin* (annually, in English and French).
*Human Rights Information Bulletin* (monthly, in English and French).

# ECONOMIC CO-OPERATION ORGANIZATION—ECO

**Address:** 1 Golbou Alley, Kamranieh St, POB 14155-6176, Tehran, Iran.

**Telephone:** (21) 2831733; **fax:** (21) 2831732; **e-mail:** registry@ecosecretariat.org; **internet:** www.ecosecretariat.org.

The Economic Co-operation Organization (ECO) was established in 1985 as the successor to the Regional Co-operation for Development, founded in 1964.

### MEMBERS

| | | |
|---|---|---|
| Afghanistan | Kyrgyzstan | Turkey |
| Azerbaijan | Pakistan | Turkmenistan |
| Iran | Tajikistan | Uzbekistan |
| Kazakhstan | | |

The 'Turkish Republic of Northern Cyprus' has been granted special guest status.

## Organization

(October 2003)

### SUMMIT MEETING

The first summit meeting of heads of state and of government of member countries was held in Tehran in February 1992. Summit meetings are generally held at least once every two years. The seventh summit meeting was convened in İstanbul, Turkey, in October 2002.

### COUNCIL OF MINISTERS

The Council of Ministers, comprising ministers of foreign affairs of member states, is the principal policy- and decision-making body of ECO. It meets at least once a year.

### REGIONAL PLANNING COUNCIL

The Council, comprising senior planning officials or other representatives of member states, meets at least once a year. It is responsible for reviewing programmes of activity and evaluating results achieved, and for proposing future plans of action to the Council of Ministers.

### COUNCIL OF PERMANENT REPRESENTATIVES

Permanent representatives or Ambassadors of member countries accredited to Iran meet regularly to formulate policy for consideration by the Council of Ministers and to promote implementation of decisions reached at ministerial or summit level.

### SECRETARIAT

The Secretariat is headed by a Secretary-General, who is supported by two Deputy Secretaries-General. The following Directorates administer and co-ordinate the main areas of ECO activities: Trade and investment; Transport and communications; Energy, minerals and environment; Industry and agriculture (to be renamed Human development); Project research; Economic research and statistics; and Co-ordination and international relations.

**Secretary-General:** Dr BEKZHASAR NARBAYEV (Kazakhstan).

## Activities

The Regional Co-operation for Development (RCD) was established in 1964 as a tripartite arrangement between Iran, Pakistan and Turkey, which aimed to promote economic co-operation between member states. ECO replaced the RCD in 1985, and seven additional members were admitted to the Organization in November 1992. The main areas of co-operation are transport (including the building of road and rail links, of particular importance as seven member states are landlocked), telecommunications and post, trade and investment, energy (including the interconnection of power grids in the region), minerals, environmental issues, industry, and agriculture. ECO priorities and objectives for each sector are defined in the Quetta Plan of Action and the İstanbul Declaration; an Almaty Outline Plan, which was adopted in 1993, is specifically concerned with the development of regional transport and communication infrastructure. The period 1998–2007 has been designated as the ECO Decade of Transport and Communications.

In 1990 an ECO College of Insurance was inaugurated. A joint Chamber of Commerce and Industry was established in 1993. The third ECO summit meeting, held in Islamabad, Pakistan, in March 1995, concluded formal agreements on the establishment of several other regional institutes and agencies: an ECO Trade and Development Bank, in İstanbul, Turkey (with main branches in Tehran, Iran, and Islamabad, Pakistan), a joint shipping company, airline, and an ECO Cultural Institute, all to be based in Iran, and an ECO

Reinsurance Company and an ECO Science Foundation, with head-quarters in Pakistan. In addition, heads of state and of government endorsed the creation of an ECO eminent persons group and signed the following two agreements in order to enhance and facilitate trade throughout the region: the Transit Trade Agreement (which entered into force in December 1997) and the Agreement on the Simplification of Visa Procedures for Businessmen of ECO Countries (which came into effect in March 1998). The sixth ECO summit meeting, held in June 2000 in Tehran, urged the completion of the necessary formalities for the creation of the planned ECO Trade and Development Bank and ECO Reinsurance Company. In May 2001 the Council of Ministers agreed to terminate the ECO airline project, owing to its unsustainable cost, and to replace it with a framework agreement on co-operation in the field of air transport.

In September 1996, at an extraordinary meeting of the ECO Council of Ministers, held in İzmir, Turkey, member countries signed a revised Treaty of İzmir, the Organization's fundamental charter. An extraordinary summit meeting, held in Ashgabat, Turkmenistan, in May 1997, adopted the Ashgabat Declaration, emphasizing the importance of the development of the transport and communications infrastructure and the network of transnational petroleum and gas pipelines through bilateral and regional arrangements in the ECO area. In May 1998, at the fifth summit meeting, held in Almaty, Kazakhstan, ECO heads of state and of government signed a Transit Transport Framework Agreement and a memorandum of understanding to help combat the cross-border trafficking of illegal goods. The meeting also agreed to establish an ECO Educational Institute in Ankara, Turkey. In June 2000 the sixth ECO summit encouraged member states to participate in the development of information and communication technologies through the establishment of a database of regional educational and training institutions specializing in that field. The ECO heads of state and government also reconfirmed their commitment to the Ashgabat Declaration. In December 2001 ECO organized its first workshop on energy conservation and efficiency in Ankara. The seventh ECO summit, held in İstanbul, Turkey, in October 2002, adopted the İstanbul Declaration, which outlined a strengthened and more pro-active economic orientation for the Organization

Convening in conference for the first time in early March 2000, ECO ministers of trade signed a Framework Agreement on ECO Trade Co-operation (ECOFAT), which established a basis for the expansion of intra-regional trade. The Framework Agreement envisaged the eventual adoption of an ECO Trade Agreement (ECOTA), providing for the gradual elimination of regional tariff and non-tariff barriers between member states. ECO and the International Trade Centre are jointly implementing a project on expanding intra-ECO trade. In November the first meeting of ECO ministers responsible for energy and petroleum, convened in Islamabad, adopted a plan of action for regional co-operation on energy and petroleum matters over the period 2001–05. The first meeting of ECO ministers of agriculture, convened in July 2002, in Islamabad, Pakistan, adopted a declaration on co-operation in the agricultural sector, which specified that member states would contribute to agricultural rehabilitation in Afghanistan and considered instigating a mechanism for the regional exchange of agricultural and cattle products. In December the first meeting of ECO ministers of the environment, held in Tehran, adopted an action plan for co-operation in environmental issues covering the period 2003–07.

ECO staged its third trade fair in Bandar Anzali, Iran, in July 1998. The fourth fair, scheduled to be held in Karachi, Pakistan, in May 2002, was postponed. The Organization maintains ECO TradeNet, an internet-based repository of regional trade information. ECO has co-operation agreements with several UN agencies and other international organizations in development-related activities. An ECO-UN International Drug Control Programme (UNDCP) Project on Drug Control and Co-ordination Unit commenced operations in Tehran in July 1999. ECO has been granted observer status at the UN, OIC and WTO.

In November 2001 the UN Secretary-General requested ECO to take an active role in efforts to restore stability in Afghanistan and to co-operate closely with his special representative in that country. In June 2002 the ECO Secretary-General participated in a tripartite ministerial conference on co-operation for development in Afghanistan that was convened under the auspices of the UN Development Programme and attended by representatives from Afghanistan, Iran and Pakistan. The ECO summit meeting in October authorized the establishment of a fund to provide financial assistance for reconstruction activities in Afghanistan.

# Finance

Member states contribute to a centralized administrative budget.

# Publications

*ECO Annual Economic Report.*
*ECO Bulletin* (quarterly).

# EUROPEAN BANK FOR RECONSTRUCTION AND DEVELOPMENT—EBRD

**Address:** One Exchange Square, 175 Bishopsgate, London, EC2A 2EH, United Kingdom.

**Telephone:** (20) 7338-6000; **fax:** (20) 7338-6100; **e-mail:** generalenquiries@ebrd.com; **internet:** www.ebrd.com.

The EBRD was founded in May 1990 and inaugurated in April 1991. Its object is to contribute to the progress and the economic reconstruction of the countries of central and eastern Europe which undertake to respect and put into practice the principles of multiparty democracy, pluralism, the rule of law, respect for human rights and a market economy.

## MEMBERS

Countries of Operations:

| | |
|---|---|
| Albania | Lithuania |
| Armenia | Macedonia, former Yugoslav |
| Azerbaijan | republic |
| Belarus | Moldova |
| Bosnia and Herzegovina | Poland |
| Bulgaria | Romania |
| Croatia | Russia |
| Czech Republic | Serbia and Montenegro |
| Estonia | Slovakia |
| Georgia | Slovenia |
| Hungary | Tajikistan |
| Kazakhstan | Turkmenistan |
| Kyrgyzstan | Ukraine |
| Latvia | Uzbekistan |

EU members*:

| | |
|---|---|
| Austria | Italy |
| Belgium | Luxembourg |
| Denmark | Netherlands |
| Finland | Portugal |
| France | Spain |
| Germany | Sweden |
| Greece | United Kingdom |
| Ireland | |

EFTA members:

| | |
|---|---|
| Iceland | Norway |
| Liechtenstein | Switzerland |

Other countries:

| | |
|---|---|
| Australia | Malta |
| Canada | Mexico |
| Cyprus | Mongolia |
| Egypt | Morocco |
| Israel | New Zealand |
| Japan | Turkey |
| Republic of Korea | USA |

* The European Community and the European Investment Bank are also shareholder members in their own right.

## Organization

(October 2003)

### BOARD OF GOVERNORS

The Board of Governors, to which each member appoints a Governor and an alternate, is the highest authority of the EBRD.

### BOARD OF DIRECTORS

The Board is responsible for the organization and operations of the EBRD. The Governors elect 23 directors for a three-year term and a President for a term of four years. Vice-Presidents are appointed by the Board on the recommendation of the President.

### ADMINISTRATION

The EBRD's operations are conducted by its Banking Department, headed by the First Vice-President. The other departments are: Finance; Human Resources and Administration; Evaluation, Operational and Environmental Support; Internal Audit; Communications; and Offices of the Secretary-General, the General Counsel and the Chief Economist. A structure of country teams, industry teams and operations support units oversee the implementation of projects. The EBRD has 32 local offices in all 27 of its countries of operations. At December 2002 there were 903 regular staff at the Bank's headquarters.

**President:** JEAN LEMIERRE (France).

**First Vice-President:** NOREEN DOYLE (USA).

## Activities

In April 1996 EBRD shareholders, meeting in Sofia, Bulgaria, agreed to increase the Bank's capital from ECU 10,000m. to ECU 20,000m., to enable the Bank to continue, and to enhance, its lending programme (the ECU was replaced by the euro, with an equivalent value, from 1 January 1999). It was agreed that 22.5% of the new resources, was to be paid-up, with the remainder as 'callable' shares. Contributions were to be paid over a 13-year period from April 1998. By 31 December 2002 paid-up capital amounted to €5,197m.

The Bank aims to assist the transition of the economies of central Europe, southern and eastern Europe and the Caucasus, and central Asia and Russia towards a market economy system, and to encourage private enterprise. The Agreement establishing the EBRD specifies that 60% of its lending should be for the private sector, and that its operations do not displace commercial sources of finance. The Bank helps the beneficiaries to undertake structural and sectoral reforms, including the dismantling of monopolies, decentralization, and privatization of state enterprises, to enable these countries to become fully integrated in the international economy. To this end, the Bank promotes the establishment and improvement of activities of a productive, competitive and private nature, particularly small and medium-sized enterprises (SMEs), and works to strengthen financial institutions. It mobilizes national and foreign capital, together with experienced management teams, and helps to develop an appropriate legal framework to support a market-orientated economy. The Bank provides extensive financial services, including loans, equity and guarantees, and aims to develop new forms of financing and investment in accordance with the requirements of the transition process. The EBRD's founding Agreement specifies that all operations are to be undertaken in the context of promoting environmentally sound and sustainable development. It undertakes environmental audits and impact assessments in areas of particular concern, which enable the Bank to incorporate environmental action plans into any project approved for funding. An Environment Advisory Council assists with the development of policy and strategy in this area.

The economic crisis in Russia, in August 1998, undermined the viability of many proposed projects and adversely affected the Bank's large portfolio of Russian investments. In March 1999, partly in response to the region's economic difficulties, the Board of Directors approved a new medium-term strategy for 2000–03, which focused on advancing the process of transition. Key aspects of the strategy were to develop a sound financial sector and investment climate in its countries of operations; to provide leadership for the development of SMEs; to promote infrastructure development; and to ensure a balanced and focused project portfolio. In April 1999 the Bank and the European Commission launched a new EU/EBRD SME Finance Facility, with committed funds of €125m., to provide equity and loan financing for SMEs in countries seeking accession to the EU. During 2001 the Bank directed substantial investment to the so-called accession countries, and supported the development of institutions in areas including financial regulation, competition policy and telecommunications. During 2001 the Bank also further strengthened measures to improve institutional governance, in particular to combat money-laundering. A Trade Facilitation Programme, which extends bank guarantees in order to promote trading capabilities in the region, was expanded during 1999. By the end of 2002 74 issuing banks in 20 countries of operations, together with 400 confirming banks in countries world-wide, were participating in the Programme. During 1999 the Bank participated in international efforts to secure economic and political stability in the Balkans, following the conflict in Kosovo. Subsequently the Bank has promoted the objectives of the Stability Pact for South-Eastern Europe by expanding its commitments in the region and by taking a lead role among international financial institutions in promoting private sector development. In July 2000 a US/EBRD SME Financing Facility was established for South East Europe and other early transition countries, and by early 2003 this had leveraged loans across the region to the value of $114m. During 2001 the Bank committed €678m. to 46 new projects in the six Stability Pact countries. In October the Bank development an Action Plan for Central Asia in order to accelerate development and economic stability in the countries neighbouring Afghanistan, as part of a wider objective of securing peace in the region.

In the year ending 31 December 2002 the EBRD approved 102 operations, involving funds of €3,899m., compared with €3,656m. for 102 operations in the previous year. During 2002 29.95% of all project financing committed was allocated to the financial sector and 26.3% to infrastructure. Support to micro-, small and medium-sized enterprises through financial intermediaries totalled €509m., bringing the cumulative total committed since 1991 to more than €3,900m.

A high priority is given to attracting external finance for Bank-sponsored projects, in particular in countries at advanced stages of transition, from government agencies, international financial institutions, commercial banks and export credit agencies. The EBRD's Technical Co-operation Funds Programme (TCFP) aims to facilitate access to the Bank's capital resources for countries of operations by providing support for project preparation, project implementation and institutional development. During 1991–2002 technical co-operation funding from donor countries and institutions reached a cumulative total of €100m. In 2002 the EBRD committed €101.7m. to finance some 261 consultancy assignments under the TCFP. Resources for technical co-operation originate from regular TCFP contributions, specific agreements and contributions to Special Funds. The Baltic Investment Programme, which is administered by Nordic countries, consists of two special funds to co-finance investment and technical assistance projects in the private sectors of Baltic states. The Funds are open to contributions from all EBRD member states. The Russia Small Business Fund (RSBF) was established in 1994 to support local SMEs through similar investment and technical co-operation activities over a period of 10 years. Other financing mechanisms that the EBRD uses to address the needs of the region include Regional Venture Funds, which invest equity in privatized companies, in particular in Russia, and provide relevant management assistance, and the Central European Agency Lines, which disburse lines of credit to small-scale projects through local intermediaries. A TurnAround Management Programme (TAM) provides practical assistance to senior managers of industrial enterprises to facilitate the expansion of businesses in a market economy. A Business Advisory Services programme complements TAM by undertaking projects to improve competitiveness, strategic planning, marketing and financial management in SMEs. In 2001 the EBRD collaborated with other donor institutions and partners to initiate a Northern Dimension Environmental Partnership (NDEP) to strengthen and co-ordinate environmental projects in northern Europe; the Partnership, which became operational in November 2002, includes a 'nuclear window' to address the nuclear legacy of the Russian Northern Fleet. The Bank manages the NDEP Support Fund.

### PROJECT FINANCING COMMITTED BY SECTOR

| | 2002 | |
|---|---|---|
| | Number | Amount (€ million) |
| **Financial institutions** | | |
| Bank equity | 7 | 311 |
| Bank lending | 13 | 541 |
| Equity funds | 6 | 126 |
| Non-bank financial institutions | 7 | 166 |
| Small business finance | 3 | 24 |
| **Specialized industries** | | |
| Agribusiness | 12 | 425 |
| Property, tourism and shipping | 1 | 95 |
| Telecommunications, information technology and media | 6 | 241 |
| **Infrastructure** | | |
| Municipal and environmental infrastructure | 11 | 482 |
| Transport | 9 | 543 |
| **Energy** | | |
| Energy Efficiency | 2 | 76 |
| Natural Resources | 3 | 265 |
| Power and Energy | 4 | 219 |
| **General industry** | | |
| General industry | 17 | 385 |
| **Total** | 102 | 3,899 |

### PROJECT FINANCING COMMITTED BY COUNTRY

| | 2002 | | Cumulative to 31 Dec. 2002 | |
|---|---|---|---|---|
| | Number | Amount (€ million) | Number | Amount (€ million) |
| Albania | 2 | 42 | 15 | 156 |
| Armenia | 1 | 4 | 7 | 122 |
| Azerbaijan | 1 | 52 | 12 | 358 |
| Belarus | 0 | 8 | 6 | 164 |
| Bosnia and Herzegovina | 2 | 39 | 18 | 230 |
| Bulgaria | 6 | 182 | 39 | 667 |
| Croatia | 8 | 318 | 44 | 1,180 |
| Czech Republic | 2 | 69 | 37 | 902 |
| Estonia | 4 | 73 | 42 | 446 |
| Georgia | 2 | 16 | 17 | 205 |
| Hungary | 1 | 27 | 60 | 1,326 |
| Kazakhstan | 6 | 175 | 25 | 818 |
| Kyrgyzstan | 0 | 2 | 13 | 143 |
| Latvia | 0 | 9 | 24 | 321 |
| Lithuania | 1 | 5 | 25 | 407 |
| Macedonia, former Yugoslav republic | 2 | 20 | 16 | 258 |
| Moldova | 2 | 10 | 19 | 181 |
| Poland | 9 | 463 | 118 | 2,688 |
| Romania | 6 | 447 | 63 | 2,251 |
| Russia | 25 | 1,289 | 152 | 4,818 |
| Slovakia | 4 | 121 | 37 | 952 |
| Slovenia | 1 | 181 | 25 | 588 |
| Tajikistan | 0 | 0 | 5 | 31 |
| Turkmenistan | 1 | 10 | 5 | 163 |
| Ukraine | 5 | 170 | 50 | 1,293 |
| Uzbekistan | 1 | 34 | 18 | 612 |
| Yugoslavia* | 10 | 135 | 15 | 366 |
| **Total** | 102 | 3,899 | 905 | 21,6467 |

Note: Operations may be counted as fractional numbers if multiple sub-loans are grouped under one framework agreement.
*Renamed Serbia and Montenegro in February 2003.

Source: EBRD, *Annual Report 2002*.

In 1997 the G-7, together with the European Community and Ukraine, endorsed the creation of the CSF-financed Chornobyl Unit 4 Shelter Implementation Plan (SIP) to assist Ukraine in stabilizing the protective sarcophagus covering the damaged Chornobyl (Chernobyl) reactor. The plan also provides for the construction of a new confinement structure to safely enclose the building, to be completed by 2007. In 1995 the G-7 requested that the Bank fund the completion of two new nuclear reactors in Ukraine, to provide alternative energy sources to the Chornobyl power-station. A study questioning the financial viability of the proposed reactors threatened funding in early 1997; a second survey, however, carried out by the EBRD, pronounced the plan viable, although environmental groups continued to dispute the proposals. In July 2000 donor countries committed additional funds to the SIP, raising the total pledged to €766m.

The funds have enabled the closure of nuclear plants for safety reasons in countries where this would otherwise have been prohibitively costly. In December 2000 Chornobyl unit 3 was closed, and in 2002 two units were closed in Bulgaria. The closure of a further two units in Bulgaria and units in Lithuania and the Slovak Republic are expected in the next few years. The NSA is also financing the construction of two major pre-decommissioning facilities in Ukraine, scheduled to be completed in 2003.

Throughout 2002 the EBRD was involved in negotiations over financing for the Baku-Tbilisi-Ceyhan (BTC) oil pipeline; a decision on this was expected by the end of 2003. Construction of the pipeline commenced in April of that year.

# Publications

*Annual Report.*

*EBRD Report to the Donor and Co-financing Community* (annually).

*Environments in Transition* (2 a year).

*Law in Transition* (2 a year).

*Transition Report* (annually).

# THE EUROPEAN UNION—EU*

## Permanent Missions to the European Union

### (October 2003)

**Armenia:** 157 rue Franz Merjay, 1050 Brussels, Belgium; tel. and fax (2) 346-56-67; fax (2) 346-56-67; e-mail armemel@wanadoo.be; internet www.armenian-embassy.be; Ambassador VIGEN TCHI-TETCHIAN.

**Azerbaijan:** 78 ave Gen. Lartigue, 1200 Brussels, Belgium; tel. (2) 735-98-80; fax (2) 735-92-70; e-mail azmissioneu@chello.be; Ambassador ARIF MAMEDOV.

**Georgia:** 58 ave Orban, 1150 Brussels, Belgium; tel. (2) 761-11-90; fax (2) 761-11-99; e-mail geoemb.bru@skynet.be; Ambassador KONSTANTIN ZALDASTANISHVILI.

**Kazakhstan:** 30 ave Van Bever, 1180 Brussels, Belgium; tel. (2) 374-95-62; fax (2) 374-50-91; e-mail kazakstan.embassy@linkline.be; Ambassador TULEUTAY SULEIMENOV.

**Kyrgyzstan:** 42 rue d'l'Abbaye, 1050 Brussels, Belgium; tel. (2) 640-18-68; fax (2) 640-01-31; e-mail aitmatov@infonie.be; Ambassador TCHINGUIZ AITMATOV.

**Russia:** 31–33 blvd du Régent, 1000 Brussels, Belgium; tel. (2) 502-18-55; fax (2) 513-76-49; e-mail misrusce@coditel.net; Ambassador Dr VASILY LIKHACHEV.

**Ukraine:** 799–101 ave Louis Lepoutre, 1180 Brussels, Belgium; tel. (2) 340-98-60; fax (2) 340-98-79; e-mail missionofukrainetoeu@unicall.be; internet www.ukraine-eu.mfa.gov.ua; Ambassador ROMAN SHPEK.

## Technical Assistance to the Commonwealth of Independent States—TACIS

In the late 1980s the extensive political changes and reforms in Eastern Europe led to a strengthening of links with the EC. In December 1989 EC heads of government agreed to establish a European Bank for Reconstruction and Development (EBRD, q.v.) to promote investment in Eastern Europe, with participation by member states of the Organisation for Economic Co-operation and Development (OECD) and the Council for Mutual Economic Assistance (CMEA), which provided economic co-operation and co-ordination in the Communist bloc between 1949 and 1991. The EBRD began operations in April 1991. In the same year the EC established the Technical Assistance to the Commonwealth of Independent States (TACIS) programme to assist in the development of successful market economies in the CIS and to foster pluralism and democracy, by providing expertise and training to the 12 CIS countries of the former USSR, as well as to the Baltic States of Estonia, Latvia and Lithuania. The Baltic States left the programme in 1992 (being eligible, instead, for assistance under the 'Operation PHARE' programme—Poland/Hungary Aid for Restructuring of Economies). In 1993 Mongolia became eligible for TACIS assistance. The TACIS/EBRD Bangkok Facility provides EU financing to assist in the preparation for, and implementation of, EBRD investment in the region.

Under TACIS indicative programmes lasting 3–4 years identify priorities for assistance in individual countries. Annual and biannual action programmes determine the projects to be supported and the funds to be used. In addition regional programmes and small projects programmes operate under the TACIS framework. During 1991–99 TACIS committed ECU 4,220.9m. to support transition in the former USSR and Mongolia, of which 20.2% was allocated for nuclear safety and the environment; 15.0% for the reform of education, public administration and social services; 14.1% for the restructuring of state enterprises and private-sector development; 9.0% for energy; 8.2% for agriculture and food; 8.0% for donor co-ordination; and 6.6% for transport. In January 1999 the European Commission agreed to divert ECU 20m. of TACIS funds to provide emergency assistance to eight countries affected by the Russian financial crisis of 1998. A new regulation providing the legal basis for TACIS over

the period 2000–06 was adopted in December 1999. The budget under the 2000–06 TACIS regulation was set at €3,138m., with emphasis placed on the promotion of democracy and the stimulation of investment in the region. The new regulation reduced the number of areas of potential co-operation. Each national or inter-state programme may focus on no more than three areas, which include institutional, legal and administrative reform; private-sector and economic development; environmental protection; rural economy; and nuclear safety. A TACIS Regional Co-operation Strategy Paper, adopted in December 2001, outlines a strategic framework for inter-state activities during 2002–06.

**PHARE and TACIS Information Centre:** rue Montoyer 19, 1000 Brussels, Belgium; tel. (2) 545-90-10; fax (2) 545-90-11; e-mail phare-tacis@cec.eu.int; internet http://europa.eu.int/comm/external_relations/ceeca/tacis/index.htm.

## Partnership and Co-operation Agreements

The EU has diplomatic relations with a number of countries in the region (see above). In 1992 EU heads of government decided to replace the agreement on trade and economic co-operation that had been concluded with the USSR in 1989 with new Partnership and Co-operation Agreements (PCAs), providing a framework for closer political, cultural and economic relations between the EU and the former republics of the USSR. The PCAs are preceded by preliminary Interim Agreements. An Interim Agreement with Russia on trade concessions came into effect in February 1996, giving EU exporters improved access to the Russian market for specific products, and at the same time abolishing quantitative restrictions on some Russian exports to the EU; a PCA with Russia came into effect in December 1997. In January 1998 the first meeting of the Co-operation Council for the EU–Russia PCA was held, and in July an EU–Russia Space Dialogue was established. In June 1999 the EU adopted a Common Strategy on Russia. This aimed to promote the consolidation of democracy and rule of law in the country; the integration of Russia into the common European economic and social space; and regional stability and security. At the sixth EU–Russia summit, held in October 2000, both parties agreed to initiate a regular energy dialogue, with the aim of establishing an EU–Russia Energy Partnership. The partnership would seek to improve relations in the field of energy and to pursue the opening and integration of energy markets. Improved investment would be sought for Russia, to upgrade infrastructure in the country and promote environmentally-friendly techniques. In May 2001 Russia agreed to consider a proposal by the President of the European Commission to use the euro, in place of the US dollar, as the instrument of trade between Russia and the EU. The ninth and 10th EU-Russia summit meetings were held, respectively, in May and November of that year, at which each party reconfirmed its commitment to democratic principles and human rights, and its determination to continue the fight against international terrorism, drugs-trafficking and illegal immigration. In May the EU announced that it was formally to grant Russia 'market economy status'. In November, *inter alia*, discussion centred on the issue of Kaliningrad, a Russian enclave between Poland and Lithuania, and its future status following the accession of those two countries to the EU. In the face of opposition from Russia, the EU insisted that residents of Kaliningrad would need a visa to cross EU territory; the matter was eventually resolved by a compromise agreement on a special multiple re-entry transit pass for residents of the enclave. At an EU-Russia summit meeting held in May 2003 it was agreed to launch a new strategic approach to EU-Russian relations. In this respect the decision was taken to strengthen the existing EU-Russia Co-operation Council and to redesignate it as a Permanent Partnership Council.

The EU's Northern Dimension programme covers the Baltic Sea, Arctic Sea and north-west Russia regions. It aims to address the specific challenges of these areas and to encourage co-operation with external states. The Northern Dimension programme operates within the framework of the EU–Russia PCA and the TACIS programme, as well as other agreements and financial instruments. An Action Plan for the Northern Dimension in the External and Cross-border Policies of the EU, covering the period 2000–03, was adopted in June 2000. The Plan detailed objectives in the following areas of co-operation: environmental protection; nuclear safety and nuclear waste management; energy; transport and border-crossing infra-structure; justice and internal affairs; business and investment; public health and social administration; telecommunications; and

---

*The European Union was formally established on 1 November 1993 under the Treaty on European Union; prior to this it was known as the European Community (EC).

human resources development. The first conference of Northern Dimension foreign ministers was held in Helsinki, Finland, in November 1999; a second foreign ministers' conference was convened in April 2001 and the third in August 2002. At a ministerial conference on the Northern Dimension held in October guide-lines were adopted for a second Action Plan for the Northern Dimension in the External and Cross-border Policies of the EU, covering the period 2004-2006. The second Action Plan, which was formally adopted in mid-2003, sets out strategic priorities and specific objectives in five priority areas: economy and infrastructure; social issues (including education, training and public health); environment, nuclear safety and natural resources; justice and home affairs; and cross-border co-operation.

In February 1994 the EU Council of Ministers agreed to pursue closer economic and political relations with Ukraine, following an agreement by that country to renounce control of nuclear weapons on its territory. In December EU ministers of finance approved a loan totalling ECU 85m., conditional on Ukraine's implementation of a strategy to close the Chornobyl (Chernobyl) nuclear power plant. An Interim Trade Agreement with Ukraine came into force in February 1996; this was replaced by a PCA in March 1998. In December 1999 the EU adopted a Common Strategy on Ukraine, aimed at developing a strategic partnership on the basis of the PCA. The Chornobyl plant closed in December 2000. The EU, through its Fuel Gap Programme, provided funding to cover the interim period prior to the completion of two new reactors (supported by the EBRD and the European Atomic Energy Community—Euratom) to replace the plant's generating capacity. The EU was also involved in social regeneration projects in the Chornobyl area.

An Interim Agreement with Belarus was signed in March 1996. However, in February 1997 the EU suspended negotiations for the conclusion of the Interim Agreement and a PCA, in view of serious reverses to the development of democracy in Belarus. EU technical assistance programmes were suspended, with the exception of aid programmes and those considered directly beneficial to the democratic process. Relations deteriorated further in June 1998, when the EU withdrew its ambassadors to Belarus after three EU diplomats were denied access to their residential compound by the state authorities; the ambassadors returned to Belarus in mid-January 1999. In 1999 the EU announced that the punitive measures would be withdrawn gradually upon the fulfilment of certain conditions. In 2000 the EU criticized the Belarus Government for failing to accept its recommendations on the conduct of legislative elections held in October. In September 2002 the EU condemned reported restrictions on the freedom of the media in Belarus, and in November the EU member states imposed a travel ban on President Alyaksandr Lukashenka of Belarus, as a protest against his authoritarian rule and the declining human rights situation in the country.

In May 1997 an Interim Agreement with Moldova entered into force; this was replaced by a PCA in July 1998. The first EU–Moldova Co-operation Council meeting was held in the same month in Brussels. Interim Agreements entered into force during 1997 with Kazakhstan (April), Georgia (September) and Armenia (December). An Interim Agreement with Azerbaijan entered into force in March 1999. A PCA with Turkmenistan was signed in May 1998 and an Interim Agreement with Uzbekistan entered into force in June. By the end of that year PCAs had been signed with all the countries of the CIS, except Tajikistan, owing to political instability in that country. All remaining Agreements had entered into force by 1 July 1999, with the exception of those negotiated with Belarus and Turkmenistan.

# Humanitarian Assistance

Assistance granted through the European Community Humanitarian Office (ECHO) for the new independent states of the former USSR totalled €40.5m. in 2002. ECHO was active in Armenia and Georgia (providing €2.5m.), and in Tajikistan (€10m.). In Russia and the North Caucasus ECHO provided aid totalling €28m., most of which was allocated to meet the basic needs of persons affected by the conflict in Chechnya (the Chechen Republic of Ichkeriya) or displaced in neighbouring republics.

# Regional Programmes

The TACIS programme incorporates a number of inter-state programmes. The budget for inter-state activities in 2001 included €23m. for a cross-border co-operation action programme covering Belarus, Russia, Moldova and Ukraine; €38m. for a regional action programme focusing on infrastructure networks, environment, and justice and internal affairs; €51m. for a nuclear safety programme covering Armenia, Russia and Ukraine; and €40m. for the Chornobyl (Chernobyl) Shelter Fund.

## TRANSPORT

The Transport Corridor Europe–Caucasus–Asia project (TRACECA, also referred to as the Silk Road project) was initiated in May 1993 to help to develop a transport and trade route from Central Asia to Europe, via the South Caucasus. In September 1998 the International Conference on the Revival of the Great Silk Road was held in Baku, Azerbaijan, at which it was agreed to base the secretariat of the finalized TRACECA programme in that country. The Secretariat was formally opened in February 2001. Initially covering the three South Caucasian states and the five Central Asian states of the former USSR, TRACECA extended its range in 1996 to include Moldova, Mongolia and Ukraine. By 2002 TRACECA had funded 39 technical assistance projects (totalling €57m.) and 14 investment projects (amounting to €52m.). Projects included the construction of the TRACECA Bridge, linking Azerbaijan and Georgia, which opened in June 1998; the re-opening of the Baku-Aktau road ferry service in 1999; and the inauguration of the Supsa oil terminal and ferry rail terminal in Georgia in 1999. The indicative budget for TRACECA in 2003 was €10m.

## ENERGY

The Interstate Oil and Gas Transport to Europe (INOGATE) programme aims to rehabilitate and modernize regional gas and petroleum transmission systems and to facilitate the transportation of hydrocarbons from the Caspian Sea region and Central Asia to European and Western markets. The first INOGATE meeting of senior ministers was held in 1995, in Brussels, where common issues on petroleum and gas in Central Asia were discussed. In 1997 INOGATE was allocated a five-year budget of ECU €50m. The indicative budget for INOGATE in 2003 was €2m. In February 1999 INOGATE drafted an Umbrella Agreement, setting out an institutional framework for co-operation and for the establishment of interstate oil and gas transport systems. The agreement had been signed by 21 states by February 2001. Under the TACIS Regional Co-operation Indicative Programme for 2000–03, the INOGATE programme was to focus on three priority areas in the short and medium terms: implementation of the Umbrella Agreement; development of existing energy networks; development of new strategic pipeline routes.

## NUCLEAR SAFETY

During 1991–96 the nuclear safety programme focused on the development of nuclear regulations, legislation and licensing arrangements, improved nuclear safety, and the restructuring of the sector, in particular in Ukraine. A Russian Methodological and Training Centre opened in November 1998. In that year a new programme of action for the nuclear sector, SURE, was adopted, focusing on the safe transportation of radioactive materials and the development of safeguards and industrial co-operation to promote the safety of nuclear installations. In January 2002 the EU adopted a Nuclear Safety Strategy Paper, which established a strategic framework for the allocation of assistance during 2002–06.

## ENVIRONMENT

At a meeting of ministers of the environment held in Sofia, Bulgaria, in 1995, it was agreed to establish a number of Regional Environment Centres (RECs). The first REC was established in Moldova in 1998, and has since been complemented by the establishment of a REC for the Caucasus (in Georgia), for Central Asia (in Kazakhstan), for Russia and for Ukraine. In 1999, in the third phase of development, the RECs became independent, non-profit-making organizations. A Joint Environment Programme aims to assist TACIS countries in the implementation of National Environmental Action Plans (NEAPs). All forms of technical assistance relating to the environment under TACIS are linked to these plans, which are drawn up by the governments of individual states. In addition, a Hazard Analysis Critical Control Point food-testing centre concentrates on environmental health and safety issues arising from industrial pollution, resulting, in particular, from the 1986 Chornobyl accident. It has provided assistance to Belarus, Russia and Ukraine. The TACIS Regional Sea Programme provides support for programmes in the Black Sea region, the Caspian Sea region and the Danube River Basin. Under the TACIS Indicative Programme 2002–03, €4m. was to be allocated for Caspian Sea programmes in 2002, and €3m. for Black Sea programmes in 2003.

## CROSS-BORDER CO-OPERATION

The Cross-border Co-operation (CBC) Programme was initiated in 1996 to fund co-operation between the newly independent states of Eastern Europe, Russia and Central Asia and the EU and Central Europe. The Programme's main objectives are to improve the efficiency of border controls; to facilitate local cross-border transit; to fund border crossings linking the EU, Central Europe and the newly independent states; to assist border regions in overcoming development problems; and to address trans-frontier environmental problems. Some 50 projects with a total value of €132.5m. were financed under CBC in 1996–2000. The indicative budget for CBC in 2003 was €10.8m.

## OTHER PROGRAMMES

The TACIS programme also works in the areas of telecommunications, to promote standardization and certification and, ultimately, to create an integrated European telecommunications network; and justice and home affairs, to combat drugs production and trafficking in Central Asia, strengthen the police force, improve border controls and combat money-laundering (the processing of illegally obtained funds into legitimate holdings). Other small project programmes include the Productivity Initiative Programme, the Managers' Training Programme and the European Senior Service Network, which provide training to increase efficiency in a market economy. The Joint Venture Programme aims to promote EU investment in the TACIS region, whereas the Link Inter European Non-governmental Organizations (NGOs) programme encourages co-operation between NGOs in EU and TACIS countries. TEMPUS (Trans-European Co-operation Scheme for Higher Education) assists in the provision of higher education in the region, linking institutions in participant countries and EU member states. There are additional programmes in the areas of customs co-operation, policy advice, the promotion of democracy, statistics and city twinning. An International Science and Technology Centre (ISTC) was established in March 1994 by the EU, Japan, Russia and the USA. The ISTC is jointly financed by the TACIS programme, Japan, the Republic of Korea, Norway and the USA. From November 1998 the EU has also co-operated with the Science and Technology Centre (SCTU) in Ukraine, founded in 1994 by Canada, Sweden, Ukraine and the USA. The centres aim to provide high-level work for scientists, in an effort to retain their skills and expertise within the region. In particular, the centres seek to encourage scientists who previously worked on Soviet weapons programmes to transfer their skills to other research.

# TACIS Co-ordinating Units

**Armenia:** 375010 Yerevan, Republic Sq., 1 Govt Bldg, Ministry of the Economy; tel. (2) 52-42-22; fax (2) 15-11-64; e-mail office@taciscu .airnet.am; Exec. Dir KORIUN DANIELIAN.

**Azerbaijan:** 370016 Baku, 8th Floor, Rm 851, Govt House; tel. (12) 93-95-14; fax (12) 93-76-38; e-mail jkasimov@eccu.baku.az.

**Belarus:** 220010 Minsk, Rm 115, Left Wing, Govt House; tel. (17) 276-80-61; fax (17) 227-26-15; e-mail orlov@tacis.open.by.

**Georgia:** 380004 Tbilisi, Chanturia St 12, Ministry of Economy; tel. (32) 98-85-37; fax (32) 98-84-37; e-mail cutacis@pop.kheta.ge.

**Kazakhstan:** 480083 Almaty, Rm 411, 4th Floor, 521 Seifullin St; tel. (3272) 50-76-10; fax (3272) 62-65-67; e-mail tacis.cu@asdc.kz.

**Kyrgyzstan:** 720040 Bishkek, 170 Sovietskayast; tel. (312) 22-57-89; fax (312) 62-01-21; e-mail root@tacis.bishkek.su.

**Moldova:** 2033 Chişinău, Piata Marii Aduranii Nationale 1, Rm 214–16, Ministry of Economy and Reforms, Govt Bldg; tel. (2) 23-74-58; fax (2) 23-41-43; e-mail tacisdm@moldova.md.

**Russian Federation:** 119898 Moscow, Smolenskaya bul. 3/5; tel. (095) 246-94-10; fax (095) 245-09-88; e-mail cutacis@online.ru.

**Tajikistan:** 734025 Dushanbe, pr. Rudaki 44–46, 2nd Floor, Office 103, Ministry of Agriculture; tel. (372) 221-26-09; fax (372) 221-01-00.

**Turkmenistan:** 744005 Ashgabat, ul. Kemine 92; tel. (12) 51-21-17; fax (12) 51-17-21; e-mail postmaster@taciscu.cat.glasnet.ru.

**Ukraine:** 252001 Kiev, ul. Mykhaylivska pl. 14; tel. (44) 228-30-26; fax (44) 230-25-13; e-mail postmaster@taciscu.glasnet.ru.

**Uzbekistan:** 700029 Tashkent, ul. Taras Shevchenko 4; tel. (71) 139-40-18; fax (712) 120-65-88; e-mail taciscu@tacis.uznet.uz.

# ISLAMIC DEVELOPMENT BANK

**Address:** POB 5925, Jeddah 21432, Saudi Arabia.

**Telephone:** (2) 6361400; **fax:** (2) 6366871; **e-mail:** idbarchives@isdb.org.sa; **internet:** www.isdb.org.

The Bank is an international financial institution that was established following a conference of Ministers of Finance of member countries of the Organization of the Islamic Conference (OIC), held in Jeddah in December 1973. Its aim is to encourage the economic development and social progress of member countries and of Muslim communities in non-member countries, in accordance with the principles of the Islamic *Shari'a* (sacred law). The Bank formally opened in October 1975.

## MEMBERS

There are 54 members.

# Organization

(October 2003)

## BOARD OF GOVERNORS

Each member country is represented by a governor, usually its Minister of Finance, and an alternate. The Board of Governors is the supreme authority of the Bank, and meets annually. The 28th Annual Meeting was held in Almaty, Kazakhstan, in September 2003.

## BOARD OF EXECUTIVE DIRECTORS

The Board consists of 14 members, seven of whom are appointed by the seven largest subscribers to the capital stock of the Bank; the remaining seven are elected by Governors representing the other subscribers. Members of the Board of Executive Directors are elected for three-year terms. The Board is responsible for the direction of the general operations of the Bank.

## ADMINISTRATION

In addition to the President of the Bank, there are three Vice-Presidents, responsible for Operations, Trade and Policy, and Finance and Administration.

**President of the Bank and Chairman of the Board of Executive Directors:** Dr AHMED MOHAMED ALI.

**Vice-President Operations:** Dr AMADOU BOUBACAR CISSE.

**Vice-President Trade and Policy:** Dr SYED JAAFAR AZNAN.

**Vice-President Finance and Administration:** MUZAFAR AL HAJ MUZAFAR.

## REGIONAL OFFICES

**Kazakhstan:** c/o Director, External Aid Co-ordination Dept, 93–95 Ablay-Khan Ave, 480091 Almaty; tel. (3272) 62-18-68; fax (3272) 69-61-52; Dir ZEINAL ABIDIN.

**Malaysia:** Level 11, Front Wing, Bank Industri, Jalan Sultan Ismail, POB 13671, 50818 Kuala Lumpur; tel. (3) 2946627; fax (3) 2946626; Dir SALEH AMRAN BIN JAMAN (acting).

**Morocco:** 177 Ave John Kennedy, Souissi 10105, POB 5003, Rabat; tel. (7) 757191; fax (7) 775726; Dir HANI SALIM SUNBUL.

## FINANCIAL STRUCTURE

The authorized capital of the Bank is 6,000m. Islamic Dinars (divided into 600,000 shares, having a value of 10,000 Islamic Dinars each). The Islamic Dinar (ID) is the Bank's unit of account and is equivalent to the value of one Special Drawing Right of the IMF (SDR 1 = US \$1.43686 at 10 October 2003).

Subscribed capital amounts to ID 4,000m.

## SUBSCRIPTIONS*
(million Islamic Dinars, as at 5 April 2000)

| | | | |
|---|---|---|---|
| Afghanistan . . . | 5.00 | The Maldives . . | 2.50 |
| Albania . . . . | 2.50 | Mali . . . . | 4.92 |
| Algeria . . . . | 124.26 | Mauritania . . . | 4.92 |
| Azerbaijan . . . | 4.92 | Morocco . . . . | 24.81 |
| Bahrain . . . . | 7.00 | Mozambique . . | 2.50 |
| Bangladesh . . . | 49.29 | Niger . . . . | 12.41 |
| Benin . . . . | 4.92 | Oman . . . . | 13.78 |
| Brunei . . . . | 12.41 | Pakistan . . . . | 124.26 |
| Burkina Faso . . | 12.41 | Palestine . . . | 9.85 |
| Cameroon . . . | 12.41 | Qatar . . . . | 49.23 |
| Chad . . . . | 4.92 | Saudi Arabia . . | 997.17 |
| Comoros . . . | 2.50 | Senegal . . . | 12.42 |
| Djibouti . . . | 2.50 | Sierra Leone . . | 2.50 |
| Egypt . . . . | 346.00 | Somalia . . . | 2.50 |
| Gabon . . . . | 14.77 | Sudan . . . . | 19.69 |
| The Gambia . . | 2.50 | Suriname . . . | 2.50 |
| Guinea . . . . | 12.41 | Syria . . . . | 5.00 |
| Guinea-Bissau . . | 2.50 | Tajikistan . . | 2.50 |
| Indonesia . . . | 124.26 | Togo . . . . | 2.50 |
| Iran . . . . | 349.97 | Tunisia . . . | 9.85 |
| Iraq . . . . | 13.05 | Turkey . . . . | 315.47 |
| Jordan . . . . | 19.89 | Turkmenistan . . | 2.50 |
| Kazakhstan . . . | 2.50 | Uganda . . . | 12.41 |
| Kuwait . . . . | 496.64 | United Arab | |
| Kyrgyzstan . . . | 2.50 | Emirates . . . . | 283.03 |
| Lebanon . . . | 4.92 | Yemen . . . . | 24.81 |
| Libya . . . . | 400.00 | | |
| Malaysia . . . | 79.56 | **Total** | 4,060.54 |

* Côte d'Ivoire became a member of the Bank after this date.

# Activities

The Bank adheres to the Islamic principle forbidding usury, and does not grant loans or credits for interest. Instead, its methods of project financing are: provision of interest-free loans (with a service fee), mainly for infrastructural projects which are expected to have a marked impact on long-term socio-economic development; provision of technical assistance (e.g. for feasibility studies); equity participation in industrial and agricultural projects; leasing operations, involving the leasing of equipment such as ships, and instalment sale financing; and profit-sharing operations. Funds not immediately needed for projects are used for foreign trade financing. Under the Import Trade Financing Operations (ITFO) scheme, funds are used for importing commodities for development purposes (i.e. raw materials and intermediate industrial goods, rather than consumer goods), with priority given to the import of goods from other member countries (see table). The Longer-term Trade Financing Scheme (LTTFS) was introduced in 1987/88 to provide financing for the export of non-traditional and capital goods. During AH 1419 the LTTFS was renamed the Export Financing Scheme (EFS). A special programme under the EFS became operational in AH 1419, on the basis of a memorandum of understanding signed between the Bank and the Arab Bank for Economic Development in Africa (BADEA), to finance Arab exports to non-Arab League members of the OAU (now African Union).

The Bank's Special Assistance programme was initiated in AH 1400 to support the economic and social development of Muslim communities in non-member countries, in particular in the education and health sectors. It also aimed to provide emergency aid in times of natural disasters, and to assist Muslim refugees throughout the world. Operations undertaken by the Bank are financed by the Waqf Fund (formerly the Special Assistance Account). Other assistance activities include scholarship programmes, technical co-operation projects and the sacrificial meat utilization project.

By 5 April 2000 the Bank had approved a total of ID 4,947.98m. for project financing and technical assistance, a total of ID 11,125.24m. for foreign trade financing, and ID 402.59m. for special assistance operations, excluding amounts for cancelled operations. During the Islamic year 1420 (17 April 1999 to 5 April 2000) the Bank approved a total of ID 1,522.80m., for 230 operations.

The Bank approved 39 loans in the year ending 5 April 2000, amounting to ID 179.70m. (compared with 38 loans, totalling ID 159.79m., in the previous year). These loans supported projects concerned with the construction and modernization of schools and health centres, infrastructural improvements, and agricultural developments. During the year ending 5 April 2000 the Bank's disbursements totalled ID 871m., bringing the total cumulative disbursements since the Bank began operations to ID 11,010m.

## Operations approved, Islamic year 1420
(17 April 1999–5 April 2000)

| Type of operation | Number of operations | Total amount (million Islamic Dinars) |
|---|---|---|
| Ordinary operations . . . . | 112 | 725.49 |
| Project financing . . . | 77 | 718.31 |
| Technical assistance . . . | 35 | 7.19 |
| Trade financing operations* . . | 64 | 805.85 |
| Waqf Fund operations . . . | 54 | 21.46 |
| **Total** † . . . . . . . . | 230 | 1,522.80 |

* Including ITFO, the EFS, the Islamic Bank's Portfolio and the UIF.
† Excluding cancelled operations.

## Project financing and technical assistance by sector, Islamic year 1420
(17 April 1999–5 April 2000)

| Sector | Number of operations | Amount (million Islamic Dinars) | % |
|---|---|---|---|
| Agriculture and agro-industry . . . . . | 18 | 87.51 | 12.1 |
| Industry and mining . . | 4 | 71.40 | 9.8 |
| Transport and communications . . . | 17 | 99.25 | 13.7 |
| Public utilities . . . . | 18 | 222.18 | 30.6 |
| Social sectors . . . . . | 39 | 183.74 | 25.3 |
| Financial services/Other* . | 16 | 61.41 | 8.5 |
| **Total** † . . . . . . | 112 | 725.49 | 100.0 |

* Mainly approved amounts for Islamic banks.
† Excluding cancelled operations.

During AH 1420 the Bank approved 35 technical assistance operations for 19 countries (as well as six regional projects) in the form of grants and loans, amounting to ID 7.19m.

Import trade financing approved during the Islamic year 1420 amounted to ID 651.34m. for 39 operations in 12 member countries. By the end of that year cumulative import trade financing amounted to ID 9,480.37m., of which 37.4% was for imports of crude petroleum, 26.4% for intermediate industrial goods, 7.5% for vegetable oil and 6.4% for refined petroleum products. Export financing approved under the EFS amounted to ID 61.32m. for 15 operations in nine countries in AH 1420. In the same year the Bank's Portfolio for Investment and Development, established in AH 1407 (1986–87), approved eight operations amounting to US $106.6m. (or approximately ID 79.1m.). Since its introduction, the Portfolio has approved net financing operations amounting to $1,490.1m. (or ID 1,106.0m.).

The Bank's Unit Investment Fund (UIF) became operational in 1990, with the aim of mobilizing additional resources and providing a profitable channel for investments conforming to *Shari'a*. The initial issue of the UIF was US $100m., which has subsequently been increased to $325m. The Fund finances mainly private-sector industrial projects in middle-income countries. The UIF also finances short-term trade financing operations: two were approved in AH 1420, amounting to $19.0m. In October 1998 the Bank announced the establishment of a new fund to invest in infrastructure projects in member states. The Bank committed $250m. to the fund, which was to comprise $1,000m. equity capital and a $500m. Islamic financing facility. In September 1999 the Bank's Board of Executive Directors approved the establishment of an Islamic Corporation for the Development of the Private Sector, which aimed to identify opportunities in the private sector, provide financial products and services compatible with Islamic law, and expand access to Islamic capital markets for private companies in member countries. The Bank was to retain 50% of the authorized capital of $1,000m., with the remainder owned by member countries (30%) and public financial institutions (20%). In November 2001 the Bank signed an agreement with Malaysia, Bahrain, Indonesia and Sudan for the establishment of an Islamic financial market. In April 2002 the Bank, jointly with governors of central banks and the Accounting and Auditing Organization for Islamic Financial Institutions, concluded an agreement, under the auspices of the IMF, for the establishment of an Islamic Financial Services Board. The Board, which was to be located in Kuala Lumpur, Malaysia, was intended to elaborate and harmonize standards for best practices in the regulation and supervision of the Islamic financial services industry.

During AH 1420 the Bank approved 54 Waqf Fund operations, amounting to ID 21.5m. Of the total financing, 28 operations provided assistance for Muslim communities in 18 non-member countries.

By the end of AH 1420 the Bank's scholarships programme for Muslim communities in non-member countries had benefited some 5,343 students, at a cost of ID 27m., since it began in 1983. The Merit Scholarship Programme, initiated in AH 1412 (1991–92), aims to develop scientific, technological and research capacities in member countries through advanced studies and/or research. During the second five-year phase of the initiative, which commenced in January 1997, 20 scholars each year were expected to be placed in academic centres of excellence in Australia, Europe and the USA under the programme. In December 1997 the Board of Executive Directors approved a new scholarship programme designed specifically to assist scholars from 18 least-developed member countries to study for a masters degree in science and technology. A total of 190 scholarships were expected to have been awarded by AH 1423. The Bank's Programme for Technical Co-operation aims to mobilize technical capabilities among member countries and to promote the exchange of expertise, experience and skills through expert missions, training, seminars and workshops. During AH 1420 74 projects were implemented under the programme. The Bank also undertakes the distribution of meat sacrificed by Muslim pilgrims: in AH 1420 meat from approximately 416,699 animals was distributed to the needy in 26 countries.

## SUBSIDIARY ORGANS

**Islamic Corporation for the Insurance of Investment and Export Credit (ICIEC):** POB 15722, Jeddah 21454, Saudi Arabia; tel. (2) 6445666; fax (2) 6379504; e-mail idb.iciec@isdb.org.sa; internet www.iciec.org; f. 1994; aims to promote trade and the flow of investments among member countries of the OIC through the provision of export credit and investment insurance services; auth. cap. ID 100m., subscribed cap. ID 95.0m. (March 2001); Man. Dr ABDEL RAHMAN A. TAHA; Mems: 29 OIC member states.

**Islamic Research and Training Institute:** POB 9201, Jeddah 21413, Saudi Arabia; tel. (2) 6361400; fax (2) 6378927; e-mail maljarhi@isdb.org.sa; internet www.irti.org; f. 1982 to undertake research enabling economic, financial and banking activities to conform to Islamic law, and to provide training for staff involved in development activities in the Bank's member countries; the Institute also organizes seminars and workshops, and holds training courses aimed at furthering the expertise of government and financial officials in Islamic developing countries; Dir Dr MABID ALI AL-JARHI; publs *Annual Report*, *Journal of Islamic Economic Studies*, various research studies, monographs, reports.

## Publication

*Annual Report*.

# NORTH ATLANTIC TREATY ORGANIZATION—NATO

**Address:** blvd Léopold III, 1110 Brussels, Belgium.
**Telephone:** (2) 707-41-11; **fax:** (2) 707-45-79; **e-mail:** natodoc@hq.nato.int; **internet:** www.nato.int.

The Atlantic Alliance was established on the basis of the 1949 North Atlantic Treaty as a defensive political and military alliance of a group of European states (then numbering 10) and the USA and Canada. The Alliance aims to provide common security for its members through co-operation and consultation in political, military and economic fields, as well as scientific, environmental and other non-military aspects. The objectives of the Alliance are implemented by NATO. Following the collapse of the communist governments in Central and Eastern Europe, from 1989, and the dissolution of the Warsaw Treaty of Friendship, Co-operation and Mutual Assistance (the Warsaw Pact), which had hitherto been regarded as the Alliance's principal adversary, in 1991, NATO has undertaken a fundamental transformation of its structures and policies to meet the new security challenges in Europe. NATO partner countries (of which there were 27 in 2003) are represented by heads of diplomatic missions or liaison officers, located at NATO headquarters.

### HEADS OF MISSIONS AND LIAISON OFFICERS
(at October 2003)

**Armenia:** VIGUEN TCHITETCHIAN.
**Azerbaijan:** MIR-GAMZA EFENDIYEV.
**Belarus:** IGOR FISSENKO (Chargé d'affaires).
**Georgia:** DAVID DONDUA.
**Kazakhstan:** TULELLTAI SULEIMENOV.
**Kyrgyzstan:** TCHINGUIZ AITMATOV.
**Moldova:** MIHAI POPOV.
**Russian Federation:** KONSTANTIN V. TOTSKIY.
**Tajikistan:** SHARIF RAKHIMOV.
**Turkmenistan:** NIYAZKLYCH NURKLYCHEV.
**Ukraine:** VOLODYMYR KHANDOGIY.
**Uzbekistan:** ALISHER SHAYKHOV (acting).

## Regional Relations

At a summit meeting of the Conference on Security and Co-operation in Europe (CSCE, now renamed as the Organization for Security and Co-operation in Europe—OSCE) in November 1990, the member countries of NATO and the Warsaw Pact signed an agreement limiting Conventional Armed Forces in Europe (CFE), whereby conventional arms would be reduced to within a common upper limit in each zone. The two groups also issued a Joint Declaration, stating

that they were no longer adversaries and that none of their weapons would ever be used 'except in self-defence'. Following the dissolution of the USSR in December 1991, the eight former Soviet republics with territory in the area of application of the CFE Treaty committed themselves to honouring its obligations in June 1992. The Treaty entered retroactively into full force from 17 July (Armenia was unable to ratify it until the end of July, and Belarus until the end of October). In March 1992, under the auspices of the CSCE, the ministers of foreign affairs of the NATO and of the former Warsaw Pact countries (with Belarus, Georgia, Russia and Ukraine taking the place of the USSR) signed the 'Open Skies' treaty. Under this treaty, aerial reconnaissance missions by one country over another were to be permitted, subject to regulation. At the summit meeting of the OSCE in December 1996 the signatories of the CFE Treaty agreed to begin negotiations on a revised treaty governing conventional weapons in Europe. In July 1997 the CFE signatories concluded an agreement on Certain Basic Elements for Treaty Adaptation, which provided for substantial reductions in the maximum levels of conventional military equipment at national and territorial level, replacing the previous bloc-to-bloc structure of the Treaty.

An extensive review of NATO's structures was initiated in June 1990, in response to the fundamental changes taking place in Central and Eastern Europe. In November 1991 NATO heads of government, convened in Rome, Italy, recommended a radical restructuring of the Organization in order to meet the demands of the new security environment, which was to involve further reductions in military forces in Europe, active involvement in international peace-keeping operations, increased co-operation with other international institutions and close co-operation with its former adversaries, the USSR and the countries of Eastern Europe. The basis for NATO's new force structure was incorporated into a new Strategic Concept, which was adopted in the Rome Declaration issuing from the summit meeting. The concept provided for the maintenance of a collective defence capability, with a reduced dependence on nuclear weapons. Substantial reductions in the size and levels of readiness of NATO forces were undertaken, in order to reflect the Alliance's strictly defensive nature, and forces were reorganized within a streamlined integrated command structure. A new Strategic Concept, which confirmed NATO to be the principal generator of security in the Euro-Atlantic area, was approved at a special summit meeting, convened in Washington, USA, in April 1999, to commemorate the 50th anniversary of the Alliance. A separate initiative was approved to assist member states to adapt their defence capabilities to meet changing security requirements, for example improving the means of troop deployment and equipping and protecting forces.

The enlargement of NATO, through the admission of new members from the former USSR and Eastern and Central European countries, was considered to be a progressive means of contributing to the enhanced stability and security of the Euro-Atlantic area. In December 1996 NATO ministers of foreign affairs announced that invitations to join the Alliance would be issued to some former Eastern bloc countries during 1997. The NATO Secretary-General and member governments subsequently began intensive diplomatic efforts to secure Russia's tolerance of these developments. It was agreed that no nuclear weapons or large numbers of troops would be deployed on the territory of any new member country in the former Eastern bloc. In May NATO and Russia signed the Founding Act on Mutual Relations, Co-operation and Security, which provided for enhanced Russian participation in all NATO decision-making activities, equal status in peace-keeping operations and representation at the Alliance headquarters at ambassadorial level, as part of a recognized shared political commitment to maintaining stability and security throughout the Euro-Atlantic region. A NATO-Russian Permanent Joint Council (PJC) was established under the Founding Act, and met for the first time in July; the Council provided each side the opportunity for consultation and participation in the other's security decisions, but without a right of veto. In March 1999 the Czech Republic, Hungary and Poland became members of NATO. In the following month the NATO summit meeting, held in Washington, DC (USA), initiated a new Membership Action Plan to extend practical support to aspirant member countries and to formalize a process of reviewing applications. In March 2003 protocols of accession, amending the North Atlantic Treaty, were adopted by the 19 NATO member states with a view to admitting Bulgaria, Estonia, Latvia, Lithuania, Romania, Slovakia and Slovenia to the organization in May 2004.

In March 1999, as the result of escalating tensions in the Serbian province of Kosovo and Metahija, between the Kosovo Liberation Army and Serbian security forces, and the failure of intensive diplomatic efforts to implement a political settlement, NATO initiated an aerial offensive against the Federal Republic of Yugoslavia (FRY, now Serbia and Montenegro). Russia, which was pursuing diplomatic efforts to secure a peaceful resolution of the conflict, condemned the military action and announced the suspension of all relations within the framework of the Founding Act, as well as negotiations on the establishment of a NATO mission in Moscow. The airstrike campaign was finally suspended in June, following the signature of a Military Technical Agreement between NATO and the FRY, and a UN-authorized international security presence under NATO, the Kosovo Peace Implementation Force (KFOR), entered the province. An agreement was subsequently concluded with Russia, which had also sent troops to Kosovo and taken control of Priština airport, providing for the joint responsibility of the airstrip with a NATO contingent and for participation of Russian troops in KFOR. The NATO force was demilitarized in September.

In May 1997 NATO ministers of foreign affairs, meeting in Sintra, Portugal, concluded an agreement with Ukraine providing for enhanced co-operation between the two sides; the so-called Charter on a Distinctive Relationship was signed at the NATO summit meeting held in Madrid, Spain, in July. In May 1998 NATO agreed to appoint a permanent liaison officer in Ukraine to enhance co-operation between the two sides and assist Ukraine to formulate a programme of joint military exercises. The first NATO-Ukraine meeting at the level of heads of state took place in April 1999. A NATO-Ukraine Commission met for the first time in March 2000.

### EURO–ATLANTIC PARTNERSHIP COUNCIL (EAPC)

The EAPC was inaugurated on 30 May 1997 as a successor to the North Atlantic Co-operation Council (NACC), which had been established in December 1991 to provide a forum for consultation on political and security matters with the countries of Central and Eastern Europe, including the former Soviet republics. The Partnership for Peace (PfP) programme, which was established in January

1994 within the framework of the NACC, was to remain an integral element of the new co-operative mechanism, incorporating practical military and defence-related co-operation activities that had originally been part of the NACC Work Plan. In June 1994 Russia, which had previously opposed the strategy as being the basis for future enlargement of NATO, signed the PfP framework document, which included a declaration envisaging an 'enhanced dialogue' between the two sides. Despite its continuing opposition to any enlargement of NATO, in May 1995 Russia agreed to sign a PfP Individual Partnership Programme, as well as a framework document for NATO-Russian dialogue and co-operation beyond the PfP. During 1994 a Partnership Co-ordination Cell (PCC), incorporating representatives of all partnership countries, became operational in Mons, Belgium. The PCC, under the authority of the North Atlantic Council (NAC), aims to co-ordinate joint military activities and planning in order to implement PfP programmes. The first joint military exercises with countries of the former Warsaw Pact were conducted in September. In December 1997 NATO ministers of foreign affairs approved the establishment of a Euro-Atlantic Disaster Response Co-ordination Centre (EDRCC), and a non-permanent Euro-Atlantic Disaster Response Unit. The EDRCC was inaugurated in June 1998. During 2000 *ad hoc* working groups were convened to consider EAPC involvement in global humanitarian action against mines, addressing the challenge of small arms and light weapons, and prospects for regional co-operation in South-Eastern Europe and in the Caucasus. The EAPC Action Plan for 2002–04 aimed to promote new approaches to co-operation in the combating of international terrorism.

In September 2001 the EAPC condemned major terrorist attacks against targets in the USA, allegedly perpetrated by militant Islamist fundamentalists. Meanwhile the NAC, for the first time in the history of the Organization, invoked Article 5 of the founding treaty, concerning collective self-defence, which stipulates that an armed attack against one NATO member on European or North American territory is considered as an attack against all the allies. In December NATO ministers of defence initiated a review of military capabilities and defences with a view to strengthening the Organization's ability to counter international terrorism.

### NATO-RUSSIA COUNCIL

In December 2001 an agreement was concluded by NATO ministers of foreign affairs and their Russian counterpart to establish a successor body to the Permanent Joint Council (PJC), with a greater decision-making role. The NATO-Russia Council, which replaced the PJC, was inaugurated in May 2002 at a meeting of heads of state and of government. The Council was to provide a framework for consultation, consensus-building, co-operation, joint decisions and joint actions on a range of issues of common interest, with NATO member states and Russia working as equal partners. The Council was to meet at ambassadorial level each month, and at the level of ministers of foreign affairs and of defence twice a year. The following were identified as priority areas for co-operation: measures to combat terrorism, including joint assessments of specific terrorist threats; crisis management; non-proliferation of weapons of mass destruction and other arms control and confidence-building measures; consideration of theatre missile defence; search and rescue at sea; enhanced military-to-military co-operation and defence reform; and a strengthened joint approach to civil emergencies. In October a joint NATO-Russia conference, focusing on aspects of defence reform, was held at the NATO Defense College in Rome, Italy.

**NATO Information Office in Moscow:** 1174049 Moscow, ul. Mytnaya 3, Russia; tel. (095) 937-36-40; fax (095) 937-38-09; e-mail office@nio-moscow.nato.int; opened Feb. 2001.

# ORGANIZATION FOR SECURITY AND CO-OPERATION IN EUROPE—OSCE

**Address:** 1010 Vienna, Kärntner Ring 5–7, Austria.

**Telephone:** (1) 514-36-180; **fax:** (1) 514-36-105; **e-mail:** info@osce .org; **internet:** www.osce.org.

The OSCE was established in 1972 as the Conference on Security and Co-operation in Europe (CSCE), providing a multilateral forum for dialogue and negotiation. It produced the Helsinki Final Act of

1975 on East–West relations (see below). The areas of competence of the CSCE were expanded by the Charter of Paris for a New Europe (1990), which transformed the CSCE from an *ad hoc* forum to an organization with permanent institutions, and the Helsinki Document 1992 (see 'Activities'). In December 1994 the summit conference adopted the new name of OSCE, in order to reflect the Organization's changing political role and strengthened secretariat.

## PARTICIPATING STATES

| | | |
|---|---|---|
| Albania | Greece | Romania |
| Andorra | Hungary | Russia |
| Armenia | Iceland | Serbia and |
| Austria | Ireland | Montenegro |
| Azerbaijan | Italy | Slovakia |
| Belarus | Kazakhstan | Slovenia |
| Belgium | Kyrgyzstan | Spain |
| Bosnia and | Latvia | Sweden |
| Herzegovina | Liechtenstein | Switzerland |
| Bulgaria | Lithuania | Tajikistan |
| Canada | Luxembourg | Turkey |
| Croatia | Macedonia, former | Turkmenistan |
| Cyprus | Yugoslav republic | Ukraine |
| Czech Republic | Malta | United Kingdom |
| Denmark | Moldova | USA |
| Estonia | Monaco | Uzbekistan |
| Finland | Netherlands | Vatican City (Holy |
| France | Norway | See) |
| Georgia | Poland | |
| Germany | Portugal | |

# Organization

(October 2003)

## SUMMIT CONFERENCES

Heads of state or government of OSCE participating states normally meet every two to three years to set priorities and political orientation of the Organization. The most recent conference was held in İstanbul, Turkey, in November 1999.

## MINISTERIAL COUNCIL

The Ministerial Council (formerly the Council of Foreign Ministers) comprises ministers of foreign affairs of member states. It is the central decision-making and governing body of the OSCE and meets every year in which no summit conference is held.

## SENIOR COUNCIL

The Senior Council (formerly the Council of Senior Officials—CSO) is responsible for the supervision, management and co-ordination of OSCE activities. Member states are represented by senior political officers, who convene at least twice a year in Prague, Czech Republic, and once a year as the Economic Forum.

## PERMANENT COUNCIL

The Council, which is based in Vienna, is responsible for day-to-day operational tasks. Members of the Council, comprising the permanent representatives of member states to the OSCE, convene weekly. The Council is the regular body for political consultation and decision-making, and may be convened for emergency purposes.

## FORUM FOR SECURITY CO-OPERATION—FSC

The FSC, comprising representatives of delegations of member states, meets weekly in Vienna to negotiate and consult on measures aimed at strengthening security and stability throughout Europe. Its main objectives are negotiations on arms control, disarmament, and confidence- and security-building; regular consultations and intensive co-operation on matters related to security; and the further reduction of the risks of conflict. The FSC is also responsible for the implementation of confidence- and security-building measures (CSBMs); the preparation of seminars on military doctrine; the holding of annual implementation assessment meetings; and the provision of a forum for the discussion and clarification of information exchanged under agreed CSBMs.

## CHAIRMAN-IN-OFFICE—CIO

The CIO is vested with overall responsibility for executive action. The position is held by a minister of foreign affairs of a member state for a one-year term. The CIO may be assisted by a troika, consisting of the preceding, current and succeeding chairpersons; *ad hoc* steering groups; or personal representatives, who are appointed by the CIO with a clear and precise mandate to assist the CIO in dealing with a crisis or conflict.

**Chairman-in-Office:** JAAP DE HOOP SCHEFFER (Netherlands) (2003).

## SECRETARIAT

The Secretariat comprises two principal departments: the Conflict Prevention Centre (including an Operations Centre), which focuses on the support of the CIO in the implementation of OSCE policies, in particular the monitoring of field activities and co-operation with other international bodies; and the Department of Management and Finance, responsible for technical and administrative support activities. The OSCE maintains an office in Prague, Czech Republic, which assists with documentation and information activities, and a centre in Tashkent, Uzbekistan.

The position of Secretary-General was established in December 1992 and the first appointment to the position was made in June 1993. The Secretary-General is appointed by the Ministerial Council for a three-year term of office. The Secretary-General is the representative of the CIO and is responsible for the management of OSCE structures and operations.

**Secretary-General:** JÁN KUBIŠ (Slovakia).

**Co-ordinator of OSCE Economic and Environmental Activities:** MARCIN SWIECICKI (Poland).

## HIGH COMMISSIONER ON NATIONAL MINORITIES

POB 20062, 2500 EB The Hague, Netherlands; tel. (70) 3125500; fax (70) 3635910; e-mail hcnm@hcnm.org; internet www.osce.org/hcnm.

The establishment of the office of High Commissioner on National Minorities was proposed in the 1992 Helsinki Document, and endorsed by the Council of Foreign Ministers in Stockholm, Sweden in December 1992. The role of the High Commissioner is to identify ethnic tensions that might endanger peace, stability or relations between OSCE participating states, and to promote their early resolution. The High Commissioner may issue an 'early warning' for the attention of the Senior Council of an area of tension likely to degenerate into conflict. The High Commissioner is appointed by the Ministerial Council, on the recommendation of the Senior Council, for a three-year term.

**High Commissioner:** ROLF EKÉUS (Sweden).

## OFFICE FOR DEMOCRATIC INSTITUTIONS AND HUMAN RIGHTS—ODIHR

Aleje Ujazdowskie 19, 00-557 Warsaw, Poland; tel. (22) 520-06-00; fax (22) 520-06-05; e-mail office@odihr.pl; internet www.osce.org.odihr.

Established in July 1999, the ODIHR has responsibility for promoting human rights, democracy and the rule of law. The Office provides a framework for the exchange of information on and the promotion of democracy-building, respect for human rights and elections within OSCE states. In addition, it co-ordinates the monitoring of elections and provides expertise and training on constitutional and legal matters.

**Director:** CHRISTIAN STROHAL (Switzerland).

## OFFICE OF THE REPRESENTATIVE ON FREEDOM OF THE MEDIA

Kärntner Ring 5–7, 1010 Vienna, Austria; tel. (1) 512-21-450; fax (1) 512-21-459; e-mail pm-fom@osce.org; internet www.osce.org/fom.

The office was founded in 1998 to strengthen the implementation of OSCE commitments regarding free, independent and pluralistic media.

**Representative:** FREIMUT DUVE (Germany).

## PARLIAMENTARY ASSEMBLY

Rädhusstraede 1, 1466 Copenhagen K, Denmark; tel. 33-37-80-40; fax 33-37-80-30; e-mail osce@oscepa.dk; internet www.osce.org/pa.

The OSCE Parliamentary Assembly, which is composed of 317 parliamentarians from 55 participating countries, was inaugurated in July 1992, and meets annually. The Assembly comprises a Standing Committee, a Bureau and three General Committees and is supported by a Secretariat in Copenhagen, Denmark.

**President:** BRUCE GEORGE (United Kingdom).

**Secretary-General:** R. SPENCER OLIVER (USA).

# OSCE Related Bodies

## COURT OF CONCILIATION AND ARBITRATION

266 route de Lausanne, 1292 Chambésy, Geneva, Switzerland; tel. (22) 7580025; fax (22) 7582510; e-mail cca.osce@bluewin.ch.

The establishment of the Court of Conciliation and Arbitration was agreed in 1992 and effected in 1994. OSCE states that have ratified the OSCE Convention on Conciliation and Arbitration may submit a dispute to the Court for settlement by the Arbitral Tribunal or the Conciliation Commission.

**President:** ROBERT BADINTER.

## JOINT CONSULTATIVE GROUP—JCG

The states that are party to the Treaty on Conventional Armed Forces in Europe (CFE), which was concluded within the CSCE framework in 1990, established the Joint Consultative Group (JCG). The JCG, which meets in Vienna, addresses questions relating to compliance with the Treaty; enhancement of the effectiveness of the Treaty; technical aspects of the Treaty's implementation; and disputes arising out of its implementation. There are currently 30 states participating in the JCG.

### OPEN SKIES CONSULTATIVE COMMISSION

The Commission represents all states parties to the 1992 Treaty on Open Skies, and promotes its implementation. Its regular meetings are serviced by the OSCE secretariat.

# Activities

In July 1990 heads of government of the member countries of the North Atlantic Treaty Organization (NATO) proposed to increase the role of the CSCE 'to provide a forum for wider political dialogue in a more united Europe'. The Charter of Paris for a New Europe, which undertook to strengthen pluralist democracy and observance of human rights, and to settle disputes between participating states by peaceful means, was signed in November. At the summit meeting the Treaty on Conventional Armed Forces in Europe (CFE), which had been negotiated within the framework of the CSCE, was signed by the member states of NATO and of the Warsaw Pact. The Treaty limits non-nuclear air and ground armaments in the signatory countries. In April 1991 parliamentarians from the CSCE countries agreed on the creation of a pan-European parliamentary assembly. Its first session was held in Budapest, Hungary, in July 1992.

The Council of Foreign Ministers met for the first time in Berlin, Germany, in June 1991. The meeting adopted a mechanism for consultation and co-operation in the case of emergency situations, to be implemented by the Council of Senior Officials (CSO, which was subsequently renamed the Senior Council). A separate mechanism regarding the prevention of the outbreak of conflict was also adopted, whereby a country can demand an explanation of 'unusual military activity' in a neighbouring country. These mechanisms were utilized in July in relation to the armed conflict in Yugoslavia between the Republic of Croatia and the Yugoslav Government. In mid-August a meeting of the CSO resolved to reinforce considerably the CSCE's mission in Yugoslavia and in September the CSO agreed to impose an embargo on the export of armaments to Yugoslavia. In October the CSO resolved to establish an observer mission to monitor the observance of human rights in Yugoslavia.

In January 1992 the Council of Foreign Ministers agreed that the Conference's rule of decision-making by consensus was to be altered to allow the CSO to take appropriate action against a participating state 'in cases of clear and gross violation of CSCE commitments'. This development was precipitated by the conflict in Yugoslavia, where the Yugoslav Government was held responsible by the majority of CSCE states for the continuation of hostilities. It was also agreed at the meeting that the CSCE should undertake fact-finding and conciliation missions to areas of tension, with the first such mission to be sent to Nagornyi Karabakh, the largely Armenian-populated enclave in Azerbaijan.

In March 1992 CSCE participating states reached agreement on a number of confidence-building measures, including commitments to exchange technical data on new weapons systems; to report activation of military units; and to prohibit military activity involving very large numbers of troops or tanks. Later in that month at a meeting of the Council of Foreign Ministers, which opened the Helsinki Follow-up Conference, the members of NATO and the former members of the Warsaw Pact (with Russia, Belarus, Ukraine and Georgia taking the place of the USSR) signed the Open Skies Treaty. Under the treaty, aerial reconnaissance missions by one country over another were permitted, subject to regulation. An Open Skies Consultative Commission was subsequently established (see above).

The summit meeting of heads of state and government that took place in Helsinki, Finland, in July 1992 adopted the Helsinki Document 1992, in which participating states defined the terms of future CSCE peace-keeping activities. Conforming broadly to UN practice, peace-keeping operations would be undertaken only with the full consent of the parties involved in any conflict and only if an effective cease-fire were in place. The CSCE may request the use of the military resources of NATO, the CIS, the EU, Western European Union (WEU) or other international bodies. (NATO and WEU had recently changed their Constitutions to permit the use of their forces for CSCE purposes.) The Helsinki Document declared the CSCE a 'regional arrangement' in the sense of Chapter VIII of the UN's Charter, which states that such a regional grouping should attempt to resolve a conflict in the region before referring it to the Security Council. In 1993 the First Implementation Meeting on Human Dimension Issues (the CSCE term used with regard to issues concerning human rights and welfare) took place. The Meeting, for which the ODIHR serves as a secretariat, provides a now annual forum for the exchange of news regarding OSCE commitments in the fields of human rights and democracy.

In December 1993 a Permanent Committee (now renamed the Permanent Council) was established in Vienna, providing for greater political consultation and dialogue through its weekly meetings. In December 1994 the summit conference redesignated the CSCE as the Organization for Security and Co-operation in Europe—OSCE and endorsed the role of the Organization as the primary instrument for early warning, conflict prevention and crisis management in the region. The conference adopted a 'Code of Conduct on Politico-Military Aspects of Security', which set out principles to guide the role of the armed forces in democratic societies. The summit conference that was held in Lisbon, Portugal, in December 1996 agreed to adapt the CFE Treaty, in order to further arms-reduction negotiations on a national and territorial basis. The conference also adopted the 'Lisbon Declaration on a Common and Comprehensive Security Model for Europe for the 21st Century', committing all parties to pursuing measures to ensure regional security. A Security Model Committee was established and began to meet regularly during 1997 to consider aspects of the Declaration, including the identification of risks and challenges to future European security; enhancing means of joint co-operative action within the OSCE framework in the event of non-compliance with OSCE commitments by participating states; considering other new arrangements within the OSCE framework that could reinforce security and stability in Europe; and defining a basis of co-operation between the OSCE and other relevant organizations to co-ordinate security enforcement. In November 1997 the Office of the Representative on Freedom of the Media was established in Vienna, to support the OSCE's activities in this field. In the same month a new position of Co-ordinator of OSCE Economic and Environmental Activities was created.

In November 1999 OSCE heads of state and of government, convened in İstanbul, Turkey, signed a new Charter for European Security, which aimed to formalize existing norms regarding the observance of human rights and to strengthen co-operation with other organizations and institutions concerned with international security. The Charter focused on measures to improve the operational capabilities of the OSCE in early warning, conflict prevention, crisis management and post-conflict rehabilitation. Accordingly, Rapid Expert Assistance and Co-operation (REACT) teams were to be established to enable the Organization to respond rapidly to requests from participating states for assistance in crisis situations. The REACT programme became operational in April 2001. At the İstanbul meeting a revised CFE Treaty was also signed, providing for a stricter system of limitations and increased transparency, which was to be open to other OSCE states not currently signatories. The US and EU governments determined to delay ratification of the Agreement of the Adaptation of the Treaty until Russian troop levels in the Caucasus had been reduced.

In April 2000 the OSCE High Commissioner on National Minorities issued a report reviewing the problems confronting Roma and Sinti populations in OSCE member states. In April 2001 the ODIHR launched a programme of assistance for the Roma communities of south-eastern Europe. The OSCE and UN Office for Drug Control and Crime Prevention (ODCCP) jointly organized a conference in October 2000, supported by the Governments of Kazakhstan, Kyrgyzstan, Tajikistan, Turkmenistan and Uzbekistan and attended by representatives of 67 states and 44 international organizations, which aimed to promote co-operation, democratization, security and stability in Central Asia and to address the threat of drugs-trafficking, organized crime and terrorism in the sub-region. In November an OSCE Document on Small Arms and Light Weapons was adopted, aimed at curtailing the spread of armaments in member states. A workshop on implementation of the Document was held in February 2002. In mid-November 2000 the Office of the Representative on Freedom of the Media organized a conference, staged in Dushanbe, Tajikistan, of journalists from Kazakhstan, Kyrgyzstan, Tajikistan and Uzbekistan. In February 2001 the ODIHR established an Anti-Trafficking Project Fund to help to finance its efforts to combat trafficking in human beings. In July the OSCE Parliamentary Assembly adopted a resolution concerned with strengthening transparency and accountability within the Organization.

In September 2001 the Secretary-General condemned the major terrorist attacks perpetrated against targets in the USA, allegedly by militant Islamist fundamentalists. In early October OSCE member states unanimously adopted a statement in support of the developing US-led global coalition against international terrorism. Meanwhile, the Organization determined to establish a working group on terrorism to draft an action plan on counter-terrorism measures. In December the Ministerial Council, meeting in Romania, approved the 'Bucharest Action Plan' outlining the Organization's contribution to countering terrorism. A Personal Representative for Terrorism was appointed by the CIO in January 2002 to co-ordinate the implementation of the initiatives. Later in December 2001 the OSCE sponsored, with the ODCCP, an International Conference on Security and Stability in Central Asia, held in Bishek, Kyrgyzstan. The meeting, which was attended by representatives of more than 60 countries and organizations, was concerned with strengthening efforts to counter terrorism and providing effective support to the Central Asian states. In October 2002 the ODIHR and the Government of Azerbaijan organized an international conference on religious freedom and combating terrorism. At a Ministerial Council meeting held in Porto, Portugal in December the OSCE issued a Charter on Preventing Terrorism, which condemned terrorism 'in all its forms and manifestations' and called upon member states to work together to counter, investigate and prosecute terrorist acts. The charter also acknowledged the links between terrorism, organized crime and trafficking in human beings. At the same time, a political declaration entitled 'Responding to Change' was adopted, in which member states pledged their commitment to mutual co-operation in combating threats to security. At the OSCE's first Annual Security Review Conference, held in Vienna, in July 2003, a range of practical options for addressing the new threats and challenges to security were set out. These included the introduction of common security features on travel documentation, stricter controls on manual portable air defence systems, and the improvement of border security and policing methods. Security issues were also the subject of the Rotterdam Declaration, adopted by some 300 members of the Parliamentary Assembly in July, which stated that it was imperative for the OSCE to maintain a strong field presence and for field missions to be provided with sufficient funding and highly trained staff. It also recommended that the OSCE assume a role in unarmed peace-keeping operations.

During July 2003 the first OCSE conference on the effects of globalization was convened in Vienna, attended by some 200 representatives from international organizations. Participants called for the advancement of good governance in the public and private sectors, the development of democratic institutions, and the creation of conditions that would enable populations to benefit from the global economy.

## OSCE MISSIONS AND FIELD ACTIVITIES IN EASTERN EUROPE, RUSSIA AND CENTRAL ASIA

At mid-2003 there were long-term OSCE missions in Bosnia and Herzegovina, Croatia, Georgia, the former Yugoslav republic of Macedonia, Moldova, Serbia and Montenegro and Kosovo. The OSCE was also undertaking field activities in Albania, Armenia, Azerbaijan, Belarus, Kazakhstan, Kyrgyzstan, Tajikistan, Turkmenistan and Uzbekistan. The OSCE has institutionalized structures to assist in the implementation of certain bilateral agreements. At mid-2003 there were OSCE representatives to the Russian-Latvian Joint Commission on Military Pensioners and to the Estonian Government Commission on Military Pensioners.

In August 1995 the CIO appointed a Personal Representative concerned with the conflict between Armenia and Azerbaijan in the Nagornyi Karabakh region. The OSCE provided a framework for discussions between the two countries through its 11-nation Minsk Group, which from early 1997 was co-chaired by France, Russia and the USA. In October 1997 Armenia and Azerbaijan reached agreement on OSCE proposals for a political settlement; however, the concessions granted by the Armenian President, Levon Ter-Petrossian, which included the withdrawal of troops from certain strategic areas of Nagornyi Karabakh, precipitated his resignation in February 1998. The proposals were rejected by his successor, Robert Kocharian. Nevertheless, meetings of the Minsk Group continued in 1998 and both countries expressed their willingness to recommence negotiations. The then CIO, Bronisław Geremek, met with the leaders of both countries in November and persuaded them to exchange prisoners of war. In July 1999 the OSCE Permanent Council approved the establishment of an Office in Yerevan (Armenia), which began operations in February 2000. The Office works independently of the Minsk Group, to promote OSCE principles within the country in order to support political and economic stability. It aims to contribute to the development of democratic institutions and to the strengthening of civil society. An Office in Baku (Azerbaijan) opened in July 2000. In November 2001 the Office in Yerevan presented a report on trafficking in human beings in Armenia, which had been compiled as a joint effort by the OSCE, IOM and UNICEF. In March 2002 the CIO visited the region to discuss prospects for peace, and the OSCE's role in the process. In that year a programme on military and security issues was initiated in Armenia which was to enhance the OSCE's role in police-related activities in conflict prevention, crisis management and post-conflict rehabilitation. In July 2003 the Armenian police service signed a Memorandum of Understanding with the OSCE, launching a major police assistance programme with the particular aim of creating a constructive partnership between the police and the general population.

In January 1995 Russia agreed to an OSCE proposal to send a fact-finding mission to assist in the conflict between the Russian authorities and an independence movement in Chechnya (the Chechen Republic of Ichkeriya). The mission criticized the Russian army

for using excessive force against Chechen rebels and civilians; reported that violations of human rights had been perpetrated by both sides in the conflict; and urged Russia to enforce a cease-fire to allow the delivery of humanitarian supplies by international aid agencies to the population of the city. An OSCE Assistance Group to Chechnya mediated between the two sides, and, in July, brokered a cease-fire agreement between the Russian military authorities in Chechnya and the Chechen rebels. A further peace accord was signed, under the auspices of the OSCE, in May 1996, but the truce was broken in July. A more conclusive cease-fire agreement was signed by the two parties to the conflict in August. In January 1997 the OSCE assisted in the preparation and monitoring of general elections conducted in Chechnya. The Assistance Group remained in the territory to help with post-conflict rehabilitation, including the promotion of democratic institutions and respect for human rights. In December 1998, however, the Assistance Group relocated from its headquarters in Groznyi (also known as Dzokhar from March of that year) to Moscow, owing to security concerns. It continued to co-ordinate the delivery of humanitarian aid and implementation of other assistance projects. In September 1999, in response to resurgent separatist activity, Russia launched a military offensive against Chechnya. In early November an OSCE mission arrived in the neighbouring Republic of Ingushetiya to assess the condition and needs of the estimated 200,000 refugees who had fled the hostilities; however, the officials were prevented by the Russian authorities from travelling into Chechnya. The issue dominated the OSCE summit meeting held in İstanbul, later in that month. The meeting insisted upon a political solution to the conflict and called for an immediate cease-fire. An agreement was reached with the Russian President to allow the CIO to visit the region, and on an OSCE role in initiating political dialogue. In February 2000 the CIO welcomed the Russian Government's appointment of a Presidential Representative for Human Rights in Chechnya. In June 2001 the Assistance Group to Chechnya resumed operations inside the territory from a new office in Znamenskoye. An OSCE/ODIHR delegation visited Chechnya during that month to evaluate the prevailing humanitarian and human rights situation. In December 2001 the mandate of the OSCE in Chechnya was extended for one year; the mission was withdrawn on 31 December 2002, owing to failure by the OSCE and Russia to agree on a further extension of the mandate.

In December 1999 the Permanent Council, at the request of the Government of Georgia, expanded the mandate of the existing OSCE Mission to Georgia to include monitoring that country's border with Chechnya. The first permanent observation post opened in February 2000 and the monitoring team was fully deployed by July. In December 2001 the Permanent Council approved an expansion of the monitoring mission to cover the border between Georgia and Ingushetiya. This took effect in January 2002. In December of that year the mission was further extended to include the country's border with Dagestan. The OSCE Mission to Georgia was established in 1992 to work towards a political settlement between disputing factions within the country. Since 1994 the Mission has contributed to efforts to define the political status of South Ossetia and has supported UN peace-keeping and human rights activities in Abkhazia.

In late 1996 the OSCE declared the constitutional referendum held in Belarus in November to be illegal and urged that country's Government to ensure political freedoms and respect for human rights. In September 1997 the Permanent Council determined to establish an OSCE Advisory and Monitoring Group to assist with the process of democratization; the Group commenced operations in February 1998. It was subsequently active in strengthening civil society, organizing training seminars and workshops in electoral practices, monitoring the human rights situation, including the registration of political parties and the development of an independent media, and in mediating between the President and opposition parties. In October 1998 the OSCE Parliamentary Assembly formed an *ad hoc* Committee on Belarus, to act as a working group to support and intensify the Organization's work in the country. The OSCE/ODIHR declared legislative elections staged in Belarus in October 2000 not to have been conducted freely and fairly, and pronounced that presidential elections held in September 2001 had not met the standards required by the Organization. In December 2002 the decision was taken to terminate the Group and to establish in its place an OSCE Office in Minsk; the Office was opened in January 2003. In May the OSCE Representative on Freedom of the Media requested urgent clarification on a decision by the Belarus Government to ban publication of two independent newspapers. In September the ODIHR entered into dialogue with the Belarus authorities on reforming electoral legislation. In the same month the Minsk Office expressed its concern at the recent closure of non-governmental organizations in Belarus for alleged violations of the law.

An OSCE Mission to Moldova was established in February 1993, in order to assist the conflicting parties to pursue negotiations on a political settlement, as well as to observe the military situation in the region and to provide advice on issues of human and minority rights, democratization and the repatriation of refugees. In December 1999 the Permanent Council, with the approval of the Russian Government, authorized an expansion of the Mission's mandate to ensure the full removal and destruction of Russian ammunition and armaments and to co-ordinate financial and technical assistance for the withdrawal of foreign troops and the destruction of weapons. In June 2001 the Mission established a tripartite working group, with representatives of the Russian Ministry of Defence and the local authorities in Transdniestrian, to assist and support the process of disposal of munitions. Destruction of heavy weapons began in mid-2002, under the supervision of the Mission. In May 2003 a seminar on federalism, organized by the OSCE Parliamentary Assembly, was held further to promote negotiations between Moldova and the Transdniestrian region on the development of a new Moldovan constitution, based on the principles of federalism. A second parliamentary conference on federalism was convened in September.

In 1999 an OSCE Project Co-ordinator in Ukraine was established, following the successful conclusion of the OSCE Mission to Ukraine (which had been established in November 1994). The Project Co-ordinator is responsible for pursuing co-operation between Ukraine and the OSCE and providing technical assistance in areas including legal reform, freedom of the media, trafficking in human rights, and the work of the human rights Ombudsman. In April 2002 an ODIHR Election Observation Mission monitored parliamentary elections held in Ukraine. In July 2003 the Project Co-ordinator and the Ukrainian defence ministry launched a joint programme to assist former military personnel with adaptation to civilian life.

In December 2000 the Permanent Council renamed the OSCE Liaison Office in Central Asia the OSCE Centre in Tashkent. The Centre aims to promote OSCE principles within Uzbekistan; it also functions as an information exchange between OSCE bodies and participating Central Asian states and as a means of liaising with OSCE presences in the region. In July 1998 the Permanent Council determined to establish OSCE Centres in Bishkek (Kyrgyzstan), Almaty (Kazakhstan), and Ashgabad (Turkmenistan), all of which opened in January 1999. In general the Centres were to encourage each country's integration into the OSCE, and implementation of its principles, and to focus on the economic, environmental, human and political aspects of security. In January 2000, for the first time, the OSCE refused to dispatch official observers to monitor presidential elections in a member state, owing to concerns about the legitimacy of elections held in Kazakhstan. Subsequently the Centre in Almaty, with the ODIHR and the OSCE Parliamentary Assembly, initiated a round table on elections project to improve electoral legislation, thus strengthening the political system. The project concluded in January 2002, when participants presented a list of recommendations to the national parliament.

The OSCE Mission to Tajikistan was established in December 1993, and began operations in February 1994. The Mission worked with the UN Mission of Observers to Tajikistan (UNMOT) to promote a peace process in that country, and was a guarantor of the peace agreement concluded in June 1997. The Mission remained actively concerned with promoting respect for human rights, assisting the development of the local media, locating missing persons, and the fair distribution of humanitarian aid. Following multi-party parliamentary elections, held in February 2000, the Mission's focus was to be on post-conflict rehabilitation. In April 2002 the Mission initiated a one-year project to promote access to environmental information and network-building among young people concerned with ecology. In October the Permanent Council, taking into account the progress made in Tajikistan since the end of the civil conflict, decided to adapt the OSCE's mandate in the country and to replace the mission with a Centre in Dushanbe, with effect from the beginning of November.

The OSCE was actively involved in co-ordinating the Stability Pact for South-Eastern Europe, which was initiated, in June 1999, as a collaborative plan of action by the EU, Group of Seven industrialized nations and Russia (the G-8), regional governments and other organizations concerned with the stability of the region. (This can be accessed at www.stabilitypact.org.) In March 2000 the OSCE adopted a Regional Strategy for South-Eastern Europe, aimed at enhancing co-operation amongst its presences in the region.

Japan, the Republic of Korea and Thailand have the status of 'partners for co-operation' with the OSCE, while Algeria, Egypt, Israel, Jordan, Morocco and Tunisia are 'Mediterranean partners for co-operation'. Regular consultations are held with these countries in order to discuss security issues of common concern.

**OSCE Mission to Georgia:** Tbilisi, Kristanisi Governmental Residence 5; tel. (32) 98-99-04; fax (32) 94-23-30; e-mail pm@osce .georgia.ge; internet www.osce.org/georgia/; Head of Mission ROY STEPHEN REEVE (United Kingdom).

**OSCE Mission to Moldova:** 2012 Chişinău, str. Mitropolit Dosoftei 108; tel. (2) 22-34-95; fax (2) 22-34-96; e-mail secretary@osce.md; internet www.osce.org/moldova/; Head of Mission WILLIAM H. HILL (USA).

**Personal Representative of the OSCE Chairman-in-Office on the Conflict in Nagornyi Karabakh:** Tbilisi, Zovreti 15, Georgia; tel. (32) 37-61-61; fax (32) 98-85-66; e-mail persrep@access.sanet.ge; Personal Rep. ANDRZEJ KASPRZYK (Poland).

**OSCE Advisory and Monitoring Group in Belarus:** 220116 Minsk, pr. Gasety Pravda 11; tel. (17) 272-34-97; fax (17) 272-34-98; e-mail office-by@osce.org; internet www.osce.org/belarus/; Head of Mission Dr EBERHARD HEYKEN (Germany).

**OSCE Project Co-ordinator in Ukraine:** 01054 Kiev, vul. Striletzka 16; tel. (44) 238-04-06; fax (44) 238-04-08; e-mail ocwohlmuther@osce.kiev.ua; internet www.osce.org/ukraine/; Senior Project Officer CORDULA WOHLMUTHER.

**OSCE Centre in Tashkent:** 70000 Tashkent, ul. Khamid Alimdjain, 2nd Floor, Uzbekistan; tel. (71) 132-01-52; fax (71) 120-61-25; e-mail oscecao@online.ru; internet www.osce.org/tashkent/; Head of Mission AHMET KAMIL EROZAN (Turkey).

**OSCE Office in Yerevan:** 375019 Yerevan, 60 Zarobyan, Armenia; tel. (1) 54-58-45; fax (1) 56-11-38; e-mail osce@osce.am; internet www.osce.org/yerevan/; Head of Office MICHAEL WYGANT (USA) (acting).

**OSCE Office in Baku:** 370004 Baku, 4 Magomayev Lane, 2nd Floor, Azerbaijan; tel. (12) 97-23-73; fax (12) 97-23-77; e-mail office@ osce.baku.org; internet www.osce.org/baku/; Head of Office PETER BURKHARD (Switzerland).

**OSCE Centre in Almaty:** 480091 Almaty, Tole bi 67, 2nd floor, Kazakhstan; tel. (3272) 62-17-62; fax (3272) 62-43-85; e-mail osce@ nursat.kz; internet www.osce.org/almaty/; Head of Mission ANTON RUPNIK (Slovenia).

**OSCE Centre in Ashgabat:** 744005 Ashgabat, Turkmenbashy Shayoly 15, Turkmenistan; tel. (12) 35-30-92; fax (12) 35-30-41; e-mail info@oscetm.org; internet www.osce.org/ashgabad/; Head of Mission PARASCHIVA BADESCU (Romania).

**OSCE Centre in Bishkek:** 720001 Bishkek, Toktogula 139, Kyrgyzstan; tel. (312) 66-41-260; fax (312) 66-31-69; e-mail bd@osce .elcat.kg; internet www.osce.org/bishkek/; Head of Mission AYDIN IDIL (Turkey).

**OSCE Office in Dushanbe:** 734017 Dushanbe, Zikrullo Khojaev 12; tel. (372) 21-40-63; fax (372) 24-91-59; e-mail office@osce .tojikiston.com; internet www.osce.org/tajikistan/; Head of Office YVES BARGAIN (France).

# Finance

All activities of the institutions, negotiations, *ad hoc* meetings and missions are financed by contributions from member states. The budget for 2003 amounted to €185.7m., of which some 84% was allocated to OSCE missions and field activities.

# Publications

*Annual Report of the Secretary-General.*
*The Caucasus: In Defence of the Future.*
*Decision Manual* (annually).
*OSCE Handbook* (annually).
*OSCE Newsletter* (monthly).

# ORGANIZATION OF THE BLACK SEA ECONOMIC CO-OPERATION—BSEC

**Address:** İstinye Cad. Müşir Fuad Paşa Yalısı, Eski Tersane 80860 İstinye-İstanbul, Turkey.

**Telephone:** (212) 229-63-30; **fax:** (212) 229-63-36; **e-mail:** bsec@turk.net; **internet:** www.bsec.gov.tr.

The Black Sea Economic Co-operation (BSEC) was established in 1992 to strengthen regional co-operation, particularly in the field of economic development. In June 1998, at a summit meeting held in Yalta, Ukraine, participating countries signed the BSEC Charter, thereby officially elevating BSEC to regional organization status. The Charter entered into force on 1 May 1999, at which time BSEC formally became the Organization of the Black Sea Economic Co-operation, retaining the same acronym.

## MEMBERS

| | | |
|---|---|---|
| Albania | Georgia | Russia |
| Armenia | Greece | Turkey |
| Azerbaijan | Moldova | Ukraine |
| Bulgaria | Romania | |

Note: Observer status has been granted to Egypt, France, Germany, Israel, Italy, Poland, Slovakia and Tunisia. The BSEC Business Council, International Black Sea Club, and the Energy Charter Conference also have observer status. Iran, the former Yugoslav republic of Macedonia, Serbia and Montenegro and Uzbekistan have applied for full membership.

## Organization

(October 2003)

### PRESIDENTIAL SUMMIT

The Presidential Summit, comprising heads of state or government of member states, represents the highest authority of the body.

### COUNCIL

The Council of Ministers of Foreign Affairs is BSEC's principal decision-making organ. Ministers meet twice a year to review progress and to define new objectives. Chairmanship of the Council rotates among members; the Chairman-in-Office co-ordinates the activities undertaken by BSEC. The Council is supported by a Committee of Senior Officials.

### PARLIAMENTARY ASSEMBLY

**Address:** 1 Hareket Kösku, Dolmabahçe Sarayi, Besiktas, 80680 İstanbul, Turkey.

**Telephone:** (212) 227-6070; **fax:** (212) 227-6080; **e-mail:** vdeiv@pabsec.org; **internet:** www.pabsec.org.

The Parliamentary Assembly, consisting of the representatives of the national parliaments of member states, was created in February 1993 to provide a legal basis for the implementation of decisions within the BSEC framework. It comprises three committees concerning economic, commercial, technological and environmental affairs; legal and political affairs; and cultural, educational and social affairs.

### PERMANENT INTERNATIONAL SECRETARIAT

The Secretariat commenced operations in March 1994. Its tasks are, primarily, of an administrative and technical nature, and include the maintenance of archives, and the preparation and distribution of documentation. Much of the organization's activities are undertaken by 15 working groups, each headed by an Executive Manager, and by various *ad hoc* groups and meetings of experts.

**Secretary-General:** Valeri Chechelashvili (Georgia).

## Activities

In June 1992, at a summit meeting held in İstanbul, heads of state and of government signed the summit declaration on BSEC, and adopted the Bosphorus statement, which established a regional structure for economic co-operation. The grouping attained regional organization status in May 1999 (see above). The Organization's main areas of co-operation include transport; communications; trade and economic development; banking and finance; energy; tourism; agriculture and agro-industry; health care and pharmaceuticals; environmental protection; science and technology; the exchange of statistical data and economic information; collaboration between customs authorities; and combating organized crime, drugs-trafficking, trade in illegal weapons and radioactive materials, and terrorism. In order to promote regional co-operation, the organization also aims to strengthen the business environment by providing support for small and medium-sized enterprises; facilitating closer contacts between businesses in member countries; progressively eliminating obstacles to the expansion of trade; creating appropriate conditions for investment and industrial co-operation, in particular through the avoidance of double taxation and the promotion and protection of investments; encouraging the dissemination of information concerning international tenders organized by member states; and promoting economic co-operation in free-trade zones.

In recent years BSEC has undergone a process of reform aimed at developing a more project-based orientation. In April 2001 the Council adopted the so-called BSEC Economic Agenda for the Future Towards a More Consolidated, Effective and Viable BSEC Partnership, which provided a roadmap for charting the implementation of the Organization's goals. In 2002 a project development fund was established and a regional programme of governance and institutional renewal was launched. Under the new orientation the roles of BSEC's Committee of Senior Officials and network of country-co-ordinators were to be enhanced.

BSEC aims to foster relations with other international and regional organizations, and has been granted observer status at the UN General Assembly. In 1999 BSEC agreed upon a Platform of Co-operation for future structured relations with the European Union. The main areas in which BSEC determined to develop co-operation with the EU were transport, energy and telecommunications infrastructure; trade and the promotion of foreign direct investment; sustainable development and environmental protection, including nuclear safety; science and technology; and combating terrorism and organized crime. BSEC supports the Stability Pact for South-Eastern Europe, initiated in June 1999 as a collaborative plan of action by the EU, the Group of Seven industrialized nations and Russia (the G-8), regional governments and other organizations concerned with the stability of the region. The Declaration issued by BSEC's decennial anniversary summit, held in Istanbul in June 2002, urged that collaboration with the EU should be enhanced.

A BSEC Business Council was established in İstanbul in December 1992 by the business communities of member states. It has observer status at the BSEC, and aims to identify private and public investment projects, maintain business contacts and develop programmes in various sectors. A Black Sea Trade and Development Bank has been established, in Thessaloníki, Greece, as the organization's main funding institution, to finance and implement joint regional projects. It began operations on 1 July 1999. The European Bank for Reconstruction and Development (EBRD) was entrusted as the depository for all capital payments made prior to its establishment. A BSEC Co-ordination Centre, located in Ankara, Turkey, aims to promote the exchange of statistical and economic information. In September 1998 a Black Sea International Studies Centre was inaugurated in Athens, Greece, in order to undertake research concerning the BSEC, in the fields of economics, industry and technology. The transport ministers of BSEC member states adopted a Transport Action Plan in March 2001, which envisaged reducing the disparities in regional transport systems and integrating the BSEC regional transport infrastructure with wider international networks and projects.

BSEC has supported implementation of the Bucharest Convention on the Protection of the Black Sea Against Pollution, adopted by Bulgaria, Georgia, Romania, Russia, Turkey and Ukraine in April 1992. In October 1996 those countries adopted the Strategic Action Plan for the Rehabilitation and Protection of the Black Sea (BSSAP), to be implemented by the Commission of the Bucharest Convention.

# ORGANIZATION OF THE ISLAMIC CONFERENCE—OIC

**Address:** Kilo 6, Mecca Rd, POB 178, Jeddah 21411, Saudi Arabia. **Telephone:** (2) 690-0001; **fax:** (2) 275-1953; **e-mail:** oiccabinet@arab.net.sa; **internet:** www.oic-oci.org.

The Organization was formally established in May 1971, when its Secretariat became operational, following a summit meeting of Muslim heads of state at Rabat, Morocco, in September 1969, and the Islamic Foreign Ministers' Conference in Jeddah in March 1970, and in Karachi, Pakistan, in December 1970.

## MEMBERS

| | | |
|---|---|---|
| Afghanistan | Indonesia | Qatar |
| Albania | Iran | Saudi Arabia |
| Algeria | Iraq | Senegal |
| Azerbaijan | Jordan | Sierra Leone |
| Bahrain | Kazakhstan | Somalia |
| Bangladesh | Kuwait | Sudan |
| Benin | Kyrgyzstan | Suriname |
| Brunei | Lebanon | Syria |
| Burkina Faso | Libya | Tajikistan |
| Cameroon | Malaysia | Togo |
| Chad | The Maldives | Tunisia |
| Comoros | Mali | Turkey |
| Côte d'Ivoire | Mauritania | Turkmenistan |
| Djibouti | Morocco | Uganda |
| Egypt | Mozambique | United Arab |
| Gabon | Niger | Emirates |
| The Gambia | Nigeria | Uzbekistan |
| Guinea | Oman | Yemen |
| Guinea-Bissau | Pakistan | |
| Guyana | Palestine | |

Note: Observer status has been granted to Bosnia and Herzegovina, the Central African Republic, Thailand, the Muslim community of the 'Turkish Republic of Northern Cyprus', the Moro National Liberation Front (MNLF) of the southern Philippines, the United Nations, the African Union, the Non-Aligned Movement, the League of Arab States, the Economic Co-operation Organization, the Union of the Arab Maghreb and the Co-operation Council for the Arab States of the Gulf.

## Organization

(October 2003)

### SUMMIT CONFERENCES

The supreme body of the Organization is the Conference of Heads of State, which met in 1969 at Rabat, Morocco, in 1974 at Lahore, Pakistan, and in January 1981 at Mecca, Saudi Arabia, when it was decided that summit conferences would be held every three years in future. Ninth Conference: Doha, Qatar, November 2000. An extraordinary summit conference was convened in Doha, Qatar, in March 2003, to consider the ongoing situation in Iraq.

### CONFERENCE OF MINISTERS OF FOREIGN AFFAIRS

Conferences take place annually, to consider the means for implementing the general policy of the Organization, although they may also be convened for extraordinary sessions.

### SECRETARIAT

The executive organ of the Organization, headed by a Secretary-General (who is elected by the Conference of Ministers of Foreign Affairs for a four-year term, renewable only once) and four Assistant Secretaries-General (similarly appointed).

**Secretary-General:** Dr ABDELOUAHED BELKEZIZ (Morocco).

At the summit conference in January 1981 it was decided that an International Islamic Court of Justice should be established to adjudicate in disputes between Muslim countries. Experts met in January 1983 to draw up a constitution for the court; however, by 2003 it was not yet in operation.

### STANDING COMMITTEES

**Al-Quds Committee:** f. 1975 to implement the resolutions of the Islamic Conference on the status of Jerusalem (Al-Quds); it meets at the level of foreign ministers; maintains the Al-Quds Fund; Chair. King MUHAMMAD VI OF MOROCCO.

**Standing Committee for Economic and Commercial Co-operation—COMCEC:** f. 1981; Chair. AHMET NECDET SEZER (Pres. of Turkey).

**Standing Committee for Information and Cultural Affairs—COMIAC:** f. 1981; Chair. ABDOULAYE WADE (Pres. of Senegal).

**Standing Committee for Scientific and Technological Co-operation—COMSTECH:** f. 1981; Chair. Gen. PERVEZ MUSHARRAF (Pres. of Pakistan).

Other committees comprise the Islamic Peace Committee, the Permanent Finance Committee, the Committee of Islamic Solidarity with the Peoples of the Sahel, the Eight-Member Committee on the Situation of Muslims in the Philippines, the Six-Member Committee on Palestine, and the *ad hoc* Committee on Afghanistan. In addition, there is an Islamic Commission for Economic, Cultural and Social Affairs and OIC contact groups on Bosnia and Herzegovina, Kosovo, Jammu and Kashmir, and Sierra Leone.

## Activities

The Organization's aims, as proclaimed in the Charter that was adopted in 1972, are:

(i) To promote Islamic solidarity among member states;

(ii) To consolidate co-operation among member states in the economic, social, cultural, scientific and other vital fields, and to arrange consultations among member states belonging to international organizations;

(iii) To endeavour to eliminate racial segregation and discrimination and to eradicate colonialism in all its forms;

(iv) To take necessary measures to support international peace and security founded on justice;

(v) To co-ordinate all efforts for the safeguard of the Holy Places and support of the struggle of the people of Palestine, and help them to regain their rights and liberate their land;

(vi) To strengthen the struggle of all Muslim people with a view to safeguarding their dignity, independence and national rights; and

(vii) To create a suitable atmosphere for the promotion of co-operation and understanding among member states and other countries.

The first summit conference of Islamic leaders (representing 24 states) took place in 1969 following the burning of the Al Aqsa Mosque in Jerusalem. At this conference it was decided that Islamic governments should 'consult together with a view to promoting close co-operation and mutual assistance in the economic, scientific, cultural and spiritual fields, inspired by the immortal teachings of Islam'. Thereafter the foreign ministers of the countries concerned met annually, and adopted the Charter of the Organization of the Islamic Conference in 1972.

At the second Islamic summit conference (Lahore, Pakistan, 1974), the Islamic Solidarity Fund was established, together with a committee of representatives which later evolved into the Islamic Commission for Economic, Cultural and Social Affairs. Subsequently, numerous other subsidiary bodies have been set up (see below).

### ECONOMIC CO-OPERATION

A general agreement for economic, technical and commercial co-operation came into force in 1981, providing for the establishment of joint investment projects and trade co-ordination. This was followed by an agreement on promotion, protection and guarantee of investments among member states. A plan of action to strengthen economic co-operation was adopted at the third Islamic summit conference in 1981, aiming to promote collective self-reliance and the development of joint ventures in all sectors. In 1994 the 1981 plan of action was revised; the reformulated plan placed greater emphasis on private-sector participation in its implementation. Although several meetings of experts were subsequently held to discuss some of the 10 priority focus areas of the plan, little progress was achieved in implementing it during the 1990s.

The fifth summit conference, held in 1987, approved proposals for joint development of modern technology, and for improving scientific and technical skills in the less developed Islamic countries. The first international Islamic trade fair was held in Jeddah, Saudi Arabia, in March 2001.

In 1991 22 OIC member states signed a framework agreement concerning the introduction of a system of trade preferences among member states. It was envisaged that, if implemented, this would represent the first step towards the eventual establishment of an

Islamic common market. In May 2001 the OIC Secretary-General urged increased progress in the ratification of the framework agreement. An OIC group of experts was considering the implications of the proposed creation of such a common market.

## CULTURAL CO-OPERATION

The Organization supports education in Muslim communities throughout the world, and was instrumental in the establishment of Islamic universities in Niger and Uganda. It organizes seminars on various aspects of Islam, and encourages dialogue with the other monotheistic religions. Support is given to publications on Islam both in Muslim and Western countries. The OIC organizes meetings at ministerial level to consider aspects of information policy and new technologies.

## HUMANITARIAN ASSISTANCE

Assistance is given to Muslim communities affected by wars and natural disasters, in co-operation with UN organizations, particularly UNHCR. The countries of the Sahel region (Burkina Faso, Cape Verde, Chad, The Gambia, Guinea, Guinea-Bissau, Mali, Mauritania, Niger and Senegal) receive particular attention as victims of drought. In April 1999 the OIC resolved to send humanitarian aid to assist the displaced ethnic Albanian population of Kosovo and Metohija, in southern Serbia. Several member states have provided humanitarian assistance to the Muslim population affected by the conflict in Chechnya. During 2001 the OIC was providing emergency assistance to Afghanistan, and in October established an Afghan People Assistance Fund. The OIC also administers a Trust Fund for the urgent return of refugees and the displaced to Bosnia and Herzegovina.

## POLITICAL CO-OPERATION

Since its inception the OIC has called for vacation of Arab territories by Israel, recognition of the rights of Palestinians and of the Palestine Liberation Organization (PLO) as their sole legitimate representative, and the restoration of Jerusalem to Arab rule. The 1981 summit conference called for a *jihad* (holy war—though not necessarily in a military sense) 'for the liberation of Jerusalem and the occupied territories'; this was to include an Islamic economic boycott of Israel. In 1982 Islamic ministers of foreign affairs decided to establish Islamic offices for boycotting Israel and for military co-operation with the PLO. The 1984 summit conference agreed to reinstate Egypt (suspended following the peace treaty signed with Israel in 1979) as a member of the OIC, although the resolution was opposed by seven states.

In August 1990 a majority of ministers of foreign affairs condemned Iraq's recent invasion of Kuwait, and demanded the withdrawal of Iraqi forces. In August 1991 the Conference of Ministers of Foreign Affairs obstructed Iraq's attempt to propose a resolution demanding the repeal of economic sanctions against the country. The sixth summit conference, held in Senegal in December, reflected the divisions in the Arab world that resulted from Iraq's invasion of Kuwait and the ensuing war. Twelve heads of state did not attend, reportedly to register protest at the presence of Jordan and the PLO at the conference, both of which had given support to Iraq. Disagreement also arose between the PLO and the majority of other OIC members when a proposal was adopted to cease the OIC's support for the PLO's *jihad* in the Arab territories occupied by Israel, in an attempt to further the Middle East peace negotiations.

In August 1992 the UN General Assembly approved a non-binding resolution, introduced by the OIC, that requested the UN Security Council to take increased action, including the use of force, in order to defend the non-Serbian population of Bosnia and Herzegovina (some 43% of Bosnians being Muslims) from Serbian aggression, and to restore its 'territorial integrity'. The OIC Conference of Ministers of Foreign Affairs, which was held in December, demanded anew that the UN Security Council take all necessary measures against Serbia and Montenegro, including military intervention, in order to protect the Bosnian Muslims.

A report by an OIC fact-finding mission, which in February 1993 visited Azad Kashmir while investigating allegations of repression of the largely Muslim population of the Indian state of Jammu and Kashmir by the Indian armed forces, was presented to the 1993 Conference. The meeting urged member states to take the necessary measures to persuade India to cease the 'massive human rights violations' in Jammu and Kashmir and to allow the Indian Kashmiris to 'exercise their inalienable right to self-determination'. In September 1994 ministers of foreign affairs, meeting in Islamabad, Pakistan, agreed to establish a contact group on Jammu and Kashmir, which was to provide a mechanism for promoting international awareness of the situation in that region and for seeking a peaceful solution to the dispute. In December OIC heads of state approved a resolution condemning reported human rights abuses by Indian security forces in Kashmir.

In July 1994 the OIC Secretary-General visited Afghanistan and proposed the establishment of a preparatory mechanism to promote national reconciliation in that country. In mid-1995 Saudi Arabia, acting as a representative of the OIC, pursued a peace initiative for Afghanistan and issued an invitation for leaders of the different factions to hold negotiations in Jeddah.

A special ministerial meeting on Bosnia and Herzegovina was held in July 1993, at which seven OIC countries committed themselves to making available up to 17,000 troops to serve in the UN Protection Force in the former Yugoslavia (UNPROFOR). The meeting also decided to dispatch immediately a ministerial mission to persuade influential governments to support the OIC's demands for the removal of the arms embargo on Bosnian Muslims and the convening of a restructured international conference to bring about a political solution to the conflict. In December 1994 OIC heads of state, convened in Morocco, proclaimed that the UN arms embargo on Bosnia and Herzegovina could not be applied to the Muslim authorities of that Republic. The Conference also resolved to review economic relations between OIC member states and any country that supported Serbian activities. An aid fund was established, to which member states were requested to contribute between US $500,000 and $5m., in order to provide further humanitarian and economic assistance to Bosnian Muslims. In relation to wider concerns the conference adopted a Code of Conduct for Combating International Terrorism, in an attempt to control Muslim extremist groups. The code commits states to ensuring that militant groups do not use their territory for planning or executing terrorist activity against other states, in addition to states refraining from direct support or participation in acts of terrorism. In a further resolution the OIC supported the decision by Iraq to recognize Kuwait, but advocated that Iraq comply with all UN Security Council decisions.

In July 1995 the OIC contact group on Bosnia and Herzegovina (at that time comprising Egypt, Iran, Malaysia, Morocco, Pakistan, Saudi Arabia, Senegal and Turkey), meeting in Geneva, declared the UN arms embargo against Bosnia and Herzegovina to be 'invalid'. Several Governments subsequently announced their willingness officially to supply weapons and other military assistance to the Bosnian Muslim forces. In September a meeting of all OIC ministers of defence and foreign affairs endorsed the establishment of an 'assistance mobilization group' which was to supply military, economic, legal and other assistance to Bosnia and Herzegovina. In a joint declaration the ministers also demanded the return of all territory seized by Bosnian Serb forces, the continued NATO bombing of Serb military targets, and that the city of Sarajevo be preserved under a Muslim-led Bosnian Government. In November the OIC Secretary-General endorsed the peace accord for the former Yugoslavia, which was concluded, in Dayton, USA, by leaders of all the conflicting factions, and reaffirmed the commitment of Islamic states to participate in efforts to implement the accord. In the following month the OIC Conference of Ministers of Foreign Affairs, convened in Conakry, Guinea, requested the full support of the international community to reconstruct Bosnia and Herzegovina through humanitarian aid as well as economic and technical co-operation. Ministers declared that Palestine and the establishment of fully-autonomous Palestinian control of Jerusalem were issues of central importance for the Muslim world. The Conference urged the removal of all aspects of occupation and the cessation of the construction of Israeli settlements in the occupied territories. In addition, the final statement of the meeting condemned Armenian aggression against Azerbaijan, registered concern at the persisting civil conflict in Afghanistan, demanded the elimination of all weapons of mass destruction and pledged support for Libya (affected by the US trade embargo). Ministers determined that an intergovernmental group of experts should be established in 1996 to address the situation of minority Muslim communities residing in non-OIC states.

In December 1996 OIC ministers of foreign affairs, meeting in Jakarta, Indonesia, urged the international community to apply pressure on Israel in order to ensure its implementation of the terms of the Middle East peace process. The ministers reaffirmed the importance of ensuring that the provisions of the Dayton Peace Agreement for the former Yugoslavia were fully implemented, called for a peaceful settlement of the Kashmir issue, demanded that Iraq fulfil its obligations for the establishment of security, peace and stability in the region and proposed that an international conference on peace and national reconciliation in Somalia be convened. The ministers elected a new Secretary-General who confirmed that the organization would continue to develop its role as an international mediator. In March 1997, at an extraordinary summit held in Pakistan, OIC heads of state and of government reiterated the organization's objective of increasing international pressure on Israel to ensure the full implementation of the terms of the Middle East peace process. An 'Islamabad Declaration' was also adopted, which pledged to increase co-operation between members of the OIC. In June the OIC condemned the decision by the US House of Representatives to recognize Jerusalem as the Israeli capital. The Secretary-General of the OIC issued a statement rejecting the US decision as counter to the role of the USA as sponsor of the Middle East peace plan.

In early 1998 the OIC appealed for an end to the threat of US-led military action against Iraq arising from a dispute regarding access granted to international weapons inspectors. The crisis was averted by an agreement concluded between the Iraqi authorities and the UN Secretary-General in February. In March OIC ministers of foreign affairs, meeting in Doha, Qatar, requested an end to the international sanctions against Iraq. Additionally, the ministers urged all states to end the process of restoring normal trading and diplomatic relations with Israel pending that country's withdrawal from the occupied territories and acceptance of an independent Palestinian state. In April the OIC, jointly with the UN, sponsored new peace negotiations between the main disputing factions in Afghanistan, which were conducted in Islamabad, Pakistan. In early May, however, the talks collapsed and were postponed indefinitely. In September the Secretaries-General of the OIC and UN agreed to establish a joint mission to counter the deteriorating security situation along the Afghan–Iranian border, following the large-scale deployment of Taliban troops in the region and consequent military manoeuvres by the Iranian authorities. They also reiterated the need to proceed with negotiations to conclude a peaceful settlement in Afghanistan. In December the OIC appealed for a diplomatic solution to the tensions arising from Iraq's withdrawal of co-operation with UN weapons inspectors, and criticized subsequent military air-strikes, led by the USA, as having been conducted without renewed UN authority. An OIC Convention on Combating International Terrorism was adopted in 1998. An OIC committee of experts responsible for formulating a plan of action for safeguarding the rights of Muslim communities and minorities met for the first time in 1998.

In early April 1999 ministers of foreign affairs of the countries comprising OIC's contact group met to consider the crisis in Kosovo. The meeting condemned Serbian atrocities being committed against the local Albanian population and urged the provision of international assistance for the thousands of people displaced by the conflict. The group resolved to establish a committee to co-ordinate relief aid provided by member states. The ministers also expressed their willingness to help to formulate a peaceful settlement and to participate in any subsequent implementation force. In June an OIC Parliamentary Union was inaugurated; its founding conference was convened in Tehran, Iran.

In early March 2000 the OIC mediated contacts between the parties to the conflict in Afghanistan, with a view to reviving peace negotiations. Talks, held under OIC auspices, ensued in May. In November OIC heads of state attended the ninth summit conference, held in Doha, Qatar. In view of the significant deterioration in relations between Israel and the Palestinian (National) Authority during late 2000, the summit issued a Declaration pledging solidarity with the Palestinian cause and accusing the Israeli authorities of implementing large-scale systematic violations of human rights against Palestinians. The summit also issued the Doha Declaration, which reaffirmed commitment to the OIC Charter and undertook to modernize the organization's organs and mechanisms. Both the elected Government of Afghanistan and the Taliban sent delegations to the Doha conference. The summit determined that Afghanistan's official participation in the OIC, suspended in 1996, should not yet be reinstated. In early 2001 a high-level delegation from the OIC visited Afghanistan in an attempt to prevent further destruction of ancient statues by Taliban supporters.

In May 2001 the OIC convened an emergency meeting, following an escalation of Israeli-Palestinian violence. The meeting resolved to halt all diplomatic and political contacts with the Israeli government, while restrictions remained in force against Palestinian-controlled territories. In June the OIC condemned attacks and ongoing discrimination against the Muslim Community in Myanmar. In the same month the OIC Secretary-General undertook a tour of six African countries—Burkina Faso, The Gambia, Guinea, Mali, Niger and Senegal, to promote co-operation and to consider further OIC support for those states. In August the Secretary-General condemned Israel's seizure of several Palestinian institutions in East Jerusalem and aerial attacks against Palestinian settlements. The OIC initiated high-level diplomatic efforts to convene a meeting of the UN Security Council in order to discuss the situation.

In September 2001 the OIC Secretary-General strongly condemned major terrorist attacks perpetrated against targets in the USA. Soon afterwards the US authorities rejected a proposal by the Taliban regime that an OIC observer mission be deployed to monitor the activities of the Saudi Arabian-born exiled militant Islamist fundamentalist leader Osama bin Laden, who was accused by the US Government of having co-ordinated the attacks from alleged terrorist bases in the Taliban-administered area of Afghanistan. An extraordinary meeting of OIC ministers of foreign affairs, convened in early October, in Doha, Qatar, to consider the implications of the terrorist atrocities, condemned the attacks and declared its support for combating all manifestations of terrorism within the framework of a proposed collective initiative co-ordinated under the auspices of the UN. The meeting, which did not pronounce directly on the recently-initiated US-led military retaliation against targets in Afghanistan, urged that no Arab or Muslim state should be targeted under the pretext of eliminating terrorism. It determined to establish a fund to assist Afghan civilians. In February 2002 the Secretary-General expressed concern at statements of the US administration describing Iran and Iraq (as well as the Democratic People's Republic of Korea) as belonging to an 'axis of evil' involved in international terrorism and the development of weapons of mass destruction. In early April OIC foreign ministers convened an extraordinary session on terrorism, in Kuala Lumpur, Malaysia. The meeting issued the 'Kuala Lumpur Declaration', which reiterated member states' collective resolve to combat terrorism, recalling the organization's 1994 code of conduct and 1998 convention to this effect; condemned attempts to associate terrorist activities with Islamists or any other particular creed, civilization or nationality, and rejected attempts to associate Islamic states or the Palestinian struggle with terrorism; rejected the implementation of international action against any Muslim state on the pretext of combating terrorism; urged the organization of a global conference on international terrorism; and urged an examination of the root causes of international terrorism. In addition, the meeting strongly condemned Israel's ongoing military intervention in areas controlled by the Palestinian (National) Authority. The meeting adopted a plan of action on addressing the issues raised in the declaration. Its implementation was to be co-ordinated by a 13-member committee on international terrorism. Member states were encouraged to sign and ratify the Convention on Combating International Terrorism in order to accelerate its implementation. In June ministers of foreign affairs, meeting in Khartoum, Sudan, issued a declaration reiterating the OIC call for an international conference to be convened, under UN auspices, in order clearly to define terrorism and to agree on the international procedures and mechanisms for combating terrorism through the UN. The conference also repeated demands for the international community to exert pressure on Israel to withdraw from all Palestinian-controlled territories and for the establishment of an independent Palestinian state. It endorsed the peace plan for the region that had been adopted by the summit meeting of the League of Arab States in March.

In June 2002 the OIC Secretary-General expressed his concern at the escalation of tensions between Pakistan and India regarding Kashmir. He urged both sides to withdraw their troops and to refrain from the use of force. In the following month the OIC pledged its support for Morocco in a territorial dispute with Spain over the small island of Perejil, but called for a negotiated settlement to resolve the issue.

An extraordinary summit conference of Islamic leaders convened in Doha, Qatar, in early March 2003 to consider the ongoing Iraq crisis, welcomed the Saddam Hussain regime's acceptance of UN Security Council Resolution 1441 and consequent co-operation with UN weapons inspectors, and emphatically rejected any military strike against Iraq or threat to the security of any other Islamic state. The conference also urged progress towards the elimination of all weapons of mass destruction in the Middle East, including those held by Israel. In May the 30th session of the Conference of Ministers of Foreign Affairs, entitled 'Unity and Dignity', issued the Tehran Declaration, in which it resolved to combat terrorism and to contribute to preserving peace and security in Islamic countries. The Declaration also pledged its full support for the Palestinian cause and rejected the labelling as 'terrorist' of those Muslim states deemed to be resisting foreign aggression and occupation.

# Finance

The OIC's activities are financed by mandatory contributions from member states. The budget for 2002/03 totalled US $11.4m.

## SUBSIDIARY ORGANS

**Islamic Centre for the Development of Trade:** Complexe Commercial des Habous, ave des FAR, BP 13545, Casablanca, Morocco; tel. (2) 314974; fax (2) 310110; e-mail icdt@icdt.org; internet www.icdt.org; f. 1983 to encourage regular commercial contacts, harmonize policies and promote investments among OIC mems; Dir-Gen. ALLAL RACHDI; publs *Tijaris: International and Inter-Islamic Trade Magazine* (bi-monthly), *Inter-Islamic Trade Report* (annually).

**Islamic Jurisprudence (Fiqh) Academy:** POB 13917, Jeddah, Saudi Arabia; tel. (2) 667-1664; fax (2) 667-0873; internet www.fiqhacademy.org.sa; f. 1982; Sec.-Gen. SHEIKH MOHAMED HABIB IBN AL-KHODHA.

**Islamic Solidarity Fund:** c/o OIC Secretariat, POB 178, Jeddah 21411, Saudi Arabia; tel. (2) 680-0800; fax (2) 687-3568; f. 1974 to meet the needs of Islamic communities by providing emergency aid and the finance to build mosques, Islamic centres, hospitals, schools and universities; Chair. Sheikh NASIR ABDULLAH BIN HAMDAN; Exec. Dir ABDULLAH HERSI.

*Organization of the Islamic Conference*

**Islamic University in Uganda:** POB 2555, Mbale, Uganda; Kampala Liaison Office: POB 7689, Kampala; tel. (45) 33502; fax (45) 34452; e-mail iuiu@info.com.co.ug; tel. (41) 236874; fax (41) 254576; f. 1988 to meet the educational needs of Muslim populations in English-speaking African countries; mainly financed by OIC; Principal Officer Prof. Mahdi Adamu.

**Islamic University of Niger:** BP 11507, Niamey, Niger; tel. 723903; fax 733796; f. 1984; provides courses of study in *Shari'a* (Islamic law) and Arabic language and literature; also offers courses in pedagogy and teacher training; receives grants from Islamic Solidarity Fund and contributions from OIC member states; Rector Prof. Abdelali Oudhriri.

**Islamic University of Technology—IUT:** GPO Box 3003, Board Bazar, Gazipur 1704, Dhaka, Bangladesh; tel. (2) 980-0960; fax (2) 980-0970; e-mail vc@int-dhaka.edu; internet www.iutoic-dhaka.edu; f. 1981 as the Islamic Centre for Technical and Vocational Training and Resources, named changed to Islamic Institute of Technology in 1994, current name adopted in June 2001; aims to develop human resources in OIC mem. states, with special reference to engineering, technology, tech. and vocational education and research; 224 staff and 1,000 students; library of 23,000 vols; Vice-Chancellor Prof. Dr M. Anwar Hossain; publs *News Bulletin* (annually), annual calendar and announcement for admission, reports, human resources development series.

**Research Centre for Islamic History, Art and Culture—IRCICA:** POB 24, Beşiktaş 80692, İstanbul, Turkey; tel. (212) 2591742; fax (212) 2584365; e-mail ircica@superonline.com; internet www.ircica.org; f. 1980; library of 50,000 vols; Dir-Gen. Prof. Dr Ekmeleddin Ihsanoğlu; publs *Newsletter* (3 a year), monographical studies.

**Statistical, Economic and Social Research and Training Centre for the Islamic Countries:** Attar Sok 4, GOP 06700, Ankara, Turkey; tel. (312) 4686172; fax (312) 4673458; e-mail oicankara@sesrtcic.org; internet www.sesrtcic.org; f. 1978; Dir-Gen. Erdinç Erdün; publs *Journal of Economic Co-operation among Islamic Countries* (quarterly), *InfoReport* (quarterly), *Statistical Yearbook* (annually).

## SPECIALIZED INSTITUTIONS

**International Islamic News Agency—IINA (IINA):** King Khalid Palace, Madinah Rd, POB 5054, Jeddah 21422, Saudi Arabia; tel. (2) 665-8561; fax (2) 665-9358; e-mail iina@ogertel.com; internet www.islamicnews.org; f. 1972; distributes news and reports daily on events in the Islamic world, in Arabic, English and French; Dir-Gen. Abdulwahab Kashif.

**Islamic Educational, Scientific and Cultural Organization—ISESCO:** BP 755, Rabat 10104, Morocco; tel. (7) 772433; fax (7) 772058; e-mail cid@isesco.org.ma; internet www.isesco.org.ma; f. 1982; Dir-Gen. Dr Abdulaziz bin Othman al-Twaijri; publs *ISESCO Newsletter* (quarterly), *Islam Today* (2 a year), *ISESCO Triennial*.

**Islamic States Broadcasting Organization—ISBO:** POB 6351, Jeddah 21442, Saudi Arabia; tel. (2) 672-1121; fax (2) 672-2600; e-mail isbo@isbo.org; internet www.isbo.org; f. 1975; Sec.-Gen. Hussein al-Askary.

## AFFILIATED INSTITUTIONS

**International Association of Islamic Banks—IAIB:** King Abdulaziz St, Queen's Bldg, 23rd Floor, Al-Balad Dist, POB 9707, Jeddah 21423, Saudi Arabia; tel. (2) 651-6900; fax (2) 651-6552; f. 1977 to link financial institutions operating on Islamic banking principles; activities include training and research; mems: 192 banks and other financial institutions in 34 countries; Sec.-Gen. Samir A. Shaikh.

**Islamic Chamber of Commerce and Industry:** POB 3831, Clifton, Karachi 75600, Pakistan; tel. (21) 5874756; fax (21) 5870765; e-mail icci@icci-oic.org; internet icci-oic.org; f. 1979 to promote trade and industry among member states; comprises nat. chambers or feds of chambers of commerce and industry; Sec.-Gen. Aqeel Ahmad al-Jassem.

**Islamic Committee for the International Crescent:** POB 17434, Benghazi, Libya; tel. (61) 95823; fax (61) 95829; f. 1979 to attempt to alleviate the suffering caused by natural disasters and war; Sec.-Gen. Dr Ahmad Abdallah Cherif.

**Islamic Solidarity Sports Federation:** POB 5844, Riyadh 11442, Saudi Arabia; tel. and fax (1) 482-2145; f. 1981; Sec.-Gen. Dr Mohammad Saleh Gazdar.

**Organization of Islamic Capitals and Cities—OICC:** POB 13621, Jeddah 21414, Saudi Arabia; tel. (2) 698-1953; fax (2) 698-1053; e-mail secrtriat@oicc.org; internet www.oicc.org; f. 1980 to promote and develop co-operation among OICC mems, to preserve their character and heritage, to implement planning guide-lines for the growth of Islamic cities and to upgrade standards of public services and utilities in those cities; Sec.-Gen. Omar Abdullah Kadi.

**Organization of the Islamic Shipowners' Association:** POB 14900, Jeddah 21434, Saudi Arabia; tel. (2) 663-7882; fax (2) 660-4920; e-mail oisa@sbm.net.sa; f. 1981 to promote co-operation among maritime cos in Islamic countries; In 1998 mems approved the establishment of a new commercial venture, the Bakkah Shipping Company, to enhance sea transport in the region; Sec.-Gen. Dr Abdullatif A. Sultan.

**World Federation of Arab-Islamic Schools:** POB 3446, Jeddah, Saudi Arabia; tel. (2) 670-0019; fax (2) 671-0823; f. 1976; supports Arab-Islamic schools world-wide and encourages co-operation between the institutions; promotes the dissemination of the Arabic language and Islamic culture; supports the training of personnel.

# OTHER REGIONAL ORGANIZATIONS

## Agriculture, Food, Forestry and Fisheries

(For organizations concerned with agricultural commodities, see Commodities)

**International Baltic Sea Fishery Commission:** 00-528 Warsaw, 20 Hozastr., Poland; tel. (22) 6288647; fax (22) 6253372; e-mail ibsfc@polbox.pl; internet www.ibsfc.org; f. 1973 by the Convention on Fishing and Conservation of the Living Resources in the Baltic Sea and the Belts (the Gdansk Convention) to protect the living marine resources of the Baltic Sea and to make rational use of such resources; mems: Estonia, the EU, Latvia, Lithuania, Poland and the Russian Federation; several international organizations have observer status; Chair. L. VAARJA (Estonia).

**International Centre for Agricultural Research in the Dry Areas—ICARDA:** POB 5466, Aleppo, Syria; tel. (21) 2213433; fax (21) 2213490; e-mail icarda@cgiar.org; internet www.icarda.cgiar .org; f. 1977; aims to improve the production of lentils, barley and faba beans throughout the developing world; supports the improvement of on-farm water-use efficiency, rangeland and small-ruminant production in all dry-area developing countries; within the West and Central Asia and North Africa region promotes the improvement of bread and durum wheat and chick-pea production and of farming systems; undertakes research, training and dissemination of information, in co-operation with national, regional and international research institutes, universities and ministries of agriculture, in order to enhance production, alleviate poverty and promote sustainable natural resource management practices; member of the network of 16 agricultural research centres supported by the Consultative Group on International Agricultural Research (CGIAR); Dir-Gen. Dr ADEL EL-BELTAGY; publs *Annual Report, Caravan Newsletter* (2 a year).

**North Pacific Anadromous Fish Commission:** 889 W. Pender St, Suite 502, Vancouver, BC V6C 3B2, Canada; tel. (604) 775-5550; fax (604) 775-5577; e-mail secretariat@npafc.org; f. 1993; mems: Canada, Japan, Russia, USA; Exec. Dir VLADIMIR FEDORENKO; publs *Annual Report, Newsletter* (2 a year), *Statistical Yearbook, Scientific Bulletin, Technical Report.*

**Rural Enterprise Adaptation Program International— REAP:** 1427 Fourth St, Cedar Rapids, IA 52404, USA; tel. (319) 366- 4230; fax (319) 366-2209; e-mail 000651.3571@mcimail.com; internet www.reapintl.com; f. 1991; aims to aid agriculturalists in Latvia, Lithuania and Russia in the transition to a market economy; promotes the exchange of expertise, provides training and technical assistance to farms; Dir WILLIAM MÜLLER.

## Arts and Culture

**Baltic Music Network:** Willemoesgade 52, 2100 Copenhagen Ø, Denmark; tel. 35-26-49-07; fax 33-93-44-13; internet www.sjoki.uta .fi/&ub.nft;latvis/TBMN; f. 1991 to encourage the international exchange of culture, particularly music, in the Baltic Sea region; Mems: organizations and individuals in nine countries; Co-ordinator IB JENSON.

**International Centre for the Study of the Preservation and Restoration of Cultural Property—ICCROM:** Via di San Michele 13, 00153 Rome, Italy; tel. (06) 585-531; fax (06) 5855-3349; e-mail iccrom@iccrom.org; internet www.iccrom.org; f. 1959; assembles documents on the preservation and restoration of cultural property; stimulates research and proffers advice; organizes missions of experts; undertakes training of specialists; mems: 104 countries; Dir-Gen. Dr NICHOLAS STANLEY-PRICE (UK); publ *Newsletter* (annually, in English and French).

**Organization of World Heritage Cities:** 56 Saint-Pierre St, Suite 401, Québec, QC G1K 4AI, Canada; tel. (418) 692-0000; fax (418) 692-5558; e-mail secretariat@ovpm.org; internet www.ovpm.org; f. 1993 to assist cities inscribed on the UNESCO World Heritage List to implement the Convention concerning the Protection of the World Cultural and Natural Heritage (1972); promotes co-operation between city authorities, in particular in the management and sustainable development of historic sites; holds a General Assembly, comprising the mayors of member cities, at least every two years; mems: 187 cities world-wide; Sec.-Gen. D. S. MYRVOLL (acting).

## Commodities

**International Cadmium Association:** 12110 Sunset Hills Rd, Suite 110, Reston, VA 22090, USA; tel. (703) 709-1400; fax (703) 709- 1402; f. 1976; covers all aspects of the production and use of cadmium and its compounds; includes almost all producers and users of cadmium; Chair. DAVID SINCLAIR (USA).

**International Cotton Advisory Committee—ICAC:** 1629 K St, NW, Suite 702, Washington, DC 20006-1636, USA; tel. (202) 463- 6660; fax (202) 463-6950; e-mail secretariat@icac.org; internet www .icac.org; f. 1939 to observe developments in world cotton; to collect and disseminate statistics; to suggest measures for the furtherance of international collaboration in maintaining and developing a sound world cotton economy; and to provide a forum for international discussions on cotton prices; mems: 43 countries; Exec. Dir Dr TERRY TOWNSEND (USA); publs *Cotton This Month, Cotton: Review of the World Situation, Cotton: World Statistics, The ICAC Recorder.*

**International Grains Council—IGC:** 1 Canada Sq., Canary Wharf, London, E14 5AE, United Kingdom; tel. (20) 7513-1122; fax (20) 7513-0630; e-mail igc@igc.org.uk; internet www.igc.org.uk; f. 1949 as International Wheat Council, present name adopted in 1995; responsible for the administration of the International Grains Agreement, 1995, comprising the Grain Trade Convention (GTC) and the Food Aid Convention (FAC, under which donors pledge specified minimum annual amounts of food aid for developing countries in the form of grain and other eligible products); aims to further international co-operation in all aspects of trade in grains, to promote international trade in grains, and to secure the freest possible flow of this trade, particularly in developing member countries; seeks to contribute to the stability of the international grain market; acts as a forum for consultations between members; provides comprehensive information on the international grain market; mems: 28 countries and the EU; Exec. Dir. G. DENIS; publs *World Grain Statistics* (annually), *Wheat and Coarse Grain Shipments* (annually), *Report for the Fiscal Year* (annually), *Grain Market Report* (monthly), *IGC Grain Market Indicators* (weekly).

**International Lead and Zinc Study Group—ILZSG:** 1 Mill St, London, SE1 2DF, United Kingdom; tel. (20) 7740-2750; fax (20) 7740-2983; e-mail root@ilzsg.org; internet www.ilzsg.org; f. 1959 for intergovernmental consultation on world trade in lead and zinc; conducts studies and provides information on trends in supply and demand; mems: 28 countries; Chair. A. IGNATOW (Canada); Sec.-Gen. DON SMALE; publ. *Lead and Zinc Statistics* (monthly).

**International Silk Association:** 34 rue de la Charité, 69002 Lyon, France; tel. 4-78-42-10-79; fax 4-78-37-56-72; e-mail isa-silk .ais-sole@wanadoo.fr; f. 1949 to promote closer collaboration between all branches of the silk industry and trade, develop the consumption of silk, and foster scientific research; collects and disseminates information and statistics relating to the trade and industry; organizes biennial congresses; mems: employers' and technical organizations in 40 countries; Gen. Sec. X. LAVERGNE; publs *ISA Newsletter* (monthly), congress reports, standards, trade rules, etc.

**International Sugar Organization:** 1 Canada Sq., Canary Wharf, London, E14 5AA, United Kingdom; tel. (20) 7513-1144; fax (20) 7513-1146; e-mail exdir@isosugar.org; internet www.isosugar.org; administers the International Sugar Agreement (1992), with the objectives of stimulating co-operation, facilitating trade and encouraging demand; aims to improve conditions in the sugar market through debate, analysis and studies; serves as a forum for discussion; holds annual seminars and workshops; sponsors projects from developing countries; mems: 63 countries producing some 80% of total world sugar; Exec. Dir Dr PETER BARON; publs *Sugar Year Book, Monthly Statistical Bulletin, Market Report and Press Summary, Quarterly Market Review*, seminar proceedings.

**Organization of the Petroleum Exporting Countries—OPEC:** 1020 Vienna, Obere Donaustrasse 93, Austria; tel. (1) 211-12; fax (1) 214-98-27; e-mail prid@opec.org; internet www.opec.org; f. 1960 to unify and co-ordinate members' petroleum policies and to safeguard their interests generally; holds regular conferences of member countries to set reference prices and production levels; conducts research in energy studies, economics and finance; provides data services and news services covering petroleum and energy issues; mems: Algeria, Indonesia, Iran, Iraq, Kuwait, Libya, Nigeria, Qatar, Saudi Arabia, United Arab Emirates, Venezuela; Sec.-Gen. Dr ALVARO SILVA CALDERÓN (Venezuela); publs *Annual Report*, *Annual Statistical Bulletin*, *OPEC Bulletin* (monthly), *OPEC Review* (quarterly), *Monthly Oil Market Report*.

# Development and Economic Co-operation

**Asia-Pacific Mountain Network—APMN:** c/o International Centre for Integrated Mountain Development, POB 3226, Kathmandu, Nepal; tel. (1) 525313; fax (1) 524509; e-mail baden@zhk.l-card.msk; internet www.apmn.mtnforum.org; f. 1995; forum for the production and dissemination of information on sustainable mountain development, reducing the risk of mountain disasters, economic development, the elimination of poverty, and cultural heritage; mems: about 1,000, including mems from Russia and Central Asia.

**Council of Baltic Sea States—CBSS:** Strömsberg, POB 2010, 103 11 Stockholm, Sweden; tel. (8) 440-19-20; fax (8) 440-19-44; e-mail cbss@cbss.st; internet www.cbss.st; f. 1992 as a forum to strengthen co-operation between countries in the Baltic Sea region, including Russia; Sec.-Gen. HANNU HALINEN (Finland); publ. *Newsletter* (monthly).

**Pacific Basin Economic Council—PBEC:** 900 Fort St, Suite 1080, Honolulu, HI 96813, USA; tel. (808) 521-9044; fax (808) 521-8530; e-mail info@pbec.org; internet www.pbec.org; f. 1967; an assen of business representatives aiming to promote business opportunities in the region, in order to enhance overall economic development; advises governments and serves as a liaison between business leaders and government officials; encourages business relationships and co-operation among members; holds business symposia; mems: 20 economies (Australia, Canada, Chile, People's Republic of China, Colombia, Ecuador, Hong Kong, Indonesia, Japan, Republic of Korea, Malaysia, Mexico, New Zealand, Peru, Philippines, Russia, Singapore, Taiwan, Thailand, USA); Chair. SUCK-RAI CHO; Pres. DALTON TANONAKA; publs *Pacific Journal* (quarterly), *Executive Summary* (annual conference report).

**Pacific Economic Co-operation Council—PECC:** 4 Nassim Rd, Singapore 258372; tel. 67379823; fax 67379824; e-mail peccsec@pecc.net; internet www.pecc.net; f. 1980; an independent, policy-orientated organization of senior research, government and business representatives from 25 economies in the Asia-Pacific region; aims to foster economic development in the region by providing a forum for discussion and co-operation in a wide range of economic areas; holds a General Meeting every 2 years; mems: Australia, Brunei, Canada, Chile, the People's Republic of China, Colombia, Ecuador, Hong Kong, Indonesia, Japan, the Republic of Korea, Malaysia, Mexico, Mongolia (assoc. mem.), New Zealand, Peru, Philippines, Russia, Singapore, Taiwan, Thailand, USA, Viet Nam and the Pacific Island Forum; French Pacific Territories (assoc. mem.); Dir-Gen. DAVID PARSONS; publs *Issues PECC* (quarterly), *Pacific Economic Outlook* (annually), *Pacific Food Outlook* (annually).

# Economics and Finance

**Bank for International Settlements—BIS:** Centralbahnplatz 2, 4002 Basel, Switzerland; tel. (61) 2808080; fax (61) 2809100; e-mail email@bis.org; internet www.bis.org; f. pursuant to the Hague Agreements of 1930 to promote co-operation among national central banks and to provide additional facilities for international financial operations; mems: central banks in 50 countries, incl. the Russian Federation; Chair. and Pres. NOUT WELLINK (Netherlands); publs *Annual Report*, *Quarterly Review: International Banking and Financial Market Developments*, *The BIS Consolidated International Banking Statistics* (every 6 months), *Joint BIS-IMF-OECD-World Bank Statistics on External Debt* (quarterly), *Regular OTC Derivatives Market Statistics* (every 6 months), *Central Bank Survey of Foreign Exchange and Derivatives Market Activity* (every 3 years).

**Central Asian Bank for Co-operation and Development—CABCD:** 115A Abay, Almaty, Kazakhstan; tel. (2) 422737; fax (2) 428627; f. 1994 to support trade and development in the sub-region; mems: Kazakhstan, Kyrgyzstan, Tajikistan, Uzbekistan.

**International Bank for Economic Co-operation—IBEC:** 107815 GSP Moscow B-78, ul. Masha Poryvaeva 11, Russia; tel. (095) 975-38-61; fax (095) 975-22-02; f. 1963 by members of the Council for Mutual Economic Assistance (dissolved in 1991), as a central institution for credit and settlements following the decision in 1989–91 of most member states to adopt a market economy, the IBEC abandoned its system of multilateral settlements in trans-

ferable roubles, and (from 1 January 1991) began to conduct all transactions in convertible currencies; provides credit and settlement facilities for member states, and also acts as an international commercial bank, offering services to commercial banks and enterprises; capital ECU 143.5m., reserves ECU 164.8m. (Dec. 1998); mems: 10 states, incl. Bulgaria, Czech Republic, Hungary, Poland, Romania and Slovakia; Chair. VITALII S. KHOKHLOV; Man. Dirs V. SYTNIKOV, A. ORASCU.

**International Investment Bank:** 107078 Moscow, ul. Masha Poryvaeva 7, Russia; tel. (095) 975-40-08; fax (095) 975-20-70; f. 1970 to grant credits for joint investment projects and the development of enterprises following the decision in 1989–91 of most member states to adopt a market economy, the Bank conducted its transactions (from 1 January 1991) in convertible currencies, rather than in transferable roubles; focuses on production and scientific and technical progress; mems: Bulgaria, Cuba, Czech Republic, Hungary, Mongolia, Poland, Romania, Russia, Slovakia and Viet Nam.

# Education

**Comparative Education Society in Europe—CESE:** Institut für Augemeine Pädagogik, Humboldt-Universität zu Berlin, Unter den Linden 6, 10099 Berlin, Germany; tel. (30) 20934094; fax (30) 20931006; e-mail juergen.schriewer@educat.hu-berlin.de; internet www.ceseurope.org; f. 1961 to promote teaching and research in comparative and international education; organizes conferences and promotes literature; mems: in 49 countries; Pres. Prof. DONATELLA PALOMBA (Italy); Sec. and Treas. Prof. MIGUEL A. PEREYRA (Spain); publ. *Newsletter* (quarterly).

**European Association for the Education of Adults:** rue Liedts 27, 1030 Brussels, Belgium; tel. (2) 513-5205; fax (2) 513-5734; e-mail eaea@eaea.org; internet www.eaea.org; f. 1953; aims to create a 'learning society' by encouraging demand for learning, particularly from women and excluded sectors of society; seeks to improve response of providers of learning opportunities and authorities and agencies; mems: 100 organizations in 34 countries; Pres. JÁNOS TÓTH; Gen. Sec. ELLINOR HAASE; publs *EAEA Monograph Series*, newsletter.

**European Cultural Foundation:** Jan van Goyenkade 5, 1075 HN Amsterdam, Netherlands; tel. (20) 6760222; fax (20) 6752231; e-mail eurocult@eurocult.org; internet www.eurocult.org; f. 1954 as a nongovernmental organization, supported by private sources, to promote activities of mutual interest to European countries on aspects of culture; maintains national committees in 23 countries and a transnational network of institutes and centres: European Institute of Education and Social Policy, Paris; Institute for European Environmental Policy, London, Madrid and Berlin; Association for Innovative Co-operation in Europe (AICE), Brussels; EURYDICE Central Unit (the Education Information Network of the European Community), Brussels; European Institute for the Media, Düsseldorf; European Foundation Centre, Brussels; Fund for Central and East European Book Projects, Amsterdam; Institute for Human Sciences, Vienna; East West Parliamentary Practice Project, Amsterdam; and Centre Européen de la Culture, Geneva. A grants programme, for European co-operation projects is also conducted; Pres. Princess MARGRIET OF THE NETHERLANDS; Sec.-Gen. GOTTFRIED WAGNER; publs *Annual Report*, *Newsletter* (3 a year).

**European Union of Arabic and Islamic Scholars** (Union Européenne des Arabisants et Islamisants—UEAI): c/o Prof. S. Naef, Univ. de Genève, Faculté des Lettres, 3 place de l'Université, 1211 Geneva 4, Switzerland; tel. (081) 5517840; fax (081) 5515386; e-mail silvia.naef@lettres.unige.ch; f. 1964 to organize congresses of Arabic and Islamic Studies; holds congresses every two years; mems: 300 in 28 countries; Pres. Prof. URBAIN VERMEULEN (Belgium); Sec. Prof. SILVIA NAEF (Italy).

**European University Association—EUA:** 42 rue de la Loi, 1040 Brussels, Belgium; tel. (2) 230-55-44; fax (2) 230-57-51; e-mail info@eua.unige.ch; internet www.unige.ch/eua/; f. 2001 by merger of the Association of European Universities and the Confederation of EU Rectors' Conferences; represents European universities and national rectors' conferences; promotes the development of a coherent system of European higher education and research; provides support and guidance to its mems; focuses policies and services on the creation of a European area for higher education and research. mems: 37 collective and 8 assoc. universities and rectors' conferences in 45 countries; Sec.-Gen. LESLEY WILSON; publs *Thema*, *Directory*, *Annual Report*.

# Environmental Conservation

**Baltic Marine Environment Protection Commission (Helsinki Commission)—HELCOM:** Katajanokanlaituri 6B, 00160 Helsinki, Finland; tel. (9) 6220220; fax (9) 62202239; e-mail helcom@helcom.fi; internet www.helcom.fi; f. 1980 to combat regional pollution; reorganized in Sept. 1999; mems: Denmark, Estonia, European Community, Finland, Germany, Latvia, Lithuania, Poland, Russia and Sweden; Exec. Sec. ANNE CHRISTINE BRUSENDORFF; publ. *Baltic Sea Environment Proceedings*.

**Regional Environmental Centre for Central and Eastern Europe:** 2000 Szentendre, Ady Endre ut. 9–11, Hungary; tel. (26) 311–199; fax (26) 311–294; e-mail rec-info@rec.org; internet www .rec.org; f. 1990; aims to assist in the solution of environmental problems in Central and Eastern Europe through the promotion of co-operation between non-governmental organizations, governments and businesses, the free exchange of information and public participation in decision-making; provides grants and training and facilitates networking; 15 local offices; Exec. Dir JERNEJ STRITIH.

**World Conservation Union—IUCN:** 28 rue Mauverney, 1196 Gland, Switzerland; tel. (22) 9990000; fax (22) 9990002; e-mail mail@hq.iucn.org; internet www.iucn.org; f. 1948, as the International Union for Conservation of Nature and Natural Resources; supports partnerships and practical field activities to promote the conservation of natural resources, to secure the conservation of biological diversity as an essential foundation for the future; to ensure wise use of the earth's natural resources in an equitable and sustainable way; and to guide the development of human communities towards ways of life in enduring harmony with other components of the biosphere, developing programmes to protect and sustain the most important and threatened species and eco-systems and assisting governments to devise and carry out national conservation strategies; maintains a conservation library and documentation centre and units for monitoring traffic in wildlife; mems: government agencies in 98 countries and national and international non-governmental organizations in 128 countries; 37 non-voting affiliate mems; Pres. YOLANDA KAKABADSE NAVARRO (Ecuador); Dir-Gen. ACHIM STEINER; publs *World Conservation Strategy*, *Caring for the Earth*, *Red List of Threatened Plants*, *Red List of Threatened Species*, *United Nations List of National Parks and Protected Areas*, *World Conservation* (quarterly), *IUCN Today*.

**World Wide Fund for Nature—WWF:** ave de Mont-Blanc, 1196 Gland, Switzerland; tel. (22) 3649111; fax (22) 3643239; e-mail kevans@wwfnet.org; internet www.panda.org; f. 1961 (as World Wildlife Fund); aims to stop the degradation of the natural environment, conserve bio-diversity, ensure the sustainable use of renewable resources, promote the reduction of pollution and wasteful consumption; mems: 27 national organizations, five associates, c. 5m. individual mems world-wide; Pres. Chief EMEKA ANYAOKU (Nigeria); Dir-Gen. Dr CLAUDE MARTIN.

# Government and Politics

**Central European Initiative—CEI:** CEI Executive Secretariat, Via Genova 9, 34121 Trieste, Italy; tel. (040) 7786777; fax (040) 360640; e-mail cei-es@cei-es.org; internet www.ceinet.org; f. 1989 as 'Quadrilateral' co-operation between Austria, Italy, Hungary and Yugoslavia, became 'Pentagonal' in 1990 with the admission of Czechoslovakia, and 'Hexagonal' with the admission of Poland in 1991, present name adopted in 1992, when Bosnia and Herzegovina, Croatia and Slovenia were admitted; the Czech Republic and Slovakia became separate mems in January 1993, and Macedonia also joined in that year; Albania, Belarus, Bulgaria, Romania and Ukraine joined the CEI in 1995 and Moldova in 1996; the Federal Republic of Yugoslavia (now Serbia and Montenegro) was admitted in 2000; aims to encourage regional and bilateral political and economic co-operation, working within the OSCE; Dir-Gen. Dr HARALD KREID.

**GUUAM:** internet www.guuam.org; f. 1997 as a consultative alliance of Georgia, Ukraine, Azerbaijan and Moldova (GUAM); Uzbekistan joined the grouping in April 1999, when it became known as GUUAM; GUUAM Charter adopted June 2001, defining a framework for co-operation; secretariat to be established in Ukraine; objectives include the promotion of political co-operation; participation in conflict resolution and peace-keeping activities; economic development, including the creation of an East–West trade corridor and transportation routes for petroleum; and integration with organizations such as NATO; also aims to combat religious intolerance and extremism, the proliferation of weapons of mass destruction, international terrorism and drugs-trafficking; in July 2002 heads of state, meeting in Yalta, Ukraine, signed a Declaration on Common Efforts to Ensure Stability and Security in the Region, an agreement on co-operation in the fields of terrorism, organized and other crime, and an agreement to establish a free trade area; also approved the establishment of an information office in Kiev, Ukraine.

**International Federation of Resistance Movements—FIR:** c/o R. Maria, 5 rue Rollin, 75005 Paris, France; tel. 1-43-26-84-29; f. 1951; supports the medical and social welfare of former victims of fascism; works for peace, disarmament and human rights, and against fascism and neo-fascism; mems: 82 national organizations in 29 countries; Pres. ALIX LHOTE (France); Sec.-Gen. OSKAR WIESFLECKER (Austria); publs *Feuille d'information* (in French and German), *Cahier d'informations médicales, sociales et juridiques* (in French and German).

**International Institute for Democracy and Electoral Assistance—IDEA:** Strömsborg, S-103 34 Stockholm, Sweden; tel. 8-698-3700; fax 8-20-2422; e-mail info@idea.int; internet www.idea.int; f. 1995; aims to promote sustainable democracy in new and established democracies; provides world-wide electoral assistance and focuses on broader democratic issues in Africa, the Caucasus and Latin America; 21 mem. states; Sec.-Gen. KAREN FOGG (United Kingdom).

**International Institute for Peace:** Möllwaldplatz 5, 1040 Vienna, Austria; tel. (1) 504-43-76; fax (1) 505-32-36; e-mail iip@aon.at; internet www.iip.at; f. 1957; non-governmental organization with consultative status at ECOSOC and UNESCO; studies conflict prevention; new structures in international law; security issues in Europe and world-wide; mems: individuals and corporate bodies invited by the executive board; Pres. ERWIN LANC (Austria); Dir PETER STANIA (Russia); publs *Peace and Security* (quarterly, in English), occasional papers (2 or 3 a year, in English and German).

**International Peace Bureau (IPB):** 41 rue de Zürich, 1201 Geneva, Switzerland; tel. (22) 7316429; fax (22) 7389419; e-mail mailbox@ipb.org; internet www.ipb.org; f. 1892; promotes international co-operation for general and complete disarmament and the non-violent solution of international conflicts; co-ordinates and represents peace movements at the UN; conducts projects on the abolition of nuclear weapons and the role of non-governmental organizations in conflict prevention and resolution; mems: 220 peace organizations in 53 countries; Pres. CORA WEISS; Sec.-Gen. COLIN ARCHER; publs *IPB News* (quarterly), *IPB Geneva News*.

**Inter-Parliamentary Union—IPU:** CP 438, 1211 Geneva, Switzerland; tel. (22) 9194150; fax (22) 9194160; e-mail postbox@mail .ipu.org; internet www.ipu.org; f. 1889 to promote peace, co-operation and representative democracy by providing a forum for multilateral political debate between representatives of national parliaments; mems: national parliaments of 142 sovereign states, incl. Armenia, Azerbaijan, Belarus, Georgia, Kazakhstan, Kyrgyzstan, Russia, Tajikistan, Ukraine and Uzbekistan; Sec.-Gen. ANDERS B. JOHNSSON (Sweden); publs *Chronicle of Parliamentary Elections* (annually), *The World of Parliaments* (quarterly), *World Directory of Parliaments* (annually).

**Non-aligned Movement—NAM:** c/o Permanent Representative of South Africa to the UN, 333 East 38th St, 9th Floor, New York, NY 10016, USA (no permanent secretariat); tel. (212) 213-5583; fax (212) 692-2498; e-mail soafun@worldnet.att.net; internet www.nam .gov.za; f. 1961 by a meeting of 25 Heads of State, with the aim of linking countries that had refused to adhere to the main East-West military and political blocs; co-ordination bureau established in 1973; works for the establishment of a new international economic order, and especially for better terms for countries producing raw materials; maintains special funds for agricultural development, improvement of food production and the financing of buffer stocks; South Commission promotes co-operation between developing countries; seeks changes in the United Nations to give developing countries greater decision-making power; holds summit conference every three years; 13th conference (2003): Kuala Lumpur, Malaysia; mems: 113 countries.

**Organization for the Prohibition of Chemical Weapons (OPCW):** Johan de Wittlaan 32, 2517JR The Hague, Netherlands; tel. (70) 4163300; fax (70) 3063535; e-mail inquiries@opcw.org; internet www.opcw.org; f. 1997 to oversee implementation of the Chemical Weapons Convention, which aims to ban the development, production, stockpiling and use of chemical weapons; the Convention was negotiated under the auspices of the UN Conference on Disarmament and entered into force in April 1997, at which time the OPCW was inaugurated; governed by an Executive Council, comprising representatives of 41 States Parties, elected on a regional basis; undertakes mandatory inspections of member states party to the Convention (151 at March 2003); provisional 2003 budget: €68.6m; Dir-Gen. ROGELIO PFIRTER.

**Shanghai Co-operation Organization—SCO:** f. 2001, replacing the Shanghai Five (f. 1996 to address border disputes); comprises People's Republic of China, Kazakhstan, Kyrgyzstan, Russia, Tajikistan and Uzbekistan; aims to achieve security through mutual co-operation; promotes economic co-operation and measures to eliminate terrorism and drugs-trafficking; agreement on combating terrorism signed June 2001; an SCO anti-terrorism centre was to be established in Bishkek, Kyrgyzstan; holds annual summit meeting (2003: Moscow, Russia).

**Unrepresented Nations' and Peoples' Organization—UNPO:** Eisenhowelaan 136, 2517 KN The Hague, Netherlands; tel. (70) 360-3318; fax (70) 360-3346; e-mail unpo@unpo.nl; internet www.unpo

.org; f. 1991 to provide an international forum for indigenous and other unrepresented peoples and minorities; provides training in human rights, law, diplomacy and public relations to UNPO members; provides conflict resolution services; mems: 52 organisations representing occupied nations, indigenous peoples and minorities; Gen. Sec. MICHAEL VAN WALT; publs *UNPO News, UNPO Yearbook*.

## Industrial and Professional Relations

**General Confederation of Trade Unions—GCTR:** 42 Leninsky Prospekt, 119119, Moscow, Russia; tel. (095) 938-79-15; fax (095) 938-21-55; e-mail mail@vkp.ru; internet www.vkp.ru; f. f. 1992; congress convenes every five years (4th congress: Moscow, Russia, Sept. 2002); mems: 48 trade union organizations from CIS countries, comprising about 75m. workers; Pres. VLADIMIR SCHERBAKOV.

**World Federation of Trade Unions—WFTU:** Branická 112, 14701 Prague 4, Czech Republic; tel. (2) 44462140; fax (2) 44461378; e-mail wftu@login.cz; internet www.wftu.cz; f. 1945 on a world-wide basis; mems: 132m. in 121 countries; Gen. Sec. ALEKSANDR ZHARIKOV (Russia); publ. *Flashes from the Trade Unions* (every 2 weeks).

## Law

**International Institute of Space Law—IISL:** c/o IAF, 3–5 rue Mario Nikis, 75015 Paris, France; tel. 1-45-67-42-60; fax 1-42-73-21-20; e-mail iaf@wanadoo.fr; internet www.iafastro.com; f. 1959 at the XI Congress of the International Astronautical Federation; organizes annual Space Law colloquium; studies juridical and sociological aspects of astronautics; makes awards; Pres. NANDASIRI JASENTULIYANAARBOSA (USA); publs *Proceedings of Annual Colloquium on Space Law, Survey of Teaching of Space Law in the World.*

**International Nuclear Law Association—INLA:** 29 sq. de Meeûs, 1000 Brussels, Belgium; tel. (2) 547-58-41; fax (2) 503-04-40; e-mail aidn.inla@skynet.be; internet www.aidn-inla.be; f. 1972 to promote international studies of legal problems related to the peaceful use of nuclear energy; holds conference every two years; mems: 500 in 30 countries; Sec.-Gen. V. VERBRAEKEN; publs *Congress reports, Une Histoire de 25 ans.*

## Medicine and Health

**Association of National European and Mediterranean Societies of Gastroenterology—ASNEMGE:** c/o Andrea Bauer, Vereinsmanagement Lassingleithnerplatz 2/3, 1020 Vienna, Austria; tel. 1-533-35-42; fax 1-535-10-45; e-mail info@asnemge.org; internet www.asnemge.org; f. 1947 to facilitate the exchange of ideas between gastroenterologists and to disseminate knowledge; organizes International Congress of Gastroenterology every four years; mems: in 37 countries, national societies and sections of national medical societies; Pres. Prof. PETER FERENCI (Austria); Sec. Prof. JØRGEN RASK-MADSEN (Denmark).

**Balkan Medical Union** (Uniunii Medicale Balcanice—UMB): POB 149, 1 rue G. Clémenceau, 70148 Bucharest, Romania; tel. (1) 3137857; fax (1) 3121570; f. 1932; studies medical problems, particularly ailments specific to the Balkan region; promotes a regional programme of public health; facilitates the exchange of information between doctors in the region; organizes research programmes and congresses; mems: doctors and specialists from Albania, Bulgaria, Cyprus, Greece, Moldova, Romania, Turkey and the former Yugoslav republics; Pres. Prof. H. CIOBANU (Moldova); publs *Archives de l'union médicale Balkanique* (quarterly), *Bulletin de l'union médicale Balkanique* (6 a year), *Annuaire.*

**European Association for Studies on Nutrition and Child Development:** 9 blvd des Capucines, 75002 Paris, France; tel. 1-44-73-67-39; fax 1-44-73-67-39; e-mail ade.paris@wanadoo.fr; f. 1969; conducts research and humanitarian work in Albania, the People's Republic of China, Georgia, Poland, Russia, Sudan and Uganda; Pres. Z. L. OSTROWSKI; publ. *Newsletter.*

**European Health Management Association—EHMA:** Vergemount Hall, Clonskeagh, Dublin 6, Ireland; tel. (1) 2839299; fax (1) 2838653; e-mail pcberman@ehma.org; internet www.ehma.org; f. 1966; aims to improve health care in Europe by raising standards of managerial performance in the health sector; fosters co-operation between health service organizations and institutions in the field of health-care management education and training; mems: 225 in 30 countries; Pres. Dr ROBERT F. KONING; Dir PHILIP C. BERMAN; publs *Newsletter, Eurobriefing* (quarterly).

**World Self-Medication Industry—WSMI:** Centre International de Bureaux, 13 chemin du Levant, 01210 Ferney-Voltaire, France; tel. 450-28-47-28; fax 450-28-40-24; e-mail dwebber@wsmi.org; internet www.wsmi.org; Dir-Gen. Dr DAVID E. WEBBER.

## Posts and Telecommunications

**European Conference of Postal and Telecommunications Administrations:** Ministry of Transport and Communications, Odos Xenofontos 13, 10191 Athens, Greece; tel. (1) 9236494; fax (1) 9237133; internet www.cept.org; f. 1959 to strengthen relations between member administrations and to harmonize and improve their technical services; set up Eurodata Foundation, for research and publishing; mems: 26 countries; Sec. Z. PROTOPSALTI; publ. *Bulletin.*

**European Telecommunications Satellite Organization—EUTELSAT:** 70 rue Balard, 75015, Paris Cédex 15, France; tel. 1-53-98-47-47; fax 1-53-98-37-00; internet www.eutelsat.com; f. 1977 to operate satellites for fixed and mobile communications in Europe; EUTELSAT's in-orbit resource comprises 18 satellites; commercialises capacity in three satellites operated by other companies; mems: public and private telecommunications operations in 47 countries; Dir-Gen. GIULIANO BERRETTA.

**Internet Corporation for Assigned Names and Numbers—ICANN:** 4676 Admiralty Way, Suite 330, Marina del Rey, CA 90292-6601, USA; tel. (310) 823-9358; fax (310) 823-8649; e-mail icann@icann.org; internet www.icann.org; f. 1998; non-profit, private-sector body; aims to co-ordinate the technical management and policy development of the internet; comprises three Supporting Organizations to assist, review and develop recommendations on internet policy and structure relating to addresses, domain names, and protocol; Pres. and CEO STUART LYNN.

## Press, Radio and Television

**Asia-Pacific Broadcasting Union—ABU:** POB 1164, 59700 Kuala Lumpur, Malaysia; tel. (3) 22823592; fax (3) 22825292; e-mail sg@abu.org.my; internet www.abu.org.my; f. 1964 to foster and co-ordinate the development of broadcasting in the Asia-Pacific area, to develop means of establishing closer collaboration and co-operation among broadcasting orgs, and to serve the professional needs of broadcasters in Asia and the Pacific; holds annual General Assembly; mems: 102 in 50 countries and territories; Pres. KATSUJI EBISAWA (Japan); Sec.-Gen. HUGH LEONARD; publs *ABU News* (every 2 months), *ABU Technical Review* (every 2 months).

**Broadcasting Organization of Non-aligned Countries—BONAC:** c/o Cyprus Broadcasting Corpn, POB 4824, 1397 Nicosia, Cyprus; tel. (2) 422231; fax (2) 314050; e-mail rik@cybc.com.cy; f. 1977 to ensure an equitable, objective and comprehensive flow of information through broadcasting; Secretariat moves to the broadcasting organization of host country; mems: in 102 countries.

**European Alliance of Press Agencies:** Norrbackagatan 23, 11341 Stockholm; tel. (8) 301-324; e-mail erik-n@telia.com; internet www.pressalliance.com; f. 1957 to assist co-operation among members and to study and protect their common interests; annual assembly; mems: in 30 countries; Sec.-Gen. ERIK NYLÉN.

**European Broadcasting Union—EBU:** CP 45, Ancienne-Route 17A, 1218 Grand-Saconnex, Geneva, Switzerland; tel. (22) 7172111; fax (22) 74740003; e-mail ebu@ebu.ch; internet www.eurovision.net; f. 1950 in succession to the International Broadcasting Union; a professional asscn of broadcasting organizations, supporting the interests of members and assisting the development of broadcasting in all its forms; activities include the Eurovision news and programme exchanges and the Euroradio music exchanges; mems: 71 active (European) in 52 countries, and 45 associate in 28 countries; Pres. ARNE WESSBERG (Finland); Sec.-Gen. JEAN STOCK (France); publs *EBU Technical Review* (annually), *Diffusion* (2 a year).

**Organization of Asia-Pacific News Agencies—OANA:** c/o Xinhua News Agency, 57 Xuanwumen Xidajie, Beijing 100803, People's Republic of China; tel. (10) 3074762; fax (10) 3072707; internet www.oananews.com; f. 1961 to promote co-operation in professional matters and mutual exchange of news, features, etc. among the news agencies of Asia and the Pacific via the Asia-Pacific News Network (ANN); mems: Anadolu Ajansi (Turkey), Antara (Indonesia), APP (Pakistan), Bakhtar (Afghanistan), BERNAMA (Malaysia), BSS (Bangladesh), ENA (Bangladesh), Hindustan Samachar (India), IRNA (Iran), ITAR-TASS (Russia), Kaz-TAG (Kazakhstan), KABAR (Kyrgyzstan), KCNA (Korea, Democratic People's Republic), KPL (Laos), Kyodo (Japan), Lankapuvath (Sri Lanka), Montsame (Mongolia), PNA (Philippines), PPI (Pakistan), PTI (India), RSS (Nepal), Samachar Bharati (India), TNA (Thailand), UNB (Bangladesh), UNI (India), Viet Nam News Agency, Xinhua (People's Republic of China), Yonhap (Republic of Korea); Pres. GUO CHAOREN; Sec.-Gen. MIKHAIL GUSMANN.

# Religion

**Aid to Believers in the Soviet Union—ABSU:** 91 rue Olivier de Serres, 75015 Paris, France; tel. 1-42-50-53-46; fax 1-42-50-19-08; e-mail acerus@club-internet.fr; f. 1961; supports Christianity, in particular the Russian Orthodox Church, in the countries of the former USSR; Pres. A. VICTOROFF; publ. *Bulletin de l'Aide aux Chretiens de Russie*.

**Conference of European Churches—CEC:** POB 2100, 150 route de Ferney, 1211 Geneva 2, Switzerland; tel. (22) 7916111; fax (22) 7916227; e-mail cec@cec-kek.org; internet www.cec-kek.org; f. 1959 as a regional ecumenical organization for Europe and a meeting-place for European churches, including members and non-members of the World Council of Churches; holds assemblies every six years; mems: 128 Protestant, Anglican, Orthodox and Old Catholic churches in all European countries; Gen. Sec. Rev. Dr KEITH CLEMENTS; publs *Monitor* (quarterly), CEC communiqués, reports.

**European Baptist Federation—EBF:** Postfach 610340, 22423 Hamburg, Germany; tel. (40) 5509723; fax (40) 5509725; e-mail office@ebf.org; internet www.ebf.org; f. 1949 to promote fellowship and co-operation among Baptists in Europe to further the aims and objects of the Baptist World Alliance; to stimulate and co-ordinate evangelism in Europe; to provide for consultation and planning of missionary work in Europe and elsewhere in the world; mems: 49 Baptist Unions in European countries and the Middle East; Pres. DAVID COFFEY; Sec.-Treas. Rev. KARL-HEINZ WALTER (Germany).

**Muslim World League—MWL** (Rabitat al-Alam al-Islami): POB 537–538, Makkah, Saudi Arabia; tel. (2) 5422733; fax (2) 5436619; e-mail mwlhq@aol.com; internet www.arab.net/mwl; f. 1962; aims to advance Islamic unity and solidarity, and to promote world peace and respect for human rights; provides financial assistance for education, medical care and relief work; has 30 offices throughout the world; Sec.-Gen. Dr ABDULLAH BIN ABDULMOSHIN AL-TURKI; publs *Majalla al-Rabita* (monthly, Arabic), *Akhbar al-Alam al Islami* (weekly, Arabic), *Journal* (monthly, English).

**Slavic Gospel Association:** 6151 Commonwealth Dr., Loves Park, IL 61111, USA; tel. (815) 282-8900; fax (815) 282-8901; e-mail sga@sga.org; internet www.sga.org; f. 1934; runs Regional Ministry Centres in Belarus, Russia and Ukraine; sponsors bible and ministry training to church pastors and workers in CIS countries; provides Russian-language bibles and Christian literature; sponsors national church-planting missionaries and humanitarian aid; Pres. Dr ROBERT W. PROVOST; publs *Insight* (monthly newsletter), *Prayer and Praise* (calendar).

**Union of Councils of Soviet Jews:** 1819 H St, N.W., Suite 230, Washington, DC 20006, USA; tel. (202) 775-9770; fax (202) 775-9776; e-mail ltaxman@ucsj.com; internet www.ucsj.com; f. 1970; supports the Jewish community in the former USSR through eight bureaux in Moscow, St Petersburg, Almaty, Bishkek, Lviv, Riga, Tiblisi and Minsk; co-ordinates the Yad L'Yad partnership programme, linking Jewish communities in the former USSR with participating schools and synagogues in the USA; Pres. YOSEF I. ABRAMOWITZ; Sec. MICHA H. MAFTALIN.

**World Council of Churches (WCC):** Route de Ferney 150, Postfach 2100, 1211 Geneva 2, Switzerland; tel. (22) 7916111; fax (22) 7910361; e-mail info@wcc-coe.org; internet www.wcc-coe.org; f. 1948 to promote co-operation between Christian Churches and to prepare for a clearer manifestation of the unity of the Church; Activities are grouped into four 'clusters': Relationships, Issues and Themes, Communication, and Finance, Services and Administration; mems: 342 Churches in more than 120 countries, incl. Armenia and Russia; Gen. Sec. Rev. Dr KONRAD RAISER (Germany); publs *Current Dialogue* (2 a year), *Ecumenical News International* (weekly), *Ecumenical Review* (quarterly), *International Review of Mission* (quarterly), *WCC Yearbook*.

# Science

**European Association of Geoscientists and Engineers—EAGE:** c/o EAGE Holdings, 3990 DB Houten, Netherlands; tel. (30) 6354055; fax (30) 6343524; e-mail eage@eage.nl; internet www.eage.nl; f. 1997 by merger of European Asscn of Exploration Geophysicists and Engineers (f. 1951) and the European Asscn of Petroleum Geoscientists and Engineers (f. 1988); these two organizations have become, respectively, the Geophysical and the Petroleum Divisions of the EAGE; aims to promote the applications of geoscience and related subjects and to foster co-operation between those working or studying in the fields; organizes conferences, workshops, education programmes and exhibitions; seeks global co-operation with organizations with similar objectives; mems: approx. 5,400 in 95 countries; Exec. Dir A. VAN GERWEN; publs *Geophysical Prospecting* (6 a year), *First Break* (monthly), *Petroleum Geoscience* (quarterly).

**Federation of European Biochemical Societies:** c/o Institute of Cancer Biology and Danish Centre for Human Genome Research, Danish Cancer Society, Strandboulevarden 49, 2100 Copenhagen Ø, Denmark; tel. 3525-7364; fax 3525-7376; e-mail secretariat@febs.org; internet www.febs.org; f. 1964 to promote the science of biochemistry through meetings of European biochemists, advanced courses and the provision of fellowships; mems: 40,000 in 34 societies; Chair. Prof. C. RODRIGUES-POUSADA; Sec.-Gen. Prof. JULIO E. CELIS; publs *European Journal of Biochemistry*, *FEBS Letters*, *FEBS Newsletter*.

**International Council for Science—ICSU:** 51 blvd de Montmorency, 75016 Paris, France; tel. 1-45-25-03-29; fax 1-42-88-94-31; e-mail secretariat@icsu.org; internet www.icsu.org; f. 1919 as International Research Council; present name adopted 1931; new statutes adopted 1996; to co-ordinate international co-operation in theoretical and applied sciences and to promote national scientific research through the intermediary of affiliated national organizations; General Assembly of representatives of national and scientific members meets every three years to formulate policy. The following committees have been established: Cttee on Science for Food Security, Scientific Cttee on Antarctic Research, Scientific Cttee on Oceanic Research, Cttee on Space Research, Scientific Cttee on Water Research, Scientific Cttee on Solar-Terrestrial Physics, Cttee on Science and Technology in Developing Countries, Cttee on Data for Science and Technology, Programme on Capacity Building in Science, Scientific Cttee on Problems of the Environment, Steering Cttee on Genetics and Biotechnology and Scientific Cttee on International Geosphere-Biosphere Programme. The following services and Inter-Union Committees and Commissions have been established: Federation of Astronomical and Geophysical Data Analysis Services, Inter-Union Commission on Frequency Allocations for Radio Astronomy and Space Science, Inter-Union Commission on Radio Meteorology, Inter-Union Commission on Spectroscopy, Inter-Union Commission on Lithosphere; national mems: academies or research councils in 98 countries; scientific mems and assocs: 26 international unions and 28 scientific associates; Pres. W. ARBER; Sec.-Gen. H. A. MOONEY; publs *ICSU Yearbook*, *Science International* (quarterly), *Annual Report*.

# Social Sciences

**Association for the Study of the World Refugee Problem—AWR:** Piazzale di Porta Pia 121, 00198 Rome, Italy; tel. (06) 44250159; f. 1951 to promote and co-ordinate scholarly research on refugee problems; mems: 475 in 19 countries; Pres. FRANCO FOSCHI (Italy); Sec.-Gen. ALDO CLEMENTE (Italy); publs *AWR Bulletin* (quarterly, in English, French, Italian and German), treatises on refugee problems (17 vols).

**European Association for Population Studies—EAPS:** POB 11676, 2502 AR The Hague, Netherlands; tel. (70) 3565200; fax (70) 3647187; e-mail contact@eaps.nl; internet www.eaps.nl; f. 1983 to foster research and provide information on European population problems; organizes conferences, seminars and workshops; mems: demographers from 40 countries; Exec. Sec. GYS BEETS; publ. *European Journal of Population/Revue Européenne de Démographie* (quarterly).

**European Co-ordination Centre for Research and Documentation in Social Sciences:** 1010 Vienna, Grünangergasse 2, Austria; tel. (1) 512-43-33-0; fax (1) 512-53-66-16; f. 1963 for promotion of contacts between East and West European countries in all areas of social sciences; activities include co-ordination of international comparative research projects; training of social scientists in problems of international research; organization of conferences; exchange of information and documentation; administered by a Board of Directors (23 social scientists from East and West) and a permanent secretariat in Vienna; Pres. ØRJAR ØYEN (Norway); Dir L. KIUZADJAN; publs *Vienna Centre Newsletter*, *ECSSID Bulletin*, and books.

**International Peace Academy—IPA:** 777 United Nations Plaza, New York, NY 10017, USA; tel. (212) 687-4300; fax (212) 983-8246; e-mail ipa@ipacademy.org; internet www.ipacademy.org; f. 1970 to promote the prevention and settlement of armed conflicts between and within states through policy research and development; educates government officials in the procedures needed for conflict resolution, peace-keeping, mediation and negotiation, through international training seminars and publications; off-the-record meetings are also conducted to gain complete understanding of a specific conflict; Chair. RITA E. HAUSER; Pres. DAVID M. MALONE; publs *Annual Report*, *Newsletter* (2 a year).

# Social Welfare and Human Rights

**European Federation of Older Persons—EURAG:** Wielandg-asse 9, 1 Stock, 8010 Graz, Austria; tel. (316) 81-46-08; fax (316) 81-47-67; e-mail eurag.europe@aon.at; internet www.eurag-europe.org; f. 1962 as the European Federation for the Welfare of the Elderly (present name adopted 2002); serves as a forum for the exchange of experience and practical co-operation among member organizations; represents the interests of members before international organizations; promotes understanding and co-operation in matters of social welfare; draws attention to the problems of old age; mems: organizations in 33 countries; Pres. ÉDMÉE MANGERS-ANEN (Luxembourg); Sec.-Gen. Dr ULLA HERFORT-WÖRNDLE (Austria); publs (in English, French, German and Italian) *EURAG Newsletter* (quarterly), *EURAG Information* (monthly).

**International Federation of Red Cross and Red Crescent Societies:** 17 Chemin des Crêts, Petit-Saconnex, CP 372, 1211 Geneva 19, Switzerland; tel. (22) 7304222; fax (22) 7330395; e-mail secretariat@ifrc.org; internet www.ifrc.org; f. 1919 to prevent and alleviate human suffering and to promote humanitarian activities by national Red Cross and Red Crescent societies; conducts relief operations for refugees and victims of disasters, co-ordinates relief supplies and assists in disaster prevention; Pres. JUAN MANUEL SUÁREZ DEL TORO RIVERO (Spain); Sec.-Gen. DIDIER CHERPITEL (France); publs *Annual Report, Red Cross Red Crescent* (quarterly), *Weekly News, World Disasters Report, Emergency Appeal*.

**International Organization for Migration—IOM:** 17 route des Morillons, CP 71, 1211 Geneva 19, Switzerland; tel. (22) 7179111; fax (22) 7986150; e-mail info@iom.int; internet www.iom.int; f. 1951 as Intergovernmental Cttee for Migration; name changed in 1989; a non-political and humanitarian organization, activities include the handling of orderly, planned migration to meet the needs of emigration and immigration countries and the processing and movement of refugees, displaced persons etc. in need of international migration services; mems: 71 countries; an additional 46 countries and 49 international governmental organizations hold observer status; Dir-Gen. BRUNSON MCKINLEY (USA); publs include *International Migration* (quarterly) and *IOM News* (quarterly, in English, French and Spanish).

**International Society for Human Rights:** 60388 Frankfurt-am-Main, Borsigallee 9, Germany; tel. (69) 4201080; fax (69) 420108-33; e-mail is@ishr.org; internet www.ishr.org; f. 1972; promotes fundamental human rights and religious freedom; mems: 30,000 in 25 national sections (incl. Azerbaijan, Belarus, Moldova, Russia, Ukraine, Uzbekistan) and three regional sections; Pres. ALEXANDER FRHR. VON BISCHOFFSHAUSEN (Germany); publs *Für die Menschenrechte* (every two months), *Newsletter* (quarterly).

**Médecins sans frontières—MSF:** 39 rue de la Tourelle, 1040 Brussels, Belgium; tel. (2) 280-18-81; fax (2) 280-01-73; internet www.msf.org; f. 1971; independent medical humanitarian org. composed of physicians and other members of the medical profession; aims to provide medical assistance to victims of war and natural disasters; operates longer-term programmes of nutrition, immunization, sanitation, public health, and rehabilitation of hospitals and dispensaries; awarded the Nobel peace prize in Oct. 1999; mems: national sections in 18 countries in Europe, Asia and North America; Pres. Dr NORTEN ROSTRUP; Sec.-Gen. RAFAEL VILASANJUAN; publ. *Activity Report* (annually).

# Sport and Recreations

**International Gymnastic Federation:** rue des Oeuches 10, CP 359, 2740 Moutier 1, Switzerland; tel. (32) 4946410; fax (32) 4946419; e-mail gymnastics@fig.worldsport.org; f. 1881 to promote the exchange of official documents and publications on gymnastics; mems: in 122 countries and territories; Pres. BRUNO GRANDI; Gen. Sec. NORBERT BUECHE (Switzerland); publs *FIG Bulletin* (quarterly), *World of Gymnastics Magazine* (quarterly).

**International Olympic Committee—IOC:** Château de Vidy, 1007 Lausanne, Switzerland; tel. (21) 6216111; fax (21) 6216216; internet www.olympic.org; f. 1894 to ensure the regular celebration of the Olympic Games; the IOC is the supreme authority on all questions concerning the Olympic Games and the Olympic movement; mems: 125 representatives; Dir-Gen. URS LACOTTE; publ. *Olympic Review* (6 a year).

**International Skating Union—ISU:** chemin de Primerose 2, 1007 Lausanne, Switzerland; tel. (21) 6126666; fax (21) 6126677; e-mail info@isu.ch; internet www.isu.org; f. 1892; holds regular conferences; mems: 73 national federations in 57 countries; Pres. OTTAVIO CINQUANTA; Gen.-Sec. FREDI SCHMID; publs Judges' manuals, referees' handbooks, general and special regulations.

**International Ski Federation** (Fédération internationale de ski—FIS): 3653 Oberhofen am Thunersee, Switzerland; tel. (33) 2446161; fax (33) 2446171; internet www.fis-ski.com; f. 1924 to further the sport of skiing to prevent discrimination in skiing matters on racial, religious or political grounds; to organize World Ski Championships and regional championships and, as supreme international skiing authority, to establish the international competition calendar and rules for all ski competitions approved by the FIS, and to arbitrate in any disputes; mems: 100 national ski asscns; Pres. GIAN-FRANCO KASPER (Switzerland); Sec.-Gen. SARAH LEWIS (UK); publ. *FIS Bulletin* (quarterly).

**International Tennis Federation:** Bank Lane, Roehampton, London, SW15 5XZ, United Kingdom; tel. (20) 8878-6464; fax (20) 8878-7799; e-mail communications@itftennis.com; internet www.itftennis.com; f. 1913 to govern the game of tennis throughout the world, promote its teaching and preserve its independence of outside authority; produces the Rules of Tennis; promotes the Davis Cup Competition for men, the Fed. Cup for women, the Olympic Games Tennis Event, wheelchair tennis, 16 cups for veterans, the ITF Sunshine Cup and the ITF Continental Connelly Cup for players of 18 years old and under, the World Youth Cup for players of 16 years old and under, and the World Junior Tennis Tournament for players of 14 years old and under; organizes tournaments; mems: 141 full and 57 associate; Pres. FRANCESCO RICCI BITTI; publs *World of Tennis* (annually), *Davis Cup Yearbook, ITF World* (quarterly), *ITF This Week* (weekly).

**Union of European Football Associations—UEFA:** route de Genève 46, 1260 Nyon 2, Switzerland; tel. (22) 9944444; fax (22) 9944488; internet www.uefa.com; f. 1954; works on behalf of Europe's national football asscns to promote football; aims to foster unity and solidarity between national asscns; mems: 51 national asscns; Pres. LENNART JOHANSSON; CEO GERHARD AIGNER; Publ *Magazine* (available online).

**World Chess Federation** (Fédération internationale des echecs—FIDE): POB 166, 1000 Lausanne 4, Switzerland; tel. (21) 3103900; e-mail fide@fide.ch; internet www.fideonline.com; f. 1924; controls chess competitions of world importance and awards international chess titles; mems: national orgs in more than 160 countries; Pres. KIRSAN ILYUMZHINOV; publs (annually), *International Rating List* (2 a year).

# Technology

**Regional Council of Co-ordination of Central and East European Engineering Organizations:** c/o MTESZ, 1055 Budapest, Kossuth Lajos tér 6–8, Hungary; tel. (361) 353-4795; fax (361) 353-0317; e-mail mtesz@mtesz.hu; f. 1992; Hon. Pres. JÁNOS TÓTH.

**World Association of Industrial and Technological Research Organizations—WAITRO:** c/o SIRIM Berhad, 1 Persiaran Dato' Menteri, Section 2, POB 7035, 40911 Shah Alam, Malaysia; tel. 5544-6635; fax 5544-6735; e-mail info@waitro.sirim.my; internet www.waitro.org; f. 1970 by the UN Industrial Development Organization to organize co-operation in industrial and technological research; provides financial assistance for training and joint activities; arranges international seminars; facilitates the exchange of information; mems: 200 research institutes in 80 countries; Pres. BJORN LUNDBERG (Sweden); Contact MOSES MENGU; publs *WAITRO News* (quarterly), *WAITRO News*(quarterly).

**World Association of Nuclear Operators—WANO-CC:** Kings Bldgs, 16 Smith Sq., London, SW1P 3JG, United Kingdom; tel. (20) 7828-2111; fax (20) 7828-6691; internet www.wano.org.uk; f. 1989 by operators of nuclear power plants; aims to improve the safety and operability of nuclear power plants through the exchange of operating experience; operates four regional centres (in France, Japan, Russia and the USA) and a co-ordinating centre in the UK; mems: in 34 countries; Dir (Co-ordinating Centre) V. J. MADDEN.

# Tourism

**International Tourist Association (ASTOUR):** 113532 Moscow, Ozerkovskaya 50, Russian Federation; tel. (095) 235-36-88; fax (095) 230-27-84; f. 1992; promotes travel to Russia and other member countries of the CIS; Exec. Dir JANNE ANDRIANOVA; Publ. *Journal* (monthly).

**World Tourism Organization:** Calle Capitán Haya 42, 28020 Madrid, Spain; tel. (91) 5678100; fax (91) 5713733; e-mail comm@world-tourism.org; internet www.world-tourism.org; f. 1975 to promote travel and tourism; co-operates with member governments; secures financing for and carries out tourism development projects; provides training in tourism-related issues; works for sustainable and environmentally-friendly tourism development; encourages the liberalization of trade in tourism services; considers health and safety issues related to tourism; collects, analyses and disseminates data and operates a Documentation Centre; mems: governments of 138 countries and territories, also associate members, observers and over 300 affiliated mems; Sec.-Gen. FRANCESCO FRANGIALLI; publs *Yearbook of Tourism Statistics, Compendium of Tourism Statistics, Travel and Tourism Barometer, WTO News, Tourism Market Trends, Directory of Multilateral and Bilateral Sources of Financing for Tourism Development*, guide-lines and studies.

## Trade and Industry

**Association of European Chambers of Commerce and Industry—EUROCHAMBRES:** 5 rue d'Archimède, 1000 Brussels, Belgium; tel. (2) 282-08-50; fax (2) 230-00-38; e-mail eurochambres@eurochambres.be; internet www.eurochambres.be; f. 1958 to promote the exchange of experience and information among its members and to bring their joint opinions to the attention of the institutions of the European Union; conducts studies and seminars; coordinates EU projects; mems: 15 full and 18 affiliated mems; Pres. JÖRG MITTELSTEN SCHEID (Germany); Sec.-Gen. ARNALDO ABRUZZINI (Italy).

**International Co-operative Alliance—ICA: Regional Office for Europe:** 15 route des Morillons, 1218 Grand-Saconnex, Geneva, Switzerland; tel. (22) 9298888; fax (22) 7984122; e-mail ica@coop.org; internet www.coop.org/europe; f. 1994; promotes the role of co-operatives and supports their development in Central and Eastern Europe, and aims to establish centres to process data and to provide expertise, training and other resources; in 1998 a Plan of Action on Gender Equality was adopted; a Regional Assembly is usually held once every two years (Oct. 2002: Lisbon, Portugal); mems: 92 orgs in 37 countries; Regional Dir GABRIELLA SOZÁNSKI (Hungary).

**World Federation of Trade Unions (WFTU):** Branická 112, 14701 Prague 4, Czech Republic; tel. (2) 44462140; fax (2) 44461378; e-mail wftu@login.cz; internet www.wftu.cz; f. 1945 on a world-wide basis; mems: 132m. in 121 countries; Gen. Sec. ALEKSANDR ZHARIKOV (Russia); publ. *Flashes from the Trade Unions* (every 2 weeks).

**World Trade Organization:** Centre William Rappard, rue de Lausanne 154, 1211 Geneva, Switzerland; tel. (22) 7395111; fax (22) 7314206; e-mail enquiries@wto.org; internet www.wto.org; f. 1 Jan. 1995 as the successor to the General Agreement on Tariffs and Trade (GATT); aims to encourage development and economic reform among developing countries and countries with economies in transition participating in the international trading system; mems: 144 countries at mid-2002, incl. Georgia, Kyrgyzstan and Moldova; Observer countries include Armenia, Azerbaijan, Belarus, Kazakhstan, Russia, Ukraine and Uzbekistan, all of which have applied to join the Organization; Dir-Gen. SUPACHAI PANITCHPAKDI (Thailand); publs *Annual Report* (2 volumes), *WTO Focus* (monthly).

## Transport

**Danube Commission:** Benczúr utca 25, 1068 Budapest, Hungary; tel. (1) 352-1835; fax (1) 352-1839; e-mail secretariat@danubecom-intern.org; internet www.danubecom-intern.org; f. 1948; ; supervises implementation of the Belgrade Convention on the Regime of Navigation on the Danube; approves projects for river maintenance; supervises a uniform system of traffic regulations on the whole navigable portion of the Danube and on river inspection; mems: Austria, Bulgaria, Croatia, Germany, Hungary, Moldova, Romania, Russia, Serbia and Montenegro, Slovakia, Ukraine; Pres. Dr S. NICK; Dir-Gen. Capt. D. NEDIALKOV; publs *Basic Regulations for Navigation on the Danube, Hydrological Yearbook, Statistical Yearbook*, proceedings of sessions.

**European Civil Aviation Conference—ECAC:** 3 bis Villa Emile-Bergerat, 92522 Neuilly-sur-Seine Cédex, France; tel. 1-46-41-85-44; fax 1-46-24-18-18; e-mail ecac@compuserve.com; internet www.ecac-ceac.org; f. 1955; aims to promote the continued development of a safe, efficient and sustainable European air transport system; mems: 41 European states; Pres. ALFREDO ROMA; Exec. Sec. RAYMOND BENJAMIN.

**European Conference of Ministers of Transport—ECMT:** 2 rue André Pascal, 75775 Paris Cédex 16, France; tel. 1-45-24-82-00; fax 1-45-24-97-42; e-mail ecmt.contact@oecd.org; internet www.oecd.org/cem; f. 1953 to achieve the maximum use and most rational development of European transport; aims to create a safe, sustainable, efficient, integrated transport system; provides a forum for analysis and discussion; holds round tables, seminars and symposia; shares Secretariat staff with OECD; mems: 43 member countries, 6 associate mems, 2 observer countries; Sec.-Gen. JACK SHORT; publs *Activities of the Conference* (annually), *ECMT News* (2 a year), *Catalogue of Publications*, various statistical publications and surveys.

**Organisation for the Collaboration of Railways:** Hoża 63–67, 00681 Warsaw, Poland; tel. (22) 6573600; fax (22) 6573654; e-mail osjd@osjd.org.pl; f. 1956; aims to improve standards and co-operation in railway traffic between countries of Europe and Asia; promotes co-operation on issues relating to traffic policy and economic and environmental aspects of railway traffic; ensures enforcement of a number of rail agreements; aims to elaborate and standardize general principles for international transport law. Conference of Ministers of mem. countries meets once a year; Conference of Gen. Dirs of Railways meets at least once a year; mems: ministries of transport of 27 countries world-wide; Chair. TADEUSZ SZOZDA; publ *OSShD Journal* (every 2 months, in Chinese, German and Russian).

## Youth and Students

**WFUNA Youth:** c/o Palais des Nations, 16 ave Jean-Tremblay, 1211 Geneva 10, Switzerland; tel. (22) 7985850; fax (22) 7334838; internet www.wfuna-youth.org; f. 1948 by the World Federation of United Nations Associations (WFUNA) as the International Youth and Student Movement for the United Nations (ISMUN), independent since 1949; an international non-governmental organization of students and young people dedicated especially to supporting the principles embodied in the United Nations Charter and Universal Declaration of Human Rights; encourages constructive action in building economic, social and cultural equality and in working for national independence, social justice and human rights on a world-wide scale; maintains regional offices in Austria, France, Ghana, Panama and the USA; mems: asscns in 53 countries world-wide; Pres. ALYSON KELLY.

**World Federation of Democratic Youth—WFDY:** POB 147, 1389 Budapest, Hungary; tel. (1) 3502202; fax (1) 3501204; e-mail wfdy@mail.matav.hu; internet www.wfdy.org; f. 1945 to strive for peace, disarmament and joint action by democratic and progressive youth movements and for the creation of a new and more just international economic order; promotes national independence, democracy, social progress and youth rights; supports the liberation struggles in Asia, Africa and Latin America; mems: 152 members in 102 countries; Pres. IRAKLIS TSAVDARIDIS (Greece); publ. *WFDY News* (every 3 months, in English, French and Spanish).

# RESEARCH INSTITUTES

## ASSOCIATIONS AND INSTITUTES STUDYING EASTERN EUROPE, RUSSIA AND CENTRAL ASIA

### ARGENTINA

**Centro de Estudios de Europa Central y Oriental (CEECO)** (Centre for East and Central European Studies): Blanco Encalada 3225 D 8, 1428 Buenos Aires; tel. and fax (11) 4541-8676; e-mail ceeco@mail.fsoc.uba.ar; f. 1992; researches current and regional affairs, such as devts in the petroleum sector, economic reform, ethnic, religious and national problems, migration and border demarcation, organized crime, peace-keeping and post-communist issues; affiliated to the Argentine Council for Int. Relations (CARI) and the School of Social Sciences of the Univ. of Buenos Aires; Dir Prof. JUAN BELIKOW; publs *Cuadernos de Trabajo CARI-UBA, Serie T y C*.

**Centro de Estudios Internacionales para El Desarrollo (CEID)** (International Research Centre for Development): San José de Calasanz 537 P B, 'A', 1424 Buenos Aires; tel. and fax (11) 4686-0212; e-mail admin@ceid.edu.ar; internet www.ceid .edu.ar; f. 1998; civil society, education, ecology and international relations in Central and South-Eastern Europe, the Russian Federation and the Commonwealth of Independent States (CIS), Central and Eastern Asia, Africa and Central America; international electronic symposiums; Pres. Lic. MARCELO JAVIER DE LOS REYES; publ. *Revista del CEID* (2 a year).

### ARMENIA

**Armenian Society for Friendship and Cultural Relations with Foreign Countries:** Yerevan, Abovian St 3; tel. (1) 56-45-14; publ. *Armenia Segodnia* (2 a month).

**Institute of Economics:** 375001 Yerevan, Abovian St 15; tel. (1) 58-19-71; attached to the Armenian Nat. Acad. of Sciences; Dir M. KOTANIAN.

**International Centre for Human Development (ICHD):** Yerevan, Sayat Nova St 19; tel. (1) 58-26-38; fax (1) 52-70-82; e-mail mail@ichd.org; internet www.ichd.org; f. 1999; research and public-policy institution, with a particular focus on regional co-operation; Chair. ARMEN R. DARBINIAN; Exec. Dir TEVAN POGOSIAN.

### AUSTRALIA

**Research Unit for Russian and Euro-Asian Studies:** Contemporary Europe Research Centre (CERC), Univ. of Melbourne, 2nd Floor, 234 Queensberry St, Carlton, Vic 3052; tel. (3) 8344-9502; fax (3) 8344-9507; e-mail cerc@cerc.unimelb.edu .au; internet www.cerc.unimelb.edu.au/russian; f. 1989; interdisciplinary research on Europe and the former USSR; library and database; Dir Dr PHILOMENA MURRAY; Deputy Dir Prof. LESLIE HOLMES; publ. *CERC Working Paper Series*.

**Ukrainian Studies Association of Australia:** Ukrainian Section, Dept of European Languages, Division of Humanities, Macquarie Univ., NSW 2109; tel. (2) 9850-7034; fax (2) 9850-7054; e-mail hkoschar@pip.elm.mq.edu.au; Pres. Dr HALYNA KOSCHARSKY; publ. *Biuleten/Newsletter*.

### AUSTRIA

**Institut für Osteuropäische Geschichte, Universität Wien** (Institute for East European History): 1090 Vienna, Spitalgasse 2/Hof 3, Universitätscampus; tel. (1) 427-74-11-01; fax (1) 427-79-41-1; e-mail suedosteuropaforschung@univie.ac.at; internet www.univie.ac.at/iog; f. 1907; education and research; Chief Profs H. HASELSTEINER, A. KAPPELER, M. PEYFUSS, A. SUPPACH.

**International Institute for Applied Systems Analysis (IIASA):** 2361 Laxenburg, Schlossplatz 1; tel. (2) 236-80-70; fax

(2) 236-71-31-3; e-mail inf@iiasa.ca.at; internet www.iiasa.ac.at; f. 1972; scientific studies on environmental, social and technological issues and economics, incl. the transition of Eastern European economies; Dir ARNE B. JERNELÖV.

**Internationales Institut für den Frieden** (International Institute for Peace—IIP): 1040 Vienna, Möllwaldplatz 5; tel. (1) 504-64-37; fax (1) 505-32-36; f. 1957; peace research and studies on interdependence as a strategy for peace, future tasks for the UN, the security structure of Europe in the post-Cold War era, reconstruction of countries in Central and Eastern Europe, and prevention of conflict; Pres. ERWIN LANE; Dir PETER STANIA; publs *IIP Occasional Papers*, *Peace and Security* (quarterly), other publications and reports.

**Österreichisches Institut für Internationale Politik (OIIP)** (Austrian Institute of International Affairs): 1040 Vienna, Operngasse 20B; tel. (1) 581-11-06; fax (1) 581-11-06-10; e-mail info@oiip.at; internet www.oiip.at; f. 1978; independent research studies on national and international foreign and security policy, European integration, Central and Eastern Europe, Russia, the Near East and the Balkans; international environmental and development policies; foreign-policy conferences and workshops; library; Dir Prof. Dr OTMAR HOELL; publs working paper series and *Wiener Schriften zur Internationalen Politik*.

**Österreichische Ukrainistenverband:** Institut für Geschichte Ost- und Südeuropas, 9020 Klagenfurt, Universitätstr. 65-67; tel. (463) 270-06-21-7; fax (463) 270-04-15; e-mail andreas.moritsch@uni.klu.ac.at.

**Österreichisches Ost- und Südosteuropa-Institut** (Austrian Institute of East and South-East European Studies): 1010 Vienna, Josefsplatz 6; tel. (1) 512-18-95; fax (1) 512-18-95-53; e-mail sekretariat@osi.ac.at; internet www.osi.ac.at; f. 1958; research and information centre; devt and cultural politics, ecology, geography, history, nationality and minority studies; library of 47,000 vols and 2,400 periodicals and documents; Chair. of Exec. Bd Prof. Dr ARNOLD SUPPAN; Dir Dr PETER JORDAN; publs *OSI-Aktuell* (newsletter), *Österreichische Osthefte* (quarterly), *Schriftenreihe des Österreichischen Ost- und Südosteuropa-Instituts*, *Wiener Osteuropastudien*.

**Wiener Institut für Internationale Wirtschaftsvergleiche (WIIW)** (Vienna Institute for International Economic Studies): 1010 Vienna, Oppolzergasse 6; tel. (1) 533-66-10-11; fax (1) 533-66-10-50; e-mail wiiw@wsr.ac.at; internet www.wiiw.ac.at; f. 1974; focuses on Central and Eastern Europe, the CIS and the Balkans; analyzes economic devts of countries in transition, studies East-West European integration and the comparative aspects of global economic trends; reference library of over 13,000 vols and 350 periodicals; Dir MICHAEL LANDESMANN; Admin. Dir INGRID GAZZARI; publs research reports, working papers and a monthly database.

### AZERBAIJAN

**Institute of Economics:** 370143 Baku, Narimanova Ave 31; tel. (12) 39-34-57; attached to Azerbaijan Acad. of Sciences; Dir A. A. MAKHMUDOV.

**Institute of History:** 370143 Baku, Husein Javid Ave 31; tel. (12) 39-36-15; fax (12) 39-36-19.

### BELARUS

**Association of Political Science of Belarus:** 200672 Minsk, pr. Partizanski 26; tel. (17) 249-41-34; fax (17) 227-83-05; f. 1993; conducts research in the fields of economics, industrial relations, politics and social affairs; Pres. V. A. BOBKOV; Vice-Pres. A. V. SHARAPO.

**Belarusist International Association for Belarusian Studies:** 20050 Minsk, vul. Revolutionnaya 15.

**Belarusian Association for Ukrainian Studies:** 220002 Minsk, vul. Starozhovskaia 8/175; tel. (17) 233-64-51; Dir TETIANA KOBRZHYTSKA.

**Development and Security Research Institute of Belarus:** 220050 Minsk, vul. Babruiskaya 11.

**Economic Research Institute of the Ministry of the Economy:** 220086 Minsk, vul. Slavinskaga 1; tel. (17) 264-02-78; fax (17) 264-64-40; f. 1962; library of 51,425 vols.

**Institute of Economics of the National Academy of Sciences of Belarus:** 220072 Minsk, ul. Surganova 1, Korpus 2; tel. (17) 284-24-43; fax (17) 284-07-16; e-mail medvedev@economics.avilink.net; internet economics.avilink.net; f. 1931; areas of interest include the dynamics and structure of the Belarusian transition economy, industrial economics and policy, international economic relations, the privatization of state enterprises, and regional and urban economics and policy; library of 1,400 vols; Dir Prof. PETR G. NIKITENKO.

## BELGIUM

**Centre de Recherches Interdisciplinaires sur la Transition des Pays de l'Est vers l'Economie de Marché (CRITEME)** (Centre for Interdisciplinary Research on the Transition of Eastern Countries to a Market Economy): Université Libre de Bruxelles, Institut de Sociologie, 44 ave Jeanne, bte 124, 1050 Brussels; tel. (2) 650-33-60; fax (2) 650-34-27; research on socio-economic devts in Central and Eastern Europe and the former USSR.

**Centre for the New Europe (CNE):** 23 rue de Luxembourg, 1000 Brussels; tel. (2) 506-40-00; fax (2) 506-40-09; e-mail info@cne.org; internet www.cne.org; f. 1993; conducts research to develop and promote policies favouring a market-oriented economy and individual, rather than collectivist, values; Pres.and Dir-Gen. Dr TIM EVANS; publs *CNE Newsletter* (on-line, two a week), research papers.

**Institut Royal des Relations Internationales** (Royal Institute of International Relations): 69 rue de Namur, 1000 Brussels; tel. (2) 223-41-14; fax (2) 223-41-16; e-mail info@irri-kiib.be; internet www.irri-kiib.be; f. 1947; research on international relations, economics, politics and international law, particularly with regard to the European Union (EU), the World Trade Organization (WTO) and European security; library of 700 vols and 200 periodicals; Dir-Gen. FRANÇOIS DE KERCHOVE D'EXCERDE; Chair. Vicomte ÉTIENNE DAVIGNON; publs *Studia Diplomatica* (every 2 months); *Internationale Spectator* (monthly, in collaboration with Instituut Clingendael).

**International Centre for Caspian Studies:** 304 ave Louise, bte 5, 1050 Brussels; tel. (2) 640-24-85; fax (2) 647-65-93; non-governmental research organization; examines economic, geo-political and social issues in the Caspian Sea region; Pres. RZA IBADOV.

## BULGARIA

**Bulgarian Association for Ukrainian Studies:** 1000 Sofia, Faculty of Slavic Philologies, Rm 130, Blvd Tsar Osvoboditel 15; tel. (2) 85-83-07; e-mail ter@slav.uni-sofia.bg; Dir Dr LIDIA TERZIISKA.

## CANADA

**Canadian Institute of Ukrainian Studies:** Univ. of Alberta, 450 Athabasca Hall, Edmonton, Alberta, T6G 2E8; tel. (780) 492-2972; fax (780) 492-4967; e-mail cius@ualberta.ca; internet www.ualberta.ca/CIUS/; Dir ZENON E. KOHUT.

**Centre for Russian and East European Studies:** Univ. of Toronto, c/o Munk Centre for Int. Studies, 1 Devonshire Place, Toronto, Ontario, ON M5S 3K7; tel. (416) 946-8938; fax (416) 946-8939; e-mail janet.hyer@utoronto.ca; internet www.utoronto.ca/crees/; f. 1963; conducts research to promote a broad and integrated understanding of the nations and peoples of the region, past and present; includes the Stalin-era Research and Archives project, the Petro Jacyk Programme for the Study of Ukraine, and the Research Programme on Russian and Soviet Mennonite Studies; forms part of the School of Graduate Studies; Russian and East European library collection of 400,000 vols (approx.); Dir Prof. PETER H. SOLOMON, Jr; publs working papers.

## PEOPLE'S REPUBLIC OF CHINA

**Chinese Association for Ukrainian Studies:** 48 Xintaicang Yixiang Donzhimen, Beijing 100007; tel. (10) 4031547; fax (10) 4074077; Dir Prof. JIANG CHANGBIN.

**Eastern Europe and Central Asia Studies Institute:** Renmin Univ., 175 Haidian Rd, Haidian District, Beijing 100872; tel. (10) 82656672; fax (10) 62566374; f. 1937 as Eastern Europe and Soviet Union Studies Institute, renamed 1991; study of the situation in Eastern Europe, Russia and Central Asia and analysis of its history, with a particular focus on international economics and politics; Prof. ZHOU XINCHENG; Deputy Dirs Prof. ZHONG YAPIN, GUAN XUELIN.

**Soviet and East European Studies Institute:** 3 Zhanzhizhong Rd, Beijing 100007; tel. (10) 64014020; f. 1976; attached to Chinese Acad. of Social Sciences; Dir XU KUI.

## CHINA (TAIWAN)

**Graduate Institute of Russian Studies:** National Chengchi Univ., 64 Chih-nan Rd, Sec. 2, Wen-Shan District, Taipei 116; tel. (2) 29363413; fax (2) 29387124; e-mail russia@nccu.edu.tw; internet www.cc.nccu.edu.tw/nccucd/263/index.htm; f. 1994; research on international politics and economics, to further diplomatic and economic relations; Associate Prof. WU-PING KWO.

**Graduate Institute of Slavic Studies:** Tamkang Univ., 151 Ying-Chuan Rd, Tamshui, Taipei 251; tel. (2) 26215656; fax (2) 26209908; e-mail tisx@www2.tku.edu.tw; internet www2.tku.edu.tw/~tisx; f. 1990; historical research, as well as diplomacy, economics, military issues, politics and society in Russia and the other independent states of the former USSR, with particular emphasis on the devt of Sino-Russian bilateral relations; library of 4,500 vols; Dir ALEXANDER A. PISSAREV.

**Institute of International Relations:** 64 Wan Shou Rd, Wen Shan, Taipei 11625; tel. (2) 9394921; fax (2) 9378609; e-mail scchang@cc.nccu.edu.tw; f. 1953; research on international relations and mainland Chinese affairs, as well as Eastern Europe and the former USSR; affiliated to National Chengchi Univ.; library of 100,000 vols, 985 periodicals and 704 vols of Russian-language newspaper cuttings; Dir YU-MING SHAW; publs *America and Europe* (monthly), *Chinese Communist Affairs* (monthly).

## COLOMBIA

**Instituto de Estudios Politicos y Relaciones Internacionales (IEPRI)** (Institute of Political Studies and International Relations): Universidad Nacional de Colombia, Edificio Manuel Ancizar, Of. 3026, Ciudad Universitaria 14490, Santafé de Bogotá, DC; tel. and fax (1) 316-5217; e-mail iepri@bacata.usc.unal.edu.co; internet www.unal.edu.co/institutos/iepri; international relations, incl. European Studies; Dir WILLIAM RAMÍREZ TOBÓN; Co-ordinator of European Section HUGO FAZIO VENGOA.

## CROATIA

**Institut za Medunarodne Odnose (IMO)** (Institute for International Relations): 10000 Zagreb, POB 303, Lj. Farkaša Vukotinovića 2/2; tel. (1) 4826522; fax (1) 4828361; e-mail ured@mairmo.irmo.hr; internet www.imo.hr; f. 1963; attached to Univ. of Zagreb; principal fields of research include economic devt and transformation, international economic and cultural co-operation and international relations; library of 9,000 vols and 400 periodicals; Dir Prof. Dr MLADEN STANIČIĆA; publs *Croation International Relations Review* (quarterly, in English), *Culturelink* (quarterly, in English), *Euroscope* (6 a year), *Euroscope Reports* (quarterly, in English).

## CZECH REPUBLIC

**Czech Association for Ukrainian Studies:** Benediktsa 16, 110 00 Prague 1; tel. 222318302; Pres. Dr VACLAV ZIDLICKY.

**Institute for East-West Studies:** Rasinova nábreží 78/2000, 120 00 Prague 2; tel. 2296759; fax 2297992; f. 1981; research into East-West relations, incl. economic and devt questions; Pres. JOHN EDWIN MROZ; Dir STEPHEN HEINTZ; publs annual report, conference reports.

**U'stav mezinárodních vztahů** (Institute of International Relations): Nerudova 3, 118 50 Prague 1; tel. 251108111; fax 251108222; e-mail umv@iir.cz; internet www.iir.cz; f. 1957; research on international relations and foreign and security policy, publishing, training and education; Dir JIŘÍ ŠEDIVÝ; publs *International Relations* (quarterly), *International Politics* (monthly), *Perspectives—The Central European Review of International Affairs*(2 a year).

## DENMARK

**Center for Russiske og Østeuropæiske Studier** (Dept of Russian and East European Studies): Syddansk Universitet, Campusvej 55, 5230 Odense; tel. 65-50-10-00; fax 65-15-78-92; e-mail bro@litcul.sdu.dk; internet www.sdu.dk/hum/studier/slavisk/index.html; f. 1966; Soviet-Danish relations, history of Soviet/Russian society, culture and literature, Russian language; library of 15,000 vols; Dirs Prof. ERIK KULAVIG, Prof. BENT JENSEN.

**Centre for East European Studies (CEES):** Copenhagen Business School, Howitzvej 60, 2000 Frederiksberg; tel. 38-15-30-30; fax 38-15-25-00; e-mail mail.cees@cbs.dk; internet www.econ.cbs.dk/institutes/cees/sider/; f. 1996; transition in Eastern Europe; Dir NIELS MYGIND; publs working papers.

**Danish Centre for International Studies and Human Rights:** Copenhagen; internet fusion.humanrights.dk; f. 2003, through the merger of existing research institutes; comprises:

> **Danish Institute for Human Rights:** S. H. Wilders Plads, 1403 Copenhagen; tel. 32-69-88-88; fax 32-69-88-00; e-mail center@humanrights.dk.

> **Danish Institute for International Studies:** Strandgade 56, 1401 Copenhagen K; tel. 32-69-87-97; internet www.diis.dk; library of some 100,000 vols and 100 periodicals.

**Institute of History and Area Studies:** Aarhus Univ., Slavic Dept, Jens Chr. Skous Vej 5, 8000 Aarhus C; tel. 89-42-64-70; fax 89-42-64-65; e-mail slavisk@au.dk; internet www.hum.au.dk/slavisk/web.

**Institute of Political Science:** Univ. of Copenhagen, Rosenborggade 15, 1130 Copenhagen K; tel. 35-32-33-66; fax 35-32-33-99; e-mail polsci@ifs.ku.dk; general and comparative political science, information technology, international relations and organization, public administration, policy studies, sociology and statistics.

**Østeuropainstitutett** (Institute of East European Studies): Univ. of Copenhagen, Snorresgade 17-19, 2300 Copenhagen S; tel. 35-32-85-40; fax 35-32-85-32; e-mail osteuro@hum.ku.dk; internet www.ku.dk; f. 1992; history, linguistics, literature, and social and political science in Russia and the CIS, the Baltic states (Estonia, Latvia, Lithuania), Central and Eastern Europe and Greece; library of 50,000 vols; Dir LARS NØRGAARD.

**Thorkil Kristensen Institutett (TKI)** (Thorkil Kristensen Institute): Sydjysk Universtitetcenter, Niels Bohr Vej 9, Esbjerg 6700; tel. 79-19-11-11; fax 79-14-11-99; e-mail fla@suc.suc.dk; f. 1971; research into events in Central and Eastern Europe, the former USSR and the People's Republic of China, and their effects on Western Europe; also concerned with relations between the EU and Central and Eastern European countries, incl. the CIS; centre for East-West research; Dir Prof. FINN LAURSEN; publs working papers.

## ESTONIA

**Estonian Institute for Futures Studies:** Lai 34, Tallinn 10133; tel. 641-1760; fax 641-1759; e-mail eti@eti.online.ee; devt scenarios for Estonia and its neighbouring areas; Dir ERIK TERK.

## FINLAND

**Aleksanteri Institute Finnish Centre for Russian and East European Studies (FCREES):** Univ. of Helsinki, 6th Floor, Yliopistonkatu 5, POB 4, Helsinki 00014; tel. (9) 19124175; fax (9) 19123822; e-mail aleksanteri@helsinki.fi; internet www.helsinki.fi/aleksanteri; f. 1996; national co-ordinating unit and research institute; Dir Prof. MARKU KIVINEN.

**Bank of Finland Institute for Economies in Transition (BOFIT):** POB 160, 00101 Helsinki; tel. (9) 1832287; fax (9) 1832294; e-mail bofit@bof.fi; internet www.bof.fi/bofit; f. 1991; specializes in high-level study and academic analysis of individual national economies involved in the transition from a command to a market economy; Dir Dr PEKKA SUTELA; publs *Russian and Baltic Economies—The Week in Review, Russian Economy—The Month in Review, Baltic Economies—Bimonthly Review, BOFIT Discussion Papers, BOFIT Online.*

**Elinkeinoelämän Valtuuskunta (EVA)** (Centre for Finnish Business and Policy Studies): Yrjönkatu 13A, 00120 Helsinki; tel. (9) 6869200; fax (9) 608713; e-mail postmaster@eva.fi; internet www.eva.fi; f. 1974; policy research group; fields of interest include Finland's relations with the Russian Federation and international economic comparisons; Man. Dir PENTTI VARTIA; publs reports.

**Institute for East-West Trade:** Business Research and Development Centre, Turku School of Economics and Business Administration, Lemminkäisenkatu 14-18c, POB 110, 20521 Turku; tel. (2) 3383569; fax (2) 3383268; e-mail sari.soderlund@tukk.fi; f. 1987; research focuses on the foreign economic relations of transitional economies, in particular the Russian Federation, the Baltic States and the Baltic Sea economic area; Dir Prof. URPO KIKIVARI.

**Ulkopoliittinen instituutti (UPI)** (Finnish Institute of International Affairs—FIIA): Mannerheimintie 15A, 00260 Helsinki; tel. (9) 4342070; fax (9) 43420769; e-mail firstname.lastname@upi-fiia.fi; internet www.upi-fiia.fi; f. 1961; research into Russia-European Union (EU) relations; the security of Nordic countries and the Baltic states; European foreign affairs and security issues; EU expansion; democracy and globalization; Dir TAPANI VAAHTORANTA; publs *Ulkopolitiikka* (quarterly), *Yearbook of Finnish Foreign Policy, FIIA Report*, UPI Working Papers.

**Venäjän ja Itä-Euroopan Instituutti** (Finnish Institute for Russian and East European Studies—FIREES): Annankatu 44, 00100 Helsinki; tel. (9) 22854434; fax (9) 22854431; e-mail bibliotek@rusin.fi (library); internet www.rusin.fi; research into Russia and Eastern Europe; focuses on basic and applied research in social sciences and humanities, especially culture, population and social structures; library of more than 90,000 vols, 300 journals and maps; Dir WALDEMAR MELANKO; publ. *Studia Slavica Finlandensia* (annually).

## FRANCE

**Association d'Etudes et d'Informations Politiques Internationales** (Association for International Political Study and Information): 86 blvd Haussman, 75008 Paris; f. 1949; Dir G. ALBERTINI; publs *Est et Ouest / Este y Oeste* (2 a month), *Documenti sul Comunismo*.

**Centre d'Etudes du Monde Russe, Soviétique et Post-Soviétique** (Centre of Russian, Soviet and Post-Soviet Studies): Ecole des Hautes Etudes en Sciences Sociales (EHESS), 54 blvd Raspail, 75006 Paris; tel. and fax 1-49-54-25-58; e-mail centre.russie@ehess.fr; internet www.ehess.fr/centres/cemrsps; f. 1995; history of Russia and the USSR from the 17th century; social and demographic studies, diplomacy and cultural contacts between Russia, the West and the rest of the world, and ethnography, historiography, social sciences and statistics; library of 22,000 vols, 115 periodicals and 700 microfilms; Dir VLADIMIR BERELOVITCH; publs *Bibliographie Européenne des Travaux sur l'ex-URSS et l'Europe de l'Est, Cahiers du Monde Russe, Revue d'Etudes Comparatives Est-Ouest.*

**Centre de Documentation Internationale (CEDUCEE)** (Centre of International Documentation): 29 quai Voltaire, 75344 Paris Cédex 07; tel. 1-40-15-72-18; fax 1-40-15-69-93; e-mail cdi@ladocumentationfrancaise.fr; internet www.ladocumentationfrancaise.fr; f. 1967; political, economic and social affairs in 27 countries of Eastern Europe and the CIS; library of 13,000 vols, 330 periodicals and 400 statistical yearbooks; Dir MARIE-AGNÈS CROSNIER; publ. *Courrier des Pays de l'Est* (10 a year).

**Institut d'Etudes Slaves:** 9 rue Michelet, 750006 Paris; affiliated to Centre Nationale de Recherche Scientifique; publ. *Revue d'Etudes Slaves* (in French and Russian).

> **Association Française des Etudes Ukrainiennes** (French Association of Ukrainian Studies): e-mail fouchard@ehess.fr; Dir Prof. DANIEL BEAUVOIS; publ. *Bulletin de l'Association Française des Etudes Ukrainiennes.*

**Institut Français des Relations Internationales (Ifri)** (French Institute of International Relations): 27 rue de la Procession, 75740 Paris Cédex 15; tel. 1-40-61-60-00; fax 1-40-61-60-60; e-mail accueil@ifri.org; internet www.ifri.org; f. 1979; international politics and economy; security issues; regional studies; library of 32,000 vols, 250 periodicals; Pres. Prof. THIERRY DE MONTBRIAL; Exec. Dir PIERRE LEPETIT; publs *Politique étrangère* (quarterly, in French), *Notes de l'Ifri, Publications du CFE à l'Ifri, Travaux et recherches de l'Ifri, Rapport annuel mondial sur le système économique et les stratégies (RAMSES)* (annually, in French), *Cahiers du Centre asie ifri cahiers et conférences de l'Ifri.*

## GEORGIA

**Caucasian Institute for Peace, Democracy and Development (CIPDD):** 380008 Tbilisi, POB 101; tel. (32) 33-40-81; fax (32) 33-41-63; e-mail cipdd@cipdd.org; internet www.cipdd.org; f. 1992 to promote democratic and free-market values and to encourage the impartial theoretical analysis of the post-communist transition process in Georgia and the Caucasus region.

**Centre for Peace and International Relations Studies (CPIRS):** Tbilisi; e-mail cpirs@ip.osgf.ge; internet www.cpirs.org.ge; f. 1998 to promote democratic and free-market values and to encourage peace and international co-operation in the Caucasus region.

**International Centre for Geopolitical and Regional Studies (ICGRS):** Tbilisi, POB 158, M. Aleksidze 3; tel. (32) 98-40-34; fax (32) 93-26-70; e-mail vasitar@caucasus.net; Dir GIORGI TARKHAN-MOURAVI.

**Research Centre of National Relations:** 380007 Tbilisi, Leselidze 4; attached to Georgian Acad. of Sciences; Dir G. V. ZHORZHOLIANI.

## GERMANY

**Deutsche Gesellschaft für Osteuropakunde eV** (German Society for East European Research): 10719 Berlin, Schaperstr. 30; tel. (30) 21478412; fax (30) 21478414; e-mail info@dgo-online.org; internet www.dgo-online.org; f. 1913; concerned with research into all areas of Central and Eastern Europe, with particular emphasis on economic issues; Pres. Prof. Dr RITA SÜSSMUTH; Dir Dr HEIKE DÖRRENBÄCHER; publs *Osteuropa* (monthly), *Osteuropa-Recht, Osteuropa Wirtschaft* (quarterly).

**Deutsches Institut für Internationale Politik und Sicherheit, Stiftung Wissenschaft und Politik:** 10719 Berlin, Ludwigkirchplatz 3-4; tel. (30) 88007301; fax (30) 88007598; e-mail dietrich.seydel@swp-berlin.org; internet www.swp-berlin.org; f. 2001 by merger of Forschungsinstituts der Stiftung Wissenschaft und Politik (Ebenhaüsen) and Bundesinstitut für Ostwissenschaftliche und Internationale Studien (Köln).

**Forschungstelle Osteuropa an der Universität Bremen** (Research Centre for East European Studies at Bremen University): 28359 Bremen, Klagenfurter Str. 3; tel. (421) 2183687; fax (421) 2183269; e-mail anlorenz@osteuropa.uni-bremen.de; internet www.forschungsstelle.uni-bremen.de; f. 1982; concentrates mainly on culture, politics and society in the Czech Republic, Poland, the Russian Federation and Slovakia; Dir Prof. Dr WOLFGANG EICHWEDE; publs *Dokumentationen zu Kultur und Gesellschaft im Östlichen Europa, Forschungen zu Osteuropa, Veröffentlichungen zur Kultur und Gesellschaft im Östlichen Europa,* catalogues, working papers.

**Frankfurt Institute for Transformation Studies (FIT):** European Univ. Viadrina, 15207 Frankfurt (Oder), POB 1786;

tel. (335) 55342861; fax (335) 55342807; e-mail elange@euv-frankfurt-o.de; internet fit.euv-frankfurt-o.de; research on cultural dimensions of political and economic systems in Eastern Europe; transformation, and capital markets and banking reform; Exec. Dir Prof. Dr DETLEF POLLACK; publs *Annual Report,* discussion papers.

**George C. Marshall Center for Security Studies:** 82467 Garmisch-Partenkirchen, Gernackerstr. 2; fax (8821) 750452; e-mail webpage@marshallcenter.org; internet www.marshallcenter.org; f. 1993; includes College of Int. and Security Studies and a conference centre; long-term interdisciplinary research on transatlantic-Eurasian security and defence; a German-US joint initiative; library of 40,000 vols and 500 periodicals; Dir Dr ROBERT KENNEDY; publs *Marshall Center Papers Series, Quarterly Update.*

**Institut für Friedensforschung und Sicherheitspolitik (IFSH)** (Institute for Peace Research and Security Policy): Universität Hamburg, 22587 Hamburg, Falkenstein 1; tel. (40) 8660770; fax (40) 8663615; e-mail ifsh@rrz.uni-hamburg.de; internet www.ifsh.de; f. 1971; focuses on the establishment of security structures and projects dealing with conflict settlement and prevention; library of 24,000 vols and 150 periodicals; Dir Prof. Dr DIETER S. LUTZ; publs *Hamburger Beiträge zur Friedensforschung und Sicherheitspolitik, Hamburger Informationen zur Friedensforschung und Sicherheitspolitik, IFSH Aktuell, Pädagogische Informationen zur Friedensforschung und Sicherheitspolitik, OSCE Yearbook.*

**Institut für Slavistik** (Institute for Slavonic Studies): University of Regensburg, 93053 Regensburg, Universitätsstr. 31; tel. (941) 9433362; fax (941) 9431988; internet www.uni-regensburg.de/Fakultaeten/phil_Fak_IV/Slavistik/; research on the culture, languages and literature of Central and Eastern Europe.

**Institut für Wirtschaft und Gesellschaft Ost- und Südosteuropas** (Institute for East and South-East European Economics and Society): Ludwig-Maximilians-Universität München, 80799 München, Akademiestr. 1-3; tel. (89) 21802278; fax (89) 21806296; f. 1964; concerned with economic and social questions relating to South-Eastern Europe, the countries of the former USSR and the People's Republic of China; fields of interest include devt, economic integration, energy and trade; library of 6,500 vols and 100 periodicals; Dirs Prof. Dr FRIEDRICH HAFFNER, Prof. Dr WERNER GUMPEL.

**Osteuropa-Institut der Freien Universität Berlin** (Institute of East European Studies of the Free University Berlin): 14195 Berlin, Garystr. 55; tel. (30) 53380; fax (30) 53788; e-mail oei@zedat.fu-berlin.de; internet www.oei.fu-berlin.de; f. 1951; engaged in contemporary and historical cultural studies, economics, history, jurisprudence, philosophy, political science and sociology; library of 360,000 vols; Dir Prof. Dr KLAUS SEGBERS; publs *Berliner Osteuropa Info* (2 a year), *Forschungen zur Osteuropäischen Geschichte,* working papers.

> **Deutsche Assoziation der Ukrainisten eV:** tel. and fax (30) 8231006; Pres. Prof. BOHDAN OSADCZUK.

**Osteuropa-Institut München** (Munich Institute of East European Studies): 81679 München, Scheinerstr. 11; tel. (89) 9983960; fax (89) 9810110; e-mail oeim@lrz.uni-muenchen.de; internet www.lrz-muenchen.de/~oeim; f. 1952; observation and analysis of economic devt in Eastern Europe and the former USSR; library of over 160,000 vols and 600 periodicals; Dir Prof. Dr LUTZ HOFFMANN; publs *Economic Systems* (quarterly, in English with German abstracts), *Jahrbücher für Geschichte Osteuropas* (quarterly), working papers (irreg.).

**Ost-West Institut an der Universität Koblenz-Landau** (East-West Institute at the University of Koblenz-Landau): 56016 Koblenz, Postfach 201 602, Abteilung Koblenz; tel. (261) 2871590; fax (261) 2871591; e-mail owi@uni-koblenz.de; internet www.uni-koblenz.de; f. 1996; focuses on Central and Eastern Europe, incl. the Asian states of the former USSR.

**Zentralinstitut für Mittel- und Osteuropastudien (ZIMOS) der Katholischen Universität Eichstätt** (Central Institute for the Study of Central and Eastern Europe of the Catholic University of Eichstätt): 85072 Eichstätt, Ostenstr. 27; tel. (8421) 931717; fax (8421) 931780; e-mail chiara.savoldelli@

ku-eichstaett.de; internet www.ku-eichstaett.de/zimos/body
.htm; f. 1994; research includes the study of the history of
communism in Russia and the former USSR, the Czech
Republic, Hungary, Poland and Slovakia; financed by sponsors;
library of 4.5m. vols (approx.); Dir Prof. Dr NIKOLAUS LOBKOWICZ;
publs *Forum für Mittel- und Osteuropäische Zeit- und Ideenge-
schichte* (2 a year), book series.

## GREECE

**Hellenic Foundation for European and Foreign Policy
(ELIAMEP):** Odos Xenophontos 4, 105 57 Athens; tel. (1)
3315022; fax (1) 3642139; e-mail eliamep@eliamep.gr; internet
www.eliamep.gr/; f. 1988; forum for the understanding of issues
relating to foreign and security policy, European affairs and
international relations; Pres. PARIS KYRIAKOPOULOS; Dir-Gen.
THEODORE COULOUMBIS; publs *Agora Choris Synora/Market
without Frontiers* (quarterly), *ELIAMEP Newsletter*, *Journal of
Southeast European and Black Sea Studies*, *Greece and the
World* (annually).

## HUNGARY

**Institute for Strategic and Defence Studies:** Miklós Zrínyi
National Defence Univ., 1241 Budapest, POB 181; tel. (1) 432-
9092; fax (1) 432-9058; e-mail ssvki@mltc.hu; internet www.svki
.hu; 3,000 vols; Dir Prof. FERENC GAZDAG; publ. *Defence Studies* (6
a year).

**Ukrán és Ruszin Filológiai Tanszék** (Dept of Ukrainian and
Rusyn Philology): 4400 Nyíregyháza, Nyíregyházi Főiskola,
Sóstói u. 31B; tel. (42) 599-400; fax (42) 404-092; e-mail udvarii@
zeus.nyf.hu; f. 1992; the history of Ukraine, Rusyn-Hungarian
interethnic relations, and Ukrainian-Hungarian lexicography
and word formation; library of 5,000 vols; Dir Dr UDVARI ISTVÁN;
publs *Glossarium Ukrainicum 1-7*, *Studia Ukrainica et
Rusinica Nyíregyháziensia 1-12*.

## INDIA

**International Institute for Non-Aligned Studies (IINS):** A-
2/59 Safdarjung Enclave, New Delhi 110 029; tel. (11) 6102520;
fax (11) 6196294; e-mail iins@iins.org; internet www.iins.org; f.
1980; has consultative status with the UN's Economic and Social
Council (ECOSOC); works in the fields of international relations, social devt and human rights, and has a Centre for
Human Rights; Dir Dr PRAMILA SRIVASTAVA; publs *News from the
Non-Aligned World* (every 2 weeks, in English and Hindi), *Non-
Aligned World* (quarterly) and selected publs on Indo-Soviet
relations.

## IRAN

**Centre for the Study of Central Asia and the Caucasus
(CSCAS):** Institute of Political and International Studies, POB
19395-1793, Shahedd Aghaei St, Tehran; tel. (21) 230267175;
fax (21) 2802649; e-mail ipis@www.dci.co.ir; f. 1983; research
and information on economics, international relations, Islamic
studies and law; library; publs *AMU DARYA: Iranian Journal of
Central Asian Studies*, *Caucasus Review* (quarterly), *Central
Asia*.

## ISRAEL

**Cummings Centre for Russian and East European
Studies:** Tel Aviv Univ., Ramat Aviv, Tel-Aviv 69978; tel. 3-
6409608; fax 3-6409721; e-mail crees@post.tau.ac.il; internet
www.tau.ac.il/~russia; f. 1971; carries out research, study and
documentation and publishes information on the history and
current affairs of Russia, the former Soviet republics and the
countries of Eastern Europe; Dir Prof. YAACOV RO'I.

**Israeli Association of Ukrainian Studies:** Centre of Slavic
Languages and Literatures, Hebrew Univ. of Jerusalem, POB
7823, Jerusalem 91078; tel. and fax 2-5634073; e-mail jeremy@
vms.huji.ac.il; Pres. Prof. WOLF MOSKOVICH.

**Marjorie Mayrock Centre for Russian, Eurasian and East
European Research:** Faculty of Social Sciences, Hebrew
Univ., Mount Scopus, Jerusalem 91905; tel. 2-5883180; fax 2-
5882835; e-mail msrussia@mscc.huji.ac.il; internet pluto.huji.ac
.il/~msrussia/general.html; f. 1969; holds seminars and confer-

ences; Dir STEFANI HOFFMAN; publ. *CIS Environment and Disarmament Yearbook*.

## ITALY

**Associazione Italiana di Studi Ucraini** (Italian Association
of Ukrainian Studies): Dipartimento di Studi Letterari, Linguis-
tici e Filologici (Sezione Slavistica), Università di Milano, Piazza
S. Alessandro, 20123 Milan; tel. (02) 50313628; fax (02)
50313632; e-mail gbrogi@mailserver.unimi.it; internet www
.aisu.it; f. 1993; colloquia and conferences devoted to Ukrainian
culture; approx. 60 mems; Pres. Prof. GIOVANNA BROGI BERCOFF.

**Istituto di Studi e Documentazione sull'Europa Comuni-
taria e l'Europa Orientale (ISDEE)** (European Community
and Eastern Europe Study and Documentation Centre): Corso
Italia 27, 34122 Trieste; tel. (040) 639130; fax (040) 634248;
e-mail isdee@spin.it; internet www.isdee.it/; f. 1969; documentation, study and research on economic, institutional, political and
social devt in Europe and on relations between Western Europe
and Central and Eastern Europe; Chair. FULVIO DEGRASSI; Dir
TITO FAVARETTO; publ. *Est-Ovest* (6 a year, in English, French and
Italian).

**Osservatorio sull'Evoluzione nei Paesi dell'Europa Ori-
entale (EUROEST)** (Centre for Evolution in Eastern European
Countries): c/o Dipartimento di Economia, Università degli
Studi di Trento, Via Inama 5, 38100 Trento; tel. (0461) 882162;
fax (0461) 882222; e-mail euroest@risc1.gelso.unitn.it; internet
euroest.gelso.unitn.it; f. 1992; monitors and analyses devts in
Eastern Europe, in particular economic transformation; Dirs
Prof. GIOVANNI PEGORETTI, Prof. BRUNO DALLAGO, GIANMARIA AJANI,
RICARDO SCARTEZZINI; publs *Blue Series* and *Green Series* of
working papers.

## JAPAN

**Centre for European Studies:** Nanzan Univ., 18, Yamaza-
tocho, Showa-ku, Nagoya 466-8673; tel. (52) 832-3111; fax (52)
831-2741; e-mail cfes@ic.nanzan-u.ac.jp; internet www.ic
.nanzan-u.ac.jp/%7Ecfes/cesj.html; f. 1991; the study of contemporary European affairs (incl. Belarus, the Russian Federation and Ukraine), primarily in the field of social sciences;
library of 3,500 vols and 155 periodicals; Dir TOSHIAKI TOMOOKA;
publ. *Nanzan Daigaku Yoroppa Kenkyu Senta-ho/Bulletin of
the Nanzan Centre for European Studies* (annually).

**Centre for Northeast Asian Studies:** Tohoku Univ.,
Kawauchi, Aobaku, Sendai, Miyagi Prefecture 980-8576; tel.
(22) 217-6009; fax (22) 217-6010; e-mail www@cneas.tohoku.ac
.jp; internet www.cneas.tohoku.ac.jp/index-e.html; f. 1996; integrated area studies on culture, economics, environment,
resources and society in the North-East Asia region (North Asia,
from Siberia to the Bering Strait, East Asia and Japan); library
of 12,000 vols; Dir Prof. Dr MASANORI TOKUDA; publs *Northeast
Asian Alacarte*, *Northeast Asian Studies*, *Northeast Asian Study
Series*.

**Centre for Russian Studies:** Japan Institute of International
Affairs, 11th Floor, Kasumigaseki Bldg, 3-2-5, Kasumigaseki,
Chiyoda-ku, Tokyo 100-6011; tel. (3) 3503-7261; fax (3) 3503-
7292; e-mail info@jiia.or.jp; internet www.jiia.or.jp; comprehen-
sive research concerning the former USSR, the CIS and Eastern
Europe; library of 20,000 vols and 470 periodicals; Pres. HISASHI
OWADA; Dir TOSHIRO OZAWA (acting); publs *Japan Review of
International Affairs* (quarterly, in English), *JIIA Newsletter*,
*Kokusai Mondai/International Affairs*, *Roshia Kenkyu/Rus-
sian Studies* (2 a year).

**Economic Research Institute of Northeast Asia (ERINA):**
6th Floor, Nihonseimai Masayakoji Bldg, 6-1178-1, Kamioka-
wamae, Niigata 951-8068; f. 1993; focuses on north-eastern
China, Japan, the Republic of Korea, the Democratic People's
Republic of Korea, Mongolia and Far Eastern Russia; Chair.
HISAO KANAMORI; publs *ERINA Report*, *Journal of Econometric
Study of Northeast Asia*, *Northeast Asia White Paper*.

**Hokkaido Daigaku Surabu Kenkyu Senta** (Slavic Research
Centre, Hokkaido University): Kita-9, Nishi-7, Kita-ku, Sapporo
060-0809; tel. (11) 706-2388; fax (11) 706-4952; e-mail src@slav
.hokudai.ac.jp; internet src-h.slav.hokudai.ac.jp/; f. 1955;
national centre for interdisciplinary research activities on Slavic

Eurasian countries; areas of research include economics, ethnology, geography, humanities, international relations and political-social systems; library of 162,000 vols and 1,200 periodicals; Dir OSAMU IEDA; publs *Acta Slava Iaponica* (annually), *Suravu Kenkyu/Slavic Studies* (annually), *SRC Newsletter*, *SRC Occasional Paper Series*.

**Japanese Association for Ukrainian Studies:** Univ. of Tokyo, 3-8-1, Komaba, Meguroku, Tokyo 153; tel. (3) 5454-6487; fax (3) 5454-4339; e-mail nakai@waka.c.u-tokyo.ac.jp; Pres. Prof. KAZUO NAKAI; publ. *Ukuraina Tsushin*.

**Shadan Hojin, Russia To-Oh Boekikai (ROTOBO)** (Japan Association for Trade with Russia and Central and Eastern Europe): Kaneyama Bldg, 1-2-12, Shinkawa, Chuo-ku, Tokyo 104-0033; tel. (3) 3551-6215; fax (3) 3555-1052; e-mail rotobo@root.or.jp; internet www.root.or.jp/rotobo_inst.

### KAZAKHSTAN

**Central Asia Agency of Political Research:** 480100 Almaty, Dostyk 85A, Office 309; tel. (3272) 91-12-78; fax (3272) 91-15-09; e-mail apr@lorton.com; internet www.caapr.kz; independent, non-governmental research institution.

**Institute of Economics:** 480100 Almaty, Kurmangazy 29; tel. (3272) 93-01-75; fax (3272) 62-78-19; e-mail ieconom@academset.kz; f. 1952; research and training; attached to the Ministry of Education and Science; library of 900 vols; Dir M. B. KENZHEGUZIN; Deputy Dir N. K. NURLANOVA; Sec. V. V. SHEVCHENKO; publ. *Izvestiya NAS RK/News* (annually).

### REPUBLIC OF KOREA

**Institute for Far Eastern Studies (IFES):** Kyungnam Univ., 28-42, Samchung-dong, Chongro-ku, Seoul 110-230; tel. (2) 735-3202; fax (2) 735-4359; f. 1972; affiliated to the Institute of Oriental Studies (Russian Federation); research programmes on developing countries; annual conference on Korean-Russian relations; research seminars; library of 10,000 vols; Dir Dr JO YUNG-HWAN; publs include *Asian Perspective* (2 a year), *Korea and World Politics* (2 a year), *Research Series of North Korea* and *Research Series of the Third World* (annually).

### KYRGYZSTAN

**Centre for Economic Research:** 720071 Bishkek, pr. Chui 265A; tel. (312) 25-53-90; fax (312) 24-36-07; e-mail tdyikanbaeva@hotmail.com; f. 1956; researches the mechanisms of forming, and the devt of, the market economy, analyses the limits, structure and legalization of the shadow economy and macroeconomic aspects of social economic policy, and advises the Kyrgyz Govt; library of the Acad. of Sciences of some 1m. vols; Dir TOKTOBIUBIU SAYAKBAEVNA DYIKANBAEVNA.

**Institute for Regional Studies:** 720000 Bishkek, POB 1880; e-mail ifrs@elcat.kg; internet eng.gateway.kg/ngo_ifrs; f. 1994 as the Kyrgyz Peace Research Centre; supports democratization in Central Asia; runs Programme on Sustainable Development in Central Asia, the Civic Education and Training Programme, and a Gender Studies Unit; research, seminars and conferences; library.

### LITHUANIA

**Institute of International Relations and Political Science:** Vilnius Univ., Didlaukio 47-205, Vilnius 2057; tel. (527) 62672; fax (527) 00779; e-mail tspmi@tspmi.vu.lt; internet www.tspmi.vu.lt; research on international relations and political science, including regional security and foreign policy issues, democratization during transition, nationalism, the rule of law and the free market economy; Dir Prof. RAIMUNDAS LOPATA.

**Lietuvos Ukrainistu Asociacija** (Lithuanian Association of Ukrainian Studies): Vysniu 4-6, Vilnius 2038; tel. (2) 265-513; e-mail jaroslava@takas.lt; Pres. NADIA NEPOROZHINA.

### MOLDOVA

**Academy of Economic Studies:** 27005 Chişinău, str. Bănulescu-Bodoni 61; tel. (2) 22-98-80; fax (2) 22-19-68; e-mail rectorat@ase.md; internet www.ase.md; f. 1991; Rector BELOŞTECINIC GRIGORE; Pro-rector COJOCARU VADIM; publ. *Economica*.

**Institute of Economic Research:** 2012 Chişinău, bd Ştefan cel Mare 1; tel. (2) 26-24-01; e-mail 231sii@math.moldova.su; f. 1960; attached to the Acad. of Sciences of Moldova; conducts research on economic devt in Moldova; Dir V. CIOBANU; publs research reports.

### MONGOLIA

**Institute of Oriental and International Studies:** c/o Acad. of Sciences, Sühabaataryn Talbay 3, Ulan Bator 11; f. 1968; research on oriental and international affairs, in particular Mongolia's relations with the People's Republic of China and the Russian Federation; Dir A. OCHIR; publs *Dorno-Örno* (2 a year), *Mongolian Journal of International Affairs* (annually).

### NETHERLANDS

**Instituut voor Oost-Europees Recht en Ruslandkunde** (Institute of East European Law and Russian Studies): Leiden Univ., Faculty of Law, Hugo de Grootstraat 32, POB 9521, 2300 Leiden; tel. (71) 5277814; fax (71) 5277732; e-mail ieelrs@law.leidenuniv.nl; internet www.leidenuniv.nl/law/ieelrs; f. 1953; from 1993 involved in assisting the legal community of Eastern Europe to draft legislation and new civil codes; library of 40,000 vols and 350 periodicals; publs *Law in Eastern Europe Series*, *Review of Central and East European Law* (quarterly).

**Slavische Talen, Russisch, Midden- en oost Europakunde:** Rijksuniversiteit Groningen, POB 716, 9700 AS Groningen; tel. (50) 3636061; fax (50) 3635821; e-mail cet@let.rug.nl; internet www.odur.let.rug.nl/slav.

### NORWAY

**Fridtjof Nansen Institute (FNI):** Fridtjof Nansens vei 17, POB 326, 1324 Lysaker; tel. 67-11-19-00; fax 67-11-19-10; e-mail sentralbord@fni.no; internet www.fni.no/; f. 1958; social-science research on international issues concerning energy, the environment and resource management; research programmes on European energy and environment, multilateral assistance, ocean mining, the Northern Sea Route and Russia and Eastern Europe; Dir KÅRE WILLOCH; publs *Energy, Environment and Development Reports*, *Green Globe Yearbook*, *Nansen News*.

**Institutt for Forsvarsstudier (IFS)** (Institute for Defence Studies): Tollbugt 10, 0152 Oslo; tel. 23-09-31-05; fax 23-09-33-79; e-mail rolf.tamnes@ifs.mil.no; internet www.ifs.mil.no; f. 1980; research programmes on civil-military relations, Norwegian and Atlantic security policies after 1945, Russian studies, and UN forces; also conducts research into Norwegian foreign policy, Russian-Norwegian relations and Norway's role in US strategy; library of 7,500 vols; Dir Prof. Dr ROLF TAMNES; publs *Defence Studies* (6 to 10 a year), *IFS-Info* (6 to 10 a year).

**International Peace Research Institute, Oslo (PRIO):** Fuglehauggata 11, 0260 Oslo; tel. 22-54-77-00; fax 22-54-77-01; e-mail info@prio.no; internet www.prio.no; f. 1966; the research programme follows three broad themes: the conditions of war and peace, ethnic and nationalist conflicts and foreign and security policies; library of 13,000 vols and 400 periodicals; Chair. FRIDA NOKKEN; Dir DAN SMITH; publs *Journal of Peace Research* (6 a year), *Security Dialogue* (4 a year).

**Norsk Utenrikspolitisk Institutt (NUPI)** (Norwegian Institute of International Affairs): POB 8159, 0033 Oslo; tel. 22-05-65-00; fax 22-17-70-15; e-mail info@nupi.no; internet www.nupi.no; f. 1959; research and information on political and economic issues, focusing on international security policy, the long-term political devt of Europe and Russia, international economic and devt issues, conflict resolution and peace operations; library of 25,000 vols and 400 journals; Pres. AGE DANIELSEN; Dir SVERRE LODGAARD; Head of Centre for Russian Studies HELGE BLAKKISRUD; publs *Hvor Hender Det* (weekly newsletter), *Internasjonal Politikk* (quarterly), *Nordisk Ostforum* (quarterly), *Forum for Development Studies* (twice yearly journal), *NUPI Rapport* (research report) and monographs.

### PAKISTAN

**Institute of Regional Studies:** 56-F, Nazimuddin Rd, Blue Area, F-6/1, Islamabad; tel. (51) 9203974; fax (51) 9204055; e-mail irspak@isb.comsats.net.pk; internet www.irs.org.pk; f.

1982; covers a wide range of research into economics, industry, international and internal affairs, science and technology, and security-related and socio-cultural issues, extending studies to incl. Central Asia and the People's Republic of China; Pres. Maj.-Gen. (retd) JAMSHED AYAZ KHAN; Editor ABUL BARAKAT; publs include *Regional Studies* (quarterly), *Spotlight* (monthly).

**Pakistan Institute of International Affairs:** Aiwan-e-Sadar Rd, POB 1447, Karachi 74200; tel. (21) 5682891; f. 1947 to study international affairs and to promote the scientific study of international politics, Pakistani foreign policy, economics and jurisprudence; library of 29,740 vols, 42 microfilms, 126 tapes; Chair. FATEHYAB ALI KHAN; publ. *Pakistan Horizon* (4 a year).

## POLAND

**Central and East European Economic Research Centre (CEEERC):** Joint Graduate Instruction Centre, Dept of Economics, Univ. of Warsaw, 02-097 Warsaw, ul. Banacha 2B; tel. (22) 8227404; fax (22) 8227405; e-mail wisniewski@ceeerc.wne .uw.edu.pl; internet www.ceeerc.wne.uw.edu.pl/; f. 1998; centre for policy-relevant issues critical to the devt of open and competitive economies in the post-communist countries of Central and Eastern Europe; Dir Dr MARIAN WISNIEWSKI.

**Centre for Eastern Studies:** 00-564 Warsaw, ul. Koszykowa 6A; tel. (22) 5258000; fax (22) 6298799; e-mail info@osw.waw.pl; internet www.osw.waw.pl; f. 1990; monitors and analyzes the political, economic and social situation in the countries of the Commonwealth of Independent States and in Central and South-Eastern Europe; Dir MAREK KARP; Deputy Dir JACEK CICHOCKI; publs *Annual Report*, *CES Studies* (every two months), *Week in the East* (weekly), *Policy Briefs* (occasional).

**Centre for Eastern Studies of the University of Warsaw:** 00-046 Warsaw, ul. Nowy Świat 69; tel. (22) 6200381; fax (22) 267520; f. 1990; an interdisciplinary science and research unit on subjects relating to the Baltic Republics, Belarus, the Russian Federation and Ukraine, in particular questions of economics, ethnicity, law, sociology and socio-political systems; Dir Prof. MICHAŁ DOBROCZYŃSKI; publ. *Polityka Wschodnia/Eastern Politics* (2 a year).

**Instytut Slawistyki, Polska Akademia Nauk (PAN)** (Slavonic Institute, Polish Acad. of Sciences): 00-337 Warsaw, ul. Bartoszewicza 1B m. 17; tel. and fax (22) 8267688; e-mail iwona@ ispan.waw.pl; internet www.ispan.waw.pl; f. 1954; research into, and study of, Slavonic history, literature and linguistics; library of 120,000 vols; Dir Prof. dr Hab. ZBIGNIEW GREN; publs *Acta Baltico-Slavica*, *Slava Meridionalis* (annually), *Studia Literaria Polono-Slavica* (annually), *Studia z Filologii Polskiej i Slowanskiej* (annually), *Slavica* (annually).

**Instytut Studiów Politycznych PAN** (Institute of Political Studies): 00-625 Warsaw, ul. Polna 18/20; tel. (22) 255221; fax (22) 252146; e-mail politic@isppan.waw.pl; f. 1990 to develop theoretical work and empirical studies of post-communist societies; attached to Polish Acad. of Sciences; library of 16,500 vols; Dir Prof. JERZY HOLZER; publs *Culture and Society*, *Polis*, *Political Studies*, *Civitas* (all quarterly).

**Polski Instytut Spraw Międzynarodowych (PISM)** (Polish Institute of International Affairs): 00-032 Warsaw, ul. Warecka 1A; tel. (22) 5568000; fax (22) 5568099; e-mail pism@pism.pl; internet www.pism.pl; f. 1996; research, courses, conferences; library of 150,000 vols; Dir Prof. RYSZARD STEMPLOWSKI; publs *Polski Przeglad Dyplomatyczny* (every two months), *Polish Digest of International Affairs* (quarterly), *Europe* (quarterly, in Russian), *Raporty* (in English and Polish), *Conferences* (in English and Polish), *Collections* (in English and Polish), *Polskie Dokumenty Dyplomatyczne* (in English and Polish).

**Polskie Towarzystwo Ukrainoznawcze** (Polish Association for Ukrainian Studies): Univ. of Warsaw, 02-678 Warsaw, ul. Szturmowa 4; Pres. Prof. Dr STEFAN KOZAK; publ. *Yearbook Warszawskie Zeszyty Ukrainoznawcze-Varshavki Ukrainoiznavchi Zapyski*.

## RUSSIA

**Carnegie Endowment for International Peace Center for Russian and Eurasian Programs:** 103051 Moscow, Sadova Samatiochnaya 24-27; tel. (095) 258-50-25; fax (095) 258-50-20;

e-mail carnegie@glas.apc.org; f. 1993; promotes intellectual collaboration between academics in Russia, the USA and the successor states of the USSR on issues of international peace and understanding; research programmes on conventional arms control and security, and ethnicity and nationality; Dir RICHARD BURGER; publs *Nuclear Non-Proliferation: A Compilation of Materials and Documents* (6 a year), *Nuclear Successor States of the Soviet Union* (2 a year).

**Central Economics Research Institute:** 119898 Moscow, Smolenski bul. 3/5; tel. (095) 246-84-63.

**Centre for Applied Political Studies (INDEM):** 121914 Moscow, ul. Novyi Arbat 15; tel. (095) 202-32-14; fax (095) 202-31-69; e-mail indemglas@apc.org; publ. *Russian Monitor: Archive of Contemporary Politics* (quarterly).

**Centre for Black Sea and Mediterranean Studies:** Russian Acad. of Sciences, 103873 Moscow, ul. Mokhovaya 8/3; tel. (095) 203-73-43; fax (095) 200-42-98; f. 1989 under the auspices of the Institute of Europe of the Russian Acad. of Sciences; research into Black Sea and Mediterranean countries and into Russian policy towards those countries; Dir NIKOLAI A. KOVALSKI.

**Centre for Caucasian Studies:** 117133 Moscow, ul. Akademika Vargi 24, kv. 9; tel. and fax (095) 339-13-23; e-mail iskand@glas.apc.org; f. 1992; research on political and economic issues of the North Caucasian and Transcaucasian regions; projects include the effects on Europe of the instability in the Caucasus and democratic institutions and systems in the region; Dir ALAN C. KASAYEV.

**Centre for National Security and International Relations:** 121069 Moscow, per. Khlebnyi 2-3; tel. (095) 291-20-52; fax (095) 202-90-00; e-mail srogov@rambler.ru; f. 1992; research into Russian civil-military relations, ethnic conflicts in Eastern Europe, peace-keeping and US and Russian strategy; Dir SERGEI M. ROGOV; publ. bulletin on security issues in countries of the former USSR (monthly).

**Centre for Policy Studies (PIR Centre):** 103001 Moscow, Trekhprudny per. 9; tel. (095) 234-05-25; fax (095) 234-95-58; e-mail info@pircenter.org; internet www.pircenter.org; f. 1994; non-profit, independent research and public education organization, which focuses on international security and arms control, and non-proliferation issues linked directly to Russia's internal situation; Dir Dr VLADIMIR ORLOV; publs *PIR Study Papers*.

**Centre for Political and International Studies:** 129090 Moscow, pr. Mira 36; tel. (095) 280-35-36; fax (095) 280-02-45; e-mail cpis@orc.ru; internet isn.rsuh.ru/cpis/index.htm.

**Centre for Strategic and Global Studies (CSGS):** Russian Acad. of Sciences, 103001 Moscow, ul. Spiridonevka 30/1; tel. (095) 290-63-85; fax (095) 202-07-86; e-mail csgs@inafr.msk.su; f. 1991; conducts research on economic and political issues, incl. global and political economic trends, environmental issues, geopolitical issues, the new world order, the devt of the CIS, and Mediterranean and Black Sea Studies; Dir Prof. Dr LEONID L. FITUNI.

**Centre for Strategic and International Studies:** 103753 Moscow, ul. Rozhdestvenka 12; tel. and fax (095) 924-51-50; f. 1991; research and training on Central Asia and Transcaucasia, ethnic relations, Eurasian studies, international relations, Islamic studies, the Middle East and North Africa, military and strategic studies, and politics; holds conferences and undertakes consultancy work; Pres. Prof. VITALII V. NAUMKIN; Exec. Dir Dr ALEKSANDR FILONIK.

**Gorbachev Foundation:** 125167 Moscow, pr. Leningradski 39; tel. (095) 945-59-99; fax (095) 945-78-99; f. 1992; research on the economic and political problems faced by the countries of the former USSR during the transition to democracy, incl. national and regional politics, European security and arms control; Pres. MIKHAIL S. GORBACHEV.

**Institut Mezhdunarodnych Ekonomicheskikh i Politicheskikh Issledovanii** (Institute of International Economic and Political Studies): 117418 Moscow, Novocheremushkinskaya 46; tel. (095) 128-91-54; fax (095) 120-83-71; e-mail imepi@transecon.ru; internet www.transecon.ru/; f. 1960 as the Institute for the Economy of the World Socialist System, name changed as above in 1990; forms part of the Russian Acad. of Sciences; research on political and economic reform, and international relations in post-communist countries of Central and Eastern Europe, in particular the former Soviet republics; Dir Prof. ALEKSANDR DMITRIEVICH NEKIPELOV; publs *Bulletin of Research Information, Politekonom* (jt German/Russian publ.), scholarly articles and monographs.

**Institut Mirovoy Ekonomiki i Mezhdunarodnykh Otnoshenii (IMEMO)** (Institute of World Economics and International Relations): 117589 Moscow, ul. Profsoyuznaya 23; tel. (095) 120-52-36; fax (095) 310-70-27; e-mail imemeoran@glasnet.ru; f. 1956; attached to Russian Acad. of Sciences; research into issues of global economy and international relations, including economic relations and the conversion of military economies; library; Dir V. A. MARTINOV; publs *Disarmament and Security Yearbook, Russia and Post-Soviet States Today* (monthly), *Mirovaya Economika I Mezhdunarodnye Otnosheniya* (monthly).

**Institut Slavianovedenia i Balkanistiki** (Institute of Slavonic and Balkan Studies): 125040 Moscow, pr. Leninskii 32A; tel. (095) 938-17-80; fax (095) 938-22-88; f. 1946; part of the Russian Acad. of Sciences; the major centre of Slavic and Balkan research in the Russian Federation, it also studies the relationship of the Slavs and other neighbouring ethnic groups with the Russian people; Dir VLADIMIR K. VOLKOV; publs monographs and periodicals.

**Institute for Comparative Political Studies:** 101831 Moscow, Kolpachnyi per. 9a; tel. (095) 916-37-03; fax (095) 916-03-01; f. 1966; attached to Russian Acad. of Sciences; library of 50,000 vols; Dir T. T. TIMOFEYEV; publs *Forum* (annually), *Polis* (6 a year).

**Institute for Current International Problems:** 119021 Moscow, ul. Ostozhenka 53/2; tel. (095) 208-94-61; fax (095) 208-94-66; Dir BAJANOV EUGUENI; publ. *Diplomatic Yearbook.*

**Institute for the Study of the Russian Economy:** 121854 Moscow, ul. Bolshaia Nikitskaya 44-2, Rm 26; tel. (095) 290-51-08; fax (095) 291-15-95; e-mail economic@clcp.co.ru; internet www.inme.ru.

**Institute of Economic Transition:** 103918 Moscow, ul. Ogareva 5, str. 3; tel. (095) 202-42-74; e-mail e40102@sucemi .bitnet; publ. *Russian Economy: Trends and Prospects.*

**Institute of Economics:** Russian Acad. of Sciences, 117218 Moscow, pr. Nakhimovski 32; tel. and fax (095) 129-52-28; e-mail vopreco@opc.ru; publ. *Voprosi Ekonomiki / Problems of Economics* (monthly).

**Institute of Socio-Political Research:** Russian Acad. of Sciences, 117334 Moscow, pr. Leninskii 32A; tel. (095) 938-19-10; Dir G. V. OSIPOV.

**International Foundation for Economic and Social Reforms (Reforma):** 109240 Moscow, nab. Kotelnicheskaya 17; tel. (095) 926-77-52; fax (095) 975-23-73; f. 1990; research into economic transition, CIS integration, ethnic conflict and the Russian Constitution; several brs thoughout the Russian Federation and rest of the CIS; publ. *Reforma Monthly.*

**Moskovskii Gosudarstvennii Institut Mezhdunarodnykh Otnoshenii (MGIMO)** (Moscow State Institute of International Relations): 117454 Moscow, pr. Vernadskogo 76; tel. (095) 434-91-58; fax (095) 434-90-66; f. 1944; studies international political and economic relations; areas of interest include Central Asian security, Russian policy in Central Asia and Moldova, CIS affairs and nuclear non-proliferation; Rector ANATOLII V. TORKUNIV; publ. *Moscow Journal of International Law.*

**Russian Association for Ukrainian Studies:** Institute of Slavonic and Balkan Studies, 117334 Moscow, Leninskii pr. 32; Pres. Dr LIUDMILA A. SOFRONOVA.

## SLOVAKIA

**Asociatsia Ukrainistiv Slovachchyny** (Slovakian Association for Ukrainian Studies): Filozofická Fakulta Presovskej Univerzity, Novembra 17 c. 1, 08078 Presôv; tel. (91) 7723-641; fax (91) 7733-231; e-mail babotova@unipo.sk; internet www .unipo.sk; f. 1991; studies Slovak-Ukrainian cultural and histor-

ical relations; Head of Section MIKULÁS MUSINKA; publs monographs.

**Vedeckovyskumné oddelenie ukrajinistiky, Katedra ukrajinského jazyka a literatúry** (Ukrainian Research Section, Dept of Ukrainian Language and Literature): tel. (91) 7723-424; fax (91) 7733-268; f. 1966; research on ethnography, folklore, children's literature and youth and minority issues affecting Ruthenians-Ukrainians in Slovakia; library of over 3,000 vols.

## SLOVENIA

**Slavistično društvo Slovenije** (Slovene Slavonic Studies Society): 1000 Ljubljana, Aškerčeva 2/II; tel. (1) 2411320; fax (1) 4257055; e-mail center-slo@ff.uni-lj.si; internet www.neticom.si/kronika; f. 1935; a forum for professional Slavists, to provide a link between research and professional practice and to organize support for, and to publish, Slavic research; Pres. ZOLTAN JAN; publs *Language and Literature / Jezik in slovstvo* (10 a year), *Slavonic Studies Journal / Slavistična revija* (quarterly).

## SWEDEN

**Central Asia and the Caucasus Centre for Social and Political Studies:** Rodhakegrand 21, 97 454 Luleå; tel. and fax (920) 62-016; e-mail murad@communique.se; internet www.ca-c .org; f. 1998 to study and review the social and political situation in Central Asia and the Caucasus from an academic point of view, to create a database and to distribute information; Dir Dr MURAD ESENOV; publ. *Central Asia and the Caucasus: Journal of Social and Political Studies.*

**Centre for Russian and East European Studies:** Centre for European Research, Göteborg Univ., Pilgaten 19, 1st Floor, POB 720, 405 30 Göteborg; tel. (31) 773-43-16; fax (31) 773-44-61; e-mail crees@crees.gu.se; internet www.host.gu.se/crees; f. 1991; cross-disciplinary centre to promote contacts between the Univ., the public sector, the business communities of western Sweden and the countries of the region; Dir Prof. RUTGER LINDAHL.

**Stockholm Institute of Transition Economics (SITE):** Stockholm School of Economics, POB 6501, 113 83 Stockholm; tel. (8) 736-96-70; fax (8) 31-64-22; e-mail site@hhs.se; internet www.hhs.se/site/; f. 1989; conducts economic research on issues facing countries in transition and contributes to the development of economic research institutions in those countries; Dir Prof. ERIK BERGLÖF; publs *Transition Economics Abstract Series (TEASE), Baltic Economic Trends,* working papers, newsletters and reports.

**Stockholm International Peace Research Institute (SIPRI):** Signalistgatan 9, 169 70 Solna; tel. (8) 655-97-00; fax (8) 655-97-33; e-mail sipri@sipri.org; internet www.sipri.org; f. 1966; scientific research into the conditions for peaceful solutions to international conflicts and a stable peace focusing, in particular, on arms control and disarmament; library of 40,000 vols; Dir ALYSON J. K. BAILES; publs *SIPRI Yearbook,* monographs, occasional papers and research reports.

## SWITZERLAND

**Institut für Internationales Recht und Internationales Beziehungen** (Institute of International Law and International Relations): Universität Basel, Maiengasse 51, Basel 4056; tel. (61) 2673011; fax (61) 2673035.

**Institut Suisse de Recherche sur les Pays de l'Est** (Swiss Eastern Institute): Jubiläumsstr. 41, 3000 Bern 6; tel. (31) 431212; fax (31) 433891; f. 1959; study of, and information on, the devt of former communist countries; library; Dir Dr GEORG J. DOBROVOLNY; publs *Le Périscope* (monthly), *Schwejzarskij Vestnik* (monthly, in Russian), *SOI-Bilanz* (monthly), *Swiss Press Review* (every 2 weeks), *Zeit-bild* (every 2 weeks).

## TAJIKISTAN

**Institute of World Economics and International Relations:** 734000 Dushanbe, ul. Aini 44; tel. (372) 23-27-32; fax (372) 22-57-65; f. 1964; attached to Acad. of Sciences; conducts research into economic devt in Tajikistan and other countries, with particular attention to transitional economies and the process of integration into the global economy; Dir RASHID K. RAKHIMOV; publ. *Ekonomiko-Matematicheskie Metody v Planirovanii Narodnogo Khozyaistva.*

## TURKEY

**Karadeniz ve Orta Asya Ülkeri Arastirma Merkez** (Black Sea and Central Asian Countries Research Centre): Orta Dogu Teknik Üniversitesi, Ismet Inönü Bul., 06531 Ankara; tel. (312) 2101204; fax (312) 2101105; e-mail kora@rorqual.cc.metu.edu.tr; internet www.metu.edu.tr/home/wwwkora; f. 1992; data analysis and economic and political forecasting; Dir Dr ALI RIZA GÜNBAK.

## TURKMENISTAN

**Institute of Economics:** 744032 Ashgabat, Bikrova sad keshi 28; tel. (12) 24-02-52; Dir G. M. MURADOV.

## UKRAINE

**Centre for Peace, Conversion and Foreign Policy of Ukraine (CPCFPU):** Kiev, POB 101; tel. and fax (44) 484-38-19; f. 1992 as the Ukrainian Centre for Peace, Conversion and Conflict Resolution Studies; international relations, security and foreign policy.

**Institute for Economic Research:** 01023 Kiev, bul. Druzhby Narodiv 28; tel. (44) 269-96-33; e-mail sas@niei.kiev.ua; part of the Ministry of the Economy and Progress towards European Integration; areas of research have included analysis of the most important trends in Ukrainian economic and social devt and the state of Ukraine's economy during the transition to a market economy.

**Institute of Economics:** 01011 Kiev, vul. Panasa Mirnoho 26; tel. (44) 290-84-44; fax (44) 290-86-63; f. 1992; attached to the Acad. of Sciences; conducts research into transitional economies, theory of political economy and the devt of agro-industrial complexes in Ukraine; library; Dir I. I. LUKINOV; publs *Ekonomika Ukrainy* (monthly), *Istoriya Narodnoho Hospodarstvo Ta Ekonomichnoi Dumki Ukrainy* (annually), research reports.

**Institute of International Relations of Kiev National Taras Shevchenko University:** 04119 Kiev, ul. Melnikova 36/1; tel. (44) 213-09-90; fax (44) 213-07-67; e-mail long@iir.kiev.ua; internet www.iir.kiev.ua; Dir Prof. Dr LEONID GUBERSKY.

**Institute of the World Economy and International Relations:** Nat. Acad. of Sciences, 01030 Kiev, vul. Leontovicha 5; tel. (44) 235-70-22; fax (44) 235-51-27; f. 1992; research and studies on European and national economic, political and social problems; transitional societies and world civilization processes; global, national and regional interdependence in the contemporary world; US and trans-Atlantic economic and policy studies; political culture of Afro-Asian societies; Dir A. N. SHLEPAKOV.

**Mizhnarodna Asotsiatsiia Ukrainistiv** (International Association of Ukrainian Studies): 01001 Kiev, vul. Hrushevskoho 4; tel. and fax (44) 229-76-50; e-mail iaus@gilan.uar.net; Pres. Prof. YAROSLAV ISEYEVICH; publ. *Biuleten Respublikans'koi Asotsiatsii Ukrainoznavtsiv.*

**Ukrainian Centre for International Security Studies (UCISS):** 02023 Kiev, POB 541; tel. and fax (44) 212-58-37; e-mail globus@uciss.freenet.kiev.ua; internet www.isn.ethz.ch/uciss/uciss.htm; f. 1991 to study national, regional and global security issues; Pres. Dr LEONID BELOUSOV; Exec. Dir OLEKSANDR PARFIONOV; publs occasional papers.

## UNITED KINGDOM

**Bakhtin Centre:** Arts Tower, Univ. of Sheffield, Sheffield S10 2TN; tel. (114) 222-7415; fax (114) 222-7416; e-mail bakhtin.centre@sheffield.ac.uk; f. 1994 to promote multi and interdisciplinary research on the work of the Russian philosopher and theorist, Mikhail Bakhtin, and the Bakhtin Circle, and on related areas of cultural, critical, linguistic and literary theory.

**Centre for Central and East European Studies:** Univ. of Liverpool, Liverpool L69 7WZ; tel. (151) 794-2422; fax (151) 794-

2366; e-mail swainnj@liverpool.ac.uk; internet www.liv.ac.uk/history/centres/cehome.html; Deputy Dir Dr NIGEL SWAIN.

**Centre for Defence and International Security Studies (CDISS):** Dept of Politics and Int. Relations, Cartmel College, Univ. of Lancaster, Lancaster LA1 4YL; tel. (1524) 594-254; fax (1524) 594-258; e-mail cdiss@lancaster.ac.uk; internet www.cdiss.org; f. 1990 by merger of the Centre for Defence and Security Analysis and the Centre for the Study of Arms Control and Int. Security; research programmes on military technology, European security, and Russia and related studies etc; holds conferences and seminars; Dir Dr MARTIN EDMONDS; publs *Bailrigg Papers, Bailrigg Memoranda, Bailrigg Debating Points, Bailrigg Studies, Defense Analysis* (quarterly).

**Centre for East European Studies:** Univ. of Sheffield, Sheffield S10 2TN; tel. (114) 222-2000; fax (114) 273-9826.

**Centre for Economic Reform and Transformation (CERT):** School of Management, Heriot-Watt Univ., Riccarton, Edinburgh EH14 4AS; tel. (131) 451-3485; fax (131) 451-3498; e-mail s.a.ashby@hw.ac.uk; internet www.som.hw.ac.uk/cert/; f. 1990; tracks and analyses economic transformation in Central and Eastern Europe and the CIS; Dir Prof. MARK E. SCHAFFER; publ. *Journal: the Economics of Transition.*

**Centre for Research into Post-Communist Economies (CRCE):** 57 Tufton St, London SW1P 3QL; tel. (20) 7233-1050; fax (20) 7233-4299; e-mail crce@crce.freewire.co.uk; internet www.crce.org.uk; f. 1984; research into issues affecting communist economies and those economies making the transition from communism to a market economy; publ. *Post-Communist Economies*; Dir LJUBO SIRC; Administrative Dir LISL BIGGS-DAVISON.

**Centre for Russian Studies:** Univ. of Aberdeen, King's College, Aberdeen AB24 3FX; tel. (1224) 272465; fax (1224) 272203; e-mail p.dukes@abdn.ac.uk; f. 1989; specializes in Siberia and the Russian Far East, comparative Russian-US studies, Russian-Scottish connections; Dir Prof. PAUL DUKES; publs occasional papers.

**Centre for Russian and East European Studies:** School of Social Sciences, Univ. of Birmingham, European Research Institute, Edgbaston, Birmingham B15 2TT; tel. (121) 414-6346; fax (121) 414-3423; e-mail crees@bham.ac.uk; internet www.crees.bham.ac.uk; f. 1963; a multidisciplinary centre focusing on the social sciences and history, incl. studies of Central European, Russian and Ukrainian politics and society, post-communist economic transformation, the history of Russia and the USSR, and security studies, Russian language and literature, Polish and Ukrainian languages; Baykov Library of 90,000 vols; Dir Prof. HILARY PILKINGTON; publs *Research Papers on Russian and East European Studies (ResPREES), Birmingham Slavonic Monographs.*

**Centre for Russian and East European Studies:** Singleton Park, Swansea SA2 8PP; tel. (1792) 205678; fax (1792) 295710.

**Centre for Russian, Soviet and Central and East European Studies:** Univ. of St Andrews, St Andrews, Fife KY16 9AL; tel. (1334) 462938; fax (1334) 462937; internet www.st-and.ac.uk/institutes/crscees/; f. 1990; Dir Dr RICK FAWN.

**Centre for the Study of Public Policy:** Univ. of Strathclyde, Livingstone Tower, 26 Richmond St, Glasgow G1 1XH; tel. (141) 548-3217; fax (141) 552-4711; e-mail o.j.robertson@strath.ac.uk; internet www.cspp.strath.ac.uk; f. 1976; undertakes international policy research, with particular emphasis on mass-behaviour in post-communist societies and regional devt in Eastern Europe; Dir Prof. RICHARD ROSE; publ. *Studies in Public Policy* (16 a year).

**Centre of International Studies:** Univ. of Cambridge, Fitzwilliam House, 32 Trumpington St, Cambridge CB2 1QY; tel. (1223) 741311; fax (1223) 741313; e-mail intstudies@lists.cam; internet www.intstudies.cam.ac.uk; f. 1977; research and postgraduate courses on international relations and European studies; Dirs Prof. J. B. L. MAYALL, Dr G. EDWARDS, Dr C. JONES, Dr P. TOWLE, Dr J. HASLAM, Dr M. EILSTRUP SANGIOVANNI, M. WELLER; publ. *Cambridge Review of International Affairs* (2 a year).

**Conflict and Security Studies Programme, University of Aberdeen:** King's College, Aberdeen, AB24 3FX ; tel. (1224)

272-725; e-mail j.h.wyllie@abdn.ac.uk; internet www.abdn.ac.uk/pir/css.

**Institute for Slavonic Studies:** Univ. of Oxford, Rewley House, 1 Wellington Sq., Oxford OX1 2JA; tel. (1865) 515635; fax (1865) 270708; internet units.ox.ac.uk/departments/Slavonic/research/institute.html; f. 1988 as the Institute of Russian, Soviet and East European Studies, name changed as above in 1994; member of the Consortium for Russian and East European Studies; Dir CHRISTOPHER DAVIS.

**Institute of Central and East European Studies:** Univ. of Glasgow, Rm 5602, Adam Smith Bldg, Glasgow G12 8RS; tel. (141) 330-4579; fax (141) 330-5594; e-mail j.lowenhardt@socsci.gla.ac.uk; internet www.gla.ac.uk/icees; f. 1999; inter-faculty research on culture, economics, history, politics and society in Central and Eastern Europe, Russia and other CIS member states; host to the website of the British Association for Slavonic and East European Studies (BASEES), the Scottish Society for Russian and East European Studies (SSREES) and the European Centre for Occupational Health, Safety and the Environment; Glasgow Univ. Library holds 75,000 to 80,000 vols on Central and Eastern Europe and Russia; publs *Europe-Asia Studies*, *The Glasgow Papers*.

**Institute of Russian, Soviet and East European Studies:** Dept of Slavonic Studies, Univ. of Nottingham, Univ. Park, Nottingham NG7 2RD; tel. (115) 951-5824; fax (115) 951-5834; e-mail slavonic.studies@nottingham.ac.uk; internet www.nottingham.ac.uk/slavonic/general/iscees.html; f. 1986; interdisciplinary research in the fields of Central and East European, Russian and Soviet studies; holds seminars, workshops and conferences; Dir Prof. LESLEY MILNE.

**Keston Institute:** 38 St Aldate's, Oxford OX1 1BN; tel. (1865) 792929; fax (1865) 240042; e-mail keston.institute@keston.org; internet www.keston.org; f. 1970; charity studying religious affairs and promoting religious freedom in post-Communist and Communist countries; Dir Dr DAVORIN PETERLIN; publs *Frontier* (quarterly), *Religion, State and Society: the Keston Journal* (quarterly).

**Leeds University Centre for Russian, Eurasian and Central European Studies (LUCRECES):** c/o School of Politics and Int. Studies, SS Bldg, Univ. of Leeds, Leeds LS2 9JT; tel. (113) 343-6869; fax (113) 343-4400; e-mail j.f.sutton@leeds.ac.uk; internet www.leeds.ac.uk/lucreces; Dir JONATHAN SUTTON.

**Pan-European Institute:** Univ. of Essex, Wivenhoe Park, Colchester, Essex CO4 3SQ; tel. (1206) 873976; fax (1206) 873965; e-mail pei@essex.ac.uk; internet www.essex.ac.uk/centres/pei; f. 1997; PEI's interests incorporate the whole of 'new' Europe, as far as the Russian Far East; Dir ALASTAIR MCAULEY.

**Royal Institute of International Affairs (RIIA):** Chatham House, 10 St James's Sq., London SW1Y 4LE; tel. (20) 7957-5700; fax (20) 7957-5710; e-mail contact@riia.org; internet www.riia.org; f. 1920; an independent body, which aims to promote the study and understanding of international affairs, incl. international security and economics; the Russia and Eurasia Programme serves as a forum for debate and research on the foreign and domestic policies of Russia and the Commonwealth of Independent States, focusing specifically on security, peacekeeping, conflict prevention, energy and economics; publishes extensively and holds regular seminars and study groups to address topical issues; library of 140,000 vols and 650 periodicals; Chair. Dr DEANNE JULIUS; Dir Prof. VICTOR BULMER-THOMAS; Contact JAMES NIXEY; publs *International Affairs* (5 a year), *The World Today* (monthly).

**Russian and Eurasian Studies Centre:** St Antony's College, Oxford Univ., 62 Woodstock Rd, Oxford OX2 6JF; tel. (1865) 284728; fax (1865) 310518; e-mail study.enquiries@sant.ox.ac.uk; internet www.sant.ox.ac.uk/russian; f. 1953; multi-disciplinary research; library of 24,000 vols; Dir ALEX PRAVDA.

**Russian and East European Research Centre:** Univ. of Wolverhampton, Molyneux St, Wolverhampton WV1 1SB; tel. (1902) 321000; fax (1902) 322680.

**School of Slavonic and East European Studies (SSEES):** Univ. College London, Senate House, Malet St, London WC1E 7HU; tel. (20) 7862-8000; fax (20) 7862-8641; e-mail ssees@ssees.ac.uk; internet www.ssees.ac.uk; f. 1915; multi-disciplinary research into the culture, economics, geography, history, international relations, language, politics and sociology of Eastern Europe and Russia; has a Centre for Russian Studies and a Centre for South-East European Studies; library of 350,000 vols and 1,200 periodicals; Dir Prof. GEORGE KOLANKIEWICZ; publs *Slavonic and East European Review* (quarterly), *Slovo: An Interdisciplinary Journal of Russian, East European and Eurasian Affairs* (2 a year), *Solanus* (annually), occasional papers.

**School of Oriental and African Studies (SOAS):** Univ. of London, Thornhaugh St, London WC1H 0XG; tel. (20) 7637-2388; fax (20) 7436-3844; internet www.soas.ac.uk; f. 1916; library of over 750,000 vols; Dir Prof. COLIN BUNDY; publ. *Bulletin*.

**Ukraine Centre:** Learning Centre, Univ. of North London, 236-250 Holloway Rd, London N7 6PP; tel. (20) 7753-3273; fax (20) 7753-5015; internet www.unl.ac.uk/ukrainecentre; f. 1997; Dir Dr MARKO BOJCUN; publs online working papers.

## USA

**American Association for Ukrainian Studies:** 211 Sparks Bldg, Pennsylvania State Univ., Univ. Park, Johnstown, PA 16802; tel. (814) 865-1675; e-mail rdelossa@fas.harvard.edu; Pres. MICHAEL M. NAYDAN; publ. *AAUS Newsletter*.

**American Enterprise Institute for Policy Research (AEI):** 1150 17th St, NW, Washington, DC 20036; tel. (202) 862-5800; fax (202) 862-7177; f. 1943; conducts research into economic policies, Eastern European affairs, international trade and finance, regional devt and social and political issues; Pres. CHRISTOPHER C. DEMUTH; publs *American Enterprise* (6 a year), monographs.

**Brookings Institution:** 1775 Massachusetts Ave, NW, Washington, DC 20036-2188; tel. (202) 797-6000; fax (202) 797-6004; e-mail brookinfo@brook.edu; internet www.brookings.edu/; f. 1916; education, research and publishing in the fields of economics, and foreign and government policy; foreign-policy research focuses on co-operative security, global sustainability, conflict resolution, international devt and the Russian Federation; library of 80,000 vols; Pres. MICHAEL H. ARMACOST; publs *Brookings Papers on Economic Activity* (3 a year), *Brookings Review* (quarterly), policy briefs and individual reports.

**Center for East Asian Studies (CEAS):** Monterey Institute of International Studies, 460 Pierce St, Monterey, CA 93940; tel. (831) 647-4100; fax (831) 647-4199; e-mail info@miis.edu; internet www.miis.edu/centers-ceas.html; projects examine issues such as the role of Pacific Rim countries in the devt of the Russian Far East and the regional security implications of North-East Asian economic devt; library of 77,000 vols and 565 periodicals; Dir Dr TSUNEO AKAHA.

**Center for European and Russian Studies (CERS):** Univ. of California, 11367 Bunche Hall, POB 951446, Los Angeles, CA 90095-1446; tel. (310) 825-4060; fax (310) 206-3555; e-mail vwheeler@isop.ucla.edu; internet www.isop.ucla.edu/euro/; library of over 250,000 vols and 1,000 periodicals; Dir IVAN BEREND; publs *Communist and Post-Communist Studies* and working papers.

**Center for Foreign Policy Development:** Thomas J. Watson, Jr Institute for International Studies, Brown Univ., 2 Stimson Ave, POB 1948, Providence, RI 02912; tel. (401) 863-3465; fax (401) 863-7440; e-mail cfpd@brown.edu; f. 1981; global security issues; particularly concerned with relations between the USA and countries of the former USSR; Dir P. TERRENCE HOPMANN; publ. *Watson Institute Briefings Newsletter*.

**Center for Nations in Transition (CNT):** Univ. of Minnesota, 230 Hubert H. Humphrey Center, 301 19th Ave S., Minneapolis, MN 55455; tel. (612) 625-3073; fax (612) 626-9860; e-mail thageman@hhh.umn.edu; internet www.hhh.umn.edu/centers/cnt/main.htm; involved in research and institutional design for sustainable devt, and educational activities in Central and Eastern European countries; Russian and Central European Area Studies library, available on-line at www.lib.umn.edu/rce; Dir ZBIGNIEW BOCHNIARZ.

**Center for Nonproliferation Studies (CNS):** Monterey Institute of International Studies, 460 Pierce St, Monterey, CA 93940; tel. (831) 647-4154; fax (831) 647-3519; e-mail cns@miis.edu; internet www.cns.miis.edu; f. 1989; library of 77,000 vols and 565 periodicals; Dir Dr WILLIAM C. POTTER; publs *CNS Forum, Inventory of International Nonproliferation Organizations and Regimes, Nonproliferation Review, Status Report: Nuclear Weapons, Fissile Material and Export Controls in the Former Soviet Union*, occasional papers.

**Center for Russian and East European Studies:** Univ. of Kansas, 1440 Jayhawk Blvd, Lawrence, KS 66045-7574; tel. (785) 864-4236; fax (785) 864-3800; e-mail crees@ukans.edu; internet www.ukans.edu/~crees; f. 1960; language and area studies in Polish, Russian, Ukrainian and general Central and Southern European affairs; special programmes for US Army Foreign Area Officers; library of 350,000 vols and 3,000 periodicals (current and out of print); Dir Dr MARIA CARLSON.

**Center for Russian and East European Studies (CREES):** Univ. of Michigan, 1080 South Univ. Ave, Suite 4668, Ann Arbor, MI 48109-1106; tel. (313) 734-0351; fax (313) 734-4765; e-mail crees@umich.edu; internet www.umich.edu/~iinet/crees; US Dept of Education National Resource Center for Eastern Europe, Russia and Central Asia; Dir BARBARA A. ANDERSON; publs newsletters.

**Center for Russian and East European Studies (REES):** Univ. of Pittsburgh, 4G15 Posvar Hall, Pittsburgh, PA 15260; tel. (412) 648-7407; fax (412) 648-7002; e-mail crees@ucis.pitt.edu; internet www.ucis.pitt.edu/crees; f. 1965; a US Dept of Education Title VI National Resource Center; areas of research include contemporary Russian culture, societies in transition, foreign policy, Balkan and Slovak studies; library of 361,000 vols; Dir Dr ROBERT M. HAYDEN; publs *Carl Beck Papers, Pitt Series in Russian and East European StudiesEast European Politics and Societies*.

**Center for Russian and East European Studies (CREES):** Univ. of Virginia, 223 Minor Hall, POB 400167, Charlottesville, VA 22904-4167; tel. (804) 924-3033; fax (804) 924-7867; e-mail crees@virginia.edu; internet minerva.acc.virginia.edu/~crees; Dir ALLEN C. LYNCH.

**Center for Russian and Eurasian Studies (CRES):** Monterey Institute of International Studies, 460 Pierce St, Monterey, CA 93940; tel. (831) 647-4154; fax (831) 647-3519; e-mail cres@miis.edu; internet cns.miis.edu/cres.htm; f. 1986; interdisciplinary study and research on Russia and the newly independent states, in the fields of contemporary politics and society, regional security and Russian foreign policy; library of 8,000 vols and 130 periodicals; Dir Dr WILLIAM POTTER; publs *NIS Environmental Watch* and occasional papers.

**Center for Russian, East European and Central Asian Studies (CREECA):** Univ. of Wisconsin-Madison, 210 Ingraham Hall, 1155 Observatory Dr., Madison, WI 53706-1397; tel. (608) 262-3379; fax (608) 265-3062; e-mail creeca@intl-institute.wisc.edu; internet www.wisc.edu/creeca; f. 1993; a US Dept of Education Title VI National Resource Center; forms part of the Int. Institute, Univ. of Wisconsin-Madison; library of 600,000 vols; Dir ROBERT J. KAISER.

**Center for Russian, East European and Eurasian Studies:** Stanford Univ., Bldg 40, Main Quad, Stanford, CA 94305-2006; tel. (650) 723-3562; fax (650) 725-6119; internet www.stanford.edu/dept/CREES; f. 1966; the promotion and support of the interdisciplinary study of the region; Dir Prof. NANCY S. KOLLMANN; publs newsletter and conference papers.

**Center for Russian, East European and Eurasian Studies (CREEES):** Univ. of Iowa, Int. 22, Iowa City, IA 52242-1802; tel. (319) 335-3584; fax (319) 353-2033; e-mail uicreees@uiowa.edu; internet www.uiowa.edu/~creees; f. 1997; the centre provides support to the schools of business, education, law and medicine, and in the fields of humanities and social sciences for the devt of courses focusing on Eastern Europe, Russia and Central Asia; Russian, East European and Eurasian Studies collection of approx. 140,000 vols; Dir RUSSELL SCOTT VALENTINO.

**Center for Russian, East European and Eurasian Studies (REENIC):** Univ. of Texas at Austin, Geography 106 A1600, Austin, TX 78712; tel. (512) 471-7782; fax (512) 471-3368;

internet reenic.utexas.edu/reenic/online.html; Dir JOAN NEUBERGER.

**Center for Slavic and East European Studies:** Ohio State Univ., 303 Oxley Hall, 1712 Neil Ave, Columbus, OH 43210-1219; tel. (614) 292-8770; fax (614) 292-4273; e-mail wolf.5@osu.edu; internet www.cohums.ohio-state.edu/slavicctr; f. 1965; a US Dept of Education Title VI National Resource Center; Dir IRENE MASING-DELIC.

**Center for Slavic and East European Studies:** Univ. of California, Berkeley, 361 Stephens Hall, Rm 2304, Berkeley, CA 94720; tel. (510) 642-3230; fax (510) 643-5045; e-mail csees@uclink4.berkeley.edu; internet socrates.berkeley.edu/~csees; f. 1957; Berkeley main library includes Slavic and East European collections comprising 750,000 vols and 10,000 serial titles.

**Center for Slavic, Eurasian and East European Studies (CSEEES):** Univ. of North Carolina at Chapel Hill, 223 E. Franklin St, POB 5125, Chapel Hill, NC 27599-5125; tel. (919) 962-0901; fax (919) 962-2494; e-mail slavic@email.unc.edu; internet www.unc.edu/depts/slavic; f. 1991; operates jointly with Duke Univ; a US Dept of Education Title VI National Resource Center; undergraduate education, graduate student and faculty research, conferences and seminars; Dir Dr ROBERT M. JENKINS (Univ. of North Carolina), EDNA ANDREWS (Duke Univ.); publ. *Inflections* (quarterly newsletter).

**Center for Strategic and International Studies (CSIS):** 1800 K St, NW, Washington, DC 20006; tel. (202) 887-0200; fax (202) 775-3199; e-mail jgeis@csis.org; internet www.csis.org; f. 1962; public-policy research institute dedicated to analysis and policy impact; Russian and Eurasian programme; Chair. SAM NUNN; Programme Dir CELESTE WALLANDER; publs *Washington Papers* (monographs), *Washington Quarterly, PONARS Policy Memos*, newsletters.

**Center for the Study of Foreign Affairs:** Foreign Service Institute, 4000 Arlington Blvd, Arlington, VA 22204; tel. (703) 302-7137; research on Russian foreign-policy issues, foreign policy in the Persian Gulf, arms control, conflict resolution and trade policy; diplomatic training; holds conferences and seminars; Dir DENNIS H. KUX; publs various monographs.

**Center of International Studies:** Woodrow Wilson School of Public and Int. Affairs, Princeton Univ., 116 Bendheim Hall, Princeton, NJ 08544-1022; tel. (609) 258-4851; fax (609) 258-3988; internet www.wws.princeton.edu/~cis; f. 1951; international relations and national devt research, incl. analysis of international security and the political economy; Dir MICHAEL DOYLE; publs *World Politics* (quarterly), books, occasional papers.

**Central Asia-Caucasus Institute:** Paul H. Nitze School of Advanced Int. Studies, Johns Hopkins Univ., 1740 Massachusetts Ave, Washington, DC 20036; tel. (202) 663-5624; fax (202) 663-5656; internet www.sais-jhu.edu/caci; f. 1996; Dean PAUL WOLFOWITZ; publ. *Central Asia-Caucasus Analyst* (available online, every 2 weeks).

**EastWest Institute:** 700 Broadway, 2nd Floor, New York, NY 10003; tel. (212) 824-4100; fax (212) 824-4149; e-mail iews@iews.org; internet www.iews.org; f. 1981; the study of conflict prevention and democracy in Eastern Europe, Russia and Central Asia; Pres. JOHN EDWIN MROZ.

**Harriman Institute:** Columbia Univ., 420 West 118th St, New York, NY 10027; tel. (212) 854-4623; fax (212) 666-3481; e-mail harriman@columbia.edu; internet www.columbia.edu/cu/sipa/REGIONAL/HI; f. 1946; publ. *Harriman Review*.

**Hudson Institute:** Herman Kahn Center, 5395 Emerson Way, POB 26919, Indianapolis, IN 46226-0919; tel. (317) 545-1000; fax (317) 545-9639; f. 1961; studies Central and Eastern Europe, global food issues and US strategic issues; library of 13,000 vols; Pres. Dr LESLIE LENKOWSKI; publs *Hudson Opinion* (monthly), *Hudson Report* (quarterly).

**Institute for Democracy in Eastern Europe (IDEE):** 2000 P St, NW, Suite 400, Washington, DC 20036; tel. (202) 466-7105; fax (202) 466-7140; e-mail idee@idee.org; internet www.idee.org; f. 1985; supports independent human-rights, political and social movements, and publications independent of government control, in Central and Eastern Europe and the countries of the former USSR; library of 1,000 vols; Pres. IRENA LASOTA; publ. *Centers for Pluralism Newsletter* (quarterly, in English and Russian).

**Institute for East-West Studies:** 700 Broadway, 2nd Floor, New York, NY 10003, USA; tel. (212) 824-4100; fax (212) 824-4149; e-mail iews@iews.org; internet www.iews.org; f. 1981; has a particular focus on economic and regional devt, international security, the Russian regions, and transfrontier co-operation; Chair. DONALD M. KENDALL; Pres. JOHN EDWIN MROZ; publs *Annual Report, Russian Regional Report* (weekly), conference papers and regional reports.

**Institute for European, Russian and Eurasian Studies:** George Washington Univ., Stuart Hall, 2013 G St, NW, Suite 401, Washington, DC 20052, USA; tel. (202) 994-6340; fax (202) 994-5436; e-mail ieresgwu@gwu.edu; internet www.gwu.edu/~ieresgwu; f. 1961 as the Institute of Sino-Soviet Studies; name changed as above 1992; Dir JAMES M. GOLDGEIER; publ. *Problems of Post-Communism*.

**Institute for the Study of Conflict, Ideology and Policy (ISCIP):** Boston Univ., 141 Bay State Rd, Boston, MA 02215; tel. (617) 353-5815; fax (617) 353-7185; internet www.bu.edu/iscip; f. 1988; focuses on conflict-prone societies in crisis, especially Russia and other post-Soviet republics, paying particular attention to destabilizing factors of a political, ethnic or international nature; Dir Prof. URI RA'ANAN; publs *NIS Observed: An Analytical Review* (every 2 weeks), *Perspective* (every 2 months), ISCIP publication series; database of political and security devts in the post-Soviet republics.

**Institute of Slavic, East European and Eurasian Studies:** 260 Stephen's Hall, Berkeley, California, CA 94720-2304; tel. (510) 642-3230; fax (510) 643-5045; e-mail iseees@uclink4.berkeley.edu; Dir VICTORIA E. BONNELL.

**Kathryn W. and Shelby Cullom Davis Center for Russian Studies:** Harvard Univ., 625 Massachusetts Ave, Cambridge, MA 02139; tel. (617) 495-4037; fax (617) 495-8319; e-mail daviscrs@fas.harvard.edu; internet www.daviscenter.fas.harvard.edu; f. 1948; advanced study of the experiences and problems of Russia and adjacent regions of Europe and Asia; library; Dir TIMOTHY J. COLTON; publ. monograph series (100 vols).

> **Ukrainian Research Institute:** 1583 Massachusetts Ave, Cambridge, MA 02138; tel. (617) 495-4053; fax (617) 495-8097; Dir ROMAN SZPORLUK.

**Kennan Institute for Advanced Russian Studies:** Woodrow Wilson Center, One Woodrow Wilson Plaza, 1300 Pennsylvania Ave, NW, Washington, DC 20004-3027; tel. (202) 691-4100; fax (202) 691-4247; e-mail kiars@wwic.si.edu; internet wwics.si.edu/kennan/index.htm; f. 1974; Russia and the former USSR; Dir BLAIR A. RUBLE.

**Matthew B. Ridgway Center for International Security Studies:** Univ. of Pittsburgh, 3J01 Posvar Hall, Pittsburgh, PA 15260; tel. (412) 648-7408; fax (412) 624-7291; e-mail goldy@pitt.edu; research into organized crime; the non-proliferation of weapons of mass destruction; regional conflict; and new dimensions of international security, including the environment, chemical and biological weapons, terrorism, information warfare, etc; Dir DONALD GOLDSTEIN (acting); publs *Ridgway Newsletter, Transnational Organized Crime*.

**National Bureau of Asian Research (NBR):** 4518 University Way NE, Suite 300, Seattle, Washington 98105; tel. (206) 632-7370; fax (206) 632-7487; e-mail nbr@nbr.org; internet www.nbr.org; research on security issues, economic growth, politics and international relations in East, Central and South Asia, and Russia; publs *NBR Book Series, NBR Analysis, NBR Briefing,*

*NBR Bulletin, NBR Special Reports, AccessAsia Review*; Pres. RICHARD J. ELLINGS.

**National Council for Eurasian and East European Research (NCEEER):** 910 17th St, NW, Suite 300, Washington, DC 20006; tel. (202) 822-6950; fax (202) 822-6955; e-mail dc@nceeer.org; internet www.nceeer.org; f. 1978; covers economic, political and social developments and trends in the post-communist countries of Asia and Europe; Chair. NANCY CONDEE; Editor ROBERT HUBER.

**Russian and East European Center (REEC):** Univ. of Illinois at Urbana-Champaign, 104 Int. Studies Bldg, 910 S. Fifth St, Champaign, IL 61820; tel. (217) 333-1244; fax (217) 333-1582; e-mail reec@uiuc.edu; internet www.uiuc.edu/unit/reec; f. 1959; houses the American Association for the Advancement of Slavic Studies; interdisciplinary research; Slavic and East European Library of 676,000 vols and 4,000 periodicals; Dir Prof. MARK STEINBERG; publ. *Slavic Review*.

**Russian and East European Institute:** Indiana Univ., 565 Ballantine Hall, Bloomington, IN 47405-6615; tel. (812) 855-7309; fax (812) 855-6411; e-mail reei@indiana.edu; internet www.indiana.edu/~reeiweb; f. 1958; interdisciplinary training and research; main library holds 600,000 vols on Slavic and East European issues; Dir DAVID RANSEL; publ. *REEIfication* (quarterly newsletter).

**Russian and East European Studies Center (REESC):** Univ. of Oregon, Eugene, OR 97403; tel. (541) 346-4078; fax (541) 346-5041; e-mail Russian@darkwing.uoregon.edu; internet darkwing.uoregon.edu/~reesc; Knight Library of 180,000 vols and 100 serial titles; Dir ALAN KIMBALL.

**Russian, East European and Central Asian Studies Center at the University of Washington's Jackson School of International Studies:** Thomson Hall, Rm 203, POB 353650, Seattle, WA 98195-3650; tel. (206) 543-4852; fax (206) 685-0668; e-mail reecas@u.washington.edu; internet depts.washington.edu/reecas; a US Dept of Education Title VI National Resource Center; Dir STEPHEN HANSON.

**Shevchenko Scientific Society** (Naukove Tovarystvo im. Shevchenka): 63 Fourth Ave, New York, NY 10003-5200; tel. (212) 254-5130; fax (212) 254-5239; e-mail info@shevchenko.org; internet www.shevchenko.org; f. 1947; Pres. LARISSA M. L. Z. ONYSHEKEVYCH.

**UCLA Center for European and Eurasian Studies (CEES):** 11367 Bunche Hall, POB 951446, Los Angeles, CA 90095-1446; tel. (310) 825-4060; fax (310) 206-3555; e-mail vwheeler@international.ucla.edu; internet www.international.ucla.edu/euro; f. 1993; multidisciplinary teaching and research; especially concerned with the EU and in the framework of the new East-West connection.

**US Institute of Peace:** 1200 17th St, NW, Suite 200, Washington, DC 20036-3011; tel. (202) 457-1700; fax (202) 429-6063; e-mail usip_requests@usip.org; internet www.usip.org; f. 1984 by US Congress; aims to promote conflict resolution by peaceful means; Chair. CHESTER A. CROCKER.

**World Association of International Studies:** Hoover Institution, Stanford Univ., Stanford, CA 94305-6010; tel. (650) 322-2026; fax (650) 723-1687; e-mail hilton@stanford.edu; internet wais.stanford.edu; f. 1965; performs a continuous on-line discussion of international affairs; Pres. RONALD HILTON; Chair. MAURICE HARARI; publ. *World Affairs Report*.

## UZBEKISTAN

**Institute of Economics:** 700060 Tashkent, ul. Borovskogo 5; tel. (712) 33-86-03; attached to Uzbek Acad. of Sciences; Dir O. KHIKMATOV.

# SELECT BIBLIOGRAPHY (PERIODICALS)

*American Bibliography of Slavic and Eastern European Studies (ABSEES).* University of Illinois Library at Urbana-Champaign, 128 Observatory, 901 South Mathews Ave, Urbana, IL 61801, USA; tel. (217) 333-0284; fax (217) 333-7011; e-mail absees@uiuc.edu; internet www.library.uiuc.edu/absees; f. 1956 under the auspices of the American Asscn for the Advancement of Slavic Studies; covers US and Canadian scholarship on Central and Eastern Europe and the former USSR; contains bibliographic records, book extracts and reviews, dissertations, on-line resources and selected government publs; available on-line; Exec. Editor AARON TREHUB; in English.

*Annual Report of the East-West Institute.* 700 Broadway, 2nd Floor, New York, NY 10003, USA; tel. (212) 824-4100; fax (212) 824-4149; e-mail iews@iews.org; internet www.iews.org; f. 1981; East-West relations and economics; Editor ELIZABETH BELFER; in Russian and English; circ. 3,000.

*Arab Strategy.* Arabian Establishment for Strategic Affairs (AESA), Hadda St, POB 11612, San'a, Yemen; tel. (1) 207720; Russian-US relations; in English.

*Armenian Review.* Armenian Review Inc., 80 Bigelow Ave, Watertown, MA 02172, USA; tel. (617) 926-4037; fax (617) 926-1750; f. 1948; Editor Dr HAYG OSHAGAN; quarterly.

*Armenya Segodniya* (Armenia Today). Armenian Society for Friendship and Cultural Rels, Yerevan, Abovian St 3, Armenia; tel. (2) 56-45-14; Armenian international relations and foreign affairs; 2 a month, in Armenian.

*A-P Blitz.* Dushanbe, 35/1 ul. Bokhtar, 8th Floor, Tajikistan; tel. and fax (372) 21-72-20; e-mail info@asiaplus.tajik.net; internet www.asia-plus.tajnet.com; f. 1996; 190 a year (in Russian), 485 a year (in English).

*Asia-Plus.* Dushanbe, 35/1 ul. Bokhtar, 8th Floor, Tajikistan; tel. and fax (372) 21-72-20; e-mail info@asiaplus.tajik.net; internet www.asia-plus.tajnet.com; f. 1996; culture, economics, education, health care, politics, reform, regional news and social security; Editor-in-Chief UMED BABAKHANOV; weekly.

*Ayna.* Sita Politik Tanitim Danismanlik Hizmetleri AŞ, Abide-I-Hürriyet Cad. 78-15, 80260 Sisli, İstanbul, Turkey; tel. (212) 2472157; fax (212) 2255623; f. 1993; issues concerning the Turkic-speaking nations of Central Asia; Editor O. SUAT OZCE-LEBI; quarterly, in English and Turkish.

*Azerbaijan International.* POB 5217, Sherman Oaks, CA 91413, USA; tel. (818) 785-0077; fax (818) 997-7337; e-mail ai@artnet.net; internet www.azer.com; f. 1993; an independent magazine committed to the discussion of issues relating to Azerbaijanis around the world; features culture, language, music, art, literature, international relations and petroleum; Editor BETTY BLAIR; quarterly.

*Aziya I Afrika Segodnya* (Asia and Africa Today). Institute of Oriental Studies, Russian Acad. of Sciences, 103777 Moscow, ul. Rozhdestvenka 12, Russia; tel. (095) 925-29-42; fax (095) 975-23-96; f. 1957; Russian policy in the Asia-Pacific region; affiliated to the Institute of Africa; Editor MICHAEL L. KAPITSA; monthly, in Russian; circ. 2,000.

*Bailrigg Memoranda.* Centre for Defence and Int. Security Studies (CDISS), Dept of Politics and Int. Relations, Cartmel College, Univ. of Lancaster, Lancaster LA1 4YL, United Kingdom; tel. (1524) 594254; fax (1524) 594258; e-mail cdiss@lancaster.ac.uk; internet www.cdiss.org; f. 1980; security, defence and change in Eastern Europe, Russia and Ukraine; Editor HUMPHRY CRUM EWING; irreg., in English; circ. 500.

*Belarusian Review.* Belarusian-American Association Ltd, POB 10353, Torrance, CA 90505, USA; tel. (310) 373-0793; fax (310) 373-0793; e-mail belreview@aol.com; internet members.aol.com/belreview/index.html; f. 1989; quarterly; in English.

*Biuletyn Kalinigradzki.* Centre for Eastern Studies, 00-564 Warsaw, ul. Koszykowa 6A, Poland; f. 1993; information on economic, political and social policy in the successor states to the USSR, in particular Belarus, the Russian Federation and Ukraine; monthly, in Polish.

*BNA's Eastern Europe Reporter.* Bureau of National Affairs, 1231 25th St, NW, Washington, DC 20037, USA; internet www.bna.com; current news arranged by country, industry and topic; every 2 weeks.

*Bulletin of the Asia Institute.* 3287 Bradway Blvd, Bloomfield Hills, MI 48301, USA; e-mail bai34@aol.com; internet www.bulletinasiainstitute.org; publishes studies in the art, archaeology, history, languages and numismatics of ancient Iran, Mesopotamia and Central Asia; Editor CAROL ALTMAN BROMBERG.

*Business and Politics.* Russian Foreign Policy Foundation, 107078 Moscow, per. Bolshoi Kozlovski 4, Russia; tel. (095) 924-72-70; fax (095) 208-08-06; Russian business, economic relations and foreign policy; monthly, in English.

*Business Eastern Europe.* Economist Intelligence Unit, Economist Bldg, 111 West 57th St, New York, NY 10019, USA; tel. (212) 554-0600; fax (212) 586-0248; e-mail newyork@eiu.com; internet www.eiu.com; commercial and business information; Editor JOHN REED; weekly, in English.

*Business Week—Russia.* McGraw-Hill Inc, 1221 Ave of the Americas, New York, NY 10020, USA; tel. (212) 512-2000; fax (212) 512-6111; f. 1991; articles on business, economics and industry of particular interest to the Russian Federation; monthly, in Russian; circ. 50,000.

*Cahiers d'études sur la Méditerranée orientale et le monde tur-coiranien (CEMOTI)* (Journal of Studies on the Eastern Mediterranean and Turkish-Iranian World). 56 rue Jacob, 75006 Paris, France; tel. 1-58-71-70-56; fax 1-58-71-70-90; e-mail vaner@ceri.sciences-po.org; internet www.ceri-sciencespo.com/publica/cemoti/presente.htm; f. 1985; published by l'Association française pour l'étude Méditerranée orientale et du monde tur-coiranien (AFEMOTI); covers the geographical zone from the Balkans to ex-Soviet Central Asia, incl. the Caucasus; utilizes all aspects of political science, among other disciplines, to analyse the complexity of the region's current affairs, as well as looking to other disciplines; Editor SEMIH VANER; 2 a year, in French and English.

*Canadian-American Slavic Studies.* Charles Schlacks, Jr, POB 1256, Idyllwild, CA 92549-1256, USA; tel. (909) 659-4641; e-mail schslavic@tazland.net; quarterly, in English, French, German and Russian; Editor CHARLES SCHLACKS, Jr.

*Canadian Slavonic Papers.* Canadian Association of Slavists, Univ. of Alberta, Dept of Modern Languages and Cultural Studies, 200 Arts Bldg, Edmonton, Alberta, T6G 2EG, Canada; tel. (780) 492-2566; fax (780) 492-9106; e-mail gustolson@ualberta.ca; internet www.ualberta.ca/~csp; Man. Editor EDWARD MOZEJKO.

*Caucasian Regional Studies.* Vrije Universiteit Brussel (Free Univ. of Brussels), Centre for Political Science, Brussels 1050, Belgium; tel. (2) 629-21-11; fax (2) 629-22-82; e-mail bruno.coppieters@vub.ac.be; internet poli.vub.ac.be; f. 1995; published by the Int. Association for Caucasian Regional Studies; articles on a wide variety of topics, incl. civil society, collective security, democratization, economics, ethnic conflict and inter-state relations; Editor ALEXANDER KUKHIANIDZE; in English (on-line version) and Russian (print version).

*CaucasUS Context* (incorporating *Profile*). Georgian Foundation for Strategic and International Studies, 380008 Tbilisi, Niko Nikoladze 7, 380008 Tbilisi, Georgia; tel. (32) 93-13-35; fax (32) 98-52-65; e-mail gfsis@gfsis.org; internet www.gfsis.org; Pres. Dr ALEKSANDR RONDELI; Editor ZURAB KARUMIDZE.

*Central and Eastern Europe Business Information Center.* Market Access and Compliance Group, US Dept of Commerce, 1401 Constitution Ave, NW, Washington, DC 20230, USA; internet www.mac.doc.gov; business information, including information on US companies in the region and market research.

*Central Asia and the Caucasus: Journal of Social and Political Studies.* Central Asia and the Caucasus Center for Social and Political Studies, Rodhakegrand 21, 974 54 Luleå, Sweden; tel. and fax (920) 62-016; e-mail murad@communique.se; internet www.ca-c.org; f. 1995; covers economics, human rights, parties and movements, politics, religion and society, and culture and the arts; Editor Dr MURAD ESENOV; every 2 months, in English and Russian.

*Central Asia Monitor.* 560 Herrick Rd, Benson, VT 05743, USA; e-mail cam@chalidze.com; internet www.chalidze.com; f. 1992.

*Central Asian Survey.* Taylor & Francis Group, 4 Park Sq., Milton Park, Abingdon, Oxford OX14 4RN, United Kingdom; fax (1235) 829003; e-mail enquiry@tandf.co.uk; internet www.tandf .co.uk/journals/carfax/02634937.html; f. 1982; economics, history, politics and religions of the Central Asian and Caucasus region; Editor MARIE BENNIGSEN BROXUP; quarterly, in English; circ. 600.

*Central Asiatic Journal.* Harrassowitz Verlag, 65174 Wiesbaden; tel. (611) 5300; fax (611) 530570; e-mail verlag@ harrassowitz.de; internet www.harrassowitz.de; f. 1955; archaeology, history, languages and literature of Central Asia; Editor Prof. GIOVANNI STARY; 2 a year, in English, French and German; circ. 320.

*Chechnya Weekly.* Jamestown Foundation, 4516 43rd St NW, Washington, DC 20016, USA; tel. (202) 483-8888; fax (202) 483-8337; e-mail pubs@jamestown.org; internet chechnya .jamestown.org/pub-chweekly.htm; Editor LAWRENCE A. UZZELL.

*Chinese Communist Affairs Monthly.* Institute of Int. Relations, 64 Wan Shou Rd, Mucha, Taipei 11625, Taiwan; tel. (2) 9394921; fax (2) 9378609; countries of the former USSR and East European issues, in addition to Chinese affairs.

*CIS Environment and Disarmament Yearbook.* Marjorie Mayrock Centre for Russian, Eurasian and East European Research, Faculty of Social Sciences, Hebrew Univ. of Jerusalem, Mount Scopus, Jerusalem 91905, Israel; tel. 2-5883180; fax 2-5882835; e-mail msrussia@mscc.huji.ac.il; internet pluto .huji.ac.il/~msrussia; focuses on the ecological aspects of nuclear and chemical disarmament and examines other areas of environmental concern in the former USSR; Editor ZEʿEV WOLFSON; annually, in English.

*Classical Russia: Literature and Culture.* Charles Schlacks, Jr, POB 1256, Idyllwild, CA 92549-1256, USA; tel. (909) 659-4641; e-mail schslavic@tazland.net; annually, in English, French, German and Russian.

*Communist and Post-Communist Studies.* Center for European and Russian Studies (CERS), Univ. of California, 405 Hilguard Ave, Los Angeles, CA 90095-1446, USA; tel. (310) 825-4060; fax (310) 206-3555.

*Contemporary Security Policy.* Frank Cass and Co Ltd, Crown House, 47 Chase Side, Southgate, London N14 5BP, United Kingdom; tel. (20) 8920-2100; fax (20) 8447-8548; e-mail info@ frankcass.com; internet www.frankcass.com; a forum to discuss the broadening spectrum of security issues emerging in the post-Cold War world and the security implications of economic decline, ethnic conflict, environmental degradation, nationalism and underdevt, etc.; Editors STUART CROFT, TERRY TERRIFF; 3 a year, in English.

*Controversia: A Journal of Debate and Democratic Renewal.* International Debate Education Association, Open Society Institute, 400 West 59th St, New York, NY 10019, USA; tel. (212) 547-6918; fax (212) 548-4610; e-mail nwatkins@sorosny.org; f. 2002; Editors DAVID CRATIS WILLIAMS, MARILYN J. YOUNG.

*Country Profiles.* Economist Intelligence Unit, 15 Regent St, London SW1Y 4LR, United Kingdom; tel. (20) 7830-1007; fax (20) 7830-1023; e-mail london@eiu.com; internet www.eiu.com; individual reports on Armenia, Azerbaijan, Belarus, Georgia, Moldova, the Russian Federation, Tajikistan, Turkmenistan, Ukraine and Uzbekistan; annually, in English.

*Country Reports.* Economist Intelligence Unit, 15 Regent St, London SW1Y 4LR, United Kingdom; tel. (20) 7830-1007; fax (20) 7830-1023; e-mail london@eiu.com; internet www.eiu.com;

reports on each of the member countries of the Commonwealth of Independent States (CIS); quarterly, in English.

*Courrier des Pays de l'Est* (Journal of East European Countries). La Documentation Française, 29 quai Voltaire, 75344 Paris Cédex 07, France; tel. 1-40-15-71-48; fax 1-40-15-67-88; e-mail cpe@ladocumentationfrancaise.fr; internet www .ladocumentationfrancaise.fr; f. 1967; analyses the political and economic evolution of the countries of the CIS and Central and Eastern Europe; Editor MARIE-AGNÈS CROSNIER; 10 a year, in French; circ. 1,500.

*Current Digest of the Post-Soviet Press.* 3857 N. High St, Columbus, OH 43214, USA; tel. (614) 292-4234; fax (614) 267-6310; e-mail fowler.40@osu.edu; internet www.currentdigest .org; f. 1949; translations and abstracts from Russian-language press materials; Editor FRED SCHULZE; weekly, in English; circ. 1,000.

*Current Politics and Economics of Russia.* Nova Science Publishers, 227 Main St, Huntington, NY 11743, USA; tel. (631) 424-6682; fax (631) 424-4666; e-mail novascience@earthlink .net; internet www.nexusworld.com/nova; f. 1990; changing political and social issues; Editor G. T. SHALTILIS; quarterly, in English.

*Defence Studies.* Institute for Strategic and Defence Studies, 1241 Budapest, POB 181, Hungary; tel. (1) 262-1920; fax (1) 264-9623; e-mail h9315gaz@huella.bitnet; the armed forces, conflict resolution and security; 6 a year, in English.

*Defense Analysis.* Centre for Defence and Int. Security Studies (CDISS), Cartmel College, Univ. of Lancaster, Lancaster, LA1 4YL United Kingdom; tel. (1524) 594254; fax (1524) 594258; e-mail cdiss@lancaster.ac.uk; internet www.cdiss.org; f. 1985; defence theory and analysis; Editor Dr MARTIN EDMONDS; quarterly, in English.

*Delovaya Ukraina* (Business Ukraine). 01133 Kiev, vul. Kutuzova 18/7, Bldg 2, Ukraine; tel. and fax (44) 201-03-90; e-mail delukr@email.kiev.ua; internet www.delukr.kiev.ua; f. 1992; business issues; Editor ALLAL KOVTUM; two a week, in Ukrainian and Russian.

*Delovie Lyudi* (Independent People). Press Contact, 117342 Moscow, ul. Profsoyuznaya 73, Russia; tel. (095) 333-33-40; fax (095) 330-15-68; f. 1990; business, management and economics, for those interested in the economic situation in the Russian Federation and Eastern Europe; Editor VADIM BIRYUKOV; monthly, in Russian and English; circ. 130,000.

*Democratization.* Frank Cass and Co Ltd, Crown House, 47 Chase Side, Southgate, London N14 5BP, United Kingdom; tel. (20) 8920-2100; fax (20) 8447-8548; e-mail info@frankcass.com; internet www.frankcass.com; f. 1994; contemporary emphasis and a comparative approach, with special reference to democratization in the developing world and in post-communist societies; Editors PETER BURNELL, PETER CALVERT; 6 a year.

*Demokratizatsiya* (Demography and Democracy in Russia). Harley D. Balzer, Georgetown University, 37th and O. Sts, NW, Washington, DC, 20057; tel. (202) 687-0100; e-mail balzerh@ georgetown.edu.

*Diplomatic Yearbook.* Institute for Current Int. Problems, 119021 Moscow, ul. Ostozhenka 53/2, Russia; tel. (095) 208-94-61; fax (095) 208-94-66; international relations and diplomatic history.

*Disarmament and Security Yearbook.* Institute of World Economy and Int. Relations, Russian Acad. of Sciences, 117859 Moscow, ul. Profsoyuznaya 23, Russia; tel. (095) 120-43-32; fax (095) 310-70-27; e-mail ineir@sovam.com; f. 1987; foreign policy, international relations and strategic studies; in English.

*Donald W. Treadgold Papers in Russian and East European and Asian Studies.* HMJ School of Int. Studies, Univ. of Washington, POB 353650, Seattle, WA 98195-3650, USA; tel. (206) 221-6348; fax (206) 685-0668; e-mail treadgld@u.washington.edu; internet depts.washington.edu/reecas; f. 1969 as *Publications on Russia and Eastern Europe*; name changed as above in 1993; Editor GLENNYS YOUNG.

*Dostoevsky Journal: an Independent Review.* Charles Schlacks, Jr, POB 1256, Idyllwild, CA 92549-1256, USA; tel. (909) 659-

4641; e-mail schslavic@tazland.net; Editor SLOBODANKA VLADIV-GLOVER; annually, in English, French, German and Russian.

*East Central Europe.* Charles Schlacks, Jr, POB 1256, Idyllwild, CA 92549-1256, USA; tel. (909) 659-4641; e-mail schslavic@tazland.net; Editor JULIA SZALAI; 2 a year, in English, French and German.

*East Europe Monographs.* Governmental Research Bureau, Park College, Kansas City, MO 64152, USA; tel. (816) 741-2000; f. 1969; Editors JERZY HAUPTMANN, GOTTHOLD RHODE; irreg., in English.

*East European Politics and Societies.* Univ. of California Press, 2000 Center St, Suite 303, Berkeley, CA 94704-1223, USA; tel. (510) 643-7154; fax (510) 642-9917; e-mail journals@ucop.edu; internet www.ucpress.edu/journals/eeps; f. 1986; economic, political and social issues in Eastern Europe; Editor VLADIMIR TISMANEANU; 3 a year, in English; circ. 650.

*East European Quarterly.* Regent Hall, Univ. of Colorado, POB 29, Boulder, CO 80309, USA; tel. and fax (941) 753-4782; e-mail eeqeem@web.tv.net; f. 1967; publishes articles on the civilization, culture, economics, history and politics of Eastern Europe; Editor STEPHEN FISCHER-GALATI; quarterly, in English; circ. 1,000.

*East-West Business and Trade.* Welt Publishing LLC, Suite 1400, 1413 K St, NW, Washington, DC 2005, USA; tel. (407) 279-095; fax (407) 278-8845; f. 1972; business relations, economic devt, political stability and international organizations; Editor JOHN JUSTIN FORD; 2 a month, in English; circ. 3,500.

*East-West Digest.* Foreign Affairs Publishing Co, 139 Petersham, Richmond, Surrey, United Kingdom.

*Eastern Europe and the Political Briefing.* Eastern Europe Newsletter Ltd, 4 Starfield Rd, London W12 9SW, United Kingdom; tel. (20) 8743-2829; fax (20) 8743-8637; e-mail 100316.1530@compuserve.com.

*Eastern European Analyst.* World Reports Ltd, 108 Horseferry Rd, London SW1P 2EF, United Kingdom; tel. (20) 7222-3826; fax (20) 7233-0185; East European economies and their effect on Russian foreign policy; Editor CHRISTOPHER STOREY; quarterly, in English.

*Eastern European Consensus Forecasts.* Consensus Economics Inc., 53 Upper Brook St, London W1K 2LT, United Kingdom; tel. (20) 7491-3211; fax (20) 7409-2331; internet www.consensuseconomics.com; f. 1998; economic forecasts for the East European region, incl. Turkey; Editor CHE-WING PANG; 6 a year, in English.

*Eastern European Constitutional Review.* 161 Ave of the Americas, 5th Floor, New York, NY 10013, USA; tel. (212) 998-6562; fax (212) 995-4769; e-mail ar55@is8.nyu.edu; internet www.law.nyu.edu/eecr/volumes.html; published by New York Univ. Law School and Central European Univ. (Budapest, Hungary); East European constitutional law and post-communist politics; Editors STEPHEN HOLMES, ALISON ROSE, AVIEZER TUCKER; quarterly, in English and Russian; circ. 7,000.

*Eastern European Economics: a Journal of Translations.* M. E. Sharpe Inc., 80 Business Park Dr., Armonk, NY 10504, USA; tel. (914) 273-1800; fax (914) 273-2106; e-mail custserv@mesharpe.com; internet www.mesharpe.com; f. 1962; macroeconomic and microeconomic analysis of Eastern European transitional economies; Editor JOSEF C. BRADA; 6 a year, in English; circ. 400.

*East European Jewish Affairs.* Frank Cass and Co Ltd, Crown House, 47 Chase Side, Southgate, London N14 5BP, United Kingdom; tel. (20) 8920-2100; fax (20) 8447-8548; e-mail info@frankcass.com; internet www.frankcass.com; f. 1970; interdisciplinary journal dealing with the position of Jews in both the former USSR and the countries of East-Central Europe, from an historical perspective and in the context of general, social, economic, political and cultural developments in the region; Editors ROBERT BRYM, GENNADY ESTRAIKH, ZVI GITELMAN, JOHN KLIER, MIKHAIL KRUTIKOV, HOWARD SPIER; 2 a year, in English.

*Economic Survey of Europe.* Economic Commission for Europe, United Nations, Palais des Nations, 1211 Geneva 10, Switzerland; tel. (22) 9172606; fax (22) 9170027; e-mail unpubli@unog.ch; economic analysis, incl. statistical information; 2 a year, in English and Russian.

*Economic Systems.* Osteuropa-Institut München, 81679 München, Scheinerstr. 11; tel. (89) 9983960; fax (89) 9810110; e-mail rfrensch@lrz.uni-muenchen.de; internet www.lrz-muenchen.de/~econsys; f. 1970; international economics, the theory of economic systems and comparative economics; published in collaboration with the European Association for Comparative Economic Studies; Man. Editor R. FRENSCH; quarterly, in English with German abstracts; circ. 450.

*Economics of Planning* (incorporating *MOCT-MOST: Economic Policy in Transitional Economies*). Kluwer Academic Publishers BV, van Godewijckstraat 30, POB 17, 3300 AA Dordrecht, Netherlands; tel. (78) 6576116; fax (78) 6576377; e-mail services@wkap.nl; internet www.kluweronline.com; Editors ROBERTA BENINI, WOJCIECH W. CHAREMZA.

*Economics of Transition.* Blackwell Publishers Ltd, 108 Cowley Rd, Oxford OX4 1JF, United Kingdom; tel. (1865) 791100; fax (1865) 791347; e-mail subscrip@blackwellpub.com; internet www.blackwellpublishers.co.uk; published for the European Bank for Reconstruction and Development (EBRD); transition economies; Editors PHILIPPE AGHION, WENDY CARLIN; 3 a year, in English.

*Ekho Planety* (Echo of the Planet). 125993 Moscow, Tverskou bul. 10-12, Russia; tel. (095) 290-59-11; fax (095) 202-67-48; e-mail echotex@itar-tass.com; internet www.explan.ru; f. 1988; cultural, economic and social international affairs; Editor VALENTIN VASILETS; weekly, in Russian; circ. 12,000.

*Ekonomika i Matematicheskie Metody* (Economics and Mathematical Methods). Central Mathematical Economics Institute, Russian Acad. of Sciences, 117418 Moscow, ul. Krasikova 32, Russia; tel. (095) 129-16-44; fax (095) 310-70-15; f. 1965; journal of the Central Mathematical Economics Institute and of the Institute of Market Problems; theoretical and methodological problems of economics and econometrics; Editor V. L. MAKAROV; quarterly, in Russian; circ. 3,500.

*Ekonomika i Zhizn* (Economics and Life). 127994 Moscow, pr. Bumazhnyi 14, Russia; tel. (095) 250-57-93; fax (095) 200-22-97; e-mail gazeta@ekonomika.ru; internet www.akdi.ru; f. 1918; fmrly *Ekonomicheskaya Gazeta*; international and domestic economic and business activity in the former USSR; Editor YURII YAKUTIN; weekly, in Russian; circ. 1,100,000.

*Ekonomika Ukrainy* (Economy of Ukraine). 01015 Kiev 15, vul. Moskovska 37/2, Ukraine; tel. (44) 290-32-71; fax (44) 290-86-63; f. 1958; published by the Ministry of the Economy, Ministry of Finance and National Academy of Sciences of Ukraine; credit policy, management, state of the national economy in sectoral and territorial aspects, taxes, and theoretical and applied economics; Editors Prof. IVAN I. LUKINOV, I. P. VUSYK; monthly, in Ukrainian and Russian; circ. 3,900.

*Emerging Europe Monitor (EEM).* Business Monitor International, 179 Queen Victoria St, London EC4V 4DU, United Kingdom; tel. (20) 7248-0468; fax (20) 7248-0467; e-mail subs@businessmonitor.com; internet www.businessmonitor.com; macroeconomic performance, outlook and political risk; Marketing Man. JENNIE BEEBEE; monthly, in English.

*Emerging Markets Finance and Trade.* M. E. Sharpe Inc., 80 Business Park Dr., Armonk, New York, NY 10504, USA; tel. (914) 273-1800; fax (914) 273-2106; e-mail custserv@mesharpe.com; internet www.mesharpe.com; f. 1965; tracks the most critical questions facing emerging market economies; Editor ALI M. KUTAN; 6 a year, in English.

*Est-Ovest* (East-West). Istituto di Studi e Documentazione sull'Europa Comunitaria e l'Europa Orientale (ISDEE), Corso Italia 27, 34122 Trieste, Italy; tel. (040) 639130; fax (040) 634248; e-mail isdee@spin.it; internet www.isdee.it; f. 1970; institutional, political and socio-economic aspects of Eastern Europe and of East-West relations; 6 a year, in Italian, English and French; circ. 400.

*Eurasian Geography and Economics.* Bellwether Publishing Ltd, 8640 Guilford Rd, Suite 200, Columbia, MD 21046, USA; tel. (410) 290-3870; fax (410) 290-8726; e-mail subs@bellpub.com; internet www.bellpub.com/psge; f. 1960 as *Soviet Geography*, and subsequently renamed *Post-Soviet Geography and Economics*; economics, geography and urban affairs in the countries of Central and Eastern Europe, the former USSR and the socialist countries of Asia; Editor-in-Chief RALPH S. CLEM; 8 a year, in English.

*Eurasian Politics.* Institute for Current Int. Problems, 119021 Moscow, ul. Ostozhenka 53/2, Russia; tel. (095) 208-94-61; fax (095) 208-94-66; Eurasian international affairs and politics; monthly, in English.

*Eurazja* (Eurasia). Centre for Eastern Studies, 00-564 Warsaw, ul. Koszykowa 6A, Poland; f. 1994; economic, political and social issues, in particular in Central Asia; in Polish.

*Europe-Asia Studies.* Hetherington Bldg, Bute Gardens, Glasgow G12 8RS, United Kingdom; tel. (141) 330-5585; fax (141) 330-5594; e-mail europe-asia@gla.ac.uk; internet www .carfax.co.uk/eas-ad.htm; f. 1949; economics, history, politics and society and history of the former USSR, and comparisons with Asian communist countries; Editor ROGER A. CLARKE; 8 a year, in English; circ. 1,400.

*European Policy Research Papers.* European Policies Research Centre, Univ. of Strathclyde, 40 George St, Glasgow G1 1QE, United Kingdom; tel. (141) 548-3908; fax (141) 548-4898; e-mail eprc@strath.ac.uk; internet www.eprc.strath.ac.uk; Editors JOHN BACHTLER, PHILIP RAINES; 4 a year, in English.

*European Security.* Frank Cass and Co Ltd, Crown House, 47 Chase Side, Southgate, London N14 5BP, United Kingdom; tel. (20) 8920-2100; fax (20) 8447-8548; e-mail europeansecurity@ku .edu; internet www.frankcass.com; f. 1992; reviews new concepts, institutions, problems and prospects for European security in the wake of the end of the Cold War, to explore the possibilities and dangers of creating an alternative security system for Europe; includes cultural, economic, environmental, ethnic, political and social dimensions; Editors PAUL D'ANIERI, CHRISTOPHER DONNELLY, PAUL D'ANIERI; quarterly, in English.

*Expert.* Izdatelski Dom Commersant, pr. Kozhnovskii 3, Moscow, Russia; tel. and fax (095) 152-11-61; f. 1995; business news from Russia and the CIS, financing, politics, privatization, science and technology, and the stock market; Editor GELENA SAYOT; monthly; circ. 100,000.

*Experiment: a Journal of Russian Culture.* Charles Schlacks, Jr, POB 1256, Idyllwild, CA 92549-1256, USA; tel. (909) 659-4641; e-mail schslavic@tazland.net; Editor JOHN E. BOWLT; annually, in English and Russian.

*Forschungen zu Osteuropa* (Research into Eastern Europe). Edition Temmen, 28209 Bremen, Hohenlohestr. 21, Germany; tel. (421) 348430; fax (421) 348094; e-mail ed.temmen@t-online .de; f. 1986; publication of Forschungstelle Osteuropa an der Universität Bremen; irreg., in German.

*Forschungen zur Osteuropäischen Geschichte.* Osteuropa-Institut der Freien Universität Berlin (Institute of East European Studies of the Free University Berlin), 14195 Berlin, Garystr. 55, Germany; tel. (30) 83852076; fax (30) 83854036; e-mail oei@ zedat.fu-berlin.de; internet www.oei.fu-berlin.de; f. 1954; Editor HOLM SUNDHAUSSEN.

*From the Other Shore: Russian Writers Abroad, Past and Present.* Charles Schlacks, Jr, POB 1256, Idyllwild, CA 92549-1256, USA; tel. (909) 659-4641; e-mail schslavic@tazland.net; Editor LEONID LIVAK; annually, in English, French and Russian.

*Give and Take: A Journal of Civil Society in Eurasia.* Initiative for Social Action and Renewal in Eurasia (ISAR), Suite 301, 1601 Connecticut Ave, NW, Washington, DC 20009; tel. (202) 387-3034; fax (202) 667-3291; e-mail membership@isar.org; internet www.isar.org; quarterly.

*Global Newsline: Former Soviet Union and Central Asia.* BBC Monitoring, Caversham Park, Reading RG4 8TZ, United Kingdom; tel. (118) 948-6289; fax (118) 946-3823; e-mail marketing@mon.bbc.co.uk; internet www.monitor.bbc.co.uk; political and economic e-mail news service; in English.

*Global Studies: Russia, the Eurasian Republics, Central and Eastern Europe.* Dushkin Publishing Group, Sluice Dock, Guilford, CT 06437-9989, USA; tel. (203) 453-4351; fax (203) 453-6000; internet www.dushkin.com; f. 1990; every 2 years, in English.

*Harriman Review.* Harriman Institute, Columbia Univ., 420 West 188th St, New York, NY 10027, USA; tel. (212) 854-6218;

fax (212) 666-3481; e-mail harriman@columbia.edu; internet www.columbia.edu/cu/sipa/regional/hi; f. 1994; Eastern and Central Europe; Editor RONALD MEYER; quarterly, in English; circ. 1,500.

*IIP Occasional Papers.* Internationales Institut für den Frieden (Int. Institute for Peace—IIP), 1040 Vienna, Möllwaldplatz 5, Austria; tel. (1) 504-64-37; fax (1) 505-32-36; f. 1989; security and conflict resolution, and reconstruction; Editor PETER STANIA; irreg.; circ. 400.

*Inside Central Asia.* BBC Monitoring, Caversham Park, Reading RG4 8TZ, United Kingdom; tel. (118) 948-6289; fax (118) 946-3823; e-mail marketing@mon.bbc.co.uk; internet www .monitor.bbc.co.uk; an overview of key political and economic news reports from the Central Asian area; weekly, in English.

*International Affairs.* Royal Institute of Int. Affairs (RIIA), Chatham House, 10 St James's Sq., London SW17 4LE, United Kingdom; tel. (20) 7957-5700; fax (20) 7957-5710; e-mail contact@riia.org; internet www.riia.org; 5 a year.

*International Affairs.* Russian Foreign Policy Foundation, 107078 Moscow, pr. Bolshoi Kozlovski 4, Russia; tel. (095) 924-72-70; fax (095) 208-08-06; internet www.mosinfo.ru/news/ int-aff/subintaf.html; f. 1992; 6 a year, in English.

*International Journal.* Glendon Hall, 2275 Bayview Ave, Toronto, ON M4N 3M6, Canada; tel. (416) 487-6830; e-mail fraser@ ciia.org/ij.htm; internet www.ciia.org/ij.htm; f. 1946; mix of commentary and articles on international affairs; quarterly, in English.

*International Peacekeeping.* Frank Cass and Co Ltd, Crown House, 47 Chase Side, Southgate, London N14 5BP, United Kingdom; tel. (20) 8920-2100; fax (20) 8447-8548; e-mail info@ frankcass.com; internet www.frankcass.com; f. 1994; examines the theory and practice of peace-keeping; Editor MICHAEL PUGH; quarterly, in English; circ. 1,500.

*International Security Review.* Royal United Services Institute (RUSI), Whitehall, London SW1A 2ET, United Kingdom; tel. (20) 7930-5854; fax (20) 7321-0943; internet www.rusi.org/subs1 .html; f. 1992; international and regional security; annually, in English; circ. 1,500.

*Internet Resources for Eurasia.* Civil Society International, 2929 NE Blakeley St, Seattle, WA 98105, USA; tel. (206) 523-4755; fax (206) 523-1974; e-mail ccsi@u.washington.edu; internet www.friends-partners.org/~ccsi; annually.

*Istoriya Narodnoho Hospodarstvo Ta Ekonomichnoi Dumki Ukrainy: respublikanskii mizhvidomchyi zbirnik naukovykh prak* (History of National Government and Economic Thought in Ukraine). Institute of Economics, Ukrainian Acad. of Sciences, 252011 Kiev, vul. Panasa Mirnogo 26, Ukraine; tel. (44) 290-84-44; fax (44) 290-86-63; f. 1965; economic history, systems and theories; Editor I. I. DEREV'YANKIN; annually, in Ukrainian with summaries in Russian.

*Izvestiya NAS RK* (News). Institute of Economics of the Ministry of Science and Higher Education, Kazakhstan Acad. of Sciences, 480100 Almaty, Kurmangazi 29, POB 137; tel. (3272) 62-87-88; fax (3272) 63-12-07; e-mail adm@econ.academ.south-capital.kz; social science and economic issues; incl. articles concerning the problems faced by Kazakhstan during the transition to a market economy; Editor Prof. A. K. KOSHANOV; annually, in Kazakh; circ. 500.

*Johnson's Russia List.* Center for Defense Information, 1779 Massachusetts Ave, NW, Suite 615, Washington, DC, 20036-2109; tel. (202) 332-0600; fax (202) 462-4559; e-mail davidjohnson@erols.com; internet www.cdi.org/russia/johnson/ default.cfm; f. 1997; daily e-mail digest on Russian and post-Soviet politics, and US, British and Russian culture and society; English; monthly Research and Analytical Supplement (Editor Stephen D. Shenfield; Dir DAVID JOHNSON.

*Journal of Communist Studies and Transition Politics.* Frank Cass and Co Ltd, Crown House, 47 Chase Side, Southgate, London N14 5BP, United Kingdom; tel. (20) 8920-2100; fax (20) 8447-8548; e-mail info@frankcass.com; internet www.frankcass .com; f. 1985; devotes particular attention to the process of regime change and also to the effects of this upheaval on Communist parties, ruling and non-ruling, in Europe and the wider world; Editors Stephen White, Ronald J. Hill, Paul G. Lewis, Margot Light, Richard Sakwa; quarterly, in English.

*Journal of East-West Business.* Int. Business Press (IBP), POB 399, Middletown, PA 17057, USA; tel. (717) 566-3054; fax (717) 566-8589; e-mail k9x@psu.edu; f. 1994; business studies, devt, practice and strategies, focusing on Russia, the CIS and Central and Eastern European countries; Editor-in-Chief Dr Erdener Kaynak; quarterly, in English; circ. 500.

*Journal of European Integration.* Univ. of Essex, Dept of Govt, Wivenhoe Park, Colchester CO4 3SQ, United Kingdom; tel. (1206) 872749; fax (1206) 873598; e-mail emil@essex.ac.uk; internet www.tandf.co.uk/journals/titles/07036337.html; f. 1978; publishes articles with a focus on pan-European integration from an interdisciplinary perspective, integrating economics, history, law, politics and sociology; Exec. Editor Emil Kirchner; Editors Hans Michelmann, Reimund Seidelmann, Mario Telò; quarterly, in English and French.

*Journal of Islamic Studies.* Oxford Univ. Press, Gt Clarendon St, Oxford OX2 6DP, United Kingdom; tel. (1865) 267907; fax (1865) 267485; e-mail enquiry@oup.co.uk; internet www3.oup.co.uk/islamj; all aspects of Islam; Editor Dr Farhan Ahmad Nizami.

*Journal of Muslim Minority Affairs.* Taylor & Francis Group, 4 Park Sq., Milton Park, Abingdon, Oxford OX14 4RN, United Kingdom; fax (1235) 829000; e-mail enquiry@tandf.co.uk; internet www.tandf.co.uk/journals; Editor Saleha S. Mahmood; 2 a year.

*Journal of Russian and East European Psychology.* M. E. Sharpe Inc., 80 Business Park Dr., Armonk, New York, NY 10504, USA; tel. (914) 273-1800; fax (914) 273-2106; e-mail custserv@mesharpe.com; internet www.mesharpe.com; f. 1962; translations of both new and published academic articles; Editor Pentti Hakkarainen; 6 a year, in English.

*Journal of Slavic Military Studies.* Frank Cass and Co Ltd, Crown House, 47 Chase Side, Southgate, London N14 5BP, United Kingdom; tel. (20) 8920-2100; fax (20) 8447-8548; e-mail rzhev@aol.com; internet www.frankcass.com; f. 1988; investigates all aspects of military affairs in the Slavic nations of Central and Eastern Europe, in an historical and geopolitical context; Editors David M. Glantz, Christopher Donnelly; quarterly, in English.

*Journal of Southeastern European and Black Sea Studies.* Frank Cass and Co Ltd, Crown House, 47 Chase Side, Southgate, London N14 5BP, United Kingdom; tel. (20) 8920-2100; fax (20) 8447-8548; e-mail info@frankcass.com; internet www.frankcass.com; f. 2001; covers the politics, political economy, international relations and modern history of South-Eastern Europe and the Black Sea region; Editors Franz-Lothar Altmann, Theodore Couloumbis, Jonathan Eyal, Shireen Hunter, Thanos Veremis; three a year, in English.

*Kino: Russian Film, Past and Present.* Charles Schlacks, Jr, POB 1256, Idyllwild, CA 92549-1256, USA; tel. (909) 659-4641; e-mail schslavic@tazland.net; annually, in English, French, German and Russian.

*Kyiv Post.* 252133 Kiev, bul. Lesya Ukraina 34, Rm 606, Ukraine; tel. (44) 296-94-72; fax (44) 254-31-13; e-mail editor@thepost.kiev.ua; internet www.thepost.kiev.ua; Editor Greg Bloom; weekly, in English; circ. 20,000.

*Main Economic Indicators.* Organisation for Economic Co-operation and Development (OECD), 2 rue André-Pascal, 75775 Paris Cédex 16, France; tel. 1-45-24-16-93; fax 1-45-24-17-13; e-mail kei.contacts@oecd.org; internet www.oecd.org/std/dnm; f. 1999; covers the Russian Federation, Ukraine, and the Baltic states (Estonia, Latvia and Lithuania), Bulgaria, Romania and Slovenia; monthly, in English.

*Medjunarodni problemi* (International Problems). 11000 Belgrade, Makedonska 25, Yugoslavia; tel. (11) 3373824; fax (11) 3373835; e-mail branam@eunet.yu; internet www.diplomacy.bg .ac.yu; f. 1948; review of the Institute of International Politics and Economics; covers international law, international organizations, international political relations and the world economy; Editor Brana Marković; quarterly, in Serbian and English; circ. 1,000.

*Mezhdunarodnaya Zhizn* (International Life). 103064 Moscow, pr. Gorokhovski 14, Russia; tel. (095) 265-37-81; fax (095) 265-37-71; e-mail inter_affairs@mid.ru; f. 1954; problems of foreign policy in Russia and other countries; Editor-in-Chief Boris Pyadishev; monthly, in English and Russian; circ. 30,000.

*Military Thought: a Russian Journal of Military Theory and Strategy.* East View Publications Inc., 3020 Harbor Lane N., Minneapolis, MN 55447, USA; tel. (612) 550-0961; fax (612) 559-2931; e-mail periodicals@eastview.com; internet news.mosinfo .ru/news/2000/mth/index; f. 1918 in Russian; English version from 1992 (Russian version now published by Russian Ministry of Defence); global military devts, issues affecting the Russian Armed Forces, military theory and planning in Russia; Editor P. Ilyin; 6 a year, in Russian and English; circ. 200.

*Mirovaya Economika i Mezdunarodnye Otnoshenii* (World Economy and International Relations). Institute of World Economy and Int. Relations, Russian Acad. of Sciences, 117859 Moscow, ul. Profsoyuznaya 23, Russia; tel. (095) 128-08-83; fax (095) 120-14-17; e-mail ineir@sovam.com; f. 1957; world economy and international relations, and political and economic devt of the contemporary Russian Federation; Editor German G. Diligenski; monthly, in Russian; circ. 5,000.

*Moldovan Economic Trends.* Ministry of Economy and Reform, Govt Bldg, 2033 Chişinău, Rm 219, Piaţa Marii Adunări Naţionale, Moldova; tel. (2) 23-40-13; fax (2) 23-40-57; e-mail currie@moldova.md; internet www.moldova.md/met.htm; published by the Govt of Moldova and the European Expertise Service; quarterly.

*Monitor.* Centre for Eastern Studies, 00-564 Warsaw, ul. Koszykowa 6A, Poland; f. 1991; responsible to the Ministry of Foreign Economic Relations; economic, political and social information and analysis on the countries of the former USSR, in particular Belarus, the Russian Federation and Ukraine; in English.

*Moscow Journal of International Law.* Moskovskii Gosudarstvennii Institut Mezhdunarodnykh Otnoshenii (MGIMO—Moscow State Institute of Int. Relations), 119454 Moscow, pr. Vernadskogo 76, Russia; tel. and fax (095) 434-93-13; e-mail mjl@mgimo.ru; internet www.mgimo.ru; f. 1990; all branches of international law, in connection with contemporary international relations and Russian foreign policy; Editor-in-Chief Yurii M. Kolosov; quarterly, in Russian and English; circ. 1,000.

*Moscow Magazine.* 121019 Moscow, Rm 303, Dom Journalista, Suvorovski bul. 8A, Russia; tel. (095) 291-17-87; fax (095) 973-21-44; 6 a year.

*Moscow Times Business Review.* 125212 Moscow, ul. Vyborgskaya 16, Russia; tel. (095) 937-33-99; fax (095) 937-33-93; e-mail businessreview@imedia.ru; internet www .businessreview.ru; business and current affairs; Editor Florence Gallez; monthly.

*Moskovskii Universitet Vestnik, Seriya 7: Ekonomika* (Moscow University Herald, Series 7: Economics). Moscow M. V. Lomonosov State Univ., 103009 Moscow, ul. Gertsena 5-7, Russia; tel. (095) 939-53-40; f. 1966; one of 14 series, which cover a wide range of academic subjects; includes bibliographical information, book reviews and indexes; 6 a year, in Russian; circ. 2,200.

*Muzyka: Russian Music, Past and Present.* Charles Schlacks, Jr, POB 1256, Idyllwild, CA 92549-1256, USA; tel. (909) 659-4641; e-mail schslavic@tazland.net; annually, in English, French, German and Russian.

*Nationalities Papers.* Carfax Publishing, Taylor & Francis Group, 4 Park Sq., Milton Park, Abingdon, Oxford OX14 4RN, United Kingdom; tel. (1235) 828600; fax (1235) 829000; e-mail enquiry@tandf.co.uk; internet www.tandf.co.uk/journals/carfax/00905992.html; publ. of the Association for the Study of Nationalities; non-Russian nationalities of the former USSR and national minorities in Central and Eastern Europe; Editor-in-Chief Dr Nancy M. Wingfield; quarterly.

*Nep Era: Russian Politics and Culture.* Charles Schlacks, Jr, POB 1256, Idyllwild, CA 92549-1256, USA; tel. (909) 659-4641; e-mail schslavic@tazland.net; Editor Alexis Pogorelskin; annually, in English, French, German and Russian.

*New Zealand Slavonic Journal.* Australia and New Zealand Slavists Association, Russian Section, Victoria Univ. of Wellington, POB 600, Wellington, New Zealand; tel. (4) 463-5322; fax (4) 463-5419; e-mail russian-section@vuw.ac.nz; f. 1967; culture, history, language and literature of Russia and other countries; Editor IRENE ZOHRAB; annually, in English and Russian.

*News Review on Europe and Eurasia.* Institute for Defence Studies and Analyses, Sapru House Annexe, Barakhamba Rd, New Delhi 110 001, India; tel. (11) 3317189; fax (11) 3319717; f. 1972; Editor Air Commdr JASIT SINGH; monthly, in English.

*Nova Přítomnost* (New Presence). Národní 11, 110 00 Prague 1, Czech Republic; tel. (2) 22075600; fax (2) 22075605; e-mail ainfo@vydavatelstvimjs.cz; internet www.pritomnost.cz; f. 1996; culture and politics, incl. art, ecology, economics, history and science, with a general focus on Central and Eastern Europe and Russia; Editors COILIN O'CONNOR, LIBUŠE KOUBSKÁ, DAVID SVOBODA; quarterly, in English and Czech; circ. 1,500.

*Novoye Vremya* (New Times). 103782 Moscow, pl. Pushkina 5, Russia; tel. (095) 229-88-72; fax (095) 200-41-92; f. 1943; foreign and Russian affairs; Editor A. PUMPY; weekly, in Czech, English, French, German, Greek, Italian, Polish, Portuguese, Russian and Spanish; circ. 25,000.

*Novyi Zhurnal* (New Review). 611 Broadway, Suite 842, New York, NY 10012, USA; tel. and fax (212) 353-1478; e-mail newreview@msn.com; internet magazine.russ.ru/nj; f. 1942; covers general cultural topics, incl. literature; Editor-in-Chief Prof. VADIM KREYD; quarterly, in Russian; circ. 600.

*Obshchestvennye Nauki v Uzbekistane* (Social Sciences in Uzbekistan). Fan (Science Publishing House), 700047 Tashkent, ul. Gulyamova 70, kv. 102, Uzbekistan; tel. (71) 133-69-91; fax (71) 133-49-01; f. 1957; publication of the Uzbek Acad. of Sciences; fields covered include economics and oriental studies; monthly, in Russian.

*Ost-Wirtschaftsreport* (Eastern Economic Report). Verlagsgruppe Handelsblatt GmbH, 40213 Düsseldorf, Kasernenstr. 67, Germany; tel. (211) 8870; fax (211) 326759; f. 1973; Editor JULIANE LANGENECKER; every 2 weeks, in German; circ. 1,200.

*Osteuropa* (Eastern Europe). Editorial Office, Deutsche Gesellschaft für Osteuropakunde eV (German Soc. for Eastern European Research), 52062 Aachen, Grosskölnstr. 32-34, Germany; tel. (241) 32707; fax (241) 405879; e-mail oe@rwth-aachen.de; internet www.rwth-aachen.de/ipw/ww/osteuropa/index.html; f. 1925; information about Central and Eastern Europe, incl. culture, economy, education, literature, new trends and devts, politics and society; Editor Dr A. STEININGER; monthly, in German; circ. 2,350.

*Osteuropa-Wirtschaft* (Eastern Europe Economy). German Soc. for East European Research, Güllstr. 7, 80336 München, Germany; tel. (89) 74613321; fax (89) 74613333; e-mail u9511aa@mail.lrz-muenchen.de; f. 1956; economic issues relevant to Central and Eastern Europe, incl. new trends and devts, and problems of transformation; also includes book reviews, indexes and statistical information; Editor Dr F.-L. ALTMANN; quarterly, in German and with abstracts in English; circ. 750.

*Oxford Slavonic Papers.* Oxford Univ. Press, Great Clarendon St, Oxford OX2 6DP, United Kingdom; tel. (1865) 267907; fax (1865) 267485; e-mail enquiry@oup.co.uk.

*PIR Study Papers.* Centre for Policy Studies in Russia (PIR Centre), 103001 Moscow, Trekhprudny per. 9, Russia; tel. (095) 234-05-25; fax (095) 234-95-58; e-mail info@pircenter.org; internet www.pircenter.org; f. 1996; arms control, international security, low-intensity conflict and Russian strategy; Editor ROLAND TIMERBAEV; 3 a year, in Russian and English; circ. 900.

*Political Crossroads.* James Nicholas Publishers, POB 244, Albert Park, Vic 3206, Australia; tel. (3) 9696-5545; fax (3) 9699-2040; e-mail custservice@jamesnicholaspublishers.com.au; internet www.jamesnicholaspublishers.com.au; cultural ideology, economic and administrative organizations, international relations, leadership and political theory; Man. Editor JOSEPH ZAJDA; annually, in English.

*Political Thought.* Ukrainian Centre for International Security Studies (UCISS), 252023 Kiev 23, POB 541, Ukraine; tel. and fax (44) 212-58-37; e-mail globus@uciss.freenet.kiev.ua; cofounded with the Asscn for Middle East Studies (AMES) and the Atlantic Council of Ukraine; in English, Russian and Ukrainian.

*Politika I Chas* (Politics and Times). 02160 Kiev, Vosyednania pr. 15/17, Ukraine; tel. (44) 550-31-44; organ of the Ministry of Foreign Affairs; Ukrainian international relations and foreign affairs; Editor-in-Chief LEONID BAIDAK; quarterly, in Ukrainian and English; circ. 6,000.

*Polityka Wschodnia* (Eastern Politics). Centre for Eastern Studies of the Univ. of Warsaw, 00-046 Warsaw, ul. Nowy Swiat 69, Poland; tel. (22) 6200381; fax (22) 267520; relations between Belarus, the Russian Federation, Ukraine and the former Soviet Baltic states (Estonia, Latvia and Lithuania); 2 a year, in Polish.

*Post-Communist Economies and Economic Transformation.* Centre for Research into Post-Communist Economies (CRCE), 57 Tufton St, London SW1P 3QL, United Kingdom; tel. (20) 7799-3745; fax (20) 7233-1050; e-mail journals.orders@tandf.co.uk; internet www.tandf.co.uk/journals/carfax/14631377.html; f. 1989 as *Communist Economies and Economic Transformation*; transformation economics of communist and former communist countries, in particular in Eastern Europe, Russia and Central Asia; Editor ROGER CLARKE; quarterly, in English.

*Post-Soviet Affairs.* Bellwether Publishing Ltd, 8640 Guilford Rd, Suite 200, Columbia, MD 21046, USA; tel. (410) 290-3870; fax (410) 290-8726; e-mail bellpub@bellpub.com; internet www.bellpub.com; f. 1985; economics, foreign policy, nationality issues and political science in the countries of the former USSR; Editor GEORGE W. BRESLAUER; quarterly, in English.

*Pro and Contra.* Carnegie Moscow Center, Carnegie Endowment for International Peace, 16/2 Tverskaya, 103009 Moscow, Russia; tel. (095) 935-89-04; fax (095) 935-89-06; e-mail timofei@carnegie.ru; internet www.carnegie.ru; f. 1996; quarterly policy journal in Russian.

*Problems of Economic Transition.* M. E. Sharpe Inc., 80 Business Park Dr., Armonk, NY 10504, USA; tel. (914) 273-1800; fax (914) 273-2106; e-mail custserv@mesharpe.com; internet www.mesharpe.com; f. 1958; translation of selected articles from economic journals in the former USSR; includes indexes and statistical information; Editor BEN SLAY; monthly, in English.

*Problems of Post-Communism.* National Council for Eurasian and East European Research, 910 17th St, NW, Suite 300, Washington, DC 20006, USA; tel. (202) 822-6950; fax (202) 822-6955; e-mail dc@nceeer.org; internet www.nceeer.org; f. 1951; publ. by M. E. Sharpe, Inc.; covers economic, political and social devts and trends in the post-communist countries of Asia and Europe; Editor ROBERT HUBER; 6 a year, in English.

*Pushkin Journal: an Independent Review.* Charles Schlacks, Jr, POB 1256, Idyllwild, CA 92549-1256, USA; tel. (909) 659-4641; e-mail schslavic@tazland.net; Editor ALEXANDRA SMITH; annually, in English, French, German and Russian.

*Reforma Monthly.* Int. Foundation for Economic and Social Reforms (Reforma), 109240 Moscow, nab. Kotelnicheskaya 17, Russia; tel. (095) 926-77-52; fax (095) 975-23-73.

*Religion in Eastern Europe.* Christians Associated for Relations with Eastern Europe, AMBS 3003, Benham Ave, Elkhart, IN 46517, USA; tel. (219) 296-6209; fax (219) 295-0092; e-mail waltersawatsky@cs.com; internet ree.georgefox.edu/; f. 1981; insight into the religious situation in Eastern Europe; Editor Dr WALTER SAWATSKY; 6 a year; circ. 850.

*Religion, State and Society: the Keston Journal.* 38 St Aldate's, Oxford OX1 1BN; tel. (1865) 792929; fax (1865) 240042; e-mail keston.institute@keston.org; internet www.keston.org; all aspects of religious life and religion-state relations in communist and post-communist countries, and issues of current common concern to religious communities, East and West; Editor Dr PHILIP WALTERS; quarterly, in English; circ. approx. 500.

*Review of Russian Periodic.* Continent (Kontinent), 217 Fourth Ave, Garwood, NJ 07027, USA; e-mail continent@comcast.net; politics, history, philosophy, religion; also Continent (quarterly); Representative MARINA ADAMOVICH.

*Revolutionary Russia.* Frank Cass and Co Ltd, Crown House, 47 Chase Side, Southgate, London N14 5BP, United Kingdom; tel. (20) 8920-2100; fax (20) 8447-8548; e-mail info@frankcass.com; internet www.frankcass.com; f. 1988; concentrates on the two

Russian revolutions, with an interdisciplinary and international approach; Editor JONATHAN SMELE; 2 a year.

*Revue d'Etudes Comparatives Est-Ouest.* Centre National de la Recherche Scientifique, 44 rue de l'Amiral Mouchez, 75014 Paris, France; tel. 1-43-13-56-69; fax 1-43-13-56-70; e-mail receo@ivry.cnrs.fr; f. 1970; economics, history of ex-communist and communist countries, law, politics and sociology; Editor MARIE-CLAUDE MAUREL; 4 a year, in French, with summaries in French and English; circ. 800.

*RFE/RL Newsline, Part One: Russia, the Transcaucasus and Central Asia.* Radio Free Europe/Radio Liberty, 110 00 Prague 1, Vinohradská 1, Czech Republic; tel. (2) 21122407; fax (2) 21123013; e-mail carlsone@rferl.org; internet www.rferl.org; f. 1949; analysis of political events and trends across the region; Editor ELIZABETH FULLER; daily.

*RFE/RL Newsline, Part Two: Central, Eastern and South-eastern Europe.* e-mail maksymiukj@rferl.org; daily; Editor JAN MAKSYMIUK.

*RFE/RL Russian Political Weekly.* e-mail corwinj@rferl.org; Editor JULIE CORWIN.

*Romantic Russia: Literature and Culture.* Charles Schlacks, Jr, POB 1256, Idyllwild, CA 92549-1256, USA; tel. (909) 659-4641; e-mail schslavic@tazland.net; Editor (vacant); annually, in English, French, German and Russian.

*Rossiiski Ekonomicheski Zhurnal* (Russian Economic Journal). 109542 Moscow, pr. Ryazanski 99, Russia; tel. (095) 377-25-56; e-mail rem@energosvjaz.ru; internet www.energosvjaz.ru/rem; f. 1958 as Ekonomicheskiye Nauki, name changed as above 1992; theory and practice of economics and economic reform; Editor A. Y. MELENTEV; monthly, in Russian; circ. 6,000.

*Rusia Hoy* (Russia Today). Institute of Latin American Studies, Russian Acad. of Sciences, 113035 Moscow, ul. Bolshaya Ordynka 21, Russia; tel. (095) 233-43-40; fax (095) 233-40-70; monthly, in Spanish.

*Russia and Eurasia Review.* Jamestown Foundation, 4516 43rd St NW, Washington, DC 20016, USA; tel. (202) 483-8888; e-mail pubs@jamestown.org; internet russia.jamestown.org/pubs_russia.htm; f. 2002; Editor PETER RUTLAND; every two weeks.

*Russia and Euro-Asia Bulletin.* Contemporary Europe Research Centre, Univ. of Melbourne, 2nd Floor, 234 Queensberry St, Carlton, Vic 3052, Australia; tel. (3) 9344-9502; fax (3) 9344-9507; e-mail cerc@cerc.unimelb.edu.au; internet www.cerc.unimelb.edu.au/bulletin; f. 1994; current economic trends; every 2 months, in English.

*Russia Briefing.* Eastern Europe Newsletter Ltd, 4 Starfield Rd, London W12 9SW, United Kingdom; tel. (20) 8743-2829; fax (20) 8743-8637; e-mail 100316.1530@compuserve.com; Editor CHARLES MEYNELL; 3 a year.

*Russian and Baltic Economies—Week in Review.* Bank of Finland Institute for Economies in Transition, POB 160, 00101 Helsinki, Finland; tel. (9) 1832268; fax (9) 1832294; e-mail bofit@bof.fi; internet www.bof.fi/bofit; f. 1997; two-page review of the previous week's focal events in Russia and the Baltic states, incl. key financial-market figures; Editor TIMO HARELL; weekly, in English; circ. 1,500.

*Russian Economy—Month in Review.* Bank of Finland Institute for Economies in Transition, POB 160, 00101 Helsinki, Finland; tel. (9) 1832268; fax (9) 1832294; e-mail bofit@bof.fi; internet www.bof.fi/bofit; f. 1998; Editor SEIJA LAINELA; monthly, in English; circ. 1,000.

*Russian Economy: Trends and Prospects.* Institute of Economic Transition, 103918 Moscow, ul. Ogareva 5, str. 3, Russia; tel. (095) 202-42-74; e-mail e40102@sucemi.bitnet.

*Russian Education and Society: A Journal of Translations.* M. E. Sharpe Inc., 80 Business Park Dr., Armonk, New York, NY 10504, USA; tel. (914) 273-1800; fax (914) 273-2106; e-mail custserv@mesharpe.com; internet www.mesharpe.com; f. 1958; post-Soviet writing on pedagogical theory and practice, education policy, youth and the family; Editor ANTHONY JONES; 12 a year, in English.

*Russian Environmental Digest (RED).* Transboundary Environmental Information Agency (TEIA), 190000 St Petersburg, POB 105, Russia; tel. (812) 323-4089; fax (630) 604-9463; e-mail majordomo@teia.org; internet www.majordomo.teia.org; environmental issues; in English and Russian.

*Russian History.* Charles Schlacks, Jr, POB 1256, Idyllwild, CA 92549-1256, USA; tel. (909) 659-4641; e-mail schslavic@tazland.net; Editor RICHARD HELLIE; 4 a year, in English and Russian.

*Russian Linguistics: International Journal for the Study of the Russian Language.* Kluwer Academic Publishers BV, van Godewijckstraat 30, POB 17, 3300 AA Dordrecht, Netherlands; tel. (78) 6576116; fax (78) 6576377; e-mail services@wkap.nl; internet www.wkap.nl; Editors R. COMTET, W. LEHFELDT, J. SCHAEKEN; 3 a year, in English and Russian.

*Russian Monitor: Archive of Contemporary Politics.* Centre for Applied Political Studies (INDEM), 121914 Moscow, ul. Novyi Arbat 15, Russia; tel. (095) 202-32-14; fax (095) 202-31-69; e-mail indemglas@apc.org; quarterly.

*Russian Politics and Law: a Journal of Translations.* M. E. Sharpe Inc., 80 Business Park Dr., Armonk, New York, NY 10504, USA; tel. (914) 273-1800; fax (914) 273-2106; e-mail custserv@mesharpe.com; internet www.mesharpe.com; f. 1962; analysis of past and contemporary issues, such as constitutionalism, foreign relations, ideology, imperialism, nationalism, party devt and state-building; Editor NILS H. WESSELL; 6 a year, in English.

*Russian Public Opinion Monitor.* Aspect Press Ltd, per. Gagarinski 25, Moscow, Russia; tel. (095) 241-22-06; Editor YURI LEVADA; every 2 months, in Russian.

*Russian Regional Report.* ETH Zentrum, Leonhardhalde 21, 8092 Zürich, Switzerland; tel. 16326379; fax 16321413; e-mail rorttung@att.net; internet www.isn.ethz.ch/researchpub/publihouse/rrr; political development in the constituent units of the Russian Federation; Editor-in-Chief ROBERT ORTTUNG; every two weeks.

*Russian Review.* Blackwell Publishers Ltd, 350 Main St, Malden, MA 01248, USA; tel. (781) 388-8200; fax (781) 388-8232; e-mail subscrip@blackwellpub.com; internet www.blackwellpub.com; Editor EVE LEVIN; quarterly.

*Russian Social Science Review: a Journal of Translations.* M. E. Sharpe Inc., 80 Business Park Dr., Armonk, New York, NY 10504, USA; tel. (914) 273-1800; fax (914) 273-2106; e-mail custserv@mesharpe.com; internet www.mesharpe.com; f. 1960; presents essays and studies in a range of fields, incl. anthropology, economics, education, history, literary criticism, political science, psychology and sociology, for insights into the problems of post-Soviet society; Editor PATRICIA A. KOLB; 6 a year, in English.

*Russian Studies in History.* M. E. Sharpe Inc., 80 Business Park Dr., Armonk, New York, NY 10504, USA; tel. (914) 273-1800; fax (914) 273-2106; e-mail custserv@mesharpe.com; internet www.mesharpe.com; f. 1962; translations of Russian history articles; Editors JOSEPH BRADLEY, CHRISTINE RUANE; 4 a year, in English.

*Russian Studies in Literature.* M. E. Sharpe Inc., 80 Business Park Dr., Armonk, New York, NY 10504, USA; tel. (914) 273-1800; fax (914) 273-2106; e-mail custserv@mesharpe.com; internet www.mesharpe.com; f. 1964; translations of Russian literary criticism and scholarship; Editor JOHN GIVENS; 4 a year, in English.

*Russian Studies in Philosophy.* M. E. Sharpe Inc., 80 Business Park Dr., Armonk, New York, NY 10504, USA; tel. (914) 273-1800; fax (914) 273-2106; e-mail custserv@mesharpe.com; internet www.mesharpe.com; f. 1962; translations of Russian articles on philosophy; Editor TARAS D. ZAKYDALSKI; 4 a year, in English.

*Russland und Wir* (Russia and Us). Verlag und Handlung, 61350 Bad Homburg, Sindlinger Weg 1, Germany; tel. (6172) 35191; f. 1961; economic, political and social issues affecting Russian-German relations; Editor SIEGFRIED KEILING; quarterly, in German; circ. 2,000.

*Sankt-Peterburgskii Universitet Vestnik, Seriya: Ekonomika* (St Petersburg University Herald, Series: Economics). Sankt-Peterburgskii Universitet, 199034 St Petersburg, Universitetskaya nab. 7-9, Russia; tel. (812) 218-20-00; fax (812) 218-13-46; e-mail office@inform.pu.ru; f. 1946; one of eight series; quarterly, in Russian, with summaries in English.

*Science and Global Security: the Technical Basis for Arms Control and Environmental Policy Initiatives.* Harwood Academic Publishers, POB 32160, Newark, NJ 07102-0301, USA; tel. (973) 643-7500; fax (973) 643-7676; internet www.gbhap .com/science_global_security; f. 1989; scientific analyses relating to arms control and global environment policy; Editors H. A. FEIVESON, STANISLAV N. RODIONOV; quarterly, in English and Russian.

*Short-Term Economic Indicators: Transition Economies.* OECD, 2 rue André-Pascal, 75775 Paris Cédex 16, France; tel. 1-45-24-16-93; fax 1-45-24-17-13; e-mail kei.contacts@oecd.org; internet www.oecd.org.

*Silver Age: Russian Literature and Culture.* Charles Schlacks, Jr, POB 1256, Idyllwild, CA 92549-1256, USA; tel. (909) 659-4641; e-mail schslavic@tazland.net; Editor ERIC LAURSEM; annually, in English, French, German and Russian.

*Slavic and Eastern European Journal.* American Association of Teachers of Slavic and Eastern European Languages, POB 7039, Berkeley, CA 94707-2306, USA; tel. and fax (510) 526-6614; e-mail aatseel@earthlink.net; research studies in all areas of Slavic culture, language and literature; Editor Dr GERALD JANECEK.

*Slavic Review.* Univ. of Illinois at Urbana-Champaign, 57 E. Armory Ave, Champaign, IL 61820-6601, USA; tel. (217) 333-3621; fax (217) 333-3872; e-mail slavrev@uiuc.edu; internet www.econ.uiuc.edu/~slavrev; f. 1941; formerly *The American Slavic and East European Review*; covers art, history, humanities, literature, linguistics and social sciences in Eastern Europe, Eurasia and Russia; Editor DIANE P. KOENKER; quarterly, in English; circ. approx. 4,500.

*Slavic Review: American Quarterly of Russian, Eurasian and East European Studies.* American Association for the Advancement of Slavic Studies Inc., 8 Story St, Cambridge, MA 02138, USA; tel. (617) 495-0677; fax (617) 495-0680; e-mail aaass@fas .harvard.edu; internet www.fas.harvard.edu/~aaass; Editor DIANE P. KOENKER.

*Slavistična revija* (Journal for Linguistics and :Literary Studies). 1000 Ljubljana, Aškerčeva 2, Slovenia; tel. (1) 2411306; fax (1) 4259337; e-mail natasa.logar@ff.uni-lj.si; internet www.ff.uni-lj.si/sr/index.html; f. 1948; quarterly.

*Slavonic and East European Review.* School of Slavonic and East European Studies (SSEES), Univ. College London, Senate House, Malet Street, London WC1E 7HU, United Kingdom; tel. (20) 7862-8536; fax (20) 7862-8641; e-mail seer@ssees.ac.uk; internet www.ingenta.com; available on-line; Editor Dr MARTYN RADY; quarterly.

*Slavonica.* Sheffield Academic Press Ltd, Mansion House, 19 Kingfield Rd, Sheffield S11 9AS, United Kingdom; tel. (114) 255-4433; fax (114) 255-4626; e-mail sales@sheffac.demon.co.uk; internet www.sheffieldacademicpress.com; f. 1995; culture, history, language and literature in Central and Eastern Europe and Russia; Editor JEKATERINA YOUNG; 2 a year, in English; circ. approx. 150.

*Slovo.* School of Slavonic and Eastern European Studies (SSEES), Univ. College London, Senate House, Malet Street, London WC1E 7HU, United Kingdom; tel. (20) 7862-8619; fax (20) 7862-8641; e-mail slovo@ssees.ac.uk; internet www.ssees.ac .uk/slovo.htm; f. 1988; interdisciplinary journal of East European, Eurasian and Russian affairs, covering the fields of anthropology, art, economics, film, history, international studies, linguistics, literature, media, philosophy, politics and sociology; Man. Editor SERGIU TROIE; annually, in English; circ. 4,000.

*Socialist Realism: Literature and Culture.* Charles Schlacks, Jr, POB 1256, Idyllwild, CA 92549-1256, USA; tel. (909) 659-4641; e-mail schslavic@tazland.net; annually, in English, French, German and Russian.

*Solanus. An International Journal for Russian and East European Bibliographic, Library and Publishing Studies.* c/o Dr Christine Thomas, Slavonic and East European Collections,

British Library, 96 Euston Rd, London NW1 2DB, United Kingdom; tel. (20) 7412-7587; fax (20) 7412-7554; e-mail chris .thomas@bl.uk; internet www.sseees.ac.uk/solanus/solacont .htm; publ. of the School of Slavonic and East European Studies, Univ. College London; Editor Dr CHRISTINE THOMAS; annually.

*Soviet and Post-Soviet Review.* Charles Schlacks, Jr, POB 1256, Idyllwild, CA 92549-1256, USA; tel. (909) 659-4641; e-mail schslavic@tazland.net; 3 a year, in English, French, German and Russia.

*Stanford Slavic Studies.* Dept of Slavic Languages and Literature, Stanford Univ., c/o Berkeley Slavic Specialities, POB 3034, Oakland, CA 94609-0034, USA; tel. (510) 653-8048; fax (510) 653-6313; Editors LAZAR FLEISHMAN, GREGORY FREIDIN, RICHARD SCHUPBACH.

*Statistical Co-operation with Central and Eastern Europe and Central Asia.* Dept for Int. Development, Statistics Dept, 94 Victoria St, London SW1E 5JL, United Kingdom; tel. (20) 7917-7000; fax (20) 7917-0019; e-mail enquiry@dfid.gov.uk; internet www.dfid.gov.uk.

*Statutes and Decisions: the Laws of the USSR and its Successor States.* M. E. Sharpe Inc., 80 Business Park Dr., Armonk, New York, NY 10504, USA; tel. (914) 273-1800; fax (914) 273-2106; e-mail custserv@mesharpe.com; internet www.mesharpe.com; f. 1964; translations from the Russian; Editor SARAH J. REYNOLDS; 6 a year, in English.

*Symposium: A Journal of Russian Thought.* Charles Schlacks, Jr, POB 1256, Idyllwild, CA 92549-1256, USA; tel. (909) 659-4641; e-mail schslavic@tazland.net; annually, in English, French, German and Russian.

*Teatr: Russian Theatre, Past and Present.* Charles Schlacks, Jr, POB 1256, Idyllwild, CA 92549-1256, USA; tel. (909) 659-4641; e-mail schslavic@tazland.net; Editor (vacant); annually, in English, French, German and Russian.

*Theory and Practice of Foreign Policy.* Institute for Current Int. Problems, 119021 Moscow, ul. Ostozhenka 53/2, Russia; tel. (095) 208-94-61; fax (095) 208-94-66; Russian foreign policy and international diplomacy; monthly.

*TOL Annual Survey.* Chlumova 22, 130 00 Prague, Czech Republic; tel. (2) 22780805; fax (2) 22780804; e-mail transitions@tol.cz; internet store.tol.cz; English; available on CD-ROM.

*Tracking Eastern Europe—Executive Business Guide.* AMF Int. Consultants, 812 N. Wood Ave, Suite 204, Linden, NJ 07036, USA; tel. (098) 486-3534; fax (098) 486-4084; f. 1990; foreign investment in Eastern Europe and the former USSR; Editor FRED T. ROSSI; 2 a month, in English.

*Transition.* Institut de Sociologie, Université Libr de Bruxelles, 44 ave Jeanne, CP 124, 1050 Brussels, Belgium; tel. (2) 650-34-42; fax (2) 650-35-21; e-mail adesmarl@ulb.ac.be; internet www .ulb.ac.be/is/revtrans.html; f. 1960; 2 a year, in French and English.

*Transition Report.* EBRD, One Exchange Square, 175 Bishopsgate, London EC2A 2JN, United Kingdom; tel. (20) 7338-6000; fax (20) 7338-6100; e-mail pubsdesk@ebrd.com; internet www .ebrd.com; annually.

*Transitions Online.* Chlumova 22, 130 00 Prague 3, Czech Republic; tel. (2) 22780805; fax (2) 22780804; e-mail transitions@tol.cz; internet www.tol.cz; f. 1999; culture, economy, media and politics in the Balkans, East-Central Europe and the former USSR; on-line only; Editor JEREMY DRUKER; daily, in English and Russian.

*Transnational Organized Crime.* Frank Cass and Co Ltd, Crown House, 47 Chase Side, Southgate, London N14 5BP, United Kingdom; tel. (20) 8920-2100; fax (20) 8447-8548; e-mail info@ frankcass.com; internet www.frankcass.com; f. 1995; a multidisciplinary journal that identifies and explores cross-border criminal activities, the threats posed by such crime to national and international security and government responses to it; Editors PHIL WILLIAMS, RENSSELAER LEE III, ERNESTO U. SAVONA, DILYS HILL, FRANK GREGORY; quarterly, in English.

*Ukrainian Economic Monitor.* Ukrainian Research Institute, Harvard University, 1583 Massachusetts Ave, Cambridge, MA

02138, USA; tel. (617) 495-4053; fax (617) 495-8097; e-mail huri@fas.harvard.edu; internet www.huri.harvard.edu/prog .monitor.html; trade, investment, economic performance and politics of Ukraine. Also reports on recent developments in political reform and privatization; monthly, in English.

*Ulkopolitiikka* (Finnish Journal of Foreign Affairs). Ulkopoliittinen Instituutti (UPI—Finnish Institute of Int. Affairs), Mannerheimintie 15A, 00260 Helsinki, Finland; tel. (9) 4342070; fax (9) 43420769; e-mail ulkopolitiikka@upi-fiia.fi; internet www.upi-fiia.fi; f. 1972; presents recent research findings and background discussions relevant to foreign-policy and security-policy issues; Editors Dr Tuomas Forsberg, Maarika Toivonen; quarterly, in Finnish; circ. 2,000.

*Venäjän aika.* Novomedia Oy, Näyttelijäntie 14B, 00400 Helsinki, Finland; tel. (9) 8545320; fax (9) 85453250; e-mail novomedia@novomedia.fi; internet www.novomedia.fi.

*Vneshnyaya Torgovlya* (Foreign Trade). 121108 Moscow, ul. Minskaya 11, Russia; tel. (095) 145-68-94; fax (095) 145-51-92; e-mail vneshtorg@mtu-net.ru; f. 1921; Editor Y. M. Deomidov; every two months, in Russian and English; circ. 8,000.

*Voprosy Ekonomiki* (Problems of Economics). Institute of Economics, Russian Acad. of Sciences, 117218 Moscow, pr. Nakhimovski 32, Russia; tel. and fax (095) 124-52-28; e-mail mail@ vopreco.ru; internet www.vopreco.ru; f. 1929; covers problems of economic theory, monetary and fiscal policies, social issues, structural and investment policy, technological change, transitional economics; Editor L. I. Abalkin; monthly, in Russian; circ. 7,000; (2002).

*Yaderny Kontrol* (Nuclear Control). Centre for Policy Studies in Russia (PIR Centre), 103001 Moscow, Trekhprudny, Russia; tel. (095) 234-05-25; fax (095) 234-95-58; e-mail info@pircenter.org; internet www.pircenter.org; f. 1994; arms control, nuclear non-proliferation and dual-use technologies; Editor Vladimir A. Orlov; monthly, in Russian, with English summaries; circ. 1,000.

*Za Rubezhom* (Abroad). 125865 Moscow, ul. Pravdi 24, Russia; tel. (095) 257-23-87; fax (095) 200-22-96; f. 1960; international press review; Editor S. Morozov; weekly, in Russian.

*Zakon* (Law). Izvestiya, 103798 Moscow, Pushkinskaya pl. 5, Russia; tel. (095) 299-74-55; f. 1991; legislation relating to business and commerce, and legal issues for the business community; Editor Yurii Feofanov; in Russian.

*Zeitschrift für Ostmitteleuropa-Forschung* (Journal of East Central European Studies). 35037 Marburg, Gisonenweg 5-7, Germany; tel. (6421) 184125; fax (6421) 184139; e-mail vertrieb@ mailer.uni-marburg.de; internet www.uni-marburg.de/ herder-institut; f. 1952; history of East Central Europe (the geographical area covered by Poland, Estonia, Latvia, Lithuania, the Czech and Slovak Republics, western Belarus and western Ukraine); Editors Dr Winfried Irgang, Marko Wauker; quarterly, in German and English; circ. 650.

# SELECT BIBLIOGRAPHY (BOOKS)

For books on individual countries see the Bibliography at the end of each Country Survey in Part Two.

Acar, Feride, and Gries-Ayata, Ayse (Eds). *Gender and Identity Construction: Women of Central Asia, the Caucasus and Turkey.* Leiden, Brill, 2000.

Adshead, Samuel Adrian Miles. *Central Asia in World History.* London, Macmillan, 1993.

Aganbegyan, A. *The Challenge: Economics of Perestroika.* London, Hutchinson, 1988.

Akiner, Shirin. *Islamic People of the Soviet Union: an Historical and Statistical Handbook, with an Appendix on the non-Muslim Turkic peoples of the Soviet Union.* London and New York, NY, Kegan Paul International, 1986 (2nd edn).

*Cultural Change and Continuity.* London, Kegan Paul International, 1991.

Allcroft, Edward (Ed.). *Central Asia: a Century of Russian rule.* New York, NY, and London, Columbia University Press, 1967.

Alleg, Henri. *Etoile rouge et croissant vert, l'Orient sovietique / Red Star and Green Crescent.* Moscow, Progress Publishers, 1985.

Allen, W. E. D., and Mouratoff, Paul. *Caucasian Battlefields: History of the Wars on the Turco-Caucasian Border 1828–1921.* Cambridge, Cambridge University Press, 1953.

Allison, Roy (Ed.). *Challenge for the former Soviet South.* Washington, DC, Brookings Institution Press, for the Royal Institute of International Affairs, 1996.

Allison, Roy, and Bluth, Christoph. *Security Dilemmas in Russia and Eurasia.* London, Royal Institute of International Affairs, 1998.

Allworth, Edward (Ed.). *Central Asia: 130 Years of Russian Dominance, a Historical Overview.* Durham, NC, Duke University Press, 1994.

Amirahmadi, Hooshang. *The Caspian Region at a Crossroad: Challenges of a New Frontier of Energy and Development.* Basingstoke, Macmillan, 2000.

Anderson, John. *The International Politics of Central Asia.* Manchester, Manchester University Press, and New York, NY, St Martin's Press, 1997.

*Religion, State and Politics in the Soviet Union and Successor States.* Cambridge, Cambridge University Press, 1994.

Andrew, C., and Gordievsky, O. *KGB, the Inside Story.* London, Hodder and Stoughton, 1990.

Applebaum, Anne *Between East and West.* Chippendale, New South Wales, 1995.

*Gulag: A History of the Soviet Camps.* London, Allen Lane, 2003.

Åslund, Anders. *Building Capitalism: The Transformation of the Former Soviet Bloc.* Cambridge, Cambridge University Press, 2002.

Atabaki, Touradj, and O'Kane, John (Eds). *Post-Soviet Central Asia.* London, Tauris Academic Studies (in association with the International Institute for Asian Studies), 1998.

Aves, Jonathan. *Post-Soviet Transcaucasia.* London, Royal Institute of International Affairs, 1993.

Banuazizi, Ali, and Weiner, Myron (Eds). *The New Geopolitics of Central Asia and its Borderlands.* London, I. B. Tauris, 1994.

Barth, Urban Joan, and Solovei, Valerii D. *Russia's Communists at the Crossroads.* Boulder, CO, Westview Press, 1997.

Batalden, Stephen K., and Batalden, Sandra L. *The Newly Independent States of Eurasia: Handbook of Former Soviet Republics.* Phoenix, AZ, Oryx, 1997 (2nd edn).

Bertsch, Gary Kenneth. *Crossroads and Conflict: Security and Foreign Policy in the Caucasus and Central Asia.* New York, NY, Routledge, 1999.

Bertsch, Gary K., and Potter, William C. (Eds). *Dangerous Weapons, Desperate States: Russia, Belarus, Kazakhstan and Ukraine.* London, Routledge, 1999.

Blaney, John W. (Ed.). *The Successor States to the USSR.* Washington, DC, Congressional Quarterly Inc., 1995.

Boobbyer, Philip. *The Stalin Era.* London, Routledge, 2000.

Bourdeaux, Michael (Ed.). *The Politics of Religion in Russia and the New States of Eurasia.* Armonk, NY, M. E. Sharpe, 1995.

Bremmer Ian, and Taras, Ray (Eds). *Nation and Politics in the Soviet Successor States.* Cambridge, Cambridge University Press, 1993.

*New States, New Politics: Building the Post-Soviet Nations.* Cambridge, Cambridge University Press, 1997.

Brown, Archie. *The Gorbachev Factor.* Oxford, Oxford University Press, 1996.

Brown, Archie (Ed.). *The Soviet-East European Relationship in the Gorbachev Era.* Boulder, CO, Westview Press, 1990.

Brown, Archie, Kaser, Michael, and Smith, Gerald (Eds), and Brown, Patricia (Assoc. Ed.). *The Cambridge Encyclopaedia of Russia and the Former Soviet Union.* Cambridge, Cambridge University Press, 1994.

Buckley, Mary (Ed.). *Post-Soviet Women from the Baltic to Central Asia.* Cambridge, Cambridge University Press, 1997.

Buttino, Marco (Ed.). *In a Collapsing Empire: Underdevelopment, Ethnic Conflicts and Nationalisms in the Soviet Union.* Milan, Feltrinelli, 1993.

Brzezinski, Zbigniew, and Sullivan, Paige (Eds). *Russia and the Commonwealth of Independent States: Documents, Data and Analysis.* Armonk, NY, M. E. Sharpe, 1996.

Cambridge International Reference on Current Affairs. *A Political and Economic Dictionary of Eastern Europe.* London, Europa Publications, 2002.

Campbell, K. M., and MacFarlane, S. N. (Eds). *Gorbachev's Third World Dilemmas.* London, Routledge, 1989.

Capisani, Gianpaolo R. *The Handbook of Central Asia: a Comprehensive Survey of the New Republics.* London, and New York, NY, I. B. Tauris, 2000.

Carrere d'Encausse, Helene. *The End of the Soviet Empire: The Triumph of the Nations.* New York, NY, Basic Books, 1994.

Chervonnaya, Svetlana M. *Conflict in the Caucasus: Georgia, Abkhazia and the Russian Shadow.* Glastonbury, Gothic Image Publications, 1995.

Childs, David. *The Two Red Flags—European Social Democracy and Soviet Communism since 1945.* London, Routledge, 2000.

Christian, David. *A History of Russia, Central Asia and Mongolia: Inner Eurasia from Pre-history to the Mongol Empire.* Oxford, Blackwell Publishers, 1999.

Chuvin, Pierre, and Gentile, Pierre. *Asia Centrale: l'Indépendence, le Pétrole et l'Islam.* Paris, Le Monde Poche, 1998.

Clarke, R. A., and Matko, D. J. I. *Soviet Economic Facts, 1917–81.* London, Macmillan, 1983.

Cockerham, William C. *Health and Social Change in Eastern Europe.* London, Routledge, 1999.

Cox, Michael (Ed.). *Rethinking the Soviet Collapse: Sovietology, the Death of Communism and the New Russia.* London, and New York, NY, Pinter, 1998.

Crockatt, Richard. *The Fifty Years War: The United States and the Soviet Union in World Politics, 1941—1991.* London, Routledge, 1996.

Cummings, Sally. *Power and Change in Central Asia.* Routledge, London, 2001.

D'Agostino, Anthony. *Gorbachev's Revolution 1985–1991.* London, Macmillan, 1998.

Dahrendorf, Ralf. *After 1989: Morals, Revolution and Civil Society.* Basingstoke, Macmillan (in association with St Antony's College, University of Oxford), 1997.

Danber, Rachel. *The Soviet Nationality Reader: The Disintegration in Context.* Boulder, CO, Westview Press, 1992.

Daniels, Robert Vincent. *The End of the Communist Revolution.* London, Routledge, 1993.

D'Anieri, Paul. *Economic Interdependence in Ukrainian-Russian Relations.* New York, NY, State University of New York Press, 1999.

Dannreuther, Roland. *Creating New States in Central Asia: The Strategic Implications of the Collapse of Soviet Power in Central Asia.* London, Brassey's (for the International Institute for Strategic Studies), 1994.

Dawisha, Karen. *Eastern Europe, Gorbachev and Reform: The Great Challenge.* Cambridge, Cambridge University Press, 1988 (2nd edn).

Dawisha, Karen (Ed.). *The International Dimension of Post-Communist Transitions in Russia and the New States of Eurasia.* Armonk, NY, M. E. Sharpe, 1997.

Dawisha, Karen, and Parrott, Bruce (Eds). *Democratic Changes and Authoritarian Reactions in Russia, Ukraine, Belarus and Moldova.* New York, NY, Cambridge University Press, 1997.

*Democratisation and Authoritarianism in Post-Communist Societies*, in four vols. Cambridge, Cambridge University Press, 1998.

*The End of Empire? The Transformation of the USSR in Comparative Perspective.* Armonk, NY, and London, M. E. Sharpe, 1997.

*Conflict, Cleavage and Change in Central Asia and the Caucasus.* Cambridge, Cambridge University Press, 1997.

Dawisha, K., and Valdes, J. 'Socialist Internationalism in Eastern Europe', in *Problems of Communism*, Vol. 36, No. 2 (March/April). 1987.

Desai, P. *The Soviet Economy.* Oxford, Basil Blackwell, 1987.

Dienes, Leslie. *Soviet Central Asia: Economic Development and National Policy Choices.* Boulder, CO, Westview Press, 1987.

Diuk, Nadia, and Karatnycky, Adrian. *New Nations Rising: the Fall of the Soviets and the Challenge of Independence.* New York, NY, and Chichester, John Wiley and Sons, 1993.

Djalilli, Mohammad-Reza, and Kellner, Thierry. *Géopolitique de la Nouvelle Asie Centrale.* Paris, Presse Universitaires de France, 2001.

Drobizheva, Leokadia (Ed.). *Ethnic Conflict in the Post-Soviet World: Case Studies and Analysis.* New York, NY, M. E. Sharpe, 1996.

Dudoignon, Stephane, and Komatsu, Hisao (Eds). *Islam in Politics in Russia and Central Asia (Early Eighteenth to Late Twentieth Centuries).* London and New York, NY, Kegan Paul International, 2001.

Dunlop, John B. *The Rise of Russia and the Fall of the Soviet Empire.* Princeton, NJ, Princeton University Press, 1994.

Ebel, Robert E., and Menon, Rajan (Eds). *Energy and Conflict in Central Asia and the Caucasus.* Lanham, MD, Rowman and Littlefield, 2000.

Ehteshama, Anoushiravan (Ed.). *From the Gulf to Central Asia: Players in the new Great Game.* Exeter, University of Exeter Press, 1994.

Eickelman, Dale F. *Russia's Muslim Frontiers: New Directions in Cross-cultural Analysis.* Bloomington, IN, Indiana University Press, 1993.

Erturk, Korkut A. (Ed.). *Rethinking Central Asia: Non-Eurocentric Studies in History, Social Structure and Identity.* Reading, Ithaca Press, 1999.

Esposito, John L. *Oxford History of Islam.* Oxford, Oxford University Press, 2000.

European Bank for Reconstruction and Development (EBRD). *Financing with the EBRD: A Guide for Companies and Entrepreneurs considering Financing Projects or investing in the Countries of Central and Eastern Europe and the CIS.* London, EBRD, 1998.

Ferdinand, Peter (Ed.). *The New Central Asia and its Neighbours.* London, Royal Institute of International Affairs/Pinter, 1994.

Fitzpatrick, Sheila (Ed.). *Stalinism.* London, Routledge, 2000.

Forbes Manz, Beatrice. *The Rise and Rule of Tamerlane.* Cambridge, Cambridge University Press, 1999.

Fowkes, Ben. *The Disintegration of the Soviet Union: a Study in the Rise and Triumph of Nationalism.* Basingstoke, Macmillan, 1997.

Frucht, Richard (Ed.). *The Encyclopedia of Eastern Europe—From the Congress of Vienna to the Fall of Communism.* New York, NY, Garland Publishing, 2000.

Galeotti, M. *Gorbachev and His Revolution.* London, Macmillan, 1997.

Gleason, Gregory. *The Central Asia States: Discovering Independence.* Boulder, CO, Westview Press, 1997.

Glenn, John. *The Soviet Legacy in Central Asia.* New York, NY, St Martin's Press, 1999.

Goldenberg, Susan. *Pride of Small Nations: The Caucasus and Post-Soviet Disorder.* London, Zed Books, 1994.

Gorbachev, Mikhail. *Perestroika.* London, Fontana Collins, 1988 (2nd edn).

Grancelli, B. *Soviet Management and Labor Relations.* Boston, MA, Unwin Hyman, 1988.

Gray, K. R. (Ed.). *Soviet Agriculture: Comparative Perspectives.* Ames, IO, Iowa State University Press, 1990.

Grousset, Rene. *The Empire of the Steppes: A History of Central Asia.* Piscataway, NJ, Rutgers University Press, 1989.

Hagendoorn, Louk, Linssen, Hub, and Tumanov, Sergei. *Intergroup Relations in the States of the Former Soviet Union.* London, Psychology Press, 2001.

Haghayeghi, Mehrdad. *Islam and Politics in Central Asia.* Basingstoke, Macmillan, 1995.

Hanson, P. *Trade and Technology in Soviet-Western Relations.* London, Macmillan, 1981.

Hedlund, Stefan. *Crisis in Soviet Agriculture.* London, Croom Helm, 1984.

*Private Agriculture in the Soviet Union.* London, Routledge, 1990.

Herzig, Edmund. *The New Caucasus: Armenia, Azerbaijan and Georgia.* London, Royal Institute of International Affairs, 1999.

Hewett, E. A. *Reforming the Soviet Economy: Equality versus Efficiency.* Washington, DC, Brookings Institution Press, 1989.

Hiro, Dilip. *Between Marx and Muhammad: The Changing Face of Central Asia.* London, HarperCollins, 1994.

*War Without End: The Rise of Islamist Terrorism and Global Response.* London, Routledge, 2002.

Holden, G. *The Warsaw Pact: Soviet Security and Bloc Politics.* Oxford, Basil Blackwell, 1989.

Hopkirk, Peter. *Setting the East Ablaze: Lenin's dream of an Empire in Asia.* Oxford, Oxford University Press, 1986.

*The Great Game.* Oxford, Oxford University Press, 2001 (new edn).

Hosking, Geoffrey. *Russia—People and Empire.* London, HarperCollins, 1997.

Hosking, Geoffrey, and Service, Robert (Eds). *Russian Nationalism, Past and Present.* Basingstoke, Macmillan, 1997.

Hudson, G. E. (Ed.). *Soviet National Security Policy under Perestroika,* Mershon Center Series on International Security and Foreign Policy (Vol. IV). Boston, MA, Unwin Hyman, 1990.

Humphrey, Caroline. *The Unmaking of Soviet Life: Everyday Economies after Socialism.* New York, NY, Cornell University Press, 2002.

Hunter, Shireen. *Central Asia since Independence.* Westport, CT, Praeger, 1996.

Ito, Takatuki, and Tabata, Shinichiro (Eds). *Between Disintegration and Reintegration: Former Socialist Countries and the*

*World Since 1989*. Sapporo, Slavic Research Centre, Hokkaido University, 1994.

Jackson, Nicole J. *Russian Foreign Policy and the CIS: Theories, Debates and Actions*. London, Routledge, 2003.

Jonson, Lena. *Keeping the Peace in the CIS: The Evolution of Russian Policy*. London, Royal Institute of International Affairs, 1999.

Jonson, Lena, and Archer, Clive (Eds). *Peacekeeping and the Role of Russia in Eurasia*. Boulder, CO, Westview Press, 1996.

Kaariainen, Kimmo. *Religion in Russia After the Collapse of Communism: Religious Renaissance or Secular State?* Lewiston, NY, Edwin Mellen Press, 1998.

Kaiser, Robert John. *The Geography of Nationalism in Russia and the USSR*. Princeton, NJ, Princeton University Press, 1994.

Kalyuzhnova, Y., Jaffe, Amy Myers, Lynch, Dov, and Sickles, Robin C. *Energy in the Caspian Region: Present and Future*. Basingstoke, Palgrave Macmillan, 2002.

Kaminski, Bartlomiej (Ed.). *Economic Transition in Russia and the New States of Eurasia*. Armonk, NY, M. E. Sharpe, 1996.

Karam, Patrick. *Asie Centrale—Le Nouveau Grand Jeu (Les Vraies Raison de la Guerre Américaine)*. Paris, L'Harmattan Edition, 2002.

Karny, Yo'av. *Highlanders: A Journey to the Caucasus in Quest of Memory*. New York, NY, Farrar, Straus and Giroux, 2000.

Kaufmann, R. F., and Hardt J. P. (Eds). *The Former Soviet Union in Transition*. London, Armonk, 1993.

Kazemzadeh, Firuz. *The Struggle for Transcaucasia (1917–1921)*. Westport, CT, Hyperion Press, 1981.

Keep, J. *Last of the Empires: A History of the Soviet Union 1945–1991*. Oxford, Oxford University Press, 1996.

Kennedy-Pipes, C. *Stalin's Cold War: Soviet Strategies in Eastern Europe, 1943 to 1956*. Manchester, Manchester University Press, 1996.

Khazanov, Anatolii M. *After the USSR: Ethnicity, Nationalism and Politics in the Commonwealth of Independent States*. Madison, WS, University of Wisconsin Press, 1995.

Kim, Young C., and Sigur, Gaston J. (Eds). *Asia and the Decline of Communism*. New Brunswick, NJ, and London, Transaction, 1992.

Kittrie, N., and Volgyes, I. (Eds). *The Uncertain Future: Gorbachev's Eastern Bloc*. New York, NY, Paragon House, 1988.

Kleveman, Lutz. *The New Great Game: Blood and Oil in Central Asia*. New York, NY, Atlantic Monthly Press, 2003.

Knight, Amy W. *Spies Without Cloaks: The KGB's Successors*. Princeton, NJ, Princeton University Press, 1996.

Kolstoe, Paul. *Russians in the Former Soviet Republics*. London, Hurst, 1995.

Kostecki, Wojciech, Zukrowska, Katarzyna, and Goralczyk, Bogdan J. *Transformations of Post-Communist States*. Basingstoke, Macmillan, 2000.

Kotkin, Stephen. *Armageddon Averted: The Soviet Collapse, 1970–2000*. Oxford, Oxford University Press, 2001.

Kozlov, V. I. *The Peoples of the Soviet Union*. London, Hutchinson, 1988.

Krag, Helen, and Funch, Lars. *The North Caucasus: Minorities at a Crossroads*. London, Minority Rights Group International, 1995.

Kulchik, Yurii, Fadin, Andrei, and Sergeev, Victor. *Central Asia After the Empire*. London, Pluto Press (in association with the Transnational Institute), 1996.

Laird, R. F., and Hoffman, E. P. (Eds). *Soviet Foreign Policy in a Changing World*. New York, NY, Aldine de Gruyter, 1986.

Laitlin, David G. *Indentity in Formation: the Russian-speaking Populations in the Near Abroad*. New York, NY, Ithaca, and London, Cornell University Press, 1998.

Landau, Jacob M., and Kellner-Heinkele, Barbara. *Politics of Language in the Ex-Soviet Muslim States: Azerbaijan, Uzbekistan, Kazakhstan, Kyrgyzstan, Turkmenistan, Tajikistan*. London, Hurst, 2001.

Lapidus, Gail W., and Zaslavsky, Victor (Eds), with Goldman, Philip. *From Union to Commonwealth: Nationalism and Separatism in the Soviet Republics*. Cambridge, Cambridge University Press, 1992.

Lee, Stephen. J. *Stalin and the Soviet Union*. London, Routledge, 1999.

Lee, Rensselaer W. *Smuggling Armageddon: The Nuclear Black Market in the Former Soviet Union and Europe*. New York, NY, St Martin's Press, 1998.

Lewis, David Christopher. *After Atheism: Religion and Ethnicity in Russia and Central Asia*. New York, NY, St Martin's Press, 1999.

Lewis, David W. P., and Lepesant, Gilles (Eds). *What Security for which Europe?* New York, NY, Peter Lang, 1999.

Lieven, Anatol. *Ukraine and Russia: A Fraternal Rivalry*. Washington, DC, Carnegie Endowment for International Peace, 1997.

Light, Margot. *The Soviet Theory of International Relations*. Brighton, Wheatsheaf, 1988.

Lightbody, Bradley. *The Cold War*. London, Routledge, 1999.

Linden, R. H. (Ed.). *Studies in East European Foreign Policy*. New York, NY, Praeger, 1980.

Litvin, V. *The Soviet Agro-Industrial Complex*. Boulder, CO, Westview Press, 1987.

Lubin, Nancy. *Central Asians take Stock: Reform, Corruption and Identity*. Washington, DC, US Institute of Peace, 1995.

Lynch, A. *The Soviet Study of International Relations*. Cambridge, Cambridge University Press, 1988.

Lynch, Dov. *Russian Peacekeeping Strategies in the CIS: the Case of Moldova, Georgia and Tajikistan*. Basingstoke, Macmillan, 1999.

McChesney, Robert Duncan. *Central Asia: Foundations of Change*. Princeton, NJ, Darwin Press, 1996.

McGwire, M. *Perestroika and Soviet National Security*. Washington, DC, Brookings Institution, 1991.

McKee, Martin, Healy, Judith, Falkingham, Jane. *Health Care in Central Asia*. Maidenhead, Open University Press, 2002.

Malcolm, N. *Soviet Policy Perspectives on Western Europe*, Chatham House Paper. London, Routledge (for the Royal Institute of International Affairs), 1989.

Malik, Hafeez (Ed.). *Central Asia: its Strategic Importance and Future Prospects*. Basingstoke, Macmillan, 1994.

Mandelbaum, Michael (Ed.). *Central Asia and the World: Kazakhstan, Uzbekistan, Tajikistan, Kyrgyzstan and Turkmenistan*. New York, NY, Council on Foreign Relations Press, 1994.

*The Rise of Nations in the Soviet Union: American Foreign Policy and the Disintegration of the USSR*. New York, NY, Council on Foreign Relations, 1991.

Mason, John W. *The Cold War—1945–1991*. London, Routledge, 1996.

Medvedev, Z. A. *Soviet Agriculture*. New York, NY, and London, Norton, 1977.

Mellor, R. E. H. *The Soviet Union and its Geographical Problems*. London, Macmillan, 1982.

Melvin, Neil. *Russians beyond Russia: The Politics of National Identity*. London, Royal Institute of International Affairs, 1995.

Melvin, Neil, and King, Charles (Eds). *Nations Abroad: Diaspora Politics and International Relations in the Former Soviet Union*. Boulder, CO, Westview Press, 1998.

Menashri, David (Ed.). *Central Asia meets the Middle East*. London, Frank Cass, 1998.

Menon, R., and Nelson, D. (Eds). *Limits to Soviet Power*. Lexington, MA, Lexington Books, 1989.

Menon, Rajan, Fedorov, Yuri E., and Nodia, Ghia (Eds). *Russia, the Caucasus, and Central Asia: the 21st Century Security Environment*. Armonk, NY, M. E. Sharpe, 1999.

Mesbahi, Moniaddin (Ed.). *Central Asia and the Caucasus after the Soviet Union: Domestic and International Dynamics*. Gainesville, FL, University Press of Florida, 1994.

Metge, Pierre. *L'URSS en Afghanistan, de la Coopération á l'Invasion: 1947–1984*. Paris, Cirpes, 1984.

Miller, J. *Mikhail Gorbachev and the End of Soviet Power*. New York, NY, St Martin's Press, 1993.

Milor, Vedat (Ed.). *Changing Political Economies: Privatization in Post-Communist and Reforming Communist States*. Boulder, CO, and London, Lynne Rienner, 1994.

Minorsky, Vladimir F. *The Turks, Iran and the Caucasus in the Middle Ages*. London, Variorum Reprints, 1978.

   *Studies in Caucasian History*. London, Cambridge Oriental Series, 1953.

Moskoff, W. (Ed.). *Perestroika in the Countryside: Agricultural Reform in the Gorbachev Era*. Armonk, NY, M. E. Sharpe, 1990.

Motyl, Alexander J. (Ed.). *The Post-Soviet Nations: Perspectives on the Demise of the USSR*. New York, NY, Columbia University Press, 1992.

Mozaffari, Mehdi (Ed.). *Security Policies in the Commonwealth of Independent States: The Southern Belt*. Basingstoke, Macmillan, and New York, NY, St Martin's Press, 1997.

Mullerson, Rein. *International Law, Rights and Politics: Developments in Eastern Europe and the CIS*. London, Routledge, 1994.

Nahaylo, Bohdan, and Swoboda, Victor. *Soviet Disunion: A History of the Nationalities Problem in the USSR*. London, Hamish Hamilton, 1990.

Naumkin, Vitalii V. (Ed.). *Central Asia and Transcaucasia: Ethnicity and Conflict*. Westport, CT, Greenwood, 1994.

   *State, Religion and Society in Central Asia*. Reading, Ithaca Press, 1993.

Nelson, D. N. 'Europe's Unstable East', in *Foreign Policy*, No. 82 (Spring), 1991.

de Nevers, R. 'The Soviet Union and Eastern Europe: The End of an Era', in *Adelphi Papers*, No. 249. London, Brassey's and International Institute for Strategic Studies, 1990.

Nichol, James P. *Diplomacy in the Former Soviet Republics*. Westport, CT, Praeger, 1995.

Nielsen, Jürgen S. (Ed.). *The Christian-Muslim Frontier: Chaos, Clash, or Dialogue?* London, I. B. Tauris, 1998.

Nogee, J. L., and Donaldson, R. H. (Eds). *Soviet Foreign Policy since World War II*. Oxford, Pergamon, 1988 (3rd edn).

Nove, A. *An Economic History of the USSR*. Harmondsworth, Penguin, 1982 (revised edn).

O'Ballance, Edgar. *Wars in the Caucasus, 1990–1995*. New York, NY, New York University Press, 1997.

Odom, William E., and Dujarric, Robert. *Commonwealth or Empire? Russia, Central Asia and the Transcaucasus*. Indianapolis, IN, Hudson Institute 1995.

Olcott, Martha Brill. *Central Asia's new state: Independence, Foreign Policy and Regional Security*. Washington, DC, US Institute of Peace, 1996.

Olcott, Martha Brill, Aslund, Anders, and Garnett, Sherman. *Getting it Wrong: Regional Co-operation and the Commonwealth of Independent States*. Washington, DC, Carnegie Endowment for International Peace, 1999.

Olivier, Roy. *The New Central Asia: The Creation of Nations*. London, Tauris, 1999.

Olson, James S. (Ed.). *Ethnohistorical Dictionary of the Russian and Soviet Empires*. Westport, CT, and London, Greenwood Press, 1994.

Organisation for Economic Co-operation and Development (OECD). *Assistance Programmes for Central and Eastern Europe and the Former Soviet Union*. Paris, OECD, 1996.

Painter, David. *The Cold War—An International History*. London, Routledge, 1999.

Painter, David, and Leffler, Melvyn (Eds). *The Origins of the Cold War—An International History*. London, Routledge, 1994.

Paksoy, H. B. (Ed.). *Central Asia Reader: the Rediscovery of History*. Armonk, NY, M. E. Sharpe, 1994.

Parrott, Bruce (Ed.). *State Building and Military Power in Russia and the New States of Eurasia*. Armonk, NY, and London, M. E. Sharpe, 1995.

Pipes, Richard *The Formation of the Soviet Union: Communism and Nationalism, 1917–23*. Cambridge, MA, Harvard University Press, 1964.

*Communism: A History*. New York, NY, Modern Library, 2001.

Polokhalo, V. (Ed.). *The Political Analysis of Post-Communism: Understanding Post-Communist Societies*. Kiev, Political Thought, 1995.

Pomfret, Richard W. T. *The Economies of Central Asia*. Princeton, NJ, Princeton University Press, 1995.

   *Asian Economies in Transition: Reforming Centrally Planned Economies*. Cheltenham, Edward Elgar Publishing, 1996.

Ponton, G. *The Soviet Era: Soviet Politics from Lenin to Yeltsin*. Oxford, Basil Blackwell, 1994.

Prizel, Ilya. *National Identity and Foreign Policy: Nationalism and Leadership in Poland, Russia and Ukraine*. Cambridge, Cambridge University Press, 1998.

Pryce-Jones, D. *The War That Never Was: The Fall of the Soviet Empire, 1985–1991*. London, Weidenfeld and Nicolson, 1995.

Quester, George (Ed.). *The Nuclear Challenge in Russia and the New States of Eurasia*. New York, NY, M. E. Sharpe, 1995.

Raack, R. C. *Stalin's Drive to the West 1938–45: The Origins of the Cold War*. Cambridge, Cambridge University Press, 1996.

Rashid, Ahmed. *The Resurgence of Central Asia. Islam or Nationalism?* London, Zed Books, 1994.

   *Taliban: Islam, Oil and the New Great Game in Central Asia*. London, I. B. Tauris, 2001.

   *Jihad: The Rise of Militant Islam in Central Asia*. New Haven, CT, and London, Yale University Press, 2002.

Reese, Roger R. *The Soviet Military Experience—A History of the Soviet Army, 1917–1991*. London, Routledge, 1999.

Remington, Thomas F. (Ed.). *Parliaments in Transition: The New Legislative Politics in the Former USSR and Eastern Europe*. Boulder, CO, Westview Press, 1994.

Remnick, David. *Lenin's Tomb: The Last Days of the Soviet Empire*. London, Viking, 1993.

   *Resurrection: The Struggle for a New Russia*. New York, NY, Random House, 1997, and London, Picador, 1998.

Renata, Dwan (Ed.). *Building Security in the New States of Eurasia: Subregional Co-operation in the Former Soviet Space*. New York, NY, M. E. Sharpe, 2000.

Roberts, Geoffrey. *The Soviet Union in World Politics—Coexistence, Revolution and Cold War 1945–1991*. London, Routledge, 1998.

Roeder, P. G. *Red Sunset: The Failure of Soviet Politics*. Princeton, NJ, Princeton University Press, 1994.

Ro'i, Yaacov. (Ed.). *Muslim Eurasia: Conflicting Legacies*. London, Frank Cass, 1995.

Ronnas, Per, and Sjoberg, Orjan (Eds). *Economic Transformation and Employment in Central Asia*. Ankara, International Labour Office, 1994.

Roux, Jean-Paul. *L'Asia Centrale, Histoire et Civilizations*. Paris, Fayard, 1997.

Roy, Olivier. *The New Central Asia: The Creation of Nations*. New York, NY, New York University Press, 2000.

Rubin, Barnett R., and Snyder, Jack (Eds). *Post-Soviet Political Order*. London, Routledge, 1998.

Rubin, Barnett R., Lubin, Nancy, and Martin, Keith. *Calming the Ferghana Valley*. New York, NY, Century Foundation, 2000.

Ruffin, M. Holt, et al. *Post-Soviet Handbook: a Guide to Grassroots Organisations and Internet Resources*. Seattle, WA, Center for Civil Society International, 1999 (2nd edn).

Ruffin, M. Holt, and Waugh, Daniel C. *Civil Society in Central Asia*. Seattle, WA, University of Washington Press, 1999.

Rumer, Boris Z. *Soviet Central Asia: 'A Tragic Experiment'*. Boston, MA, Unwin Hyman, 1989.

Rumev, Boris (Ed.). *Central Asia in Transition: Dilemmas of Political and Economic Development*. Armonk, NY, M. E. Sharpe, 1996.

Rumev, Boris, and Zhukov, Stanislav (Eds). *Central Asia: The Challenge of Independence*. Armonk, NY, M. E. Sharpe, 1998.

Ryan, M. (Ed.). *Contemporary Soviet Society: A Statistical Handbook*. Aldershot, Edward Elgar, 1990.

Sagdeev, Roald Z., and Eisenhower, Susan (Eds). *Islam and Central Asia*. Washington, DC, Eisenhower Institute, 2000.

Saikal, A., and Maley, W. (Eds). *The Soviet Withdrawal from Afghanistan*. Cambridge, Cambridge University Press, 1989.

Sakwa, Richard. *Soviet Politics in Perspective*. London, Routledge, 1998 (2nd edn).

　*The Rise and Fall of the Soviet Union*. London, Routledge, 1999.

Sandle, Mark. *A Short History of Soviet Socialism*. London, UCL Press, 1998.

Shalin, Dmitri N. (Ed.). *Russian Culture at the Crossroads: Paradoxes of Post-Communist Consciousness*. Boulder, CO, Westview Press, 1996.

Shlapentokh, Vladimir. *Public and Private Life of the Soviet People*. New York, NY, Oxford University Press Inc., 1989.

　*A Normal Totalitarian Society: How the Soviet Union Functioned and How it Collapsed*. Armonk, NY, M. E. Sharpe, 2001.

Skajkowski, Bogdan (Ed.). *Political Parties of Eastern Europe, Russia and the Successor States*. London, Longman, 1994.

Smith, Adrian, and Pickles, John (Eds). *Theorizing Transition*. London, Routledge, 1998.

Smith, Graham (Ed.). *The Nationalities Question in the Soviet Union*. London, Longman, 1996 (2nd edn).

Smith, Graham, et al. *Nation-Building in the Post-Soviet Borderlands: The Politics of National Identities*. New York, NY, Cambridge University Press, 1998.

　*The Post-Soviet States: Mapping the Politics of Transition*. London, Arnold, 1999.

Snyder, Jed C. (Ed.). *After Empire: The Emerging Geopolitics of Central Asia*. Washington, DC, National Defence University Press, 1995.

Soucek, Svatopluk. *A History of Central Asia*. Cambridge, Cambridge University Press, 2000.

Srivastava, Vinayak Narain. *The Separation of the Party and the State: Political Leadership in Soviet and Post Soviet Phases*. Aldershot, Ashgate, 1999.

Starr, S. Frederick (Ed.). *The Legacy of History in Russia and the New States of Eurasia*. Armonk, NY, M. E. Sharpe, 1994.

Suny, Ronald Grigor. *The Revenge of the Past: Nationalism, Revolution, and the Collapse of the Soviet Union*. Stanford, CA, Stanford University Press, 1993.

　*The Soviet Experiment: Russia, the USSR, and the Successor States*. Oxford, Oxford University Press, 1997.

Suny, Ronald Grigor (Ed.). *Transcaucasia, Nationalism and Social Change: Essays in the History of Armenia, Azerbaijan and Georgia*. Ann Arbor, MI, Michigan Slavic Publications, 1983.

Suny, Ronald Grigor, and Kennedy, Michael D. (Eds). *Intellectuals and the Articulation of the Nation*. Ann Arbor, MI, University of Michigan Press, 1999.

Swietochowski, Tadeusz. *Russia and Azerbaijan*. New York, NY, Columbia University Press, 1995.

Szelenyi, Ivan (Ed.). *Privatizing the Land: Rural Political Economy in Post-Communist and Socialist Societies*. London, Routledge, 1998.

Szporluk, Roman (Ed.). *National Identity and Ethnicity in Russia and the New States of Eurasia*. London, M. E. Sharpe, 1994.

　*Russia, Ukraine and the Breakup of the Soviet Union*. Standford, CA, Hoover Institution Press, 2000.

Taras, Ray. *Post-Communist Presidents*. New York, NY, Cambridge University Press, 1997.

Taubman, William. *Krushchev: The Man and His Era*. New York, NY, W. W. Norton, 2003.

Terry, S. M. *Soviet Policy in Eastern Europe*. New Haven, CT, Yale University Press, 1984.

Tismaneanu, Vladimir (Ed.). *Political Culture and Civil Society in Russia and the New States of Eurasia*. Armonk, NY, and London, M. E. Sharpe, 1995.

Tolz, Vera, and Elliot, Iain (Eds). *The Demise of the USSR: From Communism to Independence*. Basingstoke, Macmillan, 1995.

Turnbull, Mildred. *Soviet Environmental Policies and Practices: The Most Critical Investment*. Aldershot, Dartmouth, 1991.

Turnock, David (Ed.). *East Central Europe and the Former Soviet Union*. London, Hodder Arnold, 2001.

Twining, David Thomas. *Guide to the Republics of the Former Soviet Union / The New Eurasia*. Westport, CT, and London, Greenwood Press, 1993.

Urban, George R. *End of Empire: The Demise of the Soviet Union*. Washington, DC, American University Press, 1993.

Wädekin, K.-E. (Ed.). *Communist Agriculture*. London, Routledge, 1990.

Wagener, Hans-Jürgen (Ed.). *Economic Thought in Communist and Post-Communist Europe*. London, Routledge, 1998.

Waller, Michael, Coppieters, Bruno, and Malashenko, Alexei (Eds). *Conflicting Loyalties and the State in Post-Soviet Russia and Eurasia*. London, Portland, 1998.

Warikoo, K. Kulbhushan (Ed.). *Central Asia: Emerging New Order*. New Delhi, Har-Anand Publications/Himalayan Research and Cultural Foundation (India), 1995.

Webber, Mark. *CIS Integration Trends: Russia and the Former Soviet South*. London, Royal Institute of International Affairs, 1997.

Wegren, Stephen K. (Ed.). *Land Reform in the Former Soviet Union and Eastern Europe*. London, and New York, NY, Routledge, 1998.

Wheeler, Geoffrey. *The Modern History of Soviet Central Asia*. Westport, CT, Greenwood Press, 1975.

White, Stephen. *Gorbachev in Power*. Cambridge, Cambridge University Press, 1990.

　*Communism and its Collapse*. London, Routledge, 2000.

White, Stephen, Gill, Graeme, and Darrell Slider. *The Politics of Transition: Shaping a Post-Soviet Future*. Cambridge, Cambridge University Press, 1993.

White, S., di Leo, R., and Cappelli, O. (Eds). *The Soviet Transition: From Gorbachev to Yeltsin*. London, Frank Cass, 1993.

White, S., Pravda, A., and Gitelman Z. (Eds). *Developments in Soviet Politics*. London, Macmillan, 1990.

Whiting, A. S. *Siberian Development and East Asia*. Stanford, CA, Stanford University Press, 1981.

Williamson, John (Ed.). *Economic Consequences of Soviet Disintegration*. Washington, DC, Institute for International Economics, 1993.

Woff, Richard. *The Armed Forces of the Former Soviet Union: Evolution, Structure and Personalities*, 3 vols. London, Brassey's, 1996.

Wood, Alan. *Stalin and Stalinism*. London, Routledge, 1990.

World Bank. *Energy in Europe and Central Asia: A Sector Strategy for the World Bank Group*. Washington, DC, IBRD, 1990.

　*Trade in the New Independent States*. Washington, DC, IBRD, 1994.

Zevelev, Igor. *Russia and its New Diasporas*. Washington, DC, United States Institute of Peace, 2001.

Zviagelskaia, Irina Donovna. *The Russian Policy Debate on Central Asia*. London, Royal Institute of International Affairs, 1995.

# INDEX OF REGIONAL ORGANIZATIONS

(Main reference only)

Greenland
Sea

Denmark Strait
Arctic Circle

Laptev
Sea

Barents
Sea

Kara
Sea

Norwegian
Sea

Central
Siberian Plain

Khrebet Cherskorgo

Lena

West
Siberian
Plain

Ural Mountains

Yenisey

Ob

Siberia

ASIA

Scandinavia

North
Sea

Baltic Sea

Volga

British
Isles

North European Plain

EUROPE

Carpathian Mts

Alps

Lake
Baikal

Manchurian
Plain

Bay of
Biscay

Danube

Balkan Mts

Altai

Gobi
Desert

Black Sea

El'brus
5642m

Aral
Sea

Sea of
Japan

Iberian
Peninsula

Anatolia

Caspian
Sea

Pamirs

Tien Shan

Kunlun Mountains

Yellow River

Japan

Mediterranean Sea

Hindu Kush

Atlas Mts

Zagros Mountains

Iranian
Plateau

Plateau
of Tibet

Himalayas

Yangtze

East
China
Sea

Sahara

Hoggar

Libyan Desert

The Gulf

Mt Everest
8848m

Sea of
Okhot

Philippine
Sea

Tropic of Cancer

Nile

Red Sea

Arabian
Peninsula

Thar
Desert

Ganges

Deccan

AFRICA

Tibesti

Sahel

Niger

Lake Chad

Ethiopian
Highlands

Gulf of Aden

Horn of
Africa

Arabian
Sea

Western Ghats

Eastern Ghats

Bay of
Bengal

South
China
Sea

Mekong

Adamawa
Highlands

Sri
Lanka

Equator

Gulf of
Guinea

Congo
Basin

Congo

Rift Valley

Lake Victoria
Kilimanjaro
5895m

Borneo

New
Guinea

Mt W
450

ATLANTIC

Rift Valley

Lake Tanganyika

INDIAN

Timor
Sea

OCEAN

Zambezi

Lake Malawi

Mozambique Channel

OCEAN

Great
Sandy Desert

AUSTRALIA

Grea

Tropic of Capricorn

Namib Desert

Kalahari
Desert

Drakensberg

Great Victoria Desert

Nullarbor
Plain

Darling

Cape
Basin

Antarctica

Antarctic Circle